W9-AFE-390

#27.25

THE

HISTORIC NOTE-BOOK:

WITH AN

APPENDIX OF BATTLES.

BY THE

REV. E. COBHAM BREWER, LL.D.,

AUTHOR OF "THE DICTIONARY OF PHRASE AND FABLE," "THE READER'S
HANDBOOK," "DICTIONARY OF MIRACLES," ETC.

51333

PHILADELPHIA:
J. B. LIPPINCOTT COMPANY.
1891.

REPUBLISHED BY GALE RESEARCH COMPANY, BOOK TOWER, DETROIT, 1966

St. Thomas Aquinas College Library

Library of Congress Card Number 66-23191

PAPER USED IN THIS EDITION IS
A FINE ACID FREE PERMANENT/DURABLE PAPER
COMMONLY REFERRED TO AS "300-YEAR" PAPER

St. Thomas Aquinas College Library

TO THE

RIGHT HON. THE COUNTESS MANVERS

WHOM TO KNOW

(TO USE THE WORDS OF SIR RICHARD STEELE)

'IS A LIBERAL EDUCATION'

These 'Historic Notes' are with permission Dedicated

BY

THE AUTHOR

R
903
B

PREFACE

THIS volume, entitled 'The Historic Note-Book,' is the third and last of a series. The first was the 'Dictionary of Phrase and Fable,' the object of which was to explain the meaning of words and expressions in which an allusion is made to some fable, custom, or character, more or less familiarly known.

The 'Reader's Handbook,' the second of the series, undertook to unfold in a few lines the tale of the best known epic poems of ancient and modern times, the plots of novels and plays, ballads and romances, and to give short biographical sketches of their respective authors.

The present book does for history what the first of the series did for phraseology, and the latter did for poetry and romance. It is purely historical, and explains with the utmost possible brevity allusions to historical events, acts of parliament, treaties, and customs, terms and phrases, made in books, speeches, and familiar conversation.

Probably no one could turn over a couple of pages of this book and not find some item which he would be at a loss to explain or to find in any book near at hand. It may be hidden in some corner of history, some modern or ancient encyclopædia, some law dictionary, periodical, or book of antiquities; but, being neither tabulated nor inserted in the index, would be as hard to light upon as the traditional grain of wheat in a bushel of chaff. It might require hours, perhaps days, of research to hunt out, and the handling of many books. This is the sort of lore here set down. Some items have been kept by the author in the form of queries for many years waiting for solution, and those solutions have been ultimately found in most unexpected places.

I have been an author for sixty years, have written many books, and of course have been a very miscellaneous reader. In my long experience I have remarked how little the range of 'literary' reading has varied, and how doubt still centres on matters which were *cruces* in my early years. So that a work of this kind is of as much usefulness in 1891 as it would have been in 1830. I always read with a slip of paper and a pencil at my side, to jot down whatever I think may be useful to me, and these jottings I keep sorted in different lockers. This has been a life-habit with me, and the compiling of them into a subjective volume consists chiefly in selecting, sorting, explaining, correcting, and bringing down to date. What I myself have wanted to know, I presume others younger than I am may wish to know also; and what I have found difficult to discover, I presume others with fewer books may find difficult also. I know that many a time and oft I should have been most thankful if I could have laid my hand on a book, and found, without much tedious research, the explanation of some item in this book at the time unknown to me; and I judge others by myself. This very unromantic way of looking at a big book has been the secret of my success as an author. It was begun at the age of eighteen, and my first book of note was the 'Guide to Science,' the sale of which has been almost fabulous. The 'Dictionary of Phrase and Fable ' was more than twenty years in hand, and has had a very wide circulation; the present book cannot fail to be equally useful, and I hope will not be less acceptable to the general.

In these 'Historic Notes' I have had the advantage of two press-readers of unusual learning, judgment, and wide reading—one in London and one in Philadelphia. With a diligence and discrimination beyond all praise, they have called attention to every doubtful statement, date, or proper name, and much of the accuracy of the book is undoubtedly due to their painstaking co-operation. For myself I am under unbounded obligation to them, and hope they will accept my thanks thus publicly acknowledged and without stint.

Little more need be said. The arrangement is somewhat different to that usually followed in Historical Dictionaries. The items are not set under the ruling word, but generally under the first noun or adjective of the phrase. Thus under ' Massacre ' will be found all articles of that category, massed together, and not distributed under the name of the place where the deed of blood was committed. This has been done to bring the subject together in a compact form. Similarly with Church Councils, Literary Forgeries, and so on. When this allocation has been found impracticable, as in ' Irish Associations,' ' Monastic Orders,' ' Sunday Fête Days,' and so on, then under the general heading will be found an alphabetical list of all the articles in the book on the subject, which may be turned to if required.

Some antiquated customs have been pointed out, and a suggestion has been occasionally made which may possibly direct attention to what appears to the author of these ' Notes ' a national want or national defect. See p. 697, article Poets' Corner, and p. 115, article Borromeo.

In one instance, that of ' Abigail,' in which a word has an ancient and modern history, the recent revival of the word in the reign of Queen Anne has been thought more consistent with the scope of this book than the well-known tale in the life of David. Those, however, who prefer the older story may, if they think proper, consult the ' Dictionary of Phrase and Fable.'

Finally the book here offered to the public is not a ' Book of Dates,' though dates have been added whenever required. Inventions and Discoveries, the great staple of a book of dates, find no place here; and hundreds of the articles here inserted are wholly independent of dates.

Similarly, the book is not an 'Historic Dictionary,' but a dictionary of historic terms and phrases, jottings of odds and ends of history, which historians leave in the cold or only incidentally mention in the course of their narratives. If I might borrow the motto of 'Notes and Queries,' 'When found make a note of,' it would most aptly describe the end and object of these 'Historic Notes.'

THE AUTHOR.

If I might make the suggestion without being impertinent, I think the book would be admirably adapted to the upper forms of Ladies' Schools, and to those in private life who seek to extend their general knowledge, after having laid aside their elementary books. Of course, these Historic Notes are mainly designed and were specially written for the general public, and this, their educational use, is a mere afterthought.

HISTORIC NOTE-BOOK

———◇———

A *Etre marqué à l'A*, of first-class quality. A is the distinctive mark of money minted in Paris, which is purer and more free from alloy than any other money in the French dominions. For A 1 see *Dict. of Phrase and Fable*, p. 1.

Aarau (*Peace of*), 3, 9, 11 Aug., 1712. This treaty concluded the war of Toggenburg.

Aaron's Breastplate, 4 rows.

1. Reuben, *sardius*; Simeon, *topaz*; Levi, *carbuncle*.
2. Judah, *emerald*; Dan, *jacinth*; Naphtali, *agate*.
3. Gad, *amethyst*; Asher, *beryl*; Issachar, *sapphire*.
4. Zebulon, *diamond*; Joseph, *onyx*; Benjamin, *jaspar*.

Abbasides (3 syl.). Califs of Bagdad, so called from Abul Abbas (Abdallah ben Mohammed), who defeated Mervan II., and became calif, 18 Feb., A.D. 750; ceased 1258, by the overthrow of Mostasem, put to death by Hulakou or Hulagu, a Mogul prince. The Abbasides succeeded the Ommaïades.

The Abbaside califs were, Aboul-Abbas (750); Abou Giafar Almanzor (754); Mohammed Mahdi (775); Hadi (785); Haroun al Raschid (786); Amyn (809); Al Mamoun (813), and 30 more.

Abbate (2 syl.). A young Italian clergyman who has received the tonsure, but has not taken full orders.

Abbates Milites, or Abba-comités. 10th cent. Lay abbots, who deputed deans or priors to the spiritual oversight of their abbeys.

Pronounce Ab'-a-teez Mil'-i-teez.

Abbaye de Monte à Regret. .The guillotine. What is now the *Rue des*

Bourses, in Paris, was formerly the *Monte à Regret*, the place for public executions.

Pronounce Ab-bay-d' Mŏnt ah Ra-gra'.

Abbés Commendataires. The 225 abbots appointed by the king of France. The office was a perfect sinecure, but the abbé commendataire drew one-third of the revenues of his convént. Many of these abbots were laymen, but generally they were literary men, often noblemen's sons included under laymen.

Pronounce Ab-bay Com-men-da-tares. •

Abbey. In Scotland, a sanctuary for debtors against legal process afforded by the abbey of Holyrood.

Abbots in commendam. Abbots commended to hold an abbey and its dignity in charge till a regular abbot has been appointed. In the Reformation several abbots and other ecclesiastics were allowed to enjoy their livings for life, or for a time. By 6, 7 Will. IV. c. 77, s. 18, no ecclesiastical dignity, office, or benefice, after the living possessors, was allowed to be held *in commendam*.

Abbeys and other Catholic livings held *in commendam* were mere sinecures for life.

Abbotsford Club (*The*). A literary club founded in Edinburgh (1835) for the publication of works belonging to Scotch history, literature, and antiquities. Above 30 quarto volumes were published. The club no longer exists.

Abbott Scholarships. I. In the University of *Cambridge*: two for classics and mathematics, for undergraduates in

B

their first year. Value about 60*l.* a year, tenable for three years; founded by John Abbott of Halifax, Yorkshire, 1871.

II. In the University of *Oxford*: three for the sons of poor clergymen; founded the same year by the same founder.

Abdicated Monarchs. The following monarchs of Europe have abdicated:

Amadeus I. (duke of Aosta) Spain	...	...	...	1873
Charles IV. of Spain (forced)	...	...	...	1808
Charles V. of Spain and Germany	...	...	...	1556
Charles X. of France (forced)	...	...	...	1830
Charles Albert of Sardinia (forced)	...	...	...	1849
Charles Emmanuel of Sardinia	...	...	...	1802
Christina of Sweden	...	...	...	1654
Diocletian and Maximian	...	...	...	305, 308
Felipe V. of Spain	...	...	...	1724
Francis II. of the Two Sicilies (forced)		...		1860
James II. of England (forced)	...	...	...	1689
Louis Bonaparte of Holland	...	...	...	1810
Louis Philippe of France (forced)	...	...	...	1848
Ludwig of Bavaria (forced)	...	...	...	1848
Matilda (Lady of England)	...	...	...	1154
Milan of Servia	...	...	...	1889
Napoleon I. of France (forced)	...	...	...	1814
Napoleon III. of France (forced)	...	...	...	1870
Otho of Greece (forced)	...	...	...	1863
Pedro II. of Brazil (forced)	...	...	...	1889
Poniatowski of Poland (forced)	...	...	...	1795
Richard II. of England (forced)	...	...	...	1399
Stanislaus Leszczinski (forced)	...	...	...	1735
Victor Amadeus of Sardinia	...	...	...	1730
Victor Emmanuel	...	...	...	1819

Several dethroned without even the mocking show of abdication, like Edward II. of England (1327); Henry VI. of England (1471); &c.

Abeceda'rians.

Anabaptists who set their faces against all human learning, lest it should impede the progress of the soul in its apprehension of Divine truth. The Catholics at one time opposed all learning except what they called sacred literature, such as the lives of the saints, and other religious books.

Abel'ians or Abelo'nians.

A sect of the ancient Christian Church which married, but lived in continence, as they assumed Abel did (4th cent.).

Abenzerraghes.

A wealthy and powerful family of Spanish Moors, descended from Yusef ben-Zerragh. The word divided is A-ben-Zerragh[es], and is pronounced Ah'-ven-zerark'-ey. Their struggles with the family of Zegris, and destruction in the palace of the Alhambra, in Granada (fifteenth century), have furnished the subject of a charming Spanish romance, ' The History of the Civil Wars of Granada.' Chateaubriand made it the subject of his 'Adventures of the Last Abenzerraghe,' and it furnishes the text of one of Cherubini's operas. The feud began 1474.

Often written Abencerragos.

Ab'erdeen' (*University of*), 1500;

founded by James IV. It was originally founded in 1494, by W. Elphinstone, bishop of Aberdeen, and called King's College. In 1858 Marischal College (*q.v.*) was united to the University of Aberdeen. (21, 22 Vict. c. 83).

Aberdeen man's privilege (*An*).

To alter or change one's mind on second thoughts.

These good folks, Alan, make no allowance for what your good father calls the Aberdeen man's privilege, of ' taking his word again,' or what the wise call ' second thoughts.'—Sir W. SCOTT, *Redgauntlet*, Letter 7.

Ab'garus, king of Edessa (A.D. 13–50).

Is said by Eusebius to have written a letter to Christ asking Him to cure his disease, pronounced by his physicians to be incurable. Christ replied, after His ascension, that one of His disciples should be sent to effect the cure. Thaddeus was the apostle selected, and Abgärus was restored to perfect health. Of course this is only tradition. (Euseb. i. 13.)

Abhorrers.

A political party in England, in the winter 1679–1680. They looked with ' abhorrence' on Lord Shaftesbury's proposal to set aside not only James, who was a Roman Catholic, but also his daughter Mary, who was a Protestant, married to the Prince of Orange. *See* 'Petitioners,' &c.

Macaulay says, they were a church and state party which declared their abhorrence of those who sought to dictate to the king (Charles II.) as to the routine of the new parliament in 1680.

Ab'igail (*An*).

A woman of low degree and intriguing character, so called from Abigail Hill, a niece of Sarah, Duchess of Marlborough, introduced into the court of Queen Anne as a bedchamber woman. Abigail took the fancy of the queen, became prime favourite, and ousted the duchess from her high position in 1707. Harley was Abigail's uncle, as the duchess was her aunt, and Abigail had been privately married to Mr. Masham, groom of the bedchamber of George, prince of Denmark, the queen's consort. (*See* 1 Sam. xxv. 3).

Her (the Duchess of Marlborough) indignant mind instantly attributed this omission to the contrary advice of the queen's Abigail, and . . . she broke loose on Anne without regard to the presence of the public.—HOWITT, *Hist. of Eng.* (Anne, 251).

Ab'igail Earwig (*Mrs.*). Mrs. Masham, the favourite of Queen Anne, on the downfall of the Duchess of Marlborough.

Abingdon Hospital, 1689; founded by John Mason of Abingdon, for the infirm, aged, and indigent.

Abingdon Law. First hang the offender, then try him. So called from Major Brown of Abingdon, an officer in the parliamentary army.

Abjuration Bill (*The*), 1690. A bill which required of everyone who took any public office or trust to swear by oath to recognise the right of the reigning sovereign to the crown under the Act of Settlement, promising to disclose any traitorous conspiracy, and abjuring the right of the Pretender. Enforced 1701, altered in the reigns of Anne, George I., and George III.; and repealed in 1858.

Abjuration Oath (*The*). Formerly there were three oaths required of all persons before admission to any public office, viz. The Oath of Allegiance, The Oath of Supremacy, and The Abjuration Oath. The Abjuration Oath is that no foreign prince, state, or potentate, hath or ought to have any jurisdiction, power, superiority, or authority, ecclesiastical or civil, within the British realm. Enforced by Act 13 Will. III. c. 6 (1701). The three oaths amalgamated into a declaration by Act 21, 22 Vict. c. 48 (July 13, 1858).

Abjuration of Henri IV., 1593. The renunciation of Protestantism by Henri IV., for the purpose of securing the crown of France, and putting an end to civil war.

Abo. I. (*Peace of*), 17, 18 Aug., 1743, between Sweden and Russia, effected by the mediation of England.

II. (*The Treaty of*), 28 Aug., 1812, between Bernadotte, king of Sweden, and Alexander, the czar of Russia; effected by a personal conference of the two sovereigns.

Abraham's Call. His *first* call was out of Haran, which, according to Clinton, was in the autumn B.C. 2093. His *second* call was 4 May, B.C. 2055 (Gen. xii. 1). The reason why Abraham was called by God to leave Chaldea was because that country was greatly polluted with idolatry, which was less prevalent at the time in Egypt. *See* ' Era of Abraham.'

Abrahamites (4 syl.). I. A sect which, in the 9th cent., sprang up in the East, and revived at Antioch the tenets of the Paulicians. The founder was Ibraim or Abraham of Antioch. Cyriacus opposed the heretics while Charlemagne was in power.

Pronounce A'-bram-mites.

II. Bohemian deists (1782), who professed to be followers of John Huss, but reduced their religion to what they supposed was that of Abraham before his circumcision. The only part of the Bible which they retained was the Lord's Prayer. They were banished from Bohemia in 1783, and were scattered abroad in various parts of Hungary, Transylvania, and Slavonia. *See* above.

Abraham-men. A class of sturdy beggars who simulated lunacy, and wandered about the country extorting money by working on the compassion or fears of those who passed by. A ' Tom o' Bedlam' was an Abraham-man or 'Abram Cove.' So called from the Abraham ward in the Bethlehem Hospital.

Pronounce A'-brum-men.

Abrantes (*Treaty of*), 6 June, 1801, between Spain and Portugal. Signed at Abrantes, Estremadura, in Portugal.

Absolute Loyalists. In the middle of the 17th cent. meant the friends and followers of the Duke of Montrose. The Engagers (*q.v.*) and the Whiggamors (*q.v*) were also in a measure supporters of the king; but there was no possibility of united action between them, and they only weakened the royal cause.

Absolute Wisdom, 1821. Alderman Wood was so called. He was a staunch supporter of Queen Caroline, and being charged with having ill-advised the queen, he admitted that his advice might not be 'absolute wisdom,' and he was jocularly called 'Absolute Wisdom Wood.'

Absolution Thursday. In French ' Jeudi Absolu,' the day before Good Friday, when the priest recites the seven penitential psalms, gives a sermon, and then pronounces the ' Misereatur' and the ' Indulgentiam.'

B 2

Absolutists (*The*), 1819. The monarchical party of Spain, opposed to the radical 'Exaltados' (*q.v.*). They wished to restore the absolute power of the king, and consisted of the nobility in general, the clergy, and, what seems somewhat inconsistent, the lower orders. Of course the Absolutists wanted to abrogate the Constitution of 1812.

Abstainers. Teetotalers, or those who abstain from alcoholic drinks. Abstinence societies are now generally called temperance societies. Established in America, at Boston, in 1826; in London (The British and Foreign Temperance Society) 1831; the National, in London, 1842.

Abyssin'ian War (*The*). Between the British and Theodore, king of Abyssinia. This expedition (for the release of missionaries, Capt. Crawford and others) was under Sir R. Napier, who joined the army at Senafé, Jan. 1868. Col. Phayre defeated Theodore at Magdala 10 April, which was bombarded and taken on 13 April. The return of the British army commenced 18 April, 1868.

Academic School of Philosophers (*The*). Founded by Plato the Athenian (B.C. 429–347), who taught in the Academy, a garden about a quarter of a mile from the city, in the north-western suburb. It belonged originally to Acadēmos, and was adorned by Cimon, son of Miltiădês, the great general. Plato's disciples were called the Academ'ics, or Garden sect. Plato was the disciple of Socrătês.

Academ'ics (*The*). One of the Grecian sects in the early ages of Christianity. They maintained the total uncertainty of all sensuous impressions, and, therefore, the impossibility of man's knowing anything for certain. They doubted the existence of a God, they doubted the immortality of the soul, and doubted whether virtue was better than vice, or vice better than virtue.

Academy (*The*). A London weekly journal, chiefly of reviews, commenced 9 Oct., 1869.

Ac'amoth Plero'ma. With the ancient Gnostics, *plerōma* meant the fulness of knowledge, and *acamoth*, inferior wisdom.

Accord' (*The*). So the Treaty of Edinburgh is called. This treaty was between Queen Elizabeth and the Scots for the evacuation of Scotland by the French; concluded 6 July, 1560.

Accusative (*The*). John Calvin was so called by his companions (1509–1564). Also 'The pope of Geneva.'

Acemetes (*The*), or 'Accœmeti' (i.e. *Watchers*), 5th cent. A religious order founded by St. Alexander, an Asiatic (died 430). So called because one of them was always to be on the 'watch.' That is, one of the three classes was to be in rotation performing service all day and all night (Greek, *a-koimētos*, sleepless).

Pronounce As-se-me'-teez.

Aceph'ali (*The*), 482. A faction among the Eutychians—heretics who denied the true manhood of Christ. Their founder was Peter Mongus, bishop of Alexandria, who renounced his error, and then his followers were 'without a head' (Greek, *a-kephalê*, headless). They were reconciled by Mark I. in 799.

Subsequently those Christians who belonged to no special church, and acknowledged no ordained chief, like the Vaudois, were called Acephali (men without a head to their church).

Pronounce A-sef'-fa-le (*see below*).

Acephalites (*The*). Certain levellers in the reign of Henry I., who acknowledged no leader (*see above*).

Pronounce A-sef'-fa-lites.

Achæ'an League (*The*). A confederacy of the twelve towns of Achæa. It was dissolved by Alexander the Great, but reorganised B.C. 280, and again dissolved B.C. 147. The second of these leagues, founded at Megalopŏlis, contained all the chief cities of Peloponnesus. It contended with the Macedonians and the Romans for the liberty of Greece; but, being beaten at Scarphēa by Metellus, and at Leucopetra by Mummius, it caved in soon after the taking of Corinth.

The twelve cities of Achæa, in Ionia, wer founded by the Heraclĭdæ.

Achæ'an War (*The*). Roman ambassadors at Corinth enjoin the dismemberment of the Achæan League and are insulted (B.C. 147). Kritolāos, general of the league, at once besieged Heracleia (B.C. 146), but was defeated at Scarphēa by Metellus, and slew himself. Diæos, successor of Kritolaos, was defeated at Leucopĕtra by Mummius (B.C. 146); Corinth was then destroyed; and all Greece was erected into a Roman province, Sept. 146.

Achæmenides (*The*), also called Kai-anians, the sixth dynasty of Persia. The first four were fabulous, the fifth or Pishdadian dynasty was mythic, the sixth is semi-historic. It gave fourteen sovereigns, and lasted 329 years (B.C. 660–331), when Persia fell under the Greeks. Seat of government Ispahan.

Kai-anians. Kai (mighty) called by the Greeks Kur[os], and by the Latins Cyr-us, grandson of Achæmenês. The founder was Kai-Kobad or Cyrus I.
    Pronounce Ak-ke-men'-e-deez.

Achilles (*The English*). John Talbot, first Earl of Shrewsbury, 1373–1453.

The Duke of Wellington is represented by a statue of Achilles of gigantic size once in Hyde Park, London, close to Apsley House (1769-1852).

Achilles (*The Second*). Dentātus, the Roman tribune. It is said that he slew at different times 300 of the enemy; and when treacherously set upon by twenty-five of his countrymen, although, at the time, he was more than sixty years of age, he killed fourteen of them before he was slain.

Achilles of Germany (*The*). Albrecht, elector of Brandenburg (1470-1487), was called the Achilles and also the Ulysses of Germany. He was the third son of Friedrich I., elector of Brandenburg.

Achilles of Rome (*The*). Sicinius Dentātus (put to death B.C. 450).

Achiropoetos. A picture of Christ and the Virgin made without human hands, *i.e.* miraculously (Greek, *a-cheiro-poiētos*). One of the best known is the picture of Christ preserved in the church of St. John of Lateran, at Rome. This picture is said to have been begun by St. Luke, and finished by angels; a Catholic tradition.
    Pronounce A-kĭ'-ro-po-e'-tos.

Acil'ian Law (*The*). I. B.C. 197, by C. Acilius, tribune of the people, about planting colonies on the coast.
    II. B.C. 101, by the tribune M. Acilius Glabrio, respecting extortion.

Acolytes. Their original duties were to help the deacons or sub-deacons at the altar service, to prepare the wine and water for the communion, to light the lamps, to hold the candles, and to carry from place to place the consecrated elements. The word meant *followers* or *attendants*. These duties are now for the most part assigned to the sacristans.
    Pronounce Ak'-ko-lites.

Acre-fight (*An*). A sort of duel by single combatants (English and Scotch) between the frontiers of the two kingdoms. (Cowell, 'Institutiones &c.')

Act for Uniformity (*The*), 1549 (2, 3 Edw. VI. c. 1), meaning 'uniformity of public worship.' It commanded the adoption of the new Liturgy throughout the kingdom, in place of the Latin Mass Book. Those who neglected to comply were liable to imprisonment for six months for the first offence, loss of their benefices for the second offence, and imprisonment for life for the third offence.

Other Acts of Uniformity are 5, 6 Edw. VI. c. 1; 1 Eliz. c. 2; 13, 14 Car. II. c. 4.

Act in pais. A thing done out of court, and not a matter of record. (*Pais* is the French word 'pays,' meaning in old law *où l'on suit le droit*.)

Act of Cura'tory (in Scotch law). Extracted by the clerk upon anyone's acceptance of being curator.

Act of Explanation (*The*), 1664. For the removal or modification of some of the most obnoxious clauses of the Act of Settlement in Ireland (*q.v.*). See 'Magna Charta of the Protestants of Ireland.'

Act of Grace (*The*), 1696. Provides maintenance for debtors imprisoned by their creditors (Scotch law).

In England it is usually applied to insolvent acts and general pardons at the beginning of a new reign, or on some very special occasion.

Act of Oblivion (*The*). I. In 1653 procured by Cromwell himself, abolishing the memory of all offences committed before the battle of Worcester. This act relieved the minds of royalists from the fear of further forfeitures. After the conspiracies of 1654 all who had ever borne arms for the king were decimated —that is, were fined one-tenth of all the estates then in their possession the fine to be spent in recouping the state the expenses it had been put to by the royalist rebellions.

II. In 1660 (12 Car. II. c. 11). Indemnity for treason and state offences committed between 1 January, 1637, and 24 June, 1660.

Act of Safety (*The*), 1789, in Swedish history. When Gustavus III. was abandoned by his nobles and chief military officers, he threw in his lot with the other three orders. These orders passed the Act of Safety, which conferred on the King of Sweden the same powers which are enjoyed by the English crown, viz. that of making peace and war. At the same time they granted him liberal supplies, and raised the army to 50,000 men.

Act of Security (*The*), 1704. Passed by the Scotch parliament in the reign of Queen Anne, to the effect that 'unless a satisfactory settlement of the rights, liberties, and independence of Scotland should be obtained in the course of the present reign, the Scotch parliament would, on the queen's decease, meet and name a successor different from the person who succeeded to the English throne.' This led to the Act of National Union, which was ultimately carried 16 Jan., 1707. The first united parliament 23 Oct., 1707.

Act of Separation (*The*), 1843. A voluntary resignation of livings and professorships signed by 470 of the Scotch presbyters, who protested against any interference with the free choice of ministers by their respective congregations. *See* ' Free Church of Scotland.'

Act of Settlement (*The*). I. In 1653 an Act for the settlement of Irish confiscated estates. All Irish landowners charged with participation in the massacre of 1641 (*q.v.*) were absolutely deprived of all their lands. Those who had taken part with Charles in the civil war were deprived of two-thirds of their estates. The rest was partitioned among three classes of claimants, viz. the soldiers who had been in service before Cromwell arrived—the adventurers who had advanced money on the understanding that they were to be repaid in Irish land—and Cromwell's own army. A portion of Wicklow and its vicinity was assigned to the first of these, nine counties were

divided between the other two classes of claimants. Connaught was reserved for the Irish. The counties of Dublin, Kildare, Carlow, and Cork, with the lands of bishops, deans, and chapters, were kept at the disposal of parliament. One county was set aside for Cromwell himself.

II. In 1662 passed by the Irish parliament. First, all the confiscated lands of Ireland were vested in the hands of King Charles II., and were then confirmed to the adventurers and soldiers to whom they had been granted. All officers in the king's service before 1649 were to receive their arrears in land at the rate of 12*s.* 6*d.* in the pound. Protestants and innocent Papists, whose estates had been given to adventurers, were to have those estates restored, and the present holders were to be granted lands elsewhere of equal value. Those who had joined the king in exile were in like manner to be restored to their estates, and the present holders were to be 'reprised' by other holdings. *See* ' Settlement, Act of.'

When James II. landed in Ireland, one of his first acts was to abolish this Act of Settlement so as to displace the Protestant holders in favour of the Catholic claimants, 1689.

Act of Succession (*The*). I. A.D. 1534 (25 Hen. VIII. c. 22), ordaining that the succession should descend with the issue of Anne Boleyn ; thus setting aside Mary, the daughter of Katharine.

II. In 1537 (28 Hen. VIII. c. 7), by which both the preceding marriages of the king were declared void, and both Mary and Elizabeth were illegitimatised, the succession being fixed on the issue of Jane Seymour.

III. In 1701, whereby it was enacted that no Catholic should reign in England; and the succession was settled in the House of Hanover.

Act of Uniformity (*The*), 1661. An Act passed in the reign of Charles II. obliging all clergymen to subscribe to the Thirty-nine Articles, in order to secure uniformity of doctrine and discipline in the national religion. Upwards of 2,000 persons who had been ministers during the Commonwealth refused to subscribe, and either threw up their ' livings ' or were ejected from them.

Act of Union (*The*), 1648. French history. An agreement of all the parlements of France to stand fast by each other, and not suffer one parlement to be favoured more than the others. This Act was made by the lawyers because Mazarin had proposed to take back, for four years, the salaries of all the parlements except that of Paris. The object of Mazarin was to sow discord among the lawyers and then strip them of their prerogatives. This Act and the 'Arrèt' (*q.v.*) led to the Fronde war.

Act of 1870 (*The*). On the education of the children of the labouring classes. This was the first legislative provision for public elementary education in England and Wales. The Act of 1876 made it compulsory for every child to receive elementary education.

Acts of 1848 (*The*). In Hungarian history. The Acts passed into law the Hungarian ideas of liberty, fraternity, and equality. They passed the Diet without opposition, and were proclaimed at Presburg, April 11, amidst the wildest enthusiasm, in the presence of Kaiser Ferdinand V.

By these laws the privileges of the nobility were abolished, the soil was declared free, the right of free worship was accorded to all, liberty of the press was granted, and Transylvania was declared a part of the mother-country.

Acts and Opponencies abolished in the University of Cambridge, 1839. They used to be held in Latin, and in syllogistic form. A proposition was stated, as a major premise; a minor was added; and an inference drawn. The respondent denied one of the three. The opponent supported his proposition, which was again denied. This went on, say five times, and then the respondent stated the reasons of his denial. If satisfactory, the moderator complimented him with 'bene disputasti,' or 'optime disputasti,' or 'optime quidem disputasti.' If he argued badly or failed altogether, the moderator said 'descendas,' and no degree was conferred on him.

Acts of the Apostles. A book of the New Testament containing a record of what was done by the apostles between the ascension of Christ and the first imprisonment at Rome of the apostle Paul. A part of it is supposed to have been written by Luke, the evangelist, and all of it to have been edited by him. Rosenmüller says it was written about A.D. 65.

Acts of the Lords of the Council. Acts of committees of the Privy Council. If the sovereign is present the acts are called 'Orders in Council.'

Acta, in ancient Rome, were public registers kept by actuaries. In these registers were officially entered the acts of the public assemblies; the acts of the senate; the judgments of the law courts; the births, deaths, marriages, and divorces. Each register had its distinctive name, as *Acta Populi*, *Acta Senatus*, *Acta Urbana*, and so on.

Acta Diur'na. A gazette published daily in ancient Rome, both under the republic and the empire, containing an abstract of the proceedings of public assemblies and law courts, the punishment of offenders, public works, births, deaths, and marriages, and so on. Julius Cæsar, B.C. 59, had the proceedings of the senate published in the Acta Diurna, but Augustus repealed this rule. It was not finally discontinued till A.D. 328. The 'Blue Book' of old Rome has been appealed to by historians as of the highest authority (Suetonius, *In Cæsarem*, xx.).

Acta Pilati. An apocryphal report of the crucifixion, said to have been sent by Pilate to Tiberius. *See* 'Forgeries.'

Acta Sancto'rum. Many folio vols., containing, in Latin, the lives of Christian saints, and based on the *Acta Sincēra* of Héribert Rosweyde, on which he had laboured for twenty years. He died 1629, before it was printed. Father John Bolland (1596–1665) was entrusted with Rosweyde's collection, and associated with, himself ten others, who brought down the work to 1753, in 32 folio vols. This ended series 1.

In 1789 John Limpen and six others carried the work down to 1782, closing series 2.

A 3rd series was begun after the dispersion of the Jesuits, and five new vols. were added by John Baptist Fonson with four assistants, bringing down the hagiography to the year 1826, and completing the 53rd vol.

In 1837 a new society of Bollandists was organised under the sanction of the Belgian government, who brought the work down to 1855. In 1875 the 61st vol. was published and others have been added since.

There is a French hagiography, called *Les Petits Bollandistes*, in 17 large octavos, edited by Mgr. Paul Guérin, chamberlain to Leo XIII. The 7th edition was published in 1880. This compilation contains hundreds of lives not in the Latin books.

Acte Additionnel. *See* 'Additional Act,' 1815.

Pronounce Act Ad-dis'-se-o-nel.

Acte Constitutionnel (*L'*), June 24, 1793. Presented to the French nation by the Convention, and based on the 'sovereignty of the people and indivisibility of the Republic.'

Pronounce Act Con-sti-tu'-se-o-nel.

Ac'tiac War (*The*). This arose out of the rupture between Octavian and Antony, two of the Triumvirs (B.C. 33). Octavian declared war against Cleopatra, queen of Egypt, and defeated Antony at Actium, 2 Sept., B.C. 31. Both Cleopatra and Antony killed themselves. Alexandria was taken by Octavian Aug. 30 (B.C. 33), and Egypt was made a Roman province B.C. 30.

Ac'tian Years. Years in which the games at Actium were celebrated. These games were held by the Romans once in five years, and were instituted B.C. 30 by Augustus.

Actiat'ic Era (*The*). This era begins from the battle of Actium, between Antony and Octavian. The defeat of Antony made Octavian master of the Roman empire, 2 Sept., B.C. 31.

The era of Augustus was later by **four years** than the Actiatic era. It began B.C. 27.

Acton Burnel (*The Statute of*), 12 Oct., 1283. So called from the place of its enactment. It gave creditors their remedy by what is called 'Statute-merchant,' *i.e.* a bond of record under the hand and seal of the debtor, authenticated by the king's seal. If the debtor failed to pay on the date assigned, execution was summarily awarded. This was called *Pocket Judgment* (2 Edw. I.).

The Statute of Acton Burnel is sometimes called the Statute of Merchants (*Statutum Mercatorum*).

Adaman'tius. So Origen was called on account of his great perseverance and persistency (185–253).

Ad'amites (3 syl.), or Adam'ians. A fanatical sect of the second century, which wanted to revert to the life of Adam and Eve before the Fall. They rejected marriage and went about naked.

Ad'amites (*The*), or 'Brethren of the Free Spirit,' 15th and 16th cent. A religious sect that imitated Adam's nakedness before the fall, asserting that their redemption by Christ had restored their innocence. They met together quite naked to pray and preach, both men and women. This sect was propagated at Antwerp by one Tandemi, who drew after him 3000 followers; and in Bohemia by one Picard (St. Augustine, *De Hæres. et Isidor.* book viii. c. 5).

In *Notes and Queries*, Jan. 10, 1885, is given an extract of a Camisard prophetess, who, on Nov. 16 (no year stated, but about 1707), did strip quite naked, and after the ceremony of the mass, ran to the High Altar of Lincoln's Inn Fields, and in 'several strange and indecent postures . . . did hold forth in a powerful manner,' for about a quarter of an hour.

Adams Prize (*The*). For pure mathematics, astronomy, &c. Value 80*l.*; for any graduate of the University of Cambridge; awarded every two years. Founded from a fund raised by members of St. John's College in honour of Mr. Adams, who first discovered the planet Neptune, in 1848. *See* 'Regius Professor of Divinity.'

Ad'amus Magis'ter, Adam of Bremen, died 1076. He wrote a 'History of the Churches of Hamburg and Bremen' (from 788 to 1072).

Addenbrooke's Hospital. 120 beds and a children's ward. Founded, in Cambridge, by John Addenbrooke, M.D., fellow of Catharine Hall, 1766, and further endowed in 1813.

Pronounce Ad'-den-brook's.

Addison (*The American*); Joseph Dennie (1768–1812).

Addison (*The Spanish*), Benedict Jerome Feyjoo (1701–1764).

Addison of the North, Henry Mackenzie, author of the 'Man of Feeling' (1745–1831).

Addison's Disease. A bronzing of the skin which goes on till the patient assumes the appearance of a mulatto. It was first described by Dr. Thomas Addison of Guy's Hospital.

Additional Act (*An*), 1815. So Napoleon called his new constitution, granting freedom of election for the representatives, who were to be elected every five years, and to be paid stipends; it also provided for juries, for the right of petition, for freedom of worship, and for the inviolability of property.

Published April 25, 1815, and accepted at the *Champ de Mai*, May 31, 1815.

Addle Parliament (*The*). 5 April to 7 June, 1614. So called because it displayed a great spirit, pregnant with most momentous consequences, but did not pass one single bill. Its eggs were addled and produced no living creature. *See* 'Parliament.'

It remonstrated, for example, with the king (James I.) on his levying 'benevolences,' but passed no act to restrain or prevent the imposition in future.

Addressers, 1759. A knot of Irish commercial men who addressed the British Government for Catholic relief. The 'Address' was drawn up by Charles O'Conor, signed by 400 citizens of Dublin, and presented to the Speaker. The Speaker took the Address in silence, and the deputation retired. The Viceroy published it in the *Dublin Gazette*, the deputation was sent for again, and the Speaker thanked them for their Address. This being the first recognition of the Catholics, forms a political epoch in the history of Ireland.

In 1760 the Catholics drew up an 'Address' to King George III on his accession to the crown, praying for Catholic relief; and in 1793 the Catholic Relief Bill received the royal assent.

Adelantados Mayores, 1230. A new order of nobility created by Fernando III. of Castile and Leon, for the provinces of Spain, instead of counts and governors.

Pronounce Ad'-e-lan-tah'-doze May-or'-reez.

Adel'phi (*The*). A secret society of Piedmont, sprung out of the Carbonari, after the unsuccessful outbreak of 24 June, 1817.

Adiaphoristic Controversy (*The*), 1548. By what is called the 'Interim' (*q.v.*), Karl V. allowed the cup to the laity, and the clergy to marry. The Protestant party called a conference at Leipsic to consider this concession, and voted that it might serve its purpose in things *indifferent*, but did not touch upon points which were really essential. This decision caused a split in the Lutheran party, and the disputation which ensued between them was called the Adiaphoristic Controversy, or the controversy upon what the Leipsic conference called matters of indifference or of no moment. Vestments formed part of the controversy, and the famous Hooper lifted up his voice against 'Aaronical habits.'

Greek, *adiaphoros*, indifferent.

Ad'jutant-General. A military officer on the staff of the commander-in-chief, charged with all matters relating to the discipline and drill of the army.

Adju'tators, or 'Council of Adjutators,' 28 April, 1647. Two delegates from each of the eleven parliamentary regiments, summoned to a meeting at Triploe Heath, in lieu of the Council of Officers. This Council of Adjutators settled all questions of pay, disbanding, officers, and so on. It was also called the 'Council of Assistors;' and after their petition to Parliament (soon after the battle of Naseby), that Cromwell and his army should not be sent to Ireland, the Presbyterians called them the 'Council of Agitators,' which name they readily adopted. Charles I. addressed Cornet Joyce as 'Mr. Agitator Joyce,' when he came to remove him (the king) from Holmby House.

Ad'mirable (*The*), James Crichton, a Scotchman (1561–1582).

Admirable Doctor (*The*), or 'The Wonderful Doctor,' Roger Bacon, frequently called 'Friar Bacon,' born near Ilchester, in Somersetshire. He was a Franciscan, and one of the most learned men that ever lived. So great his knowledge, so numerous his discoveries, so wonderful his philosophical experiments, that he was condemned for necromancy by the Franciscan Council of Paris during his sojourn in France, and Pope Nicholas IV. commanded that he should be imprisoned. He was accordingly incarcerated at Paris from 1278 to 1289. Being released he returned to Oxford, where he died. (1214–1294.)

He has left several works behind him, which show a considerable acquaintance with the laws of mechanics, statics, optics, and the chemical properties of bodies. He was a good mathematician, and knew both Greek and Hebrew.

Admiral. The title of the highest class of British naval officer. Called a 'flag officer' from being entitled to fly a flag when in command of a squadron. Admirals formerly were distinguished by the colour of their flag, whether red, white, or blue, but these distinctions were abolished in 1864, and the ensign of all admirals is now white. There are, however, three grades, called admiral, vice-admiral, and rear-admiral. Admirals and vice-admirals must retire at the age of 65, and rear-admirals at 60.

The retiring pay of an admiral is 850*l*. per annum (30 years' service) ; half pay, 2*l*. 2*s*. a day.
The retiring pay of a vice-admiral is 725*l*. per annum (29 years' service); half pay, 1*l*. 12*s*. 6*d*. a day.
The retiring pay of a rear-admiral is 600*l*. per annum (27 years' service) ; half pay 1*l*. 5*s*. a day.
N.B.—Admirals of the fleet retire at the age of 70, and their half pay is 3*l*. 7*s*. a day.

Admiralty Court (*The*), or 'High Court of Admiralty.' Erected by Edward III. about 1350. Held before the Lord High Admiral or his deputy. There used to be two courts, viz., the Instance Court, and the Prize Court. The former was a municipal tribunal for the determination of private injuries or private rights arising at sea, or intimately connected with maritime subjects. The latter decided all matters of capture, prizes, reprisals, and so on, which were all submitted to the Admiralty laws and the law of nations. The prize court was virtually abolished by 3, 4 Vict. c. 65, s. 22 (1840), and great changes were made in 1861 and 1875.

Admiralty Droits. Derelict ships and other property picked up at sea by British vessels, if not claimed. These perquisites were formerly claimed by the Lord High Admiral; but by the Merchant Shipping Act (1854) are now placed under the control of the Board of Trade, by which all the proceeds are now paid into the public exchequer.

Seizures of property belonging to an enemy in time of war are deemed droits of Admiralty.

Admiralty Office (*The*), 1512. Instituted by Henry VIII.; business regulated by 2 Will. IV. c. 40 (1832).

Admonition of Parliament (*The*), or 'The Admonition to the Parliament,' 1571, by certain puritans in the reign of Queen Elizabeth, condemning everything in the Church of England not in accordance with Calvinism. This admonition condemned every rite and ceremony not expressly commanded in Scripture, and set at naught all general rules and church canons.

The two fundamental principles of the Admonition were these: (1) We ought to have the same kind of church government as that of the Apostolic times, to be gathered from Scripture, and Scripture only. (2) Nothing used in the Church of Rome may in any wise be continued. Wilcox and Field, the supposed authors, were imprisoned. A second Admonition by Carter called forth a reply by Archbishop Whitgift.

Admonitionists (*The*), 1571. Certain puritans in the reign of Queen Elizabeth, authors of the 'Admonition of Parliament' (*q.v.*).

Pronounce Ad-mo-nish'-shun-ists.

Adop'tian Controversy (*The*). A controversy which arose in Spain in the 8th cent., whether Jesus Christ was the Son of God by generation, or by adoption only. Elipand archbishop of Toledo, and Felix bishop of Urgel, maintained that Jesus Christ had two distinct natures, one divine and the other human. In his divine nature he is the Son of God by generation, the 'only begotten of the Father;' but in his human nature he is the Son of God by adoption only (Rom. viii. 29). Alcuin took the orthodox side. Two synods were convened on the subject : one at Ratisbon in 792, and the other at Frankfort in 794, in which Adoptianism was pronounced heretical. Duns Scotus and Durandus were Adoptianists.

Adop'tianists (*The*). 'Adoptians,' or 'Adoptiani,' 8th cent. Spanish heretics who maintained that Christ was the Son of God only by adoption. This heresy was condemned at the Synod held at Frankfort in A.D. 794.

Ador'ni and Frego'si Contests (*The*). In Genoa, 1360–1527, contests between the two powerful families of Gabriele Adorno and Domenico da Fregoso, who contended for the chief magistracy. Adorno was appointed doge and deposed, then Fregoso was appointed doge and deposed, and so it went on till 12 Sept. 1527, when Andrea Doria gave Genoa a new constitution.

Adrianites (4 syl.). Followers of Adrian Hamstedius (16th cent.). They held that the body of Christ was formed entirely of the substance of the Virgin mother.

The followers of Simon Magus are also called Adrianites.   Pronounce A'-dre-an-ites.

Adrianople, Peace of (*The*), Sept. 14, 1829. A treaty between Russia and Turkey. The war preceding this treaty was the most disastrous in which Turkey had ever been engaged, and the treaty added large territories to Russia. It acquired Anäpa and Poti, with a considerable extent of coast on the Black Sea, a portion of the pashalik of Akhilska, with the two fortresses of Akhilska and Akhilkillak, and in many other ways greatly weakened Turkey. As Lord Aberdeen said in his despatch, it gave Russia the control of Asia Minor, and the keys to the Persian and Turkish provinces whenever she may choose to extend her conquests to Teheran (Ta-rain) or to Constantinople.

Advent Sundays. Instituted 567, by the Council of Tours, to commemorate the four Advents of Christ—

1. His advent to Bethlehem, where He was born.

2. His advent to Jerusalem, where He was crucified.

3. His advent into man's heart when he believes and receives Him as a Saviour.

4. His advent in the clouds when He comes to judge the world. *See* 'Sundays.'

Adventure Bay (S.E. of Tasmania). So called by Captain Furneaux, from the ship *Adventure* in which he sailed, 1773.

Adventurers. I. 1641-1650, persons who had adventured money for the reduction of Ireland during the rebellion. Those who adventured 200*l.* were to have 1,000 acres in Ulster. Those who adventured 300*l.* were to have 1,000 acres in Connaught. Those who subscribed 450*l.* were to have 1,000 acres in Munster, and those who subscribed 600*l.* were to have 1,000 acres in Leinster.

II. 1652, those soldiers who had served in Ireland since the landing of Cromwell in 1649, and were entitled to a share of the lands in lieu of their arrears of pay.

Adversity Hume. Joseph Hume, M.P. (1777-1855). So called because he was for ever presaging the ruin of Great Britain. 'Prosperity Robinson, M.P., just before the commercial crisis of 1825, boasted that the country was never in a more prosperous condition. Cobbett gave Robinson his sobriquet, and that of Hume followed naturally.

Advocate (*Lord*). About 1500, the principal public prosecutor in Scotland. He is assisted by a solicitor-general and

four junior counsel (termed 'advocates depute'). Virtually he is secretary of state for Scotland.

Pronounce Ad'-vo-kate.

Advocates' Library (*The*), Edinburgh, 1682. By the copyright law of 1709 it obtained the privilege of receiving gratuitously a copy of every new book. This magnificent library belongs to the Faculty of Advocates (*q.v.*), and was established by Sir George Mackenzie.

It contains about 170,000 books, and of course the number increases every year.

Advoca'tus Diab'oli. One appointed to advance every conceivable reason why a person whose name is submitted for canonisation should not be admitted into the calendar of the saints.

Advowson ('Advocatio'). The right of presentation to a living. Advowsons were originally vested in those laymen who were founders or benefactors of livings; but at the dissolution of the monasteries in the reign of Henry VIII. livings were given to laymen who took the tithes and appointed vicars to represent the patrons. These vicars were paid stipends, generally 'the small tithes.' By sales the right of presentation to livings has passed into private hands.

Ægine'tan Standard (*The*). That is, the standard of weights and measures used in the island of Ægina, and introduced into Greece by Periander of Corinth (B.C. 665, 625-585).

A, E, I, O, U. The five vowels, adopted by Friedrich III., second of the Habsburg dynasty, for the imperial device: Austria Est Imperare Orbi Universo (or Imperatura). *In German:* Alles Erdreich Ist Oesterreich Unterthan.

In 1866, after the seven-weeks' war with Prussia, Austria was denuded of Germany, and in 1870 the king of Prussia became the emperor of Germany. Then the famous anagram might have been inscribed on the conqueror's banners, Austria's Empire Is Overthrown Utterly.

Æ'lian and Fuf'ian Law (*The*), B.C. 156, in ancient Rome, empowering magistrates to prevent or dissolve comitia when the auspices were unpropitious.

Æ'lian Sen'tian Law (*The*), B.C. 3, regulating the manumission of slaves.

Æmil'ian Laws (*The*). These were (1) the law by Mamercus Æmilius, dictator of Rome, to shorten the censors' term of office, B.C. 434.

And (2) the sumptuary laws of Marcus Æmilius (Scaurus), relative to the kind and quantity of food to be set on table at entertainments, B.C. 115.

Æmil'ian Road (The), between Bononia (Bologna) and Placentia; made by Marcus Æmilius Lepidus, the consul, B.C. 187. It was a continuation of the Flaminian Way.

Æolian Poets. See 'Lesbian Poets.'

Æo'lians (The) had for their possession the plain land of Thessaly, with Phocis, Bœotia, part of Peloponnesus (i.e. Arcadia and the parts near), and their colony in Asia Minor.

In Asia Minor they founded Lesbos, Smyrna, and Ælis.

Æol'ic Migration (The). In the mythic period of Greek history. According to mythic history, Æŏlos was the eldest son of Hellen and grandson of Deucalion. He spread his ancestral name through the greater part of northern Greece and along the western coast of the peninsula. In the 11th cent. B.C. some of them migrated to Asia Minor, where they founded, on the north-west coast, above thirty cities. They were ultimately absorbed in the Roman Empire.

Æra or A.E.R.A, Annus Erat (or Est) Regni Augusti. The Spaniards began their dates from the advent of the reign of Augustus, the Roman Emperor. See 'Era.'

Ae'rians or 'Aeria'ni.' A religious sect, founded by Aërius, a priest, in the 4th cent. In doctrine they corresponded with the Arians, but they also maintained that all priests are bishops. Their great 'heresy,' however, was forbidding masses for the dead.

Pronounce A-ē-ri-ah'-ne.

Aeroliths or Aerolites.

Pronounce Air'-ro-lites.

B.C. 654, a shower of stones fell on the Alban Mount (Livy).

B.C. 467, a great stone fell at Ægospotămi, on the Hellespont (Parian Chronicle). Pliny says it was about the size of a waggon.

A.D. 1492, Nov. 7, a ponderous stone, weighing 250 lbs., fell from the sky near the town of Ensisheim, in Upper Alsace. A part of it is still preserved in the parish church. The Emperor Maximilian witnessed the fall of this meteor, and had the stone placed in the church to prove that 'God insisted on a crusade against the Turks.'

A.D. 1510 there was a great fall of meteors in Lombardy, some 60 lbs. in weight, and some as much as 120 lbs. They were of a rusty colour.

A.D. 1627, Nov. 27, a stone weighing 59 lbs. fell on Mount Vassier, in Provence. This is attested by Gassendi.

A.D. 1751, May 26. Two masses fell at Agram, in Sclavonia, one weighing 16 lbs. and the other 71 lbs. The analysis of these stones by Klaproth is preserved in the Vienna museum (95 parts are iron, 3 nickel).

A.D. 1803, April 26. A shower of stones fell near L'Aigle. M. Biot was deputed by the French Government to repair to the spot and report on the phenomenon. Between 2,000 and 3,000 stones had fallen, the largest being 17 lbs. in weight.

A.D. 1807, March 13. A stone fell at Smolensk, in Russia, weighing 160 lbs. It was black and shiny.

A.D. 1813, Sept. 10. A stone, weighing 17 lbs., fell in the county of Limerick, at 10 o'clock in the morning.

A.D. 1815, Feb. 15. A stone weighing 25 lbs. fell in the town of Dooralla, in British India. The Indians consecrated it in a temple, and approach it with reverence and clasped hands.

A.D. 1822, June 2, Sunday, 3 o'clock p.m. I myself saw an aërolith fall at Gislingham, Suffolk. It made a deep hole in the earth about 3 yards from a wheat stack. It then bounded off in an opposite direction to the stack and burst. It fell with a tremendous noise, like crashing thunder. I was too young at the time to search for pieces, and not a little terrified. The window I was sitting at was some 20 yards off.

In the Imperial Museum of St. Petersburg is an immense mass. The fall was witnessed by Pallas in Siberia.

The largest aërolith known is one which fell in Brazil. It is estimated to weigh 14,000 lbs.

A.D. 1887. An aërolith fell near St. Joseph, in the West Indies. It weighs 2 tons (i.e. 2,280 lbs.), and buried itself in the earth between 15 and 18 feet.

J. Norman Lockyer says ,the number of meteors which fall daily to the earth 'exceeds twenty-one millions.'—Nineteenth Century (Nov. 1889, p. 787).

Æschylos (The French). Prosper de Crébillon (1674–1762), noted for his power in depicting rage and terror. His plays are 'Xerxes,' 'Semiramis,' 'Electra,' 'Pyrrhus,' and 'Catiline.'

Pronounce Eas'-ki-lus.

Æto'lian Confederacy (The), B.C. 323, called into existence by the Lamian war (q.v.). The states used to assemble annually in the autumn at Thermum, and the assembly was called the Panætolicon. B.C. 189 the Ætolian States were subjected to the Romans.

The object of the Lamian war was (on the death of Alexander the Great) to liberate Greece from Macedonia. The Athenians were the principal insurgents, but were defeated in 322 at Cranon, by Antipater.

Æto'lian League (The). Ætolia joined the Greek confederates in the Lamian War B.C. 313, but the Ætolian League rose into no great prominence till the Macedonian War (B.C. 214), when Sparta joined it, and it became the antagonist of the Achæan League, which sided with Philip V. of Macedon. It was the unwise policy of the Ætolian League which made Rome master of Greece.

The Ætolian Confederacy included Ætolia, Acarnania, part of Thessaly, Locris, and the island of Cephalonia.

Affshars (*The*). An eastern tribe known by the celebrated Nadir-shah, who received the crown of Persia on condition that he would compel the people to abandon the doctrines of the Sophi, and receive those of the Sonnee. After a reign of 11 years he was assassinated.

Afghan (*Treaty of*), 1881. A secret treaty between Russia and the amîr of Afghanistan. Russia on her side engaged to be the perpetual friend of the amîr, to recognise the successor appointed by the amîr, and to assist the amîr against any of his foes, if such assistance was required (the English were meant). The amîr, on his part, engaged not to wage any war without permission from Russia, and to keep Russia well informed of whatever took place within the kingdom of Afghanistan.

Afghan War (*The*). A diplomatic contest between France and Russia induced Dost Mohammed of Cabul to invite the friendship of Great Britain in 1836. This led to a diplomatic contest between Great Britain and Russia respecting Afghanistan. Dost Mohammed joined Persia, and war was proclaimed against him at Simla by Lord Auckland, governor-general of India, 1 Oct., 1838. Dost Mohammed gave himself up at Cabul to Sir W. MacNaghten, 3 Nov., 1840; but his son Akbar Khan completely outwitted General Elphinstone and the envoy, Sir William MacNaghten, both of whom were treacherously put to death. Negotiations for quitting Cabul were purposely delayed till winter had set in; and then the whole British force, which, with women and children, amounted to 20,000 souls, were as treacherously destroyed in the Khyber Pass, 1842.

No event in British history is more deplorable than this. The total incompetency of such men as General Elphinstone and Sir William MacNaghten so demoralised the soldiers under them, that every Englishman is ashamed of the miserable fiasco in which was not one single redeeming trait. Dost Mohammed and Akbar Khan, no doubt, were villains, but our 'leaders' actually invited treasonable dealings.

African Methodist Episcopal Church (*The*), 1816, seceded in Philadelphia under Richard Allen. They are coloured Methodists.

African Paris (*The*). Algiers.

African War (*The*). The *first* African war was undertaken by the Romans for the restoration of Hiempsal to the throne of Numantia. Ahenobarbus, the leader of the Marian party in Africa, had dethroned him, but Cneius Pompey slew Ahenobarbus, and restored Hiempsal B.C. 81.

The *second* African war was between Cæsar and Scipio, B.C. 46. Cæsar defeated the party of Pompey at Thapsus, in Africa, and thus put an end to the civil war.

The *third* African war was undertaken by the Romans against Tacfarînas, a Numidian, in the reign of Tiberius. Tacfarinas, having collected a large gang of freebooters, defied for some years the Roman arms in Numidia, but was ultimately overthrown and slain by Dolabella, A.D. 17–24.

The *fourth* African war was between the Romans and Vandals in Africa. The Vandals under Genseric took possession of the Roman dominions in Africa, and continued masters for 105 years (A.D. 429–534). Belisarius was sent into Africa by the emperor Justinian to win back the African dominions, and he utterly overthrew the Vandals, took Carthage in 533, and returned to Rome in triumph in the autumn of the year following, A.D. 534.

Africa'nus. Three of the Scipios were so called from their African conquests: (1) Publius Cornelius Scipio Africanus Major, B.C. 234–183; (2) Publius Cornelius Scipio Africanus, his elder son; and (3) Lucius Cornelius Scipio Africanus, younger brother of No. 2.

Africa'nus (*The Arabian*). Akbar Khan (7th cent.).

Africa'nus cf New Rome (*The*). Belisarius, Roman general in the reign of Justinian (505–565). He is called 'The Third Africanus.'

If the three Scipios were all called Africanus, Belisarius was the fourth, not the third.

Aftas'ides (3 syl.). A dynasty founded by Abdallah ben al Aftas about 1030; overthrown 26 Feb., 1094.

Agamemnon, Menela'os. Atreus had two sons—Plisthenês and Thyestês.

(Thyestês usurped the throne of Argos).

Plisthenês had two sons—Agamemnon and Menelaos.

Agamemnon married Clytemnestra, daughter of Tyndáros.
Menelaos married Helen, sister of Clytemnestra.

The two brothers married two sisters. Both the wives were false. Clytemnestra became the mistress of the regent Ægisthos, and Helen eloped with Paris, son of Priam king of Troy.

Ag'apæ. Originally love feasts, in which contributions for the poor brethren were made. These feasts were held after the communion service. Afterwards, they were degraded into wakes, took the place of the heathen Parentalia, and were held at the tombs of relatives or 'saints.' Great efforts were made to abolish these unseemly gatherings, but they continued even into the 13th cent.

Enjoined by the council of Gangra, A.D. 340; forbidden by the council of Laodicea in 366; by the council of Carthage in 397; by the council of Orleans in 533; and by the council of Aix-la-Chapelle in 816. The last mention of them is in 1250.

Agapem'one (The abode of love), in Somersetshire, 1848. Founded by Henry James Prince and a Mr. Starkey, and hence the members are called Princeites, Starkeyites, and Agapemonians. The object of this abode is perpetual joy. Pain and grief, sorrow and sickness should be banished from the abode. The Princeites are taught perfect resignation, and Prince himself tells us, 'He has no wish, no desire, no will of his own at all.' *See* 'Princeites.'

Agapemo'nians (*The*); **Agapemo'nianism.** The Agapemonians are those who dwell in Agapemonè, and Agapemonianism is their special views, social, moral, and religious.

Agape'tæ, 3rd cent. Certain ascetics who lived together as man and wife, but preserved a life of celibacy. St. Cyprian (200–258) condemned the practice, and the church generally did the same, though several of these Agapetæ are enrolled among the saints, as Cecilia and Valerian, Gombert and Bertha, Injurieux and Scholastica, Jeanne Marie de Maillé and Robert de Sillery, Julian and Basilissa, Thierry and his wife, &c.

Du Cange says (vol. i. p. 129, col. 1): So called, 'quod cum mulieribus ac virginibus, quas domi sub *agapetarum* seu dilectarum appellatione detinebant, prava commercia habere dicerentur.'

Age of Leo X. (*The*), 1513–1521. A proverbial phrase for magnificence and high art. Leo X. was a great patron of learning and art, and his court was magnificent in the highest degree.

Agents of Captain Right. *See* under ' Whiteboys.'

Ages. The Golden Age, a mythical period when the earth brought forth spontaneously, and the gods held converse with men.

The Silver Age, the second period, when the gods taught men the useful arts.

The Age of Bronze, the third or transition period, semi-historical. The age of heroes. It followed the 'Stone Age' (*q.v.*).

The Iron Age, the historic period, when wars abound, and man earns his food by labour.

The Wire Age, the present age of telegraphs and telephones.

Aggregate Bodies, 1785. Irish volunteers in favour of free trade, and the extension of the franchise to the people at large. Some of them adopted the American fashion of tarring and feathering their victims; and some, calling themselves 'houghers,' deliberately maimed their victims, especially the soldiers. The introduction of the question of Catholic disabilities broke up the associations. As Plowden says, ' at night they existed with all their attributes of power . . . but on the following day the room of their assembly was shut, their colours waved no more, their uniform was no longer seen in the streets, and the body was disbanded.' *See* 'Irish Associations.'

Ag'idæ (*Dynasty of the*), B.C. 1058–219. One of the dynasties of Sparta; the other was the dynasty of the Proclidæ. They were contemporaneous. The former was founded by Agis, son of Eurysthenes; and the latter by Proclês, son of Aristodēmos. These dynastic kings were followed in B.C. 219 by the 'Tyrants,' viz.—Lycurgos, 219; Machanïdas, 210; and Nabis, 216.

Agiosemandrum. A wooden instrument used in Christian churches in Turkey instead of a bell; because the use of bells in Turkey is forbidden.

Greek *agios semaino*, meaning the holy (service) caller. Incorrectly, but generally spelt *sy*.
Pronounce Ag'gi-os'sy-man'-drum.

Agitator (*The*). Daniel O'Connell (1775–1847). He began agitating for the Repeal of the Union in 1842, and the 'Monster Meeting' was held in 1843. He was arrested for sedition and convicted, but the judgment was reversed by the House of Lords (1844).

Agitators (*The*). The committee appointed in 1647 to manage the affairs of the army when it formed a separate body in the state. The committee consisted of two of the superior officers of each of the eleven parliamentary regiments. The secret object of the council was to get possession of the person of the king (Charles I.), and withdraw him from the power of the Parliament. Cornet Joyce was one of these agitators, and, at the head of fifty horse, actually took possession of the king at Holmby House. The real appellation of this committee was the Council of Adjutators or Assistors, but the Presbyterians nicknamed them the Council of Agitators, which they readily adopted.

Ag'labites (3 syl.). Califs of Kairwan, so called from Ibrahim ibn el Aglab, who was invested with the government by Harun al Raschid, A.D. 800. He made himself independent in 802, and founded the dynasty of the Aglabites.

Succeeded by Abu l'Abbas (811); Ziadet Allah (815); Abu Akkal (827); Abdul Abbas (837); Abu Ishak Ibrahim (874); Abd ul Abbas II., murdered by his son and successor, Ziadet Allah (906); dynasty overthrown A.D. 909.

Ag'noites or '**Agnoitæ**' (3 syl.). I. A.D. 370, followers of Theophronius the Cappadocian, who denied the omniscience of God.

II. A.D. 535, followers of Themistius, deacon of Alexandria, who denied that Christ knew the time of the day of judgment. 'Of that day and that hour knoweth no man, no, not the angels which are in heaven, neither the Son, but the Father [only].' (Mark xiii. 32.) They die out before 700.

Du Cange says (vol. i. p. 137, col. 1) 'quod novissimam horam Christo, etiam quoad divinam ejus naturam, ignotam esse arbitrarentur.'

Agnos'tic (*An*), 1885. One who maintains that there are subjects wholly beyond the scope of human thought; not subjects now unknown, but subjects actually unknowable. On the other hand, an agnostic repudiates the belief that there are propositions which men ought to believe without such logical evidence.

Agnosticism. The faith of an agnostic. The refusal to say that we know or believe what we have no scientific or experimental grounds for professing to believe or know.

Agnostics are not atheists, because they believe the question of God's existence unfathomable, and the question of his non-existence equally so. Man, they say, has no means of knowing either the one or the other. Human knowledge cannot go beyond human observation and experience. The term 'agnostic' was introduced by Professor Huxley in 1869 at a private meeting preliminary to the formation of the Metaphysical Society. Plato said, 'Speculations about the gods are speculations of man respecting the gods.'

Agonalia. A Roman festival held several times a year in honour of the guardian deities of the state. So called from Agonius, the god who presided over business. (Ovid, *Fasti* i. 331.)

Agrarian Agitation, B.C. 480. The great Roman agrarian agitation was set on foot by Spurius Cassius, who had been three times consul. To win popular favour, he told the people that the senate ought to give an account of the land taken from the Volsci, which ought to have been equally divided amongst the whole people irrespective of rank. The senate, to allay the popular clamour, promised to give the matter their best consideration, but arrested Cassius and hurled him from the Tarpeian rock. Things went on till B.C. 464, when Herdonius the Sabine got possession of the Capitol. Then the senate promised to pass an agrarian law, if the people would eject the invaders. The invaders were expelled, but it was not till B.C. 365 that Licinius Stolo, the plebeian tribune, got a law passed making it penal for anyone to hold more than 500 acres of the public lands.

Agreement of the People (*The*), 1647. A paper drawn up by the Levellers and presented to the Council of Agitators or Adjutators, for the abolition of kings and lords; biennial parliaments with six-monthly sessions; a widely-extended franchise, and a more equal distribution of representation. *See* 'Lilburne.'

'Biennial parliaments with six-monthly sessions' means the parliament was to meet for six months every two years, the other eighteen months were to be wholly under the control of the Executive Council. In 1649 Colonel John Lilburne objected to this clause, and said it was not agreed to by the people at all.

Agriculture.

The *Board of Agriculture* was incorporated in 1793, and dissolved in 1816.

The *Report* of Children's Employment Commission on Agricultural Gangs was published in 1867, and their employment was regulated by Act of Parliament the same year.

The *Royal Agricultural College* at Cirencester was chartered in 1845, and opened in 1846.

The *Royal Agricultural Society* was incorporated by charter in 1840.

The *Scotch* Society, called 'Improvers of Agriculture in Scotland,' was established in 1723.

Minister of Agriculture appointed 1889.

Agricultural Protection Society of Great Britain (*The*),

17 Feb., 1844. Founded in opposition to the Anti-Corn-Law League to advocate protection in opposition to free trade.

Agrippa. Son of Aristobūlus, who was the son of Herod the Great and his second wife Mariamne the Asmonēan. It was this grandson of Herod the Great who was made king by Caligula. He slew James the apostle. His *son*, also named Agrippa, went with his sister Berenīcē to hear Paul's defence.

Ahab of the Nation (*The*). Charles I. was so called by the Levellers.

Aids. Sums to be paid by the tenant to ransom his lord if taken prisoner, or to make his lord's eldest son a knight, or to dower at marriage the lord's eldest daughter. Subsequently aids were exacted to pay a lord's debts, or to enable a lord to pay aids to his own superior lord. Of course, those who held immediately of the king could never be called upon for this last-named contribution. Introduced by William the Conqueror, and abolished by 12 Car. II. c. 24.

Ainaly-Cavak (*Treaty of*), Jan. 8, 1784, between Turkey and Russia, whereby the Ottoman Porte abandoned the Crimēa and Kuban to Russia.

Ainslie's Supper, 1566. A supper given at Ainslie's tavern in Edinburgh by the Earl of Bothwell, at the rising of parliament, to its leading members. After the banquet Bothwell informed his guests that he was about to marry the widowed Queen Mary; and drawing forth a bond, he induced them to sign their full and entire approval of the alliance, although at the time he was married to Jane Gordon.

The tavern itself was afterwards called 'Ainslie's Supper.'

Aix-la-Chapelle (*Congress of*), from 14 Feb. to 24 Nov., 1818. To settle the affairs of Europe after the restoration of the Bourbons.

Aix-la-Chapelle (*Convention of*), 30 Nov., 1818. For the evacuation of France by the Allies. It was signed by the plenipotentiaries Oct. 9, and ratified by France Oct. 13.

Aix-la-Chapelle (*Peace of*), 2 May, 1668. Between Louis XIV. and Carlos II. respecting the Spanish Netherlands.

Aix-la-Chapelle (*Treaty of*), 1748. Between George II., Louis XV., Maria Theresa of Austria, Ferdinand VI., Charles Emmanuel III., the Republic of Genoa, and the United Provinces. Signed by England, France, and the United Provinces, 18 Oct.; by Spain, 20 Oct.; by Austria, 23 Oct.; by Modēna, 25 Oct.; by Genōa, 28 Oct.; by Sardinia 7 Nov. (1748). It was a mere truce forced on the signatories by sheer exhaustion. France still contemplated the humiliation of England; the 'Family Compact' was still maintained; Maria Theresa had still designs on Silesia. In 1755 a leagúe was secretly formed between Russia, Spain, Austria, and France for the renewal of war on the first favourable occasion; and, in 1756, the 'Seven Years' War' began.

Ajax of the East (*The*). Leo, appointed by the eunuch Eutropius to the command of the Asiatic army; called the Ajax of the East from the bulk of his body and the dulness of his mind. He was originally a wool-comber.

Akerman, in Bessarabia (*Treaty of*), 26 Oct. (4 Sept.), 1826. Between Russia and Turkey, placing Moldavia, Valachia, and Servia under the protection of Russia. This was to secure the fulfilment of the treaty of Bucharest.

Akh'shidites (3 syl.). An Egyptian dynasty, generally called 'The dynasty of the Ikhshidites,' founded by Abu Bekr Mohammed Akhshid, or Ikhshid, A.D. 936. The dynasty was overthrown in 970 by the Fatimite general Goher.

Alabama. An American state, so named, in 1817, from its principal river. The river was so called by the Indians in allusion to the well-stocked hunting-grounds. The name is properly that of an Indian band, or tribe, of the Muscogee stock.

Pronounce Al'-a-bah'-mah.

Alaba′ma (*The*). A vessel built by Messrs. Laird of Birkenhead, and known as 'No. 290.' On 31 July, 1862, it sailed surreptitiously from the Mersey and proceeded to Terceira, one of the Western islands, where she was supplied with guns, coals, and stores by a vessel sent from London for the purpose. Captain Semmes then took charge of her, named her the 'Alabama,' and hoisted the Confederate flag. She committed great damage to the American shipping, capturing 65 vessels, and destroying property to the amount of four million dollars; but in June 1864 she was sunk near Cherbourg by the United States steamer 'Kearsage.' In 1871 it was agreed to refer the question to five arbitrators, who were to decide if the English Government were responsible, and if so, what fine was to be paid by England for the damage done to the United States of North America.

Alaba'ma Claims (*The*), 1868. A money demand made by the United States of America on Great Britain for damage done by a corvette named the 'Alabama,' and built at Birkenhead for the Confederates, who were at war with the United States. The British Government, which had declared itself a neutral power, had forbidden the corvette to leave the docks; but, notwithstanding this prohibition, it put to sea, displaying a British flag, and succeeded in destroying 65 of the United States vessels; but in 1864 it encountered the 'Kearsage' off Cherbourg, and was sunk. After the war, the United States demanded compensation, and five arbitrators met at Geneva to consider the question in 1872. The sentence of these arbitrators was to award damages to the amount of 3,250,000*l.*, with interest in settlement of the American claims. The money was duly paid, and a large surplus remained in the hands of the American Government after all recognised claims had been paid in full. *See* 'Alexandra.'

The arbitrators were the king of Italy, the President of the Swiss Confederation, the Emperor of Brazil, a representative of Great Britain, and another of the United States.

Alba Comiti'va. A free company of English, also called 'Les Tards Venus,' *q.v.*

Alban Hall (*St.*), Oxford, 1549; founded by Robert de St. Alban. The head of the Hall is called the principal.

Al'bany or Albyn. The ancient name of Scotland; a corrupt spelling of Albanigh, connected with the word *Alps,*

and meaning hilly or mountainous. The Romans called the south part Caledonia. The west, now called Argyllshire, was colonised by the Scoti of Ulster, and these Irish Scots, in the time of their chief, Kenneth Macalpine, having conquered the Picts who occupied the eastern parts, added that portion to his dominion, and called the two Scot-land (*q.v.*).

Al'bany, New York, North America. So called in honour of James, duke of York and Albany (afterwards James II.), to whom Charles II. gave the proprietorship of the colony.

Alba'ti (*The*), 1399. A class of hermits who dressed in white linen. Pope Boniface IX. fancied their leader aimed at his deposition, and put him to death.

Albe or Albane'ser. Lord Byron was so called. A correspondent in 'Notes and Queries' (March 28, 1887, p. 425) says: 'Madame Cottin wrote a romance entitled "Claire d'Albé." This romance was well known to Shelley, who induced his first wife to translate it into English.' May not the intimacy between Claire and Byron have suggested the application of Albé to Lord Byron?

Mr. Forman suggests L-B (Lord Byron). Others fancy it is a contraction of Albe-marle (Street), the place of business of Murray, his lordship's publisher.

Albert I. (Albrecht I.). One of the promiscuous kings of Germany (1248, 1298–1308), son of Rudolf I. of Habsburg. In this reign is placed the tale of William Tell.

Albert (Albrecht) **II.** Founder of the present line of Austrian emperors, and first of the House of Habsburg (1394, 1438–1439), son of Albert IV., duke of Austria, and son-in-law of Siegmund, the preceding kaiser-king. He was surnamed 'the Illustrious,' 'the Magnanimous,' and 'the Grave,' but reigned only about a year and a half. Like his next two successors, Frederick III. and Maximilian, he died of dysentery brought on by eating too freely of melon.

Albert (Albrecht) the Bear, so called because his cognisance was a bear. He was a fine tall fellow with a quick eye, and so well featured that he was familiarly called 'the handsome.' He was the first margraf of Brandenburg (1106–1170).

C

Albert the Bear died the same year as Thomas Becket did.

Albertus Magnus (1193–1280), bishop of Ratisbon. A marvellous man, whose literary works cover 21 folio volumes. Thomas Aquinas was his pupil. He made a speaking head of brass, and his knowledge of chemistry was ascribed to the black art. He was the founder of the Second Age of Scholastic Philosophy, or the Aristotelian school.

Albigen′ses (*The*), 11th and 12th cent. Reformers or ‘heretics’ of mid-France, so called from Albi or Albigia, where their tenets were first condemned, in 1176. They were defended by Count Raymond of Toulouse, Roger viscount of Beziers, and the Counts of Foix and of Béarn. Alexander III. excommunicated them in 1179, and Innocent III. organised a crusade against them in 1204. It is said that 60,000 were massacred in 1209. Another crusade against them was set on foot in 1219.

The Waldenses should not be confounded with the Albigenses, although many of their religious views were the same; but the Waldenses rose in the 9th cent. under the teaching of Claudius of Turin. The peculiar faith of the Albigenses was that God the Father created the first matter; but the Evil Principle arranged it and stamped every created thing with all their present forms and attributes.

Albigen′ses (*Wars with the*). The first, 1209–1229, set on foot by Philippe Auguste of France. The second, 1226, prompted by Pope Honorius III. and set on foot by Louis VIII., called the Lion. The third, 1545–1547, set on foot by François I. of France. In the last war John, baron of Oppido, cut them off root and branch.

Alcacebas (*Treaty of*). Between Isabella of Castile and Alfonso V. of Portugal; signed at Alcacebas, in Estremadura, Sept. 24, 1479.

Alcan′tara (*Knights of*), 1212. A Spanish order, so called by Alfonso IX., king of Castile, from the city of Alcantara. It was founded in 1156 by Don Suarez and Don Gomez, but called by them ‘Knights of the Pear-tree’; which was changed in 1176 by San Julian del Pereyro into ‘Knights of San Julian.’

Alcibi′ades of Germany (*The*). Albrecht, margraf of Baireuth (1522–1555).

Aldermen. Since the Municipal Corporations Act (*q.v.*) in 1835, one third of the councillors are elected aldermen, but they are not eligible for the offices of coroner or recorder, and are exempted from serving on juries. They hold office for six years, one-half going out every three years.

Since 1889 aldermen are chosen by the new organisation called the County Council (*q.v.*), and hold office for six years in the Council. The councillors are in office for three years only, and are elected like members of parliament.

Aldine Editions. A series of books published by Aldo Manuzio (Aldus Manutius) between 1490 and 1597. During this period 908 books, chiefly Greek and Latin classics, with carefully corrected texts of Boccaccio, Dante, Petrarch, and other Italian authors, were issued. Aldo was the first to use the Italian type. His mark is an anchor entwined by a dolphin. Pickering, a London publisher, published an edition of the British poets, which he called the Aldine (2 syl.).

Aldrich′ian Professorships (*The*). One for anatomy, one for the practice of medicine, and one for chemistry, in the University of Oxford, founded by George Aldrich, M.D., in 1798.

That for anatomy is now annexed to the Linacre professorship of physiology; that for the practice of medicine is attached to the Regius professorship of medicine; and that of chemistry is incorporated with the Waynflete professorship of chemistry.

Ale-conner. A judge of ale, an annual office of great antiquity, appointed in the court leet of each manor. His duty was to taste the ale and beer, and decide if they were wholesome, sound, and sold at a proper price. Ale-conners were called *Gustatores cervisiæ*.

Alexander (*The English*). Henry V. (1388, 1413–1422). He resembled Alexander in the shortness and glory of his reign, his princely liberality, his enjoyment of life, his great military talents, and his wonderful hold on the hearts of the people over whom he reigned or whom as a general he commanded. Captain Fluellen would put it thus: Alexander was born at Macedon and Henry V. was born at Monmouth, and both begin with M.

Alexander (*The Second*). Sandjar or Mog-Eddyn-Sandjar, third son of Malek Shah, king of Persia (1118–1175). He was called Sandjar from the place of his birth, but his proper name was Abou'l Hareth Moez Eddyn.

Alexander-Newski (*Knights of*), 1725. A Russian military order. Cordon, a flame or poppy colour.

Alexander's Wine. A celebrated poison, so called from Rodriguez Borgia, historically known as Pope Alexander VI., traditionally said to have been killed by drinking one of the Borgia poisons, in a bowl of wine intended for another person.

Alexandra (*The*). A screw-steamer seized, 1863, by the government at Liverpool, during the civil war of America, under suspicion of its being a Confederate vessel (England had declared itself neutral in the war). The case was tried in the Court of Exchequer, and judgment given against the government. An appeal was made to the House of Lords, and the previous judgment being confirmed, the vessel was restored to the owners in April 1864. *See* 'Alabama.'

Alexan'drian Codex. A manuscript in Greek of the entire Bible written on parchment, and now in the British Museum. It is in uncial letters, without accents, and without spaces between the words. The probable date is about A.D. 500, or a little before. It belonged (in 1098) to the patriarch of Alexandria, and in 1621 was taken to Constantinople by Cyrillus Lucăris, the patriarch. The patriarch gave it to Charles I., king of England, in 1628, and it was placed in the Royal Library. It was transferred to the British Museum in 1753. *See* 'Bibles.'

There are two other Greek MSS., one the Codex Vaticanus, in Rome, and the other an imperfect copy called the Sinaitic Codex, in St. Petersburg. The Alexandrian Codex contains the epistles of Clemens Romănus, a third and fourth book of the Maccabees, the epistle of Athanasius to Marcellinus, a hymn to the Virgin, &c.

Alexan'drian Era (*The*). Dates creation Aug. 29, B.C. 5502.

This must not be confounded with the Era of Alexander, Nov. 12, 324. *See* under ' Era.'

Alexan'drian Library (*The*). This magnificent museum and library was begun, B.C. 204, by Ptolemy Soter, and completed by his son, Ptolemy Philadelphus. It was in the quarter of Alexandria called Bruchïon, and contained 700,000 volumes. It was burnt in the siege of Alexandria by Julius Cæsar, but partially restored and again destroyed by Theophilus, a fanatical Christian bishop, by order of the Emperor Theodosius. We are told that the library contained a copy of every known literary work in the civilised world, whether Egyptian, Jewish, Greek, Latin, Phœnician, Punic, Chaldee, Syriac, or Persian.

According to Abdallatîf (1230), Amrou, A.D. 640, burnt the library, saying: ' If the books contain truth, they are needless, being mere repetitions of the blessed Koran ; if not, they are mischievous, and better destroyed.'

Alexan'drian Massacre (*The*), A.D. 215. When Caracalla, the Roman emperor, visited Alexandria, the people made some allusion to his flagitious crimes and to those of his mother; upon which he ordered a general massacre of all the inhabitants. Many, especially of the Christians, escaped by flight, but the slaughter was immense, especially of young men of military age. *See* ' Massacres.'

Alexan'drian School (*The*). It may be divided into two periods : The *first*, or Ptolemæan period (from B.C. 323–30), was given to mathematics and poetry; the former unrivalled, the latter little better than mathematical verse, perfect in anatomy, but without a living soul. The *second* period (from B.C. 30 to A.D. 640, the fall of the Ptolemæan dynasty to the irruption of the Arabs) was the philosophic period. The introduction of Christianity produced the systems of Neo-Platonism and Gnosticism. The former was a fusion of Christian doctrines and dogmas with the ideas of Plato, the chief exponent of which was Philo the Jew ; the Gnostic school dipped into the religious tenets of Origen and other fathers of the Church. The dogmas of the *Logos* and the *Trinity* are ascribed by many to Alexandrian influence.

Alexan'drine MS. (*The*) of the Bible. *See* ' Codex Alexandrïnus.'

Alexan'drine Platonism. The philosophic system of Plato applied to the Christian system. Platonism led to mysticism, the Aristotelian philosophy led to sophistry and disputation. In the middle ages the Alexandrine Platonism, matured in Asia, adopted in the Greek Church, and afterwards introduced into the Western Church, produced much mischief. Joannes Scotus, surnamed 'Erigĕna,' was the reviver of mystic theology.

Erigena divides nature into four classes : (1) that which creates and is not created ; (2) that which is created and creates ; (3) that which is created and does not create ; and (4) that which neither creates nor is created.

Alexan'drine War *(The)*. The war between Cæsar and Pompey, from August, B.C. 48 to January, B.C. 47. After the defeat of Pompey at Pharsalia, Cesar pursued him into Egypt, where Pompey was assassinated. Cesar then placed Cleopatra and her younger brother on the throne of Egypt, and the war was over.

Alexan'drists. Disciples of Alexander of Aphrodisia, a peripatetic philosopher (2nd cent. B.C.). He was an exponent of Aristotle, and has left comments on nearly all Aristotle's works. The Alexandrists in the 12th Christian century were combated by the Averroists (*q.v.*), and for a time there were two antagonistic and concurrent sects called the Alexandrists and the Averroists.

Alex'ians, or 'Brethren and Sisters of Alexius.' Lollards, who rose at Antwerp, about 1300, and were admitted by Sixtus IV. among the religious orders in 1472. Also called Cellites (*q.v.*), and Matemans. Recognised by Pius IX. in 1870. See 'Monastic . . . Orders.'

Alfonsi'nas. The Alfon'sine tables of astronomy (1252), in which Alfonso X., 'the Astronomer,' corrected some of the errors of the Ptolemaic system. The king was assisted in this work by Isaac Hazan, a Jewish rabbi. It would be more correct to say that these tables were constructed by the order and under the patronage of Alfonso by Isaac Hazan, assisted by Christian and Arabian savants united at Tolēdo. See 'Ilkanian and Rudolfine Tables.'

These tables recognise what was called the Trepidation,' of Ptolemy's system. This was a mere cabalistic mystery, and has not the smallest foundation in any scientific observation. Milton makes Satan, in his way to earth,

Pass the planets seven ; and pass the fixed [stars] ; And that crystallin sphere, whose balance weighs The Trepidation talked [of] ; and that first moved [primum mobile].—*Paradise Lost*, iii. 481, &c.

It was Alfonso X. who (puzzled over the intricacies of cycles and epicycles) exclaimed, 'What a muddle ! I could have done creation better.'

Alfonsine Tables *(The)*. *See* above.

Alfonso the Magnanimous. Alfonso V. of Aragon (1385, 1416–1458), by far the most accomplished sovereign of the 15th cent.

Algerine Act *(The)*, 1831. So Daniel O'Connell called the prohibition of holding political meetings in Ireland.

The time at which he (O'Connell) should have been called up for judgment did not arrive till within a month or two of the expiration of the statute under which he was convicted, and which he called the ' Algerine Act.'—*Personal Recollections of Lord Cloncurry*, pp. 418-421.

Pronounce Al'-je-reen'.

Algon'quin Tongue *(The)*. The language of the native north-east Americans, dialects of which are spoken over the greater portions of eastern North America.

Mr. A. Gatschet, after a careful study of what remains of the Beothuk language, has come to the conclusion that it belongs to 'a separate linguistic family to the Innuit, Tinné, Iroquois, and Algonkin.'—Lady BLAKE, *Nineteenth Century* (Dec. 1888, p. 905).

Alham'bra of the Crimea *(The)*. Aloupka, built of rich greenstone, in various colours ; the Gothic and Saracenic being the prevailing orders of the architecture.

Alien Acts *(The)*. 33 Geo. III. c. 4, Jan. 4, 1793, and 34 Geo. III. c. 43, 67, &c., A.D. 1794, were passed on account of the great number of foreigners who came to England in the years 1792, 1793. The object of these acts was to confer on the crown the power of banishing aliens from the realm. These acts were superseded by the Peace Alien Act, 6 Will. IV. c. 11, A.D. 1836, which required the masters of ships arriving from a foreign port to declare the number of foreign passengers on their bills, and also required each passenger on landing to show his passport. As no penalty is attached to non-compliance, the provisions soon fell into neglect.

By the Junian Law, B.C. 126, all aliens were banished from Rome. In 122 the law was extended to Latins and Italiots.

All Saints' Day, Nov. 1. In commemoration of all the dead who have 'died in the Lord,' especially those for whom no special day has been appointed. Called also ' All Hallows,' and, in French, ' La Toussaint.' These terms were, in 830, substituted by Gregory IV. for the previous one of Al Martyrs.'

All Souls College, Oxford, 1437. Founded by Henry Chichele, archbishop of Canterbury.   The head-master is called the Warden.

All Souls Day. 'Festa Animārum,' Nov. 2, in commemoration of all the dead. It was instituted by Odilon, abbot of Clugny, in 998.   Till 1582 it was observed in Milan on the third Monday of October.

also called 'Animarum Commemoratio,' or 'Omnium Fidelium Commemoratio'; in French, 'Trépassés' (or *Jour des Trépassés*).

All the Hacks, 1807–1809.   An imbecile ministry which succeeded the bungling parliament called, in ridicule, 'All the Talents.'   The Duke of Portland was premier, and his chief supporters were Perceval, Castlereagh, Canning, and Hawkesbury (Lord Liverpool).   The duke died Oct. 30, 1809.

All the Talents (*Administration of*), 5 Feb., 1806, to 23 March, 1807 Formed by Lord Grenville after the death of Pitt (Jan. 23, 1806).   It consisted of Lord Auckland (President of the Board of Trade), Lane Barham, duke of Bedford (Lord-Lieutenant of Ireland), Erskine (Lord Chancellor), Sir Gilbert Elliot [Lord Minto] (President of the Board of Trade), Lord Ellenborough (Chief Justice of the King's Bench), General Fitzgerald (Secretary of War), Earl Fitzwilliam (Secretary of War), Charles James Fox (Foreign Secretary), Lord Grenville (First Lord of the Treasury), Earl Grey (Lord of the Admiralty), Earl of Moira (Master-General of Ordnance), Lord Henry Petty (Chancellor of the Exchequer), Pigott (Attorney-General), Romilly (Solicitor-General), Lord Sidmouth (Privy Seal), Lord Spencer (Secretary for the Home Department), Lord Temple (Vice-President of the Board of Trade), Windham (Secretary for the Colonies).   N.B.—Canning was not a member of this ministry.

Alleluiat'ica (*Victoria*), 30 March, A.D. 430.   A legendary victory won by St. Germānus over the Picts and Saxons at Mold.

Alliteration.
C.—Hamconius wrote a poem in which every word begins with C. It opens thus :—

Certamen Catholicum cum Calvinistis

Hucbald wrote a poem of 100 lines,

every word of which begins also with C. The last two lines are :—

Conveniet claras claustris componere cannas,
Completur claris carmen cantabile calvis.

M.—In the 'Materia More Magistralis' every word begins with M.
P.—Placentius, the Dominican (16th cent.) wrote a poem containing 253 Latin hexameters, and entitled 'Pugna Porcorum,' every word of which begins with P.   It opens thus :—

Plaudite, porcelli; porcorum pigra propago
Progreditur . . .

T.—Tusser has a poem of 12 lines in rhyme, on Thrift, every word of which begins with T.
The alliterative poem beginning 'An Austrian army awfully arrayed' contains 26 lines.   Each line in succession begins with one letter in alphabetical order. *See* 'Reader's Handbook,' p. 719.
The distich on Cardinal Wolsey is not so well known :—

Begot by butchers, but by bishops bred,
How high his Honour holds his haughty head.

Allo'dia, or 'allodial lands.'   Freeholds, that is lands held without the requirement of military service.   In times of trouble it was by no means unusual for such a tenant to place his lands under a lord, and pay him military service for protection. *See* 'Mesne lord.'

Almack's.   A suite of assembly rooms, built in 1765, in King Street, St. James's, London, by a tavern-keeper named M'Call, who inverted the two syllables of his name, Mac-call, into Allmack or Almack.   The rooms became famous for fashionable balls under the management of a committee of ladies of the highest rank.   The rooms are now called Willis's Rooms, from a proprietor named Willis.

Al'magest.   The Arabic translation of Ptolemy's 'Magna Constructio,' by command of Al Mamûn, A.D. 827.   It was retranslated by Gerard of Cremona, about 1230.   Ptolemy's 'Syntaxis of Astronomy' was written about A.D. 150.

Almiran'tê (*El*), without the adjunct of a proper name, means Columbus.

So El Marchese, among Mexicans, means Cortes; and Il Segretario, among the Florentines, means Machiavel.

Al'mohades (3 syl.).   A dynasty that ruled in Africa and Spain in the

12th and 13th cent. The word means 'The Unitarians,' and they assumed that they alone of all the earth worshipped God properly. The founder of the sect was Mahommed Ibn Toumert, of the Atlas region. The power of the Mohades was destroyed in Spain in 1257 and in Africa in 1269. (Mohades, 2 syl.)

Almo'rah, in Hindustan (*Convention of*), 27 April, 1815, for the cession of Kumaon to the British.

Almo'ravides (4 syl.). A dynasty in Africa and Spain founded by Yahia Ibn Ibrahim about 1050; driven out of Spain in 1155; suppressed in Africa 1208. The word Almoravides is a corruption of 'Al Morabeth' (the frontier people). Called in English the Marabûts.

The founder is sometimes called Abdallah Ibn Yasim, who undertook to instruct the tribes on the slopes of the Atlas range in the Mahometan faith.

Alog'ians (*The*), or 'Al'ogi.' 2nd cent. Those who denied the divinity of the Logos, and rejected the Gospel of St. John with the Apocalypse. (Greek, ἀ, negative, λόγος, the word.)

Alom'brados (*The*). Religious sectaries of Spain first mentioned in 1575, suppressed by the Inquisition in 1623. They were an early school of the Illumināti.

Alphonsine Tables. *See* 'Alfonsine' &c.

Altenberg, in Hungary (*Congress of*), 12–28 Sept., 1809. For the negotiation of peace between France and Austria.

Alter ego. Is an official title originally in use in the Two Sicilies, meaning the vicar-general of the king, to whom was deputed sovereign power. The French lieutenant-general of the kingdom was a similar officer.

It is now used to signify a very dear friend, a second self.

Altmark, in Prussia (*Truce of*), 26 Sept., 1628. Between Gustávus Adolphus of Sweden and Sigismund of Poland, for six years.

Extended to 26 years Sept. 12, 1635.

Altona, in Holstein (*Convention of*), 20 June, 1689. Between Christian V. of Denmark and Christian Albert of Holstein-Gottorp, by the mediation of the kaiser. (Al'-tŏ-nah.)

Amal (*The*). The chief or king of the Goths. The Amals, or 'sons of Odin,' were a race of heroes who reigned over the Goths in the 5th and 6th Christian centuries. The word means celestials—Amal'aric, or rather Amalric, one of this race, means 'the celestial king.' Theodorick the Great was an Amal. Kingsley in his 'Hypatia' frequently uses the word.

Amal'fian Code (*The*), or 'Tabūla Amalphitāna.' A code of maritime laws compiled by the Amalfians in the 11th cent., and observed by all Italy.

Amazo'nian Brigade (*The*), 1792. The dames de la Halle and the women of the Faubourg St.-Antoine enrolled themselves into this brigade in the French Revolution. Their head-dress was a *bonnet-rouge*, or red night-cap, with a tricolour cockade, and their arms were pikes.

Am'azons. Runjeet Singh of Lahore formed a regiment of 150 of the prettiest girls in Cashmere, Persia, and the Punjab. They were magnificently dressed, armed with bows and arrows, and appeared on horseback as cavalry. This regiment was more for the amusement of the maharajah than for war service.

Ambarva'lia, a festival in which the Romans, in solemn procession, prayed for their fields and increase of corn. (*Am*= round about, *arva*= the fields.)

It was the day of the 'little' or private Ambarvalia, celebrated by a single family for the welfare of all belonging to it; as the great college of the Arval brothers at Rome officiated in the interest of the whole city.—PATER, *Marius the Epicurean*, chap. i.

Amber Witch (*The*). A literary forgery, professing to be a 'story of the olden time.' When it first appeared the great scholars of Germany applied severe tests of historical and philological criticism to the work, and declared it to be an undoubted relic of antiquity. Even those acute neologists, the Tübingen Reviewers, found it 'hoary with the lapse of centuries.' When the wise ones had fully committed themselves, Dr. Reinhold came forward and proved beyond a doubt that he was himself the author. *See* 'Literary Forgeries.'

Amboise (*Conspiracy of*), 1560. Formed by the partisans of the Prince of Condé, to carry off François II., and to massacre the Guises, who had removed from Paris to Amboise when they gained secret information of the conspiracy. Called the Conspiracy of Amboise because the conspirators assembled there to carry out their purposes. It was betrayed to the Duke de Guise, and 27 barons, 11 counts, and 7 marquises were executed in one day.

Pronounce Ahm-bwoiz.

Amboise (*Edict of*), 19 March, 1563. It gave to the Huguenots free exercise of religion in those towns which were in the power of the Calvinists at the date of 7 March, 1563; permission to the lords *hauts justiciers* to hold assemblies throughout the whole extent of their domains; permission to the nobles of the second rank to celebrate their worship in their own houses, but only for their household; finally, permission in each bailiwick pertaining directly to the *parlements* for a single place of worship. To all other persons it accorded only the right of private worship. *See* ' Edict of January.'

Amboise, in France (*Treaty of*), 12 March, 1563. Concluding the ' Religious War ' (1562–63); signed by Charles IX. of France.

Amboy'na (*The Massacre of*), 1624. The Dutch laid claim to all the Spice Islands in the Indian Archipelago. In one of these (Amboyna) the English East India Company had established, in 1612, a small settlement at Cambello. In the whole island there were some 20 English, 30 Japanese, and 200 Dutch. The Dutch pretended that the English and Japanese had combined to expel them from the island, so they seized Captain Towerson, with 9 other Englishmen, 9 Japanese, and 1 Portuguese, and, after torturing them, cut off their heads. *See* ' Massacres.'

Ambro'sian Chant, or 'Hymn,' called ' Ambrosiānum,' mentioned by Isidore in his ' De Eccl. Offic.' Book I. c. 6. It was a chant or hymn introduced into the church at Milan in the 4th cent., now known as the ' Te Deum laudāmus,' said, as we now have it, to have been the joint work of St. Ambrose and St. Augustine.

Ambro'sian Library (*The*), at Milan, founded by Cardinal Federigo Borroméo in 1602, and plundered by Napoleon in 1796. The plunder was restored in 1816. So named in honour of St. Ambrosius, patron saint of Milan.

N.B. St. Ambrose was Bishop of Milan, A.D. 374–397.

Ambro'sian Liturgy, ' Missal,' ' Office.' So called from being edited and supplemented by St. Ambrose, bishop of Milan (340, 374–397). This liturgy is one of the most ancient; and must, of course, have been in use before the time of St. Ambrose. This is called the Liturgy of Milan, and is one of the chief liturgies of the Roman Church, the other three being the Roman, the Gallican, and the Spanish Liturgies.

Ambro'sian Mass, ' Missa Ambrosiāna.' Used at Milan, according to the service employed by St. Ambrose.

Am'brosin. A coin of the middle ages, struck by the dukes of Milan, on which St. Ambrose was represented on horseback, with a whip in his right hand.

Amedieu (2 syl.), **or** 'Friends of God,' 1400. A religious congregation who wore no breeches, but a grey cloak girded at the loins with a rope. Pius V. united them to the Cistercians and Soccolanti.

Amen Corner, London. Before the Reformation the clergy used to walk in procession every year on Corpus Christi day to St. Paul's Cathedral. They mustered at the upper end of Cheapside, and there commenced chanting the *Paternoster*, which continued through 'Paternoster Row '; at the end of the Row they said *Amen*, and the spot was called ' Amen Corner.' They then began the *Ave Maria*, turning down ' Ave-Maria Lane.' After crossing Ludgate, they chanted the *Credo* in ' Creed Lane ' (which no longer exists).

Corpus Christi Day, called in French the ' Fête Dieu,' is the Thursday after Trinity Sunday ; it was the greatest Church festival in the year.

American—

Academy of Arts and Sciences, incorporated by the legislature of Massachusetts, 1780.

Academy of Fine Arts, founded at New York, 1808.

Antiquarian Society, incorporated by the legislature of Massachusetts, 1812.

Anti-Slavery Society, formed 1833.

Association for the Advancement of Science, projected at Boston, 1847.

Bible Society, founded in New York, 1816.

Board of Commissioners for Foreign Missions, instituted 1810.

Colonisation Society, founded at Washington, 1816.

Company (of Russia) for carrying on the fur trade with the north-west coast of America, incorporated 1799.

Philosophical Society, originated by Franklin, 1743.

Temperance Society, formed at Boston 1826.

Tract Society, instituted at Boston 1814.

American Cato (*The*). Old Samuel Adams (1722–1803), who played such a patriotic part in the American Revolution, and was governor of Massachusetts.

American Fabius (*The*). George Washington (1732–1799).

American Land League (*The*), 1882. A branch of the Irish 'Land League,' suppressed the same year. The Irish league was reorganised into the 'National League' (*q.v.*). *See* 'Irish Associations.'

American Postage Stamps (*The*). Each denomination of stamp contains a different head. There are twelve denominations, and twelve heads of American worthies.

Cents.
1. Benjamin Franklin, 1706-1790.
2. Andrew Jackson, 1767-1845 (7th president).
3. George Washington, 1732-1799 (1st president).
5. Zachary Taylor, 1786-1850 (11th president).
6. Abraham Lincoln, 1809-1865 (14th president. assassinated).
7. Edwin Stanton, 1815-1869 (statesman).
10. Thomas Jefferson, 1743-1826 (3rd president).
12. Henry Clay, 1777-1852 (statesman).
15. Daniel Webster, 1782-1852 (statesman).
24. Winfield Scott, 1786-1866 (general).
30. Alexander Hamilton, 1757-1804 (statesman).
90. M. C. Perry. *See* 'Japanese Perry.'

American War of Independence (*The*), 1775–1783. The first skirmish was at Lexington, 19 April, 1775; issue doubtful, but unimportant. Terminated by the Peace of Versailles, signed at Paris 3 Sept., 1783. The object of the war was to make the United States of America independent of England. The chief battles of the war are subjoined. Those in common type were doubtful. Those in *italics* were won by the Americans. Those in *capitals* were won by the British.

Lexington, 19 April, 1775.
Bunker Hill, 17 June, 1775.
BROOKLYN, 27 Aug., 1776 (Howe over Washington).
WHITE-PLAINS, 28 Oct., 1776 (won by Lord Howe).
Trenton, 26 Dec., 1776 (won by Washington).
Princeton, 3 Jan., 1777 (Washington over Cornwallis).
Bennington, 16 Aug., 1777 (German mercenaries defeated).
BRANDYWINE, 11 Sep., 1777 (Howe over Washington).
Stillwater, 19 Sep., 1777; and 6 Oct., 1777.
Saratoga, 11 Oct., 1777 (Gates over Burgoyne).
Monmouth Court House, 28 Jan., 1778 (won by Washington).
King's Mountain, 7 Oct., 1780.
Cowpens, 17 Jan., 1781 (Morgan over Tarleton).
GUILFORD, 15 March, 1781 (Cornwallis over Greene).
HOBKIRK HILL, 25 April, 1781 (Rawdon over Greene).
Eutaw-Spring, 8 Sept., 1781 (claimed by Arnold.)
Yorktown, 19 Oct. 1781 (Washington over Cornwallis).
The war lasted eight years to a day. The battle

of Lexington was fought 19 April, 1775, and the cessation of hostilities with Great Britain was, by order of General Washington, proclaimed in the American camp 19 April, 1783.

France acknowledged the independence of the United States 16 Jan., 1778 ; Spain in 1779 ; Holland on 19 April, 1782.

England signed a provisional compact with America, 30 Nov., 1782 ; announced to Parliament, 5 Dec. ; and all hostilities ceased 20 Jan., 1783. The British troops evacuate New York, 25 Nov.; and an American detachment under General Knox took possession of the town.

American War (*The Second*), 1812–1814. The American War of Independence terminated in 1783. The second war between America and Great Britain was declared by the United States, June 18, 1812, and concluded Dec. 24, 1814, by the Peace of Ghent. The chief battles were : (*capitals*, English victories ; *italic*, American victories).

QUEENSTOWN (Sheaffe over Van Rensselaer).
STONY CREEK (Vincent over Winder), 1813.
Moravian Town (Harrison over Proctor), 5 Oct.
BLADENSBURG (Ross over Winder), 24 Aug. 1814.
Plattsburgh (Macomb over Prevost).
New Orleans (Jackson over Pakenham).

The immediate cause of this war was, that in 1811 a British ship called 'The Little Belt,' under Captain Bingham, had engaged the American frigate named 'The United States,' under Commodore Rogers, and each party laid the blame on the other. Nearly the last incident was that the President Madison, on Aug. 24, prepared a grand banquet at the White House, but General Ross took Washington by surprise, and feasted his men on Madison's banquet. (Ross killed 12 Sept. 1814.)

American Civil War (*The*), 1861–1865. Between the Federals of the Northern States and the Confederates of the Southern and slave-holding States. The total loss of life was 800,000. The Federals were the victors, and American slaveholding was abolished. Cost of the war, to the Federals, 940,000,000*l*. sterling ; to the Confederates, 460,000,000*l*. Total, 1,400,000,000*l*. sterling.

Ami du Peuple (*L'*). A scandalous democratic journal conducted by Marat in the French Revolution. Its articles were most ferocious, and no one was spared except the very scum of the people. The original name of this infamous journal was the 'Publiciste Parisien,' and its last title was 'Le Journal de la République.'

Pronounce Lah'-me du Peu'pl.

Am'iens (*Peace of*), 1 Oct., 1801. One of the most fatuous ever made by England. As Lord Grenville said : 'England gave up everything, and France nothing. France kept Savoy, Belgium, the Germanic States on the left bank of the Rhine, Upper Italy, and Holland. In Asia she was to have

Pondicherry, Cochin, Negapatam, and the Spice Islands; in Africa she was to have the Cape of Good Hope and Senegal; in the West Indies she was to hold Martinique, St. Lucia, Guadaloupe, Tobāgo, Curaçao, and most of St. Domingo; in America she was to be repossessed of St. Pierre and Miquelon; and in South America she was to keep Surinam, Demerara, Berbice, and Esse-quibo.' We had spent in the nine years 461,800,000*l.*, and retained nothing but Ceylon and Trinidad. Addington's Ministry. On 22 May, 1802, a fresh rupture put an end to the 'Peace.'

Amis des Noirs (*Société des*). The first anti-slavery society instituted at Paris by Brissot de Warville, Feb. 1788.

Pronounce Ah'·me da Nwar'.

Amnesty Association (*The*), 1870. The members were nearly all Fenians, and one of them was Mr. Parnell. Other members were Egan, Biggar, J. Nolan, John Levy, James Carey, John Sullivan, and Daniel Curley.

Amor'ian Dynasty (*The*), of the Byzantine Empire. It includes Michael II., the Stammerer, who was born at Amoria, in Phrygia, from 820–829; Theophilus, 829–842, and Michael III., the Sot, 842–867. This dynasty was then succeeded by the Macedonian under Basil I.

Michael II. conspired against Leo the Armenian, and was made emperor in 820.

Amor'ian War (*The*), A.D. 838. Between the Emperor Theophilus (son of Michael the Stammerer), and the Calif Motassem (son of Harun al Rashid). So called from Amorium, in Phrygia, the birthplace of Theophilus. The Saracens had the word AMORIUM in-scribed on their saddles, in revenge of Theophilus's siege of Sozopetra, the birthplace of Motassem. The Saracens were the victors, but the slaughter on both sides was great. Gibbon gives it as 70,000 Moslems and 30,000 Christians.

Theophilus was defeated at Dasymon, and Amorium was lost.

Amphictyon'ic Council (*The*). Established B.C. 1124 to the 2nd cent. A.D. A politico-religious court of twelve Grecian tribes held twice a year. In spring, the members met in the Temple of Apollo, at Delphi; and in the autumn they met in the Temple of Ceres, at

2

Anthēla, near Thermopylæ. Their pur-pose was (1) to determine questions of international law; and (2) to preserve the religious institutions of Greece.

Æschinēs gives the following names: the Thessalians, Bœotians, Dorians, Ionians, Perrhæ-bians, Magnetes, Locrians, Œlæans, Phthiots, Malians, Phocians, and one omitted, probably the Dolopians. In the time of Demosthenēs the glory had departed from the council.

Amphis'san War (*The*). The third sacred war of Greece, from Feb. to Aug. B.C. 338. The Locrians of Amphissa rebuilt Cirrha on the 'Sacred Land,' and the matter, B.C. 339, was laid before the Amphictyonic Council, which declares war against these Locrians. Philip II. of Macedon undertakes the war for the Council, and is joined by the Peloponnesians; but Athens and Thebes take the side of the Locrians. Amphissa is taken and destroyed in the summer of 338, and in August of the same year the Thebans and Athenians being over-thrown at Cheronēa, the war is brought to an end.

Am'pian Law (*The*), B.C. 64. A law by T. Am'pius, one of the tribunes, to allow Pompey to wear the symbols of triumph at the Circensian games.

Amyclæ'an Silence, perilous silence. It is said that the Amyclæans were forbidden to disturb the peace by raising a cry of danger from invasion. This law was passed, because the people were always crying 'wolf,' out of fear of the Spartans. It so happened that the Spartans came at last, and none durst sound a note of warning, and so the city was taken. Hence the Greek proverbs, 'Amyclæ perished through silence,' and 'more silent than the Amyclæans' (*Amyclis ipsis taciturnior*).

Anabaptists, 1521. The nickname of a religious party who maintained that, as baptism should not be administered without a personal confession of faith, the baptism of infants was worthless, and those who had so been baptized must be baptized again as adults, at their own express desire, and after a confession of faith.

In Germany, John of Leyden, Munzer, Knipperdoling, and others were called Anabaptists, and maintained that Christ was not God, that righteousness is of works, that there is no such thing as original sin, that infants ought not to be baptized, that all men are of one rank, and that civil magistrates are anti-scriptural. *See* 'Mennonites.'

The Anabaptists of Moravia called themselves *apostolical.* They went barefoot; had a community of goods; dressed in black; and had very gloomy views of future judgment, the malice of Satan, and the enduring pains of hell.

Anac'reon (*The French*). I. Pontus de Thiard, one of the 'Pleiad poets' (1521–1605).

II. P. Laiyon, perpetual president of the 'Caveau Moderne,' a Paris club noted for its good dinners. No one not a poet could be a member of it (1727–1811).

Anacreon (*The Persian*), Mohammed Hafiz. His collected poems are called 'The Divan' (1310–1389).

Anacreon (*The Scotch*). Alexander Scot (flourished 1550).

Anacreon (*The Sicilian*). Giovanni Meli (1740–1815).

Anacreon Moore. Thomas Moore of Dublin, who translated Anacreon's odes from Greek into English in the spirit of the original, and wrote numerous odes and other poems of unusual merit (1779–1852).

Anacreon of Painters (*The*). Francesco Albăno (or Albăni), 1578–1660.

Anacreon of the Guillotine. Bertrand Barère de Vieuzac, president of the National Convention in 1792. So called from the flowery language he employed in speaking on the measures of the Reign of Terror.

Anacreon of the Temple (*The*). Guillaume Amfrye, abbé de Chaulieu (1639–1720), the Tom Moore of France. Called 'of the Temple' from the place of his abode. Sometimes called the Horace of France.

Anacreon of the Twelfth Century. Walter Mapes or Map (1150–1196). His song 'Meum est propositum' has been translated by Leigh Hunt.

Anagni, in Italy (*Council of*), 24 March, 1160, in which Pope Alexander III. excommunicated Frederick Barbarossa.

Anally, in Ireland. The modern Longford.

Anatomy (*Professorship of*), in the University of Cambridge, 1707; founded by the University. Stipend 800*l.* a year. *See* 'Lowndean Professor.'

Anatomy Act (*The*), 2, 3, Will. IV. c. 75, 1832. It provides that a person must have a licence to practise anatomy; it enjoins that inspectors be appointed to visit chambers where anatomy is carried on; that any one may leave his body to be dissected, if he chooses. The law is not applicable to post-mortem examinations.

The cause of this Act of Parliament was that persons previously used to murder people and sell their dead bodies for dissection. Burke and Hare murdered sixteen persons and sold their bodies. They used to inveigle men, women, and children into a house, make them drunk, and then smother them by placing a pitch plaster over the mouth and nose.

Anatomy of Melancholy (*The*), 1621. 'A carnival of quotations, Greek, Latin, German, French, and Italian; philosophical, geometrical, medical, poetical, astrological, musical, pedagogic.' The subject is melancholy, its nature, seat, varieties, causes, symptoms, prognosis; its cure, by legitimate and forbidden means, by dietetics and by pharmacy. Author, the Rev. Robert Burton (1576–1640).

Ancenis, in France (*Treaty of*), 10 Sept., 1468. A treaty of peace between Louis XI. and François II., duc de Bretagne.

Ancient of the Mountains (*The*). Chief of the Assassins.

The Assassins settled in Persia in 1090. Murdered the Marquis of Montferrat in 1192; Louis (Ludwig) of Bavaria in 1213; the Khan of Tartary in 1254, &c. In 1257 the mischievous sect was extirpated.

Ancients. The Moravian elders who are the civil and ecclesiastical heads of the community. They preside over the education of the children, enjoin penances, pronounce excommunications, and determine the rank of each member of the community.

Between the French 'National Council' and 'Corps Législatif' were 'two councils,' one of which was called the *Conseil des Anciens* (consisting of 250 members), the other being the *Conseil de Cinq-cents*. The Florentine Council in the 13th cent. were called the *Anziăni. Senator* means 'senior,' or elder.

Andelot (*Treaty of*), 28 Nov., A.D. 587. Between Gontran of Orleans and Childebert II. of Austrasia. By this treaty Burgundy was assigned to Gontran.

Andrew (*Knights of St.*), 10 Sept., 1698. A Russian military order (founded by Peter the Great). The cordon is sky-blue. The motto is 'For Religion and Loyalty.'

The Scotch order is generally called the Order of the Thistle.

Andrews (*University of St.*). Lectures commenced here in 1410. Charter granted by Henry Wardlaw, bishop of St. Andrews, 27 Feb., 1411. Chartered 3 March, 1432, by James I. of Scotland. St. Salvátor College founded, 1455, by James Kennedy, bishop of St. Andrews. St. Leonard's College founded, 1512, by prior John Hepburn. St. Salvator's and St. Leonard's Colleges united 1747, and called the 'United College.'

The Pædagogy of Wardlaw was enlarged in 1538 by Archbishop Beaton, and called St. Mary's or New College.

Andrussow, in Russia (*Truce of*), 30 Jan., 1667. Between Alexis Michailowitz, czar of Russia, and John II., king of Poland, for fifteen years. It stipulated for the re-annexation to Russia of Smolensko, Polotsk, Mohilef, and Kief, with the abandonment of part of the Ukraine and Severia.

Ane'da or Agne'da. The modern Latin name of Edinburgh (Scotland).

Angel of the Church of Smyrna (*The*). Polycarp, the fourth of the Apostolic Fathers (*q.v.*). He is so addressed in the Book of the Revelation. It is said that he was a disciple of John, the apostle, who appointed him bishop.

Angel of the Schools (*The*). Thomas d'Aquinas, the fifth doctor (1224–1274). *See* 'Angelic Doctor.'

Angelic Doctor (*The*). 'Doctor Angelicus,' 'Angel of the Schools,' 'the Eagle of Divines,' 'the Universal Doctor,' &c. Thomas Aquinas, or St. Thomas of Aquino, in Italy, of the Dominican order (born 1227, died 1274, canonised by John XXII. in 1369, and declared by Pius V., in 1567, to be the 'Fifth Doctor of the Church'). He was a schoolman of the Aristotelian class, and a Nominalist (*q.v.*). His great opponent was Duns Scotus, a Realist (*q.v.*), of the Franciscan order; and from these two leaders

Nominalists were called 'Thomists,' and Realists 'Scotists.'

The five doctors were Ambrose (340 397); Augustine (354 430); Jerome (345-420); Gregory, and Aquinas. *See* Addis and Arnold's Dict., 'Doctors of the Church.'

It is said that Thomas Aquinas was called the 'Angel of the Schools,' or the 'Angelic Doctor,' from his controversy 'Utrum Angelus possit moveri de extremo ad extremum non transeundo per medium.' Aquinas took the negative.

Angel'ici, 1st cent. Certain Christians who worshipped angels. They were most numerous in A.D. 180. Mentioned by St. Augustine in his 'Liber de Hæresibus,' 'qui angelos cultu divino prosequebantur.' Angelolatry was forbidden by the Council of Laodicea in 366, but enjoined by the Second Council of Nice in 787. *See* 'Angelites.'

Angel'ici. An order of knighthood instituted 1191 by the Emperor Isaac II.

Angel'icus, meaning 'Hymnus Angelicus,' is the hymn sung in the Mass, 'Glory to God in the highest, &c.,' sung by the angels at the Nativity. The *Trisagion* is also called 'Hymnus Angelicus.'

The monk's dress is called 'Angelicus,' or 'Angelica Vestis,' 'quod et ipsi dicantur angeli a patribus,' as in the Revelation the ministers of the churches of Asia are addressed as 'Angels.'

An'gelites (3 syl.), A.D. 494. Monoph'ysites (4 syl.), or heretics who maintained that Christ had but one nature. They received their name from Angelius, in Alexandria, where they used to meet. *See* 'Angelici.'

Angel'ium (*The*). The annunciation. First mentioned by Gelāsius in 492.

An'gelus, 1095 (Council of Clermont). A prayer and a bell which calls to the prayer. The *Angelus* is a prayer to the Virgin Mary, instituted by Urban II. It begins with the words 'Angelus Domini nuntiavit Mariæ ' (Luke i. 28), then follows the salutation of the angel Gabriel, 'Ave Maria,' &c. The prayer contains three verses, and each verse ends with the salutation, 'Ave Maria.' The bell, which is rung three times a day, morning, noon, and evening, was instituted in 1316, by John XXII. It was Louis XI. who (1472) commanded it to be rung daily at noon.

Louis IX., in 1472, commanded all his subjects to repeat the 'Salutatio Angelica' every noon, at the sound of a bell. The Compline is about three hours after the Vespers, which are said at sunset, say 6 o'clock p.m.

Anglesea Leg (*The*). An artificial leg like that made for the Marquis of Anglesea.

Dr. Bly's leg is an improvement on the Anglesea leg.

Pronounce An'-gle-see.

Anglo-Israel Identity Society (*The*). A religious sect which holds that the inhabitants of Great Britain are none other than the lost ten tribes of the House of Israel. Some of the reasons assigned are these : (1) The children of Israel were to inhabit islands north-west of Palestine ; (2) they were to speak a language not Semitic ; (3) they were to possess colonies in all parts of the earth (Isa. liv. 3) ; (4) Israel was to have a nation from her, but independent of her (America) ; (5) Israel was to be under a monarchy ; (6) Israel was to be unconquerable, but to be a great conqueror ; (7) Israel was to be a sabbath-keeping people ; (8) Israel was to be a prolific race ; (9) Israel was to send missionaries to the end of the earth (Isa. xliii. 21).

Anglo-Israelism (19th cent., last quarter). The hypothesis that the English are the descendants of the lost tribes. *See* above.

Anglo-Saxon (*Professorship of*), in the University of Cambridge, 1878. Founded by the Rev. Joseph Bosworth, D.D., of Trinity College, and called the Ebrington and Bosworth Professorship of Anglo-Saxon. Stipend not less than 500*l.* a year.

Anne Margaret Elliot, married twice, first Colonel Ebrington, and then Dr. Bosworth.

Anglo-Saxon Chronicle (*The*). Said to have been begun at the instance of King Alfred. It begins with Cæsar's invasion, and ends with the accession of Henry II. (1154).

An'grias (*The*). The Mahratta pirates. Conaji Angria and his brothers began their piratical exploits in 1670. Angria was taken prisoner by the English in 1756, when his piratical state was overthrown.

An'ima Mundi, called by Plato, 'Psuchê tou kosmou.' Plato compared the great world to a human being (or the little world). As man is vitalised by the living soul within him, so the world itself is vitalised by its living soul, without which it would be a mere *corpus mor-*

tuum. The sun would give neither light nor heat, the vegetable world would yield neither leaves nor seed, the animal world would consist of dead bodies only. The sun would not glow, the trees would not blossom, the air would not circulate, the rivers would not run into the sea, the sea would not evaporate, and the seasons would have no succession.

Stahl (1660–1734) called this ' Psuchê ' ' Anima Mundi,' by which he meant that it is not God who vivifies and preserves all things in being, but a vital principle which dwells in the universe, as the soul dwells in man. This *anima mundi* is not material, but co-exists with all objects and quickens them :

Warms in the sun, refreshes in the breeze,
Glows in the stars, and blossoms in the trees,
Lives through all life, extends through all extent,
Spreads undivided, operates unspent.—*Pope.*

An'imism, Animists. The system which explains the phenomena of life and disease by the action of soul (*anima*), and rejects the solution of these phenomena as purely physical. Van Helmont may be called the chief advocate of animism, and the system was taken up by George Ernest Stahl in the 18th cent. Those who believe in animism are called ' Animists.' *See* Rom. i. 20.

The difference between Stahl's doctrine and Spinoza's is this. Stahl taught the existence of an independent and all-pervading ' anima ' ; but Spinoza taught the identity of phenomena and deity. Pope expresses Stahl's idea in the well-known lines—

Great in the earth, as in the ethereal frame, &c.
See above.

Annals. Registers kept in Rome from the commencement of the state down to the time of Publius Mucius ; they were made by the Pontifex Maximus, and were called ' Annâles Maximi.' Livy freely used them in his history,

Annals are bare records of events. History is tracing out the motives and consequences of these events.

Annals of Tacitus (*The*). Said to be a forgery by Poggio Bracciolini, a learned scholar of Tuscany (1381–1459), author of ' Historia Florentina ' (printed 1715), and ' De Varietate Fortunæ ' (printed 1723). The tale is that he was paid 500 gold sequins (about 250*l.*) by Cosmo de' Medici for his MS.; the original is still shown in the library of Florence. It was published in 1468, when Johannes de Spire produced 'the last six books, which he affirmed he had copied carefully from the original in St. Mark's, Venice;' but this *original* was only Bracciolini's forgery. The first six books did not appear till 1514 (*i.e.* 46 years after the last six). *See* 'Literary Forgeries,' &c.

The reply to this is that Poggio Bracciolini was a professional dealer in MSS. and purchased them if possible, or obtained permission to make transcripts. The sixteen books of Annals in MS. are not Poggio's original work, but merely a transcript of the original lent him to copy. The manifest reply is, first, that Poggio was not a mere tradesman, but apostolic secretary to Boniface IX. and seven succeeding popes (1412–1452). He attended the Council of Constance (1414–1415), most certainly not as a tradesman. He resided with Cardinal Beaufort in 1417; was chancellor of the republic of Florence in 1452, and was the author of two important works at least. Where is the original from which Poggio made his copy? And can any reference to the 'Annals' be shown before the 16th cent.?

The *Annals* consist of Books I., II., III., IV., half of V., VI., . . . XI., XII., XIII., XIV., XV., and part of XVI.

No writer has mentioned the name of the 'Annals of Tacitus' before 1533, when Beatus Rhenanus so speaks of the book, and may be said to have given it its name. See 'Tacitus and Bracciolini,' published by Diprose & Bateman, Lincoln's Inn Fields.

Annap'olis, in Maryland (U.S. America). So named in compliment to Anne (1669), afterwards Queen of England, when it was constituted the seat of local government.

An'nates (2 syl.), or 'first fruits.' In ecclesiastical law means the value of a spiritual living for a whole year. From 1260 to the time of the Reformation, the pope claimed the first fruits; but by the 26 Hen. VIII. c. 3 (1534) they were, in England, annexed to the crown, and by 2 Anne c. 11 the revenue thus arising was vested in trustees for a perpetual fund to augment poor livings. This fund is called 'Queen Anne's Bounty.' Annates were first calculated according to a rate made under Innocent IV. in 1253. This rate was augmented by Nicholas III. in 1292. The Council of Pisa pronounced them simoniacal in 1435, but Alexander VI., in 1500, doubled the rate.

It appears that these 'Annates' were not actually the whole produce of a living for a year, but a sort of property tax paid by the new incumbent on presentation.

Anne (1 syl.), Queen of England (1664, 1702–1714), sister of Mary (wife of William III.), and younger daughter of James II. Married Prince George of Denmark. She had thirteen children, only one of whom lived to the age of 11. The rest died in infancy.

Her style: Anne, D.G. of Great Britain, France, and Ireland, Queen, Defender of the Faith, &c.

Anne of Bohemia was the wife of Richard II.; Anne of Cleves was one of the wives of Henry VIII.; Anne of Denmark was the wife of James I. of England.

Anne, 'the Word.' Anne Lee (1736–1784), the apostle of the Shakers, by whom she was called ' Mother,' that is, ' the true Mother of all living in the new creation,' and ' the Morning Star of the second coming of Christ.' She was born in Toad Lane, Manchester, and her father was John Lee, a blacksmith. She married Abraham Standley, also a blacksmith, joined the Shakers, and migrated to New York in 1774.

Année Terrible (*L'*), 1870. When Paris was besieged by the Prussians from 19 Sept. to 28 Jan., 1871.

Annius of Viterbo. Nannius, or ' Giovanni Nanni,' a Dominican (1432–1502), a literary impostor. His work, entitled ' Antiquitates Variæ,' professes to contain selections from Berosus, Manetho, Megasthenes, Archilocus, Myrsiles, Fabius Pictor, Sempronius, Cato, &c., but are, for the most part, mere fabrications. *See* ' Literary Forgeries.'

Anno'næ Præfectus. An officer appointed by Augustus to superintend the corn-market (ancient Rome).

Annual Indemnity Act (*The*), 1689. A clumsy makeshift for the repeal of the Corporation and Test Acts, whereby Dissenters were admitted into office in defiance of these acts, and were legally indemnified for violating them. An Act passed in every session of Parliament to indemnify those who neglected to take the sacrament before entering parliament or accepting some civil office.

By 22 Vict. c. 15, an Act of Indemnity secures from punishment or damage all those who have neglected to take the necessary oaths of office, &c.

Annual Mass, 'Missa Annuālis,' The mass which is said daily throughout the year.

Annual Register (*The*). Commenced by Robert Dodsley for the year 1758-9, appeared in June 1759. The 'Register' is published once a year, and contains a brief abstract of every event of historical interest, during the preceding twelve months. Also notices of new books and other miscellaneous matter. The work still goes on.

Edmund Burke assisted **Dodsley in preparing** his Registers.

The *New Annual Register*, edited by Dr. Morgan, was started 1781 and came to a close in 1825.

The *Edinburgh Annual Register*, written by Sir W. Scott and afterwards by Southey, commenced 1808 and closed 1827.

Annuncia'da, 1460. A society founded at Rome by Cardinal John Turrecremata for the marriage of poor young women. It now provides, every Lady-day, 60 Rom. crowns, a dress of white serge, and a florin for slippers to above 400 persons for marriage portions.

Annun'ciades (4 syl.). The name of several religious orders instituted in honour of the Annunciation.

I. 1362, called 'The Annunciades of Savoy,' created by Amadeus VI., count of Savoy. This was a military order.

II. 1500, an order instituted at Bourges by Jeanne de Valois, daughter of Louis XI., in honour of the ten virtues of the Virgin Mary.

III. 1604, 'The Celestial Annunciades,' instituted by Maria Vittoria Fornari. They dress in a blue mantle and are therefore called 'The Blue Sisters.'

The Annunciades of Jeanne de Valois wear a grey gown, a scarlet scapular, a blue simar, and a white mantle, to prefigure penitence, the passion of Christ, heaven, and virginity.

Annunciation (*The*), 25 March, our Ladyday. Commemorates the announcement of the angel to Mary that she was to be the mother of the Messiah (Luke i. 26-38).

In the Roman Catholic Church the Annunciation, or ' Festum Campanārum, is the Monday next after Easter Monday.

The 'Annunciatio Dominica' (or) 'Beatæ Virginis Mariæ' was instituted 629. By the Twelfth Council of Toulouse it was transferred to Dec. 18; but in 691 it was restored to March 25. *See* ' Order of the Annunciation.'

Annus Deliberandi, in Scotch law, is the interval allowed to the heir from the death of a proprietor of here-ditary property to make up his mind whether he will accept the succession with its incumbrances or not. The time is now reduced to six months.

Annus Mirab'ilis, A.D. 1666. The year of the great fire of London, and of the successes of our arms over the Dutch. So called by Dryden, who has a poem on the subject.

Anomalis'tic Year. The interval between two successive times of the earth being at the least distance from the sun. It consists of 365 days, 6 hours, 13 minutes, 45 seconds, and is 25 minutes less than a mean tropical year.

Anomœans, 357. A branch of the Arian heretics, who maintained that the essence of the Son is not like the essence of God the Father (Greek *anomoios*, unlike).

They rejected the dogma called ' Homoiousian, *i.e.* that the nature of Christ was like that of God the Father. The ' heresy ' was condemned by the Council of Ancyra in 358, and some subsequent councils.

Antal'cidas (*Peace of*), B.C. 387. A peace between Persia and the different states of Greece, arranged by Antalcīdas (or Antalkidas), the Lacedæmonian, after the suicidal contest called the Corinthean war (*q.v.*).

It ran thus : ' King Artaxerxes thinks it just that the cities in Asia and the islands of Clazomēnæ and Cyprus should belong to him. He also thinks it just that all the other Grecian cities should be left independent, except Lemnos, Imbros, and Scyros, which are to belong to Athens, as of old. If any state refuses to accept these terms, I, King Artaxerxes will make war thereon, both by sea and land.

Antelu'can. The 'before daylight' service held by early Christians to avoid observation (Latin, *ante lucem*, before daylight).

Anthropol'atræ, or 'Worshippers of Man,' so the Apollina'rians called the ' orthodox ' Christians, because they worshipped Christ, who, they maintained, was ' a perfect man of a reasonable soul, and human flesh subsisting ' (Greek, *anthropos*, *latreia*, man-worship).

Anthropomor'phism, in theology, means that God is formed like man, or rather that God is man's ideal, as every man forms his own god. One man forms him revengeful, another all merciful, a third love, and so on, according to each man's notion what a god ought to be.

Anthropomor'phites (5 syl.), 4th cent. Egyptian monks who maintained that God has the human form, and is of the same substance as man, because he made man in his own likeness.

Anti-Addressers, 1759. Those Irish Catholics who disapproved of the 'address,' and therefore seceded from the Catholic Association. *See* 'Addressers.'

Anti-Birminghams, 1680. Opponents of the Birminghams (*q.v.*), or Exclusionists. They were the friends of James, duke of York, and favourers of 'the right divine' and succession of James.

Anti-Burghers, 1747. Those Scotch Presbyterians who refused to take the required oath 'that they heartily and entirely concurred in the religion as by law established.' Those who accepted the oath were called Burghers.

Anti-Corn-Law League (*The*), 20 March, 1839. An association against the corn-laws was formed in London in 1836; the Manchester Anti-Corn-law Association was formed 24 Sept., 1838; the League with Cobden at the head was formed in 1839; dissolved 2 July, 1846. The corn-laws existing prior to the repeal consisted of a sliding-scale. When, for example, corn was selling at 62s. a quarter, a duty of 24s. 8d. a quarter was imposed on imported corn; for every shilling less than 62s. a quarter an extra shilling was added to imported corn; but when corn exceeded that price the duty rapidly increased, till it reached 73s., when a minimum tax of 1s. was imposed. This minimum tax of 1s. a quarter is still paid to defray the expenses of registration.

Anti-Corn-law Wafers. Sheets of mottoes (40 for 1s.) advocating free-trade in corn. These mottoes are either original or mere extracts; some aimed at wit, some at smartness, some were political truisms, and some were satirical. During the Anti-Corn-law agitation these 'wafers' had a large sale.

Anti-Gallican Society (*The*), 1757. 'To promote British manufactures extend the commerce of England, and discourage the introduction of French modes and the importation of French commodities.' The headquarters of the society were at Lebeck's Head, Strand. St. George's Day (23 April) was the day of their anniversary feast.

It was at its best in 1771.

Anti-League League (*The*), 1844. A league formed to counteract the Anti-Corn-law League, on the supposition that the higher the price of corn, the higher the rate of wages. Chartists were anti-leaguers.

Sir Robert Peel said experience proved that the high price of corn was not accompanied by a high rate of wages, and that wages did not vary with the price of corn (1845).

Anti-Pædo-baptists, 1607, now called Baptists. Certain dissenters who object to infant or *pædo* baptism, and maintain that no one should be baptized without expressing a personal wish to undergo the ceremony, and without a personal confession of faith. They perform the rite by total immersion. (Greek *anti pais baptisma*, against child baptism.)

Anti-Popes. Popes elected in opposition to the pope of Rome.

1. NOVATIANUS, elected in opposition to Cornelius, A.D. 251.
2. FELIX II., elected on the banishment of Liberius, A.D. 355.
3. URSINUS or URSINUS, elected in opposition to Damasus, A.D. 366.
4. EULALIUS, elected in opposition to Boniface I., A.D. 418.
5. LAURENTIUS, appointed by Festus in opposition to Symmachus, A.D. 498.
6. DIOSCORUS, consecrated in opposition to Boniface II., A.D. 530.
7. VIGILIUS, appointed by Belisarius on the exile of Silverius, A.D. 537.
8. 9. PETER and THEODORUS, in the pontificate of John V., A.D. 686.
10. 11. PASCHAL and THEODORUS, elected in opposition to Sergius, A.D. 687.
12. 13. 14. THEOPHYLACTUS, CONSTANTINUS, and PHILIP, elected at the death of Paul I., A.D. 767-768.
Constantinus was deposed by Pope Stephen III., shut up in a monastery, and his eyes put out, Aug. 6, 768.
15. ZIZIMUS, elected in opposition to Eugenius II., A.D. 824
16. ANASTASIUS, who contested the election of Benedict III., A.D. 855.
17. SERGIUS, elected in opposition to Formosus, A.D. 891.
18. BONIFACE VI., chosen to succeed Formosus, A.D. 896, died a fortnight afterwards.
19. CHRISTOPHORUS, who deposed and imprisoned Leo V., A.D. 905.
20. LEO VIII., elected to succeed John XII., A.D. 964, deposed 965.
21. BONIFACE VII., elected on the death of Benedict VI., A.D. 974, deposed 975.
22. GREGORY, who unseated Benedict VIII., A.D. 1012, deposed by Kaiser Henry II., A.D. 1014.
23. SILVESTER III., elected to succeed Benedict IX. on his banishment, A.D. 1044. Benedict sold the pontificate to John, 1044.
24. BENEDICT X., who opposed Stephen IX., A.D. 1058.
25. HONORIUS, appointed by the diet of Basel in opposition to Alexander II., A.D. 1061, deposed by the council of Osbor, 1062.
26. CLEMENT III., elected at Brixen in opposition to Gregory VII., A.D. 1080. Clement was set up by Kaiser Henry IV.
27. ALBERT, appointed to succeed Clement taken prisoner by the partisans of Paschal II., A.D. 1100.

28. THEODORIC, appointed to succeed Albert, A.D. 1100.

29. MAGINUFE, appointed to succeed Theodoric, A.D. 1106.

30. GREGORY VIII., elected in opposition to Gelasius II., A.D. 1118. Gregory was set up by Kaiser Henry V.

31. CALIXTUS, elected during the pontificate of Honorius II., A.D. 1124-1130.

32. ANACLETUS, elected by a majority of the conclave in opposition to Innocent II., A.D. 1130.

33. VICTOR IV., chosen to succeed Anacletus, A.D. 1138, abdicated.

34. VICTOR (also called Victor IV.), elected in opposition to Alexander III., A.D. 1159.

35. PASCHAL III., elected to succeed Victor, A.D. 1164.

36. CALLISTUS III., elected to succeed Paschal. A.D. 1168. Abjures his schism, 1178.

87. INNOCENT III., chosen in the place of Callistus, A.D. 1178. Taken prisoner by Pope Alexander, 1180, and died soon afterwards.

38. NICHOLAS V., chosen by Louis of Bavaria in opposition to John XXII., A.D. 1328. Renounced his schism, 1330.

The Great Schism of the West, 1378-1429. When there was a pope at Rome, and another at Avignon, and sometimes three or four popes.

Presuming the French popes to be anti-popes in this schism, we have—

39. CLEMENT VII., the French pope in opposition to Urban VI., A.D. 1378.

40. BENEDICT XIII., who succeeded Clement, A.D. 1394.

41. ALEXANDER V., elected by the Council of Pisa, which took upon itself to depose the two existing popes, and to elect a third, A.D. 1254.

There were now three popes, viz. Gregory XII. at Rome, Benedict XIII. at Avignon, and Alexander V.

42. JOHN XXII., who succeeded Alexander, A.D. 1410. Was deposed by the Council of Constance 1417, and Martin V. elected.

There were now four popes: Gregory XII., Benedict XIII., John XXIII., and Martin V.

43. CLEMENT VIII., succeeded Benedict XIII., A.D. 1424. Abdicates 1429, and thus the schism ends.

Gregory XII. died 1417. John XXIII. died 1419, Benedict XIII. died 1424, Clement VIII. abdicated 1429. Martin V. was left sole pope.

44. FELIX V., elected in opposition to Eugenius IV. by the Council of Basel, A.D. 1439; abdicated 1449. Undoubtedly an excellent choice, accepted by England, France, Germany, Spain and Lombardy. Only Italy (bar Lombardy) and Venice refused to acknowledge him.

Anti-Remonstrants, or 'Gomarists,' 1611.

Ultra-Calvinists and followers of Frans Gomar, of Bruges (1563-1641), who arbitrarily laid down the dogmas of absolute predestination and reprobation in answer to the 'Remonstrance' of the Arminians presented to the states of Holland in 1610.

The word is applied to the Jansenists (q.v.); and their opponents (the Jesuits) were termed Remonstrants.

Anti-Tobacconists (The), 1848.

In Italy. The Austrians had the monopoly of tobacco in Italy, and the Liberals resolved to leave off smoking, so that a cigar became the sign of loyalty, and non-smoking of disaffection. The Austrians resented the anti-tobacco movement; and in order to put a stop to it, supplied their Italian troops with cigars, and ordered them to smoke them ostentatiously in the streets. This insult was resented by the Italians. On 17 March the Milanese rose in revolt and expelled the Austrians. Venice next rose and did the same. Sicily expelled King Ferdinand II., and elected in his stead Charles Albert (Albert Amadeus I.). At last Garibaldi appeared and liberated Italy, making it a united and independent kingdom.

Anti-Tory Association (The), 1834.

Established in Ireland by Daniel O'Connell to oppose the new Tory administration under the leadership of Sir Robert Peel. See 'Irish Associations.'

Anti-Trinita'rians.

Those who reject the doctrine of the Trinity on *philosophical* grounds.

Those who reject it on *theological* grounds are called Arians, Socinians, or Unitarians; Mohammedans are Anti-Trinitarians.

Anti-Union Society (The), 1830.

A new name for the Repeal Association (q.v.), when that association was proclaimed. Both had the same object viz. the repeal of the Union effected in 1801, or the amalgamation of the Irish and British Parliaments. See 'Irish Associations.'

Antid'ico-Mariani'tæ (4th cent.).

i.e. 'Detractors of Mary,' as the Apollinarians and Eunomians were called, who denied the perpetual virginity of Mary; in other words, believed that Mary had other children besides Jesus, who was her 'firstborn' (Matt. i. 25). The brethren of Jesus mentioned in the gospels they considered to be the other children of Mary (see Matt. xiii. 55, 56; Mark vi. 3; Matt. xii. 46; Gal. i. 19).

In English 'Antidicomarianites,' pronounce Antid'-i-co Ma'ri-an-ites (Greek, ἀντίδικος, Μαρία, (adversary [of] Mary).

Antino'mians, 1535.

A sect founded by John Agricŏla, who maintained that Christ abolished the entire law for believers. They furthermore affirmed that good works do not further salvation, which is wholly of grace. 'Not of works, lest any man should boast.' 'If (salvation) is by grace, then it is no more of works, otherwise grace is no more grace. But if it be of works, then is it no more grace, otherwise work is no more work'

(Rom. xi. 6); (Greek, *anti, nomos*, opposed to the law, i.e. of works.)

The system is called 'Antinomianism.'

The Antinomians taught that the chosen were at liberty to help themselves to such a share of this world's goods as their necessities required; and that however they might sin in their outward man, in the inner man they sinned not. (Strype, *Cranmer*, p. 178.) This is a gross perversion of Antinomianism.

N.B. In New England, Antinomians, in the 17th cent., denied the 'moral law to be the rule of Christ' (John Harvard, 1628).

The Antinomians contended that all things were free and allowable to the saints without sin.— HOWITT, *Hist. of Eng.* vol. ii. p. 262.

Antiphona'rium.

An Antiph'onary, or book containing the Antiph'onies throughout the year. Such as the 'Greater Antiphonies of O'; the 'Rogational Antiphonies'; the 'Alleluyatic Antiphonies'; the 'Antiphona ad introitum'; the 'Antiphonæ Invitatoriæ'; the 'Antiphona de Podio'; the 'Processional Antiphonies' &c. By the Constitutions of Archbishop Winchelsey, at Merton (1305), every parish church was ordered to have one.

The 'O Antiphonies' are the fifteen prayers beginning with the letter O ('Horæ Beatissimæ Virginis Mariæ'). The 'Antiphona de Podio' is the 'Salve Regina' made by Ademarus, bishop of Podium, i.e. Puy. The 'Antiphona ad introitum' was sung *in introitu Missæ*. The 'Invitatoriæ' were sung on Sunday nights.

Antiphon'eti.

An image of Christ crucified set up near the pulpit. Du Cange quotes (vol. i. p. 276, col. 2) the following words:

Visus est sibi in occiduo graduum, qui ad sacram ædem ducunt, ascensu stare, ubi præter divinam Domini imaginem quam Antiphoneti appellant, ipsius etiam Niconis effigies expressa est.— MARTEN, 10, 6, *Ampliss. Collect*, col. 880.

Antiquaries (*The Society of*).

For the cultivation and understanding of the antiquities of the chief countries of Europe and America. It was started in 1572 by Archbishop Parker and Sir Robert Cotton; but James I. dissolved this society in 1604; and it was reconstructed in 1717.

The London Society was chartered in 1572.
The Scotch Society was founded in 1780.
The Royal Irish Society was chartered in 1786.
The French Society was founded, as the *Académie Celtique* in 1805; but in 1814 it changed its name into the *Société des Antiquaires de France*.

The American Antiquarian Society was incorporated in 1812 by the legislature of Massachusetts.

Antiquitates Variæ, 1498.

A literary forgery by Annius of Viterbo (Nannius, Giovanni Nanni), a Dominican. His 17 volumes profess to be selections from Berosius, Manĕtho, Megasthĕnĕs, Archilŏcus, Myrsilĕs, Fabius Pictor, Sempronius, Cato, &c., but the selections are not genuine.

Anto'nian Laws (*The*).

The laws of Mark Antony, the Roman consul.

1. To change the name of the month *Quintīlis* into Julius (July).

2. To abolish the perpetual dictatorship.

3. To repeal the Judiciary Julian Law, commanding that the *judices* should be chosen from the senators and equitês only, and not from the *tribuni ærarii*.

The vanity of Augustus in making *Sextilis* (August) the same length as *Quintilis* (July), deranged the natural system that the *even* months, 2, 4, 6, 8, 10, 12, had thirty days each, and the *odd* numbers, 1, 3, 5, 7, 9, 11, had thirty-one days each.

Antonine Column (*The*).

A column, like that in the Place Vendôme (2 syl.), Paris. It was erected by the Roman senate in honour of Marcus Aurelius Antonīnus, to commemorate his victories over the Marcomanni and other Germanic tribes. On the shaft is represented spirally the victories of the emperor, and an inscription was cut on the pedestal. Sixtus V. had the bad taste to substitute a gilt statue of Paul, holding a Latin cross, for that of Marcus Aurelius; and to substitute a new inscription. So that now the Apostle Paul surmounts a huge column commemorating victories over Germanic tribes; and the new inscription is absolutely ludicrous. It stands on the Piazza Colonna in Rome.

Antonine's Itinerary.

Extending over the whole Roman empire, embracing all the main roads in Italy and the provinces, with the respective distances. Attached is a maritime itinerary of the distances from port to port. The distances of this itinerary were surveyed by command of Julius Cæsar. Augustus and Antony, B.C. 44, 30, 24; and A.D. 19; and the entire book was corrected and extended between 285–305.

The Peutingerian Table (*q.v.*) and the Jerusalem Itinerary are also valuable for ancient geography.

D

Antony's Fire (*St.*). A pestilence also called *feu sacré* and *mal des ardents*, especially destructive in France and Germany between 994 and 1089. It appeared in England in the years 1011 and 1012. Hugues Capet, founder of the Capetian dynasty, died of this terrible plague. *See* 'Feu Sacré,' 'Plague,' &c.

Called St. Antony's Fire, because Urban IV. in 1089 founded an order of St. Antony to take charge of those afflicted with this disorder. Never in the history of man was such a disastrous century as that which began at the close of the tenth. All Europe looked for the end of the world, which contributed not a little to the calamities which followed in battalions.

Antwerp. Fabulously derived from *hand-werpen* (hand-throwing); hence the arms of the city are two hands thrown into the Scheldt by the hero Brabo. Much more likely it is *an t' werf* (the city) on the wharf.

Anzia'ni (*The*), or seniors in Florentine history before 1282. They were twelve in number, two for each sestiere of the city. These seniors acted in concert with a foreign Podestà, and a captain of the people charged with military authority. *See* 'Ancients.'

Ape (1 syl.*).* The assumed signature of the famous caricaturist, who drew so many of our living notabilities. He was Signor Carlo Pellegrini, who died 1889.

Apega. Wife of Nabis, tyrant of Sparta. He invented an infernal machine which he called after his wife, 'Apega.' It was a box exactly resembling his wife in her royal apparel, but inside it was full of spikes which wounded the victim enclosed in almost every part of the body. The 'Iron Virgin' was a similar instrument of torture employed by the Inquisition. It represented a woman of Bavaria, and the spikes were so arranged as to pierce the least vital parts in order to prolong the sufferings of the victim inclosed. (Apega, 3 syl.)

Apellês of Europe (*The*). Antonio Allegri da Correggio (1494–1534).

Apelles of his age (*The*). Sam. Cooper is so called in his epitaph in Old St. Pancras Church (1609–1672).

Apex. In the Fenian organisation is the president of the head centres. *See* 'Bees.'

Apocryphal Scriptures, of the New Testament. From Eusebius:—
The Acts of Paul.
Pastor of Hermas.
The Revelation of Peter.
The Epistle of Barnabas.
The Institutions of the Apostles.
The Gospel according to the Hebrews.
The Gospel of Peter.
The Gospel of Thomas; Acts of ditto.
A Gospel of Matthew.
Acts of the Apostles by Andrew.
Acts of the Apostles by John.

Doubtful.
The Revelation of John.
The Epistle of James.
The Epistle of Jude.
The Second Epistle of Peter.
The Second and Third Epistle of John.
Eusebius, Book III. chap. 25. *See* ' Old Testament.'

Other books not mentioned by Eusebius. The Gnostic Scriptures were:
The Prophecies of Cain.
The Writings of Pachur.
The Psalms by Valentīnus and Bardesanês.
The Gnostic Hymns by Marcus.
The Books of Adam, of Enoch, of Moseh, of Elijah, of Isajah, and many others.
Sundry writings by Barkor, Armagil, Barbelon, Balsamum, Lensiboras, &c.—Hier, *Ad Theod.* iii. 6, &c.

Apollina'rians, 4th cent. Followers of Apollināris or Apollinarius, bishop of Laodicea, who denied that Christ had a human soul, and affirmed that the Logos or divine nature supplied the place of the reasonable soul. Condemned in the Council of Alexandria, A.D. 362, and again by the council at Rome in 375. In 378 Apollinaris was deposed.

Apologists. Those 'Fathers' who wrote 'Apologies,' or treatises in defence of the rites, doctrines, and moral conduct of Christians in the first three centuries.

APOLLINARIS (*Claudius*), 2nd cent., bishop of Hierapolis, was a Christian apologist.

JUSTIN MARTYR, 103–167. Wrote two 'Apologies,' both in Latin; one he addressed to Antonīnus Pius, in 150; and the other to the Senate, in 164. He says that the Christian religion tends to good morals and submission to rulers; shows that Christ fulfilled prophecy; and explains Christian rites and doctrines.

MEL'ITO, bishop of Sardis. Addressed his 'Apology for Christians' to Marcus Aurelius in 170.

ORIGEN, 185–254. Wrote 'An Apology for Christianity,' against Celsus. He became a Gnostic.

QUADRA'TUS, bishop of Athens. Presented his 'Apology' to Hadrian in 126.

TATIAN, born in Syria (flo. 170). Wrote his 'Apology' about 160. Afterwards he was accused of heresy, for forbidding the use of wine even in the sacrament of the Eucharist. He was a Gnostic.

THEOPH'ILUS of Antioch, 120–190. Wrote 'An Apology for the Christian Religion,' in three books.

Tertullian, 160–240. Shows in his 'Apology' that faith and patience were manifested by Christians in persecution.

Many others wrote in defence of Christianity, but not 'Apologies.' For example:

ARNOBIUS (flo. 296). Wrote a 'Disputation against the Gentiles,' in seven books.

ATHENAG'ORAS (flo. 117). Wrote a defence of Christians against the charges of atheism, incest, infanticide, and other abominations.

CYPRIAN, 200–250. Wrote on the 'Absurdity of Idolatry.'

JEROME, 345–420. Refuted the objection that no distinguished person had embraced Christianity.

MINUCIUS FELIX (flo. 250). Wrote a dialogue entitled 'Octavius,' in which the speakers represent several objections against Christianity, but are compelled to acknowledge their errors.

ORO'SIUS (flo. 415). In his 'History of the Word' he refutes the accusation that plagues, famine, earthquakes, &c., were judgments of God to show his displeasure against Christians.

Besides these, CYRIL of Alexander wrote a reply to Julian the apostate; and THEODORET, in twelve sermons shows the superiority of the prophets and apostles to the Greek philosophers.

LACTANTIUS (250–325), wrote 'Divine Institutions,' in seven books; AUGUSTINE (354–430) wrote 'On the City of God.'

EUSEDIUS (270–338), though no Apologist, wrote an 'Ecclesiastical History,' in ten books, which served the same end.

In modern times.

GROTIUS (1583–1645) defended Christianity in his 'De Veritate Religionis Christianæ,' 1686.

LARDNER (*Nathaniel*), 1684–1768, did the same in his 'Credibility of the Gospel History,' 1727–1755.

BUTLER, bishop of Durham, (1692–1752), in his 'Analogy of Religion,' 1736.

PALEY (1743–1805), in his 'Evidences of Christianity,' 1794.

WATSON, bishop of Llandaff (1737–1816), in his 'Apology for Christianity,' 1776.

.' Still more recently we have Neander, Tholuck, and Reinhard (among Protestants); with Pascal, Bergier, Mayr, and Chateaubriand among Catholics.

The branch of theology which deals with the defence of Christianity is called 'Apologetics.'

Apology of Melanchthon (*The*). That is, his Apology or defence of the Augsburg Confession (*q.v.*), one of the *Libri Symbolici Ecclesiæ Evangelicæ* of the Lutherans.

Apostle of Beauvais (*The*). St. Lucian, who died 290. His day is January 8. Also patron saint.

Apostle of Brazil (*The*). Jose de Anchieta, 1533–1597.

It must be distinctly understood there is a great difference between a patron saint and an apostle. The former protects and is generally chosen by the people. The latter converts. Occasionally an apostle is subsequently chosen by a people as their patron saint.

Apostle of England (*The*). Hugh Latimer, bishop of Worcester, 1472–1555. Burnt at the stake in Mary's reign. *See* 'Apostle of the English.'

It was Hugh Latimer who said to Ridley while being chained to the stake: ' Be of good comfort, Master Ridley, and play the man. We shall this day light such a candle in England, as I trust by God's grace shall never be put out.'

St. George is patron saint of England, and St. Paul of London.

Apostle of France (*The*). St. Denys, *i.e.* Dionysius the Areopagite, burnt to death A.D. 95. Also patron saint of France.

Apostle of Hungary (*The*). St. Stephen (I.), King of Hungary (979, 997–1038).

Apostle of Infidelity (*The*). Voltaire (1694–1778).

Apostle of Liberty (*The*). Thomas Jefferson, third president of the U.S. America (1743–1826).

Apostle of Massacre (*The*). Jean P. Marat called himself so (1744–1793).

Apostle of Presbytery (*The*). John Knox (1505–1572).

Apostle of Temperance (*The*). Father (Theobald) Mathew, a friar of Cork, who began his temperance movement in Ireland in 1837, and met with wonderful success. The movement was in full force during O'Connell's repeal agitation and even during the potato famine (1790–1856).

Apostle of Virginia (*The*). Rev. A. Whittaker, 17th cent.

Apostle of the Abyssinians (*The*). St. Frumentius, who died 360. His day is 27 Oct. Also patron saint of Abyssinia.

Apostle of the Allemanian Nations (*The*). St. Gall or Gallus, an Irishman.

Apostle of the Alps (*The*). Felix Neff (1798–1829).

Apostle of the Ardennes (*The*). St. Hubert (656–730). His days are 30 May and 3 Nov.

Apostle of the Armenians (*The*). Gregory of Armenia (256–331). Also the patron saint of Armenia. His day is 30 Sept.

Apostle of the English (*The*). St. Gregory the Great is so called by the Venerable Bede (544–604).

Apostle of the English People (*The*). St. Augustine, who died 607. *See* 'Apostle of England.'

St. George is the patron saint of England.

Apostle of the French (*The Great*). St. Remi (439–535). His day is 1 Oct. The patron saint of France is St. Denys.

The patron saint of Paris is Ste. Geneviève.

Apostle of the Frisians (*The*). St. Wildrod or Willibrod (657–738). His day is 7 Nov. Also the patron saint of Friesland.

Apostle of the Gauls (*The*). St. Denys martyred in 272. His day is 9 Oct. St. Irenæus is sometimes so called (130–200). His day is 11 Nov. *See* 'Apostle of France.'

The patron saint of Gaul is St. Martin.

Apostle of the Gentiles (*The*). St. Paul, who died A.D. 66. His days are 29 June and 25 Jan.

Apostle of the Germans (*The*). St. Boniface, an English Benedictine monk, whose name was Winfrith or Winfrid, born at Kirton or Crediton, in Devonshire, then part of Wessex, in 680. He was archbishop of Germany in 731, metropolitan at Metz in 742, and was slain 5 June, 755, aged 75. St. Martin is the patron saint of Germany.

Gregory II. consecrated him bishop of the New German churches, in 725, and changed his name to Boniface (or Well-doer).

Apostle of the Goths (*The*). Ulfilas, their first bishop (348–388). He translated the Bible into the Gothic tongue, and one copy of the four gospels (if not more) is still extant.

Apostle of the Highlanders (*The*). St. Colomb (521–597). His day is 9 June. Also the patron saint of the Highlands.

Apostle of the Hungarians (*The*). St. Anastasius (954–1044).

St. Louis is the patron saint of Hungary; and also St. Mary of Aquisgranum (Aix-la-Chapelle).

Apostle of the Indians (*The*). Bartolomé de Las Casas (1474–1566). Also the Rev. John Eliot (1603–1690).

Apostle of the Indies (*The*). St. Francis Xavier (1506–1552). His day is 3 Dec.

Apostle of the Irish (*The*). St. Patrick (372–493). His day is 17 March.

Apostle of the Lowlands (*The*). Cuthbert, Archbishop of Canterbury (741–758.)

Apostle of the Netherlands (*The*). St. Amandus (594–667). He was bishop of Maestricht. Also the patron saint.

Apostle of the New Jerusalem (*The*). Emanuel Swedenborg (1688–1772).

Apostle of the North (*The*). St. Ansgar (801–864). Also Bernard Gilpin (1517–1583).

Apostle of the Peak (*The*). William Bagshawe, of Ford Hall, a nonconformist in the reign of Charles II. (17 Jan., 1627–8—2 April, 1702).

Apostle of the Scottish Reformers (*The*). John Knox (1505–1572).

St. Andrew is the patron saint of Scotland. His day is 30 Nov. It is said that his remains were brought by Regulus to Fifeshire, A.D. 368.

Apostle of the Slavi, or Slaves (*The*). St. Cyril, who died 868. His day is 14 Feb.

Apostles (*The* 14). According to Gospel history or Church tradition—

1. ANDREW of Bethsaida, a fisherman, brother of Simon Peter, and son of Jona (bar-Jona). Bound to a cross like the letter X, called a St. Andrew's cross, by order of Ægæus, proconsul of Achaia (1st cent.). His day is 30 Nov. His symbol in paintings is a St. Andrew's cross. His scene of labour was Scythia, according to tradition.

2. BARTHOLOMEW of Galilee, a fisherman; supposed to be Nathaniel Bar-Tholemy. Flayed alive in Armenia,

A.D. 71. His day is 24 Aug. His symbol is a knife. His scene of labour was India, according to tradition.

3. JAMES I. (the Greater), of Bethsaida, a fisherman, brother of John, and son of Zebedee and Salomê. Beheaded at Jerusalem by Herod Agrippa, A.D. 43. His day is 24 July. His symbol is a pilgrim's staff and a gourd bottle.

4. JAMES II. (the Less), surnamed 'The Just,' supposed to have been a Jewish ecclesiastic. Brother of Simeon and Jude, called 'brothers of the Lord.' Son of Cleopas (or Alphæus) and Mary. Thrown from a pinnacle of the temple, and then beaten or stoned to death, A.D. 65. His day is 1 May. (See 'Philip.') His symbol is a fuller's club.

Said to be the first bishop of Jerusalem, and succeeded in 67 by his brother, Simeon or Simon.

5. JOHN (the beloved disciple, an Evangelist) of Bethsaida, a fisherman, brother of James I., and son of Zebedee and Salomê. The two brothers were called Boanerges. John was the youngest of the apostles, and died at an extreme old age at Eьhesus between A.D. 91 and 100. His day is 27 Dec. His symbol is a bowl with a winged serpent flying out of it. He wore a priest's petalon.

6. JUDAS ISCARIOT, i.e. of the tribe of Issachar. Place of birth, parentage, and vocation unknown. Hanged himself A.D. 64.

7. JUDE, Judas not Iscariot, surnamed Thaddæus, of Nazareth. Brother of James II., and son of Cleopas (or Alphæus and Mary), a 'brother of the Lord.' Occupation unknown. Shot to death by arrows in Armenia or Persia, A.D. 80. His day is 28 Oct. His symbol is a club.

8. MATTHEW, or Levi, of Galilee, a Roman revenue officer at Gennesareth. One of the four Evangelists. Slain by a sword in Ethiopia (1st cent.). His day is 27 Sept. His symbol is a hatchet.

9. MATTHIAS, elected by lot to the college, in place of Judas Iscariot. Nothing known of him. Said to have been first stoned and then beheaded in Colchis (1st cent.). His day is 24 Feb. His symbol is a battle-axe.

10. PAUL, or Saul, of Tarsus. Probably designed to be a Jewish scribe. Brother of Rufus (Rom. xvi. 13), and son of Simon of Cyrenê, who helped to carry the cross (Mark xv. 21). Beheaded at Rome, A.D. 66. His days are 29 June (death),

and 25 Jan. (conversion). His symbol is a sword.

11. PETER (Simon), or Cephas, of Bethsaida, a fisherman, brother of Andrew, and son of Jona (Bar-Jona). Crucified at Rome with his head downwards, A.D. 66. His day is 29 June. His symbol is two keys.

Called by Catholics 'the Prince of the Apostles.'

12. PHILIP, of Bethsaida, probably a fisherman. Parentage unknown. Hanged against a pillar at Hierapŏlis, a city of Phrygia, A.D. 80. His day is 1 May. (See 'James II.') His symbol is a long staff with a cross at the end.

13. SIMON or Simeon (Zealotês), probably a fisherman of Nazareth. Brother of James II. and Jude, and son of Cleopas (or Alphæus) and Mary. Crucified in Persia, A.D. 107, at the age of 120. The oldest and last of the Apostles. His day is 18 Feb. His symbol is a saw.

Said to have succeeded his brother James in 67, as bishop of Jerusalem.

14. THOMAS (surnamed Didymus), of Galilee. Probably a fisherman. Parentage unknown. He was run through the body with a spear at Coromandel (1st cent.). His day is 21 Dec. His symbol is a spear. His scene of labour was Parthia, according to tradition.

The Apostolic days are: Jan. 25, Feb. 18 and 24, May 1 (two apostles), June 29 (two apostles), July 24, Aug. 24, Sept. 27, Oct. 28, Nov. 30, Dec. 21 and 27. None in either March or April, the busy season of Lent and Easter, but two are placed in the following months of May and June.

Of the two non-apostolic Evangelists nothing is known. Probably Luke (Lucius) was a Roman by birth, and it is supposed he was a physician and an artist. Tradition says he was hanged in Greece on an olive-tree, in the 1st cent.

Mark is supposed to be John Mark, the companion of Paul. Tradition says that, being dragged through the streets of Alexandria, he was hurled from a high rock into the sea.

Apostles' Creed (The), or 'Symbol of the Apostles.' This creed is so called because each of the twelve clauses is attributed to one of the apostles. Thus:

1. PETER: I believe in God the Father Almighty, Maker of heaven and earth.

2. JOHN: [And] in Jesus Christ, His only Son, our Lord.

3. JAMES (Sen.): Who was conceived of the Holy Ghost, born of the Virgin Mary.

4. ANDREW: Suffered under Pontius Pilate ; was crucified, dead, and buried. ('Dead' not in the Oriental Creed.) 'Was dead'=was deaded.

5. PHILIP: He descended into hell. (From the Creed of Aquileia.)

6. THOMAS: The third day He rose again from the dead. (St. Augustine.)

7. JAMES (Jun.): He ascended into heaven, and sitteth on the right hand of God the Father Almighty.

8. MATTHEW: From thence He shall come to judge the quick and the dead.

9. NATHANIEL: I believe in the Holy Ghost.

10. SIMON: The Holy Catholic Church, the Communion of Saints. (Added 6th cent.)

11. MATTHIAS: The forgiveness of sins.

12. JUDE: The resurrection of the body. and the life everlasting. (Last part belongs to the 3rd cent. the first part to the 4th cent.)

These twelve articles, we are told, were suggested by the Apostles in a grotto of Mount Olivet, before their final separation, and the Apostles were anciently delineated each holding a banderole, on which was inscribed the words of the symbol attributed to him.

Apostolic Bishops (*The*). The bishops of the Apostolic Churches (*q.v.*). In 1046 the Council of Reims declared that the bishop of Rome is the sole apostolic primate of the Universal Church, and hence such terms as apostolic see, apostolic nuncio, apostolic notary, apostolic brief. apostolic vicar, &c. meaning papal nuncio, notary, &c.

Apostolic Blessing (*The*). The blessing of the pope of Rome, as successor of St. Peter.

Apostolic Brethren, or 'Aposto-lici' (1260–1368). A Christian sect founded by Girolamo Segarelli, a weaver of Parma, who went about in the dress of an apostle, preached repentance, free society, and a return to apostolic manners. From 1290 his adherents began to denounce infant baptism. the dogma of purgatory, invocation of saints, prayers for the dead, and the corrupt lives of the clergy. In 1300 Girolamo Segarelli, the founder, and many of his followers were brought to the stake.

Dolcino then became the head of the society and drew together many thousands of followers. but in 1305 a crusade was preached against him, and being captured. he was burnt alive. The brotherhood lingered on till 1368, and gradually died out. Dante refers to Dolcino in the 'Inferno,' xxviii. 55.

Volumus quod nullus clericus, nulla secularis persona, intuitu religionis eorum, ac insolito habitu, eos de cætero recipiat, aut eis alimenta ministret.—*Council of Jerusalem*, 1287.

Apostolic Chamber (*The*). A council entrusted with the care of the revenues of the see of Rome. Equal to papal chamber or board.

Apostolic Churches (*The*). Alexandria, Antioch, Jerusalem, and Rome ; sometimes Corinth and Ephesus are also included. These churches are supposed to have been founded by the Apostles themselves.

Apostolic Constitutions (*The*), or 'Apostolic Canons.' A collection of ecclesiastical laws attributed to St. Clement, a disciple of St. Peter, but proved to be not earlier than the 3rd cent. Indeed the Quini-Sext (*q.v.*) council, held at Constantinople in 690, pronounced the collection to be apocryphal. *See* 'Literary Forgeries.'

Apostolic Fathers (*The*). The immediate fellow-labourers of the apostles, born in the first century. They were: (1) Barnabas, who died A.D. 61; (2) Clement of Rome, 30–100; (3) Ignatius, who died 115; (4) Polycarp, 80–169. They were succeeded by the Primitive Fathers (*q.v.*)

Papias of Hierapolis, and Hermas, author of the 'Shepherd,' are sometimes ranked amongst the apostolic fathers. Papias died 169, Polycarp in 167, and Hermas in the 1st cent. It is doubtful whether Hermas is a proper name at all.

Apostolic Kings (*The*). Pope Sylvester II., in 1000, granted to Stephen of Hungary and his successors the right of so styling themselves. The reigning king is addressed as Your Apostolic Majesty, and referred to as H.A.M. In 1758 Clement XIII. conferred the title of H.A.M. on Maria Theresa, as queen of Hungary, and the emperor of Austria, as king of Hungary, continues the same style.

Apostolic Letter or Brief (*An*). A papal letter or brief.

Apostolic Months (*The*). The six following months: January, March, May, July, September, and November. That is, every alternate month beginning with January. It was on these months that the pope (according to the Vienna Concordat of 1448) took possession of the vacant benefices in Germany, &c.

Apostolic Party (*The*), 1819–1830. In Spanish history. Fanatical Catholics who were also absolutists. Their leaders were priests and their troops were smugglers and robbers. They ultimately merged into the Catholic party.

Apostolic See (*The*). The see of Rome, said to have been founded by the apostle Peter.

Apostolic Succession (*The*). The supposed succession of the priesthood in an unbroken line from the Apostles, by means of ordination and laying on of hands.

Apostolic Vicar (*The*), or '**Vicar Apostolic.**' The cardinal who represents the pope in extraordinary missions.

Apostolical Canons, 'Canōnes Apostolici.' Two collections of ecclesiastical rules and formularies attributed to Clement of Rome (1st cent.). This, however, has been entirely disproved, and probably they were first drafted in the 2nd and 3rd cents., and the main portion is assigned to a period close upon the great council at Nice (A.D. 325). The first allusion to these canons is in the Council of Constantinople, A.D. 394. The whole number is 85, of which 50 are regarded with respect by the Western Church, but all are accepted by the Greek Church. *See* 'Apostolic Constitutions.'

The first fifty were translated from the Greek into Latin, in the 5th cent., by Dionysius the Younger. References made in these canons to Eusebius (265–338), Athanasius (296–373), and Epiphanius (310–403), suffice to prove that parts at least of these canons cannot have been earlier than the 4th cent. (*See* 'Literary Forgeries.')

Apostolical Constitutions (*The*). In eight books, in which the Apostles are introduced as speakers. They are supposed to date from the 4th cent., but certainly much is of later date. They enjoin the duty of assembling twice a day for public praye rand psalmody; the observance of fasts and festivals; the obligation of the Jewish Sabbath and the Christian Sunday; the duty of reverencing bishops as God's anointed ones and of inferior clergy as Christian magistrates. Epiphanius (367–403) speaks of these books, and, though not genuine, they are useful in showing the religious tone and feeling of the period. *See* 'Apostolical Canons.'

The first six books contain rules for a Christian life; Book VII. is an abridgment of the preceding six books, and Book VIII. relates to priests and their duties.

Apostolical Junta (*The*), 26 Sep., 1825. Formed by Ferdinand VII. of Spain for the purpose of assisting the ministry.

Apostolicals (*The*). Members of the Apostolical Junta (*q.v.*).

Apostol'ici, or '**Apostolic'ians**,' or '**Apotac'tici**.' Heretics mentioned by Papias, who died A.D. 169. They professed to follow the Apostles in having all things in common, and renounced riches and marriage. *See* 'Apostolic Brethren.'

Epiphanius' (310–403) says these vagabonds made use of the Apocryphal Acts of St. Andrew and St. Thomas.

Apostolicians. The Waldenses, or Vaudois, were so called in the 12th cent.; so were the Apostolic Brethren (*q.v.*) of the 13th and 14th cents. *See* also '**Apostolici**.'

Apostol'icum (*The*), 7 Jan., 1765. A bull granted by Pope Clement XIII. at the solicitation of the Jesuits, confirming their institution. It was suppressed 11 Feb., 1765, by a Parlement of Paris.

The publication was forbidden in Portugal in 1765.

Apostoo'lians, or '**Apostoo'lists**,' 1664. A branch of Baptists in Holland, founded by Samuel Apostool (1638–1700). They split from the Mennonites, and were Calvinistic in their views of absolute predestination.

Apotac'tici, or **Apotac'titæ.** The same as the Apostol'ici (*q.v.*).

Apothe'ker (*The*). The Fourteen Saintly Helpers (*q.v.*).

Similar to the *Theoi Alexikakoi* of the Greeks, and the *Dii Averrunci* of the Romans.

Apparel. To give apparel was, in Ireland, a symbol of lordship. Thus our John, as lord of Ireland, being applied to by Crovderg for help against the O'Conors, gave the required aid, and sent a quantity of scarlet cloth to be presented to the king of Ireland and the provincial chiefs, who acknowledged the English supremacy. It was, in fact, a livery.

O'Donnell applied for apparel (1541), a request which the Deputy, not understanding the political meaning, thought very strange, seeing that when he made it he wore a coat of crimson velvet with twenty or thirty pair of aglets, under a double cloak of rich crimson satin corded with black velvet, and a bonnet of equal splendour.—O'CONOR, *History of the Irish People*, p. 123.

Appartements. Receptions held thrice a week by Louis XIV. at Versailles. An '**Appartement**' was an assembly of all the court in the grand saloon from seven till ten, when the king sat down to table. There was first music, then billiards, cards, dominoes, chess, and dancing. A guest was at liberty to order of the attendants anything he wished for.

Appeal (*An*). An accusation by a private subject against another for some heinous crime, demanding punishment on account of some specified injury suffered, rather than for the offence against the public. In 1386 the members of the commission appointed to regulate the affairs of the nation and the king's household (Rich. II.) appealed of high treason the Archbishop of York, the Duke of Ireland, the Earl of Suffolk, Sir Robert Tresilian, and Sir Nicholas Brembre, for disputing their authority. The appeal was sent to the king, who was obliged to give way, and the accused fled, but only Sir Nicholas Brembre and Tresilian were captured and executed. The object of the appellants was really to depose the king, and take the crown into their own custody.

Appeal (*Court of*). The Judicial Committee of the Privy Council was constituted a Court of Appeal by 3, 4 Will. IV. c. 41 (1833), and by 14, 15 Vict. c. 83 (1851).

Appeal (*Right of*). 'Provocatio ad populum' in Roman law. This right was secured to all Roman citizens by the Valerian Law B.C. 509, but was abolished by the 'Twelve Tables' (*q.v.*), B.C. 451. It was restored by the Valerian-Horatian Law B.C. 449, and confirmed by several subsequent laws.

Appeal to Cæsar (*I*). 'Appello Cæsărem.' By the law of Porcius Læca, *de capite et tergo civium*, no Roman citizen could be put to death or scourged. His appeal was to a trial before the Centuries (B.C. 256); but in the empire, Cæsar represented the Centuries. It was somewhat like our *habeas corpus*, which ensures a fair trial.

Appeals (*The Statute of*). 24 & 25 Hen. VIII., 1532, 1533, forbidding all appeal to Rome; all processes of the Court of Rome in England; and abolishing entirely the judicial jurisdiction of the papacy in any affair connected with an English subject.

Appel comme d'abus (*L'*). This right was recognised in 1329. It was an appeal to the civil powers against the *abuses* of ecclesiastical superiors, whether in contravention of the constitutions or the corcordats of the country.

Appellants, 1717. Those who appealed, or rather wished to appeal, to a general council against the bull called *Unigenitus*, issued by Pope Clement XI. in 1718, against the 'Moral Reflexions' of Quesnel. This book favoured the Jansenists and condemned the Jesuits. The bull condemns it *in globo*—that is, as a whole—without particularising any stated parts, doctrines, or dogmas, as objectionable. The archbishop of Paris, and the bishops of Mirepoix, Sénez, Montpellier, and Boulogne wished to refer the matter to a general council, but Louis XIV., in his usual overbearing manner, insisted that the bull should be accepted unconditionally. The controversy was kept alive till 1730, when the bull was registered by the Paris parlement, and the heat of the opponents cooled down; but even to this hour there are some appellants who disapprove of the bull.

Ap'pian Way (*The*), B.C. 302. A road between Rome and Capua begun by Appius Claudius Cæcus, during his consulship. The oldest and most famous of all the Roman roads.

Called the Queen of Roads (Regina Viarum).

Apple-pie Causes. Causes in which judgment is beyond the possibility of dispute. Lord Eldon used to say, 'I have often wished that all my causes were apple-pie causes.' He referred to a complaint made to him when he was resident fellow of University College. Some of the undergraduates complained to him that the cook had sent to table an apple-pie that could not be eaten. Lord Eldon ordered the cook to bring the pie before him, but the cook returning informed him that the pie was eaten; whereupon Lord Eldon gave judgment for the defendant. 'You complain,' said he to the undergraduates, 'that the pie could not be eaten, but the pie *has* been eaten, and therefore *could* be eaten.'

Apple-stall Legislation, 1851. The eviction of Ann Hicks from Hyde Park by the First Commissioner of Woods and Forests. In 1843 Ann Hicks had a little apple-stall in the Park. She obtained permission to erect a wooden stand in which to lock up her commodities. The wood was repaired by brick, then raised five feet high with a roof and chimney, then surrounded with hurdles which every few weeks encroached more and more upon the Park, and grew into a little garden. The Duke of Wellington, as Ranger of the Park, had to employ the Crown solicitors; and the commissioners had to pay Ann Hicks a sum of money by way of compensation before she could be got rid of.

Apposition Day. Midsummerday is so called at St. Paul's School, founded by Dean Colet in 1509. It was designed for 153 boys, being the number of fishes caught by the disciples, as related in the fourth gospel, and dedicated to the boy Jesus, who at twelve years of age 'apposed' the doctors in the Temple.

Apprenticeship (*Statute of*), 1562-3 (5 Eliz. c. 4). Provided that no person should exercise any trade in England who had not served a seven years' apprenticeship. Abolished in 1814, except in the legal profession, in which clerks must be ·'articled' before they can practise for themselves. *See* 'Arti.'

Appropriation Clause (*The*), 1838. A part of the 'Act for altering and amending the laws relating to the Temporalities of the Church in Ireland.' The temporalities of the Irish bishoprics were, by this clause, vested in ecclesitical commissioners for the provision of divine service, the payment of church rates, the repairs of churches, and other similar purposes.

The statute abolished ten bishoprics, and united them to the ten remaining ones. It abolished those of Dromore, Raphoe, Clogher, Elphin, Killala and Achonry, Clonfert and Kilmacduagh, Kildare, Ossory, Waterford, and Lismore, Cork and Ross.

Après nous le déluge. 'Let the flood come, for aught I care, when we are gone' was the scandalous exclamation of Madame de Pompadour, the Court favourite of Louis XV. Louis himself said to the Duc de Choiseul, when urged to attend to business, 'Bah, duke! the crazy old machine will hold out my time; and my successors must look after themselves.'

Aqua Tofa'na, 'Acqua Tofan'ica,' 1709. A liquid poison concocted by Tofana of Palermo, and called by her 'Manna of St. Nicholas of Bari,' and said to be a liquid which oozed from the tomb of that saint. Four or five drops were fatal. Tofana confessed to the

murder of 600 victims. Thought to have been a solution of arsenic.

In the 16th and 17th cents. Spara and her assistant, Gratiana, used a similar poison to kill young husbands when their wives wished to be widows. In 1659 the number of young widows in Italy excited the attention of Pope Alexander VII., and suspicion was excited against a society of young wives presided over by Spara, an old woman. Five were executed.

Aquæ et Ignis Interdictio, *i.e.* banishment.

It is somewhat remarkable that the Roman symbol of marriage was 'Fire and Water,' not, perhaps, because man and wife in old Rome led a cat and dog life, but simply because fire and water are two essentials of 'married life,' or 'home.' Bachelors could partake of the Ignis et Aqua of other men.

Aquarians. A very early section of Christians who celebrated communion with water instead of wine. St. Cyprian speaks of them with condemnation; but it is said that they drank water to prevent detection by their breath.

Aquitaine, Aquita'nia. One of the four great regions of ancient Gaul, including all the south-west part lying between the Pyrenees, the Gulf of Gascony, and the river Garonne.

Henry II. called himself 'dux Normannorum et Aquitanorum.'
Richard I., John, and Henry III. called themselves 'dux Normanniæ et Aquitaniæ.'
Edward I., II., III., dropped the former and called themselves 'dux Aquitaniæ.'
Between Edward III. and George III. *Franciæ* was substituted for 'Aquitaniæ' and *rex* for *dux.*

Arabella (*The Lady*)—that is, Arabella Stuart, 1575–1615. Cousin of James I.

She was the daughter of Charles Stuart, earl of Lennox; and Charles was younger brother of Henry Darnley, who married Mary Queen of Scots. Hence, James I. and the Lady Arabella were the children of two brothers.

Mary Queen of Scots claimed the throne of England as the grand-niece of Henry VIII. and Queen Margaret. But Charles Lennox married the *niece* of Queen Margaret, and consequently was one degree nearer to that queen than Mary was. Besides, the Countess of Lennox was a native Englishwoman. The name of the countess was Margaret, and, as Sir Walter Scott observes, if brought to a court of law, English lawyers would probably have decided against Mary Queen of Scots and her son James.

Arabian Literature in Spain (*The Golden age of*), 961–976. When

Al Hakem II. was king of Cordŏva. Al Hakem II. founded schools, endowed colleges, invited over learned men of all countries, and formed at Cordova an immense public library.

Arabian Odyssey (The). Mr.

Hole, in his remarks on the 'Contes Arabes' ('Arabian Nights'), considers 'Sinbad the Sailor' as the Arabian Odyssey.

The 'Arabian Nights Entertainments' are the 'Contes Arabes' of Antoine Galland, a French orientalist, who travelled under the patronage of Colbert. They were published in Paris in 12 vols. (1704-1717).

Arabic (Professorship of). In the

University of Cambridge, 1632 ; founded by Sir Thomas Adams, Bart., and endowed with a stipend of 40l. a year. The present stipend is 540l.

Arabic versions of the Bible.

I. The Old Testament, A.D. 925, translated by Rabbi Saadia Gaon Haphitomi.

II. The Pentateuch, translated in 1486, by Harites ibn Sina.

Ar'biter Elegantia'rum. Petro-

nius was the director-in-chief of the pleasures and amusements of Nero. Beau Nash was the 'arbiter elegantiarum' of Bath (1704, &c.).

Arbitrary Appropriation (The),

12th cent. The permission to pay tithes wherever a person thought proper. Innocent III., by a decretal epistle, abolished this liberty, and enjoined that every man must pay his tithe to his own parish church.

Arbor Day. A day set apart in

Canada and the United States for planting trees. Thus—

The 2nd Wednesday in April 1874 was Arbor Day in Nebraska, when twelve million trees were planted in that state alone.

The 15th of April, 1876, was Arbor Day in Michigan.

The 3rd Tuesday in May 1876 was Arbor Day in Minnesota, when 1,342,886 trees were planted in that State.

The 27th of April, 1882, was Arbor Day in Ohio.

The first Friday in May 1887 was Arbor Day in Canada.

The first Friday in May should be set apart by the trustees of every rural school and incorporated village (in Canada) for the purpose of planting shady trees, making flower-beds, and otherwise improving and beautifying the schoolgrounds.—*Education Department of Ontario.*

Arca'na. The secret operations of

alchemists, the chief of which was the 'Philosopher's Stone.'

The *Double Arcane*, or Arcānum, the sulphate of potash.

The *Coral Arcane*, or Arcānum, the deutoxide of red mercury, prepared by nitric acid.

The *Jovial Arcane*, or Arcānum of Jupiter, a mixture of the deutoxide of tin and nitrate of mercury.

Archangels (The Seven).

CHAMUEL, represented as bearing a cup and staff.

GABRIEL, the messenger of God ; represented as floating through the air, with his hands crossed over his breast. Also with royal robes, bearing a lily in his hand.

MICHAEL, represented in complete armour, bearing a sword. Sometimes he is represented with eyes bandaged, and bearing a sword and pair of scales, in allusion to his being the angel of the Judgment.

RAPHAEL is represented as a pilgrim with staff and gourd ; or a traveller carrying a *fish* (*Tobit*).

URIEL is represented carrying a parchment scroll, to signify his being the interpreter of prophecies.

ZADKIEL bears the sacrificial knife which he took from Abraham, when the patriarch was about to slay his son.

ZOPHIEL bears a flaming sword.

Archdeacon's Court (The). To

hear ecclesiastical causes, subject to an appeal to the bishop, 24 Hen. VIII. c. 12.

Archê and Duum'virat. The

vital principle and the soul. Terms used by Van Helmont of Brussels (1577-1644) to express the dual nature of man. By *archê* he meant the vital principle penetrating the entire body, which principle performs all the functions of nutrition and digestion. 'Duumvirat' with him meant the intellectual principle or soul. He called it *duum-vi-rat* because it resides in the 'two organs' called *vi*[scera] and *rat*[a], that is the bowels and the spleen. *See* 'Natura Naturans,' 'Anima Mundi,' and 'Pre-established Harmony.'

He did not place the soul in the *brain*, because he said the brain has no blood ; but as the digestive organs are so intimately wrapped up with the intellectuality of man, he placed the soul there.

Archestratides, B.C. 577. The

Archons of Athens.

Pronounce Ar-kes-trat'-i-deez.

Archibald Bell-the-cat. Archi-

bald Douglas, earl of Angus (died 1514).

An armed conclave was held in Lauder church (on the subject of ridding the kingdom of the upstart Cochrane, who had risen from the station of a mason to become the earl of Mar). Lord Gray reminded them of the fable of the mice which laid a project for preventing the ravages of the cat by tying a bell round her neck. ' An excellent project indeed,' said one of the conclave, 'but who would undertake to bell the cat?' 'That will I,' exclaimed Douglas, earl of Angus; and ever after he was called Archibald Bell-the-cat.— Sir W. SCOTT, *Hist. of Scotland*, xx.

Archimandrite. A father provincial of the Greek Church. The superiors of convents are Mandrites (2 syl.) or Hegumĕni.

Pronounce Ar'-ki-man'-drite.

Archon'tics. ' Archon'tici' or Valentinians, a section of the Gnostic school founded by Valentīnus in the 2nd cent. So called because they taught that ' mundum universum a Deo conditum opus esse ἀρχόντων.' They denied the resurrection of the body, the divine institution of the sacraments, and maintained that the incorporeal could not communicate with the corporeal, or that a spirit god could reveal anything to a material substance like man.

Arctic Highlands (*The*). That part of the American continent which lies between Hudson's Bay and the mouth of the Mackenzie. The general route of the explorers of a north-west passage, such as Franklin, Richardson, Back, Dease, Simpson, Rae, &c.

Areop'agites (*The*), (5 syl.). An Athenian court of judicature, which was held on the Mars Hill (in Greek, *Arês Pagos*). All wilful murders came under the cognisance of this court. The number of members varied; but on a column in the citadel of Athens, erected to Rufus Festus, the number is stated to have then been 300.

Argen'teus Codex (*The*), or ' Silver Book.' The MS. of Ulphilas's Mœso-gothic translation of the gospels, discovered in the abbey of Werden, and taken to Prague in 1597. It was captured at Prague in 1648, and presented to Christina of Sweden; subsequently, it was presented to the University of Upsala in 1662. It contains a large part of the four gospels and is written on vellum, the letters being silver, and the initials gold. (Ar-gen'-te-us, 4 syl.)

Ar'gentine Republic (*The*), 1816. Thirteen confederated provinces of Rio de la Plata, South America.

Argyll. *God bless the Duke of Argyll!* The Duke of Argyll set up rubbing-posts for cattle in the Highlands of Scotland. When the tenders of cattle used these posts for their own delectation, suffering from what they call *yuke*, they gratefully ejaculated, ' God bless the Duke of Argyll ! '

Pronounce Ar-gīle.

A'ria Cat'tiva Mala'ria. So the Italians call the emanations of the Pontine marshes, which produce fevers. The aria cattiva reaches even to the lower parts of Rome.

A'rian Controversy (*The*), 4th cent. In the time of Constantine the Arians were very numerous. They withdrew from the Trinitarians, built their own churches, and ordained their own bishops. The General Council of Nice, A.D. 325, condemned the Arians as heretics.

A'rianism, A.D, 312. The religious tenets of Arius of Alexandria (270–336), who disavowed the dogma of the Trinity, and denied that Christ, the Word, is coequal and consubstantial with God the Father. In fact, he maintained that Christ is not God at all, but was a human being, born of human parents.

The religious views of Arius were condemned in the First General Council held at Nice in 325. Arius said : If God is one, all wise, all powerful, and everywhere present, it is a contradiction of terms to suppose a second possessed of the same attributes. The party-word of the Arians was *homoiousios* not *homoousios*. That of the Athanasians was *homoousios* not *homoiousios* (*homo-ousios* = identical in nature; *homoi-ousios* = similar [but not identical] in substance).

Arios'to of the North (*The*). Sir Walter Scott (1771–1832).

Aristar'chos and Zoilos. Critics. Aristarchos (B.C. 160–88) of Samothrace revised Homer with such severity that his name is proverbial for a caustic critic. Zoïlos of Amphipŏlis also criticised Homer with equal severity and was called ' Homeromastix.'

Aristides (*The British*). Andrew Marvell (1620–1678), poet, satirist, and politician. He was the last paid M.P. for Kingston-upon-Hull.

Pronounce Ar'-ris-ti'-deez.

In 1678 the Lord Treasurer Danby paid a visit to Andrew Marvell in his humble lodging; and, at parting, slipped into his hand a cheque for 1000*l*. Marvell bade the Treasurer wait a moment, and said to the serving boy, 'Jack, child, what had I for dinner yesterday?' 'Don't you remember,

Sir? It was a shoulder of mutton?' 'Aye, true! I remember. And what am I to have to-day?' 'The blade-bone broiled.' 'So, my lord, you see my dinner is provided. I thank you, but there is the piece of paper you gave me. My services belong to my constituents.'—C. THOMSON, *Autobiography*, p. 87.

Aristi'des (*The English*). John
Pym, the republican (1584–1643). *See* above.

He sought no advantage to himself, he derived nothing from his exertions or his prominent position, but the satisfaction of seeing his country saved by his labours. He derived no influence from wealth or rank, for he had none of either; his whole prestige was intellectual and moral worth. He wore himself out for the public good, and died as poor as he commenced, the only grant which he received from the state being an honourable burial in Westminster Abbey.—HOWITT, *Hist. of Engl.*, 'Charles I.,' chap. iv. p. 242.

Aristides (*The French*). M. Grévy,
the third president of the third republic of France, from 1879 to 1884.

Aristoph'anes (5 syl.). Samuel
Foote (1722–1777) is called the English or Modern Aristophănês.

Aristophanes of his age (*The*).
J. Baptiste Poquelin de Molière, the French dramatist (1622–1673).

Aristophanes of the Revolution (*The*). Camille Desmoulins (1762–1794). *See* above.

Aristote'lian Categories (*The*).
The ten Aristotelian categories are : (1) substance; (2) quantity; (3) quality; (4) relation; (5) action; (6) passivity; (7) position in space; (8) position in time; (9) situation; (10) possession.

Aristote'lianism. The system of
Aristotle's logic and metaphysics applied to the Christian system in the middle ages. This substitution of reason for faith, and logical inferences for what are called 'inspired truths,' gave birth to the Scholastics. The tendency of Platonism was to enthusiasm and mysticism, that of the Aristotelians to subtlety and logical minuteness. Platonists tended to fanaticism, Aristotelians affected disputation. Thomas Aquinas was an Aristotelian, Duns Scotus a Platonist.

Aristotle of China. Tehuhe (3
syl.), who died A.D. 1200, also called 'the Prince of Science.'

Aristotle of Christianity.
Thomas Aquīnas, who tried to reduce the doctrines and dogmas of Christianity to syllogistic formulæ (1224–1274).

Aristotle of the nineteenth
century (*The*). George Cuvier (1769–1832), the great French naturalist.

Ark of the Covenant (*The*).
Exod. xxv. A chest of shittim wood, the lid of which was of pure gold. It contained at one time the two stone tables of the law, a pot of manna, Aaron's rod, and the book of the law. The lid was the 'Mercy Seat.' It was taken to Babylon and lost sight of.

'Shittim wood,' probably cedar.

Arkan'sas (U.S. of America). So
called in 1819 from its chief river. The inhabitants of this state are nicknamed 'Toothpicks.'

The rivers are the Mississippi, the Arkansas, the Red River, the White River, and the St. François. The Arkansas is a magnificent river, navigable for 1,980 miles, area reckoned 178,000 square miles.

Arm of Iron (*The*). Baldwin, who
married Judith, widow of Ethelbald. Judith, when she married Ethelbald, was a widow, having been previously married to his father, Ethelwulf.

Baldwin I., Bras de Fer, count of Flanders, died 877.

Arma'da (*The*), or 'The Invincible
Armada,' as the Spaniards vauntingly named it, 29 July to 7 Aug., 1588. The Armada consisted of 130 vessels, four of which were gigantic galleys, and the whole carried 2,500 cannons. Against this was opposed 50 English vessels no bigger than yachts, and 30 queen's ships, the biggest of which was smaller than the least of the Spanish ships. The Armada was so roughly handled that it tried to retreat round the Orkneys, but a storm scattered the ships and dashed them to pieces against the Irish cliffs. What escaped were 50 of the 130 ships, and 10,000 of the 30,000 men—a miserable wreck. The medal struck to commemorate this mighty overthrow had for its legend, 'He sent out his arrows and He scattered them' (Ps. xviii. 14).

Armagnacs (*Les*), 1407–1497. In
French history. The faction headed by Bernard VII., comte d'Armagnac, during the insanity of Charles VI. The other faction was that of the Burgundians led by Jean Sans-peur, duke of Burgundy. The object of each was to get possession of the king, and thus obtain mastery of France under the title of regent. The original Armagnac faction was called

the Orleanists, from Charles, duke of Orleans, who married the daughter of the Count of Armagnac and was assassinated in 1407 by the Duke of Burgundy. On the death of the Duke of Orleans the Count of Armagnac put himself at the head of the Orleanist party, entered Paris at the head of an army in 1413, and was named Constable by the Queen Isabella. He made himself odious by his exactions, and broke with the queen, who fled to the court of Burgundy in 1418. The Burgundians now entered Paris and drove out the Armagnacs. The count fled, was discovered, and assassinated with many of his adherents. The race died out with Charles I., brother of Jean IV., in 1497.

Pronounce Ar-ma′-nyak.

Armatoles (3 syl.), or ' Armatŏli.' A Thessalian militia instituted at the beginning of the 16th cent. by Selim I. to oppose the incursions of the Klephtes. In the insurrection of 1821 the Armatoles and Klephtes united against Turkey. Botzaris was the most illustrious leader of the Armatoles.

Armed Neutrality (*The*), 1780. Against Great Britain, which insisted on the right of search during the American war, to be assured that neutral vessels were not carrying to America articles reckoned contraband of war. Catharine of Russia resisted this claim, and was joined by other European states on the principle that ' free bottoms make free goods.' Denmark and Sweden joined Russia in August; the States-General on 24 Dec.; Prussia on 8 May, 1781; the Kaiser, 9 Oct.

The treaty between Russia, Denmark, and Sweden was ratified 16 Dec., 1800.

Armée de Condé (*L'*), 1789. An army collected on the banks of the Rhine by Louis Joseph, prince de Condé, to resist the Revolution. It was distinguished for its valour at Wissembourg, Haguenau, and Bentheim; but in 1800 the prince took refuge in England. He returned to Paris at the restoration, and died at Chantilly in 1818.

Arme′nian Era (*The*). Commenced 7 July, 552. Superseded by the Julian era in 1330.

Arme′nian Liturgy (*The*). Dates from the time of Gregory the Illuminator (257–331), who introduced Christianity into Armenia. It is based on the Liturgy of St. Chrysostom.

Arme′nians (*The*). Christians of Armenia, and the purest of the disciples of Eútÿches (3 syl.). They still maintain that the manhood of Christ is of a divine and incorruptible substance. The Jacobites say the Armenian Christ is a mere phantom; and the Armenians retort by saying the Christ of the Jacobites is a God with all the infirmities of the flesh, and even with the infirmities of nutrition and digestion. They are pretty numerous in Russia, Austria, and Turkey. *See* 'Arminians.'

The Armenians believe that the Holy Ghost proceeds from the Father only. *See* ' Filioque.'

Armin′ianism, 1603. The religious tenets of Dr. James Arminius, a Latinised form of Harmennsen or Hermannsen, a native of Holland (1560–1609). The following five points are the most salient: (1) God wills that all should be saved, and His predestination is only the effect of His foreknowledge; (2) Christ died for all, and God will bestow eternal life on all who repent and believe on Christ; (3) Man is of himself incapable of true faith, and hence the necessity of being born again by the Holy Ghost; (4) All good works are to be attributed to the Holy Ghost, but that Holy Ghost forces no one against his own inclination; (5) God gives to the true believer the means of continuing in grace. Condemned by the Synod of Dort in 1618.

At the present day, Arminians reject all 'creeds;' advocate the right of private judgment in the interpretation of Scripture; virtually reject the dogma of original sin; look on the sacraments as religious ceremonies; dwell on preaching more than on churchism; and are anti-Calvinists.

Armin′ians. Anti-Calvinists in the five points. *See* above.

Arms of Bourges (*The*). An ass on an arm-chair. The tradition is this: Asinius, a Roman governor of Bourges in the time of Cæsar, being too ill to stand, was carried in an arm-chair to animate his troops; and gained a signal victory. Be this as it may, the arms are a never-failing source of jests; and to honour one with the arms of Bourges is like giving Dr. Pangloss the degree of A double S.

Pronounce Bourjh.

Arms of the English sovereigns (*The*).

WILLIAM I. and II. Gules, 2 lions (*leos pardés*) passant gardant Or. And for Matilda of Flanders, gyronny of 8; in the nombril point a plain shield gules.

HENRY I. and Matilda of Scotland. England as before, and Scotland.

STEPHEN and Matilda of Boulogne. Gules, 3 sagittaries Or, 3 torteaux.

HENRY II. England as before; and for Eleanor of Aquitaine, gules, 1 lion passant gardant. His cognisances were a crescent beneath a star, an escarbuncle of 8 rays, and the broom-plant or genista for his name Planta-genet.

RICHARD I. 3 lions passant gardant for England; and for Berengaria of Navarre, a cross botonné Arg. Motto: *Dieu et mon droit.*

HENRY III. England; and for Eleanor of Provence, paly of 8, Or and Gules.

EDWARD I. England; and for Eleanor of Castile, a label of 3 or 5 q. With Margaret of France, England and semée de lys.

EDWARD II. The same with his father, but with 2 small castles on the side of his throne to show his descent through his mother, from Castile.

EDWARD III. England, within a border of France (i.e. Az. semée-le-lys, placed on his throne, between 2 fleurs-de-lys, to show his descent from France). He first quartered the arms of France in 1358. His cognisances were the sun issuing from the clouds, the stump of a tree sprouting.

RICHARD II. France and England quarterly, with a label of 3 points, the middle point charged with the cross of St. George. He was the first to bear supporters, which were 2 angels.

HENRY IV. France and England quarterly, 5 fleurs-de-lys, and the supporters of Richard II.

HENRY V. and VI. France and England quarterly, the 5 fleur-de-lys reduced to 3, in imitation of Charles VI. of France. Supporters, the black bull of Clare and white lion of Mortimer. Crest, the fleur-de-lys of France, and the lion of England conjoined. Likewise with 2 lions' supporters, and arms within the garter.

EDWARD IV. V. France and England. Supporters, a lion and a white hart.

RICHARD III. France and England, between 2 boars, or a bull on the right and a boar on the left.

HENRY VII. France and England, surrounded with a garter, and ensigned with a large crown. Crest, the portcullis, from the mother of the family of Beaufort. Supporters, a red dragon, from Cadwallader; and on the left a greyhound Arg. collared Gules, from the Somersets. Badges, the white and red rose per pale.

HENRY VIII. France and England. Supporters, a red dragon and greyhound (in the early part of his reign), afterwards a lion of England and a red dragon sinister. For Katharine of Aragon, impaling Castile and Leon, and Aragon and Sicily.

EDWARD VI. France and England. Supporters, a lion and a griffin.

MARY. A lozenge, 1 and 4 France, 2 England, 3 Spain. Supporters, an eagle dexter, and a lion rampant gardant sinister.

ELIZABETH. France and England, ensigned with imperial crowns. Supporters, a lion dexter crowned, and a red dragon sinister.

JAMES I. France, England, Scotland, and Ireland, differently blazoned. Supporters, lion and unicorn.

∴ George III. omitted France, and it has been omitted ever since.

Army Book 48.

The orderly corporal's ledger, a monthly account-book, each page of which is headed *Company Daily Messing Account*. It contains an exact account of the articles and price of every eatable served to the company, in four columns. (1) The article (as tea, sugar, oatmeal, &c.); (2) the quantity; (3) the rate charged; and (4) the sum totalised.

Army Plea (*The*).

See under 'Plea.'

Army of England (*The*), 1797.

A French army raised by the Directory and placed under the command of Bonaparte (Napoleon), for the subjugation and plunder of England. After visiting Etaples, Ambleteuse, Boulogne, Calais, Dunkirk, Furnes, Newport, Ostend, and Walcheren, Bonaparte satisfied himself that the attempt must be abandoned.

Again, 1803, when Bonaparte was first consul, he assembled a fine army on the heights above Boulogne, called the 'army of England,' and there continually exercised it, under the inspection of Soult, Ney, Davoust, and Victor; but hearing that England was one vast camp, he abandoned his projected invasion in despair.

Army of God and the Church (*The*), 1215.

The barons and their retainers who took up arms against King John when he refused, at Oxford, to sign Magna Charta.

Pandulph told the king that the primate of the kingdom ought to excommunicate the barons for daring to present the charter; but Stephen Langton replied, he ought rather to excommunicate the foreign mercenaries who overran the kingdom, and indeed would do so, unless the king ordered their instant dismissal.

Army of Reserve (*The*), 1804.

A contingent to the regular army enforced on every parish by William Pitt. The men were called out for five years' service, but were not compelled to quit the United Kingdom. The reserve were attached to the regulars as second battalions.

Army of Viscounts (*The*), 1568.

An army of Huguenots which overran Gascony, Quercy, and Languedoc. So called because it had for leaders Viscount Montelar, Viscount Bruniquel, Viscount Caumont, and Viscount Rapin.

Viscounts pronounce Vi'counts.

Army of the Cross (*The*),

and 'Soldiers of the Cross,' the crusaders. Every man wore a cross cut in red cloth either on his shoulder or on his breast. First crusade was 1096 (Rufus reigned in England at the time).

Army of the Indus (*The*), 1839.

An army under the command of Sir

John Keane, raised to restore Shah Shuja to the throne of Afghanistan, from which he had been driven by Dost Mohammed, chief of Cabul. The army consisted of a British force amounting to 28,000 men, 6,000 Sikhs of the Punjab, and 5,000 troops raised by the Shah Shuja. The shah was restored and crowned 8 May; Ghazni was taken 2 July; Jellalabad 30 July; Dost Mohammed fled to Bokhara, and Sir John Keane entered Cabul 7 Aug., 1839.

Arnaldists. A branch of the Waldenses; so called from Arnaldo of Brescia (1100–1155). This Arnaldo was a disciple of Abélard, but on his return to Italy became a monk, and introduced numerous reforms, to bring back his followers to primitive times. He was condemned by Innocent II. and the Lateran Council in 1139, after which he withdrew to Switzerland. Wishing to increase his following, he went to Rome in 1144, but was driven out by Lucius II. and Eugenius III. He was seized by Barbarossa and put to death. *See* ' Waldenses.'

Pronounce Ar-nol'dists.

Ar'naoot. An Albanian Mohammedan. A pasha's bodyguard should be composed of Arnaoots.

Arnold's Historical Essay. Oxford University. Value 42*l.* annually. Founded, by subscription, in honour of Dr. Arnold, Regius Professor of Modern History (Head-Master of Rugby), 1850.

Arpad (*House of*). The Hungarian dynasty which succeeded on the death of St. Stephen. The crown remained in the dynasty for three centuries. It began with Andrew, duke of Arpad, who reigned 1046–1061. The last of the Arpads was Andrew III. (1290–1301). This was a most heroic dynasty, still fondly remembered by the Hungarians. Andrew II., a very worthless king, like our King John, reluctantly granted the Bulla Aurea, or Magna Charta of Hungary.

Ladislaus I. (1077-1095) was the greatest of the Arpad kings. He was canonised. Bela III. (1173-1196) was an excellent king.

Arquebuses of Sancerre (*The*), 1573. Slings. When Sancerre was besieged by the French Catholics, the inhabitants, who had no firearms, defended themselves with simple slings. The town endured a long famine, and the siege is compared to that of Jerusalem by Titus and Vespasian.

Arrabbia'ti (*The*), *i.e.* ' the Enraged.' The party of the Medici opposed to that of Savonarola, called the *Piagnoni* (or the Weepers). The Arrabbiäti wanted to see an oligarchy, not a tyranny in Florence.

Arraigns (*The Clerk of*). The official who reads the indictment, and calls on the prisoner to plead.

The calling of a prisoner by his name to the bar of a law court to answer to the charge laid against him in the indictment is called ' Arraignment.'
Pronounce Ar-rains'.

Arrest of Judgment. A plea made by an unsuccessful defendant, after verdict, to arrest judgment in consequence of some error which vitiates the proceeding. By 15, 16 Vict. c. 76 (1852), omitted facts and other ' faults ' may now be corrected.

Arrest of the Five Members. I. By Charles I. 4 Jan., 1642. Charles I., supposing he had evidence of treason against five members of parliament, imparted to him by James Graham, earl· of Montrose, proceeded to the House with a band of armed attendants to arrest the members and strike terror into the rest of the House. A measure like this depends wholly on its success. Cromwell succeeded when he turned out the members and locked the doors upon them; but the five members that Charles sought, having an inkling of what was about to happen, kept away, and Charles cut a most ridiculous figure, a blusterer utterly foiled and made a fool of.

The five members were Hampden, Haslerig, Hollis, Pym, and Strode.

II. By Louis XVI., May 1789. Louis was urged by the *Parlement de Paris* to convene a States-General in order to solve the national deadlock in the ministry of Brienne. He agreed to do so, but a few days afterwards refused to do anything of the sort; and, entering the Assembly, insisted on its registering two royal edicts, one of which was for a succession of Government loans. Epréménil, Sebastian de Cabre, Fréteau and Monsabert demanded the calling of the States-General; and Louis, rising, left the assembly commanding the edicts to be registered without another word. Fréteau and

Cabre were arrested by *lettres de cachet,* and the parlement was dissolved, but it would not submit to be stamped out thus. When the parlement met, an officer was sent to arrest Epréménil and Monsabert, and the king called a *lit de justice*; but the parlement denounced the conduct of the king and the arrest of its members as unconstitutional, and refused to recognise the royal edicts; no one subscribed to the loans.

The 5th member was the Duc d'Orleans. He was not actually arrested, but banished from Paris, and commanded to confine himself to his château of Villars Cotterets.

Arrestment for founding jurisdiction, in Scotch law. By this law a foreigner (or one out of the jurisdiction of the Scotch courts) may, if he has any sort of property in Scotland, be sued in the Scotch tribunals on a warrant called ' Ad fundandam jurisdictionem.'

Arrêt d'Union (L'), 13 May, 1648.
Henri IV. of France created an impost called *paulette,* whereby members of the parlement, by paying an annual cess, could transmit their offices to their heirs. Mazarin, acting for Louis XIV. in his minority, ratified this privilege to the four chief courts, viz. the Parlement, the Chambre des Comptes, the Cour des aides, and the Grand Conseil, but with this proviso, that the last three companies ' perdraient quatre années de leurs gages.' The parlement refused to recognise this distinction, and insisted that all the four bodies should be treated alike. This ' stand,' called *l'arrêt d'union,* insisted that no one should be admitted to any office in the state without the consent of the widow and heirs of the previous deceased officer. It furthermore enacted that all the four companies should stick together ' malgré la défense qui leur en fut faite, et au mépris d'un arrêt du conseil du roi qui cassait l'édit d'union.' Mazarin arrested the president Blancménil and a councillor named Broussel. This led to a riot, and Mazarin was obliged to release his prisoners. This was the beginning of the Fronde War (*q.v.*).

Arrondissement (4 syl.). A division of a French department presided over by a sub-prefect.

Ars Sacra. Chemistry was so called in Alexandria, because only priests could study it or practise it.

Ar'sacides, or Arsăcĭdæ (*The*),
B.C. 250–A.D. 226. The Parthian dynasty of Persia, founded by Arsăcês, the Greek spelling of Ashk, a tributary chief who induced the Parthians to revolt from the Seleucidæ, B.C. 250. The first stock gave 20 kings, who ruled over Persia for 476 years; the second line, called the Ashk-anians, gave 11 kings, and ruled 221 years. Capital Ctesiphon. *See* ' Sassanides.'

Pronounce Ar'-sas-sides, Ar-sas'-ĭ-dee.

Art Unions. Institutions to promote a patronage and sale of fine art productions. The Art Union of Munich was established in 1823; that of Düsseldorf in 1829; in Edinburgh in 1834; in London 1837.

Arti, or Arts. Every burgher of Florence must belong to one of the twenty-one arts, just as, before the reform, every freeman or voter of England was obliged to rank as a tradesman. It was not necessary to follow the trade, but it was indispensable to ' matriculate' as a tradesman in order to take up your freedom.

The 7 *higher arts* were: (1) judges and notaries, (2) calimala or manufacturers, (3) exchangers, (4) wool-staplers, (5) silk mercers, (6) physicians and apothecaries, and (7) furriers.

The 14 *lower arts* were: (8) butchers, (9) shoemakers, (10) blacksmiths, (11) drapers and clothesmen, (12) masons and stonecutters, (13) vintners, (14) innkeepers, (15) oilmen, pork-butchers and rope-makers, (16) hosiers, (17) armourers, (18) locksmiths, (19) saddlers, (20) carpenters, and (21) bakers.

Each art had its guild. All other trades must unite with some one of these arts, or were not ranked as burghers or freemen.

Articles in Theology. *See* under.
Three articles; three *test* articles; *four* articles; *five* articles; *six* articles; *seven* articles; *nine* articles (under ' Lambeth Articles'); *ten* articles; *eleven* articles; *twelve* articles; *thirty-nine* articles; *forty-two* articles. Also *nine* articles of the Evangelical Alliance.

Articles of Confederation and perpetual Union (*The Thirteen*), 1777.
1. The States to be called the United States, instead of the United Colonies, as heretofore.

2. Each state to retain its sovereignty and independence.

3. All the states to league together for mutual defence.

4. The free inhabitants of any one state to enjoy the immunities and privileges of free citizens in every other state.

5. Traitors or great delinquents fleeing from a state to be delivered up to the state where the offence was committed.

6. Laws and judicial proceedings of each state to be respected by all.

7. Delegates from each state elected to meet in congress the first Monday in November.

8. No state to have less than two or more than seven delegates.

9. Each state to maintain its own delegates.

10. Each state to have only one vote in congress.

11. Freedom of speech to be allowed to all delegates, and freedom from arrest, except for treason and felony.

12. No state to enter into war or make peace without consent of Congress.

13. In times of peace no ships of war or military force to be kept in any state without consent of Congress.

Articles of Henry (*The*), or Pacta Conventa, 1573. Articles agreed to by Henry de Valois on his election to the throne of Poland.

1. That the king should not elect his successor; 2. should not declare war without the sanction of the Diet; 3. should not appoint ambassadors to foreign courts; 4. should not impose any tax; 5. should be governed by a privy council of 16 (4 bishops, 4 palatines, and 8 castellans); 6. should confer no dignity or office on any foreigner; 7. should neither marry nor divorce a wife without consent of the Diet, &c.

Articles of Reform (*The*). Ireland, 1340. By these articles Edward III. threatened to take the lands and possessions of the Anglo-Irish into his own hands, if the great landholders were not more attentive to their duties. In two centuries the English lords in Ireland had grown enormously rich, and showed symptoms of a very rebellious spirit. It had become the fashion among them to assume the dress, cut of the hair, and manners, as well as the names of the Irish.

Articles of Schmalkal'den or Smalkald (*The*), 1537. The articles of defence adopted in the city of Schmalkalden by the Protestants under the direction of Martin Luther.

Articles of Torgau (*The*), 1530.

The 17 articles drawn up by Luther at the request of the Elector of Saxony, showing the points of difference between the Reformer and the Church of Rome. The document was presented to the Elector at Torgau, whence the name.

Torgau, pronounce Tor'gow.

Articles of War. Government regulations relating (1) to the army, (2) to the navy, and (3) to the marine forces.

Articles of the Peace. The terms required from a defendant, when a person swears in court that he is in fear of damage or personal injury from the defendant. The terms set forth what security the defendant shall give that he will keep the peace, and to what length of time the terms extend.

Articlemen, 1648. Those restorable Irishmen who were promised pardon and restoration by the articles of the peace made between the Duke of Ormonde on behalf of the king (Charles II.), and confederate Catholics. The Act of Explanation shut the door of hope on more than 6,000 of the restorable Irish.

There were four classes of restorable Irish, viz. Innocents, Articlemen, Ensignmen, and the King's Nominees (*q.v.*).

Artic'uli Cle'ri, 1313. An Act for the purpose of maintaining in England certain prerogatives of the Church against the temporal power.

Artillery Company (*The Honourable*), 1537. The oldest Volunteer corps in Great Britain, being established in the reign of Henry VIII. In the Gordon riots (1780) it successfully defended the Bank of England against the rioters. The members are elected by ballot on a recommendation of five members, and pay an annual subscription of two guineas, but the uniforms are expensive: of the cavalry, 29*l.* 9*s.*; of the artillery, 18*l.* 14*s.* 6*d.*; of the infantry, 14*l.* 17*s.* 6*d.*

It consists of one squadron of light cavalry, an artillery division, six companies of infantry, and a veteran company. The Prince of Wales is captain-general and colonel of the company.

Artist of the Revolution (*The*). J. L. David (1748–1825), founder of the Statuesque School. His best piece is the 'Oath of the Horatii,' and his most popular piece is 'Napoleon crossing the Alps.' Napoleon is represented as prancing on a fiery white charger, with fluttering shawl, and in a very theatrical

3

E

attitude. Historically, he rode a patient mule, was buttoned to the chin in a large grey coat, and toiled through the deep snow doggedly.

Artists and Smiths (*Patron saint of*). St. Eloi (588–659), master of the mint in the reign of Clotaire II.

Artizo'e. The *Fatale Marmor* of the Persians, mentioned by Pliny. Elagabālus was a similar black conical stone representing the sun, and worshipped at Emĕsa.

Similar palladia were the Black Stone of the Seids: it is a huge mass of very rich grey silver ore of one of the Indian tribes of South America, which was removed from place to place, as the tribe fled from before the Spanish invaders. The Caaba of the Mussulmans, which Mahomet removed to Mecca, was another *Fatale Marmor*; so probably was the idol of Diana at Ephesus, which 'fell from heaven.' We have also the Lia Fail of Ireland; the Tanist Stone; the pillar of Shechem (2 Kings xi. 14); and so on.

Artoty'ritæ or Bread and Cheese Christians. So called from their using bread and cheese in the Eucharist. (Greek, *artos*, bread; *turos*, cheese.)

Ar'undel Marbles (*The*). 'Mar'mora Arundellia'na' or 'Marmora Oxonien'sia,' preserved in the University of Oxford, and often called the Oxford marbles, the most valuable of which is the 'Parian Chronicle' (*q.v.*). These gems of Grecian art were collected by Mr. (Sir William) Petty, who was commissioned by the Earl of Arundel to collect antiquities in Greece. Brought to England A.D. 1610; presented to the University of Oxford by his son Henry Howard, in 1667.

The entire collection originally contained 37 statues, 128 busts, and 250 inscribed marbles, besides altars, sarcophagi, fragments and gems; but part was sold in 1678. The Pomfret marbles were given to Oxford in 1756.

Arval Brothers (*College of who*). 'Fratres Arvāles,' priests of Rome who went in procession through the fields, and prayed for the increase of corn. (*Varro*.)

The little or private *Ambarvalia* were celebrated by a single family for the welfare of all belonging to it, as the great college of the Arval brothers . . . officiated in the interest of the whole state.—PATER, *Marius the Epicurean*, chap. 1.

A'ryan Languages (*The*). The different languages of the Aryan Nations (*q.v.*), which have all one common source, and bear a strong family likeness. 'They count with the same numerals, call individual speakers by the same pronouns, address parents and relatives by the same titles, call the different parts of the body by the same names, decline their nouns on the same system, compare their adjectives in the same way, conjugate their verbs alike, and form derivatives by the same suffixes.'

A'ryan Nations (*The*). The Persians, Hindûs, and all Europeans except the Basques, Turks, Hungarians, and Finns. *See* 'Semitic' and 'Turanian.'

Eastern branch: the Persians and Hindûs, which include Zend, Armenian, Kurdish, and Afghan; Sanskrit, Hindi, Hindustani; Gipsy; Pali, and the dialects of Ceylon.
Western branch (First Swarm), the Celtic. It settled in Greece; and spread into Italy, Spain, France, and the British Isles; (Second Swarm), the Teutonic, colonised Germany, and spread into Denmark, Sweden, Norway, and England; (Third Swarm), the Slavonic, settled in Bohemia, Poland, and Russia.
Pali is the sacred language of the Buddhists; Sanskrit is the sacred language of the Hindûs; Zend is the sacred language of the Persians. All now dead languages.

As = a God. The twelve Asæ or Æsir of Scandinavian mythology are Odin, Thor, Baldur, Niord, Freyr, Tyr, Bragi, Heimdal, Wedar, Wali, Uller, and Forseti.

The chief goddesses are Frigga, Freyja, Idunna, Eira, and Saga.
The twelve divine Asæ.—ERIC G. GEIJER, *Hist. of Sweden*, p. 5.

Asca'nian House (*The*). One of the most ancient families of Germany, so called from the castle of Ascania in Aschersleben. It reigned over the principality of Anhalt in the 11th cent., and gave the sovereigns of Brandenburg (1143–1320) and of Saxony. The dukes of the Ascanians of Saxony formed two branches, viz. Saxe-Wittenberg, extinct in 1422, and Saxe-Lauenburg, extinct in 1689.

Ascension Day, or 'Holy Thursday.' A religious festival held on the 40th day after Easter to commemorate the Ascension of Jesus Christ.

Beating the bounds (of parishes), called in Scotland 'riding the marches,' used to be, and still is in some places, observed on this day.

Ascet'ics (*The*), 3rd cent. Persons who devoted themselves to a solitary and contemplative life, following the system of the Essenes and Therapeutæ (*q.v.*) among the Jews. They practised great austerities for the mortifying of the flesh, withdrew the mind from worldly objects, and tried to lose themselves in God. They haunted the deserts of Egypt and Syria, and gave rise to monachism.

Asci'tes (3 syl.). From the Greek ἀσκός, a bladder, meaning ' inflated like a bladder.' Christian heretics who ' utrem inflatum et opertum solebant circumferre, tanquam ipsi essent evangelici utres novi, vino novo repleti ' (Acts ii. 13). Augustine mentions them in his book of ' Heresies ' (62).

Ascodrog'itæ, or ' Ascodrog'ili.' Christian heretics of Galatia, ' qui utrem inflatum ponunt et cooperiunt in sua ecclesia, et circumeunt eum insanientes potibus, non intelligentes quod ait Salvator '—' New wine must be put into new bladders.'—Du Cange, i. p. 408.

Ash Wednesday. First day of Lent, when at one time penitents appeared before their bishop or priest with naked feet and clad in sackcloth ready to submit to penance. The *pessimi* were first sprinkled with ashes of the palms burnt on the Palm Sunday of the preceding year, and were then driven out of the church door by the clergy, who cried after them ' In the sweat of thy brow shalt thou eat bread! ' The less offensive were signed on the forehead with the sign of the cross, and the priest or bishop said, ' Memento, homo, quia pulvis es, et in pulverem reverteris ' ! Said to have been introduced by Gregory the Great (590–604), sanctioned by the Council of Benevento in 1091.

Ashari (*The*). An Arabian sect which held that God, being the cause of *everything*, is the author of all human actions; but men, being free, acquire merit or incur guilt according as they obey or disobey the precepts of religion. Averroës, the Arabian philosopher of Cordŏva, (1149–1198), adopted the creed of the Ashari sect.

Ashbourne's Act (*Lord*), 1885. A government loan of five millions sterling set apart to be lent to Irish farmers, at the rate of 3⅛ per cent., to enable them to buy their farms of their landlords. In 1888 a second five millions was voted by parliament for the same purpose.

No landlord would, of course, join the Land League, and therefore the best plan of quieting Ireland is to multiply the freeholders, all of whom have a stake in the peace and prosperity of the island. Napoleon introduced government loans of very small value per share to induce the poorer classes of France to become holders, with the same view. Applicants for a small number of shares were first awarded their shares, and those who applied for the largest number were deferred to the last. Thousands of persons slept all night in the Piazza of the Rue Rivoli that they might be early applicants. I myself saw the thick crowd there long after midnight.

Ashbur'ton Treaty (*The*), 9 Aug. 1842. In 1842, Lord Ashburton was appointed special ambassador to the United States of North America, to settle the north-west boundary question, and other disputes which then threatened to involve the two countries in war. In August he concluded the famous Treaty of Washington, commonly called the Ashburton Treaty, by which the Oregon question was settled, and the frontier line between the state of Maine and Canada was definitely agreed to. By the 8th and 9th articles, provisions were made for putting an end to the African slave trade; and the 10th article provides for the mutual extradition of suspected criminals.

Ashmo'lean Museum (*The*). In the University of Oxford (1683); bequeathed to the university by Elias Ashmole (2 syl.). It is used to hold the collection of natural and artificial curiosities, and to aid in the study of chemistry and natural science.

This collection properly belonged to certain persons of the name of Tradescant, and is more correctly called the ' Tradescant Collection.'

Asia. From the Greek ἄσις, mud. The first part known to the Greeks was that watered by the river Caÿster, where some Ionian colonists settled. Hence, Asia means ' the land of mud,' and it is somewhat noteworthy that Paris used to be called Lutetia, which means the same thing. The mythological derivation of the word from Asia, daughter of Oceänus and Tithys, is only a poetical way of stating the fact that the river Caÿster, like any other river, is a daughter of the sea.

Asia. (Acts of the Apostles xvi. 6; compare xix. 22, 26, 27, &c.) Here Paul, who was in Phrygia or Galatia, speaks of going into Asia. To understand this it must be known that, after the battle of Magnesia, in Asia Minor, Eumĕnĕs, king of Pergämus, was rewarded by the

E 2

addition of Lydia and some other districts; and when the kingdom of Pergamus became a Roman province, it was dignified by the title of ASIA, but Galatia was still ruled by native chiefs, and formed no part of ' Asia,' in the sense alluded to. Hence Paul might leave Galatia and go to the Roman province of Asia, still travelling in Asia Minor.

Askha'nians (*The*). So the Persians call the Arsăcīdæ (*q.v.*), but there are no points of agreement. The Arsacidæ give thirty kings, the Askhanians only seven. The Arsacidæ continued 476 years, the Askhanians only 132. The Askhanians derived their name from Ask or Ashk, the father of Arduan, the founder; the Arsacidæ derived their name from Arsăcês, their founder.

Some tell us that the Askhanian was the second house of the Arsacidians, and that it gave eleven kings, who ruled 221 years.

Asmonæ'ans (*The*). So the Maccabees, rulers of the Jews, were called, because Mattathias, who first headed the revolt against Antiochus Epiphănès, was great-grandson of Asmonæos, a wealthy Jewish priest (Josephus, 'Antiquities,' book xii. chap. viii.) *See* ' Maccabees.'

Aspasia of France (*The*). Ninon de l'Enclos (1615–1705).

Ass (*The Procession of the*), 14 Jan. A mediæval religious procession, in commemoration of the Flight into Egypt.

Thus described by Ducange: 'A beautiful girl being selected, was mounted on an ass, richly decorated. An infant child was nursed on her lap, and the procession was formed by the clergy and laity, from the highest to the lowest, who walked from the cathedral to the parish church of St. Stephen. On reaching the west door, the ass, bearing the girl and infant, was led to the gospel side of the altar, and high mass was begun; but, instead of " Amen," both clergy and congregation cried " He-haw," imitating the braying of an ass. The Introit, Kyrie Eleison, the Gloria in Excelsis, the Credo, &c., were all concluded with " He-haw." At the close of the mass, the officiating priest, turning to the people, said, " Ite missa est," " He-haw, he-haw, he-haw," three times.'

Probably this was the festival of Vesta adapted to Christian history. An ass, by its braying, saved Vesta from brutal violence, and ' the coronation of the ass ' formed a ceremony in the festival of that goddess.

Ass of Mesopota'mia (*The*). Merwan II., the 14th and last of the Ommiade califs (688, 744–756). The surname (' Al Himar ') was a compliment, due to his temperance and strength.

Mesopotamia was noted for a breed of asses which never fled from an enemy. *See* Homer, λ 557, where Ajax is compared to an ass. The

poet says the Trojans beat Ajax with darts and arrows as boys beat an ass feeding in a meadow. Doubtless a compliment is intended, for, like the Mesopotamian ass, Ajax would not show his back to the foe.

Assassination Plot (*The*), 1696. A conspiracy to assassinate William III., near Richmond, on his return from the chase. The chief conspirator was the Earl of Aylesbury. It was discovered 15 Feb., the day before that fixed for its execution. On 27 Feb., 1696, an association was formed for his defence.

In May 1695 a plot was formed against him, which also proved abortive.

Assassins. A military and religious order of Persia formed in the 11th cent. They belonged to the Shiite sect of Mohammedans. Abdallah formed a party of these assassins into a secret society, ostensibly to maintain the claims of the Fatimide califs to universal dominion, and to extirpate the Sunnites (2 syl.); but it was Hassan ben Sabah, called the ' Sheik of the Mountain,' who made the name a name of terror. He died in 1124, after a ' reign ' of 35 years; and in 1256 the sect was stamped out by Hulagû.

The Syrian branch continued some fourteen years longer. It was this branch which murdered the Marquis of Montferrat in 1192; Louis of Bavaria in 1213; the Khan of Tartary in 1254; and frequently put the life of Saladin in danger. They were ultimately conquered by Bibars, sultan of Egypt.

It is supposed that the word Assassin is a corruption of *Hashishim* (eaters of *Hashish*, the hemp plant), a powerful intoxicant.

Assemblée des trois états (*L'*). The legislative assembly of Louis le Gros (1108–1137), in which the commons were allowed to take part with the *noblesse* and the clergy. They were not again convened till 1302, in the reign of Philippe IV., when the assembly was called ' Les Etats Généraux.'

Pronounce As-sahm'-blay day trwors'-a-tah'.

Assemblée Législative, 1 Oct., 1791–21 Sept., 1792. The National Legislative Assembly of France consisting of 745 members, not one of the previous house, called the Constituent Assembly, being eligible; hence such men as Robespierre, Pétion, and Danton were excluded. It consisted wholly of men unknown, but of red republican principles —low attorneys, club orators, newspaper writers, and mere adventurers. The special function of this assembly was to conform the laws to the new constitution, On 21 Sept., 1792, the Legislative Assembly gave place to the National Convention. Burke said there were '400 lawyers and 300 of no condition whatever.'

Pronounce As-sahm'blay Led'-jis-lah'tif'.

Assemblée Nationale (L'). I. 17 June, 1789–30 Sept.,1791. The National Assembly of France. The clergy and nobles having refused to sit in the same chamber with the commonalty, the deputies of the *tiers état* withdrew, constituted themselves into a deliberative body, and assumed the name of the National Assembly. On the *jeu de paume* (20 June), they swore not to separate till they had given France a new constitution, and from that day the house was called 'L'Assemblée Constituante.' Having prepared the constitution, they dissolved themselves, and gave place to the 'Assemblée Législative,' whose function was to conform the laws to the new constitution. On 21 Sept., 1792, the Legislative Assembly gave place to the National Convention.

II. 4 May, 1848, of 900 members. The most democratic form of government ever devised. Every Frenchman who was of age was an elector, and every Frenchman after the age of 25 was eligible to become a deputy. There was only one assembly. *See* above.

Pronounce As-sahm'-blay Nas-ce-o-nahl.

Assemblies of the Wilderness (*The*), 18th cent. French history. The assemblies of the restored Protestants of France. Held in open day when possible; but when dangerous, in some wild retreat or rocky nook. Summonses were issued only a few hours beforehand, and unarmed sentinels were placed on the heights to give notice of the approach of soldiers.

Assembly (*The Act of*). Enacts that no persons, professing to believe in Jesus Christ, shall be molested in respect to their religion, or in the free exercise thereof, or be compelled to the belief and exercise of any other religion against their consent.

Assembly of Divines (*The*), or 'Westminster Assembly,' 1643. Convoked by the Long Parliament in Hen. VII.'s chapel, Westminster, to reconstruct the Church of England. Episcopacy was abolished, and Presbyterianism substituted in its place. Above 3,000 of the clergy refused to submit, were ejected from their benefices, and pensioned off with a fifth part of their clerical incomes. In 1644, ten of the assembly and thirteen presbyters were told off to ordain ministers to these vacancies. The Assembly was dissolved in 1649. It was this assembly which put forth the 'Assembly's Larger and Shorter Catechisms' for the use of the people. This assembly was a spiritual court, with jurisdiction over all affairs pertaining to religion or morals.

Assembly of Notables (*The*). An assembly of the princes of the blood, and the chief nobility, magistrates, and clergy, convened occasionally in times of trouble to consult with the king on matters of state. Every member of the assembly was named and invited by the king. It possessed no legislative or executive functions. Assembled for the first time in 1369, under the summons of Charles V. of France.

They were again convoked in 1470, and met at Tours. Again in 1526, and met at Cognac Again in 1560, and met at Fontainebleau. Again in 1661, and met at St. Germain. Again in 1566, and met at Moulins. Again in 1596, and met at Rouen. Again in 1626, and met at Paris; but the two best known were those convened at Versailles 22 Feb., 1787, and 12 Dec., 1788.

Assent (*Royal*) to bills which have passed the House of Commons and House of Lords is given, either personally in the House of Lords or by letters patent. After the title of the bill has been read by the clerk of the crown, the clerk of the parliament says (if it is a bill of supply) 'Le roi' (or 'La reyne') 'remercie ses bons sujets, accepte leur bienveillence, et ainsi le veult.' If a *public* bill, not of supply, he says 'Le roi (la reyne) le veult.' If a *private* bill, he says 'Soit fait comme il est désiré.'

If the royal assent is withheld, the announcement is made by the words 'Le roi s'avisera,' but the last instance of such a refusal was by William III. in 1693.

One would think it is time for the monarchs of England to speak English, and not old French.

Assessors (*The*). Since the Municipal Corporations Act of 1835, two officers chosen by the burgesses to assist the mayor in revising the burgess lists.

Assid'ians, or 'Chasidim.' A set of zealous defenders of the unity of God, against the attempts of Antiochus Epiphanês and his successors to force the Jews into idolatry. Mattathias headed the Chasidim for four years, afterwards Judas Maccabæus assumed the chief command.

'Chasidim' means pietists.

Assien'to. A Spanish treaty conferring on some foreign nation a monopoly in the negro slave-trade. In 1713 the exclusive right of importing negroes to Spanish America was transferred from France to England, and was made over by government to the South Sea Company for thirty years. In 1748 the English company relinquished its right (which had still four years to run) on the payment of 100,000*l.*, and the concession of certain commercial advantages.

The Spanish name of this treaty is 'El Asiento de los Negros.'

Assien'to Company [*of England*], 1713. I. Under the Treaty of Utrecht. This English company had the monopoly or exclusive privilege of supplying the Spanish West Indies and the South American colonies with slaves. The quéen (Anne) had one-fourth of the profits of this traffic in human blood. Abolished (1807) by 47 Geo. III. c. 36. The word means 'a treaty,' and is applied to a compact between Spain and some foreign nation.

II. [*of France*], 1702. The French Guinea Company took the name of the 'Assiento Company,' when Philip V. of Spain granted them the exclusive right of importing 4,800 negroes of both sexes annually for ten years to the continent and islands of Spanish America.

Assignats, 9 Sept., 1790, recalled 18 July, 1796. French government notes. The National Assembly confiscated all the church lands, but being unable to sell them, kept them as national property, and issued paper money to the amount of 400,000,000 livres, making the church lands security for the repayment. These assignats were negotiable like our bank notes, and were generally for 100 francs (4*l.*) each, though some were as low as 5 francs. In June 1793, this paper money was worth only one-third of its nominal value; and in March 1796, an English sovereign would have bought 7,200 francs worth of assignats. They were then bought in by the French government at the rate of one franc in specie for 30 francs in paper.

It is said that the entire amount of assignats issued represented 45,578,000,000 francs, *i.e.* 1,823,000,000*l.* sterling.

Pronounce As'-sin-yahs'.

Assistors (*The Council of*). The same as the 'Council of Adjutators' (*q.v.*).

Assize of Arms, 1181. The substitution of the old military obligation of every freeman to serve in defence of the realm in lieu of feudal retainers. By this law, every *knight* was forced to arm himself with coat of mail, shield, and lance; every *freeholder* with lance and hauberk; every *burgess* and poorer freeman with lance and iron helmet. This universal military levy was wholly at the disposal of the king for purposes of military defence.

Assize of Battle. Trial by combat.

Assize of Bread (*The*), 1214. A public price set upon bread according to its weight, from the reign of John to that of George IV., 1824.

Assize of Clarendon (*The*), 1166. A law in the reign of Henry II. which revived the old English system of mutual security or frank pledge to provide for the good order of the realm. By this law no stranger could remain in any place more than one night, without giving sureties for his good conduct; and twelve men in every hundred, with four from each township, were sworn to report known criminals or evildoers within their district, that they might be brought to trial by ordeal. This is the foundation of our 'grand jury' system.

Assize of Jerusalem (*The*). 'Les Assises de Jérusalem,' 1099. A body of laws promulgated by Godfrey, the 'Defender and Baron of the Holy Sepulchre.' Gibbon calls it 'a precious monument of feudatory jurisprudence.'

Assize of Northampton (*The*), 1176. An expansion of the Assize of Clarendon. By this assize Henry II. divided the kingdom into six districts or circuits, to each of which he assigned three itinerant judges. Appeals from the judges might be made to the king himself in council. This is the basis of our

Privy Council, and the equitable jurisdiction of our lord chancellor.

Associate Presbytery (*The*),
1733. Those who separated from the
establishment in Scotland under Ebenezer Erskine assumed this name, but they
were generally called Seceders.

Associated Patriots (*The*), 1821.
The Carbonāri of France. After the July
Revolution, 1830, the society assumed
the name of the 'Charbonnerie Démocratique.'

Associated Synod (*The*), or 'Associate Synod,' 1740. Separatists from the
General Assembly of Scotland, led by the
Rev. Ebenezer Erskine and his brother
Ralph. They objected to the law of the
assembly made in 1732, 'that if a patron
neglected to fill up a vacancy within six
months, the elders should select a candidate, subject to the veto of the presbytery. Erskine insisted that the appointment of ministers belonged to the people,
and that heritors and elders had no right
to interfere. Now merged in the United
Presbyterian Church.

Association Bill (*The*), 1829. A
bill to suppress the Catholic Association
of Ireland preparatory to the introduction of a bill for Catholic emancipation.'

**Association for Discounte-
nancing Vice** (*The*), 1800. In Ireland.
The masters and mistresses were to be
Protestants, and the reading of Scriptures
was part of the daily curriculum. The
church catechism was taught, and no
other religious catechism was allowed.

**Association of Russian
Knights** (*The*). A secret Russian
society formed in the reign of Czar Alexander I. Its object was to put an end to
the abuses of the interior administration
of the empire. Being informed that the
Czar intended to restore Poland, the society resolved to assassinate him. On
mature reflection the scheme was abandoned, and the society was reorganised as
'the Union of Public Good.'

Association of the North (*The*),
otherwise called the 'Association of
St. Petersburg.' A secret society organised in 1823. It consisted of *believers*
and *adherents*, the former being the
founders from whom three presidents

were elected, and the latter members admitted by the believers. The object was
ultimately to convert Russia into a republic, but this was to be done gradually,
and for the nonce the czar was to be reduced to a monarch with similar powers
to the American president. The Emperor
Alexander I. was to be assassinated, and
all the rest of the royal family deported
or exiled. The assassination was fixed
for the beginning of 1826, but the czar
died 30 Nov., 1825.

Assumption Day, 15 Aug. Instituted in the 7th cent.

**Assumption of the Virgin
Mary** (*The*), 7th cent. The dogma that
the soul and body of the Virgin Mary was
carried up to heaven by Christ and his
angels.

Titian's picture of the Assumption, in Venice, is
one of the finest pictures ever painted by man.

Assyrian Canon (*The*), B.C. 909–
640. Discovered and published by Rawlinson in 1862.

Asto'ria (Oregon, U.S. America). So
called, in 1811, from Mr. Astor, merchant
of New York, who founded here a fur-
trading station. The adventure of this
merchant forms the subject of Washington Irving's 'Astoria.'

Astral Body (*The*), or *linga sharira*,
the third principle. A semblance of the
human form, fully inhabited by its higher
principles. It can migrate to any distance from the physical body. The
Scotch 'double' is a sort of *linga
sharira*.

Astral Spirits. The supposed
spirits which pervade the stars, each star
having its own spirit, (or soul). Paracelsus taught that every human being had
an astral spirit; hence the influence of a
person's particular star on his life.

Astrologers. The most noted are:
Tommaso Pisano, father of the celebrated Christina Pisano (*–1380);
Johann Müller Regiomontānus, German
(1436–1476); Johann Stöffler, German
(1452–1531); Cardan (1501–1576); Nos-
tradāmus (1503–1566); Count Cosmo
Ruggieri, astronomer to Catharine di
Medici (16th cent.); Philip and Matthieu
Laensberg (17th cent.). The chief astronomers between Ptolemy and Kepler
believed in astrology.

The rule of the triplicities, as recommended by Pythagoras, Hippocrates, Dioclés and Avicenna. Or I will begin *ab hora quœstionis*, as Haly, Massahala. Ganwehis, and Guido Bonatus have recommended.

Will you place . . . the vernacular name of Isaac Newton in opposition to . . . Dariot, Bonatus, Ptolemy, Haly, Eztler, Dieterick, Naibob, Harfurt, Zael, Taustettor, Agrippa, Duretus, Maginus, Origen, and Argol?—Sir W. SCOTT, *Guy Mannering*, chap. iii.

Astronomy and Experimental Philosophy (*Professorship of*).

In the University of Cambridge, 1704; founded by Dr. Plume, archdeacon of Rochester. Stipend 800*l*. a year, exclusive of fees. The professor is called the Plumian Professor. *See* 'Sheepshanks Exhibition.'

At'abeks (*The*), *i.e.* 'Father of the Princes,' 11th and 12th cent. A title assumed by certain emirs, governors of provinces, who, under the Seljuks, usurped supreme power. The chief were: (1) The Atabeks of Irak, founded by Omad Eddin Zenghi. This dynasty lasted from 1127 to 1218. (2) The Atabeks or Attabegs of Farsistan, who ruled over Persia (1148–1264), and were driven out by Hulagou; (3) the Atabeks of Aderbaïdjan (1169–1225); (4) the Atabeks of Laristan, the last of whom, named Rokneddin, died 1339. *See* 'Attabegs.'

Ateliers Nationaux, 1848. National workshops for unemployed operatives. The works were generally useless, badly done, and dearly paid for. In Paris they proved an utter failure; and similar attempts in England and Ireland have always been fruitful sources of discontent and rebellion.

Pronounce At-tel'-e-a Nas'-se-o-no'.

Atella'næ, 'Fab'ulæ Atella'næ,' or 'Ludi Osci.' First introduced into Rome from Atella in Campania. Called 'Ludi Osci' because the two chief characters (Macchus and Bucco) spoke Oscan and represented Oscan characters. They were, like our after-pieces, extravagant and droll.

Athana'sian Creed (*The*), between 426 and 430. Probably composed in France by Hilary, bishop of Arles. It was originally composed in Latin, but our version is from a Greek translation.

It was originally called 'the Catholic Faith,' but in 640 it was called 'the Athanasian Creed,' not meaning the creed composed by Athanasius, but the creed which sets forth the views of Athanasius, the great opponent of Arius. It was received in Italy, 700; in the churches of France in 670; in Germany about 787; in England about 800, and in Rome not before 930 or 1014.

Athana'sians. Those who, like Athanasius (296–373), believe there are three persons (the Father, Son, and Holy Ghost) in the one undivided Godhead; that all the three are co-equal and eternal, 'none afore or after other,' and that the Holy Ghost proceeded from the Father *and* the Son.

The Athanasian Creed was not composed by Athanasius, but expresses his opinions respecting the Trinity. It was not received in the Latin Church till 930 or 1014, and was never sanctioned by any council.

Athenæum. I. Founded in Rome by Hadrian A.D. 133.

II. The London weekly journal established in January 1828.

III. The club so called in Pall Mall, founded in 1824.

Athenian Confederacy (*The*), B.C. 431. It contained Thessaly and Acarnania (in northern Greece), Corcyra, Zacynthus, and Naupactus. Their allies were Chios and Lesbos, with all the other islands of the Ægean Sea, except Melos and Thera, together with the Greek cities on the coast of Asia and Thrace.

Athenian Moses (*The*). Plato (B.C. 428–347), the Greek philosopher, is so called by Numenius.

Athens of India (*The*). Benares (2 syl.), 460 miles from Calcutta, the seat of Brahminical learning.

Atlantic Cable (*The*). A cable between Valentia in Ireland and Heart's Content in Newfoundland, successfully laid in 1866. Many laid since.

Atlantic Telegraphs. Telegraphic cables used for sending telegraphic messages across the Atlantic. In communication with all the telegraphs of the two worlds.

At'omic Theory (*The*). The 'laws of combining proportion,' discovered by Dalton and expressed in four laws: (1) that of constant proportions; (2) that of reciprocal proportions; (3) that of multiple proportions; and (4) that of compound proportions.

At'tabegs (*The*). *See* 'Attabeks.'

Attabeg is from 'Atta,' a master or tutor, and 'Beg,' or 'Bey,' a lord, a kind of 'mayor of the palace.'

Attacot'ti, or 'Attacots.' The Irish of prehistoric times who paid tribute to the Scoti. The word is a Latinised form of an Irish word meaning tribute-payers. The insurgent peasantry who assassinated Frederick the Just of Ireland were Attacots, and the word is applied to disturbers of the peace even in North Britain.

Attacot'tic Rebellion (*The*). A prehistoric rebellion of the Attacotti or tributaries of Ireland against the Scoti, who were 'massacred,' and a native prince set over the island; succeeded by his son, Moran. *See* 'Irish Associations.'

Attacot'tic Wars (*The*). The two plebeian rebellions (*q.v.*).

The chief movers of those two rebellions known by the name of the Attacottic Wars.—T. MOORE, *History of Ireland*, vii. 151.

At'talic Wealth. Unexpected or unlooked for wealth. B.C. 133, Attalus, the rich king of Pergămos, made the Romans his heirs. Queen Victoria has been enriched by 'Attalic wealth.'

Atterbury's Pad. Lord Coningsby was so called. In the debate on the Occasional Conformity and Schism Bill in 1718, Atterbury, bishop of Rochester, opposed the bill, and said, 'I prophesied last winter the bill would be brought forward, and I am sorry to find my words have come true.' Lord Coningsby insolently retorted : 'The right reverend speaker has set himself forth as a prophet ; but, for my part, I know no prophet to liken him to, unless to that famous prophet Balaam, who was reproved by his own ass.' To this the bishop replied : 'I am well content to be compared to the prophet Balaam, but I am sure I have been reproved by nobody but his lordship.'

Attic Moses (*The*). Plato (B.C. 428–347).

Attic Orators (*The Ten*). i. Æschĭnês (B.C. 398–314) ; ii. Andocĭdês (467–391) ; iii. Antĭphon (died 411) ; iv. Demosthĕnês (385–322) ; v. Dinarchos (361–293) ; vi. Hyperĭdês (396–322) ; vii. Isæos (flo. 420–348) ; viii. Isocrătês (436–338) ; ix. Lycurgos, not the lawgiver (396–323) ; x. Lysĭas (458–378).

Atticus (*The Christian*). Reginald Heber bishop of Calcutta (1783–1826).

Atticus (*The English*). Joseph Addison (1672–1719).

Who but must laugh, if such a man there be ?
Who would not smile if Atticus were he ?
       POPE, *Prologue to the Satires.*

Atticus (*The Irish*). George Faulkner, printer and author (1700–1775). So called by Lord Chesterfield.

At'ticus of Midlothian (*The*). The Right Honourable W. E. Gladstone (1809–), so called for his 'Midlothian speeches,' which obtained for him the premiership in 1880.

At'tila le petit. Thiers, the French historian (1797–1877).

He was also nicknamed 'Tamerlan à lunettes' ; 'Came'léon' ; 'General Bonne' ; and 'Le Roi des Versailleux.'

Attorney-General (*The*). A ministerial officer of the crown at an annual stipend of 7000*l.* He is appointed by letters-patent, and stands in relation to the sovereign as any other attorney does to his employer. His duties are to conduct prosecutions for such grave offences as tend to disturb the state ; to advise the heads of other ministerial departments on legal points ; to conduct all suits relating to the public revenue or charitable endowments in which the crown has a right to interfere ; and, in short, to act in all things as the legal adviser of the sovereign.

The stipend of the Solicitor-General is 6,000*l.*; but both these lawyers are paid extra fees for 'contentious business,' according to the usual professional scale.

Attorney-General of the Lantern (*Procureur général de la Lanterne*). Camille Desmoulins (1762–1794), one of the chief instigators of the French Revolution, when those obnoxious to the mob were hanged on the street lamp-ropes.

Pronounce At- ur'-ney.

Attroupement (3 syl.). A political or party meeting in the public streets or squares, like those in Trafalgar Square, London, in 1887–1888. By the French law, till April 1831, they were declared unlawful, and if persisted in, after due notice, the military dispersed them. Those apprehended might be imprisoned for two years, at the discretion of the magistrates.

At'ua (plu. *Atuas*). The Elohim of the Tongans, including (1) the original gods ; (2) the souls of nobles ; (3) the souls of metabooles or vassals, which appear as ghosts to relatives; (4) the souls of attendants and serfs; (5) the Atua-pow, the mischievous gods; and (6) the Mooi, or god which supports the earth. (Mariner, vol. ii. p. 127.)

Aubaine (2 syl.). The right of French kings to the property of every foreigner who died in France without being naturalised. Abolished by the National Assembly in 1790; re-established by Napoleon in 1804; and finally annulled on 14 July, 1819.

Auchterar'der Case (*The*), 1834–1843. The great test case of the celebrated 'Voluntary Controversy' (*q.v.*) of Scotland. The question was this: Is the congregation to give a 'Call' or invitation to its pastor, or has the Kirk a right to appoint any minister it thinks proper? A vacancy occurred in the parish of Auchterarder, containing 3,000 souls. In a congregation of 300, only two persons signed 'the Call,' and the kirk pronounced it insufficient. The House of Lords was appealed to, and confirmed the decision of the kirk, but when the kirk selected a minister, the court of sessions interfered. The kirk commanded the presbytery to proceed with the presentation, and it did so, but was summoned at the bar of the civil courts, and the candidate was prohibited from preaching in the church. This controversy went on till 18 May, 1843, when 470 clergymen withdrew from the General Assembly, and constituted themselves into 'The Free Church of Scotland.'

During the controversy various other cases occurred, as those of Dunkeld, Lethendy, Strathbogie, &c.

Audæism, 338. The heresy of Audæus or Udo of Mesopotamia, who insisted that God had a human form. At that early period he accused the clergy of worldliness and impurity of morals. Udo died A.D. 370.

Audi'ans, or 'Audæans.' Same as Quartodecimans (*q.v.*).

The same capital punishment was inflicted on the Audians or Quartodecimans who should dare to perpetrate the atrocious crime of celebrating on an improper day the festival of Easter.— GIBBON, *Decline and Fall*, &c., chap. xxvii.

Audit Ale. Extra strong ale, supposed to be provided for an audit feast, when the college accounts are audited.

It is, however, sold at the butteries of Cambridge University at any time.

Audley Street, London. So named from Mr. Hugh Audley, a barrister of the Inner Temple, who bought the ground thereabouts for building purposes. He began with 200*l.*, and at death, in 1662, left a property worth 400,000*l.*

Aughton Pudding Feast. Held every twenty-one years at Aughton, near Ormskirk, in Lancashire. About a century ago a firm of wand weavers constructed for their trade an immense oblong boiler, which was inaugurated by cooking therein a large plum-pudding of a ton weight (20 feet long and 6 feet thick). In 1886 (16 June) the pudding weighed 1,000 lbs., and was provided by public subscription.

Augsburg (*Diet of*). *See* under 'Diet.'

Augsburg (*Treaty of*), 22 Sept., 1555. Also called the 'Religious Peace of Augsburg, in which full liberty of worship was confirmed. Lutherans and Catholics were declared alike eligible to all offices of state, and to seats in the imperial diets. Every ruler was allowed to sanction what form of religion he chose in his own province, but all were to tolerate those who held different views.

Augsburg Confession (*The*). The statement of the doctrines of Luther and his disciples, handed in to Charles V., who had convoked a diet at Augsburg to receive it, 8 April, 1530. The first part contained 21 articles of faith and doctrine; and the second part contained 7 articles on disputed points: as (1) on the two kinds of the eucharistic sacrament; (2) on the marriage of priests; (3) on the mass; (4) on confession; (5) on distinctions of meat; (6) on conventual vows; and (7) on the authority of bishops.

The 'confession' is no longer an exponent of the theological views of German Protestants.

Augsburg Interim (*The*). The provisionary settlement of the points in dispute between the Lutherans and Roman Catholics, till they could be finally settled by a general council. The Augsburg Interim was held at Augsburg in 1548, by order of Charles V. A compromise was agreed to, but in 1552 it was declared to be unsatisfactory, and another compromise was made at Leipsic, called the 'Leipsic Interim.'

August, 31 days. This month ought to be 30 days. Thus: March 31, *April* 30, May 31, *June* 30, July 31, *August* 30, &c.; but when the Latin month Sextilis was named August, in honour of Augustus (as the month Quintilis had been changed to July in honour of Julius), court flattery could not allow the Augustan month to be shorter than the Julian month, so the short month was shifted to Sept., and the symmetry of the Calendar was destroyed. September was the birth-month of Augustus, but August (Sextilis) was his lucky month. Thus he held his triumph for his Illyrian, Actium, and Alexandrian victories in Aug. B.C. 29, and was made emperor the same month. He died 19 Aug., 14 B.C.

August 1. The anniversary of the accession of the house of Hanover.

August 4 (1789). When the National Assembly of France, in one sitting, abolished all privileges formulated in 19 articles, and presented their measure to the king. It included:—

The abolition of all serfdom, seignorial dues, and seignorial jurisdictions.

The suppression of exclusive rights of hunting, shooting, keeping warrens, dovecotes, &c.

The abolition of tithes, sales of offices, and monopolies.

The equalisation of taxes.

The eligibility of every citizen to any civil or military office.

The suppression of all privileges granted to towns or provinces.

Such an amount of legislation in one night is wholly unparalleled.

August 10 (1792). 'La sanglante journée du 10 août,' called by Legendre 'the glorious 10th of August.' The Tuileries were stormed by the Paris mob. Mandat, commander of the National Guard, was assassinated by the mob. Danton, Tallien, Billaud-Varennes, and Collet d'Herbois usurped the municipal functions, dubbing themselves 'Les Commissaires de la Commune.' The Swiss guard was assassinated by the Paris mob. The king (Louis XVI.), the queen (Marie Antoinette), and her three children, were saved alive, for a time, by the National Assembly. They were sent to the Temple. The National Convention was formed,

consisting of Servan, (minister of war; Roland (of the interior); Clavière, (of finance); Mongé (of marine); Lebrun (of foreign affairs); and Danton (of justice). Santerre was made commander of the National Guard, in place of Mandat, and an 'Extraordinary Tribune' was appointed to examine into the offences of the Bloody Tenth of August.

August 15. French history. The birthday of Napoleon I., and while the empire lasted considered a national holiday. It was on 15 Aug., 1806, that he was surnamed 'The Great'; that he repealed the republican calendar; that he appointed the cathedral of St. Denis the place of sepulchre for the emperors of the French; that he converted the Panthéon into the church of Ste.-Geneviève; that he created his brother Joseph king of the Two Sicilies; his brother Louis king of Holland; his brother-in-law Murat grand duke of Cleves and Berg; gave his stepson Beauharnais in marriage to a Bavarian princess; and bestowed imperial fiefs on his great ministers and generals; that he united fourteen princes of the south and west of Germany into the 'Confederation of the Rhine'; and appointed the day a national festival for ever. Napoleon III. used to keep it magnificently.

Neither of the two emperors was buried in the cathedral of St. Denis. Both died in exile.

Augusta. The 2nd Roman Legion, A.D. 50. The Romans made the 'civitas Trinobantum' a station for this legion, and called the station Augusta. Tacitus in his Annals calls it Londinum. Now *din* is Keltic for town, and *Lon*, if the *o* is also corrupt for *y* or *i*, would be lyn or llyn, which means in Keltic a pool or body of water, so that Llyn-din means the water-town, or town on the pool.

Liver-pool seems to give colour to this etymology (another plausible suggestion is *Lion*, cheerful or gay).

Augustales Sodales, about A.D. 17. An order of priests instituted by Tiberius.

Pronounce Aug-us-tay'-leez So-day'-leez.

Augustan Age of China (*The*). The reign of Tae-tsong, son of Kao-tsou, founder of the 13th Imperial dynasty. Tae-tsong is called the Solomon of China (626–650).

Augustan Age of England (*The*). The reign of Queen Anne (1702–1714) also called the Silver Age, the Golden

Age being the reign of Elizabeth. By far the foremost name is that of Sir Isaac Newton, and of commanders, John Churchill (duke of Marlborough). The poets were Congreve, Garth, Gay, Parnell, Philips, Pope, Prior, Rowe, and Swift. The other authors were Addison, Barnes, George Bull, Anthony Collins, Jeremy Collier, Roger Cotes, Defoe, Dodwell, Flamsteed, George Hickes, Dr. John Jeffery, John Norris, Ray, South, Steele, &c. Wren, Archibald Pitcairn, and Sir Cloudesley Shovel also lived in this reign. Except Pope and Gay, the poets have no high standing, and of the miscellaneous class, Addison and Defoe are the best known.

Augustan Age of France (*The*). The middle period of the reign of Louis XIV., while Colbert was his chief minister (1619-1683).

Augustan Age of Germany (*The*). The 19th century.

Augustan Age of Hindûstan (*The*). The reign of Vikramáditya, surnamed S.kari (or foe of the Sakas), B.C. 56.

It is an anachronism to speak of an Augustan age before the reign of Augustus.

Augustan Age of Persia (*The*). That of Artaxerxes (B.C. 464-425), about which time historians, philosophers, poets, painters and sculptors of peculiar merit flourished.

Augustan Age of Portugal (*The*). The reign of Dom Affonso Henriquez (1094, 1137-1185). In this reign Brazil was occupied; the African coast was explored; the sea-route to India was traversed; Camoens flourished, &c.

Augustan Era (*The*). Began 14 Feb., B.C. 27.

Augustine (*The Rule of St.*)—included: absolute obedience; personal poverty; universal charity, and perfect chastity, both of mind and body.

The order first appeared in England about 1105.

Augustine (*The second St.*). Hugues de St. Victor, who died 1140.

Marcus Aurèlius (121-180) is called the 'Augustine of philosophy.'

Augus'tines (3 syl.), or 'Augustinians,' 1257. I. Some thirty monastic fraternities were so called, not because they were founded by St. Augustine, but because Pope Alexander IV. imposed on them the rule of St. Augustine (13th cent.).

II. An order of nuns which claimed descent from a convent founded by St. Augustine at Hippo, of which his sister was abbess. Till 1632 they wore a black habit, but it was then changed to a violet. Their special office was the charge of hospitals and the sick.

Augustin'ian Canons. Those who lived under the rule (*kanón*) of St. Augustine. Their dress was a long black cassock, having a white rochet over it, covered with a black cloak and hood. *See* 'Austin Friars.'

Augusti'nus, 1640. A work by Cornelius Jansen (1586-1638), just completed before he died, and which proved the occasion of a religious controversy the most important in its doctrinal, social, and political aspects since the Reformation. Its object was to show that the teaching of St. Augustine was in direct opposition to that of the Jesuits on the subjects of grace, free will, predestination, and pelagianism. It was inhibited by the Jesuits in 1641. In 1642 Pope Urban VIII. condemned it, in his bull 'De Eminenti'; Alexander VII. condemned it 1656; but the scholars and divines of Port Royal defended it.

In France, the members of Port Royal (*q.v.*) were Jansenists; those of the Sorbonne (*q.v.*) were bitterly opposed to the 'Augustinus,' and issued seven allegations to prove it to be heretical. These seven allegations were reduced to five.

Augustus and Cæsar. For above 1,000 years, from Vespasian to Alexius Comnēnus, 'Augustus' was the title given to the sons and brothers of the reigning monarch, and 'Cæsar' was the next in rank. The imperial wife, mother, sisters, and daughters were 'Augusta.' Only the emperor could assume the purple or red buskin. The buskins of a 'Cæsar' were green.

In the reign of Diocletian the two viceroys of Illyricum and Gaul were entitled 'Cæsar,' and the two emperors of Rome and Constantinople were each 'Augustus,' A.D. 292; but this arrangement soon lapsed after the death of that emperor. The Roman senate gave Octavius the title of 'Augustus.'

Auletes. Ptolemy X. of Egypt was so called for his skill in playing on the flute (B.C. 65-51.)

Pronounce Au lo'-teez.

Au'lic Council. The supreme tribunal of the German empire. It consisted of a president, a vice-chancellor, and eighteen councillors. This council always followed the court, and was hence the *aulic* or court- tribunal (Latin, *aula*, the court or palace). It was instituted in 1501 by Kaiser Maximilian, and was suppressed in 1806, when the empire was reconstructed ; but there are still ' aulic councillors ' in Austria.

Au'rea Bulla, or Golden Bull of Hungary. The Magna Charta of that kingdom, granted in 1222 by Andrew II., just seven years after King John signed the Magna Charta of England. By article 31 it was provided that, if a king violated any of the principles of the Golden Bull, his subjects might depose him, or take up arms against him without being guilty of treason. This article was cancelled in 1705 by Joseph I. Like John, Andrew was a bad king ; and, like John, he neither observed his *Aurea Bulla* nor intended so to do.

Auro'ra (*Missa de*). The second mass on Christmas Day, the first being the *Missa de nocte*, or midnight mass, and the third high mass. *See* ' Mass.'

Sir Walter Scott says, 'On Christmas Eve the mass was sung,' and he has been accused of an oversight, inasmuch as no mass is ever said or sung at nighttime. But Cassianus ('Instit.' book ii. c. 13) says, 'Quare post missam nocturnam dormire non oporteat.' Again, 'Missa de Exceptato' is defined by Du Cange as the mass ' quæ die vigiliam Natalis Domini præcedente cantatur, unde eadem *Præparatio ad vesperam Natalis Domini* vocatur in Missali Gothico.' Cassianus says again (c. 7) : 'Missa Canonica celebrata usque ad lucem post vigilias extendunt.' However, the 'Missa de nocte,' we are told, was only *begun* before midnight ; the ' sacrifice' must be in the morning after the clock has struck 12.

Austin Friars, or ' Begging Hermits,' or ' Hermits of St. Augustine.' Were not founded by St. Augustine, but had the rule of St. Augustine imposed on them by Innocent IV. in the middle of the 13th cent. In 1256 Pope Alexander IV. placed them under a superior called a ' general.' In 1570 Friar Thomas, a Jesuit, introduced a still more austere rule, forbidding his disciples to wear shoes, whence they were called ' The Barefooted Friars.'

Austria (*House of*), 1438–1745. Has given Germany fourteen kaisers, from Albert II. to Karl VII.

Sometimes the house of Hohenstaufen is called the house of Austria, and sometimes the present reigning emperors are also called the house of Austria, but ought to be called the house of Austria-Lorraine.

Austria-Lorraine (*House of*). The present reigning family of Austria. This house began in 1745 with Franz or Francis I., who married Maria Theresa.

Austrian Hye'na (*The*). Julius Jakob von Haynau, an Austrian general (1786–1853), noted for his ruthless cruelty towards the Hungarians, and his alleged flogging of women. In 1850 he visited the brewery of Messrs. Barclay & Perkins, when he was assaulted by the draymen, and barely escaped with his life. Subsequently, he received similar discourtesy in Belgium and France. Called also ' the Austrian butcher.'

Austrian Lip (*The*). A protruding under-jaw, with a heavy lip disinclined to shut close. It came from Cimburgis, a Polish princess, who married Kaiser Friedrich III., and displayed itself in their son, Maximilian (I.) Hence also called the ' Cimburgis Under-lip.'

A somewhat similar peculiarity occurs in the family of Sir Gideon Murray, of Elibank. He had taken prisoner a young gentleman named Scott, whom he was about to hang, but his wife induced him to commute the sentence into marriage with their daughter Meg, of ' muckle mouth.' Meg made a good wife, but the muckle mouth descended to their posterity for many generations.

Austrian War (*The*), 1859. To rescue Italy from the hands of Austria. The belligerents were France and Sardinia against Austria. France won the battles of Magenta and Solferino, and then made peace with Austria. Garibaldi continued the contest to a successful issue.

Rome was not added to the new kingdom of Italy till the autumn of 1870. Venetia was ceded to Italy in 1866, as the fruits of the Austro-Prussian war.

Austro-German Treaty of Alliance (*The*), 7 Oct., 1879. Between the Emperor of Austria and the Emperor of Germany. They agree, if either state is attacked by Russia, both shall unite their full strength to repel it. If either state is attacked by any nation except Russia, the other shall observe a friendly neutrality. If Russia assists any other state in an attack upon either Austria or Germany, the two allies shall consider the attack as made by Russia. Signed at Vienna.

In 1887 Italy joined the alliance.

Austro-Hungarian Empire (*The*), 14 Nov., 1868. The kaiser-king of Germany had to abandon his title of

Emperor of the West, or of the Holy Roman Empire, in 1806, and was entitled 'Emperor of Austria,' till 1868, when he styled himself 'Emperor of Austria and King of Hungary and Bohemia,' his dominion being styled the 'Austro-Hungarian Empire.'

Austro-Prussian War (*The*), 1866. Called the Seven Weeks' war. Won by Prussia. The chief victories were the battles of Custozza, Langensalza, Sadowa, and Olmutz. By this victory Prussia became the chief power of Germany, and Austria was entirely excluded therefrom. Total cost of the war 66,000,000*l.* sterling. Total loss of life 50,000.

Authentic Doctor (*The*). Gregory of Rimini (' Gregorius Ariminensis '), general of the Augustine order at Montpellier, died 1358. He wrote two books of ' Sentences.'

Pierre de Lombard, who died 1160, was the great ' Magister Sententiarum.'

Authorised Version (*The*), 1611. Means the English translation of the Bible, authorised to be read in churches by James I. Fifty-four men were appointed by the king to bring out this version, but seven died or retired from the task. This version is often called ' King James's Bible,' or the ' King's Bible.' *See* ' Bible.'

The Psalms in the Common Prayer Book are those in the Bishops Bible, and so were the epistles and gospels till 1661.
The Authorised Version was based on Tyndale's translation (*q.v.*), which passed through three stages: (1) the publication of the Great Bible (1539-1541), in the reign of Henry VIII.; (2) the publication of the Bishops' Bible (1568-1572), in the reign of Elizabeth; (3) the publication of the King's Bible, in 1611, in the reign of James I. Revised 1870-1884, in the reign of Victoria (published 1885).

Auto da Fé (plu. ' Autos da Fé '). An act of faith. In the Catholic Church a day was held by the Spanish Inquisition to examine into the faith of a supposed heretic. If innocent, the accused was absolved; if guilty, he was handed over to the secular power to be put to death, generally by burning at the stake. The sentence of the court and the session also are both called ' Autos da fé.'

Burning of heretics symbolised hell fire, to which heretics were consigned by the Church.

In Portugal it was customary to erect a vast theatre capable of holding 3,000 spectators, and the accused were brought forward one by one to hear judgment. Those who were brought in their own clothes paid a fine and were discharged; those who wore a ' Sambenito '— that is, a straight yellow coat without sleeves, charged with a St. Andrew's cross—had to forfeit all their effects, but their lives were spared; those who had their ' Sambenito ' decorated with red serge patches resembling flames, without a cross, were discharged, but warned, if ever they relapsed, they would be delivered to the flames; those, lastly, who had the ' Sambenito ' decorated with flames and devils were condemned to die. The place of execution in Portugal is called ' Roussi.'

Pronounce Awe'-to-dah-fay'.

Auxiliary War (*The*), B.C. 214-200. Between the Romans and the last Philip of Macedon. The Romans were the victors.

Avaricious Tyrant. Mauritius, emperor of the East (582-602). This was a mere pun. Mauritius refused to pay Chagan, king of the Avāri, four oboli a head for the prisoners taken by him in war, in 587. This refusal not only fixed on him the ill name, but also lost him his crown and empire.

Avengers (*The*). A Fenian society organised by Burton, of which he was himself the ' supreme head.' It consists of the most desperate of the Irish faction, bound by oath to murder any one the society wishes to be removed. Burton was condemned to penal servitude for life in May 1885. . *See* ' Irish Associations.'

Aver'roism. The doctrines of Averroës, the Arabian philosopher, that the soul is not an individual possession, but part of a Universal Intellect diffused through the whole world. A sort of pantheism. *See* ' Averroists.'

Aver'roists. Of Seville, Cordŏva, and Fez. Disciples of Averroës, the Arabian philosopher and expositor of Aristotle (1149-1225). He taught the doctrine of evolution, or that every existing form has been developed from some previous one; that each individual is a part or limb of the great mundane whole, and that this mundane whole is animated by a General Intelligence or ' Anima Mundi,' and ultimately all existences will be reabsorbed in deity.

Of course he denied what we call 'the human soul,' for the 'Anima Mundi' was general and not particular. Thomas Aquīnas combated this doctrine, which was condemned by the University of Paris in 1240, and by the Lateran Council in 1512. The Averroists were opposed to the Alexandrists (q.v.).

Avignon Captivity (The), 1309–1376. When the popes resided at Avignon in France, instead of at Rome.

Avignon, pronounce Av'-vin-yŏng'.

Avignon Obedience, in the great Western schism, means obedience to the Avignon pope. As obedience to the pope of Rome is called 'Roman Obedience.' See above.

Avocat-général (L'). A magistrate attached to the ministry of France, and charged to defend the law and public order.

Pronounce Av'-vo-kah' djen'-e-rahl

Avocats au Conseil d'Etat et à la Cour de Cassation. Ministerial officers charged to follow the procedure and plead for clients before the Conseil d'Etat and la Cour de Cassation (q.v.). These two courts since 10 Sept., 1817, have been united. Such an 'avocat' must be 25 years of age, and must have been in the profession at least two years. The number is limited to sixty.

Pronounce Av'-vo-kah' o con-say'-e da-tah'.

Avvogado'ri (The), 1178. Three Venetian magistrates whose duty it was to watch over the public interests. In the courts of justice they acted as checks upon the administration of the law, and were also public accusers. In the councils they superintended the debates, and without the presence of one of the Avvogadori no act of any session was valid. The police was under their care; the public disbursements passed through their hands; they were the guardians of the public registers. (Singular, 'Avvoga-dore,' 5 syl.)

Ayerst Hall, in Cambridge University. Named after the Rev. W. Ayerst, the first principal, 1884.

The chief object of this foundation is to reduce the expense of a college education.

Aylesbury Men (The), 1704. Mr. Ashby, a burgess of Aylesbury, and five other Aylesbury men who insisted that they had a right to vote for their own member, because they were freeholders. The House of Commons gave it against the claimants, and the House of Lords reversed the judgment. When the Aylesbury men commenced actions against the constables of their town, they were committed to Newgate for contempt of the House. The queen (Anne), to cut the knot, dissolved the parliament, the men were then set at liberty, and the matter dropped.

Ayoubites (3 syl.). Descendants of Ayoub, a Turkish dynasty which reigned in Egypt and Syria from 1171 to 1254. It was founded by Saladin, son of Ayoub, and was overthrown by the Mamelukes.

Azores (2 syl.). Martin Behem, in 1448, gave this name to these western islands, because he found them full of hawks (azor, Spanish, a goshawk).

Aztecs. The dominant tribe of ancient Mexico. Their kingdom was founded in 1325. Allied with the Toltecs, they extended their kingdom of Tenochtitlan (Mexico) to the Gulf of Mexico and the Atlantic. They were at their best in the 15th and 16th cents., when the Spaniards arrived. The supreme god of the Aztecs was Taotl, and the protector of their nation was Huitzilopochtli.

Az'ymites (3 syl.). Those who celebrated the communion with unleavened bread.

There was a tribe or province under the Saracens so called. Thus Robert the monk. in his 'History of Jerusalem,' book vi., speaks of 'Persæ et Medi, Arabes et Turci, Azymitæ et Saraceni, Curti et Publicani, et diversarum nationum alii multi.'

Babel (Tablet of the Tower of), 1876. Discovered by Mr. George Smith. A tile of burnt clay impressed while soft with an inscription. It is much broken, and only four columns of writing out of six remain. The translation runs thus :—

. . . of Babylon He hastens to the submission,
Small and great He confounded the mound.
Their walls all the day they founded.
For their destruction in the night
He did not leave a remainder.
In His anger, secret counsel He poured out
. . . to confound their speech He set His face.
He gave the command—He made strange their counsel.
They weep hot tears for Babil. . . .
Bitterly they weep. . .

Babington's Conspiracy, 1585. To murder Elizabeth, and having liberated Mary to place her on the throne instead. Pius V. excommunicated Elizabeth, and authorised all true Catholics to compass her death. Three priests—Gifford, Gilbert Gifford, and Hodgson—associated with Savage, undertook the assassination of the queen. Another priest, Ballard, afterwards joined the conspiracy; then Anthony Babington, a young man of fortune, with ten others (Windsor, Salisbury, Tilney, Tichbourne, Gage, Travers, Barnwell, Charnock, Dun, and Jones) ; last of all a man named Polly, who was, in fact, one of Walsingham's spies, who made his employer acquainted with all the proceedings. At the fulness of time all were apprehended and executed, except Salisbury, who escaped abroad (20 Sept., 1586).

Ba'bism, 1843. A new religion founded in Persia by Mirza Ali Mohammed, a young man who professed to be the real successor of Ali, the prophet of Iran. He told the people that he was the *bâb* (the door) through which all must go who enter into paradise. His followers are called *Bâbis*. He condemned polygamy; disapproved of the seclusion and veiling of women; allowed believers to mix with unbelievers ; and advocated a republican form of government. The royal troops were sent against the Bâbis, thousands were put to death, and Mirza Ali, with his 'apostles,' were publicly executed. However, Mirza Yahya, a youth of sixteen, was chosen successor, and the religion of the Bâb still continues.

It is not a little remarkable that Jesus Christ says of himself, 'I am the bâb or door. By me if any man enter in, he shall be saved ' (John x.).

Babouvism. Socialism, or the spoliation of land from landowners to distribute to those who had none; agrarian equalisation. So called from its author, Edouard Fleury Babeuf, who perished on the scaffold in 1797. The socialistic system of this Frenchman bears an extraordinary likeness to the platform of the Irish Land League (1881, &c.).

Baby Jumper (*The*). Bob Munton, who was entrusted by the Cambridge undergraduates with their business at Newmarket races (18th and 19th cent.).

Babylon. Old Cairo was so called, as well as the city on the Euphratês. Thus we read of the fourth crusade, 'Babylon was proclaimed to be the destination of the armament' (Villehardouin).

Babylonian Captivity (*The*). Lasted seventy years, from B.C. 588, when Jerusalem was taken by Nebuchadnezzar, and the people of the kingdom of Judah were deported to Babylon. On the conquest of Babylon by Cyrus, B.C. 538, the captives had permission to return. Only a few of them returned with Zerubbabel in 536, but a second migration was made B.C. 458, under the command of Ezra ; and a third, B.C. 445, under Nehemiah.

The ten tribes never returned, and they have been identified with the Kurds, the Afghans, the Nestorians, the North American Indians, the Angles, and many others.

Babylonica doctrina. Astrology in which the Chaldæans were especially skilled.

Ne Babylonios tentaris numeros means, do not pry into futurity by astrological calculations—do not consult fortune-tellers.

Bac'chiadæ. The kings of Corinth, so called from Bacchis, who, B.C. 931, succeeded his father Prumnidês, and ruled with firmness and equity. His descendants continued to reign in Corinth till B.C. 779, when the government of the Prytanês was established.

Bachardians. Pantheists, so called from one Bachardus, of whom Hermann says, ' Hujus Brunonis tempore, quidam fuit (Deo et hominibus detestabilis) Bachardus nomine, speciem gerens magnæ sanctitatis, sed plenus malitia homo' ('Chron. Comit. Schawenburg,' p. 26). This must be taken for what it is worth, but most likely the word is simply a corruption of Beghardians, Pantheists on the borders of the Rhine in the 12th cent., condemned by the Council of Vienne in 1311, and so called from the German *begehren* (to beg), their fundamental law being that ' necessaria mendicarent, quo facilius possint sua deliria divulgare.' These begging friars were also called ' Fratres Conversi, hoc est, fratres non habentes domicilia ' ('Annales Colmarienses,' year 1302). The Turlupins and German

Mystics of the 14th cent. were offshoots of the Bachards.

Back-staff (A). An instrument invented, in 1590, by Captain John Davis, and used for taking the sun's altitude at sea, before the invention of the quadrant and sextant. In using it, the observer turned his *back* to the sun.

Bacon of the Rhyming Crew (*The*). John Dryden (1631–1701); so called by Landor.

Badge.

Of *England*, a white and red rose ensigned with the royal crown. (The crown ensigned with the initial of the sovereign.)

Of *Scotland*, a thistle ensigned with a royal crown.

Of *Ireland*, either a golden harp or a sprig of trefoil, ensigned with the royal crown.

Of *Wales*, a dragon passant, wings elevated, gules, on a mount vert.

Of *Ulster*, the 'bloody hand.'

Of *France*, the fleur de lis.

The *white hart* was the badge of Richard II.; the *silver swan* of the house of Lancaster; the *bear and ragged staff* of the earl of Warwick, and so on.

Badger State (*The*). The State of Wisconsin, in North America. The natives are [Wisconsin] badgers.

Badingueux. The party of the French emperor Napoleon III. The empress's party was called 'Montijoyeux' and 'Montijocrisses.'

Badinguet was the name of the mason in whose clothes Louis Napoleon made his escape from Ham; and the empress was the second daughter of the count of Montijo of Spain. One of the nicknames of the emperor was 'Badinguet.' See 'Napoleon III.'

Bagarre (*Day of the*), 13–16 June, 1790. A scuffle at Nismes, which lasted four days, between the Protestants and Catholics. It was political under the guise of religion. As many as 134 persons lost their lives in this senseless squabble.

Bagaudæ (*The*), A.D. 287. Rebels in Gaul, consisting chiefly of Roman citizens. They rose in insurrection in 287, but were suppressed by Maximian. From the reign of Galliënus to that of Dioclétian the peasant class of Gaul was especially wretched, and, like the peasant class of France, they turned ou their

oppressors. Their numbers were so formidable that town after town opened its gates to the rebels; but, as in the Jacquerie, their hostility was mainly directed against the upper classes. For a time the bagaudæ tyrannised without control, but their power was soon crushed when the Roman legions were brought against them.

Bagaudæ, a βαγεύειν, quod est *vagari* apud Suidam. Boxhornius ab Hebræo *Bognedim* (rebelles). Altaserra sic dictos censet Bag'uudas (quasi silvicolas) a voce *gau*, quæ Gallis *silvam* sonat. A *bagad*, quæ vox Armoricis *turmam* sonat, et hominum collectionem.—DU CANGE.

Bagdad' (*Peace of*), Oct. 1727. Between the sultan, Ahmed III., and the shah, Meer Aschraf. War was renewed in 1730.

Bagford Ballads (*The*). Sixty-four folio vols. deposited among the Harleian MSS., in the British Museum, collected by John Bagford, a shoemaker, bookseller, and printer, of Great Turnstile, Holborn (1650–1716).

Bagimont's Roll, 1512. *See* 'Bajimont's Roll.'

Bagnes (1 syl.). French convict prisons. In 1748 the galleys as a punishment were abolished, and convicts were employed in hard labour on public works, and lodged in *bagnes*. The Constituent Assembly of 1791 called this public labour *travaux publics*, but in the Code Napoléon it is called *travaux forcés*.

Bagnigge Wells. The bagnios or baths established in 1708, in opposition to the cold baths of Mr. Baines. *See* 'Cold Bath Fields.'

Bagnolenses, or **Bagnolensians.** A branch of the Waldenses, so named from Bagnols, a town in France, where they sprang up.

Bahar'ites (3 syl.). The first of the Mameluke dynasty in Egypt. These Mamelukes were Egyptian slaves. Malek Saleh bought 1,000, trained them to the use of arms, and placed them in a fortress on the seacoast (called in Arabic *bahar'*). They succeeded in usurping the sovereign power, and Noureddin-Ali in 1254 called himself Sultan of Egypt. In 1382 the Baharite Mamelukes were succeeded by the Borgites or Bordjites.

Baharites in 3 syl. Borgites in 2 syl.

F

Bailies in Scotland correspond to aldermen in English corporations, and provost corresponds to our mayor. The Scotch Municipal Reform Bill was passed 18 Aug., 1840, and rendered this office unnecessary.

Bailiwick (*A*). A district within which the sheriff's bailiffs may execute their office. A sheriff is the king's or queen's bailiff. The corresponding French word is *bailliage*.

Bairak-tar (*i.e.* standard bearer). The title of the Grand Vizier Mustapha (1755–1808).

Bairam (2 syl.). A Moslem festival in the month Shawall or Chaval, and following the Ramadan (*q.v.*) or great fast of four weeks' duration. The Great Bairam is the time when all true Mussulmans are supposed to make a pilgrimage to Mecca at least once in their life. The feast of Bairam lasts four days, but it is preceded by a lesser Bairam of three days' duration, which begins on the first of Chaval, and puts an end to the fast. As the Turkish calendar consists of 12 lunar months, it follows that the months Ramadan and Chaval, in the course of 33 years, have run through all the seasons of the year.

The Great Bai'ram, or ' festival of the sacrifices,' commemorates the offering of Abraham on Mount Moriah.

Bajimont's Roll, 1512. The Valor Beneficiorum,' drawn up by the clergy in council at Edinburgh, and giving the valuation on which the ecclesiastical benefices of Scotland were taxed from the close of the 13th cent. to the Reformation, so-called from an Italian, Baiamund or Bajimont de Vinci, sent in 1276 from Rome to make the valuation, and collect the tithes for an expedition to the Holy Land.

Balaam's Ass Sunday. The second Sunday after Easter, when the story of Balaam is read in the lesson for the day   *See* ' Sundays.'

Balafré (*Le*), that is, the scarred one. So Henri, duc de Guise was called, after receiving at Dormans (1575) a frightful sword-cut on the face (1550–1588).

Ludovic Lesly, an old archer in the Scotch Guard at Plessis les Tours, one of the castle palaces of Louis IX., is called *Le Balafré* in ' Quentin Durward.' Probably Sir Walter Scott had some authority for the appellation.

Balance of Power (*The*). That limitation of the European states which forbids any one of the nations having such a preponderance as to endanger the independence of the others. In the 18th and first half of the 19th cent. it was a European principle, but is now utterly exploded.

Balance of Trade (*The*). The difference between the aggregate amount of the exports and imports of a nation ; or the difference of purchase and sale between any two nations. This calculation no longer exists, as it leads to false conclusions.

Balbus (the stammerer). The most renowned was Lucius Cornelius Balbus of Gades, in Spain, who served under Pompey the Great against Sertorius. Pompey took him to Rome, B.C. 71, and he gained the esteem of Julius Cæsar. Cicero defended him in an oration still extant. In the civil war Balbus accepted the management of Cæsar's affairs during the frequent absences of the great dictator, and to this Balbus the 8th book of the ' Commentaries ' is dedicated. After the death of Cæsar Balbus served the consulship, B.C. 40.

Balfour Studentship. For original research in biology and animal morphology, in the University of Cambridge. Value 200*l.* a year, tenable for three years. Candidates need not be members of the university. Founded from the memorial fund of Francis Maitland Balfour, fellow of Trinity, 1883.

Balia. A temporary delegation of sovereignty to a number of dictators. They named the magistrates and banished suspected individuals, in the republics of Italy. Italian, *balìa*, power.

A balìa was appointed (in Florence), for ten years to exclude all the Albizi from magistracy . . . and this was repeated six times in twenty-one years. —HALLAM, *Middle Ages*, vol. i. p. 540.
When the signory has taken its place to address the assembly the piazza is guarded by armed men, and then the people are asked if they wish to give balìa (dictatorial power) to the citizen named.— SYMONDS, *Renaissance in Italy*.

Balia (*The Council of*). The council which discussed and carried into effect every important measure of Florence during the Medici administration. They appointed eight men for criminal business, and this committee was called the ' Otto di guardia e balìa.'

In Venice was a similar council convened originally only on great emergencies, but in the time of Lorenzo di Medici, the Balia was made permanent, and became the legislative, administrative, and judicial power of the republic.

'Magistratus novem civium apud Senenses, qui rebus bellicis præfecti sunt.'—Du Cange.

Baliol. See 'Balliol.'

Ball Money. Blackmail levied on the newly married to prevent their being mobbed on leaving church. Called 'ball-money,' because it was given ostensibly to buy a foot-ball for the village green, but probably it rarely got further than the nearest public-house.

Ball put off (*A*). Andrew Marvell says, in his Satires, 'A silly fellow's death puts off the ball.' The allusion is to the death of the beadle of the ward, attacked, 1672, by the Duke of Monmouth, young Monk (Duke of Albemarle), and eight others, in a drunken brawl. Charles II. pardoned the ruffians, but deferred the ball which was to have taken place at Whitehall the same night.

Balliol (*John*). Joint claimant with Robert Bruce of the throne of Scotland, at the death of Alexander III. He was *great-grandson* of David, but in the *elder line*. Robert Bruce was *grandson*, but in the *younger* line. Edward I. decided the claim in favour of Balliol.

MALCOLM IV. had two sons, WILLIAM I. and David.

From WILLIAM I. descended ALEXANDER II. (his son), and ALEXANDER III. (his son), when issue failed.

Then comes David, who had three daughters, viz. Margaret, Isabella, and Adama.

Margaret's daughter, Devergilda, married John Balliol, and had a son called *John Balliol* (the claimant).

Isabella married Robert Bruce, and had a son called *Robert Bruce* (the claimant).

Balliol College, 1263. Founded by John Balliol of Barnard Castle, Durham, father of John Balliol, king of Scotland. The head of the college is called the Master.

Ballot (*Voting by*). Was first publicly adopted in England in the election of the school boards in 1870. In 1872 an act was passed by which ballot was applied to parliamentary and municipal elections in the United Kingdom.

In France the ballot is used in the election of members of the Chamber of Deputies, and not unfrequently in the deliberations of the legislative chambers.

In the United States of America and in the Australian colonies almost all public elections are conducted by ballot.

Baltadji. The 400 halberdiers who attend on the royal princes and princesses of Constantinople. Their colonel is called the 'Kizlar-agasi.' The name means hatchet-bearers.

Baltimore, in Maryland, U.S. America. So called, in 1634, from Lord Baltimore, who led a colony to settle there.

Bambi'no. A representation of the infant Christ in swaddling clothes, surrounded by a halo and watched over by angels. The 'Santissimo Bambino' in the church of the Ara Cœli, at Rome, is carved in wood from Mount Olivet, and the likeness is attributed to Luke the evangelist. The festival of the Bambino occurs in the Epiphany.

Bampton Lectures (Oxford University), 1779. The highest distinction the university can bestow. The lecturer must be an M.A. of Oxford or Cambridge, and is chosen annually on the fourth Tuesday in Easter term by the heads of colleges, but no one can hold the appointment twice. Founded by the Rev. John Bampton, of Trinity College, Oxford, who left 120*l.* a year for eight lectures, preached in Great St. Mary's on eight consecutive Sunday mornings between Lent term and Trinity term, on the following subjects: (1) Confutation of heresies; (2) The divine authority of the Holy Scriptures; (3) The authority of the Fathers; (4) The divinity of the Holy Ghost, and (5) The Articles of the Established Church as explained by the Apostles' and Nicene Creeds. Thirty copies of the sermons are printed within two months of their delivery. The endowment is 200*l.* for the eight printed sermons.

The Cambridge Hulsean Lectures are of a similar character to the Oxford Bampton Lectures.

Ban. An Illyrican word, *bojan*=lord, about equal to the German margraf. Croatia is still a banat. There were at one time several others, as Dalmatia, Slavonia, Bosnia, Wallachia, Bulgaria, Servia, &c. In the reign of Maria Theresa, a ban was the third dignitary of

F 2

St. Thomas Aquinas College Library

the Hungarian kingdom, but on the erection of the vassal lands into crown lands in 1849, the banat of Hungary ceased. Some say Slavonic Pan = lord.

Jellachich, the Ban of Croatia, resolved to hold a Sclavonic diet at Agram on 5 June (1848).— HOWITT, *Hist of Engl.* (year 1849, p. 56).

Ban (*A*), in French history, is a call to arms, and the 'banlieu' was the district encompassed by the call or proclamation.

Ban and **Arrière-ban.** Regulated in France by Louis le Gros, 1124, and last levied in 1672. The 'ban' was a summons of the king to his immediate vassals, calling them to his banner; the 'arrière-ban' was the summons of the suzerain to his tenants. Sometimes the levy itself was called the 'ban' or 'arrière-ban.' *See* 'Bouillet' *sub voce.*

Ban of the Empire. 'To be put under the ban of the empire,' in German history, means to be cut off from society, and deprived of rank, title, privileges, and property.

Banat (*A*). The district under a ban. The ban of Croatia is the third of the Hungarian barons. *See* 'Ban.'

Banbury Saint(*A*). An overstrained puritan. Mr. S. R. Gardiner calls Banbury the 'most puritan of all puritan towns.' It is a tradition that cats who caught mice on Sunday in Banbury were hanged on Monday.

To Banbury came I, O profane one !
Where I saw a puritane one
Hanging of his cat on Monday
For killing of a mouse on Sunday.
                Drunken Barnaby.

Banbury Story (*A*). An idle silly story. A correspondent in 'Notes and Queries' (21 May, 1887, p. 404), derives the phrase from one William Morrell, who lived at Banbury, noted for the wonderful tales which he told of his travels. He was a professor of chirurgery, and was looked on by the country people as a prodigy. (*See* Gardner, 'History and Gazetteer of Oxfordshire,' p. 432.)

Banco (*Sittings in*). Now means the sittings of judges during term-time, when the several judges sit in their respective courts; but formerly it meant those judges who held their court at Westminster, in contradistinction to judges of

the *curia* or *aula regis*, who followed the king. *See* 'Days in banc.'

Banco. The standard money in which a bank keeps its accounts, as distinguished from the current coin of the locality. Thus the Hamburg bank keeps its account in an hypothetical coin having no representative in the current coinage.

Band of Hope, 1855. Children under working age—that is, about 14—who have agreed to abstain from all intoxicating drinks. Started by the Rev. Jabez Tunnicliffe, of Leeds. First president of the union was Canon Morse, who was succeeded by Lord Ebury, and then by Samuel Morley, M.P. Stephen Shirley was one of the most active leaders, but Mr. Tunnicliffe suggested the name.

Band of the Heroine (*The*), A.D. 618. A band raised by Lee-chee, daughter of Lee-chee-min, who sold all her jewels to pay for a band of soldiers to assist her father in deposing Yang-tee, the emperor of China. The emperor was deposed, and the conqueror, after a short interval of a few months, founded the thirteenth imperial dynasty, called that of Tâng, the Augustan age of China.

Band-room Methodists, or 'The United Free Gospel Churches,' 1806. So called because they met originally in the Band-room at Manchester. They do not pay their ministers. They admit persons who are not members into their society, and ignore class-meetings.

Bandage (*The*), with which Christ was blindfolded by the soldiers, according to Mark xiv. 65, was given (we are told) by Charlemagne to St. Namphasus, who built the abbey of Marsillac (in France), where he deposited it. It is now kept in a little country church called St. Julian of Lunegarde. It is a linen bandage stained in places with blood. *See* 'Crucifixion, Relics of the.'

Asservatur in ecclesia S. Juliani de Lunegarde (cujus præsentatio ad abbatem Marciliacensem pertinet) tenue velum ex lino Ægyptio; idemque illud esse dicunt quo Christi faciem milites obduxere, dum per ludibrium colaphis cæderetur. Est et in eadem ecclesia frustum arundinis ei in signum regni affectati pro sceptro traditæ.— DOMINICY, *De Sudario Capitis Christi,* p. 47.

Bande Noire. A society of speculators which, after the French Revolution, bought up the châteaux, the abbeys, the monuments of art, not to preserve them, but to sell them as 'raw material.' These Vandals would pull down a fine building merely to sell the material, or a work of art as so much gold, silver, or marble. Hence 'Bande Noire' means Vandals who would sell a Colossus of Rhodes merely as so much bronze, or Doomsday Book as so much parchment. *See* 'Black Band.'

Bandit. In Italian *bandito*, plural *banditi*, means an outlaw or banished man; what we call *banditti* the Italians call *briganti* (brigands).

Bandoleer (*A*). A leather belt formerly slung by musketeers over the left shoulder, and to which were suspended twelve little cases, each containing sufficient powder for a charge.

Bangorian controversy (*The*). Whether or not the reigning monarch can consistently be called the 'head of the Church.' The question was raised by Dr. Hoadly, bishop of Bangor, who preached (31 March, 1717) before the king (George I.) on the text 'My kingdom is not of this world,' meaning to prove that the kingdom of Christ is spiritual, not temporal. This brought on a long paper war, but had the happy result of severing convocation from the government, for it has never since been called together by the sovereign, and has now no legal authority whatever. Hoadly's chief opponents were Dr. Sharpe and William Law.

Dr. Hoadly denied that episcopacy is a divine institution, and also denied the existence of a visible Church. He greatly objected to Articles XVIII. and XIX.; and denied wholly the divine right of kings. His opinions tended to republicanism, disestablishment, and the equality of all Christian creeds.

Bank Holidays. In 1871 an Act of Parliament (34, 35 Vict. c. 17) was passed providing that Easter Monday, Whit Monday, the first Monday in August, and the day after Christmas Day, shall be bank holidays, and that bills due on such days shall be payable the day following.

The sovereign has power to appoint any other day as a bank holiday.

Bank Restriction Act (*The*), 7 Geo. IV. c. 6 (1827). The prohibition of banknotes under 5*l*. The issue of small notes was restricted 5 April, 1826, but the Act of prohibition was deferred till the following year.

Bannatyne Club (*The*), 1823. Instituted by Sir W. Scott in Edinburgh for printing rare works illustrative of Scotch history, topography, poetry, and miscellaneous literature in a uniform size and style. Only 100 copies of each work were published, one for each member who paid 5*l*. a year. The club was dissolved in 1859.

The club was called after George Bannatyne, by whose industry much of the Scotch poetry of the 15th and 16th cents. had been preserved.

Banner (*A*). In feudal times was the square flag of a knight banneret, made by cutting off the point of the pennon of a simple knight.

Now any flag carried on a pole may be called a banner; but the royal national flag is more strictly called the Royal Standard; a bishop's banner is called a gonfalon (one is called an oriflamme); a ship's flag is a union-jack, an ensign, and the long strip of bunting is a pennon. For telegraphic uses three flags are used, viz. a square flag; a pennant or triangular flag; and a flag with two points like a <, called a burgee.
A *white* flag indicates a truce or a desire to come to terms for a truce; a *red* flag means defiance; a *black* flag indicates a pirate's vessel; and a *yellow* flag a ship in quarantine. *See* 'Labarum.'

Banner-bearer of the Church (*The*). Louis the Great of Hungary was so styled by the pope (1342–1382).

Banner of St. Ambrose (*The*). The sacred oriflamme of Milan. When taken to a battle-field, it was drawn thither in a red car, by red bullocks harnessed with red trappings.

Banneret. A higher grade of knighthood conferred by the king for some heroic deed performed in the field. So called because the knight's *pennon* was then exchanged for a *banneret*, by rending off the points and making it square. The first banneret was made by Edward I. and the last by Charles I., in 1642.

George III., at the naval review, Portsmouth, in 1773, conferred the title on Admiral Pye and some other officers.

Banns. A proclamation or public notification, as 'banns of marriage,' first enjoined by the fourth Council of the Lateran, 1215.

Bantingism, 1862. The system adopted by Mr. William Banting to reduce obesity. His system was to abstain from fat-producing foods, such as bread, sugar, fat, oil, and butter.

Breakfast: tea or coffee without milk or sugar; beef, mutton, kidneys, boiled fish, eggs, biscuit, dry toast, brown bread.
Dinner (at 1 o'clock): fish, any meat but pork,

greens, dry toast, game, poultry, sherry, claret,
but *no port or champagne.*
    Tea(at 5 o'clock): fruit, rusk, tea without milk
or sugar.
    Supper (8.30): fish, meat (not pork), claret.

Bap'homet. A small image used by
the Knights Templars in their religious
services. It had two heads, one of a
man, and the other of a woman. It held
the key of life, and was surrounded with
the sun, moon, and stars. The Gnostics
and Manichæans made use of a similar
image. It is compounded of two Greek
words, *baphê mêtes* (wisdom from baptism), meaning the wisdom which those
initiated by baptism possess.

Baptiste (*Jean*). A generic name
of French Canadians, like John Bull for
an Englishman, Sawney (Alexander) for a
Scotchman, Taffy (David) a Welshman,
Michael a German, brother Jonathan a
native of the United States of North
America, &c.

Baptists. Protestant dissenters
who baptize by immersion, and only
those of an adult age, who have made a
satisfactory personal confession of faith.
They are independent in church discipline, like the Congregationalists. Baptists are divided into General Baptists
and Particular Baptists (*q.v.*).

    There are Baptists, Baptized Believers, Cal-
vinistic Baptists, General Baptists, General
Baptist New Connection, Old Baptists, Open
Baptists, Particular Baptists, Presbyterian Bap-
tists, the Scotch Baptists, the Seventh-day Bap-
tists, the Strict Baptists, the Union Baptists, the
Unitarian Baptists, &c. *See* 'Apostoolians.'

Bar (*The Confederation of*), 29
Feb., 1768. A confederation of Polish
'patriots,' organised by Pulawski, Krasin-
ski, and others, who protested in this
city against the intermixture of the
Muscovites in the government of Poland.
In 1767 the dissidents of Poland had
organised themselves into the Confederation of Radom (*q.v.*), which called
on Russia for aid. Russia gladly responded, and this led to the partition of
Poland in 1772. *See* 'Dissidents.'

    France took the side of the Confederates of Bar,
and Turkey joined them when the War of Independence began. As a rule, the Confederates of Bar
were Catholics and the Confederates of Radom
were of the Greek Church, Calvinists, Arians, and
other anti-Catholics.

Bar of Dower (*A*). Forfeiture of
the dower which a widow would otherwise be entitled to receive out of the
lands and tenements of her deceased

husband. Elopement would be such a
bar, so would treason in the husband, by
which his property is confiscated to the
crown.

Bar of Michael Angelo (*The*).
The ridge of bone which forms the base
of the forehead, and along which the
eyebrows are traced, is called the bar,
which in Michael Angelo was well
developed. This is said to indicate
great mental power.

Barattiero (plural 'barattieri').
See under 'Bianchi.' Dante, the poet,
who sided with the Bianchi, was condemned by the Neri (*q.v.*) to be burnt
alive as a 'barattiero' in 1302.

    Dante made his escape and quitted his Guelf
connections after this, and composed his immortal
'Commedia' ('Hell,' 'Purgatory,' and 'Paradise').

Barbadoes Leg (*A*). A disease in
the leg indigenous to Barbadoes; the
limb becomes tumid, hard, and mis-
shapen. It is similar to the elephanti-
asis of the Arabs.

Barbarians. All the world except
the Greeks themselves were so called in
the time of Homer. The human race
was by the early Greeks divided into
Hellenês and Barbaroi; the ancient
Jews divided mankind into Jews and
Gentiles.

    I am a debtor both to the Greeks and to the
Barbarians.—Rom. i. 14. *See also* 1 Cor. xiv. 11.

    II. The Romans ranked as Barbarians
all people except themselves and the
Greeks; but after the fall of the Roman
empire, the Teutonic races which overran Europe were called Barbarians.

    In modern speech, the word means persons of
a low civilisation.

Barbarossa = Rufus or Red Beard.
So Friedrich I., kaiser of Germany,
was called by the Italians (1121, 1152–
1190).
    Aroodje (2 syl.), or Harudj, and Khair
Eddin, two brothers, natives of Mity-
lênê, who turned Turkish corsairs, and
were the terror of the Mediterranean in
the first half of the 16th cent., were so
called. These two brothers made themselves masters of Algeria and Tunis.
Karl V. defeated them, restored Tunis
to the dey, and set free 20,000 Christian
captives in 1535.

Barber Poet (*The*). Jacques Jasmin (1798–1864) of Gascony, a barber by trade.

Barber-surgeons. The Company of Barber-surgeons was incorporated in England by charter of Edward IV. in 1461. It was united with the Company of Surgeons by 32 Hen. VIII. c. 42 (1540); but in 1745, by 18 Geo. II. c. 15, the two were made separate corporations.

For 'Barber's Pole,' *see* 'Dict. of Phrase and Fable,' p. 65.

Barbers. Pierre la Brosse, the barber of St. Louis, was made chief minister of Philippe le Hardi; Olivier le Dain, barber of Louis XI., was the confidant of that king. Figaro, the barber of Seville, in Beaumarchais' comedy ('Le Barbier de Séville'), is the type of barber-surgeons.

Barberini Vase (*The*). So the Portland vase was called before it received its present name in honour of the Duchess of Portland. It was for two centuries the principal ornament of the Barberini palace.

Barbes. Vaudois ministers. The word is synonymous with 'uncle,' and is now no longer used except as a term of endearment to old men. A minister since 1630 has been addressed as *monsieur le pasteur*.

Barclay's Janissaries, 1696. Sir George Barclay was at the head of a conspiracy for the assassination of William III., and was aided by twenty picked men from the court of St. Germain. Others were subsequently added one by one. These were called his Janissaries. The idea being that they would help Sir George to the 'George and Garter,' by subverting the throne. (Macaulay, 'Hist. of Eng.,' chap. xxi.)

Janissaries were the infantry of the Turkish empire, 25,000 of which were massacred in 1825 by Sultan Mahmood. The word means 'new troops.'

Barclayans (*The*). A religious sect founded by the Rev. John Barclay of Perthshire (1734–1798). Also called Bere'ans (*q.v.*).

Bar Cochba (Son of the Star). The title given to Shimeon, who gave himself out to be the star spoken of by Balaam. 'There shall come a star out of Jacob, and a sceptre shall rise out of Israel,' &c. He opposed Hadrian, and A.D. 132 made himself master of Jerusalem. The Romans were driven back in all directions, and Bar Cochba occupied fifty fortified places and 985 villages At length Julius Sevērus was sent to Palestine, and, A.D. 135, we are told that 580,000 Jews perished, and Bar Cochba was among the slain.

No dependence can be placed on numbers, especially in Jewish history. Tens are made hundreds, either from the spirit of exaggeration or from carelessness.

Bard of all time. Shakespeare (1564–1616).

Bard of Avon (*The*). Shakespeare, born and buried at Stratford-upon-Avon (1564–1616).

Bard of Ayrshire (*The*). Robert Burns, a native of Ayrshire (1759–1796).

Bard of Hope (*The*). Thomas Campbell, author of 'The Pleasures of Hope' (1777–1844).

Bard of Memory (*The*). Samuel Rogers, author of 'The Pleasures of Memory' (1762–1855).

Bard of Olney (*The*). William Cowper, who lived for many years at Olney, in Buckinghamshire (1731–1800).

Bard of Prose (*The*). Boccaccio, author of the 'Decameron' (1313–1375).

Bard of Rydal Mount (*The*). William Wordsworth, who lived at Rydal Mount. Also called the 'Poet of the Excursion,' from his principal poem (1770–1850).

Bard of Twickenham (*The*). Alexander Pope, who lived at Twickenham (1688–1744).

Bard of Woodstock (*The*). Geoffrey Chaucer (1328–1400).

Bard of the Imagination. Mark Akenside, author of 'The Pleasures of the Imagination' (1721–1770).

Bardesa'nists (*The*), 2nd cent. Followers of Bardesānes (3 syl.), a Syrian heresiarch of the Valentinian or Platonic school. He also denied the doctrine of the resurrection.

Bardesanistæ, inter alia exsecranda mysteria, Christum cœleste corpus habuisse confirmant, nec adsumpsisse carnem de Virgine, sed per eam, quasi aquam per fistulam transiisse deliberant. Gloss, ' Sangerm.'

Barebone Parliament (The).

From 14 July to 22 Dec., 1653, convened by Cromwell after the dismissal of the Rump (q.v.) ; so called from one Barbon, a leather-seller of Fleet Street, a name corrupted into Barebone, and seized on as a nickname for this parliament. Cromwell named eight officers and four civilians as his council of state, and this council chose 156, or (some say) 140 men for the parliament ; six being for Wales, six for Ireland, and five for Scotland. Their first act was to elect eight of their number ' to seek the Lord in prayer,' and their wish was to substitute the law of Moses for the law of the land. This parliament or convention, however, was called together chiefly to pave the way to a parliament on a really national basis. It named a new council of state, and then the Speaker placed the abdication of the convention in Cromwell's hands. See 'Parliaments.'

The Barebone Parliament projected the abolition of the Court of Chancery ; the introduction of civil marriages ; the abolition of tithes, and lay patronage ; and parliamentary reform. Cromwell was afraid of these measures, and the dissolution of the convention was determined on.

Bare-feet (Pieds-nus), 1563.

French Catholics incited by monks and priests to put down the Huguenots. These bands consisted of persons of no calling, vagabonds and beggars, armed with reaping hooks, knives and pikes. In their attacks they respected neither law, modesty, nor pity.

The Pieds-nus fell upon the Calvinists by surprise, massacred men, outraged women, demolished houses, tore down the vines, rooted up the trees, and desolated whole districts.—FELICE, History of the Protestants of France, viii.

Barefooted Carmelites (The),

1540. Reformed Carmelites, founded by St. Theresa, and approved by Gregory XIII. in 1580.

Barefooted Friars (The), 1570.

A branch of the Austin Friars or Begging Hermits, 'reformed ' by Friar Thomas, a Jesuit, who forbade his disciples to wear shoes.

Barefooted Monks, or Feuillants.

Reformed Cistercians during the 16th cent., contemporary with the Reformation. The author of this reform was Jean de la Barrière.

Barlaam, died 1348.

Censured by the Council of Constantinople 1341. He drew upon himself the *odium theologicum* of the monks of Mount Athos by denying that the light seen on Mount Tabor was the 'light of God,'*i.e.* the uncreated essence of the Deity, or, as Milton calls it, the ' bright effluence of bright essence increate.' The monks of Mount Athos were the strenuous supporters of the divine essence of that light.

Barlaamites.

Those who entertain the same views as Barlaam respecting the light seen on the mount of transfiguration. *See* 'Palamites.'

Barlettare. *Qui nescit barlettare nescit prædicare.*

Fra Gabriele de Barletta, a preacher of the Dominican order in the 15th cent. (flo. 1450), enjoyed at Naples an immense popularity. His sermons were a mixture of pathos and burlesque, and have passed through thirty editions. No one can lay claim to be a pulpit orator who cannot preach like Barletta.

Barn-burners (The).

Ultra-Radicals or Nihilists. As the Dutchman burnt down his barn to rid himself of the rats, so these Nihilists would pull down the state about their ears in order to get rid of abuses.

Barnabas (The Gospel of).

An apocryphal book containing 222 chapters. It is held in honour by Mohammedans because it is supposed to refer to Mohammed when it speaks of a ' messenger of God who will perfect the dispensation of Jesus.' There is an Arabic version, a Spanish version, and an Italian one. The last is supposed to have been written in 1450.

There is also an epistle ascribed to Barnabas, partly doctrinal and partly practical. It is a pious work, but there is no sufficient reason to suppose it was composed by the companion of Paul the Apostle. Dr. Lardner supposes it to date from 71 or 72, whereas the Gospel of St. Barnabas is not earlier than 1211. (See p. 35, col. 2.)

Barnabites (3 syl.), 1530.

An order of monks which sprang up in Milan. So called because the church of St. Barnabas in that city was granted them to preach in. Their special duties were to attend the sick and instruct the young. In France and Austria their special duty was to convert Protestants.

Barnes Scholarship (*Thomas*). For classics and mathematics. Value 60*l.* a year, tenable for four years. Founded in the University of Cambridge for undergraduates in their first year by Thomas Barnes of Pembroke College, 1844. *See* ' Bell scholarship.'

Baron of the Holy Sepulchre. Godfrey of Bouillon, in Belgium, commander-in-chief of the first crusade (1096–1099), when the city of Jerusalem was taken. The victorious army would have created him 'king of Jerusalem,' but Godfrey refused ' to wear a crown of gold where his Master wore only a crown of thorns.'

Baron Slumber. John Wodehouse, earl of Kimberley (born 1826–   ). When secretary of state for the colonies he greatly objected to the delivery of official telegrams at night-time, for fear they should disturb his night's rest.

Barones majores we now call peers. In the time of ·John they were summoned to parliament by the king. The *Barones minores* were summoned by the county sheriffs, and called 'knights of the shires;' they sat in a different house. All Barones majores were called to the king's council, but only a few of the Barones minores, who were very numerous.

Barones, 3 syl. ; majores, 3 syl. ; minores, 3 syl.

Barons (*The 24*), 1258, &c. By this is meant the 24 barons who, in the reign of Henry III. of England, endeavoured to convert the kingdom into an oligarchy. They virtually set aside the king and placed the supreme power in the hands of twelve advisers. It was these barons that first called knights of the shires to assist in reforming abuses, and the parliament called by them at Oxford is called the Mad Parliament (*q.v.*), because their measures were so anti-aristocratical and anti-despotic.

Barons. Barons are either greater or lesser. Barones majores being peers, the Barones minores being gentry possessed of lands erected into a barony, sometimes called Free Barons. *See* Sir Robert Douglas, ' The Baronage of Scotland.'

Barons (*War of the*). An insurrection of the barons against Henry III. It broke out in 1262 and terminated in 1265.

4

when Simon de Montfort was killed in the battle of Evesham.

Sometimes the uprising of the barons, 1215–1216, to compel King John to sign Magna Charta, is spoken of as the Barons' War, or War of the Barons, likewise.

Barons of the Exchequer (*The*). Anciently the three puisné judges of the exchequer. There were besides a lord-treasurer and a chancellor. The court now consists of five judges, viz. the chief baron and four barons of the exchequer.

Puisné pronounce *pu-ne.* French *puis-né.*

Baronet. *Primus Baronetorum Angliæ.* Sir Nicholas Bacon, of Redgrave, in Suffolk, whose successors are styled so still.

Baronet. *See* under ' Knight Baronet.'

Baronial Days. Days when the barons sat to hear the complaints of their vassals.

Barracoon (*A*). A depôt on the coast of Africa for newly-captured slaves, where they were stowed till they were carried off in the slave-vessels.

Barrel-Mirabeau. Boniface Riquetti, viscount de Mirabeau (1754–1792), was so called from his huge bulk and the quantity of liquor he consumed.

Barren Periods. Plato says there are periods when inferior things are made partakers of extraordinary virtues, and celestial virtues show themselves in earthly things; and there are periods when no such virtues shine forth in them. The former he calls *Fertile* periods, the latter *Barren* periods. Miracles belong to the fertile periods, but when magical operations ceased, came a barren period.

Barricades (*Day of the*), ' Journée des barricades,'. 12 May, 1588, when the Parisians barricaded the city against the Swiss Guards sent by Henri III. to put down the populace, who were clamourous to place Henri of Guise on the throne.

(ii.) 5 Aug., 1648, when the populace barricaded the streets of Paris, because their favourites Blancmesnil, Charton, and Broussel, ' conseillers au parlement,' had been arrested.

(iii.) July 1830. July 27, 28, 29, called La Grande Semaine, when Charles X. was driven from the throne.

(iv.) Feb. 1848. Feb. 22, 23, 24, when
Louis Philippe was driven from the
throne.

(v.) June 1848. June 23, 24, 25, when
the national workshops were closed.

(vi.) 2 Dec., 1851. The *coup d'état*,
when Louis Napoleon became emperor.

A barricade is a barrique filled with sand, &c.

Barrier (*Treaty of the*), 15 Nov.,
1715. Between the Kaiser, the King of
Great Britian (George I.), and the States-
General of the United Provinces. It
was signed at Antwerp.

Barrier Act (*The*), 8 Jan., 1697.
An Act of the General Assembly of the
Church of Scotland, intended as a barrier
against innovations, and a hindrance to
hasty legislation. It provides that no
change shall be made in the laws of the
Scotch Church without being first
approved by a majority of the presbyteries. After having obtained this
approval, even then the General Assembly
had the power of *veto*.

Barrier Treaty (*The*), 1709. (i.)
Propounded by Lord Townshend to
De Torcy, the French plenipotentiary
on behalf of the Dutch. The Dutch
were to receive from France as a barrier
to their states Furnes, Fort Kenock,
Menin, Saverage, Yprès, Warneton,
Comines, Wervick, Lille, Condé, Tournay,
and Maubeuge. The French were also
to deliver back all the towns, cities, and
fortresses which they had taken in the
Netherlands. In 1712 the Tory government disallowed this treaty as injurious
to British trade.

(ii.) 5 Nov., 1713. Between the Dutch
and the king of France, shortly before
the peace of Utrecht; by which treaty,
the Dutch reserved the right of holding
garrisons in certain fortresses of the
Spanish Netherlands.

Barriers (*Battle of the*), 30 March,
1814. Between Napoleon and the
armies of the allied sovereigns, fought
under the walls or barriers of Paris.
The French army was defeated, and
Napoleon abdicated.

Barristers first acted as advocates
about 1600. The rules for admission to
the bar were adopted by all the Inns of
Court in 1762; the new rules were agreed
to in 1852.

By the new rules a student is compelled to attend
two of the five courses of lectures delivered at the
halls of the Inns of Court, during one whole year,
which is divided into three educational terms.
He may, however, avoid attendance on these
lectures by passing an examination in law.

Bartenstein, in Wurtemberg (*Con-
vention of*), 26 April, 1807. Between
Alexander I., czar of Russia, and the
King of Prussia.

Barthélemi (*The*). The slaughter
of the Huguenots on the eve of St.
Bartholomew, and some days after.

[Sully] escaped the Barthélemi, and had a command in the battles of Contras, Arques, and Ivri.
—PRINCE, *Parallel Hist.*, vol. ii., p. 164.

Barthélemite order (*The*), 1640.
An order of clerical students living in
common, and founded by Barthelemy
Holzanter.

Bartholomew's Day (*St.*), 24
Aug., 1572. When the massacre of the
French Huguenots began, at the instigation of Charles IX. and his mother. It
is said that as many as 30,000 Protestants
were murdered in France in this terrible
persecution.

Some estimate the entire massacre as high as
70,000 persons. Felipe II. of Spain warmly approved of it, and Pope Gregory XIII. went in
solemn state to the church of St. Louis to hear a
grand *Te Deum* as a public thanksgiving; he also
had a medal struck to commemorate the event,
and proclaimed the year a year of jubilee.

Bartholomew Fair, 24 Aug. (old
style). Henry I., in 1133, granted the
charter of this fair to Rayer or Rahere,
a monk. Like all other fairs, it was connected with the church, and miracle-
plays, mysteries, and moralities were
performed. In 1445 four persons were
appointed by the Court of Aldermen as
keepers of the fair. In 1661 the fair
lasted fourteen days. In 1691 the fair
was limited to three days. In 1840 the
fair was removed to Islington; and in
1855 it was discontinued.

Bartholomew's Hospital (*St.*).
Smithfield, London, originally part of
the Priory of St. Bartholomew. It was
founded in 1123 by Rahere, the first
prior (originally minstrel to Henry I.),
who had, in 1102, founded the priory.
After the dissolution of the monasteries
the hospital was, in 1544, refounded for
100 beds.

A medical school was added in 1662, and the
hospital was rebuilt by subscription in 1729. It
now contains 650 beds, and some 70,000 patients
are relieved there every year.

Bartholomew Slaughter of Ottoman History (*The*), 1513. The Sultan Selim began his reign by a general massacre of all the Schiites in Europe and Asia. 40,000 were slain, and 30,000 sentenced to perpetual imprisonment.

Bartholomists or 'Bartholomites,' 1640. Partisans of Pope Urban VI., whose name was *Bartholomæus Prignani*, or Bartholomew of Prignano, in Naples. Many of the cardinals protested against his election (in 1378), out of dislike to his severity; and these dissentients elected Robert of Geneva, who went to Avignon, under the name and title of Clement VI. This was the commencement of the 'Grand Schism of the West.' Urban was recognised by England, Germany, Bohemia, Hungary, and Sicily; but Clement was acknowledged by France, Spain, and Naples. Urban contracted the intervals of the jubilees to 33 years, and established the fête of the Visitation of the Virgin. He died 1389. The religious order so called was instituted in 1640.

Bartole, or Bartolus. *See* under 'Coryphæus,' &c.

Bas-Chevaliers. Knights bachelors, or knights holding military fees by a *base* tenure. Superior knights were termed bannerets.

Base Court (*The*). The outer court of a feudal mansion, containing the stable-yard and accommodations for servants.

Base-Empire (*The*). The Roman empire in its decadence, from Constantine; and the Eastern empire after Theodosius.

Basel (*Council of*). *See* under 'Council.'

Basel (*Treaty of*), 1795. Between the French Republic, Prussia, and Spain. By this treaty Prussia withdrew from the coalition against France, and gave up to the republic her possessions beyond the Rhine. Spain gave up to the republic St. Domingo.

Basel, Basle, or Bâle. In the vicinity is a marble monument to commemorate the battle of St. Jacob's, in 1444, when 1,600 Swiss kept a French army (twenty times their number) in check for ten hours. All the Swiss except ten were killed.

Basel Compact, 1431. Between Siegmund and the Hussites. Siegmund

consented to allow the laity the use of the cup in the Eucharist. Procop, leader after Zisca, insisted also that the 'Bible and nothing but the Bible should have any authority in religious doctrines, rites, and sacraments.' The insurgent Bohemians then split into two parties; the Calixtines or Chalice-men (*q.v.*) accepted the treaty, but the Taborites (3 syl.) stood out till both the Procops were dead, when peace was made. *See* 'Taborites,' and 'Hussite War.'

Basil (*Monks of*), 358. Founded by St. Basil, bishop of Cæsarëa, who retired into Pontus, where he founded a monastery, and gave written rules for its regulation, the first ever enacted in the Christian Church. These rules were afterwards adopted by St. Benedict. The monks call themselves of the 'Order of St. Basil.' *See* 'Basilians.'

The monks of St. Basil in Spain (suppressed in 1835) followed the Greek ritual; those of Italy follow the Latin ritual. Numerous in Russia, but never introduced into England.

Basilæon or **Basilica**. A Greek adaptation of the Pandects, Code, and Institutes of Justinian, in 60 books. It was begun 877 by Basilius I., called the Macedonian, continued by his son Leo VI., called the Philosopher, to 900, and revised by Leo's son, Constantinus Porphyrogënitus, in 945.

Basilian Race (*The*). That is the race of Basil, emperor of the East. He was born of poor parents, but on the murder of Michael III. in 867 seized the throne, and his reign was both wise and equitable. He enforced the strict administration of justice; corrected abuses, and began the famous compilation of laws called after him 'Basilics' or Basilica. He was killed by a stag when hunting, A.D. 886, and was succeeded by his son Basil II.

The Byzantine empire, since the accession of the Basilian race, had reposed in peace and dignity—GIBBON, chap. liii.

Basilians (*The*). Of Plymouth and Beaconsfield, England, of France and Canada, are a congregation of priests founded at St. Basil (Vivarrais), France, in 1800. They are *not* connected with the old order of St. Basil.

Basil'ica or 'Basil'ika.' A Greek code, commenced A.D. 876, by the Emperor Basilios I., and completed by his son Leo VI., the philosopher. It was revised by order of Constantine VII. in 945. This code contains the Institutes, the Code, the Digest or Pandect, the Novellæ, and the Imperial Constitutions, in 60 books, subdivided under titles.

The Basilica does not contain all that the Corpus Juris contains, but at the same time it contains some things which are not included in the Justinian body of laws.

Basilica. Originally the court (*stoa*) in which the basīleus (3 syl.) of Athens administered justice. In Rome the Basilica was not only a court of justice, it was also a market place and an exchange. In B.C. 182, Marcus Portius Cato erected a basilica at Rome, and later on the basilica was a synonym of forum. Many of the churches in Italy are called *basilicas*, and so are large structures erected over tombs, as the basilica of Edward the Confessor in Westminster Abbey. *See* 'Basilæon.'

Basilica Aurea. 'The Golden Basilica,' that of the Lateran, in Rome, called *Constantiana* from its builder, and 'Golden' from its superb structure and ornaments.

'Basilicon Doron.' A work composed by James I. of Great Britain, for the edification of his son, on the principles of government, describing the duties of a young prince, and the principles by which he should rule.

Basili'des (4 syl.). A famous Gnostic of Egypt in the 2nd cent. He taught the existence of two principles, one good or light, and the other evil or darkness. The good principle has seven æons, called mind, the word, the understanding, power, excellencies, princes, and angels, forming the 'blessed Ugdoad,' or combination of eight. From these æons sprang other æons, making the total of 365, the mystic number of the Gnostics (or Basileides).

It is thought that the Gospel of St. John bears a resemblance to 'Basil'idism,' ch. i. In the beginning was the Word . . . and the Light shineth in darkness . . . and the Word was made flesh, &c.

Basilid'ians, the followers of Basil-Idès, an Alexandrian Gnostic, numerous in Egypt, Syria, Italy, and Gaul (2nd 3rd and 4th cents.). They denied the doctrine of the atonement; believed in the transmigration of souls; looked on Jesus as a mere human being, on whom at baptism the æon Nous (intelligence) descended. They affirm that it was not Jesus who was crucified, but Simon of Cyrenê, who bore his cross.

Basket Processions. The procession of the basket was the chief ceremony of the 4th day of the Eleusinian mysteries. The basket was placed on an open chariot and followed by a long train of Athenian women, each one of whom also carried a basket. The procession commemorated the rape of Proserpine, and the baskets represented the basket which the maiden was filling with flowers when Pluto carried her off to the infernal regions to be his wife.

Basoche (*Les clercs de la*), that is, Clerks of the Palace. When the kings of France lived in the Palais de Justice, the judges, the barristers, the proctors, and all persons connected with these officials, were called *Clercs de la Basoche*. The president was called *Le Roi de la Basoche*. Basoche (2 syl.) is a French corruption of the Latin word basilica (a royal palace).

Basocians (*The*). The lawyers connected with the Palais de Justice, who formed themselves, in the 15th cent., into a theatrical company, to act satires on living characters and passing events. François I. was obliged to withdraw their licence in 1540.

This interdict only applied to Paris, for we read of the Basochian farces of Bordeaux for several years after.

Bastard eigné. An eldest son, born before wedlock, whose parents subsequently married each other and had other children.

Bastard of Orleans (*The*). Jean, comte de Longueville and of Dunois (1392–1470), natural son of Louis, duc d'Orléans and Marie d'Enghien.

Bastards. 'La guerre des Bâtards,' 1324, between certain seigneurs of Gascony and Charles IV. (Le Bel) of France. So called 'parce que les Gascons avaient pour chefs des bâtards de la noblesse.'

Bastille. The French prison; was founded in 1369 by Hugues d'Aubriot; four tours were added in 1383; the fosse and outer wall in 1634. It was destroyed by the Paris mob 14 July, 1789.

The 14th of July and the 20th of June (the *Jeu de paume, q.v.*), were the two great holidays in the Revolution.
The Bastille was besieged and taken three times: viz. in 1418 by the Burgundians; in 1594 by Henri IV.; and on 14 July, 1789, by the Parisians, from which day the great Revolution is generally dated.

Only seven prisoners were found within it. The site of the prison is marked by a column in the Place de la Bastille. One soldier and eighty-three insurgents fell on this memorable day.

The *prisoner* confined in the Bastille for 35 years at the instigation of Madame de Pompadour, mistress of Louis XV., was H. Mazers de Latude. He was 24 years old at his incarceration, and his offence was giving Madame de Pompadour a false report of a plot against her life. He was liberated in 1784 and died in 1805. His 'Memoirs' are very interesting. The only prisoner who escaped from the Bastille was D'Aligre.

The *governor*, when the Bastille was destroyed by the mob in 1789, was Jourdan Delaunay, who fell into the hands of the mob and was hanged on a lamp-rope.

There were only seven prisoners found in the Bastille when it was stormed ; one was Tavernier, who had been confined ten years in the Isle St. Marguerite, and thirty in the Bastille. He was more than ninety years of age and an idiot. One of the governors named St. Florentin used to boast that he had received more than 50,000 *lettres de cachet*.

Batavia, the modern Holland. The country of the Batavi, who settled in the island formed by the river Rhine and the Waal, called by the Romans *Insŭla Batavorum*.

Batāvi or Batăvi.

Batavian Republic (*The*). Proclaimed 16 May, 1795 ; raised to the 'kingdom of Holland' under Louis, brother of Napoleon Bonaparte, in 1806 ; Belgium and Holland united to form the kingdom of the Netherlands under William I. in March 1815 ; Belgium separated from Holland 1830, and Prince Leopold of Saxe-Coburg was elected king of Belgium by the National Congress 4 June, 1831.

Bath, in Somersetshire. The *Hū'dăta Therma* · (hot waters) of Ptolemy ; the *Aquæ Solis* of Antoninus ; the *Caer-Baden* of King Bladud and Geoffrey of Monmouth ; the *Caer-Ennant* (city of ointment and of healing) of a subsequent period ; the *Ack-man-chester* (the sick-man's city) of the Saxon.

Ensample of his wondrous faculty,
Behold the boiling baths at Cair-badón,
Which seethe with secret fire eternally.
SPENSER, *Faery Queen*, bk. ii., cant x. stanza 26.

Bath (*Knights of the*). An English order instituted by Richard II., but reinstituted in 1399 by Henry IV., and again in 1725 by George I. There are 26 knights. The ribbon is red, to which is attached a medal having three crowns,

with the legend 'Tria juncta in uno.' So called because the knights were required to bathe before inauguration. G.C.B. = *Grand Cross of the Bath* ; K.C.B. = *Knight Commander of the Bath* ; and C.B. = *Companion of the Bath*.

Bath Shillings. Silver tokens coined at Bath in 1811–1812, and issued for 4*s*. 2*s*. and 1*s*. by C. Culverhouse, J. Orchard, and J. Phipps.

Baths and **Spas.** Good for

Anæmia. Schwalbach, St. Moritz, Harrogate.
Articular rheumatism and gout. Aix-les-Bains.
Asthma. Mont Dore.
Atonic gout. Royat.
Biliary obstructions. Carlsbad.
Calculous disorders. Vichy, Contrexéville.
Diabetes. Neuenahr, Carlsbad.
Gouty-catarrhal dyspepsia. Homburg, Kissingen.
Obesity. Marienbad.
Plethoric gout. Carlsbad.
Scrofulous glandular affections. Kreuznach.
Skin diseases. Aix-la-chapelle, Cannstadt, Bourbonne-les-bains, Uriage.
Throat affections. Cauterets, Eaux Bonnes.
Bath and Buxton. To soften the skin, and give it tone.
Harrogate and Droitwich, brine baths for anæmia.

Baths and **Washhouses** (*Public*), 1846, were established by Act 9, 10 Vict., c. 74.

Bâton blanc (*Le*). A marshal's bâton, in France, is covered with violet-coloured velvet spangled with gold, so that a white bâton means no honour at all, or nothing whatever. Hence the phrase : ' La garnison est sortie de la place, le bâton blanc à la main,' means the garrison went forth without either arms or baggage. And ' Il est sorti de son emploi, le bâton blanc à la main,' means he left his place without a penny in his pocket or bundle of clothes at his back ; with only his walking-stick in his hand.

Bats (*Parliament of*), 1426. During the regency of Henry VI., in consequence of the brawls between the Duke of Gloucester and Cardinal Beaufort, the citizens were forbidden to carry arms ; so when parliament assembled the members of the House of Commons came armed with bats and clubs. *See* 'Parliaments.'

Battersea Training College, 1840. Instituted by (Sir) J. P. Kay Shuttleworth in conjunction with Mr. Tuffnell, for training teachers, especially those intended for our 'national' or parish schools.

Battiad (*The*), 1750. A lampoon on Dr. Battie, said to be the composition of Dr. Schomberg, Moses Mendez, and Paul Whitehead. Dr. Battie took a very active part in the College of Physicians against Dr. Schomberg. It is somewhat remarkable that Dr. Battie's father-in-law is pilloried by Pope in the 'Dunciad.'

Battie Scholarship, for Classics. Value between 30*l.* and 35*l.* a year, tenable for seven years. Founded in the University of Cambridge by William Battie, M.D., of King's College, 1747. *See* 'Regius Professor of Greek.'

Battle. The last battle in which a king of England has been allowed to appear in person on the field was the battle of Dettingen (1743), against the French on behalf of Maria Theresa of Austria. The English were led by George II. and Lord Stair. The latter was most incompetent, but George II., by courage and dash, rescued the army from most imminent peril, and repelled the French at the hazard of his life.

For battles named from the localities in which they are fought, *see* Appendix, 'Battles.'

Battle (*Trial by*), or 'Wager of Battel.' The last waged in the Court of Common Pleas, Westminster, was in 1571; the last waged in the Court of Chivalry was in 1631; and the last waged in the Court of Durham was in 1638. Abolished by 59 Geo. III. c. 46.

So late as 1818 this procedure was decided by the Court of King's Bench to be a legal mode of trial.

Battle Abbey, Sussex. Founded by William I. in 1067 in commemoration of his victory, 14 Oct., 1066. The high altar marks the spot where the standard of Harold was fixed. The town is called Battle, but was previously known as St. Mary-in-the-Wood. The ruin which now remains was the front entrance of the abbey. The abbey is now the property of the Duke of Cleveland.

It was consecrated 11 Feb., 1094, and its first inmates were Benedictine monks from Normandy. Telham Hill is where the Norman standard was raised. Locally called Tellham Hill. The Anglo-Saxon camp stood on the rising ground (called Senlac) occupied by the abbey.

Battle Field, in Shropshire. So called in commemoration of the decisive victory of Henry IV. over Henry Percy, surnamed Hotspur, in 1403.

Battle of Belahoe (*The*), 1538. This was no battle, but simply a spoiling of the spoiler. The two chieftains O'Neill and O'Donnel, having made a predatory inroad into Meath, were returning with their spoil when Lord Leonard overtook them at the Ford of Belahoe. After a feeble resistance the two Irishmen fled, leaving their spoil in the hands of the Englishman (Lord Leonard).

Battle of Bonnymuir (*The*), 2 April, 1820. A jocose phrase to express a brush which some men of Glasgow had with the military. The fact was this: the Radicals of Glasgow called a monster meeting for Sunday, 2 April, 1820, in the interest of parliamentary reform, but hearing that great preparations had been made to prevent a disturbance, the meeting was abandoned. Some fifty or sixty men, however, started on the projected expedition of destroying the Carron Ironworks, but were dispersed at Bonnymuir by the military. Nineteen were arrested and three imprisoned for a few days, but the whole affair was considered to be a storm in a teacup.

Battle of Nations (*The*). The terrible three days' conflict at Leipzig in Oct. 1813 between Napoleon and the allies. Its issue was the defeat of the French, and the deliverance of Germany. It is called 'the Battle of Nations,' not only from the number engaged, but also because it was the champion battle of the nations of Europe. *See* below 'Battle of the Nations.'

The nations engaged were the French, Austrians, Prussians, and Russians.

Battle of Wartberg (*The*). The annual contest of the Minnesingers for the prize offered by Hermann, margraf of Wartberg, near Gotha, in Germany, in the 12th cent.

Battle of the Barriers. *See* 'Barriers,' &c.

Battle of the Bastards. *See* 'Bastards,' &c.

Battle of the Blues (*The*). The annual University boat-race on the Thames, from Putney to Mortlake, the Saturday before Holy Week. Called the Blues because both crews wear blue, the Cambridge crew *light* blue, and the Oxford crew *dark* blue.

In 1840, 1841, 1842, the race was from Westminster Bridge to Putney. In 1846 and 1856, it was from Mortlake to Putney.

Battle of the British Soldiers (*The*). The battle of Inkerman, 5 Nov., 1854.

Battle of the Butchers and Carpenters (*The*), 1413. Paris. The Duke of Burgundy and the Duke of Orleans led two factions during the idiocy of Charles VI. The Duke of Burgundy armed the butchers and the faction adopted as their badge a white hood. The Orleanists or Armagnacs armed the carpenters, and this faction adopted for badge a white scarf. In 1413 a regular conflict took place between them, on the Place de Grève, Paris, and the carpenters succeeded in driving the butchers out of Paris. The Duke of Burgundy fled to Flanders, and the Duke of Orleans entered Paris in triumph.

Battle of the Diamond. The engagement between the Roman Catholics and Orangemen of Ireland in Sept. 1795. So called from Diamond, County Antrim, where it was fought.

Battle of the 5th of November (*The*), 1854. The famous battle of Inkerman, in which the Russians in far greater force were defeated by the allied English and French armies. This battle is often compared with that of Agincourt by Henry V.

The Russians had failed to raise the siege by the battle of the 5th of November.—HOWITT, *History of England* (year 1854, p. 263).

Battle of the Forty (*The*). A battle between twenty Frenchmen and twenty Italian cavaliers. A painting of this battle is in Hampton Court. It belonged to William III., and was painted by Peter Snayers or Esaias Vandervelde (1593–1670).

Battle of the Giants (*The*), 13 Sept., 1515. The battle of Marignano, in which the allied French and Venetian armies under François I. and D'Alviano defeated the allied Italian and Swiss army. The carnage was very great, 12,000 of the conquered and 4,000 of the conquering army were left on the field. Trivulzio, who had been present in eighteen pitched battles, called them all child's play compared with this ' combat of the giants.' (Guicciardini, book xii. vol. iii. p. 167.)

Battle of the Herrings (*The*), 12 Feb., 1429. In which Sir John Fastolfe defeated the French general Dunois, near Rouvray. Called in French 'La journée des harengs.' Sir John conducted the convoy of herrings in triumph to the English camp before Orleans. Sir John had 1,600 men-at-arms and archers, with some hundred carts of provisions (bread, wine, and salt herrings, for it was Lent), for the besieging force. Dunois came against him with 6,000 Scots and French. Sir John placed the carts between the attacking force and the attacked, and placed his archers between the carts. Six hundred Scots lay dead on the field, and the French fled. So the English besieging force was both strengthened and victualled.

Battle of the Kings and Nations (*The*). Leipzig, 1813. *See* 'Battle of Nations,' and ' Battle of the Nations.'

Battle of the Moat (*The*). A skirmish before Medĭna, between Mahomet and Abu Sofian, chief of the Koreishites. So called because Mahomet had a moat dug before the city to keep off the invaders; and in this moat much of the fighting took place.

Battle of the Nations (*The*), A.D. 625 ; also called ' the Battle of the Moat ' or Ditch. The third great battle of Mahomet, in which he defeated Abu Sofian and the Koreishites. *See* above, ' Battle of Nations.'

The other two great battles were those of Bedr and Ohud, both in 623.

Battle of the Peoples (*The grand*). The battle of Leipzig, 16 and 18 Oct., 1813. The ' peoples ' were the Austrians, Russians, Prussians, and Swedes, allied against the French under Napoleon. The allies numbered 240,000 men, the French 160,000. In the heat of the battle seventeen German battalions (10,000 men), in alliance with the French, deserted, and the French were utterly defeated. They lost above 40,000 men, and the allies about the same number.

Battle of the Rocks (*The*), 1814. The battle of Falkenstein, when the French mountaineers hurled rocks on the Germans and Cossacks who sought to dislodge them. Rows of fifteen or twenty men were overthrown by a single rock, and the besiegers fled in disorder to escape certain death.

This was a repetition of the battle of Morgarten (15 Nov., 1315), won by the Swiss mountaineers over the Austrians.

Battle of the Spurs (*The*).

I. A battle fought at Courtray in 1302, between the French and the Flemish. The Flemish were led by John, count of Namur and William de Juliers. The French were defeated. It is called the battle of the spurs because as many as 4,000 gilt spurs, worn by French knights, were picked up on the field after the fight was done.

II. 'Journée des esperons,' 16 Aug., 1513. Also called the battle of Guinegate. Between the French and English. The French pretended to give way to decoy the English cavalry; but by so doing they spread a p; **ni**: , and the whole French army fled in a stampede without striking a blow. When the French officers, taken captive, were brought before Henry VIII., he jocosely complimented them on the speed of their men, and the Frenchmen entering into the jest, declared with a laugh that the only weapon they used was the spur. 'Well,' said the bluff Henry, 'then we will call it the Battle of Spurs,' and so it has ever been designated. *See* 'Guinegate.'

Battle of the Standard (*The*),

22 Aug., 1138, or battle of Northallerton, in Yorkshire. David I., king of Scotland, was defeated by Stephen. The standard consisted of the consecrated banners of St. Cuthbert of Durham, St. Peter of York, St. John of Beverley, and St. Wilfrid of Ripon, fixed to a mast, and mounted on a four-wheeled carriage, wheeled into the centre of the field; and on the top of the mast was a pyx containing a consecrated host. It was lent to Stephen by Thurstan, archbishop of York. The field of the battle was Cuton or Cutton Moor, near Northallerton, and the Scotch, being defeated, fled in confusion to Carlisle.

David I. came in defence of Maud, the 'lady of England' (*q.v.*), and was joined by Archbishop Thurstan.

Battle of the Thirty (*The*), 27

March, 1351. The French general Beaumanoir, and the English general Bemborough, agreed to settle a dispute of territory by the combat of thirty knights on each side. At first the English were successful, but Bemborough being slain, the struggle was renewed,

and the French won the fight. It is still said in France, when speaking of a hard contest, it was as desperate as *le combat des Trente*. The battle was fought at the Midway Oak, between the castles of Josselin and Ploermel, in France.

Battle of the Three Emperors

(*The*), or the battle of Austerlitz, 2 Dec., 1805, when Napoleon defeated the united armies of Austria and Russia, commanded by their respective emperors. The three emperors were Napoleon emperor of the French, Francis emperor of Austria, and Alexander emperor of Russia. The result of the victory was the Peace of Presburg.

Battle of the Three Hundred,

B.C. 547. The Lacedæmonians and Argives each laid claim to Cynuria, and agreed to submit the decision to 300 champions chosen from each side. So fierce was the contest that only one Spartan and two Argives survived. The two Argives, supposing all the Spartans to have been slain, hastened home with the news of victory; but it was shown that one Spartan survived, and a general battle ensued, in which the Spartans proved the conquerors.

Battle of the West (*The great*).

The battle between King Arthur and Mordred. It was in this battle that the king received his death wound. (How far this is historic cannot be decided. And doubt rests both on the time and place of the battle.)

Battle which lasted a week

(*The*), A.D. 732. The battle of Tours between Charles Martel, leader of the Franks, and Abdalrahman, the Moslem general of Spain. The Saracen army was 400,000 strong, but Abdalrahman was slain, and his army was overthrown with great slaughter after a whole week's fighting. No other battle in all history lasted so long.

Battles (*The fifteen decisive*),

according to Professor Creasy:

1. *Marathon* (B.C. 490), in which the Greeks, under Miltiădês, defeated Darius, the Persian, and turned the tide of Asiatic invasion.

2. *Syracuse* (B.C. 413), in which the Athenian power was broken, and the

extension of Greek domination was prevented.

3. *Arbēla* (B.C. 331), by which Alexander overthrew Darius, and introduced European habits into Asia.

4. *Metaurus* (B.C. 207), in which the Romans defeated Hannibal, and Carthage was brought to ruin.

5. *Armin'ius* (A.D. 9), in which the Gauls overthrew the Romans under Varus, and established their independence.

6. *Châlons* (A.D. 451), in which Attila, 'the Scourge of God,' was defeated by Aëtius, and Europe saved from utter devastation.

7. *Tours* (A.D. 732), in which Charles Martel overthrew the Saracens, and broke from Europe the Mohammedan yoke.

8. *Hastings* (A.D. 1066), by which William of Normandy became possessed of the English crown.

9. *Orléans* (A.D. 1429), by which Jeanne d'Arc raised the siege of the city, and secured the independence of France.

10. *Armada (The)*, A.D. 1588, which crushed the hopes of Spain and of the papacy in England.

11. *Blenheim* (A.D. 1704), in which Marlborough, by the defeat of Tallard, broke the ambitious schemes of Louis XIV.

12. *Pultowa* (A.D. 1709), in which Charles XII. of Sweden was defeated by Peter the Great of Russia, and the stability of the Muscovite empire was established.

13. *Saratōga* (A.D. 1777), in which General Gates defeated Burgoyne, and virtually decided the fate of the American Revolution.

14. *Valmy* (A.D. 1792), in which the allied armies under the Duke of Brunswick were defeated by the French revolutionists, and the Revolution was suffered to go on.

15. *Waterloo* (A.D. 1815), in which Wellington defeated Napoleon, and rescued Europe from French domination.

Several of these might be changed for far more important battles, as, for example, that which gained the independence of Switzerland, that which destroyed the independence of Poland, &c., &c.

Bauern Krieg. The peasants' war of Germany at the time of the Reforma-

tion, similar to the Jacquerie of France and Wat Tyler's rebellion in the reign of Richard II.

Bavaria (*House of*). Furnished Germany with two kaisers, Ludwig V. (1314–3347), and Robert (1400–1410).

Baxter's Maxim. 'In necessary things *unity*, in doubtful things *liberty*, in all things *charity*.' Though attributed to Baxter, he was not the original author of the maxim.

Baxterians. Those who adopt the religious system of Richard Baxter (1615–1691). With the Calvinists they believe in election, but with Arminians they reject the doctrine of reprobation.

Their religious system is (1) that, although Christ died in a special sense for the elect, yet He atoned for all, and, therefore, if a man is not saved, it is his own fault.

(2) They reject the dogma of reprobation.

(3) They maintain that it is possible for saints to fall away from saving grace.

Dr. Watts and Dr. Doddridge were Baxterians. Baxter was the author of the 'Saints' Everlasting Rest,' and of the 'Call to the Unconverted.'

Bay State (*The*), Massachusetts, which before the Federal constitution was called the colony of Massachusetts Bay.

When first the pilgrims landed on the Bay State's iron shore.—LOWELL.

Bayaderes. The trained dancing girls of India, which are divided into *Devádassi* (devoted to the service of the temples), and the *Nautchis*. The former dwell within the inclosure of the temple, and never leave it without a permit from the high priest; the latter are not attached to the temples, but take part in grand processions. The Devádassi prepare garlands for the idols, dance before them, sing sacred songs, and take part in all processions; the Nautch girls go about the country and perform for pay.

Pronounce bahy-a-dairs' (3 syl.).

Bâyandourians (*The*), or 'the Bâyandouree.' The Turkoman dynasty generally called the White Sheep. Bâyandour was the founder of the line, but Ussum Kassan (the Tall) founded the dynasty, which was driven out by Ismail I. in 1499.

G

Bayard (*The British*). Sir Philip Sidney (1554–1584).

The Chevalier de Bayard (1475-1524) was called *Le Bon Chevalier, sans peur et sans reproche*. He took part in the 'Battle of the Spurs,' 16 Aug., 1513, where he was taken prisoner, but was restored to liberty by Henry VIII. without ransom.

Bayard of India (*The*). General Sir James Outram (1802–1863). In the Indian Mutiny he was sent to supersede General Havelock, but by rare chivalry he allowed Sir Henry Havelock to retain command.

Bayard of Poland (*The*). Prince Joseph Poniatowski (1763–1814).

Bayard of the Netherlands (*The*). Louis of Nassau, brother of William of Orange (founder of the Dutch republic).

Bayeux Tapestry (*The*). Discovered in the cathedral of Bayeux in 1728; removed to Paris by order of Napoleon I. in 1803; restored to the town hall of Bayeux in 1804; and copied by C. A. Stothard in 1816. Supposed to be the work of. Matilda (wife of William the Conqueror) and her maidens. It is a picture in worsted needle-work of the history of England from the mission of Harold to William, duke of Normandy, to the conquest of England by William, whereby he became king of England. It is now preserved in a glass case in the library of the town of Bayeux. It was originally one piece of cloth 227 feet long and 20 feet wide; containing 623 figures of men, 137 of birds, 49 of trees, 37 of buildings, and 41 of ships.

The Bayeux tapestry and Domesday Book are invaluable documents of the period.

Bayonne (*The Secret League of*), 1567. A Catholic league between France and Spain, to compel France, Spain, and Flanders to abandon Protestantism. Here, in 1572, Catherine de' Medici and the Duke of Alva planned together the massacre of the French Huguenots. Mary, queen of Scots, joined the league in the year of her marriage with Henry Darnley.

Bayonne (*The Treaty of*), 5 May, 1808. When Carlos IV. of Spain resigned his crown to Napoleon I.

Bayou State (*The*). Bayou means a creek. The State of Mississippi, which abounds in creeks, is so called.

Bear Flag War (*The*), 1847. In California, between General Fremont and the Mexicans, who tried to prevent the Americans from settling in California. The Mexicans were soon driven back, and the independence of California was secured.

Bear State (*The*). The State of Arkansas, the forests of which are infested by bears.

Beards.

The *Arabians* dyed their beards red, because Mahomet hated black hair.

Assyrians and *Africans* appear in soulpture and paintings with long beards.

Britons, according to Cæsar, shaved all but the upper lip. The Anglo-Saxons and Danes wore forked beards. The Normans were clean shaved. Edward III. is represented on his tomb at Westminster with a long beard. In the reign of Elizabeth beards were cut into fantastic shapes. In the reign of James I. each profession wore a differently shaped beard. In the reign of Charles I. a small pointed beard was the mode. In the reign of Charles II. only whiskers and moustaches were worn. The modern fashion of wearing beards was introduced in the Crimean War, 1854, but the habit had been creeping in ten years before. Even the clergy no longer considered it needful to follow the fashion of Catholic priests. In the reign of Elizabeth it was ordered that 'no fellow of Lincoln's Inn shall wear a beard above a fortnight's growth.'

Egyptians apparently wore beards only in mourning ; in some statues we find that they had beards enclosed in a beard-case.

France. Beards were worn till the reign of Louis XIII, who was beardless, and the custom changed. In the reign of Napoleon III. the French shaved off their whiskers, and shaved the chin, only leaving a knot of hair, called an imperial. The moustache was worn long, pointed, and waxed.

Grecian heroes are represented with short curled beards. The philosophers are for the most part represented with long beards. Alexander made his soldiers shave that the enemy might not lay hold of their beards.

Jews. In Leviticus xix. 27 the lawgiver says, 'Thou shalt not mar the corners of thy beard.' Beards were always worn by the Jews.

Lombards, or Longobards, wore long beards.

Parthians. The kings had bushy beards.

Persians entwined their beards with gold thread.

Romans, according to Pliny, began to shave A.U.C. 454. Scipio Africanus introduced daily shaving. The first fourteen emperors shaved, but Hadrian retained his beard.

Spain. Beards were worn till the accession of Felipe V., who, being beardless, like Louis XIII., set the fashion of clean chins.

Béarnaise (*Le*). Henri IV. of France, so called from 'Le Béarn,' his native province (1553, 1589–1610).

Beatification,—Canonisation.

In imitation of heathen apotheosis. When persons are *beatified*, their picture or image is allowed to be placed in some particular church, where spiritual communion may be held with them in prayer. When persons are *canonised* their image or picture may be placed in all churches, that the whole body of Christians may hold communion with them. Instead of image or picture, the names of the *beati* or canonised saints are inscribed in missals or service books.

Beauclerk, 'Good Scholar.' Henry I. of England (1068, 1100-1135).

Beau Sabreur (*Le*). General Murat, marshal of France, and afterwards king of Naples (1771-1815).

Beauté (*La dame de*). Agnes Sorel (1409-1450) was so called from the *Château de Beauté*, on the banks of the Marne. This château was given to her by Charles VII.

Beauty of Holiness (*The*). Jeremy Taylor was so called from the extraordinary beauty of his person and his great piety. He died 1667, aged 54.

Becket, in his flight from Northampton, Nov. 1164, assumed the garb of a monk, and called himself 'Dereman.' His *murderers* were four knights, viz. Richard Brito, Hugh de Morville, William de Tracy, and Reginald Fitzurse who struck the first blow. He was assassinated in Canterbury Cathedral, 29 Dec., 1170. In 1538, Henry VIII. put forth a proclamation that Becket was killed in a riot of his own provoking; and as he was a rebel and traitor, his name should be erased from all religious books and calendars.

Becket's Day was Tuesday. He was born on Tuesday, baptized on Tuesday, took flight from Northampton on Tuesday, withdrew from the realm to take refuge in France on Tuesday, had his vision of martyrdom at Pontigny on Tuesday, returned to England on Tuesday, was assassinated on Tuesday, and his body was removed from the crypt of the cathedral to the shrine on Tuesday. The new church was consecrated to him by Cardinal Manning on Tuesday (13 April, 1875).

Beckmanites (*The*), 1875. A religious sect, the followers of Mrs. Dora Beckman of Alpena, Michigan, who died 1883. Mrs. Beckman claimed to be a 'second Christ,' and gave out that Christ, in her person incarnate, 'is the bride of the Church.' In 1888 a Beckmanite of Chicago claimed to be the wife of Christ. Their midnight meetings were so disorderly, that an appeal was made to the legislature to forbid them.

Bed of Justice, 'Lit de justice.' The seat occupied by the king of France in a parlement when he enforced an edict not acceptable to the house. As the parlement derived its authority from the crown, when the king was present the power of the parlement was in abeyance. The last 'lit de justice' was held by Louis XVI. at Versailles, in Sept. 1787.

Bede (*The Venerable*). An English monk and historian of the 8th cent. There is a tradition that a monk, writing his epitaph, fell asleep without completing the verse, and when he woke discovered the word 'venerabilis' supplied by some unknown hand. The whole line then ran thus:—

Hac sunt in fossa Bædæ [venerabilis] ossa.

Bedells' (*Esquire*). In the University of Cambridge. Two officers elected by the senate to carry silver maces on all public solemnities. They precede the chancellor or his deputy in processions; receive from him all graces, and deliver them officially to the proctors; they summon members of the senate to the chancellor's court; arrange all public processions, and on all such occasions carry their maces or staffs of office.

Bedlam. A corruption of Bethlehem, formerly a hospital founded by Simon Fitz-Mary in Bishopsgate Street Without, in 1246, as 'a privy of canons, with brethren and sisters.' When the religious houses were suppressed by Henry VIII. the corporation converted it into a lunatic asylum for six lunatics, but in 1641, the funds being insufficient, partially convalescent patients were turned out to beg, and wore a badge. These were the 'Bedlam Beggars,' generally called 'Tom-o'-Bedlams.' In 1675 the old building was taken down and a new one was erected in Moorfields. In 1814 this building was also pulled down, and a new hospital built in St. George's Fields.

Bedouins of Paris (*The*). The Red Republicans and roughs who thronged the streets in every insurrection and revolution.

Bees (*The*). Candidates for 'dangerous work' in the Fenian lodges. Every seven bees is responsible to a 'centre'; each set of seven centres is responsible to the district centre; each set of seven district centres is responsible to the 'head centre,' with whom alone these district centres are allowed to communicate; and, lastly, the head centres communicate with the ' Apex ' (*q.v.*).

A circle, centre, and bee are Fenian officers, not boards. They correspond to captain, lieutenant, and sergeant. Each bee has ten members under his jurisdiction.

Bees' College (*St.*), Cumberland, 1816. Founded by Bishop Law.

Befa'na. A kind of Santa Klaus, who visits children on Twelfth Night to put presents in a stocking hung at their bed. Befana, it is said, was an old woman busy cleaning her house when the Magi passed by, but she said she would look out for them on their return. As they went home another way, she is looking out for them still, but entertains a great fondness for young children. The word is a corruption of ' Epiphania ' (Epiphany).

Begards. *See* ' Beghards.'

Begeaux (*Les*). In the reign of Charles VI. of France. Bands of free-booters, consisting of Burgundians and their butchers, predatory forces from Artois, discharged German, Lombard, and Savoyard mercenaries, with other disorderly persons, who laid waste the country round Paris and ravaged France at will. These brigands were still more demoralised than the Free Companies in the time of the Black Prince.

The two most noted of their leaders were Jean de Poix and De Sobre.

Beggars (*The*), 1566. Those Calvinists of Holland who leagued together to resist the Inquisition in their country. The term arose thus : Three hundred of the chief men of the Netherlands, all Calvinists, were deputed to demand of Margaret of Austria, the governor, the removal of the Inquisition. When Margaret inquired of the Comte de Barleymont, her counsellor, about the deputation he told her they were only a ' set of beggars ' (' Ce ne sont que des gueux '). This reply got wind, and the party assumed the title of ' Beggars ' as their distinctive badge, and from that time dressed as beggars, substituting a fox's tail for a feather, and a wooden platter instead of a brooch. Their place of rendezvous was a house called the Cock, out of whose mouth proceeded the words ' Vivent les gueux par tout le monde ! '

It is said that the count ' spat upon them, called them beggars, and dismissed them contemptuously.' ' Geus ' is still a Dutch by-word for ' Protestant.'

Beggars of the Sea (*The*), or ' Les gueux de mer,' 1566. Those Hollanders who placed themselves under Count Horn, in the Zuyder Zee, to resist the Spanish invaders. *See* below.

Beggars of the Wood (*The*), or ' Les gueux des bois,' 1566. Those Hollanders who lurked in the woods, and resisted on land the Spanish invaders. *See* ' Beggars.'

Begging Friars. The second Council of Lyons reduced them to these four orders : Franciscans or Grey Friars, Dominicans or Black Friars, Augustines (Black Friars), and Carmelites or White Friars.

Begging   Licences. Licences granted to the poor Venetian nobies to beg. These beggars were called ' I Vergognosi ' (*q.v.*).

Beghards (*The*). ' Beghardi,' or ' Begehardi,' 1065 ; ' qui vulgariter Begehardi quoad *viros*, et Beginæ quoad *feminas* nominantur ' (Conradus de Monte, ' de Erroribus Begehardorum '). Also called ' Tertiaries ' (the third order). *See* ' Beguins.'

Secta quædam pestifera illorum qui Beguini vulgariter appellantur, qui se Fratres pauperes de tertio Ordine S. Francisci communiter nominabant, ex quibus plures fuerunt tanquam hæretici condemnati et combusti.—BERNARD GUIDO, *Life of John XXII.*

Beghinæ, or ' Belgian Beguins.' Very numerous in Belgium in the 12th and 13th cent. John XXII. (7 Kal. Martii, anno 3) calls them ' Sorores de Pœnitentia.' It is said that their founder was Begha (Papini Landensis filia, S. Gertrudis Nivellensis sorore) ; but this cannot be relied on.

In Alemannia mulierum continentium, quæ se Beguinas volunt appellari, multitudo surrexit innumerabilis, adeo ut solam Coloniam mille vel plures inhabitarent.—MATTHEW PARIS (year 1251).

Begihards (*The*). ' Begihardi,' preaching friars, 1302.

Fuerunt conversi seu Begihardi, hoc est, fratres non habentes domicilia.—*Annales Colmarienses* (year 1302).

Begin with Vesta. Before the guests of a Greek banquet began to eat, an oblation was always offered to Vesta, the tutelary goddess of hospitality.

Begtashi. A religious order in the Ottoman Empire, instituted in the 14th cent., by Hadji Begtash. The members have secret signs and passwords, like freemasons, to which they bear many resemblances.

Béguins, of Flanders, 1207. Followers of Lambert le Bègue, of Liège. They believed men capable of perfection, and of obtaining so clear a view of God as to become freed from the obedience of any human laws, civil or ecclesiastical. They are now orthodox.

They were called Bizochi in Italy; Béguins in France; and Beghards in Germany.

Begums. Women of high rank in the East Indies. The charge of Warren Hastings, brought by Sheridan in his famous speech of five hours' length, referred to his treatment of the mother and grandmother of Asoff-ul-Dowlah, nabob of Oude. These ladies were very rich and kept a splendid court. Asoff-ul-Dowlah forced large sums of money from them, and the begums appealed for protection to Warren Hastings, governor-general of India (1778). Hastings commanded the nabob to abstain from further extortions, but Hastings resolved to get the begums' money for conducting the war in Madras. His plan was this: He supplied the nabob with a brigade of British soldiers to keep down his own people, and ran up so heavy a claim that the nabob could not pay it. Hastings told him to extort the money from the begums. The nabob trumped up a charge against the begums that they were concerned in stirring up the insurrection at Benares, 115 miles from their residence, and marched against them. The ladies resisted, and were taken prisoners, but had concealed their treasures (3,000,000*l.* sterling). The two chief ministers were seized and put in irons, and the two ladies were placed in rigorous confinement. As the money was not produced, torture was applied, and 500,000*l.* was produced. More severe torture forced from the ladies, another 500,000*l.* The begums and their two ministers were released, and were told that they ' owed this favour to the governor-general.' *See* 'Sheridan's Begums Speech.'

Begum is the fem. of Beg, or Bey.

Behmenists. Disciples of the German mystic Jacob Böhm or Boehm

(1575–1624). He taught that all things consist in Yes and No. The Yes is pure power, life, deity; the No is the reply to the Yes, and indispensable to the revelation of the truth. The present controversy respecting the absolute and relative is an offshoot of Behmenism (1890).

Behring. A strait, sea, bay, and island named after Captain Vitus Bering, a Dane in the service of Peter the Great. He discovered the strait in 1728. Captain Bering died in 1741 in the island which bears his name.

Belgian Lion (*Order of the*), 29 Sep., 1815. Instituted by William I., king of the Netherlands. The decoration is a white enamelled cross surmounted with the royal crown, in a blue 'ring' with the letter W and a circle of laurels; on the reverse, the royal arms with the legend 'Virtus Nobilitas.' The ribbon is blue, edged with orange.

Belgic Confession (*The*), 1559. One of the chief confessions of faith of the continental Calvinistic or Reformed churches. *See* 'Confessions.'

Belgica. That part of ancient Gaul which lay between the Seine and the Rhine.

Believers. So those were called who believed in the divine visitation of Joanna Southcott, prophetess of Exeter (1750–1814).

Believers in Christ (*The*). A sect, whose special doctrine is that their prayers alone can influence the decrees of divine providence.

Bell, Book, and **Candle.** In the ceremony of the greater excommunication by the Catholic Church, since the 8th cent., after reading the sentence a bell is rung, the book closed, and a candle extinguished; and from that moment the person excommunicated is excluded from the communion of saints, divine worship, and the sacraments.

Bell-rock. A reef of old red sandstone, 2,000 feet long, once a fruitful source of shipwreck. The abbot of Arbroath (John Gedy, 14th cent.) placed on the reef a bell fixed on a beam of wood, and the beam being agitated by the sea, kept the bell incessantly ringing. Southey, in a ballad on the subject, says that Sir Ralph the Rover wantonly cut the bell from the buoy, and on his homeward voyage was wrecked on the reef.

Bell Scholarships. For classics and mathematics. Two annually for undergraduates, worth about 5l. a year each, tenable for four years. Founded in the University of Cambridge by the Rev. William Bell, D.D., fellow of Magdalene College, 1810. *See* 'Barnes Scholarship.'

Bell the Cat. *See* p. 42.

Belle Alliance (*La*). The name of a farm some thirteen miles from Brussels; ever memorable for being the position occupied by the centre of the French infantry in the battle of Waterloo (18 June, 1815). Napoleon himself was in the vicinity of this farm, but Wellington was at Mont St. Jean, two miles further north. Between these two spots was La Haye Sainte, where were posted the French tirailleurs.

The Prussians call the battle of Waterloo the 'Battle of la Belle Alliance,' and the French call it the 'Battle of Mont Saint-Jean.'

Belle Bretonne (*La*). The Princess Eleanor, also called the Pearl of Brittany, daughter of Geoffrey, duke of Brittany, grand-daughter of Henry II., and niece of King John. She would have been heir-presumptive if her brother Arthur had succeeded Richard Cœur de Lion, but from the time of Arthur's death she had to endure a lifelong imprisonment at the hands of John.

Belle Cord·ère (*La*). Louise Labé (1526-1566), a French poetess, who married Eddemond Perrin, a wealthy ropemaker.

Belle Corisande (*La*). Diane, comtesse de Guiche et de Grammont (1554-1620).

Belle Gabrielle (*La*). Daughter of Antoine d'Estrées, grandmaster of artillery, and governor of the Île-de-France. She was the mistress of Henri IV. of France, and died from eating an orange (1565-1599). Also called 'La Belle Jardinière.'

Belle Parricide (*La*). Beatrice Cenci, executed 1599.

Belle et vertueuse Huguenotte (*La*). Rachel de Rouvigny, the mother of Rachel, who first married Francis, lord Vaughan, and afterwards Lord William Russell. She received the name of Wriothesley from Thomas Wriothesley, the mother of her first husband (an heiress).

Bellot Straits. In the Arctic ocean; so named from Mons. Joseph René Bellot, who perished in the Arctic regions, while searching for Sir John Franklin (1826-1853).

Bellum Episcopale, 1640. The convocation which met this year made canons, and gave subsidies to carry on the war against the Scots.

Beloved Merchant (*The*). Michael de la Pole was so called by Edward III. This De la Pole in the next reign was created earl of Suffolk.

Belted Will. Lord William Howard, who died in 1640. His belt used to be shown at Naworth. He was second son of Thomas Howard, fourth duke of Norfolk (beheaded in 1572). In right of his wife he succeeded to Naworth Castle, in Cumberland, and was the ancestor of the present earls of Carlisle. In 1603 'Belted Will' was restored in blood, by Act of Parliament; he died and was buried at Greystock.

Beltein, or 'Beltane.' A festival observed in Ireland and in some parts of Scotland. Sometimes fires are kindled on hills; and sometimes the young muster on some green spot, feast on a dish of eggs and milk, and go through various ceremonies. The Irish Beltein is held on 21 June, the Scotch hold theirs on May-day (old style). The Romans held the festival of Cybelê on May-day; and Gregory ch·nged the day in order to change 'Cybelê and all the gods' into 'St. Mary and all the saints.'

Beltane means Baal's fire, and probably the festival is a relic of heathen times. *See* 'Hallow Eve Fires.'

Belvedere (3 syl.) means a corridor or look-out which commands a fine view (Italian 'bel vedere,' beautiful view). The most famous is that of the Vatican, built by Bramante, but the word is associated with a statue called the Apollo Belvedere, *i.e.* the Apollo of the (Vatican) belvedere or corridor, discovered at Cape d'Anzo (Antium), in the 16th cent. It was taken from Rome to France in 1797 by Napoleon, but restored after the battle of Waterloo, in 1815.

Belzunce, bishop of Marseilles. Immortalised by his attention to the sick and dying in the plague of Marseilles in 1720. It was introduced by Captain Chataud, who brought over a Turk infected, and entered Marseilles 25 May. Above 40,000 persons within the walls of the city, and 10,000 in the suburbs, died between 25 May, 1720, and 20 Aug., 1721, when the plague ceased. *See* 'Plagues &c.'

So when Contagion, with mephitic breath.
And withered Famine, urged the work of death,
Marseilles' good bishop, London's generous mayor,
With food and faith, with medicine and with prayer,
Raised the weak head, and stayed the parting sigh,
Or with new life relumed the swimming eye.
       DARWIN, *Loves of the Plants*, ii. 433, &c.
N.B. The mayor was Sir John Lawrence, and the plague referred to was the Great Plague of London. There's many a statue to a lesser man.'

Bench. A seat of justice. There are two benches: the Crown Bench, called the Queen's or King's Bench; and the Common Bench, called the Court of Common Pleas. The former takes cognisance of crown or criminal offences; while the Common Bench or Court of Common Pleas has jurisdiction in civil matters only.

There is a plea side even in the Queen's Bench, but there is no criminal side in the Common Pleas.

Bench Warrant (*A*). A warrant signed by a superior judge or two justices of the peace, during the assizes, to apprehend a defendant against whom a bill of indictment has been found.

Benedictines (*The*), A.D. 528. Founded by St. Benedict, who drew up the 'rule' of his order in 529. They wear loose black gowns with large wide sleeves, and cowl ending in a point as a head covering. They perform their devotions seven times a day. Every monk of the order has two gowns, a table-book, a knife, a needle, and a handkerchief. The Benedictines are great agriculturists, and at one time supplied Europe with corn. The order was introduced into England by St. Augustine, archbishop of Canterbury, about 600.

The rule implied obedience to the superior, avoiding laughter, holding no private property, living sparingly, exercising hospitality, and above all great industry. They were the most gentlemanly and most literary of the monkish orders.

Benedictines (*Father of the English*). St. Dunstan, archbishop of Canterbury (925, 959–988), who enforced the Benedictine rule, and became the first abbot of that order in England.

Benefice (*A*). A church living. Estates distributed in fief by sovereigns of France and Germany among their favourite nobles were termed *beneficia*. Similarly, the temporalities of bishops are held by the bounty of the sovereign, and the temporalities of rectors and vicars are (or at one time *were*) held of the bishops.

Benefices. In England and Wales, 11,728. Of these, 9,669 are in the province of Canterbury, and 2,059 in the province of York. The number of parishes is 14,610. The entire number of incumbents in England and Wales is 11,029.

The number of churches and episcopal chapels is 11,825, but of officiating ministers, 12,332.

The income of the archbishop of Canterbury is 15,000*l.* a year; of the archbishop of York, 10,000*l.*; of the bishop of London, 10,000*l.*; of Durham, 8,000*l.*; of Winchester, 7,000*l.*; of Ely, 5,500*l.*; of St. Asaph and Bangor, 5,200*l.*; of Worcester, 5,000*l.*; of all the other bishops between 5,000*l.* and 4,000*l.*

Benefit of Clergy, or 'Privilegium clericale.' The origin of this privilege is not clear, but it was based on the text, 'Touch not mine anointed, and do my prophets no harm' (Ps. cv. 15). The privilege related to ecclesiastical places and persons. Places consecrated to religious offices were exempted from arrests, and hence became sanctuaries; and the clergy themselves were exempt from criminal processes in the civil courts. By 3 Edw. I. A.D. 1274, we find the privilege had extended to all laymen who could read, and such a criminal could not be put to death, but was branded on the brawn of the left hand. In 1691 the privilege was extended to women. By 4 Hen. VII. c. 13, A.D. 1489, it was enacted that no person should be allowed to avail himself of the benefit more than once. By 7 & 8 Geo. IV. c. 28 s. 6, A.D. 1827, the benefit was abolished.

It never at any time extended to high treason.

Benefit of Inventory (*The*). In Scotch law. A legal privilege whereby an heir secures himself against unlimited liability for his predecessor, by giving up within the year an inventory of his heritage. The heir is then liable only to the extent of this inventory. The law was virtually abolished by 10, 11 Vict. c. 47, ss. 23, 25.

Benefiziati (*The*). See 'Eighty.'

Benevolences. In English history. Were 'gratuit: ' or forced gifts exacted by a king, the loyalty of the giver being measured by the amount of the gift. These exactions, in violation of Magna Charta, had been made by Henry III. and Richard II.—Edward IV., in 1473, after the death of Henry VI., called on his subjects to replenish his purse by their benevolences. They were declared illegal by 1 Rich. III. c. 2 (1484); but were again exacted by Henry VII., Henry VIII., and James I. By the Bill of Rights (1 Will. & Mary st. 2, c. 2, 1689) they were again declared to be illegal. In the Petition of Rights (3 Car. I.) one of the articles is this, that 'No man shall be compelled to yield any gift, loan, benevolence, or tax, without common consent of the Act of Parliament.'

Bengalee' Era (*The*). Began A.D. 593.

Bennet College, Cambridge, 1352. Founded by the benevolence of two guilds, that of Corpus Christi and that of the Blessed Virgin Mary; Henry, duke of Lancaster, also assisted the endowment. It is now almost always called Corpus Christi College or C.C.C.C.

Bentham (*Jeremy*), 1748-1832. It was Bentham who said the principle of government should be 'the greatest happiness to the greatest number.'

It was Priestley who taught Bentham this political axiom.

Benthamist Doctrine (*The*). 'The greatest happiness of the greatest number.'

Beothuks (*The*). Aborigines of Newfoundland, now numbered with the great awk and dodo. They were Red Indians, who daubed their skin, canoes, garments, weapons, and almost everything they possessed with red ochre and grease. The word is said to mean 'men.'

So the Apaches, Dakotahs, and many other Indian tribal names signify 'the people.'—Lady BLAKE, *Nineteenth Century*, Dec. 1888, p. 905. Dakotah signifies 'allied.'

Bephania. See 'Befana.'

Hodierna solemnitas . . . tribus vocabulis decoratur: (1) Epiphania, (2) Theophania, (3) Bethphania . . . a *beth* quod est domus,' et *phanos*

'apparitio,' quia revolutis xxx et uno anno ad nuptias fuit invitatus (Jesus).—BARELETA, *Sermon on the Epiphany.*

Berbers. A general name for the tribes inhabiting the mountainous regions of Barbary and the northern portions of the Great Desert.

In Algeria they are termed 'Kabyles' (2 syl.); in Morocco they are called ' Shellooh' ; in the Atlas range, 'Amazirgh' or ' Timzirght.'

Bere'ans (*The*). A Christian sect founded by the Rev. John Barclay of Perthshire (1734–1798). They derive their name from the Bereans who 're-ceived the Word of Truth with all readiness of mind, and searched the Scriptures daily' (Acts xvii. 1). They are for the most part Calvinistic in doctrine, but believe that the knowledge of God, even of his existence, is a pure matter of revelation; that the Psalms refer wholly to Christ, and not to David at all; and that assurance is the outcome of faith.

They are called Barclayans from their founder.

Berengarians, 11th cent. Followers of Berenger, or Berengarius, of Tours (1000–1088), who emphatically denied the corporal presence in the Eucharist. Leo IX. procured the condemnation of Berenger's doctrine by the Council of Rome in 1049 and the Council of Vercelli in 1050. In 1079 Berenger declared his belief in transubstantiation, and was much honoured by Gregory VII.

Bergen, in Norway (*Treaty of commerce*), 1217. Between England and Norway, noteworthy as being the first treaty made by England with any foreign power. The English-Scotch traders were, however, soon displaced by the merchants of the Hanse towns, who continued to maintain their monopoly till 1560, when it was broken up by Frederick II. of Denmark.

Berkeleyism. Idealism as taught by Bishop George Berkeley. To understand this it must be borne in mind that an abstract idea is the idea of an abstract noun, as goodness, solidity, &c. apart from any object. Berkeley, abandoning this theory, maintained that all that is known is the idea; thus, all that we know of a tree is our *idea* of a tree. He does not say there is no such *thing* as a tree, but only that our *knowledge* of such an object is our idea or conception of a tree.

Dr. Johnson kicked a stone and asked if that stone were only an ideal one. It is a sorry thing that a man like Johnson should have been so foolish. What did Johnson know of a stone beyond his idea of it? The kick may have given him a more accurate idea of its hardness, but still, all he knew of it was limited to his conception or idea of a stone.

Berlin (*Peace of*), 28 June, 1742, which closed the first Silesian war, between Maria Theresa of Austria and Friedrich II., the Great, of Prussia. By this treaty Silesia was given up to Prussia.

Berlin Decree (*The*), 21 Nov., 1806. Issued by Napoleon for the ruin of Great Britain :—

1. The British Isles were declared in a state of blockade.

2. All commerce and correspondence with Great Britain were forbidden.

3. Every Englishman found on the Continent was declared a prisoner of war.

4. All British goods and merchandise were to be considered lawful prize.

5. All vessels coming from England or an English colony were to be refused admission into any continental harbour.

Bermudas (*The*). So named from Bermudez, a Spaniard, who first sighted these islands in 1527. They are also called ' Sommers Isles,' from Sir George Sommers, an Englishman, who was ship-wrecked here in 1609. Sir George's ship-wreck was the immediate reason why these islands were colonised from Vir-ginia, which, at the time (1611), was itself only four years old.

Probably the 'Bermoothes' **of** Shakespeare (' Tempest,' i. 2) is Bermudas.

Bernadotte (*The House of*). The present reigning family in Sweden and Norway. Carl XIII. died childless, and concurred with the states in choosing Bernadotte, one of Napoleon's generals, as his successor. Bernadotte proved true to his adopted country by refusing to enforce Napoleon's ' Continental Sys-tem ' on Sweden.

The Continental System was to 'boycott' Great Britain, and ruin its foreign trade. Bernadotte reigned as Carl XIV., but his name was Jean-Bap-tiste-Jules Bernadotte. He died in 1844, and was succeeded by his son, Oscar I., who died in 1872, and was succeeded by his son, Oscar II.

Bernard (*The Great St.*). The hospice on this famous mountain pass was founded in 962, by Bernard de Menthon, a Savoysien nobleman, for the benefit of pilgrims.

Bernardiani. Franciscans of the Strict Observance, so called from St. Bernardin of Sienne, of the same order (1380–1444).

Bernardines, 1115. Cistercians reformed by St. Bernard of Clairvaux (1091–1153). Called White Monks from the colour of their habit.

Also a congregation of women of the same order, who consecrated themselves to the education of girls. The chief establishments were those of the Port-Royal, and another in the Faubourg St.-Antoine.

Bernese (*The*). Henri IV. of France. Before he was king of France he was called the Bernese or Béarnese king. He was king of Navarre, sovereign prince of Béarn, and first peer and prince of France.

Bernesque Poetry, ' Poesia Ber-nesca.' Burlesque poetry, so called from Francesco Berni of Tuscany (1490–1536).

Bersærker (*The*). The bodyguards of Danish jarls and kings, noted for their dauntless daring. These military fanatics were probably so called from ' ber ' (bare), ' særker ' (garment), because they wore no armour in battle. Ogier the Dane, one of Charlemagne's paladins, was a Bersærker.

Berserkir rage means a frenzy of passion wholly beyond control. The rage of the French in the first Revolution was Berserkir rage.

Bertram (*Dr. Charles Julius*). A literary impostor. He was professor of English at Copenhagen, and professed to have discovered, in 1747, the ' De Situ Britanniæ ' of Richardus Corinensis (Richard of Cirencester), in the library of Copenhagen. In 1758 he published it with two other treatises, calling the whole ' The Three Writers on the Ancient History of the British Nations ' (' Scrip-tōres Tres '). His forgery was exposed by J. E. Mayor, in his preface to ' Richardi de Cirencestria Speculum Historiale.' *See* ' Literary Forgeries,' & .

The 'Scriptores Tres' were Richardus Corinensis (of Cirencester), Gildas Badnīcus (of Bath), and Nennīus Banchorensis (of Bangor).

Beshters. A Jewish sect, a branch of the ancient Chasidim, which take their stand on the Kabbala, but remain (ostensibly at least) within the province of rabbinical Judaism (Baal Shem Tob).

Besieger (*The*). Demetrius Polior-cetês, king of Macedonia.

Bess of Hardwick. Elizabeth, countess of Shrewsbury, to whose charge, in 1572, Mary Queen of Scots was committed. She built a former mansion of Chatsworth, the present Hardwick Hall, and founded, by her three marriages, the wealth and dignity of the Cavendish family. The countess treated Mary with great harshness and rigour, being excessively jealous of the earl, her husband.

Bethlehem Hospital. Granted to London for lunatics in 1547. The word is generally called Bedlam (q.v.), and its lunatic inmates Bedlamites. In 1814 a new building was erected south of the Thames.

Bethlehem Massacre (*A*). A murder or massacre of young children. Of course, the allusion is to the massacre of the Innocents by Herod.

These ruthless scoundrels would not scruple committing a second Bethlehem massacre.—Sir W. SCOTT, *Guy Mannering*, chap. xxxix.

Bethlemites (3 syl.), 1257. A sect of monks, of whom Matthew of Paris writes: ' Concessa est mansio Fratribus B thleemitis in Cantabrigia . . . quorum habitus similis est habitui Prædicatorum. Signatur autem capa eorum in pectore quadam stella rubra 5 radiis crinita, in cujus medio quædam rotunditas est aërei coloris propter stellam, quæ apparuit in Bethleem nato Domino.'

Beza's Codex. A Greek MS. of the four Gospels and Acts of the Apostles, with a corresponding Latin text on every opposite page. It was presented by Theodore Beza to the University of Cambridge in 1581, and is sometimes called the ' Codex Cantabrigiensis.' It is a thick quarto, written on vellum in uncial letters. Supposed to be of the 5th or 6th cent.

Bianchi (*The*). I. 1294. A political faction in Pistoia, similar to the Cenchi of Florence; favourers of the Ghibellines. The Bianchi were opposed to the Neri or faction of the Guelfs. The names Bianchi and Neri belonged to two powerful families. Bianchi = ' white '; Neri,'black.'

Dante, the poet, though of the house of Donati, joined the Bianchi faction, had his house pulled down over his ears, and was actually condemned, 'col falso pretesto d'aver egli commesso baratterie. cioè estorsioni di denaro e vendite di offici pubblici.' Dante says of *baratteria* (*Inferno*, xxi. 41):—

' Ogni uom v'è barattier. fuor che Bonturo ; Del no, per lì denar, vi si fa ita.'

II. or ' White Penitents,' 1399. Fanatics who dressed in white, and wandered about Italy crying out ' Misericordia,' with their faces covered and bent towards the ground. A great crucifix was borne before them. Their constant song was ' Stabat Mater dolorosa.' The march continued for three months at a time, and those who refused to join the procession were accounted heretics.

They appeared in France, but Henri IV. forbade any one, ' under pain of forfeiting all his goods, to receive the new sect in white clothes, pretending to great sanctity ' (Rot. Parl. vol. iii. p. 428). This was because their hiding up their faces gave great opportunity to the commission of all sorts of crimes.

Biandrate (3 syl.). Commander of the Order of St. John of Jerusalem.

Biaronne (*L'ambassade de*). The three tailors of Tooley Street, *see* ' Dict. of Phrase and Fable,' p. 875. Biaronne is a small town in Spain, the chief trade of which is in honey. The embassy referred to consisted of ' trois cents chevaux et une mule,' *i.e.* trois *sans* chevaux et une femme. Oudin, ' Curiosités Françaises.'

Bible. *See.*

Authorised Version	Manx Bible
Biblia Pauperum	Matthew Parker's Bible
Biblia Sacra	Matthew's Bible
Bishops' Bible	Mazarinian Bible
Breeches Bible	Peace-maker's Bible
Bug Bible	Printers' Bible
Codex	Polyglot Bible
Coverdale's Bible	Psalmorum Codex
Cranmer's Bible	Rhemish Bible
Cromwell Bible	Revised Version
Devil's Bible	Sacy's Bible
Dotted Bible	Silver Bible
Douay Bible	Smallest Bible
Genevan Bible	Tyndale's Bible
Golden Bible	Treacle Bible
Great Bible	Vinegar Bible
Idle Bible	Whig Bible
King James's version	Wicked Bible
Leda Bible	Wyclif's Bible

Bible. The name given by Chrysostom to the scriptures in the 4th cent. Divided into chapters in the 13th cent. either by Cardinal Hugo or by Stephen Langton (archbishop of Canterbury). The first English bible divided into verses was published at Geneva in 1560. The oldest MSS. of the New Testament are in uncial characters, and are supposed to belong to the 6th cent. The oldest modern MSS. (in cursive characters) date from the 10th cent. The most valuable MSS. are:

1. The *Codex Alexandrinus* in the British Museum. *See* ' Alexandrian Codex.'

2. The *Codex Vaticanus* in the Vatican at Rome. Considered the oldest.

3. The *Codex Ephræmi*, in the Imperial Library at Paris.

4. The *Codex Cantabrigiensis*, or 'Codex Bezæ,' given by Beza to the University.

Bible Christians, 1815. Followers of Mr. Bryan, a local preacher, who separated from the Methodist connection, and introduced a more popular element in his scheme of church government. These Methodists are great advocates of open-air preaching, and receive the Lord's Supper sitting.

Bible Clerks in Oxford University. Students on the foundation received at reduced fees. These foundations belong to five of the colleges : All Souls, Exeter, Lincoln, St. John's, and Worcester ; and to one Hall, viz. that of St. Mary. *See* 'Clerks,' 'Sizars,' 'Servitors.'

At Oriel College, Oxford, there are five bible clerks not on the foundation. At one time they had to read the bible lessons at chapel.

Bible Moths. A nickname given to revivalists, subsequently called Methodists.

Bible Orchard. A piece of ground bought for 50*l.*, the legacy of Dr. Robert Wilde, who died in Aug. 1678, and desired that the interest accruing therefrom should be expended in the purchase of six bibles not exceeding the price of 7*s.* 6*d.* each. The bibles were to be raffled for on the communion table of the parish church of St. Ives, Hunts, every year by six boys and six girls of the town. The practice of throwing dice on the communion-table has been discontinued, and now the raffle takes place on a table placed on the chancel steps.

Bible Prohibited. Innocent III. in 1199 prohibited the private possession and reading of the bible. Similar prohibitions were repeated at Toulouse in 1229; at Béziers in 1233; at the synod of Oxford in 1383.

The synod of Tarragona, in 1234, denounced as a heretic anyone who, having a translation of the bible, refused to surrender it to be burned within the space of eight days.

The bible is placed among the books forbidden in the 'Index Librorum Prohibitorum.'

Bible Society (*The*), founded in 1780. All bible societies were condemned by the bull of Pius VII., 29 June, 1817 and again by Leo XII. in 1824. The society of Biblical Archæology was instituted in London, in 1871. The object of the Bible Society is the diffusion of the bible without note, comment, expurgation, or addition to the text.

The *American* Bible Society, founded at New York in 1817.

The *British and Foreign* Bible Society, founded in London in 1802, issues annually 1½ million copies of the bible.

The *Edinburgh* Bible Society, 1860. Also a Bible Society at Glasgow.

The *French* Bible Society, founded in London, 1792.

The *Hibernian* Bible Society, 1806.

The *Naval and Military* Bible Society, 1781. The first ship in which bibles were distributed by this society was the ill-fated ' Royal George,' which went down at Spithead, 29 Aug., 1782.

The *Prussian* Bible Society, founded at Berlin in 1814.

The *Russian* Bible Society, founded at St. Petersburg by Dr. Paterson, in 1813.

Biblia Pauperum. The leading events of 'human salvation through Christ' in pictures with text in Latin. This picture-book bible and the 'Mirror of Salvation' were immensely popular in the 13th cent. The pictures were copied by artists and sculptors, and were text-books with the Franciscans, Carthusians, and others. *See* 'Bibles.'

Biblia Sacra Latina (about 1455). A folio bible, printed in double columns, the initial letter of each chapter being 'illuminated' by hand with a pen in colours and gold. Unhappily the book bears no date. The first book printed with moveable metal types by John Gütenberg and Fust. *See* 'Psalmorum Codex.'

Not to be confounded with *Biblia Latina*, which bears the date 1462.

Bicêtre. The grand hospice in the department of the Seine on the road to Fontainebleau. This hospice derives its name from John, bishop of Winchester, who built and fortified a castle on the spot in 1204. There is no w in French, so the letter is supplied by ou, v or b, and *cêtre* (the French form of ' cester '). Hence Winchester becomes Vincêtre or Bincêtre, softened into Bicêtre. In 1632 the castle was converted by Louis XIII. into a hospital for military invalids, and was so used till the Hôtel des Invalides superseded it. It is now used for incurable lunatics, strangers, and a poor-house, a prison for vagrants and for criminals condemned to the galleys, or men condemned to death awaiting execution.

Biela Comet. Discovered in 1826 by William, baron von Biela, astronomer; discovered at Josephstadt, in Bohemia. It separated into two in Dec. 1845.

Bien fortuné (*Le*), *i.e.* the Lucky, so Philippe VI. was called. The reason is this : when Charles died in 1328, his cousin Philippe de Valois was chosen regent, because the royal widow was expected to give birth to a posthumous child. The child proved to be a girl, which by the Salic law was disqualified, and so the regent by ' good luck ' became the king (1293, 1328–1350).

Bigi (*The*). The friends of the Medici in Florence opposed to Savonarola.

Bill. ' The bill, the whole bill, and nothing but the bill,' 1831. The cry arose on the motion of General Gascoyne, who moved, as an amendment, that the number of representatives for England and Wales should not be diminished. The amendment was carried by a majority of eight, the bill was abandoned, and the parliament dissolved.

Bill Chamber. A department of the Court of Session in Scotland in which one of the judges officiates at all times, during session and vacation. The youngest judge is lord ordinary on the bills during session; and the duty is performed during vacation by the other judges, with the exception of the two presidents.

Bill of Adventure (*A*). A writing to signify that the goods shipped by a merchant in his name are the property of another, whose *adventure* it is; but the shipping merchant undertakes to account to the adventurer for what the goods produce.

Bill of Attainder (*A*). A bill in Parliament, introduced for penally enacting the *attaint* and punishment of a person or of persons who have criminally offended against the state and public peace.

Bill of Complaint (*A*), or 'bill in Chancery.' The formal statement in writing by which a plaintiff in the Court of Chancery seeks equitable redress or relief.

Bill of Costs (*A*). An account stating articulately and in detail the charges and disbursements of an attorney in the conduct of his client's business.

Bill of Exceptions (*A*). A statement of objections against the ruling of a judge in a civil cause. This is done by way of appeal against the judgment.

Bill of Indemnity (*The*), 1660. All the injuries and offences against the crown or against individuals, arising out of quarrels between political parties since 1 June, 1637, shall be and are forgiven. Except (1) the 51 individuals actually concerned in the death of the king's father; (2) Vane and Lambert; (3) Lord Monson, Hazlerig, and five others, as far as regards liberty and property; (4) all judges in any high court of justice, together with Hutchinson, Lenthall, St. John, and 16 others (named), who shall not be eligible to hold any office, civil, military, or ecclesiastical. The 19 regicides who have voluntarily surrendered, shall not be put to death without a special Act of Parliament, passed expressly for that purpose.

Bill of Rights (*The*), 2 Nov., 1689. By which William and Mary, being called to the throne, bound themselves to rule on the constitutional principles set forth in the bill. It stated that it is contrary to law for the king to suspend the laws, or interfere with them without consent of parliament; that it is contrary to law for the king to erect commission boards, levy money, or impose fines without consent of parliament; that it is contrary to law for the king to keep a standing army in times of peace without consent of parliament. It provided for freedom of speech in parliament, disallowed excessive bail and fines, enjoined the due impanelling of juries, forbade grants and promises of fines before conviction, and insisted that parliament only shall be empowered to amend the laws and redress grievances.

Bill of Sales (*The*), 1660. Passed by the Convention Parliament (*q.v.*). This was for the restoration of all crown lands. Church lands were not included, so that many church livings remained to the Presbyterians.

This must not be confounded with a 'bill of sale,' or assignment of chattels-personal.

Billets, 1796. Royal missives granted to the Vaudois to repair and enlarge their temples, or even to remove their sites, provided notice was given to the intendant of the province.

Billy Blue. Lord Admiral St. Vincent (John Jervis), 1734–1823. Admiral of the Blue, 1795. Called Lord St. Vincent from his victory over the combined French and Spanish fleets off Cape St. Vincent in 1795.

Bi-metallism. The employment of two metals, like gold and silver, of fixed legal relative value. Till 1873 this had been the custom for nearly 200 years. One ounce of gold was then equal to 15½ ounces of silver. Up to 1873 silver was the standard of Germany, as it is still of India, China, and Japan; but in 1873 gold was made the sole standard of Germany, and silver became a mere article of commerce and circulating counter, which varied in value according to circumstances. The relative value might be one ounce of gold worth twenty ounces of silver, or any other difference; and those countries which pay in silver pay more as the relative value of silver declines. Bi-metallists want to restore the fixed relative value of these metals.

Birdcage Walk (St. James's Park, London). Here Charles II. made an aviary.

Birmese War. *See* 'Burmese.'

Birmingham Political Union (*The*), 1 Feb., 1830. Members paid from 4s. to 2 guineas a year. There were several affiliated unions for the dissemination of Radical principles, such as free trade, manhood suffrage, shorter parliaments, the ballot, and so on.

Birminghamers, 1680. Opponents of the Court, or adherents of the Exclusion Bill—that is, a bill to exclude James from succeeding Charles II. The Court party were called Anti-Birminghamers. The Birmingham manufacturers had become notorious as coiners of base money, so the Tories and 'Catholics' nicknamed the Exclusionists 'Birminghamers,' *i.e.* men who preferred a base or usurping king to one of the real stamp of right divine.

The Whigs were Birminghamers, Petitionists, and Exclusionists (*see* these words).
The Tories were Anti-Birminghamers, Abhorrers, and Tantivies (*see* these words).

Biron's Conspiracy, 1602. The conspiracy of Charles de Gontaut, duc de Biron, to dethrone Henri IV. This was a conspiracy with Spain and Savoy. Biron was to receive in marriage the daughter of the Duke of Savoy and the full sovereignty of Burgundy. Biron was betrayed and beheaded.

Birthday. The following, among many others, died on the anniversary of their birthday.

ALEXANDER the Great, 24 July (B.C. 356-324).
ANTIPATER, died B.C. 44.
BROWNE (*Sir Thomas*), 19 Nov. (1605-1682); his 77th birthday.
CARACALLA, 8 April (188-217).
DIGBY (*Sir Kenelm*), 11 June (1603-1665).
ELIZABETH, wife of Henry VII., 11 Feb. (1466-1503).
GARSIAS, grandfather of Petrarch, at the age of 104.
GREGORY the Great, 12 March (540-604).
HILARUS (*M. Ofilius*), the comedian.
HOLLAND (*Sir Henry*), born 1788.
PLATO, 21 May (B.C. 430-347).
RAPHAEL, 6 April (1483-1520).
SANDFORD (*John*), died 1850.
SHAKESPEARE, 23 April (1564-1616).
WILLIAMS (*John*), archbishop of York, 25 March (1582-1650). *See* Pliny, *Nat. Hist.* vii. 53.

Bishop in partibus, 1623. A vicar apostolic, vested with episcopal authority by the pope over a church in want of a bishop, but which, for some reason, cannot have one of its own. In such a case a bishop is consecrated to some see, *in partibus infidēlium*, which had formerly a bishop, but has now no church. These bishops in partibus were created only during the pope's pleasure, and might be removed at any hour. They are now called titular bishops.

Bishop of the English (*The*). Augustine (597-604). Sent over by Gregory the Great. He is called 'The Apostle of the English.'

Bishops (*Commitment of Twelve*), 1641. Williams, archbishop of York, prevailed on eleven other prelates to join him in a declaration stating that they could no longer, without danger to their lives, attend their duty in parliament, and that therefore they protested against the validity of any votes or resolutions during their absence. The Lower House impeached the twelve prelates of high treason for this declaration, and ten were committed to the Tower. The bishop of Lichfield and the bishop of Durham, on account of their great age and infirmity, were given in charge to the usher of the Black Rod.

Bishops' Bible (*The*), 1568–1572. The corrected edition of the G eat Bible (*q.v.*) in the reign of Elizabeth. Archbishop Parker engaged the bishops and other learned men to take each a portion for revision ; the different portions were printed with short annotations, and the whole called 'Parker's Bible' or the 'Bishops' Bible.' It was based on Tyndale's translation. *See* 'Bibles.'

Bishops' Book (*The*) 1537. Or 'The godly and pious Institution of a Christian Man, &c.,' compiled by the bishops and dedicated to the king. Quoted in brief as the 'Institution.' *See* 'King's Book.' It was founded on the 'Ten Articles' (*q.v.*), and explained such matters as the Apostles' Creed, the Ten Commandments, the Lord's Prayer, Ave Maria, the seven sacraments, infant baptism, baptismal regeneration, confession, absolution, the apostolic succession, and the real presence. Two articles, published in 1536, were appended, one on Justification and the other on Purgatory.

Bishop's Eye (*The*). So the archdeacon is called in canon law.

Bishops' War (*The*) 1640. The contest of the Scotch against the appointment of bishops in their country, which Charles I. tried to force upon them. It terminated in the conference held at Repton, October 1640.

Charles I. was urged to stand to his ground by Laud and the Earl of Strafford. The Scotch had petitioned for triennial parliaments and freedom of election and debate. Strafford said the rascals ought to be 'whipped' into their senses. When the parliament refused to vote supplies without redress of grievances, Strafford told the king he was entitled to help himself, and he advanced to the North with an army. The Scots crossed the Tyne, occupied Newcastle, and despatched proposals of peace. Charles, to evade calling a parliament, summoned at York a 'Great Council of Peers,' but the council was obstinate, and the king after all was forced to call a parliament. Laud called these Scots 'the rascal riotous multitude.'

Bissextile Year. Leap year was so called, because Julius Cæsar ordained that the 23rd Feb. should be counted twice on leap years ; and by the Roman calendar the 23rd Feb. was the sextile or vi. Kal. Martii, *i.e.* the sixth day before the Kalends, or 1st of March.

Bizochii, or Fratricelli, 1189. A sect of Minorites condemned by Boniface VIII. (1294–1303), by John XXII., and by Martin V. in 1418.

Nonnulli viri pestiferi, qui vulgariter Fratricelli, seu Fratres de paupere vita, aut Bizochi, sive Bichini, vel aliis fucatis nominibus nuncupantur.—JOHN XXII. (year 6), *Epist. Communium.*

Black. The colour consecrated to the Abbassides (3 syl.). Their turbans and garments were black ; and two black standards (called *Night* and *Shadow*) were borne aloft on pike-staves nine cubits long in the van of their army. The 'Black and White Factions' were the factions of Abu Moslem the Abasside, and Merwan II. the Ommiade calif.

The Fatimites (3 syl.) colour was *green*; the Ommiades (3 syl.) *white*; the Abbasides, *black.*

Black and White Cockade (*The*). The allied American and French badge in 1780.

Washington directed all his continental troops to adopt the black and white cockade, as a sign of amity (between America and France).—HOWITT, *Hist. of Engl.* (Geo. III. p. 264).

Black and White Faces. *See* under ' White, &c.'

Black and White Factions (*The*). I. Of Florence, called the Neri and Bianchi. Rival factions towards the close of the 13th cent., and for the first five years of the 14th. The Blacks were the noblesse, and the Whites the rich merchants. The Whites joined the Ghibellines. Dante was a White, and was banished in 1302.

II. That of the *Abbassides and Ommiades.* The colour of the Abbassides (3 syl.) was black, and of the Ommiades (3 syl.) was white.

The colour of the Fatimites (3 syl.) was green.

• Black Act (*The*), 1722 (9 George I. c. 22). Is so called because it was directed against the Waltham deer-stealers, who blackened their faces for disguise, and under the name of 'Blacks' appeared in Epping Forest. This act was repealed in 1827.

It made it felony to appear with the face blackened or otherwise disguised in any park, warren, &c., for the purpose of hunting or stealing deer, &c.

Black Acts. Acts of the Scottish parliament from the reign of the first James to 1587 (James VI.) were so called because they were printed in black letter.

Black Agnes. Wife of the Earl of Dunbar, famous for her defence of

Dunbar Castle, when in 1337 it was besieged by Lord Salisbury. See 'Sow.'

Came I early, came I late,
I found Black Agnes at the gate.
                              Sir W. Scott.

Black Arrow (*The Band of the*). A fraternity of freebooters at the time of the war of the Two Roses. The arrows used by the band left a black mark on those wounded by them.

Black Assize (*The*). The assize held at Oxford, 6 July, 1577. So called from the fatal pestilence which broke out at the time. It is said that it broke out in the court-house just as the judge was passing sentence on Richard Jencks, a bookbinder, who was condemned to lose his ears for sedition; and it was popularly called a divine judgment for the cruelty or injustice of the sentence.

Another 'Black Assize' was that held at Cambridge in the Lent term of 1521, when a similar putrid fever broke out.

Black Band (*The*). I. A body of German foot-soldiers employed by Louis XII. in the Italian wars. So called because they carried black ensigns after the death of their favourite commander.

II. A body of Italian troops in 1526 was also called the Black Band because they also carried black ensigns on the death of their leader, Giovanni de' Medici.

III. A French regiment of Piedmont, who had served for a long while in Italy for the same reason, was called the Black Band in 1596, on the death of Comte de Brissac. See 'Black Brunswickers' and 'Bande Noire.'

IV. *Saxon* mercenaries in the employ of Denmark. The Black Band employed by John I., king of Denmark, to enforce on Sweden the 'Union of Calmar,' in 1497, had served under the kaiser Maximilian in the wars of Flanders.

Black Bartholomew's Day. I. *French* history, 24 Aug., 1572. Noted for the great Huguenot slaughter in France.

II. *English* history, 24 Aug., 1662. When, by the Act of Uniformity, some 2,000 ministers in England and Wales resigned their benefices, or were ejected from them for conscience sake.

Who so active as he to execute the fatal edict of Black St. Bartholomew's day, when so many hundreds of gospel-preachers were expelled from house and home, from hearth and altar, from church and parish.—Sir W. Scott, *Peveril of the Peak*, chap xiii.

Black Belt (*The*). A part of Alabama where the negro population has always been very dense.

Black Book (*The*), 1536. A book containing the reports of two royal commissioners, named Legh and Leyton; appointed by Thomas Cromwell, chief minister of Henry VIII., to visit the religious houses of England. About a third of them are charged in these reports with drunkenness, simony, and crimes perfectly revolting. In consequence of the charges all houses were suppressed whose income fell below 200l. a year, and their revenues were confiscated to the crown. The great abbeys were still suffered to remain.

Called 'Black Books' because they *blackened* the practices of the religious houses in England when Henry VIII. designed their dissolution.

Black Book of the Exchequer (*The*). 'Liber Niger Scaccarii,' 1175 (Henry II.). Said to have been the work of Gervase of Tilbury; contains an account of the exchequer and its officers. It describes the ranks and privileges of those officers, their wages, perquisites, and jurisdiction; with the revenues of the crown in money, grain, and cattle. Called black from their black leather covers. See 'White, Red, Yellow Books.'

There are two Black Books of the Exchequer preserved in the Public Record Office. The smaller one was bound by William Caxton the printer, and had at one time two stamps for the decoration of the leather cover. These stamps, being Caxton's, prove the book to have been bound by the great printer. —James Wheale, *Book-binders and Book-binding* (1880).

Black Breeches. See 'Procession of the Black Breeches.'

Black Broth (μέλας ζωμός). The chief food of the Spartans, who dined in public.

A citizen of Sybaris said: 'He no longer wondered why the Lacedæmonians were the most valiant soldiers of the world; seeing that any man of sound mind would rather die a thousand times than devour such nastiness.' And Glaucos, the Locrensian, declared that it is unfit food for the meanest of the free-born.

Black Brunswickers (*The*), 1806 The 700 hussars under the command of Frederick William, duke of Brunswick, son of Charles William Frederick, duke of Brunswick, who made the foolish manifesto against the French republic, was driven by the republican army from Valmy, and mortally wounded at Auerstadt. His son Frederick William took part in the campaign of Waterloo, and was slain at Quatre-Bras (1815). The Duke Frederick William, at the death of his father, clothed his hussars in black, with lace disposed like the ribs of a skeleton. Their caps and helmets, moreover, bore in front the device of a skull and cross-bones, and instead of feather, long flowing black horse-hair was adopted. It was Charles, son of Frederick William, who two days after the battle of Quatre-Bras joined in the battle of Waterloo.

Black Bull's Head (*The*). The sign of death. It is repeatedly mentioned in Highland tradition, and seems to have been a Celtic custom. When William, son of the fifth earl of Douglas, and his younger brother David, were inveigled, in 1440, to Edinburgh Castle, as they sat at meat, the black bull's head was placed before them. The two boys were forthwith dragged from table and cruelly beheaded.

Black Cabinet (*The*). 'Le Cabinet Noir.' The secret apartment where (in continental countries) letters of political importance, or such as are supposed to be so, are opened by government agents. Some are copied, and the copy sent to the address given ; others are impounded and find their way to the head of the police.

Black Califs (*The*). The Abbassides (3 syl.), whose uniform and standards were black.

As subjects of the *White* party, *i.e.* the Ommiades (3 syl.), they might lawfully invade the dominions of the Black Califs.—GIBBON, chap. lii.
The standard of the Fatimites (3 syl.) is green.

Black Camisards (*The*), 1703. Huguenots. So called in contrast to the White Camisards (*q.v.*), who were Catholic auxiliaries in Montrevel's army.

Camisard is used in two senses; sometimes the Protestant insurgents of the Cevennes are so called.
∴ *Camisard* should not be confounded with *Camisade* (an attack by night).

Black Canons (*The*). The Canons Regular of St. Augustine were so called from their black cloaks. The 'Black Friars' were Dominicans. *See* 'White Canons.'

Black Captain (*The*). Lieutenant-Colonel Davidoff, an officer in the Russian army in the time of the French invasion,

was called by the invaders 'Le Capitaine Noir,' from the terror of his name, like our 'Black Prince.'

Black Charlie. Sir Charles Napier (1786–1860).

Black Clergy (*The*). Monks in Russia are so called in contradistinction to the *white* clergy, or parish priests.

Black Code (*The*), of Louis XIV., 1685. Colbert's code relating to the African slave-trade.

Black Colin Campbell. General in the army of George III.

Introduced by Sir W. Scott in 'Redgauntlet.'

Black Country (*The*). South Staffordshire, famous for its hardware manufactures and its mines of coal and iron. The volumes of smoke thrown off all day and night cover everything with smut and destroy vegetation, so that a patch of grass or green tree can scarcely be seen. Gardens are well nigh unknown, and cleanliness is almost impossible. In this vast district, Wolverhampton (to the south-east) produces locks, tin, and japan wares; Walsall (to the north-west) saddlers' ironmongery, brass, and iron wares, &c.; West Bromwich (to the south), coal and iron; Bilston, Sedgley, Wednesbury, Dudley (chains and nails), Darlaston, &c., are all busy towns in the same district.

Black Crosses, Cruces Nigræ or Croix noires. The Greater Litany on St. Mark's Day, when the altars, crosses, and relics are covered as in mourning.

Thys letanye is sayd [called] the blacke crosse; for thenne in sygne of pestylence, wepyng, and of penaunce, they clad them [the croses, &c.] wyth blacke clothes.—*The Golden Legende* (WYNKYN DE WORDE, 1512).

Black Days. Varro (Book v.) says : 'Dies postridie Kalendas, Nonas, Eidus, appellati *atri*, quod per eos dies novi inciperent.'

Black Death (*The*), 1348–1382. The oriental plague which desolated Asia and Europe in the 14th cent. So called from the black spots which appeared at the time of death on the skin, from putrid decomposition. It broke out in China in 1333, and carried off 13,000,000 of the inhabitants, and in the rest of Asia about 24,000,000. In 1349 it reached Norway and Sweden ; in 1351 it desolated Russia. It reappeared in 1360, 1373,

1382; carrying off 30,000,000 Euro-peans. Of the 4,000,000 which formed the population of England, more than half were swept away. Labour was at a high premium, the price of food rose greatly, and a strike between capital and labour followed.

Dr. Hecker puts down the mortality of London from the Black Death at 100,000; of Norwich about 52,000 (the entire population of London at the time being 120,000, and of Norwich 60,000). The deaths at Lübeck were 90,000; at Basle 14,000; at Erfurt 20,000; **and 200 villages were quite de-populated.**

Black Dick. Richard, earl Howe (1725–1799). The English admiral sent to operate against D'Estaing, in com-mand of the French forces on the coast of America, during the war of inde-pendence.

Black Dog of Arden (*The*). So Piers Gaveston nicknamed Guy, earl of Warwick, and the earl vowed he would show the Gascon his teeth. He combined with other great barons and murdered the royal favourite.

Black Douglas (*The*), *i.e.* the for-midable or terrible Douglas (died 1390).

It is said that the name of this indefatigable chief had become so formidable that women used in the northern counties to still their froward children by threatening them with the Black Douglas.—Sir W. SCOTT, *Hist of Scotland*, xl.

Black Eagle (*Knights of the*), 17 Jan., 1701. A Prussian order instituted by Frederick, elector of Brandenburg, when he was crowned king of Prussia. Ribbon, orange; a Maltese cross, and the legend 'Cuique suum.' There are thirty knights besides those of the royal family. They are sworn to be just and chaste, and to protect widows and orphans.

Black Flag (*The*). I. Betokens a *pirate*; a white flag, *peace*; a red flag, *defiance*; a yellow flag that the vessel is in quarantine. The pirate's black flag is called the 'Jolly Rover.'

A black flag is hoisted on club-houses, &c. to indicate vexation or annoyance at some political measure thought to be destructive or injurious to their well-being; thus was it hoisted over the club-house of Liberty in Brussels, in Sept. 1884. It is set up at the corner of in-fected streets down which the public are forbidden to go. Thus was it set up in Naples in Sept. 1884, when the cholera prevailed in that city. It was hoisted on

5

the Hôtel de Ville of Paris in 1793, as a symbol of distress and a call to arms, when the city was threatened with invasion. It was carried in the insurrection of Lyons, Nov. 1831, when the silk-weavers rose *en masse*.

II. The 'national party' in Ireland, during the visit of the Prince of Wales in 1885, displayed black flags. Black was the colour of the *royal* banners of Ireland, and Cassanæus states that 'the royal arms of Ireland was a king enthroned in majesty in a field sable.' *See* 'Antho-logia Hibernica,' i. 172.

III. A black flag was displayed by Tamerlane, when a besieged city refused to surrender, meaning that he gave over the city to utter destruction and spolia-tion.

Black Flags (*The*). Mussulman soldiers, the black banner being that of the prophet of Mecca and of the faith of Islam. In the Annamite war, 1883, between the Annamese and the French, the Black Flags were political refugees from border provinces, and were by far the bravest of the Chinese (Annamite) army. Their headquarters was Laokai, on the left bank of the river, in the angle formed by the confluence of Nan-si-ho with Songkoi. *See* 'Yellow Flags,' and 'Flag of the Prophet.'

Black is the colour of the Abbasides (3 syl.), green of the Fatimites (3 syl.), and white of the Ommiades (3 syl.). Hence the banner of the kalif of Bagdad was a crescent on a black flag; that of the sultan of Damascus a crescent on a green flag.—GIBBON, ch. lii.

Black Flagellants (*The*). So called from their black masks. *See* 'Flagel-lants' and 'Blancs Battus.'

Black Friars (*The*). The Domini-cans or Preaching Friars were so called in England from the colour of their dress. They were founded in 1216, and first appeared in England in 1221.

Called 'Jacobins' in France from their establish-ment in the Rue de Jacques, Paris. The 'Black Canons' were the Augustines or Canons Regular of St. Augustine. There was also an order of Black Nuns.

Black Friday, 6 Dec., 1745. The day on which the news arrived in London that the army of Charles Edward (the Young Pretender) had reached Derby (reign of George II.).

II. 11 May, 1866. It was announced the day before that the great discounting house of Overend, Gurney, & Co. had

H

suspended payment. Only twelve months before the bank had been converted into a limited liability company, and half a million had been given for the goodwill. On the day of suspension the Bank of England raised its rate of discount to 9%. The English Joint-Stock Bank and its thirty branches closed their doors. The next announcement was that Messrs. Peto and Betts, the great contractors, had failed, their liabilities being 4,000,000*l.* Then the Imperial Mercantile Credit Association, with a capital of 5,000,000*l.*, and the Consolidated Discount Company, with a capital of 1,000,000*l.*, gave way. The panic was terrible, but it rapidly subsided, and the mischief was very much less than was apprehended.

Black George, of Servia. Kara George Petrovitsch, a Servian peasant who, in 1804, revolted against the Porte. Having defeated several armies sent against him, in 1807 he took Belgrade, and formed a military government in Servia. In 1811, Turkey acknowledged him 'hospodar of Servia,' but, in 1814, the Turks recovered the country, Black George fled to Austria, was imprisoned, and died.

Black-haired Race (*The*). The Chinese.

He (Commissioner Keshen) humbly hopes that the Holy One will look down with pity and compassion on the black-haired race . . . so that the people of the land may not be turned to ashes.—*Keshen's Dispatches,* 1841, *to the Emperor of China.*

Black Hand (*The Band of the*). A socialist society discovered in Andalusia in 1883, and consisting of about 50,000 members of all ranks. The confederacy was divided into 190 district federations and 800 local sections.

Black Hole of Calcutta (*The*), 1756. A cell, 18 feet square, in which the Nabob Suraja Dowlah confined 146 Englishmen captured by him at Calcutta. After a night of agony from heat, thirst, and want of air, only 23 survived till morning, and these 'were the ghastliest forms that ever the eye of man had seen.'

The governor Drake had imprisoned several native merchants unjustly. When the subahdar marched against the factory with 400 or 500 men, Drake fled and Howell took the command of the English. The Indians, with muskets presented, drove Howell and his 145 Englishmen into the 'black-hole prison, situated at the end of the barracks.' Mr. Howell was one of the 23 who escaped, and it is from his pen that we obtain a narrative of this disastrous event.

Black Hood House (*The*). The Non-Regent or Lower House in the University of Cambridge. So-called because its members wore black hoods. This house consisted of masters of arts of more than five years' standing and doctors of more than two. Graduates on the boards of shorter standing formed the Regents' or Upper House. *See* 'White Hood House.' Abolished in 1858. *See* 'Senate.'

Regents mean tutors, professors, and lecturers. Non-regents, those who had served their time and were exempt from these duties. Such masters of arts stripped off the white lining of their hoods.

Black Horse (*The*), or 'The Blacks.' The 7th Dragoon Guards; facetiously called, in the reign of George II., 'The Virgin Mary's Guard.' They are called the 'Blacks' from their black facings, and 'horse' because they are a cavalry regiment.

Black Indulgence. A licence to preach without interruption, granted by Charles II. to those Presbyterian ministers who complied with certain specified regulations made by parliament. This indulgence made a great schism, and those who availed themselves of it were hated with *odium theologicum.*

Of all the baits with which the devil has fished for souls in these days of blood and darkness, that Black Indulgence has been the most destructive.—Sir W. SCOTT, *Old Mortality,* chap. v.

'Presbyterian!' answered Gilfillan contemptuously; 'a wretched Erastian, or rather an obscure prelatist—a favourer of the Black Indulgence; one of the dumb dogs that canna bite.' —Sir W. SCOTT, *Waverley,* chap. xxxvi.

Black Jagers (*The*). *See* 'Black Brunswickers.'

Black John. Scottish history. John Home, the man who revealed the plot of Sir James Edmonstone to take James VI. prisoner and keep him so till he recalled the lords banished or disgraced for the part taken by them in the raid of Ruthven (*q.v.*), 1584.

Black Knight of Lorn (*The*). Sir James Stewart, who married Joanna, the widow of James I. of Scotland.

Black Legion (*The*), 1806. That of the Duke of Brunswick. After the death of his father at Jena, Frederick William put all his soldiers into mourning. Their military caps had in front for device, a skull and cross-bones, and for gay feathers were substituted flowing black horse-hair. This was because Napoleon refused to allow the dying duke to be removed to Brunswick; so the son commanded that his legion should wear mourning till the death of Napoleon. However, soon after the battle of Waterloo, the Brunswickers resumed their proper costume.

Black Legions (*The*). So the Hungarian troops were called in the 15th cent. *See* 'Black Troop.'

We generally read of the Black Legion, in the singular number, and the Black Hussars; but Godkin, in his 'History of Hungary,' says, 'the Hussites were everywhere compelled to give way before the terrible attacks of the Black Legions, as the Hungarian troops were called' (p. 127).

Black List. I. 1832. A list of all those members of the House of Commons who voted in favour of reform till the bill was thrown out by the Lords; but it was known that the (William IV.) hated the bill and wanted to shelve it. Several members shuffled and held themselves at bay. These 72 members constituted the black list, to be blackballed at the next election.

II. A printed list of bankruptcies, liquidations by arrangement, registers of protested bills, decrees of absence, offers of composition, and other matters pertaining to the credit of firms and individuals, circulated from London to subscribers for the information and guidance of men of business.

Black Lord Clifford. John, ninth Lord Clifford, son of Thomas, Lord Clifford. Also called 'the Butcher' (died 1461).

Black Lord Herbert. Edward, Lord Herbert of Cherbury (1581-1648).

Black Mail. A payment made by the Highlanders in the first half of the 18th cent. as a compromise to bandits, who promised that neither the property nor person of anyone who paid the impost should suffer injury. In 1601 (by 43 Eliz. c. 13) the levy of black mail was made felony.

Mail (Ango-Saxon *mal*, rent-tax), used in Scotland to designate every sort of periodical payment, and is still the term employed technically for rent paid by a tenant to his landlord.

Black Militia (*The*). The officials of the Jesuits.

Black Monday. I. Easter Monday, 14 April, 1360. So called because it

was so dark with mist and hail, so cold and windy, that many of the men and horses in the army of Edward III. lying before Paris perished.

See Shakespeare, ' Merchant of Venice,' ii. 5.

II. 27 Feb., 1865. So called in Victoria (Australia),from a terrible sirocco from the N.N.W. which produced frightful havoc between Sandhurst and Castlemaine.

Black Money. Base money introduced from foreign countries. By the statute of York (12 Edw. II. A.D. 1318), it was ordered that all manner of black money (*noir monnoie*) lately current in the realm shall be excluded. In 1339, a certain black money called *turneys* was made in Ireland, and circulated to the injury of the king's sterling money; and in 1341 the mayor and bailiffs of Dover made proclamation for the better observance of the statute of York respecting black money.

Camden speaks of the prohibition of black money by Edward III. (9 Edw. III. st. 2).

Black Parliament (*The*). I. In *English* history, 1529. The parliament held by Henry VIII. at his palace in Bridewell, the year of the king's divorce from Katharine. *See* 'Parliament.'

II. In *Scotch* history, 1320. The parliament which condemned to death Sir David de Brechin, Sir William Malherbe, Sir John Logie, and Richard Brown, and imprisoned for life the Countess of Strathearn and Sir William de Soulis, for a conspiracy against Robert Bruce. The plan was to put Bruce to death and make Sir William de Soulis king. The Countess of Strathearn betrayed the conspiracy. *See* 'Parliament.'

Black Prince (*The*). I. 1355. Edward, prince of Wales, son of Edward III., was first so called by the French just before the battle of Poitiers. He had won the marvellous battle of Cressy, had invaded Gascony, had carried terror through the length and breadth of France, and was called the very devil or prince of darkness. Froissart says 'he was called black by the terror of his arms'; and Strutt, in his 'Antiquities,' gives the same reason.

See this word in the ' Dictionary of Phrase and Fable,' p. 90. All the armour known of the prince was *gilt* armour.

Black Prince (*The*). I. Nicknamed by the French 'Pie-de-Plomb' (Waurin's 'Recueil,' &c. vol. i. p. 236, Rolls Series), not a leaden *pica* or *magpie*, but a draught of lead, referring to cannons first used at the battle of Cressy, by which draughts of lead were poured into the French. *Croqueter la pie* in archaic French means to drink hugely. The verb *pier* means to drink—as

Je vous prie que j'aye à pyer (to drink)
Ung coup de quelque bon vin vieulx.
　　　　　Le Testament de Pathelin, p. 120.
S'il vouloit croqueter la pie,
J'en euse volontiers coppe,
Pour rendre la soif destouree.
　　　　　Actes des Apostres (1541).

II. Fulc the Black, or 'Fulc Nerra,' the greatest of the Angevins. He burnt his wife at the stake ; waged the bitterest war against his son ; despatched twelve assassins to the murder of the minister of the French king ; and shocked even the rude barbarians of the times with his treason, rapine, and blood. It was the blackness of his deeds which procured him the sobriquet of 'Nerra'(the Black).

Black Regiment (*The*), 1863. A regiment of negroes in the Federal army, under the command of General Banks ; their prowess and courage in the storming of Port Hudson are celebrated by G. H. Boker, the war poet.

Black Rent, 1409. The tribute paid to Irish chieftains by the residents living in border counties of the Pale for peace and protection. It began in the reign of Henry IV.

Rents paid in cattle (neat-gild), or in any other way except in lawful cash are termed *redditus nigri*. Rents paid in lawful silver are called *redditus albi* (white rents).

Black Republicans. The North American republicans were so called by the pro-slavery party. These republicans resisted the introduction of negro slavery into territory where it was not already recognised. They morally hoisted the black flag of no surrender against slavery.

Black River (*The*). The river Til or Tula, so called from the deep black shade of the forests thrown on the water.

Black Rod, or, in full, 'Gentleman Usher of the Black Rod.' An officer of the crown in the House of Lords, whose duty it is to attend on the peers during the session of parliament To the care

of this officer all peers impeached for any crime or for contempt are first committed. His staff of office is a *black rod* with a golden lion in repose on the top. *See* 'Yeoman Usher.'

Black Rood of Scotland (*The*). A piece of the 'true cross' set in an ebony figure of Christ, inclosed in a cross of 'gold' elaborately wrought, about a span long. This relic was taken by Margaret, the Anglo-Saxon princess, to Scotland, when in 1070 she married King Malcolm Ceanmohr. In 1291 it was delivered to Edward I., when it was found that the casket cross was only silver gilt. Of the 'true cross' nothing is known. In 1328 it was restored to Scotland. In 1346 King David II. invaded England and took with him the black rood as an amulet ; but he was captured by Sir Ralph de Neville (lord of Raby), and the relic became part of his prize. It was then deposited in the shrine of St. Cuthbert, in Durham Cathedral, where it remained till the Reformation, when all trace of it disappeared.

Black Saturday. I. 10 Sept., 1547. When Lord Protector Somerset defeated the Scotch in the battle of Pinkie, near Musselburgh, with terrible slaughter.

II. 4 Aug., 1621, is so called in Scotland from a violent storm which occurred at the very time the parliament was sitting to enforce episcopacy on the people.

Black Sheep (*The*), 1407–1468. Certain Turkomans who, under the leadership of Kara Yussuff, made themselves masters of Azerbijan', Irak, Fars, and Kerman, but were subsequently driven out by the Turkomans of the White Sheep. Called the 'Black Sheep' from the effigy displayed on their standard.

At the decay of Timur's dynasty his empire fell into three separate parts. Hussein Mirza, a descendant of Timur, governed Khorasan and held his court at Herat ; the Turkomans of the White Sheep held Armenia, Mesopotamia, and part of Asia Minor ; the Black Sheep held the third part.

Black Soldiers (*The*), or Sidier Dhu. The independent companies raised to keep peace and law in the Highlands. So called from their dark tartans ; English soldiers are Sidier Roy, or red soldiers. *See* 'Waverley,' chap. xviii.

Black Somerset (*The*). Somerset was a negro slave brought to England and turned adrift because of ill-health. Mr. Granville Sharpe took pity on him, and by care restored him to perfect health, whereupon his master claimed him again. Mr. Sharpe resisted the claim, and it was brought into the law-courts, when it was decided that slavery could not exist in Great Britain, 22 June, 1772.

Black Spring (*The*). That of 1771 is so called in Scotland. It was followed by a famine.

Black Stone (*The*). Of the Kaaba, in Mecca. Said to have 'dropped from paradise,' and set in the silver door. A pilgrim walks round the Kaaba or mosque seven times, and each time kisses the stone or lays his hand on it. We are told that the stone was originally white, but has been turned black by the sins of man.

Black Stone Examination (*The*). In Glasgow University is the commencement of the ceremony of graduation; the conclusion being the 'act of Laureation' in the college hall, or one of the city churches.

Black Strangers, or 'Black Gentiles.' Danes were so called by the ancient Irish. They first made their appearance in Ireland in the 8th cent. From Dublin southwards was the territory of the Black Strangers. Dublin and northwards was the territory of the White Strangers.

The country south of Dublin was called Dubh-Gal, or territory of the Black Strangers. Called by the Four Masters Dubh-gentie (Black Gentiles).

Black Sunday, 20 Jan., 1837. *See* 'Russian Influenza.'

Black Thursday, 6 Feb., 1851. Is so called in the colony of Victoria from a terrific bush-fire which occurred on that day.

Black Troop (*The*), 1470. Of King Matthias of Hungary; a royal bodyguard, and, next to the French, the earliest standing army in Europe. *See* 'Black Legions.'

Black Vomit (*The*). So the plague (1348) of Florence was called. Some think it is the same as the cholera morbus, or Indian cholera. Its principal ravages were in 1736, 1737, 1761, and 1782; in this last year Mexico lost 25,000 of its

inhabitants from it. Yellow fever is so called in Mexico and tropical America.

In 1348 the plague began in China, and spread into Turkey, Egypt, Greece, Italy, France, Germany, England, and Russia. In Russia it carried off the whole royal family; in France a fourth of the inhabitants; and in Europe a third of the entire population. *See* 'Black Death.'

Black Watch (*The*). The 42nd Foot, so called from their ' black ' tartan, *i.e.* a tartan of black, dark blue, and dark green, called 'the Black Watch tartan.' It was originally a Scotch militia, dressed in tartans of very dark colours. In 1725 General Wade was their commander-in-chief. In 1730 they were formed into six companies of 100 men each, and stationed in different parts of the Highlands to enforce the 'Disarming Act,' to prevent political meetings, and to check depredations. In 1739 they were formed under the Earl of Crawford into the famous 42nd regiment, and became one of the most distinguished of the British army. Linked with the old 73rd.

Black Wind (*The*). The Sherki. An easterly wind much dreaded in Armenia, and so called by the Kurds because it is a terrible scourge.

Black Year (*The*), 1742. The driest year known in England, when all green things were dried up.

The years 1744, 1749, 1758 were very nearly as dry.

Blacks (*The*). The Waltham deer-stealers in the reign of George I. were so called because they blackened their faces for disguise. *See* 'Black Acts,' 'Black Horse.'

Blacks and Reds, or 'I Neri ' and 'I Rossi.' The Council of Ten, in Venice, were called 'I Neri' from their black official robes. The signory or privy council of the doge was called 'I Rossi' from their red robes of office.

Blacks and Whites (*The*), 13th cent. and first four years of the 14th. Rival factions in Italy. The *Blacks* were the aristocratic Guelfs, the *Whites* were the bourgeois and Ghibelins. Dante in 1302 was exiled for being a *White*, and during his exile wrote his 'Divina Commedia.'

Blackfoot. One of the disturbing factions of Ireland in the early part of the present century. The faction seems to have resembled the Terry Alts. *See* ' Irish Associations.'

And the Blackfoot who courted each foeman's approach,
Faith, 'tis hot-foot he'd fly from the stout Father Roach.—LOVER.
N.B. ' Hot-foot he'd fly,' *i.e.* quickly.

Blacksmith of Antwerp (*The*). Quentin Matsys, first a blacksmith and then a great painter (1450–1529).

Blacksmith's Apron (*The*). The standard of Kâwâh or Gawo, a blacksmith of Ispahan, who headed a rebellion against Biver-asp Zohâc, a merciless tyrant; and raised Feridoun, son of Djemchid, to the throne. The blacksmith's apron was adopted by Feridoun as the royal standard of Persia. Every king of the Djemchid dynasty (called the Pichdadians or Paisdadians) added jewels to enrich the apron-standard, called Derufsh-e-Kawânee (standard of Kâwâh). (Sir John Malcolm, ' Hist. of Persia,' vol. i. p. 13.)

It need hardly be added that the Pishdadian dynasty belongs to the mythical period of Persian history. The apron remained the royal standard till A.D. 636, when in the battle of Cadesia it fell into the hands of the Saracens.—GIBBON, chap. li.

Blackwork. That of mutes at a funeral. Waiters hired for this purpose call the employ ' blackwork,' from the black clothes and cloaks worn on the occasion.

Blanch Holding (*A*), or ' Blench holding.' A tenement held of a superior for a peppercorn or mere nominal rent.

Blanch-Lyon. At one time one of the English pursuivants-at-arms was so called. *See* ' Pursuivants.'

Blanco White of the 18th cent. (*The*). Pierre François le Courayer (1681–1776), a French divine who died in England, and is one of the ten foreigners buried in Westminster Abbey. He is so called by Dean Stanley.

Blancs Battus (*Les*). The White Flagellants ; there were also the Black and Blue orders. Henri III. joined the White order, his mother Catharine de Medicis the Black order, and Cardinal d'Armagnac the Blue. They went in procession bare-footed and bare-headed, with chaplets of death-bones at their girdles, and making blood spirt from their naked shoulders by lashing them with cords. The White Flagellants wore a whit mantle, the Black Flagellants wore a black mantle, and the Blue Flagellants a blue mantle. The mantle was thrown off when the scourging began.

Blancs et Bleus (*Les*). The Blancs (Whites) were partisans of the Bourbons, whose emblem was a *drapeau blanc.* The Bleus were republican soldiers whose uniform was blue.

Blank Bond (*A*). In Scotland. A security in which the creditor's name is left blank, the bearer being at liberty to insert his name in the blank space and sue for payment. Abolished in 1696.

Blanket Meeting (*The*), 10 March, 1817. The muster of the Blanketeers (*q.v.*) in 'St. Peter's Field, Manchester. According to government estimate the number was 10,000 ; but this seems to be a gross exaggeration, and about 5,000 is thought to be the correct estimate. The meeting was broken up by the military.

Blanketeering Expedition (*The*), 10 March, 1817. The march of certain Lancashire weavers to lay their grievances before the Prince Regent. As the way was long, each man took a blanket to wrap round him at night, and a stock of provisions. At least 5,000 met in St. Peter's Field, Manchester, but the military dispersed them ; some taking the road to Stockport. Not above 180 reached Macclesfield, in Cheshire, ' a most deplorable lot, without food and without organisation.' A score struggled as far as Staffordshire, and only six reached Ashbourne Bridge, when the expedition collapsed. *See* ' Peterloo.'

Blanketeers (*The*). The radical reformers of Lancashire, who mustered on St. Peter's Field, Manchester, with the intention of marching to London to lay a petition of grievances before the Prince Regent. Only six got as far as Ashbourne Bridge. The deviser of this expedition was Joseph Mitchell, draper of Liverpool. *See* above.

Bleu-thonge, 1189. A military order instituted by Richard I., when about to lay siege to Acre. It was in honour of St. George, and consisted of twenty-six knights, the decoration being a blue leather garter round the left leg. *See* ' Knights of the Garter.'

Blind Archbishop (The). Robert Wauchope (pronounce Vaucop), titular archbishop of Armagh, was blind from birth. He introduced Jesuits into Ireland in 1541; was appointed archbishop by Paul III. in 1543; and attended the Council of Trent in 1547.

Blind General (*The*). Zisca, the Hannibal of Bohemia. He was totally blind (1318–1424).

Blind Harper (*The*). John Parry, who died 1739.

Blind Harry. A Scotch minstrel of the 15th cent. blind from infancy, minstrel in the court of James IV. His epic of 'Sir William Wallace' runs to 11,861 lines.

Blind Inventor. Dr. James Gale, F.G.S. of Plymouth, inventor of non-explosive gunpowder, &c. *See* ' Men of the Time ' (1833-   ).

Blind Jack of Knaresborough. Lived by laying out roads.

Blind Mechanician (*The*). John Strong, blind from his birth (1732–1798).

Blind Musician (*The*). John Stanley, musician and composer, was blind from birth (1713–1786).

Blind Naturalist (*The*). François Huber of Geneva (1750–1831). His ' Observations on Bees ' was published in 1796.

Blind old Bard of Chio's rocky isle (*The*). Homer (flo. about B.C. 950).

Blind Physician (*The*). Dr. Hugh James (17th cent.).

Blind Poet (*The*). Luigi Grotto, an Italian poet, called *Il Cieco d'Adria* (1541–1585). John Milton (1608–1674).

Blind Postmaster-general (*The*). Henry Fawcett (1833–1884). An exceedingly active and efficient postmaster-general.

Blind Prebendary (of Westminster). Richard Lucas, D.D. (1648–1715), author of 'Practical Christianity,' 'Inquiry into Happiness,' 'Christian Thoughts for every Day of the Month,' ' Sermons,' &c.

Blind Scholar (*The*). Ambrose Fisher (17th cent.).

Blind Sculptor (*The*). Giovanni Gonelli, a Tuscan (1610–1664). He also made admirable likenesses; amongst others, that of Pope Urban VIII. is very celebrated.

Blind Traveller (*The*). Lieutenant James Holman (1787–1857), who walked through Russia almost to the Chinese frontier. He would have continued his tour, but the Russian government grew suspicious and sent him back.

Blockam Feast. Lynch law. Holinshed, in his Chronicles, referring to the rebellion of 1381, has this marginalia: ' Lawyers, justices, and jurors, brought to blockam-feast by the rebels under Jack Straw and Wat Tyler.'

Sir Robert Bealknap, the chief justice of the common pleas, being sent to Essex to try the insurgents, they denounced him as a traitor to the country, cut off the heads of the jurors and clerks of the commission, and carried them on poles through the neighbouring towns.

(A block-house is a prison, a block-stick is a cudgel, and a blocker is a broad axe. Blockam seems allied to these words.)

Blocking a Bill. Putting down notice of opposition to a bill before the House. The effect of this notice is that, unless the stage objected to can be reached before 12.30 A.M., the bill is blocked, as no bill objected to can be taken after that time.

Blois (*Treaty of*), 1513. A treaty of alliance between Venice and Louis XII., renewed by François I. in 1515.

Blood (*The*). It is said that when Longinus pierced the side of Jesus with a spear, about a spoonful of the blood was caught, and this blood was preserved at Billom, in France, till the Revolution, when it was thrown away. We are told that it was brought from Syria, in the first crusade, by two canons, named Durand Albanelli and Peter Barbasta. Several vouchers accompanied the vessel containing the blood, one dated in the reign of Tiberius, and another in that of Valens. A bull of Eugenius IV., in 1444, established a confraternity in honour of the blood. (*Discours historique sur le sang précieux que l'on révère dans l'église collégiale et royale de Saint-Cerneuf de la ville de Billom, en Auvergne*, 1757.)

** Some of the blood of Jesus we are assured is preserved at Mantua, said to have been preserved by Longinus, the Roman soldier who pierced the side; but it is most improbable that he would catch and preserve the blood of a despised Galilean. *See* 'Crucifixion, Relics of the.'

Blood (*The Court of*). 'The twelve judges of the Tumults,' established in the Netherlands by the Duke of Alva, in 1567 (Motley, 'Dutch Republic').

Blood Bath of Stockholm (*The*). Christian II. of Denmark, wishing to restore the Union of Calmar, was empowered by the pope to treat the Swedes as heretics. Armed with this authority, Christian invaded Sweden, was victorious, and solemnly crowned at Stockholm. Under pretence of obedience to the pope's bull, he put to death his political enemies, and executed ninety-four bishops, senators, knights, and burgomasters, amongst whom was Eric, father of Gustavus Vasa. This massacre, which occurred in Nov. 1520, is called in history 'The blood bath of Stockholm.'

Blood Book (*The*). The register of the Vehmgerichte (*q.v.*), in which was entered the judgments of the court, with the name of the crime which had called down the sentence.

Blood Council, Sept. 1567, or 'Council of Troubles' (*q.v.*).

Blood Feud. The duty of the next akin of a murdered man to slay the person who has killed him. This tit-for-tat law is well nigh universal in all nations not brought into legal civilisation. It is called *Vendetta* (*q.v.*) in Corsica and many other places, *Tar* by the Bedouins, *Talio* by the Twelve Tables of old Rome. The *lex talionis* is a similar barbarity, only the retaliation was not left in the hands of the next akin, but was administered by officers appointed by law.

Blood-money. Money paid by press-gangs to anyone who informed them of a man who had deserted from the naval service, or who was instrumental in giving up a deserter to the press-gang. The deserter ought to have been a sailor, but in a 'hot-press' landsmen were often kidnapped. 'Blood-money' now means money paid to a person for informing against a felon.

Blood-wedding (*The*). So the Germans called the massacre of the Protestants in Paris on the night of St. Bartholomew's Day (German, *Blut-hochzeit*).

Blood of Christ (*The*). At Hales, Gloucestershire; said to have been brought from Jerusalem; invisible except to absolved penitents; was shown in 1538 to be the blood of a duck ntroduced every week into a bottle transparent on one side and opaque on the other. *See* 'Rood of Grace,' 'Darvel Gatheren,' &c.

Bloodless year of '82 (*The*). That is 1782, when Holland acknowledged the independence of the United States of America, peace was negotiated, and the provisional articles were signed by Great Britain and America. It was not, however, a 'bloodless year,' for in May the British were repulsed near Savannah, and in July the last action in the war took place near Combahee Ferry.

> And when at last he had fought us thro'
> To the bloodless year of '82.
> WILL CARLETON, *How we Kept the Day.*

Bloody Assize (*The*), 1685. The infamous assize held by Judge Jeffreys, when some 300 persons were condemned to death, more were whipped or imprisoned, and nearly 1000 were sent to the plantations as slaves, because they had joined the Monmouth rebellion.

Bloody Bill (*The*). The 31 Henry VIII. c. 14, which denounces death by hanging or burning on all who denied the dogma of transubstantiation. The first of the six articles, or 'Bloody Statute.'

Bloody Bonner. Edmund Bonner, bishop of London (1500–1569), a main instrument of the religious persecutions in the reign of Mary.

Bloody Feast (*The*), A.D. 981. The Romans, anxious to free themselves from the German yoke, formed a conspiracy to establish a republic. This conspiracy was secretly revealed to Otto II. of Germany, who went to Italy, invited the chief conspirators to a banquet at the Vatican, and when the guests were seated at table, Otto, rising from his chair, stamped his foot, and the room was instantly filled with armed men. The kaiser then deliberately unrolled a paper from which he read aloud the names of those concerned in the plot; and, as each name was read, the victim was dragged from the table and strangled. This 'bloody feast' is described in Leonine verse in the 'Pantheon' of Godfrey of Viterbo.

Bloody Feast of Rouen (*The*), 1356. The young dauphin, Charles, son of Jean le Bon, gave a banquet at Rouen to his private friends and leading nobles of France, to which Charles the Bad, his brother-in-law, was invited. While the guests were seated at table King Jean entered the banquet room with a numerous escort, and, seizing Charles, shook him violently, exclaiming, 'Traitor, thou art not worthy to sit at table with my son! Guards, seize your prisoner. By holy Paul! I will not eat or drink till his head be brought me!' The dauphin threw himself at his father's feet, imploring him to desist, but the king, seizing a mace, struck one of the guests with it, and four others were cut down by the guards. Charles the Bad was shut up in the Tower of the Louvre, but was released after the battle of Poitiers, 1356.

Bloody Ledger (*The*). An account of the burnings and spoliations of Henry VIII. on the coasts of Kintyre, Kyle, and Carrick, in 1544. We find that 192 towns, villages, farms, towers, and churches were destroyed; 10,386 head of cattle were driven off, 12,492 sheep, and 1,496 horses; and an untold amount of miscellaneous plunder was taken.

Bloody Statute (*The*). The statute passed in 1541, commanding all British subjects, under pain of death or imprisonment at the king's pleasure, to subscribe to the following church dogmas: (1) The Real Presence of Christ in the Eucharist; (2) The all-sufficiency of communion in one kind only; (3) The unlawfulness of the marriage of priests; (4) The indissoluble obligation of vows of chastity; (5) The propriety of retaining private masses; and (6) The obligation of auricular confession. This statute was repealed in 1549. More authentically called 'The Statute of Six Articles.'

Bloody Sunday, 13 Nov., 1887. Noted for a Socialist riot in Trafalgar Square, London. The Socialists resolved to hold a public meeting in the square, but Sir Charles Warren commanded the police to disperse the crowd. Many severe injuries were received on each side, and one or two fatalities occurred; but it is a mere party exaggeration to call the day 'Bloody Sunday.'

Bloody Sword (*The*). In Hungary a bloody sword used to be carried through the land to rouse the people to arms in cases of great national danger. Thus Bela IV., in 1246, caused 'the bloody sword to be carried through the land according to ancient custom,' when threatened by inroads of the Mongols. The Scotch sent round a 'fiery cross' (*q.v.*). The Parisians ring the tocsin.

Bloody Theatre of Eperjes (*The*), 1684-1687. A permanent scaffold erected in the middle of the town of Eperjes, in Hungary, for the torture and execution of Hungarians suspected of being hostile to the government of Kaiser Leopold of Germany. Thirty executioners, dressed in green uniform, were employed night and day in torturing, mutilating, and beheading the victims. Count Caraffa, a foreign general of sanguinary disposition, was president of the tribunal established at Eperjes for the mockery trial of the accused. It sat from March to the end of the year, and only poverty and obscurity escaped its persecution (Godkin, 'Hist. of Hungary,' p. 234).

Bloody Thumb. This was the brand of the Irish 'National League' (*q.v.*).

Bloody Tower (*The*). So called in the reign of Elizabeth from the tradition that the two young princes were murdered there. In the reign of Henry VII. it was called the 'Garden Tower.'

Bloody Tribunal of Eperjes (*The*), 1684-1687. When Hungary was rescued from the Turks after their disaster before Vienna, Caraffa, a military commander, was appointed to reinstate the Hungarian owners. The first question Caraffa asked was whether the applicant was of the new faith (Lutheranism); if so, he was instantly put to death. This bloody tribunal was abolished by the diet which met at the opening of the year 1687.

Bloody Wedding (*The*). The wedding of Henri (afterwards Henri IV. of France) with Marguerite (daughter of Catharine de' Medici). So called because it was made the occasion of the wholesale massacre of the French Huguenots, generally called 'The massacre of St. Bartholomew's Eve.'

Blue. The Sikhs wear blue, even blue turbans; but all other Hindûs reckon blue unlucky.

Blue (*True*). True Blue principles, *i.e.* Toryism; but in 'Hudibras' we read of 'Presbyterian true blue.'

Sir Stafford O'Brien one night exclaimed in the House of Commons, 'There is no "True Blue" now. There are many Tories, but no "True Blues."'—Sir W. HARCOURT, 24 Oct., 1885.

Blue and Red Hoods (*The*). 'Mi-partie bleus et rouges,' 1356, during the captivity of Jean le Bon, was the faction livery of the dauphin (afterwards Charles V.). In 1358, on the death of the provost Marcel, this faction fell away. *See* 'Blue Hoods.'

Blue and White. The Whig cockade, in some counties. Hence the well-known song and tune 'Come wave your blue and white.'

Blue and Yellow (*The*). The 'Edinburgh Review' is so called from its cover, which is blue with a yellow back.

The Blue and Yellow speaks out with its old directness.—Newspaper paragraph, Jan. 1886.

Blue and Yellow Robes. In China. All the twelve sects wear blue robes in China; but the followers of Lamaism wear yellow robes, the imperial colour, because Lamaism was promulgated by a son-in-law of the emperor.

Yellow is also worn by Buddhist monks of the southern countries.

Bluebeard. So Giles, marquis of Laval, the French general, was called. It is said that he put to death seven of his mistresses 'to aid his incantations with their blood.' This debauched and licentious villain was at last burnt alive at Nantes by order of the Duc de Bretagne, 1440. (Nantes, pronounce *Nahnt*.)

Blue Bellies. The Federals were so called by the Confederates in the civil war of America, from the light blue cloaks worn by the northern soldiers. *See* 'Greybacks.'

Blue Blanket (*The*). The blue standard or banner of the incorporated trades of Edinburgh. When the trades-

men thought themselves aggrieved, they unrolled their standard, and the people used to say, 'Up goes the Blue Blanket;' in other words, the tradesmen are rallying their forces to resist the powers which they think have aggrieved them. It was originally called 'The Banner of the Holy Ghost;' but James III. changed its name into 'The Standard of the Crafts within Burgh.'

Blue Blood and Pigeon's Blood. 'Sangue blò' and 'Sangue colombin.' The blue blood in Venice were the wealthiest of the nobility, termed *I Signori*; the pigeon's blood were the poorest of the nobility, termed *I Barnaboti*, from the quarter San Barnabo where they resided.

There was an intervening class sometimes called *Morèl di Mèzzo*.
. The Spaniards are especially proud of their blue blood when they can trace their pedigree to the Goths.

Blue Bonnets over the Border. The reference is to the Covenanters in the year 1640, passing into England against Charles I. The whole of the infantry wore the Lowland blue bonnet.

Blue Book (*The*), of America, is similar to the English Red Book. It contains lists of all persons under government in the civil, military, and naval departments, including the law offices. Called blue from the blue wrapper.

Blue Books. I. Parliamentary reports, but not statutes. All command-papers, all returns such as import duties, export duties, returns of the names of members of parliament, all official statements, statements of accounts, &c. in Great Britain, whether in a blue wrapper or without a wrapper, are so called. Thin documents have no cover, thick ones have a blue wrapper. Blue is the only colour recognised by the British parliament.

The official colour in Spain is red, in Italy green, in France yellow (*livres jaunes*), in Germany and Portugal white.
N.B.—The reports sent annually to the colonial secretary by the governors of our colonies are officially called 'blue books.'

II. The blue books quoted by Butler are three books, stitched in dark blue wrappers, which appeared in 1789, 1791, and 1792. Charles Butler wrote the whole of the first and third, and most of the second. They contain scandalous doctrines, which no Catholic would allow. Copies may be seen in the British Museum.

Blue Boy (*Gainsborough's*). Master Jonathan Buttall (1779) (Gainsborough died 1788). Buttall's father was an ironmonger, 31 Greek Street, Soho, and died 1768. The 'Blue Boy' succeeded to the business, and carried it on till 1796, when he sold it to Sharpe and Coxe. The famous picture of the Blue Boy is in the Devonshire collection.

Blue Cap (*The*). In England a blue cap with a white border in the civil wars was the ' cap of liberty,' or anti-royalism. Britannia on some coins is represented holding such a cap on the point of her spear.

Blue-coat School (*The*). A familiar designation of. Christ's Hospital; so called from the long blue coat worn by the boys. Founded 26 June, 1553, by Edward VI. (the year of his death).

Blue Cockades, 1780. The badge of the Protestant association. In the Gordon riots everyone who wished to go abroad unmolested wore blue in some part of their dress.

Lord George Gordon appeared in the House wearing a blue cockade. Colonel Herbert, on seeing this, declared that he would not sit and vote in the House while he saw a noble lord with the ensign of riot in his hat ; and that if his lordship would not take it out, he himself would step across the House and do it for him. Lord George quietly took the cockade from his hat and put it in his pocket.—HOWITT, *Hist of England*, George III., p. 249.

Blue Flag (*A*). A warning of danger in the Roman Empire. Livy speaks of it in his ' Annals.'

Blue Flagellants (*The*). So called from their blue mantles. See ' Flagellants,' and ' Blancs Battus.'

Blue Friars (*The*), 1829–1846. A convivial and intellectual society of Plymouth, numbering many men of note. Charles Mathews, the elder, was member and was called ' Brother Prism.'

Blue-gowns. King's bedesmen, or licensed beggars who wore blue gowns. Called in Scotland gaberlunzies. *See* ' Thiggers and Sorners.'

Blue Hats (*The*), 1356–1358. The Navarrese party organised by Marcel, provost of Paris, during the captivity of Jean *le Bon* in England. The object of the provost was to place Charles *le Mauvais* on the throne. *See* ' Blue Hoods.'

Marcel, entering the palace without any regard to the dauphin, seized the two marshals and put them to death so close to the prince, that his dress was sprinkled with their blood. ' How now,' cried the dauphin, ' will you shed the blood royal of France?' ' No!' cried Marcel, and so saying he rudely snatched from the dauphin's head the embroidered hat of a pale rose colour, put it on his own head, and clapped his own blue hat on the dauphin's head. Through all the day the provost went about Paris with the dauphin's hat.—HOWITT, *History of England*, vol. i., p. 395.

Blue Hens. The natives of Delaware, one of the United States of North America. Captain Caldwell, an officer in the 1st Delaware regiment in the American War of Independence, was very fond of game cocks, but maintained that no cock was truly game, unless its mother was a blue hen. As the Delaware regiment was truly game, they were the sons of blue hens.

Blue Hoods. The party badge of Navarre; red hoods, the party badge of Paris; blue and red, the party badge of Charles [V.], when dauphin ; white hoods, the party badge of the Burgundians.

Blue Laws. The code of 1660, a compilation of the earliest laws and customs of Connecticut. It is almost verbally copied from the Mosaic Law. After the restoration of Charles II. ' Presbyterian true blue ' became a term of derision applied to anything which smattered of Puritanism, and ' blue laws ' simply meant puritanical laws, or laws with a blue tinge. These laws inflicted the penalty of death for worshipping any god but the God of the Bible ; for speaking disrespectfully of the Bible, Christ, or the Holy Ghost; for witchcraft, adultery, theft, false-swearing, and disobedience to parents. Said to have been drawn up by the Rev. Samuel Peters, but generally supposed to be apocryphal.

Blue-light Federalists. Those Americans who befriended the English in 1812, by giving them blue-light signals.

Bluemantle. One of the four pursuivants of England. *See* ' Pursuivants.'

Blue Monday. St. Crispin's Day. This is the German ' der blaue Montag.' Not 25 Oct., but holiday Monday, the day of ' blue looks.'

Blue Moon. *Once in a blue moon,* occasionally, but very seldom. In the second week of Dec. 1883 we had green, purple, and blue moons: on the 7th green, on the 10th blue. The sunset clouds were also unusually brilliant and deep-coloured. 2 Sept., 1883, the sun at Trinidad was blue, and at Panama it was green.

In England the winter 1883-4 was unusually mild and the wind south-west.

Blue Noses. The Nova Scotians are so called from a potato which they rear in great perfection, and term ' Blue Noses.'

Blue Pedigrees. Pedigrees concocted for rich nobodies by professional genealogists. Mr. Wray of Philadelphia tells us (' Notes and Queries,' 23 Jan., 1886, p. 74), that ' genealogical publications are searched for the names of families desiring information, and suitable pedigrees are constructed for them out of the visitations and county histories, and are duplicated by . . . the " blue print " process.'

Blue Ribbon Army, or ' Blue Ribbonites,' or ' Blue Ribboners.' Teetotallers who bear as a badge a small piece of blue ribbon, to remind all who see it that they drink no alcoholic liquor.

Blue Ribbon of the Turf (*The*). So Disraeli, Lord Beaconsfield, called the Derby. To win the great Derby horse-race is the greatest achievement of the year in the estimation of the turf.

The ' cordon bleu ' was the ribbon worn by the knights of the ' St. Esprit,' the highest order in France, as the blue garter is the highest distinction in British knighthood.

Blue Ring (*The*). This was a sapphire ring which Lady Scrope let down from the window of the queen's chamber to announce to her brother, Robert Carey (afterwards earl of Monmouth) the death of Queen Elizabeth. The moment he caught it he galloped off to Scotland as fast as possible, to be the first to announce the welcome news to the expecting James.

Blue Sisters (*The*) 1604. The Celestial Annunciades, a religious order instituted by Maria Vittoria Fornari. So called from their blue mantles. The Annunciades of Jeanne de Valois wear a blue simar, but white mantle.

Blue Skins. The Presbyterians were so called after the restoration of Charles II., *blue* meaning puritanical. Anything smattering of roundheadism, whether laws, institutions, sects, persons, or what not, was called in derision *blue*, that is, tinged with ' Presbyterian blue.'

Joseph Blake, an English burglar, was called ' Blue-skin ' from his complexion. He was executed in 1723.

Blue Stocking Club (*The*). Established in London in 1780. It was a society of literary ladies which lasted up to 1840. The members were supposed to wear blue stockings, and two ladies (Montagu and Stillingfleet) are said to have given name to the society. Probably it was in imitation of the ' Società della Calza ' of Venice (1400–1590).

Similar clubs have been adopted both in Germany and France. Indeed the French ' bas-bleu ' is as often heard as the phrase ' blue-stocking ' to designate a female literary pedant.

Blue Waiters. At one time waiters were dressed in blue, the badge of servitude, but the badge was discontinued in the reign of James I. Frequent reference to the blue coats of servant men will be found in old plays.

Blues (*The*). I. ' Les Bleus,' in the Vendean war, were the republican soldiers, so called by the royalists on account of the colour of their uniforms. *See* ' Whites.'

II. the police, so called from being dressed in blue. Also called the ' Blue Foot-guard.' Of course the ' wit ' lies in the allusion to the ' Blue Guards.'

Blues and Greens (*The*). In Latin ' Venĕti et Prasĭni.' Charioteer factions at Byzantium. The Venĕta factio wore a light blue livery; the Prasĭna factio wore a leek-green livery (Greek *prason,* a leek). The Emperor Justinian was a Blue, and the two factions became political. In 532 the Greens revolted, proclaimed Prince Hypatius emperor in the circus, and waylaid Justinian in his palace. Belisarius and Mundus repelled the rebels, but more than 30,000 persons fell in the sedition. Hypatius, being taken, was beheaded and his body thrown into the Bosphorus. This sedition was called the *Nika,* the rallying word of the insurgents.

Venĕtus means Venice blue, the colour of the common soldiers and seamen of Rome. There were two subordinate factions, the white and the red, but the white merged into the blue and the red into the green.

Blues and the Lilacs (*The*).

Two rival court parties in the reign of François I. The *Blues* were the partisans of Diane de Poitiers, mistress of Henri the dauphin, afterwards Henri II. The *Lilacs* were the partisans of Madame d'Etampes, mistress of the king. Both king and dauphin had a wife living at the time. Madame d'Etampes was nine years the younger. She died at the age of 67, her rival died at the age of 68.

Blues, Reds, and Whites (*The*),

in the first French Revolution. Balzac tells us in ' Le dernier Chouan : ' ' Dans ces temps de discordes, les habitans de l'ouest avaient appelé tous les soldats de la république des *bleus*,' because their ' premiers uniformes étaient bleus et rouges.' A *Bleu*, therefore, in 1793, was a republican, in opposition to a royalist or Vendean, who wore the *White* royal uniform. Dumas tells us, in his ' Vingt Ans après,' that ' blue and red is the livery of Paris.' The French tricolour is the combination of republican blue, the city of Paris, and the Bourbon white.

Bluff City.

The city Hannibal, in Missouri (North America).

Bluff Harry.

Henry VIII., who affected a bluntness of speech and manner, and delighted in being so called.

Blunden. *The thrice-buried Mrs. Blunden.*

Mrs. Blunden was buried at Basingstoke ; but some of the boys of the neighbouring grammar-school, hearing a noise underground, ran to tell their master. The coffin was disinterred, the body was found to be alive. Proper means being applied, life was fully restored, and Mrs. Blunden continued to live for several years. A second time she fell into a trance and was buried, and sounds underground again attracted attention ; the coffin was again disinterred, and it was found that the flesh had been gnawed from one of the hands by the teeth of the buried lady. Means were tried to restore life, but without success, and Mrs. Blunden was buried for the third time.

Lazarus and many others were twice buried.

Boabdil.

A corruption of Bu-abdad, which is a contraction of Abu-Abdallah. This Moorish prince of Granāda was called ' Assaghir ' (small, insignificant). His mother Ayesha said of him, when he was driven out of Spain in 1492 : ' My son, you have cause to weep like a woman, who defended not your throne either as a monarch or a man.' It was probably this littleness, and not diminutive stature, which procured him the sobriquet of Assaghir.

Board Schools, 1870.

National or parish schools under a school board or a board of directors, and supported by rates. Religious instruction forms no part of the curriculum. These schools are under government inspectors and receive government grants *per capita*, according to a scale of merit given in the inspector's report. Every parish or group of parishes must have either a voluntary school or a board school.

A voluntary school is not supported by a rate, but by voluntary contributions, children's pence, and a government grant. It is inspected by a government inspector, and those connected with the Church of England are also under diocesan inspection.

Board of Admiralty (*The*).

A government department which has the management of all matters concerning the British navy.

Board of Control (*The*), 1784.

A committee of commissioners for managing the affairs of India. Abolished 1858 (21, 22 Vict. c. 106).

Board of Green Cloth (*The*).

Consisting of the lord steward and several inferior officers. Their duty was to punish offenders within the verge of the palace and within 200 yards beyond the gates. So called because the board or table at which they sat was covered with a green cloth. It existed in the reign of Henry I., probably even earlier. Abolished 1849 (12, 13 Vict. c. 101).

Board of Ordnance (*The*).

A government department to which is committed the management of all matters relating to the artillery and engineering corps of the British army.

Board of Trade (*The*), 1786.

Has the control of all matters pertaining to our colonial trade and all matters pertaining to our mercantile marine, all railways in the United Kingdom, the fisheries, harbours, weights and measures, statistics, electric lighting, &c. All charters for incorporation are referred to this board; the Privy Council on education is under its control, &c. The board consists of a president and vice-president, the lord chancellor, the archbishop of Canterbury, the first lord of the treasury, the chief secretaries of state, the speaker, and several others.

It originated in 1660, when Charles I. created a council for trade and a council for foreign plantations; but the present constitution dates from the reign of George III.

Board of Triers (*The*), March 1653. A committee, one-fourth being laymen, appointed by Cromwell to try or examine the fitness of candidates to hold livings or take part in the church services.

Cromwell also appointed a church board in every county to see that the clergy did their duty, and to remove those who were inefficient or evil examples.

Board of Works (*The*), 1851. Constituted by the Metropolitan Management Act. It had control over the streets of London, the line of buildings, the fire brigade, the gas, drainage, bridges, parks, and commons; the tramways, artisans' dwellings, slaughterhouses, theatres, and music-halls, &c. The fifty-nine members of the board were elected by the respective vestries; the corporation and city of London used to elect three of them. Abolished 1889.

Boarian, or **Borome'an Tribute.** A heavy mulct imposed by Tuathal, overking of Ireland, on the province of Leinster for the infamous conduct of their ruler Achy. This continued from the 2nd to the 7th cent., but was dropped in 693, though the intercession of St. Moling. So called from *bo*, a cow, because beeves formed the medium of tribute. *See* 'Fine of Leinster.'

The offence was this. Achy married a daughter of Tuathal; but tiring of his wife, he went to Tara and brought home his wife's younger sister as a bride. When the bride discovered that her sister was living, she died of the shock, and the sister pined to death a few weeks after.

'This brutal sacrilege the monarch punished by putting twelve of the Lagenian chieftains to death, and exacting rigorously the Boarian tribute from the province to which they belonged.' T. MOORE, *History of Ireland*, vii., p. 133.

Boatswain Smith. G. C. Smith, pressed into the British navy in 1796, quitted the service in 1803; became pastor of a Baptist church at Penzance in 1807 (1782-1863).

Bobêche (2 syl.). A famous clown (1815-1825) who drew crowds to a small theatre on the Boulevard du Temple of Paris; his rival was Galimafré. Bobêche takes rank with the Tabarin and the Bruscambille (18th cent.). A comedian or farce-actor is complimentarily called 'un vrai Bobêche' in France. *See* 'Tabarin.'

Bocasoti. The same as 'Bizocii' (*q.v.*).

Bode's Law, of the relative distances of the planets from the sun.

Write 4 nine times.

Under the second write 3, and multiply by 2 throughout. Then add.

Thus:

4	4	4	4	4	4	4	4	4
	3	6	12	24	48	96	192	384
4	7	10	16	28	52	100	196	388
Mercury	Venus	Earth	Mars		Jupiter	Saturn	Uranus	Neptune

Between Mars and Jupiter is no planet, but Bode said there must be one in the gap, and the asteroids being discovered proved the correctness of the series.

Taking earth to be 10, the relative distances are (roughly) 3·9, 7·2, 10, 15·2, 27·4, 52, 95·4, 192, 300 (millions of miles).

Boden Scholarships. Four for Sanskrit. Value 50*l*. a year, and tenable for four years in the University of Oxford. Founded by Colonel Boden in 1830 and 1860.

Bodleian Library (*The*), 1597. The public library of Oxford restored by Sir Thomas Bodley on the site of the old University library, which had been despoiled of its contents in the reign of Edward VI. It has been added to by many magnificent gifts, and now contains above 256,000 volumes and 22,000 MSS. The Bodleian Library is one of the five depositories of copyright books. The corresponding institution in Cambridge is called the University Library.

Refounded by Sir Thomas Bodley (1597-1599). The new building commenced 17 July, 1610, and finished 1613. Augmented by the libraries of Richard Gough and Edmund Malone in 1812, and by that of Francis Douce in 1834.

Boece (*Hector*), or 'Boethius.' A literary romancer born at Dundee (1470-

1550). In his 'Scotorum Historia,' published in 1526, he has forged the names of forty-five Scotch kings with which he interpolated the Irish list of the Dalriadic rulers (*i.e.* kings of Argyllshire). *See* 'Literary Forgeries.'

Bœuf Gras (*La marche du*). The procession of the prize ox on Shrove Tuesday through the chief streets of Paris, introduced in the reign of Charles VIII. (1483–1498). The ox, with gilt horns and hoofs, a fillet on its head and decorated with ribbons, is led through the chief streets, accompanied by a host of followers dressed in ridiculous costumes, and bands of music playing on ridiculous instruments. The whole is a farcical imitation of Roman priests going to offer sacrifice. The butcher's expenses are paid by donations from ambassadors, noblemen, ministers, and wealthy citizens, on whom he calls to show his ox.

I have seen the procession six or eight times, but probably it is now (1890) shorn of its glory, if not abolished. Shrove Tuesday is called *Mardi gras* in French.
Bœuf Gras pronounce *Buh-grah'*.

Bœotian Confederacy (*The*). The confederacy of the fourteen independent states of Bœotia, with Thebes at the head. The chief magistrates of the league, called Bœotarchs, were elected annually, two for Thebes and one for each of the other states.

The number of Bœotarchs varied as the independent states were not constant; but fifteen may be roughly called the college of Bœotarchs.

Bogomiles or **Bogarmitæ**, 12th cent. Heretics of Bulgaria, who denied the Trinity, the resurrection, the institution of the sacraments, and holy orders. They were deists. The Emperor Alexis Comnēnus in 1118 burnt to death their leader. (Sing. Bogomil.)

Bog is the Sclavonic for 'God,' and *mil* is a corruption of *milotii*, 'have pity on us.'

Bohemian Brethren (*The*). The followers of Huss of Bohemia, 1457. Their great offence was allowing the cup to the laity, whence they were called 'chalice men.' They subsequently merged into the Moravians or 'United Brethren.' Their platform was : (1) the free preaching of the gospel ; (2) the administration of the eucharist in both kinds ; (3) the separation of the clergy from all secular pursuits ; and (4) the

punishment of the clergy by the civil courts.

Böhmenists. *See* 'Behmenists.'

Boiling to death. By 22 Henry III., c. 9, it was enacted that poisoners should be boiled to death. The law was repealed by 1 Edward VI. c. 12.

Bolden Book (*The*). The book containing the survey of the see of Durham, made in 1183 by order of the Bishop de Pusay. So called because the parish of Bolden is the first mentioned in the survey. It begins thus :

Incipit liber qui vocatur Bolden Book, Anno Dominice Incarnationis, 1183.
It is a small folio, and is kept in the auditor's office at Durham.

Bolivia (in South America). So called after Simon Bolivar, who liberated several of the South American provinces from Spain in 1824.

Bollandists. The compilers of the numerous folio volumes of the 'Acta Sanctōrum' (*q.v.*). So called from Father John Bolland, who with ten coadjutors brought out the first 32 volumes folio, and completed the first series. Reorganised at Brussels in 1837, and the 54th volume was published in 1845. The 57th volume brings down the hagiography to 1855 ; the 61st to 1875.

The first five vols. contained Jan. in two vols. (1643), and Feb. in three vols. (1658). The 53rd vol. appeared in 1794.
'Les Petits Bollandistes' is a French hagiography by Mgr. Paul Guérin in 17 large octavo vols., the 7th edition of which was published in 1880. The last vol. is all index.

Bolleghe, *pl.* **Bolleghes.** The herdsman and his herd in Ireland living on the mountains. The usage is called *Bollinge.*

Bologna (*Treaty of*), 1 Jan., 1530. A treaty of peace between Venice and Charles V. Charles abandoned to Venice all his conquests in Lombardy, and Venice gave up to Charles the Neapolitan ports.

Bolton Quarter. Instant death without mercy.

2 May, 1644 Bolton was taken. Colonel R.'s forces routed, and many a sweet saint slain. No quarter would be given, so that Bolton Quarter grew into a proverb.—ISAAC AMBROSE, *Media or Middle Things*, 1650, p. 72.

Bomba. A sobriquet of Ferdinand II. of Naples and Sicily, so called from his savage bombardment of Messina in Sept. 1848.

Bombalino, or ' Bomba II.' Francis II. of Naples, who bombarded Palermo in 1860. He was the son of Ferdinand II., nicknamed 'King Bomba' (*q.v.*).

Bombay (in Hindustan). A corruption of the native name into the Portuguese *Bom-bahia,* the good bay (1509).

Bona Dea. Called by the Romans Fauna, who revealed her oracles to women only, and no man was permitted to be present at her mysteries. There was a similar deity, named Faunus, exclusively confined to the other sex. Publius Clodius, in the house of Cæsar, violated the sanctuary of Bona Dea, and was brought to trial, but he was acquitted by bribery (Cicero, ' Att.' i. 12).

Bonaght (Ireland). An exaction imposed at the pleasure of the lord for the maintenance of his soldiers. There were two sorts, viz. Bonaght-bur and Bonaght-beg. The first was free quarters at discretion, the latter was a money commutation. *See* ' Coygne and Livery.'

Bonaparte's Egyptian campaign, 1799. Alexandria fell into his hands ; he won the great battle of the Pyramids ; completed the subjugation of Egypt ; passed into Syria, made himself master of Gaza and Jaffa ; won the battle of Mount Tabor ; returned to Egypt, attacked the Turks at Aboukir, and utterly destroyed their whole army, 25 June, 1799.

Bonaparte's Italian campaign, 1796-7. He was 27 years of age.

11 April, he defeated Beaulieu, the Austrian general, at Montenotte, in Sardinia.

14 April, he won the battle of Millesimo.

15 April, he won the battle of Dego.

22 April, he won a victory over the Piedmontese at Mondovi.

10 May, he defeated the Austrian general Beaulieu at the Bridge of Lodi, and entered Milan.

19 June, he occupied Bologna, Ferrara, and Ancona.

3 Aug., he defeated the Austrian general Würmser at Lonato.

5 Aug., he defeated the same general at Castiglione.

8 Sept., he defeated him again at Bassano.

17 Nov., he won the great battle of Arcōla over Alvinzi, the Austrian general.

14 Jan., 1797, he won the battle of Rivoli over Alvinzi and Würmser.

15 Jan., he won a battle at the faubourg of St. George, near Mantua.

16 Jan., he won a battle near the palace called The Favourite.

16 March, he defeated the Austrians led by the Archduke Karl at Tagliamento.

17 Oct., the treaty of Campo Formio, and in December he returned to France.

He had won 15 battles ; added Savoy and Nice to France, the Netherlands, and Italy ; had obtained vast money compensations, and returned to France laden with treasures of art.

Bonaparte's Forty Days' Campaign. He left Paris 6 May, 1800 ; marched over the Alps, and reached Aosta 23 May ; he entered Milan 2 June ; won the battle of Montebello over the Austrians 9 June, and the great battle of Marengo, 14 June ; returned to Paris 2 July.

The 40 days count from his arrival at Aosta, 23 May, to his return to Paris, 2 July.

Bones, or St. Hugh's bones. Dice. 'To rattle the bones,' to play dice. The St. Hugh referred to is St. Hugh of Lincoln, whose teeth were knocked out by Jews when he was crucified in mockery of the crucified Saviour. Of course this statement is given only as a tradition, and not as an historic fact.

Bonfire of Vanities (*The*). In Florence, 1493. Savonarola had such effect by his preaching on the people of Florence, that women, gay gallants, and grave scholars, went in throngs, and threw into a vast bonfire before the gates of the cathedral whole hecatombs of poems, works of fiction, and other works of art, and burnt them, after the example of the men and women of Ephesus (Acts xix. 19).

Bonnet-piece (*A gold*). A gold coin of James V. of Scotland, and the most beautiful of all Scottish coins. So called because the head of the king is represented wearing a bonnet instead of a crown.

Bonnet Rouge (*Un*). A red republican was so called from the red cap of liberty worn by him.

Bonnet Vert. *Prendre le bonnet vert,* to become a bankrupt. Alluding to an old law which compelled bankrupts to wear a green cap. This custom continued down to the 17th cent.

Bononcinists, 1720-1730. A musical faction in London opposed to the Handelists. The Prince of Wales led the Handel party, supported by Pope and Dr. Arbuthnot; the Duke of Marlborough led the Bononcinists, supported by many others of the nobility. For about twelve years the Italian school was so strongly supported that Handel could not resist the tide; but in 1742 his popularity returned.

Bonzes. Priests of Fo, founder of a reformed Buddhism in China. Born about B.C. 1027. He taught the equality of man; the love of others; the love of truth; honest dealing; the sin of murder; abstention from all intoxicating drinks; the love of purity; recompense or punishment after life according to one's deeds. Bonzes live in monasteries.

Book. I. The *first book printed in German* (1461) was the 'Edelstein' (or 'precious stone') by Ulrich Boner. A collection of fables, tales, and maxims in reproof of evil ways and for the encouragement of piety and virtue.

The first printed book was the Psalter of Mainz, 1457; the next was William Durand's 'Holy Office' ('Rationale divinorum officiorum libris viii distinctum'), printed 1459; the third was Balbis's 'Catholicon, a sort of dictionary, 1460; then comes the 'Edelstein,' in German.

II. The *highest price* ever offered for a book was 20,000*l*. It was a Hebrew Bible in the possession of the Vatican. In 1512, the Jews of Venice wished to buy this book, but though Julius II. was greatly pressed for money in order to keep up the Holy League against Louis XII. of France, he declined to part with the volume.

The German Government paid 10,000*l*. for the missal given by Leo X. to Henry VIII., along with the parchment conferring on him the right to assume the title of 'Defender of the Faith.' Charles II. gave these relics to the ancestor of the famous Duke of Hamilton, whose library was sold by Messrs Sotheby, Wilkinson, and Hodge of London.

III. The *largest book* on one subject is the 'Acta Sanctorum' of the Bollandists, not yet completed (1890). The 61st vol. was published in 1875.

IV. The *oldest book* in the world is a papyrus containing the proverbs of Ptah-hotep, an Egyptian king, who reigned some 3000 B.C., which was before the birth of Abraham. It has been in part translated by Chabas and others; and may be seen in English dress in J. D. Heath's 'Record of the Patriarchal Age.'

Book of Advertisement (*The*), 1565. The book containing the canons and articles drawn up by the Court of Ecclesiastical Commission appointed by Queen Elizabeth. The object of the book was to secure uniformity of doctrine and discipline throughout the realm.

Sampson, dean of Christchurch, and Humphrey, regius professor of divinity at Oxford, with many others, refused to conform, and were called Non-conformists.

Book of Common Order (*The*), 1562. A liturgy drawn up by John Knox for the use of the Scotch church. It was in general use for nearly a century, and contained forms for the Sunday services, for week days, for the sacraments, and for some other occasions. The people took no part in the liturgy.

All saints days were ignored.

Book of Common Prayer (*The*). Based on the 'King's Primer' (*q.v.*), was published by Henry VIII. in 1546. In the reign of Edward VI. it underwent two revisions, and 'The Second Prayer Book of Edward VI.' approaches very near to the one now used in the Church of England. In the reign of James I. was introduced a collect in the daily morning and evening service, the prayer for the Royal Family in the Litany, and that part of the catechism about the sacraments. It was revised in 1662, and from time to time special prayers have been introduced which are not now included in the Common Prayer Book.

Cranmer appointed in 1548 twelve commissioners to assist him in compiling the Book of Common Prayer in the reign of Edward VI. They were Goodrich (bishop of Ely), Holbeach (bishop of Lincoln), Day (bishop of Chichester), Skip (bishop of Hereford), Thurlby (bishop of Westminster), Ridley (bishop of Rochester), May (dean of St. Paul's), Taylor (dean of Lincoln), Haynes (dean of Exeter), Redmayn (master of Trinity, Cambridge), Coxe (dean of Christ Church, Oxford), and Robertson (archdeacon of Leicester).

The service books consulted by them were these eleven: the Antiphonarium, the Finale, the Graduale or Grayle, the Legenda, the Manuale, the Missal, the Ordinale, the Pica or Pie, the Pontificale, the Portiforium or Breviary, and the Processionale. Cranmer presided.

I

Book of Discipline (*The*), 1560. A digest of the forms by which the reformed church in Scotland was to be governed. Both in doctrine and discipline the church was modelled on the Geneva or Calvinistic plan.

Book of Leinster (*The*). An Irish MS. compiled 1000–1100.

Book of Mormon (*The*), 1830. The 'revealed' history of America from its first settlement by a colony dispersed at the confusion of tongues to the 5th cent. of the Christian era. Joseph Smith professed that this information was obtained by him in September 1827 in a volume of metal plates engraved in reformed Egyptian, and discovered by revelation 'on the west side of a hill, not far from the top, about four miles from Palmyra, in the county of Ontario.' As Smith could not decipher the writing, a pair of magic spectacles, which he called his Urim and Thummim, were given to him, and one Oliver Cowdery wrote down on paper what Smith professed to translate. It is said that the 'Book' is a mere plagiary of a MS. romance by the Rev. Solomon Spalding in 1816. Certainly the plates and spectacles have disappeared. *See* 'Literary Forgeries.'

Book of Sentences (*The*). By Pierre Lombard (1100–1164). A compilation of the leading arguments of the fathers upon moot points of divinity, arranged and digested under heads. Above 244 commentators have written annotations on this book; among others, Thomas Aquinas, Guillaume Durand, St. Bonaventure, &c.

Book of Sports (*The*), 1618. A declaration issued by James I. of England, signifying his pleasure that on Sundays, after divine service, ' no lawful recreation should be barred to his good people.' The sports more especially mentioned were dancing, archery, leaping, vaulting, May-games, Whitsun-ales, morrice-dances, and setting up of Maypoles. The declaration was appointed to be read in the parish churches. In 1633 the declaration was again published. In 1644 the Long Parliament ordered all copies of the declaration to be burned. It was again reprinted in Arber's ' English Garner.'

The following sports were forbidden on Sundays: bear and bull baiting, bowling, and interludes. Those who had not attended church were forbidden to join in the sports, and no one could go out of his parish to join the sports of another parish.

Book of Torgau (*The*), 1576. A famous confession of faith by the Reformers, the object of which was to produce unity and uniformity among the divergent sects. From this was developed 'The formula of concord' (1580).

Booted Mission (*The*). 'La Mission bottée,' the dragonnade of Louis XIV. Trench, speaking of the Ephesian Church, refers to ' the French Protestant refugees, who had found shelter from the dragonnades, the " Mission bottée," as it is so facetiously called by some Roman Catholic writers, of Louis XIV.' (' Commentary on the Epistles to the Seven Churches of Asia,' p. 73.)

None of the infinite abuses which might arise from this ' Mission bottée ' (as the rude and fierce body of instructors were called, either in bitter sportiveness or contempt) was likely to be diminished by the temper of the officer to whom its direction was entrusted.—SMEDLEY, *History of the Reformed Religion in France*, vol. iii. p. 250, chap. xxiv., of A.D. 1681.

Boot-jack. John, earl of Bute (1713–1792) ; a pun on John-Bute, whence Jack-Bute, and by metathesis Boot-jack.

Booth's Expedition (*Felix*), 1829. He equipped the ' Victory' steamer at his own cost and sent it under the command of Captain Ross to discover whether there is a north-west passage from the Atlantic to the Pacific. Mr. Booth has his name perpetuated in the words Boothia, Boothiana, and Point Felix; and William IV. made him a baronet; but no passage could be discovered. Captain Ross returned in 1832.

Border (*The*). The frontier of England and Scotland. The Tweed for about sixteen miles, the Cheviot hills for about twenty-five miles, then the Kershope Water (a tributary of the Esk), then the ' Debatable Land ' and the river Sark, to the Solway Firth.

Border-thief School (*The*). Those novelists who took for their heroes border thieves, or for their subjects the adventures of border chiefs. Sir W. Scott and his poetical imitators are meant.

With your Lake Schools, and Border-thief Schools, and Cockney and Satanic Schools, there has been enough to do.—CARLYLE.

The 'Lake School,' such as Wordsworth, Southey, and Coleridge, who 'haunted the lakes of Cumberland' and Westmoreland.

The 'Cockney School,' such as Leigh Hunt, Hazlitt, Shelley, Keats, &c.

The 'Satanic School,' such as Byron, Moore, Bulwer, Rousseau, Victor Hugo, Paul de Kock, and George Sand. So called because they show no deference to the conventionalities of religion and morals.

Border Warrant (*A*). A warrant issued by a Scotch sheriff or county-court judge to arrest a debtor on the English side, and detain him till he produces bail for his appearance when called on within six months.

Borgites (2 syl.), or '**Bordjites.'** A dynasty of Mamelukes in Egypt (1382–1517), which succeeded the Baharites (3 syl.). Every one of these rulers, except Barkuk the founder, was either deposed or met with a violent death. Touman-Bey (the last of them) was hanged by Selim, sultan of the Ottomans.

Boromé (*The*), or Leinster tribute. An annual tribute paid by the King of Leinster to Tuathal, overlord of Ireland, for causing the death of Tuathal's two daughters, whom he had inveigled into his power under the promise of marriage.

Boromean Tribute (*The*). *See* '**Boarian.'**

His (Leogaire's) war upon the Lagenians, or people of Leinster, to enforce the payment of the Boromean tribute, seems worthy of notice.— T. MOORE, *Hist. of Ireland*, xi. 232.

Borough English. The law by which the youngest son is the heir, from the supposition that he is less able to maintain himself than his elder brothers.

Borough-mongers. A term applied by Cobbett to those who were 'mongers' of boroughs; that is, had property in parliamentary seats, which seats they could sell or bestow on whom they thought proper.

Borrome'o (*Charles*), archbishop of Milan, and Augustin Valerio, bishop of Verona, have won to themselves immortal fame by their intrepidity in visiting the plague-stricken in 1576. This terrible pest depopulated Venice, Verona, Milan, and Trent. The great Titian fell a victim to it. It was attributed to the miasma rising from stagnant water and bad drainage. *See* '**Plagues,'** &c.

We have an Englishman fully worthy of being placed with these philanthropists. During the great plague of London in 1665, Sir John Lawrence, then Lord Mayor, continued the whole time in the city; heard complaints and redressed grievances. The day after the disease was known to be the plague, 40,000 servants were dismissed and turned into the streets, for no one would take them in. Sir John supported them all at first from his own private fortune, till subscriptions came in to help him in his benevolent work.—*Journal of the Plague*, printed by E. Nutt, 1722.

Query.—Is there a statue to this great man in the City? If not, for the honour of our Lord Mayors, there ought to be. The John Lawrence in Westminster cloisters was a 'short-hand writer.' I can call to mind no public monument to one of the greatest of England's worthies.

Boscobel. So celebrated for the concealment of Charles II., was originally the property of a Mr. Giffard, who built there a small mansion, which he called 'Bosco-bello,' fair wood. When Charles took refuge there the farmer's name was Penderell.

Bosphorus (*The*). Means the ox or cow ford. So called because Io, transported into a cow, forded or swam across it. So, at least, we are told in Grecian fable.

Bosporic Era (*The*). Commenced B.C. 297.

Boston Bard (*The*). Robert S. Coffin, born in Boston, Massachusetts (1797–1857).

Boston Massacre (*The*), 5 March, 1770. A ridiculously grand phrase for a petty squabble between the British soldiers quartered in Boston and the men employed in Gray's rope-walk. Some of the soldiers mockingly asked to be employed in the rope-walk; a row ensued, which was renewed for two or three days, and at last some of the officers drew up a company of soldiers to overawe the men. The workmen began to taunt the 'lobsters,' and struck one of them. The soldiers fired. Three of Gray's men fell, and eight were wounded. The funeral of the three men was made a public protest, and its anniversary was kept for 14 years.

Boston News Letter (*The*). Appeared 24 April, 1704. It was the first American newspaper.

Boston Port Bill (*The*), March 1774. A bill by Lord North to take away from Boston (Massachusetts) the customs, the courts of justice, and the government offices, and transfer them to New Salem, in consequence of the rebellion of the Bostonians, especially their wanton destruction of tea to the value of 18,000*l.*, to show their hatred of England.

Boston Tea-party (*The*), 16 Dec., 1773. Those citizens of Boston who, disguised as Indians, boarded the three English ships, which had just come into the harbour, and threw into the sea several hundred chests of tea, by way of protest against English taxation of America without a representation in parliament.

Botany (*Father of*). Tournefort (1656–1708).

Botany (*Professorship of*). In the University of Cambridge, 1724, founded by the university. Stipend 300*l.* a year.

Botany Bay, 1770. So called by Captain Cook, who discovered, on entering the bay, the epăcris (a sort of heath), which, though very brilliant, will grow in the poorest soil.

Bottle Riot (*The*), 1822. In Dublin theatre. Someone (12 June, 1822) daubed the equestrian statue of William III., on College Green, with lampblack. The Orangemen had been accustomed for many years to whitewash it and decorate it with yellow ribbons on the anniversary of the battle of the Boyne (1 July, 1690). As these pranks caused great riots, the Marquis of Wellesley, the lord-lieutenant, forbade any unauthorised person to interfere with the statue at all. This offended the Orangemen, who clubbed together to mob him in the theatre. During the National Anthem, someone threw a bottle at the marquis; a riot ensued, and some of the offenders were prosecuted; but the bills were thrown out, and when government took the matter up, the jury would not agree, and the prosecution was dropped.

Bottomless Pitt (*The*). William Pitt (1759–1806), the statesman, a very thin man, with no 'fall' in his back.

Boulden Book (*The*). A book recording the inquisition made by Hugh Pudsey, bishop of Durham, in 1183, still extant. It shows that the villeins of Bolden held each thirty acres of land, which they paid for partly in service, partly in land, and partly in money. It is valuable for throwing light on the subject of villeinage in England in the

12th cent., and for other incidental information on the social state of the people.

Bourbon Dynasty, of France. Began with Henri IV. the Great, and continued in a direct line to the Revolution. Louis XVIII. and his brother Charles X. were also in the direct line. Louis Philippe was of the Orleans branch.

The Bourbons were descended from the sixth son of St. Louis, brother of Philippe III. The dynasty (with the interruption of the Revolution and Empire) continued from 1589 to 1848.

Bourbon Orleans branch of the Bourbon dynasty. Gave to France one king, Louis Philippe, called *Le Roi Citoyen* (1773, 1830–1848, died 1850).

Bourguignons (*The*), 1407. The faction of the Duke of Burgundy (Jean-sans-Peur), opposed to the Armagnacs or Orleanist party, during the imbecility of Charles VI. of France. The cognisance of the Bourguignons was a St. Andrew cross on a red scarf.

The cognisance of the Armagnacs was a St. George's cross on a white scarf.
Bourguignons (pronounce *Boor-gwin'-yohn*).
Armagnacs (pronounce *Ah-man'-yaks*).

Bow-street Runners (established 1749). Nicknamed Robin Redbreasts from their scarlet waistcoats. The Bow-street officers were a brave resolute set of men, nimble of foot like a proctor's 'bull-dog,' skilled to run down offenders and 'bring them to book.'

Bowdlerise. To expurgate a book in editing it. Dispatches are bowdlerised by government, or 'edited,' that objectionable statements may be omitted, before the dispatches may be given to the public. Bowdler gave to the world an expurgated edition of Shakespeare's works, in which, as he tells us, 'nothing is added to the original text, but all words and expressions are omitted which cannot with propriety be read aloud in a family.' *See* 'Grangerise.'

Bowdlerite (*A*). An abridger, so called from Thomas Bowdler (1754–1825). The opposite of a Grangerite (*q.v.*).

We have also Bowdlerise, Bowdleriser, Bowdlerism, Bowdlerisation, &c.

Bowides (2 syl.) or 'Bouides,' 10th and 11th cents. A Mussulman dynasty, under the califs, in Irak Adjěmi, in Persia, offspring of Bouyah of Dilem.

This Bouyah had three sons, viz. Imad-Eddaula, Rockn-Eddaula, and Moez-Eddaula, who rose to sovereign power, reigning at Bagdad and over Persia (932–1055). These three brothers were called the pillars of the state, and under their vigorous reign the language and genius of Persia revived. The Seljuks succeeded them.

The Bouides (2 syl.) were not shahs, but *emirs.*

Box-days, 1690. Two days (one in the spring and one in the autumn vacation) appointed by the Scotch judges of the Court of Session, when law papers may be filed.

For preventing [private solicitation], and for easeing the leidges themselves, and the lawyers, they . . . have appointed boxes for every one of the lords, to stand on a bank in the Session-house from 3 o'clk till 7 o'clk at night, each box having a slitt in which the informations or bills, may be lett in, and cannot be drawn out untill the box be opened; the key whereof is to be kept by every judge himself, and to be committed to no other.

Boxers. There were two schools of boxing during the regency, the Bristol school and the Hebrew school, the chief exponents being Tom Cribb of Bristol and Mendoza the Jew. *See* 'Broughtonian.'

The chief boxers have been:
Jim Belcher (Bristolian), who had but one eye (champion), and Tom Belcher, his brother; Bendigo; Cohen; Thomas Cribb, the champion; Figg; Gardolio, of the Hebrew school; Bob Gregson (the Pot of Pork); Gully; John C. Heenan, the Benicia Boy; Humphries; Gentleman Jackson (Lord Byron was his pupil; Jim Mace; Oliver; Painter; Randal (the Nonpareil), noted for his pink cheeks; Caleb Rann (Mendoza's favourite pupil, and called the Pink [of Bow]; Richmond; Scroggins, a sailor; Tom Sayers (who fought the Benicia Boy in 1860); Cyrus Smalley (the Sprig of Myrtle), Cribb's favourite pupil; Spring, so called by Cribb, but his real name was Thomas Winter; Sutton; Tomkins; Jem Ward, the Nestor of the ring, &c.
Daniel Mendoza published in 1799 the 'Art of Boxing,' in which he gives particulars of his match with Humphries. The era of boxing was 1719–1860.

Boy Bachelor (*The*). Thomas [cardinal] Wolsey (1471–1530), of Magdalen College, Oxford. He took his degree before he was fifteen years of age. He told Sir William Cavendish that he was usually so called at Oxford.

Hugo Grotius, 1600, pleaded his first cause when only seventeen years of age; Francis Bacon, born 1561, entered Trin. Coll. Camb. at the age of twelve, and was called to the Bar before he was twenty-one. Edward Herbert matriculated at University College, Oxford, at the age of twelve.

Boy Bishop (*The*). Mentioned as early as 1290. Prohibited by the council of Sens in 1485. The election of a boy-bishop prohibited in England by proclamation in 1542 (reign of Henry VIII.).

The election revived by an edict of the bishop of London, 13 Nov., 1554. Custom abolished by Queen Elizabeth in 1558.

The boy-bishop was elected on St. Nicholas's Day (Dec. 6), and the office lasted till Holy Innocents Day (Dec. 28). He was chosen from the cathedral choir or grammar-school, and when elected was arrayed like a bishop, and, attended by his chapter, went about the streets blessing the people in ridicule. He took possession of the church and performed all services except mass.

Boy Bishops. A child of only five years old was made archbishop of Reims. The see of Narbonne was purchased for a boy of ten. *See* 'Boy Popes.' (Hallam, 'Middle Ages,' vol. ii. p. 248.)

Boy Crusades. *See* 'Child Pilgrimages.'

Boy Martyr (*The*). St. Pancras, who suffered martyrdom under Diocletian (293–303).

Boy Patriots (*The*), 1742. So Walpole, after his fall, called Pitt, Lyttelton, Grenville, and their party of ambitious young men opposed to him and his measures (temp. Geo. II.).

Boy Popes. John XII. was made pope at the age of eighteen (956–963). Benedict IX. was made pope at the age of ten (1033–1054). Both these lads were licentious, extravagant, and profligate. One died at the age of twenty-five, having been pope for seven years, and the other died at the age of thirty-one, having been pope for twenty-one years. *See* 'Boy Bishops.'

Boys (*The*). I. So Walpole called the young 'Patriot' faction (1733), at the head of which was the young cornet of horse, William Pitt, the future earl of Chatham. In 1739 Walpole was obliged to bow to the faction, and consent against his better judgment to a war policy, and in 1742 he was compelled to resign.

II. The Irish Land-leaguers (*q.v.*) are generally called 'The Boys.'

III. *See* 'Wonderful Boys.'

Boycott (*To*). To ostracise. A word adopted from a Mr. Boycott, who was ostracised in 1881 by the Irish Land League. The principle is old enough, as the proverbs *Damner une boutique*, and *Damner une ville*, will show.

One word as to the way in which a man should be boycotted. When any man has taken a farm from which a tenant has been evicted, or is a grabber, let every one in the parish turn his back on him; have no communication with him; have no dealings with him. You need never say an unkind word to him; but never say anything at all to him. If you must meet him in the fair, walk away from him silently. Do him no violence, but have no dealings with him. Let every man's door be closed against him; and make him feel himself a stranger and a castaway in his own neighbourhood.—J. DILLON, M.P., *Speech to the Land League*, 26 Feb., 1881.

Boyle's Law. The volume of a portion of gas varies inversely as the pressure (1662). Thus if we double the pressure, the gas will be reduced one-half; if we treble the pressure, the volume of gas will be reduced to one-third, and so on.

Called by Continental writers Mariotte's Law (1676).

Boyle Lectures. Eight lectures in one year in defence of Christianity against heterodoxy, infidelity, or objectors. Bentley preached the first series. Established by Robert Boyle, son of the Earl of Cork (1627–1691).

Brabançons. Bands of mercenaries or brigands, chiefly from Brabant, who overran France, in the middle ages, and committed frightful disorders. John king of England and Philippe (II.) Auguste draughted them off into their armies, and trained them.

Brabant Screen (*The*), 1720. A caricature in which the Duchess of Kendal, from behind a screen, is supplying Knight, treasurer of the South Sea Company, with money to effect his escape, when the bubble bursts.

Knight, with all the documents, books, and secrets of the directors, effected his escape to Calais. He was apprehended near Liège, and lodged in the citadel of Antwerp; but the States of Brabant refused to give him up, and he was allowed to make his escape. The Duchess of Kendal was the mistress of George I., the reigning king, and the caricature implies that the royal family was involved in the iniquity of the scheme. The Prince of Wales was certainly one of the governors of the Company.

Bracceschi (*The*), 1409. The party of Braccio, formed into a company on the death of Barbiano. *See* 'Sforzeschi.'

Bracciolini (*Poggio*), of Tuscany (1381–1459), secretary to seven popes. Said to be the author of the 'Annals of Tacitus' (*q.v.*), for which 'forgery' he received from Cosmo de' Medici 500 gold sequins. We are told that the original MS. of Bracciolini's forgery is still preserved in the library of Florence. *See* 'Literary Impostors, &c.'

If this is true, then the quotations given by Paley and others from Tacitus in testimony of Christ are utterly worthless for they are extracts from the 'Annals': thus 'Christians took their name from their founder, one Christ, put to death in the reign of Tiberius by his procurator Pontius Pilate' is from the 'Annals' xv. 44.

Bradford Law. Hang first and try afterwards. A summary way of dealing with marauders, especially in border laws and in times of general turbulence.

There are many similar expressions: as Lydford Law, Halifax Law, Cupar Justice, Jedburgh Justice, Burslem Club Law, Abingdon Law (*q.v.*), Mob Law, &c.

Brahminism. It includes a belief in a Supreme Being, the doctrine of immortality, that of a Trinity, and also of an Incarnation. It teaches a belief in a heaven and hell, and of a divine revelation. The Brahmins have their sacred scriptures (viz. the Vedas, the Vedentas, the Upanishads, and the Puranas), and two sacred poems of immense length. The present number of Brahmins is 139,000,000.

Brandanes (2 syl.). The name given to the 1,000 Scotch archers, exceptionally tall and handsome men, who, in 1298, followed Sir John Stewart to the battle of Falkirk. In that fatal engagement, Sir John was slain and the 'Brandanes' were annihilated.

Brandons and 'St. Brandon's day.' Valentine's day is called 'Dominica de brandonibus.' A brandon is a lighted torch, like Cupid's torch of love; and boys used at one time to carry about brandons on Valentine's eve and Valentine's day, collecting largesses.

Bras-de-Fer. François de Lanoue, a Calvinist of the 16th cent., and most distinguished chief after the death of Coligny.

Brasenose College, Oxford, 1509. Founded by William Smith, bishop of Lincoln, and Sir Richard Sutton of Prestbury, Chester. The head-master is called the principal.

The origin of the word is doubtful. There is a brazen nose over the great gateway, 'a sign,' as Anthony Wood calls it; but there is a legend that the site of the college was an old brew-house or brasserie.

Bravest of the brave (*The*), 'Le brave des braves.' Michael Ney, marshal of France, so called for his services at the terrible battle of Moskowa in Russia, in 1812, which procured him the title of 'duc de la Moskowa' (1769–1815).

Brazen Horses of St. Mark (*The*). Four horses of gilt bronze removed by the Venetians from the Hippodrome at Constantinople, and placed over the western porch of the Basilica of St. Mark. No one knows the artist or date of these horses. Augustus brought them from Alexandria, after the conquest of Antony, and set them on a triumphal arch in Rome; they were removed by Nero, Domitian, Trajan, and Constantine to other arches. Constantine removed them to Constantinople. When Bonaparte took Venice in 1797 he removed the four horses to Paris, but in 1815 they were restored to Venice, which was allotted to the Austrian Government.

Brazen Wall (*The*). A horse regiment of Cromwell's republican party, so called because it was never broken. *See* 'Stonewall Jackson.'

Bread and Cheese. The shibboleth of Tyler's rebels, 1381, whereby he detected Flemish merchants.

Bread-and-cheeseland. Twenty acres of land left by Mary and Elizabeth Chukhurst of Biddenden (in the 12th cent.) for the benefit of the poor of their parish. The rent of this land was to be laid out in bread and cheese, to be distributed on Easter Sunday. The parish poor were to have 270 three-and-a-half pound loaves, with cheese in proportion; and 600 rolls were to be given to non-parishioners.

Breaking Money. To break a piece of money at parting, each keeping a part, was a bond of fidelity at one time among lovers. This came from very remote times, before inns and houses of public accommodation were known. Travellers had then to trust to the hospitality of strangers living on the road, and it was customary at parting to divide some article, such as a white stone or small coin, and for the host and guest each to take a part, that if the host required similar hospitality from his guest, he might claim it by showing the token. In the Revelation of St. John this custom is referred to (ii. 17), where Christ says, 'To him that overcometh will I give a white stone,' so that at the day of judgment he may demand admission into heaven.

It stares, beckons, points to the piece of gold
We brake between us.—*The Vow Breaker*, iii. 1
(1636).

Breast-laws. The common law of the Isle of Man. The code being a *jus non scriptum* is deposited in the heart or breast of the deemsters and keys (*q.v.*).

Breda (*Compromise of*), 1566.
(*Peace of*), 31 June, 1667, between England, France, and Denmark.

Breeches. *See* 'Procession of the Black Breeches.'

Breeches Bible (*The*), 1557. Printed by Whittingham, Gilby, and Sampson. So called because Gen. iii. 7 runs thus: 'The eyes of them bothe were opened. . . . and they sewed figge-tree leaves together and made themselves breeches.' Also called the 'Geneva Bible.'

Breeches Martyrs. O'Brien, M.P. and several other Irishmen imprisoned in 1889 for exciting the Irish to rebellion during the turbulent times of the Land League, refused to put on the prison dress, and went without their breeches, shivering with cold. Ridiculed by the general public as the 'breechless martyrs.'

Breeches Review (*The*). The 'Westminster Review,' so called from Francis Place, a West-end breeches-maker who had a considerable share both in the property and also in its conduct.

Breffni. Comprised the present Irish counties of Cavan and Leitrim. Cavan was called Breffni O'Reilly; and Leitrim was Breffni O'Ruark.

Dermot MacMurrogh, king of Leinster, eloped with the wife of O Ruark of Breffni, who appealed to the monarch.—O'CONNOR, *Hist. of the Irish People*, p. 48.

Brehon Laws. In Ireland. Unwritten or traditional laws. These laws were reduced to writing about 440. As, not unfrequently, the Brehon laws were repugnant to the laws of God and man, they were abolished in Anglo-Ireland by the Statute of Kilkenny 40 Edw. III., 1366; and the abolition was extended to the whole island by James I.

Brehon in Ireland meant a 'judge,' and Brehon law was justice administered by the chief of a clan to those of his own tribe. The Brehon sat in the open air on a stone or mound. Spenser calls the Brehon laws 'a rule of right unwritten.' That is, not deriving its authority by written statutes. The *writing* was simply a record of existing laws. So with the 'common law' of England.

Brennus. No proper name, but a corrupt Cymric word, *brenhin* meaning 'king.' It was a Brennus who sacked Rome in the days of Camillus, B.C. 390. Another Brennus invaded Greece, and was defeated B.C. 280.

Brethren, Brethrenism, 1832. The Plymouth Brethren call themselves only 'Brethren,' and their religious system they call 'Brethrenism.' They practise no rites and have no ministers. According to the teaching of these Christians, to preach the Gospel is to deny that the Saviour's work is finished.

However, they baptize one another, which is a rite. *See* 'Brothers.'

Brethren of Good Will (*The*). *See* 'Brethren of Social Life.'

Brethren of Our Lady of Mount Olivet, or Olivētans, 1272. An offset of the Benedictines, founded by John Tolomei. The brethren devoted themselves chiefly to teaching and the cultivation of sacred science.

Brethren of St. Alexius. *See* 'Alexians.'

Brethren of St. George (*The*), 1472. *See* 'Brotherhood of St. George.'

Brethren of Social Life (*The*), 1376. Founded in Holland by Geert Groote and Florentius Radewin, not unlike the subsequent society known as the 'United Brethren' or Moravians. They enjoined a community of goods, ascetic habits, the use of the vernacular tongue in all religious services, and acknowledged no conventual distinctions ('all ye are brethren'). In 1430 they numbered 130 societies.

Brethren of the Christian Schools. 'Frères des écoles chrétiennes,' 1681, instituted at Reims by Canon J. B. de la Salle, for the gratuitous education of children in the elements of religion. The brethren wore a large black robe and square cap. This order survived the Revolution, and was legalised in 1808.

Brethren of the Common Lot (*The*). *See* 'Brethren of Social Life.'

Brethren of the Free Spirit, 1065, or 'Fratricelli.' Censured by the Council of Vienna in 1311, and persecuted by Karl IV. in 1369. They took their name from Rom. viii. 2. 'The law of the spirit of life in Christ Jesus hath made us free from the law of sin and death.'

Their doctrine was a sort of pantheistic mysticism. They said that all things emanate from God, and will revert to Him again; that rational souls are part of God, that the whole universe is God, that by divine contemplation the soul is converted into the divine essence and becomes free from sin.

Brethren of the Holy Cross (*The*), 17th cent. The Rosicrucians, said to have been founded by Christian Rosencreutz, who died 1484, and bound his disciples not to make public any of his doctrines till 120 years after his death, The Rosicrucians were credited with possessing the secret of gold-making, keeping lights burning for centuries, and other alchemic secrets.

Brethren of the Passion (*The*). A company of pilgrims authorised to represent dramatically in cathedrals and other churches religious *mysteries*, such as the Incarnation, the Crucifixion, the Holy Trinity, the Real Presence, the Resurrection, &c. (13th to 15th cent.).

Brethren of the White Caps, 13th cent. The followers of one Durand, a carpenter, so called because their headgear was of white linen. They bound themselves not to play dice, not to frequent taverns, to wear no affected clothing, to avoid perjury and all vain swearing. They also forbade the lords from taking 'dues' from their vassals.

Bretigny (*Treaty of*), 8 May, 1360. Between France and England, in which Edward III. renounced all pretensions to the crown of France; abandoned his claim to Normandy, Anjou, and Maine; but, on the other hand, his duchy of Aquitaine (including Gascony, Guienne, Poitou and Saintonge) remained to him, not as a fief, but in full sovereignty; while his new conquest of Calais continued till the reign of Queen Mary a possession of the English crown.

King Jean was taken captive and brought to London, when his ransom was fixed at 8,000,000 gold crowns (about 1,500,000*l*. sterling). When he went to France to collect the money, he left his son, the Duc d'Anjou, as a hostage; but the duke ran away, and Jean returned to London, where he died in 1864.

Breton Club (*The*), 1789. Founded at Versailles at the instigation of Lafayette by the deputies of Brittany. It was subsequently transferred to Paris, and became the famous 'Club des Jacobins.'

The Breton club was formed because the king (Louis XVI.) over and over again refused to see their deputations, sent to remonstrate against his arbitrary conduct.

Bretts and Scots. Bretts were the remains of the British or Welsh people in Scotland. At one time the 'British' were the chief inhabitants of Dumbarton, Renfrew, Ayr, Lanark, Peebles, Selkirk, Roxburgh, Dumfries, and Cumberland; and this province was called 'Cambria,' 'Cumbria,' and 'Strathclyde.' In the middle of the 10th cent. it was a tributary to England, and continued so into the 12th cent., when Cumberland became a part of England.

The Scots were a Keltic people dwelling in the western and northern parts, and were called the 'wild Scots,' the 'Irishry of Scotland,' and 'Scotch Highlanders.'

The 'Laws of the Bretts and Scots' were abolished by Edward I.

Bretwalda. An Anglo-Saxon chief chosen to command the army (*Bretwald*, British ruler).

I. Ella of Sussex, 491-514.
II. Ceawlin of Wessex, 584-592.
III. Ethelbert of Kent, 597 to Feb. 616.
IV. Redwald of East Anglia, 616.
V. Edwin of Northumbria, king of all England except Kent, 620 to Oct. 633.
VI. Oswald of Northumbria, 635 to 5 Aug., 642.
VII. Oswy (his brother) of Northumbria, 651 to 15 Feb., 670.
VIII. Egbert of Wessex, 827-837. Also king.
IX. Alfred the Great, 871. Also king.
X. Edgar the Pacific, 958. Also king.

Breviarium Alaricianum, A.D. 506. An abridgment of the Theodosian Code by Alaric II., king of the Visigoths.

Breviary (*The*), 494. A book containing the canonical hours of the Latin church, viz. Matins, Lauds, Prime, Tierce, Sexte, None, Vespers, and Compline. It is called a breviary because it contains in a brief or abridged form the several offices. An ecclesiastic ought to go through his breviary daily. The original breviary was the work of Pope Gelasius, A.D. 494, but it has been often modified. The Greek breviary is called '*Eucology*,' and is more ancient than the Latin, going back to the time of Chrysostom, who died 409.

Originally it consisted of the Lord's Prayer and extracts from the Psalms. Subsequently short readings (lessons) from the Scriptures were added.
∴ The Breviary is quite a distinct book from the Missal (*q.v.*).

6

Brian (Boru) king of Munster, in the 10th cent. He was slain in the battle of Clontarf on Good Friday 1014.

Bridewell, 1522. Was built by Henry VIII. for a royal palace, for the reception of Karl V. and his retinue, but sometimes the king himself lived there; in 1553 the palace was given by Edward VI. to the city of London for a workhouse and house of correction. In 1666 it was burnt down in the fire of London. Bridewell is the name of the parish, so called from a well dedicated to St. Bride.

Bridge of Sighs (*The*), or Ponte dei Sospiri, Venice. Connecting the Prigioni Sotterraneo with the judgment hall of the doge's palace. Those who passed over it after their trial were prisoners on their way to execution.

Ruskin says it is renaissance of the 16th cent. After the great fire of 1574 the prisons previously connected with the palace were moved to the other side. Whether Niccolo da Ponte, the doge, who died in 1578, had any connection with the word 'Ponte' in the phrase I cannot determine. The bridge was the work of Jacopo Tatti Sansovino, the architect (1479-1570).

Bridge of Straw, Venice, (*The*). 'Ponte della Paglia.' One of the bridges which connected the prisons with the doge's palace. So called because when the nobles rode to the council they left their horses at the foot of this bridge in charge of grooms, and they were either stabled or baited, or both.

Bridgewater Canal (*The*), 1760. From Worsley to Manchester, cut by Brindley under the direction of the Duke of Bridgewater.

Bridgewater Collection (*The*), 1829. In the MS. department of the British Museum. Collected by the last earl of Bridgewater. Chiefly MSS. relating to French history.

Bridgewater Treatises (*The*), 1829. Francis Henry Egerton, 8th and last Earl of Bridgewater, placed 8,000*l.* at the disposal of the president of the Royal Society to be paid to eight persons appointed by him to publish 1,000 copies of a work on the goodness of God manifested in his works, from eight standpoints. WHEWELL was appointed to take general physics considered in connection with natural theology. BUCKLAND, geology and mineralogy. BELL, the human hand. ROGET, animal and vegetable physiology. PROUT, chemistry and the functions of digestion. CHALMERS, external nature adapted to man's moral and intellectual constitution. KIDD, on the adaptation of nature to man's physical condition. And KIRBY, the history, habits, and instincts of animals.

Brigandage of Ephesus (*The*), A.D. 449. A council of Ephesus, which condemned Theodoret, one of the Christian fathers, and defended Eutyches the heresiarch, who maintained that the humanity of Christ was absorbed in his divine nature. The Council was called 'Latrocinium,' the assembly of thieves and robbers.

Briggs's Logarithms. Constructed by Henry Briggs, a contemporary of Baron Napier (1556–1630).

Bright's Disease. A fatty degeneration of the tissues of the kidneys. So called from Dr. R. Bright, who was the first to investigate the character of the disease in 1837.

Brighton of the Riviera (*The*) or 'Brighton of the South,' Nice.

Brilliant Madman (*The*). Charles XII. of Sweden (1697–1710). He compelled the Danes to make peace, dethroned the king of Poland, and waged war with Russia for a time with success; but, being defeated by Czar Peter the Great at Pultowa, Sweden fell from her high estate as a first-class power.

Brinvilliers, the poisoner, was Marie Madeleine d'Aubray, marquise de Brinvilliers (1630–1676). She poisoned her father, her two brothers, and a sister. She was tortured, beheaded, and then burnt to ashes in Paris, 16 July, 1676.

Brissot (*Jean-Pierre*). The French revolutionist (1754–1793); was the first to abandon the use of hair-powder, and was the first victim of Robespierre. He assumed the dress of a quaker, and the name of De Warville.

Brissotins. The followers of Jean-Pierre Brissot in the first French revolution. Brissot was editor of the journal called 'Le Patriote Français,' and was one of the moving spirits of the times. He was a member of the Convention, but was opposed to the Montagnards, which drew upon him the wrath of Robespierre, who caused him to be proscribed 31 May, and he was put to death 31 Oct., 1793.

Bristol Fashion (*In*). Methodical, in apple-pie order. In the great mass meeting, 18 Oct., 1884, a route of above three miles was observed in one unbroken line. No cheering disturbed the stately solemnity; no one ran to give any direction; no noise of any kind was heard; but on, in one unbroken line, steady and stately, marched the throng in 'Bristol fashion' ('Daily News,' 20 Oct., 1884).

Bristol Riots (*The*), Sunday, 29 Oct., 1831, on the visit of Sir Charles Wetherell. It was during the excitement of the Reform Bill, which had been thrown out by the House of Lords. Sir Charles, a tory, entered with a cavalcade in a kind of triumph, and the mob rose in rebellion. The bridewell, the new gaol, the Gloucester county prison, several of the toll-houses, the bishop's palace, the mansion-house, the custom-house, the excise-office, and several private houses were set on fire. About 110 persons were killed, and three of the ringleaders were executed. The loss of property sustained was over half a million sterling.

Bristolians or Bristolites (3 syl.). Prize-fighters in the regency, of the Bristol school. Bristol was famous for the three pugilists, Jem Belcher (who had lost one eye), Thomas Cribb (once a coal-porter), and Molineux. The other school of boxers was called the 'Hebrews,' of which Mendoza was the chief exponent. The Prince Regent was a Bristolian, and his brother Frederick, duke of York, was a partisan of the Hebrew rivals. Much to the annoyance of the general public, the Prince Regent actually attached Thomas Cribb to his household. *See* 'Boxers.'

Britain (*Rulers of*), before Egbert.

(Those in italics were prætors, proprætors, or præfects of Rome.)

Segōnax	B.C. 38–20
Temantius	20 to A.D. 2
Cunobelini (Cymbeline) (at Camelodūnum)	2–31
Adminius	31–40
Caractacus and Togodumnos (sons of Cunobelin)	40–51
Pub. Ostorius Scapula, prætor	50–53
Didius, proprætor	53–57
Veranius	57–58
Paulīnus Suetonius	58–62
Boadicēa, queen of the Icēni	60–62
Petronius Turpilidnus	62–70
Petilius Cereālis	70–78
Cnæus Julius Agricŏla	78–85
Gladus, king of the Icēni	79

Trebellius	...	...	...	...		A.D. 86-120
Hadrian, emperor	...	...	...	...		120
Sevẽrus, prætor	...	...	...			120-138
Lollius Urbicus	...	...	...			138-161
Calpurnius Agricola		...	...			161-183
Ulpius Marcellus	...	...	...			183-186
Pertinax	...	...	...	...		186-192
Clodius Albinus	...	...	••	...		192-196
V. Lupus	...	...	...	...		196-206

(Sevẽrus, the emperor, died at York 211)
(No names given till 257)

Posthumus, proprætor	...	...	...		257-276
Bonõsus ...	...	...	...		276
Marcus Aurelius Carausius	...	...			287-293

(Revolts, and assumes the title of Augustus,
in Britain)

Alectus, emperor of Britain	...	...		293-296

(He murdered Carausius)

Asclepiodõtus, captain of the guard	...		296-304

(Slew Alectus ; and acted as prætor)
Britain joined to the præfecture of Gaul ...   304
Constantius Chlorus, with imperial power   304-306

(Died at York)

Constantine the Great	...	...	...		306-335
Constantine II.	...	...	...		335-340
Constans	...	...	...	...	340-350
Constantius	...	...	...		350-360
Julian and Lupicus, prætors	...	...		360-361
Lupicus alone ...	...	...	...		362
Nectaridius	...	...	...		362-367
Theodocius the Ancient, proprætor	...		367-378
Gratian (emperor) ...	...	...	...		378-395

(Revolt of Maximus 381)

Victorīnus	...	...	...		395-403
Stilicho, prætor	...	...	...		403-408
Constantine, præfect...	...	...			408-421

(Romans recalled 421)
Vortigern, king of the Britons   ...   445

(Dethroned 454)
Ambrosius and Vortimer   454-457

(Vortigern restored 454 ; deposed by
Hengist 455)

Ambrosius sole nominal king...	...	...		508
Hengist	...	...	...	...	457-488
Ella, bretwalda of Britain ! ...	...	...		491-519
Cerdic	...	...	...		519-534

(Arthur is said to have reigned 518-542)

Kenric ...	...	...	...	...	534-560
Cœline ...	...	...	...		560
Chevline	...	...	...	...	560-589
Ethelbert, king of Kent ..	...	...		580-616

(St. Augustine arrives)

Redwald of East Anglia	...	...		616-624
Edwin the Great of Mercia	...	...		624-635
Oswald of Northumbria ...	...	...		635-642
Oswy of Northumbria	...	...	...	642-670
Wolfhere of Mercia	...	...	...	670-675
Ethelred of Mercia	...	...	...	675-704
Cenred of Mercia ...	...	...	...	704-716
Ethelbald of Mercia	...	...	...	716-757
Offa of Mercia	...	...	...		757-794
Egfryd of Mercia	...	...	...	704-795
Cenolf of Mercia	...	...	...		795-829

Egbert sole king
(He was bretwalda in 827)

Britain. The Romans divided it
into five parts :

1. *Britannia Prima :* all the southern
counties from Kent to Cornwall.

2. *Britannia Secunda :* Wales, Hereford, Monmouthshire, with parts of Shropshire, Worcestershire, and Gloucestershire.

3. *Flavia Cæsariensis :* all between
the north of the Thames and the wall of
Sevẽrus, and between the Mersey and
the Humber, *i.e.* Lincoln, Nottingham,
Leicester, Cheshire, and part of Shropshire.

4. *Valentinīa :* Northumberland, part
of Cumberland, and the south of Scotland.

5. *Maxima Cæsariensis :* Lancashire
and Yorkshire.

Britain (*Little*), Aldersgate Street,
London. So called from the Earl of
Breton, whose mansion stood on the
site. Brittany is so-called by Waller.

Britain of the South. New
Zealand.

Britannia on the copper coins was
first adopted by Charles II. The academy
figure of Britannia was Louise de Querouaille, created by the king duchess of
Portsmouth. The general design was
copied from the coins of Antonīnus Pius,
in which is a female figure holding a
sceptre, and sitting on a rock, the whole
encompassed by the word BRITANNIA.

Some say that Britannia is meant for Frances
Theresa Stuart, duchess of Richmond ; others say
it is meant for Barbara Villiers, duchess of Cleveland. The probability in favour of Louise de
Querouaille is this : the coinage dates from 1672,
and a son by Louise was born the same year, and
she was created duchess of Portsmouth in 1673 ;
so that at the time she was the reigning favourite.
Querouaille, pronounce *Ker-wail.*

Britannia Prima. One of the
five provinces into which Britain was
divided in the reign of the Emperor
Sevẽrus. It included all the country
south of the Thames and the estuary of
the Severn. It had its own ruler (called
præses), who was subject to the præfect
or governor-general of the island.

Britannia Rediviva. A birthday
ode by Dryden. His Pollio, who was
to usher in the Golden Age, was the son
of James II. and Mary of Modẽna, known
in history as that very poor creature
called ' The Old Pretender.' Dryden
might be a good poet, but certainly he
was no prophet.

Britannia Secunda. One of the
five provinces into which Britain was
divided in the reign of the Emperor
Sevẽrus. It included that part of the
island lying between the Severn and the
sea, now called Wales. It had its own
ruler (called *præses*), who was subject to
the præfect or governor-general of the
island.

British Association (*The*). I.
In 1831. To give a stronger impulse
and more systematic direction to scientifio
inquiry ; to promote the intercourse of

scientific men generally; to obtain more general attention to objects of science, and a removal of whatever impedes its progress. First meeting was held at York.

II. In 1846–1847, for the relief of the starving Irish and Scotch during the potato famine. It was under the direction of Mr. Jones Lloyd (Lord Overstone) and Mr. Thomas Baring, and the collection was 269,302*l.*, to which was added collections made in churches of 209,738*l.*, total 470,041*l.*, of which one-sixth was sent to the highlands of Scotland and the rest to Ireland.

British Columbia, 1859. A territory about 420 miles in length (extending from the Rocky Mountains on the east to the Pacific), with an average breadth of 300 miles from the American frontier northwards. It includes Vancouver's Island.

British Kings. According to the 'Chronicles of the Celtic Kings,' Japhet was the first British king. This is not given as history, but it is worth knowing as a tradition.

British Legion in Spain (*The*), 1838. The 1,200 men under the command of Colonel Evans which Lord Palmerston permitted to serve the Queen of Spain in the Carlist civil war, by doing which he suspended the Foreign Enlistment Act.

British Lion (*The*). Richard Cœur de Lion (1157, 1189–1199).

So early were his heroic energies displayed, that he was called 'The British Lion' before he began his reign.—SHARON TURNER, *Hist. of England*, vol. i. p. 301.

British Museum (*The*), 1753. Began with the library and curiosities of Sir Hans Sloane, purchased for 20,000*l.*, and deposited in Old Montague House, Bloomsbury (the house was built by the first Duke of Montague for his residence). Townley's collection of marbles was purchased by the nation in 1805; his gems, coins, and bronzes in 1814. The Elgin Marbles were purchased for the nation in 1816; and Blacas's collection of antiquities in 1867. *See* 'Townley Marbles,' 'Elgin Marbles.'

British Museum Library (*The*), 1753. The library of Sir Hans Sloane, and the MSS. collected by Harley (earl of Oxford) and his son, were purchased by the British Museum. In 1757 George II.

presented to the Museum the 'Royal library,' and the Cottonian library was then transferred thither (the Cottonian library was collected by Sir R. B. Cotton, who died in 1631). In 1823 the splendid library of George III. was presented to the Museum by George IV. In 1847 the Grenville library was bequeathed to the Museum. In 1857 the new reading-room was opened, and the military guard was discontinued in 1863.

British North America Act (*The*), 1867. The instrument of Federation, constituted as the 'Dominion of Canada.'

British Solomon (*The*). James I. (1566, 1603–1625). Sully called him 'the most learned (not the *wisest*) fool in Christendom.' The poet Hawes calls Henry VII. the 'British Solomon.'

British Thaumaturgus (*The*). St. Cuthbert, who died 688.

Broad Bottom Administration (*The*). From Aug. 1743 to March 1754, formed by Pelham and dissolved at his death. It succeeded the Grenville administration. It was called 'Broad Bottomed' because it included both Whigs and Tories. Lord Hardwicke (chancellor), Pelham (first lord, &c.); Duke of Newcastle and Earl Harrington (secretaries of state); Duke of Devonshire (steward of the household); Bedford and Sandwich (admiralty); Earl Gower (privy seal); Lyttelton, Marquis of Tweeddale, Earl Harrington, Mr. Grenville, Sir John Hynde Cotton, Bubb Dodington, Cobham Hobart, and the Duke of Dorset were the other members. It contained nine dukes, seven of whom were in the cabinet, viz.—Argyll, Bedford, Dorset, Grafton, Montagu, Newcastle, and Richmond. *See* 'Unionists.'

Broad Church School (*The*). Of German theology, headed by Neander, a converted German Jew. His 'Universal History of the Christian Religion and Church' has superseded Mosheim's 'Ecclesiastical History.'

Bromsberg (*Treaty of*), 23 Aug., 1645. Between Sweden and Denmark. In 1643 Oxenstiern, chancellor of Sweden, invaded the duchies of Holstein and Sleswig, because Christian IV., jealous of Sweden, had secretly tried to ruin its trade. After a war of two years, a conference for peace was opened at Bromsberg, through the mediation of France, and in Aug. 1645 a treaty was duly signed. This treaty secured to Sweden exemption from the payment of the Sound duties; and the isles of Gothland and Oesel were ceded in perpetuity to Sweden.

Bronze Age. That period when a people or race use chiefly bronze for tools and weapons. Byron calls the era of Napoleon Bonaparte 'the Age of Bronze.'

Brook Farm. A socialistic society which had its *locale* in the vicinity of Boston, U.S. Every member contributed to the general fund or paid his quota in manual or other work. The idea was suggested by Margaret Fuller, but the society was organised by the Rev. W. H. Channing. The members boarded in common, dressed most economically, bought at their own stores, and reduced the price of living to the lowest point. The evenings were spent in intellectual amusements or social gatherings. The speculation was an utter failure, and after six years the 'Farm' was broken up. Emerson often visited the Farm, and Hawthorne lived there for twelve months.

Broom (*Van Tromp's*). Dr. Lingard, in his 'Hist. of Engl.,' viii. 5, tells us that in 1652, while Admiral Blake (supposing the naval operations for the year to be over) had detached a large part of his fleet, Van Tromp came into the Downs with a fleet double the size of that commanded at the time by Blake. A battle ensued, but at night Admiral Blake ran up the river as far as Leigh. Van Tromp insulted the coast as he sought to renew the fight, cruising backwards and forwards from the North Foreland to the Isle of Wight. Intoxicated with his success, he now fastened a broom to the head of his mast to indicate that he had swept the English from the sea; but next year, 18 Feb., Blake met Van Tromp on an equal footing, when the victory rested with the English, the loss of the Dutch being 11 men-of-war and 30 merchant-men.

He gives as his authorities: Heath, p. 335; Whitelock, p. 551; Leicester's 'Journal,' 138; Le Clerc, i. 328, and Basnage, i. 298–301.

Brother Protectors (*The*). A secret republican society of France and Lombardy, sprung from the Carbonari, after the unsuccessful outbreak of 24 June, 1817.

Brothers and Sisters of the Free Spirit, 13th cent. Sprang up in the Rhine country and spread into France and Italy. As the 'Spirit had made them free,' they claimed perfect civil, moral, and religious freedom. They set aside the marriage tie and acknowledged no church. Their religion was a mixture of pantheism and antinomianism. They were condemned by the synod of Cologne in 1306, and by that of Trèves in 1310.

Brothers of Charity, 1520. Established for visiting and administering to the sick. Approved by Paul V. in 1621, and subjected to the rule of St. Augustine. In Europe they dress in black, in America in brown. *See* 'Brethren.'

Brothers of the Cross. I. A name adopted by the Jesuits after the society was suppressed by Clement XIV. in 1773. *See* 'Paccanarists.'

II. The Flagellants. *See* 'Brotherhood of the Cross.'

Brothers of the Pen (*The*). A trade-guild at Brussels, in the middle of the 15th cent., for the copying of manuscripts, and their illuminations, hitherto confined to the scriptoria of religious houses. Some twenty years later the introduction of printing revolutionised the literary world of Europe.

Brothers of the Teutonic House of our Lady of Jerusalem (*The*). The 'Teutonic knights' (*q.v.*).

Brotherhood of St. George (*The*), 1472–1494. A short-lived fraternity of arms constituted by Act of Parliament in the reign of Edward IV., and consisting of 13 gentlemen chosen from the four counties of the Pale: for Kildare 4; for Dublin 3, one of which was the lord mayor of the time being; for Meath 4, one of which was the seneschal ; and for Louth 2, one of which was the mayor of Drogheda. They met annually to elect a captain on St. George's Day and maintained 120 mounted archers, 40 horsemen, and 40 pages, for the protection of the English border.

Brotherhood of St. Patrick
(*The*), about 1863. An Irish secret society, a branch of the Ribbon association (*q.v.*), their platform being similar to that of the Fenians. *See* 'Irish Associations.'

Brotherhood of Thomas à Becket (*The*), 1300. A merchants' company chartered in 1406 by Henry IV.

Brotherhood of the Cross (*The*). The Flagellants (*q.v.*) so called themselves. They wore a cross on their breast, another on their back, and a third on their hat; and took upon themselves to do penance for the sins of the people. All who joined the brotherhood had full forgiveness of sins for 33 days, a day for a year of Christ's sojourn upon earth.

Broughtonian (*A*). A boxer, so called from Broughton the beefeater, who was the best boxer of his day.

Brown Monarch of Ireland (*The*). Rotherick O'Conor, called don, dun, or dhu, king of Connaught (1116–1198).

Browne Scholarship, for classics. Value 21*l.*, tenable for seven years. Founded in the University of Cambridge, by Sir William Browne, M.D., 1774. *See* 'Regius Professor of Greek.'

Browne's Medals (*Sir William*). (1) For a Greek ode in imitation of Sappho ; (2) for a Latin ode in imitation of Horace ; (3) for a Greek and Latin epigram. Each medal to be gold, worth 5*l.* For undergraduates in the University of Cambridge. Founded by Sir William Browne, M.D., in 1774. *See* 'Regius Professor of Greek.'

Brownists, 1580. The followers of Robert Brown, educated at Corpus Christi College, Cambridge. He maintained that the Scriptures ought to be followed in all matters of discipline, as well as in matters of doctrine. That every congregation is a church, independent, and with power to settle its own discipline and government. Whence they were called 'Independents' and 'Congregationalists.'

The Brownists were rigid Separatists, the Robinsonians only semi-separatists. The Brownists, as ultra-puritans, looked on the Established Church as unchristian, and refused communion with it. Thacker and Copping, two Brownists, suffered death.

Bruno (*Giordano*), 1530–1600. He was burnt to death for what was called 'heresy,' but his heresy consisted in his belief that this earth of ours is not the only part of the universe inhabited by intelligent beings ; that the temporal power of the pope is an anomaly ; and that thought should be free. In 1889 the Italians, Germans, Swiss, and some others, erected a bronze statue to the 'martyr,' executed by Signor Ettori Ferrari. It stands on a granite pedestal, adorned with bas-reliefs. The ceremony of unveiling took place on Whitsun Day, 9 June ; a procession of above 3,000 took part in it, and 200 flags were carried. The statue stands in the Campo dei Fiori, on the spot where Bruno was burnt to death.

Brunswick (*Line of*). See 'Hanover &c.'

Brunswick Clubs and 'Brunswickers,' 1828. Clubs organised to counteract the Catholic Association (*q.v.*). Called Brunswick because George III. was most resolute against any concessions to the Roman Catholics. Frederick, duke of York, shared his father's hostility, and so did George IV. Members of these clubs were called 'Brunswickers.' The Duke of Newcastle, Lord Winchelsea, and Lord Kenyon led the way to the formation of Brunswick clubs in England.

The Catholic Association led to a counter-organisation of the Protestants, in the form of Brunswick clubs. This organisation embraced the whole of the Protestant peasantry (of Ireland), north and south, the Protestant farmers, and many of the gentry. They held their regular meetings . . . and had their 'rent' to bear the expense of the agitation.—HOWITT, *Hist. of England* (year 1828, p. 125).

Brunswick Manifesto (*The*), 25 July, 1792. A manifesto of the Duke of Brunswick, commander-in-chief of the united armies of Prussia and Austria, sent to put down the French revolution. The duke stated in this foolish and insulting document that he had been sent by the sovereigns of Europe 'to lay Paris in the dust, and to crush the republican vipers under his heel.' Brunswick was thoroughly beaten by the revolutionists.

Bryanites (3 syl.), 1815. The followers of William Bryan, a local preacher, who separated from the Methodist connection, and introduced a more popular element in his scheme of church government. Like the Methodists they are great open-air preachers, and receive the Lord's Supper sitting.

Bryce, or **Brice** (*St.*). Bishop of Tours; he succeeded St. Martin about 400, but was driven from his see by the mob, and took refuge in Rome. Subsequently he returned to Tours, where he died in 444. His day is 13 Nov.

Bryce's Day (*St.*), 13 Nov., 1002. Memorable for the massacre of the Danes in England. They had accepted heavy bribes time after time from Ethelred II. the Unready to quit the kingdom, but always returned again to commit further devastation. At length, by unwise policy (un-ready policy), it was resolved to massacre all the Danes in the kingdom. As might have been expected, this roused the vengeance of the Danes, and next year Sweyn appeared with a more formidable army to avenge his countrymen.

Bubble Act (*The*), 1719. 6 George I. c. 18; to punish the promoters of bubble schemes. Repealed 5 July, 1825.

Buccaneers, 1526–1697. In French 'Flibustiers.' An association of seamen whose object was to effect landings forcibly on the shores of the New World, locked against them by Spanish *guarda-costas*. Originally the English and the French united for the purpose, and were afterwards joined by the Portuguese and the Dutch. Thomas Tyson was the first to fit out a fleet which ravaged several of the West India Islands (1526); but the most renowned buccaneer was Henry Morgan, a Welshman. In the reign of William III. the French flibustiers were the sworn enemies of the British buccaneers; and at the treaty of Ryswick, in 1697, all these piratic expeditions were suppressed.

Bucentaur (*The*). The state barge of the Venetians. A flashy cumbersome 'Lord Mayor's Coach,' some 100 feet long and 21 broad, with 32 banks of oars, manned by 168 rowers. All the fittings were gorgeous in the extreme. It was employed every year when the doge 'married the Atlantic,' and also to conduct guests whom the republic delighted to honour to the doge's palace. *See* 'Espousal of the Adriatic.'

The barge was broken up by the French when Venice in 1797 fell into the hands of Bonaparte.

Buchanists, 1783. A Scotch sect, extinct in 1846. *See* 'Buchanites.'

Buchanites (3 syl.), 1776, &c. Followers of Mrs Buchan (*née* Elspeth Simpson, 1738–1791), a native of Banff. She was called by her disciples 'Our Lady,' and had rather a numerous following, who lived in common, were industrious, and paid their way. They neither married nor were given in marriage, and believed that they would be taken to heaven without dying. On her deathbed she told her disciples she would rise again within six days, ten years, or fifty years, according to the strength of their faith. Andrew Innes was her first disciple, and died at the age of ninety, a few days after the expiry of the 50th anniversary of Mrs. Buchan's death.

Bucharest (*Treaty of*), 28 May, 1812. Between Russia and Turkey, signed while Napoleon with his grand army was in Russia, and meditating a descent on Moscow.

Buckeye State (*The*). The State of Ohio is so called because the buckeye tree (*æsculus flava*) abounds there.

Buckingham House, London. So called from John Sheffield, duke of Buckingham, who built it in 1703. Bought by government for Queen Charlotte, in 1761. It was taken down in 1825, and the present palace raised on the site in the same year, but enlarged by Queen Victoria in 1853.

Buckingham's Flood, Oct. 1483. The Duke of Buckingham, having ratted from Richard III. to the Duke of Richmond's party, set out to join his forces with the other leaders; but there fell such heavy and continuous rains during his whole march from Brecon through the Forest of Dean to the Severn, that the bridges were carried away, and all the fords were rendered impassable. Such rains and floods had not been known in the memory of man; and the inundation of the Severn was called 'Buckingham's Flood.'

Buddhist St. Augustine (*The*) of Japan. Shodo Shonin, who, in 767, erected the Buddhist temple of Nikko.

Buffon. The supplemental works of Buffon's 'Natural History' are—

Daubenton (1716-1800), the anatomy of animals.
Lacépède (1757-1825), oviparous animals, serpents, whales and fishes. Published 1789.
Gueneau de Montbeillard (1720-1785), birds.
Sonnini (1751-1811), foreign birds. He published an edition of Buffon in 127 vols.
Daudin (1774-1804), reptiles.
Latreille (1762-1833), insects.

Bug Bible (*The*), 1551. Matthew's bible is so called because verse 5 Psalm xci., 'Thou shalt not be afraid of the terror by night,' is there translated 'Thou shalt not be afraid of the bugges by night.' *See* 'Bibles.'

Building Act Committee (*The Metropolitan*). Responsible for the carrying out of the different acts regulating the height of buildings in the metropolis, the materials used in their construction, the thickness of the party walls, and (in cases of theatres and other places of public entertainment) the facilities afforded for ingress and egress.

For these purposes London is divided into 74 districts, each under the charge of a district surveyor appointed by the board, but paid by fees.

Building Bess of Hardwick. She was thrice married. She built a former Chatsworth, the existing Hardwick Hall, and added 'a great parlour,' and the chapel of Sutton Court, in Somersetshire.

Bulgarians (*The*). The Cathäri (*q.v.*) were so called sometimes from their connection with the Bulgarian Paulicians.

Bull Run. *See* Appendix.

Bull against Luther (*The*). By Leo X., 1521. 'In the name of the Father, and of the Son, and of the Holy Ghost, the Blessed Virgin, St. Peter and St. Paul, we do curse him and those who are led astray by him; and we cut off both him and them from all communion of the saints. Cursed be they in prayer, cursed in speech and in silence, in eating and in sleep, in taste, in hearing, and in all the other senses. Cursed in the eyes, the head, and the whole body, from the crown of the head to the sole of the foot. I conjure Satan and his imps to torture them both day and night, till they perish by water, by fire, or the cord.' As this bull was read in the churches, the officiating priest, after the lights had been extinguished, said aloud, 'As I blow out these lights, may the light of life be for ever hidden from their eyes. So be it. Amen and amen.'

See a similar bull in 'Notes and Queries,' 21 Jan. 1832, p. 44.

Bull of Pius V. (*The*), 27 April, 1570 Commanding all the faithful to break with the Anglican Church, to abandon and dethrone Elizabeth, and to subject England to a foreign invader. *See* 'Cœna Domini.'

The words ran thus : ' Declaramus Elizabetham hæreticam . . . eique adhærentes . . . anathematis sententiam incurrisse esseque a Christi corporis unitate præcisos . . . prout nos illos præsentium autoritate absolvimus, et privamus eamdem Elizabetham prætenso jure regni aliisque omnibus supradictis. Præcipimusque et interdicimus universis et singulis proceribus, subditis, populis, et aliis prædictis, ne illi, ejusve monitis, mandatis, et legibus, audeant obedire. Qui secus egerint, eos simili anathematis sententiâ innodamus.
.·. In 1576 Gregory XIII. supplemented the bull of his predecessor by declaring that Elizabeth had forfeited the crown of Ireland.

Bulla Aurea of Hungary, 1222. The Magna Charta of that kingdom, exacted from Andrew II., a feeble, self-willed, worthless king, not unlike our King John.

Bulla Cœnæ Domini. A bull of excommunication and anathema against heretics, read before the people on Holy Thursday. Those offences which are condemned by this bull can be absolved only by the pope.

Buller of Brasenose. John Hughes is so called in Wilson's ' Noctes Ambrosianæ.' Hughes, however, was not of Brasenose, but Oriel College, Oxford.

Bullies. F. J. Gall noticed that all bull-eyed boys are overbearing and quarrelsome. By bull-eyes he meant full prominent eyes. As an historical pun this connects bull-eyes with our word ' bullies,' but whether the connection is of any philological worth is quite another matter. *See* ' Nab.'

Bulwer Clayton Treaty (*The*), 1850. Between Great Britain and the United States of North America, respecting the ship-canal between the Atlantic and Pacific Oceans. Signed at Washington. This treaty bears upon the canal through Lake Nicaragua.

Bund (*The*) of Germany. A confederation of the thirty-five sovereign states, which had every variety of government. from absolutism to democracy, all independent. It was represented by a Diet, *q.v.*

Bundesrath (*The*), 1871. The delegates of the confederated governments of the German empire.

The twenty-five states confederated with Prussia are Alsace-Lorraine (taken from France), Anhalt, Baden, Bavaria, Bremen, Brunswick, Hamburg, Hesse, Lippe, Lübeck, Mecklenburg-Schwerin, Mecklenburg-Strelitz, Oldenburg, Reuss (elder branch), Reuss (younger branch), Saxe-Altenburg, Saxe-Coburg and Gotha, Saxe-Meiningen, Saxony, Schaumburg-Lippe, Schwartzburg-Sondershausen, Schwartzburg-Rudolstadt, Waldeck, Würtemburg.

Bills which have passed the Reichstag and Bundesrath, after being signed by the emperor, are binding on all the empire.

Bungtown Coppers (*American*). Counterfeit English ha'pennies manufactured at Bungtown (now Barneysville), Mass. (Bartlett, 'Dictionary of Americanisms,' 1877).

Buoy (*The Mystery of the*), 14 Sept., 1854. When the combined French and English army resolved to land on the Crimea, the spot selected was the 'Old Fort Bay,' *i.e.* the southern bay; and to prevent confusion a buoy was to be placed in the centre of the bay. The French were to debark on the left of this buoy, and the English on the right. During the night, three French officers placed coloured buoys as the limits for the French landing, taking up the whole south bay, and leaving Admiral Lyons to improvise a new arrangement as a landing place for the English. This was a dodge that the French might be the first to land.

Burchardicum, Burchardic. Beyond dispute. Burchard, who died 1026, bishop of Worms, compiled a huge volume which long enjoyed unbounded repute. It was a 'compte rendu' of edicts and decretals, so admirably set forth that an appeal to his book was considered final. Hence 'Burchardicum' came to mean a dictum beyond dispute.

Burchardicum has not an English timbre, but Burchardism, Burchardic, Burchardise, might be admitted and prove useful.

Burchell (*Old*). The pen-name of Elihu Burritt, the 'learned blacksmith,' an American linguist and author (1810-1879).

Burdett Riot (*The*), 1810. This arose out of the arrest of Gale Jones, president of a debating society called the 'British Forum.' The question of debate was, 'Which was the greater outrage upon public feeling: Mr. Yorke's enforcement of the standing order, or Mr. Windham's attack on the liberty of the press on the same occasion?' Sir Francis Burdett moved in the house that Gale Jones should be discharged, as the 'British Forum' was a private debating society; and Cobbett, in his 'Weekly Register,' took Burdett's side of the question. Sir Francis, in a letter published by Cobbett, spoke contemptuously of the House of Commons, and Mr. Lethbridge moved that he should be committed to the Tower. This led to a riot, in which the soldiers were called out, and two men were shot dead. The question now was whether the soldier who killed one of the men should not be tried for murder. Ultimately the contention drifted into this question; Is not the House of Commons so one-sided that it needs a radical reform?

Burdett-Coutts Scholarships. Two for geology in the University of Oxford, each tenable for two years. Founded by the Baroness Burdett-Coutts, 1860.

Bureau. Not unlike our board of Green Cloth in the history of the name. A bureau meant originally a coarse woollen cloth. Hence Boileau says of Damon, the author, 'n'étant vêtu que de simple bureau, passe l'été sans linge, et l'hiver sans manteau.' It then came to mean the cloth on the board table, then the officials who sit at the board.

Bureau d'Esprit. Literary reunions, such as those held in the Hôtel Rambouillet, in the hotel of the Duchesse du Maine, of Madame de Tencin, of Mesdames du Châtelet and du Boccage, of Deffand and Geoffrin, of Madame Doublet, &c.

In the reign of Louis XV. the three 'bureaux d'esprit' were presided over by Madame de Deffand, Mademoiselle de Lespinasse, and Madame Geoffrin. The first embraced the élite of the literati; the second, the leading political reformers; and the last, professed sceptics. Madame Deffand was noted for her caustic wit; Mademoiselle de Lespinasse for the charms of her conversational power; and Madame Geoffrin for her practical benevolence.

Burgess Oath (*The*), administered in royal boroughs of Scotland, ran thus: 'I protest before God and your lordships that I profess and allow with my heart the true religion now at this present professed within this realm, and authorised by the laws thereof. I will abide in the same and defend it to my life's end, renouncing the Roman religion called popery.' Those who saw no inconsistency in taking this oath were called burghers, those who refused to take it were called anti-burghers.

K

Burgess Roll (*The*), 1832. An alphabetical list of the burgesses entitled to vote for municipal officers or borough members, made out by the respective town clerks. There was also for a time another list called the Freeman's Roll (*q.v.*), but this list is no longer required (5, 6 Will. IV. c. 76, amended by 20, 21 Vict. c. 50).

Burgesses of the Palisades Aliens who sought the sanctuary of fortified towns in the middle ages, especially in Germany, where they were called 'Palburgers.' These aliens were allowed to dwell in the suburbs between the city walls and the palisades which bounded the territory of the corporation. Hence the name. *See* 'Outburgers.'

It must be remembered that there was a constant collision between the feudal barons and the corporate towns; and therefore offenders of the one sought refuge with the other, and it was a point of honour or policy not to give up the refugee.

Burgh Schools, 1696. Founded by the General Education Act in Scotland. They were of the same character as English grammar schools; of a higher grade than the parochial schools, founded by the same Act, and existing in burghs or towns, managed by the town councils, and supported by grants from the 'Common Good,' *i.e.* the public funds of the burgh.

Burghers and Anti-Burghers, 1745. Seceders from the Kirk of Scotland. The burghers are those who saw no inconsistency in taking the 'Burgess Oath' (*q.v.*). Those who refused to take it were anti-burghers.

The two parties were united in 1820, and called the 'United Presbyterians.'

Burgundian Code (*The*), or 'Loi Gombette,' published in 502 by Gundibald, at Lyons. *See* 'Gombette.'

Burgundians *The*). The followers of the Duke of Burgundy, in the early part of the 15th century, opposed to the faction of the united Orleanists and Armagnacs (*q.v.*). Headed by Jean Sans Peur, duke of Burgundy. He got the Duke of Orleans assassinated at Paris 23 Nov., 1407, and became reconciled with the Orleans family in 1409; but after the marriage of the young Duke of Orleans with the daughter of the Count of Armagnac in 1411, the feud broke out again: the Orleanists and Armagnacs against the Burgundians. The Duke of Burgundy in 1417 led an army to Paris, liberated the queen at Tours, and was by her named governor of the kingdom 10 Jan., 1418; but in 1419 he was assassinated at the bridge of Montereau.

Burkers' Hole. Formerly called 'Nova Scotia Gardens,' a part of Bethnal Green now occupied by St. Thomas's Church and Baroness Burdett Coutts's model lodging-houses. It was the residence of May, Bishop, and Williams, the infamous 'burkers,' who procured subjects for dissection by secret assassination. They were convicted of the murder of a poor friendless Italian boy in 1826. Burke (who gave his name to the words *to burke, burker,* &c.) used to place a pitch plaster over the mouth of his victim to smother his cries. He was an Irishman, and was hanged in 1829.

Burmese Wars (*The*). I. 1826. Arakan and Tenasserim were acquired by the treaty of Yandabo, and annexed to our province of Lower Bengal. II. 1851–1853. Martaban stormed 5 April, 1852; Rangoon stormed 14 April, 1852; Pegu taken 4 June, 1852, and annexed to our province; Prome taken 9 July, 1852. III. Upper Burmah was annexed to our Indian empire 26 Feb., 1886. The population of this province is about 3,500,000, and the territory (including the Shan States) about 200,000 square miles.

Burnbill. Henry de Londres, archbishop of Dublin, in the reign of Henry III. He fraudulently procured the archiepiscopal estates, and burnt all the deeds by which the lands were held.

Burlington Fine Arts Club (*The*). London, established 1867.

Burnett Prizes (*The*). Allotted every forty years to the authors of the two best essays on the 'Evidence that there is a Being all-powerful, wise, and good, by whom everything exists, &c.' First award, 1815, to Dr. William Lawrence Brown 1200*l*., and the Rev. J. B. Sumner (archbishop of Canterbury) 400*l*.; the next award, 1855, was to the Rev. R. A. Thompson, 1800*l*., and Dr. J. Tulloch 600*l*. The third award should be in 1895. Founded by Mr. Burnett of Dens, Aberdeenshire. The judges are three.

Burney Collection (*The*), 1818. In the MS. department of the British Museum. Collected by the Rev. Dr. Charles Burney, and consisting of 520 volumes, chiefly Greek and Roman classics. Amongst these is the Townley 'Homer,' a MS. of the 'Iliad' similar to the 'Odyssey' in the Harleian collection; a Greek MS. of Ptolemy's 'Geography,' adorned with maps of the 15th cent., &c.

Burney Prize (*The*). For an essay on some moral or metaphysical subject on the existence, nature, and attributes of God. For graduates of the University of Cambridge of not more than three years standing, value 105*l.* annually. Founded by Richard Burney of Christ's College, Cambridge, 1845. *See* 'Mathematics,' &c.

Burning and Starving Act (*The*). The Commutation Act passed by William Pitt, greatly reducing the duties on excisable articles, enabling the lawful dealer to compete with smugglers. These smugglers in Galloway and Dumfriesshire, being ruined by the Act, called it the Burning and Starving Act.

Burnt Candlemas (*Day*), 2 Feb., 1356. The day when Edward III. marched through the Lothians with fire and sword. He burnt to the ground Edinburgh and Haddington, and then retreated for want of provisions. The Scots call the day 'Burnt Candlemas.'

Burnt Pillar (*The*), or 'Tchernberle Tash.' A column in the centre of the forum of Constantinople. It was raised by Constantine on a pedestal of white marble twenty feet high. The pillar was composed of ten pieces of porphyry, each eleven feet in height and thirty-three in circumference. It was surmounted with a colossal statue of Apollo in bronze, said to have been the work of Phidias. This statue was thrown down in the reign of Alexis Comnenus.

Burschenschaft, 1813. A secret society of Germany, established by the students for the defence of the country. The Grand Burschenschaft of Jena, in Saxe-Weimar, was established 12 June, 1815, and soon absorbed all the others. In 1818 the government declared the association to be illegal, and it gradually dropped off.

Burschen. pl. of 'Bursch,' a student, and 'schaft, an association.

Burton Arch (*The*). The marble arch formerly at Hyde Park Corner, in imitation of the arch of Titus at Rome, on the top of which was placed, in 1846, a huge equestrian statue of the Duke of Wellington, the work of Mr. C. Wyatt. This hideous deformity was removed in 1883.

> 'Hail to the statue!' people cry—
> In justice there they fail;
> But let it have the Burton arch,
> If we've the Burton ale.
> *Newspaper Epigram,* 1846.

Butcher (*The*). I. Dante, in his 'Purgatory' (canto xx.), makes Hugh Capet say, 'I was the son of a butcher of Paris.' Pasquier told François I. that Dante meant by 'butcher' a formidable warrior.

II. Olivier de Clisson, constable of France (1320–1407), who never spared the life of any Englishman who fell into his hands.

III. John de Clifford, called the 'Black Clifford,' the ninth baron, died 1461.

IV. Ahmed Jezzar, pacha of Acre, which he defended against Napoleon. He struck off the heads of his nine wives at one and the same time (1735, 1775–1804).

Butcher (*The Bloody*). William Augustus, duke of Cumberland (1721–1765), son of George II., so called for his cruel treatment of the Jacobites, whom he defeated at Culloden, 16 April, 1746. Also called the 'Butcher of Culloden.'

He (Cumberland) seemed to revel in blood, and to be ambitious of earning the name he there (at Culloden) won of THE BUTCHER. ... When the wounded had writhed in their agonies all night they were despatched by the bayonets of the Butchers. They were hunted out of their hiding-places in the woods and moors, and massacred in cold blood. Twenty wounded men, who had crept into a farmhouse, were shut up and deliberately burnt in it. The prisoners in Inverness were treated with equal cruelty.—HOWITT, *Hist. of England,* (George II. ch. xi. p. 525).

Butcher of England (*The*). John Tiptoft, earl of Worcester, lord deputy, who died 1470. On one occasion, in the reign of Edward IV., he ordered Clapham (one of Lord Warwick's squires) and nineteen other gentlemen to be impaled. This bloodstained leader of the Wars of the Roses was a great patron of Caxton, and one of the earliest scholars of the revival of letters.

Butcher of Vassy (*The*). François, duc de Guise (1519–1563), was so called by the Huguenots. *See* 'Massacre of Vassy.'

Butchers and Carpenters' Insurrection, 1413. This was the great

K 2

nsurrection of the White Hoods and White Scarfs. The Butchers or White Hoods were the Burgundian faction; the Carpenters or White Scarfs were the Orleans or Armagnac faction. The Carpenters or White Scarfs prevailed, and after the bloody fray in the Place de Grève, the White Hoods were driven out of Paris, and disappeared.

Butcher's Dog (*The*). Cardinal Thomas Wolsey, son of a butcher of Ipswich (1471–1530). After he brought Edward Stafford, duke of Buckingham, to the block in 1521, it was wittily said of him, 'The butcher's dog has pulled down the fairest buck in Christendom.'

Many efforts have been made to give Wolsey a more aristocratic birth. One is this: that he was a bourgeois' son, and that *bourgeois* was corrupted into *butcher*; but there would be no point then in the witticism above referred to. Another is this: that the Emperor Charles V. called Henry VIII. the *butcher* and Wolsey was the 'butcher's dog'; but Henry was by no means a butcher when a young man, and at the death of Buckingham he was under thirty, and called 'a gentle, merciful, and pleasure-loving prince.' Buckingham was executed in the 12th year of Henry's reign; and Wolsey must have been known before then as a *butcher's son*, or there would have been no wit in the remark. Skelton, a contemporary, speaking of Wolsey, says he 'was cast out of a butcher's stall,' and William Roy, another contemporary, calls him 'the vile butcher's sonne.'

Begot by butchers, but by bishops bred;
How high his honour holds his haughty head!

Butcher's Shambles (*The*). An old oak tree in Birkland, a part of Sherwood Forest. It is now a mere shell, but in this tree a butcher named Hooton used to conceal the carcases of sheep or deer till he could dispose of them. There used to be a beam across the tree with hooks, on which three sheep could be suspended. Old men can still (1890) remember this arrangement. In the hollow of this tree fourteen or fifteen persons could stand, and its girth at the height of a man was certainly thirty feet or more; but now half even of the rind is gone, and the other half is a mere shell.

Buttermere (*Mary of*). Daughter of an innkeeper, called the 'Beauty of Buttermere,' married a man who came to the vicinity for fishing, and passed himself off as the Hon. Augustus Hope. It turned out he was a married man, whose name was Hadfield, a notorious swindler, who was ultimately executed for forgery. At the beginning of the 19th cent. this romantic tale caused a very great sensation. It is said that Mary afterwards married a substantial farmer.

Buttoners (*The*). A branch of the Strict Mennonites (3 syl.), which split from the general body in 1554, and were so called because they used buttons in their dress instead of hooks-and-eyes. *See* 'Mennonites.'

Buttons. In China there are nine official buttons worn in the cap, each one denoting a special rank. 1. the plain red; 2. the red figured with the character SHOU (longevity); 3. the clear blue; 4. the opaque blue; 5. the crystal; 6. the opaque white; 7, 8, 9. buttons of brass.

By this conquer, A.D. 312. The inscription said to have been annexed to the cross seen in the sky by Constantine when about to encounter Maxentius. According to tradition it was the cause of his conversion to Christianity.

Of course the words were Greek, Ἐν τούτῳ νίκα.

Bye Conspiracy (*The*), 1603. A conspiracy of Roman Catholics, Puritans, and Presbyterians, who thought that James I. would favour their own special religious party, but found that he threw himself entirely into the hands of the High Church of England party. Clarke and Watson, two Catholic priests, were the heads of the conspiracy. Their plan was to seize the king, proclaim Arabella Stuart queen, and to place the government in the hands of the chief conspirators. Lord Cecil was to be put to death, and Watson to be made lord chancellor. The plot was revealed to Cecil, the leading conspirators were tried for treason, and Watson, Clarke, and Brooke were executed. The conspiracy was called the 'Bye' because it was simultaneous with another conspiracy called the 'Main' (*q.v.*).

Byng (*To*), or 'make the Byng of the day,' to sacrifice one as a scapegoat. The reference is to Admiral John Byng, who was shot at Portsmouth by sentence of court martial, 14 March, 1757. He was sent to relieve Minorca, besieged by the French, and after a partial action sheered off, declaring that the ministry had not supplied him with a sufficient fleet. The ministry and the public were furious, and Byng was brought before a court martial.

Precisely the same thing occurred in the Crimean war. The ministry and officers were blamed for not taking Sebastopol sooner, and the Duke of Newcastle, minister of war, was made the 'Byng' or scapegoat of the day.

Byzantine Historians (*The*). Greek historians who lived under the Eastern empire between the 6th and 15th cents. They consist, 1. of historians who continue the history of the Byzantine empire; 2. of general chroniclers; and 3. of authors who wrote on the antiquities, politics, manners and customs of the Romans. The whole of the works were compiled and published by order of Louis XIV., and ran to thirty-six volumes folio (1644–1711).

The most noted are Zonaras, Nicetas Acominatus Chon'atês, and Nicephorus Gregoras, who form a complete *corpus historiæ* to the close of the 15th cent. Then comes Laonicus Chalcondylas, and then follow a host who wrote detached parts of history.

Ca'aba, or 'Kaaba.' A stone which Mahomet removed to Mecca, where it was inserted in the walls of the sacred shrine built by Abraham and Ishmael. The angel Gabriel presented Mahomet with this stone, which was originally a petrified angel, and quite white. It is now black from the kisses of sinners.

The site of this shrine is where repentant Adam stood, after wandering for 200 years, when he received pardon for his disobedience in Paradise.

Cabal' Ministry (*The*), 1667–1674. A ministry under Charles II., so called because the initial letters of the cabinet happened to form the word *cabal* : they were Clifford, Ashley, Buckingham, Arlington, and Lauderdale.

The French 'cabale' means a party who seek to gain their object by underhand or unscrupulous means, and the Spanish 'cabala' means intrigue. The word was not therefore first coined from Clifford's ministry, although it was not used in the English language before. Dryden uses the word.

Thomas Clifford (first commissioner of the treasury, afterwards Lord Clifford).
Lord Ashley (chancellor of the exchequer, afterwards Earl of Shaftesbury).
Duke of Buckingham (master of the horse), Earl of Arlington (secretary of state). Duke of Lauderdale.

Caballarii. Feudal tenants bound to serve on horseback, equipped with coat of mail. This service implied no personal merit and gave no civil privileges. It was a mere duty or knight's fee.

Cabbala. Jewish tradition said to have been handed down from Moses.

The first book, on cosmogony, is attributed to the 7th cent. ; but from the 12th to the 15th cent. numerous cabbalistic writings were added, teaching the esoteric meaning of 'the Law,' the method of performing miracles, incantations, &c.

The 'Sohar' (13th cent.) in Aramaic may be called the bible of the Cabbalists.

Cabinet Council. Lord Clarendon says the term originated thus : In the reign of Charles I. the affairs of state were controlled by the Archbishop of Canterbury, the Earl of Strafford, and the Lord Cottington; to these were added 'for ornament' the Earl of Northumberland, the Bishop of London as lord treasurer, and Vane and Windebank (two secretaries) for service and intelligence. The Marquis of Hamilton 'meddled just so far and no further than he had a mind.' These persons made up the committee of state, reproachfully called the *junto*, but 'enviously' called afterwards the 'cabinet council.' In cabinet councils the royal presence is not necessary, as it is in 'privy councils.' When George I. was king, as he was ignorant of the English language, he took no part in state councils; and ever since cabinet councils have dispensed with the sovereign's presence.

Cabinet Noir (*The*). The secret offices where all the correspondence of the French nation used to be handled during the monarchy.

Cabi'ri. Ancient Pelasgian deities.

Cabochienne (*La*), 1413. An ordinance for the reform of the state forced from the Dauphin of France by the White Hoods or Cabochians (*q.v.*).

Cabochiens (*Les*), 1413–1422. A gang organised by Jean Sans Peur, duke of Burgundy, and placed under the command of Simonet Caboche, a butcher. It numbered 500 vagabonds, and kept Paris in terror by its massacres and plunder. In 1422 the Parisians rose *en masse*, fell upon the gang, Jean Sans Peur fled from the city, and the Armagnacs or Orleans faction remained in the ascendent. *See* 'French Brigands.'

Cacciatori. The Chasseurs of the Alps, or 'Cacciatori delle Alpi.' (Italian, *cacciare* to hunt, *cacciatore* a hunter).

We have already referred to Garibaldi as general of the Cacciatori.—HOWITT, *Hist. of England*, year 1859, p. 552.

Caddée or **Cadée** (*The*), or ' League of God's House,' 1400–1419. *See* ' Cadeian, &c.'

Cade (*Jack*). Ringleader of the insurrection which broke out in Kent, 1450. He was an Irishman, and called himself Mortimer, because he was a natural son of the Duke of York. He marched to London at the head of 20,000 armed men, who encamped at Blackheath, 1 June, 1450. Being slain by Alexander Iden, 11 July, his head was stuck on London Bridge.

Cade's Insurrection. *See* above.

Cadeian League (*The*), 1400–1419, *i.e.* the league of *Casa-dei*, or God's house; in German, Gotteshausbünd. One of the three unions of the canton of the Grisons.

The other two leagues were the 'Ligue Grise,' formed in 1424; and the 'League of the Ten Jurisdictions,' formed in 1436. All three were admitted into the Helvetic Confederation in 1798.

Cadets of the Cross, 1703. Catholic auxiliaries in the army of Marshal Montrevel, sent to extirpate the Camisards of the Cevennes. Also called ' White Camisards.'

Cadjahs. *See* ' Dynasty of the Kadjahs,' or Kujurs.

Cadmean Letters. Sixteen Greek letters said to have been introduced into Thebes (in Bœotia) by Cadmus, son of Agēnor, king of Phœnicia. The letters are a, b, g, d, ĕ, i, k, l, m, n, ŏ, p, r, s, t, u. These letters were subsequently increased by 8 Ionic letters, z, ē, th, x, ph, ch, ps, and ō. Simonĭdēs of Cos is credited with the 4 letters th, z, ph, ch, and Epicharmos the Sicilian with the 4 letters x, ē, ps, ō. The Ionians were the first to employ all the 24 letters, whence the 8 added were called Ionic letters.

Cadmean Victory (*A*). A victory purchased with great loss. The reference is to the armed men who sprang out of the ground from the teeth of the dragon sown by Cadmus. These men fell foul of each other, and only five escaped with their lives. Hence the Greek ' Kadmeia nikê,' and Latin ' Cadmēa Victoria.' The victories of Boadicea sowed her kingdom with dragon's teeth, and the Romans were roused by them to most vindictive fury

Cærite Franchise (*The*). The franchise of a Roman subject in a pre-

fecture. These subjects had the right of self-government, were registered by the Roman censor as taxpayers, but enjoyed none of the privileges of a Roman citizen. Cærê was the first community placed in this dependent position, whence the term *cærite* franchise.

Cæsar, as a title, varied in its force. I. The first twelve emperors were all entitled Cæsar in compliment to Julius Cæsar. Thus Octavius or Octavianus Cæsar (better known as Augustus); Tiberius Cæsar; Caligula Cæsar; Claudius Cæsar; Nero Cæsar; Galba, Otho, Vitellius, whose united reigns lasted only one year; Vespasian Cæsar; Titus Cæsar; and Domitian Cæsar.

II. After the death of Domitian, A.D. 96, the word as a title dropped out of use till the reign of Hadrian (14th emp. 117–138), who called the heir presumptive *Cæsar*.

III. In the reign of Diocletian, A.D. 292, the two emperors of Constantinople and Rome were each styled *Augustus*, and the two viceroys of Illyricum and Gaul were each styled *Cæsar*. This arrangement, however, soon dropped after the death of that emperor.

The wife of a Roman emperor was entitled *Cæsara*, and probably all imperial princes were by courtesy addressed as *Cæsar*. Czar and Kaiser are modified forms of Cæsar.

Cæsarean Era of Antioch (*The*). This era began 1 Sept., B.C. 48, to commemorate the victory of Julius Cæsar over Pompey.

Cage (*The*). The little hut built of sticks, heather, and moss, in a thicket of trees on the rocky face of a high mountain, called Letternilinchk, in Benalder, to which Charles Edward was taken for concealment by Lochiel and Macpherson, after the fatal battle of Culloden (1746).

Cameron had been one of those who assisted Charles Edward to escape, and had lived with him in the ' Cage.'—HOWITT, *Hist. of England*, (George II. ch. xii. p. 549).

Cagliari. Generally called Paul Veronese (1530–1588).

Cagliostro of Literature (*The*), 1835. Comte de Courchamps, the most unblushing literary thief on record. He stole the two novels of John Potocki, a Polish count, and published them as his own. The ' National ' exposed the theft, and ferreted out all the falsehoods of De Courchamps, establishing his infamous piracy beyond a shadow of doubt. Comte de Courchamps called his book 'The Inedited Memoirs of Cagliostro,' and hence the quack of literary quacks was stigmatised with the name of the quack of quacks. See 'Literary Forgeries.'

Joseph Balsamo, the prince of quacks, assumed the title-name of Comte de Cagliostro (1743-1795).

Cagots. A tribe of men in France akin to the gipsies. Some think the word is compounded of *Caas-goths* (dogs of Goths), and that they are remnants of the Teutons who overran the south of Europe at the fall of the Roman Empire. Others quote the synonyms *Caqueux, Cacous, Capos,* and *Gaffos,* meaning 'lepers,' to prove that they were Jewish lepers. They are often called 'Canards,' because they were obliged to carry as a badge 'une patte de canard.'

It is in Brittany that they are called *Caqueux.* In Poitou, Maine, and Anjou they are called 'Colliberts.' In Auvergne, 'Marrons.'

Cainites (*The*), 2nd cent. A Christian sect which held that the books of the Old Testament were inspired by the Demiurge, or son of darkness and chaos; and that the real worthies were Cain, Esau, the men of Sodom, Korah, and so on; and the only spiritual apostle was Judas Iscariot, who betrayed Christ lest he should lead men into darkness. These 'heretics' say Judas Iscariot left a gospel, which is the only true one.

Ça Ira (It will succeed). The 'Carillon National' of the French Revolution. The refrain is:

Ah ! ça ira, ça ira, ça ira !
Les aristocrates à la lanterne !

Cairns' Act (*Lord*), 1882. Called 'Cairns' Settled Lands Act,' to allow the sale of entailed estates, but not the 'family mansion.'

Caius College (generally called Keys), in Cambridge University. Originally called Gonville Hall (*q.v.*); changed in 1353 by William Bateman, bishop of Norwich, into 'The Hall of the Annunciation, &c.'; and in 1558 by the third founder, John Caius, M.D., into 'Gonville and Caius College.'

Calasirians and **Hermotybians.** The Egyptian military, an hereditary caste spoken of by Herodotos (ii. 166). He numbers the former at 250,000 men, and the latter at 160,000. Their settlements were in Lower Egypt, the Calasi-

rians in eleven nomes and the Hermotybians in five. Herodotos speaks of linen tunics fringed about the legs, οὕς καλέουσι καλασίρις (Coptic *kali*, a leg). The derivation of the other word is extremely doubtful.

Cala'thumpian (*A*). A nothingarian, or anythingarian, or what you please in regard to the question 'What religion are you of ?' From *calathus,* a waste basket for all sorts of odds and ends.

Calatrava (*Knights of*), 1158. A Spanish military order founded by Sancho III. of Castile, when he took from the Moors the strong fort of Calatrava. The mantle is white, decorated with a red cross cut out in the form of lilies.

Calcuith, in Lancashire (*The Council of*), 785-787. I. By this council a third archbishopric of England was made, viz. Lichfield, and Higbert was appointed primate. The authority and decisions of the first six general councils were also adopted. In 803 Lichfield was again reduced to its original rank of bishopric.

II. A.D. 816, decided that the saint, in honour of whom a church was dedicated, might be pictured on the walls; that no Scotch clergyman shall officiate in an English church, because they refused to admit the primacy of the bishop of Rome; that no private monastic institution shall be allowed; and that baptism shall be by immersion, and not by sprinkling.

Caleb d'Anvers. The pen-name of Nicholas Amhurst, a noted political writer who conducted a paper called the 'Craftsman,' and died in 1742 in most miserable circumstances.

Caledonia. A name given by the Romans to that part of Scotland lying between the Forth and the Clyde; so-called from the tribe of the Caledonii. The name disappears in the 4th cent., and the people of Scotland began to be called Picts (to the east) and Scots (to the west). In more modern times Caledonia is a poetical name for Scotland.

What the Romans called Caledonii were the Celyddones, *i.e.* dwellers in the woods.

Caledonia. The Irish race of kings in Caledonia are said to have been—

Eder	...	...	...	...	B.C. 55-71
Evenus ...	...	...	...	B.C. 71 to A.D. 1
Metellan	...	...	...	...	1-35
Caractacus	...	...	...	...	35-57
Colbrede I.	...	...	...	...	57-74
Dardanes	...	...	...	...	74-78
Colbrede II., with Galgacus	...	...	...	78-84

(Agricola was prætor and defeated Galgacus	A.D. 84)
Colbrede alone	113
Lugtace...	113-118
Mogal ...	118-160
Conar ...	160-162
Argade ...	162-166
Ethode I.	166-199
Satrahal	199-203
(Marcellus was prætor)	
Donald I.	203-224
Erode II.	224-240
Atirgo ...	240-252
Natholic ...	252-263
Findoc ...	263-273
Donald II.	273-274
Donald III.	274-284
Cratlini .	284 303
Fincormac	303 355
Romac ...	355-358
Augusian	358-360
Fetelmac	360-363
Eugene I.	363-395
Fergus (the restorer)	440
Eugene II.	440-461
Dongard	461-465
Constantine I. king of Scotland.	

Caledonian War (*The*), A.D. 208·
When the Roman emperor Sevērus was
sixty years old, he went with his two sons,
Caracalla and Geta, into Scotland to repel
an invasion. He marched to the northern
extremity without meeting an enemy, but
it cost him the loss of 50,000 men. At
length the Caledonians sued for peace,
but the moment the Roman legions were
withdrawn they were up in arms again.
While Sevērus was preparing to extirpate
the Caledonians, he died.

If Ossian is historic, it was Fingal who opposed
Severus, and Caracalla is called by Ossian 'Caracul,
son of the king of the world ' (Poems, i. p. 175).
Strange that Ossian should call Antonīnus by a
nickname not used even in Rome till four years
after the war !

Calendar. The French Republican
calendar was the work of Fabre d'Eglantine and M. Romme.

Autumn months: Vendémiaire, Brumaire, Frimaire.
Winter months: Nivôse, Pluviôse, Ventôse.
Spring months: Germinal, Floréal, Prairial.
Summer months: Messidor, Thermidor, Fructidor.
　1. *Wheezy, Sneezy, Freezy.*
　2. *Slippy, Drippy, Nippy.*
　3. *Showery, Flowery, Bowery.*
　4. *Wheaty, Heaty, Sweety.*

Calenders, 13th cent. The 'Purists,'
a species of Moslem hermits, founded by
Youssouf, an Arab of Andalusĭa. They
have no fixed abode, but lead a vagrant
life under the vow of poverty. They
have proved themselves dangerous
sectaries, who have always taken an
active part in all Oriental revolutions.
See 'Santons.'

Calends. *See* 'Dict of Phrase and
Fable,' p. 132.

Ausonian Calends (Ausoniæ Calendæ),
the Roman Calends.

Greek Calends (Græcæ Calendæ), never;
there were no Greek Calends.

Intercalary Calends (Intercalares
Calendæ), February.

Calends of Janus (Jani Calendæ), New
Year's day (Statius).

The Women's Calends (Fœmineæ Calendæ), the 1st of March (Juvenal, ix. 53)

Tristes Calendæ, pay-day. The
Romans paid on the 1st of every month.

Calif. The successor of Mohammed
the prophet, both in temporal and spiritual power. At first there was but one
calif, whose empire was called the califate,
which for three centuries exceeded the
Roman empire in extent; but in 970
there were three califates, viz. one at
Bagdad, one at Cairo, and one at Cordŏva.

In 1031 the califate of Cordŏva ceased.

In 1158 the calif of Bagdad fled to
Egypt before the sword of the Mongols.

In 1517 the Turks conquered Egypt,
and the sultan thus became the one and
only calif.

In 800 Tunis and Fez made themselves independent for a time, and in 821 Taher established for a
time an independent califate at Khorassan.

Calif of the West (*The*), A.D. 756.
So Abd-el-Ramah, founder of the Cordŏva
califate, styled himself (781–787). This
califate lasted till 1031.

The calif of Bagdad was then called Calif of the
East. Since 1517 the sultan has been the only
calif.

California (U.S. America). The
inhabitants are called 'gold-hunters.'

Caligula. Caius, son of Germanicus,
and successor of his uncle Tiberius, in the
empire of Rome. So called because he
wore the calīga or clouted shoe of the
common Roman soldier. The caliga was
a close shoe, studded with nails, and
bound on the foot and ankle by straps.
It was not worn by the superior officers,
but Caius was an insane fool.

Caligātus meant 'a common soldier,' one of the
rank and file. It was this monster who said ' Oh,
that all the Roman people had but one neck, that
I might decapitate Rome at a blow !'

Calixtins (*The*), or 'Calixtines' (3
syl.), 1424. Bohemians in the Hussite
war. These were for the most part the
gentry and better classes. So called
because they insisted on retaining the
calix or cup in the Eucharist. The priests
had only very recently withheld the cup
from the laity. The more violent party
were called Ta'borites (3 syl.).

Calixtines' Confession of Faith (*The*).

1. The Word of God ought to be freely and regularly preached thoughout all Bohemia.

2. The Eucharist ought to be administered to all communicants.

3. The clergy ought to follow no secular occupation.

4. All crimes ought to be punished by those in lawful authority, whether committed by clerks or laymen.

Call of Abraham (*The*), B.C. 1921.

The command from God to Abraham to leave the land of his birth and sever himself from his relations, friends, and neighbours, who were idolaters, and to go afar off to live among strangers, that he might be the founder of a people which would serve God and abjure idolatry. He was 75 years old at the time; the land he left was Ur of the Chaldees; the land he went to was Canaan, 'the land of promise;' and the son of promise was Isaac, father of the twelve patriarchs.

Call of the Abbasides (3 syl.).

Abu Moslem, A.D. 750, the founder of the Abbaside califs, who removed the seat of empire from Damascus to Bagdad.

Call of the House (*A*).

An imperative summons to every member of parliament to be present in his place, when the sense of the whole house is deemed necessary.

In 1820 such a call was made to pass an opinion respecting the trial of Queen Caroline. On the day appointed the Speaker (in the House of Commons) calls over the names of the county members first, and then of the borough members, both in alphabetical order. Absentees are committed to the custody of the serjeant-at-arms.

Callias (*Peace of*), B.C. 371.

Between Sparta, Athens, and their allies. Thebes was excluded. Callias was the Athenian representative.

Callippic Cycle (*The*).

Meton's cycle corrected by Callippus, B.C. 330. In B.C. 432 Meton set up a column in Athens which recorded that 235 lunar months corresponded to 19 solar years. This was too long, and made an error of nearly a day and a half in a century. Callippus discovered that a year consists of 365¼ days, and proposed a cycle of 76, or 4 Metonic cycles (19 × 4 = 76). A further correction was made in 1512, whereby the error of a day requires the lapse of 3,000 years.

Callippic Period (*The*).

Began with the new moon of the summer solstice, B.C. 330.

Calojoannes.

John II. (Comnēnus), emperor of the East, so called from his extremely handsome person. Reigned 1118–1143.

Calottistes (3 syl.), or 'Le régiment de la Calotte,'

in the time of Louis XIV. A society of satirists, headed by Torsac and Aimon, who sent a ' calotte ' (or small cap) to any public character who had exposed himself to ridicule. The ' calotte ' was worn by monks over their tonsure, and was to cover the 'weak part of the head ' of the receiver. The armorial bearings of the Calottistes consisted of various symbols of folly, and their motto was ' C'est régner que de savoir rire.'

Calvary (*A*).

A chapel with a cross, generally placed, in Catholic countries, on an eminence, or at the meeting of two or more roads. The calvary of Montmartre and of Mont Valérien, near Paris, are well-known examples. The latter still attracts many persons during Holy Week. The approach to a calvary is called the 'Via Dolorosa,' and at each stone which marks a station a prayer should be said.

A little farther on . . . is a colossal wood-carved calvary, and beside it a small but very rich chapel.—OUIDA, *Bimbi*, The Nürnberg Stove.

Calvinism, 1561.

The religious tenets of John Calvin of Picardy. They are generally called the five points : (1) Predestination and reprobation ; (2) original sin ; (3) particular redemption ; (4) irresistible grace ; (5) the perseverance of the saints.

Calvinist.

A Christian whose tenets are Calvinistic. *See* ' Calvinism.'

There are Calvinistic Baptists, Calvinistic Methodists, Welsh Calvinists, and even in the Episcopal Church there are some few of a Calvinistic tendency.

Calvinistic Methodists, 1741.

A body which seceded from Wesley, especially on the doctrine of election. Whitefield was the leader of the Calvinistic Methodists. After Whitefield's death they divided into two ; (1) Lady Huntingdon's Connexion, and (2) the Tabernacle Connexion.

Calvin's Daily Offices.

For family prayer, as well as for morning

and evening services, in the reformed churches. It was used in the reformed churches of France after their organisation in 1555. Various modifications have been introduced from time to time. It was at one time much used in Scotland, and John Knox died repeating words of Calvin's 'Daily Offices.'

Camal'dolites (4 syl.). *See* below.

Camaldulensian Order (*The*).
'Camaldules,' or 'Camal'dolites' (4 syl.), 1010. A very austere religious order first established in the vale of Camaldöli by Romuald, a Benedictine monk; and approved by Alexander II. in 1072. The order is almost extinct.

Camarilla (*A*).
A royal clique, junto, or secret council, composed of the sovereign, the priests, and the intriguing ladies of the court. It was for a long time part of the Austrian government. Some of the sovereigns of France and England too had their camarillas.

Cambray (*League of*), 1508.
Between the pope, Louis XII. of France, and the Duke of Ferrara, 'to blot out the Republic of Venice from the map of Europe.' The Venetians, however, bribed off the pope, who promised to break up the league. To this end he made a compact with the Swiss to chase the French out of Lombardy; and then Venetia, Spain and England joined the league, which was called 'The Holy Alliance' (1513).

Cambray (*Peace of*), or 'Paix des Dames,' 5 Aug., 1529.
Between France and the Kaiser. So called because its terms were settled by two ladies, viz. the mother of François I. on behalf of France, and Margaret of Austria, the aunt of Karl V., on behalf of Germany. By the terms of this scandalous treaty, François stipulated to renounce the lordship of Flanders and Artois; to pay 400,000*l.* for the ransom of his two sons; to abandon Venice and all his other allies to the vengeance of Karl V.; and to marry Eleonore, sister of the emperor.

Cambria, Wales.
The Welsh call their country 'Cymru,' 'Cymro' is a Welshman, 'Cymraes' a Welsh woman, 'Cymraeg' the Welsh language, and 'Cymruain' the adjective Welsh.

Cambria, or Cumbria, was also the country of the Bretts or Welsh in Dumbarton, Renfrew, Ayr, Lanark, Peebles, Selkirk, Roxburgh, Dumfries, and Cumberland, which formed a separate kingdom.

Cambridge Colleges.
N.B.—The head of King's is a *provost*, of Queen's a *president*, and of all others a *master*.

			Called	
Catherine Hall or College ...	...	...	Cat's	1475
Christ's	...	...	...	1505
Clare Hall or College	...	...	...	1326
Corpus Christi ...	...	...	C.C.C.C.	1351
Downing ...	...	...	...	1800
Emmanuel	...	...	...	1584
Gonville or Caius	...	...	Keys	1348
Jesus	...	...	...	1496
John's (St.)	...	...	...	1511
King's	...	...	...	1441
Magdalene	...	...	Maudlin	1519
Pembroke	...	...	...	1343
Peter's (St.)	...	...	...	1257
Queen's	...	...	1446, refounded	1465
Sidney Sussex ...	...	...	...	1598
Trinity	...	...	...	1546
Trinity Hall	...	...	...	1350

All these 17 are corporate bodies.

HOSTELS

Ayerst Hall	...	...	...	1884
Cavendish College	...	...	...	1876
Selwyn College and Ridley Hall	...	1882

In 1873 Girton, and in 1880 Newnham, colleges for ladies.

Cambridge Platonists (*The*).
The Whig party opposed to the Oxford Anglicanism of which Laud was the exponent. The leaders were Whichcote, Cudworth, Henry More, Culverwell, Rust, Glanvil, and Norris. They succeeded the puritan divines, and were succeeded by the school of Sherlock, Law, and Paley, who in turn gave way to the evangelical school of Berridge, Milner, and Simeon; and still later came the school of Trench and Hallam.

Camden and Powis Medals.
For a poem in Latin hexameters. Founded by the Marquis of Camden, chancellor of the University of Cambridge, and called, from 1841 to 1866, the Camden Medal. On the death of the marquis, the Earl of Powis, high steward of the University, continued the medal, since called the Powis Medal. For undergraduates of not more than two years' standing.

Camden Professorship of Ancient History (*The*), in Oxford University.
Stipend 600*l.* a year. Founded by William Camden, Clarencieux King of Arms, in 1622.

Came with a lass and will go with a lass (*It*).
The words uttered by James V. of Scotland on his dying bed, when informed of the birth of a daughter.

' God's will be done. It came with a lass and will go with a lass.' Marjory Bruce, daughter of Robert Bruce, married Walter, the 6th steward of Scotland, and this alliance eventually brought the crown into the Steward family (called Stuart in French). The daughter born to James V. on his death-bed was Mary (Queen of Scots), whose son James removed to England, and called himself James I. of England and VI. of Scotland.

Camel-driver of Mecca (The).
Mahomet the prophet of Arabia (570–632).

Camel People (The).
So the Arabs call the inhabitants of the Sahara. The inhabitants of the towns of Barbary they call the *Gold* people, and those of the Tell, or cultivated lands, they call the *Silver* people.

Caméléon.
A nickname given in France to Thiers the historian (1797–1877). *See* 'Attila le Petit.'

Cameron Highlanders (The).
The 79th regiment in the British service, raised by Allan Cameron of Erroch in 1793.

Now called the Queen's Own Cameron Highlanders.

Cameronians (The).
I. *Scotch Covenanters*, 1680. So called from Richard Cameron, who was slain at Airdsmoss, Ayrshire, 20 July, 1680. Richard Cameron disowned Charles Stuart (II.) for having violated the Engagement (*q.v.*), and his brother James as a papist. He collected some six-and-twenty horse and forty foot, which he called ' the host of Israel,' was attacked and fell. His followers hold the perpetual obligation of the Solemn League and Covenant (*q.v.*); they stoutly resisted the introduction of the English Church into Scotland, and continued to preach in the open air in violation of the Act against ' Field Conventicles ' (*q.v.*). The party still exists in Ireland and North America, but is very small.

Graham of Claverhouse, viscount Dundee, has obtained dishonourable notoriety for his slaughter of the Cameronians.

II. *The Scottish Rifles.* Originally formed from the Glasgow Cameronian guard, raised in 1786 from the followers of Richard Cameron, the puritan preacher. The first battalion is the 26th foot, and the second battalion the 19th.

Camisards (The), 1688.
Calvinists of the Cevennes, who, after the Revocation Edict, took up arms under their leaders Cavalier and Roland, and defeated the French troops sent against them by Louis XIV. again and again. At last the Duke of Berwick extirpated them and desolated the whole province of the Cevennes in 1705. Called Camisards from the *camise* or smock which they wore. Clement VI. said they were ' a cursed brood from the execrable race of the Albigenses.'

Dr. Emms died 22 Dec., 1707, and the Camisards of England staked their reputation that he would return to life on 25 May. Guards were set over his grave ; but it is needless to add that Dr. Emms slept on the sleep which knows no waking.
N.B. Any military surprise by night is a Camisade. Thus the taking of Pontoise in 1419 was a camisade, and the battle of Pavia in 1524 commenced with a camisade.

Camp of Boulogne (The), 1802.
Preparations made by the Consul Bonaparte, at Boulogne, for the invasion of England. It contained a vast number of gunboats and flat transports, military stores and munitions of war ; but it came to nothing.

Campbell's Acts.
Two Acts of Parliament introduced by Lord Campbell (9, 10 Vict. c. 93) 1846, and (20, 21 Vict. c. 83) 1857, against the sale of obscene publications, prints, &c.

Campbellites (3 syl.).
Reformers of New America, 1823, so called from Alexander Campbell of Bethany, U.S. He was a Baptist ; protested against all creeds, and professed subjection to the Bible only. The Campbellites reject all school theological terms and doctrines attached to names such as Regeneration, Trinity and Trinitarian, Unitarian, Calvinism, Arianism, Arminianism, using only the words and phrases of Scripture. They baptize by immersion, and employ the word immerse instead of baptize.

Campo-Formio (*Peace of*), 17 Oct., 1797.
In which Austria recognised the Rhine as the boundary of France ; and ceded to that nation Milan, Mantua, and the Netherlands. France, on the other hand, restored to Austria the city of Venice, Istria, Dalmatia, and the left bank of the Adige.

Campus Martius.
A vast plain to the west of Rome where was a temple of Mars. Here the assemblies of the people were held, here magistrates were

elected, and here the young Romans held their athletic sports. In the latter times of the republic porticoes, triumphal arches, and magnificent public monuments were erected round the Campus Martius. At Paris a vast plain was laid out in 1770, which was called the Champ de Mars; it is south-west of the city, between the Ecole Militaire and the river Seine. And here in 1815 was held the federation of the Champ de Mai.

Champ de Mars (pronounce *sharnd Marz*), Champ de Mai (pronounce *sharnd May*).

Canadian O'Connell (*The*). Papineau, leader of the democratic party of Lower Canada, in the rebellion of 1836. He was made attorney-general when the two Canadas were united in 1840.

Canal Navigation (*Parent of*). Francis Egerton, 6th earl and 3rd duke of Bridgewater (1729–1803).

Candiotes (3 syl.). Natives of Candia or Crete.

Candle Hymn (*The*). The hymn sung at the kindling or lighting of the lamp at sunset.

Just then the voices of the singers . . . concentrated themselves . . . into an evening or 'candle hymn.'—PATER, *Marius the Epicurean*, chap. xxi.

Candlemas Day, 2 Feb. The feast of the Purification of the Virgin Mary, observed by Catholics with a procession of lighted candles. On this day the candles required for the services of the ensuing year are consecrated.

In Scotland Candlemas-day is one of the four term days, for the payment of rents, interest, taxes, &c. The other three term-days are Whitsunday, Lammas-day, and Martinmas-day.

Candle Rent. A rent given for an out-let or out-drift before the passing of the Enclosure Act in 1811. Those who liked met at a given time and place, and perfect silence was exacted. An inch of candle being lighted, one of the party named what he would give for the plot, and laid a shilling near the candle. If another would give more he stated it, and laid a shilling near the candle, returning the deposit to the first bidder. This went on till the candle had burnt out, and the last depositor rented the land at his own price for the year.

Canicular Period (*A*). 1,461 Egyptian years, which began with the heliacal rising of the dog-star. Also called a Sothic Period.

The first Canicular period was B.C. 2785. In 1461 Egyptian years, the sum of the deficits of the Canicular years equals one entire year. *See* 'Dog Days.'

Cannonade of Valmy (*The*), 20 Sept., 1792. The attack of General Kellermann on the Duke of Brunswick at Valmy was so called, because as many as 20,000 cannon shots were exchanged between the French and Prussians.

Not above 400 men on either side were slain in this battle, notwithstanding these 20,000 cannon shots. In Kellermann's army were the young Duke de Chartres (Louis Philippe), and his brother the Duke of Montpensier, then only 17 years of age.
Kellermann was afterwards created by Napoleon 'duc de Valmy'; and on his deathbed he requested to be buried in the field of Valmy.

Canon (*A*). A cathedral dignity (Greek 'kanôn,' a rule), originally a Cenobite living under a certain rule, as the rule of St. Augustine, the rule of St. Francis, the canonical rule, &c. By the rule of Chrodegang (763) canons were bound to manual labour, silence, and confession twice a year. Later on the canons formed the bishop's council, and were paid by the bishops. The dean and canons of a cathedral form what is called 'the dean and chapter.' *See* 'Canons.'

Canon Law (*The*). 'Corpus Juris Canonici' (1151), a body of rules for ecclesiastical government compiled by Gratian, an Italian monk, from Scripture, the Latin Fathers, the decrees of general councils, decretals, and bulls; together with the decrees of Gratian, the decretals of Gregory IX. &c., the Clementine constitutions, and the Extravagants of John XXII. (20 in number), drawn up by John Lancelot in the time of Pope Paul IV. (1555–1559). *See* 'Civil Law.'

In 1603 Convocation was ordered to draw up a new body of canons, and 141 canons were decided on, which make the present code of ecclesiastical law in England. They were compiled by Bancroft from the articles, injunctions, and synodical decrees published in the reigns of Edward VI. and Elizabeth.

Canonical Hours (*The Eight*). Four great (in capitals), and four little (in italics).

MATINS or Nocturns before break of day. On festivals and Sundays they consist of 3 psalms, 3 anthems, and 3 lessons.

LAUDS, at dawn. They consist of 5 psalms, 2 or more capitules (*i.e.* Scripture extracts), prayers, and canticles.

Prime, at 6 o'clock in the morning, called the *first* hour of the day.

Tierce, at 9 o'clock in the morning, called the *third* hour of the day.

Sext, at mid-day or noon, called the *sixth* hour of the day.

Nones, at 3 o'clock in the afternoon, called the *ninth* hour of the day.

VESPERS, at sunset, or after 3 o'clock. They consist of 5 psalms, a capitule or extract from Scripture, a hymn, the *Magnificat,* one or more anthems, and prayers.

COMPLINE, at bed-time. Consisting of confession, one lesson, 3 psalms, one anthem, one capitule, one short 'response,' the *Nunc Dimittis,* and prayers.

Canonical Obedience.

The obedience which the inferior clergy owe to the diocesan bishop, which bishops owe to the metropolitan, and the metropolitans to the pope in the Roman Catholic Church.

Canons.

Means *rules* (Greek *kanôn*). The 'Canons of the Church' are the laws and regulations of ecclesiastical discipline, the decrees and decisions of the councils, and the creeds to which Christians should conform. *See* ' Canon.'

Canons (The Book of).

In Scotch history. A code of the rules for the guidance of the Scotch Church, prepared by the Scotch bishops, in obedience to the command of Charles I.; revised by Laud, and confirmed by letters patent 23 May, 1635. The influence has been to widen the breach between the Scotch and Anglican Churches.

Canons Apostolic.

A collection of ecclesiastical laws attributed to St. Clement, a disciple of Peter the apostle. This tradition requires proof; the probability is that these canons are of Eastern origin, and of the 3rd or 4th cent.

Canons Penitentiary.

Rules enjoined on penitents for different sins, drawn from different councils, papal rescripts, and the writings of the Fathers.

Canons Regular of St. Geneviève,

1615. Confirmed 1622 by Gregory XV.

Canons Regular of St. Victor,

1113. Established in Paris by Guillaume de Champeaux, abbot of St. Victor.

Canons of Scripture.

Those books of the Old and New Testament contained in our ordinary Bible, regarded by the church as authentic in contradistinction to the Apocryphal Books.

The books accepted by the church are called the canonical books.

Canons of the Church of England (The).

Agreed upon in the synod held in London 1603–4. They are 141 in number.

Canonical obedience means obedience to these canons of the Anglican Church.

Canons of the Mass (The).

Secret or inaudible words, and certain ceremonies employed by the priest between the *Sanctus* and the *Pater,* in which interval the elements are consecrated. Attributed to St. Jerome and Pope Sevērus.

In the Protestant Common Prayer Book this part of the communion service begins with ' We do not presume to come to this Thy table. . . .'

Canons of the Saints.

A catalogue of the saints recognised by the Catholic Church. Hence canonisation, *i.e.* insertion of a name in the canon of saints ; and to canonise is to insert the name in the list or canon.

Canossa.

'Has the Czar gone to Canossa ? ' This was part of a leader in the ' Standard ' newspaper in Nov. 1887, referring to the visit of the czar to Berlin to visit the Emperor of Germany, with whom relationships had not been friendly. The meaning is, ' has he gone to eat humble pie ? ' Canossa, in the duchy of Modĕna, is the place to which Kaiser Heinrich IV. went in the winter of 1076–7 to humble himself before Pope Gregory VII. (Hildebrand).

Canōsa, or Cannæ, in the south of Italy, is quite another place.

Canteen (A).

A licensed store within a barrack, under the superintendence of a committee of officers and the charge of a sergeant. Here the best ale, beer, porter, tea and coffee, tobacco, with ginger-beer, soda-water, flour, bacon, bread, butter, and sweets, together with tapes, needles, buttons, marbles, tops, and a hundred other things are sold at less than half the price they would cost in any shop, and all of the very best quality. These canteens are very profitable, and the surplus is applied to the reduction of the cost of other charges to the men.

Canter of Coltbridge (The),

1745. The retreat of the dragoon picquets, immediately the Highlanders under Charles Edward fired their pistols. These rascal dragoons, not waiting to

return the fire, rode off towards Colt-
bridge, nearer to Edinburgh. Fowkes
and Gardiner now ordered a retreat, and
the men went helter skelter through
New Town towards Leith. Still dreading an attack, they made off to Preston,
six miles further, and stopped not till
they reached Dunbar. This is certainly
one of the most dastardly actions on
record.

Canterbury Riots (*The*), 1838.
Caused by a Cornishman, named John
Nicholl Thom, who went to Kent, and
passed himself off as Sir William
Courtenay. He said he was the Messiah,
invulnerable, and immortal. Strange as
it may appear, hundreds of respectable
persons followed him. At length the
military being called out the 'lunatic'
was shot. No such absurd delusion and
infatuation had been known for centuries.

Cantred (*A*), of land contained 100
towns; so that an Irish cantred (says
Ware) corresponded to the Saxon
hundred. In the registry of Duisk
Abbey, Connaught is said to contain only
twenty-six cantreds (*i.e.* 2,600 towns).

Canuleian Law (*The*), B.C. 445.
A law projected by Caius Canulēius, a
Roman tribune, to allow patricians and
plebeians to intermarry, and legitimise
their offspring. This wise law utterly
broke down the absurd caste of old
Rome.

Canute the Great (995, 1016–
1035).

Canute was called 'the Great' from the extent
of his dominions (six kingdoms); he was called
'the Brave' for his military prowess: he was
called 'the Rich' from his wealth and liberality,
and 'the Pious' for his devotion.

Canute's Law, or 'Cnut's Law.'
The laws enforced by King Canute, and
the mode of government which then prevailed.

When the people clamoured for Canute's law,
they meant that they wished to be governed in
the same way as Canute governed the nation
(1014-1036).

Cap. *See* also :—

Blue cap (republican)
Cardinal's red hat
City flat cap
Episcopal cap
Greek cap
Green cap (bankrupt's)
Mortar-board

Phrygian cap
Pope's cap
Purple caps (religious
  virgins)
Square caps
Statute caps
Yellow cap (Jews' badge)

Cap of Liberty (*The*). In the
French Revolution was not like the cap

worn by manumitted slaves in Roman
history, but a red cloth
Phrygian cap, properly with
two pointed ends behind.
The annexed engraving is
taken from a 25 centime-piece
in the year 3 (*i.e.* 1794-1795).
See 'Phrygian Cap.'

It was and still is called 'Le bonnet rouge.'
'Bonnet' means a woollen cap, 'mortier' a velvet
one.

Cap of Liberty (*The*). Worn in
the Roman states by manumitted slaves ;
was made thus, according to a coin of
Brutus, after the death of
Cæsar. It was made of red
cloth, and those who wore it
were called 'pileāti,' *i.e.* wearers
of the 'pileus.' In revolutionary
émeutes at Rome the pileus was
sometimes hoisted on a spear.
After the murder of Cæsar, Brutus and
his rebels adopted the red cap as a
token of their republican sentiments.

The pileus was commonly worn at games and
festivals. The sick also wore it as more convenient
than the 'gelārus' or the broad-brimmed 'pe-
tāsus.'

Cap of Maintenance (*The*). One
of the regalia of state belonging to the
British sovereigns, and carried before
them at the coronation and other national
solemnities. Caps of
maintenance are also
carried before the
mayors of several cities
in England. It is made
of crimson velvet lined with ermine, and
has two points behind. Most of the
reigning dukes of Germany and various
families of the British peerage bear their
crests on a cap of maintenance.

'Mantenementum' (says Ducange) means ' ad-
ministratio '; and the cap of maintenance, without doubt, is the symbol of administrative power.

Caps (*The*), 1738–1771. The popular
faction of Sweden under Frederick and
Adolphus Frederick. They upheld the
treaty with Russia, and wore the Russian
cap as a badge of their proclivities ; they
were also friendly to England. The
opposite faction were called the Chapeaux or Hats, and wore the French
'chapeau' as their badge, to show their
French proclivities. They wanted to
roll back the government into an oligarchy. The leader of the Caps was
Count Horn; the leader of the Hats
was Count Syllenborg. Gustavus III.

prohibited the names and broke up the factions, 1771.

Gustavus courted the Caps, that is, the citizens and the people, and thus received the services of the burgher guard of the capital. The Caps were only too ready to assist in pulling down the haughty and oppressive aristocracy.—HOWITT, *Hist. of Engl.*, 'George III.,' chap. iv. p. 95.

Carlyle says: 'Faction of Caps, that is night-caps, as being somnolent and disinclined to France and war. Seldom has a valiant nation sunk to such depths.'

Capability Brown. Lancelot Brown, the landscape gardener, was so called from his constant use of the word in regard to the sites submitted to his skill (1715–1783).

Bute . . . employed Capability Brown (1771) . . . to sound Chatham as to a coalition.—HOWITT, *Hist. of Engl.*, 'George III.,' chap. iv. p. 87.

Capetian Dynasty (*The*). The third race of French kings (987–1848). In 1270 the Philippine or elder branch succeeded, and in 1328 the younger branch, called the Valois. In 1848 Louis Philippe abdicated, and the line ended.

Huguet Capet appeared in public in an abbot's cope, for he was abbot of St. Martin de Tours, but never crowned. He was called Capet-us, which means one who wears a capot, or abbot's cope. In 1792 the monarchy was interrupted by the First Republic. In 1804 Napoleon I. became Emperor of the French. The monarchy was restored in Louis XVIII., Charles X., and Louis Philippe. In 1848 the Second Republic was introduced. From 1852 to 1873 the Empire was restored in Napoleon III., after whose captivity the Republic was again restored.

Capitoline Games (*The*), A.D. 86. Instituted by the Emperor Domitian to commemorate the saving of the Capitol by the sacred geese when Rome, B.C. 390, was invaded by the Gauls.

Capitularies. The laws of the Frankish kings are so called because they are subdivided into 'capitula' or chapters. Ducange says any laws reduced into a code may be so called; but the most famous are the Capitularies of Charlemagne (827) compiled by the Abbot Angesius of Fontenelles (3 syl.), and those of his son Louis le Débonnaire.

Capitulation Resolution (*The*), 1612. Granting absolute religious liberty and equality, because the estates of Austria, leagued in the Union of Horn, refused otherwise to do homage to Mathias, the new kaiser. Ferdinand II., who succeeded Mathias in 1619, wholly disregarded the capitulation, and acted on the motto, 'Better a desert than a country full of heretics.'

Capitulation of Dantzig (*The*), 26 May, 1807.

Capon Tree (*The*). An oak on which six followers of Charles Edward were hanged on Tuesday, 21 Oct., 1746, viz. Colonel James Innes, Peter Lindsey, Ronald Macdonald, Thomas Park, Peter Taylor, and Michael Delard. Called the Capon Tree because under it the judges and their retinue regaled themselves with capons on their way from Newcastle to Carlisle. The tree no longer exists.

Cappel (*Wars of*), 1529, 1531. These were religious wars between the adherents of Zwingli the Swiss reformer and the Catholics. The Zürichers sided with Zwingli, but the Catholics of Lucerne, Schwyz, Uri, Unterwalden, and Zug opposed them. On 11 Oct., 1531, in a conflict at Cappel, in Switzerland, Zwingli the reformer was slain.

The war of 1529 was patched up by a peace.

Capriana (*Peace of*), 1441, between Venice and Milan. Celebrated by the marriage of Sforza with Bianca, only child of Filippo Maria Visconti, duke of Milan.

Captain Cobbler. An insurgent leader in 1536, who with Dr. Mackrel headed a rising in Lincolnshire. Some 20,000 followers presented a petition to Henry VIII. complaining of extortion and misgovernment. The King replied : ' Ye are presumptuous—the rude commons of one shire, and that the most brute and beastly of the whole realm—ye would rule your prince whom ye are bound to obey and serve with your lives, your lands, and your goods. Mind your own business and leave government to your betters.' Captain Cobbler (Melton) and Dr. Mackrel, with thirteen others, were executed.

' Captain' Grant, sometimes called ' Cooney.' A famous Irish burglar, executed 29 Aug., 1816. He was profusely liberal, most polite, and an incomparable dancer. He never injured anyone except in self-defence, and on no account allowed those who paid him blackmail to be robbed of anything. He was a great favourite with Irish farmers, and a welcome guest at every fair. His first operations were in Queen's County, his last in the county of Wexford.

'Captain Grant' being surprised by the military, was committed as 'Cooney.'

Captain Moonlight, 1878.

The name assumed by some unknown leader of Irish Fenians, who wrote threatening letters to those who resisted or refused to join their league. The following was received in May 1889 by a tenant on the Kenmare estate for being on friendly terms with the bailiff.

> Feniun Lodge, Castle island.
> . . . I give you till Tuesday evening to let the people know you repent mending a cooler, receiving the milk and butter, and taking tea with 'Gloster.' If you don't ask pardon . . I will take your life within a week. . . .
> (signed) CAPT. MOONLIGHT.

A diagram below of a coffin, a rifle, and a skull with cross-bones. (See 'Irish Associations.')

Captain Rag.

Edmund Neale Smith, the poet (1668-1710), so dubbed at Oxford.

Captain Swing (1830-1833).

An assumed name adopted by the writer of threatening letters to those who used threshing instruments instead of flails. As the letter was generally followed by the burning of ricks, the 'captain' was called 'Swing the Rick-burner.' There was a life published by Carlile, Fleet Street, of 'Francis Swing, the Kent burner,' in 1830, pp. 24. Another, published by Rooke & Varty, Strand (? 1831), called 'The Life and Death of Swing the Rick-burner.'

Captains of Liberty, 1270-1291.

Oberto Spinola and Oberto Dona of Genöa, who seized the supreme power from the podesta, and ruled the state for 21 years. Under them was a magistrate called the Abbate del Popolo.

Captivity of the Popes (The),

1309-1377. The time that the popes held their court and resided at Avignon, instead of Rome. It was followed by 'the Great Schism of the West,' when there were two or more popes, one at Rome and one at Avignon or Basel (Bâle).

Boniface VIII. anathematised Philippe IV., le Bel, of France; whereupon the king seized him, and the pope, angry and vexed, fretted himself into a fever and died. Philippe then secured the papal chair for Bertrand de Goth (Clement V.), on condition that he stigmatised the memory of Boniface, assisted in suppressing the Knights Templars, and consigned to the king for five years the tithes of all the church property in France. In order to carry out these conditions Clement V. took up his residence in Avignon. The time that the popes resided in France is called 'the seventy years' captivity.'

Captivity (Popes of the).

(1) Clement V. (1305-1314), who removed his court from Rome to Avignon.

(2) John XXII. (1316-1334). Louis of Bavaria set up Nicholas V. in opposition to John, but John called him antipope, and succeeded in imprisoning his rival.

(3) Benedict XII. (1334-1342).

(4) Clement VI. (1342-1352),

(5) Innocent VI. (1352-1362),

(6) Urban V. (1362-1370).

(7) Gregory XI. (1370-1378), who removed his court back to Rome in 1376.

These are not anti-popes. The anti-popes followed the popes of the captivity. See 'Antipopes,' p. 31.

Capucins, or 'Capuchin Friars,'

1528. Reformed Franciscans established in Italy by Matteo Baschi; established in France at Meudon in 1585; in Spain 1606. So called from the cappucio, capuche, their head-dress. See 'Franciscans.'

Capulets and Montagues (3 syl.),

or Capuletti and Montecchi. Two noble families of Verona, whose feuds have been rendered familiar by Shakespeare's tragedy of 'Romeo and Juliet,' 1303. Dante in his 'Purgatorio' (VI.) alludes to the same. The story of Romeo and Juliet forms one of Bandello's famous tales (1554).

Caput (The).

The council of the Senate in Cambridge University, consisting of the vice-chancellor, one doctor in each of the three faculties, and two masters of arts. This caput represents the senate. A muster, called a 'congregation,' is held once a fortnight. A measure passed or licence granted by the Caput is called a Grace, and a Grace for a degree, duly signed by the prælector of the college to which the candidate belongs, is called a Supplicat.

Caqueux.

So the Cagots (q.v.) are called in Brittany.

Caracalla.

A Roman emperor (211-217), so called because on his visit to Gaul he brought home a number of Gaulic garments, called caracalla, which he both adopted himself and compelled all about his person to adopt also. Caracalla's name was Bassiänus, and he was usually called Antoninus.

The caracalla was like what we now call a frock coat, much more convenient than the Roman toga.

Caracci of France (*Le*). Jouvenet (1647–1707), being paralysed on the right side, he painted with the left hand.

Caracci School of painting. *See* 'Incamminati.'

Caraites (Kara-ites), 8th cent. Those Israelites who reject the authority of the Talmud. Those who admit it are called Talmudists. They were textualists, confining their faith to the text of scripture, and rejecting tradition.

Caravats. The Ribbonmen of Tipperary, Kilkenny, Cork, and Limerick. Organised in 1808. *See* 'Irish Associations.'

The Caravats had been called 'Pauddeen Gar's-men,' till one of their number, prosecuted (in 1810) by the Shanavests for burning the house of a man who had taken land over his neighbour's head, was hanged, and Pauddeen Gar declared he would not leave the place of execution till he saw *caravat* about the fellow's neck.—BROWNE, *Narrative of State Trials in the Nineteenth Cent.* (1882), vol. i. p. 400. (Quoted in 'Notes and Queries,' 1882, p. 446.)

Carbonari (*The*). 'The charcoal burners,' 19th cent. A secret political and 'religious' society of Italy, having for its object the expulsion of Austria and the establishment in Italy of a democracy. It spread into France in 1818, where it aimed at the downfall of the restored Bourbons. The society was organised into companies of twenty called *vendita*, and the central assembly was called the *alta vendita*; and the united lodges, the *republic*. The name originated with the Guelfs, who, in order to elude the Ghibellines (masters of Italy), met in the woods in the cabins of the charcoal-burners.

It is said that the Carbonari established themselves in the Forest of Ardennes as far back as A.D. 445, but in the reign of Charlemagne became incorporated with the French nation. They were noticed at Naples in 1327 as a dangerous political association, and Pope John XXII. tried to put down their gladiatorial contests.

Carbonarism, or 'The Rule of the Carbonari,' 1808. Scarcely known till 1815, when Maghella, the Genoese, established affiliated lodges in Naples and the Roman States. The ostensible object of the society was the suppression of vice, the real object the establishment of republicanism. The initiated, called *Good Cousins*, were divided into apprentices and masters. In 1821 Paris was made the head-quarters, but the society was called 'The Associated Patriots.' After the July revolution (1830), a split was made in the society; the French portion

called itself the 'Charbonnerie Démocratique,' and the Italian portion called itself 'Young Italy.' *See* 'Santa Fedists.'

The lodge of the Carbonari was called 'a hut.' Inside was 'the place for selling charcoal;' outside was 'the forest.' The political opponents were called 'Wolves.' Carbonari meant 'charcoal-burners.' All the insurrections between 1819 and 1822 were instigated by the Carbonari. The 'Secret Association of the Holy Faith' (*q.v.*) declared war to the knife with the Carbonari.

Carders, 1808. The Ribbonmen of East and West Meath, Roscommon, and part of Mayo. *See* 'Irish Associations.'

Cardinal Canons. Canons attached, *in cardinali*, to a church, as a priest is to a parish.

Cardinal Carstairs, 1649–1715. Born at Cathcart near Glasgow; was no cardinal, but a great friend and adviser of the Prince of Orange. It was by the advice of William Carstairs that William planned his invasion in 1688. He was made chaplain to William III., and it was from his enormous influence in church and state that he was popularly called Cardinal Carstairs.

Cardinal de l'Ignominie (*Le*). Cardinal de Loménie, finance minister of Louis XVI. He was so hated by the people that they burnt him in effigy. He took the oath to the civil constitution of the clergy, and being proscribed by Robespierre and sent to prison, died in 1794, as it is supposed, by his own hand.

Cardinal Mass, 'Missa Cardinalis.' A mass 'quæ in ara cardinali celebratur.' *See* 'Mass.'

Cardinal's Red Hat, 1244. Directed to be worn, instead of mitre, by Innocent IV., in the Council of Lyons. Twelve cardinals were then created in honour of Christmas day. As 25 Dec. was called the 'Sun's annual birthday,' and red was the symbolic colour of the sun, the reason and connection are obvious. The notion of martyrdom is wholly erroneous.

Galerus cardinalium rubeus, iis ab Innocentio IV. primum concessus in Concil. Lugd. ann. 1244, in previgilio Natalis Domini, creatis 12 cardinalibus. —DU CANGE, vol. iii. p. 730.
∴ Before the Council of Lyons cardinals wore mitres.

Cardinalists, 1643. Adherents of Cardinal Richelieu when Cinq Mars headed the royalist faction to assassinate him.

Cards. P. A. Prince, in his 'Parallel History' (vol. i. p. 673) says : Cards were the invention of the Spanish Moors, and represented the seasons. Two colours represent the two equinoxes, and the four suits the four seasons. Spring was designated by a rose (now a diamond); summer by a trefoil (a club) ; autumn by an acorn (a spade) ; and winter by a cup (now a heart). There are twelve court cards to represent the twelve months and 52 cards to represent the 52 weeks in a year.

After the expulsion of the Moors, the Spaniards changed the original symbols, and made the four suits represent the four castes or grades of society—*Chori*, the ecclesiastics (called by the French *cœurs*, hearts); *Spada*, swords, the military rank (corrupted into spades); *Dineros*, coins to represent the merchant class (our diamonds); and *Basta*, clubs to represent the agricultural class. There are traces both in India and Egypt of this quadripartite division of society.

The French call spades *pique*, *i.e.* pikemen ; clubs they call *trèfle*, *i.e.* clover ; diamonds they call *carreaux*, *i.e.* square pavements.

In French cards the four kings are representatives of the four kingdoms: France, Judæa, Macedonia, and Rome. Thus Charlemagne (*hearts*) stands for France; David (*spades*) for Judæa; Alexander (*clubs*) for Macedonia; and Cæsar (*diamonds*) for Rome. In English packs *hearts* stand for England ; *spades* for France ; *clubs* for the pope : and *diamonds* for Spain.

In the reign of Charles VI. of France the four queens represented Isabeau (*clubs*), the queen-mother ; Jeanne d'Arc (*spades*) ; the queen herself was *hearts* ; and Agnes Sorel was *diamonds*.

The four knaves were Hogier the Dane, La Hire, Lancelot, and Hector de Galard.

Carême. A perversion of Quaresme, which is a French contraction of Quadragesima (Qua'r'es'm'), the season of Lent which begins with Ash Wednesday, forty days before Easter.

Caricaturists (*English*). It is said that Hogarth and Cruikshank are our best ; that Gillray exaggerated, and animal Rowlandson was a humourist ; it was elegant Leech; Bunbury ('H.B.') was gaseous ; 'genteel' Sayer was vulgar ; Collet stupid ; and that Seymour excelled in cockney foolery. John Doyle was the reputed author of the 'H.B.' sketches in 'Punch.'

Carizmians (*The*), or 'Chorasmims,' or 'Kharizms,' or 'Khovaresmians,' inhabitants of Kharizm or Chovaresm in Turkestan, south of the Aral. From 994 to 1231 this province was independent, and in 1193 the Carizmians ruled over Persia. Genges-Khan overturned the dynasty. A dynasty of Carizmians reigned in Delhi from 1213 to 1398, when it was succeeded by the Patans.

Carl X. of Sweden, 1622, 1655-1660. First of the 7th dynasty, called Deux-Ponts, succeeded his cousin Christina, who had abdicated.

Father, John Casimir ; *mother*, Catharine (daughter of Carl IX., and sister of Gustavus Adolphus); *wife*, Hedwig ; *son*, Carl XI.

Contemporary with Cromwell and Louis XIV.

Carle Sunday. The Sunday before Palm Sunday, from an ancient practice of eating *carlings* (gray peas) fried in butter, with pepper and salt, on that day. Perhaps the more orthodox food would be hallowed beans fried. *See* 'Sunday.'

It will be remembered that Twelfth Day was the bean feast, and the person who drew the bean was bean king for the nonce.

Carlists (*The*), 1833, of Spain, adherents of Don Carlos, brother of Ferdinand VII. Up to 1830 the Salic law prevailed in Spain; but Ferdinand VII., having no child except a daughter, announced that the succession would in future pass to both male and female. He thus set aside the succession of his brother Carlos for Isabel, an infant girl not three years old. Carlos resisted, and a civil war ensued from 1833 to 1839. In 1845 Don Carlos abandoned his claim, and died at Trieste in 1855 at the age of 67.

Don Carlos the younger (Count of Montemolin), after an unsuccessful struggle, was arrested in France, 1860, and renounced his claim. He also died the following year.

In 1871 the nephew of young Carlos renewed the struggle, but after five years' desultory fighting, he fled to France, and the contest ended.

** The 'Pragmatic Sanction' of Austria made Maria Theresa the heir of Karl VI. and set aside the Duke of Bavaria, who raised a civil war.

Carlo Khan, 1784. A name given to Charles James Fox from a popular caricature during the progress of his first India Bill. Fox is represented as the Great Mogul riding into Delhi on an elephant ; Lord North and Burke are represented as leading the elephant. Burke has a trumpet, to indicate that he is Carlo Khan's trumpeter. It is supposed that Fox aimed at being khan or dictator of the East Indies, and this supposition is supported by a bill which, in 1783, he brought before parliament.

Carlovingians (*The*), 715–987. The 2nd French dynasty. So called from Charles (Carolus) Martel, maire-du-palais, and son of Pepin d'Héristal.

* Charles Martel, king 715–741; his son Pepin le Bref, 752–768; Charlemagne, 768–814, who was king of France and emperor of the West. He was succeeded by Louis le Débonnaire, 814–840.

In 840 a separation took place; the French kings were CHARLES LE CHAUVE, Louis le Bègue, Louis III., and Carloman, CHARLES LE GROS, Charles le Simple, Louis d'Outremer, Lothaire, Louis V. called *Le Fainéant*, 986–987.

The emperors were Lothaire, Louis his son, CHARLES LE CHAUVE, CHARLES LE GROS, Guy of Sopeto, Lambert, *Arnould of Carinthia*, Louis son of Boson, and Berenger, 906–924.

The kings of Germany were Louis the Germanic, Louis the Young, CHARLES LE GROS, *Arnould of Carinthia*, and Louis the Infant, 899–911.

The kings of Italy were for the most part the same as the emperors up to Louis son of Boson; but then follow Hugh of Provence, Lothaire, Berenger II., and Adelbert, 950–961.

Carlowitz (*Peace of*), 26 Jan., 1699. Between Venice, Kaiser Leopold, and the Turks. By this treaty the Turks ceded to Germany Hungary, Transylvania, and Sclavonia; and Turkey ceded to Venice the Morea, in honour of Morosini, surnamed Peloponnesiacus. This peace was effected by the mediation of England.

The Turks reconquered the Morea in 1715, and it was made part of the kingdom of Greece in 1830.

Carmagnole. I. A revolutionary *dress* worn in France, especially during the reign of terror. It consisted of a blouse, a red cap, and a tricoloured girdle.

Blouse, pronounce *blaze*.

II. A street *dance*, in which men, women, and children promiscuously took hold of hands, danced in a ring, ran butting down the street, broke into small parties, and danced vehemently like Bedlamites, till ready to drop.

III. A *song*, 'Madame Veto' (*q.v.*), the refrain of which was 'Dansons la Carmagnole! Vive le son, vive le son du canon!'

IV. Sometimes red republicans were called Carmagnoles, and M. Barère designated the speeches made against Marie-Antoinette as 'Des Carmagnoles.'

V. Bombastic and fanatical reports of the successes and glory of the French arms. These were tried in the Franco-Prussian War (*q.v.*), but were found to be wind-bladders.

Carmagnole, pronounce *kar-man-yole*.
The word is from Carmagnola, in Piedmont, the great nest of the Savoyards, noted for their street music and dancing.

Carmathians (*The*), or 'Carmathites' (3 syl.), A.D. 890–951. The followers of Carmath, the Mussulman reformer, who called himself 'the guide, the director, the demonstration, the Word, the Holy Ghost, the camel, the herald of the Messiah, and the representative of Mahomet, John the Baptist, and Gabriel. He relaxed the duties of ablution, fasting, and pilgrimage, allowed the indiscriminate use of wine and food, and enjoined the daily repetition of fifty prayers. His twelve apostles by the success of their preaching seemed to threaten Arabia with a revolution. The Carmathians were a secret society united and concealed by an oath of secrecy.

Carmelites (3 syl.), 1171. One of the four orders of begging friars and nuns founded by a Calabrian monk on Mount Carmel in Syria, and established in England in 1240. They dress in white and are called 'White Friars' from the colour of their dress, as the Dominicans are called 'Black Friars,' and the Franciscans are called 'Grey Friars.' The Carmelites abstain from animal food.

St. Theresa in 1540 established a reformed order called the Carmes-déchaussés, or Barefooted Carmelites. *See* 'Monastic . . . Orders.'

Carmental Gate (*The*), or Carmentālis Porta. One of the eight gates of Rome, very celebrated because it was the gate through which the Fabian clan (consisting of 306 men) passed, when the patricians rejected their agrarian law. They were all cut off by Veientines, and the gate was nicknamed *Scelerata* or cursed.

Carmenti Portæ dextro via proxima Jano est;
Ire per hanc noli, quisquis es: omen habet.
         OVID, *Fasti*, ii. 201.

Carmes. *See* 'Carmelites.'

Carolin Books (*The*). Containing the judgments of the general council of the bishops of the West on certain religious questions which were mooted in the time of Charlemagne, especially the desirability of having pictures and images in churches as aids to devotion. Alcuin induced Charlemagne to submit the question to a general council, and the practice was condemned. *See* 'Iconoclasts.'

Carolina. So called in 1562 by Jean de Ribault in honour of Charles IX. of France, whose envoy he was. He settled in the south, but in 1565 the colony was massacred by the Spaniards. In 1663 some English settled there, and renewed the name in compliment to Charles II. of England, who granted the whole country to eight English adventurers. The nicknames of the North Carolinians are *tar-boilers, tar-heels, buffaloes,* and *tuckoes;* of the Southerners *weasels.*

Caroline of Brunswick. The divorced wife of George IV., and mother of the Princess Charlotte. It was Bergami, her chamberlain, with whom the queen's name was so slanderously connected.

Carolus. A silver coin worth ten deniers, struck in the reign of Charles VIII. of France (1483–1498). It bore the letter K, the initial of Karl. Hence the phrase 'Il a des Carolus '—he has lots of money. This word is quite common in French comedy, and is called sometimes a *carle, charle,* or *carlo.*

The English Carolus was what we now call a sovereign. It was a gold coin struck in the reign of Charles I.

Carosse à cinq sous, 1662. A French omnibus introduced by Colbert. Seven were started, each containing eight seats, and they were compelled to start at fixed times whether full or not. Three started in Paris from the Porte St.-Antoine, and four from the Luxembourg.

The modern omnibus, 'Entreprise Générale des Omnibus,' was established in 1827; and Shillibeer introduced the omnibus into London three years later, in 1830; the fare was 6d.

Carpenters' and Butchers' Insurrection (*The*), 1413. This was the great insurrection in Paris of the White Scarfs and White Hoods. The Carpenters or White *Scarfs* were the Orleans or Armagnac (Ar-man′-yak) faction; the Butchers or White *Hoods* were the Burgundians. The Carpenters prevailed, and after the bloody fray in the Place de Grève, the White Hoods were driven out of Paris and soon wholly disappeared.

Carpet-bag Régime (*The*), 1866–1876. When the Southern States of America were practically disfranchised after the rebellion, there grew up swarms of adventurers who went down to the Southern States and organised the negro voters, who got elected to all the chief offices, plundered the state treasures, contracted huge state debts, and stole the proceeds. Government in the South Carolina and Mississippi states was a mere caricature. When, in 1876, President Hayes refused the 'carpet-baggers' the protection of Federal troops, the *régime* fell to pieces, and the rule fell again into the hands of the whites.

Carpocratians (*The*). Disciples of Carpocratès, who flourished under Hadrian (A.D. 130) at Alexandria. Carpocratès taught that the world was made by angels; that Jesus was the son of Joseph and Mary, and that his body after his burial remained in the grave; he denied the doctrine of the resurrection of the body, but seems to have believed in the transmigration of souls.

Carrickshock Affray (*The*), 1832. An anti-tithe affray. A number of writs against defaulters having been issued by the court of exchequer, the process-servers, with a strong body of police, proceeded on their mission with secrecy and dispatch; but the Irish were in waiting, and suddenly a vast number armed with 'pitchforks and scythes attacked the yeomen.' A terrible hand-to-hand fight ensued, and in a few minutes eighteen of the police, with their commanding officer, were slaughtered; the remainder fled. The coroner's verdict was 'wilful murder,' but not one single conviction was obtained.

Carrier of Europe (*The*). Denmark, which lets out for hire her merchant ships and men to foreign states.

Carrier's Battues, 1794. A device by Carrier for clearing Nantes of persons suspected of being disaffected towards the republic. Some 500 persons were placed on a bridge near Nantes (1 syl.), and shot down by cannons.

Carrier's Vertical Deportation, 1794. A scheme devised by Carrier to clear Nantes of persons suspected of not being red republicans. He confined 150 persons at a time in the hold of a ship, and drowned them in the Loire by scuttling the vessel. We are told that the number of persons thus 'deported' amounted to 32,000.

Carroll (*Lewis*). The pen-name of C. Lutwidge Dodgson, author of 'Alice in Wonderland,' 'Through the Looking-glass,' 'Phantasmagoria,' 'Hunting the Snark,' &c.

Carrousel. A species of tournament at one time very common and very popular in all the courts of Europe. It was not known in France till the reign of Henri IV. (1589–1610); but there were such sports in Italy before that time. The most famous carrousels in history were that of Louis XIII., and the two given by Louis XIV. in honour of Mademoiselle de la Vallière (one in Paris, 1662, and the other at Versailles in 1664). The 'Place de Carrousel' in Paris is the place where these fêtes were usually held. In 1750 a revival of the carrousel was attempted at Berlin, and in 1828 the cavalry school at Saumur held one in honour of the Duchesse de Berry. The Eglinton tournament was the last carrousel held.

Running with a lance at the pasteboard head of a Turk, or cutting it down with a sword, or firing at it with a pistol, were favourite tests of horsemanship in France.

Cartesians. Partisans of René Descartes, the French philosopher (1596–1650). Gisbert Voët charged him with atheism, and some of his books were placed in the Roman 'Index,' especially his 'Meditations.' Descartes said he could find only one thing that was not doubtful, and that was that he existed because he thought (*cogito, ergo sum*). From this he inferred that whatever 'thought' must also *exist*, hence God must exist. Now spirit cannot act on matter without a concursus on the part of God, the true cause of the action of mind on matter.

It is absurd to call Descartes an atheist. He was not orthodox, but a God was absolutely essential to his system. Of course, his axiom is a *petitio principii*. Why not 'ambulo, ergo sum'?

Carthu'sians (*The*), 1084. A monastic order founded by Bruno of Cologne. So called because their chief institution was at Chartreuse (in Latin *Cartūsia*), near Grenoble, in France. Their establishments, wherever situated, were called 'Chartreuse Houses,' corrupted into *Charter Houses.* They were introduced into England in the reign of Henry II., A.D. 1180. They adopted, in a great measure, the Benedictine rule, with additional austerities.

The *Carthusian Rule* was as follows: To fast all Lent till six at night; never to eat meat at any time; and three days a week to fast on bread, salt, and water.

Each monk to have a separate cell, where he was to sleep and take in silence his solitary meals. Every monk to wear a hair-shirt at all times. All to work at agriculture, to be hospitable, and given to works of charity.

Cartoon of Pisa (*The*), by Michel Angelo. It represented some soldiers bathing, and suddenly disturbed by the appearance of the enemy. It was torn to pieces by Baccio Bardinelli out of envy of the young artist. An old copy of this cartoon is in the possession of the Earl of Leicester.

Carus Greek Testament Prizes. In the University of Cambridge, 1853. Two prizes of books, raised by subscription in honour of the Rev. William Carus, Fellow of Trinity.

Casa de Pila'tos. In Seville. It is a Moorish house said by tradition to have been removed from Jerusalem by angels. Murray's 'Handbook for Spain' tells us 'it was built (1533) in imitation of Pilate's house at Jerusalem by Fredrique Enriquez de Ribera, in commemoration of his having performed the pilgrimage to Jerusalem in 1519.' Others say it was built by Moorish captives for a duke of Medīna Cœli. *See* 'Santa Casa.'

Cassation (*Court of*). France. For *quashing* the decision of other courts (*casser*, to annul). The only question this court has to decide is whether the tenor of the law and its administration have been correctly observed by the court from which the appeal is made.

Cassin'ians. In Latin Cassiāni. A law school which took its name from Cassius Longīnus, governor of Syria, A.D. 50. He wrote ten books on the civil law, and was a follower of the Sabinians (*q.v.*), or imperial party.

Caste. In India, a social class, to each of which certain pursuits are limited by the *Laws of Manu*, B.C. 900.

1. The *Brahmans* or sacerdotal class, which 'issued from the *mouth* of Brahma.'

2. The *Chuttree* or military class, which 'sprang from the *arm* of Brahma.'

3. The *Baïs* or mercantile class, which 'sprang from the *thigh* of Brahma.'

4. The *Sudras* or servile class, which 'sprang from the *foot* of Brahma.'

The *Parīahs* and *Chandalas* are nobodies, or worse, for it is pollution to be touched by such 'scum of the earth.'

Castle (*The*), Dublin. The town residence of the lord-lieutenant. It is the headquarters of the principal public departments, and contains an armoury, an arsenal, and a chapel. Here are the offices of the chief secretary, who is practically the prime minister of the lord-lieutenant or viceroy, but he has nothing whatever to do with the police. His office is divided into two departments, each presided over by one of the two permanent under-secretaries. The lord-chancellor of Ireland and the law officers of the crown have offices in a wing of the castle. Prosecutions are initiated in the law-rooms of the Castle, and both the attorney-general and the solicitor-general of Ireland have their offices here.

Cat (*The*). So James I. used to call Chief-Justice Sir Edward Coke (1549–1634), noted for his 'Commentary on Littleton's Treatise on Tenures.' James called him 'the Cat,' because he always fell on his legs when he got into trouble. Thus, in 1616 he was removed both from his office of chief-justice and the council, because he refused to favour certain views of Villiers (the king's new favourite) on money matters; but in 1616 he married his youngest daughter to Villiers' brother, and was restored. Again in 1621 (27 Dec.) he was imprisoned in the Tower for supporting the privileges of the Commons, but was liberated 6 Aug., 1622.

Cat Hoax (*The*), 1815. When Napoleon was about to depart for St. Helēna, some wag in Chester had a number of handbills distributed, stating that the island was so overrun with rats that 16s. would be given for every full grown tom-cat, 10s. for every full-grown tabby, and 2s. 6d. for every kitten able to feed itself. The city on the day fixed was crowded with men, women, and children carrying cats. A riot ensued, the cats broke away and infested the private houses; 500 were killed, others were drowned, and many infested the neighbouring sheds and barns for many weeks afterwards. *See* 'Cats,' p. 152.

Catamaran' Admiralty (*The*), 1804. The English Admiralty which employed a catamaran to destroy the French flotilla at Boulogne.

The catamaran referred to was a machine invented by Fulton to be sent against an enemy's ship with a view of blowing it into the air. The machine employed on this occasion blew itself up with the commander and thireeen sailors, amidst the jeers of the French and the sarcasms of our own people. This was the first and last time that such a machine was employed by our navy.

Cateau Cambre'sis (*Peace of*), 2 April, 1559. Between France, England, and Spain, called in French history *La Paix Malheureuse*, because, after 65 years of war in Italy, the French had to renounce all their conquests in that peninsula and also Corsica.

Catechumens' Mass, 'Missa Catechumenōrum.' The part of the liturgy which precedes the 'Missa Fidēlium,' *i.e.* the consecration of the elements and the communion. That is the epistle and gospel, after which the catechumens were dismissed, the deacon saying 'Si quis non communicat, det locum.' *See* 'Mass.'

Caterans (Scottish history), outlaws, freebooters. Thus Sir Robert Graham, the outlaw who murdered James I. at Perth, was the leader of a band of caterans. (Gaelic, *ceatharnach*, a soldier.)

Iron stanchions on the lower windows . . . to repel any roving band of gipsies, or resist a predatory visit from the Caterans of the neighbouring Highlands.—Sir W. SCOTT, *Waverley*, chap. viii.

Cath'ari, 'Cathărēs,' or 'Cathăr-ists' (about A.D. 255), similar to the Waldenses (12th cent., latter part). A plain, unassuming, harmless, and industrious race of Christians, who placed their religion in faith, and entertained supreme reverence for the Bible. They rejected the dogmas of apostolic succession, purgatory, and papal supremacy; accepted only two sacraments; believed in only one Mediator, and therefore disavowed the advocacy of the Virgin Mary and of saints, and disbelieved in masses for the dead, the adoration of images and relics, and, of course, in indulgences also; and set their faces against second marriages. Sometimes called *Bulgarians*, sometimes *Patarenes* or *Patarines*, sometimes *Popelitans* or *Poplicans*, and in the Low Countries *Piphles.*

The word Cathări is the Greek *katharoi*, puritans. Their religious tenets were very similar to those of the 'Poor Men of Lyons,' and the Waldenses. Probably they rejected infant baptism, but it is a gross slander to call them Manichæans. Of course they were persecuted as Luther was in later times.

Catharine's College (*St.*). In Cambridge University, founded by Robert Wodelarke, D.D., chancellor of the University, 1473.

Familiarly called Cat's.

Catharine de' Medici of Africa
(*The*). Sophonisba, queen of Numidia (died B.C. 203).

Catharine de' Medici of China
(*The*). Voo-chee, who married Kao-tsong. As François I., the father-in-law of Catharine de' Medici, was called *Le Père des Lettres*, so Tae-tsong, the father-in-law of Voo-chee, was called the 'Solomon of China,' and the greatest patron of letters of all the emperors of the celestial kingdom. As Catharine, on the death of her husband, ruled her sons like puppets, so Voo-chee ruled her son, and usurped the whole power. As the conduct of Catharine demoralised society and impoverished France, so Voo-chee demoralised and impoverished China. As Catharine alienated from her all France, so Voo-chee exhausted the patience of her subjects, who at last deposed her. *See* also ' Catharine.'

Cathedra Petri
means Roman supremacy, or the supremacy of the Church of Rome, 'founded' by St. Peter. Hence the Church of Rome is styled ' Ecclesia Apostolica.'

Cathedral Beard
(*The*). A long square-cut beard peculiar to ecclesiastics.

The fashion of his beard was just, for all the world, like those upon Flemish jugs, bearing in gross the form of a broom, narrow above and broad beneath.—BULWER, *The Artificial Changeling,* 1653.

Cathedral Builders of Florence.
Arnolfo, Giotto, Ghiberti, Donatello, Brunelleschi, and Agnolo.

Cathedrals of the New Foundation.
Those to which Henry VIII., after the dissolution of the monasteries, gave a new dean and chapter.

Catherine of Aragon.
Wife of Prince Arthur and afterwards of Henry VIII. of England, was lineal descendant of John of Gaunt, whose fourth child and second daughter married Alfonso V. of Castile. *See* also ' Catharine.'

John of Gaunt; his daughter Joanna married Alfonso V. of Aragon, and their son was Juan II. of Aragon.
The son of Juan II. was Ferdinand V., who married Isabella of Castile, and the daughter of Ferdinand and Isabella was Katharine or Catherine, who first married Arthur (eldest son of Henry VII.), and then his younger brother, Henry VIII., by whom she was divorced.

Catholic Association
(*The*), 1824. In Ireland. Abolished by Act of Parliament in 1825. It still existed in 1828.

when the Brunswick clubs were formed ; but after the passing of Catholic emancipation the association dissolved itself, 1829.

Catholic Emancipation,
1829 (10 Geo. IV. c. 7). The repeal of all laws which disqualified Roman Catholics from the enjoyment of civil rights and the free disposal of their property. The Corporation and Test Acts had been repealed in 1828. In 1832 Jews were admitted to their elective franchise, in 1845 were admitted to municipal offices, and in 1858 were made eligible for seats in Parliament.

Catholic Epistles
(*The*). Those seven epistles of the New Testament, not addressed to particular churches or persons. They are the Epistle of James, the three Epistles of John, the Epistle of Jude, and the two Epistles of Peter. Originally only 1 John and 1 Peter were accepted as apostolical, but in the 4th cent. the other five epistles were read as 'lessons,' and therefore received as canonical epistles.

The 2 and 3 John are anything but 'catholic.'

Catholicos.
The primate of the Armenian Church, and of the Christians of Georgia and Mingrelia.

Catilines and Cethēgi
(*The*). Conspirators who hope to mend their fortunes by rebellion. Cethēgus was one of Catiline's crew, a kind of O'Donovan Rossa of ancient Rome.

The intrigues of a few impoverished Catilines and Cethēgi.—MOTLEY, *Dutch Republic.*

Catnach Press
(*The*). The press which published 'last dying speeches and confessions,' with accounts of executions of notorious criminals, such as Thurtell and Greenacre, Bishop and Williams, Fauntleroy and Corder. So called from ' Jemmy ' Catnach, the printer of ' patter songs ' and ' last dying speeches and confessions,' &c. One of his chief assistants was John Morgan, the 'last of the Catnach bards.'

Cato
(*The Polish*). Thaddeus Reyten, deputy of Novogrodek, who in 1773 resisted the partition of Poland.

Cato the Younger.
Sir John Barnard (1685-1764), the firm and upright patriot. A statue was erected to him in the Royal Exchange, after

which he never transacted business within the edifice, but always in the front of it.

Cato-street Conspiracy (The),
22 Feb., 1820. A conspiracy devised by Arthur Thistlewood to assassinate Lord Sidmouth, Lord Eldon, Lord Castlereagh, and all the other cabinet ministers at the great ministerial dinner to be given at the house of Lord Harrowby. One of the conspirators was to call with a note, and then the rest were to rush in and put the ministers to death. This done the conspirators were to fire the cavalry barracks by throwing fireballs into the straw-sheds. Then they were to take the Bank and the Tower. Two spies, Edwards and Hidon, kept the ministers well posted in all the plans. Thistlewood and four others were executed on May day (1820).

The conspirators met in a stable in Cato Street, near Edgware Road, London.

Catochiens, 1413. French rebels
so called from their leader Catoche, a butcher. Like the Jacquerie (1357), they insisted, amidst blood and rapine, on stamping out the privileged classes and abolishing royalty in France.

Catskin Earls. Earls who wore
catskin trimmings instead of ermine—that is earls prior to 1520, as Shrewsbury, Derby, and Huntingdon.

Some period subsequent to 1520, the catskin trimmings of earls was changed to ermine. The earls, however, created before that period were allowed to wear their catskin trimmings. The only ones existing are those of Shrewsbury, Derby, and Huntingdon.—*Notes and Queries,* 5 Sept., ix. 214.

Cats' Raffael (The). Gottfried
Mind of Berne, in Switzerland (1768–1814). *See* 'Cat,' p. 150.

Caucasians (The). An ethnological
division adopted by Blumenbach, including all the inhabitants of Europe (except the Fins); with the Hindûs, Persians, Assyrians, Arabians, Jews, and Phœnicians, of Asia; and in Africa, the Egyptians, Abyssinians, and Moors.

Dr. Prichard says this division includes two separate groups; language, not the form of the skull, being now considered the philosophical basis of ethnological groups.

Caucus, 1774. A meeting got to-
gether at Boston (Massachusetts) by Samuel Adams to resist the British Government and especially the Boston Port Act (*q.v.*). He induced thirty persons

to join him, and appointed a committee of five to meet the provincial committees of Philadelphia 1 Sept. The scheme was kept a profound secret from the government, and 500*l.* was voted for the expenses of the delegates. The committee met in a *calker's* shed in Boston, called a *calk-house,* hence calk-hus, Caucus. *See* 'Patres Patriæ.'

Caudine Forks (The). 'Furcŭlæ
Caudĭnæ,' two mountain gorges near the town of Caudium, in ancient Samnium, where the Roman army was entrapped by Pontius in the second Samnite war (B.C. 321). Four legions under Titus Veturĭus and Spurius Posthumius, locked in these gorges by the Samnites, were obliged to surrender. They passed, as was customary, under the yoke. Terms were made by the Roman consuls, but the senate basely repudiated them. The consuls were sent back prisoners to Caius Pontius, the Samnite general, but he refused to accept them.

The phrase has become proverbial for a strategic trap.

Cauldron of Slaughter (The).
In the Teutoberger Wald, where the Roman legions under Varus were cut to pieces by the Germans under Hermann in the reign of Augustus.

Cautionary Towns. Briel,
Flushing, Rammekens, and Walcheren, which were placed in the possession of Queen Elizabeth (1585), as security for the payment of troops furnished by her to the Netherlands. Only one-third of the sum was ever refunded; but the 'Cautionary' towns were delivered back 14 July, 1616.

Cavaliere. In Venice was a title
given to a noble who had been an ambassador. He wore a gold star embroidered on his robe. Thus Antonio Foscarĭni, ambassador to the court of France, was on his return to Venice in 1662 styled a 'cavaliere.'

Cavaliers and Roundheads,
1641. The royalists and puritans in the reign of Charles I. The royalists wore their hair long, flowing over their shoulders; the puritans cropped their hair short, and were called crop-haired or 'Roundheads.' The terms sprang up 25 Nov., 1641, on the return of Charles I. to London, when the parliament greeted

him with a 'remonstrance' on his evil doings. The royal party had long hair falling in ringlets over their shoulders, the remonstrants wore their hair cropped short, studiously avoided all ornaments, and affected a very sober style of dress.

Cavalry (*The British*) is divided into mediums, heavies, and light cavalry. The *mediums* consist of 13 regiments; the *heavies* of 2 regiments; and the *light* of 13.

(1) The mediums contain the 7 regiments of Dragoon Guards (numbered 1, 2, 3, 4, 5, 6, 7); 5 regiments of Lancers (numbered 5, 9, 12, 16, 17); and the 6th Inniskilling Dragoons.

(2) The heavies consist of the 12th Royal Dragoons and 2nd Royal Scots Greys.

(3) The light contains the 3, 4, 7, 8, 10, 11, 13, 14, 15, 18, 19, 20, 21 Hussars.

There are no Light Dragoons now.

Cavendish College. In Cambridge University. Founded by the County College Association, and named from William Cavendish, duke of Devonshire, chancellor of the University at the time, 1882.

The chief objects are (1) economy; (2) to train for schoolmasters; (3) to enter at a somewhat younger age.

Cavendish's Creed (*Mr.*), 1769. 'I do, from my soul, detest and abjure, as unconstitutional and illegal, that damnable doctrine and position, that a resolution of the House of Commons can make, alter, suspend, abrogate, and annihilate the law of the land.' This was spoken in reference to Mr. Wilkes, who was returned to parliament time after time by the freeholders of Middlesex, but not allowed to take his seat.

A little more than a century later a similar contest arose between the Commons and Mr. Bradlaugh, junior member for Northampton. Ostensibly the cause of objection to Mr. Bradlaugh was his slighting the obligation of the required oath; but the real objection was his unorthodox opinions disseminated, like those of Wilkes, in a journal.

Cavendish Experiment (*The*). To discover the weight of our earth. Cavendish makes it 5·480 times the weight of water, and the total weight to be 6,000,000,000,000,000,000,000 tons (*i.e.* 6,000 trillions).

Cavendish Laboratory (*The*). For physical researches. Founded in Cambridge by William Cavendish, duke

of Devonshire, Chancellor of the University from 1861 to

Cavour Federation (*The*). 'La Federazione Camillo Cavour,' July, 1888. A political association in Italy for carrying out the great programme of Camillo Cavour: viz. monarchy, liberty, progress, and a parliamentary government. It may be called a progressive Tory policy, similar to the Primrose League in England.

Caxton Society (*The*), 1845–1854. For the publication of the literature of the middle ages. It published 16 vols. Named in honour of William Caxton (1412–1491), the first English printer.

Caymes Castles or 'Cayms Castles (Caym = Cain). Monasteries were so called by Wyclif.

Wyclif called monks 'devil's kitchens.'

Ceada. The deep pit into which the Spartans threw criminals condemned to death.

Cecilite Order. Founded by Lord Adelbert Cecil. The tenets resemble those of the Plymouth Brethren.

Celestial Empire (*The*), China. The emperor is called 'the Son of Heaven.' The first hypothetical sovereign was Puon-ku, *i.e.* Highest Eternity, and the second was Tien-hoâng = emperor of Heaven. Then followed Ti-hoâng = emperor of the earth; and then Gine-hoâng = emperor of the race of man.

Celestial Indexes. So the Irish round towers were called by some Irish annalists. Whence it is supposed their object was astronomical observations connected with sun-worship.

Celestial Judgments ('Breathe Neimidh'). The code of Forchern, A.D. 40, was so called by the Irish. It was a digest of the ancient laws greatly venerated.

Celestians. Pelagians (*q.v.*), so called from Celestius, a disciple of Pelagius (5th cent.). Condemned by the Council of Carthage in 412, and again in 430 by the Council of Ephesus.

Celestines (*The*), 1254. A religious order, a branch of the Benedictins founded by Pietro da Morone (Celestine

V.). Suppressed in 1778. The 'Quai des Célestines' of Paris was so named because the chief house of the Celestines was behind the arsenal on the Quai called after the order. They adopted the Rule of St. Benedict.

Cellamare's Conspiracy, 1718.

This was a conspiracy to outwit the Quadruple Alliance, by ousting Philippe, duc d'Orléans, from the regency of France, and giving it to Felipe V. of Spain. Cellamare was the Spanish ambassador at Paris, and acted on the instructions of Alberoni. The conspiracy being discovered, Cellamare was conducted to the frontiers, and others concerned in the plot were sent to the Bastille.

Cellites (2 syl.) or 'Celli.' Lollards, Matemans, Alexians or Brethren and Sisters of Alexius, who rose in Antwerp about 1300, and were admitted by Sixtus IV. amongst the religious orders in 1472.

Nullus Christianus ad fana, vel ad petras, vel ad fontes, vel ad arbores, aut ad cellos [i.e. lucellos, *groves*], vel per trivia luminaria faciat, aut vota reddere præsumat.—ST. AUDOËNUS, *Life of St. Eligius*, bk. ii. chap. 15.

Celts or Kelts (*The*). A race which at one time peopled almost all Western Europe. They possessed France, much of Germany, most of Spain and Portugal, Ireland, Wales, Cornwall, and Brittany. The Celts of France were called Gaels (Gauls), those of Britain and Belgica Cymri. Druidism was properly Cymric. After the Saxon and Danish invasions England largely became Teutonic, and after the Norman Conquest still more so.

In Ireland and the Highlands of Scotland we still find Gaels; but in Wales and Low Brittany we find Cymri. Kelt and Gael are mere varieties of the same word Kelt-ai, Galat-ai, Gall-i, Gaul, Gael.

Cenchi (*The*), 1293. A faction in Florence opposed to the Donati. So named from two powerful houses. At first both these factions were Guelfs, but later on the Cenchi were Ghibellines, and the Donati Guelfs.

In Pistoia, an ally of Florence, there were two similar factions called the Bianchi (= Cenchi, Ghibellines), and the Neri (=Donati, Guelfs), Dante the poet, though of the house of Donati, joined the Bianchi, and had his house pulled down over his ears.

Cenchi, pronounce *Chen'-ke*.

Central Committee of Insurrection (*The*), 1792.

A committee of five (afterwards nineteen) federates which sat daily in one of the Jacobin club-rooms. The object of these five villains was to assassinate the king (Louis XVI.).

Their names were Vaugeois (grand vicar), Debessé of La Drôme, Guillaume of Caen, Simon (editor of newspapers, a native of Strasburg), and Galissot of Langres. These five were soon joined by fourteen others, such as Santerre, Camille Desmoulins, and Danton, &c.

Central Committee of the Communists (*The*), 1871.

The insurgents' government, in opposition to the Republic with M. Thiers at the head, appointed after the Franco-Prussian war. It had nine sub-committees to superintend the several departments of finance, public instruction, foreign affairs, home matters, the army, the municipalities, and so on. The Hôtel de Ville was the seat of government. It lasted nine weeks, when it was stamped out by Marshal Mac-Mahon, with much bloodshed.

Centuria'ni. So the primitive Christians were called from their ceintures or broad belts by which they were distinguished.

In ista autem Babylonia habitant . . . multitudo christianorum, qui dicuntur *Centuriani* . . . quia cingulum portant latum, vestimentum per quod recognoscuntur ab aliis.—ORDERICUS.

Cercle de Bourgogne (*Le*).

The duchies of Brabant, Limbourg, and Luxembourg; the Franche Comté; the Comté Palatin; the counties of Flanders, Hainaut, Namur, Artois, Holland, and Zealand; the marquisate of Antwerp; and the seignory of Mechlin.

Ceremonial (*The*). The service book for the pope, embracing all that pertains to the various functions of his office. *See* 'Pontifical.'

Cerinthians (*The*). Followers of Cerinthus contemporary with the apostles. He maintained that Jesus was a proper man, the son of Joseph and Mary, but that, at baptism, God sent the first of the Æons named Christ, in the shape of a dove, upon him. He further taught that this Æon left the body of Jesus before death on the cross, for the Christ could not die, though the man Jesus, like other men, was mortal. Cerinthus considered the Mosaic law binding on all Christians.

According to Cerinthus the Saviour referred to this Æon when on the cross He cried, 'My God (or Æon), my God, why hast Thou left or forsaken Me?'

Cerinthus, the heresiarch, wrote a book on the millennium. Dionysius of Alexandria says ('On Promises,' book ii.)

that 'Cerinthus affixed the name of John to his forgery.'

Irenæus ('Against Heresies,' book 1.), says that 'John the apostle once entered the public baths, but ascertaining that Cerinthus was within the same building, he (John) rushed out of the door, not enduring to be under the same roof with Cerinthus; and, as he fled, he cried to his companions, "Flee! Flee! Let us flee, lest the bath fall in, for Cerinthus is within."'—EUSEBIUS, book iii. 28.

Certiora'ri. A writ issued from a superior court to an inferior one to remove a cause depending in it. The writ commands the judges &c. of the inferior court 'to certify,' *i.e.* return, the records of the depending cause, that the party may be 'more fully assured,' or may have more speedy justice.

Cessation (*The*), 1645. In the Irish rebellion (*q.v.*), Charles I. being at war with the Parliamentarians, was greatly in want of money, and under hope of obtaining a subsidy from Ireland, commanded the Marquis of Ormond to treat with his Majesty's subjects in arms, and agree with them for a cessation of hostilities for one year. This was called the king's new and favourite expedient. The Irish insurgents granted the king 30,000*l.*, one half in cash and the other moiety in beeves. Never did any project encounter such a storm of opposition, indignation and rage, as broke out in Great Britain and Ireland at the proclamation of the cessation, especially from the English and the Scotch.

Cestui que trust (*A*). A person for whose benefit a trust is created. For example : if A founds and endows a professorship at Cambridge University, the professor who receives the endowment is the *cestui que* trust. Or, if A founds a church, the vicar is the *cestui que* trust, or, in old French, the *fidei commissaire*.

Chain of Silence (*To shake the*). In the tribal assemblies of the Scots in Ireland. It is mentioned in the celebrated Eric Fine case of the children of Turenn, cited in an article on the 'Ancient Irish Eric Fine' by R. R. Cherry, in the 'Law Magazine and Review,' No. 255 (Feb. 1885).

A celebrated contention between Goll and Finn MacCumhail had risen to such a pitch, that it could only be appeased by the intervention of the bards, who, shaking the Chain of Silence between the chiefs, succeeded in calming their strife.—T. MOORE, *Hist. of Ireland*, viii. p. 135.

Chaldaic Targums. Paraphrastic versions of the Old Testament in Chaldee for the use of the Jews, who, after the captivity, did not understand Hebrew (Neh. viii. 3). The oldest and best is that of Onkelos on the pentateuch, in the 3rd Christian cent. Next in value and age is that by Jonathan Ben Uzziel on the prophets.

Chaldee MS. (*Translation from an ancient*). A skit published in 'Blackwood's Magazine' in 1817. The authors were Hogg (the Ettrick Shepherd), Professor Wilson, and Mr. Lockhart. It really is a chronicle of the strife of Whiggism and Toryism in Edinburgh. The following persons are introduced : John Ballantine, Blackwood and Constable (publishers), Sir David Brewster, Professor Jameson, Lord Jeffrey, Professor Leslie, J. G. Lockhart, Henry Mackenzie (novelist), Macvey Napier, Professor Playfair, Sir Walter Scott, Charles Kirkpatrick Sharpe, Fraser Tytler, and Professor Wilson.

Chalk Sunday. The first Sunday in Lent is so called in Ireland from the common practice indulged in by young women on that day, of chalking the backs of young men who have not plighted troth to any one. *See* 'Sunday.'

Chamanism, or 'Shamanism.' A religious cult which spread among the Samovedes (3 syl.), Bouriates (3 syl.), and in the islands of the Pacific. The chief doctrines are that God is one whose habitation is the sun, and under whom are a host of ministering angels and genii, benevolent and malignant. The great evil spirit they call *Chaïtan,* and their priests they call *chamans.* The priests carry a horse's tail as a talisman. Their women, they say, have no souls; certainly they have no modesty.

Chamber of Liquidation (*The*), 1686. Erected by Carl XI. of Sweden for the purpose of liquidating the public debt by raising the nominal value of money, without increasing its real worth. Thousands were reduced to poverty by this arbitrary act.

Chamberlain (*The Lord*). A member of the privy council with a salary of 2,000*l.* a year. He has control over all the officers and servants of the royal chambers, except those of the bedchamber; over the physicians, surgeons, and apothecaries of the royal household; over the musicians, comedians, trumpeters, and messengers; over all tradesmen and officers employed, and over the state robes. All theatres in towns in which there is a royal palace must be licensed by him, and no new play can be acted without his licence. He issues also all royal invitations.

N.B. The lord great chamberlain is quite another officer. *See* below.

There is a vice-chamberlain, whose salary is 924l. a year.

Chamberlain (*The Lord Great*).

An hereditary officer who has the government of the palace of Westminster. At coronations and state trials or banquets the fitting-up of the hall devolves on him; and when the sovereign goes to parliament he delivers the sword of state to any member of the administration he thinks proper, to be borne before the sovereign, he himself walking on the right-hand side. During the sitting of Parliament he has charge of the House of Lords, and issues tickets of admission on the opening or prorogation of parliament. The lord chamberlain is quite another officer, not hereditary, but dependent on the choice of the chief minister or premier of the time being.

Chamberlainars in Scotch history were courts of justice held by the chamberlain in the royal boroughs. There lay appeal from this court to the 'Court of the Four Boroughs' (*q.v.*).

Chamberlaine's Riot, 1288.

Thomas Chamberlaine, a gentleman of fortune, under pretence of holding a tournament, assembled a number of associates at Boston, in Lincolnshire; their secret understanding being a raid on the town during a fair. In order to create confusion the conspirators set the town on fire, broke into the booths, and carried off the goods. Chamberlaine was arrested and hanged, but refused to implicate any of his companions (Edw. I.).

Chambre à crucer, the torture chamber. It was a chest lined with sharp stones or nails, in which the victim was fastened up.

Chambre Ardente (*La*). 'The lighted chamber.' A court for the investigation of 'heretics' established in 1525 by François I. Also an extraordinary commission nominated in 1680 by Louis XIV., to judge Brinvilliers, La Voisin, and La Vigoureux (Italian exiles). Also the chamber under the regency, in 1716,

to verify the accounts of the *fermiers généraux*. So called because they were quite dark and lighted only by torches.

The ' Chambre Ardente ' of 1680 is also called ' La cour des poisons ' (the court for the poisoners); and the ' Chambre Ardente ' of 1716 is also called ' La chambre du visa ' (the court of the endorsements).

Chambre Introuvable (*La*), 7 Oct., 1815. The French 'Mad Parliament' (*q.v.*), only the reverse of our house so called. It was ultra-royalist, and in its zeal for the aristocracy and clergy it tried to roll back the government into the ancient régime or the state before the revolution. It pronounced the banishment of all the conventionnels who voted for the death of Louis XVI., and went to such outrageous extremes that Louis XVIII. was obliged to dissolve it 5 Sept., 1816.

Chambre des Députés (*Le*), 4 June, 1814. The French House of Commons. It took the place of the Corps Législatif of the French empire, and at the accession of Napoleon III. the term Corps Législatif was restored (1852). It consisted at first of 430 members; was increased 'in the monarchy of July' to 459 deputies, but reduced to 260 deputies, 5 Sept. (1814). At first the office was for five years, and one-fifth retired annually; each deputy must be at least forty years of age, and pay a direct contribution of 1000 francs (40l.). But after 1830 the age required was reduced to thirty years, and the contribution to 500 francs (20l.). The king called the assembly every year, and if he dissolved it he must reassemble another within three months.

The upper house was called the ' Pairie' or Chambre des Pairs'' (*q.v.*), which in 1852 was replaced by the Senate.

Chambre des Pairs (*Le*), 4 June, 1814. The French House of Lords. The peerage abolished in 1789 was restored by Louis XVIII., and the Chambre des Pairs, formed, with the Chambre des Députés, the French legislature. In 1831 hereditary peerages were abolished and peers were named by the king. The Chamber of Peers was abolished in 1848 and in 1852 was replaced by a Senate.

Chambre du Visa, 1716. To verify and endorse the accounts of the *fermiers généraux* of France.

Chambres de Réunion (*Les*), 1679. Commissions formed by Louis XIV. to search into the ancient dependencies of the countries ceded to France by the treaties of Westphalia, Aix-la-Chapelle, and

Nimeguen (2 syl.) : viz. Vaudemont, Saarbourg, Saarbruck, Salm, part of Luxembourg, Homburg, Deux-Ponts, Montbéliard, Wissembourg, Strasbourg, and part of Alsace Inférieure. The Peace of Ryswyk (1697) compelled him to restore a large part of these acquisitions ; but he retained Strasbourg and Alsace.

Champ de Boulogne (Le), 1803–4.
The wonderful preparation of Bonaparte at Boulogne for an invasion of England. A large army was collected, and above 2,000 flat-bottomed vessels, built for transports, were moored at Boulogne, Etaples, and Ambleteuse. When all was ready the descent was deferred to the spring of 1804. In the meantime other matters diverted the attention of the First Consul, and in 1804 he was crowned emperor, so the invasion came to nothing.

The Column of Boulogne commemorates this 'Champ de Boulogne.'

Champ, pronounce *sharn*, the *r* silent.

Champ de Mai, or 'the Field of May.'
After A.D. 755 the Champs de Mars were held in May. June 1, 1815, was held in Paris, in a large *campus martius*, the famous assembly called the 'Champ de Mai' during the 'Hundred Days' when Napoleon proclaimed, in the presence of the deputies, the electoral colleges, and the army, *L'Acte additionnel aux constitutions de l'Empire*. *See* below.

It was called 'the Field of May,' but was held 1 June.

Champ de Mai, pronounce *Sharnd May*.

Champ de Mars, or 'the Field of March.'
A grand general assembly of Frank warriors held from time to time in Gaul from the 5th cent. till the time of Charles le Chauve (877), when all trace of them disappears. The objects of these conventions were twofold : (1) that of military reviews in which the freemen came to pay homage to their chief and bring their annual gifts ; and (2) consultative deliberations upon what expeditions should be made, what should be done for the defence of the nation, and what laws should be passed for the better government of the state. From 755 these assemblies were held in May. *See* above.

Napoleon I. announced a Champ de Mai to be held in the great plain called the Champ de Mars ['Sharnd Marz'] of Paris, on 26 May; but it was not held till 1 June, 1815. The object was to proclaim *L'Acte additionel aux constitutions de l'Empire.*

Champagne Speech (The), 1767.
A speech made by Charles Townshend, chancellor of the exchequer, after a dinner party in his own house, which astonished the whole country.

Horace Walpole says it was 'a torrent of wit, parts, humour, knowledge, absurdity, vanity, and fiction, brightened by all the graces of comedy, the happiness of allusion and quotation, and the buffoonery of farce.' He adds that it gave him the most singular pleasure he ever enjoyed.

Champion of the Cross (The).
Prince Edward (Edward I. of England), who led a crusade (1269–1272). So called mainly from the wound he received from a poisoned dagger. The Emir of Jaffa pretended to be converted, and sent a letter to Edward, but while the prince was reading it the messenger stabbed him. The tradition is that Eleanor sucked the poison from the wound, but, like so many other pretty stories, this is only a troubadour's tale.

Chancellor (The), of our Universities.
The nominal head, but his duties are deputed to the vice-chancellor (*q.v.*). The first chancellor, in Oxford, elected for life was John Russell, bishop of Lincoln, in 1483. In Oxford the chancellor is elected by the House of Convocation (*q.v.*), in Cambridge by the Senate (*q.v.*). In both cases the office is practically held for life. The chancellor is expected to be present at his installation and on occasions of a royal visit.

The chancellor has power to deal with all offences, short of mayhem and felony, between members of the university.

*** Mayhem is mutilation of an arm, leg, finger, eye, or fore-tooth. It takes no cognisance of a broken nose or broken jaw, or loss of an ear.

Chancellor (The Lord), 1079.
Head of the Court of Chancery; lord keeper, holding the royal signet, which it is his duty to impress on all documents issued in the name of the sovereign. The lord chancellor is the highest lord in the realm ; he appoints all justices of the peace, is a privy councillor, and *ex-officio* Speaker of the House of Lords. He is keeper of the king's conscience, visitor of all royal hospitals and colleges, and patron of all royal benefices, which in the king's book are stated to be not more than 20*l.* a year. He is also guardian of infants and lunatics, and has the general superintendence of all charitable foundations in the nation.

Chancellor of Scotland (The).
Had duties in Scotland similar to

those of the lord high chancellor of England; but on the union of the two kingdoms in 1707 the office was abolished, and the lord high chancellor of Great Britain is chancellor of both kingdoms.

Chancellor of a Cathedral (*The*). An officer who superintends the arrangements for the celebration of the religious services. The chancellor of a diocese is quite another officer.

Chancellor of the Diocese (*The*). Vicar-general to the bishop. An ecclesiastical judge appointed to assist the bishop in questions of ecclesiastical law, and to hold his courts for him. He may be a layman, but must be a doctor of the civil law.

Chancellor of the Exchequer (*The*). The highest finance minister of the British government.

Chancellor of the Order of the Garter (*The*). An officer who seals the commissions and mandates of the chapter, &c.

Similarly there is a chancellor to every other military order.

Chancellor's Classical Medal (*The*). In the University of Cambridge, 1751. Two gold medals. First given by his grace Thomas Holles, duke of Newcastle. *See* 'Regius Professorship of Greek.'

Chancellor's English Medal (*The*). For English heroic verse. A gold medal for any undergraduate of the University of Cambridge. Founded (1812) by the Duke of Gloucester, chancellor, and continued by his successors in the office. In Oxford this competition is called the Newdigate (*q.v.*).

Chancellor's Medal for Legal Studies. In the University of Cambridge. First awarded in 1857. Instituted by Prince Albert, chancellor of the University. *See* 'Regius Professor of Civil Law.'

Chancery (*The Court of*), 1070. Next in power to the House of Peers. It exercises jurisdiction in cases of equity, to abate the rigour of common law. Its head is called the lord 'chancellor' (*q.v.*).

Called 'Chancery' from the *cancelli* or latticework to keep off public intruders.

Chandos Clause of the Reform Bill (*The*), 18 Aug., 1831. That tenants

at will (*i.e.* from year to year) paying an annual rent of 50*l.* have a county vote, regardless of the tenure by which the land is held, or the interest derived from it.

Chang or Shang Dynasty (*The*), B.C. 1766–651. The second Imperial dynasty of China, of the semi-historic period. It gave twenty-eight emperors, whose chief city was Yang-tching. The 17th emperor of this dynasty (Poan-keng) changed the name of the dynasty to that of Yn, in which city he held his court (B.C. 1401–1373).

Chanzos. Poems of love and gallantry by the Provençals or troubadours of France. Those of war and chivalry were called 'Sirventes.'

Chapeaux (*Les*), 1738–1771. The oligarchical party of Sweden, in the reigns of Frederick and Adolphus Frederick. So called because they adopted the French chapeau as their badge, to show their French proclivities. They were bitterly averse to the late treaty with Russia, and openly avowed their desire to recover all the provinces which had been ceded to the czar. The faction opposed to the Chapeaux or Hats were called the Caps (*q.v.*). The leader of the Hats was Count Syllenborg. The leader of the Caps was Count Horn.

The Hats were composed chiefly of the remains of the late king's military officers and servants; and entertained principles favourable to the old system of administration.

Chaperons. Many popular factions have been distinguished by the colour of their hoods. The 'chaperon rouge' was the Paris colour, the 'chaperon blue' was the Navarre colour. In 1356 the commune of Paris adopted a 'red and blue hood.' In 1379 the workmen of Gand in their revolt against the Duke of Burgundy adopted 'white hoods.'

Chapter of Mitton (*The*), or 'White Battle.' Between the English and the Scotch, 20 Sept., 1319. *See* 'White Battle.'

Chapter-house (*The*). A house contiguous to a cathedral or collegiate church, where, in Catholic times, the monks and canons of monastic establishments, with the dean and prebendaries, used to meet for the management of their society. They are now used for the dean and chapter as their official chamber.

Char'egites, (3 syl.). Moslem fanatics, who classed themselves with the free-born Arabs, and disclaimed the yoke of subordination and reason. These enthusiasts agreed that there would be no peace and unity till Ali, Moawiyah, and Amrou (viceroy of Egypt) were dead; so three of their number were told off and furnished with poisoned daggers to despatch the three. The viceroy of Egypt escaped, because the assassin mistook the deputy for the viceroy, and slew the wrong person. Moawiyah (prince of Damascus) was wounded, but not killed. Ali, the calif, received a mortal wound from the third assassin in the mosque of Cufa.

Charge of the Light Brigade (*The*), or 'Death charge of the 600 at Balaclava' 26 Sept., 1854. It was the 13th Light Dragoons, the 17th Lancers, the 11th Hussars commanded by Lord Cardigan, the 8th Hussars, and the 4th Light Dragoons. The Russians were advancing in great strength to cut off the Turkish force from the British. Lord Raglan sent an order to Lord Lucan to advance, and Lord Lucan, not understanding what was intended, applied to Captain Nolan, who brought the message, and Nolan replied 'There, my lord, is your enemy.' Lucan then gave orders to Lord Cardigan to attack, and the 600 rode forward into the jaws of death. In twenty minutes 12 officers were killed and 11 wounded; 147 men were killed and 110 wounded, and 325 horses were slain. The blunder must be shared by Lord Lucan, General Airey, and Captain Nolan. However, never victory was more glorious to the devoted men than this useless charge. 'It was magnificent, but it was not war.' When Lord Cardigan rallied the scattered remnants, and said 'My men, someone has blundered,' they replied, 'Never mind, my lord, we are ready to charge again, if it is your lordship's command.'

Charing Cross. Not from *chère reine* in honour of Eleanor, the 'dear queen' of Edward I., for it was so called before Edward's time. In the Close Roll, 6 Rich. II., p. 1 (1382), we read that the custody of the falcons 'at Charryng, near Westminster,' was granted to Simon Burley, who was to receive 12*d.* a day from the Wardrobe.

Charitable Corporation Fund (*The*), 1731. A horrible swindle which numbered on the board six members of Parliament and several noblemen. The scheme was to lend money to the poor upon small pledges at 5 per cent. interest. When the capital reached 600,000*l.* the board decamped with all the money. It was a most disgraceful transaction.

Charity (*Brothers of*), 1520. A religious order instituted to relieve the indigent, ratified in 1621 by Paul V. Another order called 'The Sisters of Charity' was instituted by Vincent de Paul, 8 Aug., 1655.

Charlemagne. A French compound for *Charles-magnus*. Called by the Germans Karl the Great, or Karl I. The English usually adopt the French compound (born 742, king of the Franks 768–814, emperor of the West, 800–814). He was the third and youngest son of Pepin le Bref. Charlemagne was the founder of the Carlovingian dynasty, which followed the Merovingian in 'France' and was succeeded by the Capetian.

Pronounce *shar'-le-mah'n'*.

The pedigree runs thus from father to son: Pepin d'Heristal; Charles Martel (his son); Pepin le Bref (his son); Charlemagne.

The son of Charlemagne was Louis le Débonnaire, and his grandson was Charles II. le Chauve.

Charlemagne, emperor of the West and king of France, was son of Pepin le Bref (742, 771–814). His nine wives were

1. Hamiltrude, a poor Frenchwoman, who bore him several children.
2. Desiderata, who was divorced.
3. Hildegarde (died before him), daughter of Hildebrand, count of Suabia, mother of Charles (king of Italy) and of Louis le Débonnaire.
4. Fastrade, daughter of Count Rodolph the Saxon (died before him).
5. Liutgarde the German (died before him).
6. Maltegarde.
7. Gersuinde the Saxon.
8. Regina.
9. Adalinda.

Charlemagne (*The Second*). Karl V. of Spain and Austria, called by the French Charles-quint (1500, 1519–1556, abdicated, and died 1558).

Charles. For those of Germany *see* 'Karl,' of Sweden 'Carl,' of Spain 'Carlos,' of Italy 'Carlo.' *See* also 'Charlemagne.'

ENGLAND.

Charles I. of ENGLAND. Son of James I., born at Dunfermline, in Scotland (1600, 1625–1649); beheaded for treason against his parliament by making war upon their army. He married Henrietta Maria, daughter of Henri IV. of France. His sons Charles and James succeeded to the crown, and his daughter Mary married William II. of Orange.

His style was: Charles D.G. of Great Britain, France, and Ireland, King, Defender of the Faith, &c.

The chief *battles* were Edgehill (Warwickshire) 23 Oct., 1642, won by Rupert and lost again; Newbury (Berkshire) 20 Sept. 1643, in which Charles lost his general Cary, lord Falkland; Marston Moor (Yorkshire), 2 July, 1644, in which Cromwell defeated Prince Rupert; and Naseby (Northamptonshire) 14 June, 1645, won by Fairfax and Cromwell. This victory closed the contest.

The *servants* who followed the body from London to Windsor were Herbert and Captain Anthony Mildmay, his sewers; Captain Preston; Joyner, the king's cook; and Murray, his coachman, who drove the hearse.—TIGHE and DAVIS, *Annals of Windsor.*

Charles II., of ENGLAND. Son of Charles I., born 1630, dates his reign from 1648-9, restored Saturday 29 May, 1660, died 1685. Married Catharine or Katerine, Infanta of Portugal, had no legitimate offspring, but many children by mistresses.

His style was: Charles D. G. of Great Britain, France, and Ireland, King. Defender of the Faith. Head of the Anglican and Hibernian Church.

Wife, &c. of Charles II. His wife was the Infanta Katerine of Portugal; but his wandering fancy fell on Nell Gwynne; Davies; Roberts; Louise Renée de Querouaille, created duchess of Portsmouth; Barbara Villiers, created duchess of Cleveland, &c. These women were thrown in his way for political ends, answered their purpose, and were successively supplanted by others. Probably, Nell Gwynne came the nearest to his true affection, if such a volatile heart was capable of such a passion.

Charles II. was a traitor to his country, being the mere tool of Louis XIV.; a man of the loosest morals; a 'heretic' under false colours; and faithless in every stage of life. We have had some bad monarchs, but it would be hard to find one worse than Charles II.

Escape of Charles II. After the battle of Worcester, 3 Sept., 1651, he first went to White Ladies, in Staffordshire, but the family being away, Mr. Giffard disguised him as a servant, and he remained all the next day with Richard Penderell at Boscobel, near White Ladies. At night they tried to reach the house of Mr. Wolfe, Shrewsbury, and next day returned to Boscobel. Being told that the soldiers were searching for him, he concealed himself, with Major Carlis, in a polled oak, and at night sought refuge seven miles off in the house of Mr. Whitegreave Next day Mrs. Lane, the

sister of Colonel Lane, took him as a groom to Bristol. From Bristol he went to Lyme, riding before Mrs. Judith Connesby, and thence to Bridport, and from Bridport to Shoreham, where (17 Oct.) he embarked on a merchant vessel and was landed at Rouen.

Issue of Charles II. (none by his wife).

James, duke of Monmouth, by Lucy Walters.

Charlotte, countess of Yarmouth, by Lady Shannon.

Charles (duke of Southampton), Henry (duke of Grafton), George (duke of Northumberland), and Charlotte (countess of Lichfield), by the Duchess of Cleveland (Lady Castlemaine, or Mrs. Palmer, *née* Barbara Villiers).

Charles, duke of St. Albans, by Nell Gwynne.

Charles, duke of Richmond, by the Duchess of Portsmouth (Louise de Querouaille). (Pronounce *Koo-rah'e.*)

Mary, countess of Dumbarton, by Mary Davies.

FRANCE.

Charles II. (*le Chauve*), of FRANCE (823, 840-877), grandson of Charlemagne.

Father, Louis I., le Débonnaire; *Mother,* Judith of Bavaria; *Son,* Louis II., le Bègue. He died while Alfred the Great was king of England.

Charles I. was 'Charlemagne' (*q.v.*).

Charles III. (*le Simple*), of FRANCE (879, 887-929). Posthumous son of Louis II., le Bègue, and brother of Louis III.

Charlemagne (Charles I.); whose son was Louis I., *le Débonnaire*; Louis's son was Charles II., *le Chauve*, whose son was Louis II., *le Bègue.* Louis II., *le Bègue,* had two sons, viz. Louis III. and Charles III. From the latter the line was continued in his son Louis IV., &c.

Charles IV., (*le Bel*), of FRANCE (1294, 1322-1328). Third son of Philippe IV., *le Bel,* and last of the Capetian dynasty.

Contemporary with Edward II., who was his brother-in-law, having married Isabelle, 'the she wolf of France.'

Hugues Capet; Robert, his son; Philippe I., his son; Louis VI., his son; Louis VII., his son; Philippe II., his son; Louis VIII., his son; Louis IX., his son; Philippe III., his son; Philippe IV., his son; whose three sons were Louis X., Philippe V., and Charles IV. *See* 'Fatal Three.'

Charles V. (*le Sage*), of FRANCE (1337, 1364-1380). Grandson of Philippe V., and third of the Valois line.

Father, Jean II., le Bon; *Mother*, Bonne, daughter of the blind king of Bohemia slain at Crécy; *Wife*, Jeanne, daughter of the Duc de Bourbon.

Contemporary with Edward III. and Richard II. of England.

The Valois line was from Philippe III., son of St. Louis [IX.], whose second son was Charles de Valois.

Charles VI. (*le Bien-aimé*), of FRANCE (1368, 1380–1422). An imbecile, who resigned his kingdom to Henry V. of England, after the battle of Agincourt. He was the fourth of the Valois line.

Father, Charles V.; *Mother*, Jeanne, daughter of the Duc de Bourbon; *Wife*, Isabelle of Bavaria. One of his daughters, Isabelle, married Richard II. of England, and another, Catherine, married Henry V., and afterwards Owen Tudor of Wales.

Contemporary with Richard II., Henry IV., and Henry V. of England.

Charles VII. (*le Victorieux*), of FRANCE (1403, 1422–1461). So called because he succeeded in wresting France from the hands of the English. His first success was due to Jeanne d'Arc.

Father, Charles VI., the Imbecile; *Mother*, Isabelle of Bavaria; *Wife*, Marie d'Anjou, daughter of Louis II. of Naples; *Son*, Louis XI.

Contemporary with Henry VI. of England.

Charles VIII. (*l'Affable*), of FRANCE (1470, 1483–1498), last of the Valois line.

Father, Louis XI.; *Mother*, Charlotte of Savoy; *Wife*, Anne of Brittany. All his children died young.

Contemporary with Edward V., Richard III., and Henry VII. of England.

Charles IX., of FRANCE (1550, 1560–1574), of the Valois-Angoulême line. Notorious for the St. Bartholomew slaughter (*q.v.*).

Father, Henri II.; *Mother*, Catharine de' Medici; *Wife*, Elizabeth, daughter of Maximilian II. of Austria; no issue.

Contemporary with Elizabeth of England. His mistress was Marie Touchet, who afterwards married François de Balzac, whose younger daughter was the Marchioness of Verneuil, mistress of Henri IV. It was Henri IV. who made the anagram on the name of 'Marie Touchet,' *Je charme tout.*

CHARLES V. had two sons, CHARLES VI. and Louis, duc d'Anjou.

The elder branch of the Valois line, viz. CHARLES VI.; CHARLES VII., his son; LOUIS XI., his son; CHARLES VIII., his son; no surviving issue.

The younger branch or second son of CHARLES V., viz. Louis, duc d'Anjou; Louis, duc d'Orléans, who had two sons, viz. Charles, duc d'Orléans, and Jean, comte d'Angoulême.

First take Charles, duc d'Orléans: his son was LOUIS XII., no son.

Next take Jean, comte d'Angoulême: his son was Charles, duc d'Angoulême, whose son was FRANÇOIS I.; then comes HENRI II., his son, who had three sons, all crowned, viz. FRANÇOIS II., CHARLES IX., and HENRI III., with whom the dynasty became extinct. *See* 'Fatal Three.'

Charles X., of FRANCE (1757, 1824–1830; abdicated and died in 1836). The fourth son of Louis the Dauphin, grandson of Louis XV., and last of the Bourbon dynasty. The only king of France who reached his 80th year.

Father, Louis the Dauphin; *Mother*, Marie Leczinska; *Wife*, Maria Theresa of Savoy; *Son*, Henri [V.] never crowned, lived at the castle of Frohsdorf in Austria, where he died in 1883. His eldest son Louis-Antoine married Marie-Thérèse (his cousin, daughter of Louis XVI.), 'the modern Antigone.'

Contemporary with George IV.

Charles X., on abdicating, assumed the title of Comte de Marnes. He first retired to Holyrood in Scotland, then to Hradschin near Prague, and lastly to Göritz, where he died.

The Bourbons: HENRI IV.; LOUIS XIII., his son; LOUIS XIV., his son, died 1715; [Louis, le grand dauphin, his son, died 1711; Louis, duc de Bourgogne, dauphin, his son, died 1712]; LOUIS XV., his son, died 1774 [Louis, the dauphin, died 1765], leaving three sons, LOUIS XVI., LOUIS XVIII., and CHARLES X. *See* 'Fatal Three.'

(Louis XVII., the son of Louis XVI., *le Martyr*, was never crowned, but as he survived his father he received the empty title, like Henri V. (*see* above), and Napoleon II.).

Charles le Téméraire or the Bold, duke of Burgundy (1433–1477). 'Bold' he was not; foolhardy or self-willed would be nearer the mark.

Charles's Law (1787). The volume of a gas under constant pressure expands when raised from the freezing to the boiling point, by the same fraction of itself, whatever be the nature of the gas.

Citizen Charles lived 1746-1823. This law is also called 'Dalton's Law,' who published it in 1801, and 'Gay-Lussac's Law,' who published it in 1802. Charles did not publish it at all, but it is mentioned in his Memoir.

Charlotte (*The Princess*), daughter of George IV. Her mother's name was Caroline (afterwards the wife of George IV.); her husband was Prince Leopold of Saxe-Coburg (afterwards King of the Belgians). She was married 2 May, 1816, at Carlton House. Her town residence was Camelford House; and her country residence was Claremont, not long ago

M

the property of Lord Clive. She was born 7 Jan., 1796, and died in childbirth 6 Nov., 1817. The name of her accoucheur was Croft.

Charte Constitutionnelle (of France), 1814. Granted by Louis XVIII., and re-formed in 1830 after the abdication of Charles X.

Charter of Community (*A*). A charter of corporate rights, a French term. *See* 'Chartered Towns.'

Charter of 1830 (France). The charter granted by Louis-Philippe when he was made King of the French. This was a modification of the Constitutional Charter granted in 1814 by Louis XVIII. Its chief item was changing the line of monarchs into the family of Louis-Philippe, Duc d'Orléans, and his decendants.

M. Guizot said: 'The Charter of 1830 would be transmitted to future generations as an inviolable deposit; and would secure for France the alliance of order and liberty, the most invaluable co-heritance which a nation could receive ' (1847).

Charter of Liberties (*Henry I.'s*), 1100. This charter was the re-establishment of the laws of Edward the Confessor. Magna Charta is for the most part a mere renewal of the same.

Charter of Louis XVIII. (*The*). *See* above, ' Charte Constitutionnelle.'

Charter (*The People's*), 1838–1848. It consisted of these six items : (1) Manhood Suffrage, (2) Annual Parliaments, (3) Stipendiary Members, (4) Vote by Ballot, (5) Electoral Districts, and (6) No Property Qualifications for members. It was drawn up by William Lovett, a working man, but the preamble was written by Mr. Roebuck, M.P. In 1848 the monster petition was taken to the House of Commons in three cabs, but being examined, was found to contain the name of the Duke of Wellington 15 times, with whole strings of fictitious names, such as Snub-nose, Hook-nose, Long-Nose, Short-nose, &c. It was a complete failure, and brought the Chartists into such ridicule that the society fell to pieces. *See* ' Chartists.'

Their first petition was presented to Parliament by Attwood, 14 June, 1839.

Charter-house (*The*). A corruption of *Chartreuse, i.e.* Carthusian house —in Aldersgate Street. It was originally founded by Sir Walter de Manny, in 1371,

as a monastery ; but, on the suppression of monasteries in 1537, it was used by Henry VIII. as a depôt for his nets and pavilions. It was next sold to the Duke of Norfolk, and sundry other persons. In 1611 Thomas Sutton bought it for 13,000*l.* of Lord Suffolk, and endowed it with the revenues of more than twenty manors, lordships, and other estates, for eighty *poor brethren* over 50 years of age ; and the free education of forty-four boys, ' sons of poor gentlemen,' admitted at the age between 10 and 14.

The following were educated at this school: Dr. Barrow, Judge Blackstone, Addison, Sir Richard Steele, John Wesley, Bishop Thirlwall, George Grote, Thackeray, Sir Charles Eastlake, and many others. Removed to Godalming, Surrey, in 1872.

Charter Schools (*The*), 1733. In Ireland. Schools chartered by government for the education of the Irish poor on the principles of the Established Church. Grant withdrawn in 1832. *See* ' Incorporated Society for Promoting English Protestant Schools in Ireland.'

Chartered Towns. According to feudal law, towns (like all the rest of the soil) pertained to the feudal lords ; and the inhabitants, together with their shops and houses, were the property of these lords ; but when a town was chartered it was emancipated and set free. It then chose its own magistrates, had its own guild, its own police, and its own byelaws. The bailiff or steward hitherto appointed by the feudal lord to collect his dues was then superseded by a mayor and other civic officers, elected by the townsmen. The feudal lord had no longer any legal authority in the town, which was wholly governed by its own magistrates and the king.

Louis VI. (1108–1137) was the first to grant charters of community in France ; but Henry I. in 1100 granted such charters in England, and probably Edward the Confessor did the same.

Charters of Inspeximus or of ' Vidimus.' Charters reciting previous charters and confirming them, with the addition of some new privilege. ' Inspeximus' or ' Vidimus,' *i.e.* we have inspected or seen the old charter, and confirm it.

Chartists. Organised 1838, but the word was in use in 1832. The most seditious speakers were Stephens (a dissenting minister), Oastler, and Feargus O'Connor. Charles Ernest Jones, barrister-at-law, was also a great Chartist advocate (1819–1869).

The Rev. Joseph Rayner Stephens, of Hyde, Chester, was in 1839 imprisoned in Knutsford gaol for 18 months.
For the six points *see* above, 'Charter (*The People's*).'

Chartist Constitution (*The*). It contained six items. *See* under ' Charter (*The People's*).' The Chartists intended to march to the House of Commons on 10 April, 1848, to place Feargus O'Connor in the chair, and pass their charter; but the whole scheme fell through.

Chartist Convention (*The*), 1839. Also called by them the 'National Convention' (*q.v.*).

Chartist Riots in Birmingham (*The*), 1838. Of these riots the Duke of Wellington said in the House of Lords : 'I have seen as much of war as most men; but I have never seen a town, carried by assault, subjected to such violence as Birmingham has been in one single hour by its own inhabitants.'

Chartist Riot at Newport (*The*), 29 Sept., 1839. Led by John Frost (linendraper, a magistrate), Williams, and Jones. Upwards of twenty persons were killed in this riot. The three leaders were condemned to be hanged. Sentence of death was commuted into transportation for life; but in May 1856 the three were pardoned and returned to England.

Chartreux. A religious order, called in English 'Carthusians' (*q.v.*). La Grande Chartreuse is a celebrated French monastery in the department of Isère, which owes its origin to St. Bruno, who settled there in 1084. The monks were despoiled in the revolution of 1789.

Chasidim, *i.e.* Pietists. I. Those who resisted the efforts of Antiochos·Epiphanês and his successors to lure the Jews into idolatry.
II. Jewish ascetics who studied the Kabbala, and sought by mortifying the flesh to come into closer communion with God and his angels.
III. In 1750 Israel Baal Shem pretended to work miracles, and the revived Chasidim became numerous, but at his death in 1760 they died out again.
IV. In 1760, among the Jews of the Ukraine. The sect spread rapidly through Poland and other parts of Russia. They are very strict observers of the law ; believe in the miracles of their saints, and in their power of curing bodily ailments.

Joyfulness is insisted on by these Pietists, but it is said to tend to Epicureanism.

Chasles Forgeries (*The*). M. Chasles, a member of the French Academy of Sciences, gave out that he had bought 27,000 MSS. for 5,000*l.*, but would not tell where, ' lest others should go and spoil his market.' Amongst these MSS. was a correspondence from Alexander the Great to Aristidês, several letters from Attila, king of the Huns, and from the widow of Martin Luther. Several also from Judas Iscariot to Mary Magdalene, and from Lazarus to St. Peter. What, however, more nearly concerns Englishmen was a faded yellow MS., purporting to be letters from Pascal to Sir Isaac Newton, to prove that Newton had pilfered his system of gravitation. The tale was that this MS. belonged to the Abbey of Tours; came into the possession of Comte de Boisjourdain, who in 1791 was wrecked on his way to America. The MS. was sold, and the purchaser gave it to M. Chasles. Another letter was produced from Galileo, stating that the discovery had been made known to him. A committee was formed to examine into the matter, when a poor tool named Vrain Lucas was discovered to be the forger, and, after conviction, was severely punished. *See* ' Literary Forgeries.'

Chassepot Rifle, 1866. A breechloading rifle invented by M. Chassepot, and adopted by the French government. It was largely used by the French in the Franco-Prussian War, 1870–1871.

Chasseurs de Vincennes, or ' Tirailleurs,' *i.e.* sharp-shooters, 1835. A corps in the French army organised by the Duke of Orleans, and armed with the new rifle. They were first garrisoned at Vincennes; but now a whole battalion has been organised.

Chaste Week (*The*). Hebdomăda Casta. The week preceding Lent ; so called because the faithful vowed in that week to observe inviolable chastity throughout the coming Lent.

Chateaubriand (*Edict of*). In France, 27 June, 1554. Published by Henri II., renewing the persecution of the Huguenots, and referring cases of 'heresy' to the civil as well as to the ecclesiastical judges. The edict prohibits all books of an unorthodox tendency.

Chatterton (*Thomas*). 'The marvellous boy.' A literary impostor. He began in 1768 to produce poems which he professed to be from the pen of Thomas Rowley, a monk of the 15th cent. Chatterton was born at Bristol, and committed suicide (1752–1771). *See* 'Literary Forgeries.'

Chattertonian Controversy (*The*), 1770. This controversy was whether the poems said by Thomas Chatterton to be Rowley's were forgeries or not. Rowley was said by him to have been a priest of Bristol in the reigns of Henry VI. and Edward IV. The forgery was exposed by the poets Mason and Gray. The wonder is how anyone the least acquainted with the literature of the period referred to could be deceived. Modernise the spelling, and the deception is manifest. The boy, however, was a true poet and great genius.

Chaucer of Artists (*The*). Albert Dürer, of Nürnberg (1471–1528), called by his countrymen the 'prince of artists.'

A contemporary artist was Lucas Kranach (1472-1553), famous for his portraits of Luther, Melanchthon, and other reformers. These portraits are as celebrated as the portraits of Charlemagne and his successors by Albert Dürer.

Chaucer of France (*The*). Clément Marot, valet to François I. (1484–1544).

Chaucer of Scotland (*The*). William Dunbar (1465–1530). His 'Thistle and Rose,' an allegory, celebrates the marriage of James IV. (the Thistle) with Margaret, daughter of Henry VII. (the Rose), and is a rich specimen of poetical allegory worthy the bard of Woodstock.

Chaucer's Inn, the 'Tabard,' was burnt down in the Great Fire of London, 1666. Rebuilt and called the 'Talbot' or 'Dog' till 1873, when it was converted into a gin-shop.

Chaumont (*Treaty of*), 1 March, 1814. A treaty of alliance against Napoleon, between Great Britain, Austria, Prussia, and Russia. The allies bound themselves to pursue without relaxation war against France, till Napoleon consented to renounce all the acquisitions made by France since the commencement

of 1792, and to abandon all interference with any state except France.

Chauvinism originally meant extravagant admiration of Napoleon; but now it means *jingoism*. Chauvin is a character in Scribe's *Soldat Laboureur*, an intense admirer of Napoleon Bonaparte.

Cheapside Knight (*The*). Sir Richard Blackmore, who resided at Sadlers' Hall, Cheapside, and was knighted by William III. (1650–1728).

Chefs Plaids (*The*). The parliament or general assembly of Sark, convened by the 'Seigneur' (*q.v.*). The members consist of the seneschal, the prévot, the greffier, and the tenants of the forty farms.

Chelsea Philosopher (*The*), or 'The Sage of Chelsea.' Thomas Carlyle (1795–1881); he was born at Ecclefechan, in Dumfriesshire, but settled in Chelsea.

Chemistry (*Father of French*). Arnaud de Villeneuve (1238–1314).

Chemistry (*Professorship of*). In the University of Cambridge, 1709; founded by the University. Stipend, 50*l*. a year.

Cherubim. Ezekiel's cherubim is identical with the four standards stationed at the four sides of the Tabernacle in the Wilderness: the Lion for Judah, Man for Reuben, Ox for Ephraim, and the Flying Eagle for Dan (Gen. xxx. 14). According to Dante the Cherubim inhabit the Fixed Stars, and the Seraphim the Primum Mobile. *See* 'Evangelical Symbols.'

Cheruscan League (*The*), A.D. 9. A league of German tribes each side of the Weser to drive out the Romans from their territory. Hermann, called in Latin Arminius, was chosen chief; and succeeded in destroying the army of Varus, and driving the Romans beyond the Rhine.

Chestnut Bells. In 1886, in New York, and some other large cities in the United States, the gallery gods carried little bells when the theatres, and rang them when a stale witticism (or 'chestnut') was uttered by the actors. These bells soon became a stale nuisance, and were called 'chestnut bells.'

Chestnut is an Americanism for a stale joke or witticism.

Chevalier de St. George (*The*), 1708. The name and title assumed by James the Pretender, just as he was about to cross over to Scotland as its king. This son of James II. is generally called the ' Old Pretender.' *See* ' Warming-pan.'

His son was Charles Edward [Stuart], the ' Young Pretender,' who, on the death of his father, laid claim to the throne of Great Britain; but, being signally defeated at Culloden in 1746, he fled to the continent.
⁂ He assumed the name of Betty Blake, an Irishwoman, when he escaped to Skye, accompanied by Flora Macdonald. The sum of 30,000*l.* was set on his head.

Chevalier sans peur et sans reproche (*Le*). The Chevalier de Bayard (1476 – 1524). Like Horatius Coclès, the Roman, he defended alone a bridge (*Garigliano*) against a whole army; and, like Fabricius, he rejected with indignation the offer of a villain to poison Pope Julius II., with whom he was at war.

Chevaliers de Livonie (*Les*). The same as the ' Frères de la milice du Christ,' or the ' Chevaliers Porte-glaive ' (*q.v.*).

Chevaliers du Poignard (*Les*), 28 Feb., 1791. Certain royalists who, being . alarmed at the attack of the French mob on the prison of Vincennes (called the Second Bastille), rushed to the Tuileries to defend the king and royal family. La Fayette, with his guards, searched the courtiers, and took from them a large basket full of poniards, daggers, pistols, and sword-canes. The courtiers were very roughly handled. Marat declared in his journal, *L'Ami du Peuple*, that 5,000 poniards had been manufactured against the patriots; but, after a strict search, only thirty-six were found in the whole city, and those belonged to persons engaged in the slave-trade. *See* ' Day of the Poniard.'

Chevaliers Porte-glaive (*Les*). In Latin ' Ensiferi,' 1201. A religious military order founded by Albert d'Apeldorn, bishop of Livonia, to subdue countries still pagan. They were first called ' Les Frères de la milice du Christ,' and were sometimes called ' Les Chevaliers de Livonie.' They wore a white robe with two red swords on the breast. In 1237 the order was amalgamated with the Teutonic Knights, and remained so

till 1525, when the original order was reconstructed.

Chevy Chase. A British ballad based on the story of the battle of Otterburn, Aug. 1388. This battle was declared by Froissart to have been the bravest and most chivalrous ever fought in his day. The two chieftains were Percy and Douglas; and, if the ballad so named can be trusted, Douglas was slain by an English arrow, which pierced his heart, and Percy was slain by Hugh Montgomery. Probably a mere tale. (*Chevaucher*, to ride; *chevauchage*, a riding out; *chevauchée*, chased.)

Chicard. A French harlequin, so called from Mons. Chicard, the originator. His costume consists of a helmet, a postilion's wig, a flannel shirt, and cavalry trousers. His arms are half-bare, and his hands are thrust into buff gloves with large cuffs.

Chichele Professorships (*The*). One for International Law, and one for Modern History, in Oxford University. Formed out of five suppressed fellowships in All Souls, 1854. Stipends, 750*l.* a year each.

Henry Chicheley, or Chichele, archbishop of Canterbury, founded All Souls College in 1437.

Chicken (*The*). Mr. Michael Angelo Taylor was so called because, in the debate on the Westminster scrutiny in 1785, he said, ' I always deliver my legal opinion in this house with great diffidence, because I am young—a mere chicken in the profession of the law.'

Chief Secretary of Ireland (*The*). Practically the prime minister of the lord-lieutenant. He advises and directs the viceroy, and is responsible to parliament for every act of the Irish Administration; but to the viceroy belongs the prerogative of pardon. The chief secretary is president of the Local Government Board, and can be called to account for every detail connected with the poor law. As head of the civil service he can be interrogated in parliament upon well nigh everything which takes place in Ireland; the police (both the Royal Irish Constabulary and the Dublin Metropolitan Police) are not under him, both being self-governed. The chief secretary's office has two departments, each presided over by one of the permanent under-secretaries.

Child of Fortune (*The*). So Napoleon called Marshal Masséna after the battle of Rivoli, 14 January, 1797, and created him ' duc de Rivoli.'

Child of Hale. John Middleton, the giant, born at Hale, in Lancashire, in 1578. His height was 9 feet 3 inches. Dr. Plott tells us that John Middleton wanted only 6 inches to equal Goliath in size.'

Goliath was 6 cubits and a span.

Child of the Cord (*The*). The prisoner summoned to appear before the Vehmgerichte (*q.v.*), who was always dragged bound before the tribunal. If found guilty the president said to him: ' Prisoner . . . I devote your neck to the rope, your body to the birds of prey, and may God have mercy on your soul.' He was then dragged bound out of the court and hanged on the nearest tree. *See* ' Free Bench.'

Child Pilgrimages (13th cent.). A religious epidemic which broke out in Europe in 1212, but the last boy crusade was in 1459. Threats and persuasions, love and fear, had no effect upon the boys, who wept day and night, pined, and trembled in every limb. There was no difference in the social scale, the children of counts and barons ran away from home as well as the sons of shepherds and tradesmen.

Childermas, or 'Holy Innocents' Day,' 28 Dec. In commemoration of the children slain by Herod.

The coronation of Edward IV. was put off till the Monday, because the preceding day was 'Childermas Day.'

Children's Crusade (*The*), 1212. Preached in France by Stephen, a peasant boy, and in Germany the same year by Nicholas, also a peasant boy. Some 90,000 children left their mothers and schoolmasters in the spring ' to rescue the Holy Land from the infidels,' and ships were placed at their disposal. The French contingent embarked at Marseilles in August; part perished the same month by shipwreck on the island of San Pietro, and the rest were sold into slavery to Mohammedans. The German contingent reached Genoa in August, and was utterly dispersed by various disasters before the next spring.

Children's Employment Commission (*The*), 1841. To inquire into the employment of children in mines, cotton mills, and other industries. In 1842 they laid before Parliament a statement of the employment of children in coal-mines which greatly shocked the moral sense of the country, and Lord Ashley took the subject up.

Children of Rebecca, 1843. Welsh rioters whose object was to destroy toll-gates. So called from Gen. xxiv. 60. Laban said to Rebecca or Rebekah, ' Let thy seed possess the gate of those that hate thee.'

Chiliasm. The belief that Christ will come to earth and rule the world from Jerusalem for 1,000 years. The Latin word ' millennium ' means the same thing. The Revelation of John is the chief authority of the Chiliasts.

Papias, Justin Martyr, Irenæus, Tertullian, and Lactantius were Chiliasts, but Origen was opposed to the notion. Papias, bishop of Hierapolis, says, in the millennium 'every vine will bear 10,000 branches, every branch 10,000 shoots, every shoot 10,000 sprigs, every sprig 10,000 bunches, every bunch 10,000 berries, and every berry 36 times 25 gallons of wine; and if a saint comes to pluck a berry it will cry out, "Pluck me, O saint! I am better for being plucked, praise the Lord." '

The Fifth Monarchy Men were, of course, Chiliasts, only they maintained that the golden age had begun, and that they were of it.

Chilly Saints (*The Three*). St. Pankratius, St. Liberatus, and St. Servatius, whose anniversaries are the three cold days of May the 11th, 12th, and 13th. Some substitute St. Mamertus for St. Liberatus.

Chiltern Hundreds. There are three, viz. Stoke, Desborough, and Bonenham or Burnham. At one time the Chiltern Hills between Bedford and Hertford, &c., were covered with beech trees, which formed shelter for robbers ; so a steward was appointed by the crown to put down these marauders and protect the inhabitants of the neighbourhood from their depredations. The necessity of such watch and ward has long since ceased, but the office remains ; and when a member of parliament wishes to vacate his seat, one way of doing so is by accepting the office of steward of the three Chiltern Hundreds. Being thus advanced to a government office, his seat is *ex officio* vacated. Immediately the member has effected his object he resigns his office again. The gift is in the hands of the chancellor of the exchequer. In 1842 it was refused to the member for Reading. This acceptance began in 1750.

Similar crown offices are the Stewardship of the Manor of Poynings, of East Hendred and North-stead, and the escheatorship of Munster. The holder of these sinecures is party to a contract between the crown and certain hypothetical con-tractors. One farthing suffices to make the con-tract.

Chiminage. Toll for passing through a forest. Those who carried brushes, timber, bark, or coal on their backs to sell, paid no chiminage. Also called 'pedagium' (French *chemin*, a road or way, *chiminus reginæ*).

Chimney-tax. 'Hearth-money,' or 'Chimney-money.' A tax of 2s. a chimney levied by 13, 14 Car. II. c. 10 (1662), but abolished by 1 Will. & Mary, c. 10 (1689).

Chinese Bible (*The*). Compiled and partly composed by Confucius, di-vided into five books :—

1. Called the *Yih-King*, a treatise on cosmogony.

2. Called the *Shu-King*, the acts and maxims of Yaou, Shun, and other ancient kings held in religious veneration.

3. Called the *Shi-King*, which contains 311 sacred poems.

4. Called the *Ee-King*, or book of rites, containing maxims and directions for everyday life and all conditions of men.

5. Called the *Chun-tsien*, a history of Confucius's own times.

Chinese Cæsar (*The*). Kao-hoang-ti, founder of the Han dynasty, one of the most illustrious that ever occupied the Chinese throne (dynasty lasted B.C. 202–A.D. 226).

Chinese Wars (*The*) with Great Britain. The *First* War 1834–1842; the *Second* War 1855–1858. The cause of the first war was the prohibition of the opium trade by the Chinese Government. When this prohibition was disregarded the British boats were fired on from the Chinese forts. Commissioner Lin was sent to adjust the dispute, and his first demand was that all the opium in store, whether in factories or boats, should be given up to him to be burnt. This was done. Then Lin forbade all trading whatsoever between Great Britain and China. This provoked hostilities, and after several successes the British at-tacked Nanking ; whereupon the Chinese concluded a treaty of peace 26 Aug.,

1842, in which Hong Kong was ceded to Britain.

The *Second* War broke out (1855) in consequence of the bad faith of the Chinese, who violated the treaty. The English now demanded free access to Canton, and, this being refused, they pro-ceeded to besiege that city. A second treaty of peace at Tientsin was at once concluded, and the war ceased in 1858.

The first treaty of peace stipulated (1) the surrender of Hong Kong ; (2) 21 million dollars [about 5 millions sterling] for war indemnity ; (3) free trade between Britain and China, and (4) the following to be open ports, in each of which a British consul was to reside, viz. Canton, Amoy, Foo-chow-foo, Ningpo, and Shang-hae.

Napoleon, by the Berlin Treaty (*q.v.*), boycotted Great Britain as the Chinese did, and both at-tempts failed. Any individual may refuse to deal with any other, but no one has a right to enforce that prohibition on another against his will.

Chivalrous Madman (*The*). James IV. of Scotland (1473, 1488–1513), slain at Flodden Field.

Cholera [Morbus]. An epidemic which appeared in Bengal, the Isle of France, and the Ile de Bourbon in 1818, 1819, and 1820. It appeared in Sunder-land 26 Oct., 1831, in Edinburgh 6 Feb., 1832, and in March had reached Dublin. In Paris the deaths between March and Aug., 1832, were 18,000. It raged in Rome and in the Two Sicilies, Genoa, and Berlin from July to Aug., 1837. In 1848, 1849 it again appeared in England, and the death-rate of September was 3,183, and from 17 June to 2 Oct. it was 13,161. In 1866 it appeared again in Great Britain, and in fifteen weeks above 5,000 persons in London were carried off by it. It re-turned to Germany in 1883, 1884.

Chopping with the Whittle. An ancient tenure. 'Walter de Aldeham holds land of the king in the More in the county of Salop by the service of paying to the king yearly at his Exchequer 2 knives [whittles], whereof one ought to be of that goodness that it would cut, at the first stroke, into the middle of a hasle rod of a year's growth, and of a cubit in length. The same service ought to done in the middle of the Exchequer in the presence of the treasurer and barons on the morrow of St. Michael ; and the said whittles are to be delivered

to the Chamberlain for the king's use.'
Blount, *Ancient Tenures*, 1815.

Chorbishops, or 'Chorepiscopi.'
Suffragans, or rural bishops, delegated
by the diocesan. In 846, at the Council
of Sens, Andrad Modicus was appointed
chorbishop; but in 849 the Council of
Paris deposed all the chorbishops of
France.

Pronounce Kor-bishops.

Chouans. I. *First Period.* Were
bands of insurgent royalists who, during
the first French Revolution, organised a
reactionary movement against the Blues
(or Republicans). The original Chouan
was Jean Cottereau, a maker of sabots,
near Laval, who turned smuggler. He
was called Chouan, or screech-owl [*chat-
huant*], because he rallied his men, or
warned them of danger by imitating the
cry of that bird, and all his gang went
by the name of Chouans. In 1791 several
'trees of liberty' were destroyed in Brittany, and other outrages were fomented
by seditious priests. In 1792 an insurrection was planned by the Marquis de
la Rouarie, under the sanction of the two
brothers of Louis XVI. The marquis
entered into communication with Jean
Cottereau, who, with his Chouans, carried on successfully a guerilla war with
the Blues, till he fell, 28 July, 1794.

II. *Second Period.* George Cadoudal
was the next leader of the Chouans, or
royalist insurgents of Brittany. He was
born in 1771 near Auray, where his
father was a miller. He was captured
by the Blues in 1794, but made his escape, and became more active than ever
in the royalists' cause. Annoyed at the
dissensions of the Vendean generals, he
organised an army in which no aristocrat
was permitted to hold command. So
brave, so well drilled, and so well officered was this Chouan army that General
Hoche was unable either to subdue or
to disperse it. In 1799 George Cadoudal
was the soul of the conspiracy to overthrow the First Consul (Bonaparte), but
on the 18 Brumaire he was forced to renounce the war, and took refuge in
England. In 1803 he joined Pichegru's
plot against the First Consul, but the
conspiracy being discovered, Cadoudal
was apprehended and put to death,
25 June, 1804.

III. *Third Period.* Many petty
spurts of Chouannerie broke out after

1799, when George Cadoudal was obliged
to give up the struggle. In 1803 it
ceased for a while. In 1814–1815 it
again started into life on both banks of
the Loire, but Lamarque stamped it out.
In the July Revolution (1830) the Duchesse de Berry tried to revive Chouannerie on behalf of the Duc de Bordeaux,
but it was soon crushed out by the ener-
getic measures of M. Thiers.

Chouans, pronounce Shwahng.

Chouannerie. Guerilla warfare by
volunteers on behalf of a royal cause. The
word is from *Chouans*, the insurgents
of Brittany, who rose on behalf of Louis
XVI., and also against the First Consul
(Bonaparte). Sometimes the word means
devotion to the kingly cause in France,
as *chauvinism* means enthusiastic devotion to Napoleon I. and the Imperial
cause.

Chow, or Tchow *dynasty* (*The*).
The third Imperial dynasty of China. It
gave 34 sovereigns, and lasted 866 years
(from B.C. 1122 to 256). Yn was the seat
of government. This dynasty is called
that of the 'Kings Combatant,' being a
period of almost unvarying contention
and feudal strife.

Confucius and Mencius, the Chinese philoso-
phers, were both born under this dynasty.

Chremonidean War (*The*), B.C.
268 or 263. When Athens was taken by
Antigōnus Gonātus. So called from Chre-
monidês, the Athenian, who distinguished
himself in the defence of the city.

Christ (*Knights of*), 1318. A military order, founded in Portugal by King
Dionysius; also founded in Brazil in 1813.

Christ (*Order of*), 1205. In Livonia,
instituted by Albert, bishop of Riga. The
popes also confer the 'order of Christ.'

Christ's Birth.

Idler fixes it in	.	. Dec.	B.C. 7
Petavius and Usher	.	25 Dec.	„ 5
Bengel	. .	25 Dec.	„ 4
Anger and Winer	.	. March	„ 4
Scaliger	. .	. Oct.	„ 3
St. Jerome	.	25 Dec.	„ 3
Eusebius (Bk. i. 6.)	.	. 6 Jan.	„ 2

(Dr. Geikie, 'Life of Christ,' i. p. 559.)

Bunsen shows, on the authority of Irenæus, that
Jesus was born some fifteen years before the time
assigned, and that he lived to be about fifty years
of age.
Basnage, the Jew, in his 'Hist. des Juifs,' placed
the birth nearly a century sooner than A.D. 1.
According to Luke ii. 1-7, it was about A.D. 10.

Christ Church, 1526. Founded by Cardinal Wolsey. The most aristocratic and wealthy of all the colleges of Oxford. The head-master of this college only is called the Dean.

Christ's College. In Cambridge University, founded by the Lady Margaret, countess of Richmond and Derby, mother of Henry VII., in 1505.

The founder of St. John's College also. Surely this college ought to be Christ College, as Christ Church in Oxford. What would be said of Trinity's College, Peter's House, or Corporis Christi College? Bishop Latimer, Milton, and Cudworth were of this college.

Christ's Hospital (The Blue-coat School), London, 1553. Founded by Edward VI. (the year of his death).

Called Blue-coat from the blue woollen coat fastened round the waist with a narrow red leather girdle. The boys wear yellow breeches and yellow stockings, bands, and a very small blue worsted cap.

Christadelphians (The), 1st cent. Brethren *of* Christ, not brethren *in* Christ. Revived by Dr. Thomas in the 19th cent. The immortality of the soul, the theory of hell, the devil, disembodied spirits, and the Trinity they utterly disbelieve; but the millennium they believe in fully. The Holy Ghost is not a distinct *person*, they say, but simply the instrumental power of the Father. And Jesus Christ is God, only because the Spirit of God dwelt in Him fully and without measure. Dr. Thomas died in 1871, but the Thomasites continue still.

Christian Advocate (The). In the University of Cambridge, 1789; founded by the Rev. John Hulse, of St. John's College. In 1860 converted into the Hulsean Professor of Divinity (*q.v.*).

Christian Brethren (The), 1525. An association chiefly of London tradesmen and citizens, who smuggled over and circulated the Gospels and Epistles translated by Tyndale, and reprinted at Cologne or Worms the tracts of Wyclif and Luther.

Christian Charity (*Knights of*), 1578. Instituted by Henri III. of France for the benefit of poor military officers and maimed soldiers. It resembled our 'Poor Knights of Windsor' (*q.v.*).

Christian Cicero (The). Lactantius, first of the Latin fathers (*q.v.*). About 250–330. Converted 301.

8

Christian Club (*The*), 1768. A political union in the borough of Shoreham, where the burgesses agreed to sell their borough to the highest bidder, and share the proceeds equally. Called the 'Christian' club because, like the early Christians, they agreed to have all things [*i.e.* the proceeds of the bribe] in common.

Christian Connexion (*The*), 1800. Chiefly in the United States of America. They recognise no leader, no creeds, no forms of prayer. The Bible is their code, and each man is his own interpreter. Their great law is universal toleration. The general creed is this: There is one God; Christ the Son of God is the Mediator between God and man. The Holy Ghost is the power and energy of God. Of course the table of communion is open to all who choose to attend.

Christian Eloquence (*Founder of*). Bourdaloue (1632–1704). Especially famous for his 'Lent Sermons.'

Christian Era. It was Dionysius 'Exiguus,' in the 6th cent., who introduced the felicitous custom of dating from the birth of Christ. He, however, was incorrect in fixing the Nativity after the death of Herod; and indubitably it was not in December, but either in the spring or autumn.

Irenæus (ii. 22, 5) tells us that Jesus was between 40 and 50 when he was put to death, but the general opinion is that he was between 33 and 34 years of age.

Christian Era (*The*).

Fixed by Dionysius Exiguus at zero A.D. 1

Eusebius	?	B.C 2
Jerome and Scaliger		„ 3
Anger, Bengel, Petavius, Winer, Usher		„ 4
Ewald		„ 5
Idler		„ 7
Bunsen		„ 15
Irenæus apparently		„ 20
Luke ii. 1–7		A.D. 4 or 5

(*See* Josephus,' Ant.' xvii. 1. 1, and Eusebius, i. 6.)

(On the authority of Irenæus Jesus was 50 at his crucifixion.)

In regard to the month of the Nativity, Eusebius places it in January; Anger and Winer in the spring; Scaliger in Oct.; Bengel, Idler, Irenæus, Petavius, and Usher in Dec.

The Christian Era, suggested by Dionysius Exiguus, began to be used A.D. 526. Christmas Day was celebrated in the reign of Antoninus Pius (138–161), and the festival is attributed to Telesphorus. (See 'Dec. 25.')

Christian Era (*The*). This era begins Jan. 1, A.D. 1, or A.U.C. 753. First used by Dionysius *Exiguus* in 526. Introduced into Italy in the 6th cent. ; into France in the 7th cent. ; ordained by the Council of Chelsea in 816. Not generally used in Spain till the 11th cent. ; not in Portugal till 1415 ; not in the Eastern Church till 1453.

Called the 'Year of Grace'; the Year of the Incarnation ' ; ' Annus Trabeationis ' ; and sometimes ' Recapitulatio Dionisii ' [sic]. It is generally thought that A.D. 1 should be A.D. 4, in order to bring in Herod the Great, who died that year ; but the government of Cyrenius, mentioned by Luke, requires an adjustment in the opposite direction, as he was proconsul of Syria 4-5, according to the calculation of Dionysius.

Christian Fathers (*The*), 3rd

cent. Irenæus, Pantæus, Clemens Alexandrīnus, Tertullian (*Latin*), Minucius Felix (*Latin*), Hippolytus, Origen, Gregory Thaumaturgus,Cyprian, and Methodius (10 altogether). *See* ' Doctors.'

Christian Forgeries (*The*). Of

Brahmanic writings printed in French at Yverdun, in 1778, imposed even on Voltaire. A Carmelite missionary justifies the forgery, as the object was laudable. Origen thought that a good aim or end justifies the means. *See* ' Literary Forgeries.'

Christian Sen'eca (*The*). Joseph

Hall, bishop of Norwich (1574–1656).

Christian of the Cleek, 1335,

&c. A Scotchman who, in the early part of the reign of Edward III., used to catch men with a ' cleek,' or hook, for food. Sir Walter Scott gives us a heartrending picture of the miserable condition of the people who saved life by devouring their fellows.

Christians. Believers in Christ

were so called first at Antioch in apostolic times. In modern times the sect so called own no name or founder but the Lord Jesus.

The following sects keep the word with a difference : Christian Believers, Christian Brethren, Christian Connexion, Christian Disciples, Christian Eliasites, Christian Israelites, Christian Mission, Christian Teetotalers, Christian Temperance Men, Christian Unionists, The Free Catholic Christian Church, The Free Christians, The Free Christian Association, The Free Evangelical Christians, The Free Grace Gospel Christians, The Rational Christians, The Unitarian Christians, The United Christian Church, The Universal Christians, The Christians of St. John (*q.v.*), The Christians of St. Thomas (*q.v.*), &c.

Christians are subdivided into three general categories:
1. Those who admit the authority of tradition and of the Pope, as Roman and Greek Catholics.
2. Those who acknowledge some authority besides the Bible: The Greek Church, which acknowledges the authority of the patriarchs of Con-

stantinople, Jerusalem, Antioch, and Alexandria. The Russian Church, which acknowledges the Czar as ' head of the Church.' The Chaldæan Church, or Nestorians ; the Monophysites or Eutycheans, as the Copts, Jacobites, and Armenians.
3. Those which acknowledge no authority except the Bible. They are (*a*) Unitarians, (*b*) Trinitarians: as the Arians and Socinians; the Anabaptists, the Anglican Church or Church of England, Arminians, Baptists, Calvinists, Congregationalists, Enthusiasts, Episcopalians or those Protestants who have an order of Bishops, Evangelicals, Hernhütters, Huguenots or French Calvinists, Lutherans, Mennonites, Methodists, Moravians, Mormons, Mystics, Nonconformists, Presbyterians, Puritans, Quakers or Friends, Remonstrants, Shakers, Swedenborgians, Wesleyans, Zwinglians, &c. These and many others will be found under their distinctive name.

Christians of St. John (*The*), 1st

cent. A sect which recognised John the Baptist as their head. They repeated their baptism annually ; denied the divinity of Christ ; attributed a body to God ; called Gabriel God's son, and declared that God created the world by the instrumentality of Gabriel and 50,000 angels. At death, they asserted that the soul went to different spheres.

Christians of St. Thomas (*The*),

A.D. 883. Said to have been founded by Thomas the Apostle. In 883 ambassadors of Alfred visited the shrine of the founder in the neighbourhood of Madras. They were then governed by the bishop of Angamala, who exercised jurisdiction over 1,400 churches and 200,000 souls. In 1500 the Portuguese inquisitors accused them of the Nestorian heresy, and after a fierce persecution Malabar was reduced under the dominion of the Pope of Rome. They remained sixty years in this servitude (1599–1663), when, the Portuguese empire being shaken, the Malabar Christians asserted their independence and relapsed into their Nestorianism (*q.v.*).

The 'Thomists' were Roman Catholics. The disciples of Thomas Aquinas were quite another class of Christians.

Christi'na of Sweden. Crowned

under the title of ' king,' was born 1626, reigned 1633–1664, abdicated, and died 1689. She was the daughter of the great Gustavus.

Christinos and Carlists, 1833,

&c. In Spanish history. The partisans of Donna Maria Christina (regent for her daughter, Isabella Maria II.) and Don Carlos, brother of the late king. A salique law had been passed in Spain by Felipe V., but was repealed by Carlos IV., as he had only a daughter. Don Carlos claimed his right of succession, on the

salique law. His partisans were called
Carlists, and for seven years a tedious
guerilla war ensued. It was renewed 1873,
and ended in 1876.

Christmas Day. Now held on 25
Dec. The early Christians held it, some
in May, some in April, and some in June.
It could not have been in December, as
shepherds would not be in the fields
watching their flocks by night in that
month. Most likely it took the place of
the Yule-feast and Roman festivals held
during the winter solstice. The festival
of the Nativity was introduced at Antioch
in 375, but in the forged Isidorian
Decretals (*q.v.*) Telesphŏros (who lived
in the 2nd cent.) is said to have instituted it.

The Puritan Parliament abolished the Christmas
festival; and the decoration of churches and
houses was made an act of sedition.

Christmas Day, 1684. Eight of
the British sovereigns were all living.
1. Richard Cromwell, born 4 Oct.,
1626–1712.
2. Charles II., born 29 May, 1630–1685.
3. James II., born 14 Oct., 1633–1701.
4. William III., born 4/14 Nov., 1650–
1702.
5. Q. Mary II., born 30 Apr., 1662–1694.
6. Q. Anne, born 6 Feb., 1664–1714.
7. George I., born 28 May, 1660–1727.
8. George II., born 30 Oct., 1683–1760.
(*See* 'Notes and Queries,' Dec. 28, 1889,
p. 505.)

Christmas Eve. Sir Walter Scott
says, 'On Christmas Eve the mass is
sung.' Strictly speaking, this is not
correct, as no mass is celebrated on the
vigil of Christmas Day, or indeed on any
vigil; but it is usual in Rome to celebrate
a midnight mass, *i.e.* a mass in the small
hours of the morning of Christmas Day.
The service may commence before midnight, but it cannot be finished till after
midnight. It is absolutely necessary that
the elements be taken in the morning,
i.e. between midnight and midday. On
Christmas Day or any other day any
number of masses may be said in a church
at different altars by different priests,
but no priest should celebrate more than
one mass in a single day. This is not
strictly observed.

Christmas Prince (*A*). A Lord
of Misrule.

The High and Mighty Prince, Henry, prince of
Purpoole [? Poole Park], archduke of Stapulia and

Bernardia [Staples and Barnard's Inn], duke of
High and Nether Holborn, marquis of St. Giles and
Tottenham, count palatine of Bloomsbury and
Clerkenwell, great lord of the cantons of Islington,
Kentish Town, Paddington, and Knightsbridge.—
Notes and Queries, 17 March, 1888 (quoted from the
'Book of Christmas,' by T. K. Hervey, 1835).

Christopher North. The pen-
name assumed by John Wilson (1785–
1854).

Christot'okos, Theot'okos,
Theoph'oron. Nestorius (5th cent.)
taught that Mary was not θεοτόκος
(mother of God), but only χριστοτόκος
(mother of Christ), for God cannot be
born of a woman. Jesus of Nazareth he
called θεοφόρον (possessed of God). These
distinctions were condemned by the
Council of Ephesus in 431.

Chronicle of St. Neots (*The*).
The Chronicle of Asser is so called because it was discovered in the monastery
of St. Neots.

Asser, bishop of St. David's, Wales, died 910. His
chronicle goes down to 893, and has been continued by other hands.

Chronicles of Denis (*The*), or
'Chronicles of France.' The lives of St.
Louis (IX.) and his brothers (Robert,
Alphonse, and Charles), and the sons of
St. Louis, Philippe III. *le Hardi*, and
Robert de Clermont (the root of the
Bourbon dynasty of France). It was
written by Guillaume de Nangis, who
died in 1300, and was a Benedictine
monk of St. Denis.

Suger (1092–1152), the wise minister of Louis VII.
le Jeune, is called the precursor of the Chronicles
of St. Denis. [Pronounce *Sahn Dnee.*]

Chronology (*Father of*). Scaliger
the younger (1540–1609).

Chrysostom, or Golden-mouth.
John, patriarch of Constantinople, was
so called, but not till long after his death.
His oratory was very attractive, appeal-
ing more to the feelings and passions
than to the reason (347–407).

Dion, the rhetorician, was surnamed Chrysostom
before the patriarch (A.D. 50–117).

Chupattie Mystery (*The*), Feb.
1857. Just before the Indian mutiny, a
native policeman entered a village of
Oude, carrying two chupatties, or cakes,
and ordered the person who took them
to make ten more and distribute two to
the five contiguous villages. In a few
hours the whole country was alive with
watchmen running from place to place
with these cakes. The mystery has not

yet been solved, but two facts are known: (1) that soon all India was in mutiny; and (2) that five centuries previously a similar distribution of cakes in China led to the mutiny which overthrew the dynasty of the Moguls.

Church (*Orders of the*). The sacrament of orders is only one; but it is divided into seven grades in the Roman Catholic Church.

I. Latin Church : *Seven* clerical orders (or grades) : Ostiarius, exorcist, reader, acolyte, subdeacon, deacon, priest. The last three are called the greater orders; the other four are called the lesser orders. The priesthood completes the grades; the dignitaries being only priests.

Subdeacons have been classed with the higher orders only since the time of Innocent III. (1193-1216).

Bishops, priests, and deacons are said to be of divine institution.

The five orders of ostiarius, exorcist, reader, acolyte, and subdeacon are human institutions, which (we are told) have existed from apostolic times.

Ten clerical orders. Those who insist that there are ten clerical orders in the Latin Church reckon these three amongst the grades : the tonsure, the office of precentor, and episcopal consecration.

II. Greek Church : Either *Four* clerical orders: reader, subdeacon, deacon, and priest;

Or *Eleven*. Those who maintain that there are eleven clerical grades in the Greek Church recognise the following : sexton, confessor, singer, ostiarius (or doorkeeper), exorcist, acolyte, reader, subdeacon, deacon, priest, and bishop.

III. Anglican Church : *Three* clerical orders: deacon, priest, and bishop.

Church-ale. A wake to commemorate the dedication of a church. These revels consisted of drinking and sports, especially dancing.

In 1634 Denham issued an order in the western circuit to put an end to the disorders attending church-ales, bid-ales, and clerk-ales.—HOWITT, *Hist. of England* (Charles I. ch. iii. p. 159).

Church Army (*The*), 1882. A home missionary society for the conversion of the masses by out-door and indoor meetings, and by personal influence.

Church Catechism (*The*). Strype assigns it to Nowell ('Ecc. Mem.' ii. 368) ; but Churton, in his 'Life of Dean Nowell,' attributes it to Poinet, afterwards bishop of Winchester (pp. 403, 407). The 'Church Catechism' must not be confounded with what is called 'Cranmer's Catechism' (*q.v.*), which was originally German.

Church-cess (Ireland). Same as church-rate in England, for the general expenses connected with the parish (Protestant) church, such as clerk's salary, washing the surplice, cleaning the church, buying the sacramental bread and wine. Levied in Ireland on Catholics as well as Protestants, and in England on dissenters as well as church-goers. Church-rates abolished 1868 (31, 32 Vict. c. 31); but the Irish church-cess was abolished in 1833. It amounted to 80,000*l.* a year. *See* 'Irish Church Temporalities Bill.'

Church Cities. In feudal times, were those built on church lands; and in these the abbot or bishop was chief magistrate. Generally speaking these cities were much more free than 'Ducal Towns' (*q.v.*).

Church Education Society (*The*). In Ireland, 1839. Supported wholly by voluntary subscriptions. This society was started by those who disapproved of Mr. Stanley's 'National Schools' (*q.v.*), because religious instruction was disallowed, and because any person, of any persuasion, at certain hours, might give special instruction to the children whose parents sanctioned it. The Church Society insisted that the Bible should be taught, and that religious instruction should be given to the children in conformity with the principles of the Established Church.

Church Forgeries. Mosheim says (vol. ii. 17): 'Acts of councils, records, epistles, and whole books were forged by these zealous fanatics [the monks], in order the more easily to rob and plunder the credulous, on whom they imposed their glaring and fraudulent absurdities.' *See* 'Literary Forgeries.'

Church-scot. The same as church-rate, a tax levied as far back as 692 for the repair of churches, and the supply of what was needful for divine worship. It was paid at Martinmas, according to a rate made at Christmas. In case of failure to pay the rate, a fine of twelve times the amount was imposed. In 1868 Mr. Gladstone virtually abolished parish church rates by making the payment voluntary.

Church Temporalities Act
(*The*). Ireland, 1834 (3, 4 Will. IV. c. 37). Investing the revenues of the suppressed bishoprics of Ireland (about 50,000*l*.) in the Board of Ecclesiastical Commissioners, to be applied by them to the erection and repairs of churches, church-rates, and other ecclesiastical purposes. The archbishoprics of Cashel and Tuam were reduced to bishoprics, the total number of sees being 10, instead of 21 as heretofore, with 2 archbishops instead of 4.

The suppressed sees were Ardagh, Clogher, Clonfert with Kilmacduagh, Cork with Ross, Dromore, Elphin, Kildare, Killala with Achonry, Ossory, Raphoe, Waterford with Lismore. Value in 1833 of the 11 sees, 61,521*l*. Of these Clogher was 10,560*l*. a year, and Elphin 9,484*l*.
There are now (1890) 4 Catholic archbishops and 24 Catholic bishops in Ireland.

Church of Christ (*The*). *See* 'Disciples.'

Cicero (*The British*). William Pitt, earl of Chatham (1708–1778).

Cicero (*The Christian*). Lucius Cælius Lactantius (died 330). Tutor of Crispus, son of Constantine.

Cicero (*The German*). Johann Sturm, printer and scholar (1507–1589).

Cicero of France (*The*). Massillon, bishop of Clermont (1663–1742). The conclusion to his sermon called 'The Day of Judgment' is sublime and harrowing.

Cicero of Germany. John elector of Brandenburg (1486–1499).

Cicero of Latin Christianity (*The*). Augustine (354–430).

Cicero of the British Senate. George Canning (1770–1827).

Cicero's Mouth. Philippe Pot, prime minister of Louis XI. (1428–1494).

Cicero's Murderer was Popilius Lænas.

Cid el Campeador (4 syl.). Don Roderigo Ruy Diaz de Bivar [*i.e.* Roderic, son of Diego of Bivar], a nobleman of Castile (1040–1099).

'Cid' is an Arabic word meaning *lord*, and 'campeador' = champion.

Cid'aris. The head-dress of Persian monarchs, not unlike the French cap of liberty, or Phrygian cap. Only the king is allowed to wear the top of the cap erect. The cidaris of Darius was blue and white, or purple and white (Quintus Curtius, book iii. ch. 3, and vi. chap. 6).

Cimbri. The inhabitants of the Chersonesus Cimbrica. Confederated with the Teutŏnês, they invaded the Roman dominions, and were overthrown by Marīus in the battle of the Campi Raudii, B.C. 101.

Cimbrian Panic (*The*). B.C. 105. A Roman panic after the annihilation of five armies by the Cimbrians. This panic rose to its climax after the terrible defeat of Cæpio, the consul in Gallia Narbonensis.

Cimburgis Lip (*The*). A protruding under-jaw, with a heavy lip indisposed to shut close, often called the 'Austrian Lip.' It came from Kaiser Maximilian I., and was inherited from his grandmother, Cimburgis, a Polish princess, who married Kaiser Friedrich III.

Cimon (*Peace of*), B.C. 447. Which brought to a close the hostility between Persia and Greece.

This treaty of peace was made by Anaxicrătês, not Cimon, who had lately died.

Cincinna'ti (*The*), or 'Cincinnātuses,' 1783. An order in the United States of N. America, established by the officers of the anti-British army 'to perpetuate friendship, and to raise a fund for the relief of the widows and orphans of those who fell in the War of Independence.' Their badge is Cincinnatus receiving the ensigns of dictator, and the motto is 'Omnia reliquit servare rempublicam.'

Cinerarians, 'Cinerarii.' So Christians were called by their enemies, because they reverenced the ashes or bones of the dead.

Reliqua SS. Mirac. S. Ursinari, sumptis de concineratione sanctissimi corporis in sepulcro ejus duobus dentibus. Hinc 'cinerarios' catholicos appellabant heretici.—DU CANGE, vol. ii. p. 619, col. 2.

Cinq Mars (*Conspiracy of*), 1642. A conspiracy secretly fomented by the king himself, Louis XIII., 'to get rid of Richelieu, whose domineering spirit was most hateful to him. Those who favoured the conspirators were called 'Royalists,' the adherents of Richelieu were called 'Cardinalists.' The object of the conspiracy was to dismiss Richelieu and make Cinq Mars chief minister. The plot being discovered, and it being known that Cinq Mars had made a treaty with Spain, the leading conspirators were

arrested. Cinq Mars and other noblemen were beheaded; the Duc de Bouillon was deprived of his principality, which was confiscated to the throne; and the infamous Duc d'Orléans turned king's evidence.

Richelieu brought to the block at least six noblemen: Marillac, Cinq Mars, De Thou, Châlais, Bouteville, and Montmorency.

Cinque Centisti. Those Italian artists of the 16th cent. who formed the Cinque Cento school. See 'Seicentisti,' and ' Trecentisti.'

Cinque Cento (2 syl. each), 500. Used to designate the style of art which rose in Italy after 1,500.

The Golden Age of Italian art, containing the immortal five, who all died after 1500, viz. :

Leonardo da Vinci ... ... who died	1520	
Raphael ... ... ,,	1520.	
Correggio ... ... ,,	1534	
Michel Angelo [*Michelagnoio*]* ,,	1564	
Titian ... ... ,,	1576	

* His name was Michel Angelo Buonarroti.

*** In *literature* Italy produced at the same period :

Machiavelli ... ... who died	1527	
Ariosto (*Orlando Furioso*) ... ,,	1533	
Tasso (*Gerusalemme Liberata*) ,,	1595	

All these, except Tasso, were born in the century before, so that many use the word 'Cinquecento' to denote the sensuous school that followed the immortal five—a school which borrowed their subjects from heathen mythology.

Pronounce *Chin-kwa Chento.*

Cinque Ports (*The*). Incorporated in 1212 by King John. The five ports are Dover, Hastings, Sandwich, Romney, and Hythe. Three other ports, viz. Rye, Winchelsea, and Seaford, were subsequently added. The governor is entitled lord warden.

Cinque in English is pronounced *Sink.*

Circè of the Revolution (*The*). Madame Roland (1754–1793). The most fascinating woman of the period. As she was led to the guillotine she exclaimed, bowing to the statue of Liberty, 'O Liberty, how many crimes are committed in thy name!'

Circle of Popilius (*The*). The necessity of explaining your intentions without hesitation or delay. The tale is that Popilius was sent by the Roman Senate as envoy to Antiochus, king of Syria, and was commissioned to forbid the king making war on Egypt, or harassing the children of Ptolemy. Antiochus replied that he would think about the

matter, when Popilius drew a circle round the king, and said: ' Prince, you must reply before you leave this circle.' Antiochus, taken by surprise at this boldness, replied at once, ' Tell the Senate I will do what they demand of me.' Having so said, Popilius saluted him, and offered him the friendship of the Roman people.

Circle of Stennis (*The*), or ' Circle of Odin.' A circular hole in one of the huge Standing Stones of what is called the Orcadian Stonehenge. This Standing Stone was at one time used by rustics for plighting troth. The lovers joined hands in this hole, and swore by Odin to be faithful to each other. This plight is called the ' promise of Odin,' and making the plight is 'taking the promise of Odin.'

We were wedded after the ancient manner of the Norse, our hands were clasped in the circle of Odin, with ... vows of eternal fidelity.—Sir W. SCOTT, *The Pirate,* chap. xxxiii.

Circles of Germany (*The*). Departments or districts. In 1887 Kaiser Wenceslaus divided Germany into *four* circles, viz. (1) Saxony; (2) the Rhine provinces; (3) Austria, Bavaria, and Suabia; and (4) Franconia and Thuringia.

In 1438 Kaiser Albert II. increased the number to *six*, each of which had a right to be represented on the diet or national assembly. The circles were : Franconia, Bavaria, Suabia, Westphalia, Upper Rhine, and Saxony.

In 1512, under Maximilian I., the number of circles was increased to *ten*, viz. Austria, Bavaria, Burgundy, Franconia, Lower Rhine provinces, Upper Rhine provinces, Lower Saxony, Upper Saxony, and Westphalia.

Each circle had an ecclesiastical and lay prince, with a military chief.

At the Reformation the circles were divided into Catholic, Protestant, and Mixt. The *Catholic Circles* were Austria, Bavaria, and Burgundy ; the *Protestant Circles* were those of Upper and Lower Saxony; and the *Mixt Circles* were the other five. In 1806 the division into circles was broken up by the ' Confederacy of the Rhine.'

Circular Coin. 'When English coin is made circular the prince of Wales shall be crowned in London.' This ' prophecy ' is attributed to Merlin. In 1281 Edward I. issued a new coinage of round halfpence and farthings, and forbade the penny to be divided into four quarters. David, thinking this to be the thing predicted, invaded England 22 March, 1282, and, being joined by Llewellyn, brought Edward I. into the field and led to the conquest of Wales. In 1284 Edward's son was born at Carnarvon, and was presented to the Welsh as the 'prince of Wales.' When Llewellyn's head was placed on the Tower of London it was crowned with a willow-wreath in derision of the 'prophecy.' The circular coin and coronation of the Welsh prince synchronised, but the prophecy brought about its own accomplishment.

Circumcellians (*The*), or 'The Circumcelliones,' A.D. 317. A kind of 'Salvation Army' organised by the Donatists, which marched from town to town with staves in their hands, to redress wrongs, and propagate their own religious views. They set slaves at liberty, released debtors from prison, and called themselves 'The Saint's Chiefs.' They were very zealous, and courted martyrdom, but were at last put down by the magistrates. (Lat. *circumcello*, to beat about, to go about. *Excello*, to excel, is to go beyond others).

The leaders were called Captains ; the 'soldiers' (who were peasants) carried huge clubs called *Israelites*; their war-cry was 'Praise be to God.'

Circumspecte Agatis (*The Statute of*), 13 Edw. I. st. 4 c. 1, A.D. 1285. Defining more strictly the power of the clergy, and directing the bishops to see that the parishioners kept their parish churches in repair.

The statute is called ' **Circumspecte Agatis**,' from the first two words.

Cirrhæan War (*The*), B.C. 595–586. This was the First Sacred War. *See* 'Sacred War.'

Cisalpine Republic (*The*), 1797. Bonaparte, after the battle of Lodi, organised two states in Italy, one on the south and the other on the north side of the river Po. These two states were united next year into one under the title of the Cisalpine Republic, with Milan for the capital.

Cistercians, 1098. Reformed Benedictines, founded by Robert, abbot of Molême, in Burgundy, who retired with some twenty monks to Citeaux, in the diocese of Châlons. His order rapidly increased, and acquired the form and privileges of a religious republic, which exercised a sort of dominion over other monastic orders. The Cistercians were great graziers and wool-growers.

Cities of Great Britain.

Aberdeen, *the granite city.*
Birmingham, *the midland capital.*
Brighton, *the queen of watering-places.*
Edinburgh, *the modern Athens.*
Liverpool, *the modern Tyre.*
Manchester, *Cottonopolis.*
Worcester, *the faithful city,* so called from its motto : ' Floreat semper civitas fidelis.'

Brighton is often called ' London-super-mare.'

Citizen King (*The*). 'Le roi citoyen ' Louis Philippe of France (born 1773, reigned 1830–1848, died 1850). He was a member of the Jacobin Club, the son of Philippe Egalité, and one of the leaders of the revolutionary party. As a king he was most despotic and autocratic.

Servius Tullius of Rome was called the ' People's King.'

Cittadini (*The*). The Venetian bourgeois, between the popolari and gentiluomini.

City Flat Cap (*The*). The cap of Edward VI.'s reign, similar to the cap of the Blue-coat Boys. Subsequently called the Statute cap (*q.v.*). *See* ' Cap.'

City of Brotherly Love (*The*). A translation of Philadelphia, the chief city of Pennsylvania, U.S. of America.

City of David (*The*). Mount Zion, the fortified part of Jerusalem, where David had his palace.

City of Elms (*The*). New Haven, Connecticut, the streets of which are thickly shaded with elm-trees.

When happier days shall return . . . the South . . . will rear a monument of gratitude in the beautiful City of Elms, over the ashes of her greatest benefactor (Eli Whitney).—EDW. EVERETT, 1861.

City of Magnificent Distances (*The*). Washington, chief city of the U.S. of America, intersected with fifteen avenues from 130 to 160 feet wide. It was designed to cover a space of four and a half miles long by two and a half wide.

City of Notions (*The*). Boston, Massachusetts, ' the metropolis of Yankeedom.'

City of Peace (*The*). I. Jerusalem. The word Salem means *peace.* Jesus,

'King of the Jews,' was called the 'Prince of Peace' (Salem).

II. Bagdad, the capital of the Abbassides (3 syl.).

The calif retired from Bagdad, and established his residence at Samara on the Tigris, about twelve leagues above the City of Peace.—GIBBON, ch. lii.

City of Rocks (*The*). Nashville, in Tennessee.

City of St. Mark (*The*). Venice.

City of Spindles (*The*). Lowell, in Massachusetts, the largest cotton city of the U.S. of America.

City of Victory (*The*). Cairo, which means victory. The Arabic name is *El Kahira* (the Victorious). Founded 969 by Gohar, lieutenant of Moez (the first Fatamite kalif).

City of the Golden Gate (*The*). San Francisco in California.

City of the Seven Hills (*The*). Both Rome and Constantinople stood on seven hills.

City of the Seventy Isles (*The*). Venice.

City of the Straits (*The*). Detroit, which means a *strait*. It is situated on the west bank of the strait connecting Lake St. Clair with Lake Erie.

City of the Violated Treaty (*The*). Limerick, in Ireland; so called from the repeated violations of the treaty signed Oct. 1691, granting to Roman Catholics the same privileges in the exercise of their religion as they enjoyed in the reign of Charles II.

Years of unjust and vindictive penal laws show that the name, 'City of the Violated Treaty,' was well bestowed.—KNIGHT.

City of the Violet Crown (*The*). Athens. Aristophanês (*Equites*, and *Acharnians*) calls it ἰοστέφανος. Ion [meaning a *violet*] was a representative king of Athens, whose four sons gave names to the four Athenian classes. It was Ion's city, the city of the violet, the city of King Ion or king of the Violet Crown.

Similarly, Paris, the city of Louis or Lys, is the city of the lily.

[Pitt] loved England, as an Athenian loved the City of the Violet Crown.—MACAULAY.

Civil Era of Constantinople (*The*). This era began 1 Sept. B.C. 5508.

Civil Jewish Era (*The*). This era began Oct. B.C. 3761.

Civil Law (*The*), or 'Corpus Juris Civilis.' A collection of the laws, edicts, and imperial decrees of the Roman Empire; first compiled by private individuals, afterwards by Theodosius, A.D. 438, and finally by Justinian, A.D. 533. It comprises (1) The Institutes or first principles of Roman Law; (2) The Digest or Pandects in 50 books, being the opinions of eminent lawyers; (3) a new Code or collection of Imperial Constitutions in 12 books, and (4) the Novels, or new constitutions of succeeding emperors. This body of laws was unknown in feudal times till a copy was discovered at Amalfi, in Italy in 1130, and produced a greater effect on the laws, pursuits, and characters of the Middle Ages than any book ever published before or since.

The Corpus Juris Civilis, with certain modifications, restrictions, and additions, is still an authority in our Ecclesiastical, Admiralty, and University Courts.

Civil List (*The*). The yearly sum of money granted by the British government for the support of the household of the reigning monarch and the dignity of the crown.

It used to include the royal household, the privy purse, the royal palaces, the salaries of the chancellor, judges, great officers of state, and ambassadors, the incomes allowed to the several members of the royal family, secret service money, pensions, and other irregular claims. The army and navy, with the interest of the national debt, have been separate charges since the accession of James I.

At the beginning of the reign of Victoria the Queen surrendered the hereditary revenues of the crown, and received from parliament a yearly stipend of 385,000*l.*, with 1,200*l.* a year for pensions 'to those who have just claims on the royal bounty.' Her Majesty pays her own household, but all other national expenses are paid by parliament as separate items.

Civil Marriage Act. 6, 7 Will. IV. c. 85. 17 Aug., 1836. Provided for the celebration of marriage without religious service, before a registrar, or with religious service in any certified place of religious worship, leaving it optional with the parties concerned to be married, as aforetime, in a parish church, by licence, or after banns. By this Act marriage is constituted a civil compact consummated before witnesses, with or without religious service.

Civil Oath (*The*), 13 July, 1790. Taken in the Champ de Mars, first by Lafayette on behalf of the National Guards, then by the President of the Assembly, and then by the king himself (Louis XVI.), who said 'I, king of the French, swear to use all power delegated to me by the constitutional law of the State to maintain the Constitution (*q.v.*) decreed by the National Assembly, and accepted by me.' The oath taken by Lafayette and the President was : 'We swear to be faithful to the nation, the law, and the king. To maintain with our utmost power the Constitution decreed by the National Assembly, and to remain united to all Frenchmen by the indissoluble bonds of fraternity.'

Champ de Mars, pronounce *Sharnd Mars.*

Civil Service (*The*). The duties rendered by those in government appointments, and paid for by the State. The whole list would be over 15,000 names, including the officers of the royal household, the officers of the House of Lords and House of Commons, all such offices as the Treasury, Home, War, Foreign, Admiralty, Post, &c. (but not policemen, postmen, and such other employés as receive weekly wages). In 1855 a law was made for the examination of candidates for the Civil Service, who enter generally as clerks and rise by seniority, the age at entrance being between eighteen and twenty-five, and the first year's stipend about 80*l.* Of course the more important departments are not included.

The Civil Service Estimates are between seven and eight millions sterling annually.

Civil Wars of Rome (*The*). In their widest extent they began with Tiberius Gracchus, and terminated with the election of Octavius Augustus to the empire, B.C. 133-31. In a more limited sense, they mean the contest between Caius Marius and Cornelius Sylla, or Sulla (B.C. 88-78).

The original cause of the civil war was the struggle between the oligarchy and the democracy of Rome. This struggle lasted till Sylla restored the Senate to sovereignty; but this sove-

reignty was soon disturbed by Julius Cæsar.

Clan-na-Gael (*The*), 1870. An Irish Fenian organisation founded in Philadelphia, and known in secret as the 'United Brotherhood.' Its avowed object is to secure 'the complete and absolute ird ipendence of Ireland from Great Britain; and the complete severance of all political connection between the two countries, to be effected by unceasing preparation for armed insurrection in Ireland.' *See* 'New Departure.'

In 1883 Alexander Sullivan was elected one of the three heads of this murder club. His colleagues were Colonel Michael Boland, and D. C. Feely (or, as some say, Michael Kirwin). To this club the dynamite outrages in London are due, the designs to murder the Queen's ministers, and all the outrages of 1883 connected with 'Home Rule' (*q.v.*).

Clare College, Cambridge, 1326. This is University Hall, founded by Richard Badew, chancellor of the University. It was destroyed by fire, and on its restoration by Elizabeth de Clare, countess of Ulster, changed its name to Clare Hall; since 1857 called Clare College.

Clare Election (*The*), 1828. An epoch in the history of Ireland. Daniel O'Connell was elected M.P., although, being a Catholic, he was disqualified from taking his seat. So popular was he, and so powerful the Catholic Association, that the Duke of Wellington (the premier), and Sir Robert Peel (leader of the House of Commons) did not dare to resist the movement; and in 1829 Sir Robert brought in his bill for Catholic Emancipation, which was carried.

The Clare election was the harsh prelude to Catholic Emancipation and civil equality.— HOWITT, *History of England* (year 1828, p. 125).

Clarenceux King-of-arms. English herald of the southern provinces. That of the northern provinces is called Norroy (*q.v.*). Clarenceux king-of-arms, like Garter king-of-arms, was first appointed by Henry V.

Clarendon, in Wiltshire (*The Council of*), A.D. 1164. It comprised the king (Henry II.), the 2 archbishops, 11 bishops, 40 of the higher nobility, and a host of barons. It was convened in consequence of the conduct of Thomas Becket, and its judgments are comprised in the 16 canons called 'The Constitutions of Clarendon' (*q.v.*).

N

Clarendon Press (*The*). University of Oxford. The building was erected by Lord Clarendon, partly out of the profits of his 'History of the Rebellion,' 1713–1830. On the south side Bibles and Prayer-books are printed, on the north side general literature. Ten delegates have the management of the press, the vice-chancellor being one. The corresponding foundation in Cambridge is the Pitt Press (*q.v.*).

Clarisses, or 'Poor Clarisses,' 1224. Founded by St. Francis of Assisi, and placed under the charge of Clara, or Clarissa, of Assisi, his favourite nun. *See* under 'Franciscans.'

Clarty Hole. Muddy hole or slough, the site of Abbotsford, on the south bank of the Tweed, the residence of Sir W. Scott.

Claude (*The English*). Richard Wilson (1713–1782).

Clayton-Bulwer Treaty, 1850. *See* 'Bulwer-Clayton,' &c.

Clean-the-Causey Riot, 1515. The street riot between the rival factions of Angus and Arran. The former represented the Douglas party, and the latter the Hamiltons. The partisans of the Earl of Angus were swept from the causeys or streets like dirt.

Cleanest City in the World (*The*). Broeck, in Holland. It is 'painfully clean and neat.'

Cleanse the Causeway (*The Battle of*), 1522. A skirmish between the Douglases and Hamiltons in the High-street, Edinburgh. The Douglas party occupied the High-street, and attacked their opponents as they issued in disorder from the narrow closes or lanes. The Hamiltons were driven out of the city, leaving upwards of 70 men dead.

Their strife had been appeased since the battle of Cleanse-the-Causeway, and Arran drew out his forces in support of Angus, and not in opposition to him.—Sir W. SCOTT, *Hist. of Scotland*, xxii.

Clear the Causeys. *See* 'Cleanse the Causeway' and 'Clean the Causey.'

Clearing-House (*The*), 1775. A building in Lombard Street, where debit and credit cheques from different banks are balanced by *transfer tickets*. These tickets are white and green; the *white* being used when the bank has to *pay* a balance to the Clearing-house, and the

green when it has to *receive* one. By this means transactions to the amount of several millions daily are settled.

There is a Railway Clearing-house in Seymour Street, London (adjoining the Euston Station), which enables different companies to carry on a through traffic. The Railway Clearing Act was passed in 1850. Most large commercial cities have clearing-houses.

Clem's Day(*Old*). St. Clement's day, the blacksmiths' day (23 Nov.). St. Clement is patron saint of blacksmiths, as St. Crispin is of shoemakers, St. Winifred of bakers, St. Louis of barbers, St. John Port Latin of booksellers, St. Lucy of candle-makers, St. Joseph of carpenters, St. Christopher of ferrymen, St. Peter of fishermen, St. Sever of fullers, St. Eloy of goldsmiths, St. William of hatters, St. Yves of lawyers, St. Arnold of millers, St. Florian of mercers, St. Cloud of nailers, St. Luke of painters and sculptors, St. Cosmo of doctors, St. Sebastian of pinmakers, St. Gore of potters, St. Nicholas of seamen, St. Gwendoline of shepherds, St. Hubert of sportsmen, St. Peter of stonemasons, St. Goodman of tailors, St. Urban of vintners, St. Boniface of wheelwrights, St. Blaise of woolcombers &c. &c.

Clementi'na. A spurious account of the journeys of Clemens Romānus with the Apostle Peter. The Apostolic Canons and Constitutions attributed to him are also spurious. Clemens is said to have died in 102. *See* 'Literary Forgeries.'

Clementine Liturgy (*The*). The oldest liturgy extant. It directs that two deacons shall stand, one on each side of the altar, holding their fans of vellum, fine linen, or peacock's feathers, to wave off the flies, and prevent their defiling the sacred elements. *See* 'Liturgy.'

Clementine Museum (*The*), of the Vatican, 1773. Founded by Clement XIV. It was improved by Pius VI., and then called Museo-Pio-Clementino.

Clementines (*The*). Nineteen discourses, preceded by two letters. One of Peter to James, bishop of Jerusalem, and the other of Clement to the same. The discourses are spurious Christian stories, but the work was esteemed next to the Holy Scriptures. There is no reason to believe it to have been the work of Clemens Romānus. On these fictitious homilies rests the sole evidence that St.

Peter ever was in Rome. *See* 'Literary Forgeries.'

What is usually understood by Clementines is the third part of the Decretals of Raimond de Pennafort, a continuation of the text (*q.v.*) together with the rescripts since Boniface VIII. Undertaken by the order of Clement V. The Clementines of Clement I. are homilies, and wholly apocryphal. The Clementines of Clement V. are 'constitutions,' decrees, or rescripts of Roman pontiffs, forming the seventh volume of the Decretals. The Extravagantes Joannis (XXII.) form what was the 'Extravagantes Communes' of the Corpus Juris Canonici.

Clementines and Urbanists,
1378. The followers of Clement VII., pope in Avignon, and Urban VI., the simultaneous pope in Rome. France and Spain were Clementines. The split lasted fifty-one years, during all which time there were always two popes.

Cleomen'ic war (*The*). The war waged by Cleomĕnês III., king of Sparta (225–222), against the Achæans, aided by Antigonus Doson, king of Macedonia. Cleomenês was completely defeated at the battle of Sellasia, B.C. 222, and in B.C. 220 put an end to his life.

Cleopatra's Needles. Two obelisks of the time of Thothmes III., who reigned in Egypt some 1,500 years before Cleopatra was born.

Clerical Titles. The English clergy first assumed their honorary titles at the beginning of the 18th cent. Every clergyman is called 'Reverend.' Addressed in letters by strangers 'Rev. Sir.' An archbishop is styled, 'Most Reverend Father in God,' or 'The Most Reverend Arbp. of —.' Addressed as 'Your Grace,' 'May it please your Grace.' A bishop is styled 'The Right Reverend Father in God,' or 'The Right Reverend the Bishop of —.' Addressed as 'My Lord.' Deans are called 'The Very Reverend the Dean of —.' Addressed in letters 'Mr. Dean,' or 'Dear Mr. Dean.' Archdeacons are called 'The Venerable.' Addressed in letters by strangers 'Rev. Sir.'

The title of Canon was assumed by canons and honorary canons in the last quarter of the 19th cent. They are addressed as Canon —, or the Rev. Canon —. *See* 'Church Orders.'

Cler'ici Regula'res (4 syl.). Monks ordained to the priesthood, and who lived in monasteries (10th cent.).

Cler'ici Secula'res (4 syl.). Parish clergymen who lived in their own houses and might marry (10th cent.).

'Clericis Laicos' (*The Bull*). **I.**

1074. By which Gregory VII. forbade prelates to receive investiture from secular princes. This bull gave rise to the long contention about investitures.

II. Of 1160. Directed against Kaiser Friedrich I.

III. Of 1227, 1246. Directed against Friedrich II., *Barbarossa.*

IV. Of 1263. Directed against Manfroi, king of Naples.

V. Of 1294. Issued by Pope Boniface VIII., forbidding Edward I. and all other princes, under pain of excommunication, to tax church property without permission from Rome. In 1296 Edward, in defiance of this bull, did tax church property, and that severely; nay, more, he outlawed all those ecclesiastics who refused to pay the levy, and then confiscated their whole property.

VI. Of 1327, 1346. Directed against Ludwig of Bavaria.

Clerk of Assize. A salaried officer attached to each circuit, who accompanies the judge at the assizes, to issue subpœnas, orders, writs, and other processes.

Clerk of the Pipe. An exchequer clerk for making out leases for crown lands, sheriffs' accounts, and so on. The Pipe Office was abolished in 1833.

The office is so called (says Lord Bacon) because the whole receipt of the court is finally conveyed into it by means of divers small pipes or quills, as water into a cistern.

Clerks in Oxford University. Students on the foundation, received at reduced fees. These foundations belong to the five colleges: Magdalen, Merton, New College, Queen's, and Wadham. *See* 'Bible Clerks,' 'Sizars,' 'Servitors.' At Jesus College, Oxford, there are three 'clerks' not on the foundation.

Clerk-ales. A festive meeting in the house of the parish clerk, celebrated with drinking, dancing, and sports.

The ordinary amusements (1632) in country parishes were church-ales, clerk-ales, and bid-ales.—T. V. SHORT, D.D., *Hist. of the Church of England*, p. 392.

Climacteric Years. Certain years in the life of man which were at one time considered to be turning-points in his health and fortune. They were 7 and its multiples. The Grand Climacteric was 63, which consists of 3 times 3 multiplied by 7, all 'sacred' numbers.

Clinic Baptism. Baptism administered to a *clinicus*, or one on a sick-bed. No clinicus could enter holy orders.

Clinicus. One who has received *clinic baptism*—that is, one who has been baptized on a sick-bed.

Cliquot. The sobriquet given by *Punch* to Frederick William IV. of Prussia (1795, 1840–1861), who was fond of champagne with the 'Cliquot' brand.

Clog Almanac (*The*). A square stick of some hard wood about 8 inches long, which might either be hung up in a room or be fitted into a walking-stick. It was a 'perpetual almanac,' showing the Sundays and other fixed festivals. Used in Denmark, and brought to England by the Danish invaders.

Close Communionists, or 'Strict Communionists.' Those Baptist dissenters who admit no one to partake with them of the Lord's Supper who is not one of their special persuasion. Dr. Doddridge says, 'They most inconsistently avow that they hope to sit all together in the great Marriage Supper of the Lamb, but refuse to sit together at the table of a little Bethel.'

Closelings, 1687. Private conferences in which James II. sought to win over men of influence and men in office to aid him in the abolition of the Test Acts, which excluded Catholics from office. He said, of course, men must act as they think proper, but, at the same time, they could not expect to continue in his favour or employ while they acted in direct violation of his wishes. The Lords Derby, Thanet, Shrewsbury, Lumley, and Newport, with Vice-admiral Herbert and many others, at once resigned their respective offices.

Closter Seven (*Convention of*), 10 Sept., 1757. Concluded with the French by the Duke of Cumberland, but disavowed by the British parliament. By this most disgraceful compact Hanover was left in the hands of the French, and it was agreed that England and France should take no further part in the Seven Years' War.

Clothier of England (*The*). Jack of Newbury—that is, John Winchcomb—the greatest clothier in England in the reign of Henry VIII. He kept 100 looms in his own house at Newbury.

Cloveshoo, in Kent (*The Council of*), 747. Called by Cuthbert, arch-bishop of Canterbury, in deference to a request of Pope Zacharias. It was decided in this Council that bishops should visit their dioceses every year; that the people should be taught the Creed and the Lord's Prayer in the vulgar tongue, and have the two sacraments explained to them; prayers for the dead were enjoined. The great historical value of this council is, however, that there is no indication that the English Church was at the time under submission to the See of Rome, although Wilfrid, an ultra-partisan of the Roman pontiff, and friend of Cuthbert's, was certainly present.

Club (*The*), 1689. A league of discontented Whigs in the Scotch Convention of Estates, at the beginning of the reign of William and Mary. The leaders were Montgomery, the Lords Annandale and Ross, and the factious Sir Patrick Hume. These clubbists caused for a time great trouble. They opposed every measure which the ministers introduced in the Scotch 'Convention of Estates,' refused all supplies, and claimed for the convention a veto on the nomination of Scotch judges, by which they put a stop to the business of the Court of Session. They tried to ruin the Dalrymples, and succeeded in carrying an act to incapacitate all who had served James II. from holding office under the new sovereigns. The government of Scotland was at a deadlock; both the legal and legislative business was at an end. The object of the clubbists was to compel the king to give them posts in the government of Scotland. By the end of the year their influence declined, and the nation insisted that business should be obstructed no longer.

Club des Enragés (*Le*), 1789. A political club which acted with the Breton club (*q.v.*) at the outbreak of the Great French Revolution. When the States-General was about to be convened, these two clubs vehemently insisted that the Tiers Etat should outnumber the other two orders together.

Club Monarchique (*Le*), 1790. A nickname of the 'Feuillants Club' (*q.v.*).

Club Parliament (*The*), 1426. So called because, arms being prohibited, the retainers of the barons appeared with clubs on their shoulders. This prohibition was made in consequence of the brawls of the Duke of Gloucester and Cardinal Beaufort. *See* 'Parliaments.'

Club of Equality and Freedom
(*The*), 1793. A Scotch club in sympathy with the French revolutionists.

Club of '89 (*The*).
A branch of the Jacobin Club (*q.v.*). It held its meetings in the Palais Royal. Lafayette, Bailly the mayor of Paris, the Abbé Sieyès, and Mirabeau were members of this club. Though called the 'Club of '89,' it was not founded till 1790. It was nicknamed Le Club Monarchique, being friendly to the monarchic constitution. It changed its quarters from the Palais Royal to a convent of the Feuillants, near the Tuileries, and was then known at 'The Feuillants.'

Clubbists.
See above, 'The Club.' 1689.

Clubmen, 1644.
A society formed for self-defence against Maurice's and Goring's armies in the west. They were yeomen and others, who armed themselves with clubs to resist military marauders. They were not political, and being between two stools, were befriended by neither. The king's party hated them because they hindered their movements; and the parliamentary party called them 'traitors to the commonwealth' because they opposed the depredations of Fairfax's army. They were strong in numbers (some 10,000 in all), but want of discipline was their weakness. Their badge was a white ribbon.

The republican party had cause to be suspicious if it is true that 'after the battle of Naseby there was found on Sir Lewis Davis a royal commission for raising clubmen to aid the king's party.'

Cluniac Order (*The*), or 'Cluniacs,'
942. A branch of the Benedictine monks reformed by Odo abbot of Cluny, in Normandy. Introduced into England by William earl of Warren, in 1077.

Coal Burner (*The*).
Edmund king of Sweden (1026–1051) was called *Kolbrenner* because he enacted 'If anyone injures his neighbour's goods, he shall have goods to the same value burnt in a coal-fire.'

Coalition Ministry (*The*).
The ministry formed under Lord North and Charles James Fox, from 5 April, 1783, to 19 Dec. same year.

Also the Aberdeen Administration, 28 Dec., 1852, to 30 Jan., 1855.

Coalitions against France.
First coalition 1793, made by England and all the powers of Europe, except Sweden and Denmark. Napoleon Bonaparte won the battles of Montenotte, Milesimo, Dego, Mondŏvi, Lodi, Lonato, Castiglioni, Bassano, Arcŏla, Rivoli, Tagliamento. The Treaty of Campo Formio was made 17 Oct., 1797.

Second coalition 1799, by Russia, Austria, England, Naples, Portugal, Turkey, &c., a year and a half after the Treaty of Campo Formio; 1800 famous for Bonaparte's 'Forty Days' Campaign,' in which he won the battles of Montebello and Marengo; and Moreau won those of Hochstädt, Hohenlinden, and Traun. Peace of Luneville, 9 Feb., 1801.

Third coalition 1805, consisting of England, Austria, Russia, and Sweden. Napoleon won the battle of Austerlitz. Peace of Presburg, 26 Dec., 1805.

Fourth coalition 6 Oct., 1806, to the Treaty of Tilsit, 8 July, 1807, consisting of Prussia, Saxony, Great Britain, and Russia. Napoleon won the battles of Schleitz (9 Oct.), Saalfeld (10 Oct.), Jena and Auerstadt (14 Oct.), Potsdam (16, 17 Oct.), Berlin (28 Oct.), Eylau, the most bloody of all his victories (8 Feb., 1807), Heilsberg (10 June), and Friedland (14 June, 1807).

Fifth coalition of April 1809, to the battle of Wagram (6 July, 1809). Napoleon won the battle of Ingolstadt (20 April), Eckmühl, in Bavaria (22 April), and Wagram (6 July).

He was wounded in the heel at Ratisbon 23 April; was defeated by the Archduke Karl at Aspern 21 May, and at Essling 22 May; and was excommunicated by the pope 10 June, 1809.

Sixth and last coalition, consisting of Prussia, Russia, Austria, Sweden, and Great Britain, 3 March, 1813 to the banishment of Napoleon to St. Helena, 18 Oct., 1815.

Napoleon *won* the battles of Lützen 2 May, 1813, Bautzen (in Saxony) 19 May, Wurschen 20 May, Hochkirchen 21 May, Dresden 27 Aug. (here Marshal Moreau was slain), St. Dizier 27 Jan., 1814, Brienne 29 Jan., Champ-Aubert 10 Feb., Montmirail 11 Feb., Château-Thierry 13 Feb., Champ-Aubert (a second time) 14 Feb., Méry-sur-Seine 24 Feb.; and after his escape from Elba he won the battle of Ligny 16 June, 1815.

He *lost* the battles of Leipzig 16, 18, 19 Oct., 1813; Rothière 1 Feb., 1814; Laon 7 March, Quatre Bras 16 June, and WATERLOO 18 June, 1815.

Coastguard. A force originally established to prevent smuggling. In 1856 it was placed under the Admiralty, and is now divided into eleven districts, each under a captain of the navy, and the whole under a commodore. The number is 4,000.

Coat and Conduct Money. Money required for the equipment and transport of the militia. This tax was extorted by Charles I. ('Fairfax Correspondence,' vol. ii. p. 2.)

Cobden Prize (*The*). For an essay on political economy. For members of the University of Cambridge who have not graduated more than three years. Value 50*l*. Founded by the Cobden Club in 1876. *See* 'Political Economy.'

Cochrane-plack. Debased coin issued in Scotland in the reign of James III. by Cochrane, the royal mason, on whom the king conferred the earldom of Mar, lately made vacant by the murder of the king's brother. When Cochrane was told that the base coin would certainly be called in, he answered incredulously, 'Yes, on the day when I am hanged.' But so it turned out—Cochrane was hanged, and the Cochrane-plack was called in.

Cockade City (*The*). Petersburg, in Virginia.

Cockburn's Act. The Act of Sir Alexander Cockburn in 1853 to abolish 'list offices,' set up after the Act of 1845 to abolish sweepstakes. In list offices money was staked in advance on an adventure, and they proved to be most disastrous of all the methods of gambling, especially among clerks, shopboys, and servants, who were induced to rob their employers under the promise of certainly winning.

Though betting-houses were abolished in 1853 (16 & 17 Vict. c. 119), yet Tattersall escapes the law because he himself has direct personal interest in a bet, like a ' bank '; and gentlemen there bet with each other freely, without any interference whatever. No bet can be recovered as a debt in any court of law. They are 'debts of honour' only. Gambling was prohibited by law even in the reign of Henry VIII. (1541).

Cock Lane Ghost (*The*). Near West Smithfield, London, 1760–1762. The Duke of York, with Lady Northumberland, Lady Mary Coke, Lord Hertford, and Horace Walpole, all in one hackney-coach, drove to the 'haunted house,' while the rain fell in torrents. The house was crammed full, above fifty people having crowded into the room, lighted with one tallow candle, and stayed from seven till half-past one in midwinter, to witness the knockings and scratchings of the ghost, which refused to make any manifestations. But such a company tells plainly what hold the imposition had taken on the public. The case was this : Kent, a broker, having lost his wife, was visited by his sister-in-law Fanny, with whom he fell in love. They took lodgings with Parsons, parish clerk of St. Sepulchre's, and each made a will leaving all to the survivor. Fanny died suddenly, and Parsons gave out that Kent had murdered her. In proof of this, certain knockings and scratchings were heard every night in the chamber lately occupied by Fanny, and these were attributed to her ghost. When questions were asked ' the ghost knocked once to signify *yes*, twice to signify *no*, and scratched to indicate displeasure.' Parson's daughter, a child of 12, took a board into her bed, and made these knockings and scratchings, which for many months set all London agog, and even made matter for sober history.

Cock-pen Tree. A large hollow oak in that part of Sherwood Forest called Birkland, from the number of silver birches. In the hollow of this tree game cocks were penned for the Shrove Tuesday sports, to keep them well out of the way of dunghill poultry. The tree is now called 'The Major,' or the ' Major's Oak,' from Major Rooke, the antiquary.

This tree is very large, fifteen persons can be packed inside it. The bole grips the earth with a circumference of 90 feet; 6 feet above the ground its girth is 30 feet; and its branches cover a circumference of 240 feet. It stands in a part of the forest belonging to the Earl Manvers, and is almost always called the 'Major Oak.'

Cockpit, Whitehall, the Privy Council Office. Also a locality where persons lived, for George duke of Albemarle died ' at his apartment in the Cockpit;' and the Princess Anne, we are told, 'left the Cockpit ' to live ' at Zion House.'

After the Restoration, the Treasury Board sat at a place called the Cockpit.—COX, *Inst. of Eng. Govern.* ii. vii. 682 (1863).

Cockpit of Europe (*The*). Belgium is so called because it has been the site of more battles than any nation in Europe.

Cocles, or Horatius Cocles, of Horn. John Haring, of Horn, who defended the Diemerdyke against 1,000 Spaniards, and made his escape unwounded by either spear or gun.

Cocles, or Horatius Cocles, of the Tyrol, 1793. Alexander Davy Dumas, father of the novelist, who, at Brixen, defended the passage of a bridge on which Dumouriez's success wholly depended.

Code Henri (*The*). That is the code of Henri, king of Hayti (1767, 1811–1820). Joining the black insurgents against the French, he became head of the Haytian army in 1806, president of Hayti for life in 1807, and king of Hayti in 1811. He was a giant in stature, and his courage was indisputable.

Code de Napoléon (*Le*), 15 Mar., 1803 to 17 Sept., 1804. A French code of laws regulating all that pertains 'aux droits civils, à la personne et à la propriété des citioyens.'

There are several other codes used in France, as Le Code de Commerce, Le Code de Procédure Civile, Le Code d'Instruction Criminelle, Le Code Pénal, Le Code Rural, Le Code Forestier, Le Code de la Pêche fluviale; all except the last two are Napoleonic codes. There are also Le Code Militaire, Le Code Maritime, Le Code de l Enregistrement, &c.

Code Noire (*Le*). That is, a code of laws for the negroes in the French colonies, made by Colbert, in the reign of Louis XIV.

Code of Lanego (*The*). An excellent code of laws drawn up at Lanego, in Portugal, by order of King Alfonso I. (1139–1185).

Code of Melrose (*The*). A collection of laws compiled at Melrose Abbey; the work of many learned jurisconsults, appointed for the purpose by David I. of Scotland, who reigned 1114–1143.

Codex Alexandri'nus. Long supposed to be the oldest MS. of the Bible extant. It is preserved in the British Museum, and was published in facsimile under the care of Charles Godfrey Woide, in 1786 (London). It contains all the New Testament, except Matt. i., xxv. 5; John vi. 50, viii. 52; and 2 Cor. iv. 13, xii. 6. This valuable MS. was found in Alexandria,

and was presented to Charles I. in 1628 by Cyril Lucar, at one time patriarch of Alexandria. It is in four vols., size 10 in. by 13, in double columns, and in uncial or capital letters. The Codex Vaticanus (*q.v.*) is older. *See* 'Sinaitic MS.'

Supposed to be of the 5th cent., towards the close.

Codex Argen'teus, or rather ' Argenteus Codex.' A MS. of the Gospels in Mœso-Gothic, by Ulfilas bishop of the Goths (348–388). It was discovered by Arnold Mercātor, in the abbey of Werden, and taken to Prague in 1597, where it remained till 1648, when it was captured and presented to Christina of Sweden. Finally, it was presented to the University of Upsala in 1662 by Count Magnus Gabriel de la Gardie. Called Argenteus, or the Silver MS., from its silver letters.

Codex Augiensis. Purchased by Richard Bentley, and presented, after his death, to Trinity College, Cambridge, by Thomas Bentley. It contains most of the Pauline Epistles, in Greek and Latin.

Codex Basiliensis. A MS. copy of the four evangelists, with a few gaps, attributed to the close of the 10th cent. Belonging to the library of Basel, or Basle.

Codex Bezæ, or ' Cantabrigiensis,' A Bible MS. of the middle of the 6th cent., once in the possession of Beza, and sent by him as a gift to the University of Cambridge. It contains the Gospels and the Acts. Edited in 2 vols. folio by Thomas Kipling in 1793.

Codex Claromonta'nus. Containing the Pauline Epistles. This MS., which belongs to the latter half of the 6th cent., was edited in facsimile by Tischendorf in 1852 (Lips.)

Codex Coislinia'nus. Belonging to the Imperial Library of Paris. It is a MS. of the 6th cent.

Codex Cyprius. Formerly Colbertinus. Containing the four Gospels. The MS. belongs to the 9th cent.

Codex Damasce'nus. A Greek MS. of the Old and New Testament, with the Epistle of Barnabas and part of ' Shepherd' of Hermas. It was discovered in 1889 by M. Papadopulos in the vaults of the Arabic library of Damascus.

From the extremely meagre description given of this new-found MS., it seems to be a copy of the Sinaitic Codex. The doubt might easily be settled by referring to the 'Shepherd,' which in the Sinaitic MS. lacks the conclusion.

'Codex Diplomat'icus Siciliæ,' 1791. A literary forgery, by Abbé Giuseppe Vella, who confessed his frauds, and was sentenced to fifteen years' imprisonment. He died 1814. *See* 'Literary Forgeries.'

His other book is *Libro del Consiglio di Egitto,* 1793.

Codex Dubliniensis. A palimpsest belonging to Trinity College, Dublin. It belongs to the close of the 6th cent., and was edited in facsimile by Dr. Barrett in 1801.

Codex Ephra'imi. The Parisian palimpsest, so called because over the original Bible MS. some treatises of Ephraim the Syrian have been inscribed. It is preserved in the Royal Library at Paris. Edited in facsimile by Tischendorf, 1843 (Lips.) Latter part of 5th cent.

Codex Sinait'icus. A Greek MS. of the Old and New Testament, with the Epistle of Barnabas, and part of the 'Shepherd' of Hermas, discovered in 1859 by Tischendorf in the Convent of St. Catherine. This codex, supposed to belong to the 4th cent., is one of the oldest in the world. In 1868 it was acquired by the Imperial Library of St. Petersburg.

Codex Theodosia'nus. A *recueil* of the Roman laws since the reign of Constantine, reduced by the order of Theodosius II., and promulgated in the East in 438. Valentinian III. introduced the codex into the West.

Codex Vaticanus. The oldest MS. of the New Testament, containing the four gospels, the Acts, the Catholic Epistles, and the Pauline Epistles. A facsimile of this MS., comprising the LXX. version of the Old Testament, was issued at Rome (edited by Cardinal Mai), and published in 1858, 4 vols. folio. Called 'Vaticānus' because it is preserved in the Vatican Library at Rome. Its date is supposed to be of the 4th cent. It does not contain the Revelation of John the divine. Copies are to be found in all the chief libraries of Christendom.

This MS. contains 700 leaves of the finest vellum, about a foot square, bound together.

It is very doubtful which codex is the older, the Vaticānus or the Sinaiticus. The secretary of the Bible Society (18 April, 1890) writes to me that the latter is 'regarded as the oldest MS. of the New Testament.'

Cœ'nobites (3 syl.). Those who lived in community, having all things in common. The locality where they dwelt was called the Cœnobium, and the first was built by Pachomius in Egypt A.D. 340. The cœnobium was subsequently called a 'monastery,' and the Cœnobite a 'monk.' It was St. Basel who reduced monachism into a system A.D. 378.

Of course the word is compounded of the two Greek words κοινός, βίος common life, or living in common), in contradistinction to Anchorites or Hermits, who lived solitary lives.

Cœur de Lion, 'Lion's-heart.' Richard I. of England (1157, 1189–1199). Probably so called from his generosity, magnanimity, and bravery.

It is said by the troubadours that Richard acquired the name of Lion's-heart from a contest he had with a lion, like David, the son of Jesse, and in the contest, thrusting his mailed arm down the lion's throat, he tore out its heart.

Cogito, ergo sum. Because I think, therefore I must exist. Descartes's axiom (1597–1650). He argued thus: 'I think, but thought cannot proceed from nothing; if therefore I think, I must be something.' Pushing the argument further back, as *ex nihilo nihil fit*, if something cannot proceed from nothing, and I myself am something, there must be a something from which I proceed, and that something is God.

Of course the fallacy of this argument is patent, for it makes cogitation the proof of what is required to be proved, and Descartes (2 syl.) is hopelessly involved in a vicious circle. Ice is cold, therefore there is such a thing as ice.

Descartes furthermore said : 'I can think of eternity and infinity, subjects beyond a finite mind ; and as no man can think beyond himself, man must possess a soul, "spark of the Deity." But can a man think of either eternity or infinity ? Does he not think instead of time without dimension, and the finite multiplied ?'

Cognac (*Treaty of*), 22 Mar., 1526. Between Leo X., François I., Henry VIII. of England, Venice, Florence, and Switzerland.

Cognizances of English Kings. The Cross of St. George has been the royal badge since its introduction by Edward III., but all the kings up to the time of Henry VII. (inclusive) had their private cognizance also.

STEPHEN, a sagittary.
HENRY II., an escarbuncle.
RICHARD I., JOHN, and HENRY III., a star above a horned crescent.

EDWARD I., a golden rose.
EDWARD II., a castle, in allusion to his mother's arms (Castile).
EDWARD III. had several badges, as a falcon, the ostrich feather, a griffin, and the stump of a tree.
RICHARD II. adopted the stump and the falcon, but added the hart couchant, the peacock, and the sun behind a cloud.
HENRY IV., the ermine, the eagle, and the panther crowned.
HENRY V., a lighted beacon, an antelope and swan chained, with crowns round their necks.
HENRY VI., the antelope, panther, and double ostrich feather.
EDWARD IV., the falcon within a fetterlock, the rose and sun, a white hart, a white wolf, and a sable dragon and bull.
EDWARD V., the falcon and fetterlock.
RICHARD III., the rose and sun, a white boar; or boar and thorn-tree.
HENRY VII., a hawthorn bush crowned, a grey-hound, the red dragon of Wales, a portcullis, red and white rose combined.

Coiffure à la serviette (La). A
head-dress devised by Léonard, hair-dresser of Marie Antoinette. It consisted of a coarse whity-brown table-napkin twisted into the hair amidst real vegetables, such as artichokes, cabbage-leaves, carrots, turnips, and radishes.

Coincidences—
I. The fall of Robespierre was 1794, which added together = 21. Now add the two together thus, 1794+21=1815, the fall of Napoleon.

II. 1815 added together = 15, which two added together, thus 1815+15=1830, the fall of Charles IX.

It would be remarkable if 1902 were to complete the triad so striking in French history.

III. It is curious about Louis Philippe. The year of his birth, or the year of the queen's birth, or the year of his flight, added to the year of his coronation, will give 1848, the date of abdication (this is another French triad—*q.v.*). He was born 1773; his queen was born 1782, and his flight was 1809; the sum of each is 18. And 1830 + 18 = 1848.

IV. Charles I., Louis XVI. each contains 8 letters.

Charles was decapitated January, Louis was guillotined January.

The sum of the day of the month in each case is 3. Thus Charles was executed January 30, Louis January 21.

The sum of the year in each case is 20. Thus 1649 = 20; and 1793 = 20.

Hence, finally, the entire summation is identical, 8 letters in the names, month January, sum of the days of the month 3, sum of the year 20; and total 31 + January.

V. Louis XIV. The number 14 is the sum of the figures of his age, 77 = 14;

the sum of the figures which make the date of his coronation 1643 = 14; and the sum of the figures which make the date of his death 1715 = 14.

Coining Machine of the Revolution (*The*). The guillotine, so called by Fouquier Tinville, the public accuser, because the wealthy were always suspected when money was needed.

Cold shade of the aristocracy (*The*). It was Colonel Napier, in his 'History of the Peninsular War,' who said the people were doomed 'to wither in the cold shade of the aristocracy.'

Cold Year (*The*), 1614.

Collar of Tomar (*The*). A golden torque which Malachy, monarch of Ireland, took from the neck of a Danish chieftain whom he had conquered.

Let Erin remember the days of old,
  Ere her faithless sons betrayed her,
When Malachy wore the collar of gold
  Which he won from the proud invader.
                T. MOORE, *Irish Melodies.*

Collection des Deux-Ponts (*La*). A collection of the Latin classics published at Deux-Ponts, or Zwey-brücken in Bavaria, towards the close of the 18th and in the first quarter of the 19th cent.

Colliberts. So the Cagots (*q.v.*) are called in Poitou, Maine, and Anjou.

Colloquy of Poissy (*The*), 1561. A synod of Catholics and Calvinists held at Poissy to settle the religious controversies by which France was molested. The end of this colloquy was to make each party more fiercely hostile than before, and their animosity broke out into a desolating religious war.

Collyrid'ians (*The*), or 'Collyridian Christians,' A.D. 373. Heretics abundant in Arabia, who invested the Virgin Mary with the name and honours of a goddess. They were so called because they offered to the goddess virgin a κολλύρα or cake. The heresy was carried from Thrace to Arabia by some women.

Colonisation of Ulster (*The*), 1610. A measure introduced in the reign of James I. for the pacification of Ireland. It was a vast measure of spoliation. Two-thirds of the north of Ireland was confiscated to the crown, and the land was allotted to Scotch and English

settlers. The Corporation of London undertook the colonisation of Derry. Without doubt this 'plantation of Ulster' was a brilliant success; but its injustice has not even yet been condoned by the Irish.

An attempt was made, in 1889, to 'colonise' evicted farms, in Ireland, by English and Scotch tenants.

Coloquint'ida (*St.*). So Charles I. was called. Coloquintida is colocynth (or 'bitter apple'), which is extremely bitter and nauseous. To say Charles was to the Levellers a Coloquintida is about equivalent to saying he was to them 'a very bitter pill.' See Clarendon's 'Rebellion,' book iii. p. 91 (Oxford edit. 1839). In 2 Kings iv., 'Death in the pot,' or 'wild gourds,' is in the old versions translated ' coloquintida,' whence the Levellers obtained their comparison.

The Levellers styled him [Charles I.] an Ahab and a Coloquintida, a man of blood, and the everlasting obstacle to peace and liberty.—HOWITT, *Hist. of Eng.* (Charles I., chap. vi. p. 284).

Colora'do (U. S. America). So called from Rio Colorado or coloured river (Red River) which falls into the Vermilion Sea. The inhabitants are nicknamed *Rovers*.

Colossus of Danish Literature (*The*). Baron Ludwig Holberg (1684–1754). One of the greatest authors of comedy that ever lived. He was also an historian and satirist.

Colossus of the 19th cent. (*The*). Napoleon Bonaparte (1769–1821).

Colours for Church Decorations.
White for festivals of our Lord, for Easter, and for all saints except martyrs.
Red for martyrs, for Ash Wednesday, the last three days of Holy Week, and Whitsuntide.
Blue for all week days after Trinity Sunday.
Blue or *green*, indifferently, for ordinary Sundays.
Violet, brown, or *grey* for Advent and Lent.
Black for Good Friday.

Colours for the Days. An effort was made in France to introduce letterpaper of a special colour for each day of the week.
For *Sunday*, a delicate mauve.

Monday, pale green.
Tuesday, pink.
Wednesday (an unlucky day), sombre grey.
Thursday, blue.
Friday, white.
Saturday, straw-colour.

Colours in China.
Yellow is the imperial colour, restricted to the emperor and his sons. Symbolical of faith.
Purple is the colour worn by the emperor's grandsons.
Red is the symbol of virtue, truth, and sincerity.
Vermilion is the colour in which imperial edicts are written.
Black denotes guilt and vice.
White denotes moral purity. The colour of mourning indicative of hope.

Colours. *See* ' Military Colours.'

Colston's Day, or 'The Colston Day,' 13 Nov. The anniversary of the birth of Edward Colston (1636–1721), merchant, and M.P. for Bristol (1710). He founded and endowed schools and almshouses in Bristol, and on the anniversary of his birthday the four following societies dine together :—
The Colston, established 1726.
The Dolphin, established 1749 (the Colston crest is two dolphins).
The Grateful, established 1758.
The Anchor, 1769.
Large sums of money are collected at these dinners for annuities to aged persons, relief for lying-in women, apprenticing boys, and money gifts. In 1886 the subscription amounted to 3,534*l.*

Columbia. America is so called from Columbus, who discovered it. A part is still called British Columbia. It was called America from Amerigo Vespucci, the pilot who accompanied Alonzo de Ojeda in 1499 and published an account of the voyage. This book first made the New World popularly known.

Columbia, Columbia, to glory arise,
The queen of the world, and the child of the skies.
Dr. T. DWIGHT.

Hail, Columbia, happy land !
JOSEPH HOPKINSON, 1789.

Column of Antoninus (*The*). At Rome; made of marble, 176 feet high, in memory of the Emperor Marcus Aurelius Antoninus. Like that of Trajan, this column is covered externally with spiral bas-reliefs representing the wars carried on by this emperor. As Sixtus V. caused the original statue of Trajan to be supplanted by that of St. Peter, so he caused the original statue of Antoninus to be supplanted by that of St. Paul.

The spiral staircase has 106 steps, and the column has 56 windows to let in light. This pillar is very inferior to Trajan's Column. The column in the Piazza Colonna at Rome, called the Pillar of Antoninus, is really one raised by the senate to Marcus Aurelius, after his victory over the Marcomanni.

Column of July (*The*), 1832. Paris. Made of bronze, erected on the Place de la Bastille, to commemorate the Revolution of July (*q.v.*), 1830, when Charles X. abdicated. It is surmounted with a statue of Liberty standing on one foot. In 1840 the bodies of the victims of that revolution, which had been thrown into a ditch, were disinterred. A monster hearse being provided, 50 coffins (each containing ten bodies), drawn by 24 black horses, were buried in the vault under this column.

Column of the Place Vendôme (*The*), 1806–1810. Paris. Made of bronze, erected in honour of Napoleon I., and containing, in a spiral, pictorial representations of his victories in a series of bas-reliefs, 900 feet long, and terminating with the battle of Austerlitz in 1805. This magnificent column, made of cannons taken from enemies, the facsimile of Trajan's famous column, was surmounted with a statue of Napoleon himself.

On 17 May, 1871, it was hurled to the ground by the Communists out of hatred to Napoleon III. It was re-erected in 1874, but the statue of Napoleon was replaced with another standing on one leg, infinitely inferior in every respect to the original one.

Columns. *See* ' Pompey's Column,' ' Trajan's Column.'

Columns of Hercules (*The*). Two large pyramidal columns set up by the Phœnicians as lighthouses and landmarks, dedicated one to Hercules (the sun) and the other to Astarte (the moon). By the Greeks and Romans the two pyramidal mountains at the Straits of Gibraltar, viz. Calpe and Abўla, the former in Europe and the latter in Africa, were termed *Columnæ Herculis* from their resemblance at a distance to the Phœnician columns.

Calpe (2 syl.), Ab'-y-lah, *i.e.* Ce-u'-ta.

Combat of the Thirty (*The*). ' Le Combat des Trente,' 1351. Thirty

Bretons against thirty Englishmen. It was the defiance of Jean sire de Beaumanoir to the English chatelain of Ploër-mel. Eight of the English being slain, the combat was brought to a close. It is said that Beaumanoir, exhausted by fatigue and heat, drank the blood which flowed from his wounds. *See* ' Battle.'

Combative Kings (*The*). The dynasty of Tcheou-kue of China, from the tenth to the third cent. B.C., when China was broken up into a multitude of minor states always at war with each other. In B.C. 247 Thsin-chi-hoang-ti (of the dynasty of Tsin) united all the states under one sovereign; pushed back the Moguls; and built the Great Wall.

Combination Laws (*The*), 1360. The Statute of Labourers enacted ' that all alliances [combinations] of masons, carpenters, and other artificers,' be annulled and declared unlawful. Abolished in 1824, since which times Trades-Unions (*q.v.*) have become very general. *See* ' Criminal Law Amendment Act.'

Comedy (*Father of French*). Molière (1622–1673).

Comité de Surveillance, 1792. A committee in the French Revolution whose function was to examine the denunciations received by the Committee of General Safety. After the butcheries of 2 Sept. this committee drew up an address, recommending all the communes in France to follow the same example. *See under* ' Committee.'

This address was signed by Duplain, Panis, Sergent, Lenfant, Marat, Lefort, Jordeuil, administrators of the Comité de Surveillance, constituted at the Mairie, 2 Sept. 1792.

Commandery (*A*). A district containing estates with a revenue annexed, belonging to a military order, and governed by a knight-commander, or the whole body of knights subject to a knight-commander, as the Commanderies of Malta, of St. Lazare, of Calatrava, of Alcantara, of St. Bernard, and of St. Antony. Till 1267 Commanderies were called Preceptories.

Commenda, or ' Ecclesia Commendāta.' A living commended by the crown to the charge of a clergyman to hold till a person is duly provided for it. It may be either temporary or perpetual.

Commendam (*In*). A living is held

'in commendam' when (to prevent its becoming void) it is committed (*commendatur*) to the charge of a clergyman till it can be conveniently provided with a pastor. Thus when a rector or vicar is made a bishop his benefice becomes void from the moment of consecration, but, being 'commended' to a commendatory, the bishop retains the income till his successor is provided.

Commendators. A Scotch term meaning secular persons upon whom church benefices are bestowed. The livings are commended, *i.e.* entrusted to their care and keeping. They are, *pro tempore*, trustees of the priories, abbeys, or dioceses committed to them. The living thus held in trust was called a *commendatory*.

Commendatory Abbot (*A*). Was a secular clerk provided by the pope to enjoy the fruits of an abbey, generally for life, without being saddled with clerical duties.

Commendatory Letters. Letters written by one bishop to another on behalf of a clergyman or layman going to the diocese.

Commenda'tus [*pl.* Commendāti]. In baronial times was a person who lived under the protection of some great man. He was a voluntary vassal, and paid voluntary homage for the sake of protection.

Commerce (*Father of English*). Edward III. (1312, 1326–1377).

Commissaires de la Commune (*Les*), 10 Aug., 1792. A title assumed by Danton, Tallien, Billaud-Varennes, and Collot d'Herbois, who usurped on this day the municipal functions of Paris.

Commissary (*The*). In the University of Cambridge. An executive officer appointed by the chancellor by letters patent to hold a court of record for all privileged persons and scholars under the degree of M.A.

Commission (*The Parnell*), 1889. *See* 'Parnell,' &c.

Commission of Innocency (*The*), 1663. A commission appointed by the Duke of Ormond, lord-lieutenant of Ireland, to inquire into the guilt or innocency of those Catholics whose estates

had been forfeited by Cromwell. The cases were so numerous that the session was limited, and only a fourth of the cases were adjudicated. The other three-fourths (about 3,000 in number) were stripped of their estates whether they were innocent or not.

Commission of Inquiry (*The*), 1623. A commission appointed by James I. to examine into the titles of holders of land in the province of Leinster and the adjoining districts. The commission adjudged 82,500 acres of land to be crown land, and James tried to plant it with Englishmen and Scotchmen, as he had done Ulster.

Commission of Twelve (*The*), 1793. An extraordinary board appointed by the National Convention to watch over the commune, arrest those who interrupted the business of the house, and to judge traitors. It forthwith arrested Hébert; whereupon a riot ensued, and the Convention was obliged to dissolve the commission.

Commissioners of Delinquency, 1650. Commissioners appointed after the rebellion of Ireland to decide what lands were forfeited by the rebellion, and what Catholics were entitled to receive compensation. Those Catholics who in the lifetime of Charles I. had served the king against the rebels, and would be entitled to retain any part of their estates, were to resign that part and receive an equivalent in the waste lands of Connaught; but no Catholic, under any condition, was to reside in any town or within a certain fixed limit of a town. There were commissioners to decide on the qualifications of Catholics, others to arrange the details of those to be transplanted to Connaught, and others to receive and hear claims. The first sat in Athlone, the second in Loughrea, and the third in Dublin.

Commissioners of Innocency. *See* 'Commission of Innocency.'

Commissioners of National Education (*The*). In Ireland. 1833. The board appointed to carry out the plan of national education introduced by Mr. Stanley, chief secretary. *See* 'National Schools, Ireland.'

The first commissioners were the Duke of Leinster, Archbishop Whately, Archbishop Murray, Rev. Dr. Sadlier, Rev. James Carlile (*Presbyterian*), A. R. Blake (*Catholic*), and Robert Holmes (*Unitarian*).

Commissioners of Parliament.
Part of the civil government of Cromwell,
appointed to grant commissions by letters
patent, and to examine into the legality
of those holding any public office. In
Ireland their chief duty was to adjust and
apportion among the claimants confiscated estates.

Commissioners of Trust (*The*),
1647. Twelve persons appointed by the
general assembly of confederates and
Protestants in Ireland to guard the treaty,
and vested with powers to levy soldiers,
raise money, and perform all acts of supreme authority in Ireland. The arrangement fell through because the king was
beheaded before he had signed it.

The Catholics were granted by the treaty freedom of religion, seminaries for the education of
their children, admission to Parliament, and an
amnesty for the late rebellion.

Committee of Estates (*The*),
1640. A committee appointed by the
Scotch Parliament which had been prorogued by Charles I., but which refused to
obey, declaring the warrant to be informal.
They instantly voted a tax of 10 per cent.
on rents, and 5 per cent. on interest of
money, and appointed a Committee of
Estates to act in the place of the king in
giving assent to their measures.

Committee of Evils (*The*), 1625.
A committee of the House of Commons in
the second year of the reign of Charles I.
for the remedy of grievances and abuses.
The Committee of Grievances brought
forward to the notice of the house what
were national grievances, and the Committee of Evils suggested remedies. Thus
the Committee of Grievances complained
of purveyance [collecting provisions at a
set price], tonnage and poundage, and so
on; and the Committee of Evils, attribut-
ing these grievances to the Duke of Buckingham, insisted on his being punished.

Committee of Grievances (*The*),
1626. A committee of the House of Commons to check the encroachments of the
young king Charles I. It was especially
directed against the Duke of Buckingham, the king's favourite, whose insolence, extravagance, incapacity, and
licentiousness were a great scandal.

Committee of Murder (*The*),
1690. A committee appointed by the
Whigs, in the reign of William and Mary,
to inquire into the concern of sundry in-

dividuals in the deaths of Lord Russell,
Algernon Sidney, and others of the Whig
party. John Hampden (grandson of the
great patriot) and John Howe were the
most violent, and would have inundated
the nation with blood if William had not
stoutly resisted the persecution.

Committee of Nine (*The*), 6 April,
1793. The Committee of Public Safety
(*q.v.*) in the French revolution. It consisted of nine members.

Committee of Public Safety
(*The*). 'Le Comité du Salut Publique,'
formed in the French revolution, 6 April,
1793, by a decree of the Convention.
For a year it was omnipotent, and had
under it the 'Revolutionary Tribunal,'
the 'Revolutionary Committees,' and the
Committee of General Security.' It originally consisted of nine members chosen
from the Convention, the leaders being
Danton, Barère, and Cambon. Three
more were added in June; and, after the
fall of the Girondists, Robespierre and
Carnot belonged to the committee. It
was this committee which inaugurated
the *Reign of Terror*, and filled France
with scaffolds. It was broken up 27 July,
1794. *See* 'Committee of the Two
Kingdoms.'

Revolutionary committees and Committees of
General Safety were also appointed in every commune of France. The former to receive denunciations and the latter to look after the police.

Committee of Purchases, 1792.
A committee of Frenchmen, under Bider-
mann, the banker, and consisting of Jews
and speculators, whose function was to
make bargains for the army under Du
mouriez and pay the soldiers. The soldiers were paid in cash, but all bargains
were paid for in assignats. All emigrants
were plundered of their money, jewels,
furniture, and works of art; and the
people of Belgium were treated as aristocrats. Plunder and robbery were thus
made a very profitable trade.

Committee of Religion. I. 1626.
A committee of the House of Commons,
in the second year of Charles I., to put
down the growth of popery, which had
become aggressive from the large suite
of Roman Catholics introduced by the
queen. The committee presented its
report 25 Feb., 1629. It complained that
the bishops licensed the circulation of
books favourable to popery. It advised

that such books as those of Mainwaring and Montague should be burnt; that candlesticks should be removed from communion-tables, now impiously called high-altars; that pictures, lights, and images should be removed from churches; that crossing and turning to the east in prayer should be forbidden; that better and more learned men should be preferred to church livings; and better provision be made for the supply of holy ministers to the several parishes.

II. 6 Nov., 1640, a committee of the whole house appointed by the Long Parliament for providing preachers, and removing ministers of scandalous character.

Committee of Safety. I. In the civil wars of Charles I. was a supreme council which sat in the Painted Chamber, Westminster. Pym was president, and among the members were Lord Saye and Sele, Sir Harry Vane, Harry Marten, Selden, St. John, and others.

II. Oct. 1775. A committee formed from the congress convened by Governor Gage at Salem, and adjourned by the 'patriots' to Concord, a town about 25 miles from Boston. Here a standing committee was appointed, which assumed the name of 'The Committee of Safety,' with authority to call out the militia when they thought it necessary for the defence of the province. The French afterwards adopted the same idea in their Comité du Salut Publique.

Committee of Secresy (*The*), 6 Jan., 1721. A committee appointed by the House of Commons to examine into the South Sea Company's failure. The committee was appointed merely to soothe the angry feelings of the public. The directors in the service of the crown were discharged 11 Jan., and the rest were examined before the House of Lords. Knight, the company's cashier, absconded 22 Jan., was imprisoned at Antwerp, 3 Feb.; escaped, and was pardoned 18 Oct. the same year. It was not till 1 June, 1733, that an inquiry into the conduct of the company was made in the House of Lords. Broderick was chairman of the committee, and Jekyll, Molesworth, &c. were members put upon it.

Committee of Supplies (*The*), 1774. To purchase ammunition, ordnance, and other military stores, when the Committee of Safety (*q.v.*) thought it advis-

able to call out the militia in defence of the province of Massachusetts.

Committee of Twelve (*The*), 1793. A committee appointed by the Convention, through the influence of the Girondists, to watch over the designs of the commune and to arrest those persons who were dangerous to the public peace. The Twelve were the sworn enemies of the Jacobins.

Committee of the Protestant Interest (*The*), 1780. Formed to resist any relaxation of the penal code against the Catholics. The synod of Glasgow was especially rancorous, but the synod of Edinburgh favoured measures of relief.

Committee of the States, 1777. Appointed by Congress to sit during their recess. It consisted of one delegate from each state; nine to form a quorum. This committee exercised such powers as Congress thought fit to vest them with.

Committee of the Two Kingdoms (*The*), Dec. 1643. So the Committee of Public Safety was called, when Scotland joined the Parliamentary party. This was after the death of Pym. It was again called into active service in 1647.

Committee of the whole House (*A*). All the members of the House of Commons in attendance, presided over by a chairman for the nonce instead of the Speaker. After a public bill has been printed and distributed to the members, it is read for the second time and then 'committed.' When the day for 'committing' has arrived, the Speaker moves 'that I do now leave the chair,' and the bill is read clause by clause, and line by line, till every part has received the approval of the house, and then the Speaker resumes his chair to receive the report.

Committees of Correspondence, 1779. To carry out reform in Parliament; organised in twenty-one counties, and in the towns of York, Bristol, Cambridge, Nottingham, Newcastle, Reading, and Bridgwater. The chief promoters of these committees were Lord Rockingham, in Yorkshire; Lord Shelburne, in Buckinghamshire; Lord Mahon (son-in-law of Chatham), in Kent; the Duke of Richmond, the Marquis of Carmarthen, Sir George Savile, Edmund Burke, and Charles James Fox.

In 1780 Committees of Correspondence were organised by the Protestant Association in numerous towns to resist any relaxation of the penal acts against the Catholics. The anti-Catholic furore culminated in the Gordon riots.

Committees of General Security, or 'Comité de Sûreté Générale' (1793).

Appointed by the Convention to act under the Committee of Public Safety to look after the police.

Common Good (*The*).

A Scotch phrase meaning the public funds of a burgh.

Common Prayer Book (*The*).

Was drawn up chiefly by Goodrich bishop of Ely, and Ridley bishop of Rochester. Their coadjutors were Skyp bishop of Hereford, Thirlby bishop of Westminster, Day bishop of Chichester, Holbeach bishop of Lincoln, Dr. May dean of St. Paul's, Dr. Taylor dean of Lincoln, Dr. Haynes dean of Exeter, Dr. Redmayne dean of Westminster, Dr. Cox the king's almoner, and Dr. Robertson archdeacon of Leicester. In the communion office there were added the Archbishop of York and the Bishops of Durham, Worcester, Norwich, St. Asaph, Lichfield, Salisbury, Carlisle, Bristol, and St. David's.

Common Recovery.

A legal fiction practised in the reign of Edward IV. for cutting off entails. The estate being forfeit to the crown was granted to a person by private agreement. This person brought an action against the grantor for unjustly claiming such estate. Of course the suit was permitted to go by default, and the entail, being declared lost, the fee simple of the property recurred to the possessor, to be disposed of as he thought proper.

Common Sense, 1776.

A pamphlet by Thomas Paine, then living in Philadelphia, urging the Americans to claim independence. It ridiculed the idea of a small island, 3,000 miles off, ruling the immense continent of America, and threatening three million men, more vigorous and more virtuous than their would-be enslavers. This spark was sufficient to rouse the Americans, who at once signed their Declaration of Independence.

Commoners.

The ordinary students of the University of Oxford, called 'pensioners' in the University of Cambridge.

In the University of Cambridge 'Fellow Commoners' are pensioners who dine at the Fellows'

or Masters' table. They are generally married men, noblemen, and elderly men. They wear a gold tassel on their cap instead of a silk one, and have the privilege of paying higher fees.

Commons' King (*The*).

The Commons' King of Rome was King Servĭus Tullius, sixth king of Rome. His mother was a captive taken at Cornubium, and became the female slave of Tanaquil, wife of Tarquin I. Servĭus was by birth a slave also, but married the king's daughter and succeeded to the throne.

Louis Philippe of France was called 'Le roi citoyen.'

Commons Spiritual (*The*).

The Proctors of Convocation, who, in the reign of Richard II., were elected as knights of the shire were.

Commonwealth, or Free State, 19 March, 1649.

So the government of the United Kingdom was called, as soon as it was constituted after the execution of Charles I.

Commonwealth (*The*).

Lasted in England eleven years (1649–1660). During which period, Cromwell was Lord Protector for about four and three-quarter years (16 Dec., 1653, to 3 Sept., 1658), and was styled 'his highness.' During the Commonwealth, the recognised government superscription ran thus: 'Keepers of the liberties of England by the authority of Parliament.'

Commonwealth of Babina (*The*), 16th cent.

A society founded in Poland in the time of Sigismund Augustus, last male heir of the house of Jagello (1548–1572), so called from Babina, the place of meeting. They had a regular mock government, under king, senate, and magistrates. The executive was elected from something which appeared ridiculous in the member elected. Thus, an officious man was made archbishop, a disputatious one was made speaker, a boaster was made commander-in-chief. To decline to serve was to be outlawed. Thus every foible was held up to observation, and Babina was a word of terror. Without doubt the society did a vast amount of good. It gradually died out.

Commorantes in Villa.

Graduates of the University of Cambridge, not on any of the college staffs, but members of the Regent's House (called the White Hoods). When the university was re-organised in 1858, the term was abolished and the Regent's House formed part of the Senate.

Commune of Paris (*The*), 14 July, 1789. A municipal revolutionary board, which took the place of the ' Conseil de Ville' and held its sessions in the Guild Hall (Hôtel de Ville). It had the supreme government of the city, the appointment of the civil officers, and the magisterial duties. It was presided over by a provost—Chaumette was the first provost, and the next was Robespierre, at whose fall the commune was abolished (27 July, 1794).

Com'munes (2 syl.). Chartered towns were so called in France. The first was the commune of Mans, in 1066.

Commu'nes (3 syl.). A supplement, in five books, to the Corpus Juris Canonici, being the Extravagantes of popes subsequent to John XXII. Not unfrequently called ' Extravagantes Communes.'

Communion Service (*The First*), 1548. By a committee of bishops and other clergy, appointed by Cranmer. It made auricular confession optional ; appointed that the eucharist should be given in both kinds ; that the Host should not be elevated ; that the chief part of the service should be in English ; that the bread should be of the same form and kind as heretofore ; and that the words used should be those printed in our Common Prayer Book, now in use.

Communism. A scheme for associating men and women together without recourse to the laws of social and political economy, usually resorted to. The representatives of communism are Robert Owen, St. Simon, Fourier, Proudhon, and Enfantin.

(1) Owen published his scheme in 1813, and tried it in 1825, at Orbiston, in Lanarkshire. This scheme failed, and in 1843 he opened his ' Harmony Hall,' in Hampshire ; but this also was a failure.

(2) St. Simon established a corporate society at Menilmontant, but Louis Philippe charged it with immorality and irreligion. The readers were imprisoned and the commune dissolved.

(3) Fourier established his ' phalanstery' at Rambouillet, but it proved a total failure.

(4) Proudhon is noted for his axiom, 'La propriété, c'est le vol,' 1848, and for

his *Banque du Peuple*, 1849, which had for its object the suppression of capital. It was closed by authority, and Proudhon fled to Geneva.

(5) Enfantin, a partisan of St. Simon, advocated the abolition of marriage ties, and was prosecuted on the grounds of public decency. *See* ' Socialism,' ' St. Simonianism,' ' Supreme Father.'

Communists (*The*). A secret society, which the report of the Government of Zürich, 1844, says was then in existence in Switzerland. Its object was ' the enfranchisement of all humanity ; the abolition of property, of heritage, of money, of wages, of laws, and of punishments.' They also insisted on an equal distribution of labour and enjoyment. *See* 'Communism.'

Commutation Act. *See* ' Tithes Bill.'

Comneni (*The*), or ' The Comnēnians.' A family of Roman origin which furnished six Byzantine emperors, one Heraclēan, and three of Trebizond. The six of Constantinople are : Isaac (1057-1059), Alexis I. (1081-1118), John (1118-1143), Manuel (1143-1180), Alexis II. (1180-1183), and Andronīcus (1183-1185), who was dethroned.

The one of Heraclēa was David, grandson of Andronicus.

Alexis III., who founded a dynasty at Trebizond, which lasted from 1204 to 1462.

The rest of the Comnēni migrated to the Morea and Corsica. Napoleon used to claim descent from these Comneni.

Comorbans, or Corbes. Lay dignitaries who held in Ireland church lands. If not dignitaries, they were called Erenachs. Like lay-abbots, they appropriated to themselves the revenues, leaving the clergy the fees and tithes. (From the 9th to the 17th cent.)

Compagnacci (*The*). A set of foolish youths in Florence, during the palmy days of Lorenzo de' Medici ; who, laying aside all sense of shame, gave themselves up to every sort of wickedness, emulating each other in the depths of naughtiness to which they could attain.

Compagnies (*Les*). Often called 'Les grandes compagnies.' Bands of troops composed of different nations, and led by a general whose device was ' L'ami

du Dieu et l'ennemi du tout le monde.'
See 'Companions' League,' 'Condottieri.'

<small>One of them called himself 'The enemy of God,
of pity, and of mercy.'</small>

Companions' League (*The*),
1360. A confederacy of the mercenary
troops disbanded by Edward III. after
the battle of Poitiers (1356). The league
mustered 40,000 soldiers, and fought
several pitched battles with the French
troops. In 1366 they joined Duguesclin's
army levied to aid Henry da Trastamare
against his brother Pedro the Cruel.
This league was a confederacy of Les
grandes compagnies (*q.v.*).

Companions of Jehu (*The*). The
Chouans, a royalist faction in France in
1800. Louis XVIII. being *Jehu*, whose
'companions' were bound to aid him in
'cutting off, root and branch, all who had
taken part in the assassination of his royal
brother' (Louis XVI.). *See* 2 Chron.
xxii. 7.

Company of 1789 (*The*). The
club of the Feuillants was originally so
called. Its platform was the support of
the constitution against the ultra party.
They took the constitution of England for
their model. On 28 March, 1791, the club
was forcibly dispersed by a raging mob.

Company of St. George (*The*),
1379. A company of adventurers under
Alberic di Barbiano. This company was
a most famous school of great generals
from its formation to the 16th cent.

Compassionate Allowance. A
government gratuity to the widows and
children of those in the British army
slain in the Crimean War (1855–1856).

Compassionate Brothers (*The*),
1540. Founded at Seville, in Spain, by the
Portuguese John di Dio, who had served
in Africa under Charles V. They obtained their funds by begging. Their
chief functions were nursing the sick and
reforming immoral women. The brothers
were laymen under no rule till 1572, when
the pope subjected them to the rule of
St. Augustine.

Competitive Examination for
the Civil service, introduced in 1855.
Every candidate is required to pass first
a preliminary examination.

Compitalian Lares. Gods who
presided respectively over the several

quarters of the city (Rome). Comp*ī*tum
was the place where two or more roads
met, as *Trivium* was the place where two
or more streets met. It was customary
with the Romans to erect altars, shrines,
and small temples at these spots, as
Roman Catholics used to erect on such
spots crucifixes. The *Larês Compitalês*
were the deities who presided over cross
roads (Propertius, iv. 3, 54). Varro
tells us the word *compītum* comes from
the verb *competo*, to agree in one.

Complaint (*The*), 1450, or, in full,
'The Complaint of the Commons of Kent.'
The petition of grievances presented by
John Cade, calling for administrative
and economical reforms, a change of
ministry, a more careful expenditure of
the royal revenue, and the restoration of
freedom of election, which had been
broken in upon both by the crown and
by the great landlords.

Compline. The last of the eight
daily services of the Catholic Church and
of the four greater ones. At bed-time.
The word means complete. *See* 'Canonical Hours.'

**Complutensian   Polyglot
Bible** (*The*), 1502–1517. Printed under
the patronage and at the expense of
Cardinal Ximenês at Complûtum (*i.e.*
Alcala de Henarês in New Castile, about
nineteen miles from Madrid, in Spain).

Comprehension (*A*), 1670. A
decree by Leighton to pacify the Scotch
clergy irritated by the Act against Field
Conventicles (*q.v.*). It required that they
should attend presbyteries as they were
established before the year 1638. The
bishops were required to waive their
claim of a negative voice, and all who
pleased were to be at liberty to protest
against it. (*See* Lingard, ix. 4.)

Compromise (*The*), 1567. The
league between the Protestants and
Catholics of the Netherlands, headed by
the Prince of Orange, the Count Egmont,
and the Count Horn, to put down the
Inquisition, introduced into their country
by Philip II. of Spain. The Duchess of
Parma, who governed the country, gave
way to the storm, and abolished the Inquisition; by which wise concession she
broke up the league.

Compur'gators. Twelve persons
who swore that they believed an accused

person who pleaded 'not guilty' to be innocent of the crime charged against him. The finding was called 'compurgation.' This basis of our common jury system existed in the Saxon times, and is generally placed to the credit of Alfred the Great.

Comte's Three States. The theological state, the metaphysical state, and physical state. 'Chacun de nous, en contemplant sa propre histoire, ne se souvient-il pas qu'il a été successivement, quant à ses notions les plus importantes, *théologien* dans son enfance, *métaphysicien* dans sa jeunesse, et *physicien* dans sa virilité?' In the infancy of thought the mind attributes changes in phenomena to the overruling will of some divinity which shapes them. In the next stage the mind attributes changes of phenomena to some hypothetical abstract principle. In the third, or mature stage, the mind clings to facts, and attributes phenomena to those agencies which experience or experiment teaches us to have been in operation.

Comuneros, 1520–1521. A Spanish party opposed to the appointment of Karl V. of Germany to the Spanish crown. Padilla, a young nobleman of Toledo, was at the head of the insurgents. They were defeated by the royalists at Villalar in 1521, and Padilla was executed. This civil war is called the 'Guerra de las Comuniades.'

Conacre System (*The*). The system of subletting small patches of land, consisting of from 1 to 5 acres, for a single potato crop. Thus, in Ireland, a landlord of, say, 100,000 acres, would farm it to a middleman, and live in England or abroad. The middleman will divide this large tenement into several smaller ones, which he will let out to tenants, say from 100 to 500 acres each. These tenants will sublet a part (say in parcels of from 10 to 50 acres) to other tenants; and, lastly, these farmers will 'conacre' small patches to some peasant to grow on it a crop of potatoes for the current year. So that sometimes six or eight persons under the landlord make a profit of the land, and the last occupant pays at the rate of 8*l.* or 10*l.* per acre for his little patch of land.

Conception of the Virgin Mary (*The*), or 'Festum Beatæ Mariæ de Adventu,' 8 Dec. Instituted 1356.

There is an order of nuns, which was founded in 1484, entitled 'The Conception of Our Lady.' Their dress is a white gown, a blue mantle, and a scapulary.

Conceptualism. Abelard's *tertium quid* (*q.v.*).

Concord of Madrid (*The*), 1526. Extorted by Karl V. from François I., his captive. François consented to give up all claims to Flanders and Artois, the possession of Naples, Milan, Genoa, and all other Italian territories, to deliver the dauphin and Duc d'Orléans into the hands of Karl as hostages, and bound himself to return into captivity if these conditions were not fulfilled within four years. François also promised to marry Queen Eleonora (sister of Karl V.), to restore Bourbon and the rest of the rebels to their estates and honours, to pay Henry VIII. all the money which Karl owed him, to lend Karl his whole navy, with 500 men-at-arms and 6,000 foot soldiers, to put down the princes of Italy, and to use his influence with the King of Navarre and Duke of Gueldres to get Karl appointed heir to their dominions. The pope absolved François from his obligation to observe this scandalous exaction.

Concordat of 1801 (*The*). Between Pius VII. and Napoleon Bonaparte, then first consul. It put an end to the anarchy introduced by the revolution in the Gallican Church, and re-established the French hierarchy. The appointment of bishops was left in the hands of the temporal power, but their institution was reserved to the pope.

A new division of the dioceses of France was made. The appointment of curés or vicars was left to the bishops. Napoleon said to Cabanis: 'Do you know what this Concordat really is? It is the vaccination of religion. In fifty years there will be no more religion in France than small-pox.'

Concordat of 1855 (*The*). Between Pius IX. and the Emperor Francis Joseph of Austria. This concordat was abrogated in 1870.

Concordat of François I., A.D. 1515. A repeal of the Pragmatic Sanction, which the pope had condemned, and the substitution of a compromise. By the Pragmatic Sanction the independence of the Gallican Church was secured, and its freedom from all papal encroachments; by the Concordat the pope and king made a partition of the spoil. The king appointed to vacant bishoprics within six months; if the nominee was objected to by the pope, three months more were allowed, and if then the appointment was objected to, the pope made the appointment. By this foolish arrangement annates or first fruits were again rendered to the pope. Of course the French parliament and council greatly objected, but the king carried his point.

Concordat of Vienna (*The*), 1448.

Drawn up by Kaiser Friederich III., and approved of by Czar Nicholas V., establishing the canonical election, abolishing the Acts called 'Provisiones' for curbing the arbitrary power of the crown, abolishing pontifical expectatives, determining in what cases the pope could dispose of German benefices, and substituting a tax spread over two years for annates.

Concordat of Worms (*The*), 1122.

Between Pope Calixtus II. and Heinrich V. of Germany. This instrument put an end to the long contention about investitures. The pope recognised the right of the monarch to give *temporal* investitures, and reserved to himself the right of spiritual investitures.

A concordat is a contract between the pope and a temporal potentate to fix their respective rights in matters pertaining to the Church and State.

Condignitism.

A doctrine taught by Thomas Aquinas (1224–1274), who contended that man in his natural state cannot so live as to *merit* or earn God's grace; but that with Divine assistance he could do so, and render himself worthy (*condignus*) of salvation. This sort of merit is called the 'merit of condignity.'

The 'merit of congruity' is the possibility of so ordering our lives as to *deserve* grace, and with the desert, of course, follows the grace. *See* 'Congruism.'

Condottie'ri.

Either free-lances, or bands of adventurers, who for hire entered the service of anyone who would pay them. Hawkwood's condottieri hired themselves into the Venetian service in the 14th cent., and were called the English condottieri. A condottiere is not a captain or leader of a band, but a free-lance, or a company of free-lances under a leader. Thus Hawkwood collected a band of condottieri, and made the best bargain he could with those who were willing to pay for their services. At the same time Francesco Sforza was a condottiere; so also Angelo de la Pergola,

Nicolo Piccinino, and Guido Torello were noted condottieri.

Of course the word *condottie're* means a captain or leader, and *condottieri* those under a leader.

Confarrea'tion.

A species of marriage in ancient Rome; so called because the chief ceremony was partaking of the *panis farrĕus* (bread made of spelt) in the presence of ten witnesses. This was the highest form of marriage; and certain offices in the state, such for example as the *Flamen Diālis*, could be held only by those who were born of parents thus married.

Our bridecake is a relic of the *panis farreus*.

Confederacy of Delos (*The*), B.C. 477.

A league to place Athens, instead of Sparta, at the head of Greece, chiefly brought about by the treason of Pausanias. Called the Confederacy of Delos, because the deputies of the allies were to meet annually in Delos in the temple of Apollo and Artĕmis.

Confederate Catholics (*The*), 1641.

An Irish secret society formed in Ulster, where 50,000 Englishmen were assassinated. 'Husbands were cut to pieces in the presence of their wives; children's brains were dashed out before their parents; women were brutally violated, and driven naked to perish in the woods. Some were burned; others drowned for sport; many were buried alive. The contest was that of Catholic against Protestant; and the rebels, believing that Charles I. really befriended them, called themselves 'the king's army,' and claimed to be acting on the king's commission. *See* 'Irish Associations.'

Confederates (*The*), 1861–1865.

The Southern States of North America, in the American civil war, consisting of South Carolina, Georgia, Florida, Virginia, North Carolina, Alabama, Mississippi, Louisiana, and Texas. These states were utterly opposed to what was called the Garrison school, which considered American slavery a scandal. Sumner and Seward took up the question, and organised an anti-slavery party. The Southerners confederated, and resolved to separate from the Union, the federalists or unionists armed to preserve the Union. As the war went on the slavery question was thrust to the forefront. The Southerners were vanquished, slavery was abolished, and the Union was preserved.

Confederation (*The Irish*), 1846. Formed by the Young Ireland party when it separated from the old Repealers, led by Daniel O'Connell. The meetings were held in the Music Hall, Abbey Street. *See* 'Irish Associations.'

Confederation of Bar (*The*), 1768. Formed by the Catholics of Poland against the dissidents (*q.v.*). It was dissolved in 1773.

Bar is a town of Podolia. The confederation was supported by Russia. *See* 'National Confederacy of Poland.'

Confederation of the Rhine (*The*), 1806. The German states confederated by Napoleon. As allies of France each state was bound to furnish a contingent to the French army. In 1808 the number of Germans yielded 120,000 men to Napoleon's call. Bavaria and Würtemburg allied themselves to France in 1805, and in reward of this unpatriotic conduct these electorates were raised into kingdoms. In 1806 fourteen other German princes signed an act of alliance, and in 1808 other princes did the same. After the disaster of Moscow in 1813 the confederation broke up, and the German princes allied themselves against their common enemy.

The fourteen were, the Elector (now called the Grand-Duke) of Baden, the new Grand-Duke of Cleves (Napoleon's brother-in-law), the Landgraf (now called Grand-Duke) of Hessen-Darmstadt, the Prince of Nassau-Usinges, the Prince of Nassau-Weilburg, the Prince of Hohenzollern-Hechingen, the Prince of Isenberg-Birstein, the Prince of Liechtenstein, the Duke of Aremberg, the Count of Lagen. Subsequently, the Duke of Würzburg, the King of Saxony, the King of Westphalia, the Duke of Mecklenburg, and some other small princes.

Conference (*The*), 1661. Held at the Savoy, in the residence of the Bishop of London (Dr. Sheldon). Four months were awarded to it (25 March–25 July). Between twenty-one Episcopalians and twenty-one Presbyterians. After long dispute, the nonconformists reduced their grievances to these eight : The sinfulness

1. Of wearing a surplice.
2. Of the cross in baptism.
3. Of calling the baptized regenerate.
4. Of kneeling at the Lord's Supper.
5. Of administering the Lord's Supper to the sick and impenitent.
6. Priestly absolution.
7. Returning thanks promiscuously in the Burial Service.
8. Subscription to the Thirty-nine Articles.

Conference of London (*The*), 1826. A diplomatic congress held in London to determine on the fate of Greece.

Confession of Augsburg (*The*), 1530. A summary of faith drawn up by Melanchthon, and presented to the Emperor Charles V. at the Diet of Augsburg. This confession is based on 'The Articles of Torgau' (*q.v.*), and contains twenty-one articles on doctrine, and seven on practical matters. They very much resemble the Thirty-nine Articles of the Church of England.

Torgau, pronounce *Tor-gow*.
The last 7 are these :—22 : of both kinds, *see* Art. xxx. ; 23 : of the marriage of priests, *see* Art. xxxii. ; 24 : of the sacrifice of the mass, *see* Art. xxxi. ; 25 : of oral confession ; 26 : of distinction of meats ; 27 : of conventual vows ; and 28 : of the authority of bishops. Compare also the 21 Articles of the Confession with the Articles of the Church of England, viz. : 1 : of God with Art. i. ; 2 : of original sin with Art. ix. ; 3 : of the Son of God with Art. ii. ; 4 : of justification with Art. xi. ; 5 : of preaching with Art. xxiv. ; 6 : of obedience ; 7, 8 : of the Church with Art. xix. xx. ; 9 : of baptism with Art. xvii. ; 10 : of the Lord's Supper with Art. xxviii. xxix. xxx. ; 11 : of confession ; 12 : of penance ; 13 : of the use of the sacraments with Art. xxvi. ; 14 : of church government with Art. xx. ; 15 : of church order ; 16 : of secular government with Art xxxvii. ; 17 : of Christ's second coming ; 18 : of free will with Art. x. ; 19 : of the cause of sin with Art. ix. ; 20 : of faith and good works with Art. xii. xiii. ; and 21 : of the worship of saints.

Confession of Bâle (*The*), 1534. The first Helvetic confession of faith, drawn up by Zwingli in 1530, was so called because it was ratified at Bâle.

Confession of Brandenburg (*The*). The confession of faith drawn up in the city of Brandenburg by order of the elector, with a view to reconciling the tenets of Luther with those of Calvin, and to put an end to the disputes occasioned by the Confession of Augsburg.

Confession of Bullinger (*The*). The *Expositio Simplex* of Heinrich Bullinger, the successor of Zwingli, at Cologne, 1566.

Confession of Emden (*The*), 1562. By the Belgian reformers.

Confession of Würtemburg (*The*), 1551. A Lutheran confession of faith.

Confession of Zwingli. In 1523 the government of Zürich invited the Protestants and Catholics to a conference, in the hope of adjusting their religious difficulties. Zwingli drew up his arguments under sixty-seven heads, and the council gave their vote in his favour. These sixty-seven articles he afterwards submitted to François I. of France, and called them his *Confession*. They are worthy to be compared with the twenty-eight articles of the *Confession of Augsburg*, drawn up by Melanchthon, or the *Thirty-nine Articles* of the Church of England.

Confession of the Druses (*The*),

11th cent. (1) The Unity of God. He manifested himself to man seven times, the last being in the person of Hàkim; (2) there are five superior ministers who have all manifested themselves to man—the chief of them were Hamza and Christ; (3) the transmigration of souls; (4) Hàkim shall by-and-bye reign on earth, and all its kingdoms shall be subject to him; (5) the seven points are truth, mutual aid, renunciation of all other religions, belief in one Hàkim (as God), contentment, submission, and separation from heretics.

Confessions of the Reformed Churches.

(1) The Helvetic Confessions, as that of Basel in 1530, and that of Bullinger, called *Expositio Simplex*, in 1566; (2) the Tetrapolitan Confession in 1531; (3) the Gallic Confession in 1559; (4) the Palatine, or Heidelberg, Confession in 1575; and (5) the Belgic Confession in 1559. *See* each of these *in loco.*

See also 'Westminster Confession of Faith.'

Confessor of the Household.

One of the twelve royal chaplains, whose office it is to read prayers every morning to the family, to visit the sick, to prepare communicants, and give advice on points of religion to those who desire information.

Confirmatio Charta'rum, 25

Edw. I. A.D. 1297. By which Magna Charta was directed to be allowed at the common law, all judgments contrary thereto were declared void, copies of the charter were directed to be read in all cathedral churches twice a year, and sentences of excommunication were denounced against all those who infringed the charter.

Conflans (*Treaty of*),

1465. A treaty of peace after the battle of Montlhéry (*q.v.*).

Confrères de la Congrégation de

Notre-Dame de Miséricorde, 1223. A religious order instituted in Barcelona by Pierre de Nolasque, a Frenchman, for the redemption of slaves. Till 1308 it was chiefly supported by the laity. The members went barefoot.

Confucianism.

Called 'Yu,' the orthodox, or state, religious system of China, devised by Confucius.

The other two systems are *Taoism* (Rationalism), and *Fo* or Buddhism. Confucius is *Kûng-fu-tsu*, Kûng the philosopher. His three chief books are (1) the *Lûn-yu* or sayings; (2) the *Ta-hio* or Great Lesson; and (3) the *Chúng-yúng*, or doctrine of the mean.

Congé d'élire (*A*),

25 Hen. VIII. c. 20, A.D. 1534. A licence sent to the chapter to elect one of the persons named by the crown to a vacant bishopric. If the chapter refuses to elect within twenty days, it incurs the penalty of præmunire.

Pronounce *cŏnjay day-leer'*.

Congesta Mendve'dii.

A collection towards the history of Denmark by Eric VI. or VIII. (Mendvedius), 1274, 1286-1319.

Congested Districts of Ireland.

Those parts of Donegal and Kerry which are mere mountain or bog lands. The population is so thick that, even if cabins and holdings were free, the people could not earn a living.

Dillon says he 'would include Leitrim, Galway, Roscommon, and western half of Cork also' (April 1890). A line drawn down the map fifteen miles from the sea would about enclose this area.

Congregation (*The*),

1559. A name assumed by the Protestants of Scotland in the regency of Marie de Guise. The leaders, called the 'Lords of the Congregation' (*q.v.*), pledged themselves to see the 'Solemn League and Covenant' (*q.v.*) carried out.

The Duke of Châtelherault abandoned the congregation [reform party]. In this predicament the Lords of the Congregation made still more impassioned appeals to Cecil.—HOWITT, *Hist. of Eng.*, vol. ii. p. 405.

Congregation de Propaganda Fide (*The*).

A Board of high church dignitaries in the Catholic Church which consult on the propagation of the Catholic religion throughout the world.

Congregation of France.

See 'Génovéfains.'

Congregation of Relics (*The*).

A board of high Catholic dignitaries whose duty it is to enquire into the genuineness of supposed relics.

Congregation of St. Maur (*The*),

1621. Reformed Benedictines.

Congregation of the Holy Office (*The*).

The congregation at Rome

to which the direction of the tribunal of the Inquisition is subject. It was established in 1542 by Paul III., and consists of twelve cardinals, a commissary, several 'theologians,' 'consulters,' and 'qualifiers' whose duty it is to report on each case for the information of the cardinals. *See* 'Holy Office.'

Congregation of the Index

(*The*). A committee appointed by Pope Pius V. to read books and state which should be prohibited to Catholic readers. Those prohibited were published from time to time in what was called the 'Index.' We find the following prohibited: Milton's 'Paradise Lost,' Goldsmith's 'History of England,' Bacon's 'De Augmentis Scientiarum,' Locke 'On the Human Understanding,' Cudworth's 'Intellectual System,' Whately's 'Logic,' 'Little Henry and his Bearer' (a child's tale), Gibbon, Robertson, Sismondi, Hallam, J. S. Mill, Addison, Kant, parts of Descartes, Malebranche, Fleury, Fénelon, Dante; all Calvin's Luther's and Voltaire's works; all works of heresiarchs on any subject whatsoever, and every book which threw doubt on Catholicism.

Congregation of the Lord (*The*),

Scotland, 1557. Consisted of a band of Protestants who met at Edinburgh. They were led by the Earls Argyll, Morton, and Glencairn. They covenanted to stand together in mutual defence of faithful ministers, gospel truths, and the holy sacraments. The Established Church was styled 'The Congregation of Satan.'

The Book of Common Prayer of Edward VI. was ordered to be used in the parish churches of Scotland.

Congregation of the Oratory

(*The*), 1558. Founded by Philip de Neri. Confirmed by the pope in 1575. Established in France in 1611 by Father de Berule. Introduced by Newman into England in 1847.

Congregation of the University of Oxford (*The*), 1854. Consists

of the heads of colleges, professors, examiners, and university officials, with all members of the Convocation who have resided 140 nights within a mile and a half of the university. Duties are, to deliberate and vote on statutes proposed by the Hebdomadal Board (*q.v.*), and to submit their deliberations to the House of Convocation (*q.v.*) to be accepted or rejected as the case may be.

Congregation of the Visitation (*The*), 1610. Under the rule of

St. Augustine, founded by the Baroness of Chantal at Annécy. Confirmed by Urban VIII. in 1626.

Congregations of Aids (*i.e.* 'de

Auxiliis'). Began 2 Jan., 1598. Polemical consultations or conferences between the Dominicans and the Jesuits. The fourth was held in 1601, opened in Jan. and closed in July. The last began 14 Sept., 1605, and went on to 1 March, 1606. Paul V., in Aug. 1607, prohibited its renewal.

Congregationalists or 'Inde-

pendents,' 1580. Those dissenters who maintain the right of each separate congregation to choose its own minister and lay down laws for its own government. They are all trinitarians and pædobaptists, and thus differ from the Unitarians and the Baptists.

Called Independents because each congregation is independent, and admits neither bishops, elders, nor any other board, not of their own choosing, to interfere with their choice of ministers or church government. Mr. Robinson or Mr. Jacob founded the sect.

Congregationists, 1557–1638. The

Scotch reformers. The whole body was called the Congregation; but from 1638, when they bound themselves by oath to adhere to the Solemn League and Covenant (*q.v.*) the reformers were called Covenanters. Not unfrequently the Congregationists are called Covenanters also, but this is not strictly correct.

In the spring of 1562 Elizabeth became engaged to the support of the Huguenots . . . against their government as she had supported the Covenanters of Scotland.—HOWITT, *History of England*, vol. ii. p. 418.

Congress. The American Senate

and House of Representatives. The Senate is elected for six years, the President for four years, and the Representatives for two years.

Congress of Carlsbad (*The*),1819.

For regulating the affairs of Germany.

Congress of Laybach (*The*), 1820.

For deliberating on the condition of Spain, Portugal, and Naples.

Congress of Vienna (*The*), 2 Oct.,

1814, to 23 March, 1815, at the close of the great war. By this congress the Cape of Good Hope, the Mauritius, Malta, and Corfu were assigned to *England*; Finland and Poland to *Russia*; Lombardy and the Venetian States to *Austria*; Saxony, Franconia, and Swedish Pomerania to *Prussia*; Tuscany to the Archduke *Ferdinand*; Genoa to the King of *Sardinia*; Parma and Placentia to *Marie Louise*, the wife of Napoleon; Norway to *Sweden*; and the Two Sicilies to *Ferdinand* VI. of the Bourbon dynasty.

Congress of the United Colonies (*The*), 10 May, 1775.

The style assumed by the second congress of Philadelphia, in revolt from Great Britain. They issued a prohibition of the export of provisions to any British colony or fishery, or of any supply to the British soldiers in Massachusetts, or of the negotiation of any bill drawn by a British officer. *See* ' Thirteen United Colonies.'

Congress's Own, 1776.

Hazen's Canadian regiment, kept up by recruiting in the States. It was on the side of the Americans in the War of Independence.

Congruism.

A doctrine taught by Duns Scotus (1265–1308), who maintained that man in his natural state can so regulate his life as to *deserve* God's grace, and this natural fitness or congruity for grace obliges the Deity to grant it. *See* ' Condignitism.'

Molinism (*q.v.*) is a modification of this.

Conjuration de l'Epingle Rose (*La*), 1816.

A French secret society which ' prit pour signe de ralliement une épingle rose.' *See* ' Society of the Black Pin.'

Pronounce : *Con-ju-rah'-se-on'g dla-pâhn-gl*, &c.

Connecticut (U.S. America).

So called from its river of the same name, which enters the state about twenty miles north of Hartford. The nickname is ' the Wooden Nutmeg State,' or ' Nutmeg State,' from a trick played by one of its 'cute ones, who sold imitation nutmegs made of wood as real nutmegs, and realised by his dishonesty a pot of money.

Connétable [Lord High Constable of France].

First appointed by Henri I., from which reign to that of Louis XIII. he was the highest dignitary of the crown. In times of *war* he was commander-in-chief of the army, with absolute power; even the king himself at such times was wholly under his commands. In *peace* he was war minister,

and took precedence of all other ministers of the crown. The office was abolished in 1627, but was nominally restored by Napoleon I. in favour of his brother Louis. The most noted of the Connétables were :—

CHÂTILLON (1250–1329) under Philippe le Bel and Louis X.

DU GUESCLIN (1314–1380) under Charles V.

CLISSON the Butcher (1320–1407) under Charles VI.

BOURBON (1489–1527) under François I.

MONTMORENCY (1493–1567) under Henri II., François II., and Charles IX.

LESDIGUIÈRES (1543–1626) under Henri IV. and Louis XIII.

Conqueror (*The*), 1027, 1066–1087.

In English history means William I., duke of Normandy, who conquered Harold II. in the battle of Senlac, and obtained the English crown thereby.

Conqueror of the Danes.

Brian Boru, monarch of Ireland. It was in the battle of Clontarf, 1014, that the Danes in Ireland were so utterly defeated that they never more made head in that island; but such as remained mixed with the natives and became one people with them. Brian was assassinated on the day of conquest, aged 88.

Brian has been made a parallel to our Alfred the Great, but in moral greatness never king equalled our Alfred.

Conrad. *See* Konrad.

Con's Half, and Mogh's Half.

Con of the hundred battles was king of Meath, and Mogh Nuad was king of the province of Leinster. Mogh overcame Con in ten fights, and claimed half of Con's kingdom.

Conscript Fathers. 'Patres Conscripti.'

After the expulsion of Tarquin a new element was introduced into the Roman Senate. The new senators were called *conscripti*, while the original 300 patricians were still called *patres*. So that the senate then consisted of *patres et conscripti*, and was addressed by speakers as *patres, conscripti*, or conscripts, fathers, perverted into the compound word Conscript Fathers.

Conseil des Anciens (*Le*), 23 Sept., 1795–10 Nov., 1799.

In French history. Consisted of 250 members, whose function was to elect the directors, and to ratify or reject the resolutions of the 'Conseils des Cinq-cents' (*q.v.*). One-third of the council retired annually. Both these councils were created by the constitution of Year III. (*q.v.*). Each member must be at least forty years of age, married or a widower, and have been a householder for fifteen years. They sat in the Tuileries.

Conseil des Cinq-cents (*Le*),

23 Sept., 1795—10 Nov., 1799. One of the two councils created by the constitution of Year III. (*q.v.*). It consisted of 500 members, elected for three years. Each member must be at least thirty years of age, and have been a householder for ten years. This assembly proposed the laws, which were then submitted to the 'Conseil des Anciens' (*q.v.*). They held their sessions in the Salle de Manège (rue Rivoli).

Conseil d'Etat (*Le*), of Year

VIII. (1799). Modified in 1814, 1815; reorganised by the law of the 19th July, 1845; greatly modified by the constitution of 1848 and by the law organic of 1849; but in 1852 it was restored to its original state. It is an assembly of magistrates to prepare the laws and give advice on all questions of national importance. It consists of councillors, masters of requests, and auditors; and is divided into six sections, viz. the legislative section, the section of foreign affairs, the section du contentieux, de l'intérieur, de l'instruction publique, and the section des cultes.

Conseils des Prud'hommes

(*Les*). Municipal tribunals to arbitrate in disputes between masters and workmen. The council is composed of merchants, master-workmen, common workmen, and manufacturers, all elective except the president, who is named by the government. In all disputes not exceeding 200 francs (8*l.*) their judgment is final. There was such a Council at Marseilles in 1452, called the *Prud'hommes Pêcheurs*. Louis XI. in 1464 established such a council at Lyons. In 1806 was established a modern council at Lyons, and similar ones have since been instituted all over France. In 1844 a council of Prud'hommes was organised for the metal trade, and in 1847 for manufacturers of all sorts of tissues. chemists,

and all other trades. In 1853 these councils were recognised by law.

Prud'hommes, according to Bouillet, is from the Latin *prudens homo*, but Scheler disputes this.

Conservative and Radical.

These terms were substituted in 1832 for Tories and Whigs; it was soon after the passing of the Reform Bill. The partisans of Sir Robert Peel adopted the appellation, and gave out that their platform was to *conserve* or maintain the constitution against the inroads of democracy, which were 'destructive.' Radicals are those who would *eradicate*, or pull up by the roots, the monarchy, and establish instead a democracy, or republic. The term 'Radical' is older than that of Conservative, being applied in 1818 to the party headed by Henry Hunt and Major Cartwright, who advocated a *radical reform*; but since 1832 its meaning has been changed. The Tories were averse to change, the Conservatives were willing to amend, the Whigs would preserve the monarchy, the Radicals would convert it into a democracy.

Lord Eldon always manfully adhered to the old word Tory; the word respected, time honoured of his party; under which for near two centuries they had so gallantly defended the altar and the throne—talking rather contemptuously of the upstart appellation of 'Conservatives,' among whom, he foretold, would be introduced some very lax notions of religion and politics.—Lord CAMPBELL, *Lives of the Chancellors*, xvii. p. 580.

Conservatoire, or 'Conservatorio.'

An Italian school for the study of music, its advancement, and purity. In Naples there was at one time three such schools, and in Venice four. In 1818 the Neapolitan conservatoires were reduced to one, called the Real Collegio di Musica, and the Venetian schools were similarly reduced. In 1808 a grand Conservatorio was founded at Milan. In 1842 a school for music was established by Mendelssohn at Leipsic; and one was founded at Cologne in 1849.

In 1784 was established a similar school called *L'Ecole Royale de Chant, &c.*; and in 1793 was founded the *Institut National de Musique*, which in 1795 was changed into the *Conservatoire de Musique*.

Consiglio Maggiore (*The*). The

lower house of legislature in the republic of Florence, which in the time of Savonarola consisted of 3,200 members, divided into three sections, each of which held office for six months. This council did not originate laws, but had the power of veto, and voted without discussion. All laws were proposed by the Signoria, were discussed by the upper chamber, called the Ottanta, and were then sent to the great council to be accepted or rejected.

Consistoires Isra'élites (*Les*), 15 March, 1808 (France). Reorganised 5 May, 1844; distinguished into the Consistoires *Départmentaux* and the Consistoire *Central*, which sits in Paris.

Consistorial (*A*). In the Protestant communion of France means an assembly for the regulation of all things bearing on the discipline and temporalities of the Protestant churches. It appoints pastors and supplies vacancies. In the Calvinist communion a synod consists of five consistorial churches. In the Lutheran communion five consistorial churches constitute an *Inspection.* In Strasburg there is a General Consistory, which has authority over all other consistories and inspections. In Paris, since 1852, has been instituted a ' Conseil Central ' of the two churches.

Consistorial Phrases. Certain Bible phrases learnt by Catharine de Medicis with which to beguile the Consistorials who had joined the Huguenots. These were common in her mouth : *To approve of the counsel of Gamaliel; Beautiful are the feet of those who preach the Gospel of Peace ;* the king she called *the Lord's anointed,* or *the image of the living God; I call the Eternal to witness; Before God and His angels.*

Consistorialists, 1574. French malcontents of the tradesmen and merchant class, as opposed to the nobles, magistrates, and councillors of towns. Many of the clergy were Consistorialists. These malcontents were very unwilling to take up arms, but once in the battlefield they insisted on sufficient guarantees for the liberty of the reformed church. The nobles, on the contrary, were ever ready for a compromise if they benefited thereby. The malcontents were Catholics, but many joined the Huguenots so long as they found it to their advantage to do so.

Consistory (*A*). In Roman history. A secret council of the Roman emperors (*Consistorium*).

Consistory (*The*). In Church history, the college of cardinals or council of the Pope. There is a public and a secret consistory. The *public* consistory meets in the great room of the palace of St. Peter, and the pope in his pontifical robes, seated on a throne, and attended by his court, presides. In this court judicial causes, the canonisation of saints, &c., are determined. The *secret* consistory is held in the chamber called the ' Chamber of Papogay ' (*q.v.*), and only cardinals are admitted. In this court the election of cardinals and bishops is determined.

Consistory Court. The prætorium of a diocesan bishop, held in his cathedral, for the trial of ecclesiastical matters arising within his jurisdiction. The judge is the bishop's chancellor, or his commissary, and the appeal is to the archbishop of the province.

In Scotland a large portion of the Consistory Court of Edinburgh was transferred to the courts of the sheriffs by 11 Geo. IV. and 1 Will. IV. c. 69.

Consolati. The Consoled, a name by which the Waldenses (*q.v.*) are sometimes called, on account of the consolation and peace of mind which they derived from their views of gospel Christianity.

Consolidated Fund (*The*), 1787 (27 Geo. III. c. 13). The union of the Aggregate, General, and South Sea Funds. In 1816, that of Ireland was combined with it. This fund is pledged for the payment of the whole interest of the national debt of Great Britain and Ireland.

Consolidation Acts. Acts of Parliament which combine different provisions of separate clauses into one act. Thus we have—

The Companies' Clauses Consolidation Act of 1845 (8, 9 Vict. c. 16).

The Lands' Clauses Consolidation Act of 1845 (8, 9 Vict. c. 18).

The Railways' Clauses Consolidation Act of 1845 (8, 9 Vict. c. 20).

This is done to save the repetition, in each special act, of the clauses introduced.

Consols. The different government stocks consolidated into one fund. The Consolidated Annuity Act was passed in 1757.

Conspiracy of Pazzi (*The*). The Pazzi was the rival power of the Medici in Florence. Lorenzo de' Medici used all his efforts to keep his rivals out of power, and Sixtus IV., the pope, who hated the Medici, leagued with Francesco Pazzi and Salviati (archbishop of Pisa) to murder Lorenzo and his brother, and place the Pazzi in the chief offices of Florence. The plan was to murder the two brothers while bent in adoration at high mass. The elevation of the host by the Archbishop of Pisa was to be the secret sign of the attack. Bandini was to murder the younger brother, and two ecclesiastics were to despatch Lorenzo. The younger brother, Giuliano, was murdered, but Lorenzo escaped, and the conspirators were all put to death.

Conspiracy of 1618.

Well known to English readers by the tragedy of 'Venice Preserved' by Otway (1682). The Abbé St. Real says that the Duke d'Os-suna, the Marquis de Bedmar, and Don Pedro di Toledo, governor of Milan, concerted a plan for the destruction of Venice, and entrusted to Pierre and Renault the chief execution. On the eve of its maturity, Antoine Jaffier, a French captain, one of the conspirators, peached, and the conspiracy was dissolved. Pierre and forty-five of his accomplices were drowned, and Jaffier, being found to hold communications with the conspirators whom he had denounced, was drowned also.

Belvidera is a wholly imaginary character. Pierre was not stabbed by Jaffier, and Jaffier did not kill himself. Breaking on the wheel was a punishment wholly unknown in the Republic of Venice. Probably the whole conspiracy was altogether a mare's-nest.

Constance (Treaty of), 1183.

A model of future treaties between the German empire and the North Italian states. By this treaty, signed by Frederick Barbarossa, after his defeat at Legnano in 1176, the Italian cities were confirmed in their independence; they had the right of declaring war, of coining money, &c. See Hallam, 'Middle Ages,' vol. i. p. 355.

Constantine of Gaul (The).

Clovis was sometimes so called, as Gibbon informs us (465, 481-511). Constantine was the father of the Christian Church in the East, and Clovis was the father of the 'Orthodox' Church in Gaul.

Constantine Cross (A).

The inhabitants of Dakóta were treated to a sub-lime . . . display on the morning of 9 January,

1889, at nearly the time of sunrise. Three gorgeous prismatic columns . . . shot up from the verge of the prairie into the heavens in intense brilliancy, equalling the light of the sun itself. . . . These prismatic columns extended one-third of the way to the zenith, and at the upper end gradually blended with the sky. What made the phenomenon remarkably striking was that the centre column assumed the form of a cross, from a small cloud which hung directly athwart the centre, and was illuminated by the light of the sun, still below the horizon, and forming the transept of the figure of the cross.—The Leeds Mercury (quoted in 'Notes and Queries,' 22 Jan., 1889, p. 483).

Constantinople (Convention of), 1784.

Between Catherine II. of Russia and the Porte, confirming to Russia the sovereignty of the Crimea.

Constituent Assembly (The), 27 June, 1789.

'L'Assemblée Constituante.' The name assumed by the National Assembly (q.v.) after it was joined by the Duke of Orleans and forty-seven other members of the aristocracy, with a large number of the clergy. So called because the work they set themselves to perform was to get France a constitution.

In 1848 the Legislative Assembly of France was again called L'Assemblée Constituante, because it set itself to give France another constitution, a democratic republican one, with a four-years president and universal suffrage. It met 4 May, finished its labours 4 Nov., on 12 Nov. proclaimed the republican constitution, and gave place to the Legislative Assembly.

In the first of these were three parties, the right, the left, and the centre. The right were the ministerial party, the left the republican party, the centre the moderate party, or trimmers.

Constitution (A).

The cudgel carried by a Muscadin (q.v.).

Constitution de la République (La).

I. 26 Feb., 1848-14 Jan., 1852. The Second Republic of France. This constitution was even more democratic than that provided by the Acte Constitutionnel (q.v.). Every Frenchman in France, who had attained the age of 21, was an elector, and everyone who was 25 years old was eligible to be a deputy in the National Assembly, which consisted of 900 members. There was only one assembly, the members of which were elected by universal suffrage, the age of 21 being the one and only restriction. The motto of this constitution was 'Liberty, Fraternity, and Equality.'

II. 13 Feb., 1871. This was the fifteenth change since the reign of Louis XVI.,

30 Sept., 1791. Represented by a president and National Assembly.

The National Assembly nominally consists of 700 members, but as any deputy can represent more than one constituency, the number does not exceed 670.

Constitution Française (La), 30 Sept., 1791.

Decreed by the National and Constituent Assembly, and accepted by Louis XVI. It was monarchical and representative. The previous form of government was thenceforward called the 'Ancien Régime.' In 1793 the *Acte Constitutionnel (q.v.)* introduced a purely democratic government, called the ' Constitution of '93 ' (q.v.).

Constitution of '93 (The).

The constitution given to France by the ' Acte Constitutionnel' presented to the nation by the Convention 21 June, 1793, and based on the sovereignty of the people, and the indivisibility of the republic. On the death of Robespierre in 1794 the Thermidorians had the chief power, and set about abolishing the Constitution of '93, and on 24 June, 1795, they created an executive director, assisted by two councils.

Constitution of the President (The), 14 Jan., 1852.

See ' Constitution of the Second Empire.'

Louis Napoleon was elected president of the French Republic 10 Dec., 1848; he re-established universal suffrage 2 Dec., 1851 ; he was made president for ten years, by plébiscite, 20, 21 Dec. 1851; the Second Empire was established 7 Nov., 1852; Louis Napoleon was elected emperor by plébiscite 21, 22 Nov., 1852; and he assumed the title of Napoleon III. Dec. 2, 1852.

Constitution of the Second Empire (The).

Much the same as that of the president, 14 Jan., 1852. It consisted of an emperor, a senate, and a legislative chamber. The *senate* consisted of 150 members chosen by the emperor, and each member had a stipend equal to 1,200l. a year. The deputies of the *corps législatif* were elected for six years by universal suffrage, and received a salary equal to 100l. a month during the time of session. In case of a dissolution, a new corps législatif was to be in sessions within six months. The number of deputies fluctuated with the population, each of the eighty-nine departments having one representative for every 35,000 inhabitants. There was also a *council of state* composed of the emperor, all members of the imperial family, a president, vice-president, and about 150 councillors; acting as a high court of appeal. In 1870 the emperor resigned the right of proposing laws, and made himself a ' constitutional emperor.'

Constitution of the Second Republic (The), 13 Feb., 1871.

M. Thiers being the first president and minister of war, with a stipend of 2,000l. a year. *See* ' Constitution de la République,' II. (Thiers, pronounce *Tear*.)

Constitution of Year III. (The), 24 June, 1795—24 Dec., 1799.

This form of government was adopted in France after that called ' The Constitution of '93,' which after the reign of terror was impracticable. The *legislative* power was vested in two houses, called the Council of Elders and the Council of 500. The former contained 250 members. The *executive* was entrusted to five directors, called the Directory. All laws were to emanate from the 500, the elders rejected or ratified them, and the directors saw that they were carried out.

Constitution of Year VIII., 24 Dec., 1799—2 Aug., 1802.

It vested the power of government, in France, in 3 consuls, 60 senators, 100 tribunes called the tribunate, and 300 legislators called the *corps législatif.*

The 1st and 2nd consuls were to hold office for 10 years, the 3rd for only 5. The 1st consul was almost absolute. In 1802 the consular office was for life. In 1814 the conservative senate became the ' Chamber of Deputies.' In 1807 the tribunate was suppressed, and the corps législatif was addressed by the *Conseil d'Etat.*

In 1814 the corps législatif was replaced by the Chamber of Deputies. During the ' Hundred Days' the Chamber of Deputies was called the 'Chamber of Representatives;' in 1815 it was again called the ' Chamber of Deputies;' and in 1852 it resumed its name of the *corps législatif.*

Constitution of Year X. (The), 2 Aug., 1802—18 May, 1804.

Bonaparte was made consul for life, and the entire executive power was vested in his hands. The act which established this constitution was the *Sénatus-consulte organique de la constitution (Year X).*

Constitution of Year XII. (The), 18 May, 1804—4 June, 1814.

Conferring on Napoleon I. the title of emperor. The act which created this constitution was the *Sénatus-consulte organique de l'Empire Français (Year XII).*

Constitutions were the edicts of the Roman emperors. The first compilation of these edicts was by Theodosius the younger, from Constantine to A.D. 438; but the great compilation was the Imperial Constitutions of Justinian, A.D. 529.

See 'Apostolical Constitutions.'

Constitutions (*The*). That is, the Constitutions of Clarendon (*q.v.*).

The pope advocated the side of the primate [*i.e.* Becket], and condemned 'the Constitutions.' —PINNOCK, *Analysis of the Early Church*, p. 82.

Constitutions of Clarendon (*The*), 1164. Sixteen ordinances agreed to in the General Council assembled by Henry II. at his palace of Clarendon, Wiltshire. The objects of these ordinances were to define the limits between civil and ecclesiastical jurisdictions, to abolish the abuses arising from the encroachments of the popes, and to limit the papal patronage and jurisdiction in the realm.

These enactments provide that the clergy shall be amenable to the king's courts; that no appeal shall in any case be carried from the king's courts to the pope; that no dignitary of England shall quit the kingdom without the king's permission; that no officer or tenant of the crown shall be excommunicated without the king's sanction; that presentations to all royal livings shall be with the king; that the revenues of vacant livings still accrue to the crown; that all bishops shall be made by the king's writ; and before consecration every nominee shall pay homage and fealty to the crown.

Constitutions of King Half (*The*). Regulations for pirates: (1) No one to wear a sword more than an ell long; (2) each pirate must be able to encounter twelve ordinary men; (3) no boys or women to be made prisoners; (4) no wounds to be bound till after the lapse of twenty hours. (Bartholinus, 'De Causis Contemptæ a Danis Mortis,' book ii. 9.)

Constitutions of Otho (*The*), 1237. Passed by a council held in London by Otho, the papal legate, forbidding the clergy to keep concubines 'openly in their houses,' or to visit them 'openly, to the great scandal of religion.' The same constitutions forbade the clandestine marriages of priests, which were declared to be very common.

Constitutional Agitation Act (*The*), 1792. A mere mask to mislead the loyalists of Ireland, by giving out that Irish agitation should be carried on by constitutional means.

It is a plan that has proved eminently successful in preventing the Government from grappling with the beginning of sedition . . . it is a game of masked sedition.—*Irish Seditions*, 1792-1880, p. 34.

Constitutional Assembly of Rome (*The*), 30 March, 1848. A republican assembly of deputies established in Rome by the triumvirate Mazzini, Armellini, and Suffi.

Constitutional Charter (*The*), 4 June, 1814. Given by Louis XVIII. to France. It established a representative government, composed of two houses, one of hereditary peers (a house of lords) and the other of elective deputies (a house of commons). The franchise he restricted to persons above 30 years of age who paid annually at least 12*l.* of direct taxes.

He thus disfranchised about three and a half millions of his subjects.

Constitutional Society (*The*), 1769. A society founded by Horne Tooke and Wilkes for supporting the Bill of Rights. In 1775 Lord North commented sharply on the conduct of this society, and Tooke was prosecuted for circulating letters of the society denouncing the skirmish of Lexington (America) 'as a bloody murder on our own part of British subjects.' The society voted the sum of 100*l.* for the relief of the widows and children of those who fell at Lexington on the American side.

Constitutionalists *The*), 1814, of Spain. The Exaltados or radicals were so called, because they wanted to restore the constitution given to Spain in 1812, but abolished by Ferdinand VII. in 1814.

In 1820 Ferdinand swore adherence to the constitution, and for two years matters went on more smoothly; but then civil war broke out afresh, Louis XVIII. interfered, and for many years Spain, from one cause or another, was in almost ceaseless broils.

Consubstantialists (*The*). Those who maintained what was called the *homo-ousion, i.e.* that the Father, Son, and Holy Ghost are all of the same nature. Aristotle says the stars are consubstantial or homo-ousian. So men are consubstantial or homo-ousian.

Consulate (*The*), of France, from 10 Nov., 1799–18 May, 1804. *See* 'Constitution of Year VIII.'

Continental System (*The*). A pet system of Napoleon's to ruin England by ruining her trade. He prohibited any

nation over which he had control or influence to trade with Great Britain ; he
enjoined that every subject of the British
kingdom who set foot on the continent
should be accounted a prisoner of war, and
all British merchandise be considered lawful prize. The folly of boycotting England
was this: as Great Britain was the best
customer of these continental nations,
they ruined their own commerce in seeking to ruin that of England.

The first announcement of this system was made
9 Feb., 1801; the 'Berlin decree' was made 21 Nov.,
1807. Austria acceded to the system 24 Nov., 1807;
Sweden 17 Sept. 1809; the Roman States in Dec.
Russia relaxed 31 Dec., 1810. Strenuous efforts were
made by France to enforce the system in 1812, but
after the Moscow expedition in the autumn of that
year the system was wholly abandoned.

Continental Troops (The), 1775.
A body of men maintained by the
united colonies of North America, in
the War of Independence, and placed
under George Washington. The continental troops must not be confounded
with the provincial militia.

Continual Council (The). Certain
great prelates and lords, who combined
together in the reign of Edward I. to
control the king and overpower the parliament. Edward II. tried to oust them
by choosing his council from men of inferior rank, but the 'continual council'
then formed themselves into a standing
committee of bishops, earls, and barons,
for the government of the realm, and
drew up certain 'articles of reform,'
which transferred the power of the crown
into the hands of the 'Lords Ordainers,'
as the committee called themselves. Edward II. resisted for a time, but was
ultimately compelled to take some of the
most powerful of the barons into his
privy council.

Contra-Remonstrants, or 'Anti-
Remonstrants,' 1611. The Calvinists, or
Gomarists(q.v.), who opposed the Remón-
strants or Arminian party. This party
became more violent after the Synod of
Dort, 1619.

It is said that the Socinian bias of Vorstius
greatly weakened the Arminian party.

Conventicle Acts (The). I. The
First, 16 Car. II. c. 4 (1664). By this act,
every person found at any dissenting meeting, where more than five persons were
present, was punishable by fine, or three
months' imprisonment. For a third

offence a person might be transported for
seven years.

In 1670 (22 Car. II. c. 1) this act was
enlarged. Children above 16 years of age
were to be fined 5s. each for attending
such meetings for the first offence, and
10s. for every subsequent offence. The
preacher was to be fined 20l. for the first
offence, and 40l. for every subsequent
one. The master of the house where the
meeting was held was to be fined 20l. for
each offence. Repealed by the Toleration
Act, 1 Will. & Mary, c. 18 (1689).

II. The Second, 1670 (22 Car. II.). By
which it was furthermore enacted, that
all incumbents who had been admitted
by the kirk-sessions and lay-elders during
the interregnum in England must receive
a presentation from the patron of the
living, and be instituted afresh by the
bishop of the diocese, under pain of deprivation. In consequence of this law
350 parishes were declared vacant.

Convention Nationale (La), 10
Aug., 1792. Succeeded the 'Assemblée
Législative.' The first sessions held
21 Sept., when royalty in France was
abolished, and France was declared a republic. 17 Jan., 1793, they condemned
Louis XVI. to death. 1 Feb., 1793, they
declared war against England, Spain, and
Holland. 5 Oct., 1793, they introduced the
Revolutionary Calendar. 16 Oct., 1793,
they condemned to death Mary Antoinette. 31 Oct., 1793, they condemned to
death twenty-one of the Girondin deputies. 5 April, 1794, they condemned to
death Danton, Camille Desmoulins, and
several members of the club of the Cordeliers. 27 July, 1794, they outlawed
the two Robespierres and their chief
partisans. 31 May, 1795, they suppressed
the Revolutionary Tribunal. 22 July,
1795, they concluded peace with Spain.
26 Oct., 1795, they passed a decree of
general amnesty, and declared its sessions terminated. They met in the
Tuileries. Chief members were Brissot,
Collot d'Herbois, Condorcet, Couthon,
Danton, Gensonné, Marat, Péthion,
Robespierre, St. Just, Tallien, and
Vergniaud.

Convention Parliament (The).
I. 1660. The first parliament after the
restoration, consisting of both houses. It
was not called together by order of the
sovereign, but was merely convened by

Monk. Passed an act restoring the ancient general constitution of kings, lords, and commons, and was legalised by Charles II. The Convention Parliament was certainly the most bloodthirsty and infamous of all the parliaments in the annals of English history. Even John Milton, the immortal poet, was condemned by it to death; but the fame of his great genius saved him, and England was spared the scandal of so great a shame. First met 25 April, 1660; dissolved 29 Dec., 1660.

II. 22 Jan., 1689, dissolved 29 Jan., 1691, under William III. (prince of Orange). Conferring the crown on William and Mary. *See* 'Parliament' and 'Geneva Convention.'

Convention of Cintra (*The*), 30 August, 1808. This was really the convention signed at Torres Vedras, when Junot agreed to quit Portugal; but the despatch of Sir Hew Dalrymple, inclosing a copy of the treaty, was dated from Cintra, 13 miles from Torres Vedras. Sir Arthur Wellesley was so disgusted with the treaty that he requested to be recalled.

The French ought to have been made to disgorge all their spoil. The Russian fleet ought to have been given up to England; and Junot, with his army, ought to have been forbidden to take any further part in the war.

Convention of Estates. The Scottish Parliament was so called between the removal of a king from Scotland and the Union. Convention is a word applied to a parliament not summoned by the king. Sometimes spoken of as 'The Estates,' and sometimes as 'The Convention.'

Convention of St. Cloud (*The*), 5 July, 1815. A military convention signed at St. Cloud by Davoust, Wellington, and Blücher, to put an end to further hostilities. The next day the allies entered Paris for the 2nd time, and Louis XVIII. followed on the 8th.

Convention of Sempach (*The*), 1393. The act of confederation between the Swiss and the Austrians. The two memorable battles of Morgarten and Sempach, won by the Swiss, had lowered the pride of Austria, who concluded peace with Switzerland for twenty years.

Convention of the Irish Rule (*The*). According to their own circular, the object of this association was 'to promote the confederation of every body

in America, and, if possible, in the whole world, to advance the welfare of a wretched, oppressed, plundered, and misgoverned people [the Irish], and to awaken the long-suspended conscience of a powerful and brutal foe [the English].'

Converters, or 'Propagators of the Faith,' 1630. Missionaries, or rather ambulating controversialists — monks, Capuchins, and Recollets (*q.v.*)—with others of meaner sort, paid for every convert they made to the Catholic faith.

Fénelon says many were cordwainers, brokers, tailors, itinerant grinders, and little shopmen, who, without any study, abandoned their trade to convert the Huguenots; but they drew down upon the Converters universal contempt by their ignorance and fanaticism.

Convertisseur. A title given to Pélisson, the great converter of the French Huguenots in the reign of Louis XIV. In 1677 Louis devoted a secret fund for the conversion of these 'heretics,' the price paid per head was about 5*s*. (6 livres), and Pélisson was the chief instrument in distributing this fund.

The French livre = a franc. The *livre tournois* was a little less, but in each case 20 sous = 1 livre. The exact deficit of the *livre tournois* was: 81 such livres were equal to 80 francs.

Convocation, 12th cent. An assembly of the archbishops, bishops, and canons, summoned by the king's writ for the purpose of assessing themselves in levies of taxes. Subsequently other church questions were discussed in these meetings, but the crown had the power of proroguing and dissolving them. In 1665 the clergy gave up the power of taxing themselves, and Convocation lost its *raison d'être*. Now, Convocation consists of two houses; in the upper house sit the prelates; in the lower house deans, archdeacons, canons, and proctors. Both are mere debating societies without one jot of authority.

In the Convocation of York the same distinction exists, but the business has generally been conducted in one assembly (1890).

Convocation. In England. A synod of clergymen dating from 8 Hen. VI. c. 1, A.D. 1429. Reconstituted by 25 Hen. VIII. c. 19, A.D. 1533, but greatly changed in the reign of Queen Elizabeth, A.D. 1600.

The Convocation of Canterbury was then made to comprise all the bishops of the province, who compose the upper house. While the lower house consists of 22 deans, 53 archdeacons 24 proctors of chapters, 44 proctors of the parochial clergy, and one precentor (of St. David's).

The Convocation of York is of much smaller extent. Occasionally the two act together. *See* 'House of Convocation.'

In 1870 the Convocation of Canterbury appointed the Committee of Revisers of the Authorised Version of the Bible.

Convulsionists, 1632. I. The convulsion epidemic broke out in whole nunneries about Bordeaux, especially in the convent *des Ursulines* of Loudun, an educational establishment. In 1686, the French refugees, driven from house and home in the infamous dragonnade expeditions, were affected by the same epidemic. *See* 'Convulsionnaires' and 'Plagues,' &c.

II. 1882. An extreme democrat or radical, whose platform is convulsion, or plucking up the established order of all things by the roots.

Convulsionnaires, 1730. Certain Jansenists of France who met in St. Medard's churchyard, in the suburbs of Paris, where was the tomb of the Abbé François de Paris, who had died in 1727, where numberless miracles were alleged to have been done. These fanatics 'threw themselves into the most violent contortions of body; rolled about on the ground, imitated birds, beasts, and fishes; and when utterly exhausted went off in convulsions or a swoon.' Louis XV. ordered them to be imprisoned in 1733, but it was not possible to stamp out the fervour altogether. In the revival meetings in the last quarter of the 19th cent. similar exhibitions have been recorded in the daily papers.

When the king commanded the cemetery gates to be closed, a wit wrote over them :

De par le roi, défense à Dieu
De faire miracle en ce lieu.

Henceforth the king forbids God's grace
To show His wonders in this place.

Co-operative Stores. Retail stores for the sale of groceries, drapery-goods, shoes, and even butcher's meat and poultry, of the best quality at the lowest profitable price. The movement began at Rochdale in 1843. In London the Civil Service Co-operative Store does an enormous business, insomuch that an original 1*l.* share is worth 200*l.* (1890), and the capital of the stores is worth seven millions sterling. The next largest is the Army and Navy Stores. Every customer must be a member by the pay-

ment of 20*s.*, and all sales are strictly for ready money. A member may hold as many as 200 shares.

Copenhagen (*Peace of*), 10 June, 1660. Between Denmark and Sweden, effected by the Swedish Government on the death of their king Carle X. By this treaty the district of Trondhjem and the island of Bornholm were restored to the Danes. *See* 'Treaty of Roskilde.'

Trondhjem, pronounce *Tron-yem.*

Copley Medal (*The*), 1709. Instituted in the Royal Society of London by Sir Godfrey Copley for scientific discoveries.

Copts, or 'Copti.' Egyptian Christians of the Eutychian heresy. They continue the practice of circumcision. Their patriarch lives in Cairo, and is called the Patriarch of Alexandria and Jerusalem.

Copyright. *See* 'Lord Mahon's Act.'

Coqueluche (*The Great Plague of*), 1580. Was so called in France 'parce que les malades à l'agonie rendaient des sons enroués, comme le fait un coq.' A sort of *catarrhe convulsif,* or hooping-cough.

Cordeliers. I. The French name for the strictest branch of the Franciscan friars, who wore a girdle of knotted *cord.*

II. 1790. A republican club which held its sessions in the convent of the Cordeliers, Paris. It was opposed to the Jacobins (*q.v.*), and affected extreme poverty. It was this club which demanded the abolition of royalty and the institution of a free republic. Closed by the Convention at the death of Danton in 1794.

The chief members were the giant Danton; the scarcely less notorious Camille Desmoulins, Hébert, the editor of 'Père Duchêne,' and Marat, the bloodthirsty young surgeon. Camille Desmoulins was the editor of a popular journal called *Le Vieux Cordelier.*

Corinthians. I. Prize-fighters. Falstaff calls himself 'a Corinthian . . . . a lad of mettle' (1 *Hen. IV.* act ii. 4). So called from the Isthmian games held by the Greeks on the Isthmus of Corinth every alternate spring. In these games boxing formed a prominent part, and St. Paul, in his first epistle to the Corinthians (ix. 26), alludes to the racing and boxing so famous in Corinth, when he says, 'I, therefore, so run, not as uncertainly; so fight I, not as one that beateth the air.'

A Corinthian, a swell of the first water.

> Brave Tom, the champion, with an air
> Almost Corinthian took the chair.
>   CRIB, *Memorial.*

II. In the days of the Regency, Corinthians meant London bloods, or, more strictly speaking, members of the Pugilistic Club, in Bond Street, London, of which both George the prince regent and his brother Frederick duke of York were distinguished members. The Prince Regent was the chief champion of the Bristoleans (Belcher, Cribb, and Molineux), the Duke of York was leader of the Hebrew school, of whom Mendoza was the principal. Thomas Cribb was actually attached to the household of the Prince of Wales, much to the annoyance of the general public.

Cork, in Ireland, is the Irish *corcah,* a marsh.

Cork-boys, 1762. A political Irish association, a Cork branch of the Whiteboys (*q.v.*). Their especial grievance was the payment of tithes. *See* ' Irish Associations.'

Corn Importation Bill (*The*), 1846. When wheat is 48s. the duty shall fall by 1s. with every shilling in price till it touches 53s., when the fixed duty shall be 4s. This scale to last for three years, and to disappear on 1 Feb., 1849, leaving from that date only a normal rate of duty. All colonial wheat and flour to be admitted at once at a nominal rate.

Corn-law Rhymer (*The*). Ebenezer Elliott (1781–1849); born near Rotherham, in Yorkshire. His Corn-law Rhymes were published in 1831.

Corn Laws (*The*). Laws to regulate the exportation and importation of corn date as far back as 1360, which prohibited the exportation of corn except to Calais and Gascony. In 1393 the right to export was granted. In 1436 the right to export was granted only when wheat did not exceed 6s. 8d. a quarter. From that time sundry laws were made, till 1828, when the sliding scale was 'perfected.' By this law, if wheat was selling at 62s. a quarter, a duty of 24s. 8d. a quarter was imposed on imported corn; for every shilling less than 62s. a quarter

an extra shilling was added to the import duty; but when corn exceeded that price, the import duty rapidly decreased, till the price of corn reached 73s. a quarter (famine price), when a minimum duty of a shilling was imposed on imported corn.

Cornage. A kind of tenure in grand sergeanty. The service in this tenure was the blowing of a horn to warn the subjects of the king when any invasion of the Scots was detected or apprehended (Latin, *cornu,* a horn).

Corn-cracker State (*The*). The State of Kentucky. The inhabitants are called Corn-crackers.

Corneille du Boulevard (*Le*). Guilbert de Pixérécourt (1773–1844).

Cornwallis (*A*). A sort of Guy Fawkes procession once held in the U.S., to commemorate the struggle for independence, typified by the surrender of Lord Cornwallis at York Town in 1781 to the united American and French army. Prior to this he had rendered himself formidable to the Americans in the battle of Brandywine, by the reduction of Charleston, and his victories at Camden and Guilford. Now obsolete.

Coro'na (*The Roman*). 1. ' *Corōna Castrensis,*' or ' *Corona Vallaris,*' a gold crown, ornamented with palisades (*valla*), bestowed on the soldier who first surmounted the stockade, and forced his way into an enemy's camp.

2. *Corona Civica* (a civic crown), a chaplet of oak-leaves and acorns, bestowed on the Roman soldier who saved the life of a comrade in battle and slew the antagonist.

3. *Corona Classica,* or *Corona Navalis,* or *Corona Rostrāta,* a gold chaplet designed to imitate the beaks of ships (*rostra*), presented to the admiral who had destroyed an enemy's fleet (*classis*).

4. *Corona Longa,* a festoon of flowers hung round the neck on festive occasions, as on the feast of Bacchus, &c.

5. *Corona Murālis* (or mural crown) decorated with the towers and turrets of a battlement, and bestowed on the soldier who first scaled the walls of a besieged city.

7. *Corona Natalitia,* a wreath of laurel, ivy, or parsley, hung over a door to announce the birth of a child. In

Holland a rosette of lace is the natal symbol.

8. *Corona Obsidionālis*, a garland of grasses and wild flowers presented to a commander who came to the relief of a besieged army. The least in value, and highest in honour, of all crowns.

9. *Corona Oleagina*, a wreath of olive-leaves, presented to all those by whose counsel or instrumentality a triumph was obtained, whether present or not in the action.

10. *Corona Ovālis*, a chaplet of myrtle won by a general in an ovation.

11. *Corōna Pactĭlis*, or *Plectĭlis*, a wreath of natural flowers with their leaves and stalks, worn on festive occasions.

12. *Corona Radiāta*, for gods and emperors. A band of gold set round with conical rays, tapering upwards.

13. *Corona Sutĭlis*, a wreath of roses without their stalks, worn by the Salii at their festivals.

14. *Corona Triumphālis*, worn by a general in a triumph. Some were laurel leaves without their berries, some were gold leaves in imitation, and some were of gold, not worn, but presented as a valuable gift.

Corona never meant a royal crown. No. 12 was worn by emperors not as *imperator* but *divus*. The royal head-dress was a white band tied behind the head in a bow with long ends. Asiatic monarchs wore a blue and white fillet.

Besides the corona mentioned above, there were others not honorary, but only emblematical, such as the *Corona Sacerdotālis*, worn during sacrifice, both by priests and people.

Corona Funēbris, or *Sepulchrālis*, with which the dead were crowned.

Corona Convivālis, the *Corona Nuptiālis*, and the *Corona Natalitia* over the door of the vestibule where a child was born.

Coro'na Sacerdota'lis.

A crown of flowers worn by the clergy on certain high festivals, when they walked in procession from the monastery to the parish church. Thus, in the fifteenth century, Roger de Walden went to St. Paul's to be enthroned bishop, crowned with a wreath of red roses. Polidore Vergil (sixteenth century) refers to the same custom at the feast of St. Paul. Stow speaks of 'the dean and chapter issuing from the west door with roses on their heads.'

The tonsure was called the 'corona clericālis,' meant to symbolise the crown of thorns.—BEDE, v. 22.

Coronation of English Queens

(*The*). The queen of William I. crowned two years after the coronation of the king; the queen of Henry I. ditto; the queen of John not crowned with him, but alone; the queen of Henry III. not crowned with him, but afterwards alone; the queen of Edward III. crowned alone; the queen of Henry IV. not crowned with him, but alone; the queen of Henry V. ditto; the queen of Henry VI. ditto; the queen of Henry VII. crowned long after him; the queens of Henry VIII. some crowned and some not crowned; the queen of Charles I. never crowned; the queen of Charles II. ditto; the queen of George I. ditto; the queen of George IV. never crowned.

Coronation of the Ass (*The*).

An important ceremony in the Festival of Vesta, to commemorate the following incident: Vesta was once brutally assaulted by some Roman ruffians, who would have offered her indecent violence, but were alarmed by the sudden braying of an ass. *See* 'Feast of the Ass.'

Coroners,

1079, were originally state officers with authority to determine felonies; but now they only take inquisitions of death. They are elected for life, and have authority to assemble juries. When a jury is assembled, it is charged and sworn by the coroner to inquire, upon view of the dead body, how the party came by its death. Recently, the coroner has been empowered to order the attendance of a legally-qualified medical attendant to make a post-mortem examination if required. The fee is one guinea for attendance without a post-mortem, and two guineas for attendance with post-mortem examination.

Corporal D'Epré,

1814. A sobriquet under which the imperialists toasted Napoleon while he was in Elba. D'Epré is a pun on the word *dépré*, parted [from us].

Corporal Violet,

1814. The sobriquet under which Napoleon was toasted during his stay in Elba. The violet is and was the floral emblem of the French empire. Napoleon left for Elba in May, but it was generally thought by the imperial party that he would return the spring following 'with the violets,' and so he did.

The Government of Louis XVIII. never paid the money promised to the 'Emperor of Elba,' and therefore broke the contract which bound the exile to his abdication of the throne of France.

Corporation Act (*The*), 1661. This act, passed in the reign of Charles II., compelled everyone, before being admitted to any office in any municipal corporation, to take the sacrament in the Established Church, to subscribe the declaration abjuring the Solemn League and Covenant, and also that against the lawfulness of taking up arms against the ruling sovereign on any pretence whatsoever. *See* 'Test Act' and 'Municipal Corporation Act.'

Corporation and Test Act Repeal Bill (*The*), 9 Geo. IV., May 1828. To repeal the 'Corporation' and 'Test' Acts (*q.v.*). *See* 'Municipal Corporation, &c.'

Corporation Oath (*The*), 1661. Passed by the Pension Parliament (*q.v.*) to this effect : 'I do declare and believe that it is not lawful upon any pretence whatever to take arms against the king; and I do abhor that traitorous position of taking arms by his authority against his person, or against those commissioned by him.'

Corps Législatif (*Le*), of the Consulate, 24 Dec., 1799. Consisting of 300 deputies. The Tribunate acted as a legislative grand jury, deciding what laws and bills were to be laid before the Corps Législatif. In 1807 the Conseil d'Etat took the place of the Tribunate. In 1814 this body was replaced by the 'Chamber of Deputies.' During the 'Hundred Days' the 'Chamber of Deputies' was called the *Chamber of Representatives*. In 1815 it was again called the 'Chamber of Deputies.' In 1852 it resumed the name of the *Corps Législatif*.

Pronounce *Cor lay-jis-lah'-teef*.

Corpus Christi College. I. Cambridge [C. C. C. C.], 1352. Founded by the guilds of Corpus Christi and of the Blessed Virgin Mary, assisted by Henry duke of Lancaster, and originally called 'Benet College.' The head is called 'master.'

II. Oxford, 1516. Founded by Fox, bishop of Winchester. The head is called 'president.'

Corpus Christi Festival (*The*). Called by the French *Fête Dieu*, 1264, in honour of the consecrated host or wafer. It is held on the Thursday following Trinity Sunday, and is the most splendid festival of the Catholic Church.

Corpus Juris Canon'ici. A summary of the legal responses and papal rescripts respecting the jurisdiction of the Church of Rome. It contains three parts : viz. (1) The Decretals, in 5 books; (2) The Text, in 5 books ; and (3) The Extravagantes Communes.—The Decretals, compiled by Raimond de Pennafort, by order of Gregory IX., contain the rescript of the popes Alexander III., Innocent III., and Gregory IX., and was published in 1234. The Text was compiled by order of Boniface VIII., and continued the Decretals to the reign of the living pope. The Extravagantes Communes contained the 'Clementines,' or constitutions of Clement V. and the Extravagantes Johannis (XXII.).

Corpus Juris Civi'lis. The summary of Roman laws made in the reign of the Emperor Justinian. It consisted of four parts : (1) The Code, in 12 tables; (2) The Digest or Pandects, in 50 books ; (3) The Institutes, a *précis* of the Digest to teach the rudiments of Roman law, in 4 books ; and (4) The Novels, containing 16 edicts and 168 new laws by Justinian himself. The first three published A.D. 533, the last in 534.

Correggio. The best pictures of Correggio were actually used in the royal stables in the North to keep the wind from the backs or tails of the horses.

> Well then, the Charles of Mr. West
> And Oliver, I do protest,
>   And eke the witnesses of resurrection (Peter
>   and John)
> Will stop a hole, keep out the wind,
> And make a properer window-blind,
>   Than great Correggio, used for horse-protection.
>
>   PETER PINDAR, *Lyric Odes*, ii.

Correggio of Sculptors (*The*). Goujon (1515–1572), slain in the massacre of St. Bartholomew.

Corresponding Society (*The*), 1792. A society in London in strong sympathy with the French revolutionists, which corresponded with the National Convention of France. The object of the society was to establish a republic in Great Britain.

Corrupt Practices Act (*The*), 1854 (21, 22 Vict. c. 87). Relating to bribery, treating, and undue influence at the election of members of parliament.

Numerous additions and amendments of the original act have been made. The New Act came into force in 1883.

Corruptibles (*The*), or 'Corruptibilists, 537. A party of the Monophysites of Alexandria, supported by Justinian, and led by Theodosius, a disciple of Sevērus. This party, favoured by the Empress Theodora, and the arms of the eunuch Narses, were called by their opponents *Imperialists* or *Melchites*. It was opposed to the 'Corruptibles' (*q.v.*), and so bitter was the animosity that the streets of Alexandria were deluged with blood. It is said that 200,000 Christians were slaughtered in one day at the installation of Apollinarius as patriarch of Alexandria. This, of course, is a gross exaggeration.

The Corruptibles were Nestorians, who insisted on the perfect manhood of Christ. The Incorruptibles were Eutychians, who insisted that the body of Christ was not, like ours, corruptible, but was a celestial body.

Corse Present. An oblation made at funerals. *See* 'Soul-shot.'

Corsica Paoli. Pasquale de Paoli, a native of Corsica, leader of the war in Corsica against Genoa. When the island was conquered by the French, Pasquale de Paoli took refuge in England.

Corsican Ogre (*The*). Napoleon I., who was a Corsican by birth and family (1769, 1804–1814; died 1821).

Corsican Sesostris (*The*). Napoleon Bonaparte (1769–1821, reigned 1804–1814).

Cortes (2 syl.). The representative assembly of the estates of Spain and of Portugal.

Corvée. Gratuitous work enforced by feudal tenure. It consisted either of personal labour or the gratuitous loan of horses and oxen. The usual work was to cut down and stack the lord's hay, to lop and cut his firewood, to dig and plough his land, to keep his ditches and hedges in order, and to sweep and repair his chimneys. Turgot, the French minister, abolished much of this enforced labour, 27 June, 1787, and the rest was abolished by the Constituent Assembly and the Convention.

Still used in Egypt, &c.

Corvi′nus. János Hun′yadi was so called (1400–1456). The tale is that his

mother, Elizabeth Morsiani, was a paramour of the Emperor Sigismund, who gave her a ring, and promised to load her child with honour if she presented this ring. Elizabeth was on her road to the king's palace when a crow snatched the ring from her son's hand and flew up with it to a neighbouring tree. Her brother shot the bird and restored the ring. When her son, who was named János, was grown to man's estate, the king bestowed on him the domain of Hunyad, with 60 villages, and gave him as coat-of-arms a crow carrying a ring in its beak. Whence his name, John of Hunyad, Corvīnus.

Coryphæus of the Interpreters of Law (*The*). Bartōlus of Sasso-Ferrato, in Umbria (1313-1356). He practised law in Pisa and Perugia, and is known for his commentaries on the Corpus Juris Civīlis. A French proverb runs thus: 'He knows his Bartolus as well as a cordelier knows his Dormi.' (Il sait son Bartole comme un cordelier son Dormi.)

The Dormi was a celebrated recueil of sermons of the fourteenth century. The words 'Dormi securé' are the first two words of the book.
** The coryphēus was the leader and chief speaker of the chorus in Greek dramas. Hence, a leader, chief, best of the kind.

Cosherers. Irish vagrants who lived by preying on their neighbours. There were always in Ireland a number of ' young gentlemen' who lived by 'coshering' on the country with their horses and hounds, preying on the farmers, drinking, gambling, and running into debt.

Coshery. An Irish custom which entitled the chief lord or dynast to exact from his tenants provisions and lodging for himself and his retinue.

These dynasts used to come with a great multitude of people to monasteries and gentlemen's houses, and there continue for two days and two nights, taking meat and drink at their pleasure, while their horses and servants were quartered upon the poor farmers of the neighbourhood, and nothing was paid for their entertainment.—T. MOORE, *Hist. of Ireland*, ch. xlv.

Coterie, 1770. The first English female club. Amongst other members were the Duchess of Bedford, Lady Betty Delmé, the Countess of Pembroke, Mrs. Fazakerly, Lady Molyneux, Miss Pelham, &c. Play was both deep and constant.

Though called the Female Coterie, 'Ladies might ballot for gentlemen;' hence Sir T. Tancred was a member, so was George Augustus Selwyn.

Cottereaux (*The*). A band of brigands organised in 1792 by John Cottereaux, a cobbler of Laval. He rallied his men by screeching like an owl, and hence these desperadoes were nicknamed Screech-owls or Chouans. John Cottereaux was slain in 1794 in an encounter with the French Republican army. *See* 'French Brigands.'

Pronounce *Cot'-ro'*, and *Shwân*.

Les coteraux, ou Routiers, ou Brabançons, étaient des misérables de la secte de Pierre de Bruys, espèce de Manichéens, qui avait surtout infecté de ses erreurs le Languedoc et la Gascogne. Ils faisaient profession de ne craindre ni Dieu ni les hommes. Ils se mettaient aux gages de tous ceux qui voulaient commettre quelque crime, et ils se signalaient par toutes sortes de brigandages. Henri II., roi d'Angleterre, les avait pris à son service en 1174 pour combattre son fils Richard.—*Les Petits Bollandistes*, vol. vi. p. 350.

(The word coteraux in this extract is an anachronism, as John Cottereaux died in 1794.)

Cottesmore Pack (*The*). Rutlandshire. One of the three packs of the old 'Melton-Mowbray Hunt,' established in 1759. They were the Earl of Lonsdale's hounds. The other two packs were the Duke of Rutland's and Mr. Osbaldiston's, called the Quorn pack, of Leicester. The 'Melton-Mowbray Hunt' is now a thing of the past, but the Duke of Rutland's hounds, the Quorn, and the Cottesmore hounds are still celebrated (1890).

Cottonian Library (*The*), 1753. In the British Museum, but purchased for the use of the public in 1700. It was collected by Sir Robert Cotton (1570–1634), and consisted originally of 958 volumes; but part was burnt by a fire which broke out in Ashburnham House, and the present collection consists of 746 entire volumes and 98 defective ones. It is rich in historical documents, from the Saxon times to the reign of James I. It also contains numerous registers of English monasteries, the charters of Edgar and of Henry I. to Hyde Abbey, near Winchester, written in gold letters, and the MS. called the 'Durham Book,' which is a copy of the Latin Gospels, with an interlinear Saxon gloss, written before the year 800, and reputed to have belonged to the Venerable Bede.

COUNCIL OR COUNCILS.

A complete list of the 2,730 Church councils, with a brief summary of the subjects of debate in each, would fill at least fifty pages of this Dictionary. Those here given require to be known by all students of Church history. *See* p. 218, col. 2, 'Councils (*contradictory*),' and 'General Councils.'

Council, PARLIAMENT. In the early times of parliaments we frequently meet with the word 'council,' especially in the reigns of Edward III. and Richard II. After the Leicester Parliament (*q.v.*), a parliament was an assembly of the commons with the clergy and barons. A great council was an assembly to which the commons were not summoned. Strictly speaking, a parliament had the power of granting taxes, and a council was called merely to consult with the king on matters where taxes were not concerned.

Council (*A Civic*). 'Concilium Civile,' in which a local bishop meets the clergy of his diocese.

Council (*A Great*). 'Concilium Magnum,' an œcumenical council or great synod. The Council of Nice is called 'Magnum et Universale Concilium.' The whole college of bishops dispersed throughout Christendom ought to be convened to an œcumenical or general council.

Council (*The Palace*). 'Concilium palatinum,' 859. These councils were held biennially in the royal palace of the Carlovingian kings, and were conventions of the bishops—'generales episcoporum conventus.'

Council (*A Plenary*). 'Concilium Plenarium' is one to which a metropolitan invites all the bishops under his jurisdiction.

Council (*A Provincial*). 'Concilium Provinciale.'

Sunt et provincialia Concilia quæ post illa universalia necessario recipere debemus, quia et in illis multa ecclesiasticis negotiis necessaria reperimus.—BERNALDUS CONSTANTIENSIS PRESBYTER, *De Reconciliatione lapsorum*, p. 267.

Council (*Privy*). *See* 'Privy Council.'

Council for the Propagation of Faith and the Extirpation of Heretics (*The*), 31 May, 1650. At Turin. Designed for the extirpation of the Vaudois. If the council could not convert the Vaudois to the 'Catholic' faith, they were to extirpate them as heretics.

Council of Aix-la-Chapelle (*The*), Nov. 809. An ecclesiastical council, held at Aix-la-Chapelle, on the 'Procession of the Holy Ghost.' The 'Filioque' controversy, which long disturbed the church, was this: Did the

Holy Ghost proceed from the Father only, or from the Father and the Son (*filioque*)? The Greek Church maintained the former, the Roman Church the latter dogma. The Council of Aixla-Chapelle condemned the Greek dogma.

Council of Albi (*The*), in Lent 1255. That is the Council held at Albi, in France, for the final extirpation of the Albigensian heresy.

Council of Ariminium (*The*). That is, Rimini, in Italy, A.D. 359; convened by the Emperors Constans and Constantius to decide upon the Arian controversy.

This council condemned as heretics Arius, Ursacius, Valens, and others.

Councils of Arles (*The*). I. A.D. 814, assembled by Constantine against the Donatists (*q.v.*).

II. A.D. 353. Against Athanasius and others.

III.-VII. On discipline : viz. A.D. 442, 452, 524, 554, 813.

VIII A.D. 1059. Against the Archbishop of Narbonne.

IX. A.D. 1205. Respecting church government.

X. A.D. 1211. To excommunicate the Count of Toulouse, the great defender of the Albigenses.

XI. A.D. 1234. Against heretics.

XII. A.D. 1260. Against the followers of Joachim, abbot of Flores, called 'The Prophet.' It was his 'Everlasting Gospel' which was condemned in the council.

XIII. A.D. 1274. Respecting church discipline.

Council of Basel (*The*), 1431-1443. *The Ninth General Council of the Western Church* (eighteenth), convened for the reunion of the Eastern and Western Churches, and for general reform. It declared the authority of a general council superior to that of the pope, and that appeals lay from the pope to a general council ; it abolished annates or first-fruits, and wrested from the pope the right of electing to vacant bishoprics and benefices. Pope Eugenius was so disgusted that he set up an opposition council; whereupon the Council of Basel cited him to appear before them, but he refused, and declared the council dissolved. The council now deposed the pope, and elected Felix V. in his place,

thus making a new schism. Eugenius died in 1447, Felix resigned, and Nicholas V. remained sole pope.

Eighteenth if numbered from the Council of Nice, A.D., 325, when the Eastern and Western Churches were not divided.

Council of Blood (*The*). So the council established in the Netherlands by the Duke of Alba was called by the Brabançons, in consequence of the numerous executions which it ordained. The Counts of Egmont and of Horn were two of its victims. *See* under 'Conseil.'

Councils of Carthage (*The*). I. A.D. 200. Respecting the rebaptism of heretics.

II. A.D. 251. To confirm the election of Cornelius as pope ; to regulate the readmission of apostates ; and to condemn the schism of Felicissimus.

III. A.D. 252. Respecting the treatment of apostates.

IV. A.D. 253. Respecting the baptism of infants.

V. A.D. 254. Respecting the deposition of Basilides and Martial, Spanish bishops.

VI. A.D. 255. Respecting rebaptism.

VII. A.D. 256. To confirm the previous council.

VIII. 312. To elect Cæcilianus as bishop of Carthage. He was deposed by the Donatists.

IX. A.D. 397. To abolish love feasts. It declared the Apocryphal writings of equal authority to other scriptures. *See* 'LAODICEA.'

X. A.D. 401-411. Respecting the Donatists.

XI. A.D. 412. Against Celestius.

XII. A.D. 416-418. Against Pelagius and Celestius.

XIII. A.D. 419-425. On the appeal of Apiarius to the pope.

XIV. A.D. 484. A conference appointed by Hunneric between the Catholics and Arians. The Catholic bishops exiled.

XV. A.D. 525. On the liberties of monasteries.

XVl. A.D. 535. For the restitution of the rights and possessions of the church usurped by the Vandals.

Council of Chalce'don (*The*), 451. *The Fourth General Council*, convened by the Emperor Marcian to condemn the heresy of Eutyches. This council confirmed the condemnation of the Nestorians.

The *Eutychian* heresy merged the human nature of Christ in his divine nature. The *Nestorians* divided the Godhead and manhood of Christ into two distinct persons and natures.

The *First* General Council was held at Nice 325 and condemned the Arian heresy. The *Second* General Council was held at Constantinople in 380 and condemned the Macedonian heresy. The *third* General Council was held at Ephesus, and condemned the Nestorian heresy. The *Fourth* condemned the Eutychian heresy. Arius denied the divinity of Christ. Macedonius denied his humanity. Nestorius maintained that Mary was not the mother of God but of Jesus, for God could not be born. And Eutyches maintained that the human nature was merged in the Divine and there lost. *See* ' General Councils.'

Council of Cloveshoo (*The*). In

Kent, A.D. 747. Convened by Cuthbert, archbishop of Canterbury. It enacted that every bishop should visit his diocese at least once a year; that the people should be taught the Creed and the Lord's Prayer in English, and should have the nature of the sacraments explained to them in English. Other canons were passed for the correction of morals and discipline.

Prayers for the dead were enjoined in this council.

Councils of Constanee (*The*).

I. A.D. 1043. To establish ' public and universal peace ' in Germany.

II. A.D. 1094. To reprobate simony and incontinence, and to regulate the time of Easter and Whitsuntide.

III. A.D. 1153. For the divorce of Frederick Barbarossa and Adelaide.

IV. *The Eighth General Council of the Western Church* (seventeenth), A.D. 1414–1418. Against Wyclif, Huss, and Jerome of Prague. With impotent rage this council not only condemned the opinions of Wyclif, but ordered his bones to be exhumed and burnt. Thirteen years afterwards his bones were actually exhumed and burnt, and the ashes thrown into the river Swift. This council deposed the three contemporary popes (Gregory XII., Benedict XIII., and John XXIII.), and elected Martin V. pope. Gregory died first, and no other was elected in his place : then John, and then Benedict, leaving Martin V. the sole pope, and thus closing the Great Schism which had lasted from 1378 to 1429.

Seventeenth if reckoned from the Council of Nice, A.D. 325, when the Eastern and Western Churches were not divided.

Councils of Constantinople

(*The*). Those of 336, 339, and 360 were in favour of Arius.

The Second General Council, May to July 381. Called by Theodosius. It condemned appeals to Rome, and determined the limits of the Metropolitan provinces. It also condemned Macedonius, who denied the divinity of the Holy Ghost.

The councils of 382, 383, 394 were convened to pacify the schismatics, if possible.

The council of 403 was in favour of Chrysostom, and that of 404 deposed him.

The council of 448 condemned Eutyches. *See* ' Eutychians.'

The council of 450 condemned the dogmas of Nestorius and Eutyches. *See* ' Nestorians.'

The council of 459 condemned the Simoniacs.

The council of 492 confirmed the Council of Chalcēdon.

The council of 495 or 496 deposed Euphemius.

The council of 516 condemned the Council of Chalcedon.

The council of 518 reversed the condemnations of Euphemius and Macedonius, and restored their exiled partisans.

The councils of 520, 531, 532 were in favour of Euphemius, who was ordained patriarch.

The council of 536 condemned ' heretical ' bishops.

The councils of 543, 547, 551 condemned Origen.

The Fifth General Council, 553, also condemned Origen. So did the councils of Constantinople of 588, 626.

The council of 638 was in favour of the Monothelites (*q.v.*).

Sixth General Council, 680–681, condemned the Monothelites (*q.v.*).

The councils of 712, 715, 730 were in condemnation of the ' Sixth General Council.'

The councils of 786, 806, 809, 812, 814 condemned the Iconoclasts (*q.v.*).

The council of 815 deposed Nicephorus. In this council the Iconoclasts had it all their own way.

The councils of 821, 829 were called to reconcile the Catholics and Iconoclasts, but the Catholics refused to attend.

The councils of 842, 847 condemned the Iconoclasts.

The council of 858 deposed Photius (the *fons et origo* of the separation of the two churches).

The council of 861 restored Photius and deposed St. Ignatius.

The council of 867 reversed the decision of the previous council 861, and deposed Photius again.

Eighth General Council, 869–870, deposed Photius and condemned the Iconoclasts.

The council of 1054 anathematised the pope's legates.

The councils of 1066, 1067 were against incestuous marriages.

The council of 1110 condemned the Bogomiles or Bogarmitæ (*q.v.*).

The councils of 1140, 1143, 1144, 1147, 1157 condemned the works of Constantine Chrysomale.

The council of 1170 was to effect the union of the Eastern and Western Churches.

The councils of 1277, 1280 excommunicated the opponents of the union.

The council of 1283 condemned Veccus.

The councils of 1284, 1285 reversed the judgments of 1277, 1280, and condemned those who sought the union of the two churches.

The council of 1341 condemned Barlaam, the opponent of Palamas.

The council of 1345 condemned the doctrine of Palamas, the opponent of Barlaam; he was imprisoned 1346, but in 1349 was created patriarch of Constantinople, and in 1351 a synod in the same city confirmed his doctrine.

The council of 1450 was also against the union.

The councils of Constantinople give a lamentable picture of the Eastern Church, which seems to have had no fixed principle.

Council of Eanham (*The*).
In Oxfordshire, 1008, convened on the subject of church government. It decreed that tithes of produce should be paid at Allhallows, but tithes of *young* at Whitsuntide. That Rome-shot should be paid at St. Peter's mass, soul-shot immediately the grave was opened, light-shot thrice a year, plough-alms a fortnight after Easter. That on Sunday no trade should be carried on.

Council of Elders (*The*), or 'Conseil des Anciens,' 23 Sept., 1795.
One of the two Legislative Councils of Year III. in French history. The other council was 'Le Conseil des Cinq-cents,' which had the sole right of initiating laws; the Elders had the power of veto or approval.

The executive was placed in a board of five directors called the Directory.

Le Conseil des Anciens consisted of 250 members.

Councils of Ephesus (*The*).
I. A.D. 245. Condemned Noetus.

II. A.D. 401. For the election of a bishop.

III. A.D. 431. *The Third General Council*, condemned Nestorius and Pelagius. It laid down this canon, that every diocese and province shall exercise the right of ordaining unmolested and inviolable, and no bishop shall occupy another's diocese. Each province is 'Autocephälus,' and each diocese independent.

IV. A.D. 449. Called the *Latrocinium*, or 'Robber Synod' (*q.v.*).

V. A.D. 476. Respecting Basiliscus and the Council of Chalcēdon.

Council of Holy Martyrs (*A*).
'Concilium Martȳrum Sanctorum,' a place where many martyrs or holy men lie buried.

Council of Laodicea (*The*), A.D. 360.
Excluded the apocryphal writings from the canon of Scripture; but the Council of Carthage, in 397, declared them to be 'of equal authority with the other scriptures.'

Councils of the Lateran (*The*).
I. A.D. 649. To condemn the Monothelites (*q.v.*).

II. Nov. 864. To depose and excommunicate the Bishop of Porto.

III. Aug. 900. To restore the Bishop of Langres.

IV. Jan. 993. To canonise Udalric, bishop of Augsburg.

V. Feb. 1111. Respecting investitures. Pope Pascal II. compelled by Kaiser Heinrich V. to concede the right.

VI. March 1112. To revoke the concession of Pope Pascal II.

VII. March 1116. To excommunicate Kaiser Heinrich V.

VIII. A.D. 1123. *The First General Council of the Western Church*, held by Callixtus II. (*Ninth*).

IX. A.D. 1139. *The Second General Council of the Western Church*, for the reunion of the Eastern and Western Churches (*Tenth*).

X. A.D. 1179. *The Third General Council of the Western Church*. It placed in the cardinals the sole right of electing the pope. Decided on the crusade against the Albigenses. Anathematised the Albigenses as heretics, and forbade their interment in consecrated ground (*Eleventh*).

XI. Nov. 1215. *The Fourth General Council of the Western Church*. Held by Innocent III. to deprive Raymond count of Toulouse of his dominions for protecting the Albigenses. To anathematise the English barons for forcing Magna Charta on King John, and declaring the charter null and void. To vote for the extermination of heretics. And to declare transubstantiation to be a tenet of the 'Catholic' Church.

XII. July 1511 (The Fifth General Lateran). *The Tenth General Council of the Western Church*. By Julius II. to declare void the Council of Pisa.

XIII. March 1517. To abolish the Pragmatic Sanction. To confirm the concordat with François I. To impose a tax of one-tenth for war with Turkey. And to issue a decree against the printing of 'dangerous books.' (This was in fact a part of the preceding council.)

If reckoned from the Council of Nice, when the Eastern and Western Churches were not divided, these general councils would be numbered thus: A.D. 1123 (the Tenth), A.D. 1139 (the Eleventh), A.D. 1179 (the Twelfth), A.D. 1215 (the Thirteenth), and A.D. 1511-1517 (the Nineteenth).

Council of Lyons (*The*), 1245. *The Fifth General Council of the Western Church* (Fourteenth), held by Innocent IV., to depose the Kaiser Friederich II.

A.D. 1274. *The Sixth General Council of the Western Church* (Fifteenth), held by Gregory X. Respecting the election of bishops, the reunion of the Eastern and Western Churches, the reduction of the Begging Friars, and the reformation of the clergy.

The Council of 1528 was against Lutheranism.

Fourteenth and *Fifteenth*, if reckoned from the Council of Nice, A.D. 325, when the Eastern and Western Churches were not separated.

Council of Mantua (*The*), 1536. Summoned by Paul III., who cited Henry VIII. to appear before it. Henry VIII. of course denied the authority of the council.

Council of Nice, or 'Nicæa.' Called *The First General Council*, A.D. 325. Assembled by Constantine against the Arians. The sentence runs thus :—
'The Catholic and Apostolic Church anathematises all who say that there was

a time when the Son did not exist; that He had no existence previous to his birth in Bethlehem; that He was created out of nothing; or who say that He was formed from another substance or essence; or who say that He is capable of change.' It also condemned the Melesian schism (*q.v.*), and 'settled' the Paschal or Easter Controversy (*q.v.*).

The Nicene Creed, as it now stands, was not published by this Council, but by the Council of Constantinople in 381. It was drafted at Nice, approved of by the Council of Milan in 846, by the Council of Sardica in 347, and the Council of Rimini in 360; but it was completed by the Council of Constantinople.
The *Seventh Ecumenical Council* was also held at Nice A.D. 787.

Council of Officers (*The*), 1647. Officers elected from each of the parliamentary regiments to examine into and rectify the 'distempers' of the parliamentary army. To this upper council was added a lower one, consisting of two privates or officers not higher in rank than ensigns, and called the adjutants or adjutators or adjuvants, and afterwards Agitators, because, like the Roman tribunes, they were ceaseless disturbers of the peace. This lower council soon became the Aaron's rod of all the other national assemblies, and dominated even the parliament itself. Charles I. called Cornet Joyce 'Mr. Agitator Joyce,' not by way of reproach, but as a usual method of address.

Council of Peers (*The*), 24 Sept., 1640, or 'Great Council of Peers.' Convened at York by Charles I., who was unwilling to summon a parliament, because his parliaments always insisted on redress of grievances before they would vote supplies. The object for which the Council of Peers was convened was to grant supplies in order to raise an army against the Scotch, who had encamped on Dunse-law hill, and threatened to advance.

Council of Pisa (*The*), 1409. Convoked by the cardinals of the rival popes (Gregory XII. and Benedict XIII.). The two popes were summoned to appear, but refused, and were declared contumacious, schismatic, heretical, and perjured. They were both deposed, and Alexander V. elected pope. The condemned popes treated the decrees of the council with supreme contempt; and all the council effected was to make three popes instead of two, all of whom hurled curses, calumnies, and excommunications at each other. Declared void by the Fifth General Lateran Council.

Council of Sar'dica (*The*), or 'Sardia,' in Thrace, A.D. 347; to settle the controversy between the Arians and Athanasius. It condemned the Arians.

Councils of Toulouse (*The*).

I. 13 Sept., 1056. Against simony, the marriage of ecclesiastics, and other abuses.

II. 1068. Against simony.

III. 1118. Against the Manichæans.

IV. Nov. 1229. To establish the Inquisition.

Council of Trent (*The*), or 'Tridentum,' 1545–1563. Assembled by Paul III., and continued under Julius III. and Pius IV., to fix what should be admitted as orthodox doctrine. Its main object was to condemn the Reformation.

Council of Trouble (*The*), 1567. The organisation, under Margaret, governor of the Netherlands, under which 18,000 persons in three years were put to death. Also called 'The Tribunal of Blood.'

Council of Trullo (*The*), A.D. 692. *The Fifth and Sixth General Council*, which confirmed the decree of the Council of Ephesus, that every bishop shall ordain unmolested in his own diocese, and no bishop shall interfere in another's diocese or province.

In the language of the council, each province is Autocephalous, and each diocese independent and free except to its own metropolitan.

Council of War (*A*). A conference of officers on some matter in which the chief commander, pending war, wishes to state his own opinion upon some military or naval matter, and hear what his officers think about it. In the navy the council of war usually consists of flag officers, assisted sometimes by other officers of lower rank. In the army the commander-in-chief can call whom he thinks proper to confer with him.

Council of the Earthquake (*The*), 1382. The council, held at Blackfriars, and headed by Courtenay, archbishop of Canterbury, to condemn Wyclif and his teachings. The archbishop submitted twenty-four allegations drawn

10

from Wyclif's works; but an earthquake in the midst of the proceedings terrified every prelate present, except the primate, who declared that the earthquake was a good omen, signifying that God would expel from the church the ill humours of heresy.

Council of the Senate (*The*). University of Cambridge, established in 1857 (19, 20 Vict., c. 88), which must send a 'grace' to the senate before that legislative body can move in any matter. The council consists of the chancellor and vice-chancellor, with eight other members of the senate chosen from the electoral roll (*q.v.*). The eight members hold office in the council for four years.

The eight members of the council consist of 2 heads of colleges, 2 of the professors, and 4 other members.

Council of the Troubles (*The*). So the Spaniards called the 'Council of Blood' (*q.v.*).

Council of the 6 (*The*). For the exclusion of the Stuart dynasty and the restoration of Great Britain to a republic. Of this council four were beheaded, viz. Russell, Algernon Sidney, Monmouth, and Argyll; Essex died in the Tower by his own hand; and Howard of Escrick (a traitor and sad villain) perished in great poverty, deserted and hated by all men.

Hampden said 'that the coming into England of King William was nothing else but the continuing of the council of six.'—HOWITT, *Hist. of England*.

Council of the 10 (*The*), 'I Dieci,' 1310. A secret tribunal of the republic of Venice, armed with unlimited powers in watching over the safety of the state. It punished at discretion all secret enemies of the republic. At first it was prorogued annually, but in 1325 it was made perpetual, and continued as long as the Venetian republic endured.

Council of the 13 (*The*), 1653. A council of state, with Cromwell at the head, appointed after the dissolution of the Long Parliament. The council selected a parliament of 156 members; 139 for England, 6 for Wales, 6 for Ireland, and 5 for Scotland. It was to last fifteen months, when they were to choose successors and disperse. It was called the 'Little Parliament' (*q.v.*).

Some proposed that the council of state should consist of 10 members; some of 70, after the model

of the Jewish sanhedrim; others of 13, in imitation of Christ and his apostles. The last suggestion was adopted.—Dr. LINGARD, *Hist. of Eng.*,
viii. 6.

Council of the 16 (*The*), 'Conseil
des Seize,' 1585. A committee of sixteen
members of the Catholic League of
France to prevent the crown descending
to Henri of Navarre, a Protestant, on the
death of the reigning king, Henri III.,
who was childless. The plot was to proclaim the old Cardinal de Bourbon king.
This, however, was a mere bait, for if they
had succeeded, they would have given the
crown to Charles de Lorraine, duc de
Mayenne.

On the death of Henri III. in 1589 the old cardinal was actually proclaimed Charles X., but Henri
of Navarre, by his victories of Arques and Ivry,
secured the crown to himself, and in the interim
the old cardinal died.

Council of the 38 (*The*), 1649. The
government of England was vested in a
council of thirty-eight members, with
Cromwell at the head, after the execution
of Charles I.

Council of the 40 (*The*.) *See*
'Forty.'

In 1653 Cromwell intended to dissolve the Long
Parliament, and substitute a ' Council of Forty,'
with himself at the head. But after dismissing the
parliament he appointed instead a ' Council of
Twelve,' with himself at the head (making 13), in
imitation of Christ and his twelve apostles.

Council of the 100 (*The*). The
great legislative and executive council of
ancient Carthage, which concentrated in
itself all the real power of the state. The
two elective magistrates called ' Suffètes '
were amenable to the council of the self-
elected hundred, who held office for
life, and so was the senate, which consisted of 300. Similarly in Venice the
doge and senate were amenable to the
Council of Ten.

Council of the 400 (*The*), B.C. 594.
Instituted by Solon of Athens. *See*
' Government of the 400.'

Council of the 500 (*The*). I. In
Greek history. Βουλὴ τῶν πεντακοσίων.
The Athenian Senate. Solon divided the
people into four tribes, each of which
chose a representative. Klisthenês increased the number to ten, and then the
senate was increased to 500.

II. In *French* history. ' Conseil des
Cinq-cents,' from 27 Oct., 1795 to 14 Dec.,
1799, was one of the two councils, the
other being called the ' Conseil des
Anciens,' consisting of 250 members.

Both these were legislative bodies like
our lords and commons. The executive
was placed in a board of five directors
called the ' Directory.' The 500 had the
exclusive power of the initiative; the
elders only vetoed or confirmed the measures.

Councils (*Contradictory Church*).

A.D. *Council of* :—

310. ARLES condemned Athanasius, so
in 385 did the Council of Tyre, and
in 354 the Council of Milan; but in
325 the Council of Nice confirmed
the tenets of Athanasius, and so did
the Council of Sardica in 347.

325. NICE condemned Arius as a heretic;
but three Councils of Constantinople (*q.v.*), the Council of Arles in
353, and the Council of Milan in 354,
declared Arianism to be the orthodox faith. Eusebius, bishop of
Nicomedia, sided with Arius. When
Julius, in 336, succeeded Mark, he
called a council at Sardica, but it was
so divided on the subject that each
party excommunicated the other.

357. SIRMIUM condemned the dogma of
Homoiousion (*q.v.*); but the Council of Ancy'ra and that of Constantinople confirmed it.

360. LAODICEA excluded the Apocrypha
from the canon of scripture; but
in 397 the Council of Carthage
declared it to be equal in every
respect to all other scripture.

382. CONSTANTINOPLE confirmed the
Council of Calcium; but in 516
another Council of Constantinople
reversed the previous decision.

403. CONSTANTINOPLE was in favour of
Chrysostom; but that of 404 deposed him.

492. CONSTANTINOPLE confirmed the
Council of Chalcēdon; but in 516
another Council of Constantinople
condemned it.

495. CONSTANTINOPLE deposed Euphemius; but that of 518 reversed the
decree, and restored him.

638. CONSTANTINOPLE confirmed the
doctrine of the Monothēlites (4 syl.),
as the true faith; but in 680 another
Council of Constantinople condemned it as heresy. Three other
councils condemned that of 680.
The Lateran Council of 648 also
condemned it.

712. CONSTANTINOPLE condemned the Sixth General Council.

730. CONSTANTINOPLE approved of Iconoclasm; but in 814 condemned it. In 815 approved of it; but in 842, 869, 870 condemned it. In 787 it was condemned by the council held at Nice.

754. CONSTANTINOPLE condemned the worship of images. In 766 the Council of Jerusalem favoured images, so did the Council of Nice in 787. In 829 the Council of Constantinople again condemned them, but in 842 another Council of Constantinople reversed the judgment of the previous one.

852. CONSTANTINOPLE deposed Photius; 861 it restored him and deposed Ignatius; in 867 it reversed the judgment of 861.

1112. LATERAN revoked the 5th Lateran of the previous year.

1284, 1285. CONSTANTINOPLE reversed the judgments of 1277, 1280.

1341. CONSTANTINOPLE condemned Palamas; but in 1345 another council reversed the judgment.

1511. IV. LATERAN declared the Acts of the Council of Pisa null and void.

N.B.—A complete list of all the Contradictory Councils would require several pages of this NOTE-BOOK.

Councillors (*The*). Since the Municipal Corporations Act of 1835, every burgess is qualified to be elected who was of full age on the last day of August preceding the election, provided (1) he has occupied premises within the borough continuously for three preceding years, and has for that time resided within seven miles of the borough; (2) provided also he has been rated to the poor-rate, and has paid both poor-rates and borough-rates. In the council is vested the entire deliberative and administrative functions of the corporation. They appoint the town-clerk (*q.v.*), the treasurer (*q.v.*), the mayor (*q.v.*), and aldermen, all from their own body. They control the police, the watch, and the lighting; make bye-laws, impose fines for nuisances, and are responsible for the government of the borough. They control the burgess fund, and appoint the salaries of police magistrates.

Counter-Remonstrance (*The*), 1611. The counterblast put forward by Frans Gomar of Bruges against the Remonstrance (*q.v.*) of the Arminians, presented to the States of Holland in 1610, and dogmatically laying down the dogmas of absolute predestination and reprobation.

Counter-Remonstrants. Ultra-Calvinists or Gomarists who put forward the Counter-Remonstrance (*q.v.*). The States tried to reconcile the Remonstrants and Counter-Remonstrants in 1614, but wholly without effect, and so violent did the contest grow that the Remonstrants had to be protected by a military guard. In 1619 the Synod of Dort was convened, and the Arminians were excluded from pleading their cause. Since then the Remonstrants have become more temperate and less Calvinistic.

Countess of Huntingdon's Connexion (*The*), 1770. A sect of Calvinistic Methodists founded by Selina countess of Huntingdon, widow of Theophilus earl of Huntingdon. They use the English Prayer-book.

Counties Corporate. Twelve cities and five towns in England with territories annexed, governed by their own sheriffs, who are quite independent of the county sheriffs.

The twelve *cities* are Bristol, Canterbury, Chester, Coventry, Exeter, Gloucester, Lichfield, Lincoln, London, Norwich, Worcester, and York.

The five *towns* are Kingston-upon-Hull, Newcastle-upon-Tyne, Nottingham, Poole and Southampton.

In 1889 London was erected into a county of itself.

There are some in Ireland.

Country (*The*), 1620. The anti-Court party. The terms 'Court and Country' to express the royalists and anti-royalists first arose in the parliament assembled 30 Jan., 1620, by James I.

In 1678 the 'Country' was the opposition party, bent on overturning the government of Lord Danby, and on the exclusion of the Duke of York from the succession. After the death of Charles II., the Dukes of Buckingham and Shaftesbury (who were in the 'Cabal') were its leaders.

In 1692 they were often called the 'Grumbletonians,' and were opposed to what was called the 'Patriot party.' They were the 'outs' in Walpole's ministry. The 'ins' or 'let alones' were the Patriot party, called formerly the 'Court party.'

In the latter part of the reign of George I., and in the reign of George II., the Court party meant the Whigs, and the Country party the Tories. In the early part of George I.'s reign the Whigs, or Court party, were called the Hanoverians.

Country Pastor (A). The penname of Archbishop Whately (1787–1863).

Country of the Three Mountains (*The*), and of four rivers, Hungary. The mountains are the Tátra, Fátra, and Mátra. The rivers are the Danube, the Theiss, the Drave, and the Save. The last three are tributaries of the Danube, which empties itself in the Black Sea.

County Councils, 1889.

1. They have charge of the public buildings, such as the shire-hall, the police-courts, the bridges, the lunatic asylums, &c. in the county.

2. They appoint the public analyst, the inspector of weights and measures, the county surveyor, the county treasurer, and the county coroner.

3. They have to keep up the highways (*i.e.* the disturnpiked roads).

4. They carry out the regulations connected with the Contagious Diseases (Animals) Act, the compensation to those who have to destroy their infected animals, and the restrictions to be placed on the importation of cattle.

5. They make regulations, &c. to preserve the purification of rivers.

6. They, in union with the justices of peace, have the charge and appointment of the county police.

7. They are bound to put in force the Allotment Act, and to enable labouring men, according to the council's discretion, to obtain allotments.

8. They are, at their discretion, to assist emigrants from this country to other places of settlement.

9. All local taxes are handed over to them, whether from probate duties or the consolidated funds.

The councils are elected for three years; and they appoint the aldermen who hold office for six years.

County Courts, 1846. Originally established for the recovery of small debts under 20*l*., subsequently extended to 50*l*., and in 1865 to 500*l*. They now take cognizance not only of debts to the amount stated, but of all personal actions, not criminal, where the amount does not exceed 50*l*.; and exercise all the functions of the High Court of Chancery in suits by creditors, legatees, devisees, heirs-at-law, &c., in which the estate and personals do not exceed 500*l*. They also take cognizance of the dissolution of partnerships; but the vice-chancellor has the power of removing a suit from a County Court to the Court of Chancery.

Coup de Bourguignon (*Un*). A blow given from behind; a cowardly blow; the blow of an assassin. The origin of this phrase is as follows: The Duc de Biron, who was beheaded in the reign of Henri IV., was told by an astrologer, ' de se garder d'un coup de Bourguignon par derrière.' When brought to the block he asked who was to be his headsman, and was told ' a man from Burgundy.' Then the words of the astrologer flashed into his memory : ' Beware of the blow of a Burgundian,' and the words became proverbial.

Coup d'état. I. 23 *de Juin*, 1789. After the Séance Royale, the master of the ceremonies commanded the Tiers état to retire as the other two classes had left and the assembly was over. Then Mirabeau, one of the deputies, told the Tiers not to leave : ' Nous sommes ici ' (he exclaimed in a voice of thunder), ' nous sommes ici par la volonté du peuple, nous n'en sortirons que par la force des baïonnettes.' He then made the deputies swear not to part till they had given the nation a constitution. Finally he declared the person of a deputy inviolable. (This was carried by 493 against 34 voices.)

Pronounce *Coo da-tah' de Ju'ah'n* (*n* slight and nasal).

II. *De* 18 *Fructidor*, 4 Sept. 1797. By the Directory. The royalists had made great head in the elections. They had returned 42 new deputies, and had succeeded in getting Pichegru appointed president of the 'Five Hundred,' Barbé Marbois as chief of the Elders, and Barthélemy as the new director. At midnight 12,000 armed men, with 40 pieces of cannon, were stationed round the Tuileries; 52 of the deputies, including Pichegru, Barbé Marbois, and Barthélemy, were arrested and transported to Cayenne; the elections of 48 of the departments were cancelled; and 35 of the journals were suspended.

Coup de Jarnac. A treacherous blow, a stab in the dark. In 1547, in the presence of Henri II. of France, La Châtaigneraie, a favourite of the king's, and Guy Chabot, lord of Jarnac, fought a duel at St. Germain. After a few sword strokes Châtaigneraie fell in a very suspicious manner, being wounded, it was supposed, by some secret emissary of the king, and not by his adversary.

Coupe-tête. Mathieu Jouve Jourdan (1749-1794). So called because he boasted that he had cut off the head of De Launay, governor of the Bastille. He also cut off the heads of two of the body-guards at Versailles (6 Oct., 1789), and stuck them on pikes, reproaching the people because they had allowed him to cut off the heads of only two of the guards.

Pronounce Coop-tait.

Cour de Poison (*Le*), 1680. A court of justice to try the poisoners Brinvilliers, La Voisin, and La Vigoureux.

Court and Country (*The*), 1620. *See* ' Country.'

Court Fools. A long list is given in the ' Readers' Handbook,' pp. 344, 345, 346. The following have obtained an historical reputation:—

ARCHIE ARMSTRONG, jester to James I. and Charles I. He died 1646.
BRUSQUET, ' who never had his equal in repartee ' (1512-1563).
CHICOT, jester to Henri III. and IV. of France.
COULON, ' prince of mimics.' He died 1858, and was jester to Louis XVIII.
DUFRESNOY, the ' Joe Miller ' of France. Jester in the court of Louis XIV.
KLAUS NARR, jester in the court of the Elector Friedrich the Wise of Prussia. His jests have been frequently printed.
SCOGAN, court fool to Edward IV.
TRIBOULET, court jester to Louis XII. and François I. (1487-1536).

Court-leet. The same as ' Court of Frank-pledge ' (*q.v.*).

Court-Martial. A military tribunal for trying military or naval men for offences of discipline : such as mutiny; abandonment of a post, guard, or fortress; desertion, &c. The president of the court should be a field officer, and in no case may be inferior in rank to a captain. It has even the power of life and death, but the offender is shot, not hanged.

Court of Arches (*The*). The supreme court of appeal in the archbishopric of Canterbury, formerly held in St. Mary-le-Bow. In 1567 it was removed to the Common Hall of Doctors' Commons, but since 1867 the sittings have generally been held at Westminster.

The court used to be held in the church of St. Mary-le-Bow (*Sancta Maria de Arcubus*), so called because the steeple was raised on pillars built archwise, like bent bows.

Court of Audience (*The*), or ' Audience Court.' Belonging to each of the archbishops, and having the same authority as the Court of Arches (*q.v.*), but inferior to it in dignity and antiquity. The Dean of the Arches was the official auditor of the Audience.

Court of Augmentations (*The*). 27 Hen. VIII., c. 27, A.D. 1536, established for managing the revenues of the lesser monasteries given to the crown.

The annual revenues of the 375 smaller monasteries was 30,000*l*. The wages of an ordinary workman in the reign of Henry VIII. was 3*d*. a day, and of a master workman 4*d*. The wages in 1890 of a labourer is 2*s*. 6*d*., and of a gardener 3*s*. 6*d*. That is, ten times the price of wages in the reign of Henry VII. So 30,000*l*. would equal 300,000*l*. of money in 1890.

Court of Cassation (*The*). An ancient French court of appeal, having the power to quash (*casser*) the judgments of all inferior courts. It was divided into three chambers, called La Chambre des Requêtes, La Chambre de Cassation Civile, and La Chambre de Cassation Criminelle. In 1790 the court was replaced by the ' Tribunal de Cassation,' but in 1804 the old title was restored.

Court of Claims (*The*). I. A court established in the early part of the reign of Charles II. to decide on the rival claims or titles of estates in Ireland confiscated by Cromwell. It will be remembered that Cromwell confiscated many of the estates of the ancient Irish nobility who had joined the rebellion, and bestowed them on his own adherents. When Charles II. was restored the evicted noblemen applied for the recovery of their estates, and this court was established to settle the rival claims. The restorable Irish were divided into Innocents, Ensignmen (*q.v.*), and Articlemen (*q.v.*).

II. A court established in the reign of William III. to investigate the claims and dispose of the lands forfeited in

Ireland by the adherents of James II. The chief sufferer by this court was the Earl of Clancarty.

Court of Commissioners of Review (*The*). To revise the sentence of the court of 'Delegates' (*q.v.*). Both this court and the High Court of Delegates are abolished.

Court of Conscience. For the recovery of small debts. These courts, of which there were several in London, Westminster, and other trading districts, were superseded by county courts in 1846.

Court of Ecclesiastical Commission (*The*), 1686. Instituted by the lord chancellor under the advice of Jeffries. It had supreme power to decide dogmatically on all ecclesiastical matters, without restraint of laws, canons, or customs. The commissioners consisted of three divines and three laymen. The archbishop (Sancroft) refused to sanction the commission, and was set aside by Cartwright, bishop of Chester.

The three clerics were the archbishop of Canterbury (*Sancroft*), the bishop of Durham, and the bishop of Rochester.
The three laymen were the lord chancellor (*Jeffries*), the lord treasurer, and the chief justice of the King's Bench.

Court of Exchequer (*The*), 1357. A court of appeal (31 Edw. III. st. 1, c. 12), consisting of a court of revenue and a court of common law. Its equity jurisdiction was, by 5 Vict., c. 5 transferred to the Court of Chancery; and by 19, 20 Vict. the Court of Exchequer was abolished, and its jurisdiction transferred to the Court of Session (*q.v.*).

A Court of Exchequer was established in Scotland by 6 Anne c. 26.

Court of Faculties (*The*). Established by 25 Hen. VIII. c. 21, s. 4, transferring to the two archbishops certain fees and prerogatives previously claimed by the pope of Rome. The chief officer is called 'Magister ad facultâtés.' Of late years the court is mainly occupied in granting licence to marry without publication of banns.

By 25 Hen. VIII. this court was given dispensing power in regard to pluralities—eating meat in Lent, pew rights, monuments, modes of burial, erecting organs in churches, levelling churchyards, removing buried bodies, and so on.

Court of Frank-pledge (*The*), or 'Court-leet.' A court of record held annually within a hundred, lordship, or

manor, which every resident freeholder was bound to attend in order to take an oath of allegiance. It took cognisance of all crimes committed within its jurisdiction. The business is now performed by the quarter sessions and justices of the peace.

Court of High Commission (*The*), 1559. Established by 1 Eliz. c. 1 for the settlement of ecclesiastical offences. It became most obnoxious in the reign of Charles I., as it assumed unwarrantable proportions, almost all offences of a political tendency being construed as ecclesiastical. Established in Scotland by James I. in 1610. Abolished in 1641 (16 Car. I. c. 11).

Court of Love (*The*), 12th to 14th cent. A tribunal of ladies established to decide metaphysical questions of gallantry. André le Chapelain has collected the rules of this court in his 'De arte amatoria et reprobatione amoris.'

Court of Peculiars (*The*). An annex of the Court of Arches (*q.v.*), having jurisdiction over those parishes which are exempt from the jurisdiction of the Ordinary. Superseded by the Court of Probate.

Court of Pie-powder. 'Curia pedis pulverizati,' so called from the dusty feet of the suitors; is a court of record, incident to every fair and market. The steward of the owner of the market is *ex officio* judge, and has power to administer justice for all commercial injuries in that fair or market. *See* Stephen, 'Commentaries,' iii. 321 *n* (1830).

Pipowders est un Court qui est incident a chescune faire, pour le determination de differences sur contract et touts disorders en ceo commis.—*Termes de la Ley*, p. 478.

Court of Session (*The*), 1532. In Scotland, established by James V. of that nation. A central and supreme tribunal of justice. In 1808 the Court of Session was divided into two separate courts called the First and Second Divisions.

Court of Tynwald (*A*). The Manx court of legislature, consisting of the Council and the House of Keys (*q.v.*).

The court at Tynwald Hill was formed by King Orry, who gave the Manx their legislative government about the time of the emigration of Rollo to Normandy, and of Ingolf to Iceland, during the reign of Harald Harfager, 872-933.

Court of the Four Boroughs

(*The*). In Scotch history, a high court of appeal, to which Edinburgh, Stirling, Roxburgh, and Berwick sent commissioners. When Berwick fell into the hands of the English, either Lanark or Linlithgow was substituted.

Courts of Requests. Established

by Cardinal Wolsey for the recovery of small debts. They were abolished in 1846, when the Small Debts Act was introduced.

There was a Court of Requests of the king in person; but the court was virtually abolished by 16 Car. I. c. 10.

Courte-heuse. Robert, eldest son

of William the Conqueror, was so called on account of the shortness of his legs.

Courtenay (*Peregrine*). The pen-

name of W. M. Praed (1802–1839).

Courtenay Riots (*The*), 1832.

One John Nicholls Thom, of Truro, assumed the name of Count Rothschild, of Rose Hill, Herne Bay; and afterwards as Sir William Percy Honeywood Courtenay he laid claim to the old seats of Hales Place and Powderham Castle. He was now called 'King of Jerusalem' and 'Knight of Malta.' Being found to be insane, he was confined for a little time, but in 1838 made his escape, called himself the 'Saviour of the World,' and with a large following, carrying a blue and white flag, surmounted with a rampant lion, proceeded to various farmhouses. At Bossenden three constables attempted to arrest the madman, but one being shot, the other two fled. A hundred and fifty of the 45th regiment were then sent against the rebels, when ten were shot, amongst whom was Courtenay himself.

Cousin (*Trusty and well-beloved cousin*).

So the monarchs of Great Britain address every peer of the degree of earl, in formal instruments such as writs, commissions, and so on. The style of address runs back to the time of Henry IV.; and Blackstone tells us that this king, either by his wife, his mother, or his sisters, was actually related or allied to every earl in the realm, and, being a usurper, never ceased reminding his peers of their connection with the crown in his own person. The custom remains, though the *raison d'être* has long since ceased ('Commentaries,' i. 398).

Cousinhood (*The*). The Grenville

family, in the reign of George II., was so called from its 'many flourishing branches,' which have furnished in 150 years 3 first lords of the treasury, 3 secretaries of state, 2 keepers of the privy seal, and 4 lords of the admiralty, all sons or grandsons of the first Countess Temple.

In Pitt's administration, 1756, there were, four of the Grenville family. Pitt was first lord; his brother-in-law (Lord Temple) was first lord of the admiralty; his next brother, George Grenville, was treasurer of the navy; the third brother, James Grenville, was at the Treasury Board. Horace Walpole sarcastically remarked, 'Tis a pity that Pitt has not Grenville cousins enough to fill the whole administration.'

Covenant (*The*), 1643. An agree-

ment between the English and Scotch parliamentarians, to do all in their power to bring the churches of the three kingdoms into a uniformity of faith, church government, and form of worship; to extirpate popery, prelacy, schism, and profaneness; to preserve intact the rights and privileges of the parliament, and the liberties of the kingdom; to punish malignants; to unite England and Scotland in lasting union; and to lead, both in private and public, lives consistent with a God-fearing and God-loving people. *See* 'National Covenant,' 'Solemn League and Covenant,' &c.

The first 'Covenant' was subscribed 3 Dec., 1557, pledging the subscribers to 'maintain and set forward the Word of God.' Another was subscribed in 1580, abjuring the tenets of the Church of Rome. The Covenant of 1638 was provoked by Archbishop Laud. *See* 'National Covenant.'

Covenanters, 1557. Scotch re-

formers, who subscribed to the Solemn League and Covenant (*q.v.*), or to the National Covenant (*q.v.*). It was first introduced in the reign of James V. In 1581 the General Assembly of Scotland drew up a Confession of Faith, and this covenant was signed by James VI. of Scotland and I. of England. In 1590 and 1596 it was again subscribed to. In 1638 it was renewed, and the Covenanters bound themselves by oath to preserve religion in the same state in which it existed in 1580. Strictly speaking, the Covenanters date from the time of this oath (1638), but the 'congregation' (*q.v.*) are sometimes called covenanters, because they bound themselves to the Solemn League and Covenant.

In the spring of 1562 Elizabeth became engaged to support the Huguenots against their government, as she had supported the Covenanters of Scotland.—Howitt, *Hist. of Eng.*, vol. ii. p. 418.

Coventry Act (*The*), 22, 23 Car. II. c. 1, making cutting and maiming a capital offence. So called from the ill usage of Sir John Coventry by some of the life-guardsmen, in revenge of something he said in parliament respecting the king's theatrical amours.

The tale is that Sir John Coventry, Oct. 1670, rose in his place in parliament, and asked a question which was considered to be a reflection on the king's amours. Charles was furious, and Sir John was attacked one night in the streets, when his nose being cut to the bone, he ever after wore a patch. It became a common jest for courtiers to put a patch on their nose, and strut about in mimicry of Sir John, in order to divert the king.

I will have his nose slit as wide as Coventry's.—Sir W. Scott, *Peveril of the Peak*, chap. 37.

Coverdale's Bible, 1535. This translation of the Bible by Miles Coverdale, afterwards Bishop of Exeter, was dedicated to Henry VIII., and was the first English Bible sanctioned by royal authority. *See* ' Bibles.'

Coxians and Knoxians, 1556. The followers of Dr. Coxe, dean of Christ Church (Oxford), and John Knox, who left England during the reign of Mary, and retired to the Continent. Dr. Coxe insisted on the use of the English Liturgy and made a point of repeating the responses aloud; but Dr. Knox (backed by Calvin) objected to the Common Prayer-book, and insisted on the use of the Genevan service. The altercation became so noisy that the magistrates had to interfere. Coxe retired to Strasburg, and settled there; Knox retired to Geneva.

C. P. pricked against a sailor's name in the muster-roll of a man-of-war stood for ' civil power,' meaning that the man had been sentenced by the civil power to serve in the fleet. It was equivalent to rogue or vagabond. Such men were nick-named ' Newgate birds,' *i.e.* they had flown out of prison aboard ship.

Cracovia. *Avoir ses lettres de Cracovie*, to be recognised and pro-claimed a liar. The Hôtel de Cracovie is in ' Moncorbeau,' in the département de Lot-et-Garonne. The master, who is a café-tier, ' délivre, moyennant quelques sous, des brevets de hâbleurs, que les mauvais plaisants envoient, par la voie de la poste, aux menteurs de leur connaissance.'

PATENT OF MEMBERSHIP.—Nous ayant fait savoir que depuis longtemps vous vous étiez exercé dans le noble art de maltraiter toute sorte de vérités, à amplifier les récits, en augmentant et diminuant aux faits qui arrivent en ce monde terrestre, et que par des succès heureux, fruit d'une imagination féconde et brillante, vous étiez parvenu à inventer des vérités qui n'ont jamais existé, à créer des histoires qui, sans vous, auraient resté éternellement dans l'oubli. . . . Nous, toujours zélés à maintenir et accroître la haute réputation de notre ordre . . . avons jugé à propos de vous incorporer dans notre diète, et vous recevoir en frère bien-aimé. . . . Fait et passé dans notre diète générale.—Signed by the secretary.

Cracovia. *L'arbre de Cracovie.* A tree in the garden of the Palais Royal was so called ' à cause des menteries débitées sous son ombrage, ou parce que les nouvellistes se réunissaient là pendant les troubles de Pologne' (Quitard, *Dictionnaire des Proverbes Français*, p. 273).

Je donne sept-mille livres . . . . au baron de Kniran, à condition qu'il se rendra, tous les lundis et vendredis . . . . au Palais Royal, sous l'arbre de Cracovie, et que là il lira des nouvelles supposées à cette multitude de faux politiques et de vrais désœuvrés, qui gobent tout ce qu'on leur dit.—*Le Livre des Quatre Couleurs*, p. 109.

Craft-gilds. Clubs of tradesmen in contradistinction to merchant-gilds. These gilds were all-powerful with apprentices, who were required to carry their work to the craft-box to be inspected by the committee of masters, bad work being punished by fines. Any workman who proved refractory might be expelled, in which case he was not allowed to exercise any trade within the limits of the gild. Our ' Livery Companies ' are relics of the craft-gilds.

Edward III. was a member of the Armourers' craft-gild.

Craftsman (*The*), 1724. A very celebrated journal planned and established in the reign of George I. by ' the Patriots,' in opposition to the ministry of Walpole. Bolingbroke and Pulteney were the chief organisers of this paper.

Crane's Charity. For the relief of sick scholars. To pay nurses, medicine, medical attendance, and give money grants to sick scholars in the University of Cambridge, or one of the following grammar-schools, that of Wisbeach, Cambridge, Lynn, and Ipswich. The proceeds of the gift received in order by the five aforestated institutions. Founded by John Crane in 1654.

Cranmer's Bible, 1539. This was Coverdale's Bible (*q.v.*), examined and corrected by Archbishop Cranmer, who also wrote the preface. It was printed by Grafton in 1540, and every parish was obliged by royal proclamation to have a copy in the parish church under a penalty of 40s. a month. *See* ' Bibles.'

Cranmer's Catechism was not composed by Cranmer, but only adopted by him. It was originally written in German for the youth of Nürnburg; was translated into Latin by Justus Jonas, the friend of Luther; was brought to England in 1548, and translated by Rowland Taylor, one of Cranmer's chaplains. It insists on Three Sacraments—baptism, absolution, and the eucharist—and states that those who have heathen parents and die without baptism are ' damned eternally.' Our Church Catechism is quite another thing, probably the work of Nowell or else of Poinet.

It was not originally written in question and answer. It contained a third sacrament, called the ' Sacrament of Reconciliation.'

Crannoges (2 syl.), or ' Crannogs.' Fortified islands in the Irish or Scotch lakes, in common use as dwelling-places among the ancient Celtic inhabitants. Herodotos (v. 16) speaks of the lake-dwellings of Lake Prasias. A crannoge was generally approached by a boat. In the Irish annals frequent mention is made of these lake-dwellings between the 9th and 17th cent. That at Lough Lynch, in Antrim, was the birthplace of Colkitto; and that of Roughan Lake was the last retreat of Sir Phelim O'Neil in 1641. In 1853-4 similar dwellings were found in Lake Zürich (Switzerland), in Lake Constance, and at Morges, on the Lake of Geneva; and since 1857 lake dwellings have been discovered in Savoy, Hanover, Denmark, Borneo, New Guinea, Burmah, and Siam.

Craven Fund. For researches in the languages, literature, history, archæology, and arts of ancient Greece and Rome, or for the comparative philology of the Indo-European languages. Value 40l. a year. Left to the University of Cambridge by John lord Craven, and founded in 1886.

Craven Scholarships. For classics. I. Two for undergraduates in the University of Cambridge. Present value 50l. a year, tenable for seven years. Founded by John lord Craven. *See* ' Regius Prof. of Greek.'

In 1861 new rules were made for these scholarships.

II. Six in the University of Oxford of the value of 80l., and tenable for three years. Founded by Lord Craven in 1647.

Craven Studentship. Philology. Value 200l. for one year, but the holder eligible for re-election. The funds for this studentship were left by John lord Craven, but it was not founded till 1886. Cambridge University.

Subjects : Languages, literature, history, archæology, and arts of ancient Greece and Rome, or else the comparative philology of the Indo-European languages.

Crazy Jane. Joanna la Loca, daughter and heiress of Isabella of Spain. She was born to vast dominions, but was imbecile, and spent her time in watching the coffin of her husband Philip, who she believed would come to life again (1479-1555).

Crazy Poet (*The*). Nathaniel Lee, the dramatic poet, who was confined four years in Bedlam (1657-1690).

Cream-coloured Parasite (*The*), 1770. Bradshaw, one of Bute's agents with the king (George III.).

Credenza di Sant' Ambrogio, 1198. The House of Commons in the Milanese republic.

S. Ambrogio, *i.e.* St. Ambrose, patron saint of Milan.

Crédit Foncier, 1852. A French method of borrowing money on real property. Its peculiarity is that the repayment of the loan is by an annuity terminable at a certain date—the date and annuity being so calculated that when the last payment is made, the loan and interest are both extinguished.

In England, loans advanced from the Queen Anne's bounty are of a similar character. A clergyman borrows a sum of money on the security of his ' living,' and either he or his successor pays annually a sum of money equal to the interest and part of the principal, so that in twenty years both are extinguished.

Creed of Pope Pius IV. (*The*). In Latin, ' Professio Fidei Tridentina,' A.D. 1564 : (1) the seven sacraments; (2) the Trent doctrine of justification and original sin ; (3) the propitiatory sacrifice of the mass ; (4) transubstantiation ; (5) communion in one kind only ; (6) purgatory; (7) invocation of saints ; (8) veneration of relics ; (9) image worship ; (10) the Roman Church is the mother of all Christian

Q

churches; (11) obedience to the pope is obligatory ; (12) the decrees of all synods, Trent included, must be accepted. This oath is to be taken by all priests and all members of a monastic order. ' Hanc veram catholicam Fidem, extra quam nemo salvus esse potest, voveo, spondeo, et juro.' *See* ' Confession ' and ' Symbol.'

Crem'era (*The*). A river which flows into the Tiber below Veii. It was here that the Fabian clan marked out their place of abode when they quitted Rome.

Creole State (*The*). Louisiana. The original settlers were French and Spanish.

Crescent and the Cross (*The*). Mahometanism and Christianity. The Saracenic symbol is a crescent; the Christian symbol is the cross.

The battle of Tours was to decide whether or not the Cross was to sink under the Crescent.—*Chroniques de St. Denys*, book v. 26.

Crescent as a Turkish Symbol (*The*). The Sultan Othman (1259–1326), founder of the Othman or Ottoman dynasty, saw in a vision a crescent moon which went on increasing till it reached from furthest east to furthest west. This led him to adopt the symbol which had been in use by the Janissaries at least half a century previously, and he took for his motto 'Donec totum compleat orbem.'

Philip, father of Alexander, meeting with great difficulties in the siege of Byzantium, set workmen to undermine the walls; but a crescent moon discovered the design, which miscarried. Consequently, the Byzantes erected a statue to Diana, and the crescent became the symbol of the state. This legend reminds us of the Thistle of Scotland.

Crespi (*Treaty of*), 17 Sept., 1544. Between Karl V. and François I., binding the two sovereigns to unite for the defence of Christendom against the Turks, and to unite their families by the marriage of the second son of François with a daughter of Karl.

Henry VIII. was allied with Karl in an invasion of France, but while Henry was besieging Boulogne François broke up the alliance by a separate treaty.

Crests of the Kings of England (*The*).

Richard I., a lion, assumed in the crusade. The same was borne by Edward III., Henry VII., Edward VI., James I., and has since been recognised as the crest of the royal family of England.

Edward III. sometimes bore a white raven crowned.

Alexander the Great assumed a *ram's head* under pretence of being sprung from Jupiter Ammon.

Julius Cæsar adorned his helmet with a star to denote his descent from Venus.

Crime'an War (*The*), 1853–1856. In 1852 Napoleon III. demanded that the protectorate of the Holy Places in Turkey should be restored to the Latin Church, according to the treaty of 1740, called 'The Charter of the Latins.' The Greek Church, supported by Russia, had gradually ousted the Latin Church ; and Turkey, wholly indifferent to the religious question, but fearing to offend either France or Russia, swayed backwards and forwards according to the pressure made to bear upon her. Threatened by Russia, the sultan at last declared war in Oct. 1853, and, being supported by England and France, hostilities were carried on till 1855, when Russia sued for peace, and a treaty of peace was signed by all the belligerents 30 March, 1856. The secret object of Napoleon III. was to divert the attention of the French from home politics.

Criminal Law Amendment Act (*The*), 1871. Provides 'that no person shall be liable to punishment for doing any act on the ground that it tends to cripple or restrain the free course of trade.'

Crimson and White. In the Valois-Angoulême dynasty, the Catholic soldiers wore crimson jackets and scarfs; but the soldiers of the Protestant faction wore white jackets and scarfs. The Swiss guard wore a grey livery.

Crofters. Descendants of the Highland clansmen dwelling in the Western Isles, and the counties of Ross, Argyll, Sutherland, Inverness, and the islands of Orkney and Shetland. They occupy small farms or crofts. In 1745 the chiefs claimed the ownership of the lands, and during the present century have made large clearances for sheep-walks.

Crofters' Act (*The*), 1886. Provides (1) security of tenure for the crofters; (2) fixed reasonable rents ; (3) compensation for improvements ; (4) enlargement of holdings ; and (5) bequest of holdings.

By this Act a crofter is a yearly tenant of a holding not rented at more than 30*l.* a year.

Cromnyo-mantia. A kind of divination with onions laid on the altar on Christmas Eve. *See* Burton, 'Anatomy of Melancholy,' vol. ii. p. 341.

Cromwell Grandison. So Lafayette was called by Mirabeau. The Grandison referred to was Sir Charles Grandison, the hero of a novel by Samuel Richardson, so faultless a gentleman that Sir W. Scott wrote of him as 'the faultless monster that the world ne'er saw.' Lafayette was as dogmatic and dictatorial as Cromwell, and assumed all the French suavity and finesse of a Sir Charles.

Cromwell of France (*The*). François Maximilien Joseph Isidore Robespierre (1759-1794). Both were main instruments in bringing their respective kings to the block, and both after the death of their king rose to supreme power; but in other respects there was very little resemblance between them.

Tallien was one of the first to denounce him [Robespierre] from the tribunal; and the whole assembly shouted, 'Down with the tyrant! Down with the Cromwell!'—PRINCE, *Parallel History*, vol. iii. p. 98.

Cromwell of the Jews (*The*). Judas Maccabæus, died B.C. 160.

Cromwell's Mad Chaplain. Hugh Peters (1599-1660). His favourite text was Psalm cxlix. 6-9, 'To bind their kings with chains, and their nobles with fetters of iron.'

Cromwell's Trench. A woody dell about half-a-mile from Lathom, in Lancashire. So called because the parliamentary army made their camp there when they besieged the Countess of Derby in her castle.

'Cromwell's Stones' are two circular holes in a large stone which evidently once contained nodules of iron. It is said that the parliamentary besiegers used these holes as moulds for casting balls during the siege.

Cromwellians. The partisans of Oliver Cromwell (1599, 1653-1658).

Cronbane Halfpenny, 1789. A token of the Associated Irish Mine Company, payable at Cronbane Lodge, Wicklow. It had on one side the head of a mitred bishop (perhaps meant for St. Patrick), with the legend CRONBANE HALFPENNY.

Croppies (*The*). So the Irish insurgents were called in derision, when, in 1796-97, soldiers and yeomanry marched over the country to put down the various societies which kept the island in continual terror. They were so called because of their short-cut hair. In 1798 Ireland was in revolt. Some 15,000 'rebels' mustered on Vinegar Hill, near Enniscorthy; the camp was stormed by English troops under General Lake, and the revolt stamped out. *See* 'Irish Associations.'

Croppers, 1812. The tag-rag of 'General Lud,' who went about destroying the new frames for the finish of woollen goods. These Croppers were the men hitherto employed to finish the woollen goods; and the new frames, which did the work better, faster, and cheaper, threw them out of employ. The chief ringleader was a man named Mellor. These riots broke out from time to time for four or five years.

Croquants (*Les*). Peasants of Guyenne, who revolted in the reign of Henri IV. and in that of his son Louis XIII. They were reduced to submission in 1595, and again in 1636, by the Duc d'Epernon.

It is said they were so called from the town Crocq (*Creuse*). The word is used as a verb: 'Les gens de guerre qui de toutes parts croquaient le peuple.'— BORDIER and CHARTON, *Histoire de France*, vol. ii. p. 107, col. 2.

Cross.

Agnus Dei 9.	Holy Rood 12.
Altar cross 5.	Lambeaux 15.
Austral cross 18.	Latin cross 12.
Cardinal s cross 13.	Maltese cross 7.
Constantine's cross 16.	Marking cross 11.
Croix de Bourgogne, 10.	Moline cross 2.
Cross crosslet 6.	Patriarch's cross 13.
Cross patonée 5.	Pectoral cross 4.
Cross pattée 8.	Pope's cross 14.
Cross pendant 5.	Reliquary cross 10.
Cross potent 4.	Rood 12.
Cross of the Passion 12.	St. Andrew's cross 10.
Cross of the Resurrection 9.	St. Anthony's cross 11.
Cross of Victory 9.	St. George s cross 1.
Crux decussata 10.	St. Patrick's cross 10.
Crux immissa 12.	Saltire 10.
Egyptian cross 11.	Southern cross 18.
Fitchée 17.	Spire cross 8.
Fleury cross 3.	Tau cross 11.
Greek cross 1.	Teutonic cross 7.
	Triumphant cross 12.

(1) ✚ *Greek* cross. The basis of all others. Two straight lines bisecting each other at right angles. *St. George's* cross, red on white.

(2) ✪ Cross *moline*. A Greek cross with the ends turned round both ways.

(3) ✤ Cross *fleury*. A Greek cross with a *fleur-de-lis* on each end.

Q 2

(4) Cross *potent*. A Greek cross with each end crutched. The *Pectoral* cross.

(5) Cross *patonée*. A Greek cross with three points at each extremity. The cross *pendant* or *Altar* cross.

(6) Cross *crosslet*. A Greek cross with a cross at each extremity.

(7) *Maltese* cross. A Greek cross narrowing towards the centre, with two points at each extremity. The Teutonic knights wore a black Maltese cross.

(8) Cross *pattée*. A Maltese cross without the points at the extremities. The *Spire* cross.

(9) *Agnus Dei*. A Spire cross on the top of a blunt spear. The cross of the *Resurrection*. The cross of *Victory*.

(10) **X** *St. Andrew's*. The capital letter **X**. White on blue. *St. Patrick's* cross, red on white. *Crux decussáta*. The *Reliquary* cross. In heraldry called a *Saltire*. *Croix de Bourgogne*.

(11) **T** *Tau* cross. A Greek letter **T**. *St. Anthony's* cross. An *Egyptian* cross. The *Marking* cross, or *Crux Ansáta*.

(12) **†** *Latin* cross. A Greek cross with the stem lengthened. *Crux immissa*. Cross of the *Passion*. The *Triumphal* cross. When placed on the chancel screen and made large, it is called the *Rood* or the *Holy Rood*.

(13) *Cardinal's* cross, carried before a cardinal. A double Greek cross. A *Lorraine* cross. The *Patriarch's* cross in the Greek Church.

(14) *Pope's* cross, carried before the pope. A triple Greek cross.

(15) The *Lambeaux*. A Maltese cross on a Latin stem, set on a lambel with three pendants.

(16) *Constantine's* cross. A cross with a Greek P [R] = Chr, *i.e.* Chr[istos].

(17) A cross *crosslet* with the lower stem pointed, technically called *fitchée*.

(18) The *Austral* or *Southern* cross. A constellation consisting of four bright stars disposed in a cruciform fashion, the upper and lower stars pointing to the south pole.

Cross (*The sign of the*). This is made by carrying the right hand to the forehead, the stomach, the left shoulder, and the right shoulder, thus forming the four points of a Latin cross. It is said that this was a secret sign practised by Christians for mutual recognition, and that it may be traced back to the 2nd cent.

Cross of Christ (*The*). The Empress Helĕna, mother of Constantine, is supposed to have found the cross hidden in a cave, near the Temple of Venus, at Jerusalem. We are told that she cut it up into three unequal pieces, one of which she enshrined in a silver casket, and gave it to Macarius, patriarch of Jerusalem; another part she sent to Constantinople, and the rest she sent to Rome, where it was deposited in the church of the Holy Cross. This part is now enclosed in one of the four pillars which support the dome of St. Peter's Church. The part sent to Constantinople was given by Baldwin II. (king of Jerusalem) to St. Louis [IX.] of France, and it is kept in Notre-Dame de Paris. The part sent to Jerusalem was, in 636, subdivided into nineteen pieces, four of which were kept at Jerusalem, and the rest were sent, three to Antioch, three to Constantinople, two to Cyprus, two to Georgia, and one to each of the five following places: Alexandria, Ascalon, Crete, Damascus, and Edessa. *See* 'Crucifixion,' *Relics of the*.

Macarius was the person who suggested to Helĕna that the true cross of the three discovered should be tested by touching with the crosses a woman ready to die. The two crosses of the two thieves produced no effect, but the moment she felt the touch of the true cross she leaped up, restored to perfect health. As Helĕna was eighty years old at the time, one is rather surprised that she parted with so valuable a treasure.

Calvin says that 'fifty men could not carry the wood of what is called the true cross.' Luther thinks there was wood enough 'to build an immense house.' Cyril of Jerusalem tells us the wood was multiplied 'like the loaves and fishes when Jesus fed the multitude in the desert'.

and St. Paulinus tells us that, although chips were cut from it daily, 'yet the wood never suffered diminution.'

By a diligent search I find the following places are said to possess parts of the cross :—Aix-la-Chapelle, Amiens, Angers, Arles, Arras, Autun, Avignon, Baugé, Bernay, Besançon, Bologna, Bonifacio, Bordeaux, Bourbon-Larchambault, Bourges, Brussels, Chalinargues, Châlons, Chamirey, Châtillon, Cheffes in Anjou, Chelles, Compiègne, Conques, Cortona, Courtray, Denmark, Dijon, Donawert, England, Faphine, Fiume, Florence, Gand, Geneva, Grammont, Jaucourt, Jerusalem, Langres, Laon, Libourne, Lille, Limbourg, Longpont, Lorris, Lyons, Mâcon, Maestricht, Marseilles, Milan, Mount Athos, Montepulciano, Naples, Nevers, Norway, Nuremberg, Padua, Paris, Pisa, Poitiers, Pontigny, Ragusa, Rielles-Eaux, Rome, Royaumont, St. Dié, St. Florent, St. Quentin, St. Sepulchre, Sens, Siena, Tournay, Trèves, Troyes, Turin, Valcourt, Vamback, Venice, Venloo. These I have traced, but doubtless there are several others.

Mount Athos has 878,360 cubic millimètres of the cross ; Rome has 537,587 ; Brussels 516,090 ; Venice 445,582 ; Ghent 436,450 ; and Paris 237,731.

Cross of Shame (*The*).

The 'Fiery Cross' (*q.v.*) was so called, because disobedience to its summons was deemed infamy.

Crosses on Tombs.

Seven crosses designate the tomb of a bishop, who alone can administer all the seven sacraments.

Five crosses designate the tomb of a priest, who can administer five out of the seven sacraments.

One cross marks the tomb of an ordinary Christian, to indicate his faith in the cross as his one hope of salvation.

Crosse Scholarships.

For Theology. Three in the University of Cambridge for Bachelors of Arts ; value 20*l.* a year each, and tenable for three years. Founded by the Rev. John Crosse, vicar of Bradford, Yorkshire, 1832. *See* 'Regius Professor of Divinity.'

Crossing the Line.

The first authentic account of the ordeal observed on board ship dates 1702. One sailor represents Neptune and another his wife Amphitrite ; another his barber, and the rest his suite. All dress in the most grotesque raiments they can obtain. A tarred topsail is formed into a bath, and a throne is provided for Neptune and his wife. Those midshipmen who have never crossed the line are then brought forth, while the men pour over them buckets of water, or play the fire hose into their faces. Their faces being tarred are scraped by the barber, and the victims are then soused into the bath provided. Here they are left to struggle out and make their escape as they best can. This horse-play is now almost entirely, and in most cases wholly, abolished.

Crossman's Catechism.

This is Robert Nelson's 'Whole Duty of a Christian,' edited and abridged by Crossman. Nelson lived 1656–1715, and was a non-juror, but the intimate friend of Tillotson.

Crouchback.

Edmund Plantagenet, 2nd son of Henry III., and first earl of Lancaster. Next brother to Edward I. (1241–1296).

Crown (*The*).

It was Walter Walker, grocer, at the sign of the Crown, who said he would make his son heir of the crown. When Edward IV. was told of this merry jest, he ordered Walker to be arrested and put to death for treason (1461).

Crown.

A crown is the circlet of gold, &c., ornamented, placed over the cap represented in England by a border of ermine and a silk or velvet loose cap. The crown of the sovereign and Prince of Wales has a jewelled diadem of gold arched over the cap, surmounted with a ball and cross pattée. Cap velvet, turned up with ermine.

The sovereign's crown has two diadems crossed at right angles. The crown of the Prince of Wales has only one diadem. The coronet has a fleur-de-lis, and 4 crosses pattée, alternately. A cross pattée stands in full-front midway between the spring of the diadem.

The robe of state of the Prince of Wales is of purple velvet, lined with ermine, and trimmed with a deep ermine cape reaching to the elbows. Its speciality is five rows of ermine tails.

Baron's crown. A velvet cap with ermine border similar to that of other peers, but the coronet differs from that of a viscount by having only 8 round pearls on

the upper rim instead of 14. In France
' une torsade en perles.'

His robe of state is similar to that of a viscount,
but the cape has only 2 rows of black spots. A
prince has 5 rows, a duke 4 rows, a marquis half 4
and half 3, an earl 3, a viscount half 3 and half 2,
a baron 2.

A prince's coronet bears on the upper rim
4 fleurs-de-lis and 4 crosses pattée, a duke's
6 strawberry leaves, a marquis's 4 strawberry
leaves alternating with 4 golden balls, an earl's
4 points surmounted with balls alternating with
4 strawberry leaves, a viscount's with 14 golden
balls, a baron's with 8 golden balls.

Duke's crown consists of a velvet cap
with a border of ermine, and the coronet
over it is a circle of gold with jewels, the
upper rim being set with 8 gold strawberry leaves. In France the leaves were
' fleurs de persil.'

His state robe is a crimson velvet mantle lined
with white taffeta (not ermine), but the cape is
ermine, reaching to the elbows, having 4 (instead
of 5) rows of ermine tails.

His parliamentary robe is scarlet cloth, lined
with white taffeta, and the ermine cape.

Earl's crown. A velvet cap with a
border of ermine, with a circlet of gold
enriched with jewels, from the upper
rim of which rise 8 points, each surmounted with a round pearl, towering
somewhat above the cap, and between
these points 8 small gold strawberry
leaves. In France the leaves were
omitted.

His robe of state is crimson velvet, like that of
a duke, but the cape has only 3 rows of black spots
instead of 4.

Marquis's crown. A velvet cap with
a border of ermine, and a coronet of gold
jewelled like that of a duke, but with
this difference, instead of eight strawberry leaves on the upper rim, the rim is
surmounted with 4 strawberry leaves and
4 round pearls. In France they were
parsley leaves.

His state robe is a crimson velvet mantle, and
the cape has 4 rows of black spots on the *right*
shoulder, and only 3 rows on the *left*.

Prince's crown (except the Prince of
Wales). A velvet cap turned up with
ermine and surmounted with a gold ball.
The gold and jewelled circlet has
4 crosses pattée and 4 fleur-de-lis alternately, but there is no diadem, nor ball
and cross.

The princesses' crown is like that of
the princes'.

The nephews and nieces have strawberry leaves in the place of fleurs-de-lis
and crosses pattée.

Viscount's crown. The cap is the same
as that of a duke, marquis, or earl; but
the gold and jewelled coronet has 14

round pearls on the upper rim, quite
close together. In France the pearls
were arranged in sets of three.

His state robe is the same as that of an earl,
with this difference, instead of 3 complete
rows of black spots, there are 3 rows on the *right*
shoulder and only 2 on the *left. See* 'Marquis,'
above.

Crown (*A*). In the Catholic Church
is the subjective recognition of superior
Christian merit: as the crown of virginity,
the crown of humility, the crown of learning, the crown of martyrdom, &c. St.
Peter of Ravenna received the 'triple
crown of virginity, doctorate, and martyrdom.' St. Angelus, in 1225, received ' the
triple crown of virginity, preaching, and
martyrdom.' St. Cecilia received the
double crown of virginity and martyrdom.

Crown (*The English*). It is said
that Alfred, in 872, was the first English
sovereign to wear a symbol of regal
authority.

In 929 Athelstan wore a coronet not
unlike that of our earls.

William the Conqueror added a coronet
with points to his ducal cap.

In 1483 Richard III. introduced the
crosses, and Henry VII. the arches in
1485.

The oldest crown now existing in
England is that of Charles II., 1660.

The present crown was made in 1838,
the jewels being taken from old crowns
broken up. It contains a large ruby and
a large sapphire.

The smaller stones are 1,363 brilliants, 1,273 rose
diamonds, 273 pearls, 147 table diamonds, 16 sapphires, 11 emeralds, 4 rubies, and 4 drop pearls.

In 1386 Richard II. pawned his crown and regalia for a loan of 2,000*l.*

Crown (*The Papal*). In 593 Pope
Hormisdas wore a cap of state.

In 1053 Pope Damasus II. followed the
same example.

Hildebrand (1073–1083) wore a royal
crown, with the legend, *Corona regni de
manu Dei.*

In 1160 the papal cap was encircled
with a crown.

Boniface VIII. (1294–1303) added a
second crown, with this legend, *Diadema
imperii de manu Petri.*

It is very doubtful who introduced the
third crown. Some say it was John XXII.
(1316–1334), some say it was Benedict
XII. (1334–1342), and some ascribe it to
Urban V. (1362–1370). It indicates su-

premacy in temporal power, in spiritual power, and in ecclesiastical power, in Europe, Asia, and Africa.

Crown and Anchor Association (*The*), 1795. For the 'protection of liberty and property from republicans and levellers.' The chairman was Mr. Reeves, M.P.

Crown and Government Securities Bill (*The*), 1848. To facilitate prosecutions for political offences. The bill was especially directed against the war party of Ireland urged on by Mr. Mitchel, M.P., editor of the 'United Irishman' (*q.v.*).

Crown Oration (*The*), B.C. 330. Soon after the battle of Chæronēa, Ctesiphon proposed that Demosthenês should be presented with a golden crown in the theatre, during the great Dionysiac festival, for his services to Athens. Æschinês indicted Ctesiphon for this proposal, and Demosthenês spoke in his defence. The oration of Æschinês is called the 'oration against Ctesiphon'; that of Demosthenês is called his oration 'on the Crown,' or his 'Crown oration.' Æschinês failed to secure a fifth part of the votes, and quitted Athens to live in Rhodes.

Crown of Thorns (*The*). Placed on the head of Jesus; was not found in the cave with the cross, and there is no record extant of its discovery. In the thirteenth century Baldwin II., king of Jerusalem, gave it to St. Louis [IX.] of France, who built in Paris a holy chapel for its depository. It is devoid of thorns now, for they have been given away to a vast number of churches, and parts have been set in rings. I myself have seen and handled one of these rings. This relic and fragments of the Cross are borne in procession by twelve canons at 8 o'clock every Good Friday night through Notre Dame de Paris. At least this was the case when I lived in Paris. See 'Crucifixion,' *Relics of the.*

In the Hôtel de Cluny, Paris, is a ring said to contain a small part of one of the thorns.

Crowns. The kaiser-kings of Germany received three crowns. I. The silver crown, as king of Germany. II. The iron crown of Lombardy, as king of Italy; and III. The imperial crown as kaiser of the Holy Roman Empire. The

first he received at Aix-la-Chapelle, the second at Monza, and the third at Rome ; but Karl V. (Charles-quint) was the last kaiser-king who received the imperial crown at the pope's hands.

The imperial crown was a small mitre, cleft in the front instead of at the sides.

Crown of St. Stephen (*The*). The crown of Hungary. Stephen I. (979, 997–1038), called 'the Apostle of Hungary,' received a crown from Pope Sylvester II., with which the emperor of Austria is still crowned as 'king of Hungary.' *See* 'Corona.'

If Hungarian independence should be secured through the help of Prince Napoleon, the prince himself should accept the crown of St. Stephen.— KOSSUTH, *Memoirs of my Exile* (1883).

Crucifixion (*Relics of the*). *See* under

The Bandage.	The Robe.
„ Blood.	„ Spear.
„ Cross.	„ Sponge.
„ Crown of Thorns.	„ Staircase.
„ Cup.	„ Table.
„ Grave clothes.	„ Title.
„ Handkerchief.	„ Tunic or Shirt.
„ Nails.	„ Whipping-post.
„ Reed.	

Crusades, from 11th to 13th cent. Expeditions to recover Palestine from the Moslems. So called because the soldiers wore a cross on the shoulder or breast as a badge of their religious faith.

1st, in 1096–1099; decreed by Urban II. It ended in the capture of Jerusalem by the crusaders.

2nd, in 1147–1149; led by Louis VII. and Konrad III. Its object was the relief of Christians oppressed by the Moslems. It was a complete failure. The Christians had to surrender Jerusalem.

3rd, in 1189–1192. This crusade was the most heroic. Frederick Barbarossa of Germany, Philippe Augustus of France, and Richard Cœur de Lion of England were among the crusaders, while the renowned Saladin was on the other side. It was brought to an untimely close, on Saladin's agreeing to allow pilgrims free access to the Holy Sepulchre.

4th, in 1198–1204. Constantinople was taken.

5th in 1216–1221. The sultan recovered Damietta.

6th, in 1215–1229. Kaiser Friederich II. proclaimed King of Jerusalem; but in 1244 Jerusalem was retaken by the Turks.

7th, in 1248–1253. A truce of ten years concluded. (Led by St. Louis of France.)

8th, in 1270–1272. Nazareth taken, truce

of ten years concluded. (Led by St. Louis, who died at Tunis, on his way, 25 August, 1270.)

Crusca (*Accademia della*), 1582. The famous Florentine Academy, instituted to enrich the literature and improve the language of Tuscany. So named because it discarded as *bran* all words not purely Tuscan. The great Italian dictionary was produced by this Academy, 1612. *See* 'Della Crusca.'

Crusoe's Island. Juan Fernandez is so called by sailors, from a persuasion that it was the island of Defoe's famous story.

Crusty Christopher. So Tennyson called Professor Wilson, who noticed the works of the young poet in 'Blackwood's Magazine' with praise not unmixed with censure, 1830.

Crystal Palace (*The*), 1851. A large building almost entirely of iron and glass constructed in Hyde Park, London, as an exhibition room for all nations in the world. It was 1,848 feet long, 408 feet wide, and 66 feet high, crossed by a transept 108 feet high and 408 feet long, enclosing several noble elms. It was nearly four times the length of St. Paul's and twice the width. It contained 34 miles of gutter to carry off the rain, 900,000 feet of glass, and covered over 18 acres of ground. The designer was Mr. Joseph Paxton, and the contractors were Messrs. Fox and Henderson; their contract being 79,800*l.* and the material, or 150,000*l.* without it. The actual cost was 176,030*l.* It was begun 26 Sept., 1850, and opened 1 May, 1851. It realised a profit of 150,000*l.* in 144 days.

Cuckoo Ale. Ale drunk the first day one hears the cuckoo. In Shropshire it was at one time customary for the labouring classes, as soon as the cuckoo was heard by them for the first time in the year, to leave off work, and spend the rest of the day in merry-making, a main part of which was drinking cuckoo ale. This was drunk out of doors to welcome the cuckoo.

Cuckoo Day, 14 April. The birthday of the Princess Beatrice. The tradition is that the old woman let the cuckoo out of her bag at Heathfield Fair.

Cuentas del Gran Capitan. A ridiculous pretence of an account of money spent. Gonsalvo, the great captain, was accused by Ferdinand of misappropriating the public money, and was commanded to produce his accounts. Gonsalvo read aloud: 'Item the first, 200,763 ducats and 9 reals to friars, nuns, and mendicants, to offer up prayers for the success of his majesty's arms. Item the second, 700,494 ducats and 10 reals to spies.' Here Ferdinand, who had never sent Gonsalvo money enough to pay the soldiers, seeing the jest, and fully ashamed of the accusation, interrupted the captain by a burst of laughter which was echoed by the whole court.

Cuirassiers. Heavy horsemen wearing, in the time of Queen Mary, body-armour over their buff coats. They carried sword and pistol. Napoleon had twelve regiments of cuirassiers. The Russian cuirassiers are armed with lances. In England, at the present day, the Life Guards and Horse Guards wear cuirasses.
Pronounce *Kŭĕ-ras-seeah.*

Culdees. Secular clergy attached to cathedrals and performing the office of dean and chapter to the episcopate. They were pretty numerous, and made their first appearance in the 9th cent. Nothing is heard of them after the 14th cent. The word seems to be Irish, and to mean 'Attendants of God' (*ceile De*).

Cum Occasione (*The Bulls*), 1653. By which Innocent X. condemned the five famous propositions of Jansen. In 1665, Alexander VII. prescribed a formula for the condemnation of Jansen and the Jansenists, which all ecclesiastics were required to sign.

Cumean Sibyl. Amalthæa offered 9 vols. of prophecies on the future of Rome to Tarquinius *Superbus*, who refused to purchase them. Having destroyed three of them, she returned the following year, asking the same price for the remaining six. Tarquin again refused to purchase them; whereupon Amalthæa destroyed three more, and demanded the original price for the three left. The books were bought, placed in a coffer, and stowed away in the crypt of the capitol under the charge of two patricians. The custodians were afterwards increased to ten, and then to fifteen. In the reign of Honorius they were burnt by Stilico, his master of the horse. (Varro, ' Antiquities,' vol. ii.)

It is rather remarkable tnat Tarquinius Superbus died at Cumæ, the home of the famous sibyl.

Cup or **Chalice** (*The*) used by our Lord at the Last Supper has been preserved, according to tradition; but there are two cups which profess to be the genuine one. Some affirm that it is the silver chalice at Valencia, in Spain; but others insist that it is the green glass cup at Genoa, which was taken to Paris in 1816, and broken in the transit. This cup has two handles and is of hexagonal form. Its diameter a-top is 326 millimètres, and it will hold three litres of liquor. *See* ' Crucifixion,' *Relics of the.*

The ' Sacro Catino ' is sometimes identified with the ' Holy Graal ' of the romances of the middle ages; but many consider the Holy Graal to be the paten and not the cup. In Arthurian romance it seems to be a *golden vessel*, not silver or glass, and suits the idea of a paten with the consecrated bread far better than that of a chalice. Thus we read (part iii. chap. 3, 4, 85, 102), ' immediately the bread had been distributed the graal vanished.'

Cupid's Gardens. A corruption of Cuper's Gardens. Public gardens laid out by Boydell Cuper, gardener to Thomas, earl of Arundel. Boydell Cuper, when Arundel House was taken down, obtained numerous mutilated marbles, which he erected in these gardens. They were opposite Somerset House, were opened to the public in 1678, and ceased to exist in 1753. These gardens were famous for fireworks, but no less notorious for licentiousness.

Curfew Bell (*The*. A corruption of *couvre-feu*, ' put out tne fire.' William the Conqueror ordered the bell to be rung at eight o'clock every night in every city and town in England, when every fire and every lamp and candle was to be put out. This was not to annoy the English, but to prevent fires and conspiracies. William had enforced the same in Normandy as an act of police before the battle of Hastings.

Curia Regia (*The*), 1860. The supreme court of judicature in Hungary.

Curia Regis, or **Council of the Realm,** 1172. A sort of parliament held by Henry II. at Lismore for the purpose of conferring with the prelates and magnates on the government of Ireland. Henry determined to extend to his English subjects in Ireland the laws and

usages they were accustomed to while they lived in England. These laws and usages extended over what was called the Pale (*q.v.*), but all the rest of Ireland continued to observe their own laws and usages.

Sir John Davies informs us that no legislative council was held in Ireland for 140 years after the council at Lismore, but that Irish representatives attended the English parliaments.

Curlew Mountains (*The*). The county of Leitrim was so called even in the reign of Queen Elizabeth.

Curop'alate. One who had charge of the palace in the Eastern Empire, called in the Frankish kingdom ' Maire du Palais,' by the Romans ' Major domus,' and in English ' Steward of the Household.' Michael I. was called ' Curopalātus,' because he was Mayor of the Palace to Stauracius, whom he deposed and succeeded 2 Oct., 811. Being himself deposed by Leo, he turned monk and died about 845.

Curry-powder Duke (*The*). The Duke of Norfolk, who, during the corn-law agitation, said in a speech he was surprised that the poor did not put a pinch or two of curry-powder in their stews, as it gave the meat such a piquant flavour.

I remember Sir Robert Harvey saying in a public speech that he was surprised the poor did not more frequently eat a red herring at breakfast, as it gave such a piquant flavour to bread and butter. In ridicule of this speech, a red herring was often carried on a pole in political elections. The remark of the Princess Lamballe was of a similar character. She was surprised the poor did not eat *brioches*, as bread was so dear. And our Princess Charlotte said she would rather eat beef than starve.

Curse of Cromwell (*The*), 1650. His campaign in Ireland, which certainly was stained with revolting cruelty. Witness the massacres of Drogheda and Clonmel. He was lord-lieutenant at the time.

This bloody campaign has always been remembered in that country as the ' Curse of Cromwell.' —HOWITT, *Hist. of Eng.* (Commonwealth, p. 315).

Curse of Scotland (*The*). The Nine of Diamonds is so called from its resemblance to the nine lozenges in the heraldic bearing of John Dalrynple, first earl of Stair, so scandalously concerned in the massacre of Glencoe (*q.v.*).

Curtmantle. The surname of Henry II. of England. He wore the Anjou mantle, which was shorter than the robe worn by his predecessors (1133, 1154–1189).

Curule Magistrate (*A*). A Roman state officer, such as dictator, consul, prætor, &c., who sate on an ivory chair at the head of public assemblies. All the children of such a magistrate became nobles [*nobiles*]. The Curule chair was like a camp-stool, which could easily be moved about, and was placed in the chariot of the magistrate when he rode in state.

Curūlis is connected with *currus*, a chariot; hence *equus curūlis* (a carriage-horse), *triumphus curūlis* (a carriage triumph), in contradistinction to an ovation which was made on foot.

Custos Rotulo'rum. The chief officer of the court of Quarter Sessions (*q.v.*), who has custody of the records or rolls ; he must be a justice of the peace of the county, nominated by the crown, and appointed by the commission.

Cynic Philosophers (*The*) of ancient Greece. Founded by Antisthênês the Athenian (B.C. 440–376). Cynic is an adjective from κυνὸς (gen. of κύνων, a dog) ; so called because Antisthênês taught in the gymnasium called Cynosargês (*the White Dog*). He was a censor of public morals and manners. Diogênês of Sinôpê (B.C. 412–323) affected to be surly like a dog, and like a dog snarled at every one. The Athenians raised to his memory a pillar of Parian marble surmounted with a dog. The substance of the inscription being—

Say, dog, I pray, what guard you in that tomb ?
  'A dog.' His name? 'Diogenês.' From far ?
'Sinope.' He who made a tub his home?
  'The same. Now, dead, among the stars a star.'

Cyclic Poets (*The*). The epic poets who sprang up after Homer, and confined themselves to the same cycle of events, viz. the Story of Troy. Stasīnos of Cyprus chose for his subject events immediately *preceding* the Trojan war. Arctīnos of Milêtus related the story of the *wooden horse*. Agīas of Trœzênê took for his subject the return from Troy. And Eugāmon of Cyrênê made a continuation of the Odyssey.

Nec sic incipies, ut scriptor cyclicus olim.
  HORACE, *Ars Poetica*, 137.

Cy-près Process (*The*). The process of approximation. Where a literal execution is inexpedient or impracticable, the court will execute a devise as nearly as it can, according to the spirit of the devisor's words, or, to speak technically, cy-près. For example : if there are no objects remaining to take the benefit of a charity, the court will dispose of the revenues by a new scheme on the principles of the original trust.

As in law, a cy-près or approximate administration of an obsolete devise is admissible, so in reference to the Bible, is it not incumbent upon you to apply what seems obsolete to cases analogous to those originally intended ?—Dr. HESSEY, *Moral Difficulties connected with the Bible* (1871), p. 112.

Cyrena'ic Sect (*The*). Founded at Cyrênê, in Africa, by Aristippos, who studied under Socratês. He taught that pleasure is the ultimate object of human pursuit, but that virtuous motives and virtuous conduct are indispensable to true pleasure. Aristippos died B.C. 380.

Cyzicēnus. Antiochus IX., king of Syria, who was educated at Cyzicos (B.C. 112–96).

Czar (Cæsar or Kaiser), 1237. A title first conferred on Dimitri I., son of Yaroslaf, by the Greek emperor. Before then the sovereign was called *Kniaz* (grand-duke) or *Welik Knez* (great prince), a title which ran on concurrently with czar till 1545. After the battle of Pultowa, in 1709, the head of the Russian empire was also styled emperor and autocrat.

The monarch of Casan was called *tzar*. This monarchy was conquered, in 1545, by Ivan Vassilivich (the Terrible) ; and it is said that Ivan then dropped the titles of *Kniaz* and *Welik Knez*, and retained only that of ' tzar ' or ' czar.'

D. By the Mutiny Act, 21 Vict. c. 9 (1858) it was enacted that, ' on the first, and on every subsequent conviction for desertion, the court-martial . . . may order the offender to be marked on the left side, two inches below the armpit, with the letter "D" (deserter), not less than an inch long, with some ink, or gunpowder, or other preparation not liable to be obliterated.'

For other brands, *see* 'F' ('Dict. of Phrase and Fable,' p. 281), 'V,' and 'S.'

Dacoits. Brigands, so called in Oude, Burmah, &c. But sometimes the Dacōtah Indians of North America are incorrectly called Dacoits.

Dacoity. Brigandage.

Dactyls, or 'Idêan Dactyls.' Priests of Cybêlê, Saturn, and Jupiter, dwelling in Crete, on Mount Ida.

Said to be called 'Dactyls' from the Greek word *δακτυλος*, a finger, because they were ten in number.

Dagger-ale. A very celebrated ale sold at 'The Dagger' ordinary, in Holborn. The dagger refers to the City arms.

Dagger-money. A tax to provide arms and police, when judges entered a town, to prevent their being molested or attacked by highwaymen.

Dagger-scene in the House of Commons (*The*). During the French Revolution, Edmund Burke on one occasion threw a dagger on the floor of the house, vociferating 'There is French fraternity for you! Such is the poignard which French Jacobins would plunge into the heart of our sovereign.' Canning spoilt this bunkum by saying: 'The gentleman has brought his knife with him, but where is the fork?'

Dague de la Miséricorde (*La*), or the 'Mercy of God.' A broad strong poniard, which was hung on the right side of the Scottish-French archers. *See* Sir W. Scott, 'Quentin Durward,' chap. v.

Daguerreotype (*The*), 1825. The production of permanent pictures on plated copper by Louis Jacques Mandé Daguerre (1789–1851).

Daibutsu. The great statue of Buddha, in Japan. It is about 600 years old, 50 feet in height, and 100 feet in girth; it is made of bronze and silver, but the eyes are of gold. The proportions are exquisite, and probably it is the finest idol in existence.

Daily Courant (*The*), 11 March, 1702. Called the first daily newspaper in England.

Daily News (*The*). Commenced 21 Jan., 1846, London.

Daily Paper (*First English*), 11 March, 1702. The 'Daily Courant.' *See* 'English Mercurie.'

Daily Paper (*First French*), 1777. Called the 'Journal de Paris.'

It contained an article on the 'Almanach des Muses,' a short letter by Voltaire, the advertisement of a library, two or three miscellaneous articles, and a pun; the pun was the chief attraction, and continued so for some time.

Daily Telegraph (*The*). A London newspaper, commenced 29 June, 1855.

Daisy League (*The*), 1887. A league formed at Belfast for the promotion of women's rights, and for Home Rule in Ireland under imperial control. Not independent Home Rule or separation from Great Britain. The badge of the league is a daisy, and the motto is 'Faith, Hope, and Charity.' Of course the idea was suggested by the Primrose League (*q.v.*)

Dalcassians, or Dalgais. The people of North Munster, including Clare, Limerick, and the country about Cashel as far as the mountains of Sliablama, in Ossory. The people of South Munster were called Eugenians (Eoganachts, or sons of Eogan).

Dalreudi'ni. Natives of Ulster, same as Dalriads (*q.v.*).

Dalriada. Antrim in Ireland is so called from Cairbre Riada, on one of whose descendants the country was settled by the arbitration of St. Colman, A.D. 572.

Carbre, or Cairbre, was generally called Carbre 'of the Long Arm.'

Dalriadic Rulers (*The*). The kings of Argyllshire. Dalrīada is the ancient name of the northern half of Antrim, in Ireland. Cairbre (of the Long Arm) of the race of Riada, who lived in the 3rd cent., planted a colony on the shores of Argyllshire, in Albany, and in 506 some of his descendants founded there the kingdom of 'Dal-riada in Albany.' In 843 Kenneth MacAlpin united the Dalriads and Picts under one sceptre, and became the first king of Albany.

About two centuries afterwards Albania began to be known as Scotia, or Scotland.
'Hector Boece added by interpolation from forty to forty-five Scotch kings to the authentic Irish list of Dalriadic rulers.'—T. MOORE, *History of Ireland*, chap. viii. p. 137.

Dalriads (*The*). The Irish-Scots, who possessed themselves of a part of Argyllshire, in the middle of the 3rd cent.

Damage-cleer (*i.e. damna clericorum*). A fee paid to the clerks of courts before judgment was executed. It was the *tenth part* in all Common Pleas, and a *twentieth part* in the King's Bench and Exchequer courts, of all damages exceeding five marks. Abolished in 1665.

Dame de Beauté (*La*). Agnes Sorel, the mistress of Charles VII. of France (1410–1450). So called from the 'Château de Beauté,' on the banks of the Marne, given her by the king.

Damianists. Those nuns of the Order of St. Claire who followed the most austere rule of St. Francis. Those who followed the modified rule introduced by Urban IV. in 1264 were denominated *Urbanists.*

Damien (*Father*). A Belgian Catholic missioner (1839–1889) who devoted his life to the care of the lepers at Molokai. He caught the disease, and speedily fell a victim, at the age of 49.

Damiens (*Robert François*), Jan. 1757. Attempted the life of Louis XV. as he was stepping into his coach to return to the Trianon, by stabbing him between the fourth and fifth rib. The devilry of the French in torturing this creature is wholly without precedent. First incisions were made in his arms and thighs, into which boiling oil was poured. He was next chained on an iron bed, and the torture again applied. On 28 March, amidst a vast crowd of people, he was taken to the Place de Grève, and being fastened by iron gyves to a scaffold, one of his hands was burnt in liquid flaming sulphur. His thighs, legs, and arms were then excoriated with red-hot pincers, and boiling oil, molten lead, hot resin, and sulphur were poured over the wounds. Next, tight ligatures being tied round his wrists and ankles, four young horses were fastened to the ropes to pull the limbs asunder. This lasted an hour, when the medical attendants ordered the tendons to be cut. Again the horses were lashed, and one arm and leg were severed. After a few more pulls the other members were pulled off, and the man expired. In 1764 Goldsmith published his 'Traveller,' and at the conclusion alludes to 'Damiens' bed of steel.' *See* Smollett's 'History of England,' vol. v., chap. 12, p. 3.

Dan. So Daniel O'Connell was lovingly designated by the Irish.

Danaanian Dynasty (*The*). A dynasty said to have reigned in Ireland, and to have been succeeded by the Milesians. They were descendants of Tuatha na Danaan (*q.v.*), who had migrated to Scotland, and had been led back by Nuad of the 'Silver Hand.' *See* 'Silver Hand.'

Danans (*The*). Invaders of Ireland in prehistoric times, who overthrew the Belgæ settlement in one great battle and the 'Irish' in another, and made themselves masters of the island. The Belgæ were allowed by them a free territory in Connaught.

By the 'Irish' must be understood the Fomorians and Partholanians (*q.v.*).

Dance of St. Guy (*The*), 1378. An epidemic in Germany; also called the 'Dance of St. Witt.' It was supposed that the victims of this disease were possessed, and therefore they were exorcised by the priests.

Pausanias tells us that the daughters of Prœtus and the women of Argos fancied they were cows, and ran about the meadows under this hallucination. Compare *Dan.* ii. 32, 33.

Dancing Mania (*The*), 1374. A strange disease, which pervaded different parts of Germany, and first broke out in the neighbourhood of Aix-la-Chapelle. Persons would join hands, forming large circles, and dance like mad people till they fell exhausted to the ground. The magistrates of the Rhenish cities were obliged to put down the mania by an armed force. In the French Revolution a similar mania prevailed, the 'Carmagnole' being the name of the dance and song which then moved men, women, and children to a temporary frenzy.

Called in Holland 'St. John's Dance;' in Germany 'St. Witt's Dance;' in Strasburg 'St. Guy's' or 'St. Vitus's Dance.'

Dancing-masters (*Father of all*). Beauchamps, who died 1695. Louis XIV. took lessons of him for twenty years.

Dando (*The*), Sept. 1427. A kind of influenza which affected nearly everyone in France. It began with pains in the shoulders and loins, shivering fits followed, and then a tearing cough. It lasted fifteen or sixteen days. A chronicler says during the dando not a man or woman could be found who had not a large pimple either on the mouth or on the nose.

Dandy. For the different names of French dandies, *see* 'Incroyables.'

Dandy King (*The*). Joachim Murat, king of Naples, called by Napoleon 'Un roi de théâtre.' He used to parade the streets of Paris dressed like a stage king in silks and satins (1771–1815).

Egan says the word 'dandy' was first used in 1820; this requires confirmation, for velocipedes, invented in 1779, were called 'dandy-horses,' and were common in 1818. I myself rode one at the time.

Dane Territory. In England. At the Peace of Nottingham, 868, Alfred the Great divided England into two parts, the larger of which he assigned to the Danes; but he kept London in his own portion. The boundary ran along the Thames to the mouth of the Lea; then by Bedford and the river Ouse to the old Roman road called 'Watling Street.' *See* 'The Five Burghs.'

Danebrog (*The Order of*), 1219. Instituted in Denmark by Waldemar the Victorious. Revived in 1671 by Christian V. To recompense services rendered to the state, whether military or civil. The decoration consists of a cross of gold *patiée*, enamelled with white, and suspended with a white ribbon edged with red.

Brog = flag. The order is in honour of the national flag of Denmark.

Danegelt. A tax first levied in 991 by Ethelred the Unready to bribe the Danes, who had invaded the kingdom, to quit it. Several times during the reign of Ethelred the Danes returned, and received fresh bribes. It is said that he paid them altogether 150,000*l.* (fully four and a half millions according to the present value of money). The tax was from time to time levied by subsequent kings, under pretence of fortifying the kingdom or maintaining a fleet or army against the Danes. Edward the Confessor abolished it; but it was again collected, under the name of 'Heregeld' (army tax), in the reigns of William I., William II., Henry I., and Stephen.

In 991 the tax was 1s. for every hide of land, but the tax was soon doubled.

Danelagh. Means the 'Danes' law,' but the word is applied to the 'Five Burghs' given by Alfred to the Danes at the Peace of Nottingham in 868. The 'Five Burghs of the Danes' were Derby, Leicester, Lincoln, Nottingham, and Stamford.

According to the 'Bromton Chronicle,' the Danelagh contained fifteen counties (not five), viz. Essex, Middlesex, Suffolk, Norfolk, Hertfordshire, Cambridgeshire, Hampshire, Lincoln, Nottinghamshire, Derbyshire, Northamptonshire, Leicestershire, Buckinghamshire, Bedfordshire, and all that vast territory called Northumbria.

Danish Butler (*The*). Baron Ludvig Holberg (1684–1754), author of the heroi-comic Hudibrastic poem entitled 'Peder Paars.'

Danites (*The*). Sometimes called 'Destroying Angels.' The more violent members of the Mormon community who carried out the decrees of the Elders on recalcitrant brethren. A number of them, disguised as Indians, massacred a party of Mormons withdrawing from the Utah settlement. Brigham Young was accused of complicity.

'P'r'aps you've heard tell of Danites?' I had heard . . . of that spiritual police of Mormondom, of those fierce zealots who obey their prophet blindly . . . Seth's right; we don't want to set up any chaps to paint Injun on our account, as Angel Brown, and young Harris, and the Danites did.'—CHARLES DICKENS, Christmas Number, 1861, *All the Year Round*, p. 41 (*Tom Tiddler's Ground*).

Dante of Philosophy (*The*). John Baptist Pico, professor of rhetoric in Naples (1688–1740).

Danton of the Gironde (*The*). Isnard, son of a perfumer at Grasse; a literary man, formed on the old Grecian and Roman model. He was a thorough republican of very impetuous character.

Dantonists. The followers of Danton, one of the three leaders in the Reign of Terror, the other two being Hébert and Robespierre. When Danton thought that blood enough had been shed, he halted and advised moderation, but was trampled in the dust by those less scrupulous than himself. Robespierre accused him of monarchical proclivities, and he was condemned to death by the Revolutionary Tribunal.

Danubian Principalities (*The*). Moldavia and Wallachia, constituted into independent states by the Convention of Paris, 19 Aug., 1858. They were united provisionally by a firman of the Sultan, 12 Nov., 1861. United under the title of Roumania 23 Dec., 1861.

Darbyites (Dar'-by-ites), **Darbyism,** 1832. A split from the Plymouth Brethren on the doctrine of the humanity of Christ. So called from John H. Darby.

Darg. The regulation enforced by the trades union among colliers, that no workman shall raise in a day more of the mineral than could be easily raised by the most inexperienced and unskilful of the colliers.

Darg = day: contract work by the day.

Darien Scheme (*The*). The Darien Company was projected by William Paterson (founder of the Bank of England) in 1694. Incorporated by Act of Parliament in Scotland, 1695. Settlement abandoned in 1699, and finally in 1700. The scheme was to colonise the Atlantic side of the Isthmus of Panama, in order to form a commercial *entrepôt* between the eastern and western hemispheres; and a monopoly of all the trade of Asia, Africa, and America was granted to the company. The ground, however, belonged to Spain, and the climate was fatal to the colonists. Many having died and more sickened, a Spanish force was sent against the new-comers, which broke up the company entirely.

> Then there were malcontents [in Scotland] created by the government opposition to the Darien scheme. ... The Darien malcontents were for the most part revolutionists.—HOWITT, *History of England* (Anne, p. 182).

Dark Ages (*The*). From the fall of the Roman empire, A.D. 475, to the revival of literature on the discovery of the Pandects at Amalfi in 1137. Not to draw the limits too finely, say 700 years (450 to 1150). The Middle Ages (*q.v.*) may be extended to about 1550, covering from ten to eleven centuries.

Darling of Mankind (*The*). Vespasian the Roman emperor (9, 70–79). Titus was called the 'Delight of Mankind' (40, 79–81).

Darvel Gatheren. A great wooden idol in Wales, held in great veneration. There was a legend that one day Darvel would burn a forest. When Friar Forrest, in 1538, the confessor of Queen Katharine, was burnt for denying the king's supremacy, this image was cast on the pile.

> David Darvel Gatheren,
> As saith the Welshmen,
> Fetched outlaws out of hell;
> Now is he come, with spear and shield,
> In harness to burn in Smith-field,
> For in Wales he may not dwell.
> And Forrest, the friar,
> That obstinate liar,
> That wilfully shall be dead,
> In his contumacy
> The gospel doth deny
> The king to be supreme head.

Darwinism. So called from Charles Darwin. Is the theory that species owe their origin to natural selection, or the survival of those best adapted to the surroundings, &c.

> Evolution is the development of new species of animals and plants by a natural process, of which the chief factors are heredity, variation, and adaptation. Hence Darwinism and evolution are quite distinct ideas.

Daughter of Jerusalem. Mount Zion, the fortified part of Jerusalem. Here David had his palace, and hence it was also called 'The City of David.'

Dauphin of France (*The*), 1349. Heir apparent of the crown, like our 'Prince of Wales.' Humbert II. count of Dauphiny, by the Treaty of Vincennes (30 May, 1349), ceded Dauphiny to the crown of France, and from that time to the first Revolution the eldest son of the reigning king was entitled 'The Dauphin.' The wife of a dauphin was entitled *Dauphine* (2 syl.).

The *Grand Dauphin* means the eldest son of Louis XIV., named 'Louis de France' (1661–1711). The son of the Grand Dauphin also died before his grandfather (1682–1712).

David Dale's People. Scotch Independents. So called from David Dale of New Lanark, the philanthropist (1738–1806).

Davidians, or the 'Family of Love.' So called from David George, who made himself sometimes Christ and sometimes the Holy Ghost. *See* Strype, 'Cranmer,' p. 291. Their tenets are touched upon in the preface to the 'Ecclesiastical Polity,' and a short account of them is given in Sir W. Scott's 'Woodstock,' ii. p. 218.

> David George published an account of his visions in 1542, under the title of the 'Book of Wonders.' He died in 1556.

Davies Scholarship. For Classics. Value about 30*l*. a year, tenable for seven years. Founded in the University of Cambridge by the Rev. Jonathan Davies, D.D., provost of Eton, 1804. *See* 'Regius Professor of Greek.'

Davis Chinese Scholarship. Tenable for two years. Founded in the University of Oxford by Sir John F. Davis, F.R.S.

Davis Strait. So called from John Davis, an English navigator of the 16th cent.

Day of Adoration (*The*). 'Dies Adoratus,' 14 Sept. Called also 'L'exaltation de la Sainte Croix,' 'en mémoire de ce qu' Héraclius rapporta sur le Calvaire en 642 la vraie croix que Chosroès, roi des Perses, avait enlevée 14 ans auparavant.'

Day of Federation (*The*), 14 July, 1790. The anniversary of the storming of the Bastille, when the people swore 'to defend the liberty of France.'

Day of Ferdinand (*The*), 27 May, 1800. By a most disgraceful trick, Napoleon Bonaparte persuaded the old king of Spain to abdicate, and then he set his own brother Joseph on the vacant throne. The Spaniards, disgusted at this treachery, rose as one man, massacred the French garrison at Madrid, and cut to pieces the squadron at Cadiz. This, of course, led to reprisals, and the result was the long Peninsular War (*q.v.*), so glorious to the Duke of Wellington, ending with the battle of Waterloo, 18 June, 1815, and the banishment of Napoleon to St. Helena.

Day of July (*The*). 'Journée de Juillet,' 14 July. Noted for the insurrection of the people of Paris in 1789, and the taking of the Bastille. Between 1790–1792 the anniversary was called the 'Fête de la Fédération. *See* 'Days of July.'

Day of New Cloaks (*The*). Old Christmas Day was at one time so called in France, from the custom of giving on that day a new robe to each courtier.

On Christmas Eve, 1245, the king [Louis IX.] bade all his court be present at early morning mass. At the chapel door each man received his new cloak, put it on, and went in. . . . As they rose, each man saw on his neighbour's shoulder the cross which betokened the crusading vow.— KITCHIN, *History of France*, vol. i. p. 328.

Day of Poniards (*The*), 28 Feb., 1791. The day of the attack on the prison of Vincennes (2 syl.), called 'the Second Bastille.' On this day a large number of courtiers rushed to the Tuileries to defend the king and royal family. Lafayette with the National Guards disarmed them, and they were very roughly handled by the mob. This day was called 'the Day of Poniards' because Marat, in his journal, *L'Ami du Peuple*, declared that 5,000 poniards had been manufactured in Paris for the use of the aristocrats against the patriots. A diligent search was made by order of the National Assembly, but only thirty-five poniards could be found, and those were for persons engaged in the slave trade.

A number of the king's friends . . . had flocked to the palace, as on the Day of Poniards.—HOWITT, *History of England* (George III., p. 418).

Day of Reason (*The*), 8 June, 1794. When the bishops and clergy of Paris, decorated with caps of liberty, renounced their sacerdotal office and publicly declared : ' We now abjure the trade of superstition, and are resolved henceforth to be men instead of Christians ; to own no temple but the sanctuary of the law ; no divinity but liberty ; no object of worship but our country ; and no gospel but the constitution.'

The Bishop of Moulines trampled on his cross and mitre, and, taking up a pike and cap of liberty, preached to the people that ' death is an eternal sleep.'

Day of Rest (*The*).
Christians set apart 1st day of the week (Sunday).

Greeks	"	2nd	"	"	(Monday).
Persians	"	3rd	"	"	(Tuesday).
Assyrians	"	4th	"	"	(Wednesday).
Egyptians and Jesids }	"	5th	"	"	(Thursday).
Turks	"	6th	"	"	(Friday).
Jews	"	7th	"	"	(Saturday).

See ' Sunday.'

Day of St. Ferdinand (*The*). A repetition of the ' Sicilian Vespers.' *See* ' Day of Ferdinand.'

Day of the Barricades. *See* ' Barricades.'

Day of the Bastille (*The*), 14 July, 1789. The day on which the Bastille was demolished by the French rabble.

Day of the Buræ (*The*). The first Sunday of Lent is so called by the Lotharingians, from the custom of carrying *bandons* or torches on that day, first observed in 1249. The day is known as the ' Buræ ;' hence we read such phrases as these :—' Die crastina burarum,' or ' Feria quinta post buras.' *See* ' Sunday.'

Day of the Camel (*The*), ± Nov., A.D. 657. The famous battle of Bassörah, in which Ali defeated Ayesha, Telha, and Zobeir. It was the first civil war of the Moslems, and received its name from the following circumstance : Ayesha, the prophet's widow, who hated Ali (son of Fatima), went to the battle on a camel, with seventy men to hold her bridle. All the seventy men were slain, and the cage or litter in which Ayesha rode was struck with so many darts and javelins that, as Gibbon says, it was like a porcupine with its quills.

Day of the Dupes (*The*), 11 Nov., 1630. Marie de Medicis, the queen mother, hating Richelieu, induced her son, Louis XIII., to dismiss him ; and the king, unable to resist his mother, commanded the cardinal to resign his portfolio. The lady was triumphant, her friends were loud in their congratulations, and all thought the influence of the queen mother was paramount. Next day Richelieu waited on the king to place in his hands the seals of office ; Louis relented, refused to accept the resignation, and Richelieu became more powerful than ever. This day is called in French history 'La Journée des Dupes.' The dupes were the queen mother, her younger son the Duke of Orleans, Michel and Louis de Marillac, and all their clique.

Day of the Millers (*The*). 'Journée des Farines,' 3 Jan., 1591. When some of the partisans of Henri IV., disguised as millers, attempted to get possession of the barrier de St. Honoré, in Paris, with the view of making themselves masters of the city. In this they failed.

Days. *See* also

Baronial days.	Red-letter days.
Black days.	Scarlet days.
Egyptian days.	Sundays.

Days in Banc. Days appointed by the courts, or fixed by statute, when process must be returned, or when parties served with writs are to make their appearance in full court.

Days of Grace. The three days beyond the time at which a 'bill' is actually due. Sunday, Good Friday, and Christmas Day do not count.

Days of Ill-name. 'Dies maledicti,' also called 'Dies Ægyptiaci' and 'Dies Ægri.' Two days in every month held unlucky by the Egyptians, because they fancied 'quod in aliqua hora dierum illorum non erat bonum sanguinare (id est sanguinem minuere), nec aliquod opus incipere.' On these days they would commence no new work, nor start on a journey. St. Augustine refers to this in his 'Commentary on Epistle to the Galatians,' chap. iv.

Days of July (*The*). 'Journées de Juillet,' the 27, 28, 29. When the people of Paris rose and drove Charles X. from the throne for suppressing the liberty of the press, 1830. *See* 'Day of July.'

Days of June (*The*), 5, 6. I. An émeute provoked in Paris by the Republicans at the funeral of Lamarque, deputy of the Opposition, 1832. Barricades were thrown up in the quarters of St. Antoine, St. Martin, St. Denis [*Sahn Dnee*], &c. The troops were called in, and on the 6th put down the disturbance by taking the church of St. Merry by storm.

II. 23, 24, 25, 26. A bloody insurrection by the party styled the 'Démocratique et Sociale' against the republic established in France 24 Feb., 1848. It was aroused by the dissolution of the ateliers nationaux. St. Jaques, St. Marceau, and St. Antoine were besieged, and it was only put down by calling out the soldiers under the direction of Cavaignac. Seven generals were killed, and Mgr. Affre (archbishop of Paris) was shot on the 25th, attempting to stop the slaughter. The loss of life was enormous, but the number of slain was not allowed to be published.

De Donis Conditionalibus (*Statute*). The statute of Westminster which established in England the power of creating an entail (13 Edw. I. c. 1).

De Eminenti, 1642. The bull of Urban VIII. against Jansen and his book 'Augustinus.'

De Hæretico Comburendo (*The*), 2 Hen. IV. c. 15, A.D. 1401. An Act forbidding all unlicensed preaching ; authorising bishops to arrest anyone suspected of propagating unsound doctrines; and all persons arrested were to be kept in prison till they abjured their errors, or in default thereof were to be handed over to the secular power, which 'shall forthwith do them to be burnt.' Repealed by 29 Car. II. c. 9, A.D. 1677.

William Sawtrey, a London clergyman, was the first to suffer. He was arrested by Archbishop Arundel, and burnt alive for refusing to adore the cross.

De Officiis. By Cicero, 1466. Printed by Fust and his son-in-law Peter Schœffer. The first secular book ever printed in moveable metal types. The three books previously printed were *Biblia Sacra Latina*, *Biblia Latina*, and *Psalmorum Codex*.

De Profundis. The first two words of the Psalm cxxx. in Latin, sung by Catholics in the funeral service.

Deacon. A deacon must be 22 years of age. His duties in the Greek and Latin Churches are : (1) to administer the alms to the poor, and to administer the Eucharist, but not to consecrate.

Deacons were prohibited from celebrating the Holy Communion by the Act of Uniformity (*q.v.*), 1662, 14 Car. II. c. 4.

Dead-cart (*The*). A cart which traversed London from nightfall to daybreak during the plague. It was accompanied by two men, one with a bell, and the other with a long pitchfork. The bell was rung from time to time to give notice that the cart was at hand, and when the dead were pushed into the street, they were tossed by the pitchfork into the cart, and carried to a great pit, where they were shot down wholesale (1665).

The pit in Aldgate was 40 feet by 16 feet, and 9 feet deep. Above 400 bodies were shot into it between the 6th and 20th of Sept.

Dead Hand (*The*). Mortmain, *i.e.* the possession of lands and tenements in 'dead hands,' or hands which cannot alienate.

These may have been his reasons for seeking the protection of the 'dead hand.'—H. HAYMAN, D.D.
A corporation is a 'dead hand' because it cannot alienate. So is the Church.

Dead's Part (*The*). That portion of the moveable estate of a deceased person which remains over, after satisfying the legal claims of wife and children. In Scotland the surplus is the only part which the deceased could dispose of by will or testament. Abolished by 19, 20 Vict. c. 94.

Dead Reckoning. A term in navigation, signifying the calculation of a ship's place at sea, made independently of celestial observations.

Dead Weight Annuity (*The*). 4 Geo. IV. c. 22. Military and naval pensions, and pensions given to civil supernumeraries. They expired in 1867.

Dead Woman Crowned (*A*), 1357. Ines de Castro, wife of Pedro (I.) of Portugal. Pedro had clandestinely married Ines de Castro, and his father Affonso, king of Portugal, had her privately assassinated. In 1357 Affonso died, and Pedro succeeded to the crown. He then had the corpse disinterred, sumptuously arrayed, and crowned. Pedro stood beside the corpse, and the nobles did homage to it by kissing the hand. The ceremony being over, the dead body was restored to its sepulchre again.

Dean. In Oxford University; the title of the master of Christ Church, which is a cathedral.

Dean Ireland Exegetical Professorship (*The*). In Oxford University. Stipend 800*l.* a year. Founded by Dr. John Ireland, of Oriel College, dean of Westminster, 1847.

Dean Ireland's Scholarships. Four for Latin and Greek, tenable for four years. Founded in the University of

11

Oxford by Dr. John Ireland, of Oriel College, dean of Westminster, in 1825.

Dean of Faculty (*The*). President of the incorporation of advocates or barristers in Scotland ; elected annually.

Dean of Guild. In Scotch burghs was head of the mercantile body called the 'Guild brethren.' At one time he was a judge in mercantile and maritime causes within the burgh, but is now a kind of city edile.

Dean of University College, London. The principal or head of a faculty chosen for a limited period.

Deans (*Honorary*). Without jurisdiction, such as the dean of the Chapel Royal, of St. James's Palace, &c.

Deans (*Rural*). Are deputies of the bishop, planted all round his diocese, to inspect the conduct of the parochial clergy, inquire into and report dilapidations, and armed with judicial authority in matters not of serious importance.

Deans of Chapters. Are either of cathedral or collegiate churches. Such as the dean of Canterbury and the dean of St. Paul's, who are governors over the canons. It is a crown appointment, and the dean must reside eight months in the year, and may hold a living with his deanery. The office in Durham is worth 3,000*l.* a year ; of St. Paul's, of Westminster, of York, and of Manchester is worth 2,000*l.* a year; of most other cathedrals about 1,000*l.* a year ; but from agricultural depression in the last ten years (1890) the value of all church benefices dependent on tithes has much depreciated.

Deans of Peculiars, or 'Deans in Peculiar.' Have sometimes jurisdiction and cure of souls, and sometimes jurisdiction only. Of this nature is the dean of Battle in Sussex, founded by William I., the dean of Westminster, the dean of the chapel of St. George of Windsor, and the dean of King's Chapel. The following have jurisdiction but no cure of souls, viz. the dean of Arches in London, the dean of Bocking in Essex, the dean of Croydon in Surrey, and the dean of Christ Church, Oxford.

Deans of Provinces, or 'Deans of Bishops.' Like the bishop of London, who is ' dean of the province of Canter-

R

bury.' The archbishop sends to him his mandate for summoning the bishops of his province when a convocation is to be assembled.

Deans of the Chapel Royal (*The*). In Scotland there are three such deans appointed by the crown; the duties are quite nominal, being limited to an occasional sermon before the sovereign when in the neighbourhood.

Deasy's Act, 1860. An Irish land act, which reduced the question to a mere matter of contract. So that the tenant's house, the out-offices, the fences and drains, made or paid for by the tenant, were the property of the landlord. This continued till 1870, when an act was passed to provide compensation for improvements and prevent capricious evictions.

Death Rate. The number of inhabitants at present on the earth is 1,300 millions.

The *annual* death rate is 33 millions; 92 thousand daily: nearly 4 thousand every hour,* 60 every minute, and 1 every second.

Only 1 in 1,000 reach the age of 100, 1 in 500 reach the age of 80, 6 in 1,000 reach the age of 65.

   * In round numbers: More exact, 33,033,033 die annually, 91,824 daily, 3,730 hourly.

Death with Music. Leopold I., the kaiser (1658–1705), on his death-bed requested that the court musicians might be introduced, that he might die to the sounds of sweet music. Mirabeau's last words were 'Let me die to the sounds of delicious music.'

Deaths (*Registration of*). *See* 'Registration,' &c.

Debarring. In the Scotch church, means excluding from communion all those deemed by the minister and his lieutenants unworthy to 'partake of that feast.'

Debased Style (*The*), 1600. Applied to architecture means that which followed the Reformation period. Called debased, because the designs were inferior to the previous styles, and the execution by no means good. There was no unity, but different schools and different periods were mixed together.

   The first was the Early English or Lancet style, the second the Decorated, the third the Florid or Perpendicular, and the fourth the Debased.

Debateable Land (*The*). 'The space between the Esk and the Sark, bounded on the third side by the march dike. It seems properly to belong to Scotland, but having been disputed by both crowns, was styled "The Debateable Land." In the reign of James VI. (I. of England) Sir Richard Graham, obtaining from the Earl of Cumberland a lease of this tract, bought it of James, and got it united to the county of Cumberland.' (Pennant, 'Tour in Scotland,' vol. ii. p. 82.)

Decadence. In *ancient* art applied to works subsequent to the reign of Augustus. In *modern* art the term is applied to the post-renaissant period, or the rococo style introduced in the reign of Louis XV.

   In Greece the term is applied to art subsequent to the time of Periclés, the turning point of Greek art. In England art reached its lowest point in the reign of George IV.

Dec'adists. Those who observed the new French Calendar introduced by Fabre d'Eglantine in 1793. So-called because the year was divided into decades (10 days instead of weeks), the 10th decade being called *décadi*.

   There were 860 decades in a year, and these made up 360 days, the odd 5 (to make up 365 days) were called Sans-culottides, or holidays for the sans-culottes or operatives.

Decalcea'ti, 1570. The barefooted friars. They were Augustine and Franciscan friars of the stricter rule, which forbade the wearing of boots or shoes.

Deccan (*i. e.* the south). The country between the river Nerbuddah and the river Krishna.

Decelæan War (*The*), B.C. 413. Decelëa was a demus of Attica on the borders of Bœōtia. In the nineteenth year of the Peloponnesian war (B.C. 413) the Peloponnesians, under Agis, seized and fortified the demus, and thereby greatly annoyed the Athenians. It was held till the close of the Peloponnesian war (B.C. 404).

December 25. The time of the winter solstice has been held in high festival by well nigh all the nations of the earth, and probably our festival of the Nativity was fixed to this day in order to divert a long and general pagan practice to the birth of Christ in Bethlehem. The 25 Dec. was chosen for the festival in the reign of Antonīnus Pius

(138–161), and is attributed to Telesphŏrus.

CHINA.—The birth of Buddha, son of Mâya, is celebrated 25 Dec.—BUNSEN, *The Angel Messiah*; LILLIE, *Buddha and Buddhism*, p. 73.

DRUIDS.—The festival called 'Nolagh' was celebrated at the winter solstice.—HIGGINS, *Anacalypsis*, vol. ii. p. 99.

EGYPT.—Horus, son of Isis, is said to have been born at the close of Dec.—M. LE CLERK DE SEPTEHENES, *Religion of the Ancient Greeks*, p. 214; BONWICK, *Egyptian Belief*, p. 157.

GREECE.—The birth of Demēter (*Cerēs*), Dionysos (*Bacchus*), and Herāklês (*Hercules*), were all celebrated during the winter solstice. Just as that of Osiris was in Egypt. The Greeks called 25 Dec. 'The Triple Night.'—*Religion of the Ancient Greeks*, p. 213; *Anacalypsis*, vol. ii. p. 99.

INDIA.—Monier Williams (*Hindústan*, p. 181) tells us that numerous Indian tribes keep Yule as a religious festival, decorate their houses with garlands, and make presents to their friends at this festal season.

MEXICO.—The festival called 'Capacrame' was held in the winter solstice.—*Hist Indies*, vol. ii. p. 354.

ROME.—The festival called 'Natālis Solis Invicti' was celebrated on 25 Dec. with public games.—Rev. J. B. GROSS, *The Heathen Religion*, p. 287.

PERSIA.—The great festival in honour of the birth of Mithras was at the same period—*Celtic Druids*, p. 163; GROSS, &c., p. 287.

SCANDINAVIA.—The festival called Jul, in honour of Freyr, son of Odin, was our Yule.

GERMANY.—The Yule-feast; the French Noël, the Scandinavian Jul, the Druidical Nolagh.

. On this day [25 Dec.] the birth of Christ was lately fixed at Rome, in order that, while the heathen were busy with their profane ceremonies, Christians might perform their holy rites undisturbed.—CHRYSOSTOM.

December Laws (*The*), 1867, which gave to Hungary its present form of government.

Decembrists (in Russian history), 1825. Revolutionists who, at the death of Czar Alexander I., on 1 Dec., tried to introduce a constitutional government in Russia. This revolution was headed by some of the chief military and naval officers in the empire. It came to naught, and multitudes were imprisoned for long periods. Thus Colonel Battenkoff was imprisoned in the fortress of Petropavlovsk, in St. Petersburg, from Dec. 1825 to Feb. 1846, when he was exiled to West Siberia.

Decemviral Tribunal (*The*). Of Venice. Called in English the 'Council of the Ten,' or 'The Ten' (*q.v.*).

Decemvirs (*The*), or Council of Ten, B.C. 451. Appointed both to administer justice, conduct the government, and command the armies of Rome, as well as to draw up a new body of laws. Their code was called 'The Twelve Tables,' or *Leges Duodecim Tabularum*, the Magna Charta of old Rome. Abolished B.C. 449.

There were ten curators of the Sibylline Books called the *Decemviri*. Originally the curators were only two, called the *Duumviri*, appointed by King Tarquin. The number was increased to ten by the Licinian Laws, B.C. 366. Sulla added five more B.C. 82, and Julius Cæsar in about B.C. 46 augmented the number to sixteen.

Decided (*The*). A secret society sprung from the Carbonāri after the unsuccessful outbreak of 24 June, 1817. They were the Guelphs of the papal states, the republican 'Brother Protectors' of France, the 'Adelphi' of Piedmont, and the 'Society of the Black Pin.'

Decimation Tax (*The*), 1654. 'That all who had ever borne arms for the king, or had declared themselves to be of the royal party, should be decimated; that is, should pay a tenth part of all the estate which they had left to support the charge which the commonwealth was put to by the unquietness of their temper, and the just cause of jealousy which they had administered.'

The decimation tax was denounced as unjust, because it was a violation of the Act of Oblivion (*q.v.*).—DR LINGARD, *Hist. of Eng.* viii. 7.

Declaration for refuting Four Scandals (*A*), 6 Dec., 1662. The four scandals which Charles II. abjured were these :—

I. That the Act of Indemnity was intended to be merely temporary.

II. That he intended to keep a large standing army.

III. That he was a persecutor.

IV. That he favoured popery.

Declaration at the Savoy, London (*The*), 29 Sept., 1658. A declaration of faith drawn up by the Independents in the Savoy, London; not unlike the Confession of Faith of the divines at Westminster. The chief difference is in the church government, which is wholly democratic.

The Church of England is governed by parliament and bishops, assisted by the deans and other ecclesiastics. The Presbyterian Church is governed by the presbyter and elders. The Independents leave all government to the discretion of each individual congregation.

Declaration of Breda, in Holland (*The*), 1660. In which Charles II., then in exile, promised a general amnesty to all concerned in the parliamentary wars, religious toleration, and satisfaction to the army. Sometimes called the 'Declaration from Breda.' There was this proviso—'unless parliament in its wisdom sees fit to determine otherwise.'

Declaration of Charles II.

(*The*). I. 25 Oct., 1660. A declaration having for its professed objects ' the promotion of godliness, the encouragement of public and private religious services, the observance of the Lord's day, and the holiness of ministers.' It promised that all holy offices should be filled with holy men, that confirmation should be carefully performed, that bishops should have no civil power, that the liturgy should be revised, that the cross in baptism and bowing at the name of Jesus should be left free, and that only the oaths of allegiance and supremacy should be required, without subscription and canonical obedience.

II. *For the Settlement of Ireland,* 28 Nov., 1660. Whereby soldiers and adventurers who had been planted on the estates of the Irish by the Commonwealth were to retain them, except they had belonged to persons who had remained entirely neuter in the civil war. In such cases the soldiers and adventurers were to give back the estates to the Irish, and were to receive compensation from the ' fund of reprisals.'

Declaration of Cromwell (*The*),

1654. Forbidding any clergyman or fellow of a college to preach, be an instructor of youth, or administer the sacraments, under pain of imprisonment or exile. This prohibition continued in force till the Restoration.

Declaration of Dunfermline

(*The*), 1650. In this instrument Charles II. was called upon by the Scotch presbytery to lament his father's opposition to the work of God and to the ' Solemn League and Covenant ' (*q.v.*), which opposition had caused the blood of the Lord's people to be shed. He was called upon also to deplore the idolatry of his mother, the toleration of which in the king's house could not fail to provoke the anger of a jealous God, who visits the sins of the fathers on the children. He declared that he subscribed the covenant in sincerity of heart, and would in future have no friends but those who were friends to the covenant, and that such friends should in no wise be held his enemies. He acknowledged the sinfulness of the treaty with the bloody rebels of Ireland, which he now declared to be null and void. He de-

clared his detestation of both popery and prelacy, as well as of idolatry and heresy, schism and profaneness. He promised to reform the Church of England and conform it to the Church of Scotland, according to a plan to be drawn out by the Assembly of the Divines of Westminster.

Declaration of George I.,

in 1728. George I. was a Lutheran, and in order to conform church and state to his own views, prohibited the clergy touching on politics in their sermons, but allowed Convocation to transact ecclesiastical business and make church canons.

Declaration of Independence

(*The*). Signed 4 July, 1776, by the American Congress, declaring the ' United States of North America' independent and separated entirely from the British crown. The Independence was acknowledged by France 16 Jan., 1778, and by Holland 19 April, 1782 ; provisional articles of peace were signed by England 3 Sept., 1782. The Declaration was drawn up by Thomas Jefferson, of Virginia ; John Adams, of Massachusetts; Roger Sherman, of Connecticut ; Robert R. Livingstone, of New York ; and Benjamin Franklin, of Pennsylvania. It was signed by eleven states, and the name American Colonies was changed into ' The United States ' (of North America).

Provisional articles of peace were signed by England at Paris 3 Sept., 1782; the definitive treaty was signed at Paris 3 Sept., 1783 ; and John Adams was received by George III. as ambassador of the United States 2 June, 1785.

Declaration of Indulgence

(*The*). I. 26 Dec., 1672. Published by *Charles II.* of England, ' by virtue of his ecclesiastical powers, suspending all penal laws against Nonconformists. The real object was to legalise the Catholic religion. In virtue of this edict John Bunyan left his prison at Bedford. The declaration was a mere political ruse whereby the ' traitor king ' hoped to play into the hands of Louis XIV., and it was immediately followed by a dissolution of the triple alliance against France, and a declaration of war with Holland. The Commons, suspecting the villainy of the king, passed the Test Act ; and the Duke of York, the Lord High Treasurer, and many high officers in the army, were obliged to retire from public life.

For the Declaration in the reign of James II. *see* p. 245.

II. 8 April, 1687, by *James II.* He removed the oaths and penalties from Dissenters, that Roman Catholics might be eligible to places of emolument and influence on his privy council, the two houses of parliament, the corporations, universities, the church, and even in the army and navy. It ran thus:—'We have thought fit, by virtue of our royal prerogative, to issue forth this our Declaration of Indulgence, making no doubt of the concurrence of our two houses of parliament when we shall think it convenient for them to meet.' *See* 'Declaration of Indulgence 1688.'

III. 1688, by *James II.* Commanding the bishops to instruct their clergy to read in their respective churches, in London on 20 May, and elsewhere on 27 May, the Declaration of 1687, with this additional clause, stating the king's unalterable resolution to secure to his subjects 'freedom of conscience for ever,' and of rendering merit henceforth the sole qualification for office. *See* 'Seven Bishops.'

Declaration of Jamestown

(The), 1650. By ten Irish bishops and ten other clergymen, charging Ormond, the lord-lieutenant, with negligence, incapacity, and perfidy. They protested, however, that although they were compelled to withdraw from the government of the king's viceroy, they had no intention of disputing the royal supremacy; but under present circumstances the Irish were no longer bound by the articles of pacification. Next day they appended a form of excommunication against all those who abetted either Ormond or Ireton, in opposition to the interests of the Catholic confederacy.

Declaration of Liberty of Conscience

(The), 27 April, 1688. Ordered to be read in all churches, 4 May. Seven bishops (*q.v.*) petitioned against the order May 18, and were committed to the Tower June 8. This Declaration, sometimes called a 'Declaration of Indulgence,' annulled the penal laws against Roman Catholics as well as against Nonconformists, and abrogated the Test Act. The object of James II. was to introduce popery, and to appoint papists to all offices of state, magistracies, and military posts.

Declaration of Rights *(The)*.

I. Tendered by the Convention to William and Mary, and accepted 13 Feb., 1689. This Declaration set forth how King James II. tried to subvert the laws and liberties of the kingdom by levying money without consent of parliament, by persecuting those who petitioned him, by keeping a standing army in time of peace, by violating freedom of election, by returning corrupt jurors, by excessive bail, fines, and punishments. And 'they do claim and insist on all and singular the premises, as their undoubted rights and liberties.' The Declaration, being accepted, was formed into a 'Bill of Rights.'

II. Sept. 1774. Passed by the first American Congress, which met in Carpenters' Hall, Philadelphia. It was attended by deputies secretly sent from twelve different states. The Declaration set forth that the colonists had lost neither the rights of nature nor the privileges of Englishmen by emigration, and consequently, that the late acts of the British Parliament were gross violations of their rights, especially as affecting Massachusetts. They resolved, therefore, to suspend all imports, or all use of imported goods, till harmony was restored between Great Britain and her American colonies.

III. May, 1776 (United States) :—

I. All men are born equally free, possessing natural rights which no compact can deprive them of.
II. All power is vested in the people, from whom it is derived.
III. The people have an inalienable and indefeasible right to reform, alter, or abolish any form of government at their pleasure.
IV. The idea of an hereditary first magistrate is unnatural and absurd. [True, but popular elections are great evils.]

Declaration of Sports *(The)*,

1617. Issued by James I. of England, to signify his pleasure that on Sundays, after divine service, 'no lawful recreation shall be barred to his good people. Nonconformists and others not attending divine service at church shall be prohibited from taking any part in the sports, nor shall anyone be allowed to go out of his own parish.' The sports specified in the Declaration as fit for Sunday are 'dancing, archery, leaping, vaulting, May-games, morrice-dances, and the setting-up of May-poles;' but bear and bull baiting, bowling, and interludes were forbidden. Charles I. (1633)

also caused the Declaration to be read from the pulpit of parish churches.

Declaration of Toleration
(*The*), 15 March, 1672. Suspending all penal laws on account of religion ; promising licences and places of worship to Protestants, provided they met together with open doors; and granting liberty of private worship to all papists.

Declaration of Vienna (*The*),
13 March, 1815. An act published by the allies declaring Napoleon I. an outlaw.

Declaration of the Clergy.
'Déclaration du Clergé' 'or 'Libertés Gallicanes.' Insisting on a distinction between spiritual and temporal power ; and placing infallibility not in the pope, but in the whole episcopal body united under the pope. This Declaration furthermore recognised the supreme authority of the general councils and of the sacred canons. As drawn up by Bossuet in 1682 it may be thus summarised :—

Que l'église doit être régie par les canons; que saint Pierre et ses successeurs n'ont reçu de puissance que sur les choses spirituelles ; que les règles et les constitutions admises dans le royaume doivent être maintenues, et les bornes posées par nos pères demeurer inébranlables ; que les décrets et jugements du pape ne sont irréformables qu'autant que le consentement de l'église est intervenu, &c.

Declaration of the Rights of Man (*The*).
In French history. 1 Oct., 1789. Adopted by the Assemblée Constituante of Paris, setting forth all the new liberties, equality of imposts, and the eligibility of anyone and everyone to public offices. Called in French, ' La Déclaration des droits de l'homme et du citoyen.' It was drawn up by Comte Emanuel Sieyès, better known as l'Abbé Sieyès.

The Abbé Sieyès was a monarchist, and declared a monarchy to be more favourable to liberty than a republic. He opposed the licentiousness of the press, declined sitting in the Convention, opposed the Jacobins throughout, and declared that the Convention could not constitutionally try Louis XVI. for his life, because such a proceeding would make the Convention both accuser and judge. Sieyès was one of the few prominent men who survived the Revolution, and died in his bed at the age of 88.

Declaratory Act (*The*), 1766.
An act declaratory of the supreme power of parliament over the colonies. This act the Americans objected to, although the Stamp Act was repealed.

Decorated English, 1275–1375.
In architecture ; succeeded the Early English or Lancet style. It is more ornamental, and the principal lines run pyramidically rather than horizontally or vertically.

Decoration or Memorial Day,
30 May. An annual holiday in the United States of America to honour those deceased soldiers of the north who took part in the war between the Federals and Confederates. The cemeteries are visited and decorated with wreaths of flowers.

In the extreme south, where spring comes in earlier, an earlier day is taken.

Decree of Berlin (*The*), 21 Nov.,
1806. Also called the Continental System, which declared the British Isles in a state of siege, and prohibited all commerce and correspondence with the hated nation. Every Englishman found in a country occupied by France was declared a prisoner of war. All merchandise belonging to an Englishman was lawful prize. All trading in British goods was forbidden. And, by a subsequent addition to this decree, all English goods, wherever found, were to be burnt.

Decree of Fontainebleau (*The*),
18 Oct., 1810. Ordering that all English goods wherever found should be burnt in all countries directly or indirectly belonging to France.

Decree of 3 Ventôse, Year III.
(*The*), 21 Feb., 1795. The state undertakes to pay salaries to the Catholic clergy ; but any persons may freely exercise any other form of religious worship, provided they violate no law, and pay their own expenses. *See* the 'Law of Germinal.'

Decretals.
The second volume of the canon law, containing the responses of sundry popes and church councils to questions put to them. The first collection was made by Dionysius Exiguus somewhere about 550 ; but what is generally understood by the word is the compilation made by Gratian, a Benedictine monk, in 1151. This was supplemented by Pope Gregory IX. about a century later, and the supplement was called *Extra*. Boniface VIII. supplied a sixth volume, called *Sexte*, and the letters of Clement V., called *Clementines*, make two more volumes. The last volume, called *Extravagantes* contains the decisions of the popes between Urban IV. and Sixtus IV. both included. *See* ' False Decretals.'

Decretum of Gratian (*The*), 1151. A compilation by Gratian, an Italian monk, of canons, papal epistles, and patristic sentences, arranged into titles and chapters, like the Pandects.

This decretum gives authority to the False Decretals of Isidore. It was supplemented in 1234 by the decretals of Raimond de Pennafort, which consist almost entirely of the rescripts issued by the later popes, especially Alexander III., Innocent III., Honorius III., and Gregory IX. The decretum is nearly obsolete.

Dec'uman Gate (*The*). The rearward gate of a camp. The opposite or front gate was the prætorian gate. In a Roman camp there were always four gates. The *prætorian* gate faced the enemy; the decuman gate was the furthest from the enemy, and was called *dec'uman*, because the tenth legion were posted near it. The gate on the right side of the camp was the *porta principalis dextra*, and the one opposite to it on the left side was *porta principalis sinistra*.

Decŭmus is another spelling of *decimus* (tenth), as maxŭmus is of *maximus*.

Dee's Speculum (*Dr.*). In which persons were told they could see their friends in distant lands, and how they were occupied. It is generally said that this speculum was a ' polished piece of cannel coal,' but this is a mistake, as it was a piece of solid pink-tinted glass about the size of an orange. It is now in the British Museum.

Deed-bote. Amends for misdeeds, sometimes substantial and sometimes only chastisement or punishment; satisfaction. (*Dæd-bót*, an act of atonement.)

Confession, restitution, deed-bote, and penance were strictly enforced [by St. Dunstan].—*Early English Church.*

Deemsters. In the Isle of Man. There are two judges so called, whose courts are held weekly, alternately at Douglas and Castletown, by the deemster of the *southern* division, and at Ramsey and Peel (or Kirk Michael) by the deemster of the *northern* division. An appeal from the deemster's judgment may be made to the staff of government.

In the Isle of Man and in Jersey, deemsters decide disputes without process or charge. They are chosen by the contending parties (Ang.-Sax., *dema*, an umpire). At one time there was a deemster, or demster, attached to the High Court of Justiciary in Scotland, who pronounced the ' doom ' or sentence

of condemned persons ; the office was attached to the executioner, but has been long abolished.

Referred to in Scott's ' Old Mortality ' and ' Heart of Mid-Lothian.'

Deev-bend (devil-binder). Tah-Omars was so called from his victories over his enemies (deevs). A mythic shah of Persia placed B.C. 870–840. His successor was his nephew, the famous Jam-sched.

Defender of the Faith. I. John de Torquemada (1388–1468). He was a Dominican, born at Valladŏlid, and received in 1437 the honour of ' Defender of the Faith' from the Council of Basle. He denounced the heresies of Wyclif and of Huss. He was finally made a cardinal.

II. 'Fidĕi Defensor,' 1521. A title conferred by Leo X. on Henry VIII. of England in grateful acknowledgment of a book written in Latin against Martin Luther, entitled ' A Defence of the Seven Sacraments' (*Assertio Septem Sacramentorum adversus Martinum Lutherium*). The pope subsequently withdrew the title, but in the thirty-fifth year of the king's reign the parliament legally confirmed it, and it still remains.

The title had been assumed by Richard II. in his proclamation against Wyclif. Henry IV. in 1411 had been styled ' The Chief Defender of the Orthodox Faith,' and Henry III. was called ' Defender of the Church.' The bull of Leo X. was preserved by Sir Robert Cotton, and is signed by the pope, 4 bishop-cardinals, 15 priest-cardinals, and 8 deacon-cardinals. Henry's book is now in the Vatican, and contains this inscription in the king's handwriting: 'Anglorum rex Henricus Leoni X. mittit hoc opus et fidei testem et amicitiæ.'

* The title ' Defender of the Faith ' seems to have been given to advocates of ecclesiastical suits who defended the Church against those who opposed its doctrines, rules, and discipline.

Defenders. I. A.D. 407. Ecclesiastical history. Church officers. In 420 one or more were appointed to each patriarchal church.

II. 1690. An Irish secret association formed after the battle of the Boyne in defence of the Catholics. Opposed by the Orangists. They were very active in the uprisings between 1798–1803.

III. 1795. An Irish Roman Catholic association organised in self-defence against the Peep-o'-Day Boys, a Presbyterian association which arose in Ireland in 1790. In 1688 all the Catholic property of Ireland was confiscated. In the latter part of the 18th cent. some attempts were made to ameliorate this injustice, and the Protestants of the north clamouring for 'Protestant ascendency' associated themselves into a society called 'The Peep-o'-Day Boys,' whose object was to maintain the Protestant ascendency, and resist all Catholic encroachment. The Roman Catholics then organised themselves into a society called 'The Defenders,' and collisions became common, but the principal aggressions of the Defenders were nocturnal plunder, house-breaking, and murder. In 1795 a pitched battle was fought in the county of Armagh, attended with much bloodshed. Ultimately the Defenders amalgamated with the United Irishmen (*q.v.*), and the great opponents were the Orangemen, a Protestant association. *See* 'Irish Associations.'

The battle of the Diamond, in which the Catholics of Ireland sustained great loss, was fought 21 Sept., 1725, and the first Orange lodge was formed later in the same day.

Defenestration of Prague (*The*), 23 May, 1618. That is, the ejection out of windows by the Bohemians. The Bohemians had two Protestant churches, one in the diocese of Prague, and the other in the territory of the abbot of Braunau. The archbishop of Prague and the abbot pulled down these reformed churches, and when the Protestants remonstrated they were told it was the king's pleasure. So Count Thurn of Bohemia headed a deputation which went to the royal castle of Prague to lay their grievance before the king. Being admitted into the council hall, they were so insolently received that they *threw* two of the councillors and the king's private secretary *out of the windows* into the moat. This was the beginning of the Thirty Years' War.

Precisely the same thing occurred at Prague in 1419, when someone from the royal castle threw a stone at a procession of Bohemian reformers. Instantly a rush was made into the council hall, and thirteen of the magistrates were thrown out of the windows into the streets.

Degree of Meridian. First measured by Eratosthênês between Syênê and Alexandria, about B.C. 196; next by Posidonius between Alexandria and Rhodes, A.D. 112–150; then by the brothers Ben Shaku by order of the calif Al Mamûn, on the plain south of Damascus, A.D. 813–833. It was measured from London to York by Norwood in 1633–1635. It was measured in France by the Abbé Picard, between Amiens and Malvoisine,

in 1669–1671. It was measured in Lapland by Maupertius, Clairaut, and others in 1735; in Peru by Bouguer and others in 1735; at the Cape of Good Hope by Lacaille in 1752.

Dei Gratia. Introduced into English charters in 1106. It continued in the British coinage up to 1849, when it was discontinued in the florins, thence called the 'graceless florins.' These coins were recalled the same year, and the letters D.G. were restored.

It is in reality a relic of the exploded doctrine of the 'divine right of kings.' Thus M.N. is king by divine right, or *Dei gratia*, and not by human appointment, or *hominum gratia*.

Deilemites. *See* 'Di'-le-mites.'

De'ipassia'ni or 'Patripassionists.' Certain Unitarians who maintained that God is one and indivisible, and denied the three personalities of the Trinity. Hence, said they, the being crucified on Calvary was not God the Son (for there is no such being), but God the Father, or the one and only God. St. Augustine refers to these 'heretics.'

Dek'abrist. A Decembrist, from Dekaber, the Russian for December. It denotes those persons who suffered death or captivity for the part they took in the military conspiracy which broke out in St. Petersburg in December 1825, on the accession of Czar Nicholas to the throne.

Delaval Papers (*The*). A large collection of letters, state papers, and old records belonging to the Delaval family of Seaton Delaval, discovered by John Robinson in 1888 in certain store-rooms of the disused Royal Northumberland Glass Works, Hartley, near Seaton Delaval Hall, and presented to the museum of the Society of Antiquaries. See 'Notes and Queries,' 1889, May 25, pp. 415, 416.

Delaware (Pennsylvania). The English name of an Indian tribe (the Lenäpe) with which William Penn chiefly negotiated.

Delaware (U.S. North America). A river and a state so called from Lord Delaware, governor of Virginia under James I. He rendered the colony great services (died 1618). The nickname of the inhabitants of this state is *Musk-rats*.

Visited by Lord Delaware in 1610; was settled by Swedes in 1627; passed to the Dutch in 1655; was ceded to England in 1664; made into a separate colony in 1704 (but was attached to Pennsylvania); and became one of the United States 'n 1776.

Delegates (*The High Court of*), 1533. Established by Act of Parliament (25 Hen. VIII. c. 19) as a tribunal of appeal from the Ecclesiastical and Admiralty Court. The jurisdiction was transferred to the Privy Council in 1832 (2, 3 Will. IV. c. 92).

Delegation (*The*), 1867. A body of delegates in the Austro-Hungarian kingdom, in which both states are equally represented; the house acts in matters which affect both the kingdoms, such as relations with foreign countries, army and navy, peace and war, &c. Besides this house each kingdom has its own legislative chambers, consisting of an upper and lower house.

Delenda est Carthago. Carthage must be destroyed, or wiped out of the nations of the earth. The words with which old Cato used to finish his speeches. Alexander said to the same effect, ' No world two suns can bear '—that is, Persia and Macedonia cannot both exist together. Napoleon said that London must be stamped out.

Delicate Investigation (*The*), 1806. This was a closed-door investigation by the four lords, Erskine, Grenville, Spencer, and Ellenborough, into the conduct of the Princess Caroline, cousin and wife of George, prince regent of Wales, with the view of a separation for alleged adultery. The real cause of offence was the intimacy of the prince with Lady Jersey, whose dismissal, demanded by Caroline, was refused. The four lords gave a very unsatisfactory verdict of ' Undue levity,' and the princess was banished from the receptions at Windsor. A trial was afterwards arranged, called ' a Bill of Pains and Penalties,' 1820. Denman and Brougham undertook the defence, and the Bill was abandoned—*i.e.* the queen was acquitted —in November. She was refused admission into Westminster Hall at the coronation of her husband (July 1821) and died the following August.

Delight of Mankind (*The*). Titus the Roman emperor (40, 79–81).

Delinquents, 1641. Those proceeded against for having exercised illegal powers in levying arbitrary taxes, and in the sentences of the Star Chamber, High Commission, and so on.

There was an order of Parliament directing the confiscation of their estates. In this order certain bishops and other of the clergy are named. We constantly find them coupled with Papists.

Della Crusca (*L'Accademia*), or ' Della Cruscan School,' 1582. Instituted at Florence; but in 1785 a number of English residents at Florence assumed the name of ' Della Cruscans,' and amused themselves by writing verses which they published in the ' Florence Miscellany.' These verses were conspicuous for affectation and insipidity, but got introduced into two daily English newspapers, ' The World ' and ' The Oracle.' Gifford says the epidemic spread ' from fool to fool '; but in 1794 Gifford's ' Baviad,' and in 1796 his ' Mæviad,' so mauled these simpletons that the name of ' Della Cruscan ' became a by-word for literary puerility.

Gifford's Della Cruscan bookworm, who ' lives upon a *whilome* for a week,' has become proverbial.

Delphine Classics (*The*), 1670–1680. ' In usum Delphini.' The chief Latin authors, edited by Pierre Huet for the French dauphin. They contain, in the margin of the text, the ' interpretatio ' in italic type, and at the bottom of each page a commentary which explains every allusion and difficulty. At the close is a verbal concordance of great value, added chiefly by the Daciers (husband and wife).

They were republished by Valpy in 183 volumes, 1819–1830.

Delta of 'Blackwood's Magazine' was David Macbeth Moir, 1798–1851. He was author of ' Casa Wappy.'

Deluge. *See* 'Flood.'

Demagogische Umtriebe, 1817. An attempt of demagogues in Germany to stir up the people against the governments. In 1819 a committee was appointed to examine into it, and in 1834 a tribunal of arbitration was constituted.

Democratic Labour Association, 1890. Organised by Michael Davitt in Ireland, in opposition to Mr. Parnell's notion of peasant proprietorship. Davitt insists that there should be neither landlords nor proprietors of land, under any kind of denomination, whether farmers or independent gentlefolk, but that the people of the soil have each a natural right to ' a man's full share ' of the land, which he has as much right to take from the farmer proprietor as from the landed proprietor. Mr. Parnell's platform is that farmers should be proprietors, not tenants. *See* 'Irish Associations.'

Démocratique et Sociale. *See* 'Days of June, II.,' p. 240.

Democritus Junior. Rev. Robert Burton, author of the 'Anatomy of Melancholy' (1576–1640).

Demon of the South (*The*). Philip II. of Spain (1527, 1555–1598).

Demosthenês (*The High-born*). William the Silent, prince of Orange.

The High-born Demosthenês electrified large assemblies by his indignant invectives against the Spanish Philip, 1568.—MOTLEY, *The Dutch Republic*, pt. iii. 2.

Demosthenes of America (*The*). Daniel Webster, the statesman. Like Demosthenês, he was neither florid nor impassioned, but he reasoned with irresistible force, and his language was terse, well chosen, and telling. He had the power of sarcasm, but seldom used it. His face, figure, and voice made him master of his audience.

Demosthenes of France (*The*). Comte de Mirabeau (1749–1791); also called 'The Hurricane,' from the overpowering force of his eloquence and irresistible audacity. He was so corpulent that he was jocosely called the *Tub*.

Demosthenes of the Pulpit. Dr. Thomas Rennell, dean of Westminster, was so called by William Pitt (1753–1840).

Demy' (plu. *Demies*). A 'scholar' of Magdalen College, Oxford.

Denmark, *i.e.* dain-mark. Dain means *flat*, hence the German *danieder*, on the ground, &c. The Danskir occupied the flat or low lands between Gothland hills and the sea.

Denyer and Johnson Scholarships. Two for theology. Value 50*l.* a year each, tenable for one year. Founded in Oxford University from the revenue of the scholarship founded by John Johnson, D.D., fellow of Magdalen College, and the prizes offered by Mrs. Denyer for two theological essays. Incorporated in 1878.

Denys (*St.*). Martyred 251. The tradition is that after being beheaded he walked from Paris four miles to found an abbey, where now stands the town of St. Denys, carrying with him his head under his arm, and resting seven times on the way at equal distances to bless and console his followers. Crosses were erected at these seven places, and it was long customary to lay the dead which passed by on one of these crosses for a few minutes.

St. Denys, pronounce *Sahn dnee.*

Deodand. A chattel or chattels forfeited as a peace-offering to God for causing the death of a human being, as when a brick or tile falls on him, or the wheel of a cart runs over him. When the forfeit was transferred from the church to the crown, instead of the chattel being forfeited, a money-fine was imposed. Abolished 18 Aug., 1846 (6, 10 Vict. c. 62).

Deontology, 1830. Jeremy Bentham's system of the science of morality or *Maxima felicitas* doctrine. *Deon*, a Greek word, means 'right' or 'fit,' and the great aim of deontology is to secure the 'greatest happiness to the greatest number.' There can be no doubt that Bentham was in advance of his age, and many points once considered utopian are now established by law.

Departments, 1790. Territorial divisions of France made by the Constituent Assembly.

The 'Départements Maritimes' (3 syl.) are the five great ports, viz. Lorient, Brest, Toulon, Cherbourg, and Rochefort.

Deposed Kings of England.

I. *Before the Conquest.*
Sigebert of Wessex, A.D. 755.
Alcred of Northumbria, 774.
Ethelred I., 779.
Eardwulf and Ethelwulf, 857.
Edwy, 957.
Ethelred II., 1013.
Hardicanute, son of Canute, 1037.

II. *Since the Conquest.*
Edward II., 1327.
Richard II., 1399.
Henry VI., 1460.
James II., 1688. Euphemistically called his 'abdication.'

Charles I. was not only deposed but tried for treason against his parliament and beheaded; Charles II. was not exactly deposed, but he was kept from the crown during the Commonwealth.
The most absolute and tyrannical of our sovereigns have been the Welsh and Scotch dynasties, but Wales and Scotland are eminently democratic.

The Stuarts claimed the 'right divine' of kings, but James I. and Charles II. did no honour to the claim.

Deposed Kings of France.

Louis XVI., like Charles I., was not only deposed but executed, 1793.

Napoleon I. (emperor) was twice deposed, 1814, 1815.

Charles X. (1830), like James II., is said to have 'abdicated.'

Louis-Philippe (1848), also said to have 'abdicated.'

Napoleon III., 1872.

Déprêtrisation, 7 Nov., 1793. When Mgr. Gobel, archbishop of Paris, and hundreds of the clergy appeared at the bar of the Convention, and declared they would henceforth acknowledge no master, in heaven or earth, except the sovereign people. They renounced their ministry, and abandoned the Christian religion.

Derby Day. The Wednesday of the great spring meeting which takes place at Epsom, in Surrey, in the month of May. The Derby week is the week succeeding Trinity Sunday, and Derby Day, which is the second day of the races, is the most important horse-race day in the kingdom and the greatest English holiday.

Derby is generally pronounced Dar'-be.

Derby Scholarship. In Oxford University. The recipient must have highly distinguished himself either in the final examination or as the winner of university scholarships and prizes. Founded in honour of Edw. Geoffrey S. Stanley, earl of Derby, chancellor of the university, by subscribers in Lancashire. Value, the interest of 4,300l. Founded 1870.

Derbyites or 'Darbyites.' A split from the Plymouth Brethren, under a Mr. Darby, on the subject of the human nature of Christ.

Derbyshire Hudibras (*The*). George Eyre.

Derbyshire Insurrection (*The*), 1817. Stirred up by Jeremiah Brandreth, a framework-knitter of Nottingham who induced 300 Derbyshire and Nottingham men, chiefly miners, to march with him to London and overturn the government. At Eastwood, some three miles from Nottingham, they were overtaken by a troop of horse-soldiers, and fled in all directions. Several were taken prisoners and three executed at Derby, one of whom was Brandreth the leader.

Derbyshire Neck (*The*). Goître or swelling in the throat produced, some think, by excess of lime in the water used for drinking.

Dervises, *i.e.* paupers, A.D. 759. A species of Moslem monk, of which there are thirty-two sects. They live in convents, the principal establishment being at Konieh, in Caramania. They fast every Thursday. They are great opium eaters and are given to strong drinks. The dancing dervises twist themselves round with extended arms for hours together, all the while repeating the name of Allah. Persia is noted for its dervises.

Descartes. See 'Cogito, ergo sum.'

Despairing Shepherd (*The*). Addison is meant, and the lady was the dowager Countess of Warwick. The ballad is by Nicholas Rowe (1716).

Despard's Conspiracy, 1803. A very foolish plot devised by Colonel Edward Despard of Ireland to assassinate the king (George III.), and establish in Great Britain and Ireland a republican form of government. Despard and six others were executed on Kennington Common. If Despard was not partly insane, this silly plot was out of revenge for being superseded in office on the Mosquito Shore in consequence of having got into some squabble with the colony.

Destroying Prince (*The*). Tamerlane or Timur the Tartar (1336, 1870-1405). So called in India because in 1396 he made in Delhi a general massacre of the inhabitants. It is said that 100,000 were put to death in a single hour (!)

Destructionists. Those Christians who believe that after the wicked have suffered in hell in proportion to their sins they will be destroyed. The Rev. Mr. Bourne of Norwich is the founder of this sect.

They deny that they teach the doctrine of annihilation; assert that *destruction* is the scripture term, and say they are not bound to be wise above what is written.

Determinists. Those who believe that the actions of men are not predetermined by God, but are determined by the nature which they inherit and surrounding circumstances.

Detroits (*Treaty of*), 13 July, 1841. Between England, Austria, France, Prussia, Russia, and Turkey; by which the sultan engaged to close the Bosphorus and the Dardanelles to all nations without distinction or favour; revoking the privilege accorded to Russia by the treaty of Unkiarskelessi.

Deus Vult. The war-cry of the first crusade (1096–1099). At the Council of Clermont in France, after Pope Urban had finished his address in favour of a crusade against the Saracens, the assembly shouted *Deus vult* (God wills it), the crowd outside took up the cry, and Urban, crossing his arms over his breast, and bending to the rails of the altar, said with deep emotion, ' God wills it, God's will be done.'

Deux-Ponts (*The Dynasty of the*). 'Deux-Ponts' is the French form of Zweibrücken in Bavaria. After the abdication of Christina, last of the dynasty of Gustavus Vasa, in Sweden, Charles X., of the principality of Deux-Ponts, was elected king of Sweden. The dynasty lasted from 1654 to 1751. Charles X. was cousin of Christina, but is generally called Charles the Aggressor. The successor of Charles X. was Charles XI. (1660–1697), 'The Golden Era of Art.' Then followed Charles XII., surnamed the Warlike, or 'Brilliant Madman.'

Deux-Ponts pronounce *deh pŏ'n*, 'n' very slight and nasal.

Devadassi (*The*). Indian girls attached to the temples. They prepare the garlands, dance and sing before the idols, and take part in all public processions. *See* 'Bayaderes.'

Devil (*The*). I. ' Le Diable.' Olivier Ledain, the tool of Louis XI., and once the king's barber. So-called from his malice and mischief-making.. He was executed in 1484.

II. John Hunyades, surnamed Corvin (1400–1456), called 'The Devil' by the Turks, from the terror of his name. Called Corvīnus from his crest, which was a crow with a gold ring in its beak.

Hunyades pronounce *Hu'-ne-a-dee*.

III. Giovanni de' Medici was called *Le Grand Diable* (1498–1526). So-called

by the French on account of his horrible cruelties at Caravaggio and Biagrasso in 1524.

IV. A noted public-house (No. 2, Fleet Street), purchased in 1788 by Child's Bank firm. Here the original Apollo Club was held, and here lawyers of the neighbourhood used to dine, sticking up a notice on their doors ' Gone to the Devil,' that those who wanted them might know where to find them. *See* the 'Heaven.'

Devil (*Robert the*). I. Robert of Normandy, surnamed the Magnificent, father of William the Conqueror (1028–1035).

II. Robert François Damiens, who attempted to assassinate Louis XV. (1714–1757). *See* 'Damiens.'

Devil (*Son of the*). Ezzelīno, chief of the Ghibellins, governor of Vicenza. So called on account of his diabolical cruelties (1215–1259).

Devil (*The French*). Jean Bart, an intrepid French sailor born at Dunkirk (1650–1702).

Devil (*The White*). George Castriot, called 'The White Devil of Wallachia' (1404–1467).

Devil Dick. Richard Porson, the Greek critic (1759–1808).

Devil of Arras (*The*). Cardinal d'Alibi, sent in 1418 to negotiate a peace between the Armagnacs and Burgundians. The cardinal offered fair terms, but while the Count of Armagnac was signing the treaty the soldiers of Louis XI. massacred both him and his followers.

Devil of Vendée (*The*). J. Antoine Rossignol, the commissioner in the Vendéan War (1759–1802).

Devil's Bible (*The*). An exquisite MS. Bible, inscribed on 300 asses' skins, and taken to Stockholm after the 30 years' war. The tradition is that a poor monk was condemned to death, but was told that the sentence would be commuted if he would copy out on asses' skins the whole Bible in a single night. At night he made a compact with the devil to exchange his soul for the required transcript. The writing is exquisite, and every letter is a model. *See* 'Bibles.'

Each of the many editions of Tyndale's New Testament possesses some distinct characteristic by which it may be recognised. The edition of 1552 has a woodcut of the Devil with a wooden leg, sowing tares.—DORE, *Early English Bibles.*

Devil's Bridge (*The*). I. Over a precipice of Mount St. Gothard. It has only one arch.

II. In Cardigan, Wales. Over a precipice at the base of which flows Monk's brook.

Devil's Parliament (*The*). The parliament assembled by Henry VI. at Coventry, in 1459. So called because it passed attainders on the Duke of York and his chief supporters. *See* 'Parliament.'

Devil's Staircase (*The*). General Wade's road up the Corry Arrack, constructed after the rebellion of 1715. It wound up the mountain by seventeen zigzags, or traverses, and down the other side.

If this road you had seen before it was made,
You'd hold up your hands and bless General Wade.

Devil's Wall (*The*), in Germany, which extends from the Danube to the Rhine; built by the Romans to preserve the possessions south of Germany from the incursions of the Teutons and Germans. It was begun by Hadrian.

Devoirs of Calais. Customs due to the king for merchandise brought to Calais or exported therefrom while our staple was there.

A staple is a mart or place where goods are stored or exposed for sale. There were courts of staple, statutes of staple, and a mayor of the staple.

Devolution (*The War of*). *See* 'War of Devolution.'

Dewanny Adawlut (*Court of*). An Indian court for trying revenue and other cases. 'Adawlut' means a court of justice, and 'Dewanny' the jurisdiction of a *dewan*, a minister of the revenue department.

Dey. The chief of Algiers before the French conquest. The Algerian militia was under a pacha sent from Constantinople, but in 1600 permission was obtained from the sultan to elect a dey, to counteract the tyranny of the pacha-governors. The power of the deys grew rapidly, and in 1710 the dey Baba-Aly actually deposed the pacha and obtained from the sultan the investiture of regency. As the deys were always elected from Constantinople, they were always under the power of the sultan. In 1732 six deys were installed and assassinated in one day. The last dey of Algiers was Hussein, who reigned twelve years, up to the occupation of the French in 1830.

Dgelallian Era (*The*). The Persian era followed to this day, and begun in 1075. Dgel-al-Eddin, son of Alp-Arslan (the valiant lion), called Malek-Shah (1071–1092), appointed eight astronomers to reform the calendar.

Dharina Subha (*The*), 1830. A Hindu society formed at Calcutta for the purpose of keeping up the ancient usages of the Hindu faith, and especially of the Suttee, which the 'Company' had made illegal.

Diadem. A diadem was anciently a fillet worn round the head, and tied behind with a bow having long ends.

In *Egypt*, the diadem bore the symbol of the sacred serpent.

In *France*, Clovis wore a diadem; and François I. was the first to adopt a crown.

In *Greece*, Alexander the Great adopted the Persian diadem.

In *Persia*, the diadem was a blue fillet worked with white, and bound round the tiara or turban.

In *Rome*, Julius Cæsar bound his head with a diadem of laurel leaves. Diocletian introduced the Persian diadem. Constantine the Great habitually wore it ornamented with precious stones. Subsequent emperors adorned it with single or double rows of pearls and precious stones.

*** What we now call a diadem is the gold and jewelled band springing from the coronet and arched over the cap. The Prince of Wales has one diadem to his crown, the sovereign has two crossing each other at right angles.

Dialogue with Trypho. By Justin Martyr, A.D. 156, in Latin. Trypho is a Jew supposed to be travelling in Greece, having been driven out of Palestine during the insurrection of Barchocab; and Justin Martyr is supposed to convert him. He shows from the Old Testament that Jesus Christ is the Messiah, and confutes the usual charges of the Jews against this theory. The disputations of the first and second day are lost.

Diamonds of note.   (N.B. 151½ *carats* = 1 *oz.*)

Carats (uncut)	Carats (cut)	Name	Discovered	Possessor
1680 (?)	*Never cut*	Braganza	1741	King of Portugal
787½	367 9/16	Rajah of Mattan	1756	Rajah of Mattan (Borneo)
—	194½	Orloff	—	Czar of Russia (sceptre)
—	139½	Florentine	—	Emperor of Austria
242½	—	Tavernier	1668	Stolen in 1792
150	138½		1775	King of Portugal
410	136¾	Pitt or Regent	1702	King of Prussia
254	1 7/10	Star of the South ...	1853	*A Brazilian diamond*
186½	1 6 7/16	Koh-i-noor	B.C. 56	Queen of England
—	86	Shah	—	Czar of Russia
80¾	78¾	Nassac	—	Lord [Marquis of] Westminster
288½	—	*Light yellow*	—	Stewart (diamond)
150	—	Porter Rhodes	1872	*Found in South Africa*
112	67½	*Blue*	—	
82	53½	Sancy...	15th cent.	Czar of Russia
—	49	Pigott...	—	Bought by Messrs. Rundell and Bridge
83½	46½	Star of South Africa ...	1867	
88½	44½	Dudley	—	Earl of Dudley
—	49½	Hope	—	Mr. Henry Hope's family
—	40	Pacha of Egypt ...	—	Khedive of Egypt
—	28	Charles the Bold ...	—	

The Great Mogul is the Koh-i-noor.

The Braganza diamond was discovered in Brazil, and is now among the Portuguese State jewels. It is the size of a hen's egg, and is valued at 58 million pounds sterling. It has never been cut, and many fancy it must be a White Topaz; if so, the diamond of the Rajah of Mattan is the largest known. E. W. STREETER, in his 'Precious Stones and Gems' (p. 111), says it is valued at 58,350,000*l.*

✱ *For the history of these diamonds see under the respective names.*

Diamond Necklace (*The*), 1785. A necklace presented through Madame de Lamotte by Cardinal de Rohan, as he supposed, to Marie Antoinette. It was a swindling transaction of the Countess de Lamotte. The fact is this. The Cardinal de Rohan, a profligate churchman, entertained a love passion for the queen; and the Countess de Lamotte induced him to purchase for 85,000*l.* a diamond necklace, made for Madame Dubarry, and present it to the queen. The cardinal handed the necklace to the countess, and when the time of payment arrived Boehmer, the jeweller, sent his bill in to the queen. Marie Antoinette denied all knowledge of the matter, and in the trial which ensued it was proved that the countess had sold the necklace to an English jeweller and kept the money. The trial lasted nine months, and created immense scandal.

Diane de France. The Duchess of Angoulême (1538–1619). She married François de Montmorency, and in 1572 contrived his escape from the massacre of St. Bartholomew. She exercised great influence over Henri III. and Henri IV. of France.

Diane de Poitiers (1499–1566). Married Louis de Brézé. Her influence in the court of Henri II. of France was paramount. The king created her Duchesse de Valentinois. Even Catherine de Medicis, the queen, was under the thumb of the court favourite. At the death of Henri II. she retired to Anet, and disappeared wholly from public life.

Diapason. *See* 'Musical Scale,' &c.

Diapente (4 syl.). *See* 'Musical Scale,' &c.

Diatessaron. *See* 'Musical Scale,' &c.

Diatessaron (*Tatian's*). An heretical *précis* of Four 'Gospels,' ascribed to Tatian, and supposed to confirm the existence of four gospels, and only four, received by the church at the time. There were three or more Tatians in the first four centuries of some celebrity:

I. The Platonic philosopher (born in Syria, A.D. 130), a disciple of Justin the Martyr, author of 'Discourses to the Greeks' (published by C. Gessner in 1546, and by Otto, Iéna, 1851). He became a Gnostic and chief of the *Encratistês*, or total abstainers.

II. Tatian of Mesopotamia, who lived in the 5th cent., author of the 'Diatessaron' in bad Greek; a Latin translation by Victor of Capua is inserted in the 'Library of the Fathers.'

III. A martyr who suffered death in the reign of Julian. His day is 12 Sept., &c.

Many erroneously ascribe the 'Diatessaron' to the Platonic Tatian, but the Greek of the 'Discourses' is far better than that of the 'Diatessaron,' and the style of thought is widely different.

Dickon of the Broom. Richard *Cœur de Lion*. So called from the *genista* or broom plant worn by his ancestors, as pilgrims, symbolical of humility; whence the name Plantagenet. Strange as it may seem, never was there so proud and overbearing a line of princes as these self-styled 'humble ones.'

Dictator. The first dictator of Rome was Titus Lartius, created dictator B.C. 498, about nine years after the expulsion of the 'kings.' The cause was the fear of a domestic sedition. Cincinnatus was dictator B.C. 458; Mamercus Æmilius in 437, 433, and 426; Quintus Servilius, B.C. 439; Camillus was five times dictator, B.C. 396, 390, 389, 368, 367; Papirius about 320; and Fabius Maximus 315. After B.C. 202 the office fell into abeyance; but in B.C. 82 it was revived by Sulla; in B.C. 48 Julius Cæsar was dictator. The office was offered to Augustus B.C. 23, but declined. *The office was formally abolished by Antony B.C. 44.*

Dictator of Letters (*The*). Voltaire (1694–1778).

Dictum of Kenilworth (*The*), 15 Oct., 1266. After the battle of Evesham and death of Simon de Montfort, Montfort's younger son shut himself up in Kenilworth Castle, and there sustained for six months a siege from the royal forces of Henry III., but at the end of six months he surrendered. A decree was then enacted that hereafter all who took up arms against the ruling sovereign shall pay to the crown five years' value of all their lands and possessions. This is called 'The Dictum of Kenilworth.'

Dido, niece of Jezebel.
ITHOBAL I., king of Tyre (1 Kings xvi. 13) had for children, BEL[US], Margenus, and Jezebel.
Belus was the father of PYGMALION and Dido (of Carthage).
Hence Jezebel was Dido's aunt.

Dies Fasti. Business days. On these days, marked F, the prætor administered justice, and assemblies of the people might be held. Subsequently a law was passed forbidding the holding of a comitia upon certain of the *dies fasti*.
Fasti dies, quibus certa verba legitima, sine piaculo, prætoribus licebat fari. Erant hæc tria,

do [actionem], dico [jus], addico [aliquid mea sententia].'—VARRO.

Dies Intercisi. Half-holidays. On these days it was lawful to administer justice one part of the day, but not for the other half.

Dies Iræ. A famous medieval hymn on the Last Judgment, beginning with the line 'Dies iræ, dies illa,' supposed to be the work of Thomas of Cela'no, a native of Abruzzi, in Naples, who died about 1255. It forms a portion of the service of the mass. The first and third stanzas are:

I.
Dies iræ, dies illa,
Solvet sæclum in favilla,
Teste David cum Sibylla.

III.
Tuba mirum spargens sonum
Per sepulcra regionum,
Coget omnes ante thronum.

I.
That day of wrath, that fearful day,
Shall melt both heaven and earth away,
As David and the Sibyl say.

III.
The trumpet by the angel blown
Shall wake the dead, bring bone to bone,
And summon all before the throne.

Dies Nefasti. Holidays. On these days it was unlawful to administer justice, and assemblies of the people could not be held. Marked N.
Numa nefastos dies fastosque fecit.—LIVY, bk. i. 10.

Diet (*The*). I. Of the old *German Empire*. It was summoned by the emperor twice a year, and oftener if needful, and met usually at Ratisbon. The emperor and his diet levied taxes, enacted laws, declared war, and made peace. The diet consisted of three chambers, that of the electors, that of the princes, and that of the Imperial cities. Each chamber deliberated separately, and then the electors and princes ratified or refused the proposition. If they ratified it, the emperor was asked to sign it, and it became law.
Switzerland and Poland had their diets. Greek διαιτα, the diet of the Διαιτηται, or justices-in-eyre.

II. Of the *German Bund*. A permanent assembly containing the plenipotentiaries of the thirty-five sovereign states. The place of meeting was the free city of Frankfort-on-the-Main. The diet might be either a plenum of seventy representatives, or a federative council of seventeen. Every state of the Bund has at least one vote in the *plenum*; Austria, Prussia, Bavaria, Saxony, Hanover, and Würtemberg had four votes each, five other states had three votes each, and three other states had each a double vote. In the minor or federative council the eleven principal states had one vote each, and all the rest of the states six votes amongst them. Austria always presided. Superseded in 1848 by the National Assembly. *See* ' Reichstag.'

This was all changed in 1871. As to Hanover, it is now only a geographical name. It was attached to Prussia in 1866.

Diet of Augsburg (*The*). I. 1530. Convened by Karl V. to put an end to the Lutheran controversy. At this diet the Protestant party presented and read out their ' Confession,' or summary of their faith. This summary spread over twenty-eight chapters, and had been drawn up by Melanchthon. A confutation on behalf of the Romanists was put in, and met the emperor's approval. It was therefore decreed that all Protestants shall forthwith return to their allegiance to the see of Rome on pain of the emperor's severe displeasure. This decision led the Reformers into an alliance, called ' The League of Smalkald' (*q.v*). *See* ' Augsburg Confession.'

There were three other diets, so-called, in 1500, 1518, 1548 (*see* ' Interim '); and 1555, which conceded to the Lutherans liberty of conscience. *See* next article.

II. 26 Sept., 1555. Also called ' The Religious Peace of Augsburg.' According to the treaty of Passau (1552) an imperial council was called for the autumn of 1555. Karl V. would take no part in it; he was disgusted at the turn of affairs, and deputed his brother Ferdinand, ' king of the Romans,' to represent him. The diet was held at Augsburg, and full liberty of conscience was confirmed. Lutherans and Catholics were declared alike eligible to all offices of the state, and to seats in the imperial diet. Every ruler in Germany might sanction in his own province whatever form of religion he chose, but all were to tolerate those who held different views.

Diets of Compearance. Scotland. The days on which a party to a civil or criminal process is cited to appear in court. Till 1823 there were two such diets, because there were two summonses, but since then only one summons and one diet to a process.

Diet of Hungary (*The*). Is composed of the king (*i.e.* Emperor of Austria) and two chambers. The upper chamber consisting of the higher clergy, the magnates, the two courts of appeal, and two representatives from each chapter, county, city, and privileged district.

Diet of La Magione (*The*), 1502. The confederacy of Cardinal Orsini, his brother Paolo, Vitellozzo Vitelli, and other magnates, to assassinate Cesare Borgia. Cesare by craft managed to assemble all the lords of this conspiracy, apart from their troops, in the castle of Sinigaglia, where he had them all strangled.

Diet of Roncaglia (*The*), 12 Nov., 1158. It declared Italy to pertain to the empire of Germany.

Diet of Spire or Speyer (*The*). In Bavaria. I. A.D. 1526. Called by the German princes to terminate the religious differences stirred up by Martin Luther. It was resolved to request the Emperor Karl V. to call a general council, and in the interim each individual state in Germany was to regulate its own church matters.

II. A.D. 1529. In which the decrees of the previous diet were revoked and declared to be illegal. The Edict of Worms was directed to be put in full force; and the Gospels were not to be preached except in the sense approved of by the Church. The Lutheran princes *protested* against this decision of the diet, and appealed to the emperor (Karl V.) and to the next general council. Hence arose the name of *Protestants*. *See* ' Diet of Worms.'

Diet of Switzerland (*The*). Is composed of the representatives of the several cantons, and is held every two years, alternately at Zürich, Berne, and Lucerne. Each canton has a vote.

Diet of Worms (*The*). I. 1495. Maximilian asked for troops against Charles VIII. of France; but instead of troops the diet proclaimed a *perpetual peace*, by which decree private feuds were stamped out; for instead of appeals to arms the angry barons were commanded to refer their grievances to courts of law.

II. The Diet of 1521, to which Charlesquint (Karl V.) cited Luther, and commanded him to recant. Luther made answer: 'Whatsoever can be shown in my writings contrary to the Word of God I will freely retract; but he who shall take away from that book or add thereto, God will take away his part from the Book of Life.' Luther was then dismissed. This is what is generally meant by the ' Diet of Worms.'

The other diets of Worms were those of 1547 and 1578.

Dietrich. A German way of spelling Theodoric, the great Gothic hero.

Dieu et mon Droit. Assumed as a motto by Richard Cœur de Lion (1189-1199). It was revived by Edward III. in 1340.

Diffusion of Useful Knowledge (*Society for the*), 1825. Consisting chiefly of eminent public characters and men of distinguished literary and scientific merit. The object was the diffusion of useful knowledge to all classes of society, by periodical literature. Mr. Henry (afterwards Lord) Brougham was the leader, and published the first book, on ' The Objects, Advantages, and Pleasures of Science,' in 1827.

Digest. The Pandects of Justinian, in fifty books, containing the opinions of eminent lawyers on points of Roman law, digested or arranged in systematical order by Tribonian and sixteen assistants. It was finished in three years, A.D. 533. *Digesta* is the Latin term; the proper Greek title is *Pandectæ*. The symbol is ff, a corruption of the Greek π (p). A manuscript copy of Justinian's Digest was discovered at Amalfi in 1137, and was carried from Pisa to Florence in 1411.

Dilemee (*The*). The middle part of Ghilan, raised into a separate government by Abu Shujah ul Buiyah, a fisherman, while Persia was under the califs (10th cent.). The government of the Dilemee included Irak, Fars, Kerman, Khuzistan, and Laristan.

Dilemites (3 syl.) or ' Bouides,' (2 syl.). A Mussulman dynasty (932-1055) in Fars, Kerman, Khuzistan, Laristan, and part of Irak, contemporary with the Samanides (*q.v.*), while Persia was a province of the califs. Founded by Abu Shujah ul Buiyah, a fisherman of Dilem in Mazanderan. He had three sons, and

an astrologer told him all his sons should be kings, and so it was: Ali, his eldest son, was king of Fars and Irak Adjemî. Dying childless, he was succeeded by his brother Ruken u Dowlut Hussein Buiyah. The third of the fisherman's sons was virtually king of Bagdad. Persia was at the time a province of the Califs.

The Samanides (*q.v.*) were contemporary from 902 to 999.

Dilettanti Society (*The*). A society of some sixty gentlemen for the study of antique art, formed into a club in 1734, and holding its meetings in the Thatched-house Tavern, St. James Street. In 1764 three members were sent to the East to make drawings: they were Mr. Chandler for the literary part, Mr. Revett for the architectural part, and Mr. Pars to take drawings of bas-reliefs and views. They returned in 1766, and published two magnificent volumes. In 1811 another expedition was sent out, viz. Mr. Gill (Sir William), Mr. Francis Bedford, and Mr. John Gandy, who visited Asia Minor, and published two volumes of drawings, one in 1817 and the other in 1835. These are all first-class works. The following gentlemen were members of the society: Sir Joshua Reynolds, Charles James Fox, the Duke of Norfolk, George Selwyn, David Garrick, George Colman, Lord Holland, Sir Joseph Banks, and Sir George Beaumont.

Dinner Bell (*The*). Edmund Burke (1729-1797), though a great orator, was, especially in the latter part of his life, most prolix. General Fitzpatrick said of him :—

Ask any person in the house who is the best-informed man, and the answer will certainly be Mr. Burke. Ask who is the greatest wit, and the answer will be Mr. Burke. Who is the most eloquent? Mr. Burke. Who is the most tedious? Mr. Burke.

Dionysian Cycle (*The*). The cycle harmonising the Alexandrine and Roman usage. It was Dionysius Exiguus who constructed this table, which was in use till the reform of the calendar by Gregory XIII., in the latter half of the 16th cent.

Dionysian Period (*The*), or ' Great Paschal Period,' 532 years. The Ethiopians, who use the ' Era of Diocletian,' do not date as we do, consecutively from one period, but after the lapse of 532 years begin again. This is called the 'Dionysian Period.'

S

Dionysius the Areopagite (Acts xii. 34). The books called the 'Celestial Hierarchy,' 'Mystical Theology,' and the 'Name of God,' ascribed to him, are spurious, and certainly are not earlier than the 5th cent. *See* 'Literary Forgeries.'

Diploma (*A*). A 'libellus duorum foliorum,' written on one side, granted by a magistrate either for a passport or to confer some privilege or favour on the person named therein. Greek δίπλόος double, δίπλόω to double, δίπλωμα.

Diploma Leopoldinum. The constitution of Transylvania, granted by Leopold I.—the Magna Charta of Transylvanian freedom. It guaranteed religious toleration, the existence of Hungarian laws, and the reservation of offices and appointments of state to natives only, and a large number of minor immunities.

Directions (*The*), 1695. For the unity of opinion in the doctrine of the Trinity, issued by command of William and Mary under the advice of Archbishop Tenison. It followed the *Injunctions* for the maintenance of church discipline.

Directory (*The*). 'Le Directoire,' the executive of the Constitution of Year III. (27 Oct., 1795—9 Nov., 1799). The legislature consisted of two houses, the Council of Elders and the Council of 500. The number of the directors was five, named by the two councils, and they were elected for five years, without power of re-election. They appointed the ministers and les généraux-en-chef. Abolished by Napoleon in Nov. 1799.

The military glory of France was never greater than in the Directory. It had for its commanders Bonaparte, Kléber, Desaix, Masséna, and Moreau.

Directory for Public Worship (*The*), or 'The Directory,' 1645. A book put forth by the Westminster Assembly of Divines (*q.v.*) to supersede the Book of Common Prayer. The Creed, the Lord's Prayer, the Ten Commandments were omitted; the sign of the cross in baptism, private and lay baptism, and the use of the ring in matrimony were disallowed; the Confession, the absolution in the 'Visitation of the Sick,' the Burial Service, saints' days, and Christmas Day were dispensed with; the Apocrypha, vestments, crosses, crucifixes,

roodscreens were forbidden. For the use of the people the Assembly put forth their 'Larger and Shorter Catechisms.' The Directory contained directions, but no prayers. It is almost obsolete.

Disastrous Peace (*The*). 'La Paix Malheureuse,' 1558. Made after the battle of Gravelines. It was signed at Cateau-Cambrésis. By this treaty Henri II. of France renounced all claim to Genoa, Naples, Milan, and Corsica. Thus ended the Italian war, which had lasted for sixty-five years (1483–1559).

Discalceati of the Augustine Order were reformed by Friar Thomas of Jesus, a Portuguese, in 1570.

Disciples of Christ (*The*), or the 'Disciples.' Members of the 'Church of Christ,' or 'Campbellite Baptists.' Organised by Alexander Campbell, who emigrated to America early in the 19th cent. They are Baptists, and think all Christians have departed from the simplicity of the gospel. They ignore all creeds, and take the Bible as their only rule of faith and practice.

Discipline (*The First Book of*), 1560. Was drawn up by John Knox and four other ministers, laying down rules for the Scotch, for the election of their church ministers by the congregation, for their examination by the elders, for the election of elders, the way of dealing with ecclesiastical offenders, and other matters of discipline.

THE SECOND BOOK OF DISCIPLINE, 1578. An exposition of Presbyterianism by the Committee of the General Assembly, in which Andrew Melville took a leading part. It sets forth the line of demarcation between the civil and ecclesiastical powers, the platform being Presbyterianism.

Discoverers, 1623. Agents employed by the English government, in the reign of James I., to scrutinise Irish titles to estates, and to discover flaws if possible. Their reward was a part of the lands discovered to have faulty titles.

The disturbed state of Ireland, and the law fluctuating between English and Irish tenure, caused great laxity in the enrolment of patents and rights of all sorts in Ireland, and full 500,000 acres were added to the crown by the Discoverers.

Dispersion (*Day of the*), 5 July. Instituted 1098, in commemoration of the dispersion of the apostles, each of whom then went to a specific field of labour.

Dissenters' Acts (*The*). In the reign of Charles II.

The Corporation Act (*q.v.*), excluding dissenters from municipal offices, 1661 (13 Car. II. st. 2, c. 1).

The Act of Uniformity (*q.v.*), 1662 (14 Car. II. c. 4).

The Conventicle Acts (*q.v.*) of 1664 (16 Car. II. c. 1) and 1670 (22 Car. II. c. 1), forbidding conventicle assemblies.

The Five Mile Act (*q.v.*), 1665 (17 Car. II. c. 2).

The Test Act (*q.v.*), 1673 (25 Car. II. c. 2), excluding dissenters from government offices.

See also the Toleration Act, exempting dissenters from certain penalties, 1689 (1 Will. & Mary, c. 18); the Savoy Conference (*q.v.*), 1661; and the 'Seven Bishops.'

Dissidents (*The*), of Poland, 1548. The Greek Church party, with the Calvinists, Arians, and other Protestants. In 1573 Henry of Valois, by the 'Pacta Conventa,' gave freedom of worship and equality of rights to all Poles, regardless of their religious creeds; but still the Catholics persecuted and oppressed the dissidents. In 1736 the 'Pacta Conventa' was repealed. Russia interfered on behalf of the dissidents (for Russia belonged to the Greek Church), and was supported by England, Prussia, Sweden, and Denmark, but without success. In 1767 the dissidents united into what was called the Confederation of Radom, and applied to Russia to support their cause. Next year the Catholics of Poland, calling themselves 'patriots,' combined into the Confederation of Bar. Poland was divided. Russia interfered, and this led, in 1772, to the partition of Poland.

Dissidents. In Polish history. Originally the Polish Christians generally spoke of themselves as 'nos dissidentes in religione' from the Catholic Church; but in 1572 the Catholics called the Lutherans 'dissidents' and the Greek Church 'schismatics.'

Dissolution of Monasteries (*The*). The lesser monasteries, entirely dissolved in 1539 (31 Hen. VIII. c. 13), were restored by Queen Mary, but again suppressed, and the property vested in the crown 1559 (1 Eliz. c. 24).

Distinguished Service Order (*The*), Nov. 1886. A naval and military order founded by Queen Victoria for distinguished merit in the United Kingdom.

Ditch (*The*), 625, or 'Expedition of the Nations.' The great defeat of the Koreish tribe by Mohammed; after which the tribe concluded a truce and then surrendered Mecca to him.

Dithmarschen War (*The*). Count Gerhard VII. of Holstein attempted to subjugate Dithmarsch, but the inhabitants resisted, and defeated the count with considerable loss (1386). In 1500 John I. of Denmark resolved to subjugate the rebels, and marched into Dithmarsch with an army of 30,000 men; but he was utterly defeated, and the sacred banner called 'the Dannebrog' became the trophy of the conquerors.

Diversions of Purley (*The*). A philological treatise by John Horne Tooke (Pt. I., 1786; Pt. II., 1805), to prove that all words were originally formed from objects of external perception. Called 'Purley' from the residence of William Tooke, his benefactor. The title of the work is headed by the Homeric phrase ἔπεα πτερόεντα.

The persons of the dialogue are: *B* (for Dr. Beadon, afterwards bishop of Gloucester); *H* (for Horne Tooke), and *T* (for William Tooke).

Divine Aspasia. 'Whom to know is a liberal education.' (Steele, 'Tatler,' No. 49; Lady Elizabeth Hastings, 1682–1739).

Divine Doctor (*The*), or the 'Ecstatic Doctor.' Johan van Ruysbroeck, the mystic, born at Ruysbroeck, near Brussels (1294–1381).

Divine Legation (*The*), or, in full, 'The Divine Legation of Moses demonstrated.' By William Warburton, bishop of Gloucester (1738), to prove that the Pentateuch must be a divine revelation, because it is silent on the subject of a future state. This extraordinary production has laid under tribute such a parade of learning as was never equalled, except, perhaps, in Burton's 'Anatomy of Melancholy.' Everyone is aghast at the learning, but no one is convinced.

Divine Right of Kings (*The*). A 17th cent. dogma, implying the belief that kings hold their office by divine appointment, and are the earthly representatives of deity. So they are in a theocracy like Judæa and the popedom. The dogma was sanctioned in the book of the Canons of Convocation, 1604; but in the Bill of Rights, 1689, the right of the people to depose the monarch, to change the order of succession, and to confer the throne on whom they think proper is distinctly set forth. In Great Britain the monarch has only parliamentary right, and the parliament that makes a sovereign can unmake also.

In Russia the Czar still claims the 'divine right to govern wrong,' and, accordingly, in 1883, Alexander insisted on placing the crown on his own head.

Divorce *a mensa et thoro* (Latin). A partial divorce, severing wife and husband 'from board and bed,' but not annulling the marriage. In this sort of divorce neither husband nor wife could marry again so long as both remained alive. Divorces *a mensa et thoro* were granted by the ecclesiastical court when man and wife could not, from incompatibility of temper or ill-usage, live under the same roof.

Now called 'judicial separation'; the court has power to order alimony for the wife. The new law of divorce dates from 1857. In 1878, by the 'Matrimonial Causes Amendment Act,' a wife can plead cruelty as a sufficient cause for judicial separation.

Divorce *a vinculo matrimonii.* A total divorce 'from the bond of matrimony,' in consequence of some canonical impediment existing before marriage, such as bigamy, kinship within the prohibited degrees, &c. The children of such parents are illegitimate.

By the law of 1857 adultery is made a valid plea for an entire dissolution of marriage; but the Council of Trent, which closed in 1563, pronounced marriage to be absolutely indissoluble.

Divorce Court, 1857 (23, 24 Vict. 144). A court which takes the jurisdiction of divorce out of the ecclesiastical courts. It is composed of a judge ordinary, the three chiefs in the courts of common law, and three present judges. After divorce the offending party is free to marry again.

Dix-huit Brumaire. Year VIII. The *coup d'état* of Bonaparte, when the Directory was overthrown, and the supremacy of Bonaparte established (9 Nov. 1799).

Dixie Professorship. Of ecclesiastical history. Stipend 500*l.* a year and a fellowship at Emmanuel College. Founded in the University of Cambridge by Sir William Dixie, of Emmanuel College, 1884.

Djezzar, *i.e.* Butcher. Achmed Pacha (1735–1804). He was originally a slave, and rose to the pashalic of Acre. He is noted for his dogged defence of Acre against Napoleon I. in 1799. His cruelty was a monomania, for at times he was both tender-hearted and charitable. *See* 'Butcher.'

Djoubanians (*The*). A dynasty which reigned in Irak and Khorassan from A.D. 1335 till 1378, founded by Djouban, tutor of Behader-Khan. He married the khan's sister and revolted. Tamerlane conquered this part of Persia, and made his son governor thereof.

Doce'tæ (*The*), or 'Docētes' (3 syl.). A sect ascribed to Simon Magus. They believed that the body of Christ was a sort of phantom body, like that which had appeared to Adam and Eve, Cain and Abel, Noah and Abraham, and therefore that the sufferings and death of Christ were not real. Supposed to be referred to in 2 John vii. (Greek δοκέω, to seem, to appear.)

The Docetæ were a Gnostic sect, and, like the Gnostics generally, considered matter the opposite of spirit, and evil the opposite of good. As God is spirit and only good, evil must be resident in matter, and it would be no more possible for a divine nature to take a material body than for good to mix with evil.

Doce'tism. The doctrine of the Docetæ (*q.v.*), which was this, that the humanity, the actions, and the sufferings of Christ were only phenomenal and not real.

Doctor Doctorum. Alexander of Hales, Gloucestershire, the 'Irrefragable Doctor,' a friar minor, who applied the rules of Aristotle to school philosophy. His chief work is 'Summa Theologiæ.' He died in 1245.

Doctor My-book. John Abernethy (1764–1831). So called because he said to so many of his patients, 'I must refer you to my book; there are only about a dozen pages you need read. Begin at p. 73, and you will soon find all that I can tell you or you need know.' He was not a physician, but a surgeon. His fundamental principle was that most ailments, whether of the legs or eyes, feet or head, are due to deranged digestion, and that a 'blue pill,' with 4 ozs. of food three times a day, will prove a panacea.

Doctor of Asia. POLYCARP, bishop of Smyrna, in Asia; or 'Doctor of the Holy Church of Smyrna' (26 Jan.), 72-167.

Doctor of Dancing (*The*). Beauchamps, of whom Louis XIV. took lessons for twenty years. Beauchamps died 1695.

Doctors (*Scholastic*) who bear complementary titles. Those marked with a * are 'Doctors of the. Church.' The rest are, for the most part, Mediæval Schoolmen.

, *Those without a date have been borrowed from a list sent from America to the publishers.*

Doctor Admirabilis	...	...	...	BACON (*Roger*)...					...	1214-1292
„ Angelicus...	...	...	...	AQUINAS (*Thomas*)*	...	...	...	...	...	1224-1274
„ Authenticus		...	...	GREGORY of Rimini					...	died 1357
„ Bonus		...	...	BRINKEL (*Walter*)	...				...	
„ Christianissimus		...	...	GERSON (*John Charlier de*)				...	...	1363-1429
„ Collectivus		...	...	CARACCIOLI (*Lardolpho*)	...				...	
„ Communis	...	...	...	AQUINAS (*Thomas*)*	...	...	...	...	...	1224-1274
„ Difficilis	...	...	...	JOHN of Ripatransone					...	
„ Divinus	...	...	...	RUYSBROECK (*Jan de*)	...				...	1294-1881
„ Doctorum...	...	...	...	HALES (*Alexander of*)					...	died 1245
„ Dulcifluus		...	...	ANDREÆ or ANDREAS (*Antonius*]					...	died 1320
„ Dulcissimus		...	...	„					...	
„ Ecstaticus...	...	...	...	RUYSBROECK (*Jan de*)	...	...			...	1294-1381
„ Evangelicus		...	...	WYCLIF (*John*)	...				...	1324-1384
„ Facundus		...	...	PETER AUREOLUS	...				...	14th cent.
„ Famosissimus		...	...	INNOCENT V.	...				...	1225-1276
„ Famosus	...	...	...	TORRE (*Bertrand de la*)					...	*
„ Fertilis	...	...	...	FRANCIS of Candia	...				...	*
„ Fundatissimus	...	...	...	ÆGIDIUS or GILES of Colonna...				...	...	1247-1816
„ Fundatus	...	...	...	VARRO (*Gulielmus*)	...				...	13th cent.
„ „ et Copiosus		...	MIDDLETON (*Richard*)		...	...			...	died 1364
„ Illibatus	...	...	...	ALEXANDER Alemanicus					...	
„ Illuminatus	...	...	...	LULLY (*Raymond*)	...				...	1235-1315
„ „ et Acutus...		...	MAIRONE (*François de*) (docteur éclairé)				...	...	died 1327
„ Illustratus		...	...	MARCA (*François de*)	...				...	*
„ „		...	...	ADAM de Marisco (bishop of Ely)					...	died 1237
„ Ingeniosissimus...		...	...	ALPHONSO de Novo Castro					...	
„ Invincibilis		...	...	OCCAM (*William*) (excommunicated by John XXII).			...	1276-1347
				TOME (*Peter*)	...				...	*
„ Irrefragabilis	...	...	...	HALES (*Alexander of*) (Gloucestershire)				...	died 1245
„ Marianus...	...	...	...	DUNS SCOTUS (founder of the Scotists)				...	1265-1308
„ Mellifluus...	...	...	...	BERNARD of Clairvaux*	...				...	1091-1153
„ Methodicus		...	...	BASSOL (*John*), a Scot	...				...	died 1347
„ Mirabilis	...	...	...	BACON (*Roger*)	...				...	1214-1292
„ Notabilis	...	...	...	PETER de l'Isle	...				...	*
„ Optimus		...	...	ANTONY of Padua	...				...	1195-1231
„ Ordinatissimus	.	...	...	BASSOL (*John*), a Scot					...	died 1347
„ Perspicuus		...	...	BONET (*Nicholas*)	...				...	died 1360
„ Planus et Clarus		...	BARLEY (*W.*)	...					...	
„ „ et Perspicuus ..		...	BURLEY (*Walter*)					...	1275 1357
„ Profitabilis		...	...	BONET (*Nicholas*)	...				...	died 1360
„ Profundissimus	.	...	...	ÆGIDIUS or GILES of Colonna				...	1247 1316
„ Profundus...		...	...	JACOBUS de Ascoli	...				...	*
„ „		...	...	BRADWARDINE (*Thomas*) (bishop of Chichester) ...				...	1290-1849
„ „		...	...	MIDDLETON (*Richard*)					...	died 1364
„ Refulgidus		...	...	ALEXANDER V. (pope)	...				...	1339-1410
„ Resolutissimus		...	...	DURAND de St. Pourçain (*Guillaume*) (bishop of Meaux)			...	1267-1333
„ Resolutus...	...	...	...	BACONSTHORP (*John*)	...				...	died 1346
„ Sapiens		...	...	WESSEL (*Jan Hermann*)	...				...	1419-1489
„ Scolasticus		...	...	ALFRED, the Philosopher	...				...	died 1270
„ „		...	...	ANSELM, archbishop of Canterbury*					...	1033-1109
„ „		...	...	ANSELM of Laon	...				...	1050 1117
„ „		...	...	BURIDAN	...				...	1295 1360
„ „		...	...	CASTRO NOVO (*Hugh de*) (an Englishman) ...				...	died 1310
„ „		...	...	ODON (*Gerard*)	...	...	...			...	*

[John of Antioch, *Climacus* (525 600), and Epiphanus were also surnamed 'Scolasticus.']

„ Seraphicus		...	...	BONAVENTURA (*Giovanni di Fidenza*)*					...	1221-1274
„ Singularis		...	...	OCCAM (*William*) (excommunicated by John XXII.)			...	1276-1347
„ Solemnis ...		...	...	GOETHALS (Henry of Ghent)				...	...	1217 1293
„ Solidus		...	...	MIDDLETON (*Richard*)					...	died 1364
„ Sublimis et Illuminatus		...	TAULER (*Johann*)				...	...	1290 1361
„ Sublilis	...	...	...	DUNS SCOTUS	...			...	...	1265-1308
„ Subtilissimus				„					...	„
„ Sufficens		...	...	PIETRO Aquila	...				...	1350-1420
„ Theologicus		..	...	CLEMENGES (*Matthieu Nicholas de*)				...	1360-1440
„ Ultimus Scholasticorum		...	BIEL (*Gabriel*)					...	1420-1495
„ Universalis		...	...	AQUINAS (*Thomas*)*					...	1224-1274
„ „		...	...	ALAN de l'Isle	...				...	1114-1203
„ Utilis	...	...	...	LYRA (*Nicholas de*)					...	1270-1340
„ Venerabilis		...	...	HILDEBERT	...				...	1055-1133
„ „		...	...	OCCAM (*William*)	...	...	...	...	...	1276-1347

Doctor Venerabilis	PIERRE de Cluny	died 1156
[Bede the Anglo-Saxon historian (673-735) is also called the 'Venerable.']		
Doctor Venerandus	GREGORY of Fonts	• •

II. A SUPPLEMENTAL LIST. Other complementary titles.

Aquila Doctorum	AILLY (Pierre d')	1350-1420
,, ,, ,,	AQUINAS (Thomas)	1224-1274

[J. B. Bossuet, bishop of Meaux (1627-1704) was called the 'Eagle of Meaux,' and also the 'Rhone of Christian Eloquence.']

Augustine of his Age (The)	FULGENTIUS, bishop of Ruspina	464-533
Chrysologus (Golden Speech) ...	PIETRO, bishop of Ravenna	433-450
Chrysostom (Golden Mouth)	JOHN, patriarch of Constantinople	344-407
Deacon (The)	EPHREM, one of the Fathers of the Greek Church	320-379
Deacon (The Little)	JOHN of Salisbury	1110-1182
Fifth Doctor of the Church (The) ...	AQUINAS was so called by Pius V.	1224-1274
Fons Vitæ	HALES (Alexander of)	died 1245
Mangeur or Comeston	PIERRE, author of 'Historia Scholastica'	died 1180
Magister Abstractionum	MAIRONE (François de)	died 1327
,, Contradictionis	GROSSETESTE (Robert)	1174 1253
,, Scolarum	,, ,, excommunicated	
,, Sententiarum...	LOMBARD (Pietro)	1100-1164
Malleus Arianorum	HILARY, bishop of Poitiers (The Rhone of Latin	
	Eloquence)...	300-367

[J. B. Bossuet was called the 'Rhone of Christian Eloquence.']

Malleus Hereticorum	AILLY (Pierre d')	1350 1420
Princeps Theologorum	ÆGIDIUS of Colonna	1247-1816
Scotus Minor	PIETRO Aquila	1350-1420
Theologian (The)	GREGORY of Nazianzus	329-390
,, ,, ...	ISIDORE of Seville	570-636
Thorough Doctor (The)	VARRO (Gulielmus)	• •

Doctors (*Ubiquist*). 'Docteurs Ubiquistes' are doctors not members of the Sorbonne, the college of Navarre, or the Cholets.

Doctors of Reason (*The*). Members of the Chinese sect of Tao or Taou, a kind of rationalistic religious sect.

Tao, one of the Chinese names of the Supreme Being, is identified by some missionaries with the 'Logos' of St. John's Gospel. *See* 'Tao.'

Doctors of the Church. Certain canonised authors of the early and mediæval Christian Church whose works have been accepted as authority on doctrine, dogma, and discipline. There have been hundreds and thousands of Theological Doctors, but the following list contains all those distinctively recognised by Catholics as 'Doctors of the Church,' and must not be confounded with the 'Scholastic Doctors.'

To make this list as correct and perfect as possible, I have been carefully over all the many thousand names of the Bollandists, with those contained in the 'Dictionnaire Hagiographique' of the Abbé Migne.

(*Greek*, *Latin*, signify the language in which the works were written). The *month* shows the 'Saint's day.'

ALFONSO Maria of Liguori, Naples, Founder of the Order of Liguorians or Redemptorists. Called by Pius IX. 'one of the doctors of the Church' (2 Aug.) ... ... *Latin*	1696-1787
AMBROSE, archbishop of Milan (7 Dec.) *Latin*	340-397
ANSELM, archbishop of Canterbury (21 April) ... ... *Latin*	1033-1109
AQUINAS. *See below*, 'Thomas.'	
ATHANASIUS, patriarch of Alexandria (2 May)... ... ... *Greek*	296-373

AUGUSTINE, bishop of Hippo, in Africa (28 Aug.) ... ... *Latin*	354-430
BASIL the Great, archbishop of Cæsarea, in Cappadocia (14 June) ... *Greek*	329-380
BERNARD, abbot of Clairvaux, 'the Mellifluous or Most Mellifluous Doctor' (20 Aug.) ... ... *Latin*	1091-1153
BONAVENTURA (*Giovanni di Fidenza*), a cardinal-bishop, 'the Seraphic doctor' (14 July; ... ... *Latin*	1221-1274
CHRYSOLOGUS. *See below*, 'Pietro Chrysologus.'	
CHRYSOSTOM. *See below*, 'John Chrysostom.'	
CLEMENS or CLEMENT of Alexandria (*Titus Flavius Alexandrinus*) (4 Dec.) *Greek*	150-207
CYPRIAN (*Thascius Cæcilius*), bishop of Carthage, and one of the 'Fathers' (16 Sept.) ... ... *Greek*	210-258
CYRIL, patriarch of Alexandria, and one of the 'Fathers' (28 Jan.) ... *Greek*	died 444
EPHREM, 'the Deacon' of Odessa. One of the 'Fathers' (1 Feb.) ... *Greek*	320-379
EPIPHANIUS, bishop of Constantia, in Cyprus. One of the 'Fathers' (12 May) ... ... *Greek*	310-403
FULGENTIUS (*Fabius Claudius Gordianus*), bishop of Ruspina, in Africa, the 'Augustine of his age' (1 Jan.) *Latin*	464-533
GREGORY the Great, pope (12 March) *Latin*	544-604
GREGORY of Nazianzus, in Cappadocia, 'the Theologian.' One of the 'Fathers,' and archbishop of Constantinople (9 May) ... *Greek*	329-390
GREGORY of Nyssa, brother of S. Basil (9 March) ... ... *Latin*	331-396
HILARY, bishop of Poitiers, 'Malleus Arianorum' and the 'Rhone of Latin Eloquence.' One of the 'Fathers' of the Church (13 Jan.) ... *Latin*	300-367
HIPPOLYTUS, bishop of Portus, in Rome, author of the 'Refutation of all Heresies' (22 Aug.) ... ... *Greek*	died 238
ISIDORE, archbishop of Seville, 'the Theologian' (4 April) ... *Latin*	570-636
JEROME, 'Father of the Latin Church' (30 Sept.) ... ... *Latin*	331 420
JOHN CHRYSOSTOM (*Golden Mouth*), patriarch of Constantinople, and one of the 'Fathers' (27 Jan.) ... ... *Greek*	344-437

JOHN DAMASCENUS or 'Joannes Damascēnus (6 May) ... *Greek* 696-756
LEO I. the Great, pope (11 April) *Latin* 390-461
MANAHEN, prophet of Antioch (24 May.) (*See* Abbé Migne, 'Dictionnaire Hagiographique') ... *Greek* • •
NIL of Ancyra, of Galatia. A disciple of St. Chrysostom. (*See* Migne, 'Dictionnaire Hagiographique') (12 Nov.) *Greek* died 1005
ORIGEN of Alexandria (22 April) *Greek* 185 247
PANTENUS or Pantænus of Alexandria (7 July) ... *Greek* 155-216
PIETRO CHRYSOL'OGUS (*Golden Speech*), archbishop of Ravenna (2 Dec.) *Latin* died 450
PROSPER AQUITANAS (25 June) ... *Latin* 408-464
SATYRUS, brother of S. Ambrose (17 Sept.) *Latin* 338-378
THOMAS of Aquino or THOMAS AQUINAS, 'Angel of the Schools,' 'Eagle of Divines,' 'Universal and Angelic Doctor,' 'The Fifth Doctor of the Church,' 'The Dumb Ox' (7 March) ... *Latin* 1224-1274

. The four preceding doctors of the Latin Church were—

1. AMBROSE of Milan 340-397
2. AUGUSTINE of Hippo 354-430
3. JEROME, 'Father of the Latin Church' 345-420
4. GREGORY the Great... 544-604

When Pius V. in 1567 declared Aquīnas to be the 'Fifth Doctor of the Church,' he did not ignore those between Gregory and Aquīnas, but spoke of S. Thomas as we speak of the Tenth Muse, or Eighth Wonder of the World, meaning some one or some wonder of striking excellence. There may have been others more learned than Aquīnas, as there are poets superior to Marie Lejars de Gournay, surnamed 'the Tenth Muse,' and buildings more marvellous than the palace of the Escurial of Toledo, called the 'Eighth Wonder.' Such phrases are merely complementary hyperbole.

Doctors of the Sorbonne. 'Docteurs en Sorbonne.'

The Sorbonne is a secular ecclesiastical college founded in Paris by Robert de Sorbon in 1252. The members live in common, and are provided with everything necessary for life and well-being. The head of the college is called the *Proviseur*, and his assistant is called a *Prior*. The buildings were restored by Richelieu in the 17th cent. Since 1821 these buildings have been the seat of the University of Paris, consecrated to humanity studies, the arts, sciences, and theology

The following doctors of the Sorbonne are placed in the 'Petits Bollandistes' among the saints. They were 'Martyrs of the Revolution' (M. R.).

BURTE (*Jean François*), whose day is 2 Sept.
MEUR (*Vincent de*),   „   „   26 June
THORAME (*Jules de Pazery de*) „   „   2 Sept.

Doctors' Commons.

A college of doctors in the civil law, London, wherein the Court of Admiralty and the principal ecclesiastical courts were held. Founded by Dr. Henry Harvey, dean of the Arches. The original house was destroyed by the great fire of London in 1666. Building taken down in 1867.

Doctrinaires.

I. or 'Prêtres de la Doctrine,' 1592. Founded by Cæsar de Bus of Avignon, and confirmed by the pope in 1597. The object of the society was to instruct the poor, especially in rural districts, in religious matters. Many schools were under them. Cæsar de Bus also established a female society for women called 'Filles de la Doctrine.'

II. 1815. A political party in France favourable to a constitutional government, and hoping to combine perfect liberty with regality. Royer-Collard was the chief, or père de la doctrine. *See above.*

The following were eminent doctrinaires, viz. Camille Jordan, De Broglie, De Serre, Duchâtel, Duvergier, De Hauranne, Guizot, Jaubert, and Rémusat.

Doctrine of Signatures (*The*).

The doctrine that visible signs indicate the virtues and uses of natural objects. Thus white was cold, and red hot. Hence in fever red medicines, such as mulberries and pomegranates, were prescribed. For liver complaints yellow substances were recommended. Malignant plants, says Coles, have a sad or evil appearance, either in their leaves, flowers, or fruit. Euphrasia, or 'eye-bright,' has a spot like the pupil of the eye ; walnuts, which represent the human brain, are good for idiocy ; nettle-tea for the nettle-rash ; bilberry and turmeric, being yellow, are good for jaundice ; liver-wort, which is spotted like tubercles on the liver, is good for liver complaints. So throughout Nature puts her label on everything, if men were but wise enough to read her writing.

Doctrines of Port Royal.

The community of Port Royal, in Paris, were the most strenuous defenders of the famous book called 'Augustīnus' by Cornelius Jansen, which was designed to show that St. Augustine was unsound on the doctrines of grace, free-will, predestination, and universal redemption. Jansen's book was condemned by Pope Urban VIII., and the school of Port Royal was suppressed in 1660.

[She] had adopted the tenets of the Jansenists, with perhaps a still further tendency towards the reformed doctrines than those of Port Royal.—Sir W. SCOTT, *Redgauntlet*, chap. xvii.

Dodd, D.D. (*William*), 1753–1777.

Hanged at Tyburn for forging the name of Lord Chesterfield to a bond for 4,200*l.*

Dodo (*The*). This bird, now extinct, was seen by the Portuguese in the Mauritius in 1499; it was seen by the Dutch in 1598; it was figured by De Bry in 1601, by Clusin in 1605, and by Bontius in 1658; the bones of a dodo were discovered in the Mauritius by Clark in 1805.

There is a dodo's foot in the British Museum; a head and foot in the Ashmolean Museum, Oxford.

Dog, or 'Dog Steenie.' George Villiers duke of Buckingham. When first made the king's favourite [James I.], the queen said 'Now you must be my watchdog, and whenever the king is inclined to make a fool of himself, you must pull the old sow by the ear.'

Buckingham wrote from Madrid to James to send over jewels: 'first your best hatband, the Portugal diamond, the rest of the pen nt diamonds to make up a necklace to give the Infanta, and the best rope of pearls, with a rich chain or two for myself to wear, or else your dog will lack a collar' (1623).

Dog-days, or 'Canicular Days.' The forty days beginning with 3 July and ending 11 Aug. So-called from Caniculus, the Dog-star, or Sirius, in the constellation called Canis Major, the brightest of the fixed stars. The Egyptians had the beginning of their year dependent on the heliacal rising of the Canicula, coinciding with the flood of the Nile.

Dogs, or Barbets. So the Vaudois were usually called by the Catholics. The Vaudois employed by gentlemen as footmen to stand behind a carriage were called barbets.

The Marquises Fleury and Angrogna, fearing the bite of the dogs (*barbets*), were not the last to run away.—LÉGER (quoted by Ant. Monastier, *Hist. of the Vaudois Church*, p. 304).

Dogado. The territory of the doge of Venice, comprising the city of Venice, the isles of Malamocco, Chioggia, and Brondolo, with a narrow slip of coast between the mouths of the Adige and the Musone. By a law in 1367 neither the doge nor any of his family could hold any estate beyond the dogado, and if before raised to the office any doge happened to have any estate or fief beyond this territory, he was obliged to sell it.

Doge, *i.e.* duke. The chief magistrate of several Italian republics. In Venice (697) and Amalfi (897) the office was held for life; in Genoa from 1528 the office was limited to two years; in Ragusa from 787 it was monthly, so that

there were twelve doges a year. The doge was both general and judge, ruling in concert with a representative council of the chief citizens. The first doge of Venice, 697, was Paulucci Anaferto; the last was Ludovico Marini, for in 1795 Napoleon I. abolished the office. Marini was elected in 1789, and died 1803. The doge was 'rex in foro, senator in curia, captivus in aula.'

The constitution of Venice was a pyramid, resting on the basis of the grand council, and rising through the senate and the college to the doge, the ornamental apex. In 1172 the election of doge was transferred from the people to the grand council.

Dogget's 'Coat and Badge,' 1715. The prize of a rowing match on the Thames, instituted by Thomas Dogget, an actor. The race day is 1 Aug., the day of the accession of George I. The race is from London Bridge to the 'Old Swan' at Chelsea, when the tide is strongest against the rowers.

Dogmael's Stone (*St.*). A stone in Pembrokeshire with an inscription in Ogham. *See* 'Golspie Stone.'

There is another near Margam in Glamorganshire, and one near Crickhowel, in Brecknockshire. The town is called St. Dogmell in Bartholomew's Gazetteer.'

Dogmatists and Empirics. Two schools of medicine in Alexandria which prevailed during the three centuries preceding the birth of Christ. The Dogmatists or Methodists were those who followed certain prescribed rules; the Empirics were those who trusted to experiment and experience. The chief of the Dogmatists were Erastratos, Themison, and Cœlius Aurelianus.

The chief of the Empirics were Philinos of Cos, Sextus *Empiricus*, and Heraclides of Tarentum.

Dom-Boc. A book of dooms or 'Liber Judiciālis.' A code of laws compiled by Alfred the Great from the West Saxon collection of Ina, the Kentish collection of Ethelbert, and the Mercian laws of Offa.

It begins, 'The Lord spake all these words, saying. . . .' Then follow the Ten Commandments, part of the Mosaic Law, and the Golden Rule; then the ecclesiastical and civil laws.

Dome of Chosroes (*The*). A magnificent edifice in Modain, one of the wonders of the East, built in the 6th cent. by Chosroes the Great of Persia.

Domesday Book. *See* 'Doomsday Book.'

Domicellæ Cameræ Reginæ. Ladies of the bedchamber; generally, if not always, married ladies.

Domicellæ Reginæ. Maids of honour, and of course unmarried.

Domiciliary Canons. Canons not in holy orders, and therefore having no right to any particular chapter.

Domina Anglorum. Maud, daughter of Henry I., and mother of Henry II., by Geoffrey Plantagenet, count of Anjou.

Domingo (*Revolt of Santo*) from the French yoke.

(*a*) The revolt of the slaves broke out 22 Aug., 1791, and Toussaint Louverture, a negro chieftain, was proclaimed governor for life in 1801, but he died in 1803.

(*b*) Another revolt, to expel the French from the island, broke out in 1803. The revolters put themselves under British protection; D'Essalines (originally a slave) was appointed governor, and the ancient name of Hayti was restored. In 1804 the governor declared himself emperor of the whole island, but in 1806 he was assassinated, and the French part of the island was divided into two parts—a negro republic and a mulatto commonwealth. In 1822 Peter Boyer, a man of colour, reduced the whole island under one government—a representative republic—but he abdicated in 1843, and retired to Paris, where he died in 1850.

(*c*) In 1844 the Spanish portion of the island was seized by the blacks, and formed into a republic under Santana, and in 1849 Faustin Soulouque, a negro, proclaimed himself Faustin I. emperor of Hayti, but he abdicated in 1861. Salnave was declared president 11 Jan., 1870, but was shot by the French on the 15th of the same month.

At present (1890) the island is divided into two republics: one (Hayti) French-speaking, and the other (Santo Domingo) Spanish-speaking.

Dominica Bran'donum. Properly was the Sunday preceding Quadragesima Sunday (1st in Lent). *See* 'Sundays.'

Brandones appellabant Galli primam quadragesimalis jejunii hebdomadam, quod hujus prima die sub vesperum pueri *brandonibus*, seu facibus accensis februare solerent. Dominica brandonum Quadragesimam præcedit. — DUCANGE, *Glossary* (BRANDO).

Dominica de Rosa, or 'Lætare Sunday' (*q.v.*). The fourth Sunday in

12

Lent, when the pope blesses the golden rose. *See* 'Sundays.'

Domin'ical Letters (*The*). From Dominĭca (dies), *i.e.* Sunday; the Sunday Letters. They are A B C D E F G, used in almanacs to mark the Sundays throughout the year. The 1st, 8th, 15th, and 22nd days are marked A; the 2nd, 9th, 16th, 23rd, &c., are marked B, and so on. Hence, on whatever day the first Sunday of the year falls, the letter which marks it will mark every other Sunday in the year. If it is A (the 1st of the month) every Sunday will be A, and so on, because there are seven days and seven letters.

Dominicans, or Preaching Friars, 1215. A religious order of the rule of Augustine, founded by St. Dominic at Toulouse for preaching and the conversion of heretics. In 1233 the function of Inquisitors was added. They had several houses in Italy, Spain, Portugal, France, Germany, and England. In 1218 the Dominicans of Paris were called Jacobins, because their convent was in the Rue St. Jacques. Among the most famous of the order were Albert the Great, St. Thomas Aquinas, Raymond of Penafort, Vincent of Beauvais, Caïetan, Dom Soto, &c. They sustained a long rivalry with the Franciscans, but were suppressed in France in 1790 by the National Assembly. Their outer dress is a black garment with a scapulary and capuchin of the same cloth. They also carry a rosary suspended from their girdle.

By the Second Council of Lyons the Begging Friars were limited to the Dominicans or Black Friars, the Franciscans or Grey Friars, the Augustines (also Black Friars), and the Carmelites or White Friars.

There are Dominican nuns and Dominican tertiaries, &c.

Dominicans, 1793, &c. Those Frenchmen who observed Sunday after the introduction of the new French Calendar, which abolished the week of seven days and introduced a decade of ten days instead. The Dominicans had, of course, fifty-two weeks in the year, the Decadists had thirty-six decades.

Dominion Day. Canada, 2 July.

Dominus. Ds. on tombstones, in the middle ages, indicates either a clergyman or a knight. Clergymen were then addressed as knights.

Dominus ac Redemptor Noster, 1773. The famous brief of Clement XIV. suppressing 'for ever the society of the Jesuits, out of regard to the peace of the church.'

Domitian Road (*The*), B.C. 122. Constructed in Gaul by Cnæus Domitius (Ahenobarbus).

Don, Dom, Dona. Don is *Do[mi]nus*, Dom is *Dom-inus*, Dona is *Do[mi]na.* Don and Dona are Spanish forms, Dom is Portuguese. At one time these were given only to princes, bishops, and seniors, then to hidalgos; but now-a-days they are very often mere polite forms of address, like our esquire.

Donald Ballach, *i. e.* the Freckled. Cousin-german of Alexander lord of the Isles.

Donati (*The*), 1293. A faction in Florence opposed to the Cerchi. So named from two powerful houses. Dante, the poet, was connected with the house of the Donati. *See* 'Donātists.'

In Pistoia, an ally of Florence, there were two similar factions, the Neri and the Bianchi. The Neri sided with the Donati, and the Bianchi with the Cerchi. The Neri were zealous Guelfs, and the Bianchi were of the Ghibelline party. When Dante was in Pistoia he joined the Bianchi, and his house was pulled down about his ears by the Neri zealots. (Cerchi pronounce *Cher-kē*.)

Donation of Constantine (*The*). The tale is that Constantine the Great (306–337) was healed of leprosy by the water of baptism under St. Silvester, the Roman bishop. In reward of this service the emperor withdrew from Rome, and founded a new capital in the East. The Roman capital he resigned to St. Silvester and his successors for ever ('palatiam nostrum, et urbem Romam, et totius Italiæ civitates'). If this tale is accepted, the 'Donations of Pepin and Charlemagne' were no donations at all, but simply restitutions of a part of Constantine's Donation. The deed has been proved to be a gross and impudent forgery. *See* 'Literary Forgeries.'

In Ariosto we read that the Deed of Constantine's Gift was found in the Moon with other rubbish—

> Di varii fiori ad un gran monte passa,
> Ch' ebbe già buono odore, or putia forte.
> Questo era il dono (se però dir lece)
> Che Costantino al buon Silvestro fece.
>   *Orlando Furioso*, xxxiv. 80.

Donation of Pepin (*The*). By the liberality of Pepin and Charlemagne the ancient patrimony of farms and houses of the popes was transformed into the temporal dominion of cities and provinces. This first-fruits of the conquests of Pepin, called his donation, was the germ of the temporal dominions of the pope of Rome ('Liber Pontificalis,' p. 171).

The 'donation' included the territories of Ravenna, Bologna, and Ferrara, taken from Astolphus. The donation was greatly enlarged by Charlemagne.—*Codex Carolinus.*

The 'Donation of Constantine' was a forgery probably of the notorious Riculfe, who is supposed to have forged the 'Decretals' (8th cent.).

Donatism, A.D. 311. The religious tenets of Donātus, the Numidian bishop, who insisted that personal holiness made a Christian; and that the apostolic succession of bishops did not of itself form the necessary medium of communication with Christ; that, in fact, Christianity is a personal matter more than a matter of pedigree. At one time Donatism ran Catholicism very hard indeed, and at the present day there are not many who would not subscribe to this fundamental doctrine of Donatus, 'that he who by faith and works shows himself an approved Christian, is to be accounted a Christian, whether that grace has been communicated by apostolic succession or not.'

Don'atists. I. A.D. 311. A religious sect founded by Donat, bishop of Casa Nigra, in Africa. Donātus declared that Cæcilianus, bishop of Carthage, was not duly elected, and that all those in his obedience were heretics. His heretical doctrines were these: that baptism administered by heretics is null and void; and that the church is not infallible, seeing it had erred in the case of Cæcilianus. The Council of Arles, held A.D. 314, acquitted Cæcilianus and condemned Donatus. Donatus and his followers now seceded from the church and formed a new sect which, in 330, had as many as 172 bishops. The fundamental doctrines of the new sect were these: (1) that the Son is inferior to the Father, and the Holy Ghost is inferior to the Son; (2) that personal holiness is far more important than apostolic succession, and (3) when any member is excommunicated for offences, he must be rebaptized before he can be again admitted into church membership.

II. A.D. 316. The followers of Donātus, bishop of Carthage, who, being condemned by pope and emperor as a schismatic, revolted, and carried with him a large following of reformers, who lighted a civil war and desolated Africa in the reigns of Constantine and his successors till the Vandal invasion. St. Augustine combated these 'sectaries.'

Donnellan Lectureship (*The*), 1794. Instituted in Dublin University under the will of Anne Donnellan.

Dooms of Ethelbert (*The*), A.D. 597. Giving a legal status in England to the Christian church.

Doomsday Book, or 'Domesday Book,' 1085-1086. A statistical survey of that part of England which was under the sway of William the Conqueror. So called, probably, because it was of authority in all dooms, *i.e.* judgments in disputed questions which afterwards arose on matters contained therein. It was anciently known as the 'Liber de Wintonia' (Book of Winchester), because at one time it was preserved in the royal treasury of that city, under three locks and keys. It was printed and published in 1783 in two folio volumes. In 1816 two supplementary volumes were published. *See below* 'Supplementary Volume.' N.B. The counties of Durham, Northumberland, Westmoreland, and Cumberland are omitted.

There are two volumes: one called the Great Domesday Book and the other the Little Domesday Book. The great book contains 382 double pages of vellum, each page having a *double* column. Some of the capital letters are in red ink, and some passages are touched with red ink. It contains a survey of thirty-one counties. The Little Domesday Book contains 450 double pages of vellum in *single* column. It contains the counties of Essex, Norfolk, Suffolk, part of Rutland, part of Lancashire, York, and Chester.

Contents : The name of the place; the present tenant; the tenant in the time of Edward, 1041; how many hydes of land in the manor; how many ploughgates in demesne (*i.e.* reserved in the lord's own hand); how many homagers or vassals; how many villeins; how many cottars; how many serfs; what freemen; how many tenants in socage (*i.e.* by hereditary right); how much wood; how much meadow and pasture; what mills and fishponds; how much has been added or taken away since 1041; what the present value. The return was three-fold: (1) As these details were in 1041; (2) As they had been given by William; and (3) As they were when the survey was made.

Doomsday Book (*Supplementary Volumes*). Vol. i. contains an introduction by Sir Henry Ellis, and indices of the names contained in Doomsday Book. Vol. ii. contains (1) the Exon Domesday (*q.v.*); (2) the Inquisitio Eliensis, or survey of the lands of the monastery of Ely, *i.e.* of the counties of Cambridge, Hertford, Essex, Norfolk, Suffolk, and Huntingdonshire; (3) the Winton Domesday, containing two surveys of the city of Winchester : one made between 1107 and 1128, and the other made in 1148; and (4) the Bolden Book (*q.v.*), or survey of the see of Durham made in 1183.

Dorian Mode (*The*). In music is our scale of D played entirely on white notes of the piano, with the minor seventh so characteristic of Greek music. Practically singers began their scale with A instead of D.

Dorians. One of the four distinctive people of old Greece, who conquered Peloponnesus and settled there. This is called 'The Return of the Heraclidæ.' There were also Dorian settlements in Asia Minor and the neighbouring islands. They were a sturdy unpolished race. In architecture it was the strongest, simplest, and plainest of the three orders; in philosophy it was of the Pythagorean school; in politics highly aristocratic; in dialect harsh and rough. Scotch is often called the British Doric.

The three orders were the Ionic, the most chaste and elegant ; the Corinthian, the most ornate ; and the Doric, the most plain and the strongest.

Doric School of Greek Poets (*The*). Founded by Alcman and Stesichŏros. Alcman of Lydia (B.C. 660–600) was a Spartan slave, emancipated. He wrote in the Doric dialect; most of his poems are erotic, but very few fragments remain. In one of his odes he exclaims, ' Oh that I were a seamew, which wings its flight among the halcyons, and runs on the surface of the sea-waves. Bird of spring with radiant plumage, and heart that knows no sigh!' This is not unworthy to be compared with that beautiful verse of the psalmist, ' Oh that I had wings like a dove, for then would I flee away and be at rest!'

Stesichŏros (B.C. 632–552) was a native of Sicily, and was the father of the choral epode. His poems are in irregular verse, and the subjects are 'The Labours of Herculês,' the ' Return of the Heraclidæ,' the ' Siege of Troy,' ' Return from Troy,' and the ' Calydonian Hunt.'

Alcman wrote in Old Doric ; but Theocrĭtos, Bion, and Moschos wrote in New Doric.

Dorislaus (*Dr.*), in 1649. Was sent by the British parliament as envoy to the States of Holland, while Charles II., in exile, was holding his court at the Hague. The very evening of his arrival, while he sat at supper in the inn, six gentlemen with drawn swords dragged him from his chair, and murdered him on the floor. These assassins were Scotchmen, followers of Montrose, and Dorislaus had been recently employed 'to draw the charge against the king.'

As long as he (William II. prince of Orange) lived, no atonement could be obtained for the murder of Dorislaus.—Dr. LINGARD, *Hist. of Engl.*, viii. 5.

It must be remembered that William II. had married a daughter of Charles I., and all the partisans of the stadtholder were rabid royalists.

Dorsetshire Labourers (*The*), 1834. At the Dorchester assizes six agricultural labourers were tried and convicted of being members of an illegal society, and for administering illegal oaths. They belonged to a trades-union in which those initiated were admitted blindfold into a room where was the picture of a skeleton and a skull. These labourers were sentenced to transportation for seven years.

It was now proposed that, as the Orange leaders had violated the law as much as the Dorsetshire labourers, they should be dealt with in the same manner, and that if evidence could be obtained, the Duke of Cumberland [grandmaster], Lord Kenyon, the Bishop of Salisbury [chaplain], Colonel Fairman, and the rest should be prosecuted in the central criminal court.—HOWITT, *Hist. of Engl.* (year 1836, p. 273).

Dort (*Synod of*). Held between 13 Nov., 1618, and 25 May, 1619. It was an assembly of Protestant divines to consider the nature and tendency of the doctrines of Arminius, professor of divinity in Leyden. The synod decided in favour of Calvinism, and excommunicated Arminius and his adherents.

Dotation of Pepin (*The*). *See* 'Donation,' &c.

Dotted Bible (*The*). An edition of the Bible printed in 1578, page for page with that of 1574. *See* 'Bible.'

Douay Bible (*The*), 1581. A translation made by the professors connected with the College of Douay, founded in 1568 by Dr. William Allen for the education of English boys designed for the Romish priesthood. These students were to be sent into England as itinerant preachers, with the view of creating a reactionary feeling and upsetting the Reformed Church. Dr. Allen himself worked on the translation. *See* 'Bible.'

Double Procession (*The*). That is the *Filioque* dogma. Did the Holy Ghost proceed from the Father AND the Son, or from the Father BY the Son? The former is the dogma of the Western Church; the latter is the belief of the Eastern Church.

Doublement du Tiers (*Le*), 27 Dec., 1788. When the commons or deputies of 'Le Tiers' were made equal in number to the deputies of the *noblesse* and clergy both together. There were 572 of the Tiers, 572 of the other two estates, and a chairman.

Doubling Ordinance (*The*), 1662. A law that whoever advanced one-fourth more than his original share for land in Ireland should be entitled to double the quantity of land; but if any 'adventurer' refused to make such advance, any other person might reap the benefit, provided he repaid the 'adventurer' the sum originally subscribed.

Those who subscribed 200*l.* were to have 1,000 acres in Ulster; those who subscribed 300*l.* were to have 1,000 acres in Connaught; those who subscribed 450*l.* were to have 1,000 acres in Munster; and those who subscribed 600*l.* were to have 1,000 acres of the forfeited land in Leinster. The subscribers were called 'The Adventurers.'

Douglas's Larder (*The*), 1307. 'James Douglas penetrated into his own country in disguise, and, collecting some of his ancient followers, surprised the English garrison placed by Lord Clifford in Douglas Castle, and putting the garrison to the sword, he mingled the mangled bodies with a large stock of provisions which the English had amassed, and set fire to the castle. The country people to this day call this " Douglas's Larder." ' (Sir W. Scott, 'History of Scotland,' ix.)

Having set fire to his castle, he fled to the mountains, saying that he liked better to hear the lark sing than the mouse cheep.

Douglas Wars (*The*), 1572, 1573. Skirmishes in the regency of James earl of Morton, in which prisoners were relentlessly executed on both sides.

Douloir (*The*). An instrument of death resembling the more modern guillotine. It was used in the reign of Henri IV. for the execution of his godson, the Duc de Montmorenci.

Dover (*Treaty of*), 22 May, 1670. A secret compact between Charles II. of England and Louis XIV. of France, negotiated through Henrietta duchess of

Orléans, and providing that Charles should publicly announce his conversion to Romanism; and if any disturbance ensued, that Louis should send to his aid a French army and a subsidy of three million francs.

Doves' Dung (2 Kings vi. 25). Sold in the siege of Samaria at the rate of half a pound for twelve shillings, does not mean the droppings of pigeons, but the plant called by botanists 'ornithogallum,' from two Greek words, ὄρνιθος γάλα, bird's milk, and known as 'the Star of Bethlehem'—*i.e.* the star-shaped flower of Bethlehem. The roots of these plants are white, edible, and in some English counties are sold for 'French asparagus.' They are much eaten in the Levant, where the plant abounds, roasted like chestnuts or boiled. The plant sold in Samaria would be better understood by the equivalent, 'A bunch of asparagus or half a pint of chestnuts for twelve shillings.'

Dow Purse. The money anciently given by the bridegroom to his bride on their wedding day. It was a Roman custom, but obtained among the Greeks, the Jews, and almost all the northern parts of Europe.

The Greeks called it ορθριον δωρον. In Germany it is called *Morgengabe*, *i.e.* morning present.

Downing College. In Cambridge University, founded by Sir George Downing, of Gamlingay Park, Cambridge, in 1800, opened in 1821.

Downing Professorship of the laws of England. Stipend 200*l.* a year. Founded 1800, in the University of Cambridge, by Sir George Downing, Bart., founder of Downing College, Cambridge, and of the Downing Professorship of Medicine. *See* 'Regius Professorship of Civil Law.'

Downing Professorship of Medicine (*The*), in the University of Cambridge, 1800. Founded by Sir George Downing, Bart., the founder of Downing College, Cambridge, and of the Downing Professorship of the Laws of England. Stipend 200*l.* more than a Fellow of Downing receives. *See* 'Regius Professorship of Physic.'

Doxology (*The*). In the reign of Constantine the Great there were four forms of the doxology in use:—

1. Glory be to the Father, *and* to the Son, *and* to the Holy Ghost.
2. Glory be to the Father, *and* to the Son, *in* the Holy Ghost.
3. Glory be to the Father, *in* the Son, and *in* the Holy Ghost.
4. Glory be to the Father, *by* the Son, and *in* the Holy Ghost. (Philostorgius, Book III., chap. xiii.)

Doyen des Rois (*Le*). So Louis XIV. used to style himself in the latter years of his long reign. He reigned 72 years, and it will not be easy to find in history a reign of equal length.

Dozen Peers (*The*). The 12 peers assembled at the instance of the barons, in the reign of Henry III., to be privy councillors, or rather conservators of the kingdom.

Dozsa Rebellion (*The*), 1513–1514, Hungary. Also called the Kurucz Rebellion, that is the rebellion of the Cruciferi, because the original insurgents were intended to be 'soldiers of the cross.' It was a peasants' uprising against the oppressions of the upper class. Of course the rebels were defeated immediately they came into conflict with the better trained, and George Dozsa was put to death with the most savage cruelty. He was seated on a red-hot iron chair, a red-hot iron crown was placed on his head, and a red-hot sceptre in his hand, and to add to his tortures his flesh was then torn from his bones. *See* 'Damiens.'

Draco Regis. The standard borne in war anciently by our kings. It had the figure of a dragon wrought on it.

Dragonnades (3 syl.), 1685. An armed expedition to stamp out Protestantism in France. Each expedition was led by a bishop, who demanded that every Protestant should abjure Protestantism, and those who refused to do so were left to the tender mercies of the dragoons who accompanied him. Hundreds were thrown into dungeons; hundreds who fled were hunted down like wild beasts; many were gibbeted or sent to the galleys; and not a few were cut down by the sword.

The persecutions were renewed in 1723 and 1724.

Drama (*Father of the French*). Jodell (1532–1573).

Drama (*Father of the modern German*). Andreas Greif (1616–1664).

Drama (*Father of the Greek*). Thespis, 6th cent. B.C.

Drama (*Father of the Spanish*). Lopé de Vega (1562–1635).

Drapier's Letters, 1724. A series of letters by Dean Swift on the halfpence and farthings coined for Ireland by William Wood, iron and copper founder of Wolverhampton. Drapier is represented as a poor but independent-spirited shopkeeper, utterly unskilled in law, but who did not mean to be ruined if he could help it. In these letters the Irish were told that Wood's patent was iniquitous, and that the contract had been infamously carried out. Wood was called a 'wood-louse,' and his copper was declared to be vile brass, 20 of which coins were not worth 10 honest ones. The Irish refused to take Wood's halfpence, and the government was compelled to withdraw the coinage. Swift became immensely popular in Ireland, but Sir Isaac Newton, master of the mint, examined the coin, and declared it to be rather above the terms of the contract.

Dreadful Woman (*The*). Caroline, the wife of George prince regent. Married 1795, separated the year her daughter was born, 1796, died 1821.

The Whigs threatened to espouse in a body the cause of the Dreadful Woman, and bring her to the front again.—WINGFIELD, *Abigail Rowe*, vol. i. p. 169.

Dresden (*Treaty of Peace at*). 25 Dec., 1745, was signed at Dresden the treaty which concluded the second Silesian war between Maria Theresa of Austria and Frederick II. the Great of Prussia. By this treaty Silesia was again restored to Prussia. *See* 'Berlin,' treaty of.

Drinking in Belgium. The Belgian labourer spends one quarter of his wages in dram-drinking. On ordinary days he requires six drams a day, and on festal ones more. The first, called a *Worm-killer*, is taken at 5.30 a.m.; the second, called an *Eye-opener*, at 8 a.m.; the third, called a *Whip*, at 11 a.m.; the fourth, called a *Digester*, at 2 p.m.; the fifth, called a *Soldier*, at 5 p.m.; and the sixth, called a *Finisher*, at 7.30 p.m.

Drinks of Great Men.

BRAHAM, the singer—Bottled porter.
BYRON—Port wine.
CHARLES V.—Alicante.
CROMWELL—Malvoisie.
FRANÇOIS I.—Sherry.
FREDERICK THE GREAT—Tokay.
FREDERICK WILLIAM IV. of Prussia—Cliquot.
GLADSTONE—Egg beaten up in sherry.
GOETHE—Johannisberg hock.
HENRI IV.—Surènes.
HUMBOLDT—Sauterne.
KEAN (Edmund), the actor—Beef tea for breakfast, cold brandy.
NAPOLEON I.—Chambertin.
PETER THE GREAT—Madeira.
RABELAIS—Old Chablis.
RICHELIEU (Cardinal)—Romanée.
RICHELIEU (Marshal)—Médoc.
RUBENS—Marsala.
SAXE (Marshal de)—Champagne.
TALLEYRAND—Château-Margaux.

Driving for Rent (Ireland). Driving the cattle of a defaulting tenant into a pound, there to be kept till the rent is paid, or sold by auction till the money due to the landlord is realised.

Droits of Admiralty. Derelict ships and other property picked up at sea and unclaimed. These possessions at one time were the perquisites of the lord high admiral; but by the Merchant Shipping Act of 1854 they were placed under the control of the Board of Trade.

Droughty Year of '26 (*The*), *i.e.* 1826. The prevailing wind was north. Corn ceased to grow, and grass was dried up. The hottest day of the year was 28 June, when the thermometer in England stood at 90° in the shade.

Drum (*The Sacred*). An object of religious veneration and instrument of magical incantations among the Laplanders in former times. It was hollowed out of a piece of pine or birch, and covered with skin like a kettledrum. The drumstick was a reindeer's horn. Every family had its sacred drum, and the movement of certain rings attached to it was the domestic Urim and Thummim.

Drunken Parliament (*The*). The parliament assembled at Edinburgh 1 Jan., 1661, the members of which, says Burnet, 'were almost perpetually drunk.' It annulled, in a single act, all the proceedings of its predecessors during the last twenty-eight years. By this measure the whole church system of Scotland fell to the ground. *See* 'Parliament.'

Druses (*The*) of the Lebanon. The seven heads of their religious creed are:

1. Speak the truth to a Druse ; 2. Every Druse must stand fast to every other Druse; 3. The religious creed of a Druse must be exclusive; 4. A Druse must believe in the unity of Hakem as God ; 5. A Druse must be contented with his lot; 6. he must submit his own will wholly ; 7. he must eschew the devil and all false doctrine.

Hakem (the sixth Fatimite calif of Egypt) taught that he himself was the tenth and last revelation of God to man. He was therefore a sort of Christ or God manifest in the flesh. The chief is always called the *Hakem.*

Dry Mass. 'Missa Sicca,' mass without the elements. The Introitus, Collect, Epistle, Gospel, and Canticles constitute the entire service. This sort of mass was performed when 'sacerdos non potest conficere, quia forte jam celebravit, vel ob aliam causam, potest, accepta stola, Epistolam et Evangelium legere, et dicere Orationem dominicam, et dare benedictionem.' This mass was not allowed in the Netherlands, and was vehemently objected to by the Jansenists. It is now quite obsolete.

Dryden of Germany (*The*). Martin Opitz of Silesia (1597–1639). No more like the Duke of Buckingham's poet 'Squab' than Beau Brummel is like Dr. Samuel Johnson.

Duad. According to Pythagoras is the second mathematical quantity, viz. length. The point is the monad, length the duad, breadth the triad, and depth the tetrad. Physically, intellectual capacity is the monad, scientific knowledge is the duad, opinion the triad, and perception by the senses the tetrad.

Dualism. Same as Manicheism. So-called because it teaches the twofold nature of everything, one evil and the other good. Thus there is a principle of good and a principle of evil in soul and matter, male and female, and even in deity. The correlative of dualism is monism.

Dublin Castle. I. A collection of public government offices, such as the Privy Council Chamber, the Chief Secretary's Office, the Prisons Office, the bureau of the Constabulary and Metropolitan Police, the Record Tower, &c., conjoined in one block of buildings, with the lord lieutenant's official residence, where he dispenses hospitality.

II. 1880. A convenient but not very precise phrase to express the policy introduced in the Gladstone administration of arresting men known to the agents of government 'for inciting to any act of violence or intimidation, and tending to interfere with or to disturb the maintenance of law and order ' (in Ireland).

Dublin University. In 1591 (at the especial direction of Queen Elizabeth) the first stone of Trinity College, Dublin, was laid. This university has a chancellor, vice-chancellor, provost, vice-provost, and nineteen professors. The students may, if they choose, take an *ad eundem* at either Cambridge or Oxford. That is a graduate of Trinity College, Dublin, may take the same degree at Cambridge or Oxford without being called on to pass an examination.

Duc de Roussillon (*Le*). A name and title assumed by Henri Cosprons of Perpignan, but not recognised in France. The man so-called was ' d'une famille tout-à-fait bourgeoise.' He disappeared suddenly into obscurity, and whether alive or dead in 1890 is not known.

Ducal Towns. In feudal times were those built on the domains of dukes and other princes. They were inhabited by the duke's retainers, who were subject to just such laws and service as each particular duke thought proper to impose. Generally the townsmen were obliged to ask their lord's permission even to marry or give in marriage, and the lord expected a fee for his permission. When license for a marriage was obtained, a herald announced it in the streets, and at one time the ceremony could not be performed till that day twelvemonth. *See* 'Imperial Free Cities,' and 'Church Cities.'

Duchess of Devonshire's Kiss (*The*). In 1784, the Duchess of Devonshire, with Lady Duncannon, Mrs. Crewe, Mrs. Damer, and some others, dressed in blue and buff, the colours of the American Independents, canvassed personally for Mr. Fox. In the purlieus of Westminster a butcher, in his sleeves and apron, stoutly refused his vote except on the condition that he might give her grace a kiss. The request was granted, and the vote secured.

Duchoborzes (*The*), or 'Duchobortzi.' A sect of the Russo-Greek church (18th cent.). They believe that human souls existed before the creation of the world, and, like the Swedenborgians, ascribe hidden mysterious meanings to Bible language, which only inward light can unfathom. They reject the use of pictures, and observe neither the rite of baptism nor of the eucharist. During the reign of Alexander I. an impostor, named Kapustan, who called himself a prophet, taught them the transmigration of souls. Disputes arose, many were burnt alive, many others were put to death in other ways, and in 1841 almost all the residue were transferred to the provinces beyond the Caucasus.

Dudley Diamond (*The*). A Cape diamond weighing 46 carats, triangular in shape, and of great brilliancy. It was bought by the Earl of Dudley, and has been set in a beautiful head ornament (1872).

Duke, 1337. The first English duke was Edward the Black Prince, created by his father (2 Edward III.), 1327.

Duke of Exeter's Daughter (*The*). The famous rack in the Tower of London is so called, because it was invented by the Duke of Exeter when he was high constable, 1447.

Duke of Thunder (*The*). Horatio Nelson, in allusion to his Sicilian title 'Duke of Brontë' (in Sicily). •

Brontë is the Greek for *thunder*

Duke of York's School (*The*). The 'Royal Military Asylum' at Chelsea is so called because, in 1800, Frederick duke of York was the chief instrument in founding the soldiers' orphan asylum at Chelsea. In 1803 schools were opened for 700 boys and 300 girls, children of deceased soldiers. The girls' school is abolished.

Duke with the Silver Hand. Nuad, who led the tribe of the Danaans from Scotland back to Ireland. Having lost his hand in the great battle of Moytura, Cred a goldsmith made him a silver one, which the surgeon Miach, son of Dian Kect, fixed on his wrist. *See* 'Golden Hand,' 'Iron Hand' (Keating, 'Ogygia,' part iii. chap. 10).

In this phrase duke = king, as in dukes of Edom (1 Chron. i. 51-54). Shakespeare calls the king of Athens 'Duke Theseus'; Horace calls Laomedon king of Troy, 'the fraudulent duke' (Odes III. iii.

24), because he borrowed money from the temples and never restored it. Then we have the dukes of Parma, of Holstein, of Savoy, &c.; and several grand-dukes.

Dulceans or Dulcinists (*The*), 1300. Heretics, so called from Dulcin (*—1308), an Italian, who gave out that his was to be the third reign: first, the Father, from the beginning to the coming of Christ; then the son to the year 1300; and then the reign of Dulcin, the Holy Ghost, when the authority of the pope was to cease. He and his wife were burnt to death, in 1308, by Pope Clement IV.

Dulcifluous Doctor (*The*). 'Doctor Dulcifluus' or 'Dulcissimus,' Antonius Andreas or Andrea, a scholastic philosopher, who died 1320.

Dulwich College, 1619. Founded by Edward Alleyne, a tragic actor.

Pronounce *Dul'-litch*.

Dulwich Gallery (*The*). A collection of pictures in a gallery constructed by Sir John Soane, and connected with Dulwich College. It was opened to the public in 1812. The collection originated with M. Noel Desenfans, a picture dealer, agent to Stanislaus king of Poland; and bequeathed to Sir Francis Bourgeois, who left it to the trustees of Dulwich College.

Dumas (*Alexandre*). A French novelist (1803–1870). According to the *Times* newspaper (13 Dec., 1870, p. 6) Alexandre Dumas wrote 1,200 vols. His memoirs take up thirty volumes. In his heyday he made 30,000*l.* a year.

Dumb Ox of Sicily (*The*). Thomas Aquīnas (1224–1274), so called by his fellow-students at Cologne; but Albertus Magnus, his tutor, said, The dumb ox will one day fill the world with his lowing.' Longfellow, in 'The Golden Legend,' calls him 'the dumb ox of Cologne,' from the monastery of Cologne. He was born in Naples.

Dunces' Day. In the University of Cambridge, Ash Wednesday, 18th cent., &c. Eight by-term men received their degrees as *baccalaurei ad baptistam* in the following Michaelmas term; and eight more as *baccalaurei ad diem cinerum* on Ash Wednesday, or 'Dunces' Day' (W. W. Rouse Ball, 'Hist. of the Study of Mathematics,' &c., 1889).

Dunkers, or 'Tunkers.' A sect of German-descended Baptists founded in Pennsylvania in 1724. They are divided into several minor sections, chiefly differing in points of discipline. To this sect may be assigned the German Seventh-day Baptists. They believe that salvation is to be obtained only by penance and mortification of the body and live in meditation. They deny the eternity of future punishment, and believe that the dead have the gospel preached to them. They are sometimes called 'Pennsylvanian Baptists,' and dress like Dominican friars, in *black* gowns. The word Dunker or Tunker is from *tunken*, to dip.

Hannah Adams, in her 'Religious World Displayed,' calls the Dunkers 'a medley of the Baptists, Universalists, Calvinists, Lutherans, Jews, Methodists, and Roman Catholics.' They are, however, **distinguished for their piety and benevolence.**

Dunmow Flitch (*The*). A custom of the manor of Little Dunmow, of uncertain origin, of giving a flitch of bacon to any married couple who would take oath that for a year and a day since they were wed they never once wished themselves unmarried. During six centuries only seven persons have claimed the prize; the last claimants were John and Susan Gilder, of Tarling, Essex, in 1772. Harrison Ainsworth tried to revive the custom, but without success.

Dunse (*Pacification of*), 18 June, 1639. Between Charles I. and the Scots.

Dunse Law. Is no legal enactment or legal custom at all, but a beautiful little hill close by the town of Dunse on which the Covenanters encamped when Charles I. invaded Scotland with a view of forcing episcopacy and the Church of England Prayer-book on the people of Scotland. *See* 'Pacification of Dunse.'

Durani Dynasty (*The*). Founded in Afghanistan by Nadir Shah in 1747.

Durham (*University of*). Patent granted by Cromwell, 15 May, 1657. Incorporated by royal charter, 1837.

Durham Book (*The*). A copy of the Latin gospels with an interlinear Saxon gloss, written before the year 800, illuminated in the most elaborate style of the Anglo-Saxons, and reputed to have once belonged to the Venerable Bede. It is in the Cottonian collection of the British Museum Library. *See* 'Lindisfarne MS.'

Durham Letter (*The*), Oct. 1850. A letter written by Lord John Russell to the Bishop of Durham on the subject of 'Papal Aggression' (*q.v.*), which contained these words : 'The Roman Catholic religion confines the intellect and enslaves the soul.' This letter caused great excitement for a few weeks. A bill passed through both houses with large majorities against the establishment of a Catholic hierarchy in England and Ireland, but it proved a dead letter. The hierarchy continued, and soon the angry feeling of the nation subsided.

Duri Durani (Pearl of Pearls). The title assumed by Shah Ahmed, founder of the Kaubul empire. He died 1773, after a reign of twenty-six years.

Dutch School (*The*) of painting. The golden age was the 17th cent. Faultless in drawing, arrangement, colour, and also for texture of garments, hair of the head and beard, skin, &c.

CUYP, head of all animal painters	...	1605-1691
DOUW (*Gerard*)	...	1613-1675
HALS (*Franz*), unsurpassed in portraits	...	1584-1666
HOBBEMA, famous for tree-foliage	...	1638-1709
LIEBENS	...	1607-1633
MIÉRIS	...	1635-1681
METSU (*Gabriel*)	...	1630-1680
OSTADE	...	1610-1685
PAUL POTTER, famous animal painter		1625-1654
REMBRANDT, one of the greatest artists of all time	... ...	1607-1669
RUYSDAEL	...	1625-1682
STEEN (*Jan*)	...	1626-1679
TERBURG, called 'White Satin' ...	...	1608-1681
VAN DER HELST	...	1610-1670
VAN DER HEYDEN, architectural artist		1637-1712
VAN DER WELDE (*Adrian*)	...	1629-1672
,, (*William*), in the service of Charles II.		1633-1707
WEENIX, famous for still life	...	1640-1719
WOUVERMANS (*Philip*)	...	1620-1668
,, (*Jan*)	...	1624-1666
WYNANTS	...	1605-1691

Dutch Toys. Not toys made by the Dutch, but by the Germans (*Deutsche*). They are chiefly made at Sonneberg in Saxe Meiningen.

Dutch War (*The*). I. 1652-1654. Carried on chiefly by Admiral Blake and the Dutch admiral Van Tromp in Cromwell's time. Several engagements took place with varying success, and at last the Dutch sued for peace.

II. 1666-1668. Carried on by Louis XIV., and terminated by the Peace of Aix-la-Chapelle, between Louis XIV. and Carlos II.

III. 1672-1674. Carried on by Louis

T

XIV., and terminated by the Peace of Ryswick, signed by France, Austria, Spain, and Holland.

Duumviri. The two chief magistrates in Roman colonies who represented consuls. The two officers originally appointed in charge of the Sibylline books were also called *duumviri.*

There were duumviri whose duty it was to distribute corn to the people, duumvirs charged with the temple edifices and their services, as well as the colonial duumvirs, and many others.

Dyeing. In the dark ages the Jews were the only dyers. Hume says that the English, in the reign of Henry II., wore their robes white because they knew not the art of dyeing; but Hallam proves that woad was imported in the reign of John for dye. We also find allusions to a vegetable substance called 'folium,' used by the English for dyeing wood red or purple, in the 13th century. In 1628 two dyers of Exeter were flogged for teaching the art of dyeing in the North of England.

Dynamite Saturday, 24 Jan., 1885. When great damage was done to the Houses of Parliament and the Tower of London by explosions of dynamite. The Law Courts and some other public buildings were to have been attacked, but were happily too well guarded. *See below.*

Dynamiters, 1882. Irish rebels who used dynamite to destroy the public buildings of the English and destroy the private property of those obnoxious to them. In 1883 t ese Fenians were especially active, being urged to mischief by the money and encouragement received from the Irish in North America.

Dynast. A provincial ruler of Ireland, king in his own province, but subject to the Ard-righ, or supreme lord of the island. From the 5th to the 12th cent. Ireland was a pentarchy. Roderic O'Conor, who died in 1198, was the last Ard-righ, or Milesian over-lord. In 1175, by a treaty signed at Windsor, he became the liegeman of Henry II. *See* Rymer, 'Fœdera,' vol. i. p. 31.

Not one seventh part of the kings of Ireland, before its conquest by Henry II., died a natural death. This applies not only to the monarchs, but also to the dynasts and even to the heads of septs. Ireland was never so ill governed as when under the rule of Irishmen.

Dynasty danced out (*A*), 1760. Mr. Hawkins Brown (aged 80), in his travels, danced one evening at the court of Naples. His dress was a 'volcano silk with lava buttons,' and his dancing was with 'such agility and vigour' that the queen laughed till she was in convulsions, which terminated in a miscarriage, and changed the dynasty of the Neapolitan throne.

Dyvour (Scotch). A bankrupt.

Dzat and Bedagat. The sacred books of the Buddhists.

Eagle (*An*). As an ensign.

An eagle stripped of its feathers, emblematic of the Nile, was the ensign of the ancient Egyptians.

An eagle was adopted as an ensign by ancient Rome, B.C. 104. Marĭus confined the golden eagle to the legions. It had wings displayed and a thunderbolt in one of its talons.

The head of a white eagle, stripped of feathers, was the ensign of the Lagĭdês.

A gold or silver eagle at the end of a pike (with wings displayed), emblematic of the sun, was the Persian ensign in the time of Cyrus.

The Teutonic knights in 1148 adopted an eagle as their cognizance.

In MODERN times: the eagle was adopted, as a *Russian* symbol, by Ivan Vassilivich (who died 1584).

It was adopted by the *United States* of North America in 1783.

It was adopted in *France* by Napoleon I. in 1804 (superseded by the Fleur-de-lys in 1815), and restored by Napoleon III. in 1852.

Eagle (*The Double-headed*). Appears on the arms of the *Holy Roman Empire* under Kaiser Siegmund or Sigismund, 1433. *See* 'Eagle of Austria.'

Eagle and Child in the eagle's nest (*The*). Crest of the Earl of Derby. The tradition is that Sir Thomas Lathom, in the reign of Edward III., had only a daughter by his wife, and, wishing for a son, had a natural son whom he wished to make his heir. His difficulty, of course, was his wife, and this difficulty he surmounted thus: he conveyed the infant boy to an eagle's nest, and leading his lady to the spot, she heard the cries of a child in the tree. Her pity was moved, and the child was adopted. This child was afterwards Sir Oskytel. The daughter Isabella married Sir John

Stanley, who adopted the crest of *Eagle and Child*, with the motto *Sans changer* (J. Roby, 'Traditions of Lancashire ').

Eagle of Austria (*The*). Kaiser Ludwig V. (1814–1347) chose two black eagles for the national device; but Karl IV. (1347–1378) changed the device into a black eagle with two heads.

Eagle of Christ (*The*). St. John the Evangelist is called by Dante *l' aquila di Cristo* (' Paradiso,' xxvi. 53). It was St. Augustine who changed the ancient symbolism of the Four Evangelists derived from Ezekiel's cherubim. Irenæus says John was the *lion*, and Mark the *eagle*; others make the lion symbolise Matthew, and the *man* symbolise Mark; but now the *man* represents Matthew, the *lion* Mark, the *ox* Luke, and the *eagle* John. *See* 'Evangelical Symbols.'

Unde mihi videntur qui ex Apocalypsi (iv. 7) illa quatuor animalia ad intelligendos quatuor Evangelistas interpretati sunt, probabilius aliquid attendisse, illi qui leonem in Matthæo, hominem in Marco, vitulum in Luca, aquilam in Joanne intellexerunt, quam illi qui hominem Matthæo, aquilam Marco, bovem Lucæ, leonem Joanni tribuerunt.—*De Consens. Evang.* i. 6.

Eagle of Divines (*The*). Thomas d'Aquinas, the 5th doctor (1224–1274).

Eagle of Doctors, 'Aquila Doctorum.' Pierre d'Ailly, called the ' Eagle of France,' and the ' Hammer of Heretics ' (1350–1420).

Eagle of Meaux (*The*). Bossuet (1627–1704), bishop of Meaux, a great pulpit orator, especially famous for his ' Funeral Orations.'

Meaux, pronounce *Mo.*

Ear of Dionysius (*The*). The second of the ' latŏmiæ,' or quarries of Syracuse, used as prisons. The Athenians were confined therein, and subjected to all the torments of hunger, filth, and foul air. Capt. William Henry Smyth (1824) describes this cavern, and says amidst its many grottoes is one resembling the tympanum of the human ear, which is remarkable for its echoes. It is 64 feet high, varies from 17 to 35 feet in breadth, and is 187 feet long. It is said that Dionysius the tyrant had it constructed that its guardsman might overhear the conversation of the prisoners confined therein.

At one time the grotto was 72 feet high and 219 feet long, but Capt. Smyth says a part of it has been filled up, and that if two persons speak together the report is ' a confused clamour.' Without doubt the shape resembles the hollow of the human ear, and without doubt it was used at one time as a prison.

Earl Marshal's Court (*The*). Abolished in 1641 by the Long Parliament (*q.v.*). The earl marshal used to preside (jointly with the constable) over the Court of Chivalry. The last proceedings of the court were in 1631.

There is still an earl marshal, head of the College of Arms.

Earl of Aberdeen's Act (*The*), 1843. Determining questions respecting ' calls,' and the election of pastors in the church of Scotland.'

No legislation can possibly settle such questions finally.

Earl of Flint (*The*). The inexorable chief justice, George Jeffreys, was so called by the people after James II. made him a peer (Baron Jeffreys of Wem), 1640–1689.

Early English. Applied to architecture 1190. Distinguished by the Pointed arch, which was either lancet-shaped, equilateral, or obtuse-angled. Merged in the Decorated or Geometrical in 1275.

Early English Text Society (*The*). Established in London 1864.

Earth Houses. Underground buildings called 'Picts' Houses,' ' Weems,' and ' Caves.' Little stone houses built underground to hide people in time of war. Sometimes forty or fifty are found in Scotland clustered together.

East Country Company (*The*). Called by Elizabeth ' The Royal East Company,' the company which traded with the Baltic. The woollen cloths were principally made in Suffolk and Yorkshire. Ipswich, having the noblest harbour on the east, was most prosperous. Laud ruined the company by his religious dogmatism, and drove the workers in woollen goods to Holland, ' whereby the Dutch became instructed in a manufacture which before they knew nothing of.'

East Hendred, Northstead, and Hempholme Manors. The stewardship of which serves the purpose of the Chiltern Hundreds when the Buckinghamshire office is not vacant.

East Hendred is in Berkshire ; post town Wantage. Hempholme is in Yorkshire, near

Beverley. The Escheatorship of Munster serves for a similar purpose. *See* 'Chiltern Hundreds.'

East India Company (*The*), 1599. A company of merchants who sent out four ships to trade with the East Indies. In 1600 it was chartered by Queen Elizabeth, and in 1624 was vested with powers of government. Other companies were chartered in 1657, 1688, 1698, &c. In 1702 the companies were united. In 1773 a governor-general was appointed at Bengal. The charter ceased in 1833, but was renewed the same year. In 1858 the government of India was transferred to the crown.

In 1853 the number of directors was reduced from 24 to 18.

East India Company (*The Danish*), 1616. Dissolved in 1634. New one formed in 1670, a third in 1686, and a fourth in 1731. In 1777 the rights of the company were purchased by the king.

East India Company (*The Dutch*), 1595. Several companies united by the States in 1602.

East India Company (*The French*), 1664. Dissolved 1770. A new company formed 1785, but dissolved in 1790.

East India Company (*The Ostend*). Formed by Leopold in 1718, dissolved by Charles VI. in 1731.

East India Company (*The Swedish*), 1741. Reorganised in 1806.

Easter Eggs (*Serving one with*). Pelting one in the pillory with rotten eggs. In 1565 a Catholic priest in Scotland was seized in the service of the mass at Easter. Being seized he was dragged to the market-cross of Edinburgh, and there pelted with mud, filth, and rotten eggs. This was called 'serving him with his Easter eggs.'

Easter Limit (*The*). 'Termĭnus Paschālis.' From 8 March to 5 April. It begins with the vernal full moon, or that which immediately follows it. The earliest possible Easter Sunday is 22 March, and the latest possible is 25 April. Easter Sunday in 1943 will fall on 25 April, as it did in the year 1886.

The Easter *new* moon must fall somewhere between 8 March and 5 April. If on 8 March Easter Iay would be 21 March, if on 5 April it would be on 18 April. Now if 21 March happens to be Saturday, Easter Sunday will be the next day (March 22), the earliest possible. If, on the other hand, 18 April

should happen to be Sunday, then Easter Sunday would be postponed a week, viz. to 25 April, the latest day possible.

..* If the full moon fell on a Sunday, Easter day was postponed for a week, to prevent the coincidence of the Jewish passover and the Christian Easter being on the same day.

Easter Week. 'Hebdomăda Paschālis.' The week beginning with Easter Monday, and ending with the following Saturday, and therefore containing only 6 days. The next week following it was 'Hebdomada in Albis' (*q.v.*), which contained 8 days; and the week before it was the Great Week or Passion Week (*q.v.*), which contained 13 days.

Easterlings (*The*). 15th cent. Mariners of the Hanse-towns, as terrible at sea as the pirates of Algiers were afterwards. Spelman derives our word sterling [money] from these traders.

In the time of Richard I. monie coined in the east parts of Germany began to be of especiall request in England for the puritie thereof, and was called Easterling monie. Shortly after, some of that countrie skilful in mint matters and in all dies, were sent for into this realm to bring the coine into perfection, which since that time was called of them *sterling*, for Easterling.—CAMDEN.

Eastern Church (*The*). Separated from the Western or Latin Church about 324–334, and a rivalry began in 341. In 451 the Council of Chalcēdon conferred on the bishop of Constantinople equal rank and power with the bishop of Rome. John in 588 assumed the title of 'Œcumenical Patriarch.' The bishop of Constantinople is now generally called 'the Patriarch,' or 'the Patriarch of Constantinople.' *See* 'Patriarch.'

Eastern Empire (*The*). The eastern portion of the old Roman empire after its division by the brothers Valentinian and Valens, A.D. 364. Valens took the eastern part, with Constantinople for its capital; and Valentinian the western part, with Rome for his capital. The Eastern empire ended in 1453, when Mahomet II. warred against Constantine, who was slain, and the Eastern empire fell to the Ottomans or Turks.

The Western empire fell much sooner, viz. in A.D. 476.

Eating Fruit (*Death from*). Anacreon died from eating grapes. La Belle Gabrielle died from eating an orange. Kaiser Albert II., Friedrich III., and Maximilian I. all died from eating melons. Gen. Knox (U.S.) from eating raisins.

Eau de Brinvilliers, 1718. A poison made by Godin de Sainte Croix, who lived in scandalous intimacy with the Marchioness Brinvilliers, and furnished her with the means of poisoning her father, her two brothers, and several others. The marchioness chiefly employed a powder, called 'le poudre de succession.'

Eb'ionites (4 syl.). Judaising Christians of the 1st cent. They insisted on circumcision, despised the prophets, accepted only the gospel of St. Matthew, and that they interpolated ; looked on Jesus only as a human being, but believed that Christ descended on him at his baptism. Paul's *Epistles* they rejected as antinomian. The Ebionites continued to exist as a sect after 300.

M. Guizot says the first Christians of Jerusalem were called Ebionites, on account of their poverty; called in Rom. xv. 26 'the poor saints.' These 'poor saints' were afterwards accused of the heresy of denying the divinity of Christ. (ήβαιοί, poor, insignificant.)

Eblana, *i.e.* Dublin in Ireland.

Ecclesia Apostolica. The Church at Rome, called 'Cathedra Petri,' as having been founded by St. Peter.

Ecclesiastical Commission (*The*). I. 1583. A permanent commission, consisting of 44 members, established by Queen Elizabeth to decide on all questions respecting supremacy and uniformity. It had power to deprive any clergyman of his benefice without appeal. Heresy, schism, nonconformity, and even incest and adultery, fell within the pale of this court. Practically the whole power of the court rested with the bishops, and as there was no code to refer to, each question as it arose had to be left to the private judgment of the court or bishop appealed to. Parker deprived a vicar of his benefice for denying the verbal inspiration of scripture. Whitgift tried to force on the church the Calvinistic supralapsarian dogma. Bancroft was hot for the divine right of bishops. Abbot had no mercy on Erastians; Laud none for anti-Erastians.

'Supralapsarianism,' the doctrine that the fall of Adam and Eve, as well as the salvation or rejection of every living being, was predestined from all eternity.
'Erastianism,' the dogma that the church is, and ought to be, wholly dependent on the State.

II. 1686. Appointed by the advice of Jeffreys, the lord chancellor, with full authority, and without appeal, to decide on all ecclesiastical matters, without restraint of canon, civil, or municipal law. The commissioners were three divines and three laymen, all tools of the king (James II.), and their first act was to suspend Compton, bishop of London, because he would not favour the Romish party.

Ecclesiastical Commissioners (*The*), 1840. Amended from 1836. *Ex officio* the two archbishops and all the bishops of England and Wales, the deans of Canterbury, St. Paul's, and Westminster, the lord chancellor, the two chief justices, the master of the rolls, the chief baron, and the judges of the prerogative and admiralty courts, the president of the council, first lord of the treasury, chancellor of the exchequer, and one of the secretaries of state. Also nine laymen, not *ex officio*, seven appointed by the crown, and two by the archbishop of Canterbury. Five commissioners make a quorum, the highest in rank or else the senior commissioner to take the chair.

Ecclesiastical Courts. To decide on matters exclusively pertaining to the clergy and the established religion. Bacon enumerates ten such courts in his time :—

1. Convocation (*q.v.*).
2. The Court of Arches (*q.v.*).
3. Prerogative Court (*q.v.*).
4. Court of Audience (*q.v.*).
5. Court of Faculties (*q.v.*).
6. Court of Peculiars (*q.v.*).
7. Consistory Court (*q.v.*).
8. Archdeacon's Court (*q.v.*).
9. Court of Delegates. See 'Delegates.'
10. Court of Commissioners of Review (*q.v.*).
⁎ In 1857 the Prerogative Court was merged in the Court of Probate.
. In 1832 the Commission of Delegates was superseded by the Judicial Committee of the Privy Council.

II. In Scotland there have been three ecclesiastical courts—(1) the General Assembly ; (2) the Commissary Court ; and (3) the Court of Teinds.

Ecclesiastical Era of Antioch (*The*). This era began 1 Sept., B.C. 5492.

Ecclesiastical Era of Constantinople (*The*). This era began 1 April, B.C. 5508.

Ecclesiastical Titles Assumption Act (*The*), 1851. To prohibit the pope of Rome from conferring on ecclesiastics titles connected with the names of places in the United Kingdom, such as

Westminster, Nottingham, and so on. This act was provoked by what is called the 'papal aggression' of the court of Rome, which, 30 Sept., 1850, had divided Great Britain into territorial bishoprics under the Catholic archbishop of Westminster. Lord John Russell introduced the Ecclesiastical Titles Bill. Repealed 1867.

Ecclesiasticum Reservatum.

A provision made in 1555 whereby it was stipulated that if any of the German clergy abandoned the Roman Catholic Church hereafter, his benefice should be forthwith filled up by a Catholic successor. With this exception, the alienation of all ecclesiastical property, secularised before the Treaty of Passau in 1552, was confirmed by the Diet of Augsburg in 1555.

Passau, pronounce Pas-sow, as in now.

Eclectic School (*The*).

I. Of *Italian* painting, succeeded the *cinque cento* (*q.v.*). The Carracci headed the movement. Domenichino (1581–1641) and Guido Reni (1575–1642) were exponents also of the same school.

II. Of *French* painting, founded by Paul Delaroche (1797–1856). He selected from the *Classic* and *Romantic* schools.

Eclectics (*The*).

Alexandrine philosophers. Potamon and Ammonios Saccas (2nd cent.) were the first who attempted to fuse Platonism and Aristotelianism into one consistent system. The Neo-Platonic school was founded by Plotinus (205–270).

Modern eclecticism was founded by Victor Cousin, the French philosopher.

École Polytechnique (*The*), 1795.

France. For the education of young men for the army, navy, civil engineering, and telegraphy.

Écoles Centrales, 2 Feb., 1795.

Established by the National Convention for teaching sciences, arts, and letters. There must be 300,000 inhabitants in order to have such an institution. In 1802 many of these schools were converted into 'grammar schools' (*Lycées*), and in 1808 many ceased to exist.

Pronounce A-coal sen-trahl.

Écoles Chrétiennes (*Frères des*),

1681. Instituted at Reims by J. B. de la Salle for the gratuitous instruction of children in the elements of religion and in elementary instruction. ' Les Frères portent une grande robe de bure noire et un chapeau à cornes.' This order was not suppressed at the Revolution, and still flourishes in France and other Christian countries.

Pronounce A-coal kra-te-en.

Écoles Pieuses (*Les*).

The 'homes' of the waifs and strays brought under the care of the Piaristes (*q.v.*).

Pronounce A-coal pe-uze.

Écoles Primaires, 1802.

To give children elementary instruction, as reading, writing, arithmetic, and the elements of French grammar. In some elementary schools geography and history are taught. They subdivide into *écoles publiques* (or *communales*), and *écoles privées*; the former are directed by laymen and the latter by ecclesiastics. They are under the inspection of the bishops, pastors, rectors, prefects, sub-prefects, and mayors.

Pronounce A-coal pre-mair.

Écoles Secondaires, 1802.

For teaching ancient and modern languages, geography, history, and the elements of science. They include grammar schools (*lycées*), colleges, boarding schools (*pensions*), and so on.

Pronounce A-coal skone-dair.

Economists.

Christians who take for their rule of life 1 Cor. ix. 20: 'All things to all men.' In other words, 'Do as Rome does,' that is, adapt yourselves in every respect, as far as possible, to the society in which you are thrown.

Economists (French *économistes*).

A name given to certain French writers of the 18th cent., who maintained that agriculture is the only fountain of wealth, and therefore clamoured for a land-tax. They were usually called ' Physiocrates ' (*q.v.*).

Écorcheurs (*Les*), 1437.

A gang of adventurers who committed great ravages, chiefly in Hainault, during the revolt of the Low Countries against the Duke of Burgundy. The best known of their leaders were Villandras and Chabannes the bastard. They were called the Skinners (*écorcheurs*), says Bouillet, ' parce qu'ils se composaient pour la plupart de bouchers ou d'écorcheurs de bêtes,' or else because they stripped those who fell into their hands of all their clothes, even their body-linen. *See* ' French Brigands.'

Pronounce *Lays a-kor-shure.*

Écrasez l'infâme. A party watchword among the Encyclopædists, meaning Down with superstition, or Down with senseless mummery. In full it would be *Écrasez l'infâme superstition* (' Walpoliana,' ii. 88).

Pronounce *A-krah-zay lahn-fahm.*

Ecstasy of Plotinus. A rapture in which he lost his personal consciousness and became part of the ' universal mind.' Plotīnus says this ecstasy may be attained by music, by love, or by meditation. Paul speaks of such rapture in 2 Cor. xii. 2.

Ecstatic Doctor (*The*). *See* ' Divine Doctor.'

Ec'thesis of Heraclius. Published 638. Heraclius was emperor of the East, and the Ecthēsis was the famous edict in favour of the Monoth'elites (4 syl.), *q.v.*

Ecumenical Bishop, A.D. 592. John, bishop of Constantinople, assumed this title, but Gregory I. of Rome induced Mauritius, emperor of the East, to insist on his dropping the title.

Ecumenical Councils (*The Eight*).

I. At NICÆA in Bithynia, held 325, to condemn the doctrine of Arius, who denied the divinity of Christ. Present 318 bishops.

II. At CONSTANTINOPLE, held 381, to condemn the heresy of Macedonius, who denied the divinity of the Holy Ghost. Present 150 bishops.

III. At EPHESUS, held 441, to condemn Nestorius, who denied the divinity of the Virgin Mary. Present 200 bishops.

IV. At CHALCE'DON, held 451. to condemn the Monophysite heresy, Present 630 bishops.

(N.B.—The Anglican Church admits these four.)

V. At CONSTANTINOPLE (*the second*), held 553, to condemn the Nestorians. Present 165 bishops.

VI. At CONSTANTINOPLE (*the third*), held 680, to condemn the Monothelites. Present 170 bishops. *See* ' Synods.'

VII. At NICÆA (*the second*), held 787, to condemn the Iconoclasts and re-establish images.

VIII. At CONSTANTINOPLE (*the fourth*), 869, to depose Phocius and reinstate Ignatius. In this council the Monoth'elites and the Iconoclasts were both anathematised.

Monophysites (Greek μονος, φύσις, one nature), the human raised to the divine.

Nestorians allow the co-existence of the two natures of Christ, but not their union.

Monothelites, that is Μονοθελῆται (Greek μονος, θέλημα, one will), the human will of Christ being absorbed, as they supposed, in the Divine will.

Edda. A collection of mythic and heroic songs of Scandinavia. The *Poetic* or elder Edda was compiled by Sæmund

Sigfusson, and the songs compiled by him are supposed to belong to the 8th cent.; the oldest copy of Sæmund's Edda is of the 14th cent. It is from the original MS., and is preserved in the Royal Library of Copenhagen. Published by Resen in 1665, and edited by Rask in 1818.

The *Prose* or younger Edda was compiled by Snorro Sturleson, the Scandinavian Livy (1178–1241). It is supposed to have been compiled from posthumous papers left by Sæmund, Icelandic sources and traditions, and treats of Scandinavian mythology. This is sometimes called the Resenian Edda, because it was translated by Resen, in 1640.

Sæmund hinn Froda, Sigfusson, lived 1054-1133. Snorro Sturleson, 1178-1241. The *elder Edda* consists of two parts, the first mythological and the second heroic. The Sæmund Edda contains the famous poems of the Nibelungen cycle.

Edgar's Law. This was no law in the ordinary acceptation of the word, but the English constitution as it shaped itself in the hands of his minister Dunstan.

When the people clamoured for Edgar's law they meant they wished to be governed in the same way as Edgar governed the nation (959-975).— FREEMAN.

Edict (*The Perpetual*). I. Of Hadrian, A.D. 132. A compilation of all the edicts of preceding ediles and prætors, made by Salvius Juliānus.

II. 1611. The forty-seven articles published by Albrecht, archduke of Austria, for the administration of justice in his dominions.

Edict of Berlin (*The*), or ' Decree of Berlin,' 21 Nov., 1806. Issued by Napoleon I., declaring the blockade of the British Isles, and ' boycotting' the English.

Edict of Chateaubriant (*The*), 1551. By Henri II., against the Calvinists.

Edict of Crémieu (*The*), 1536. By François of Crémieu, to regulate the jurisdiction of bailies, seneschals, and presidents (*présidiaux*).

Edict of Grace (*The*), July 1629. A treaty granted ' by grace ' to the Huguenots soon after the capture of La Rochelle. By this treaty the reformers were reinstated in the possession of their places of worship, their cemeteries, and the exercise of their religion in the places they had before used, 'pending their return to the Catholic Church.'

By what has been said we may judge of the condition of the Reformed after the Edict of Grace.—FÉLICE, *Hist. of the Protestants of France*, book iii. 7.

Edict of January (*The*), 1562. Provided that those reformers who had taken possession of churches and ecclesiastical property in France should restore them without delay. It forbade reformers to destroy images or crosses, to meet within the walls of any town, or to go armed to any meeting (unless, indeed, they were of the privileged classes).

Edict of July (*The*), 1561. Granting toleration in France to domestic gatherings of reformers, but forbidding public meetings. See ' Edict of January.'

Edict of June 20 (*The*), 1730. A confirmation of the edict of 1620, granting to the church members of the three Vaudois valleys the right of working in their houses (with closed doors) on Catholic feast-days, of being employed on public works, and of acquiring real property. See 'Edict of Pacification.'

Edict of May 13 (*The*), 1694. In favour of the Vaudois, recognising their lawful establishment in the land of their ancestors, from which they had been expelled, their right to their hereditary possessions, and the revocation of the edicts of January and April 1686.

Edict of Melun (*The*), 1580. Redressing the complaints of the clergy.

Edict of Milan (*The*), March, 313. Published by Constantine in favour of Christians.

Edict of Nantes (*The*), 1598. An edict published by Henri IV. granting toleration ·to all Huguenots or Protestants, and placing them on entire equality with his Catholic subjects. Revoked by Louis XIV. (1685).

Pronounce Nantes to rhyme with *aunt, can't.*

Edict of Pacification (*The*), 1694. Granting full toleration not only to the Vaudois who belonged to the reformed religion from birth, but also to converts from Catholicism. This edict, as far as proselytes were concerned, was revoked by Victor Amadeus, and at the beginning of 1730 the exiles went to Geneva.

These edicts are very numerous in the 16th cent., with a view of putting an end to the religious wars. The most celebrated are—

The Edict of 19 May, 1563, by Charles IX., permitting Huguenots to assemble and worship in their own way.
The Edict of Nantes. *See above.*

Edict of Petites-Dates (*The*). 'L'Edit des Petites-Dates,' 1550. By Henri II., for the repression of abuses introduced ' dans la collation des bénéfices ecclésiastiques.'

Edict of Restitution (*The*), 1630. A foolish edict by Kaiser Ferdinand II. in the Thirty Years' War, after the retirement of the Danes. It enjoined restoration to the Catholics of the two archbishoprics, the twelve bishoprics, and all the parish churches, lands, and other property, which had been confiscated by the Protestants since the Treaty of Passau (7 Aug., 1552, *i.e.* 78 years ago). Compliance with this edict was well-nigh impossible, and at the Peace of Westphalia (24 Oct., 1648) the edict was cancelled.

Passau, pronounce *Pas-sow,* as in *now.*

Edict of Revocation (*The*), 1685. That is the Revocation of the Edict of Nantes (*q.v.*) by Louis XIV.

It was he [Louis XIV.] who in 1635 signed the fatal Edict of Revocation.—FÉLICE, *Hist. of the Protestants of France*, bk. iii. 7.

Edict of Romorantin (*The*), May 1560. Proposed by the French chancellor, Michel de l'Hôpital, restoring to the bishops the adjudication of the crime of heresy. This edict was prodigal of the most scandalous penalties, but it saved France from the establishment of the Inquisition which Cardinal de Lorraine laboured hard to introduce.

Edict of Theodoric (*The*), A.D. 500. Promulgated in Italy, but superseded by Justinian's laws in 554.

Edict of Toleration (*The*), 1787 (102 years after the Revocation). The Huguenots or Protestants are spoken of in this edict as ' non-Catholics.' It granted to non-Catholics the right of living in France and of exercising any vocation ; permission to marry before justices ; and the right of interment without calling in a Catholic priest. As no penalty was mentioned for nonconformity, of course perfect toleration was tacitly granted to all religionists.

Edict of Union (*The*). I. A.D. 405. Published by Honōrius against the Donātists and Manichæans, with a view of 'uniting' them with the Catholic Church.

II. 21 July, 1588. The edict by which Henri III., who had been driven out of Paris, was supported by the League, and declared *s'unir à elle.*

Edict of 1693 (*The*), 13 April. French history. This edict solemnly confirmed the Revocation of the Edict of Nantes, and enjoined that new means should be employed for the better instruction of the people in the true religion.

Nantes (1 syl.), to rhyme with *aunt, jaunt.*

Edict of 1724 (*The*), or 'The Royal Declaration of 1724,' 14 May. By Louis XV. on the advice of Cardinal Dubois. This was the last law against the French Protestants, and the most severe of all. It declared the punishment of perpetual imprisonment at the galleys for men, and life seclusion for women, with confiscation of property, if they attended any religious service except those of the Catholics. The galleys or imprisonment for all who sheltered or omitted to denounce a 'heretic.' All children to be baptized by a Catholic priest within twenty-four hours of their birth, and to be sent to a Catholic school till fourteen years of age. Notice to be given to the parish priest of illness. No marriage to be legalised unless solemnised by a Catholic priest. No child to be sent out of France to be educated. No office whatever to be held except by Catholics. All mulcts to be for the relief of necessitous new converts.

Ediles (2 syl.). Annual magistrates in Rome whose duty it was to see to the edifices (*ædes*), especially the public baths, aqueducts, and market-places. There were curule ediles and plebeian ediles, the latter instituted B.C. 493. They ceased to be created in the reign of Constantine.

Edinburgh is Edwins-burgh, so called from Edwin, who founded the castle in the 6th cent. In Notts is a village called Edwin-stowe, where Edwin was buried. Here Robin Hood was married.

Edinburgh (*Treaty of*), 6 July, 1560. Between Queen Elizabeth and the Scots for the evacuation of Scotland by the French. By this treaty François II. and Mary fully recognised the right of Elizabeth to the English crown, and agreed that Mary, in time to come,

should neither assume the title nor bear the arms of England.

At their coronation in Paris François and Mary were proclaimed king and queen of France England, and Scotland. The princes of Lorraine had money struck in France bearing the arms of England; and proclamations were made in the names of François and Mary, king and queen of the three realms.

Edinburgh (*University of*), 1582. Founded by James VI. (James I. of England). Reconstituted in 1858.

Edinburgh Review (*The*). Commenced in Oct. 1802. The political views were those of the Whig party.

Edmund Crouchback, 1241–1296. First earl of Lancaster, 2nd son of Henry III., the eldest son being Edward I.

Edmund Hall (*St.*), Oxford. Said to have been founded by Edmund archbishop of Canterbury, in the reign of Henry III. The head of the Hall is called 'the Principal.'

Edrisites (3 syl.), 785–919. A Mussulman dynasty which had Fez as the seat of government. The founder was Edris (785–793), of the race of Ali, poisoned by order of the calif Harun al Rashid.

Edris was succeeded by Edris II. (793-828); Mohammed I., Ali, Yahia I., Yahia II., Ali II., Yahia III., Yahia IV. (905-919).

Education. The first parliamentary grant for education was made in 1834. The Committee of Privy Council was appointed in 1839. Public elementary education in England and Wales was provided for in 1870 (33, 34 Vict. c. 75).

Edward I. 'Longshanks,' king of England (1239, 1274–1307). Son of Henry III. He married twice: (1) Eleanor daughter of Ferdinand III. of Castile, by whom he had four sons and eight daughters. The first two sons died young, and the last three daughters.

3rd son, EDWARD II. (the first prince of Wales) who succeeded his father.

The daughters who married are Eleanor, Joan, Margaret, Beatrix, and Elizabeth. Mary was a nun at Amesbury, and died 1286.

By his second wife he had two sons; Thomas earl of Norfolk, and Edmund of Woodstock, earl of Kent.

His style and title: 'Edwardus rex Angliæ dominus Hiberniæ et dux Aquitaniæ' (Guienne).

His title to France: On the death of

Charles IV., two claimants for the crown appeared, Philippe de Valois his cousin, and Edward I. his nephew. If the Salique law was set aside, then Blanche (sister of Charles IV.), wife of Ph')e de Valois, was the heiress; if the Salique law remained in force, Edward, who claimed through his mother Isabelle, must be set aside, and again Philippe de Valois, grandson of Philippe III. le Bel, was heir. In neither case had Edward any just claim.

PHILIPPE III. was father of PHILIPPE IV. and of Charles de Valois.

PHILIPPE IV. was father of LOUIS X., PHILIPPE V., CHARLES IV., and Isabelle (who married Edward II.). *See* 'Fatal Three.'

CHARLES IV. left a daughter, Blanche, who married PHILIPPE [VI.], son of Charles de Valois. This was after his accession to the throne; he was then son-in-law as well as cousin to the last king, CHARLES IV., and grandson of PHILIPPE III.

Edward II. ' Caernarvon,' king of England (1284, 1307–1327). This son of Edward I. was born at Caernarvon, and was the first English prince of Wales. He married Isabella, daughter of Philippe IV. of France, his cousin, by whom he had two sons and two daughters.

1. EDWARD III., who succeeded his father.

2. John of Eltham, earl of Cornwall.

3. Joan, who married David Bruce, king of Scotland.

4. Eleanor, who married Reynald count of Gueldres.

His *favourites* were Gaveston, who was twice banished—in 1297 and in 1307 —and at last executed summarily by the indignant barons in 1312. Edward's next favourite was Hugh Despenser, who was executed in 1326.

He was murdered in Berkley Castle by Maltravers and Gournay.

His style and title, up to 1326, was: ' Edwardus, D.G. rex Angliæ, dominus Hiberniæ, et dux Aquitaniæ ' (Guienne). From 1326 he discontinued the title of ' dux Aquitaniæ.'

Edward III. ' Windsor,' so called from the place of his birth (1312, 1327– 1377). Married Philippa of Hainault, by whom he had seven sons and five daughters.

                       Born

1st son. Edward the Black Prince, born at Woodstock, father of RICHARD II., who succeeded his grandfather. • •   1330
      (*Isabella*)   *

2nd son: William, born at Hatfield, who died 1336 .   1334
(*Joanna, born* 1335, *died* 1348.)

3rd son. Lionel duke of Clarence, born at Antwerp .   1338

4th son. John of Gaunt, born at Ghent, duke of Lancaster . . . . }   1339 or 1340

5th son. Edmund duke of York, born at King's Langley   1341
(*Blanche, died young; Mary and Margaret*)   * * *

6th son. William, born at Windsor, lived only from June to Sept. . .   1348

7th son. Thomas, born at Woodstock, created duke of Gloucester 1385 by Richard II., and murdered in 1397. Born, according to Stow and Dugdale . . .   1355

After the death of Philippa, Edward III. attached himself, without marriage, to Alice Perrars or Perrers, one of the ladies of the bedchamber.

His style and title, from 1327 to 1337 : ' Edwardus, D.G. rex Angliæ, dominus Hiberniæ, et dux Aquitaniæ ' (Guienne). From 1337 to 1377 : ' Edwardus, D.G. rex Angliæ et Franciæ [sometimes ' Franciæ et Angliæ '], dominus Hiberniæ, et dux Aquitaniæ.'

N.B.—All the monarchs of England from 1377 styled themselves ' king of France' up to 1800, when George III. relinquished the senseless title.

His claim to the throne of France. On the death of Charles IV. without male issue, the claimants were Philippe de Valois and Edward III. of England. The former was crowned as Philippe VI. de Valois.

PHILIPPE III. of France had two sons, viz. PHILIPPE IV. (who succeeded him) and Charles de Valois.

PHILIPPE IV. had for issue LOUIS X. (who succeeded and died without issue), PHILIPPE V. (who also died without issue), and Isabelle.

Philippe the claimant was the son of Charles de Valois, grandson of PHILIPPE III., and cousin of the last king, CHARLES IV.

Edward III. was the son of Isabelle, and great-grandson of PHILIPPE III., and nephew of the last king, CHARLES IV.

• The main argument was this: As women could not succeed to the crown, therefore Isabelle had no claim whatever, and her children could have none.

Edward III. and the two captive kings.—At the battle of Poitiers, 1355 Jean II. of France was made captive and brought to England. At the same time David II. of Scotland, defeated at Neville's Cross in 1346, was made captive. Thus were there two kings at one and the same time captives in London.

Edward IV. First of the line of York. The claim of York was undoubtedly superior to that of Lancaster, being from the third son (Lionel) of Edward III.; whereas the house of Lancaster was from John of Gaunt, the fourth son, and therefore a younger brother. The descent was from Lionel, third son of Edward III.

Lionel's daughter Philippa married Edward Mortimer. Their son was Roger Mortimer; and Roger Mortimer's daughter Anne married Richard (son of Edmund duke of York).

Richard duke of York, the *White Rose*, was slain in the battle of Wakefield; and his sons were EDWARD IV. and RICHARD III.

Edward married Elizabeth Woodville, a widow, and was the first of our sovereigns since the Conquest to marry a subject. He had ten children, but of the seven who reached maturity five were girls and two boys. Edward V. succeeded, but he and his brother Richard were both murdered in the Tower.

Elizabeth, the eldest daughter of Edward IV., and called 'The Rose of York,' or 'The White Rose of York,' married Henry VII., and thus united the rival branches of York and Lancaster.

His style and title: 'Edwardus, D.G. rex Angliæ et Franciæ, et dominus Hiberniæ.'

Edward V. Nominal king of England for about a month (1483). He was thirteen years of age, and his brother Richard was nine; both were murdered in the Tower by order of their uncle Richard [III.] duke of Gloucester. The actual assassins were Slater, John Dighton, and Miles Forest. In the reign of Charles II. the bodies of the princes were found under a staircase, and removed to Henry VII.'s Chapel in Westminster Abbey 1674.

Edward V. and Dr. Shaw.—Dr. Shaw, at St. Paul's Cross (Sunday, 22 June, 1483), preached from these words in the Book of Wisdom, 'Bastard slips shall not strike deep root,' his object being to show that Edward V. was a bastard. He said that Edward IV. was married to Lady Eleanor Butler, the widow of Lord Butler of Sudely and daughter of the Earl of Shrewsbury; consequently, Eliza-

beth Woodville (mother of Edward V.) was merely a concubine, and that Stillington, bishop of Bath, was a witness. As Edward V. was the son of a concubine, he could not come to the throne.

To set aside Edward and his brother Richard would not render Richard duke of Gloucester heir, because his elder brother Clarence left two sons behind; but Clarence having been put to death for treason barred his sons by his attainder.

Richard III. (1483) ordered Edward V. to be called officially 'Edward the bastard, lately called Edward V.'

Edward VI. Son of Henry VIII (1537, 1547–1553). He died after an attack of small-pox, leaving the crown to Lady Jane Grey. *His style* was 'Edward, D.G. of England, France, and Ireland king; Defender of the faith, and supreme head of the Anglican and Hibernian Church.'

The Pretender, Edward VI.—Lambert Simnel, son of Thomas Simnel, a joiner of Oxford, instructed by one Simons, a priest, to personate Edward Plantagenet, son of the Earl of Warwick, and become a 'pretender' to the crown, in the early part of the reign of Henry VII. (1486). He was crowned at Dublin as Edward VI. 2 May, 1487. Being defeated at Stoke by Henry VII. (16 June, 1487), he was made a scullion in the king's kitchen, but was afterwards raised to falconer.

Henry released Edward Plantagenet from prison and showed him publicly to the people, to show the imposition of Lambert Simnel. Edward VI. [Simnel] was crowned by the Bishop of Meath, with a diadem taken from a statue of the Virgin Mary, and carried to the castle on the shoulders of a chieftain named Darcy.

Edward VI.'s First Prayer Book or *The First Liturgy of Edward VI.* 1549 (2, 3 Edw. VI.). Substituted for the Latin *Mass Book*. By the Act for Uniformity all clergymen who refused to adopt the new liturgy were subject to imprisonment for six months for the first offence, loss of benefice for the second offence, and perpetual imprisonment for the third.

The DAILY SERVICE did not contain the Introductory Sentences, Exhortation, Confession, and Absolution, but began with the Lord's Prayer. There were no State prayers in this liturgy.

The LITANY contained a petition against the papacy.

The COMMUNION SERVICE did not contain the *Ten Commandments*, but enjoined that *water* be mixed with the wine.

In the BAPTISMAL SERVICE exorcism was employed to drive out the evil spirit; the child was clothed in a chrisom, and was anointed on the head.

The CATECHISM formed part of the service, but it comprised only an exposition of the Creed, the Lord's Prayer, and the Ten Commandments.

In the MARRIAGE SERVICE the sign of the cross was to be made on the forehead of the newly-married persons, and a present of money was given to the bride when the ring was put on her finger.

In the BURIAL SERVICE prayers for the dead were offered.

VESTMENTS. The priests of parish churches were to wear a surplice only; in cathedrals the hood was to be worn in preaching.

Edward VI.'s Second Prayer Book, or *The Second Liturgy of Edward VI.*, 1552. The first liturgy reformed by Cranmer under the advice of Bucer and Peter Martyr.

In the DAILY SERVICE the Introductory Sentences, the Exhortation, the Confession, and the Absolution were added.

In the COMMUNION SERVICE the Ten Commandments were added; but the Introit, prayers for the dead, the name of the Virgin Mary, the sign of the cross, and mixing *water* with the wine were all omitted.

In the BAPTISMAL SERVICE exorcism, anointing the child, chrisom, and dipping the child thrice were omitted.

In the MARRIAGE SERVICE the sign of the cross and present of money were omitted.

In the BURIAL SERVICE prayers for the dead were omitted.

VESTMENTS. The nether albe, 'vestments,' and cope were forbidden. Prelates might wear a rochet, but other clergymen '*a surplice only.*

Edward Longshanks. See 'Edward I.'

Edward of Caernarvon. See 'Edward II.'

Edward of Hampton, Edward VI. (1537, 1547–1553). Ca'led Hampton from Hampton Court, the place of his birth.

Edward of Hampton was no otherwise prince of Wales then under the general title of England, his father being king of England and Wales.—COKE, *Reports* (3 Jacobi, sect. viii.).

Edward the Black Prince (1330–1376). Son of Edward III., king of England, and father of Richard II. As he died a year before his father, he never succeeded to the crown. He was called *Black* because he was a name of terror to the French.

Similarly Lord Clifford was called *Black* for his cruelties. George Petrowitsch was called by the Turks *Black George* from the terror of his name; Agnes countess of March was called *Black Agnes* for her resistance to Edward III. at Dunbar. The Black Sea means the sea of terror, and the Black Wind the wind of terror. *See* 'Black.'

Edward the Confessor (1004, 1041–1066). A king of England before the Conquest. Canonised 1166 by Alexander III. The use of the Great Seal was first introduced by this king.

Confessores dicti qui martyrio vitam pro Christo, quem palam confessi et contestati sunt, finierunt. DU CANGE, vol. iii. p. 644, col. 1.

Edward the Elder (870, 901–925), king of England.

Edward the Martyr (961, 975–979). A king of England before the Conquest, assassinated at Corfe by order of his stepmother Elfrĭda, to make room for her own son, Ethelred the Unready.

Edward was no martyr in the ordinary sense of the word, but he was basely and treacherously murdered.

Edward the Outlaw. Son of Edmund Ironside, outlawed to Sweden by Canute.

Eelkhanee Tables (*The*). The astronomical tables of Nazir-u-Dien, produced in the reign of Hoolaku, shah of Persia (1258–1265). They are still highly esteemed, and are referred to for the latitude and longitude of places not yet fixed by European observations. *See* 'Star Tables.'

The word Eelkhanee means 'Chief of the Tribes.'

Effendi. A Turkish title of courtesy equal to our squire, and always placed after the proper name. Sometimes, however, in speaking to a Turkish gentleman the word effendi is used as the French use monsieur before a proper name. The Grand Chancellor of Turkey is called 'Reis Effendi.'

Égalité (*Monsieur*). Louis Philippe Joseph, duc d'Orléans (1747–1793). When Barère, president of the National Assembly, put the question what punishment should be accorded to the king, Louis XVI., the Duc d'Orléans rose and said, '*La mort sans phrase.*' It is somewhat strange, but the only person who voted against the sentence of death was Thomas Paine, an Englishman, who had the manhood to say to the assembly, 'The king's death, instead of an act of justice, will appear in history as an act of vengeance.' Louis Égalité was guillotined 1793.

Egypt and Bible History.

There were thirty dynasties in ancient Egypt. From B.C. 3892 to 340.

The I. dynasty began in Upper Egypt with Menês, B.C. 3892. Menês founded the city of Memphis.

No trace of the 'Flood' has yet been discovered by Egyptologists.

II. dynasty began with Boethos, B.C. 3639. The second king of this line was Kakan, who introduced the worship of Apis, the sacred bull.

III. dynasty began with Necherophês,

B.C. 3338. The Sphinx was carved in this dynasty.

IV. dynasty began with Khufu [Suphis or Cheops], B.C. 3124. Khufu built the great pyramid. His successor, Khafra or Khafren [Cephren or Kephren], built the second great pyramid; and the third king of the same line, Menkara [Mykerinos], built the third great pyramid.

V. dynasty began B.C. 2840. The VI. began B.C. 2744, the last monarch being Queen Nitocris, noted for her great beauty. VII. dynasty began B.C. 2592; the VIII. B.C. 2522; the IX. B.C. 2674; the X. B.C. 2565; the XI. B.C. 2423.

XII. dynasty began B.C. 2380 with Amen'emhat. In this dynasty were built the Temple of Amun-Ra, at Thebes, and the obelisk of Heliopôlis. Amenemhat's son was Usurtesen I.

XIII. dynasty began B.C. 2136; the XIV. B.C. 2167.

HYKSOS or 'Shepherd Kings' were probably Arabs. The XV., XVI., XVII. dynasties (B.C. 1842, 1684, 1591).

It is supposed that ABRAHAM went to Egypt in B.C. 1806, while the XVI. dynasty was regnant.

It is supposed that JOSEPH was viceroy of Sutapepe-Nubti of the same dynasty. About B.C. 1713.

Hyk = king, Sos = shepherds.

XVIII. dynasty was founded by Aahmes [Amāsis], B.C. 1591, who expelled from Egypt the Shepherd Kings.

XIX. dynasty, B.C. 1443, was the Golden Age of the Pharaohs. The XIX. began with Ramses I., who was succeeded by Seti [Sethos], who built Karnak. Ramses II. was by far the greatest of all the kings of Egypt. It is said that he had 170 children, of which 111 were sons, that he reigned 67 years, and died above 96 years of age. After his death came a period of confusion.

It is supposed that MOSES was born in the reign of the great Ramses, and that the EXODUS occurred after his death, during the reign of Arisu, a usurper and a Syrian, about B.C. 1314.

No hint can be traced by Egyptologists either of the Exodus or the Passage of the Red Sea.

XX. dynasty was founded B.C. 1269 by Set-Nekht, and Egypt was on its full decline.

XXI. dynasty began B.C. 1091.

SOLOMON married Abra, the daughter of Pfusenes II. [Pisham], last king of this line. She was 19 years of age (1 Kings iii. 1). It is supposed that 'Solomon's Song' was an epithalamium of this alliance.

XXII. dynasty was founded by Sheshouk [Shishak], B.C. 961, who received under his protection Jeroboam, and afterwards marched against Rehoboam with 12,000 chariots and 60,000 horsemen.

See 1 Kings xiv. 25, and 2 Chron. xii.

It is supposed that 2 Chron. xiv. 9-15, and xvi. 8, &c., refer to Zerah, the fourth of this dynasty, generally called Osorthon II.

XXIII. dynasty began B.C. 787. The second king of this line (Osorthon IV.) was the Egyptian Hercules.

XXIV. dynasty had only one sovereign, Bochoris, B.C. 729-716. He was deposed and put to death by Shabak.

XXV. dynasty founded by Shabak, B.C. 716.

HOSEA gave tribute to this king (2 Kings xvii. 3).

The successor of Shabak was Shabakok, called So in 2 Kings xvii. 4.

HEZEKIAH formed a confederacy with So, king of Egypt, against Sennacherib, king of Assyria, and Sennacherib marched against the allies (2 Kings xviii., xix.); but So had been succeeded by Tirhākah or Tarach.

XXVI. dynasty was founded by Psammetik [Psammetichus] the Great, B.C. 685. His son, Neku II., called Pharaoh-Nechoh (2 Kings xxiii. 29, &c.), overthrew Josiah and slew him.

Pharaoh Hophra, the seventh of this line, contemporary of Jeremiah (xliv. 30), was dethroned by Nebuchadnezzar, king of Babylon. In 525 B.C. Egypt was an appanage of Persia (dynasty XXVII.); then followed a Saite dynasty, a Mendesian, and a Sebennyte, after which the Persian power was restored. Next came the Græco-Macedonian period; and B.C. 30 Egypt became a Roman province.

Egyptian Days. Unlucky days. There are three in the year, viz. the last Monday in April, the 2nd Monday of August, and the 3rd Monday of December. Called Egyptian because ill-luck was attributed to them by the Egyptian astrologers. In the Exeter Kalendar, a MS. of the time of Henry II., there are 24 Egyptian days.

Three days there are in the year which we call 'Egyptian days.'—Saxon MS. (British Museum).

⁎ In regard to Friday, the Brahmins and Buddhists consider it a dies mala, as well as many Christians.

Egyptian Hall (The). In the Mansion House, City of London. It was built after the description of the Egyptian Hall by Vitruvius.

Egyptian Version of the Sacred Scriptures, embraces the Coptic and Memphitic, in the dialect of Lower Egypt. It is ascribed to the 3rd cent.

There is a version in the dialect of Upper Egypt, called 'Sa'hidic' or 'Theba'idic,' even more ancient. Probably close upon the 2nd cent.

Eight (The), i.e. ' Al Motamen.' So the Kalif Al Motassem was called by a play on his name, after his death. His subjects used to say he was the 8th of his dynasty, was born in the 8th month, reigned exactly 8 years, 8 months, and 8 days, had fought 8 battles, and left at death 8 sons, 8 daughters, 8,000 slaves, and 8 millions of gold.

It is possible that this may be true, just as it is possible that a dealer may hold thirteen trumps in his hand.

Eight Articles (*The*), 1555. While Cranmer, Ridley, and Latimer were in prison they drew up their confession of faith in eight articles: (1) the Scriptures are the true word of God; (2) the three Catholic creeds are to be believed; (3) justification is by faith only; (4) marriage is lawful to all men; (5) we reject the dogma of transubstantiation; (6) we reject the dogma of purgatory; (7) the cup in the Lord's Supper is to be given to the laity; and (8) public worship is not to be carried on in any foreign tongue. *See* 'Articles.'

Eight Canonical Hours (*The*). In the Catholic Church. There are four great (printed in capitals), and four little (printed in italics).

MATINS, or Nocturnes, between midnight and daybreak. On festivals and Sundays, three psalms, three anthems, and three lessons.

LAUDES, at daybreak. Five psalms, two or more capitules (scripture extracts), prayers, and canticles.

Prime, six o'clock in the morning. The first hour of the day.

Tierce, nine o'clock in the morning. The third hour of the day.

Sexte, twelve o'clock, or mid-day. The sixth hour of the day.

Nones, three o'clock in the afternoon. The ninth hour of the day.

VESPERS, at sunset. Five psalms, a capitule, a hymn, the *Magnificat*, one or more anthems, and prayers.

COMPLINE, at bedtime. Confession, one lesson, three psalms, an anthem, a hymn, a capitule, a short response, *Nunc Dimittis*, and prayers.

Eight Paradises (*The*), or 'Hesht Behesht.' Eight gardens in Ispahan, on either side of the gate called Char Baugh. Each garden has a pleasure-house.

Eighteenth Brumaire (*The Battle of the*), Year VIII. (9 Nov., 1799).

Between Napoleon Bonaparte and the Directory. The Directory was overthrown, and Bonaparte constituted 'First Consul.'

Eighth Wonder of the World (*The*). The Escurial of Spain (*q.v.*).

Eighty (*The*), or the Ottanta. The upper house of legislature in the republic of Florence, in the time of Savonarola; the lower house consisted of 3,200 *benefiziati*, divided into three sections, holding office for six months. All laws were proposed by the Signoria, discussed by the Ottanta, and voted in silence into law by the Commons.

The *benefiziati* were those who had already held office in the state, or had been proposed for office. The former were called the *Seduto*, and the latter the *Veduto*.

Eighty-six. 'The immortal 86.' The followers of C. S. Parnell in the House of Commons in 1886, &c. These 86 really ruled the House, for they voted as one man, and could overthrow or carry any measure. Home Rule was the great question. The Tory government was thrown out by the 'immortal 86,' and Mr. Gladstone, who supported Home Rule, was supported by them.

Eikon Basilike (I-kon Bă-zil-ĭ-ky). Published 1649, at one time attributed to Charles I.: but John Gauden, writing to the Bishop of Exeter, says the book 'is wholly and only my invention.' It contains a full account of the trial and condemnation of the king.

Eikonoclastes (5 syl.), 1649. Milton's reply to 'Eikon Basilikê.'

Eisteddfod (*The*), 1078. First appointed by Gryffith ap Conan to reform the Welsh bard system. In these annual meetings bards of merit rehearsed their poems, and minstrels played their harps. These bards were oral historians and genealogists. An Eisteddfod was held at Caerwys, 26 May, 1568, by proclamation of Queen Elizabeth. It was again revived by the Gwyneddigion Society in 1798; and again by the Cymrodorion Society in 1828. It lasts several days, and begins with the opening of the Gorsedd (or council of bards), and concludes with the Eisteddfod, or competition for prizes in poetry, recitation, and music.

Eisteddfod is from the Welsh verb *eistedd*, to sit, and means a session, meeting together, or muster.

El Dora'do. Manoa, the hypothetical capital of Guiana, supposed by Sir Walter Raleigh and others to be so affluent that it was called 'The Golden City,' and Guiana was called 'The Golden Empire.'

He (Sir Walter) seems to have heard many wonderful rumours of gold mines, and of cities built of gold and silver, and even embossed with precious stones: but he discovered no magnificent Manoa, with pinnacles blazing with diamonds and rubies, nor any gold mines, only signs of gold in the mountains beyond the Spanish town of St. Thomas.—HOWITT, *History of England* (James I. vol. iii. p. 74).

Elders (*The*), or 'Council of the Elders' (*Conseil des Anciens*). One of the two legislative councils of the 'Constitution of Year III.' in French history (Sept. 22, 1795). It had no power of initiating any law, but only of veto or approval. The initiative was restricted to the 'Council of 500' (*q.v.*), and the executive to the five directors.

Eldest Son of the Church (*The*). Clovis, grandson of Merwig or Merovens (465, 481–511). The first king not an Arian.

Eldon Law Scholarship. Value 200*l.*, and tenable for three years. Founded in the University of Oxford in honour of Lord Chancellor Eldon in 1830.

El'eanor Crosses. Twelve memorial crosses erected in places where the bier of Eleanor of Castile, wife of Edward I., rested on its way from Hornby, in Lincolnshire, where she died, to Westminster, where she was buried. Three still remain : viz. at Walsham, Northampton, and Geddington. Charing Cross was destroyed in 1647, but a model of it stands in the front of the South-Eastern railway station, Strand, London.

The twelve are these: Charing, Dunstable, Geddington, Grantham, Lincoln, Northampton, St. Albans, Stamford, Stoney Stratford, Walsham, West Cheap, and Woburn.

Charing cross was the work of Richard and Roger Crandale.

Dunstable cross was the work of John Battle.

Lincoln cross was the work of Richard de Howe.

Northampton cross was the work of John Battle.

Stoney Stratford cross was the work of John Battle.

Walsham cross was the joint work of Dymenge de Leger and Dymenge de Reyns.

West Cheap was rebuilt by John Hetherley, lord mayor of London.

Woburn cross was the work of John Battle.

*** Some of these crosses, but were certainly not memorial crosses, but were built by Queen Eleanor herself as works of piety.

Eleanor, Maid of Brittany. Sister of Prince Arthur, and next to

Arthur lawful successor to the crown of England. John usurped the crown, and both Eleanor and Arthur were captured by him at Mirabel 31 July, 1202. Arthur met with his death mysteriously, and Eleanor was imprisoned for life. She died in Bristol Castle 1241.

Eleatic School of Philosophers (*The*). So called from Eléa, in Italy, the chief seat of these philosophers. They were divided into the Old and New Schools. The Old School was speculative, like the Ionic sect, and taught that there is but one element. The New School confined themselves to the study of natural philosophy.

The chief of the *Old School* were Xenophãnês, the founder (B.C. 556–456); Parmenïdês (B.C. 513–430), and Zenon (B.C. 430–405).

The chief of the *New School* were Leucippos (B.C. 510–430), Democrítos (B.C. 509–400), and Protagõras (B.C. 481–411).

Xenophãnês revived the Eastern theory that God and the Universe are identical.

The Eleatic Metaphysicians were Pantheists, and the Eleatic Physicians were Atomistics.

Electoral Roll (*The*). University of Cambridge. Consists of members of the senate who have resided for fourteen weeks, at least, within 1½ mile of Great St. Mary's Church. The following are *ex officio* members : All officers of the University (members of the senate), all heads of houses, all professors and public examiners.

The Electoral Roll is published by the first Monday in October, from which day residence is calculated.

Electors (*The*). Originally the seven most powerful feudatories of Germany, who assumed the exclusive privilege of choosing the kaiser. They were (1) the king of Bohemia, (2) the duke of Saxony, (3) the margrave of Brandenburg, (4) the count palatine of the Rhine, (5) the archbishop of Mentz or *Mayence*, (6) the archbishop of Trèves, and (7) the archbishop of Cologne; the archbishop of Mentz was the official president, and 'Convener of the Electors.'

In 1618 the Duke of Bavaria was substituted for the King of Bohemia (the palsgrave), but in 1648 the palsgrave was readmitted, and in 1692 Ernest duke of Hanover was created the *ninth* elector; but in 1777 the number was again reduced to *eight*. In 1356 the Golden Bull of Karl IV. recognised the right of the electors to choose the king, but in 1806 the whole system was abolished by Napoleon Bonaparte.

The title of Elector continued to be held in Hesse-Cassel till 1866. The electoral crown was a scarlet cap turned up with ermine.

Electric Telegraph (*The*). Patented by Cooke and Wheatstone 12 June, 1837; brought into use on the Great Western Railway 1839; purchased by the postmaster-general 31 July, 1868; management of the telegraph assumed by the post-office 5 Feb., 1870.

Morse's original instrument dates from 1835. The submarine electric telegraph from Dover to Calais was laid in Aug. 1850, and purchased by the postmaster-general in 1888.

Elemental Spirits. Beings supposed in the middle ages to preside over the four elements. The elemental spirits of *fire* were called SALAMANDERS; the elemental spirits of *air* were called SYLPHS; the elemental spirits of *earth* were called GNOMES (1 syl.); and the elemental spirits of *water* were called UNDINES (2 syl.).

Elephant (*Order of the*), 1189. A Danish military order created by Knut VI. after his crusade in the East, when an elephant was killed. Revived in 1458 by Christian I. The cordon is blue moiré.

Elephants. The eight which sustain the world, according to Indian mythology, are called Achtequedjams.

Eleusin'ian Mysteries (*The*). The sacred rites with which the annual festival of Cerês was celebrated at Eleusis in Attica. '

Eleuther'ia. Games in honour of Zeus Eleuthêrios, so named from Eleuthêris, a city of Bœotia, near which the famous battle of Platæa was won B.C. 479. *See* 'Platæa.'

Eleven (*The*). Athenian magistrates who had the charge of executing criminals.

When he [Socrates] came in from bathing, he sat down, and did not speak much. For then the officer of the Eleven came in.—PLATO, *The Phaedon.*

Eleven Articles (*The*), 1560. Provisionary articles drawn up by the bishops in the early part of the reign of Queen Elizabeth for the instruction and guidance of the clergy and people till the meeting of convocation: (1) The Trinity is to be believed; (2) the holy scriptures and the three creeds are all sufficient; (3) the Church has authority to decree rites and ceremonies; (4) all persons not lawfully appointed shall be excluded from the ministry; (5) asserts the royal supremacy; (6) renounces all papal jurisdiction; (7) declares that the Common Prayer Book is according to scripture; (8) forbids exorcism, and the use of oil, salt and spittle in baptism; (9) rejects private masses, and denies the propitiatory sacrifice of the mass; (10) enjoins communion in both kinds; and (11) rejects images, relics, praying on beads, pilgrimages, miracles, and so on. *See* 'Articles.'

Eleven Members (*The*), 1647. When the army presented their ' Humble Representation' to parliament, it demanded the expulsion of eleven members, with H)lles at their head. The army charged these members with stirring up strife between them and the parliament, and with a secret design of renewing the civil war. The eleven members were not expelled, but were induced to withdraw. A London mob forced the House to recall the eleven, and fourteen peers with 100 commoners fled to the army. Cromwell in two days took London, restored the 114 fugitives, and expelled the obnoxious eleven.

Elgin Marbles (*The*), 1816. So called from Lord Elgin, who collected them during his mission to the Porte in 1802. They were chiefly derived from the Parthenon, a temple of Minerva, on the Acropolis of Athens, of which they formed part of the frieze and pediment built by Phidias about B.C. 500. They were purchased by the British government for 35,000*l.*, and placed in the British Museum.

Elgin, pronounce *gin* as in the word ' begin,' not like the monosyllable.

Elijahs of Mosul (*The*). One of the three branches of the Nestorians. The other two are the ' Josephs of Ami'da' and the ' Simeons of Ormia.'

Eliot (*George*), the pseudonym of Miss Marian Evans (afterwards Mrs. Cross), a novelist (1819–1880).

Elisabeth (*Mad.*), sister of Louis XVI., who shared the captivity of the Royal family, and was scandalously guillotined in 1794.

Elizabeth, daughter of Henry VIII. (1533, 1558–1603). Katharine was divorced 23 May and Elizabeth born 7 Sept. the same year. Elizabeth is called 'The Virgin Queen of England,' because she was never married.

Her style was: 'Elizabeth, D.G. of England, Fian e, and Ireland queen; Defender of the Faith ; Supreme Governor of the Church of England and Hibernia.'

Elizabeth (1 Eliz. c. 1) insisted that the title 'Supreme Governor of the Church' should be substituted for 'Supreme Head of the Church.'

** *Elizabeth and Mary queen of Scots.* Elizabeth was not the cousin of Mary queen of Scots, but the cousin of Mary's father.

HENRY VII. had issue HENRY VIII. (who succeeded him) and Margaret (who married James IV. of Scotland).

ELIZABETH was a daughter of HENRY VIII. Margaret's son was James V. of Scotland, and Mary queen of Scots was the daughter of James V. (she married Henry Stuart, lord Darnley).

Her favourites were, first, Robert Dudley (earl of Leicester), who died 1588; then Robert Devereux (earl of Essex), executed for treason in 1601.

Elizabethan Architecture.

A style of domestic architecture which prevailed in the reign of Elizabeth, especially used in mansions and palatial buildings. Its gables are most characteristic.

Ellerton Theological Essay.

Oxford University. Value 21*l.* annually. Founded by Dr. Ellerton, fellow of Magdalen College, 1825.

Ellison Gallery (*The*)

of water-colour paintings. Presented to the nation by Elizabeth Ellison, and placed in the South Kensington Museum, May 1860.

Elms (*The*).

The place of execution in Smithfield previous to the reign of Henry IV., when the gibbet was erected at Tyburn, which continued to be the chief place of execution in London till 1783.

Eloquence (*Father of French*).

Alain Chartier, secretary to Charles VI. and VII. He was both poet and prose writer (1386-1458).

Eloquent Doctor (*The*).

Peter Aureŏlus, archbishop of Aix. There was a Peter of Ravenna surnamed Chrysologos, or Golden-speech, who died 450, and was canonised. And two Chrysostoms or Golden-mouthed, viz. Dion and John. Dion was born in Bithynia A.D. 80 and died 116, and John was born at Antioch 347 and died 407. It is this latter who is generally known as St. Chrysostom (the saint with the golden mouth).

Elrington and Bosworth Professorship. *See* 'Anglo-Saxon, &c.'

13

Elzevirs.

Books printed by a celebrated family of printers in Holland between 1533 and 1680. The 12mo and 16mo classics are beautifully and correctly printed. The Virgil, Terence, and other Roman classical authors, the New Testament and the Psalter, have an unrivalled reputation.

For *Greek* printing the ALDINES are wholly unrivalled.

Emancipation Act (*The*), 13 April, 1829.

The act which emancipated Catholics from religious and civil disabilities in the United Kingdom of Great Britain and Ireland. It was framed by Sir Robert Peel, in the ministry of the Duke of Wellington, and signed by George IV.

Emancipation of Slaves (*The*),

28 August, 1833 (3, 4 Will. IV.). By this act slavery was abolished throughout the British colonies, and slave-owners were compensated by a grant from parliament of 30 millions sterling.

In 1861 Alexander II. of Russia emancipated 50 million serfs, but 'it has proved a gigantic failure, as the wretchedness of the peasantry is greater, the cultivation of the soil inferior, and much of the land is little better than waste. They cannot pay the interest of the money, which is 95 millions sterling, and hundreds are knouted every year. The result is the irrepressible Nihilists, by whom Alexander was blown to pieces.'—*Nineteenth Century,* June 1889.

Emania (*The Kings of*).

King Kimboath of Ireland built the palace of Emania in Ulster, an epoch from which Tigernach dates the dawn of authentic Irish history. From this splendid palace the princes of Ulster were called the 'kings of Emania.' The princely palace of Emania was utterly destroyed when Muredach [Emain Macha] Tirech invaded Ulster, and dispossessed his cousin, the usurper Colla, of his kingdom (A.D. 327).

It was Colla himself and his brothers who burnt Emania after their return from banishment.

Embargo Act (*The*), 22 Dec., 1807,

of President Jefferson, forbidding American vessels to leave their ports. This was, in fact, a measure preparatory to war, allowing merchants to call home their ships, and the country to put itself into a posture of defence. Repealed 3 Feb., 1809, 'as ruinous to the States, unsatisfactory to France, and ineffectual as a retaliation upon England.'

Embassy of the Three Philosophers (*The*), B.C. 151.

An embassy sent by the Athenians to the Roman senate to obtain a mitigation of the fire

(500 talents) imposed on them for attacking Orŏpus. The fine was reduced to 100 talents. The three philosophers sent were Diogenês the Stoic, Critolaŏs the Peripatetic, and Carucadês (founder of the third academy).

Embassy to China (*The*), 1793. (George) lord Macartney was sent by George III. on a friendly embassy to Kien Lung, emperor of China, who was at the time in his summer residence, Zhe-hol, in Tartary. His journey from Pekin to Zhe-hol was most gratifying, and more information of this ancient people was gained in this embassy than in all preceding ages put together. He tells us that white is worn in mourning, but never by brides; that the left is the side of honour; that titles of honour never descend; and that all ranks, except that of emperor, depend on competitive examination. Yellow is the imperial colour.

Ember Days, 1095. Four times a year: the *spring* being the Wednesday, Friday, and Saturday of Ember week, or the week after the first Sunday in Lent; the *summer* being the same days after Whit-Sunday; the *autumn* the same days after the feast of Holy Cross (14 Sept.); and the *winter* the same days after the feast of St. Lucia (13 Dec.). These seasons in the Western Church are appointed for the ordination of the clergy.

German *quatember*, i.e. 'quatuor tempora,' or four seasons. Consult Skeat's Dictionary.

Emerald Club (*The*), 1882. A branch of the Fenian Brotherhood whose object was to work by force alone for the freedom of Ireland. Dynamite and other compounds of nitro-glycerine were freely employed. The Emerald Society was organised in the United States of North America, and was contemporary with the Dublin 'Invincibles.' The principal of the Emerald Society was O'Donovan Rossa. *See* 'Irish Associations.'

Emerald of the Green Vault (*The*). An immense uncut Peruvian emerald given by Randolph II. to the Elector of Saxony, and kept in the Green Vault (*grünes Gewölbe*) at Dresden.

This 'vault' is in the Zwinger, a group of buildings erected by Augustus II. as a vestibule to his new palace. It is called 'Green' from the colour of the paper or hangings with which it was originally covered. The regalia used at the coronation of Augustus (a present of Karl V.) are still kept in the seventh apartment. The Emerald is in the eighth or last apartment.

Émeute. A riot of a political character, the result of what the French call 'attroupement' or party meetings in the public streets and squares. These public musters were first declared illegal in France in 1791; the law was confirmed 24 May, 1834, and again 7 June, 1848, when the pillagers of shops, breakers of windows, plunderers of arms, stump orators, and leaders of riots were most severely handled.

The Great Three Days Émeute of 1830 occurred on Tuesday, Wednesday, and Thursday, 27, 28, 29 July, when Charles X. was obliged to flee and abdicate.

Emil'ian Provinces (*The*). The northern part of the States of the Church (*i.e.* the Romagna), with the duchies of Parma and Modĕna, which in 1860 were attached to Sardinia, but now form part of the kingdom of Italy.

In 1796 Napoleon Bonaparte called Emilia the 'Emilian Republic.' NEW EMILIA comprehends Bologna, Ferrara, Forli, Massa and Carrara, Modĕna, Palma, Placentia, Ravenna, and Reggio.

Emilie (*The Divine*), to whom Voltaire wrote verses, was Madame Châtelet, with whom he lived at Cirey for ten years. Her palfrey was called 'Rossignol.'

Emir al Omra. Commandant of commandants; a military rank and title created by the Calif Rhadi (936) as a sop to the Turkish guards, a constant terror of the Abbasides (3 syl.), as the Pretorian guards were of the Roman emperors. This great officer had the sole management of all military matters; officiated for the calif in the mosque of Bagdad; and had his name mentioned in the public prayers. The French 'Mayor of the Palace' resembled in rank and power the Emir al Omra of the Abbaside califs.

Imperator imperatorum would be the Latin equivalent.

Emma. So Harold called his coat-of-mail.

And he put on his coat-of-mail which he called Emma, and which was so strong that no man could pierce it.—FREEMAN, *Old English History*, &c. p. 314.

Emmanuel College. n Cambridge University. Founded by Sir Walter Mildmay in 1584.

Emmett's Insurrection. In Dublin 23 July, 1803, in which Lord Kilwarden and several other persons were assassinated by the insurgents. It received its distinctive name from Robert Emmett, a young enthusiast, who headed this outbreak, and only arrived in Dublin the previous year (1802). Emmett had manufactured a large number of arms, and heaped together a vast amount of ammunition. He expected 2,000 rebels to meet him at Contigan's mills before nine o'clock on Wednesday morning, 23 July, 1803, but everything went wrong. The man who was to turn the fuzees and rammers for the beams had forgotten them, the jointed pikes were all lost by an explosion in Patrick Street, the slow matches got mixed with others, the fuzees of the grenades were nowhere to be found, the scaling-ladders were not finished, and of the 2,000 men only eighteen put in an appearance. However, Emmett, with five or six others, in their green uniforms, marched towards the Castle, and were informed that Lord Kilwarden's carriage had been stopped, and that both his lordship and his nephew had been murdered. A company of soldiers soon dispersed the insurgents, and Emmet, being arrested, was tried, condemned, and executed 19 Sept. the same year.

Thomas Moore refers to Robert Emmett in his 'Irish Melodies,' 'O breathe not his name'; and again, 'She is far from the land where her young hero sleeps.' Emmett was engaged to a daughter of Curran.

Emoraim (*The*). Jewish doctors who assisted in composing the Gema'ra, which took about 311 years. It contains annotations, discussions, and amplifications of the Mishnah. There are two Gemaras —that of Babylon, completed A.D. 500, and that of Jerusalem, finished in the middle of the 4th cent. The Mishnah and Gemara together make what is called the Talmud.

Empecinado (*The*). Juan Martin Diaz of Spain, the Spanish guerilla chief (1775–1825), so called from *pecina*, a pool or marsh; the villagers of Spanish marshes were nicknamed Empecinados. Diaz was a man of enormous muscular strength. George III. gave him a sword which no man could wield but himself. When captured in 1825 he burst the cords which bound him, threw from him

five men, and was only captured by casting a cloak over him. Thus entangled he was hanged on a tree.

Another derivation of the name is this : 'El Empecinado, c. a. d. *l'empoissé*, qui lui fut donné, parce qu'il était d'un village de cordonniers, état où l'on fait, comme on sait, grand usage de la poix.'—*Bouillet*.

Emperor Elect of the Romans. Maximilian, who failed to get himself crowned kaiser, in 1508 assumed the title of 'Emperor Elect of the Romans.' Till then the 'emperors elect' were only called ' Kings of the Romans ' (*q.v.*).

Emperor of Elba (*The*), 1814. Napoleon I., after his abdication. Elba is an island 20 leagues in extent, with 12,000 inhabitants. Napoleon was allowed an annual income of 240,000*l.*, and Josephine, with other members of his family, were allowed 80,000*l.* more. He entered Elba 10 May, and left it 26 Feb., 1815 (298 days).

Emperor of the German Kingdoms (*The*), 'Kaiser der deutschen Reiche,' 18 Jan., 1871. William I., king of Prussia, during the siege of Paris was created ' German Emperor.' In the preceding Nov. he was made head of the German Confederation (*q.v.*). The Austrian monarchs were only kings of Germany and emperors of the West, *i.e.* the Holy Roman Empire, and hence were kaiserkings. They were sometimes called emperors, a title which did not belong to them as sovereigns of Germany, but as sovereigns of the West.

'Emperor of Germany' is not a correct designation, but either 'Deutscher Kaiser' (*German Emperor*) or 'Kaiser der deutschen Reiche.'

Emperor of the Romans. 'Emperors of Rome,' ' Emperors of the Holy Roman Empire,' or ' Emperors of the West,' all titles equivalent to kaiser, borne by Charlemagne and his successors. Otto the Great, king of Germany, revived the title. From 1508 the king of Germany was *ex officio* emperor of the Romans, and the king elect was emperor elect of the Romans, and continued so till his coronation; previously the king elect of Germany had been entitled 'king of the Romans.'

Emperor of the Romans, *i.e.* king of Germany after his coronation.

Emperor Elect of the Romans, the king elect of Germany from the time of Maximilian.

King of the Romans, the king elect of Germany between Otto I. and Maximilian I.

Empire State (*The*) of North America. New York, which has thirty-six votes in the Electoral College of 401.

Empirics and **Dogmatists.** Two schools of medicine in Alexandria in the three centuries preceding the birth of Christ. The Empirics took *experience* as the only base of curing maladies. The Dogmatists, or *Methodists*, were the regulars who treated diseases according to rule. The chiefs of the Empirics were Philīnos of Cos, Sextus *Empiricus*, and Heraclīdês of Tarentum.

The chief of the Dogmatists were Erasistrătos, Themĭson, and Cœlius Aureliānus.

Empirics and **Rationalists.** Two rival schools of philosophy. The Empirics insist that our sole knowledge of the material world depends upon our senses. The Rationalists or Idealists contend for an innate sense or perception. Chief of the Empiric philosophers are the Peripatetics, the disciples of Democrĭtos, Epicūros, and Aristotle, among the ancients; and the disciples of Hobbes, Locke, Condillac, and Diderot, among the moderns.

The chief of the Rationalists or Idealists are Plato, Malebranche, Kant, Schelling, and Hegel. There was also another school of Idealists, the exponents of which were Berkeley, Hume, Fichte, &c.

Empress of India, 1877. Queen Victoria assumed the title in addition to her other titles.

Enabling Statute (*The*), 1540 (32 Henry VIII. c. 28). I. Enabling a tenant-in-tail to make a lease for three lives, or twenty-one years, to bind his issue.

II. Enabling a husband seised in right of his wife in fee-simple, or fee-tail, to make a similar lease to bind his wife and her heirs, provided she joined therein.

III. Enabling ecclesiastics seised of an estate of fee-simple in right of their churches, to make leases to bind their successors. Repealed by 19, 20 Vict. c. 120, s. 35.

There are other enabling acts by which ecclesiastical lands may be leased.

Enactments (*Russian*). The old form used in Russia was *Boiare prigovorili, i czar prikazal* (The seniors are of opinion, and the czar has enacted). The seniors were called *boyars* = Latin *majores*, or *primores*, till Peter the Great abolished the title.

Encke's Comet. Recurs in about 1,200 days. It was not discovered by Encke (2 syl.), but its periodicity was.

Seen by Méchain 17 Jan., 1786.

Seen by Caroline Herschel 7–27 Nov., 1795.

Seen by Bonvard, Huth, and Pons 20 Oct. to 19 Nov., 1805.

Seen by Pons 25 Nov., 1818, to 12 Jan., 1819.

Johann Franz Encke (2 syl.) was born at Hamburg in 1791, and died in 1865.

Encratistes (3 syl.). *See* 'Encratites.'

Encratites (*The*), or Abstainers, A.D. 173. A religious sect founded by Tatian, one of the Greek Fathers. They abstained from marriage, meat, wine, and indeed all bodily indulgences. They distinguished between God and the Creator, and they denied the reality of Christ's body.

Encumbered Estates Act (*The*), 14 Aug., 1848. Ireland. To enable persons whose estates were encumbered by mortgages, chancery suits, or otherwise, to sell them at once, without delay or expense, either wholly or in part, with 'a parliamentary title,' which is given at the time of sale.

The *Court* was established 28 July, 1849, and closed 31 Aug., 1858. A similar Court was established in the West Indies 11 Aug., 1854.

Encumbered Estates of Ireland. Estates under the Court scattered all over Ireland, with deserted mansions and empty houses. Receivers take the place of the non-resident landlords, and, of course, are able to do nothing to help the tenants or pay for improvements.

Encyclical Letter (*An*). A letter from the pope or church council addressed to a whole nation or the whole of Christendom. In 1884 the French nation was addressed by an encyclical letter.

Encyclopædists, 18th cent. Leaders of thought who, in a publication entitled the 'Encyclopædia,' popularised enquiry into the Christian religion, politics, science, and government. No doubt these writers prepared the way for the Great Revolution.

The chief were D'Alembert (1717–1783), joint editor with Diderot of the famous 'Encyclopædia,' in 28 vols., to which Voltaire and other living savants contributed, Diderot (1712–1783), a materialist, who made the 'Encyclopædia' a vehicle for the diffusion of materialistic and atheistic opinions. **J. J. Rousseau, Grimm, Dumarsais, Voltaire, Baron d'Holbach, and Jancourt. (N.B. Biography and history were excluded.)**

End of the World. Nostradamus said, in 1566:

> Quand Georges Dieu crucifera,
> Que Marc le ressuscitera,
> Et que St. Jean le portera,
> La fin du monde arrivera.

That when Good Friday falls on 23 April (St. George's Day), and Easter Sunday on 25 April (St. Mark's Day), and Corpus Christi falls on 24 June (John the Baptist's Day), the world will come to an end. This coincidence of dates occurred in 1886, but the world still wags. The same coincidences occurred in 1734, 1666 (Great Fire), and, what is strange, in 1546, in 1451, 1421, 1204, 1109, 1014, 919, 672, 577, 482, 387, 140, and in 45. So will it be in 1943.

*** Sir Isaac Newton calculated (so says the critic Corneille de Pauw) ' qu'une comète heurtera si violemment notre soleil en l'an 2255, qu'il n'y a plus aucune espérance qu'il soit encore en état d'éclairer les habitants de notre monde après cet accident.'

Endless Peace (The), A.D. 533.
Purchased by Justinian of Kosroës or Chosroës I. the Great, king of Persia, for 11,000 pounds of gold (about 440,000*l.* sterling). It lasted barely seven years (Gibbon, 'Decline and Fall,' xli.).

Enfans sans Souci (Les). A
volunteer theatrical company of young tradesmen in Paris, in the 15th cent., for the representation of satirical farces, in which living characters and current events were introduced. There was another company formed of lawyers and called the 'Basocians' (*q.v.*).

Pronounce *Ahn-fahn sahgn soo-see.*

Enfant de Miracle (L'). Napoleon I.
' They flit like phantoms about the mimic court of the "Enfant de Miracle." '—*The Oracle,* 1885.

Enforcing Act (The). Passed Congress 9 January, 1809. Its object was to preserve strict neutrality between England and France. All vessels from these two countries were, by this act, excluded from the United States.

Engagement (The). I., or *Scottish Covenant,* 1643. The agreement of the Assembly of Divines met in Henry VII.'s Chapel at Westminster, to maintain Presbyterianism. The whole clergy were required to submit; and 3,000 were ejected from their livings for refusing to do so.

II. In 1647. A secret treaty between Charles I. and the ' Solemn League and Covenant' (*q.v.*). Charles engaged to establish Presbyterianism in Scotland and extirpate the sectaries; and the league engaged to restore the king by force of arms. See 'Engagers.'

III. In 1649. The new oath substituted by the Long Parliament, after the execution of Charles I., for the oaths of *Supremacy* and *Allegiance*: ' I swear to be true and faithful to the government established without king or house of peers, and never to consent to their re-admission.'

Some doubt may be raised of the policy of the 'Engagement.' . . . As long as it was confined to those who held office under the government, it remained a mere question of choice; but when it was exacted from all Englishmen above 17 years of age . . . it became to many an act of necessity, and served to irritate rather than to produce security.—Dr. LINGARD, *History of England,* viii. 5.

Engagers (The), 1649. Or the party
of Hamilton, pledged to support ' the Engagement.' The Duke of Hamilton collected some 15,000 men, tumultuary and ill-disciplined, on the king's (Charles I.'s) behalf; but they were utterly routed by Cromwell near Warrington, and Hamilton surrendered. The Engagers were the moderate Presbyterian party; the rigid Presbyterians, called ' Whigamores,' had the Duke of Argyll for their leader, and were the dominant party in the middle of the 17th cent.

If the Covenanters got the upper hand . . . he [Montrose] must abandon his most devoted followers, the old Royalists and Engagers, and take the covenant himself.—HOWITT, *History of England* (Commonwealth, p. 815).

England. Its Sovereigns and Dynasties since the Conquest :—
NORMAN line—Four kings (1066–1154): William I. the Conqueror; William II. Rufus (son); Henry I. Beauclerc (brother); Stephen of Blois (nephew).

PLANTAGENET line—Eight kings (1154–1399): Henry II. (grandson of Henry I.); Richard I. Cœur de Lion (son); John Lackland (brother); Henry III. (son); Edward I. Longshanks (son); Edward II. (son); Edward III. (son); Richard II. (grandson).

House of LANCASTER—Three kings (1399–1461): Henry IV. (son of John of Gaunt duke of Lancaster); Henry V (son); Henry VI. (son).

House of YORK—Three kings (1461–1485): Edward IV. (son of Richard duke of York); Edward V. (son); Richard III. (brother of Edward IV.).

TUDOR line—Five sovereigns (1485–1603): Henry VII. (son of Edmund Tudor and Margaret Beaufort); Henry VIII. (son); Edward VI. (son); Mary (daughter of Henry VIII. and Katharine of Arăgon); Elizabeth (daughter of Henry VIII. and Anne Boleyn). Lady Jane Grey not reckoned in the list.

STUART Dynasty (*sovereigns of Great Britain*)—Four sovereigns (1603–1689): James I. (son of Mary queen of Scots); Charles I. (son); [COMMONWEALTH: Cromwell, Lord Protector]; Charles II. (son of Charles I.); James II. (brother); Anne (daughter of James II.).

House of ORANGE (Revolution), 1689–1714: William III. (prince of Orange) [grandson of Charles I.] and his wife Mary (daughter of James II.), conjointly.

House of HANOVER—At present (1890) five sovereigns (1714–*): George I. (elector of Hanover); George II. (son); George III. (grandson, son of Frederick prince of Wales); George IV. (son); William IV. (brother); Victoria (niece of William IV., daughter of Edward duke of Kent). *See* 'English Sovereigns.'

The Saxon race, which dominated 827–1013, gave fourteen sovereigns. The Saxons and Danes gave eight sovereigns (1013–1066).

N.B.—The English monarchs descend through the female line from King Egbert, the first king of England; and trace back in the male side up to William the Conqueror, whose son, Henry I., married Matilda, daughter of Margaret and Malcolm III. of Scotland. Margaret was the daughter of Prince Edward, and granddaughter of King Edmund, lineally descended from Egbert. *See* 'Victoria.'

England's Darling. Herëward the Wake, lord of Burn in Lincolnshire, famous for his resistance to William the Conqueror. He established his 'camp of refuge' in the Isle of Ely, where, in 1071, he was joined by Earl Morcar. Morcar surrendered and was imprisoned in Normandy, but Hereward escaped.

'England's Standard Advanced,' 1 May, 1649. A manifesto ssued by Captain Thompson demanding the completion of public freedom, vowing justice on the murderers of Arnold and Lockyer, and threatening, if a hair of Lilburne's head was touched, to avenge the wrong seventy-and-sevenfold. This party was put down on 17 May by Fairfax and Cromwell, who shot Cornet Thompson (brother of Capt. Thompson) and two corporals in Burford churchyard; the rest promised to return to Ireland.

Lockyer, a trooper, a brave young fellow of 23, was shot by Fairfax and Cromwell, 26 April, 1649, for mutiny. He was buried with military honours, followed by thousands with sea-green and black ribbons on their hats.

English Aristophanês (*The*). Samuel Foote (1722–1777).

English Chrysostom (*The*). Jeremy Taylor is so called by Coleridge in 'Table Talk' (4 June 1830).

English Church Union (*The*), abbreviated into E.C.U. Formed in 1859 'for the purpose of uniting churchmen in defence of the doctrine and discipline of the Church of England, and of the rights and liberties of her faithful children.' It is what is called a high-church or 'ritualistic' association.

The 'Church Association' represents the 'moderate' or 'Evangelical' party.

English Claude (*The*). Thomas Gainsborough (died 1788 at the age of 61).

English Crown (*The*). Contains the following jewels:

1 large ruby, irregularly polished.	4 rubies.
1 large broad-spread sapphire.	1,363 brilliants.
	1,272 rose diamonds.
16 sapphires.	147 table diamonds.
11 emeralds.	4 drop-shaped pearls.
	273 pearls.

The gross weight of the crown made in 1838 by Messrs. Rundell & Bridge is 39 oz. 5 dwts. Troy.

The famous ruby was given to Edward the Black Prince by Don Pedro of Castile in 1367. Henry V. wore it in his helmet at the battle of Agincourt in 1415.

English Ennius (*The*). *See* 'Ennius.'

English Garrison (*The*). So the Irish landlords were denominated by the partisans of the Irish Land League (*q.v.*). The third allegation of the *Times*, in their charge called 'Parnellism and Crime,' 17 Sept., 1888.

We [the three Royal Commissioners] find that the respondents did enter into a conspiracy to a system of coercion and intimidation to promote an agrarian agitation . . . for the purpose of impoverishing and expelling from the country the Irish landlords, who were styled the 'English Garrison.'—*Verdict* (1890).

English Justinian (*The*). Edward I. (1239, 1272–1307). So called because, like Justinian, he codified the laws, and reduced to practical shape the institutions of his predecessors. Edward I., in fact, begins a new epoch; all before him was ancient England, all from his accession is modern England. He defined the limits of civil and ecclesiastical jurisdiction, instituted the appointment of ' Conservators of the Peace,' now called 'Justices of the Peace,' organised into their present shape the superior courts (the Queen's Bench, the Exchequer, and the Common Pleas), and instituted the 'Court of Appeal,' the basis of our 'Court of Chancery.'

In this reign were passed the 'Statute of Mortmain,' 1279, and the 'Statute of Rhuddlan,' 1284. And both Magna Charta and the Charter of the Forest were confirmed.

English Language (*The*). Ordered to be used in all courts of law, 1362 (36 Edw. III. st. i. c. 15).

It is a pity that the sovereign still uses Norman French, instead of English, in expressing the royal assent or dissent to Acts of Parliament.

English Language, how derived.

ARYAN family has six branches	1. *Indian* (Sanskrit).
	2. *Persian* (Zend).
	3. *Slavonic* (Russian).
	4. *Celtic* (Gaelic and Cymric).
	5 *Græco-Latin* (Greek).
	6. *Gothic* (German).
TEUTONIC Gothic has three groups	1. *Mæso-Gothic*.
	2. *Low German* (English, Dutch, Flemish).
	3. *High German* (German).

See ' Erse.'

English Martyr (*The first*), 10 March, 1401. William Sawtre, rector of Lynn, Norfolk, who was burnt at the stake in the reign of Henry IV.

'**English Mercurie** ' (*The*), 1588. Was for many years considered to be the oldest English newspaper, but in 1839 Mr. Thomas Watts of the British Museum proved it to be an impudent forgery, as the paper on which it is printed bears the arms of the House of Hanover, and the initials ' G. R.' *See* ' Literary Forgeries.'

English National Anthem. ' God save the King ' (or Queen).

English Pale (*The*). In Ireland. The five districts of Cork, Drogheda, Dublin, Waterford, and Wexford. Generally called ' the Pale ' (Henry II.).

There was an ' English Pale ' about Calais.

English Pope (*The*). Adrian IV. (1100, 1154–1159). His name was Nicholas Breakspear.

English Sovereigns do not succeed to the crown by hereditary right, but by parliamentary authority. A crooked sort of descent is preserved, but not like that of our hereditary nobility.

WILLIAM I. had no hereditary right at all. The heir (though not of royal descent) was Harold.

WILLIAM II. had no hereditary right. The heir was his elder brother Robert duke of Normandy.

HENRY I. had no hereditary right. The heir was Robert.

STEPHEN, the nephew of Henry I., had no hereditary right. The heir was Maud.

JOHN had no hereditary right. The heir was Arthur, son of Geoffrey, 4th son of Henry II. John was the 5th son.

HENRY II. had no hereditary right. The heir was Eleanor, damsel of Brittany, heiress of William I.

HENRY IV. had no hereditary right after Richard II. ; the heir was Edward Mortimer, earl of March, by descent from Lionel (3rd son of Edward III.). Henry IV. was the son of John of Gaunt (4th son of Edward III.).

HENRY V. and VI. were out of the direct line, which was continued in the line of Mortimer earl of March.

RICHARD III. had no right to the crown while Edward V. was alive, and after the death of his nephew Edward the direct heirs were the sons of George duke of Clarence, his elder brother.

HENRY VII. had no right in descent ; he was the son of Edmund Tudor, whose only pretence to ' royal descent ' was that his grandmother was the widow of Henry V. (daughter of Charles VI. king of France). The heir was Elizabeth of York, whom he married after he became king.

There was another equally shadowy 'claim.' His paternal grandmother, Margaret, was the granddaughter of an illegitimate son of John of Gaunt (*i.e.* John Beaufort earl of Richmond had a natural son by Katharine Swynford).

WILLIAM III. and MARY had no hereditary right. The heir was the Old Pretender.

ANNE had no hereditary right. The heir was the Queen of Sardinia, by Henrietta Anne, daughter of Charles I.

GEORGE I. had no hereditary right.

This line was chosen by parliament because the Brunswickers were the nearest Protestant relatives to their predecessors. *See* 'England,' its sovereigns and dynasties.

English Sweat (*The*), Sept. 1482. So called because those attacked were covered from head to foot with a profuse perspiration. It lasted twenty-four hours, and sometimes longer, but left an extreme languor with palpitations for three years, and in some cases till death. Some 600 persons were attacked daily, and ninety out of a hundred died. It reappeared in the years 1485 and 1486. *See* 'Plague,' &c.

From 1506 to 1551 a modification of this disease appeared in Great Britain and in France. It was attributed to bad drainage, and was especially fatal to the fat and non-industrial class. Twelve hours decided whether it would prove fatal or not. In 1533 it broke out in Germany and the Netherlands, and again appeared in England in 1542 and 1551, since which time it has not recurred.

English Twenty Club (*The*). A club restricted to twenty of the best shots amongst the English volunteers. In 1884 Albert Victor, son of the prince of Wales, joined the club.

English in the Pale. The English settled in Ireland, holding the estates of native chiefs expelled by Strafford. These colonists kept themselves apart not only from the Irish proper but also from the Anglo-Irish. Many of the Pale were Catholics. *See* 'English Pale.'

Enne'ades (3 syl.). The great work of Plotīnus, the neoplatonic philosopher, edited by Porphyry his disciple. It consists of six sections each divided into nine parts; hence the name Ennēades or Nines.

Ennius (*The English*). Layămon, who wrote a translation in Saxon of 'The Brut' of Wace (13th cent.).

Ennius (*The Spanish*). Juan de Mena of Cordŏva (1412–1456).

Ennius of France (*The*). Jehan de Meung (1260–1320), surnamed *Clopinel*, because he was lame and hobbled in his gait. He added 1,280 verses to the 'Romance of the Rose,' begun by Lorris.

Enoch (*The Book of*). Referred to by Jude, supposed to have been written about A.D. 40. Three Ethiopic versions were brought to Europe by Bruce in 1773; and a translation of it into English

by Dr. Laurence was published in 1821; and much more recently Dr. Kenealy published a translation 'illustrated.'

It is divided into five parts: (1) the fall of the angels and the journey of Enoch through the earth under the guidance of an angel; (2) the revelation made to Enoch, as that of the revelation of St. John; (3) astronomy and the phenomena of the seasons; (4) the prophetic vision of the Messiah's kingdom till the Last Judgment; (5) exhortations and moral reflections.

Bruce presented one of his MS. copies to the Bodleian Library, Oxford.

Ensign of the British Navy (*The*). The Union Jack. It consists of three crosses, the blue field of St. Andrew is the *field* ; then the white saltire of St. Andrew and the red saltire of St. Patrick, joined together, with a white edging to the latter, to express the field ; over all is charged the red cross of St. George fimbriated with white.

The *white* ensign of the British or Royal Navy is the banner of St. George, with the 'Jack' cantoned in the first quarter.

The *red* ensign is that of the merchant service.

The *blue* ensign is that of the naval reserve.

Ensignmen, 1662. Those evicted Irishmen who joined the ensigns of Charles II. in Flanders, and after his return were entitled to have their estates restored to them by the Act of Settlement. To prevent injustice the then holders were 'reprised' by the grant of land elsewhere of the same value.

The claimants fared but badly. One of them was Lord Castleconnell, who had served Charles II. for five or six years as a common soldier in the Netherlands, in the Duke of York's regiment. Another was Colonel Charles MacCarthy Reagh, once the owner of a principality. It was found impossible to carry out the Restoration Settlement.

Enthusiasts (*The*). A sect of the Independents which sprang up during the civil war between Charles I. and the parliament. The word was applied to all those who insisted that the Scriptures must be interpreted by the light of private inspiration.

Under the head of Independents . . . . were the Arminians, Millenaries, Baptists, Anabaptists, Familists, Enthusiasts, Seekers, Perfectists, Socinians, Arians, and others.—HOWITT, *Hist. of Eng.* (Charles I., chap. vi. p. 273).

Eolic Dialect. The Eolians formed one of the four great divisions of Greece, and dwelt originally north of Thessaly, but pushed their way southwards. Their dialect was distinguished by an aspiration of initial vowels, called the digamma. Alcæos, Sappho, Corinna, and Pindar wrote in the Eolic dialect. One of the *modes* of music was called Eolic; it was less grave than the Doric, and less effeminate than the Lydian and Ionian.

Eon de l'Étoile, 12th cent.

A religious impostor who gave himself out to be the Son of God, and drew around him a host of followers. In 1148 he was taken before the Council of Reims, and pronounced to be an idiot, but was thrown into prison and died there. He used to pervert '*Eum* qui venturus est' into 'Eon qui venturus est.'

Eons. Intermediaries between the Supreme Being and the Jewish Jehovah; or, according to the Gnostic theory, between God and man. Wisdom is an Eon, so is Faith, so is Prudence. Basilîdês says there are 365 such beings, but Valentin admits only thirty.

In modern phraseology the word 'Eon' (from the Greek *aion*, for ever) means an interminable period. Thus Eternity is said to be 'eon upon eon.'

Ephesian Letters. Magical letters from an inscription of the statue of Diana in the temple of Ephesus. These letters were looked on as an amulet or charm. They were ascribed to the Dactyli or priests of Cybelê. The letters were *Askion, Kataskion, Tetras, Dam-nameneus, Aisia.*

When Milesius contended with Ephesius at the Olympic games, Ephesius proved the successful competitor, because he had the *Ephesian letters* attached to his heels. When these were removed Milesius was the winner.

Ephors. Five contemporary Spartan magistrates of almost unlimited civil power. The two contemporary kings were, for the most part, only generals of the army.

Ephtalites (3 syl), or White Huns (*q.v.*).

Epicureans (*The*).

Ancient Greek philosophers, so named from Epicûros of Samos, the founder. He taught in his own private grounds in Athens, and his disciples, like the Academics, were called the 'Garden sect.' His system was that the chief aim of life should be enjoyment; that the highest degree of enjoyment is perfect repose; and that is to be obtained only by keeping a sound and healthy mind in a sound and healthy body. Epicuros lived B.C. 342–270. His disciples were Metrodōros, Polyænos, and Hermăchos. His successors were Polystrătos, Basilîdês, Protarchos, and others of less note.

Heraclîtos of Ephesus (B.C. 543-483) taught that happiness is the end and aim of life.

Epicure'ans (*The Sect of the*).

One of the Grecian sects in the early ages of Christianity. They denied that God troubles Himself about mundane matters, and taught that the world was made by the chance conflux of atoms. They disbelieved in a resurrection; held that man consists only of a material body, and as this life is his end-all and be-all, his duty is to make the best of it, without taking any thought of a state after death.

Epicu'rus of China (*The*).

Tao or Taou, generally called by the title Laou-keun. He is mentioned by Kong-foo-tse (*Confucius*), with whom he was contemporary (about 5th cent. B.C.). *See* 'Tao' and 'Taoism.'

Epidemics.

Such diseases as attack a large number of persons at the same time. The following have been noted:—

Year	Popular Name	Scientific Name	Affected	Authority
1374	Dancing mania	*Chorea-mania*	Hundreds	Hecker
1523	Wolf madness	*Lycanthropia*	,,	Calmiel
1642, &c.	Demoniacal possession ...	*Demono-mania*	,,	,,
1731	Convulsionaries of St. Médard	*Theo-mania*	,,	,,
1800	Incendiarism	*Pyro-mania*	Many	Marc
Various	Witchcraft	*Demono-pathia*	Thousands	*Various*
—	Suicide	*Melancholia*	,,	Esquirol
—	Visions	*Delusions*	Many	Boismont
1845	Panic	*Pan-phobia*	,,	'Edin. Review,' 1849.

Asiatic cholera appeared in England in 1831 and several times since. Russian influenza was very fatal in London in 1729, and has frequently appeared in England since 1782.

Epiph'anes (4 syl.). Ptolemy V. This surname seems to have been given in irony. Similarly Ptolemy II., called 'brother-lover,' murdered all his brothers, and Ptolemy IV., called ' father-lover,' murdered both father and mother. So Ptolemy V., who began to reign at the age of 4, was poisoned at the age of 28, having distinguished himself in nothing. He was simply a commonplace villain.

Epiphany (*The*). A season kept in remembrance of the visit of the Magi to the infant Jesus in Bethlehem. First celebrated in 360. Twelfth day (or 6 Jan.).

It was not held as a separate festival till 813.

Episcopacy in Scotland. The three old women who hurled their stools at the head of the dean of Edinburgh, 22 July, 1637, for attempting to read the Anglican service in St. Giles's Church, were Euphemia Henderson, Bertha Craig, and Elspa Craig. The congregation shouted, ' A pope! a pope! Antichrist! Stone him! stone him! '

Episcopal Cap (*The*). A cap adorned with cordels and silk threads of a green colour. ' Pileus pontificalis cordulis ac floccis sericis coloris viridis ornatus.' *See* Du Cange, vol. v. p. 300. *See* ' Caps.'

'Cordula' means little cords or threads, a word not to be found in Latin dictionaries.

Episcopalians. Properly means those who accept the institution of bishops as rulers of the Church, but in modern parlance the term is restricted to the Church of England, and those churches which are associated with it, as *Catholics* is to the Church of Rome and *Presbyterians* to the Church of Scotland. The words are convenient and only perversely distorted to their etymological meanings.

It is puerile to contend against the ordinary acceptance of these words. They speak with sufficient preciseness for ordinary language, and if more is required we must indeed ' speak by the card or equivocation will undo us.'

Episcopi Vagan'tes (3 syl.). Free bishops. They had no diocese, but received the title for their learning. They were almost entirely Irish, and assumed the power of ordaining, till a Council called in 816 decreed that no Scot (Irishman) so ordained should be admitted into the ministry.

Epoch of the Building of Solomon's Temple (*The*), May B.C. 1015.

Era—Epoch. An era is a series of years beginning from an epoch. An epoch is an important event which constitutes the starting point of the series. Thus the birth of Christ was the epoch from which the Christian era begins to count, either backwards or forwards, or both.

Before the Nativity there was no general starting point of historic dates, but each nation chose its own epoch; generally the foundation of a city, the commencement of a dynasty, or some famous victory. These eras can easily be reduced to B.C. or A.D. if required, according to the notes appended to several of the following eras. The Catholic Church divides the whole history of man into six epochs or ages of unequal length, viz.:—

1. From Adam to Noah;
2. From Noah to Abraham;
3. From Abraham to David;
4. From David to the Babylonish captivity;
5. From the captivity of Judah to the birth of Christ;
6. From the birth of Christ to the end of the world.

But independent of these epochs there are numerous other events which have been made *points de départ* by different people:—

The Era of the Greek Olympiads	B.C. 776
The Era of the Foundation of Rome	753
The Era of Nabonassar	747
The Era of Alexander the Great	324
The Era of the Seleucidæ	312
The Julian Era	45

and so on. *See* ' Æra.'

Era (*The Mundane*). Many chronologists date from the foundation of the world, at any rate up to the Nativity; but great diversity of opinion exists on the subject. The chief authorities are: ' The Benedictines,' Calmet, The Greek Church, Professor Hales, and Archbishop Usher.

The BENEDICTINES' system is better known as ' L'Art de Vérifier les Dates.'

Dom Augustin CALMET (1672-1757) was a learned theologian of Lorraine, author of a ' Dictionary of the Bible,' in French.

The GREEK CHURCH based its calculation on the Septuagint.

HALES (Prof. William) of Dublin University, author of a ' New Analysis of Chronology ' (1809-1814).

Dr. James USHER, archbishop of Armagh, was born in Dublin (1580-1656); and is the author of ' Annales Veteris et Novi Testamenti,' and a book of universal Chronology.

NUMBER OF YEARS BETWEEN THE CREATION
AND THE NATIVITY.

According to the modern Greek Calendar	7388
According to Josephus	7282
According to Scaliger	5829

According to the ancient Greek Church ...	5508
According to Professor Hales	5411
According to ' L'Art de Vérifier les Dates' ...	4963
According to Archbishop Usher	4004
According to Calmet	4000
According to the Jews	3760

See 'Era of Antioch,' 'Era of Constantinople,' ' Era of Alexandria,' &c.

Prof. William Hales, the Chronologist, who died in 1831, must not be confounded with Alexander de Hales, who died in 1242, and was called the 'Irrefragable Doctor.'

Era of Abraham (*The*).

Those who make the patriarch Abraham the epoch of their chronology begin their era 1 Oct., B.C. 2016.

To reduce the era of Abraham to the Christian era, subtract 2,015 years and three months. The remainder will be the year and the month.

Era of Actium (*The*), or 'the Actiatic Era.'

Began 1 Jan. B.C. 30. It commemorates the victory of Octavianus (Augustus Cæsar) over Antony.

We ourselves often speak of events as occurring before or since the Conquest.

Era of Alexander (*The*), or Era of the Lagidæ,

that is of Ptolemy son of Lagus, a general of Alexander the Great, who reigned in Egypt after the death of the Macedonian. The era here referred to was that which began with the death of Alexander, and was used in Egypt after the accession of Ptolemy. It began 12 Nov., B.C. 324.

Called in Latin *Æra Philippi* or *Æra Bicornis*.

Era of Alexandria (*The*).

A computation of Julius Africanus adopted by the Christians of Alexandria, who reckoned the interval between Adam and Christ to be 5,500 years, or rather 5,502. In the reign of Diocletian ten years were deducted, and 5,787 was called 5,777 of the world, or 277 of the incarnation.

Era of American Independence (*The*), 4 July, 1776.

Era of Antioch (*The*).

According to Panodorus of Antioch, the chronologist, who lived in the 5th cent., the world was created 1 Sept., B.C. 5492.

This differs from the Mundane Era of Alexandria, which was fixed at 5502 ; but in A.D. 285, ten years being subtracted from the Alexandrian calculation, both the eras were alike. *See* ' Era, The Mundane.'

Era of Augustus (*The*), or of ' the Empire,'

adopted by the Romans. It began B.C. 27.

Era of Bengal, or ' The Bengalee Era.'

Measured by solar time, and not by lunar, like the Mohammedan year. It is supposed, however, to be derived from the Hegira, and in the middle of the 16th cent. the two correspond.

Era of Bithynia (*The*).

An era adopted by the Bithynians, who took for their starting point the year when they threw off the Macedonian yoke, and became independent ; that is, B.C. 288.

This means that the year B.C 288 of the Christian Era was the year 1 of the Bithynian Era.

Era of Constantinople (*The*).

Adopted in the Eastern Empire in the 7th cent. Like the Era of Antioch (*q.v.*), it began from the creation of the world. According to this calculation, the interval between the Creation and the Nativity was 5,508 years, and the birth of Christ occurred in the 5,509th year. The Russians followed this era till the reign of Peter the Great.

The civil year of Constantinople began 1 Sept.; the ecclesiastical year either 21 March or 1 April. So in the Church of England the civil year begins on New Year's Day, but the ecclesiastical year in the preceding Advent, four weeks before Christmas Day.

Era of Creation (*The*).

See ' Era, The Mundane.'

Era of Diocletian (*The*).

Began 29 Aug. A.D. 284, when Diocletian was proclaimed emperor of Rome. This era was used by Christians till the introduction of the Christian era. *See* next article.

Era of Jesus Christ (*The*), or the ' Christian era,' the ' Year of Grace,' or ' the Incarnation.'

Begins 1 Jan. in 4714 of the Julian period. This era was first used in 527 by Dionisius Exiguus, a monk of Scythia, and a Roman abbot, but was not generally adopted till long after that. In France in the 8th cent., in England in July 816, in Spain in the 11th cent., in Portugal in 1415, in the Eastern empire in 1453. It was in use in England as far back as A.D. 680.

Herod the Great died A.U.C. 750, and the era of Jesus Christ is A.U.C. 753. There must be an error of three years or more, for Herod not only died A.U.C. 750, but he spent the last forty days of his life at Jericho.

Regnante in perpetuum ac gubernante Domino nostro Salvatore secula universa, anno recapitulationis Dionisi, id est ab Incarnatione Christi, sexcentesimo octuagessimo [680]. . . . Ego Oshere Rex. . . .

Sometimes called 'Annus Trabeationis'; and sometimes 'The Circumcision.'

Era of Julius Cæsar (*The*), or ' the Julian Era.'

It was B.C. 46 when

Julius Cæsar reformed the calendar, and Julian's system prevailed in England till 1752, when it was superseded by the Gregorian year. What we call the 'Old Style' is that according to the Julian system : and what we call the 'New Style' is the Old Style corrected. In 1752 the difference was twelve days.

Russia still adheres to the 'Old Style.'

Era of Kings (The). See 'Era of the Seleucĭdæ.'

Era of Nabonassar (The). This era began on Wednesday, 26 Feb., B.C. 747. Nabonassar was the founder of the kingdom of Babylon. The Jews at this era made their year consist of 365 days instead of 360.

Famous in astronomy, being the era followed by Hipparchus and Ptolemy. It was used by the Chaldæan astronomers, and was transmitted by Callisthenés to Greece.

Era of Pisa (The). Much used in France in the 12th cent. ; it preceded our common era by one year.

Era of Rome (The). See 'Era of the Foundation of Rome.'

Era of Salivâhana Saka (The), or 'The Saka' (i.e. the year), began A.D. 78. Named after Salivahan, a king who reigned many years in the Deccan, and was a great encourager of the arts and sciences. This era is much used in the southern provinces of Hindûstan. The years are called 'Saka.'

Era of Spain (The). Began 1 Jan., B.C. 38, and was in commemoration of the conquest of Spain by Augustus the year preceding. This era was long followed in Spain and Portugal.

Era of Tyre (The). Began 19 Oct., B.C. 125 ; the year when the Tyrians obtained their autonomy from the Syrian kings. This era was used in Syria.

To reduce the Tyrian Era to the Christian Era, subtract 124, and if the given year is less than 125, deduct it from 125, and the remainder will be the year B.C.

Era of Vicramâditya is reckoned from B.C. 56, and prevails chiefly in the northern provinces of India, and in Guzerat. It is called after a sovereign of Malwa, who defeated Soka king of Delhi, and acquired possession of the most important throne of India. The years are called 'Samvat.'

According to Indian mythology the world is to last for 4 yugs [ages], three of which are past already.

The fourth, called the Kali-yug, is the last and worst.

Era of Yezdegird (The). A Persian era which began on the accession of Yezdegird III. to the throne of Persia, 16 June, A.D. 632. Also called 'the Gelalæan era.'

To reduce the Persian to the Christian era, add to the Persian era 630.

Era of the Arabians (The). See 'Era of the Hegïra.'

Era of the Armenians (The). This era began Tuesday, 9 July, A.D. 552, when the Council of the Armenians confirmed the condemnation of the Council of Chalcedonia, pronounced in 536, and thus completed their 'schism.'

Era of the Ascension (The). The era was used only by the author of the 'Chronicle of Alexandria,' who dates the martyrdom of Menas, 'Anno CCLVII Domini in cœlos assumptionis.'

To reduce this era to our A.D. add 38. Thus the martyrdom of St. Menas of Cotys is given in the 'Chronicle' : 'Anno CCLVII Domini in cœlos assumptionis.' Which would be A.D. 295.

Era of the Chinese (The). Begins B.C. 2697. The Chinese begin their era with the accession of the Emperor Yao, a semi-historical monarch of the Tenth Ki (or race). Yao was the traditional author of the Chinese calendar, who first divided the year into 365 days, with an extra day every fourth year.

It is said that on one occasion, during the reign of Yao, the sun did not set for ten days. Some persons quote this, but not wisely, in confirmation of Joshua x. 12.

Era of the Foundation of Rome (The). A.U.C.

According to Varro	21 April, B.C.	753
According to the Capitoline Marbles		752
According to Polybius	. .	751
According to Archbishop Usher	.	748
According to Fabius Pictor	.	747
According to Newton	. .	627

Cato, Dionysius of Halicarnassus, Solinus, and Eusebius follow the date given by the Capitoline Marbles.

The Roman emperors, with Plutarch, Tacitus, Dion, Aulus Gellius. Censorïnus, Onuphrius, Baronius, Prof. Hales, Bishop Beveridge, Strauchius, Dr. Playfair, &c. follow the computation of Varro.

Era of the French Republic (The). Began 22 Sept., 1792, the day of the foundation of the French Republic, and terminated 31 Dec., 1805.

The following table will show the correspondence between the foolish French system and the ordinary Christian era

Year				
I.	From 22 Sept., 1792	to 21 Sept., 1793		
II.	„	„	1793	„	„	1794
III.	„	„	1794	„	„	1795
IV.	„	„	1795	„	„	1796
V.	„	„	1796	„	„	1797
VI.	„	„	1797	„	„	1798
VII.	„	„	1798	„	„	1799
VIII.	„	„	1799	„	„	1800
IX.	„	„	1800	„	„	1801
X.	„	„	1801	„	„	1802
XI.	„	„	1802	„	„	1803
XII.	„	„	1803	„	„	1804
XIII.	„	„	1804	„	„	1805
XIV.	„	„	1805	to 31 Dec., 1805	

Era of the Heg'ira (The).

Adopted by all Mohammedans. It began with the 'flight' of Mohammed from Mecca, 16 July, 622.

The *i* of 'Hegira' is generally pronounced long, but it would be more correctly written and pronounced 'Hedj'rah.' The word does not mean *flight* but *emigration*. Some place the Hedjrah on Thursday, 15 July.

Era of the Jews (The).

The Jews now date from creation, which they place B.C. 3760, and they begin their year with the new moon next after the autumnal equinox.

Era of the Maccabees (The).

Began B.C. 166, when Judas Maccabæus took the command of the insurgent Jews who sought to throw off the yoke of Antiochus Epiphănês. His arms were successful, he destroyed every vestige of the heathen religion, restored the Mosaic law, and established a Jewish dynasty called the Asmonæan which lasted to B.C. 37, when Herod the Great was made king of Judæa by the Romans. This era of the Maccabees is called by the Jews 'the Era of Kings.'

In 2 Maccabees vii. we read of a mother and her seven sons who were martyred by Antiochos Epiphănês, because they refused to eat swine's flesh at the king's command. This massacre is said to have occurred B.C. 166, and is celebrated in the Catholic Church on 1 August. These seven brothers were not related to the great Asmonæan family, but it is rather remarkable that both the events referred to occurred in the same year.

Era of the Martyrs (The).

Began 23 Feb., 303. It was the tenth and last persecution of Diocletian, the Roman emperor, to which he was instigated by his colleague Galērius. Diocletian died A.D. 313.

The 'Era of Diocletian' (*q.v.*) and the 'Era of the Martyrs' are often used as synonymous terms, but the former began 29 August, 284, and the latter 23 Feb., 303. Without doubt Christians used the era of Diocletian in consequence of the persecutions which rendered the reign so memorable.

Much error prevails on the subject of these persecutions. We are apt to forget that Christians in power instituted the crusades, the wars of the Waldenses and of the Albigenses, the Dragonnades, the Thirty Years' war, the Bartholomew slaughter, the fires of Smithfield, and all the horrors of the Inquisition. All religious persecutions arose from a conviction that there is only one right religion; and those in power think that religion which is sanctioned by the state is the right one.

Era of the Olympiads (The).

Began 1 July, B.C. 776. The era of the Olympiads is a system of dates adopted by the ancient Greeks. An Olympiad was the interval of four years between two consecutive celebrations of the Olympic games. These games were trials of strength and agility tested by running, boxing, leaping, wrestling, and so on, held at Olympia, a plain of Elis, every fourth year. They were first employed for chronological purposes, when Chorœbos won the foot-race, the principal match before chariot-races were introduced.

By this system of dates, events were said to have occurred on the 1st, 2nd, &c. year of the so-and-so Olympiad, mentioning the number of celebrations since the establishment of the era in B.C. 776.

Era of the Persians.

See 'Era of Yezdegird.'

Era of the Seleu'cidæ (The).

Began 1 Oct., B.C. 312, when Seleucus Nicätor, king of Syria, took possession of Babylon. The dynasty lasted 247 years, to B.C. 64.

Seleucus Nicätor, one of the best generals of Alexander the Great, was a native of Macedon, and therefore the era which he founded is sometimes called the 'Macedonian Era.'

It was called by the Jews the *Era of Contracts*, certainly a very apt appellation.

Erasmus's Paraphrase.

This was a paraphrase of the Scriptures, in 1547, placed with the Bible in parish churches.

Erastianism.

The religious tenets of Thomas Erastus, a physician of Baden (1524–1583), who asserted that the church is a civil institution, subordinate to and dependent on the civil power. Thus it is said that the Church of England is Erastian or a parliamentary church, and that its articles and discipline depend on acts of parliament. Erastus taught that the Christian ministry is not a divine institution, that Christ and his apostles prescribed no particular form of church government, and that the punishment of all offences belongs to the magistrate. Of course he denied the dogmas of apostolical succession, the power of the keys, and ordination. He taught that anyone might preach who liked, and that the success of preaching depended solely on moral suasion.

The Scotch Covenanters called submission to the civil powers 'Erastianism.' The book of Erastus is entitled 'De Excommunicatione ecclesiastica.'

Eremites of St. Paul (*The*), or 'Frères de la Mort,' 13th cent. A religious order under the patronage of St. Paul the Anchorite. Their special duty was to attend to the sick and preside at funerals. They wore on their scapulary a death's head and cross-bones.

Erenachs. Laymen who held in Ireland church lands. If dignitaries they were called Comorbans. They appropriated the revenues, like lay abbots, leaving to the clergy only the tithes and fees. (From the 9th to the 17th cent.)

Erfurt (*Treaty of*), 27 Sept., 1808. Between Napoleon I. and Alexander of Russia. Napoleon agreed to recognise as parts of the Russian empire Finland (taken from Sweden), and Moldavia and Walachia (taken from Turkey); and Alexander promised to support Joseph Bonaparte as king of Spain.

Eric. Blood-fine which the kindred of a layman convicted of homicide were compelled to pay to the family of the slain (Ireland).

Eric's Law. The ancient laws of Sweden collected into a single volume by orders of Eric IX., who reigned 1150–1162.

Eri'gena means 'the Irishman.' Joannes Scotus, the Schoolman, is so called. Scot and Irish were at one time synonymous terms; so that John Erigēna and John Scotus mean the same thing. (Died 875.)

He must not be confounded with Duns Scotus, the Schoolman (1265-1308).

Erlau (*He has won the fame of*). An Hungarian proverb. In 1552 Erlau was besieged by the Turkish army of Solyman the Magnificent. Women joined the men in its defence, and so obstinately resisted that the Turks raised the siege, and Erlau was saved. This was one of the noblest defences in history. (Erlau, -lau to rhyme with *now*.)

Ernest of Hanover. Called the Confessor on account of his having introduced into his dominions the 'Augsburg Confession' (*q.v.*).

Erse. The native Irish language. Celtic is divided into Cymric and Gaelic.
Cymric is Welsh, old Cornish, and Armorican or Breton.
Gaelic is Highland Scotch, Erse, and Manx. *See* 'English Language,' &c.

Escalier des Malheureux (*L'*). A back or private staircase in the palace by which the boon companions of Pharamond entered into his sanctum sanctorum. When Pharamond wanted a little relaxation he made a well-known sign, and entering this apartment, 'on admettait ceux à qui les ministres avaient refusé leur audience, ou que la garde avait rebutés; et cet escalier, par lequel le monarque et eux passaient également, s'appelait "l'escalier des Malheureux"' (*Dictionnaire Historique,* &c., par C. S. des R . . . .).

Escu'rial (*The*). A famous monastery in New Castile called 'the eighth wonder of the world.' It is a pile of granite of great magnificence.

The tale is that Felipe II. of Spain in the battle of St. Quentin vowed to St. Lorenzo (on whose day, 15 Aug., 1557, the battle was fought) that if he would grant him the victory he would build a monastery to his honour. As St. Lorenzo was burnt to death on a gridiron the monastery was built in the form of a gridiron, long courts representing the bars of the gridiron. It was begun in 1563, and finished in 1584, and was intended for palace, mausoleum, and monastery. It has 14,000 doors, and 11,000 windows.

Es'karites (3 syl.). Mohammedan Platonists, who place the *summum bonum* in the 'Contemplation of the Great Omnipotent.' They are moral and of most placid temper.

Eskimo. Is derived from Ashkimai, and means 'eaters of raw flesh.' A term applied to them in contempt by the Indians of Algonkin stock.

Espousal of the Adriatic (*The*). An annual ceremony on the feast of Ascension in Venice from 1177 to the end of the republic, when the doge went in his state barge, the 'Bucentaur,' to the shore of Lido, near the mouth of the harbour, and dropped a gold ring into the sea, saying, 'We wed thee with this ring in token of our true and perpetual sovereignty.' The origin of this custom is as follows : When Pope Alexander III. was driven out of Rome by Frederick Barbarossa, he took refuge in Venice, and was honourably entertained in the doge's palace. Ziani, the doge, sent an embassy

to the kaiser demanding the restitution
of the pope, but Barbarossa replied,
'Unless the Venetians will deliver the
fugitive into my hands a captive in chains
I will utterly extirpate the republic.'
War was the inevitable consequence.
The Venetians proved the victors, and
the kaiser's son Otto fell into their hands.
Pope Alexander went forth to meet the
victorious fleet, and, giving the doge a
gold ring, said to him, 'With this ring
take, on my authority, the lordship of
the sea,' and the anniversary was kept
ever after.

Essays and Reviews, 1860. By
several Oxford scholars on ecclesiastical
subjects. Condemned by the Conference
of Clergy at Sion House, 25 Jan., 1861.
The judgment of the Court of Arches
against Williams and Wilson was reversed by the Judicial Committee of the
Privy Council, 18 Feb., 1864. Synodical
judgment on the book passed 24 June,
1864.

Essenes (2 syl.). A very ancient
Jewish sect who maintained that the
essence of religion is silence and contemplation. Many passed their life in celibacy; they looked on the Mosaic law as
an allegorical system of mysterious
truths, and renounced the outward letter.
'The letter killeth, it is the spirit [or
spiritual meaning] which giveth life.'

Essex Junto (*The*), 1812. A certain
party of the federalists of the United States
imbued with Anglomania, and favourable
to monarchy and separation. All the
federalists were opposed to war with
England, and favourable to a war with
the French republic. The American
government stigmatised the platform of
the junto as treason, and as tending to a
dissolution of the union.

At the head of this minority (said Jefferson) is
what is called the Essex Junto of Massachusetts,
but the majority of these leaders do not aim at
separation. In this they adhere to the known
principle of General Hamilton—never, under any
views, break the union. Anglomania, monarchy,
and separation, then, are the principles of the
Essex federalists; Anglomania and monarchy
those of the Hamiltonians; Anglomania alone
that of the people who call themselves federalists
(vol. iv. p. 188).

Est-il Possible? Nickname of
Prince George of Denmark, given him by
his father-in-law, James II. He was the
consort of Queen Anne, and his everlasting exclamation was 'Est-il possible?'

Estates of the Realm. Not king,
lords, and commons, but lords spiritual,
lords temporal, and the commons. Hence
we read of the 'king and the three
estates of the realm.'

Esther. The Persian word is Ar-
tishona. Her real Hebrew name was
Hadassah.

Estrith'sonides (4 syl.). The
second dynasty of Denmark (1047-1375).
So-called from the founder, Svend, son
of Estritha, sister of Canute the Great
of England.

Estrapa'do (*The*). A punishment
in which the victim was raised by his
hands tied behind him, and then let fall
once, twice, or more, with a concussion.
The French called the suspension of a
victim on a movable gibbet which (rising
and falling alternately) plunged him into
a fire and pulled him out, the 'punishment of the estrapade.' This was also
sometimes repeated twice, thrice, or more
times.

Établissements de St. Louis
(*Les*), about 1255. A recueil of laws and
ordinances under the direction of Louis
IX., especially aimed at the venality of
justice, the harsh treatment of creditors,
and the extravagant rate of interest.
The code is still extant, and shows both
wisdom and a love of justice. Published
in Paris 1786.

États Généraux (*Les*). A French
deliberative assembly, consisting of all
the three states, viz. the noblesse, the
clergy, and the commons. The first was
convoked by Philippe IV., in 1302, and
the last by Louis XVI. in 1789, when the
total number of deputies was 1,145. That
is, 572 commons, 572 noblesse and clergy,
and a chairman.

Louis le Gros (1108-1137) admitted the commons
into the Legislative Assembly, and called the name
l'Assemblée des Trois Etats. The commons were not
again called till 1302.
Pronounce *A-tah' jen-a-ro'*.

Et-cetera Oath (*The*), 1641. An
oath imposed by Charles I. upon the
clergy, who were required to swear that
they 'would not consent to alter the
government of the church by archbishops, bishops, deans, archdeacons, &c.,'
and to give a fixed declaration of opinion
respecting church dogmas, government,
rites, and ceremonies.

Eternal City (*The*). Ancient Rome.

Ethelred the Unready. That is, the Unwise (*, 978–1016). His great unwisdom was shown in the massacre of the Danes on St. Bryce's Day, 13 Nov., 1002, in warding off the Danes by bribes rather than by war, and in his most unfortunate choice of ministers to execute his commands.

He bribed the Danes time after time. In 991 he paid them 10,000*l.* to retire, in 997 he paid them 16,000*l.* to leave the country. In 998 he increased his bribe to 20,000*l.*, in 999 to 24,000*l.*, then 36,000*l.* In 1002 he tried secret massacre, and in 1008 he bribed Sweyn, who had come over to avenge the blood of his countrymen, with 14,000*l.* in money and sixteen counties.

Ethelwolf's Charter. An erroneous term for 'Ethelwolf's Grant.' This king of Wessex gave a tenth part of his private estate to ecclesiastical purposes; and, in return, the churches gifted were to perform weekly certain 'religious' services. He ordained that one poor man on every ten hides of his own land should be maintained in food and clothing. He released from all payment (except the *trinoda necessitas, q.v.*) a tenth part of the folkland.

Selden, Hume, and others quote this as the legal origin of tithes; but tithes were established in the 8th cent., if not before. Ethelwolf reigned in Wessex 836–858, and hoped to avert invaders and bring peace on his kingdom by giving largely to the church.

Ethiopic Version (*The*) of the Bible, supposed to be of the 4th cent. This version is printed in Walton's Polyglot, but with many inaccuracies. *See* 'Scriptures.'

Eton School, or College, 12 Sept., 1440. Founded by Henry VI. as the 'College of the Blessed Marie of Eton, by Wyndesore.' The 'Montem' was abolished in 1847.

The Montem was a kind of 'black mail' exacted by the boys triennially on Whit Tuesday from all who passed the mound (or montem) called Salt Hill, and the 'gratuities,' called *salt*, sometimes amounted to 1,000*l.* The last 'Montem' exaction was made in 1844.

Ettrick Shepherd (*The*). James Hogg, born at Ettrick, a shepherd and poet. Died 1835.

Eubages (*The*). The 2nd order of Druids—they may be called the working clergy. The Druids were the high priestly party, a princely order. The inferior order were called Bards. Hence the three classes were Druids, Eubãges (3 syl.), and Bards.

Eudoxian Heresy (*The*). Promulgated by Eudoxius, patriarch of Antioch, in the 4th cent.—That the Son had an independent mind, and, therefore, might differ from the Father; so that Father and Son might be at variance.

Eu-er'getes (4 syl.). The well-doer, or benefactor. Ptolemy III., king of Egypt, was so called after ravaging Syria and Persia, when he brought back 2,500 statues of Egyptian gods carried away by Cambyses (B.C. 246–221).

Eugene Aram. A market gardener's son, of Newby, in Yorkshire, who set up a school at Knaresborough. In 1745 one Daniel Clarke, a shoemaker, was missing, and thirteen years afterwards Richard Houseman dropped a remark about a skeleton in St. Robert's Cave, which caused him to be apprehended. Houseman on his trial accused Aram, who was apprehended and executed in 1759.

Euge'nians. The people of South Munster, *i.e.* Waterford, Cork, and Kerry, so called from Prince Eogan. Those of North Munster were called Dalcassians.

Eu'gubine Tables (*The*). Seven bronze tables with inscriptions, discovered at Gubbio (Eugubium), where they are still preserved. The literal characters on four of the tables are Umbrian, on two of them Latin, and on the remaining one partly Umbrian and partly Latin. The inscriptions are supposed to date between three and four hundred years before Christ. [Eugŭbine 3 syl.]

The subjects are directions respecting sacrifice and forms of prayer.

Euhe'merism, 4th cent. The teaching of Euhemerus or Evemerus, who taught that the heathen gods—Mars, Bacchus, Apollo, and so on—were either kings or noted worthies in the fabulous island of Panchæa, which he placed in the Southern Ocean. Some explain miracles by euhemerism.

Eulo'gia. Is bread blessed by the priest at the time of mass, for the benefit of those unable to attend, or for communicants who were allowed to take it home with them. The custom gave rise to the *panis beatus* (pain bénit), or Holy Bread (*q.v.*).

Food blessed by the priest is sometimes called Eulogia.

Eunom'ians, 4th cent. Disciples of Eunomius, bishop of Cyzīcum, who maintained that God the Father could not be of the same nature as Jesus Christ, because no creature can be equal to the Creator. He also denied the proper humanity of Christ, disbelieved the dogma of the Trinity, and believed that the Virgin Mary had other children besides Jesus her ' first-born.'

European Wars. The two greatest of modern history are the Seven Years' War and the War of Europe against Napoleon I. In the Seven Years' War (q.v.) England, Sweden, and Prussia opposed Russia, Austria, Saxony, and France. In the Napoleonic war England, Russia, Prussia, Austria, Spain, Portugal, &c., combined to dethrone the ' disturber of nations.'

Euse'bians. Another name for Arians, so called from Eusebius, bishop of Nicomedea, who supported Arius, condemned by the Council of Nice A.D. 325.
This was not Eusebius the historian.

Eutych'eans, or ' Monoph'ysites,' A.D. 448. Followers of Eutychês the archimandrite, who maintained that Christ was not man, but God only ; and that his humanity was absorbed in his divine nature, ' as a drop of rain by the sea.' His heresy was condemned by the Council of Chalcêdon in 451.

Euxine Sea (The). The hospitable sea. Originally called ' the Axine,' or inhospitable sea. Similarly, the Cape of Good Hope was first called ' the Cape of Despair ' ; Beneventum was originally called ' Maleventum ' ; and Dyrrachium was called ' Epidamnus,' till the Romans thought *-damnus* too much like *damnum* to be lucky.

Evangelic League (The), 1613. A confederacy of the Lutherans and Calvinists of Bohemia against the Kaiser Mathias. It was counterbalanced by another confederacy, called ' the Catholic League,' and the contests of the two leagues kept Germany in a most disturbed state through the entire reign. Mathias died in 1619, and was succeeded by his cousin Ferdinand II., when the Thirty Years' War between Catholics and Protestants deluged Germany in blood. See next article.

Evangelical Alliance (The).
I. 1608. An alliance of the Protestant states of Germany in self-defence. It was opposed by the Holy Alliance, formed in 1609.
The chief Protestant states of the alliance were the Electoral Palatinate, Würtemberg, Hessen-Cassel, and the margraviate of Baden-Durlach.

II. 1845. The alliance of all Christians without regard to denominational distinctions ; for the advancement of ' evangelical ' religion ; the counteraction of infidelity, romanism, and mere ritualism ; and for the strict observance of the Christian sabbath. See ' Nine Articles.'

Evangelical Community (The). The Moravian Association so called themselves. It was a kind of social republic. The chief ecclesiastics, called ' the Ancients ' (elders), regulated all the acts, both civil and religious ; presided over the education of the children, enjoined penances, pronounced excommunications, and determined the rank of each member of the community.

Evangelical Doctor (The). John Wyclif (1324–1384). Called a heresiarch by Catholics, but ' the morning star of the Reformation' by Protestants. Bouillet numbers among his sins : ' Wiclef exaspéré attaqua dès lors la puissance papale au spirituel et au temporel, et traita le pape d'*Antéchrist*. Il niait la transsubstantiation ; la nécessité de la confession pour qui a la contrition ; la damnation des enfants morts sans baptême [!!] ; l'efficacité des indulgences ; la primauté du siège de Rome ; la hiérarchie ; le droit des clercs et des moines aux biens temporels,' &c. (' Dictionnaire Universel,' p. 2010, col. 2.)
, No doubt Wyclif was morally aided in his work by the ' Great Schism of the West ' (q.v.), when the pope of Rome and pope of Avignon never tired of cursing and excommunicating each other.

Evangelical Prophet (The). Isaiah is so called from his clear and constant allusions to the Messiah. Isaiah was cut to pieces by a wooden saw, B.C. 698, aged 60.

Evangelical School (The). Of Germany under the leadership of Schleiermacher, whose ' Discourses on Religion,' 1804–1828, made a new era in German theology ; but his greatest work is ' Christian Faith ' (1768–1834).

x

Evangelical Symbols. The symbols of the four Evangelists, taken from Ezekiel's cherubim (*see* 'Cherubim') are—a man, a lion, an ox, and an eagle, mentioned in Rev. iv. 6–7 as supporting the throne of God. Jerome was the first to give the present appropriation of the *man* to Matthew, the *lion* to Mark, the *ox* to Luke, and the *eagle* to John. Matthew begins with the human descent of Christ from David, and Luke has the ox because his gospel begins with the account of Zacharias serving in the temple. The eagle refers to the doctrine of the *logos*, and the lion to the beasts in the desert where Jesus was tempted with which Mark begins his gospel. The union of the four symbols in one creature is called a TET'RAMORPH.

Often the four Evangelists bear four bannerols on which are respectively inscribed the initial sentence of each gospel. Perhaps the oldest symbol is a mountain from which issues four streams, and a lamb standing at the top.

In frescoes, windows, &c.
Matthew is represented with a pen, writing at the dictation of an angel.
Mark is represented writing, and with a winged lion at his feet.
Luke has a pen, but is not writing. He is studying a scroll.
John is represented as a youth rapt in thought, and an eagle about to take flight to heaven stands by him.

Evangelical Union (*The*), 1608. An alliance of the Protestant states of Germany formed at Auhausen in Bavaria; it was opposed in 1609 by the Holy Union, formed at Würzburg.

Evangelical Unionists (*The*), 1840. A religious sect founded in Scotland by James Morison, who taught that the greatest sin is want of belief in the universal atonement of Christ—*i.e.* that Christ, by his death, saved all men, past, present, and yet unborn.

There are also the Evangelical Free Church, the Evangelical Mission, the Free Evangelical Christians, the Working-man's Evangelical Mission, and, in the middle of the 19th cent., the 'Low Church party' of the Anglican Church were called 'Evangelical' (Churchmen), and the German Protestant Church is called officially the 'Evangelical Church.'

Evangelics and Papalins. So Strype designates the Protestants and Papists at the accession of Queen Elizabeth. By 'Papalins' he means, not Roman Catholics, but the half-and-half Papists, the compromisers of a papistic bias.

Evans Prize for Theology. Value about 9*l.* Founded in the University of Cambridge by the friends of the Venerable Robert Wilson Evans, D.D., archdeacon of Westmoreland 1869. (*See* 'Regius Professor of Divinity.')

Evem'erism. *See* 'Euhemerism.'

Ev'erest (3 syl.), probably the highest mountain in the world, is named after Sir George Everest, surveyor-general of India. The mountain, which is in the Nepaul range of the Himalayas, is 29,002 feet above the level of the sea (nearly 5½ miles).

Evergreen Pam. Lord Palmerston, or Henry John Temple, third Viscount Palmerston, 1784–1863. He was born 20 Oct., died 18 Oct., was buried in Westminster Abbey 27 Oct., entered Parliament 1807. Was M.P. 56 years, and died at the age of 79.

Everlasting Aris'teas (*The*). A mythical character of ancient Greece, like the Wandering Jew of more modern times. He taught Homer (about B.C. 900), and reappeared in sundry places 400 years afterwards.

Exalta'dos (*The*) of Spain, 1819, &c. The extreme radical party in the reign of Ferdinand VII.; they were especially irate because the Inquisition was restored. The Exaltados were composed of disbanded soldiers, with a sprinkling of Spanish dons. The high tory party were called 'Absolutists' (*q.v.*).

The Exaltados were called 'Constitutionalists' because they wanted to restore the constitution given to Spain in 1812, abolished by Ferdinand VII. in 1814.

Exaltation of the Cross (*The*). 'Exaltatio Crucis.' A festival held 14 Sept. Instituted in 642 in memory of 'la vraie croix que Chosroës, roi des Perses, avait élevée 14 ans auparavant.'

Ex Apostolatus Officio. A bull by Paul IV., wherein 'by his apostolic authority' he ratifies 'all and singular sentences, censures, and penalties of excommunication, suspension, interdict, deprival, at any time decreed or promulgated by pope, council, decree of the fathers, canons, apostolic constitution, or ordinance, against heretics and schismatics.'

Exarch. I. A viceroy of the Byzantine empire in the West. He had the government of a province, as the exarch of Rome, the exarch of Africa, the exarch of Italy, and the exarch of Ravenna.

II. The *Ecclesiastical* exarchs were delegates of the patriarch of Constantinople or of some synod, charged to visit a diocese and see to the moral conduct of the clergy. At the present day an exarch of the Greek Church is tantamount to a legate of the Western Church.

Many bishops and archbishops of the Greek Church are called exarchs

Exchequer (*The*). Low Latin *scaccarium*, Norman French *eschequier*. The word is generally ascribed to a ' chequered table, much like a chessboard, at which the barons sat,' and in defence of this etymology it is said that the use of this ' chequered table ' was to assist the board in its calculations. This is Camden's suggestion. Chevellet connects the word with the German *Schatz* (a treasure), and the Court of the Exchequer would then mean the court of the royal revenues; but Scheler says of this suggestion: ' C'est incontestablement une erreur.' The court was established by William the Conqueror in the Aula Regis, and its chief work lay in the assessment and collection of the revenue.

Exchequer (*Court of*). *See* under ' Court.'

Exchequer Bills, 1696. Bills for money, or promissory bills issued from the exchequer by authority of parliament. They vary from 100*l*. to 1,000*l*., and bear interest at 2½*d*. per cent. per diem. They form the chief part of the unfunded debt of the nation. Government from time to times gives the holders of these bills the option of having the bills paid off at par or of receiving new bills. Charged on the Consolidated Funds from 18 April, 1861.

Excise—Customs. Excise is a duty imposed on home goods, made, manufactured, or grown. This sort of tax was first imposed on beer 1648. It was introduced by Pym, the republican (German *accise*, ' tribute '). *Customs*, an impost on things of foreign growth or manufacture.

Exclusion (*The Bill of*), 11 Nov., 1680. To exclude James duke of York from the throne after the death of his brother Charles II. The bill passed through the Commons, but was thrown out by the Lords.

James duke of York did succeed to the throne, but being a Papist William and Mary were invited over by the Protestant party. James fled, and it was declared that he had abdicated.

Exclusionists, 1680. Adherents of the Exclusion Bill (*q.v.*). They were the Whig party.

Excommunication — Interdiction. Excommunication is exclusion from Christian fellowship. Interdiction is a prohibition to perform a religious rite, service, or ceremony. In mediæval times the excommunication of a king absolved his subjects from allegiance.

Execra'bilis (*The Bulls*), 1460. In which Pius II. forbids appeals to a future council.

1530, in which Clement VII. condemns the divorce of Henry VIII.

1606, by which Paul IV. forbids the Catholics of England to take the oath of allegiance.

10 June, 1809, launched by Pius VII. against Napoleon I. This was avenged by the captivity of the pope.

Executive Council of the State (*The*), 1648. The Council of Forty, with John Milton the poet for secretary. Appointed to govern the nation after the execution of Charles I. There was to be a parliament convened for six months every two years, and for the other eighteen months the council was without control.

Executive of the University of Cambridge (*The*). The Chancellor, the High Steward, the Vice-Chancellor, a Commissary, the Sex Viri, the Public Orator, the Librarian, the Registrary with his assistant, the two Proctors, the two Pro-proctors with their two assistants, the two Esquire Bedells, the University Marshal, the two Members of Parliament for the University, the Counsel, the Solicitor, and the Syndics. *See* each.

Exempt Lords. In the Commonwealth meant lords suspended or debarred from exercising the functions of their office.

' 14 May, 1660. The Lords passed a vote for calling on all those lords who had formerly been exempted for siding with the king.'

Exeter College, Oxford, 1314. Founded by Walter de Stapledon, bishop of Exeter. The Head-master is called the Rector. See 'Pusey and Ellerton Scholarships.'

Exeter Hall is quite another place. It is a large proprietary building on the north side of the Strand, London, completed in 1831, and used for concerts and public meetings. The Handel festivals and the 'May Meetings' (*q.v.*) have rendered the place famous. It is 131 feet long, 76 feet wide, and 45 feet high.

Exhibition, London. I. *The World's Fair,* opened 1 May, 1851, and closed 15 Oct., 1851. The building was a monster glass palace, and the exhibition consisted of manufactured articles, works of art, jewellery, and curiosities.

II. *The International Exhibition* was opened 1 May, 1862, and closed 1 Nov., 1862.

Similar exhibitions have been since opened in numerous places. The first in Paris, called 'the Universal Exhibition,' was opened 1 April, 1867, and closed 1 July, 1867. The Paris Exhibition of 1889 surpassed all the others for splendour of design and variety of exhibits. The Eiffel Tower was a prominent feature.

Exhibitioner. In Oxford University one who holds an exhibition; a kind of scholarship in Corpus Christi; and in Worcester College. Exhibitioners are now called scholars.

Exon. A title applied to certain officers of the Yeomen of the Guard. Latin *exon-erarius, i.e.* one relieved from work or active service, but still remaining in a position of dignity and ease. Exons are also called exempts.

Exon Domesday. The statistical survey of the Conqueror's commission for the monastery of Exeter, containing the counties of Wiltshire, Dorsetshire, Somersetshire, Devonshire, and Cornwall. This survey contains, what is omitted in the great Domesday Book, the tally of live stock, as well as the names of landowners, the amount of land held by each, the number of vassals, villeins, cottars, and serfs, the amount of pasture land and arable land, the number of mills and fishponds, &c.

Exorcist. This officer of the Greek and Latin churches had nothing to do with the act of exorcising, but only to discriminate between the really possessed and those who pretended or were supposed to be so. In the fourth Council of Carthage it was prescribed that the bishop, when he ordained an exorcist, should place a book in the hand of the aspirant, and say to him, 'Take this book, study it, and receive power to lay hands on the possessed, whether they be baptized or only catechumens.' The exorcism itself was delegated to certain priests by the bishop of the diocese.

Ex-oukontians. Arians were so called by their opponents, because by their tenets Christ was created out of nothing (*ex-ouk-onta*), in which respect alone He differed from man.

Expectation Sunday. The Sunday before Whit Sunday. Acts i. 4, Christ commanded the disciples 'that they should not depart from Jerusalem, but *wait* for the promise of the Father.' They waited till the day of Pentecost and the promise was fulfilled. See 'Sundays.'

Expectation Week. The week preceding Easter, commemorative of the waiting or expectation of the apostles for the outpouring of the Spirit, which came at Pentecost.

Expectative Canons. Canons without revenue or prebend, but possessing the title of canon, with a voice in the chapter, and a place in the choir till a prebend became vacant.

Expectatives (4 syl.), or 'Mandates.' Letters of request from the pope praying that benefices be conferred on certain individuals nominated in the letters.

Experimental Physics (*Professorship of*). In the University of Cambridge, 1871, founded by the University. Stipend 850*l.* a year.

Explanation (*Act of*), 1649. A bill brought into parliament by the Duke of Ormond, lord-lieutenant of Ireland, to confirm the Protestants in the estates confiscated from Irish Catholics, after what is called the 'Irish Rebellion.' This act was quaintly called the 'Magna Charta of the Protestants of Ireland.'

Expositor (*The*). Averroës, the Moorish expositor of Aristotle; born at Cordŏva, in Spain, 1120; died between 1196 and 1206.

Exsurge, Domine (*The Bulls*). I.
1377. By Gregory XI. against Wyclif.
II. 1520 by Leo X. against Luther. This
bull was publicly burnt 10 Dec., 1520, at
Wittenberg by Luther.

Pronounce *Ex-sur'-ge Dom'-i-ne.*

Extension Teaching, 1887. Extending the voluntary popular education
to a regular course of instruction covering between two and three years. The
instruction to contain two groups—(1),
natural, physical, and mathematical
science; and (2) history, political economy, mental science, literature, and art.
It requires the students to attend a
consecutive series of lectures for six
terms in a group of subjects, and an
examination proof of efficiency either
in Latin or some modern language, the
first three books of Euclid, and algebra
as far as quadratic equations.

Extradition Treaty. For the
mutual surrender of criminals (not political) who have taken refuge in another
kingdom. Concluded between England
and France 13 Feb., 1843, and the same
year between England and the United
States of America.

Since 1843 similar treaties have been made with
other nations, so that now we have extradition
treaties with Austria, Belgium, Brazil, Denmark,
[France], Hayti, Italy, Luxemburg, Netherlands,
Prussia, Salvador, Spain, Sweden and Norway,
Switzerland, Tonga [the United States], &c.

Extravagants or 'Extravagantes
Constitutions,' in canon law are decretals or constitutions published after the
Clementines (*q.v.*), not at first included in
the Corpus Juris Canonici, but forming a
supplementary volume. They consist of
the Extravagants or papal constitutions
of John XXII. and a few of his successors. They were added to the Corpus
Juris Canonici by John Lancelot in the
time of Paul IV. (1555–1559).

The whole Corpus Juris Canonici consists of (1)
the Decretals of Raymond of Penaforte (1234), in
5 books; (2) the Sixt, or continuation of the
Decretals, also in 5 books; and (3) the Extravagantes Communes, consisting of the Clementines,
in 5 books, and Extravagantes Joannis in 1 book.
Subsequently 5 books of Communes were added,
being the rescripts of later popes.

Ezra. Same as Esdras, Zoroaster,
or Zerdusht. The last is the Persian
translation of Ezra, which means 'help.'
He died B.C. 440, aged 99.

F. *The three F's.* Mr. Butt's Irish
platform (1876) : F[ixity of tenure], F[ree
sale], F[air rent]. The principle of com-

pensation for unexhausted improvements
was introduced in Ireland in the Land
Act of 1870 ; that of the Three Fs in the
Land Act of 1881.

Fabian Method (*The*). Delay.
Fabius Maximus, instead of attacking
Hannibal, harassed him by marches and
countermarches. Hence the proverb, 'To
win, like Fabius, by delay.'

Fabius of America (*The*). George
Washington (1732–1799).

Fabius of Austria (*The*). Marshal
Daun, able and cautious (1705–1766).

Fabius of France (*The*). Anne
Montmorency (1493–1567), so called from
the way he conducted his expedition
against Kaiser Karl V.—annoying him
in every way, alluring him from place
to place, and never coming to a general
battle.

Fable of Jenkins' Ear (*The*),
1738. Capt. Robert Jenkins, master of a
sloop trading from Jamaica, was boarded
and searched by a Guarda Costa (Spanish
coastguard), and barbarously ill-treated.
He affirmed that the Spanish captain had
cut off one of his ears, and Jenkins
carried about with him an ear wrapped
in wadding. On 16 March he appeared
at the bar of the House of Commons, and
Pulteney, Barnard, Wyndham, and Pitt
made political capital out of the story to
embroil the nation with Spain ; but Burke
dubbed the whole story a fable. This
incident or fable led to a declaration of
war with Spain.

Fabliaux, 1150–1350. Short fables
or tales in verse, such as 'Reynard the
Fox' and Parnell's 'Hermit.' The fabliaux
poets were wandering minstrels very inferior in position to the Troubadours and
Trouvères. The best of all this immense
pile of French verse which has come
down to us is the fabliau of 'Aucassin
and Nicolette,' which is tender, natural,
and full of interesting situations.

Fabulæ Atella'næ. A species of
farce written in the Oscan language,
which was spoken in all the south of
Italy, and, from its resemblance to Latin,
was understood by educated Romans.

Atellanæ, from Atella, a city of the Oscans, in
Campania, where these farces were performed.

Fact and Right. *See* 'Right and
Fact.'

Factory Act (*The*), 9 Aug., 1870 (33 & 34 Vict. c. 62). Working hours, 6 to 6 or 7 to 7, except Saturdays, when work is to close at 2 p.m. Extra hours 6 to 8 p.m., 7 to 9 p.m., or 8 to 10 p.m., not more than five days in any week, and not more than forty-eight days in any year. This not to be allowed in anywise except two hours are allowed for meals, at least half an hour of the time being at five o'clock p.m. The Factory and Workshop Act of 1878 (41 Vict. c. 16) repealed all previous acts, and consolidated them into one comprehensive statute. It was amended in 1883 (46 Vict. c. 53).

In 1890 there was a European clamour for higher wages and a reduction of working time to eight hours a day.

Factory King (*The*). Richard Oastler (1789–1861).

Faculty (*A Grant of*). Is an order by the bishop of a diocese to do something or enjoy something not permitted by common law ; such as an alteration in a church, the erection there of a gallery or organ, to place a tablet on the church walls, to obtain a particular seat in a church, and so on.

Faculty of Advocates (*The*), 1424. Scotland. The college or society of advocates who plead in all actions before the courts of sessions, justiciary, and exchequer.

The statute runs : 'Gif there bee onie pure creature, for faulte of cunning or dispenses, that cannot or may not follow his cause, the king . . . sall ordaine the judge before quhom the cause sulde be determined, to purvey and get a leill and a wise advocate to follow sik pure creatures' causes ; and gif sik causes be obteined, the wranger sall assyith baith the partie skaithed and the advocatis coastes and travel.'

Fagot Votes. *See* 'Dictionary of Phrase and Fable,' p. 283. From the following quotation it would seem that this term is literal, and that buying a few fagots and hiring for a few pence a room in a hut gave a person a vote at elections for members of parliament.

Faggot voters were there in plenty, renting a room of some old crone at a penny or so a week, lighting a fire with a small faggot of sticks, and thus standing in freedom's might an elective burgess.—C. THOMSON, *Autobiography*, p. 58.

Fainéants, *i.e.* worthless. A term applied to the latter Merovingian kings of France, in which reigns the mayors of the palace really governed the kingdom, and the kings were mere puppets.

They were Thierry III., Clovis III., Childebert III., Dagobert III., Chilperic II., Thierry IV.,

and Childéric III., dethroned in 730. Of these seven kings, five were the *third* of their name. *See* 'Fatal Three.'

. Louis V. was also called 'le Fainéant.'

Fair Maid of Galloway (*The*). Margaret, sister of Earl William of Douglas, on whom descended the estates of Galloway, Wigton, Balvenie, Ormond, and Annandale, after the execution of William in 1440. She married William, heir of James the Gross, her cousin-german.

Fair Maid of Kent (*The*). Joan, daughter of the earl of Kent. She was the wife of the Black Prince, and mother of Richard II., born 1326, married 1361, died 1385.

The Black Prince was born in 1330. At his marriage he was 31 and his wife 35 years of age. Edward died 1376, so his widow survived him nine years. Her son was crowned 1377.

Faire Ruelle. To receive guests in one's bedchamber.

Armande Béjart had made a start by receiving her guests, sumptuously attired and reclining on a state-bed. The guests passed on both sides of the bed. This was called *faire ruelle.—Nineteenth Century* (June 1889, p. 79b).

Faithful Norman (*The*). Prendergast (in the reign of Henry II.). When MacGallapatrick of Ossory sought a safe-conduct to the Norman camp in Ireland to exculpate himself from treason his friend Prendergast was appointed his escort. On his reaching the camp, O'Brien insisted on his death, but Prendergast, drawing his sword, swore on the cross that no harm should befall the man who had confided in his honour ; and he was allowed to conduct his friend back again in safety.

Fakirs (Fa-keers'). Paupers ; a species of religious recluse common in India and the East generally. They live on alms, but subject themselves to great hardships to earn eternal happiness. Some neither lie nor sit for years together. Some hold their hands over their heads all life long. Some go about well-nigh naked, exposed to heat, cold, and the stings of insects. Some live in ditches. Some carry fire on their heads. Some condemn themselves to perpetual silence. And all live an ascetic life.

Falaise (*The Treaty of*), 1174. William king of Scotland (brother of Malcolm IV.) invaded Northumberland, but was made prisoner at the battle of

Alnwick and taken to Henry II., who was at Northampton. The Scotch redeemed their king by making him liegeman to Henry, and the treaty was signed at Falaise. in Normandy. This treaty is important, as it made the king of England the overlord of the king of Scotland. Richard I. cancelled this treaty for a sum of money equal to 100,000*l*. of the present day.

Falczy (*Peace of*). 24 July, 1711. Between Russia and Turkey, by which Czar Peter I. the Great agreed to restore Azof to the Porte.

Falk Laws (*The*), 1873. So called from Dr. Falk, who insisted on the compulsory education of the clergy of Prussia. The laws are four in number : (1) The first was directed against the abuse of ecclesiastical discipline for political purposes, such as 'boycotting,' excommunication, and anathemas ; (2) the next regulated the effect of secession from the Church on the obligation to meet certain taxes; (3) the third law was directed at the evasions of Roman Catholics of State education incumbent on all Germans ; and (4) abolished the legality of papal tribunals, recognising the judgments of the German ecclesiastical courts as the only authority on Church matters. In 1874 these four laws were supplemented by others to ensure more perfect obedience.

Dr. Adalbert Falk was appointed by Prince Bismarck 'Minister of Public Worship' 22 Jan., 1872. In 1872 Prince Bismarck carried through the Prussian Houses a bill to transfer the control of primary education from the Church to the State authorities.

Falkenstein (*Battle of*), 1814. Called 'The Battle of the Rocks'; in which a party of French mountaineers defended themselves from an army of Germans and Cossacks by hurling rocks upon them.

Fall of the Leaf (*The*), 1712. The Act 10 Anne, c. 19, A.D. 1712 imposed a stamp-duty on newspapers, and so many were consequently discontinued that it was called the 'Fall of the Leaf.'

False Coiner (*The*). Philippe III. 'Le Hardi' of France was so called because he debased the coin. (1245, 1270–1285.)

False Decretals (*The*), 835–845. A shameless forgery purporting to be forty-nine rescripts of bishops in the first four centuries. Signed by such names as St. Anaclêtus (who died 78), St. Alexander (who died 109), St. Fabian (who died 236), Julius (who died 337), and St. Athanasius (who died 373). The object of the Decretals is to diminish the authority of metropolitans over their suffragans, by establishing an appellant jurisdiction of the Roman See in all causes, and by forbidding national councils to be holden without its consent. Every bishop is made amenable only to the tribunal of the pope. Every accused person might appeal to the pope from any civil sentence. The pope only could make new sees or translate from one see to another. Upon these spurious decretals has been built the great fabric of papal supremacy. Koch says that this book ' produced enormous changes in the Roman hierarchy, doctrine, and discipline; and has to an incalculable extent raised the authority of the pope.'

They assume to have been compiled by St. Isidore of Pelūsium, who died 450, but certainly had no existence for nearly 400 years later.

The ' False Decretals ' are subdivided into three parts :

Part I. contains 61 decretals of popes in the first three centuries (from Clement, A.D. 91, to Sylvester, A.D. 314).

Part II. contains the Canons of the Councils.

Part III. contains the decretal epistles from Sylvester to Gregory the Great (34-590).

The False Decretals assert that Constantine the Great ceded to Pope Sylvester and his successors the empire of the West, and that the Church of Rome has the charge of the whole flock of Christ, as the successor of St. Peter. That every bishop emanates from Rome, and that the power of the pope overrides that of the councils.

** It is passing strange that a vile forgery should have been accepted and appealed to as authority by the Catholic Church for nearly 1,000 years. It was appealed to in 865 by Nicholas I. ; by the Ecumenical Council in 870; again by Leo. IX. (1048-1054). It was made the basis of the Hildebrandine system (1073-1080) ; was referred to as authority by the Abbot Barlaam in 1341; by the Council of Florence, 7 May, 1437; and was confirmed by the Council of Trent in 1564.

They were proved to be forgeries by Nicolas Cusanus in 1432; by Laurentius Valla in 1457; by Contius in 1586, but his evidence was suppressed; and by Blondel in 1628, but his book was placed in the 'Index.' At length, Pope Pius VI., in 1789, had the honesty and courage to declare the author of the book *Impostor Nequissimus*, and the decretals ' infamous forgeries.' *See* 'Literary Forgeries.'

The author of these decretals was either Isidore Mercator a Cenobite, or Benedict Levita of Mentz, or Riculfe archbishop of Mentz who brought them to France in 811.

False Hermit (*The*). Enrico the Italian was so called by the Catholics because he was a hermit of the 'heretical' Waldenses. He was condemned to death in 1134 by the Council of Pavïa, but escaped and died in 1147.

Families (*The*). A secret society founded by Auguste Blanqui and Bernard, chiefs of the French Socialists and Communists. This red republican party were greatly instrumental in bringing about the revolution of 1830.

Familist. 1540. One of the religious sect called ' the Family of Love ' (*q.v.*).

Under the head of Independents . . . . were the Arminians, Millenaries, Baptists, Anabaptists, Familists, Enthusiasts, Seekers, Perfectists, Socinians, Arians, and others.—HOWITT, *History of England* (Charles I., ch. vi. p. 273).

Familists. A religious sect in New England in the 17th cent. This sect looked for rare revelations and forsook the revealed word (JOHN HARVARD, 1628).

The Davidians (*q.v.*) are so called in England and Holland.

Family Feud, or 'Blood Feud.' *See* 'Vendetta,' 'Rimbecco.'

Family Pact (*The*), 'Pacte de Famille,' 15 Aug., 1761. A secret compact made at the instigation of the Duc de Choiseul by all the crowned heads of the Bourbon race to stand together in defence of each other, and put an end to the British maritime supremacy. The family consisted of Louis XV. of France, Carlos III. of Spain, Ferdinand IV. of Naples, and Filippo of Parma. Spain bound herself to deprive Great Britain of her commercial privileges in America, and to transfer them to France. France bound herself to aid Spain in the recovery of Gibraltar. The 'Pact' was quite effete, and was broken up by the revolution in 1789.

Louis XV. was the fourth of the Bourbon dynasty (founded by Henri IV.); Carlos III. was the fifth of the Bourbons in Spain (founded by the grandson of Louis XIV.); Ferdinand IV. was Carlos's son ; and Filippo of Parma was son of Charles de Bourbon.

Family of Love (*The*), or 'Familists, 1540. A religious sect founded by Henry Nicholas, a mercer of Delft, and introduced into England in 1570 by Vitells. These sectaries made all religion consist of inward love to Christ They rejected infant baptism, the divinity of Christ, and original sin.

Fanariotes (4 syl.). Greek dragomans residing at Fanar, in Constantinople, and exercising considerable influence in Turkey in the 17th and 18th centuries. The insurrection of the Greeks in 1821 put an end to their power.

Faneuil Hall. In Boston, Massachusetts. Built in 1742 by Peter Faneuil and presented by him to the town for public meetings, &c.

Fanny (*Lord*). John lord Hervey (1696–1743). Lord Privy Seal in 1740; ' half wit, half fool ; half man, half beau.' It is said that he used rouge, drank asses' milk, and took Scotch pills.

These lines are weak, another's pleased to say,
Lord Fanny weaves a thousand such a day.
POPE, *Sat. and Ep.*, i. 6.

Like gentle Fanny's was my flowery theme,
A painted mistress or a purling stream.
POPE, *Prologue* (*Sat. and Ep.*), line 149.

Far'andole (3 syl.), or ' Faran'dola.' A sort of country dance peculiar to the South of France and North of Italy, akin to the Carmagnole (*q.v.*). It was under the excitement of this dance that Maréchal Brune was murdered at Avignon in 1815.

Farmer George, or ' The Farmer King.' The sobriquet of George III.

Farmer Godric and his Cummer Godgifu. Henry I. of England and his wife Matilda (daughter of King Malcolm of Scotland and Margaret sister of Edgar the Atheling). By this marriage the blood of Cerdic and Alfred was blended with that of Rolf and the Conqueror.

Farmers General. In French ' Fermiers Généraux.' Those in the ancient *régime* of France who farmed the public revenues, such as tallage, gabelle (or tax on salt), the tax on tobacco, the octrois, and so on. Originally forty in number, but afterwards increased to sixty. They were immensely rich, and were appointed by the 'ministre de finances,' who expected his *pot-de-vin* for the appointment. Suppressed by the Assemblée Constituante in 1790.

Farnese (3 syl.). A princely Italian family, famous for their patronage of the arts. In their palace at Rome they possessed some of the finest sculptures of the world, as the Farnese *Bull*, now at Naples; the Farnese *Flora, Herculés*, and *Gladiator.*

Fast Days. In the Catholic Church Wednesday was a fast in commemoration of the day when Jesus was betrayed and taken prisoner, and Friday the day of his crucifixion. To these was added Saturday to commemorate the entombment.

The quadrigesimal or Lent fast commemorates the forty days passed by Jesus in the wilderness; it was originally only forty hours.

There are four different sorts of fast: (1) *Jejunium generālé* (binding on all); (2) *Jejunium consuetudinarium* (a local fast); (3) *Jejunium pœnitentiālé* (by way of penance); and (4) *Jejunium votivum* (consequent on a vow).

The Mohammedans fast the whole month of Ramadan, when the Prophet brought the Koran from heaven.

Fasti. In ancient Rome days when the law-courts were open; 'Nefasti' days when they were closed. Also public registers. These registers were of two sorts, *Fasti Kalendārés* (or *Sacri*) and *Fasti Annālés.* The Fasti Kalendares were almanacs. The Fasti Annales were chronicles of the year containing the names of the consuls and other magistrates for the current year, and a brief notice opposite each day of some past historic event in Roman history.

Ovid's *Fasti* is a poetical companion to the calendar published by Julius Cæsar.

Fat Thursday. *See* 'Zobia grassa.'

Fat Tuesday. *See* 'Mardi Gras.'

Fatal Stone (*The*). A palladium, as the 'Fatalé Marmor' or 'Stone of Destiny' (*q.v.*) of Scotland. The Fatal Stone of Artizoe, of the Persians, mentioned by Pliny. The 'Black Stone' of the Seids. The 'Fatal Stone' is described as a large mass of very rich grey silver ore of an Indian South American tribe, removed from place to place, as the tribe fled before the Spanish invaders. *See* 'Caaba.'

Probably the 'Great Goddess Diana which fell from heaven' was a meteoric stone, like the 'Fatal Stone' referred to above.

Fatal Three. The succession of three brothers has been singularly fatal in France. The CAPETIAN dynasty terminated with the three succeeding brothers (sons of Philippe IV. *le Bel*), viz. Louis X., Philippe V., and Charles IV. The Valois line came to an end by the succession of the three sons of Henri II., viz. François II., Charles IX., and Henri III. Similarly, the Bourbon dynasty terminated with the three sons of Louis the Dauphin, viz. Louis XVI., Louis XVIII., and Charles X. The empire also

14

consisted of Napoleon I., Napoleon II., and Napoleon III.

After Charles IV., the third brother of the Capetian dynasty, came Philippe de Valois, a collateral branch. After Henri III., the third brother of the Valois dynasty, came Henri de Bourbon, a collateral branch. After Charles X., the third brother of the Bourbon dynasty, came Louis Philippe, a collateral branch. And with the third of these triplets monarchy in France died out. Of the seven Rois Fainéants of France, five were the third of the name—Thierry III., Clovis III., Childebert III., Dagobert III., and Childéric III. And after Napoleon III. the empire was converted into a republic.

Fatale Marmor, the 'Lia Fail' (*q.v.*), or 'Stone of Destiny.' *See above,* 'Fatal Stone.'

Fatale, pronounce *Fay-tā'-le.*

Father and Friend of the People (*The*). Henri IV. of France (1553, 1589–1610).

Il fut de ses sujets le vainqueur et le père.— VOLTAIRE.

Father and Mother of his People (*The*). Kang Hi (1653, 1661–1724). One of the best of the Chinese emperors.

Father Fritz. The name of endearment given to Friedrich II. the Great by his Prussian subjects (1712, 1740–1786).

Father Violet. Napoleon I. (1769–1821, emperor 1804–1815). So called after his banishment to Elba, because he assured his partisans that he would 'return to France with the violets.' Violets are still the symbol of imperial proclivities in France.

Father of Biblical Criticism (*The*). Orĭgen is called the father of Biblical criticism and exegesis (185–254).

He was accused and tortured for heresy. He denied the inspiration of scripture, rejected much of the historical portions of the Bible, and disbelieved in eternal punishment.

Father of Botany (*The*). Tournefort (3 syl.), 1656–1708. Linnæus followed him in all the main parts of his system.

Father of British Inland Navigation (*The*). Francis Egerton, duke of Bridgewater (1736–1803). Brindley constructed for him a canal between his coal pits at Worsley to Manchester, which reduced the carriage of coals from 12s. to 6s. a ton, and their price from 7d. to 3d. a cwt.

The 'Bridgewater Canal,' commenced in 1758, was by no mean the *first* canal in the British Isles.

The New River Canal was begun in 1608, the Carmarthenshire Canal in 1755, the Droitwich to the Severn in 1756, &c. But it was the first *great* navigable canal.

Father of Burlesque Poetry (*The*). Hippōnax of Ephesus (B.C. 566–520), a Greek poet.

Father of Chronology (*The*). Josephus Justus Scalĭger (1540–1609). His great work is ' De Emendatione Temporum.'

Father of Church History (*The*). Eusebius, first of the Greek Fathers (*q.v.*) and author of an Ecclesiastical History in ten books (Greek) from A.D. 1 to 324. Also called ' Father of Christian History ' (265–338).

Father of Cruelty. Alhakem I. of Cordŏva who exiled to Africa 40,000 of his own subjects for rebellion A.D. 818. He was also called ' He of the Suburbs,' because he razed to the ground the suburbs in which the above-mentioned rebels resided.

Father of English Poetry (*The*). Geoffrey Chaucer, the greatest English poet up to the time of Shakespeare. There were English poets before him, but Chaucer was *inter ignes Luna minores*.

Father of French Chemistry (*The*). Arnaud de Villeneuve (1238–1314). He discovered sulphuric, muriatic, and nitric acids; obtained alcohol from fermented liquors; and procured the spirit of turpentine by dissolving in alcohol the juice of pine-wood.

Father of French Eloquence (*The*). Alain Chartier (1386–1458), secretary to Charles VI. and Charles VII.

Father of French Philosophy (*The*). D'Alembert, mathematician, littérateur and encyclopædist (1717–1783). Called the ' Mazarin of Letters.'

Father of French Poetry (*The*). Thibault (1210–1253), comte de Champagne, and afterwards king of Navarre. He introduced the alternate masculine and feminine rhymes.

Feminine rhymes for the most part end in *e* or *es*; silent in prose, but pronounced slightly in poetry at the end of a line.
　　　　Thibault, pronounce *Tee'-bo*.

Father of French Satire (*The*). Mathurin Regnier (1573–1613).
　　Regnier, pronounce *Rain'-yca*.

Fathers of French Sculptors (*The*). Goujon and Pilon (16th cent.). The former, called the Correggio of sculptors, was slain in the Bartholomew massacre.

Father of French Surgery (*The*). Ambroise Paré (1517–1590), author of a treatise on Gunshot Wounds.

Father of French Tragedy (*The*). Robert Garnier (1534–1590). The foreboding dream in his ' Hippolyte ' has nothing superior in Corneille or Racine. However, Corneille is generally looked on as ' the Father of French Tragedy.'

Father of Grace and Elegance (*The*). So the French style Du Bellay, one of their Pleiad poets, also called ' the French Ovid ' (1524–1560).

Father of Landscape Gardening (*The*). Lenôtre (1613–1700). He laid out the gardens of Versailles, the Tuileries, St. Cloud, St. Germain, Fontainebleau, Clugny, Chantilly, Meudon, and Sceaux. He died at the age of 88, never having had a day's illness in his life.

Father of Letters (*The*). Louis XII. (1462, 1498–1515).
François I. (1494, 1515–1547).
Lorenzo de Medicis of Florence (1448–1492).
Mæcenas, the Roman statesman, was called the Patron of Letters (B.C. 73–8).

Father of Medicine (*The*). Hippocrătĕs, B.C. 460–357.

Father of Mesmerism (*The*), or ' Animal Magnetism.' Mesmer (1734–1815). He taught that there exists a force in man which he could communicate to others, and that this force was of a sedative character, inducing sleep or alleviating pain.

Father of Modern French Literature (*The*). Claude de Seyssel (1450–1520), celebrated for being the first prose writer in French with any degree of purity.

Father of Modern German Poetry (*The*). Martin Opitz of Silesia (1597–1639).

Father of Modern Philosophy (*The*). Roger Bacon, a friar, author of ' Opus Majus ' (1214–1292).

Father of Modern Scepticism (*The*). Bayle (1647–1706), author of a French 'Historical and Critical Dictionary.'

Father of Modern Swedish Poetry (*The*). Stjernhjelm (*Shearnyelm*), 16th cent., contemporary with Shakspeare, Lopë de Vega, &c.

Father of Parody (*The*). Hippŏnax of Ephesus (B.C. 566–520), a Greek poet.

Father of Physiology (*The*). Haller (1708-1777). He wrote eighty-six books on medicine and physiology.

Father of Political Dissenters (*The*). Sir John Oldcastle, commonly called Lord Cobham (1360–1417). Burnt to death in the reign of Henry V. He was condemned by Archbishop Arundel in 1413, but the sentence was carried out by Henry Chicheley, Arundel's successor, 14 Dec., 1417. Lord Cobham was said to be unsound on these four points : Transubstantiation, penance, pilgrimages, and image-worship.

Father of Satire (*The*). Archilŏchos of Paros (B.C. 710–690), a Greek poet. He inveighed against Paros, against Thasos, and against Lycambês, who promised to give him his daughter in marriage, but afterwards retracted his word. Lycambês was so pricked to the heart by the satire of the poet that he hanged himself.

Archilochum proprio rabies armavit iambo,
HOR. *De Arte Poetica*, 79.

Father of Waters. The Irrawaddy (Burmah). Johnson, in his 'Rasselas,' calls the Mississippi 'the Nile of the Father of Waters.'

Father of his Country.
ANDRONICOS *Palæolŏgos* assumed the title (1260-1332).

AUGUSTUS ('Pater atque Princeps'— HORACE), B.C. 63, 31–14 A.D.

CICERO, who broke up the Catiline conspiracy (B.C. 106–43).

The Romans offered the same title to Marius after his annihilation of the Teutŏnês and Cimbri, but he declined to accept it.

COSMO DE' MEDICI is so designated on his tombstone.

' *Cosmus Medici* | *Hic situs est*, | *Decreto publico*, | *Pater Patriæ* (1519-1574).

DORIA (*Andrea*) is so called on his statue at Genŏa (1468-1560).

JULIUS CÆSAR was so styled after he had quelled the Spanish insurrection (B.C. 100–44).

LAURENCE O'TOOLE, archbishop of Dublin, who died 14 Nov., 1180 : he was of the illustrious house of O'Tuathal, and was canonised in 1226 by Honorius III.

LOUIS XVIII. of France (1755, 1814–1824).

WASHINGTON (*George*), 'Defender and Paternal Counsellor of the American States ' (1732–1799).

See also 1 Chron. iv. 14.

Father of his People (*The*). Louis XII. of France (1462, 1498–1515).

Even Louis XI. was so called. The French, as a rule, have not been happy in their royal appellatives.

Father of the English Unitarians (*The*). John Biddle of Gloucestershire (1615–1662). He was thrice imprisoned by the Long Parliament, and was at last liberated in 1652 by the Act of Oblivion. He was again arrested in 1655, but Cromwell discharged him in 1658; he was again arrested in 1662, and fined 100*l*. Not being able to pay the fine, he died in prison within five weeks.

Father of the Forest (*The*). It stands in California in Tulare County, is 450 feet high, and 138 feet round the trunk.

Father of the French Drama (*The*). Rotrou (1609–1650) was so called by Corneille. If not the 'father of the drama,' he was doubtlessly the 'founder' of the French theatre ' so far as scenery is concerned and the general conduct of the stage.

Father of the German School (*The*). Albert Dürer (1471–1528).

Fuseli says of Albert Dürer, 'though called the Father of the German School, he neither reared scholars, nor was he imitated by German artists of any age.'

Father of the Land League. Ireland. Michael Davitt, 1879.

Father of the Modern Drama (*The*). In Germany. Andrew Gryph (1619–1664), prince of the Silesian poets. Shakspeare died the very year that Gryph was born. He wrote both tragedies and comedies, but is pompous, declamatory, and overstrained.

Father of the People (*The*). Christiern III. of Denmark (1502, 1534-1559).

Gabriel du Pineau, a French lawyer (1573–1644).

Fathers (*Last of the*). St. Bernard (1091–1153).

The 'Fathers of the Church' were followed by the 'Schoolmen.'

Fathers of the Greek Church.

Those Christian writers of the Greek Church who succeeded the Primitive Fathers (*q.v.*), and lived in the 4th and 5th cents.:

Died
342 Eusébius of Nicomedia.
873 Athanásius.
379 Ephrem of Edessa (the deacon).
— Basil the Great.
386 Cyril of Jerusalem.
390 Gregory of Nazianzus in Cappadocia.
396 Gregory of Nyssa.
403 Epiphanius.
407 Chrysostom.
444 Cyril of Alexandria.

Fathers of the Latin Church.

Contemporary with those of the Greek Church (*q.v.*).

Died.
317 Lactantius.
397 Ambrose of Milan.
420 Jerome (2 syl.).
430 Augustin of Hippo.
467 Hiláry.
St. Bernard (1091-1153) is called the Last of the Latin Fathers, and was followed by the Schoolmen.

Fatherland. Germany.

What is the German fatherland?
Is't Prussia's realm or Suabian-land?
Is't where the Rhenish red-grapes hang?
Or where the Baltic sea-mews clang?
Oh! nay, nay, nay, so cribbed a strand
Is not the German fatherland.

Our fatherland all Germany—
Who speak the tongue our sons must be.
God give us courage, will, and strength,
To free it in its breadth and length;
Join every heart, join every hand
Till Germany's one fatherland.
         ARNDT (*translated by E. C. B.*).

Fatigue Party. Men of the rank and file employed on works, such as making roads, digging trenches, moving guns, pitching camps, &c., not their special military work. They are said to be 'men on fatigue.'

Fatimites (3 syl.). An Arabian dynasty in Egypt, founded by Mahadi Obaidallah, a descendant of Fatima, daughter of Mohammed 'the prophet' (910–1171). On the death of Adhid (last of the Fatimites) the dynasty of the Ayubides (3 syl.) succeeded. The Fatimites of Egypt wore red turbans.

The princes of the Fatimites were called Allades (3 syl.), from Ali, cousin of Mohammed. Ali married Fatima, the Prophet's daughter, and was proclaimed kalif in 656.

Faust (*The English*). Dr. Dee, the astrologer (1527–1608).

Favoured Child of Victory (*The*). Marshal Masséna, duke of Rivoli (1758–1817), so called because his whole career in Italy, Switzerland, Germany, and Poland had been an unbroken series of victories. He was foiled by Viscount Wellington (Duke of Wellington) at Busaco 27 Sept., 1810.

Fawkes (*Guy, i.e.* Guido). Was at the taking of Calais by Archduke Albrecht in 1598. He took part with Catesby and the other conspirators in Gunpowder Plot, 1604-5, was arrested 5 Nov. 1605, and executed at Westminster 31 Jan., 1606.

In 1850, the year of 'the Papal aggression,' the figure of Cardinal Wiseman was substituted for Guy Fawkes in the street processions.

Fealty was performed standing; *homage* was performed kneeling. Fealty was sworn to by oath; homage required no oath. In fealty the vassal stood before his lord, and laying his right hand on the Bible, said aloud : 'Know ye this, my lord, that I swear to be faithful and true to you, and to bear faith to you for the lands that I shall hold of you. And I will lawfully do unto you the customs and services which I ought to do, and at the times assigned. So help me God and his saints.' Then taking up the book he kissed it, and put it back again. *See* 'Investiture of Vassals.'

Feast, Feasts. *See* also 'Festa,' 'Festum,' and 'Fête.'

Christian Feasts are (a) Fixed; (b) Movable.

(a) The Fixed Christian Festivals are

All Saints or All Hallows, 1 Nov.
All Souls in honour of all the faithful dead, whether canonised or not, 2 Nov.
Candlemas Day or the Purification of the Virgin Mary, 2 Feb.
Christmas Day or the Nativity, 25 Dec.
Circumcision, 1 Jan.
Epiphany or Twelfth Day, 6 Jan.
Innocents' Day, 28 Dec.

Lady Day or Annunciation of the Virgin Mary, 25 March.

The following are also called Saints' Days, or Red Letter Days :—

S. Andrew	...	...	...	...	30 Nov.
Barnabas	...	...	...	...	11 June
James the Elder		...	...	...	25 July
John the Baptist (his Nativity)			...	24 June
John the Evangelist		...	...	27 Dec.
Luke the Evangelist		...	...	18 Oct.
Mark the Evangelist		...	...	25 April
Matthew the Evangelist			...	21 Sept.
Matthias	...	...	...	...	24 Feb.
Michael (Michaelmas Day)			...	29 Sept.
Paul (his Conversion)		...	...	25 Jan.
Peter (by Catholics Peter & Paul)			29 June
Philip and James the Less			...	1 May
Simon and Jude			...	28 Oct.
Stephen (the first martyr)		...	26 Dec.
Thomas (the shortest day)		...	21 Dec.

(b) Movable Christian Feasts :—

Ascension Day or Holy Thursday, ten days before Whit Sunday.

Ash Wednesday, the first day in Lent.

Easter Sunday (q.v.).

Good Friday, the Friday before Easter Day.

Palm Sunday, the Sunday before Easter Day.

Pentecost or Whit Sunday, the seventh Sunday after Easter.

Sexagesima Sunday, (about) sixty days before Easter, second Sunday before Lent.

Trinity Sunday, the Sunday following Whit Sunday.

See each of these *in loco*. They all depend on Easter Day.

Feasts (*Grecian*), or Grecian Festivals.

Agraulia, or Agrauria, held at Athens in honour of Agraulos or Agrauros, daughter of Cecrops.

Artemisia in honour of Artěmis [Diana]; the bread offered to the goddess was called *lochia*, and the women who performed the sacred rites were called *lombai*.

Diony'sia in honour of Dionÿsos [Bacchus], observed in Athens with great splendour and numerous ceremonies.

Eleusinia, the most celebrated and most mysterious festival of any in Greece. The greater mysteries were celebrated at Eleusis, in the month Boëdromion (the latter half of Sept. and the former of Oct.).

Panathenaia in honour of Athěnê [Minerva], protectress of Athens. It lasted several days and was celebrated with great magnificence.

The festivals of Greece were very numerous. There were fifty beginning with the letter A. And besides these special festivals there were the

times set apart for the Isthmian, Němēan, Olympian, and Pythian games.

Feasts (*Roman*), or Roman Festivals.

1. In January : The *Agonālia* in honour of Janus on the 9th ; and *Carmentālia* in honour of Carmenta (mother of Evander) on the 11th.

2. In February : The **Faunālia** in honour of Faunus on the 13th; the *Lupercālia* in honour of Pan, on the 15th ; the *Regifugium* on the 24th, to commemorate the flight of Tarquin ; and two or three others.

3. In March : the *Matronālia* to commemorate the termination of the Sabine war on the 1st; the *Liberālia* in honour of Bacchus on the 18th ; the *Quinquatrīa* in honour of Minerva, on the 19th ; and two others.

4. In April : the *Megalēsia*, on the 4th and 5th, in honour of the mother of the gods ; the *Cereālia* in honour of Cerês, on the 9th ; and three others.

5. In May : on the 1st the sacred rites of the *Bona Dea* were performed by the vestal virgins ; the *Lemuria*, to the souls of the deceased, on the 9th ; and two others.

6. In June : On the 1st were several festivals, one of which was that of *Juno monēta*. Other festivals were held on the 4th, 7th, 9th, and 10th.

With the festivals of this month the *Fasti* of Ovid end. The other six books are lost.

7. In July were seven festivals.

8. In August were four festivals.

9. In September : the *Ludi Magni* were held on the 4th in honour of the great gods ; and on the 13th the consul fixed a nail in the temple of Jupiter.

10. In October were two festivals.

11. In November were two festivals.

12. In December : the Saturnālia were held on the 17th, the most celebrated festival of the whole year, when all persons of every rank gave themselves up to feasting, frolic, and fun.

Besides the time devoted to the games.

Feast of Fools, or ' Festum Fatuorum.' The Christian substitute of the Roman Saturnalia. The same as 'Festum Kalendarum' (q.v.), 1 Jan. Abolished in Germany by the Council of Basel (1431–1449) ; in France by Charles VII. in 1444. Observed at Antibes (2 syl.) as late as 1644. See ' Festum Asinorum.'

This was not the Ass's Festival, as many assert. The Ass's Festival was the 14th of Jan., and commemorated the ' Flight into Egypt,' whereas the

Feast of Fools was New-year's day, and thence called 'Festum Kalendarum.' It was called *Festum hypodiaconorum*,' non quod revera soli Subdiaconi has scelestas choreas ducerent; sed quod hac joculari appellatione indicare voluerint festivitatem hanc fuisse ebriorum clericorum vel diaconorum.' DU CANGE, vol. iv. p. 298, article 'Kalendæ.' It was a day of drunkenness and debauchery, in which the clergy took a leading part.

Feast of Liberty (*The*). A festival held by the Athenians every five years, in commemoration of the victory of Salamis over Xerxes and his host. It was celebrated on the battle-field of Platæa.

Feast of Nature (*The*), 10 Aug., 1793. To celebrate the 'perfected constitution.' Séchelles and David the painter were the chief devisers. A plaster statue of Nature was erected on the Place de la Bastille, having two streams of water sprouting from her breasts. The front of the pedestal bore the words, 'We all are her children.' Other mottos were 'Hell vomits kings,' and 'Hell vomits priests.' The chief members of the Convention, public committees, and commune kneeled in adoration to this plaster image, praying her to receive the eternal devotion of the French. Then followed firing of cannon, scattering of flowers, kissing, and dancing. The nurses of the foundling hospital brought their children to 'Mother Nature,' and the Dames de la Halle were crowned with wreaths. In the Place de la Révolution (now ' de la Concorde ') was a gigantic statue of Liberty with a forest of poles bearing red caps, and inscribed, 'Imitate us; we are free.'

Feast of Pikes (*The*), 14 July. So the 'Feast of the Federation ' is called by Carlyle, because the Bastille was taken on 14 July, 1790, by the mob, for the most part armed with pikes.

France roared simultaneously to the welkin, bursting forth into sound and smoke at its Feast of Pikes.—CARLYLE, *French Revolution*, vol. iii. bk. ii. 1.

Feast of Reason (*The*), 10 Nov., 1793. Celebrated by decree of the Convention at Paris.

Feast of Reconciliation (*The*), 25 Jan., 1555. A grand religious procession in London, in the reign of Queen Mary, to commemorate the return of England to the See of Rome. It was to be held annually on St. Andrew's day (25 Jan.).

The bishops were empowered to ' reconcile ' all to the Catholic Church, and enter their names in registers. Those who did not give in their names were to be proceeded against as heretics. This was followed by four years of persecution, when about 300 suffered death.

Feasts of the Être Suprême (*The*), 8 June, 1794. Celebrated by decree of the Convention at Paris. *See* also ' Festa,' ' Festum,' and ' Fête.'

Feathers Tavern Association (*The*), 1771. An association opposed to the abolition of subscription to the Thirty-nine Articles and confessions of faith. Its name is derived from the place of meeting. In 1772 the association presented a petition to parliament on the subject. It was signed by 200 clergymen and 50 laymen, chiefly lawyers.

Febron'ianism, anti - papalism. John Nicholas von Hontheim, who assumed the pen-name of Justīnus Febronius, wrote a book, ' De Præsenti Statu Ecclesiæ,' published in 1767, to prove the independence of national churches, and the ' home rule ' of diocesan bishops. It met with the severest censures of the Roman tribunals.

February Patent or Ordinance (*The*), 1861. Promulgated for the establishment of a central Reichsrath, consisting of a house of lords and house of representatives from all the provinces of the Austrian empire. Hungary refused to send any representative, and in 1867 Hungary was granted its present form of government.

February Revolution (*The*), 1848 (22, 23, 24). In which the government of Louis Philippe of France was overthrown. It began at a reform banquet with the cry of *Vive la Réforme !* and ended in three days with the cry of *Vive la République !* The king fled, and a republic was proclaimed 24 Feb.

Fedavees. A company of young men, agents of the Chief of the Assassins, a secret society of Asia. They dressed in white, with red bonnets and girdles, and were armed with daggers; but they assumed all sorts of disguises.

Federalism, 1792, 1793. A scheme proposed by the Girondists (*q.v.*) to form the different departments into a federacy, like the United States of America.

Federalists (*The*), 1841. Ireland. When the House of Commons decided that demands for the repeal of the Union were unconstitutional, the repealers called themselves 'Federalists,' and declared that their platform was not identical with the repeal for which Daniel O'Connell had previously been agitating. They said they were opposed to the dismemberment of the Imperial Parliament, but favoured the idea of an Irish Parliament to have jurisdiction in exclusively local affairs. O'Connell accepted the new programme.

Federals *(The)*, 1861–1866. In the American Civil War the Federalists were those who armed to preserve the Union against the Confederates *(q.v.)* or Southern States.

Federate Republicanism, 1793. A French federation against the Convention. The chief league consisted of Lyons, Marseilles, and Toulon. Kellermann was sent with 30,000 troops to reduce Lyons to obedience, and the siege lasted from 19 Sept. to 9 Oct., 1793, when the city surrendered, and 2,000 of the inhabitants were put to death. Toulon was set on fire, and the federation was stamped out.

Federation of the Champ de Mars, or 'Fête of the Federation,' 14 July, 1790. The first anniversary of the taking of the Bastille in Paris, when 60,000 persons assembled, and Louis XVI. swore to preserve the constitution worked out by the Constituent Assembly.

A second federation was held 14 July, 1792.

A third was held during the famous Hundred Days *(q.v.)*, 26 May, 1815. This is more properly called the Champ de Mai, but it was held in the Champ de Mars of Paris. Here Napoleon the Great proclaimed what is called 'L'Acte Additionnel'—that is, the act which Napoleon, during the Hundred Days, 'ajouta aux Constitutions de l'Empire.' This assembly, announced for 26 May, did not really take place till 1 June.

Fee-penny *(The)*. A fine paid or exacted of a debtor if his debt was not paid to time. Sir Thomas Gresham, writing from Flanders, frequently requests the English government to settle its debts ' to save the fee-penny.'

Fehmgerichte (4 syl.), or the ' Holy Fehm.' A secret tribunal of the middle ages, in Westphalia. Its object was especially to terrorise the barons, whose lawless conduct was the curse of the land. These tribunals were at their climacteric in the 14th and 15th cents.

The members of the tribunal were called ' Wissende ' (3 syl.), the initiated.

The district over which it exercised judicial authority was called the ' Red Land.'

The assessors of the court and executors of its sentences were called ' Freischöffen ' (free justices).

The presiding judge was the ' Freigraf ' (free count).

The kaiser (king of Germany) was *ex officio* one of the ' Wissende.'

Felix'ians, 8th cent. A Spanish sect so called from Felix bishop of Urgel. He taught that Christ in respect of his divine nature was the Son of God by generation; but in respect of his human nature was only the adopted Son of God, like other holy men. ·This was called the ' Adoption Controversy.'

Elipandus (archbishop of Toledo) was a Felixian.

Fellow Commoners, in Cambridge University, are students who pay higher fees, wear a distinctive costume, and ' common' or dine at the Fellows' Table. They were called in Oxford University ' Gentleman Commoners.' They are generally either noblemen or married men.

Female High Sheriff *(The)*. Anne countess of Pembroke, a staunch royalist in the reigns of Charles I. and II. On the death of her father, the Earl of Cumberland, in 1643, she succeeded to the hereditary office of Sheriff of Westmoreland, attended the judges of assize, and sat with them on the bench at Appleby.

Fencing the Tables. Keeping from the eucharist all whom the ' Fencers' thought unworthy to be communicants. One clergymen of Dumfries forbade from the table all who used minced oaths, such as ' heth, teth, feth, fegs, losh, gosh, and lovenenty.'

Fénelon of Germany *(The)*. Lava'ter (1741–1801). Born at Zürich; the founder of physiognomonie, or the art of reading character by physiognomy.

Fénelon of the Reformation. Johann Arnd of Anhalt (1555–1621).

Fenian Heroes (*The*). The heroes of Finn, called by Ossian 'Fingal.' 'Gal' means the alien or foreigner, as Wales, &c.

Fenians, or Fenian Brotherhood. An association of Irish rebels ill-disposed to the British government, and bent on a separation of Ireland from England. It was organised in America by James Stephens in 1858. The leaders were called 'Head-Centres,' and their subordinates were called 'Centres.'

It was introduced into Ireland in 1865 by James Stephens, the 'head-centre,' who was imprisoned in Dublin, 11 Nov., but made his escape, 24 Nov., by the connivance of the turnkey.

This society, which made the most reckless attacks on life and property, was condemned, 12 Jan., 1870, by Pope Pius IX., and on 14 Oct. by General Grant, president of the U.S. of America; but it still remains active for mischief.

18 Sept., 1867, Sergeant Brett was killed ; and on 13 Dec. the wall of Clerkenwell House of Detention was blown up by these miscreants. The attack on Clerkenwell prison was for the rescue of Richard Bourke.
12 March, 1868, O'Farrell, a Fenian, made an attempt to assassinate in Sydney the Duke of Edinburgh, the second son of Queen Victoria.
In May 1882 Lord Frederick Cavendish (the newly-appointed viceroy of Ireland) and Thomas A. Burke, under-secretary, were savagely assassinated while walking in Phœnix Park, Dublin.
In March 1883 simultaneous attempts were made to blow up the offices of the Local Government Board and the office of the *Times'* newspaper.
In 1884 the Fenians attempted to blow up with dynamite four of the chief railway stations.
_{*} The name 'Fenian' is a base dishonour to the famous national militia, the Fianna Eirin, whose achievements formed a source of song and romance honourable to Ireland. Fingal, son-in-law of King Comhal or Combal (A.D. 213-353), little thought his name would be so degraded in the 19th cent.
Sir Walter Scott alludes to the Fenians in 'The Antiquary,' but not the Fenians condemned by every right-thinking man, under the patronage of Michael Davitt.

Fer, aut feri ; feri, ne feriare (Suffer or strike; strike lest you be stricken), or thus, 'Aut fer, aut feri; ne feriare, feri.' The jingling words incessantly muttered by Queen Elizabeth while she remained in doubt whether to sign the death-warrant of her cousin Mary or not.

Ferdinand I. Kaiser-king of Germany of the house of Austria (1503, 1556–1564).

Father, Philipp the Handsome ; *Mother*, Juaña, daughter of Ferdinand and Isabella; his elder brother was KARL V., and his grandfather was Kaiser

MAXIMILIAN I.; *Wife*, Anna Jagellon of Bohemia; *Son* and successor, MAXIMILIAN II. Contemporary with Mary and Elizabeth.

Ferdinand II. Kaiser-king of Germany of the House of Austria. He was son of Karl duke of Styria, and succeeded his cousin Mathias on the throne of Germany (1608, 1637–1657). He began the infamous thirty years' religious war against the Protestants.

Father, Karl archduke of Styria ; *Mother*, Maria of Bavaria; *Son* and successor, FERDINAND III. Contemporary with James I. and Charles I.

FERDINAND I. had two sons, viz. MAXIMILIAN II., who succeeded him, and *Karl*, who died duke of Styria.
Karl of Styria (the 2nd son of Kaiser Ferdinand I.) had for issue FERDINAND II., who succeeded his cousin Mathias on the throne of Germany.

Ferdinand III. Kaiser-king of Germany (1608, 1637–1657).

Father, FERDINAND II.; *Mother*, *; *Wives* (1) Mary-Anne of Spain, mother of LEOPOLD, his successor; (2) Mary Leopoldina of Austria, and (3) Eleanora of Mantua. Contemporary with Charles I. and the Commonwealth.

Ferdinand the Summoned. Ferdinand IV. of Castile and Leon (1285, 1295–1312). So called because, when he ordered two noblemen, the brothers Carvajal, to execution without trial, they summoned him to appear before the tribunal of God within thirty days, and within the allotted time he died.

Fergus MacIvor (*Sir W. Scott's Waverley*). The original was Major Donald Macdonald, executed on Saturday, 18 Oct., 1746, with eight others.

Feringhee (Afghanistan). A European.

Fermiers Généraux. A name given in France, before the Revolution of 1789, to a privileged association who 'farmed' the public revenues. It was a shocking jobbery, the *fermiers* being selected either by the minister of finance (who made his selection for a money consideration) or by the king's mistresses. The number was forty, but rose to sixty a little before the revolution. These farmers paid the king a fixed sum and made what profit they could out of the taxpayers.

Pronounced *Fair'-me-ay jen-e-ro'*,

Ferney (*The Patriarch of*). Voltaire (1694-1778). After his departure from Prussia he retired to Ferney, a quiet little spot near Geneva. He died at the age of eighty-two.

Ferocious Beast of Auso'nia (*The*). So Caracalla, the Roman emperor, was called by the Alexandrians. It is said that the tyrant was pleased with the name, and boasted of it.

Ausonia means Italy.

Ferra'ra (*Peace of*), 26 April, 1433. Between Venice and Milan, brought about by Nicholas marquis d'Este, the 'Pacificator of Italy.'

Ferry of Death (*The*). The ferry of the Irtish, leading to Siberia. So called because it leads the Russian exile to political death.

To cross the Ferry of Death, to be laid on the shelf in political life.

Fertile Periods. Plato tells us there are times when the powers of minerals, vegetables, and animals sympathise magically with superior natures, and have a greater aptitude to participate in those superior powers. At those periods 'miracles' abound, for inferior things partake of the Divine powers. When no such celestial powers are inherent in minerals, vegetables, and animals, Plato says it is a 'barren period.'

Festa Brachio'rum, or 'Festa Manuälia,' 1493. Days on which no works requiring the aid of horse and cart might be done. Manual labour means such as is done by the skill of the hands; but brachial labour is such as is done by the muscular force of the arms.

[Festa] 'Manuälia' seu 'Brachiörum' vulgo appellantur, in quibus videlicet ipsa prohibitio per totam diem ad ea duntaxat opera et negotia quæ sine equis et carrucis fieri possunt se extendebat.' —*Statuta Ecc. Meldens.* 1493. See *Historia Meldens. inter Instrum. p.* 542.

Festa Capit'uli, *i.e.* those fête days 'quæ Capitulum habent': as All Saints', Annunciation, Ascension, Assumption, Epiphany, Michaelmas Day, Nativity of Christ (Christmas Day), Nativity of John the Baptist, Pentecost, Purification of the Virgin Mary, and the Resurrection. Add to these the fête day of Mary Magdalene, and that of Hugh of Lincoln.

Festa Domin'ica. Sacred festivals set apart in honour of some saint,

martyr, or confessor of the Christian Church, called in English a saint's day.

Festival of St. Napoleon (*The*), 1806. 15 Aug., the birthday of Napoleon, was so designated by the first Emperor of the French.

Festival of the Sacrifices (*The*). 'Id-al-Azha,' or 'Kurbân Bairâm,' the second or Great Bai'râm, is observed by Mohammedans in commemoration of Abraham offering his son. It is observed seventy days after the Lesser Bairâm, and lasts four days.

Festum Ar'chitricli'ni. The second Sunday after Epiphany, the gospel of which day is John ii.; the marriage feast, when the Architriclinus wanted wine and Jesus miraculously supplied it. *See* 'Sundays.'

Festum Asino'rum. 14 Jan., to commemorate the 'Flight into Egypt.' Several rituals of this *festum* are extant. That of Beauvais, in France, has a rubric which orders the priest to bray three times, and the congregation to bray three times in answer. As the ass was led to the altar a hymn of nine stanzas was sung, each stanza ending with *hee-haw, hee-haw!* The first runs thus (*see* 'Feast of Fools') :—

Orientis partibus, Adventavit Asinus, Pulcher et fortiss'imus, Sarcinis aptissimus. *Hé, sire Âné, hé!*	From out the East Came forth the beast, Both strong and fair, Its packs to bear. *Hee-haw! Sir Ass, hee-haw!*

Festum Bea'tæ Mari'æ de Adventu, *i.e.* the Conception of the Virgin Mary, 8 Dec. Instituted 1356.

Festum Broncher'iæ, *i.e.* Festum Brancher'iæ, or Palm Sunday (the Feast of Branches). *See* 'Sundays.'

Festum Campana'rum. The festival of the Annunciation; the day after Quasimodo Sunday; that is, the Monday next after Easter Monday. So called because on this day 'ad Salutationem-angelïcam solemnius pulsantur campanæ' (DU CANGE).

With us the Annunciation is called 'Lady Day,' celebrated on 25 March.

Festum Canaba'rum. The Feast of Tabernacles (Lev. xxiii.).

Festum Cande'læ. The founder's day of any church or religious institution when candles were lighted in honour

Y

thereof. This festival used to be called in old English *Lichtmesse*.

Festum Compassio'nis Bea'tæ Mari'æ. Instituted 1423, and held the Friday before Palm Sunday.

Festum Coro'næ Christi. Instituted 1357. Innocent VI. appointed it to be held as the 'Feria 6 post octavam Resurrectionis Dominicæ.'

Festum Corporis Christi, or at full 'Festum Consecratiōnis Corpŏris Christi,' or in brief 'Festum C.C.C.' Instituted 1371. The great C.C.C. festival is '5 feria post Octavam Pentecostes.'

Another festival of 'Corpus Christi' was that called 'Festum Sacrosancti Sacramenti,' in German *Frohnleichnamsfest*, instituted by Urban IV. in 1264; it followed the octave of Pentecost.
The 'Festum Eucharistiæ,' instituted in 1856, was another 'Festum Corporis Christi.'

Festum de Clav'ibus, 1355. Instituted by Innocent VI. in honour of the nails used in the crucifixion of Christ.

Festum Divisio'nis Apostolo'-rum, 5 July. When Bede, Usuard, and others say the apostles parted company, and each went into his special field of labour. Also called the Festival of the Dispersion; instituted 1098.

Festum Duplex. When two fêtes occur on the same day. In which case the greater festival is observed and the lesser one is deferred to the day following.

Festum Fatuo'rum. *See* 'Fête des Fous.'

Festum Florum. 'Nono Kalendas Junii' (May 24).

Festum Herba'rum. Assumption Day (15 Aug.). This was the day when Roman women carried bundles of herbs to the temples, as offerings to their gods. The [Roman] Catholic Church preserved the custom, but changed the object of veneration.

The Assumption is the act of taking up to heaven the Virgin Mary bodily without dying. This change was made in the 5th cent.

Festum Hypapantes, or 'Purification of the Virgin Mary,' Feb. 2. Also called 'Festum Lumĭnum.' Instituted 542.

Hypapantè means 'meeting together.' It was on this day that Mary met Simeon and Anna the Prophetess.

Festum Hypodi'acono'rum. The fête of the Subdeacons, a part of the Saturnalia, when archbishops and bishops, with all the inferior clergy, played practical jokes on each other, and all forms of distinction were, for the time being, held in abeyance. The general character of the feast was gross drunkenness, and the name was a satire on the worldly lives of the general clergy. As Belētus says, 'hac joculāri appellatione indicare voluerint, festivitatem hanc fuisse ebriorum clericorum.'

Festum Kalenda'rum. A Christian substitution of the Roman Saturnalia, at the close of the old year and beginning of the new. It was a time of unbridled license, when slaves and servants were on equal footing with their masters. Men, women, and children dressed up as beasts, and ran about the streets braying, roaring, barking, and indulging in the coarsest practical jokes. The early Church, unable to abolish the custom, tried to divert its object, and introduced innovations scarcely less objectionable than the old Roman licentiousness. One day of the feast was a satire on the drunkenness of the clergy, and was called 'Festum Hypodiacono-rum' (*q.v.*), or the Subdeacons' Fête, where subdeacon included all ecclesiastics, from the archbishop to his curate.

Augustine refers to the feast in his 'Sermo de Tempore,' 215; and in the 'Life of Eligius,' bk. ii. chap. 15, we read 'Nullus in Kalendis Januarii nefanda et ridiculosa, vetulas, aut cervulos, aut jotticos [practical jokes] faciat.'

Festum Lu'minum, or 'Festum Hypapantes.' The Feast of Purification (Greek ὑπαπαντή), from the meeting of Simeon and Anna with Christ, whom they had long waited for in the Temple

Also called 'Festum St. Simeonis.'

Festum Oliva'rum. The Sunday before Easter day, generally called Palm Sunday. *See* 'Sundays.'

Festum Sancti Petri ad Vin'-cula, 1 Aug. Instituted by the order of Eudoxia, wife of the Emperor Theodosius. This was the continuance of an old heathen festival in honour of the victory of Actium, in which Octavius overcame Antony. The festival was continued, but its object was changed.

Festum Translatio'nis Jesu, or the 'Day of Transfiguration.' Instituted 6 Aug., 1498. (Matt. xvii. 1-13.)

See also under the word 'Feast.'

Fête Days. *See* 'Holy Days.'

Fête de l'Âne. Introduced into Paris in the 15th cent.; was a ridiculous caricature of the Flight into Egypt. A young woman with an infant in her arms was seated on an ass, led by an old man representing Joseph, and followed by a long procession to the cathedral church, accompanied by bishops and their clergy. As it went along, chanting the appointed canticles, the crowd responded *hinha ! hinha !* imitating the bray of an ass. It was not discontinued till the close of the 16th cent.

Other similar processions were the 'Marche du Bœuf Gras' (*q.v.*), 'La fête de la Bouteille,' 'La fête des Cornards,' 'La fête des Fous' (*See* Fools, Feast of '), and ' La fête du Géant aux Ours ' (on 3 July).
Pronounce *Fate de lahn, Fate d'la Bou-tay'-e, Fate dé Foo.*

Fête des Fous. January, in commemoration of the Flight into Egypt. This profane exhibition was immensely popular in France from the 12th to the 16th cent.

Fête-Dieu, 1246. A festival instituted by Urban IV. in honour of the host or consecrated wafer, called 'Festum Corpŏris Christi,' and held in France on the Sunday following Trinity Sunday. At one time it was celebrated with street processions and great pomp, but the street processions ceased in 1830.

Except in France the festival is held on the Thursday following Trinity Sunday.

Fête of the Federation. *See* under ' Federation.'

Fêtes. *See* 'Holy Days.'

Fetichism. An idolatry of the grossest sort. The name was given by the Portuguese to the adoration paid by negroes in Africa to the fetiches, such as fire, water, animals, trees, stones, and invisible beings such as the *Grisgris* of Central Africa, the *Manitous* and *Ockis* of America, the *Burkhans* of Siberia.

The priests of this idolatry are called *griots* in Africa, *jongleurs* in America, and *shamans* in Central Asia.
If a worshipper does not get what he prays for, he will address his idol thus: ' How now, dog of a spirit! We give you lodging in a magnificent temple, we gild you handsomely, feed you well, and offer incense; yet, after all this, you are so ungrateful as to refuse us what we ask.'—ASTLEY, *Collection of Voyages.*

Fetters of Greece (*The*). Demetrias, Chalcis, and Corinth were so called by Demetrius Poliorcētês of Macedon.

' The freedom promised,' said the Ætolians,

' was an illusion . . . The fetters of Greece would only be clasped lighter by a stronger hand.'—*The Students' Rome,* p. 336.

Feu Sacré, or 'Mal des Ardents.' A terrible malady which appeared in Paris A.D. 945; in Scotland in 954; and in Italy and Germany in 985. 'Ce mal [says Sauval] brûlait à petit feu, et consumait sans qu'on y pût remédier . . . elle brûlait les entrailles ou toute autre partie du corps, qui tombait en lambeaux. Sous une peau livide, elle consumait les chaires en les séparant des os. Ce que ce mal avait de plus étonnant, c'est qu'il agissait sans chaleur, et pénétrait d'un *froid glacial* ceux qui en étaient atteints ; et qu'à ce froid mortel succédait une ardeur si grande dans les mêmes parties, que les malades y éprouvaient tous les accidents d'un cancer.'

Feudal System (*The*). Holding estates by military service. William I. divided the kingdom of England into 700 fiefs and about 60,000 knights' fees (or holdings). These knights' fees or secondary holdings were held, not of the crown immediately, but of one of the 700 crown vassals under similar service. The 700 vassals were bound to supply the crown with soldiers according to a fixed scale, and the secondary holders supplied the vassals under whom they held in a similar way. Bishops and abbots were bound, in times of war, to supply the king with soldiers in proportion to their possessions.

Feuillantines (4 syl.), 1583. Reformed Feuillants, an order founded by Marguérite de Polastron. Anne of Austria, in 1622, founded a house of Feuillantines in the Faubourg St. Jacques, Paris.

Feuillantism. The political principles of the Feuillants in the French revolution. It was reformed monarchism.

Feuillantism—that party which loves liberty yet not more than monarchy.—CARLYLE, *French Revolution,* vol. ii. bk. v. 10.

Feuillants (*The*), 1577. Reformed Benedictines, founded by Jean de la Barrière, Abbé de Notre Dame de Feuillant, in France. They go about bareheaded and bare-footed, sleep upon wooden pallets, eat kneeling, and impose on themselves incredible austerities. Their robe is white, with a white hood. In 1630 Urban VIII. separated the

Feuillants of Italy, and called them 'Reformed Bernardins.' The Feuillans or Feuillants are often called the Bare-footed Monks.

Pronounce *Fuh'e-yahn'*.

Feuillants' Club (*The*), or 'Club des Feuillants,' 1790. The more moderate of the Jacobins. So called because they held their meetings at a convent of the Feuillants (*see above*), near the Tuileries. The chief of the club were Lafayette, Bailly, Duport, and the brothers Lámeth. Their enemies nicknamed them the 'Club Monarchique.' Extinguished Nov. 1791.

The original name of the club was the 'Company of 1789.'

Fez (*The*), or 'Council of Tara,' in Ireland. The triennial meeting of the subordinate chieftains, priests, and bards, held at Tara in Ireland, and instituted by Ollav Fola about 900 years B.C. Ollav Fola reigned forty years and died in peace.

In the second year of his mission Patrick presented himself before the Fez . . . and Logary the king declared himself a convert.—*The Britannica* (article 'Ireland,' p. 465).

ff for Pandects. ff is a corrupt way of making the Greek Π, *π*, the initial letter of Pandects.

Fiacre. A French cab, so called because the first fiacres were made in the Hôtel St. Fiacre, Rue St. Martin.

St. Fiacre is the patron saint of gardeners.

Fian'a Er'ion (*The*). A very celebrated Irish militia commanded by Fingal (or Fein M'Cooil), in the reign of Cormac, grandson of Conn. It consisted of 9,000 men of great strength, activity, and intelligence, who were bound to choose wives solely for their merits, never to ill-treat a woman, and never to turn their backs on a foe. This force was annihilated at the battle of Gabra, or Gawra, in Meath, where Oscar, the son of Ossian the poet, fell.

Fiann (*The*). An ancient order of warriors in Ireland. No man of the order was allowed to marry a dowered wife, lest he might choose her for her money and not for her merits. No man of the order might use his strength against a woman. None might assert his own rights selfishly against another's wants.

Fief or Feud. Conquered land let out, not for money, but military service. The Romans let out conquered land for usufruct, called Emphyteusis (grafting), the grantor was the 'stock,' the tenant was only the graft. Feud is a corrupt contraction of 'phūt', fūt, feud. And fee, fief are variants of the same Latinised Greek word.

Field Conventicles (*Act against*), 1670. A field conventicle is 'any unauthorised meeting for religious worship, even in a private house, if any of the hearers stand in the open air.' Every minister who preaches and prays on such occasion during the three following years shall incur the forfeiture of his property and the punishment of death.

Field Fortification has for its object the protecting of camps, villages, posts, passages of rivers, and the construction of such works as may be required to aid the operations of an army in the field. Trenches and offensive works executed on the spot in carrying on a siege also belong to 'field fortification.'

Field of March (*The*), or 'Champ de Mars.' A national convention or assembly held during the first dynasty of France. It was revived by Pepin d'Héristal, but after A.D. 755 was held in May, and called *Champ de Mai*. Napoleon I. revived these assemblies in the 'Hundred Days' (June 1, 1815).

Pronounce *Sharnd Marz, Sharnd Ma'-e.*

Field of the Cloth of Gold (*The*). Called in French history *Le Champ du Drap d'Or*. The site between Guisnes and Ardres, where in June 1520 was held an interview between Henry VIII. and François I. of France. So splendid and gorgeous was this *fête*, that the site where it was held was called 'The Field of the Cloth of Gold.'

Fiery Cross (*The*). A blazing torch in the form of a cross, carried from hill to hill to summon the clans to battle. Sir Walter Scott speaks of it in 'The Lady of the Lake.' He says the chaplain slew a goat, and dipped the cross in its blood. It was then delivered to a swift runner, who ran with all his speed to the next hamlet, where he presented it to the principal person, who was bound to send it on. Every man, from 16 to 60 years of age, was expected instantly to repair fully equipped for war to the place of rendez-vous on pain of 'fire and sword.' In the civil war of 1745–6 the Fiery Cross was sent round thus.

The 'fiery cross' was borne swiftly through the townships and parishes (of Upper Canada), calling forth a levy *en masse* of the loyal inhabitants, who rushed to the defence of the capital.—HOWITT, *Hist. of Eng.*, 1837, p. 389.

Fiery Tears of St. Lawrence
(*The*). The shooting stars which appear with considerable regularity between the 9th and 14th of August. The festival of St. Lawrence is the 10th August.

Fieschi Laws, 1837. Some very
stringent laws against the French press, published after the attempt of Fieschi on the life of Louis Philippe, king of the French, by the 'infernal machine' (*q.v.*). Enormous fines were imposed on those who ridiculed the king, or disputed the wisdom of any act of his government, or who avowed themselves republicans, or who published a print of any sort without subjecting it first to the minister of the interior.

The fines were from 400*l.* to 2,000*l.* sterling for the first offence, double that for a second offence, and so on.

Pronounce *Fe-esk'ke.*

Fifteen (*The*). The judges of the
Supreme Court of Session in Scotland.

Fifteen (*Out in the Fifteen*). A
partaker in the Derwentwater rebellion, 1715. *See* 'Forty-five.'

Is it so singular that a man should have been out in the forty-five ? . . . your father, I think, . . . was out with Derwentwater in the fifteen.—Sir W. SCOTT, *Redgauntlet,* chap. vii.

Fifteen Mysteries (*The*), in Catho-
lic theology. *See* 'Five Joyous Mysteries,' 'Five Dolorous Mysteries,' and 'Five Glorious Mysteries.' Observe the triplet.

Fifteen Years' Farce (*The*). The
Great French Revolution which ended in the coronation of Napoleon I. (1789–1804).

La comédie de quinze ans was admirably played in France . . . but what have been the results ?—MAZZINI, *Faith of the Future.*

Fifth Doctor of the Church
(*The*). So Pius V. called Thomas Aquinas (1224–1274).

The Four Doctors of the Latin Church, emphatically so called, were St. Ambrose (340-397), St. Jerome (345 420), St. Augustine (354 430), and St. Gregory. The fifth doctor was similar to such phrases as the 'Tenth Muse,' the 'Eighth Wonder of the World,' &c., meaning one of super-eminent merit.

Fifth Monarchy Men appear in
1654. They believed in the four great monarchies of Antichrist, marked out by the prophet Daniel (ch. vii.), viz. the Assyrian, Persian, Macedonian, and Roman, the fifth being that of Christ on earth. In politics they were republicans, acknowledging no earthly king but Christ; and they conspired to murder Cromwell, the lord-protector. In the reign of Charles II., led by one Venner, a wine-cooper, they proceeded to 'take the kingdom of heaven by force, without waiting for Christ'; the king sent the military against them, and after some severe fighting, the ringleaders were taken captive and executed 1660, and the sect died out.

Filibuster. A corrupt spelling of
the French 'flibustier,' called in English a buccaneer (*q.v.*). Filibusters were piratical seamen, resolved to force their way into the New World jealously guarded by the Spanish. The most famous were Morgan (a Welshman), who took Panama in 1670; Pierre Legrand of Dieppe, who with twenty-eight men took the ship of a Spanish admiral; Nau l'Olonnais, Michel a Basque, who made themselves masters of Vera Cruz in 1683; and Monbars the Exterminator, who in 1683 took Vera Cruz. After the accession of William III. the French flibustiers and the English buccaneers were in deadly antagonism; but after the Treaty of Ryswick in 1697, the piratical expeditions were put an end to.

Filio'que Controversy, which long
disturbed the Church, was this : ' Did the Holy Ghost proceed from the Father *by* the Son, or from the Father *and* the Son (*filioque*)? The Greek Church maintained the former, the Latin Church the latter dogma. The phrase was added to the Creed by Recared in the Council of Toledo A.D. 589 ; was adopted by Charlemagne in 788 ; and by Benedict VIII., at the instance of Kaiser Heinrich II., in 1014. This question is often called ' the Procession of the Holy Ghost.'

It must be confessed that the authority is not very satisfactory. Recared, Charlemagne, and Heinrich II. of Germany are not the names we should select to settle a point in divinity. Recared, or Recarede, was the seventeenth king of the Visigoths in Spain, who compelled his subjects to embrace the Christian faith, and was therefore called 'The Catholic.' He was converted only two years and a few months before the Council of Toledo was convened. The addition of *filioque* to the Nicene Creed created a flame of discord between the Eastern and Gallic Churches. Pope Leo III. was averse to the addition.

Filius Nullius, or 'Filius pŏpuli,' a bastard. In the eyes of the law an illegitimate son is nobody's son ; and as such a son has no 'blue blood' he is only a commoner, or one of the *ignobile vulgus.*

Filles Bleues (*Les*), 1604. Also called the 'Celestial Annunciades' (4 syl.). A religious order instituted by Maria Victoria Fornaro. They wore blue mantles, and hence their name.

Pronounce *Fee-yd bluh.*

Filles de Sagesse (*Les*). The grey nuns of St. Laurent.

A host of other religious communities might be added, as :

Filles de Ste Geneviève	Filles Repenties
Filles de la Providence	Filles St. Thomas, &c.
Filles du Calvaire	*See* 'Founders.'

Filles-Dieu. Hospitallers, at one time called *Sœurs de St. Gervais,* because in 1300 they were charged with the hospital of that name. Their dress is a white gown and black mantle.

Filmerite (3 syl.), 17th cent. A disciple of Sir Robert Filmer (*—1688), author of 'The Anarchy of a Limited and Mixed Monarchy,' opposed to a Williamite or adherent of the House of Orange. The Filmerites, like Archbishop Sancroft and Dean Hickes, believed in the 'divine right of kings,' and were therefore zealous Jacobites and advocates of the political doctrine of 'Passive Obedience' or 'Non-resistance' (*q.v.*).

Fine of Leinster (*The*). Exacted for more than 500 years, and paid by more than forty kings to the king of Meath. It consisted of 3,000 cows, 3,000 hogs, 3,000 sheep, 3,000 copper caldrons, 3,000 ounces of silver, and 3,000 mantles, and was paid every second year till A.D. 963, when it was remitted. For the reason of this fine see 'Boärian . . . Tribute.'

Fines (*Statute of*), 4 Henry VIII. This was a renewal of the law of Edward IV., by which entails could be cut off at pleasure, and thus the great landowners were enabled to divide their estates amongst their children, bequeath them, or sell them.

Fingal. The Territory of the Fingal or White Strangers, consisting of Dublin and certain parts to the north thereof. *See* 'White Strangers.'

Staffa is called 'Fingal's cave ;' or, more strictly speaking, the cave in the Isle of Staffa is so called.

Macpherson's Fingal was Finn, rig [king] of the Leinster Finns or Finians, who resided at a dun or fort at Almhain [Allen] in Kildare. Transferred by Macpherson to Morven in Scotland.

Finn's Fingers. Five enormous stones, each about 5 feet in height, and some 4 tons in weight, on the top of the hill of Shanthamon, in the county of Ca'van, Ireland.

Finns, the *Fenni* of Tacitus, and *Phinni* of Ptolemy, belonging to the Ugrian race or Ogres, probably of Mongolian origin. They were divided into five groups : the Finns of Finland ; the Lapps ; the Permian Finns ; the Volga Finns ; and the Ugrian Finns, to which group the Magyars [*Mard'-yahs*] belong.

Firbolgs (*The*). The remnant of the old Thracian Nemedians which returned to Ireland under the conduct of the five sons of Dela. The tribe had been driven from the island by the Fomorians, said to be African pirates, descendants of Ham. The sons of Dela, according to Irish tradition, divided the island into the five kingdoms of Leinster, Munster, Ulster, Connaught, and Meath, each of the sons being ruler of one of these principalities. The rule of these princes continued forty, or, as some say, eighty years, when they were dispossessed by the Danaans under Tuatha-na-Danaan (*q.v.*), a people famed for necromancy.

The Irish still call strangers 'Fawmorries (Fomorians). The Nemedians are said by chroniclers to have been descendants of Japhet, through Nemedius. Of course all this is only Bardic history. The Firbolgs were probably Belgæ, or Belgæ who migrated from Britain.

Fire and Water Interdicted. 'Aquæ et Ignis Interdictio.' The judicial form of words used to signify that the person referred to was banished from Italian soil. He might go where else he liked, but must not remain in Italy.

Fire Brigade Committee (*The Metropolitan*). Responsible for the management of the 700 men and the state of their 150 fire-engines, 150 fire-escapes, 150 horses, and 28 miles of hose. Since 1889 the number of fire-engines has been increased in London to 170. The whole city and county of London is divided into four districts, A, B, C, D, each district being under a separate superintendent, who is paid 195*l.* a year.

All the districts are connected by telegraphs and telephones.

The average number of fires in the metropolis is about 2,000 a year.

Fire Cross (The). See 'Fiery Cross.'

'Fire First.'
'Gentlemen of the French Guard, fire' (said Lord Charles Hay); to which the Comte d'Auteroche replied, 'Fire yourselves, gentlemen of England; we never fire first.' The battle of Fontenoy, 10 May, 1745.

Quant à moi, je tiens le mot de M. d'Auteroche, 'Messieurs les Anglais, tirez les premiers,' très authentique. . . . Les deux troupes sont en présence. Lord Hay crie, s'avançant hors des rangs: 'Messieurs les gardes françaises, tirez.' M. d'Auteroche alors va à sa rencontre, et le saluant de l'épée: 'Monsieur (lui dit-il), nous ne tirons jamais les premiers; tirez vous-mêmes.' —M. E. FOURNIER (an eye-witness).

Cet engagement se fit à distance si rapprochée que les officiers anglais, au moment d'arrêter leur troupe, nous saluèrent le chapeau à la main; les nôtres ayant répondu de même à cette courtoisie. . . . Lord Charles Hay sortit de son rang, et s'avança; le comte d'Auteroche, lieutenant des grenadiers, se porta alors au-devant de lui. 'Monsieur (dit le capitaine, lord Hay), faites donc tirer vos gens;' 'Non, Monsieur (répondit d'Auteroche), nous ne tirons pas les premiers;' et s'étant de nouveau salués, ils rentrèrent chacun à son rang.—L'Esprit dans l'Histoire, chap. lii. pp. 348, 349 (Paris, 1883).

Lord Charles Hay gives a different version: 'When we came within 20 or 30 paces of [the French], I advanced before our regiment, drank to them, and told them we were the English guards, and hoped they would stand still till we came up to them, and not swim across the Scheldt, as they did the Mein at Dettingen. Upon which I immediately turned about to our regiment, speeched them, and made them huzzah, I hope with a will. An officer [d'Auteroche] came out of the ranks, and tried to make his men huzzah; however, there were not above three or four of the brigade that did so.'—Letter (now in the possession of the Marquis of Tweeddale, at Yester House).

Fire of Antwerp (The), 29 July, 1588.
So the Spaniards called the fire-ships sent by Drake and Hawkins into the Armada. The eight vessels, under charge of Capt. Young, ran right into the Spanish fleet in full blaze, sending forth explosion after explosion. The Spaniards, remembering the Dutch fire-ships, shouted, 'The fire of Antwerp! The fire of Antwerp!' and every vessel was put in motion to escape in the darkness as best it might. The confusion was terrible, ships running foul of each other, and escaping from Ostend to Calais. A thunderstorm, with a furious gale of wind from the south-west, added to the terrors of that terrible night.

Firman (A).
A decree issued by the sultan, signed with his cipher, and sealed with his signet. Also a passport given to travellers by a pacha.

First Book of Discipline (The), 1561.
A book of church polity drawn up by John Knox and five others for the use of Scotland.

First Book of Homilies (The), 1547.
In which is comprised the doctrines of the Church of England, as established in the reign of Edward VI., declaring that salvation rests solely on a lively faith in the merits of Jesus Christ; and that no works without such faith are good works in a scripture sense.

First Communion Office (The), 1548.
In the reformed Church of England.

First Day of the Republic (The).
French history. 20 Sept., 1792. When the National Assembly at the proposal of M. d'Herbois rose en masse, and, waving their hats, shouted, 'We declare royalty in France abolished for ever.'

First English Liturgy (The), or
'Book of Common Prayer,' 1548. The Second Liturgy was in 1552. The Forty-two Articles in 1553; reduced to Thirty-nine in 1563; and modified to their present form in 1571.

First English Martyr (The), 1401.
William Sawtre, rector of St. Oswyth, London, a Lollard, in the reign of Henry IV., was the first person who suffered at the stake in England for religious opinions.

There is a tradition that St. Alban fell a martyr in the persecution of Diocletian A.D. 305. The tale is that he served in the Roman army, but, having offered an asylum to Amphibalus, a Christian priest, in order to save his guest he changed dresses, and being apprehended was beheaded at Verulamium. It is said that a church was afterwards erected on the spot, and the name of the town was changed to St. Albans.

First-fruits, or 'Annats.'
The first year's income of a church living paid to the pope, forbidden in 1534 (by 25 Hen. VIII. c. 20). Granted to the crown in 1534 (26 Hen. VIII. c. 3); restored to the church in 1555 (by 2, 3 Phil. & Mar. c. 4); again granted to the crown in 1559 (by 1 Eliz. c. 4); restored to the church by

letters patent of Queen Anne, 3 Nov., 1703.
See 'Queen Anne's Bounty.'

Abolished in *France* in 1438 by the
'Pragmatic Sanction,' under Charles VII.

Abolished in *Ireland* in 1833 (3, 4 Wm.
IV. c. 37).

Ceased in *Spain* under Carlos V.
(1519–1558).

In Germany it formed one of the *Centum gravāmina* presented to the emperor in 1521, and the claim ceased.

When Dr. Benson in 1883 was made archbishop of Canterbury his fees amounted to 885l. 5s. The amount for this presentation has now been reduced to 281l. 5s. 6d.

First Gentleman of Europe.
George IV. (1762, 1820–1830).

Louis d'Artois of France was so called also.

First Martyr of Liberty (*The*),
1770. North America. Christopher Snider,
a Boston lad. Theophilus Lillie, a Boston
shopkeeper, persisted in selling English
goods after they were tabooed. His
shop was attacked by the mob, and one
of his shopmen, named Richardson, fired
on the mob and killed the boy Snider,
who was followed to the grave by a procession reaching a quarter of a mile, and
the boy was exalted into a martyr.

First Year of Equality (*The*),
1792, beginning 22 Sept. The address
Monsieur was abandoned, and the word
Citizen substituted in its stead.

Fishing Inquiry (*A*). In parliamentary language means an inquiry at
large; an inquiry into a given question
not for the sake of solving that question,
but with the hope that something may
turn up.

This is what is called in the familiar language of lobbies of parliament 'a fishing inquiry.' Fishing for something to say about the matter; but you cannot get your fish if the fish will not come into your net.—W. E. GLADSTONE, *Speech at Calder*, 17 Nov., 1885.

Fitzwilliam Museum (*The*). Of
books, paintings, illuminated MSS., engravings, &c. in Cambridge; to which
has been added, in 1834, the Mesman collection; in 1850 eighty-three ancient
marbles collected by John Disnay. In
1861 John Ruskin gave twenty-five watercolours by J. M. W. Turner, R.A.; and
in 1862 Mrs. Elizabeth Ellison presented
to the museum thirty pictures of modern
English masters. Since then many other
valuable presents have been added by
different donors, and the university has
purchased numerous rarities. Founded

by Viscount Fitzwilliam of Trinity Hall
in 1764.

Five (*Council of*), 1722. The Earl of
Arran, the Earl of Orrery, Lord North,
Lord Gower, and Atterbury bishop of
Rochester. A junto constituted to bring
back the Stuart dynasty after the birth
of Charles Edward.

Five Acts (*Sidmouth's and Castlereagh's*), 1819. After the Manchester
Massacre (*q.v.*) Lord Sidmouth brought
in three bills in the House of Lords, and
Lord Castlereagh two bills in the House
of Commons to prevent large gatherings
of a political character and political
articles like those of Hone calculated to
disturb the public peace. The five bills
all passed, and were

(1) An Act to prevent the training of
persons to the use of arms (*Sidmouth*).

(2) An Act to prevent and punish
blasphemous and pernicious libels (*Sidmouth*).

(3) An Act to authorise justices of the
peace to seize arms collected for riotous
purposes (*Sidmouth*).

(4) An Act to impose stamp duties on
newspapers (*Castlereagh*).

(5) An Act to prevent blasphemous
and seditious meetings (*Castlereagh*).

Five Articles (*The*), 1559. Drawn
up by Convocation at the beginning of
Queen Elizabeth's reign, and forwarded
by Bonner to the lord keeper to be laid
before parliament. They were these:
(1) The corporal presence to be maintained; (2) the elements after consecration are no longer bread and wine; (3)
the mass is a propitiatory sacrifice; (4)
the lawful successor of St. Peter is the
supreme head of the Church; and (5) the
clergy only are to settle all matters bearing on doctrine and church discipline.
No notice was taken of this petition.
See 'Articles.'

Five Articles of Dort (*The*), 1618–
1619. Calvinistic views of (1) absolute
predestination and election; (2) redemption only through the death of Christ;
(3) original sin and human corruption;
(4) conversion not of ourselves, but the
gift of God; (5) the final perseverance of
the saints.

In church government the Synod of Dort decidedly preferred Presbyterianism to Episcopacy.

Five Articles of Perth (*The*),
1618. (1) The communion shall be

received kneeling, and not sitting; (2) in extreme cases the communion may be privately administered; (3) in extreme cases baptism may be privately administered; (4) young people, when advanced to a suitable age, shall be confirmed by the bishop; (5) the five following days shall be holidays—viz. Christmas Day, Good Friday, Easter Day, Ascension Day, and Pentecost. These five enactments were passed by a parliament held at Perth, in the reign of James I. of England, and were designed as the thin edge of a wedge to introduce into Scotland a form of worship similar to that of the Anglican Church.

Five Burghs of the Danes (*The*). Derby, Leicester, Lincoln, Nottingham, and Stamford. These five burghs were called the 'Danelagh' (Dane-Law), because they were ruled by Danish and not by English law. Recovered from the Danes in 941 by Edmund.

Five Christian Verities (*The*). In Catholic theology.

1. The child Jesus, conceived in the womb of the Virgin Mary, was verily and indeed the Son of God, and the second person of the Trinity.

2. This Jesus is true God, one with the Father and the Holy Ghost.

3. The two perfect natures exist in one only person. The divine nature received from God the Father, and the human nature from his mother Mary.

4. All that pertains to the *person* of Christ as a substance is *unique*; but all that pertains to his *nature* is *double*.

5. The Virgin Mary is veritably and properly the Mother of God.

(Mgr. Guérin, *Vies des Saints*, vol. iii. pp. 625, 626.)

Five Dolorous Mysteries (*The*). In Catholic theology.

1. The agony of Christ in the olive garden.

2. The scourging.

3. The crowning with thorns.

4. The burden of the cross borne to Calvary.

5. The crucifixion.

Five Glorious Mysteries (*The*). In Catholic theology.

1. The Resurrection.

2. The Ascension.

3. The descent of the Holy Ghost on the day of Pentecost.

4. The assumption of the Virgin, body and soul, to heaven.

5. The consummation of her glory by her triple coronation of grandeur, power, and goodness. *See* 'Crowns.'

Five Good Emperors (*The*) of Rome. They succeeded the Flavian Emperors (*q.v.*). They were Nerva, Trajan, Hadrian, Antonīnus Pius, and Marcus Aurēlius.

Five Hundred (*The*). *See* 'Council of 500.'

Five Hundred (*The*), or Les Cinq-cents, 1795. One of the two legislative councils of the 'Constitution of Year III.' in French history. Dispersed by Napoleon I. in 1799. *See* 'Council of 500.'

Five Hundred of Athens (*The*). The original number of the senate appointed by Solon was 400, a hundred for each tribe, but Klisthenês increased the number to 500. B.C. 401 the constitution of Athens was changed into an oligarchy of 500, but this state of things only lasted from March to June, when the democracy was restored.

Five Joyous Mysteries (*The*). In Catholic theology.

1. The annunciation and conception of the Word or Logos in the Virgin's womb.

2. The visitation and influence of grace on John the Baptist, who 'leaped in the womb.'

3. The birth in Bethlehem.

4. The purification and offering made by Mary in the temple.

5. Christ's visit to the temple at the age of twelve, when he was found by his mother among the doctors.

Five Kings (*The*). I. B.C. 2598–2205, preceded by the three emperors, and forming the tenth or mythic period of Chinese history. The names were Chao-hao, Chouan-hio, Ti-ko, Yao, and Shun. In the reign of Shun is placed the great flood or inundation of China. Next followed the semi-historic period.

II. In A.D. 990, five kings were simultaneously converted to Christianity—viz. Olaf king of Sweden, Harold king of Denmark, Miczyslaf sovereign of Poland, Vladimir grand-duke of Muscovy, and

Geisa prince of Hungary. A European panic, that the world was coming to an end, some time between 901 and 1000, may account for the religious fervour of the times. Never were there so many kings entitled ' pious ' before or since.

Five Kings of France (*The*).
The five Directors, 1795.

The five kings of France sit in their curule chairs with their flesh-coloured breeches and regal mantles.—*Atelier du Lys*, ii.

Five Members of the General Assembly (*The*).
In 1605 James I. of England asserted his right to call and dissolve the General Assembly of the Church of Scotland; but several of the Scotch clergy resisted this innovation, and five of them were punished by banishment. *See* ' Arrest of the Five Members ' by Charles I. in 1642.

Five Mile Act (*The*),
17 Car. II. c. 2, A.D. 1665. This act subjected every Nonconformist minister who approached within five miles of any corporate town, or other place where he had been used to preach, to a penalty of 40*l*., or six months' imprisonment, unless he would take the oath that ' he deemed it unlawful, under any pretext, to take up arms against the king, and that he would in no wise seek to bring about any alteration of government either in church or state.' Abolished by the ' Act of Toleration ' in 1689.

The act aimed at those who had been driven from their livings by the ' Act of Uniformity,' as well as at Nonconformists.

Five Nations (*The*).
The Iroquois, afterwards called ' The Six Nations,' *q.v.* *See also* ' Pentapŏlis,' ' History of the Five Nations ' (N.Y. 1727, 1866; London 1747, 1755).

Five Orders of the Clergy
(*The*), 3rd cent. Subdeacons, Acolyths, Exorcists, Readers, and Ostiarii, said by the Church of Rome to be apostolic institutions. The duty of *sub-deacons* is to wait upon the deacons in divine service. In the Roman Church there are seven, in some churches many more. Acolyths did the menial work, such as lighting the candles, carrying the sacred vessels, bread and wine, &c. *Exorcists* had charge of the dæmoniacs. *Readers* read the scriptures in that part of the service in which the catechumens were admitted. *Ostiarii* were the doorkeepers.

Five Points (*The*), 1536.
The five points of Calvinism are—(1) Absolute election and reprobation; (2) particular and not universal redemption; (3) the grace of God is irresistible; (4) the will is not free to choose or reject God's grace; (5) the final perseverance of the saints.

Or in brief thus: (1) Absolute election and reprobation; (2) particular redemption; (3) irresistible grace; (4) the will is not free; (5) the perseverance of the saints.

Five Propositions of the Jansenists (*The*).
The bishops of France subscribed a letter to Pope Innocent X. in condemnation of five heretical propositions said to be contained in the ' Augustīnus ' of Jansenius. They are these:

1. Some of God's commandments are impossible to be kept by the righteous.
2. A man doth ever resist inward grace in the state of fallen nature.
3. In order to merit, or not merit, it is *not* indispensable to have a freedom of will, but only freedom from restraint.
4. The semi-Pelagians were heretics, because they maintained the necessity of an inward preventing grace.
5. It is heretical to say that Jesus Christ died for *all* mankind.

Five Races (*Period of the*),
or in Chinese Woo-tae, 420–618. This period includes the 8th, 9th, 10th, 11th, and 12th imperial dynasties, called Tsong, Tsee, Lĕang, Tchin or Chin, and Swi. From 420 to 534 the empire was divided into southern and northern, the former being the imperial line. From 534 to 618 it was divided into the southern, eastern, and western empires. In 618 the three empires were united again under the Swi dynasty.

Five Sacraments (*The*).
(1) Confirmation; (2) Penance; (3) Orders; (4) Matrimony; (5) Extreme Unction. Article xxv says ' these five are not to be counted [by the Anglican Church] for sacraments of the gospel, being such as have grown partly of the corrupt following of the apostles, partly are states of life allowed in the scriptures.'

Five Successions (*Period of the*),
or Heehoo-Woo-tae. This includes the 14th, 15th, 16th, 17th, and 18th imperial dynasties of China, called Hehoo-Lĕang, Hehoo-Tång, Hehoo-Tsĭn, Hehoo-Hàn, and Hehoo-Chew. The seat of empire

was at Kai-fong-foo. It lasted from 907 to 960. During all this period the Tartars held the north of the empire. The Five Successions gave way to the Song or Tsong dynasty, called the 19th, but the Tartars continued to occupy the north. In 1206 the Monguls established themselves in the west, and Temou-gin assumed the title of Genghis Khan (*i.e.* supreme khan or over-lord).

Five Thousand (*The*), B.C. 411. A nominal distinction which included all the citizens of Athens. In contradistinction to the 500 oligarchs. 'It meant that Athens was to be governed by all the citizens, and not by 500 only; that its government should be democratic, and not oligarchical.

Fives Court (*The*). The headquarters of the 'fancy,' during the regency. It was in the neighbourhood of the Haymarket. There was another in St. Martin's Lane. In 'fancy' slang the hand is called ' a bunch of fives.'

Flag Captain, Flag Lieutenant. A captain or lieutenant in a flag ship. A flag lieutenant in the navy is about tantamount to the aide-de-camp of a general in the army. It is his duty to see that the admiral's orders are communicated to the various ships of the squadron. *See* ' Flag Officers ' in ' Dict. of Phrase and Fable.'

Flag of the Prophet (*The*), or ' Sanjak-Sheriff,' 632. The sacred banner of the Mohammedans. Originally the white turban of the Koreish, captured by Mohammed. Subsequently a green flag was substituted, being the curtain which hung before the door of Ayesha, one of the prophet's wives. It is preserved most carefully in a chapel of the seraglio, and watched over by several emirs.

Flags (*Modern National*).

America, field with seven red and six white stripes, and a blue canton with stars. ' Stars and Stripes.'

Austria, red, white, and red (horizontally). A shield and crown in the white stripe.

Belgium, black (next the staff), yellow, and red (vertically disposed). A device in the yellow stripe.

Denmark, a red field, with a white cross cutting it into quarters.

France, blue (next the staff), white, and red (vertically disposed).

Greece, a blue field with a white cross in the canton, and four white stripes.

Holland, red, white, and blue (horizontally disposed).

Mexico, a white flag with a black spread eagle, holding in its beak a green serpent.

Norway, a red flag, quartered by blue and yellow stripes, and the first quarter crossed.

Portugal, blue and white, vertically disposed (blue next the staff). Shield and crown in the centre.

Prussia, a white flag with a black eagle and a small black Maltese cross in the top corner next the staff.

Russia, a white flag with two blue stripes running from corner to corner like a St. Andrew's cross.

Spain, red, yellow, and red (horizontally disposed).

Sweden, a blue flag, quartered with yellow stripes. In the first quarter several crosses.

Switzerland, a red flag with a white cross in the centre.

Turkey, a red flag with a silver crescent and star with eight points.

Venezuela, yellow, blue, and red (horizontally). A device in the yellow stripe.

See ' Standards,' and ' Black Flag,' ' Red Flag,' ' White Flag,' ' Yellow Flag.'

Flagellants. Fanatics who appeared at sundry times in Europe, and marched about in procession along the streets and public roads to appease the wrath of God. They marched two and two, singing dolorous hymns, mingled with groans; and every now and then stopped to whip each other with scourges to 'atone for the sins of the people.' They first appeared in the 11th cent. under St. Peter Damian. Again in 1268, when Reinier, a Dominican, formed them into a sect. Again in 1349, when Germany was attacked with the pestilence, called the Black Death (*q.v.*). Again in 1574, when Henri III. of France joined the sect. They still exist in Italy, France, Mexico, and New Mexico, but their number is small.

The Flagellants were naked to the waist, but on march threw over their shoulders a white cloak, hence they were called 'Blancs-battus.' They threw off the cloak when the scourging began, and insisted that ' Without shedding of blood there was no remission.' They called themselves the

Brotherhood of the Cross (*q.v.*), and wore a cross on their breast, another on their back, and a third on their hat.

Black Flagellants were so called from their black masks.

Blue Flagellants were so called from their blue mantles.

White Flagellants were so called from their white mantles. *See* 'Blancs-battus.'

Flamin'ian Way (*The*). The great high road made by Flaminius, the Censor, from Rome, through the Sabine country to Ariminium, B.C. 220.

Flammock's Rebellion, 1495, in behalf of Perkin Warbeck. The most formidable danger which ever threatened the throne of Henry VII. The rebellion was crushed out by the king's artillery at Blackheath. Thomas Flammock, the leader, was hanged at Tyburn in 1497.

Flanders. In 862 erected into a county under Baldwin 'Bras-de-Fer,' continued to 1119. Then follow Charles I. of Denmark, 1119-1127, and William Clinton of Normandy, 1127-1128.

The dynasty of Alsace and Hainault, 1128-1405.

The dynasty of the dukes of Burgundy, 1405-1482.

The Austrian dynasty, 1482-1506.

Charles Quint in 1659 incorporated it with the seventeen provinces called 'The Circle of Burgundy.' Since 1830 it has belonged to Belgium.

Flanders Mare (*A Great*). So Henry VIII. called Anne of Cleves, who was married to him by deputy, and separated by mutual agreement. Born 1515, married 6 Jan., and divorced 12 July, 1540, died at Chelsea 1557, aged 42.

Fla'via Cæsarien'sis. One of the five provinces into which Britain was divided in the reign of Sevērus. It consisted of the western portion of the island. It had a separate ruler, but that ruler was subject to the prefect, or governor-general, of the island.

Flavian Emperors (*The*) of Rome. The successors of the Cæsars, of whom Nero was the last. After a year of anarchy, order was restored by Titus Flavius Vespasian, who gave his name of Flavian to the new dynasty, which consisted of Vespasian, Titus, and Domitian, the 12th emperor. *See* 'Five Good Emperors.'

Flaxman Gallery (*The*). A collection of some 140 plaster casts modelled by John Flaxman, R.A., and presented by Miss Denman to the council of University College, London.

Fleet Marriages. Fictitious, clandestine, or irregular marriages, in the 17th and 18th cents., solemnised without banns or licence in the Fleet chapel, or in some 'marriage-room,' dignified for the nonce with the name of chapel, generally some tavern. These marriages were performed by disreputable parsons who lived in the purlieus of Fleet Prison, which were not under the jurisdiction of the bishop. They were declared illegal by Lord-Chancellor Hardwicke's Act, which came into operation 26 March, 1754.

March 25, the day before these marriages became illegal, as many as 217 marriages were celebrated and entered in one of the Fleet register books.

Fleet Prison. A metropolitan prison abolished in 1842, and pulled down in 1845. It was situated on the side of the river Fleet, and was used for persons committed by the Ecclesiastical Courts, the Court of Equity, the Exchequer Court, and the Common Pleas.

It was burnt by Wat Tyler in the reign of Richard II., 1381; again in the great Fire 1666; and again in the Gordon Riots 1780.

Flemish Painters.

Called	Name	
Albrecht DÜRER	. . . .	1471-1528
Lucas van LEYDEN	(*Lucas Dammesz*)	1494-1533
Hans HOLBEIN	. . . . .	1495-1554
Otho van VEEN	(*Otto-Venius*)	1548-1588
Sir Peter Paul RUBENS	. .	1577-1640
David TENIERS	. . . . .	1582-1649
Jacob JORDAENS	. . . . .	1594-1678
Sir Antony VANDYCK	. . .	1599-1641
Hermanszoon REMBRANDT van Ryn	. . . . .	1606-1674

Snyders (1579-1657) the great animal painter was contemporary with Rubens.

Fleshly School (*The*), 1871. A school of English poetry, of which the chief exponents are D. G. Rossetti, Swinburne, Whitman, and Baudelaire. It means sensuous, voluptuous, amorous poetry, 'verging on nastiness.' The term was given to this school of writers by Robert Buchanan in the 'Contemporary Review,' Oct. 1871.

Fleur-de-lis (*The*), or 'Lily of France,' first adopted by Louis VII. le Jeune (1120, 1137-1180) as a symbol of the French monarchy. The royal standard was thickly charged with the flower, but Charles VI. (1380–1422) reduced the number to three. The nature of the emblem is uncertain. Some think it is a bee, the emblem of the early kings—Clovis and his successors. Some fancy it is a toad or frog, whence Nostradamus calls the French *crapauds*. Some think it is the flower of the reed placed in the hands of Christ by the soldiers when they crowned him with a diadem of thorns. And some think it is an emblem of the Trinity, ' tria juncta in uno,' which probably is the basis of the symbol.

Some heralds tell us that when the Franks chose a king they raised him on their shields, and placed a reed, for sceptre, in his hand; hence the ancient kings are represented holding a fleur-de-lis.

Flight into Egypt (*The*), 14 Jan. The flight of the Holy Family from Bethlehem to Egypt, in order to escape the slaughter of the Innocents about to take place under the orders of Herod the Great.

Flint Jack. A notable forger of prehistoric implements.

Floating Debt. Government loans not funded, but to be paid off in full at a stated time. If the government is unable to meet the demand, the floating debt, or such part of it as cannot be met, is converted into funded debt—that is, a debt on which interest is paid by government either for a fixed term of years or for ever. The former is called *terminable* annuities, and the latter *perpetual* annuities.

Flogged by Deputy. When Henri IV. of France abjured, and was received into the Catholic Church in 1595, two ambassadors were sent to Rome to do penance for him. They knelt in the portico of St. Peter's and sang the ' Miserēre,' a blow being given on their shoulders with a switch at each verse.

Lesage, in his ' Gil Blas ' (v. 1) makes Raphael the deputy of the marquis's son ; but Raphael, not seeing the justice of the substitution, ran away. Strange as it may seem, yet is it sanctioned by both God and man. Thus for the sin of David thousands of his subjects were ' scourged ' by a plague. And what else is the entail of Adam's disobedience ?
N.B. Flogging in both services was abolished in England in 1882.

Flood (*Date of the*). According to

	B.C.		B.C.
Septuagint	. 3246	Persian	. 3103
Jackson	. . 3170	Hindû	. . 3102
Hales	. . 3155	Samaritan	. 2998
Josephus	. . 3146	Howard	. . 2698

	B.C.		B.C
Clinton	. . 2482	Petavius	. . 2329
Playfair	. . 2352	Strauch	. . 2293
Usher	. . 2348	Hebrew	. . 2288
Marsham & Calmet	2344	Vulgar Jewish	. 2104

Floral Games of Toulouse (*The*), 1 May, 1322. A literary contest instituted at Toulouse for the encouragement of poetry. The prizes consisted of flowers made of gold or silver, chiefly the violet, eglantine, marigold, amaranth, and lily. The poets who belonged to the institution were called ' The college of the gay science.' The games still exist, and the prizes are given away every year on 3 May.

Florentine Diamond (*The*). Weighs 139½ carats, and is among the crown jewels of the Emperor of Austria. It has a slight citron tint, and is valued at 105,000*l*. It belonged to Charles the Bold, and after the battle of Granson was picked up by a Swiss, who thought it was a bit of glass, and sold it to a priest for a gulden. The priest sold it for 3 francs, and it was next bought for 200*l*. by Bartholomew May, a merchant who lived in Berne. May sold it to a Genoese for a large sum of money; Ludovico Sforza bought it of the Genoese for double what he had given; it then came into the possession of Pope Julius II., and Pope Julius presented it to the Emperor of Austria.

Flores Historia′rum, or ' Flowers of History,' by Matthew Paris, is in reality the work of Wendover continued by Matthew Paris. It begins at creation and goes down to 1238. Matthew Paris brought it down to 1259, and William Rishanger continued it still further.

Florid or Perpendicular Style. Succeeded the Decorated English in the 14th cent., as the Decorated had succeeded the Early English or Lancet style in the 13th cent. The Florid style is so called from its profusion of ornamental detail. It is called Perpendicular from the perpendicular mullions of the windows, the lines of the panel-work, and the Tudor arch. One of the finest specimens is Henry VII.'s Chapel, Westminster. Its best period was between 1375 and 1598.

The Tudor arch was four-centred. St. George's Chapel, Windsor, and the nave of Canterbury Cathedral are good specimens of this style of architecture.

Florida (U.S. North America). So called by Juan Ponce de Leon, in 1512, because it was discovered on Palm

Sunday, called in Spanish '[Pascua] Florida.' The nickname of the inhabitants in this state is *Fly-up-the-Creeks*.

Flower Badges. Of Families.

Blue cornflower, the badge of William king of Prussia.

Erica cinerĕa, the five-leaved heath, the badge of the Macalisters.

Erica Tetrălix, the cross-leaved heath, the badge of the Macdonalds.

Genista, the badge of the Plantagenets.

Primrose, the badge of the Primrose League, in honour of Lord Beaconsfield.

Rose (red), the badge of the Lancastrians.

Rose (white), the badge of the Yorkists.

Violet, the badge of Napoleon and the French imperialists.

Wild Strawberry, the badge of the Frasers.

Flower Badges. Of Nations.

Athens	. .	. The Violet.
Canada	. .	. Sugar-maple.
England	. .	. Red Rose.
Florence	. .	. Giglio (Lily).
France	. .	. Iris Lily.
Ireland	. .	. Shamrock-leaf.
Prussia	. .	. Linden.
Saxony	. .	. Mignonette.
Scotland	. .	. Thistle.
Wales .	. .	. Leek-leaf.

As in England the Lancastrian badge was a *red* rose, and the Yorkist a *white* one, so in Florence the Guelfs (or papal party) adopted the *red lily*, and the Ghibellines (or imperial party) a *white* one.

Flower Symbols. Of Moral qualities.

Box	a symbol of	Immortality.
Cedar	,,	Fidelity.
Corn-ears	,,	Holy Communion.
Dates	,,	Faith.
Grapes	,,	The blood of Christ.
Holly-berries	,,	The Resurrection.
Ivy	,,	"
Olive	,,	Peace. "
Orange-blossom	,,	Virginity.
Palm	,,	Victory.
Rose	,,	Incorruption.
Vine	,,	Christ our Life.
White Lily	,,	Purity.
Yew	,,	Death.

The amaranth, cypress, laurel, myrtle, oak, olive, asphodel, and rosemary are funereal plants.

Flower of the Levant (*The*). 'Il fiore di Levante,' Zantè.

Flower of the Sun (*The*). The

Elixir of Life. The alchemists called all sorts of flocculent substances obtained by distillation *flower*, hence we have 'flowers of sulphur,' 'flowers of benzoin.' The flower of the sun was a bright ruby stone called the 'philosopher's stone.'

He that has once the 'Flower of the Sun,'
The perfect ruby which we call *elixir*,

Can confer honour, love, respect, long life;
Give safety, valour, yea, and victory
To whom he will. In eight-and-twenty days
He'll make an old man of four score a child.
BEN JONSON, *The Alchymist*, ii. 1.

Flower-pot Plot (*The*), 1692. An

infamous imposition got up by Young and Blackhead, who hoped to make money by it, like Titus Oates. These villains wrote an engagement to bring back James II. and seize William. Having forged the signatures of Marlborough, Cornbury, Sancroft (the ex-primate), and Sprat bishop of Rochester, they secreted the document in a flower-pot at the bishop's house at Bromley. The bishop was arrested, but denied all knowledge of the plot, and then Black-head confessed the forgery.

Flower Sermon (*The*), May 1851.

Established by W. M. Whittemore, D.D., rector of the united parishes of St. Katherine Cree and St. James. It is usual to present nosegays, which are then sent to hospitals.

Flowers. According to Herrick the

ancient inhabitants of this island used to adorn their houses all the year round with green boughs. At *Christmas* with bay, rosemary, and mistletoe, up to Candlemas day (2 Feb.); from *Candlemas to Easter* with box; at *Easter* with yew; at *Whitsuntide* with birch and flowers, oaken boughs, and bent (a kind of grass).

Flowers dedicated to Saints.

Baneberry to ...	St. Christopher.
Bean (the common) to	St. Ignatius.
Corn-feverfew to ...	St. Anne.
Spider-wort to	St. Bruno.

Toywort to the shepherds, for their purses.
Valerian (blue) to Jacob, for his angels' ladder.

Flowers referring to Saints.

Briony (black)	Our Lady's seal.
Clematis	The Virgin's bower.
Hyacinth (blue) ...	St. Dorothy's tears.
Lily of the Valley ...	Madonna's tears.
Oleander	St. Joseph's nosegay.

Flowery Kingdom (*The*). China.

Flowery Land (*The*), or 'Hwa

Kwoh.' China; meaning the 'flower of the world.' Certainly no land is more productive.

It justifies the long-existent and always increasing hope of foreigners that the Flowery Land would eventually adopt this most speedy and effectual mode of locomotion.—FUNG YEE, *Nineteenth Century*, Feb. 1890, p. 225.

Flowery Land Pirates (*The*),

1864. 'The Flowery Land' was the name of the pirates' cutter. The captain, the mate, and several others were murdered in the passage from London to Singapore. Five Spaniards were publicly executed at Newgate for this outrage.

Fly (*Killed by a*). Adrian IV., the only Englishman who has been pope. He was Nicholas Breakspeare of Langley, and succeeded to the papal throne in 1151; died, being choked by a fly, in 1159.

Flying Company (*The*), 1561. Chosen troops of 100 musketeers for constant service, destined to act in defence of the Vaudois at any point where an attack was threatened by their Catholic persecutors. Two pastors always attended the 'company.'

Flying Dutchman (*The*), 1806, or 'Ship of Doom.' The reflection of a vessel off the Cape of Good Hope, occasionally seen at a considerable distance, and regarded by sailors with superstitious terror. The tale is that this mirage is the ship of Vanderdecken, who in 1806 tried in vain to enter Table Bay, and swore he would do so, if he 'beat about the Cape till the day of doom.' Out of punishment his ship and crew were turned into phantoms, 'beating about the bay,' and bringing evil to all who view the vessel.

Flying Highwayman (*The*). Richard (Dick) Turpin, 1711–1739. To-day in town, to-morrow at York, the next day at Chester, 'an *alibi* personified.' Hanged at York 1739.

Flying Roll (*The*), 1175. A book compiled by James Jershom White from the writings of Joanna Southcott and John Wroe. It is a jumble of texts from Genesis to Revelation, supposed to have a meaning known only to the initiated.

Flying Squadron (*The*), 1705. Those members of the Scotch Parliament who professed to act independently, but sought their own ends by joining one of the other two parties (Jacobites and revolutionists) as suited them. Their leader was the Marquis of Tweeddale.

Fo, or Foë. The founder of a religious system in China which may be called Buddhism, or reformed Brahmanism. His birth is placed B.C. 1027. He taught as his fundamental principles truth and altruism, to take the life of no living creature, to abstain from wine, not to steal or covet, to keep the body in chastity and temperance, and to believe in a future state. The priests are called 'Bonzes,' and live in monasteries.

The orthodox or state religion of China is Confucianism (Yu); and there is a third system called Taoism, or rationalism.

Fodrum Rega'le (3 syl.). Certain customary supplies of provisions, at the expense of the city where the German emperor resided when he visited Italy. *See* Hallam, 'Middle Ages,' vol. i. p. 346.

Folio (*Tom*). Thomas Rawlinson, a bibliophilist, who flourished 1681–1725.

Folk Mote. The Court of the Hundred in Saxon England. It was held once a month, and was presided over by the alderman and bishop of the diocese. This mote was superior to the Hall Mote and inferior to the Shire Mote.

In the Folk Mote all contracts for the sale of land were made; and such crimes were tried as could not be judged by the lord of a tithing or town.

Folkungs (*The*). A race of administrators in Sweden, somewhat like the French 'Mayors of the Palace.' They called themselves *Jarls*, and were in power from 1250 to 1387, when the regency of Sweden was given to Margaret, queen regent of Denmark and Norway. In 1397 by the 'Union of Calmar' the three kingdoms were nominally united in Eric, grand-nephew of Margaret; but Sweden had separate administrators from 1471 to 1523, when Gustavus broke from Denmark, and erected Sweden into an independent kingdom.

Folkungs of Norway (*The*), from 1319 to 1387. Like the Folkungs of Sweden these rulers were not kings, but resembled the 'Mayors of the Palace' in French history. The Norwegian Folkungs were Magnus VIII., also Folkung of Sweden (1319–1350), Hako VIII. (1350–1380), and Olaf V. (1380–1387).

Folly of Spain (*The*), or 'Folies d'Espagne.' A lively dance tune. The dancers used castanets. The measure was *à trois temps*, and the movement moderately fast.

Fomo'rians (*The*). According to Keating (p. 116), the original owners of Ireland. They supported themselves by fishing and fowling. When Partholan and his four sons, some 2,200 years before the Christian era, visited Ireland, these

Fomorians were found in the island. It is said they were an Iberian or Basque colony. Moore, in his 'History of Ireland,' calls the Fomorians 'African sea-rovers, who infested the coasts of Ireland *after* the extirpation of Partholan's race.' He says they stamped out the Nemedians, held the island for 200 years, and were succeeded by the Firbolgs. Of course, this is only 'bardic history,' but the storming of Tor Innis by the Nemedians is the subject of a very famous Irish poem.

Fondation Montyon (*La*), 1825. Founded by J. B. Robert Auget baron de Montyon, who gave 5 million francs *aux convalescents sortant des hôpitaux de Paris, qui auraient le plus besoin de secours*. The money was invested, and brings an annual interest of 10,000l. sterling. Everyone who has been in a hospital for five days receives 1 franc, and the bounty rises to 25 francs.

Pronounce, *Lah fone-dah'-se-on Moan-te'-yone.*

Fondeurs, or 'Clippers.' Bands of robbers which disturbed France in the unsettled times of Charles VI. and VII. They were often accompanied by the *écorcheurs* and other vagabonds.

Fontainebleau (*Treaties of*).
(1) 1542. A treaty of alliance between François I. and Gustavus Vasa.
(2) 2 Sept., 1679. A treaty of peace between France, Denmark, and Sweden.
(3) 10 Nov., 1785. A treaty of peace between Austria and Holland, by the mediation of France.
(4) 27 Oct., 1807. A secret treaty between Napoleon I. and Carlos IV. of Spain, for the deposition of the House of Braganza for refusing to accept the 'Continental System.' By this compact, Portugal was partitioned between the Prince of Asturias and a young libertine named Godoy, chief minister of Spain.

In 1640, Portugal threw off the Spanish yoke and recalled the Duke of Braganza. The concordat between Napoleon and Pius VII. at Fontainebleau took place 25 Jan., 1813.

Fontanges (*À la*). A style of head-dress in the reign of Louis XIV., in which long streaming ribbons were introduced. Mlle. Fontanges (2 syl.) was maid of honour to Mme. de Montespan, and was a court favourite for a few months; but she died at the age of 20.

Fontenoy (*Battle of*). See 'Fire First.'

Fonthill Abbey. Was commenced by Beckford in 1795, and sold by him in 1822.

Foolish. *More foolish than Abu Gabshan.* An Arabian proverb. Kofa made Abu Gabshan intoxicated, and induced him to deliver up the keys of the temple of the Kaaba. When he grew sober he saw the full evil of his folly, but it was too late. The tribe of Khozaab, which had been in possession of Mecca and its temple, were deprived of both by the Koreish, who retained possession till the time of Mahomet.

Fools (*Last of the titled*) of France was L'Angély (1620–1679), court fool of Louis XIII. He was of good family, but very poor. His satire was so caustic that he grew rich by the blackmail given him to purchase exemption from his sallies.

Armstrong, court jester to James I. and Charles I., was the last of the titled fools in England. He died 1672.

Fools' Fair, 14 Sept. Held in the Broad Gate, Lincoln, for the sale of cattle. Licensed by William and Mary. Called 'Fools' Fair' because the time is so unsuitable for the purpose. Being harvest time, very few can attend it, and Lincoln at the time had no special trade or manufacture. See 'Fête des Fous.'

Fool's-cap Livery (*The*), 1563. A badge livery adopted by the Calvinists of the Netherlands to show their contempt and abhorrence for Cardinal Granvelle, a pompous, arrogant, bigoted churchman, sent by Philip II. of Spain to introduce Roman Catholicism into Holland and stamp out Calvinism. A party of young nobles, to show their contempt for this churchman, assumed a dress in ridicule of the cardinal's finery. It was something like that of a poor monk, of the coarsest grey cloth, without any ornament except that of a fool's cap and bells embroidered on the sleeves. This was in allusion to the cardinal's custom of calling the Flemings 'fools.' In a few days all the Flemings assumed the new livery.

Foolscap Paper. The smallest folio-sized paper. It used to have the royal arms in the water-mark, but the Rump Parliament ordered the water-mark to be changed for a fool's cap and bells. There seems to be a pun in the device from the Italian *foglio capo* (chief or full-sized sheet of paper).

Foot of a Fine (*The*). The fifth or last part of a fine, containing all the matter, the day, year, and place, and before what justices the fine was levied. A corruption of the old French *la pée* or *la pés = paix*. After proclaiming the fine in the Common Pleas, the justice said, ' Criez la pees ' (*i.e.* Proclaim the peace), and the serjeant read the concord or agreement between the parties. The foot of the fine is, therefore, the *paix* or final agreement as stated by the countor or serjeant.

Foot-page, or ' Foot-bearer.' An attendant in olden times whose duty it was to squat under the table of kings and other great men, and keep his master's feet warm, by rubbing them with his hands, nursing them in his lap, and even cherishing them in his bosom.

The foot-bearer shall hold the feet of the king in his lap. from the time he [the king] reclines at the board till he goes to rest ; and he [the foot-page] shall chafe them with a towel, and during all that time shall watch that no harm befalls the king. He shall eat of the same dish from which the king takes his food ; and shall light the first candle before the king.—SOUTHEY, *Madoc* (note).

Fops' Alley. A railed-off passage in front of the pit of the Italian opera-house, where dandies lounged who thought their figures showed more to advantage in a standing posture than in a sitting one. They wagged their *chapeaux bras*, and dropped their canes, and hallooed to their friends in the boxes, being thus an intolerable nuisance.

Forbes Mackenzie Act (*The*), 1853. For the regulation of public-houses in Scotland (16, 17 Vict. c. 67). Its object was to prevent grocers from being secret publicans, for no liquor is to be drunk on the premises where groceries are sold. No liquor is to be sent out from any hotel or inn on Sundays before six in the morning, nor after eleven at night. Some grace was allowed to travellers journeying either on pleasure or business.

Foreign Canons. Such as did not officiate in the canonries to which they were attached. They were the non-residentiary canons.

15

Foreign Enlistment Acts (*The*). In 1605 British subjects were prohibited from entering foreign service (3 Jac. I. c. 4, s. 18). In 1835 the prohibition was suspended by order in council.

The enlistment of foreigners into the British service was permitted in 1854 (18 Vict. c. 2).

Foreigners' Friend (*The*). Dermot king of Leinster, who brought over English and Welsh allies to assist him in regaining his throne, from which he had been driven by Tiernan O'Ruarc, lord of Breffny, in 1168.

Forest Cantons of Switzerland (*The*), or the 'Waldstetten,' that is, Schwitz, Uri, and Unterwalden.

Forester (*Fanny*). The pen-name of Emily Judson (Chubbock), an American author.

Forester (*Frank*). The pen-name of Henry William Herbert, an English-born American author.

Forfeiture and Corruption of Blood. A law which existed before the Conquest, that a man guilty of treason forfeits his estates to the crown, and can transmit no title of dignity to his heirs.

In America the law of ' Corruption of Blood' cannot exist, for there are no titles of dignity transmittable.

Forgeries (*Literary*). *See* under ' Literary Forgeries.'

Fork-Beard. Sueno (*Swe-no*) king of Denmark (985-1014).

He exacted the tribute called Danegeld, and in 1013 was crowned king of England. Tyfve-skeg or Fork-Beard was succeeded by his son Canute.

Form of the Beads (*The*), 1538. Certain instructions for praying drawn up by Browne, archbishop of Dublin.

Forma Pau'peris (*In*). By statutes passed in the reigns of Henry VII. and VIII., if a plaintiff swore he was not worth 5*l.* beyond the clothes he was wearing, he had counsel and attorney assigned him by the court gratuitously, and all court-fees were excused him.

Formula of Concord (*The*), or ' Consensus,' 1576. Drawn up at Torgau ; suppressed at Brandenburg in 1614 ; re-published in Switzerland in 1675.

Torgau, pronounce *Tor-gow.*

Formulary, or ' Formula.' I. 1653. In which Innocent X. condemned the five propositions of Jansen taught in his

Z

famous book entitled ' Augustīnus ' (*q.v.*). He commanded the Jansenists to subscribe to it, but they refused to do so.

II. The formulary of 1665, in which Alexander VII. confirmed the formulary of Innocent X. The Jansenists still refused subscription. In 1668 Pope Clement, to prevent a schism, withdrew the formulary, and this is called the 'Peace of Clement IX.'

Fort Adjutant (*A*). A staff-officer in command of a fortress. They have an extra pay of 4s. 9d. daily.

Forties (*The*), 1826. The forty shilling franchise of Ireland, repealed 1829. See ' Forty-shilling Freeholders.'

Mr. O'Connell at the head of the priests and the ' Forties ' was declared by the sheriff duly elected. —HOWITT, *Hist. of Eng.*, year 1828, p. 117.

Mr. O'Connell had repeatedly declared that he would not accept emancipation if the faithful ' Forties ' were to be sacrificed. He would rather die on the scaffold than submit to such a measure. —*Ibid.* year 1829, p.142.

Fortification (*Permanent*). The art of shutting in a circumscribed piece of ground, or a city, by defensive masses of earth and ditches, to resist the attacks of an enemy. Every plot of ground so fortified is supposed to be surrounded by a polygon of fortification, and the works constructed on any one side of this polygon constitute a *front of fortification.* The great mass of earth thrown up from the ditch inwards is the *rampart*; and the covering shot-proof mass of earth on the outer edge of the rampart is the *parapet*. The step of earth behind the parapet (about a foot high) is called the *banquette*.

A rampart is about 7½ feet high.

Fortunate (*The*). So Philippe VI. de Valois was called, but his whole reign was a series of calamities. In this reign the French lost the battles of Sluys (*Slu'iz*) and Crécy.

The French have been singularly unhappy in their royal ' pet ' names.

Forty. This number is very conspicuous in the Bible and Christian Church.

1. It rained forty days and forty nights in the Flood.—*Gen.* vii. 12.
2. Moses twice fasted for forty days and forty nights.—*Exod.* xxiv. 18, &c.
3. The spies sent to Canaan were forty days in searching the land.—*Num.* xiii. 35.
4. The Israelites wandered forty years in the wilderness.—*Ps.* xcv. 10.
5. Goliath defied the armies of Saul for forty days.—1 *Sam.* xvii. 16.
6. Elijah fasted forty days.—1 *Kings* xix. 8.

7. Ezekiel bore the iniquities of the house of Jacob forty days, a day for a year.
8. Jonah cried to the Ninevites, ' Yet forty days and Nineveh shall be overthrown.'—*Jonah* iii. 4.
9. Jesus fasted and was tempted forty days in the wilderness.—*Matt.* iv. 2.
10. Jesus tarried on earth forty days after his resurrection.—*Acts* i. 3.
11. Jerusalem was destroyed by Titus forty years after the Ascension.
12. According to Church tradition Jesus was forty hours in the tomb.
13. The Lenten Fast continues for forty days, from Ash Wednesday to Easter Sunday. Introduced into England by order of Ædbald king of Kent, A.D. 640.
14. One of the saints of the Catholic Church is called ' Quadragesimus,' said to have been a shepherd, and under-deacon of Pavia. His day is 26th Oct.
15. St. Swithin's days of rain are forty.
16. The Jews were forbidden to inflict more than forty stripes on an offender.
17. The martyrdom. See ' Forty Martyrs.'

Forty (*The*). I. ' I Quarantia.' A council of state, in Venice, between the Six Sages and 450 representatives, of whose origin and positive duties very little is known. It was a permanent body, which seems to have represented the chief families of Venice, and exercised criminal justice. In the best days the doge had a Council of Six, to which every bill was first submitted. The Six sent it to the Forty, or council of state, and then it was sent to the legislative assembly, consisting of 450 representatives.

The 40 electors of the doge were in 1249 increased to 41 to prevent an equal division. The nomination of these electors was very complex. The Grand Council first selected 30, who were reduced by ballot to 9. These 9 nominated 40, who were reduced by ballot to 12. These 12 elected 25, who were reduced by ballot to 9. These 9 elected 45, who were reduced by ballot to 11. These 11 elected the 41 electors, and the 41 electors chose the doge out of the Grand Council.

II. Besides the council of state in Venice, there were three tribunals, each of which was composed of forty members. (1) The tribunal of appeal from the city magistrates; (2) Another tribunal of appeal from the suburban magistrates; and (3) a high court of assize which took cognisance of all criminal offences except treason.

III. The Académie Française, founded by Richelieu in 1635, consists of forty members, neither more nor less. Its original intention was to fix and purify the French language. Membership is now the highest literary distinction which the nation can bestow.

The election of the ' head administrator ' of the Théâtre Français to a seat among the ' Forty ' of the Académie is, after the lapse of 200 years, in atonement for the non-election of the founder himself [M. Claretie elected 22 Feb., 1889].—*Nineteenth Century*, July 1889, p. 85.

IV. The English Academicians are called 'The Forty.'

Mr. Faed lacked not backers all the way up and down among the 'Forty,' and Sir Frederick's threat of resignation had no terrors.—*Truth*, 13 Jan., 1887.

V. One of the inferior courts of Athens consisted of 40 magistrates (οἱ τεσσαρά-κοντα), who went on circuit to settle controversies about money, actions of assault and battery, and neglect in attending the public assemblies.

Forty Columns (*The*), or 'Chihel Sutun.' A lofty erection still existing, but in a somewhat dilapidated condition, in 41° N. lat., on the route of the caravans from Bokha'ra to China (HEEREN, 'Asiatic Nations,' vol. iii. p. 389).

This is the 'Stone Tower' of Ptolemy.—*Geographia*, bk. i., ch. 12.

'Forty-five (*The*). The rising which took place in Scotland in 1745. It was an attempt on the part of Prince Charles Edward Stuart to regain the throne of James II. Lewis Gordon, brother of the Duke of Gordon, was one of the adherents.

'Forty-five (*Out in the*). One of the Jacobites who had taken part in the rebellion of 1745, when the anti-Hanoverian furore ran very high not only in the Highlands of Scotland, but also in England.

He designated the rebellion of 1745 as the *affair of '45*; and spoke of one engaged in it as a person who had been *out in the forty-five*.—Sir W. SCOTT, *Redgauntlet*.
In the 'forty-five, that is, concerned or involved in the rebellion of 1745.
I suffered in the forty-five.—*Ib*. ch. x.
An old 'forty-five man, one formerly concerned in the rebellion of 1745.—*Ib*.

Forty-hour Prayers, 1560. Made before the 'saint sacrement' in the times of public calamities, jubilees, 'les jours gras,' and so on. At one time they lasted forty hours without interruption, because Christ was 'forty hours in the tomb.' Indulgences were granted by Pius IV. to those who observed these *prières de quarante heures*.

Forty Martyrs (*The*), 320. The martyrs of the famous Thundering Legion, condemned to death by Agricolaus for refusing to offer sacrifice at Sebasté, in Lesser Armenia, in obedience to their commander Licinius. It is said that they were exposed naked on the surface of a pond frozen over, and St. Basil tells us that they lay there for three days, and all their limbs were mortified by the cold (St. Basil, 'Homily' 20, vol. i. p. 452).

Forty-nine Men, or 'The Forty-nine Officers.' Protestant royalist officers who had served Charles I. in Ireland before 1649. These officers by a declaration of Charles II. were to receive their arrears in lands at the rate of 12*s*. 6*d*. in the pound, and an equal dividend of whatever should remain of their security.

Forty - shilling Freeholders (*The Irish*), 1826. Men entitled to the elective franchise who swore that their tenement was equal to them in value to 40*s*. a year. A hut and small potato plot were sufficient to give a vote. In order to multiply votes farms were cut up into small holdings, whereby a large constituency was created scarcely removed from actual pauperism, and almost entirely under the command of the parish priest. Repealed 1829 (10 Geo. IV. c. 8), after the Bill for the Emancipation of Catholics had passed.

Till 1429 universal suffrage prevailed, but votes were then confined to 40*s*. freeholders in the counties, and the qualification of a county member was the possession of a freehold worth 40*l*. a year, equal to 400*l*. at the present time.

Forty-times Forty Churches (*The City of*), Moscow.

Forty-two Articles (*The*), 1552, 1553. The original number of the Articles of the Church of England. In 1562 seven were omitted, and the number was reduced to thirty-nine by the substitution of four new articles.

THE ARTICLES OMITTED.

1. (Art. x.) Of Grace. No man is constrained to sin.
2. (Art. xvi.) Of Blasphemy against the Holy Ghost. That is, perversion of 'God's Word,' or malignant opposition to it.
3. (Art. xix.) All men bound to keep the moral law.
4. (Art. xxxix.) The resurrection of the dead is not past.
5. (Art. xl.) The soul does neither sleep nor perish with the body.
6. (Art. xli.) Of the millenarians. Declaring the dogma a fable derived from Jewish tradition.
7. (Art. xlii.) Not all men will be saved.

The new articles are the v., xii., xxix., and xxx.

Foss of Ma'rius (The), B.C. 103.

A canal cut by the soldiers of Marius when encamped against the Cimbrians. It ran from the rear of his camp on the right bank of the Rhône to the coast. Its object was to secure ready access to the sea.

Foujdarry Court (The). In India,

the court of criminal law. The 'foujdar' is a magistrate of police who takes cognisance of criminal matters.

Foul Raid (The), 1417. The dis-

honourable inroad; referring to the raid of the Regent Albany on Roxburgh Castle and the town of Berwick while Henry V. was in France. The Dukes of Exeter and Bedford, with an English army, compelled Albany to raise both the sieges.

The Duke of Albany was prime minister of Scotland to Robert I., Robert II., and James I. (fifty years); he was above eighty at his death (1419).

Foul-weather Jack. The Hon.

John Byron, admiral and navigator, who was noted for the tempestuous weather which pursued him in all his voyages (1723–1786).

Founder of Christian Eloquence (The). Bourdaloue (1632–

1704), unrivalled for argument, method, and depth of thought. His 'Lent Sermons' are the best known of his works.

Founders of Religious Orders.

Annunciades (numerous)		
— Celestes	...	Maria Vittoria Fornari
— of Bourges	...	Jeanne de Valois
— of Savoy	...	Amadeus VI.
Augustines	...	Augustine of Hippo
Barefooted Friars (numerous)		
Barefooted Alcantarines		Ferdinand Gomez
— Augustines		Tommaso da Jesu
— Carmelites		Theresa of Avila
— Eremites or Ermites (several)		
— Franciscans	...	Paolo of Foligno
— Trinitarians	...	Jean Baptiste de la Conception
Benedictines	...	Benedict of Nursia
Bernardines	...	Bernard of Clairvaux
Brigettines or Nuns of our Holy Saviour		Brigitte or Bridget of Sweden
Brothers of Charity	...	Vincent de Paul
Camaldules	...	Romualdus
Capucins or Capuchins	...	Matteo Baschi
Carmelites (White Friars)		John of Jerusalem
— of Mâcon	...	Margaret of St. Joseph
Several others		
Carthusians	...	Bruno
Celestines	...	Pierre de Moron [Celestine V.]
Christian Doctrine	...	Ippolite Galantini
Cistercians	...	Robert de Molesme
Clarisses or Poor Clares		Clare of Assisi
Clercs Mineurs	...	Francesco Caracciolo
— Reguliers (Theatins)	...	Gaetano of Chieti (Latin Theate)
— of the Mother of God		Giovanni Leonardi

Clercs Somasques	...	Geremia Emiliani
Cluniacs	...	Bernon abbé de Cluny
Congregation of the Holy Heart of Mary		Frances Mary Paul Liebermann
— Holy Hearts	...	Marie Joseph Coudrin
— Holy Trinity	...	Marie de la Croix
— Son of Mary	...	Louis Marie Baudouin
— Very Holy Sacrament		Louis Agut
— Very Holy Trinity	...	Philip Neri
And several others		
Cordonniers	...	{ Gaston de Rente and { Henri Michael Buch
Daughters of Calvary	...	Antoinette d'Orléans
— Charity	...	Vincent de Paul
— Providence	...	Marie de Lumagne
And several others		
Doctrinaires	...	Cæsar de Bus
Dominicans	...	Dominic
Feuillants	...	Jean de la Barrière
Filles Dieu (originally Sœurs de St. Gervais)		
Franciscans	...	Francis of Assisi
Fratres Cellitæ or Mexians	...	Mexius
Frères des Ecoles Chrétiennes		Jean Baptiste de la Salle
— Mineurs	...	Francis of Assisi
Gilbertines	...	Gilbert bishop of Meaux
Hieronimites of Fiesole		Charles de Rumène
— of the Observance		Loup of Olmedo
— of Spain	...	Thomas of Siena
— of Umbria	...	Pietro of Pisa
Hôpital de Mouze	...	Gerard Teinturier
Hospitallers	...	Gerard Tom
Jesuits	...	Ignatius Loyola
Lazarists	...	Vincent de Paul
Liguorians	...	Alfonso of Liguori
Minims	...	Francis of Paula
Minorites	...	Francis of Assisi
Missionaries of the Precious Blood		Gaspard del Bufalo
Norbertines	...	Norbert archbishop of Magdeburg
Notre Dame de Réfuge	...	Elizabeth of Ranfaing
There are thousands of institutions entitled Notre Dame		
Oratorians	...	Philip Neri
Order of France	...	Pierre de Bérulle
— Mercy	...	Pierre de Nolasque
— Our Holy Saviour	...	Brigitte or Bridget of Sweden
— the Holy Cross	...	Theodore of Celles
— the Incarnate Word		Jeanne Marie de Matel
— the Perpetual Adoration		Catherine Mechtilda de S. Sacrement
— the Very Holy Trinity		Felix de Valois
And many others		
Ordre de Flore		
— de l'Œuvre de la Jeunesse	...	S. Joachim
— de Pulsano	...	John Joseph Allemand
— des Servites	...	John of Mathera
		Manetto, Sostenus, and five others
— de Très-sainte Trinité		Jean de Matha
Penitents	...	Angela countess of Civitella
Picpus	...	Abbé Condrin
Preaching Friars of S. Dominic	...	Dominic de Gusman
Premonstratensians	...	Norbert archbishop of Magdeburg
Priests of the Mission, or Lazarists		Vincent de Paula
Récoilets, reformed Franciscans		John of Guadalupe
Redemptorists	...	Alfonso of Liguori
Reformed Bernardines	...	Louis Perrucard de Ballon
Religieuses Auxiliatrices des âmes du Purgatoire		Marie de la Providence
Religious Hospitallers	...	John de Dieu
St. Fintan of the Order of St. Jerome		Mary Garcias
Second Founder of the Filles de Ste. Geneviève		Marie Bonneau

Séminaires de la Providence	François de Chanciergues
Sisters of Charity of St. Joseph	Elizabeth Anne Bayley
— of Mercy	Marie Thérèse Charlotte de Lamourous
— of Ste. Anne	Jeanne de la Noue
— of St. Gervais	François Armand Gervais
— of the Hermitage ...	Ursula Benincasa
— of the Holy Family ...	Marie de Rodat
— of the Presentation of Mary, &c.	Marie Anne Rivier
Society of French Missions	John Baptist Rauzan
Sœurs Grises	Marie Marguerite Dufrost de Lajemmerais à' Youville
Sylvestrians	Sylvester Gozzolini
Tabennites	
Templars	Hugues des Payens, Geoffrey de St. Adhemar, and 7 others
Trappists	Rotrou count of Perche
Tertiaries of St. Francis	Francis of Assisi
Teutonic Knights	Frederick duke of Suabia
Third Order of the Humble	Jean de Méda
Urbanists	S. Isabelle (confirmed by Urban II.)
Ursulines	Angela of Merici

Foundling Hospital (*The*). London, 1739. Founded by Capt. Coram.

One established at Milan in 787.
" " at Paris in 1640.
, " at Stockholm in 1753 by the Freemasons.

Four Ancient Books of Wales (*The*). 'The Black Book of Carmarthen,' 'The Book of Aneurin,' 'The Book of Taliesin,' and the poetical portion of 'The Red Book of Hergest' (*q.v.*). It was published in 1868, with an English translation, by the Rev. Canon Williams and the Rev. D. Silvan Evans.

Four Articles (*The*). Drawn up by Bossuet in the reign of Louis XIV.
1. The ecclesiastical power shall be subordinate to the civil power in France.
2. The decision of a general council shall supersede the dictum of a pope.
3. The church shall at all times conform to local usages and municipal laws.
4. The judgment of the pope even in matters of faith shall not be binding unless ratified by a general council. *See* 'Articles.'

Four Attributes of Glorified Bodies (*The*). In Catholic theology: Subtlety, agility, luminosity, and immortality (Mgr. GUÉRIN, 'Vies des Saints,' vol. ix. p. 559).

Four Burghs (*The*). Edinburgh, Stirling, Berwick, and Roxburgh; noted for their 'Court of the Four Burghs,' superseded by the 'Convention of Royal Burghs,' 1487.

Four Cardinal Virtues (*The*). In Catholic theology: Fortitude, justice, prudence, and temperance.

Four Credenze (*The*). After the treaty of Constance (*q.v.*), 1183, Frederick Barbarossa introduced a podesta or dictator into Milan, not a native, and under him were four estates or credenze: (1) the old consuls and their officers; (2) the capitani or higher nobles, with the archbishop of Milan at their head; (3) the popolani or burghers; and (4) the valvassori or inferior nobles. Soon these four estates practically resolved themselves into the aristocracy and proletariat or popolani.

Four Creeds (*The*). Of the Catholic Church of Rome: The Apostles' Creed, the Nicene Creed, the Athanasian Creed, and the Creed of Pius V.

Four Days' Battle (*The*), 1–4 June, 1665. Between the English fleet under the joint command of Prince Rupert and the Duke of Albemarle, and the Dutch fleet under the command of De Ruyter and De Witt off the North Foreland. The English lost ten ships and 1,700 men killed and wounded; the Dutch lost two admirals, seven captains, and 1,800 men, with fifteen vessels of all sorts. The Dutch claimed the victory, and without doubt had the advantage.

Four Hundred (*The*), B.C. 411. The oligarchical legislature of Athens. This body formed an irresponsible government, and held its sittings in the senate house. In four months the constitution of the 400 was overthrown, and the government placed in the hands of 5,000 citizens instead of the entire male population.

A committee of five was first chosen; this committee chose ninety-five members; and each of the hundred chose three.

Four Hundred and Fifty (*The*). The legislative assembly of ancient Venice, chosen from the six quarters of the city. The privy council of the doge consisted of the Six Sages; the great council of state of forty members.

Four Masters (*The*). Rhyming annalists of Ireland. The annals were compiled in the 17th century (1636) by Michael O'Clery, with the assistance of three other antiquaries. Harris tells us they are 'chiefly drawn from the annals of Clonmacnois, Inisfail, and Senat, as well as from other approved and ancient chronicles of Ireland.' A full account may be found in Mr. Petrie's 'Remarks on the History and Authenticity of the Autograph Original of the Annals of the Four Masters.'

Four Points (*The*), 1854. (1) The cession of the Russian protectorate in the Principalities, and establishment of a European protectorate in its stead; (2) the free navigation of the Danube; (3) an arrangement to put an end to Russian preponderance in the Black Sea, and for bringing the Ottoman government into harmony with European governments; and (4) the renunciation by Russia of a protectorate over the Christian subjects of the sultan.

Four Symbols (*The*), or standards in Catholic theology.

(1) The Apostles' Creed; (2) the Nicene Creed; (3) the symbol of Constantinople; and (4) the Athanasian Creed.

The Constantinople formulary was made at the Council of Constantinople in 331, and is recited at mass. It is identical with the Nicene Creed, except in the one article about the procession of the Holy Ghost from the father (*filioque*).

Four Vows of the Order of St. Francis of Paula. Poverty, chastity, obedience, and the quadragesimal life (*i.e.* the Lenten fast of 40 days).

Fou'rierism. The social system devised by Charles Fourier. He would divide men into groups of 400 families, and these groups into series, and these series into phalanxes. A single group he would place under one immense roof, and there should be supplied every appliance of industry and art. No army would be required, no wars could ever break out, as all the world would be one great family.

Fourteen Saintly Helpers (*The*). The fourteen saints to whose churches, between Bamberg and Coburg, annual pilgrimages were made, viz. George, Blaise, Erasmus, Vitus, Pantaleon, Christopher, Denys or Dionysius, Cyriacus, Acnatius, Eustace, Giles or Ægidius, Margaretha, Catharine, and Barbara.

Fourth Estate (*The*). The newspaper press. The 'three estates of the realm' in the legislature are the lords spiritual, the lords temporal, and the commons. The newspaper press as a power may well be called 'the fourth estate,' with a moral power far greater than the other three.

Fourth of July (*The*), or 'The glorious Fourth of July.' In American history is glorious as being the day of the Declaration of Independence (1776).

Fowler (*The*). Heinrich I. of Germany is so called, because he was flying his hawks on the slopes of the Harz mountains when the messengers came to tell him he had been chosen king.

Fox (*A*). An old English broadsword. So called because it bore the figure of a fox, the rebus of a famous sword-maker.

Come, come, comrade, . . . put up your fox, and let us be jogging.—Sir W. Scott, *Kenilworth*, ch. iv.

On point of fox. 'By the sword's point.'

Thou diest by point of fox, if thou comest a-prying to this tower once more.—*Ibid.* ch. xxix.

(Probably, 'fox' is the Latin *falx*, which is the Greek πέλεκυς, a hatchet, axe, or pruning-knife.)

Fox (*The*). A vessel of 170 tons burden, fitted out by Lady Franklin, and committed to the charge of Capt. McClintock, to go towards the North Pole to ascertain if anything could be learned of the fate of Sir John Franklin or his two ships, the 'Erebus' and 'Terror.' On 6 May, 1859, was discovered in a cairn a document stating that Sir John Franklin had died 11 June, 1847. Numerous relics of the two crews were brought home and publicly exhibited in London. It was also ascertained that Sir John had discovered the long-sought-for North-west Passage.

'Fox's Martyrs.' The 120 supporters of Charles James Fox who lost their elections when parliament was dissolved 25 March, 1784.

Foxites (2 syl.). Quakers, followers of George Fox, founder of the sect (1624–1690).

His muzzle, formed of opposition stuff, Firm as a Foxite, would not lose its ruff. Peter Pindar, *The Razor-seller*.

Fra Diavolo. Michele Pezza, one of the leaders in the Calabrian insurrection. In 1799 Cardinal Ruffo made him a colonel. He was taken captive by the French, and was hanged at Naples in 1806.

Fra Moria'le (4 syl.). Montréal d'Albano, provençal condottiere, died

1354. Being sentenced to death by Rienzi, he 'summoned' the tribune to follow him within a month, and within a month Rienzi was killed by the fickle mob.

France. (a) *The three Royal dynasties of France :—*

I. The Merovingian race (420–752), gives 34 sovereigns (including Pharamond).

II. The Carlovingian race (752–987) gives 16 sovereigns.

III. The Capetian race (987–1848) gives 37 sovereigns. But the Republic was 1792–1804; the Empire of Napoleon I. was 1804–1814. In 1848 Louis Napoleon was president, and emperor 1852–1871. In 1871 a republican form of government was established.

The Capetian dynasty was often indirect. The first nine kings were in direct descent. Then came Philippe III. *Le Hardi,* called the Philippine line, 1270–1285; the elder branch gave five kings, 1285–1328; the Valois branch gave seven kings, 1328–1498; then followed the Valois-Orléans branch, Louis XII., 1498–1515; then the Valois-Angoulême dynasty of five kings, 1515–1589; then the Bourbon race from 1589. Louis-Philippe was Bourbon-Orléans.

(b) *The six great peers of France.* In the time of Henri I. (1031–1060). The Duke of Burgundy, the Duke of Aquitaine, the Duke of Normandy, the Count of Champagne, the Count of Flanders, and the Count of Toulouse. Each of these peers had almost equal power with the king himself.

According to Ronsard (*Franciade*), the Franks were so called from Francion, son of Hector of Troy. Of course this is a poet's fable.

Franchi (*Ausonio*). The pseudonym of Francesco Bonavino, the Italian philosopher.

Francis II. (Fränz). Emperor of the Romans and king of Germany. From 6 Aug., 1806, called 'emperor of Austria'; born 1768, died 1835. He reigned as kaiser-king of Germany, 1792–1806; as emperor of Austria, 1806–1835.

Father, LEOPOLD II.; *Mother,* the Infanta Maria Louisa; *Wives,* Elizabeth of Würtemberg, mother of FERDINAND his successor, who abdicated; Maria Theresa, mother of Maria Louisa, who married Napoleon I.; Maria Louisa of Austria; and Charlotte Augusta of Bavaria. Francis II. was brother of Marie Antoinette, the unhappy wife of Louis XVI. of France, both of whom were guillotined.

He gave up the Netherlands and Lombardy by the treaty of Campo Formio, but received Venice 17 Oct., 1797.

Gave up all his possessions on the left bank of the Rhine by the treaty of Lunéville, 8 Feb., 1801.

Gave up all his Italian states, Suabia, and the Tyrol, by the treaty of Presburg, 26 Dec., 1805.

Renounced the dignity of emperor of Germany, but retained that of emperor of Austria, 6 Aug., 1806.

End of the Holy Roman Empire, 1806, after lasting 1006 years.

Francis - Joseph (Franz-Joseph), Emperor of Austria and king of Hungary and Bohemia. Born 1830, reigned 1848–

He succeeded his uncle FERDINAND, who abdicated in 1848. *Father,* Francis (younger brother of Kaiser FERDINAND), son of Francis II.; *Wife,* Elizabeth of Bavaria; contemporary with Victoria.

His son Rudolph, heir apparent to the throne, was born 1858, married Stephanie of Belgium 1881, and put an end to his life in Feb., 1889.

Franciscans (*The*), or 'Fratres Minores,' 1209. Followers of the rule of St. Francis of Assisi, originally divided into 'Conventuals' and 'Observantins.' The Conventuals lived in convents and monasteries; the Observantins (*q.v.*) were hermits, and in France were called *Cordeliers,* from the cord which they used for belt. The strictest of the Observantins were barefooted.

Récollets of Spain were formed in 1500 by Father John of Guadalupe. 'Le nom *Récollets* fut donné à ces religieux, parce qu'ils vivaient dans des couvents solitaires, et qu'ils faisaient une profession plus spéciale de la pratique de la retraite et de recueillement' (GUÉRIN, 'Pet. Boll.' xii. p. 43).

Reformed *Capucins* of Tuscany, 1525; formed by Matteo Baschi of Urbano.

The Capucins 'ont une pièce sur le derrière de leur habit, comme S. François le recommande dans son testament.' They have long beards, but St. Francis himself had a very short beard. Both the Récollets and the Capucins wear a brown dress, but Cordeliers a black one.

SECOND ORDER of St. Francis: The *Clarisses,* or followers of St. Clair. They were called, in France, 'Urbanists,' because they obtained their constitution from Urban IV. (in 1263), but generally they went by the name of 'The poor sisters Clarisses,' or the 'poor Clarisses.'

The Minories of London were so called from the Minory convent of Clarisses.

The *Grey Sisters* of Flanders were Franciscans who originally dressed in grey, but subsequently adopted either white, black, or dark blue. They took on themselves the vows of poverty, chastity, and obedience.

THIRD ORDER, instituted by St. Francis in 1221, for both sexes. These Franciscans followed their own vocations, married and were given in marriage. The Dominicans, Augustines, Minims, Carmelites, and Servites, all had a similar order.

Penitents were of this order, instituted in 1397 by Angela countess of Civitella. 'Récollettines' are reformed Penitents.

Nurses of hospitals, asylums, &c., who took on themselves the vows of chastity, poverty, and obedience to the bishop of the diocese. They went by various names. In Spain, *Minimes infirmiers*, or *Obregons*, from Bernardin Obregon of Madrid. In Flanders, *les Bons-Fieux* or *Bons Fils*.

Mgr. Guérin (vol. xii. p. 44) tells us there were 1,500 'maisons de Franciscains' and 430.000 *religieux* in England in 1380. Introduced into England in 1224. Some Franciscan tertiaries live in convents.

They were called 'Grey Friars' from the colour of their dress, as the Dominicans were called 'Black Friars,' and the Carmelites were called 'White Friars.' They were in everlasting antagonism with the Dominicans ever since 1250.

Franco-Austrian War (*The*),
1859. Between France and Austria, to deprive the latter of Italy. France was victorious. Total loss of life, 40,000. Cost of the war, 60,000,000*l*. sterling.

Franco-Prussian War (*The*),
1870, 1871. Between Napoleon III. emperor of France, and William I. king of Prussia. The French were defeated in every great battle and in every siege. The chief battles were those of Weissenburg, Wörth, Saarbrück, Vionville, Gravelotte, Beaumont, and Sedan. By these victories William I. became German emperor. This is called 'The Six Months' War' (from 28 July, 1870, to 28 Jan., 1871). Total cost of the war, 500,000,000*l*. sterling. Total loss of life, 225,000. William I., who was king of Prussia, added to his titles 'German emperor' (*Deutscher Kaiser*).

François I. le Grand.
Also called 'Le Père des Lettres.' Of the Capetian dynasty, and second of the Valois-An-

goulême line (1494, 1515-1547). The Renaissance period. François I. 'had the largest nose in France, except his jester' (Triboulet).

Father, Charles comte d'Angoulême (great-grandson of Charles V. and cousin of Louis XII., whom François succeeded); *Mother,* Louise of Savoy; *Wives,* Claude, daughter of Louis XII., mother of HENRI II. his successor, and Eleanore, widow of Emmanuel of Portugal, and sister of Charles-Quint, emperor of Germany. *Contemporary* with Henry VIII. and Leo X. His first *mistress* was the Countess of Châteaubriant; his second was Mdlle. Heilly, created duchesse d'Etampes (that is, she was married, under cover, to Jean de Brosse, who was requited by being made duc d'Etampes). Another of his mistresses was La belle Ferronnière, the nominal wife of one Ferron, an ironmonger.

CHARLES V. had two sons, CHARLES VI. and Louis duc d'Orléans.
From the former descended in direct line CHARLES VII., LOUIS XI. his son, and CHARLES VIII. No surviving issue.
Louis duc d'Orléans had also two sons—viz. Charles duc d'Orléans and Jean d'Angoulême.
LOUIS XII. was son of Charles duc d'Orléans. Jean d'Angoulême had for son Charles d'Angoulême, whose son was FRANÇOIS I.

François II. of FRANCE
(1543, 1559-60). Was son of Henri II. and grandson of François I. While dauphin he married Mary Stuart, daughter of James V. of Scotland. After his death the widow became queen of Scots and married her cousin Henry Darnley. *Contemporary* with Elizabeth.

Franco'ni (Roi).
Joachim Murat. So called by Napoleon for his theatrical display. Franconi was a pompous, conceited director of one of the minor theatres of Paris. Murat, though undoubtedly intrepid, was extremely vain, and used to parade the streets of Naples in silks and satins like a theatre king (1771-1815).

Franco'nia.
A large district of Germany lying north and south of the river Main, originally peopled by the Franks. In the early part of the empire this province enjoyed the privilege of electing the king of Germany within its own territory, and of crowning him by the hands of its own archbishop (Mainz), primate of the empire. In 912 Konrad I., count of Franconia, succeeded the Carlovingians in Germany, but gave them only

one king; but after the extinction of the Saxon dynasty, the house of Franconia succeeded in the person of Konrad II., and supplied Heinrich III., IV., and V. The house of Hohenstauffen was a branch of the same powerful line. At the close of the Hohenstauffen dynasty Franconia rapidly declined, and now forms a part of the kingdom of Bavaria.

Franconia (*House of*). Represented in Germany by one king, Konrad I. of Franconia (912-918). Succeeded by the house of Saxony. Another house of Franconia reigned in Germany (1024-1106), represented by Konrad II., Heinrich III., and Heinrich IV.

Frangistan. The country of the Franks. Europe generally was so called by the Saracens.

Others have made private offers . . . to disjoin their forces from the camp of the kings of Frangistan.—Sir W. SCOTT, *The Talisman*, chap. xv.

Frank Pledge. A law which prevailed in England before the Conquest, whereby every member of a tything was held responsible for the good conduct of everyone within the tything. Hallam says 'ten men in a village were made answerable for each other.'

Frank Tenements, or 'Freeholds.' Lay tenements which were divided into knight-service and free-socage. The former of these was divided into knight-service proper, grand-sergeanty, cornage, &c. Free-socage was divided into petit-sergeanty, tenure in burgage, and gavelkind.

Sergeanty means service rendered to the king. Grand-sergeanty was personal service, petit-sergeanty was a money or other payment as rent. This payment might be merely nominal, as the delivery of a corn of wheat or small tuft of grass, a fish, a flag, and so on.

Franks of Walla'chia (*The*), 1750. A politico-religious secret society, founded by Frank, a neophyte of Wallachia. He preserved the Jewish doctrines and the Roman-Catholic ritual. He was interred at death with royal honours, and his daughter became the Sovereign of the Faithful. The members of this sect are very numerous.

Frankfort (*Treaty of*), 10 May, 1871. A treaty of peace between Germany and France after the terrible Franco-German war.

Franking Letters. Sending letters by post free of charge. This pri-

vilege was claimed by the House of Commons in 1660, when the post-office was first legally established. Each member of parliament was entitled to send ten letters a day (not exceeding an ounce in weight) to any part of the United Kingdom, and to receive fifteen free. Members used to give franks to their friends, relations, and constituents. Abolished in 1840, when the uniform penny-post was introduced.

Cabinet ministers still send letters free of post, and letters from and to the post-office general are all free.

Franklin (*Benjamin*), 1706-90. Aged 84. Turgot happily said of him:

Eripuit cœlo fulmen, sceptrumque tyrannis.

'Eripuit cœlo fulmen' refers to his lightning conductor, and the latter clause to the part he took in American independence.

Fraternelle (*La*), 1793. A society of Parisian women, which met under the roof of the Jacobins. Each woman carried a dagger.

These were female patriots, whom the Girondins called 'Megæras,' and count to the extent of 8,000; with serpent-hair all out of curl, who have changed the distaff for the dagger. They are of the Society called *Fraternelle*, which meets under the roof of the Jacobins.—CARLYLE, *French Revolution*, vol. iii. bk. iii. 7.

Fraternity of St. George (*The*). A military order established in the reign of Edward IV. for the defence of the Irish Pale, or the four counties of Dublin, Meath, Kildare, and Louth. It consisted of 40 knights, 40 squires, and 120 archers.

In the time of John the Pale contained twelve counties.

Frates'chi (*The*), or 'Piagno'ni.' The disciples and friends of Savonarol'a, or the republican party of Florence.

Fraticelli (*The*). A section of the Italian Franciscans, founded by Father Maurato and Father de Fossombroni, who lived as hermits, and observed the rule of St. Francis in all its rigour. The Fraticelli gave out that the Church of Rome is the Babylon spoken of in the Book of the Revelation; that the rule of St. Francis was the rule observed and enjoined by Christ; that the sacraments are inutile; and that the perfection of the Christian régime is absolute poverty. This schism had a material tendency to lower the temporal authority of the papacy, and helped greatly to pave the way to the Reformation. They were joined by the Beghards (*q.v.*).

Sometimes the Fratres Minores are called Fraticelli, which means about the same thing. The term is also applied by way of contempt to the Catharists, Waldenses, and other 'heretics.'

Fratres Cellitæ. A religious order pretty common in Germany and the Netherlands ; sometimes called Mexians, from Mexius, their founder.

Fratres Conversi. Lay monks (*q.v.*).

Conversi proprie dicebantur, qui a sæculari vita, quam aliquandiu professi fuerant, vitam monachicam amplectabantur, et ad morum conversionem veniebant. Differebant a *Nutritis*, qui scilicet ab infantia in monasteriis enutriti eandem vitam amplexati erant.—DU CANGE, vol. ii. p. 703, col. 1.

Fraunhofer's Lines. The dark lines of a solar spectrum, first carefully observed and measured by Fraunhofer in 1815.

Frederick. For German kings *see* Friedrich.

Frederikshamn, in Finland (*Treaty of*), 17 Sept., 1809. A treaty of peace between Sweden and Russia, by which Sweden ceded Finland to Russia. Charles XIII. of Sweden also promised his adhesion to the 'continental system,' and closed her ports to British commerce.

Free Bench (*The*). I. The place where a lodge of the Vehmgericht (*q.v.*) was held. *See* 'Frei-grafs.

II. A widow's dower in a copyhold.

Free Burghers. Judges, with the Frei-grafs, in the Vehmgericht (*q.v.*). The president was called the grand master.

Free Church of Scotland (*The*), 1843. That part of the Presbyterian Church which resists all interference with the free choice of ministers by the congregations over which they are called to preside. No patron, no board, no trustees can present. They may nominate, but cannot over-ride the will of the congregation. Between 18–30 May as many as 470 ministers and professors signed an Act of Separation, thus renouncing all claim to the benefices which they held. *See* 'Seven Ministers,' 'Veto,' 'Voluntary Controversy,' 'Non-Intrusionists.'

The chief leaders were Drs. Chalmers, Chandler, Candlish, Welsh, Buchanan, and Gordon, with Messrs. Guthrie, Cunningham, and Dunlop.

Free Communionists, or 'Open Communionists.' Those Baptist dissenters who admit other orthodox Christians to partake with them of the Lord's Supper. John Bunyan, author of 'Pilgrim's Progress,' was a 'Free Communionist.' *See* 'Close Communionist.'

Free Coup. A term applied in Scotland to a piece of waste land where rubbish may be deposited free of charge.

Free Lances [Middle Ages]. Military rovers collected together under a free captain, and hired out by any government which wanted a ready-made army. In Italy they were called *condottieri*; in France they were called *Compagnies Grandes*.

Free Methodist Church (*The*), 1860. Their distinctive points are simplicity in dress, free pews, extempore preaching, no instrumental music, no choir. They are Wesleyans in doctrine.

Free Socage. Free tenure of land. It was divided into petit-sergeanty, tenure in burgage, and gavelkind.

Free Trade, 1779. This phrase was coined by Grattan in the Irish Parliament, and referred to the restrictions placed on the Irish trade by the British Parliament.

In the reign of Charles II. acts were passed prohibiting the Irish from sending to England either cattle, provisions, or manufactures. As labour was cheaper in Ireland, the English tradesmen, farmers, and manufacturers thought they would be ruined by Irish competition. Free Trade meant the liberty of trading freely with England.

Free Trade Battle (*The*). The struggle for the reform of our customs and excise laws, which culminated in the abolition of the corn laws in 1846. The battle may be divided into four periods : (1) From 1822 to 1830, in which Huskisson was the moving spirit ; (2) from 1830 to 1840 ; (3) from 1840–1846, when Villiers, Cobden, Sir Robert Peel, John Bright, and Lord John Russell were the most prominent characters ; and (4) from the repeal of the corn laws in 1846 onwards.

No nation has followed suit, although Cobden predicted all would within twenty years. On the contrary, all nations of Europe, America, and even our own colonies, think Free Trade a great political mistake (1890).

Free Will. The Arminians insisted on the freedom of the will to choose the right and reject the wrong. Calvinists are what is called 'Necessitarians,' *i.e.* they deny that the will is free. If the propensities of a man are evil, his will is enslaved by his evil propensities; if his heart has been changed by conversion, his will acts in obedience to the Spirit of God within him.

Freeman (*Mr. and Mrs.*). The Princess Anne and Duchess of Marlborough mutually agreed to abandon all formalities and court etiquette in their intercourse with each other. To this end Anne and her husband were to be called ' Mr. and Mrs. Morley,' while the Duke and Duchess of Marlborough were to be called ' Mr. and Mrs. Freeman.'

Freeman's Roll (*The*), 1832. A list of the Freemen (*q.v.*) made out by the town-clerk of a borough or municipal town (5, 6 Wm. IV. c. 76). As the Reform Bill did not disfranchise the freemen, a list was kept of those then living that they might still retain their municipal rights; but no new freeman was admitted, and the old 'citizens' gradually died out. *See* ' Burgess Roll.'

Freemason (*The Female*). The Hon. Mrs. Aldworth of Newmarket, co. Cork, the youngest child and only daughter of the Right Hon. Arthur St. Leger (created Viscount Doneraile 23 June, 1703). The lady concealed herself, it is said, in a clock-case, got frightened, and thus revealed her presence. It was resolved by the brotherhood, to prevent further mischief, to receive Mrs. Aldworth into the craft (*née* Elizabeth St. Leger).

In 1882 Mdlle. Marie Deraismes was received into the Grand Orient Lodge of Paris.

Freemasons. Grand Lodge held at York, under the patronage of King Edwin, A.D. 926. Henry VI. entered the order in 1442. Duke of Sussex was grand master 1813 to 1843. Besides Edwin and Henry VI., Edward the Confessor, Henry VII., William III., and George IV. were 'free accepted masons.' So were St. Dunstan, William of Wykeham, Sir Thomas Gresham, Inigo Jones, Sir Christopher Wren, and a host of others whose names are household words.

First French Lodge, at Paris   1725
First American Lodge   1730
First German Lodge, at Hamburg   1735
Grand Lodge of Scotland   1736

Freemasonry. The tenets and system of the Freemasons: 'l'exercice de la bienfaisance, l'étude de la morale universelle, et la pratique de toutes les vertus.' In French Masonry, in which I was accepted, the initiatory steps are called *Voyages*, the club-houses are called *Lodges*, and the head of a lodge is called

The Venerable (in English lodges the Master). A lodge formed is called a *Temple*. There are thirty-three degrees, but the three early ones are most important, called Apprentice, Companion, and Master. (In England the Companion is called the Craftsman or Fellow-craft.) The initiated form a council called *The Great East*, or *Grand Orient*; in England the *Grand Master*. In France there are two annual banquets to celebrate the winter and summer solstice. In England banquets are more frequent, but less significant. French Master Masons wear a highly decorated pale blue scarf, on which are hung the masonic jewels.

Freemasonry is generally traced to the building of Solomon's Temple. It was introduced into England in A.D. 674. The grand lodge at York was founded in 926. In France each lodge has an Orator, and when I was made a Master Mason in Paris the oration made to me was ' On the Immortality of the Soul.' I found the French lodges less social than those of England, but never once entered a lodge without being expected to contribute freely to some charity.

Freemen. Persons in boroughs or municipal towns who had by birth, marriage, adoption, purchase, or apprenticeship the right of citizen, from which right they were the sole electors of the municipality and members of parliament for such town or borough. At the time of the Reform Bill (1831) many of these freemen were in almshouses, many were paupers, many were in workhouses, and many in gaol, but still retained their votes, which were bought for a sum of money varying from 5l. to ten times that sum, and in some cases even more.

Freethinkers. Those who are not in bondage to any church formulary, such as creeds, articles of religion, and confessions of faith. They hold themselves free to think for themselves, and feel themselves not bound to think as councils, states, or churches think for them. Their thoughts on religious subjects are not bound, but free.

Freethinking Christians, 1799. They acknowledge no law of church government and no doctrine of faith binding but such as the New Testament teaches. They may be called Unitarians, or Deists, in that they reject the divinity of Christ, the doctrine of the atonement, the notion of original sin, the dogmas of election and reprobation, eternal punishment, angels, the immortality of the soul, and the inspiration of the Bible.

Frei Grafs. The judges of the Vehmgericht (*q.v.*). *See* 'Free Burghers.'

French Art¡sts.

1. The *Florentine* school : Jean Cousin (1492–1570), Nicolas Poussin (1594–1665), &c.

2. The *Italian-French* school : Vouet (1589–1649), Lesueur (1617–1655), Lebrun (1619–1690), Pierre Mignard (1610–1695), Jouvenet, called the ' Carracci of France ' (1647–1707), &c.

3. The *Romantic* school : Greuze (1726–1805).

4. The *Statuesque* school : J.-L. David (1748–1825).

5. The *Realistic* school : Carle Vernet (1758–1836), Horace Vernet (1789–1863), Géricault (1791–1824), &c.

6. The *Eclectic* school : Paul Delaroche (1797–1856), Delacroix, Hersent, Prudhon, Ary Scheffer, &c.

French Assembly (*The*). The legislative assembly of France is divided into Right and Left. The Right includes the Legitimists, the Orleanists, and the Imperialists. The Left includes the Republicans and the Radicals. The Legitimists are those who favoured the fortunes of the older branch of the Bourbon family, represented till 1883 by the Comte de Chambord, who was called by them 'Henri V.' The Orleanists favoured the Louis Philippe branch of the Bourbon family. On the death of the Comte de Chambord, in 1883, the Legitimists and Orleanists became united. The Imperialists favour the family of Napoleon. The Legitimists used to constitute the 'Extreme Right,' the Orleanists the 'Right Centre.' The Radicals sit in the 'Extreme Left,' and the Republicans in the ' Left Centre.'

French Brigands and insurgents. *See*

Cabochiens.	Jacquerie.
Chaperons-blancs.	Maillotins.
Communists.	Pastoureaux.
Cottereaux.	Routiers.
Ecorcheurs.	

French Byron (*The*). Alfred de Musset (1810–1857).

Paul de Musset has gone to rejoin his brother, the French Byron—a less powerful Byron than yours, yet a poet to the tips of his fingers.—ED. ABOUT, *To the Athenæum*, 3 July, 1880.

French Club (*The*), 1792. A federation of artisans and soldiers of the national guard, who had weapons concealed in the building where they met (near the Tuileries), with which they were to arm themselves and rush to the defence of the king if his life was threatened by any of the desperadoes of the Paris mob. This club cost the court 10,000 francs a day (400*l.*).

French Crown (*The*). Made in 1791, contained the following diamonds : The Regent, the Blue Diamond, the Sancy, the Golden Blies, the Crown diamond, the Ebenda, the Mirror of Portugal, the Tenth Mazarine, and a large number of others without specific names. Valued at 588,112*l.* when, in 1810, Napoleon commanded the crown jewels to be re-valued ; but in 1791 they were supposed to be worth 807,808*l.*

French Ennius (*The*). Guillaume de Lorris (1235–1265), author of the first part of the ' Roman de la Rose ' (*q.v.*).

French Florentine School of Painters (*The*). Includes Cousin (1492–1570) and Nicolas Poussin (1594–1665).

French Fury (*The*), 1582. The Duke of Anjou and Brabant had been recently raised to the sovereignty of the Netherlands; but, finding the Prince of Orange a great check on his actions, resolved to make himself in one day master of all the towns in which were French garrisons. The seizure of Antwerp fell to the Duke's lot, and he assembled his soldiers in the city, ostensibly for a review. At a given sign the French troops fell on the burghers, and set fire to the city. The burghers drove the French soldiers out of the city. Above 1,500 fell, among whom were 260 of noble rank. The biter was bit, and the French were victims of their own ' Fury.'

French Iso′cratês (*The*). Fléchier, bishop of Nismes (1632–1710). Florid, antithetical, and elegant in style. His masterpiece is his oration over Marshal Turenne.

French Maccabæus (*The*). Simon de Montfort (1150–1215), the most celebrated military genius of the 12th cent Entrusted by Philippe II. (Auguste) with the crusade against the Albigenses in the south of France (1208–1218).

French Ovid (*The*). Du Bellay, one of the *Pléiade Française* (1524–1560), called also the 'Father of Grace and Elegance.' Spenser speaks of him as 'first garland of free poesy that France brought forth.'

The word *Olive*, the title of his 115 sonnets, is an anagram of Viole, the name of the lady whom he celebrates, as Petrarch shadowed forth his Laura under the figure of a laurel.

French Painters (*Mediæval*).

Nicolas Poussin	1594–1665
Claude le Lorrain [*Claude Gelée*].	1600–1682
Bourdon	1616–1671
Le Sueur	1617–1655
Le Brun	1619–1790

French Peasant Relief Fund (*The*). Originated by the 'Daily News' Sept. 1870 and closed April 1871.

French Phidias (*The*). J. B. Pigalle (2 syl.), 1714–1784.

His nude statue of Voltaire is, however, well-nigh ridiculous.

French Pindar (*The*). Two of the French poets are so designated: (1) Jean Dorat (1507–1588); and (2) Ponce Denis Lebrun (1729–1807).

French Pléiade (*The*). 'La Pléiade Française' in the reign of Henri III. (1574–1589), composed of the seven poets Ronsard, Du Bellay, Remi Belleau, Jodelle, Baïf, Pontus de Thiard, and the seventh was either Dorat or Amadis Jamyn.

Under Louis XIII. (1610–1643) was a second batch called *La Pléiade Française*, and consisting of Rapin, Commire, Larue, Santeuil, Ménage, Dupérier, and Petit.

The term is borrowed from the Alexandrians under Ptolemy Philadelphos, who so called seven contemporaneous poets, viz. Lycophron, Theocrites, Arâtos, Nicander, Apollonios, Callimachos, and Philiscos (called Homer the younger).

French Propertius (*The*). Antoine Bertin, who died 1790, at the age of 38. He possessed the brilliant imagination and also the licentiousness of the Latin poet.

French Raphael (*The*). Lesueur (1617–1655).

French Revolution. I. John Karrion, elector of Brandenburg, more than two centuries before the French Revolution, says (in his journal (still in MS.): 'Alors sera l'une des plus grandes conjonctions et la dixième totale rénantion (*sic*) de Saturne, laquelle, après la Nativitey de Nostre Seigneur, mil vii cents et lxxxix, sera totalement accomplie; et si le monde doit après plus durer, nul ne scait (*sic*) sinon Dieu. O quelles grandes merveilles l'on verra ad'onc (*sic*), tant de variations et destructions, principalement ès constitutions et ordinances chrestiennes . . . &c.'

Against the year 1525 he has these words: 'Il y auroit grand effusion de sang des chrestiens, et grandes oppressions d'aulcuns grands fiefz.'

II. Between 1719 and 1889 there have been seventeen revolutions in France. The Reign of Terror and that of Napoleon were terrible for their slaughter.

The accumulated deficit of France in ten years, ending 1889, was 240 millions sterling. The revenue has fallen short of the expenses about 24 millions sterling annually.

The financial embarrassment which led to the Great Revolution was a little over two millions sterling.

The financial embarrassment in 1889 was, in round numbers, 1,686 millions sterling.

The public debt of Great Britain in 1890 was 599 millions; of France 1,286 millions.

In ten years the public debt of Great Britain (1889) has decreased 68 millions sterling; of France it has increased 240 millions. Mr. Goschen in 1889 reduced it 20 millions.

French Revolution (*The First*). From 5 May, 1789, to 27 July, 1794.

Chief Leaders of the First French Revolution :—

Comte de Mirabeau, 1789 1791.
Danton, from the death of Mirabeau to 1793.
Robespierre, from June 1793 to 27 July, 1794.
Next to these three were St. Just, Couthon, Marat, Carrier, Hébert, Santerre, Camille Desmoulins, Roland and his wife, Brissot, Bernave, Sieyès, Barras, Tallien, &c.

Great Days of the First French Revolution :—

1789. 17 June. The *Tiers Etat* constituted itself into the 'National Assembly'; 20 June, the day of the *Jeu de Paume*, when the Assembly took an oath not to separate till it had given France a constitution; 14 July, Storming of the Bastille; 5, 6 Oct., the king and National Assembly transferred from Versailles to Paris. This closed the ancient *régime* of the court.
1791. 20, 21 June. Flight and capture of the king, queen, and royal family.
1792. 20 June, attack on the Tuileries by Santerre; 10 Aug., attack on the Tuileries and downfall of the monarchy; 2, 3, 4 Sept., massacre of the state prisoners.
1793. 21 Jan., Louis XVI. guillotined; 31 May, commencement of the Reign of Terror; 2 June, the Girondists proscribed; 16 Oct., Marie Antoinette guillotined; 31 Oct., the Girondists guillotined.
1794. 5 April, downfall of Danton; 27 July, downfall of Robespierre.

French Revolution of Feb. 1848. See under Revolution,' &c.

French Revolution of July 1830. *See* under ' Revolution,' &c.

French Roscius (*The*). François Talma (1770–1826), the greatest of French tragedians. Roscius the great actor was a comedian.

French Theatre (*Founder of the*). Rotrou (1609–1650). Corneille calls him his *father.*

French Triumvirate (*The*), 1560. François duc de Guise, Marshal St. André, and the Comte de Montmorency, who leagued together against the queen mother Catherine de' Medici. They were leaders of the high Catholic party, and irreconcilable enemies of the Huguenots.

French Vegetius (*The*). The Chevalier de Folard, born at Avignon (1669–1752).

French of the East (*The*). The Persians. ' Vanity ' (says James Morier) ' is their besetting sin, and that alone will account for the lust of compliment which prevails in both nations.'

French of the North (*The*). The Poles. So called from their vivacity, fickleness, love of society, and quickness of parts.

Frenchmen. It was Voltaire who described his countrymen as ' half monkey and half tiger.'

Frères Bleus (*Les*). Affiliated Philadelphians, whose object was the restoration of the Bourbons. They were organised by Lieut.-Colonel Oudet. *See* ' Philadelphic Society.'

Frères Mineurs. *See* ' Fraticelli.'

Frères Prêcheurs, or ' Preaching Friars.' Dominicans (*q.v.*).

Frères de la Milice du Christ. *See* ' Chevaliers Porte-glaive.'

Pronounce *Frair d'lah me-leece; She-val-le-ay port glaiv.*

Frères de la Mort (*Les*). The Eremites of St. Paul, 13th cent., whose special province was to look after the sick and preside at funerals. They had on their scapulary a death's head, which they kissed by way of grace before meat, and laid beside them.

Friar Bacon's Study. On Folly Bridge, Oxford. A gateway tower to defend the passage and keep out undesirable intruders.

Friars (*The Four Branches of*). (1) Augustine Friars, or mendicants; (2) Franciscans, or Grey Friars ; (3) Dominicans, or Black Friars; (4) Carmelites, or White Friars.

The Franciscans and Dominicans were always ' cat and dog.'

Friars Conventual. The first order of St. Francis of Assisi was divided into ' Conventuels ' and ' Observatins.'

On les appela conventuels parce qu'ils vivaient dans de grands couvents, au lieu que ceux qui suivaient la régle dans toute sa pureté demeuraient dans des ermitages, ou dans des maisons basses et pauvres.—Mgr. GUÉRIN, *Les Petits Bollandistes*, vol. xii. p. 42.

Friars Observant. Those Franciscans who dwelt in hermitages or huts, observing the rule of St. Francis in all its length and breadth. Those who dwelt in convents were called ' Conventuals ' (*see above*). There were four classes of Observants : (1) the Observatins, constituted in 1363 ; (2) those who followed the strict observance ; (3) those of the Order of Mercy, called ' the Great Observants' ; and (4) the Preaching Friars of the primitive observance who were reformed Dominicans.

All the Friars Observant were [1535] ejected from their monasteries and dispersed. Some were thrust into prisons, and others were confined in the houses of the Friars Conventual.—HOWITT, *History of England*, vol. ii. p. 215.

Friars Minor (*The*), or ' Minorites ' (3 syl.), 1209. Founded by St. Francis of Assisi. They arrived in England in 1224, and were called ' Grey Friars ' from the colour of their dress.

Subsequently divided into Observants, Conventuals, Capuchins, Récollets, Cordeliers, &c.

Friday Lucky to the United States. On Friday, 21 Aug., 1492, Christopher Columbus sailed on his great voyage of discovery. On Friday, 12 Oct., 1492, he first discovered land. On Friday, 4 Jan., 1493, he sailed on his return voyage to Spain. On Friday, 14 March, 1493, he arrived at Palos in safety. On Friday, 22 Nov., 1493, he arrived at Hispaniola in his second voyage to America. On Friday, 13 June, 1494, he discovered the continent of America. On Friday, 5 March, 1496, Henry VIII. gave John Cabot his commission. On Friday, 7 Sept., 1565, Melendez founded St. Augustine, the oldest town in the U.S. On Friday, 10 Nov., 1620, the ' Mayflower,' with the Pilgrim Fathers, made the harbour of Provincetown. On Friday, 22 Dec., 1620, the Pilgrim Fathers landed at Plymouth rock. On Friday, 22 Feb., George Washington was born. On Friday, 16 June, Bunker Hill was seized and fortified. On Friday, 17 Oct., 1777, the surrender of Saratoga was made. On Friday, 22 Sept., 1780, the treason of Arnold was laid bare. On Friday, 19 Sept., 1791, was the surrender of York Town. On Friday, 7 July, 1776, the motion was made by John Adams that the U.S. are and ought to be independent. The 'Great Eastern' sailed from Valentia on Friday, 13 July, 1866, and landed safely at Heart's Content (Newfoundland), with the 'cable,' Friday, 27 the same month ('Norfolk Beacon,' U.S.).

Aurengzebe considered Friday a lucky day, and used to say in prayer, 'O that I may die on a Friday, for blessed is he who dies on that day!'

Friday (*Unlucky*). Friday, 5 Oct., B.C. 105, was marked *nefastus* in the Roman calendar, because on that day Marcus Mallius and Cæpio the consul were slain, and their whole army was annihilated in Gallia Narbonensis by the Cimbrians.

Considered very unlucky in Spain.

It is deemed an unlucky day by Buddhists and Brahmins.

The reason given by Christians for its ill-luck is because it was the day of Christ's crucifixion; but surely that is not an 'unlucky' event to Christians.

A Friday moon is unlucky for weather.

Friedrich I. Barbarossa, or Red Beard. 'The father of his country.' Kaiser-king of Germany (1121, 1152–1190). Drowned while fording the Selef, a river of Cilicia. Second of the house of Hohenstauffen or Suabia. He was the first king to set pendant seals to diplomas.

Father, Friedrich duke of Suabia, brother of KONRAD III., founder of the dynasty. *Mother*, Agnes sister of Heinrich the Proud. *Wives*, Adelaide, repudiated; Beatrice of Burgundy, mother of his son and successor HEINRICH VI. *Contemporary* with Stephen, Henry II., and Richard I. (Cœur de Lion).

Of course, KONRAD III. was his uncle.

Friedrich II. Iron Tooth, son of Friedrich I. count of Hohenzollern,

elector of Brandenburg. So called because he showed his teeth to the unruly barons who presumed on his youth to rebel against him. He abdicated in 1470 in favour of his brother Albert [Albrecht], the Achilles and Ulysses of Germany.

Friedrich II. The Wonder of the World. Kaiser-king of Germany (1194, 1215–1250). Probably poisoned by his son Manfroi, who poisoned his brother Konrad in 1254.

Father, HEINRICH VI. *Mother*, Constance, heiress of the Two Sicilies. *Wives*, Constance of Aragon; Yolande, or Iolanthe, daughter of the king of Jerusalem, mother of KONRAD IV., who succeeded him; and Isabella daughter of Henry III. of England. *Contemporary* with John and Henry III.

Kaiser Otto III. (983-1002) was also called 'The Wonder of the World.'

Friedrich III. the Pacific, or, rather, 'the Indolent.' Second of the Habsburg line of kings (1415, 1440–1493), the longest reign of the kaiser-kings of Germany. Emperor of the Romans 1452, and this was the last time that any German king was crowned at Rome. It was this *roi fainéant* that adopted the five vowels for the imperial device, meaning 'Austriæ Est Imperare Orbi Universo,' or 'Alles Erdreich Ist Oesterreich Unterthan'; in English, 'Austria's Empire Is Overall Universal.' Like his predecessor and successor Maximilian, he died of dysentery by indulging too freely in a melon. Three successive kings died of melon-colic.

Father, Ernst duke of Austria. *Mother*, Cimburgis, a Polish princess. *Wife*, Eleonore daughter of Edward king of Portugal. *Son* and successor, Maximilian I. *Contemporary* with Henry VI., Edward IV., Edward V., Richard III., and Henry VII.

** Ernst father of Friedrich III. was cousin of Kaiser ALBERT II., who married Elizabeth daughter of Kaiser SIEGMUND or SIGISMUND.

Friedrich III. kaiser-king of Germany reigned 53 years (1440 1493), and died at the age of 78.
George III. of Great Britain reigned 60 years (1760-1820), and died at the age of 82.
Louis XIV. of France reigned 72 years (1648-1715), and died at the age of 77.

Friedrich the Handsome. A rival claimant of the German throne with Ludwig V. Both were elected and both crowned, but Friedrich, being defeated at the battle of Mühldorf in 1322, was imprisoned, and Ludwig remained king.

Friedrich Wilhelm IV. of Prussia (1795, 1840–1861); son of Frederick William III. *Father*, FRIEDRICH WILHELM III.; *Mother*, Louisa Augusta of Mecklenburg-Strelitz; *Wife*, Elizabeth Louisa of Bavaria; *Son*, Wilhelm I. king of Prussia and German emperor. *Contemporary* with Queen Victoria.

Friends (*The Society of*), 1624. Quakers, a sect founded by George Fox, of Drayton, in Leicestershire, a shoemaker. They believe in the main fundamental principles of what is called 'Orthodox Christianity,' but they express their religious creed in the very words of the New Testament Scripture, and each member has the liberty of interpreting the words. Their main speciality is the belief of 'the Light of Christ in man,' and hence they entertain a broader view of the Spirit's influence than other Christians.

In morals, propriety of conduct, good order, and philanthropy, the Quakers are a pattern society.

Friends of God (*The*), 1370–1400. A brotherhood formed by Nicholas of Basel, which protested against the sacerdotalism of Germany and Switzerland.

Friends of Liberty and Equality (*The*), 1794. An Hungarian secret society, organised by Martinovics for the purpose of introducing the principles of the French Revolution. The society had not been in existence many months when it was stamped out, Martinovics and six others being executed by the sword in a field near Buda, still called 'the field of blood.'

Friends of Truth (*The*). Quakers were so-called in the seventeenth century. They are now called 'Friends.'

Friends of the People (*The*), April 1792. A political association formed in London for the purpose of obtaining a reform in the representation of the people. Headed by Gray, Baker, Whitbread, Sheridan, Lambton, and Erskine.

Frith Gild. A peace-club or voluntary society pledged to the maintenance of peace and mutual security. A member of the gild was called a 'Frith-man,' and a breaking of the peace was a 'Frith-breach.' These Frithgilds were very general throughout Europe in the 9th and

10th cents. Our friendly societies are 'Frith-gilds.'

Fronde (*La*), 1648–1653. A French insurrection provoked by the meanness and arrogance of Mazarin, the chief minister, while Louis XIV. was still a minor. At length the chief nobility united in a grand council, and insisted on a reform, such as the abolition of monopolies, the reduction of taxes, the examination of public expenditure, prohibition of arrest without assigning a cause, and so on. Mazarin resisted, and even arrested Blancménil (president of the council), and Broussel, a conspicuous member. All Paris rose in insurrection, and compelled Mazarin to release his prisoners. Mazarin and the queen-mother fled, and both parties prepared for war. The insurgents soon disagreed among themselves, and Mazarin, at the head of 8,000 men, returned to Paris in triumph. The insurgents in this riot were called *Frondeurs*, and the court party were called *Mazarinians* (*q.v.*).

Monglat thus explains the term. He says that the Paris parlement forbade boys to sling stones, and one day a young barrister said, 'Quand ce sera mon tour, je *fronderai* bien l'opinion de mon père.' Here *fronderai* means to combat, to oppose; but the whole point of the remark was in allusion to the Fronde war, and therefore it could not have originated the term.

The word became popular slang for several years. Everything was *à la Fronde*. There were Fronde hats, coats, and gloves; Fronde muffs and fans; Fronde dishes and loaves of bread; Fronde songs and tunes

Fronde (*The Little*), 1650. The great Condé, in the guerre de la Fronde, was originally of the court or Mazarin party, but he quarrelled with the party, and made a split called 'the Little Fronde.' This was a third party, for though Condé hated Mazarin much, he hated the parliamentarians more.

Frondeurs. Slingers, common in the Spanish armies in the 13th and 14th cents. The natives of the Balearic Isles were most noted slingers. The Greeks, Romans, and Carthaginians had companies of slingers; so had the French and German. But the word is chiefly associated with the insurgents of the Fronde war, called les Frondeurs, who were opposed to the court party called Mazarinians (*q.v.*).

Fruc'tidor (*Dix-huit*), *i.e.* 4 Sept., 1797. A noted *coup d'état*, by the majority of the Directory against Barthélemy and Carnot, and against those members, both of the Conseil des Cinq-cents and of the Conseil des Anciens, thought to be favourable to royalty. The three directors were Barras, Laréveillère-Lepaux, and Rewbell. The result of this revolution was the deportation of the two directors, 11 members of the Conseil des Anciens, 42 members of the Conseil des Cinq-cents, 35 journalists, a host of priests, and numerous others called 'conspirators.'

Fuero Jusgo (*The*). The code of the Visigoths in Spain.

Fueros (*The*). The written laws of Jaca (Spain), the most ancient of Europe. They were confirmed by Alfonso III., and called 'the Ancient Usages of Jaca.' Fuero = charter, statute, or code of laws.

There were the 'Fuero of Leon,' the 'Fuero of Naxera,' the 'Basque fueros,' &c., which were charters. These charters were abolished by Espartero, but restored in 1844 by Queen Isabella.

Fugger (*Antony*). A modern Crœsus. When Charles-Quint was shown by François I. the royal treasury in Paris, he said to the king, 'There is a linen-weaver in Augsburg that could pay for all this out of his own purse.'

Fuh-he. First of the five emperors of China. Like the old kings of Rome, the mythological kings of China represent five periods and not five persons. To Fuh-he is attributed the invention of writing, and he is said to have taught the people the art of rearing cattle, fishing, &c., and to have instituted the rite of marriage. Musical instruments are also attributed to this mythical king.

Fullers and Weavers of Ghent (*The*), 1344. A trade dispute, in which Jacob von Artevelde, the great brewer, sided with the fullers, and Gerrard Denys with the weavers. In a battle fought in the market-place as many as 1,500 fullers were slain, and trade was utterly ruined. Artevelde (4 syl.) was assassinated 9 July, 1345.

Fum. A kind of cock, often represented on Chinese works of art, and embroidered on the dresses of mandarins of a certain rank. Like the roc of the Arabs and the phœnix of the Egyptians, the Chinese 'fum' is mythological. It is a salamander, with the head of a goose, the hindquarters of a stag, the neck of a snake, the tail of a fish, the forehead and beak of a cock, and the back of a tortoise.

It is about 6 cubits high, and is called 'the mandarin of time.'

Fum (*George IV.*). Fum 'the Chinese bird of royalty' was represented on the ceiling of the staircase at the north end of the main corridor of the Brighton Pavilion (then called the Chinese Gallery).

And where is Fum the Fourth, our royal bird,
Gone down, it seems to Scotland. . . .
         BYRON, *Don Juan*, xi. 78.
One day the Chinese bird of royalty—Fum,
Thus accosted our own bird of royalty—Hum,
In that palace or china-shop, Brighton, which is it?
When Fum had just come to pay Hum a visit.
     THOMAS BROWN (MOORE), *The Fudge Family in Paris*.

Here, 'Fum' seems to mean **Louis of France**, and 'Hum' **George IV.**

Fundamental Law (*The*), 29 Sept. (Oct. 11), 1862, Russia. The whole judicial system of Russia was then settled on a new basis, securing the independence of the courts of justice, the limitation of the courts of appeal, the introduction of the jury system in criminal cases, and the appointment of judges by the state. It is framed in three parts, the first treating of the constitution of the courts in 91 articles; the second of criminal procedure in 157 articles; and the third of civil procedure in 138 articles. By the first, judicial power is vested in justices of the peace, with the senate as a final court of appeal. By the second, prosecution is placed under the control of a public prosecutor. By the third, it was decreed that there should be in future two courts of appeal.

Fuor-Usciti (*The*), or the 'turned-out ones.' So were called those persons of the Neri and Bianchi (Blacks and Whites) who were exiled by the faction which for the time being had the upper hand. Dante, a White, was one of the *Fuor-Usciti* (1302). Singular of *Fuor-Usciti* is *Fuor-Uscito.*

Let Florence perish, so long as the *Fuor-Usciti* get back to the city; let her streets run with blood, her treasure be exhausted, her foes victorious, until the *Fuor-Usciti* be within her walls again.—Mrs. OLIPHANT, *Makers of Florence*, p. 54.

Furies of the Guillotine (*The*). The Tricoteuses, or women who frequented the public clubs and revolutionary tribunal of France, where they sat knitting, and openly expressed their approval or disapproval of the proceedings. With the fall of the Jacobins they disappeared.

A A

They were called *Tricoteuses* from their knitting, and *Furies* from their violence.

Furor Berser'kicus. An artifice of battle among the Danes, like the Indian war-whoop. In this furor the men tried to resemble wild beasts, such as wolves and dogs. They bit their shields; they howled; they threw off their clothing; they rushed about frantically; they made hideous faces. It was at length made penal.

Eric earl of Norway *Omnes berserkos Norwegia exulare jussit* (Grettis Saga, p. 142).

Furry Dance (*A*). A processional dance in May consisting of thirty or more couples, who danced to the ancient Celtic Furry tune in at the front door of houses and out at the back door. It differed from the May dance, which was round a May-pole. In Lithuania processional dances on the octave of May-day have existed from time immemorial.

Sometimes, but erroneously, called the 'Flora Dance,' or Floralia.

Fürstenbund (*The*), March 1785. The alliance of Friedrich II. (the Great) of Prussia with the Electors of Saxony and Hanover, for the maintenance of the German constitution. By this masterstroke of policy Friedrich defeated the kaiser's plot of adding Bavaria to Austria.

Fuste et bac'ulo. 'By staff and bâton,' commonly called 'tenure by the verge.' A mode of tradition or delivery of *real property* where there is no house. In France, seisin was made by delivery of a bâton or pair of gloves; in Lombardy by a spear; in Germany by a clod or twig; in Scotland by a pen.

Fuste (Latin) in 2 syl.

Fyzoola Khan. The charge brought by Mr. Wyndham against Warren Hastings, governor-general of India, was his conduct to Fyzoola Khan, the Rohilla chief, 1787. The basis of the charge was this: The Nabob of Oudh wanted to seize certain lands belonging to the Rohilla chief, and gave Hastings 100,000*l.* to help him in this seizure. Hastings now told the Rohilla chief if he would give him one and a half million sterling he would guarantee his retention of these lands. Fyzoola (3 syl.) replied he did not possess so much money, and the matter was allowed to drop.

G. Cornwall. George IV. so signed his private letters to his personal friends. *See* 'N. & Q.,' 19 April, 1884, p. 305.

G of Edward's Race. There was a 'prophecy' afloat in the reign of Edward IV. that the king's son would perish by the hands of a person whose name began with G. Clarence, the king's brother, was named George, and Edward, with the Woodvilles, always suspected him of aiming at the crown. Fabyan says that Clarence was drowned in the Tower in a butt of Malmsey wine, but he left behind a brother Richard duke of Gloucester, who was generally credited with the death of Edward V. as well as with that of Margaret's son Edward, the Duke of Clarence, Henry VI., and many others.

Gabelle. From the German *gabe*, tribute, impost, was a tax imposed on salt by Philippe IV. le Bel in 1286, and was one of the causes of the revolution. There were many other gabelles, as the *gabelle des draps*, *gabelle des vins*, *gabelle de tonlieu* (standing in the markets for sale), &c.; but when used alone it always means the tax on salt. The king had the monopoly of this article, and every person was compelled to buy at least 7 lbs. of it yearly, whether wanted or not. Heads of families had to buy the same quantity for each member of their establishment; but no one was allowed to use this salt for pickling or corning beef. Another injustice was this: the price varied in different provinces; thus, what would cost 32*s.* in other provinces, was sold by government in Auvergne for 8*s.* As many as 8,000 persons were annually imprisoned in France for infringing the salt laws. *See* 'Pays de Grande Gabelle,' 'Pays de Petite Gabelle.'

Not till 1340 was the tax extended to all France. Edward III. with a pun called it *La Loi Salique*.

HISTORY OF LA GABELLE.

Imposed by the Etats Généraux in 1353, and abolished by the Assemblée Constituante 10 May, 1790. It brought into the revenue at one time as much as 60,000,000 livres, and in the reign of Louis XVI. 38,000,000 francs. Some provinces redeemed the tax, others obtained (from sundry causes) exemption from additions to the original levy, so that the greatest inequality existed, and at the time of the revolution one-third of the country paid two-thirds of the tax. Between 1549 and 1553, Poitou, Saintonge, Aunis, Anjou, Limousin, La Marche, Périgord, and Upper Guienne, redeemed the tax; other provinces bought off a partial exemption; while Artois, Flanders, Hénault, Calais, the Boulonnais, Alsace, Béarn, Lower Navarre, and other modern acquisitions of the crown were, like Brittany, wholly exempt from the tax. This inequality of necessity was the cause of smuggling, and we are told that every year there were more than '4,000 saisies domiciliaires, plus de 3,400 emprisonnemens, et plus de 500 condamnations à des peines capitales ou afflictives.' It seems that a temporary tax on salt was imposed by an ordinance of Louis IX. as far back as 1246, by Philippe le Bel in 1286, again by Philippe VI. de Valois in 1340, and in 1353 by the Etats Généraux ' pour des besoins momentanés.' Discontinued in 1358; but Charles V. (1364–1380) made it a permanent tax. Wholly suppressed 28 March, 1790.

Gaberlun′zies. Licensed beggars who were compelled to wear a badge to distinguish themselves from the Thiggers and Scorners (*q.v.*). Gaberlunzies were called blue-gowns in England.

Gadel′ian Conquest of Ireland (*The*). Gadelus or Gathelus, an Egyptian and contemporary of Moses, was the son of Scota (daughter of a Pharaoh of Egypt). He descended on Ireland under the conduct of two sons of Milesius (king of Spain), B.C. 1372, and utterly subdued the race of Tuath. From these Gadelians all the kings of Ireland, down to the English conquest in A.D. 1172, descended, and in Irish history are called the ' princes of the Milesian race.'

We are also told that the Irish are called *Scots* from Scota, the Egyptian princess. Of course these traditions must not be accepted as historical facts, but they are necessary to be known.

Gaelic. Comprehends the Irish, the Highland-Scotch, and the Manx languages.

Gagging Act (*The*). In England, 1795 (36 Geo. III. cc. 7, 8), for treason and sedition.

Gaisford Prizes (*The*). One for Greek prose and one for Greek verse. Oxford University. Founded by subscription in memory of Dr. Thomas

Gaisford, dean of Christ Church, regius professor of Greek, 1856.

Galeazzo's Lent. A system of torture calculated to prolong the victim's life for forty days. It was the invention of Galeazzo Visconti, lord of Milan (1277, 1322–1328).

Galenists. A branch of Mennonists, founded by Galenus in 1664. They advocate freer views both in doctrine and discipline than the strict Mennonites. *See* 'Mennonites.'

Galile′ans. Those Jews who held it unlawful to obey a heathen magistrate. Josephus says they agreed in all things with the Pharisees, but insisted that they owed subjection and obedience only to God. When (Luke xxiii. 5) Jesus was represented to Pilate as a Galilean, an insinuation was made that he acknowledged no obedience to Cæsar.

Probably all that was meant is that he was a native of that province. Julian said in his dying moments, ' Thou hast conquered, O Galilean !' The disciples of Jesus were called Galileans (Acts ii. 7).

Galley Ha′pence (*The*). Genoan coins brought into England by the galleymen who came hither with wine and other merchandise. They were broader than the English ha'penny, but not so thick. They were prohibited by Henry IV. as a legal tender.

Galleys (*The*). As a punishment in France was fixed by an ordinance of Charles IX. in 1564, to be not less than ten years. The bagnes were substituted for the galleys in 1748 ; and the name was changed to *travaux forcés* by the Constituent Assembly in 1798. By the Code Napoléon in 1810, the sentence of *travaux forcés* included forfeiture, infamy, and branding. Branding was abolished in 1832, and *travaux forcés* in 1852.

Gallia. The country of the Galli or Gauls. The Latin *Galli* and Greek Γαλ-λάται are classic forms of the word *Keltai* (Celts). The German form is *Waelchs*, whence our word *Welch*. Gallia, Wales, and Walloon, all mean the ' land of the Celts.'

For a familiar instance of the interchange of G and W compare Guillaume and William.

Gallia Bracca′ta. Later on, Gallia Narbonensis. Called ' Braccāta ' from the *braccæ* or trousers worn by the natives.

Gallia Coma'ta. All Transalpine Gaul except Gallia Braccāta (*q.v.*). So called from the long hair worn (*coma*). It included Belgĭca, Celtica, and Aquitanica.

Gallia Narbonensis corresponded with the ancient provinces of Languedoc, Provence, and Dauphiné.

Gallic Cæsar (*The*). Napoleon I.

Galli·can Church (*The*). The *liberties* of the Gallican Church were asserted in 1438 in the Pragmatic Sanction (*q.v.*); and in 1512 by the Concordat (*q.v.*) between Pope Leo X. and François I.; and were distinctly defined by Bossuet in 1682 in his famous 'Four Articles' (*q.v.*).

Galli·c Confession (*The*), 1599. One of the chief continental confessions of faith by the Calvinistic or Reformed Church of France. *See* 'Confessions.'

Gallican Liberties, 1682. As opposed to Ultramontanism (*q.v.*) were thus summarised by Bossuet:—

Que l'Eglise doit être réglé par les canons ; que saint Pierre et ses successeurs n'ont reçu de puissance que sur les choses spirituelles ; que les règles et les constitutions admises dans le royaume doivent être maintenus, et les bornes posées par nos pères demeurer inébranlables ; que les décrets et jugements du pape ne sont irréformables qu'autant que le consentement de l'eglise est intervenu . . . &c.

.·. The defenders of the *libertés gallicanes* were Hincmar, Gerson, Bossuet, the Abbé Fleury, the Cardinal de la Luzerne, Bausset, Frayssinous, Guillon, Boyer, Affre, &c.

Gallican Liturgy (*The*). Dates from before the time of Pepin (9th cent.). It is based on the Oriental liturgies, because the first missionaries of Gaul were from Greece. It remained in use till Charlemagne introduced the Gregorian liturgy. The liturgy now used in France is the Roman, with some slight alterations. *See* 'Ambrosian Liturgy,' 'Spanish Liturgy,' &c.

Gallican Missal. *See above.*

Gallicans (*The*). Catholics who insist on what they call the *libertés gallicanes,* one of which is the distinct separation of the spiritual and temporal powers. They place 'infallibility' not in the pope, but in the whole church presided over by the pope. They acknowledge the authority of General Councils. *See* 'Gallican Liberties.'

Gal'lowglasses and Kernes. 'Gallowglasses' were ancient Irish heavy-armed foot-soldiers ; but 'Kernes' were Irish foot-soldiers of very mean condition, and without armour. *See* the 'Cent. Mag.' 1890, p. 296.

Game Chicken (*The*). Pearce, the prize-fighter. He fought with John Gully, who was taken out of the debtors' prison by Colonel Mellish to fight this champion of the ring. Gully was beaten, but afterwards fought Gregson twice, and then retired, to settle at Newmarket.

Game Laws. Before the *Carta de Foresta,* 1224, the killing of game was punishable with death. Qualifications to kill game were introduced in 1389. Annual certificates required by 25 Geo. III. c. 50 (1785). Permission to sell game given by 1, 2 Will. IV. c. 32 (1831).

I⸱ France game laws were abolished in 1789.
(a ᵔe includes hares, pheasants, partridges, g o⸱s⸳, heath and moor fowls, black-game, and bi se⸳rds. The close season is their respective times of breeding and rearing.

Gangway. *To sit below the gangway* in the House of Commons, to sit among the independent members. The gangway is a passage running across the house, which separates the supporters of the government and the opposition from the independent members.

In a ship the gangway is the way out or into the ship. Ang.-Sax. *gangan,* to go. ●

Gants Glacés (*Les*). The Black Mousquetaires during the Fronde war. Very dandified, but brave and daring. *See* 'Mousquetaire.'

Gaoler of Napoleon at St. Helena (*The*). Sir Hudson Lowe, military governor of St. Helĕna while Napoleon was there in banishment.

Gaping Gulf (*The*). A book published by John Stubbs, a student of Lincoln's Inn, showing how undesirable it was that Queen Elizabeth should marry the Duc d'Anjou, especially after the frightful massacre of the Huguenots on St. Bartholomew's eve. Stubbs and his publisher were seized and taken to the market-place of Westminster, where both had their right hand cut off by driving a cleaver through the wrist with a mallet. The moment Stubbs lost his hand, he waved his cap with his left hand, crying 'Long live the queen!'

Garde Doloureuse. A castle in the marches of Wales, so called because it was greatly exposed to attacks by the Welsh.

Garde Impériale (*La*), 1804. Called before the *Garde Consulaire*, and organised in 1799. It first consisted of 9,775 men, but in 1814 the number was increased to 102,706 men. In 1809 it was subdivided into the *Vieille Garde* and the *Jeune Garde*, and admission into it was given only as recompense for merit, and after having served in three campaigns.

It was re-established in 1856 by Napoleon III.

Garde Mobile (*La*), 1848. Composed chiefly of young soldiers, and ranking between the *Garde Nationale* and the general army. It was a species of *Garde Nationale Mobile* for Paris only. It consisted of 24 battalions of 1,000 men each.

Garde Municipale de Paris (*La*), 1802–1813, and again 1830–1848. The guard charged with the preservation of good order in the city of Paris. In the old monarchy this guard was called the *guet*, suppressed in 1792, when it was supplanted by the *gendarmerie*, changed in 1795 into the *Légion de police générale* of 5,844 men. In 1813 it took the name of the *Gendarmerie Impériale de Paris*, and in 1816 the *Gendarmerie Royale de Paris*, and consisted of 1,021 men and 471 mounted police. From 1830–1848 it was called the *Garde Municipale*, and consisted of twelve companies, four of which were mounted. It was suppressed in 1848, and its place supplied by the *Garde Républicaine* and the *Gendarmerie Mobile*. It next became *la Garde de Paris*, and in 1852 the *Gendarmerie de Paris*.

Garde Nationale (*La*), 1789. Improvised by the municipality of Paris on 13 July, and called at first the *Garde Bourgeoise*. Its badge was a blue and red cockade (the colours of the city); white, the royal colour, was afterwards added by its general, Lafayette. Charles X. disbanded the guard in 1827 for insubordination. It was reorganised in 1830. In 1848 it became a mere mob army of some 200,000 volunteers, but Napoleon III. reduced it to order in 1852, and gave it for motto 'Liberté, ordre public.'

Garde Royale (*La*), 1815. A corps instituted by Louis XVIII., and consisting of picked men, to which were added two *régiments Suisses*. Dissolved in July 1830, when they tried in vain to defend Charles X.

Gardes de la Marche (*Les*), who accompanied the king wherever he went. They consisted of 24 picked noblemen from the *Gardes du Corps du Roi* (*q.v.*). See 'Gold Stick.'

Gardes du Corps du Roi (*Les*), or 'Garde Ecossaise,' 1448. Organised by Charles VII. of France. They consisted of 300 archers, all of whom ranked as gentlemen, and were sumptuously armed, equipped, and mounted. Each one was allowed a squire, a valet, a page, and two yeomen, with corresponding equipage ; so that cadets of the best families in Scotland were sent to serve in this honourable corps. They wore the Scotch bonnet and feather, and, in the reign of Louis XI., a massive silver brooch, called a 'Virgin Mary,' the Virgin Mary being made by him their colonel. They wore a loose surcoat of rich blue velvet, with a large white St. Andrew's cross of silver bisecting it before and behind. Suppressed in 1791, but restored by Louis XVIII. in 1814, and formed into six companies, called the *Corps Ecossaise*, the *Corps de Gramont*, the *Corps de Poix*, the *Corps de Luxembourg*, the *Corps de Wagram*, and the *Corps de Raguse*. Finally disbanded in 1830.

One of the two yeomen attached to these guardsmen was called his 'knife-man' (*coutelier*), from a large knife which he carried to despatch those whom his master had thrown to the ground in a *mêlée*.

Gardes-côtes (*Les*). French coast-guards, created in 1791; reorganised in 1799; suppressed in 1814; and re-established in 1831. 'Ils se forment six compagnies de canoniers.'

Gardes Françaises (*Les*), 1553. Formerly a part of the royal household troops, consisting of ten companies of 100 men each, and having barracks in the faubourgs of Paris. This guard took rank above all the rest of the army. In 1789 it fraternised with the insurgents, and became a part of the *Garde Nationale de Paris*.

Garden of *England*. Worcestershire and Kent. Both so called.

Garden of *Erin.* Carlow, in Leinster.
— *Europe.* Italy and Belgium.
Both so called.
— *France.* Amboise, in the *département* of Indre-et-Loire.
— *India.* Oude.
— *Italy.* Sicily.
— *South Wales.* The southern division of Glamorganshire.
— *Spain.* Andaluci'a.
— the *Argentine.* Turcuman, a province of Argentinia.
— the *East.* Ceylon and Burmah. Both so called.

> Ceylon is also called 'The Resplendent'; the 'Jewel of the Eastern Sea'; the 'Gem of Paradise.' Its climate and productions are quite unrivalled.

— the *West.* Illinois and Kansas. Both so called.
— the *World.* The region of the Mississippi.

Garden and the Lane (*The*). Covent Garden Theatre and Drury Lane Theatre.

> The old-fashioned friendly rivalry between the Garden and the Lane is renewed this year [Dec. 1887].—*Newspaper paragraph.*

Garden of the Mid-West (*The*). Evesham, in Worcestershire. Famous for table-fruit and kitchen produce.

Garden Sect (*The*). The disciples of Plato were so called because they attended his lectures in the Academy, a garden in the suburbs of Athens which once belonged to Académos. Epicūros taught in his own private garden.

Garigliano (*Rout of the*), 1503. The rout of the French, led by Saluce and Bayard (the *chevalier sans peur et sans reproche*), by Gonsalvo the Great Captain. Above 4,000 French fell in this rout, with all their standards and baggage, tents, provisions, stores, and splendid artillery. A capitulation was signed the next day. In 1860 (Nov. 3) Francis I. king of Naples was routed on the banks of the same river by Victor Emmanuel.

Garrick Fever (*The*), 1742. A contagious disorder which broke out in Dublin, ascribed to the heat of the theatre crowded to hear Garrick during unusually hot weather.

Garter King of Arms (*The*), 1417; also 'Principal King of Arms.' Two separate offices held by the same person. It was Henry V. who instituted the Garter King to attend upon knights at their solemnities, call them to their installation, see that their arms are hung over their stalls, to grant arms, and to marshal national funeral processions. *See* 'Heralds.'

> There are altogether four Kings of Arms for England: Garter and Bath; and the two provincial kings CLARENCEUX and NORROY: the former having jurisdiction over all parts *south* of the Trent, and the latter over all parts *north* of that river. BATH King of Arms, though not a member of the college, takes precedence next to Garter. The office was created in 1725 for the service of the Order of the Bath. The King of Arms of Scotland is 'Lyon,' and for Ireland 'Ulster.'

Gas from coal. Described by Clayton in 1739. First applied to illumination in 1792 by Murdoch. Introduced into Paris in 1802, into London by Winsor in 1803. Came into general use in *London* in 1814, and in *Paris* about 1820. The Gas Company was chartered in 1810 (50 Geo. III., c. 163).

> The meter was invented by Crossley in 1815, Clegg's meter in 1816.

Gastein Convention (*The*), 1865. In which Austria and Prussia agreed to a joint occupation of Schleswig, Holstein, and Lauenburg. *See* 'Schleswig-Holstein Question.'

Gate of France (*The Iron*) Longwy, a strong military position.

Gate of Italy (*The*). That part of the valley of the Adige (3 syl.) which is in the vicinity of Trent and Roverēdo. It is a narrow gorge between two mountain ranges.

Gate of Science (*The*), or 'Daur ul Ilm.' Shiraz was so called of old. Sadi and Hafiz were both born in Shiraz.

Gate of Tears (*The*). Babelmandeb, the passage into the Red Sea.

> Like some ill-destined bark that steers
> In silence through the Gate of Tears.
> MOORE, *Lalla Rookh* (The Fire Worshippers).

Gate of the Mediterranean. Gibraltar.

Gates (*The*). In Scripture language means the towns and fortresses.

> Thy seed shall possess the gate of his enemies.
> —*Gen.* xxii.
> ∴ Gates of Hell = the power or dominion of Satan.
> Gates of the Grave = the brink of death.

Gates or Mountain Passes of ASIA MINOR.

The *Albanian Gates.* Either the pass

of Derbend along the Caspian Sea or else the Sarmatian Pass.

The *Amanian Gates.* Tamir Kapu (or the Iron Gate of the Turks), a Cyclopean arch, where the hills come down to the sea-beach at the head of the gulf.

The *Cappadocian Gates.* The pass described by Strabo and explored by the Euphratês expedition, leading through Taurus to Marash (ancient Germanica).

The *Caspian Gates,* 'Caspiæ Portæ' or 'Caspiæ Pylæ,' a defile near Teheran [Teh-ran'], in ancient Media.

The *Caucasian Gates.* A defile in the Caucāsus range leading from Mosdok to Tiflis. In this narrow valley Strabo tells us the river Arāgon flows. Now called 'Dariel.'

The *Cilician Gates.* The Taurus Pass (Kulak Bughaz or Gülek Bógház).

Darius's Pass. Across the Amānus, north of Issus, and near the Amanian Gates.

The *Gates of Syria.* The Pass of Ballan. Pictānus of the 'Jerusalem Itinerary'; Erāna of Cicero. Near this pass was the battlefield of Issus.

Thermop'ylæ, or ' the Hot Gates,' generally called 'Pylæ' or 'The Gates.' The celebrated pass between Thessaly and Locris, immortalised by the heroic defence of Leonīdas and 300 Spartans against the enormous host of Xerxês.

Gates of China *(The).* The cluster of rocky islets called 'the Ladrones.'

Gates of the Caspian, or 'Pylæ Caspiæ.' *See above,* 'Caspian Gates.'

Gates of the Occult Sciences *(The).* Forty, or as some say forty-eight, books on magic in Arabic. The first twelve on sorcery and enchantment; the thirteenth on disenchantment.

Gatton and Old Sarum. Although without inhabitants, had the right, before 1831, of returning two members of parliament. In the reform agitation 'Gatton and Old Sarum' proved a *tour de force.*

Gaudents (*Les Chevaliers*), 1204. A religious order of Italy, whose special work is to protect the widow, the orphan, and the poor. They wear a white dress with a red cross, surmounted with two stars, and follow the rule of the Dominicans, but may marry if they like. Both father and mother must be of noble birth.

Gaul. *See* ' Gallia.'

Gaultier. 'As aspish as Gault.er. Claude Gaultier was a French advocate (1590–1666), referred to by Boileau.

Dans vos discours chagrins plus aigre et plus
    mordant
Qu'une femme en furie, ou Gaultier en plaidant.
                                        Sat. ix.

Gaurian Dynasty *(The).* So called from Gaur in West Afghanistan, because Hussein Mahmoud Ghori was governor of Gaur under the Gaznevides (3 syl.), before he declared himself independent in 1155. He overthrew them in 1158, and usurped the kingdom; but the Gaurians were in turn overthrown by the Khans of Kharism in 1213.

The *second* Gaurian Dynasty was the 'House of Khilji,' which succeeded in 1288. The last of the house (Khusru) was dethroned and put to death, 22 Aug., 1321, by Ghâzi Khan Toghlak, who founded 'The House of Toghlak.'

Gau'tama *(Prince).* Prince Siddâr'tha, born on the borders of Nepaul B.C. 600, died B.C. 543 at Kusinag'ara in Oudh. He became a Buddh, and was the founder of the Buddhists, which embrace more than a third of the human race.

Father, Suddhôd'ana king of Sâk'ya. *Mother,* Queen Maya. *Wife,* Yasôd'hara. *City,* Kapilavas'tu. *Son,* Rahūla.

His horse was Kantāra; his pleasure-palace Vish'ramvan'; his charioteer Channa.

As Buddha he dwelt first on the rock Munda by the village of Dâlidd'; then in the solitudes of Senâ'ni; his dress a yellow robe.

** Buddhism consists of four truths and eight precepts which lead to Nirvâ'na, *i.e.* sinless rest which never changes. The four truths are: Sorrow; desire the *cause* of sorrow; the conquest of self; and the victory over sorrow. Eight precepts lead to victory. The five commandments of Buddha are: (i.) Kill not; (ii.) Give freely; (iii.) Bear no false witness; (iv.) Shun intoxicating drinks; (v.) Touch not thy neighbour's wife. The eight precepts are: Right doctrine, right purpose, right converse, right conduct, right purity, right thought, right lowliness, and right rapture. (Sir Edwin Arnold, ' The Light of Asia,' bk. i.)

'Lord Buddha — Prince Siddârtha styled in
    earth.'

Gavelkind. A law whereby all the sons succeed alike. By this tenure an estate does not escheat to the lord (in case of felony), the maxim being 'The father to the bough [gallows], the son to the plough [land].' In default of sons the property descends to daughters.

Suppose A, B, C, to be three sons, and A dies, leaving a daughter; then A's daughter takes her third with B and C.

Gay (*Joseph*). The pen-name of Captain John Durant Breval, who wrote 'The Confederates,' 1717; 'The Progress of a Rake,' 1733; 'The Lure of Venus,' 1733; &c.

The fabulist and author of the 'Beggars Opera' was John Gay (1688-1732).

Gay Science (*The*), or 'The Joyous Science,' that of minstrelsy. In Norman French, the *Joyeuse Science.*

'[I am] an unworthy graduate of the Gay Science, my lord,' said the musician, 'yet let me say for myself, th t I will not yield to the king of minstrels, Geoffrey Rudel, though the king of England hath given him four manors for one song.'—Sir W. SCOTT, *The Betrothed*, ch. xix.

Gazari, Gazeri, or Gacari. The same as the Cathāri or Paterīni, meaning Puritans. Called in Italy 'Paterini,' 'Cathari,' or 'Gazari'; in France, 'Les Vaudois,' and 'Les Pauvres de Lyon.'

The Albigenses were quite another sect, although both protested against the dogmas of the Catholic Church, and the evil lives of its clergy.

Gazette (*The*). Published at Venice in 1563.

Published at Paris by Renaudot, 25 May, 1631.

Published at Oxford 1665. *See* 'Pall Mall.'

The gazette now means with us an official newspaper in which proclamations, notices of appointments, bankruptcies, dissolutions of partnership, and so on are published by government. It is issued every Tuesday and Friday.

Gaznevides (3 syl.). A Tartar and Musulman dynasty which lasted 184 years (999-1183), so called from Gaznĕ, the birthplace of Alp Tekin the founder. It succeeded the Samanides (3 syl.). The greatest of the Gaznevides was Mahmoud, who reigned in the eastern provinces of Persia (967, 927-1030). He was 'the slave of the commander of the faithful,' and was the first who was ever called *sultan.*

Gelal'ean Era (*The*). This era began 15 March, A.D. 1079. So called

from Gelal Eddin Malek Shah, who reformed the old Egyptian calendar.

The reign of Malek was illustrated bythe Gelalean Era, which surpasses the Julian and approaches the accuracy of the Gregorian style. GIBBON, chap. lvii.

Gelosi (*I.*). A celebrated troop of Italian comedians who acted in Venice. They went to Blois in 1577, and then to Paris. In 1588 a fresh company of Gelosi appeared at Blois, and then at Paris, where they acted till 1604.

Gema'ra (*The*). The second part of the Talmud, or commentary on the Mishna, regarded as the text. There are two commentaries—viz. the Babylonian Gemāra (completed A.D. 500), and the Jerusalem Gemāra (middle of the 4th cent.), the former of which is by far the better one.

Gemblours (*Battle of*), Jan., 1578. In which Don John of Austria defeated the Dutch, and spread consternation throughout the Netherlands.

Gemon'iæ Scalæ. The staircase in Rome down which criminals condemned to death descended from their prison cells to execution. It was near the Tiber.

Gemotes (2 syl.). There were several in the Saxon period, as—

The *Shire-gemote,* or county court, which met twice a year.

The *Burg-gemote,* met thrice a year.

The *Hundred-gemote,* met monthly.

The *Halle-gemote* or ' court-baron.'

The *Witena-gemote,* which corresponded to the Reichstage (2 syl.) of the Franks. A national assembly.

Gendarme (2 syl.), *i.e. gens armāta.* The men who accompanied a feodal lord to battle. In 1453 Charles VII. appointed a permanent gendarmerie. In the reign of Louis XVI. it was replaced by the *Gendarmerie de Lunéville.* In 1791 the Constituent Assembly converted it into the *Gendarmerie départementale;* under Napoleon I. it was called the *Gendarmerie d'élite*; at the restoration it was called the *Gendarmerie Royale;* in 1830 it was replaced by the *Garde Municipale,* called in 1848 the *Garde Républicaine,* and in 1852 the *Gendarmerie de Paris.*

General (*The*). Of religious orders in the Catholic Church. The supreme head (under the pope) of each of the leading religious orders.

The Superior of an individual convent, &c., is an abbot, prior, rector, superior, &c.
A Provincial has authority over all the convents, &c., of a province.
A General has authority over all provinces.

General Assembly (*The*), 1689.

The supreme court of the Scotch Kirk, composed of delegates from every presbytery in the church. Two elders are elected by the Town Council of Edinburgh, one by each burgh, a representative is elected by the senate of each of the four universities, and an elder by the church in India. It meets annually in May, and sits for ten days; and if any business is left over it is settled by a commission nominated by the General Assembly.

General Assembly of the Presbyterian Church of Ireland

(*The*), 1840. The union of the General and Secession Synods. It contains about 500 congregations under forty presbyteries.

General Baptists. Those dis-

senters of the Baptist connection who uphold the doctrine of general redemption in contradistinction to the Particular Baptists, who maintain the Calvinistic doctrines of election, predestination, and reprobation. *See* 'Free Communionists.'

General Boum. Nickname of

Mons. Thiers the French historian (1797–1877). *See* 'Attila le Petit.'

Thiers, pronounce *Te-air*.

General Councils. The *first* at

Nice, A.D. 325, against Arius, who denied the divinity of Christ. The *second* at Constantinople, 381, against Macedonius, who denied the true humanity of Christ and the Holy Ghost. The *third* at Ephesus, 431, against Nestorius, who said the Virgin Mary was the mother of Jesus, but not θεοτόκος (the mother of God). The *fourth* at Chalcêdon, 451, against Eutychês, who maintained that the human nature was merged in the divine nature. The *fifth* at Constantinople, 553, which condemned Origen's doctrine that parts of the scripture are either allegorical or figurative. The *sixth* at Constantinople, 680, against the Monoth'elites (4 syl.), who maintained that, although Christ had two natures, He had but one *will*, that of his divine

16

nature. These are the only councils of acknowledged authority.

Council 1 declared Christ to be God ἀληθῶς (truly). Council 2 declared Him to be God and Man τελίως (perfectly). Council 3 declared Him to be God and Man ἀδιαιρέτως (indivisibly). And Council 4 declared him to be God and Man ἀσυγχύτως (distinctly). The decisions of these four councils are acknowledged by the Church of England. *See* 'Ecumenical Councils.'

Of the Western Church:

1, 2, 3, 4. All of the Lateran in Rome, A.D. 1123, 1139, 1179, 1215 (or 10, 11, 12, 13).

5, 6. Both at Lyons, A.D. 1245, 1274 (or 14, 15).

7. Council of Vienne in France, A.D. 1311 (or 16).

8. Council of Constance, A.D. 1414 to 1418 (or 17).

9. Council of Basel, Ferrara, Florence, A.D. 1431 to 1443 (or 18).

10. Council of the Lateran, A.D. 1511 to 1517 (or 19).

11. Council of Trent, A.D. 1545 to 1563 (or 20).

12. Council of the Vatican, 1869–1870.

Numbered from 10 to 20 if taken from the Council of Nice, A.D. 325, when the Eastern and Western Churches were not divided.

General Non - subscribing Presbyterian Association (*The*),

Ireland, 1850. The union of the three non-subscribing presbyteries of Ireland—viz. 'The United Presbytery or Synod of Munster,' 'The Presbytery of Antrim,' and 'The Remonstrant Synod of Ulster.' They claim the right of private judgment and non-subscription to creeds or confessions of faith.

General Privilege of Peter III. The Magna Charta of Aragon,

1283. The Fueros de Aragon contain a series of provisions against tallages, spoliations of property, sentences of the justiciary without assent of the Cortes, appointments of foreigners to judicial offices, trials of accused persons in places beyond the kingdom, the falsification of the coin, bribery of judges, absolute power, and so on. It was an improvement on our own charter.

Generalissimo Procession (*A*).

An extraordinary religious procession, in which all the chief men of the state took part. In the Generalissimo Procession of Paris, 29 Jan., 1535, the king, François I., all the clergy, ambassadors, lords, presidents of the courts of justice, and all the notables took part. The reliquary of the

St. Chapelle was carried through the streets; the head of St. Louis; a piece of the true cross, the crown of thorns, a real nail, the spear-head, and the shrine of Ste. Geneviève. The king went bare-headed, holding a lighted torch. Every house passed by was lighted with tapers, and the inmates holding lighted candles sank on their knees.

Généralité, in the ancient régime of France, was the jurisdiction of an intendant-general of finance. The number of these généralités varied. In the 14th century there were four; under François I. the number was increased to sixteen; in 1787 there were thirty-two. Abolished in 1789.

Geneva—Rome, Protestantism—Catholicism. Strictly speaking, Geneva means Calvinism.

I would have you know I care as little for Geneva as for Rome; as little for homilies as for pardons. —Sir W. Scott, *The Abbot*, ch. xvi.

Gene'va Bands, 1652. Clerical bands in imitation of those worn by the Calvinistic Protestants of Geneva. Till the last quarter of the 19th cent. they were worn by the clergy of the established church and university men; but since the Oxford Tract movement both the bands and the black gown have been almost entirely abandoned by clergymen.

Gene'va Bible (*The*), 1560. The Bible translated by the English exiles at Geneva. The exiles who assisted in this translation were Knox, Coverdale, Goodman, Gibbs, Samson, William Cole, Whittingham, and Gilery. It was the first Bible in Roman letter, divided into verses. This is the famous 'Breeches Bible,' based on Tyndale's translation. *See* 'Bibles.'

Coverdale had already produced his own translation in 1535, and had superintended the production of the 'Great Bible,' 1539.

Geneva Catechisms (*The*), 1536. A larger and shorter formulary, the work of Calvin. A standard work in Switzerland, the Netherlands, France, and Hungary.

Luther published a larger and smaller catechism 1529; and a larger and shorter catechism were compiled in the reign of Edward VI., the shorter one by Cranmer, and the larger one by Poynet or Ponct. There is also a larger and shorter catechism of the Presbyterian Churches, the shorter one published in 1647, and the larger one in 1648. These form part of the 'Westminster Confession of Faith.'

Geneva Convention (*The*), 1863. An international agreement to respect the persons and property of those who give voluntarily their services in times of war to attend on the sick and wounded. They must have a recognised costume, flag, and arm-badge (a red cross on a white ground). If taken prisoners they are to be discharged without ransom. Often called 'The Red Cross Society.'

First brought into operation in the Franco-German War 1870-71. The idea was popularised by a book written by M. Durant, *Un Souvenir de Solferino*, 1862, and the Convention was held the following year at Geneva, attended by delegates from Austria, Baden, Bavaria, Belgium, France, Great Britain, Hanover, Hesse-Darmstadt, Italy, Prussia, Russia, Spain, Saxony, Sweden, Switzerland, and Würtemberg.

Gene'va Formula (*The*), 1543. Published six years before the First Book of Edward VI. It was the first to originate the idea of making the singing of psalms take the place of vocal response on the part of the people. Provision was made for extemporaneous prayer, and for prayer on special occasions.

Geneviève (*Canons Regular of Ste.*), 1615. Ratified by Gregory XV. The abbey of Ste. Geneviève was built by Eugenius III. in 1148.

Pronounce *Jhan'-ve-ave*.

Gengiskha'nians (*The*), or 'Gengisk'hanides'. (4 syl.). A Persian dynasty (1225–1258), which supplanted the Khariz'mians (*q.v.*).

The four kings were Gengis Khan, 1225; Oktai, 1229; Kaiouk, 1242; and Mangou, 1250. Mangou sent his younger brother Houlagou to conquer the west of Asia. This done, the conqueror fixed his residence at Tauris, in Persia; took Bagdad in 1258 from the Califs; and carried his conquests into Syria. He succeeded Mangou in 1258, and formed a branch line of the Gengiskhanians, which continued to 1336, when it gave place to the Ilkhanians.

Genoese War (*The*), 1378–1381. The Venetians call the 'War of Chiozza' (*q.v.*) the 'Genoese War.' And the new nobles aggrandised after the war they call 'The Nobles of the Genoese War' ('I Nobili della Guerra di Genova.') *See* 'Nobles of the, &c.'

Genovefains. Canons of the abbey de Ste. Geneviève, which formed what is called the 'Congrégation de France,' instituted by Clovis in 500. They followed the rule of St. Augustine, and wore a white robe with a rochet, but when abroad a black cloak.

Gente Grassa (*The*). The substantial tradesmen of Italy, like the Medici.

Gente (2 syl.).

Gentilhomme de la Peinture (*Le*). Rubens (1577-1640) is so called by Charles Blanc.

Gentiluom'ini (*The*). The masters of Venice both by sea and land, corresponding with the burghers of Florence. The lowest class was the popolari or plebeians, then the cittadini, then came the gentiluomini, about 3,000 in number.

Gentle (*The*). Izaak Walton, the Angler (1593-1683). Angling is called ' The Gentle Craft.' Probably there is something of a pun in the phrase, referring to the bait of gentles used by anglers.

Gentle Shepherd. George Grenville (1712-1770).

In 1763 Sir Francis Dashwood proposed a tax upon cider and perry, which Pitt (Earl Chatham) objected to. Whereupon George Grenville declared the tax inevitable, and added, if Pitt objected to it, ' Let him tell me where the money is to be raised', let him tell me where,' he repeated. Pitt, who sat opposite, hummed, in tone mimicking Grenville, the beginning of a popular tune of the day, ' Gentle Shepherd, tell me where ? ' The House was convulsed with laughter, and Pitt walked out.

Gentleman George. George IV., also called Handsome Al Raschid. *See* ' Fum.'

Gentleman Highwayman(*The*). I. Tom King, friend of Richard . (Dick) Turpin; the ' Pyladês and Orestês of the road.' Accidentally shot by Turpin in a scuffle, in 1739.

II. Claude Duval, executed 1670.

Gentleman's Magazine (*The*), 1731. Originated by Cave.

Gentlemen Commoners. Students in the Oxford University who dine at the Fellows' table, and wear a distinctive college costume. Called in Cambridge University Fellow Commoners (*q.v.*). They are generally either noblemen or married men.

· Gentoo. An obsolete term at one time applied to the natives of Hindûstan.

It is the Portuguese *gentio*, meaning a Gentile.

Geology (*Professorship of*). In the University of Cambridge, 1727, founded by Dr. Woodward; and hence the professor is also called the Woodwardian professor. Stipend, 500*l.* a year.

George I. First of the Hanoverian dynasty in England. He died on his road to Osnaburg, and was buried in Hanover (1660, 1714-1727). He could not speak a word of English, and looked on Great Britain only as a useful appendage to Hanover.

Father, Ernestus duke of Brunswick, &c.; *Mother*, Sophia daughter of Elizabeth, granddaughter of JAMES I. of England ; *Wife*, Sophia Dorothy of Zell, only daughter of George William duke of Brunswick and Zell ; *Issue*, GEORGE [II.], his successor, and Sophia, who married Frederick William of Prussia, and was the mother of Frederick II. the Great.

His style.—George, Dei Gratia, of Great Britain, France, and Ireland, king ; Defender of the Faith.

His *Mistresses* were the Countess Platen and Madame Herrengard Melusina von Schlemberg, who said to the London rabble: ' Mein people, why do ye abuse us thus ? We do be come here to England only for all your goods.'

. Of course George I. had no hereditary right to the throne of England, but only a parliamentary right. His mother was a granddaughter of James I., and the line of his father runs back to Maud, daughter of our Henry II.

George II. King of Great Britain, second king of the House of Hanover (1683, 1727-1760). He died on Saturday, 25 Oct. Like his father, he looked on Great Britain only as the appendage of Hanover.

Father, GEORGE I. ; *Mother*, Sophia Dorothy daughter of George William duke of Zell ; *Wife*, Caroline Wilhelmina of Anspach ; *Issue*, three sons and five daughters. Frederick Lewis (Prince of Wales), father of GEORGE III., died about ten years before his father, George II. His *nickname* was Prince Tite.

His style and title.—George, Dei Gratia, of Great Britain, France, and Ireland, king ; Defender of the Faith.

From Frederick Lewis prince of Wales the Princess Alexandra is descended, thus : His youngest daughter, Caroline Matilda, married Christian VIII. of Denmark, the son of whom was FREDERICK VI. of Denmark ; the son of Frederick VI. was FREDERICK VII.; the son of Frederick VII. was CHRISTIAN IX., whose daughter is Alexandra princess of Wales (great-great-great-grandchild of George II.)

George III. Son of Frederick Lewis prince of Wales, and grandson of George II. (1738, 1760-1820), born in London, and the first of the line of Brunswick who was a Briton born. He married Charlotte daughter of Charles duke of Mecklenburg-Strelitz, by whom he had fifteen children, viz. nine sons and six daughters. The eldest son George [IV.] succeeded to the throne, but he had previously been prince-regent. Familiarly called ' Farmer George,' or ' the Farmer King.'

Style and title.—From 1760 to 1800:

George, D.G. of Great Britain, France, and Ireland, king; Defender of the Faith. From 1800 to 1820: George, D.G. of the United Kingdom of Great Britain and Ireland, king; Defender of the Faith.

GEORGE III. was the father of GEORGE IV., WILLIAM IV., and Edward duke of Kent (the father of Queen VICTORIA.)

George IV. King of Great Britain, &c., Electoral Prince of Brunswick-Luneburg, Duke of Cornwall and Rothsay, Earl of Chester and Carrick, Baron of Renfrew, Lord of the Isles, hereditary Grand Steward of Scotland, &c. Born 1762, regent from Feb. 1811, king 1820, died Saturday, 26 June, 1830.

Father, GEORGE III.; *Mother,* Sophia Charlotte of Mecklenburg-Strelitz; *Wife,* his cousin Caroline, daughter of the Prince of Brunswick; *Issue,* Charlotte, who married Leopold (afterwards king of Belgium). *Nicknames :* The Magnificent (from his love of gorgeous apparel), Prince Florizel, Fum the Fourth, The Fat Adonis of Fifty, the First Gentleman of Europe. *Style and title,* as George III. after 1800.

At the age of sixteen he fell in love with Mrs. Robinson, an actress, who received an annuity of 500l. a year; in 1785 he married Mrs. Fitzherbert, a widow, but the marriage was a 'German one.' After his marriage with Caroline of Brunswick his favourite lady was the Countess of Jersey.

George (*A St.*). A badge worn over the armour by every English soldier in the 14th cent., and subsequently. On the invasion of Scotland by Richard II., in 1386, and at the battle of Agincourt, it was ordained that

Everi man, of what estate, condicion, or nation they be of, so that he be of oure partie, shall bere a signe of the armes of St. George, large (bothe before and behynde) upon parell that yf he be slayne or wounded to deth, he that hath so doon to hym shall not be putte to deth for defaulte of the crosse that he lacketh. And that non enemy do bere the same token or crosse of St. George, notwithstandyng if he be prisoner, upon payne of deth.

** The St. George is a red cross on a white field. In the Order of the Garter it is a figure of St. George on horseback piercing the fallen dragon, on a mount.

George (*Knights of St.*), I. 1201. A military order of *Alfana,* in Spain. Confirmed by John XXII. in 1317; united to the order of Montesa by Benedict XIII. in 1399. Extinct.

II. In *Burgundy,* 1400, founded by Philibert de Miolans. Extinct.

III. 1273, in *Carinthia,* founded by Rudolf of Hapsburg. Revived in 1468 by Frederick III. Extinct in 1598.

IV. 1470, in *Austria,* founded by Fre-

derick III. to guard the frontiers of Bohemia and Hungary.

V. 1492, at *Rome,* instituted by Alexander VI., and abolished in 1578 by Gregory XIII.

VI. 1500, in *Germany,* founded 1500. Extinct.

VII. 1535, at *Ravenna,* founded by Paul III., and abolished in 1578 by Gregory XIII.

VIII. 1729, in *Bavaria,* refounded by Karl VII.

IX. 1769, in *Russia,* founded by Catherine II.; and restored by Alexander I. in 1801.

X. 1819, in *Sicily,* instituted by Ferdinand I.

XI. 1833, in *Lucca,* instituted by Duke Charles Louis.

XII. 1840, in *Hanover,* instituted by Ernest Augustus.

George the Magnificent. *See above,* George IV.

Georgia, in N. America. So named in honour of George II., in whose reign the first white settlement there was effected (1733). The nickname of the inhabitants is *Buzzards.*

Geougen (*The*). A gang of Tartar robbers, enlisted under Moko, slave of a Topa prince. The gang swelled into a camp, then into a tribe, and then into a numerous people. The posterity of Moko assumed the title of Khan or Cagan A.D. 400.

German Athens. Wittenberg was so called by Giordano Bruno.

German Catholics. A religious party in the German Catholic Church with independent congregations. They call themselves 'Christian Catholics.' They are not Protestants. This party sprang into being in 1844, when Bishop Arnoldi appointed a pilgrimage to the Holy Coat at Trèves, which called forth a protest from J. Ronge (2 syl.), a priest of Silesia, who characterised the relic as the 'coat of idolatry.'

German Confederation (*The*). I. 'Der Deutsche Bund,' 8 June, 1815; constituted by treaty of Vienna, after the battle of Waterloo, to create a barrier against French aggression. Its object was to grant to the thirty-nine states of Germany external and internal security. Of the states Austria and Prussia were large kingdoms, and Bavaria, Saxony,

Hanover, and Würtemberg were minor kingdoms; the other thirty-three states were grand duchies, free cities, &c. Each state was bound to supply 1 per cent. of its population to form an army in time of war. Austria presided, but in 1866 was excluded from the Bund by the treaty of Prague.

The princedom of Gotha became extinct in 1826; the duchy of Anhalt-Cothen was annexed to Anhalt-Dessau in 1847; the principalities of Hohenzollern-Hechingen and of Hohenzollern-Sigmaringen were annexed to Prussia in 1849; the duchy of Anhalt-Bernberg became extinct in 1863; and in 1866 Hanover, Hesse-Cassel, Nassau, Frankfort, and part of Hesse-Darmstadt were annexed to Prussia.

II. 1871. During the Franco-Prussian war (Nov. 1871), Bavaria, Würtemberg, Baden, Hesse-Darmstadt, and Saxony joined the North German Confederation, which consisted of Prussia and the states north of the Main. By this extension the *North* German Confederation was changed to the 'German Confederation,' and on 18 Jan., 1871, the king of Prussia was elected German emperor.

After the Seven Weeks' War, 1866, the following states formed a part of Prussia:—The kingdom of Hanover (annexed); Hesse-Cassel, Nassau, and Frankfort (annexed); Lauenburg (since 1865), Schleswig and Holstein (annexed); Kaulsdorf, Gersfeld, and Orl (ceded by Bavaria); Hesse-Homburg, Amt-Homburg, Amt-Meisenheim (ceded by Hesse-Darmstadt).

German Emancipation War (*The*), 1813. That is, to emancipate Germany from the hands of Napoleon. The battles fought in 1813 were Lützen and Bautzen, Grossbeerin, Katzbach, Dresden, Culm, Dennewitz, Leipzig, and Hanau. The last of the battles was that of Waterloo in 1815.

German Emperor. Not 'Emperor of Germany,' but either ' Deutscher Kaiser ' or 'Kaiser des Deutschen Reiches ' (Kaiser of the German Dominion). *See* 'Prussia (*King of*) ' for his various titles.

German Florence (*The*). Dresden, noted for its architecture and collections of art.

German Herrick (*The*). Paul Flemming of Silesia (1609–1640). Some of his Anacreontic odes are equal to those of the great Greek erotic poet. His sonnet on ' Myself,' and his ' Epitaph,' are gems of heaven-born poetry.

German Iliad (*The*). The Nibelungen Lied, the most important poem of the middle ages. It is in thirty-nine books, and is about as long as Milton's 'Paradise Lost.' The poem is divided into two parts. The first part contains the marriage of Siegfried and Kremhild, and ends with the death of the bridegroom; the second part is the marriage of the widow with Etzel, in order to revenge the murder of her first husband.

German Knights of the Cross (*The*). The 'Teutonic knights ' (*q.v.*).

German Literature (*Father of*). Gotthold Ephraim Lessing (1729–1781).

German Nestor of Philosophy (*The*). Ernst Platner (1744–1818).

German Odyssey (*The*). 'The Kudrun,' and second best poem of the Hohenstauffen school. It is divided into three parts. (1) The Hagen; (2) the Hildê; and (3) the Hedel; so called from the chief characters.

German Pliny (*The*), or 'the Pliny of Germany.' Konrad von Gesner of Zürich (1516–1565). So called from his ' Catalogue of Plants,' in four languages, and his 'History of Animals ' (in Latin), a marvellous production, which from that day to this has been accounted a memorable treatise.

German School of Painting (*The*), 1490–1520. Founded by Holbein, Albrecht Dürer, and others.

German Strabo (*The*). Sebastian Munster of Ingelheim (1489–1521), author of a ' Universal Cosmography.'

German Version of the Bible (*The*). Old Testament, at the expense of the Kaiser Wenceslaus, 1405, first printed in 1466 ; Luther's version, 1522–1530.

German'icus (*The French*). Louis the dauphin, son of Louis XV. (1729–1765), father of three kings; Louis XVI., Louis XVIII., and Charles X.

Gesta Romano'rum. A legendary book of the middle ages, in Latin. The stories are short, with religious morals. The compiler was Elinandus, a monk, and the morals were added subsequently by Peter Bercheur of Poitou.

Ghauts. Buildings on the banks of the Ganges and other rivers of Northern Hindûstan for the use of bathers. The steps down to the river form lounging places where the idle or devout pass their happiest hours.

Ghaz'nevides (3 syl.). A Tartar Musulman dynasty, which reigned over a large part of Persia and Hindûstan. So called from Ghazna or Gazna, the birthplace of Alp-Tekin, who drove the Samanides (3 syl.). There were ou.y four kings of this dynasty—viz. Alp Tekin (960–975), Sebek Tekin (975–999), Mahmoud (999–1028), and Masoud (1028–30).

The Ghaznevides, called the sixth dynasty, contemporary with the Califs, reigned only over a part of Persia. It was succeeded by the Seldjûks of Persia.

Ghib'ellines (3 syl.). A political party in Italy which maintained the supremacy of the German kaiser-kings over the Italian states in opposition to that of the pope. The Guelfs were supporters of the pope and of Italian independence. The Ghibellines were the imperial party, the Guelfs were the papal party. The strife began with a dispute about investiture between Gregory VII. and the kaiser-king Heinrich IV. The first time the names were used as a battle-cry was at the combat of Weinsberg, between Konrad of Franconia and Heinrich the Lion, in 1140. The names continued in use till 1450.

The commander of the Imperialists at the battle of Weinsburg was Friedrich duke of Suabia (the king's cousin), who lived at Weblingen, corrupted into Ghibelline. Guelf was the name of the leader of the papal army.

Ghebres (The), i.e. infidels. All non-Musulmans except Jews and Christians. The appellation is more especially applied to the followers of Zoroaster t... fire-worshipper. Also called Parsees, from Farsistan, their original locality. They are gentle, faithful, benevolent, and hospitable. (Persian ghebr, an infidel.)

Ghebres, pronounce Ge'-bers (hard g).

Ghengis Khan (Dynasty of), 1222–1259. Ghengis (the Great Warrior) is a Chinese title given to Temudgin for his vast exploits. His empire included Persia. In 1250 his fourth son, Mangou, succeeded his brother in China, and for eight years Persia had no separate sovereign.

Ghent. Notorious for its rebellions. In the public library of Flanders is a book entitled 'The 120 revolts of the good city of Ghent.'

Ghent, pronounce Gah n (with n nasal).

Ghent (Peace of). 24 Dec., 1814. Between Great Britain and the United States, bringing to an end the second American War.

Ghorides (2 syl.), 'Gaurides,' or 'Ghorians.' A dynasty which reigned in Persia from 1158 to 1213, founded by Hussein Mahmoud Ghori, governor of Gaur or Ghor in Afghanistan. Under Ala Eddin they conquered all Persia and drove out the Ghaznevides (3 syl.) in 1158 ; but in 1213 they were supplanted by the khans of Kharizm.

A branch of the House of Ghor reigned in Hindûstan from 1152 to 1215, when the Kharismians drove them out ; but the Kharismians, in 1398, were in turn supplanted by the Pathans.

Giants' Stairs of Venice. A flight of forty-five stone steps leading to the doge's palace at Venice. Marino Falie'ri was beheaded on the landing of the staircase Friday, 16 April, 1355. On the same landing the doge was accustomed to take the oath after his election, before he entered the palace. The giant stairs are guarded by two noble statues of Mars and Neptune, emblems of the military and naval power of Venice ; the works of Sansovi'no of Florence (1479–1570).

Giaour, a corruption of the Turkish 'Yaoor,' is applied by Moslems to a Christian, and means an infidel.

Pronounce, djowr.

Gibraltar (Siege of), Sept. 1782. Gibraltar was taken by Sir George Rooke in 1704, and ceded to the English in 1713 by the treaty of Utrecht. Several efforts have been made to wrest it from our hands, but the most serious was the siege in Sept. 1782, when the Spaniards invested the fort, which was gallantly defended by General Elliott. When all hope of reducing the place was abandoned, the Spaniards determined to intercept the supplies and starve the garrison into a surrender ; but Lord Howe succeeded in supplying abundant food, and the Spaniards raised the siege.

Gibraltar of America, or the **New World.** Quebec, a city on Cape Diamond in the province of Quebec.

Gibraltar of Greece. A precipitous rock 700 feet above the sea.

Gibraltar of the West Indies (The). The Bermudas.

These islands were discovered by Juan Bermudez, a Spaniard, in 1552 ; but, being colonised by Sir George Somers, they are sometimes called ' Somers Isles.'

Gilbert's Act, 1782. To incorporate parishes into unions, whereby parishes under the power of landlords were not depopulated in order to save poor rates.

Gil'bertines (3 syl.). A religious order founded by St. Gilbert of Sempringham in England, who lived 1084–1190.

Gilded Youth (*The*). *See* 'Jeunesse Dorée.'

The prisons of Lyons, Avignon, Marseilles, Tarascon, and Toulon were no sooner filled with Jacobins than they were broken open by what were called the 'gilded youth,' and the prisoners massacred.—HOWITT, *Hist. of Engl.* (Geo. III. 1795, p. 143).

Gillies' Hill (*The*), 1314. The hill behind which the gillies were stationed at the battle of Bannockburn to guard the luggage. When they saw the battle was going in favour of the Scotch, they could restrain themselves no longer, but rushed forwards to share the victory and the booty. The English, thinking them to be a body of reserves, lost heart and fled, and the Scotch obtained a complete and signal victory.

The *g* of 'Gillies' is hard, and not like *j*, as in *gin*.

Gilt Lance (*A*). A symbol of vassalage. A royal vassal, when he first paid homage, received a gilt lance to denote that he was henceforth the king's man [*puer regis*].

Gin Act (*The*), 1736. Sir Joseph Jekyll, greatly concerned at the excess of gin drunk by the poor, proposed to put a heavy tax on it, so as to put it out of the reach of the operative. The duty he suggested was to be 20s. a gallon on all gin sold retail, and 50l. yearly for the licence to a retailer.

Gipsy (*The*). I. Dudley earl of Leicester (1532–1588).

II. Antonio Sola'rio, the painter and illuminator, was called '*Zingaro*' (1382–1455).

The favourite greyhound of Charles I. was named 'Gipsey.' *See* 'Memoirs,' 829.

Giraldus Cambrensis, *i.e.* Gerald the Welshman. His father was a Norman and his mother Welsh. His name was Gerald or Girauld de Barri (1147–1222).

Gir'lingites (3 syl.). The followers of Mary Ann Girling, of Tiptoe, Hordle, Hampshire. According to her manifesto, dated 1883, Jesus Christ was not only God and man, but man and woman; the only visible part being the man nature. Mrs. Girling says: 'I am the second appearing of Jesus, the bride, the Lamb's wife, the God-mother, and there will not be another.' This crazy woman had some thousands of deluded followers.

Girls' Friendly Society (*The*), 1875. The objects are (1) to band together in one society ladies as associates, and girls as members, for mutual help, sympathy, and prayer. (2) To encourage purity of life, dutifulness to parents, faithfulness to employers, and thrift. (3) To provide the privileges of the society for its members, wherever they may be, by giving them an introduction from one branch to another.

Giron'dins (*Les*). In English 'The Giron'dists.' The pure republican party in the National Assembly and National Convention of the first French revolution. So called because it consisted mainly of the deputies of the Gironde. This party was distinguished for its oratory, and for a time dominated the assembly; but, horrified at the September massacres, they condemned the Reign of Terror, and tried to bring in more moderate measures. This drew upon them the hatred of the demagogues; and on 31 May, 1793, some twenty-nine of the Girondists were arrested at the instigation of Robespierre, and on 31 Oct. twenty of them were guillotined, amongst whom were Brissot, Gensonné, Vergniaud, Ducos, and Silléry. Valazé stabbed himself while he stood in the dock under his mockery trial.

They were called *Federalists*, because they wanted to unite all the departments of France into a *Federacy* like that of the United States of America.

Girton College, 1873. A college for ladies, about two miles from the town of Cambridge.

Gisors', in Normandy (*Peace of*), March 1114. A treaty between Henry I. of England and Louis VI., in settlement of certain disputes respecting the rights of William the son of Henry I. to certain territories in France. By this treaty Maine and Brittany were ceded to Henry.

Giunta (*The*). Of Venice. Consisted originally of ten patricians, but at a later period of twenty. It was sometimes called 'The Twenty.'

Gladiatorial War (*The*), B.C. 73. Headed by Spartăcus, a Thracian, who had served in the Roman army, but had turned brigand, and, being captured, was made a gladiator. Crassus brought this war to an end at Brundusium, but Pompey claimed the honour because he accidentally intercepted 5,000 fugitives and put them to the sword. Crassus hanged 6,000 of the captives along the road from Rome to Capua.

Glasgow Arms (*The*). A tree, a bird, a bell, and a ring. For the legend *see* 'Phrase and Fable,' p. 345.

> Here is the tree which never grew;
> Here is the bird which never flew;
> Here is the bell which never rang;
> Here is the fish which never swam.

The *tree* is the hazel, which supplied St. Kentigern with the torch with which he lighted the lamps of Culross Cathedral.

The *bird* is St. Serf's robin-redbreast restored to life by St. Kentigern.

The *bell* is the one brought by the saint from Rome, and hung in the tree to summon the people to prayer.

The *fish* is the salmon caught in the Clyde, containing the ring given to Oina, the faithless queen, as a love-token by the king (7th cent.).

Glass Houses. *Those who live in glass houses should not throw stones.* When the Scotch came over in throngs with James I., the English were greatly enraged against them; and, instigated by the Duke of Buckingham and others, the windows of the houses occupied by these interlopers were broken in all directions. A party of Scotchmen combined and retaliated by smashing the windows of Buckingham's mansion, which was called 'the Glass House,' and the duke brought his complaint to the king, who answered, 'Those who live in glass houses, Steenie, shouldn't throw stones.'

Glassists or 'Glassites' (*The*), 1728. Followers of John Glass, afterwards called 'Sandemanians' (*q.v.*). This Scotch sect was founded in the 18th cent. Members are admitted by a holy kiss, and abstain from all animal food that has not been well bled. John Glass condemned all national establishments of religion, and maintained the 'congregational system.'

Robert Sandeman was a disciple of John Glass.

Glencoe. *See* 'Massacre of Glencoe.'

Glipping. Eric V. or VII. king of Denmark was so called because of his incessant habit of winking (1249, 1259–1286); murdered 22 Nov.

Globe Theatre (*The*). Of which Shakespeare was a shareholder; was built in 1593, and a patent for it was granted in 1603 by James I. It was burnt down in 1613, rebuilt in 1614, and demolished somewhere between 1640–1650.

Glomerel Schools, 14th cent. Grammar schools in Cambridge connected with the University. In these schools the lads were taught the elements of Latin. A dozen glomerel schools were under the inspection of a Master of Glomery (*Magister Glomariæ*), who had a bedell to attend him. On these glomerels the University conferred the degree of 'Master in Grammar.'

Gloria (*The*), or 'Great Doxology' (Luke ii. 14). 'Glory to God in the highest, and on earth peace, good will towards man.' The 'Gloria in excelsis,' sung in the Latin Church after the introïtus (except on the penitential days of Advent and during Lent).

Called the 'Great Doxology' to distinguish it from the 'Glory be to the Father, and to the Son, and to the Holy Ghost,' sung at the end of each psalm.

Glorieuse Rentrée (*La*). The 'Glorious Return,' 1689. The return of certain of the Vaudois under the leadership of Arnaud. They had been driven from their homes by Duke Victor Amadeus, at the command of Louis XIV., who threatened to invade Savoy if the Vaudois were not driven out. Most of them took refuge in Switzerland, and about 800 contrived to get back.

Glorious First of June (*The*).
I. In *English* history, 1 June, 1794. The victory of Lord Howe, with 25 ships, over the French fleet, with 26 ships. Probably the phrase is French, and refers to the sinking of 'Le Vengeur.'

II. In *French* history, 1 June, 1794. When it is said that 'Le Vengeur' refused to surrender to Lord Howe, but, instead of so doing, the crew sank the ship, and all went alive into the deep, shouting, 'Vive la République!' Villaret de Joyeuse had command of the vessel.

The English version is that Lord Howe, with 25 ships, encountered the French fleet of 26 ships off Ushant. In less than an hour the French admiral fled. The English captured two ships of eighty guns, and four seventy-fours. Another seventy-four sank immediately after it was captured. As for the 'Le Vengeur,' the crew craved help, and many were picked up by the victorious English. All London was illuminated for three nights for this victory, and King George visited Lord Howe personally on board his flag-ship, gave him a sword, and made him a Knight of the Garter.

Glorious Fourth (*The*), *i.e.* of July. The day on which Americans celebrate the anniversary of their independence (1776).

Glorious Three Days (*The*). In French history. Tuesday, Wednesday, and Thursday, 27, 28, and 29 July, 1830, when Paris rose in arms against Charles X., compelling him to flee and abdicate. Thursday the 29th is called 'The Glorious Third.'

Glory and Sun of the East (*The*). Kharim Khan, vakel (regent), 1753–1779. He constituted Shiraz the capital of Persia, and restored peace to the country.

He never would take the title of shah.

Glory of Bristol (*The*). The 'Great Britain,' an iron steamship built at Bristol. Its dimensions were 1,795 tons register, and 3,270 tons burden. Launched in 1845. The engineers were I. Brunel, jun., and Mr. Bremner.

Gloucester. Called the 'Good Duke of Gloucester,' Lord Protector of England. Was born 1391 and 'found dead' in 1447. He was the brother of Henry V., and named protector during the minority of his nephew Henry VI. He married Eleanor Cobham in 1435, who was accused of witchcraft and imprisoned in 1441. Gloucester was arrested for high treason 11 Feb., and found dead (probably the work of Cardinal Beaufort) 28 Feb., 1447.

Glover's Roll, 1586. A copy of the famous Roll of Arms made by Glover, Somerset Herald, and preserved in the College of Arms. It goes back to the reign of Henry III. The original vellum roll is lost.

Gloves. Bishops, in the Catholic Church, wear violet gloves, cardinals scarlet, and popes white.

In maiden assizes, both in England and Scotland, the presiding judge is presented with a pair of white kid gloves.

Women first used gloves in France in the reign of Henri III. They were knitted gloves. Leather gloves were not introduced till the reign of Louis XIV. Their importation into England was forbidden in 1766 (6 Geo. III. c. 19).

The Greeks and Romans did not wear gloves, but used an armour to protect their hands in war.

Gluckists, 1774–1780. Followers of Johann Christoph von Gluck, of Bohemia, in the great musical war between Piccini and Gluck. Gluck tried to reform the Neapolitan school, in which the dialogue and business of opera were wholly subsidiary, and the music was the only thing regarded. The scenes were unconnected, and only served as vehicles for the airs and orchestra. Those who thought Gluck's reform an improvement were called Gluckists, but those who thought the music only was worth consideration in opera were called Piccinists, from Nicolo Piccini of Naples, a contemporary composer.

Piccini's fame rests on his 'Didon,' 1783, and 'Roland,' 1778; Gluck's fame rests on his 'Orfeo,' 'Alceste,' 'Armida,' 'Iphigénie en Aulide,' and 'Iphigénie en Tauride.' The 'Alceste' (of Euripedes), 'Iphigénie en Aulide' (of Racine), and the 'Iphigénie en Tauride,' are in the French language. The 'War' in France was musico-political. Marie Antoinette, a German by birth, was a Gluckist, and therefore all her enemies were Piccinists. Wagner followed Gluck in his operatic reforms.

A free translation of a French squib:—

One day the Muses had a quarrel
To whom they should present the laurel—
Whether to Gluck or to Piccini;
They could not for the world agree
'Twixt tweedledum and tweedledee;—
  'There's not a pin to choose between ye.
So Pic or Gluck (say I) or neither,
Or both, for aught I care, or either;
More undecided than Babouc,
Here's heads for Pic, and tails for Gluck.'

Glutton-masses. Celebrated five times a year. The people in the vicinity brought to the secular clergy all sorts of roast and boiled meats, with pasties and other viands, with strong drinks of every sort. As soon as mass could be despatched, the clergy and people of the different parishes set to in good earnest to see who could devour and drink the most in honour of the Blessed Virgin.

Gnosticism. The Gnostics taught that God lived in divine light, called πλήρωμα, and was all in all. The next stage was a long succession of æons, in which the *Demiurgos*, or Creator, appeared. Then followed *Man*, an earthy

B B

compound with an imprisoned soul. Those souls which shall be able to throw off corruption will join the pleroma, the rest will pass into other bodies. They supposed man to be tripartite, having a πνεῦμα or spirit derived from the pleroma, a ψυχή or soul bestowed by the Demiurgos, and a body or ὕλη of matter. Christ came to liberate the pneuma from the psyche and hyle. They despised the body and mortified it, and of course preferred celibacy to wedlock. For the same reason they denied the resurrection of the body, and maintained that its only resurrection was in baptism. They rejected the divinity and humanity of Jesus. His divinity, in that He was inferior to God; his humanity, in that his body was only a sort of phantom. All diseases they ascribed to malignant imps who had power over nature.

Evil, say the Gnostics, is the opposite of Good, and therefore of God. If God is a spirit, matter is the opposite, and evil must be in matter, and hence the antagonism between matter and God.

Of Gnostics there were more than fifty sects, of which the chief were the Basilidians, Valentidians, Marcionites, and later on the Manichæans. They flourished in the 3rd cent., and disappeared in the 5th.

Gnostics. All those multifarious sects which welded Greek, Roman, and other philosophies with Christianity. Such as the systems of Aristotle, Plato, Pythagŏras, Heraclītos, Empedoclês, Mysticism, Demonology, and the science of Cabbala. Thus, accepting the person of Christ, the Gnostics taught that he was an æon sent from heaven to reclaim the better part of the human race. Some maintained that the divine and human nature of Christ united at baptism, and separated at the crucifixion, when 'God forsook him.' Others maintained that his humanity was a mere illusion. Their canonical books are widely different to those received by the Christian Church in our days.

They are the 'Prophecies of Cain,' the 'Writings of Pachur,' the 'Psalms of Valentinus and Bardesanês,' 'Gnostic Hymns by Marcos,' the 'Books of Adam, Enoch, Mosch, Eliah, Isajah,' with books called 'Barkor,' 'Armagil,' 'Barbelon,' 'Balsamum,' 'Lensiboras,' &c.

Gnostics. Of *Syria*: Saturninus, Bardesanês, Tatian, and Severus.

Of *Asia*: Cerdo, Marcion, Lucian or Lucan, and Apellês.

Of *Alexandria*: Valentīnus, Basilidês, Carpocrātês, Heracleon, Ptolemæus, Secundus, Marcus, Colobarsus.

Lesser *Gnostic Sects*: Sethians, Cainites, and Ophites.

All in the first two centuries.

Gobbo (*It*). The Hunchback. I. Peter Paul Bonzi of Cortōna, the famous painter (1580–1640).

II. Lonati of Milan, the famous violinist (17th–18th cents.).

Gobelin Tapestry, or 'Tapestry of the Gobelins.' A famous tapestry made in the Faubourg St.-Marcel, Paris, and so called from the brothers Gobelin, dyers from Reims, who made a fortune by their scarlet dye in the reign of François I. Louis XIV. in 1667 converted the business into a royal manufacture, and employed eminent artists, like Lebrun, to invent designs. It was then designated 'The Royal Hotel of the Gobelins,' and the manufactures produced were called 'The Tapestry of the Gobelins.'

The tale is that a dyer of Leyden one day left on a window seat lined with tin a bottle of aqua regia near some cochineal which he was using. The bottle was accidentally thrown down, and mixing with the cochineal produced an exquisite scarlet dye. The man thought the tin had something to do with it, and by mixing in cream of tartar first some finely-powdered cochineal and then some tin in solution succeeded in discovering the famous dye.

God of Flowers (*The*). So Simon Varelst, the great flower-painter, called himself.

God save the King. The national anthem of Great Britain and of Prussia. Was (according to Cappell) the work of Dr. Henry Carey, both words and music (1696–1743). Cappell says it was composed as a birthday hymn for George II., and performed for the first time in 1740 at the Mercers' Company.

The words are an imitation of the 'Domīnĕ salvum fac regem' of the Catholic Church service. Some still ascribe the words and music to Dr. John Bull (1563–1591), professor of music in Gresham College, and chamber-musician to James I.

God-Bote. An ecclesiastical fine paid for offences against God.

Man-bote was a fine paid for slaying a man.

God's Congregation of poor unarmed Christian Brothers, 1537. So Simon Menno of Friesland called his followers. *See* 'Mennonites.'

God's House (*The League of*). 'La Ligia de la Chiada.' Switzerland; for the independence of the territory previously subject to the Bishop of Coire. Formed between 1424–1436.

God's Peace, 1035. *See* 'Holy Peace.'

God's Truce, 1040. A suspension of arms from sundown on Wednesday till sunrise on the Monday following, and on all festivals. It superseded the 'Holy Peace' (*q.v.*), 1035, which was an entire cessation of arms. All princes and barons bound themselves to abstain from feuds and spoliation on the days prohibited.

Goddess of Liberty (*The*), 10 Aug., 1793. The Goddesses of Liberty and of Reason were enthroned by the French Convention at the suggestion of Chaumette, and the cathedral of Notre Dame de Paris was desecrated for the purpose. The wife of Momoro the printer was the best of these 'goddesses.' The procession was attended by the municipal officers and national guards, while troops of ballet girls carried torches of truth. Incredible as it may seem, Gobet (the archbishop of Paris), and nearly all the bishops, vicars, canons, priests, and curés of Paris, stripped themselves of their canonicals, donned the red nightcap, and joined in this blasphemous mockery. So did Julien of Toulouse, a Calvinistic dissenting minister. *See* 'Goddess of Reason.'

Mrs. Momoro, it is admitted, made one of the best goddesses of Reason, though her teeth were a little defective.—CARLYLE, *French Revolution,* vol. iii. bk. v. 4.

Goddess of Reason (*The*), 10 Nov., 1793. A festival was given at Notre Dame, Paris, in honour of the 'Goddess of Reason,' who was personated by Mlle. Candeille of the Opera, one of the earliest of these 'goddesses.' She wore a red Phrygian cap, a white frock, a blue mantle, and tricolour ribbons. Her head was filleted with oak-leaves, and in her hand she carried the pike of Jupiter-Peuple. In the cathedral a sort of temple was erected on a mound, and in this temple (called the Temple of Philosophy) Mlle. Candeille was installed. Young girls crowned with oak-leaves were her attendants, and sang hymns to her honour. *See* 'Goddess of Liberty.'

The two goddesses—one of Liberty and one of Reason—have caused some confusion of names; and similar installations were repeated at Lyons and other places, as well as at Notre Dame and St. Sulpice.

Mlle. Maillard, the actress, is mentioned by L martine as one of the goddesses, who was compelled, much against her will, to play the part.

And Mlle. Aubray was one of the goddesses of Reason.

A new religion. Demoiselle Candeille, of the Opera; a woman fair to look upon when well rouged. She, borne on palanquin, shoulder high, with red woollen nightcap, in azure mantle, garlanded with oak, holding in her hand the pike of the Jupiter-Peuple, sails in, heralded by white young women girt in tricolor. This . . . . is our new divinity—Goddess of Reason, worthy, and alone worthy of revering.—CARLYLE, *French Revolution,* vol. iii. bk. v. 4.

Goderic. A nickname given by the Normans to Henry Beauclerc. They called his wife Matilda by the nickname of Godithe or Godiva, because, as Wace says, they 'tint la terre si sagement.' The sneer would be better understood by 'The goody king and queen.'

Gold Coined. By Darius, son of Hystaspês, B.C. 521–485. First coined at Rome A.D. 207. First coined in England by Henry III. in 1257.

Gold Keys (*The*). The badge or token of office given to the groom of the stole and mistress of the robes.

The queen [Anne] had repeatedly insisted to Marlborough that the duchess should deliver up the gold keys . . . . but that resolute woman refused to comply.—HOWITT, *Hist. of England* (Anne, 274).

Gold Mine of Europe (*The*). So Transylvania was once called; but the supply of gold now obtained thence is so much decreased that the title is no longer applicable.

Gold People (*The*). So the Arabs style the people of the towns of Barbary; the inhabitants of the Tell or cultivated lands they call the *Silver* people; and the inhabitants of the Sahara they call the *Camel* people.

Gold Purse of Spain (*The*). Andalūsia, the city from which Spain derives her chief wealth.

Gold Rings. By Roman law, were restricted by Tiberius (A.D. 22) to citizens with certain property qualifications. Severus (193–211) conferred the privilege on the army. Justinian in 529 removed all restrictions, and allowed any one who liked to wear them.

Gold Stick. The colonel of the 2nd Life Guards, who stands next to the sovereign on state occasions, and carries an ebony staff surmounted with a gold head engraved with the royal cypher and crown. He is assisted by another officer called the Silver Stick. The following extract from the standing orders of the 2nd Life Guards was supplied to me direct from the Lord Chamberlain's Office, St. James's Palace, July 1890.

'In consequence of a conspiracy existing in 1528, the king's person [Henry VIII.] was supposed to be in danger. It was, therefore, ordered that one of the captains commanding the Life Guards should wait next to his Majesty's person, before all others, carrying in his hand an ebony staff with a gold head engraved with his Majesty's cypher and crown. Another principal officer, carrying an ebony staff with a *silver* head, was ordered to be near the captain to relieve him occasionally. They were to be in attendance on the king's person whenever he walked, from his rising to his going to bed, except in the royal bedchamber.' See 'Golden Staff.'

The 'Morning Post,' describing the investiture of the royal princes in 1890, says: 'General Earl Howe, C.B., was introduced to her Majesty's presence by the Lord Chamberlain, and received from her Majesty the gold stick of office as colonel of the 2nd Regiment of Life Guards.'

Gold of Affliction (*The*). A personal tribute in the Eastern empire on the industry of the poor. Abolished by Anastas'ius about 500.

Timotheus of Gaza chose this tax as the subject of a drama. He made it necessary for a father to send out his own daughter to earn money to pay the tax by the wages of unrighteousness. This play contributed in no small measure to the abolition of the tax.

Gold of Tolo'sa, or Toulouse Gold, ill-gotten and ill-starred wealth. It is said that Cæpio the consul, on his march against the Cimbrians, stole from the temple of Tolosa the gold and silver deposited there. His subsequent defeat was regarded as a divine punishment for this sacrilegious act; and hence arose the Latin proverb, *Aurum Tolosānum habet*, meaning ' his ill-gains will never prosper.'

Golden Age (*The*). The Greeks and Romans placed their golden age under the rule of Saturn.

Hesiod described five ages, and Byron adds a sixth, the ' Age of Bronze.' Hesiod's five ages:—
The *Golden* Age, or patriarchal, under the rule of Saturn.
The *Silver* Age, or voluptuous, under the rule of Jupiter.
The *Brazen* Age, or warlike, under the rule of Neptune.
The *Heroic* Age, or renaissant, under the rule of Mars.
The *Iron* Age, or utilitarian, under the rule of Pluto.
The *Bronze* Age (of Byron), under Napoleon Bonaparte.

Golden Age of England (*The*). The reign of Queen Elizabeth (1558–1603).

Statesman : William Cecil lord Burleigh		1520–1598
Dramatists : Shakespeare (wrote 85 plays)		1564–1616
Ben Jonson (' Rare Ben ')		1574–1637
Beaumont (1586–1607) and Fletcher	...	1576–1625
Massinger	... ...	1585–1639
Poets not dramatists :		
Spenser, 'Faëry Queen '	... ...	1553–1599
Tusser, ' 500 points of Good Husbandry'		1515–1580
Buchanan (elegant Latin verse)	..	1506–1582
Ecclesiastics : John Knox (Scotch Reformer)		1505–1572
Hooker, 'Ecclesiastical Polity'	...	1553–16 0
Historians : Camden, ' Britannia '	...	1551–16 3
Stow, 'Chronicle,' &c.	... ..	1525–1605
Holinshed, 'Chronicles '	...	died 1580
Scholar : Sir Philip Sidney, 'The Marcellus of England,' Author of 'Arcadia '		1554–1586

To these add ' The Admirable ' Crichton, a universal genius (1551–1583), Sir Thomas Gresham, the great merchant, and a host of others not so well known.

. It is rather remarkable that our three chief queens have all marked epochs in English history.

Elizabeth : The Golden Age.
Anne : The Silver Age.
Victoria : The Iron Age and Age of Science.

Golden Age of France (*The*). Louis XIV. It contained the following great men :—

Army : Turenne, Condé, Luxembourg, Catinat, Créquy, Vendôme, and Villars.
Navy : Duquesne, Tourville, and Duguay Trouin.
Ministers : Colbert, Louvois, and Torcy.
Clergymen : Bossuet, Bourdaloue, and Massillon.
Statesmen : Molé, Lamoignon, Talon, D'Aguesseau.
Military Engineer : Vauban.
Architects : Mansard and Perrault.
Artists : Pujet, Girardon, Le Poussin, Le Sueur, and Le Brun.
Landscape Gardener : Le Vautre.
Poets : Racine, Corneille, Molière, Quinault, Lafontaine, La Bruyère, and Boileau.
Tutors to his children : Montausier, Fénelon, Huet, Fléchier, and De Fleury.
This galaxy gave him a title to be called ' Le grand monarque.'

Golden Age of German Literature (*The*), 1750–1850. It contained :—

Klopstock, author of ' Messiah '	1708–1803
Lessing, poet and prose writer	1729–1781
Herder, ' Outlines of the Philosophy of the History of Man'	1744–1813
Wieland, the ' Voltaire of Germany ' ...	1733 1813
Goethe, author of ' Faust'	1749–1832
Schiller, the poet	1759–1805
Kant, the philosopher	1724–1804
Fichte, ,, ...	1762–1814
Schelling, ,, ...	1775–1854
Hegel, ,, ...	1770 1831

Bürger, Voss, Kotzebue, Schlegel, Gesner, Zimmermann, Sturm, Richter, &c.
Baumgarten, Moses Mendelssohn, Hamann, Haller, Winckelmann, Mesmer, Sir William Herschel, Lavater, Pestalozzi, Hahnemann, Gall, &c.
With the musical composers, Beethoven, Hummel, Meyerbeer, Spohr, Weber, and others.

Golden Age of Italian Art (*The*). See ' Cinque Cento.'

Golden Age of Poland (*The*). That of Sigismund I., the Great, and his son Sigismund II., *Augustus* (1506–1572).

Golden Age of the Roman Empire (*The*). The age of Antonīnus Pius (138–161).

The reign of Augustus is called the Augustan Age.

Augustus	...	...	...	B.C. 63—A.D. 14
Livy (historian)	...	...	...	... 59-17
Ovid (' Metamorphoses ')	...	...	· 43-18
Horace (poet)	...	...	...	65-B.C. 8
Virgil (poet)	...	...	...	70-B.C. 19

And many others. *See* 'Augustan Age.'

Golden Angel, Golden Fleece, Golden Spurs. *See under* 'Order,' &c.

Golden Ass (*The*). A romance by Appulēius. It is the adventures of Lucian, a young man, metamorphosed into the form of an ass, but still retaining his manly intelligence. This satire contains the exquisite episode of Cupid and Psyche (*Si'-ke*).

Golden Book (*The*). 'Il Libro d' Oro.' The register of Venetian nobility. Anyone enrolled in the 'Golden Book,' if 25 years old, was a member of the Grand Council.

When Bonaparte took possession of Venice in 1797, the 'Golden Book' was burned at the foot of a Tree of Liberty.

The attainment of the chancellorship was more than once preferred to inscription in the 'Golden Book.'—*History of Venice*, vol. i. p. 206 (Murray, 1831).

Golden Bull (*The*).
I. Of *Hungary*, 1222. Wrung from King Andrew II. by his nobles, just as Magna Charta was extorted from John. Andrew II. of Hungary, surnamed 'Hi'erosolymitānus,' was a feeble, self-willed, worthless king, like our John.

The nobles and the church were to be exempt from taxes.
The daughter of a noble without male heir shall inherit one-fourth of his property.
No noble shall be obliged to follow the king in any foreign war.
The palatine (*i.e.* mayor of the palace) shall be the supreme judge.
No foreigner to hold office or dignity without consent of the council of the realm.
The King shall not grant counties or offices of any kind in perpetuity.
If the king violates any of the laws in this bull, it shall not be treason to levy war on him.
Called the 'Golden Bull' because the attached seal was enclosed in a golden case or box.

* *It is rather remarkable that one of the very first countries in Europe to effect the liberty of subjects should have been one of the last-born nations, the Huns of Hungary.*

II. Bulla Aurea of the *Empire*, 1356. Published by Kaiser Karl IV. at the Diet of Nürnberg. Considered the Magna Charta of Germany. It prevented a repetition of the contests which had hitherto arisen whenever a vacancy in the throne occurred; and regulated the functions, number, and privileges of the electors. Called 'golden' because the seal attached to the parchment was of gold instead of lead, or else that it was enclosed in a golden case.

Since 1440 the electorate has been merely nominal, as the House of Rudolph has been permanently established.
It limited the number of electors to seven (three prelates and four lay princes). The prelates were the three Archbishops of Mainz, Cologne, and Trèves; the lay princes were the King of Bohemia, the Duke of Saxony, the Margraf of Brandenburg, and the Pfalzgraf of the Rhine. Their persons were declared sacred. Every question was to be decided by majority and without appeal. Frankfort was appointed the place of session, and Aix-la-Chapelle the place of coronation.

Golden Cord (*The Society of the*), 1888. Organised by Mr. Scadding, an American minister, among the boys of his parish. The majority of the members are newsboys, from nine to thirteen, and they are pledged to keep five rules: (1) To be loving and lovable; (2) to be pure in heart, mind, and body; (3) to pity and help the poor and weak; (4) to be kind to dumb creatures; (5) to hate all shams, meanness, and dishonesty. Having signed this pledge, the boy receives the badge—a knot of golden cord.

Golden Dragon of Bruges (*The*). Taken in one of the crusades from St. Sophia, in Constantinople, and placed on the belfry of Bruges (1 syl.).

Philippe van Artevelde transferred it to Ghent, where it is still.

Golden Election (*The*). The election of Addison, Hugh Boulter (afterwards primate of Ireland), and Wilcox, as demies of Christ Church, Oxford.

Addison was born 1672, Boulter 1671, Wilcox 1673.

Golden - footed Dame (*The*). Leader of a troop of women who rode in the attitude and armour of men, under the banner of Conrad, in the second crusade. The leader of the Amazonian band wore buskins and gilt spurs.

Golden Gate (*The*).
I. The entrance of the land-locked bay on which San Francisco is seated.
II. Or 'Gate of the Seven Towers' (Jedicula Kapi) of Constantinople. Dr. Smith says that over this gate was the following inscription:

Hæc loca Theudosius decorat post fata Tyranni
Aurea secla gerit, qui portam construit auro,

and adds, 'cited by Sirmond, in his notes upon *Sidonius*.' It still exists; and near it is a smaller arch, also called the Golden Gate.

Golden Gate of Constantinople (*The*).
The entrance of the Golden Horn (*q.v.*) or port of Constantinople. It has no connection whatever with the Lofty Gate or *Sublime Porte* of the vizier's official residence.

The Bosphorus and the Hellespont may be considered as the two gates of Constantinople. . . . When these gates were shut, the capital still enjoyed every production which could supply the wants or gratify the luxury of its inhabitants . . . but when the passages of the straits were thrown open, they admitted the natural and artificial riches of the north and south, the Euxine and Mediterranean.—GIBBON, xvii.

Strange, after this, that Gibbon should more than once speak of 'battering the Golden Gates of Constantinople with axes.'

Golden Gate of Salo'na (*The*).
A gate in the palace of Diocletian, in Dalmatia. It was to his palace in Dalmatia that the emperor retired after his abdication. The gate, which still opens into the market-place, was probably gilt when it was first built.

Golden Girdle.
Louis VIII. made an edict that no courtesan should be allowed to wear a golden girdle under very severe penalties. Hence the proverb: 'Bonne renommée vaut mieux que ceinture dorée.'

Golden Hand.
General Zelislaus lost his right hand in battle, and Boleslaus III. gave him a gold hand. *See* 'Silver Hand,' 'Iron Hand,' and 'Steel Hand.'

Zelislaus ducis pariter atque militis officio functus contra Moravos dextram amisit. Eum Boleslaus III., Polonorum rex, collaudatum pro meri is et virtute, aurea manu donavit.—*Hist. Polon.* book v.

Golden Hind (*The*).
Sir Francis Drake's ship, on board which Queen Elizabeth on one occasion dined.

Golden Horde (*The*), or 'La Horde d'Or.'
The Tartars of the Kaptschak, who established themselves in 1463 in the Crimea, the chief city of which peninsula was called Or or Perekop, the Greek Taphros. The Tartar word Or, the Slavonic word Perekop, and the Greek word Taphros, all mean the same thing, that is, a 'ditch or trench.' The Horde d'Or simply means the 'Horde of the Isthmus.' Our 'Golden Horde' is a blundering translation of *La Horde d'Or*, which should be the Horde of Or, or of

Perekop. Compare Greek οὐρός, ὅρος (a channel, a boundary).

The usual explanation is this. The horde was called 'the golden' from the gorgeous tapestry of the Khan's tent, and that a present of the emperor of China to Ghengis Khan of a rich tent suggested the title. The suggestion is utterly worthless.

Golden Horn (*The*).
A branch or gulf of the Bosphorus, called also the Port of Constantinople. It runs from Galata north-westward, and is called golden from its great beauty and the wealth of the cities on each side.

The harbour of Constantinople obtained, in a very remote period, the denomination of the *Golden Horn*. The curl which it describes might be compared to the horn of a stag or of an ox. The epithet of *golden* was expressive of the riches which every wind wafted into the capacious port. GIBBON, ch. xvii.

Golden Legends (*The*), 13th cent.
A collection made by James de Voragine (3 syl.), a Dominican. There are 177 sections, each of which is devoted to a particular saint. That of Felix listening to a bird, rendered into verse by Longfellow in 1851, is what is distinctively meant by 'The Golden Legend.'

Golden Mass.
'Missa Aurea,' a mass in celebration of the Virgin Mary; so called from its great pomp and magnificence. *See* 'Mass.'

Golden Mouth (*The*).
I. John of Antioch, called Chrysostom (A.D. 347-407). He was archbishop of Constantinople.
II. Dion the rhetorician (90-117).

Golden Number (*The*).
The 'Meton'ic Cycle' or 'Cycle of the Moon,' B.C. 432, devised by Meton. It ranges from 1-19, because 19 years make a cycle. The number used to be engraved in letters of gold on pillars of marble.

Add 1 to the date of the year, and divide by 19. The remainder is the golden number. If no remainder, then 19 is the golden number. This number determines the epact, and the time of Easter. Thus the epact for 1890 is 9.

Golden Rose (*The*).
A rose wrought of gold, and blessed by the pope on Mid-Lent Sunday (Lætare Sunday, *q.v.*), and presented to some Catholic whom the pope thinks proper to honour. Du Cange fixes the origin to Innocent IV. (1243-1254).

Isabella of Spain, and Eugénie the wife of Napoleon III., have both received the Golden Rose. Isabella of Spain was certainly no model queen. Henry VIII. also received one from Clement VII. (! !)

Golden Rule (*The*).
In *Arithmetic*, the Rule of Three.

In *Morals*, 'Do unto others as you would be done by.'

Golden Shield (*Knights of the*). A French military order instituted by Louis II. for the defence of the country. Motto : ' Allons.'

Golden Spears (*The*). The title and ornament of the best army of the Persians, consisting, in the days of Chosroes II., of 50,000 men. Cut to pieces in the great battle of Nineveh, 1 Dec. A.D. 627 (Gibbon, xlvi.).

Golden Speech, or Chrysologus, Pietro bishop of Ravenna (*433–450).

Golden Spurs (*Order of the*), 1539. Instituted by Pope Paul III. Regulated anew by Gregory XVI. in 1840.

Golden Staff. Thomas Mowbray first earl marshal of England was so created by Richard II. He and his successors were authorised by charter to carry before the king a gold staff surmounted with the royal arms, and having the Mowbray arms at the lower end. All other marshals carry a wooden staff. *See* ' Black Rod,' ' Gold Stick,' &c.

It is said that William Marshall, who married Isabel daughter of Strongbow, by whom he came into possession of the palatinate of Leinster held by her father, carried a gold staff at the coronation of Richard I.

Golden State (*The*). California, in North America.

Golden Stream (*The*), or ' Chrysorroas,' Joannes Damascēnus (676–756). The first to apply the logic of Aristotle to Christian dogmas and doctrines.

Golden Tongued (*The*). *See* ' Golden Speech.'

Golden Valley (*The*). The eastern part of Limerick is so called from its great fertility.

Golden Veil (*The*). The Khalif of Bagdad was inaugurated by a golden veil, strongly perfumed with musk, being thrown over his head.

Golden Verses of Oppian (*The*). The Κυνηγετικά, a Greek poem on hunting, for which the Emperor Caracalla paid him a piece of gold for every line. He also wrote a poem on fishing. Oppian died A.D. 213, aged 30.

Golden Verses of Pythagoras (*The*). May be thus rendered into English :—

Ne'er suffer sleep thine eyes to close
  Before thy mind hath run
O'er every act, and thought, and word,
  From dawn to set of sun ;
For wrong take shame, but grateful feel
  If just thy course hath been :
Such efforts day by day renewed
  Will keep thy soul from sin.

Golden Violet (*The*). The original prize given by the ' Gaie Société des Sept Troubadours de Toulouse,' founded in 1328, for the best poem sent in by Mayday every year. This society was the origin of the ' Academy of Floral Games,' in France.

Goldsmiths' Company (*The*). London, 1393. Incorporated by Richard II.

Goldsmiths' Notes. Bank-notes were originally so called, because the bankers were all goldsmiths.

Golspie Stone (*The*). A stone in Sutherland, with an Ogham inscription. *See* ' Dogmael's Stone.'

Other stones in Scotland with inscriptions in Ogham are the Newton Stone and Logie Stone in Aberdeenshire, and the Bressay Stone in Shetland.

G. O. M. ' The Grand Old Man.' So W. E. Gladstone, in his last premiership (1881–1885), was called, half in ridicule and half in admiration. Born 1809.

Go'marists or ' Anti-Remonstrants,' 1611. Calvinists, so called from Frans Gomar of Bruges (1563–1641), who put forth a strong ' Counter-Remonstrance ' against the Arminian ' Remonstrance ' (*q.v.*) presented to the States of Holland, in 1610. This Counter-Remonstrance dogmatically affirmed the dogmas of absolute predestination and reprobation.

Gombette (*La loi*), A.D. 502. A Burgundian code of considerable repute, often printed, even so late as 1855. It was so called from Gombaud or Gondebaud, the third king of Burgundy, who died A.D. 516. A second part was added in 519 by Sigismond, the son and successor of Gondebaud. Gombette (2 syl.).

I observe that this code is often erroneously called by English authors La loi Gourbelic, originally, without doubt, a typographical error.

Gonfalon'iere (*The*), 1292. The title given to the chief magistrate of Florence. Subsequently, a gonfalonier of justice, with eight priors, constituted the Signoria, held office for two months, and lived in the palazzo at the public charge. In other Italian republics the gonfaloniers were officers of justice, varying in number, and commanders of regiments. In France, a gonfalonier was the person who carried the gonfalon, or grand banner of the church. This sacred flag was always committed to the charge of the *avoués*, or temporal defenders of the churches and abbeys.

Gon'falons (*The*). Of Florence, were the sixteen standards of the four quarters of the city. The quarters were named from the four chief churches (Santo Spirito, Santa Croce, Santa Maria Novella, and San Giovanni); the gonfalons were named after the devices blazoned on them.

The four gonfalons of the Santo Spirito quarter were the Ladder, the Shell, the Whip, and the Dragon.

The four gonfalons of the Santa Croce quarter were the Car, the Ox, the Golden Lion, and the Wheels.

The four gonfalons of the Santa Maria Novella quarter were the Viper, the Unicorn, the Red Lion, and the White Lion.

The four gonfalons of the San Giovanni quarter were the Black Lion, the Dragon, the Keys, and the Vair.

The standard-bearers were called the 'Sixteen,' and next to the Signory the office was the most honourable in Florence.

Gongor!s'n. A stilted bombastic style, called sometimes *Estilo culto*. The word is derived from Luis de Gongora y Argotê, a Spanish poet born at Cordŏva (1561–1627).

G. H. Lewes, speaking of Calderon, says: 'I seriously declare that his poetry does not seem to me a whit richer in thought or feeling than that of Lopé de Vega, while it is even more defaced by hyperbolical conceits and frigid Gongorisms.'

Gonville Hall, Cambridge, 1348. Founded by Edmund Gonville, rector of Terrington and Rushworth, in Norfolk. *See* 'Caius College' (Keys College), by which name it is now generally called.

Gonville Hall was enlarged by Bishop Bateman in 1353.

Gonza'ga (*The House of*). A long line of sovereign dukes of Mantua and Montferrat (1328–1665), when the territory was taken possession of by the kaiser-king Joseph I.

Good Bishop of Marseilles (*The*). Henri François Xavier de Belsunce (1671–1755), who night and day, with heroic courage, exerted himself to succour the dying during the plague of 1720–21, to cheer the despairing, to comfort the afflicted, and to point all to that source of help which alone holds the issues of life and death.

A similar devotion was shown in the 19th cent. by Father Damien, a Belgian priest, who spent sixteen years at the leper settlement at Molokai, a Hawaiian island. This devoted priest caught the disease, and died from it in May 1889.

Good Cousins, 1808. The initiated of the Carbonari. There were (1) apprentices, (2) masters.

Good Duke (*The*). Edward duke of Somerset, lord Seymour, governor of the person of the king's [Edward VI.] Majesty and protector of all his realms; lieutenant-general of all his armies, both by land and sea; lord high treasurer, earl marshal of England, knight of the most noble order of the garter, &c. If honours make goodness, he must have been 'good' indeed. Yet all his greatness and goodness did not save him from a traitor's death. He was made lord protector in 1547, and was beheaded on Tower Hill 22 Jan., 1552.

Good Duke Humphrey (*The*). Brother of Henry V. and lord protector of England during the minority of Henry VI. His brother John duke of Bedford was regent of France (1391–1447).

He was arrested for high treason 11 Feb., 1447, and found dead 28 Feb. Probably murdered by Cardinal Beaufort.

Good Duke of Argyll (*The*). John Campbell, duke of Argyll (1678–1743).

Good Friday. The Friday before Easter Day. Kept sacred in commemoration of the crucifixion on Calvary. It seems to have been set apart by Constantine the Great, who forbade 'the holding of law-courts and markets' on that day. In England and Ireland it is a *dies non*.

The day of the Crucifixion is by no means certain. Supposing the 'Last Supper' to be the pascha, the three synoptists say that the Crucifixion took place the day *after*, *i.e.* 15th Nisan; but John informs us that the pascha occurred *after* the Crucifixion.

Good Friend, 1854. A nickname given to Napoleon III., from a letter which he wrote to the Emperor Nicholas of Russia. The letter began ' Sire,' and not ' Sire, my brother,' and ended ' Your Majesty's good friend.' The letter was published in the ' Moniteur,' and was like a red flag to the Russian autocrat.

Good Lord James (*The*) of Douglas, the friend of Bruce (died 1330). He was entrusted with the heart of Bruce, to carry it to the Holy Land and bury it there ; but, on reaching Seville, he entered the service of Alfonso against the Moors, and was slain. The heart was brought back and buried in Melrose Abbey.

Goodman of Ballengeich. The name assumed by James V. of Scotland when he made his disguised visits in the districts round Edinburgh and Stirling.

Goodman's Fields, Whitechapel, London. So called from a large farmer of the name of Goodman.

At this farm I myself in my youth have fetched many a ha'p'orth of milk, and never had less than three ale-pints in summer and one in winter, always hot from the kine and strained. One Trolop, and afterwards Goodman, was the farmer there, and had thirty or forty kine to the pail.— STOW, *Survey of London* (1598).

Good Men. So the Waldenses (*q.v.*) were called in Germany, from the sincerity of their persuasion and purity of their lives.

Good Men of St. Martin (*The*). ' Buonomini di San Martino.' A charitable society of twelve men, founded in the middle of the 15th cent. by Antonino (afterwards archbishop of Florence, and known as St. Antonio). Called ' San Martino ' from the little homely church of St. Martin, the headquarters of the brotherhood. It still exists in Florence. The object of this charity was the relief of those who had fallen into poverty, but were unable to earn their bread, and were ashamed to beg.

Dante was married in this church, and was born within sight of it.

Good Parliament (*The*), 1376. In the reign of Edward III. So called from its sturdy opposition to the illegal government of the Crown, or royal council. The speaker was Sir Peter de la Marc, and the Black Prince most heartily supported the Commons. It denounced the mismanagement of the French war, the oppressive taxation, and John of Gaunt the duke of Lancaster, who was obliged

to withdraw from the council. It demanded a strict account of how the public money had been expended. It exposed a terrible list of abuses ; not sparing the king himself and his mistress Alice Perrers. Alice was driven from the court, and made to swear never to return again. It impeached Lord Latimer and William Lyons ; and presented 160 petitions of grievances. It demanded the annual assembly of parliament and freedom of election ; denounced the papal aggressions, and demanded a more vigorous prosecution of the war. *See* ' Parliament.'

The taxes levied for the pope were five times those levied for the king.

Good Queen Anne (*The*). The wife of Richard II. of England. On her marriage she was 15 and Richard 16. She was the daughter of Karl VI. kaiser of Germany, who attended his father, the blind old King of Bohemia, at the battle of Crécy, and was granddaughter of Sigismund. Anne of Bohemia was good looking and most amiable. She married Richard 14 Jan., 1382, and died at Sheen 7 June, 1394, aged 27.

Many suppose the phrase is meant to apply to Anne daughter of James II., because she transferred to the church the money called ' Queen Anne's Bounty ' (*q.v.*) ; but Anne Stuart was the mere tool of stronger minds.

Good Queen Maud. First wife of her cousin Henry I. of England, and daughter of Malcolm of Scotland. Married 1100, died 1118.

Good Regent (*The*). James Stewart, earl of Murray (or Moray), natural son of James V. of Scotland, by Margaret, daughter of John 4th lord Erskine. Assassinated by Hamilton of Bothwellhaugh 21 Jan., 1570.

Good Swordsman (*The*). ' Le bon sabreur,' Joachim Murat, marshal of France (1771-1815).

Good Templars (*The Independent Order of*). This order is pledged to total abstinence. It was formed in New York in 1851, and introduced at Birmingham in 1868. The president is styled the ' Grand Worthy Chief.'

This order has no connection with the ' Knights Templars ' (*q.v.*).

Goody Palsgrave. So Anne (wife of James I. of England) used to call her daughter Elizabeth, after her marriage with Frederick elector palatine and ' king of Bohemia.' She had eight sons and five daughters. 'Goody' was a term of contempt. Elizabeth is often called 'queen of Bohemia.'

Grave Maurice [*i.e.* the Graf Moritz] and Prince Rupert, so celebrated in the wars of England between Charles I. and his parliament, were her sons; and Sophia, the mother of George, was her daughter.

Goorkha (India). A cow-herd; a name applied to every native of Nepaul. It properly belongs to the Gorkhalis, a Hinduised and warlike race of Nepaul.

Goose Moon (*The*). So the North American Indians call the month in which the flocks of geese from the Arctic shores arrive. These geese supply the Indians with a much-coveted food in winter.

Goose Tower (*The*). The tower of the Castle of Gurve, built by Valdemar I. of Sweden in 1166. In this tower captives taken in war, called geese, were confined.

Gordon Riots (*The*), 1778. Riots organised by Lord George Gordon as a protestation against the relaxation of the penal code against English Roman Catholics. 2 June, 1780, Lord George Gordon, with some 100,000 followers, left St. George's Fields, with the view of presenting a monster petition (containing 120,000 names) for the repeal of the late act. The soldiers were called out; only eight persons in the House voted with Lord George; but the mob were riotously inclined, and went about destroying Roman Catholic chapels, the shops of Roman Catholics, and molesting those who resisted their foolish fanaticism. This went on for six days; on the ninth Lord George Gordon was apprehended on a charge of high treason. Twenty-one of the rioters were executed in July 1780, but Lord George was acquitted as of unsound mind. He ultimately died in Newgate of a fever in 1793.

On 2 June, 1780, the chapel of the Sardinian minister was razed to the ground.
On 5 June a Catholic school and three priests' houses were destroyed.
On 6 June Newgate was forced, and 300 prisoners were released; and in the evening several houses were set on fire.
On 7 June King's Bench Prison, the Fleet Prison, Bridewell, and several private houses were destroyed.

Gorham Case (*The*). A dispute between the Rev. George C. Gorham and the Bishop of Exeter, who refused to institute him to the vicarage of Bramford Speke in Devonshire, in 1848. Gorham applied to the Court of Arches, and his application was dismissed by Sir Herbert Jenner Fust (2 Aug., 1849). An appeal was then made to the Privy Council, which reversed the order of the Court of Arches (8 March, 1850). The bishop then applied to the Court of Queen's Bench, but was cast (15 April, 1850). Another application by the bishop to the Court of Common Pleas also failed (2 May, 1850). Ultimately Gorham was instituted, 7 August, 1850. The case created an immense sensation, as it was a combat between the Evangelical Church party, represented by Gorham, and the High Church party, represented by the Bishop of Exeter.

A somewhat similar contest occurred in 1889, when the Bishop of Lincoln was summoned to appear before the Archbishop of Canterbury for what were called 'Rubrical offences.' *See* 'Lincoln Impeachment,' &c.

Görlitz Process (*The*), 1850. A celebrated trial which took place in Germany. The Countess of Görlitz was strangled by a servant named Johann Stauff, whom she had caught stealing articles from a desk in her sitting-room. The case was tried at Darmstadt, and the prisoner pleaded 'Not guilty,' but was imprisoned for life. The main interest of the case rested on this point: the body of the countess was burnt, and Dr. von Siebold maintained it was destroyed by spontaneous combustion, while the chemists Bischoff and Liebig denied the possibility of such combustion.

Gortonists. A religious sect in New England, so-called from Samuel Gorton (1600–1677), a sectary who denied the humanity of Christ. Extinct.

Go'schens, 1888. A Stock Exchange term for the new 2¾ per cent. stock, which was for the first time officially quoted 30 March, 1888. Named after George Joachim Goschen, chancellor of the exchequer, who projected the conversion.

Gospellers, 1549. A religious party in England, said to have been very profligate in their lives, and thus to have brought scandal on the Reformed Church. Article 38 of the Church of England is aimed at these men: 'The goods of Christians are not [in] common . . . as certain Anabaptists do falsely boast.'

When two ministers read the communion service, the one who stands on the north side of the table is called the Gospeller because he reads the Gospel.

Gospels (*Spurious*).

The Gospel of	The Gospel of
Andrew	Matthias
Apelles	Marcion
Barnabas	Nicodemus
Cerinthus	Peter
Eve	Philip
James the Greater	Tatian *the Diatessaron*
Judas Iscariot	Thaddeus
Lucianus	Thomas
Lucius	Valentinus
Matthew (*false*)	

The Gospel of Perfection
The Gospel of the Ebionites (4 syl.).
The Gospel of the Infancy of Christ
The Gospel of the Nativity of Mary *
The Gospel of the Twelve Apostles
The Gospel according to the Egyptians
The Gospel according to the Hebrews
The Gospel according to the Syrians
The Everlasting Gospel (13th cent.)
The Four Gospels of the Manichēans
The History of Joseph the Carpenter
The Protevangelium of James [Toldoth Jeschu]
* *It is from these that Mohammed derived his knowledge of the Saviour.*

Irenæus (i. 17) tells us that the Gnostics, in the 2nd cent., had an innumerable multitude of spurious books ; and in the following age the number greatly increased. In the 4th cent. there were at least 80 gospels. *See under* ' Gnostics.'

Gotescalc, surnamed *The Second Effulgence*. A German heretic (806–868). His 'heresy' seems to have been the Calvinistic doctrines of absolute election and reprobation. He was condemned by the Council of Mayence in 848, imprisoned by the order of Hincmar archbishop of Reims, and died in gaol in 868.

Go'thamite. A New Yorker.

Gothamist, a man of Gotham, in Nottinghamshire.

Gothic Architecture (*Pointed style*). Originated about 1190.

Gothic Code (*The*), or ' Codex Legum Barbarorum.' The laws of the barbarians codified by Alaric, king of the Visigoths, and augmented by his successors. *See* ' Codex.'

Gothic Liturgy (*The*). Same as the 'Mozarabic Liturgy' (*q.v.*).

Gothic War (*The*), A.D. 331. The Sarmatians being threatened by Alaric, king of the Goths, applied to Constantine the Great for protection. The emperor gladly responded to the request, and after three or four engagements of varying success, the Goths retreated across the Danube, and Constantine received the honours of a triumph.

Goth'icus. Claudĭus II. of Rome was so called because he defeated the Scythians, Herŭli, and Goths, who had invaded

Mœsia, A.D. 269. In the great battle at Naïssus there were more than 320,000 Goths, and as many as 50,000 were slain.

Goths (*The*). Part of the great Teutonic swarm at one time dispersed about the southern and eastern shores of the Baltic. Afterwards they moved towards the Black Sea, where, in the middle of the 3rd cent., they split into two parts. Those who remained in the east of Europe were called the Eastern [Ostro] Goths ; and those who journeyed westwards were called the Western [Visi] Goths.

Gottesfreunde (*The*), or ' Society of the Friends of God,' who strove to establish the *unio mystĭca*, or loving intercourse with deity.

Gourides (2 syl.). A dynasty which reigned in Persia in the 12th cent., founded by Hussin Mahmoud Gouri, governor of Gour under the Gaznevides. He declared himself independent in 1155. Under Alah Eddyn the Gourides conquered all Persia, and drove out the Gaznevides in 1158 ; but in 1213 they were in turn driven out by the Carizmians.

Government (*The Act of*), 1657. The act which made Cromwell the Lord Protector. The Speaker, in the name of the Commons, invested him with a mantle of state, placed the sceptre in his hand, and girt the sword of justice by his side. By this act of government Cromwell was allowed to name his successor, but in all after cases the office was to be elective.

The Commons had previously offered Cromwell the title of king, but the army disapproved ; and Cromwell told the Commons he could not undertake the government burdened with such a title.

Government of July (*The*). The Royal Republic, with Louis Philippe, an elective king, called ' King of the French,' not ' King of France.' From 9 Aug., 1830, to 24 Feb., 1848.

Government of the Cortês (*The*), 1814–1823. The constitutional monarchy established in Spain after the fall of Napoleon.

Government of the National Defence (*The*), 2 Sept., 1870, to 13 Feb., 1871. After the battle of Sedan, when the French emperor (Napoleon III.) yielded up his sword to William king of Prussia, certain persons arrogated to themselves the offices of state under the title of ' The Government of the National

Defence'; but they resigned their office to the National Assembly, when M. Thiers was appointed president of the new republic. (Thiers, pronounce *Te-air*.)

Government of the 400 (*The*),

B.C. 411. An oligarchy instituted in Athens for the democracy, by the persuasion of Alcibiadês. The 400 were chosen by five presidents, and in them was lodged absolute power. This form of government lasted only four months.

Governor-General of India, or

'Governor-General of the United Colony,' *i.e.* Bengal, Bombay, and Madras, 1786. Each of these provinces has a governor, but that of Bengal has precedence.

Gower.

A part of Glamorganshire, colonised by Flemings in the reign of Henry I. These colonists did not speak Welsh.

Gownsmen.

Men who had risen by their wise counsel in civil affairs; in contradistinction to military heroes, called Men of the Sword. The terms were common in Queen Elizabeth's reign. We still use the phrase 'Carpet Knights' for lord mayors and other civil officers who receive the order of knighthood.

Gowrie Conspiracy (*The*),

5 Aug., 1600. The king's version is that during a hunting expedition Alexander Ruthven informed him that a mysterious stranger with stores of gold was in Ruthven Castle, and that it would be desirable for the king to see him. The king went to the castle with a few attendants, and was taken by Alexander to a high tower, where, instead of a stranger, he found Henderson, one of Gowrie's servants. He says that Alexander tried to murder him, but he called out 'Treason,' and, some of his attendants coming to his rescue, Alexander was slain. The noise of the scuffle roused the house, and the Earl Gowrie, with seven retainers, rushed into the tower, whereupon a scuffle ensued, and Gowrie fell dead at the hand of Sir John Ramsay. Some say the whole tale is most improbable, and that it is more likely that James was the aggressor, and murdered the two brothers to avenge an insult offered to him by their father, in the 'Raid of Ruthven' (*q.v.*). The clergy generally disbelieved the king's version, and refused to offer up thanks to God for his deliverance; but a day was,

nevertheless, set apart for the purpose. The truth of the matter seems to be that the two brothers wanted to kidnap the king, but met with their death and the king escaped.

Graal (*The*), or 'The Holy Graal.'

A miraculous chalice made of a single emerald, which possessed the power of preserving chastity and prolonging life. Said to have been the cup from which Christ drank at the last supper, and in which Joseph of Arimathea caught the last drops of blood as Christ was taken down from the cross. In 1170 Chrétien of Troyes sang of the search by knights for this miraculous cup, which was a very favourite subject in the middle ages.

Grace

was the title assumed by Henry IV. of England on his accession in 1399. 'Excellent Grace' was assumed by Henry VI. in 1425, and was retained till Henry VIII. adopted the word 'Majesty' (*q.v.*). An archbishop or duke of the United Kingdom is still addressed as 'Your Grace.'

Grace (*A*).

In the University of Cambridge means a proposal by the Council offered to the Senate to be confirmed. All laws, all degrees, all permits, all licences, connected with the University are graces before they take effect by the authority of the Senate (*q.v.*).

A grace for a degree is called a supplicat.

Grace (*The Act of*), 1696.

Provides maintenance for debtors in Scotland when imprisoned by their creditors.

In England general pardons at the beginning of a new reign, or on other special occasions, are called Acts of Grace. In the reign of William and Mary, at the dissolution of the United Ministry of Whigs and Tories, a general pardon for all political offences, called an Act of Grace, was sent down to the House, 1689.

Grace (*Days of*).

See 'Days of Grace.'

Grace Darling, 6 Sept., 1838.

The 'Forfarshire' steamboat, with sixty persons on board, was wrecked on its passage from Hull to Dundee. A few escaped in the larboard quarter-boat, but the vessel itself went to pieces on a rock near the Farne Islands. Half the ship was carried away, with all the persons in the cabin or on the stern and quarterdeck, but the other half stuck fast on the rock. Grace Darling, who was living with her father in the Longstone lighthouse, heard the screams, and induced her father to go with her in a lifeboat to the rock. The sea was very rough, the wind high, and the rain heavy, but Grace and her father saved nine persons. This heroic maiden died 20 Oct., 1842, of consumption, aged 25.

Graceless and Godless Florins

(*The*). The florins struck in 1849 by Mr. Sheil, Master of the Mint. The legend was only 'Victoria Regina,' both F.D. (*fidei defensor*) and D.G. (*Dei gratia*) being omitted. This gave great offence, and the coins were called in the same year.

Graces (*The*).

Articles of the covenant between Charles I. and the great landed proprietors of Ireland. Charles had quartered a large military force on the Irish; and the chief proprietors agreed to pay the king 120,000*l.* to be secured in their rights and properties.* The Graces provided: That the king's claim to lands in Ireland should be limited to sixty years; that the proprietors of Connaught should receive new patents; that the exactions of the soldiery should be restrained; that the fees of the king and the powers of the court should be defined; and that a general pardon for past offences should be granted. The articles were never carried into effect.

* That is, that the Discoverers (*q.v.*) should not be sent to examine the titles of their estates.

Gradual.

That part of the Mass which intervenes between the epistle and the gospel; it consists of a few verses of the psalms chanted on the steps (*gradus*) of the altar.

Gradual Psalms.

'Psalms of the Steps,' 'Songs of Degrees,' Psalms 120-134. The meaning is uncertain. Probably they were the psalms sung during the time of burnt-sacrifice, called *olut*, *m-olut* (of degrees).

Graf.

In Germany a reeve, as in our word *sheriff*, *i.e.* shire-reeve. Subsequently it was a mere honorary title, somewhat like the French count. The original function of the reeve was to collect the revenues of his district. The word is very old, and occurs in the *Lex Salica* (5th cent.). Charlemagne divided his vast empire into grafschaften or districts, over each of which was a chief magistrate called a graf. *See* 'Margraf,' 'Pfalzgraf.'

Graham's Dyke.

The rampart running along the line of the detached forts which Agricola planted A.D. 81 between the firths of Clyde and Forth, to serve as a defence against the Picts and Scots. Also called the 'Wall of Antonīnus.'

Called the 'Wall of Antonīnus' because it was made by Lollius Urbĭcus, general of the Emperor Antonīnus. The 'Dyke of Urbĭcus' connects these forts together. *See* 'Grimes Dyke.'

Grahamise.

To open letters at the post office in order to trace crime. 'Harcourting' is a word of the same meaning, introduced while Sir William Harcourt was home secretary (1880-1885).

Grammarians, or 'Grammatĭci.'

Philologists of ancient Rome. Suetonius has written a history of the Grammatici. The most famous were Aristarchus, Dionysius, Didymus, Flaccus, and Quintilian. But of the second century of the Christian era the following names are well known: Pollio, Eutychius, Athenæus, Julius Pollux, Macrobius, and Aulus Gellius.

Gramota Soudebnaia.

The code of laws drawn up for the people of Novogorod by Jaroslaf I. of Russia (1015-1055). The code is still in force.

Granary of Athens (*The*).

The district about Kertch. The buckwheat of this district carried off the prize in the Great Exhibition of London in 1851.

Granary of Europe (*The*).

Hungary, famous for its cereals. Sicily was so called at one time.

Granary of Turkey (*The*).

So Egypt used to be called.

Grand Alliance (*The*).

I. Of Kaiser Leopold and Holland against Louis XIV., signed at Vienna 12 May, 1689. Joined by England 20 Dec., 1689; by Spain 6 June, 1690; and by Saxony 2 June, 1694.

II. Against Louis XIV. and the Spanish Succession. Between the kaiser, Great Britain, Holland, Prussia, and Hanover; signed at the Hague 7 Sept., 1701.

III. Against Napoleon I., 3 March, 1813. This was the 6th and last coalition against Napoleon, encouraged by the disastrous Moscow expedition. The alliance, signed at Reichenbach, consisted of Prussia and Austria, Russia, Sweden, and Great Britain. Denmark joined 14

Jan., 1814. Before this Denmark had thrown in her lot with Napoleon.

Grand Assize (*The*). Appointed by Henry II. to supersede trials by battle. A freeholder might refer his dispute to twelve legal knights, and, if they agreed in their verdict, their judgment was final; if not, others were selected till the verdict was unanimous.

Grand Climacteric (*The*) of man's life is 63, the compound of the two mystic numbers 7 × 9. Of course it needs hardly be added that this year is not more fatal to man than any other.

Certainly 9 × 9 is far nearer the psalmist's 'fourscore' years. As a rule, five times the years of full growth is the natural term of animal life.

Grand Companies (*The*), or 'Free Companies.' Troops of adventurers that desolated France in the reign of Jean II. le Bon, and the first part of the reign of Charles V., his son. The nucleus of these bandits was the disbanded German mercenaries after the battle of Poitiers (1356). Being without employment, they enlisted under any daring leader that would hire them, and spread themselves abroad as a desolating scourge. To free the country of this pest Charles induced them to take service under Duguesclin, and sent them to the Spanish war, where they were either slain or took service under the Black Prince (1367–1369).

Grand Corneille (*Le*). Pierre Corneille (1606–1684). Thomas Corneille was also a dramatist (1625–1709).

Grand Corrupter (*The*). Sir Robert Walpole (1676–1745). He was expelled the House 17 Jan., 1712, being found guilty of 'a high breach of trust, and notorious corruption.' There is no doubt that he always had a profound faith in bribery, and never scrupled to exercise it.

Grand Council (*The*). 'Consiglio Grande.' An assembly of Venetian noblemen over the age of 25. All persons eligible were inscribed in the Golden Book. The Grand Council chose a committee of 11 to elect the members of the Grand Council; the Grand Council, after 5 ballots and 5 scrutinies, elected the Council of Forty; and the Council of Forty elected one of the Grand Council for doge.

Grand Coutu'mier of Normandy (*The*). A collection of the ancient laws of Normandy, compiled in the 3rd year of Henry III., and containing the laws and customs prevailing in the reigns of Henry II., Richard I., and John.

Grand Days. Those days in the term which are 'dies non juridici,' in the Inns of Court and Chancery, as Candlemas day in Hilary—Ascension day in Easter—St. John the Baptist's day in Trinity—and All Saints' day in the Michaelmas term.

In the French monarchy the annual assizes were called the *Grand Jours*, especially the extraordinary assizes of the kings of France in the provinces. In the reign of François I. there were many such, *e.g.* in Poitiers 1531, and again 1541; at Moulins in 1534, 1540, 1545; at Troyes in 1535; at Angers in 1539, &c. The last Grand Jour was held by Louis XIV. in 1665 at Clermont-Ferrand.

Grand Duke of the West (*The*). The Duke of Burgundy. Philippe III. le Bon (1396, 1419–1467) was 'duc de Bourgogne, de Lorraine, de Brabant, de Limbourg, et de Gueldres; comte de Flandre et d'Artois; comte-palatine de Hainault, de Zeeland, de Namur, et de Zutphen; seigneur de la Frise, de Salins, et de Malines.'

Grand Master. The head of the Hospitallers, Templars, Teutonic Knights, and Freemasons respectively.

Grand Monarque (*Le*). Louis XIV. (1638, 1643–1715). He was for twenty years the pupil of Môns. Beauchamp, the dancing-master, and in his wars with Marlborough reduced France to the verge of bankruptcy. His religious persecutions were almost as disastrous to France as his wars with England. It is well for a nation not to have such 'great kings' as Louis XIV.

It is truly pitiable to call such a man as George IV. 'the First Gentleman of Europe,' or Louis XIV. the 'Grand Monarque' of France. Henri IV. was twice as 'Great' as the pupil of M. Beauchamp.

Grand Old Man (*The*), or G.O.M. I. William Ewart Gladstone was so-called in his last administration, 1881–1885. Lord Rosebery first used the expression 26 April 1882, and the Right Hon. Sir W. Vernon Harcourt repeated it, 18 Oct. the same year.

II. **Dr.** Hook, when vicar of Leeds (1837–1859), addressing a working class, said, in reference to the 'Messiah,' Handel, 'the Grand Old Man,' entertained the town with that oratorio for a whole week (*Leeds Weekly Express*, 9 Nov., Local Gossip).

Grand Pensionary (*The*). In Holland, or 'Assessor juris perītus,' the chief minister of the States, and chancellor of the exchequer. The office lasted for five years, but the same person was eligible for re-election. The most famous were Jean de Witt (died 1672) and Heinsius (1689–1720). Office abolished by Napoleon I. in 1795.

There used to be a pensionary in each of the main cities of Holland.

Grand Privilege (*The*). 'Groot Privilegie.' The Magna Charta of Holland, granted 1477 by Mary duchess of Burgundy.

Grand Remonstrance (*The*), 22 Nov., 1641. Adopted by the Long Parliament against the measures of Charles I. It was brought in by Pym, who declared it was not the intention of the parliament to abolish episcopacy, but only to limit and reduce the power of the bishops. It repudiated the charge of being revolutionary. It demanded the observance of the laws against papistry ; securities for the even administration of justice ; and the employment of ministers who had the confidence of parliament.

Grand Serjeanty. An ancient English tenure by which a man holds his lands and tenements of the king by service, such as carrying the royal banner or king's lance ; leading an army ; carrying the coronation sword ; being the king's carver, butler, chamberlain, and so on.

Grand Tour (*The*). The tour made by wealthy Englishmen through France, Switzerland, Italy, and home by Germany.

Grand Vizier. Chief minister of the Ottoman empire, introduced by Amurath I. in 1386 ; abolished by Mahmoud II. in 1838 ; but restored by Abdul Medjid in 1839.

In 750 the chief minister of the kalif was called vizier.

Grande Mademoiselle (*La*). Anne Marie Louise d'Orléans, duchess of Montpensier, and first cousin of Louis XIV. She was the daughter of Gaston duc d'Orléans, and Marie de Bourbon-Montpensier. Louis XIII. was her uncle. La Grande Mademoiselle was one of the richest heiresses in Europe.

Grande Semaine (*La*), 27, 28, 29 July, 1830. Tuesday, Wednesday, and Thursday of the Insurrection of Paris which drove Charles X. from the throne, and substituted for him Louis Philippe, called the Citizen-king. Semaine (2 syl.).

Grandees, 1648. So the members of the council of officers were called in the reign of Charles I. The members of the inferior council were called Adjutors, and subsequently Agitators.

Grandes Compagnies (*Les*), 14th cent. Gangs of adventurers which desolated France in the reigns of Jean II. and Charles V. They were recruited by strangers of all nationalities, especially by the Germans whom Edward III. had set at liberty after the treaty of Brétigny in 1360. The populace rose up against them and put them down for a time, but they reappeared in 1361 under the name of Tards-Venus. Duguesclin had the wit to enrol them in the army of Enrique of Trastamare, and employed them in the Spanish war against Pedro the Cruel.

Grandes Précieuses (*Les*). The learned women of the Hôtel Rambouillet, in contradistinction to the Précieuses Ridicules.

Les Grandes Précieuses sont de ces choses excellentes aptes à être imitées par de mauvais singes.—MOLIÈRE.

Grandison-Cromwell. So Lafayette (1754–1834) was called by Mirabeau. He wanted to appear a Christian gentleman, like Richardson's 'Sir Charles Grandison,' but in his heart of hearts he had the ambition of a Cromwell.

[Paris rang] with endless talk about English Monk, nay about Cromwell. O thou poor Grandison-Cromwell !—CARLYLE, *French Revolution*, vol. ii. bk. vi. 1.

Grangerite (*A*). One who extends and supplements a book by collateral matter culled from all sorts of sources, as prints, maps, newspaper cuttings, selections from other books, pamphlets, autograph letters, and so on. So called from the Rev. J. Granger (1710–1776), who 'grangerised' a biographical history of England (1769) with 'supplement' (1774).

See BOWDLERISE. There are also the words

'Grangerise,' 'Grangerism,' 'Grangerisation,' &c. Forster's 'Life of Dickens,' 3 vols. was 'grangerised' to 9 vols. in America, by playbills, engravings, portraits, views, catalogues, illustrations, and other supplemental matter.

Granite City (*The*). Aberdeen, Scotland. Many of the houses are built of the granite which abounds in the neighbourhood.

Granite Redoubt (*The*), 14 June, 1800. The grenadiers of the Consular Guard of Bonaparte (First Consul) were so called from the stand which they made at the battle of Marengo against the Austrians.

Granth. The sacred book of the Sikhs. There are really two Granths: one the *Adigranth* by Arjunmall, and the other by Guru Govind Sinh. Both are metrical and very bulky.

Under me (Govind) the bows of the Singhs have proved triumphant over the sabres of the Moslems; and the precepts of the Granth over the cowardly doctrines of the Vedas and Shastras.—GOVIND, *History of his Wars.*

Grape-stone (*Killed by a*). Anacreon the poet was choked by a grape stone, B.C. 478, aged 85. The favourite concubine of Yezid II., kalif of the Saracens, was also killed in the same manner, A.D. 726. *See* 'Eating Fruit.'

Grasshopper (*The*). Callimīdês, an Athenian, in the time of Philip of Macedon; so called on account of his vivacious wit and liveliness.

Grateful Order of St. Catherine (*The*), 1712. A Russian order founded by Peter the Great, in gratitude to his wife for delivering him from captivity by bribing the Turkish vizier.

Grateley (*Synod of*). During the reign of Edgar. Made ten regulations for the Church, by far the most important ever passed:

1. Regulated tithes.
2. Authorised judges to execute sentence on those condemned by the trial of ordeal.
3. Against witches and highwaymen.
4. Names the towns authorised to coin money.
5. Awards the punishment for debasing coin.
6. Regulates ordeals.
7. Forbids buying and selling on Sundays.
8. Against perjury.

9. Commands bishops to assist the judges.
10. Against remiss and negligent magistrates.

Gratian's Decretal, or 'Decrētum Gratiani.' A part of the 'Corpus Juris Civīlis' collected by Gratian, a Benedictine monk of the 12th cent. in Tuscany. The collection took him twenty-four years to compile.

Grattan's Parliament. Consisted of a house of lords and house of commons. It was altogether Protestant, and was elected exclusively by Protestants till towards the close of its career, when Catholics were admitted to the franchise. It was eminently the representative of the property class of Ireland, and many of its members were the nominees of the British government. Pitt based his argument for the Union mainly on the ground that the Irish Parliament was not workable. In 1780 Grattan proposed in the Irish Parliament the abolition of 'Poyning's Act' (*q.v.*). It was not then carried, but in 1782 he moved what is called the 'Declaration of Rights'—that any claim out of Ireland to bind the kingdom of Ireland is illegal. In April the same year he assumed the question to be carried, and declared that henceforth no body of men, except the Irish Parliament, has any right to make laws by which Ireland shall be bound. In May C. J. Fox repealed the bill of 6 Geo. I., and Ireland was set free. Grattan was rewarded by a grant from the Irish Parliament of 50,000*l. See* 'Parliaments.'

Grattan's Parliament passed 54 coercion acts. It began in one revolution, and ended after the putting down of an insurrection. The Irish parliament was united to that of Great Britain in 1800, by what is called the 'Act of Union.' Grattan's statue in Dublin was erected in 1876.

Grave of the Russians (*The*), 1733. On the death of Augustus II. of Poland, Stanislaus Leczinski was elected king, but his election was opposed by Austria and Russia. Stanislaus fled, and shut himself up in Dantzic, where he was besieged by the Russian army, but made so stout a defence that a place is still shown on the fortifications of Dantzic called 'The Grave of the Russians.'

Grave-clothes (*The*), in which the body of Christ was wrapped after the crucifixion, are thus tabulated by hagiographers: Aix-la-Chapelle contains some;

the parts deposited at Besançon were thrown away at the Revolution ; Cadouin, in the diocese of Périgueux, claims to possess a cloth, somewhat more than two yards and a half in length, and a yard and a quarter in breadth ; Cahors is especially rich in the sacred grave-clothes, it claims to possess the cloth which covered the head of Jesus, it is of Egyptian linen ' trois doubles superposés ' ; Carcasso, in Italy, contains some of them ; Chambéry has one beautiful bit of linen cloth, said to have been employed on the occasion ; Mayence has some of the grave-clothes ; in Rome several churches profess to contain some of these relics ; Toulouse has some ; and in Turin is a square of linen four and a half yards long, spotted with blood, and said to be the napkin wrapped round the head. *See* ' Crucifixion, *Relics of the.*'

If all the grave-clothes said to be relics were used, it must have taken considerable time to have folded them up neatly and placed them on the seat where the body was laid.

Grave-stones (*Jewish*). An image or effigy with uplifted hands, signifies a Jewish priest. A vase of water delineated on a grave-stone signifies a Levite, who bathed the hands of priests or poured water over them.

In Catholic symbolism figures with their hands on their breasts, and chalices, denote *priests*.
Figures with crozier, mitre, and pontificals, represent *prelates*.
Figures with armour represent *knights*.
Figures with legs crossed represent either *crusaders* or *married* men.
Figures with mantle and large ring represent *nuns*.

Gray. *See* ' Grey.'

Gray's Inn. One of the four Inns of Court, having the sole power of calling persons to the degree of barrister.

The four Inns of Court are the Inner Temple, the Middle Temple, Lincoln's Inn, and Gray's Inn. New Inn is affiliated to the Middle Temple ; Thavies Inn and Furnival's Inn to Lincoln's Inn ; Clifford's Inn and Clement's Inn to the Inner Temple ; Barnard's and Staple's to Gray's Inn.

Greased Cartridges, 1857. In January, a man employed in India in making cartridges for the new Enfield rifles just supplied to our native soldiers, asked a sepoy of the 2nd Grenadiers for a draught of water from his drinking-pot. The high-caste sepoy was indignant, for if the pot but touched the lips of the artisan, it would have been polluted for ever. The man replied with a sneer that the sepoy need not be so squeamish, as the new cartridges were greased with bullock fat, and every sepoy would lose caste in biting off the end. The horrible tale spread like wildfire. The Hindûs were told the grease was that of the sacred cow, the Moslem soldiers were told it was the grease of the unclean swine. Others asserted it was a mixture of cow and pig fat. And this led to the Indian Mutiny (*q.v.*).

Great Antiquity (*The*). The revised records and chronicles of Ireland by the suggestion of St. Patrick. Parts existed for many centuries, as ' The Book of Armagh,' ' The Psalter of Cashel,' ' The Book of Glandaloch,' ' The Leabhar Gabala,' and others, from which much of the ancient history of Ireland is derived.

' The Psalter of Cashel ' was compiled by King Cormac. It was a book of annals, very valuable, but unhappily lost.

Great Bear (*The*), or ' Ursa Major.' The finest of the northern constellations, consisting of seven great stars. Called ' Ceorl's Wain ' (the churl's waggon), corrupted into King Charles's Wain. Also called the plough. The figure of a bear with a fox's tail is certainly a funny anomaly.

Great Beds. I. Deut. iii. 11. The bedstead of Og king of Bashan was 9 cubits long and 4 cubits wide, after the cubit of a man, *i.e.* 18 in. In English measure the length was 13 ft., and the width 6 ft.

II. The Great Bed of Ware is 12 ft. long and 12 ft. wide, said to have been made for Warwick, ' the King-maker.'

III. The bed of Reims Cathedral in which Louis XVI. and Marie Antoinette slept at their coronation was 7 ft. 10 in. long, and 7 ft. 8 in. wide. Its height was 8 ft. from the ground, which must have been most inconvenient.

Great Bible (*The*), or ' Great English Bible,' 1539-1541. Published in the reign of Henry VIII. A translation under Archbishop Parker, who induced the bishops and other learned men to undertake it in portions. The different parts were afterwards joined together and printed with short notes in folio. In 1589 an octavo edition was brought out. In 1572 another folio edition was printed with corrections, and several prolegomena. This was called ' Matthew Parker's Bible.' *See* ' Bibles.'

The Great Bible was based on Tyndale's translation.

17

Great Britain. A name adopted on the legislative union of Scotland and England by the Act of Union passed 16 Jan., 1707. It was provided by this act that the two kingdoms of England and Scotland should be united into one under the name of Great Britain.

Great Bullet-head (*The*). George Cadoudal, the French royalist (17C9–1804). He was head of the Chouans after the death of Jean Cottereau, and in 1802 joined Pichegru's conspiracy (*q.v.*).

Great Captain (*The*). I. Hernandez Gonzalo de Cordŏva y Aguilar (1443–1515). Called *El Gran Capitan* in 1496 after reducing Upper Calabria, surprising Laino, and going to the aid of Ferdinand at Atella in the first half of the year 1496.

He finished up the year by expelling the French from Naples.

II. Manuel I. emperor of Trebizond (1120, 1143–1180).

Great Cham of Literature (*The*). Dr. Samuel Johnson (1709–1784).

Great Civil War (*The*). The war in the reign of Charles I.

Nor was he less affected when his aunt narrated the sufferings and fortitude of Lady Alice . . . during the Great Civil War.—Sir W. SCOTT, *Waverley*, chap. v.

Great Commoner (*The*). I. Sir John Barnard, who, in 1717, proposed to reduce the interest of the National Debt from 4 to 3 per cent. Any creditor, however, was at liberty to receive his principal in full, if he liked. It was William Pitt (Lord Chatham) who gave this designation to Sir John Barnard.

Mr. Goschen in 1888 reduced the interest from 3*l.* to 2¾*l.* per cent.

II. William Pitt (afterwards Earl of Chatham), 1708–1778. Buried in Westminster Abbey.

Great Company (*The*). I. 1343. The first was commanded by the German Guarnieri or Duke Werner, who wrote on his corslet ' Enemy of God, of Pity, and of Mercy.' It was employed against the Visconti by the league of the Montferrat, La Scala, Carrara, Este, and Gonzaga houses.

II. 1353. Bands of adventurers under the command of Fra Moriale, and afterwards of Conrad Lando. It consisted of 40,000 men, of whom 5,000 were cuirassiers. It hired itself out to anyone who wanted

a ready-made army, and exacted blackmail from cities and castles to be secure against depredations. *See* 'Pind'aris.' (*See* Hallam, ' Middle Ages,' vol. i. p. 498.)

Les Compagnies Grandes were the condottieri or free-lances of France; thé chief were under Sir Hugh Calverley, Sir Matthew Gournay, and the Chevalier Verte. Under Duguesclin they enlisted in the Spanish army, and disappeared from history 1360.

Great Condé (*The*). Louis prince de Condé. Died 1674, aged 65.

Great Council (*The*), 1173. A Venetian council of 480 members, who represented the general assembly of the whole people, and was renewed every year. The electors were a committee of twelve, two from each of the six districts or *Sestieri*. From this body a committee of sixty formed the senate, and assisted the doge.

Great Council of the Peers (*The*), 24 Sept., 1640. Assembled at York by Charles I., who was unwilling to summon a parliament because the parliament always insisted on redress of grievances before they would grant supplies. This great council was called to grant supplies to raise an army to resist the Scots, who had recently encamped on a hill called Dunse Law, and threatened to advance.

Great Council of the Realm (*The*). The witenagemote, or parliament of the Norman kings of England. All tenants who held directly of the crown, all bishops, and the greater abbots, with the great officers of the court, constituted this council. It was not so much an assembly of ' wise men ' as an assembly of feudal vassals. In the reign of Henry I. the lesser barons were excused attendance, though their right of doing so remained. In 1265 Simon de Montfort summoned knights from each county and two burgesses from each town to his parliament. From 1295 the great council had become the parliament of the realm, in which every order of the state was represented, and having the control of the legislation and executive government of the nation.

Great Cromwell Bible (*The*), 1538–39. The first edition of the folio Bible, printed in the reign of Henry VIII. The edition contained 2,500 copies, one of which was set up in every church in England, and secured to a desk by a chain. Within three years seven editions were published. *See* 'Bibles.'

This was not Oliver Cromwell, but Thomas Cromwell, who was beheaded in 1540.

Great Dauphin (*The*). Louis, son of Louis XIV. (1661–1711).

The son of the Great Dauphin was called ' The Little Dauphin.' Both died before Louis XIV.

Great Disease (*The*). Leprosy.

Great Duke (*The*). The Duke of Wellington (1769–1852).

Bury the Great Duke
With an empire's lamentation ;
Let us bury the Great Duke
To the noise of the mourning of a great nation.
           TENNYSON.

Great Earl of Cork (*The*). Richard earl of Cork, lord high treasurer of Ireland in the reigns of James I. and Charles I.

Great Eastern (*The*). The iron 'leviathan' steamship built by Brunel in 1857. It made its first voyage across the Atlantic in 1860. It was broken up in 1888.

Great Elchi (*The*). Stratford Canning (Lord Stratford de Redcliffe), ambassador to the Ottoman Porte 1841–1858; born 1787, died 1880.

The Turks called him the 'Padishah of the Padishah.'

Great Elector (*The*). Frederick William elector of Brandenburg (1620–1688).

Great Fire (*The*), or 'The Great Fire of London,' 1666, the year after the Plague, which it put an end to. It broke out at a bakehouse near London Bridge. Only six persons perished in the fire, though 600 streets, 13,000 houses, 80 churches, St. Paul's Cathedral, the Custom-house, Guildhall, and 4 stone bridges were destroyed. The people, to the amount of 200,000, camped out in the fields of Islington and Highgate.

Great Harry (*The*), 1509. The first double-decker built in England ; it had three masts. It was 1,000 tons burden, and cost 14,000*l.* This ship was built by order of Henry VII., and was completed in the year of his death. It was accidentally burnt at Woolwich in 1553. (*See* 'Archæologia,' vol. iii. p. 266.) *See* 'Henri Grâce à Dieu.'

The second great ship was the 'Henri Grâce à Dieu,' and the third was the 'Sovereign of the Seas.' *See* 'Great Michael.'

Great-head, or 'Caenmore.' Malcolm III. of Scotland, who married Margaret sister of Edgar Atheling (1024, 1057–1093). *See* also 'Grostête.'

Great King (*The*). The King of Persia was so called during the prosperity of that empire.

Great Light (*The*), or *Llever Mawr*. Cyllin or Linus (2 Tim. iv. 21), brother of Claudia (wife of the senator Pudens, and grandfather of King Lleirwg [*Lucius*], who is said by some to have introduced Christianity into Britain A.D. 59).

Of course the introduction of Christianity into Britain by King Lucius is generally denied ; but other conjectures, no less fanciful, are : St. James the son of Zebedee (*Ussher*); Simon Zelôtês (*Caw*) ; Joseph of Arimathea (*Gildas*); St. Paul (*Eusebius*); St. Peter ; Aristobûlus, &c. All that is certain is this : Christianity was introduced by someone, probably in the 1st or 2nd cent. In the Council of Arles, 314, the British Church was represented by three bishops (York, London, and Lincoln).

Great Magician of the North (*The*). Sir Walter Scott is so called by Professor John Wilson (1771–1832).

Great Marquis (*The*).

I. James Graham marquis of Montrose (1612–1650).

II. Dom Sebastiano Jose de Carvalho marquis of Pombal, the greatest of all the Portuguese statesmen (1699–1782).

Great Michael (*The*). A monster ship constructed by James IV. of Scotland. Its sides were 10 ft. thick ; its length was 240 ft., breadth 36 ft. It required 300 mariners to work her, and would hold 1,000 soldiers. A cannon ball would not pierce her sides. *See* 'Great Harry,' and ' Henri Grâce à Dieu.'

Great Mogul (*The*), 1526. A title first assumed by Baber, fifth in descent from Tamerlane. The sovereigns of Delhi continued the title.

Great Mogul Diamond (*The*). The history of this diamond runs back to B.C. 56, but little is known of it till the 14th cent., when it was held by the rajah of Malwa. Later on it fell into the hands of the sultans of Delhi, after their conquest of Malwa. Tavernier tells us he saw it among the jewels of Aurengzebe, and says in the rough state it weighed 793⅝ carats. The Shah Djihan sent it to Hortensio Borgio, a Venetian lapidary, to be cut, when it was reduced to 186 carats. Djihan was so enraged at this great waste that he not only refused to pay the lapidary, but he also fined him 1,000 rupees. This is all that is known of the 'Great Mogul Diamond,' but it is supposed that the Koh-i-noor is the same stone—under which name the rest of its history will be found. *See* 'Diamonds.'

Great Moralist (*The*). Dr. Samuel Johnson (1709–1784).

Great O (*The*). Daniel O'Connell (1775–1847).

As to O'Connell, depend upon it that whatever Mr. Stanley may wish to do, Mr. Stanley's masters have other uses to make of the great O than to gag him.—GLEIG, *Life of Wellington* (year 1830).

Great Pan (*The*). Voltaire (1694–1778). Also called the 'Dictator of Letters.'

Great Paschal Period (*The*). 532 years. *See* the 'Dionysian Period.'

Great Peace (*The*), 8 May, 1360. The peace-treaty of Brétigny between France and England, whereby Edward III. renounced his pretension to the crown of France, and his claim to Normandy, Anjou, and Maine. He still, however, retained Calais, Guisnes, Guienne, and Poitou.

Great Plague (*The*). In French, 'La Grande Peste,' 1580. It began in Portugal, and Lisbon was well-nigh depopulated. It was very fatal in Provence and Aix. In 1581 it appeared in Marseilles, where it carried off all the inhabitants, except 3,000. In Paris it appeared, and the city was overrun with thieves. *See* 'Plagues.'

Great Power of God (*The*). Simon Magus (Acts viii. 10).

Great Rebellion (*The*). The civil war in England which broke out between Charles I. and the Parliament. It began 22 Aug., 1642, and practically terminated with the defeat of the king at Naseby in 1645.

Great Roll of the Pipe (*The*). A record made up year by year of the revenue accruing to the crown in the different counties of the realm. The *certain* revenues consisted of farms, fees, castleguard, and other rents; the *casual* revenues consisted of fines, amercements, wards, marriages, reliefs, and other profits which fell to the crown by virtue of its prerogatives. The series of these pipe rolls, according to Madox ('History of

the Exchequer') goes back to 1155, continues unbroken to 1834, and contains invaluable notices of distinguished persons in English history through all that time by contemporaries. There is *one* roll of a still earlier date. It has been printed, and Mr. Hunter has shown that it belongs to the 31st year of Henry I. These records and 'Domesday Book' are documents unequalled for antiquity in all Europe.

The office (Clerk of the Pipe) is so called because the whole receipt of the court, says Lord Bacon, is finally conveyed into it by divers small pipes, as water is conveyed into a cistern.

Great Sabbath (*The*), or Holy Saturday. The day between Good Friday and Easter Sunday.

Idem dicitur SABBATUM LUMINUM, in Chronico Orientali (page 125), quod in eo baptismi fierent quos φωτισμους vocant Græci.—DU CANGE.

Great Schism of the West (*The*), 1378–1429. The time when there were two or more contemporary popes, one chosen by French cardinals and the other by Italians. On the death of Gregory XI. the Italians chose Urban VI., a Neapolitan, for his successor; but the French cardinals, who were far the greater number, nominated one of their own countrymen, who was crowned by them as Clement VI. (1378). Urban held his court at Rome, and Clement at Avignon. England, Italy, Bohemia, Germany, Prussia, Poland, and the Scandinavian kingdoms acknowledged the Roman pope; but France, Scotland, Spain, Sicily, and Cyprus acknowledged the French pope.

In this unseemly schism sometimes there were three contemporary popes, as for example Gregory XII., Benedict XIII., and Alexander V.; and sometimes as many as four, as John XXIII., Gregory XII., Benedict XIII., and Martin V.; and again John XIII., Gregory XII., Clement VIII., and Martin V. This disgraceful schism continued for more than half a century.

Great Sea (*The*). The Mediterranean was so called by the ancient Jews, Greeks, and Romans.

Great Storm (*The*), 27 Nov., 1703, in the south of England. The damage in London was some two millions sterling, and at Bristol about a quarter of a million. In Little Wild Street chapel, Lincoln's-Inn Fields, a sermon is annually preached on the 27th Nov. to commemorate this national calamity.

It suggested to Addison that happy line—
Rides on the whirlwind and directs the storm.

Great Unknown (*The*). Sir Walter Scott. So called because his principal romances and novels were not issued under his name, and speculation was agog as to the real author (1771–1832).

Great Unpaid (*The*). Justices of the peace, whose sentences on offenders have given great dissatisfaction to those who love even-handed justice. Thus at Dulverton, March 1886, Sarah Ann Blackmore was sentenced to 12 months' hard labour for stealing turnips to the value of 4*d*. The very same week Riva Eugene, accused of stealing a policeman's cape, was dismissed, 'because the weather was cold, and policemen should not leave their capes about to tempt cold people.' In the same week William Maltby, aged 10, was sentenced to one month's imprisonment and four years in a reformatory for stealing a shillingsworth of onions, at Southampton.

Great Unwashed (*The*). The artisan class were first so called by Sir Walter Scott.

Great Wall of China (*The*). Completed B.C. 214 by Chi-Hwang-Ti of the Tsin dynasty. Every third man of the whole empire was employed on the work, and half a million of them died of starvation. All the houses of Great Britain would not suffice to build such a wall, the contents of which would be enough to build two walls 6 ft. high and 2 ft. thick round the equator.

Great Week (*The*). Hebdomada Magna. The 13 days between the 5th Sunday of Lent and Easter Sunday (neither of the Sundays included). These 13 days were called Passion Week (*q.v.*).

Great Western (*The*). A steamship which sailed from Bristol to New York in 1838. *See* 'Great Eastern.'

Grecian Year of the World (*The*). This was 1 Sept., B.C. 5598.

Grecizing Jews. Descendants of Abraham born in foreign countries where Greek was spoken. They were the Greek Hebrews, in contradistinction to the Hebrew Hebrews, who spoke Aramaic or debased Hebrew.

Greco. An Italian who made an attempt on the life of the Emperor Napoleon III. (*q.v.*), 14 Dec., 1863.

Greek (*The Pronunciation of*). *See* 'Greeks and Trojans.'

Greek Cap (*The*). Was egg-shaped; made, according to a bust of Ulysses, thus :—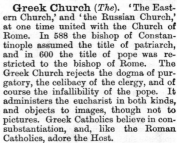

See 'Caps,' and 'Hats.'

Greek Church (*The*). 'The Eastern Church,' and 'the Russian Church,' at one time united with the Church of Rome. In 588 the bishop of Constantinople assumed the title of patriarch, and in 600 the title of pope was restricted to the bishop of Rome. The Greek Church rejects the dogma of purgatory, the celibacy of the clergy, and of course the infallibility of the pope. It administers the eucharist in both kinds, and objects to images, though not to pictures. Greek Catholics believe in consubstantiation, and, like the Roman Catholics, adore the Host.

What is absurdly called *The Schismatic Greek Church* is that which denies the procession of the Holy Ghost from the Father and the Son, called the *Filioque* (*q.v.*), introduced into the creed in 589 by Recared, and sanctioned by the Council of Toledo. Of course, if there is any schism at all about the matter, it was not by those who adhered to the old creed, but by those who introduced the new departure and their followers.

Greek Church Catechism (*The*), 1642. Prepared by Peter Mogilas. It received authority as a standard or symbolical book from the synod of Jerusalem in 1672, and is often called the 'Larger Russian Catechism,' to distinguish it from the Smaller Russian Catechism prepared by the order of Peter the Great.

Greek Fathers (*The Ten*). Called, with five Latin ones, the 'Later Fathers' (4th cent.), viz.: Eusebius, Athanasius, Basil, Gregory Nazianzen, Gregory of Nyssa, Cyril of Jerusalem, Chrysostom, Epiphanius, Cyril of Alexandria, and Ephrem the Syrian. *See* 'Latin Fathers.'

Greek Fire. A terrible weapon invented by Callinīcus, a native of Heliopōlis in Syria, who imparted the secret to the Greek government. It was used in battles and sieges, by sea and land. It was either poured from the ramparts from large boilers, or hurled in red-hot balls of stone or iron. Sometimes fire-ships were charged with it, and sometimes it was blown through long copper tubes from the prows. We are told it was made of naphtha, that it caught fire immediately it came in contact with the air, and that it produced a great smoke, a loud explosion, and a fierce flame.

It seems to have been rock oil, as the inflammable liquid sprang from the earth, and to have been mixed with sulphur and pitch from evergreen fir-trees. It was treason to reveal the secret. It continued in use till the 14th cent., when gunpowder took its place.

Greeks and Trojans (*The*). I. The advocates of Greek literature in the reign of Henry VIII. were called the Greeks, and those who held fast to the old Latin schoolmen were called the Trojans. Both Oxford and Cambridge furiously resisted the introduction of Greek literature, and denounced the Greek Testament as heterodoxy. It was prohibited in the University of Cambridge under very severe penalties. Henry VIII. commanded Greek to be taught in Oxford, and established a Greek professorship at Cambridge. Erasmus tried to teach it, but was unable to resist the opposition he met with.

II. A fiery contest respecting the pronunciation of Greek introduced by Sir John Cheke (1514–1557), Regius Professor of Greek in the University of Cambridge. Sir John (then a Protestant) introduced a new pronunciation of Greek which Gardiner, the chancellor, condemned. Sides were chosen by the scholars: those who supported Sir John were called 'Trojans,' those who opposed him called themselves 'Greeks.' As Gardiner was a Catholic the contention was really Protestants *v.* Catholics. Many a street fight was fought by the scholars; but at length the king in council commanded the innovation of the regius professor to be discontinued. *See* 'Ramists.'

Green was the colour consecrated to the Fatimites; *White* to the Ommiades; *Black* to the Abbassides (each 3 syl.).

Green-aprons (*The*). Nonconformist preachers.

Unbeneficed Noncons that live by alms, and no Paternoster no penny, say the Green-aprons.— HICKERINGILL, *Priestcraft*, pt. i. p. 21.

Greenbacks. A popular name for the paper currency of the United States, from the colour of the printing on the backs of the notes.

Green Bag Inquiry (*The*). I. On 3 Feb., 1817, the celebrated green bag was sent by the Prince-regent to the Lords, and another on the following day to the Commons. These green bags (always referred to as one), stuffed with documents regarding the occurrences in the Midland counties, as the Derbyshire insurrection (*q.v.*), the Blanketeers (*q.v.*), &c. were to be examined by secret committees in both houses. The Lords committee produced their report on 23 Feb., the Commons produced theirs on the 27th. From documents dated 1816 they said there could be no doubt that schemes of conspiracy were in agitation, and the events in 1817 in Derbyshire and Yorkshire confirmed these averments. The insurrections, however, were not formidable, and the mass of the people took no part in them. The committee condemned the ministry for their arbitrary measure in suspending *Habeas Corpus*, for having executed three men at Derby, and for imprisoning or transporting twenty others. Mr. Tierney called the whole affair 'absurd, contemptible, and ludicrous.' *See* 'Spencean Philanthropists.'

II. 1820, an inquiry into the conduct of Queen Caroline, the wife of George IV., accused of adultery with Bergami, her chamberlain. The evidence was inclosed in sealed green bags, which were laid on the table of the House of Lords and Commons for investigation. The bags contained documents connected with a commission sent to Milan in 1818; but as far back as 1806 the queen was charged with having given birth to a child at Blackheath, after her separation from the king. The queen was tried and acquitted.

Sir Samuel Romilly says the boy was Billy Austin, son of Sophia Austin, born in Brownlow Street Hospital 11 July, 1802, and taken by the [queen], then Princess of Wales, into her house the same year.

Green Book (*The*). The register of the South Sea Company, so called from the colour of its covers. When the bubble exploded, Mr. Knight, the cashier, fled to France, carrying the green book with him. General Ross declared the swindle to be 'the greatest villany and fraud ever contrived to ruin a nation.'

Green Books (*The*). In Italy. Corresponds to our blue-books (*q.v.*). They contain all sorts of government reports, papers, and other documents.

Green Cap. *To wear a green cap,* to be a bankrupt. In France, 'porter le bonnet vert.' This phrase rose from an ancient custom which was common even in the 17th cent. of compelling bankrupts to wear a green cap, out of disgrace, and to put men on their guard against them.

Green Cloth (*Board of*). A court of justice held in the counting-house of the British monarch's household, and composed of the lord steward and inferior officers. To this court is committed the charge and supervision of the royal household in matters of justice and government, with power to correct offenders, and to maintain the peace of the jurisdiction of the court-royal, which extends 200 yards, every way, from the gates of the palace. Without a warrant from this court no servant of the household can be arrested for debt. It takes its name from the green cloth spread over the board at which it is held (Wharton, 'Law Dictionary ').

The Board of Green Cloth executed in 1849 the remaining functions of the 'Marshalsea Court.'

Green Cockade (*The*), 1789. The cockade worn by the French insurgents at the commencement of the Great Revolution. Camille Desmoulins, on one occasion, snatching a green twig from a tree after addressing the mob, stuck it in his hat as a cockade. The whole mass of people followed his example, and a woman brought out a great roll of green ribbon and cut it into bows as far as it would go. This was the revolutionary cockade till the militia of 48,000 was embodied, when a cockade of red and blue (the Parisian colours) was substituted instead.

Green Count (*The*), 1348. Amadeus VI. count of Savoy (1334, 1343–1383) was so called because he appeared in green at a tournament and was so announced.

Green Crescents. The symbol of the orthodox Moslems. *See* ' Green Turbans.'

Green Flags (*The*). The soldiers of the Fatimites. Hence the banner of the sultan of Damascus was a crescent on a green flag. The Abbassides (3 syl.) have a crescent on a black flag, and the Ommiades (3 syl.) a crescent on a white flag. Ordinarily by ' green flags ' we mean the Arab troops.

As a railway signal a green flag signifies *caution*.

Green Isle (*The*). Ireland is so called from its brilliant verdure.

Green-Mountain Boys (*The*), 1775. Three hundred men, led by Ethan Allen, who, in the American war of independence, joined the volunteers, who undertook to secure the passes into Canada. They came from the Green Mountains which run through a large part of Vermont.

Green-ribbon Club (*The*). An anti-popery club held at the club-house in Fuller's Rents, London, in the reign of Charles II., known in history chiefly by its procession on 17 Nov., 1680, organised under the auspices of the Earl of Shaftesbury. It went from Moorgate to Temple Bar, where, in front of the club-house, the whole array of popish effigies which had been carried in the procession were burnt amid fireworks and tremendous shouts. It is said there were at least 100,000 spectators.

The club-house, says Roger North, was a sort of carrefour at Chancery Lane.

Green Room (*The*). The actors' muster-room in theatres. So called because it is painted green to relieve the eyes of the actors distressed with the glare of the foot-lights. To this room they retire when they make their exit from the stage.

Green Scarfs (*The*). The badge of Mazarin, Isabella, and the family of Condé.

Red Scarfs, the badge of Henri III. and Charles IX.; White Scarfs, the badge of Crusaders. Armagnacs, and Huguenots ; Tricolour Scarfs still worn in France by the municipal magistrates and commissaire of police. White *Hoods*, the badge of the Burgundians.

Green Silver. A halfpenny tax paid yearly to the feudal lord, as rent, by every tenant in the manor of Writtel, Essex, whose front-door opens on Greenbury.

Green Spectre (*The*). Irish Rebellion. *See* ' Irish Associations.'

It is worth while to consider what means can be adopted to prevent the periodical reappearance of the Green Spectre of Ireland.—*Irish Seditions from 1792 to 1880*, p. 64.

Green Standard (*The*). Of the Turks; never unfurled except in danger. Said to have been given to Mohammed by the Angel Gabriel, and hence called ' The celestial standard.'

Green Thursday, or 'Dies Viridium' (Luke xxxiii. 31). Maundy Thursday, the day of absolution in the Lutheran Church, preparatory to the Holy Communion, which is celebrated the day following (*i.e.* on Good Friday). In German called ' Gründonnerstag.'

Green Turbans. The descendants of Fatima, in Turkey, called emirs or shereefs, wear green turbans; but the Fatimites of Egypt wore *red* ones, like the unorthodox Persians.

In Afghanistan every synd, or Afghan descendant of the Prophet, is entitled to wear a green turban.

Green Vault of Dresden (*The*). Grüne Gewölbe'; is in the Zwinger, a group of buildings erected by Augustus II. as a vestibule to his new palace. It is called ' Green ' from the colour of the paper or hangings with which it was originally covered. The regalia used at the coronation of Augustus (a present of Karl V.) are still kept in the seventh apartment. The ' Emerald of the Green Vault ' is in the eighth or last apartment.

Greens and Blues (*The*). The livery colours of opposed charioteer factions in Constantinople, which in the time of Justinian verged on sedition. Like our Light and Dark Blue, which are the livery colours worn by the contending Universities of Cambridge and Oxford in athletic contests such as the boat race. The Blues in Constantinople denoted the votaries of Justinian, and the Greens those of Anastasius.

Cambridge is Light Blue, Oxford is Dark Blue. In Constantinople there were two minor factions, called the Whites and the Reds; but these merged into the other two, the Whites into the Blues, and the Reds into the Greens.

Gregorian Calendar (*The*), 1582. The calendar reformed by Pope Gregory XIII. by expunging ten days, in order to restore the equinox to March 21, the day on which it fell in the Council of Nice in A.D. 325. In order to prevent the recurrence of a like error in future, he ordered that of years ending centuries only those divisible by 400 should be accounted leap years (excepting 400, and all multiples of 400). Introduced into Italy, Spain, and Portugal in 1582; into France a few months later; into Catholic Switzerland, Germany, and the Netherlands in 1583; into Poland in 1586; into Hungary and Denmark in 1700; into Protestant Switzerland in 1701; into England in 1752; into Sweden in 1753; but Russia still retains the old style.

The centuries 1700, 1800, 1900 are not leap years, because 17, 18, 19 will not divide by 4; but the years 1600, 2000, and 2400 are leap years, because 16, 20, 24 are multiples of 4.

Gregorian Chant (*The*). The chant of Ambrose (bishop of Milan), which had only four tones, extended to eight tones by Gregory the Great (591–604). It was taken from the Greek chant used in the mysteries of Eleusis.

The Ambrosian chant had four tones or modes, called the Dorian, Phrygian, Lydian, and Mixolydian.

Gregorian Epoch (*The*). Begins March 1582, when the New Style or Reformed Calendar was introduced by Gregory XIII.

Gregorian Liturgy (*The*). This is the Roman liturgy (*q.v.*).

Gregorian Mass. ' Missa S. Gregorii,' a mass ' quæ juxta ritum Gregorianum celebratur.' *See* ' Mass.'

Gregorian Year (*The*). The civil year of the Gregorian Calendar.

Gregorians (*The*), 1376. A religious society named after Gregory the Great, founded in Holland by Geert Groote and Florentius Radewin. Not unlike the subsequent society known as Moravians or the United Brethren. They acknowledged no conventual distinctions, and enjoined community of goods, ascetic habits, and the use of the vernacular tongue in all religious services.

Gregory Act (*The*). By which tenants in Ireland could not get relief from the workhouse if they held more than a quarter of an acre of land, without surrendering their holding.

Grenville Collection (*The*), 1846. Added to the British Museum Library by the Right Hon. Thomas Grenville. It consists of 20,240 volumes, and cost about 54,000*l*. It contains the Mazarine Bible (2 vols. 1455), a copy of ' Livy ' on vellum (1469), the Aldine ' Virgil ' (1505), a Shakespeare (1623), Azzoduidi's ' Ovid,' a series of early editions of ' Orlando Furioso,' &c.

Gresham Lectures (*The*), 1575. Lectures on the seven sciences (divinity, astronomy, music, geometry, law, physic, and rhetoric), delivered in Gresham

College, and founded by Sir Thomas Gresham, the merchant. The lectures were neglected from 1700 to 1762, and then the building was sold to the government for the site of an excise office. Some attempts have been made to revive the lectures, which were delivered in the Royal Exchange till the fire of 1838. The new buildings were opened in 1843.

The lectures were established in 1575, but the college was not completed till 1579.

Gretna Green Marriages.

When Lord-Chancellor Hardwicke, in 1754, brought in his bill for the virtual abolition of Fleet marriages by compelling the publication of banns on three successive Sundays, or else an expensive licence; he wished to extend the operation of the bill to Scotland also; but, failing in this, marriages at Gretna Green without banns, notice, or licence continued to the close of the year 1856, when by 19 & 20 Vict. c. 96, s. 1, they were declared to be irregular.

Grey (Lady Jane), 1537-1554.

Reigned ten days, and was beheaded. She was persuaded or forced by her father-in-law (the Duke of Northumberland) to usurp the crown. Her name is not received in the list of English monarchs.

HENRY VII. was the father of HENRY VIII. and Mary.

HENRY VIII. was the father of EDWARD VI., MARY, and ELIZABETH (no issue).

Now take Mary, Henry VII.'s daughter: her second husband was Charles Brandon duke of Suffolk, by whom she had Frances [Brandon], who married Henry Grey; and the Lady Jane was their daughter.

Lady Jane Grey married Lord Guilford Dudley (fourth son of the Duke of Northumberland), aged sixteen.

. Lord Guilford Dudley was the grandson of the scandalous lawyer of the firm Empson and Dudley so notorious in the reign of Henry VII.

Grey Friars (The).

So the Franciscans were called from the colour of their dress, as the Dominicans were called 'Black Friars,' and the Carmelites were called 'White Friars.'

Grey League (The), 1424.

'Graubünden' or 'Lia Grescha,' one of the three unions of the Grisons. So called from the grey homespun worn by the unionists, whence the word 'Gris-ons' and the German 'Graubünden.' In 1427 the three leagues united into a general federation, and formed an alliance with the Swiss cantons.

The other two unions are the Cadeian League (q.v.) and the League of the Six Jurisdictions.

Grey Sister of Hearts (The).

Julienne Wittinghoff, baroness von Krudener (1764-1824), a mystic, credited with prophesying Napoleon's flight from Elba and his fall at Waterloo. Alexander I. of Russia was one of her disciples; and when she went to Paris during its occupation by the allies, her religious 'drums' were the fashion of the hour.

The baroness promoted the 'Holy Alliance' in 1815, and died in the Crimea, 13 Dec. 1824.

Grey Sisters (The), 1634.

Sisters of Charity, so called from their grey dress. A society of unmarried women, whose functions are to nurse the sick, and do what they can to relieve the sufferings of all inmates of hospitals. The society was founded in France by Vincent de Paul and the widow Legras. Suppressed at the Revolution, but restored by Napoleon in 1807, under the presidency of the empress-mother.

Greysteil.

Lord Ruthven, son of the Lord Ruthven who murdered David Rizzio, was so called from Sir Greysteil, the hero of a metrical romance very popular at the time. He was honoured for his courage and hardihood, in which respect he resembled Greysteil.

Griffith's Valuation, 1826.

To provide for the more equal levying of grand jury cess and county charges. Made by Richard Griffith, the commissioner appointed under Act 7 Geo. IV. c. 62, for Ireland.

The Tenement Valuation, 1846-7, amended by Act (1852) was used for all public and local assessments, as well as for all imperial purposes, till the new assessment came into operation.

Grimes Dyke, A.D. 140-141.

A rampart and ditch formed by Lollius Urbicus, general of Antonīnus Pius, from Dunglass Castle (on the Clyde) to the heights above Caer Ridden Kirk. It had nineteen forts, with an average interval of two miles. Also called Graeme's and Graham's Dyke.

Grimes is Keltic for 'great.'

Grimm's Law.

The formula of Jacob Louis Grimm, the philologer, for the variation of consonants as a word passes out of one country into another.

For example: the Latin, Greek, or Sanskrit p becomes f in English: thus *pater* becomes *father*, &c.

Grise League (*The*), 1424. The second league of the Grisons for independence.

Grisognel the Grey Cloak. Geoffrey of Anjou, father of Henry II. (1113–1151).

His son was called ' Curtmantle.'

Grist Tax (*The*), 1815. An absolute prohibition on the delivery of wheat out of warehouse, and its importation for home consumption till the price reached 80s. per quarter was imposed. In 1822 this act was amended, and in 1828 a sliding scale was established ('Notes and Queries,' 2 May, 1889, p. 180).

Groans of the Britons (*The*), A.D. 426. A letter addressed to Aetius, the popular captain of the day, to come and help the English against the constant irruptions of the Picts and Scots. But the Romans were at the time dreading the advance of Attila; and the Britons, left to the tender mercies of their ravagers, invited over the Saxons.

Grostête or **Grosseteste.** Robert Copley, bishop of Lincoln (1175, 1235–1253). Sometimes Anglicised into ' Greathead.'

Grub Street Journal, London. Grub Street is now called Milton Street, famous at one time for trashy literature. The journal was a folio in size, and continued to be issued to the end of the year 1737. It then became a quarto, and was entitled ' The Literary Courier of Grub Street.'

He, honest man, was deep in Grub Street and polemical divinity.—ANDREW MARVELL, *The Rehearsal*, &c. *See also* ' Dunciad,' i. 38.

Grumbletonians, 1692. The anticourt party, or out-of-office party. By a refined euphemism the court party was called ' The Patriot Party ' and the Grumbletonians the ' Country Party.' Bolingbroke and Walpole were the two representative men in 1723 (MACAULAY, ' Hist. of Eng.,' chap. xix.).

Grypus (*γρυπός, Hooked Nose*). So Antiochus VIII., king of Syria, was called (B.C. 141–196).

Guard. *See* ' Garde.'

Guardian and Lieutenant of the Realm. So George I. called the Prince of Wales, when left in charge of the United Kingdom, in 1716. He was extremely jealous of his son, and would not hear of his being called regent. It was not, however, a new title, as the Black Prince had borne it in 1338, &c.

Guebres [*Infidels*]. So the Moslems call all, except Jews and Christians, who do not profess Islamism; but generally the Parsees are meant. *See* ' Giaours.'

Guelf Fund. A considerable amount of money which falls annually to the emperor of Germany, and is not dependent on the consent of parliament. A part is paid to subsidise newspapers, and 50,000*l.* is spent yearly in secret service. It is called the ' Guelf Fund ' because it arises from the interest of the sequestered property of the Hanoverian dynasty.

Guelfs and Ghibellines (*The*), 12th cent. The Guelfs were dukes of Bavaria, who contended with the house of Hohenstauffen for pre-eminence. From a mere German feud the contention advanced to a long and bitter struggle between the civil and spiritual powers. The Guelfs were the pope's party, and laboured to set the pope above the crowned princes. The Ghibellines were the imperial or civil party, and tried to set the kaiser above the pope.

In consequence of this rivalry, we find two rival contemporary popes, Alexander III. (A.D. 1159) the Guelfic pope, and Victor IV. (A.D. 1159) the kaiser's pope. Of course the latter was called an antipope by the Roman party. Guelf was duke of Saxony ; Ghibelline, or rather Waiblingen, is a town of Würtemberg, the patrimonial seat of the Hohenstauffen family. . . . The words were first used as the battle cries in 1188 when Guelf, the brother of Henry the Proud, was defeated by Konrad of Hohenstauffen at Weinsberg.

₊ [After the reign of Kaiser Heinrich VII., in 1313, the terms ' Guelf ' and ' Ghibelline ' completely changed their original meaning. The Ghibellines were originally the imperial party, but from 1313 Italian rebels were called Ghibellines. This was because the German emperors were for ever disturbing the government of the Italian states ; and as these emperors were Ghibellines, so the word came to denote a disturber of the state, a rebel, or insurgent. Of course, the insurgents were not slow to retort on the government party the nickname of Guelfs. The Hanoverian British line is that of the Guelfs. *See* ' Tories.'

Guercino (*Squint Eye*). Gian Francesco Barbieri, a famous painter of the

Bolognese school. His masterpieces are the fresco of 'Aurora' in the Villa Ludovisi, the 'Persian Sibyl,' and 'St. Petronilla' (1590–1666).

Gue'rinets (*The*), 1684. Enthusiasts and visionaries in France; a sort of Illuminati.

Guerra de las Comunerades (5 syl.), 1520–1521. The insurrection of the Comuneros under Padilla, a young nobleman of Toledo. The insurgents were defeated at Villala, and Padilla was executed. *See* 'Comuneros.'

Guerra di Candia (*Una*). 'War to the knife.' A Venetian expression alluding to the siege of Candia by the Turks (1667–1668). This siege cost the lives of 30,000 Christians and 120,000 Turks. Candia was ultimately obliged to surrender.

Guerrillas. Petty wars, or partisan warriors; armed bands of peasants are so called in Spain. The insurrections of Jack Cade, Wat Tyler, and Robert Kett would be so called in Spain. From 1808 to 1814 guerrillas were regularly organised against the French, and the names of Empecinado, the Pastor Merino, and Mina, as leaders, are well known.

Mina's band joined Wellington, and did good service in the Peninsular war. The guerrillas also joined the Carlists, and distinguished themselves.

Guet (*Le*). The police of the old *régime* of France, changed, in 1789, into the *Garde Municipale de Paris*. It was reorganised in 1254 by St. Louis [IX.], who subdivided the corps into the *Guet Royal*, and the *Guet assis* or *des mestiers*. The Guet Royal consisted of twenty sergents à cheval and twenty sergents à pied. The Guet assis consisted of bourgeois and artisans, the former being the night watch, and the latter orderlies of the Guet Royal. The Constituent Assembly replaced the *Guet* by the Gendarmerie.

Pronounce *Gu-ay*.

Gueux. 16th cent. ragamuffins. The revolutionists in Spain and the Netherlands in 1566. There were 300 deputies of the Calvinistic party, headed by H. de Brederode (a descendant of the counts of Holland) and Louis count of Nassau, who demanded of Margaret, the governor, the abolition of the Inquisition. When Margaret seemed about to give way the Count of Barleymont, her counsellor, re-

commended her to dismiss the deputation, saying to her, 'Ce ne sont que des gueux.' The word was caught up; they called themselves 'Les Gueux,' and took for their badge a wallet and porringer. The 'Gueux des bois' combated on land, the 'Gueux de mer' sought a refuge at sea.

Pronounce *Lay geuz* ; *Gewda bwă* ; *Gewd mair.*

Guillemites (3 syl.), 1153. A religious congregation founded at Pescara by St. Gulielmus of Malaval. They soon spread over Italy, France, and Germany. From 1256 they had a monastery at Montrouge, near Paris. They were called White Mantles (*Blancs-Manteaux*) from the great white mantles which they wore. They ceased to exist long before the Revolution.

Guillotine (*The*), 31 May, 1791. Joseph Ignace Guillotin, M.D., induced the Legislative Assembly of France to adopt the machine which bears his name for the execution of criminals condemned to death. But it was not till 20 March, 1792, that a special decree was made for its universal use. It was not the invention of Dr. Guillotin, for a like instrument was used in England in the time of Edward III. 'The Maiden' of Scotland was used in 1578. The Halifax 'Maiden' was well known. And a similar instrument had been used in Germany, Bohemia, and Italy.

The Regent Morton, who introduced the 'Maiden' into Scotland, was (according to tradition) the first to suffer by it.

Guinea. The English gold coin, equal to 21s., first coined in 1662. Withdrawn from circulation in 1817.

Physicians, barristers, schoolmasters, clergymen in temporary office, artists, &c., still preserve the word 'guinea,' and are paid by guineas instead of sovereigns. Honoraria and many subscriptions to charities are also paid in guineas. In fact, it is esteemed a more 'aristocratic' payment. The gold of the first specimens came from the coast of Guinea.

Guinegate, or 'Guinegatte.' In France. Noted for the 'Battle of the Spurs' [p. 80, col. 1], won by Henry VIII. over the French. Here, on 7 Aug., 1479, had been fought another battle, between Louis XI. and Maximilian of Austria, to which Philippe de Comines (2 syl.) refers :—

Remember Guynegate, a warning against the allurements either of plunder or of prisoners; for Guynegate was lost in the very moment of victory by our too great eagerness for pillage.

Guinever (*The Canons Regular of St.*). *See* 'Genevieve.'

Guirlande de Julie. This Julie was the celebrated Julie Lucie d'Angennes, daughter of the Marquis de Rambouillet, who presided over the society called L'Hôtel de Rambouillet, and married the Duc de Montausier. When the duc was paying his court to the witty Julie, he made her a present of a MS. book of select poems, which he called the 'Guirlande de Julie,' illuminated with flowers painted by Robert. The poems were in the handwriting of Jarry. The book was in the family of the Duc d'Uzès in 1870, and probably is there still, but it has been printed and published.

Pronounce *Gir-land d'zhu-le.*

Gulistan (*Peace of*), 1813. Between Persia and Russia.

Gunpowder Plot, 1605. A conspiracy to destroy the king, lords, and commons, by springing a mine secreted under the houses of parliament, on 5 Nov., the day of the king's speech. The plot was projected by Robert Catesby, who was joined by many Roman Catholics of high rank. Guido Fawkes (Guy Faux) was employed to fire the train, but was apprehended in the vaults under the houses of parliament. Sir Everard Digby, Rockwood, Winter, Garnet (a Jesuit), Guy Faux, and some others were executed 31 Jan., 1606. Robert Catesby was shot 8 Nov., 1605, while attempting to raise an insurrection in Worcestershire; and Thomas Percy, of the family of Northumberland, was shot at Holbeach the same day.

Gunter's Chain, 1624. A chain used for land-measuring. It is 22 yards long, the square of which is 484. Now an acre is 4,840 square yards, and therefore a square chain is a tenth of an acre, or 10 = 1 acre. Again, a chain contains 10,000 square links, and, as 10 chains = an acre, it follows that 100,000 square links = an acre. So that, in measuring a field by a Gunter's chain, all that is required is to divide the result by 100,000, or (which is the same thing) to cut off the last five figures, to obtain the area in acres.

Gunter's Line. A logarithmic line engraved on scales and sectors, serving to perform the multiplication and division of numbers instrumentally.

Gunter's Quadrant. A quadrant for finding the hour of the day, the sun's azimuth, and other problems of the sphere.

Gunter's Scale. For resolving questions in navigation by the aid of a pair of compasses. Called by seamen 'The Gunter.'

Gurgoyles (2 syl.), familiarly called 'The Gurgs,' 1775–1855. A society which flourished for eighty years at Lincoln's Inn, being a revival of the old Cambridge Shakespeare Society. It was never formally dissolved.

Guy's Hospital, 1721. Founded by Thomas Guy, a London bookseller, who was M.P. for Tamworth (1694–1707).

Gwynn (*Nell,* or *Eleanor*). It is said that her real name was Margaret Symcott. The dukes of St. Albans are descended from this mistress of Charles II.

Gymnos'ophists (4 syl.), or 'Naked Philosophers.' Indian philosophers, so called by the Greeks because they went about naked. The two best known are Calānus and Zarmenochegas. The former followed Alexander the Great from India, and, being taken ill, burnt himself alive in the presence of the Macedonian army, B.C. 323. The latter burnt himself alive at Athens in the presence of Augustus.

They are now represented by the 'sky-clad' branch of the Jains. At present they eat their meals without any clothing.

Gypsy (*plu.* **Gypsies**). Called also 'Egyptians,' 'Bohemians,' 'Gitanos,' 'Zingari,' or 'Zingali.' Are mentioned in 1122 in the German paraphrase of Genesis. They appeared in Hungary, Wallachia, and Cyprus in 1320; in Germany between 1416–1420; at Zürich in 1418; in Italy in 1422; at Paris in 1427; in Scotland in 1506.

Gypsies forbidden to dwell in the land:—

1492, by Ferdinand the Catholic of	*Spain.*
1500, by the Diet of Augsburg .	*Germany.*
1530, by Henry VIII. .	*England.*
1540, by James V. .	*Scotland.*
1560, by the States of Orleans	*France.*
1740, by Friedrich II.	*Prussia.*

H, on pennypieces, 1875, &c., stands for H[eaton]—the firm of Ralph Heaton & Sons of Birmingham, which supplied the mint with 100 tons of the bronze pennypieces. Their first issue was 1875;

and the officers of Tower Hill, in order to identify the coin, had the letter H impressed on the dies.

Habeas Corpus (*Suspension of the*). In times of great political excitement the operation of the Habeas Corpus Act is usually suspended, by which persons committed are not allowed to be bailed. The committing magistrate has to bear, in such cases, all the responsibility of the commitment.

Habeas Corpus Act (*The*), 1679, (31 Car. II. c. 2), securing English subjects against arbitrary imprisonment.

This is provided for by the writ called 'Habeas Corpus ad Subjiciendum' which is addressed to any person who detains another in custody, commanding him to produce the body of the prisoner, and to state the day and cause of his capture and detention. This done, the court decides whether the prisoner shall be liberated, admitted to bail, or remanded.

Habsburg (*House of*). Incorrectly written 'Hapsburg.' I. Furnished Germany with Rodolf I., Adolf of Nassau, and Albert I. of Austria (1273-1308).

The word Habsburg or Habichts-burg, built in the 11th cent., means 'hawk's castle.' The castle stood on the right bank of the Aar, in the Swiss canton of Aargau.

II. Of Austria. Began with Albert [Albrecht] II. the Illustrious (son of Albert IV. duke of Austria), and son-in-law of Siegmund the preceding kaiser. Albert was also called 'the Magnanimous' and 'the Grave.' This line of kaisers began in 1438, and still continues in that part of Germany called Austria and Hungary.

The Habsburgers of direct male descent ceased in 1806; Karl VII., son of Maria Theresa, was a Habsburger on his mother's side only.

Hadith. Traditions about Mohammed the prophet, complementary to the Koran.

Hadrian's Rescript. A letter to Serēnius Graniānus, proconsul of Asia, respecting the way he was to treat Christians. 'If anyone shall prove any offence against the laws to have been committed by Christians, proceed against them as the law directs; but if the charge brought against them be mere calumny, then punish the accuser as he deserves.' *See* 'Trajan's Rescript.'

Hæcceity. A term in school divinity meaning the principle of individuation. The Realists maintained that universals only were real, and that they formed individuals by the intervention of the principle of hæcceity.

Hæret'ico comburendo (*De*). A writ against heretics, who, being convicted of heresy by a bishop abjured it, but afterwards relapsing, were delivered over to the secular power to be burnt alive. Abolished by the pension parliament in 1677 (*tempore* Charles II.).

Hag'gada. The rabbinical interpretation of scripture for homiletical purposes. *See* 'Midrash.'

Haileybury College, 1806. Founded by the East India Company at Great Amwell, Herts, for the education of 105 students intended for the civil service in India.

Hair.

GREEKS. The Spartans combed and dressed their hair carefully, especially when about to encounter any great danger; as Leonīdas and his 300 did before starting for Thermopўlæ. Sailors both in Greece and Rome shaved off their hair after a shipwreck or other calamity, and dedicated it to some deity. In mourning, Greek and Roman women cut their hair short, but the men in both countries left their hair rough and unkempt, as if their grief was too great for their concerning themselves about personal adornment.

In childhood both Greeks and Romans wore long hair, but the boys, on reaching puberty, had their hair clipped and dedicated to some river-god. At Athens this ceremony took place on the third day of the festival called 'Apaturīa.'

Slaves, both in Greece and Rome, were always shaved, and vestal virgins, like Catholic nuns, cut off their hair when they took their vows.

One way of supplicating was pulling out one's hair. After this manner Agamemnon presented himself before Zeus, when Hector had given the Greeks an overthrow.—*Iliad*, xx. 15.

ROMANS. Men wore their hair long till about B.C. 300, when short hair and shaving came into vogue. Scipio Africānus (B.C. 234-183) was the first Roman who shaved. Under the empire the style of dressing the hair was extremely finical. Mark Antony (B.C. 80-30) is represented as wearing his hair in sausage curls arranged in rows all round his head. The Emperor Galliēnus (A.D. 260-268) had his hair powdered with gold-dust.

In Hadrian's time (76, 117–138) full beards and short hair were in vogue, and this fashion continued to the end of the empire.

The GAULS and ancient BRITONS. The Teutonic tribes wore their hair long, as did the ancient Gauls and Britons. That part of Gaul the furthest remote from Roman influence was called *Gallia Comāta* (long-haired Gaul), to distinguish it from the half-Romanised *Gallia Togāta.*

The SAXONS and DANES wore long hair and long beards, but the NORMANS shaved their chins, and sometimes the back of their heads also.

ENGLAND. In the reign of Henry I. (1100–1135) the gentlemen rivalled the ladies in the length of their hair, and long hair prevailed till the time of Henry VIII. (1509–1547), when short hair came into vogue. In the reign of Charles I. (1625–1649) ringlets and love-locks were affected by the Cavaliers, but Puritans cropped their hair close to the head. In the reign of Charles II. (1661–1685) enormous wigs flowing over the shoulders were worn, and this fashion continued up to the reign of George III. (1760–1820).

In 1765 the wig-makers petitioned the king against the discontinuance of wigs, praying for their reintroduction. An excellent satire was set on foot praying his Majesty to introduce the fashion of wooden legs for the benefit of carpenters.

At the close of the 18th cent. the disgusting habit of plastering the hair with flour, powder, and pomatum, to the amount of 2 lbs. or more, was introduced. My father used to tell us how, when he was a young man, and was going to a public entertainment, the hairdresser was generally obliged, from stress of business, to come the day before 'to make his head,' which was the usual phrase ; and that he was obliged to sleep in an armchair for fear of deranging his hair. When the head was 'unmade' the lard and powder taken out would fill a small basin. He said that every gentleman used to carry a 'scratcher,' with an ivory hand at one end to scratch the back, and a sharp point at the other to scratch the head, because the parasites were so troublesome. In my young days, gentlemen wore their hair smooth, with a pig-tail and bag or pig-tail and knocker. Not long after William Pitt introduced his

tax on hair-powder, the hair was cut short as it is at present (1890).

The style of dressing hair among ladies is far too long a subject for this note-book, but foolery reached its climax in the time of Marie Antoinette. My mother says that in her days the hairdresser was provided with steps, that he might pile up the hair high enough.

Hair as a sign of Rank.

The PARTHIANS and ancient PERSIANS of high rank wore long flowing hair.

Homer speaks of the 'long-haired GREEKS' by way of honourable distinction. Subsequently, the Athenian cavalry wore long hair, and all the Lacedæmonian soldiers did the same.

The GAULS considered long hair a mark of honour, for which reason Julius Cæsar obliged them to cut off their hair in token of submission, for all slaves were shorn.

The FRANKS and ancient GERMANS considered long hair a mark of high birth. Hence Clodion, the Frank, was styled ' the Long-haired,' and his successors were spoken of as *les rois chevelures.*

The GOTHS considered long hair a mark of honour, and short hair a mark of thraldom.

For many centuries long hair was in FRANCE the distinctive mark of kings and nobles, and in the time of Charles II. the Cavaliers gloried in long hair.

Hair shaved off.

MOHAMMEDANS shave the scalp, but leave a tuft of hair for the 'angel to lay hold of when he carries the dead to paradise.'

The CHINESE shave all the head except the top, where the hair is suffered to grow into a long pig-tail. This was a Tartar custom.

The Buddhist priests shave all the head.

Catholic priests shave their head more or less. The part shaved is called the 'tonsure.' St. Peter's tonsure is quite round the head, to indicate the crown of thorns. St. Paul's tonsure is the whole head shaved like a Buddhist priest's. Simon Magus's tonsure is a semicircle shaved from ear to ear above the forehead, but not extended to the back of the head. This sort of tonsure is natural baldness.

Catholic priests shave their faces quite clean, and the same custom is affected by the 'High Church party' of the Anglican Church. However, Christ and his apostles are always represented with moustaches and long beards.

Hair Powder, 1590. An aristocratic badge of the Guise party, opposed to Henri IV. The Guise party put forward the old Cardinal de Bourbon whom they called king, and in courtly flattery whitened their hair, and wore white plumes or white cockades. Originally hairpowder was an aristocratic distinction of the high church and state party in France. It was taxed in England in 1795 (1*l.* 3*s.* 6*d.*), which brought in 20,000*l.* a year. Nowadays hair-powder is worn only by some of the footmen of the nobility and higher commoners. The number of powdered footmen in 1890 was under 900.

Hakem (*A*). A Musulman magistrate under a cadi.

Hal′danites (3. syl.). Followers of James Alexander Haldane (1768–1857) of Aithrie, near Stirling. They are the Scotch Baptists, commonly called ' Maclean's People.'

Halifax, capital of Nova Scotia, 1749. So named in honour of the Earl of Halifax, then president of the Board of Trade in England. When the army was reduced in consequence of the peace of Aix-la-Chapelle, a great number of soldiers and sailors were thrown out of employment. It was resolved, therefore, to grant to every settler in Nova Scotia a free passage, 50 acres of freehold land, and another 10 acres for each child. Some 4,000 men with their families accepted the offer, sailed to Nova Scotia under Colonel Cornwallis, and founded the town of Halifax, now the capital of the province.

Halifax Law. Whoever committed a theft exceeding 13*d.* in value in the liberty of Halifax was summarily executed on the 'jyn' of Halifax, a kind of guillotine. Taylor the Water-poet (1630) refers to this law and this jyn.

Hall—College. Colleges are corporate bodies. Halls are not incorporated.

Hall Marks of gold and silver articles.

Silver articles have now four marks and a cartouch. Beginning on the left hand we have (1) the head of the reigning sovereign ; (2) the date-letter ; (3) the leopard's head, the company's mark ; (4) the lion passant, the national mark ; and (5) the cartouch containing the initials of the manufacturer.

The head of the sovereign was first added to the marks in 1784.

The leopard's head was adopted as the company's mark in 1300.

The date-letters have been in use since 1438. The custom for the last 200 years has been to use capitals and small letters alternately every twentieth year.

As all common alphabets have been exhausted, the shape of the shield will distinguish a modern mark from a more ancient one of the same character. Thus in 1876 Roman capitals were employed ; so they were in 1796. But the shields were different ; the shield of 1876 being

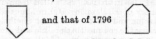

and that of 1796

and of course the sovereign's head differs.

A is the 1st year, B the 2nd year, C the 3rd year, and so on, omitting J and the last six letters.

The character of letters hitherto used are as follows :—

1438-1457 Lombardic, simple, small letters.
1458-1477   „   with external cusps.
1478-1497   „   with double cusps.
1498-1517 Black letter, small.
1518-1537 Lombardic, simple, capitals.
1538-1557 Roman caps, with border.
1558-1577 Black letter, small.

From this date the letters are placed in shields.

1578-1597 Clarendon caps, in shield.
1598-1617 Lombardic, with external cusps, in shield.
1618-1637 Italic, small, in shield.
1638-1657 Court hand   „
1658-1677 Black letter caps   „
1678-1696 Black letter, small „
1696-1715 Court hand   „
1716-1735 Clarendon caps   ‚
1736-1755 Clarendon, small letters, in shield.
1756-1775 Old English caps   „
1776-1795 Clarendon, small letters   „

From this date caps and smalls alternate.

1796-1815 Roman capitals, in shield, flat bottom.
1816-1835 Roman small letters „   „
1836-1855 Old English caps, in shield, pointed bottom.
1856-1875 Old English smalls, in shield, pointed bottom.
1876-1895 Roman caps, in shield, pointed bottom.
1896-1915 Roman smalls   „   „

Clarendon, *i.e.* Roman letters with no fine strokes, but all black alike.

** *The assay-marks* guarantee the exact proportion of alloy contained in the article. The standard of perfect purity being assumed to be 24 carats ; the figures —such as 12, 15, 18, 20, &c.—marked on gold and silver articles mean that 12, 15,

18, or 20 carats of the 24, are pure metal, and the rest is alloy.

Some silver has been assayed out of London, and instead of the leopard's head the following marks are used :—

For Birmingham	...	An anchor.
" Chester	...	... Three garbs and a dagger (the City arms).
" Exeter	...	... A castle with 3 towers.
" Newcastle-on-Tyne		Three castles.
" Sheffield	...	... A crown.
" Edinburgh	...	... A thistle.
" Glasgow	...	... Tree, fish, and bell (the City arms).
" Dublin	...	... A harp crowned.

(A garb in heraldry is a sheaf of grain.)

Hall Mote. The court held in Saxon times in the castle hall of the lord of a town or tithing, to punish by fines thieves, vagrants, and disorderly persons. It was inferior to the ' Folk Mote ' (*q.v.*).

Hallamshire. So called from the manor of Hallam, or Hallun, north of Rivelin, and ' in the parish of Sheffield.' Before the conquest Attercliffe and Sheffield were integral parts of Hallam manor, but after the conquest the manors of Hallam, Ecclesfelt, Bradfield, and Hansworth were all occupied by one baron, and called the Manor of Sheffield. Leland says:—' Halamshire beginneth a ii mile from Rotheram. Sheffield iii miles from Rotheram, wher the lord of Shreusbyre's castle is, the chese-market towne of Halamshire. And Halamshire goith one way vi or vii miles above Sheffilde by west, yet as I here say, another way the next village to Sheffilde is in Derbyshire. Al Halamshire go to the sessions of York, and is counted as a membre of Yorkshire. Æglesfild and Bradfield ii townelettes or villages long to one paroche chirche. So by this meanes ther be but iii paroches in Halamshire that is of name, and a great chapelle ' (' Itin.,' vol. v. f. 94). *See* ' Hoyland.'

Hallelujah Band (*The*). A Protestant religious sect whose services consist entirely of thanksgiving.

Hallelujah Victory (*The*), or 'Victoria Alleluiatica,' 30 March, A.D. 430. A legendary victory of St. Germanus bishop of Auxerre and Lupus bishop of Troyes over the Picts and Saxons at Mold in Flintshire. So called because the Britons led by them shouted ' Hallelujah ' so loudly that the enemy was panicstruck and fled.

St. Germānus was chosen commander against the Saxons; and not by the clang of trumpets and clash of arms, but by singing hallelujah, he routed the foe, and they perished in the sea.—NENNIUS, *Hist. of the Britons*, § 47.

Halley's Comet, 1682. Dr. Halley determined the recurrence of this comet by supposing it to be the same as that which appeared in 1607 and 1531. If so it would appear again in 1759, and so it did. M. Damoiseau calculated that it ought to appear again in 1835, and so it did.

It will be seen that these intervals vary from 70 to 80 years ; the variation is occasioned by the attraction of the planets on the motion of the comet.

Hallow Eve Fires, 1 Nov. The bonfires kindled in Scotland for the harvest-home festival. The Highlanders keep their bonfire festival, called Beltein (*q.v.*), on May-day, old style. Gregory IV. changed the feast of All Saints or All Hallows from May-day to 1 Nov. Hence the double feast. The Romans held the festival of Cybelê on May-day, and Gregory IV. changed the day for the sake of changing ' Cybelê and all the gods ' into ' St. Mary and all the saints.'

Hallow-e'en. The eve of All Hallows (31 Oct.), or day before All Saints', which is 1 Nov.

Halt (*Robert*). The pen-name of M. Vieu.

Hamadanites (4 syl.), 892–1001. Of the tribe of Hamadan. A dynasty of Mesopotamia, including Mosul and Aleppo, occupied by Arabian princes of the tribe of Hamadan. Their history is a tissue of treachery, parricide, and assassination.

The poets of their court said the Hamadanites were formed with beauty of person, eloquence of speech, and arms of valour.

Hamadites (3 syl.), 1015–1091. A Spanish dynasty, established by Soliman, after the defeat of Mohammed II. of Cordōva.

Hamburg (*Treaty of*), 22 May, 1762. A treaty of amity between Sweden and Russia, on the death of the Czarina Elizabeth.

Hamilton (*Patrick*), 1504–1528. A Scotch reformer and martyr, of whom it was said, ' The reik of Patrick Hamilton will infect as many as it blows upon.'

This sentiment was like that uttered by Bishop Latimer, at the stake, 1555: ' We shall this day light up such a blaze in the land as shall never be put out.'

Hammer and Scourge of the English (*The*). William Wallace, the Scotch patriot (1270–1305), is so called by Fordun.

Hammer of Scotland (*The*). So Edward I. is styled on his tomb in Westminster Abbey.

Hampden Clubs, 1816. To prosecute the cause of parliamentary reform, and to unite the reformers in one system of action. These clubs were established in every town in the kingdom, and in many villages; but the great central club was held at the ' Crown & Anchor,' Strand, the president being Sir Francis Burdett. The leading members were William Cobbett, Major Cartwright, Lord Cochrane, and Henry Hunt.

Hampton Court Conference (*The*), 12 to 18 Jan., 1604. Between prelates and Puritans; James I. presided. This conference was convened to take into consideration the ' Millenary Petition ' (*q.v.*), and it was decided that no change was required. On 16 Jan. the petitioners were called before the king, and, according to the account of James himself, he ' peppered them soundly.' On the 18th judgment was given adverse to the petitioners and the Puritan party.

Han Dynasty (*The*), B.C. 202—A.D. 25. The second historical and fifth imperial dynasty of China. It was divided into two parts : the first sixteen emperors being Si-Hân or Western Hân, and the last fourteen being Tong-Hân or Eastern Hân. It was preceded by the Tshin dynasty, and succeeded by the Sân-Kuo or Three States. It gave 16 emperors, lasted 227 years, and held its seat of government at Yn.

From A.D. 25 the dynasty was called Tong-Han, which gave 14 emperors and continued to A.D. 220. So that some say the dynasty of Han lasted 422 years and gave 30 emperors.

This was one of the most illustrious of all the dynasties of China.

Hanaper. A treasury, answering to the modern term exchequer. From *hanaperium*, a hamper or basket used anciently by our sovereigns for holding their money when they journeyed from place to place.

' Hanap ' is French for a goblet or cup, and these gold and silver vessels being packed in hampers, like the coined money, was the origin of the word *hanaperium*.

Hanaper Office. An office belonging to the common-law jurisdiction of the Court of Chancery. So called because all writs relating to the business of a subject, and their returns, were formerly kept in a hamper [*in hanaperio*].

Hand (*The*). The hand engraved on the keystone of the arch of the Gate of Justice in the Alhambra, and on several Mahometan mausoleums, signifies the five prophets—Mahomet, Ali, Hassan, Hosein, and Fatama.

Handelists. . A musical faction in England in 1720–1730, opposed by the Bononcinists or the Italian school. The Prince of Wales was a leader of the Handelists, supported by Pope and Dr. Arbuthnot ; while Marlborough and many others of the nobility were adherents of Bononcini and the Italian music. Some of the admirers of Handel erected an academy in the Haymarket, to secure a supply of operas by Handel, and under his direction. It succeeded for about ten years, when it was closed, because the rage for Italian music was so great that Handel could not resist it. In 1742, however, his popularity returned.

Handkerchief (*The*) with which Seraphia is said to have wiped the face of Jesus on his way to Calvary, and on which was miraculously impressed a likeness of the sufferer, is preserved at Rome. It was placed in the Vatican by John VII. in 707 ; and it is now enshrined in one of the four huge supports of St. Peter's dome. *See ' Crucifixion, Relics of the.'*

Philip of Bergamo says that Tiberius Cæsar sent his friend Volusian, a valiant soldier of the imperial guards, to escort Seraphia to Rome. The emperor was ill at the time, but the moment he set his eyes on the handkerchief he was completely cured. This miracle, he adds, made so great an impression on Tiberius, that he wanted to enrol Jesus among the Roman gods ; but the senate would not listen to the proposal, so the emperor was obliged to content himself with a statue of the Nazarene in his palace. Of course the tale is a mere myth.

Handsome Al Raschid. George IV., also called Gentleman George. Called Al Raschid on account of that oriental toy palace built by him at Brighton.

Handsome Englishman (*The*). John Churchill duke of Marlborough was so called by Turenne, 'and his manners were as winning as his person' (1650–1722).

Hanging Hill. On Haywood Oaks Manor, near Black Gate, is where forest dogs were 'expeditated,' and forest offenders were 'swung to death.'

Expeditate is to cut out the balls or claws of a dog's forefeet for the preservation of the king's game.—*Old Forest Law.*
The 'canes Leporarii,' which as our record sings, 'Might never be expeditate,—they are our lord the king's.'
　　　　　The Regarde of Brian d'Insula, 1202.

Hanging Judge (*The*). I. Sir Francis Page (1718–1741).

II. John Toler earl of Norbury, Chief Justice of the Common Pleas in Ireland from 1820 to 1827.

Hango Massacre (*The*), 5 June, 1855. By Russians, on a party covered by a white flag. While the allied fleet of Great Britain and France was off Cronstadt, certain prizes had been made by the allies, who agreed to set at liberty seven of the prisoners. These were sent in a boat under a flag of truce to Hango; but no sooner had they been set ashore, than a party of Russians from ambush fired on the defenceless crew, spite of the white flag, killed 6 and wounded 4 of the crew, and 4 of the Russian liberated captives. The entire crew consisted of only 11 men. *See* 'Massacre.'

Hanifites, or Hanefites (3 syl.). The most ancient of the four principal orthodox sects of the Musulmans, founded by Abou-Hanifa, called the Socrates of the Musulmans, put to death in 767.

Hannibal of Batavia (*The*). Civilis (1st cent.).

Hannibal of China (*The*). Cheewang-tee the Great, who reigned thirty-seven years (B.C. 246–209). He completely reorganised the Chinese empire, and finished the great wall begun by Tchao-siang-wang. Chee-wang was contemporary with Hannibal.

Hannotin of Flanders. The nickname given to Jean Sans-Peur duke of Burgundy by his Flemish subjects.

Hanover (*Line of*). George I., George II., George III., George IV., William IV., Victoria.
George I. was the son of Sophia and Ernest Augustus duke of Brunswick, both descendants from Henry II. of England
SOPHIA **thus:** HENRY II., JOHN,

HENRY III., EDWARD I., II., III., Lionel duke of Clarence, Philippa, Roger Mortimer, Ann Mortimer, Richard duke of York, EDWARD IV., Elizabeth wife of HENRY VII., Margaret wife of James IV. of Scotland, James V. of Scotland, Mary queen of Scots, JAMES I. of England, Elizabeth wife of Frederick king of Bohemia, Sophia.

ERNEST AUGUSTUS thus: Maud daughter of HENRY II., Otto duke of Brunswick, Albert I., Albert II., Magnus, Bernard, Frederick, Otto II., Henry, Ernestus, William, George, Ernest Augustus, who married Sophia.

All either sons or daughters of the name preceding.

Hanover (*Treaty* or *Convention of*), 3 Sept., 1725. Signed at Hanover between Great Britain, France, Prussia, and afterwards by Denmark and Holland, to balance the alliance recently made between Spain, Austria, and Sweden. It protected England from the demand of Spain to surrender Gibraltar; and it defended Hanover from the aggressions of Russia. (*Tem.* Geo. I.)

Maria Theresa refused to join the treaty, and Prussia withdrew in 1727.

Hanover Rat (*A*). Originally meant a partisan of the first George elector of Hanover. As these partisans were converts from the true royal line to the German indirect line, a rat soon became a contemptuous word for a turncoat.

The origin of the term was this. About the time of the Hanoverian succession it was observed that the English black rat was being supplanted by the larger and fiercer grey rat from Astrakhan, which first appeared in Europe at the beginning of the 18th cent., and reached Britain about the middle of the cent. The Jacobites chose to associate the Hanover kings and the grey rat together, for both came into England at the same time.

Hanoverian Succession (*The*). The crown of Great Britain settled on Sophia duchess dowager of Hanover in 1702 (by 13, 14 Will. III., c. 6). Further secured by 6 Anne cc. 41 and 66.

Hanoverian Tories, 1705. A party bent on securing their interest with the house of Hanover, after the Hanoverian succession was resolved on. The Jacobites, strange to say, joined this party, to weaken the government and strengthen the chance of the Pretender.

Hanoverians (*The*). So the Whigs or Court party were called in the early part of the reign of George I., because they were favourable to the Hanoverian section. Those opposed to them were called Jacobites or favourers of James II., who had abdicated.

The whole history of England shows that our kings owe their accession to the sanction of parliament only, and not to the 'divine right,' blood inheritance, or royal succession. *See* 'English Sovereigns.'

Hanoverians and Jacobites. So Whigs and Tories were called in the reign of George I. The Whigs or Hanoverians supported George I. and the Hanoverian succession. The Jacobites supported Jacobus (or James) the Pretender (son of James II.).

Hanse Parisienne (*La*). An association of Paris 'marchands d'eau,' constituted under Philippe Auguste. It had a monopoly of the navigation of the Seine. Suppressed in 1672 by Louis XIV.

Hanse Towns (*The*). The three republics of Hamburg, Bremen, and Lübeck. Hanse means a league or union. *See below.*

Hanseat'ic League (*The*), 1241. A trades-union to protect merchandise from pirates and the pillage of nobles. It began with the three towns of Hamburg, Bremen, and Lübeck, but ultimately contained 85 trading towns. The league was divided into four colleges, viz. Lübeck, Cologne, Brunswick, and Dantzig. Of these Lübeck was the chief, and presided in all the conferences. The league had four principal factories in foreign parts, viz. at London, Bruges, Bergen, and Novogorod.

In the 15th cent. it reached its culminating point; in 1598 it came into collision with England; in 1630 most of the cities fell off.

Harakiri. Disembowelling oneself; either by legal sufferance, to prevent a public execution, whereby a man's goods are confiscated and his family attainted,— or to save the dishonour of failure, the scandal of insult, or the sickness of disappointed hope. A Japanese custom (*hara* = the belly, *kiri* = cutting open). *See* R. M. JEPHSON, &c., 'Our Life in Japan,' pp. 392, 393 (1869). Abolished.

The practice of harakiri in duelling had a quaint touch of humour. The challenger and challenged went home, arranged their affairs, and then disembowelled themselves.

Harcourt's Round Table. A private conference in the house of Sir William Harcourt, 14 Jan., 1887, with the view of reuniting, if possible, the Liberal party, broken up by Mr. Gladstone's Irish policy. In March a quarrel between Mr. Gladstone and Mr. Chamberlain broke up the conference.

The phrase 'Round Table' is American, meaning what the French call a *cercle*, or club meetings at each other's houses.

Har'courted. Letters secretly opened at the Post Office to learn their contents. The word was adopted by the Parnellites when Sir William Harcourt was secretary for the home department (1880–1885). The word 'Grahamise' means the same thing.

It was not unusual for the Parnellites to write on their letters 'Not to be Harcourted.' The subject of Harcourting letters was brought to the attention of parliament.

Hardham's No. 37. A particular mixture of snuff made by John Hardham, tobacconist and snuff merchant, Fleet Street, London. This Hardham, by a puff of Garrick, realised in a few years a fortune of 22,000*l.*, which at death he left to the poor of Chichester, his natal town. The interest amounts to 682*l.* yearly.

. . . Each connoisseur, a transient heaven
Finds in each pinch of Hardham s 37.
COLTON, *Hypocrisy.*

Hardwicke's Act (*Lord*), 1753. Directing all marriages to be by licence or banns, and to be solemnised in some church or chapel where banns are usually published.

By this act St. Paul's Cathedral and Westminster Abbey were excluded, as no banns are ever published in these places. It also rendered Fleet marriages unlawful, and thus abolished an abominable church scandal.

Hare (*Knights of the*). A military order of twelve knights instituted by Edward III. while he was in France. It is said that a hare ran before the French camp, when the soldiers raised a loud shout. Edward thought it was the cry of battle, and hence the order. Obsolete.

Hare Prize (*The*). For an essay on Greek or Roman history or philosophy. Given once in four years to any member of the University of Cambridge who has not graduated more than ten years. Value about 50*l.* Founded by the University in honour of Archdeacon Hare, of Trinity College, Cambridge, in 1861.

Hargrave Collection of MSS. (*The*), 1813. Purchased for the library of the British Museum for 8,000*l.* of the representatives of Francis Hargrave. It

D D 2

consists of 500 volumes, chiefly belonging to the faculty of law.

Harklensian Version. *See* 'Philoxenian,' &c.

Harkness Scholarship. For geology and palæontology. Value 250*l.*, tenable for one year by any member of the University of Cambridge. Founded in honour of Robert Harkness, professor of geology at Queen's College, Cork, 1887.

Harlaw (*The*). I. A municipal regulation made after the battle of Harlaw (24 July, 1411), in which the provost of Aberdeen was killed—that the chief magistrate of Aberdeen should in future leave the precincts of the liberty only a very brief space.

II. The battle of the Harlaw.

James I. also reduced to obedience the Highland chiefs who . . . had forgotten the terrors of the Harlaw.—Sir W. SCOTT, *Hist. of Scotland*, xviii.

Harleian MSS. (*The*). A collection of MSS. formed by Robert Harley earl of Oxford (1661–1725), and purchased by government in 1754 of the Duchess of Portland (his grand-daughter) for 10,000*l.* There are 14,236 original rolls, charters, and other deeds, besides 7,639 volumes. The collection is very miscellaneous, but its main character is historical. It is rich in heraldic and genealogical MSS., in county visitations, parliamentary and legal proceedings, original records and calendars, abbey registers, missals, antiphonaries, and other Catholic service-books, ancient English poetry, and works on arts and sciences. It is kept in the British Museum library.

It also contains the oldest known MS. of Homer's 'Odyssey,' two very early copies of the Latin Gospels in gold letters, 300 MS. Bibles or Biblical books, 200 volumes of the Fathers, &c.

Harmony (*The Patriarch of*). Nicholas Porpora of Naples (1685–1767), author of thirty-eight operas. He was a pupil of Scarlatti, and Farinelli (the best male singer on record) was his pupil.

Harmony Hall, 1844. A building and family collected together in Hampshire by Robert Owen, organised on his socialistic principles. Religion, marriage, competition, rivalry, were either abolished or remodelled, and all the inmates were to live in perfect harmony, seeking only the general good, without regard to personal or individual ambition or indulgence. The scheme proved an utter failure.

Harmony of the Spheres (*The*). Pythagoras taught that the motions of the stars through space must of necessity produce sounds, like the motion of any body through the air. As the stars differ in size and velocity, the sounds must differ in tone, and these different notes produce a harmony called the 'Music of the Spheres.'

Harness Prize (*The*). For the best essay on some subject connected with Shakespearian literature. Value about 50*l.*, and given once in three years to any member of the University of Cambridge who has not graduated more than three years. Founded by subscribers to a memorial fund of the Rev. William Harness, of Christ's College, Cambridge, in 1870.

Harold Blue-tooth (*Blaatand*). The 31st king of Denmark, descendant of the mythical Skiold, founder of the Skioldung dynasty (B.C. about 60 to A.D. 1044). Harold was the son of Gorm, and succeeded him to a peaceful and undivided kingdom, so that he is often called the 'first of the Skioldungs,' or the first who reigned over all Denmark (A.D. 930–980).

Harold Harefoot (*, 1035–1040). Harold I., a king of England before the Conquest. Swiftness of foot is often spoken of by Homer as a great military virtue. Thus his great hero was called by him 'The swift-footed Achillês.'

Harp (*Cradled in a*). Aslauga, wife of Ragner Lodbrok the sea-king, was cradled in a golden harp.

Etenim tractus illius incolæ constanter referunt, seque a majoribus suis accepisse perhibent, inventam apud se in exiguo sinu angulove maris citharam auream, cujus cavitati inclusa fuerit parvula virgo.—*Series Reg. Dan.* iv. chap. 4.
** Ragner or Regenfrid was surnamed Lodbrok (*Hairy-breeches*) from the magical garment (daubed with sand, pitch, and hair) which he wore when he slew the guardian serpent of the Princess Thora, his first wife.

Harp Lords (*Cromwell's*). Those soldiers and partisans of Cromwell put into the Irish confiscated estates after the 'Irish Rebellion' had been crushed out in 1648. On the return of Charles II. these lords of the soil were turned out, and the estates restored to their original possessors. Called Harp lords from the Irish harp; meaning Brummagem lords, as Harp shillings (worth about 9d. each) mean counters current for a time and then called in. Lords in this phrase do not mean noblemen, but lords of the confiscated soil.

Harp of Ireland (*The*). One of the very early lords of Ireland was named David, who took for his cognisance a harp, in honour of the harp of the sweet singer of Israel.

Harrisburg (Pennsylvania). So named from Mr. Harris, by whom it was first settled, in 1733, under a grant from the Penn family.

Harry (*Blind*), 15th cent. Author of a poetical romance entitled 'Sir William Wallace,' 1488. It contains 11,861 lines of ten syllables in rhyming couplets.

Harvard University, 1639, New England. Founded by John Harvard, whose father carried on his business at the Boar's Head, exactly opposite St. Mary Overies, in London (1607-1688).

Harvest Months.
JANUARY.—The greater part of Chili, portions of the Argentine Republic, Australia, and New Guinea.
FEBRUARY to MARCH.—The East Indies.
APRIL.—Mexico, Egypt, Persia, and Syria.
MAY.—Japan, China, Northern Asia Minor, Tunis, Algiers, Morocco, and Texas.
JUNE.—California, Spain, Portugal, Italy, Sicily, Greece, and some of the southern departments of France.
JULY.—The larger part of France, Austria, Southern Russia, and the larger part of the United States of America.
AUGUST.—Germany, England, Belgium, Netherlands, part of Russia, Denmark, part of Canada, and the N.-E. States of America.
SEPTEMBER.—Scotland, the larger part of Canada, Sweden, Norway, and the north midlands of Russia.
OCTOBER.—The northern parts of Russia, and the northern parts of the Scandinavian peninsula.

Hash'emites (3 syl.). The followers of Haschem the Scherif, who declared himself to be of the issue of Mahomet. He was king of Fez in 1508, and founded the dynasty of the Scherifs in 1509.

Hassan ben Sabah. 'The Old Man of the Mountain,' founder of the Assassins or Hassanis.

Hastings (*Impeachment of Warren*), from Feb. 1786 to April 1795. Warren Hastings was governor-general of India 1774-1785. He was born 1732, and died 1818. Burke brought before the House of Commons the first charge against Hastings Feb. 1786. Sheridan the third charge (Hastings's treatment of the Begums). This speech lasted five hours, and produced such a sensation that the House arose after it and adjourned till the next day. The fourth charge (Hastings's selfish contracts and high salaries) was made by Sir James Erskine. The sixth charge (Hastings's conduct to Fyzoola Khan the Rohilla chief) was brought before the House by Wyndham. Sheridan made the seventh charge (Hastings's receipt of bribes). Francis, the supposed author of 'Junius's Letters,' made the eighth charge (Hastings's mismanagement of the revenues). The case being carried to the House of Lords, it was appointed to begin at Westminster 13 Feb., 1788. The defence began 2 June, 1791. The trial terminated in an acquittal 23 April, 1795 (having lasted over six years). *See* ' Sheridan's Begum Speech,' ' Begums,' and ' Fyzoola Khan.'

Hate of Englishmen (*The*). So Shane O'Neill, lord of Ulster, called the fortress which he built on his border.

Hats. I. *The Petăsus.* A felt hat with broad brim and low crown, used by

the ancient Greeks and Romans. It was very much like the felt hat still worn by agricultural labourers, only it was fastened with a thong either under the chin or round the back of the head. In the British Museum the horsemen in the Panathenaic procession are represented wearing these sorts of hats. *See* Caps.'

II. *The Pilĭos.* The ancient Greeks wore a close-fitting skull-cap called a

'pilĭos.' Ulysses is generally represented wearing such a cap.

III. *The Galērus.* The Romans wore a skull-cap of some animal with the hair

left on, outside, called 'galērus.' The pontifical galērus had a spike of olive wood at the top, and strings. *See* 'Caps.'

Hats and Caps (*The*), 1738. Two political factions which arose in Sweden in the reign of Adolf Frederick (1720–1771). The *Hats* were the anti-Russian party, who were violently opposed to the late treaty with Russia, and wanted to recover all the provinces ceded to that power. This was the French or *Chapeau* party. The *Caps* were for peace with Russia, economy, and retrenchment. This was the Russian party, and the distinguishing characteristic of a Russian was the Muscovite *cap.* The accession of Gustavus Vasa in 1771 put an end to these factions. No king of Sweden since the time of Charles XII. (1697–1719) to that of Gustavus III. (1771–1792) could speak the language of the country.

Count Gyllenborg was the leader of the Hats, and Count Horn of the Caps.

Hatted King (*The*). Kaiser Joseph II., son of Maria Theresa, was so called by the Hungarians, because he refused to be crowned.

Hatti-sheriff, or 'Scherif.' An irrevocable order issuing immediately from the sultan. A Turkish word brought into use at the time of the battle of Navarino (1827).

Lord John Russell in 1828 said : 'The government issued a sort of hatti-sheriff for the purpose, calling upon everyone within their influence who possessed the faith of a true Mussulman to follow them in opposing the measure' [*i.e.* the repeal of the Test Act].

Haudriettes (3 syl.). Religious Hospitallers who followed the rule of St. Austin ; so called from their founder, Etienne Haudri, secretary of Louis IX. Haudri followed his master to the Holy Land. He abandoned his house to twelve religious paupers, and endowed the society.

Haute Justice (*La*). The gallows-tree.

Romsey Abbey possessed many extraordinary privileges, amongst others the rare and anomalous right of *la haute justice,* or gallows-tree ; a privilege of which the records do not mention any use having been made.—*Cassell's History of England,* vol. i. p. 149.

Haw'kubites (3 syl.). A turbulent set of young men in the reign of Queen Anne, whose delight was to molest and ill-treat the old watchmen, women, children, and feeble old men found after sunset in the ill-lighted streets of London. The Mohocks, Scourers, and Hawkubites were contemporaneous, about 1711–1714. Hawkubites, an Indian tribe of savages. *See* 'Street Bullies.'

'From Mohock and from Hawkubite,
　Good Lord deliver me,
Who wander thro' the streets at night
　Committing cruelty :
They slash our sons with bloody knives,
　And on our daughters fall ;
And if they murder not our wives
　We have good luck withal.
Coaches and carts they overturn . . .'

An Argument to prove the present race of Mohocks and Hawkubites are the Gog and Magog mentioned in the Revelation.

Head-Centres. The leaders of the Fenian Brotherhood of Ireland ; their lieutenants were called 'centres.' James Stephens was appointed the first head-centre of Ireland 11 Nov., 1865. O'Mahoney was the first head-centre of the brotherhood in America, 1858.

Head Pacificator (*O'Connell's*). Tom Steel, who looked up to his hero with the veneration of Boswell for Dr. Johnson.

Heads of Houses or Colleges (*The*).

In Cambridge : The Head of King's is styled the *Provost*; of Queens', the *President*; of all other colleges, the *Master*.

In Oxford : The Heads of University College, Balliol, and Pembroke are styled the *Master*; of Oriel, Queen's, and Worcester, the *Provost*; of Trinity, St. John's, Magdalen, and Corpus, the *President*; of Merton, All Souls', Wadham, New College, and Keble, the *Warden*; of Jesus, Brasenose, and Hertford, the *Principal*; of Lincoln and Exeter, the *Rector*; of Christ Church, the *Dean*.

Healing Declaration (*The*), 6 Nov., 1660. The declaration of Charles II. for the settlement of most Church matters by 'competent persons' approved of by the king. The idea was to have a united convention of suffragan bishops and synods, or presbyterians; but the bishops refused to meet the synod. It was ultimately decided to unite the presbyterian and episcopal establishments, and of these the king was to select a certain number to revise the liturgy, and consider such moot points as standing or kneeling to receive the sacrament, signing infants with a cross, bowing at the name of Jesus, and wearing surplices. The bill was thrown out by the parliament, which re-assembled 6 Nov.

Heart of Midlothian (*The*). The Tolbooth (a prison), of Edinburgh, is popularly so called. Sir Walter Scott's novel of the same name gives a graphic description of the Porteous riot, and the execution of Capt. Porteous by the mob. *See* ' Mids of Mar.'

Hearts of Steel, 1764. Irish insurgents in Ulster, roused to rebellion by high rents and the rapacity of the agents of absentees. It was a part of the great southern brotherhood called Whiteboys. *See* ' Irish Associations.'

Hearth-tax (*The*), 1662. A tax of two shillings for every fire-hearth and stove, ' payable on the feast of St. Michael and the feast of the Blessed Virgin Mary ' (13 & 14 Car. II. c. 10). Repealed by the special desire of William III. in 1689. A hut with two chimneys paid as much as a house or hall with the same number. The hearth-tax and the window-tax were certainly

the worst and most oppressive taxes ever laid on the people.

Heaven (*The*). A public-house in Whitefriars, kept in the reign of Charles II. by Bradley. Charles, with Buckingham, Monmouth, Lord Howard, and other debauchees, visited this house, and drank punch there till their wits were out. Colonel Blood and Titus Oates also frequented the house. *See* ' Gone to the " Devil." '

Heaven-born Minister (*The*). William Pitt was so called in a parliamentary oration by Mr. Drake. Prime minister 1783-1801, and again 1804 ; died 1806.

Heavy Peg, 1412, &c. A heavy cannon by which Friedrich count of Hohenzollern, who had lately bought Brandenburg of the Kaiser Siegmund, reduced the turbulent barons to order by blowing up their castles.

Hebdom'ada. For other weeks *see* the English equivalent. For example—

For Hebdomada	Casta	*see* Chaste Week
,,	Crucis	,, Week of the Cross
,,	Expectationis	,, Week of Expectation
,,	Magna	,, Great Week
,,	Muta	,, Silent Week
,,	Paschalis	,, Easter Week
,,	Passionis	,, Passion Week
,,	Penitentialis	,, Penitential Week
,,	Pentecostes	,, Whitsun Week
,,	Trinitatis	,, Trinity Week

Hebdom'ada de Excepto. The last week in Advent is so called in the Ambrosian ritual.

Hebdom'ada Grassa(Meat Week). The week preceding Quinquagesima Sunday, the last week before Lent. The third day after Quinquagesima Sunday is Ash Wednesday, therefore the week preceding was the last in which meat was allowed to be eaten.

Hebdom'ada in Albis. An octave, beginning the Sunday after Easter and ending the following Sunday, when those baptized on Palm Sunday laid aside their white stoles.

Hebdom'ada Indulgentiæ, or Absolution Week. Between Palm Sunday and Holy Saturday, when penitents received indulgence or absolution.

Hebdóm'ada Major. Same as Holy Week (*q.v.*). Passion Week, which lasted thirteen days, was Hebdomada

Magna; but the last seven of these days constitute Holy Week, or the ' Greater Week' of the 'Great Week.'

Hebdom'ada Mediana. Beginning with the third of Lent, called in French Mi-carême (Mid Lent). In this week some slight relaxation was allowed of the long Lenten fast.

Hebdom'ada Pœna'lis, 'Laboriosam Hebdomadam' vocant Latini Patres. Also called Hebdomada Pœnosa. Du Cange says: ' Illa qua Christus crucem subiit, et quod jejuniis et laboribus transigatur ad memoriam passionis Christi.'

Hebdom'adal Council (*The*), 1631. Oxford University. So called because it assembles weekly. This weekly board discusses all measures of reform before they are sent to the House of Congregation (*q.v.*). The *ex-officio* members are the chancellor, vice-chancellor, ex-vice-chancellor, and the two proctors. There are also eighteen members—viz. six heads of houses, six professors, and six members of Convocation, of not less than five years' standing. The council meets every Monday during term time.

Hébertists. The followers of Hébert, the coarsest and most vulgar-minded of the three leaders in the Reign of Terror, the other two being Danton and Robespierre. It was Hébert who instituted *le culte de la raison*.

Anacharsis Clootz, Ronsin, Vincent, and Momoro were Hébertists.

Hebrew of the Hebrews (*A*). A descendant from Abraham.

Hebrew Prize. Worth about 20*l.* Founded in the University of Cambridge by subscription, 1866 ; increased 1867. *See* 'Tyrwhitt Scholarship.'

Hecatæos the Abderite (3 syl.). Said to have been the author of a 'History of the Jews,' frequently referred to by Josephus, but pronounced by Origen to be spurious. *See* 'Literary Forgeries.'

Hec'atomphon'ia. A sacrifice made to the Ithomæan Jupiter by such as had slain 100 men in battle. Aristomēnês of Messēnia thrice offered this sacrifice.

Hectors. Street bullies and brawlers who succeeded the 'Titÿre tu-s,' and

delighted to be as rude as possible to women and the defenceless. Robbery was not their object, but simply to annoy and get talked about. *See* 'Street Bullies.'

To hector is to bully or treat with insolence; but the noble Hector of Troy was as unlike a bully as possible.

Hedgebote (2 syl.), or 'Haybote ' in English law. The right of a tenant to cut wood on the farm to repair his hedges, gates, and fences, to make rake-handles and handles for forks, &c.

Hedonism. The system of Aristippus, the Cyrenaïtic philosopher, born at Cyrēnê about B.C. 435. He said that the aim of life should be ἡδονή (*hēdonê*, pleasure), and he passed his life in the court of Dionysius the Tyrant amidst delicacies and indulgences.

He was very witty. One day being rebuked for casting himself at the feet of Dionysius he replied, ' Well, it is not my fault if his ears are in his feet.'

He'donists. Philosophers who placed the *summum bonum* in pleasure (ἡδονή), before Epicurus improved upon their teaching by the dogma that psychic pleasure is superior in degree and duration to physical enjoyments.

Hegelianism. The philosophical system of Wilhelm Friedrich Hegel of Stuttgart (1770–1831). It may be called an idealistic pantheism. In the Spinozan system God is a substance ; in the Hegelian system God is spirit. In the Spinozan system God is endowed with both matter and mind—the phenomena of the material and spiritual universe may be compared to two parallel streams. In the Hegelian theory God objectifies Himself in nature, rises out of nature, and returns to Himself.

Heg'ira (*The*), 16 June, 622. The day that Mahomet fled from Mecca to Medina. The people of Mecca were exasperated because those of Medi'na believed him to be a prophet. From this day the Mahometan era begins.

Generally called Hegira. The Arabic word is ' Hijra,' and means the 'flight' or emigration.

Hegu'meni or Mandrites (2 syl.). Superiors of convents in the Greek Church.

Hehoo-Woo-tae, or the Five Hehoo races, being the 14th, 15th, 16th, 17th, and 18th imperial dynasties of China, called Hehoo-Lĕang, Hehoo-Tâng,

Hehoo-Tsin, Hehoo-Hân, and Hehoo-Chew. From 907 to 960. During this period the Tartars held the north of the empire. The 'five successions' terminated with the 19th or Tsong dynasty.

Hehoo, sometimes written in English 'Heou' or 'How'; and Chew is written 'Chow.'

Heidelberg Catechism (*The*), or the 'Palatinate Catechism,' 1563. A religious formulary compiled by the Heidelberg theologians—Caspar, Olivetan, and Zacharias Ursīnus—at the request of the Elector Friedrich III. of the Palatinate. This catechism was sanctioned by several synods, and was revised by the Synod of Dort.

Heidelberg Confession (*The*), 1575, or the 'Palatine Confession.' One of the chief confessions of the continental Calvinistic or Reformed Churches. *See* 'Confessions.'

Heiltum (*Hile-tum*), or 'Heiligthum.' That is, holy relics of Nuremberg, exhibited the second Friday after Easter, and consisting of the insignia of the city; the sword, sceptre, and crown of Charlemagne; a piece of the true cross, part of the manger of Bethlehem, Longinus's spear, and portions of the respective chains with which Peter, Paul, and John were bound, with many other relics. The church of the Holy Ghost at Nuremberg, in which the Heiltum was formerly kept, was recently restored; but Nuremberg is now a Protestant city.

Heinel (*Mlle.*). A famous dancer in London in the last quarter of the 18th cent. *See* 'Walpole's Letters,' vol. v. pp. 327, 355, 383, 431.

Dotes upon dancing, and, in all her pride, Swims round the room, the Heinel of Cheapside.
Epilogue to *She Stoops to Conquer*.
Pronounce *High′nel.*

HEINRICH OF GERMANY.
(Heinrich, pronounce *Hine-reek*.)

Heinrich I., or 'Henry I. the Fowler,' surnamed 'the father of his country.' Founder of the Saxon dynasty of Germany. He succeeded Konrad of Franconia (876, 918-936). This dynasty gives five kings—viz. Heinrich I., Otto I., II., III., and Heinrich II. His father was Otto the Illustrious, duke of Saxony. His empire embraced Holland, Flanders, and Switzerland, as well as Germany. With Heinrich I. the Fowler the modern

18

history of Germany begins, as that of France with Hugues Capet, and that of England with William the Conqueror. *See* 'Fowler.'

Father, Otto the Illustrious. *Wife*, Mechtildes. *Contemporary* with Edward the Elder and Athelstan.

Heinrich II., called 'The Saint' and 'The Lame.' Was the cousin of Otto III., the grandson of Heinrich the Quarrelsome, and great-grandson of the Fowler. As he died without issue, in him the Saxon dynasty of Germany came to an end. It was Heinrich II. who founded Strasburg Cathedral.

HEINRICH I. (Henry the Fowler), founder of the Saxon dynasty.
OTTO I. the Great and *Heinrich the Quarrelsome*, sons of the Fowler.
OTTO II. son of Otto I.
OTTO III. son of Otto II.

HEINRICH the Fowler
|

OTTO I.	Heinrich the Quarrelsome
OTTO II.	Heinrich the Regent
OTTO III.	HEINRICH II.

Both Otto III. and Heinrich II. were great-grandsons of the Fowler.
Father, Heinrich duke of Bavaria (late regent). *Wife*, Cunegunda (no children). *Contemporary* with Ethelred, Edmund Ironsides, and Canute.

Heinrich III. the Black King. Second of the house of Franconia (1017, 1039-1056). He died at the age of 39. In 1056 he created the title of 'King of the Romans' for the heir-elect of the throne. Called 'Black' from the colour of his hair. He was an excellent king.

The kings of Germany were elective, but a father before death generally got his son elected. Heinrich III. was elected in 1026.
Father, Konrad II. *Mother*, Gisela of Burgundy. *Wives*, (1) Kunihild daughter of Canute; (2) Agnes mother of HEINRICH IV. *Contemporary* with Hardicanute and Edward the Confessor.

Heinrich IV. kaiser-king of Germany (1050, 1056-1106). Died at Liège of starvation at the age of 56. The whole reign was one incessant struggle with the pope for mastery. He was three times excommunicated, and once his kingdom was put under the ban of Rome. His eldest son Konrad revolted against him, and died 1101. His second son Heinrich [V.] then revolted, arrested his father, and confined him in a castle. The kaiser made his escape, and died at Liège on the doorstep of a religious house, 'clemmed with hunger and starved with cold.'

Father, Heinrich III. *Mother*, Agnes of Aquitaine. *Wives*, (1) Bertha; (2) Adelaide of Russia. *Contemporary* with Edward the Confessor and William the Conqueror.

Heinrich V. the Parricide, kaiser-king of Germany. Fourth and last of the house of Franconia. Son of Heinrich IV. the kaiser-king, and son-in-law of Henry I. of England (1081, 1098–1125).

Father, Heinrich IV. *Mother,* Bertha. *Wife,* Maud daughter of Henry I. of England.* *Contemporary* with Rufus and Henry I.

* *Soon after the death of her royal husband, Maud married Godfroi earl of Anjou, by whom she became the mother of our Henry II. surnamed ' Curtmantle.'*

Heinrich VI. the Cruel, kaiser-king of Germany, son of Friedrich I., called Barbarossa (1163, 1190–1197). He was poisoned by his wife Messina, Sunday, 28 Sept., 1197, at the age of 32. This was the dastard who imprisoned Richard Cœur-de-Lion in 1192, and kept him captive for two years.

KONRAD III., founder of the royal house of Hohenstauffen.
FRIEDRICH I., Barbarossa, Konrad's nephew.
Father, Friedrich I., Barbarossa. *Mother,* Beatrice of Burgundy. *Wife,* Constance of Sicily. *Contemporary* with Richard I. and John.

Heinrich VII. of Luxemburg. One of the promiscuous kaiser-kings of Germany (1263, 1309–1313). Said by a Dominican monk to have been poisoned by Politian (a Dominican monk), by the sacramental wine, administered to him in the House of God. The only *kaiser* since the time of Friedrich II. (1220).

. Horrible as this appears, it was not uncommon. At least nine other monarchs, we are told, were despatched in the same way. *Wife,* Margaret of Brabant. *Contemporary* with Edward II.

Heir.

I. *Apparent.* The eldest son is heir apparent, because he is certain to succeed if he outlives his father.

II. *Presumptive.* The person who would succeed under present conditions, but who may be set aside if the *statu quo* is altered. Thus a daughter is heir presumptive, but if a son is born later on the daughter does not succeed.

Heirs to the Crowns of Europe.
AUSTRIA-HUNGARY, Prince Imperial.
ENGLAND, Prince of Wales. The heir or heiress presumptive is the Prince or Princess Royal.
GERMANY, Crown Prince.
ITALY, Prince of Naples.
PORTUGAL, Prince or Princess Royal.
RUSSIA, Czarevich and his wife Czarevna.
SPAIN, Prince of Asturias ; the heiress is called the Princess Royal.

SWEDEN and NORWAY, Crown Prince or Princess.

Helena (*The Tyrian*). The mistress of Simon Magus. They called themselves Jupiter and Minerva, and gave out that those who believed in them were absolved from all obligations to the moral law, seeing they would be saved by grace and not by works. Epiphanius tells us that Simon Magus claimed to be the Messiah, and Heléna, he said, was the Holy Ghost.

Heliæa, or ' Court of Heliæa.' An Athenian tribunal, fluctuating in number, but usually consisting of several hundreds, chosen by lot from the whole body of citizens. It was before this tribunal that Socratês was brought, and by it was he condemned to death.

Heliastæ (*The Tribunal of the*). An Athenian tribunal which assembled at Heliæa. It took cognisance of only very grave offences. The ordinary number of members was 200, but in some cases it amounted to 500, 1,000, and even 1,500 members.

Heliogab'alus. A Roman emperor (204, 218–222), who had been from infancy high priest in the Temple of the Sun at Emissa, in Syria, where he received the title of Heliogabaal (Lord of the Sun).

It will be remembered that Samuel, like Heliogabalus, was consecrated to the Temple from infancy.

Heliop'olis. The City of the Sun. Baalbek in Syria was so called by the Greeks ; so was On in Egypt, noted for the temple of Actis.

Hell. Called by the ancient *Egyptians* 'Amenthês'; by the *Gauls* 'Ifurin'; by the *Greeks* 'Tartăros'; by the *Indians* 'Patala' and 'Naraka'; by the *Jews* 'Sheôl'; the *Mohammedans* believe in seven infernos; by the *Persians* 'Douzakh'; by the *Romans* 'Avernus'; by the *Scandinavians* 'Niflheim.'

Hell (from the verb *hélian,* to cover) means a place covered over, hence a grave. 'Helings' means the eyelids or covers for the eyes ; 'hellier' is a thatcher or one who covers with thatch. Chaucer calls Elysium 'Helise.' Then there is the participle 'helling' or 'heling' = hidden, 'helen' = caves; and many other similar words more or less archaic. *See below.*

Hell. So the cellar under the House of Commons, in the reign of Charles I., was called. *See* 'Pride's Purge.'

Hellenists. Those Jews who spoke the Greek language, chiefly resident in Asia Minor, Greece, and Egypt. The Jews of Jerusalem spoke Aramaic, a bastard Hebrew; whence Paul, when he was permitted to address the Jewish mob, spoke to the people in the Hebrew [Aramaic] tongue. They could hardly be called a sect, although without doubt they corrupted the pure Jewish faith with Greek philosophy and mythology. They had a temple of their own certainly at Leontopolis.. (*See* JOSEPHUS, 'Antiquities,' xiii. 3, 1–3.)

The Hellenists were certainly looked on by the strict Jews as unsound, and were accused of ' reading the Scriptures in the Egyptian manner.'

Hell-fire Club (*The*), 1721. President, the Duke of Wharton, a most profligate young nobleman. The central club was in London, but it had affiliated clubs both in Edinburgh and in Dublin. The members were of both sexes, and had such nicknames as Pluto, the Old Dragon, the King of Tartarus, Lady Envy, Lady Gomorrah, and so on. Their toasts were revoltingly blasphemous, and sulphurous flames were raised at their meetings. Suppressed by royal proclamation the same year (1721).

This was the Medmenham Club, originally held in Medmenham Abbey. It consisted of wild spirits, euphemistically called ' wits and humorists,' who assumed the name of ' Monks of St. Francis.' The inscription over the club door was *Fais ce que tu voudras*. Langley gives an account of it. When I lived in Paris there was an important street called 'Hell Street' (Rue d'Enfer). The name is changed now.

Helluo Libro'rum (Cicero). A devourer of books ; a great reader.

Charles in Fletcher s 'Elder Brother' is a mere ' helluo librōrum,' who falls in love with Angelina.

Helmets. The helmet of a king has six bars over the face. (Full faced, gold.)

The helmet of a noble has five bars over the face. (In profile, steel with gold bars.)

The helmet of a knight has the visor thrown back. (Full faced, steel.)

The helmet of a squire has the visor closed. (In profile, steel.)

The helmet is placed above the escutcheon and supports the crest.

Helvetia. The modern Switzerland, the country of the Helvetii. Helvetia is not classic Latin ; the country was never so called, but *Ager Helvetiorum*.

Helvetic Confederation (*The*). I. After the battle of Morgarten, in 1315, the three cantons of Uri, Schweiz, and Unterwalden formed themselves into a perpetual league, and declared themselves free from Austria. In 1332 Lucerne joined the confederacy; in 1351 Zürich ; in 1352 Zug and Glaris ; in 1353 Berne. Two other victories over the dukes of Austria (one at Sempach in 1386, and the other at Naefels in 1388), made the name of Switzerland respected in Europe ; and the two subsequent battles of Granson and Morat in 1476 greatly added to this renown. Five other cantons joined the confederacy in 1841; Bâle and Schaffhausen in 1501, and Appenzell in 1513, completed the thirteen cantons. In 1648, at the peace of Westphalia, the Helvetic Confederacy was declared by Austria and all the rest of the European powers to be independent of the empire.

II. 1814. The old constitution of Switzerland, restored after the banishment of Napoleon to Elba. Each canton enjoys ' home rule,' but all unite in matters pertaining to the confederacy.

Helvetic Confessions (*The*). Are those of Bâle in 1530, and of Bullinger in 1566. The former was an exposition of faith drawn up by Zwingli, and being solemnly sworn to at Bâle in 1534, was called the ' Confession of Bâle.' The other was the exposition drawn up chiefly by Theodore Beza and Bullinger. In this ' confession ' images were proscribed, predestination was acknowledged, only two sacraments were admitted, and the eucharist was regarded as commemorative only. The phrase ' Helvetic Confession ' is sometimes used to designate ' Calvinism ' ; and sometimes the ' Reformed Church of Germany.'

The religion of Calvin, or the Helvetic Confession, had such a hold on the Hungarians that it was soon designated . . . the Hungarian faith.— VAMBERY, *Hungary*, ch. xii.

Helvetic Republic (*The*), 12 April, 1798–1814. A kind of polyarchy vested in French officers and their partisans by Napoleon Bonaparte, who compelled Switzerland to become virtually a French province.

Heno'ticon (*The*), A.D. 482. A concordat published by the Emperor Zeno for the reconciliation of the churches of Constantinople and Alexandria. It was issued at the solicitation of Acacius patriarch of Constantinople. Whatever its merits, it proved no better than ecclesiastical dynamite, by exciting in the Eastern Empire angry disputes and relentless persecutions. In 484 Pope Felix III. condemned it. In 496 the Emperor Anastasius confirmed it. In 519 it was revoked by Justin I. (Greek ἑνωτικόν).

Gibbon says, xlvii.: 'The Henoticon was most pleasing to the Egyptians; yet the smallest blemish has not been descried by the jealous and even jaundiced eyes of orthodox schoolmen, and it accurately represents the Catholic faith of the incarnation without adopting or disclaiming the peculi r terms or tenets of the hostile sects.' Petavius says, *Chalcedonensem ascivit*, but, adds Gibbon, this proves ' he had never read it' (Greek ἑνότης, unity).

Henri Grâce à Dieu (*The*).

Was built at Erith in 1515. It measured 1,000 tons, had four masts, and was the first three-decked ship built in England. It carried 80 guns of various calibres.

This ship appears in a list of 1552 as 'The Edward,' and all trace of her then ceases. The next British ship of note was 'The Soveraigne of the Seas,' built at Woolwich Dockyard in 1637 by Mr. Phineas Pett. She also was a three-decker. James, in his ' Naval History of Great Britain,' says : 'There is reason to believe that Richard III. owned a few of the ships which he employed; the rest were either hired of merchants, or supplied under a law of the state by the Cinque Ports.'

The 'Great Harry' and 'Henri Grâce à Dieu' were two entirely distinct ships.

The 'Great Harry' was built in the third year of Henry VII., 1488; the 'Henri Grâce à Dieu' was built at Erith in 1515.

The 'Great Harry' was a *two*-decker, with three masts; the ' Henri Grâce à Dieu' had three decks and four masts.

The 'Great Harry' was accidentally burnt at Woolwich in 1553; the 'Henri Grâce à Dieu' was renamed ' Edward' after the death of Henry VIII. in 1547, and there is no record of its destruction.

I hope this will settle the question of historians on the moot point of the identity of these two vessels.

HENRI KINGS OF FRANCE.

Henri I. of France (1011, 1031–1061).

Third of the Capetian dynasty.

Father, Robert le Pieux; *Mother*, Constance of Arles; *Wife*, Anne of Muscovy; son and successor, Philippe I. l'Amoureux. *Contemporary* with Edward the Confessor.

Henri II. le Belliqueux, of France (1519, 1547–1559).

Of the Capetian dynasty, and of the Valois-Angoulême line.

Father, FRANÇOIS I.; *Mother*, Claude, daughter of LOUIS XII.; *Wife*, Catharine de' Medici, daughter of Lorenzo de' Medici; son and successor, FRANÇOIS II. *Contemporary* with Edward VI. and his sister Mary. His *mistress* was Diane de Poitiers, whose colour was blue. The colour of her rival, the Duchesse d'Etampes, was lilac. Diane de Poitiers was created duchesse de Valentinois.

CHARLES V. had two sons, CHARLES VI. and Louis duc d'Orléans.

From the first came, in regular succession, CHARLES VII.: LOUIS XI. his son; and CHARLES VII. his son, who left no issue.

The second son, Louis duc d'Orléans, had also two sons, viz. Charles duc d'Orléans and Jean d'Angoulême.

LOUIS XII. was son of Charles duc d'Orléans, but left no male issue.

From the second son, Jean d'Angoulême, came FRANÇOIS I., and HENRI II. was the son of François.

Henri III. le Mignon, of France (1551, 1574–1589).

Third son of Henri II. (*q.v.*). Weaker than woman, and worse than harlot.

Father, HENRI II.; *Mother*, Catharine de' Medici, daughter of Lorenzo de' Medici; *Wife*, Louise de Vaudemont; no issue. *Contemporary* with Elizabeth. *See* 'Fatal Three.'

Henri IV. le Grand, first of the Bourbon kings of France (1553, 1589–1610).

He was the tenth in descent from Robert, the sixth son of St. Louis (IX.), and was related to the last king (Henri III.) only in the eleventh degree. He is generally spoken of as *le bon roi Henri*.

Father, Antoine duc de Vendôme; *Mother*, Jeanne d'Albret, queen of Navarre; *Wives*, Marguerite de Valois, daughter of HENRI II. (she was divorced); Maria de' Medici, daughter of the duke of Tuscany and mother of LOUIS XIII. his successor; *Mistress*, La belle Gabrielle, daughter of Antoine d'Estrees, created duchess of Beaufort. *Contemporary* with Elizabeth and James I. *Life* attempted by Pierre Barrière in 1593, by Jean Châtel in 1597, by Jean de l'Isle in 1605, and fatally by Ravaillac in 1610.

. Robert comte de Clermont (sixth son of ST. LOUIS) married the heiress of the Sieur de Bourbon, and died 1311, leaving Louis duc de Bourbon his son and heir.

The third son of this Louis was Jacques, whose son Jean (Comte de la Marche) married the heiress of the Duc de Vendôme; and their second son, Louis (Comte de la Marche), died 1446, leaving issue Jean comte de la Marche.

The son of this Jean was François (who married Marie de Luxembourg), and their son was Charles, who died 1537.

The son of this Charles was Antoine duc de Vendôme (who married Jeanne d'Albret, queen of Navarre), and these were the parents of HENRI IV.

Henri V. of France,

like Louis XVII. and Napoleon II., was a mere nominal king. He was born 1820, after the assassination of his father, Charles Ferdinand duc de Berry (son of Charles X.). When Charles X. abdicated, the next heir to the throne was Henri his grandson, who assumed the title of Henri V., but the French people chose Louis Philippe for their king instead.

Charles X. died 1836; the Duc de Berry was assassinated by Louvel in 1820; and Henri V. (Comte de Chambord) died 1883, at the age of 63.

Henricians (*The*), 1140.

Followers of Henry of Italy, called ' the false hermit,' who was given up in chains to the bishop of Toulouse, and died 1147. They rejected the Apocrypha; would have no churches; administered baptism only to adults; denied the real presence and the existence of purgatory; suppressed masses; proscribed crucifixes, adoration of saints, relics, images, and prayers for the dead; they rejected also the separate order of the priesthood and the lawfulness of oaths. The Henricians, chiefly confined to Switzerland and Germany, merged soon after.1150 in the Albigenses.

Pronounce *Hen-ris'-si-ans.*

HENRY KINGS OF ENGLAND, ETC.

(For those of France, *see* 'Henri'; for those of Germany, *see* 'Heinrich.')

Henry I. 'Beauclerc' (good scholar), third son of William the Conqueror (1068, 1100–1135). He married Maud daughter of Malcolm III. of Scotland, and niece of Edgar Atheling, heiress of the Saxon line. He had two children by Maud: William, who died at sea 26 Nov. 1119; and Maud, who married (at the age of 6) Heinrich V. kaiser of Germany. Heinrich died 1126, and the widow married, the same year, Geoffrey Plantagenet, from whom descend our long line of kings.

His style and title: 'Henricus rex Anglorum et dux Normannorum.' After 1106 we find 'Dei Gratia' introduced in charters.

Henry I. had three natural children: two sons, Robert and William, and one daughter. Robert's son was William of Gloucester, whose daughter Avisa married King John (Lackland).

Henry II. First of the Plantagenet dynasty (972, 1002–1024).

Father, Geoffrey Plantagenet; *Mother,* Matilda daughter of HENRY I.; *Wife,* Eleanor, the divorced wife of Louis VII. of France (she was divorced 18 March, 1152, and married Henry six weeks afterwards); *Mistress,* the Fair Rosamond [Clifford]. He had three sons and three daughters:—

1. William, died in infancy.
2. Henry, died before his father, without issue.
3. RICHARD [I., Cœur de Lion], died without issue.
4. Geoffrey, who married Constantia, daughter of the Duke of Brittany, by whom he had two children, Eleanor and Arthur. Arthur, heir to the English crown, was murdered by his uncle John, 1230; and Eleanor was confined in Bristol Castle for 40 years.
5. JOHN.

His style and title.— 'Henricus rex Anglorum, et dux Normannorum et Aquitannorum, et comes Andegavorum, or 'Henricus rex Angliæ, dux Normanniæ et Aquitaniæ, et comes Andegaviæ.' Aquitania is now called Guienne, and Andegavia is Anjou.

Maud the eldest daughter of Henry II. married Henry V. duke of Saxony and Brunswick, from whom our present royal family is descended. [Thus: (1) Otto duke of Brunswick and Lunenburg, her son; (2) Albert I., his son; (3) Albert II., son; (4) Magnus, son; (5) Bernard, son; (6) Friedrich, son; (7) Otto II., son; (8) Heinrich, son; (9)

Ernestus I., son; (10) Wilhelm, son; (11) George, son; (12) Ernestus II., son, who married *Sophia,* daughter of the Princess Elizabeth, and granddaughter of James I. of England, whose son and heir was GEORGE I. of England.]

Eleanor, another daughter of Henry II., married Alfonso VIII. of Castile.

Joan, his youngest daughter, married William II. of Sicily.

Henry III. of England, called 'Winchester' from the place of his birth (1206, 1216–1272).

Father, JOHN; *Mother,* Isabelle of Angoulême. *Wife,* Eleanor of Provence, by whom he had nine children, five of whom died in infancy.

The four who lived to grow up were:
1. EDWARD I., who succeeded to the crown; he was earl of Chester.
2. Edmund, surnamed Crouchback, earl of Leicester and king of Sicily.
3. Margaret, who married Alexander III. of Scotland. She had a daughter who married Eric king of Norway; and this daughter, also named Margaret, was the famous 'Maid of Norway,' who succeeded her grandfather (Alexander III.) in Scotland, but died on her passage from Norway to Scotland, Sep. 1290.
4. Beatrix, who married John duke of Brittany.

His style and title from 1216 to 1259 was: 'Henricus, D.G. rex Angliæ, dominus Hiberniæ, dux Normanniæ et Aquitaniæ [*Guienne*], et comes Andegaviæ [*Anjou*].'

From 1259 to 1272: 'Henricus D.G. rex Angliæ, dominus Hiberniæ, et dux Aquitaniæ.' He therefore dropped the titles of 'dux Normannorum' or 'dux Normanniæ,' and of 'comes Andegaviæ.'

Henry IV. of England, called Bolingbroke because he was born at Bolingbroke Castle, in Lincolnshire (1367, 1399–1413). First of the line of Lancaster, which contained the three Henrys—IV., V., and VI.—

HENRY III., son of John.
EDWARD I. and *Edmund duke of Lancaster,* sons of Henry III.
EDWARD II., son of Edward I.
EDWARD III., son of Edward II.
Edward the Black Prince, William, Lionel, and *John of Gaunt,* sons of Edward III.
RICHARD II., son of Edward the Black Prince and grandson of Edward III.

Philippa (daughter of Lionel), *Roger Mortimer* (son of Philippa), *Edmund Mortimer* (son of Roger Mortimer, and heir to the throne on the death of Richard II.)—descendants of Lionel, third son of Edward III.

HENRY IV. was son of John of Gaunt duke of Lancaster (4th son of EDWARD III.).

** Henry IV. had no hereditary right to the crown. The legal heir, on the death of Richard II., was Edmund Mortimer earl of March. Henry was duke of Lancaster in right of his mother Blanche, heiress of Edward duke of Lancaster.

Father, John of Gaunt. *Mother,* Blanche, heiress of Edmund duke of Lancaster. *Wives:* I. Mary daughter of Humphrey de Bohun, by whom he had six children; II. Joan (daughter of Charles II. of Navarre), no issue.

His sons were HENRY [V.], his successor; Thomas duke of Clarence; John duke of Bedford, regent of France; and Humphry duke of Gloucester. His daughters were Blanche and Philippa. Philippa married Eric X. of Denmark.

Henry IV. was first of the Lancaster line, and his usurpation brought about the War of the Roses in the reign of Henry VI.

His style and title.— 'Henricus D.G. rex Angliæ et Franciæ, et dominus Hiberniæ.'

Henry V., 'Monmouth,' from the place of his birth (1389, 1413–1422), 'the English Alexander.'

Father, HENRY IV. *Mother,* Mary daughter of Humphry de Bohun. *Wife,* Catherine daughter of Charles VI. of France, by whom he had one child, HENRY VI., who succeeded him. (After the death of Henry his widow married Sir Owen Tudor, captain of the guards. Their grandson was Henry VII., first of the Tudor line).

His style from 1413 to 9 April, 1420, was : 'Henricus D. G. rex Angliæ et Franciæ, et dominus Hiberniæ.' From 1420 to his death it was : 'Henricus D. G. rex Angliæ, hæres et regens Franciæ, et dominus Hiberniæ.' HENRY V. was heir to the French crown.

.·. The place of his traditional riotous court and merry doings, when Prince of Wales, was Cheylesmore, near Coventry, an estate belonging to the duchy of Cornwall.

Henry VI., 'Windsor,' from the place of his birth (1421, 1422–1471).

Father, HENRY V.; *Mother,* Catherine daughter of Charles VI. of France; *Wife,* Margaret of Anjou daughter of René or Reni titular king of Naples and duke of Provence and Anjou. He had one son (Edward), murdered by the York party after the battle of Tewkesbury, 1471

Prince Edward was 18 years old at his death; he was at the time married to Anne daughter of the Earl of Warwick. Soon after the prince's death his widow married Richard III.

The regents and guardians of Henry VI. were the Dukes of Bedford, Gloucester (the good duke), and Exeter, with the Bishop of Winchester.

Henry VII. His right to the throne was shadowy indeed. He was the son of Edmund Tudor, who married Margaret countess of Richmond, daughter of John Beaufort. This John Beaufort was a natural son of John of Gaunt by Catherine Swynford, the governess of his children, expressly by law disqualified for the succession. Another shadowy claim was that his grandfather, Sir Owen Tudor, captain of the guards, married Catherine, the widow of Henry V. Neither of these, nor both together, could give Henry Tudor the slightest hereditary right. Besides, at the time of his coronation his mother was alive, who, of course, had a prior claim to her son. However, at the death of Richard III., the legitimate heir was Elizabeth, who subsequently married Henry VII. Next to Elizabeth daughter of Edward IV. came Edward earl of Warwick, then Margaret countess of Salisbury.

It is somewhat remarkable that John Beaufort, through whom the father of Henry VIII. laid claim to the crown, had been expressly set aside, and the two daughters of Henry VIII. (Mary and Elizabeth) were also expressly set aside.

Father, Edmund Tudor. *Mother,* Margaret Beaufort. *Wife,* Elizabeth of York (the White Rose). *His style and title* : 'Henricus D.G. rex Angliæ et Franciæ, et dominus Hiberniæ.'

Henry VII. had two daughters and two sons who lived to maturity.

His eldest daughter, Margaret, was married to James IV. of Scotland, and it is by this marriage

that their descendant James VI. of Scotland became JAMES I. of England.

His other daughter, Mary, was married twice—first to Louis XII. of France, and secondly to Charles Brandon duke of Suffolk, by whom she had two daughters. Frances and Eleanor. Frances was married to Henry Grey marquis of Dorset (and afterwards duke of Suffolk), and it was their child which was the unfortunate Lady Jane Grey.

Henry VII. of Japan (*The*) was Iyeasu, who, in the name of the Mikado, gave peace, prosperity, and laws to his distracted country, after centuries of civil war (17th cent.).

Henry VIII. (1491, 1509–1547). *Father,* Henry VII. *Mother,* Elizabeth of York (the White Rose). *Wives:*

1. (1509) Catalina (daughter of Ferdinand and Isabella of Spain), widow of his brother Arthur; mother of Queen Mary. This wife was divorced. Shakespeare spells the name 'Katharine.'

Arthur survived his marriage only a few months.

2. (1533) Anne Boleyn (daughter of Thomas Boleyn, of Hever Castle, Kent, earl of Wiltshire). Mother of Queen Elizabeth. Beheaded 1536.

3. (1536) Jane Seymour (sister of Somerset the protector); mother of Edward VI. Died two days after the birth of her son.

4. (1540) Anne of Cleves. Divorced.

5. (1540) Catherine Howard (granddaughter of John Howard duke of Norfolk). Beheaded.

6. (1543) Catherine Parr (daughter of Sir Thomas Parr). Twice a widow, first of Edward Burghe, and next of John Neville lord Latimer. On the death of Henry VIII. Catherine married Sir Thomas Seymour, uncle of Edward VI. If Henry had six wives, Catherine had four husbands.

None of his children had any issue.

His style and title from 1509 to 1521 was : 'Henry, D.G., of England. France, and Ireland, King.'

From 1521 to 1534 it was : 'Henry, D.G., of England, France, and Ireland, King. Defender of the Faith.'

From 1534 to 1547 it was : ' Henry, D.G., of England. France, and Ireland, King. Defender of the Faith, and Supreme Head of the Church of England.'

Henry VIII.'s Walking Stick. A spiked mace in the Tower of London. In the head of the mace are four barrels, which could be charged with gunpowder. The spikes are formidable triangular knives.

Henry IX. of England, 1788. Henry Benedict Maria Clement (last of the Stuarts). He was the younger brother of Charles Edward, the Young Pretender. Henry [IX.] was a cardinal, but on the death of Charles Edward he succeeded to the mock dignity of king of Great Britain and Ireland, and had coins cast with the inscription, 'Henricus nonus Angliæ rex,' and on the obverse, 'Gratia Dei, non voluntate hominum.' Forgetting in such cases that 'Vox populi est Dei vox.'

Henry (*Knights of St.*), 7 Oct., 1736. A military Saxon order. A cross attached to a crimson ribbon.

Henry Beauclerc. Henry I. (*q.v.*).

Henry Fitz-Empress (*The Statute of*), 1172. An enactment of Henry II. and his council in Ireland that, in case of the death of any chief governor, the chancellor, treasurer, chief justices, and certain other officers should be empowered (with the assent of the lords spiritual and temporal) to proceed to the election of a successor to that office (Ireland).

Henry 'Longsword' (1519, 1547-1559). Henry II. king of England, grandson of Henry I., his mother being Maud daughter of Henry I.

Also called CURTMANTLE and FITZ-EMPRESS. The Anjou sword was longer and mantle shorter than the sword and mantle of the Norman kings.

Henry Town-bull. St. John (Henry Viscount Bolingbroke, 1678-1751). (DR. ARBUTHNOT, 'John Bull.')

Henry of Monmouth. Henry V. of England, born at Monmouth Castle, belonging to the great estates of his mother, Mary de Bohun, daughter of the Earl of Hereford (1388, 1413-1422).

Henry of Windsor. Henry VI. of England, who was born at Windsor.

On the news of the birth of a son being brought to Henry at Meaux, he eagerly demanded where the boy was born, and on being told at Windsor, he appeared greatly vexed, and repeated to his chamberlain, Lord Fitzhugh, the following lines:—

I, Henry, born at Monmouth,
    Shall small time reign, and much get;
But Henry of Windsor shall long reign, and lose
    all.—
        But as God wills,
            So be it.

Heou-Woo-tae Dynasties (*The*). Five dynasties of China. The 14th Imperial dynasty was Heou-Woo-tae Lĕang or L'ang; the 15th was Heou-Woo-tae Tang; the 16th was Heou-Woo-tae Tsin; the 17th was Heou-Woo-tae Hân;

and the 18th was Heou-Woo-tae Tche-u. These five dynasties lasted only from 907 to 960, and from 927 a warlike Tartar horde established itself in the north of China, under Tae-tsong.

These dynasties are called 'The Five Successions.' The seat of government was Kai-fong-foo.

Heptarchy (*The*). The seven kingdoms founded in England by seven different Saxon invaders. See 'Bretwalda.' They are:—

1. KENT	founded by	Hengist	455
2. SUSSEX	„	Ella	477
3. WESSEX	„	Cynric	519
4. ESSEX	„	Erkinwin	526
5. NORTHUMBRIA	„	Ida	547
6. EAST ANGLIA	„	Offa	571
7. MERCIA	„	Crida	584

Northumbria was divided at Ida's death into Bernicia and Deira, and Deira was absorbed into Bernicia by Oswy in 655.

Egbert, of the Wessex race of kings, united in his own person all the separate kingdoms, and called the united kingdoms ENGLAND 800.

Heraclĕa (*Table of*), or 'Lex Julia Municipālis,' which was passed B.C. 45, discovered in 1732 at Heraclĕa, in Lucania.

Heralds. I. Of *England.*—There are 14—viz. 4 kings-of-arms, 6 heralds, and 4 pursuivants.

The 4 kings-of-arms are Clarenceux (having power over all parts of England *south* of the Trent); Norroy, *i.e.* Northroy (who has power over all parts *north* of the Trent); and the 2 who serve the Orders of the Garter and the Bath: the former called Garter King-of-arms, and the latter Bath King-of-arms. *See* 'Garter King-of-arms.'

The 6 heralds are Somerset, Chester, Windsor, Richmond, Lancaster, and York.

The 4 pursuivants are Rouge Dragon, Portcullis, Blue Mantle, and Rouge Croix.

There are seven colours in English heraldry, and nine in French. The seven English colours are *or* (gold), *argent* (silver), *gules* (red), *azure* (blue), *sable* (black), *vert* (green), and *purpure* (purple). The two extra colours are *tenne* (orange), and *sanguine* (murrey).

II. Of *Ireland.*—Consists of 5 members. The king-of-arms is styled Ulster king-of-arms.

The 2 heralds are Cork and Dublin.

The 2 pursuivants are Athlone (the senior) and St. Patrick.

III. In *Scotland.*—The Lyon Court consists of 12 members.

The king-of-arms is styled Lord Lyon, or Lyon king-of-arms.

The 6 heralds are called Albany, Islay or Ilay, Marchmont, Ross, Rothesay, and Snowdoun.

The 5 pursuivants are called Bute, Carrick, Kintyre, Ormond, and Unicorn.

Heralds' College (*The*), or 'College of Arms.' Incorporated and chartered in 1483 by Richard III.

Herbs (*The Feast of*), or 'Festum Herbarum.' In German 'Krautweihe.' When women carried herbs and sweet spices to commemorate the anointing after the Sabbath of the Crucifixion week.

Hercules. Almost every nation has its Hercŭlês, or man of marvellous strength, some fabulous and some more or less historical. Diodōrus mentions three, Cicero ('De Natura Deorum') six, and Varro as many as forty-three. Thus Bel is called the *Syrian* Hercŭlês, Melkart the *Tyrian*, Chon the *Egyptian*, Dorsănês the *Hindû*, and Ogmios the *Gaulic* Herculês. The following are well known:—

The Attic Herculês: Theseus (2 syl.), who went about performing exploits similar to those of Herăklês or Hercūles.

The Barbaric Herculês: Simeon of Bulgaria (883–927).

The Greeks were defeated, and their horn was broken by the barbaric Herculês.—GIBBON, lv.

The Egyptian Herculês: (1) Sesostris or Ramses II. the Great, of the XIX. dynasty. A sculptured head of this hero is in the British Museum. (2) Chon or Son, called by Pausanias 'Macĕris son of Ammon.'

The English Herculês: Guy earl of Warwick.

Warwick ... thou English Herculês. — DRAYTON, *Polyolbion*, xiii.

The French Herculês: Jean-Baptiste Kléber, the French general, a man of prodigious strength and stature (1754–1800).

The Greek Herculês: Alkīdês, *i.e.* Herăklês, who was grandson of Alkæos.

The Indian Herculês: Dorsănês, who married Pandæa and became the founder of a race of Indian kings.

Sometimes Belus is called 'The Indian Hercules.'

The Jewish Herculês: Samson, the judge of Israel, who died B.C. 1113.

The Persian Herculês: Rustum son of Zâl, prince of Sedjistan. Matthew Arnold has a poem entitled 'Sohrab and Rustum,' which gives an account of Rustum slaying his son Sohrab.

The Roman Herculês: Commŏdus the emperor called himself 'Herculês Secundus.' He was a gigantic idiot who killed 100 lions and overthrew 1,000 gladiators in the amphitheatre (161, 180–192).

The Swedish Herculês: Starchatĕrus (1st cent. A.D.).

Hercules (*The Farnese*). A famous statue, the work of Glykon, copied from one by Lysippos; called 'Farnese' (3 syl.) from being placed in the Farnese Palace at Rome, but now at Naples. The hero is represented leaning on his club, and holding an apple in his left hand, which rests on his back. There is a copy of this statue in the Tuileries garden of Paris.

Farnese, pronounce *Far-nay'-ze*.

Hercules (*Pillars of*). Calpê and Abўla; one at Gibraltar and the other at Ceūta. Torn asunder (according to fable) by Alcīdes on his route to Gades (*Cadiz*).

Hercules of Music (*The*). Christoph von Gluck (1714–1787).

Herdsman (*King Alfred's*). It is said that the name of the herdsman in whose hovel King Alfred was sheltered for six months was Dunulf, who was afterwards educated, ordained, and made bishop of Winchester.

Hereditary Union (*The*), 1540. An act by which the crown of Sweden was declared hereditary in the House of Vasa.

Heregeld, or 'Heregyld' (3 syl.). An army tax. It was first imposed by Ethelred II. under the name of 'Danegelt,' a war tax to resist the invasions of the Danes and buy them off. It was afterwards called 'Here-gyld,' from the Anglo-Saxon words *here* (2 syl.), an army, and *gyld*, a tax. See 'Danegelt' and 'Hidagium.'

Heremo'nian Line [of Kings] (*The*). Descendants of Heremon (3 syl.) son of Milesius king of Ireland.

Heretical Baptism. The baptism of heretics (3rd cent.). The controversy was this: Is baptism valid only when administered in the orthodox church? If so, baptism by heretics is no baptism at all, and those so baptized must be baptized again in order to be members of Christ's Church. This was the view of the Eastern Church. The Western Church considered any baptism valid if administered in the name of the Father, Son, and Holy Ghost; so that whether performed by heretics or on heretics it mattered not if the orthodox words were uttered when the rite was administered.

The Synod of Iconium and the Synod of Synnāda in Phrygia decreed that 'heretical baptism is no baptism at all.' Some eight or ten councils confirmed this view of the question. The Western Church would not give way, and council after council decreed that heretical baptism is valid. This is still the belief of Western churches, whether affiliated with Rome or not.

Heretics are those who differ from the dominant power in some religious point or points which those who condemn them deem essential for the 'true faith.' Thus Jesus Christ was considered a heretic by the Pharisees and Sadducees. The Buddhists are considered heretics by the Brahmins. The Shiites are considered heretics by the Sunnites.

SECTS are those who differ from a main religious body in some point or points less grave than heresy. Thus the Jansenists and Jesuits, the Dominicans and Franciscans, always antagonistic to each other, are virtually sects of the Catholic Church—Nonconformists of the Anglican Church—and Ismaëlians of the Shiites.

In a word, orthodoxy is the doxy of the judge; heterodoxy is the doxy of those condemned by the judge. Both change places as opinions change or the dominant power changes. Thus Mary considered Protestantism heretical, but Elizabeth called it orthodox. Laud condemned the Puritans, and, like Ferdinand II., would have stamped them out if he could; whereas the Puritans were every bit as intolerant during the Commonwealth. See the following *in loco* :—

ALBIGENSES. Condemned by the Third Lateran 906.

APOLLINARIANS. Condemned by the Council of Alexandria in 362, and the Council of Constantinople in 381.

ARIANS. Condemned by the Council of Nice 325.

ARMENIANS. Condemned by the Council of Chalcedon 451.

BARDESANISTS.

BASILIDIANS. A branch of the Gnostics. *See below,* 'Marcionites.'

BOGOMILES. Condemned by the Council of Constantinople 1110.

BUDDHISTS. Called heretics by the Brahmins.

CALVINISTS. Condemned by the Council of Trent 1545.

CELESTIANS. Condemned by the Council of Carthage 412, and again by the Council of Ephesus 430.

CERINTHIANS. A branch of the Gnostics. Cerinthus denied that John was the author of the Fourth Gospel.

CHRISTIANS. Called heretics by Moslems.

CHYITES or SHIITES (2 syl.). Called heretics by the Sunnites (2 syl.).

COPTS or COPTI, the Monophysites or Jacobites of Egypt.

DOCETÆ. A branch of the Gnostics.

DONATISTS. Condemned by the Council of Arles 314.

DRUSES.

EBIONITES (4 syl.). Supposed to be condemned in the Fourth Gospel.

EUTYCHIANS. Condemned by the Council of Chalcedon 451. They affirmed that Christ was one thing and the Logos another; that there were two natures in Christ before the hypostatical union, but after that the two were amalgamated into one.

GNOSTICS.

GREEK CHURCH. Condemned by the Council of Aix-la-Chapelle 809.

HERMESIANS. Condemned by a papal brief in 1835.

HUGUENOTS of France.

HUSSITES. Huss was excommunicated by Alexander V.

ICONOCLASTS. Condemned by several councils.

ISMAELIANS (5 syl.). Deemed heretics by the Sunnites (2 syl.).

JA'COBITES (3 syl.) or JACO'BIANS, of Syria. So called from Jacob, a disciple of Eutyches. In the 7th cent. the Eutychians, Copts, and Monophi'o-sites (4 syl.), who acknowledged but one nature in Christ, all merged in the Jacobites or Jacobians.

JAN'SENISTS. Condemned by Innocent X.

LUTHERANS. Condemned by the Council of Lyons 1528, and again by the Council of Trent 1545.

MACEDONIANS. Condemned by the Council of Constantinople 381.

MANICHE'ANS. Condemned by several councils.

MAR'CIONITES (4 syl.). Similar to the Basilidians. Perhaps the same.

MONOPH'YSITES (4 syl.). A general term for those sectaries of the Levant who believe that Christ had only one nature. *See above.* 'Jacobites.' Condemned by the Council of Chalcedon 451.

MONOTH'ELITES (4 syl.). Condemned by the Council of Constantinople 680.

MON'TANISTS. Condemned by the bishops of Asia.

NAZARE'ANS (3 syl.). A Jewish sect. Acts xxiv.

NESTORIANS. Condemned by the Council of Ephesus 431, and again by the Council of Constantinople 448.

PAT'ERINS. Condemned by the Council of Lateran 1179.

PAULIANISTS. Condemned by the Council of Antioch 270.

PAULICIANS.

PELA'GIANS. Condemned by the Council of Ephesus 418, and again by the Council of Carthage 46.

PRISCILLIANISTS. Condemned by the Council of Saragossa 381.

PROTESTANTS. *See* 'Calvinists' and 'Lutherans.'

REFORMATION. Condemned by the Council of Trent 1545.

SABELLIANS. Condemned by the Council of Alexandria 261.

VAUDOIS. Condemned by the Council of the Lateran 1179; by the bull of John XXII. in 1332; and by Innocent VIII. in 1487.

WYCLIFITES (3 syl.). Condemned by the Council of Trent 1545.

Heresy, in Greek αἱρεσις, simply means a choice, or something chosen. A heretic is one who chooses

E E

his own religious opinions, and does not accept blindly those chosen for him by others.

Heretics (*Laws against*).

The first laws against heretics, on which all subsequent ones were founded, originated in 1220 by the Kaiser Friedrich II. They were for the extermination of heretics, and had been dictated by Pope Honorius III. Confirmed by Innocent IV. in 1243, by Alexander IV. in 1253, by Urban IV. in 1262, and by Clement IV. in 1265 (four popes, all the IVths of the name).

'These laws' (says the pope), 'published by our dearest son Friedrich emperor of the Romans, we praise and approve, so as to be valid for all time. And if anyone attempt to infringe them . . . he will incur the wrath of Almighty God. . . . As for the persons of heretics, they are all to be burnt alive without appeal or possibility of pardon . . . all their goods are to be confiscated, and never restored to their posterity. Their children and grandchildren shall be held incapable of holding any public office, with this one exception, viz. if a son informs against the secret heresy of a father. Persons only suspected of heresy shall be put to death unless they can clear themselves within a year and a day. Repentant heretics to be imprisoned for life.'

The bull of Paul III., published in 1538 against Henry VIII., contains some new enactments against 'the accomplices of heretics.'

In Section XII. all the faithful are admonished, under pain of excommunication, 'to avoid and cause others to avoid' all adherents of the king, and to 'have no commerce, conversation, or communion' with him, his household, vassals, and subjects; they are strictly enjoined not 'to buy or sell, exchange, deal, or chaffer, in any town, fort, castle, or city' in his dominion, nor 'cause wine, grain, salt, victuals, arms, clothes, wares, or other articles of commerce, to be brought by ship, trireme or other vessel, by mule, horse, or other animal,' to any part of his dominion; and 'stoutly to refuse all assistance, counsel, or favour to those who, directly or indirectly, secretly or openly, presume to traffic with them.'

Section X. enjoined 'all who possess armed forces to set them on the king and his adherents.'

Section XVII. gives everyone full liberty of appropriating to himself all goods belonging to the king or any of his subjects.

In a word, the bull of Paul III. states :—
1. That no man who refuses to believe all the articles of the Catholic Church has any right to life or property.
2. No Christian has any right to respect the life or property of a heretic.
3. Christian governments are bound to burn

alive all heretics and to confiscate all their property.
4. Children are bound to pry into the secret belief of their parents, and denounce them if heretical.
5. Error in faith is infinitely worse than moral turpitude.
6. Anyone may appropriate to himself the goods of a heretic.
7. Every heretic is virtually an outlaw, and all contracts made with heretics or debts owing to them are null and void.
8. Slavery and the slave-trade should be kept up, if the slaves are heretical.

(Abridged from a letter sent to the 'Times' from an English Catholic, and published in that journal under the title of 'Papal Infallibility and Persecution.')

Heretics (*The Statute of*), 1401.

By this infamous act priests were allowed to arrest and imprison all heretical preachers in England, all schoolmasters tainted with Lollardry, all owners and writers of heretical books; and, on refusal to abjure, or relapse after abjuration, to send the heretic to the stake, 'to be burnt to death on a high place in the sight of the people.' The first victim of this iniquitous statute was William Sawtre of Lynn, in Norfolk. Next followed John Badbie, for denying the dogma of transubstantiation.

This statute, often called 'The Statute of Heresy,' was revived by Mary in 1555; but it was the first act of Elizabeth to repeal it. Constantine, in 325, passed a penal edict against heretics; and the Council of Laodicea, in 372, forbade marriages between heretics and orthodox Christians. But what was heresy and what orthodoxy in the 4th cent. is impossible to determine.

Heretics of Brixen.

In 1486 the magistrates of Brixen refused to burn heretics, on the ground that heresy being an ecclesiastical offence, civil magistrates could take no cognizance of it. Innocent VIII. forthwith excommunicated them, 'without appeal, unless within six days they carried out the sentences of the Inquisition.'

In 1520 Leo X. condemned the proposition, 'Hæreticos comburi est contra voluntatem spiritus.'

Heretics of Périgord and Périgueux.

The Waldenses were so called because they abounded in Périgord and Périgueux in the 12th cent.

Heretoga (4 syl.).

A Saxon word meaning a general or commander; from *here* (2 syl.), an army, and *toga*, a leader. Latin *comes*, our *earl*, the continental *count*. German Herzog = duke; Graf = earl or count.

Her'mandad (*The Santa*),

or 'Holy Brotherhood.' An association of the

principal cities of Castile and Aragon, bound together by a solemn league for mutual defence. The first hermandad in Aragon was established in 1264, that of Castile in 1295. These associations were defences against the barons, whose unruly conduct and depredations were the curse of the middle ages.

Hermann the Cripple (1013-1054).
One of the most marvellous of men. His body was wholly paralysed, so that he could not move without assistance, and could scarcely speak so as to be understood; yet was his society sought by men from all quarters of the globe. He has left a book of great merit behind, entitled 'A Chronicle of the Six Ages of the World,' containing a history of Germany during the 10th and 11th cents.

Paul Scarron, the French poet, was a similar cripple (1610-1660).

Herme'sian Heresy (19th cent., about 1828).
The substitution of conviction for faith. By conviction is meant the persuasion which results from judgment and sound reason ; by faith is meant the persuasion of authority. One is belief in what sound reason convinces the mind is true ; the other is belief in what the church pronounces to be true. Hermes of Westphalia was divinity professor in the University of Münster, and thought by his teaching to amalgamate Catholics and Protestants, as well as Calvinists and Lutherans, but his doctrine was condemned by a papal brief in 1835.

Hermippic School (The).
Hermippus, the Greek philosopher, placed the *elixir vitæ* in the health-bestowing breath of youth.

Hermit of Lathom (The).
Robert Swarsbrick (1740-1824), who lived first in a one-roomed and then in a two-roomed hut at the bottom of the 'Ladies' Walk' at Lathom. He wrote a journal, and was fond of gardening.

Hernhutters, or 'Hernhutes,' 1721.
The Moravians or 'United Brethren' were so called, because after the Thirty Years' War they found refuge in Hernhutt, under the protection of Count Zinzendorf. They profess to take the pure precepts of the gospel as their rule of conduct, choose their ministers by lot, wash each other's feet, celebrate agapæ or love-feasts, and address prayer to the Saviour only.

Héro de la Fable (Le).
Charles de Lorraine, duc de Guise (1571-1640), the implacable foe of the Protestants. He bore arms against Henri IV., but tendered his submission; he conducted a fleet against Rochelle, but incurred the displeasure of Richelieu, and retired to Italy, where he died.

Héro de l'Histoire (Le).
The Duc d'Enghien. Ever since 1485, when the house of Enghien passed into that of Bourbon, some member of the family has become historic. Amongst others we have François de Bourbon-Vendôme, brother of Prince Louis I. de Condé (1519-1544) ; the Grand Condé (1621-1659) ; Louis Antoine Henri de Bourbon, last of the Condés (1772-1804).

Hero of Modern Italy (The).
Garibaldi (1807-1882). Certainly the most disinterested hero that ever lived, but treated with scant honour.

Hero of Rora (The).
Joshua Janavel, who lived at Rora, and with seventeen companions put to flight a troop of Irishmen led on by Mario against the Vaudois in 1655.

Hero of the Nile (The).
Horatio viscount Nelson; so called for his great naval victory over the French, 1 August, 1798, for which he was created 'Baron Nelson of the Nile' (1758-1805).

Hero of the Nine Hostages (The).
Nial the Great, who was succeeded in A.D. 406 by Dathy, last of the pagan kings of Ireland. Nial was killed by a flash of lightning.

Hero of the Peninsula (The).
The Duke of Wellington, who, between 21 August, 1808, and 10 April, 1814, defeated five French marshals in the Peninsula of Spain and Portugal, won nine battles, and made three successful sieges.

A rare hero indeed. Napoleon's prevailing fault was the exaltation of himself and family. Wellington's great merit was modest patriotism. Being asked in 1806 how he could condescend to lead a brigade after commanding large armies, he replied : ' I am *nim-muk-wallah*, as we say in the East; that is, I have eaten the king's salt, and think it my duty to serve him faithfully, wherever he finds it convenient to employ me.' This is magnificent magnanimity ; more honourable to a hero than the slaughter of Austerlitz.

Herod the Great.
Son of Antipăter, prime minister of Hyrcănus. He married ten wives.

1st. Doris, by whom he had *Antipater*.

2nd. Mariamne the Asmonæan, by whom he had *Alexander, Aristobūlus,* Herod, Salampso, and Cypros [Aristo-bulus].

King Agrippa, who put James to death, was son of Aristobulus. Agrippa's son and daughter (Agrippa and Berenice) heard Paul make his defence (Acts xxv., xxvi.). This was Herod II. of Judæa.

3rd. Mariamnê, daughter of Simon the high-priest, by whom he had PHILIP (whose wife was Herodias).

4th. Malthacê, by whom he had ARCHE-LA'US, Philip, and Olympias.

5th. Cleopatra, by whom he had HEROD ANTIPAS and Philip.

6th. Pallas, by whom he had Phasaël, in honour of whom he built Phasaëlis.

7th. Phædra, by whom he had Roxana.

8th. Elpis, by whom he had Salômê. (Names of the other two wives not known.)

N.B.—Italics, put to death; capitals, the tetrarchs.

At the death of Herod the Great the Romans divided the Jewish state into four parts, called tetrarchies—viz. Judæa, Galilee, Ituræa, and Samaria. The first three they gave to the sons of Herod the Great. To Herod Archelaus was given Judæa; to Herod Antipas was given Galilee (this is the man who slew John the Baptist); and to Herod Philip was given Ituræa (he married his niece Herodias, who lived in adultery with her brother-in-law Herod Antipas). The tetrarchy was abolished A.D. 56, and Herod II. (Agricola) became sole king of Judæa. Samaria was ruled by Roman governors. For table of affinity, *see* 'Maccabees.' *See* also next article.

Hero'dians. A Jewish sect in the time of Herod. Dr. Prideaux reduces their tenets into two heads : (1) a belief that the dominion of the Romans over the Jews was lawful, and it was their duty to submit to it; (2) that, under present circumstances, they might follow many heathen usages. In fact they were trimmers between political policy and religious obligations.

Herod'otos of China (*The*). Sse-ma-Thsian, author of the Sse-ki, or Annals of China. He lived in the reign of Hàn Ho-tee, who reigned 89–106.

Herodotos of Old London (*The*). John Stow (1525–1605), author of 'Summary of the Chronicles of England,' 1561, 'Annals of England,' 1580, and 'Survey of London,' 1598.

Heroes scratched off the Church Doors. So Sheridan called Militia officers who had served four years. An act of parliament enjoined that a list of all persons between 18 and 45 should be affixed in each parish to the church doors

three clear days before the day of appeal, Sunday being one of the days. Commissioned officers who had served four years in the Militia were exempt, and their names were ' scratched off the doors.'

Heroic Age (*The*). The semi-historic age preceding the historic. The heroic age of Greece dates from the arrival of the first colony under Inachos, and goes to the 19th cent. B.C., the return of the Hera-clīdæ. China, Persia, and all other civi-lised countries have passed through their mythical age and their heroic age, before they came to their historic period.

England, Wales, Scotland, and Ireland have had their heroic ages. Brute, Colbrand, Guy of Warwick, Arthur, &c., will readily recur to the mind.

Herrings (*Battle of*), Feb. 1429. Sir John Fastolfe carrying provisions, much of which was salt fish, to the English army before Orleans, was intercepted by an allied army of French and Scotch. Sir John succeeded in vanquishing his opponents near Rouvrai and reaching the English army.

Herrying of Buchan (*The*). The ravaging of the country of Comyn earl of Buchan, in 1307, by Robert Bruce, in revenge for the pertinacity with which the earl had pursued him when, wasted by sickness, he had retreated before him.

Sir Alexander and Sir Simon Fraser took a very prominent part with Bruce in this expedition. To herry is to plunder or spoil.

Hertford College, Oxford, 1282. Founded by Elias de Hertford, and called ' Hertford Hall '; but the word ' college ' was substituted in 1740. It was dissolved in 1805, but in 1874 was re-established. The head-master is called the Principal.

Hertford Scholarship. For Latin, value about 30*l.,* and tenable for one year only. The funds are derived from the interest of 1,100*l.* made over to the University of Oxford at the dissolution of the College in 1834. *See above.*

Hes'ychasts or 'Hesicastæ.' Mystics of the Greek Church, very similar to the Quietists (*q.v.*). They either came into being or revived in the 14th cent.

Anachoretæ dicuntur quoque hesicastæ tam-quam *quiescentes, ἡνυχαζω* enim quiesco significat. —DU CANGE, vol. iv. p. 53, col. 2.

Hetaireia (*The*), 1820. The Greek confederates, whose resolve was to liberate Greece from the slavery of the Moslem. The leader of the confederates was Prince Alexander Ypsilanti.

The confederacy was formed by Rhigas before 1798, but made small progress till 1816. In 1821 it brought about the Greek Revolution.

Hexapla (*The*). Origen's Old Testament in six columns, each column being a different language. (1) Hebrew, (2) Hebrew in Greek characters, (3) the Septuagint, (4) the text of Aquila, (5) that of Theodotian, and (6) that of Symmachos. The book no longer exists. It disappeared in the 7th cent.

Hia Dynasty, B.C. 2205–1766. The first Imperial dynasty of China, and the first of the semi-historic period. It gave 18 emperors, and lasted 440 years. Their capital was Yang-tching.

It was followed by the Châng dynasty. Yoo the Great, founder of the Hia dynasty, is the first monarch mentioned in the 'Shoo-king' of Confucius.

Hialmar's Ordinances for pirates. His men were forbidden to rob women of their money, or to carry them off against their consent. They were also forbidden to eat raw flesh. (BARTHOLINUS, 'De Causis Contemptæ a Danis Mortis,' bk. ii. 9.)

Hialtland (3 syl.). The Norse name of Shetland or Zetland Islands, or rather of the mainland of that group.

Or shall Hialtland's minstrel own
One note to rival glorious John ?
Sir W. SCOTT, *The Pirate*, xxi.

Hibernia. The Roman name for Ireland. Diodōrus Siculus calls it Irin; Erin is the modern name. Ire-land is Iren-land; and Hibernia is another form of Iernia or Irinia. It is called the Holy Island, and Irin or Erin is connected with the Greek *ἱερός* (sacred or holy), Hebrew *Ira* (to revere).

Hibernian Rescius (*The*). Gustavus Vaughan Brooke (1819–1862).

Hickesites (2 syl.). Non-jurors were so called after Dr. George Hickes, a non-juror and learned Saxonist (1642–1716).

Hicksites (2 syl.), 1827. Rationalistic Quakers; so called from Elias Hicks, spoken of by Mr. Conway, 'a sort of mystical and eloquent Thomas Paine.' Walt Whitman wrote in 1887 a life-sketch of this mystic.

Elias Hicks denied the miraculous conception, the divinity of Christ, the doctrine of the atonement, and the inspiration of Scripture.

Hidage (2 syl.), or 'Hidágium.' A tax paid to Ethelred II. for every hide of land ; levied in money, provisions for the army, armour, ships, &c. By this tax every 310 hides were required to furnish one ship in defence of the kingdom against the Danes, and every 8 hides had to supply 'one jack (foot-soldier) and one saddle (horse-soldier),' fully armed and equipped, in defence of the kingdom. *See* 'Danegelt.'

Hieronymites (5 syl.). I. A religious society founded in Holland in 1376 by Geert Groote and Florentius Radewin, who named the society after St. JEROME. Very similar to the subsequent society known as the Moravians or the United Brethren. They owned no conventional distinctions, enjoined community of goods, ascetic habits, and the use of the vernacular tongue in religious services. In 1430 the Hieronymites numbered 130 societies.

II. Hermits of St. Jerome, founded in 1380 in Umbria by Pietro of Pisa. The austerity of these hermits is almost incredible.

III. The Hieronimites of the Observance, instituted in Lombardy by Loup d'Olmédo in 1424 under the reformed rule of Thomas.

High and Low Church, 1700. The favourers of the doctrine of divine right were the High Churchmen, and they, of course, were Jacobites. The friends of William of Orange and the Hanoverian succession, who denied the doctrine of divine right, were the Low Churchmen.

At the present day High Churchmen are those who exalt the priestly office and church rites. *See below*, 'High Church Principles.' The Low Churchmen are what may be called the Evangelists or Simeonites, whose creed is 'by grace are ye saved, through faith; and that not of yourselves, it is the gift of God.'

High and Mighty States (*The*), 20 Nov., 1789. The title assumed by the States of Brabant when they threw off their allegiance to Austria (Kaiser Joseph II.).

High Church Principles. These seven doctrines may be termed essentials. *See* 'High and Low Church.'

1. Baptismal regeneration.
2. The Apostolic succession of ordained ministers.
3. The power of absolution in priests.
4. The eucharistic sacrifice.
5. The real presence of Christ in the elements of bread and wine.

6. The communion of saints, militant and triumphant.
7. The authority of the Church, as a Church.

High Church and Sacheverell!

So shouted the London mob in 1709, after
the trial of the doctor in the House of
Lords. His offence was alluding to Lord
Godolphin as 'Volpone' in the sermon
preached by him in St. Paul's, London.
See 'Volpone.'

High Commission Court (*The*),

1 Eliz. c. 1, A.D. 1559; abolished by 16
Car. I. c. 11, A.D. 1641. This court was
instituted to vindicate the dignity and
peace of the church by reforming, ordering, and correcting the ecclesiastical
state and persons, as well as all manner
of errors, heresies, schisms, abuses,
offences, contempts, and enormities. The
commission was directed in the reigns of
James I. and Charles I: to tyrannical and
unconstitutional purposes, and therefore
the court was abolished. There was no
appeal from the judgments of this court.
James II. partially restored it.

Not unfrequently called 'The Court of High
Commission.' The test of heresy was the Four
Gospels and first four General Councils. Dr. Alexander Leighton, for his pamphlet, entitled 'An
Appeal to Parliament, or Zion's Plea against
Prelacy,' was thus sentenced by Archbishop
Laud, in the High Commission Court: 'To be
imprisoned for life, and to pay a fine of 10,000*l.*; to
be degraded from his ministry; to be whipped,
set in the pillory, have one ear cut off, and one
nostril slit up; then to be branded on the forehead
with S.S. (seditious slanderer), and carried back to
prison. After a few days to be again pilloried, to
lose his other ear, to have his other nostril slit,
and being whipped, again to be restored to his
dungeon till his death.'

High Constable (*Lord*) of Eng-

land. The seventh great officer of the
crown. The office existed before the
Conquest, when it went by inheritance
to the earls of Hereford and Essex, and
next fell into the line of Stafford. In
1522 it became forfeited by the attainder
of Edward Stafford duke of Buckingham.
Abolished 1869 (32, 33 Vict., c. 47).

High Constable (*Lord*) of Scot-

land. Keeper of the king's sword, and
commander of the army. Instituted by
David I. in 1147, and made by Robert
Bruce hereditary in the family of Errol.
The title is only honorary, but it makes
the earl of Errol the hightest peer in
Scotland.

High Court of Justice (*The*). A

court formed for trying Charles I. for
'treason against the sovereign majesty of

the people.' Bradshaw was the president.
The king was found guilty by the court,
and condemned to death.

High Mass, 'Missa alta.'

The cele-
bration of the Eucharist in the Catholic
Church, performed musically, and *alta
voce*, with a loud voice. Low mass is
merely read, *submissa voce*, with a low or
subdued voice. *See* 'Mass.'

High National Court (*The*), 179).

A court which the National Assembly
substituted for the court of justice at the
Châtelet. This court was to try all treasons
against the nation. Barnave was the first
president of this High Court.

High School (*The*), of Edinburgh,

1577. Founded by the magistrates of
that city.

High Steward (*The*).

I. At one
time the first great officer of the crown.
Established before the Conquest, but
abolished in 1265. The office is still
revived at a coronation, or may be so if
a peer is charged with high treason.
II. Of the Universities of Cambridge and
Oxford. Adjudicates in all cases of felony
charged against a member of the university if committed within the limits thereof.
He is also empowered to hold a leet; but
he appoints a deputy, subject to the
approval of the senate in Cambridge,
and Convocation in Oxford. Appointed
in Cambridge by the senate; in Oxford
by the chancellor. In both universities
there is a deputy steward.

The limit of the university is one statute mile
from any of the suburbs. Stipend of the high
steward, in Oxford, is 5*l.*, and of his deputy 2*l.*

Highfliers and Moderates, 1835.

In the Scotch Presbyterian Church.
They were also called 'Non-intrusionists'
—that is, those who looked on the veto law
(*q.v.*) passed by the General Assembly as
an illegal intrusion or interference with
the patron's rights. The Highfliers were
the High Church party. *See* 'Free Church
of Scotland.'

The leaders of the Non-intrusion party were Dr.
Chandler, Dr. Candlish, Dr. Gordon, and Messrs.
Guthrie, Cunningham and Dunlop.

Highgereve, or 'Shire-reeve,' we

now call a viscount, not meaning a count's
deputy or vice, but simply the peer next
in dignity to a count or earl.

Our high sheriff is of course the same word, but
its modern meaning is quite different to that of
viscount.

Highgate Prophet (*The*). William Powell (died 1803). For many years he walked from Sloane Street to Highgate Hill, then started off at a run to the top of the hill. Being asked why he did so, he replied, that if he ceased to do so, the world would be no more. Hence he was called 'The prophet.'

Highland Host (*The*), 1679. A scandalous raid against what was called Scotch heretics. Some 8,000 Highlanders were let loose by the English Government upon the Presbyterians, who refused to accept the prelacy which the government of Charles II. tried to force upon them. The savagery of these Highlanders was quite equal to that of the French dragonnades. Neither age nor sex was spared, and Alva or Torquemada never showed more diabolical ingenuity of torture than these 'brither Scots' did to their own countrymen.

Highland Plot (*The*), 1704. A plot in which Simon Fraser and Athol were deeply concerned. The plot was to raise a rebellion in Scotland, to invade England with French soldiers, and having subverted the government of Queen Anne, to bring back James, who called himself Prince of Wales, but is better known as the Old Pretender.

Bishop Burnet [being told of the plot] remarked to the queen that .. they did not mean her to live any longer than till they thought their designs for the prince were well laid; on which the queen answered very quickly, 'There is no manner of doubt about that.—HOWITT, *Hist. of Eng.* (Anne), p. 180.

Highness (*His*). A title given to princes not sovereigns. 'His Royal Highness' or 'His Imperial Highness' is given to royal or imperial princes. 'His Most Serene Highness' is given to the collateral branches of the blood royal in Germany. The Sultan of Turkey is entitled 'His Highness.'

Till the reign of James I. in England kings were generally addressed as 'His Highness'; so were they in Spain till the reign of Charles V. In France, the Duke of Orleans was called 'His Highness.' In 1633 the elder sons of the cadet branch of the Bourbons took the title of 'His Royal Highness.' Under Louis XIV. all legitimate princes were addressed as 'His Highness,' and the Prince of Condé as 'His Most Serene Highness.'

In addressing the
Sultan of Turkey we say 'Your Highness';
Royal princes we say 'Your Royal Highness';
Imperial princes we say 'Your Imperial Highness';
The collateral branches of the blood royal of Germany we say 'Your Serene Highness.'
⁂ The king or queen is addressed as 'Your Majesty.' *See* 'Majesty.'

Hil'ary Term. One of the four legal terms of England. It used to be from 11 Jan. to the end of the month. It now terminates the Wednesday before Easter. St. Hilary's day is the 13th Jan., whence the name.

The other three terms are called **Easter Term**, Trinity Term, and Michaelmas Term.

Hildebrand (*The Hymn of*), 8th cent. A popular German legend in metre, without rhymes. The story is this. Hildebrand thought his father was dead, and one day, as he was riding in full armour, he was encountered by another knight, and said to him : 'Sir Knight, tell me thy name and country, but an ye refuse to do so, ye shall not pass this way.' The stranger replied, 'Wit you well, I am Sir Hildebrand of Lombardy.' 'Knave,' cried the younger man, 'thou liest'; and so saying he let drive at him, and knocked him off his horse. Then going to unlace his helm, he discovered that it was his father whom he had thus slain.

Hill Coolies. Hindoo highland labourers.

Hill-men. The Cameronians.

The religious sect called Hill-men, or Cameronians, was at that time noted for austerity and devotion, in imitation of Cameron, their founder.—Sir W. SCOTT, *Old Mortality* (Introduction).

Hillside Men. Old Nationalists (about 1881). So called because they believed that one day they would be in a position to fight for their country [Ireland] on the hillside. They had, however, an utter abhorrence of assassination. They were not members of the Land League (*q.v.*). *See* 'Irish Associations.'

Hippoc'ratês (*The British*). Thomas Sydenham, M.D. (1624–1689). So called over and over again by Boerhaave.

Hippoc'ratês (*The Roman*). Aulus Cornelius Celsus (1st cent.) was so called because for the most part he followed the great father of medicine.

Hiram [exalted]. The common title of the kings of Tyre, as Pharaoh [the sun] is that of the kings of Egypt. The Hiram, in Solomon's days, was by name Abibalus.

Historic Register (*The*). A quarterly publication containing an abstract of historical events for three months. Begun 1716, discontinued 1738. *See* 'Annual Register.'

History (*The Father of*). Herodotus, the Greek historian (B.C. 484–408).

History of Formosa (*The*), 1704. By George Psalmanasar, a Frenchman, who pretended to be a Japanese, and published an 'Historical and Geographical Description of Formosa, an island belonging to the empire of Japan.'

The real name of this literary impostor is not known. It seems that he was born in France in 1679, and died in London 3 May, 1763.

His'triomas'tix. A huge volume by William Prynne, of 1,000 pages, against the stage. He says 'theatres are the chapels of Satan, the players his ministers, and that their frequenters are rushing headlong into hell.' He not only denounces theatres, but also dancing, music, village sports, and even chanting in churches.

Hobbe (*King*). So Edward I. called Robert Bruce. In the statutes of Kilkenny (1367) the new arrivals from England were nicknamed 'English Hobbes.' (*See* Du Cange, art. 'Hobellarii.')

Equi quos Hobinos sive Hobbyes vocant ob mollem gressum.—*Antiquitates Hibernicæ*, p. 38.

Hohenstauffen (*House of*). The 3rd German dynasty: 1, the Saxon; 2, the House of Franconia. It gave five kings, viz. Konrad III., Friedrich I. (Barbarossa), Heinrich VI. the Cruel, Friedrich II. and Konrad IV.

Konrad III. was the son of Friedrich of Hohenstauffen, who was son-in-law of Heinrich IV.

On the death of Heinrich VI. there were three contemporary kings of Germany. As Friedrich his son was only two years old the Ghibelline barons elected Philip, and the Guelfic barons elected Otto (son of Heinrich the Lion); but as Friedrich had been created already 'king of the Romans,' or kaiser elect, of course the other two were usurpers.

Friedrich von Buron or Stauffen, born 1015, the founder of this house, lived in the castle of Hohenstauffen, and married the half-sister of Konrad II. kaiser-king of Germany.

Pronounce *Ho-hen-stowf'-fen.*

Holding by the Straws. Similar to the old English custom of 'holding by the verge,' *i.e.* by a rod or stick handed to the tenant, whereby he is admitted into the occupation of a copyhold estate. There was at one time a large number of these symbolic transfers. Thus a clergyman was presented by one of the churchwardens with a sod from the churchyard, whereby the freehold was conferred on the clergyman so long as he remained incumbent of the parish.

Holland. Was an independent country from 863 to 1433; when Philippe of Burgundy united it to his vast estates. In 1477 Mary of Burgundy married Maximilian, and Holland, with many other estates, was united to Austria. After Karl V. it passed into the Spanish branch of the house, and in 1523, under the influence of Luther, it became Protestant. In 1579 Holland united with six other provinces in the 'Union of Utrecht,' threw off the Spanish yoke, and became a republic, called 'The Seven Provinces,' with William of Orange as stadtholder. In 1621 Holland was united to France. In 1806 it was erected into the *kingdom of Holland* by Napoleon I. and given to his brother Louis Bonaparte. In 1810 it was again united to France, but after the battle of Waterloo (1814) it was united to Belgium and formed 'The Kingdom of the Netherlands.' In 1830 Holland and Belgium were divided into two kingdoms, called the 'Kingdom of Holland' and the 'Kingdom of Belgium'; the king of Holland still calls himself the 'King of the Netherlands.' *See* 'Netherlands.'

Holland. One of the three districts of Lincolnshire. Where Boston stands used to be called 'High Holland.' The other two districts are Lindsey (the highest land) and Kesteven (the western part). 'Holland' is the south-eastern part or fen district. *See* 'Hallamshire.'

And for that part of me [*Lincolns.*], which men
'High Holland' call,
Where Boston seated is, by plenteous Wytham's
fall . . .
No other tract of land doth like abundance yield.
DRAYTON, *Polyolbion*, xxv.

Holliglasses (buffoons). A word derived from Howle-glass = Eulen-spiegel, the famous jester, the hero of a popular German tale, translated into English in the time of Shakespeare.

Mr. Black, speaking of the council, called them holiglasses, cormorants, and men of no religion.—Sir W. SCOTT, *Hist. of Scotland*, xxxix.

Holstein-Gottorp (*The Dynasty of*). I. SWEDEN. It succeeded that of Deux-ponts, and lasted from 1751 to 1818. Adolf Frederik was of the house of Holstein-Gottorp, and was pressed on the nation by Russia. It was in this reign that the factions of the Hats and Caps arose (*q.v.*).

II. RUSSIA. The fourth dynasty, 1762 ——* It has given Peter III. (*assassinated*); Catherine II. his widow; Paul I. their son (*assassinated*); Alexander I.; Nicholas I., who died during the Crimean war ; Alexander II. (*assassinated* in 1881); Alexander III.

Holy Alliance (*The*). I. 1511–1512.

Not holy meaning pious and godly, but holy meaning in the temporal interest of the pope. In 1509 the pope (Julius II.) had joined the 'League of Cambray' (*q.v.*), the object of which was to seize Venetia and divide it between the leaguers. Louis XII., being first in the field, won the brilliant battle of Agnadello, by which Venice fell into his hands. The pope, being thus outwitted, formed a new league to oust Louis, but died the following year, 1513. The holy alliance of the pope, Spain, Venice, and Switzerland.

II. In 1609, formed at Würzburg, in opposition to the Evangelical Alliance (*q.v.*) formed by Protestant states of Germany in 1608.

III. The alliance entered into 26 Sept., 1815, between the Czar of Russia, the Emperor of Austria, and the King of Prussia. It was agreed by the three contracting parties to pursue no policy in future which had not for its object the maintenance of christianity, justice, and peace. The three crowns contracted to stand fast to each other, and to suffer no other power to touch any portion of their respective dominions. France entered the alliance 26 Sept. It was under the strength of this alliance that Austria laid claim to Italy. England held aloof, feeling the scheme to be Utopian. Only think of Metternich, Talleyrand, and Castlereagh joining hands to bring peace on earth and good-will towards men. The inconsistency became a matter of ridicule, and fell powerless and abortive.

Holy Bread.

Not the eucharist, which is a wafer in the Catholic Church, but bread brought to the church to be blessed by the officiating priest on Sundays and feast-days at the time of mass. The 'pain bénit' is distributed to the heads of families and taken home with them. The custom dates from 655, and was instituted by the great council of Nice. Du Cange (vol. v. p. 122) calls it ' Panis Beatus, eulogia, panis a sacerdote benedictione consecratus ' ; but *panis beatus* is not the synonym of Eulogia (*q.v.*).

Hallowed Bread would be a better translation of ' Panis Beatus ' than Holy Bread.

Holy Brotherhood (*The*), or

' Santa Hermandad.' An association which executed summary justice on all offenders without distinction of rank. It was established in Spain by Ferdinand the Catholic for the suppression of high-road robbery (1481, 1516).

Holy Cities of the Islam (*The Four*).

Jerusalem, Mecca, Medīna, and Damascus.

Holy Coat of Trèves (*The*).

See ' Dict. of Phrase and Fable,' p. 411. Said to be spun from the wool of a lamb by the Virgin Mary, and woven in a grey coat by St. Helēna on the Mount of Olives. Christ wore it at the crucifixion. It came into the hands of a Jew, who threw it into the sea because the blood-stains would not wash out, and a whale swallowed it. The whale being caught by a fisherman, the grey coat found in its belly was sold for thirty pieces of silver to Orendel, son of Eygel, a Christian king of Trèves. Orendel deposited the coat in a stone coffin, where, being discovered, it became a venerable relic exhibited to the faithful every twenty-five years.

Holy Constitution (*The*), 'La

Sainte Constitution,' 817. The division by Louis I. le Débonnaire of his kingdom between his three sons. Lothaire he associated with himself in the empire, to Pepin he gave the government of Aquitaine, and to Louis that of Bavaria.

Lothaire, associated with his father, was charged with the vice-royalty of Italy. This ' holy constitution ' was certainly most impolitic, and proved to be an Iliad of woes.

Holy Days observed in the Catholic

Church. Some are more or less observed in the Church of England, and used to be marked in the Book of Common Prayer either with red letters or italics. Sundays are not included in this list except they happen to be fête days. (*Those without a date are movable.*)

All Saints	1 Nov.
All Souls	2 Nov.
Andrew	30 Nov.
Annunciation (The), or Lady Day	25 March.
Ascension Day, or Holy Thursday. The fortieth day after Easter.	
Ash Wednesday. The first day of Lent.	
Assumption (The), or Ascension of Mary	15 Aug.
Barnabas's Day	11 June.
Bartholomew's Day	24 Aug.
Christmas Day...	25 Dec.
Circumcision of Jesus. New Year's Day	1 Jan.
Commemoration of the Passion.	
Conception of Mary	8 Dec.
Conversion of Paul	24 Jan.
Epiphany, or Twelfth Day	6 Jan.
Fat Ox (The). Called in French Mardi Gras. The day before Ash Wednesday.	
Fête Dieu, or Corpus Christi Day. The Sunday next after Trinity Sunday.	
Good Friday. The Friday before Easter Day.	
Grave-Clothes (The). In French the Très-saint Suaire. The Friday next to Good Friday.	
Holy Cross	14 Sept.
Holy Relics of Nevers (The)	30 Oct.
Innocents' Day	28 Dec.
James the Elder	25 July.
John the Baptist's Day	24 June.
Beheaded	29 Aug.
John the Evangelist's Days ...	{ 6 May & 27 Dec.
Lammas Day ...	1 Aug.
Lord's Prayer (The). Called in French L'oraison de Notre Seigneur. Shrove Tuesday.	
Luke's Day	18 Oct.
Mark's Day	25 Apr.
Matthew's Day...	21 Sept.
Michaelmas Day	29 Sept.
Miracles of the Virgin Mary of Déols	21 May.
Name of Jesus (The Holy) ...	1 Jan.
Name of Mary (The Holy). The second Sunday in Sept.	
Nativity (The), or Christmas Day ...	25 Dec.
Nativity of Mary mother of Jesus ...	8 Sept.
Patronage of Joseph husband of Mary. Fifth Sunday of Oct.	
Patronage of Mary wife of Joseph. The third Sunday after Easter.	
Paul's Day ...	29 June.
Pentecost, or Whitsunday. The seventh Sunday after Easter.	
Peter ' prince of the Apostles'	29 June.
Petit Fête Dieu	2 Feb.
Philip and James	1 May.
Presentation of Mary	21 Nov.
Purification of Mary ...	2 Feb.
Relics (The). The Sunday in the Octave of Ascension.	
Resurrection of Jesus Christ. Uncertain. Mgr. Guérin says: 'Il n'y a point de jour que Dieu n'ait fait, et qui ne reconnaisse ce grand ouvrier ' (vol. xvi. p. 60). This fête is not the same as Easter Day.	
Seven Sorrows of Mary	1 Sept.
Shrove Tuesday.	
Simon and Jude	28 Oct.
Stephen the first Martyr	26 Dec.
Stigmata of Francis of Assisi ...	17 Sept.
Thomas's Day (the shortest of the year)	21 Dec.
Transfiguration (The)	6 Aug.
Trinity Sunday. The Sunday next after Whitsunday.	
Vigils. (These are numerous.)	
Visitation of Mary to her cousin Elizabeth	2 July.

See 'Sundays' and 'Saints' Days.'

Holy Directing Synod (*The*). A college of bishops established in Russia by Peter the Great, having supreme control and judgment in all matters ecclesiastical. The only appeal from this synod was to the czar himself.

Holy Fair (*The*). A Scotch custom of celebrating the eucharist in the open air. Burns has a poem on the subject. This led to such immorality that it was abolished.

Holy Ghost (*Knights of the*).

I. A *Neapolitan* Order, instituted by Louis of Anjou, king of Naples, 1352.

II. A *French* Order, instituted 1198 at Montpellier by Comte Guy. In 1672 it was united to the Order of St. Lazarus.

III. A French military order instituted (1578) by Henri III., who was both born and crowned on Whitsunday. Ribbon, blue moiré. Abolished in 1789 ; re-established in 1815, and again abolished in 1830.

Holy Island. I. Lindisfarne, about eight miles from Berwick-upon-Tweed, in the German Sea. Once the see of the famous St. Cuthbert, but now in the bishopric of Durham.

II. Ireland was so called at one time from its numerous saints.

III. Guernsey was so called in the tenth century from the great number of monks residing there.

IV. Rügen was so called by the Slavonic Varini.

Holy League (*The*). **I. 1511–1512.** Between the pope (Julius II.), Ferdinand of Aragon, Venice, and Switzerland, against Louis XII., to dispossess him of Venice and drive him out of Italy. Louis now placed a formidable army under the command of Gaston de Foix, his nephew, who gained three victories over the league in as many months, viz. at Bologna, at Brescia, and at Ravenna. In this last victory Gaston de Foix was left dead on the field, and the success of Louis terminated.

II. **1565.** The league of BAYONNE (*q.v.*).

The Holy League was directed against Scotland as well as against heretical nations, and how ready soever the Catholic princes might be to avenge the death of the Catholic Mary, they could not be supposed to entertain much zeal in the cause of the Protestant James.—Sir W. SCOTT, *Hist. of Scotland,* xxxvii.

III. **1576.** The high Catholic party of France, taking umbrage at the 'Paix de Monsieur' (*q.v.*), which gave the Protestants the free exercise of their religion in every part of the kingdom except Paris, formed themselves into a 'Holy League' in defence of the 'Holy Catholic Church' against the encroachments of the Huguenots. The objects of the league were (1) to exterminate the Calvinists; (2) to shut up the king Henri III. in a monastery; and (3) to crown the duc de Guise. The pope gave it his sanction, but its true strength lay in Felipe II. of Spain, who supported it with both men and money.

Holy Maid of Kent (*The*). Elizabeth Barton of Aldington, Kent, a religious enthusiast, executed in the reign of Henry VIII. She entered the convent of St. Sepulchre, Canterbury, and was then called 'The Nun of Kent.' In 1531 the parish priest gave out that the nun was inspired. Elizabeth Barton raved against the divorce of Queen Katharine, and threatened the king with deposition and death. She was brought before the Star Chamber, condemned, and executed at Tyburn in 1534.

Holy Mother of the Russians. Moscow; celebrated before its destruction for its number of churches and religious houses.

Holy Mountain (*The*). Athos, called by the Franks *Monte Santo*, and by the Greeks Ἅγιον ὄρος, for its numerous monasteries, convents, chapels, and other sacred edifices. It is said that above 8,000 monks reside on Mount Athos. It rises abruptly from the sea to the height of 6,349 feet. (Almost a mile and a quarter.)

Holy Office (*The*). The examination and extermination of heretics by the Catholic Church. The Inquisition was so called. The Holy Office existed in A.D. 382, when Theodosius I. appointed inquisitors to search out and punish heretics, and the first person put to death by them was Priscillianus of Aragon in 385. The epoch of the modern Inquisition was 1203, when Innocent III. was pope; but 'the modern Spanish Inquisition' dated from 1480, was suppressed in 1813, restored by Ferdinand VI. in 1814, and finally suppressed in 1820.

Holy Peace (*The*), or 'Peace of God,' 1035. An agreement of the princes and barons to cease from feuds, spoliation, and wars of aggression.

The priests read from the churches daily after the gospel this bull: 'May they who refuse to obey be accursed, and have their portion with Cain the first murderer, with Judas the arch-traitor, and with Dathan and Abiram who went down alive into the pit. May they be accursed in the life which now is: and may their hope of salvation, like the light of these candles, be put out.' So saying the lights were put out, and the people said 'Amen.' In 1040 the Holy Peace was superseded by 'God's Truce' (*q.v.*).

Holy Roman Empire (*The*). The western part of the old Roman empire, which was severed from the eastern part in 800, and was given by the pope to Charlemagne, who was crowned 'Emperor of the Romans.' When Charlemagne's empire was divided, Ludwig the German became kaiser; but on the death of Karl the Fat the title fell into abeyance for 70 years. In 962 John XII. gave the title to Otto I. the Great, and changed it into 'The Holy Roman Empire.' Francis II. renounced the titles of king of the Romans and emperor of the Romans in 1806, and Napoleon added the Italian states to France 17 May, 1809.

Holy Sabbath (*The*). Sabbatum Sanctum, the Saturday next before Easter Sunday.

Holy Sea (*The*). Ἅγιον πέλαγος, the Archipelago. This is D'Anville's etymology (vol. i. p. 281). It is, however, as old as Æschylus and Plato. Vossius says Ἅγιος is a corruption of αἰγαῖος, and that the Dorians called the bounding waves αἶγες, goats. We call them *horses*.

The fifty islands of the Holy Sea.—GIBBON, chap. lli.

Holy Sepulchre (*Defender and Baron of the*). Godfrey, first Latin king of Jerusalem. He rejected the title of king, and refused to wear a diadem 'where Christ was crowned with thorns' (1061, 1099–1100).

Holy Sepulchre (*Knights of the*), 328. A military order founded by St. Helĕna on the discovery of the Holy Sepulchre. Revived by Godfrey of Bouillon 17 July, 1099, again by Baldwin in 1103, and confirmed 1114 by Pascal II.

Holy Union (*The*), 1609. A confederation organised at Würzburg of Roman Catholics against the Protestants.

The counter league was called the 'Evangelical Union,' which was formed in 1608.

Holy Wars (*The*). The Crusades.

Holy Week. The last seven days of Passion Week (*q.v.*), or the Great Week. It begins on Palm Sunday, and ends with Holy Saturday (the day preceding Easter Sunday). The 4th day is Spy Wednesday, the 5th Maundy Thursday, the 6th Good Friday, and the last Holy Saturday, or the Great Sabbath. *See* 'Hebdomada Major.'

Holy Week has been called the Silent Week (*Hebdomada Muta*), the Week of the Holy Passion (*Hebdomada Passionis*), the Vacant Week (*Hebdomada Inofficiosa*), the Penitential Week (*Hebdomada Penitentialis*); also Hebdomada Indulgentiæ, Hebdomada Luctuosa, Hebdomada Nigra, and Hebdomada Ultima.

Homage was either *liege* or *simple*. 'Liege homage' implied an obligation of *service* to the lord. 'Simple homage' was a mere symbol of feudal dependence. VILLARET, vol. xii. p. 82; vol. xv. p. 199. Abolished in England 1660 (12 Car. II. c. 24).

In liege homage the vassal, kneeling on both his knees, and placing his two hands between those of his lord, spoke thus: 'I confess myself your man from this day forward to life and limb, and to all earthly worship. Unto you will I be true and leal, and will bear you faith for the lands and tenements I shall hold of you.' Having thus said, the king (without rising from his seat) bent forwards and kissed him on the forehead and on both cheeks.

Homburg (*Synod of*), 1526. The First General Reformed Synod, preceding the Diet of Augsburg about four years. It was convened by the Landgraf of Hesse to consider an order for the conduct of worship in conformity with the new religious views. By order of this synod a commission of ecclesiastics and laymen was appointed to draw up a directory for Divine worship and Christian instruction on the base of Melanchthon's 'Book of Visitation,' which formed the 'First Confession of Faith' of the reformed church.

Home Rule Federation, 1884. 'The objects of the Home Rule Federation of Great Britain were to organise the Irish vote in the various constituencies of Great Britain, and to influence the elections by the Irish vote.' Hor Secretary Frank Hugh O'Donnell. Alfred Henry Ruegg counsel for O'Donnell in the 'Parnellism and Crime' libel case, 2 July 1888 (*q.v.*).

Home Rule League, 1870. Projected by Mr. Butt, who stoutly opposed the repeal of the Union, but agitated for an Irish parliament which should have no power to touch upon imperial matters, but should be empowered to deal with matters of Ireland of a purely local character. On the death of Mr. Butt in 1879 his scheme passed into the hands of the Land League, and their watchword 'Ireland for the Irish' meant separation from Great Britain. The term Home Rule survived the death of Mr. Butt, and in 1886 Mr. Gladstone, then prime minister, brought in a bill to give Ireland Home Rule, and exclude Irish members from Westminster. The measure broke up the great Whig party under the leadership of Lord Hartington, supported by Mr. Chamberlain (a Radical), Mr. Goschen, and others, who called themselves Unionists, and joined the great Tory party under the government of Lord Salisbury. *See* 'Irish Associations.'

Mr. Gladstone's measure was to give to Ireland 'effective self-government in affairs properly and exclusively Irish, subject to the supremacy of the Imperial parliament.' In fact, it was Mr. Butt's scheme.

'The objects of the Home Rule League were to obtain for Ireland the right and privilege of managing its own affairs by a parliament assembled in Ireland, and to secure for the Irish parliament the right of legislating and regulating all matters relating to the internal affairs of Ireland.'—ALFRED HENRY RUEGG, counsel for O'Donnell, July 2, 1888 ('Parnellism and Crime' libel case).

⁎⁎ Imperium in imperio is proverbially a dangerous hazard.

Homer, Homêros. Everyone knows that it is somewhat doubtful if Homêros is a proper name or not. It is said that the Iliad and Odyssey were not continuous poems by one man, but ancient lays welded together under the direction of Pisistratos. It is not a little remarkable that the Greek word Homêros [ὄμηρος] means *united* or joined together. The great inequality of the poems has also been noticed by critics. Thus the interview between Priam and Achilles is admirable, but the death of Hector is contemptible, and the reconciliation of Agamemnon and Achilles, which ought to have exhibited magnanimity and generosity, is absolutely puerile.

Homer and Virgil of Portugal (*The*). Luis de Camoens (1522–1579), author of 'The Lusiads,' *i.e.* the Lusitanians or Portuguese; a poetic history of the people, the hero being Vasco da Gama.

The subject of the Lusiads resembles that of the Æneid, but bears no resemblance to the epics of Homer.

Homer (*The British*). Milton, 1608–1674.

No more the Grecian muse unrivalled reigns;
  To Britain let the nations homage pay :
She felt a Homer's fire in Milton's strains,
  A Pindar's rapture in the lyre of Gray.
        Westminster Abbey (Gray's Monument).

Homer (*The Keltic*). Ossian, son of Fingal king of Morven.

Homer (*The Oriental*). Firdusi (940–1020). *See below*, ' Homer of Khorasan.'

Homer (*The Prose*). Henry Fielding the novelist, called by Byron ' The Prose Homer of Human Nature' (1707–1764).

Homer (*The Scottish*). William Wilkie, author of 'The Epigoniad' (1721–1772).

Homer of Ferra'ra (*The*). ' *Omero Ferrarēsē.*' Ariosto is so called by Tasso (1474–1533).

Homer of Khorasan (*The*). Abul Casim Firdusi (940–1020), author of ' Shâh Nâmeh,' an historical romance of the Kings of Persia (from Kayomurz to Yezdijird), begun by Dukiki, who was assassinated when he had written only 1,000 lines. It was the labour of 30 years.

The chief characters in this poem are Rustem (the Persian Achilles); Feridun, the model king; Zohak, the cruel and impious tyrant; Kavah the blacksmith, an intrepid patriot, whose leather apron, set with jewels, became the banner of the empire till it fell into the hands of Kudsiah. The poem runs to 120,000 lines. The characters are bold and various, the diction polished and noble, the narrative especially perspicuous, and individual parts are of surpassing beauty.

Homer of Modern Days (*The*). Sir Walter Scott (1771–1832).

Homer of Persia (*The*). Firdusi, 941–1020. *See* ' Homer of Khorasan.'

Homer of Philosophers (*The*). Plato (B.C. 429–347).

Homer of our Dramatic Poets. So Shakespeare (1564–1616) is called by Dryden.

Shakespeare was the Homer or father of our dramatic poets; Jonson was the Virgil. I admire rare Ben, but I love Shakespeare.—DRYDEN.

Homer of the Franks (*The*). Angilbert, who died 814, was so called by Charlemagne.

Homer of the French Drama. Pierre Corneille (1606–1684) is so called by Sir Walter Scott.

Homer the Younger. Philiscos of Corcȳra, one of the seven poets of Alexandria, who, in the reign of Ptolemy Philadelphos, formed the Tragic Pleiad.

His six contemporary poets were Lycophron, Theocritos, Arātos, Nicander, Apollonios, and Callimāchos.

Home'rides (4 syl.), ὁμηρίδης. Those poets who succeeded Homer and either followed his style or took analogous subjects to the Iliad and Odyssey. Also called ' Cyclic Poets ' (*q.v.*).

Homerites (3 syl.). A people of ancient Arabia dwelling in Arabia Felix. Gibbon (ch. l.) says the first silk veil of the Caaba or temple of Mecca was an offering by a pious king of the Homerites 700 years before the birth of Mahomet.

Ho'meromas'tix. Zoïlos of Amphipŏlis (B.C. 259–336). So called for his caustic criticism on Homer.

Homilia'rium. A collection of homilies. Fifty homilies of the Venerable Bede in general use for a long time. The deacon Paul Warnefried, by the command of Charlemagne, compiled into a volume homilies for every Sunday in the year (8th cent.); it was printed at Speyer in 1482, and again at Cologne in 1557. A collection of English homilies in verse was composed in the 13th cent. It contained a sermon for every Sunday and every festival throughout the year. It is still extant in MS., and a part of it was published by Mr. Small, librarian to the University of Edinburgh. *See* ' Homilies.'

Homilies (*The*). Vol. i. (1547). On ' Salvation,' on ' Faith,' and on ' Good Works ' are attributed to Cranmer; that on ' Brawling and Contention ' is Latimer's, as appears by internal evidence; that on ' Adultery ' is by Thomas Becon, one of Cranmer's chaplains; that on ' The Misery of Mankind ' is ascribed to Bonner; of the rest nothing is known. Vol. ii. published 1562; thought to be by Bishop Jewell.

Some think Latimer was the author of the homilies on the ' Nativity' and on ' Whit-Sunday.'

Homme du Lit de Fer (*L'*). Henri Eugène Philippe Louis d'Orléans, fourth son of the Citizen King (Louis Philippe of France), born 1822, died *.

Pronounce *Hom deh leed-fair.*

Homœopathy (*The Creator of*). Hahnemann (1755–1843). That is, the art of curing diseases by medicines which in healthy bodies would produce like diseases. His motto is *Similia similibus curantur*, or ' Like cures like.'

Homoi'an theological party allied to the Arians, before 359, founded by Acacius, bishop of Cesarēa. These Christians were called ' Acacians,' from their founder.

Homoi-ousion means ' of a similar nature, essence, or state.' *Homo-ousion* (*q.v.*) means ' of equal essence or consubstantiate.' Applied to the nature of Christ, what is called the orthodox faith is that He is *homo-ousios* or consubstantiate with the Father. The semi-Arians maintain that He is only *homoi-ousios* or of similar essence, while strict Arians affirm He is neither one nor the other.

Arius declared that Jesus Christ might be *homoi-ousios* (of a similar nature) to the Father; but could not be *homo-ousios* (of the *same* substance).

Homo-ous'ion (*The*). Consubstantial, of the same nature. According to Aristotle, the stars are homo-ousian to each other; but the word is mainly connected with a theological controversy of the 4th cent. between Arius and Athanāsius. The Arians were *homoi-ousians*, the Athanasians were *homo-ousians*. That is, the Arians believed the nature of Jesus Christ to be god-*like*, but not *divine*; the Athanasians believed it to be very God of very God. As party words the ' orthodox' were *homo-ousians*, the non-orthodox were *homoi-ousians*.

Five times was Athanasius expelled from his (archiepiscopal) throne, and almost every province of the Roman empire was witness to his sufferings in the cause of Homo-ousion.—GIBBON, xxi.

Hone (*William*), 1817. The trial of William Hone for publishing parodies on Scripture or church subjects was, in reality, an attempt to put down the free expression of political opinions. His first trial was 18 Dec. before Mr. Justice Abbot, and the charge was that Hone had published parodies on the Catechism, the Lord's Prayer, and the Ten Com-

mandments. Hone showed that the editor of 'Blackwood's Magazine' had parodied part of Ezekiel; that Martin Luther had parodied the 1st Psalm; that Bishop Latimer, Dr. Boys dean of Canterbury, the author of the ' Rolliad,' and Mr. Canning were parodists, but were never accused of blasphemy. The jury acquitted Hone. The second trial was on 19 Dec., before Lord Ellenborough, and the charge was a parody on the Litany. Hone followed the same line of defence and was again acquitted. The third trial was 20 Dec., for a parody on the Athanasian Creed. Hone showed that Lord Ellenborough's own father, the bishops Warburton and Tillotson, with hosts of others, dissented from this creed, and he was again acquitted. So ended this government attempt to gag the press.

There is but little wit and little worth in these literary trifles, which often offend against ' good taste '; but the trials were an outrage on the liberty of free thought.

Honest Lawyer (*The*). The tablet to Edward Trelawny, in Pelynt Church, ends with these two lines:—

Here lyes an honest lawyer, wot you what,
A thing for all the world to wonder at.
(Died 7 June, 1630).

In St. Dunstan's in the West is a tablet to Hobson Judkins ' the honest solicitor,' who died 30 June, 1812.

Honest Man (*The*). A man of Burton (name . unknown), an agent in 1586 of Throckmorton, Gifford, and Walsingham, and spy upon Mary queen of Scots.

' The honest man' was in communication with the brewer who supplied the castle of Chartley with beer, and agreed to carry letters to and from Mary. Those intended for Mary were enclosed in a water-tight bottle, which floated inside the beer-cask ; the answers were deposited in a hole in the castle wall, where they were covered by a loose stone. The brewer and ' the honest man' were both in the pay of Walsingham. The letters were all broken open and read, after which they were resealed and despatched to their address.— HOWITT, *History of England*, ii. p. 509, &c.

Honorary Canons and honorary prebends, 1838—that is, canons or prebends without any stipend—were created by what is called the ' Oxford Movement' (*q.v.*). ' Canon' is now used as an ordinary title of address, as ' Canon A or B,' and on letters ' The Rev. Canon A or B.' Each bishop has the power of conferring a certain number of these honorary titles to clergymen within his diocese. Generally four.

Hono'rians (*The*), A.D. 408. Barbarian auxiliaries in Gaul and Britain, consisting of two bands of Scots or Attacotti, two of Moors, two of Marcomanni, Ascarii, Gallicani, and Victores. So named from Honorius the emperor.

Honourable. The younger sons of earls, and all the children of viscounts and barons.

'The Right Honourable' is added to the title of peers and peeresses below a marquis. All the younger sons of dukes and marquises, all privy councillors and ex-privy councillors, all the three lord mayors (London, York, and Dublin) are so styled.

'The Most Honourable' is added to the title of a marquis and marchioness. *Not* 'Most Noble.'

Dukes and archbishops are styled 'His Grace,' and addressed as 'Your Grace.'

Honours of Scotland (*The*). The Scotch regalia, consisting of the crown, sceptre, and sword of state, regarded by the Scotch with superstitious veneration.

Honours of War (*The*). The privilege accorded to a garrison surrendering after a very brave defence. It permits them to carry away their arms, and in some cases to march out with drums beating and colours flying.

Honveds (*The*), or 'Defenders of home,' 1848–1849. Ten battalions of Hungarian insurgents who organised themselves for the defence of house and home.

Hoods. As a badge. Red hoods the party badge of Paris. Blue hoods the party badge of Navarre. Red and blue the party badge of Charles [V.] when dauphin. White hoods the party badge of the Burgundians.

Hoods. *See* Chaperons.

Hoods. I. BLACK *without* lining.

Hood	Trimmed			
	Black silk	...	...	B.D.	Oxford or Cambridge
silk	Blue	...	...	LL.B.	London
	Gold-coloured	...	...	B.Sc.	London
silk	Mauve	...	...	A.K.C.	London
	Purple	...	...	L.Th.	Durham
	Russet-brown	...	...	B.A.	London
	Trimmed with white fur			
corded silk	narrow	...	...	B.A.	Oxford
stuff	broad	...	...	B.A.	Cambridge

II. *Black with* silk lining.

Hood	Lining			
velvet	Black	...	...	D.D.	Glasgow
cloth	Blue	...	...	LL.D.	Edinburgh
silk	,, dark	...	...	M.A.	Dublin
,,	,, ,, (white fur border)	...	LL.B.	Edinburgh
velvet	Gold-coloured	...	D.Sc.	Glasgow
cloth	Green	...	D.Sc.	Edinburgh
,,	,, (white fur border)	B.Sc.	Edinburgh
silk	Puce	...	...	B.D.	Lampeter
,,	Purple	...	...	M.A.	Durham
,,	,,	...	...	B.D.	Glasgow
cloth	,,	...	...	D.D.	Edinburgh
silk	Red	...	...	B.D.	Aberdeen
,,	,, dark	...	...	M.A.	Oxford
,,	,, ,,	...	...	LL.B.	Glasgow
velvet	,, ,,	...	...	LL.D.	Glasgow
silk	,, heather-bell	M.A.	Glasgow
,,	Russet	...	...	M.A.	London
,,	White	...	...	M.A.	Cambridge
,,	Yellow	...	...	B.Sc.	Glasgow

BLUE HOOD.

Pale blue silk hood (with white fur border)	B.C.C. or LL.D.	Oxford

PURPLE HOODS.

Hood	Lining		
cloth	Blue (pale)	...	LL.D.	Aberdeen
silk	,, (bound with white fur)	B.C.L.	Durham
,,	Blue (pale) (bordered with white fur)	...	B.D.	Edinburgh
cloth	White	...	...	D.D.	Aberdeen

SCARLET HOODS.

Hood	Lining		
cloth	Black	...	...	D.D.	Oxford
,,	Blue	...	...	LL.D.	London
,,	Crimson	...	...	D.C.L.	Oxford
,,	Gold-coloured	...	D.Sc.	London
,,	Pink	D.D. or LL.D.	Cambridge
cashmere	Purple	...	...	D.D.	Durham
cloth	Russet	...	...	D.Lit.	London
cloth or silk	White satin	...	LL.D.	St. Andrews
cashmere	White silk	...	D.C.L.	Durham

VIOLET HOODS.

cashmere	White satin	...	D.D.	St. Andrews
silk	White silk	...	B.D.	St. Andrews

*** Hoods for medical, musical, civil engineering, &c. not included.

Hook-and-Eye-ers. A branch of the strict Mennonites who split off from the general body in 1554. So called because they employed hooks-and-eyes in their dress instead of buttons. *See* Mennonites.

Hope Professorship (*The*) of Zoology, in Oxford University. Founded by the Rev. Frederick William Hope of Christ Church, 1861.

Hopkins Prize (*The*). For mathematico-physical or mathematico-experimental science. Founded in the University of Cambridge in memory of W.

Hopkins, and adjudged every three years. First adjudged in 1867.

Horace of France (*The*). Béranger (1780–1857).

He was called 'The Poet of St. Honoré,' from the street in which he lived, and 'The French Burns.'

The English Horace. I. Ben Jonson (1574–1637) is so called by Dekker the dramatist.

II. Cowley (1618–1667) is preposterously called by George duke of Buckingham 'The Pindar, Horace, and Virgil of England.'

The French Horace. Jean Macrinus or Salmon (1490–1557).

The Portuguese Horace, Antonio Ferreira (1528–1569).

The Spanish Horace, Lupercio Argensóla and also his brother Bartolome are both so called.

Horatius Cocles of the Horn.

John Haring, who defended a dyke against 1,000 Spaniards, till all the men under the governor Sonoy, who were put to flight, had made good their escape. After which he threw himself into the sea and effected his escape untouched by either spear or gun.

Horatius Cocles of the Tyrol.

Alexander Davy Dumas, father of the novelist. So called because in 1798, while in Dumouriez's army, he alone defended at Brixen the passage of a bridge on which depended the success of the day.

Horn Fair.

An annual fair granted by Henry III. (1268) to Charlton in Kent, for three days, viz. the eve, the day, and the morrow of Trinity, for the sale of winding horns, horn cups, and other vessels or implements made of horn. This fair was abolished in 1872. At horn fair it was usual for all persons to wear some horn ornament, generally on the headgear.

Horned-Cattle Session (*The*),

1770. So called because the first and chief item of the king's speech was in allusion to a murrain among horned cattle, though questions of enormous magnitude required attention. Earl Chatham in his speech drew a dismal picture of the domestic condition and foreign relations of the country. By the abandonment of Prussia the nation was without an ally. The internal affairs were even worse. The people were partly starving and wholly murmuring. John Wilkes was invading the ancient institutions, Spitalfields was in semi-rebellion, Ireland was netted with Whiteboys, Cork-boys, Levellers, and Hearts of Steel; America was on the verge of war; and yet, as Junius says, the ministers make the king a half-ruined grazier rather than the monarch of a vast empire.

Horse decides who is to be king of Persia (*A*).

Cambyses was followed on the throne of Persia by Smerdis the pretender, put forward by the Magi, but he was put to death by Otānês. Otānês then called a council of the chief men to determine on a successor, and agreed to meet on horseback at sunrise next morning, and he whose horse neighed first they agreed should be king. When Æbarês, the groom of Darius Hystaspês, heard this he took a mare to the spot the preceding evening, and showed it to his master's horse, which of course neighed next morning as soon as it came to the spot. So Darius was elected king.

Horsenails (*Counting*).

By the City officers at Westminster Hall. 'Walter le Brun, farrier, in the Strand, was to have a piece of ground in the parish of St. Clement to place a forge there, for the nominal sum of 6 horseshoes. This rent was paid every year to the Exchequer . . . and it is still rendered at the Exchequer by the mayor and citizens of London, to whom in process of time the said piece of ground was granted' (Blount, ' Ancient Tenures,' 1815).

In the reign of Edward I. Walter Marescallus paid at the *crucem lapideam* six horseshoes with nails for a certain building which he held of the king *in capite* opposite the stone cross.
A similar entry occurs in the 15 Edw. II. &c.

Hospit'allers, or 'Knights Hospitallers,'

or 'Knights of St. John of Jerulem,' or 'Knights of Malta,' 1050, established to protect pilgrims in the Holy Land. Confirmed by statute in 1118. They made themselves masters of the Isle of Rhodes in 1310, but were driven from the island by the Turks in 1522, and established themselves at Malta in 1530. Their dress is black, with a white cross of eight points. Established in England in 1100. Suppressed in England in 1540, in France

1792. Dispersed on the capture of Malta by Napoleon I. in 1798.

Called Hospitallers because they built at Jerusalem an hospital for the entertainment of pilgrims. The order still exists, and its flag is still seen in Mediterranean commerce.

Hospitallers of St. Lazarus, 1119.

A religious military order established at Jerusalem by Crusaders, and confirmed, in 1255, by the Pope. Its special duty was to take charge of lepers. Introduced into France by Louis VII., but in 1490 united in *Italy* to the order of the Knights of Malta; in *Savoy* (1572) to the Knights of St. Maurice; and in *France* (1693) to the Knights of St. Michel. There were 100 chevaliers, who might both marry and hold property. Their medallion was a cross with eight points, alternately green and purple, and adorned with images of the Virgin Mary and St. Lazarus.

Hospitals and Asylums.

We have mention of hospitals in Athens five centuries before the Christian era, and dispensaries long before that time supported by the state.

The Romans had public physicians at a very early date.

The ancient Mexicans had hospitals in all their principal cities.

India, however, seems to be the nursery of hospitals. King Asoka, B.C. 325, commanded that hospitals should be built for the poor, sick, and distressed, at each of the four gates of Patna, and throughout his whole empire. Fa Hian, a Chinese pilgrim (A.D. 400), says: ' The nobles and landlords founded hospitals for the poor in all places, and thither the poor, the cripple, and diseased might freely repair. They receive every kind of help gratuitously. Physicians attend to their diseases, and order them medicine, food, and drink, according to their judgment. Even when cured they may remain till it is convenient for them to retire.'

The first Christian hospital was built by a Roman lady named Fabiola, in the 4th cent.

In regard to asylums: The Egyptians and Greeks took charge of them in their temples. The Mohammedans built asylums for the insane at Fez in the 7th cent. The first Christian asylum was built at Valencia, in Spain, A.D. 1409.

Hospodar, 13th cent.

The sovereigns of Walachia and of Moldavia. In 1391 the hospodar of Walachia fell into the dependence of the Turks, and in 1536 the hospodar of Moldavia did the same, and the sultan nominated the hospodar. In 1821 the hospodars were nominated by the boïards under the investiture of the Porte. In 1829 the Hospodar of the Danubian Principalities was appointed for life by the Treaty of Adrianople. Since 1861 these provinces have formed (with the Dobrudscha) the kingdom of Roumania.

Host of Israel (*The*), 1681.

The armed Cameronians so styled themselves. They took up arms to dethrone Charles II. and set aside James his brother.

Hostings [of the lord deputies of Ireland].

Circuits or progresses for the display of military force *in terrorem*. They were more precautionary than hostile. In some a collision took place, but very many were mere displays or military progresses through the Pale (*q.v.*). Sometimes a hosting was made into the territory of a rebellious Irish chief.

Hot Gospeller (*The*).

Edward Underhill of Worcestershire, an ardent Protestant, but yet a devoted partisan of Queen Mary.

Hot Potatoes, 1782.

So the British sailors called the red-hot balls fired from Gibraltar into the combined French and Spanish fleet sent to take the Rock from the English. This magnificent defence by Gen. Elliot is wholly without a parallel in all history, and the humanity of Capt. Curtis, in saving 250 Spaniards at the peril of his life, is an achievement which every Englishman must be proud of.

The girl Campen, daughter of a Tyrolese tailor, sent with a load of hay while the Bavarians and French were fighting against Hofer, kept crying ' Come on! Come on with ye! Who cares for Bavarian dumplings?'

Hôtel Rambouillet (*L'*).

Very influential soirées held at the château of Charles d'Angennes marquis of Rambouillet, who married (in 1600) Catherine de Vivonne. Their daughter was the celebrated Julie [*i.e.* Julie Lucie d'Angennes] who married the Duc de Montausier. It was Julie who presided over these soirées, which were attended by Mme. de Sévigné and Mme. de Lafayette.

Pronounce *Lo-tel Rham-boo-yea*.

Houghers, 1785. Irish Volunteers belonging to the 'Aggregate Bodies' (*q.v.*), who went about maiming the soldiers and other persons obnoxious to them. The platform was universal suffrage. The introduction of the question of Catholic disabilities broke up the associations, and, as Plowden says, 'they disappeared like a bubble on the face of a stream.' *See* 'Irish Associations.'

[Houghers, pronounce *hok'-kers.*

House of Congregation (*The*), in Oxford University, consists of all masters of arts and doctors of every faculty of less than two years' standing. Called *Necessario Regentes.* Heads of colleges, masters of schools, and deans of colleges are called *Regentes ad placitum.* Duties are almost entirely confined to granting degrees and the appointment of public examiners. In Cambridge University 'The Electoral Roll' corresponds in a great measure with the Oxford House of Congregation.

House of Convocation (*The*), in Oxford University, consists of all persons who have taken the degree of M.A. or of doctor, provided their names remain on the boards of their college. All the business of the university as a corporate body is transacted by Convocation, and no statute is binding till it has received the assent of this house. It also confers honorary degrees and degrees of diploma, affixes the common seal to all documents, and elects all offices in the gift of the university. No proposition of legislation originates in this house, nor can it amend any proposition submitted to it; it can only accept or reject. The Council of the Senate in Cambridge corresponds to the Oxford 'House of Convocation.'

House of Keys (*The*), in the Isle of Man, consists of twenty-four representatives formerly selected by their own body, vacancies being filled up by the House presenting to the governor 'two of the oldest and worthiest men of the land,' one of whom the governor nominates, and he takes office for life. But since 1866 they have been elected by the people (male and female freeholders voting).

The civil government of the island is vested in three estates: the king or queen in council, the governor and council, and the House of Keys. The latter two constitute a court of Tynwald. To the 'Keys' or wardens all doubtful and important matters of law are referred.

Houses of Parliament (*The Burning of the*), 16 Oct., 1834 (Will. IV.). Caused by overheating the flues with old tallies with which the fires were lighted.

Household Troops (*The*). Those troops whose especial duty it is to attend the sovereign and to guard the metropolis. They are the 1st and 2nd Lifeguards, the Royal Horse-guards, and the three infantry regiments called the Grenadiers, the Coldstream Guards, and the Scots Fusiliers.

Howard (*Sister*). So Queen Caroline used to call Mrs. Howard (afterwards countess of Suffolk), mistress of George II. She even employed 'Sister Howard' at her toilet, and otherwise about her person.

Howard of Russia (*The*). John Venning.

Howard-Arundel Collection (*The*), 1831. In the MS. department of the British Museum, and consisting of about 600 volumes of interest in almost every branch of learning, especially connected with the history and language of our own country.

Hubert (*Knights of St.*), 1414. A military order of Bavaria founded by Guerhard duke of Juliers. Revived in 1709 by the Elector Palatine.

Hubertsburg (*Treaty of*), 15 Feb., 1763. A treaty of peace at the close of the Seven Years' war between the Kaiser, Prussia, and Saxony.

Hudson's Bay Company (1670). A corporation chartered by Charles II. It consisted at first of Prince Rupert and certain specified associates, who were invested with the absolute proprietorship of 'Rupert's Land,' which consisted of all the regions then discovered and hereafter to be discovered within the entrance of Hudson's Bay. The great traffic of the company was in beaver furs. In 1783 was formed the North-west Company of Montreal, which in 1821 coalesced with the Hudson's Bay Company. Surrendered to the crown in 1868, and ceded to the Dominion of Canada in 1869.

It still exists as a commercial corporation.

Hugh Wolf, or 'Hugh Lupus.' Hugh d'Avranches, a near relative of the Conqueror. His device was a wolf's head, and William gave to his kinsman almost all Cheshire.

Huguenots (U-gen-oze, *g* hard). Members of the reformed church of France, as Protestants are members of the reformed church of Germany, England, America, and other countries. The Huguenots are called 'French Calvinists.'

Les uns font dériver ce nom d'un certain *Hugues* [Hugon], chef d'un parti religieux et politique à Genève; les autres, avec plus de raison, de l'allemand *Eidgenossen* (associés par serment), nom donné d'abord aux habitants de Genève soulevés et ligués contre le duc de Savoie.—BOUILLET.
Another derivation is Hugon, a gate in Tours, near which, it is said, the Huguenots assembled. 'Les huguenots avoient pris leur nom à cause de la tour Hugon [in Tours] où ils s'assemblaient.'— D'AUBIGNÉ, *Hist.* i. 96.

Hul'sean Lecturer or Christian Preacher (*The*). In the University of Cambridge, 1789, established by the Rev. John Hulse of St. John's College. The subject to be on the evidence for revealed religion and exegesis of obscure texts. Four sermons.

Hul'sean Prize (*The*). For an essay on miracles for any member of the University of Cambridge under the degree of M.A. Value between 70*l.* and 80*l.* annually. Founded by the Rev. John Hulse of St. John's College, 1789. *See* 'Reg. Prof. of Divinity.'

Hul'sean Professor of Divinity (*The*). In the University of Cambridge, 1728. So called because it was endowed by eight-tenths of 1,000*l.* left by the Rev. John Hulse of St. John's College. The professor must print and publish six lectures in the course of every six years. Till 1860 the Hulsean Professor was called the Christian Advocate. *See* 'Regius Professorship of Divinity.'

The 1,000*l.* has to be divided thus: one part to maintain two scholars at St. John's College; another part to found a prize for dissertation; a third part to support the office of Christian Advocate; and the fourth part to support the Hulsean Lecturer or Christian Preacher.

Hu'manists, 16th cent. A literary set which devoted themselves to the cultivation of classical literature (*litĕræ humaniōres*). They not only set themselves in opposition to classical professors, they also wanted to reform theology.

Humanita'rians. I. Those Christians who deny the divinity of Christ.

The primitive Ebionites (4 syl.) and the Cerinthians were Humanitarians, but not the Arians.

II. The disciples of St. Simon, who believe in the perfectibility of human nature, and ignore the dependence of man-upon supernatural aid.

Humanity Martin. Richard Martin, of Ballinabench Castle, M.P. for Galway, so called from the Martin Act (1822) for the prevention of cruelty to animals (1754-   ).

If all had been like me, in fact,
There'd been no need for Martin's Act.
If I had a donkey that wouldn't go.

Humble Petition and Advice (*The*), 1656. A petition from parliament entreating the lord protector to take a royal title. A blank was left in the petition for the exact designation, which was ultimately filled up with the word 'Protector.'

Humble Representation (*The*), 1647. After Charles I. fell into the hands of Cornet Joyce, the army presented to the parliament an 'humble representation,' stating : 'We desire a settlement of the peace of the kingdom, and of the liberties of the subjects. We desire no change in the civil government, but we demand toleration in religion. We demand the repeal of all acts enforcing the use of the prayer-book, attendance at church, and the enforcement of the covenant. We ask for triennial parliaments, the reform of the franchise, and the readjustment of taxes.' These petitions, with a simplification of law proceedings, constituted the 'Humble Representation.' Charles, however, resisted.

Hume, *Mr. Hume's motion carried without a division,* 16 Oct., 1834, by the utter destruction of the two houses of parliament by fire. Mr. Hume had been noted for his efforts to get rid of the old houses, and to have new ones more worthy of the British Legislature.

Humiles (*Ordre des*), 1134. A religious confraternity of both sexes, founded at Milan by St. John of Meda. It was in a great measure of the Benedictine rule, but had its own badge. Suppressed in 1571.

Hundred (*A.*) A county division mentioned in Domesday Book, and generally supposed to include a hundred families. Northumberland, Cumberland, Westmoreland, and Durham are not subdivided into hundreds, but *wards* ; Yorkshire, Lincolnshire, and Nottinghamshire are subdivided into *wapentakes*. York.

shire is likewise divided into three parts, called *Ridings*. Kent is divided into five *laths*, and these laths into sixty-three hundreds. Sussex is divided into six *rapes*, with subordinate hundreds.

Hundred Days (*The*). From 29 March to 22 June, A.D. 1815. From the time that Napoleon quitted Elba (breaking his parole) to his abdication.

In this period occurred the battle of Ligny (16 June); the battle of Quatre Bras (16 June); and the battle of Waterloo (18 June).

Hundred Grievances of Germany (*The*), 1522. Presented to Pope Adrian VI. by the Diet of Nuremberg. During the contention between Luther and the pope, Adrian sent a brieve to the Diet of Nuremberg, calling on the princes of Germany to stamp out the plague of heresy. The diet, in reply, sent to the pope a memorial of a 'hundred grievances' which they besought the holy father to redress, and that too without delay, as the nation neither could nor would endure them any longer.

Hundred Isles (*The*). Venice.

Hundred Years War (*The*), 1336–1431. Between England and France. From Edward III. to Joan of Arc. The origin of this long war was Edward's claim to the crown of France. Philippe le Bel left three sons, all of whom died without male issue, and the nearest male heirs were Edward III. (who was the nephew of the three sons), and Philippe de Valois (who was their cousin). The flaw in Edward's claim is the Salic law, which passed over women, and Edward owed his blood relationship to his mother. Edward maintained that, though his mother was cut off, being a woman, the Salic law could not apply to him, being a man; but Philippe answered, if the mother was cut off, the son was cut off also. On this dispute began the war which lasted above a century.

Hun'dreders. The impanelling of 'hundredors' on juries in civil actions abolished 1705 (4, 5 Anne c. 16).

Hung, Drawn, and Quartered. The punishment of traitors. It is an error to suppose that 'drawn' means dragged on a hurdle by a horse to the place of execution. It means disembowelled. The first instance in English history is that of David the Welsh prince,

20 Sept., 1283. He was 'hung' for causing the murder of the knights in Hawarden Castle; he was 'drawn' because he had profaned Palm Sunday by committing the murder on that day; he was 'quartered' for conspiring against the king (Edward I.). This was the precedent in cases of high treason.

It is misleading and a falsifying of history to reverse these words into 'drawn, hung, and quartered,' as some historians do, to intimate that 'drawn' means dragged on a hurdle to execution.

Hungarian Anjous (*The*). Succeeded the Arpad dynasty. Charles Robert was the founder (1309–1342), Louis the Great his son (1342–1382), and Sigismund, in virtue of his wife (1386–1437). Succeeded by the house of Hapsburg.

Sigismund or Siegmund was king of Hungary, king of Bohemia, and kaiser-king of Germany. He will always be remembered for violating his royal word of safe-conduct, and afterwards assenting to the martyrdom of Huss and Jerome of Prague.

Hungarian Compromise (*The*), Feb. 1868. Providing the new army organisation.

Hungarian National Anthem. Rakolski's March.

Hungarian Revolution (*The*), 1848–1849. Under Kossuth. Kossuth resigned 11 Aug., 1849.

8 June, 1867, Francis Joseph of Austria was crowned king of Hungary.

Hungarian Sea (*The*). Lake Balaton, forty-seven miles long and nineteen miles wide. Famous for the savoury *fogas* fish.

Huns (*The*). A people driven out of China by Vou-ti (*i.e.* Hiong-nu). Many left the steppes of Tartary, and made their way to the Caspian Sea. A part, crossing the Caucasus, came into collision with the Eastern Goths in A.D. 375.

Hunter's Mass. Missa Venatīca.' Celebrated very early in the morning for those about to spend the day in hunting, hawking, or the chase. A greatly shortened mass, gabbled over as fast as possible.

Hunter's Moon. The moon next after the harvest moon, where, as in 'honey-moon,' the word 'moon' stands for month. The harvest moon is that immediately *before* the vernal equinox, and the hunter's moon that which follows *after* the vernal equinox. The harvest being over, hunting may begin.

Hurricane (*The*). Comte de Mirabeau (1749–1791). Also called 'the Demosthenês of France,' from the overpowering force of his eloquence. He was so corpulent that he was jocosely called the *Tub*.

Huss (*John*), 1376, 1415. The great charge against Huss was his insistence on faith. 'Faith, not in the Virgin, not in the saints, nor yet in the pope, nor in baptism, nor in holy water and oil, but in Christ.' He was burnt alive by order of the Council of Constance, though the kaiser himself (Siegmund) had given him safe conduct. 'I came here' (he said to the council) 'under the public faith of the kaiser, here present.' In so saying he fixed his eyes on Siegmund, 'who blushed scarlet at the just but unexpected rebuke.'

Hussite War (*The*), 1419–1436. Siegmund was elected kaiser 1410, and in 1415–1416 Huss and Jerome were burnt to death. The Hussites were indignant that the kaiser should have pledged his royal word for the safety of Huss and Jerome, and yet should have presided at the council which condemned them both to death. In 1419 they put themselves under Ziska the One-eyed and prepared for war. Siegmund also prepared to put down the insurgents, but was defeated over and over again. Ziska died in 1424, and Procop (both the elder and the younger) led the insurgent Bohemians, and no longer stood on the defensive, but carried the war beyond the boundaries of Bohemia with wonderful success; but at the death of the two leaders peace was made, and Siegmund acknowledged king of Bohemia (1437).

The Hussites' platform was: (1) Freedom to preach the gospel; (2) administration of the eucharist in both kinds to laity as well as clergy; (3) prohibition to the clergy to follow secular pursuits; and (4) submission of the clergy to the civil power. Their symbol was a chalice. The more moderate were called 'Calixtines' (3 syl.), and the more extreme 'Taborites' (3 syl.).

Hussites (2 syl.). Followers of John Huss of Bohemia (1376–1415), who was condemned to be burnt alive by the Council of Constance. He was a Wyclifite of most unimpeachable character, and his murder is one of the blackest stains in the history of the Roman Catholic Church.

Hutcheso'nians, 1729. Followers of Dr. Francis Hutcheson, whose 'System of Moral Philosophy' was based on the ethical notions of Lord Shaftesbury. He deduces all our moral ideas from an innate moral sense, or instinct, which leads us to perform certain acts and to avoid others.

Dr. Hutcheson, professor of philosophy at Glasgow, died 1747, aged 53.

Hutchinsonianism, 1724. The doctrines of John Hutchinson of Yorkshire, author of 'Moses' Principia,' in which he defends the Mosaic cosmogony and assails Newton's 'Principia.' He maintained that the Holy Scripture is the only divine revelation of true religion and true science, and that all science not in conformity with Scripture is 'philosophy falsely so called.' He substitutes 'a plenum and air' for Newton's 'vacuum and gravity.'

John Hutchinson must not be confounded with Dr. Francis Hutcheson.

He said that the air from the earth *to the sun* grew more and more rarefied till it became pure light; but from the sun to the *fixed stars* it grew denser and denser, till it stagnated into 'outer darkness,' the very 'blackness of darkness.'

Hutin (Louis X. of France, 1314–1316) means 'headstrong' or 'obstinate,' but applied to Louis it was a mere pun. He was sent by his father against the Hutins, a seditious set of people of Navarre and Lyons, and this expedition gained for him the sobriquet.

Hydro-parasta'tæ, or 'Aquarii.' The followers of Tatian (born 130), who forbade the use of wine even in the eucharist. (Greek, ὕδωρ, water; παρίστημι, I present.)

Hyksos (*The*), or Shepherd Kings of Lower Egypt. A race of Arabs which invaded ancient Egypt, and continued dominant, according to Manêtho, for 500 years, but according to others about half that time (B.C. 1842–1591). They formed or were contemporary with the 15th, 16th, and 17th dynasties of Upper Egypt. Amôsis drove them out and established the 18th dynasty in Thebais, contemporary with the 19th and 20th. They were driven from the Thebais by Totmosis or Thotmosis, but continued to hold certain cantons of Egypt long afterwards.

It is supposed that Abraham went to Egypt in B C. 1806, while the 16th dynasty was regnant; and that Joseph was viceroy about B.C. 1713, in the same dynasty.   (*Hyk*=king, *Sos*=shepherd.)

Hylo-idealism, 1883. A system thought out by Dr. Lewins, and given to the world in 1882-1883. It is not idealism, but objective or hylo-idealism. The fundamental principle is this: Objects or objective phenomena must be made subjective or mental concepts before they are cognisable. The object is the stimulus and the perceiving brain the response. The two are like the two clocks of a telegraphic wire. The object works one clock, sends it to the brain, and the brain works the other clock. If either clock is out of order, or the telegraphic wire is broken, no message is received, and the objective world is cut off from all cognisance or even existence as far as the person in question is concerned.

Hymnus S. Mariæ, *i.e.* the 'Magnificat.'

Hymnus S. Trinitatis. In Latin: 'Sanctus Deus, Sanctus fortis, Sanctus immortalis, miserere nobis.' In Greek: Ἅγιος ὢ θεὸς, Ἅγιος ἰσχυρὸς, Ἅγιος ἀθάνατος, ἐλέησον ἡμᾶς.

Hypapanti (Greek, ὑπαπαντὴ, a meeting together). It means the meeting of Christ in the Temple by Simeon and Anna, who had long waited for Him. The Feast of Purification is called 'Festum Hypapanti,' 'Festum S. Simeonis,' 'Festum Purgationis Mariæ Virginis,' or 'Festum Luminum.'

'Hypapanti' is barbarous Greek, and undeclinable.

Hypos'tasis, in divinity, means 'person'; as the Trinity has one essence or nature, but three hypostases or persons.

'Person' is not a good word, as it is so closely allied to a phenomenon, whereas hypostasis is mere noumenon without phenomenon. The basis or substratum of personality. The plural is 'hypostases.'

Hypostat'ic Union (*An*). A union of two or more natures so intimate as to constitute one person. Thus the union of man and God in Christ is an hypostatic union.

The Nestorians held that the union of humanity and Deity in Christ was a mere moral union, and not an hypostatic one.

Hypothetical Universalism. A doctrine taught by Moïse Amyraut (1596-1664), professor of Saumur: that the death of Jesus Christ was *sufficient* for all men, but *efficacious* for the elect only.

Iambic Poets of Greece (*The*). The three principal were Archilŏchos of Paros (B.C. 710-690), inventor of iambic verse, and father of satire; only a few fragments are extant. Simonĭdês of Samos (flourished B.C. 660); the chief fragment extant is a satire on women. He says a *slattern* has something of the swine in her composition; a *cunning* woman something of the fox; a *stupid* one shares her nature with the ass, the *headstrong* with the weasel, the *vain* with the horse, the *malicious* with the monkey, &c. The third of this class of poets was Hippōnax of Ephesus (B.C. 566-520), father of parody and burlesque.

The *latter Iambic* poets were Nicander (B.C. 200-120), and Meleāger of Gadăra (B.C. 135-60), who wrote 130 epigrams and a collection of poems called 'The Garland,' which no longer exists.

Simonĭdês of Ceos (B.C. 566-520), the great lyric poet, was quite another person.

Ibe'ria. The Latin name of Spain, the people dwelling about the river Ibērus (*i.e.* the Ebro).

Ica'rians. The colonists led by Cabet, a French communist (1788-1856), to Icaria, in Iowa, with a view of forming them into a model community. In this community there is no money, no buying and selling, but all work for the community, and all are provided by the community with everything required. All manufactures and industries are national property, and the executive determines what each individual is to do. In regard to religion all worship the 'unknown God,' but there are no creeds, ceremonies, or rites.

Edward Bellamy of America has a novel called 'Looking Backward' which embodies this idea.

Ich Dien (I serve). The motto chosen by the Black Prince when he was knighted by his father after the battle of Crécy. (1) It was the motto of the king of Bohemia, who fell in battle by the hand of the young prince, and served to commemorate that achievement; (2) the prince had just been made his father's 'man' by knighthood, and no words could better express his acknowledgment of service and duty to his liege lord.

Pronounce *Eek-deen.*

Icil'ian Law (*The*), B.C. 454. A law for the parcelling out the Aventine Hill among the plebeians of old Rome, proposed by Lucius Icilius the tribune.

Here the people lived in flats without any ground rent.

Icoglans. Children who attend the sultan as pages.

Ico'nia (*The*). A sacred ensign of the emperors of Constantinople. It consisted of a tall pole surmounted by a cross, from which, attached to a cross-bar, hung a large flag with a Latin cross. On another cross-bar on one end hung the Virgin Mary with several relics; to the opposite end a string was attached, and held in the hand of some ecclesiastic. Amongst the relics were a piece of the lance which pierced the side of the Saviour, and a tooth shed by him in childhood. It first belonged to the Cistercians, fell into the hands of the Venetians in 1204, and was then deposited in the treasury of St. Mark.

Icon'oclasts, or ' Image Breakers,' A.D. 485. A religious sect which considered crucifixes, images of saints, statues, and pictures in Christian churches as idolatrous, and went about destroying them. They became very active in the 8th cent. under Leo the Isaurian. Iconoclasts were condemned by the Councils of Constantinople held in 786, 806, 809, 812, 814, but these judgments were reversed in 815. They were again condemned in the Councils held in 842, 847, and 870. The Lombards were strenuous opposers of images and pictures in churches.

'Iconoclast' is εἰκών (image), κλάζω (I break).

Iconodu'li (*The*). Those who advocated and reverenced images and pictures in churches. Those who broke them and discarded them were called Iconoclasts (6th and 7th cents.). *See* ' Iconolatrists.'

Εἰκών (image), δουλεία (an inferior reverence paid to saints, images, and relics, in opposition to λατρεία).

Iconolatrists. Worshippers of images. Applied to those Christians who admit crucifixes, material symbols of deity, and pictures into churches and houses, either for direct adoration, as aids to religion, or as ' outward visible signs of an inward invisible faith.' Iconoclasts, or image-breakers, were those Christians who opposed iconol'atry, and broke to pieces all such material symbols in churches, &c. *See* ' Iconduli.'

Idæan Boy (*The*), or *Idæus Puer.* Ganymede is so called because it was from Mount Ida, in Asia Minor, that Zeus or Jupiter seized on him and carried him to Olympus to be his cup-bearer.

Idæan Dactyls (*The*). Mythical priests and priestesses of Cybele, and said to have been the original discoverers of iron. Called *Idæan* from Mount Ida, in Asia Minor, their hypothetical seat; and *Dactyls*, or fingers, because they were ten in number (five males and five females).

Idæan Judge (*The*), or *Idæus Judex.* Paris, who decided from Mount Gargarus, a part of Ida, between the rival claims of Juno, Minerva, and Venus. All the goddesses offered bribes to influence the award, which the shepherd gave in favour of Venus. Cicero calls Paris the ' Idæan Shepherd ' (*Idæus Pastor*).

These 'dactyls,' like the ' Idæan Boy ' and ' Idæan Judge,' belong more to mythology than to *history*, as we now understand the word.

Idealism. Two different systems of philosophy are so called :—

I. A system which considers absolutes or universals as subjective realities. Thus *white, black, tree*, &c., were supposed to have a subjective existence independent of any special object. Plato is the exponent of this system, supported in modern times by Malebranche, Kant, Schelling, Hegel, and others.

II. Those who deny the reality of the world, and maintain that everything is only an idea ; or at any rate, so far as any individual is concerned, that his senses make his world, and if he had no senses there would be, to him at least, no external world. Bishop Berkeley, Hume, Fichte, &c. were exponents of this system.

Idle Bible (*The*), 1809. In which the ' idol shepherd ' (Zech. xi. 17) is translated ' idle shepherd,' in the new version ' worthless shepherd,' which does not mean the same thing. An idol is a counterfeit, and an ' idol shepherd ' is a counterfeit or false shepherd, who sets up himself for his people's adoration, and not God. The Pharisees of old, who did their good deeds to be seen of men, were ' idle shepherds.' *See* ' Bible.'

The Hebrew word is of ambiguous meaning.

Ignatian Controversy (*The*). Whether the Epistles ascribed to Ignatius, who died 115, are genuine and authentic. This is very important, as these writings are the battle-ground of Episco-palians and Presbyterians. They favour the hierarchical system, and therefore are strenuously defended by Episcopalians, but the present opinion of scholars such as Daillé, Semler, Hermann, Ernesti, Neander, &c., is that much is spurious, and the rest has been greatly tampered with. *See* ' Literary Forgeries.'

The works of Ignatius are a *Liturgy*, a little book calle1 *Didaché* (quoted by Chrysostom), and 15 epistles (12 in Greek and 3 in Latin). The 7 follow-ing epistles—to the Ephesians, Magnesians, Phila-delphians, Trallians, Smyrnæans, Romans, and to Polycarp—were long accepted as genuine and authentic, but are now suspected. Bunsen thinks three may be accepted, but condemns the rest. Probably all have been interpolated. It is a very sad thing, but too true, that no church lite-rature which passed through the hands of the monks can be relied on.

Ignora'mus Jury (*An*). A grand jury was so called because they wrote *Ignoramus* instead of 'no true bill,' when sufficient evidence was wanting to send the case to the common jury.

If you find that anything proceeds from malice . . . you may acquit the person that is so wrong-fully prosecuted, and so . . . an Ignoramus jury may be of no use.—*Judge Allibon's charge at the Croydon Assizes in 1688.*

Ignoran'tines (4 syl.). The ' Con-gregation of the Ignorantines ' was founded in 1724 in France by the Abbé de la Salle (1 syl.). It was suppressed in 1789, but re-established by Napoleon in 1806.

Ik'shidites (3 syl.), 933–968. A dynasty of califs ruling in Syria and Egypt founded by Abubekr Mohammed Ikshid, a Turkish slave.

Il Regno. The half-mocking name of the kingdom of Naples. It was so called for centuries by all the republics of Italy.

Il'derim (lightning). So Bayazid I. of Turkey was called from the extreme rapidity with which he executed all his designs. He reigned 1389–1403.

Île du Palais (*L'*). The larger of the two little aits or islets in the river Seine (Paris) ; the smaller one is called L'Île St. Louis, the two are connected by the Pont de la Cité. The Île du Palais for many centuries constituted the whole city of Paris. Here a tribe of the Celtic Gauls, called the Parisii, built their mud huts of a circular form, and thatched them with reeds from the river. Here Clovis built his palace, and here the kings of France resided up to the time of

Philippe II. Auguste (1180–1223), who resided in the old Louvre. The palace of Clovis was converted by Charles V. into the Palais de Justice. Notre Dame de Paris stands on the Île du Palais, or cité.

Île du Palais is so called because of the palace built there by Clovis, and used by the early kings of France.

Iliad (*The French*). The ' Roman de la Rose ' (*q.v.*) by Guillaume de Lorris (1235–1265). A ' continuation ' was sub-sequently added by Jehan de Meung (1260–1318).

One might just as well call the ' Faëry Queen ' an Iliad. The ' Romance of the Rose ' is a love alle-gory in verse: The Rose is the poet's lady-love, and the subject matter is the course of true love does not run smoothly. Fully described in the ' Reader's Handbook,' p. 842.
The ' Chanson de Roland,' containing upwards of 1,500 verses, is called the ' Iliad of France.'

Iliad (*The German*). The Nibel-ungen Lied, 1210.

The plot and tale of this epic are fully described in the ' Reader's Handbook,' p. 684.

Iliad (*The Portuguese*). The ' Lu-siads ' by Camoens. Fully described in the ' Reader's Handbook,' p. 580.

Iliad (*The Scotch*). The Epigoniad, by William Wilkie. Fully described in the ' Reader's Handbook,' p. 297.

Ilkha'nian Tables (*The*), 13th cent. The astronomical tables and ob-servations of Nazir Eddin, the great Persian astronomer, in the reign of Houlagou Khan, son of Ghengis Khan, who reigned 1259–1265. Nazir Eddin lived 1201–1274.

Hassan Bouzrûk Ilkani did not found the Ilkanian dynasty till 1336, sixty-two years after the death of Nazir Eddin.

Ilkha'nians (*The*). A Mogul dy-nasty of Persia, founded by Hassan Bouzrûk, or Ilek-khan, who made Bagdad his capital. His dynasty only lasted 65 years (1336–1401), when it was overthrown by Tamerlane.

Illinois (*U. S. America*). So called, in 1809, from an Indian tribe of that name. The natives are nicknamed ' Suckers.' Discovered by the French in 1670 ; ceded to England in 1763 ; and admitted as a state of the Union in 1818.

Illiterate Parliament (*The*), 1404. From which all lawyers were ex-cluded. *See* ' Parliaments.'

It advised the king, Henry IV. to seize the re-venues of the clergy, which were more than one-third of all the land of England, and to repeal the statute ' De Hæretico Comburendo ' ; but the king feared to offend the clergy.

Illuminated Doctor (*The*). 'Doctor Illuminātus,' or 'Most Enlightened Doctor.' Raymond Lully, born in Majorca (1234–1315). He entered the Franciscan order, and set himself to convert the Moslems, was stoned at Bugia [in Algeria], and supposed to be dead (30 June, 1315). Some looked on him as a saint, others considered him 'un insensé et un hérétique.'

He was the best chemist of his age, but spent his time in searching for the philosopher's stone by distillation.

Illuminati (*The*), 16th cent. A religious sect, founded by Jacob Boehmen, or Boehm, a shoemaker of Lusatia. He averred that he was often carried up to heaven, like the Apostle Paul. Swedenborgians and Quietists were in a great measure 'Illuminati'; that is, they professed to have an inner light which illuminated them. *See* 'Martinists,' 'Guerinets,' and 'Alombrados.' Also next article.

Illumina′tists (*The*), or The Society of Illuminatists,' 1776. A secret society founded by Dr. Adam Weishaupt, professor of canon law at Ingolstadt, his avowed aim being 'to illuminate the world with a higher philosophy.' This society was joined by Mesmer, Cagliostro, Condorcet, the Duc d'Orléans, Mirabeau, and the Abbé Sieyès. The real objects were to crush priestly intolerance and superstition, to stamp out feudalism, and to limit regal authority to the popular will. In a word, the 'Illuminatists' were the midwives of the first French Revolution, though, without doubt, the revolution far outran their programme. Suppressed in 1785.

Also called 'Illumināti.'

Illyr′ian Conservatives (*The*), 19th cent. The Croatian party which sought the establishment of an independent Slav nationality (about 1847).

Illyr′ian Provinces (*The*), 1809. So named by Napoleon's decree. They consisted of Carinthia, Carniola, Istria, Austrian Friūli, the Hungarian littoral, and Southern Croatia. In 1810 it was augmented; but after the battle of Waterloo (1815) the provinces were restored to Austria by the Congress of Vienna, and, in 1849, were subdivided into duchies and counties.

Image Worship, introduced into Christian churches, was condemned by the Council of Illiběris (Elvira in Gra-

nāda) between 300 and 305. Calif Yezid II. in 723 commanded the destruction of all 'religious' images. *See* 'Iconoclasts.'

Images were denounced in *Germany* by Carlstadt in 1522.

In *Switzerland* by Zwingle in 1523, and removed from the churches of Zürich.

In *England* by act of parliament 1549, and removed from all churches in England.

In *Austria* by Joseph II., 1782. *See* 'Iconduli' and 'Iconolatrists.'

In the Second Council of Nice, 787, a distinction was drawn between *latreia* (worship) and *douleia* (reverence). The adoration of God is *latreia*, the reverence paid to images and saints is *douleia*.

Imam, or 'Imaum.' The chief supreme of the Moslem faith. The Sunnites, or orthodox Moslims, use the title of 'Imam' as a synonym of calif, their spiritual and temporal head; but the Shiītes maintain that the true Imam was Ali, son-in-law of Mohammed, and his direct descendants: as Ali, Hassan, Hussein [sons of Ali], Ali-Seinolabiddin, Mohammed-Bakr, Giafar-el-Sadic, and Ismael, who died 730, leaving an infant son, named Mohammed, who was set aside for his uncle Mousa. This departure created a new schism. Those who followed the direct line called themselves Ismaelites, who separated from the Shiites or followers of Mousa. The Ismaelites maintain that Mohammed, one of these days, will manifest himself, but till then they will acknowledge no one as Imam.

The ordinary ministers of the Moslims are calle1 'Imams.' In Arabia certain chiefs are enti led Imams, and their territory an Imamat. *See* 'Mahdi.'

Imaum′ians (*The*). One of the numerous Shiite sects. They ins:st that the chief point of religious observance is to distinguish who is the true imaum or head of the Mohammedan Church. The people have no will in the matter. *See* 'Imam,' 'Khallabians,' 'Zeyds.'

Immaculate Conception (*The Religionists of*). Were a branch of the Franciscans, founded in Toledo, in 1484, by the venerable Beatrice of Sylva. They followed the rule of the Clarisses, with certain mitigations.

Immaculate Conceptionists. *See under* 'Franciscans.'

Immortal Princ:ples of 1789 (*The*). So the French denominate the principles enunciated by the Constituent

Assembly in their Declaration of Rights (*q.v.*), ' Déclaration des droits de l'homme et du citoyen,' 1 Oct. 1789. The chief were equal taxation for all classes; equal eligibility of all citizens to hold office in the state; unrestricted liberty to all.

As principles, these are anything but immortal. A tax of 4s. in the pound to all alike would be anything but equality of taxation. To a man who earns a pound a week it is a fifth of his earnings, to another who earns 40s. a week, it is a tenth part. To one who earns 4l. a week it is only a twentieth part, and so on. Equal objection lies against the other two 'immortal principles,' which would be more correctly denominated ' mortal folly.'

Impannation, *i.e.* ' consubstantiation.' Luther taught that the bread of the eucharist remained bread after consecration; but that by consecration the body of Christ was imparted to the bread, so that the communicants ate both bread and Christ at one and the same time. Catholics maintain that the bread is transmuted, and no longer remains bread at all. Most Protestants believe that no change takes place in the bread by consecration, but being devoted to God, like a church, it cannot be used for secular or ordinary purposes.

Krauth, in his 'Conservative Reformation,' affirms that Luther entertained the same views as the High Anglican party.

Imperial Chamber (*The*), 1495. The first law-court established in Germany. Instead of settling differences by the sword, the barons were commanded by the Diet of Augsburg (1495) to submit their grievances to the Imperial Chamber, which consisted of a president named by the crown, four judges, and fifty assessors.

The Aulic Council was instituted to prepare matters for the Council; but in 1654 the Aulic Council was recognised as equal to the Imperial Chamber.

Imperial Federation League (*The*), 28 July, 1884. For securing a permanent unity of the United Kingdom and its colonies.

Imperial Free Cities, in feudal times, were those built on the royal demesnes. In Germany they owed their origin to Heinrich I. (the Fowler), who granted them special privileges. *See* ' Church Cities ' and ' Ducal Towns.'

No one could open a shop in these towns without a licence, which was never granted to any except ' free burghers.' Those who were not town-free could only have their shops beyond the city walls.

Imperial Parliament (*The*), 22 Jan., 1801. George III. so called the parliament after the union with Ireland. *See* ' Parliament.'

Imperialists, or ' Melchites,' 537. A party of the Monoph´ysites (4 syl.) of Alexandria, supported by Justinian and favoured by the Empress Theodōra. *See* ' Corruptibles.'

They have ceased to be Monophysites, and are now Orthodox Greeks. They are still found in Egypt, but are very few.

Importants (*Les*), 1643. A political faction formed at the death of Louis XIII., consisting of those who had been ill-used by Richelieu, in the hope of obtaining justice under the new king. The chiefs were Les Guises, Les Vendômes, the Duc d'Epernon, the Duchess de Chevreuse and the Duchess de Montbazon. Besides these there were Potier bishop of Beauvais, and the Duc de Beaufort. To break up this cabal many of them were sent into exile, Beaufort was imprisoned, and the bishop was sent to his diocese. Most of the Importants took part in the Fronde (*q.v.*).

In Cam´era. With closed doors, the public not being permitted to be present.

It was directed that the inquiry should be conducted *in camera.—The Royal Liver Friendly Society*, Jan. 1886.

In Cœna Dom´ini, 1568. The famous Bull of Pius V. anathematising everyone who dared to question, limit, or abjure the absolute authority of the Holy See. It was specially directed against the League of Schmalkalden, a German Protestant association. Next year (1569) the pope excommunicated Queen Elizabeth, and absolved her subjects from their allegiance.

Thomas Erastus wrote a book entitled ' De Cœna Domini,' in which he contended for the figurative interpretation of the words ' This is My body,' &c. This Bull was read on Holy Thursday, called ' The day of the Lord's Supper,' whence its name.

In Eminenti (*The Bull*), 1642. By Urban VIII. in condemnation of the ' Augustinus ' of Cornelius Jansen.

The work was designed to prove that (judged by the Jesuit s standard) St. Augustine was unsound on the points of Grace, Free-will, and Predestination.

In Usum Sarum, 1078. The Salisbury Missal, drawn up by Oswald or Osmund bishop of Salisbury in the reign of Rufus. It is in Latin, and based on the Roman Missals.

There were numberless ' Uses' or Missals employed before the introduction of the Book of Common Prayer. Hence in the Introduction of that book we read : ' There hath been great diversity in saying and singing in churches within this realm : some following *Salisbury* Use, some *Hereford* Use, some the Use of *Bangor*, some of *York*, and some of *Lincoln*. But from henceforth all the whole realm shall have but one Use.'

Ina (*Laws of*), A.D. 692. Ina was king of Wessex, and promulgated a code of laws which was received over the whole heptarchy. By these laws the British proprietors were allowed to retain their lands; and alliances by marriage were encouraged between the natives and the Saxons.

Incammina'ti (*The*). The school of painting formed by the Carracci. The word means ' progressive,' and the Carracci school was eclectic, seeking to stamp out the exaggerations and mannerism of contemporary artists. It directed art to the study of nature and the best masters. The good taste of the Carracci is proverbial.

The Carracci were Ludovico (1554-1619), and his two cousins Annibale and Agostino ; the former died in 1609 at the age of 48, and the latter in 1602 at the age of 45. Annibale was the best artist of the three.

Incas. A Peruvian dynasty (1130-1571) which succeeded the Aymara dynasty, and was reigning when (in 1533) Pizarro conquered Peru. The Incas called themselves descendants of the Sun. The first Inca was Manco-Capac 1130, and his successors were Sinchi-Roca, Lloqui-Yupanqui, Mayta-Capac, Capac-Yupanqui, Roca, Yahuar-Huacac, Viracocha, Pachacutec, Yapanqui, Tupac-Yupanqui, Huayna-Capac, Huascar and Atahualpa (taken prisoners by the Spaniards and put to death in 1533). Tupac-Amaru was beheaded in 1571.

Incident (*The*), 1641. A supposed plot of Charles I. to kill or kidnap the Marquis of Hamilton and the Earl of Argyll, at the instigation of James Graham earl of Montrose. Charles I. contrived to win over James Graham, Earl of Montrose ; but when the Scotch Covenanters got wind of this treachery they arrested the earl and imprisoned him. While in prison he revealed to the king certain treasonable plots which he alleged were set on foot by Hamilton and Argyll, and he advised the king to summon the two Scotch noblemen ostensibly ' to a consultation ' ; but when they entered the ante-room armed men (headed by the Earl of Crawford) were to kidnap them, and carry them beyond the seas. If they resisted they were to be slain. The two noblemen escaped to their castles, and the king denied the scandal. The matter was privately investigated, and it was given out that the whole tale was a mare's nest ; but instead of punishing the supposed traitors the king created Hamilton a duke and Argyll a marquis. This strange ' Incident ' will be found in the ' Hardwicke Papers.'

Income Tax (*The*). Proposed by Pitt Dec. 1798, repealed 1802. Reimposed as a property tax 1803, abandoned 1816. Reimposed by Sir Robert Peel, 22 June, 1842, for three years, but continued at varying rates, from 2*d*. to 8*d*. in the pound, according to the exigencies of government.

The triennial renewals from 1842 were 1845, 1848, and 1851. In 1853 it was renewed for seven years and extended to Ireland. It was doubled in 1854, but in 1857 it was reduced, and incomes under 150*l*. a year were relieved.

Incorporated Society for Promoting English Protestant Schools in Ireland (*The*), 1733. Established by royal charter, for the education of the poor in Ireland in the principles of the Established Church. Grant reduced in 1824, and wholly withdrawn in 1832.

Incorruptible (*The*). I. Robespierre (1759, 1793-1794). Bouillet says : ' Robespierre était un homme froid, caché, tenace dans ses opinions, et dominant. Il affectait le plus pur patriotisme et tous les dehors de la vertu, ce qui l'avait surnommé par ses partisans *l'Incorruptible*.'

· Probably called the Incorruptible from his denunciations against corruption at the outbreak of the Revolution.

II. Fabricius the Roman hero, of whom Pyrrhus said : ' It would be easier to turn the sun from its course than Fabricius from his path of duty.'

III. William Shippen, of whom Horace Walpole said, ' he is the only man proof against a bribe.'

IV. Andrew Marvell, who refused a cheque for 1,000*l*., slipped into his hand by the Lord Treasurer Danby in 1673. The anecdote is given on p. 43, under the title of ' Aristides (*The British*).'

Incorruptible Lucas (*The*). Charles Lucas, who in 1746 (George II.'s reign) tried to abrogate the law of Charles II., which took the power of choosing the city magistrates of Ireland from the Irish commons, and vested it in the aldermen, thus virtually giving the election to the crown, because the aldermen were chosen by the privy council.

Incorruptibles (*The*), or 'Incorruptibilists,' 537–568. A branch of the Monoph'ysites of Alexandria which arose on the death of the patriarch Timothy. The leader was Gaian, a disciple of Julian—whence his followers were called *Gaianites*—a party supported by the monks and senators, the city and provinces. The Incorruptibles were opposed to the Corruptibles (*q.v.*), and so bitter the animosity between them that Alexandria was filled with the dead bodies of the factionists. Women from housetops hurled missiles against their religious opponents, and it is said that 200,000 Christians fell by the sword when Apollinarius was installed patriarch of Alexandria.

The Incorruptibles insisted that the body of Christ was a celestial body, and not a body of corruptible flesh like ours. The Corruptibles insisted on the perfect manhood of Christ.

Incroy'ables (*Les*). A class of young dandies during the time of the Directory. They affected great care in their dress, a refined manner of speech, and elegance of deportment—the very opposite of the sansculotte style of dress and manner affected by the revolutionary party. The Incroyables represented the reactionary party.

Under the Regent 'un Incroyable' was called *un talon rouge*; under Louis XIV., *un libertin*; under Henri III., *un mignon*; under Charles IX., *un raffiné*; under François I., *un muguet*. In 1886 he was called *un bécarre*; in 1887 *un copurchic*.

Indemnity (*Bill* or *Act of*). 12 Car. II. c. 11, 1660. A bill for the indemnity of all acts of treason and all state offences committed between 1 Jan., 1637, and 24 June, 1660.

II. 2 William and Mary c. 10, 20 May, 1690. Indemnity for the adherents of James II.

III. 7 Geo. III. c. 7, 16 Dec., 1766. Indemnity for the advisers of the embargo on the exportation of corn.

IV. 41 Geo. III. c. 66, 23 June, 1801. Indemnity for protecting authorities from penalties in respect to proceedings during the suspension of the Habeas Corpus Act.

V. 21 Vict. c. 1, 12 Dec., 1357. Indemnity for the infringement of the Currency Acts.

Independence (*Declaration of*), 4 July, 1776. *See* under 'Declaration.'

Independence Day, July. The Great National Holiday in the U.S. of North America.

Independent Methodists, 1810. Separatists from the old Methodist connection. Chiefly distinguished by their rejection of a paid ministry.

Independent Order of Good Templars (*The*), 1852. Seceders from the 'Order of Good Templars,' whose motto is 'Faith, Hope, and Charity.' It is a total abstinence society.

Independents, 1580. Those Christians who, in the reign of Elizabeth, protested against a state church. They maintain that each congregation is independent in the selection of its own minister and the laws of church membership and government; in contradistinction to Roman Catholics, Episcopalians, Presbyterians, and Methodists, who have no such freedom.

They were at first called Brownists from Robert Brown, a clergyman, 1580, and were not called Independents till 1610; but they attracted very little attention before the opening of the Long Parliament, when Hugh Peters returned from New England. The first Independent Synod was held in the Savoy (Strand) 29 Sept., 1658. *See* 'Brownists' and 'Congregationalists.'

. Besides Independents (who are more or less Calvinistic), there are the Independent Methodists, the Independent Religious Reformers, the Independent Unionists, &c. In 1730 was formed the association of the *Three Denominations*: Independents, Presbyterians, and Baptists.

Independents and Presbyterians, 1647. Two political parties in English history which sprang up during the Civil war. The Independents were the parliamentarians, but the Presbyterians were disposed to make terms with the king and the royalists. In 1680 the Independents were called Whigs and the royalists Tories. Since the middle of the 19th cent. the words Liberal and Conservative have well-nigh superseded those of Whig and Tory.

Independents' Declaration of Faith (*The*). Their confession of faith, contained in 33 articles, 12 Oct., 1658.

Index. The first index to a book was by Valerius Soranus. Pliny says that he himself gave an index to his 'Natural History,' adding these words: 'Valerius Soranus, one of our Latin authors, had done the like before me.'

Index Expurgato'rius, or 'Index Librorum Expurgandorum,' 1557. Issued by Paul IV. A list of books forbidden to be read by Catholics. The books of all heresiarchs, whatever the subject, are forbidden; all books of an heretical tendency, and all versions of the Bible by 'heretics.' The list was made out originally by the Congregation of the Inquisition of Rome, but Pius V. appointed a special 'Congregation of the Index.' *See* next article.

Index Librorum Prohibitorum. In May 1825 Sir Robert Inglis, speaking in the House of Commons, said : 'I hold in my hand the "Index Librorum Prohibitorum" (a list of books proscribed by the Catholic Church under the penalties of the Inquisition). It was printed at Rome by authority in 1819, and I bought it there in 1821.' The first book on the list is 'Bacon, De Augmentis Scientiarum.' Then follow 'Locke, on the Human Understanding,' Cudworth's 'Intellectual System,' Milton's 'Paradise Lost' . . . 'Algarotte On the Newtonian System,' &c. This is also called the 'Index of the Court of Rome,' or briefly the 'Index.' Many of the books of Descartes, Malebranche, Fleury, Fénelon, with all Calvin's, Luther's, and Voltaire's, are in the Index—Gibbon, Robertson, Sismondi, Hallam, Goldsmith's 'History of England,' Kant, T. S. Mill, Whately's 'Logic,' Dante, Addison, &c. Some little tales for children are banned in the Index, as, for instance, 'Little Henry and his Bearer.'

Sir Robert says that Jacquier, the editor of Newton's 'Principia,' wrote on the fly-leaf 'Newtonus, in tertio libro, Telluris motæ hypothesim assumit . . . Cæterum latis a summis pontificibus contra. telluris motum decretis nos obsequi profitemur. 1739.'

Indian File (*In*). In single file; one at a time; as North American Indians go on an attack, the one behind treading exactly in the footsteps of the man before him, the last man carefully obliterating the footprints.

Indian Mutiny (*The*), 1857, 1858. It began by mutinies of the Sepoys at Barrackpore and Berhampore, between 24 Jan. and 6 May, 1857; the Meerut massacre (*q.v.*) occurred 10 May, the mutiny at Delhi 11 May, the mutiny at Lucknow 30 May, at Benares 4 June, at Allahabad and Cawnpore 5 June. War over June 1858. Also called the 'Sepoy War.' *See* 'Greased Cartridges.'

In fact, the mutiny was virtually crushed in seven months, and by the close of 1857 the Bengal Army and East Indian Company ceased to exist.

India'na (U.S. America). So called in 1802 from the number of Indians who had flocked thither. A French settlement in 1702; a separate territory in 1800; admitted to the Union in 1816. The nickname given to the inhabitants o Indiana is *Hoosiers.*

Indiction. I. In *chronology* means a period of fifteen years. The Indiction of Constantinople begins 1 Sept., 312, the date of Constantine's victory over Maxentius. This epoch is still preserved in papal bulls, because then Christianity was first recognised by the state. But the Papal Indiction begins on 1 Jan., 313.

Divide the date by 15 and it will give the number of indictions, the remainder being the years over. Thus 1890 ÷ 15 gives 126 indictions exactly.

II. In *political history* it means the recurrence of 15 years when the emperor of the East revised and reimposed the imposts of his empire. The word means the imperial *edict.*

Indolent Dick. Richard Cromwell, son of Oliver Cromwell (1626–1712).

Induction—Institution. Induction is the investing of a clergyman with the *temporalities* of a benefice or living. Institution is the investing him with its spiritualities. If a bishop is the patron of a benefice the two ceremonies are united in what is termed 'collation' to the living.

Inductive Philosophy (*The Father of*). Francis Bacon lord Verulam (1561-1626).

'Inductive philosophy' is inferring general principles from data. *Deductive* philosophy goes the other way about; it begins with general principles and then presumes what these principles involve. One is the *à posteriori* process, and the other is the *à priori* one. All 'science' follows the *inductive* or Baconian plan. 'Theology' still adheres to the *deductive* system.

Indulgence (*An*). A Papal Indulgence was a grace given or sold by the pope, or someone authorised by him, granting either partial or plenary immunity of sin for some meritorious act, on payment of a sum of money. The price of these notes-of-hand varied from 20*d*. to 10*l*. In a captured vessel 500 bales of indulgences, each containing a million, were found during the Reformation period in Germany. Tetzel, the great hawker of indulgences, went about like a cheap Jack, crying in the streets of German towns: 'The very moment the ring of the cash is heard in the basin St. Peter will throw open the gates of paradise to the buyer; and if for the dead, the soul will be instantly taken from purgatory to Abraham's bosom.' We first hear of indulgences in Nov., 1095, granted by the Council of Clermont to crusaders. Next on 2 Feb., 1300, granted by Pope Boniface VIII. to pilgrims visiting Rome at the Jubilee. Again 27 Jan., 1343, granted by Clement VI. Again in 1411, granted by John XXIII. to those who joined the crusade against Ladislaus king of Naples. But the sale of indulgences authorised by Leo X. for raising money to complete the cathedral of St. Peter at Rome was so barefaced a traffic in sin that Luther made capital out of it for his reformation plea; and no worse agent could have been employed than the charlatan Tetzel. The Council of Trent in Dec. 1563 restricted the grace by fixed laws.

Samson, a hawker of indulgences in Switzerland, roused the indignation of Zwingli the reformer, just as Tetzel roused Luther. The following is an exact translation of one of these diplomas, a few words being omitted where the dots are made for the sake of brevity: 'May the Lord have mercy on thee, and absolve thee by the merits of his most holy passion! And I, by God's authority, do hereby absolve thee from all ecclesiastical censures . . . and from all sins . . . how enormous soever they may be . . . and I remit to thee all the punishment which those sins have deserved. I restore thee to the holy sacraments of the church, to the communion of saints, and to perfect innocence of life; so that when thou diest, the gates of hell shall be shut, and those of paradise be thrown open to these . . . In the name of the Father, and of the Son, and of the Holy Ghost.'
The enormous impudence of this traffic almost exceeds belief. Through the Netherlands the price current of these indulgences was published in every town and village. God's pardon for crimes already committed, or about to be committed, was advertised according to a graduated tariff. Poisoning was absolved for eleven ducats (about 50s.).—MOTLEY, *Dutch Republic*, vol. i. p. 73.

Indulgence to Scotch ministers, 1668, whereby the ejected ministers were readmitted to their livings if they accepted collation from the bishop, and would attend the presbyteries and synods. This was the Earl of Tweeddale's Act.

1670. Lauderdale offered indulgence to all ministers who would take the oath of supremacy and acknowledge the bishops.

1673. Lauderdale named eighty ejected ministers, and ordered them to officiate

in their own churches, but nowhere else; but one-fourth of them refused the offer. *See under* 'Declaration.'

Indulgences (*Tariff of*). From 'The Tax of the Sacred Roman Chancery' :—

Adultery 40s. (joint pardon).
Arson, or setting fire to a house, 11s.
Forgery 8s.
Fornication 8s.
Incest by a priest 40s. (joint pardon).
Keeping a concubine, a priest 9s.
Murder of a layman 4s.
Perjury or lying 8s.
Procuring abortion 6s.
Rape 40s. (joint pardon).
Robbery 12s.
Robbing a church 8s.
Striking a priest 11s.

Of this list 'Robbery' and 'Robbing a church' seem the most extraordinary.

Industrial Schools. Generally means 'Ragged Schools,' in which writing, reading, and arithmetic are taught, with mechanical arts, and in which the children are clothed and fed. They scarcely existed till 1857, and were not finally established till 1866.

In *Scotland* they were established by act of parliament in 1861.

In *Ireland* in 1868.

Private enterprise opened such schools before these dates, but the first act of parliament bearing on the subject was 20, 21 Vict. c. 48.

Indus'trialists (*The*), about 1800. A school founded by St. Simon for the amelioration of the people. He taught that producers are the only aristocracy, and if men would not work neither should they eat. After the death of St. Simon in 1825 the society became political and communistic. In 1825 they called themselves 'St. Simonians,' and in 1833 were abolished by law.

Inexpiable War (*The*), or 'The War without Truce' (B.C. 240–236). A war which sprang up immediately after the First Punic War. It was headed by Matho, a Libyan, who had been very forward in urging the Carthaginian soldiers to demand their pay. The insurgents kept the Carthaginians at bay for more than three years, when Hamilcar reduced them to famine in Tunis; a *sortie* was made, Matho was taken prisoner and put to death, and the war was brought to a close.

Infallibility of the Church of Rome means the moral impossibility of the church ever sanctioning the introduction of a false doctrine, as well as perfect immunity of all errors at all times. Our Lord said (Matt. xvi. 18), ' Thou art Peter, and upon this rock will I build my church; and the gates of hell shall not prevail against it.' Not only is the church the *fons et origo* of doctrine, but it is deputed to carry its teaching throughout the world (Matt. xxviii. 19, Mark xvi. 15, Eph. iv. 11–16).

Of course the main question is what is meant by the Catholic Church ? And the answer is the consensus of the pope and bishops either expressly delivered by ecumenical councils, or tacitly accepted on questions of doctrine or discipline, no matter from whence they originally emanated.

What is called the Infallibility of the Pope, or, in other words, whether the pope alone, as pope, is capable of pronouncing an infallible judgment, was a moot point for many hundreds of years between Gallican and Ultramontane divines. The right was first claimed in 750, but was not made an article of faith till 1870, when it caused a rift in the Catholic Church.

In the 19th Art. of the Church of England we read : 'As the Church of Hierusalem, Alexandria, and Antioch have erred, so also the Church of Rome hath erred—not only in their living and manner of ceremonies, but also in matters of faith.'

⁂ The Catholic Church distinctly repudiates any infallible judgment in historical and scientific matters.

Infallibility of the Pope. This dogma in 1870 was rejected by a party which termed themselves ' Old Catholics.' They also denied the ecumenical character of the Vatican Council, and rejected the Vatican decrees.

Infant Stockbroker (*The*). Sidney Herbert Cronmire, aged twenty in 1886, when he was charged with misappropriating cheques which had been sent him for specified investments by gentlemen residing at Bridgewater. The ' Infant ' was arrested in Spain, and pleaded guilty.

Infant of Lübeck (*The*). Christian Heinrich Heinecken (1721–1725). If what is told us of this unhappy child is true, it is the most pitiable instance of precocity on record. His life was written by his tutor Schöneich.

We are told that he spoke when only a month old; that at twelve months of age he knew the chief events of the Pentateuch; at thirteen months he knew the history of the whole Old Testament; at fourteen months the history of the New Testament; at two and a half years he could answer any general question of history or geography; at three years old he knew French and Latin as familiarly as he knew German, although he was not then weaned (!!). He died between four and five.

⁂ More marvellous still, the infant prodigy John Philipp Baratier was born at Schwabach near Nürnberg the same year (!!), 1721–1740. Of this latter prodigy there is no doubt.

Infante (mas. 3 syl.), **Infanta** (fem.). Titles given in Spain and Portugal to all the princes and princesses of the blood royal, except the heir or heiress apparent.

The heir apparent of Spain is called the Prince of Asturias. The heiress *presumptive* is entitled Infanta. In Portugal the heir or heiress apparent is called the ' Prince ' or ' Princess Royal.'

Infantry. Foot soldiers. 'Infantry' originally meant a particular army of foot soldiers, raised by the *Infante* or heir-apparent of Spain to rescue his father from the Moors, and is about equal to our phrase 'the Prince of Wales's Own.' The infantry was the Infante's own. We have applied the particular term to foot soldiers generally. Like calling all foot soldiers 'the Prince of Wales's Own.'

Infernal Columns (*The*), 1793. Republican detachments in the Vendéan war. So called from their diabolical barbarity. They murdered all, even children at the breasts, and as they advanced set the houses and country on fire.

Infernal Machines.

I. 21 Dec., 1800. A machine planted by the Chouans in the Rue St. Nicaise to blow up Napoleon Bonaparte on his return from Italy. As Bonaparte drew near, the barrel hung fire; but scarcely had he passed the spot when it exploded, shattered the windows of his carriage, and injured several persons in the crowd.

II. 28 July, 1835. Discharged from a window at Louis-Philippe king of the French as he was riding on horseback with his three sons down the Boulevard du Temple (Paris). Marshal Mortier, General de Virigny, and twelve others, including a child, were killed, but Louis-Philippe was uninjured. The assassin was Fieschi. a Corsican, formerly a soldier and a police spy. Fieschi, Peppin, and Morey were executed; Boireau was sentenced to imprisonment for twenty years, but Bescher was acquitted.

The projectile of Orsini thrown at Napoleon III., 14 Jan., 1858, was a species of bombshell; that which assassinated Czar Alexander II., 13 March, 1881, was a dynamite bomb, thrown at his carriage by Nihilists.

Infrancesa'dos, 1808. Those Spanish grandees who traitorously favoured the French usurpation of the Spanish crown and the appointment of Joseph Bonaparte as his brother Napoleon's viceroy king. Also called 'Josephi'nos' (*q.v.*).

Influenza. An epidemic catarrh. Appeared in Europe in 1510, 1557, 1580.
Very fatal in *London* in 1729, and in Russia in 1781, 1782.
It has appeared in England in 1782, 1803, 1831, 1833, 1836, 1837, 1889.

The word means an epidemic due to the influence of the planets; under the notion that it is connected with volcanic action.

Ing'hamites (3 syl.). Christian followers of Mr. Benjamin Ingham, son-in-law of the Countess of Huntingdon.

Injunctions (*Royal*), 1535. It was commanded that no lectures should be given in the Universities on the 'Sentences' (*q.v.*), or on Canon Law; but that Greek, Latin, and Divinity should be taught in addition to the Trivium (*q.v.*) and Quadrivium (*q.v.*).

Injunctions of Edward VI. (*The*), 1547. Commands issued to the Commissioners appointed by Cranmer to make a visitation of all England. They enjoined that all images, shrines, candlesticks, pictures, representations of miracles, &c., in windows and elsewhere, be removed and destroyed; that all processions and pilgrimages be discontinued; that the Creed, the Lord's Prayer, the Ten Commandments be repeated when there is no sermon; that the Epistle and Gospel be read in English; that the Litany be said or sung kneeling; that the bidding prayer be used as prescribed. Under penalty of excommunication, sequestration, or deprivation.

Injunctions of Elizabeth (*The*), 1559. They were fifty-three in number. Most were similar to those of Edward VI., but some new regulations were added respecting the marriage of the clergy; chanting and singing were allowed in divine services; reverence was enjoined at the name of Jesus; all were required to kneel during the Litany and all collects; the wafer in the eucharist was to be dispensed with; and the oath of supremacy was to be explained as disavowing all claim to any authority in the divine service or the sacred functions of the church.

Injunctions of Mary (*The*), 1554. Restoring to the ecclesiastical courts their jurisdictions; enforcing the celibacy of the clergy, and insisting that all married clergymen should put away their wives; abolishing the oath of Royal supremacy; restoring the Latin tongue in all church services; forbidding Protestants to be schoolmasters; and commanding that a new set of homilies be at once prepared to secure uniformity of doctrine and practice.

Injunctions of William and Mary (*The*), Feb. 1695. Under the advice of Archbishop Tenison, for the maintenance of church discipline. They were followed by 'Directions' for unity of opinion on the doctrine of the Trinity.

Innocent Papists. Those Catholics of Ireland who could prove to the satisfaction of the commissioners that they had never acted with the confederates, never adhered to the pope's nuncio, had never been absolved for taking part directly or indirectly in the Irish rebellion (*q.v.*), that they did not derive their title to the estates claimed from persons who had been guilty of the offences mentioned above, that they had never held any correspondence with any person who had concurred in the rebellion, that they never had taken any part in their councils, never employed any agent directly or indirectly to treat with a foreign power, never been a Tory, *i.e.* a marauder, &c. It was almost impossible to find such a papist in all Ireland.

Innocents. Those Irish who had been transplanted by Cromwell merely for their religion, and not for rebellion or any political offence. These Irish at the Restoration were by the Act of Settlement to be restored to their estates, and the displaced tenant was to be indemnified by some other tenement.

Innocents' Day, or 'Festum Innocentium,' 28 Dec. To commemorate the slaughter of the babes of Bethlehem by Herod the Great, with the view of killing thereby the infant Jesus.

Inns of Chancery. Ten schools between the City of London and Westminster, for law students, founded in the reign of Edward III. Originally meant for preparatory colleges for young students, and each school was attended by 100 students at least. Now they are for the most part occupied by solicitors, &c. *See* 'London University.'

Inquisitio Eliensis. The doomsday of the lands of the monastery of Ely, contained in the counties of Cambridge, Herts, Essex, Norfolk, Suffolk, and Huntingdon. Published by Sir Henry Ellis (1816) in the second of the two supplementary volumes of 'Domesday Book.'

Inquisition (*The*), or 'The Holy Office,' 1232. A tribunal erected by the popes for the examination and punishment of heretics. The chief inquisitors were the Dominicans. The Inquisition tried the suspects, and when condemned handed them over to the civil powers to be punished. Introduced into Spain in 1248; established in Portugal in 1543. Abolished in Portugal by the Cortes between 1818 and 1826. Extinguished by royal decree in Spain 1835.

Strictly speaking it originated with Innocent III., who (in 1203) granted a commission for the conversion of the Albigenses. The jurisdiction of the courts of the Inquisition were defined and regulated by Gregory IX. in 1232 or 1233. The modern Spanish Inquisition was constituted by Ferdinand and Isabella in 1480, and suppressed in 1820.

Inquisition of Goa, in the Indies (*The*). A very powerful tribunal for the trial of 'heretics.' Those sentenced to die were clad in much the same way as in Portugal. *See* 'Santo Benito.' Such as are convicted of magic wear paper sugarloafed caps covered with flames and devils. All the 'heretics' go in procession to the church chosen for the ceremony; they go barefooted, carrying lighted tapers in their hands; the least guilty go first, then comes one carrying a cross, and then those condemned to die. The day after the execution the head of each person burnt to death is exhibited in a picture rudely executed, surrounded with flames, and underneath is written the name and quality of the person thus represented. Abolished.

Inquisition of Rome (*The*), or 'The Congregation of the Holy Office,' 1543. Founded by the Bull of Paul III. It consisted of twelve cardinals and some inferior officers, but the pope himself presided. Its standard is of red damask, on which is delineated a cross, with an olive branch on one side and a sword on the other. The motto is 'Exurge, Domine, et judica causam meam' (Ps. lxxiii.).

Inquisition of Venice (*The*). Consisted of the resident nuncio, the patriarch of Venice, the father inquisitor, and two senators. This Inquisition was nothing like so severe as the Inquisitions of Spain and Portugal. It took no notice of Greeks and Armenians, and tolerated Jews, who wore a scarlet cap as a badge. Heretics were allowed to take their degrees in law and physic, and were not interfered with by this tribunal. Abolished by Napoleon in 1808.

Inquisitor of Atheists (*The*). J. André Naigeon (1738–1810), so called from his intolerance.

Inquisitori del Doge Defunto (*The*). Three magistrates of Venice whose duty was to examine into the administration of deceased doges, to compare their acts with the provisions of their oath, to inquire into charges brought against them, and if the charges were proved, to make their heirs responsible for reparations.

Inquisitors (*The State*), 16 June, 1454. Three persons chosen by the Council of Ten in Venice, with dictatorial powers; two were of *I Neri* (the Blacks, *i.e.* The Ten), and one was *Il Rosso* (the Reds, or the Council of the Doge). These inquisitors were invested with plenary authority over every person in the republic, noble or citizen, magistrate or ecclesiastic. The penalties they might inflict were wholly optional, and the trials of offenders were public or secret. They kept the keys of the treasury, and were accountable to no one for their expenditures. All commanders, ambassadors, and governors addressed themselves to the Three. They made their own laws and rescinded them as they liked; and to prevent the inviolability of secrecy, no one who had an ecclesiastic directly or indirectly among his connexions was eligible to the office of inqui-

G G

sitor. It is needless to add that the history of this Inquisition exceeds in infamy and cruelty any tribunal the world ever established.

I. N. R. I. Jesus of Nazareth, King of the Jews. Inscription over the crucifix (Jesus Nazarēnus Rex Judæōrum).

Insabbata'ti, or 'Insabbates' (4 syl.), 12th cent. The Waldenses are over and over again called 'Inzabatati' in the council held at Tarragon in 1242. Probably the word means 'shoeless.' They are also called 'Sabbatati' (*q.v.*). Eberhard de Bethune is the first authority for the word.

In opposition to the 'shoeless' explanation, Father Natalis says, they [the Waldenses] celebrate no sabbath or feast day, and do not abstain from work even on days consecrated to the Virgin and the blessed saints.—P. NATALIS ALEXANDER, vol. vii. pp. 94, 95.

Inspection (*An*). In the Lutheran communion means. a synod of five consistorial churches; called a synod in the Calvinist communion. *See* 'Consistorial.'

Instance, in French law, means *stare in judicio*, to be under judgment (*instantia*); and a process is *en instance* when it is brought before a jurisdiction.

First Instance is the jurisdiction 'qui doit connaître en premier ressort de la décision d'une affaire'; whence the civil tribunals before which processes are first brought are called 'Courts of First Instance' (*tribunaux de première instance*).

Second Instance means the jurisdiction of the appeal, or of the second degree.

Reprise d'instance is resuming a suit which has been interrupted by the death of one of the parties, the retirement or withdrawal of the advocate, or some such cause.

We also find the phrases *L'instance liée contradictoirement* (qui a lieu lorsque les *deux* parties comparaissent ensemble); and *L'instance par défaut* (qui se poursuit lorsque le *défendeur* ne se présente pas sur l'assignation qui lui a été donnée).

Institute of France. Constituted in 1795 as the 'Institut National' by the union of the French Academy, the Academy of Inscriptions, and the Academy of Arts and Sciences. The constitution was revised in 1803 by Napoleon Bonaparte. Louis Philippe in 1832 added to it a class of moral and political sciences.

Institutes (3 syl.). The elements of Roman law, composed by Tribonian, Theophilus, and Dorotheus, A.D. 533. Divided into four books, each book subdivided into chapters, and each chapter into paragraphs.

Institutes of Ghazan or Kasan (*The*), 1295–1304. The 'commentary' of Ghazan, or Kasan, sultan of Persia, compiled from several sources. These Institutes are still held in honour in the East.

Institution, Induction, and Collation. Institution is investiture of the spiritualities of a benefice. Induction is investiture of its temporalities. Collation is the union of the two investitures. Thus a person collated to a living is both instituted and inducted.

Instrument of Government (*The*), 1653. Spoken of generally as 'The Instrument.' A new English constitution drawn up by the Council of State nominated by the Barebone Parliament (*q.v.*), and accepted by the Council of Officers. The house was to consist of 400 members from England, 30 from Scotland, and 30 from Ireland. The seats hitherto assigned to small and rotten boroughs were transferred to larger constituencies; all special rights of voting for members were abolished, and the franchise was given to holders of property to the value of 200*l.* and upwards. Catholics and Malignants (*q.v.*) were excluded. Cromwell was made Lord Protector, but his power was strictly limited. The members of the council were all named by him, but no member could be removed except by the consent of the council itself. With the council rested the power of peace and war, the choice of all officers civil and military, and the election of protectors. Parliaments were to last three years, and three years only. All taxes were to be imposed by parliament only.

*** The *conditions* which Cromwell swore to observe when appointed the Lord Protector were as follows: (1) The legislative power to be vested in a lord protector and parliament; (2) the executive power to reside in the lord protector acting with the advice of his ·council; (3) no laws to be made or taxes to be levied without consent of parliament; (4) the civil list to be fixed at

200,000*l.* a year, and the army to be 30,000 men, two-thirds of which to be infantry; (5) all religious persuasions to be protected except prelatists and papists; (6) the successor of Cromwell to be selected by council.

They proceeded with the revision of 'the Instrument'; and their labours were embodied in a bill, which was read a third time 1655. — Dr. LINGARD, *History of England*, viii. 6.

Insulated Abbots. Abbots of independent or liberated abbeys, who acknowledged no lord but the pope. In the middle ages these abbots frequently enjoyed episcopal titles, but very few had dioceses.

Insurrection Act (*The*) of 1796. Giving the lord-lieutenant of Ireland power to proclaim any county or district of Ireland, on the requisition of seven magistrates; and to seize, imprison, and send on board His Majesty's fleet persons found in an unlawful assembly or in any way imperilling the public peace.

Insurrection of June (*The*), 23, 24, 25 June, 1848. This was a war against society, against law, against property; and was produced by the closing of the national workshops of Paris, the expense of which cost the government 40,000*l.* a week. Two million and eighty thousand pounds annually to maintain lazy, worthless operatives, who planned rebellion and diffused discontent!

Insurrection of La Vendée (*The*), March 1793. The Vendeans, a very primitive people, had no sympathy with the French Revolution, so the gentry and clergy organised an army to resist the dangerous innovations. They defeated every army sent against them for a time, but at length were obliged to succumb. All who took part in the insurrection were outlawed, and their property confiscated. M. Prudhomme informs us that 937,000 persons perished in this savage butchery.

Insurrection of Ragots'ki (*The*), 1703–1713. He declared himself protector of Poland and prince of Transylvania; but in 1713 the Austrians compelled him to retire. He died 1735.

Insurrection of the Duchesse de Berry (*The*), 1832. The last Chouan *émeute* made with a view of placing Henri [*Cinq*] on the throne of France.

The duchess was the widow of the assassinated Duc de Bordeaux and mother of Henri V. Her insurrection was very romantic, and the duchess, being taken prisoner, would have been put to death had she not been *enceinte*.

Insurrection of the Yellow Caps (*The*), A.D. 220. Tchang-kio of China persuaded the multitude that he could cure them of a pestilential disease which was then prevalent. He thereby soon acquired a large following of some 500,000 men. These he persuaded to adopt as a badge the yellow cap, and then he assumed regal power. The whole military strength of China was sent against the rebels; and though at first the mob gained certain advantages, ere long the regular troops prevailed, and the insurgents were routed with great slaughter.

Intellectual Artist (*The*). Nicolas Poussin (1594–1665). Famous for his classic costumes.

Intendants Militaires. A corps charged with all things which concern the administration and ' comptability' of war. They are named by the minister of the war department. They were established in France in 1817 in substitution of the inspectors of revenue and commissioners of war. The corps consists of 28 intendants (who rank next to generals) and 140 sub-intendants.

Pronounce *Ahn-tahn-dahn me-le-tair.*

Intendants of a Province (*The*). Magistrates, administrative, judicial, and financial, who exercise their functions in each *généralité* (*q.v.*). The chamber in which they meet is called the 'Intendance. ' The first intendants of a province were established by Henri II. in 1551. They were suppressed in 1790.

A ' generality' is the jurisdiction of an intendant-general.

Intercursus Magnus. The treaty made by Henry VII. with the Flemings. In 1496 Henry made a less liberal treaty, which was branded as the Intercursus Malus.

Interdiction of Fire and Water. ' Aquæ et ignis interdictio.' The form used by the Romans in their judicial sentence of banishment from Italy; the person thus interdicted might go anywhere he chose provided he left Italy.

Interim (*The*), or 'Formula ad Interim,' 1548. When Charles V. saw that the pope removed the Council of Trent to Bologna, he believed that he only sought time to stave off a decision on the knotty points of the day; and, in order to preserve peace in his kingdom, he made a provisionary arrangement with the Protestants appointed, which was to be in force till the council was actually summoned. By this 'Interim' or provisionary arrangement, the cup was allowed to the laity in the Lord's Supper, and the clergy were allowed to marry. This concession pleased neither party, and the Interim fell through by the 'Treaty of Passau,' which secured full and perfect liberty to all in matters of religion (1552).

Passau, pronounce *Pas-sow*—'ow' as in 'now.'

International Law (*Professorship of*), 1867. Founded by Dr. Whewell, master of Trinity College. Salary 500*l*. See 'Regius Professorship of Civil Law.'

Whewell, pronounce *You'-el.*

Interregnum (*The English*). From 23 Dec., 1688 (the abdication) to 13 Feb., 1689, when parliament assented to the accession of William and Mary.

William III. was son-in-law and Mary was daughter of James II.

Introit, or 'Introïtus.' The psalm or passage of scripture chanted in the Catholic Church while the priest is entering the chancel to celebrate mass. Such terms as *Reminiscere* Sunday, *Oculi* Sunday, *Lætare* Sunday, *Quasimodo* Sunday, &c. are so called from the beginning words of the introitus.

Intrusionists and Non-Intrusionists, 1835. The two Scotch parties called into existence by the 'Veto Act,' passed by the General Assembly, whereby the nomination of a patron to a living might be voided by veto. They were also called 'Highfliers,' and 'Moderates.' Intrusionists are those who regarded the veto as an illegal intrusion or interference with the rights of a patron to present to a living. See 'Veto Act.'

Invasion of England (*Threatened*).

1386. Charles VI. of France was persuaded by his uncles to invade England, and a formidable army of 40,000 men was assembled in Flanders for the purpose. Every knight provided himself with a pillard, or man to collect pillage for him, and an enormous tent called a cité was constructed under the direction of Oliver de Clisson, the lord high constable. This monster tent, which took to pieces, would enclose a space of 8,000 sq. ft. and required 72 vessels to convey it across the Channel. When all was ready for sailing the king was wasting his time in dissipation. When the king arrived he had to wait for his uncle the Duc de Berry. And when the duke arrived the king changed his mind and gave up the expedition. The army was disbanded, the stores were pillaged, and the monster tent, having drifted to the Thames, became the prey of English mariners.

1803. Bonaparte, mad with England for daring to beard him, and determined to make a descent on the island, assembled a formidable army on the northern coast, where he formed his famous 'Camp de Boulogne,' constructed above 2,000 gun-boats and flat transports, and increased his military stores and munitions of war, but ultimately deferred his descent till the next spring (1804). When next spring arrived Bonaparte had changed his mind, and the invasion of England was set aside for his coronation as Emperor of the French.

The Column of Boulogne was erected to perpetuate the memory of this grand preparation. There is a wonderful resemblance in these two threatened invasions, that of Charles VI. in 1386, and that of Bonaparte in 1803. *See* 'Armada.'

Invention of the Cross (*The*). An annual fête (3 May) held in the Catholic Church to celebrate the 'discovery of the true cross' in a cave by Helēna mother of Constantine. She was 80 years of age at the time, and was told where to find the three crosses by one Judas, a monk of Jerusalem. The true cross of the three was discovered because when a sick woman was touched by the other two the contact had no effect on her, but immediately the true cross touched her she was restored to perfect health. This 'Invention' dates from 326.

Investiture, 1052–1122. Kaiser Heinrich III. was the first to give a ring and crozier to a bishop on his consecration, as a symbol of investiture, or grant of episcopal temporalities in his dominions. The innovation was like a bombshell, and for seventy years pope and king contended about the prerogative. No pope can give away lands and buildings in another man's empire, and no king can confer office in a 'kingdom not of this world.' At last, in 1122, the moot point was settled thus: the pope was to consecrate, and then the bishop was ·to do homage to the king for the temporalities of his diocese. The pope invested with ring and crozier, and the king with a sceptre.

Investiture in Carinthia. This was a nominal purchase, and evidently referred to a time when the land belonged to the people. On the day of inauguration the peasant appointed for the purpose seated himself on a marble block beneath a tree, and the new duke, dressed as a countryman, approached on foot, carrying a crook, a spade, and a wallet of bread and cheese. Two noblemen on foot attended as his sponsors. 'Who are these?' asked the peasant of the crowd. 'The prince of the country,' was the reply. 'Is he a good man and true?' demanded the peasant. 'He is,' was the answer. 'Then, by what right will he push me from my stool?' asked the peasant. 'He will buy it of thee,' said the crowd. 'For how much?' 'For sixty pence.' Whereupon the peasant rose, and the duke took his place, paying sixty pence into the hand of the peasant, who also received as a perquisite the clothes worn by the duke, and was exempt from rent and taxes. Soon as the duke was seated, his vassals paid him homage, and the duke promised to deal even justice to all. The duke then proceeded to church to hear mass, and ended the day with a banquet.

Investiture of Vassals (*The*). The lord having received homage and the oath of fealty (*q.v.*) invested his 'man' with the fief by delivering to him the old banners belonging thereto. There were often several of these banners, because every large fief contained several smaller ones, each of which had its own banner. The chief threw the old banners into the crowd to be torn to pieces, and then presented his dependents with new ones emblazoned with arms of the new fief, by accepting which the dependents acknowledged the suzerainty of their new lord.

Invincible (*The*). Cosmo de' Medici was called 'the Great and the Invincible' (1389–1464). He was also called the 'father of his country.'

Invincible (*The*). The Russian general Suwarof or Suworof (1730–1800). His full name, &c. was Alexander Vassilivich Suwarof-Rymnikski, count, prince Italinski, field-marshal, generalissimo of the Russian army.

Invincible Doctor (*The*). 'Doctor Singularis et Invincibilis,' William of Occam, in Surrey (1270–1347), Provincial of the English Cordeliers. He was excommunicated by Pope John XXII. for writing a book against the secular power of the pope, 'Super potestate summi pontificis.' *See* 'Doctors,' &c.

Peter Tome was also called 'Doctor Invincibilis.'

Invincibles (*The*). I. The French legion, whose exploits in Italy under Bonaparte were so astounding. This legion was almost annihilated in Egypt by Abercrombie in 1801.

II. Irish sicārii. *See* 'Irish Invincibles.'

Invisible Commander (*The*). Lord Raglan commander-in-chief of the British army in the Crimean war. The sufferings of the soldiers in the winter of 1854–5 were very great, and the anger of the nation was bitter against Lord Raglan, but somewhat unjustly so.

Invisible Prince (*The*). William John Cavendish Scott Bentinck 5th duke of Portland (1800–1879), famous for his enormous excavations and palatial buildings underground. At one time he employed 1,000 artificers on his estate to make himself invisible. A tunnel was made across the park for the workmen to pass to and fro without intruding on his seclusion. He also constructed tunnels in the abbey, by which he could pass from one building to another without being seen, and a tunnel leads to the riding school.

Invisible Three (*The*), or State Inquisitors of Venice. *See* 'Inquisitors,' &c. Called 'invisible' because no inquisitor was publicly known. All its citations and acts were done in the name of the Ten. All its judgments were pronounced by the mouths of the secretaries.

Invisibles (*The*). I. The Rosicrucians. So called because they never showed themselves in public in open day.

II. The disciples of Illyricus, Flaccus, Osiander, &c., who denied the perpetual visibility of the church.

Io'nian Republic (*The*). Founded 1815; consisting of the seven islands: Cephalonia, Cerigo, Corfu, Paxo, Santa Maura, Theaki, and Zantè; all placed under the protection of Great Britain by treaty with Russia. Ceded to Greece 1864.

Cerigo, pronounce *Cherry-go*. Corfu, pronounce *Kor-foo'*.

Io'nian War(*The*),B.C.501–492. Began with the revolt of Aristagŏras, who obtained help from Athens and Eretria in 500. Athens and Eretria left the confederacy B.C. 499. Aristagoras was slain in Thrace B.C. 497. And in 492 Ionia was completely subjugated by Persia.

Io'nians (*The*). Had twelve great cities on the north coast of the Peloponnesus and twelve colonies in Asia Minor, with several islands. Ephesus, Smyrna, Milētus, and Samos belonged to the twelve confederated Ionian colonies.

Ion'ic Letters. The four added to the Greek alphabet by Simonīdês of Cos ($ζ$, $θ$, $φ$, $χ$), and the four added by Epicharmos the Sicilian ($ξ$, $η$, $ψ$, $ω$). Called Ionic, because the Ionians were the first to adopt all the 24 letters. (N.B. The other 16 are called Cadmēan letters.)

Ionic Poets of Greece (*The*). Those poets who wrote in the Ionic dialect or the Greek of Asia Minor.

Homer wrote Ionic Greek; but of the lyrists the two most eminent are Anacrěon (B.C. 563–478) and Simonīdês (B.C. 556–467). The elegy of the latter on Leonīdas and his 300 has no superior in the world; and his ' Lament of Danäe ' is a model of pathos. As for Anacrěon, his odes are quite unrivalled. There never were odes more inimitable than his ' Cupid dripping wet ' (Ode 3), ' To my dove ' (Ode 9), and ' The Rose ' (Ode 53) (' Barnes's edition ').

The following is a literal translation of the elegy. 'How glorious their fate who fell at Thermopylæ! How beautiful their death! Their tomb an altar! We give them not our tears, but cherish them in immortal memory. The manner of their death is their funeral song. Rust nor destroying time shall efface the memorial of the brave. This mound is the archive of Grecian glory. Leonidas lies here; Leonidas the king of Sparta; Leonidas who left behind him a monument of praise, a trophy of glory which no time shall destroy.

.•. Simonīdês the lyric poet must not be confounded with Simonīdês the satirist who wrote in Iambic verse, and lived a century earlier.

Ionic Sect (*The*) of ancient Greek philosophers. Founded by Thālês, the sage, and father of speculative philosophy (B.C. 611–547). He taught that all bodies are compounded of atoms; that the earth is round; that the sun is a sphere of fire; and that the moon is lighted by the sun. His most noted disciples were Anaximander (B.C. 611–547); Anaximĕnês (B.C. 558–460); Anaxagŏras (B.C. 500–428); Heraclītos of Ephesus (B.C. 543–483); and Diogĕnês of Crete (B.C. 539–465).

Archeläos of Milētus joined together the two systems of Anaximander and Anaxagŏras. He held with the former that the elements of all things are eternal, and admitted with the latter the existence of a Supreme intelligence, independent of matter.

.•. Diogĕnês of Crete must not be confounded with Diogĕnês of Sinŏpé the cynic.

I'owa (U.S. America). So called from an Indian tribe, and from a river of the same name. The inhabitants are nicknamed *Hawkeyęs*.

Iphicra'tians. The mercenaries of Iphicrătês the Athenian general (B.C. 419–348).

Ille pedestria arma mutavit. Quum ante illum imperatorem maximis clypeis, brevibus hastis, minutis gladiis uterentur; ille, e contrario, peltam pro parma fecit, ut ad motus concursusque essent leviores. Hastæ modum duplicavit, gladios longiores fecit. Idem genus loricarum mutavit, et pro ferreis atque aeneis linteas dedit.—NEPOS, *Iphicrates.*

Ireland (*King of*). Edward Bruce, brother of Robert Bruce, was crowned king of Ireland at Dundalk in 1316, but was slain by the English under Sir John Bermingham at Faughart, near Dundalk, 5 Oct., 1318. Henry VIII. was the first English sovereign who called himself ' King of Ireland.'

Ireland (*Samuel William Henry*). A literary impostor (1777–1835). He published in folio, 1795, ' Miscellaneous Papers and Instruments under the hand and seal of William Shakespeare, including the tragedy of "King Lear," and a small fragment of "Hamlet," from the original,' price 4*l*. 4*s*. On 2 April, 1796, he produced the play of ' Vortigern and Rowena ' from the pen of Shakespeare. It was actually represented, and drew a most crowded house. Dr. Parr, Dr. Valpy, James Boswell, Herbert Croft, and Pye the poet-laureate, signed a document certifying their conviction that Ireland's productions were genuine; but Malone exposed the imposition of the tragedy, and Ireland publicly confessed that all his publications from beginning to end

were impositions. *See* 'Literary Forgeries,' &c.

For my own part I cannot imagine how anyone
could be deceived.

Ireland of Austria (*The*). Hun-
gary, which struggled long for home
rule, and obtained it in 1867. In 1868
the empire of Austria was designated the
'Austro-Hungarian Monarchy.'

Irish American Land League
(*The*), 1879. Organised by C. S. Parnell
and affiliated with the Irish National Land
League (*q.v.*). *See* 'Irish Associations.'

Irish Army of Liberation
(*The*), 1848. The war party of Ireland,
who had both commissions and uniforms
to fight against soldiers of Great Britain
on behalf of the Irish rebels. *See* 'Irish
Associations.'

Irish Associations. *See* under

Agents of Captain Right.	Kilkenny Convention.
Aggregate Bodies.	Lady Clares.
American Land League.	Ladies' Irish Land
Anti-Tory Association.	League.
Anti-Union Society.	Ladies' Land League.
Attacottic Rebellion.	Ladies' Labour and In-
Avengers.	dustrial Union.
Black Foot.	Land Grabbers.
Boys (*The*).	Land Grabbers League.
Brotherhood of St. Pa-	Levellers.
trick.	Loyal Irish Brethren.
Captain Right.	Loyal National Repeal
Caravats.	Association.
Confederate Catholics.	Martyrs' Meeting.
Confederation.	Massacre of Scullabogue
Cork Boys.	Barn.
Daisy League.	Molly Maguires.
Defenders.	Moonlighters, Captain
Democratic Labour As-	Moonlight.
sociation.	M. W. S.
Emerald Club.	National Association
Federalists.	for the Repeal of the
Fenians.	Union.
Green Spectre.	National Association of
Hearts of Steel.	Ireland.
Hillside Men.	National Land League.
Home Rule League.	National League.
Houghers.	Nationalists.
I. N. B.	New Fenians.
Invincibles.	Night Boys.
I. R. B.	No. 1.
Irish American Land	Oak Boys.
League.	Our Boys.
Irish Army of Libera-	Orangemen.
tion.	Peep o' Day Boys.
Irish Confederation.	Phenicians.
Irish Invincibles.	Philadelphia Conven-
Irish Labour and Indus-	tion.
trial Union.	Phœnix Park Murder.
Irish Land League.	Phœnix Society.
Irish Loyal and Patrio-	Redpath Boys.
tic Union.	Remonstrants.
Irish Massacre.	Repeal Agitation.
Irish National Brother-	Repeal Association.
hood.	Repeal of the Union.
Irish National Land	Repeal Year.
League.	Revolver Boys.
Irish Republican Bro-	Ribbon Men.
therhood.	Right Boys.
Irish Revolutionary	Rockites and Captain
Brotherhood.	Rock.
Irish Tenant League.	Rory of the Hills.
Irish Tenants' Defence	Separatists.
League.	Shanavests.

Society of United Irish-	Tithe Agitators.
men.	Tithe War.
Sons of Freedom.	United Brotherhood.
Steel Boys.	United Irishmen.
Tenants' Defence Asso-	V. C.
ciation.	Vigilance Society.
Tenants' Defence	White Boys.
League.	Young Irelanders.
Terryalts.	Young Ireland's Ris-
Threshers.	ing.

Irish Church (*The*). The papal
authority in Ireland was recognised by the
Synod of Kells in 1152.

The Catholic Church was abolished by Henry
VIII. in 1539, and the English reformed liturgy
was introduced in 1550.

Catholic priests were expelled, under penalty of
death, by James I. in 1605 ; and the Articles of the
Church of England were introduced in 1635.

Intermarriages between Catholics and Protestants in Ireland were forbidden by William III.
in 1697.

Catholics were declared disqualified to sit on
the grand jury in 1705.

The disestablishment and disendowment of the
Anglican Church in Ireland date from 1871.

Irish Church Temporalities
Bill (*The*). A bill to abolish the col-
lection of tithes and firstfruits, and to
substitute a rent-charge, 30 July, 1833.
Amended in 1834, and again in 1836. A
Sustentation Fund was originated in
1870, and its union with the Protestant
Church of England was dissolved in 1871.

The Act of 1833 abolished the church-cess,
reduced the four archbishops and eighteen
bishops to two archbishops and ten bishops, and
appropriated the revenues thus obtained to
general church purposes.

Irish Confederation (*The*), 1845.
The Young Ireland party headed by
William Smith O'Brien, a split from the
great Repeal party of Daniel O'Connell.
The Young Irelanders were for enforcing
their charter at the sword's point, but
O'Connell was opposed to any such mad
measure. In 1848 they sent a deputation
to France craving aid for 'the oppressed
nationality of Ireland,' and organised an
insurrection, but just before the time of
uprising O'Brien was arrested, and, being
convicted, was exiled to Van Diemen's
Land for life. In 1856, having obtained
a free pardon, he returned home, and
died in 1864. *See* 'Irish Associations.'

Irish Crisis (*The*), 1846, 1847.
During the potato famine.

Potato famines have not been uncommon in
Ireland : Thus in 1822 Parliament voted 300,000l. for
relief purposes, and subscriptions to the amount
of 310,000l. were raised. In 1831 the crop in the
West of Ireland failed, and so on.

Irish Invincibles (*The*). An or-
ganisation started in Dublin in Dec.

1881 (organised fully in the spring of 1882), the members of which bound themselves by oath to 'remove all tyrants from the country,'—in other words, to 'assassinate the executive council of Ireland, the chief secretary, and all government officers.' McCafferty, with others, established the society. It was limited to 250 members, and was under the control of a committee of five Fenians, viz. James Mullett, Edward McCafferty, Daniel and James Curley, and James Carey, who were paid by the Land League. The first person on the list for removal was the Right Hon. W. E. Forster, chief secretary for Ireland; the second was Earl Cowper, the lord-lieutenant of Ireland. These gentlemen resigned and left the island. The first officials who fell to the assassins were Mr. Thomas Burke, perpetual under-secretary, and Lord Frederick Cavendish, who succeeded Mr. Forster, 6 May, 1882. They fell on a Saturday, in full daylight, in Phœnix Park. The trial of these 'Invincibles' took place in Dublin, 1883. *See* 'Irish Republican Brotherhood' and 'Irish Associations.'

Irish Land Acts.

I. An Act was passed in 1858 (21, 22 Vict. c. 72) to facilitate the sale and transfer of land in Ireland.

II. Deasy's Act, 1860, limiting the power of a landlord to the terms of his contract, but not giving a tenant any compensation for improvements on eviction.

III. The Act of 1870 remedied this, and provided that a tenant on eviction might demand of his landlord just compensation for all improvements made by himself [the tenant] during his term of tenancy.

IV. The Act 1881 set up a tribunal to fix a 'fair rent'; and legalised the tenant's interest in his holding, which was saleable in open market, so that virtually the Irish tenant by this Act was a co-partner in the soil.

V. The Ashbourne Act, 1885, placed five million pounds sterling at the disposal of Irish tenants who desired to purchase the fee simple of their holdings, the loan to be repaid by instalments in forty-nine years. In 1888 another similar sum was granted for the same object. And in 1890 Mr. Balfour introduced a bill for a much larger loan on very easy terms enough by principal and interest

to buy up any number of farms which the tenants would be likely to desire.

VI. The Act of 1887, subjecting the rents judicially fixed in 1881-85 to revision, by which rents were again reduced about 10 per cent. ; and to give county-court judges the power of staying eviction, and of spreading arrears over a discretionary number of years.

These several Acts give to tenants in Ireland—
(1) Compensation for improvements.
(2)   "   disturbance.
(3) Security of tenure, subject to payment of rent.
(4) A 'fair rent' tribunal.
(5) The right of selling their interest.
(6) The revision of judicial rents.
(7) The right of having eviction stayed on good cause shown.
(8) Facilities for acquiring the fee simple of a holding.

** Lower Beltoney, in far-off Gweedore, is now (under the Purchase Act) a real garden, while Keeldrum, on the other side of the road [under the Plan of Campaign, *q.v.*], is a waste wilderness. Again, the barony of Farney in Monághan, once the most blood stained spot in all Ireland, has, with the sale of the Marquis of Bath's property, become quite a model district (1890).

Irish Legion (*The*), 1803.
An army of Irish refugees in Paris raised by Bonaparte, with the intention of invading England through Ireland.

Irish Liberator (*The*).
Daniel O'Connell (1775-1847).

Irish Loan (*The*), 1885.
Five millions sterling set apart, to be lent to Irish farmers by government at $3\frac{1}{2}$ per cent., to enable them to buy their farms of their landlords. *See above*, 'Irish Land Acts,' No. V.

Irish Loyal and Patriotic Union (*The*), 1885.
To unite the loyalist party into one body irrespective of class, party, or creed. This union was to counteract the 'National League' (*q.v.*). *See* 'Irish Associations.'

Irish Massacre (*The*), Oct. and Nov., 1641.
Not the massacre of Irishmen, but the massacre of forty or fifty thousand Englishmen by the Irish secret society called 'The Confederate Catholics.' In this massacre husbands were cut to pieces in presence of their wives, children's brains were dashed out in the face of their parents, women were brutally violated, and driven naked into the woods to perish. Some were burned to death, others were drowned, and many were buried alive. Nothing like it has

been known except the outrage of Cawnpore.

The instigator of this massacre was Sir Phelim O'Neil of Ulster. In July 1648 a Bull was received from the pope granting a jubilee and plenary absolution to all those who had taken up arms in the cause of the Catholic faith. Horrible and incredible as it may seem, Gregory XIII. proclaimed the slaughter of St. Bartholomew as the 'Year of Jubilee,' and went in full procession to celebrate a public thanksgiving service for the massacre.

Irish National Brotherhood

(*The*), 1881. I. I.N.B. This was an offshoot of the Clan-na-Gael, or United Brotherhood. It began in 1880 under what was called the New Departure (*q.v.*). A union of the murderous violence of the Clanna-Gael, the constitutional craft of the Land League, and the spoliation of the No Rent party.

II. I.N.B., 1886, at Chicago. An offshoot of the U.B. or 'United Brotherhood.' *See* 'Irish Associations.'

Irish National Land League

(*The*), Oct. 1879-1881. The object of this conspiracy was to establish the absolute independence of Ireland as a separate nation. To effect this object, agrarian agitation against the payment of agricultural rents was resorted to, in order to secure the co-operation of the tenant farmers of Ireland, and to impoverish and ultimately drive from the country the Irish landlords, styled by the leaguers 'the English garrison.' Suppressed 1881. *See* 'Irish Associations.'

The confederation was called the Land League, the Irish National Land League, and the Labour and Industrial Union. There were also Ladies' Leagues, and affiliated societies in Great Britain and America.

Irish Night

(*The*), 13 Dec., 1688, when a cry arose in London that the Irish (disbanded on the flight of James II.) were up, and were going to cut the throats of all Protestants. At one in the morning the drums collected the militia and the train bands, and 100,000 men kept the streets in a state of terror and anarchy. It was called the 'Irish Night,' though no Irish put in an appearance, the panic being created by a false alarm.

Trenchard was brother-in-law to the unprincipled agitator Hugh Speke, who by his trumped-up lies had occasioned the 'Irish Night. —HOWITT, *Hist. of Engl.* (Will. and Mary, p. 69).

Irish Parliament

(*The*), or Grattan's Parliament (1782-1800). Two independent parliaments in the same kingdom being found pregnant with perpetual danger both from within and from without, the Dublin parliament, by the Act of Union, in 1800, was abolished, and a large number of Irish representatives, out of all proportion to the rest of the kingdom, were admitted to the Westminster parliament. In England and Wales it is one in 6,000. In Ireland one in 5,000.

To the Irish parliament no Catholic was admitted. To the representatives admitted into the Westminster house no such restriction exists.

The proximate cause of the abolition of the Irish Parliament was this : In 1789 the Prince of Wales was made regent. The English parliament restricted his powers, but the Irish parliament granted him the regency of Ireland without restrictions. This was a warning of the mischief which might hereafter occur from two legislatures, and convinced the British cabinet that the Irish parliament, like that of Scotland, must be united to the one general house of legislature in London. The Irish rebellion of 1798, in which the French were invited over, brought the matter to a head, and in 1801 the union was effected. *See* 'Parliaments.'

Grattan stated in 1793 that of the 300 members of the Irish house, 200 were nominees of private individuals, and 50 were returned by constituencies of not more than ten electors in each, and several boroughs had not more than one elector. In 1890 about 50 of the Irish deputies in the House of Commons were, for the most part, the nominees of C. S. Parnell.

Irish Rebellion.

I. In 1565 occurred the rebellion of Shan O'Neal, who applied to France for soldiers. O'Neal was assassinated in 1567.

II. In 1594 occurred the rebellion of Hugh O'Neil, earl of Tyrone, who assumed the title of *The O'Neil.* This 'patriot' (!) offered the crown of Ireland to the king of Spain in 1597, and the Spaniards actually sent an army into Ireland to obtain the promised crown. O'Neil, with his Spanish army, was defeated at Kinsale ; he surrendered to Mountjoy, was pardoned, and went to Rome, where he died in 1616.

III. In 1608 occurred the rebellion of O'Dogherty, in Ulster. James I. then parcelled out the north of Ireland to Scotch and English settlers. This confiscation is known as the 'Plantation of Ulster' (*q.v.*).

IV. In 1641, while the English were in civil war, the Irish rose in rebellion under Roger More and Sir Phelim O'Neil, and massacred the Protestants to the number of 40,000.

20

V. In 1649 Cromwell, having taken the cities of Drogheda, Wexford, and Clonmel, left Ireton to carry on the war. Ireton reduced place after place, and soon after the death of Ireton the rebellion was quite stamped out (1652).

VI. In 1789 the Great Rebellion broke out. It was caused by the creation of numerous Irish societies hostile to England, especially that called the 'United Irishmen' (q.v.).

VII. In 1796 the Irish concluded a secret treaty with the French Directory, but the treasonable plot was utterly frustrated by the battles of Bantry Bay in 1796, and the battle of Camperdown in 1797.

1 Jan., 1801, the union of Great Britain and Ireland was effected, and since then the Irish have had no opportunity of offering 'their crown' either to France or Spain.

VIII. 1848. The nation was more or less disturbed from April to the middle of Sept. William Smith O'Brien was the chief disturber, and his lieutenants were Meagher and M'Manus. All three being arrested were condemned to death, but were transported to Van Diemen's Land. Meagher and M'Manus escaped to America, and O'Brien, in 1856, having obtained a free pardon, returned home and died at Bangor in 1864.

William Smith O'Brien was joint deputy from the Irish Confederation to the French republic, 3 April, 1848.

IX. The Home Rule faction, under the leadership of Charles S. Parnell, began in 1870, and disorganised Ireland with numberless disorderly associations, some of an anti-landlord character, others more criminal still. Boycotting (q.v.) was introduced. Shooting men through the legs, pouring hot pitch on the heads of women, maiming cattle, and the most reckless destruction of property, intimidated all who resisted the rebels. See 'Plan of Campaign,' 'Irish Associations,' &c. &c. In 1890 the disturbance was not wholly stamped out.

When Ireland had its own rulers the civil and moral condition of the country was so bad that Pope Adrian IV. authorised Henry II. to undertake the conquest of it, hoping that a strong arm might do something to settle the country.

When Grattan had his parliament he passed fifty-four coercion acts, 1782, &c.

Whatever may be said respecting 'the plantation of Ireland' by James I., one thing is certain : No part of Ireland is so wealthy, and no part of Ireland so loyal and industrious, as Ulster.

Irish Reproductive Loan Fund (*The*), 1822. Originated in the excess of subscription to what was expended in the relief of sufferers from the famine. The surplus was entrusted to a committee in London, and called the Irish Reproductive Loan Fund, under which small sums are advanced to industrious individuals of the working classes, to be repaid by instalments, with interest at 6d. in the pound, reduced afterwards to 4d.

Irish Republican Brotherhood (*The*), 1869. The Dublin contingent of the 'Irish Invincibles' (q.v.). It consisted of fifty of the most desperate of the gang. They were sworn 'to remove all tyrants from the country.' This meant they were to murder or drive out of Ireland all the constituted administrators and guardians of the law and of order, together with all owners of land The Phœnix Park murder (q.v.) was their first and most notorious achievement. See 'Irish Associations.'

Irish Revolutionary Brotherhood (*The*), or I. R. B. The Irish branch of the American V.C. (i.e. United Brotherhood), for the purpose of making Ireland an independent republic by force of arms. See 'Irish Associations.'

Irish Society (*The*), 1619. Certain London merchants incorporated by charter, who contracted for large tracts of land in Tyrconnel (q.v.), when James I. planted the territory with Scotch and English tenants. See 'Plantation of Ulster.'

Irish Tenant League (*The*), 1850. Pledged to oppose all Governments which did not recognise the principle of Tenant Right (q.v.) for all Ireland. The league broke up in 1858, and was replaced by Fenians (q.v.). See 'Irish Associations.'

Irish Tenants' Defence League (*The*), 1889. To supersede the 'Plan of Campaign' (q.v.), declared to be illegal. The object of the 'Defence League' is to supply tenants with money and legal advisers to fight their landlords and weary them out with the infinite shifts of law. During the process an evicted tenant is to be furnished by the League with a home and needful support. Mr. C. S. Parnell was the *primum mobile* of the scheme. See 'Irish Associations.'

Irishmen of Islam (*The*). So the Moors of Morocco have been called.

Irmin-sul. Herman's Column. Erected to commemorate the victory of Herman over Varus the Roman. It was long considered a palladium of the Saxon nation. Charlemagne destroyed the temple of Eresburg, and transferred the pillar to Corbey.

Iron Age (*The*). The era between the death of Charlemagne, 814, and the accession of Hugues Capet, 987, is so called from its constant civil wars. Also called the 'leaden age' from its worthlessness, and the 'dark age' from its barrenness of learned men.

The present has often been called 'The age of steel.' Hugues Capet, pronounce *U Cap'-pay*.

Iron Arm.
I. Guillaume *Bras de fer* (*-1046). First of the twelve sons of Tancrède de Hauteville.
II. Capt. François de Lanoue, a Huguenot, who died at the siege of Lamballe (1531–1591).

Iron Calvinist of Rosny (*The*). Maximilien de Béthune, duc de Sully (1560–1641), born at Rosny; chief minister of Henri IV., and the greatest of all French statesmen.

Iron Chancellor (*The*). Prince Otto von Bismarck of Prussia (1813), Chancellor of the North German Confederation 14 July, 1867. He retired from public life in 1890.

Iron Chest (*The*). A secret closet in the wall of the king's bedchamber in the Tuileries. Made by Gamain, a locksmith who had been employed by Louis XVI. to construct it. It was behind the wainscot, and so well concealed that no one could have discovered it without being first shown it. Gamain betrayed it to the Convention, and amongst other papers were several from Mirabeau which were so damnatory that the Convention ordered his bust to be removed from the hall and stamped to powder.

Iron-clad Oath (*The*). An act passed, in 1867, by the United States of North America, excluding from the franchise all those who had borne arms against the United States, and even all who had directly or indirectly given aid to the Southerners. It was practically the temporary disfranchisement of the Southern whites.

Iron Crown. Several examples occur of traitors or aspirants to a crown being put to death by a mockery red-hot iron crown. Take the two following:—
1. Walter earl of Athol murdered James I. of Scotland in Perth, hoping to usurp the crown; but he was crowned only with a red-hot iron diadem which ate to his brain and killed him (1437).
2. Doza or Dosa the Hungarian was put to death by a similar torture, for heading the peasant rebellion against the nobles (1514).

Iron Crown of Lombardy (*The*). Not an iron crown, but a magnificent gold diadem, containing a narrow iron band about ⅜ths of an inch broad, and ¹⁄₁₀th of an inch in thickness. This band was made out of a nail given to Constantine by his mother, and said to be one of the nails used in the crucifixion. The outer circlet of the crown is of beaten gold, set with large rubies, emeralds, and sapphires, and the iron band is within this circlet. The first Lombard king crowned with it was Agilulph, at Milan, in 591. Charlemagne was crowned with it in 774; Friedrich III. in 1452; Karl V. in 1530; and Napoleon I., 23 May, 1805, crowned himself with it as 'king of Italy' in Milan Cathedral. It was given up to Victor Emmanuel on the conclusion of peace with Austria in 1866. The motto on the crown is 'God has given it me; beware who touches it.'

According to a tradition Gregory the Great gave this crown to Queen Theodelinda. The first kaiser who wore it was Henry of Luxemburg in 1311.

Iron Duke (*The*). Arthur Wellesley duke of Wellington (1769–1852). His statue, made of bronze by M. C. Wyatt, was mounted on the marble arch opposite his house in 1846. This hideous deformity, removed in 1882, had a share in establishing the eponym of the 'Iron' duke.

An Achilles in bronze, by Westmacott, was erected in Hyde Park from subscriptions contributed by the ladies of England in honour of the duke.

Iron Emperor (*The*). Nicholas of Russia (1796, 1826–1855).

Iron Hand. Götz von Berlichingen, immortalised by Goethe (16th cent.), is so called from his iron hand. The hand weighed 3 lbs., and was so constructed as to grasp a sword or lance. It was invented by a mechanic of Nuremberg, and is preserved at Jaxthausen, near

Heilbronn. A duplicate is in the Schloss at Erbach, in the Odenwald. Götz von Berlichingen lost his right hand at the siege of Landshut.   See 'Duke with the Silver Hand'; 'Golden Hand.'

The family of Clephane of Carslogie are in possession of a steel hand conferred by one of the kings of Scotland on a laird of Carslogie, who had lost his hand in his country's service.—SCOTT, *Border Antiquities*, vol. ii. p. 206.

Iron Mask (*Man in the*). A mysterious prisoner in the reign of Louis XIV., condemned at all times to wear a black velvet mask. He was confined in 1662 in the château of Pignerol; and died in the Bastille in 1703, at the age of 63. He went by the name of L'Estang, but who he was nobody knows; and Louis XIV., when the captive was dead, commanded that his face should be beaten to a pulp and cut to pieces to prevent recognition.

Iron Tooth. 'Dent de Fer.' Friedrich II. elector of Brandenburg (1657, 1688–1713).

Iron Virgin (*The*). An instrument of torture. It was a hollow wooden figure representing a woman. The figure opened like a cupboard, and the front of it was studded with long sharp iron spikes. The victim being placed in the figure, the front or lid was gradually closed upon him, and the spikes were so arranged as to pierce the eyes and least vital parts. When quite closed the victim was crushed, and lingered in horrible torture till actual agony exhausted his vital powers. *See* 'Nabis.'

Ironside. Edmund II. king of the Anglo-Saxons was so called from his iron armour (989, 1016–1017).

Sir Richard Steele signed himself 'Nestor Ironside' in the 'Guardian' (1671–1729).

Ironsides (*The*). Cromwell's brigade was so called for their irresistible obstinacy in fight.

Sir Philip Warwick says: 'The regiment of 1,000 men which Cromwell raised for the Association of the Eastern Counties, and which soon became known as his *Ironsides*, was formed strictly of religious fanatics, for Cromwell told Hampden that the one weapon which could meet and turn the chivalry of the cavalier was religious enthusiasm.'

Iroquois. A confederation of five American-Indian States, partly in Canada and partly in the United States. They were the Mohawks, the Oneidas, the Onondagas, the Senecas, and the Cayugas.

They were proud, brave, hospitable, faithful, and melancholic.

When the Tuscaroras joined them they were increased to six states.

Irrefragable Doctor (*The*). 'Doctor Irrefragabĭlis,' Alexander of Hales, of the Order of Friars Minor, Paris (died 1245). He was an Englishman, and was called Hales from a monastery in Gloucestershire where he was brought up. He wrote a commentary on the famous 'Sentences' of Pierre Lombard, and was the master of Duns Scotus. *See* 'Doctors.'

There was a John Hales who was called 'The Ever Memorable,' who was born at Bath (1584–1656). Professor William Hales, the chronologist, is quite another person. He died in 1831.

Irregulars (*The*). We have no Irregulars in the British army; but in the Indian army we have Irregulars among the black troops, such as Hodson's Horse, Probyn's Central India Horse, &c.

The Militia, the Yeomanry, and the Volunteers are not regulars (*q.v.*), but yet they are not called Irregulars. In France the 'troupes irregulières' are those who do not belong to the line (*q.v.*).

Ir'vingites (3 syl.), 1826. Followers of Edward Irving, a Scotch minister, whose most striking peculiarity was the expectation of the speedy advent of Christ and the beginning of the millennium. His followers claimed the miraculous gifts of tongues, prophecy, healing, and raising of the dead, though Irving himself never laid claim to any powers. He died in 1834.

They call themselves the 'Apostolic Catholic Church,' and have four ministries : (1) Apostles; (2) Prophets; (3) Evangelists; and (4) Pastors or Angels.

Isau'rian War (*The*), 492–498. Tarcalissæus, or Zeno, invited over a formidable band of Isaurians, but his successor Anastasius suppressed their pensions, banished them from Constantinople, and prepared war for their extermination. Some 150,000 barbarians, headed by a fighting bishop, flew to arms, and a war of six years' duration ensued. The Isaurians retired to their fastnesses in the mountains, but fort after fort fell; their communication with the sea was cut off; the bravest of their leaders died in arms; those who survived were dragged in chains to the hippodrome, and those of their young men who refused to submit to the Romans were banished to Thrace.

Is'iac Table (*The*). A flat rectangular bronze plate, about 4 ft. 8 in. long, containing three rows of figures of Egyptian emblems and deities. It was sold by a soldier to a locksmith, and the locksmith sold it to Cardinal Bembo in 1527. It is now at Turin, but it is a general opinion that the table is spurious. *See* 'Literary Forgeries.'

Isidore of Seville. One of the doctors of the church (570–636) : his day is 4 April. Author of 'Commentaries on the Old and New Testament,' a 'Treatise on the Ecclesiastical Writers,' 'A Chronicle from Adam to 626,' &c. *See* 'Doctors of the Church.'

Isido'rian Decretals (*The*), 820–836, or 'The False Decretals.' Fifty-nine decretals palmed off as the work of St. Isidore of Seville (570–636). They aim at the exaltation of the Roman pontiff and the depreciation of the civil power, the infallibility of the pope, and the justification of certain 'Catholic' practices, such as the rite of chrism, and so on. *See* 'Literary Forgeries.'

The collection consists of three parts : (1) contains 61 decretal epistles from popes of the first three centuries, Clement to Sylvester (91–314) ; (2) canons of the councils ; (3) decretal epistles from Sylvester to Deodatus (314–615). Of these 35 are certainly spurious, and yet for nearly 1,000 years they were appealed to by popes and councils as authority. In 1789 Pope Pius VI. admitted them to be iniquitous forgeries.

⁎⁎ Some attribute these decretals to Riculfe archbishop of Mentz ; others to Isidore Mercator, or 'Peccator,' as some surname him, a Cenobite ; others again to Benedict Levita, a Gallican monk.

Islam. The Mohammedan creed ; a believer in the creed is a Moslem, Mussulman, Islamite, or Mohammedan.

Isle des Chevaux (*The*). The Isle of May, in the throat of the Firth of Forth. It is about a mile in length and encloses some 70 acres of pasture land much prized for grazing horses.

Pronounce *Eel' da'Sha-vo'*.

Isle of Destiny (*The*). Inisfail.

Isle of Mist (*The*). The Isle of Skye, its high hills being almost always shrouded in mist.

'Nor sleep thy hand by thy side, Chief of the Isle of Mist.'—OSSIAN, *Fingal*, i.

Isle of Saints (*The*). Ireland was so called after the conversion of the people to Christianity ; before that time it was called the Sacred Isle. It was as distinguished for being the school of

Druidism or sun-worship as it was subsequently for being the school of Christian scholars.

Isma'elites (4 syl.), or 'Ismael'ians.' Separatists from the Shiites, a Moslem sect. The Shiites believe that there have been twelve true Imams. The Ismaelites believe in only seven : Ali (son-in-law of Mohammed) and his six regular descendants. The seventh was Ismael, who died 730, leaving an infant son Mohammed. This infant was set aside, and his uncle Mousa was made kalif or imam (*q.v.*). This caused a split in the party, and those who followed the infant Mohammed called themselves Ismaelites. No one knows what became of the infant, but the Ismaelites assert that he will appear in the fulness of time, and restore the true faith. These Ismaelites were very influential from 730 to the 12th century, and from them sprang the Karmathians who ravaged Persia and Syria in the 8th century ; the Fatimite kalifs who reigned in Egypt from 909 to 1174 ; the Assassins (*q.v.*) 1090–1258 ; the Druses, the Nosaïris, and the Wahabites (3 syl.).

The Ismaelites were materialists, and symbolised away all those parts of the Koran opposed to their own views. Their missionaries are called 'dais,' and a good Ismaelite should pray fifty times a day.

Ismaelites of the East (*The*). The Assassins, an order of the Ismael'ians or Isma'elites (*q.v.*). Their great aim was to stamp out the Sunnites and assassinate the Sunnite kalif.

Isoc'rates (*The French*). Fléchier (1632–1710). A great pulpit orator. Noted for his 'Funeral Orations,' especially one pronounced over Marshal Turenne.

Israelites' Clubs. *See* note after 'Circumcellians,' p. 175, col. i.

Isth'mian Games (*The*). In ancient Greece held in the Isthmus of Corinth every alternate spring, the 1st and 3rd of each Olympiad. The games began at sunrise with the foot-match, and the victor gave his name to the Olympiad. Wrestling was the next match, then boxing, then leaping, then the chariot race. The only prize was a wreath of parsley or green pine-leaves.

The *pancra'tion* was a combination of wrestling and boxing. The combatants tried their strength first by squeezing each other's hands. Sostratos of Sicyon gained twelve prizes for crushing his opponent s hand in the preliminary grip.

Italian Architecture. Renaissance, or 'Classical Revival.' It commenced in Italy at the beginning of the 15th cent., was introduced into France about a century later, and into England 1560–70.

Italian Confederacy (*The*), 1526. Consisting of the pope, the Italian princes and states, and François I. of France, against Karl V. The allies engaged to raise 30,000 foot soldiers, 3,000 horse, and a sufficient fleet. Henry VIII. of England did not join the league, but he favoured it, for Wolsey hated Karl.

Italian Confederation or League (*The*). The eight allied nations in the Social War (B.C. 90–89).

Italian French School of Painting (*The*). Called the 'Sophoclês of Art,' because the exponents drew their human beings models of perfection. This school

included Vouet (1582–1649), Mignard (1610–1695), Lesueur (1617–1655), Lebrun (1619 – 1690), Jouvenet (1647 – 1707), Rigaud (1659–1743), and Lemoine (1688–1737).

Italian League (*The*), 1511–1512. Set on foot by Pope Julius II. against Louis XII. of France. Henry VIII. of England and his father-in-law Ferdinand V. of Aragon joined the pope. Julius laid the kingdom of France under an interdict, and convened a general council at Rome (the Fifth General Council of the Lateran), chiefly for the reproof of Louis XII. Pope Julius died in 1513, and the league was dissolved.

Louis XII. and Maximilian had convened the Council of Pisa to depose the pope. The real cause of contention was this. The Pope, the Kaiser of Germany, and the King of Aragon had formed a league for seizing Venetia and parcelling it out between them; but Louis contrived to be in the field first, won the battle of Agnadello, and Venice fell into his hands. This was not what the pope wanted, so he broke the league and formed a new one to drive the French out of Italy.

Italian Painters of *Lombardy*.

CALLED						NAME					
Correggio	...	...	...	...	...	*Antonio Allegri*	...	...	...		(1494–1534)
Annibale Carracci	...	...	...	...	...	*Annibale Carracci*	...	...	...		(1560 1609)
Michel Angelo da Caravaggio		...	...	...		*Amerighi or Merighi*	...	...	...		(1569 1609)
Guido ...	...	...	...	...	...	*Guido Reni*	...	...	...		(1575 1642)
Albano	...	...	...	...	...	*Francesco Albani*	...	...	...		(1578 1660)
Domenichino	...	...	...	...	...	*Domenico Zampieri*	...	...	...		(1581–1641)
Lanfranco ...	...	...	...	...	...	*Giovanni Lanfranco*	...	...	...		(1581–1647)
Guercino	...	...	...	...	...	*Giovanni Francesco Barbieri*	...			(1590 1666)

Italian Painters, &c. of *Rome*.

CALLED				NAME				
Leonardo da Vinci	...	...	...	*Leonardo da Vinci* ...	...	...		(1445–1519)
Il Perugino	...	...	...	*Pietro Vanucci*	...	...	...	(1446–1524)
Michel Angelo	...	...	...	*Michelagnolo Buonarroti* ...		...		(1474 1564)
Sanzio Raphael	...	...	...	*Raphael, or Raffaelo*	...	...		(1483 1520)
Andrea del Sarto	...	...	...	*Andrea Vannucchi* ...	...	...		(1486 1530)
Francesco Primaticcio	...	...	...	*Francesco Primaticcio*	...	...		(1490 1570)
Giulio Romano	...	...	...	*Giulio Pippi* ...	...	...		(1492–1546)
Polidoro Caldara	...	...	...	*Polidoro da Caravaggio*	...	...		(1495–1543)
Il Parmigiano	...	...	...	*Girolama Francesco Maria Mazzuoli*			(1504–1540)
Daniele Ricciarelli	...	...	...	*Daniele da Volterra...*	...	...		(1509 1566)
Cecchino del Salviati	...	...	...	*Francesco de' Rossi* ..	...	...		(1510–1563)
Berrettini	...	...	...	*Pietro da Cortona* ...	...	...		(1596–1669)
Il Lucchesino	...	...	...	*Pietro Testa* ...	...	...		(1611 1648)

Italian Painters of *Venice*.

CALLED						NAME.				
Giambellini	...	...	...	...	...	*Giovanni Bellini*	...	...		(1426–1516)
Giorgione	...	...	...	...	...	*Giorgio Barbarelli*	...	...		(1477 1511)
Titian	...	...	...	...	...	*Tiziano Vecellio*	...	...		(1477 1576)
Jacopo da Ponte il Bassano	...		...	...						(1510–1592)
Il Tintoretto	...	...	...	...	...	*Jacobo Robusti*	...	...		(1512–15 '4)
Paul Veronese	...	...	...	...	...	*Paolo Cagliari*	...	...		(1530–1588)
Il Giovane	...	...	...	...	...	*Jacobo Palma* (of Venice)	...		(1544–1628)
Il Vecchio	...	...	...	...	...	*Jacobo Palma*	...	...		(1548–1588)

Italian Republic (*The*), 1802. So Napoleon called the Cisalpine Republic.

In 1801 Savoy and Piedmont were united to France; Milan taken from Austria formed the Cisalpine Republic.

Italian War (*The*), 1483–1549. Begun in the reign of Charles VIII. and

ended in the reign of Henri II. It was an attempt of France to become master of Italy. After sixty-five years of war, Henri signed at Cateau Cambrésis the Paix Malheureuse, by which he renounced Genŏa, Naples, Milan, and Corsica.

Though the Italian war brought no material

advantage to France, indirectly it was beneficial and brought about the renaissance, which made itself conspicuous in the literature, architecture, and taste of the nation.

Italian of Asia (*The*). Persian, noted for its harmonious sound, its facility of versification, and its adaptation to music of the lighter forms.

Malay is 'the Italian of the East'; and Telugu 'the Italian of India.'

Italic School (*The*) of Philosophy. The Pythagorean school, which arose in Italy about 540 B.C. In this school almost all things are explained by relative numbers. The chief of the disciples are Ocellus, Timæus, Archȳtas, Alcmæon, Philolãos, and, somewhat later, Apollōnius of Tyãna.

Italics. Sloping type. Originally called *cursiveti*, or 'cursive letters,' afterwards 'Venetian letters,' because they were used by the great Venetian printers, Aldo Manuzio (1447–1515), Paolo Manuzio (1512–1574), and Aldo Manuzio the younger (1547–1597). The classical authors issued by these printers are called the 'Aldine editions.' It was silly to adopt the French word *Italique* instead of Venetian type, but custom has established the word too firmly to be displaced. *See* 'Roman Type.'

Cursive letters are now employed to mark emphatic words or words of a foreign language.

Iva'rian Dynasty (*The*). Improperly called 'The Skioldung Dynasty' (*q.v.*), and sometimes 'The Race of Lodbrok.' The founder was Ivar Vidfadmê, who is said to have reigned from A.D. 647 to 735. The Ivarian dynasty gave fourteen kings, and lasted from 647 to 1056 ; it followed the Ynglings, and was succeeded by the race of Stenkil. The Ivarian was the second Swedish dynasty, and is sometimes called the 'Race of Sigurd,' from Sigurd-Ring, the 3rd of the line. The reason is this: Harald Hildeτand, the grandson and successor of Ivar, lived in Denmark, and sent his nephew Sigurd-Ring to Upsa'la as his viceroy. Sigurd rebelled against his uncle, who was slain in battle, and succeeded him. Lodbrok was the son of Sigurd-Ring.

Jack Boot (*A*), 1763. The mocking emblem of John . . . Bute, the chief minister of George III. A jack-boot was carried in procession, and burnt in the cider riots raised by Sir Francis Dashwood's unpopular tax on cider and perry.

When No. 45 of 'The North Briton' was condemned to be burnt by the common hangman in 1763, the mob rescued the paper and burnt a jack-boot instead.

The scandal was that the Earl of Bute was the paramour of the Dowager Princess of Wales, and the rioters therefore carried a petticoat on a pole as well as a jack-boot, and both were burnt together. John Stuart earl of Bute (1713–1792).

Jack Straw. A priest who, with John Ball of Kent, took a leading part in Wat the Tyler's rebellion of 1381. He was executed the same year.

Jack the Ripper. An unknown person who so called himself, and committed a series of murders in the east end of London on common prostitutes.

The first was 2 April, 1888, when he murdered and mutilated a woman in a most barbarous manner ; the next was 7 Aug. ; the third was 31 Aug. ; the fourth was 8 Sept. ; the fifth was 30 Sept., when two women were murdered, one of whom was brutally mutilated; the sixth was 9 Nov. ; the seventh was 20 Dec., in a builder's yard ; the eighth was 17 July, 1889, at Whitechapel ; the ninth was 17 Sept., when the mutilated trunk of a woman was found in Pinchin Street, Whitechapel. The perpetrator of these murders fearlessly announced that he was Jack the Ripper, and the series of murders created quite a panic in Whitechapel. For a parallel case, *see* 'Monster' (*The*).

Jackmen. Military retainers dressed in jacks or doublets quilted with iron. These partisans in the middle ages conducted themselves with great insolence towards the industrious part of the community, lived by plunder, and were ready, at the command of their master, for any act of violence.

It is Christie of the Clinthill, the laird's chief jackman ; ye know that little havings [behaviour] can be expected from the like o' them.—Sir W. Scott, *The Monastery*, chap. ix.

Jacksonian Professor of Natural and Experimental Philosophy, in the University of Cambridge. Stipend 500*l.* a year. Founded by the Rev. Richard Jackson, 1783.

Jacob's Stone. The stone used in our coronation service, brought from Scotland by Edward I., and transferred from Ireland to Scotland by one of the Milesian kings.

The 'stone of destiny' is said to have been the stone set up by the patriarch Jacob to commemorate his dream, in which he saw a ladder reaching from earth to heaven. The stone is historic, but the tradition connecting it with Jacob is mythical.

Jaco'bi or **Jacobe'ans**, 1358. French rebels under the leadership of Guillaume Caillet, surnamed Jacques Bonhomme. Their rebellion is known in history as 'La Jacquerie' (*q.v.*). ('Froissart,' vol. i. chapters 187,188,189.)

Jac'obins, 1207. I. In *Church history*. The Dominicans of Paris were popularly so called from St. James's Hospital for Strangers assigned to them in 1207 by Alberic. The street in which the hospital stood was in 1219 called the Rue St. Jacques. The Dominican convent subsequently occupied by the Breton Club was not the original hospital referred to above, but an affiliated convent in the Rue St. Honoré. *See* ' Jacobins, a political club.'

II. A *political club* in the first French Revolution formed at Versailles in 1789, and at first called the Club Breton, because it was organised by the deputies of Brittany. When the National Assembly was moved to Paris the club followed, and called itself La Société des Amis de la Constitution; but the general public called it the ' Jacobins' Club,' because it held its meetings in the ancient convent of the Jacobins in the Rue St. Honoré. The opinions of this club were very radical and Robespierre was its chief leader. On the fall of Robespierre the club was dissolved, 11 Nov., 1794.

The original platform of the Breton Club was to dethrone Louis XVI. and place the Duke of Orleans on the throne.

Jac'obites (3 syl.). I. Pilgrims to the shrine of St. James of Compostella in Spain (ad Jacobum Compostellanum).

II. In *Church history*, 541. An oriental sect of Monoph'ysites called after Jacob Zanzale, surnamed Baradæus (*i.e.* Al Baradas, the ragged) bishop of Edessa. They prevailed especially in Egypt, Syria, Mesopotamia, and Chaldæa. The chief of the sect is called patriarch of Antioch, and lives at Diarbekir, and the next in rank is the maphrian. They recognise only one nature in Jesus Christ, and they used to brand their foreheads with a cross.

III. In *British history*. The partisans of James II. after his abdication in 1688, his son James called the Old Pretender, and his grandson Charles Edward (the Young Pretender). Many believed at the time in the divine right of kings, and that this right was inalienable. The unpopularity of the first two Georges, whose love was bound up with Hanover, contributed to popularise the Jacobite party.

Jaco'byns. A word applied in newspapers to the ultra-radical party, first in 1889 when Mr. Jacoby was appointed their ' whip.'

This will, of course, have the support of the Jacobyns, the Irish, and the peace-at-any-price faction of the English radicals.—*Newspaper leader,* 13 Feb., 1890.

Jacquerie (*La*), 1358. A faction of the revolted peasants of Picardy, who for about six weeks went about in monster gangs attacking all the well-to-do without distinction of sex. Their leader was Guillaume Caillet, the ' Jack Cade ' of France, and with 20,000 followers he destroyed thirty castles. He led his gang to Meaux [*Mo*], where the Duchess of Orléans with some fifty ladies of rank had fled for security. The rebels reached the city gates, and prepared to break them down, when the Captal de Buch, with forty followers, sallied out upon them. The insurgents fled in all directions; 7,000 of them were slain or trampled to death, and Caillet, falling into the hands of Charles the Bad, was beheaded summarily with a sword.

Wat Tyler's insurrection was in 1381. Jack Cade's was 69 years later, in 1450.
Pronounce *Zjah-ke-re.* Caillet, pronounce *Ki-yea.*

Jacques Bonhomme. The name assumed by Guillaume Caillet, leader of the revolt called after him ' La Jacquerie ' (*q.v.*).

Pronounce *Zjark Bun-num' ; Ghu'yum Ki'yea.*

Jactitation of Marriage. A false pretension to marriage. The person who utters the pretence is called in law the ' boaster ' (jactātor). This pretence is now actionable at law.

Jaffa Massacre (*The*), 1799. Bonaparte had taken about 2,000 prisoners in his Egyptian campaign ; they were a mixed body of Egyptians, Turks, and others. Thinking they would encumber his army, he marched them out to the sandhills, south-east of Jaffa (Joppa), had them all shot, and piled the dead bodies into a pyramid.

Jagello (*Dynasty of the*), 1386–1572. Succeeded in Poland the House of Anjou. Hedviga, the youngest daughter of Louis the Great king of Hungary and Poland, married Jagello of Lithuania, and thus the dynasty was founded. It gave six kings.

Jagello was the thirteenth son of Gedymin duke of Lithuania.

Jago (*Knights of St.*). A Spanish military order instituted under Alexander III., the grand-master.

Jain'as, A.D. 500. A very numerous heterodox sect of Hindûs. So called from *Jina* (deified saint). Like the Buddhists, they deny the divine authority of the Veda; but, with the Brahmans, they admit the institution of 'caste.' The Jainas declined in numbers after 1200.

Sometimes they are called 'Arhatas,' from *arhat*, another word for 'deified saint.'

Jalès. A borough and château of Languedoc. In Sept. 1790 was formed the *Camp de Jalès*, consisting of French nobles whose object was to overthrow the Constituent Assembly. The château was burnt to the ground in 1792, and the 'camp' was scattered to the winds.

The camp, which was really 2,000 strong, boasted of being able to bring 70,000 men into the field to put down the revolutionary party.—CARLYLE, *French Revolution*, vol. ii. bk. v.

James I. of Great Britain, first of the Stuart dynasty (1566, 1603–1625).

Father, Henry Stuart lord Darnley. *Mother*, Mary queen of Scots, daughter of James V. of Scotland. James I. was great-grandson of the Princess Margaret, a daughter of Henry VII. *Wife*, Ann daughter of Frederic II. of Denmark. *Court favourites*, Robert Carr, whom he made duke of Somerset, and George Villiers, whom he created duke of Buckingham.

HENRY VII. was the father of HENRY VIII. and Margaret.
HENRY VIII. was the father of his three successors, EDWARD VI., MARY, and ELIZABETH (all without issue).
Margaret married James IV. of Scotland—the parents of James V. And James V. was the father of Mary queen of Scots,
** CHARLES I. succeeded his father JAMES I.; and Elizabeth daughter of James I., who married the Elector Palatine, was called 'queen of Bohemia.' Their daughter Sophia was the mother of GEORGE I.
Style and title : 'James D.G. of England, Scotland, France, and Ireland king; Defender of the Faith; and Supreme Head of the Anglican and Hibernian Church.'

James II. (1633, began to reign 1685, abdicated 1688, died at St. Germains 1701).

Father, CHARLES I. *Mother*, Henrietta Maria of France. *Wives* (i.) Anne Hyde, who died 1671; (ii.) Marie Beatrix d'Este, who died 1718.

By Anne Hyde he had four sons and four daughters, six of whom died young and two (viz. MARY and ANNE) were queens of England.
The Pretender, James Francis Edward, was the only surviving son of the second wife (1688–1766).
His style and title was : 'James. D.G. of England, Scotland, France, and Ireland king; Defender of the Faith,' &c.
Mary was born 1662, *married William prince of Orange* 1677, *died* 1694.
Anne was born 1664, *married George of Denmark* 16.., *died* 1714.

James III. (of England). So Louis XIV. recognised the Old Pretender, James son of James II., who had been set aside by the nation over whom he ruled. Louis XIV. insisted that kings reigned 'by divine right,' and, being appointed by God, only God could rightfully depose them.

James VIII., 6 Sept., 1714. James the Pretender, son of James II. of England, was proclaimed at Castleton 'James VIII. of Scotland'; but he was never crowned, and the battles of Preston and Sheriffmuir in 1715 put an end to his hopes of supplanting George I.

James of the Iron Belt. James IV. of Scotland, who fell at Flodden Field (1473, 1488–1513).

James the Conqueror. James I. of Aragon (1206, 1213–1276). So called from his numerous victories over the Moors.

James the Just. James II. of Aragon (1261, 1285–1327). So called from his just and strictly legal dealings with his subjects.

James with the Fiery Face. James II. of Scotland, son of James I. So called from a fiery red stain on his face (1430, 1437–1460).

Jane (*Three Heroic Contemporaries named*), 1342, &c. Jane wife of De Clisson, Jane wife of De Montfort, and Jane wife of Charles de Blois. Three of the most heroic women that ever lived. All antagonistic to the French and allies of Edward III. The wife of De Blois was called 'Jane the Lame.'

Jan'izary. A corruption of *yengicheri*, new soldiers. Ottoman infantry, who, in times of peace, acted as a police force, but proved a most unruly lot, their whole history abounding with conspiracies and the assassinations of sultans and viziers. The force was dissolved in 1826, but 15,000 of them were executed and 20,000 were exiled.

The new militia was consecrated and named by a celebrated dervish, who said: 'Let them be called *yengi-cheri*; may their countenance be ever bright; and, wherever they go, may they return with *white* [joyous] faces.—GIBBON, lxiv.

Jan'senism, 1640. The tenets of Cornelius Jansen bishop of Ypres, opposed to those of the Jesuits. Jansen was a disciple of St. Augustine, whose religious views were very similar to those

H H

of Calvin. He wrote a book called 'Augustīnus,' published in 1640; and from this book the following five points were deduced : (1) It is not possible to keep some of God's commandments ; (2) Inward grace is irresistible; (3) Man has liberty free from restraint, but not free from predestination, or there could be no such things as sin and merit; (4) The *Semi-Pelagians* were heretical, because they asserted the necessity of an inward preventive grace ; (5) It is heresy to say that Jesus died for all. The book was very severe against the Jesuits, who induced Urban VIII. to condemn it 1642.

Jan'senists, 1640. Disciples of Cornelius Jansen bishop of Ypres (1585–1638). Condemned by Innocent X. in 1653. Blaise Pascal wrote his famous 'Lettres Provinciales' in 1656, in their defence and against the Jesuits, whom he charged with immorality, equivocation, mental reservation, and simony. A formulary was issued by Innocent X. which the Jansenists were required to sign. This they refused to do. Alexander VII. in 1656 issued another bull of condemnation, and again commanded the Jansenists to sign the formulary. Still they refused, and to prevent a split in the church the next pope compromised the matter by withdrawing the formulary. This is called 'The Peace of Clement IX.' 1668. Clement XI. in 1713 issued his bull called 'Unigenitus' in condemnation of the Jansenists, who appealed to a general council, and were therefore called 'Appellants.' In 1720 the Jansenists were banished from France by the Regent Orléans.

The Jansenists were Calvinistic Catholics who maintained the doctrines of grace, predestination, and non-freedom of the will.

Janua'rius's Blood (*St.*). Januarius bishop of Benevento was beheaded in the tenth and last Roman persecution, about 303. It is said that a lady of Naples caught about an ounce of his blood at the moment of decapitation (!), and this blood, preserved in a phial, from that day to this has lost none of its weight. Three times a year this phial in Naples is brought near the head of the saint, and the blood, which before was congealed, liquefies.

It appears to me that catching the blood [in the phial] was the greatest miracle. The liquefaction is a small affair. Any chemist could manage that.

January 1. Made in England New Year's Day in 1751. (24 Geo. II. c. 23.)

March indubitably is the proper beginning of the year. And our calendar still recognises it as such in the names of the last four months.

January (*Edict of*), 1562. Which granted to the Huguenots of France full liberty of conscience, provided they held their meetings beyond the barriers of Paris. *See* 'Edict of Amboise.'

The judge pleaded the Edict of January. 'The Edict of January!' said Guise, laying his hand upon his sword. 'This steel shall speedily cut asunder that edict, however tightly bound.'— G. DE FELICE, *History of the Protestants of France*, v.

January 21 (1793). Memorable for the decapitation of Louis XVI. The place of execution was what is now called the 'Place de la Concorde.' It is a *fête* day with Napoleonists.

He gave a jovial supper to his companions on the 21st of January, the anniversary of the execution of Louis XVI.—*The Czar*, ch. xxxii.

HISTORICAL COINCIDENCES:—

1. The number of letters in Charles I. and Louis XVI. is in both cases 8.
2. The sum of the dates 1649 and 1793 is in both cases 20.
3. The sum of the days 30 and 21 is in both cases 3.
4. The month in both cases is January.
5. Both were Christian kings ; both were tried by their subjects ; and both were decapitated by judicial sentence.

January 25 (*The Manifesto of*), 1655. By Gastaldo, 'conservator-general of the holy faith.' 'It is enjoined and commanded on all persons of the pretended reformed religion of every state, inhabitants of Lucerna, Lucernetta, San Giovanni, La Torre, Bibbiana, Fenile, Campiglione, Bricherasco, and San Secondo, to withdraw from the aforesaid places within three days. . . . Those who disobey this edict will incur the penalty of death, and the confiscation of all their property not disposed of to Catholics.

January 30, 1649. Memorable for the decapitation of Charles I. at Whitehall. *See* 'January 21 *n*.'

January 31 (*Edict* or *Decree of*), 1686. Abolishing the religious services of the Vaudois, or any other form of religious teaching except the Roman Catholic, under pain of death and confiscation of property. It commanded the instant demolition of all houses of worship in which 'the reformed religion' was observed, the banishment of all Vaudois ministers and schoolmasters, the compulsory baptism of all children by Catholic priests, and their education in the Catholic faith.

Janus. One of the gods of old Rome, represented with two faces. Numa Pompilius, according to LIVY, built a gate which was to be closed in time of peace. It was closed four times: once B.C. 235, in the consulship of Titus Manlius; again B.C. 29, by Augustus Cæsar; a third time B.C. 25, also by Augustus; and finally A.D. 71 by Vespasian.

St. Augustine says:—

The gates of Janus were not the gates of a temple, but the gates of a passage called Janus, which was used only for military purposes. 'Shut,' therefore, in peace; open in war.—*The City of God*, vol. i. p. 98.

Japan in 1889 received a new constitution, two chambers being established on the German model.

Japanese Martyrs, 5 Feb., 1597. A number of Franciscan friars crucified near Nagasa'ki. They were beatified in 1627, and canonised by Pius IX. in 1862.

Japanese Perry of the United States, America, whose head is represented on the 90-cent stamps, is Commodore Matthew Calbraith Perry (1795–1858), who made the treaty for the United States with Japan. Both he and his father were celebrated naval officers. *See* 'American Postage Stamps.'

There was another of the name, also an American naval officer, viz. Oliver Hazard Perry (1785–1820).

Ja'redites (3 syl.). The first American colony, according to the Book of Mormon. They were led from the Tower of Babel, at the dispersion, by Jared. The Jaredites were a wicked and bloody people, who utterly extirpated themselves by war. In B.C. 600 Nephi brought over a new colony from Jerusalem, and these new settlers were called Nephites.

Jarvey (*A*). A hackney coachman of the olden times. So called from Jarvis, one of the fraternity, who was hanged (BALLANTINE).

Jasher (*The Book of*). Quoted twice in the Old Testament (Jos. x. 13, and 2 Sam. i. 18). Nothing more is known about it. *See* 'Literary Forgeries'

In 1751 Jacob Ilive published a forged book so called, but the forgery was exposed in the 'Monthly Review' Dec. 1751. It was republished by Donaldson in 1854.

Jasper. The first foundation of the celestial city, represented the tribe of Gad in the pectoral of the high priest, and as a zodiacal sign it stands for Pisces. Symbolically it means 'lucky,' or 'win at last.'

Jassy (*Treaty of*), 9 Jan., 1792. A treaty of peace between Russia and the Porte, which fixed the Dniester as the boundary between Russia and Turkey.

Jaunot. The European Chinaman. His real name is M. Lemaire. He was consul-general of Shanghai, and in 1884 was appointed minister plenipotentiary at Hué. Lemaire was nicknamed Jaunot at school from his singularly yellow complexion. He married a Cochin-Chinese lady, and was appointed interpreter of the French Consulate.

Pronounce *Zjone-o*.

Jean I. Though enrolled among the kings of France, like Napoleon II., is a *vox et præterea nihil.* Jean I. was the posthumous son of Louis X. by Clementia his wife; but the child died three weeks after its birth.

Jean le Bon or **John the Good.** Jean II. of France (1319, 1350–1364). He was brought captive to England after the battle of Poitiers, and remained in captivity from 1357 to 1361, when the French agreed to pay a million and a half sterling for his ransom. Jean returned to Paris and sent his two sons as hostages till the ransom was paid. The two princes violated their parole and escaped to France; whereupon Jean returned to his captivity, saying, ' Good faith must never be violated by a king.' It was this which gained for him the name of ' Le Bon.'

Jeanne d'Arc. The University of Paris condemned her on twelve charges:

I. *Her apparitions,* inspired by Belial, Satan, and Behemoth.

II. *Her sign to the king,* a lie.

III. *The visits of St. Catherine,* a rash belief injurious to the faith.

IV. *Her predictions,* mere superstitious divination.

V. *Her wearing male attire by command of God,* blasphemy.

VI. *The letters written to the English to depart from France,* traitorous, bloodthirsty, and blasphemous.

VII. *Her leaving Chinon,* filial impiety.

VIII. *Her attempt to escape from the tower at Beaurevoir,* cowardice.

IX. *Her confidence in her salvation,* presumption.

X. *Her assertion that St. Catherine and St. Margaret do not speak English,* blasphemy, and violation of love to our neighbour.

XI. *Paying honour to saints,* idolatry.
XII. *Refusal to submit to the Church (i.e.* **her tribunal),** schism.

The judgment was reversed in 1246, and the former record of the University of Paris torn out of the register and destroyed.

Jedburgh Justice ; also called ' Jeddart Justice ' and ' Jedwood Justice,' Jeddart and Jedwood being local variations of Jedburgh, in Roxburghshire, Scotland. A summary proceeding against mosstroopers, who were punished without trial if taken *flagrante delicto.*

Somewhat similar expressions are the following: Cupar Justice. Bradford Law, Jedburgh Law, Halifax Law, Abingdon Law (*q.v.*), Burslem Club Law, Mob Law, Lynch Law, &c.

Jeddart Staff (*A*). A species of battle-axe, especially used in the ancient borough of Jeddart. The armorial bearings of Jeddart are an armed horseman brandishing a battle-axe.

The tongue of a tale-bearer breaketh bones as well as a Jeddart staff.—Sir W. SCOTT, *The Abbot,* chap. iv.

Jeffreidos (4 syl.). A mock epic by William Davenant, the subject of which is the combat of Sir Jeffrey Hudson, the dwarf, with a turkey-cock.

Jeffreys' Bloodstone. So the ring presented in 1684 by Charles II. to Chief Justice Jeffreys was popularly called, because he received it just after the execution of Sir Thomas Armstrong.

Jeffreys' Campaign, 1685. So James II. called the circuit of Judge Jeffreys, through Dorchester, Exeter, Taunton, and Wells, after Monmouth's rebellion. As many as 251 persons were condemned to death as partisans of Monmouth.

Jefume, *i.e.* ' treading on the crucifix.' The Dutch were allowed to traffic in Japan provided they would trample on the crucifix to show they were not Roman Catholics. From 1586 to 1637 Spaniards and Portuguese freely traded in Japan ; but at the latter date a Dutchman revealed to the Emperor of Japan a conspiracy formed by the Spaniards and Portuguese to murder him. Both of these people were expelled, and no Roman Catholic was allowed to trade in the country. The Jefume was abolished in 1854, when the ports were thrown open.

Jellale'an Era (*The*), 1074. The calendar of the Seleucidês, reformed in the reign of Malek Shah by an assembly of sage astronomers. At this epoch the Persian year was nearly 112 days before the sun, and to make the Persian calendar coincide with the Julian the assembly commanded that the vernal equinox should always be on the fourteenth day of what we call March, and that the intercalary days should be six instead of five every fourth year.

Sir Harris Nicholas calls the word Jelaledin, and says he was a sultan. James B. Fraser calls the word Jellalean, and says that the calendar was reformed, not by a sultan, but by sage astronomers when Malek Shah was sultan.

Jemmy Twitcher. John earl of Sandwich, one of the New Franciscans, an obscene and impious club, of which Wilkes was also a member. Sandwich was especially forward in condemning No. 45 of the ' North Briton,' and in denouncing Wilkes the editor. As Sandwich was just as lewd and blasphemous as Wilkes, this was like the pot calling the kettle ' Black-face.' The ' Beggar's Opera ' was running at the time at Covent Garden, and when Macheath uttered the words, ' That Jemmy Twitcher should peach, I own surprises me,' all the theatre applied the words to Sandwich, amidst most tumultuous applause, and ever after the earl went by the name of Jemmy Twitcher.

Jenner'ian Institution (*The Royal*). Founded in London 1803. In 1808 it merged in the National Vaccine Establishment.

Dr. Edward Jenner in 1798 published his treatise ' An Enquiry into the Causes and Effects of the Variolæ Vaccinæ,' after his first 'experiment of vaccination in May 1796; and in 1802 received a grant of 10,000*l.* from parliament.

Jenny Geddes (1 syl.). The name of Robert Burns's mare. It was so called after Jenny Geddes of Edinburgh, who took up her stool to throw at the bishop's head when trying in the High Church to introduce the Anglican service.

Jenny mistook the meaning of collect for colic. And when the bishop from the pulpit implored the riotous congregation to hear the collect, she exclaimed, ' Colic, d' you say ? Deil colic the wame o' thee ! '—*i.e.* the devil send the colic into thy stomach.

Je'ofail (*Statutes of*). Statutes for the remedy of slips or accidental errors in a law proceeding. ' Jeofail ' is corrupt for *J'ai failli,* I have made a mistake (in Latin, *Lapsus sum*).

Jer'emie's Prizes (*Dr.*). For proficiency in the Septuagint version of the Old Testament and other Hellenistic literature. Two prizes annually in books for undergraduates. Founded in the University of Cambridge by the Very Rev. James Amiraux Jeremie, D.D., dean of Lincoln, in 1870. *See* 'Regius Professor of Divinity.'

Jerome of Prague (1378–1416).

Jerome (2 syl.) was charged with heresy, and, asking what heresy, was told that, lecturing at Heidelberg, he had likened the Holy Trinity to a liquid in three states: water, vapour, and ice. 'Away with him! Away with him! To the stake! To the stake!' roared the council with one voice, and he was burnt to death. *See* 'Huss.'

St. Patrick's illustration, a leaf of shamrock, was quite as objectionable. Abelard and Jeremy Taylor were equally unorthodox in their attempts to illustrate the 'Three-in-One.' In all these cases the fundamental error is the assumption that the three hypostases are three personal objects or phenomena, which would necessitate their creation. The whole of which supposition is bad philosophy and bad theology.

Jerry-building. Worthless or in-

secure building; cheap contract work, flimsy and showy. So called from the firm of Jerry, Brothers, Liverpool, house contractors, notorious for their unsubstantial edifices (19th cent., latter half).

The falling-in of two villas at Chalk Farm, while in course of erection, will, I hope, call attention to the system of jerry-building so much in vogue.—*Truth*, 29 Oct., 1885.

Jerusalem (*The Destruction of*).

This epoch began with the taking of Jerusalem by Titus, Sept. A.D. 70.

Jerusalem Jump (*The*). A negro

religious service, or 'awakening.' While the negro preacher is still ranting, two concentric circles are formed round him. The outer circle is of men, and the inner one of women, facing the men. Each man then takes hold of the opposite woman, and the two jump together violently, shaking hands and shouting at the top of their voices. After about a minute the two circles move, one one way and one another, so that each brother faces a different sister, and again the jumping is repeated. *See* 'Jumpers.'

This really is not more absurd than the dancing of dervishes.

Jerusalem of Russia (*The*).

Moscow, the 'sacred city.' Close by is the 'Mount of Salvation,' where the natives, coming in full view of their beloved city, kneel and cross themselves.

Jesids (*The*), or 'Devil Worshippers.'

In Russian and Turkish Armenia, the valley of the Tigris, &c. Their holy city is Ba-Hasani. It is said their name is compounded of Jesu (their founder) and Jesid a town. They pray to the rising sun, worship Allah, reverence Mahomet, and deem Christ a great angel ('the son of light'). Their chief concern is to conciliate Shaitan, the devil, whose name they never utter. Thursday is their Sabbath, and they fast forty days in the spring of the year. Their children are baptized, and their ecclesiastical orders consist of sheikhs, fakirs, and djirs (*elders*). They abhor the colour blue, show the greatest respect to women, widows dress in white, and the dead are buried with their faces turned to the pole-star.

Jes'uates (3 syl.), 1355. A religious

order founded by St. John Colombine, and confirmed by Urban V. in 1367. Suppressed in 1668, when all their possessions were given to the Hospitallers of Italy. The object of the order was to administer to the sick and needy. They were suppressed because they were manufacturers of strong drinks. They had popularly the name of 'Aqua Vitæ Fathers.'

Ainsi appelé parce que ses fondateurs avaient toujours le nom de Jésus à la bouche.—BOUILLET.

Jesuits, founded 1538. A religious

society founded by Ignatius Loyola, and confirmed by Paul III. in 1540. It was monarchical in its constitution and secular, while all other Catholic societies are more or less democratic and regular. The head of the society is called the General, or 'Præpositus Generalis,' and holds his office for life. This General has absolute command over the whole society, and from his decisions there is no appeal.

The four objects of the society are: (1) the education of youth; (2) the education of others by preaching, &c.; (3) the defence of the Catholic faith against all heretics and unbelievers, and (4) the propagation of the Catholic faith among the heathen. The Jesuits wear no monastic garb, but dress like any other of the 'secular clergy' (*q.v.*), and live in no religious house, but in private dwellings. Banished from England by 27 Eliz. c. 2 A.D. 1584, banished from France in 1594, expelled from Portugal in 1759, expelled

from Spain in 1767, expelled from Naples
1767, expelled from Parma 1768, expelled from Malta 1768, dissolved by
Clement XIV. in 1773, expelled from
Russia 1820, expelled from Switzerland
1847, expelled from Genŏa 1848, expelled
from Naples, the Papal States, Austria,
Sicily, 1848. Still they survive.

They are accused of being accessories to the
Gunpowder Plot, the Popish Plot, the Thirty
Years' War, and almost all the political troubles
of Europe.

Jesuits of the Revolution (*The*).
The Girondins are so called by Dumouriez, ' Mémoires,' iii. 314.

Jesuitesses (*The*), 1534. An order
of religious women, founded by two Eng-
lishwomen, Warda and Tuittia, in imitation of Loyola's foundation. Abolished
by Urban VIII. in 1631.

These women were street preachers. Surely
Warda and Tuittia are not English names, but so
is the record.

Jesus College. I. In Cambridge
University, founded by John Alcock
bishop of Ely, in 1496.

II. In Oxford, 1571. Founded by Queen
Elizabeth. The head-master is called the
principal.

Jesus Paper. Paper bearing the
letters I.H.S. for the water-mark. It is
of large size.

Jeu de Paume (*Day of the*),
20 June, 1789. When the States-General
assembled 5 May, 1789, to investigate
the wrongs of France and adjust the
finances, the nobles and clergy snubbed
the Tiers Etat; whereupon the Tiers Etat
left the Salle de Menu, retired to the
tennis court, and constituted themselves
the ' National Assembly,' wholly ignoring
the nobles and clergy, who refused to join
them. They then took an oath not to
separate till they had given France a
constitution. Seven days afterwards the
Duc d'Orléans, with forty-seven of the
noblesse and a large number of the clergy,
joined the Tiers Etat in the tennis court,
and declared themselves the national
parliament under the name of the ' Constituent Assembly ' (Assemblée Constituante).

Jeu de Paulme (*Jeud pome*), tennis. The Day of
the Jeu de Paume (June 20) was the great holiday
during the Revolution.

Jeune (*Le*). Louis VII. was so
called, not for his youth, but for his

puerile policy, as Ethelred of England was
called the ' Unready,' *i.e.* the impolitic.

1. Louis VII. began his reign with quarrelling
with his clergy, for which he was excommunicated.
2. He interfered with the Count of Vermandois,
whereby he got into hot water with the Count of
Champagne, and setting fire to the count's castle
burnt down the whole town of Vitry.
3. He left his kingdom to conduct an absurd expedition to the Holy Land, which failed throughout.
4. He divorced his wife Eleonore, who married
Henry II. of England, whereby France lost Poitou
and Aquitane.
5. He went to Palestine by land and not by sea,
contrary to the advice of his best counsellors.
6. His wars with England were perfidious and
most short-sighted in policy.
Though amiable enough, he failed in everything
from want of worldly wisdom, manly energy, and
state prudence.

Jeunesse Dorée de Fréron (*La*),
1794. Those young men of the Thermidorian faction who armed themselves
according to the advice of Fréron, given
in his journal ' L'Orateur du Peuple.'
These were violent against the Jacobin
Club, with whom they had frequent
skirmishes.

Jew of Tewkesbury (*The*). This
was Salomon, a Jew whom Richard earl
of Gloucester, in 1260, offered to pull out
of a cesspool into which he had fallen
one Saturday; but the Jew refused the
proffered aid, saying: ' Sabbata nostra
colo; de stercore surgere nolo.' Next
day [Sunday] the earl passed again, and
the Jew cried to him for help. ' No,
no, friend!' replied the earl, ' Sabbata
nostra quidem, Salomon, celebrabis ibidem.' This story occurs twice in the
' Chron. Monast. de Melsa,' ii. pp. 134, 137.

Eodem tempore apud Theokesbury, quidam
Judæus cecidit in latrinam, sed quia tunc erat
sabbatum, non permisit se extrahi, nisi sequente
die Dominica, propter reverentiam sui sabbati,
quamobrem Judæum contigit mori in fœtore.—
Rolls Series.

Jews of Damascus (*Persecution
of the*), 1840. A Catholic priest named
Thomaso of Damascus, having disappeared suddenly in February, a Jew
barber at whose house he was seen was
examined by torture, when he accused
seven of the most wealthy Jewish merchants of being concerned in the murder.
The seven merchants were apprehended ;
two died under torture, the other five
pleaded guilty. A dreadful persecution of
the Jews followed, and the absurd notion
was confirmed that human blood was
necessary for the paschal feast. The
English and French interfered, repre-

sented to Mehemet Ali the absurdity of the notion, and the persecution ceased.

Jews' Parliament (*The*), 1243. Six of the richest Jews from each large town of England, and two from each small town, sent by the county sheriffs to meet Henry III. at Worcester, on Quinquagesima Sunday 1248, 'to treat with him for their mutual benefit.' *See* 'Parliaments.'

The king informed his Jewish advisers that they must raise without delay 20,000 marks (200,000*l.* of money at its present value), one half to be ready by Midsummer day, and the other moiety by Michaelmas day.

Jewel of Europe (*The*). Sicily. According to legend, God plucked a jewel from his crown out of which he formed Sicily.

Jewel of Seville (*The*). The Giralda is so called. It is the most beautiful and largest specimen of Oriental architecture of its kind.

Jewish Disabilities Act (*The*). 21, 22 Vict. c. 49, 22 July, 1858. By this act the oath administered to members of parliament was modified to suit the religious faith of Jews. Baron Rothschild was member for Hythe, and Alderman Salomons for Greenock in 1858.

Jewish Emancipation. Jews emancipated in the United Kingdom from disabilities of holding municipal offices and voting as members of parliament.

1. Naturalised without being required to take the sacrament 1753 (26 Geo. I. c. 26).
2. Admitted to the elective franchise 1832 (2 Will. IV. c. 45).
3. Liberty of religious worship granted as to dissenters, 1855 (19 Vict. c. 86).
4. Made eligible to seats in parliament 1858 (21, 22 Vict. c. 49).
5. All disabilities removed, and the oath 'On the true faith of a Christian' omitted 1860.

Jewish Mundane Era (*The*), B.C. Commences with the vernal equinox 3761. *See* 'Era.'

Jewish Plato (*The*). Philo-Judæus of Alexandria, who endeavoured to weld Platonism and the Mosaic institutions together ; B.C. 20, died about A.D. 61.

Jewish Sects. *See* each *in loco.*

Chasidim	Hero'dians
Beshters	Karaites *
Essenes (2 syl.)	Masboth'eans
Galilēans	Meristes *
Gaulanites (3 syl.), probably Rabbinists of extreme views	Pharisees
	Sad'ducees
	Shebsen
Hellēnians *	Therapeutæ
Hellenists	Zealots or Zelotes
Hem'erobap'tists *	

Nothing beyond the names is known of those sects to which a * is attached.

Jewish Soc'rates (3 syl.). Moses Mendelssohn, the modern Jewish philosopher (1729–1785). So called for his 'Phædon,' a dialogue on the immortality of the soul in imitation of Plato.

One would think the better appellative would be the 'Jewish Plato.'

Jewry (*Statute of*). Forbade usury by Jews, and provided that the Jews should live in 'the king's own cities and boroughs where the Chest of Chirographs of Jewry are wont to be.' They were permitted by this statute to buy houses and farms, and to hold them for fifteen years.

Jezebel, Aunt of Dido. *See* 'Dido.'

Jezre'elites (4 syl.), 1884, or 'The New and Latter House of Israel.' A religious sect founded by James Jershom White, a private of the 16th regiment, who compiled from the works of Joanna Southcott and John Wroe a book which he called 'The Flying Roll.' He called himself Jezreel, and gave himself out to be the spiritual child of Joanna Southcott, the Joshua of Christ, and the Immortal Spirit who held the last message of God to man. White erected a temple 144 feet in length, breadth, and height, at Gillingham, near Chatham. The great hall would hold 5,000 persons. He died 1885, but his wife gave herself out to be Esther the queen, the virgin, and mother of Israel, sent to prepare the people for Christ's second advent in 1895.

Jin'goes (2 syl.), 1877. Russophobists. Those who supposed that Russia would take Constantinople and then our Indian empire; but any Bobadil or warlike blusterer was afterwards called a Jingo. The word was adopted from ' M'Dermott's War Song'—that is, the song sung in music halls by M'Dermott and very popular at the time. The chorus runs thus :—

We don't want to fight, but, by Jingo ! if we do,
We've got the ships, we've got the men, we've got the money too.

Jin'goism, 1877. Warlike bluster and Bobadilism. The French *chauvinism* (*q.v.*) is now used in much the same sense. *See* 'Jingoes.'

J. J. In Hogarth's 'Gin Lane,' written on a gibbet, is Sir J[oseph]

J[ekyll], obnoxious for his bill to increase the duty on gin.

J. K. L. That is, Dr. Doyle, unquestionably the most accomplished polemical writer of his time, died 1834. The letters stand for James Kildare Leighlin—that is, his Christian name and his see as Catholic bishop.

He [Mr. Stanley] made an exception in favour of the then [1832] celebrated J. K. L. He acknowledged a letter from Dr. Doyle . . . with warm expressions of thanks . . . and expressed a wish to see him on his arrival in Dublin.—HOWITT, *History of England* (year 1832, p. 215).

Joan Makepeace, 1328. Joan sister of Edward III., who at the age of seven was affianced to David son of Robert Bruce, aged five. This betrothal was brought about by Mortimer (the paramour of Isabella the queen dowager), to cement the peace made between the English and Scotch in the year 1328.

Joan of Arc. Called ' La Pucelle,' ' the Maid of Orleans ' (1412–1431). Her sword was the mystic sword of St. Catherine.

Joan of Kent. Joan Bocher, an Anabaptist who was burnt at Smithfield 2 May, 1550. Some say she was convicted and sentenced by Archbishop Cranmer, and others say when Edward VI. was called on to sign the writ of her execution his eyes were full of tears. Others affirm that the writ was issued by the Court of Chancery and that Cranmer had no part in the matter. ' Sir Thomas Browne, who wrote against vulgar errors, influenced the jury to give their verdict against the woman ' (' Parr's Works,' iv. 181). *See* ' Van Paris.'

Blunt ('Reformation in England,' p. 260) says she was condemned, 'probably under the law against Anabaptists, who advocated community of goods.'

Joan the Fair Maid of Kent was quite another person. She married Edward the Black Prince, and died 1385. See ' Pope Joan.'

Joanna and Isabella, 1468–1479. Names which produced a civil war in Castile. The question was, which of these two should succeed Enrique on the throne. Isabella was his sister (wife of Don Ferdinand, who was son of Juan II. king of Navarre), Joanna was the natural daughter of Enrique. The Archbishop of Toledo took the part of Isabella, and undertook to dethrone Enrique, but war for ten years desolated the kingdom. Enrique died, his daughter Joanna retired to a convent, and

Isabella with Ferdinand became sovereigns of Aragon and Sicily, Leon and Castile.

Joanna Southcott (1750–1814). The mission of this ' prophetess ' began in 1792, when she declared herself to be ' the woman driven into the wilderness ' of Rev. xii. Her prophecies are in prose and wretched doggrel, and she gave her followers her *seals*—that is, bits of paper sealed to insure them against the wrath of God. In 1814 she announced she was about to be the mother of Shiloh the Prince of Peace, but she died the same year of dropsy.

Joanna Southcott was born in Devonshire of humble parents, and was in youth a domestic servant.

Joanna the Mad, Queen of Castile (1479, 1504–1555). She married Philip archduke of Austria, and was the mother of Kaiser Karl V., emperor of the Romans, king of Castile, afterwards of Spain, &c.

Joan'nites (3 syl.). The adherents of John Chrysostom, who stood firmly on his side when Theophilus of Alexandria charged him with heresy and misdemeanour. *See below,* ' Johannists.'

Jockey of Norfolk. Sir John Howard, a firm adherent of Richard III. On the night before the battle of Bosworth field he found a warning couplet in his tent, running thus :—

Jocky of Norfolk be not too bold,
For Dicon, thy master, is bought and sold.

** Dicon or Dickon of course means Richard III., and Jocky or Jacky = Jack, Jock, or John.

Jockies. Superior sort of vagrants, perhaps a relic of the ancient bards or minstrels. They were well versed in the slogan or gathering-cries of Scotland, and being full of observation, and very entertaining, were admitted into the houses of the well-to-do as guests. The race is now extinct.

The well-remembered beggar was his guest.
GOLDSMITH, *Deserted Village.*

(Here ' well-remembered ' means having a good memory.)

Johannists. A sect which refused to acknowledge the successor of John surnamed Chrysostom, who died in 407. The Johannists refused to return to the general communion till 438, when the body of Chrysostom was brought back to Constantinople and solemnly interred, the emperor himself (Theodosius the Younger) taking part in the service.

John. The hated name of kings in England, France, and Scotland. The English king John was certainly as bad a king as ever reigned. In France John I. reigned only a few days, and John II., having lost the battle of Poitiers, died in captivity in London. In Scotland John [Baliol] was a mere tool of Edward I. So greatly was the name disliked in Scotland that John son of Robert II. reigned under the designation of Robert III.

Popes named John. There have been twenty-three popes of this name. One *abdicated* (John XVIII.); four were *deposed* (John XII., XIII., XIV., XIX.); two were *expelled* (John XVI., XVII.); two were charged with *heresy* (John IV., XXII.); four were *imprisoned* (John I., VIII., X., XI.); seven were *nonentities* (John II., III., V., VI., VII., XV., XX.); one was *killed accidentally* (John XXI.); and one had Sergius III. for a *rival pope* (John IX.).

JOHN I. (523-526). *Imprisoned* at Ravenna by Theodoric, and died in prison.
— II., III. *Nonentities.*
— IV. (640-642). Accused of *heresy.*
— V., VI., VII. *Nonentities.*
— VIII. (872-882). *Imprisoned* by Lambert duke of Spoleto ; made his escape to France, and was poisoned.
— IX. (898-900). Had Sergius III. for a *rival pope.*
— X. (914-928). Cast into *prison and murdered* by order of Guido and Marozia.
— XI. (931-936). *Imprisoned* with his mother by Alberic, and died in the castle of St. Angelo.
— XII. (956-964). A most profligate libertine. Was *deposed* and died suddenly, probably by *assassination.*
— XIII. (965-972). *Imprisoned* by his nobles and *deposed.*
— XIV. (983-995). *Deposed; imprisoned* by Boniface VII., an antipope, and died in the castle of St. Angelo.
— XV. A *nonentity.*
— XVI. (985-996). Driven from Rome by Crescentius.
— XVII. (997-998). Antipope. *Expelled* by Otto III., and barbarously treated by Gregory.
— XVIII. (1003-1009). *Abdicated.*
— XIX. (1024-1033). *Deposed* and expelled by Konrad.
— XX. A *nonentity.*
— XXI. (1276-1277). *Crushed to death* by the falling in of his palace at Viterbo.
— XXII. (1316-1334). Charged with *heresy*, and recanted.
— XXIII. (1410-1419). *Deposed*, and afterwards imprisoned for three years.

. A very sad list indeed.

John Amend-all. John Cade, an Irishman, who gave himself out to be the son of Sir John Mortimer, and heir to the English throne. In May 1450 he encamped on Blackheath with 20,000 followers ; but he was captured and killed on 1 July the same year.

John called Robert. John earl of Carrick, eldest son of Robert II. of Scotland, was crowned 1390 as Robert III., because John had proved an ill-omened name in England, France, and Scotland.

John Company. The old East India Company. Also called 'Mother Company.'

In 1857 the 19th Native Infantry feasted the 11th Irregulars, and told them that John Company had sent out Lord Canning to convert India to Christianity.—HOWITT, *Hist. of Eng.* (year 1857, p. 407).

John Free-born. John Lilburne (1618–1657). So called from his intrepid defence, before the tribunal of the Star Chamber, of his rights as a free-born Englishman.

John-Jacob Christians. A branch of the strict Mennonites, which split from the general body in 1554. So called from their founder. *See* 'Mennonites' (3 syl.).

John Knox's Liturgy. The Book of Common Prayer used in the Presbyterian Church of Scotland.

Extempore prayer is also used.

John 'Lackland' king of England, (1166, 1199–1216). *Father*, Henry II.; *Mother*, Eleanor of Aquitaine; *Wives* (1) Alice; (2) Avisa daughter of William earl of Gloucester, divorced; (3) Isabelle daughter of Aymer count of Angoulême, by whom he had five children (none by the other two) :—

1. HENRY III., his successor.
2. Richard earl of Cornwall, chosen King of the Romans, and crowned at Aix-la-Chapelle in 1257.
3. Jane, married Alexander II. of Scotland in 1221.
4. Eleanor, married first William earl of Pembroke, then Simon de Montfort earl of Leicester, by whom she had two sons, who with their mother were banished for rebellion.
5. Isabella, who married Friedrich II. the Kaiser. She died 1241.

His style and title.—John, D.G. rex Angliæ, dominus Hiberniæ [Iberniæ or Yberniæ], dux Normanniæ. They addressed him 'Rex Anglorum.' This was the first of our kings called 'Dominus Hiberniæ,' which title continued till Henry VIII. changed it into 'King of Ireland.'

John Lackland alone of all the sons of Henry II. had no territory or land left him. Henry, the eldest son, was associated with his father in the government, but died before him ; Richard Cœur de Lion had Poitou and Guyenne; Geoffrey had Brittany in right of his wife.

N.B. The first *Henry*, 'lord of Ireland,' was Henry III. son of John, and in Rymer's 'Fœdera' Dr. Clarke has erroneously ascribed to Henry II. a document belonging to Henry *dominus Hyberniæ*.

John of Gaunt, fourth [not third] son of Edward III. Was born at Ghent in Flanders, whence he was called John of Gaunt (Ghent). His first wife, Blanche, was daughter of the Duke of Lancaster.

John of Gaunt received his title of duke of Lancaster from his father-in-law.

Henry VII. claimed his title of the crown through John Beaufort, a natural son of John of Gaunt.

John o' Groat's to Land's End
(*From*). Through the entire length of the kingdom. John o' Groat's is furthest north and Land's End, Cornwall, is furthest south of the mainland of Great Britain.

John of Jerusalem (*Knights of St.*), 1120. So called from John patriarch of Alexandria and the place of their abode. The knights subsequently resided at Rhodes (1310–1523). When driven from Rhodes by the Turks they made their abode at Malta, and were called 'Knights of Malta.'

John the Furious. A Norwegian chieftain who went to Ireland (1170) to restore Hascult to his throne of Dublin. He was felled to the ground and slain by Walter de Riddlesford, an English knight, the same year.

John with the Leaden Sword.
John duke of Bedford (1424) was so called by Archibald Douglas (*Tineman*).

John duke of Bedford sent a herald to the Scottish chief [in France] to say he was coming to drink wine and revel with him. The Earl of Douglas returned answer that the duke would be most welcome, and that he had come from Scotland to France on purpose to carouse in his company. Under these terms a challenge to combat was understood to be given and accepted.—Sir W. SCOTT, *History of Scotland*, xviii.

Johnnie Cope's Salve, 1745. So the Highlanders called the chocolate taken from the tent of Sir John Cope after the battle of Prestonpans.

Some of the luxuries which the Highlanders found they did not comprehend the use of, and chocolate was soon after cried in the streets of Perth as 'Johnnie Cope's Salve.'—HOWITT, *History of England* (George II. p. 501).

John's College (*St.*).
I. In Cambridge University. Founded by Lady Margaret countess of Richmond and Derby, mother of Henry VII., in 1511.

The founder of Christ's College also.

II. In Oxford, 1555. Founded by Sir Thomas White, a London alderman. The head-master is called the president.

Johns (*Sir*). The poor clergy were so called before the Reformation. 'Babbling Sir Johns' (Wordsworth, 'Ecclesias-

tical Biography,' i. 265). 'Blind Sir Johns' (Jewel, Sermon on Haggai i. 2). Strype speaks of 'Lack-Latin Sir Johns' ('Annals,' 177), and of 'Mumble-matins Sir Johns' ('Annals,' 181).

Johnson Scholarship for theology. Founded in the University of Oxford by John Johnson, D.D., fellow of Magdalen College. In 1878 this scholarship was united to Mrs. Denyer's two theological prizes, and formed into two scholarships called the 'Denyer and Johnson Scholarships' (*q.v.*).

Johnso'nians, as a religious sect, are the followers of the Rev. John Johnson (1662–1725), a nonjuring divine of Liverpool, and author of 'The Unbloody Sacrifice.' They deny the pre-existence of Christ, the three Persons of the godhead, original sin, and the natural immortality of the soul. They baptize by immersion, and believe in the perseverance of the saints.

John-William, or *Jean-Guillaume*, the French Jack Ketch. Jean-Guillaume was the executioner of Paris under Louis XIII., and numerous allusions are made to him by French authors both in prose and verse.

Et personne de mon royaume
Ne se fera pas Jean-Guillaume,
Pour étrangler à belles mains
Ce larron des plus inhumains?
Virgile travesti, bk. iv. (Dido speaks).

** The French have the verb *Jeanguillaumer*, to John-William [you].

Jomsvi'kings (*The*). In Danish, *Jomsvikingr*. The piratical republic of Joms-borg, in the island of Wollin. It was a nest of pirates founded by Danish sea-rovers in the reign of Harald Blaatand (991–1014). This piratical republic continued till the last quarter of the 12th cent., when it was put an end to by Valdemar I. of Denmark (1182–1202).

Jongleurs. 'Joculatõrès,' instrumentalists who accompanied the troubadours to fairs and gentlemen's houses in the middle ages. After the crusade against the Albigenses, the troubadours gradually disappeared, and the jongleurs joined singing to instrumental music, and many danced, juggled, and made fun in all sorts of ways.

Jonköping (*Treaty of*), 10 Dec., 1809. A treaty of peace between Sweden and Denmark.

Jordan (*Mrs.*). The actress to whom the Duke of Clarence (William IV.) was virtually married; eight children survived the king, four sons called Fitzclarence and four daughters. The real name of Mrs. Jordan was Dorothy Bland. Her connection with William was suddenly broken off in 1811 ; she returned to the stage, but she subsequently retired to France, and died at St. Cloud 3 July, 1816. In 1830 William married Adelaide of Saxe-Meiningen, but her two children died before their father did, so the crown went to his niece Victoria, daughter of Edward duke of Kent.

Joseph I. the Victorious. Son of Leopold I. kaiser-king of Germany, of the house of Austria (1676, 1705–1711).

In this reign three great victories were won by Marlborough over the French : 1706 the battle of Ramillies, in 1708 the battle of Oudenarde, and in 1709 the battle of Malplaquet.

Joseph the Unfortunate, kaiser, son of Maria Theresa, who always tried to do right and was always disappointed in all his plans. He wrote, half in jest and half in earnest, what he termed his epitaph : ' Here lies Joseph, unfortunate in all his undertakings ' (1741, 1765–1790).

Josephs of Amida (*The*). One of the three branches of the Nestorians. The other two are the ' Elijahs of Mosul ' and the ' Simeons of Ormia.' The Josephs are now reconciled to the Church of Rome, and are called ' Chaldean Christians.'

Josephinism. Oppression of the Church by the State, so-called from Joseph II. of Austria.

Josephi'nos, 1808. Those Spanish grandees who had traitorously sided with Napoleon in his scandalous usurpation of the Spanish crown. So called because they supported Joseph Bonaparte, his brother's viceroy-king of Spain, and fled with Joseph to Vittoria for safety on the first reverse of the French arms, at the battle of Baylen, on 16 July. In this defeat Castaños was the Spanish general and Dupont the French.

Jo'sephins, 1885. Followers of Joseph Chamberlain, an advanced Radical.

Jos'ephites (3 syl.). The Mormons who disallow polygamy. So called from Joseph Smith, son of Joseph Smith the founder of Mormonism. These are called the ' Reorganised Church of Jesus Christ of Latter Day Saints.'

There are now one or two other non-polygamous sects.

Joshua of Scotland (*The*). Robert Bruce king of Scotland (born 1274, king 1306–1329, died 1329).

Josiah of his Country (*The*), or 'The Josiah of England.' Edward VI. was generally so called in his own day.

Joule's Equivalent. That if a pound of water falls to the ground through 772 feet, and is then suddenly arrested, its temperature will be raised one degree; and, conversely, the heat that would raise the temperature of a pound of water one degree would (if applied to a steam engine) raise 772 lbs. one foot high.

Jour de Rois (*Le*). The Epiphany. (Twelfth Day), meaning the hypothetical ' Kings ' of Cologne. Voltaire has a satire on the three kings—the Pretender (rejected by England, telling his beads in Italy), Stanislaus (ex-king of Poland, smoking his pipe in Austrasia), and the emperor, or King Charles of Bavaria (living at an inn in Franconia), while Maria Theresa is laughing at this Epiphany.

Journal de Paris (the first French daily paper), 1777.

Journal de Trévoux (*Le*). Published by Jesuits in 1701–1704.

Journal des Révolutions de Paris (*Le*). A vile republican newspaper in the French Revolution, conducted by Prudhomme. If possible it was even more inflammatory than the ' Ami du Peuple ' by Marat. It advocated the murder of Louis XVI., and of all other crowned heads; and recommended the organisation of 100 young men into a band, sworn to assassinate all tyrants, in emulation of Harmodios and Aristogīton of Greece, and of Scævola and the Brutuses of Rome.

Journal des Savants (*Le*). Commenced 5 Jan., 1655.

Journals. Of the House of Lords commenced 1509; that of the House of Commons in 1547.

Journée des Dupes. *See* ' Day of the Dupes.'

Journée des Epérons, 1302. The bloody battle of Courtray, in which the French left on the field about 4,000 knights' spurs.

Another Journée des Epérons was in 1513, the battle of Guinegate, in which the French used their spurs in flight more than their swords in fight.

Journée des Farines, 3 Jan. 1591. When the besiegers attempted to surprise St. Denis, occupied by the troops of Henri IV. This was two days after the Béarnais had attempted to surprise Paris. It was called the ' Journée des Farines ' because the officers disguised themselves as millers leading horses, asses, carts, and so on, and demanded entrance into the town. Their design was to enter the gates and keep them open till the arrival of the troops ; but entrance was denied them, and the alarm given.

Journée des Maubrulés. ' The day of the unburned,' 27 April, 1562. Faveau and Mallart, two Protestants of Brussels, were condemned to be burnt to death. As the executioner was binding Simon Faveau to the stake a woman threw her shoe into the funeral pile. This was a preconcerted signal, and immediately the mob rushed forward, scattered the faggots in all directions, rescued the two victims, and succeeded in sending them out of the country. *See* ' Rise of the Dutch Republic,' by Motley.

Journées de Juillet. *See* ' Days of July.'

Journées de Septembre (*Les*), 2, 3, 4, 5 Sept., 1792. *See* ' Massacre of September.'

Journées des Barricades. *See* 'Barricades.'

Jovinian, 4th cent. A heresiarch, and monk of Milan. He rejected fasts, penance, and celibacy, denied the virginity of Mary, and entertained other 'heretical views.' He was condemned by the Council of Milan in 390, and banished by Theodosius.

Joyous Entry (*The*), 'La Joyeuse Entrée,' 1430. The charter given by Philip the Good to the states of Brabant on his entry into Brussels. On this charter nearly all their privileges rested. In 1789 Kaiser Joseph II. annulled this charter, because the States refused to grant a subsidy. On 20 Nov. Brabant threw off allegiance to Austria, and assumed the title of ' The High and Mighty States.'

The emperor [Joseph II.] on 1 Jan., 1787 (?), published several sweeping edicts, annihilating the most ancient municipal privileges, remodelling the courts of justice, and introducing a totally new system of judicature, in direct violation of the celebrated compact made by Charles V. (?), called ' The Joyous Entry.'—HOWITT, *Hist. of Eng.* (Geo. III. p. 387).

Joyous Science (*The*), or ' The Gay Science.' Minstrelsy (*Joyeuse Science*).

The Joyous Science, as the profession of minstrelsy was called, had its various ranks, like the degrees in the church and in chivalry.—Sir WALTER SCOTT, *The Betrothed*, chap. xix.

Jubilee (*The*), 21 June, 1887, when the 50th anniversary of Queen Victoria's accession to the crown was celebrated in the United Kingdom. The colonies and India, for convenience sake, celebrated the anniversary some weeks before 21 June.

There was a Jubilee in the reign of George III., 25 Oct., 1809. He came to the crown 25 Oct., 1760. Queen Victoria succeeded to the throne 21 June, 1837. Hence it will appear that George celebrated his jubilee at the commencement, and Victoria at the completion of the 50th regnal year.

.* There are scores of Jubilees of divers sorts, as the Handel Jubilee, the Shakespeare Jubilee, the Jubilee of the Reformation, and the Jubilees of the Catholic Church first proclaimed by Boniface VIII. in 1300, &c.

Judaising Teachers. Compromising Jews who mingled the observance of the law with that of the Gospel. They insisted on the rite of circumcision. Peter and John were for a time at least Judaising teachers.

Judaists. Those Christians who insisted on the perpetual obligation of the Jewish law. All the apostles who were the companions of Jews were Judaists. Paul insisted that the Gospel was meant for all men, and those who thought with him were called Paulinists or Universalists.

Judas (*The Irish*). Colonel Blood (1628–1680).

Judge-Advocate-General(*The*). The supreme judge, under the Mutiny Act and Articles of War, of the proceedings of courts-martial. He receives a salary of 2,000*l.* a year, and is a member of the ministry.

Judges. The ancient Carthaginians were ruled by a senate of 300, out of which thirty were selected for the council, and two of the council were *suffetes* or judges. So the Hebrews, before the appointment of Saul as king, appointed *shofetim* (judges or bret-waldas) in times of trouble, who were sometimes women. The judges or bret-waldas were—

				B.C.
Othniel	...	...	...	1554—1514
Ehud	...	...	...	1496—1416
Shamgar		...	...	1416—1396
Debôrah (a woman)		...	...	1396—1356
Gideon		...	...	1349—1309
Abimelech (his son)	...	...	...	1309—1306
Tola	...	...	...	1306—1283
Jaïr	...	...	...	1283—1261
Jephthah	...	...	...	1243—1237
Abêsan or Ibzan	...	...	...	1237—1230
Ahiâlon or Elon	...	...	...	1230—1220
Abdon	...	...	...	1220—1212
Samson	...	...	...	1172—1152
Eli (the high priest)	...	...	...	1152—1112
Samuel (priest and prophet)		...	...	1092—1080

Judges of Assize. In 1284 superseded justices in eyre (*q.v.*). Judges of the superior courts commissioned to hold courts or assizes in each county town twice a year.

Judgment and Declaration (*A*), 1683. Passed in the Oxford Convocation, maintaining the doctrine of non-resistance, and enjoining: ' All and singular the readers, tutors, and catechists, diligently to instruct and ground their scholars in that most necessary doctrine . . . of submitting to every ordinance of man for the Lord's sake, teaching that this submission and obedience is to be clear, absolute, and without exception of any state or order of men.'

Judgment of the Cross (*The*). Introduced during the reign of Charlemagne. The plaintiff and defendant of a suit were required to cross their arms upon their breast, and he who could hold out the longest gained the suit.

All ordeals and all oaths are appeals to the judgment of God. Ordeals have been abolished in England ever since 1219, but oaths are still administered (1890). The notion is that God will supplement man's ignorance and idleness by a miraculous interference on the side of what is right. In regard to oaths, as the law stands, to violate an oath is perjury, whereas to violate one's word is only a lie.

Judicial Mass, ' Missa Judicii.' An ordeal mass, in which a person charged with an offence appealed to the ' Judgment of God' in proof of his innocence. *See* ' Mass.'

Judicious (*The*). Richard Hooker, author of the ' Laws of Ecclesiastical Polity' (1554–1600).

Jugurtha (*The Modern*). Abd-el-Kader, bey of Mascara, afterwards sultan (1808–1883). He was no Jugurtha in his moral character, although there was some resemblance in his chivalry, bravery, and misfortunes. Jugurtha, taken captive by the Romans, was thrown into a dungeon at Rome and starved to death ; Abd-el-Kader, taken captive by the French, was imprisoned first in the castle of Pau, then in the castle of Amboise ; but, instead of being starved to death, he was released by Napoleon III. in 1852, retired to Damascus, and died in 1883 at the age of 76.

Jugurthan War (*The*). War between Jugurtha king of Numidia in Africa and the Romans (B.C. 111–104). Jugurtha, being taken prisoner, was sent to Rome and starved to death in the Mamertine prison, a horrible underground dungeon.

Julian Period (*The*). Commenced 1 Jan., 4713 B.C.

Julian Year (*The*). Began 1 Jan., B.C. 45.

Julien the Apostate. Simon Julien, a French painter, pupil of Carlo Vanloo, at Paris. Called the ' Apostate' because he forsook the French school of painting for the Italian.

The Emperor Julian is called the ' Apostate' because he abandoned Christianity for ' the old religion' (331, 361–363).

July Cross (*The*). ' Croix de Juillet,' 1830. Instituted to decorate those Frenchmen who distinguished themselves in chasing Charles X. from the throne. It is a star of three rays, with the legend ' 27, 28, 29 July, 1830,' and the motto ' Patrie et Liberté.' The ribbon is blue edged with red.

July 4 (American history). Declaration of Independence, 4 July, 1776. A national holiday.

July 14. Called, in French history, ' the great day,' in commemoration of 14 July, 1789, the day of the storming of the Bastille. This and June 20 (*q.v.*), the two great days of the Revolution, were made annual festivals.

The disturbed state of Paris since that ' great day,' the 14th of July, had suspended the activity of the National Assembly.—HOWITT, *History of England* (George III., p. 459).

* * For 27, 28, 29 July, when Charles X. was driven from his throne (1830), *see* ' Days of July.'

Jumpers, 1760. Welsh Methodists who jump during religious worship. They are the followers of Harris, Rowlands, Williams, and others. The sermon being over, the preacher begins to jump and the congregation joins in—sometimes for two or three hours. When quite exhausted, they take hold of hands, kneel down, and pray. *See* 'Jerusalem Jump.'

David danced before the ark, and the lame man, on being cured, leaped and praised God.

Jumping-cat School (*The*). Turncoats who run on the winning side. A. B. is 'one of the most notorious examples of the jumping-cat school . . . and is always on the winning side.' (Newspaper paragraph, March 1886).

June 1, 1774. I. In North American history, the day on which the Boston Port Bill (*q.v.*) was to take effect. Selected by the Virginians, Patrick Henry and Thomas Jefferson, as a day of fasting, humiliation, and prayer, 'that the evils of civil war might be averted, that the American colonists might be inspired with firmness in support of their rights, and that the hearts of the British king and parliament might be turned to moderation and justice.'

II. 'The Glorious First of June' is 1 June, 1794, when Lord Howe gained a signal victory over the French off Brest.

June 3 (*Victory of*), 1665. A great naval victory gained by James duke of York over Van Tromp, the Dutch admiral, near Lowestoft. The duke commanded the red, Prince Rupert commanded the white, and the Earl of Sandwich the blue. This was the greatest naval victory hitherto gained by the English. The Dutch lost four admirals, 7,000 men, and eighteen sail. The English only one ship and 600 men killed or wounded.

June 5, 6, A.D. 1832. An émeute in Paris by the republican faction at the funeral of General Lamarque, deputy of the opposition. Barricades were thrown up at St. Antoine, St. Martin, St. Denis (*Sahn-dnee*), and other parts of Paris. The troops were called out, and the combat was brought to a close on the 6th, after taking the church of St. Merry (or Méderic).

June 20. The anniversary of the foundation of the National Assembly.

This and the anniversary of 14 July (*q.v.*) were the two great festivals of the French Republic.

June 23, 24, 25, 26, A.D. 1848. A bloody insurrection of the French republican faction called 'Démocratique et Sociale' against the constitution of 24 Feb. the same year. It made for its pretext the dissolution of the *ateliers nationaux*, and was most rife in the faubourgs St. Jacques, St. Marceau, and St. Antoine. The *garde nationale* and *garde mobile* were employed to suppress the insurrection under General Cavaignac. Seven generals were slain, and representatives, the Archbishop of Paris (Mgr. Affre), and an enormous number of citizens and soldiers. Those insurgents who were taken prisoners were transported.

June 26, and 10 April, 1846. The great Chartist festivals. On 10 April the monster petition was presented, and on 26 June the Corn-laws were repealed.

Junius (*Letters of*), 1769. A series of political letters signed 'Junius,' dissecting the conduct and characters of public men—the Duke of Grafton, the Duke of Bedford, Lord Mansfield, and others, not excepting the King himself. These letters caused the utmost consternation amongst the ministry, and were immensely popular for their caustic satire, just censure, clear reasoning, their great knowledge of the secret government movements, and the brilliancy of their style. It is not known who was the author of these letters, but perhaps the most weighty evidence points to Sir Philip Francis.

The 'North Briton,' under the auspices of Wilkes, and the commencement of the American War, increased the ferment. The letter, 18 March, 1769, to the Duke of Grafton on the 'murderers' of Clarke, and the 14th letter (against Blackstone) are most scathing.

Junto (*The*). I. 1694. A Whig ministry in the reign of William III., the chief members of which were Admiral Russell, the victor of the great battle of La Hogue; Somers, who successfully defended the 'Seven Bishops'; Lord Wharton; and Montague, the great financier. This was the first ministry ever made of one and the same party politics. It was the suggestion of Robert earl of Sunderland to William III., who shrewdly said, if all the ministers

were of one party they would pull together, and if that party represented the
majority they would be able to pass their
measures.

II. 1727. A club formed by Benjamin
Franklin for mutual improvement.
Morals, politics, and natural philosophy,
as well as the social well-being of man,
were the main subjects discussed. It
continued for about thirty years.

Jus Ælia'num. The law books of
Sextus Ælius Catus. These law books
explained the meaning of the mystic
ciphers employed by the lawyers to conceal the laws from the ignoble common
people. Much the same as medical prescriptions are still written, sometimes
by symbols, sometimes by contractions,
sometimes by a single arbitrary letter, or
per siglas. Ælius wrote them out in full,
so that all could read them.

Gibbon, chap. xliv., gives some of these symbols:
Fire and water=married life; resignation of keys
=divorce; casting a stone=prohibition; clenched
fist=a deposit; broken straw=broken covenant,
&c.

Jus Cyp'rium, 431. That each
province is *autocephalous* and each
diocese independent, no one except the
metropolitan having any right to interfere. Called Jus Cyprium because the
canon was laid down in the Council of
Ephesus A.D. 431 in regard to the province of Cyprus, which was declared free
and independent of the province of Antioch.

Jus Devolu'tum, 1712. An act
which provided 'if a patron neglected for
six months to fill up a vacant charge, the
presbytery should fill it up' (Scotland).

Jus Honora'rium. The edicts of
the Roman prætors; written in white
ink. The imperial rescripts were in
purple, and the Jus Civile in red ink.

Jus Ital'icum. All Italian land
was tax free, all provincial land paid
land-tax. Hence the exemption of land
from taxation was called 'The Italian
Right.'

Jus La'tii conferred on cities the
right of electing their own magistrates.
These magistrates took rank and enjoyed
privileges next in degree to Roman
citizens.

Jus Trium Libero'rum. Granting to those who had three children

exemption from the trouble of guardianship, priority in bearing offices, and a
treble proportion of corn.

Just (*The*). Louis XIII. was so
called, but no one knows why. He was
a good shot, and a wit said, 'Il étoit
juste à tirer de l'arquebuse' (1601, 1610–
1643).

Louis XII. was with more reason called
'Le Juste' as well as the 'Father of his
People' (1462, 1498–1515).

Justice-airs. In Scotch history,
were courts of justice held twice a year
in each county by the Justiciar-general.

Air is eyre, French for *iter* a journey. Justice-
airs are *justiciares itinérantes, i.e.* judges to travel
from county to county.

Justices in eyre (air), 1176, *i.e. in
itinere,* 'on journey.' Henry II. divided
England into circuits, and justices went on
these circuits once in seven years. The
courts in which they sat were called
'assizes,' from a law-Latin word *assisa* a
session, from the verb *assideo* to sit down
(supine *assisum*). Magna Charta provided for annual visits (1215). In 1284
justices in eyre were superseded by
judges of assize.

Justinian (*The English*). Edward I. (1239, 1272–1307). Sir Edward
Coke says, 'The statutes passed in this
reign were so numerous and so excellent
that they deserve the name of establishments, being more durable than any made
since.' And Sir Matthew Hale says,
they were so 'excellent as scarcely to
need revision or addition.'

Juvenal (*The English*). I. John
Oldham (1653–1683).

II. Joseph Hall, bishop of Norwich.
Pope affirms Hall's 'Satires' to be 'the
best poetry and truest satires in the English language.'

Juvenal (*The Young*). Dr. Thomas
Lodge (1555–1625). So called by Robert
Green.

Juvenal des Ursins. A French
magistrate born at Troyes (1350–1431),
who enjoyed the confidence of Charles VI.,
and was *prévot de marchands* of Paris
in 1388. He opposed the Duc de Bourbon;
and, having saved the king from falling
into the hands of the duke, was given
the Hôtel des Ursins in reward of his services.

Juvenal of Painters (*The*). William Hogarth (1697–1794).

Juzail (Afghanistan). A very long rifle; those armed with the juzail are Juzailchees.

Jy-anian Dynasty (*The*). The second fabulous dynasty of Persia. Jy means *pure, holy*. The only two names known are Jy-Affram and Jy-Abad his son, who suddenly disappeared. It followed the Mahabadean, and was succeeded by the Kuleev dynasty.

K. 'The Three bad K's.' The Karians, Kappadokians, and Kilikians; generally spelt Carians, Cappadocians, and Cilicians.

Kaaba, or 'Caaba.' Was taken possession of by Cossai about 455, and was restored in 1630 by the sultan Mustapha. The word means 'the square house,' and it designates a stone building in the great mosque at Mecca. Next the silver door is the famous Black Stone, 'dropped from Paradise.' It was originally quite white, but the sin of the world has turned it black. In pilgrimages the devotee walks round the Kaaba seven times, and each time he passes the stone either kisses it or lays his hand thereon.

According to Arabian legend Adam, after his expulsion from the garden, worshipped Allah on this spot. A tent was then sent down from heaven, but Seth substituted a hut for the tent. After the flood Abraham and Ishmael rebuilt the Kaaba.

Kabyles (2 syl.). Another name for Berbers, a mountain tribe which dwell on the Atlas range of Algeria and Morocco. They are neither Arabs, Moors, nor Turks. They live in villages which they call 'gourbis,' and several of these villages would constitute a kabyle. Their government, like that of Switzerland, is a democratic confederation. They are a sober people, brave and hospitable, but vindictive and superstitious. As with the Swiss, love of independence is their dominant characteristic.

Kadjahs (*Dynasty of the*). A Turkoman dynasty, which now occupies the Persian throne. Founded in 1748 by Mohammed Hassan, son of the governor of Mazanderan. The word means 'fugitives' or 'deserters,' and was applied to those deserters of the Ottoman army to whom Abbas I. had in the 16th cent. given asylum.

The shahs of this line have been Mohammed Hassan, 1748; Futeh Ali Shah (his nephew), 1797; Mohammed Shah, 1834; Nasser Eddin Shah, 1848 (who visited London in 1873) and again in 1889.

The dynasty was interrupted by Kurem Khan Zend, the Walik, and restored in 1794.

Kaianides (*The*), or 'Kaianian dynasty.' The second dynasty of the Persians, called by the Greeks Achemenîdès. It consisted of Kai-Kaous (Astyagês); Kai-Kosru (Cyrus), B.C. 536; Lohrasp (Cambyses, or Ahasuërus of Scripture), B.C. 530; Gouchtasp (Darius), 521; Xerxes, 486; Ardechir Diraz Dest, or long-handed (Artaxerxes *Longimanus*), B.C. 471; Xerxes II. Sogdian and Darab (Darius *Nothos*), B.C. 424; Artaxerxes *Mnemon*, B.C. 404; Artaxerxes Ochos, B.C. 362; Arses, B.C. 338; Darab II. (Darius *Codomanus*), B.C. 336, dethroned by Alexander the Great in 331; and thus the dynasty ended after enduring 206 years. It succeeded the Pishdadian dynasty.

Achæmenès was an ancestor of Cyrus. Zoroaster or Zerdusht, who wrote the Avesta in the Zend tongue, lived in the reign of Cyrus (Κϋρος). At the death of Alexander there was an interval from B.C. 323 to A.D. 226 filled by the *Seleucïdès* and the *Arsacïdès*. (Kaianides, 3 syl.)

Kaimacan. A deputy or governor in the Ottoman empire. There are generally two, one residing at Constantinople, and the other attending the grand vizier as his lieutenant.

Kainardji, or **Kutchuk Kainardji** (*Treaty of*), 21 July, 1774. A treaty of peace between Russia and Turkey, in which Turkey opened to Russia the Black Sea, ceded Azof and Taganrog, and assured the independence of the Crimēa. In 1784 the sovereignty of the Crimea was confirmed to Russia (Catherine II).

The Treaty of Kutchuk Kainardji gave to Russia the protectorate of two chapels in Turkey, one in the Russian Legation, and one about to be built in Galâta. It was on this treaty that, in 1853, Russia claimed the protectorate of the holy places in Turkey, against France, who rested her right on a treaty as far back as 1740. This contention was made the pretext of the Crimēan War (*q.v.*).

Kaioma'rian Dynasty (*The*). Same as 'Pishdadian' (*q.v.*). Succeeded by the Kaianian dynasty. Kai-Omar was the first of the Pishdadides, and the Pishdadians were first of the mythic period of Persia, placed by some as far back as B.C. 2340, and by others as low down as B.C. 940. (Pishdadides, 3 syl.)

Omar was the hypothetical founder of the dynasty. Pishdad or Paishdad (just lawgiver) was the title given to the third of the line, named Hūshung or Iran.

Kaffirs. So Mussulmans call unbelievers.

Kaiser = Cæsar. Used as a title. The Roman Empire in its decline was divided into east and west. The popes of Rome ignored the east, and assumed that the title of the old Roman emperor belonged exclusively to the west.

Charlemagne restored Leo III. to the papal chair, and out of gratitude Leo gave to Charlemagne the empty title of 'Carolus Cæsar Augustus,' or 'Karl Kaiser Augustus of the Romans.' Keyser is Low German for Cæsar, and the title given by Leo becomes in Low German 'Karl, Keyser Wehzen desz Reichs.' So says Selden, 'Titles of Honour,' chap. v. p. 47 (1673).

This title was continued in the German successors of Charlemagne till the death of Charles le Gros, when it fell into abeyance for 74 years.

In 962 Pope John XII. restored the title with a slight alteration, and crowned Otto I. the Great (king of Germany) 'Kaiser of the Holy Roman Empire'; and till 1056 his successors went to Rome, after their coronation as kings of Germany, to receive the additional title of 'kaiser' [of the Holy Roman Empire, or of the West].

Heinrich III., just before his death, invented a new title, 'King of the Romans,' to be borne by the kings *elect* of Germany, and then the reigning king was kaiser or 'Emperor of the Romans,' and the king *elect* was 'King of the Romans.'

In 1338 the electors decreed that it was not needful for a king of Germany to undergo a second coronation at Rome; But inasmuch as from the moment of his election he was 'King of the Romans,' he became *ex officio* 'Emperor of the Romans' or kaiser the moment he was crowned. From that time till 1508 the king regnant was *ex officio* 'Emperor of the Romans,' and the crown prince or king elect was 'King of the Romans.'

In 1508 Maximilian intended to go to Rome to get crowned, but was prevented, and he assumed a somewhat new departure. Being king, he called himself 'Emperor-elect of the Romans,' and henceforth the crown prince was 'King of the Romans,' but after the death of his father he became 'Emperor-elect of the Romans,' and as soon as he was crowned he became King of Germany and Emperor of Rome.

In 1806 Napoleon, having mutilated the German empire, Francis II. was obliged to abandon the title of 'Emperor of the West,' and assumed instead the title of 'Emperor of Austria and King of Hungary,' and that dominion is now styled 'the Austro-Hungarian empire.'

Kalandos Society (*The*), 1518. An Hungarian league which met on the kalends or 1st of every month. The object of the league was to depose John Szapolyai from the office of treasurer, and restore Stephen Verboczy. It succeeded, and Szapolyai fled to Transylvania.

Kalapos King (*The*), the 'hatted king.' Kaiser Joseph II., son of Maria Theresa, was so called by the Hungarians because he refused to be crowned.

James V. of Scotland, in his famous gold coin, is represented as wearing a bonnet instead of a crown.

Kali'lah and Dimnah. A Sanscrit book of fables, extant in 500. It was translated into Pehlevi about 550. A copy was discovered in 1870 by Dr. Socin in the monastery at Mardin. *See* 'Academy,' 1 Aug., 1871.

Kali-yuga. The 4th and last of the Yugas or ages of Hindû chronology, corresponding to the 'Iron Age' of the Greeks and Romans.

It consists of 432,000 solar-sidereal years, and began B.C. 3102.

Kalpa. In Hindû chronology means a day and night of Brahma, equal $4\frac{1}{2}$ billions of solar-sidereal years.

Some geologists seem to think 'the evening and the morning' of Genesis i. mean a 'Kalpa.'

Kant's Four Categories. Immanuel Kant generalises the fundamental modes of conception into—

1. *Quantity*, including unity, multeity, and totality;

2. *Quality*, divided into reality, negation, and limitation; .

3. *Relation*, that is, substance and accident, cause and effect, action and reaction;

4. *Modality*, subdivided into possibility, existence, and necessity.

Regarding the outside world, he says our perception thereof is merely representative; and it is not possible for man to know what any object really is. All he can possibly know is what his senses represent them to be.

Of deity, immortality, &c., he says,

human reason can decide nothing, because these subjects are not cognisable by the senses.

Revelation, or the exercise of man's moral nature, can alone cope with such subjects.

Ka'raites (3 syl.), A.D. 580. A sect of the Jews who rejected the traditions of the Talmud and adhered to the Kara (Aramaic word for ' Scripture '). There are many Karaites still in Poland, Crim Tartary, Egypt, and Persia. The Jews perform their public religious services in Hebrew, but the Karaites use the language of the state in which they live. The sect was founded by Anan ben David.

Kardis (*Treaty of*), 1661. A treaty of peace between Sweden and Russia, based on the conditions of the treaty of Stolbowa.

Karl III. the Fat of Germany is the same as Charles le Gros of France. He was the youngest of the sons of Ludwig the German ; and as he survived his two brothers, he united the three kingdoms of Germany, Italy, and France in his own person (832, 881–888).

CHARLEMAGNE was the father of LOUIS I. le Débonnaire.
LOUIS le Débonnaire was the father of Lothaire (king of Italy), LUDWIG (the German), and KARL II. (called in French Charles le Chauve).
KARL II. was the father of Louis II. le Bègue ; and LUDWIG the German was the father of KARL III.
*** Karl and Ludwig for German kings ; Charles and Louis for French kings.
Contemporary with Alfred the Great.

Karl IV. of Luxemburg. One of the promiscuous kaiser-kings of Germany. Nominated to the throne by Pope Clement VI., without consulting the electors, and therefore called the ' Pope's kaiser ' (1316, 1347–1378). He was son of that John of Bohemia who fell at Crécy in 1346, and grandson of Kaiser Heinrich VII.

Father, John king of Bohemia. *Wives,* (1) Anne princess palatine and (2) Anne Schweidwitz. *Contemporary* with Edward III.

No reign ever embraced so many interesting historical events in the same space of time.
1347. Rienzi was tribune of Rome; assassinated 1354.
1348. The plague referred to by Boccaccio in his ' Decaměron.'
1349. Edward III. of England instituted the order of the Garter.
1351. The Great Helvetic Confederation was instituted.
1354. Marino Falieri was elected doge of Venice at the age of 80.
1356. Karl IV. submitted to the Diet of Nürnberg the famous Golden Bull.
1356. Sept. 19 was fought the battle of Poitiers.

1357. David Bruce was set at liberty.
1363. Timur the Tartar began his wonderful career.
1371. The Stuart dynasty began in Scotland.
1374. The poet Petrarch died.
1376. Edward the Black Prince died.
1377. Edward III. of England died.

Karl V. (Charles V.), called by the French ' Charles Quint,' son of Philipp and grandson of Kaiser Maximilian I. the Pennyless. His son Philipp married Mary queen of England (born 1500, reigned 1519–1556, died 1558).

Father, Philipp. *Mother,* Juaña, daughter of Ferdinand and Isabella of Castile and Aragon. *Wife,* Isabella, daughter of Emmanuel king of Portugal. He *died* at the convent of St. Juste in Spain. *Contemporary* with Henry VIII., Edward VI., and Mary.
*** In this reign the reform under Luther occurred, and Magellan made the first voyage round the world.

Karl VI., kaiser-king of Germany (1683, 1711–1740). He was brother of Joseph I. his predecessor, and son of Leopold I. of the house of Austria. As he had no son he drew up the ' Pragmatic Sanction ' in favour of his daughter Maria Theresa. The Duke of Bavaria objected, but Maria Theresa succeeded her father notwithstanding.

This was the last king of the house of Habsburg. *Father,* Leopold I. *Mother,* Eleanor Anne. *Wife,* Elizabeth Christina, daughter of Rudolf of Brunswick-Wolfenbüttel. *Contemporary* with George I. and George II.

Karmathians. A Mohammedan sect which arose in Irak during the 9th cent. It took its name from Karmath, its founder, a poor labourer, who assumed the rank of a prophet. The Karmathians, who maintained bloody wars with the kalifs for nearly a century, advocated community of goods and wives, rejected all revelation, fasts, prayer, alms, and abstinence. Karmath died A.D. 900. The sect was stamped out in 982.

Katerfelto. A celebrated quack, and a generic name for a quack. He practised on the people of London in the influenza of 1782. In 1790 he visited Durham, and sent his coach round the town with trumpeters. His *pièce de résistance* was a solar microscope showing the animalcules in water, &c.

Katerfelto with his hair on end
At his own wonders wondering.
COWPER, *The Task,* bk. iv. (Winter Evening.)

Kaye Prize (*The*). For an essay connected with ecclesiastical history, biblical criticism, or the canon of scripture. Given once in four years to a graduate of the University of Cambridge of not more than ten years' standing. Value about 50*l.* Founded by subscribers to Bishop Kaye's memorial 1861. *See* 'Regius Professor of Divinity.'

Keble College, Oxford, 1870. Founded by subscription in memory of John Keble, professor of poetry in the university. The head-master is called the warden. There are no fellowships (1890).

Keel-hauling. A punishment practised at one time in the Dutch and English navies, but now never resorted to. The offender was let down by ropes on one side of the ship, and after being dragged under the keel, was hauled up on the other side.

Keening (*A*). An Irish word for that wild song of lamentation poured forth over a dead body during the 'wake ceremony' by certain mourners employed in Ireland for the purpose.

Keeper of the Forest (*The*). Chief warden of the forest, who has the superintendence over all the other forest servants (MANWOOD, 'Forest Law,' part i. p. 156).

Keeper of the Great Seal (*The*). A judicial officer, who used to be appointed (5 Eliz. c. 18) in lieu of the lord chancellor. Abolished.

Keeper of the King's Conscience (*The*). The lord chancellor. The early chancellors being ecclesiastics were probably the 'father confessors' of the sovereign. The lord keeper is now the officer who presides in the court of chancery.

Keeper of the Privy Seal. Now called 'the Lord Privy Seal,' through whose hands all charters, &c., must pass before they come to the 'Great Seal.'

Keeper of the Signet. An officer in Scotland, appointed by the crown, who appoints one of the Writers of the Signet (*q.v.*), and presides at the meetings of the society.

Keeper of the Touch. The Master of the Assay in the Mint.

Keepers of the Liberties of England (*The*). Custodians of the new great seal after the abolition of royalty 1648. The first three keepers were Whitelock, Keble, and Lisle.

Kee-tan Dynasty (*The*). A Tartar dynasty which established a footing in the north of China during the 14th imperial dynasty. It gave nine kings and lasted 211 years (907–1118). Kao-tsu II. purchased peace of this troublesome horde by giving to it 16 cities in the province of Pecheli'.

Also called the Leao dynasty.

Kellgrenism, 1889. Curing diseases by manipulation. So called from J. Henrik Kellgren.

The idea is that disease arises from a surcharge of some gaseous matter, which passes into the operator, and thus relieves the patient. Sometimes the operator himself suffers, but for the most part the 'broach' passes through the operator, either into the air or into the earth. Of course, the cure of diseases by the laying on of hands is mentioned in the New Testament, but whether this was a 'special gift' *pro tempore* is beyond the scope of this Dictionary.

Kempenfelt, 1782. The 'Royal George' was the finest ship in the British service, carrying 108 guns, and was the flag-ship of Admiral Kempenfelt. It was lying off Portsmouth, crowded with its own crew and a vast number of visitors, before starting for Gibraltar. On 29 Aug. the carpenters were busy caulking the seams, and the ship was laid somewhat on her side. Kempenfelt was writing in his cabin, and the bulk of the people were between decks. A sudden squall plunged the open port-holes under water on the lowered side, and the ship went down in a minute. The admiral, the officers, and all between decks, to the number of 1,000 persons, perished. Cowper has a poem on the subject.

Kenilworth (*Dictum of*). *See* under 'Dictum.'

Kennicott Scholarship. Two for Hebrew. Value about 60*l.*, tenable for one year. Founded (1831) in the University of Oxford by Anne Kennicott, widow of Dr. Benjamin Kennicott, canon of Christ Church.

Kensington Martyr (*The*). Caroline, wife of George prince regent. She was spoken of by the friends of the regent as the 'Dreadful Woman.' Married 1795, separated soon after the birth of her child in 1796, died 1821. The regent and his friends called her the 'Kensington Megæra.' She resided at Kensington, and was certainly persecuted to death by her royal husband, but she was no 'martyr.'

Kent (*Holy Maid of*). See 'Holy Maid,' &c.

Kentish Fire. Vehement protracted cheering. So called from the cheering in Kent in the 'No popery' meetings, got up to oppose the Catholic Emancipation Bill of 1829.

Kentish Petition (*The*), 29 April, 1701. Signed at Maidstone and presented to the House of Commons 8 May. It prayed that the house would not waste their time in party quarrels, but attend to the public business. It was signed by grand jurors, magistrates, and freeholders. Those who presented it were sent to the Gate House, under the plea that the petition was 'scandalous, insolent, and seditious.' When parliament was prorogued they were liberated.

The Tories . . . accused Thomas Bliss and Thomas Culpepper, two of the gentlemen concerned in the Kentish petition, of having been guilty of corrupt and scandalous practices in a contested election at Maidstone.—HOWITT, *Hist. of Eng.* (William III. p. 166).

Kepler's Laws.

1. The planets revolve about the sun in

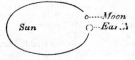

ellipses, having the sun in one of the foci.

2. If a line is drawn from the centre of the sun to any planet, this line (as it is carried forward by the planet) will sweep over equal areas in equal portions of time.

3. The square of the periodic times of the planets are as the cubes of their mean distances from the sun.

The second law is 'the radius vector sweeps over equal areas in equal times.'

Keri-Chetib [*Keri* what is read, *Chetib* what is written]. There are some 1,000 passages in the Hebrew Bible where the 'Keri' differs from the 'Chetib.' Kennicott tells us in all these instances the *false* rendering is the one inserted in the text, or written [chetib], and the *true* one is that given in the margin. It is thought that Ezra made the marginal readings. 'Dissertatio Generalis.'

Kesteven. The south-west part of Lincolnshire. The north-east part is

called Lindsey, and the south-east part is called Holland.

Kett (*Robert*). A tanner of Wymondham, near Norwich, and a man of substance, headed a rebellion in July 1549. His forces were dispersed by the Earl of Warwick, and Kett was hanged in Nov. the same year [1549]. See 'Reformation Tree.'

Wymondham, pronounce *Win'-dum*.

Kett's Rebellion, 1549. The suppression of monasteries had caused a great deal of temporary distress, and given birth to many insurrections, by far the most important of which was that of Norwich, headed by Robert Kett, a tanner, in the summer of 1549, who encamped on Mousehold Heath near the city. A petition of grievances was first sent to the king, praying that the bondmen might be set free, that the rabbits might be reduced in number, and that a uniform bushel measure might be established by law. Kett held his court under the 'Oak of Reformation,' and here a chaplain duly read the liturgy. The king promised to submit the petition to parliament in October, but the herald ordered Kett to be arrested. This was the signal for war, and Kett made himself master of Norwich, where he won several victories over the king's troops; but at length the Earl of Warwick defeated the insurgents at Dussinsdale, and Kett was hanged in chains on Norwich Castle.

Norwich, pronounce *Norridge*, to rhyme with porridge. Mousehold, pronounce *Mussle*.

Key of Russia (*The*). Smolensko. Taken by Svatoslas in 1232; taken by the Lithuanians in 1413; taken by Vassili in 1514; taken by the Poles in 1611; taken by the Russians in 1654; burnt by Napoleon in his Moscow expedition in 1812.

Key of Spain (*The*). Ciudad Rodri'go, taken by Lord Wellington (the Duke of Wellington), 19 Jan., 1812.

Key of the Mediterranean (*The*). The fortress of Gibraltar, which commands the entrance and exit of that sea. See 'Gates.'

Keys (*The House of*). In the Isle of Man. It consists of twenty-four persons, to whom all doubtful and important matters of law are referred. They are chosen from the chief landed proprietors of the

island. If a vacancy occurs two names
are sent to the governor, who nominates
one of them. All freeholders, men and
women, elect.

Keys (*The Power of the*), 'Potestas
Clavium' (Matt. xvi. 19). The supreme
power of church government vested in
the pope of Rome as the professed successor of St. Peter.

Keystone State (*The*). Pennsylvania, one of the original thirteen states
of North America. Called the Keystone
State from its position and importance.

Khan. A noble, a gentleman; about
equal to the Egyptian effendi and
English esquire (Afghanistan).

Khariz'mians (*The*), 1213–1223. A
people of Western Turkestan, which from
994 to 1231 formed an independent principality. In 1193 they invaded Persia,
but their power was overthrown by
Ghengis Khan in 1225.

A branch of the Kharizmians reigned at Delhi,
Hindûstan, from 1213, after having chased out
the Ghorians; but in 1398 they were superseded by
the Patans.

Khatta'bians (*The*). One of the
numerous Shiite sects, disciples of Abdúl
Khattáb. They maintain that the prophet
meant by *paradise* 'the good things of
this world.' So they indulge in wine,
music, and other things forbidden by
the imaums. They may be called the
Epicurean Moslems. *See* 'Imaumians,'
'Zeyds.'

Khilji (*The House of*). The second
Gaurian dynasty of Delhi, founded by
Jelal-u-din in 1288. It continued to reign
till 1321, when it was overthrown by
Tóglak.

Khyber Pass (*The*), 1842. Has obtained great notoriety because a British
army of 16,000 men was here annihilated
in the month of January, during the retreat from Kaubul. The only persons
who escaped were Dr. Brydon (a regimental surgeon) and a private soldier.
In 1838 Lord Auckland, governor-
general of India, declared war against
the Afghanistans because their ruler,
Dost Mohammed, had unlawfully attacked a British ally, and because Dost
Mohammed had usurped the throne of
Shah Sujah, who was under British protection. On 21 July Shah Sujah was re-

stored to the throne of Kaubul, and the
British thought the matter was ended.
This was a grand mistake, for at the beginning of winter Akbah Khan, the son
of Dost Mohammed, attacked the British
army in Kaubul, and slew several of the
officers. A capitulation was made, and
when the British army were in the
Khyber Pass on their way home they
were cut to pieces. (With women, children, and camp followers 20,000 were
slain in the Pass.)

Ki in Chinese history. There were
ten of these races [Ki] before even the
semi-historical period which began with
Hia, B.C. 2205. The first Ki or fabulous
age embraces a period of 300,000 years.
The mythic period is the tenth Ki; the
three emperors were Fo-hi, Chin-nōng,
and Hoângti. These were followed by
five kings.

The first Ki consisted of (1) Puon-ku (*highest eternity*); (2) Tiën-hoâng (*emperor of heaven*); (3) Ti-
hoâng (*emperor of earth*); and (4) Gine-hoâng (*emperor of men*). Evidently allegorical. The historical period begins B.C. 256 with the dynasty of
Tsin.

Kidnapping. Entrapping children,
either for reward or to serve some object
of the kidnapper. Also entrapping slaves
or men to serve aboard ship. It is now
a felonious act (24, 25 Vict. c. 100).

Kiel, in Holstein (*Treaty of*),
14 Jan., 1814, between Great Britain,
Sweden, and Denmark, for the transfer
of Norway from Denmark to Sweden.
The 'War of Liberation' in Germany
ends with this treaty.

Kildare Insurrection (*The*), 23
May, 1798. The commencement of the
great rebellion, not finally quelled till
the following year.

On 23 May Lieutenant Gifford of Dublin and a
number of other gentlemen were assassinated by
the insurgents.

Kildare Place Society (*The*), 1833.
See 'Society for Promoting the Education
of the Poor.' In 1830 government withdrew its grant to this society, and the
schools gradually declined.

Kileh-Shergat Cylinder (*The*).
The earliest historical document pertaining to Assyria yet discovered in Mesopotamia. The characters are cuneiform,
and the fifth king inscribed on the cylinder
is the well-known name of Tiglath-pilēser
[Tukulti-pal-zira], 'son of Asshur-rish-ili,
who reduced the Magian world, grandson

of Mutaggil-nebu, offspring of Asshur-dapal-il, who held the sceptre of Bel.'

Kileh-Shergat is the modern name of Asshur.

Kil'hamites (3 syl.), or 'New Connection Methodists,' 1797. Seceders from the Methodists, led by Alexander Kilham. Their doctrinal views are those of Wesley, but their polity is Presbyterian. The people choose their own officers, and send representatives to all the synodical meetings of the denomination.

Kilkenny(*The Catholic Confederacy of*), 1641. Never to lay down their arms till they had obtained an acknowledgment of the independence of the Irish; the repeal of all degrading disqualifications on the ground of religion; the free exercise of the Catholic worship; and the exclusion of all but natives from civil and military offices within the kingdom. See 'Irish Associations.'

If 'Home Rule' is effected, what would the Irish say if no office of Great Britain could be held by an Irishman?

Kilkenny (*The Constitutions of*). Certain privileges granted by Edward III. to the Irish in a parliament held at Kilkenny.

Kilkenny was the seat of several Irish parliaments.

Kilkenny (*Convention of*), 1342. A parliament held at Kilkenny to remonstrate with Edward III. against his threat of excluding in future from all share in the government of Ireland those who held estates in Ireland or had married Irish wives. It was thought that the allegiance of such persons would be weakened by their private interest in Ireland. See 'Irish Associations.'

Kilkenny (*Statute of*), 40 Edw. III. 1366. For the abolition of the Brehon or common law of Ireland. Lionel the second son of Edward III., who married the heiress of the Earl of Ulster, and thus became entitled to the lordships of Ulster and Connaught, was made by his father lord-lieutenant of Ireland. In 1366 he summoned a parliament at Kilkenny, in which this statute was passed.

The object of this statute, passed by Edward III., was to prevent the amalgamation of the English and Irish chiefs, which would render them too formidable to be controlled. It forbade any Englishman, on pain of imprisonment and forfeiture of his estates, to use an Irish name, to speak the Irish language, to adopt the Irish dress, or to permit the cattle of an Irishman to graze on his lands; and made it high treason to marry a native. Brehon is the Irish for a judge.

Killala (*Battle of*), 23 Sept., 1798. The French, being invited over by the Irish insurgents, landed under General Humbert (22 Aug., 1798) from three frigates. Several battles were fought, as those of Castlebar, Colooney, and Ballinamuck, but at Killála the insurgents were defeated with great slaughter.

General Humbert surrendered to General Lake after the battle of Ballinamuck, 8 Sept. Some French frigates on their way to aid the Irish were captured, 12 Oct., by Sir J. B. Warren, and Wolfe Tone was among the prisoners.

'Killing no Murder,' 1657. A pamphlet printed in Holland, which caused an immense sensation at the time. After an address to Cromwell and another to the army, it divides itself into three parts: (1) Is the lord protector a tyrant? (Yes, because he has arrogated to himself regal power and state.) (2) Is it lawful to kill a tyrant? (Yes. Example: Brutus killed Cæsar and was deemed a patriot.) (3) Will the removal of Cromwell be for the well-being of the three nations? (Yes. For his misrule is full of mischief.) It then concludes by warning Cromwell that his life is not worth an hour's purchase. This book created quite a *furore*, and was distributed by thousands. Sexby avouched that he was the author of it, but Clarendon tells us that Sexby was an illiterate man. Evelyn and others think the author was Captain Titus, who resided in Holland at the time ('Diary,' ii. 210). Some ascribe it to Willan, and others to Allan.

There was a similar pamphlet published in France in 1658 entitled 'Tuer un tyran n'est pas un crime.' It was issued by Carpentier de Marigny, the avowed enemy of Mazarin.

Kilmainham Treaty (*The*), 1882. A supposed compact made by Mr. Gladstone, the prime minister, with Dillon, Parnell, and O'Kelly, when in April they were unexpectedly released from Kilmainham jail, where they had been confined for exciting the Irish to resist the payment of rent, and to prevent new tenants from taking the farms from which persons had been evicted. The tale is that the three gentlemen promised to exert themselves to pacify Ireland if they were set free, and so they were released; but most certainly they have done nothing since to pacify Ireland, but quite the contrary (1890).

Kin (*The*), or the Golden Race. So the Niu-tchin Tartars of China called themselves (1188–1235).

Kinconghish. A statute in Ireland which provides that every head of a sept is to be charged with any treason, felony, or heinous crime committed by any one of the sept.

King (*The Black*). Heinrich III. of Germany (1017, 1046–1056).

King (*The Red*). I. The king of Persia was so called from his red turban.

Credo ut Persam nunc propter rubea tegumenta capitis *Rubeum Caput* vocant, ita reges Moscoviæ propter alba tegumenta *Albos Reges* appellari.—SIGISMUND.

II. William II. was called *Rufus*, or the Red King, from the colour of his hair (1057, 1087–1100).

III. Otto II. kaiser of Germany was called the Red King for a similar reason (955, 973–983).

IV. Amadeus VII. count of Savoy was called 'The Red' also (1360, 1383–1391).

Kaiser Friedrich I. was called 'Barbarossa' from his red beard.

King (*The Summer*). Amadeus of Spain.

King (*The White*). The king of Muscovy was so called from his 'alba tegumenta.' *See* 'King (*The Red*)'.

Muscovy was called *White Russia*, and probably this was the reason why the Muscovite king was called the White king, or king of White Russia. Poland was *Black Russia*. *See* 'Russia.'

King (*The Winter*). Friedrich V., the rival of Ferdinand II. of Germany. He married Elizabeth daughter of James I. of England, and was king of Bohemia one winter, 1619–20. His wife was called the 'Winter Queen.'

King Becold. John of Leyden the tailor, who headed the Anabaptists of Germany, and arrogated to himself the name and title of 'King John of Leyden.' His name was John Becold (1510–1536).

His name is sometimes written Boccold and Bockholdt.

King Bomba. Nickname of Ferdinand II. of Naples, who bombarded Messīna in 1848.

'Bomba' is the noise made when the cheeks are blown out and compressed by the fingers and thumb. Ferdinand II. of Naples was a great *Vox et præterea nihil*, and his son Francis II. was only a 'Bombalino,' or *Vocicŭla et præterea nihil*.

King Edward's Law. The laws enforced by Edward the Confessor, and the mode of government which then prevailed.

When the people clamoured for King Edward's laws, they meant that they wished to be governed in the same manner as Edward the Confessor governed the nation (1041-1065).

King Henri's King. Chicot the jester (1553–1591), who ruled Henri III.; but, to his honour be it spoken, he loved him and served him faithfully. It would be well if some wise ones took counsel from the 'fool.'

King Hob. Robert Bruce was so called by Edward I., meaning 'king churl.' Hob was a common name for a villager or half-serf, as Hodge still is for a farm-labourer. Du Cange (art. 'Huba') says *Hovia* means a village, German *hof*, and the following from 'Chron. Mortis S. Agnetis,' chap. xxvi.:—'Damnum magnum habuimus in hovia nostra ex inundatione aquarum.'

Perhaps 'Hob' is a mere variant of 'Rob,' or 'Bob,' *i.e.* Robert.

King Hulan. King Alfonso XII. of Spain was called 'Roi Hulan' in 1883, because he had recently accepted a colonelcy of a Uhlan regiment in Prussia.

King James's Bible. *See* 'King's Bible' and 'Bible.'

'**King Jesus.**' William Hacket, in the early part of Elizabeth's reign, gave himself out to be King Jesus. His two 'prophets' were Arthington and Coppinger. Hacket was executed in 1592, Coppinger starved himself to death in prison, and Arthington was subsequently pardoned.

King-Maker (*The*). Richard Neville earl of Warwick (1428–1471). When Henry VI. was king he defeated the Lancastrians, captured the king at Northampton (10 July, 1460), and proclaimed Edward IV. king (4 March, 1461).

Subsequently he quarrelled with Edward, made a compact with Margaret (wife of Henry VI.), married his daughter Anne to Prince Edward (son of Henry VI. and Margaret), landed at Dover (13 Sept., 1470), drove Edward IV. from the throne, and restored Henry VI. *See* next article.

Richard Neville was slain by Edward IV. at the battle of Barnet 14 April, 1471, when Edward became king again.

King-Maker (*The Roman*). Ricĭmer (*— A.D. 472). In 456 he deposed the Emperor Avītus, and made Majorian emperor. As Majorian proved too independent and virtuous for Ricimer's liking, the Suevian put him to death (A.D. 461), and raised Libius Sevērus to the purple. On the death of Libius Severus in 465 Ricimer kept the government for sixteen months in his own hands, but in 467 the emperor of the east appointed the western emperor, and Ricimer acquiesced in the appointment. In 472 the new emperor was slain in battle, and Ricimer appointed Olybrĭus emperor. This was the third emperor which the barbarian made.

King Matthias is dead. This Hungarian proverb is the greatest compliment ever paid to a crowned head. It means 'justice no longer holds the balance,' as it did when Matthias was king. It appears that Matthias son of Hunyadi was indeed a model king, who never had his equal on any throne (1443, 1458-1490).

King Robert's Bowl. Said to be the bowl which the wife of Mark Sprotte set before King Robert. It is still preserved in the family of the Sprottes of Urr. One day King Robert was attacked by a Southron on the banks of the Urr, near the cottage of Mark Sprotte a shepherd; the wife of the shepherd caught hold of the Southron, pulled him to the ground, and he was obliged to yield. She then set before the king a bowl of porridge. Bruce said he would give her for reward all the land she could run round while he ate it, and she ran round Sheeling Hill. The land was given her, she was called the heroic dame of Galloway, the hill was called the King's Mount, and the family has been called the Sprottes of Urr for about 500 years.

King Smith. Louis Philippe of France, who escaped from France in 1848 under the assumed name of Mr. Smith.

'Mr. Smith!' exclaimed the king, 'that is curious indeed; and it is very remarkable that the first to welcome me should be a Mr. Smith, since the assumed name by which I escaped from France was *Smith*. Look, this is my passport, made out in the name of Smith.'—*The Times*, 6 March, 1848.

King Tom. Sir Thomas Maitland, the first Lord High Commissioner of the United States of the Ionian Islands, so called from his arbitrary manners. He was an excellent governor, but ruled the islands as an autocrat, and left a full exchequer at his death.

King of Arms. The title dates from the reign of Henry IV., but Henry V. created the Garter King in 1417, and George IV. the Bath King in 1725. The GARTER King of Arms now serves the Order of the Garter, and the BATH King of Arms the Order of the Bath. The two provincial kings for England are CLARENCEUX (named after Thomas duke of Clarence, brother of Henry V.), with jurisdiction over all parts of England *south* of the Trent; and Norroy [North roy], with jurisdiction over all parts *north* of the Trent.

The King of Arms for Scotland is called LYON, and for Ireland ULSTER.

King of Bath (*The*). King Richard [of Bath], Beau Nash, master of the ceremonies, or Social Premier of Bath (1674-1761).

King of Bourges. Charles VII. of France was so called by the English in France because he returned to Bourges when he fled from Paris.

On the death of Charles VI. the kingdom of France descended to Henry V. of England. Charles VII. refused to allow the claim, and for a time took refuge in Bourges. Jeanne d'Arc turned the scale, and the King of Bourges became Charles le Victorieux.

King of England. A title first assumed by Richard I. *See* 'King of the English.'

King of Fire (*The*), or Sultan Kebir. Napoleon was so called by the Orientals (1769, 1804-1814, 1821).

King of France (*The*). So the monarchs of France were called till Oct. 1789, when the National Assembly ordained that Louis XVI. should not be styled 'King of France,' but 'King of the French.' The royal title was abolished in France in 1792, but was restored in 1814. When Louis Philippe was invited in 1830 to take on himself the government he was styled 'King of the French.'

King of Ireland, 1541. A title assumed by Henry VIII. to combat a notion that the regal dominion of Ireland was vested *ex officio* in the pope, and that the king of England held from the pope his lordship of Ireland. In the reign of Mary and Philip, Paul IV. formally raised the lordship of Ireland into a kingdom, 1557.

John was 'dominus Hiberniæ,' and from John to 1541 the kings of England were styled 'lords of Ireland.' The Irish *Ard-righs* were undoubtedly kings; and Henry VIII. had no effective sway beyond the English pale. James I. of England was in reality the first king of all Ireland, when in 1603 Hugh O'Neill submitted to Mountjoy.

King of Kent. Hengist, first of the kings of the Heptarchy, was king of Kent, A.D. 455. His dominion comprehended Kent, Norfolk, Suffolk, Essex, Middlesex, &c. In 526 the foundation of the kingdom of Essex diminished that of Kent.

King of Paris (*The*), 1588. So Henri duc de Guise was called by Henri III. after the day of the barricades (the 12th May), when the king fled disguised as a rustic to Chartres.

After the murder of Balafré Henri III. left the room and visited his mother, who was ill in bed. 'The King of Paris lives no longer, madam,' said he; 'henceforth I shall reign alone. I have now no rival.' 'It is a clean cut, my son,' replied Catherine, 'but it must be sewn up again.'—FÉLICE, *Hist. of the Protestants of France*, xvii.

King of Prussia (*The First*). FRIEDRICH I. son of the Great Elector (1657, 1701–1713). *See* 'Prussia,' &c.

King of Rome, 1811. A title given by Napoleon I. to his infant son at birth, when 'he associated the child in his empire.' Probably he meant to revive the title invented by Kaiser Heinrich III.; if so the title was a blunder; but if he only meant to imitate the kaiser, he was quite at liberty to adopt any title not already appropriated.

King of Sion (*The*). John Becold, Boccold, or Bockholdt, tailor, the Anabaptist (1510, 1534–1536). Better known as John of Leyden, the name he took after his 'coronation.' He was sensual, vain, and bloodthirsty, fond of regal pomp, and introduced polygamy. John was executed by lingering tortures in 1536, at the age of 26.

King of Slops. Louis XVIII. of France (1755, 1814–1824).

King of Suffolk. *See* 'Kings of Norfolk and Suffolk.'

King of Terror (*The*). Robespierre was the 'King of Terror,' and the Committee of Public Safety his executive for 420 days, from 31 May, 1793, to 27 July, 1794.

Death is poetically so called.

King of the Barricades (3 syl.). Louis Philippe of France (1773, reigned 1830–1848, died 1850), so called because he assisted in the revolution of 1830 to barricade Paris and resist the royal troops.

King of the Baso'cians (*The*). President of the clerks of the Basoche or Basilica of Paris—*i.e.* the judges, the barristers, the proctors, and other officials of the Palais de Justice. He had his court, his great officers, his coin, and his armorial bearings. Henri III. suppressed the title, and transferred to the chancellor all the rights and privileges of this 'king of the lawyers.'

King of the Butchers (*The*). The lad who at one time rode on the Bœuf Gras through the streets of Paris on Shrove Tuesday. He was a son of one of the three great butcher families (Gois, St. Yon, or Caboche), was dressed as an eastern monarch, carried a naked sword in one hand and a sceptre in the other, and rode on the back of the prize ox. He also enjoyed certain privileges in his year of office. The procession of Bœuf Gras had no king in my time—*i.e.* the middle of the 19th cent.

In New Orleans Rex is still (1890) the central figure of the *Mardi Gras* festivities.

Bœuf gras, pronounce *Buh-grah'*.

King of the English. A title assumed in 828 by Egbert.

Every king from William to Henry II. called himself 'king of the English' (*rex Anglorum*). Richard I. was the first to call himself 'king of England' (*rex Angliæ*).

King of the French. So Louis-Philippe entitled himself in 1830. Similarly, the two Napoleons called themselves 'emperors of the French,' and not 'emperors of France.'

Of course, the notion was that the *land* called France belonged to the people, and that the king or emperor disavowed all right to it. There seems now (1890) a radical notion that all the land of the nation should be vested in the sovereign and not be held by private landlords. Strange how radicals should wish to roll back the tide of history to the time of the Conquest! Funny advancement this!

King of the Hills. Vincent the Chartist, 1839. The hill district of Wales is about five miles from Newport, and abounds in coal and iron.

King of the Markets (*The*), or 'Le Roi des Halles.' François de Vendôme duc de Beaufort (1616–1669), natural son of Henri IV. and Gabrielle d'Estrées. So called because he was very popular with the French proletariat.

Lagrange-Chancel asserted, in the 'Année Littéraire,' 1759, that the duc was the 'Iron Mask,' but this has been fully disproved. He was slain in a sortie at the siege of Candia.

King of the Peak (The), 1515.
Sir George Vernon of Haddon Hall was twice cited to appear in London for the murder of a pedlar hanged by his order on a tree. When in the court he was summoned as 'King of the Peak' he vouchsafed no reply, but on the third summons as 'Sir George Vernon' he instantly presented himself. The pedlar had committed murder and Sir George 'lynched' him. The case was dismissed.

King of the Poor.
William Fitz-Osbert, called 'Longbeard,' from the length of his beard. Executed with great barbarity in 1199.

King of the Ribalds (The).
'Le Roi des Ribauds' [Re-bo]. The captain of the militia created by Philippe II. Auguste of France in 1189. Charles V. united the captaincy of the Ribalds to the 'provost of the hôtel.'

King of the Romans, 1056.
Heinrich III. the Black King of Germany invented this title for the heir-elect of Germany, and the title was continued till he was crowned. Till 1339 the king of Germany went to Rome to receive from the pope the title of 'kaiser of the Holy Roman Empire,' but after that date the king at his coronation in Germany assumed the title ex-officio.

If a father made his son joint-king, the father was *kaiser* and the son *King of the Romans*. The successor of a kaiser was only 'King of the Romans' till he was actually crowned. In 1508 Maximilian, who failed to get himself crowned kaiser, called himself 'Emperor-elect of the Romans.'

King of the Sea.
Edward III. A title given him in 1353.

He won the great naval battle of Sluys (2 syl.) over the French in 1340, and beat the Spanish squadron off Winchelsea in 1350.

King's and Queen's Counties
(Ireland). The territory belonging to the septs of Leix and Offaly, who resisted the forfeiture of their lands and took up arms; but the septs were exterminated, and their territory formed into two counties named King's and Queen's, in honour of Philip and Mary, and the assize towns of the counties were called Philipstown and Maryborough after the names of the king and queen.

King's and Queen's Men, 1571.
The factions of James VI. of Scotland and his mother Mary queen of Scots, a prisoner at the time in England. In 1573 the queen's faction was stamped out and the reign of Mary was virtually at an end.

King's [or Queen's] Bench.
An English law court where the sovereign is supposed to occupy the *lit de justice*. It was originally the Aula Regia which followed the king in all his travels. By 1 Will. IV. c. 70 the number of judges was raised from four to five, viz. the chief justice and four puisné or younger judges. This court has control over all other law courts by a process technically called *certiorāri*, by virtue of which proceedings may be removed to it from inferior courts. It can also prohibit other courts from proceeding when it is' thought that they are exceeding their jurisdiction. It has jurisdiction over every species of criminal offence committed in Middlesex.

King's (or) Queen's Plates.
Purses of money for races, not all the gifts of the reigning sovereign. In the reign of Queen Anne a gentleman left 1300 guineas for 13 plates or purses to be run for at such places as the crown should appoint; the condition being that each horse shall carry 12 stone weight the best of three heats over a four-mile course.

King's Bible (The), 1611.
The 'Authorised Version' is so called because it was undertaken by the command of James I., to whom also it was dedicated. King James disliked the 'Great Bible' (*q.v.*) because of its annotations. He also extremely disapproved of the Geneva Bible (*q.v.*). See 'Bibles.'

King's Bishop (The), 1317.
William Sinclair bishop of Dunkeld. Edward II. sent a fleet to the Frith of Forth; and the sheriff, with 500 Scottish horse, seeing the fleet, retreated precipitately. On their road the bishop met them, and cried, 'Out on you for false knights, whose spurs should be knocked from your heels! Who loves Scotland follow me!' The bishop made a desperate charge against the English, who were driven to their ships with loss. When Bruce heard thereof, he said Sinclair should be *his* bishop, and the Bishop of Dunkeld was called 'The king's bishop' for many years.

King's Book (*The*). I. 'Liber Regis,' A.D. 1534. A schedule of the valuation of all church property in England made after the separation of the English Church from the Church of Rome.

II. 1543. ' Necessary Doctrine and Erudition for any Christian man,' a book published by Henry VIII. as a substitute for the Bible, which he forbade the general public to read. Teachers of religion, nobles, and those of gentle birth might read it, but if any artificer, apprentice, journeyman, labourer, or servant read it, the punishment was a month's imprisonment. The ' King's Book ' was far more Catholic than Protestant. Indeed Henry was a Catholic in all things except his own supremacy. *See* 'Bishops' Book.'

The ' King's Book' is quoted in brief as the 'Erudition.' It is in great measure copied from the 'Bishops' Book (*q.v.*), but leans more to Romanism. It explains the Creed, the Seven Sacraments the Ten Commandments, the Lord's Prayer, the Ave Maria, and finishes with an exposition of Freewill, Justification Good Works, and Prayers for the Dead. It accepts the Apocrypha, and the first four ecumenical Councils. *See* p. 277.

King's Collection (*The*), 1823. The Royal Library of George III. given to the nation by George IV., and added to the library of the British Museum. The Royal Library consists of the library of Mr. Joseph Smith, British consul at Venice, bought by the king in 1762 for 10,000*l.*; a collection of books bought up when the order of Jesuits was suppressed; and the library of Charles II. The number of volumes added to the library by this royal gift is somewhat more than 50,000.

King's College. I. Aberdeen, 1494. Founded by King James IV.

II. Cambridge, 1441. Founded by King Henry VI. The chapel was finished in 1530. The head of the college is called the provost.

III. London. Incorporated 1828.

King's Confession (*The*). The Scotch Covenant of 1580. So called because signed by King James VI. (afterwards James I. of England). It abjured the tenets of the Church of Rome; bound the subscribers to defend the tenets of the Reformed Church of Scotland, and to guard with goods and lives the person and authority of the king.

King's Evil (*The*). Scrofula, so called because it was supposed to be cured by the king's touch. Touching for scrofula was practised by Edward the Confessor

(1043–1066); by Louis IX. of France in 1480; by the kaiser-king Karl VIII. at Rome and Naples in 1495; by François I. in 1527; by Charles II., and Queen Anne.

It was attempted by Prince Charles Edward the Pretender, at Holyrood, in 1746; by Louis XVI. at Reims in 1775.

King's Hall, Cambridge, 1337. Founded by King Edward III. In 1546 this college was, with other foundations, consolidated into Trinity College.

King's Lieutenants (*The*). Noblemen commissioned by the three Lancastrian kings to put into military order their respective counties, and levy fines on those incapable of bearing arms. These gentlemen are now called 'Lords Lieutenants of Counties.'

King's Nominees (*The*). Thirty-six Irish noblemen and gentlemen, whose estates had been confiscated by Cromwell, named in the Declaration of Indulgence (1662) to be restored to their estates without further proof, by the special favour of the king [Charles II.]

King's Pamphlets (*The*). 30,000 tracts and pamphlets relative to the history of England during the civil wars, bound in 2,000 volumes, of which 100 were printed (but never published). The pamphlets were commenced for the use of Charles I. by a clergyman named Thomason, kept in the collector's warehouses, and at length lodged at Oxford under the care of Dr. Barlow. They were bought for Charles II. by Samuel Mearke, stationer, but Mrs. Mearke, the widow, tried to dispose of them by the desire of Charles II. George III. bought them, and in 1763 presented the whole to the British Museum.

King's Preachers. Six able divines appointed by Edward VI., four of whom were itinerant, publicly to maintain the doctrines of the Reformation.

King's Primer (*The*), 1546. Published by command of Henry VIII. It contained the Creed, the Lord's Prayer, the Ten Commandments, the Litany, the 'Venite,' and the 'Te Deum,' with some few collects. It was twice revised in the reign of Edward VI., and again in the reigns of Elizabeth and James I., being ultimately made into our present 'Book of Common Prayer.'

King's Quair, *i.e.* King's Book. A poem in six cantos (197 stanzas of seven lines each) by James I. of Scotland. It is the story of his courtship of Jane Beaufort, who became his wife.

King's Stone (*The*), 1513. An unhewn column erected on Flodden Field to mark the spot where King James IV. fell.

Kings. A Chinese word equivalent to *books*, but emphatically applied to five, as our word Bible (a book) is applied to our Sacred Scriptures. The five sacred books of the Chinese are: 1. *Y-King* (cosmogony); 2. *Chi-Kinz* (hymns); 3. *Chou-King* (annals); 4. *Li-Ki* (religious rites and ceremonies); and 5. *Tchun-Tsieou* (chronology of the kingdom of Lou, the country of Confucius). To these is sometimes added the *Tao-te-King*.

Kings. *The average length of the reigns* in the three countries of England, France, and Germany.

ENGLAND from the accession of the Conquest 23½ years.

FRANCE from the accession of Hugues Capet 20 years.

GERMANY from the accession of Charlemagne 18 years.

The long reign of Queen Victoria will considerably raise the average of the sovereigns of England.

The average length in Scotland from Malcolm I. to James VI. was 21 years.

Kings and Popes. The era of impious kings and impious popes. *See* 'Popes and Kings.'

Kings and Queens of England.

VICTORIA, who was the *niece* of WILLIAM IV., who was the *brother* of GEORGE IV., who was the *son* of GEORGE III., who was the *grandson* of GEORGE II., who was the *son* of GEORGE I., who was the *cousin* of ANNE, who was the *sister-in-law* of WILLIAM III., who was the *son-in-law* of JAMES II., who was the *brother* of CHARLES II., who was the *son* of CHARLES I., who was the *son* of JAMES I., who was the *cousin* of ELIZABETH, who was the *half-sister* of MARY, who was the *half-sister* of EDWARD VI., who was the *son* of HENRY VIII., who was the *son* of HENRY VII., who was the *cousin* of RICHARD III., who was the *uncle* of EDWARD V., who was the *son* of EDWARD IV., who was the *cousin* of HENRY VI., who was the *son* of HENRY V., who was

the *son* of HENRY IV., who was the *cousin* of RICHARD II., who was the *grandson* of EDWARD III., who was the *son* of EDWARD II., who was the *son* of EDWARD I., who was the *son of* HENRY III., who was the *son* of JOHN, who was the *brother* of RICHARD I., who was the *son* of HENRY II., who was the *cousin* of STEPHEN, who was the *cousin* of HENRY I., who was the *brother* of WILLIAM RUFUS, who was the *son* of WILLIAM THE CONQUEROR, who was the son of his mother.

Kings Combatant (*The*). The kings of the Tsheu or Chou dynasty of China. The third Imperial dynasty, and the last of the semi-historic period. The 'fighting kings' were the feudatories who ruled over petty neighbouring states, and were continually at war with each other.

The most powerful of the kings combatant were the founders of the following states: Yen, Oey, Tchao, Hân, Tsee, and Tsin.

Kings of Arms, 1483. There are four in England: Clarenceux (who has power over all parts of England *south* of the Trent); Norroy, *i.e.* North-roy (who has power over all parts *north* of the Trent), and two other kings, called Garter King of Arms and Bath King of Arms. *See* ' Heralds.'

Garter is the principal King of Arms, higher in rank than the others. He serves the Order of the Garter. Bath King of Arms serves the Order of the Bath.

Kings of France. Their *residences*.

CLOVIS resided in what is now called the Palais de Justice, which he built in the Ile du Paris, in the Seine.

PHILIPPE II., Auguste, removed to the old Louvre.

LOUIS IX. resided in the Bastille.

PHILIPPE VI. de Valois lived at Vincennes.

CHARLES V. le Sage lived in the Hôtel de St. Paul.

CHARLES VI. le Bien Aimé lived in the Palais des Tournelles.

CHARLES IX. lived in the Tuileries.

LOUIS XIII. le Juste lived in the Palais de Luxembourg.

LOUIS XIV. le Grand Monarque lived at Versailles.

LOUIS XVI. le Martyr lived at the Palais Royal.

NAPOLEON I. and III. lived in the Tuileries.

The Presidents of the Republic have lived in the Palais de l'Elysée.

Kings of Leire. So the old Danish rulers were styled, because they resided at Leire, in Seeland.

Kings of Norfolk and Suffolk, 1381. So Lester and Westbroom styled themselves in the rebellion of Wat the Tyler and Jack Straw. They were both executed in June the same year.

Kingdom of Al Garb, or *Algarve.*
Founded by Shahpoor about 1008; set
aside in 1031 by the dynasty of the Aftas-
ides (3 syl.), so called from Al Aftas.

Kingdom of Italy (*The*). I. Lombardy was so called in the reign of
Charlemagne, and when Charlemagne
and his successors are called 'kings of
Italy,' the meaning is Lombardy.
II. 1806; the union by Napoleon
Bonaparte of Lombardy and the Venetian
territories. Though the title was so pre-
tentious, the new state did not comprise
above a third of the peninsula. After
the battle of Waterloo (1815) this geographical arrangement was set aside.
The present kingdom of Italy was created in
1861, but Rome was not added till 1870.

Kingdom of Scone (*The*). Scot-
land was so called so long as the 'Lia
Fail' (*q.v.*) remained in that city, and
Scone was the *Sedes Principalis* of
North Britain.

Kingdom of Sion (*The*), in Münster, set up by John of Leyden, and
meant to be a theocracy. John appointed
twelve judges over the 'tribes,' and
Matthiesen the baker had before him
sent out 'apostles' to preach the Anabaptist doctrines (1534–1536).

Kingdom of Westphalia (*The*),
1807. Carved by Napoleon out of Hesse
Cassel and part of Hanover, and given
to Jerome Bonaparte, his youngest
brother. Abolished after the battle of
Waterloo in 1815.

Kingston, in Surrey. So called
because, in 901, Edward the Elder was
crowned there.

Kingstown (Ireland). So named
in honour of the visit made by George
IV. to Ireland soon after his coronation
in 1821. The town had been previously
called Dunleary, then a mere fishing
village on the coast of Dublin Bay, about
seven miles from the city. Kingstown
is now a large and beautiful town, with
commodious quays, magnificent piers,
railway to Dublin, mail boats, &c., and
handsome villas all about the neighbourhood.

Kirillit'za. The Russian alphabet
is so called because it was arranged by
Bishop Cyril.
[The Bible] will soon be turned into Russ and put
into a printed book which any poor man will
be able to read if only he knows his kirillitza.
The Czar, chap. xl.

Kirk (*The*). The Presbyterian Church
of Scotland (1689).

Kirk of Field (*The Tragedy of the*).
The murder of Henry Darnley, husband
of Mary queen of Scots, who was blown
up with gunpowder in a mansion called
Kirk of Field, belonging to James Ken
nedy archbishop of St. Andrews.
On the Monday before his [Darnley's] murder
the queen passed the evening with him till it was
time to attend a masque which was to be given
in the palace. . . . About two in the morning of
Tuesday Bothwell, with a selected party of desperate men, opened the under apartments of the
Kirk of Field by means of false keys, and laid a
lighted match to a quantity of gunpowder which
had been previously placed beneath the king's
apartment.—Sir W. SCOTT, *Hist. of Scotland*, xxviii.

Kirk Session (*The*), 1689. The lowest judicatory in the Presbyterian Church
of Scotland. It is composed of the
parish minister and ruling elders, to
assist in superintending the social, moral,
and religious condition of the parish,
judge of the fitness of those who wish to
become members of the church, to exercise discipline on those guilty of scandalous offences, and to grant certificates
to worthy members who remove to
another parish. The other three courts
are the Presbytery, the Synod, and the
General Assembly. *See* 'Presbytery.'

Kirkland's Plot (*Moses*), 1776.
Kirkland, a native of South Carolina,
was employed by Stuart and other
Royalists to concert measures with
General Gage for a joint attack, by sea
and land, on the southern states of N.
America, while the savages fell on their
rear. The plot was discovered, and the
Americans endeavoured to win over the
savages, but without success; so the
Americans entered their country, laid
waste the cornfields, and almost extirpated the Cherokees.

Kirkpatrick Crest and Motto.
A bloody hand holding a dagger, and
the motto 'I make sicker.' When Robert
Bruce had stabbed Comyn in the
cloisters of the Minorites, Dumfries
(1305), Sir Roger Kirkpatrick asked if he
was sure the traitor was slain. ' I doubt
so,' replied Bruce. ' Aye ? do you
doubt ? ' exclaimed Kirkpatrick, 'then
I'll make sicker.' So saying he thrust
his dagger into Comyn's heart.

Kislar Aga. Chief of the black
eunuchs. About equal in patronage to
our lord chancellor. The revenues, &c.

of all religious foundations are at the disposal of the Kislar Aga.

Kissing the Pope's Foot. Kissing the foot of a Roman emperor was a method of adoration paid to him as a god, and Diocletian (284–305) had his shoes studded with gems to render the ceremony less obnoxious.

When popes assumed regal powers they adopted the same custom, and some had crucifixes wrought in their shoes as a salve to tender consciences. It is not possible to state with certainty when the custom began, but in the ritual ascribed to Pope Gelasius (492–496) mention is made of deacons 'kissing the pope's feet before they began reading the Gospel.'

Not only were the feet of the pope kissed, but so were the feet of the mule or ass on which he happened to be riding.

The Romans certainly kissed the feet of their idols, and thought it derogatory to touch their mouths. The Persian method of adoration, introduced by Cyrus, was falling on the face at a prince's feet and kissing the ground on which he stood. Conon refused to perform this ceremony to Artaxerxes, and Callisthênês refused to prostrate himself before Alexander the Great.

Kissing the cheek was a Jewish, Greek, and Roman custom of salutation, still continued in France and some other modern nations of Europe. Kissing the hand of a liege lord was a ceremony of homage, and subsequently was adopted by sovereigns as a part of court etiquette.

'Kissing hands' or to 'Kiss-hands' is a synonym of being introduced to court in England, Spain, Russia, and Turkey. In Catholic cathedrals and other important churches on Holy Thursday the officiant who celebrates the mass washes and kisses the feet of thirteen old or thirteen young persons, in commemoration of the act of Christ mentioned in the Fourth Gospel.

Kitchen Cabinet (*The*). The private advisers of President Jackson, who used to summon Francis P. Blair and Amos Kendal (editor of the ' Globe ') and others, to consultation by a back door, or the kitchen door, to avoid observation.

The members of Jackson's Cabinet were not high-caste statesmen, but they were too high-caste to be congenial counsellors of Jackson. Behind them he kept a 'Kitchen Cabinet,' of creatures selected for their servile devotion to his person, including a representative of the domesticated press.—The *Nineteenth Century*, Aug. 1888. p. 272.

Kit-Kat Club (*The*), or ' Kit-cat Club,' 1688–1720. Composed at first of thirty members, originated chiefly by Dr. Garth the poet, author of ' The Dispensary,' in imitation of Boileau's 'Lutrin,' to ridicule the apothecaries, who were at war with the physicians about the establishment of dispensaries. The apothecaries strenuously opposed the design. Garth was a Whig and Hanoverian, and the club, which was held in King Street, Westminster, was supplied with pastry by Christopher Kat, a pastrycook near by. Its toasts were engraved on the drinking-glasses, that no Jacobite sentiment might be insinuated. Dissolved in 1720.

Addison and Steele were members of the club.

Kit-Kat, or ' Kit-cat,' **Pictures.** Oil paintings of the members of the Kit-Kat Club, by Godfrey Kneller. They were the natural size, but only down to the knees. These and all similar ' three-quarter likenesses ' are called Kit-Kat pictures.

Klephtes (1 syl.). Brigands of Thessaly, for a long time opposed to the Armatoles (3 syl.), but in the insurrection of 1821 they united against the Turks for the independence of Greece.

Knærod (*Treaty of*). A treaty of peace, after the war of Calmar, signed in 1613 at Knærod by Christian IV. king of Denmark and Gustavus Adolphus king of Sweden. Gustavus Adolphus consented to ransom the provinces which the Danes had taken, and to abandon his claim to the island of Oesel, and to the coasts of the Arctic Ocean as far as the Bay of Waranger.

Knife for the Academic Knots (*The*). Chrysippos the Stoic (B.C. 280–297). He was the keenest disputant of his age. It was said of him, ' If the gods make use of dialectics, it must be the logic of Chrysippos.'

Knight Bachelor (*A*). The lowest grade of knighthood; conferred on civilians as well as on military and naval officers. The recipient kneels before the sovereign, who says to him ' *Sois chevalier au nom de dieu,*' and then adds, ' Rise, Sir —— ' (naming the *Christian* name).

Knight Baronet. An English order instituted 22 May, 1611, by James I. Instituted in Ireland 30 Sept., 1619; and in Scotland by Charles I. in 1625.

Knight-errantry. The practice of knights wandering from place to place to redress wrongs, and especially to release young women taken captive by the unruly barons of England, Spain, France, and Germany.

They engaged themselves to redress those wrongs which laws were too feeble to remedy, and for redressing which honour, plunder, or rich donations became usually their compensation.— TURNER, *History of England during the Middle Ages*, chap. xiii.

Probably there is a basis of truth in this statement; but, without doubt, the rules of knight errantry are gross exaggerations.

Knight Service, or 'Knights' Service.' Serving the king on horseback in his military expeditions. This service was paid in consideration of lands held under the crown, and was at one time considered the most honourable of all tenures.

Knight of Liddesdale (*The famous*). William Douglas (*—1353).

Knights. Anglo-Saxon *cniht*, a military attendant who paid service to some chieftain as a rent for land. Called in French *Chevaliers*, and in German *Ritters*, because they served on horseback. It was common to create knights before and after a battle. Thus 500 French knights were created before the battle of Agincourt; similar honours were conferred on great festivals, such as a coronation or royal marriage. The apprentice of a knight was called a squire, which means a shield-bearer (French *écuyer*). Not only kings could create knights, but knights themselves could dub others. The chief ceremony was for the knight to touch with his sword the neck of the person as he knelt before him, saying these words: 'Arise, Sir Knight.'

Alfred gave Athelstan a belt and robe, and girded him with a sword, A.D. 900.

The women who distinguished themselves by preserving Tortôsa from the Moors in 1149 were knighted.

Knights Baronets of Nova Scotia, 1621. A title conferred by James I. on a number of Scotch adventurers whose object was to colonise North America.

Knight's Fee, or 'Feodum Militare.' A portion of land held by a knight for military service. William the Conqueror had an army of 60,000 knights in virtue of such fees.

Knights Hospitallers. 'Knights of St. John of Jerusalem,' or 'Knights of Malta,' 1048. Organised to guard and entertain pilgrims to the Holy Sepulchre at Jerusalem, and hence called *hospitallers*. Their monastery at Jerusalem was dedicated to St. John the Baptist, hence their second name. When expelled from Judæa they were allowed by Karl V. (1530) to settle in Malta, and hence their third title. Suppressed in England 1540, in France 1792, and dispersed by Napoleon in 1798.

Knights Sword-bearers. Founded in 1201 by the bishop of Livonia for the defence of that see. They were originally called 'Knights of Livonia,' but received the name of sword-bearers from two cross-swords embroidered in red on the breast of their white mantles. These knights were masters of Livonia and Esthonia. Gothard Kettler, the 50th grand master, became a Lutheran, and in 1561 the sovereignty of the Knights Sword-bearers was split up into five parts: (1) One part went to Ivan Vassilievitch czar of Russia; (2) Esthonia and Revel swore fidelity to Eric XIV. king of Sweden; (3) Livonia was attached to Sigismund II., called Sigismund Augustus of Poland; (4) Arensberg and the isle of Oesel went to Magnus duke of Holstein; and (5) Gothard Kettler kept for himself the provinces of Courland and Semigaglia [*Semigalia*], of which he was created duke by the king of Poland.

Knights Templars (*The*), 1118. A military order of monks organised to protect pilgrims on their road to the Holy Land. Subsequently their chief office was to protect the Holy Sepulchre at Jerusalem against the Saracens. They followed the Benedictine rule and took the vows of poverty, chastity, and obedience; but they became immensely rich, worldly, and tyrannical. The order was suppressed in 1311–1314, and in England in 1322.

Called Knights Templars or Knights of the Temple because Baldwin II. king of Jerusalem gave them a house built on the site of Solomon's Temple. Their costume was a long white robe decorated with a red cross.

Knights of Glyn and Kerry (Ireland). The heads of two ancient families named Fitzgerald. The titles still continue.

Knights of Labour (*The*), 1834. United States. The trades union committee which regulates the amount of wages to be demanded by workmen, the degree of skill to be exacted from them, and the length of time they shall work for a master. It enjoins when a strike shall be made and when workmen of the union may resume labour.

THE KNIGHTS OF LABOUR. — Philadelphia, 17 Jan.—The 'Philadelphia Press' states that a gigantic scheme of general reorganisation, by which all coal miners and mine labourers in the United States will be placed under one banner, is being accomplished by the Knights of Labour, in order to secure concerted action in their interests. —*Reuter.*

Knights of our Lady of Mount Sion (*The*). Approved 1191 by Kaiser Heinrich VI. and Pope Celestine III. All of noble birth, bound to celibacy and to the defence of the Christian church. Their dress was a white mantle and black cross; their rule that of St. Augustine. Their original number was 24 lay members and 7 priests; subsequently increased to 40. Conrad regent of Poland gave them the territory of Culm and all the country between the Vistula and the Druentsa.

Knights of Rhodes (*The*), 1314. Villaret, grand-master of the Knights Hospitallers, removed from Jerusalem to Rhodes. Andronīcus urged the Saracens to drive him out of the island, but Villaret, by a succession of conquests, made himself master of it, and then changed the name of his order into that of the 'Knights of Rhodes,' a title which was retained till 1530. The order was called that of

Knights Hospitallers 1048–1120.
Knights of St. John of Jerusalem 1120–1134 (driven out).
Knights of Rhodes 1314–1530 (driven out).
Knights of Malta 1530–1798. The order still exists, and its flag still flies on some Mediterranean vessels (1890).

Knights of St. George in Ireland (1472–1494), or 'Brotherhood of St. George.' Thirteen gentlemen chosen from the four counties of the Pale (Kildare, Dublin, Meath, and Louth). They met annually to choose a captain, and maintained 120 mounted archers, 40 horsemen, and 40 pages for the protection of the English border (WALPOLE, 'Kingdom of Ireland,' 1882).

Knights of St. Margaret, 1786. The mayors knighted for congratulating

George III. on his escape from assassination when Margaret Nicholson, a mad woman, attacked him as he descended from his carriage in St. James's Park.

Knights of the Dagger. *See* 'Chevaliers du Poignard.'

Knights of the Garter, 1346. An English military order founded by Edward III. It is under the patron saint of England, 'St. George,' an image of whom is attached to a blue ribbon, and the ribbon is passed over the left shoulder. Round the left leg is a blue garter containing the motto ' Honi soit qui mal y pense.' *See* ' Blue Thonge.'

Edward III. only 'perfyted substanegally what kynge Richarde had begunne at the sege of the cyte of Acres, wher, in his great necessyte, there were but 26 knyghtes that firmly and surely abode with the king; when he caused all them to wear thonges of blew lcyther about the legges; and afterwarde they were called the knyghtes of the blew-thonge.'—RASTEL, *Chronicle.*

Knights of the Round Table. Asser in his ' Life of Alfred' says these knights were created by Arthur A.D. 528. The order was revived in 1344 by Edward III. at Windsor, on New Year's Day.

Knights of the Shire were gentlemen chosen by the freeholders of each county to represent them in parliament, now called county members. They were paid according to the Act 12 Rich. II. c. 12 (1388); but the payment of members has long been discontinued. By Act 9 Anne c. 5 (1710) no member whose income was under 600*l.* a year was eligible for election. This restriction was abolished in 1858 (21, 22 Vict. c. 26).

Knights of the Virgin Mary (*The*), 1190. The original name of the ' Teutonic Knights' (*q.v.*).

Knighten-gild (*The*). The chief of the London gilds, dating back to the reign of King Edgar. It stood at the head of all the gilds, and its alderman or master was the grand-master of all other gilds. It consisted of 19 knights, to whom the king gave a portion of void ground lying within the walls of the city, afterwards called Portsoken ward.

A soke is a lordship enfranchised by the king, with liberty of holding a court of the lord's socmen or socagers (*i.e.* tenants). ' Knighten-gild' also written ' Cnihtena-gild.'

Knot (*The Cromwell*), 1659. This term was given by the exiled Charles Stuart to a secret council of Royalists who were working in his cause in England against the government of Cromwell. The head of the *Knot* was Sir Richard Wallis, who was proved to be a traitor to both Charles and Cromwell.

Know-nothings (*The*), or 'Natives,' 1853. A political society in the United States of America who declared that the right of citizenship should be restricted to 'natives,' or those born of American parents in America. They were opposed to Catholicism, as inconsistent with the spirit of republicanism. When asked any question respecting their society, their only reply was 'I know nothing.' They split on the slave question and died out.

Knox's Blast. 'The First Blast of the Trumpet against the monstrous Regiment of Women' is the title of a tract published by John Knox in 1558 against Mary queen of England and Mary queen of Scots. The object was 'against the political government of women.'

The words 'Regiment of Women' we should now call the 'Regimen or Rule of Women.'

Knox's Liturgy, or 'The Book of Common Order,' 1562. In 1564 its use was enjoined on the Scotch Kirk by the General Assembly. It was based on the Genevan Formula (*q.v.*), but soon went out of use when the living influence of Knox declined.

Knoxians and Coxians (*The*), 1556. The followers of John Knox and Dr. Coxe dean of Christ Church, Oxford, who left England during the reign of Mary and retired to the Continent. Knox, backed by Calvin, objected to the English Liturgy, and insisted on the use of the Genevan service; but Dr. Coxe insisted on the English Liturgy, and made a point of repeating the responses aloud. The altercation became so noisy that the magistrates had to interfere. Knox retired to Geneva, and Coxe settled in Strasburg.

Kockbunds (*The*). The Thugs of Hyderabad. Also called 'Phanseegurs.'

Koh-i-noor (*The*), *i.e.* 'Mountain of Light,' one of the largest diamonds in the world. Came into the possession of Ala-u-din soon after 1300. It fell to Baber in 1526, and subsequently to Mahommed Shah, great-grandson of Aurengzebe, who kept it hidden in his

turban; but when Nadir Shah took possession of Delhi, Mahommed had to give the diamond to the conqueror. It passed in succession to Shah Shuja, and when driven from Cabul he carried it to Lahore, when Runjeet Sing got possession of it and had it set in a bracelet, 1813. After the annexation of the Punjaub by the English the crown jewels of Lahore were confiscated, and the Koh-i-noor was presented to Queen Victoria by the East India Company and delivered into her hands 3 June, 1850. In 1889, in a most insolent letter, Runjeet Sing demanded its restitution. Its weight was 186½ carats. It was exhibited in the Great Exhibition of 1851, and valued at 140,000*l*. By order of the Queen it was cut into a brilliant by Herr Voorsanger, whereby the weight was reduced to 106$\frac{1}{16}$ carats. If this diamond is the 'Great Mogul' its previous history will be found under that name. *See* 'Diamonds.'

Konrad I. First king of Germany after the Karlovingian race. He was previously count of Franconia (911–918). Contemporary with our Edward the Elder.

Konrad II., founder of the second line of kings in Germany, was duke of Franconia. Heinrich III., IV., V. followed in regular descent. Konrad II. was crowned king of Germany 1024, and kaiser of the Holy Roman Empire 1027; he died 1039, at the age of 53. He was a descendant of Konrad the Wise, son-in-law of Otto I. the Great. However, the kings of Germany were elected or chosen, originally by the great nobles, and subsequently by a board called the 'Electors,' and were not kings by hereditary descent.

Father, Heinrich duke of Franconia. *Wife*, Gisela, a widow. *Contemporary* with Canute and Harold Harefoot.

Konrad III., founder of the House of Hohenstauffen, was grandson of Heinrich IV. (of the previous dynasty called the 'house of Franconia'). He was king of Germany from 1138 to 1152, but never kaiser or emperor of the Holy Roman Empire (1093, 1138–1152).

Konrad III. was the first of the kings of Germany who was elected by seven princes. In 1356 Karl IV. made seven the legal number of electors by what is called the 'Golden Bull.' In 1648 the number of electors was raised to eight; in 1692 it was nine; but in 1777 the number was again reduced to eight. In 1806 Napoleon swept away the whole system and introduced the law of inheritance.

Father, Friedrich Hohenstauffen nephew of

K K

Kaiser Heinrich V. *Mother*, Agnes daughter of Kaiser Heinrich IV. *Contemporary* with Henry I. and Stephen.

Konrad IV. Son of Friedrich II. and great-grandson of Barbarossa. He was king of Germany between 1250 and 1254, but never kaiser. Konrad IV. was a *roi fainéant*, and in him expired the royal house of Hohenstauffen.

The next dynasty was the house of Guelf or D'Este, which gives only one king, Otto IV., who abdicated.

Ko'raichites (3 syl.). An Arabian tribe and the principal one of Mecca up to the time of Mohammed. This tribe in A.D. 460 acquired the custody of the Kaaba, or Temple at Mecca, and, of course, most violently opposed the pretensions of Mohammed (613–622). In 623 they were defeated by him at Bedr and Ohud, and again in the 'Expedition of the Nations' in 625. They then concluded a truce, and in 629 surrendered to him the holy city of Mecca. The Koraichites professed to be the issue of Ishmael. Mohammed and his first wife (Kadijah) were Koraichites.

Koran' (*Al*). The Mohammedan Scriptures. The scattered leaves of it were collected into a volume A.D. 634 by Abubekr; it was revised and sanctioned by the calif Omar in 652; was first printed at Rome in 1530; and was burnt by order of Pope Clement VII. Sale's English translation with numerous notes was printed in 1734, and a French translation was made in 1783 by Savary.

The Koran is divided into 114 sections, and contains 3,000 paragraphs or verses.

Koreish (*The Tribe of*). *See* 'Koraichites.'

Körner of Italy (*The*)—that is, the Tyrtæus or war-poet, Godfredo Mameli. His great song was composed in 1848, the refrain of which is—

Together we stand, or together we fall;
We are ready for either at Italy's call!

The great war-song of Körner is 'The Sword Song' (1791-1813).

Koscius'ko (*Insurrection of*), 1794. He was leader of the Poles in revolt against Russia, and won the battle of Wraclawice, near Cracovia; but (2 Oct.) four months later he was attacked at Maciejowice (about 50 miles from Warsaw) and was taken prisoner, exclaiming, 'Finis Poloniæ.' He remained prisoner at St. Petersburg for two years, when he was liberated by the czar Paul I. and died in Switzerland in 1817.

Kosciusko indignantly denied ever uttering the words popularly ascribed to him.

Kremlin, *i.e.* citadel. The palace and citadel of Moscow, at one time the residence of the czars. It was originally constructed of wood, but was rebuilt of stone by Dmitri Donskoï. In 1487 Pietro Antonio, an Italian, built the towers which flanked the enceinte. It was not set on fire by Rostopchin in 1812, and was occupied by the French. The Kremlin also contains the palace of the archbishop, the Cathedral of the Assumption where the czars were crowned, the belfry of Ivan Veliki with 32 bells, one of which is the biggest in Europe.

Kufic Coins. The earliest Mohammedan coins inscribed with Kufic (or ancient Arabic) characters. The first was struck A.D. 638 under Calif Omar.

Kufa, in the pashalic of Bagdad, contained the most expert writers of the Koran', and hence the term 'Kufic writing,' to express 'old Arabic.'

Ku-Klux Klan (*The*), 1868-1871. A secret society of ex-Confederate soldiers in North America. 'Ku-Klux' is meant to represent the click in cocking a rifle. The 'Klan' was an offset of the 'Loyal League,' and its ostensible object was to 'repress crime and preserve law in the disturbed Southern States.' In 1871 Congress, resolved to put down the association, suspended the *Habeas Corpus Act* (under what is generally called 'The Ku-Klux Law') in nine counties of South Carolina. This law and the employment of the military brought the 'Klan' to an end.

Kuleev Dynasty (*The*). The third fabulous dynasty of Persia, the second being the Jy-anian and the fourth the Yassanian dynasty. The only three names of the third dynasty known are Shah Kuleev the founder, with Shah Aboul and Shah Mah-aboul, the last two of the line.

Ku'risers. Irish refugees formed into two regiments, in the pay of the Duke of Savoy, to put down the Vaudois in Piedmont. The word is a corruption of *cuirassiers* (1655).

Kurucz-Labancz Era (*The*), 1672-1681. The period in Hungarian history of the contest between the Kuruczes (*i.e.* the insurgents) and the Labanczes or Austrians. This was in a measure a 'religious war,' the insurgents being the Protestant party and the Austrians the Catholic faction.

> To cut tobacco on the bare back of the opposite faction, or to cut strips from his quivering skin, to drive iron spikes under the finger nails, and to bury an adversary in the ground up to the head and then fire at him, were everyday courtesies exchanged between these two belligerents. — VAMBÉRY, *Hungary*, ch. xiii.

Kuthans, or 'Kuthe'ans.' The Samaritans were so called by the Jews because they were carried captive by Salmanazar to Kutha, a town of Susiana, not far from Babylon. It is said that the inhabitants of Kutha went to Palestine and colonised Samaria.

L. The three L's, Lords, Levites, Lawyers. Hugh Peters said, It will never be well with England till the three fifties are abolished. L=50.

Labourers (*The Statute of*). I. In feudal times forbade a husbandman, whose land had been bought by another, leaving the estate. He was obliged to remain with his family as a villein regardant (*q.v.*) to cultivate the land.

II. 23 Edw. III. c. 1, A.D. 1349, for the regulation of wages, consequent upon the strife between labour and capital which resulted from the Black Death (*q.v.*). The act ordained that the wages of labourers shall be the same as they were 'two years before the plague began'; but, as the price of food had risen enormously, this law was a gross injustice, and led naturally to the 'Peasant Revolt' (*q.v.*). Repealed 1826.

III. Numerous acts of parliament from the reign of Edward IV. have been made to compel persons having no visible means of livelihood to go out to service either in husbandry or trade to gain an honest living.

Labyrinth of Egypt (*The*). This most magnificent edifice had 3,000 chambers; . and the gallery containing the statues of the gods was entered by a flight of ninety marble steps. The porch was of Parian marble. It was destroyed by the people of Heracleopŏlis, who worshipped the ichneumon or water-rat, the natural enemy of the crocodile, the great god of the Labyrinth. It was a theological war—the god water-rat against the god crocodile. The former prevailed, and the beautiful Labyrinth was levelled to the ground. It seems like a satire on other religious wars.

The Cretan and Samian labyrinths are also celebrated.

Laced Shoe (*The*), 1502. In German 'Bundschuh,' the peasants' rebellion in the Rhine countries. So called from its cognizance.

Lacedæmonian League (*The*), B.C. 431. The Lacedæmonian league, at the outbreak of the Peloponnesian war, comprised all the states of the peninsula except Argos and Achaia (which were neutral), and all northern Greece except Thessaly and Acarnania (which sided with Athens). *See* 'Athenian Confederacy.'

Lack-learning Parliament (*The*), 1404, from which all lawyers were excluded. *See* 'Parliament.'

> The Unready Parliament would be a better phrase; that is, the parliament lacking counsel or advice (A.-S. *ræd*, counsel, advice, as in 'Ethelred the Unready').

Laco'nia, the country of the Lacedæmonians. The ancient inhabitants were the Cynurians and Selēgês, who were expelled by the Achæans. The Dorians subsequently invaded Peloponnesos, and became the ruling race.

Laconisers, B.C. 458, &c. Those Athenians who supported the power of Sparta, after Athens by the confederacy of Delos was declared the head of Greece.

Laconisms. When Philip of Macedon wrote to the Spartan magistrates, 'If I enter Laco'nia I will level Lacedæmon to the ground,' the ephors wrote back the single word 'If.'

In 1490 O'Neill wrote to O'Donnel, 'Send me the tribute, or else—;' to which O'Donnel returned answer, 'I owe none, and if—.'

Lacustrian Period (*The*). An extremely remote period when human habitations, for the sake of security, were built in the midst of lakes. Remains of such habitations exist in certain lakes of Switzerland, Scotland, Ireland, &c.

Ladan-Thora and Ladan Bareseid. The two readers of the Pentateuch on the eighth and last day of the Feast of Tabernacles. One reads the first half and the other the latter half.

Ladder of Acesius (*The*). Sectarian exclusiveness. Acesius was bishop of Constantinople and a Novatian. Constantine the Great excepted him from the

K K 2

tribe of 'heretics,' and invited him to attend the Council of Nice. Novatian taught that the lapsed (*i.e.* those who denied the faith through fear of persecution) can never be received again into the communion of the faithful. This exclusion he afterwards extended to all guilty of 'mortal sins.' Constantine said jocosely to Acesius, 'Take a ladder, Acesius, and climb to heaven by yourself.'

Ladder of St. John. Surnamed Clīmācus, or rather Klīmăkos, 526.

PARADISE.

30.	Faith, Hope, Charity.
29.	Peace of God.
28.	Prayer without ceasing.
27.	Solitude.
26.	Inner Light.
25.	Death of the Natural Man.
24.	Single-mindedness, or only one affection, and that for God.
23.	Abandonment of false humility and doubt.
22.	Pride utterly crushed out.
21.	Self-glorification cast out.
20.	Conquest of fear.
19.	Watchfulness; the lamp always burning.
18.	Psalmody.
17.	Death of the Carnal Mind.
16.	Poverty, or loss of the love of accumulating.
15.	Chastity.
14.	Temperance.
13.	Conquest of indolence of mind and body.
12.	Restraint of exaggeration and false representation.
11.	Silence.
10.	Shunning slander and idle talk.
9.	Forgiveness of injuries.
8.	Equanimity.
7.	Sorrow the seed of joy.
6.	Constant thought of death.
5.	Penitence.
4.	Obedience.
3.	Giving up father and mother.
2.	Giving up all earthly goods and hopes.
1.	Renouncement of th world

THE WORLD.

Ladislaus' Wagon (*St.*). A two-wheeled cart drawn by men. In the reign of Ladislaus IV. of Hungary (1272–1290) the country was so impoverished by domestic wars 'that the two-wheeled cart got the name of *St. Ladislaus' wagon*; for, owing to the universal plundering of draught-cattle, the people themselves were compelled to draw the carts.'—VAMBÉRY, 'Hungary,' chap. vii.

Lady (*The*). Castlemaine *née* Barbara Villiers, wife of Mr. Palmer, and mistress of Charles II., who created her duchess of Cleveland.

The Duke of Buckingham had a quarrel with 'the Lady,' and the Lady prejudiced the king against him; and the duke was determined to have his revenge by exposing 'the Lady.'—HOWITT, *Hist. of Engl.*, Charles II., ch. xi. p. 442.

Lady Bountiful. So Joanna Baillie the poetess was called (1762–1851).

Lady Clares (*The*). An Irish association so called from the county of Clare, the nucleus being formed of Claresmen. They rose about the same time as the Terryalts (*q.v.*), and were especially conspicuous in the sanguinary tithe war (1830–1832). See 'Irish Associations.'

Lady Day. 25 March, the day of the Annunciation.

Lady Huntingdon's Connexion, 1770. A split from the Calvinistic Methodists, after the death of George Whitefield. It preserved substantially the liturgy of the Church of England. Half Presbyterian and half Independent.

Lady Selina countess of Huntingdon (1707-1791).

Lady Jane Grey. Grand-daughter of Mary youngest daughter of Henry VII. The Princess Mary and the Princess Elizabeth (though both illegitimáted by their father Henry VIII.) were by his last will acknowledged, and would naturally succeed in turn their brother Edward VI., provided there was no issue to prevent it.

HENRY VII.—His son HENRY VIII. succeeded him. The youngest daughter was Mary.
HENRY VIII.—EDWARD VI., MARY, and ELIZABETH (all children of Henry VIII.).
Mary, daughter of Henry VIII.) had a daughter named Frances, who married Henry Grey marquis of Dorset and duke of Suffolk.
Lady Jane Grey was the daughter of Frances and her husband Henry Grey.

The pedigree runs thus :—

HENRY VII.
|
Mary
|
Frances, wife of Henry Grey
|
Lady Jane Grey

Lady Margaret Preacher (*The*) in the University of Cambridge, 1504. Founded by Lady Margaret, mother of Henry VII., with a stipend of 8*l*. He has to preach one sermon on the first Sunday in Nov. in Great St. Mary's Church.

Lady Margaret Professorship of Divinity (*The*) in the University of Cambridge, 1502. Founded by Lady Margaret mother of Henry VII. Original stipend 20 marks a year. *See* ' Regius Professorship of Divinity.'

Lady of Christ College (*The*). John Milton, so called because he was fair and his features effeminate ; his hair was fine, light brown, and flowing, his constitution delicate, and his health anything but robust. (1608–1674.)

Lady of England. Matilda or Maud, daughter of Henry I. of England. She married the kaiser-king Heinrich V. of Germany in 1114, but was left a widow 1125 (aged 23). She then married Geoffrey of Anjou in 1127, but was driven from Anjou by her husband in 1129. Her son Henry [II. of England] was born in 1133. After the death of her father, Matilda made war on Stephen the usurper, and having obtained some advantages was recognised as ' Lady of England ' in 1141 ; but her imperious arrogance so disgusted the English that they drove her from London in five months, and her adherents were excommunicated. She died at Rouen in 1165, aged 63.

Lady of Mercia (*The*). Ethelflæda daughter of King Alfred. She married Ethelred, and after his death continued to reign (913–918). She conquered the ' Five Boroughs ' (*q.v.*).

Ladies' Irish Land League, Ladies' Labour and Industrial Union (between 1879 and 1888), formed in affiliation with the Irish Land League, the Land League, and the Labour and Industrial Union (*q.v.*). Its nominal object was ' the relief and sustentation of Land League prisoners.' *See* ' Irish Associations.'

Ladies of the Queen's Household (*The*). They consist of the Mistress of the Robes, the Ladies of the Bedchamber, the Bedchamber Women, and the Maids of Honour. The Mistress of the Robes has the superintendence of the personal attendants on the queen.

Lady's Gown [Scotland]. A present made by the purchaser to the wife of the man who has sold to him his estate.

Lætare Sunday. The fourth Sunday in Lent. So called from the first word of the introït of the Mass (Isa. lxvi. 10), ' Rejoice ye with Jerusalem, and be glad with her, all ye that love her' [Lætare Hierusalem . . .]. As on this day the Pope blesses the golden rose, it is also called ' Dominïca de Rosa.' It is a day of rejoicing in the middle of mournful Lent. *See* ' Sundays.'

The *introit* [introitus] is the passage of Scripture chanted while the priest is entering the chancel to celebrate mass.

Lagenians. The people of Leinster in Ireland.

Lagides (3 syl.). The Ptolemys of Egypt. *See* ' Lagos.'

Lagoon (*The*), Venice, or rather the marsh round the city. Strictly speaking, the Gulf between the Piave and the Adige. The lagunas are the canals, too deep for cavalry and too shallow for vessels.

In no place did the Inquisition obtain so little footing as in the Lagune.

The Lagune, which cannot justly be considered either sea or land, is navigable only by skiffs drawing a few inches of water.

The Rialto is the very centre of the Lagune.

After the capture of 100 ships he returned to the Lagune with his booty.

Petrarch had occasionally visited the Lagune, and was profoundly impressed with the singularity and beauty of Venice.—*History of Venice* (Murray, 1831).

Lagos. Ptolemy I. king of Egypt, the adopted son of Lagos the Macedonian. All his descendants on the Egyptian throne were called Lagídês.

La Hire, *i.e.* the growler. So Etienne Vignoles [*Vin-yole*] was called on account of his deep baying voice [1387–1442]. One of the knaves on a pack of French cards is meant for La Hire [*Here*].

Lahore (*Treaty of*). (1) 26 June, 1838, between Great Britain, Runjeet Singh, and Shah Shuja.

(2) March 8, 1846, between Great Britain and Dhuleep Singh.

Laird of Cockpen (*The*). The Duke of Buccleuch.

Laish. While Othniel was judge (B.C. 1394–1354) the tribe of Dan, finding their mountain territory too small, made an incursion into the plain beyond Mount Ephraim, and seized the city of Laish. Here they established a priesthood of their own, because Shiloh was so far distant. This worship continued for nearly 300 years, *i.e.* till the capture of the ark by the Philistines in Samuel's time.

Lake Dwellings. Human habitations in the midst of lakes. Those in Switzerland were discovered in 1854. *See* 'Lacustrian Period.'

Lake Poets (*The*). Wordsworth, Coleridge, and Southey, who resided in the lake district of Cumberland and Westmoreland. They were so named by the 'Edinburgh Review.'

Lali'ta Vistara. One of the nine chief works of the Buddhists. It contains the life and doctrines of Sakyamuni (*i.e.* St. Sak'ya).

Lamaism. Buddhism corrupted by Sivanism (*q.v.*) or Shamaism or spirit worship. It prevails in Thibet and Mongolia. The essence of it is contained in three *jewels*, called 'the Buddha jewel,' 'the Doctrine jewel,' and the 'Priesthood jewel.' The first person of the triad is Buddha, the second is the incarnation of Buddha, and the third is the church.

Lambeth (*Treaty of*), 1217. By which Louis the dauphin consented to withdraw from England on payment of a sum of money which he claimed for expenses. He had been invited over by the English barons to assist them in resisting John; but as John was just dead, the services of Louis were no longer needed, and the barons had no intention of placing a Frenchman on the throne.

Lambeth Articles (*The*), 1594. Proposed by Archbishop Whitgift; suppressed by Queen Elizabeth in 1595; rejected in 1604 at the Hampton Court Conferences; adopted by the Irish Church in 1615. These articles were nine in number, and were designed to be added to the 39 Articles.

1. God hath from all eternity predestined some to life and reprobated others to damnation.

2. This election does not proceed from God's foreknowledge of the faith and good works of his elect, but solely from his own good will.

3. The number of the elect is fixed, and can be neither increased nor diminished.

4. Those not predestined to everlasting life will of necessity be damned.

5. True faith and holiness in the elect will never fail.

6. Justifying faith is certain of remission of sins and eternal salvation through Christ.

7. Saving grace is not conferred on all.

8. No man can come unto Christ except God the Father draws him.

9. It is not in the will or power of every man to be saved. *See* 'Nine Articles.'

Lambmas Brother and Sister (*A*). A lad and his lass at St. Olla's Fair at Kirkwall, associated together as long as the fair lasted.

> Ye gallanty Lambmas lads appear,
> And bring your Lambmas sisters here.
> Sir WALTER SCOTT, *The Pirate*, ch. xxxii.

Lame Peace (*The*), 20 March, 1568. The peace of Longjumeau between the Huguenots and French Catholics. It was called 'the lame and badly-seated peace,' because one of the queen's negotiators was lame, and the other was the lord of *Malassise*. But it was otherwise lame and badly seated, inasmuch as it left the Huguenots at the mercy of their enemies, with no surety except the word of an unprincipled Italian woman. It lasted only six months, and never existed except on paper. *See* 'Paix Boiteux.'

Lamian War (*The*), B.C. 323–322. The war between Antipáter and the allied Greeks after the death of Alexander the Great. So called because Antipater threw himself into Lamia, a strong fortress on the Malian Gulf, which was besieged by the allies. Antipater succeeded in breaking up the alliance, and Athens was left completely at his mercy.

Lammas-day, 1. Aug. The feast of St. Peter ad Vincula. The word is a corruption of loaf-mass, referring to the firstfruits of harvest offered on that day. (Ang.-Sax. *hlafmæsse*).

Lamourette's Kiss, 1792. A momentary reconcilement followed by greater hostility than ever, in the French revolution. When the Prussian army was on the move towards Paris Condorcet proposed to the Assembly a reconcilement of the Jacobins and Girondists. Lamourette (bishop of Lyons) seized on the idea and exclaimed : ' He who succeeds in reconciling you will be the real conqueror of Austria and Coblentz ! ' His words had a magic effect; the most hostile members threw themselves into each other's arms and kissed each other frantically ; but ere sunset the emotion had effervesced, and Jacobins and Girondists were more bitter than ever against each other.

This is sometimes called the Judas Kiss, but most improperly so, as no betrayal was even dreamt of by the excitable Frenchmen.

Lamp of Lothian (*The*). The abbey church of Haddington was so called from the extreme beauty of its architecture. It was burnt down in 1356 on ' Burnt Candlemas' (*q.v.*).

Lamp of Wisdom (*The*). Aben Ezra, called by the Jews ' Hechachan.' They used to say, if knowledge had put out her candle it might be lighted again at the brain of Aben Ezra.

Lampeter (*College of*), 1822. Founded by Thomas Burgess bishop of St. David's, for the better and inexpensive education of Welsh candidates for ordination.

Lampeter Brethren (*The*), 1832. A society of young men, members of St. David's College, Lampeter, who met together as a praying and revival order. Henry James Prince was the most prominent of them, and he afterwards founded the Abode of Love, called Agapemonê (*q.v.*).

Lancaster (*The Line of*). Part of the Plantagenet dynasty of England, consisting of Henry IV., V., and VI. Henry IV. dethroned Richard II., but was a usurper, for (on the deposition of Richard) the rightful heir was Edmund Mortimer. *See* ' York.'

EDWARD III. His sons were (1) Edward the Black Prince, (2) William, (3) Lionel, (4) John of Gaunt. (5) Edmund Langley duke of York.

Son of Edward the Black Prince was RICHARD II. (no issue, and deposed).

Next comes Lionel (the third son), whose daughter Philippa married Edward Mortimer. Their son was Roger Mortimer, and the children of Roger were Edmund and Ann. Edmund was heir on the death of Richard II.

From Ann Mortimer proceeds the House of York. Her son Richard duke of York was the White Rose. He had two sons, both of whom reigned, viz. EDWARD IV. and RICHARD III.

The fourth son of EDWARD III. was John of Gaunt duke of Lancaster, whose son was HENRY IV., grandson HENRY V., and great-grandson HENRY VI., the Red Rose.

Lancaster Gun *The*). A species of rifled cannon invented by Mr. Lancaster, who dispensed with grooves, and instead of a strictly circular bore adopted an elliptical one.

Lancaster Herald (*The*). One of the six heralds of England, and the second in point of seniority. *See* ' Heralds,' &c.

Lancasterian Schools, 1798. So called from Joseph Lancaster. Not much known in our islands till 1808, but in 1818 they became very numerous. The idea was to save expense by means of mutual instruction. Joseph Lancaster was indebted to Dr. Bell of Madras for the idea, and for a time Bell and Lancaster were rivals, the former being supported by churchmen and the latter by dissenters. Dr. Bell called his system ' Mutual Instruction,' Lancaster called his the ' Monitorial System.' *See* ' Mutual Instruction.'

Lancasterism, 1844. Destroying wheat-stacks in order to raise the price of wages. So called from Joseph Lancaster, who was arrested for firing corn-stacks, and pleaded in excuse that his object was to improve the rate of wages.

Land.

William the Conqueror nationalised the land, himself being the sole owner.

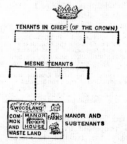

He let it out to king's or chief tenants, on certain conditions, and looked to these tenants only for the fulfilment thereof.

The chief tenants subdivided their holdings among mesne tenants on similar conditions.

The mesne tenants subdivided their holdings into manors, and the manors were parcelled into farms, with a certain portion called common.

Land Bank (*The*), 27 April, 1696. A bank of England chartered by William III. for the benefit of the landed gentry, according to a scheme projected by Hugh Chamberlayne. The Tonnage Bank (*q.v.*) lent William only a million, and that at 8 per cent. This new bank lent him double the sum at 7 per cent., but it proved to be a mere bubble.

Land-Grabber (*A*), between 1879 and 1890. In Irish history it means one who takes a plot of land from which a tenant has been evicted. *See* 'Irish Associations.'

Prior to the establishment of the Land League, 'land-grabbing' in Ireland was called 'Saintough' (covetousness), 'one of the seven deadly sins.'— *Parnell Commission* (Father Hewson, 27 June, 1889).

Land League (*The*), 1879–1881, Ireland. Michael Davitt's development of Mr. Butt's Home Rule policy, after the death of Mr. Butt, in May 1879. Ostensibly it aimed at 'the abolition of the monopoly of land,' by giving to tenants as a free gift part of the land belonging to the Irish landlords. It tried to carry out its object by defiance of the law and resistance to its execution. Suppressed in 1881, when the National League was established in its place.

The North American Land League (Ireland) was organised 11 March, 1880. The first meeting of the League was held in Philadelphia 25 April, 1883. *See* 'Irish Associations.'

In August 1879 Michael Davitt negotiated a small loan from the Fenian war-chest to start the constitutional movement. Patrick Ford was 'the honest broker' between the Fenian trustee and the Land League financier. That body held its first meeting 31 Oct., 1879, and Mr. Parnell was appointed president.—*Cashman's Life*, pp. 218, 219; *Parnellism and Crime*, p. 8.

'The objects of the Land League were to bring about a reduction of rack-rents; and to facilitate the ownership of the soil by the occupiers of the soil. —ALFRED HENRY RUEGG, counsel for O'Donnell, in the 'Parnellism and Crime' libel case, 2 July, 1888.

Land Purchase Bill (*The*), 1890. A bill projected by Mr. Balfour, chief secretary for Ireland, to enable Irish tenants to purchase their farms at the value of twenty years' rent, if they chose so to do. To enable them to make the purchase, thirty millions sterling was lent by Government at 2½ per cent. plus a fiftieth part of the principle, so that the purchase money and interest would all be paid off in fifty years. As ten millions had been hitherto advanced for the same purpose, the whole loan amounted to forty millions; and, as the money paid by tenants to the New Land Department was made eligible for the same purpose, the loan was virtually an 'endless band' available till every farmer in all Ireland had become his own landlord.

Land of Ireland (*The*). From 1280, for several centuries after, the district occupied by the English, and known at a later period as the Pale.

Edward I. in 1280 called upon the lords spiritual and temporal . . . in the 'Land of Ireland' to assemble and deliberate upon the prayer of the natives praying to be admitted to the privileges of English law.—MOORE, *Hist. of Ireland*, chap. xxxv.

Land of Storms (*The*). Tierra del Fuego, an island-group at the southern point of South America. It is separated by the Straits of Magellan. Few ships have ever passed it without observing the forked lightning playing on its cliffs, and hearing the most terrific thunders roll.

Land o' the Green. Ireland, also called the Emerald Isle, from the exquisite green colour of its meadows, &c.

Lands of the Sacred Crown (*The*). Hungary. Each of its nobles was 'Membrum Sacræ Coronæ.' The sacred crown was the crown given by the Pope to St. Stephen king of Hungary (979, 997–1038).

Landlord's Hypothec (*The*). In Scotch law. A lien on the tenant's goods as a security for his rent.

Landscape Gardening (*Father of*). Lenotre (1613–1700). He laid out the gardens of Versailles, the Tuileries, St. Cloud, St. Germain, Fontainebleau, Clagny, Chantilly, Meudon, and Sceaux.

Landseer (*The Liverpool*). William Huggins, animal painter (1821–1844).

Landseer of Sculpture (*The*). Alfred Gatley (1816–1863).

Landwehr and **Landsturm**, 1805. Land defence and land assault levies. German militia, called into service in times of war. The most complete organisation was that of Prussia in

1813. The landwehr consists of men from 26 to 40; the landsturm of men from 40 to 60. The former is part of the regular army, the latter is enrolled for home work.

Napoleon restricted the Prussian army to 42,000 men; so as soon as 42,000 men were well disciplined a new batch was brought to drill, and in this way all the people were trained for war, and the restriction was evaded.

Lane (*The*). Drury Lane Theatre.

Whenever the Lane tried Shakespeare,
    I was one of the leading men.
SIMS, *Ballads of Babylon* (' Forgotten ' &c.).

L'ang, or Le-ang Dynasty (*The*). The tenth Imperial dynasty of China. Like the eighth, ninth, and eleventh dynasties, it had dominion only over the south of China, the court being at Nanking. It gave four kings, and lasted 55 years (502–557).

Language of Canaan (*The*). Bible phrases learnt by rote by the gay ladies in the suite of Catharine de Medicis, to be used in talking with consistorials, or Catholic malcontents who had joined the Huguenots. *See* ' Consistorial Phrases.'

Languages, A.D. 1890. It is estimated that there are 3,064 languages in the world; and above 1,000 different religions, including what are called ' sects.' English is spoken by above 130 millions of the human race; German by 100 millions; Russian by 70 millions; French by 45 millions; Spanish by 40 millions; Italian by 30 millions; and Portuguese by 13 millions.

English is spoken by 4 million Canadians; 3,700,000 West Indians; 3 million Australians; 1 million East Indians; 38 millions in the British Isles, and 57 millions in America: besides Africa, Jamaica, &c.

German is spoken by 2 millions in the United States and Canada; 2 millions in Switzerland; 40,000 Belgians; 46 millions in the German empire, and 10 millions in the Austro-Hungarian empire.

French is spoken by 2¼ million Belgians; 1 million in the United States and Canada; 1 million in Algiers, India, and Africa; 600,000 Swiss; 600,000 in Hayti; 200,000 in Alsace-Lorraine; and 38 millions in France.

Langue d'oc and Langue d'oil. When the Romans reduced Gaul to a province, the native language became imbued with Latin, and this mixed language was called ' Romance.' When the Franks and Germans poured into Gaul they also corrupted the language, and this mixed language was called ' Germanised Romance ' or ' Walloon.' As far the larger number of Franks and other Germans settled north of the Loire, Walloon pre-

22

vailed in the north, and was hardly known in the south of France, where Romance continued to prevail. Now the Romance or southern word for yes is ' oc,' but the Walloon or northern word was ' oil '— (*i.e.* ' o-e ' now *oui* (pronounce *we*); hence the Langue d'oc means that south of the Loire, and the Langue d'oil that used the the river. The Troubadours north of Langue d'oc, and the Trouvères the Langue d'oil.

Lansdowne Collection of MSS. (*The*), 1807. Purchased by government, and added to the library of the British Museum. It is divided into two parts: (*a*) 121 volumes of state papers and correspondence of William lord Burghley, during the reign of Queen Elizabeth; (*b*) 50 volumes of the papers and letters of Sir Julius Cæsar, judge of the admiralty and master of the rolls; the correspondence of Henry Cromwell, as chief governor of Ireland ; and numerous other historical, genealogical, and topographical MSS. of great importance. Collected by the first marquis of Lansdowne.

Lantern of Demosthenes (4 syl.). A shrine built by Lysicrātês, the chorāgos, over the tripod which he received as a musical prize. It stood in the ' Street of Tripods ' (*q.v.*), in Athens.

Laodiceans (*The*). Those of no party ; ' neither hot nor cold ' in religious matters ; the laisser-aller or indifferent (Rev. iii. 16).

The rest were housed by Mr. Nesbitt and the local Laodiceans.—E. LYNN LINTON, *Under Which Lord,* ch. xxi.

Lapsed (*The*). Those Christians who, to avoid persecution, made a compromise with the heathen governors. They are divided into 3 classes : (1) The SACRIFICATI, who sacrificed at heathen altars ; (2) the THURIFICATI, who burnt incense to heathen gods ; and (3) the LIBELLATICI, who produced a *libellus* or certificate from a heathen magistrate of having abjured the Christian faith.

The number of the lapsed was immense, especially in Alexandria.

Larder Silver. A payment of money in lieu of provisions by the tenant farmer (14th cent.).

Lars. The leader or over-king of the 12 confederate Etrurian states. The under-king was called *lucumo*. Thus the sultan would be a *lars* and the khedive a *lucumo*. Similarly, the German emperor is *lars* and the king of Bavaria a *lucumo* (*q.v.*).

Lascars. Native East Indian and Chinese sailors employed in European ships. Also camp-followers. There are gun-lascars in the British service at Hong-Kong.

Lass of Richmond Hill (*The*). Miss Jansen. The song is by Leonard M'Nally.

Last of the Barons (*The*). Richard Neville earl of Warwick, called 'the kingmaker' (1428–1471).

Last of the Fathers (*The*). St. Bernard of Clairvaux in Champagne (1091–1153). He was the great promoter of the second crusade, as Peter the Hermit was of the first.

Last of the Greeks (*The*). Philopœmen, so called by Plutarch (B.C. 252–183).

Last of the Romans (*The*). Caius Cassius. At the battle of Philippi, B.C. 42, Cassius was defeated by Antony, and was killed by his freedman Pindārus. When Brutus was told of the death of his friend, he exclaimed, 'There lies the last of the Romans.'

This was preposterous praise. If Cassius was a type of the Roman character, then may we say with the Druid, in Cowper's 'Boadicea,'

Rome shall perish, write that word
  In the blood that she hath spilt;
Perish, hateful, and abhorred,
  Deep in ruin as in guilt.

Last of the Romans (*The*). Boethius (470–524).

Gibbon (ch. xxxix.) says, 'Boethius was the last of the Romans whom Cicero would have acknowledged as his countryman.'

Last of the Tribunes (*The*). Cola di Rienzi (1313–1354).

Lord Lytton wrote a novel, in 1835, so entitled.

Last of the Troubadours (*The*). Jacques Jasmin of Gascony (1798–1864).

Last Poet of Rome (*The*). Juvenal, the satirist, died A.D. 128, aged 80.

His Tenth Satire Bishop Burnet calls 'a store-house of moral virtues.'

Later Fathers (*The Fifteen*), 4th cent. *See* 'Greek Fathers,' and 'Latin Fathers.'

Lateran (*The*). The palace of Plautius Laterānus confiscated by the Emperor Constantine, and assigned for Christian uses. The church of St. John (Lateran) is styled 'the Mother and Head of all the churches in the city and the world'; and the first act of a new pope is to take possession thereof. From the portico, on certain days, the pope blesses the entire world. The Church has been the site of five general councils (*see below*), and till the popes returned from Avignon they resided in the Lateran palace; but in 1378 the Vatican was made the pope's residence. In the piazza of St. John Lateran stands the Scala Santa, or staircase up which it is said that Jesus passed to Pilate's judgment hall.

Lateran Councils (*The*). Five general councils have been held at the Lateran in Rome.

I. In 1123. This was the first general council of the Western Church. Under Calixtus II.

II. In 1139. To restore the union of the Eastern and Western Churches. Under Innocent II.

III. In 1179. To vest the election of popes in the cardinals. War against the Albigenses authorised. Under Nicholas III.

IV. In 1215. To sanction confession. The Albigenses condemned. Under Innocent III.

V. In 1511–1517, convoked by Julius II., and continued by Leo X. Acts of the Council of Pisa declared void. The concordat with France confirmed. Dangerous books forbidden.

Lathyros. Ptolemy VIII. king of Egypt was so called from a wen on his nose (B.C. 80–36).

It is said that the name of 'Cicero' was given to an ancestor of the great orator for the same reason.

Laticlavian. A Roman senator, so called from the broad purple stripe (*clavus latus*) which every senator was permitted to wear on his toga. Equestrian knights wore a band of two narrow stripes called *clavus angustus*.

Latin (*The Pronunciation of*). *See* 'Ramists.'

Latin (*Professorship of*). In the University of Cambridge, 1869, founded by the pupils of Dr. Kennedy. It was intended to call it the Kennedy Professorship, but the doctor gave 500*l.* towards the fund, on the condition that his name was not attached to the foundation. Salary 300*l.* a year.

Latin Church (*The*). The 'Western Church,' after its separation from the Greek Church.

Latin Cross (*The*). 'Crux immissa.' A cross with the lower limb considerably longer than the other three. *See* 'Cross.'

Latin Empire (*The*). The name given to that portion of the Byzantine empire which, in 1204, was seized by the crusaders, who made Constantinople their capital. It was overthrown by the Greeks in 1261.

Latin Fathers (*The Five*). These with the ten 'Greek Fathers' (*q.v.*) constitute the fifteen 'Later Fathers': viz. Lactantius, Hilary, Ambrose, Jerome, and Augustine (4th cent.).

Latin Ulysses (*The*). Bohemond prince of Antioch, the crusader (died 1111).

The Latin Ulysses, the artful and ambitious Bohemond, employed the arms of cunning and deceit.—GIBBON, 58.

Latin Union (*The*), 1873, consisting of France, Switzerland, Italy, Belgium, and Greece, compelled by law to coin, at a fixed legal weight and fineness, all gold and silver brought to them.

Latin War (*The*). The peasants' rebellion in Salzburg, in 1523 ; it was aimed against a very unpopular archbishop.

Latin War (*The Great*), B.C. 340–338, between the Romans and Latins. By this war all Latium was joined to Roman territory.

Latitudinarians, 1660–1670. Followers of Jeremy Taylor, who insisted that a good life was better than an orthodox faith, and that a broad-hearted toleration was the most likely means of producing Christian unity. Far from believing that salvation was limited to the Church of England, they inclined to admit the equality of all professing Christians, and that even the heathen might be saved. Hales, Chillingworth, Whichcote, Tillotson, and Burnet were Latitudinarians ; so was Hoadly bishop of Bangor.

Latrocinium. So the fourth council of Ephesus held A.D. 449 was called. It was packed by Eu'tychês the heresiarch, and condemned Theodoret, one of the Christian fathers, while it declared in favour of Eutyches, who maintained that the human nature of Christ was absorbed in his divine nature.

Spelman calls the charta of Henry I. of England 'Latrocinium' (*ius gladii*). St. Dionysius calls the charter of Louis VII., in 1144, 'Latronis Redditio.'

Latter-day Saints (*The*), or 'Mormons.' They have apostles, prophets, pastors, teachers, and evangelists ; they believe in the gift of tongues, prophecy, revelation, and visions, in healing and in the interpretation of tongues. They believe the Bible to be the Word of God so far as it is correctly rendered ; they also believe the Book of Mormon to be the Word of God. They believe in the literal gathering-in of Israel and restoration of the ten tribes ; that Zion will be built on the American continent ; that Christ will reign personally upon the earth ; and that the earth will be renewed and receive paradisaic glory.

Lauder (*William*). A literary impostor, who published, in 1751, false quotations from Masenius, a Jesuit of Cologne, Taubmann a German, Staphorstius a learned Dutchman, and others, to 'prove Milton a gross plagiarist.' Dr. Douglas demonstrated that the citations were incorrect, and that often several lines had been foisted in to make good the parallelisms. Lauder confessed the fact afterwards, in 1754. *See* 'Literary Forgeries.'

Laudian Professorship of Arabic, in Oxford University. Stipend 300*l.* a year. Founded by William Laud archbishop of Canterbury in 1636.

Lauds. One of the eight daily services of the Catholic Church, and first of the four lesser ones. At dawn. *See* 'Canonical Hours.'

Laughing Philosopher (*The*). Democritos (469–361) of Milētus. He laughed at the follies of man, whereby they were for ever involving themselves in difficulties. He was the originator of the atomic theory, taught the theory of gravitation, and that the milky way is a cluster of stars.

Laurentian System (*The*). A series of highly metamorphosed rocks (older than the Cambrian) covering the whole country north of the St. Lawrence.

Law of Admonition (*The*), 1323, in Florence, by means of which the Ghibellines were excluded from the government.

Law of Germinal (*The*). 18 Germinal Year X (7 April, 1802). The first consul (in order to secure authority over Protestants) suggested that Protestant pastors should be salaried like the Catholic clergy. This was made law, and is known by the name of the Law of Germinal. See ' Decree of 3 Ventôse.'

Law of 22nd Prairial (*The*), 10 June, 1794. Couthon, the second day after the Feast of the Supreme Being, proposed that the *Law of the Suspects* should be extended, and that there should be four revolutionary tribunals instead of one. Whereupon Robespierre with autocratic authority declared 'The Law of Prairial is law'; and 17 June a batch of 54 at once were sentenced to death. The guillotine was then shifted from the Place de la Révolution to the south-east.

The *Feast of the Supreme Being* was 8 June, 1794; the *Law of Prairial* was passed 10 June; and Robespierre was guillotined 28 July (9 Thermidor, An. II.).

Law of the Clan Macduff (*The*). Immunity for homicide anciently enjoyed by those who could claim kindred with Macduff earl of Fife within the ninth degree. Macduff's cross stood on the boundary between Fife and Strathearn, above Newburgh, and any homicide of the clan who could reach this cross was safe. He had, however, to give as a deodand nine cows and a young cow-calf to the lord of the clan.

Law of the Eric (*The*), in Ireland, A.D. 164. Compounding for murder by a money fine. Spenser gives this example : Suppose a man commits murder and is prosecuted; the murderer shall pay a fine to the friends of the murdered person, and this recompense is called an ' Eriach ' (' Views of the State of Ireland ').

Laws of the XII. Tables (*The*), B.C. 451. A famous body of laws drawn up by twelve Roman patricians at the instigation of Terentius Harsa the tribune. The commissioners were called the ' Decemviri,' appointed for one year,

and during that year all other magistrates were suspended. The two consuls (Appius Claudius and Titus Genūcius) were at the head of the commission. The original number of tables was only ten, but two new tables (respecting marriage and religious rites) were added by the second Decemvirate, and the whole, being engraved on tables of brass, was hung up in the Comitium or upper part of the Forum.

Table I., lawsuits; II., theft; III., loans : IV., rights of the paterfamilias; V., rights of guardians; VI., about property ; VII., trespasses and damages; VIII., laws regarding estates; IX., the people's rights; X., funeral rites. The two new laws were : XI., religious duties ; and XII., marriages. Each law was most briefly expressed : as, A debtor shall be dissected by his creditors; No one shall be interred or cremated within the city walls; and so on.

Law of the 40 Sous (*The*), Aug. 1793. Danton induced the committee called the *Salut Public* to decree that there should be held in Paris two meetings of sections every week, and that the poorer citizens should be paid 40 sous each day for attending them. This was a great spur to sansculottism and the extravagance of the Red Republican party.

Law of the Suspect (*The*), Aug. 1793. Introduced by Merlin of Douai, subsequently called Merlin *Suspect*. ' All are suspect (he says) who by their actions, words, or writings, have become so.' Chaumette, in his ' Municipal Placards and Proclamations,' says a ' Suspect' may be recognised in the streets and should be at once apprehended.

Law of the White Water-lotus (*The*). A brotherhood in China, associated at the close of the 18th cent. against the emperor Kea-King. It lasted eight years, and spread disaffection in Shan-tung and three adjoining provinces.

Kea-king reigned 1796-1820.

Law Terms (*The*). All the year except term-time is called ' vacation.' By canon law certain seasons are set apart as holy—viz. Advent, Lent, Pentecost, and Harvest—and these seasons were to be kept free from forensic litigations. The original term-times were : (1) *Hilary*, from 23 Jan. to 12 Feb.; (2) *Easter*, from Wednesday after Easter Day to Monday three weeks afterwards; (3) *Trinity*, beginning the Friday after Trinity Sunday and ending Wednesday fortnight; and (4) *Michaelmas*, which began 6 Nov. and ended the 28th of the same month. Since 1873 the law sessions have been :—

a. HILARY, beginning 11 Jan. and ending the Wednesday before Easter.

b. EASTER, beginning the Tuesday after Easter Week and ending the Friday before Whitsunday.

c. TRINITY, beginning the Tuesday after Whitsun Week and ending 8 Aug.

d. MICHAELMAS, beginning 2 Nov. and ending 21 Dec.

Laws (*Manx*) up to 1417 were called 'breast laws,' because the Druids objected to have their laws, customs, and traditions reduced to writing.

Something of this still exists in Freemasonry.

Laws of Blood, B.C. 618. So the laws of Draco the Athenian legislator were denominated, because the same penalty—that of death—was awarded to every offence. This is quite in accordance with the Jewish axiom, 'Whosoever shall keep the whole law, and yet offend in one point, he is guilty of all' (James ii. 10).

Laws of 1790-1791 (*The*), in Hungarian history, mean those laws which confirmed the independence of Hungary and recognised it as a state. They declared Hungary to be subject to no other country, to possess her own constitution, and secured the liberty of the Greek and Protestant Churches.

Lawless Court (*The*). An ancient court at Raley or Raleigh, in the parish of Rochford, held on the Wednesday next after Michaelmas Day. It is ' lawless ' because held at an unlawful hour at the 'King's Head.' The court was held at night and without any artificial light. The records were kept with coal and not in ink. Everything was carried on in the feeblest possible whispers. Philemon Holland states that the court owes its customs to a conspiracy held at the 'King's Head,' in the dark, and of course with bated breath. (Camden; and Dodsworth MSS., Bodleian Library).

Lay Impropriators (of tithes) date from the dissolution of monasteries in the reign of Henry VIII., when church property was given to laymen. The laymen retained the tithes and glebe land in their own possession, and appointed a clergyman to do the clerical duties at a small stipend. The person who presents is termed the patron, and the clergyman who represents him is called a ' vicar ' (*vicarius*).

Lay Titulars. Lay impropriators. (Scotch history.)

Laybach, in Austria (*Congress of*), from 17 Dec. 1820 to 6 May, 1821, of the crowned heads of Austria, Russia, and Prussia, for stamping out the revolutionary movements.

Lazaretto (*A*). A hospital for quarantine or for infectious diseases. This word is not derived from Lazarus the Bible beggar, but from the isle of St. Lazarus in Venice, where such a hospital was first built in 1484.

Lazarists, or 'Fathers of St. Lazarus,' 1624. Instituted by De Gondi; placed under the direction of Vincent de Paul in 1625, and confirmed by Urban VIII. in 1631. They were called Lazarists because their chief abode was the priory of St. Lazarus in Paris, given to Vincent de Paul by the canons regular of St. Victor. Also called ' Priests of the Mission.'

Lazarus (*Knights of St.*), 12th cent. A religious and military order of Knights Hospitallers. Confirmed by Pope Alexander IV. in 1255. United with the order of St. John in 1490. Their special office was the defence of lepers, and their title was derived from Lazarus the beggar. Abolished in France in the first revolution.

In Italy it was united to the order of St. Maurice by Gregory XII. in 1572; and in France it was united with the order of Our Lady of Mount Carmel in 1608.

Lazic War (*The*), 549-556. A contest of Rome and Persia on the Phasis. It was a profitless war, but Colchis and its dependencies were added to Justinian's empire, while Rome agreed to pay to Persia a small annual tribute. (PROCOPIUS, ' Persic.' ii. 15-30, and ' Gothic.' iv. 7-16.) This war is also called the ' Colchian War.'

Called Lazic from the Lazi, a tribe which still subsists.

Lazzaroni (*pl.* of Lazzarone). The mob of Naples, like the Sansculottes of Paris. They were proverbial for laziness, poverty, and indifference ; very few had a home; they lounged on benches about the streets all day, and slept on them at night. Those who did not live by begging were messengers, fishers, street-vendors of melons and pumpkins; they held horses, carried burdens, and so on. Every year one was chosen as their chief, called *Capo Lazzaro*. Masaniello was Capo in 1647. In 1798, stimulated by Cardinal Ruffo, and headed by Michele Sforza, they long resisted the French General Championnet. The race is now well-nigh extinct, but at the beginning of the 19th cent. they numbered at least 60,000.

So called either from the beggar Lazarus, or because they dressed like the inmates of the hospice of St. Lazare.

Lazzi. Those born to labour, those of a servile condition who could not depart from their service without their lord's leave. An old Saxon term.

The nobility were Edhilings; the middle class Frilings or free-born men.

Leaden Age *(The)*, 814–987. Between the death of Charlemagne and the accession of Hugues Capet [pron. *You Cap'-pay*]; is so called from its worthlessness. Also called the 'Iron Age' from its incessant civil wars; and the 'Dark Age' from its barrenness of learned men.

Leads of Venice *(The)*. A prison under the leaden roof of the ducal palace of St. Mark for political prisoners. Their sufferings from the heat were excruciating.

Leagh Mogha, or Mogha's share. In the reign of Conn Keadcahagh (*i.e.* Conn of the hundred fights) Ireland was divided into two parts by a rampart and fosse from Dublin to Galway. The southern part was allotted to Mogha Nuod king of Munster, and the northern part, called Leagh Cuin or Conn, was ruled over by Conn of the hundred fights.

League *(The)*, and 'Leaguers,' *i.e.* the Anti-Corn Law League and its advocates (1838–1846).

League *(The)*, or 'Sainte Union,' 1576. A union of the high Catholic party in defence of the 'Holy Catholic Church' against the encroachments of the reformers. It proposed to itself three objects: to exterminate the Calvinists; to shut up Henri III. in a monastery; and to crown the Duc de Guise king of France. It was projected by the Cardinal de Lorraine, and was sanctioned fully by the pope and Philip II. of Spain.

They proposed first to exterminate the Hugue-

nots, then the Protestants of Holland, then to invade England, then to overrun Germany.

League against Charles VIII., 31 March, 1495. Between the pope, the kaiser, Venice, the duke of Milan, and the king of Castile. This powerful combination, which sent into the field 40,000 men, was dashed to pieces by Charles VIII. in the battle of Fornovo. The allies lost 15,000 men; the French, by their own account, not above 200.

League of Argos *(The)*, B.C. 421. Formed between Argos, Corinth, Eléa, Mantinéa, and Chalcidĭcê, immediately after the peace of Niccas. This league was meant to be a combination of Greek states against Athens and Sparta. Athens joined the league in 420.

League of Augsburg *(The)*, 1687. A confederation of Holland, Germany, Spain, Sweden, and Savoy against France, to compel Louis XIV. to abide by the terms of the treaties of Westphalia and Nimeguen. By the *former* the balance of power in Europe was established, and Protestants were placed on the same platform as Catholics. By the *latter* the boundaries of France were settled, and the integrity of Holland assured. England joined the league in 1688.

Nimeguen, pronounce *Neem-gen*, with *g* hard.

League of Cambray *(The)*, 10 Dec., 1508. Between the pope (Julius II.), the kaiser Maximilian I., Louis XII., and Ferdinand the Catholic (king of Aragon) against the republic of Venice. The idea was to parcel out the republic amongst the allies; but when Louis won the battle of Agnadello, and Venice fell into his hands, the pope, seeing that he had made a false move, broke from the league, and formed the Holy Alliance, the object of which was to dispossess Louis of every inch of land in the peninsula of Italy.

League of God's House *(The)*, 1401. First of the three leagues of the canton of the Grisons to resist domestic tyranny.

The other two were the Grisons League, or Ligue Grise, formed in 1424; and the League of the Ten Jurisdictions, formed in 1436. All three were admitted into the Helvetic Confederation in 1798.

League of Malines *(The)*, 1513. Between Leo X., England, Germany, and Spain against Louis XII. of France. After the 'Battle of the Spurs' (*q.v.*) Louis made a treaty of peace.

League of Marbach (*The*), 1376. Formed between Würtemberg, Baden, and seventeen towns. It was a dead set against the Suabian league (*q.v.*). In 1404 the league was joined by France and Poland, but in 1499 Würtemberg joined the Suabian league.

League of Poor Conrad (*The*). A peasants' rebellion in Würtemberg in 1514.

League of Ratisbon (*The*), 1524. By the Catholic Powers of Germany to oppose the progress of the Reformation.

League of Smalkald (*The*), or 'The Smalkaldic League,' 1530. An alliance of all the Protestants of Germany after the imperial decree at the Diet of Augsburg. By this league the Protestants bound themselves not to help the kaiser against the Turks, who threatened invasion unless he revoked the Augsburg decree. Charles V. had gone back to Spain, and appointed his brother Ferdinand regent of Germany. There was no escape, so the decree was withdrawn, and the Protestants were allowed full liberty of worship till the next imperial diet. This is called 'The Peace of Nürnberg.' The League was dissolved in 1547 by the victory of the imperial army at Mühlberg.

League of Virtue (*The*), called in German 'Der Tugend-Bund,' was organised by German students in 1813, and had for its object the total expulsion of the French from German soil. It was joined by students and professors, patriots and fanatics, and embodied the seething hatred of Germany for France.

League of the Armed Neutrality (*The*). Between Russia, Denmark, and Sweden, ratified 16 Dec., 1800.

The first convention for this league was held 9 July, 1780; the next was held 1 Aug., 1780. The States-General joined the league 24 Dec., 1780; the king of Prussia, 8 May, 1781; and the kaiser 9 Oct., 1781.

League of the Lombard Cities (*The*), or 'Ligue Lombarde,' 1167, formed to resist the German emperors. The league was successful against Frederick Barbarossa (1175–1183), and against Frederick II. in 1225; but in the 14th cent. most of the cities submitted either to the dukes of Milan or to Venice.

League of the Public Evil (*The*), or 'Ligue du Mal Public,' 1465. Applied to the 'League of the Public Good,' because the people for whose benefit that league was ostensibly formed were entirely ignored in the treaty.

League of the Public Good (*The*), 'Ligue du Bien Public,' 1465. A league of the high feudatories of France against Louis XI. In this league were the dukes of Brittany, Burgundy, Alençon, and Nemours, St. Pol, Armagnac; and at the head was Charles duke of Berry, the king's brother. A battle was fought at Montlhéry, and though the victory was indecisive, it was sufficient to bring about the treaty of Conflans (1465). In this treaty Ponthieu was given as a bribe to the Duke of Burgundy, of which he was deprived by the States-General; Alençon was confirmed in his duchy, but it was confiscated from him by the States-General; St. Pol was made Constable of France, but deposed by the same states, and suffered death on the scaffold; Charles was made duke of Normandy, but was obliged to flee, and died, it is said of poison, at Guienne.

League of the Rhine (*The*), or 'Rhinbund,' 15 Aug., 1658. Between France, the electors of Mentz, Trèves, and Cologne, the king of Sweden, &c., for the maintenance of the peace of Westphalia.

League of the 3 Cantons (*The*), 14th cent. The Swiss cantons of Schwyz, Uri, and Unterwalden. After the battle of Morgarten in 1315 the league was joined by Lucerne, Berne, and other Helvetic cantons.

League of the 7 Catholic Cantons of Switzerland (*The*), called the Sonderbund. Formed 1846, to resist the federal diet, which had determined on the expulsion of the Jesuits, the Liguorians, and other religious congregations. Dissolved in Nov. 1847.

League of the 10 Jurisdictions (*The*), 1436. The third league of the Grisons to secure independence.

The first league was the Cadēan, 1401, and the second was the Grisons League, 1424. All three were admitted into the Helvetic Confederation in 1798.

League of the 16 (*The*), or 'Conseil des Seize.' A Protestant league formed by Henri de Bourbon [Henri IV.] against the Catholic League or 'Holy Union' of the Guise party. Henri III., who hated the Guises, joined the League of the Sixteen. Ultimately Henri de Bourbon prevailed and the Duc de Mayenne concluded peace with him in January 1596.

Leagues. *See also*—

Achæan league.	Etolian league.
Cadëan ,,	Hanseatic ,,
Holy (Louis XII.) league.	
Smalkaldic league.	*See* 'League of
Smalkald.'	
Sonderbund (*The*).	

Leagues of the Grisons (*The*), or 'Ligues Grises.' They were three in number, viz. The Cadëan League, formed in 1401; the Grisons League (Ligue Grise), formed in 1424; and the League of the Ten Jurisdictions, formed in 1436. All three were admitted into the Helvetic Confederation in 1798.

Leaguers (*The*). Adherents and partisans of the Anti-Corn-law league (*q.v.*).

Learned Painter (*The*). Charles Lebrun of Paris (1619–1690), noted for the great accuracy of his costumes. His masterpieces are the 'Five Battles of Alexander.'

Learning, says Giordano Bruno:—

First it stood in Egypt; then, under Zoroaster, in Persia; then among the Gymnosophists of India; then under Urpheus, among the Thrakians; fifthly, among the Greeks at the time of their Sages; then, under Archytas, Empedocles, and Lucretius, in Italy; and seventhly, in Germany. . . . Who is comparable to Albertus Magnus? Who can be likened to Nicolaus the Cusan—had not the priestly cowl hidden and hemmed his [Cusan's] genius, I would acknowledge his having been not similar to, but greater than, Pythagoras.

Learning (*Father of English*). So Burke called the Venerable Bede (672–735). He was the founder of mediæval history, and the first English historian.

Leather Apron (*The*). The tradition is that Kavah, an intrepid patriot, headed a rebellion against Zohak, a cruel and impious tyrant; and that he displayed his leather apron as a banner. The apron set with jewels was adopted as the national banner of Persia from that day, till it fell into the hands of Kudsiah. Historically the tale is of no more value than an incident from Homer's epics. It is recorded in the historic romance (' Shah Nameh ') of Abul Casim Firdusi (950–1039). *See* 'Homer of Khorasan.'

Le Bas Prize (*The*). For an essay on English literature. For graduates of the University of Cambridge, of not more than three years' standing. Value annually about 60*l.* Founded by subscribers to the memorial of the Rev. Charles Webb Le Bas of Trinity College in 1848.

Lectisternium. A religious ceremony observed by the ancient Romans. It consisted of a sumptuous banquet offered to certain gods, in which the images or statues of the said gods were placed on triclinary couches (*lecti*), and were bidden to ' eat, drink, and be merry.' Livy speaks of these feasts, xxii. 10, *v.* 3.

In the terrible plague at Rome A.D. 399-333, the gods were bribed by such a feast to abate the pest.

Leda Bible (*The*). The folio Bishops' Bible of 1572 and 1685. *See* ' Bible.'

Lee (*General Charles*), 1731–1782. Second in command under Washington. He lived and died in all the honours of patriotism; but in 1860 came to light his papers detailing his plan for betraying the American army to General Howe. These historic papers were kept *perdu* for eighty years among those of the secretary of Lord Clive, who took an important part in the negotiations which ended with the independence of the United States of America.

Lee-Penny (*The*). A, talisman, still in possession of the Laird of Lee. Sir Simon Lockhart of Lee brought it to this country from the East, and left it to his heirs. It is said to cure murrain and hydrophobia. It is a stone of a dark colour and triangular shape, about ½ an inch each side, set in silver like a coin of Edward I. This coin is to be dipped in water, and the water given to the diseased cattle or persons to drink. The water is still applied for. *See* ' The Talisman,' by Sir W. Scott (Introduction).

Left (*Over the*). In some parts of Germany a person when he takes an oath which he does not intend to keep puts his *left* hand on his chest or side, and this is supposed to neutralise the assertion made by putting the *right* hand on his heart. Similarly a left-handed marriage is a base injustice to the woman so dishonoured.

Left-handed Marriage. *See* ' Morganatic Marriage.'

Leg of Mutton Maniacs. The founders of 'Punch,' the periodical, who held their meetings at the 'Crown' tavern. So called from the frequency of a leg of mutton being served for their repast.

The 'maniacs' were Henry Mayhew, Horace Mayhew, Gilbert A Beckett Albert Smith, John Leech, Kenny Meadows, Ebenezer Landells, George Smith, Frederick Tomlins, Charles Tomkyns, and Joseph Allan. See 'Notes and Queries,' 25 May, 1888, p. 401.

Legal Tender Act (*The*), United States, 1862, making Treasury notes a legal tender. Proposed by Thaddeus Stevens.

Legantine Constitutions (*The*). In English history, 1237, 1268. Ecclesiastical laws enacted by the Council of London, held under Cardinal Otho, legate of Gregory IX.; and Cardinal Othobon, legate of Clement IV. in the reign of Henry III.

Legem Pone, ready money. The portion of Psalm cxix. for 25 March is entitled 'Legem Pone' (v. 33), and as Lady Day is the great pay-day, the words got applied to payment or ready cash, *pone* lay down, *legem* the legal due. It is, no doubt, a very free translation, but we have several similar perversions or adaptations. For example, 'Stir-up Sunday' (the first two words of the collect appointed for 25th Trinity) and applied by schoolboys to the rapidly approaching Christmas holidays.

In this there is nothing to be abated. All their speech is *legem pone* (ready money, cash down).— MINSHULL, *Essays in Prison*, p. 26.

Legion, or 'The Legion Memorial,' May 1701. A memorial signed LEGION, 'for we are many,' delivered by a poor woman to Harley, speaker of the Commons, to read to the House, and professing to be from 200,000 Englishmen, demanding justice and complaining of the Partition of Spain (*q.v.*), the ill-treatment of the king (William III.) and the Dutch by the House of Commons, and threatening vengeance unless the Commons behaved better. Of course the memorial was voted scandalous and seditious.

The memorial excited at first a panic in the House, but when LEGION did not appear . . . the House began to recover its senses, and it began to dawn upon them that they had been hoaxed by some clever wag. This wag was universally believed to be Daniel Defoe . . . author of 'Robinson Crusoe,' and one of the shrewdest political writers of the time . . . he must have luxuriated in the terror into which he had thrown the Commons.— HOWITT, *Hist. of Eng.* (William III., p. 155).

Legion of Honour (*The*), 19 May, 1802. An order of merit, whether military, literary, commercial, scientific, or benevolent, instituted by Bonaparte when first consul. It contained 15 cohorts, each of which had 7 grand officers, 20 commandants, 30 ordinary officers, and 350 legionaries (total 6512 members). The decoration was a star of 5 rays, white enamel, surrounded with oak and laurel branches. In the centre of the star was the figure of Napoleon Bonaparte. On one side was the legend *Honneur et Patrie* and the device was an eagle holding thunderbolts. It was suspended to a red-watered ribbon. Remodelled by Napoleon III. (22 Jan., 1853).

Badge for a *Chevalier*, a bow of red ribbon in the buttonhole of the coat, with medal attached.

Badge for an *Officer*, a rosette of red ribbon in the buttonhole of the coat, with medal attached.

Badge for a *Commander*, a collar-ribbon.

Badge for a *Grand Officer*, a broad ribbon under the waistcoat.

Badge for a *Grand Cross*, a broad ribbon with a star on the breast, and jewel cross pendant.

In the reign of Louis XVIII. the figure of Napoleon was changed for that of Henri IV., and the eagle for 3 fleurs de-lis. In 1830 the 3 fleurs-de-lis were changed for 2 tricolour flags. In 1848 the original device was restored.

Napoleon III. instituted a lower order than a chevalier, called a *Médaille Militaire*, distinguished by a yellow ribbon.

Legislative Assembly (*The*), 1 Oct., 1791. 'L'Assemblée Législative.' This assembly, consisting of 745 members, followed the Constituent Assembly. It sat till 21 Sept., 1792. It was specially appointed to alter the laws of France in conformity with the new constitution. No member of the Constituent Assembly was allowed to be appointed a member of the Legislative Assembly. The Legislative Assembly was elected by the people.

The *right* was occupied by the monarchy men chiefly *Feuillants* (*q.v.*), officers of the army, and some National Guardsmen. The *left* by Girondists and Jacobins. The *centre* by middle men.

Leicester's Parliament, June 1265. When the Commons were first summoned by him to parliament. This was in the reign of Henry III. Edward I. restored the practice. *See* 'Parliament.'

Leinster Declaration (*The*), 1828. So called from the Duke of Leinster, at that time the only duke of Ireland. It was the declaration of a medium party between the Catholic Association and the Brunswick clubs (*q.v.*). The declaration set forth that the ' disqualifying laws ' were productive of endless mischief, and were ruining Ireland; and it prayed the government without further delay to adopt such measures as would restore peace, and unite the strength of the British Empire.

Leinster Tribute. *See* ' Boromé.'

Leipzig Conference (*The*), 1519. Between Luther, Eck, and Carlstadt. This famous conference tended greatly to the promotion of the Reformation.

Leipzig Interim (*The*). A provisionary arrangement made at Leipzig, by order of Charles V., 22 Dec., 1548, between the Lutherans and the Roman Catholics, till the questions could be definitely settled by a general council. The *ad interim* compromise agreed to in this diet caused a split in the Protestant party.

Leix, Ireland, now called Queen's County, and its chief town Maryborough, in honour of Queen Mary. At the same time Offaley was called King's County, and its chief town Philipstown, in honour of her husband Philip of Spain.

Leman's Act, 1867. After the great panic of 1866, to prevent gambling in bank shares. Before this act bank shares were mere names of speculative stock, existing or non-existing, and ' bears ' by depressing the stock endangered the credit of the bank.

Lemuria. The supposed submerged equatorial continent which once covered the Indian Ocean.

Lent. The 1st Friday is dedicated to the spear and nails.
The 2nd to the holy winding-sheet.
The 3rd to the five wounds.
The 4th to the precious blood.
The 5th to the seven dolours.
The 6th is Good Friday.
' The crown of thorns ' is the Friday after Quinquagesima.

Leonard's College (*St.*). *See* ' Andrews (*University of St.*).'

Leonilas of Hungary (*The*). Nicholas count Zriny. When Solyman the Magnificent laid siege to Szigeth, and had taken the outer circle, Zriny,

with 600 men, retired to the inner circle. A mine was sprung and opened a gap in this rampart. Zriny and his 600 stood in the breach, and only two survived.

Leonine City (*The*). Leopolis in Rome (on the right bank of the Tiber), built by Leo IV. and named after him A.D. 852.
It is after this pope that Pope Joan is placed.

Leonine Verses, hexameter and pentameter. Verses which rhyme at the middle and end; invented by Leonine or Leon, a canon of the church of St. Victor, Paris, in middle of 12th cent.
His replicans *clare* tres causas explico, *quare*
   More *Leonino* dicere metra *sino*.
Let me explain to you, *therefore*, that there are
   three reasons *where ore*
Verses constructed like *mine* are to be called *Leonine*.

Leonists. A branch of the Waldenses in Leon. *See* ' Waldenses.'

Leopold I. Son of the kaiser-king Ferdinand III. of the house of Austria (1640, 1658–1705); generally called ' the Little Man in Red Stockings.' He also wore a red feather.

Leper Kings of England. Henry III and Henry IV. Leprosy was in the Angevin family. Queen Marguerite of Anjou died of the disease.
Robert Bruce of Scotland was also a leper.

Lesbian or Æolian Poets (*The*). Terpander, a native of Lesbos (B.C. 700–650); only a few fragments now remain of this poet. Alcæos of Lesbos (B.C. 624–570); only a few fragments of his odes remain, but Horace has rendered several of them into Latin verse. Arīon of Lesbos (B.C. 640–600); no specimen of this poet is extant. Sappho of Lesbos (B.C. 620–570); a few fragments of her poetry remain.
Horace, Book i. Ode ix., ' Vides ut alta,' is a translation of an ode by Alcæos; so is Book i. Ode xiv., ' O navis.'—Book i. Ode xxvii., ' Natis in usum,' and Book i. Ode xxxvii., ' Nunc est bibendum,' are either translations or imitations, &c.
Called Æolian poets because they wrote in the Æolic dialect. The other Greek dialects were Doric, Ionic, and Attic. Homer is in the Ionic dialect, and the best tragedies are in Attic Greek.

' L'État c'est moi.' So said Louis XIV. when requested to convene the States-General. This is the rule of an autocrat, but the constitution of France acknowledged at least three estates up to 1789.

L'État de la Justice, 1558. A fourth estate introduced in the States-

General by Henri II. It consisted of the chief magistracy of the country.

Letter of Attorney (A), or 'Power of Attorney.' A deed authorising the person named to act in your stead. Whatever is done by your legal substitute on your behalf has the same authority as if done by yourself personally.

Qui facit per alium facit per se.

Letter of Credit (A). An authority from one bank to another to credit the person named to a stated amount. In this case the person who gives the letter is responsible up to the amount stated in the letter.

Letter of Licence. An instrument executed by creditors whereby one who cannot pay his debts is permitted to carry on his business under surveillance, in the hope of obtaining thus a better dividend.

Letters (*Father of*). I. 'Père des Lettres,' François I. of France (1494, 1515–1547).

II. Lorenzo de' Medici the Magnificent (1448–1492).

Letters Conform. In Scotch law. A writ issued by the supreme court enforcing the judgment of an inferior one.

Letters Missive. An order from the lord chancellor to a peer to put in an appearance to a bill filed in chancery.

Letters Patent. A writing under the Great Seal, authorising the party named to do some act or enjoy some privilege, or create some office mentioned in the letter. Inventors by letters patent have a monopoly in their invention for a stated term of years.

Letters of Administration. The legal instrument granted by the Probate Court to a person appointed administrator to one who has died intestate.

Letters of Exculpation. In Scotch law. A warrant obtained by a prisoner to subpœna witnesses in his defence.

Letters of Ganganelli (Clement XIV.). Though spurious, these letters are certainly very interesting. They are said to have been the productions of Caraccioli; but Caraccioli died protesting to the last that he was only the translator of them.

(Ganganelli was born 1705, became pope in 1769, and died 1774.) *See* 'Literary Forgeries,' &c.

Letters of Horning. Warrants for charging a person in Scotland to pay or perform certain debts and duties. Wharton says they were so called because these warrants were originally proclaimed by sound of horn.

Letters of Intercommuning. By an old law in England a man accused of any crime, who did not appear to take his trial, might be intercommuned or outlawed.

These letters ran thus: 'We command and charge all our lieges and subjects that none presume to reset, supply, or intercommune with any of the aforesaid, our rebels, nor furnish them with meat, drink, house, harbour, or victuals, nor any other thing useful or comfortable to them; nor have any intelligence with them by word, writing, message, or otherwise, under pain of being repute and esteemed art and part with them in the crime foresaid.'—LAING, iv. 77.

This was like the old Roman *Aquæ et Ignis Interdictio.*

Letters of Junius (*The*). Author unknown. In 1763 appeared No. 45 of the 'North Briton,' conducted by Wilkes, member for Aylesbury. In this number the king (George III.) was charged with uttering a deliberate lie in his speech from the throne, and a 'general warrant' was issued by the home secretary for the seizure of the author, printers, and publishers. Junius supported Wilkes, and maintained that general warrants—that is, warrants in which no *names* are specified—are illegal; and generally pleading 'the people's cause' against royal prerogatives and autocracy.

The letters began to appear in the 'Public Advertiser,' 21 Jan., 1769, and continued to 21 Jan., 1772. John Taylor ascribed the authorship to Sir Philip Francis in 1816, and in 1871 the handwriting was investigated by Cabot, who confirmed the suggestion.

Letters of Mark and Reprisal. Commissions granted to individuals to fit out privateers in time of war, and to seize the bodies and goods of antagonists. Abandoned by the great powers at the Congress of Paris in 1856.

'Letters of Percy Bysshe Shelley' (*The*). Published in 1852. These forgeries were exposed in the 'Athenæum' in the months of February, March, and April, 1852. *See* 'Literary Forgeries,' &c.

'Letters of Phal'aris (*The*),' 1718. Published at Oxford. Bentley proved the letters to be forgeries. Phalăris was tyrant of Agrigentum in Sicily. Overthrown by Telemachus B.C. 550, and died B.C. 549. He is well known by the story of the brazen bull. It is said that Perillos showed the tyrant a brazen bull meant for the torture of criminals. It was an oven in which victims might be roasted alive, and tubes were so constructed as to render bellowing noises to drown the shrieks of those enclosed. Phalaris ordered the inventor to be enclosed to test the truth of what he said. *See* ' Literary Forgeries.'

Letters of Request. A writ which commences a suit in the Court of Arches against a clergyman, instead of proceeding, in the first instance, in the Consistory Court.

Letters of Safe Conduct. A writ under the Great Seal guaranteeing safety to and fro to the person named in the letter. In war, an enemy can travel to and fro without fear of molestation under such defence; and persons charged with crimes cannot legally be detained so long as they act under such authority.

Letters of Uriah. Similar to the classic ' Letters of Bellerophon '—that is, a treacherous letter of friendship, but in reality a death-warrant.

' And it came to pass in the morning that David wrote a letter to Joab, and sent it by the hand of Uriah. And he wrote in the letter, saying : Set ye Uriah in the forefront of the hottest battle, and retire ye from him, that he may be smitten and die.'—2 Sam. xi. 14, 15.

<small>However, sir, here is a guarantee; look at its contents: I do not again carry the letters of Uriah.—Sir W. SCOTT, *Redgauntlet*, ch. xvi.</small>

Letters of the Sepulchre. Two codes made by Godfrey and the patriarchs of the court of Jerusalem : one respecting the rights and duties of burghers, and the other respecting the privileges of the nobles. These two codes were laid up in a coffer with the treasures of the church of the Holy Sepulchre.

Lettre de Cachet (*Un*). A sealed letter, in virtue of which the obnoxious person named therein might be arrested and sent either to prison or into exile, without trial, or even being informed of the nature of his offence. This infamous tyranny was abolished by the revolution.

<small>St. Florentin, a governor of the Bastille, used to</small>

<small>boast that he had received 50,000 lettres de cachet. As the fortress would not hold above 70 or 80 at a time, and few were ever released, the deeds of death must have been pretty quick and numerous within those walls.</small>

Lettres Provinciales (*Les*), 1656 –1657. The famous letters of Blaise Pascal against the Jesuits and in defence of the Jansenists, written under the assumed name of ' Louis de Montalte.' The whole title is ' Lettres de Louis de Montalte à un provincial de ses amis, et aux RR. PP. Jésuites.' In these letters Pascal lashes the loose morals of the Jesuits with wonderful humour, vigour, and enthusiasm. Though condemned at Rome, they are models of their kind.

<small>There are eighteen complete letters; the nineteenth is a fragment, and the twentieth is by Lemaistre. The first three are in defence of Arnauld, who had attacked the Jesuits in a work entitled ' Moral Theology of the Jesuits '; but it is on the subsequent fifteen letters that the fame of Pascal rests. He charges the Jesuits with loose morals, mental reservation, simony, equivocation, and want of holiness.</small>

Levellers. I. April 1649. A body of men that first appeared in Surrey, and went about pulling down park palings and levelling hedges, especially those on crown property. They gave out that ever since William the Conqueror landed the native English have been oppressed. Colonel Lilburne was lodged in prison for favouring the Levellers.

II. 1647. A political party which made terms with Cromwell in November, and demanded the king's death in the November following (1648). Their platform was the perfect equality of man and the abolition of all ranks and degrees. The French Quixotic conceit of ' liberty, equality, and fraternity ' well expresses the levellers' charter. Levellers were first called Rationalists.

III. In *Irish* history, 1760, Levellers were agrarian rebels, afterwards called Whiteboys. They were called Levellers from their levelling the hedges of enclosed commons, and began their work in Tipperary. Subsequently they enlarged their programme, and set up for the general redress of agrarian grievances connected with the letting, buying, and selling of land, hiring and eviction, tithes and rates. *See* ' Irish Associations.'

'Leviathan.' Hobbes's great work is an ideal Commonwealth, called by him ' the Matter, Form, and Power of a Commonwealth, Ecclesiastical and Civil.' It fearlessly attacks early scripture authorities, and has always been one of the strongholds of sceptics. Hobbes considered the philosopher Locke a supporter of his principles.

Lex Æmilia Sumptuaria. A law by Marcus Æmilius Lepidus, consul B.C. 78, limiting both the quantity and kind of foods to be used at banquets and other entertainments. *See* 'Lex Licinia.'

Lex Carolina, 1532. A law of the German Empire passed in the reign of Charles V., whence the name. It regulated the criminal procedure, and put an end to the arbitrary processes which had hitherto prevailed. It furthermore enjoined the publicity of debates and the publication of all judicial sentences.

Lex Fabia de Plagiariis. A law against literary 'thieves' or plagiarists. The punishment was either a fine or being sent to the mines.

Lex Hortensia ordained that market days (*nundinæ*) should in future be *fasti* or court days, that country people might get their lawsuits determined when they came to town for market.

Non-court days were called by the old Romans *nefasti*; *i.e.* not *fasti* or court days.

Lex Licinia Sumptuaria, B.C. 55. A sumptuary law forbidding more than 3 lbs. of fresh meat and 1 lb. of salt meat to be served up at table on any one day.

The Fannian law, B.C. 168, forbade that more than one fowl should be served at any one table, and that not a fattened one, *quæ non altilis esset.*— Gel. ii. 24. *See* 'Lex Æmilia,' &c.

Lex non Scripta. Common law in contradistinction to statute law. It may be written or printed, but does not derive its authority thus. The written document is a mere description or memorial of the customs which have prevailed.

Lex Oppia, B.C. 213. That no woman should wear more than half an ounce of gold, nor wear a dress of two colours, nor ride in a carriage within half a mile of any city or town.

Lex Papia Poppæa, A.D. 9. To promote population. It gave rewards to marriage and imposed penalties on celibacy. Those who had three children had several privileges. *See* 'Jus Trium,' &c. Those who were bachelors could not succeed to any inheritance except of their nearest relations, and even then a part was forfeit to the state.

Lex Porcia prohibited the scourging of a Roman citizen. Paul refers to this prohibition, Acts xxii. 25.

Lex Regia of Denmark, 1665. A law to fix the order of succession in the royal house.

Lex Talionis. The law of retaliation, as an eye for an eye, and a tooth for a tooth. *See* 'Vendetta,' 'Rimbecco.'

Lexington (*The glorious Victory in the Battle of*), 19 April, 1775. This was no battle, but a mere skirmish, in which the Americans had the advantage. Its sole importance is that it was the first fight between the colonists and the British soldiers. Governor Gage had sent a detachment of 800 men to destroy a depôt of stores and arms at Concord, about twenty miles from Boston in Massachusetts. The British reached Lexington at five in the morning, but were resisted there, and at one of the bridges near Concord by the American minutemen (*q.v.*). Some 20,000 Americans came rushing to resist, and the British had to retire with the loss of 60 killed and 136 wounded. The Americans had 30 killed and about as many more wounded.

Lia Fail (*The*) of Ireland. The 'Fatale Marmor' or 'Stone of Destiny.' So called from the tradition that wherever this stone was the people would be the dominant power. Hence the Latin distich:

Ni fallat fatum, Scoti. quocunque locatum
Invenient lapidem, regnare tenentur ibidem.

It was brought to Ireland by the Tuatha na Danaan (*q.v.*) and set up in Tara, the capital of Bregia. Upon this stone the ancient Irish kings were installed. Fergus, the leader of the Dalraidic colony (*q.v.*) in Argyllshire, brought it over with him to Albany (West Scotland), but Kenneth II., the conqueror of the Picts, removed it from Argyll to Scone in 840, and Scotland was then called 'the Kingdom of Scone.' In 1296 Edward I. carried it to London, where ever since it has been in Westminster Abbey. Over it is a rude chair on which our monarchs sit to be crowned.

According to Keating ('History of Ireland'), 'Lia' means a stone, and 'Fail' is for Falias, the city whence the stone was removed to Tara in Ireland. The tradition is that this stone is the very one that Jacob used for his pillow when he had the vision about the ladder.

The Fatale Marmor does not seem to be the same stone as the Lia Fail. The Lia Fail we are told was a pillar nine feet high; but the Fatale Marmor was a syenite (like Pompey's pillar at Alexandria), 20 inches long, 10 inches thick, and about 17 broad.

Libellatici. Those Christians who had a libellus or certificate from a heathen magistrate to show that they had complied with the emperor's order in sacrificing or offering incense to idols.

Libellus Pacis, 3rd cent. A certificate of peace given by some confessor to a lapsed Christian procuring readmission into Christian communion. The form was as follows. ' Let * * be received into church communion, with all those who belong to him.'

Liber Albus, 1419. The White Book of the city of London compiled by John Carpenter, town clerk of the city of London, and one of the four executors of the famous ' Dick Whittington.' It contains the various ordinances regulating the internal trade of the city, its laws and customs. The book was edited by H. T. Riley, and printed in 1859 (' Monumenta Gildhallæ Londoniensis ').

Liber Censualis Angliæ. The ' Rate-book of England.' So Doomsday Book (*q.v.*) was sometimes called.

Liber de Wintonia. The Book of Winchester. Doomsday Book was so called because it was anciently preserved under three locks and keys in the royal treasury of that city.

Liber Niger Scaccarii (*The*). A roll of military tenants made in the reign of Henry II. of England. The tenants enrolled in this book held single knight's fees of the crown. *See* p. 95.

Books of magic and necromancy were called ' Libri Nigri,' ' Libri sacra nigredine colorati '; or rather, Books of the Black Art.

Liber Reg's. So Doomsday Book (*q.v.*) was called. *See* ' King's Book.'

Liber Vitæ, of the Middle Ages, was the Martyrology.

Liber Viventium, of the Middle Ages, was the book in which the allowances or ' commons ' of the monks were registered.

Liberal Union (*The*), 1887. An association of Unionists of all shades of ' Liberal opinion ' for the dissemination of Unionist principles, *i.e.* against the separation of Ireland from England by giving to Ireland ' Home Rule.' From 1886 they acted with Lord Salisbury's Conservative government and broke away from Mr. Gladstone's party, which advocated ' Home Rule ' (*q.v.*).

Liberator (*The*). I. Daniel O'Connell, also called ' The Agitator ' (1775–1847). He began to take a leading part in promoting the claims of Roman Catholics in 1803. Daniel O'Connell with Sheil founded the New Catholic Association in 1823 ; set up the Repeal Association in 1840 ; and held monster meetings in 1843.

II. Giuseppe Garibaldi (1807–1882). The finest character for manly independence, self-renunciation, military resources, and civil administration combined that ever existed. He liberated Sicily and Naples; and did much to unify the thirteen Italian states under the one sway of Victor Emmanuel.

Liberator Clubs, 1828. Clubs established by Daniel O'Connell in every part of Ireland, in connection with the Catholic Association (*q.v.*). Each branch had its own organisation and internal management; and all the clubs were so knit together as to insure at any time a simultaneous movement.

Liberators, 1828. A faction established in Ireland by Daniel O'Connell to prevent the formation of secret societies, and to conciliate all Ireland in one brotherhood, having in view the two great objects, Catholic Emancipation and equal civil rights for all. The Liberators were bound to prevent riots and faction fights, to protect voters from the vengeance of their landlords, to promote exclusive dealings with ' friends of religious and civil liberty,' and to use every effort to promote in Ireland the exclusive use of Irish growth, breeding, and manufacture. The force of O'Connell was moral force only.

Libertés Gallicanes. The Gallic Church insists that there are two distinct powers, one spiritual and the other temporal; that infallibility does not reside in the pope but in the church or whole body episcopal; and that the judgments of general councils are authoritative. In 1682 Bossuet reduced the Libertés Gallicanes into the following items: (1) The church must be ruled by the canons; (2) the power of St. Peter and his successors is only spiritual; (3) the laws and constitution of the kingdom are independent of the church; (4) the decrees and judgments of the pope may be reformed. Hincmar, Gerson, Bossuet, the Abbé Fleury, Cardinal La Luzerne, Bausset, Frayssinous, Guillon, Boyer, Affre, and others were great sticklers for this liberty of the Gallic Church.

Libertines. I. Acts vi. 9. Jews manumitted by the Romans, to whom probably were added those, like Paul, who were admitted to the Roman franchise. These Jews and proselytes had a synagogue of their own.

II. 1525. A religious sect in the reformed church founded by Quintin, a tailor of Picardy, and a man named Copin. Their disciples were at liberty to be either Calvinists or Lutherans. Their chief tenets were (*a*) that whatever is done, God is the doer of it; and (*b*) that nothing is sinful but what you think to be so.

III. Of *Florence* were those who cared neither for a republican form of government, such as Savonarola wanted to establish; nor yet an oligarchy; nor yet for a tyranny in the hands of one of the Medici; but only for a *laissez-aller* government where every one might do as he liked.

These political quidnuncs had evidently graduated in the Abbey of Thélème, over the door of which institution was inscribed 'FAIS CE QUE VOULDRAS.'

Liberty (*The Feast of*), B.C. 479. An annual festival held on the site of the battle of Platæa, to commemorate the victory won over the Persians in that famous battle.

Liberty of December (*The*). The Feast of Fools, 28 Dec., in honour of the slaughtered Innocents of Bethlehem. Monks joined in the supreme foolery of this festival (DU TILLIOT, 'Mémoires pour servir à l'histoire de la Fête des Fous).

Liberty Tree (*The*), 1765. A tree in Boston, Massachusetts, on which the Boston insurgents hung the effigy of Mr. Oliver, the newly-appointed stamp-distributor of the British government. The effigy was subsequently burnt in a bonfire.

This was the commencement of the American revolt for independence.

'Trees of Liberty' (*q.v.*) were quite different affairs.

Libiti'na. The Roman goddess in whose temple was kept all the paraphernalia required for funerals; whence the word was used for funeral apparatus generally, and *libitinārius* in Latin means an undertaker.

Libitinæ Ratio. The register of deaths. The name of every one who died was recorded by the Romans in a register so called. *See* above.

Librarian of the Republic of Letters. John Albert Fabricius of Leipsic, who died 1736, aged 68. So called from his intimate acquaintance with books.

'Libri Symbolici Ecclesiæ Evangelicæ.' Books of faith and discipline were so called by the Lutherans. They consisted of the three Catholic creeds (viz. the Apostles', the Nicene, and the Athanasian), the Augsburg Confession, the Apology for that confession by Melanchthon, the Articles of Smalkald drawn up by Luther, Luther's Catechisms, and the Formula of Concord, called the Book of Torgau. See each of these *in loco*.

Lichfield House Compact (*The*), 1834. A caucus opposed to the government of Sir Robert Peel and the tories generally. Lord John Russell met his chief supporters at Lichfield House to initiate them into his Reform measures; and, after the fall of the Whig ministry on the resignation of Lord Grey, it is there that he laid down the tactics which the Whigs should adopt.

Lichtmesse, or 'Festum Candelæ,' The festival of a founder.

Licinian Rogations (*The*), B.C. 376. Three bills brought in by Licinius the tribune of the plebs, (1) authorising that the interest paid on loans should be deducted from the principal; (2) limiting the amount of public land held by any individual to 500 jugera (320 acres); and (3) ordaining that one of the two consuls should be a plebeian.

By public lands was meant the lands of conquered people taken possession of by the conquerors. Thus William the Conqueror parcelled the land of England into fiefs among his barons.

Lieutenant-General of France.
A temporary dignity conferred on the Duc
de Guise in 1558 and 1560; on Prince de
Condé in 1563; on the Duc d'Anjou in
1567; on the Duc de Mayenne in 1589; on
the Duc d'Orléans in 1643; on Comte
d'Artois in April 1814; and on Louis
Philippe in July 1830.

L¹ght of Greece (*The*). Corinth is
called by Cicero ' lumen totius Greciæ,'
yet it is somewhat remarkable that
Corinth has not produced one single
author whose name has come down to our
knowledge. Bœotia, proverbially dull and
stupid, was the birthplace of Pindar.

Light of the World (*The*). Siegmund (*q.v.*), or Sigismund, kaiser-king of
Germany (1368, 1410–1437), master of six
languages.

Jocosely called *Supra Grammaticam,* because on
one occasion when he had blundered in his Latin
he replied, ' Ego sum Imperator Romanorum, et
supra grammaticam.'

Light-armed Troops. The British cavalry is subdivided into light,
heavy, and medium. The *light*-armed
are the Hussars; the *heavy*-armed are
the 4th and 5th Dragoon Guards, and the
1st and 2nd Dragoons; the *medium* include the Lancers, and the rest of the
Dragoon Guards and Dragoons.

L¹ghtfoot Scholarship. For
history. One every year for undergraduates
of the University of Cambridge. Value
45*l.* a year, tenable for 3 years. Founded
by the Rev. Joseph Barber Lightfoot, D.D.,
Hulsean Professor of Divinity 1870.

Lightning or Thunderbolt (*The*).
I. Stephen II. of Hungary (1100, 1114–
1131). So called from his impetuosity.

II. Bajazet I. sultan of the Turks was
surnamed ' Ilderim ' (the Lightning) for
his fiery impetuosity (1347, 1389–1403).

Light-shot. A kind of Church
rate.

When the Danes were overthrown at Ethandune
Alfred allowed them to settle in a part of England
assigned to them, on condition of their paying
tithes, Rome-shot (*Peter's pence*), Light-shot, and
plough-alms (*rent-charge*).

Liguorists (*The*), or 'Liguorians,'
1732. Disciples of Alphonso Maria de
Liguori of Naples. His followers are
called ' Redemptorists,' and his Institute
is the ' Very Holy Redeemer.' The object
of this foundation is to supply preachers
and teachers in rural districts.

St. Alphonso Maria Liguori (1696-1787). His in-

stitution received the sanction of Benedict XIV.
and Clement XII.

Ligurian Republic (*The*), 1797.
Established by Napoleon Bonaparte.
Genoa was the principal territory of that
part of Italy called by the Romans
' Liguria.'

Ligyan, *i.e.* ' Ligurian.'

Lilacs and the Blues (*The*). Two
rival parties in the court of François I.
The lilacs were the partisans of Madame
d'Etampes; the blues were the partisans
of Diane de Poitiers. Madame d'Etampes
was the mistress of the king; Diane de
Poitiers was the mistress of the dauphin,
Henri II. Madame d'Etampes, to throw
a flimsy veil over her amours, was ' married ' to Jean de Brosse; and Diane de
Poitiers was the young widow of Louis
de Brézé. Both king and dauphin had
a wife living at the time. Madame
d'Etampes was 9 years the younger. She
died at the age of 67; her rival died at the
age of 68.

Lilburne Agreement (*The*),
1 May, 1649. Lilburne's reformed programme of 'The Agreement of the
People' (*q.v.*). (1) It protested against
the convocation of parliaments only for
six months every two years, the council
ruling without restraint the other eighteen months; (2) it insisted on an annual
parliament, with a committee during the
recess; (3) no member to be eligible for
re-election; (4) no officer to be eligible,
the term of every officer's commission in
the army to be limited; (5) the high court
of justice and council of state to be
abolished; (6) all proceedings in the law-
courts to be in English only; (7) the fees
of lawyers to be reduced; (8) excise and
customs to be abolished; (9) the religion
to be reformed; (10) tithes to be abolished,
and (11) the stipend of every minister
to be fixed at 150*l.* a year, to be raised by
the parish rates.

What would Dissenters say now to No. 11?

Lily (*Knights of the*), 1048. A military order of Navarre, founded by Garcia.

Limerick (*Treaty of*), 3 Oct., 1691.
Concluded with the Irish by General
Ginkell, in the reign of William III. By
this treaty the Catholics of Ireland were
granted freedom of worship; allowed
the use of arms; the possession of their
estates; the right to sit in parliament, to

vote at elections, to practise law and medicine, and to engage in trade and commerce. Those of the Irish soldiery who preferred it were allowed to accept service under some friendly foreign power.

The alleged violation of the treaty by the government has been the subject of frequent and acrimonious controversy by Irish demagogues.

Limitation (*The Statute of*). Came into operation 1 Jan., 1879. By this act twelve years' possession is a bar to any action for the recovery of real estate, unless the plaintiff during those years was an infant, in which case eighteen years is a bar.

For all ordinary debts the limitation is six years. After which time they are 'statute run.'

Limited Liabilities. In 1862 was passed the 'Joint Stock Limited Companies Act,' which authorised any seven persons or more to incorporate themselves with a stated nominal capital to carry on their concern ; but limited the liability of a shareholder to the nominal value of the number of shares held by him.

Limited Liability. 18, 19 Vict. c. 133 (1855). An Act of Parliament limiting the liability of subscribers to a joint-stock company to the number of shares awarded to them by the directors of the company. Before the passing of this act each shareholder was liable to an unlimited extent for all the debts of the company, whether they held few or many shares.

Lincoln. Impeachment of Dr. King bishop of Lincoln, for 'ritualistic practices,' by the Church Evangelical Society in 1889. The case was tried before the Archbishop of Canterbury, assisted by the Bishops of London, Oxford, Hereford, and Salisbury. The verdict was not given in Aug. 1890, when this article was passing through the press.

Lincoln College, Oxford, 1427. Founded by Richard Fleming, bishop of Lincoln. The head-master is called the rector.

Lincoln Green. Lincoln at one time dyed the best green in all England, Coventry the best blue, and Yorkshire the best greys. Kendal was also noted for its green.

Lindsey. The north-east part of Lincolnshire, forming an insular district, and including the wolds or chalk hills. The other two parts are called Holland and Kesteven (*q.v.*).

Lindisfarne MS. (*The*). Otherwise known as the Durham Book, now in the Cottonian collection in the British Museum. It contains the four Gospels, in Latin, with various prefatory matter by St. Jerome, and was written about the year 700 A.D., in the island of Lindisfarne, by Eadfrith, who was bishop from A.D. 698 to 721. It is remarkable for the beauty of the characters in which it is written, the unusual stoutness of the parchment, and for the coloured geometrical patterns which adorn four of its pages. Besides this it contains a gloss in the old Northumbrian dialect, written by a priest named Aldred, after A.D. 950. The Lindisfarne MS. has been printed (inaccurately) for the Surtees Society, also (partially) by Bouterwek, and (fully) by Professor Skeat for the Pitt Press.

Supplied by Professor Skeat.

Lines of Boulair (*The*), 1854, in Gallipoli. Entrenchments thrown up by the united French and English army, extending from the Gulf of Saros to the Sea of Marmora.

Lines of Torres Vedras, in Portugal, 1809–1810. Lines of defence within which Wellington took refuge in 1810, when he found it impossible to defend the frontier of Portugal against the French armies. From these lines he issued in 1811, and drove the French out of the peninsula. The *first* line extended from Alhandra to the mouth of the Sizandro, and was twenty-nine miles long. The *second* stretched from Quintella to the mouth of the St. Lorenza, and was twenty-four miles long. The *third* line, at the mouth of the Tagus, was very short, but the entire ground thus fortified was 500 square miles.

Lingerer (*The*). Quintus Fabius Maximus, who was sent against Hannibal, refused battle, and harassed the invader by cutting off his supplies, intercepting his communications, falling on foraging parties, and watching opportunities of minor attacks. Ennius says 'Unus homo nobis cunctando restituit rem,' and the well-known English equivalent is, 'Win, like Fabius, by delay.'

Lingua Franca. A medley of Italian, French, and Teutonic.

Lion (*The*). I. Heinrich duke of Bavaria and Saxony, son of Heinrich the Proud (1129-1195).

II. Louis VIII. of France, who was born under the sign *Leo* (1187, 1223-1226).

III. William of Scotland, who chose a red lion rampant for his cognizance (*, 1165-1214).

Alp Arslan, son of Togrul Bey, the Perso-Turkish monarch, was called *The Valiant Lion* (*, 1063-1072).
Arioch *al Asser* was the 'Lion king of Assyria' (B.C. 1927-1897).

Lion-hearted (*The*). Cœur-de-lion. Richard I. of England was so called (1157, 1189-1199).

It is said that a lyon was put to kynge Richarde, beying in prison . . . to devour him, and when the lyon was gapynge he put his arme in his mouth, and pulled the lyon by the harte so hard that he slewe the lyon; and therefore . . . he is called Richarde *Cure de Lyon*.—RASTALL, *Chronicle* (1532).

Lion Rouge (*Le*). Marshal Ney, famous for his large crop of red hair and red whiskers (1769-1815).

Lion Sermon (*The*). Preached in October at St. Katherine Cree, London, in memory of Sir John Gayor's deliverance from a lion 'in the deserts of Araby,' during the reign of James I. or Charles I.

This was above 250 years ago. At present there are no lions in Arabia. Sir John Gayor was a London merchant, travelling about Asia, &c. He bequeathed 200l. for the relief of the poor on condition that a commemorative sermon on his escape was preached at the time appointed. We are told that Sir John was on his knees in prayer when the lion came up, smelt about him, prowled round and round him, and then ran off.

Lion of Bohemia (*The*). A lion with two tails.

Lion of England (*The*). Napoleon said, 'Let us chase these leopards into the sea,' and Bertrand du Guesclin said that men 'devoyent bien honorer la noble Fleur-de-lis, plus qu'ils ne faisaient le félon léopard.' The English lion is what is called a *lion léopardé*. The leopard was the crest of the dukes of Normandy—as Honoré Caille du Fourni (or Fourny) says, 'le léopard ayant été pris par ces princes et seigneurs normands qui étaient souvent sortis hors mariage . . . pour représenter leur naissance par le léopard, bitard du lion'; and, continues the great antiquary, both displayed alike

'leur naturelle générosité, dont l'un et l'autre de ces animaux est le symbole.'

Lion of God (*The*). I. Ali, the cousin and son-in-law of Mohammed 'the prophet' (born 602, kalif 656-660). He married Fatima, the prophet's daughter, and left two sons, Hassan and Hosein or Hussein.

II. Hamza. Gabriel told Mohammed that his uncle Hamza was registered in heaven as *The Lion of God and his prophet*.

Lion of Janina (*The*). Ali Pasha, overthrown by Ibrahim Pasha (1741, 1788-1822).

Lion of Justice (*The*). Henry I. (Beauclerc), 1068, 1100-1135. So called from his efforts to abolish rapine, and to subject all to the government of law.

After two dragons, the Lion of Justice shall come, at whose roaring the Gallic towers and island serpents shall tremble.—*Merlin's Prophecies*.

Lion of Lucerne (*The*). Hewn out of the living sandstone rock; is 28 feet long and 18 high. It was designed by Thorwaldsen, and stands outside the city walls. This gigantic lion is in commemoration of the Swiss guards who fell at Paris in 1792, while defending the Tuileries.

Lion of St. Mark (*The*). A winged lion over the entrance to the Arsenal of Venice. Between its fore-paws is a book, with the words *Pax tibi Marce Evangelista meus*. When Napoleon Bonaparte took possession of Venice in 1797 he changed the inscription over the arsenal to these words: 'The Rights of Man and of Citizenship.'

In 1797, when Venice fell to the French, Bonaparte removed this lion to Paris. It was restored in 1815, but was injured in the transit. It has been carefully repaired.

Lion of Sweden (*The*). John von Banier (Bannier, or Baner), a Swedish general who distinguished himself in the Thirty Years' War (1595-1641).

Lion of the North (*The*). Gustavus Adolphus king of Sweden (1594, 1611-1632).

Lion's Den (*The*). The castle of Dalkeith, about six miles from Edinburgh, where Morton resided when deprived of the regency. Morton was the old lion much dreaded by the people of Scotland, and though retired into private life, everyone thought he was merely lurking in his den, waiting for a favourable opportunity.

Sir Walter Scott says of Morton, 'his ambition could hardly be gratified with power, nor his avarice with money; and he united a degree of selfish profligacy with great pretensions of religion.'

Lions' Mouths (*The*), Venice. Under the arcade at the top of the Giant's Stairs (*q.v.*) are pillar boxes formed like gaping lions, into the mouths of which it was customary to deposit anonymous charges.

Lions in Europe. Shakespeare has been blamed for introducing a lion into Greece in his 'Midsummer Night's Dream,' but Buffon says there were lions in Thrace, Macedonia, and Thessaly, even in the days of Aristotle. Herodotus says, when Xerxes led his army through Pæonia lions came and devoured his camels.

Lions of Venice (*The*), 1684. The two marble lions which sentinel the gates of the Arsenal at Venice were trophies found in the Piræus when Athens was bombarded by Francesco Moroceno, the doge, surnamed 'Peloponnesiacus.'

The inscription runs thus: Franciscus Maurocenus Peloponnesiacus expugnatis Athenis, marmorea leonum simulacra triumphali manu e Piræo direpta in patriam transtulit, futura Veneti Leonis quæ fuerant Minervæ Atticæ ornamenta.'
** In St. Mark's Square are two pillars of oriental granite, one surmounted with a statue of St. Theodore, and the other with the brazen lion of St. Mark. The brazen lion must not be confounded with the two marble lions before the arsenal.

Lions of the Punjab (*The*). The Sikhs or Singhs (*i.e.* lions); unrivalled in India for comeliness, courage, and the powers of endurance.

Lionne (*La*). Mdlle. Paulet, the lady whom Henri IV. (after he had called on Sully) was going to visit. It was in this visit that he was assassinated by Ravaillac.

Liquidated Damage. A certain fixed and *ascertained* sum, in contradistinction to a penalty which is both uncertain, dubious, and unascertained.

Lis (*St.*), or 'Liz,' is Simon Senlis, son of Landry de Senlis lord of Chantilly and Ermenonville. He was rewarded by the Conqueror with the earldom of Northampton, and the hand of Maud daughter of Judith and Waltheof.

Listerise. A verb derived from the name of Sir Joseph Lister of Edinburgh, and meaning 'to sterilise by antiseptics.'

All instruments used in any surgical operation are bathed in a carbolised bath, and so are the fingers of the operator, in order to sterilise them—that is, to sterilise any germs of disease which may happen to be on them. This is done to prevent pyæmia or blood-poisoning. *See* 'Pasteurise.'

Somewhere between 1880 and 1886.

Lit de Justice (*Le*). On désignait ainsi les séances solennelles du roi (of France) au parlement. It originally meant the throne on which the king sat in these sessions. The first *lit de justice* was held in 1318 under Philippe le Long, and the last was held at Marseilles by Louis XVI. in 1788. In a lit de justice the king's word was enough to constitute a law, and insist on its being registered by the Paris parlement.

Any 'solemn séance' over which the king of France presided was loosely called a *lit de justice*.

Litany. A prayer of supplication, each petition of which is announced by the officiating priest and then taken up by the congregation. A 'liturgy' is a Common Prayer-book containing the Litany and many other prayers. The Litany of the Anglican Church is very similar to that of the Catholic ritual, omitting all invocations to saints and the Virgin Mary.

The first litany is ascribed to St. Mamert bishop of Vienne, 469.

Litany (*The Greater*), 'Litania Major,' was instituted in 590 by Gregory the Great. Also called 'Litania Septiformis.'

Litany (*The Minor*), 'Litania Minor.' The Gallic Litany is so called.

That part of the Anglican Litany which follows ' O Christ, hear us' is called the Lesser Litany.

Litany of the Blessed Virgin (*The*), or the Litany of Our Lady of Loretto. The prayers are, for the most part, addressed to the Virgin Mary. The Litany of Aquileia was sung at St. Mark's, ' in officio hebdomadæ majoris basilicæ S. Marci.' Both were specially sung on Saturdays, Saturday being peculiarly sacred to the Virgin Mary. This litany forms no part of the ordinary ritual of the Church.

Every Dominican friar was ordered to say daily after matins seven psalms and litanies of the Virgin.—LEA, *History of the Inquisition*, vol.i. p. 283

Litany of the Name of Jesus (*The*). One of the three litanies of the Catholic Church. It consists of prayers and addresses to Jesus under his several relations to men, with references to his sufferings. Date supposed to be the 15th cent.

The litany forms no part of the ordinary ritual of the Catholic Church.

Litany of the Saints (*The*).

The most ancient of the three Catholic litanies, and the only one contained in the common service books of the church. It is used on Rogation days, in the ordination service, the consecration services, and so on.

The other two were 'The Litany of the name of Jesus' and the 'Litany of Our Lady of Loretto.'

Literary Club (*The*).

From 1764 a certain number of literary friends used to meet together pretty constantly at the Turk's Head, Garrick being one of the party. On the death of Garrick in 1779, nine of the party formed themselves into a Literary Club. Dr. Johnson, Dr. Oliver Goldsmith, Dr. Robert Nugent, Sir Joshua Reynolds, Sir John Hawkins, Edmund Burke, Anthony Chamier, M.P., Topham Beauclerk, and Mr. Langton. In 1791 the number of members was increased to thirty-nine, and the club was transferred to the Thatched House, St. James's Street, and in 1845 it had amongst its members the Earl of Aberdeen, Lord Brougham, Bishop Copleston, Bishop Blomfield, Dr. Burney, &c.

Boswell and Gibbon belonged to the club, but were not of the original nine.

Literary Forgeries and Impostors.

Acts of Pilate (*Acta Pilāti*). 1. The account said to have been written by Pilate to the Emperor Tiberius about the character and miracles of Jesus. 2. An account full of slanders against Jesus, accusing Him of 'blasphemy.' Mentioned by 'Eusebius,' book ix. 5.

Neither of these acts can be depended on. Origen tells us there were numberless other acts 'fabricated by Christians.'—*Against Celsus.*

See under

Acta Pilati.	CHATTERTON, 'Rowley's
Amber Witch.	Poems.'
Annals of Tacitus.	Christian Forgeries.
ANNIUS of Viterbo, 'An-	Chronicle of Richard of
tiquitates Variæ.'	Cirencester [*See* 'Monk
Apocryphal Scriptures.	of Westminster].
Apostolic Constitutions.	Church Forgeries.
Apostolical Canons.	Clementina.
Barnabas (*Gospel of*).	Clementines.
BERTRAM, 'De Situ Bri-	Codex Diplomaticus.
tanniæ.'	Decretals.
BOECE (Scotch Kings).	Dionysius the Areopa-
Book of Mormon.	gite.
Bracciolini.	Donation of Constan-
Cagliostro of Literature.	tine.
Chasles Forgeries.	Eikon Basilikè.

English Mercurie (a	Phœnecian Stone.
newspaper).	Pilati (*Acta*).
False Decretals.	PORPHYRY, 'Oracles of
Gospels.	Philosophy.'
Hecatæus.	Protevangelium.
History of Formosa.	PSALMANAZAR, 'History
History of the Jews.	of Formosa.'
Ignatian Controversy.	Riculfe archbishop of
Ireland (plays of Shake-	Mayence.
speare).	Sanchoniátho and Sibyl-
Isiac Table.	line Prophecies.
Isidorian Decretals.	Scriptures (*Spurious*).
Jasher (Book of).	Shapira MSS.
Lauder (Plagiarisms of	Sibylline Verses.
Milton).	SIMONIDES (*Constantine*).
Letter of St. Peter to	Squire Letters.
Pepin. *See* 'Peter,' &c.	SURTEES (Ballad).
Letters of Ganganelli.	Theodosian Code (one of
,, Percy Bysshe	the edicts).
Shelley.	Travels of C. F. Damber-
,, Phalaris.	ger [*See* Damberger in
Monk of Westminster,	Allibone's ' Dict.].
same as Richard of	VELLA, 'Codex Diplo-
Cirencester (*q.v.*).	maticus Siciliæ.'
Orphica.	Vrain Lucas Letters.

.·. Jean Hardouin, a French Jesuit (1606–1729), says that not only all the writings of the Christian Fathers, but nearly all the Greek and Latin classics, are monkish forgeries. *Ad censuram Scriptorum veterum Prolegomena.* This probably is a gross exaggeration, but no doubt the text was often interpolated in order to give colour to some religious dogma or tradition.

The 'Squire Letters' deceived Thomas Carlyle. The 'Shapira MSS.' deceived several very clever Egyptologists and other antiquaries. The 'Vrain Lucas Letters' deceived M. Michel Chasles, the eminent French mathematician. The 'Shelley Forgeries' deceived Robert Browning. The stupid 'Shakespearian Forgeries' of Henry Ireland deceived Dr. Parr the great scholar, Pye the Poet Laureate, and a host of others. The 'Surtees Ballad' deceived Sir Walter Scott. The 'Amber Witch' deceived the ripest scholars of Germany. The 'Inscription of the Phœnician Stone' deceived the learned Raoul Rochette, professor of archæology, Paris. The 'Christian Forgeries of Brahmanic Writings' imposed on Voltaire, &c. So that the verdict even of great scholars can in no wise be depended on.

However, some *authentic* writings have been pronounced spurious by scholars. Thus Henry Hallam, when he reviewed Payne Knight's book ('An Analytical Inquiry into the Principles of Taste') in the 'Edinburgh Review,' lashed most unmercifully some Greek verses inserted therein. But, alas for the critic, the verses were Pindar's! and the discovery was made too late to prevent the publication of the learned criticism.

Literature (*Father of Modern French*).

Seyssel (1450–1520), author of ' The Singular History of Louis XII.' and ' The Great Monarchy of France.'

Lithography (*Inventor of*).

Senefelder (1771–1832).

Lithuania.

Unclassical Latin for a dependency of Poland, divided into Wilna and eight other palatinates.

Litteræ Humaniores.

A phrase introduced in the renaissance period to signify the literature which mainly humanises the world, or, as Ovid says, ' Emollit mores nec sinit esse feros.'

Little Battle of Châlons (*The*),

May 1274. On the return of Edward I.

from the Crusade the Count of Châlons requested the honour of breaking a lance with the crusader. Edward accepted the challenge; but, fearing treachery, he took with him 1,000 men. The count entered, accompanied with 2,000 men, and Edward saw at once he was in a trap. A furious fight ensued, in which the count's party was put to flight, and a large number of his men were left dead.

Little Captain (*The*). George II. He was at the battles of Oudenarde and Dettingen, and when he came to the throne delighted in a sort of military precision. He was also very fond of soldiers. It was the Jacobites who nick-named him 'The Little Captain.'

Little Corporal (*The*). Napoleon Bonaparte (1769, emp. 1804–1814, died 1821).

Little Daughter of St. Mark (*The*). Brescia, which was the Vene-tians' stronghold in Lombardy. 'His-toire du Ch. Bayard,' xlviii.

Little Doomsday Book (*The*). *See* the lesser of the two volumes. It consists of 450 double pages of vellum, in single column, and contains the counties of Essex, Norfolk, Suffolk, part of Rut-land, part of Lancashire, York, and Chester. It seems to be a transcript of the original rolls; and sets forth the number of horses, oxen, sheep, goats, and pigs in each manor, which details are left out in the great volume.

Little Douglas. Cousin of George Douglas, a lad of sixteen years of age, who (2 May, 1568), while the family were at supper, stole the keys of the castle where Queen Mary of Scotland was con-fined under the charge of Sir William Douglas. The lad let Mary and her attendant out of the tower when all the household had gone to bed, locked the gates to prevent pursuit, placed the queen and her waiting-woman in a skiff, and rowed them with muffled oars to the opposite shore, throwing the keys into the castle lake. Here Lord Seaton and a party of the Hamiltons were in waiting, who placed the queen on a swift horse, hurried off to Niddry in West Lothian, and next day to Hamilton.

Little Ease. I. A cell in Newgate into which prisoners were thrust who either could not or would not pay extra 'garnish,' *i.e.* entrance money.

There is the Little Ease, for common fees of the crown, rather dark, and the common sewer runs below it. Some gentlemen object to the company, chiefly padders [footpads] and michers [skulkers, sneaks].—Sir W. SCOTT, *Peveril of the Peak*, chap. xxxiii.

II. A kind of cage, too small for the person confined therein to sit, stand, or lie in. It is in the Tower of London. I have seen a similar one in the Castle of Loches, in which Cardinal Balue was confined for ten years by Louis XI.

Little England beyond Wales. South Pembrokeshire, colonised by Fle-mings in the reign of Henry I. Welsh is not spoken in this district.

Little Gentleman in Black Velvet (*The*). The mole which threw up the hillock against which Sorrel, the horse of William III., stumbled, an acci-dent which ultimately caused the king's death. This was a Jacobite toast in the reign of Quèen Anne.

Little John. John Nailor was so called by antiphrasis, because he was above seven feet high. He was the chief of Robin Hood's band, and is said to have lived between 1160 and 1220.

Little Man in Red Stockings (*The*). Leopold I. kaiser-king of Ger-many, of the house of Austria, son of Ferdinand III. (1640, 1658–1705).

Little Parliament (*The*). From 14 July to 12 Dec., 1653, the same as the Barebone Parliament (*q.v.*). It consisted of 140 or (as some say) of 156 members, six being for Wales, six for Ireland, and five for Scotland, all selected by Crom-well's privy council. Three months be-fore its expiry, which was fixed for 3 Sept., 1654, they were to nominate their successors; but the house was dissolved because its reforms were too rapid and radical even for Cromwell and his friends. *See* 'Parliament.'

Cromwell said : 'The Long Parliament brought their dissolution upon themselves by despotism; the Little Parliament by imbecility.'—LINGARD, *History of England*, viii. 6.

Little Rome. Montague House, Southwark. The cloisters of St. Mary Overy fell to the Montagues at the Dis-solution, and took the name of 'Monta-gue Close.' Their house became the ıefuge of persecuted Catholics, and gained hence the name of Little Rome.

Liturgi, λειτουργοί. According to Papias, Christian ministers were so called. St. Basil says they were the deacons, but that priests and bishops were called λειτουργοὶ τοῦ Θεοῦ.

Liturgies, λειτουργίαι. The duties of the liturgi. of Athens. These liturgi, λειτουργοί, were public officers selected from the most opulent citizens, who had to bear, at their own cost, the chief charges of public festivals, shows, and banquets. Every state elected 120. The expenses, B.C. 271, were transferred to the state.

Liturgies (*The Six Oriental*). All in the Syriac tongue.

1. The Liturgy of Jerusalem (*q.v.*).
2.   "   of Antioch (*q.v.*).
3.   "   of Alexandria (*q.v.*).
4.   "   of Constantinople (*q.v.*).
5. The Armenian Liturgy (*q.v.*).
6. The Nestorian Liturgy (*q.v.*).

Liturgies (*Western*).

I. Of the Catholic Church.

1. The *Roman*, traditionally attributed to St. Peter. It received its final form from Gregory the Great.
2. The *Milanese* or Ambrosian, attributed to St. Ambrose.
3. The *Gallican*, supposed to have been derived from the Oriental Church.
4. The *Spanish* or Mozarabic. derived from the Greek liturgy by Isidore of Seville.

II. Of the English Protestant Church, the 'Book of Common Prayer.'

Liturgies of the Greek Church (*The*). The two chief are the liturgy of *St. Chrysostom*, said to be apostolic; and the liturgy of *St. Basil*, used on saints' days, Christmas Day, Epiphany, the four Sundays of Lent, and Good Friday.

Liturgy and 'Book of Common Prayer.'

The first compilation of a liturgy was by St. Basil in the 4th cent.

For many centuries each bishop had the right of arranging a liturgy for his own diocese.

The first liturgy of the Reformed Anglican Church was entitled 'The Godly and Pious Institution of a Christian Man.' It contained the Lord's Prayer, the Ten Commandments, several 'Godly Lessons,' and Prayers for the Dead.

1545. Appeared 'The King's Primer,' containing the Lord's Prayer, the Ave Maria, the Creed, the Ten Commandments, Graces, Matins, Seven Psalms, Collects, &c.

1548. The second year of Edward VI. was introduced 'The Order of Common Prayer,' drawn up by Cranmer archbishop of Canterbury, Goodrich bishop of Ely, Holbech bishop of Lincoln, Day bishop of Chichester, Skyp bishop of Hereford, Thirlby bishop of Westminster, Ridley then bishop of Rochester, May dean of St. Paul's, Taylor (afterwards bishop of Lincoln), Haynes master of Queens' (Cambridge), Redman master of Trinity (Cambridge), Cox dean of Christ Church, and Robinson archdeacon of Leicester (thirteen altogether). This Prayer Book was based on the books called the Use of *Sarum*, the Use of *Hereford*, the Use of *Bangor*, the Use of *York*, and the Use of *Lincoln*, and is known as the FIRST BOOK of EDWARD VI.

1549. All Antiphonals, Missals, Grails, Processionals, Manuals, Primers, Cowchers, Journals or Diurnals, and Ordinals hitherto in use were abolished.

1552. The SECOND BOOK of EDWARD VI. was introduced, and ordered to be read in all churches of the kingdom. It contained the following additions:—The Exhortation, the Confession and Absolution, the Morning and Evening Services, the Communion Service, &c., and left out 'the Mixing of Water with the Wine and the Prayer of Oblation.'

The same year was published the Forty-two Articles (reduced in the reign of Elizabeth to thirty-nine).

1559. (1 Eliz.). The Second Book of Edward VI. (revised) was restored. The rubric against the real presence was omitted, prayers for the Queen and clergy were added, and the vestments forbidden in 1552 were restored (!!).

1604. (1 James I.). Some few alterations were introduced, such as the Collects for Morning and Evening, and intercession for the Royal Family in the Litany.

1662. After the Restoration were added the Prayer for all Sorts and Conditions of Men, the General Thanksgiving, the Prayers for Ember Weeks, for Burial Service, the Office of Baptism of those of Riper Years, and the last translation of the Bible was adopted in the Gospels and Epistles (the old version of the Psalms, however, was retained). The Collects for Easter Eve, the Sixth Sunday after Epiphany, and the Third Sunday in Advent were also inserted.

1837. Was introduced a Form of Prayer to be used June 20, the day of Queen Victoria's accession to the crown.

1859. The services for 5 Nov. [Gunpowder Plot], 30 Jan. [the execution of Charles I.], and 29 May [the restoration of Charles II.] were abolished.

Liturgy (*The Ambrosian*). A Catholic missal, popularly ascribed to St. Ambrose, and used in the diocese of Milan. It is much like the Roman liturgy (*q.v.*), but is especially interesting for its allusions to ancient Christian church customs.

Liturgy (*The Armenian*). Dates from the introduction of Christianity into Armenia under Gregory the Illuminator. It is derived, for the most part, from the Liturgy of St. Chrysostom (*q.v.*).

Liturgy (*The Gallic*). Of Oriental origin, probably introduced by the Greek colony which settled in Marseilles, &c.

It is not the missal now used in the French dioceses, which is the Roman missal, varied only in slight details.

Liturgy (*The Gothic, or Mozarabic*). Used in the chapel of Toledo, founded by Cardinal Ximenes. It is the old liturgy of the Gothic church of Spain, and is of Oriental origin.

Liturgy (*The Nestorian*). The Nestorians have three liturgies: (1) the Liturgy of the Apostles; (2) the Liturgy of Theodore of Mopsuestia; and (3) the Liturgy of Nestorius. The language of all is Syriac, and the three are merely parts of one liturgy used and adapted to different occasions.

Liturgy (*The Roman*). The oldest forms of this liturgy are to be found in the three sacramentaries of Leo, Gelasius, and Gregory the Great. The last of these is most conspicuous in the modern missal shaped by the Council of Trent (15th cent.). Revised under Pius V., again under Urban VIII., and a third time under Clement VIII.

Liturgy of Alexandria (*The*). Ascribed to St. Mark; but the existing liturgy has received numberless additions and alterations, and has been modified by both the great sects of the Alexandrine patriarchate.

Liturgy of Antioch (*The*). Exists in Syriac, but it is evidently a free translation of the 'Liturgy of Jerusalem' (*q.v.*).

Liturgy of Constantinople (*The*). On some occasions the Liturgy of St. Basil is used in the Church of Constantinople, and on other occasions the Liturgy of St. Chrysostom; but what is called the 'Liturgy of Constantinople' is the Slavonic Liturgy used in the Russian and Russo-Greek Church.

Liturgy of Ireland (*The*). Assimilated to the Catholic liturgy of England by the Council of Cashel in 1172. The reformed liturgy was introduced on Easter Day 1550.

Liturgy of Jerusalem (*The*), ascribed to St. James, is of uncertain origin, and it is not known whether it first appeared in the Syriac or Greek language. It is now known only in the Greek, and it closely resembles the text of St. Cyril of Jerusalem in his 'Mystagogical Lectures.'

Liturgy of Jesus Christ (*The*). One of the twelve liturgies of the ancient Coptic Christians, but not countenanced by the patriarchs.

Liturgy of Osmund (*The*). The Sarum Missal compiled by Osmund bishop of Salisbury, and adopted generally throughout England. It is in Latin, and our Book of Common Prayer is almost a translation of it.

Liturgy of St. Basil (*The*), *i.e.* Basil of Cæsarea. One of the liturgies of the Greek Church. It is the longest and holds pre-eminence in solemnity and antiquity. The Liturgy of St. Basil is used on the great festivals, such as Christmas Day, Epiphany, Lent, and Good Friday.

The other chief liturgy of the Greek Church is that of St. Chrysostom.' The 'Liturgy of St. Basil' is also one of the twelve used by the ancient Coptic Christians.

Liturgy of St. Chrysostom (*The*). One of the three liturgies of the Greek Church. It bears the name of St. Chrysostom, but is of much later date. It is used on all days of the year except Christmas Day, Epiphany, Lent, and Good Friday, when St. Basil's Liturgy is used. *See* note above.

Liturgy of St. Cyriac (*The*). One of the twelve liturgies of the ancient Coptic Christians, but not countenanced by the patriarchs.

Liturgy of St. Cyril (*The*). One of the twelve liturgies used by the ancient Coptic Christians; but the only three sanctioned by the patriarchs are those of Basil, Cyril, and Gregory.

Liturgy of St. Epiphanius (*The*). One of the twelve liturgies of the ancient Coptic Christians, but not now countenanced by the patriarch.

Liturgy of St. Gregory (*The*). One of the three liturgies of the Coptic Christians countenanced by the patriarchs. The other two are the 'Liturgy of St. Basil' and the 'Liturgy of St. Cyril.'

Liturgy of St. James (*The*). One of the twelve liturgies of the ancient Coptic Christians.

Liturgy of St. John the Evangelist (*The*). One of the twelve liturgies of the ancient Coptic Christians, but not sanctioned by the patriarchs.

Liturgy of Theodore of Mopsuestia (*The*). One of the three Nestorian liturgies (*q.v.*).

Liturgy of the Anglican Church (*The*), 1548, in the reign of Edward VI. The Common Prayer Book, revised edition 1551. The introduction of it into Scotland caused a riot in Edinburgh 23 July, 1637; withdrawn 9 Sept., 1638. *See* 'Liturgy.'

Liturgy of the Apostles (*The*). One of the twelve liturgies of the ancient Coptic Christians, but not countenanced by the patriarchs. It is also one of the three Nestorian liturgies (*q.v.*).

Liturgy of the Fathers of the Council of Nice (*The*). One of the twelve liturgies of the ancient Coptic Christians, but not countenanced by the patriarchs.

Liturgy of the Nestorians (*The*). The Nestorians have three liturgies, viz. that of the Apostles, that of Theodore of Mopsuestia, and that of Nestorius. These, however, are combined into the Liturgy of the Nestorians and used on different occasions. They are all in Syriac.

Liturgy of the Patriarch Dioscorus (*The*). One of the twelve liturgies of the ancient Coptic Christians, but discountenanced by the patriarchs.

Liturgy of the Præsanctified (*The*), 7th or 8th cent. One of the three liturgies of the Greek Church. It is used on certain days in Lent. *See* 'Missa Præsanctificatorum.'

The other two liturgies are the 'Liturgy of St. Basil' and the 'Liturgy of St. Chrysostom.'

Livery (*The Statute of*). A statute to regulate and restrict the wearing of livery or the badge of the lord. In the 15th cent. these liveries became political badges—different factions being known by their livery. In 1377 the Commons petitioned against 'the giving of hats by way of livery for maintenance,' and it was forbidden by 1 Rich. II. In 1389 a royal ordinance forbade any servant to wear the lord's badge. In 1 Hen. IV. c. 7, A.D. 1399, it was enacted that only the

king should give either sign or livery to a company. In 1401, 1406, 1411 concessions were made to the Prince of Wales, guilds, and fraternities. By 8 Hen. VI. c. 4, A.D. 1429, allowances were accorded to the lord mayors and sheriffs of London, the serjeant-at-law, and the two Universities. In 1408 the giving of liveries involved a penalty of 5*l*. a month; but 3 Car. I. c. 4 repealed all the Statutes of Livery.

Livy (*The Greek*). Flavius Josephus the historian (37–95) is so called by St. Jerome.

Livy (*The Protestant*). John Sleidan of Cologne, who wrote a history of the Reformation in Germany (1506–1556).

Livy (*The Russian*). Nicholas Michaelovitch Karamzin (1765–1826).

Livy of Portugal (*The*). Joaõ de Barros (1496–1570), author of 'Asia Portugueza.'

Livy of Spain (*The*).
I. Juan Mariana, a Jesuit, born at Talavëra (1537–1624). He wrote a 'History of Spain' in Latin, and a treatise entitled 'De Rege et Regis Institutione.'
II. J. Ginez de Sepulvëda (1490–1572), who wrote the 'History of Charles Quint,' the 'History of Felipe II.,' the 'History of the War in India,' &c.

Lloyd's, 1772. A set of rooms on the first floor of the Royal Exchange, London, frequented by merchants, shipowners, underwriters, &c., for the purpose of obtaining shipping intelligence and transacting marine insurances. Two enormous ledgers lie constantly open, one containing a list of vessels *arrived*, and the other a record of *disasters* at sea.

Lloyd's (*Austrian*), 1833. Founded in Trieste by Baron Bruck, to supply the want felt by maritime insurance companies of that port of a central administration to attend to their common interests. Their 'list' is called the 'Giornale del Lloyd Austriaco.'

Lloyd's List. Shipping intelligence published every afternoon at Lloyd's in the Royal Exchange, London. First published in 1716, and daily since 1800.

Lloyd's Register of British and Foreign Shipping. A volume published annually, and containing information respecting vessels—their age, their materials, their repairs, their owners, captains, and so on. This information is supplied by salaried agents at the different ports. The office of the 'Register' is quite distinct from Lloyd's rooms in the Royal Exchange.

Local Government Act (*The*), 1888. Prepared by Charles Thomson Ritchie, president of the Local Government Board, whereby London was constituted a separate county. The council hold office for three years, but the aldermen for six years (half to retire every third year). The County Council controls the borrowing of money, pays the county treasurer, and all the expenses of judges' lodging, assize courts, and county halls; licenses music and dancing halls, racecourses, lunatic asylums, reformatories, and industrial schools; has supreme power over bridges and roads, the appointment of coroners, &c. &c.

Local Taxation Bill, 1890. For increasing the duties on beer and spirits.

Lochlans, or **Lochlanders** (lakedwellers). So the Irish called the Danes who in 787 first invaded the island.

Locke King's Bill, 1859. *See* 'Qualification (Property).'

Loco-focos. Ultra-radicals in the United States of America. So called because in a grand meeting in Tammany Hall, New York, in 1834, the chairman left his seat, and the lights were put out under the hope of dispersing the disorderly assembly. But no: some of the radicals, expecting this movement, drew candles from their pockets, and lighted them by loco-focos (*i.e.* lucifer matches), and the hall being relighted, the business of the meeting went on.

'Loco-foco' is said to be from the Latin *loco-foci*, in lieu of fire.

Locus Pœnitentiæ. The time allowed in Scotch law for withdrawing from a bargain. Till the contract is finally settled either party may retract.

Lodbrog, *i.e.* 'Shaggy Breeches.' So Regner of Denmark was called, 'because, when he went forth to conquer an enormous serpent, he arrayed himself in lodbrogs.'

Spite of the terrors of a groaning world at the sound of 'Shaggy Breeches'' name, his kingdom could hardly be called other than the harbouring-place of freebooters and pirates.—PRINCE, *Paralle History,* vol. i. p. 403.

Lodging-money. An allowance, in the British army, granted to officers and others for whom suitable quarters cannot be provided in the barracks. It is about 8*s.* a week.

Lodi (*The House of*). Founded in Delhi by Behlol Lodi in 1450. Ala-eddyn, last king of the 'government of the Seiads,' abdicated in favour of Lodi.

Lodovico Sforza, duke of Milan (1479–1500), called 'Il Moro' because he adopted the mulberry tree for his device. He prided himself on his prudence; and Pliny calls the mulberry the most prudent of all trees, because it waits till winter is well over before it puts forth its leaves.

Logos (*The*). According to the school of Alexandria the Logos was a being begotten by God, and intermediate between Deity and man. This primary Logos was the first-born (ὁ πρεσβύτερος υἱός) of Deity, and from this first-born proceeded a second Logos (λόγος προφορικός) which acted at the creation of the world.

Of course the *Logos* of the Fourth Gospel is not suited to this dictionary.

Logothete (*A*). A keeper of accounts in the Eastern empire. He put in order the despatches of the emperor, and was keeper of the seals. There was an ecclesiastical Logothete also, keeper of the seals of the patriarch. Even to the present day such an officer exists in the Greek Church. Nicephŏrus I. emperor of the East was 'Logothēta,' when he assumed the purple in 802.

Loi Gombette (*La*), 502. The Burgundian Code, published at Lyons by Gundibald or Gombaud, the third king of Burgundy. It was based on the Theodosian Code (*q.v.*). In 519 a second part was published by Sigismund, son and successor of Gombaud. By this code one-third of the conquered land was left to the conquered people, and it accorded to the Romans the same rights as to the conquering people.

Loi Salique (*La*), 1340. The exclusion of women from the throne because they are unable to be the leaders of armies in battle.

Edward III. by a pun called the 'gabelle' or tax on salt, the Sal-ic law of France.

Loi des Suspects (*La*), 17 Sept., 1793. A law made by the Convention of France enabling the committees to seize and condemn anyone they suspected of being averse to the republican constitution, or whose death would be beneficial thereto.

Loi du Sacrilège, 20 April, 1825. Public profanation of the consecrated elements, which was made a capital offence.

Lola Montes (2 syl.). An Irish girl, native of Wexford, brought home from school to marry an old man whom she detested. She mentioned the circumstances to Captain James, who ran away with her and married her in India; but one morning Captain James eloped with the young wife of an old gentleman in whose house he and Mrs. James resided. Mrs. James returned to Europe, changed her name to Lola Montes, and went on the stage. Here Charles Louis king of Bavaria, an old man in his dotage, became captivated with her, took her for his mistress, and made her a countess of Lansfeldt in 1848. He abdicated the same year. Lola Montes went to the United States in 1859, and died in New York 17 Jan., 1861.

Lollard (*Walter*). Burnt to death at Cologne 1322. He was born in England, and was called the Morning Star of the Reformation in Germany. Lollard declaimed against the intercession of saints, the seven sacraments, the church ceremonies, and the evil lives of the clergy.

Wyclif lived 1324-1384; and John Huss 1376-1415.

Lollards. Religious reformers. The society was formed at Antwerp for ministering to the sick, in 1300. The name was probably taken from Walter Lollard the reformer, who was burnt at Cologne in 1322. In England the preachers were arrested by 5 Rich. II. c. 5 (1381), and the burning of them was enjoined by 2 Hen. IV. c. 15 (*De hæretico comburendo*). A party of them were executed by order of Henry V. in Jan. 1414. The statutes against Lollardism were repealed by 1 Edw. VI. ·c. 12 (1547). Wyclif was head of the Lollards in England (1324–1384) and was protected and supported by John of Gaunt.

Some derive the word from the Low German *lollen*, to sing slowly. Blunt, in his 'Reformation,' p. 81, derives it from *lolium*, a tare, and reminds us

that Eusebius calls heretics *tares.—Ecc. Hist.* iv. c. 24, p. 137.

Lombard League (*The*). I. 1175-1183. A league formed by several of the petty republics of Lombardy, such as Milan, Pavia, Cremona, and so on, under the sanction of Pope Alexander III.), against Frederick Barbarossa. The league succeeded in driving Barbarossa out of Italy, and making him recognise the independence of the cities of Lombardy.

II. A second league was formed in 1225 against Kaiser Friedrich II. This league also was supported by the popes of the time being, and after many victories and defeats was at length successful in 1249. Milan was the chief power and strength in both these leagues.

The league defeated Barbarossa at Legnano in 1167. Friedrich II. defeated the league at Cortenuova in 1237.

London has several sobriquets, as 'The Little Village' (a *lucus a non lucendo*); 'the Modern Babylon'; 'the City of Masts.'

Aberdeen is the *Granite City*; Bath, the *Queen of the West*; Birmingham, the *Midland Capital*; Bradford is *Worstedopolis*; Brighton, the *Queen of Watering Places*, or *London-super-Mer* [mare]; Edinburgh, the *Modern Athens*; Liverpool, the *Modern Tyre*; Manchester, *Cottonopŏlis*; Worcester, *the Faithful City*.

London (*Treaties of*). I. 29 Oct., 1516. Between the kaiser elect and the kings of England and Spain.

II. 6 July, 1829. Between England, France, and Russia, regulating the government of the kingdom of Greece. This treaty really created the modern kingdom of Greece.

III. 22 April, 1834. Between England, France, Spain, and Portugal, for the pacification of the peninsula, expulsion of Don Carlos and Dom Miguel, &c.

IV. 15 July, 1840. Between England, France, Austria, Russia, Prussia, and Turkey, for the settlement of the dispute between the sultan and Mehemet Ali.

V. 8 May, 1852. Between Denmark and the five Great Powers, respecting the duchies of Schleswig and Holstein.

VI. 13 March, 1871. Between the five Great Powers, for the deneutralisation of the Black Sea.

London Adventurers, or 'South Virginia Company.' By the charter of James I. the London Adventurers were empowered to plant the east from the 34th to the 41st deg. This includes what we now call Maryland, Virginia, and the two Carolinas.

London Conference.
1st in 1826 &c. for the regulat'on of the affairs of Greece.

2nd in 1830 to arrange for the separation of Belgium and Holland. To this the Dutch withheld their assent till 21 May, 1833.

3rd in 1840 on the Turko-Egyptian question. France refused to join.

London County Council (The), 1889.
London, having been erected into a separate county, has its County Council, which takes on itself the powers of the old Board of Works, and certain magisterial duties. To the County Council are consigned all questions relating to metropolitan improvements, the price to be paid for property bought or sold in the metropolis, and compensation to be given for injury during disturbances. Its magisterial work includes the three lunatic asylums; the Industrial School at Feltham; licences granted to music and dancing halls; appointment of coroners, public analysts, inspectors of weights and measures, &c., with all such miscellaneous work as relates to the Sessions House at Clerkenwell, the Guildhall at Westminster, the militia barracks at Dalston and Bethnal Green, three county bridges, and petty sessional courts. See 'Metropolitan Board of Works.'

London University.
In the reign of Edward III., between the City and Westminster, and called the 'Third University.' Edward III. built and founded St. Stephen at Westminster for a divinity college; it was dissolved by Henry VIII. Archbishop Bradwardine founded a theological lecture in St. Paul's Church. John of Gaunt founded a divinity college in St. Paul's Churchyard. Sir John Fortescue tells us the Inns of Court were law colleges; and that there were ten called at the time inns of chancery, in each of which there were at least 100 students.

The present London University was incorporated by royal charter in 1836, and the building was opened in 1870 by Queen Victoria.

Long Brothers (The), i.e. 'tall,' viz.
Dioscorus, Ammonius, Eusebius, and Euthymius (5th cent.). They were monks supposed to be tainted with Origenism (ROBERTSON, 'Hist. of the Christian Church,' vol. ii. p. 106).

Long Knives (The Plot or Treachery of the).
This was a treacherous conference to which Geoffrey of Monmouth tells us the chief Britons were invited by Hengist at Ambresbury; others say by Vortigern. Beside each Briton a Saxon was seated, armed with a long knife; and, at a given signal, each Saxon slew the Briton seated by his side. Geoffrey tells us the signal was the utterance of these words: NEMET OURE SAXAS, and that the number massacred was 460 (book vi. 15).

Of course Geoffrey's *Chronicle* is only *Geoffrey's* Chronicle.

Long Parliament (The).
Met 3 Nov., 1640, and was dissolved by Cromwell, 20 April, 1653, but it was not legally dissolved till the Restoration in 1660. This parliament, therefore, existed all through the civil war, and all through the protectorate; but in 1659 only a fag end remained, which was called 'the Rump.' The Long Parliament voted the House of Lords to be useless, and passed a bill that even the king should be unable to dissolve or prorogue a parliament without the parliament's consent. See 'Parliaments.'

Long Parliament of France.
The Permanent Committee, 1789.

Longbeard.
William Fitz-Osbert, who assumed to be a Saxon, and was popularly called 'The Saviour of the People' and 'King of the Poor.' He was executed with great cruelty in 1196.

Long-haired Kings (The).
The successors of Clodion are called in French history 'Les rois chevelures.' Clodion introduced this fashion into Gaul from Germany. See 'Hair.'

It will be remembered that Homer calls the magnates of the confederate Greek army 'the long-haired Greeks.'

Longiman'us.
So Artaxerxes was called, because his right arm was longer than his left. His proper name was Bahāman; his regal name in Persia was Kai-Ardeshir.

Kai means *mighty*, 'Ard' flour, and 'Shir' milk. Bahaman was so called from an offering of flour and milk made to him in his cradle. Artaxerxes is 'Arta-Ksathra,' *honoured king*.

Lonsdale's Ninepins (Lord).
The nine members sent to parliament to represent nine pocket boroughs in the extensive estates of Lord Lonsdale.

Looking-glass Drops (The).
A celebrated poison found hidden on remov-

ing the wooden lining of a looking-glass which belonged to Lucrezia Borgia.

Loose-girt Boy (*The*). Julius Cæsar. (*Supplied by A. Oldham.*)

Lord Almoner's Professorship of Arabic. Founded 1724, in the University of Cambridge, by the lord almoner. Original stipend 50*l.* a year paid out of the Almonry bounty. The professor must give at least one lecture a year on Arabic history or literature.

Lord Chamberlain (*The*). The officer who has the management of the chambers; the sixth high officer of the crown. He has the government of the palace at Westminster; disposes of the sword of state in royal processions, and on such occasions sits on the sovereign's right hand. The black rod and yeoman usher are under him.

The *Lord Chamberlain of the Household* is quite another person. This officer has the direction of all matters pertaining to the chambers of the sovereign (except the queen's bed-chamber).

Lord Chancellor (*The*). The highest temporal lord, but his office is bound up with the ministry of the time being. He reads the royal speech for the prorogation of parliament and opening of parliament when the sovereign is not present, and stands on the right-hand side of the throne. He appoints all justices of the peace; is patron of all crown livings; is guardian of infants, idiots, and lunatics; and has a retiring pension of 5,000*l.* a year.

Lord Gawkey. Richard Grenville lord Temple (1711–1779).

Lord High Admiral (*The*). First appointed 1405.

Lord-Lieutenants of Counties, 1545. The first permanent lord-lieutenants were the Duke of Norfolk, for arming the counties of Essex, &c.; the Duke of Suffolk, for arming Surrey, Sussex, &c.; and Lord Russell, for arming Dorset, &c. The commissions sent to these nobles were to be acted upon, not *pro re nata*, but perpetually for keeping a due supply of militia in the several districts named ' in the commission. The main duty of lord-lieutenants is raising and organising the militia.

Prior to 1545 the three Lancastrian kings sent commissions occasionally to experienced nobles to put into military order their respective counties, and these noblemen were called 'The King's Lieutenants.'

Lord-Lyon (*The*). Lyon king-of-arms, Scotland, head of Lyon Court, the Scotch office of arms. His appointment is for life. The office of Lyon runs back into very remote times, but the officer was not called lord-lyon till 1663. One of his pursuivants is called *Unicorn.*

The lord-lion who brought her [the queen-regent's] message was requested to wait for an answer.—HOWITT, *Hist. of Eng.* vol. ii. p. 407.
*** As this was in 1559, it is an anachronism to called him lord-lion [lord-lyon].

Lord Mahon's Act, 1842 (5, 6 Vict. c. 45). Gives to an author and his assigns the copyright of his books during life and for seven years afterwards. Whether alive or dead, the author or his assigns has a right for forty-two years from the time of publication. If the author lives for forty-two years after publication, then his right continues during his life and seven years after his death. If he dies before the expiration of forty-two years, his assigns may claim a right for the residue of forty-two years or for seven years, whichever is the longer period.

A copy of the book must be sent gratuitously to five libraries: viz. that of the British Museum, the Public Library at Cambridge, the Bodleian Library at Oxford, the Library of the Faculty of Advocates at Edinburgh, and the Library of Trinity College, Dublin.

Lord Mayors. There are three lord mayors in the British Isles, viz. the mayors of London, York, and Dublin.

I. LONDON. At the time of the Conquest the chief magistrate of London was called port-reeve (*i.e.* governor of the harbour). He is called Geoffrey, port-reeve, in the charter granted by William to the city.

In Stephen's reign Gilbert Becket, father of the archbishop, was port-reeve of London.

In the reign of Henry II. the Norman term *maire* was introduced, Anglicised into mayor. The first mayor of London was Henry Fitz-Ailwin [son of Æthelwine]. He was a descendant of Æthelwine, cousin of King Edgar, and one of the hereditary aldermen.

Richard I. granted the citizens the right of electing their own mayor, 1189.

John granted them the right of electing a mayor annually.

Henry III. permitted the corporation to use a common seal.

In the reign of Richard II. the mayor of London took the rank of an earl.

The prefix of ' lord,' and the style of

'right honourable,' was granted by Edward III. in 1354.

Sir William Walworth (in the reign of Richard II.) was the first mayor who had an official seal (1381).

Sir John Norman (1458) was the first lord mayor who went in procession by water to be sworn in at Westminster, and then began the Lord Mayor's Show.

The original seal of the corporation had Thomas Becket on the reverse, and St. Paul on the obverse; but at the Reformation (1539) the reverse of the seal was changed for the present device, the obverse remaining as before.

II. YORK. York received its charter from Richard II., and the mayor was made a 'lord' in 1389. The *ex officio* title is 'the right honourable.'

III. DUBLIN. The mayor of Dublin first appointed 1409. Styled 'lord mayor' in 1665 by Charles II.

Lord Shaftesbury. Anthony Ashley Cooper, 1st earl Shaftesbury, Lord Chancellor of England (1621-1683). He began life an aristocrat; 1644 he went over to the parliamentary side, was commander-in-chief of their forces, and sat in the Barebone parliament; in 1654 he severed himself from Cromwell's party, joined the Remonstrants, and was arrested as a royalist, but acquitted; in 1660 he was one of the commissioners who sat on the trial of the regicides; in 1670 he was a member of the Cabal; in 1680 he presented the Duke of York as a popish recusant in the court of King's Bench, was imprisoned for treason in 1682, and died at Amsterdam in 1683.

In friendship false, implacable in hate,
Resolved to ruin or to rule the state,
To compass this the triple bond he broke.
DRYDEN, *Absalom and Achitophel.*

Lord of all under Heaven (*The*). The Emperor of China.

One and all come to pay their respects and offer their tribute to the 'Lord of all under Heaven.'—J. N. JORDAN, *Modern China* ('Nineteenth Century,' July 1886, p. 49).

Lord of Ireland, 1177. John, son of Henry II. of England. On the death of Strongbow the government of Ireland was committed to William Fitz-Adelm, allied by blood to the king; but his administration was so bad that he was recalled, and Henry made his youngest and favourite son John 'lord of Ireland,' though only twelve years old at the time. The boy-governor was so insolent that he was recalled, and the government entrusted to De Lacy; but John retained the title of lord of Ireland to his death. Henry VIII., in 1541, raised Ireland from

a lordship to a kingdom, styling himself 'King of England, France, and Ireland, Defender of the Faith.' The same style was adopted by his son Edward VI.

Lord of Misrule (*The*). Called by the Scotch 'The Master of Unreason,' and by the French 'L'abbé de Liesse.' A person elected to superintend the diversions of Christmas. Discontinued since 1641.

In the feast of Christmas there was in the king's house, wheresoever he lodged, a 'Lord of Misrule,' or 'Master of Merry Disports'; and the like had ye in the house of every nobleman of honour or good worship, were he spiritual or temporal. The Mayor of London and either of the sheriffs had their several Lords of Misrule, ever contending, without quarrel or offence, who should make the rarest pastime to delight the beholders. These lords, beginning the rule at Allhallows Eve, continued the same till the morrow after the Feast of Purification, commonly called Candlemas Day.—STOW.

Lord of Regality (*A*). A nobleman in Scotland who held a regality, or sort of palatinate, where he exercised all the rights of a sovereign. Abolished by 20 Geo. II. c. 50.

Lord of his Age (*The*), or Sahibi Kiran, Solyman I. the Magnificent, Ottoman sultan (1493, 1520-1566).

Lord of the Golden Foot. The boa or king of Burmah.

In 1826 the state carriage of the boa, which fell into the hands of the English, was valued at 12,500*l.*

Lord of the Manor (*The*). The owner of a manor having copyhold tenants.

Lord of the Taps. An officer at Stourbridge fair appointed to taste the ale in the booths. This officer was characteristically dressed in a crimson coat decorated with taps, and provided at the time for the occasion.

Lords Appellants (*The*), 1386. Partisans of the Duke of Gloucester, whose object was to dethrone Richard II. They appealed of high treason a large number of magnates who opposed their authority, and constituted themselves into a permanent council to set in order the kingdom and the royal household. In 1389 the king, who was twenty-two years of age, took on his own shoulders the government, and all the lords appellants, except Norfolk and Hereford, either died or were cut off. Norfolk and Hereford were banished in 1397.

Lords Justices of the Court of Appeal in Chancery (*The*). Appointed by Act 14, 15 Vict. c. 83 (1871).

Lords Lieutenant of Ireland. The first, appointed in 1361, was Lionel earl of Ulster. The second was Edmund earl of March, 1379. Richard II. was lord lieutenant in 1394, and again in 1399 ; Henry [VIII.], when duke of York, 1501 ; and Oliver Cromwell in 1640.

Lords Marchers (*The*). The knights and barons of the 140 lordships of Wales ; the rest of Wales was subject to the English crown. These lordships were detached parcels which had been conquered by certain knights and barons, who ruled somewhat like county palatines, each having his own laws, his own courts, and his own judges. Henry VIII., in 1536, abolished this separate jurisdiction, and placed all Wales under the English crown.

Lords Ordainers, 1310, 1311. A standing committee of 7 bishops, 8 earls, and 13 barons (28 altogether), appointed in full parliament in the reign of Edward II. to reform the government and king's household. They presented to the king a list of what they called the ‘Articles of Reform,’ amongst which were these : Parliaments shall be held at least once a year ; no war shall be declared without the consent of the Lords Ordainers ; the king shall never leave the realm without the lords' consent ; the choice of all the great officers of the crown and wardens of the castles shall be made by the Lords Ordainers ; the selection of sheriffs shall be left to the Continual Council. The Earl of Lancaster (a grandson of Henry III.) and the Earls of Lincoln, Leicester, Salisbury, and Derby were on the committee. The king's infatuation for Piers Gaveston was the rock of offence.

Lords of Erection. Laymen of Scotland, to whom the church lands claimed at the Reformation by the crown were given.

These lords, who received a third part of the benefices, were nominally charged with the support of the poor, and were bound to provide competent stipends for the reformed clergy. When James VI. came to his majority the duties of these lords were abolished, and the lands were annexed to the crown. The Lords of Erection were also called ‘Titulars of Tithes.’

As a Tulchan bishop was one who received only a part of his revenue, the rest going to the person who presented him, so these Scotch titulars were only Tulchan lords, sharing their lands with the crown.

Lords of the Articles (*The*). A kind of caucus begun in Scotland in the parliaments of 1368 and 1369. They were a kind of parliamentary grand jury who prepared and arranged in secret meetings what measures should be submitted to parliament and what should be abandoned. Suppressed in 1690.

In Scotland there was only one house for the three estates.

Lords of the Congregation (*The*), Dec. 1557. The leading Protestants of Scotland who pledged themselves to carry out the ‘Solemn League and Covenant’ (*q.v.*) even to the knife. The chief were the Earls of Glencairn, Argyll, and Morton, Lord Lorn, and Erskine of Dun. The reformers were called the ‘Congregation.’

They agreed that all matters in debate between the government and Lords of the Congregation should be left to the consideration of the parliament [of Scotland].—Sir W. SCOTT, *History of Scotland*, xxiv.

Lords of the Justiciary. The judges of the court of justiciary, or criminal court of Scotland.

Lords of the Masso'rah (*The*). Learned Jews who decided what parts of the vast pile of annotations called the Massōrah (*q.v.*) should be accepted. They fixed by canon the verses, words, letters, and vowel-points of the Jewish scriptures. The scholia approved of by these rabbis were printed (along with the Hebrew text) in the year A.D. 1526.

There were two schools of Massoretic Lords from the 11th cent. ; that of Tiberias and that of Babylon. The principal of the former was Aaron ben Asher and of the latter Jacob ben Naphthali.

. There were originally no vowels in Hebrew writings. As the Massorites introduced vowel-points, Hebrew vowels are called ‘Massoretic points.’

Lost Tribes (*The*). The ten tribes which formed the kingdom of Israel.

The Rev. Dr. Joseph Wolff (1831) says they are in China.

The Rev. J. Samuels says they are in the regions of the Caspian Sea.

Dr. Grant says the Nestorians are the lost tribes.

Sir William Jones says they are the Afghans.

Mrs. Dixon thinks they are the Mexicans and Peruvians.

Dr. Claudius Buchanan thinks they are still where they were taken captive, *i.e.* in 'Halak, Habo, Hara, and Gozan, cities of the Medes.'

W. H. Poole, D.D., maintains that we of Great Britain and Ireland are the lost tribes.

And some think the North American Indians, and others that the Gipsies, are the lost tribes.

Lostic, or 'Loktek' (a cubit). So Vladislaus III. of Poland was called on account of his small stature (1260, 1296–1333).

Lotharingia, or Lorraine, was the country over which Lothaire reigned. It included the south of Holland, all Belgium, and the north-east corner of France up to the river Meuse. In 1044 this vast province was divided into Lower and Upper Lorraine, the former containing half Belgium, and the provinces of Brabant and Gelderland (in Holland) ; the rest forming Upper Lorraine.

Louis (*Knights of St.*), 1693. A French military order instituted by Louis XIV.

Louis I. *le Débonnaire,* emperor of the West and king of France (778, 814–840).

Father, Charlemagne ; *Mother,* Hildegarde ; *Wives* (1), Hermengarda, by whom he had three sons—Lothaire, Pepin, and Louis, to whom he gave parts of his empire ; (2) Judith of Bavaria, the mother of Charles le Chauve. *Contemporary* with Egbert.

<small>Louis I. was called *le Pieux* as well as *le Débonnaire.* He was the last surviving son of Charlemagne.</small>

Louis II. *le Bègue,* king of France (846, 877–879) ; he was son of Charles II. le Chauve, grandson of Louis I. le Débonnaire, and great-grandson of Charlemagne. His sister Judith was the second wife of Ethelwulf, Anglo-Saxon king of England. Louis le Bègue had three sons, all of whom reigned, viz. LOUIS III., CARLOMAN, and CHARLES III. le Simple. *Contemporary* with Alfred the Great.

Louis III. (879–882). Son of Louis II. le Bègue (*q.v.*) ; his brother was joint king with him, and died 884. He was succeeded by Charles II. le Gros, who

acted as regent during the minority of Charles III. le Simple, posthumous son of Louis II. le Bègue. *Contemporary* with Alfred the Great.

Louis IV. (d'Oûtremer) of France (921, 936–954). Son of Charles III. le Simple, who married a sister of Athelstan. On the dethronement of her husband, in 922, she fled to England with her infant son, and remained there fourteen years.

<small>He was the fifth remove from Charlemagne. (1) Louis I. le Débonnaire, son of Charlemagne ; (2) Charles II. le Chauve, son of Louis I. ; (3) Louis II. le Bègue, son of Charles II. ; (4) two brothers, Louis III. and Charles III. le Simple, sons of Louis II. ; (5) Louis IV., son of Charles III.</small>

Louis V. le Fainéant. Son of Lothaire, and grandson of Louis IV. d'Outremer (978, 986–987). The last of the Carlovingian kings.

<small>Lothaire, son of Louis IV. d'Outremer, died 986, a little before his father.</small>

Louis VI. le Gros, king of France (1078, 1108–1137).

Father, Philippe I. l'Amoureux ; *Mother,* Bertha ; *Wives,* (1) a sister of Hugues de Crécy, divorced ; (2) Adélaïde daughter of Hubert count of Savoy. *Contemporary* with Henry I. and Stephen.

<small>His eldest son Philippe died before his father, leaving his succession to Louis VII. his brother. This was from the stem of HUGUES Capet, who was succeeded regularly by (1) Robert, (2) Henri I., (3) Philippe I., (4) Louis VI., (5), Louis VII., (6) Philippe II. Auguste, (7) Louis VIII. All sons of the respective preceding king.</small>

Louis VII. le Jeune (1137–1180). Not the young, but the impolitic or unready (*i.e.* unwise) son of Louis VI. (1) His leaving his kingdom to conduct an expedition to the Holy Land was puerile ; (2) his divorcing Eléonore and giving up the two provinces of Poitou and Aquitaine was most impolitic ; (3) his going to Palestine by land rather than by sea, contrary to the advice of his best counsellors, was most imprudent ; (4) his wars with Henry II. of England were short-sighted, and he failed in every instance. Louis VII. was amiable enough, but 'what is mere good-nature but a fool' ?

Father, Louis VI. le Gros ; *Mother,* Adélaïde of Savoy ; *Wives,* (1) Eléonore of Aquitaine, (2) Constance of Castile, (3) Alice, daughter of Thibaud comte de Champagne, mother of his successor. *Contemporary* with Stephen and Henry II.

Louis VIII. (le Lion) of France (1187, 1223–1226). So called because he chose a lion for his device.

Father, Philippe II. Auguste; *Mother*, Isabelle of Hainault; *Wife*, Blanche, daughter of Alfonso of Castile, niece of Richard Cœur de Lion. *Contemporary* with Henry III. *See* 'Louis VI.'

Louis IX. (Saint Louis) king of France (1215, 1226–1270).

Father, Louis VIII.; *Mother*, Blanche of Castile; *Wife*, Marguerite daughter of Comte de Provence. *Contemporary* with Henry III.

Before the Revolution the French Academy used to pronounce annually on 25 Aug. a panegyric on this king.

Louis X. (Le Hutin) of France (1289, 1314–1316). Called Hutin because he was sent by his father against the Hutins, a seditious set of people in Navarre and Lyons. Similar to Africanus, the name given to Scipio, &c.

Father, Philippe IV. le Bel; *Mother*, Jeanne of Navarre; *Wives*, (1) Marguerite of Burgundy, and (2) Clementia of Hungary. *Contemporary* with Edward II.

Louis IX. le Saint was followed by his son PHILIPPE III., whose son was PHILIPPE IV. le Bel, whose son was LOUIS X.; and Louis X. was the oldest of three brothers who succeeded each other. *See* 'Fatal Three.'

Louis XI. 'Louis Onze,' king of France (1423, 1461–1483). Sixth of the Valois branch.

Father, Charles VII.; *Mother*, Marie d'Anjou, daughter of Louis II. of Naples; *Wives*, (1) Margaret daughter of James I. of Scotland, who died broken-hearted, and (2) Charlotte of Savoy, mother of his successor Charles VIII. *Contemporary* with Edward IV.

His chief residences were Plessis-les-Tours, the Palais des Tournelles, and the Louvre.

Louis X. was succeeded by his brothers PHILIPPE V. and CHARLES IV.

PHILIPPE VI., first of the Valois branch, was the son of Charles de Valois (son of Philippe III. and brother of Philippe IV.).

From Philippe VI. came in regular succession JEAN le Bon, CHARLES V., CHARLES VI., CHARLES VII., and LOUIS XI.

°.° The maxim of Louis XI. was 'Qui ne sait pas dissimuler, ne sait pas régner.'

His *physician* was Coitier, who kept the king on tenter hooks of hope and fear, and received from him in five months 54,000 écus (7,000*l.*). The king once asked him how long he had to live. 'I cannot tell exactly (said the wily doctor), but an astrologer told me I should die a few weeks before your majesty.' From this moment Louis watched over the health of Coitier with the utmost concern, and submitted to all his humours.

The *hermit* he sent for was Francis of Paola, in Calabria, afterwards canonised. Louis would

kneel before him in abject terror, imploring him to prolong his life even for a few days or hours.

His *astrologer* was Galiotti Martivalle, a native of Narni in Italy. All his instruments were of gold or silver, and his dress was a rich robe of Genoa velvet.

His *gossip* was Tristan l'Ermite, generally called the 'provost Tristan,' and his *barber* was Olivier le Dain, born in Flanders.

Louis XII. le Père du Peuple, first of the Valois-Orléans branch of France (1462, 1498–1515). So called on account of his wise regulations for the administration of justice, and his prudent expenditure of the public money. One day when a courtier represented to him that his economical habits were called parsimonious, he replied, 'Far better my courtiers should laugh at my parsimony than that my people should mourn for my extravagance.'

Father, Charles duc d'Orléans, grandson of Charles V.; *Mother*, Bona daughter of Comte d'Armagnac; *Wives*, (1) Jeanne de France, daughter of Louis XI., divorced, (2) Anne de Bretagne, widow of Charles VIII., (3) Mary daughter of Henry VII. of England. His *successor*, François I., was the husband of his daughter Claude (by his second wife). *Contemporary* with Henry VII., VIII.

Charles duc d'Orléans and Jean comte d'Angoulême were sons of Louis duc d'Orléans. LOUIS XII. was the son of Charles the elder brother, and FRANÇOIS I. was the grandson of Jean the younger brother.

Louis XIII. le Juste, second of the Bourbon dynasty of France (1601, 1610–1643). Why he was called 'the Just' it would be difficult to say, as he was the mere tool of his ministers. First Concini domineered over him, then De Luynes, and then Richelieu. At last he gave up all show of royalty, and retired to Chantilly, where he spent his time in hunting, fowling, and falconry, with a little music and painting.

Father, Henri IV. *Mother*, Maria de' Medici; *Wife*, Anne of Austria. His *successor*, Louis XIV., was nôt born till after he had been married twenty-three years. *Contemporary* with James I. and Charles I. *See* 'Henri IV.' for pedigree.

It is said he was called le Juste because he was born under the zodiacal sign of *Libra*, the balance.

Louis XIV. le Grand Monarque, third of the Bourbon line, and grandson of Henri IV. (1638, 1643–1714).

Father, Louis XIII.; *Mother*, Anne of Austria—she had been married twenty-three years before her first child was born; *Wives*, (1) Maria-Luisa-Teresa of Austria, infanta of Spain, and (2) Mdme. de Maintenon [Françoise d'Aubigné, marquise de Maintenon], widow of Scarron the poet and cripple; *Mistresses* (1), Mdlle. de la Vallière [Louise-Françoise de la Baume le Blanc de la Vallière], 1644–1661, (2) Mdme. de Montespan [Athénaïs marquise de Montespan, daughter of Gabriel de Rochechouart, duc de Montemart], 1668–1687. She had several children, as the Duc de Maine, the Comte de Toulouse, &c. *Contemporary* with Charles I., Cromwell, Charles II., James II., William III., and Anne.

His wife, Maria-Luisa, was well-nigh imbecile, but was the mother of Louis the Dauphin, who died before his father, leaving a son named Louis (duke of Burgundy), the father of LOUIS XV.

La Vallière retired to a nunnery in 1674, and died in 1710. In her retirement she was called 'Sœur Louise de la Miséricorde.'

. Louis XIV. was called 'the Great' on concluding the Peace of Nimeguen. Signed by Holland 10 Aug., 1678; by Spain 17 Sept., 1678; and by Germany 5 Feb., 1679. This treaty put an end to the European war against France. By this treaty Franche-Comté, and a part of Flanders, was added to France. This was the apogee of the fortunes of the *grand monarque*.

The princess palatine in her 'Correspondence' says: 'I have often seen the king [Louis XIV.] consume at one meal four full plates of various soups, a whole pheasant, a partridge, a large plate of salad, two large rashers of ham, mutton roast and pickled, a plate of pastry, and then fruit and hard-boiled eggs.'

Louis XV. le Bien Aimé, the fourth of the French Bourbon dynasty, great grandson of Louis XIV. (1710, 1715–1774). How such a sensual, heartless voluptuary, who boasted that the ' crazy old machine would last out his time, and he cared not what became of it afterwards,' could be *well-beloved*, is past understanding.

Father, Louis the little dauphin, son of Louis the great dauphin, and grandson of Louis XIV.; *Mother*, Adelaïde; *Wives*, (1) the Infanta of Spain, arranged but broken off, (2) Maria-Charlotte Leczinska; *Mistresses*, (1) Mdme. de Mailly, (2) the Countess de Vintimille her sister, (3) the Duchess of Lauragais, another sister, (4) Mdme. de la Tournelle duchesse de Châteauroux, another sister, (5) Mdme. de Pompadour, and (6) Mdme Dubarry. *Regent*, Philippe duc d'Orléans. *Contemporary* with George I., II., III.; *Daughters*, he nicknamed his three daughters Loque, Chiffe, and Graille.

Louis XIV. died 1715; his son Louis, the great dauphin, died before his father, 1711; and the son

of the dauphin, called Louis the little dauphin (duc de Bourgogne), died 1712, before his grandfather, leaving a son, LOUIS XV.

Again: Louis XV. died 1774; his son Louis the dauphin died before his father, 1765, leaving three sons, all of whom were crowned, viz. LOUIS XVI., LOUIS XVIII., and CHARLES X. *See* 'Fatal Three.'

Louis XVII. son of Louis XVI. outlived his father, but was never crowned. Like Napoleon II. he was *vox et præterea nihil* in kingship.

Louis XVI. was guillotined 21 Jan., 1793. Charles I. was executed 30 Jan., 1649. It is somewhat strange—

1. That Louis XVI. and Charles I. both contain eight letters.

2. That the sum of 21 + 1793 = the sums of 30 + 1649 (day of the month and fatal year).

3. That the month in each case was January.

Father, Louis the dauphin, and grandson of Louis XV.; *Mother*, Marie-Josephe of Saxony; *Wife*, Marie-Antoinette archduchess of Austria, guillotined 1793. *Contemporary* with George III.

His son Louis XVII. never reigned. Three brothers succeeded to the crown, LOUIS XVI., LOUIS XVIII., and CHARLES X. *See* 'Fatal Three.'

. Louis XVI. was called ' Louis the Last ' by the red republicans of France; but they were no true prophets.

Louis XVI. (son of sixty kings). He died Monday, 21 Jan., 1793, aged 30 yrs. 4 m. 28 d. His executioner was Samson. Six men were employed to seize the struggling king and bind him to the plank. His dress was a puce coat, grey breeches, and white stockings. When his coat was pulled off it disclosed a sleeved waistcoat of white flannel.

The whitesmith that instructed Louis XVI. in lockmaking,&c.was François Gamain of Versailles. It is said that the artisan often scolded the king roundly for his work. When Louis was a prisoner, this Gamain traitorously told the Convention committee of an iron press which he and the king had made and inserted in a wall of the royal chamber of the Tuileries. When this press was examined it was found to contain damnatory correspondence from Talleyrand, Mirabeau, and others. Gamain asserted that Louis tried to poison him, and the committee granted him a pension of 1,200 francs (about 48*l*.).

His father confessor, while he was a prisoner in the Temple, was the Abbé Edgeworth de Firmont, of Irish extraction.

His valet was Cléry.

Place of execution the Place de la Révolution, once called the Place de Louis-Quinze.

The brutal delegates who conveyed him to the guillotine were Jacques Leroux and Gorbeau.

Louis XVII., son of Louis XVI. and Marie-Antoinette. According to a tradition, the prince was rescued by the Chevalier de l'Œillet, and a half-witted lad (both deaf and dumb, a relative of Mdme. Richard the gaoler's wife) was substituted in his place. The lad was of a similar age and stature to the dauphin, and sufficiently like him not to excite suspicion. The bribe for this substitution was 300,000 francs (12,000*l*.). It is said that the young prince made his escape in an English cutter, and married Ida Caraccioli.

William Pitt did not think the tradition of the 'Lost Prince' a mere romance; and the Allied Powers, when framing the Treaty of 1814, allowed for the possibility of the prince's appearance. Charette, Pichegru (2 syl.), and George Cadoudal all firmly asserted that he escaped from the Temple, and numerous proclamations refer to it. In 1812 a document was signed in which Louis XVIII. calls himself regent, not king of France. Certainly the document signed Drs. Pelletan, Dumangin, and Lassas is most unsatisfactory. It runs thus: 'We proceeded to examine the corpse of a youth shown to us by the Commission, and stated by them to be the son of Louis Capet.' This document is preserved in the Imperial Library of Paris.

*** The general tale is much more sad. It is this: The young prince, only eight years old, was sent by the Convention to be brought up by a vulgar brute named Simon, a cobbler, who stripped him of his suit of mourning, and dressed him like a pauper in coarse jacket and red cap, forced him to drink intoxicating liquors, and repeat revolutionary ballads. In a few months this delicate boy became half-consumptive and half-idiot. January, 1794, the wretch locked him in an upper room, and here, without fire, without candle, and well-nigh without food, he lingered till June, 1795, when he died.

Louis XVIII. le Désiré, sixth of the French Bourbon kings, brother of Louis XVI. and of Charles X. It is absurd to call him *Le Désiré*, seeing he was thrust on the nation by the allies, and was never 'the desired' of the people (1755, 1814–1824).

Father, Louis the Dauphin, and grandson of LOUIS XV.; *Mother*, Marie Josephe of Saxony; *Wife*, Marie-Josephine of Savoy; no issue. *Called* Monsieur and the Comte de Provence till 1795; in exile he went as le Comte Delille. In England he lived at Hartwell, a seat of the Duke of Buckingham, where his wife died. *Contemporary* with George III., IV.

The Bourbons: (1) HENRI IV.; (2) LOUIS XIII.; (3) LOUIS XIV.; (4) LOUIS XV., great-grandson of Louis XIV.; (5) LOUIS XVI., grandson of Louis XV.; LOUIS XVIII. brother of Louis XVI.

*** Louis XVII. and Napoleon II. were regal fictions, so called simply because they outlived their respective fathers. Similarly the date of the reign of Charles II. is absurdly thrown back to the death of Charles I., ignoring and implying a legal right of succession; but in England the succession has been most irregular, and depends on the parliament. Thus William I., William II., Henry I., Stephen, Henry IV. V. VI., Richard III., Henry VII., William III., &c., had not the slightest legal right to the throne of England, and their invalidity invalidates the entire succession. The whole right is sufferance or parliamentary sanction.

Louis-Philippe. Citizen-king of the French (born 1773, reigned 1830–1848, died 1850).

Father, Louis-Philippe, Mons. Égalité [Duc d'Orléans]; *Mother*, Adelaïde de Bourbon - Penthièvre; *Wife*, Marie-Amélie, niece of Marie-Antoinette. *As-*

sumed names: 1793, M. Chabaud Latour, under which name he was a teacher in M. Jost's school in Switzerland; in 1794 M. Corby; in 1795 Herr Müller, under which name he travelled in the north of Europe; 1848 Mr. William Smith, under which name his passport to England was made out at Honfleur; but he and his wife fled from Paris under the name of M. and Mdme. Lebrun.

LOUIS XIII. had for sons LOUIS XIV. and Philippe de France duc d'Orléans. Philippe's son was Philippe the *Regent*, the Regent's son was Louis, whose son was Louis-Philippe. Louis-Philippe's son was Philippe *Egalité*, and Egalité's son was King LOUIS-PHILIPPE.

Louis de Male, Louis II. of Flanders. So called from Male, Marle, or Malain, in France, where he delighted to dwell. He succeeded his father in 1346, and died 1384.

Louis the German. *See* LUDWIG, &c.

Louisiana (U.S. America). So called by M. de la Sale in 1682, in honour of Louis XIV. In the minority of Louis XV. it was given to the *Compagnie du Mississippi*. The inhabitants are nicknamed *Creoles*.

Louisville, a city of Kentucky, in the United States of North America, on the Falls of Ohio. It was named, in 1780, in honour of Louis XVI. of France, whose troops were at the time assisting the Americans in the War of Independence.

Loup-Garou, a lyc'anthrope. A sort of hypochondriac who fancies himself to be a wolf, and under this impression goes about howling and attacking children. This mania occurred in Germany in the early part of the 17th cent.

The celebrated Nicolle tells us of a convent where all the nuns fancied they were cats, and at a certain hour every day ran about mewing and caterwauling. It was cured by threatening to quarter a regiment of soldiers in the nunnery. Nebuchadnezzar's madness, in which he fancied himself to be an ox, is supposed to have been a species of lycanthropy.

Louvestein (*Dutch*, Loevestein; pronounce 'Loovestine,' 3 syl.). A political or state prison during the time of the Dutch Republic. It is a castle at the confluence of the Meuse (*Dutch*, Maas) and the Waal (Rhine), and is opposite the town of Gorkum (Gorichem), about ten miles above Dort (*Dutch*, Dortrecht). Here Grotius was kept; he made his escape in a box which had been employed to bring him books. Here, too, De Witt and some other republican leaders had been imprisoned,

and hence the republican party was called the 'Louvestein.' They were discharged from the castle at the death of William II. the stadtholder.

Louvestein Faction (*The*). The republican party of Holland, led by Jan and Cornelius de Witt, in opposition to the Orange policy, which was to uphold the office of stadtholder. The Louvestein faction succeeded for several years in excluding the house of Orange from the stadtholdership in the person of William III. (afterwards king of England), but in 1672 both the brothers De Witt were murdered by an infuriated crowd.

Louis [XIV.] sent Caillières to Holland to tamper with the Louvestein faction, which had always been hostile to William [III. of Holland and of England].—HOWITT, *Hist. of Eng.* (William and Mary, 105).

Love-feasts, or Agapæ. Held in the early ages of Christianity after receiving the eucharist. The rich brought provisions, but the poor were not expected to contribute. They continued to be held for three centuries, and were ultimately forbidden by the Council of Carthage, A.D. 397.

The 'kiss of peace' was changed for a symbolical ceremony. An ivory tablet was first kissed by the minister and then circulated through the congregation for each one to kiss.

Low Mass, 'Missa bassa.' A mass without singing, 'quæ submissa voce celebratur.' *See* 'Mass.'

Low St. James. 'From low St. James's up to high St. Paul's' (Pope, 'Satires'). The allusion is to the Bangorian controversy (*q.v.*). Bishop Hoadly, the favourite of Queen Anne, was the exponent of the low church party at St. James, but his opponent, Dr. Francis Hare, dean of St. Paul's, was the leader of the high church party. We should now say 'from Charles Simeon to Dr. Pusey,' or (1890) from 'John Charles Ryle of Liverpool to Edward King of Lincoln.'

Lowndean Professor of Astronomy and Geometry. Value 450*l.* a year. Founded in the University of Cambridge by Thomas Lowndes, 1749.

If the professor superintends the observatory he receives an extra 250*l.* a year.

Loyal Association (*The*), 1792. Formed in London by John Reeves, favouring the British constitution, in opposition to the favourers of the French revolutionary spirit.

Loyal Irish Brotherhood (*The*), 1880. A group of the Land League organisation. *See* 'Irish Associations.'

Loyal National Repeal Association (*The*), 1839. Organised by Daniel O'Connell to procure for Ireland 'perfect equality with England,' and bring about the repeal of the union. *See* 'Irish Associations.'

Loyalty Loan (*The*), 1796. Subscribed in December to prepare against the threatened invasion of the French.

Lubbock's Day (*St.*). The August Bank-holiday. So called from Sir John Lubbock, who brought it about.

A Bank holiday is called 'A feast of St. Lubbock.'

Lübeck (*Peace of*), May 22, 1629. Between Kaiser Ferdinand II. and Christian IV. of Denmark. This treaty brought to a close the first part of the Thirty Years' War.

Lucanian Oxen. Elephants. The Romans had never seen elephants till Pyrrhus invaded Rome. In their ignorance they called them 'Lucanian oxen,' supposing them to be herds from the fertile meadows of Lucania. The swine of Lucania were also famous, and the

Romans delighted in the sausages, which they called *Lucanica*.

Lucasian Professor of mathematics. Stipend 850*l*. Founded in the University of Cambridge by Henry Lucas, M.P. for the university, 1663. *See* 'Mathematics,' &c.

Luciferians, 4th cent. An 'heretical' religious sect founded by Lucifer bishop of Cagliari. They taught that the soul is transmitted to the children from their parents.

Lucilius (*The French*). Béranger the poet. Lucilius was either the first or one of the first Roman satirists, followed by Horace, Persius, and Juvenal. Béranger is the French Horace rather than the French Lucilius.

Lu'cumo and Lars. A Lucŭmo was an independent king of any one of the twelve confederate states of ancient Etruria. His kingdom was called a 'Lucumy.' In time of war one of these Lucumos was appointed leader, and was called *Lars* (generally the over-king), as Lars Porsëna. Similarly, the leader of the Gauls was called Brenn [Latin *Brennus*], and the leader of the Britons was called Dragon, or Pendragon.

> And plainly and more plainly
> Now might the burghers know,
> By port and vest, by horse and crest,
> Each warlike Lucumo.
>   *   *   *
> Lars Porsëna of Clusium
> Sat in his ivory car.
> MACAULAY, *Lays of Ancient Rome* (Horatius).

Luddites, 1811–1813, and again 1816. Rioters, so named from their leader, who called himself 'General Lud.' The great year of riots was 1812–1813. There had been recently introduced machines for finishing woollen goods, formerly done by men called 'Croppers.' By these machines the croppers were thrown out of work, and formed themselves into rioters, who went about Derbyshire, Lancashire, Cheshire, Nottinghamshire, and the south-western districts of Yorkshire, breaking the machines, and threatening the owners of them. Sixty-four of the rioters were executed in 1812, and nine in the following January.

Miss Martineau says the Luddites were so called from Edward or Ned Lud of Leicestershire, who, being chased by some boys, took refuge in a factory, where he broke two stocking-frames. The chief of the Luddites was a man named Mellor.

Ludgate. Ludgate was originally built in 1215 by the barons, who entered London, destroyed the houses of the Jews, and erected this gate with the ruins thereof. It was first used as a prison in 1373, being then a free prison, but it soon lost that privilege. Sir Stephen Forster, who was lord mayor in 1454, had been a prisoner at Ludgate, and begged at the grate, where he was seen by a rich widow, who bought his liberty, took him into her service, and ultimately married him. To commemorate this eventful incident, Sir Stephen enlarged the accommodation for the prisoners, and added a chapel. The old gate was taken down and rebuilt in 1586. This new gate was destroyed in the Great Fire. Another gate was subsequently built and also used as a prison for debtors, but was pulled down in 1760, and the prisoners removed, first to the workhouse, and afterwards to the Giltspur Street Compter (Professor MORLEY, note to No. 82 of the 'Spectator').

Ludi-magister. A schoolmaster. Ludus means a school as well as a game of sports. Hence, 'ducere filium in ludum,' to take one's son to school. 'Noluit in . . . ludum me mittere' (Horace, "Sat." I. vi. 72).

Sir Walter Scott makes Erasmus Holiday say, 'He was inclined to think he bore the name of Holiday. . . because he gave such a few holidays to his school. Hence, the schoolmaster is termed classically *ludi-magister*, because he deprives boys of their play' ('Kenilworth,' chap. ix.).

Ludovico Sforza, the More, duke of Milan (died 1510). Ludovico adopted as his bearing a white mulberry tree (*moro*), the 'wisest of all plants,' in that it buds late, and does not flower till all hazard from winter frosts and winds has passed away. He was not named the Moor as most people write the name. (PAULUS JOVIUS, 'Vitæ Illustrorum Virorum,' iv.).

Ludwig I. The same as Louis le Débonnaire (778, 814–840). He was son of Charlemagne, and king both of France and Germany.

Ludwig, Clovis, and Louis are mere varieties of the same name. Clovis='lovis=louis; and Ludwig=Luwig=Louis.

Ludwig II. the Young, *i.e.* the Greenhorn (822, 855–874), son of Lothaire.

He was 33 when he succeeded his father, and 54 when he died, so he was not called the young on account of youthful age ; but like Louis le Jeune of France (1120–1180), he was ' green ' as a politician. Ludwig II. ceded part of his dominion to his brother Karl, and at the death of Karl, in 863, gave up part of Provence to his brother Lothaire.

So Louis VII. le Jeune by repudiating his wife Eléonore lost several provinces of France, which fell into the hands of Henry II. of England, who married her.

Ludwig III. the Blind (880, 890–903, died 923). He was grandson of Ludwig II., and had his eyes put out by Berenger, on whom he made war unsuccessfully, and by whom he was deposed in 903.

Ludwig IV. the Infant (893, 899–911). Not recognised by some. Last of the Karlovingian race in Germany. He was son of Arnulf of Carinthia. Too feeble to resist the Huns and oppose Otto (duke of Saxony), he fled to Ratisbon, and the throne was given to Konrad I. duke or count of Franconia.

Ludwig V. (of Bavaria). One of the promiscuous kaiser-kings of Germany (1314–1347). In 1338 the pragmatic sanction of Rense decreed that the elected king of Germany was *ex officio* kaiser, or emperor of the Holy Roman Empire.

Ludwig V. placed two black eagles on the imperial seal, but Karl IV. changed the device into a black eagle with two heads. He was the last of the emperors of Germany excommunicated by a pope.

Ludwig, called ' Louis the German,' third son of Louis I. le Débonnaire, and grandson of Charlemagne. On the division of Charlemagne's empire, by the Treaty of Verdun (843), Bavaria and the whole country to the east of France (called Germany) fell to his lot.

Louis le Débonnaire had four sons: Lothaire, Pepin, Ludwig, and Charles. Pepin died before his father.

Ludwig the Child. *See above.* ' Louis the Infant.'

Ludwig the Saxon, second son of Ludwig the German. He died 882.

CHARLEMAGNE, Karl I., or Charles I. Louis I. le Débonnaire, son of Charlemagne.

LUDWIG the German, third son of Louis I. le Débonnaire. (His two brothers were Lothaire of Italy and Pepin, who died before he did.)

KARL III. the Fat, third son of Ludwig the German. (His two brothers were Karlman of Italy and Ludwig the Saxon.)

Arnulf (who reigned 888-899) was son of Karlman or Carloman of Italy, and nephew of Karl III. the Fat. As he died before his uncle, his kingdom was joined to the dominions of Karl III. the Fat.

Arnulf's son was Ludwig the Child or Infant.

Lugdunensis. That part of Gaul which lay between the Loire and the Seine.

Luke's Iron Crown, referred to by Goldsmith in ' The Traveller,' should be ' Zeck's iron crown,' as it was not Luke but George Dosza who was tormented in the way described A.D. 1514. He was a Szekler, or peasant of Szekelyföld, a district of Transylvania. The Jack Cade of Hungary was punished by being seated on an iron throne with a fire under it, crowned with a red-hot crown, and having his flesh torn off his bones by hot pincers.

Hujusmodi libertatem propter seditionem et tumultuariam adversus universam nobilitatem, sub nomine cruciatæ, ductu cujusdam scelerati Georgii Szekelii, insurrectionem, amiserunt. — VERBOCZI, *Jus Consuetudinarium Regni Hungariæ,* 1514.

Lumley Exhibition, in the Universities of Oxford and Cambridge, 1657. The Right Hon. Elizabeth viscountess Lumley founded ten scholarships of 4*l.* per annum each for poor scholars. In 1820 the number of scholars was reduced to five, and the value of the exhibition increased to 15*l.* a year, to be held till they become graduates.

Lunéville (*Treaty of*), 9 Feb., 1801. Between France and Austria. By this treaty Belgium and the Rhenish provinces were ceded to France, and the states of Venice were given to Austria; the pope was re-established, and the Cisalpine, Ligurian, Helvetian, and Batavian republics were duly recognised.

Lurdane. A rich idle man; a corruption of ' Lord-Dane.' So the Danes who remained in England after the restoration of Danegeld by Ethelred the Unready were called by the servile English, who stood in awe of them.

More likely to be old French *lourdan,* modern French *lourdaud,* a loggerhead.

Lusitania, Portugal. The country of the Lusitāni.

It included Portugal and Estremadūra.

Lutatius says so, and 'therefore it must be true.' *Hoc verum est ; dixit* *enim Lutatius* (Cicero, 'De Oratore,' ii. 40). Quintus Lutatius Catŭlus was the colleague of Marĭus in his fourth consulate. The character of Catulus stood so high in Rome that no one disputed or doubted what he said.

Lutestring Administration *(The)*, 1765. That of Lord Rockingham, which followed the Grenville administration. Marquis of Rockingham premier and lord of the treasury; Grafton and General Conway secretaries of state; Earl of Northington chancellor; the old Duke of Newcastle privy seal; the old Lord Winchilsea president of the council; and Charles Townshend paymaster of the forces. As the ministry could not last, Charles Townshend himself said, 'It is a mere lutestring administration.' (Lutestring is a summer silk, unfit for winter wear.)

'Lutestring,' a corruption of *lustrin*, from the Italian *lustrino*, French *lustre*, a shining silk fabric, much worn at the time by ladies.

Luther *(Martin)*. Born at Eislĕben in Saxony 10 Nov., 1483; entered the Augustine monastery at Erfurt in 1505; professor of philosophy at Wittenberg in 1508; Leo X. issued a bull against him 24 June, 1520; Luther burnt the bull at Wittenberg 10 Dec., 1520; he appeared before the Diet of Worms April 1521; was seized on his journey and carried to Wartburg, where he began his version of the Bible; he returned to Wittenberg in March 1522; discarded the dress of a monk in 1524; married Catherine de Bora, an ex-nun, 27 June, 1525 [he was 42 years old at the time]; and died at Eisleben 18 Feb., 1546.

A monument was erected to him at Wittenberg in 1821, and one at Worms in 1868.

Luther *(The Danish)*. Hans Tausen. There is a stone in Viborg called 'Tausensminde,' with this inscription : ' Upon this stone, in 1528, Hans Tausen first preached Luther's doctrine in Viborg.'

Luther of England *(The)*. Archbishop Cranmer (1489–1556). He did the work of Luther, but was very unlike the rough German in character.

Luther's Catechisms. Luther published two catechisms, the shorter one in 1520 and the larger one in 1529. These religious catechisms found a place among the symbolical books of the Lutheran churches.

Lutheranism. The platform of those Protestants who, like Luther, believe in consubstantiation, the use of images as aids to devotion, private confession, the form of exorcism in baptism, and some other semi-Catholic doctrines and practices.

Luther said that Christ, in the sacrament, is present with the bread and wine, as fire is present with iron when the metal is red-hot.

Luxemburg *(House of)*. Furnished Germany with four kaisers, but other rulers intervened; as Heinrich VII. (1308–1313); Karl IV. (1347–1373); Wenceslaus (1378–1400); and Siegmund or Sigismund (1411–1437).

Lydford Law. Lydford is a village of Devonshire where we are told offenders were summarily punished.

First hang and draw,
Then hear the cause by Lydford law.

There are many similar expressions ; as ' Bradford law,' 'Halifax law,' 'Cupar justice, 'Jedburgh justice,' 'Burslem club-law,' 'Mob law,' 'Abingdon law,' &c.

Lydian Stone. So touchstone was called by the Romans, because it was found in Lydia of Asia Minor.

Lying Dick Talbot. Richard Talbot duke of Tyrconnel, lord lieutenant of Ireland (*–1691).

Lynch Law. The law of self-constituted magistrates. James Lynch was a Virginian farmer who in 1688 took upon himself to enforce better order by trying thieves, vagabonds, and other disorderly persons. This he did because there were then no magistrates or law courts in the neighbourhood. Lynch seems to have acted pretty fairly in his self-constituted office, insomuch that he was supported by his neighbours.

Lyonists. The followers of Peter Waldo of Lyons, who died 1197. Peter Waldo had the four gospels translated into French, and found the prevailing religion so different to that taught in the gospels that he became a preacher, and soon gathered round him a large following. The Lyonists rejected the dogma of apostolic succession; accepted only two sacraments; maintained the sufficiency of scripture; believed in only one Mediator, and therefore rejected the advocacy of Virgin Mary and the saints; denied papal supremacy and purgatory; rejected masses for the dead, the adoration of images and relics, indulgences, and other innovations.

The Lyonists, Waldenses, Cathari, and Albigenses had so much in common, they are very frequently confounded one with another.

Lyric Poets (*The Prince of*). Pindar (B.C. 529–435), a Bœotian.

Franz Peter Schubert, the musical composer, is called ' the Prince of Lyrists' (1797-1828).

Lysippus (*The English*). Grinling Gibbons, the carver and sculptor in the reign of Charles II. (1648–1721). His favourite wood was lime or linden. Lysippus was a Greek sculptor in the time of Alexander the Great, whose most famous works were statues of Alexander, the chariot of the sun at Rhodes, and the colossus of Tarentum.

Mabinogion (*The*). Welsh fairy tales. The MS. is of the 14th cent., and is included in the ' Red Book of Hergest' (*q.v.*). Lady Charlotte Guest published a translation of it in 1838–1849. ' Mabinogi means 'instruction for youth,' from *Maban*, a young child.

Macabre (*La Danse*). An allegory representing all ages and conditions of men engaged in dancing, with Death presiding. Very popular from the 13th to the 15th cent., and found in a large number of churches and cemeteries. The most ancient goes back to the year 1485, and the most famous are those of Minden, Lucerne, Lübeck, Dresden, and Basle. The painting in the convent of the Dominicans is attributed to Holbein.

Macadam (*John Loudon*) introduced two improvements in roads : (1) Instead of making the centre of the road the lowest part, he made it the highest, so that the centre is the crown from which the road on both sides gradually lowers ; (2) his other improvement was to employ stones broken small instead of entire stones of various sizes. By the first improvement the roads are better drained ; by the second they are smoother and more firm (1756–1836).

Macaroni Club (*The*), 1770. A club of dandies, first in Paris and then in London, in the latter half of the 17th cent. Their hair was dressed in an enormous toupee, with huge curls at the sides, and tied behind into a pigtail with a knot. A very small hat was perched on the top, and was lifted from the head by a small cane. Round the neck was a full white cravat tied in an enormous bow. Frills from the shirt-front projected from the top of the waistcoat. The coat and waistcoat were both short, reaching only to the hips. The breeches were tight, of spotted or striped silk, with enormous bunches of strings at the knees. A watch was carried in two breeches pockets, from which dangled huge bunches of seals. The shoes were small, with diamond buckles ; and a walking-stick with long tassels completed the costume. It was the delight of the exquisites to be as rude as possible to modest women, and to bully all the weak and timid.

Macaroni is an Italian cake. The slang expression ' What a cake (oaf) you are !' may have risen from these empty-headed fops, or ' toffs,' called in 1888 ' mashers' or ' dudes,' which words are still (1890) in vogue ; indeed have been appropriated by the lighter order of feminines, who talk of ' mashing ' the male sex when they are persuaded their appearance is particularly effective.
A kind of animal, neither male nor female, lately started up amongst us. It is called a *Macaroni*. It talks without meaning, it smiles without pleasantry. it eats without appetite, it rides without exercise.—*Oxford Magazine* (June 1770. vol. iv. p. 228).

Macbeth. Lady Macbeth's maiden name was Graoch. Macbeth did not murder Duncan in his castle of Inverness, but attacked and slew him at a place called Bothgowan or the Smith's House, near Elgin, in 1040. The claim of Macbeth, as grandson of Malcolm II., was (according to the rule of Scottish succession) much better than that of Duncan.

Lady Macbeth was the granddaughter of Kenneth IV., killed in 1003 fighting against Malcolm II.

MacBriar (*Ephraim*), introduced by Sir Walter Scott in ' Old Mortality,' is the young preacher Maccail, so hideously tortured in the reign of Charles II. He died in a rapture. *See* HOWITT, ' Hist. of Eng.' (Charles II. p. 442).

Maccabæan Martyrs (*Feast of the*), 1 Aug. A mother and her seven sons were put to death by Antiochus Epiphānēs. These were not Christian martyrs, but the festival was instituted by Christians.

Maccabæus (*The French*). Simon de Montfort, entrusted by Philippe II. Auguste with the first crusade against the Albigenses. He cut down 20,000 of them with the sword and burnt 450 to death (1150-1218).

Maccabees (*The*). The Asmonæan princes of Judæa were so called from

Jehu'dah or Judah, surnamed 'Maccaby,' who succeeded his father Mattathīas as leader of the Jews who revolted from Antiŏchos Epiphānês. *See* 'Asmonæans.'

The Maccabees continued to be rulers of the Jews till the appointment of Herod the Great. Mattathīas had five sons, and was succeeded by Judah ' Maccaby,' his third son ; after whom followed Jonathan, the youngest of the five ; and then came Simon, who transmitted the succession.

Mattathias (B.C. 167-166) was father of *Jochanan*, Simon (142-136), Judah ' Maccaby ' (166-161), *Eleazar*, and Jonathan the high priest (161-142).
Simon was the father of Joannes Hyrcānus (B.C. 136-107), the third son.
Joannes Hyrcānus was the father of Aristobūlus (who assumed the title of ' king' B.C. 107-106), and Alexander Jannæus (also called ' king,' 106 79).
Alexander Jannæus was the father of Hyrcānus II. (B.C. 79, deposed B.C. 40, and put to death by Herod B.C. 30),—and of Aristobūlus II. (dethroned by Hyrcānus II.).
Aristobūlus was the father of Mariamne, who married Herod the Great.
. Maccaby is probably the inscription of the Maccabæan banner, M.C.C.B.Y. (*Mi Camo-Co Belohim Yehovah — i.e.* 'Who is like unto thee, O Lord, among the gods?' Exod. xv. 11). After the same manner the Romans inscribed on their banners the acrostic S.P.Q.R. (*i.e.* Senātus Populusque Romanus). *See* the Austrian A.E.I.O.U.

MacCulloch (*Cutlar*). A corsair

who made repeated incursions on the northern shores of the Isle of Man, carrying off all that was not ' too hot or too heavy ' (16th cent.).

God keep the good corn, the sheep, and the buHock,
From Satan, from sin, and from Cultar MacCulloch.

MacDonald (*Half-hanged*), 1772.

MacDonald, a lad of 19 years, in the 42nd Royal Highlanders, being irritated in a public-house in Bigg Market, seized one Parker and slapped his face soundly. Parker and one or two others rushed from the public, and MacDonald, rushing after the fugitives, caught the wrong man, struck him, and he died. Being tried, he was condemned and executed. The body was handed over for dissection, and left on the table while the students went to dinner. A young surgeon came into the dissecting-room and saw MacDonald sitting up. He begged for life, but the surgeon struck him with a heavy mallet and effectually dispatched the half-hanged man.

Macedonian War (*The*). The

First, B.C. 211-205 Between Rome and Macedonia. Philip V king of Macedon not Alexander's father), thinking the

disastrous battle of Cannæ had established the Carthaginian supremacy, formed in B.C. 213 an alliance with Hannibal ; but both Rome and Carthage were for the time being too busy with their own affairs to attend to other matters, and left the war to allies. In this war Philip had the advantage.

In the first Macedonian war the Ætolians, Athenians, Rhodians, and Egyptians, together with Attalus king of Pergamus, took part with the Romans.
The Macedonians, Carthaginians, Acarnanians, with Antiochus king of Syria, sided with Philip of Macedon.

The *Second* Macedonian war, B.C. 200-197. Also between Rome and Macedonia. Philip of Macedon laid siege to Athens B.C. 200 ; but as Athens was an ally of the Romans, the Romans declared war against him, and entrusted the conduct of the war to Quintus Flaminīnus, who met the army of Philip in Thessaly, and gained a signal victory at Kynoskeph'alæ (the Dogshead Hills) in 197. The terms of peace were these: (1) Philip was to restore all the Greek towns to independence; (2) he was to give up his fleet, and pay a tribute to Rome for ten years; and (3) he was to give his son among the hostages for the fulfilment of these terms.

The *Third* Macedonian war, B.C. 172-168, was between the son of Philip, named Perseus, and the Romans. About twenty-six years after the second war, Philip being dead, his son Perseus (2 syl.), hoping to throw off the Roman yoke, made war with partial success for three years, but was at length utterly defeated by Æmilius Paullus, at Pydna in Macedonia, B.C. 168. Perseus was led captive to Rome, and the kingdom of Macedonia was converted into a Roman province.

The avarice of Perseus estranged from him all his allies, and though he behaved in the most abject manner to Æmilius Paullus, he was cast into a dungeon at Rome, and died of starvation and grief. His son Alexander gained his bread in Alba Longa as a turner.

Macedon'ians, or 'Pneumat'ics,'

4th cent. The followers of Macedon'ius patriarch of Constantinople (343-360), who denied the divinity of the Holy Ghost. He was condemned by the Second General Council, held at Constantinople in 381.

The First General Council—that of Nice, 325—condemned Arius, who denied the divinity of Christ; and the Second General Council condemned Macedonius, who denied the divinity of the Holy Ghost.

MacFarlane's Lantern. The moon. The clan of MacFarlane occupied the fastnesses of the western side of Loch Lomond, and were great depredators on the low country. As their excursions were made by night, the moon was proverbially called their lantern.

Machiavelism. Crooked, perfidious policy, in which expediency is the ruling principle and chicanery the chief instrument. So called from Niccolò Machiavelli of Florence, whose system is set forth in his 'Del Principe.' Cesare Borgia is his model of a perfect ruler (1469–1527).

Both Tiberius of Rome and Louis XI. of France are credited with the maxim, 'He who knows not how to deceive, knows not how to rule.'

Maclean's People. Scotch Baptists.

Macmillanites (4 syl.). Members of the 'Reformed Presbyterian Church' (*q.v.*); so called from Mr. Macmillan, one of their most distinguished preachers.

Macrea (*Jenny*), 1777. Abducted and murdered by Indians in the army of General Burgoyne. Miss Macrea was residing with Mrs. Macneil, a widow, close to Fort Edward, and her lover, Jones, was in Burgoyne's army. She was about 20 years of age, intelligent and charming. On 27th July a party of Indians assailed Mrs. Macneil's house, and carried her off with Miss Macrea. Being pursued by some American soldiers, Miss Macrea was fastened to a tree, tomahawked, and scalped. The elder lady seems to have escaped.

The burning houses, the scalped and murdered Americans, and the innocent blood of Miss Macrea made the names of the Six Nations terrible in Europe.—HOWITT, *Hist. of Eng.* (Geo. III.), p. 190.

Macrobiots. Exceeding 100 years. [Greek μακρός βίοτος.]

Age		Year of death	
102.	Hastings (*Henry*)	1639	Forester to Charles I.
	Chevreul (*M.E.*), French chemist	1889	aged nearly 103.
107.	Laugher (*Thomas*)	1807	of Markley, Worcestershire.
	Macklin (*Charles*)	1797	the actor.
108.	*The mother of Thomas Laugher.*		
116.	Alice of Philadelphia	1802	

Up to 120 the names are too numerous for insertion. There are above 1,200 of them.

Age		Year	
120.	Dragonetti, the Jesuit	1626	he lectured at Rome when 120 years old.
	Fournelle (*Pierre de*)	1819	a physician of Paris. Died 5 Oct.
	Grou (*Jean*)	1668	a surgeon and famous anatomist of Paris.
	Harp (*Frederick*)	1792	an Englishman.
	Jacot (*Jacques*)	1529	died at Neuchâtel in Switzerland.
	Lévezier (*Nicolas*)	1645	an Augustine, who had been a priest for 91 years. Died in the abbey of Claire-Fontaine.
	Piedrède (*Joanna Francesca de*)	1790	lived at Mexapao near Coimbra, on the road to Porto.
120.	A man of Rechingen	1791	having lost all his teeth, he cut a new set at the age of 116. The Prussian doctor Ufland is the authority for this statement.
	A priest of Linhares	1820	in the Serra da Estrella of Portugal.
121.	Camoux (*Annibal*)	1759	of Nice, died at Marseilles. He was a great eater and drinker His likeness, by J. Vernet, is in the Louvre.
	Malcomson (*Sarah*)	1810	an Englishwoman.
	Ponce le Page	1760	of Hampré, in Luxemburg. A little before death he could walk 6 or 7 miles. He was a labourer.
	Spicer (*Eleonore, sic.*)	1773	died at Accomack, in Virginia. Buffon says she never touched alcoholic drinks.
122.	Jacob (*Jean*)	1791	an agricultural labourer of the Jura. He presented himself to the Constituent Assembly in 1791.
	La Piole	1739	a labourer of Usquiole, in Berne. He never had a day's illness.
	Munier	1708	a schoolmaster of Paris.
123.	Barnet (*dame*)	1820	died at Charleston, in South Carolina. She spoke fluently English, French, Spanish, Italian and Moorish; and knew both Arabic and Hebrew.
	Countess of Arundel	—	in the reign of Charles I.
	Guignard (*Denis*)	1760	of Luché, in the Maine. In 1757 her white hair turned to a golden or golden yellow.
124.	Bueno (*André*)	1753	a Spanish officer, died at Badajoz.
	Schmit (*André*)	1753	died at Teschen, in Upper Silesia.
	Wakley (*William*)	1714	born at Shiffnal, and buried at Adbaston. He lived in the reign of eight sovereigns.
	Wishart (*Thomas*)	1759	a Scotchman.

It is said that Attila king of the Huns died at the age of 124, on the night of his second marriage, A.D. 453.

Age		Year	
126.	Barnesley (*William*)	1636	an Englishman. At the age of 100 he married a second wife.
	Grandez	1754	of Pradez d'Aubrac, in Languedoc, a silversmith. He never touched wine, and worked at his trade within twelve days of his death. Till then he had never suffered a day's illness.
	Martha Hannah	1808	an Irishwoman.

N N

Age				Year of death	
126. Montgomery (*Robert*)	...	...	...	1668	a Scotchman by birth, but lived chiefly at Skipton, in England. Latterly he lived by begging.
127. Carollan (*Owen*)	...	...	...	1764	an Irish labourer of Meath. He had 6 fingers on each hand and 6 toes on each foot. Was never ill.
Hughes (*William*)	...	...	...	1769	of Tadcaster, in Yorkshire.
Innes (*Mary*)	...	...	...	1814	of the Isle of Skye.
Neuwel (*John*)	...	...	...	1761	grandson of old Parr. An ostler, who died at Michaelstown, and at death no faculty had failed.
Scrimshaw (*Jane*)	...	...	...	1711	she lived in the reign of 8 sovereigns.
Yates (*Mary*)	..	...	...	1776	she walked from Shiffnal to London when she was 120, and married at the age of 92 her third husband.
129. Evans (*Henry*)	...	...	...	1771	a Welshman.
Meigham (*Mrs. Mary*)	...	...	...	1813	an Englishwoman.
Roger (*Jean*)	...	...	..	1740	of Bize, in the diocese of Comminges.
130. Bayles (*John*)	...	...	...4 April,	1706	of Northampton. Keill made the post-mortem, which is entered in our 'Philosophical Transactions.' He was a sheep-drover, and continued his occupation to the last. He was a thin and sinewy man.
Beattie (*William*)	...	...	...	1778	
Cameron (*David*)	...	...	...	1795	
Ellis (*William*)	...	...	...	1780	of Liverpool.
King (*George*)	..	...	...	1766	
Lasomel (*Jean de*)	...	...	...	1766	
Lilley (*Samuel*)	...	...	...	1753	dean of Worcester.
Macbride (*Robert*)	...	...	...	1786	
Mestauza (*Pierre*)	...	...	...	1743	of Vemil, in Murcia, Spain.
Taylor (*John*)	...	...	...	1767	
Watson (*John*)	...	...	...	1778	
131. Garden (*Peter*)	...	...	...	1775	
Taylor (*Elizabeth*)	...	...	...	1764	
132. Macculloch (*Alexander*)	...	...	...	1757	of Aberdeen. He served as a private in Monk's army.
133. Merchant (*Elir, sic.*)	...	...	...	1751	
134. Ague (*Francis*)	...	...	...	1767	
Brookey (*John*)	...	...	...	1777	
Grappin (*Anne Oudet*)	...	...	...	1641	died in Paris aged 134 years and 10 months.
Keit (*Mrs.*)	...	...	...	1772	of Newnham, in Gloucestershire. Her youngest daughter was 109 at the time. So says the German historian John Müller.
135. Harrison (*John*)	...	...	...	1744	
Lawler (*Margaret*)	...	...	...	1739	of Killevan, in Monaghan. A day or two before her death she walked 3 miles out and back again.

We are told that when Vespasian was emperor there were 45 persons in his empire of the age of 135.

136. Forster (*Margaret*)	...	..	...	1771	
Lafitte (*Jean*)	...	15 Dec.,	1766		he was called Liaroux. He died at Rouillac. He bathed always thrice a week.
Morriat (*John*)	...	...	...	1776	
Noon (*Catherine*)	...	...	...	1768	
Patter (*Margaret*)	...	...	...	1739	buried at St. Margaret's, Westminster; and a portrait of her is in St. Margaret's Workhouse.
Sheite (*James*)	...	...	...	1759	an Irish farmer.
136. Wunder (*George*)	...	12 Dec.,	1761		at Salzburg. Doctor Ufland of Prussia vouches for this fact.
137. Causeur (*Jean*)	...	10, July,	1775		at St. Mathieu, near Brest. He was a provision merchant. He drank little, but washed often. Born at Lanfeust.
Richardson (*John*)	..	...	...	1772	
Robertson (*John*)	...	...	...	1793	of Hopton Hall, near Edinburgh.
138. Clum (*Mrs.*)	...	...	...	1772	
Fairbrother (*John*)	...	...	...	1770	
M'Donough (*John*)	...	...	...	1768	
Sharpley (*William*)	...	...	...	1757	
A Pole	...	...	...	1803	who received an annual pension of 36 rix-dollars from the king of Prussia. He married for the first time at the age of 80, and two years afterwards his wife had twins.
139. Cameron (*Marie*)	...	...	...	1785	
Dobson (*Thomas*)	...	...	...	1766	
140. Desmond (*Catherine countess of*)				1752	Ireland.
Laland (*William*)	...	...	...	1752	
Polotiman	...	...	...	1825	surgeon, of Vaudemont, in Lorraine. He never left his native place, never took any sort of medicine, and never went to bed sober. The day before his death he performed with perfect success an operation on an old woman for cancer.
Ram (*Joseph*)	...	...	...	1808	a negro of Jamaica. He walked 4 miles a little before his death.
Sands (*James*)	...	...	...	1770	a Staffordshire farmer. His wife died at the age of 120, and the two lived out five leases of 21 years on the same farm.
Sury (*Rebecca*)	...	7 April,	1827		of Falmouth, in Jamaica, a negress. Testified by her master.
142. Iwarling	...	...	...	1773	a monk.
143. M'Findlay (*Charles*)	...	...	1773		
Hilario Pari	..	..	...	—	an Indian. Alex. de Humboldt conversed with him at Chiguata when he was 143 years old. His wife was 117. Up to the age of 130 Pari walked daily 4 miles.
144. Effingham (*John*)	...	...6 Feb.,	1757		of Cornwall. He was a teetotaller, rose every day at 6 A.M., and very rarely ate meat.
145. Williams (*Evan*)	...	...	...	1702	
A soldier	...	...	...	1803	died at Stazatmer, in Germany.

Age	Year of death	
146. Drahakemberg (*Christien James*)	1772	of Aarhuus, in Jutland. He was taken captive in his youth by corsairs, and was a sailor for 91 years. He never covered his head with hat or cap ; married a woman of 60 when he was 113 years of age ; and a little before his death walked 4 miles.

Mattathias died by misadventure at the age of 146, according to the Apocrypha.

Outegro (*Jean d'*)	1726	a day labourer of Galicia. He lived chiefly on Turkish wheat and cabbage ; and very rarely drank wine.
Winsloe (*Thomas*)	1766	
148. Mead (*William*) ...	1759	
149. *It is said that Antiochos Epiphanès king of Syria died at the age of 149.*		
150. Arganthonius	—	a Spaniard
Consir (*Francis*)	1768	of Burythorpe, Malton, in Yorkshire. From the age of 60 he was on the parish.
152. Bowles (*James*)	1656	of Killingworth, Warwickshire.
Newman (*Thomas*)	1542	
Parr (*Thomas*) ...	16 Dec., 1635	of Alberbury, in Shropshire. He was an agricultural labourer, and worked at his calling up to the age of 130, even as a thresher. At the age of 122 he married his second wife. His food was chiefly bread and cheese, and he drank milk. He was buried in Westminster Abbey. Old Parr lived in the reign of ten sovereigns.
West (*Henry*)	—	
154. Damme (*Thomas*)	1648	
155. Obst	1825	a villager of Zwronegoschutz, in Silesia. She worked in the fields to the day of her death. She was a large eater, and drank daily two glasses of brandy.
157. *Some say Epimenidès the Cretan poet died at the age of 157, B.C. 450.*		
160. Surrington (*Joseph*)	1797	of Bergen, in Norway. He left a son of 9 and one of 103 behind him.
168. Edwards (*William*)...	1668	
169. Jenkins (*Henry*)	1670	Ufland, Professor of Medicine in the University of Jena, searched into this, and tells us that Jenkins lived chiefly on charity, but sometimes went out to sea fishing.
172. Rowin (*John*)	1740	of Temeswar. His wife at his death was 164, and his youngest son was 90.
175. Tuisco	—	a German prince, mentioned by Tacitus.
179. Truxo (*Louisa*)	1785	a negress, who died at Tucuman, in South America.
185. Zorten (*Peter*)	1724	he was a vegetarian, and his portrait used to hang in the library of Prince Charles, Brussels. Claude Nicolas le Cat mentions him.
207. Carn (*Thomas*)	1588	according to the parish register of St. Leonard's, Shoreditch, he was born in the reign of Richard II., and died in the reign of Elizabeth.

These are the most noted of the Macrobiots. Some of the names are not worthy of credit, such as Rowin, whose wife was 164 ; Surrington, whose son was 103 ; Keit, whose youngest daughter was 109. However, the list is a long one, and it is well to have it handy.

** Of the antediluvian Macrobiots two solutions have been suggested : (1) that the years were not solar but lunar years ; thus in Ecclesiasticus (xliii. 6, 7,) we read : ' He [God] made the moon to serve in her season for a declaration of times, and from the moon is the sign of feasts.' It is also quite certain that six months is sometimes called a year ; but neither of these suggestions relieves the main difficulty. Another solution is this : the first date (Genesis, chap. v.) gives the age of the *sheik* himself, and the next the duration of his dynasty or race. Thus : Adam lived 100 years and he begat Seth. He died aged 100, but his dynasty continued altogether 930 years. Seth was also a sheik, who lived 105 years, but his race continued sheiks for 807 years. Enos lived 90 years, but his race continued 815 years ; and so on.

McWilliam (*A*). An Irish dress, the dress of an Irishman, significant of being thorough Irish, and therefore hating the English. In 1586 the Burkes said, 'they would have a McWilliam or else go to Spain'—*i.e.* they would assume the Irishman and throw off their English manners and allegiance, or else leave the country. In the 14th cent. the Burkes adopted the Irish dress and assumed the name of McWilliam.

Mad King of Lacedæmon (*The*). Cleomĕnês, who killed himself in a fit of madness, B.C. 494.

Mad Parliament (*The*). The parliament assembled at Oxford in 1258,

which provided three things : (1) The confirmation of Magna Charta ; (2) the virtual deposition of Henry III. ; and (3) the appointment of twenty-four councillors, with Simon de Montfort at the head, in whom the government of the nation was to be vested. *See* 'Chambre Introuvable,' ' Parliaments.'

This parliament ordered that three parliaments a year should in future be called in the months of Feb., June, and Oct. ; that a new sheriff should be annually chosen by the votes of the freeholders in each county ; that no English heirs shall be under the wardship of a foreigner ; that no new warrens or forests shall be created in the nation ; and that the revenues of no county shall be let to farm.

Mad Parson (*The*). Dean Swift, 1667—1783

Mad Priest of Kent (*The*). John Ball, a Wyclifite, executed in 1381. He was a leader in the 'peasant revolt,' and preached to the people the equality of man. 'If (said he) we be all come from Adam and Eve, how can our oppressors show they are better than we?' When Adam delved and Eve span, who was then the gentleman?'

Let Mr. Ball first tell us what is meant by 'better' before we answer. Abel was better than Cain in one sense.

Mad Queen (*The*). Juana, the wife and afterwards the widow of Philip of Flanders, generally called Philip the Fair of Austria. As she was queen of Castile and very rich, Henry VII. proposed to marry her in 1506, but this proposal was rejected, and Henry died in 1509.

The wife of Henry VII. died in Feb. 1503; therefore he was free to marry again.

Madame (without a name following) meant, in the reign of Louis XIV., the wife of Philippe duc d'Orléans, the king's brother (who was entitled *Monsieur*). The son of Philippe was entitled *Petit-fils de la France*, and their daughter *Mademoiselle.*

Amazing as the affectation may now appear, it is well known that in the reign of the Grand Monarque the title of *Madame* was limited to certain duly qualified bourgeoises, such as the wives of provosts, magistrates, sheriffs, and so on. Hence we read of the 'widow Mademoiselle Molière,' &c.

Madame l'Ange. Madame Du Barry, mistress of Louis XV., was so called from her extreme beauty. She succeeded Madame de Pompadour.

Madame la Duchesse (without a proper name) meant, in the reign of Louis XIV., the wife of Henri Jules de Bourbon, eldest son of the Prince de Condé. Mdme. la Duchesse was grand-child of the king by his natural daughter from La Vallière. Henri Jules de Bourbon was entitled *Monsieur le Duc.*

Madame la Princesse (without a proper name) meant, in the reign of Louis XIV., the wife of the Prince de Condé (a natural daughter of the king by La Vallière). The Prince de Condé was entitled *Monsieur le Prince.* Their eldest son was entitled *Monsieur le Duc,* and their eldest daughter *Madame la Duchesse.*

Madame Solidité. The pet name given by Louis XIV. to Madame de Maintenon (1635-1719).

Madame Veto. Marie Antoinette, wife of Louis XVI. (1755-1793). The constitution of 1791 accorded to the king of France the right of *veto*, but this veto was merely suspensive. Louis XVI. availed himself of this right from the 17 to the 29 Nov., and was nicknamed Monsieur Veto, his wife being Madame Veto.

Madame Veto avait promis
De faire égorger tout Paris;
Mais son coup a manqué,
Grâce à nos canonnié.
Revolutionary Song.

Madam Veto swore one day
All Parisians she would slay;
But the cannoneers of France,
Never gave her tl re .t the chance.

Madeleine (*La*), Paris. Napoleon I. in 1815 commenced this beautiful building over the spot where the body of Louis XVI. was buried. It was founded after the battle of Jena, and its name was to be the Temple of Glory. The Bourbons finished it, and called it 'The Madeleine.' It is a truly splendid shrine for a most ill-used body.

Louis XVI. was the 66th of the kings of France.

Madelonnettes (*Les*), 1618. A religious house in Paris in the Rue des Fontaines designed for repentant women, and founded by Robert de Montry. The direction of this penitentiary is under the Sœurs de la Visitation de St. Antoine. In the revolution it was turned into a political prison, and at the present day it is a house of detention for *les filles de mauvaise vie.*

Mademoiselle (without a proper name), the title of the eldest daughter of the king of France. Thus, in the reign of Louis XIII., the Duchesse de Montpensier, the eldest daughter of Gaston duc d'Orléans (the king's brother) was *Mademoiselle*; but in the reign of Louis XIV. she became *la grande Mademoiselle*, because the king's brother Philippe duc d'Orléans had a daughter who was *Mademoiselle.*

In the reign of Louis XIV. the king's son was *Monseigneur*; his brother (Philippe) was *Monsieur*, his wife *Madame*, and their daughter *Mademoiselle.*

Madman (*The*). Apollodōrus the Athenian painter, who was so irascible that he destroyed his own pictures upon the slightest provocation (died B.C. 440).

Shelley (in his preface to the translation of Plato's 'Symposium') says, 'To borrow an image from Italian painters, he [Apollodorus] seems to have been the St. John of the Socratic group,' in allusion to his impassioned and enthusiastic disposition.

Madman of the North (*The*). Carl XII. of Sweden (1682, 1697–1718). In 1700, with 8,000 men he overthrew 80,000 Russians at Narva, a success which made him madder than he was before.

Madonna Bianca. The Italian 'White Lady' (Rogers, 'Italy').

Madras College. *See* 'Andrews (*University of St.*).'

Madras System of Education (*The*), 1795. On the mutual instruction system. In 1807 Dr. Andrew Bell introduced his system among the poor in London. By this plan the more advanced pupils instruct the less advanced. The system was very popular for a time, and pupil teachers are still employed in our parish schools.

Madrid (*Treaty of*), 1526. Consequent on the battle of Pavïa in the year previous. By this treaty François agreed to renounce all claim to the duchy of Milan; to yield to the Emperor Karl V. Flanders, Artois, and Burgundy; to restore Bourbon to all his titles and possessions; and to send his two sons as hostages till these several conditions were fulfilled.

Mæcenas of France (*The*). François I. (1494, 1515–1547). Also called *Père des Lettres*, being a most munificent patron of literature and art.

Mænad (*A*). A bacchant. From the Greek μαίνομαι, to be mad or furious; because the gestures and shouts of these worshippers of Bacchus were like the ravings of mad women (pl. Mænădês).

Turning the current of her youth from the sweet modesty of maidenhood to the self-destroying violence of a Mænad.—E. LYNN LINTON, *Under which Lord?* chap. xxiii.

Magazine, 1731. The name first applied in England to a periodical ('The Gentleman's Magazine').

Magdalen College, Oxford, 1458. Founded by William Patten bishop of Winchester. The headmaster is called the president. [Pronounce *Maudlen.*]
William Patten is generally called William of Waynflete, from the place of his birth.

Magdalen Hall, Oxford, 1456. Founded as a preparatory school to the college, but in 1602 it became indepen-

dent, and in 1822 was removed to the seat of the former Hertford College. In 1874 Magdalen Hall was dissolved, and the college was incorporated, under the title of 'the Principal, Fellows, and Scholars of Hertford College,' in the University of Oxford.

Magdalene College, in Cambridge University. Founded by Thomas baron Audley of Walden in 1519. Familiarly called Maudlen.

Magdeburg Hemispheres (*The*), 1650. Two small brass cups (about two inches in diameter), each furnished with a brass handle. The two cups fit each other, and form a sphere. The object of this pneumatic toy is to show the pressure of air, for when the air has been pumped out of them two strong men cannot pull them asunder, but the moment air is admitted they can be parted without the slightest effort. Invented by Otto von Guericke of Magdeburg.

Maggy Lauder. This is a scurrilous song, in the time of the reformation, on the Catholic Church.

Magi of Cappadocia (*The*). These were accounted heretics by the Parsees. They worshipped in temples, and had many material symbols of their fire-god. They also offered up human victims. The high priest of the Cappadocian Magi wore a mitre. Unlike the Parsees, they bury their dead.
The Parsees neither burn nor bury their dead, but place them in circular towers where birds of prey may devour them.

Ma'gianism. The religious system of the Magi. The Magi believed in one god, or rather that the sky was all one god. No temples were built to this god, but those who wished to worship him went to the top of a mountain and prostrated themselves. The seven planets were supposed to be his seven chief ministers. At death the soul had to pass through seven gates before it reached the heaven of heavens. Brotherly love was a moral law of the Magi, and so was tenderness to dumb animals. Zoroaster reformed Magianism (B.C. 589–513).

Mag'ans (*The*), or 'Magi.' Part of the old Persian empire. Herodotus calls them 'one of the six Median tribes.' 'The Wise Men of the East' spoken of in St Matthew's Gospel were Magians.

Simon who deceived the people of Samaria (Acts viii.) and Elymas the sorcerer were both Magians. As a religious order they were organised by Zoroaster, who divided them into (1) learners, (2) masters, and (3) perfect scholars. They had three methods of divination, (1) by calling up the dead, (2) by cups and dishes, and (3) by water. Their learning was so great, and their 'tricks' so wonderful, that *magic* or Magianism became a synonym of sorcery.

Magician of the North (*The*). So Hamann (1730-1788) called himself. He was a Prussian philosopher who defended revelation against the attacks of the Rationalists.

Magister ad Faculta'tes (4 syl.). The chief officer of the Court of Faculties (*q.v.*).

Magister Glomeriæ. A non-academic functionary in the University of Cambridge, the superintendent of the masters of grammar, of which there were a dozen or more attached to different schools where youths were taught the elements of the Latin language. These schools were nurseries for the university. Glomeria, a corruption of *Gramery*, skill in grammar.

There were probably a dozen or more separate schools, each presided over by a master of grammar, while the *Magister Glomeriæ* represented the supreme authority.—MULLINGER, *University of Cambridge*, 1873, pp. 139, 340.

Magna Charta, 15 June, 1215. Based on the laws of Henry I., which embraced those of Edward the Confessor and the 'ancient customs of England,' derived mainly from the free institutions of the Saxons and Danes. Drawn up at Edmundsbury by Stephen Langton (archbishop of Canterbury) and the barons or free tenants of the king, 20 Nov., 1214, and signed by King John at Runnymede in the seventeenth year of his reign. It contains sixty-one clauses. Twenty-five of the barons were elected to see it carried out, and if any article was infringed four of the number were to lodge a complaint; and if immediate redress was not granted, the twenty-five barons were empowered to take possession of the royal castles till redress was fully obtained. A copy of the charter was sent to every cathedral. The facsimile engraved by the Board of Commissions on the public records was from the copy in Lincoln Cathedral, sup-

posed to be the most accurate. The following clauses will show the nature of the charter :—

The English *Church* is to enjoy all its rights and liberties, and all elections to benefices are to be free.

General Provisions :—
All towns to enjoy their charters.
All forests afforested in the present reign [*i.e.* John's] to be disafforested.
No officer of the crown to take corn, timber, or other goods without payment, or to borrow any man's horse or cart without the owner's consent.
No scutage to be exacted except by order of the national council.
Assizes to be held by justices in eyre four times a year, and the Court of Common Pleas to be fixed at Westminster.
No man to be condemned on suspicion, but only after a fair trial on the evidence of witnesses.
No freeman to be outlawed, except according to law.
All men to have equal justice.
Guardians to keep up the estate of their respective wards, and to deliver it over well stocked and provided.
Chattels to be seized for debt before lands or rents.
If a minor has borrowed money, and dies before he comes of age, only the principal (without interest) shall be paid to the lender.
All weights and measures in the realm shall be uniform.

Personal Provisions :—
No one to be distrained to perform more service to his lord than is due.
No vil or person but those bound to do so to be distrained for making bridges, &c.
No lord, except to ransom his person, shall levy aid on his freemen, either under pretence of making his heir a knight, or of dowering his eldest daughter at marriage.
Foreign merchants to be free to trade in the land, and all natives to go and come as they choose.
Widows to remain widows if they like, but if they marry they must give legal notice of their intention.
Every man to be at liberty to bequeath his personal property as he likes, but his real estates to descend to his widow and children.

The Four new Clauses added by Edward I., 5 Nov., 1297 :—
1. No taxes to be levied without consent of parliament.
2. No provisions to be taken for the king's service without the owner's consent.
3. No levy, under the name of custom, to be levied on wool.
4. All liberties, laws, and customs hitherto enjoyed to remain in force.
See also the 'Dictum of Kenilworth,' 15 Oct., 1266.

Magna Charta of Hungary. *See* 'Golden Bull of Hungary.'

Magna Charta of Manx (*The*), 1704. The Act of Settlement is so called. By this act the purchaser of a farm or other real property is allowed to sell, alienate, or devise his estate ; and as soon as it passes into the new hands, the former possessor loses all rights therein for ever. The land not revertable, as it was among the Jews in the year of jubilee.

Magna Charta of Ottoman Liberty (*The*), or Imperial Edict of

Gulhaneh, granted by Abdul Medjid sultan of Turkey (1823, 1839–1861). This edict equalised taxation and regulated the administration of justice in Turkey.

Magna Charta of Turkey (*The*),
21 Feb., 1856. A firman granted by the Sultan after the Crimean war. It confirmed to Christians in the sultanate full civil and religious liberty; it abolished all class distinctions, leaving every office open to every subject irrespective of birth, race, religion, or language ; all subjects admissible to the civil or military schools; flogging and torture made penal; all classes to pay their proper ratio of taxes according to a money scale; the items of national expenditure to be published; a council of delegates to meet annually; all subjects to have an equal right of holding land ; trade to be free.

Magna Charta of the Gallican Church (*The*), 1438. The Pragmatic
Sanction of Bourges enacted by Charles VII. It declared a general council of superior authority to the pope ; it freed all elections to church preferments from the control of the pope; it abolished mandats and first-fruits; and, in fact, did for France what the Constitutions of Clarendon had done for England ; that is, reserved the ecclesiastical preferments of the nation to natives, and prevented the *imperium in imperio* or collision of Italian interests with those of the kings and his subjects.

Magna Charta of the Protestants of Ireland (*The*), 1662.
The Act of Settlement and the Act of Explanation. The two together form the tenure under which most of the land of Ireland is held. The act was framed by the Duke of Ormond, lord-lieutenant of Ireland, to confirm Protestants in the estates confiscated from Irish Catholics after the ' Great Rebellion.'

By the Act of Explanation some few alterations were made in the most obnoxious of the clauses of the Act of Settlement (*q.v.*). Before the outbreak of the civil war the estates of Ormond brought him in an income of 7,000*l.* a year. After the Magna Charta they brought him in an income of 80,000*l.* a year.

Magna Græcia. Modern Calabria.

Magnanimous (*The*). Philippe
II. *Auguste* of France (1165, 1180–1223). Called ' Auguste' because he was born in the month of August (21st of the month).

Magnum Decreto'rum, seu Canonum, Volumen. A famous col-
lection of canons by Burchard bishop of Worms, a Benedictine, who died 1027 at the age of 72.

Magnus Saga (*The*). The history
and miracles of Earl Magnus, patron saint of Kirkwall Cathedral. It was printed for the Master of the Rolls in 1887, with other Sagas. It is in Icelandic and not translated.

Mag'ophon'ia, B.C. 522. An annual
ceremony observed by the Magi in remembrance of the massacre of their tribe by Darius Hystaspes, because a pretender usurped the throne of Persia while Cambyses was absent in Egypt. Cambyses heard of the plot, but died on his way back, and Darius, his successor, made a general massacre of the Magi. During the Magophonia no Magian appeared in public.

Magyarised (pron. *Mard'-yer-ised*),
1830. Made to use the language of the Magyars [*Mard-yers*] or native Hungarians, instead of the Latin tongue as hitherto. The Croats and Sclaves said *Nolumus Magyarizari* when the Hungarian diet proposed this change.

Mahabad'ian Dynasty (*The*).
An antediluvian and fabulous Persian dynasty, so called from Mah'ab'ad, said to be the first king that ever reigned. He divided the people into four classes, viz. the religious, the military, the commercial, and the servile.

According to Sir W. Jones, this dynasty was established ages before the accession of Cayumers or Kayomurz, great-grandson of Noah, some nine centuries B.C. The Pishdadian dynasty (*q.v.*) is called the first Persian dynasty by those who fear to extend the chronology of history much above 2,000 years B.C. The Mah-abad-ian dynasty was followed by the Jy-anian or Holy Dynasty. Of course Mah-abad means Great King. All the fourteen hypothetical kings of this dynasty are called Abad, and all were said to be prophets.

Mah'di (*The*). Supreme pontiff of
the Shiites. Only twelve of these imams have really appeared, viz. Ali, Hassan, Hosein, and the nine lineal descendants of Hosein. Mahommed, the last Mah'di, we are told, is not really dead, but sleeps in a cavern near Bagdad, and will return to active life before the Judgment-day to overthrow Dejal or Antichrist. In the royal stables of Persia two horses are always kept saddled, in readiness for the Mah'di and his

lieutenant Jesus the son of Mary. The Sunnites or 'orthodox' Moslems called the sultan the true imam [*e-maum'*].

Mahomed Achmet or Mohammed Ahmed of Dongōla was born about 1840. He was a carpenter, and became Mahdi in 1888. The Mahdi of the Soudan in 1881 was only a 'false prophet,' who pretended to be the sleeping imam come back to active life to overthrow the enemies of the faith and restore all things. Mahdi means the *guided one*.

** It must be remembered that the *Sunnites* are the 'orthodox' Moslems, and the Sultan of Turkey is the calif or head thereof. The Shiites are the Persian Moslems, hated by the orthodox party. The Mahdi and his party which are now (1890) disturbing Egypt are hated by the official Egyptians, who are Sunnites (2 syl.) like the Turks. Latterly even the Sunnites have been expecting a Mahdi, who is to stamp out 'the infidels.' In fact, the expectation is almost universal among Moslems.

Mahometanism. The belief that Mahomet was a prophet sent by God, and that the Koran is a revelation made to him by Gabriel in the cave Hoiâ. Mahomet or Mohammed lived 571–631.

Of course Mahometans are deists. The sultan is the calif of the orthodox Moslems or *Sunnites* (2 syl.), and the Mahdi is the head of the unorthodox Moslems or Shiites (2 syl.). The Turks and Egyptians are *Sunnites* (or 'orthodox'), the Persians and some Indians are *Shiites* (2 syl.) or heterodox Moslems.

Mahon's Act. *See* 'Lord Mahon's Act.'

Mahratta War (*The*), 1804–1818. The British declared war against Holkar 16 April, 1804 ; won the battle of Deig 13 Nov., 1804 ; of Bhurtpoor 2 April, 1805 ; of Mehudpoor 21 Dec.; and concluded peace with Holkar 6 Jan., 1818.

Mai (*A*), or 'Arbre de Mai.' A tree, bush, or branch planted before a house on May-day by those who wish to pay a compliment to the inmates thereof. In some villages of France the custom still lingers, and sometimes the 'tree' is decorated with ribbons and flowers. The *clercs de la basoche* used always to plant and dress such a tree every May-day in the *grand cour du Palais*. In the revolution trees of liberty were called *Maïs*.

Meanwhile the 20th June is nigh, anniversary of that world-famous oath of the Tennis-court, on which day certain citizens have in view to plant a *Mai* or Tree of Liberty on the Tuileries Terrace of the Feuillants.—CARLYLE, *French Revolution*, vol. ii. book v. 12.

Mai'atæ (*The*). An ancient Scottish tribe.

The Caledonians and Maiatæ, resuming courage, took up arms to recover the possessions they had lost. The enraged emperor (Sevērus), commanded his army to march into their country and to destroy it with fire and sword.—*Æra of Ossian.*

Maid (*The*). Joan of Arc (1412–1431). Also called 'The Holy Maid.' In French 'La Pucelle.'

Maid of Brittany (*The*). Eleanor sister of Prince Arthur, and niece of Richard Cœur-de-Lion.

Maid of Kent (*The*). Joan Bocher, who maintained that Jesus Christ was not truly incarnate of the Virgin Mary, or he would have been born in sin. For this opinion Cranmer condemned her to be burnt to death, but Edward VI. absolutely refused to sign the warrant for her execution. Cranmer insisted, and the young king reluctantly gave way. She was martyred in 1549.

Some time after a Dutchman was burnt to death by Cranmer for holding incorrect views of the divinity of Christ.

Maid of Norway (*The*). Margaret daughter of Eric and Margaret of Norway, and grandchild of Alexander III. of Scotland. At the death of her grandfather she was the acknowledged queen of Scotland, and had been betrothed to Edward, son and heir of Edward I. king of England. Margaret died on her passage from Norway, and consequently was neither wedded nor crowned. At her death thirteen claimants to the crown arose, but John Balliol was ultimately elected as the king.

The claim was really between Robert Bruce and John Balliol, and according to English law that of Balliol was undoubtedly the superior. He was great-grandson of David earl of Huntingdon by Margaret, the *elder* daughter ; whereas Bruce was the son of David's younger daughter Isabella. It was the grandson of this Bruce who was the great Scotch hero.

Maid of Orléans (*The*). ' La Pucelle d'Orléans.' Joan of Arc [*Jeanne d'Arc*], born at Domrémy 1412. According to one account she was burnt as a witch at Rouen 30 May, 1431. According to M. Octave Delepierre she was married to Robert des Armoises in 1438, and died in 1444. Called the Maid of Orléans because she compelled the English to raise the siege of Orléans.

In regard to the burning of Jeanne d'Arc it must be remembered that the French had every motive to represent the English in France in the blackest colours. So Richard III. was represented as deformed in body and mind to flatter Elizabeth.

** M. Delepierre cites a document discovered in the archives of Metz by Father Vignier in the 17th cent. in proof of the marriage of Robert sieur des Armoises with Jeanne d'Arcy, surnamed the Maid of Orléans.

Maids of the Cross, 1265. A community of young women who made vows of poverty, chastity, and obedience.

Maiden (*The*). A rude sort of guillotine, introduced into Scotland from Halifax by Morton the regent. Morton himself was beheaded by this machine as an accessory to the murder of Henry Darnley, husband of Mary queen of Scots (1566–1681).

Maiden Castle (*The*). Edinburgh or Dunedin.

In the engagement which ensued at Camelon (now Abernethy) in Perthshire, Druskenus the Pictish king was slain with the flower of his nobility. His chief fortress, the Maiden Castle, now that of Edinburgh, surrendered, and the main body of the Pictish people fled beyond sea (A.D. 824).—PRINCE, *Parallel History*, vol. i. p. 401.

Maiden Violin (*The*). A Stradivārius (1709) called *La Pucelle*. It was exhibited at the South Kensington Exhibition in 1872 among 'antique musical instruments.'

Maillotins (*Les*), 1382. Insurgents of Paris to resist the new tax on bread levied by the Duc d'Anjou, regent of France in the minority of Charles VI. So called because they armed themselves with *maillets de fer* when they attacked the arsenal, put to death the officers, and set at large the prisoners. After the battle of Rosebecque, the same year, this sedition was put down. *See* 'French Brigands.'

Pronounce *Lay May-o-tah'n.*

Mails. Mail coaches began to run 8 Aug., 1784; but 14 Aug., 1838 provision was made for the conveyance of mails, &c. by railways (2 Vict. c. 98).

Main Conspiracy (*The*), 1603. Set on foot by Sir Walter Raleigh out of hatred to Lord Cecil, the chief minister of James I. The object was to depose Cecil, and induce James to ally himself with Spain instead of with France. Sir Walter Raleigh, with Lord Cobham and Lord Grey, were brought to trial and condemned to death, but they were all reprieved. It was called the 'Main' conspiracy because it was simultaneous with another conspiracy called the 'Bye' (*q.v.*). Sir Walter Raleigh, Grey, and Cobham were charged with participation in the 'Bye,' but they utterly denied that they ever contemplated the elevation of Arabella Stuart to the throne and the deposition of James. *See* 'Bye Plot.'

Grey, after his reprieve, was kept in the Tower eleven years, Cobham was sent back to prison, and Raleigh was sent back for twelve years.

24

Maine (U.S. America). Said to have been so called from Maine, in France (1638), of which Henrietta Maria, wife of Charles I., was the proprietor. The inhabitants are nicknamed *Foxes*.

Maine Law (*The*), 1846. United States of N. America. The prohibition of the sale of intoxicating liquors in Maine. The original law was made more stringent in 1851, and is still in force as then amended.

Maintainers. Bands of banditti in the reign of Richard II. who subsisted or maintained themselves by robbery. They assembled in great bands, seized people for their ransoms, and carried off the daughters of men of property. They abounded in Cheshire and Lancashire in about 1380.

Maintenance. I. In *History*. The association of numbers of persons under some chief, whose badge or livery they wore, and to whom they were bound by oath to support him in his private quarrels against all other noblemen. Henry VII., after the conspiracy of Simnel (1487), insisted that the law against maintenance should be rigorously enforced.

II. In *Law*. Intermeddling in suits of law, prohibited in 1540 (32 Hen. VIII. c. 9).

Intermeddling by assisting either party with money, or otherwise, to prosecute or defend a suit. If such intermeddling is to assist another to obtain or retain land it is called *Rurālis*; if it is to assist a suit in any law-court it is called *Curiālis*.

Maires du Palais. 'Majóres domus,' officers of the crown who had at one time charge of the administration of the privy purse of the king and the general government of the palace. Subsequently they became a very great political power. From 575 Gogon maire of Austrasia was charged with the government of the country. In 614 Warnachaire maire of Burgundy compelled Clotaire II. to grant that the maires should no longer be nominated by the crown at pleasure, but by the great vassals for life. From 677 there were no longer any kings in Austrasia, but the maires under the title of dukes or princes of France reigned supreme. After the triumph of Pépin d'Héristal over the Neustrians, at Testry, in 687, the maires became hereditary. And in 752 Pépin le Bref deposed Childéric III., and proclaimed himself king of the whole kingdom, with the sanction of Pope Zacha-rias I. The office was abolished by Hugues Capet [*U Cap-pay*].

Maison de Dieu means a mon-astic hospital or almshouse. The second league of the Grisons was called La Ligue de la Maison de Dieu or La Ligue Caddée, 1401.

Maitland Prize (*The*). For an essay connected with the propagation of the gospel in India. Given once in three years to graduates of not more than ten years' standing. Value about 80*l*. Founded by the friends of Sir Peregrine Maitland, commander of the forces in South India, 1844.

Majesty, as a royal title, was as-sumed in England in 1527 by Henry VIII., and in France in 1559 by Henri II. Be-fore then the king or queen was addressed as 'Your Grace' or 'Your Highness.' Louis XI. and his successors were styled ' Most Christian Majesty' by a papal bull.

Ferdinand and Isabella of *Spain* were entitled by Pope Alexander VI., in 1491, ' Most Catholic Majesty.'

The King of *Portugal* is entitled his ' Most Faithful Majesty,' a style of ad-dress bestowed by Benedict XIV., in 1748.

Stephen duke of *Hungary* and Maria Theresa were styled 'Apostolic Majesty.'

The Emperor of *Austria* is now styled ' His Imperial Royal Majesty' ('K. K. Majestat,' *i.e. Kaiserliche. Königliche*).

The Sultan of *Turkey* is still ' Your Highness.'

Henry IV. addressed as Your ' Grace.'
Henry VI.   „   „   Your ' Excellent Grace.'
Edward IV. „   „   ' High and Mighty Prince.'
Henry VII. „   „   Your ' Grace ' or ' High-ness.'
Henry VIII. „   „   Your ' Highness' till 1527.
The Stuarts „   „   Your ' Most Sacred Ma-jesty.'

Majorats [*Mah-zjo-rah*], 1806. En-tail of property created by Napoleon. A majorat was annexed to the title of nobi-lity and passed with it to the next heir.

Major's or **Major Oak** (*The*), in Birkland. A part of Sherwood Forest near Edwinstowe in the possession of the Earl Manvers. So called from Major Rooke the antiquary. It was formerly called the ' Cock-pen Tree' (*q.v.*). An effort has been made by Lady Manvers to call it the ' Queen Oak,' but it is called generally ' The Major Oak' still. Its branches cover a space of 240 feet in cir-cumference. It has an opening into its

hollow trunk through which a man can pass and fifteen persons can be packed inside the trunk.

Inside the trunk are the letters J. R., and it is a fond belief of some that they stand for John Rex.

Mal de Siam, or 'La Maladie de Siam.' The yellow fever was so called when from 1694 to 1705 it desolated the Antilles (2 syl.).

Maladie Diplomatique (*La*). A feigned or exaggerated illness from motives of policy—as when a member of the existing cabinet is invited to address a public meeting on a subject which the cabinet does not wish to be ventilated, he sends word that he is bidden by his medical advisers to eschew speaking for the present.

Malakoff (*The*). Malakoff was the name of a man who once kept a tavern on the memorable spot which bears his name. He was a purser in the Russian navy, but, being kicked out of the service for drunkenness, swindling, and smug-gling, he started a drinkshop outside Sebastopol. As he sold drink cheaper than other men, his place was greatly fre-quented by Russian sailors, and, after a while, the stony hill where his shebeen stood became the Malakoff Redoubt.

Mal'andrins (*The*), or ' The Grand Companies,' a band of 40,000 adventurers who, towards the end of the 14th cent., pillaged Altkirch and other parts of Alsatia. The English word is ' Mallen-ders ' ('Acta Sanctorum,' Life of St. Morandus).

Malcontents (*The*), or ' Politiques ' of French history in the reigns of Charles IX. and Henri III., when the nation was divided into Catholics, Protestants, and a third party called Malcontents who were in accord with neither of the other two. They advocated mutual tolerance, and tried to find means of uniting the two communions. On the death of Henri III. they sided with Henri IV. against Philip II., a claimant of the throne of France.

The chief of the Malcontents were François d'Alençon (the king's brother), the King of Navarre (afterwards Henri IV.), the Prince de Condé, and the Montmorencys.

Malefammi (*The Baron*). Corso Donäti was so nicknamed.

The Baron Malefammi, or Do-me-harm, was Corso's nickname among the populace.—MRS. OLIPHANT, *Makers of Florence*, p. 37.

Malherbe's Canons, *i.e.* of French poetry. (1) Every word employed must be French; (2) a word ending with a vowel must be followed by a consonant; (3) no one line may run into another; (4) the rhymes must be alternately male and female; and the cæsura of every line must be rigidly maintained.

Malignants. In English history a royalist, or adherent of Charles I., so called by the Roundheads or opponents of the king.

Cromwell retorted on them [the Scotch] that, though they pretended to covenant and fight against malignants, they had entered into agreement with the head and centre of the malignants himself [Charles II.].—HOWITT, *Hist. of England* (Commonwealth, p. 817).

Malignity. The political tenets of the malignants or cavaliers in the time of Charles I. and II. Namely, the divine right of kings, the supremacy of royal prerogatives, the obligation of passive obedience, and the sinfulness of treason.

Malleteers, 1381. *See* Maillotins.

No doubt the terrors of the democrats of Flanders now again in full action, of the horrible Jacquerie and the ruthless Malleteers, at this time paralysing Paris, were present to the minds of the royal party.—HOWITT, *Hist. of England* (vol. i. p. 412).

Malleus Ariano'rum. St. Hilary, bishop of Poitiers from 350 to 367.

Mal'leus Hæretico'rum. I. Pierre d'Ailly; in Latin *Petrus de Alliaco* (1350–1425).

II. John Faber (1470–1541), so called from the title of one of his works.

St. Augustine is called by Hakewell 'that renowned pillar of truth and hammer of heresies' (395-430).

Malleus Scoto'rum. Edward I. On his tomb in Westminster Abbey is the inscription: *Edwardus longus Scotorum malleus hic est.*

Malt Silver. A payment of money instead of malt by the tenant farmer (14th cent.).

Malta (*Knights of*), 1523. *See* 'John of Jerusalem.'

Malthu'sianism. The doctrine of the Rev. Thomas Robert Malthus: That as population rapidly increases, but land is a fixed quantity, the time must come when the population will outgrow the means of food supply, and therefore government should make laws to restrict marriages and check the increase of man (1766–1834).

Mam'ertine Prison (*The*). So called from Mamers, the Oscan god of war. It was constructed of unhewn stone, underground, and had no door. It consisted of two chambers, the lower one 27 ft. by 20 ft. and 14 ft. high; the upper one 20 ft. by 10 ft. and 7 ft. high. The lower one was entered by a small hole in the ceiling, and the other one by a similar hole in the roof. Here Jugurtha was confined, and perished with cold and hunger; and here, according to church chroniclers, both Peter and Paul were confined, A.D. 68, the last year of the reign of Nero.

The *Tulliānum*, in which Catiline was confined and put to death, was probably the lower dungeon of the Carcer Mam'ertīnus.

Mam'ertines (3 syl.) A sort of free-lances or condottieri about 300 years B.C. These sons of Mamers or Mars were Campanian adventurers of Samnite origin, who took military service with any government which would pay them.

Man in the Iron Mask (*The*), 'Masque de Fer.' A state prisoner who went by the name of L'Estang. In 1662 he was confined in the Château Pignerol. In 1686 he was removed to the Ile Saint Marguerite, and in 1698 to the Bastille, where he died in 1703. So that he was a state prisoner above 40 years. He was buried under the name of Marchiali.

Voltaire says he was a twin brother of Louis XIV.; some think he was the Comte de Vermandois, a natural son of Louis XIV. and Mdlle. de la Vallière, who was thus punished for boxing the ears of the dauphin; others think he was the Duke of Beaufort, who disappeared in 1669 at the siege of Candia; or the Duke of Monmouth, nephew of James II.; or the Count Girolamo Matthioli, minister of the Duke of Mantua, who overreached Louis in a treaty for the purchase of Casal; or John of Gonzaque, Matthioli's secretary; or an adulterous son of Anne of Austria (the king's mother) either by the Duke of Buckingham or the Cardinal Mazarin.

Man of Blood (*The*). Charles I was so called by the puritans because he made war on his parliament. The allusion is to 2 Sam. xvi. 7.

Prince Bismarck of Prussia, born 1815, is sometimes called the 'Man of Blood and Iron.'

Man of Chios (*The*).   Homer. Chios [Ki-oss] was one of the seven cities which claimed to be the place of his birth (10th cent. B.C.).

Smyrna, Rhodos, Colophon, Salamis, Chios, Argos, Athenê.—VARRO.

Man of December (*The*).   Napoleon III.   So called because he was made president 11 Dec., 1848 ; he made his *coup d'état* 2 Dec., 1851 ; and he was made emperor 2 Dec., 1852.

Man of Destiny (*The*).   Napoleon I., who looked on himself as an instrument in the hands of destiny, and that all his acts were predestined.

The Man of Destiny . . . had power for a time to bind kings with chains, and nobles with fetters of iron.—Sir W. SCOTT.

Man of Ghent (*The*).   M. Guizot, who joined Louis XVIII. at Ghent in May 1815.   This was looked on by the Liberals as political treason, and called forth much controversy.

John of Gaunt was John of Ghent. The pronunciation is nearly *Gahn'*.

Man of Ross (*The*).   John Kyrle, of Ross, in Herefordshire, noted for his benevolence and public spirit (1637–1754).

Man of Sedan' (*The*).   Napoleon III. who, after his defeat at Sedan, 2 Sept., 1870, surrendered his sword to William king of Prussia, and was sent to Wilhelmshohe.

Also called ' The Man of Silence,' and 'The Man of December.'   No man was honoured with more nicknames than Napoleon III.

Man of Sedition (*The*).   So Madame de Maintenon called Jean Claude, the last of the eminent pastors of Charenton, who was born in 1619.   At the Revocation he was ordered to leave France within twenty-four hours.

Man of Silence (*The*).   Napoleon III. (born 1808, reigned 1852–1870, died at Chislehurst 1873).

France?   You must know better than I your position with the Man of Silence.—*For Sceptre and Crown*, chap. i.

Man of the People (*The*).   Charles James Fox, the Whig statesman (1705–1774).

Man without a Skin (*The*).   Richard Cumberland   (1732–1811)   so

called by Garrick from his irritable temper and dread of criticism.   Sheridan satirised him as ' Sir Fretful Plagiary.'

Manchester (*The American*).   Lowell, in Massachusetts, is so called from its numerous cotton-mills.

Manchester Martyrs (*The*).   An utterly absurd political term applied to a man named Larkin a tailor, Allen, and O'Brien, who murdered a policeman, named Brett, and after trial were duly hanged, 22 Nov., 1867.   It was the Irish Fenians who canonised these three felons.

Manchester Massacre (*The*), 16 Aug., 1819.   A most extravagant phrase to express the injuries received by the crowd which met in St. Peter's Field, Manchester, in defiance of the magistrate's orders, to hear ' Orator ' Hunt, on parliamentary reform.   About 80,000 persons assembled, and the military was sent to disperse them.   They used the flat of their swords, but about 100 persons were injured, either being knocked down in their flight or cut accidentally. It is said that six persons died or were killed—a very small number indeed in such a stampede.   *See* 'Peterloo.'

Hunt was arrested, tried, and imprisoned for three years. After his liberation he started in the blacking trade.   Hunt wore a white beaver hat, and his admirers followed the fashion.

Manchester Regiment (*The*), 1745.   A miserable squad which joined Charles Edward in his halt at Manchester.   ' The mere scum and ragamuffinism of the place.'   The Duke of Perth said of them ' If the devil would offer a shilling more than the prince, they would desert at once.'

Manchester of Austria (*The*). Brünn.

Manchester of Belgium (*The*). Ghent.

Manchester of France (*The*). Rouen.   It is said to have contained 200,000 inhabitants when it was besieged by Henry V. in 1418.   It does not now contain above 89,000.

Manchester of Negroland (*The*).   Kano, which exports annually 1,500 camel-loads of blue cotton cloth.

Manchester of Prussia (*The*). Elberfeld in Westphalia, one of the greatest centres of industry in all Germany. Velvets, lace, silk fabrics, ribbons, bed-ticking, cotton-goods, &c., are here manufactured in large quantities. Krupp's enormous works are at Essen.

Manchü Dynasty (*The*). The 22nd imperial dynasty of China, also called Tae-tsing. Began to reign 1644, deposing the Ming sovereign (Tsang-ching), and placing Shun-chi on the Chinese throne, with Peking for the capital. This dynasty still rules.

Mandarins. From the Latin *man-dāre*, to command ; a Portuguese word given in Europe to the governors of provinces in China and chief magistrates. The Chinese call them *ko-hans.* There are civil mandarins and military mandarins.

Man'dates (2 syl.) or ' Expectatives.' Letters of request from the pope praying that the benefices named in the letters may be conferred on the persons nominated therein.

Mandats, 1796. A sort of paper money issued by the French Directory for the redemption of their 'Assignats,' *q.v.* An assignat of the nominal value of 300 francs could be redeemed for a mandat of the value of 100 francs. A mandat, like an assignat, was a ' promise to pay ' in land, with this difference : an assignat was a *promise* to pay, but a mandat enabled the holder to take possession at once of public lands to the value of his mandat or mandats. As these mandats soon fell to a seventieth part of their nominal value, but might be given to government in payment of taxes, they were called in. They were called ' Mandats Territoriaux.'

Mandrites (2 syl.) or Hegumĕni. Superiors of convents in the Greek Church. General abbots are archimandrites.

Manichæans (*The*), 3rd cent. Followers of Manès or Mani (215–276), who gave himself out to be the Paraclete or Comforter that Christ promised to send ; and maintained there were two souls or spirits in man, one good and the other bad. He taught that the soul at death went first to the moon, then to the sun, and then to God. His creed was a mixture of the Persian Parseeism and Chris-

tianity. The Manichæans took for food neither eggs, cheese, milk, nor wine. Mani was put to death by Varanês or Baharam.

In fact Manes or Mani tried to weld together the doctrines of Zoroaster, the metempsychosis of the Hindûs, and the tenets of Christianity. He was put to death by Baharam I., called by the Greeks Varanês. Manichæism is also called dualism. A vast number of sects which believe in the two principles, one good and one evil, are called Manichæans.

Manifestation (*The Writ of*). The *Habeas Corpus* writ of Aragon (13th cent.), which provided that no person should be secretly incarcerated, as in France, nor smuggled out of the way, but that the body of every prisoner should be 'manifested' and publicly detained, till brought to trial publicly in a court free to all.

Man'ikin (*The*). The man so mercilessly satirised by ' Junius,' under the name of *Manikin* and *Grildig*, was Welbore Ellis, ' a pigmy in mind and body' who succeeded George Germaine, in 1782, in Lord North's ministry.

Man-rent (Scotch history). A bond between chief and vassal, in which the lord stipulated to give protection, and the vassal agreed to give personal service and fidelity.

The lords Sanquhar, Drumlanrigg, and others, finding him [Maxwell] thus indifferent, proposed to him that they should agree to grant him bonds of man-rent, and engage to follow him in his quarrels, provided he would effectually protect them by discharging his duty as warden.—Sir W. SCOTT, *History of Scotland*, xxxviii.

Mansard Ornament (*The*). Stone fretted like coral. So called from François Mansard, the French architect (1598–1666).

Mansard Roof (*The*). The roof broken into an elbow on each side, like the Tuileries, and not thus Λ.

Mansfield College, Oxford 1889. The first Nonconformist college at Oxford; for the education of young men for the Presbyterian ministry.

Manx Bible (*The*). Translated by Dr. John Kelly in 1772.

Map of Religion. A Christian society has published a map divided into squares, and the squares coloured differently so as to catch the eye. It calculates the present number of the earth's inhabitants at 1,500 millions. The heathen are represented by *black* squares, Christians by *white* ones, and each square represents a million people. Of the 1,500 squares, only one and less than a quarter [=1,200,000] represents the entire Protestant community, including all its multitudinous 'sects' (1890).

Mar'abuts (*The*). A corruption of marbûth (a Cenobite), of the Musulman faith. They still exercise spiritual power in Barbary and Guinea, in some parts of which 'The Great Marabût' ranks next to the king.

Marais (*The Marsh*), 1794. So the 'Plain,' or floor of the Convention, occupied by the Moderate party, was called in the 'Reign of Terror,' and its occupants were nicknamed *Grenouilles* and *Crapauds*, or frogs and toads. The Red Republicans occupied the elevated seats, and were called the Mountain party (*Montagnards*); the Girondists sat on the right hand of the ministerial benches.

Pronounce *Mah'ray*, *Gruh-noo'-yee*, *Kra'-po*.

Mar'athon of Switzerland (*The*). The battle of Morgarten, 1315, in which a few Swiss utterly discomfited their Austrian assailants, and confirmed the independence of the three cantons of Schwytz, Uri, and Unterwalden.

Marave'di (*The*). *See* 'Almoravides' (4 syl.).

Marbach (*The League of*), 1404. Formed by the electors of Mentz and Saxony, the duke of Bavaria, and the markgraf of Meissen, against the kaiser Rupert. Later on the king of France and the king of Poland joined the league.

Marcel's Revolt. French history, 1357-1358. When Jean was in captivity, his son Charles acted as regent, and wanting money convoked a States-General. Etienne Marcel, the city provost, said supplies should be granted if the regent promised to use them only for state purposes, and neither gave office nor pardoned crime for money. The regent made the promise, but refused to fulfil the conditions as soon as he received the subsidy. Civil war was the consequence, and the partisans of Marcel wore as their badge a chaperon or hood half red and half green. The revolters seized the regent, who escaped

injury by adopting the provost's badge. No sooner, however, did he feel himself free than he collected an army together to avenge himself on the provost. Marcel proclaimed the king of Navarre 'king of France,' and when the regent, at the head of an army, came to the city gates and promised to come to terms, Marcel went to open the gates, and was treacherously struck dead with a battle-axe by one of the regent's immediate suite. This ended the revolt; and the dauphin, entering the city on horseback, signalised his victory by a host of executions.

Marcellus of Spain (*The*). John son of Ferdinand and Isabella.

March and June Bills. Exchequer bills were so called till 1861, because they were payable, together with principal, in March and June; but in 1861 the method of payment was changed, interest being calculated half-yearly, and paid on March bills on 10 March and 10 Sept., and on June bills on 10 June and 10 Dec.

March-treason. The treason of passing the marches or boundaries of a country as freebooters or for loot.

March, pronounce *Marsh*, not like the month of March.

He knew how many of his ancestors had fallen by the sword of the English, how many in domestic brawl, how many by the hand of the executioner for march-treason.—Sir W. SCOTT, *The Monastery* (Int.).

Marche's Rebellion, 1242. The Comte de la Marche refused to pay homage to Louis IX. (St. Louis), and Louis declared war against him. He routed the insurgents in two battles on one day, one at the bridge of Taillebourg in the Lower Charente, and the other near the city of Saintes (1 syl.). The count was pardoned.

Marches. Boundaries between two neighbouring kingdoms. The *Spanish Marches* were from the Pyrenees to the Ebro. The boundaries between England and Wales, as well as those between England and Scotland, were called marches from the Saxon *mearc*, a boundary. 'Beating the bounds' of a parish is called in Scotland 'riding the marches.'

Our *Marchion-ess*, the wife of a marchion (marquis), preserves the word. The marchion or marquis was the officer set to guard a march or frontier.

Marchetta, or ' Marchet.' A money tribute paid to a feudal lord by a tenant on the marriage of his daughter. It prevailed in England, Wales and Scotland. Sometimes called gwahr-merched (maid's fee). Earl Brant, one of the earls of Crawford, was the last who claimed the *droit de jambage* (16th cent.).

Marching Watch. 'In 1547 Sir John Gresham, being lord mayor of London,' revived this picturesque and splendid pageant on Midsummer's Eve. It had been put down by proclamation in 1528 on account of the sweating sickness ; and again in 1539. Henry VIII. took his wife Jane Seymour to Mercers' Hall to see the pageant. Stow says it was finally discontinued in 1549. The marching watch in London consisted of 2,000 men decorated with flowers, wreaths, and ribbons. Kings, peers, and knights on horseback joined the procession. Cresset lights and bonfires turned night into day, and banquets in the streets were liberally supplied. The march began at sunset and continued till sunrise next morning.

Mar'cionites (4 syl.), 2nd cent. An heretical sect founded by Marcion of Sinōpê, in Paphlagonia, son of the bishop of that city. His system is very imperfectly known, but he taught that there are two principles, one the author of good and the other the author of evil. The soul, he said, emanates from the former, and the body from the latter. He rejected the Old Testament, and retained only a few of the Epistles and a part of the third gospel in the New. Marcion had a large following, which subsisted as a distinct party till the 7th cent.

Origen affirms that Marcion postulated three gods, viz. a God of the Jews, a God of Christians, and a God of the Gentiles. Tertullian makes him to have postulated *nine* Gods, and adds that the heresiarch denied the resurrection of the body, condemned marriage, and maintained that the living might be baptized for the dead.
‚ What is said by the Fathers about ' heretics ' must be received with great caution. Like the Church historians, they much distorted their lives and doctrines, looking at them only from their own standpoint.

Marcus Aure'lius of the Base Empire (*The*). John II. (Comnēnus), also called Calojoan'nes, *i.e.* John the handsome. Reigned 1118–1143.

The Base Empire, *i.e.* the Eastern Empire after Theodosius.

Mardi Gras [*Mah'-de-grah'*], or ' Fat Tuesday.' The last day of the carnival, when the prize ox of Paris is paraded in mock procession through the principal streets, and stops at the chief houses to gather contributions. The horns and hoofs of the ox are gilt, and the beast is decorated with ribbons ; beside it walk on each side men in mockery imitation of the Romish priests, and a long procession, representing in similar caricature a Roman triumph, follow with bands of music, the more grotesque the better. We are told that the procession represents a Roman saturnalia, but it seems very like those semi-religious processions of the middle ages, the Feast of Fools, the Fête of the Ass, the Fête of the Bottle, and the Fête of the Cornards or Cuckolds. In Venice for many centuries there was a similar procession of a fat ox and twelve hogs on the last Thursday of Carnival ; and there is still such a celebration at New Orleans, U.S.A. *See* ' Zobia-grassa.'

Marfo'rio. An antique marble statue of colossal size, found in the *Martis foro,* and at one time placed near the Braschi palace. As all sorts of placards, handbills, squibs, and satires used to be affixed to the statue, it was removed in 1784 to the Capitoline museum.

Margaret Professorship of Divinity (*Lady*), 1502. Founded in each of our two universities by Margaret countess of Richmond, mother of Henry VII. The professor must be a graduate in divinity, or an M.A. of at least seven years' standing in priest's orders. In Oxford all graduates in divinity and all members of the congregation (in deacon's orders) are electors. In Cambridge the office is nominally for two years, but as the professor is eligible for re-election, it is virtually for life. The electors (in Cambridge) are the vice-chancellor, all doctors, inceptors, and bachelors in divinity who have been regents in arts.

Margaret's Knights (*The*), 2 Aug. 1786. An attempt was made by a mad woman, Margaret Nicholson, to assassinate George III. as he was alighting from his carriage at St. James's Palace. Addresses of congratulation on his escape came from all parts of the kingdom, and a very large number of mayors and other functionaries, deputed to present the addresses, were knighted. These were called ' Margaret's knights,' or ' Peg Nicholson's knights.'

Margaret's Shift. The main standard of Margaret's army in the battle of Falkoping, 1397, in which Albert king of Sweden was defeated by Margaret queen-regent of Denmark and Norway. There is still preserved in the cathedral of Upsâla a ragged strip of linen fastened to a staff which tradition says was carried at this battle, to animate the troops by reminding them of the martial spirit of their leader.

Margaret of Calais, 1347. The daughter of Edward III. and Philippa, born in Calais, just after the termination of the siege.

Margites. Demosthenês called Alexander the Great ' another Margîtês,' meaning a conceited superficial dolt. Margîtês was a man against whom Homer wrote a satire to ridicule his superficial knowledge and affectations.

I'll take to writing poetry, a mock epic in 72 books . . . and take Homer's ' Margites' for my model.—KINGSLEY, *Hypatia*, ch. xiii.

Mar'grave or ' Mark-graf.' A German reeve or chief officer of a mark or march, *i.e.* a frontier; like our marquis. The original function of this reeve was to defend a borderland from incursions. *See* ' Graf,' ' Pfalz-graf.'

Marguerite des Marguerites (pearl of pearls). Marguerite de Valois queen of Navarre, sister of François I., born 1492, died 1549. It was her brother François who called her *La Marguerite des Marguerites.*

It was not Marguerite the wife of Henri IV. who was so called.

Maria There'sa, ' mother of her country,' married Francis Stephan duke of Lorraine in 1736. Born 1717, succeeded her father Kaiser Karl VI. in 1740; her husband was crowned Kaiser Franz I. 1745, and died 1765; the widow died 1780, aged 63, mother of three sons and six daughters. On the death of Franz I. the eldest son Joseph II. was made ' king of the Romans,' and associated with his mother as ruler of Germany; and at her death became kaiser-king.

It was the daughter of Maria Theresa (named Marie Antoinette) who married Louis XVI. of France, and was guillotined.

Marian Persecutions of the Protestants began in January 1555.

Instigated chiefly by Philip, the Spanish husband of Mary. In this persecution fell the Archbishop Cranmer, Hooper (bishop of Gloucester), Latimer (bishop of Worcester), Ridley (bishop of London), Ferrar (bishop of St. David's), and about 300 more. Hundreds of others were banished, imprisoned, and heavily fined.

It is much to be feared that religion and politics were so mixed up together that it was often morally impossible to separate ' heresy' from treason.

Marie-Jeanne (*Mah'-re Zjahn'*). A 12-pounder of fine workmanship which the republican party (the blues) took in the Vendéan war from the Château de Richelieu, where it had been placed by the famous cardinal. It was heroically retaken by the Vendeans (1794)

Mariotte's Law. The elastic force of gases and vapours increase directly with the pressure.

Maristes (2 syl.), 1818. A religious congregation at Bordeaux founded by the Abbé Cheminade, docteur de Sorbonne, the object being the education of the young. It has ramified into all parts of France, and into Switzerland, Germany, and the United States.

Marischal College (New Aberdeen), 1593. Founded by George Keith, Earl Marischal, and united in 1858 to the University of Aberdeen. The motto of the college—' They say. Qvhat say they? Let them say '—is that of the founder.

Market Crosses. Places under cover for the sale of country produce on market days. Chichester Market Cross stands at the point where North and South streets, East and West streets meet. There are several market crosses still standing besides that of Chichester, such as Winchester Market Cross, Malmesbury Market Cross, Aberdeen Market Cross, &c.

Marlbridge (*Statute of*), 52 Hen. III. c. 10 (1267), whereby all prelates, clergymen, peers, and women are discharged from attending court leets. The statute incorporated many of the ' Provisions of Oxford ' (*q.v.*).

Mar'onites (3 syl.) of Syria, 5th cent. Disciples of John Maron. A very large number of them live a monastic life. Since 1445 they have been united to the Church of Rome, but have some peculiar doctrines and church customs. The patriarch is always called Peter. Married men may become priests, but no priest may marry after he is in orders. The priests wear a blue scarf about their caps, but no surplice. They were massacred by the Druses in June 1860, but their present number is about 100,000. Since 1588 the Maronites have been tributary to the Porte.

Maroon Insurrection (*The*), 1795. The Maroons were the runaway slaves of Jamaica and Cuba, who congregated in the woods on the north side of Jamaica, and lived a predatory life. In 1795 two of them were punished with thirty-nine lashes for stealing pigs, and this drove the Maroons into insurrection. A bloody and successful war was waged by them, till the Assembly sent to Cuba for 100 bloodhounds. The Maroons then craved mercy, and all of them who would not promise to abandon their predatory habits were banished to Halifax, in Nova Scotia, whence in 1800 they were deported to Sierra Leone. The descendants of others have been peaceful occupants of a few towns built by themselves in the forests of Jamaica.

There are also many Maroons in Guiana.

Marprelate Tracts (*The*), 1588. Tracts written by one who signed himself 'Martin Marprelate and his sons.' The object of these tracts was to vilify the Established Church. Penry, one of the five Independents put to death by Queen Elizabeth, was supposed to have been the author of some of these tracts. *See* 'Martin Marprelate.'

The Anglican Church is called 'old rotten stuff . . . abstracted of [from] the pope's blasphemous mass book' . . . the liturgy is 'stinking patchery.' Churchmen are 'blasphemous wretches, the subjects of the kingdom of the Beast'; while the Puritans are called 'the great learned preachers,' the good men, but with counterfeit discipline and perjured elders, in fact, 'Pharisees.'

Marquis. From the Saxon and Norman *marchio*, a military officer whose duty was to protect the frontier where he was placed, and prevent inroads and invasions. A march means a frontier.

Marquis Duke of Cadiz (*The*). Ponce de Leon, marquis of Cadiz, was created by Isabella a duke; but, unwilling to resign the title under which he had won his laurels, he ever afterwards subscribed himself and was called by others the 'Marquis Duke.'

Marrani. Renegade Moors.

Marriage of the Adriatic (*The*). Instituted in commemoration of a naval victory won by Sebastian Ziani, doge of Venice, over Otto son of Frederick Barbarossa, 1174. In consequence of this victory Pope Alexander III., who had been driven to take refuge in Venice, gave to the doge the sovereignty of the sea, and every year the doge used to go in grand procession in his state barge, and threw a gold ring into the Adriatic, saying 'With this ring I thee wed.'

The Signoria leaves the palace amid a countless throng and ascends the Bucentaur. The rowers of this state barge sit below the deck. The doge sits on the deck under a magnificent canopy, having the pope's nuncio on his right hand, and the French ambassador on his left. All the magnates of Venice sit according to their rank, and arrayed in their official costumes. The great banner of St. Mark and the standard proper of the barge are displayed, and a band of trumpeters and hautboy players assist in the ceremony. When the Bucentaur reaches the mouth of the sea, the musicians begin a certain motet, and the doge drops into the sea a gold wedding-ring, saying: 'Desponsamus te Mare nostrum in signum veri perpetuique dominii.' Flowers are then thrown into the sea, and the procession returns.—VILLAMONT, *Peregrinatio Sacra*, ch. xxxiv. d. 3.

Marriages (*Close Times of*). 1. 'Ab Adventu usque ad Epiphaniam; (2) a Septuagesima usque ad octavas Pasche inclusive; (3) a secunda feria in Rogationibus usque ad primam dominicam post Pentecosten exclusive.'—*Liber Sacerdotalis . . . secundum Ritum Sanctæ Romanæ et Apostolicæ Ecclesiæ* (1537).

Married Women's Property Act. Came into operation 1 Jan., 1883, enabling married women to acquire, hold, and dispose of property as their own separate estate, just as if they were single. They may also enter into contracts to the extent of their own separate property. By this act, a wife who robs her husband, or a husband who robs his wife, may be proceeded against as if they were strangers.

The first Act was 3, 4 Will. IV. c. 74 (1833); the next was 20, 21 Vict. c. 57 (1857), amended in 1870.

Marrow Controversy (*The*), in the Church of Scotland, 1614. So called from a book entitled 'The Marrow of Modern Divinity,' written by a Puritan soldier in the time of the Commonwealth. The book was highly 'evangelical,' especially on the subject of free grace. The General Assembly condemned the book

O O

in 1720, and forbade the Scotch to read it. Twelve of the Evangelical clergy remonstrated, but, being called before the Assembly, were severely rebuked. Here the matter ended; but eleven years afterwards the Evangelical party seceded.

Marrow-men (*The*), 1721. The twelve Evangelical ministers who protested against the condemnation of the book entitled 'The Marrow of Modern Divinity.' Their names are James Hog or Hogg, Thomas Boston, John Bonner, James Kid or Kidd, Gabriel Wilson, Ebenezer Erskine, Ralph Erskine, James Wardlaw, James Bathgate, Henry Davidson, William Hunter, and John Williamson. They were called 'The Twelve Brethren,' and were held by the Evangelical party of Scotland in great veneration. *See above.*

Mars and Mahomet of Scandinavia (*The*). Odin. His true name was Sigge, son of Fridulph, but he assumed the name of Odin, chief god of the Scythians, of whom he was chief priest (B.C. 70-40).

Mars of China (*The*). Quâng-yoo, general of the Emperor Heou-tchao (who reigned 223-265). Quâng-yoo died A.D. 265, and Heou-tchao was compelled to abdicate.

Marseillais (*Les*), 30 July, 1792. So the battalion of federates from Marseilles, invited by the Jacobins to Paris, was called. They went chanting a revolutionary song composed by Rouget de Lisle, a young officer at Strasburg. The song was called 'La Marseillaise,' meaning the song of the battalion from Marseilles.

Marseilles (*Plague of*), 1720-1726. A dreadful plague brought from Syria in a merchant ship. It first appeared in Marseilles, whence it spread to Arles, Aix, and Toulon. More than 80,000 persons fell victims to it. *See below.*

Marseilles' Good Bishop. Henri François Xavier de Belsunce (1671-1755). Immortalised by the eminent services which he rendered to the city of Marseilles during the plague of 1720. He is commemorated in the town-hall of Marseilles by a painting in which he is represented in his episcopal robes, attended by his almoners, giving relief and benediction to those stricken with the plague—

Intrepido vadens per strata cadavera passu.

Marsh (*The*), 1792. The 'Centre' of the Convention which assembled in the Hall of the Hundred Swiss. The Girondins occupied the Right, the Left was nicknamed the Mountain, and the Centre (nicknamed the Plain or Marsh) was composed of the peaceably inclined and moderate party.

Marshal (*Earl*) of England. Hereditary in the duke of Norfolk, the sole judge in questions of honour and arms. He is president of the English College of Arms, and appoints the kings-of-arms, the heralds, and the pursuivants.

There is also a knight-marshal or marshal of the royal household, and a marshal (or provost-marshal) of the Admiralty, who acts under the Court of Admiralty. The Marshal of the King's Bench was abolished in 1849.

Marshal Forwards. 'Marschall Vorwärts,' Gebhard Lebrecht von Blücher (1742-1819). So called from his familiar exhortation to his hussars, *Vorwärts*. 'Forwards! my children, forwards!' in the famous campaign of 1814. So again 18 June, 1815, the war-cry was 'Vorwärts!' always 'Vorwärts!'

He crossed the Rhine 1-3 Jan., 1814; defeated Napoleon at Laon, 9-10 March; commanded the centre of the allies in the attack on Paris 30 March; entered Paris 31 March; resigned 2 April, but resumed command the following April, and contributed to the victory of Waterloo.

Marshal of France, 1185. A dignity which originated with Philippe II. Auguste; in 1627, when the office of constable was suppressed, 'marshal' was the highest dignity in the state. Suppressed in 1752, but revived by Napoleon in 1804.

Marshal of the Army of God and Holy Church. So was Robert Fitz-Walter called when he led the English barons to demand of John the Great Charter.

Marshall Prize for political economy, value 15l., to be spent in books. Founded for five years in the University of Cambridge by A. Marshall, M.A., of St. John's College. First awarded in 1887.

Marshalsea (*The*). I. The Knight Marshal's Court, commonly called the 'Palace Court,' created by Charles I., with jurisdiction within twelve miles round Whitehall. Abolished in 1849.

II. King's Bench Prison, in South-wark, where the marshal of the king's house was wont to sit, or keep his prison. Also abolished in 1849.

'Little Dorrit' was born in the Marshalsea prison, and the tale so called gives a full and graphic account of the prison and its inmates.—CHARLES DICKENS.

Marshalsea Court (*The*), or 'Board of Green Cloth' (*q.v.*), abolished with the Marshalsea Prison in 1849 (12, 13 Vict. c. 101).

Marshal is the German *marschalk* through the French, and means Master of the Horse.

Martel. A surname given to Karl or Charles, natural son of Pepin d'Hé-ristal, after his great victory over Abd-el-Rahman, the Saracen invader, on the plains of Poitiers, A.D. 732.

Dès lors tous commencèrent à le surnommer 'Martel,' parce que, comme le martel [*a hammer*] brise toute espéce de fer, ainsi Karle, avec l'aide du Seigneur, brisait ses ennemis dans toutes les batailles.—MOISSAC, *Chronique*.
Similarly Judas Asmonæus was called 'Macca-bæus' (the hammerer).

Martello Towers. 'Torri da Martello,' erected on the coasts of Sar-dinia and Corsica, 1530–1550, to defend the coast. Warning was given by striking a bell with a martello or hammer. Similar towers were erected on the Kent and Sussex coasts in 1795–1800; but coast-guardsmen have superseded their utility.

Similar towers, not now in use, have been found in Canada and in the United States.

Martin Marprelate Contro-versy (*The*), 1585. A controversy con-sequent on the dogmatism and tyranny of the Ecclesiastical Commission ap-pointed by Queen Elizabeth to settle all disputes of doctrine and practice in the Church of England. Archbishop Whit-gift tried to gag the press. Printing was restricted to London, and the two Uni-versities, and all candidates for a license to print were placed under the super-vision of the Company of Stationers. A series of anonymous pamphlets, signed 'Martin Marprelate,' had an enormous sale; but the press was seized, John Penry (a young Welshman) died in prison, and Udal, a minister, was put to death on the scaffold. But the mischief was done, synods and classes were organised, spread into the reign of James I., and led to the Civil War. *See* 'Marprelate Tracts.'

Martin's Act, for the 'better treat-ment of poor horses, dogs, and donkeys.' Introduced by Richard Martin, M.P., of

Cro Martin, Ireland. *See* 'Humanity Martin.'

Martinalia. A goose-feast. After the Gauls were foiled in their attack on the Capitol by the cackling of the sacred geese, B.C. 390, they annually sacrificed a goose to their war-god. They were converted by St. Martin, and the goose-feast was changed to honour the saint. Hence Naorgeorgus—

Altera Martinus dein Bacchanalia præbet :
Quem colit anseribus populus, multoque Lyæo.

In regard to Queen Elizabeth, it is said she was dining on 9 Aug., 1588, with Sir Nevile Umfreville at Tilbury Fort when the news was brought her of the discomfiture of the Spanish Armada. There happened to be a roast goose on the table, and the queen resolved, as long as she lived, to commemorate the day with a roast goose. St. Martin's day is 11 Nov., the Armada day was 9 Aug., but the great goose-feast is on Michael-mas day, 29 Sept.

Martinière (*La*). There are three schools so called—one in Calcutta, one in Lucknow, and one at Lyons in France. They were built and endowed by money left for the purpose by Major-General Claude Martin (1732–1800). He was the son of a Lyons manufacturer, and en-tered the English army of the Indian Company, where he rose from a private to become a major-general, and accumu-lated 396,000*l.* sterling. He died in Lucknow.

Martinists. I. Calvinists were so called from M. Martin, president of the consistory of Geneva.
II. Disciples of Martinez Pasqualis (1710–1779). He was a Portuguese Jew, and established a cabalistic rite called Cohens, which he introduced into certain masonic lodges of Marseilles, Toulouse, and Bordeaux.

Cohen is a Hebrew word meaning priest.

Martyr City (*The*). Moscow, burnt in 1812 (15–18 Sept.) by the inhabitants to prevent its giving harbourage and spoil to the invading army of Napoleon. It was a magnificent holocaust, the grandest the world has ever seen.

Martyr King (*The*). I. Henry VI. of England (1421, 1422–1461, died 1471). The crown was claimed by Edward duke of York 16 Oct., 1460, and he was declared king 3 March, 1461. Henry was declared a usurper by 1 Edw. IV. c. 1 (1461) ; placed in Hardlough Castle, Merionethshire, 1462–1464 ; taken to the Tower 1466 ; released by Warwick, and again imprisoned by Edward IV. in April 1471 ; and found dead 22 May, 1471.

Here o'er the Martyr King [*Hen. VI.*] the marble weeps,
And fast beside him once-feared Edward [IV.] sleeps ;
The grave unites where e'en the grave finds rest,
And mingled lie th' oppressor and oppressed.
POPE.

II. **Charles I.** of England (1600, 1625–1649).

After the Restoration January 30 was observed in the Church of England with a special religious service, 'Being the day of the Martyrdom of the Blessed King Charles I.,' &c. This service, with one or two others equally objectionable, were abolished by Act of Parliament in 1859.

III. **Louis XVI.** of France (1754, 1774–1793). He has as great a right to be called a 'Martyr' as Charles I., and in both cases the word is a misnomer. Both were executed by their indignant subjects, who believed that kings were made for the people, and not the people for kings. And in both cases the bolt of vengeance fell on the heads of amiable men.

Martyr means one who suffers death for the sincerity of his belief. Henry VI. believed he was lawful king ; Charles I. believed he had a right divine to the crown ; and Louis XVI. believed that he was right and the republicans wrong. They died 'martyrs' to their creed. Whether that creed was right or wrong is beside the question. The orthodoxy of one age may be the heterodoxy of another, and v.v. The Bollandists call Edwin king of Northumbria 'Saint and Martyr.'

Martyrs. *See* 'Manchester Martyrs.'

Martyrs' Era (*The*), A.D. 303, &c. The tenth and last persecution. It began in February, at the Roman Terminalia, or festival of the god Terminus. In this persecution fell, as it is said, St. George of Cappadocia, St. Januarius (patron saint of Naples), Quirīnus bishop of Siscia, &c.

It is very doubtful whether these names, and those of many other 'martyrs,' are not apocryphal.

Martyrs' Fund (*The*), 1883. This was a fund organised in New York at the suggestion of Patrick Egan, 'for the families of such convicted assassins as neither pleaded guilty nor confessed their crime.'

The relatives of Caffrey, 'who apologised' for what he had done and tried to explain it away, were excluded from its benefits by the lady distributors, Miss Ellen Ford and Miss M. Doherty, 10 Nov., 1883.

Martyrs' Meeting (*The*), 2 July, 1883. Held at New York to do homage to the twenty-one assassins who took part in the Phœnix Park (Ireland) murders of Mr. Burke and Lord Frederick Cavendish.

Of all perversions of the word martyr this is the very worst. But Ireland has done no little to degrade the term 'martyr' into a byword and a hissing.

Marvellous Boy (*The*). Thomas Chatterton (1752–1770). So called by the poet Wordsworth.

Marvellous Year (*The*), 1588. The year of the Spanish Armada's destruction.

The first number of the 'English Mercurie' (*q.v.*) is supposed to have appeared this year (10 Aug.) to announce the destruction of the Armada.

Mary Queen of England, born at Greenwich (1516, 1553–1558).

Father, Henry VIII. ; *Mother*, Katharine of Aragon ; *Husband*, Don Filippo [Philip II.] son of Karl V. of Spain. He was a widower, aged 27, and had a son named Don Carlos. Mary was eleven years his senior.

Her style and title : 'Mary, D.G. of England, France, and Ireland, queen ; Defender of the Faith, and Supreme Head of the Anglican and Hibernian Church.' After her marriage her husband was associated with her and called King Philip.
After the death of Mary Philip married Isabella of France in 1559. She died in 1568, and he married the Archduchess Anna Maria in 1570.
Philip left England in 1555, his father abdicated 5 Oct. the same year ; Mary died in 1558, his father Karl V. in Sept. 1559 ; he married his third wife in 1559, sent the Armada against England in 1588 ; his ministers tried to assassinate Elizabeth in 1594, and he died in Sept. 1598.

Mary Queen of Scots. Married François [II.] of France ; and, on the death of Mary queen of England in 1558, they assumed the title of king and queen of Scotland, England, and Ireland. The arms of England were also embroidered or painted on their equipage, furniture, and plate.

Father, James V. of Scotland ; *Mother*, Mary of Lorraine ; *Husbands*, (1) François [II.] of France ; (2) Henry Lord Darnley, her cousin ; (3) Bothwell.

Issue by Darnley, James VI. of Scotland and I. of England. Executed by Queen Elizabeth.
The claim of Mary Stuart was through her grandmother, a daughter of Henry VII. Elizabeth, the queen of England *de facto*, was daughter of Henry VIII., but had been bastardised by him.

Mary and Darnley.

HENRY VII. (Tudor) was the father of Henry VIII., and Margaret Tudor, who married twice, first James IV., and then Archibald Douglas.
HENRY VIII. was the father of Elizabeth ; his sister Margaret (as wife of James IV.) was the mother of James V. Thus Elizabeth and James V. were cousins. James V. was the father of Mary

queen of Scots, who was second cousin to Elizabeth.

By her second husband, Archibald Douglas, Margaret was the mother of Margaret Douglas, who married Lord Lennox, and their son was Lord Darnley (the husband of Mary queen of Scots). So Darnley was half cousin to Mary his wife.

. Both Mary and Darnley were second cousins of Elizabeth.

Mary Hall (*St.*), Oxford, 1333. Founded by Oriel College, to which St. Mary's Church belonged. The head of the hall is called the principal.

Maryland (U.S. America). So called in 1633 by Lord Baltimore in compliment to Henrietta Maria wife of Charles I. of England. The nickname of the Marylanders is *Craw-thumpers*.

Masaniello [*Ma-san-yel'-lo*]. A contraction of Tommaso Aniello, a fish salesman of Amalfi who in 1647 raised a revolt in Naples against the Spanish viceroy, the Duke of Arcos, in consequence of a tax levied by him on fruits and vegetables. The insurgents were successful, and for seven days Masaniello was master of Naples, when he was assassinated and his body thrown into a ditch. The seven-days' king held Naples from 10 July to 17 July, 1647.

Mason Prize for Biblical Hebrew. Value about 24*l.* a year, given to the best of the Tyrwhitt Scholars. Founded in the University of Cambridge by the friends of the Rev. Peter Hamnett Mason, M.A., Fellow of St. John's, 1883. *See* 'Tyrwhitt Scholarship.'

Maso'rah (*The*). A collection of traditionary observations (orthographical, critical, grammatical, and exegetical) which had been made by Jewish rabbins during a period of 300 years, on the Old Testament. They began to be made by a college of Jews at Tiberias, in Palestine, and were originally written on the margins of manuscripts, but were ultimately collected into separate books. Constant additions were made from the 6th to 11th cent. A.D.

There was the Great and the Little Masôrah. The Great Masorah means the entire mass given in full; also called *final*, because these annotations were added to the end of the Scriptures as a supplement. The Little Masorah is an abridgment, called the *marginal* Masorah, because it was inserted on the margins of the MSS.

Masque de Fer (*Le*). The Man in the Iron Mask. In the MS. memoirs of M. de la Reinterie we are told that while he was in command of the fortress of Pi-

gnerol, the Masque de Fer attempted to escape, but was recaptured. The officer who conducted him back drew his sword, when the Mask cried out in a very commanding voice : 'Songez à ce que vous faites, Monsieur ! Respectez le sang de vos souverains.' M. de la Reinterie adds that he told this to several persons about the court, and gives a list of the names to whom he told it.

'Détenu prisonnier en France plus de 40 ans, il portait sans cesse sur la figure un masque noir, qui était en fer selon les uns, en velours noir selon les autres. Mis sous la garde de St.-Mars, il fut conduit au château de Pignerol en 1666, puis transféré en 1686 à l'île Ste-Marguerite, et en 1698 à la Bastille, où il mourut en 1703. Il fut enterré sous le nom de Marchiali. On a dit que c'était un *frère jumeau de Louis XIV* (qui est l'opinion de Voltaire, et la plus vraisemblable), qu'on aurait fait disparaître pour prévenir la rivalité des deux frères. 2. *Le comte de Vermandois*, fils naturel de Louis XIV et de Mlle de Vallière, qui fut enfermé pour avoir donné un soufflet au grand dauphin ; 3. *Le duc de Beaufort*, qui disparut au siège de Candie en 1669 ; 4. *Le duc de Monmouth*, neveu de Jacques II, que la France aurait soustrait au supplice ; 5. *Le comte Girolamo Matthioli*, ministre du duc de Mantoue, qui aurait été enlevé de Turin pour avoir empêché son maître de vendre Casal au roi de France ; ou (6) Jean de Gonzague, secrétaire de Matthioli ; ou (7) un *fils adultérin d'Anne d'Autriche* [the king's mother] et de Buckingham ou de Mazarin. La 1e hypothèse est la plus vraisemblable ; mais il y a aussi des probabilités pour la 2e hypothèse.—BOUILLET, *Dict. Universel* (p. 1205 col. 2).

Mass. *See also—*

Ambrosian mass.	Judicial mass.
Annual mass.	Low mass.
Aurora mass.	Midnight mass.
Cardinal's mass.	Missa.
Christmas Eve mass.	Naval mass.
Dry mass.	Nuptial mass.
Golden mass.	Paschal mass.
Gregorian mass.	Peregrine mass.
High mass.	Sacrificial mass.
Hunter's mass.	Votive mass.

Mass. The celebration of the eucharist in the Catholic Church. The service-book, called a 'missal,' contains four parts : the Introïtus, the Consecration, the Communion, and the Post-Communio. The Canon of the Mass was compiled by Gregory the Great in 599.

The prayers of the mass are not generally in the vulgar tongue. In the Roman Church they are in Latin ; in the Greek Church they are in ancient Greek ; among the Maronites and Jacobites they are in Syriac. In some Eastern churches, however, and even in some Roman Catholic churches of the Eastern rites, the vulgar tongue is now used. Thus the Roumanians use the Roumanian language, and the (Roman Catholic) Melchites of Syria use the Arabic. This, however, is by a kind of toleration, and not by official sanction.

. Prohibited in England in 1548 (2, 3 Edw. VI. c. 1); in Scotland it was prohibited in 1560 under penalty of death ! !

Low mass is when a single priest simply *reads* the service in a low voice : high mass is *chanted*, and several ministers assist the officiating priest. In the celebration of the mass the priest wears five special garments, two of linen and three of silk. The colour varies according to the occasions. They are white, red, green, purple, and black.

• Pope Celestine introduced the *Introït* and the *Gloria in excelsis* ;

Gregory the Great ordained to say the *Kyrie Eleison* nine times ;

Gelasius ordained the *Epistle* and the *Gospel* ;

Damasus ordained the *Credo* ;

Alexander introduced this clause into the canon, *qui pridie quam pateretur* ;

Sixtus introduced the *Sanctus* ;

Innocent introduced the *Pax* ;

Leo introduced the *Orate Fratres*, and the words in the canon, *Sanctum Sacrificium et Immaculatam Hostiam*.

EDWARD KINESMAN, *Lives of the Saints*, 1623, p. 187 (an extremely rare old book).

Derivation of the word. Du Cange says (vol. iv. p. 698) :—

De vocabuli origine [*Mass*] variæ sunt scriptorum sententiæ. Hanc enim quidam, ut idem Baronius, ab Hebræo *Missah*, *i.e.* ' oblatio,' arcessunt ; Alii a *mittendo*, quod nos mittat ad Deum, ut est apud Alcuinum *de Divinis Officiis*. . . . Bk i. c. 2 ; Alii rursum a *missa*, quæ vox est sacrificiorum, ut scholiastes Bedanæ Historiæ Saxonicæ, p. 4 ; Verum missis ejusmodi et similibus conjecturis, constans est et recepta ab omnibus viris eruditis sententia scribentium *missam* dictam a *missa catechumenorum*, ea scilicet parte sacræ Liturgiæ, in qua finita concione, et Epistolæ ac Evangelii lectione, catechumeni exire jubebantur, diacono dicente, *Ite, Missa est.*

Mass for the Dead. ' Missa Animarum.' High mass for the repose of departed souls. *See* ' Missa.'

Mass of Lances (*The*). So Igor (913–945) son of Rurik called his massacre of the priests in Paphlagonia, Pontus, and Bithynia. He compelled them to don their richest robes, and then pierced them to death in their churches with long lances.

Mass of the Catechumens (*The*). 'Missa Cat'echumeno'rum.' All the Communion service up to the introïtus, at which point of the service the catechumens were dismissed by the deacon with these words, 'Si quis non communiat, det locum.' *See* ' Mass of the Faithful.'

Mass of the Faithful (*The*). The communion service, from the consecration of the elements to the close. *See* ' Mass of the Catechumens.'

Mass of the Presanctified (*The*), ' Missa Præsanc'tificato'rum,' celebrated on Good Friday. No consecration of the elements takes place on that day, but the priest distributes to communicants the ' host' which was consecrated on the previous day. *See* ' Missa.'

In the Greek Church all through Lent a ' Presanctified Mass' is administered every day except on Saturdays and Sundays.

Massachusetts (U.S. America). An Indian word meaning the ' Blue Hills.' The ' Blue Hills' referred to are those at Milton, near Boston.

Massachusetts was the name of one of the Indian tribes.

Massacre. *See also—*

Bartholomew's Slaughter (St.)	Irish Massacre.
Bartholomew's Slaughter (St.) of the Ottoman Empire.	Jaffa Massacre.
	Manchester Massacre
	Meerut Massacre.
Dragonnades.	Michelade.
Day of Ferdinand.	Shibboleth.
Hango Massacre.	Sicilian Vespers.
	Vendéan Massacre.

Massacre of Amboyna (one of the Moluccas), 17 Feb., 1623. The British establishment was destroyed, and the English of the island massacred, several of them being tortured first and executed afterwards. Satisfaction for this outrage was obtained by treaty between Cromwell and the United Provinces, Aug. 30, 1654.

Massacre of Antwerp (*The*), 4 Aug., 1788. Troops were drawn up and cannon planted in the public square of Antwerp to keep down the populace, which had risen in insurrection because Kaiser Joseph II. had resolved to break up the university of Antwerp as that of Louvain had been broken up. The professors were turned out of doors, and the doors of the college locked. An assault was made on the soldiery ; Dalton ordered the soldiers to fire on the people, and thirty or forty persons were killed, many more being wounded. All Netherlands was indignant, and Europe heard with horror of this wanton massacre.

Massacre of Athenry, in Ireland, 1599. In which the Irish put to the sword all the inhabitants because they were adopting English customs.

Massacre of Avignon, 30 Aug., 1792. Jourdan Coupe-tête and his accomplices closed the gates of Avignon, broke into the houses of the citizens, and massacred men, women, and children, on the pretence of taking vengeance on the enemies of the revolution.

Avignon, pronounce *A-vi-nyŏn*, with final *n* nasal.

Massacre of Belgrade (*The*), 1095. When Peter the Hermit with his rabble rout of crusaders reached Hungary a rumour was circulated that the Hungarians intended to attack them on one side of the river and the Bulgarians on the other. Some clothes belonging to crusaders were found suspended on the

walls of Semlin. Peter instantly commanded the crusaders under him to attack Belgrade, and above 4,000 of the inhabitants were barbarously massacred. The dead bodies floating down the river brought the first intelligence of this shameful outrage.

Massacre of Berwick (*The*), Good Friday, 1296. When Edward I. entered the town of Berwick he mowed down 8,000 of the inhabitants, and burnt alive the Flemish traders who held the town-hall against him. Berwick was then the chief merchant city of the north, but sank into a petty seaport.

Some say the number massacred was 17,000.

Massacre of Chataigneraie [*Shah-tain-ye-ray*], 1595. This was a repetition of the massacre at Vassy. The Duc de Mercœur fell suddenly on a congregation of Huguenots, and butchered 200 men, women, and children, wholly defenceless, and guilty of no offence.

Massacre of Corcy′ra (*The*), B.C. 425. In the Corcyrēan sedition (*q.v.*) about 500 fugitives fortified themselves on the hill Itōnē, and made a compact that 'they would abide the arbitration of the Athenians.' The terms were accepted, with this proviso, 'if any one of them attempted to escape, the compact should be void.' Now follows the villanous part. The men of Corcyra sent messages to these appellants advising them to flee, as the Athenians were ill-disposed towards them. They took the bait, and fled. The truce being thus broken, the fugitives were delivered up to the Corcyreans, who imprisoned them in a large edifice. Some 60 were marched out and slain; the rest refused to quit the building, so the Corcyreans unroofed it, and massacred them all with arrows and other missiles.

Massacre of Crowland (*The*), A.D. 870. When the Danes marched to Crowland, the old abbot, with all the inmates of the abbey either too old or too young to save themselves by flight, assembled in the choir, with the hope of disarming by their feebleness the cruelty of the invaders. Soon a furious swarm of the barbarians rushed howling into the choir, and massacred all without mercy, except only a child of ten, which Jarl Sidroc took a fancy to and saved from death. Having put all others to

the sword, the spoilers broke down the tombs and monuments, and then committed the abbey to the flames.

Massacre of Drogheda [*Dro′-e-dah*], 13 Aug., 1649. One of the most savage butcheries ever perpetrated. Cromwell gave orders to his soldiers to give no quarter and to spare no one. At least 2,000 men, women, and children were butchered. Some 1,000 of the people took refuge in the church, but it was set fire to, and all the inmates were burnt alive. Those who escaped both fire and sword were shipped off to Barbadoes.

Massacre of Glencoe (2 syl.), 13 Feb., 1692—*i.e.* the Massacre of the McDonalds of Glencoe in Argyllshire. The English government issued a proclamation that every Scotch rebel who did not come in and take the oaths of allegiance to William and Mary before 1 Jan., 1692, should be deemed a traitor and be treated accordingly. MacIan deferred doing so till 31 Dec., 1691, when he presented himself at Fort William to take the oaths. Colonel Hill said he was not a magistrate, and that MacIan must go to Inverary and swear before the sheriff. This was wholly impossible before the days of grace expired, and MacIan did not reach Inverary before 6 Jan., 1692. William signed a warrant for the extirpation of the 'rebels,' and an order was sent to Governor Hill to 'kill every man, woman, and child in the whole glen.' Colonel Hamilton was sent on the errand, and ordered Captain Campbell (better known as Glenlyon) to reconnoitre the place. Glenlyon and his men lived at Glencoe on apparently friendly terms for about a fortnight, and Lieutenant Lindsay used to play cards every night with MacIan and his sons. Having made himself fully acquainted with the glen and its inhabitants, a total slaughter was to be made on 13 Feb., early in the morning. Fortunately the treachery was discovered, and many of the glenmen escaped; but above thirty were butchered, and many of those who fled perished in the snow. In all history nothing more treacherous and brutal than this slaughter is recorded, and the names of Breadalbane, Stair, and Glenlyon are held in abhorrence for the part they took in the massacre.

Massacre of Ispahan' (*The*), 1721, by Mahmoud the Afghan invader. Mahmoud, having made himself master of Ispahan, resolved to reduce the whole male population to an insignificant number, and for fifteen days slaughter followed slaughter. He began with the massacre of 300 nobles and their children; then followed the slaughter of 3,000 of the shah's guard taken into his pay; then every person in the pay of the late shah, and then an indiscriminate butchery of the meaner sort.

Massacre of Magdeburg (*The*), 1631. In the Thirty Years' War. As many as 30,000 were killed, and upwards of 6,400 corpses were thrown into the Elbe. Tilly, by a stratagem, succeeded in forcing his way into Magdeburg, when his soldiers committed outrages which have no parallel in history except in the Sepoy insurrection in India.

Massacre of Magh-Cru, in Connaught, A.D. 90. The lower orders and old Celtic population of Ireland concerted together to cut off all the princes and chiefs while assembled at Magh-Cru for public business. The massacre succeeded, and the legitimate monarchy was overthrown. The insurgents put Carbre Catcan on the throne. He reigned five years, during all which time there was 'no grain on the stalk, no fruitfulness in the waters, the herds were barren, and but one acorn on the oak.'

Massacre of Mahmoud (*The*). This is the Massacre of Ispahan' (*q.v.*).

This Mahmoud usurped the throne of Persia, where he reigned for three years (1722-1725), when he died raving mad.

Massacre of Mérindol (*The*). Mérindol, in Vaucluse, was laid in ruins by the Président d'Oppède because it was the abode of Vaudois. The entire population was exterminated. It has since recovered, and is still a stronghold of Protestants.

Massacre of Mithrida'tês (*The*), B.C. 88. During the marriage festival of Mithridātês VI. king of Pontus with a young Greek woman of Stratonicēa, he sent forth an edict to every city in the province of Asia to massacre every Italian within its borders. In one day as many as 80,000 Italians were slaughtered in compliance with this edict.

This cannot but call to mind the Massacre of St. Bartholomew's Eve, during the marriage festivities of Henri [Henri IV.] and the Princess Marguerite.

Massacre of Muscovites by the Poles (*The*), 1611. While Vladislaus son of Sigismund III. was fighting his way to the throne of Russia, the Poles fell upon Moscow and massacred above 100,000 defenceless women, old men, and children.

Massacre of Nancy [*Nahn-see'*], Aug. 1790. The inhabitants of Nancy, having risen in rebellion, were attacked by Bouillé, commander of the royal army, who marched from Metz upon the insurgents. A fearful slaughter of rebels ensued, known in French history as the Massacre of Nancy. This was only a month after the supposed settlement of the differences between king and people by the famous 'civil oath' taken in the Champ de Mars 13 July, 1790.

Champ de Mars, pronounce *Sharnd Mar*.

Massacre of Nishapûr (*The*), 1269. We are told by several historians that the slaughter at Nishapûr by Gengis Khan was 1,747,000 human beings, and that it took twelve days to count the dead (PETIT LA CROIX and HABEEB AL SEYER).

Massacre of Nismes [*Neem*], 1 April, 1703 (Palm Sunday). Marshal de Montreuil, being informed that some 300 Camisards were assembled in a mill near Nismes for religious worship, hastened with a troop of soldiers to the place, burst open the doors, and put to the sword those assembled. The process being too slow, he set fire to the mill, and only one, a young girl, escaped, and she was hanged the next day.

In 1791 and 1815 were bloody religious and political massacres at Nismes.

Massacre of Otranto (*The*), 1480. The slaughter of 800 ecclesiastics by Mahomet II., when he took Otranto. We are told that the corpses of these martyrs, though left unburied for thirteen months, showed no signs of corruption, and were never violated by bird or beast. They were ultimately interred at Naples; but when Solyman the Magnificent, in 1537, threatened Otranto with assault, the ghosts of these ecclesiastics, with a host of angels, appeared on the ramparts and saved the city. Again, in 1644, the same ghostly army averted another

Turkish assault, and those who professed that they could not see the army of martyrs were put to death.

Massacre of Pa'via (The), Aug., A.D. 408.

As the Emperor Honorius was passing through Bologna, a mutiny of the guards gave Olympius a pretext for cutting off the friends of Stilicho, whom he sought to supplant. Accordingly, two prætorian prefects of Gaul and Italy, two generals of cavalry and infantry, the master of offices, the quæstor, the treasurer, and the count of the domestics were massacred. The lives of many others were lost also; many houses were plundered, and on the 23rd Stilicho himself was basely put to death.

The death of Eucherius the son of Stilicho followed; the Emperor Honorius had divorced his wife Thermantia daughter of Stilicho, and all the friends of Stilicho who had escaped the massacre were persecuted with relentless acrimony by Olympius. Even his wife Serēna (niece of Theodosius the Great and foster-mother of Honorius) did not escape, being absurdly accused of purloining the magnificent necklace of the statue of Vesta. When Alaric invested Rome she was strangled.

Massacre of Peterborough (The), A.D. 870.

The monastery of Peterborough was the glory of the age, and its library unequalled; but the Danes, having destroyed Crowland Abbey, marched to Peterborough bent on its destruction also. They assailed the monastery gates, they attacked the walls, they forced their way in, slew the old abbot and all the monks. Every other inmate of the place was massacred. The much-admired monastery and its valuable treasures were ruthlessly set on fire, and the conflagration continued for fifteen days.

Massacre of Rathlin (The), 22, 23 July, 1575.

The island being taken by Essex, the Scotch were massacred.

Massacre of St. George's Fields (The), 1768.

Six men shot and fifteen wounded by the soldiers in the Wilkes riots. Wilkes had been cast into the King's Bench, and the mob, demanding his release, assembled tumultuously in St. George's Fields. The soldiers being called out were violently assailed, and gave chase to a man with a red waistcoat. They shot a man with a red waistcoat, but it was not the right man. The mob became frantic, and the soldiers, being ordered to fire on them, killed six and wounded fifteen.

Massacre of Savenay [Sahvenay], 22 Dec., 1793.

Here the Vendéans were massacred by the republicans under Kléber and Marceau. The Vendéans had fled to Brittany, but most of them returned, and on their route were attacked by the republicans. They retreated to Mons, where they were defeated, and they then crossed the Loire; but the republicans wedged them in at Savenay, between the Loire, the Vilaine, and the sea, overwhelmed them with artillery, and literally cut to pieces every man, woman, and child with merciless fury. Kléber wrote to the Convention, 'The Vendéans are not only quieted, they are no more.'

This dispatch was an exaggeration, for they were in arms up to 19 Feb., 1795, when they submitted.

Massacre of Scullabogue Barn (The), 1798.

In the Great Irish Rebellion. This massacre by the rebels, and that at Wexford Bridge, were the most fearful of all the outrages in this terrible insurrection.

Wexford was the head-quarters of the rebels.

Massacre of September (The).

2, 3, 4, 5 Sept., 1792, when 300 assassins were sent by Danton, the 'minister of justice' in Paris, to the different prisons to massacre all the prisoners 'suspected of being averse to the revolution.' The prisons they were sent to were Les Carmes, the Abbaye, the Force, the Bernardins, and Bicêtre; and the number of persons massacred was about 10,000, chiefly ecclesiastics or gentry. Amongst the assassinated was the Princesse de Lamballe, the queen's friend, and superintendent of her household.

Ecclesiastics were confined in Les Carmes (a Carmelite convent). Aristocrats were confined in L'Abbaye. Among the ecclesiastics who fell were the Archbishop of Arles and the Bishop of Saintes. If the 'judge' said to the warder 'Convey the prisoner hence to some other prison,' which he named, it was a sentence of death.

Massacre of Siniga'glia (The), 1502.

Paolo Orsini, Francesco Orsini, Vitellozzo Vitelli, Oliverotto da Fermo, and some other of the great magnates of Italy conspired to assassinate Cesare Borgia; but Cesare by craft contrived to assemble them, apart from their troops, in the castle of Sinigaglia, and there every one of them was strangled.

Massacre of Smerwick (The), 1579.

In the reign of Queen Elizabeth Felipe of Spain sent an army of 700 men to Kerry, thinking that all Ireland would flock to his standard. They entrenched themselves in the fort of Smerwick; but the fort was obliged to surrender to the queen's troops, and Lord Grey, the lord deputy, ordered the whole garrison to be massacred.

Massacre of Stockholm (*The*).

Sten Sture, the administrator of Sweden, consented to the elevation of Gustavus Trolle to the see of Upsala. Gustavus was a tool of Christian II. king of Denmark, and promised to do his best to betray Sweden into his hands. His treason being found out, he was compelled to resign, and his castle was razed to the ground. Leo X. placed Sweden under an interdict, and confided to Christian king of Denmark the task of punishing the schismatics. Accordingly, the Danish king invaded Sweden and, having effected a landing, was publicly crowned at Stockholm. During the coronation festival, Gustavus Trolle demanded of the king 'justice and revenge'; and on 8 Nov., 1520, at dawn, all the gates of the city being closed, 94 of the leading men of the city opposed to the invader were massacred. The victims consisted of ecclesiastics, senators, knights, and burgomasters. In this slaughter fell the father of Gustavus Vasa.

Massacre of Thessaloni'ca

(*The*), A.D. 390. The Thessalonians, being goaded into insurrection by being deprived of their favourite charioteer, Circus, slew Botheric, the Roman governor, and several of his officers. Theodosius sent word to his ministers to avenge the death of his lieutenant, and they proclaimed a grand show in the circus, given by the emperor. When the amphitheatre was full, and the trumpet sounded for the sports to begin, a number of soldiers rushed on the assembly, and put them indiscriminately to death. The massacre was estimated to be between 7,000 and 15,000 persons (Gibbon, chap. xxvii.).

Massacre of Vassy (*The*), 1 March,

1562. A massacre of the Huguenots by the Guises. This was the beginning of that religious war which desolated France in the latter half of the 16th cent.

About 1,200 Huguenots had assembled in a large barn, and were celebrating their worship under the protection of the edict of January (*q.v.*), when the Duke de Guise with a large escort rode by shouting 'Huguenots! dogs! rebels!' Some of the Huguenots shut the doors, when the Duke's escort cried aloud, 'Kill! kill! mort dieu! Kill the rebels!' Stones were thrown, and Guise received a blow on his forehead. The fray became serious, 60 were slain and 200 wounded. Morel the minister was seized, but subsequently escaped. (*See* FELICE, 'Hist. of the Protestants of France,' v.)

Massacre of Wyo'ming (*The*).

In Pennsylvania, June and July 1778. The whole colony was either butchered or driven into exile by the British and Indians under Colonel John Butler, during the American War of Independence. Campbell has a poem on the subject, entitled 'Gertrude of Wyoming.'

Massacre of 1641 (*The*). Ireland.

The Catholics of Ulster whose estates had been confiscated entered into a general conspiracy to extirpate the English settled in Ireland. Roger More headed the insurgents, and Richelieu promised him a supply of French troops. The plot was discovered and frustrated, but O'Neale and his confederates were in arms and seized the houses, cattle, and goods of the English in Ulster. A general massacre followed; public buildings were burnt to the ground, private houses destroyed, the rebellion spread, and 40,000 persons perished before the onslaught could be stayed. It was ten years before the rebellion was stamped out, because Charles I. was too much occupied with his own affairs to attend to those of Ireland.

Massacre of the Albigenses

(*The*). 1208–1224 (Philippe II. Auguste); 1227 (Louis VIII. le Lion); 1545–1547 (François I.). The Albigenses were religious reformers, and the first massacre was entrusted by Philippe Auguste to Simon de Montfort, 'the French Maccabæus.' He massacred 20,000 of them at Beziers, and burnt 450 to death at Carcassone (3 syl.). The second massacre was urged on by Pope Honorius III., who commanded Louis le Lion to 'purge his land of heretics.' The third massacre was in the reign of François I., who commissioned John of Oppido to root out the accursed heretics, and the baron but too faithfully executed this horrible commission. All the inhabitants of 22 towns and villages were put to the sword·or burnt to death at midnight in their own houses.

How Catholics can declaim against the persecutions of the Roman emperors is past understanding. Oh! for the beam and the mote!

Massacre of the Arabian Brigands, 1302. The emirs, the kadis, and fakirs' contrived a plot to extirpate the Arabian brigands. Having got together four companies of men, they fell on the brigands north, south, east, and west simultaneously. 'And,' we are told, ' from the province of Djized on the west to that of Atfih on the east, every Arab, old or young, male or female, was ruthlessly massacred. Of these 16,000 were ripped up; and if a fugitive Arab took refuge in a town, the word *dakik* was put to him as a shibboleth, and if the Arabic word *kaf* was heard, instant death followed ' (Taki-Eddin Ahmad Makrizi, ' History of the Mamlook Sultans,' translated by M. Quatremère).

Massacre of the Armagnacs [*Ar-ma-nyak*], 11, 12, 13 June, 1418, by the Paris mob. The Parisians had been driven to madness by the Burgundian and Armagnac factions, increased by the invasions of Henry V., the scandalous conduct of Queen Isabella, and the imbecility of the king. In their fury they fell on the Orléanists and Armagnacs, hoping to extirpate them, under the belief that they were in alliance with the English. We are told that 14,000 were slaughtered in three days, beginning with Sunday, 12 June. The constable, the chancellor, six bishops, 3,500 persons of rank, besides the common people, fell in this dreadful massacre at Paris.

Massacre of the Benjamites (3 syl.). Judges xx. A Levite having lodged a complaint against the Benjamites respecting a concubine, 400,000 Israelites took up arms to punish the offending tribe. The Benjamites in self-defence flew to arms, and brought to the field 26,000 men of war, and 700 men of Gibeah (v.15). In the first day's conflict the Benjamites slew 22,000 Israelites, and on the second day 18,000 more (a total of 40,000). Finding they had no chance in open fight, the Israelites laid an ambush in the meadows of Gibeah, and pretending to flee, inveigled the Benjamites to the meadow, when the ambush fell on them and slew 25,100 of them (v. 35).

It is quite beyond the scope of this dictionary to reconcile these statements, which seem to require some amendment. All that is here set down is the fact that the Benjamites were almost extirpated in this massacre.

Massacre of the Ben-Ouffias, by the French, 6 April, 1833. The whole subjugation of Algeria by the French is marked by treachery; but none of their acts was more disgraceful than the massacre of the Ben-Ouffias by General Savary duc de Rovigo. On 6 April, 1833, he sent a battalion of the foreign legion and a squadron of chasseurs to fall on these unsuspecting victims in the dark hours of the night, and at daybreak they were all dead men, who had been massacred in their sleep. Savary returned to Paris death-stricken, and died the June following.

This calls to mind the narrative of Lactantius in his ' De Mortibus Persecutorum.'

Massacre of the Blues. All Constantinople in the 6th cent. was divided into two factions, the Greens and the Blues. Anastāsius the emperor was a Green (491–518), and the Greens, having concealed daggers, entered the hippodrome, and massacred 3000 of the Blues.

Justinian the Great was a Blue (527-565), and then the Blues were the nuisance of the streets, molesting, robbing, brawling, and even murdering those found in the streets after sunset.

Massacre of the Burgundians in Soissons [*Swossŏng*], 1414. When the Armagnacs drove the Burgundians out of Paris they marched to Compiègne and laid siege to Soissons. When the gates were opened the Armagnacs rushed in and perpetrated one of the most frightful massacres in history. Men, women, and children were slaughtered without mercy; the churches and monasteries were pillaged; the sacred vestments and ornaments were scattered; the relics and images demolished; the heads of the governor and his chief officers were cut off, and 200 Englishmen were hanged.

Massacre of the Champ de Mars, 17 July, 1791. When La Fayette and the mayor Bailly dispersed the mob assembled in the Champ de Mars to petition for the abolition of royalty. Brissot had prepared the petition, and the people were called upon to sign it on Sunday 17 July, at the wooden altar in the Champ de Mars. Brissot did not put in an appearance, and the mob, tired of waiting, drew up their own petition, still preserved in the archives of Paris. At 6 p.m. Bailly the mayor and La Fayette with his national guards arrived to disperse the crowd. The mob assailed them, and La Fayette commanded the guards to fire. Several were killed and more wounded ; some say thousands: Desmoulins put the number at 400, but probably between 30 and 40 was the real number. A terrible panic ensued, and all the 'patriots' hid themselves till the panic had passed away.

Massacre of the Danes (*The*).

St. Bryce's day, 13 Nov., 1002. On this night Ethelred the Unready caused all the Danes in the kingdom to be secretly murdered. This massacre was accompanied with circumstances of shocking barbarity. Among other cruelties, the Danish women were placed in holes in the earth as deep as their waists, and then mastiff dogs were set on them. The sister of Sweyn was not spared. Her name was Gunilda, and she is said to have been married to a noble Dane settled in England, and named Paleng. Her children were first murdered in her presence, and she herself afterwards.

Her brother Sweyn (or Sueno) *Fork-Beard* (*q.v.*) in revenge subjugated all England, and was crowned king in 1013.

Massacre of the Gothic Youths

(*The*), A.D. 378. After the battle of Hadrianople, so disastrous to the Romans, and the death of Valens, Julius mastergeneral of the troops proposed to the senate a general massacre of all the Gothic youths distributed for purposes of education through the different cities of the East. Having concerted his plans, the Gothic youths were invited to assemble on a given day in the forum 'for the purpose of receiving a grant of land.' They assembled according to the proclamation, and being assembled were all indiscriminately slaughtered.

Massacre of the Greens, A.D. 532.

Justinian (527–565) was a Blue, his predecessor Anastasius (491–518) had been a Green. The two factions united for a few days in the 'Nika Sedition' (*q.v.*), but the Blues separated again, and the two factions were as fierce as ever. The place of general assembly was the hippodrome; and one day Belisarius with his veteran troops entered the place to quell a disturbance. The Blues left in a body, and 'more than 30,000 Greens were massacred.'

Massacre of the Helots, B.C. 424.

The eighth year of the Peloponnesian War was notorious for the massacre of 2,000 Helots by the Lacedæmonians. Alarmed lest these slaves should turn against them, the ephors proclaimed that all Helots who had distinguished themselves during the war should come forward and claim their liberty. A large body appeared, out of whom 2,000 were selected as worthy of emancipation. Crowned with garlands, these unhappy Helots were secretly massacred by the ephors, to rid the state of what might prove a future danger.

Massacre of the Innocents

(*The*). At the birth of Jesus, Herod the Great, in order to destroy 'the future king of the Jews,' massacred all the infant children of Bethlehem from two years old and under.

Micah v. 2 tells us that Bethlehem was a little place; it was a suburban village. Suppose it contained a thousand inhabitants, the male infants under two years of age would be about half a dozen.

Massacre of the Italians (*The*),

by Mithridātēs, B.C. 88. Mithridātēs king of Pontus, during the solemnities of his marriage with a Greek woman of Stratonicéa, sent forth an edict to every city in the province of Asia to put to death every Italian within its borders. In one day as many as 80,000 Italians were massacred in compliance with this edict.

This reminds us of the massacre of St. Bartholow's Eve, which was also executed during the marriage festivities of Henri [Henri IV.] and the Princess Marguerite.

Massacre of the Jan'izaries

(*The*), 15 June, 1826. The janizaries were organised (1326–1359) into the sultan's body-guard by Orchan sultan of Turkey. In 1800 they were increased to 115,000 men, but became, like the Roman prætorian guard, too powerful, and Mahmoud II., who owed his throne to them, resolved to suppress such a dangerous power. A mutiny being excited, the sultan unfurled the sacred standard, and the soldiers cut down the janizaries with grapeshot in the narrow streets of Constantinople. At least 20,000 fell, and the rest were disbanded.

The Janizaries deposed Bajazet II. in 1512, and raised Selim to the throne; in 1595 they compassed the death of Amurath II.; in 1622 they deposed and slew Othman II.; the same year they elevated and deposed Mustapha; in 1649 they deposed Ibrahim; in 1703 they deposed Mustapha II.; in 1730 they procured the death of the grand vizier, imprisoned Achmet III., and elevated Mohammed; in 1816 they slew Selim III.; and in 1826 they rebelled against Mahmoud, and were stamped out.

Massacre of the Ma'gians (*The*),

B.C. 522. On the death of Cambȳses king of Persia, the Magians, one of the six tribes of the Medes, put forward one of their number, named Patizīthês, to assume the name of Smerdis son of Cyrus, who had been put to death by his brother Cambȳsês. Darius Hystaspês discovered the conspiracy and made a general massacre of the Magi.

Massacre of the Mameluke Beys, 1811.

At Cairo Egypt was governed by 300 Mameluke beys, but Mehemet Ali, pacha of Egypt, supplanted these 300, and kept the government in his own hands. Fearful of a rising, the pacha invited all the beys to a splendid procession in honour of his son Tossun being created general-in-chief. They came in all their pomp, but being within the palace court, were fired on by the pacha's soldiery and killed. Mehemet then sent to the governors of his several provinces to send the respective beys in chains to Cairo, where they were put to death. The entire number of beys thus massacred was from 600 to 700.

Massacre of the Mar'onites

(3 syl.) or Christians of Syria by the Drusês. It began 28 May, 1860; massacre at Hasbeyd 5 June, 1860; massacre at Deir-el-Kammer, 21 June; massacre at Damasus 9 and 10 July, 1860.

The Druses inhabit the range of Mount Lebanon, and divide possession of some 200 towns with the Maronites. Their religion is a mixture of the Jewish, Christian, and Mohammedan. The Maronites, since 1445, have been united to the Church of Rome. See 'Druses.'

Massacre of the Mitylenæans

(The), B.C. 427. A large number of prisoners fell into the hands of the Athenians in the Mitylenæan war. It was discussed by the conquerors how these prisoners should be disposed of, and Cleon advocated their instant massacre. After more than 2,000 had been put to death, the Athenians sickened with the whole-sale slaughter, and the massacre was stopped.

Massacre of the Monks of Bangor, A.D. 607.

Ethelfrith king of Northumbria attacked Chester. Hard by the city 2,000 monks assembled in the monastery of Bangor, and after a three days' fast, followed the British army to the field. Ethelfrith watched the wild gestures and outstretched arms of these monks as they stood apart invoking the vengeance of heaven on the foe. He took them for enchanters, and cried aloud,

'Bear they arms or no arms, they cry against us to their gods,' and as he spoke his soldiers rushed upon them, and put them all to the sword.

These monks were praying for the success of Brocmail king of Powys, but when his army saw the massacre, it fled, and the victory of Ethelfrith was complete.

Massacre of the Paulicians

(The). The Paulicians were the Huguenots of the 8th and 9th cents., and Theodora was the Catharine de Medicis who 'hated them with a perfect hatred.' In a few years this zealous empress put to death by gibbet, stake, or sword 100,000 of these Christians. See 'Slaughter,' 'Persecutions,' &c.

This is a long and sickening list, but by no means exhaustive. No mention, for example, is here made of the many massacres of the Jews, in which Russia of modern states stands sadly pre-eminent.

Massil'ianism.

The same as 'Semi-pela'gianism' (q.v.): so called from Massilia, the Latin for Marseille, whence the 'heresy' arose.

The doctrine was this: Man can go to the palace door, but must be ushered into the presence-chamber. In other words, man can repent, forsake sin, and wish to be a Christian, but having thus come to the door, God's grace must then lead him all the rest of the way till he enters into the presence-chamber of God.

Massoretes

(3 syl.). Jews who helped to fix the vowel points of the Hebrew Scriptures on the authority of tradition (massōra). The vowels added by these doctors are called the Massoretic points.

The main authority for these points is the school of Tiberius in the 5th cent.

Master.

In Oxford University, the title held by the head of three of the colleges, Balliol, Pembroke, and University College. In Cambridge University the head of King's College is called the provost and of Queen's president, but of all the other colleges he is called the master.

Master of Gray (The).

Son of Lord Gray, employed by Queen Elizabeth to undermine the influence of Stuart earl of Arran in Scotland. In 1585 Arran was driven from the royal presence and his estates were confiscated.

Master of Sentences (The),

'Magister Sententiarum.' Peter Lombard the Schoolman, who died 1164. So called from his book entitled 'Sententiarum Libri IV.,' a collection of quotations or sentences from St. Augustine and other

Fathers on sundry points of Christian doctrine, with objections and replies. It was a manual for the scholastic disputants of the middle ages.

Master of the Buckhounds.
Who has control of all matters relating to the royal hunts, with a salary of 1,700*l.* a year, but he goes out of office with a change of ministry.

Master of the Ceremonies, 1603.
Instituted for the more ceremonious reception of ambassadors and persons of distinction.

Beau Nash was called 'Master of the Ceremonies,' but all that this designation signified was that he arranged dictatorially the amusements at Bath, or was president of the Bath entertainments.

Master of the Horse.
The third great officer of the court, having the superintendence of the royal stables. He is master of the equerries, pages, grooms, coachmen, saddlers, farriers, and all artificers working in the royal stables. He is responsible for the disbursements in his department, but his accounts are audited. On state occasions he rides next to the sovereign. The salary is 2,500*l.* a year.

Master of the Household.
An officer in the lord steward's department whose duty it is to superintend the choice of servants. Salary 1,158*l.* a year.

Master of the Rolls,
in Chancery, 1286. A judge of the Court of Chancery, who ranks next to the lord chancellor. Since 1838 he has been keeper of the public records; his salary is 7,000*l.* a year.

He has a deputy-keeper, with several assistants and senior clerks.

Master-singers, 1350–1570.
The highest degree of the Guild of Rhetoric in Germany. The three degrees were apprentices, companions, and masters. The guild consisted of poets and musicians; the former were, strictly speaking, master-poets, and the latter master-singers. These literary guilds were first established in Mainz, Nürnberg, and Strasburg. They held their guild every Sunday in the cathedral of the city, and Karl IV. gave them corporate rights and a corporate seal. By far the most eminent of these master-singers was Hans Sachs (1494–1578), a cobbler by trade, but a true genius, and prince of satirists.

Sachs, pronounce *Sax.*

Master's Side (*The*),
for murderers and other capital offenders.

When Newgate was used as the chief convict prison, the 'Master's side' was the part so appropriated.

Masters (*The Four*):
1. Michael O'Clerighe, who died 1643; 2. Cucoirighe O'Clerighe; 3. Maurice Conry; 4. Fearfeassa Conry; authors of 'Annals of Donegal.'

O'Clerighe is sometimes Anglicised into *Clerkson* and Cucoirighe into *Peregrine.*

Masters and Fraternity of the Passion and Resurrection (*The*),
13th to 15th cents. A company of monks incorporated by Charles VI. of France to represent dramatically in churches religious mysteries. The most famous of their dramas were 'The Passion,' 'The Resurrection,' 'The Incarnation,' and 'St. Catherine.' The first two were performed before the king on his marriage with Isabeau of Bavaria. *See* 'Ober-Ammergau.'

Masters in Chancery.
Chief officers under the judges in the Court of Chancery, whose duty it was to take minutes of the proceedings, and tax the bills of cost. Abolished 1852.

Masters of Court.
The chief officers under the judges. Their duties are to attend the sittings of the courts during term, make minutes of the proceedings, and to tax bills of costs.

Matemans.
So the Lollards were called from their frugal lives and the poverty of their appearance. Also called 'Alexians' (*q.v.*), 'Brethren and Sisters of Alexius,' and 'Cellites' (*q.v.*). They rose in Antwerp about 1300, and were admitted by Sixtus IV. amongst the religious orders in 1472.

Materialists.
Those who believe that man has only a material nature, and that thought, conscience, intelligence, &c. are works of the brain. They deny the existence of soul or spirit, and deny also all that is supernatural, as the spirit god, miracles, and the resurrection.

Mathematicians (2nd cent.).
Astrologers, magicians, and diviners. In Justinian's code is a chapter headed *De Maleficis et Mathematicis*; and the Theodosian code enjoins the banishment of mathematicians from all Roman cities and the burning of their books.

Mathematics (*Professorship of*).
In the University of Cambridge, 1663,

founded by Henry Lucas, and endowed with an estate in Bedfordshire worth 150*l.*; but the present stipend is 850*l.* *See* ' Sadlerian Professorship, &c.,' ' Smith's Prizes,' ' Lucasian Professor,' 'Adams' Prize.'

Mathi′as, brother of Rudolf II., and son of Maximilian II.; kaiser-king of Germany of the House of Austria (1556, 1612-1619). Having no child, he adopted his cousin Ferdinand, in whose reign was the Thirty Years' War against the Protestants. Contemporary with James I.

Father, MAXIMILIAN II. [his brother RUDOLF II. preceded him on the throne] ; *Mother,* Mary, daughter of Kaiser Karl V.; *Wife,* Anne of Austria, no issue. *Contemporary* with James I.

Mathurins *(The),* or ' Maturins,' 1199. A religious order instituted by St. Jean de Matha and Félix de Valois for the redemption of Christian slaves in Barbary. They were originally called *Trinitaires,* or *Les Religieux de la Sainte Trinité.* The name ' Mathurins' was given to them in France, because in 1226 they occupied a church built in Paris in honour of St. Mathurin. The order was suppressed in 1790.

St. Mathurin (*Maturinus*) lived in the 4th and 5th cent. He was a confessor born in Sens and buried at Larchant, in the Gâtinais, where a church was erected to his honour. Another was built in Paris, which was given to the Trinitarians. His relics are preserved in the parish church of Moncontour, in Brittany, and many pilgrims during Pentecost flock to the church every year.

Matilda the Good, cousin and first wife of Henry I. of England, daughter of Malcolm king of Scotland. Married 1100. died 1118.

Matins, or ' Nocturns.' One of the eight daily services of the Catholic Church, and the first of the four great ones at daybreak. *See* ' Canonical Hours.'

Matronalia, 1 March. The festival of the Roman matrons to commemorate the reconciliation of the Sabine women with their fathers and brothers after the ' Rape of the Sabines.'

Matthew Parker's Bible, 1572. The second folio edition of the ' Great Bible ' (*q.v.*), with corrections and several prolegomena under the supervision of Archbishop Parker. *See* ' Bibles.'

Matthews' Bible, 1537. A version of the Bible in English edited by John Rogers, superintendent of an English church in Germany, and published by him under the fictitious name of Thomas Matthews. It was based on the translations of Tyndale and Miles Coverdale. ' Cranmer's Great Bible ' was a corrected edition of Matthews' Bible. *See* ' Bibles.'

Mat′urins *(The).* *See* ' Mathurins.'

Matutinal Mass. ' Missa Matutinalis,' a mass ' quæ post exactas matutinas dicitur.' The matutinæ follow the nocturns. *See* ' Mass.'

Matutinæ in profestis et dominicis, quibus tardius nocturnæ preces persolvebantur. — DU CANGE, vol. iv. p. 607, col. 1.

Matuti′nus Pater, *i.e.* ' Father of the Morning'; so Janus was called by the ancient Romans, and prayers were addressed to him by pious Romans every morning.

Our word January is derived from this mythological deity.

Mausole′um *(The),* B.C. 351, or Sepulchre of Mausōlus of Caria, built by his widow Artemis′ia, and considered one of the seven wonders of the world. A.D. 1500 the sculptures of this marvellous mausoleum were actually employed by the knights of Rhodes in fortifying Halicarnassos ! Some of the sculptures have been rescued, and in 1846 were placed in the British Museum, as the ' Budrum Marbles.'

Max O'Rell. The pen-name of Paul Blouet, author of ' John Bull and his Island,' &c. His grandfather was Max Blouet, an officer in the French army. Being taken prisoner he was sent to England, and fell in love with an Irish girl, named O'Rell, whom he married.

Maxima Cæsariensis. One of the five provinces into which Britain was divided in the reign of the Emperor Sevērus. It included the northern part of England extending to the Wall of Sevērus, between the Tyne and the Solway. It had its own ruler, but that ruler was subject to the præfect or governor-general of the island.

Maximilian I., ' the Pennyless' and ' Taciturn.' Second monarch of the house of Austria (or Habsburg). Like his father, he died from a surfeit of melons (1459, 1486-1519).

Father, Kaiser Friedrich III. the Pacific; *Mother,* Elenore of Portugal; *Wives,* (1) Mary of Burgundy, only child of Charles *le Téméraire,* and heiress of 17 provinces; (2) Bianca Maria [Sforza] niece of Ludovico Sforza *Il Moro. Contemporary* with Henry VII. and VIII.

His eldest son was Philippe the Handsome, who married the Infanta Juaña of Spain (daughter of Ferdinand and Isabella), by which marriage Spain became united to the house of Austria. Philippe died leaving issue the famous Karl V. (Charles-quint) afterwards King of Spain, Austria, and America (the Golden Age of Spain). It was the son of Karl V. who married Mary queen of England.

. It was a magnificent period of European history—the period of Luther, the Humanists, printing, and Columbus. The popes were Alexander VI., Pius III., Julius II., and Leo X. The first of these was the patron of Michael Angelo and Raphael. In Spain were Ferdinand and Isabella; in Portugal Emmanuel the Great, founder of the Portuguese navy, the Mæcenas of Arts and Sciences, and the friend of Vasco da Gama. In England were Henry VIII. and Cardinal Wolsey; and in Turkey was Bajazet II., the conqueror of Constantinople.

Maximilian II. Kaiser-king of Germany (1525, 1564–1576), nephew of Karl V. (Charles-quint), and of the house of Austria. He had fifteen children.

Father, Ferdinand I.; *Mother,* Anne; *Wife,* Mary his cousin, daughter of Karl V. *Contemporary* with Elizabeth.

May (*The Maids'*). There were four historic Mays in the eventful life of ' the Maid ' (Jeanne d'Arc).

1. At Vaucouleurs the Maid announced her mission to De Baudricourt, governor of Vaucouleurs, in May 1428.

2. At Orléans she compelled the English to raise the siege, 8 May, 1429.

3. At Compiègne she was besieged by the Duke of Burgundy and the English, May 1430; captured in a sortie against the Burgundian quarters, 24 May; given up to the English; and condemned to be burnt as a heretic by the University of Paris, 24 May, 1431.

4. At Rouen she was burned to death, 30 May, 1431.

Some say she was not burnt, but married to Robert des Armoises about 1438; that she was living in 1444; and that her sentence was reversed by the pope 7 July, 1456.

May Meetings (*The*). The great annual religious meetings held in Exeter Hall, Strand, London, during the month of May.

May 31 (*The Day of*), 1793. In the French Revolution, the commencement of the Reign of Terror, when the people of Paris, conducted by Henriot, invaded the Convention, compelled them to set Hébert at liberty, and to arrest the Girondins (*q.v.*).

The Reign of Terror was from 31 May, 1793, to 27 July, 1794 (the fall of Robespierre).

Maynooth [*The Royal College of St. Patrick*], in Ireland, 1795. Founded by Act of the Irish Parliament for the education of students designed for the Catholic priesthood. It was incorporated and endowed in 1845 by Acts 8, 9 Vict. c. xxv.; but in 1869 these acts were repealed, and the college received a large endowment in lieu of its previous annual subvention.

Mayor (*In England*). The title of Bailiff was changed to that of ' Mayor of London ' in the reign of Henry II. Richard I., in 1189, granted the citizens the right of choosing their own mayor; and the title was changed to Lord *Mayor* in 1354 by Edward III.

The chief magistrate of York was made *Lord* Mayor in 1389.

The first mayor of *Dublin* was appointed in 1409, and he was styled *Lord Mayor* in 1665 by Charles II.

The Mayor of the Palace, in *France,* existed as far back as 560, but merged into royalty on the accession of Pepin le Bref in 752.

The title of 'Right Honourable was conferred on the Lord Mayor of London by Edward III. His salary is 8,000*l.* for the year of office.

The first Lord Mayor's Show was in 1454, when Sir John Norman went by water to be sworn in at Westminster.

Mayor (*The*). Elected since the ' Municipal Corporations Act ' (*q.v.*) in 1835, from the councillors. If any councillor so elected does not choose to serve, he must pay a fine of 100*l.* The qualification of a mayor is the fact that he is a councillor, and if any other person serves in the office the fine is 50*l.* The mayor presides at all meetings of the council, and has (during his year of office) precedence in all places within the borough. He revises, with his two assessors, the burgess list, which he must sign in open court. He presides at the election of councillors, and is magistrate for the borough both during his official year and for the year following, when he is deputy mayor. He is also the returning officer at the election of members of Parliament.

Mayor of Garrett (*The*), 1741. Garrett is a hamlet between Tooting and Wandsworth in Surrey. The first mayor was the chairman of a club organised to prevent encroachments on the common. An encroachment took place not long afterwards, and the villagers won their suit, with costs, during a general election after Walpole's resignation. The event was celebrated by the election of a 'Mayor of Garrett,' who held office so long as the parliament sat, and with every new parliament a new mayor was elected, whose inauguration was celebrated with a village feast. Foote wrote a farce entitled 'The Mayor of Garrett.'

There have been several such' mockery mayors.' As the Seaside Mayor of Newcastle-under-Lyme; the mock mayor of Randwick in Gloucestershire; the mock mayor of Weston near Bath, &c.

Mayor of the Palace *(The).* 'Major domus'; in French 'Maire du Palais,' keeper of the privy purse and superintendent of the royal household in France. The Mayor of the Palace became the head of the aristocracy, and was the virtual ruler of France during the reigns of the *Rois Fainéants* (638–742). The office was curtailed by the Carlovingian kings and abolished by Hugues Capet.

Mazarin of Letters *(The).* D'Alembert (1717–1783), French mathematician, philosopher, and encyclopædist.

Maz'arinades (4 syl.), 1649–1652. Political squibs during the Fronde war. 'Près de quatre mille écrits satiriques, la plupart dirigés contre Mazarin, et dictés par la haine la plus âcre.' Motteville says, 'Never man of equal authority pardoned so many of his enemies, and never man committed so few to prison.'

Mazarine B'ble *(The).* The Gutenberg (? Schöffer) Bible, the earliest book printed in movable metal type. It contains no date, but a copy in the 'Bibliothèque Mazarine,' formed in 1648 for the Cardinal Mazarin by G. Naudé, and given to the public in 1688, contains the date of the illuminator Cremer, 1456, so that the Bible must have been printed before that date. Only seven copies in vellum exist, but there are known to be twenty-two copies on paper, some of them very imperfect. In 1855 Mr. Quaritch, bookseller, of Piccadilly (according to the 'Methodist Recorder'), gave 3,900*l.* for a copy at Sir J. Thorold's; certainly in 1887 he gave 2,650*l.* for the copy in the library of the late Earl of Crawford. One was sold in 1873 for 3,400*l.*, and a copy was sold in 1889 for 2,000*l.* *See* 'Bibles.'

A good vellum copy is worth 4,000*l.*

Of course it was called the Mazarine Bible because the copy in the Mazarine Library, Paris, gives the approximate date. There is another

25

Bible called the **Mazarine Bible, printed before** 1466 by Eggestein.

• A Psalmorum Codex (Sir J. Thorold's sale) was sold for the unprecedented sum of 4,500*l.*

Mazarin, a proper name; Mazarine, the adjective.

Mazarin'ians. Those who sided with Cardinal Mazarin in the Fronde War (1648–1653). The opponents were called the *Frondeurs.* The cause of this contention was Mazarin's prohibition of the Act of Union *(q.v.),* the 27 articles of demand by the Paris lawyers.

Such as the abolition of monopolies; the reduction of imposts; the prohibition to levy taxes without the authority of the States-General, or of arrest without assigning the cause; the obligation of bringing prisoners to trial within a given time, &c. Mazarin and the court party pronounced these demands an encroachment on royal privileges, and subversive to the government.

Maz'daas'nanism or ' Mazdaism.' The ancient Persian religion. So called from Ahura Mazdao, the all-wise spirit or supreme god of the Persians. This supreme god was supposed to be creator of the world, god of light and truth, without beginning of days or end of years. Mazdaism was reformed by Zoroaster or Zerdusht, whose disciples were called Guebres or Parsees.

Mazdaasnan means worshippers of Ormuzd. Parsees mean people of Pars or Fars *(i.e.* of Persia); and Guebre is a proper name = Cheber or Jebah. The Persian *gawr* means an infidel.

Mazzulo, 1503. A plague which desolated Italy. It carried off Philip of Burgos in 1506. Machiavel tells us in his 'Political Correspondences' that it especially attacked the head and chest, and was accompanied by a cough. It appeared in Padua in 1558, 1568, and 1580, and was most disastrous. *See* ' Plagues,' &c.

It appeared in France, and went there by the name of *Coqueluche.*

M.C. Master of the ceremonies [in court]; in the U.S.A. it means ' Member of Congress.'

Meagher of the Sword. Thomas Meagher, son of a Waterford merchant, the orator of the Young Irelanders. He emigrated to America, and became General Meagher. He obtained his sobriquet because his speeches were warlike harangues, and he himself was a dashing cavalier.

Meal-tub Plot *(The),* 1680. A supposed Presbyterian plot to seize the crown and prevent a popish succession. Revealed first to the Duke of York by a young man named Dangerfield. When the whole affair was proved to be false, and Dangerfield was committed to Newgate, he said with great seeming penitence that what he had told the duke was undoubtedly a forgery to cover a real plot. The real plot he said was a popish one, and the notes of the sham one would be found in a meal tub in the house of Mrs. Cellier, a Roman Catholic midwife. The papers were found there, and the plot was called the Meal-tub Plot.

This was the second of three plots. The first was the popish plot revealed by Titus Oates, and the third was the Ryehouse plot.

Mediator of the Helvet'ic League, 1803. A title and office assumed by Napoleon. By the treaty of Lunéville it was stipulated that the independence of Switzerland should be respected; but the French troops not being withdrawn, perpetual feuds were fomented by their instigation between one canton and another. Napoleon declared that this state of things must cease; and assuming to himself the right of arbitration, he reduced Switzerland to a kind of dep ndency under the military yoke of France. For this ' service ' the Swiss were ordered to supply 16,000 men to the French army.

Medical Rose (*The*), or ' Rosa Anglica,' about 1492. The medical work of John Gaddesden. Gaddesden was educated at Merton College, Oxford, and was thought to be the grand luminary of physic; but his prescriptions are a wonderful compound of superstitions, theological injunctions, charms, and quackery.

Medice'an Stars (*The*). Jupiter's satellites were so called by Galileo, who discovered them, but the term has not come into general use. Galileo's celebrated work, 'The Sidereal Messenger,' is dedicated to Cosmo de' Medici II. fourth duke of Tuscany.

Med'icis (*A*). A huge standing collar propped up by a wire frame, and inclosing the whole back of the head. This ugliness superseded the ruff, and was introduced by Marie de Medicis, wife of Henri IV. of France.

Mediæval History closes with the invention of printing and the discovery of America, and modern history begins

with the Lutheran reformation. All these three events occurred about 1500. So that mediæval history closes with the 15th cent., and modern history begins with the 16th cent.

Printing made generally known	... ...	1460
Columbus set sail for America		1492
Reformation begun in Germany by Luther		1517

Mediæval Schoolmen. For those bearing complementary titles *see* p. 261.

Medjidie, 1852. An order of honour instituted in Turkey by the Sultan Abdûl-Medjid for foreigners as well as natives.

Medmenham Club (*The*), 18th cent. It was held in Medmenham Abbey. The club consisted of wild spirits, called euphemistically ' wits and humourists,' who assumed the name of ' Monks of St. Francis.' The inscription over the door was ' Fais ce que tu voudras.' Langley gives an account of it, and significantly suggests that it is wise to draw a curtain over it.

Rabelais says the motto over the door of the Abbey of Thélème was FAIS CE QUE VOULDRAS.—*Gargantua* i. 52-57.

Medon'tidæ. The thirteen archons of Athens, so called from Medon son of Kodros the first archon.

Meerut Massacre (*The*), 10 May, 1857. The native troops or Sepoys revolted, shooting their European officers, firing the bungalows, and massacring the European inmates without respect to age or sex. *See* ' Indian Mutiny ' and ' Massacre.'

Megaclëan (*A*). A pertinacious and obnoxious political opponent, so called from Megaclês the Athenian archon. In the time of Cylon and Pittacos Megaclês and his adherents were for ever striving to upset the government, and restore it to an archonate.

Megale'sian Games (*The*), B.C. 206. In honour of Cybēlē, the great [megălē] goddess. They commenced 4 April, and lasted a week. During the Second Punic War an oracle had declared that the Romans would conquer the Carthaginians if they carried off their palladium, a great aerolith, sacred to Idēa or Cybēlē. The senate sent an ambassador to demand it, and it was transported to Rome in grand procession. A temple was erected and games instituted in its honour.

Meister-sänger, 14th cent. A corporation of German poets and musicians which succeeded the Minnesängers. They were for the most part artisans, by far the most celebrated being Hans Sachs [*Sax*]. In 1378 Karl IV. gave them a charter and a seal. *See* 'Mastersingers.'

Mek'hitarists. So called from Peter Mekhitar (1676–1749) of Cappadocia. While in Constantinople (1700) he joined the Armenians, and afterwards the Catholics. Being driven from Constantinople by religious persecution, Mekhitar took refuge in Smyrna, then in the Morēa. To Mekhitar we owe an Armenian Bible (1733), an Armenian grammar, and an Armenian dictionary.

His disciples, the Mekhitarists of St. Lazzaro (degli Armeni) are learned Benedictines whose publications have a European reputation.

Melancholy Isle (*The*). Tobago, in which an English colony was planted in 1737. So called because, viewed from the north, it seems only a mass of lofty and gloomy mountains, with black precipices descending abruptly to the sea. It is under a lieutenant-governor, a council of nine, and a house of assembly of sixteen members.

Melancholy Jacques (*The*). Jean Jacques Rousseau (1712–1777). He was a misanthrope and a recluse, of morbid sensibilities and unhappy spirit. The phrase is from Shakespeare's 'As You Like It.'

Melancholy Magyars (*The*), 955. The Hungarian fugitives in the great battle of Augsburg, on the river Lech. They were condemned by their countrymen to servitude.

Magyars, pronounce *Mard'-yars.*

Melbourne Ministry (*The*), 1835–1841. Called by Sir George Trevelyan 'that melancholy period.' Mr. Torrens says that Lord Melbourne was neither an orator, nor jurist, nor financier, nor great legislator, nor great leader, nor consistent politician. This is true, but he was a man of most wonderful tact. Of the Melbourne Ministry Praed says their policy was

To promise, pause, prepare, postpone,
And end by letting things alone ;
In short, to earn the people's pay
By doing nothing every day.

Melbourne's Six Acts, 1835–1841.
Corporation Reform (England), 1835.
Corporation Reform (Scotland), 1836.
New Marriage Law (by registration, &c.), 1836, 1837, 1840.
Tithe Commutation, 1836, 1837, 1839.
Poor Law Reform (Ireland), 1838.
Municipal Corporation Reform (Ireland), 1840.

Melchites (2 syl.), or 'Imperialists.' Syriac, Egyptian, and Levantine Christians generally so called in reproach on account of their implicit submission to the edict of the Emperor Marcian for the publication and reception of the doctrines and ceremonies of the Greek Church, and for submission to the decisions of the Council of Chalcēdon. Their head is called the Patriarch of Antioch, and dwells at Damascus.

They are Roman Catholics of the Eastern rite, and have a service in Arabic. The Copts of the Greek Church are called Melchites by their monophysitic brethren.

Mele'tian Schism (*The*), 4th cent. Caused by Meletius bishop of Lycopŏlis, who had been deposed for offering sacrifice to idols to avoid persecution. When Peter of Alexandra died Meletius took on himself the power of ordination, and was most relentless in rejecting the lapsed. The Council of Nice, A.D. 325, decreed him to be schismatic.

Mele'tians, 300–400. Followers of Meletius bishop of Lycopolis, in Egypt. *See above.*

Melitine (*The*). A legion, also called the Thundering or Fulminant Legion from its dash and courage. It was composed of Christians, and it is said that the army of Marcus Aurelius was saved by its prayers in 174, when on the point of perishing in the desert.

Mellifluous Doctor (*The*). St. Bernard, abbot of Clairvaux (1091–1153, canonised by Alexander III. in 1174.) It was this St. Bernard who preached up the second crusade in 1146, and was the founder of the Bernardins (*q.v.*). Called the 'Last of the Fathers' and the 'Oracle of the Church.'

St. Bernard procured the condemnation of Abelard at the Council of Sens, in 1140 ; was mainly instrumental in the death at the stake of Pierre de Bruys and Arnaud de Brescia, two religious reformers, who declaimed against the ill lives of the clergy, and vehemently opposed Gilbert de la Porree, bishop of Poitiers, who had attacked the Nominalists (*q.v.*). However, when the monk Raoul proposed to massacre all the Jews, St. Bernard resolutely opposed the suggestion.

⁎ The St. Bernard who founded the hospice was St. Bernard of Menthon, and lived about a century earlier (930-1008).

Melon Colic. The first three kaiser-kings of the house of Austria or Habsburg died from dysentery brought on by eating melons: Albert [Albrecht] II., Friedrich III., and Maximilian I.

Melton Mowbray Hunt (*The*), established 1759. The four chief members used to form a sort of authorised court in all matters connected with the chase in England. The three original packs were (1) the Duke of Rutland's; (2) Mr. Osbaldeston's, or the Quorn hounds, Leicester; and (4) the Earl of Lonsdale's, or the Cottesmore hounds, of Rutland-shire. There has been no such 'hunt' for many years, but the Leicestershire hounds are still celebrated, and the Duke of Rutland's hounds, the Quorn, and the Cottesmore hounds are well known (1890).

Member of the Sacred Crown (*A*). A nobleman of Hungary. Hungary was the Land of the Sacred Crown. The Sacred Crown was the crown given by the pope to St. Stephen, king of Hungary (979, 997–1038).

Members' Prizes (*The*). Of the University of Cambridge. Two prizes of thirty guineas each, one for a Latin essay and one for an English essay, on a subject connected with English history. Founded 1752, when there were four prizes, which in 1870 were reduced to two. Any student below the degree of M.A. may be a candidate.

Memmia or Remmia (*Lex*), or-dained that an accusation should not be admitted against those who were absent on the public service; and if anyone was convicted of false accusation, he was to be branded on the forehead with the letter K (*kalumnia*).

As for those who have calumniated you by leasing-making, I protest to heaven I think they have justly incurred the penalty of the *Memnonia Lex*, also called *Lex Riïemnia*.—Sir W. Scott, *Waverley*, chap. xii. (Abbotsford edition).

Memnon. The same as Proteus, and either of these is the same as Ramēses V. Proteus is not a proper name at all, but a Greek word equivalent to 'Egyp-tian king,' or Pharaoh. Ramēses V. died B.C. 1165.

Memorable 2,000 (*The*), 1661. The 2,000 ministers who refused to com-ply with the Uniformity Act passed in the reign of Charles II., and threw up their preferments. *See* 'Seven Bishops.'

The health of 'the Protestant dissenting ministers, the worthy successors of the memorable 2,000,' was proposed by the Chairman, the Duke of Essex.

Dinner given at the Freemasons' Hall to com-memorate the Repeal of the Test Act, 1828.

Memorial Crosses. Raised some-times where the bier of an eminent person stopped for a time, on its way to the place of burial, as the memorial crosses of Eleanor of Castile, called 'Eleanor Crosses,' as those of Waltham, Northampton, and Geddington. Charing cross was destroyed in 1647, but a model of it stands in front of the South-Eastern Railway station, Strand, London.

Memphitic Version of the Scrip-tures in the dialect of Lower Egypt. Also called the 'Coptic.' Supposed to be of the 3rd cent. *See* 'Scriptures.'

The version in the dialect of Upper Egypt, called the 'Sahidic' or 'Thebaidic,' is supposed to be the older of the two.

Men of '89 (*The*). The leaders of the French revolution, such as Mirabeau, Danton, Robespierre, Marat, St. Just, &c.

Men of the 14th of July. Red republicans of France. The reference is to the taking of the Bastille, 14 July, 1789.

A letter was handed in by Santerre to the president, stating that the petitioners wanted to be admitted to . . . prove themselves still the Men of the 14th July.—Howitt, *Hist. of Eng.* (Geo. III. p. 617).

Menageries (*Les*). The reunions of Mme. de Tencin in the regency of Louis XV. In these reunions one met with Montesquieu, author of the 'Persian Letters'; Helvetius, author of,' L'Esprit'; Fontenelle and Lamotte, Rollin, Vertot, the two Daciers, Voltaire, and Lord Bolingbroke. They were the nursery of the encyclopædists.

Menander, the Samaritan, who suc-ceeded Simon Magus, gave himself out to be one of the Æons, and that no one could be saved who was not of his baptism; but that all who were so baptized should be subject to death nor to the infirmities of old age (Eusebius, bk. iii. chap. 26).

Menandrians. Followers of Me-nander. *See above.*

Mendicants or Begging Friars (*The*). Numerous orders which truly infested the church in the 13th cent. They broke in everywhere upon the parochial clergy, usurped their office, set up altars of their own, withdrew the people from communion with their parish priests, and became so rich that they raised stately palaces, and became the most famous and most contemptible of all the clergy. In 1274 the Council of Lyons restricted them to the four orders of Franciscans, Dominicans, Carmelites, and Augustines.

Menippean Satire (*The*). A political pamphlet, partly in verse and partly in prose. The object of the satire was to show up the perfidious intentions of Spain in regard to France, and the criminal ambition of the Guise family. The chief writers were Leroy (died 1593), Pithou (1544–1596), Rapin the poet (1540–1609), and Passerat (1534–1602).

Called Menippean from Menippus, a cynic philosopher of the 1st cent.

Men'nonites (3 syl.). Followers of Menno (called *Simönis*, *i.e.* 'Son of Simon') of Holland (1496–1561). He was the founder of the reformed Anabaptist school, after the death of John of Leyden. Menno was a man of most gentle, earnest, modest, and spiritual nature, wholly unlike the wild fanatics known as Anabaptists. Like the Quakers the Mennonites will take no oath, nor will they hold office, employ force, or sanction capital punishment. They baptize by sprinkling, but only after a confession of faith. The New Testament is their only rule of faith; they object to the word 'person' as applied to the Father, Son, and Holy Ghost, and disbelieve in original sin.

In 1683 a following was established in America, where they number at least 250,000, and they are abundant in Southern Russia. They are divided into Mild and Strict Mennonites.

Mensal Lands (*The*). A grant of land from each of the provinces of Ireland to enlarge the county of Meath. Exacted by Tuathal, son of Feredach the Just, A.D. 136.

Merca'tor (*Isidore*). A Cenobite of the 8th cent. for many years supposed to be the author of the 'False Decretals' (*q.v.*), now generally assigned to Bene-

dict Levita of Mentz, or to Riculfe archbishop of Mentz, who introduced them into France in 811.

Mercator's Projection. Maps so constructed that the lines of longitude are straight and not curved. This device of representing a globe in perspective on a flat surface is due to Edward Wright, an Englishman; but the chart so arranged by Wright was printed and published by Gerard Mercātor, a printer of maps in Flanders, who died at the age of 82, in 1594.

Mercator's real name was Kauffmann, but a foolish fashion prevailed of adopting Greek or Latin names, generally translations of the German. Thus Melanchthon's real name was Schwarzerdt; Desiderius Erasmus is a classical form of Gheraerd Gheraerd; Œcolampadius is a Greek form of Hausschein. Nostradamus is a Latinised form of Notre-Dame (Michel de Notre-Dame); Joannes Stobæus is John Stubbs.

Other names not classical are Jacopo Robusti, known as Jacopo Tintoretto; François-Marie Arouet, known as Voltaire; Molière was the assumed name of Jean-Baptiste Poquelin, &c.

Merchant Adventurers (*The*), or 'Brotherhood of Sir Thomas à Becket,' 1296. A society established by John duke of Brabant, and sanctioned by Edward I., to promote woollen manufactures. Foreign merchants were allowed trial by jury, half the jury being foreigners, and they had a justiciary [consul] in London for their protection. *See* 'Merchants of the Steelyard.'

It received a patent in 1505 from Henry VII., and was incorporated by Elizabeth in 1564.

The clergy were called Sir, and addressed as 'Sir-reverence,' in the 'good old times.'

Merchant Queen (*The*). Venice.

The Merchant Queen, in order to preserve inviolate the Levantine commerce, humbled herself at the footstool of the Sultan.—*History of Venice*, vol. ii. p. 81 (Murray, 1838).

Merchant Taylors' School, 1568. Founded by the Merchant Taylors' Guild.

Merchants (*The Statute of*) 'Statutum de Mercatöribus,' 1283. The statute of Acton Burnel is so called. It was passed at Acton Burnel, in Shropshire, in the reign of Edward I., and its object was the speedy recovery of debts due to merchants and traders. The security which the merchant obtained in 1285 by a seisin of the debtor's lands, &c., was called a 'Statute Merchant.' *See* 'Statute of Acton Burnel.'

Merchants of the Steelyard. London Hanse Town merchants, formed into a company early in the 13th cent.

In 1235 they obtained privileges from Henry III., and received a charter in 1280 from Edward I., with further privileges from Edward IV. and Henry VII. Finally abolished by Elizabeth in 1578. This company in 1505 was opposed by the 'Merchant Adventurers' (*q.v.*).

Merchants' Petition *The*), 1820. Drawn up by Mr. Tooke for free trade, especially in corn. Being signed by more than half the court of directors of the Bank of England, and a large number of the chief London merchants, it was presented to the House by Alexander Baring [Lord Ashburton].

Mercia. The last formed and largest of the kingdoms, since called the Heptarchy. It was founded A.D. 582 by Crida or Creda, and included 17 counties and most of Herts.

The counties were—Staffordshire, Worcestershire, and Warwickshire ; Cheshire, Derby and Notts ; Gloucestershire, Oxfordshire, and Bucks ; Shropshire and Herefordshire ; Leicestershire and Rutlandshire ; Lincolnshire, Norfolk, Hunts, Bedfordshire, and most of Herts.

Mercian Province. So called from the river Mersey.

Merciless Parliament (*The*), or 'The Unmerciful Parliament,' 3 Feb. to 3 June, 1388. A junto or council of 14, the tools of Thomas [Plantagenet] duke of Gloucester, which assumed royal prerogatives, and attempted to depose the king [Richard II.], then nearly 21 years of age. Sir Nicholas Brembre, thrice Lord Mayor of London, was condemned for siding with the king ; the Archbishop of York fled for his life ; the king's confessor was driven from the kingdom ; several of the judges were condemned to death ; Blake the secretary, and Usk the under-sheriff, were put to death. Sir John Beauchamp, Sir James Berners, Sir John Salisbury, and Sir Simon Burley were all executed. In May 1399 the young king took the reins of government into his own hands, and Gloucester's power was shattered into dust. *See* 'Parliaments.'

Sometimes called ' The Wonderful Parliament.'

Mercu'rius Au'licus. A court journal published in the reign of Charles I. under the court's own direction.

Mère des Peuples (*La*). Marguerite de France duchesse de Berry, daughter of François I. (1523–1574).

Mer'inides or Merinites (3 syl.). A Saracen dynasty in Morocco which succeeded the Almohades in 1270, in Morocco, and were overthrown by the sheriffs or cherifs in 1516.

Descendants of Merin Abdallah king of Fez.

Mermnades (2 syl.). The third dynasty of the kings of Lydia. So named from Mermnas son of Gygês, the first king, B.C. 708–545. Crœsus was the last of this dynasty.

Merovin'gians (*The*), or the Merovingian dynasty (420–737). The first race of French kings, called Merovingian from Mer-wig or Meroveus, the third of the line, presuming Pharamond and Clodion to have preceded him. After an interregnum the second race, called the Carlovingian, succeeded.

Merwig is *mer*, great ; *wig*, warrior. If Pharamond ever existed, he was only Duke of the Francs. He is said to have been the son of Marcomir, and to have died 428. His son Clodion is said to have died 448, and Meroveus was his son. Then followed Chilpéric (448 481), and then his son Clovis [=Louis].

Merry Monarch (*The*). Charles II. of England (born 1630, crowned 1661, died 1685).

Called by Rochester ' The Mutton-eating King.'

Mersen (*Treaty of*), A.D. 870. By which the eastern part of Lotharingia (Lorraine), between the Maas and Rhine, was added to Germany.

Merton College, Oxford. Founded in 1264, by Walter de Merton bishop of Rochester, at Malden, Surrey, but removed to Oxford in 1274. The headmaster is called the warden.

Mesne Lords or Barons, *i.e.* middle or intermediate lords ; who hold their lands, not from the king, but from some subject, who in this case was the mesne lord's overlord. The vassal of a mesne lord is called an arrière vassal, the vassal of a vassal. Lands which owed no allegiance to a lord were called *allōdia* (sing. *allodium*). *See* 'Land.'

Messali'na of the North (*The*). Catherine II. of Russia (1729, 1762–1796).

Messe'nian War (*The First*), B.C. 743–724. Between the Messenians and Spartans. By the terms of peace the Messenians were reduced to the condition of helots, had to pay Sparta half the produce of their land in tribute, and to send a deputation of women to the obsequies of Spartan kings.

The Second, B.C. 685–662. The Spartans were again the victors. Aristoménês was the Messenian hero.

The Third, B.C. 490. The Spartans were again victorious, and banished the Messenians from the soil. Tyrtæus the Athenian poet inspired the Spartans with his lays.

The Fourth, B.C. 465–455. The helots revolted, and found refuge in Naupactos.

Methodism, 1729. Sprang up at Oxford under Mr. Morgan and Mr. Wesley. Whitfield joined the party in 1735. In 1738 Wesley and Whitfield separated on the 'five points.' Wesley took the Arminian views and Whitfield the Calvinistic. Wesley taught that, through the merits of Christ, man's sins are forgiven, and that conversion is a gift of God conveyed instantaneously, so that the converted know when the change takes place. The first Methodist societies were established in 1739. When in 1752 Whitfield separated from the Methodists, those who followed Wesley were called 'Wesleyan Methodists' or 'Wesleyans,' and those who followed Whitfield were called 'Calvinistic Methodists.'

Called Methodists because the societies were governed by certain rules, and the members were required 'to walk orderly and methodically under their respective leaders.' There was a college of physicians in ancient Rome called *Methodistæ*, from the strict régime which they enforced on their patients; probably this may have suggested the name to the Oxford scholars.

Methodist Episcopal Church (*The*), 1784. A society of Wesleyan Methodists in the United States of America, first formed in 1766 by immigrants from Ireland. Like Wesley, they regarded themselves as members of the English episcopal church. Wesley ordained Dr. Thomas Coke, the first Methodist bishop. They accept Wesley's abstract of the 'Thirty-nine Articles,' and use his abridgment of the Common Prayer-book. The bishops are itinerant, and ordain bishops, elders, and deacons.

Methodist Protestant Church in the U.S. of America (*The*), 1830. Seceders from the 'Methodist Episcopal Church' (*q.v.*). They objected to episcopacy, and desired a popular and independent form of church government.

Meth'uen (*Treaty of*), 6 May, 1703. A treaty of commerce between England and Portugal. By this treaty the duty on all Portuguese wines was one-third less than on French wines. Modified in 1810, and abolished in 1835.

John Methuen was the English ambassador to the court of Portugal. The king of Portugal at the time was Pedro II.

Métiers de Paris (*Statuts des*). From the 'Documents inédits sur l'Histoire de France,' recently published. These statutes are supposed to belong to the period of St. Louis (1226–1270).

Meton'ic Cycle (*The*), 19 years. About B.C. 432 Meton discovered that 235 lunar months very nearly corresponded with 19 solar years; but about a century later Callippus discovered that in a hundred years the Metonic cycle would be a day too long, as a solar year contains $365\frac{1}{4}$ days, and not 365. So Callippus suggested that a cycle should consist of (19×4) 76 years, instead of 19. *See* 'Callippic Cycle.'

Metropolitan Board of Works (*The*), transferred in 1889 to the London County Council (*q.v.*), had its standing committees and sub-committees. The former included the Bridges' Committee, the Building Acts' Committee (*q.v.*), the Fire Brigade Committee (*q.v.*), the Parks, Commons, and Open Spaces Committee (*q.v.*), and the Special Purposes and Sanitary Committee (*q.v.*), including gas and gas-meters, the Contagious Diseases Act Committee, and so on.

The nine sub-committees were (1) the Artisans' Dwellings' Act; (2) the coal and wine dues, (3) the examination of accounts, (4) the municipal government of the metropolis, (5) officers, (6) overhead wires, (7) sewer emanations, (8) supplementary main drainage, and (9) tramways.

Metternich's Maxim. 'All *for*, but not *through*, the people.' In other words, the king and his government, not the popular wish, judge what is best for the general welfare, and the people's interest. Of course, the king and his council must be absolute; popular constitutions could in no wise be conceded according to Metternich's political maxim.

In schools and private families Metternich's maxim is acted on; but nations are *clubs*, not schools or families; and in clubs the members, not the elected chairman, make the laws.

Mevela'vites (4 syl.). Dancing dervishes, so called from Mevela'va, their founder, who whirled round and round for four continuous days, without rest, food, or refreshment. While Mevelava spun round like a top, Hamsa played on a flute. After the fourth day the dervish fell into a trance, in which marvellous revelations were made to him.

Mexican Revolution (*The*), 1822, by which the republic was converted into an empire. Augustino Iturbide, the leader of the *coup d'état*, was proclaimed emperor under the name of Augustin I. of Mexico. He abdicated in March 1823, and retired to Leghorn in Italy; but returned to Mexico in March 1824, was arrested and shot.

Mezentian Thraldom, *i.e.* being fastened to a dead body. Mezentius was a king of the Tyrrhenians when Æneas invaded Italy. He was notorious for his cruelty, especially for tying an offender face to face with a dead man, and leaving him to die in his thraldom.

Divorce frees a man from that loathsome Mezentian thraldom—the chaining of a man for life to a cold putrefying corpse.—Miss ROBINSON, *Whitehall*, chap. xix.

⁎ Paul seems to refer to this sort of punishment in Rom. vii. 24: 'Who shall deliver me from this [dead body]?'

Mezuz'ah, pl. *Mezuzoth*. A piece of parchment fixed by the ancient Jews to the doorposts of a house, according to Deut. vi. 9; xi. 13. The parchment was rolled up, put in a case, and labelled *Shadai*, one of the names of God. A mezuzah was fixed not only on doorposts, but to door knockers on the right side.

The Tephelim which these pedants wore on their left wrists, and the Mezuzah which they fixed on the right side of their doors to keep off devils.—KINGSLEY, *Hypatia*, chap. v.

Micare Digitis [*Mi-cā-re didg-i-tis*]. A game played by the ancient Romans, and still common in Italy. Two players sit opposite to each other, and each one holds out a certain number of fingers, and he who guesses right the soonest is the winner. Thus, if A holds out *all* the fingers of one hand and *three* of the other, and B holds out *two* of one hand and *three* of the other, the number is 13. If done very quickly it is by no means easy to guess the right number. Our talking with the fingers is

sometimes called *mication*, from 'micare digitis.'

This game is called *morro*; it is often seen among Italian immigrants in America.

Micel Synod (*The*). The great council or Witenagemot of the Anglo-Saxons.

Michael (*Order of St.*), 1469. Instituted in France by Louis XI.; reorganised in 1661 by Louis XIV. Extinct since 1830.

Michael (*Order of the Wing of St.*). Instituted in Portugal by King Alfonso, 1172.

Michael and St. George (*Knights of St.*), 1818. A British order founded chiefly for Malta and the colonies.

Michael Angelo of Battles (*The*). M. A. Cerquozzi of Rome (1600–1660). Battles and shipwrecks were his favourite subjects. Also called *Michel-Ange des Bamboches*.

Michael Angelo of France (*The*). Jean Cousin (1500–1590). His great picture is the 'Last Judgment,' or *Le Jugement Universel*. Michael Angelo has a grand fresco on the same subject called the 'Last Judgment.'

Michael Angelo of Music (*The*). Gluck (1714–1787) is so called by Dr. Burney, and also father of modern opera.

Michael Angelo of Opera (*The*). Richard Wagner (1805–1864).

Michael Angelo of Sculptors (*The*). I. Pierre Puget (1623–1694). II. René Michel Slodtz (1705–1764).

Michael Angelo of the Lyre (*The*). Palestrīna (1529–1594).

Michael Angelo of the Reformation (*The*). Martin Luther (1483–1546).

Michael College (St.), or 'St. Michael House,' 1324. The second foundation in the University of Cambridge, founded by Harvey de Stanton chancellor of the exchequer to Edward II. This college in 1546 was with other foundations consolidated in Trinity College.

Michelade [*Mi'-kel-aid*], 1567. The massacre of 48 French Catholics at Nismes by Huguenots on St. Michael's Day. The day before they had murdered 72 of their prisoners (FELICE).

M'chigan [*Mish'-e-gan*]. In the United States of America, so called, in 1805, from the lake of the same name (Indian). The inhabitants are usually nicknamed *Wolverines*.

Miching Mallecho, Esq. The pen-name of Shelley in 'Peter Bell the Third.'

Microcosm. An epitome of all things in one. Paracelsus taught that the human body was such an epitome, containing in itself a part of all visible nature, including the sun, moon, stars, and even the poles of heaven.

Mid Lent. The Fourth Sunday in Lent, called *Lætare Sunday*, 'Refreshment Sunday,' 'Mothering Sunday,' and *Dominica de Rosa*. *See* each of the phrases and 'Bœuf-gras.'

Middle Ages (*The*). About 1000 years. Hallam in his 'Middle Ages' begins this period with the conquest of Gaul by the Franks, about A.D. 500, and terminates it with the invasion of Italy by Charles VIII. about 1500. Perhaps the most convenient landmarks would be from the fall of the Roman Empire to the Reformation, which would practically be the same thing; for Augustulus Romulus, the last of the Roman emperors, was deposed A.D. 475, and the Reformation was between 1516 and 1540. *See* 'Mediæval History.'

Middle Passage (*The*). The sea passage of kidnapped African slaves. The first passage is from their African homes to the ship, and their third passage is from the slave market to the cotton or sugar plantations.

Middle Persian Empire (*The First*), 226–642. Founded by Artaxarês, or rather Ardisheer Babigan Sassane, a common soldier of Persia who killed Artaban king of Parthia, A.D. 226, and founded the dynasty of the Sassanides (3 syl.), which lasted for 416 years.

Midnight Mass (*The*). Missa de nocte. On Christmas Day there are three masses : the midnight mass, the mass at daybreak, or *in aurora*, and high mass. There is also the vigil of Christmas Day. *See* 'Mass.'

On Christmas Eve the mass was sung.
　　　　　　　　　Sir W. SCOTT.
When the clock strikes midnight all the bells ring merrily, mass commences at the principal

churches, and at San Luigi dei Francesci and the Gesù there is a great illumination . . . and very good music.—W. W. STORY, *Roba di Roma*, vol. i. p. 63.
. . . Get shut up, as I have been, after midnight mass on a Christmas night.—R. H. BUSK, *Notes and Queries*, 6 July, 1889, p. 10.

Midrash Rabboth. A compilation of legends, allegories, and tales, commenced about A.D. 700, to explain or elucidate the Hebrew Scriptures.

Mignon (*Un*). A dandy or fop was so called in Paris under Henri III.; under Louis XIV. he was called *un libertin*; under the Regent *un beau* or *un talon rouge*; under the Directory *un incroyable*; later on *un petit maître, merveilleux, élégant, crevé, gommeux* (sing. and pl.), *bécarre*.

A *libertin* in Molière's time meant a freethinker.
Mignon, pronounce *Min'yone*.

Mignon (*Le*). Henri III. of France (1551, 1574–1589), a man-milliner, 'weaker than woman, and worse than harlot.' *See* above.

Chicot the Jester had a seat at the council board of the Minion king.—*Hist. of France*.

Migration of Nations (*The*). The migration of the northern and eastern hordes towards the civilised west and south, which brought about the fall of the Roman power.

Milan (*Edict of*). March A.D. 313. Made by Constantine the Great in favour of Christians. By this edict, the persecutions of the Roman governors against Christians ceased, and every Roman subject was free to choose his own religious faith. N.B. What were called heretics soon fell into the exception.

Much has been said about the Roman persecutions, but Buckle tells us ' It is estimated 1,000,000 persons perished during the Arian schism; 1,000,000 in the Carthaginian struggles; 7,000,000 during the Saracen slaughters in Spain ; 5,000,000 during the Crusades; 2,000 000 in the wars against the Scandinavians; 1,000,000 in the wars against the Netherlands, Albigenses, Waldenses, and Huguenots ; 100,000,000 during the Justinian wars ; about 25,000,000 Peruvians and Mexicans ; to say nothing of the dragonades, minor conflicts, secret murders, and so on ; 140 millions ! What were the twelve persecutions compared with this ?

Milan (*The League of*), 1575. A French Protestant league, the object of which was to place the Duc d'Alençon on the throne. This league was aided and abetted by Queen Elizabeth, who was attached to the duke personally. In 1577 King Henri III. put himself at the head of a Catholic league, and another religious war broke out.

Milan Decree (*The*), 17 Dec., 1807. The counterpart of the Berlin decree (*q.v.*). extending the 'continental system' to all Italy, except the pope's dominions, which followed soon afterwards. This decree ordained that 'any vessel which had been searched by an English ship, or which had submitted to be sent on a voyage to England, or had paid any duty to the English Government, should be declared denationalised, and be treated as if English.'

Most certainly Napoleon was no politician.

Milanese Liturgy (*The*), or Ambrosian Liturgy (*q.v.*).

Mile'sian Sect, B.C. 557. Originated with Anaximander, who taught that man was concocted of earth and water baked in the sun's rays; and that heaven is a solid concave in which the stars are fixed as nails to prevent its falling. However, he taught that the earth is spherical. *See* Gen. i. 24, and compare with i. 20.

Milesians (*The*). A Scotic [*i.e.* Gothic] colony which came to Ireland with Milesius and his eight sons. They landed in the south-west of the island, and dispossessed the dynasties of Tuatha-na-Danaan (*q.v.*). Five of the sons perished, and ultimately the entire island fell into the hands of Heremon or Erimhon, who furnished twenty successors, all of whom resided at Tara in Meath. About B.C. 900 Ollav Folla [Ollamh Fodhla], of the family of Ir, a collateral branch, became king. The Milesian race is the glory of Ireland. Every Irishman loves to trace his line to the Milesians, and the chroniclers strive to outvie each other in heaping glory, honour, and antiquity on the race. The Milesian kings are called the Scotic—a list of 136 is given before the advent of St. Patrick—and the race lasted 2,000 years, according to tradition; probably half that time would be more historically correct.

Anastasius, the Sinaite, says: 'Those called by the ancients Scythians or Scoti are Goths and Danes. Many Irish chroniclers tell us that the Milesians came from Spain. The Celto-Scythæ formed a part of the people of Spain.'

Military Colours. Each British regiment has a pair of colours, the *Royal* and the *Regimental*. The latter contains the names of the most important engagements in which the regiment has taken part.

Military Knights (*The*). The title given by William IV. to the 'Poor Knights' (*q.v.*). He also allowed *naval* officers to share in the benefits of the brotherhood.

Military Orders. *See under* 'Monks and Monastic Houses.'

Milkwoman of Bristol (*The*). Ann Yearsley, a poetess, died 8 May, 1806. Hannah More took an interest in her, and raised 600*l.* on her behalf; but Ann Yearsley proved very ungrateful to her benefactress.

Mill-boy of the Slashes. Henry Clay (1777–1852). So called from 'The Slashes,' a swampy country in the neighbourhood of a place in Hanover County, Virginia, where he was born, and where he worked as a mill-boy.

Millena'rians, 2nd cent. Believers in the millennium. God worked six days and rested on the seventh. Psalm xc. 4 says, a thousand years are in God's sight as one day, and therefore the working world will last 6,000 years, and then will follow the millennial rest for 1,000 years, which will be ushered in by a general resurrection. Fifth-monarchy men.

Papias, Irenæus, Justin Martyr, Tertullian, Lactantius, Nepos, and others were believers in the millennium.

Mil'lenary Petition (*The*), 1603. Presented to James I. of England on his accession by 800 clergymen, praying for a reform in the church courts, the provision and training of godly ministers, and the suppression of 'popish usages' in the Book of Common Prayer. James paid no heed to the petition, but convened the Hampton Court Conference (*q.v.*).

The petition was presented by a full tenth of all the clergy of the realm, and was called *Millenary* because, roughly speaking, it was signed by a thousand clergymen. The chief objections were the use of the cross in baptism, the interrogatories to infants answered by sponsors, confirmation, and a few minor particulars.

Miller (*A Joe*). A pun, so called from Joseph Miller (1684–1738), an actor, noted for his suppers in which wit and pun sparkled. John Mottley compiled a collection of jests which he attributed to Joe Miller, and since then any jest is called a Joe Miller, especially those anonymous and somewhat stale.

Millerism, or 'Second Adventism,' derives its name from William Miller, 'the American Prophet' (1781–1849), who fixed by minute calculation the end of the world 10 Oct., 1843 or 1844. Before his death he 'demonstrated from prophecy' that, as 1844 had failed, the years 1857, 1867, 1873, and 1889 were indubitably fatal years between 15 and 25 Oct.

In 1857 was the financial panic of America, and in 1873 the great financial crash. Between 1857 and 1867 occurred the 'great rebellion.' These, however, were not the end of the world, nor did they bring on the millennial advent, and yet Miller had a following of at least 40,000 in the Western States, New England, Middle States, and Canada.

Millioni, the millionnaire. Marco Polo was called by the Venetians ' Messer Marco Millioni' (1256–1323), and his house is still called ' La Corte del Millioni.' It is on the canal of St. Giovanni Crisostomo.

Milioni, with one 'l,' is now the more common spelling.

Milton of Germany (*The*). Friedrich Gottlieb Klopstock, author of 'The Messiah' (1724–1803).

A very German Milton indeed.—COLERIDGE.

Milton of Painting (*The*). Fuseli (1706–1781) not only because, like Milton, he united *terribiles visu formæ* with the *molle atque facetum*, but also painted and exhibited a ' Gallery of Milton.'

Mind Ether, or ' Mind Atmosphere.' An ether which produces by its undulations on the nervous tissue the sensation of light and thought. A concentration of this nervous tissue forms ganglia, and the union of ganglia forms brain. This hypothesis is made to explain ' Thought Reading' : thus : Nervous surface, it is said, transmits sensation faster than the undulations of mind ether, and therefore the thought of the thinker is communicated to the reader, who is further off from the brain, simultaneously with the impression made on the brain, which is much nearer.

Mind of the School (*The*). Aristotle was so called by Plato (B.C. 384–322).

Ming Dynasty (*The*). The twenty-first Imperial dynasty of China, preceded by the Yuen or Y'en and followed by the Manchoo dynasty. It gave seventeen emperors, and lasted 276 years (1368–1644). The seat of government was Nankin. This dynasty is celebrated for its princes, especially Hong-voo and Tchin-Tsu-wen-tee.

Minims (*The*), 1431. Founded by St. Francis de Paula. Often called 'Hermits of St. Francis' [*i.e.* of Paula].

These are not the Minorites (3 syl.) or Frères Mineurs of St. Francis [of Assisi] founded in 1221.

Ministerial Whitebait Dinner (*The*). A dinner given to the cabinet ministers at Greenwich soon after Trinity Monday, that is, a short time before the close of the session. These dinners began with Sir Robert Preston, M.P. for Dover, who invited his friend Old George Rose, secretary of the Treasury, to dine with him at Dagenham Lake, where he had a 'fishing cottage.' After a year or two Pitt was asked to join, and subsequently Greenwich was selected as a more convenient place of tryst. Lord Camden was next asked to join the trio, and then Mr. Long [Lord Farnborough]. The private dinner next became a ministerial dinner, in which each of the guests paid his quota, and the invitations were sent out by the private secretary of Lord Farnborough.

Ministers' Bill (*The*), 1660. Passed by the convention parliament (*q.v.*). By this bill all ministers installed within a stated time were to be expelled from the pulpits of the Anglican Church. This bill did not give satisfaction, because it did not go back far enough, and many pulpits remained in the occupation of Presbyterians.

Ministers' Money. A tax imposed on the householders of Dublin, Cork, &c. for the support of the Established Church. Abolished in 1857.

Minnesingers (*The*). *Minne* means love; the Minnesingers were love-poets, contemporary in Germany with the House of Hohenstauffen (*q.v.*), because these kings spoke Suabian, the richest, smoothest, and most musical of the German dialects. Though called love-singers, some of their poems were national ballads, and some were extended romances. Walter of Vogelweide was by far the best of the lyrists; Heinrich of Veldig was the most naïve and ingenious; Hartmann the most classical; Wolfram the most sublime; and Gottfried the most licentious. *See* 'Wartburg Contests.'

Minneso'ta (U.S. America). An Indian word meaning ' Sky-tinted Water.'

The state receives its name from the river. The nickname of the inhabitants is *Gophers*.

Minning Day, *i.e.* 'Reminding day.' The anniversary of a person's death, when a mass is offered up for the repose of the soul.

Mi'nors, Min'orites (3 syl.), or 'Grey Friars,' 1209. Founded by St. Francis d'Assisi; confirmed 1210; and settled in England 1224.

Minute Men, 1775. The militia of 12,000 men enrolled by the American congress adjourned from Concord to Cambridge. So called because they were to turn out at a minute's notice with musket and rifle. Soon augmented to 20,000.

Miquelets, 1675. Spanish guerillas in the Pyrenees, on the frontiers of Catalonia and Aragon, who armed themselves to push back the French invaders led by Schomberg. So called from their leader Miquelet de Prats. To combat them Louis XIV. created 100 companies of *fusiliers de montagnes*, also called Miquelets.

The mountain guides in the Pyrenees are called Miquelets. In 1808 Napoleon I. organised them to put down the Spanish guerillas.

The country swarmed with Miquelets, a sort of lawless Catalans, who declared for the Austrians. —HOWITT, *Hist. of Eng.* (Anne, p. 212).

Mirabeau of the Gironde (*The*). Vergniaud, the most eloquent man of the Second Assembly.

Mirabeau of the Sans Culottes (*The*). George J. Danton 1759–1794. Also called the 'Mirabeau of the Markets,' and the 'Mirabeau of the Mob.' He was Mirabeau cast in a more vulgar mould.

Pronounce *Me'-rah-bo*; *Sahn* [nasal] *ku-lot.'*

Miracle of the Age (*The*). So Roger Bacon is called by Dr. Freind, in his 'History of Physic.'

Miracles at St. Médard, 1690–1727. Referred to by Paley in his 'Evidences' as sufficiently grave to be worthy of his consideration. The Abbé de Paris, a very charitable man, was buried in the cemetery of St. Médard, and miracles were said to be performed at his tomb. The crowd so increased that government found it necessary to forbid anyone visiting the tomb. The abbé was a Jansenist, and all Jansenists insisted that the cures were miraculous; but their opponents attributed the cures to excitement operating on the nervous system. Convulsions were the general malady.

A wag wrote over the gates a doggerel to this effect:
The king henceforth forbids God's grace
To show his wonders in this place.

Miraculous Campaign (*The*), 1670. That of John Sobieski the Polish general, who triumphed over the allied Cossacks and Tartars, instigated to war by Louis XIV. of France.

Mirror of all Martial Men (*The*). Thomas earl of Salisbury (died 1428).

Mirror of Courtesy (*The*). Sir Philip Sidney, author of the ' Arcadia ' (1554–1586).

Mirror of Justice (*The*). Queen Victoria. In 1882 prayers were offered in the mosques of Cairo and the provinces for Queen Victoria under that appellation.

Mirror of Salvation (*The*). A sacred picture book with Bible stories and sacred legends in rhymes, with illustrative pictures. This book and the 'Biblia Pauperum' (*q.v.*) were immensely popular before the Reformation.

Mise of Amiens (*The*), 23 Jan., 1264. Louis IX. undertook to mediate between Henry III. of England and his barons, and gave his verdict wholly in favour of the king, cancelling the 'Provisions of Oxford' (*q.v.*) passed by the Mad Parliament. The verdict adjudged that the great officers of state should be appointed by the crown; and that aliens should be allowed to hold castles in England, and state offices if the king pleased, &c.   The decision of King Louis was indignantly rejected by the Londoners, and led to the battle of Lewes, in which Simon de Montfort and the Londoners proved the victors.

Mise, pronounce *meez*.

Mise of Lewes (*The*), 14 May, 1264. A truce after the battle of Lewes. By this mise [*meez*] it was provided that the king was to be supreme, but was to be assisted by a council nominated by the Earl of Leicester, the Earl of Gloucester, and the Bishop of Chichester. It was at this crisis that Simon de Montfort summoned for the first time two citizens from every borough to take their seats with the knights of the shires in the parliamentary assembly.

Mishna (*The*). A collection of the civil laws and traditions of the Hebrews. The Jews say that Moses on Mount Sinai received, besides the decalogue, many other laws which he taught the 70 elders. Judas, a learned rabbi, collected these floating traditions, and codified them. The Mishna was written in the 2nd cent. A.D. at Tiberias, and forms the first part of the Talmud (*q.v.*)

The rabbi Judas was called 'the saint.'

Missa Adventi'tia. A votive mass.

Missa Ambrosia'na. Instituted by St. Ambrose (374–397), and used in Milan Cathedral.

Missa Anima'rum. High mass for the dead.

Missa Annua'lis. Daily mass.

Missa Audi'ta. Mentioned by Robert of Gloucester.

Hora sexta pro grammatistis parva lectio fiat, ut aptius congregentur in sacello, et hora septima præcise celebretur Missa, ut loquuntur, ' Audita.'

Missa Au'rea. An unusually grand mass celebrated in mediæval times once a year in honour of the Virgin Mary.

Missa Cardina'lis. Mass celebrated by a cardinal.

Missa Cat'echumeno'rum. The mass up to the introïtus, when all catechumens are dismissed by the deacon with these words, ' Si quis non communicat, det locum.'

Missa Copeta'ta. A mass accompanied by the striking of a bell on one side with several distinct strokes. ' Campanæ alterum latus divisis et distinctis ictibus pulsare.'

Missa Die'i. The mass celebrated after the usual early mass, ' orto jam die.'

Missa Familia'ris. A private mass.

Missa de Jeju'niis. The mass which is celebrated on fast days.

Missa Judicii. A mass which is an appeal to God of a man's innocence of some charge brought against him. This is of the nature of an ordeal.

Missa Lu'minum, or ' Chandeleur.' In German ' Lichtmesse ' for the Feast of Purification (Candlemas), 2 Feb., in commemoration of the ' churching ' of the Virgin Mary after the birth of Jesus. Said to have been instituted by Justinian in 542.

Missa Lunat'ica. Mass celebrated on the day of the new moon.

Missa Matutina'lis, or ' Missa Minor,' ' quæ post exactas matutinas dicitur.'

Missa Nava'lis, or ' Missa Nautĭca.' Mass celebrated aboard ship. It is a *missa sicca* (*q.v.*), because the rolling of the ship might cause the wine to be spilt.

Missa Nova. A celebrant's maiden mass.

Missa Nuptia'lis. A mass celebrated at a wedding.

Missa Pascha'lis. The seven masses during the Easter festival.

Missa Peregrino'rum. A mass for all except the ordained clergy. After the chapter the poor are summoned by a bell to the ' Missa Matutinālis,' and the celebrant for the week sings the Greater Mass. The alms being then distributed, he proceeds with the ' Missa Peregrinō-rum,' which is said, not sung.

Peregrini dicuntur omnes qui non sunt de episcopatu ordinatis, sive sint clerici, sive laici.
DU CANGE, vol. v. p. 246, col. 1.

Missa Perfecta. A mass where both bread and wine are administered to the communicants.

Missa Præsan'ctificato'rum. A mass without consecration, as on Good Friday, when there is no consecration of the elements. They are consecrated the previous day. The Greek Church celebrates such masses in Lent, except on Saturdays and Sundays. *See* ' Mass of the Presanctified.'

Missa Sicca. A mass without the elements. This may occur when a priest has already administered a previous sacrament. ' Sacerdos non potest conficere quia forte jam celebravit, vel ob aliam causam potest accepta stola Epistolam et Evangelium legere, et docere Oratio-

nem dominicam, et dare benedictionem,'
&c. DURANDUS, ' Rationale divinorum
officiorum libris viii. distinctum ' (Book
iv. chap. 1, n 23).

Sacerdote agente quæ sunt celebrantis, cum Introitu, Collecta, Epistola, Evangelio, et Canticis ;
qui tamen, quia non vult communicare, non con-
secrat ita ut Missa sit sine corpore et Sanguine
Domini.—ECKIUS.

Missa Venat'ica. A short mass
celebrated very early in the morning for
persons about to follow the chase.

Missa Voti'va. A mass 'quæ ex
proprio voto, seu motu, peragitur et dicitur, ad differentiam Missæ quæ a Kalen-
dario præcipitur (Monachus Milstatensis,
in Miraculis B. Domitiani,' n 20).

Missa de Aguinaldo. *Aguinaldo*
is Spanish for ' New Year's gift.' Latin,
strēna. French, *étrennes* (2 syl.) This
mass is offered before daybreak.

Missæ vero quas Hispanice 'de Aguinaldo'
vocant, antequam dies illuxerit, ne celebrentur.
—*Concilium Mexicanum,* 1585.

Missa de Excepta'to. In the Ambrosian Missal, is a mass celebrated the
day preceding Christmas Day. ' Præparatio ad vesperam Natalis Domini.'

Missæ Bifaciatæ, Trifaciatæ,
&c. When the celebrant joins together
two or more masses having different
objects.

Missæ Feria'les. Seven masses
celebrated at the Festival of the Holy
Trinity. First day in honour of the
Trinity ; second day in honour of the
Logos ; third day in honour of the Holy
Ghost ; fourth day in honour of Charity ;
fifth day in honour of the Holy Angels ;
sixth day in honour of the Cross ; and
seventh day in honour of the Virgin
Mary.

Missal *(The),* 5th cent. A book
which serves for the celebration of the
Roman Catholic mass. It contains the
text of all the different masses used
during the year. Pope Gelasius, who
died A.D. 496, composed the first missal ;
it was in 2 vols., which Gregory the
Great reduced to one (died 604). Each
diocese and each religious order has its
own missal. There are also the Greek,
Spanish, Coptic, Ambrosian, and other
Missals.

The daily service book is called the ' Breviary '
(q.v.).

Missi Domin'ici. Eight commissioners sent into the provinces to inspect
the conduct of dukes and counts. They
were first organised by Charlemagne,
who divided the empire into ten *Missa-*
tica. Charles le Chauve increased the
Missatica to twelve. Each was visited
in January, April, July, and October by
two Missi (a count and an abbot). The
custom was discontinued at the close of
the Carlovingian dynasty.

Missing Link *(The).* The link
between man and the ape. According to
the theory of evolution, the lower animals
develop into the higher animals, so that the
larvæ of Ascidians (a marine molluscoid)
developed gradually into apes, and probably apes are only one link from man ;
but hitherto no trace of that link has
been discovered, unless, indeed, it be in
the Neanderthal skull found in the Rhine
province of Prussia, which seems to be
between the skull of an ape and the skull
of a human being. *See* ' Alali.'

Evolution goes much further back than this.
The condensation of nebulous vapour may be
called the first step.

Mission *(Prêtres de la),* 1632.
Established by St. Vincent de Paul.
Also called ' Lazarists.'

Mississippi (U.S. America). So
called (1800) from the river. It is an
Indian word meaning the 'long and great
waters.' The inhabitants are nicknamed
Tadpoles.

Mississippi Scheme *(The),* 1716–
1720. A financial scheme proposed by
John Law to the French government,
whereby he himself was to be the sole
creditor of the nation, and was to be
allowed to issue paper-money to ten
times the value of the national debt—
that is, he relieved the nation of 208
millions sterling on the right of issuing
paper-money to the value of 2,080
million pounds. The regent was so
charmed with the scheme that he gave
Law permission to open at once *The*
Royal Bank of France, and to issue his
notes. The bank received deposits, dis-
counted bills, gave promissory notes, all
in paper. It was a prodigious success,
and the regent gave ' the Royal Bank '
the exclusive right of coining money,
transferred to it the old East India
Company, and granted it the exclusive
trade of Louisiana on the banks of the

Mississippi. A 500*l.* share was now worth 18,000*l.*, and John Law was made Comptroller-General of France. In 1720 the scheme exploded, and 20*s.* would have purchased 160,000 pounds' worth of Law's notes. The nation was well nigh ruined. *See* ' South Sea Scheme.'

Missouri (U.S. America). So called (1821) from the river of the same name (Indian). The inhabitants are nicknamed *Pukes*, or more commonly *Pikes*.

Mr. Speaker. The office of Speaker dates back to the reign of Edward III. Sir Walter Hungerford, however, was the first to receive the title of ' Mr. Speaker,' 1414. The Speaker is addressed by members as ' Sir ' or ' Mr. Speaker.'

Mithridat'ic Wars (*The*). Between the Romans and Mithridátês king of Pontus.

1 (B.C. 89–85). Fimbria defeated Mithridátês at Pergamos.

2 (B.C. 83–81). Sulla took from Mithridátês all the Ionian cities in Asia Minor.

3 (B.C. 74–63). Pompey defeated Mithridátês VI., and the king of Pontus killed himself.

A ' mithridate,' or antidote to all poisons, is named from Mithridátês the Great, who knew the secret of such an antidote.

Mitred Abbots. Lord abbots who sat and voted in the House of Lords. So called because they wore mitres.

Moal'lakats (*The Seven*). The seven most ancient sacred poems of the Arabians, a copy of which (according to Caussin de Perceval's ' History of the Arabs ') is always suspended in the Kaaba of Mecca.

The authors are : Imroulcays, Tarafa, Labíd, Zohair-Abu-Selma, Antara, Amr-ibn-Kolthoum, and Harith. Armand Caussin has translated his father's book into French.

Mob Monday, 8 Feb., 1886. So called from the riots of the unemployed which took place in Trafalgar Square, London.

Model Prison (*The*). Pentonville, Caledonian Road, London.

Moderates (*The*). The Russell, Sydney, and Hampden factions, in the great republican plot headed by Lord Shaftesbury, in the latter part of the reign of Charles II. The more vio'ent, such as Lord Howard, Rumbold, and Colonel Rumsey, were more ' thorough,'

and would have assassinated both Charles and his brother James in order to establish a Commonwealth.

Moderates and Highfliers. 1835, in the Scotch Presbyterian Church. The Moderates were also called ' Intrusionists.' That is, they did not consider the Veto Law (*q.v.*) an arrogant intrusion of the patron's right of presentation, but only a moderate check on that right. A presentee could not be rejected from *causeless prejudice,* but only for *adequate reasons. See* ' Intrusionists.'

The leaders of the Moderates were Dr. Bryce, Dr. Cooke, and Dr. Robertson.

Modern Charlemagne (*The*). Napoleon I. (1769–1821).

Modern History begins with the 16th cent. About which time occurred the invention of printing, the discovery of America, and the Lutheran Reformation.

Printing made generally known 1460
Columbus set sail for America 1493
Reformation begun in Germany by Luther... 1517

Modern History (*Professorship of*). In the University of Cambridge, 1724, instituted by George I. Present stipend 371*l.* a year. *See* ' Prince Consort Prize.'

Modern Nimrod (*The*). Napoleon Bonaparte (1769–1821).

Modern Scepticism (*Father of*). Bayle (1647–1706). Famous for his ' Historical and Critical Dictionary.'

Modhafferians (*The*). A petty dynasty of Turkomans, which reigned over Farsistan (1335–1394), when it was overthrown by Tamerlane. It gave four princes, the founder being Modhaffer. They were contemporary with the Ilkhanians, and were always at war with other princes in Persia.

Modus (*The*), *i.e.* ' Modus decimandi.' A composition for tithes. It may either be perpetual or for the lives of the contracting parties.

Mogh's Half of Ireland. The southern half; the other moiety was called Conn's half, from the sons of a king who divided the island into two parts. This was about half a century after the death of Tuathal.

Mohammedan (*A*). This word is an insulting misnomer. The system of the prophet is Islam (submission to and faith in God), and a single adherent of that faith is a Moslem, a word from the same root as Islam. As well call a Jew a Mosaist as call a Moslem a Mohammedan.

God is most great, and there is nothing else great, is the Moslem's creed. Man must submit to God, and find in him his only true and greatest happiness in the Moslem's life. Almsgiving, fasting, prayer, and pilgrimage are his four chief duties.

Mohocks, or Mohawks, 1711–1714. A set of disorderly people who infested the streets of London at night and to< k pleasure in wounding and disfiguring those whom they met. In 1711 the government offered 100*l.* reward for the apprehension of any one of the gang. The Coxe MSS. (in the British Museum) inform us that Marlborough was advised to suborn these ruffians in 1712, ' to scour the streets by night and strike terror into the population.' This seems to be a blunder, as the scourers who scoured the streets of the Mohocks were another set of street brawlers.

These Mohawks were bands of young men, many of them of good families, who issued into the streets at night and committed all sorts of riots and brutalities, even on women and children . . . whom they met with in the badly lighted streets.—HOWITT, *History of England* (Anne, 292).

In 1712 Sir Mark Cole and three other gentlemen were tried at Old Bailey for attacking the watch in Devereux Street. They slit two persons' noses, cut a woman in the arm with a knife so as to disable her for life, and rolled another in a tub down Snow Hill. Gay, in his 'Trivia,' mentions these atrocities committed by the Mohocks. Mohocks or Mohawks were one of the five confederated nations of the Iroquois.

Moidart. *See* 'Seven Men of,' &c.

Moiley, *i.e.* Assassination, 1798. A word adopted by the 'United Irishmen.' A person obnoxious to the secret society was 'consigned to the Moiley'—that is, was doomed to assassination. When a murder became known, it was said that 'Moiley had had him,' or 'Moiley had eaten him.' *See* 'Irish Associations.'

Captain Moonlight and Rory of the Hill were the phrases used in the last quarter of the 19th cent.

Mo'linism. The doctrine of Louis Molīna the Spanish Jesuit. *See* 'Molinists.'

Mo'linists. Disciples of Louis Molīna (1535–1600), a Spanish Jesuit, who attempted to reconcile Free Grace with Free Will. He taught that God's reprobation and election were consequent on God's foreknowledge; that

God gives to all sufficient grace for their salvation if they would but accept it; but to the elect He does more—with this general grace He gives also co-operative grace. It is a shade of Pelagianism, from which, however, it differs in this : Molina distinctly presupposes the inability of man to turn to God without a supernatural act of grace.

Molīnists, or the disciples of Molīna, must not be confounded with Molīnosites (*Quietists*), the disciples of Molīnos. *See below.*

Moli'nosites (4 syl.). Disciples of Michael Molīnos (1627–1696) of Spain, author of 'Perfect Contemplation' or Quietism, for which he was imprisoned by the Inquisition in 1685. *See* 'Quietism.'

Molly Maguires. Irish Ribbonmen, named Maguire from Cornelius Maguire, baron of Inniskillen, who in 1641 took part with Sir Phelim O'Neil in the project of the Irish rebellion. Called Molly because the banded marauders conducted their forays in the guise of women's dresses. The association was planted also in Pennsylvania, where a charter was granted them under the name of 'The Ancient Order of Hibernians.' The Molly Maguires made themselves conspicuous in the sanguinary Tithe War (*q.v.*), 1830–1835. They also perpetrated many dreadful crimes in the U.S., where numbers of them were executed. *See* 'Irish Associations.'

Molly Maguires were generally stout active young men, dressed up in women's clothes, with faces blackened or otherwise disguised . . . In this state they used suddenly to surprise the unfortunate grippers, keepers, and process-servers, and either duck them in bog-holes, or beat them in the most merciless manner, so that Molly Maguires became the terror of our officials.—TRENCH, *Realities of Irish Life*, p. 82.

Momonians. Natives of Munster, in Ireland. The Irish for Munster is *Mumha* (pronounce *Mooa*). Cf. Esthonian, *Muhuma*, 'rich land'; *muhunestä*, '[men] from the rich land.' (De Kay.)

His claims were admitted after a desperate battle was fought, in which 7,000 Momonians fell, 1151.—O CONOR, *History of the Irish People*, p. 47.

Monad. According to Pythagoras, is, the impartible, a mathematical point without parts. Length is a duad, breadth a triad, depth a tetrad. Physically, he says, intellectual capacity which is impartible is a monad; scientific knowledge is a duad ; opinion is a triad ; and sense is a tetrad, because it is apprehended by the senses.

Monads (*The Theory of*). By Wilhelm Leibnitz of Germany (1646–1716). He says there are two kinds of protoplasms—spiritual monads and material monads. The former make mind, and the latter body. Spirit monads, he says, possess innate consciousness,—material monads possess innate sensibility. Spirit monads are the protoplasms of the soul, material monads are the protoplasms of the body.

A *monad* is the indivisible element of an element.
An *atom* is the indivisible element of a simple substance.
A *molecule* is the indivisible element of a compound substance.
A *microbe* is a minute *living* organism.
Protoplasm is the physical basis of life.
∵ An atom of gold is gold, but a monad is the indivisible basis of the element of gold. Zeno, Leucippos, Democritos, and Epicūros preceded Leibnitz in this theory of created things.

Monarchians, 'Monarchiani.' Those who maintained the monarchy of God (*q.v.*). Tertullian refers to them.

Monarchy of God (*The*). A phrase used by anti-Trinitarians to express the one and only supremacy of the one God, the one Ruler of the universe.

It is difficult to find words to express this oneness, but it means that God has only one personality, not three personalities, according to the Athanasian Creed.

Monarchy of the Barricades (*The*). Louis-Philippe of France, called 'Le Roi Citoyen' (1733, reigned 1830–1848, died 1850). Made king after the Grande Semaine, when Charles X. was driven from the throne of France. Louis-Philippe was 'King of the French,' not 'King of France.'

Monastery of the Curses of Ireland (*The*). The monastery of St. Ruan was so called because in 554 the abbots and monks cursed those who dragged therefrom to Tara a fugitive criminal who had fled to it for sanctuary. The criminal was put to death, and the abbot and monks went in procession to Tara and cursed it. 'From that day no king ever sat again in Tara.'

Monastic Orders. *See under* 'Monks and Monastic Houses.'

Monatti. A class of men, professed attendants on the plague, ever ready for the most dangerous and disgusting services. It was their duty to convey those sick of the plague to the hospitals, and attend them there; to watch over those who remained at home while the plague lasted, and to carry away the dead for interment.

Mondays (*Unlucky*). There are three unlucky Mondays in the year: (1) the first Monday in April, on which day Cain was born and Abel slain; (2) the first Monday in August, on which day Sodom and Gomorrah were overthrown; and (3) the last Monday in December, the day on which Judas was born. *See* 'Egyptian Days.'

Money.

ROMAN				£.	s.	d.
Teruncius	...	...	...	0	0	0¾
Sestertius or Nummus, marked H. S., a corruption of LL.S. *i.e.* 2½ lbs. (*semis*)				0	0	1¾
Silver *denarius*	...	...	...	0	0	7¾
Aureus	...	...	...	0	16	0
Great Roman talent	...	...	1125	0	0
Ordinary talent	...	...	...	90	0	0
Small talent	...	...	...	60	0	0
GREEK						
Brass *obolos*	...	...	...	0	0	1¼
Silver *drachma*	...	...	...	0	0	7¾
Golden *stater*	...	...	...	0	16	1¾
Mina	...	...	...	3	0	0
Talent ..	...	...	...	180	0	0
JEWISH						
Gerah (silver)	...	...	...	0	0	1½
Shekel (silver)	...	...	...	0	2	6
Mina	...	...	...	5	14	0
Talent of silver	...	...	...	342	0	0
Talent of gold	...	...	...	5475	0	0
PERSIAN						

Daric, worth 25*s.*, was used in Athens, and sometimes called a *stater.*

Money-bote. A commutation of punishment by a money fine. All offences except parricide, sacrilege, and the murder of a master by his slave, could be so commuted.

Mong-koo (*The*). So the Mogul Tartars are called by the Chinese. 'Koo' means dominion, power, &c., and 'Mong-koo' means 'The Mogul power or dominion,' founded by Ginghis Khan in 1206.

Mongo'lian Bonaparte (*The*). Tamerlane or Timur the Tartar (1336–1405).

Mongrel Parliament (*The*), 1681. Held at Oxford, consisting of Whigs and Tories, by whom the Exclusion Bill was passed, and all Catholics having an income exceeding 100*l.* a year were banished and their children taken from them to be educated in the Protestant faith. *See* 'Parliaments.'

Monitorial System (*The*). Mutual Instruction (*q.v.*), whereby the cleverer pupils are made to teach the less advanced, the pupil teachers being called 'the Monitors.' There are many

Q Q

objections against it : (1) a pupil so employed cannot himself make the same progress as if his time were devoted to his own advancement ; (2) the under pupils are not so well instructed as they would be by an experienced master ; (3) the respect of children to older children is very different from that which they feel to a full-grown person ; (4) unless there is some official to keep order, to watch closely what is done, and to inspire both teachers and learners with a right spirit, but little progress can be expected. The only one recommendation is economy.

Monk Lewis. Matthew Gregory Lewis, born in London, died 1818, at the age of 45. He received his sobriquet from his novel of 'The Monk,' which at the time of publication was immensely popular.

Monk of Bury (*The*). John Lydgate, poet (1375–1460).

> I am experte in poetry
> As the monke of Bury, floure of eloquence.
> STEPHEN HAWES, *The Passe-tyme of Pleasure* (1515).

Monk of Eis'leben (*The*). Martin Luther (1483–1546). He was born at Eisleben in Saxony.

Monk of Westminster (*The*). Richard of Cirencester, chronicler (14th cent.). *See* 'Literary Forgeries.'

It is generally supposed that this chronicle is a forgery by Dr. Charles Julius Bertram, professor of English in Copenhagen. He brought it to light in 1747, but never produced any 'original.'

Monk of Wittenberg (*The*). Martin Luther the reformer (1483–1546). He was professor of philosophy at Wittenberg in 1508, and preacher at the city church of Wittenberg in 1516. It was at Wittenberg that he burnt the Pope's bull in 1520, and at Wittenberg he preached against the Zwickau prophets in 1522. A monument was erected to him at Wittenberg in 1821.

Monks and Monastic Houses.
I. Originated (320–333) in the land of Egypt by Pachomius.

Introduced into Palestine by Hilarion, A.D. 328.
—— Rome by Athanasius, 340.
—— Gaul by St. Martin of Tours, 370.
—— England in 592 by Gregory the Great.

II. Suppressed 1524–1534 in the Protestant states of Germany.

Dissolution 1536 of the lesser monasteries by Henry VIII. in England, and in 1539 of the rest. Altogether 190 were suppressed in England. They contained 50,000 inmates, and their united incomes amounted to 2,853,000*l.* At the time the wages of a master workman was 4*d.* a day and of an ordinary artisan 3*d.* Beef and mutton were ½*d.* a pound.

Suppressed 1790 by the Constituent Assembly in France.
—— (1765–1790) in Austria by Joseph II.
—— 1855 in Sardinia by Victor Emmanuel.

Partly suppressed 1861 in Italy.
Suppressed 1868 in Spain.

MONASTIC ORDERS.

The chief orders are the Augustines, the Basilians, the Benedictines, the Carmelites, and the Franciscans, each of which has its special rule or system of observances. *See* 'Rule.'

I. AUGUSTINES, those who follow the rule of St. Augustine of Hippo (354–430).

Augustinians, Barefooted Augustinians, founded by Thomas of Jesus, Portugal, in 1574.
Brigittines (3 syl.), or Nuns of St. Saviour, founded by St. Brigett, in 1344.
Dominicans, or Preaching Friars, founded by St. Dominic of Calahorra in 1215.
Jacobins, the French Dominicans.
Order of Mercy, or 'of Redemption,' founded by Pierre Nolasque, for the redemption of Christian slaves, 1223.
Order of St. John of God, or 'Brothers of Charity,' founded in 1495.
Premonstratensians, or Norbertines (3 syl.), reformed canons regular of Augustine, founded by St. Norbert, in 1120.

II. BASILIANS, those who follow the rule of St. Basil. They belong to the Greek Church and the Eastern rites.

The so-called Basilians of the Latin church are not of this rule.
Caloyers, a very strict branch of the order found on Mount Athos, in the Morёa, and in Patmos.

III. BENEDICTINES, those who follow the rule of St. Benedict of Nursia, A.D. 529.

Bernardines, reformed Benedictines, founded by St. Bernard of Clairvaux in 1115.
Camaldulians, so called from the monastery of Camaldoli, 30 miles from Florence. Founded by St. Romuald in 1012.
Carthusians, founded by Bruno in 1084.
Celestines (3 syl.), founded by Pietro of Moron [Pope Celestine IV.] in 1254.
Cistercians, founded by Robert abbot of Molesme in 1098.
Cluniacs, founded by Bernon first abbot of Cluny, and reformed by Odo in 942.
Feuillants, founded by Jean de la Barrière in 1577.
Feuillantines (4 syl.), reformed Feuillant nuns, 1590.
Trappists, the most severe of the Cistercian order, founded by Rotrou comte du Perche, in 1140.

IV. CARMELITES (3 syl.), those who follow the rule of Albert patriarch of

Jerusalem, who founded a monastery on Mount Carmel in 1209.

The reformed order of Barefooted Carmelites was founded by St. Theresa in 1562.

V. FRANCISCANS, those who follow the rule of St. Francis of Assisi (1182–1228).

Beguins, founded by Lambert Begg or Lambert le Bègue, in 1170. Of the Third Order of St. Francis.

Capucins, or 'Capuchins,' so called from their *capuchon pointu*, founded by Matthew Baschi in 1525.

Clarisses, or 'Poor Clares' (1 syl.), a barefooted order of women, founded by St. Francis in 1224.

Cordeliers, bound round the waist by a *cord*. Founded by Bernardoni in 1210.

Fraticelli, founded by Father Maurato and Father de Fossombroni.

Fratres Minores, or 'Minorites,' a general name for the Franciscans.

Grey Sisters of Flanders.

Minims, or 'Hermits of St. Francis,' founded by St. Francis of Paula, in 1431.

Observants, or 'Fathers of the Observance,' barefooted Franciscans, founded by Paul of Foligno in 1368. There were other Observants.

Picpus, reformed Franciscans, so called from the monastery of Picpus, near Paris, founded in 1601.

Récollets, reformed Franciscans, founded in 1484.

Urbanists, founded for women at Longchamps by Isabelle in 1260. Named in honour of Urban II.

*** Other religious orders.

ANNUNCIADES in honour of the Annunciation.

1. The *Annunciades of Savoy*, founded by Amadeus VI. count of Savoy in 1362.

2. The *Annunciades of Bourges* (1 syl.), founded by Jeanne de Valois, daughter of Louis XI., in 1500.

3. The *Annunciades of Célestes* (2 syl.), or 'Filles Bleues,' founded by Maria Vittoria Fornari in 1604.

MILITARY ORDERS.

St. John of Jerusalem, or 'Knights Hospitallers' (11th cent.). Same as 'Knights of Rhodes' and 'Knights of Malta.'

Knights Templars, founded in 1118.

Teutonic Knights, who established themselves in Germany, conquered and converted Prussia and Pomerania, organised by Frederick duke of Suabia in 1190.

JESUITS, or 'Clerks of the Order of Jesus,' founded by Ignatius of Loyola in 1534.

*** For Orders, &c. of less note see under each name.

Monmouth (*Duke of*). Son of Lucy Walters or Barlow. His father, some say, was Charles II., but Macpherson ('Papers,' i. 77) says, 'All the knowing world, as well as myself, had many convincing reasons to believe he was not the king's son, but [Colonel] Robert Sydney's.' 'Lucy was previously the mistress of Colonel Robert Sydney; and her son bore so strong a resemblance to that officer, that the Duke of York always looked upon Sydney as the father' ('Life of James,' i. 491). Lingard calls Lucy a vile worthless woman, and Evelyn describes her as 'a browne, beautiful, bold, but insipid creature' ('Diary,' ii. 11).

Monoph'ysite Controversy (*The*), 5th and 6th cents. Respecting the nature of Christ. Arius in the 4th cent. had insisted that Christ had but one nature, the human, but in the 5th cent. Eutychês and others maintained that his humanity was merged in his divinity as a drop of rain is lost in mid-ocean. Eutyches, who published his views on the subject in 447, was condemned by the Council of Constantinople in 488—the sentence was reversed by the Council of Ephesus in 449, but he was condemned again by the Council of Chalcedon in 451. A schism was made between the eastern and western churches on the subject in 484; the Monophysites were condemned by the Council of Constantinople in 536, and again in 553; and the sect revived under Jacob Baradæus about 570.

The word monophysite is equivocal, for the Arians believed that Christ had only one nature, viz. the human; but the word is usually restricted to the Eutychêans, who denied the humanity and maintained that it was swallowed up in the divinity. The Copts and Jacobites (3 syl.) are Monophysites (4 syl.).

Monoth'elites (4 syl.), 7th cent. Those who believed that, although Jesus Christ had two natures, He had but one will, the human being absorbed in his divine will. The first person who taught this dogma was Theodore bishop of Pharan, in Arabia. The doctrine was condemned as a heresy by the Third Council of Constantinople in 680, and the sect died out. Their descendants are the Maronites (*q.v.*).

Greek, μόνος, θέλημα, one will.

Monroe Doctrine (*The*), 1823. Against European interference or intervention in American affairs. Monroe [2 syl.] was the fifth president (1816–1824). He enunciated a firm opinion that Americans should never entangle themselves in European broils, nor ever permit any state of the Old World to interfere with the affairs of the New World.

Mons Meg. An old gun of great size made of bars of hammered iron hooped together. It is still to be seen in Edinburgh Castle.

Monseigneur (*with* a name after it). A title given in the time of Cardinal Richelieu to French bishops, previously entitled 'très-saint' and 'bien-heureux.'

Pronounce Mo['n]-sen-ure.

Monseigneur (*without* a name after it) meant the king's son in the reign of Louis XIV. *See above.*

Monsieur (without a proper name after it) the French king's eldest brother. The Duc d'Alençon in the 16th cent., only surviving brother of Henri III., was 'Monsieur,' and hence the phrase *La Paix de Monsieur* given to the treaty signed at Loches in 1576. In the reign of Louis XIII. Gaston duc d'Orléans was *Monsieur*; in the reign of Louis XIV. Philippe duc d'Orléans was *Monsieur*, and his wife *Madame*; in the reign of Louis XVI. Louis comte de Provence [afterwards Louis XVIII.] was *Monsieur*, and in the reign of Louis XVIII. Charles comte d'Artois [afterwards Charles X.] was *Monsieur*.

The last two princes so called were the Comte de Provence (*i.e.* *Louis XVIII.*) in the reign of his brother Louis XVI., and the Comte d'Artois (*Charles X.*) in the reign of Louis XVIII.
Pronounce *Mŏ-se'u.*

Monsieur de Paris. The executioner.

Pronounce *Mŏ-se'u de Părré.*
Death arrives, like 'Monsieur de Paris,' to strip the criminal, to clip his collar and hair, and lop away from him life and love and delight.—E. ARNOLD, *Death and Afterwards,* p. 12.

Monsieur le Coadjuteur (without a proper name) meant, in the reign of Louis XIV., Paul de Gondi, who was afterwards Cardinal de Retz.

Monsieur le Duc (without a proper name) meant, in the reign of Louis XIV., Henri Jules de Bourbon, eldest son of the Prince de Condé and his wife (Mlle. de Nantes, eldest daughter of La Vallière, the king's mistress). The wife of Henri Jules de Bourbon was entitled *Madame la Duchesse.*

Monsieur le Grand (without a proper name) meant, in the reign of Louis XIV., the Grand Equerry.

Monsieur le Prince (without a name after it) meant, in the reign of Louis XIV., the Prince de Condé, 'premier prince du sang' (who married Mlle. de Nantes, a natural daughter of Louis XIV. by La Vallière). His wife was entitled *Madame la Princesse,* their eldest son *Monsieur le Duc,* and their eldest daughter *Madame la Duchesse* (1621-1686).

Monsieur Veto. Louis XVI. In 1789 the National Assembly resolved that there should be no second chamber, but that the king should have a 'suspensive' veto on decrees sent up to him from the Assembly. The king availed himself of this right on 17 and 29 Nov., and was nicknamed Monsieur Veto. The veto of 17 Nov. was in favour of the emigrants, that of 29 Nov. in favour of the ecclesiastics.

Many believed the veto to be a tax, others thought it was an enemy that ought to be hanged on a lamp-post. 'Don't you know what a veto is?' said one countryman to another. 'Well, I'll tell you. Suppose your pot is full of good broth, and the king bids you empty it out to the dogs, you would be forced to do it.'

Monster (*The*), 1790. Renwick Williams, who prowled the streets of London at night-time armed with a double-edged knife with which he shockingly wounded women in their breasts and thighs, and sometimes in lonely places mutilated them horribly. He was tried and convicted. Other street rowdies have occasionally 'delighted' in wounding and disfiguring women, especially the Mohocks or Mohawks in Queen Anne's reign. *See* 'Jack the Ripper.'

Monster Grievance (*The*). So O'Connell called the Established Church in Ireland, 1832. O'Connell said the 500,000 Lutherans in Ireland cost but little less than nine million Lutherans in England, and that while England had twenty-six bishops, Ireland had twenty-two.

Monster Petition (*The*), 10 April, 1848, for the repeal of the corn laws. This petition was three miles long.

Monsters (*Human*). Incredible as it may seem, St. Augustine bishop of Hippo says that *he himself* had seen in Ethiopia 'many men and women without heads, who had their two eyes in their breasts.' And furthermore, that in countries further south he *met* with a people 'who had but one eye, and that in the forehead.' 'Notes and Queries,' 3 May, 1890, p. 357.

Sir John Mandeville's accounts (A.D. 1356) of human monsters are equally incredible. The eye in the forehead (reported also by him) is a personal feature of the giant's wife in the story of Jack and the Beanstalk. Halliwell's edition of Mandeville (or Maundevile) has an engraving of a man with the eye in the forehead.

Mont de Piété. A pawnbroker's shop, or rather a loan bank for the poor, where money is advanced on pawns. The loan is for a year, and if not then redeemed or renewed the pawn is sold by auction, and whatever remains over and above the interest and expenses is handed to the pawner. In Paris the interest required is 9 per cent., but in some departments as much as 15 per cent. Introduced 1778; abolished 1789; re-established by the Directory in 1797; and reorganised in 1804.

There are forty-five monts de piété in France, and all are under the authority of the ministre de l'intérieur.

Monts de piété were introduced into France from Italy, where they are called 'Monti di Pietà,' and were established as far back as 1450.

Monts de piété were introduced into Germany in 1766, the interest being fixed at from 8 to 12 per cent. Belgium and Holland have their monts de piété also, but England has no such institution. The needy in the British Isles are handed over to the mercies of pawnbrokers and money-lenders. Pronounce *Mônt-d' pe-ey-tey*.

Montagnards. The party in the first French Revolution under the leadership of Robespierre. They occupied in the Convention the most elevated seats called *La Montagne*, in opposition to the *Plaine* or the lowest seats occupied by the moderate party called the *Girondins*. The Mountain party overthrew the Girondists on May 31, 1793, but was in turn overthrown 'le 9 Thermidor An II' when Robespierre met with his downfall (1794). Both the Mountain and the Plain were left of the Speaker.

Montalto (*Louis de*). The pen-name of Pascal in the famous 'Provincial Letters' in defence of Antoine Arnauld the Jansenist.

Monta'ni (Mountaineers). 'Heretics' similar to the Waldenses (*q.v.*), and probably a branch thereof. So called, says Eberard of Bethune, 'because, in time of persecution, they concealed themselves in the mountains.'

Another derivation is that they were Waldenses of Liguria, the inhabitants of which were called Montani.

Mon'tanists, A.D. 171. Followers of Montănus, a Phrygian who called himself the Paraclete, and said that the two ladies who went about with him (Priscilla and Maximilla) were prophetesses. The Montanists looked on marriage as a spiritual union which would continue after life, and utterly condemned second marriages. They observed rigid fasts, advocated celibacy, encouraged martyrdom, and observed three Lents every year.

Monte Gibello, or Mongibello. Mount Etna is so called by the Sicilians. Monte, 2 syl.

Monte de' Dodici (*The*), or Oligarchy of the Twelve. The Nine Oligarchs, or Monte de' Nove, having greatly abused their trust, were deposed, and the government of Siena was then committed to twelve men, also elected from plebeian families.

Monte (2 syl.), *Do'-dee-che*. Nove (2 syl.).

Monte de' Nobili (*The*). One of the five oligarchies which successively ruled in Siena. This was first of the five oligarchies, for Siena had originally been controlled by certain noble families to the exclusion of all other citizens from state offices.

Monte (2 syl.), *No-be'-le*.

Monte de' Nove (*The*), or Nine. One of the five governing bodies which ruled Siena in succession. When the Monte de' Nobili split into parties among themselves, they agreed to relinquish the government to nine plebeian families chosen from the most wealthy and influential of the non-privileged class. Nove, pronounce *No'vy*.

Monte del Popolo (*The*). The last of the five governing bodies of Siena. These five were elected from all who were eligible to a seat in the great council of the State. In the 16th cent. Pandolfo Petrucci made himself what the Greeks would call *Tyrant* of Siena.

Monte de' Sedici (*The*), or the 'Monte de' Riformatori.' Being tired of the twelve oligarchs, the Sienese next committed the government to sixteen men chosen from the very dregs of the people, who assumed the name of the Riformatori. Like all red republicans, they were too fond of bloodshed, and all parties joined together to depose them.

Monte (2 syl.) *Sey'-dee-che*.

Monteagle (*Lord*). Sir Edward Stanley, 5th son of Thomas first Earl of Derby, was at Flodden Field. By a sudden feint he induced the Scots to descend a hill, which was their strong position, and thus very greatly contributed to their overthrow. About a year after the battle, as Henry VIII. was keeping Whitsuntide at Eltham, in Kent, he spoke of Sir Edward's exploits, and especially his ruse which drew the Scots from the hill. Sir Edward's crest was an eagle, and the king created him Lord Mont-Eagle or Baron Stanley, Lord Monteagle.

Months (*Anglo-Saxon*).

January.—Se æftera Geóla (the latter yule).

February.—Sol-mónath (the soil or mud month).

March.—Hréth-mónath (the fierce month ?).

April.—Eáster-mónath.

May.—Thri-mylce (the three-milkings month).

June.—Se aerra Lítha (the former Litha, or warm month. Litha = mild).

July.—Se æftera Lítha (the latter Litha, or *warm month*).

August.—Wéod-mónath (weed month).

September. — Hálig-mónath (holy month or time of sacrifice).

October.—Winter-fylleth (winter fall).

November.—Blót-mónath (sacrifice month).

December.—Se aerra Geóla (the former yule).

('Notes and Queries,' 20 April, 1889, page 301.)

'Blot month' probably refers to the custom of slaving animals for the winter store. Hence 'Slay Fair' in Chichester and other places in this month.

Month with no New Moon (*The*), Sept. 1752. This month, in consequence of the change of style, contained only nineteen days. The New Style began on 3 Sept., which was called the 14th. The first quarter of the moon was 15 Sept., at one o'clock in the afternoon, and the full moon was on the 23rd. All days from 2 to 14 (neither included) were annihilated, consequently there was no new moon in that month. The month ran 1, 2, 14, 15, 16, and so on up to 30.

Montijoyeux, or 'Montijocrisses.' The party of the Empress Eugénie, wife of Napoleon III. of France. Before her marriage she was Eugénia de Montijo [*Mon-te'-ho*] of Spain.

Monument (*The London*). Begun 1671, and finished 1677, to memorialise the Great Fire of 1666. Pope says:—

Where London's column pointing to the skies,
Like a tall bully, lifts its head and lies.

The following ill-worded inscription was written by Dr. Thomas Gale, afterwards dean of York. 'The burning of this Protestant city was begun and carried on by the treachery and malice of the Popish faction, in order to the effecting their horrid plot for the extirpating the Protestant religion and English liberties, and

to introduce Popery and heresy.' And the Latin inscription contained this sentence: 'Sed furor papisticus, qui tam dira patravit, nondum restinguitur.' All this was erased by order of the city on 6 Dec., 1830. Not a vestige of proof was ever found to justify Dr. Gale's calumny. (*See* Howell, 'State Trials,' vi. 807–866.)

Monumental Figures.

Those in *armour* represent knights.

Those with *crosier*, *mitre*, and *pontificals* represent bishops.

Those with *hands on the breast* and a *chalice* represent priests.

Those *built into the church wall* represent founders.

Those *east of the altar* and *elevated* represent saints; those *not* elevated represent holy men not canonised.

Moollah. A Turkish scribe, a kind of D.D. and LL.D.; for Turkish law is based on the Koran, and therein differs from Christian law, which is wholly independent of the Bible.

A defendant would be laughed at who justified himself by a quotation from the Bible; but a text from the Koran would be indisputable law.

Moonlight (*Capt.*), 1878. The name assumed by some unknown Irish chief of the Land League and Fenians. He used to write warning letters to those who refused to join the league, and these letters were followed up by horrible mutilation of the person's cattle, or his being shot through the legs, or murdered, or boycotted. For several years Ireland was dominated by Capt. Moonlight, and every one was in terror of a visitation of the villain's gang. See 'Irish Associations.'

Daniel Connell was 'Lieutenant Moonlight' in 1882, and was offered a Parnell medal for bravery.

Moonlighters. Adherents of the Moonlight gang. There were Moonlighters in Scotland in the rebellion of 1745. In 'Redgauntlet' Sir W. Scott makes Maxwell say to Fairford (chap. xii.) that the passport at that moment was 'What is the age of the moon?' If the interrogator was answered 'Not light enough to land a cargo,' he was answered, 'Then plague on Aberdeen almanacs,' upon which the person would hold free intercourse with the stranger. But, he adds, these moonlight lads do not take freely to lawyers.

The Moonlighters of Ireland (1879) seem to have grown out of and succeeded the White Boys. Their chief was called 'Capt. Moonlight.' There was an inner circle of Moonlighters called ' Our Boys.' *See* 'Irish Associations.'

Mora-stone (*The*). In Swedish *Morasteen* (the stone on the moor), on which the kings of Sweden were crowned. It was, in fact, a circular range of stones in the plain of Mora, near Upsa'la. The coronation stone itself was a large round stone, but it was surrounded by twelve others of smaller size with wedge-shaped blocks. When Mr. Coxe visited Mora in 1782 he found ten of the stones, but the largest was only six spans long. Probably Stonehenge on Salisbury Plain was used for a similar purpose. The Lia Fail of Tara, in Ireland, was used as a coronation stone. It was removed to Scone in Scotland, and used as the coronation stone of Scotch kings. Edward I. brought it to London, and it is inclosed in our own coronation chair still.

Moral Gower (*The*). So John Gower, the poet, is called by Chaucer, from his 'Speculum Meditantis' and 'Confessio Amantis,' the former 'treating of the Vices and the Virtues, and of the various degrees of this age,' and seeking ' to teach by a right path the way whereby a transgressed sinner ought to return to the knowledge of his Creator.' No copy of this work is known to exist. The latter is a grave discussion of the morals and metaphysics of love. Probably Chaucer referred to the solemn sententiousness of the ' Confessio ' more than to the 'Speculum.'

Moral Philosophy (*Professorship of*), in the University of Cambridge, 1683. Founded by John Knightbridge, D.D., Fellow of St. Peter's. Stipend 700*l.*, exclusive of fees.

Moral Science Tripos (*The*). Three classes into which students in the University of Cambridge are classified who have passed with credit their final examinations in the Moral Sciences. The five Moral Sciences are : 1. PSYCHOLOGY (consciousness, feelings and movements, reflex action, instinct, sensation and perception, dreams, thought, desires and volition). 2. LOGIC and METHODOLOGY (as the laws of thought, syllogisms, induction and deduction, &c.). 3. METAPHYSICS (as what is Being, Reality, Finity and Infinity, the Ego and Non-ego, &c.).

4. MORAL and POLITICAL PHILOSOPHY (pleasure and pain, desire and aversion, conscience, judgment, happiness the end of rational action, politics, jurisprudence, forms of government, &c.). 5. POLITICAL ECONOMY (as capital and labour, rate of increase, land-rent, profit and wages, currency, monopolies, banking, &c.). *See* 'Natural Sciences.'

Moralities. Dramas of an allegorical character to encourage good morals. They succeeded the Mystery plays (*q.v.*), the subjects of which were the Religious Mysteries, interdicted in the 16th cent. The *dramatis personæ* of the Morality plays were such as Mr. Carnal-minded, Mr. Great-heart, Faithful, Hopeful, Despair, Youth, Age, and so on.

Moran's Collar. A collar worn by ancient Irish judges, which gave warning by tightening round the neck when the wearer was about to give an unjust judgment. Hence the proverb ' I swear to it by Moran's collar.' Moran was the son of the usurper Carbre Catcan; on the death of his father he refused the crown and restored to the throne the royal race in the person of Feredach, who appointed Moran judge. It is the justice of Moran which gave rise to the fable of the Iodhan Moran.

Mora'vians, or 'The United Brethren.' Said to have existed in the 9th cent., when the kings of Bulgaria and Moravia were converted, and united in communion with the Greek Church. They are episcopal in constitution, and are attached to the Augsburg Confession of Faith. They still exist in large numbers, and have exercised considerable influence on the Christian religion.

It was in 1457 that Michel Bradacz, of Bohemia, united them under the name of 'The United Brethren.' In 1721, after the Thirty Years' War, they found an asylum at Hernhutt, under Count Zinzendorf, and changed their name to *Hernhütter*.

Morbus Anglicus. The sweating sickness.

Morden College, Blackheath, 1695. Founded by Sir John Morden, a Turkey merchant, for decayed Levant merchants. There are 40 pensioners, allowed 40*l.* per annum each, and a treasurer. The pensioners have apartments, coals, candles, washing, and service found ; and dine in a common hall.

Morganat'ic Marriage. Legalised concubinage. It is a German fiction.

A person of rank 'marries' a woman of inferior social position, and gives her a dowry on the wedding day, called *mor-gangina*, Saxon for a 'morning-gift.' The offspring of this woman are not heirs, though legitimate, and the bridegroom gives her his left hand instead of his right, whence the phrase 'left-handed marriage.'

A disgrace to common honesty, to say nothing of Christianity.

Morley (*Mr. and Mrs.*). The Princess Anne and Duchess of Marlborough mutually agreed to abandon all formality and court etiquette in their intercourse with each other. To this end, Anne was to be called 'Mrs. Morley,' her husband 'Mr. Morley,' and the Duke and Duchess of Marlborough 'Mr. and Mrs. Freeman.'

Mormons, or 'The Church of Jesus Christ of Latter-day Saints,' 1830. A religious sect founded by Joseph Smith, of Vermont, who declares that he received his mission from an angel in 1823. This angel told him where to find certain plates containing the records of the ancient American prophets. These plates were about as thick as tin, and held together by three rings running through them all. The character employed was 'Reformed Egyptian,' and with the plates were deposited the 'Urim and Thummim,' or spectacles for deciphering them. The plates say that the Americans were a colony from the Tower of Babel at the confusion of tongues. The Mormonites receive their name from the prophet Mormon who wrote the plates called 'The Book of Mormon.'

Their written Scriptures are called the books of Enos, Jarom, Zeniff, Ether, &c.

Morning Star of Reformation (*The*). I. In *England*, John Wycliff (1324–1384).

II. In *France*, Pierre Waldo (1120–1170) of Lyons.

He taught that the laity might conduct the offices of religion as well as the clergy; that the doctrine of transubstantiation has no warrant from Scripture; that it is wrong to invoke saints; that there is no such place as purgatory; that there are only two sacraments; that the Pope of Rome does not hold the keys of heaven, and that he never received them from St. Peter.

Mortar Boards. *See* 'Square caps.'

Mortification, in Scotch law, means what the English call 'Mortmain.'

Infeftments of mortified lands are those which are granted to the kirk or other incorporation having no other *reddendo* than prayer and supplications. Such were the mortifications of the kirk-lands granted by the king to kirkmen, or by private men to provosts and prebendars.—STAIR, book ii. title 3, 39.

Mortimer's Hole. A subterranean passage through the soft sand rock on which Nottingham Castle stands, and leading from the castle-court to the river Leen. Through this passage Edward III. and his conspirators found access to the castle, broke open the door, seized Mortimer, and brought him before the parliament, by whom he was condemned to death. He was hanged at the Elms, near London, 29 Nov., 1330, with three others, and the queen-mother was shut up in her own house of Risings, where she lived for 27 years.

Mortmain (*The Statute of*). 7 Edw. I. c. 2, 15 Nov., 1279, forbidding the alienation in mortmain of real property to religious houses or other corporations. This statute was based on the 'constitutions of Clarendon' (*q.v.*).

Lands held by the clergy and corporate bodies were in dead hands (*mortuis manibus*) so far as the overlord was concerned, because corporations can neither fight for their overlord, nor do they die, like individuals; consequently the lord of the fee lost the *fine* which accrued to him on change of tenants. As Coke says, 'the lords lost their escheats, and the services for the defence of the realm, wards, reliefs, marriages, and so on.' As a dead hand yields the lord no service, so lands held by corporate bodies yielded the lord no services.

Morton's Fork. The wealthy can pay because they can spare something out of their superfluity. The thrifty can pay because they do not squander their money in self-indulgence. The tale is that Henry VII. in 1507 wanted money—no unusual thing—and levied a 'benevolence' on the whole realm. Cardinal John Morton, archbishop of Canterbury, was appointed chief commissioner to extort money from the clergy. The rich clergy, who tried to get exempt, he said could afford to give because they had abundance, and the poor frugal clergy could afford to give because they were thrifty. BACON, 'Life of Henry VIII.,' p. 436.

Erasmus tells a similar tale of Richard Fox bishop of Exeter (1487-1491). Ecclesiastes ii.

Morven (*Kings of*). The following are said to have rule over the north-west of Scotland, called Morven.

Trenmor began to rule .	A.D. 32
Fingal (father of Ossian) . .	210–246
Ossian I. (the poet) . . .	246–287
Oscar . . .	287–300
Ossian II. (Picts and Scots first so named)	300

Moscow Expedition (*The*), 15 Sept. to 19 Oct., 1812. The disastrous invasion of Moscow by Napoleon. The loss of the French in the expedition and retreat is set down at the enormous total of 200,000 human beings. Some estimate the loss of life as very much greater.

It was Rostopchin who set fire to the city. On the retreat Napoleon left his army at the Beresina, took his route towards Zemlin, and reached Paris 18 Dec.

Moses of Mesopota′mia (*The*). Jacōbus or St. Jacōbus, a bishop who prayed that God would protect Nisïbis when the city was besieged by Sapor II. (A.D. 350). Whereupon a swarm of gnats attacked the Persian elephants so fiercely that they ran away, and the city was saved. (*See* Gibbon, 'Decline and Fall,' xviii., and Theodoret, 'Ecclesiastical History,' ii. 26.)

Moslim (vulgarly ' Mussulman,' plu. 'Mussulmans '). A true believer in Mahomet's mission ; but Moslem or Moslemin means ' belonging to Islam or the creed issued by the prophet.'

The adjective is Moslem.

Moss (*Treaty of*), 16 Aug., 1814. A treaty of peace between Norway, Sweden, and Denmark. Prince Christian Frederick had been proclaimed king of Norway, 19 May, 1814 ; but Russia, Prussia, Austria, and Great Britain interfered, and induced the prince to abdicate. As resistance would have been madness, he had no choice left, and Norway was confirmed to Sweden according to the terms of the treaty of Kiel, 14 Jan., 1814.

Moss Backs. The Victorians, or people of Victoria, are so called by the Vancouverites, '·because they move so slowly that moss is apt to grow on their backs.'

Most Catholic King (*The*). The ruling king of Spain. The king of France was the ' Most Christian.'

Most Christian Doctor, 'Doctor Christianissimus.' Jean Charlier de Gerson, chancellor of the University of Paris, born at Gerson (Reims) (1363–1429). It is to this Gerson that many attribute ' The Imitation of Christ,' usually ascribed to à-Kempis, and certainly Gerson's ' Consolation Internelle ' resembles it in an extraordinary degree.

Most Christian King, or ' Christianissimus,' was first applied to the

26

kings of France by Paul II. in 1469. It is very strange that Louis XI. should have been the king so honoured. Henry VIII. was called ' Defender of the Faith,' for his book against Luther ; but the retention of the title after the Reformation was a mere perversion of its original meaning.

Some say that Pope Anastasius conferred the title on Clovis at his baptism, because he was not an Arian as all or almost all the Christian princes of Europe were at the time. The Spanish king received the title of ' Catholic ' for expelling the Moors ; the Portuguese kings were entitled ' Most Faithful.'

Most Enlightened Doctor (*The*). *Doctor Illuminatus*, or *Illuminatissimus*, Raymond Lully (1234–1315).

Most Methodical Doctor. John Bassol, a · Scotch savant, who died in 1347.

Most Profound Doctor, ' Doctor Fundatissimus ' and ' Theologōrum Princeps.' Ægidius de Colonna, *i.e.* Giles of Cologne (1247–1316), a disciple of Thomas Aquīnas, and archbishop of Bourges. He was a zealous Realist (*q.v.*). It is said of this scholastic, ' Lux in lucem reducit dubia.' (He was the luminary who brought dark [or abstruse] things to light.)

Probably modern scholars would say he argued so abstrusely that he did not himself understand his own expositions.

Most Resolute Doctor (*The*). ' Doctor Resolutissimus.' Guillaume Durand de St. Pourçain bishop of Meaux (1267–1332). He was at first a follower of Thomas Aquīnas, and a Nominalist, but afterwards became a Scotist and defended Realism. This gave great offence to the Thomists, and one of them wrote this epitaph :

Durus Durandus jacet hic sub marmore duro,
An sit salvandus ego nescio, nec quoque curo.

Harder than stone, hard by, lies Hardy here
If saved or not I neither know nor care.

John Baconthorpe, who died 1333, a provincial of the Carmelite Order, was called ' The Resolute Doctor.' *See* p. 261, ' Doctors, &c.'

Most Subtile Doctor, 'Doctor Subtilissimus.' John Duns Scotus (1265–1308), the great opponent of Thomas Aquīnas and defender of the Immaculate Conception. He was a Dominican, the great opponent of the Franciscans, and was born at Duns.

Mota'zalites (4 syl.). Mohamme-dan sectaries of the sect of Ali. They maintain that God has no attribute separable from his essence, and that the Korân was neither the work of God nor yet perpetual. They reject the dogma of fatalism.

Mother. Anne Lee (1736–1784). The chosen of God to reveal the mystery of iniquity, and the true mother of all living in the new creation. She was born in Toad Lane, Manchester, and her father was a blacksmith. She married Abraham Standley, also a blacksmith, and joined the Shakers, by whom she was called ' Mother,' but she called her-self ' Anne the Word.' In 1774 she went to America, and settled in New York, where she was received as the ' Morning Star of Christ's Second Coming.'

Mother Duchesse. So Carlyle calls the *Tricoteuse* of the French re-volution.

> Citoyennes who bring their seams with them, or their knitting-needles, and shriek or knit as the case needs. Famed *Tricoteuses*, patriot knitters, Mère Duchesse . . . giving the key-note.—CAR-LYLE, *French Revolution*, vol. iii. book ii. 5.
> Bull-voiced St. Huruge is heard, and the hys-teric eloquence of Mother Duchesse, chap. 6.

Mother Guilford. So Mary the sister of Henry VIII. called Lady Guil-ford, her governess, to whom she was greatly attached.

Mother Ludlam's Cauldron. Deposited in Waverley Abbey, whence (at the dissolution of the monasteries) it was removed to Frensham Church. Mother Ludlam was a white witch who assisted her neighbours by lending them such culinary utensils and household articles as they wanted for special occa-sions. The petitioner went to Mother Ludlam's cave at midnight, and pro-mised to return the loan in three days. On one occasion a cauldron was bor-rowed, but not returned at the stipulated time, and Mother Ludlam refused to take it back, and discontinued her loans.

Mother Shipton, the prophetess of South Wales, was T. Evan Preece. She predicted the death of Wolsey, Lord Percy, and others, in the reign of Henry VIII.

> She predicted that ' the end of the world would come in 1882.' This prophecy was safe enough for 300 years. The ' Prophecies' of Mother Shipton are still extant.

Mother of Universities. Bo-logna, 1088. A medal was struck in 1888 to commemorate its eight hundredth an-niversary.

Mother of her Country (*The*). Maria-Theresa of Austria (1717, 1740–1780).

Mother of the Gracchi (*The*), ' Mater Gracchōrum.' Cornelia daughter of Scipio Africanus.

> When Queen Victoria, in her childhood, read the story about Cornelia showing her sons as her jewels, the princess said to her tutor, ' Not jewels, but Cornelians.'

Mother of the People (*The*). ' La Mère des Peuples.' Marguerite of France, daughter of François I. (1523–1574).

Mothering Sunday. Mid-Lent, when children go home to their mothers and eat ' mothering cakes.' *See* ' Sun-days.'

Motu Proprio, 1816. An impor-tant measure introduced by Cardinal Ercole Consalvi, for the reform of abuses in the papal states. It suppressed all monopolies, feudal taxes, and exclusive rights.

Mount of Corruption (*The*). The Mount of Olives, east of Jerusalem. So called because thereon Solomon built temples to the gods of the Ammonites and Moabites, out of complaisance to his wives (1 Kings xi.; 2 Kings xxiii. 13).

Mountain (*The*), Sept. 1791. In the National Convention of France the *côté droit* was the constitutional party, the *côté gauche* was the democratic party. This latter party soon divided itself into two, viz. the Mountain and the Gironde. The former seated them-selves on the most elevated benches of the hall, hence their name; the Giron-dists occupied what was called the *plaine* or the floor. At first, all the *côté gauche* worked together; but 31 May, 1793, the Mountain overthrew the more moderate Gironde; and 1794 the Mountain fell to pieces with Robespierre their chief.

> Several young men of Hungary entered into correspondence with the chiefs of the Mountain. —GODKIN, *Hist. of Hungary*, p. 209.

Mountain Brutus (*The*). Wil-liam Tell (1282–1350).

Mountain Tiger of Nepaul (*The*). Runjeet Singh, who died 1839.

Mousquetaires (3 syl.). A company of horse-soldiers armed with muskets, created in 1622 in the service of the king of France. In 1661 they formed two companies—the *Grey* and the *Black* Mousquetaires, so called from the colour of their horses. Their uniform was scarlet-red, and hence that part of the palace appropriated to them was called the 'Maison Rouge.' In times of peace they followed the king *à la chasse*, but in war they fought both on horse and foot, like the French dragoons. The Mousquetaires were suppressed in 1791; they were re-established in 1814, but disappeared on the second return of Louis XVIII. *See* 'Gants Glacés.'

Mozarabic *or* **Gothic Liturgy** (*The*). Consisted of the liturgy of Rome mixed with the oriental liturgies of the Arian Goths. Its use was suspended by the Council of Braga, A.D. 772. It was reprinted in 1500 by Cardinal Ximenês. The Gothic Liturgy is used only in Toledo. *See* 'Spanish Liturgy.'

Mud-Cabin Votes, 1884. The Irish franchise extended to one-pound householders and under, the number of which was 32,829 in the county Mayo alone.

Making every allowance for the disqualification of occupiers on account of parochial relief, the 'Mud-cabin' voters in county Mayo would outnumber the existing voters at least ten to one.—*Standard,* 9 May, 1884.

Mufti. A 'doctor of the law' in the Mussulman religion. He interprets both the text and ideas of the Korân. The Grand Mufti, called the 'Sheik-ul-Islam,' resides at Constantinople, and is head of the lawyers and priests or ulêmas. His ordinances, called *fetfas*, must be blindly obeyed. It is the Grand Mufti who girds on the sultan's sword at his coronation. Every town has its mufti.

Muggleton¹ans. A religious sect which arose in England about the year 1651, and so called from Ludovic Muggleton (1609–1697), a journeyman tailor, who professed to be the mouthpiece of one John Reeve. The two gave themselves out to be the 'two witnesses' of Rev. xi., and assumed the right of 'cursing' all who opposed them. They denied the doctrine of the Trinity, held anthropomorphic opinions of deity, and believed that the devil became incarnate in Eve. They existed as a sect in the first half of the 19th cent., but the census of 1851 showed no trace of them.

Mules of Ma'rius (*The*). When Marïus, in his second consulate, raised an army to march against the Cimbrians, he found considerable difficulty in enlisting men. His sternness repelled them, his arbitrary habits were offensive, and those who submitted patiently were called 'the mules of Marius'; but the term of reproach soon became a term to be proud of.

Multipliers. Alchemists who pretended to multiply the precious metals.

Mul'vian Bridge (*The*). Outside the city, about two miles from Rome. The most northerly of the eight bridges over the Tiber. Built by Scaurus.

Mumping Day. The 21st Dec. (St. Thomas's Day). 'To mump' is *to beg*, and on St. Thomas's Day the poor used to go about the country begging corn for the Christmas feast.

Munce'rians. A sect of Anabaptists in Germany, so called from Muncerus their ringleader, who died 1525.

Mundane Era (*The*). This era begins Oct. B.C. 4008.

According to the modern Greek Calendar B.C. 7388

,,	Josephus	,,	7282
,,	Scaliger	,,	5829
,,	Professor William Hale	,,	5411
,,	'L'art de Vérifier les Dates'	,,	4963
,,	Usher	,,	4004
,,	Calmet	,,	4000

** Of course, all such speculations, in the light of modern science, are wholly worthless, except as historical landmarks, and even then they are most misleading.

Mundane Era (*The Alexandrine*), 29 Aug., B.C. 5502.

Mundane Era (*The Ecclesiastical*) of Constantinople, 1 April, B.C. 5508. (*The Civil*) of Constantinople, 1 Sept., B.C. 5508.

Mundane Era (*The Grecian*), 1 Sept., B.C. 5598.

Mundane Era (*The Jewish*). Vernal equinox, B.C. 3761. But the civil Jewish era is Oct. B.C. 3761.

Mundane Era (*The Julian*), 1 Jan., B.C. 4713.

Mundane Era of Abyssinia (*The*). Begins 29 Aug., B.C. 5493.

Mundane Era of Antioch (*The*). 1 Sept., B.C. 4592.

Municipal Corporation Act *(The)*, 5, 6 Will. IV. c. 76, 9 Sept., 1835. For the regulation of municipal corporations in England and Wales. This act abolished the 'freemen,' as they were called; the prohibition of any but freemen keeping a shop or following a trade in a corporate borough; and the power of purchasing one's freedom. Instead of freemen the burgesses were endowed with municipal powers; a burgess being any male of full age who has been an occupier for two years within the borough or within seven miles of it, and has paid poor rates, provided his name has been duly inscribed on the burgess-roll. The mayor and aldermen are to be elected annually by the council; the councillors by the burgesses; and the council from the aldermen and councillors. *See* 'County Council.'

The 'Irish Municipal Corporation Bill,' altering the entire structure of the corporations of Ireland, is 3, 4 Vict. c. 108, 10 Aug., 1840. The Municipal Corporation Act does not apply to London.

Municipal Reform Acts *(The)*, 1835. The passing of a Bill which gave the right of voting to all ratepayers in towns and boroughs, besides allowing the freemen to retain their former privileges. The lists of voters were as follows: Freemen's Roll, Burgess List, and Ward List.

Muns. A name assumed soon after the Restoration by a clique of young blades in London, whose delight was to break windows, upset the night watchers, kiss the pretty girls, molest sober citizens, render the streets somewhat dangerous, and get themselves talked about as 'impudent young dogs,' 'sowing their wild oats.' *See* 'Street Bullies.'

'Muns' means the face or mouth, and these simpletons so called themselves because they kissed the pretty young women and made mouths at the coarse and older ones. It would seem more likely to be a contraction of the French 'Muscadins,' only the Muns existed many years before the Paris Muscadins.

Münster *(Truce of)*, closing the Thirty Years' War. It led to the 'Peace of Westphalia,' 24 Oct., 1648.

Murab'itins *(The)*, i.e. devoted to religion. So the followers of Abdallah ben Yassim (1046) were called. Some say 'Al-Moravides' *(q.v.)* is a variant of the same word. 'Moravides' (3 syl.).

Murat of the Magyar Army *(The)*. Paul Kinisi (15th cent.). Like him in ostentation, like him in brilliancy, like him as a *beau sabreur*, and he was raised, like him, for his valour, from the ranks.

Murato'rian Canon *(The)*. A list of the books of the New Testament, said to have been compiled about A.D. 150, discovered in the Ambrosian library, Milan, and published by Lodovico Antonio Muratori in 1740. Its genuineness is very doubtful.

The author of the Muratorian Canon appears to take for granted that the apostle [Paul] went into Spain.—WORDSWORTH, *New Testament* (Pauline Epistles, p. 429).

Muscadins of Paris (1795). Paris dandies or exquisites, who aped London cockneys after the Reign of Terror. Their dress was top-boots with thick soles, knee-breeches, a dress-coat with long tails and high stiff collar, and a thick cudgel called a 'constitution.' They affected a huskiness of voice, bearish manners, and vulgarity both of speech and behaviour.

Littré says the affectation came into use during the Revolution, and he derives the word from *muscarde*, which he deduces from *musc*. He says: 'Petit-maître, homme qui affecte une grande recherche dans son costume. Ainsi dit du parfum des muscadins.' *See* 'Partis en France.'

Cockneys of London, muscadins of Paris, BYRON, *Don Juan*, viii. 124.

Muse of Tragedy *(The)*. Mrs. Siddons the great actress (1755–1831).

Mushroom Cities. Chicago, St. Louis.

Music of the Spheres *(The)*. The music produced by the seven planets rolling in their orbits. Pythagoras noticed that different lengths of string, stretched like those of a harp, produce different sounds, and as the seven planets revolve in seven orbits of different circumferences, they must, like an Æolian harp, produce different sounds as they whiz through space. These seven sounds or musical notes Pythagoras called the 'Music of the Spheres.'

Musical Scale *(The Greek)*.

		Called		
1 Ut	...	Hypatê	= *Principal*	
2 Re	...	Par-hypate	= *Post-principal*	A Diatessaron.
3 Mi	...	Lichânos	= *Index*	
4 Fa	...	Mêsê	= *Medium*	
5 Sol	...	Para-mese	= *Post-medium*	
6 Re	...	Tritê	= *Third*	A Diatessaron.
7 Mi	...	Para-nêtê	= *Ante-penult*	
8 Fa	...	Nete	= *Ultimate*	

The 'Diapente' is from *Ut* to *Sol*, and from *Sol* to *Fa* is the 'Diatessaron.' The 'Diapason' = the Diapente plus the Diatessaron. Similarly, from *Fa* to *Fa* is a Diapente. In both cases there are three tones and one semitone in a Diatessaron.

Musical Small-coal Man (*The*).

Thomas Britton (1650–1714). An amateur musician and antiquary, dealer in small coals in Aylesbury Street, Clerkenwell. The room of his gatherings, says Dr. John Hawkins, 'was over the coal-shop, and his weekly concerts were attended by the highest order of nobility.' Dr. Pepusch and, later on, even Handel played the harpsichord at these concerts. Here used to assemble Mr. Needler, accountant-general of the excise, the poet Hughes, Woolaston the painter, and many others. Walpole says that Britton took money from his visitors.

Musketeers (*The*).

'Les Mousquetaires,' 1622. A company of *gentilshommes à cheval* who formed the *garde du roi* created by Louis XIII. There were two companies—the Grey and the Black—so called from the colour of their horses. Being dressed in scarlet, the part of the palace where they lodged was called the *Maison-Rouge*. Suppressed in 1791; restored in 1814, but not organised again by Louis XVIII. on his second restoration.

Mutiny Bill (*The*), or 'Mutiny Act,'

1689 (1 William & Mary, c. 5). It enacted that any military offenders might be arrested by military authority, and tried and condemned by court-martial, in perfect independence of the civil courts.

This bill also provided for the better payment of the army, and for better quarters.

Mutiny of the 'Bounty' (*The*),

1789. H.M. ship 'Bounty,' commanded by Capt. Bligh, was sent to Otaheite for bread-fruit, and on the return voyage the crew rebelled, led by Fletcher Christian, the master's mate. The rebels forced Capt. Bligh and 18 of the men into a boat and set them adrift, but they landed in time at a Dutch settlement, and reached England. The British government sent Capt. Edward Edwards to seize and bring home the rebels, when fourteen were apprehended, but nine were missing. The captives were tried by court-martial, and three were sentenced to death. Twenty years afterwards the nine missing were heard of at Pitcairn's Island (1806); but only one—

viz. Alexander Smith (*alias* John Adams) —was alive. He had become a religious man, and was farmer, schoolmaster, physician, and pastor in the island, in which were 170 inhabitants, 88 being males and 82 females. He died in 1829.

Mutiny of the Nore (*The*), 22

May, 1797. Suppressed in June. This mutiny was preceded by a rebellious dissatisfaction of the seamen of the channel fleet at Spithead, who deprived their officers of command and threatened their lives. This uprising was quelled by an increase of pay; but it was succeeded by a mutiny of the fleet at the Nore, led by one Parker, and very extravagant terms were demanded. After a few weeks the men surrendered at discretion, and Parker was executed.

It was to encourage loyalty among our sailors that, at this period, Charles Dibdin wrote his sea-songs, and was rewarded with a pension.

Mutton-eating King (*The*).

Charles II. of England (1630, 1659–1685).

Here *lies* our mutton-eating king,
Whose word no man relies on
He never *said* a foolish thing,
And never *did* a wise on'.
EARL OF ROCHESTER.

Mutual Admiration Society

(*The*). In French, 'La Société d'Admiration Mutuelle.' A jocose appellative applied in Paris to the 'Société d'Observation Médicale.'

In England it has been applied to several sets; as Shakespeare, Ben Jonson, Beaumont and Fletcher, &c.

Another consisted of contributors to the 'Spectator,' such as Addison, Steele, &c.

A third was the famous 'club' of Johnson, Goldsmith, Burke, Reynolds, Beauclerc, and Boswell.

Mutual Instruction, 1795. A

system of education introduced by Dr. Bell in the Madras schools, where the more advanced pupils were set to teach the less advanced, whereby the number of the staff of paid teachers was very greatly reduced. Joseph Lancaster in 1798 caught the idea, and for a time the mutual instruction plan was largely adopted in our charity and parish schools. The only remnant now left is that of pupil teachers.

M.W.S., 1798. The legend on the

black flags of the Irish rebels in the

United Irishmen's sedition. The initials of *Murder Without Sin.*

Myrmillons (*The*), or 'Mirmillōnes' (4 syl.). Gladiators on foot who combated with the retiarii. So named from a fish, called by the Greeks μορμύρος, which surmounted their helmets.

Mysteries, 13th, 14th, 15th cents. Dramatic representations of the 'religious mysteries,' such as the Incarnation, the Crucifixion, the Holy Trinity, and the Real Presence. They were acted by monks, generally in a cathedral. At their decline they were replaced by the Moralities (*q.v.*).

The four best Mystery plays were the 'Passion,' the 'Resurrection,' the 'Incarnation,' and 'St. Catherine.' The 'Mystery of the Passion' is still (1890) performed in the Tyrol during 'Passion Week.'

Mystics. Those Christians who believe there is a natural and mystical meaning in Scripture, the latter to be gleaned only by particular inspiration and 'converse with heavenly habitants.' They are great in visions, dream revelations, and inward lights.

'Let there be light' means, in a natural sense, 'Let there be the light of day'—the light which now proceeds from the sun—but mystically it means 'Let there be divine inspiration and the light of glory; let light illumine the soul; let light be diffused in the heart, that it may know the divine mysteries, and see what is hid from the natural understanding.'

Mythical School (*The*) of Theology in Germany was founded by Strauss, who tried to prove that the gospels are not real history, but *beaux-idéals* of ancient prophecies personified. His 'Life of Jesus,' in 1840, produced an immense sensation. His 'Christian Doctrine and Faith' enters on the struggle between science and the Bible (1808–1874).

Naamans. A religious party founded by Alexander Knox and Rowland Hill, half churchmen and half dissenters. They were like Naaman in the house of Rimmon.

Nab. To seize unexpectedly. Nabis king of Sparta (B.C. 206–191) made a statue resembling his wife, and clothed it in magnificent apparel. When any-one refused to deliver up his riches to the tyrant, he was led up to the statue, and the statue by secret springs seized the victim in her arms and squeezed him to death against iron spikes secreted by

her dress. If this is not philologically tenable, it is at any rate an historical curiosity. *See* 'Bullies.'

Similarly, to Burke, to Boycott, &c. The Norwegian 'nappe' (to seize) is a cognate word. It may possibly be a contraction of *apprehend* (seize) with an initial *n*.

Nabathæan Kingdoms (*The*). The kingdoms of the east. Arabia Felix is called Nabathæa from Nebajoth the son of Ishmael (Gen. xxxvi. 3). The people of Arabia Petræa are called the Nabathæans, but the term is very widely applied.

Eurus ad Auroram Nabathæaque regna recessit
Persidaque, et radiis juga subdita matutinis.
Vesper et occiduo quæ littora Sole tepescunt,
Proxima sunt Zephyro; Scythiam septemque
triones
Horrifer invasit Boreas; contraria tellus
Nubibus assiduis pluvioque madescit ab Austro.
OVID, *Metamorphoses*, bk. i. 61, &c.

Nabonassar. *See* 'Era of.'

Naboth's Vineyard. A possession coveted by others. Thus in 1885, when half the nations of Europe were swooping down upon places for colonies or annexation, it was said that 'Germany, France, and Italy were looking about for a Naboth's vineyard,' that is, a part of the world which they could appropriate. Of course the allusion is to King Ahab in 1 Kings xxi.

Nag's Head Ordination (*The*). In 1559, 17 Dec., Matthew Parker was consecrated archbishop of Canterbury. Pennant says the ceremony was to have been performed by Anthony Kitchen bishop of Llandaff, but Bonner interfered; whereupon fourteen ecclesiastics determined to consecrate each other to the vacant sees. Scory, a deposed bishop, met the party at the Nag's Head Tavern, Cheapside, and consecrated Parker archbishop; this being done, Parker proceeded to consecrate the rest. Strype refutes this tale in his 'Life of Archbishop Parker,' and in Bennet College library is an instrument said to have been used on the occasion, and being the consecration in Lambeth chapel by William Barlow (late bishop of Bath and Wells), John Scory (late bishop of Chichester), Miles Coverdale (bishop of Exeter), and John Hodgkins (suffragan bishop of Bedford), of Parker and others. The Nag's Head tale is attributed to Father Talbot and another Jesuit named Holywood. Dr. Doyle in 1824–25, before a committee of the

House of Commons, revived the Nag's Head tale.

The story is this : the Nag's Head is the tavern where the dean of the arches and the civilians went to refresh themselves after the confirmation of a bishop, and while the ecclesiastics were there, one Neale (Bonner's chaplain) peeped through the keyhole to see what was going on. He saw Kitchen bishop of Llandaff solicited to assist in the consecration service, but he stoutly refused to take any part therein. Scory (late bishop of Chichester) then made all kneel down, and said to Parker, 'Take thou authority to preach the word of God sincerely.' This tale was accepted as an historic fact for at least forty years ; but we are told that the Earl of Nottingham was present and contradicted it, and that Archbishop Abbot produced the register of Canterbury to disprove it. Of course Neale's tale, as well as that of the earl and archbishop, are so doubtful that no reliance can be placed on either of them.

Nails (*The*), used at the crucifixion. Gregory Nazianzen asserts that there were only three nails used, but Cyprian maintains that there were four. The number of those said to have been found in the cave where the three crosses were buried is equally uncertain. One was sent to Rome, and is deposited in what was afterwards the Santa Croce; two others were sent by the Empress Helēna to her son Constantine, one of which was welded as an amulet to his helmet that he might not be slain in battle, and the other was set in his horse's headstall; a fourth the empress threw into the Gulf of Venice to allay a storm; a fifth was beaten out into a thin band, and is set in the famous 'iron crown of Lombardy,' with which Charlemagne and Napoleon were crowned. So that the find of the empress did not settle the disputed point, but only made it more doubtful. *See* 'Crucifixion, Relics of the.'

Similarly the dispute about the wood of the cross was not settled by the discovery of the 'true cross.' Was it oak, pine, cedar, gopher wood, or what ? Some affirm it was made of three or more different kinds of wood. Certainly the relics which profess to be parts of the cross vary, so that the question is still undecided.

Calvin enumerates fourteen nails : one in the Santa Croce at Rome, another in Siena, a third in Venice, a fourth in the church of the Carmelites in Paris, a fifth in the Holy Chapel, a sixth at Draguignan, a seventh at Trenaille, an eighth at Trèves, a ninth at Monza, a tenth in the crown of Lombardy, one was thrown into the Gulf of Venice, one was welded into the helmet of Constantine, one was set in the headstall of the emperor's horse (Gregory of Tours says two of the nails were set in the headstall). This would make fourteen. Not the slightest reliance can oe placed on the genuineness of any of the relics of the crucifixion, or of the 'saints.'

Nails found in Coffins. A nail was at one time placed in a coffin for luck, much as a horseshoe is nailed to a stable door. The Romans drove annually on the ides of September a nail into the side wall of the temple of Jupiter Capitolīnus (Livy, vii. 3).

It is supposed that the nails were originally a sort of tally for marking the number of years, and were continued out of reverence to an old custom (Festus). The nail driven into the temple was technically called 'Clavus annālis.'

Names Classicised. It was much the fashion, especially with German and Dutch authors who wrote in Latin, to convert their names into a Greek or Latin equivalent, or to give them a classic turn, as :—

Agricola (1492–1566) the reformer, and friend of Luther, whose real name was Schneider (a tailor). This was assuming another name.

Bucer (1491–1551), a Dominican and friend of Luther, whose real name was Kuhhorn (cow-horn), of which *bucer* is the Greek.

Desiderius Erasmus (1467–1536), a Dutchman whose real name was Gheraerd Gheraerd, of which Desiderius is the Latin, and Erasmos the Greek.

Melanchthon (1497–1560), one of Luther's friends, whose real name was Schwartzerde (black earth). Melanchthon is the Greek for a 'heap of black earth.'

Œcolampadius, the Latinised name of Johann Hausschein, the reformer (1482–1531).

Paracelsus (1493–1541), Græco-Latin for bombast, the real name being A. T. Bombast.

Porphyry, the Grecised name of Malk, the real name of the disciple of Plotin (233–304).

Regiomontānus, a Latinised form of Königsberger. So Johann Müller called himself (1436–1475). He was born at Königsberg in Franconia.

Stobæus is Stubbs Latinised (5th cent.).

Till after the reign of Friedrich II. the Great (1740-1786) the Germans were ashamed of their language, and all their standard works were written in Latin or Greek. Of course this does not apply to Porphyry, though probably he disliked the name of Malk.

Nameless Finger (*The*). The 3rd finger of the right hand. The right-hand fingers are the pointer, long finger, nameless finger, little finger ; of the left hand they are the pointer, long finger, ring finger, and little finger.

Nanekism. The religious system of Nanek, founder of the religion of the Sikhs, which is a fusion of Islamism and Buddhism. The Sikhs recognise both the Vedas and the Korân. H ɣ code is called the *Adi-granth.* Lahore is the centre of Nanekism.

Nanek was born 1469, and died 1539.
N.B.—' Sikh ' is one of a Hindú sect, and means *disciple.* ' Sheik ' is an Arab chief.

Nantes (*Edict of*), July 1591, granted by Henri IV. to the Protestants of France, was only a revival of the Edict of Poitiers conceded by Henri in 1577. The difference was this: the Edict of Nantes was enforced, that of Poitiers was a dead letter. In 1597 the edict was extended, and the Huguenots were allowed the public exercise of their religion in all places in which it had obtained a footing in 1597, and in the suburbs of towns. Permission was given to lords of high rank to hold religious services in their castles, and to noblemen of second rank to admit thirty co-religionists to their private chapels; the reformed were admitted to public offices, their children to schools, and the poor to a share of alms; the right of printing books in certain towns was conceded, equal representation in some of the palements, four academies of scientific and theological instruction, and a certain number of places of security.

Napier's Bones, 1617. A contrivance by John Napier baron of Merchiston for saving the tedious processes of multiplication and division by shifting about slips of ivory or bone, and, after the slips have been arranged, merely adding or subtracting the figures on the slips.

Thus a sum of multiplication by five figures would (after the bones are arranged) be performed by simply adding five lines of figures.

Napoleon (*The Code of*), 1803–1804. The ' Code Civil,' consisting of three books, the first of *persons*, under 11 titles; the second of *goods*, under 4 titles; and the third of the ways of *acquiring property*, under 20 titles. The whole code contains 2,281 articles. Tronchet was ' the soul of the code,' but he was assisted by Rœderer, Portalis, Thibaudeau, Cambacérès, and Lebrun.

Though the Napoleon Code means the Code Civil, yet there are several other codes for different branches of the law, as the ' Code Pénal,' the ' Code des Délits et des Peines,' the ' Code d'Instruction Criminelle,' &c.

Napoléon le Grand. Napoleon I. (1769, 1804–1814, died 1821). Banished to Elba 1814 (he was deposed 4 April, and arrived at Elba 4 May). Flight

from Elba 26 Feb., 1815; reached Paris 20 March; defeated at Waterloo 18 June. He gave himself up to Capt. Maitland of the 'Bellerophon,' 15 July; was banished to St. Helena, and arrived there in the ' Northumberland,' commanded by Admiral Sir George Cockburn, 16 Oct. He died 5 May, 1821. His remains were removed to Paris in 1840, and were deposited in the Hôtel des Invalides 15 Dec., 1840.

His ' day of the Violets ' is 1 March, the day when he reached Cannes after his escape from Elba. *See* ' Violets.'
Father, Carlo Buonaparte of Corsica; *Mother,* Maria Letizia Ramolina; *Wives* (1) Josephine, widow of Beauharnais, divorced; (2) Maria Louisa archduchess of Austria; *Son,* François Joseph Napoleon Bonaparte. *Contemporary* with George III.
Memoranda. Napoleon Bonaparte was sub-lieutenant of artillery 1785, captain 1792, commander of the National Guards 1792, brigadier-general 1794, commander-in-chief of the army in Italy 1796, First Consul 24 Dec., 1799, First Consul for life 2 Aug., 1802, Emperor 18 May, 1804. He won fifty-two victories. His life was attempted in Dec. 1800 by an 'infernal machine ' planted in the Rue St. Nicasse. The intention was to kill him on his way to the opera. He was once wounded slightly in battle, and was excommunicated by Pius VII. in 1809.

His abdications: I. Deposed by the senate, and abdicated at Fontainebleau 4 April, 1814. Sent to Elba in the British frigate called the ' Undaunted,' under the command of Capt. Usher; went on board 28 April, and arrived at Elba 4 May, 1814.

II. After the battle of Waterloo he abdicated a second time, 22 June, 1815. He gave himself up at Rochefort to Captain Maitland, commander of the ' Bellerophon.' Accompanied by Count Bertrand, Count Montholon, Count Lascases, Baron Gourgaud, a surgeon, and twelve domestics, he was then sent to St. Helena in the ' Northumberland,' under the command of Admiral Sir George Cockburn, and arrived there 16 Oct., 1815, Sir Hudson Lowe being governor of the island. He lived in Longwood House, and died 5 May, 1821, amidst a phenomenal tempest.

His crack *regiments* were the 30th, 43rd, and 96th. To belong to one of these infantry corps was a warrant of reckless courage and undaunted bravery. Napoleon and all his staff uncovered and bowed low as any one of their tattered colours filed in review before them.

Napoleon II. Son of Napoleon I. and his second wife Maria Louisa archduchess of Austria. He was created ' King of Rome ' from the moment of his birth (20 March, 1811), and, when his father abdicated in 1814, the Senate proclaimed him Napoleon II., a title which the powers of Europe would not allow. On the fall of his father in 1815, the lad retired to the court of his maternal grandfather, the emperor of Austria, and received the title of 'Duke of Reichstadt.' He died of consumption at Schönbrunn in 1832.

Napoleon III., Emperor of the French (1808, reigned 1852-1870; deposed, and died 1873).

Father, Louis Bonaparte, brother of Napoleon I : *Mother*, Hortense de Beauharnais, daughter of Josephine by her first husband (her second husband was Napoleon I.); *Wife*, Marie-Eugénie de Guzman, comtesse de Téba. *Contemporary* with Queen Victoria.

** His life was attempted six times.

1852, 24 Sept. An infernal machine was found at Marseilles designed to kill him.

1853, 5 July. His assassination was attempted as he was leaving the Opéra Comique.

1855, 28 April. Giovanni Pianóri fired at him in the Champs Elysées.

1857, 7 Aug. Barcolotti, Gibaldi, and Grillo came to London to assassinate him while he was on a visit to Queen Victoria.

1858, 14 Jan. Orsi'ni (*q.v.*) attempted his life.

1863, 24 Dec. Greco attempted his life.

Orsini organised his infernal plot in London, Pianori did the same; Mazzini, Ledru-Rollin, and Campanello in London supplied plotters with arms, &c. The French ambassador complained to the British government; and these plotters again-t the French emperor nearly dragged us into a war with France.

Special Constable in London, 10 April, 1848. Louis Napoleon, with 170,000 noblemen, gentlemen, merchants, and tradesmen, volunteered to be sworn in as special constables to prevent disturbance of the peace by the Chartists when they presented their monster petition (*q.v.*). Louis Napoleon acted under the Earl of Eglinton.

** *Nicknames* :—
COMTE D'ARENSBERG. So he called himself after his escape from the fortress of Ham.
BADINGUET. The name of the man he shot in his Boulogne escapade.
BOUSTRAPA. A compound of Bou[logne], Stra-[sbourg], and Pa[ris], the places of his no†ed escapades.
GROSBEC. So called from the rather unusual size of his nose.
MAN OF DECEMBER. So called because December was his month of glory. Thus he was elected president 11 Dec., 1848; he made his *coup d'état* 2 Dec., 1851; was chosen president for life by plebiscite 21 Dec., 1851; and was created emperor 2 Dec., 1852.

MAN OF SEDAN. So called because at Sedan he surrendered his sword to William king of Prussia, Sept. 1870.
MAN OF SILENCE. *See* p. 548.
OUI-OUI was the pet name given him by Hortense in his childhood. He was a quick, intelligent boy, beautiful as a girl.
RATIPOLE (3 syl.). The same as the West of England word *rantipole*, meaning a harum-scarum fellow, half idiot and half madcap.
SEDANTAIRE. A pun on Sedan. *See above.*
SOULOUQUE (*q.v.*).
The Little. Victor Hugo gave him this title, but the hatred of Hugo for Napoleon was a monomania.
VERHUEL. The name of his supposed father. He was born while his mother was separated from her husband. Scandal says she had been separated thirteen months.
** Whatever may be said of Napoleon III., two things deserve mention: (1) He was the only crowned head of France who visited England as a friend : and (2) all through his reign he knew his best policy was to remain friendly to England. From this wi e policy he never swerved, although sometimes goaded to animosity by his military advisers. Our relations with France have certainly not improved by the substitution of a republi c.

Napoleon of Peace (*The*). Louis-Philippe king of the French (1773-1850, reigned 1830-1848). Also called 'The Citizen King.'

Napoleon of the East (*The*). Mehemet Ali pacha of Egypt (1769-1848).

Napoleon of the Turf (*The*). Lord George Bentinck (1802-1848).

Nassac Diamond (*The*). Formerly in the possession of the East India Company; weighed 89¾ carats, but since the Duke of Westminster had it cut anew it weighs only 78⅝ carats. Its value is about 30,000*l*. *See* 'Diamonds.'

Nation of Shopkeepers (*A*). So Louis XIV. called Holland. Napoleon Bonaparte applied the phrase to England; but whether England or France is the more given to trade would be hard to determine. Probably the proportion of men independent of trade would be in favour of England; and without the least doubt the money-grabbing or commercial spirit in Frenchmen is very much stronger than it is in Englishmen. I lived eight or nine years in France, and mixed with all classes—the court, the military, the medical profession, the literati, the bourgeois, and the proletariat.

Nations (*Expedition of the*), A.D. 625. When the Koreish were defeated by Mohammed. They had been defeated by him in 623 at Bedr and Ohud. *See* 'Ditch.'

National Anthem (*The*) of Hungary is 'Rakotski's March.' *See* 'God save the King.'

Prince Franz Leopold Rakotski, a Transylvanian prince, protector of Protestantism (died 1676).

National Assembly (*The*).

I. Of *France*, 17 June, 1789. 'L'Assemblée Nationale,' the *tiers état*, which withdrew from the States-General, while the nobles and clergy were debating how the votes were to be counted, and whether they should sit in the same house with the deputies.

The nobles and clergy wanted to have three houses and to vote by houses. This, of course, would be simply to ignore the *tiers état*. The deputies, who numbered 584 members, while the two other estates numbered both together only 561, insisted on voting *per capita*.

II. Of *Germany*, 1848. It superseded the old German 'Diet' (*q.v.*), which held its meetings at Frankfort. The National Assembly met at Berlin, and offered the imperial crown to William king of Prussia, but he declined the honour. It formed a constitution with two chambers; the upper one was to contain 200 members and the lower one to consist of representatives of the people, one-third of the members to retire every two years. The kaiser was to have the absolute right of declaring peace and war, and of making treaties. Free municipal institutions were to be established; and perfect freedom in religion, education, science, and the press to be conceded. All this fell through in 1849, when a new legislative body was constituted, consisting of two chambers, which met at Brandenburg.

The National Assembly of Berlin proved so refractory that the city was deserted, trade was paralysed, and Prussia was reduced to the verge of civil war.

National Association for the Repeal of the Union (*The*), *i.e.* the union between Great Britain and Ireland. Organised in Ireland 1840, and monster meetings were held on the Hill of Tara to promote the object 15 Aug., 1843. The subject of repeal has agitated Ireland ever since 1810, and in 1886 Mr. W. E. Gladstone brought in a bill with a view of putting an end to the ever-recurring agitation. In 1840 Daniel O'Connell was the great agitator; and from 1881 to 1890, under the name of 'Home Rule' and the leadership of Charles Stewart Parnell, the question of repeal obstructed almost all parliamentary business. *See* 'Irish Associations.'

National Association of Ireland (*The*), 1864. Formed to disestablish the Irish Church, and to alter the land laws. The church was disestablished in 1869. *See* 'Irish Associations.'

National Board (*The*), Ireland. The 'Commissioners of National Education' (*q.v.*).

National Confederacy of Poland (*The*). The dissidents under Prince Radzivil. They amounted to 72,000 noblemen and gentlemen, and were opposed by a Catholic association called the 'Confederacy of Bar' (*q.v.*), which in 1774 conspired to assassinate the king (Stanislaus Augustus Poniatowski), suspected of favouring the dissidents. The king escaped in a miraculous manner, lived through the two partitions of Poland, was compelled by Catharine of Russia to abdicate in 1795, and died in obscurity in 1798, aged 66.

National Convention (*The*).

I. Of *Chartists*, 1838. Up to 12 Aug. the delegates met at the Arundel Coffee House, in the Strand, London. It was declared illegal by the Convention Act Dec. 1839, but meetings continued to be held for ten years longer.

The Chartists were strongly averse to the Anti-Corn-Law League, because, they said, it would reduce the labouring man's wages, which were virtually regulated by the price of corn.

II. Of *France*. 'La Convention Nationale' (from 21 Sept., 1792 to 26 Oct., 1795). The French legislature which succeeded the Legislative Assembly (*q.v.*). On the very first day of meeting it abolished royalty and proclaimed France to be a republic. On 17 Jan., 1793, it pronounced sentence of death on Louis XVI. On 5 Oct., 1793, it declared that all dates should be computed from the foundation of the republic (22 Sept., 1792). On 16 Oct., 1793, it brought Marie-Antoinette to the guillotine. On 21 Oct. it condemned to death twenty-one of the Girondists. On 5 April, 1794, it condemned to death Danton, Camille Desmoulins, and many others of the *Cordeliers* (*q.v.*). On 27 July, 1794, it condemned to death Robespierre. On 26 Oct., 1795, it declared itself dissolved.

On the *right* sat the Girondists, on the *left* the Montagnards, in the *centre* the middle-men. The number of members was originally 721; reduced to 500 in Year III. and to 300 in Year VIII. (21 Sept., 1792).

National Covenant (*The*), 1638.

A bond of union drawn up at Edinburgh by the leading Presbyterian ministers, embodying the Confession of 1580, and binding all who signed it to spare nothing in the endeavour to preserve their national religion. The proximate cause of this bond was the attempt of Charles I. to enforce on Scotland episcopacy and the Common Prayer Book.

National Debt (*The*), 1664.

The national debt began in the reign of Charles II., to make up the deficiencies of the revenue. In 1672 he declared that the interest could not be paid, but in 1684 the payment of interest was resumed. In 1699 the rate of interest was fixed at 3 per cent. Future sovereigns increased the debt chiefly for war expenses. The debt was highest in 1817, when it was almost 841 millions. In 1888 the interest was reduced to 2¾ per cent.

National Defects.

The special plague of CHINA is leprosy, so was it of the ancient JEWS; of JAPAN and INDIA smallpox and cholera; of SOUTHERN ITALY physical deformities; of HOLLAND spinal diseases; of GERMANY defective eyesight; of SWITZERLAND goître and rotten teeth; of NORTH AMERICA rotten teeth and early baldness; of FRANCE 'the French disease'; of ENGLAND consumption, especially among girls.

National Gallery (*The*), 1824.

The National Picture Gallery in Trafalgar Square, London. The foundation was the collection of Mr. Angerstein, purchased by government; enriched by the gifts of Mr. Vernon, Mr. Sheepshanks, Mr. J. W. M. Turner, and others.

The *building* in Trafalgar Square by Wilkins was opened 9 April, 1838, enlarged by Pennethorne in 1860. The *eastern* wing was granted to the Royal Academy of Arts for their annual exhibition of pictures, &c., formerly shown at Somerset House; and the *western* wing was set apart for national pictures of ancient and modern deceased artists, formerly exhibited in Pall Mall. In 1868 the Royal Academicians removed their exhibition to Burlington House, and left the whole of the National Gallery for the exhibition of national works.

National Land League of Great Britain, March 1881.

To abolish rent altogether in Ireland; and to make Ireland an independent nation, 'with its own flag among the nations of the world.' This league was in substitution of Michael Davitt's LAND LEAGUE

(*q.v.*), which was suppressed in 1882. Proclaimed as unlawful Aug. 1887. *See* 'Irish Associations.'

In 1885 there sprang up, in the U.S. of North America, the 'Irish National League of America.'

National League (*The*), 1882,

Ireland, had for its objects:—

1. National self-government.
2. Land law reform.
3. Local self-government.
4. Extension of parliamentary and municipal franchise.
5. The development and encouragement of native industries and manufactures.

The Land League, instituted in 1881, was suppressed in 1882. *See* 'Irish Associations.'

National School Society (*The*)

of England, 11 Nov., 1811. Parochial schools in connection with the Church of England, supported by voluntary contributions, school pence, and government grants. The schools are examined by government inspectors and are under diocesan inspection also. *See* 'Board Schools.'

National Schools (*The*), of Ireland, 1833.

Introduced by Mr. Stanley, chief secretary. These schools are under a board called the 'Commissioners of National Education in Ireland' (*q.v.*). The schools are strictly undenominational, and no pupil need attend any religious instruction which the parents or guardians do not approve; but any pupil may receive special religious instruction at a fixed appointed time. No book to be introduced without the express approval of the commissioners.

National Subsidy (*The English*), 1770.

The interest of the large subscriptions made in Great Britain for the augmentation of the pastors' salaries in the Piedmontese valleys. This was in addition to the 'Royal Subsidy' (*q.v.*).

Nationalists (1886).

An Irish party led by C. S. Parnell, M.P., which wanted to secure for Ireland a separate parliament, with the ulterior view of separating Ireland from England, and making it an independent kingdom. In 1886 Mr. Gladstone brought in a bill for Home Rule in Ireland. Those Whigs who favoured this bill were called Separatists, and those who opposed it were called Unionists. *See* 'Irish Associations.'

Natura Naturans. 'Nature operating is Nature's creator.' Bruno's phrase (1550–1600), by which he meant that it was not God who created all things out of nothing, but that ' energising Nature ' was the true creative force. Not ' Deus creavit omnia ex nihilo,' but ' Natura naturans naturavit naturam.'

Spinoza taught that God and Nature are identical ; and Stahl taught that God is the *anima mundi*, or its vital principle, as the soul is of the body.

Natura Naturata. Nature made Nature ; or Nature is the outcome of natu al en rgy.

Natural Experimental Philosophy. *See* ' Jacksonian Professor.'

Natural Science Tripos. Three classes into which students in the University of Cambridge are divided who have passed with credit their final examinations in the Natural Sciences. The Natural Sciences include (1) CHEMISTRY (the laws of heat, and the laws of metallic and non-metallic bodies) ; (2) BOTANY (the structure, &c. of vegetable cells, the vessels of plants, the functions of their organs, their means of reproduction, and their classification) ; (3) ZOOLOGY (the genera of animals, their special forms and skeletons, nervous system, digestive system, circulatory system, organs of respiration, ova, and embryo) ; (4) GEOLOGY (the leading facts of Physical Geography, the order of the stratified rocks and their general character). And these six other subjects : Biology, Physics, Mineralogy, Comparative Anatomy, Human Anatomy, and Physiology. Of course, no examination includes all these nine subjects. *See* ' Moral Sciences.'

Nautch Girls (*The*). *See* under ' Bayaderes ' (3 syl.).

Naval Mass. The mass celebrated on board ship, when the rolling of the vessel might cause the wine to be spilt or the ' bread ' to be scattered. In this mass the oblation, the consecration of the elements, and the communion are all omitted.

Navarrais (*The*), 1357–1364. Charles the Bad of Navarre, son-in-law of Louis X. of France, who conspired with the dauphin against Jean II. le Bon. He was imprisoned, but made his escape after the battle of Poitiers. In 1357 he joined the English, and while Jean was in captivity in London, laid claim to the crown of France (1358). At the death of Jean, his son and successor Charles V. sent Bertrand du Guesclin against these invaders and marauders. He encountered them in Normandy, routed them utterly, and slew their leader the Captal de Buch.

Charles the Bad met with a very singular death. He was advised by his medical attendant to sleep in a nightdress steeped in spirits of wine. He did so, his dress caught fire, and he was burnt to death.

Navigation Act (*The*), 1651. Promulgated by Cromwell. Its object was to exclude all foreigners from English ports, and to secure to England and its colonies all the carrying trade. Hitherto Holland had been the great carrying state, but by this act it was ordained that no goods from Asia, Africa, or America should be imported to Great Britain except in ships belonging to England or its colonies. Abolished in 1849. *See* ' Reciprocity Act.'

Nazarenes (3 syl.), or **Nazaræans.** A sect mentioned by Tertullus in Acts xxiv. 5. The Christians were so called insultingly ; but the word was subsequently applied to Judaizing Christians, who demanded exact conformity to the Mosaic ritual. The only gospel they accepted was ' an heretical gospel ' ascribed to Matthew.

In Evangelio juxta Hebræos, quod Chaldaico quidem Syroque sermone, sed Hebraicis literis conscriptum est, quo utuntur usque hodie Nazareni.—JEROME, *Dialog. adv. Pelagianos*, book iii. 2.

Nazarites (3 syl.). Persons separated or consecrated to God (Numb. vi.). (1) They abstained not only from wine, but even from the grapes of which wine is made ; (2) they were never allowed to cut their hair ; (3) they were never allowed to defile themselves by contact with a dead body, not even if that body was the nearest and dearest, as husband or wife, father or mother, son or daughter, brother or sister.

Nazoreans. ' Nazireans,' ' Nazareans,' or ' Nousaïeriens,' a sect (mentioned by St. Epiphanius), and said to have been in existence before the Christian era. They had a scripture called the ' Book of Adam,' containing most of our ' Book of Genesis.' When Christ came, they abjured his mission, and called their own founder the real Messiah (' Anacalypsis,' p. 657).

Nebraska (U. S. America). So called from the river Nebraska (Indian), now the River *Platte*. The inhabitants are nicknamed *Bug-eaters*; they are said to have once eaten locusts during a visitation of those insects.

Necessary Doctrine or Erudition *(The)*, 1543. A book of directions drawn up in convocation by the bishops inclined to the reformation. This book was of authority in the English Church during the remainder of Henry VIII.'s reign.

Necessitarians. Those who deny the freedom of the will, such as Augustine and Calvin. Thus Augustine insisted that conversion is solely by free grace, independent of the human will; and Calvin insisted that those saved were predestined to be saved. Pelagius and Arminius insisted that man is free to accept or reject the gospel.

Negative Elements of our Belief *(The)*. The Unitarian Confession of Faith, contained in four articles (Martineau, ' Studies,' p. 77).

The *Positive* Ones, as described by Dr. Beard, are about eight or nine.

Negative Oath *(The)*, 1641. An oath imposed on the clergy in the reign of Charles I., that they ' would not consent to alter the government of the Church.' The University of Oxford protested against this oath.

Neill of the Showers *(King)*, 795– So called because on the night he was born three showers fell in Ireland : a shower of honey, a shower of silver, and a shower of blood.

Nelson *(The Danish)*. Peter Tordenskiold (1691–1720). He was a tailor's apprentice in Trondhjem, and raised himself to the rank of vice-admiral.

Trondhjem, pronounce *Tron-yem.*

Nelson's Column, in Trafalgar Square, was erected in 1843; the four lions by Landseer were added in 1867.

The design of the column was furnished by W. Railton, who took for his model a column of the Temple of Mars Ultor at Rome. The order is Corinthian, and the material Devonshire granite.

Nelson's Eye. August 1794, at the siege of Calvi, a very strongly situated and fortified place in Corsica, Nelson lost the sight of one of his eyes by gravel

driven into it by a shot which fell near him (age 36).

He lost his arm in July 1797, in an attack on Santa Cruz, Teneriffe (age 39).

Neme'an Games. Held in Neme'a, in Argŏlis. Instituted by the seven heroes on their return from Thebes; but historically B.C. 575. Philip of Macedon presided at the opening games. They were held four times a year, and the original prize was an olive wreath. Eleven of the Odes of Pindar are in celebration of victors in these games.

Nemedians *(The)*. Invaders of Ireland under Nemedius, who compelled the subjugated Fomorians *(q.v.)* to build forts for them, and afterwards put the architects to death. They were driven out of the island by the natives, but a few left behind had a district awarded them (Keating, p. 121).

Moore, in his 'History of Ireland,' says the Fomorians were African pirates who overcame the Nemedians, dispersed them, and destroyed them.—Chap. v. 76.

Nemours *(The Treaty of)*, 1585, in which Henri III. of France engaged to deprive the Huguenots, not only of the public exercise of their religion, but also of liberty of conscience. It was ordered by this treaty that all the Calvinistic clergy should quit the kingdom within a month, and that all Huguenots, who would not abjure, should emigrate before six months under penalty of confiscation of goods and death. This term of six months was afterwards reduced to fifteen days.

Neo-Fenians, 1878–79. Founded by John Devoy. His ' new departure ' had for its object the ' uniting of the forces of revolution and constitutional agitation, with a view of advancing the aims of the separatist party.' *See* ' Irish Associations.'

Neolo'gians, Neol'ogy. A rationalistic form of Christianity introduced in the 18th cent. by Eichhorn and Paulus, who denied the divine origin of the Scripture; maintained that the Old Testament is like any other history; that clergymen are mere professors of theology, as lawyers and medical men are professors of their respective professions; and that miracles, if worthy of any credit, are only natural occurrences.

Neoplat'onism. This philosophy developed itself in Alexandria, and its object was an amalgamation of Plato's philosophy with Eastern mysticism. The Neoplatonists gave objective reality to abstract ideas. Thus Wisdom was made a person, and it is thought by some that 'The Word' referred to in the gospel of St. John is an instance in point. The Trinity of the Neoplatonists consists of Unity, Wisdom or the Word, and the Mundane Soul. The chief exponents are Ammonius Saccas, Plotīnus, Porphyry, Jamblichus, Proclus, and Julian the Apostate.

Neoplatonism, in Alexandria, originated with Philo about A.D. 35 or 40; but was more definitely constituted by Ammonius Saccas about 190-240.

Neph'ites (2 syl.). The second American race according to the Book of Mormon. The first were Jaredites, so called from Jared, who led a colony to America at the dispersion when God confounded the tongues of the builders of the Tower of Babel. The first colony were all slain by internecine war. The Nephites were so called from Nephi (youngest of the four sons of Lehi), who led the second colony, and was appointed by God to rule over the colony settled in Chili.

As the brothers of Nephi opposed this decree of God their skins were blackened, and they became the founders of the American Indian tribes. Nephi heard the earthquake at the crucifixion, and Christ himself appeared to him forty days and revealed to him the truths of Christianity. In A.D. 384 the race of Nephi was annihilated. *See* 'Book of Mormon.'

Neri (*The*), 1294. A political faction in Pistoia, similar to the Donāti of Florence, and favourers of the Guelfs. Their opponents were the Bianchi (*q.v.*).

The names were derived from two powerful families; the Neri represented the high aristocratic class, and the Bianchi the rich merchant class. *See* the 'Blacks and Whites.'

Nero of Persia (*The*). Sefi or Sophi, grandson of Abbas the Great (1628–1642). This tyrant had not one redeeming quality.

Nero of the North (*The*). Christiern II. of Denmark (1480, 1513–1523).

Nero's Torches. Christians smeared with oil or tar, stuck in the ground, and set alight. It is said that the Emperor Nero threw on the Christians the charge of setting fire to Rome,

and thus tortured some of them in public thoroughfares A.D. 64.

It must not be forgotten that religion and politics were united in the Roman empire, and that the persecution of Christians was in all cases more a matter of civil policy than of aversion to Christian dogmas.

Nertschinsk (*Treaty of*), 1689. Between Russia and China, fixing the boundary line between the two countries. The river Kerbeschi (the Gorbitza) was made the line of separation.

Nestor of Europe (*The*). Leopold king of Belgium (1790, 1831–1865).

Nestor of German Poesy (*The*). Christoph August Tiedge (1752–1841).

Nestor of German Sculptors (*The*). John Heinrich Dannecker (1758–1841).

Nestorian Liturgy (*The*). No Nestorian liturgy has been printed, but probably the Anglican missionaries sent to the Assyrian Church in 1887 will make it a part of their duty to print these service-books. The Nestorians teach that there are two persons, not two natures, in Christ. Their chief bishop used to be called the Catholicos, but is now called the Patriarch. They do not accept the canon of Scripture as authorised in the Council of Rome 494. They have seven sacraments, but these are not identical with the sacraments of the Western Church. They are rigid sabbatarians, and acknowledge three orders of the ministry.

Nestorians, A.D. 428. The followers of Nestorius patriarch of Constantinople (died 439). He maintained that Jesus Christ was the union of two persons, the Divine Word and the man Christ Jesus. The former dwelt in the latter as in a temple, and Mary was not the mother of God, but only the mother of the man Christ Jesus, for 'God' could not be born, neither could He die. This heresy was condemned by the General Council of Ephesus in 431. There is a Nestorian Liturgy. *See* 'Theophoron,' &c.

Theodore of Mopsuestia first broached this heresy, which still subsists in Persia and Turkey.
One party insisted that the Virgin Mary was 'Theotocos' (mother of God), another insisted that she was 'Anthropotocos' (mother of man); Nestorius devised a middle term, 'Christotocos' (mother of Christ), and thus offended both sects.

Netherlands (*The*), 1548. The seventeen provinces which under Charles V. formed the 'circle of Burgundy.' They passed to Spain in 1556. Seven of the northern provinces in 1579 leagued together in what is called the ' Union of Utrecht,' threw off the Spanish yoke, and became in 1594 'the Republic of the Seven Provinces.'

Under Louis XIV. of France Artois, with parts of Flanders, Hainaut, and Namur were united to France, and the rest was called the ' Spanish (or Catholic) Netherlands.' By the peace of Rastadt, in 1714, these provinces were ceded to Austria, and received the name of the ' Austrian Netherlands.' In the French Revolution, France took these provinces from Austria ; and in 1814 sixteen French departments were formed into the ' kingdom of the Netherlands,' and given to William I. of the house of Nassau. In 1830 the kingdom was divided into ' the kingdom of the Netherlands ' (Holland) (north), and the 'kingdom of Belgium' (south).

The king of Holland still calls himself the ' king of the Netherlands.' *See* ' Holland.'

Neustria. The ancient name of Normandy.

Neva'da (U.S. America). So called from the Sierra Nevada, or ' snowy mountain chain,' which traverses the state. The nickname of the inhabitants is *Sage-hens.*

Neuters. Presbyterians to be added to the Rump. They would have no power and no influence against the satellites of Cromwell, who would form an overwhelming majority.

Scarcely had they met the next morning, when Colonel Ingoldsby hastened in and informed them that the Commons were hard at work pushing forward their bill for increasing their own numbers by the introduction of the neuters.—HOWITT, *Hist. of England* (Commonwealth), p. 329.

Neutralisation of the Black Sea (*The*), 30 March, 1856. All ships of war (with recognised exceptions) prohibited from entering the waters of the Black Sea, but it was free to the mercantile marine of every nation.

The exceptions were that Russia and Turkey might each have six steamships of 800 tons and four light vessels of 200 tons each.

New and Latter House of Israel (*The*). *See* ' Jezreelites.'

New Church (*The*). The Swedenborgians.

New College, Oxford, 1386. Founded by William of Wykeham, bishop of Winchester. The head-master is called the warden.

New Connection (*The*), 1797. Seceders from the Methodist Connection led by Alexander Kilham. In doctrine they follow Wesley, but in discipline they resemble the Presbyterians. The people choose their own officers, and send representatives to all the synodical meetings of the denomination. They seceded because they thought the conference is not sufficiently representative; and they give an equal share in all administrative affairs to laymen and ministers.

New Departure (*The*), 1880. In Irish history, commenced on the visit of Mr. Parnell to North America. It combined the murderous violence of the Clan-na-Gael or United Brotherhood with the craft of the ' constitutional agitation in Ireland,' and the craze of the peasantry (stirred up by the Land League at the suggestion of Michael Davitt) of paying no rent for their farms. *See* ' Irish National Brotherhood.'

New Franciscans (*The*), 1763. A club of twelve profligates who met in an old Cistercian abbey at Medmenham on the banks of the Thames, and there caricatured the rites and processions of the Catholic brotherhood by obscene rites and profane imitations. Over the portal they inscribed the motto which Rabelais says was placed over the gate of Theleme Abbey : FAY CE QUE VOUDRAS. They rivalled in licentiousness and profanity the Hell Fire Club.

Amongst the members were Wilkes (editor of the ' North Briton '), Sir Francis Dashwood (chancellor of the exchequer), Paul Whitehead, Lord Sandwich, &c. Called ' Franciscans ' from Francis the Christian name of Dashwood, who had his likeness taken in the habit of a Franciscan friar.

New General Baptist Association (*The*), 1770. Seceders on the question of the divinity of Christ.

New Hampshire, in N. America, previously called ' Laconia,' received its present name from Captain John Mason of Hampshire, to whom it was conceded in 1629 by the Plymouth Company. It is a state of mountains and lakes, and called ' the Granite State ' and the ' Switzerland of America.' The inhabitants are nicknamed ' Granite Boys.'

New Inn Hall, Oxford, 1383. Founded by Dr. Cramer dean of Carlisle. The head of the hall is called the principal.

New Jersey (U. S. America). So called, 1664, in compliment to Sir John Carteret, who had defended Jersey (in the British Channel) against the Parliamentarians in 1642. Charles II. gave the territory to his brother James, and James gave it to Lord Berkeley and Sir George Carteret. Lord Berkeley resigned his right to Penn and others, but Philip Carteret the governor divided the territory with them by a straight line from north-west to south-east. Carteret took the east side and Penn the west. The inhabitants are nicknamed *Jersey Blues, Spaniards, Crows,* and *Clam-catchers.*

New Jerusalem Church (*The*). The Swedenborgians (*q.v.*).

New Method (*The*), 1720–1724. The work of John Wesley was so called at Oxford. His 'method' was to visit the sick, and go from place to place preaching. Methodism as a system arose in December 1739.

New Model (*The*), 1645. The re-organised army according to Cromwell's plan. Essex, the leader of the parliamentary army, 'who was afraid to conquer his king,' was replaced by Sir Thomas Fairfax. Cromwell said, 'If I met the king in battle, I would as soon fire my pistol at him as at any other man.' No officer of either House was to command the new-modelled army, for the tenure of military and civil offices in the same person is incompatible. The army must be wholly severed from the parliament. The soldiers must be picked men, honest and God-fearing. Young men are to be preferred. In a word, the aristocratic element was to be eliminated, and the whole army to be constructed on the model of Cromwell's 'Ironsides.' They were volunteers, not pressed men, men who left their farms and shops for a purpose, and would return to them when that purpose was accomplished.

New Moral World (*The*). The 'model parallelogram' of Robert Owen; established at Orbiston, in Lanarkshire, 1825. Only one corner of the parallelogram was ever built, and only 200 inmates were ever collected together at any one time. It was treated as a great moral nuisance, and the building was soon levelled to the ground. Owen's next scheme was in 'Harmony Hall,' Hampshire, 1844, where

he was president. This, like the Orbiston parallelogram, was an utter failure, and Owen was deposed by his own disciples. He went to Paris in 1848, but made no mark, and died in 1858.

Beside the Orbiston parallelogram and the Harmony Hall, he had a place in Indiana (America) which he called New Harmony, also an utter failure.

New Republic (*The*). The following names in Roman letters are supposed to be the academy figures of the characters in italics, introduced into the novel entitled 'The New Republic' by William Hurrell Mallock. *Donald Gordon,* Thomas Carlyle; *Lady Grace,* Mrs. Mark Pattison (Lady Charles Dilke); *Herbert,* Professor Ruskin; *Dr. Jenkinson,* Professor Jowett; *Leslie,* Mr. Hardinge; *Luke,* Matthew Arnold; *Rose,* W. Pater; *Saunders,* Professor Kingdon Clifford, or else F. Harrison; *Seydon,* Dr. Pusey; *Mrs. Sinclair,* Mrs. [Violet Fane] Singleton; *Stockton,* Professor Tyndall; *Storks,* Professor Huxley. The 'Historian,' chap. ii. bk. 3, is Professor Freeman.

New River (*The*). The united streams of two rivulets in the parishes of Ware and Amwell (Hertfordshire), brought by Hugh Myddelton through a course of twenty miles, to supply London with water. Begun 1609, completed and opened in 1613.

New Style. The reformed calendar introduced by Gregory XIII. in 1582. It was at once adopted in Italy, Spain, and Portugal by abridging October eleven days, and calling 5 Oct. the 15th. France adopted the reform the same year by calling 10 Dec. the 20th. *Catholic* Switzerland, Germany, and the Netherlands adopted the new style in 1583; Poland in 1586; Hungary in 1587; *Protestant* Germany, Holland and Denmark in 1700; Protestant Switzerland in 1701; England in the reign of George II., 1752, when Wednesday 2 Sept. was followed by Thursday 14 Sept.; that is, 3 Sept. was called 14 Sept. (Holy-rood day). In Sweden the new style was adopted in 1753; Russia alone of European nations retains the old style.

In all cases such rules have been adopted as to prevent the recurrence of any appreciable error; but the change is observable in our quarter-days: thus new Midsummer day is 24 June, but old Midsummer day is 6 July; new Christmas day is 25 Dec., but old Christmas day is 6 Jan.; new Lady day is 25 March, but old Lady day is 6 April;

so new Michaelmas day is 29 Sept., but old Michaelmas day is 11 Oct.

New Testament (*The*),

was originally written on Egyptian papyrus; but in the 12th cent. it was written on silk paper.

From the 5th to the 8th cent. it was written in uncial letters (*i.e.* inch-large letters), but from the 9th cent. *cursive* letters were employed.

At first there were no divisions of words. Euthalius (a deacon at Alexandria), in the 5th cent., divided the words into stichs (στίχα), that is, paragraphs. In the 6th cent. the text was divided into *breves*. In the 13th cent. Hugo de Santo Caro (a French cardinal, Hugues de St. Cher) divided the gospels into chapters and verses, and Robert Stephens in the 16th cent. extended the division and introduced the chapters and verses still in general use.

The earliest MSS. of the New Testament are in uncial letters. And the oldest known MS. is the 'Codex Vaticanus' (*q.v.*).

New Year's Day.

The Franks began the day on 1 March, the day of their *Champ de Mars* or national assembly. In the reign of Charlemagne it was shifted to Christmas day, and continued so till the 16th cent., when 1 Jan. was constituted New Year's day. There are numerous relics of the custom of beginning the year on 1 March.

March is a repetition of January. The moon repeats itself, thus if it is new on 1 Jan. it will be new on 1 March, &c.

New York (U. S. America).

Received its present name in 1664, in compliment to James (afterwards James II. of Great Britain and Ireland) duke of York, to whom the territory was given by his brother Charles II. The inhabitants are nicknamed *Knickerbockers.*

It had previously been called New Amsterdam.

Newdigate (*The*).

A prize for English verse given in the University of Oxford annually, value 21*l.* Founded by Sir Roger Newdigate in 1808. In Cambridge a medal is given called 'The Chancellor's English Medal' (*q.v.*).

Newmanism.

The proper adjustment of Christianity and the world according to the opinions of the Oxford Tractarians.

The Oxford Tractarians (1833-1841) were 'A,' *i.e.* Rev. John Keble, professor of poetry; 'B,' the Rev. Isaac Williams; 'C,' the Rev. E. B. Pusey, D.D., regius professor of Hebrew; 'D,' the Rev. John Henry Newman, author of 'Tract No. 90' (he subsequently joined the Catholic Church, and was made a cardinal; died in 1890); 'E,' the Rev. Thomas Keble; 'F,' Sir John Provost, Bart.; 'G,' the Rev. R. F. Wilson.

The Rev. John Henry Newman, born in London 1801; seceded from the Established Church in 1845; was made a cardinal in 1879; and died in 1890.

Newmarket Oracle (*The*).

Ogden, a professional betting-man, who rose from nothing (18th cent.).

Newnham College,

1880 (Cambridge), for the residence and instruction of ladies. Miss Fawcett's position in the Mathematical Tripos of 1890, ' above the senior wrangler ' of Cambridge, put this college in the first rank.

Newspapers.

In ancient ROME an official gazette, called 'Acta Diurna' (*q.v.*), was issued under the management and authority of the government, and posted up daily in some prominent place in the city.

In VENICE a paper of public intelligence, called 'Gazzetta,' was published in... ...	1620
In ENGLAND the first *weekly* newspaper was published by Nathaniel Butler in	1622
,, the first *daily* newspaper in ...	1709
In FRANCE the first *weekly* newspaper was published in	1631
,, the first *daily* in	1777
In AMERICA, at Boston, a newspaper was published in	1690
In IRELAND the first newspaper, called 'Pue's Occurrences,' appeared in	1700
,, the oldest Dublin newspaper, 'The Freeman's Journal,' in	1755
In GERMANY the first newspaper was published in	1715
In HOLLAND the first newspaper was published in	1732
In TURKEY the first newspaper was published in	1795
In AUSTRALIA the first newspaper was published in	18.3

. For particular newspapers see each under its own title.

Newton (*The American*).

David Rittenhouse (1732-1792) of Pennsylvania.

Newton and the Apple, 1666.

It is Voltaire who states that Mrs. Conduit, Newton's niece, told him the story. Newton, she said, was at Woolsthorpe, and, seeing an apple fall, was led into a train of thought which resulted in his discovery of gravitation.

The story is discredited by Martin Folkes, Hegel, Gause, and many others. And certainly neither Whiston nor Pemberton mentions it.

Newton of Harmony (*The*).

Rameau (1683-1764), the most philosophical musician of France. His great work is a 'Dissertation on the Principles of Harmony.'

Newtownbarry Riot (*The*), 18 June, 1831. On the occasion of a seizure of stock for tithes, a conflict ensued between the yeomen and the people, in which 35 persons were wounded or killed. The jury could not agree, and was discharged without coming to a verdict.

Niag'ara Falls Association (*The*), 1883. To promote legislation and other measures for the restoration and preservation of the natural scenery at Niagara Falls in accordance with the plan proposed by the Commissioners of the State Survey in their special report on the subject. The State of New York gave a million and a half (dollars) for the purpose, and the 'Falls' were made free to all mankind for all time to come. The bill was signed in 1885 for the payment of the 'Falls' in state bonds, and on 15 July, 1885, the Niagara Falls, including Goat Island and the lands contiguous (on the American side), were declared free to the world for ever.

Nicæan Barks. The ships of Alexander the Great. They were under the command of Nearchos, and sailed from the Indies to the Persian Gulf and to Susa. They were called Nicæan barks because they were built at Nicæa.

Nicene Creed, or 'Symbŏlum Nicænum,' 325, concocted at the First General Council of Nicæa, but completed by the Council of Constantinople in 381. This is the creed in the Communion Service.

The Apostles' Creed in its present form was adopted in the Church in the 11th cent. ; but a formula containing some of the articles existed in the 2nd cent.
The Athanasian Creed was adopted in the Latin Church in 673 ; in *France* in 850 ; in *Spain* and *Germany* a century later ; in *England* about 1000. It was not the work of Athanasius, who lived 296-372, but was supposed to incorporate what he taught on the subjects contained in the Creed.

Nicholites (3 syl.), or 'New Quakers.' An extinct sect of liberal Quakers, once found in Maryland, but long since united with the Hicksites (2 syl.).

Nicias (*Peace of*), B.C. 421. A peace for 50 years, in the eleventh year of the Peloponnesian war, between Sparta and Athens. By this treaty each party agreed to restore all the prisoners and places mutually taken during the war. The signatories were the Athenian Nicias and the Spartan king Pleistoanax.

Nickers. London night-larkers of the 17th and 18th cent., whose delight was to *nick* or hit a pane of glass and break it, by flinging a copper at it. He was the best nicker who nicked the highest panes. *See* 'Street Bullies.'

His scattered pence the flying Nicker flings,
And with the copper shower the casement rings.
                    GAY, *Trivia*, iii.

Nicode'mus (*Gospel of*), or 'Acta Pilāti.' An apocryphal gospel supposed to have been forged somewhere between 320-376. *See* 'Spurious Gospels.'

By 'Acta Pilati' is generally meant an apocryphal account of the Crucifixion, said to be the despatch of Pilate to the Emperor Tiberius. Eusebius, book ix. chap. 5, speaks of another 'Acta Pilati' 'full of every kind of blasphemy against Christ, which, with the consent of the emperor, was circulated throughout the whole Roman empire.' In these Acts Christians are charged with the most revolting crimes.

Nicola'itans (5 syl.). Condemned in Rev. ii. 6, 15. They taught the lawfulness of a community of wives; that Christians might partake of the heathen feasts; and maintained that God dwelt in the body of Jesus as in a temple, but was not united like body and soul.

Nicolas was one of the first seven deacons.—Acts vi. 5. Peter is supposed to refer to this heresy in 2 Epis. ii. 15-20.

Night of Al Kadr (*The*), 24 Ramadān. The night when Mohammed received his first revelation from Gabriel.

Verily we sent down the Korân in the Night of Al Kadr.—*The Korân*, chap. xcvii.

Night - boys. Same as Moonlighters (*q.v.*). *See* 'Irish Associations.'

Nightingale of Twickenham (*The*). Alexander Pope, who lived at Twickenham (1688–1744).

For my own part I abhor your irregular geniuses, and I love to listen to the little nightingale of Twickenham.—DISRAELI, *Venetia*, bk. vi. c. 8 (Cadurcis).

Nightingale of Wittenberg (*The*). So Hans Sachs [*Sax*] the mastersinger (*q.v.*) in 1523 calls Luther in a poem addressed to the reformer. It seems a strange comparison, but Sachs means that Luther was a bird which sang in moral darkness, as a nightingale sings at night.

Nihilism started into existence in 1848 under Herzen, a radical philosopher of the Hegel school. He was joined by Bakunin, and the two became joint editors of a communistic journal called the 'Bell' (Kolokol), published in London, but widely circulated in Russia. In 1866 the emperor was shot at by a young man, and the danger of Nihilistic teaching roused the serious attention of the Russian authorities. Soon after the death of Bakunin the secret Nihilistic societies greatly multiplied till 1881, when the Emperor Alexander II. was horribly assassinated. Since then the dogmas of the Nihilists have been gradually spreading, especially among the common people.

In 1868 the following manifesto was circulated : (1) Tear out of your hearts the belief in the existence of God, or you can never know what freedom is ; (2) the second lie to get rid of is *Right*, which is only the bastard of Might. Might makes Right. Without Might there is no such thing. Away with it ! (3) having got rid of these two lies, civilization, property, marriage, morality, and justice will snap like pack-thread ; (4) let your own happiness be your only law ; but, in order to enjoy this law, you must destroy everything that exists in the shape of government and social organisation. Annihilate everything as it now exists—the good with the bad—make a clean sweep of all ; for if but one atom of the old leaven is suffered to remain, it will corrupt the new order, and all the work will have to be done again.

It is said that this manifesto was drawn up by Bakunin, who died between 1876 and 1878.

Nika Sedition (*The*), Jan. A.D. 532. A sedition between the Greens and the Blues (*q.v.*), which lasted five days, and almost laid Constantinople in ruins. It occurred in the 5th year of Justinian on the ides of January. The Greens appealed to the emperor for protection, when the Blues rose up against them like raging lions. Seven of the ringleaders were condemned to death, but, being rescued by the mob, were carried in triumph through the streets, and as they were Greens and Blues, the two factions united for the nonce against the magistrates, and used for their watchword NIKA, that is *Victory*. The military were called out, and, hurling firebrands against the insurgents, set fire to the city, burning down the cathedral of St. Sophia, the baths of Zeuxippus, a part of the imperial palace, a hospital, and many churches, edifices, and private houses. Some 30,000 Greens fell in this sedition.

Nimbus in Christian Art (*The*). The representation of a glory round the head.

For ANGELS, the nimbus consists of rays, surrounded by a circle of quatrefoils, like pearls and roses.

For APOSTLES, MARTYRS, and CONFESSORS, the nimbus is golden.

„ CHRIST, the nimbus is more or less cruciform. Sometimes the glory, called aureola, envelops the whole figure.

„ GOD the FATHER, the nimbus is triangular, or a circle with hand in the act of blessing. Sometimes the glory, called aureola, envelops the whole figure.

„ PENITENTS, the nimbus is yellow, more or less shaded.

„ PROPHETS and PATRIARCHS, the nimbus is white or silver.

„ SAINTS (1) *living*, a square nimbus.

„   „ (2) *married*, the nimbus is green.

„ • „ (3) *who have struggled hard with temptation*, the nimbus is red.

" VIRGIN MARY, the nimbus consists of small stars. Like God the Father and God the Son, her whole body is sometimes inclosed in an aureola.

5th to 12th cent., a disc over the head.

14th cent., the triangular nimbus was introduced.

15th cent., a broad band behind the head, and the inscription of the name of the saint in the nimbus was introduced.

17th cent., the nimbus was discontinued.

19th cent., it was introduced again.

A SQUARE NIMBUS indicates that the person was living, a square being the symbol of the earth.

A CIRCULAR NIMBUS indicates that the person is gone to heaven, a circle being the symbol of eternity.

A BLACK NIMBUS is given to the traitor Judas.

GOLD NIMBUS, awarded to saints of the highest order.

GREEN NIMBUS, assigned to married persons (Hope, not Certainty).

RED NIMBUS, awarded to those who were tried as by fire, fighting against sin.

SILVER NIMBUS, next in honour to the golden nimbus.

YELLOW NIMBUS, given to sinners who by prayers and penance had become saints.

Nimeguen, in Holland (*Treaty of*), 1678, 1679. This was a great peace congress of the European powers, to put an end to the wars which had embroiled France, Germany, Spain, Holland, and Sweden. The treaty was first agreed on between France and Holland, 10 Aug. ; then between France and Spain, 17 Sept. ; then between France and Germany, 5 Feb., 1679. Next, Denmark, Sweden, and the Elector of Brandenburg agreed to the peace. By this treaty Sweden was put into possession of all it had at the commencement of the war.

Pronounce *Neem-gen*, with *g* hard.

Nine Articles of the Evangelical Alliance (*The*). To be held by those who belong to the society.

1. The divine inspiration, authority, and sufficiency of the Holy Scriptures,
2. The right and duty of private judgment in the interpretation of the Holy Scriptures.
3. The unity of the Godhead and the Trinity of persons therein.

4. The utter depravity of human nature in consequence of the fall.

5. The incarnation of the Son of God, his work of atonement for sinners, and his mediatorial intercession and reign.

6. The justification of the sinner by faith alone.

7. The work of the Holy Spirit in the conversion and sanctification of the sinner.

8. The immortality of the soul, the resurrection of the body, the judgment of the world by Christ, the eternal blessedness of the righteous and eternal punishment of the wicked.

9. The divine institution of the Christian ministry, and the obligation and perpetuity of the ordinances of Baptism and the Lord's Supper.

Our creeds are: the Apostles', the Nicene, and the Nine Articles of Faith adopted by the Evangelical Alliance.—M. McLean, *Echoes from Japan* (1889, p. 24).

See ' Lambeth Articles.'

Nine Days' Queen (*The*). Jane Dudley, better known as Lady Jane Grey ; but she was married to Lord Guilford Dudley, son of John [Dudley] duke of Northumberland (1537-1554). Proclaimed queen 10 July, and Mary was proclaimed queen by the Earl of Arundel 19 July, 1553.

Nine European Heroes of Delhi (*The*), 11 May, 1857. Lieutenants George Willoughby, Forrest, and Raynor ; Conductors Buckley, Shaw, and Scully; Sub-conductor Crow; and Sergeants Edwards and Stewart. These nine men defended the magazine against a swarm of Sepoy mutineers. Edwards and Crow were killed, then Scully fired the mine, and, as the building blew up, the surviving seven effected their escape. A trooper cut down Scully and a marauder slew Willoughby on the road to Meerut. Forrest, Raynor, Stewart, and Buckley escaped, and lived to receive the Victoria Cross.

We are not told what became of Conductor Shaw.

Nine Gems (*The*). The nine wise or learned men of Hindostan in the reign of Vikramáditya, B.C. 56, &c.

Nine Kingdoms of the Latin World (*The*). (1) England, France, and Scotland (more ancient than the reign of Charlemagne) ; (2) Castile, Aragon, and Navarre (created by the sword); (3) Sweden, Denmark, and Hungary (created by their baptism).

The Nine Kingdoms of the Latin World disclaimed their new associate (Sicily).—GIBBON, chap. lvi.

Nine Orders of Angels (*The*). Disposed in three circles. Three × three = nine, the most sacred number.

Novem vero angelorum ordines dicimus . . . scimus (1) Angelos, (2) Archangelos, (3) Virtutes,

(4) Potestates, (5) Principatus, (6) Dominationes, (7) Thronos, (8) Cherubim, et (9) Seraphim.—GREGORY, *Homily* 34 (A.D. 381).

Nine Worthies (*The*). Hector of Troy, Alexander the Great of Macedon, Julius Cæsar emperor of Rome, Joshua leader of the Israelites, David king of the Jews, Judas Maccabæus, Charlemagne, Arthur king of the Britons, and Godfrey baron of Jerusalem.

One naturally looks for the name of Moses.

Nisi Prius. A trial by jury in some civil action. A judge sitting at *nisi prius* means a judge presiding at a jury trial in a civil cause. The phrase is borrowed from the first two words of the old writ for summoning juries.

By 13 Edw. I. c. 30, juries were summoned to appear at the courts of Westminster 'in Octabis Sancti Michaelis NISI PRIUS ' the judge on circuit came to hold his court in the assize town where the jury lived. This *nisi prius provisio* has been disused (in England) since 1852, and all trials, as a matter of course, take place on circuit.

Nizam'-gedittes' (2 syl.), 1807. An army of 10,000 Turks raised by the Sultan Selim, clad in European costume, and officered by European soldiers, chiefly French. The old Turkish janissaries, jealous of these new troops, deposed the sultan and placed his cousin Mustapha on the throne.

No. 1, organiser of the Irish Invincibles, 1881, was a man named P. J. Tynan. He was a handsome man, about five and a half feet high, and wore spectacles. He went about in various disguises. All Invincibles were Fenians of the better class. See ' Irish Associations.'

No. 45 (*of the North Briton*), 1763, in which Wilkes said the words in the king's speech that the peace of Paris ' is honourable to the crown and beneficial to the nation' are false. This being deemed an insult to the king (George III.), Wilkes was arrested 30 April, and committed to the Tower. When brought to trial the bench declared that the arrest could not be sustained on account of Wilkes's privilege as a member of parliament, for nothing short of treason could interfere with that privilege. Wilkes was accordingly at once discharged. His release was celebrated, especially in the cider counties, with processions, in which a jack boot, a petticoat, and the king led by the nose by Bute, were carried. *See* 'Jack Boot.'

In 1772 George prince of Wales, having been chid for some boyish fault, stole into the king's apartment and shouted, 'Wilkes and No. 45 for ever!' George III. only laughed at the boy's impudence.

No. 61. The 'Secret Select' (*q.v.*) of the Glasgow Trades Union, 1837.

No. 90 (*Tract*). One of the 'Tracts for the Times,' written by John Henry Newman, D.D., Fellow of Oriel, Oxford. This was the last of these famous religious tracts issued 1833–1841. Dr. Newman subsequently joined the Church of Rome, was made a cardinal, and died in 1890.

No. 290. The 'Alabama' (*q.v.*).

'No Popery' Riots. In Edinburgh and Glasgow, January 1779. In London, June 1780, called the 'Gordon Riots' (*q.v.*).

Noach'idæ. Those proselytes who refused to be circumcised. They bound themselves to observe the precepts of Noah, but not the law of Moses.

Noble Lesson (*The*), 1100. A metrical production consisting of 479 lines in the Romance or Vaudois language. It is chiefly an abstract of the Old and New Testament history. It refers to the corruptions introduced into the church since the days of the Apostles. It begins thus:—

O brethren, give ear to a noble lesson: (*nobla leyczon*)
We ought often to watch and pray,
For we see this world is near its end ; . . .
Eleven hundred years are fully accomplished,
Hence it was written 'We are in the last times.'

Noble Proclamation (*The*), 980. The proclamation of Malachy monarch of Ireland after his conquest of the Danes. It was in substance as follows: 'Let all the Irish who are now in servitude return to their respective homes, and enjoy themselves in peace and gladness.' The number released by the Northmen was upwards of 2,000.

Nobles of the Genoese War (*The*), 1381. When Venice was threatened with utter destruction by the Genoese, the Venetian Grand Council announced that, at the termination of the war, The Forty (*q.v.*) would elect thirty of the citizens by ballot into their own council. These new nobles were to enjoy all the rights, privileges, and immunities of the original nobles. At the close of the war the promise was fulfilled, and among those aggrandised was 1 banker, 5 tradesmen, 6 simple citizens, 1 merchant, 5 of the lower order, and 8 operatives. Four centuries later only eight of 'I Nobili della Guerra di Genoa' had representative survivors.

Nobody's Club, 1800. A club consisting of the friends of William Stevens (1732–1807), who assumed the pseudonym of 'Oudeis' (nobody). They met at the Freemasons' Tavern, London, once a year. The original number was fifteen.

Nobs [*In the Glasgow Trades Union*], 1837, were employers who had made themselves obnoxious to the workmen, and were appointed to be dealt with by the 'Secret Select' (*q.v.*). The names of these 'Nobs' were enrolled in a book, and every sort of annoyance was offered to them.

Nocturns. Same as Matins. One of the eight daily services of the Catholic Church, and the first of the four great ones at break of day. *See* 'Canonical Hours.'

Noel's Catechism, or 'Nowel's,' &c. 1563. Alexander Nowel or Noel, dean of St. Paul's, at the recommendation of Cecil revised the 'Larger Catechism,' but his book was not published till 1570.

Noetians. Heretics of the 2nd cent., also called Patripassians, whose doctrines resembled those of the Sabellians. Founded by Praxeas, who was succeeded by Noëtus. If Jesus was verily the 'Everlasting Father,' then when Jesus suffered on the cross God the Father was crucified. (*Pater-passus*, the Father suffered.)

I consider that he had Noetian tendencies.—*We Two*, xxiv.

No-flint General (*The*). Major-General Grey, afterwards Lord Grey of Howick, and finally Earl Grey, who in the American war, 1778, ordered his men to take the flints out of their guns and trust wholly to their bayonets; also called 'No-flint Grey.'

Nolan (*The*). Giordano Bruno (1550–1600), born at Nola in Naples. He was burnt to death as a heretic.

Nol'umus leges Angliæ mut'-ari. This celebrated answer was made by the lay lords in the famous parliament held at Merton the day after the coronation of Henry III., and was given in answer to a motion of the bishops for legitimatising natural children provided, after the child was born, the father and mother married (1216).

Nominalism and Realism. Terms used in scholastic divinity during the Middle Ages to express the nature of abstract ideas, such as *circle*, *beauty*, god, &c. The question was this : is there such a thing as abstract beauty, or must not our idea of beauty be allied to some object ? Nominalism is the system adopted by nominalists, and realism is the system adopted by realists. Aristotle was a nominalist, and Plato a realist. *See* next article.

Nominalists. Those who believed in nominalism. They were the disciples of Roscelin (1040–1120), canon of Compiègne, and denied the existence of universals. Take a tree in the abstract; this is a universal, and a nominalist would say such has no existence. Take an oak tree, an elm tree, a fir tree, &c.; these are particular objects which stimulate in us certain ideas. Well, say the nominalists, our idea of a tree must be limited to particular trees, and our concept of tree in the abstract must be derived from such particular objects. It is *universalia post rem*, tree in the abstract formed *post rem*, after the concrete has been formed. It is altogether *à posteriori*, an inference of a universal or abstract idea from particular objects cognised beforehand. Of course, according to nominalism, the abstract idea of God is impossible; all we can know of God is from his works, &c.

In theology there is another sort of nominalism. We are taught that Father, Son, and Holy Ghost are one God. Well, as three persons cannot really be one, the nominalist contends that these 'three persons' are only different names (*nomina*) of the same being, just as father, son, and husband may be three distinct names of the same individual.

Abelard, William Occam, Buridan, Hobbes, Locke, Bishop Berkeley, Condillac, and Dugald Stewart were nominalists.

St. Anselm of Canterbury, Albertus Magnus, Thomas Aquinas, and Duns Scotus were realists (*q.v.*).

Roscelin seems to have raised the question whether the personal distinctions of the Deity are real or nominal only.

Nominees (*The King's*), 1662. Thirty-six of the Irish nobility and gentry specially nominated by Charles II., after his restoration, to be restored to their Irish estates, from which they had been banished by Cromwell.

About 6,000 of the restorable Irish were never restored to their estates. There were four classes, viz. Innocents, Articlemen, Ensignmen (*q.v.*), and the King's Nominees. Of the 7,778,000 acres forfeited in the Commonwealth, 68,360 statute acres were awarded to the Nominees.

Non-Catholics, *i.e.* Protestants. *See* 'Edict of Toleration.'

Nonconformists, 1565. Those who refused to conform to the 'Book of Advertisements' drawn up by order of Queen Elizabeth by the Court of Ecclesiastical Commission for the sake of securing uniformity of doctrine and discipline in the kingdom.

Now nonconformist is a synonym of *dissenter*, one who does not conform to the State Church.

Non-importation Act (*The*), 26 March, 1806. Passed by Congress to prohibit the importation of British manufactures into the United States. The immediate cause of this prohibition was the annoyance caused by the British ship 'Leander' cruising off New York and insisting on searching American vessels under pretence of looking for deserters. In one of these searches an American sailor, named Pearce, was killed, and the hostility of the States, which had long been smouldering, burst into a blaze.

Non-intercourse Act (*The*), U.S. Passed Congress 27 Feb., 1809, suspending all trade between the U.S. and either France or England. The offence of England was its claim of the right of search, which compelled American vessels to surrender any British subjects who formed part of their crew. The offence of France was the Continental system (*q.v.*). Napoleon, having removed all obstructions to American trade, Congress renewed intercourse with France 2 Nov., 1810; but the breaking out of the second American war with Great Britain in May 1812 continued the non-intercourse till after the battle of Waterloo, when friendly relations were restored.

Non-intrusion Controversy (*The*), 1838–1843. A controversy in the

Presbyterian Church of Scotland respecting the right of the State to interfere in ecclesiastical matters. It began with the question, Have patrons the right of presenting to livings or does the choice rest with the congregation? In 1833 Dr. Thomas Chalmers suggested that a patron should nominate, but the people should have the right of veto. This was accepted by the Assembly in 1834. In 1838 the Veto Act was ruled to be illegal, and the Assembly declared that the Church is wholly free and independent. Several appointments by patrons were made and disputed, and the result was a split in 1843, which gave birth to the 'Free Church.'

Non-Intrusionists (*The*). Those who separated from the Presbyterian Church of Scotland at the Non-Intrusion controversy. The split consisted of 470 ministers, with their office-bearers, elders, and communicants, and in 1843 the separatists formed the 'Free Church of Scotland.' They did not consider the veto proposed by Dr. Chalmers any intrusion or illegal interference with the right of a patron.

The chief leaders were Drs. Chalmers, Chandler, Candlish, and Gordon, with Messrs. Guthrie, Cunningham, and Dunlop. Dr. Thomas Chalmers was elected president of the new 'Free Church.'

. The law was that a congregation has the power of rejecting a presentee for 'adequate reasons.'

Non-juring Clergy of France, 28 Jan., 1791. Those clergymen who refused to take the 'civil oath' to accept the new constitution concocted by the Assemblée Constituante. *See* 'Prêtre Insermenté.'

The constitutional members of the late assembly . . . . drew up an address to the king [Louis XVI.], urging him to refuse his sanction to the decree against the non-juring priests.—HOWITT, *Hist. of England* (Geo. III. p. 586).

Non-jurors (*The*), 5 March, 1689. Those episcopal clergymen who refused to take the oath of allegiance to William and Mary, according to a clause in the Convention parliament that 'after 1 March no person shall sit or vote in either house till he has taken the new oath of allegiance to their majesties William and Mary.' The non-jurors comprised the Archbishop Sancroft, seven bishops, and about 400 of the inferior clergy. As they believed in 'the right divine,' and that the king was 'the Lord's anointed,' they could not possibly believe

that James was justly and lawfully set aside.

The six bishops were Ken bishop of Bath and Wells; Turner bishop of Ely; Frampton bishop of Gloucester; Lloyd bishop of Norwich; White bishop of Peterborough. The Bishop of Worcester and Bishop of Chichester died before the Act took effect.

Dr. Tillotson was made primate of All England in place of Dr. Sancroft.

Non Obstante (*The Bull*). By Innocent IV. sent to Robert Grosted or Grosteste commanding him to bestow a valuable benefice on an infant and that infant an Italian. The honest bishop tore up the bull, and wrote back to the pope that such practices were 'shaking the very foundations of the church.'

At this time the money paid to Italian priests in England was 60,000 marks per annum, a greater revenue than that of the crown. The barons remonstrated, and to that the words of the bull refer. Non obstante, *i.e.* notwithstanding [this remonstrance I require you to do what is set forth in the bull].

Non Possumus (*A*). Something not possible to be done, either because the person is unwilling to do it or thinks it inexpedient. Your prayer or petition cannot possibly be granted. The words used by the pope when he negatives a suit or request.

They opposed a *non possumus* to the Irish demand.—*Newspaper paragraph*, Jan. 1886.

Non-Regents. Masters of arts and doctors in a university no longer bound to give lectures. Regents were at one time the lecturers or professors. The terms regent and non-regent were retained in the University of Cambridge till 1858, though the duty of lecturing had long before passed to professors.

Non-Regent's House (*The*). The Lower or Blackhood House of the University of Cambridge, consisting of masters of arts of more than five years' standing and doctors of more than two. Abolished in 1858. *See* 'Senate.'

Non-resistance (*The Doctrine of*). That is, passive obedience to every ordinance of man and to the king—for those 'who resist the power shall bring to themselves damnation.' When the divine right of kings was maintained in the Stuart dynasty, those who took this view, of course, insisted on the doctrine of non-resistance. It was most clearly set forth in 1683 by Oxford, in what is called a 'Judgment and Declaration' (*q.v.*).

Enforced by the Homilies 1569; by the Canons of Convocation in 1609; the Oath of Non-resistance was imposed in 1661 (13 Car. II. s. 2, c. 1). The act was repealed 1718 (5 Geo. I. c. 6).

Non-resisting Test (*The*), 1675. To be taken by all members of parliament, privy councillors, magistrates, and persons holding office under the crown: 'I [A. B.] do declare that it is not lawful on any pretence whatever to take up arms against the king; and I do abhor the traitorous position of taking arms against his person, or against those that are commissioned by him according to law, in time of rebellion or war, and acting in pursuance of such commission. I [A. B.] do swear that I will not endeavour any alteration of the Protestant religion now established by law in the Church of England; nor will I endeavour any alteration in the government in church and state as it is by law established.'

Nones (1 syl.). One of the eight daily services of the Catholic Church, and one of the four lesser ones. At 3 o'clock in the afternoon, the ninth hour of the day. *See* ' Canonical Hours.'

Norbertines (3 syl.), 1119. An order of Canons Regular founded by St. Norbert. *See* ' Premonstratensians.'

Nore (*The Mutiny of the*), 22 May, 1797. A mutiny of the fleet; suppressed in June; Parker, the ringleader, was executed at Sheerness 30 June, 1797.

Norfolk Commotion (*The*), 1549. So Ket's or Kett's Rebellion (*q.v.*) is called by the old chroniclers.

Normal or **Training Schools.** To train teachers in the principles and art of teaching. First organised in Prussia. The following dates give the order in which they have been established: at Stettin, in Prüssia, 1735; at Berlin by Frederick the Great 1748; at Hanover 1757; the Borough Road school for teachers founded by Joseph Lancaster 1805; French training schools for teachers 1810; in Holland 1816; Normal Schools for England and Wales 1838; at Framingham and Westfield, in Massachusetts, North America, 1839; Battersea training school for teachers, 1840. *See* 'Ecoles.'

Norris'ian Prize (*The*). For an essay on some sacred subject. Prize given once in five years to any graduate of the University of Cambridge of not more than thirteen years' standing. Value 60*l.*, a part of which is to be expended on a gold medal worth seven guineas. Founded, in 1777, by John Norris, who also founded the Divinity professorship, when 12*l.* was given annually, altered in 1858. *See* ' Regius Professorship of Divinity.'

Norris'ian Professorship of Divinity. Founded 1777 in the University of Cambridge, by John Norris, of Witton, Norfolk. Original stipend 150*l.* a year, but now considerably augmented. *See* ' Regius Professorship of Divinity.'

Norroy King-of-arms. English herald of the northern provinces, first appointed by Edward IV. The herald of the southern provinces is called Clarenceux (formerly *Surroy*) King-of-arms (*q.v.*).

Norroy, of course, is Nor[th]roy. We still speak of a Nor' West wind or Nor' Wester. Surroy is South-roy.

North Briton (*The*), a newspaper edited by John Wilkes; was started in 1762. The printers and publishers were prosecuted for No. 45 in 1763; Wilkes was sent to the Tower in April, but discharged in May. The paper (15 Nov., 1763) was ordered by the House of Commons to be burnt by the hangman.

19 January, 1764, Wilkes was expelled from the House of Commons; but in March 1768 was elected M.P. for Middlesex. He was again arrested in the spring of 1768, and his imprisonment occasioned a riot in St. George's Fields. He was again expelled the House in 1769, but was again re-elected for Middlesex. He was made Lord Mayor of London in 1774, and Chamberlain of the City of London in 1779.

North German Confederation (*The*), 1866. After the famous ' Seven Weeks' War' and the ' Peace of Prague,' when Austria was entirely excluded from Germany. The confederation included Hanover, Hesse-Cassel, Nassau, and Frankfort (all incorporated with Prussia), and the states north of the Main united to Prussia in a bund. Strictly speaking, therefore, the confederation was Prussia and the states north of the Main. In 1870, during the Franco-German war, the ' North German Confederation,' being joined by Bavaria, Würtemberg, Baden, and Hesse-Darmstadt, became the ' German Confederation,' and two months afterwards (18 Jan., 1871) the King of Prussia had the title of ' German Emperor ' given him.

Austria with Bohemia and Hungary form no part of the modern German empire.

North-West Company (*The*), 1783. The North-West Company of Montreal was formed in opposition to a French company confirmed in 1697 by the treaty of Ryswick, abandoned in 1713 by the treaty of Utrecht, but still continued by adventurers, till the formation of the North-West Company. This company in 1821 coalesced with the Hudson's Bay Company. Its great traffic was furs or peltry.

North-West Passage (*The*). That is, a passage from the Atlantic to the Pacific by way of the Polar Sea, to the north of America. Above 200 voyages have been made in search of such a passage. Sir John Franklin reached N. Lat. 77° in 1847. Although much has been added to our geographical knowledge by these expeditions, they have clearly proved that such a passage is useless for mercantile purposes.

Northampton (*The Treaty of*), 4 May, 1328, between Edward III. and Robert Bruce, whereby the independence of Scotland was formally recognised, and Bruce was acknowledged to be its king.

A marriage was agreed upon between the Princess Joanna (sister of Edward III.) and David son of Robert Bruce (both infants). Bruce renounced all intentions of aiding the rebels of England, and Edward of abetting the rebels of the isles of Scotland. All charters and documents carried from Scotland by Edward I. to be restored. Scotland to pay 20,000*l.* to the King of England.

Northern Télémaque (*The*). Alexander I. of Russia, 1777 (1801–1825).

Northmen (*The*). Came from Scandinavia (Norway, Sweden, and Denmark). Karl III. the Fat bribed them to peace; but his nephew Arnulf attacked them boldly and drove them back.

Norwich Rentys. The London house or place of the bishop of Norwich, known subsequently as York House. In 1535 Norwich House passed by a special act of parliament into the hands of Charles Brandon earl of Suffolk. The lands ran westward as far as Hungerford Market.

No'sarites (3 syl.). A people of Syria so called from the town of Nosar. Their religious creed, like that of the Druses, is a mixture of Paganism, Judaism, Mohammedanism, and Christianity. Their chiefs are entitled 'Mekuddem.'

Nose-tax (*The*). A tax of one ounce of gold from every householder of Ireland, exacted by the Danes in the 9th cent., the non-payment of which was punished by slitting up the nose. This continued for thirteen years, when a general massacre of the Danes in Ireland put an end to the tax.

Probably the nose-tax was merely a poll-tax. We still retain the phrase to 'count noses,' and in Sweden the people paid Odin a 'scot-penny for each nose.'

Nosey. Wellington was so called lovingly by his soldiers.

'Notes and Queries.' A London weekly journal chiefly to furnish enquirers with information by correspondents on literary, biographical, and heraldic difficulties. Commenced 3 Nov., 1849.

Nothing from Nothing. 'Ex nihilo nihil fit.' The axiom of Xenophănês, founder of the Eleatic school (B.C. 619, died after 476).

Notre Dame. In the 'Petits Bollandistes,' by Mgr. Paul Guérin, chamberlain of Leo XIII., there are 2,011 articles headed 'Notre Dame,' one headed 'Jesus,' and one headed 'Christ,' and not a single one 'Notre Seigneur.' Notre Dame is called the 'Mother of God,' and Joseph the carpenter is called the 'Husband of God's Mother' (*époux de la Mère de Dieu*). This may be logical, but it looks more like Mariolatry than Christianity.

Under the words 'Passion de Notre Seigneur Jésus Christ' will be found the whole of 'Passion Week.'

Nottingham (*Peace of*), 868. Between Alfred and his brother Ethelred on one side, and the Danes on the other. By this treaty England was divided into two parts, one of which remained to Alfred and the other was assigned to the Danes. The Danish portion was Northumbria, East Anglia, and the bulk of Mercia, called 'Danelagh,' because this part was subject to Danish law. The Danish portion was the larger of the two, but Alfred kept London.

Nottingham Captain (*The*), 1817. Jeremiah Brandreth, a framework knitter of Nottingham and fiery agitator, who collected some three hundred people, whom he persuaded to 'march from Derby to London and overturn the government.' At Eastwood, about three miles from Nottingham, they were stopped by a troop of horse from Nottingham, and fled in all directions, but many were made prisoners, and three executed, viz. Brandreth, Ludlam, and Turner, 7 Nov., 1817.

Nou'menon. What Aristotle called the *hypokimenon* (ὑποκείμενον), an imaginary something which underlies all visible phenomena—the ghost of a thing, immutable and unaffected by those logical accidents, colour, odour, growth and decay, shape, size, &c. We can gain some idea of this hypostasis if we fix our thought on 'identity.' The infant man and decrepit eld have an identity, though no part of the man is common with that of the child or eld. That identity is the *noumenon* or *hypokimenon*. Again, no two persons see the same tree; no individual sees the same tree twice. It grows and decays, shoots out leaves and sheds them—is for ever changing, but remains the same. It is the phenomenon which changes; the noumenon is changeless. Kant introduced the word to express the real object, or the essence of an object, divested of its substance or phenomenon.

Noushir'wan [*The Magnanimous*]. So Chosroes the Great was called (A.D. 531–579). The Arabs called him Al Malek.

Novæ Tab'ulæ (New Tables). 'Turning over a new leaf'—that is, abolishing old debts and beginning afresh.

Nova'lis. The pseudonym of Friedrich von Hardenberg (1772–1801).

Novatians (*The*), 3rd cent. Followers of Novātus, who insisted that no lapsed Christian should be received again into communion with the church. He denied the power of the church of absolving 'mortal sin,' and his followers opposed the lawfulness of second marriages. They called themselves *Cathări*, or Puritans.

Novels (*The*), or 'Novellæ.' The fourth part of the 'Corpus Juris Civīlis,' compiled A.D. 534, and containing the new constitutions made by Justinian himself, with the emendations of the

errors detected in the other three parts. Extracts made from these novels were called 'Authentics.' *See* 'Corpus Juris Civilis.'

The novels are cited by number and chapter, thus: *Nov. 115, 3,* or *Nov. 115, c. 3.* If the chapter referred to is subdivided into paragraphs, then a third figure is added.

Noyades, 1793. A method of wholesale drowning adopted by Carrier to purge Nantes of anti-revolutionists. He murdered about 30,000 men, women, and children in a few months in Nantes alone. The boats employed had movable bottoms, so constructed as to let the victims through without admitting sufficient water to sink the boats. This method of wholesale murder was a 14th cent. invention. *See* 'Purgers.'

Also called 'Carrier's Vertical Deportation.' Noyades, pronounce *Nwoi-yahd.*

Noyon (*Treaty of*), 13 Aug., 1516. A treaty of peace between Charles V., Pope Leo X., and François I., after the brilliant victory at Marignano, the 'combat of the giants.' Charles V. engaged to marry the daughter of the king, whose dowry was to be Naples; and he engaged to restore Navarre to the house of Albret. Neither of these stipulations was carried out.

Nullity Bilson (*Sir*). A nickname given to the son of Thomas Bilson bishop of Winchester, knighted by James I. for his scandalous sycophancy in the matter of Sir Thomas Overbury, or (more strictly speaking) the divorce of the Earl and Countess of Essex in consequence of a *liaison* with Robert Carr, the king's favourite.

Robert Carr was at that time Viscount Rochester, and subsequently Earl of Essex. The famous Rochester was John Wilmot, quite another person.

Nullum Tempus Act (*The*) 1769. An act to abolish the custom of *Nullum tempus occurrit regi*—that is, no length of tenancy can bar lands which once belonged to the crown. The 'Nullum Tempus' Act limited the time to sixty years of adverse possession, *i.e.* if a person has been in possession of crown land for sixty years, the crown cannot reclaim it.

In 1772 Mr. Henry Seymour introduced a 'Nullum Tempus' Bill to apply to church property, but it was thrown out.

Number of Members in the House of Commons. The present number (1890) is 670 members. Of these 465 are for England, 30 for Wales, 72 for Scotland, and 103 for Ireland.

Of the 670 members 86 are 'Nationalists,' and about 74 or 75 are 'Liberal Unionists.'

Numbers. Symbolism of the first 13.

1 the unity of deity; 2 the hypostatic union of Christ; 3 the Trinity; 4 the Evangelists and great Prophets; 5 books of Moses and wounds of Christ; 6 the creative week; 7 times Christ spoke on the cross; 8 beatitudes; 9 orders of angels; 10 commandments; 11 apostles after the apostasy of Judas; 12 minor prophets and the original apostolic college; 13 the complete college including Matthias and Paul.

Numerical Coincidence. I.

1794 Climax of the French Revolution.
1
7
9

1815 Battle of Waterloo.
1
8
1
5

1830 Revolution of July.
1
8
8
0

1842 Death of the Duc d'Orléans.

II. A still more remarkable coincidence is 1869, the last year of the third Napoleon's glory. This is obtained by adding either his *birth* or his *marriage* to the year of his coronation, or the birth of Eugénie, or the capitulation of Paris. Thus 1852 he was crowned; he was born 1808; he was married 1853; Eugénie was born 1826; Paris capitulated 1871.

Then	1852	1852	1852	1852
	1	1	1	1
	8	8	8	8
	0	5	2	7
	8	3	6	1
	1869	1869	1869	1869

Nuptial Mass. 'Missa Nuptialis.' The mass celebrated in the marriage service. See 'Mass.'

Nuremberg Nimbus (*The*). A cruciform nimbus with finials resembling the fleur-de-lis. See 'Nürnberg.'

Nürnberg (*Peace of*). See *under* 'Peace.'

Nürnberg Eggs, *i.e.* watches. 'Dans cette ville les montres furent inventées vers 1500, ce qui les fit d'abord

nommer *œufs de Nuremberg* ' (Bouillet, 'Dict. Hist.' &c. p. 1365). They were like eggs in shape.

Nystadt, in Finland (*Treaty of*), 13 Sept., 1721. A treaty of peace between Russia and Sweden, after the death of Charles XII. 'the Brilliant Madman.' By this treaty Sweden lost Livonia, Esthonia, Ingermania, and Carelia.

O. Before the time of Brian king of Munster (978–1014), every Irishman took the name of his father or grandfather as a surname. The prefix *Mac* stood for ' son of ' and the prefix *O* for ' grandson of.' Brian established the arrangement that the patronymics thus formed should be permanent in families.

Of course nowadays O' means a descendant of some chief whose name is appended to the patronymic, as O'Brien or O'Brian, a descendant of Brien king of Munster; O'Neills, descendants of the king of Ulster; O'Connors, descendants of the kings of Connaught.

O's (*The Great*). Thirty-one antiphons for the 'Magnificat' and 'Benedictus' from the 'Proper' of Advent and of St. Thomas, all beginning with ' O,' as ' O admirabile commercium'; ' O Adonai'; ' O beata Infantia,' &c. See ' Notes and Queries,' 31 Dec., 1887, p. 527.

Oak (*The Parliament*). An oak still standing in 'Clypston' (Clipstone) in Sherwood Forest, Notts, under which Edward I. in 1282 held a parliament. He was hunting in the forest, and, being told of the revolt of the Welsh, hastily convened his nobles under the tree, and resolved to march at once against Llewellyn, who was defeated and slain the same year.

Oak Boys (*The*). I. 1549, the insurgents in Ket's rebellion. See 'Oak of the Reformation.'

II. 1757. Protestants in the North of Ireland who rose in insurrection against the Road Act, which threw the burden of making roads and keeping them in repair on the payers of poor-rates, instead of on the landed proprietors. Called 'Oak Boys' from a sprig of oak stuck in their hats.

III. In 1760. This association was a revival of the preceding, with a small difference. In 1757 the grievance was that the burden of keeping the roads in repair was thrown on the ratepayers; the new grievance was that those who complained of want of work were set to make

s s 2

a road through a part of Armagh. It did not please them to be made to work, and they vowed that they would not work like slaves to please anyone. *See* 'Irish Associations.'

Oak of Reformation (*The*). The oak on Mousehold Heath, near Norwich, under which Ket, the Norfolk farmer, held his court, and administered justice, 1549. When the rebellion was crushed out by the Earl of Warwick nine of the ringleaders were hanged on this tree.

One of the Kets was hanged on the top of Warwick Castle, and the other on the top of Wymondham church, near Norwich. (Wymondham=*Win'-dum*.)

Oath of Abjuration (*The*), 1701 (13 Will. III. c. 6). Aimed against Papal aggression. Abolished 1858 (21, 22 Vict. c. 48).

This oath abjured the pope and the pretender, denying the authority of the former and the claims of the latter to the British throne. On the death of Cardinal York there remained no descendant of James II., and the oath so far as the pretender was concerned was a dead letter.

Oath of Allegiance (*The*). From feudal times. Like the oath of a vassal to his lord : ' I (A. B.) do promise to be true and faithful to the king and his heirs, and truth and faith to bear of life and limb and terrene honour, and not to know or hear of any ill or damage intended him without defending him therefrom.'

The oath remained in force above 600 years. The Convention Parliament (*q.v.*) changed the oath to the following words : ' I (A. B.) do sincerely promise and swear that I will be faithful, and bear true allegiance to H. M. * * *.' 1 Will. & Mary, c. 1 & 8, A.D. 1689. It was again altered by 1 Geo. I., stat. 2, c. 13, A.D. 1714–15, and modified by 1 Vict. c. 24, A.D. 1838.

Oath of Supremacy (*The*), 1 Eliz. c. 1, A.D. 1559; abolished in 1858. This was not an oath acknowledging the king's supremacy, as it was wholly silent on that point, but an oath against the non-supremacy of the pope in England. The form established by William and Mary 1694 is as follows : ' I, * *, do swear that I do from my heart abhor, detest, and abjure . . . . that damnable doctrine . . . . that princes excommunicated by the pope may be deposed or murdered by their subjects. . . . And I declared that no foreign. . . . potentate hath or ought to have any jurisdiction . . . . ecclesiastical or spiritual within this realm.'

Oath of the Jeu de Paume (*The*), 20 June, 1789. Three days after the Tiers Etat formed themselves into the National Assembly (*q.v.*), several members of the two other estates joined them, and they all met in the tennis court, at Versailles. Having sent an invitation to the nobles and clergy to join them there, Bailly rose, bade the whole assembly follow his example, and then, raising their right hands, the entire assembly joined in the oath never to part till they had given France a constitution.

Jeu de paume (the hand-game) means tennis, and the oath of the Jeu de paume [*pome*] means 'the oath taken in the tennis court.'

Oath of the Vehmgerichte (4 syl.). Every person brought before the secret tribunal was sworn to profound secresy . . . . ' Not to divulge to wife or child, father or mother, friend or confessor, not to tell in words, or express in writing, or signify by symbols, or dress in parable, or hint at by sign, or communicate by look, anything done or heard or seen in the tribunal, if he would sleep in an unbloody grave.'

Obedience (*An*). The instrument containing the written precept of the superior in any religious order to the persons in subjection, to undertake a specific office, to proceed on a stated mission, to relinquish a certain appointment, and so on.

Obedience in canon law means the duty by which the various grades in the ecclesiastical system are held subject.

Avignon Obedience during the great schism of the West meant the acknowledgment of the popes of Avignon.

Roman Obedience, during the same period, meant allegiance to the Roman pontiff.

Obédience (*Pays d'*). The territory where the pope nominates to vacant benefices. During the great schism of the West, each contemporary pope had his own 'pays d'obédience.' Thus, in the 14th cent. we had 'The Obedience of Urban VI. ' (comprehending North Italy, Germany, Bohemia, Hungary, Poland, Prussia, Denmark, Sweden, Norway, and England), and the 'Obedience of Clement VII.,' comprehending all the rest of Europe.

Obedience of Benedict XIII. (*The*). Means, in the great schism of the

West, obedience given to Benedict XIII. by the supporters of the French pope, in opposition to the contemporary Roman pope(first Boniface IX., then Gregory XII., then the double popes Gregory XII. and Alexander V.).

At the death of Gregory XI. the Italians insisted that an Italian only could be pope, but as most of the cardinals were Frenchmen, they stoutly resisted this dogma. Neither would give way, so the Italians elected Urban VI., who resided at Rome, and the French elected Clement VII., who resided at Avignon (1378). As death occurred in either chair, the respective partisans elected a successor; thus Urban was succeeded in Rome by Boniface IX. and Gregory XII.; while Clement, the Avignon pope, was succeeded by Benedict XIII. See 'Great Schism of the West.'

Obedience of Gregory XII.
(*The*). Means the acknowledgment of the authority of Gregory XII., the Roman pope, in opposition to Benedict XIII., the Avignon pope, in the great schism of the West (*q.v.*).

Obelisk of Constantius (*The*),
i.e. the Egyptian obelisk which Constantius II. presented to the city of Rome when he went to visit that ancient capital. It was 115 feet in length and had been transported from Heliopolis by Constantine the Great to adorn his new city of Constantinople, A.D. 354.

Obelisk of Heliop'olis (*The*), or
'Matarieh,' erected by Osortesen I. about B.C. 1900. The oldest of the large obelisks.

An obelisk which Ramêses II. erected at Heliopolis was removed to Alexandria. The 'Flaminian Obelisk' begun by Sethos I. and finished by Rameses II. was removed to Rome by Constantius. In the pontificate of Gregory XIII. this obelisk was found buried 16 feet under the surface, and was set up by Fontana, the architect.

Obelisk of Karnac (*The*), or large
obelisk erected by Thothmes I. before the granite sanctuary of Karnac.

His daughter Hatasu erected two obelisks before the second propylæon of the same sanctuary.

Obelisk of London (*The*), or Cleo-
patra's Needle on the Thames Embankment. *See* 'Cleopatra's Needle.'

The Arabs call obelisks 'Pharaoh's needles'; the Egyptian priests called them 'Sun fingers,' because they acted as gnomons to mark the hour on the ground.

Obelisk of Paris (*The*). In the
Place de la Concorde is one of the obelisks of Ramêses II., originally erected at Luxor (Thebes). Removed to France in 1833, and called *l'Obélisque de Louqsor*.

Obelisk of St. John Lateran
(*The*). The highest in the world. It

was removed from Thebes, and was erected by Thothmes IV., some 35 years after the death of Thothmes III.

Obelisk of the Atmeidan (*The*),
or of the Hippodrome of Constantinople. The oldest of the obelisks of Thothmes III., erected to record his conquest of Naharānia or Mesopotāmia.

Obelisk of the Upper Alps
(*The*). Felix Neff, also called 'The Apostle of the Upper Alps' (1798–1829).

Ober - Ammergau (*Ammergow*),
in Upper Bavaria. Rendered specially famous of late for its Passion Play, representing in 18 acts the last days of Jesus Christ. Act i. Entry of Christ into Jerusalem, and his purging of the Temple; Act ii. The Sanhedrim; Act iii. The Leave-taking at Bethany; Act iv. The Last Journey to Jerusalem; Act v. The Last Supper; Act vi. Judas receiving the Blood-money; Act vii. Jesus in the Garden of Gethsemane; Act viii. Jesus before Annas; Act ix. Jesus before Caiaphas; Act x. The Despair of Judas; Act xi. Jesus before Pilate; Act xii. Jesus before Herod; Act xiii. Jesus scourged and mocked; Act xiv. Jesus condemned to Death; Act xv. The Via Dolorōsa; Act xvi. The Crucifixion; Act xvii. The Resurrection; Act xviii. The Ascension.

History of the Play.—As far back as the 12th cent. there had been a Passion Play performed in the little village, but in the 16th cent. a plague carried off 80 of the inhabitants, and the survivors made a vow, if the plague was stayed, to perform the Passion Play every ten years. Daisenberger, a priest, converted the 'miracle play,' which was a farce, into the present drama. In 1890 it attracted great attention, and throngs from America and Europe went to the Tyrolean Alps to witness the performance.

Obi, or Obe (2 syl.). Witchcraft or
sorcery. An O'beah man is a wizard, an O'beah woman a witch, among the negroes of the West Indies.

O'bit. In the Latin church means
the service for the dead. One *de die obītus*, one on the day of the funeral, and a third on the 30th day. It consists of the matins and lauds of the Officīum Defunctōrum, and a mass for the dead.

Oblates, 'Oblāti.' I. Those who, on
entering a monastic order, abandon their

worldly goods for the benefit of the society, or who offer themselves for any work that may be put upon them.

II. Those offered to God from birth, or consecrated from birth to a 'religious life.'

III. Those laics who pay to live in an abbey.

IV. Invalid soldiers who, before the foundation of the *Hôtel des Invalides*, were quartered by the kings of France on religious houses.

Oblates of Mary Immaculate

(O. M. I.), 1815. A congregation of priests established by the Abbé Mazenod, whose special mission is the supervision of schools and prisons ; many are missionary priests. America, more especially Canada, is full of them.

Oblates of St. Ambrose, 1578.

A congregation of secular priests established at Milan by Charles Borroméo, their special mission being the supervision of schools and colleges.

Oblivion (*Bill* or *Act of*), 12 Car. II. c. 11, 1660. An act of indemnity for treason and state offences committed between January 1, 1637 and June 24, 1660.

Oblivion (*The Committee of*). When the American trouble began, in 1775, petitions from trading companies in the United Kingdoms poured into the House of Commons, urging the ministers to abstain from coercive measures against America. A committee was appointed to report on these petitions, but so long was the report delayed that the merchants thought their petitions were forgotten, and the committee appointed to consider them was facetiously called 'The Committee of Oblivion.'

Obregons. Nurses of hospitals, &c., were so called in Spain from Bernardin Obregon (1540–1599). Called in France 'L'ordre des Frères-infirmiers Minimes.' *See* 'Franciscans (*Third Order of*).'

Obscurantism, Obscurants.

The word *obscurant* was in Germany applied to those writers who endeavoured to stem the tide of the French Revolution. Obscurantism means the doctrine, or policy, of non-progressive conservatives, fossil politicians. It also means opposition to popular enlightenment, or the progress

of knowledge. Matthew Arnold expressed this idea by the words 'Philistines' and 'Philistinism.'

Cimmerian obscurantism and this thrice-glorious revolution shall wrestle for it then.—
CARLYLE, *French Revolution*, vol. ii. bk. v. 9.

Obscure Philosopher (*The*). Heraclitos the Ephesian, who died B.C. 495, aged 60. Called ' obscure ' because he was *vir obscurus*, a very reserved man. Also called the 'weeping philosopher' (*q.v.*).

Observance (*The Religionists of the*). Persons who imposed on themselves the obligation to *observe* rigorously every item of the rule of the order to which they belonged. They are :

1. ' Les Pères de l'Observance,' or the 'Observantins ' (*q.v.*), Reformed Franciscans.

2. Those who followed the 'Strict Observance' of the Cistercian Order.

3. Those who followed the 'Great Observance ' of the Order of Mercy.

4. Preaching Friars of the ' Primitive Observance.' They were Reformed Dominicans. The other congregations of Observants are Franciscans, Cistercians, Carmelites, and Observants of the Order of Mercy.

Observantins (*Les*), or 'Les Pères de l'Observance regulière,' 1363. Reformed Franciscans, of which St. Bernardin of Sienne was the author. In 1517 they were called Reformed Franciscans by order of Leo X. The Observantins of France were called 'Cordeliers,' from the cord which they used for belt. The Strict Observantins were barefooted Franciscans.

Observer (*The*). A London weekly journal, commenced 1792.

Obstructionists, 1879. Obstruction to the business of the House of Commons began with the Home Rule party soon after the death of Mr. Butt in May 1879. Their object was to prevent legislation by the dog-and-manger process. In October 1882 Mr. Parnell was elected president of the National League, which arose on the suppression of the Land League, and the obstructionists were also called Parnellites. A reign of terror was then established in Ireland.

Obstructionists (*Parliamentary*), 1889, 1890. A parliamentary junto, chiefly of the Irish Home Rule party (*q.v.*), who set themselves to block or talk down every measure of importance introduced by the ministers of the day, regardless of the merit thereof. Night after night was wasted by the dreary drip of dilatory debate, which degenerated into absolute rudeness and unmannerly behaviour. *See* ' Kentish Petition.'

In six months, 1890, twenty opponents of the Government asked 1,768 questions, and made 1,326 speeches. There were 669 members, and just 669 hours available for public business.

Occamists. Followers of William Occam, who revived Nominalism, which was violently opposed by the Scotists. Roscelin (who died 1106) founded the sect of the Nominalists, who maintained that universals have no real existence except in the thought. There is no such thing as tree in the abstract, though there are such things as special trees, as oaks, firs, birches, and so on. The Realists denied this. The disciples of Duns Scotus were Realists, and Occam was a pupil of Scotus, but became a Nominalist, and the revived sect were called Occamists.

Occam was called the 'Invincible Doctor' and the 'Prince of Nominalists.'

Occasional Conformity Bill (*The*), 1711. A bill to evade or revoke the act of toleration granted by William III. Three times in Anne's reign was the Bill introduced, and though passed by the Commons was rejected by the Lords. Bishop Burnet resisted it. Dr. Sacheverel (1709) created riots in London against the Act of Toleration. When the Tories succeeded the Whigs, under the administration of Harley, they passed the Conformity Bill and the Schism Bill (*q.v.*), both of which were repealed in 1718 (5 Geo. I. c. 4).

The Occasional Conformity Bill was an attempt to crush opinion instead of influencing understanding; to convict when they could not proselytise; to swell the nominal numbers of churchmen with slaves and hypocrites.—HOWITT, *Hist. of Eng.* vol. iv. p. 589.

Occasionalism, or 'The Doctrine of Occasional Causes.' A doctrine which sprang from a dogma of Descartes (2 syl.), that spirit cannot act on matter without the concursus of God. By this theory the action of the mind cannot be the cause of the action of the body, and therefore whenever the action of the body follows that of the mind, God must interfere to produce the effect. This is called the Cartesian system, from Descartes, the French philosopher.

Occupation of Moscow (*The*), September 1812. The occupation by Napoleon and his army. Moscow was set on fire 15 Sept., and was burning a whole week. When Napoleon quitted the city, a month afterwards, 19 Oct., he had the Kremlin undermined and blown up with gunpowder, though hundreds of the French sick and wounded soldiers had been carried there as to an hospital.

Ocean's Queen (*The*). England. So called for the daring and valour of her navy, more than for the number and tonnage of her ships.

Ockhamists. The disciples of William of Ockham or Occam, who in the 14th cent. revived Nominalism (*q.v.*), *i.e.* that abstract ideas are obtained only by comparing a number of real phenomena or real facts. Thus the abstract idea of tree could not exist at all unless we knew real trees.

O'Connell's Tail. His henchmen or parliamentary following. So called because they had no opinions of their own, but followed O'Connell's dicta as a tail follows its owner.

O'Connor of the Bloody Hand. Cathal O'Connor was so called from the number of battles which he fought (12th and 13th cents.).

Octaeteris. A space of eight years added to the cycle of Calippus, making that cycle to consist of 84 years, instead of 76. When Dionysius of Alexandria calculated his Easter he made use of the *Octaeteris,* or cycle of 84 years, which continued in use till Gregory XIII. reformed the calendar.

Octavian War (*The*), or ' Bellum Octaviānum,' B.C. 87. Part of the social war of Rome, so called from Cneius Octavius, the consul. It was caused by the opposition of Cornelius Cinna his colleague. A battle ensued between the partisans of the two consuls, in which 10,000 men were slain. Cinna was driven from the forum, deprived of his consular office, quitted Rome, put himself at the head of an army of insurgents, and was joined by Caius Marius.

Octavians (*The*), 12 Jan., 1595 to 1596. The eight commissioners to whom James VI. of Scotland committed the care of his finances. They were all lawyers, and were responsible for the receipts and expenditure of the government. On them devolved the settling of accounts, making grants, and, in short, every national expense. Five made a quorum.

The Octavians used the trust reposed in them with as much moderation, perhaps, as could possibly have been expected ; and by their knowledge of business, and the exercise of a rigid economy, they brought the affairs into much better order than they had ever been during James's reign.—Sir W. SCOTT, *History of Scotland*, xxxviii.

October 5, 6, 1789. Noted for the great insurrection of Paris, when a mob of men and women made their way to Versailles, massacred the guard, and compelled Louis XVI. with his wife and family to go to Paris.

October Diploma (*The*), 1860. Introducing a constitutional form of government for Hungary, and vesting the power in the provincial Diets of Austria and the National Diet of Hungary.

Octonary (*The*). A name given to the Calif Motassem. He was the 8th of the Abbasside califs ; he reigned 8 years, 8 months, and 8 days ; won 8 battles ; left 8 sons, 8 daughters, 8 thousand slaves, and 8 millions of gold. (Gibbon, with notes, ch. 52.)

Oculi. The third Sunday in Lent. So called from the introït which begins thus : ' Oculi mei semper.' *See* 'Sunday.'

The 'Introit' is the psalm or passage of Scripture chanted in Catholic churches while the priest enters the chancel.

Od Force. An all-pervading force. A term introduced by Baron Reichenbach to express that luminosity which is said to be manifested at the poles of magnets, and wherever chemical action is going on. It has negative and positive poles.

In animal magnetism it is said that od force is transmitted from the magnetiser to the magnetised.

Odal Tenure. In the Orkney and Shetland Islands. The right to land without any written deed, based solely on possession. Absolute possession before the introduction of feudalism.

Odalisks. Female slaves of the Turkish harem attached to the service of the women. They are ordinarily either Circassians or Georgians, and are generally selected for their beauty.

Odomb'ian Legstretcher(*The*). Thomas Coryat of Odcombe, Somersetshire, traveller, and author of ' Coryat's Crudities ' (1577–1617).

O'Donnell Rebellion (*The*), in Spain, 1841. The object was to restore the queen-mother, Maria Louisa, who had been compelled by Espartéro to abdicate, that he himself might be regent. The revolt failed in its object, and in 1854 Espartero joined O'Donnell, who was made minister of war. O'Donnell now effected Espartero's dismissal and was named president of the council. He resigned in 1866, and died the following year (5 Nov., 1867).

Odour of Sanctity (*The*). *To die in the odour of sanctity.* It was and perhaps still is a prevalent notion among Roman Catholics that when the body of a good man dies, God will not suffer his holy one to see corruption, and that it exhales a sweet odour ; but that the body of the wicked gives forth at death a stench increasing in foulness in proportion to the scale of crime. Of course, there is a sort of truth in this notion, for the bodies of holy men were embalmed, and the swinging censers filled the room with sweet odour. Besides, monks and nuns lived so in the odour of the censers that their clothes and skin got impregnated with the perfume. Bad men, on the other hand, were neither embalmed nor incensed. Shakespeare speaks of the stench exhaled by Antiochus and his daughter, who were killed for their wickedness by lightning :

A fire from heaven came, and shrivelled up
Their bodies, e'en to loathing ; for they so stunk
That all those eyes adored them ere their fall
Scorned now the hand which gave them burial.
Pericles Prince of Tyre.

Odour of Nations (*The*). Maxime du Camp says :—

Chaque pays a une odeur spéciale qui le fait reconnaître : l'Egypte sent la fleur des fèves, l'Italie sent la cire et l'encens, l'Angleterre sent la fumée de houille, la Grèce sent l'araki, la France sent le pain de munition, la Hollande a aussi son parfum à elle et tout à fait distinct—elle sent la tourbe humide.

Certainly, a French crowd ' a une odeur spéciale,' unlike any crowd that I ever mixed in.

Odyssey (*The German*). 'The Kudrun,' in three parts: (1) 'The Hagen'; (2) 'The Hilde'; and (3) 'The Hedel.'

Œcumenical Councils. Only seven are recognised by Russia.

1. The Council of Nice, A.D. 325, in which the Arian heresy was condemned.

2. The First Council of Constantinople in 381.

3. The Council of Ephesus in 431.

4. The Council of Chalcēdon in 451.

5. The Second Council of Constantinople in 553.

6. The Third Council of Constantinople, in 680, against the Monoth'elites (*q.v.*), who recognize in Christ but one will in his two natures, the human will being merged in his divine nature.

7. The Second Council of Nice in 787.

An Œcumenical Council should be called by the pope, presided over by the pope, and attended by bishops from all parts of Christendom.

Œdipus. Caracalla was so called because, like Œdipus, he married his own mother. The people of Alexandria gave him this sobriquet, and the emperor in revenge slaughtered many thousands of them.

Œil de Bœuf (*L'*), 17th and 18th cents. A large reception room [*salle*] in the palace of Versailles, lighted by a round window [*œil de bœuf*] from the king's bedroom. The ceiling had been decorated by Van der Meulen, and on the walls were represented the children of Louis XIV.

Three short years ago there was still Versailles and an Œil-de-Bœuf.—CARLYLE, *French Revolution*, vol. iii. bk. i. 1.

Œillet (*Chevaliers de l'*), or 'Knights of the Pink,' 1793. A society organised to rescue the queen Marie Antoinette and her young son (Louis the Dauphin) from the hands of the revolutionists. It had its ramifications in Austria and Prussia, but its headquarters were in Paris. Their attempt to save the queen failed, and the failure was announced to the Parisian conspirators by one of the members pulling a pink to pieces and flinging the stalk on the ground.

Offa's Dyke. An immense trench and rampart extending from the estuary of the Dee to the mouth of the Wye. It was carried through marshes and over mountains and rivers for 100 miles. Its remains are still visible. It was used for the boundary which determined the confines of England and Wales. Every Briton found with a weapon on this side of the dyke was to have his hand cut off (Sharon Turner, 'Hist. of the Anglo-Saxons,' p. 171).

This dyke was made by Offa king of Mercia A.D. 777.

Offaley, Ireland, was called 'King's County,' and its chief town 'Philipstown,' in honour of Philip of Spain, the husband of Queen Mary. At the same time Leix was called 'Queen's County,' and its chief town 'Maryborough,' in honour of Queen Mary.

Ogdoad, or Combination of Eight. Meaning the Good Principle and his 7 æons (Mind, the Word, the Understanding, Power, Excellencies, Princes, and Angels), from each of which sprang other æons amounting to 365, the mystic number of the Gnostics. The Greek expression for the 7 æons is *Abraxas* (7 letters), each æon being supposed to govern a world. *See* 'Basilides.'

Ogham Character (*The*). A species of old Irish writing. It seems to have been either a cipher or shorthand, consisting of certain lines and marks bearing a relative value to a principal horizontal line. The word is Irish.

I shall certainly find you exerting your poetical talents in elegincs upon a prison, or your anti-quarian researches in detecting the Ogham character.—Sir W. SCOTT, *Waverley*, ch. xxviii.

Ogy'gian Flood (*The*), B.C. 1759. A great flood said to have taken place in the reign of Ogȳgês, a mythical king of Attica and Bœotia.

Bœotia was called Ogȳgia.

Ohio (U.S. America). So called, in 1802, from its river of the same name (Indian). The inhabitants are nicknamed *Buck-eyes.*

Oil (*The Sacred*). For anointing the kings of France. Kept in a phial of antique form, about an inch and a half high. The oil is reddish, not unlike thin liquid glue, and the phial is kept in the tomb of St. Remi at Reims. When a king of France was to be anointed, the tomb was opened and the phial taken out. We are told that it shrinks visibly in quantity when a dying king is to be anointed, but assumes its normal volume when a new king is to be anointed with it. According to legend it was brought to St. Remi by a pigeon when Clovis was baptized.

Trained pigeons played a very prominent part both at the death and baptism of those whom the Catholic Church delighted to honour.

Old and New Irish (*The*). The descendants of the Milesians and the Anglo-Irish settled in the Pale (*q.v.*).

Old and New Learning (*Men of the*). So Catholics and the Reformers were called in England after Henry VIII. broke from the pope.

The leaders of the Old Learning were Lee, archbishop of York; Stokesley, bishop of London; Tunstall, bishop of Durham; Gardiner, bishop of Winchester; Sherbourne, bishop of Chichester; Nix, bishop of Norwich; and Kite, bishop of Carlisle. These prelates were countenanced by the Duke of Norfolk, and by Wriothesley, the chief secretary.

The leaders of the New Learning were Cranmer, archbishop of Canterbury; Latimer, bishop of Worcester; Shaxton, bishop of Salisbury; Hilsey, bishop of Rochester; Fox, bishop of Hereford; and Barlow, bishop of St. David's. These prelates were supported by Cromwell, the vicar-general.

Old Bags. I. A nickname given to Nicholas Vansittart by William Hone in one of his political squibs, called 'The Political Showman,' published in 1821. In this satire Lord Sidmouth figures as the *Doctor*, his father having been a medical man.

II. John Scott lord Eldon was so called because he carried home with him in sundry bags the cases pending his judgment (1751-1838).

Old Bullion. Colonel Thomas Hart Benton, advocate of the gold and silver currency in the U.S. of N. America (1783-1858).

Old Catholics, 1870. Those Romanists who deny the ecumenical character of the Vatican Council of 1869, and reject the Vatican decrees, especially those concerning the pope's infallibility.

Old Fox (*The*). Marshal Soult was so called from his strategic abilities and never-failing resources (1769-1851).

Old Glory. Sir Francis Burdett (1770-1844). At one time the glory of the radicals, but subsequently he became a Tory.

Old Gravity. Lord Chancellor Thurlow (1732-1806).

So much for Old Gravity.
PETER PINDAR, *Great Cry and Little Wool*, epist. ii.

Old Grog. Edward Vernon the admiral (1684-1757). So called by British sailors from his grogram cloak, which he wore in foul weather.

Old Hickory. President Jackson of U.S. of America. So called because in his contest with the Creek Indians (1813) on one occasion he was so destitute of provisions that he and his men fed on hickory nuts.

There can be no doubt that 'Old Hickory' possessed animal force and courage in a high degree . . . [but] it is not surprising to learn that his reign was a period of general lawlessness and rowdyism, outrages being committed in the streets of the capital of which Jackson refused to take notice.—*Nineteenth Century*, August 1888, pp. 272, 273.

Old Ireland Party (*The*). The followers of Daniel O'Connell, as opposed to 'Young Ireland' led by Smith O'Brien. Both sought repeal, but the old party was Catholic, and the young party wanted to unite all Irishmen, irrespective of creed, into one union. The two parties hated each other.

Old Learning (*The*). The Catholic faith, in contradistinction to the Reformed faith.

Old Man Eloquent. President John Quincy Adams (1767-1848). President 1825-1829.

Isocrates, the Athenian orator, is generally meant by 'The Old Man Eloquent' (B.C. 436-338). It is to him that Milton refers

. . . . that dishonest victory
At Cheronæa, fatal to liberty,
Killed with report that Old Man Eloquent.

When Isocrates heard of the defeat of the Athenians at Cheronæa, it had such an effect on his spirits that he drooped and died within four days. He was nearly 99 years of age.

Old Man of the Mountain (*The*). King of the Assassins, whose name was Hussun Subah sheik ul Gebel (1090-1258). He was a convert to the doctrines of the Ismaelians (*q.v.*). He ruled over a tribe called the Aschischi in the northern mountains of Persia. The word Aschischi is from *haschish*, an intoxicating substance that produced delirium, in which the imagination had very enthusiastic views of eternal happiness. Hussun reared his young disciples into absolute obedience, so that they were fearless of man of any rank, and the greatest princes trembled at his name. Houlagou or Houlaku extirpated the order in Persia in 1258, but it lingered in Syria till 1280, when the Mamelukes stamped it out.

Old Man of the North (*The*). Christian Jacques Drahakemberg, of

Aarhuus, in Jutland. Died 1772, aged 146. See ' Macrobiots.'

Old Noll. Oliver Cromwell (1599–1658).

Old Patch. A great banknote forger. In 1784, by making his own paper and ink, and working off the notes on his own private press, he managed to get into circulation false notes to the value of 200,000*l*.

Other great forgers of Bank of England notes have been Mathison, 1783; Vincent Alessi (the Italian); and the Duke of Rovigo and Desnouettes (of Hamburg). Vincent Alessi was betrayed by a confederate; the Duke of Rovigo and Desnouettes made their notes in Hamburg, and employed agents to circulate them in England.

The name of Old Patch was Charles Price, but he had many aliases, as Wigmore, Wilmott, Brank, Bond, Parks, Powel, Schutz, &c.

Old Pretender (*The*). Francis Edward James [Stuart] son of James II. He claimed the British throne by right of birth, but as his father had abdicated the right fell through (1688–1765).

Old Public Functionary, or O. P. F. President James Buchanan (1791–1868). So called from the following words in his message to Congress in 1859: ' This advice proceeds from an old public functionary.'

Old Rowley. Charles II. was so-called from his favourite racehorse (1630, 1660–1685).

A part of Newmarket racecourse is still called 'the Rowley mile.'

Old Sarum. Marchioness of Salisbury, grandmother of the prime minister, burnt to death in 1835, at the age of 86. She used to drive in the park in a low phaeton with four black ponies and outriders in splendid liveries; always went to court in a sedan-chair, her footmen carrying flambeaux at night; she hunted till she was past 70, wearing a sky-blue habit with black velvet collar, and a jockey-cap; was a bold rider, and no fence ever stopped her.

Old Style and New Style (*The*). Old Style, computing according to the old calendar. New Style, computing according to the reformed calendar. Hence we have Lady Day 25 March, and Old Lady Day, 6 April. Midsummer Day, 24 June, and Old Midsummer Day, 6 July. Michaelmas Day, 29 Sept., and Old Michaelmas Day, 11 Oct. Christmas Day, 25 Dec., and Old Christmas Day, 6 Jan.

Old Testament (*The*). The language of the Old Testament is a composite of Aramaic, Arabic, and Hebrew. Ezra (who died B.C. 459) declared what books were to be considered canonical.

The following portions are in Chaldaic, viz. :—
Ezra iv. 8, vi. 18, and vii. 12-26.
Jer. x. 11.
Dan. ii. 4 and vii. 28.

The Hebrew Scriptures were translated into Greek in the 3rd cent. B.C.; but parts seem to be as late as the time of Antiochus Epiphanès, who died B.C. 164.

It was first *printed* in 1488, at Soncino. In 1526 the Rabbinical Bible was printed at Venice.

Esdras, *i.e.* Ezra, says : ' Behold, Lord, . . . thy law is burnt, therefore no man knoweth the things that are done of thee . . . . but if I have found favour before thee, send the Holy Ghost to me, and I will write all that hath been done in the world since the beginning, [all] that was written in thy Law. . . . And I took five men, as the Lord commanded me, and we went into a field and remained there. And the next day, behold a voice called me, saying, " Esdras, open thy mouth, and drink what I give thee." . . . So I opened my mouth, and, behold, he reached me a full cup, which was full as it were with water, but the colour of it was like fire. And I took and drank it. And when I had drunk of it, my heart uttered understanding, and wisdom grew in my breast, for my spirit strengthened my memory. . . . And the Highest gave understanding to the five men, and they wrote the wonderful visions of the night which were told [and] which they knew not. And they sat forty days, they wrote in the day, and at night they ate [their] bread. In the forty days they wrote 204 [*margin* says 904] books. And it came to pass when the forty days were fulfilled, that the Highest said to me, " The first [book] which thou hast written publish openly, that the worthy and the unworthy may read it; but keep [back] the 70 last [books], and deliver them only to such as be wise among the people, for in them [*i.e.* the 70 books] is the spring of understanding, the fountain of wisdom, and the stream of knowledge." And I did so.'—2 *Esdras* xiv. 21, 22, 37-48.

*** It is very difficult to understand what is meant by ' the first book '; still more what is meant by the ' 70 books '; and why should these books, in which were ' the fountain of wisdom and the stream of knowledge,' be kept back from the public eye?

Old Testament. Books referred to, but not in the canon.

The Book of the Wars of the Lord (*Numbers* xxi. 14).

The Book of the Covenant (*Exodus* xxiv. 7).

The Book of Jasher (*Joshua* x. 13, and 2 *Sam.* i. 18).

The Book of the Acts of Solomon (1 *Kings* xi. 41).

The Book of the Chronicles of the Kings of Israel (1 *Kings* xiv. 19; 2 *Chron.* xx. 34, xxxiii. 18; and 18 other places).

The Chronicles of the Kings of Judah (1 *Kings* xiv. 29; and 12 other places).

The Book of the Kings of Judah and Israel (2 *Chron.* xvi. 11; and 6 other places).

The Book of Samuel the Seer (1 *Chron.* xxix. 29, and 2 *Chron.* ix. 29).

The Book of Nathan the Prophet (1 *Chron.* xxix. 29).

The Book of Gad the Seer (1 *Chron.* xxix. 29).

The Chronicles of King David (1 *Chron.* xxvii. 24).

The Prophecy of Ahijah the Shilonite (2 *Chron.* ix. 29).

The Visions of Iddo the Seer against Jeroboam (2 *Chron.* ix. 29).

The Book of Iddo the Seer concerning Genealogies (2 *Chron.* xii. 15).

The Story of the Prophet Iddo (2 *Chron.* xiii. 22).

The Book of Shemaiah the Prophet (2 *Chron.* xii. 15).

The Book of Jehu (2 *Chron.* xx. 34).
The Memoirs of Hircănus (mentioned in 2 *Maccabees* ii.).
The Books of Jason (mentioned in 2 *Maccabees* 11).
The Acts of Uriah (2 *Chron.* xxvi. 22).
The Three Thousand Proverbs of Solomon (1 *Kings* iv. 32).
A Thousand and Five Songs of Solomon (1 *Kings* iv. 32).
The Prophecy of Jeremiah, torn in pieces by Jehoiakim (*Jeremiah* li.).
The Prophecy about the city of Babylon (*Jeremiah* li.).
The Memoirs of Jeremiah (mentioned in 1 *Maccabees* ii.).
The Prophecy of Jonah (*Jonah*).

Old Testament. Books supposed to be lost.

The Generation of Adam.
The Revelation of Adam.
The Genealogy of the Sons and Daughters of Adam.
Cham's Book of Magic.
A Treatise called 'Seth.'
The Assumption of Abraham.
The Jetsira, ascribed to Abraham.
The Book of the Twelve Patriarchs.
The Discourses of Jacob and Joseph.
A Prophecy of Habakkuk, and some by Ezekiel.
The Prophecy of Eldad and Medad.
The Treatise of Jannes and Jambres.
The Book of Og.
Jacob's Ladder, and several others.

See 'Apocryphal Scriptures' (New Testament).

Oldenburg (*The House of*). The present reigning house of Denmark, founded in 1448 by Christian I. of the house of Oldenburg.

Ol'eron (*Laws of*). Maritime laws chiefly borrowed from the 'Consolato del Mare,' compiled in the middle of the 13th cent. The story runs that the Laws of Oleron were enacted by Richard I. while his fleet lay at anchor there on his expedition to the Holy Land. The Ordinances of Wisby in Gothland were compiled from the Laws of Oleron before 1400.

Other traditions ascribe these laws to the Flemings, to Otto the Saxon, to the Seigneur of Oleron in 1196, to Eleonore of Guyenne, and some others.

Olim. The most ancient registers of the Parlement de Paris, from 1254 to 1318, comprehending the reigns of St. Louis, Philippe le Hardi, Philippe le Bel, Louis le Hutin, and Philippe le Long. These valuable registers contain, not only reports of the administration of justice in that period, but also the organisation of the parlement and contemporary events of all sorts. They were published in 1840.

Oliva (*Peace of*), 3 May, 1660, between Sweden, Poland, the kaiser, and the elector of Brandenburg; signed soon after the death of Charles X. of Sweden. This treaty, and that of Kardis (with the Czar of Russia), put an end to the wars in which Charles X. had involved the Swedes. The Peace of Oliva ensured the integrity of Poland, but in 1773 the first partition of Poland between Russia, Prussia, and Austria was effected.

Olive Branch (*The*), 8 July, 1775. The petition of the American Congress to King George III. after the battle of Bunker's Hill, expressive of an earnest desire for an honourable peace. The petitioners vowed that this petition if not successful should be the last.

Oliver Optic. The pen-name of William Taylor Adams, an American novelist.

Oliver's Fiddler. Sir Roger L'Estrange (1616–1704). So called because at one time he was playing a fiddle with others, in the house of John Hingston, when Oliver Cromwell was for a time one of the guests.

Roger L'Estrange, who used to be called 'Oliver's Fiddler,' formerly in danger of being hanged for a spy, and about this time the admired buffoon of High Church.—CALAMY.

Olive'tans (4 syl.), or 'Brethren of Our Lady of Mount Olivet,' 1272. A religious order in the Catholic Church, an offshoot of the Benedictines (*q.v.*), founded by Bernard Tolomei and others on Monte Olivēto in Tuscany, whence the name.

Olmütz (*The Camp at*), Sept., 1850. A military political display for the sake of averting the Crimēan War. Austria assembled at Olmütz 50,000 men 'for field exercise.' The Emperor of Russia, the Emperor of Austria, the King of Prussia, Count Buol chief minister of Austria, the British and French ministers, all met and conferred on the war. Russia suggested that the 'Vienna Note' (*q.v.*) drawn up by Count Buol should be accepted, and that the Four Powers should guarantee the good faith of Russia. Austria and Prussia agreed, but England scouted such sponsorship after the deception of Russia during many months, and France stood firm beside England. It really was most unsatisfactory and unbusiness-like, but Prussia and

Austria separated from the Western Powers.

Russia has always adopted that vile maxim of Prince Metternich : ' He who knows not how to deceive, knows not how to rule.' As if lying was the divine right of kings, instead of being the prerogative of ' the father of lies.'

Olympiad. In ancient Greece meant the space of four years between one celebration of the Olympic games and another. As a system of chronology it began from B.C. 776.

The games were held at Olympia, in Elis, dedicated to Zeus, called by the Romans Jupiter Olympus.

Olympic Games (*The*). Said to have been instituted by Herăklês. They were held on the plains of Olympia every fifth year, and constituted the most splendid national festival of the ancient Greeks. Dates were reckoned from these games, and the five intervening years made an Olympiad.

Olyn'thiac Orations (*The*), B.C. 350. The three orations of Demosthenês against Philip king of Macedon, who had captured a town of Chalcidĭcê in the sacred war. Olynthus, the head of 32 Greek towns, trembled for its own safety. Demosthenes tried to arouse the Athenians to take part with the Olynthians against Philip; but the Athenians made no great stir, and in 347 Olynthus fell into the hands of Philip.

Olyn'thian War (*The*). I. B.C. 382–379, between Sparta and the Olynthians.

II. B.C. 349–346, between Philip of Macedon and the Olynthians. The Olynthians were defeated in two battles, and their city taken.

Ommi'ades (3 syl.), 661–750. An Arabian dynasty, so called from Ommīah grandfather of Abou Sofyan, chief of the temple of Mecca before Islamism was known. This Ommiah the Koreishite was father of Moaviah, who founded the dynasty. The seat of empire was Damascus. The Ommiades were dethroned by the Abbassides in 749 or 750.

The Ommiade califs were Moaviah I. (661), Yezid I. (680), Moaviah II. (683), Merwan I. (684), Abdel Malek (685), Walid I. (705), Soliman (715), Omar II. (717), Yezid II. (720), Hescham (724), Walid II. (743), Yezid III. (744), Ibrahim (744), Merwan II. (744).

Omnibus, 1829. Introduced into London by Mr. J. Shillibeer. The first omnibus ran from the ' Yorkshire Stingo,' in the New Road, to the Bank of England, the fare being one shilling. In 1830 the fare was reduced to sixpence, and since then other reductions have been made.

Omnibus Bill (*An*). A general bill in parliament promoted by some public body (such as the Ecclesiastical or Charity Commissioners, the Board of Works, &c.), who for economy sake include in one application to the legislature several schemes or projects, mostly by way of schedule.

Omnibus Order (*An*), in law. A single order made by a judge for dealing with several applications pending before the court. All the applications are put in one omnibus or order.

Omnibus Section of the Russian Penal Code. Revised in 1885. Section 249 is so called from its wide scope and sweeping applicability. It drags into its clutches all revolutionists of every shade and degree; even thoughts are not free; and as to words, paragraphs in newspapers, advice, hints and expressions of discontent, they are all treasonable, and render the offender liable to exile for life and the forfeiture of all his goods.

Omri (*Statutes of*), B.C. 920. King of Israel, founder of Samaria. He compelled by severe laws the worship of the Israelitish idols, and these laws are still called by the Jews 'The Statutes of Omri.'

One-Sandalled Man(*The*). Jason was so called because on his way back to Iolcus he lost one of his sandals in crossing the river Anaurus.

One Thousand Eight Hundred and Sixty-seven (1867). A Fenian toast and catchword : as ' Three cheers for 1867 ! ' This was the date of the Fenian rising.

Onion Pennies. Certain Roman coins found pretty abundantly at Silchester in Hampshire. So called from one ' Onion,' said to be a giant who dwelt in this city.

On'kelos. The supposed author of an Aramäie version of the Pentateuch.

O. P. Riots, 1809. Covent Garden having been destroyed by fire during the management of John Kemble, a new house was erected in the course of a year, and the prices of admission raised. The theatre-going public took this in dudgeon, and night after night crowded the house with cries of 'O. P.' (old prices). They danced on the pit-benches and sometimes on the cushions of the boxes to the harsh music of cat-calls, and to tunes written for the occasion. O. P. music and dances were to be seen in every music shop. When at last the benches began to be torn up, the cushions demolished, and the decorations destroyed, the magistracy interfered.

Sir Vicary Gibbs, being employed to conduct the prosecution, convulsed the court with a happy quotation : 'Opes [O.Ps.] irritamenta malorum.'

Open Sea of Kane (*The*). A sea supposed by Elisha Kane the traveller (1822-1857) to surround the North Pole.

Oph'ites (2 syl.), 2nd cent. A Christian sect. So called from the Greek word ὄφις (a serpent). They maintained that the serpent (Gen. iii.) was the Logos or Christ, who came into Eden to deliver man from that ignorance to which the Creator or Demiurge had doomed him, and to make him 'wise unto salvation.' (From 2nd to 6th cent.)

Oppian Law (*The*). 'Oppia Lex,' a law by C. Oppius, the tribune, forbidding any woman to wear more than half an ounce of gold, to have parti-coloured garments, or to be carried more than a mile except for the purpose of celebrating some religious festival or solemnity.

Optime (3 syl.). The second class of the Mathematical Tripos is called 'The Senior Optimes,' and the third class is called the 'Junior Optimes.' These phrases are derived from the 'Acts' which used to be held in the schools before degrees were conferred. The compliment of the moderator paid to an opponent who had answered very well was *Optime quidem disputasti*, or *Domine opponens, optime disputasti*, and to the respondent who had disputed pretty well, *Domine respondens, satis et optime quidem et in thesi et in disputationibus tuo officio functus es*. *See* 'Wrangler.'

Optimism. The doctrine that whatever is in its best possible state, for God would not have made anything otherwise. What we call evils are needful for our conservation, and all odds will be made even in the life hereafter. Malebranche taught optimism, and Leibnitz in his 'Essais de Théodicée'; Bolingbroke adopted the same theory, and Pope in his 'Essay on Man' says, 'Whatever is, is right.' *See* 'Pessimism.'

Opus Majus [not ' Opus Magnum']. The title of the great work of Roger Bacon the Franciscan. It contains the results of his researches, and he tells us that he spent above 2,000*l.* in twenty years on apparatus for his experiments [equal to 30,000*l.* of our money at present]. His discoveries were in geometry, astronomy, physics, optics, mechanics, and chemistry.

Opus Operan'tis, in theology, means that the effect is due not to the *opus* or act itself, but to the disposition of the *operans* or operator. *See next article.*

There is no virtue in kissing the crucifix *per se*, but the mind of the devotee may by its fervour and devotion bring grace to the person who kisses it. Of course the Catholics never apply the term to sacraments, but the Anglican Church seems to imply it in the words ' feed on Him in thy heart by faith.'

Opus Opera'tum, in theology, means that the rite or sacrament itself conveys grace independently of the mind of the recipient. The *opus* is the efficient cause of grace.

Thus when the sacrament is administered *in articulo mortis*, though the recipient is moribund, yet it conveys grace.

Opus Triparti'tum (1514). The ancient customs and royal decrees of Hungary compiled by Verboczi, and divided into three parts. A second volume was added, and the whole was entitled 'Jus Consuetudinārium Regni Hungāriæ.'

Or (gold). One of the colours in heraldry of the escutcheon, expressed by dots.

There are seven colours employed in England, and nine by foreign heralds. *See* 'Heralds.'

Oracle of Delft (*The*). Hugo Grotius was called the ' Oracle of Delft, the Phœnix of his Country ' (1583-1645).

Oracle of Delphi (*The*). On the south slope of Parnassos ; founded in honour of Apollo, surnamed Pythĭos, because he slew the serpent python. The ravings of the priestess were due to a mephitic gas which issued from a hole in the earth over which the tripod was placed. Men held the woman down till the gas had intoxicated her, and her ravings were then taken down by priests and turned into verse. The priestess was called the Pythĭa.

Certainly some of the Delphic responses were most witty equivokes. Thus:

1. When Pyrrhos consulted the oracle respecting his war with the Romans, he received for answer: 'Credo te, Æacide, Romanos vincĕre posse,' *i.e.* 'The Romans, I believe, you will conquer.' Which may mean either you will conquer the Romans, or the Romans will conquer you.

2. Another response was ' This, redĭbis nunquam per bella peribis.' [You shall return never by war shall you perish.] Whether the comma is placed before or after *never* makes all the difference.

3. When the allied Greeks demanded of the oracle what would be the issue of the battle of Salămis, they received for answer—

Seed-time and harvest, weeping sires shall tell How thousands fought at Salamis and fell;

but whether the weeping sires were to be Greeks or Persians was not stated.

4. When Crœsos demanded what would be the issue of the battle against the Persians headed by Cyrus, the oracle replied: ' Crœsos will behold a mighty empire overthrown'; but which empire is left doubtful.

5. When Philip of Macedon sent to inquire if his Persian expedition would prove successful, he received for reply: 'The ready victim crowned for sacrifice stands before the altar.' Philip took it for granted that the 'ready victim' was the King of Persia, but it was he himself.

When Maxentius was about to encounter Constantine he consulted the guardians of the Sibylline Books as to the fate of the battle, and the prophetess told him : 'Illo diehostem Romanorum esse periturum '; but whether Maxentius or Constantine was 'the enemy of the Roman people' the oracle left undecided.

In the Bible we have a similar equivoke : When Ahab king of Israel was about to wage war on the king of Syria, and asked Micaiah if Ramoth Gilead would fall into his hands, the prophet replied, 'Go! for the Lord will deliver the city into the hands of the king' (1 Kings xxii. 15, 35). Ahab thought that *he* was the king referred to, but the king into whose hands the city fell was the king of Syria. *See* p. 650, *n.* to ' Orleton's Message.'

Oracle of Dodo'na (*The*), in Epĭros. The most ancient oracle of Greece, dedicated to Zeus (1 syl.). Its responses were made by women called *pigeons* (*q.v.*), who derived their responses from four sources: (1) The cooing of doves ; (2) the bubbling of a spring of water which rose at the foot of the sacred oak ; (3) the rustling of the leaves of the oak ; and (4) the tinkling of a gong hung in the branches of a tree. The gong was struck by knotted cords hung on the branches of the tree. In B.C. 219 the Ætōlians destroyed the temple and cut down the sacred grove. *See* ' Pigeons.'

Oracle of France (*The*). St. Bernard of Clairvaux. *See* 'Oracle of the Church.'

Oracle of the Church (*The*). St. Bernard, abbot of Clairvaux (1091–1153), also called the ' Mellifluous Doctor,' the ' River of Paradise,' and the 'Last of the Fathers.' He was the founder of the Order of Bernardines, but not of the Hospice. The founder of the Hospice was St. Bernard of Menthon, who lived about a century earlier (923–1008).

Orange (*Prince of*). Orange, a corruption of Arausio, in the department of Vaucluse, some sixteen miles from Avignon. The town was the capital of a principality from the 11th to the 16th century ; its last sovereign being Philibert de Châlons, whose sister married William count of Nassau. This count was the father of William I. the stadtholder- of the United Provinces, and grandfather of William II. stadtholder. This William II. married Mary eldest daughter of Charles I., whose eldest son was our William III., who married Mary eldest daughter of James II. while he was Duke of York.

William count of Nassau married Philibert's sister, and was the father of William I. stadtholder.

William I. the stadtholder was the father of William II. the stadtholder, who married Mary daughter of Charles I.

William II. was the father of WILLIAM III. of Great Britain, who married Mary daughter of James II.

Or'angeists (3 syl.), 1785. The Orange faction of Holland opposed to the French faction. The former stood by the stadtholder, and accused their opponents of democratic principles and a tendency to French influence. The democrats accused the Orange party of aiming at monarchy or oligarchy, and trampling on the ancient liberties of the people. The French faction prevailed, and the country was laid at the feet of France.

Or'angemen (3 syl.). A development of the Peep-of-day Boys in Ireland, consisting of rich and influential Irish Protestants in defence of Protestant ascendency in Ireland. So called from William of Orange, whose name and reign are associated with the Protestant ascendency in the island. The first Orange lodge was founded in the village of Loughgall, county Armagh, 21 Sept., 1795. As many as twelve or fourteen Roman Catholics would be ejected in a single night by these Orangemen. By 1798 the Orangemen were a very powerful society, having a ' grand lodge,' extending over the entire province of Ulster, and ramified through all the centres of Protestantism in Ireland. In 1808 a grand lodge of Orangemen was opened in Manchester, in 1821 it was transferred to London, and in 1827 the Duke of Cumberland was elected Grand Master. In 1835 the number of members was 200,000. *See* ' Irish Associations.'

There are **Orange** lodges **in Canada and the Colonies** also.

Orateur du Genre Humain.
See below, ' Orator of the Human Race.'

Orator Henley (1692–1756). Called
by Pope ' the Zany of his age' ('Dunciad'), and introduced by Hogarth into two of his humorous pieces. In one he is christening a child, and in the other he is represented on a scaffold with a monkey at his side, and the motto ' Amen.' His periodical called the ' Hip Doctor ' is a farrago of nonsense.

Orator of Nature (*The*). Patrick
Henry of Studley, Hanover, in Virginia, who advocated the cause of the people against the claims of the clergy of Virginia. He was highly distinguished in the war of independence, and contributed greatly to the carrying of the Declaration of Independence. ' If we would be free,' he said over and over again, ' we must fight. Yea, I repeat it; we must fight ! we must fight ! ' (1736–1799).

Orator of the Human Race
(*The*). The not very modest title assumed by Anacharsis Cloots [Baron Jean Baptiste Cloots], a Prussian by birth, brought up in Paris, where he adopted the revolutionary principles (1755–1794). So called because he appeared at the bar of the National Assembly accompanied by deputies from all the nations of the civilised world who had chosen him for speaker. He was guillotined by the French republicans.

The next day this deputation of all nations was found to be a hoax, and the deputies were merely vagabonds hired for the nonce at 12 livres apiece. One of the rascals went to the Marquis de Biancourt for the money, and said he had been the Chaldean. 'Mr. Chaldean,' said the Marquis, 'you have come to the wrong person.' M. de Biancourt made no secret of the visit, and next day it was duly reported in the daily papers. Hunt was called Orator Hunt (1773-1835).

Orators (*The*). Mark Antony and
Licinius Crassus. Cicero says, ' Crassus is the greatest orator Rome had ever seen except Antony, and Antony the greatest except Crassus.'

Mark Antony the ' Orator ' was not the triumvir, but the grandfather. Thus : Mark Antony the ' Orator,' whose eldest son was Mark Antony surnamed Creticus, and the triumvir was the son of Creticus.

Oratorians. *See below*.

Oratory (*Congregation of the*),
1550. Founded by Philip de Neri, at Rome, under the name of the ' Confraternity of the Trinity.' Introduced into Paris in 1611; and into England by Cardinal Newman in 1847. The fathers of the Oratory live in community without any special vows. Oratorians are so called ' parce qu'ils se placaient devant l'église pour appeler le peuple à la prière.'

Suppressed in France in 1790, but restored in 1853 by the Abbé Pétetot, under the title of the ' Oratory of the Immaculate Conception.'

Orbis Sensualium Pictus, 1654.
The first picture-book or illustrated manual for the young by J. Amos Comenīus, and published at Nürnberg. Object lessons in infant schools are of a similar character.

Ordainers, 1310, 1311. A council
of 28 noblemen appointed to reform the government and the king's [Edward II.] household. These lords were empowered to enact ordinances which should have the force of laws. The cause of this junto was the infatuation of the king for Piers Gaveston, a Gascon, on whom he lavished lands and honours with most wanton profusion. The ordainers revoked all the grants of the king to his favourite, demanded the removal of all foreigners from high offices, and took from the king the power of making war or peace without the consent of his barons.

Ordeal. An appeal to the judgment
of God made known by the success or failure of certain acts performed by the accused. Hebrew women accused of adultery appealed to the ' water of jealousy.' There are nine different ordeals in use among the Hindûs. In Africa a men who fancies himself bewitched by his wife sends for the o'beah woman, who administers to her a drink made of

'goho'; if she vomits it, she is pronounced innocent; if not, she is put to death. In Europe the ordinary ordeals were those of fire, water, and wager of battle (q.v.).

Ordeal by Fire. In this ordeal the accused was required to carry a piece of red-hot iron in his hand a given distance, or to tread blindfold and barefoot amongst nine red-hot ploughshares without setting his foot on any one of them. If the accused escaped unhurt he was pronounced innocent. This ordeal was reserved for the wealthy, and as priests were the adjudicators, they could easily instruct those they wished to befriend how to escape unhurt.

Ordeal by Water. Chiefly for the lower orders. There was the ordeal of hot water and the ordeal of cold water. Athelstane's law was for the accused to pick a stone out of a tub of boiling water, the arm being quite bare, and water up to the wrist, in some cases up to the elbow. The ordeal of cold water was to be flung into a pond or river; if the accused sank he was pronounced innocent, if he floated he was pronounced guilty. See 'Wager of Battle.'

Order 14. The Judicature Act which provides that when a writ has been served and duly appeared to, if the creditor makes an affidavit that his claim is for a definite sum of money of which there is no dispute, and respecting which the debtor makes no defence, then the creditor may issue a summons calling the debtor at two days' notice to appear before a Master in Chambers, and, if all is satisfactory, the creditor is allowed to obtain immediate execution, saving thus the delay and expense of going to trial in the ordinary way. A summary process of exacting payment of a debt.

Order in Council (An) is an order by the sovereign under the advice of the privy council.

Order in Council (The), 7 Jan. 1807. Ordained that all neutral vessels shall be prohibited from entering any port belonging to France, or her allies, or under her control. If any vessel violates this order, both the vessel and its cargo may be confiscated by the English Government.

11 Nov. 1807 another order was issued, by which all harbours and places of France, her allies, and colonies were placed under the same restrictions as if they were strictly blockaded.

Order of Alcan'tara (The), 1156. Instituted by Don Suarez and Don Gomez, entrusted with the defence of Alcantara, in Spain. They were first called 'Knights of the Pear Tree,' then 'Knights of St. Julian,' from San Julian del Pereyro.

Order of Argonauts (The), 1382. Instituted by Charles III. of Naples.

Order of Assassins (The). See 'Assassins.'

Order of Aviz. An order of knighthood in Portugal, instituted by Sancho the first king, in imitation of the order of Calatra'va, and having for its object the subjugation of the Moors (1146).

Order of Bernar'dines (3 syl.), 1115. Reformed Benedictines, founded by St. Bernard of Clairvaux.

Order of Calatra'va (The), 1158. Instituted in Spain by Sancho III. of Castile. When Sancho took from the Moors the strong castle of Calatrava he committed its defence to the Knights Templars, who declined to undertake it. Whereupon Don Raymond of the Cistercian order, with several caballeros of quality, volunteered to defend it, and were created 'Knights of Calatrava.'

Order of Celes'tines (3 syl.), 1274. Founded by Celestine V. (Pierre de Moron), but suppressed in 1776 by Pius VI.

Order of Christ (The), 1205. Instituted in Livonia by Albert bishop of Riga, and incorporated with the Order of Teutonic Knights in 1237. Also called 'The Short Swords of Livonia.'

Not to be mistaken for 'The Order of the Knights of Christ' (q.v.).

Order of Christ (The), 1318. A religico-military order instituted by Dionysius I. of Portugal to guard the frontiers of Algarve from invasions of the Moors. It is now only an order of honour. See 'Chevaliers Porte-glaive.'

This order was simply that of the Templars expelled from France by Philippe le Bel [IV.], and received into Portugal under a new name. A branch of the same was admitted by John XXII. into the Papal States. Another branch subsisted in Brazil until the revolution of 1890.

Order of Christian Charity (The), 1578. Instituted by Henri III. of

T T

France for the benefit of poor military officers and maimed soldiers. It was instituted at the same time as the Order of the Holy Ghost, meant for princes and men of distinction.

Order of Civil Merit (*The*), 1815. Founded in Saxony by Frederick I. [Augustus] on his being allowed by Alexander of Russia (who had taken him prisoner at Leipsic) to return to Dresden. He died in 1827, at the age of 76.

He celebrated the fiftieth year of his accession in 1818, and the fiftieth year of his marriage in 1819.

Order of Fidelity (*The*).
I. 1701. A Prussian order instituted by Frederick III. elector of Brandenburg, and better known as 'The Order of the Black Eagle.'
II. In 1715. Instituted by Charles William margraf of Baden Durlach, on his founding Carlsruhe.

Order of Fontevrault (*The*), 1100. A religious order founded by Robert d'Arbrissel. The abbey of Fontevrault was transformed into a prison in 1804.

Order of Fools (*The*). Instituted 12 Nov., 1381, by Adolphus count of Cleves, under the title of *De Order van't Gekkengezelschap*, and composed of noblemen and gentlemen of rank and renown for humane and charitable objects. Their insignia was the figure of a court fool on the left side of their mantles, cap and bells, yellow stockings, a cup of fruit in the right hand, and a gold key in the left. A grand court was held on the first Sunday after Michaelmas Day. It is alluded to in Brand's 'Navis Stultifera,' 1520. *See* 'Respublica Binepsis.'

Order of Grandmontines, or 'Grammontines' (3 syl.), 1026, founded in Limousin by Etienne de Grammont. Suppressed in 1769.

Order of Hieron'ymites (5 syl.), 1373, approved by Gregory XI.

Order of Isabella the Catholic (*The*), 24 March, 1815. Founded in Spain by Ferdinand VII. as a reward for loyalty and for the defence of the possessions of Spanish America.

Order of Jesuits (*The*), or 'Order of the Society of Jesus,' 1534. Founded by Ignatius Loyōla. Sanctioned in 1540 by a bull of Paul III. Established in France, Spain, Portugal, and Germany in 1556. Missionaries were sent to England by Gregory XIII. in 1580, but banished from the kingdom in 1584 (27 Eliz. c. 2). Banished from France in 1594; from Venice in 1606; from Turkey in 1628; from Abyssinia in 1632; from Spain in 1767; from Naples in 1767; from Parma in 1768; from Malta in 1768; from Russia in 1817; from Genŏa in 1848; from Austria in 1848.

Order of Jesuates (3 syl.), 1367. Founded in Italy by Urban V. Suppressed in 1668, and their possessions given to the Hos'pitallers of Italy.

This Order must not be confounded with the 'Order' or 'Society of Jesuits' founded by Loyōla in 1534. *See* p. 469.

Order of Jesus and Mary (*The*), 1615. Instituted in Italy by Paul V.

Order of Lazarists (*The*), or 'Fathers of St. Lazarus,' 1625. Instituted by De Gondi, and placed under the direction of Vincent de Paul.

Order of Leopold (*The*), 1808. Created by Francis I. of Austria in honour of his father Leopold II., for civil or military merit, without regard to birth. The decoration is a cross with eight points. The motto is 'Integritati et merito.' The legend on the reverse is 'Opes regum, corda subditorum.'

Order of Louisa (*The*), 1814. Instituted in Prussia.

Order of Maria Theresa (*The*), 1757. A military order instituted by Maria Theresa of Austria in memory of her victory over the Prussians at Kollin the same year. All the brave, without distinction of birth, were eligible. The decoration is a cross of gold and the motto 'Fortitudini.' The ribbon is white and red.

Order of Mercy (*The*), or 'The Religious Order of Mercy,' 1218. An order under the rule of St. Augustine, founded for the redemption of captives. Confirmed by Gregory IX. in 1235.

Order of Monte'sa (*The*), 1317. A Spanish order instituted by James II. of Aragon.

Order of Nova Scotia. An order of baronets created by James I. of England. These baronets wore a ribbon of an orange tawny colour. There are still a few surviving Nova Scotia baronetcies, all or nearly all being Scottish.

Order of Our Lady of Mercy (*The*), 1218.
Founded by Jayme I. of Aragon. Women were admitted to this order in 1261.

Order of Our Lady of Montesa (*The*), 1317.
Founded by Jayme II. of Aragon.

Order of Our Lady of Mount Carmel (*The*), 1607.
Instituted by Henri IV. of France, and consisting of 100 French gentlemen.

Quite a different order to the *Car'melites* (3 syl.) or *Ordre des Carmes*. Founded in 1156.

Order of Preachers (*The*), or 'Fratres Predicatōres,' 1216.
Sanctioned by Innocent III., who gave instructions to the people utterly to extinguish heresy; and by an official bull allowed the Dominican Order to be founded under the direction of Dominic de Guzman, a Spanish presbyter.

Called *Black Friars* in England from the colour of their dress; and *Jacobins* in France from their establishment in the Rue de Jaques, Paris.

Order of Rougemont (*The*), 1400.
A military order of Burgundy founded by Philibert de Miolans. Extinct.

Order of St. Alexander Newsky (*The*), 1714.
Instituted by Peter the Great, the insignia being a red cross with golden eagles. In the midst of the cross is St. Alexander on horseback slaying a dragon at his feet.

St. Alexander Newsky was grand-duke of Russia and son of Jaroslav II. (1218-1246), called Newsky from a battle which he gained over the Swedes, Danes, and Teutonic knights in 1240. Newsky is a title derived from the name of the river Neva, near which the battle was played.

Order of St. Andrew (*The*), 1698.
A Russian order founded by Peter the Great, and given only for high merit. The ribbon is blue, and the legend is 'Pour la Foi et la Fidélité.'

For the Scotch order *see* 'Order of the Thistle.'

Order of St. Anne (*The*), 1735.
A Russian order first instituted in Holstein by Duke Frederick in honour of his wife, who was daughter of Peter the Great. It was established in Russia by Paul I. in 1756. The ribbon is red edged with yellow, and in the centre of the cross is an image of St. Anne.

Order of St. Basil (*The*), 358.
Founded by St. Basil in Pontus; introduced into the Western Church in 1057.

Order of St. Caroline (*The*), 1816.
Instituted by Caroline, the separated wife of George prince regent, afterwards George IV. It was founded for the sake of decorating Bartolomeo Bergami, an Italian, first her footman and afterwards her chief adviser. The Emperor of Austria objected to the cross of Malta which was the badge of the order. Of course the order was never recognised.

Order of St. Christopher (*The*), 1517.
Founded in Austria for the purpose of checking intemperance and profane swearing.

Order of St. Genette (2 syl.), 782.
Instituted by Charles Martel after his victory over the Saracens, where a vast number of *gennets*, like Spanish cats, were found in the enemy's camp. The most ancient order of knighthood in France. Extinct.

Order of St. George (*The*).
BAVARIA. Instituted during the crusades, but refounded by Charles VII., 24 April, 1729.

ENGLAND. *See under* 'Garter.'

HANOVER, 1 January, 1840, founded by Ernest Augustus.

LUCCA, 1 June, 1833, founded by Duke Charles Louis.

RUSSIA, 26 Nov., 1769, founded by Catharine II. Similar to the 'Poor Knights of Windsor.' The cordon is yellow and black.

SICILY, 1 January, 1819, founded by Ferdinand I.

The following are extinct: The order of St. George in Burgundy, Carinthia, Constantinople, Germany, Ravenna, and Rome. *See* these under the national name.

Order of St. Jago (*The*).
A Spanish order instituted under Pope Alexander III. in 1175, the grand-master of which is next in rank to the sovereign.

Santiago or St. James the Greater is the patron saint of Spain.

Order of St. John of Jerusalem, 1120.
Called 'John' from John 'the patriarch of Alexandria, and 'Jerusalem' from the place of their abode. They subsequently resided at Rhodes (1310-1523), when, being driven out by the Turks, they took up their abode in Malta, and were called 'Knights of Malta.'

Order of St. Lazare, or St. Lazarus.
The knights driven from Palestine who followed St. Louis to

France. Suppressed by Innocent VIII. and united with other orders : to the order of St. John in 1490, and in France to the order of Our Lady of Mount Carmel in 1608. Abolished in 1795.

Order of St. Louis (*The*), in France, 1693. Founded by Louis XIV.

Order of St. Magdalene (3 syl.). A French order instituted by St. Louis to suppress duels, 1270. Extinct.

Order of St. Maria de Mercede (3 syl.). A Spanish order for the redemption of captives. Extinct.

Order of St. Maurice (*The*), 1434. Created by Amadeus VIII. of Savoy. Having lost his wife, Maria Beatrix of Burgundy, he retired to the hermitage of Ripaille, on the Lake of Geneva, with six of his nobles, whom he created knights of St. Maurice. In 1572 the order was united to that of St. Lazarus.

Order of St. Michael the Archangel (*The*). 'Ordre de St. Michel,' 1469, instituted by Louis XI. of France. ' St. Michel est regardé comme le protecteur et l'ange tutélaire de la France.'— BOUILLET.

Order of St. Patrick (*The*), 1783. Instituted by George III. The ruling sovereign of Great Britain and Ireland and also the lord-lieutenant of Ireland are ex-officio members.

Order of St. Stephen (*The*), 1764. Instituted by Maria Theresa of Austria for civil merit, but only nobles are eligible. The decoration is the Hungarian crown surmounted with a white cross. The motto is *Publicum meritorum præmium.*

Order of San Salvador' (*The*), 1118. Instituted in Aragon by Alfonso I.

Order of the Amaranth (*The*), 1653. Instituted by Christina of Sweden.

Order of the Annunciation.
I. A religious order, 1500, instituted at Bourges by Jeanne de Valois, daughter of Louis XI., in honour of ' the Ten Joys of the Virgin Mary'; confirmed by Pope Alexander VI. and Pope Leo X.

II. A religious order, 1604, instituted at Genoa by Maria Victoria Fornāri, called the ' Celestial Annunciades,' or

Blue Nuns, from the colour of their dresses.

There was an order of knighthood called 'Annunciada' instituted in 1362 by Amadeus VI.; reformed in 1434 by Amadeus VIII.

Order of the Augustines. *See* p. 60, ' Augustines.'

Order of the Bath. *See* ' Bath.'

Order of the Belgian Lion (*The*), 1815. Founded by William I.

Order of the Benedictines (*The*). *See* p. 67, ' Benedictines.'

Order of the Black Eagle (*The*), 1701. A Prussian order instituted by Frederick III. elector of Brandenburg. Also called ' The Order of Fidelity.'

Order of the Blood of Our Saviour (*The*), 1608. Instituted in Mantua by Duke Vincent Gonçaga. The name originated in the belief that in St. Andrew's Church, Mantua, drops of our Saviour's blood are preserved.

Order of the Burgundian Cross (*The*), 22 July, 1535. Instituted by Charles V.

Order of the Capucins (*The*). *See* p. 144, ' Capucins.'

Order of the Carmelites (*The*). *See* p. 147, ' Carmelites.'

Order of the Carthusians (*The*). *See* p. 149, ' Carthusians.'

Order of the Cincinna'ti (*The*), 1783. Established in the United States of North America, it was originally designed as an order for American officers in the War of Independence (*q.v.*), and for their eldest sons, the title to descend by primogeniture. Another purpose was the relief of the widows and orphans of those who fell in the war. The decoration is a medal representing the old Roman leaving his plough to serve the State. The order still exists.

Order of the Cistercians (*The*). *See* p. 175, ' Cistercians.'

Order of the Cordeliers (*The*). *See* p. 207, ' Cordeliers.'

Order of the Crescent. I. 1448. Instituted by Renātus of Anjou, king of Sicily.

The device of Renatus was a crescent.

II. Instituted 1799 by the sultan after the battle of the Nile. Rear-Admiral Nelson was the first knight-companion of the order.

Order of the Dannebrog (*The*), 1219. Founded by Waldemar II.; restored in 1671 by Christian V.; reconstructed 28 June, 1808, by Frederick VI.

Order of the Day (*The*). In parliamentary usage is a method of superseding a question before the house by moving that its attention be directed to the questions in the same order as they stand. Thus if the order is A, B, C, D, and the question before the house is C, a member who wants to burke the question moves that A and B be taken before C, or that the questions be taken according to 'the order of the day.' Of course, obstructionists can debate on A and B without committing themselves on C, and push C on one side.

Order of the Dominicans (*The*). *See* p. 265, 'Dominicans.'

Order of the Dove (*The*), 1379. Instituted by John I. of Castile.

Order of the Dragon (*The*), 1410. Established by Sigismond of Hungary on his marriage with Barbara his second wife. The insignia was a red cross and a gold dragon with its tail twisted round its neck.

Order of the Eagle (*The*), 1433. Founded by Kaiser Albrecht (*Albert*) II. *See* 'Order of the Black Eagle, Golden Eagle, and White Eagle.'

Order of the Elephant (*The*), 12th cent. Instituted in Denmark by Knute IV. in honour of a crusader who in a battle against the Saracens slew an elephant (1189). The order was restored in 1478 by Christian I. The decoration is an elephant carrying a tower, and the ribbon is blue moiré, passing from the right shoulder to the left side. It is reserved for princes and others of regal rank.

Order of the Franciscans (*The*). *See* p. 343, 'Franciscans.'

Order of the Garter. *See* p. 496, 'Knights of the Garter.'

Order of the Golden Angel (*The*), 312. A military order of Constantinople, instituted by Constantine. Extinct.

Order of the Golden Eagle (*The*), 1702. Instituted by Duke Eberhard Ludwig at Würtemberg. United with the Order of the Crown of Würtemberg in 1818.

Order of the Golden Fleece (*The*). Founded by Philippe III. duke of Burgundy, 10 Jan., 1429. The grandmastership of the order was disputed for twenty-four years (1700–1724) between Kaiser Karl VI. and Felipe king of Spain; but when Louis XV. of France sent back the infanta, to whom he was betrothed, the Spaniards were so indignant that they broke off their French alliance and joined Austria, and Felipe yielded to Karl the moot point. When the house of Burgundy became extinct, the grand-mastership of the order passed to the house of Austria—Karl V. transmitted it to his successors in Spain. When the dynasty failed, Philippe of Bourbon, king of Spain, with a disputed title, claimed the mastership, but the kaiser refused to renounce his prior right. This was the sore point which was healed by the alliance of Spain with Austria.

Order of the Golden Shield (*The*). Instituted by Louis II. of France (about 878) in defence of the country. The motto was *Allons!* (a call to arms). Extinct.

Order of the Golden Spur (*The*), 1534. A Roman order established by Paul III.; or, as some say, restored by him, but founded in 312 by Constantine in honour of his victory over Maxentius. Gregory XVI. reformed the order in 1841 and called it 'The Order of St. Sylvester,' or the 'Golden Spur Reformed.' The decoration is a cross of eight points, suspended on a black and red ribbon, and between the arms of the cross is a little golden spur.

Order of the Guelfs (*The*), or 'The Guelfic Order,' in Hanover, 1815. Instituted by George prince of Wales, the prince regent of England. Extinct.

Order of the Hare (*The*). Instituted by Edward III. The French raised a tremendous shout, and Edward thought it was the shout of onset, but it was occasioned by a hare running between the two armies. Extinct.

Order of the Holy Faith of Jesus Christ (*The*), 1221. A military order for a crusade against the Albigenses. Extinct.

Order of the Holy Ghost (*The*).
I. NEAPOLITAN, 25 May, 1352, instituted by Louis of Anjou, king of Naples.

II. FRENCH, 1198, instituted by Count Guy at Montpellier.

Another, 1578, instituted by Henry III. Abolished 1789; re-established in 1815, and again abolished in 1830.

Order of the Holy Phial (*The*), or 'Sainte Ampoule,' in the province of Champagne. The four barons of this order were entrusted with the care of the holy phial, in which the coronation oil of the kings of France was preserved. According to legend this phial was brought from heaven by the Holy Ghost in the form of a dove, and placed in the hands of St. Remy at the coronation of Clovis. The phial was smashed to pieces by Ruhl in 1793.

Order of the Holy Sepulchre (*The*). I. In A.D. 328. Instituted by St. Helĕna on her visit to Jerusalem at the age of 80, when the three crosses of Calvary were said to have been discovered in a cave under the temple of Venus.

II. 17 July, 1099, instituted by Godfrey of Bouillon.

Order of the Iron Crown (*The*), 1805. Instituted by Napoleon when crowned with the iron crown of Lombardy, in Milan Cathedral, king of Italy. This order in Italy corresponded with the Legion of Honour in France, also instituted by Napoleon. The number of members was at first 620, increased afterwards to 985. The badge was the iron crown (*q.v.*), in the middle the French eagle. The motto was *Dio me la diede, guai a chi la tocca* (God gave it me, woe to him who touches it).

Order of the Jacobins (*The*). *See* p. 464, 'Jacobins.'

Order of the Jesuits (*The*). *See* p. 469, 'Jesuits.'

Order of the Knights of Christ (*The*), 1317. Instituted by Dionysius king of Portugal. It acquired the possessions of the Templars in 1319, and the Grand-master was vested with the crown

by Julius III. in 1551. *See* p. 641, 'Order of Christ.'

Order of the Legion of Honour (*The*). *See* p. 513, 'Legion,' &c.

Order of the Lily (*The*), 1048. Founded in Navarre by Garcia.

Order of the Lion and the Sun (*The*), 1808. In Persia, founded by Feth Ali Shah.

Order of the Lion of Zähringen (*The*), 1812. Founded in Baden by the Grand Duke Karl.

Order of the Mathurins (*The*). *See* p. 566, 'Mathurins.'

Order of the Polar Star (*The*). A Swedish order designed for cabinet ministers, ambassadors, magistrates, and literary celebrities. The decoration is a golden cross of eight points, with a blue pole star in the centre of a medallion. The motto is *Nescit occasum*. The origin of the order is not known, but it was reorganised in 1748 by Frederick I. of Sweden.

Order of the Porcupine (*The*). A French order of knighthood. The original motto was *Cominus et eminus*, which was changed by Louis XII. into *Ultus avos Trojæ*.

Order of the Premonstratensians (*The*). *See* 'Premonstratensians.'

Order of the Red Eagle (*The*), 1705. Instituted as the 'Ordre de la Sincérité' by the margraf of Baireuth. Reconstructed as the 'Brandenburg Red Eagle' in 1734. Made the second Prussian order in 1791.

Order of the Red Staff (*The*), 1330. Instituted by Alphonso XI. of Castile and Leon.

Order of the Seraphim (*The*). Sweden, 1334. An order of chivalry instituted by Magnus II., and renewed in 1748. It is the highest order in Sweden. The badge consists of the anagram I.H.S. and a cross decorated with the winged heads of seraphs.

Order of the Servites (*The*). *See* 'Servites.'

Order of the Ship (*The*). Founded by St. Louis (IX.) on his expedition to Egypt.

Order of the Southern Cross

(*The*), 1 Dec., 1822. Created by Pedro I., first emperor of Brazil, to commemorate the independence of Brazil and the coronation of Pedro. The ribbon is light blue, and the legend *Benemerentium premium*. On the reverse is the portrait of Pedro in a cross, enamelled in white, with the southern constellation in its centre figured by 19 stars.

Order of the Star (*The*),

'Ordre de l'Etoile,' 1350. Founded in France by Jean II. le Bon for those wounded in battle or tournaments. These knights made a vow never to retreat more than a mile before an enemy, when they were to turn at bay and either conquer or die. It was well nigh extinct in 1460.

Order of the Star of India

(*The*), 1861. Instituted by Queen Victoria for conspicuous merit and loyalty. The Viceroy of India is *ex officio* grandmaster, and several native princes are knights of the order.

Order of the Swan (*The*), 1443.

Instituted by the elector Friedrich II. of Brandenburg, and restored in 1843 by Friedrich Wilhelm IV. of Prussia.

Order of the Sword.

I. Created in Sweden, 1522, by Gustavus I., and reconstructed in 1748 by Frederick I., for fidelity to the king and the Lutheran faith. The decoration is a St. Andrew's cross formed by two swords, and an azure globe with three crowns.

II. An order of chivalry instituted in 1449 by Alfonso V. of Portugal.

Order of the Theatins (*The*).

See 'Theatins.'

Order of the Thistle (*The*), 809.

Said to have been instituted by Archaïcus king of the Scots. It was renewed in 1540 by James V. of Scotland; again in 1687 by James II. of Great Britain; and again by Queen Anne.

The rue mixed with the thistles is a pun on the word Andrew. That is: 'Thistles and Rue.'

Order of the Trappists (*The*).

See 'Trappists.'

Order of the Virgin's Looking Glass (*The*), 1419. Instituted by

Ferdinand of Castile.

Order of the White Eagle

(*The*), 1325. Instituted by Ladislaus V. in Poland. Suppressed in 1638. Restored by Augustus II. in 1705. Included in the Russian orders 1832.

Order of the White Falcon,

1732. Instituted by Ernest Augustus of Saxe-Weimar. The idea is expressed in the motto *Vigilando ascendimus*.

See under 'ORDRE.'

Orders (*Holy*).

The profession of a clergyman. Every clergyman, after ordidation, is said to be in holy orders. In the Scotch and other Presbyterian churches ministers 'licensed to preach the gospel' are called *licentiates* or *probationers* till they are ordained over some pastorate.

Orders (*Social*), or 'Castes.'

At one time it was well nigh impossible to rise out of the social order in which one was born, and marriages were, of course, restricted to castes also.

In ancient EGYPT there were four social orders: priests, the military, the merchant class, and the artisans.

In FRANCE [*ancient régime*] there were only three recognised orders: the clergy, the noblesse, and the tiers état.

In INDIA the four great castes are: (1) the *Brahmans* or the sacerdotal order; (2) the *Chutria* or the military order; (3) the *Vaisya* or the mercantile class; and (4) the *Sudras* or working class.

In ancient ROME we find only three recognised social orders: senators, the equestrian order, and the plebeians.

In SWEDEN the four social orders are: the nobles, the clergy, tradesmen, and peasantry.

Orders in Council

are acts of the Privy Council made by the sovereign (who is personally present) by advice of the privy council. If the sovereign is not present, they are called 'Acts of the Lords of the Council.'

Orders of Mendicants (*The*).

See p. 571, 'Mendicant.'

Orders of the Church.

See under 'Church' and 'Monastic Orders.'

Ordinaires (*Les*).

The French royal bodyguard which, in the reign of Henri III. (1574–1589), supplanted the Scottish Archers, and were by Louis XIII. (1622) changed into the celebrated Musketeers (*q.v.*).

Of course the word has other meanings, as the ecclesiastical superior who has ordinary jurisdiction; the book which indicates the church service for each day in the year; the *ordinaire de la messe*, and so on. 'Ordinaires' (3 syl.)

Ordinance for the State of Ireland (*The*), 1289.

Vindicates the right of the English Parliament to bind Ireland (17 Edw. I.).

Ordinance for the Suppression of Blasphemies and Heresies, 1647. A statute passed with triumphant majorities after King Charles I. was made prisoner by Colonel Hamilton, governor of the Isle of Wight. It was aimed at Cromwell and his favourers, and provided that any one who denied the doctrine of the Trinity, the divinity of Christ, or that the Bible is the word of God, or anyone who denies the resurrection of the body, or a future day of judgment, shall suffer death. Anyone who denies man's free will to turn to God, anyone who affirms that there is a purgatory, that images are lawful, or that infant baptism is unlawful, shall be committed to prison. Anyone who denies the obligation of observing the Lord's Day, or that church government by presbytery is unlawful, shall be committed to prison.

Ordinance of the 5th September, 1815. Reducing the number of French deputies from 459 to 260, and declaring that no article of the ' Charte Constitutionelle' (*q.v.*) should be revised.

Ordinanze della Giustizia, 1282. A law of Florence excluding all nobles from the government.

Ordinary (*The*), in church matters means the bishop of the diocese; but in emergency a rector or vicar of a parish may act as ordinary. It means one who in ecclesiastical matters has chief authority in a parish.

The word has several other meanings: as the soldier who waits on an officer ; a daily meal at a fixed price, or the place where it is given; part of an escutcheon, &c.

Ordnance. A name given to whatever concerns artillery.

Board of Ordnance. In 1683 the board consisted of five principal officers, besides the master-general, a lieutenant-general, the surveyor-general, clerk of the ordnance, storekeeper, and clerk of deliveries. It deliberates, regulates, and orders everything relating to the artillery and garrison.

Master-General of the Ordnance. Commander-in-chief of the artillery corps. He used to have the sole command of the Royal Regiment of Artillery, but was assisted by a lieutenant-general. The office was abolished 25 May, 1855, and the duties transferred to the secretary of state for war.

Ordnance Select Committee (*The*). A committee of officers who advise the secretary of state for war on all inventions submitted to them. Their office is at Woolwich, near the headquarters of the Royal Artillery. The committee contains 2 artillery officers, 1 officer of the engineers, and 1 officer of the line, with secretary and assistant secretary both in the artillery.

Ordnance Survey. The survey of the British dominions by the Ordnance Department, who also prepare maps and plans both of the whole kingdom and also of its parts.

Of Great Britain: England commenced by Roy in 1784 ; Scotland in 1809 ; England and Wales completed January 1870.

Of Ireland: commenced 1824, and completed in 1840.

Of India, commenced by Lambton in 1801.

Ordonnances. Laws made by the French king, beginning with the words, *Au nom du roi*, and ending with the clause *car tel est notre plaisir.* The three famous ordinances of Charles X. led to the revolution of 1830: (1) Abolished the liberty of the press ; no journal might be issued before being submitted to government inspection ; (2) the chamber of deputies was dissolved; and (3) two-thirds of the electors were disfranchised; and the number of deputies was reduced nearly one-half.

Ordre de Léopold (*L'*), 1832. A Belgian order created by King Leopold for patriotic services. The decoration is a white cross. The motto is *L'union fait la force.* The ribbon is red moiré.

Ordre de l'Epic (*L'*), 1450. Instituted by François I. duc de Bretagne. The collar was of gold braid representing *ears of corn* in saltire, at the end of which hung an ermine, with the legend *A ma vie.* The order expired when Britanny was annexed to the crown of France. *See* ' Ordre de l'Hermine.'

'Epic ' here means a spike or ear of corn. Old French épic=*spica*.

Ordre de la Geneste (2 syl.), 1234. Instituted by St. Louis (IX.) on his marriage with Marguerite of Provence. The collar was decorated with broom

flowers and *fleurs de lis* in gold. *See*
p. 643, ' Order of St. Genette.'

Ordre de l'Hermine, 1381. Instituted by Jean V. duc de Bretagne, on
his reconciliation with the French and
with Clisson. The insignia was a collar
of gold charged with ermines, and the
motto *A ma vie.*

Ordre de la Toison d'Or. *See*
p. 636, ' Order of the Golden Fleece.'

Ordre de St. Michel (*L'*), 1 Aug.,
1469. A military order instituted by
Louis XI. at Amboise, in honour of St.
Michael, the patron saint of France. At
first the chevaliers were limited to 36, but
they were subsequently increased to 100,
the reigning king being the grand-master.
It ceased to exist in 1830.

Ordre des Humiliés, 1134. A
religious confraternity of Milan, instituted
by St. John de Méda, of the rule of St.
Benedict. Suppressed in 1571.

Ordre du Mérite Militaire
(*L'*), 1759. Instituted by Louis XV. to
honour Protestants of the French army
disqualified by their religious tenets
for being 'Chevaliers de St. Louis.'
Their decoration was a star of eight
points *cantonnée de fleurs de lis.* The
motto was *Pro virtute bellica.* It was
abolished in 1830.

Ordre du St. Esprit (*L'*), 1578. An
order of chivalry instituted by Henri III.
in memory of his being elected King of
Poland on the day of Pentecost. The
chevaliers were limited to 100, of which 9
were ecclesiastics. The cross bore the
image of the Holy Spirit, and was suspended on a blue ribbon. Every member
must be a Catholic, and a Knight of St.
Michael. Suppressed in 1789. Revived
at the Restoration, but again suppressed
in 1830.

Orebro, in Sweden (*Treaty of*),
6 July, 1812, between Great Britain and
Sweden. Its object was to circumvent
Napoleon, who had invaded Russia with
450,000 men.

Oregon (U.S. America). So called,
in 1846, from its river of the same name.
The inhabitants are nicknamed *Webfeet*
and *Hard-cases.*

Oriel College (*Oxford*), 1326.
Founded by Edward II. The head of the
college is called the provost

28

Oriental France. So Germany
was called in the time of Charlemagne,
still preserved in the name Franconia, a
circle of Germany containing nearly 9,000
square miles.

Orientation, in churches, means
their position more or less correctly due
east and west. Very few churches stand
due east and west, but the deviation seems
owing to the carelessness of the builders
or to some local cause.

It cannot be due to the position of the sun on
the day of the patron and saint, as churches dedicated to the same saint do not occupy the same
p sition.

Similarly it cannot typify the bending head of
the crucified Saviour, because no uniform rule is
observed in church orientation.

Oriflamme (*The*). The flag of St.
Denis, made by Philippe I. in 1082 the
standard of France. A phonetic form
of the Latin *Auri-flamma*, or flame of
gold. The oriflamme was a large red
banner mounted on a gilt staff, the loose
end of the flag being cut into three
tongues resembling flames, between each
of which was a green silk tassel. When
the counts of Vexin became possessed of
the abbey of St. Denis, the oriflamme
passed into their hands, but in 1082
Philippe I. united Vexin to the crown,
and the oriflamme became a royal banner. (St. Denis = *Sahn Dnee*.)

The first time it was displayed in a battlefield
was in 1119, when war was declared with England;
and the last time was at the battle of Agincourt
in 1415. On both occasions the French were compelled to sue for peace. It was made of red taffeta,
and was without device. Called golden from the
gilt staff.

Orkney Islands (*The*). The Or-
kejar or Orkeyjar, the Northern Islands
of the Norwegians, as distinguished from
the Sudrejar or Southern Islands, now
called Sodor (*q.v.*), and the Western, or
Hebrides.

Orkney, Latin *Orcădes*, is probably connected
with the Norwegian *orcan* or *orken*, a hurricane.

Orkneyinga Saga (*The*). History
of the men of Orkney. This saga was
printed among the Icelandic Sagas for
the Master of the Rolls in 1887. It is in
Icelandic and not translated.

Orleanists (*The*). *See* ' Armagnacs.'

Orléans (*House of*). A younger
branch of the Bourbons represented in
France by Louis-Philippe (1830–1848).

The Orléans-Orléans was Louis XII. (1498-1515),
and the Orléans-Angoulême consisted of François
I., Henri II., François II., Charles IX., and Hen
III. (1515-1589).

Orléans. *The Plot of Gaston duc d'Orléans,* 1632. This was a plot to murder Richelieu, the obnoxious minister of Louis XIII. The duke induced Henri de Montmorency to join it, and they succeeded in raising a revolt in Languedoc. The cardinal sent troops to quell the revolt; a battle was fought; the insurgents were defeated; and Montmorency, being taken prisoner, was beheaded.

Orleton's Message. Adam Orleton, bishop of Hereford, sent this ambiguous message to the keeper of Berkeley Castle, 21 Sept., 1327 : ' Edwardum occidere nolite timere bonum est.' This may be either a command to murder the king, or not to murder him, according to the way the words are pointed. Thus : ' Edwardum occidere nolite timere,— bonum est ' (to kill Edward fear not, it is right); or, ' Edwardum occidere nolite, —timere bonum est ' (do not kill Edward; it is right to dread doing so). *See* p. 638, ' Oracle of Delphi.'

Wolsey, in early life. was cautioned to ' beware of Kingston.' The warning made a great impression on his superstitious mind, and he would never enter the town of Kingston (on the Thames). When he was confined to his cell by order of Henry VIII. a blare of trumpets announced the approach of armed officials, and Sir William Kingston entered. Then the warning of his younger days flashed across him in a new light, and, bowing his head, he uttered those memorable words, ' If I had served my God as faithfully as I have served my king, He would not have forsaken me in my grey hairs.'

HENRY IV. of England was told he should ' die in Jerusalem,' which he took for granted meant the Holy Land ; but he died in the Jerusalem Chamber, London, the chapter-house of Westminster Abbey.

CAMBYSES, son of Cyrus, was told that he should die in Ecbatâna, which he supposed meant the capital of Media. Being wounded accidentally in Syria he asked the name of the place, and being told it was called Ecbatana, he replied, ' Here, then, I am destined to end my life.'

When in 1568 the Countess of Egmont implored Alva to spare the life of her husband, he replied, ' Certainly, madam, he shall be released to-morrow morning.' The countess thought the duke meant her husband would be released from prison, but Alva meant that he would be executed and released from life.

Jourdain the wizard told Somerset, if he wished to live, to ' avoid where castles mounted stand.' The duke died in an alehouse called ' the Castle,' which stood in St. Albans.

. These punning prophecies are very numerous, and somewhat amusing.

Orloff Diamond (*The*). Weighs 194¾ carats, and is set on the top of the imperial sceptre of Russia. It is of pure water, and about the size of a pigeon's egg. It is said to have been one of the eyes of an idol in a temple in India. Subsequently it came into the possession of Shah Nadir of Persia ; and, when the Shah

was murdered, it was stolen by a French grenadier, who sold it to an English sea-captain for 2,000*l.* The captain brought it to England, and sold it to a Jew merchant for 12,000*l.* The Jew sold it to Shafras, an Armenian merchant, and in 1775 Catharine II. of Russia bought it of Shafras for 90,000*l.*, and a pension for life of 4,000*l.* per annum. *See* ' Diamonds.'

Ormond Crown (*The*). A silver 5*s.* piece coined in Dublin 1643 for circulation in Ireland. Called Ormond from the proclamation of the Duke of Ormond, then lord-lieutenant of Ireland, establishing its currency.

Orphanites (3 syl.). A sect of Hussites (2 syl.) who professed unbounded admiration of Ziska, their chief, and after his death, thinking no one worthy to succeed him, wanted to place the government of affairs in the hands of a council. They were annihilated in 1434 by the Calixtines (*q.v.*).

Orphica. An enormous mass of literature which in the 3rd and 4th centuries grew out of the old Orphic myths and songs, not dissimilar to the Ossian of Macpherson, based, it may be, on some threads of older literature. Not only the Hellenists but the church fathers referred to those forgeries as to primitive and authentic sources of Greek religion, from which Pythagoras, Heraclîtos, and Plato had drawn their theological philosophy. Wesseling and Lobeck have demonstrated that these writings are forgeries of the 3rd and 4th cents.; and that, so far from being the sources of the Greek mythology, they are wholly deduced from Hesiod and Homer. *See* ' Literary Forgeries.'

Orry King, or ' Ree Gorree,' of Manx. There was in the island at one time a ' King Orry's Tower,' now the residence of the lord bishop. It is supposed that Orry was a Norwegian who fled to Man during the desolating wars of Harold Harfaga ; that he succeeded in establishing his sway over the island, and was a wise, vigorous, and politic ruler. To him Man is indebted for its legislative government. He held his court at Tynwald Hill, and his descendants continued to rule the island till 1077, when Godred IV. routed the islanders, and established a new dynasty.

Orsini Conspiracy (*The*), 14 Jan., 1858. A most infamous attempt was made to assassinate Napoleon III., as, with the Empress, he was driven to the French opera. The carriage (8·30) had just arrived at the door of the Italian Opera, in the Rue Lepelletier, when a bomb was thrown at it which exploded and killed twenty persons. A second was then thrown which killed one of the imperial horses. A third burst under the carriage; but, though the carriage was shattered, one of the horses was killed, and the aide-de-camp in the same carriage, the Emperor and Empress escaped with very slight injuries. Count Felix Orsini, Colonel Pierri, Gomez a domestic, and Rudio were arrested. The first three were executed, and Rudio was transported for life. The French ambassador remonstrated with the British Government for harbouring such villains, and Lord Palmerston brought in a bill for the punishment of conspiracy to murder. In the meantime the French colonels demanded to be allowed to extirpate the English nation. This, of course, roused a strong feeling, and the bill was lost by a majority of 19.

The life of Napoleon III. was attempted six times. *See* 'Napoleon III.' The silly bluster of the French colonels was called at the time 'Cock-a-doodle-do.'

Ortliebians (4 syl.), 1212. A branch of the 'Brethren of the Free Spirit' (*q.v.*) in Alsace, whose leader was a fanatic named Ortlieb. They spread into Thurgau and the Upper and Lower Rhine. They were pantheists, and in France were popularly called Turlupins.

Osmanlee, 1300. A Turk, or follower of Othman, founder of the Turkish empire. Othman interpreted Islam (the Mohammedan creed) in his own way. To call an Osmanlee a Turk is considered an insult.

Osman or Othman is a contraction of Al Thaman (the Bone-breaker). That is O'thaman, O'th'man, Osman.

Ossorian Wolves. Giraldus Cambrensis tells us of a certain race in Ossory who were transformed every seven years into wolves. This is not given as history, but as the statement of an historian.

De quodam hominum genere . . . . Ossyriensium, unde quolibet septennio per imprecationem sancti cujusdam Natalis . . . . formam . . . . humanam prorsus exuentes, induunt lupinam.—GIRALDUS.

Osso'rians (*The*). The inhabitants of Ossory, which comprised the present county of Kilkenny, with parts of Tipperary and Queen's County.

Os'suary of Morat, Switzerland (*The*), 1416. Made of the bones of the Burgundians slain by the Swiss in the battle of Morat, 22 June, 1476. It was destroyed by the French in 1798, and in 1822 a stone obelisk was erected on the spot.

Ostiarius. St. Ignatius in his letter to the faithful of Antioch mentions this church officer. His duties were to open the book for the officiating priest; to keep the keys of the church, and to be responsible for the cleanliness and good order of the church and its furniture; to open and close the doors at the right time; to maintain good order in the congregation; and to prevent the entrance of any Jew or heathen. They were always elderly men.

Our beadle has many of the duties of the more ancient ostiarius.

Ostrogoths. Goths of the East, in opposition to the Visigoths or Goths of the West. They disappear from history in 553.

Oswald's Law, A.D. 962. The law of Oswald archbishop of York that all collegiate chapters be turned into Benedictine fraternities, and if any chapter refused to make this change, then was an opposition church, under the special patronage of the Virgin, to be set up.

Otrepieff the Pretender. Gregory Otrepieff, a runaway monk of Ischoudoff, in Russia, was the first of the impostors who impersonated Dmitri V. son of Ivan the Terrible, put to death in his infancy by Boris Godounoff, in 1591. Supported by Sigismund II. king of Poland, he overthrew Boris and reigned at Moscow in 1605. His marriage to a Pole and a Catholic led to his massacre by the multitude in 1606. *See* 'Pougatcheff.'

Ottanta (*The*). *See* 'Eighty.'

Otta'va Rima. The stanza of the later Italian writers like Boccaccio. Byron's 'Don Juan' is an English example. Lines 1, 3, 5 rhyme, and lines 2, 4, 6 rhyme, while 7, 8 rhyme independently. Called *ottava* because it is an eight-line stanza. *See* 'Terza Rima.'

Ottima'ti (*The*). The aristocracy of Florence.

Otto I. the Lion, and 'the Great King' of Germany. The second of the Saxon dynasty (912, king of Germany 936–973, emperor of the Romans 961–973).

Father, Heinrich I. the Fowler; *Mother*, Mechtildis; *Wives*, (1) Eadgyth daughter of Edward the Elder, and granddaughter of Alfred the Great; (2) Adelheid widow of Lothaire king of Lombardy. *Contemporary* with Athelstan, Edmund, Edred, Edwy, and Edgar the Peaceful.

Otto II. of Germany. 'The Red,' 'the Bloody,' 'the Pale Death of the Saracens' (955, 973–983).

Father, Otto I. the Great; *Mother*, Eadgyth granddaughter of Alfred the Great; *Wife*, Theophānia daughter of Romānus II. emperor of the East. *Contemporary* with Edgar, Edward the Martyr, and Ethelred the Unready.
** Called 'the Bloody' from the Bloody Banquet. *See* 'Otto's Bloody Banquet.'

Otto III. the Wonder of the World. Born 980; king of Germany 983–1002; kaiser of the Holy Roman Empire 996–1002.

Father, Otto II.; *Mother*, Theophānia; *Wife*, Mary daughter of the king of Aragon, burnt to death for adultery. *Contemporary* with Ethelred.

Otto's Bloody Banquet, 981. The Romans, desirous of freeing themselves from the German yoke, formed a conspiracy to make Rome a republic. This conspiracy was revealed to Otto II. of Germany, and the kaiser, pretending to know nothing about it, invited the chief of the conspirators to a banquet. When the guests were seated, Otto stamped with his foot, and the hall was filled with armed men. The kaiser then deliberately unrolled a paper, and as he read aloud the names the victims were dragged from table and strangled.

Ottoman Empire (*The*). The 'empire of the Osmanlis,' *i.e.* all those countries under the Turkish sultan. So called from Ottoman or Othman (1289–1326), who had laid the foundation of the independent sovereignty of the Turks.

Otway the poet, we are told, being in a starving condition, had a guinea given him. He went immediately and bought a loaf of bread, but died swallowing the first mouthful. Allusion to this tale is often made.

Ouida. The pen-name of Miss Louise de la Ramé. The name was suggested by a little girl who said Weeda for Louisa.

Our Boys. An inner circle of Moonlighters (*q.v.*), who had their own captains, subservient to Captain Moonlight. They were armed, some with revolvers, and some with other weapons. Their objects were to compel men to belong to the Land or National League, to terrorise those who took evicted farms or who dealt with persons boycotted. *See* 'Irish Associations.'

Our Lady of Mercy. Mme. Tallien (1774–1831), daughter of Cabarrus, a Spanish banker. Called 'Our Lady of Mercy' because she was always pleading for the life of some one condemned to death by the revolutionary tribunal.

Our Lady of Walsingham. An image of the Virgin Mary in the abbey of Little Walsingham, Norfolk. This was the most famous image in all England. Persons of all degrees paid their vows and made offerings to it, and the most extravagant miracles were ascribed to it. It was burnt at Chelsea in 1538.

In the last age, whoever had not made a visit and an offering to the Blessed Virgin of this place [Walsingham] was looked upon as impious.—CAMDEN.
Henry VIII., when a boy, walked from Barham barefoot to the shrine, and presented to the image a necklace of great value. Its secret springs were exposed to the public before it was destroyed.

Out in the '15, *i.e.* in the rebel army of the Pretender in 1715 (Geo. I.). *See below.*

Anderson of Whitburgh, a gentleman whose father had been out in the '15.—HOWITT, *Hist. of Eng.* (Geo. I., p. 500).

Out in the '45, *i.e.* in the rebel army of the Young Pretender in 1745. *See above.*

Outburgers. Called in German 'Ausburgers.' Aliens who had been admitted to privileges of citizenship, though resident at a distance from the city. In consequence of this 'privilege' they claimed exemption from all dues to their feudal lord; and if the lord resisted this unreasonable claim, he had to do battle with the city which threw its shield over the Outburger.

Outed Prelates (*The*). The Scotch episcopate disestablished in 1689.

Alexander Rose, the last survivor of the outed prelates.—ROBERT CHAMBERS, *The Threiplands of Fingask.*

Ovate. A kind of Druidical curate or deacon. The heads of the hierarchy were *Druids*, the next in rank the *Bards*, and the third order was that of *Ovates*. Old English *ofydd*, a sapling or young shoot.

Overthrow of the Geraldines (3 syl.) in Ireland (*The*), 1535. The Geraldines were great Norman lords in the south of Ireland. They had been suffered by Henry VII. to govern Ireland in the name of the English crown; but when Henry VIII. was king, he resolved to be supreme in Ireland, and Lord Thomas Fitzgerald revolted. Skeffington, the new lord deputy, levelled to the ground Maynooth, the stronghold of the Geraldines, and wholly extirpated the family, leaving only a single boy to preserve the name.

Ovid (*The French*). Du Bellay (1524–1560). Also called the 'Father of Grace and Elegance.'

Ovid of the English Nation (*The*). Michael Drayton (1563–1631). So called by Dr. Heylin in his 'Cosmographia,' p. 303 (1637).

Ovid's Tower. About two leagues from Karansebês, upon a steep hill, stands a small square tower so called; and tradition asserts that the Roman poet was confined there by Augustus for having written his 'Art of Love.' This is most improbable. No doubt the poet was banished from Rome for some offence, but not for writing shaky poetry, and the place of his banishment was most likely Tomi in Thrace.

Owen Meredith. A pen-name assumed by Lord Lytton, British ambassador in Paris; under which name he published a number of poems. One of the windows in Knebworth Church is that of Owen Tudor, and the other is that of Ann Meredith. These windows are memorials of Lord Lytton's family on the paternal side.

Lord Lytton, *i.e.* the Right Hon. Edward Robert Bulwer-Lytton, created earl in 1880; son of Edward Lytton Bulwer 2nd Baron Lytton, the novelist, who died 1873. Owen Meredith was born 1831.

Owlglass the Jester, 1493; but the earliest copy now known is dated 1540. Thyl Owlglass was the son of a poor Brunswick peasant who lived by his wits, and was cramful of practical jokes—half knavery and half fun. He was servant, charlatan, lansquenet, artist, disputant, monk, blacksmith, cook, miller, and so on. He died 1350. Thyl was a little squat figure, with sharp keen eyes, red beard and hair. The American Clockmaker is not unlike Thyl Owlglass. Called in Germany ' Eulenspiegel.'

Ox (*The*). Domenichi'no (1581–1641). When so called by his fellow-students on account of his plodding slowness, Annibal Carracci remarked that the ' Ox will plough a fruitful field.' *See below.*

Ox (*The Dumb*). Thomas Aquinas the ' Angelic Doctor' (1224–1274). So called by his fellow-students at Cologne on account of his taciturnity and dulness; but Albertus said, ' We call him the Dumb Ox, but he will one day give such a bellow as shall be heard from one end of the world to the other.'

Also called ' the Great Sicilian Ox.' The family was allied to the kings of Sicily. He was also of unusual size, very tall and stout in proportion.

Oxford Act of 1665 (*The*). The act of parliament more usually called ' The Five-mile Act,' which banished nonconforming ministers five miles from any parliamentary town.

Oxford Colleges. (Those in italics are halls.)

	Head	When founded
Alban's (St.) Hall ...	...	1550
All Souls ...	Warden ...	1437
Balliol	Master ...	1263
Brasenose ...	Principal ...	1509
Christ Church ...	Dean ...	1525
Corpus Christi ...	President ...	1516
Edmund (St.) Hall	...	1559
Exeter	Rector ...	1314
Hertford ...	Principal ...	1282
Jesus	Principal ...	1571
John's (St.) ...	President ...	1557
Keble	Warden ...	1870
Lincoln ...	Rector ...	1427
Magdalen ...	President ...	1458
Magdalen Hall (dissolved 1874)	...	1487
Mary (St.) Hall	...	1239
Merton	Warden ...	1264
New College ...	Warden ...	1386
New Inn Hall	...	1438
Oriel	Provost ...	1326
Pembroke	Master ...	1624
Queen s	Provost ...	1340
Trinity	President ...	1554
University	Master ...	872
		restored 1240
Wadham	Warden ...	1613
Worcester	Provost ...	1714

And two private halls : Charsley and Turrell.

** Magdalen Hall was incorporated with Hertford College in 1874.

Mansfield College, 1889. The first Nonconformist college at Oxford, The chief object of the college is the education of young men for the congregational ministry; the first '*Principal*' being Dr. Fairbairn.

To these may be added Lady Margaret Hall and Somerville Hall for ladies.

Oxford's Masterpiece (*The Earl of*). The monopoly of trade to the South Seas granted to a company of merchants incorporated as the South Sea Company.

Oxford's Miss (*Lord*). Elizabeth Davenport, actress, called by Pepys 'Roxalana,' from a favourite character in 'The Siege of Rhodes.'

Oxford of Belgium (*The*). The University of Louvain founded 1834 at Malines for the union of divine and secular knowledge. The following year it was transferred to Louvain.

Oxford of Holland (*The*). Leyden.

Oxford Tract Movement, 1833–1841. A religious revival which originated at Oxford by the publication of certain pamphlets called 'Tracts for the Times,' chiefly by Pusey, Newman, and Keble. These tracts taught the dogmas of the divine origin of the church, the apostolic order of the clergy, and the high church doctrines. Church architecture, church renovation, clerical dresses, and all externals of religion were more carefully attended to; but, at the same time, it must be confessed that an enormous accession to the Roman Catholic Church was the result, and a long disputation about such things as vestments, candles, genuflexions, and so on.

Oxford University. The heads of the several colleges have the following titles.—

Of 1 he is called the *Dean*, viz. the head of Christ Church.

Of 3 he is called the *Master*, viz. of Balliol, Pembroke, and University College.

Of 4 he is called the *President*, viz. of Corpus, Magdalen, St. John's, and Trinity.

Of 3 he is called the *Principal*, viz. of Brasenose, Jesus, and Hertford; and of the 4 halls (New Inn, St. Alban's, St. Edmund, and St. Mary). To these add Mansfield.

Of 3 he is called the *Provost*, viz. of Oriel, Queen's, and Worcester.

Of 2 he is called the *Rector*, viz. of Exeter and Lincoln.

Of 5 he is called the *Warden*, viz. of All Souls, Keble, Merton, New College, and Wadham.

In Cambridge University the head of every college except two is called the *Master*, that of King's is called the *Provost*, and that of Queens' is called the *President*.

Oyer and Terminer, to hear and determine. A commission granted by the crown to judges of assize, &c., to 'hear and determine' all cases of treason, felony, and trespass brought before them on their respective circuits.

Pacata, or Pezade (2 syl.). *Un impôt de la paix*, 1040. Levied during the 'Truce of God' for the establishment of a militia to enforce obedience to the truce.

Paccanarists, followers of Paccanari. Paccanari was a Tyrolean priest who died about 1802. He founded the order called 'Les Pères de la Foi' after that of the Jesuits was abolished by Clement XIV. in 1773.

Pacha of Egypt (*The*). A diamond cut on eight sides. It weighs 40 carats, and cost 700,000 francs [28,000*l.*]. *See* 'Diamonds.'

Paciferes (3 syl.), 14th cent. Armed peasantry of France, associated together to resist the Grand Companies which plundered and oppressed the people.

Pacific Parliament (*The*). A triennial parliament dissolved 8 Aug., 1713. A Tory parliament noted for the treaty of peace signed at Utrecht after a war of eleven years. Bolingbroke and Oxford were its chief members. *See* 'Parliaments.'

No assembly but one composed as this was could have sat quiet under such a peace.—BURNET, *Own Time*.

Pacificateur de la Vendée (*Le*). Lazarus Hoche (1768–1797). So called because in 1796 he brought the Vendéan war to an end.

Pacification (*Edict of*). The same as the 'Edict of Amboise' (*q.v.*). Called the 'Edict of Pacification' because it closed the first religious war of France (19 March, 1563).

Pacification of Dunse (*The*), 18 June, 1639. The arrangement made with the Covenanters who had encamped on a hill called Dunse Law, when

Charles I. tried to enforce episcopacy and the English Prayer Book on the people. Charles, fearing the result of a battle, proposed terms of peace, and agreed to leave to a convocation all church matters. By this convocation presbytery was restored, episcopacy in Scotland was abolished, and the existing bishops were deprived of their titles and sees.

Dunse Law is an elevated spot some 630 feet high, north of the town.

Pacification of Ghent (The).
Signed 8 Nov., 1576. An accommodation between Holland *cum* Zealand and the Catholic states of the Netherlands, providing that no foreign soldiers should be permitted in the states, and that all the signatories should help each other against all opponents. This treaty was known as 'The Perpetual Peace.'

Pacification of Passau, in
Bavaria (*The*), 7 Aug., 1552. Securing freedom of religion to Protestants. This 'pacification' led to the 'Religious Peace of Augsburg,' 26 Sept., 1555.

Passau pronounce *Pas-sow* (ow as in 'now').

Pacification of Vienna (The),
23 June, 1606. Concluded between the Archduke Mathias of Austria and the ministers of Botskai of Hungary. By this treaty Hungary was split into three parts, of which Turkey possessed 1,859 square miles, Botskai in Hungary and Transylvania 2,082 square miles, and Austria 1,222 square miles.

Pacificator of Europe (The).
Benedict XIII. (1724–1730). He pacified the angry antagonists of the bull Unigenitus (*q.v.*) by his bull Pretiosus (*q.v.*). He pacified the Sicilians, who were in contention about the 'Tribunal de Monarchia.' He settled the controversy with the king of Sardinia respecting the right of nomination to certain abbacies and benefices in Piedmont And he brought about the treaty of Seville in 1729 between England, France, Spain, and Holland, thereby settling the succession of Tuscany and Parma.

Pack-Monday Fair. Held the
first Monday after 10 Oct. at Sherborne. It was held in the churchyard, and blowing cows' horns was a distinguishing feature of it. Said to be in commemoration of the completion of the church.

Pacta Conventa. Polish covenants
between the nobles and the person nominated for the crown. The first was in 1355, between the Polish nobles and Louis I. of Hungary, who was invited to accept the crown of Poland. These pacts made Poland virtually an oligarchy, and were the real cause of its downfall. Of 1573. Passed by Henry of Valois, securing freedom of worship and equality of rights to all Poles. Formally abolished in 1736. These covenants were signed by every king of Poland at his coronation. They not only disavowed all religious distinctions, but also strictly limited and defined the powers and prerogatives of the crown.

Pacte de Famille (La), 15 Aug.,
1761. Signed at the instigation of the Duc de Choiseul by the king of France, the king of Spain, and the duke of Parma, all of whom were of the Bourbon family. Its object was to break down the maritime superiority of England, but it was an utter failure. The king of the Two Sicilies refused to subscribe the treaty, and in 1789 other affairs superseded it in interest.

Pacte de Famine (La), 1765–1789.
Monopolists of corn who brought great misery on France, especially in the years 1767–1769, 1775–1778, 1788–1789. The events of 1789 put an end to this abominable traffic.

Pædagogy (The). See p. 27, 'Andrews (University of St.).'

Pædobaptists. Those Protestant
dissenters who practise infant baptism, in contradistinction to the Baptists, who allow adult baptism alone, and that after a personal confession of faith.

The Church of England and the Presbyterians are Pædobaptists, but applied to these churches the word only denotes a practical doctrine carried out by these Christians. As a distinctive title it is opposed to Baptists, and applies chiefly, if not entirely, to the Independents or Congregationalists (*q.v.*).

Pains and Penalties. Acts of
parliament to attaint particular persons of treason or felony, or to inflict pains and penalties beyond or contrary to common law, to serve a special purpose. They are new laws *pro re nata.* When Queen Caroline wife of George IV. was tried, she was proceeded against by a 'Bill of Pains and Penalties,' but was acquitted.

Painted Chamber (*The*). *Chambre peinte*. Anciently St. Edward's Chamber. It was destroyed by fire with the houses of Parliament in 1834. When, at the beginning of this cent., the tapestry and wainscoting were taken down, it was discovered that the interior had been originally painted with single figures and historical subjects, arranged round the chamber in six bands, somewhat like the Bayeux tapestry. Careful drawings were made at the time by J. T. Smith, and drawings by Charles Stothard were engraved in 1819 for the 'Vetusta Monumenta.'

Painter of Nature (*The*). So the French called Belleau, one of their Pleiad poets (1528–1577). His chief poem is entitled 'Loves and Transformations of the Precious Stones.'

Painters (*Father of Modern*). John Cimabue of Florence (1240–1300).

Paire de Gants. *Donnez-nous notre paire de gants.* Famous royalist song during the 'Hundred Days' in the mouths of all the *dames des halles* of Paris. It was a pun on 'Donnez-nous notre père de Ghent,' referring to Louis XVIII., who was residing at Ghent.

Pairs de France (*Les*). Philippe Auguste fixed the number at twelve, half of whom were seculars and half ecclesiastics. The secular peers were the duc de Normandie, the duc de Bourgogne, the duc de Guyenne, the comte de Flandre, the comte de Toulouse, and the comte de Champagne; the ecclesiastical peers were the archbishop of Reims, and the bishops of Laon, Langres, Beauvais, Châlons, and Noyon. Subsequently, the number was unlimited. All princes of the blood were *pairs-nés*. Peers were abolished in 1798, but were re-established in 1814 at the Restoration. In 1831 the heredity of peerage was abolished, and all peers were nominated by the crown. The Chamber of Peers was called the *Cour des pairs*, and at the Restoration formed a corps législatif with the House of Deputies, but in 1848 the House of Peers was superseded by the Senate.

Paishdadians. *See* 'Pishdadian Dynasty.'

Paix Boiteuse (*La*), 1570. There was signed at St. Germain in 1562 an edict which forbade the Calvinists to levy troops and preach against the Roman Catholic religion, but it authorised their holding religious services in country places. In 1570 a peace was signed between the Catholics and Protestants; but it was neither sincere nor durable. It was called 'La Paix Boiteuse et Malassise,' because its terms were drawn up by H. Mesmes and signed by Biron. Biron was *boiteux*, and Mesmes was seigneur de Malassise, but the insincerity of the affair gave point to the puns *boiteux* and *mal assise* (lame and unstable).

Paix Fourrée (*La*), 9 May, 1409. Between the children of the Duc d'Orléans (recently assassinated) and Jeansans-Peur duc de Bourgogne.

Paix Malheureuse (*La*), 1559, which closed the Italian war between France and Italy (1483–1559). By this treaty Henri II. renounced all claim to Genoa, Naples, Milan, and Corsica.

Paix de Dieu (*La*), 1035. A suspension of arms brought about by the clergy to put a stop to the depredations of the barons. From every pulpit in France was read this command and malediction:—

'May they who refuse to obey be accursed, and have their portion with Cain the first murderer, with Judas the arch-traitor, and with Dathan and Abiram who went down alive into the pit. May they be accursed in the life which now is; and may their hope of salvation be put out, as the light of these candles is extinguished from their sight.'

At the last words the priests extinguished their tapers, and the people responded, 'So may God extinguish the joy of those who violate this peace. Amen.' *See* 'Trève de Dieu.'

Paix de Longjumeau (*La*), 1568. Between the Catholics and the Calvinists, preparatory to the Paix de St. Germain. This peace is called 'La Paix Fourrée' (*q.v.*), and sometimes 'La Petite Paix.'

Paix de Monsieur (*La*), 1575. Monsieur, the title of the king's eldest brother. This peace was signed at Loches in Touraine by François duc d'Alençon, the only surviving brother of Henri III.

By this treaty the appanage of 'Monsieur' was tripled, and he assumed the title of 'duc d'Anjou,' heretofore borne by his brother the king.

Paix des Dames (*La*), or 'La Paix de Cambray,' 1529. The pope, jealous of the power of Charles V., formed a league with France, England, Venice, and Milan; but Charles at once laid siege to Rome; 8,000 Romans perished, and the pope fled for safety to the castle of St. Angelo. A capitulation followed which was signed at Cambray 5 Aug., 1529, and was called 'La Paix des Dames,' because it was negotiated by Margaret of Austria (aunt of Charles V.) and Louise de Savoie (mother of François I. of France). The hollow peace was broken in 1536.

Palace of Ice (*The*), 1739. Built by the direction of Anne empress of Russia, to honour the nuptials of Prince Galitzin with a peasant girl. The bride and bridegroom had to pass their wedding night in a room the walls of which, all the furniture, and even the bed itself, were wholly of ice.

Palais Bourbon. Now called the *Palais du Corps Législatif*, between the Quai d'Orsay and the Rue de Bourgogne, and opposite the Pont de la Concorde. It was at one time the residence of the Bourbon princes, but was confiscated at the revolution. Under the Directory it was the Chamber of the Conseil des Anciens; under the first empire it was the house of the Corps Législatif; at the restoration it was the Chambre des Députés; under the republic of 1848 it was the seat of the Assemblée Nationale; since 1852 it has been the seat of the Corps Législatif. The *Salle des Séances* was reconstructed by M. de Joly (1828-1832).

Palais Cardinal (*Le*). Now called 'Le Palais Royal' of Paris. It was built by and for the Cardinal Richelieu in the reign of Louis XIII., and was divided into an outer and inner court. The gardens extended over several acres and were the wonder of Europe.

Palais Royal (*Le*). *See above*, 'Palais Cardinal.'

Palais de Justice (*Le*). In the cité de Paris. Here, at one time, dwelt the kings of France, up to the reign of Charles VII. (1422-1461), who resided at the Palais des Tournelles. It has often been reconstructed; the last time was in 1787. The *Salle des Pas-Perdus*, origi-

nally called the *Grande Salle*, was constructed by J. de Brosse in 1622.

Pal'amites (3 syl.). The followers of Gregory Palāmas, who maintained that there were two sorts of light, one increate and one create. The former the light of Deity, who said, 'I am the Light of the world,' the latter the light of the Sun. This distinction from 1341-1351 caused a schism in the Greek Church. The monks of Mount Athos insisted that the light seen on the mount of Transfiguration was the increate light of Deity; but Barlaam insisted, in that case that there must be both a visible and an invisible God. The upshot of the matter was this—the synod presided over by the Greek emperor determined the opinion of the monks of Mount Athos to be an article of faith, and Barlaam was obliged to quit the country.

Palatinate. 'Pfalz,' Germany. The ancient empire had two palatinates, the upper and the lower. The Upper or Bavarian Palatinate, in the circle of Bavaria; and the Lower Palatinate or Palatinate of the Rhine. At the Peace of Westphalia Karl Ludwig was made elector, which increased the number of electors from seven to eight.

Palatinate (*War of the*), 1688-1697. It was occasioned by Louis XIV. in favour of the Duchess of Orleans, sister of the last elector-palatine, against Philipp Wilhelm prince palatine of Neuburg. The dauphin conquered the palatine in less than two months. In 1689 Marshal Duras made such brutal ravages in this country as called forth the indignation of all Europe, and caused a new coalition to be formed against Louis XIV. In 1697 the Peace of Ryswick gave possession of the palatinate to Johann Wilhelm son of Philipp Wilhelm.

Palatine. So the governor of Poland was formerly called, and his dominion was a palatinate or vayvody. The crown was not hereditary, but elective.

Palatine (*Count*). 'Comes Palatinus,' a high judicial officer, generally near a frontier, with *jura regália*. The district over which he had jurisdiction was called a *palatinate* or *county palatine*.

I. In *England* there were three such

U U

counties: Lancaster, Chester, and Durham, frontiers of Wales. Lancaster was made a palatinate by Edward III., but the crown is now 'palatine of Lancaster.' Chester was made a palatinate by William the Conqueror, but was annexed to the crown in the reign of Henry III., and is now vested in the prince of Wales. Durham was also made a palatinate by William the Conqueror, but in 1836 this also was vested in the crown.

II. In *France*, under the Merovingian kings.

III. In *Germany* the 'Pfalz-graf' was far more powerful than a simple *graf*. He superintended the royal revenue, and took part in the government. Originally the palatine was named by the kaiser, but in time the title and office became hereditary. The chief palatines were the counts of Lotharingia, Saxony, Bavaria, Swabia, and later on Burgundy. Of these the palatine of Lotharingia was the chief, being the first prince of Germany, and afterwards called the *Palatine of the Rhine*. In 1315 this nobleman was called the *Elector-Palatine*.

Palatine (*Princesses*). Anna di Gonzâga (1616–1684); Elizabeth granddaughter of James I. of England (1618–1680); and Charlotte Elizabeth of Bavaria (1652–1722).

Palatine (*The Great*). Foremost of the Hungarian magnates; he was first minister of the crown, head of the army, lord chief justice, and regent when a regency was required. He was elected by the National Assembly, who sent up four names, from which the king selected one.

Palatine of Heidelberg (*The*). A large library, museum, and botanical garden.

Palatines of the County of Limerick (*The*), 1709. Some 3,000 Protestants, driven from their homes, and sent by the English government to Limerick in the reign of Queen Anne. They are generally called Methodists, and are supposed to have been driven from the palatinates by the remorseless persecutions of Louis XIV. Many emigrated to America, and were called the American Palatines. Many Palatines and other continental Protestants

had, before this, joined the army of William III.

The Rev. MATTHEW HENRY in his 'Commentary' refers to them (pp. 88, 89). 'When many of the poor Palatines, driven from their country by persecution, visited Chester in the year 1709, to the discontent of the High Church party, though only going to Ireland, I lent them my stable to sleep in.' The editor adds this note: 'The number who arrived in Chester within three weeks was about 3,140. The women and children and goods travelled in 109 waggons, for which Mr. Henry was informed by the mayor that the queen paid carriage, besides two shillings per week subsistence for each head.'—HENRY, *Diary*.

Pale (*The*). In Irish history means that portion of the island over which the English rule and English law were acknowledged. It was an ever-varying quantity. In Henry II.'s reign it meant Dublin, Wexford, Waterford, and the chief part of Leinster. John distributed the Pale into twelve counties palatine, viz. Dublin, Meath, Kildare, Louth, Carlow, Kilkenny, Wexford, Waterford, Cork, Kerry, Tipperary, and Limerick. In Edward III.'s reign, after the statute of Kilkenny, the Pale was limited to four counties (Dublin, Carlow, Meath, and Louth). Richard II. increased the palatinate to nine. In Henry VI.'s reign it was again contracted. Roughly the Pale means Dublin, Meath, Carlow, Kilkenny, and Louth. Except in the Pale the king's power was only nominal.

Palestro (*The Hero of*). Victor Emmanuel II. king of Sardinia and afterwards of Italy (1820–1878). The Sardinians and French defeated the Austrians at Palestro 31 May, 1859.

Come, one and all, cluster closely round the hero of Palestro.—*Garibaldi to his soldiers*, 1860.

Pali. A trans-Gangetic idiom from the Sanskrit in Burmah, Siam, and Ceylon. In this idiom the sacred writings of the Buddhists are written. Like Sanskrit, Hebrew, Latin, and several other sacred languages, Pali is not now spoken.

Pall Mall Gazette (*The*). A London daily newspaper commenced 7 Feb., 1865.

Palles'chi (*The*). The Medicean party devoted to the ruling house of Florence, or desirous of establishing in that city an oligarchy or tyranny.

Pallikars. A national militia of Greece organised to stamp out the Klephts (1 syl.) or brigands. The Armatōlẽs formed a principal part of the militia.

Palm the Bookseller, shot by court-martial 26 Aug., 1806. This was a most unjustifiable murder. Napoleon wanted to overrun Prussia, and Palm published a pamphlet entitled ' L'Allemagne dans son profond abaissement,' for which he was tried by court-martial, and, as he refused to give up the author, was ordered to be shot. England, Russia, and other free countries were loudly indignant ; and in 1813 when the Germans rose against Napoleon, many regiments emblazoned on their banners the bloody figure of Palm the Bookseller.

Palm Sunday. 'Festum Broncheriæ,' or ' Festum Palmarum,' ' Dominĭca in Palmis.' The Sunday next before Easter Day, in commemoration of Christ's triumphal entry into Jerusalem, when the people strewed palm branches in the way. Instituted in 1106. In the Catholic Church palms, being blessed and sprinkled thrice with holy water, are distributed first to the clergy present and then to the laity, who receive them kneeling. A procession is then made, and at the mass all the communicants hold palms in their hands during the ' Passion' and the Gospel. *See* ' Sunday.'

Dies palmarum, sive florum atque ramorum appellatur.—RUPERT, *De Divin. Offic.*, chap. vii.

Palmers. Pilgrims who brought home a branch of palm in proof of their having been to Palestine. This palm-branch was deposited in the church of the pilgrims' town. Sometimes the palm-branch was wreathed round the pilgrim's staff.

Palmyra's Queen, or ' Queen of Palmyra.' So Lady Hester Stanhope was called (1770–1839). She took up her residence at Djouni, in Syria. The last and one of the most noted queens of Palmyra was Zenŏbia.

Palsgrave [Pfalzgraf]. The reeve or president of the pfalz or palace-court, the highest court of the realm, which originally moved from place to place with the monarch. In France called ' Le Maire du Palais.' When the court became stationary, the presidency was given to a ' judge '; but the king could, if he chose, confer the judicial honour on a ' man of a fief ' or province, who then became a pfalzgraf or vice-roi.

There were two German reeves possessed of this judicial power, and their districts or provinces were called ' palatinates.' There was the Upper Palatinate (which was Bavaria), and the Lower Palatinate on the Rhine; but the word pfalzgraf, unqualified, always means the count-palatine of the Rhine.

The pfalzgraf of the Rhine was one of the seven original electors of the German kings; but in the tenth year of the Thirty Years' War he was deposed from the college of electors, and his place given to the duke of Bavaria.

At the Peace of Westphalia, in 1648, it was settled that the dignity of elector could not be alienated, so the pfalzgraf was restored, and the number of electors raised to eight. When, in 1692, the electorate was conferred on Ernest duke of Hanover the electoral college contained nine members ; but in 1777 the number was again reduced to eight by the amalgamation of the two palatinates of Bavaria and the Rhine ; the duke of Bavaria being also pfalzgraf of the Rhine. The title was abolished (except for Hessen-Cassel) by Napoleon in 1806.

Panard of the 19th century. Armand Gouffé, born at Paris (1775–1845), founder of the *Caveau Moderne*.

Panare'ton. The book of Ecclesiasticus, by Jesus son of Sirach, an Alexandrian, was so called because it was a complete breviary of all the moral virtues. It lays down rules for the daily regulation of life. Jesus died B.C. 150.

Pan'athenæ'a, B.C. 1495. A great Athenian fête in honour of Athēnê [Minerva], instituted by Erichthŏnios. Athēnê was goddess of all [*pan*] Attica. The Great Pan-Athenæa was celebrated every fifth year, and the grand ceremony was carrying the peplum or veil of Athēnê to the citadel. The prize in the games was a wreath of olives and cruse of oil.

Panda'vas (*The*). The descendants of Pandû. Five princes whose contest for regal supremacy with their cousins, the Kurûs, forms the subject of the great Indian epic poem entitled the ' Mahabharata.'

Pandu means ' white.' The elder of the two princes was excluded from the throne for his whiteness, probably some disease, but his five sons were the Pandavas.

Pandects (*The*). The Greek word for the Roman Digest compiled in the reign of the Emperor Justinian A.D. 533.

U 2

The entire Corpus Juris Civilis contained (1) the Code in twelve tables; (2) the Digest or Pandects in fifty books; (3) the Institutes, a summary of the Digest to teach the elements of Roman law, in four books; and (4) the Novels or new laws, containing sixteen edicts and 168 laws published by Justinian.

The Pandects or Digest are in fifty books: each book is subdivided into *Titles*; each title into *Laws*; and sometimes a law is subdivided into paragraphs. Thus D 50. 17. 30 means Digest Book 50, Title 17, Law 30. D 12. 2. 5. 3 means Digest Book 12, Title 2, Law 5, Paragraph 3. The symbol ff for Pandects is a corrupt form of the Greek π (*i.e.* P. initial of Pandect).

Pandours (*The*). The ferocious hordes of irregular troops by which Austria for a long time spread terror among her neighbours, and which, even so late as 1849, played an important part in the army of the Ban Jellachich. .

When leagued oppression poured to northern wars
Her whiskered pandours and her fierce hussars.
       CAMPBELL, *Pleasures of Hope.*

Panic Sunday, 10 May, 1857. The day of the Sepoys' outbreak. It was about five o'clock in the evening when a rocket gave the signal of uprising. The Sepoys seized their arms and set upon their officers, released the convicts, and killed all the Europeans they chanced to meet. The bungalows were set on fire, the European dwellings were plundered. Ladies and children were brutally treated. The mutiny began at Barrackpore, spread to Delhi, Oude, Lahore, Lucknow, Jhansi, and Cawnpore. *See* ' Sunday.'

Pan-ionia, B.C. 777. Fêtes in honour of the patron god of the Ionian cities, the object being to bind together the twelve confederate cities. *See below.*

Pan-ionium. A confederation of twelve Ionian cities:—Ephesus, Melētos, Smyrna, Phocæa, Colŏphon, Teos, Erȳthræ, Clazomĕnæ, Priēnē, Lebĕdos, Samos, and Chios. The place of muster was a building on Mount Mykălĕ.

Panno′nia. Latin name for Hungary, the country of the Pannonii.

Ancient Panonnia included, besides Hungary, the eastern part of Austria, a part of Croatia and Bosnia, with Styria, Carinthia, Carniŏla, and Slavonia.

Pannus Nebula′tus. The veil used to cover the pyx containing the consecrated host.

Panontism. The deification of instinct. It teaches that instinct is the force of nature, and that creation was the work of irresistible instinct and not of all-wisdom and all-power. All wisdom, power, and love would have provided against the evils which abound, but instinct is blind, and simply follows a masterless impulse.

Panslav′ism, 1831. The confederation or union of all the Slavic branches into one great nation, including Russia, Poland, Hungary, Bohemia, &c. This scheme was advocated by the Hungarian poet Kollar (1793–1852).

Eastern Slavs: The Russians, the Serbs and Hungarian Serbs, Bosnians, Herzegovinians, Montenegrins, Slavonians, Dalmatians, Croats, Winds, and Bulgarians.
Western Slavs: Poles, Silesians, Bohemians, Moravians, Slovaks (of Hungary), and the Wends or Slavs of N. Germany.

Pantheism. Either the ultimate absorption of all things in deity, when ' God will be all in all '; or else the identification of deity with the phenomenal world, in which case God is simply the force behind everything, that which glows in the sun and blossoms on the trees. In India the Brahmins and Buddhists are Pantheists—the latter teach the ultimate absorption of everything in God. In Greece the Stoics and Eleatics, and in Italy the Pythagorĕans, were Pantheists. In Alexandria the Neo-Platonists and Gnostics. In the 7th cent. John Scotus Erigĕna taught that ' God is everything and everything is God.' In the 12th cent. Amalric de Bena and David de Dinante taught the same system. Giordano Bruno was burnt to death in 1600 for Pantheistic notions; Spinōza of Holland followed in his footsteps. In modern Germany Fichte, Hegel, and Schelling were Pantheists.

If God is everything, and everything is God, then all-worship is simply God worshipping himself.

Pantisoc′racy. A visionary scheme of Coleridge for a society where all the virtues were to thrive, and all the vices to be rooted out.

Papa Angel′ico. An ideal pope, emblem and impersonation of all virtues. Dante not only advocated a Papa Angelico, but also a Universal Overlord, who was to reign over the whole world, to redress grievances, punish offenders, administer justice, defend the weak, redeem all wrongs, be the father of the fatherless, and an ideal God on earth.

Papal Aggression, Sept. 1850. The establishment by Pope Pius IX. in England of a papal hierarchy. Dr. Wiseman was appointed vicar apostolic of the London district and lord archbishop of Westminster, with the title of cardinal. Dr. Ullathorne was appointed Roman Catholic bishop of Birmingham. In 1851 Dr. Briggs was enthroned bishop of Beverley, Dr. Brown of Clifton, and Dr. Burgess of Shrewsbury. Lord John Russell fumed furiously, and brought in a bill to prohibit the aggression. His bill was pared down to a fine of 100*l*. to any one who assumed such titles in England, but the fine was never enforced.

Pap'alins. Those of a papistic bias, little papists. Strype calls the two parties in England at the accession of Queen Elizabeth 'Evangelics and Papalins,' those who would drive post speed to Protestant doctrines and discipline, and those who would retain a spice of Romanism.

Paper Duty. The paper duty repealed in 1861 was the tax imposed in the reign of Queen Anne (1711) to meet the expenses of Marlborough's wars. There was, however, a duty on paper so far back as 1694.

Paper King (*The*). John Law (1671–1729), the projector of the Mississippi Bubble (1716–1720).

Papy'ri. Rolls made of the papy'rus plant. The Egyptian papyri are of very great antiquity, some of them running back to B.C. 2000 or more. Some have been found deposited with mummies; others, of a civil nature, have been found in jars or boxes.

1. The *Hi'eroglyph'ical* papyri, accompanied with pictures, are solar litanies, books ' of the empyreal gate,' or rituals.

2. The *Hieratic* papyri, written in the cursive Egyptian hand, are mixed civil and religious writings.

3. The *Demotic* papyri, in enchorial character, consist of rituals, contracts, and miscellaneous documents.

The papyri of Pompēii and Herculāneum are numerous. They are rolled on a stick and placed in a cylinder.

Papy'rus Prisse. The most ancient MS. in existence, said to be before Abraham's time. It is occupied with a plaint on the degeneracy of the manners and rueful decadence of man since the good old times. The MS. derives its name from M. Prisse d'Avennes, by whom it was procured at Thebes and given to the Bibliothèque Nationale, Paris. It consists of eighteen pages, was published in 1847, and is the most perfect specimen extant of the Hieratic writing. ('Notes and Queries,' 12 Feb., 1887, p. 127.)

Paques Véronaises (*Les*), 17 April, 1797. For political ends compared by Bonaparte to the ' Sicilian Vespers,' (*q.v.*). A considerable number of Italian and Slavonian troops, and mere armed peasants, made an attack on the French under the charge of Junot, sent by Bonaparte into Verona. As many as 500 French, scattered in different forts or lying in hospitals, were put to death, while the citadel fired red-hot balls upon the town. A powerful reinforcement from the French head-quarters in Italy put an end to the fray, and Verona submitted with humility to the French.

Pronounce *Lay Park Ver'ro-naze'*.

Parabola'ni (*The*), 5th cent. A charitable corporation of Alexandria instituted during the plague of Galliēnus. Their duty was to visit the sick and bury the dead, but they were so mercenary under St. Cyril the patriarch that the emperor restricted the number to five or six hundred; even then they were a canker in the empire.

Paracelsus. The knob of his staff was said to inclose the four elemental spirits—Kobold (*earth*), Salamander (*fire*), Undine (*water*), and Sylph (*air*). *See* p. 607, ' Names Classicised.'

Paraclete. The oratory erected at Troyes by Abelard after his condemnation by the Council of Sens. He made his paramour Héloïse (3 syl.) head of the oratory, and there, at death, his ashes were deposited.

In 1817 the remains of both Abelard and Héloïse were removed to Père-la-Chaise, in Paris, and interred in one sepulchre.

Paradise of Bohemia (*The*). The district round Leitmeritz.

Paradise of Central Africa (*The*), Fatiko. (Sir S. Baker, ' Exploration of the Nile Sources,' 1866.)

Paradise of Europe (*The*). The valley of the Arno in Tuscany.

Paradise of Holland (*The*), or 'The Dutch Paradise.' The province of Gelderland.

Paradise of Portugal (*The*), or 'The Portuguese Paradise.' Cintra, north-west of Lisbon.

Paradise of the Indies (*The*). Ceylon.

Paradise of the Jews. Poland was so called before its partitions.

Paraschistes. One of a low class employed in embalming, and, singularly enough, held in abhorrence by the Egyptians. They lived in the cemeteries or their neighbourhood. A scribe marked a line with a reed pen on the left side of the body of the corpse, beneath the ribs, down which line the paraschistes made a deep incision with a rude knife or Ethiopian stone, probably flint. He was then pelted by those around with stones, and pursued with curses. The *taricheutes* or preparer removed the entrails and lungs, with the exception of the heart and kidneys. The *cholchytæ* were the custodians of the mummies. As all classes were embalmed, including malefactors, the paraschistes, in spite of the disgust he inspired, was probably in as good case as the public executioners in Europe. Embalming cost from about 750*l.* to a mere trifle. *See* 'Chambers's Encyclopædia,' and Rawlinson's 'Herodotus.'

Paravail, or 'Tenants' Paravail.' The lowest tenant. The tenants of the king were the highest tenants. If these tenants let out their tenements they were overlords; and if these overlords let out their tenements their tenants were mesne lords; and the tenants of mesne lords were paravails (French *per, avayler*).

The tenants of kings were *overlords* to their own tenants; and these tenants were *mesne lords* to the tenants under them; and the tenants of mesne lords were 'tenants paravail.'

Parian Chronicle (*The*), B.C. 264. Certain pieces of marble containing inscriptions in Greek capitals. These inscriptions are chronological lists of Grecian events from Cecrops down to the archonship of Diognētos (B.C. 1556–264), and supposed to have been executed about the year B.C. 264. They are the principal part of the Arundelian

marbles (*q.v.*), and are preserved in Oxford University. Called Parian because they were made in the Isle of Paros about A.D. 250.

Paris (*François de*). A celebrated deacon born at Châtillon in France (1690–1727), and celebrated for the numberless 'miracles' said to have occurred at his tomb at St. Médard, Paris. This cemetery was so crowded day after day, and the scenes of the convulsionists there were so scandalous, that in 1732 the government closed the cemetery, and this epigram was by some wag attached to the gates:—

> De par le roi défense à Dieu
> De faire miracle en ce lieu.
>
> *It is forbidden to God's Grace*
> *To work more wonders in this place.*

Paris (*Little*). Brussels. So called from its brilliant shops, its numerous cafés, and its general gaiety.

Paris (*Patron Saint of*). Ste. Geneviève (423–512). Born at Nanterre.

Paris (*Treaties of*).

1. 12 April, 1229. Between Raymond VII. count of Toulouse, St. Louis, and the Pope, for the cession of Provence.

2. 10 May, 1303. Between France and England, for the restoration of Aquitaine to Edward I.

3. 24 May, 1515. Between Karl of Austria (sovereign of the Netherlands) and François I. of France.

4. 15 Aug., 1761. (Called the FAMILY COMPACT.) Between the different branches of the House of Bourbon.

5. 10 Feb., 1763. *Peace* between France, Spain, Portugal, and Great Britain. By this treaty Canada was ceded to England.

6. 6 Feb., 1778. Between France and the United States of North America, recognising their independence after the British overthrow at Saratoga.

7. 20 June, 1784. Between Great Britain and Holland.

8. 15 May, 1796. Between the French Republic and the King of Savoy, for the cession of Savoy and Nice to France.

9. 10 Oct., 1796. Between Ferdinand IV. king of Naples and France.

10. 8 Oct., 1801. Between France and Russia.

11. 29 July, 1806. Between France and Russia; signed but not ratified.

12. 10 Nov., 1807. Between France and Holland, by which Flushing was ceded to France.

13. 6 Jan., 1810. Between France and Sweden.

14. 14 March, 1812. *Alliance* between France and Austria.

15. 11 April, 1814. Between Napoleon I. and the allies. Napoleon was deposed and banished to Elba.

16. 23 April, 1814. *Convention* between the Comte d'Artois and the allies for the cessation of hostilities and evacuation of French territory.

17. 30 May, 1814. Between France and the allies, whereby it was stipulated that France should return to its ancient boundaries with the exception of Avignon, the Comtat Venaissin, Mulhouse, and a small part of Savoy. Malta was confirmed to England, and the three French colonies (viz. the Mauritius, St. Lucia, and Tobăgo) were ceded to our dominion. The French troops were

recalled from fifty-three garrisons, and all fortresses were restored to their respective claimants.

18. 20 July, 1814. Between France and Spain, confirming previous treaties.

19. 2 Aug., 1815. *Convention* between Great Britain, Russia, Austria, and Prussia, charging the British government with the safeguard of Napoleon.

20. 26 Sept., 1815. The *Holy Alliance*. Between Russia, Austria, and Prussia.

21. 20 Nov., 1815. Between Great Britain, Russia, Austria, and Prussia, defining the boundaries of France, &c.

22. 10 June, 1817. Between Great Britain, France, Spain, Russia, and Prussia, to fulfil the articles of the Congress of Vienna.

23. 28 Aug., 1817. Between France and Portugal, for the cession of Guiana to France.

24. 25 Aug., 1818. *Convention* between France and the allies.

25. 25 April, 1818. *Convention* between Great Britain and France respecting debts to British subjects.

26. 1 Feb., 1856. *Peace,* after the Criměan war, between Russia on one part, and Great Britain, France, Austria, and Turkey on the other. It stipulated for the independence of the Ottoman empire; the neutralisation of the Black Sea, that no arsenal was to be maintained on the Black Sea coast, and that neither Russia nor Turkey should maintain more than six steamships of 800 tons.

27. 3 March, 1857. *Peace* between Great Britain and Persia.

28. 26 May,1857. Between the Great Powers of Europe, respecting Neuchâtel.

29. 19 Aug., 1858. *Convention* between the Great Powers of Europe, to constitute the Danubian principalities.

30. 25 March to 16 April, 1865. *Congress* to arrange terms of peace between Russia and the allies.

31. Jan., 1868. *Conferences* between the Great Powers respecting the Turkish difficulty.

Paris Club (*The*). Called the *société mère* or mother society of the Jacobin clubs. The Jacobin clubs contained 400,000 members, and their platform was 'anarchy and revolution.' As Michelet ('Hist. Fr. Rev.' pp. 476, 485) says, the Jacobin clubs ' soon became a vast committee of revolutionary police.'

Paris Garden. A bear-garden on the bank of the Thames. Blount in his 'Glossographia' says that Richard de Paris had a house and garden there in the time of Richard II., and he quotes as his authority the Close Roll 16 Rich. II.; but the words of the Roll are ' domum Roberti de Parys.'

It was originally a copyhold manor which fell to Robert Marmion, after the Conquest, and was given by his son to the monks of Bermondsey Priory.

Paris of Japan (*The*). Osăka.

Parishes. In England and Wales 14,610, of which 550 are in two counties. Benefices 11,728; of these 9,669 are in the province of Canterbury, and 2,059 in the province of York.

In Ireland 2,500.

In Scotland a parish is merely an ecclesiastical division.

By the Poor-law Amendment Act, 13,964 of the parishes were amalgamated into 585 unions, but besides these there are 21 unions by Local Acts, 12 by Gilbert's Act (*q.v.*), and the 89 parishes of the Scilly Isles united.

Parisian Wedding (*The*). The massacre in Paris begun on St. Bartholomew's Eve during the wedding festivities of Henri of Navarre and Marguerite of France.

Charles IX., although it was not possible for him to recall to life the countless victims of the ' Parisian Wedding,' was ready to explain those murders to the unprejudiced mind.—MOTLEY, *Dutch Republic,* iii. 9.

Parker (*Admiral*). Richard Parker, an able seaman, was called by his comrades ' Admiral ' because he was the ringleader of the mutiny of the fleet in the Nore. He was hanged at the yard-arm of a man-of-war off Sheerness in June 1797.

Parker Society (*The*), Cambridge. Established in 1840 for reprinting the works of the early English Reformers. Dissolved 1853 or 1854. Fifty-three works were published under its auspices, equal to four every year.

Parker's Bible (*The*), 1572. The second folio edition of the ' Great Bible ' (*q.v.*), with corrections and several prolegomena, under the supervision of Archbishop Parker. See ' Bibles.'

Parks, Commons, and Open Spaces Committee (*The Metropolitan*) has under its charge about 3,000 acres or 4 square miles of the metropolitan area. Some 300 bailiffs, gardeners, and labourers are constantly employed.

Parlamento is a meeting of the Florentine people on the piazza of the Signory.

Parlement de St. Louis (*Le*), 13th cent. A law court where causes were tried by evidence. It had no fixed locality, but followed the king wherever he went. The staff consisted of 3 high barons, 3 prelates, 19 knights, and 18 councillors. Its chief business was to register the royal decrees; it had no legislative power of its own.

These parlements had no point of resemblance to our *parliament,* but though they did not *make* laws, they had to *register* the royal edicts and ordinances before they became law. The Paris parlement was formally abolished in 1790. *See* ' Olim.'

Parlement of France. Originally an ambulatory court of justice which followed the king and administered justice in his name. Philippe le Bel in 1302 was the first to fix a 'parlement' in Paris. It held sessions, at first, only twice a year; but in 1380 it was made permanent. There were 13 other parlements in France. That of Toulouse was established in 1302; of Grenoble in 1451; of Bordeaux in 1462; of Dijon in 1477; of Rouen in 1499; of Aix in 1501; of Rennes in 1553; of Pau in 1620; of Metz in 1633; of Besançon in 1676; of Trevoux in 1696; of Douay in 1713; and of Nancy in 1775.

Parlement of Paris (*The*), 28 Jan., 1226. Was called to excommunicate Raymond VII. count of Toulouse. Another was called on 29 March, 1226, to arrange a crusade against the Albigenses.

Parliament. *See*

Addle parliament	Obstructive
Barebone ,,	Pacific parliament
(of) Bats	*Parliament* (longest)
Black parliament	,, (shortest)
Club ,,	Parliament oak
Convention ,,	Pensionary parliament
Devil's ,,	
Drunken ,,	Pride's purge
(of) Dunces	Rowdy parliament
Good parliament	Rump ,,
Grattan's ,,	Running ,,
Illiterate ,,	Septennial ,,
Imperial ,,	Session of 41 hours,
Irish ,,	*see* p. 665
Jews' ,,	Shortest parliament, *see* p. 664
Lack-learning parliament	Triennial parliam't
Leicester's parliament	Unlearned ,,
Little parliament	Unmerciful ,,
Long ,,	Useless ,,
Longest ,,(p. 664)	Wonderful or Wonder-making parliament
Mad ,,	(of) 1654
Merciless ,,	*See* 'Parliamentary,'&c.
Mongrel ,,	

Parliament. Edward the Confessor called his witenagemots *parlements*.

1164. Henry II. called together at Clarendon, in Wiltshire, the prelates and nobles to pass the famous 16 ordinances to limit the power of the church.

1265. Simon de Montfort, summoned, in the king's [Hen. III.'s] name, two knights for each county, two citizens for each city, and two burgesses for each borough, to a national council.

1274. The national council was first called a parliament (Edw. I.).

1330. (4 Edw. III. c. 14) Parliaments were ordered to be held annually.

1377. (Rich. II.) The first Speaker elected. It was Peter Delamere.

1694. The Triennial Act was passed (6, 7 Will. & Mary). Similar acts had been passed by Charles I. & II.

1716. The Septennial Act was passed (1 Geo. I. c. 38).

Bills in the form of acts were first introduced in the reign of Henry VI. In the reign of Edward V. there was no parliament.

Parliament (*Irish*). The first regular parliament of Ireland was held 1295, and the great officials of the Pale (*q.v.*) were summoned to England to consult on the crisis. In 1459 the Irish parliament insisted on complete legislative independence and sovereignty. In 1780 Henry Grattan moved that 'the king, lords, and commons of Ireland are alone competent to enact laws to bind Ireland.' In 1782 Poyning's Act (*q.v.*) was repealed in the Irish parliament and Ireland was declared free. In 1800 the Irish parliaments were united with those of Great Britain. See 'Parliaments.'

Mr. Gladstone and his party have pleaded for an 'Irish parliament for purely Irish affairs,' but Grattan honestly confessed that the Irish alone should make laws for Ireland, and that the Irish ought not to be subject to the laws of England. This is the true Irish doctrine for better or for worse.

Parliaments (*The Four Longest* 1575–1586 (Q. Eliz.); by 18 prorogations it lasted 11 years.

The 'Long parliament,' including the 'Rump,' 19 years 132 days, from 3 Nov., 1640 to 16 March, 1660. The Rump began 1653, so that though the original long parliament was 12 years 168 days, from 3 Nov., 1640 to 20 April, 1653 (Charles I. and Cromwell).

The 'Pensionary parliament,' 16 years 260 days, from 8 May, 1661 to 24 Jan., 1678 (Charles II.).

The fourth Long parliament lasted 13 years 252 days, from 14 Nov., 1816 to 24 July, 1830 (George IV.).

The Pension or Pensionary parliament was followed by the Ten-week parliament, from 6 March to 24 May, 1679.

The longest parliament up to the reign of Edward IV. was convened in 1472 and lasted 2 years.

Parliaments (*The Eight Shortest*).

Days A.D.	King	From
7	1681	Chas. II.	21 to 28 Mar.* (Oxfd.)
12	1625	Chas. I.	1 to 13 Aug. (Oxfd.)
14	1658	Cromwell	21 Jan. to 4 Feb.†
20	1640	Chas. I.	13 Apr. to 3 May.‡

30	1536	Hen. VIII.	8 June to 18 July.
30	1553	Edw. VI.	1 to 31 Mar.
33	1510	Hen. VIII.	21 Jan. to 23 Feb.
33	1554	Mary	2 Apr. to 5 May.

* The fifth and last convened by Charles II.
† The last convened by Cromwell.
‡ Called the 'Short Parliament.' It was the last dissolved by Charles I. and was followed by the 'Long Parliament.'

*** The following may be added :—

1806. 4 months 5 days. From 25 Dec., 1806 to 29 April, 1807 (Geo. III.).
1830. 5 months 27 days. From 26 Oct. 1830 to 20 April, 1831 (Will. IV.).
1886. 5 months 14 days. From 12 Jan., 1886 to 26 June, 1886 (Victoria). This was the Gladstone ministry, broken up by his Home Rule Bill (Ireland).

Parliament of Bats (*The*), 1426. During the regency in the reign of Henry VI. In consequence of the litigious character of the Duke of Gloucester the citizens were forbidden to carry arms; so when parliament assembled the members of the House of Commons came armed with bats or clubs. *See* 'Parliaments.'

Parliament of Dunces (*The*), 1404. Convened by Henry IV. at Coventry. So called because all lawyers were excluded from it. *See* 'Parliaments.'

Parliament of 1654. One of the most memorable parliaments in English history. It was the first in which Scotch and Irish members took part. There were no members for rotten and pocket boroughs. It was the freest of all elections hitherto known. The 'Instrument' (*q.v.*) or New Constitution was carried through, and Cromwell was acknowledged Lord Protector. It was dissolved by Cromwell in Jan. 1655. *See* 'Parliaments.'

Parliament Oak. Within the ancient park of Clipstone Palace. As Edward I. with his retinue, in 1294, was chasing the deer in Sherwood Forest, a messenger arrived in breathless haste to announce that the Welsh were in revolt. The king instantly summoned his knights around him under this oak, and the unanimous voice was for war. The oak is still standing (1890).

Parliamentary Candidate Society (*The*), 1831. To supply informa-

tion to electors of the political opinions of candidates, by extracts from their speeches, their votes, and their public conduct. If new candidates, their characters and connections were given.

Parliamentary Reform. The Bill passed 7 June, 1832, for the adjustment of the inequalities of the representative system and an extended franchise. Fifty-six boroughs in England and Wales were entirely disfranchised; 30 which had previously returned two members were restricted to 1; 42 new boroughs were created, of which 22 boroughs returned 2 each, and 20 boroughs returned 1 each. Four members were assigned to the city of London, 2 to each of the Universities of Oxford and Cambridge, and 1 to each of 133 cities or boroughs. Lancashire was allotted 5 members; the West Riding of Yorkshire 4 members; 25 counties 4 members each; 7 counties 3 members each; 9 counties and the East and North Ridings of Yorkshire 2 members each; and 10 counties 1 member each. Total 658 for the United Parliament.

The numbers for Scotland were increased from 45 to 53, and for Ireland from 100 to 105. The qualifications of electors were made to be 40s. freeholders, 10l. general leases, and 50l. annual rent. The old freemen were wholly set aside.

Parliamentary Reform Agitation.

1776. (20 March.) The motion of John Wilkes for parliamentary reform negatived without division.
1782. (7 May.) 7 May, 1783, and 18 April, 1785, motions by W. Pitt negatived.
1784. Horne Tooke and Mr. Hardy tried for high treason and acquitted.
1810. (21 May.) Brand's motion for parliamentary reform negatived. The same year Cobbett was fined 1,000l. and sent to Newgate.
1817. As many as 600 petitions were presented to the house in favour of reform. 20 May Sir Francis Burdett's motion in favour of reform was negatived.
1818. (3 June.) Sir Francis Burdett was sent to the Tower for exciting to agitation.
1819. Hunt, a Wiltshire farmer, was sentenced to imprisonment for haranguing multitudes at Birmingham.
1822. (29 April.) Lord John Russell's motion for parliamentary reform was negatived.
1826. Major Cartwright was fined for inciting to agitation.
1829. (3 June.) The Marquis of Blandford's motion for reform was negatived.

Parliamentary Session of 41 Hours. The longest session was in 1881, when on one occasion the house sat continuously for 41 hours. The session began on Monday afternoon, 31 Jan., at four o'clock, and went on without a break till Wednesday morning, 2 Feb., after the clock had struck nine. Mr. Gladstone was prime minister.

The subject was leave to bring in a bill for the 'Protection to Person and Property' in Ireland, against the Land League (*q.v.*), and Mr. Forster, the secretary for Ireland, moved for the petition. It was the Irish members who tried to weary out the house by obstructing business. The obstruction was closed by the Speaker forbidding any more speaking on the subject, and the Bill was carried by 164 against 19.

Parliamentary Trains. Trains established by Act of Parliament for the benefit of third-class passengers, at the rate of one penny a mile. In France the *traine parlementaire* means a train reserved for the use of members of both the houses of legislature (1840).

Parliamentary Undertakers. The little group of nobles who, till William Pitt's administration, returned fully half the members of the House of Commons. More than sixty seats were in the hands of Lord Downshire, the Ponsonbys, and the Beresfords alone. 'They undertook to manage parliament in their own way and on their own terms.'

Parnassus of Germany. Blocksberg.

On Blocksberg we'll find room enough;
The wide Parnassus 'tis of Germany.
        GOETHE, *Faust* (Dr. Anster).

Parnassus of Japan. Fusiyama. (Gibson, 'Gallery of Geography,' p. 921; 1872.)

Parnell Commission (*The*). Sat for 200 days in 1889, and its report was issued 13 Feb., 1890, consisting of 121 closely printed pages of the Blue Book. The Commissioners were Sir James Hannen and Justices Day and Smith, and the object of inquiry was whether and how far Charles Stewart Parnell and his Irish party were connected with the crimes of the Irish Land League, which Mr. Gladstone asserted 'dogged it throughout.' The report was divided into nine charges, and the general tenour was that Mr. Parnell and his 'lieutenants' were at least morally responsible for much of the mischief, inasmuch as they did nothing to repress it, much to foment it, but adroitly avoided mixing up themselves with the misdemeanants.

Lord Selborne says the Irish members as individuals and politicians are cleared of charges against them, but as a political body they are proved beyond a doubt of being agents of disturbance and centres of disaffection.

The 'Standard' acknowledges that the defendants are exonerated from direct complicity with crime, but 'the report shows Mr. Parnell to

have been the leader of men devoted to the treasonable design of separating Ireland from England; to have been implicated in the whole system of crime, outrage, and lawlessness which has so long prevailed in Ireland; and to have been closely connected with foreign mercenaries who made no secret of their being the enemies of the Queen [Victoria].'—14 Feb., 1890.

Parnellism and Crime, 1888. A pamphlet published by the editor of the 'Times' newpaper to show that the Home Rule and Land League Irish party, of which Charles S. Parnell was the head, was, as Mr. Gladstone stated, 'dogged by crime in all its steps.' It appeared anonymously, but was written by Woulfe Flanagan, son of the Right Hon. Judge Flanagan, who had been judge of the Irish Land Estates Court. This pamphlet was made the basis of a trial before three commissioners in 1889.

Mr. Gladstone, 11 July, 1882, says of the Parnellite policy, 'It means the destruction of the peace of life; it means the placing in abeyance of the most sacred duties, of the most cherished duties; it means the servitude of good men, and the supremacy of bad men'; and on 28 Jan., 1882, he said, 'With fatal and painful precision the steps of crime have dogged the steps of the Land League.'

Sir William Harcourt said of the Land League, 'The doctrine so expounded is the doctrine of treason and assassination. To-morrow the civilised world will pronounce its judgment on this vile conspiracy.'

Those who read the Report of the Commissioners will see clearly that the extreme party—the party ruled by the Clan-na-Gael—has been the real motive power, in the hands of which the Irish Land League and Mr. Parnell and his friends have been nothing but tools and puppets. Wherever the Land League has been most active in its operations, whenever what is called coercion has fallen into abeyance, the increase of crime in Ireland has been something fearful. This has been proved to demonstration by the report of the Commissioners. While, therefore, it must be deplored that, in the matter of the forged letters, the authorities of the 'Times' did not exercise more care and greater vigilance, and therefore are open to grave censure; yet, in unearthing this great conspiracy which has prevailed so long in Ireland, they deserve the sincere thanks of all good and all honest men in the United Kingdom.—*Newspaper leader*, 14 Feb., 1890.

Parnellites. The followers of Charles Stewart Parnell, M.P., who in the election of 1885 contrived to bring to the English House of Commons eighty-five Irish members, who agreed to vote solidly with Mr. Parnell, member for Cork. This large contingent, thrown into either the Tory or Liberal side, was sufficient to secure a majority, consequently the Irish party ruled the British parliament. The object of Mr. Parnell was to secure to Ireland 'Home Rule,' or the right of controlling the legislature of Ireland. The weak point was this: they wanted to establish a Dublin parliament, and yet to sit in the British house at Westminster.

Parochial Charities (*The City*), *i.e.* of London. In 1887 an act, passed in 1883, came into operation, which invested the money of these charities in the Ecclesiastical Commissioners in behoof of the more populous districts of 'Greater London' for the following purposes :—

The education of the poorer inhabitants of the metropolis.

The establishment of libraries, museums, and art collections.

The preservation, &c., of open spaces for recreation, &c.

Provident institutions and convalescent hospitals.

** A permanent Board of 21 Trustees was added to the Charity Commissioners. The charities were, in 1887, worth 118,000*l*. a year, of which sum 85,459*l*. was applicable to ecclesiastical purposes.

Parsee. A disciple of Zoroaster. A fire-worshipper is so called in the West Indies; in Persia the Mohammedans call fire-worshippers *guebres* (Persian *ghebr*, infidel). In Bombay they are wealthy and influential. In 1852 an association was formed for the restoration of the creed of Zoroaster, which had been much corrupted. The Zend Avesta is the book containing the sacred writing of Zoroaster. The original, 'received from heaven,' is lost; but copies exist.

Parson Garlic. Joseph Tucker, D.D., dean of Gloucester (1711–1799), so called in the effigy burnt near his own door by a mob enraged against him for his essay in support of the Hessians who had come to settle in England.

Par'tholan Race (*The*). A fabulous race of people said by the bards to have taken possession of Ireland at the beginning of the 4th century after the flood. Partholan was of the race of Japhet. He landed on Wednesday, 14 May, at Imbersceine, in Kerry, and fixed his residence in the province of Ulster, on the island of Inis-Samer, in the river Erne. After holding possession of the island for 300 years his race was extirpated by a plague.

Parthola'nians (*The*). The second colony of Ireland, who came to the island some 2,200 years before Christ, and found it inhabited by the Fomorians. The chroniclers inform us that the Fomorians were a Basque or Iberian colony, and the Partholanians an Aryan colony, so named from Partholan, who came to Ireland with his four sons and a number of followers. The tradition is of small historic value, but the Irish boast of their Iberian descent, and scorn the notion of being Scotic.

No doubt the dark complexion, the short stature, and gracefulness of manners give colour to their Iberian descent.

Particular Baptists. Those Baptist Dissenters who hold the Calvinistic views of election, predestination, and reprobation, in contradistinction to the General Baptists, who maintain the doctrine of universal redemption. *See* 'Free Communionists,' 'Close Communionists.'

Partidas (*Las*). A code of laws established by Alfonso X. 'The Wise,' of Leon (1203, 1252–1285).

Partis en France, between 1793–1795.

Alarmistes.

Apitoyeurs, those who sympathised with the royal family.

Brissotins (*q.v.*).

Buveurs de Sang, those who revelled in blood and slaughter.

Chevaliers du Poignard (*q.v.*).

Chouans (*q.v.*).

Compagnons de Jéhu (*q.v.*).

Contre-Révolutionnaires, the anti-revolutionary party.

Crapauds du Marais. See 'Marais.'

Egorgeurs, those who were for death and slaughter without end.

Emissaires de Cobourg, the 'Suspects' supposed to be influenced by emissaries of Friedrich prince of Saxe-Coburg.

—— *de Pitt,* those who attributed the anti-revolutionary movement to bribes given by William Pitt. This silly notion was very general.

Endormeurs, poisoners. In ancient jurisprudence an Endormeur was one 'qui pour dépouiller ses victimes, mêle dans leurs aliments une drogue somnifère.'

Fédéralistes. See 'Federalism.'

Girondins (*q.v*).

Habitans de la Crête.

Hébertistes, partisans of Hébert surnamed 'Le Père Duchêne' (*q.v.*).

Hommes d'Etat.

—— *de la Plaine,* the Yea-nay party or Trimmers.

—— *du 10 Août. See* 'August 10.'

—— *du 31 Mai,* those who took an active part in 'the Reign of Terror.

Jeunesse dorée de Fréron (*q.v.*).

Maratistes, partisans of Marat.

Ministériels.

Modérés.

Montagnards (*q.v.*).

Muscadins (*q.v.*).

Partisans de la vie civile.

Patriotes de 1789, those who had taken part in the storming of the Bastille.

Sans-culottes (*q.v.*).

Septembriseurs (*q.v.*).

Suspects (*q.v.*).

Terroristes (q.v.).
Thermidoriens (q.v.).
 ⁂ Veut-on savoir, pendant ces deux ans, c'est-à-dire de '93 à '95, combien il y a eu de partis en France ? Il y en a eu trente-trois.—DUMAS, *Les Blancs et les Bleus.*

Partition (*Treaty of*). I. Signed at the Hague by France, England, and Holland, 11 Oct., 1698. It stipulated three things : (*a*) That at the death of Carlos II. the kingdom of Spain should not be absorbed by Germany, but should be given to the electoral prince of Bavaria, son of the elector ; (*b*) that Naples, Sicily, Sardinia, the province of Guipuzcoa, Fontarabia, St. Sebastjan, Ferrol, and certain towns on the Tuscan coast owned by Spain, should be settled on the Dauphin; (*c*) that Milan should be settled on Karl the second son of the kaiser. Frustrated by the death of the electoral prince of Bavaria in 1699, aged eight years.
II. The same contracting parties agreed to confer the crown of Spain, when vacant, on the Archduke Karl, son of the kaiser ; the Italian States were to be the dauphin's portion. Signed 13 March, 1700. Set aside by the will of Carlos II. of Spain in 1701, in which the whole Spanish monarchy was bequeathed to the duke of Anjou, second son of the dauphin.

Partition of Poland (*The*). *First Partition*, 1772, planned by Frederick II., was between Russia, Austria, and Prussia. Russia took 42,000 square miles, Austria took 27,000, and Prussia 13,000.
The *Second Partition*, 1790, was between Russia and Prussia; Russia took 96,000 square miles and gave Prussia 22,000 as a sop, but left Austria in the cold.
The *Third Partition*, 1795. Austria thought the Second Partition unfair, and a third spoliation was agreed upon, in which Russia took 43,000 square miles, Prussia 21,000, and Austria 18,000.

In 1847 Austria occupied Cracow, and thus seized the last remainder of independent Poland.

Altogether, Russia took 181,000 square miles, Prussia 56,000, and Austria 45,000. The nominal cause of this spoliation was a religious difference, the reigning powers being Protestants and the 'patriots' being Catholics.

Party Volant (*The*). Those who, in the reign of Charles I., fluctuated in political principles from parliament to king. Nominally parliamentarians, they hankered after the court. The heads of the Party Volant were the Earl of Northumberland, the Earl of Holland, the Earl of Clare, the Earl of Portland, Waller the poet, and the widowed Countess of Carlisle (daughter of Northumberland).

Parvula Evangel'ia. Extracts from the Gospels worn as an amulet.

Quo loco [Jerome] comparat pharisæos certis superstitiosis mulierculis, quæ inani fide inductæ, circumferebant tum temporis *Parvula Evangelia*, hoc est, excerptas ex evangelio sententias. . . . Eadem superstitio apud multos ultimis sæculis invaluit, qui collo appendebant Initium Evangelii Johannis.—SCALIGER.

Pascal of Germany (*The*). Novālis, *i.e.* Friedrich von Hardenberg of Saxony, a lyric poet, and chief of the Romantic school (*q.v.*). He is so called by Carlyle, but 'the Keats of Germany' would have been more appropriate (1772–1801).

Paschal Canon (*The*). A table of the movable feasts, showing the day of Easter, and all other feasts depending on Easter, for a cycle of nineteen years.

Paschal Controversy (*The*), or 'Easter Controversy' (162–673). A controversy about the time of keeping Easter—whether the right time is the fourteenth day of the moon, or the Sunday following the fourteenth day. The former is the practice of the Eastern Church, the latter of the Western Church. Victor bishop of Rome excommunicated the churches of Asia in 190 for keeping Easter as they did. The two churches, however, continued to disagree upon the question.

The Council of Nice (325) determined that Easter day should be the Sunday following the Jewish feast of the Passover, which was kept the fourteenth day (or full moon) of the month Nisan ; that is the full moon *on* or *next after* 21 March. In 532 Dionysius Exiguus proposed a new method of reckoning the feast. The British Church did not conform till 673, at the Council of Hertford. Iona later still.

Paschal Mass. ' Missa Paschalis.' The Mass 'quæ in singulis septimanæ Paschalis feriis agitur.' *See* ' Mass.'

Pas'chites (2 syl.), 2nd cent. Those Christians who celebrate Easter on Jewish paschal day, which was the 14th of the moon. In 196 Pope Victor excommunicated those who kept Easter on any day but Sunday. The controversy was not finally settled till the Council of Nice, A.D. 325.

Pasha is a ruler of a province in the Turkish empire. A three-tailed pasha is of the highest rank; his standard is decorated with three tails, which are its pennons.

Pass of Brander (*The*). The famous dark gorge which narrows into the Pass of Awe, the scene of the desperate engagements between Wallace and the caterans of Macfarlane, and Bruce and the Macdougalls of Lorn.

Pass of Plumes (*The*), 1599. A pass in Leinster, where the Earl of Essex was attacked by the O'Moores; so called from the number of plumes of which the soldiers of Essex were despoiled.

Pass under the Yoke (*To*). The yoke under which the Romans made a vanquished army pass, in sign of subjugation, consisted of two upright spears stuck in the ground, with a third spear fastened transversely atop, thus Π (Livy, iii. 28; Florus, i. 11, 13.)

The custom was adopted by other nations with whom the Romans made war. Thus Pontius the Samnite, the Numantians, and Jugurtha the African, made the Roman army pass under a yoke. Of course the men laid down their arms before they passed *sub juga*.

Passagins. So the Waldenses (*q.v.*) were sometimes nicknamed, meaning men of passage, or missionary vagrants.

Passar'owitz, in Servia (*Peace of*), 21 July, 1718. Between the kaiser, the Porte, and Venice. By this treaty the Morēa was confirmed to Turkey.

Passau, in Bavaria (*Treaty of*), 22 May to 7 Aug., 1552. Moritz, the new elector of Saxony, rebelled against Charles V., drove him from place to place, till at length he signed the treaty of Passau, granting full liberty to all Protestants to worship in any way they chose, free of all interference and restraint. This is called 'The Religious Peace.'

Passau, pronounce *Pas-sow* (ow as in *now*).

Passion Sunday. The 5th Sunday of Lent, 'Dominīca in Passiōne Domini.' This Sunday began 'Passion Week' (*q.v.*). *See* 'Sunday.'

Passion Week, or the Great Week, was originally a parson's week—that is, as many days as can be massed together with only one Sunday; of course, this may be thirteen days. It began the Monday following the 5th of Lent, and ended on Holy Saturday (the day preceding Easter Sunday). The last seven days of this period constitute Holy Week. The first day of Holy Week is Palm Sunday, the fourth day is Spy Wednesday, the fifth Maundy Thursday, the sixth Good Friday, and the last Holy Saturday or the Great Sabbath. When the Great Week is reduced to seven days, as it usually is by Protestants, then Passion Week and Holy Week are commensurate terms; but those who seek to restore the ancient ritual call Passion Week the period between the 5th of Lent and Palm Sunday (not included), and Holy Week from Palm Sunday to Holy Saturday. Strictly speaking, Passion Week covers thirteen days, the last seven of which constitute Holy Week.

Passionists, 1741. A religious order founded by Paul de la Croix. They dress in black and go about bareheaded and barefooted, but wear sandals.

Passive Obedience, or 'Non-resistance,' is the political doctrine that subjects are bound to obey those in authority, whether right or wrong, good or bad. Applied to kings it includes also the dogma that the king, being the Lord's anointed, must not only be obeyed, but that he cannot be deposed. The doctrine is based on Romans xiii. 1, 2 : 'Let every soul be subject unto the higher powers. For there is no power but of God; the powers that be are ordained of God. Whosoever therefore resisteth the power, resisteth the ordinance of God. And they that resist shall receive to themselves damnation.'

It is hard to see how those who allow the authority of these words can resist the dogma of 'passive obedience.' Of course those who set aside the authority of St. Paul assert that 'the powers,' being civil rulers, are the servants of the state, and like other servants can be dismissed if they neglect their duty or are incompetent to perform it. This, however, is setting aside the dictum of St. Paul for the doctrine of expediency.

Pasteurienne Inoculation, 1885. Inoculation first suggested by M. Pasteur of Paris, to cure persons bitten by mad dogs or wolves, or to prevent their becoming rabid. In 1887, out of 3,020 patients treated by M. Pasteur, only 34 died, and out of 3,852 treated by M. Pasteur and nine others, 54 died; a little over 4 per cent.

Pas'teurise (3 syl.). A verb derived from the name of M. Pasteur, the Parisian chemist, who introduced the process of and art of sealing up wines and beers in air-tight casks, to prevent the entrance of ferment or germs to deteriorate the liquors. *See* 'Listerise.'

Somewhere between 1880 and 1886.

Paston Letters (*The*). A series of letters and other documents collected by members of the Paston family, to whom most of them are addressed (1564–1700). The Pastons lived in Norfolk during the time of the Wars of the Roses, and these letters throw much light on the customs and incidents of the period. Four vols. were published between 1787 and 1789 by Mr. [Sir John] Fenn of Norfolk, but the originals have not been discovered. A fifth vol. was published in 1823 by Mr. Serjeant Frere, the originals of which were presented to the Antiquarian Society, and 95 were discovered in Roydon Hall in 1875.

These letters reveal to us various modes by which the strong man was enabled to turn the scale against the weak one at law ; but the most extraordinary relation concerning the family itself is one which occupies more than a volume, and details the actual war made upon them by the Duke of Norfolk. The celebrated general Sir John Fastolf left Sir John Paston the estate of Caistor in 1459 ; but the duke declared that Sir John had *given* it to him . . . and he laid siege to it . . . and took it.—HOWITT, *Hist. of England* (vol ii. p. 44).

Pastoral Poets of Greece (*The*). Theocrítos of Syracuse, the father of pastoral poetry. Thirty of his idyls and several of his epigrams are still extant (B.C. 300–230). Bion of Smyrna (B.C. 295–238), author of a poem on the 'Death of Adonis,' and Moschos of Syracuse (B.C. 289–200), the friend of Bion.

Pastoral Romance (*Father of*). Honoré d'Urfé (1567–1625), author of 'Astrea.'

Pastoreaux (*Les*), 1250. Politico-religious insurgents in Flanders during the captivity of St. Louis in Egypt. From Flanders the insurrection spread through France, and soon swelled to a mass of 100,000 men, divided into companies, with banners bearing a cross and a lamb. Their leader was a Cistercian monk named Job or Jacob, from Hungary, who gave out that he was commissioned by the Virgin Mary to preach a crusade to the poor against their oppressors. This Job was received at Amiens,

Bourges, Orléans, and Paris as a prophet. His wrath was mainly directed against the idleness and corruption of the clergy, some monasteries were plundered by him and their inmates put to the sword. In 1251 government interfered, and the rabble was dispersed or cut to pieces at Berry and Beaucaire. *See* 'French Brigands.'

Seventy years afterwards another insurrection broke out, and these insurgents called themselves by the same name. The object of this second 'crusade' was the general massacre of the Jews. They were called Shepherds because they assumed to be the Shepherds of the Lord who protected the 'lambs ' from the 'wolves,'

Du Cange says :—' Pastoureaux, quod pastorem infimæque plebis hominem significat, cujusmodi erant plerique ex Pastorellis, ut testatur continuator Nangii vernaculus sub 1251.'

Pastoreaux, pronounce *Pastor-o.*

Patans (*The*). So the Afghans were called in the middle ages. A dynasty of Patans reigned in India from 1205 to 1398, and succeeded the Gaurides (2 syl.). Delhi was their capital. Tamerlane overthrew the Patans, and established the dynasty of the Timorides (3 syl.).

Pat'erins, or **Patarins** (*The*). A branch of Paulicians who said that creation was the work of the Spirit of Evil. They were pretty abundant in Illyria and Bosnia in the 12th cent. Called Paterins because they taught that prayer should be addressed to the Father only. The Waldenses were sometimes called Paterins or Paterīni, as well as Cathari and Gazari (in Italy). In France they were called Albigenses and Vaudois. Condemned by the Council of Lateran in 1179.

Du Cange says : 'A loco urbis Mediolani, qui *Patarea* vel *Pataria* vocabatur.'

Apollo was called 'Paterinus,' from Patara, now Patera, a town of Lycia, which had an oracle of Apollo.

Pâtre de Montalte (*Le*). The swineherd of Montalte, Sixtus V., the 'second founder of Rome.' Born at Montalte (1521, 1585–1590).

Patres Conscripti [Fathers and Conscripts]. The Patres of Rome were the patrician senators ; but when some of these were slain at the expulsion of Tarquin, Junius Brutus selected others to fill the vacant seats ; and as these names were enrolled in the senate with the patres or previous senators, they were called the *Conscripts*, and the house was addressed as 'Patres [et] Conscripti.'

Pat'res Pat'riæ, 1774. The delegates to the first American Congress which met at Philadelphia on 14 Sept. representing twelve different states: The four New England states, with those of Virginia, Pennsylvania, Maryland, New York, New Jersey, Delaware, and the two Carolinas. They assembled for business in Carpenters' Hall. The congress sat till 26 Oct., and then adjourned till 10 May, 1775.

Patrician of Rome. A title conferred by Pope Adrian I. on Pepin le Bref, which made him the representative of the imperial power in the West. Charlemagne continued the title.

Patrimony of St. Peter (*The*), 'Estates of the Church,' 1077. The dotation of the Countess Matilda of Tuscany to the Holy See of Modĕna, Parma, and Mantua. It was united to the new kingdom of Italy in 1870.

Between Orvieto in the north, Umbria in the east, the champaign of Rome and the Tyrrhenian Sea.

This dotation was only a part of the Papal States. The Exarchate of Ravenna was given to the Holy Church by Pepin king of the Franks; Benevento was given to it by Heinrich III.; Forli and the Romagna were added in 1297; Bologna in 1364; Ferrâra in 1598; Urbino in 1626; Orvieto [*Or-vee-a'-to*] in 1649.

Patriot King (*The*). George III. was so styled by Bolingbroke.

Patriot Party (*The*), 1692. The ' Ins ' or ' Let-alones,' formerly called the Court party. They were in opposition to the Country party or ' Outs,' called the ' Grumbletonians,' in Walpole's ministry. *See* next article.

Patriots (*The*), 1724. A political party organised by Bolingbroke and Pulteney against Sir Robert Walpole, chief minister of state in the reigns of George I. and George II. Their organ was ' The Craftsman,' a journal which they started to air their opinions in.

George II. hated ' the rogue ' (Walpole), but being henpecked he was a nonentity; and Walpole, who had gained the queen, remained in office for ten years after the accession of George II.

Patriots of '89 (*The*). Those Frenchmen who assisted in storming the Bastille.

Patriotic Brotherhood (*The*), 1881. A ' gang of murderous conspirators' in Ireland, some of whom were brought to trial at the Antrim assizes in March. P. J. Sheridan was the chief

organiser in Mayo, and took a leading part in forming the association.

Patripassionists, or 'Patripassians.' Certain Monoph'ysites (4 syl.) who admit the divinity of Christ, but maintain that He was the indivisible God the Father, and that it was this God, the one and only God, who was crucified on Calvary. St. Augustine refers to them. They were also called *Deipassionists*.

Patrius Sermo. The language of the fathers and of fatherland.

Patron Saints of—

	Fête day
ABERDEEN, St. Nicholas (died 342)	6 Dec.
ABYSSINIA, St. Frumentius (died 360)	27 Oct.
ALEXANDRIA, St. Mark, who founded a church there (died 52)	25 April
ALPS (*The*). Felix Neff (1798-1829).	
ANTIOCH, St. Margaret (died 275) ...	20 July
ARDENNES (*The*). St.Hubert (died 730)	{30 May {and 3 Nov.
ARMENIA, St. Gregory of Armenia (died 332)	30 Sept.
BATH, St. David, from whose benediction the waters of Bath received their warmth and medicinal qualities (died 544)	1 March
BEAUVAIS, St. Lucian (died 290)	8 Jan.
BELGIUM, St. Boniface (died 755) ...	5 June
BOHEMIA, St. John von Pomuk (d. 1393)	16 May
BRUSSELS, St. Gudule (died 712) ...	8 Jan.
CAGLIARI, in Sardinia, St. Eficio (died 286)	15 Jan.
CAPPADOCIA, St. Matthias (died 62)	24 Feb.
CARTHAGE, St. Perpetua (died 208) ...	7 March
COLOGNE, St Ursûla (died 452) ...	21 Oct.
CORFU, St. Spiridion (4th cent.) ...	14 Dec.
CREMO'NA, St. Margaret (died 275) ...	20 July
DENMARK, St. Anscharius (died 864) ...	3 Feb.
And St. Canute (died 1086) ...	19 Jan.
EDINBURGH, St. Giles (died 550) ...	1 Sept.
ENGLAND, St. George (died 290) ...	23 April
ETHIOPIA, St. Frumentius (died 360) ..	27 Oct.
FLANDERS, St. Peter (died 66) ...	29 June.
FLORENCE, St. John the Baptist (d. 32)	{24 June {and 29 Aug.
FRANCE, St. Denis (died 272) ..	9 Oct.
FRANCONIA, St. Kilian (died 689) ...	8 July
FRIESLAND, St. Wilbrod (died 738) ...	7 Nov.
GAUL, St. Irenæus (died 200) ...	28 June
And St. Martin (died 397) ...	11 Nov.
GENOA, St. George of Cappadocia (died 361)	23 April
GEORGIA, St. Ninian (4th cent.) ...	16 Sept.
GERMANY, St. Martin (died 397)... ...	11 Nov.
And St. Boniface (died 755) ...	5 June
GLASGOW, St. Kentigern (died 601) ...	13 Jan.
HIGHLANDERS (*The*), St. Columb (d. 597)	9 June
HOLLAND, the Virgin Mary :—For	
The *Nativity*	21 Nov.
,, *Visitation*	2 July
,, *Conception*	8 Dec.
,, *Purification*	2 Feb.
,, *Assumption*	15 Aug.
HUNGARY, St. Anastasius (died 628) ...	22 Jan.
INDIA, Francis Xavier (died 1552) ...	3 Dec.
IRELAND, St. Patrick (died 493) ..	17 March
ITALY, St. Antony (died 356) ...	17 Jan.
LAPLAND, St. Nicholas (died 342) ...	6 Dec.
LICHFIELD, St. Chad (died 672) ...	2 March
LIÉGE, St. Albert (died 1195) ...	21 Nov.
LISBON, St. Vincent (died 304) ...	15 Sept.
LONDON, St. Paul (died 64) ...	25 Jan.
MILAN, St. Ambrose (died 397) ...	7 Dec.
MOSCOW, St. Nicholas (died 342) ...	6 Dec.
NAPLES, St. Januârius (died 291) ...	19 Sept.
NETHERLANDS, St. Amand (died 679) ..	6 Feb.

			Fête day
NORWAY, St. Anscharius (died 864)	...		3 Feb.
OXFORD, St. Frideswide (died 760)	...		16 Oct.
PADUA, St. Justina (died 304)	...	...	7 Oct.
PARIS, St. Geneviève (died 512)	...		3 Jan.
PEAR (*The*), Derbyshire. W. Bagshaw (died 1702)			
PICTS (*The*), St. Ninian (4th cent.)	...		16 Sept.
PISA, San Ranieri.			
POITIERS, St. Hilary (died 367)	...	...	14 Jan.
POLAND, St. Hedviga (died 1243)	...	...	15 Oct.
PORTUGAL, St. Sebastian (died 288	...		20 Jan.
PRUSSIA, St. Andrew (1st cent.)	...	...	30 Nov.
ROCHESTER, St. Paulinus (died 431)			22 June
ROME, St. Peter and St. Paul (1st cent.)			29 June
RUSSIA, St. Nicholas (died 342)		...	6 Dec.
SARAGOSSA, St. Vincent (died 304)		...	22 Jan.
SARDINIA, the Virgin Mary. *See* 'Holland.'			
SCOTLAND, St. Andrew (1st cent.)			30 Nov.
SEBASTIA, in Armenia, St. Blaise (died 316)	...	...	3 Feb.
SICILY, St. Agatha (died 251)		...	5 Feb.
SILESIA, St. Hedviga (died 1243)	...		15 Oct.
SLAVI (*The*), St. Cyril (died 868)	...		14 Feb.
SPAIN, St. James the Greater (died 44)			24 July
SWEDEN, St. Anscharius (died 864)	...		3 Feb.
SWITZERLAND, St. Gall (died 646)	...		16 Oct.
UNITED STATES, the Virgin Mary.			
VENICE, St. Mark (died 52)	...	...	25 April
VIENNA, St. Stephen (died 34)	...	...	26 Dec.
WALES, St. David (died 544)	...	...	1 March
(*He was the uncle of King Arthur*)			
YORKSHIRE, St. Paulinus (died 431)	...		22 June

Paul (*The German*). Martin Luther (1483–1546).

Paul (*The Second St.*). St. Remi or Remigius, 'the Great Apostle of the French' (439–535).

Paul Lorrain's Saints. Convicts said to have died penitent. Paul Lorrain was ordinary of Newgate, and died in 1719. He always represented his convicts as dying penitent. 'The Tatler,' No. 63. See also Note to 'Spectator,' No. 338 (Morley's edit.).

Paul Veronese of France (*The*), Delacroix (1799–1863). Sometimes called the *Rubens* of France from his rich colouring.

Paul's School (*St.*), 1509. Founded by Dean Colet for the gratuitous instruction of 153 boys in humane letters. This number was selected in accordance with that of the miraculous draught of fishes mentioned in the Gospel of St. John. This was the first public school in England in which Greek was taught. William Lilly was master of St. Paul's.

Paul's Walkers. Loungers in St. Paul's Cathedral in the Commonwealth and afterwards.

The young gallants .... used to meet at the central point, St. Paul's; and from this circumstance obtained the appellation of 'Paul's Walkers,' as we now say 'Bond Street Loungers.' —*European Magazine* (July 1807).

Paulette, 1604. A tax imposed by Henri IV. of France to supply him with ready money. It granted to members of parlement the right of transmitting their office to their heirs on payment of an annual fee 'au 60ᵐʳ de la valeur présumée de la charge.' It received its name from Henri's secretary the Chevalier Paulet, who suggested the impost.

Paulianists (*The*). 260 disciples of Paul bishop of Samisat, and afterwards patriarch of Antioch. He denied the doctrine of the Trinity and the divinity of Jesus Christ. Condemned by the Council of Antioch in 270.

Paulicians. The 'Waldenses' of the Greek Church (660–845), so called because they formed their religious views from the Pauline epistles. They rejected the worship of the Virgin, disbelieved the intercession of saints, the sanctity of relics, and the material presence in the Eucharist.

One Constantine of Mananalis, near Samosâta, had a Greek New Testament given him by one who had been a captive among the Mahometans. He studied it, and formed his own religious views therefrom. The sect was almost stamped out by the persecutions of Theodora, who massacred 100,000 of them, if Porphyry is to be believed.

Paulicians (*The*). 'Heretics' of the 10th and 11th cents. A branch of the Manichéans, who believed in two principles, a good one and an evil one. So called from Paul of Armenia (born 844).

Petrus Sicŭlus says the Paulicians believed in an evil and a good God; the former they say was the Creator of the world, the latter is the author of that which is to come, πατὴρ ἐπουράνιος.

Pauli'na Potio (Paulinus's draught). A deadly poison concocted by Paulinus, a Dominican monk, by which Kaiser Heinrich VII. was poisoned.

In grandi stat tristitia
Exercitus militia,
De principis ruina,
Quam feritas damnabilis
Manusque detestabilis
Coagulat Paulina.
　　Rythmi in obitum Henrici VII.

Paulinists, or 'Universalists.' Those who believe that the gospel system is meant for all, both Jew and Gentile. Those who insisted that it was meant for the Jews and Jewish proselytes only are called by Dr. Baur 'Judaites' or 'Apostolites.' By the latter word he means that the apostles were Judaites. The theory of the universality of the Gospel system is called 'Pau-linism' by the Tübingen school of theologians. 'I am of Paul [a universalist], and I of Apollos [a Judaist],' a distinction which lasted till the close of the 2nd cent.

When Christ told his Apostles to go into all the world and preach the gospel to every creature, the Tübingenists tell us he meant the Jews and the Jewish proselytes scattered abroad.

Pau'peres Com'milito'nes.
Pauper soldiers of the Holy City, *i.e.* the 'Knights Templars' (*q.v.*), or Red Cross Knights.

Pauvres de la Mère de Dieu (*Les*). See 'Piarists.'

Pawnees.
A nation of North American warriors (Nebraska; now removed to the Indian territory). Their divinity is the planet Venus, which they call the Great Star; but they are rapidly dying out.

Pays de Franc-salé (*Les*).
Provinces exempt from the salt tax in France. See 'Gabelle.' Some were redeemed provinces, having given Henri II. a large sum of money for the redemption; others were maritime, in which it was not possible to prevent the smuggling of salt. The *redeemed* provinces were Angoumois, parts of Poitou, Aunis, and Saintonge, Limousin, parts of Auvergne, Quercy, Périgord, Guyenne, and the counties of Foix, Bigorre, and Cominges. The *free* provinces were Flanders, Artois, Hainaut, Calaisis, Boulonnaise, principalities of Sedan, Arles, Rançon, and Brittany, and the isles of Oléron and Ré, with parts of Poitou, Saintonge, and Aunis. In the redeemed provinces salt was sold from 6s. to 12s. the cwt. In the free provinces it was sold from 2s. to 9s. per. cwt.

Pronounce *Pay'-e d' Frahnk sah'-ley.*

Pays de Grande Gabelle (*Les*).
Gabelle (*q.v.*) was the salt tax in France before the revolution. There were the provinces of Grande Gabelle, the provinces of Petite Gabelle, the provinces of Quart-bouillon, and the free provinces or Pays de Franc-salé. The *Pays de Grande Gabelle* paid the maximum impost. The capitation was 9 lbs. per head yearly, and the price was 62 francs per cwt. or quintal. These were the Ile de France, Orléans, Maine, Anjou, Touraine, Berri, Bourbonnais, Burgundy, Picardy, Champagne,

29

Perche, and part of Normandy. See 'Pays de Petite Gabelle.'

Pronounce *Lay pay'-e d' grahnd' Gah-bell'.*

Pays de Petite Gabelle (*Les*).
Gabelle (*q.v.*) was the salt tax in France before the revolution. All France was sub-divided into four parts, those called the provinces of the Grand Gabelle, the provinces of the Petite Gabelle, the provinces of Quart-bouillon, and the free provinces. The *Pays de Petite Gabelle* paid the minimum impost. The capitation was 11 or 12 lbs. per head yearly, and the price was 33s. the cwt. or quintal. These *pays* were Lyonnais, Mâconnais, Forez, Beaujolais, Bugey, Bresse, Dauphiné, Gévaudan, Languedoc, Provence, Roussillon, Rouergue, and parts of Auvergne.

Les pays de Grande Gabelle qui payaient le maximum de l'impôt; les familles étaient dans ces pays taxées à 9 livres de sel par tête, et le prix du quintal s'élevait à 62 liv. (or francs).

Les pays de Petite Gabelle, qui payaient le minimum: le prix du quintal y était de 33 livres 10 sous (about 33 shillings), mais la consommation était réglée à 11 ou 12 livres par tête.

Pronounce *Lay pay'-e duh teet Gah-bell'.*

Pays de Quart-bouillon (*Les*).
Lower Normandy was so called in reference to the gabelle or salt tax. There were salt-works here, 'où l'on faisait *bouillir* un sable mouillé d'eaux salines, et versaient le *quart* du produit de leur fabrication [in return for this privilege] dans les greniers du roi.' The capitation was 25 lbs. of salt per head yearly, and the price was 16s. a cwt. or quintal. See 'Pays de Grande Gabelle,' and 'Pays de Petite Gabelle.'

Pronounce *Lay pay'-e d'kar' boo'-yone'.*

Peace (*The Perpetual*), 24 Jan., 1502.
Concluded between England and Scotland, a few years after the battle of Flodden Field (*q.v.*).

Peace of Antal'cidas (*The*), B.C. 387.
Concluded by Antalcīdas the Spartan and Artaxerxes.

Peace of Clement IX. (*The*), 1669.
An attempt to reconcile the Jansenists and Jesuits by virtually abolishing the formulary (*q.v.*).

Peace of Durham (*The*), 1139.
After the battle of Caton Moor or North-allerton, in which the Scots under Prince Henry were routed by Stephen. In this peace Stephen surrendered to Prince Henry the whole ea ldom of Northum-

X X

berland, with the exception of the two castles of Newcastle and Bamborough, as a bribe that he might use his influence with his niece Maude, who was in arms against Stephen.

Peace of God (*The*), 1035. A command by papal bull for all men to lay down their arms, under the expectation of the second advent of Christ, 'the Prince of Peace.' Five years later, 1040, the prohibition was modified by the 'Truce of God,' which did not forbid all military contentions, but commanded all men to cease from hostilities on Thursday, Friday, Saturday, and Sunday.

After the Gospel of the day the officiating priest read from the pulpit these words: 'May they who refuse to obey be accursed, and have their portion with Cain the first murderer, with Judas the arch-traitor, and with Dathan and Abiram, who went down alive into the pit. May they be accursed in the life which now is; and may their hope of salvation be put out, as the light of these candles is extinguished from their sight.' At which words the priests extinguished their tapers.

Peace of Monsieur (*The*), 6 May, 1576. So-called because it was signed at Chastenoy by *Monsieur*, *i.e.* the brother of Henri III. It granted to the Huguenots the free exercise of their religion throughout the kingdom of France, Paris only excepted; admission to all public offices; equal numbers with the Catholics in the various parlements; eight places of surety; the right to open schools and to convoke synods; and restoration of their estates, appanages, and governments. The terms of this treaty were never carried out.

Peace of Nicias (*The*), B.C. 421. The fifty years' truce in which the Lacedæmonians engaged to give up Amphipōlis.

Peace of Nürnberg (*The*), 1532. By the Diet of Augsburg, held in 1530, the Emperor Charles V. pronounced the Protestants contumacious heretics, and commanded them to return to mother church on pain of his great displeasure. At the time Solyman II., at the head of a large army, was in Hungary, and threatened Vienna. The princes of Germany were asked to assist in driving back the Turkish invaders, but the Protestant princes united in a league (called the Smalkaldic league) not to stir unless the decree of Augsburg was revoked. In this dilemma there was no choice left, so the decree was withdrawn, and the Protestants were allowed full liberty of worship till the next imperial diet. This ad interim concession was called the 'Peace of Nürnberg,' because it was signed in that city.

Peace of Religion (*The*), 1555. The treaty of Passau confirmed by the Diet of Augsburg the foundation of religious freedom in Germany. Protestants were allowed the free exercise of their religion in their respective dominions (Karl V.).

Passau, pronounce *Pas-sow* (ow as in *now*).

For others see under the special name, because most of these treaties are differently called by different writers. Sometimes they are called *Treaties*, sometimes *Treaties of Peace*, sometimes only *Truces*, &c.

Peacock of the North (*The*). Robert Neville, who beautified Middleham Castle in 'a very peacocky style.'

Peacock's Feather. The badge of the Chinese general.

Let the peacock's feather be plucked from the cap of Yihshan for his imbecility and tardiness in bringing up his forces . . . and let every officer in the province of Canton . . . be deprived of his official button.—*The Emperor's despatches in the first Chinese war.*

Pearl of Brittany (*The*). The Princess Eleanor, daughter of Geoffrey duke of Brittany, granddaughter of Henry II. and niece of King John; confined in Bristol Castle because she was next heir to Arthur to the crown of England (1184–1241). She was starved to death.

Pearl of Ireland (*The*). St. Bridget, born in Ulster, lived in a cell in an oak called *Kill-dara*, or the 'cell of the oak,' 6th cent.

Pearl of Normandy (*The*). Emma, sister of Richard II. duke of Normandy, and wife of Ethelred the Unready (died 1046).

Pearls are next in value to diamonds. The following are historic :—

'La Peregrina' weighed 126 carats, and was pear-shaped. Gongibus of Calais brought it from India in 1620. When laid before Felipe II. of Spain, he said : 'How could you concentrate all your fortune on so small a thing ?' To which the merchant replied : 'Because I knew the world contained a king who would buy it of me.' This gem came into the possession of Princess Youssopoff, and is valued at 37,000*l.*

Felipe II. had another pearl, about the

size of a pigeon's egg, and weighing 134 grains. It came from Panăma, and was valued at 23,000*l*.

The Kaiser Rudolf II. possessed a pearl of 180 grains; and Napoleon I. had one about the same size.

The pearl which Louis XIV. gave to Madame de Maintenon, and which was offered for sale in 1819, weighed 27⅞ carats.

The Shah of Persia has a pearl an inch in diameter. In 1633 it was valued at 64,000*l*.

The pearl in the possession of the Arabian imam of Muscat is valued at 32,000*l*.

The Crown Prince of Prussia gave to the Princess Royal of England a necklace of thirty-two pearls valued at 20,000*l*.

The pearl which Cleopatra melted and drank in health to Antony was valued at 80,000*l*.
The Romans called the large bell-shaped pearls *Uniones*, the pear-shaped pearls they called *Elenchi*, the half-ball-shaped *Tympania*, and the whitest *Exaluminatæ Margaritæ*.

Peasant Bard (*The*). Robert Burns (1759–1796).

Peasant Painter of Sweden (*The*). Peter Hörberg, who died in 1814.

Peasant Poet of Northampton (*The*). John Clare (1793–1864).

Peasant Poet of Suffolk (*The*). Robert Bloomfield, author of 'The Farmer's Boy' (1766–1823).

Peasant Revolt (*The*), 1381. Under Wat Tyler, who had been a soldier in the French wars. A spirit of discontent had long been seething; it was aggravated by the Statute of Labour, which most unjustly fixed the price of labour to what it was two years before the Black Death, although the price of food had risen greatly. The discontent came to a head by a poll-tax for the prosecution of the French war, and this poll-tax was the same to the poor as to the rich. All the eastern counties rose in revolt, but Kent took the lead. Wat Tyler being stabbed to death by William Walworth the lord mayor, the young King Richard II. by a happy address promised to be the new leader, and the revolt was easily put down

Peasant of Cotignola (*The*). Sforza, whose name was Giacomuzo d'Attendolo, born at Cotignola, a village of Romagna. He was an agricultural labourer, but at the age of 12 entered the army as groom to Count Alberic, who gave him the pseudonym of Sforza, because he 'gained his own way by force.' His grandson, Francesco Sforza, married the only child of Francesco Maria Visconti duke of Milan, and succeeded to that dukedom, thus transferring its crown to the line of 'The Peasant of Cotignola' [*Co-tin'-yo-lah*].

Peasant of the Danube (*The*). 'Le Paysan du Danube,' Louis Legendre, a member of the French National Convention, famous for his 'éloquence sauvage' (1755–1797).

Peasants' War (*The*), in Germany, or 'War of the Rustauds,' 1524–1525. The grievances were these: (1) The people demanded the free election of their parish clergy; (2) the appropriation of the tithes of grain, after deducting therefrom the suitable maintenance of the parish clergy—this 'appropriation' was to be set aside for the support of the poor; (3) the total abolition of serfdom, hunting and fishing rights, and game laws; (4) throwing open of forests and other lands tied up to secular and ecclesiastical nobles; (5) equal administration of justice; and (6) the abolition of certain odious exactions made by the clergy. In 1525 the rising was stamped out with terrible cruelty, and more than 150,000 of the insurgents perished.

Pecquigny (*Treaty of*), 1475. Louis by bribes induced Edward IV. to sign this treaty, and withdraw his army from France.

Pronounce *Pe-keen'-yĕ*.

Peculiar Church, or **Parish** (*A*). Church or parish having special jurisdiction of its own, and exempt from the ordinary. There are royal peculiars, archbishops' peculiars, bishops' peculiars, and the peculiars of deans and chapters.

Peculiar People (*The*). A Protestant religious sect who trust in Providence to cure their sick of all diseases. They anoint the sick with oil and pray over them, but give no medicine and call in no medical adviser.

Pecu'lium. The plot of land given in feudal times to a slave, the produce of which helped to supply him and his family with food. When the *peculium* was more than the man could manage, he might employ a drudge, who was called *Servus servi.*

Pedobaptists. *See* 'Pædobaptists.'

Pedro the Cruel, King of Castile (1319, 1350–1369). He began his reign by murdering his father's mistress, Leonora de Gusman; daily his nobles fell his victims; he put to death his cousin and one of his natural brothers; he caused his queen (Blanche de Bourbon) to be cast into prison and there poisoned. A second queen suffered in the same way.

Pedro, pronounce *Pay-dro.*

Peel's Hundred Days. Sir Robert Peel held the seals of office from Nov. 1834 to May 1835, between the first and second administrations of Lord Melbourne.

Peel's Velveteens, 1842. Velveteens containing as design wheat-ears on a scroll on which was the word 'Free.' A specimen was sent to Sir Robert Peel and accepted by him, but afterwards returned. *See* 'Velveteen Plot.'

Peep-o'-day Boys. An Irish Presbyterian party, organised in 1790. In 1688 the whole Catholic property of Ireland was confiscated; and when in the 18th cent. William Pitt made some attempts to mitigate this injustice, the Irish Protestants took alarm, regarding 'Protestant ascendency' endangered. Acts of violence against the Roman Catholics were organised, and as they were perpetrated at the *peep of day*, the party was called 'The Peep-o'-day Boys.' *See* 'Defenders' and 'Irish Associations.'

The Peep-o'-day Boys in 1795 became the Orangemen, and the Roman Catholics the 'Defenders.'

Peers of France (*The Twelve*). There were six lay and six ecclesiastical peers. The lay peers were the duke of Normandy, the duke of Burgundy, the duke of Aquitaine, and the three counts of Flanders, Toulouse, and Champagne; the ecclesiastics were the archbishop of Reims, the archbishop of Sens, and the four bishops of Noyon, Langres, Beauvais, and Châlons.

All Brittany, for a time, did homage to the Duke of Normandy.
Aquitaine included Poitou, Limousin, most of Guienne, and the feudal superiority of Angoumois.
The feof of Flanders stretched from the Scheldt to the Somme.

The Count of Flanders possessed Languedoc, with Quercy and Rouergue, and feudal superiority over Auvergne.

Peg Nicholson's Knights. *See* 'Margaret's Knights.'

Pegas'ians. In Latin Pegasiāni. A law school so called from Pegăsus, a jurist, and follower of the Procu'lians (*q.v.*) of the republican or popular party.

Pehle'vi Dynasty. *See* 'Pishdadian dynasty.'

Peine Forte et Dure. Being pressed to death. Remanded to a low, dark chamber in a prison, the victim was laid on his back on the bare floor, naked; then on his body was placed a great weight of iron. On the first day he received three morsels of the coarsest bread: on the second day three draughts of stagnant water; and so on alternately till he died. Abolished.

Pronounce *Pain fort a dure.*

Pela'gian Heresy (*The*), or 'Pelagianism,' 5th cent. The doctrines of Pelagius, whose religious views were opposed to those of St. Augustine. He denied the dogma of original sin, and declared man to be a free agent capable of himself, without the aid of the Holy Ghost, of receiving or rejecting the proffered salvation, and of performing good works. His doctrines were condemned by the two councils of Carthage and Milevium or Milevia, in Numidia, A.D. 416. Pelagius was anathematised by Innocentius in 417, and expelled from Jerusalem in 424.

It is said that Pelagius is a Greek translation of the Welsh name Morgan (sea-born). He was a man of rank, and his life was most exemplary. It is generally supposed that he was a monk of Bangor in Wales, but it is far more likely the monastery was Bangor or Banchor, in Carrickfergus, Ireland.

Pells (*Clerk of the*). From the Latin *pellis*, a skin [*i.e.* of parchment]. An officer of the exchequer whose duty it is to enter on the pells or parchment rolls every bill sent in for payment, with the receipt thereof when discharged, and all disbursements. Hence there are pells or rolls of receipts, and pells or rolls of disbursements.

Peloponnesian War (*The*), B.C. 431–404. A war for supremacy between Athens and Sparta, which lasted 27 years. It may be divided into three parts: (1) From the commencement of the Nician truce; (2) from the truce to the Sicilian expedition; and (3) from that catastrophe to the surrender of Athens. The proximate cause of the war was this: The republican party of Epidamnus rose in rebellion against the rulers, drove them from the town, and then applied to Corinth for protection. The exiled rulers applied to Corcyra. Whereupon the Corcyræans laid siege to Corinth, and obtained aid from Athens. The Corinthians applied to Sparta for assistance, and thus Athens and Sparta were drawn into the quarrel, which ended in the ruin of Athens.

Pembroke College. I. *Cambridge*, 1347.

Founded by Mary de St. Paul, widow of Aymer de Valence earl of Pembroke, in honour of her husband, who was killed in a tournament soon after his marriage. It was originally called the 'Hall of Valence and Mary.' Subsequently Pembroke Hall; and now Pembroke College.

II. *Oxford*, 1624. Founded by James I. It was originally called Broadgates Hall, but was renamed after the Earl of Pembroke, chancellor of the university. The head of the college is called the master.

Penal Laws (against Catholics).

These existed before the Treaty of Limerick, 1691.

An act subjecting all who maintain the supremacy of the Church of Rome to the penalties of *præmunire*, and requiring the oath of supremacy as a qualification for office of any kind.

An act imposing fines on absence from the parish church on Sundays.

An act authorising the chancellor to appoint a guardian to the child of a Catholic.

An act to prevent Catholics from being private tutors without a bishop's licence.

These were added in 1695 (Will. III.):—

An act to disarm Catholics; to banish Catholic priests and prelates; to prevent the intermarriages of Protestants and Catholics; to prevent Catholics from being either solicitors or gamekeepers.

These were added in Queen Anne's reign, 1703:—

The father of a papist who conformed to the established religion was incapacitated from disposing of his property by sale, mortgage, or bequest.

A papist was prohibited from being guardian even to his own child. The child on conforming was to be given in charge to a Protestant.

Papists were incapacitated for holding land for more than 31 years; and if at any time the profit of the land exceeded one-third of the rent, the lease was to be transferred to the Protestant who made the discovery.

Papists were not allowed to inherit the lands of Protestant relatives, nor to keep any horses above the value of 5*l.* each.

In 1709 an Act was passed prohibiting Catholics from holding life annuities; to assist in schools; to act as sheriffs; to sit on grand juries.

Repealed 1861 (24, 25 Vict. cc. 95, 101). Some mitigation had been made in 1778 (18 Geo. III. c. 60).

Peninsular War (*The*), 1809–1813.

Against the French in the peninsula of Portugal and Spain. Arthur Wellesley [duke of Wellington] was the British commander-in-chief who landed in Portugal 12 July, 1808, and by April 1814 had expelled the French from the peninsula. The following year he won the great battle of Waterloo.

The battle of VIME'IRA (Portugal), 21 Aug., 1808. Marshal Junot was defeated. For this victory Wellington was highly censured by Sir Hew Dalrymple, the commander-in-chief, for fighting without orders.

The battle of DOURO, 12 May, 1809, in which Wellington defeated Marshal Soult.

The battle of TALAVE'RA (Spain), 27, 28 July, 1809. Joseph Bonaparte and Marshal Victor were defeated by Wellington, who was made in April commander-in-chief of the British forces in the Peninsula.

Battle of BUSA'CO (Portugal), 27 Sept., 1810. Marshal Masséna was repulsed by Wellington, and on 3 and 5 May, 1811, the French marshal was utterly foiled at FUENTES DE OÑORO (Spain).

1812. Wellington invested CIUDAD RODRI'GO (Spain), and on 19 Jan. took it from the French by storm, and 6 April he took BA'DAJOZ by storm.

Battle of SALAMANCA (Spain), 22 July, 1812. Marshal Marmont was defeated by Wellington.

The battle of VITTORIA (Spain), 21

June, 1813. Joseph Bonaparte and Marshal Jourdan were defeated by Wellington.

Battles of the PYRENEES, 27 to 31 July, 1813. Marshal Soult was defeated by Wellington; and SAN SEBASTIAN was stormed 31 Aug., 1813.

The battle of ORTHEZ (Pyrenees), 27 Feb., 1814. Marshal Soult again defeated by Wellington; and again, 10 April, at TOULOUSE.

General Graham defeated Marshal Victor (5 March, 1811) at Barossa in Spain; and Marshal Beresford defeated Soult at Albuēra 16 May, 1811. And 11 Jan., 1809, Sir John Moore fell at Corunna. In Nov. 1813 Sir John Murray defeated Soult's army on the Nivelle.

⁎⁎⁎ Between 21 Aug., 1808, and 10 April, 1814 (less than five and a-half years), Wellington had defeated six French marshals : Jourdan, Junot, Marmont, Massena, Soult, and Victor, together with Joseph Bonaparte. He had won the battles of Vimēira, Douro, Talavēra, Busāco, Fuentes de Oñoro, Salamanca, Vittoria, the battles of the Pyrenees, Orthez, and Toulouse, besides the sieges of Ciudad Rodrīgo, Badājoz, and San Sebastian.

⁎⁎⁎ After the victory at the *Douro*, Sir Arthur Wellesley was created 'Baron Douro '; after the battle of *Talavēra*, he was made ' Viscount Wellington '; after the siege of *Ciudad Rodrīgo*, he was made 'Earl of Wellington '; after the battle of *Salamanca*, he was made ' Marquis of Wellington' ; and for his victory at *Vittoria* he was created 'Duke of Wellington.' We had no honour left for his victory at Waterloo.

Penitent (*A*). A man whose duty it was (before the introduction of safety lamps) to descend into a coal mine, early every morning, to explode the fire-damp which had accumulated during the night. So called because he was dressed like a religious 'penitent,' in a woollen dress, which covered his face and body.

Penitents of Love (*The*), 13th cent. A fraternity established in Languedoc consisting of knights and esquires, dames and damsels, whose object was to prove their love by bearing the extremes of heat and cold. Many perished, but what matter ? 'They received the crown of martyrdom.'

Penitentes. Fanatics of New Mexico, who, during Lent, not only fast, but subject their bodies to the most horrible tortures. On Good Friday they go in procession from their lodge to a cross, with their skin cut into furrows, and as they march scourge themselves or each other over the shoulders till their bodies are completely covered with blood. Sometimes one or more will then volunteer to be crucified. They may be seen even in the streets on Good Friday with a huge wooden cross strapped on their back, their arms drawn up and fastened

to the cross-bar, and a spear fastened to their body, so that the point touches the arm, and if in walking over the road strewed with potsherds, sharp stones, and thorny plants the foot flinches or stumbles, the spear point wounds the flesh of the arms.

Penitential Week. *Hebdomada Pœnitentialis.* The same as ' Hebdomada Pœnalis ' (*q.v.*).

Penitentiary of England. A lucrative office for granting papal dispensations.

Pennsylvania (U.S. America). The 'Penn Forest.' So called from William Penn, who in 1681 founded the colony. The inhabitants are sometimes called *Pennamites*, and were once locally nicknamed *Leather-heads.*

Pennsylvanian Bonds. Kites, or waste-paper bonds. In 1843 Pennsylvania, the richest state in America, repudiated its debt, having borrowed money for the construction of roads and canals. No transaction in history is more disgraceful than this, as the state was well able to pay, but would not.

Pennyless (*The*). Kaiser Maximilian I. (1459, 1493–1519). Called in Italian ' Massimiliāno Pochidanārio.'

Pensionary Parliament (*The*). From 8 May, 1661 to 24 Jan., 1678, *i.e.* 16 years and 260 days. It was convened by Charles II., and was so called because it had so many pensions to grant to Royalists impoverished by the late troubles. *See* ' Parliaments.'

Pensioners (*The*). All the ordinary students of the University of Cambridge who are *in statu pupillari.* There are a few fellow commoners, either sons of the nobility, sons of men of fortune, or married men, who dine at the fellows' table (whence their name). These students wear a special costume, and have certain exemptions; and there are a few sizars, sons of men of small means, most of them clergymen's sons. The sizars have their commons free, and have other emoluments which vary in different colleges. Like the fellow commoners, they are not called 'pensioners.' In Oxford the ordinary students are called ' commoners.'

Pensioners are those who pay a pension. Commoners are those who 'common' or dine at a general table.

Pentap'olis.
1. The Five Cities of Cyrenaica, near Egypt: Apollōnia, Arsinōê, Berenīcê, Cyrēnê, and Ptolemãis.
2. The Dorian Pentapolis: Camīros, Cnidos, Cos, Ialÿsos, and Lindos.
3. The Five Cities of Italy in the exarchate of Ravenna: Ancōna, Fano, Pesăro, Rimĭni, and Sinigaglia.
4. The Five Cities of the Philistines: Ascalon, Ashdod, Ekron, Gath, and Gaza.
5. The Five Cities of the Plain: Admah, Gomorrah, Sodom, Zoar, and Zeboim.

Pentarchs (*The*). The French Directory, composed of five members.

The astonishing man whom the 18th Brumaire had placed alone on the tottering throne of the Pentarchs, conceived the idea of detaching the emperor of Russia from the cause of his allies.— DUNCAN, *History of Russia*, vol. i. p. 288.

People of the Book (*The*)—*i.e.* the Koran. The four 'people' are Christians, Jews, Magians, and Sabians, who are more tolerantly treated by Mahometans than idolaters.

The People of the Book were permitted to redeem their adherence to their ancient law by the payment of tribute.—HALLAM, *Middle Ages*, vol. ii. p. 167.

People's Charter (*The*), 1838. Consisting of these six demands: (1) Universal suffrage; (2) annual parliaments; (3) stipendiary members; (4) vote by ballot; (5) equal electoral districts; and (6) abolition of monetary qualification.

The Ballot Bill passed in 1872.

People's Friend (*The*). Marat. So called from his journal 'L'Ami du Peuple.'

The People's Friend is evidently rising in importance as his befriended people rises. — CARLYLE, *French Revolution*, vol. iii. bk. iii. 3.

People's William (*The*). William Ewart Gladstone (1809-). He began his political career as a Tory, but turned Whig, and became a Radical towards the close of his life.

Between 1885 and 1886, being nearly 80 years old at the time, his political views, especially in regard to the Irish Land League, the Plan of Campaign, Boycotting, and other revolutionary subjects, underwent a complete change. In 1885 he said that 'Crime dogged the Irish Land League in all its steps;' and Sir William Harcourt spoke still more strongly against the League; but in 1886 both Mr. Gladstone and Sir William Harcourt defended the Parnellites through thick and thin, and found excuses for boycotting, the refusal to pay rent, and even for open resistance of the law. They blamed the Irish Constabulary, which a few months before they most highly praised, and seemed politically to have made a *volte face.*

Peppercorn Rent (*A*). A mere nominal rent, like the delivery of a grain

of wheat or corn of pepper, in acknowledgment of the rights of the landlord.

Perceval (*Mr.*) **Assassinated.** Spencer Perceval, second son of Lord Egmont, prime minister of England, was shot in the lobby of the House of Commons 11 May, 1812, by Bellingham, who mistook him for Lord Levĕson Gower, late ambassador to the court of St. Petersburg, who (he said) had refused him redress after acting in a diplomatic matter. He was executed for murder. Mr. Perceval was fifty years of age.

Père Duchêne [*Du-shane*].
I. James René Hébert, the French revolutionist, was so called from his obscene journal of that name (1755-1794).
II. A journal during the French Revolution conducted by Hébert. This scandalous red republican newspaper contained the most exaggerated democratic sentiments, and circulated the most horrible innuendos against the queen.

Père des Lettres (*Le*). François I. of France (1494, 1515-1547).

Pères de la Foi (*Les*). The French Jesuits, readmitted at the Restoration, so called themselves. They had flourishing colleges at Montrouge and St. Acheul; but these were closed in 1828, and declared to be in violation of the law. Since 1848 there has been a slight revival of Jesuitism in France. *See* 'Paccanarists.'

Peregrine Mass. 'Missa Peregrinōrum.' After the chapter the bell announces the Matutinal Mass for the approach of paupers, and the priest, who had celebrated high mass for the last seven days, says the 'Missa Peregrinōrum.' *See* 'Mass.'

Perfecti (The Perfect Men). So the Waldenses (*q.v.*) were sometimes nicknamed, from their professed puritanism.

Perfectibilists (*The*), 1776. An order created by Adam Weishaupt, afterwards called the 'Order of the Illuminati.' A secret society, organised on the plan of the Order of the Jesuits. Persons of any religious creed were admitted members, but passive obedience was a *sine quá non.* It greatly flourished, but became political, and was interdicted in Bavaria in 1784.

Perfectists (*The*). A sect of the Independents which rose up during the

civil war between Charles I. and his parliament. The Franciscans, Jesuits, and
Molïnists believed in the perfectibility of
man; and the Wesleyan Methodists teach
that Christian perfection is attainable,
according to the exhortation contained in
Heb. vi. 1.: 'Let us go on to perfection';
and our Lord himself says : 'Be ye perfect, as your Father in heaven is perfect.'

Under the head of Independents . . . were the
Arminians, Millenaries, Baptists, Anabaptists,
Familists, Enthusiasts, Seekers, Perfectists, Socin-
ians, Arians, and others.—HOWITT, *History of
England* (Charles I., ch. vi. p. 273).

Perfidious Albion. A favourite
expression of Napoleon I., but not of his
invention. Probably it referred originally
to the homage paid by Edward III. to
Philippe VI. of France in 1329 (*see*
Rymer, 'Fœdera,' i. p. 260). Edward
paid the homage exacted of him, but resolved upon vengeance, and executed it
to the bitter end. Napoleon talking of
'perfidy' is like the pot calling the kettle
'black-face.'

'L'Angleterre, ah! la perfide Angleterre, que
le rempart de ses mers rendoit inaccessible
aux Romains, la foi du Sauveur y est abordée.'—
BOSSUET, *A Sermon preached at Metz.*

Peripatetics (*The*). A sect of philosophers of ancient Greece, founded by
Aristotle of Stagïra in Macedonia, a pupil
of Plato (B.C. 384-322). He used to lecture in a covered walk of the Lycĕan
gymnasium in Athens, and hence his
disciples were called the 'Walking Sect,'
or 'Sect of the Walk.' His favourite
pupil was Theophrastus (B.C. 394-287).

Aristotle was called the Stagïrite (3 syl.) from
Stagïra, his native place.
The proper name of Theophrastus (*the divine
speaker*) was Tyrtämos, but Aristotle called him
'the divine speaker' from his grace and fluency of
speech.

Peronne (*Treaty of*), 1468. Between
Louis XI. and Charles le Téméraire of
Burgundy. Louis agreed by this treaty
to abandon his suzerainty over the fief of
Burgundy.

**Perpetual Council of the
Gallic Nation** (*The*). The Sorbonne
(*q.v.*).

Perpetual Edict (*The*). I. *Edictum Perpetuum*, A.D. 132. The various
edicts of Roman prætors, compiled and
arranged by Salvius Julian, a lawyer, by
order of the Emperor Hadrian. Previous
to this C. Cornelius got a law passed to prevent prætors from altering their edicts.
'Ut Prætores in Edictis suis Perpetuis
jus dicerent.' A.U. 686 (B.C. 69).

This was the first general code of Roman law
published by authority.

II. The 'Pacification of Ghent' (*q.v.*),
12 Feb., 1577. By which William prince
of Orange gained nearly all he asked for.
See above.

Perpetual Peace (*The*). I. 31 May,
1419. Between the French and Henry V.
of England. It was signed at Troyes, and
ratified by Isabella (wife of Charles VI.)
and Philip the Good of Burgundy. It
made Henry the successor of Charles VI.
at death, and regent of France till then.
It also gave him the Princess Catherine
for his wife.

II. 'La Paix Perpétuelle,' Sept. 1515,
after the battle of Marignano, or 'Combat
of the Giants.' Between François and
the Swiss, signed at Freyburg. It formed
the basis of all subsequent relations between France and Switzerland till 1789.

Perse Free Grammar School.
For 100 scholars, now enlarged to admit
190 boys. Founded by Stephen Perse, M.D.
Fellow of Caius College, 1615, reorganised
in 1873 (Trumpington Road, Cambridge).

Fees for the junior department 5*l.* a year, and 14*l.*
a year for the senior department.

Persecution in Lyons (*The*),
A.D. 177. Under Marcus Aurelius the
Christians were hunted from their houses,
expelled from the public baths and
markets, insulted, stoned, and plundered.
No distinction of nationality, sex, or age
was made. Marcus Aurelius being applied
to, gave instruction that all 'who confessed themselves to be Christians should
be put to death.'

Persecution of the Jews, in
1348-1349. I. During the prevalence of
the Black Death (*q.v.*) the Jews were the
scapegoats in Germany, and their treatment was revolting. The notion got
abroad that the wells were poisoned, and
that the Jews had poisoned them to extirpate the Christians. Men bound themselves by oaths to stamp out the cursed
race which had crucified Jesus Christ.
Some were torn to pieces; some were burnt
alive. At Speyer the Jews in despair set
fire to their own houses rather than fall
into the hands of the mob. In Mainz
10,000 Jews were massacred. At Eslingen
the whole Jewish population burnt themselves in their synagogue. At Strasburg
2,000 were burnt in their cemetery. Anyone who protected a Jew was put to the

rack and executed without mercy. *See* also under 'Milan, *Edict of*.'

The report was that the Jews obtained the poison from some remote parts of the earth and mixed it with the venom of spiders, owls, adders, and toads. No doubt the Flagellants (*q.v.*) were the chief instigators of this horrible persecution.

II. By *banishment*.

From ALEXANDRIA, by Cyril, in 415.
From ENGLAND, by EDWARD I., in 1290.
From FRANCE, by Philippe Auguste, 1182; by Philippe le Bel in 1301, 1306; by Charles VII. in 1394; by Louis XIII. in 1615.
From MEDI'NA, by Mohammed, 623.
From NAPLES and SICILY in 1504.
From the PAPAL STATES, by Pius V., in 1569.
From PORTUGAL, by Emmanuel the Fortunate, 1496.
From PRAGUE in 1520.
From ROME, B.C. 16.
From RUSSIA, by the Czarina Elizabeth, 1795, and often since.
From SPAIN, by Ferdinand and Isabella, 1492.

III. By *massacre*.

In ENGLAND, pillaged and massacred in 1264.
In FULDA in 1236.
In GERMANY, pillaged and massacred by the Crusaders in 1096: as authors of the Black Death in 1348, 1349.
In JERUSALEM, by Florus, B.C. 16.
In LONDON in 1189.
In SPAIN, at the instigation of the Archbishop of Seville, in 1391.
In YORK and other places 1190.

Persecutions by Christians (*The*).

I. Against the Albigenses, 1179–1235; most bitter, bloody, and relentless.

II. Against the Moslems, in eight crusades, 1095–1274. These wars cost the lives of 5 millions of human beings.

III. Against the Huguenots, in the Dragonnades, under Louis XIV., in 1685.

IV. Against the Protestants of Germany, in the Thirty Years' War, 1618–1648.

V. Against the Waldenses, or Vaudois, 1179–1848. *See* Félice, 'History of Protestants,' &c.

VI. Against the Jews by Christians generally.

VII. The Inquisition, 1203–1814, was a series of persecutions against 'unorthodox Christians.'

VIII. The Reformation introduced a series of persecutions by Protestants against Catholics, and Catholics against Protestants.

IX. St. Bartholomew massacre of the French Huguenots, in 1572, was a frightful affair.

X. The Smithfield fires. Speed says, 'More bloud was spilt in that short time of [Mary's] raigne, than had been shed for case of christianity in any kings time since Lucius the first establisher of the

Gospell in this realme.' 'Hist. of Great Britaine,' p. 1151 (1623).

To these may be added the general persecutions of different sects, whether that between the Eastern and Western Churches, that between Catholic sects, or that between Protestant sects. All who think differently to the established or 'orthodox' system being held 'heretics.' Buckle estimates the loss of life by these Christian persecutions at 140 millions of human beings. That would be about a tenth part of the entire present inhabitants of the earth, and most frightful to think of. *See* p. 585, 'Milan, *Edict of*.'

Orthodoxy means simply the doxy of might. In one country it is Brahmanism, in another Buddhism, in a third Zoroasterianism, in a fourth Druidism, in another Paganism; in the Eastern Church it differs from the Western; in England it is Protestantism, with the Jews Mosaicism, and so on. It is then divided into sects, and only that sect sanctioned by the state is orthodox. Hence the mutual persecutions of Arians and Trinitarians, the Jesuits against the Jansenists, the Church of England and Church of Scotland, the Sadducees and Pharisees, and so on throughout. There is no such thing as absolute orthodoxy, it is simply the power to enforce certain religious views.

Persecutions of Christians (*The*), by Roman emperors. Called 'The Ten Persecutions.'

(I.) under Nero, 64–68; (II.) under Domitian, 95; (III.) under Trajan, 106; (IV.) under Marcus Aurelius, 166–177; (V.) under Septimus Sevêrus, 199–204; (VI.) under Maximinus, 235–238; (VII.) under Decius, 250–252; (VIII.) under Valerian, 258–260; (IX.) under Aurelian, 275; and (X.) under Dioclesian, 303–313. The last is called 'The Era of the Martyrs.'

Christians were not persecuted by the Roman emperors for their faith in Christ, but for their '*lawlessness*' or infidelity to the state religion and national law. Of the religious creed, as Paley said, the Roman emperors and Roman senate were supremely indifferent, but the religion of the country was an integral part of the law of the land, which it is *not* in Protestant England, Prussia, or America.

Persia (*Golden Age of*), 1253–1335. From Hulaku to Abu Seyd, distinguished for those celebrated names Naser-ud-din, Jelal-ud-din, Sadi, and Hafiz.

Persian Punishment (*The*). Flaying alive. *See* Rawlinson's note to 'Herodotus,' v. c. 25 (vol. iii. p. 191).

Persian War (*The*). I. A.D. 337–360. In the reign of Constantius II., son of Constantine the Great. In this war the armies of Rome and Persia encountered each other in nine bloody fields, in two of which Constantius commanded in person. In all these battles the Persians were the superiors.

II. A.D. 502–505, between Cabades or Kobad the Persian and Anastasius emperor of the East. The Huns and Arabs marched under the Persian standard. Amïda stood a siege of three months, in which the Persian general lost 50,000 men; but Persia expiated her loss with the slaughter of 80,000 of the adversary, and peace was concluded in 505 (Gibbon, 'Decline and Fall,' chap. xl.).

Persic Version (*The*) of the Scriptures. A version of the Pentateuch by Jacob ben Joseph, 9th cent. *See* 'Scriptures.'

Perspicuous Doctor (*The*). Walter Burley, born 1275, died 1338. Flourished 1320. He was preceptor to Edward III. Burley attacked the dogmas of Duns Scotus.

Perth (*Convention* or *Treaty of*), 18 Aug., 1305. Between Edward I. and the regents of Scotland. This convention, which apparently settled the affairs of Scotland, was scarcely signed when Robert Bruce threw the two countries into war again by the murder of Comyn lord of Badenoch.

Peschit'o (*The*), or 'Peshitto,' meaning *literal* or *simple*. An old Syriac version of the Bible, supposed to have been made in the 2nd and 3rd cents. A.D. by Jewish Christians. It omits the Book of Revelation and four of the Epistles. Ephrem Syrus (who died 378), is supposed to refer to this book when he speaks of ' Our Version.' *See* ' Bible.'

Pessimism. The doctrine that nothing can be worse than things now are. The chiefs of this school are Schopenhauer, Lucretius in his poem ' De Natura,' and Voltaire in his 'Candide.' *See* ' Optimism.'

Pet'alism. Writing the name of a person on an olive-leaf. If 600 signatures were thus obtained in Athens the person was banished. *Ostracism* was exile by writing the name on a tile or oyster-shell.

Peter (*Letter of St.*) to Pepin. Forged by Pope Stephen III., rendered desperate by the siege of Rome by Astolph the Lombard king. *See* Milman, 'Latin Christianity,' vol. iii. book iv. chap xi. pp. 21–23. *See* ' Literary Forgeries.'

Peter ad Vincula (*Saint*), or ' Festum S. Petri ad Vincula,' 1 Aug. (Lammas), the day when, it is said, St. Balbina found St. Peter's Neronian chains.

Peter Porcupine, 1784. A pen-name adopted by William Cobbett after his flight from England to avoid appearing before a court-martial for charging four of his officers with peculation. He died 1835 at the age of seventy.

Peter the Thaumatur'gus. Bishop of Argos (date unknown).

Peter the Wild Boy. Discovered in the fields near Hameln in July, 1724, and supposed to be eleven or twelve years of age. He was placed by George III. under the charge of Dr. Arbuthnot. All the words he could utter were Ke Sho (*King George*), Que Kaa (*Queen Caroline*), and Hom Hen (*Thomas Fen*), the name of the farmer, at Northchurch, Hertfordshire, under whose charge he was placed. He went about with a collar on his neck, bearing his name and address. Government allowed Mr. Fen 35*l*. a year for his maintenan e. Peter died 1785, being, it is supposed, about seventy-two years old.

Peter's College (*St.*). Cambridge University, founded by Hugh de Balsham bishop of Ely, 1257.

This is the oldest foundation in the University. It used to be called Peter House.

Peterloo, 16 Aug., 1819. The area before St. Peter's Church (called St. Peter's Field), Manchester, was so called from the monster meeting held there on that day, and presided over by ' Orator' Hunt, against the strict prohibition of the magistrates.' The ostensible reason of the meeting was to favour parliamentary reform. Hunt had scarcely begun his speech when several troops of soldiers, with 400 special constables, and the Cheshire and Manchester Yeomanry, appeared. The crowd fled in disorder, many were thrown down, 100 were more or less injured, and six persons were accidentally killed. Hunt and nine others were brought to trial, and charged with treasonable conspiracy. Called ' Peterloo' from the words of Hunt, who said, ' The magistrates desired nothing so much as an opportunity of letting loose the bloody butchers of Waterloo upon them.'

Peter-pence, or ' Rome-scot,' 720. First paid by Ina king of Wessex, discontinued by Edward III. in 1365, and prohibited by act of parliament in 1534

(25 Henry VIII. c. 21). It was one penny per family collected for the pope of Rome. An enormous tax, if we consider the value of money at the time, and to the poor almost crushing. Half-a-crown would have bought a horse or cow, and about 1s. would have bought a sheep. Wages for a labourer 1d. a day.

At present Peter-pence is a voluntary contribution to the pope.

Petit Fils de la France. Son of Philippe duc d'Orléans, brother of Louis XIV. Philippe himself was entitled *Monsieur*, his wife *Madame*, and their daughter *Mademoiselle* (all without a proper name).

Petit Manteau Bleu (*Le*). Edme Champion (1764–1853). A man of unbounded benevolence, called Le Petit Manteau Bleu by the poor, from his habit of wearing a short cloak of blue cloth, fastened at the neck by a clasp, and reaching to the loins.

Petit Roi de Bourges (*Le*). Charles VII. of France (1403, 1422–1461). Called afterwards 'The Victorious,' because he reconquered France from the English. When he succeeded to the crown Bourges was about all that acknowledged his sovereignty.

Petite Paix (*La*), also called 'La paix fourrée,' and sometimes 'La paix de Longjumeau,' 1568, between the Roman Catholics and the Calvinists. This peace was preparatory to the 'Paix de St. Germain' (*q.v.*).

Petits Maîtres, 1649. The party of Condé was so called 'parce qu'ils voulaient être maîtres de l'état' (' Siècle de Louis XIV.').

Petition (*The Monster*), 10 April, 1848. Said to have been signed by six million Chartists. Some 50,000 Chartists, led by Feargus O'Connor and Ernest Jones, intended to march to the House of Commons to present it. About 170,000 special constables were sworn in to prevent a disturbance. When the petition was examined it was found that it did not contain two million names. Many of these names were palpably forgeries, many were mere nicknames, and thousands were copied in the same hand from a directory. The petition altogether was a monster swindle.

Petition and Advice (*The*), or 'The Humble Petition and Advice,' 1657. Presented by the parliament to Cromwell, praying him to assume a higher title than that of Lord Protector, to govern, as had been done in times past, with the advice of two houses of parliament, and to abolish the odious existing institution of majors-general. Cromwell refused to take the title of king, but consented to establish a second estate, the members of which he addressed as 'My lords,' although only two real peers attended the summons. The petition was first entitled 'A Humble Address and Remonstrance.'

On former occasions he [Cromwell] had relieved himself from [money] embarrassments by the imposition of taxes by his own authority, but this practice was strongly reprobated in 'The Petition and Advice.'—Dr. LINGARD, *Hist. of Eng.*, viii. 7.

Pétition de Droit. One of the common law methods of obtaining possession or restitution from the crown of either real or personal property. It owes its origin to Edward I.

Petition of Right (*The*), 28 May, 1628, made law by 3 Car. I. c. 1, 7 June, 1628. It prayed that no man hereafter be compelled to give any gift, benevolence, or tax without consent of parliament. That the commissions for proceeding by martial law be annulled. That the king will in future declare his will and pleasure to be that all his officers and ministers obey the laws and statutes of the realm. That no freeman be imprisoned by the king's arbitrary will, but only according to established law. That no householder be compelled to receive any soldier or mariner into his house. *See* 'Bill of Rights.'

Petitioners. By 13 Charles II. it was enacted that not more than ten persons should be allowed to approach the sovereign or either House of Parliament for delivering a petition, making a complaint, or suing for redress of grievances.

Petitioners and Abhorrers, 1679–1680. Two political parties in the reign of Charles II., the germs of the Whigs and Tories. Lord Shaftesbury, by intrigue, procured from the counties a host of petitions to set aside not only James the brother of Charles II., but also his daughter Mary, who was a Protestant, married to William prince of

Orange; and to fix the succession on the Duke of Monmouth, a bastard son of the king (?) A strong party revolted at this injustice, and obtained a host of counter petitions declaring their 'abhorrence' of Shaftesbury's scheme. So that the 'Petitioners' were for setting aside the Prince of Orange, and the 'Abhorrers' were in favour of the prince.

Petrobrusians. The disciples of Pierre de Bruys (2 syl.), who was burnt alive as a heretic at St. Gilles in 1147. They denied the doctrine of transubstantiation, rejected crucifixes, baptized adults who had been already baptized in infancy, and forbade prayers for the dead. The Henricians (*q.v.*) joined this sect in 1127.

Petroleum Vesuvius Nasby. A pen-name of D. R. Locke. 'Nasby' refers to the battle of that name; 'Petroleum' to the rock-oil fever raging in Pennsylvania at the time when the 'Nasby Letters' were begun; and 'Vesuvius' to the outburst of the petroleum fever.

Pe-tse Dynasty (*The*). The 2nd dynasty of the Goli Tartars in Eastern China. It gave five kings, and lasted 28 years (550–578), when both the Eastern and Western kingdoms were again united in the imperial line.

Petticoat (*A*). Carried in the cider riots, 1763. *See* 'Jack Boot.'

Petty Bag Office (*The*). In the common law jurisdiction of the Court of Chancery. So called because all original writs relating to the business of the crown were, at one time, kept in a little sack (*in parva baga*).

Peu'tinger'ian Table (*The*). 'Tabula Peutingeriāna.' A map of the Roman world constructed about A.D. 226, some say as early as 161. It was discovered at Spires (1500) in an old library by Conrad Celtès, who sent it to Conrad Peutinger the antiquary to publish; but his death occurred before this was done. It was ultimately published in 1598 at Venice under the care of Marcus Welsen. The original is in the Imperial Library of Vienna. *See* 'Antonine's Itinerary.'

Pezade (2 syl.). *See* 'Pacata.'

Phalansterians. Disciples of Charles Fourier (1768–1837), who

grouped all men in *phalanxes*. Each phalanstery was to consist of 400 families or 1800 persons, to live under one roof in the centre of workshops, studios, places of amusement, and so on. The whole earth being grouped in phalansteries, the phalansteries themselves are to be united in larger groups under a unitary government. There is to be only one language and one government, and the only army is to be a great industrial army.

Bellamy's 'Looking Backward,' or state of society in 2000, is a slight modification of Fourierism. *See* 'Communism.'

Phal'aris. The famous controversy between Richard Bentley and Robert Boyle began thus: Mr. Boyle borrowed a MS. from St. James's Library, where Bentley was librarian. It was borrowed that Mr. Boyle might complete his 'Epistles of Phalaris.' Bentley was angry because it was kept so long, and Boyle taking offence, a paper war arose, noted for wit and satire. In 1699 Bentley published a book to prove that Phalaris was not the author of these epistles, to which Boyle replied; but all scholars side with Bentley, who was appointed Master of Trinity for his admirable criticisms. *See* 'Literary Forgeries.'

Phantastic System (*The*). Taught by the Docētes (3 syl.). It was this: that Christ was only a phantom, and not a real human being. Like the God which appeared to Adam and Eve, like the Moses and Elijah on the mount, the man Christ was palpable to the eyes, but not to the touch, and his words, like those of the beings referred to, were only 'airy words.'

Pharaoh. Another spelling of Phra, Egyptian for the sun.

Pharaohs of the Bible (*The*). Josephus ('Jewish Antiquities,' viii. chap. 6) says: 'The title of Pharaoh was applied to the kings of Egypt from Menês to Solomon, but not afterwards.' This does not correspond with the Bible; for Jeremiah, xliv. 30, speaks of Pharaoh Hophra, and Pharaoh Necho invaded Judea in the reign of Josiah (2 Kings xxiii.).

According to the tablets discovered in different parts of Egypt, the following seem to illustrate the Bible narratives:

1. The *Good Pharaoh* seems to be

Sutapepe-Nubti, one of the Hyksos, or shepherd kings; but some Egyptologists think it was Osirtesen II., and say there is a tablet in the sixth year of his reign which records the advent of several Semitics resembling Jews both in dress and physiognomy. Supposed to be Jacob and his household.

2. The *Bad Pharaoh* seems to be Amen'ophis III. of the nineteenth dynasty, who introduced the heretical worship of Typhor; but after Rameses II. the Great came a period of confusion, and the Exodus is supposed by many to have occurred in the reign of Arisu, a usurper and a Syrian, about B.C. 1314. No hint of the Exodus, however, can be traced by Egyptologists.

3. Solomon married Abra, the daughter of Pfusenes [Pisham] last of the twenty-first dynasty (1 Kings iii. 1).

4. Shishak (1 Kings xiv. 25), who came against Jerusalem in the reign of Rehoboam, was obviously Shashank I., or Sheshouk, who with 12,000 chariots and 60,000 horse-soldiers invaded Judea. The record may still be seen on the portico of the Bubastis at Karnak.

5. 2 Chron. xiv. 9–15 and xvi. 8, &c., it is supposed, refer to Zerah, fourth of the twenty-second dynasty.

6. Hosea paid tribute to Shabak, founder of the twenty-fifth dynasty, B.C. 716.

7. Shabakok, called 'So' in 2 Kings xvii. 4, was the successor of Shabak. With this king Hezekiah formed a confederacy against Sennacherib, king of Assyria, 2 Kings xviii. xix. 'So' was succeeded by Tarach or Tirshatha.

8. Pharaoh Necho who invaded Judea in the reign of Josiah was Nechos II. He defeated Josiah, but was himself defeated by Nebuchadnezzar (617–601), 2 Kings xxiii. 29, &c.

9. Pharaoh Hophra is supposed to be Apries, which without the vowel points is PR or PhR (Jer. xliv. 30).

The Sphinx was carved in the third dynasty, founded by Necherophes. The great pyramid was built by Khufu [*Suphis* or *Cheops*] who founded the fourth dynasty; his successor Khafra or Khafren [*Cephren*] built the second pyramid; and his successor Menkâra [*Mycerinus*] built the third great pyramid.

Ramses II. the Great was the Sesostris of Egypt whose reign is fixed by the calendars representing the heliacal rising of the dog-stars, B.C. 1322.

*** Goshen was in Lower Egypt, nearer Palestine than Upper Egypt. There was much marshland there, and both grass and corn would grow.

Pharisees (*The*), B.C. 160. An ancient Jewish sect who by their verbal criticisms, mystical interpretations and traditions, engrafted on the Mosaic law a host of precepts and observances. They believed in a resurrection, in angels, and spirits; placed great reliance on fastings, ablutions, and long prayers; and paid great attention to their garments, especially affecting very large borders, fringes, or hems. Their chief was Hillel.

'Pharisee' from *pharash*, to separate.

Phenicians (*The*), about 1863. An Irish secret society, a branch of the Ribbon Societies (*q.v.*), their platform being similar to that of the Fenians. *See* 'Irish Associations.'

Phenomenon, Noumenon (plu. Phenomena, Noumena). Kant used the two words to express object and subject. The Greek word φαίνομαι means to appear, and phenomenon is what our senses cognise. Noumenon is from the Greek word νοῦς, 'pure intelligence'; and a noumenon is an object pure and unbodied, that is divested of everything cognisable by the senses.

Fichte used the words ego and non-ego for subject and object. What the senses cognise as part of ourselves is, of course, part of ourselves; but what exists independent of our senses is no part of ourselves, and this he called non-ego.

Phe'si, φησί (It says). An ecclesiastical school. Hippolytus speaks of Basilidês, and Isidore, with πᾶς ὁ τούτων χορός, as 'Phêsi'; and again he speaks in the same manner of Valentînus, Heraclêon, Ptolemy, and πᾶσα ἡ τούτων σχολή. The term is used as significant of the scripture interpretation of a certain school. The Phêsi say so and so = the Ipse-dixit school.

Phid'ias (*The French*). Pigalle, died 1796. His best pieces are 'Venus,' 'Mercury,' and the tomb of Marshal Saxe.

Phid'ias (*The Northern*). Albert Thorvaldsen the Danish sculptor (1770–1844).

Philacte'rians or **Phylacterians.** Necromancers, condemned by the Church A.D. 692. The phylacteria were ancient amulets for keeping off or curing diseases. 'Philacteria, id est, X verba legis, aut scriptura vana, quod ligat homo super caballum aut super caput suum' (Du Cange; article 'Phylacteria').

Phil'adelphes (3 syl.). An association of old republicans to which Talleyrand and Fouché belonged, even while they were in the service of the Emperor Napoleon.

Philadelphia Convention (*The*) 1883, consisting of dynamitards, Fenians, murderers, and all sorts of disturbers of the public peace. Paid agents were continually sent to England to terrorise the British Parliament into granting 'Home Rule' (*q.v.*) to Ireland for peace sake. *See* 'Irish Associations.'

Philadel'phians (*The*), 1821. A branch of the Carbonāri in Calabria, also called the 'Reformed European Patriots.'

Philadel'phic Society (*The*). A literary and philosophic association at Besançon at the close of the 18th cent. One of its members, General Mallet, made this society a political instrument for the restoration of the Bourbons. Lieut.-Colonel Oudet, another member, classified the Philadelphians into three ranks, each of which was profoundly ignorant of the functions of the other two; then introduced the scheme into the army, and established affiliated societies called 'Les Frères Bleus.' The first movement was the conspiracy of Adjutant-General Arēna. This was crushed, but without Bonaparte being able to trace out the instigators of it. Now Moreau, Lahorie, Cadoudal, and Pichegru joined, and the last two concocted a plan to assassinate the first consul. Several persons were arrested, and Cadoudal, with some few subordinates, was executed. In 1813 the Philadelphians were no longer wanted, and the society lost its political power.

Philadel'phos (Brother-lover). Ptolemy II. of Egypt, so called, murdered all his brothers in order to secure the throne (B.C. 284–246). *See* 'Philopater.'

Phil'anthrop'ic Society (*The*), 1788. For the reformation of young criminals. It originated with Robert Young and was incorporated in 1806. Reformatory schools were established at Redhill, in Surrey, in 1849.

Philipp king of Germany (1178, 1197–1208). Brother of Heinrich VI.;

succeeded by Otto IV. (son of Heinrich the Lion) who abdicated.

Father, Friedrich I. Barbarossa; *Mother,* Beatrice daughter of Renaut III. of Burgundy; *Wife,* Irene Angela, widow of Roger of Sicily. No son. *Contemporary* with John.

Philippe I. l'Amoureux, of France (1052, 1060–1108). Fourth king of the Capetian dynasty.

Father, Henri I.; *Mother,* Anne of Muscovy; *Wives,* Bertha daughter of the count of Holland (mother of Louis VI.), and Bertrade of Montford. *Contemporary* with Edward the Confessor, Harold, and William the Conqueror.

Hugues Capet was the father of Robert le Pieux; Robert was the father of Henri I.; and Henri I. was the father of Philippe I.

Philippe II. Auguste, of France (1165, 1180–1223). So called because he was the real founder of the French monarchy, as Augustus Cæsar was the real founder of the Roman empire. When Philippe ascended the throne, his whole kingdom was not larger than the county of Yorkshire; but ere he died he had extended its frontiers from the Scheldt to the Mediterranean and from the Rhine to the Atlantic.

Father, Louis VI.; *Mother,* Alice daughter of Thibaud comte de Champagne; *Wives,* Isabelle daughter of the Duke of Hainault (mother of Louis IX.), Ingelburge, who was divorced, and Agnes de Meranie. *Contemporary* with Henry II., Richard, John, and Henry III.

. When Philippe Auguste began to reign all the *West* of France belonged to England or to Prince Arthur; the *South* belonged to Aragon; and the *East* to Germany. All that pertained to France was the Ile-de-France, with portions of Picardy and Orléannois.

Philippe Auguste was the 7th king of the Capetian dynasty: 1. Hugues Capet; 2. Robert le Pieux his son; 3. Henri I. his son; 4. Philippe I. l'Amoureux his son; 5. Louis VI. le Gros his son; 6. Louis VII. le Jeune his son; 7. Philippe II. Auguste his son.

Philippe III. le Hardi, of France (1245, 1270–1285). *See* 'Philippe le Bel.'

Le fils de S. Louis que, par un caprice inexplicable, ses contemporains surnommèrent le Hardi [the bold], n'avait des qualités de son père que la douceur et la piété. Il pratiquait le jeûne et l'abstinence, et vivait en moine plutôt qu'en chevalier.—BORDIER ET CHARTON, *Histoire de France,* vol. i. p. 879.

Father, St. Louis (Louis IX.); *Mother,* Marguerite daughter of the comte de Provence; *Wives,* Isabel daughter of the king of Navarre, who bore him four sons, and Marie daughter of the Comte de Brabant, who bore him two daughters. *Contemporary* with Edward I.

Philippe IV. le Bel, of France (1268, 1286–1314). Eleventh king of the Capetian dynasty, in direct descent.

Father, Philippe III. ; *Mother,* Isabel daughter of the king of Navarre ; *Wife,* Jeanne countess of Champagne and queen of Navarre. *Contemporary* with Edward I., Edward II.

1. Hugues Capet ; 2. Robert le Pieux ; 3. Henri I. ; 4. Philippe I. l'Amoureux ; 5. Louis VI. le Gros ; 6. Louis VII. le Jeune ; 7. Philippe II. Auguste ; 8. Louis VIII. le Lion ; 9. Louis IX. (St. Louis) ; 10. Philippe III. le Hardi ; 11. Philippe IV. le Bel.
All the three sons of Philippe IV. reigned in succession, as Louis X., Philippe V., and Charles IV., when the elder branch died out. *See* 'Three Fatal to France.'

Philippe V. le Long (1294, 1316–1322). Brother of his predecessor Louis X. and of his successor Charles IV.

He was the last Capetian king of the direct line, and his reign was a wretched failure.

Father, Philippe IV. ; *Mother,* Jeanne countess of Champagne ; *Wife,* Jeanne de Bourgogne. No son. *Contemporary* with Edward II.

Philippe VI. de Valois, of France (1293, 1328–1350). Succeeded his cousin Charles IV. le Bel.

Father, Charles comte de Valois, second son of Philippe IV. le Bel ; *Mother,* Jeanne countess of Valois ; *Wives,* Jeanne of Burgundy (mother of Jean), Blanche. *Contemporary* with Edward III.

. PHILLIPE III. le Hardi had three sons, viz. PHILLIPE IV. le Bel who succeeded him, Charles comte de Valois, and Louis. Philippe VI. de Valois was the son of Charles de Valois, the second son of Philippe III.

Philippe Égalite (1747–1793), duc d'Orléans, guillotined by the Committee of Public Safety. Though a royal duke, he had sided with the Jacobins ; though a relative of Louis XVI., he had voted for his execution ; and though professing republican principles, he aimed at the crown.

Philippæan Era (*The*). This era began in June B.C. 323.

Philip'pics. Three orations of Demosthenês the Athenian against Philip king of Macedonia. The *first* was spoken during the sacred war, when Philip took on himself to be the champion of the Delphic god. Demosthenês wanted the Athenians to side with the Locrians against Philip, but he produced no practical effect.

The *second* Philippic was soon after the Sacred War, when Philip had become the head of Greece. Demosthenês charged him with perfidy. Philip sent an embassy to complain of this insult, and then it was that Demosthenês delivered his second Philippic directed against the supporters of the Macedonian king (B.C. 344).

The *third* Philippic was delivered B.C. 341, and was to show the best means of resisting the encroachments of Philip.

Philistines. The inhabitants of the sea-coast of Palestine from Phœnicia to Egypt are always meant when this word is used in Scripture.

Philop'ator (Father-lover). Ptolemy IV. of Egypt, so called, assassinated his father ; just as Ptolemy II., called Philadelphos, or Brother-lover, murdered his brothers in order to secure the throne. Philopător reigned B.C. 221–204.

This madman not only assassinated his father, he also murdered his mother, sister-wife (Arsinoé), and brother.

Philosopher (*The*). I. Marcus Aurelius Antoninus the Roman is so called by Justin Martyr (121, 161-180).
II. Porphyry the neoplatonist (223–304).
III. Leo VI. emperor of the East (866, 886–911).
IV. Alured Anglicānus (died 1270).

Philosopher of Chelsea (*The*). Thomas Carlyle, who lived at Chelsea (1795–1881).

Philosopher of China (*The*). Confucius (B.C. 551–479).

Philosopher of Ferney (*The*). Voltaire, who lived at Ferney, near Geneva, for the last twenty years of his life (1694–1778).

Philosopher of Malmesbury (*The*). Thomas Hobbes, author of 'Leviathan,' who was born at Malmesbury (1588–1679).

Philosopher of Persia (*The*). Abû-ebn-Sina of Shiraz (died 1037).

Philosopher of Sans Souci (*The*). Frederick the Great of Prussia (1712, 1740–1786).

Voltaire calls him over and over again the philosopher prince.

Philosopher of Wimbledon
(*The*). John Horne Tooke, author of
the 'Diversions of Purley,' who lived at
Wimbledon, near London (1736–1812).

Philosophers (*The Five English*).
(1) Roger BACON, author of 'Opus
Majus' (1214–1292).

(2) Sir Francis BACON, author of 'No-
vum Orgănum' (1561–1626).

(3) The Hon. Robert BOYLE (1627–
1691).

(4) John LOCKE, author of a treatise
on the 'Human Understanding and Innate Ideas' (1632–1704).

(5) Sir Isaac NEWTON, author of 'Principia' (1642–1727).

Philosophers (*The French*). 'At
the close of the 18th cent. were mere exponents of public opinion, which they
popularised and vitalised. They were
preceded by Descartes (2 syl.) the Frenchman, and Leibnitz the German, who
taught that all which is real is *spirit*,
soul, or *self*, and that matter (or the
external world) is either a succession
of notions impressed on the mind by
deity, or unsubstantial images due to
the five senses. Locke taught the latter.
Early in the 18th cent. the French taught
the doctrine of *materialism*, making the
soul a mere function of matter, as light is
an effect of fuel in combustion. Helvetius
showed the moral tendency and practical
bearing of materialism. Still later the
existence of the soul was discarded, with
the notion of a future state; and the
pleasure arising from the practice of
virtue was looked on as the great end of
man. The name of God was changed
into *Nature*, and the equality of man
was made 'an immortal principle.'

The chief 'Philosophers' were Malebranche
(1638–1715), whose great work is 'The Search after
Truth.' He denied that *matter* could produce
ideas, and taught that intelligence is the function
of *deity within us*.

Condillac (1715–1780) abbé de Mureaux, chief of
the *Sensational School* of philosophy; that is, that
intelligence is admitted through the five doors
of knowledge called the senses. His chief works
are an 'Essay on the Origin of Human Knowledge,'
a treatise on 'Sensations,' and another on
'Animals.'

Helvetius (1715–1771) maintained that 'self-
interest is the spring of all our actions.' D'Alembert, Diderot, &c., were *Encyclopædists*.

Philosophic Schools of Greece
(*The*). The Academic, the Cynic, the
Cyrenäic, the Eleatic, and the New Eleatic, the Epicurean, the Ionic, the Hera-
clitian, the Megaric, the Peripatetic, the
Pythagorean, the Sceptic, the Socratic,
the Stoic, and the New Stoic. The *Old*
Eleatic school consisted of speculative
philosophers, the *New* of natural philosophers; the New Stoic school consisted
of Christian philosophers. See each *in
loco*.

Philosophical College (*The*).
Wadham, Oxford, was so called when
John Wilkins was warden, not only because he himself was a philosopher, but
because he invited to it men of a similar
turn of mind as Wallis, Wren, Boyle,
&c., who met together in his rooms.

Philosophical Radicals (*The*).
The political economists who advocated
free trade. Jeremy Bentham was at the
head of this school, which was supported
by Adam Smith, General Perronet
Thompson, C. P. Villiers, John Stuart
Mill, Richard Cobden, Sir William Molesworth, the Rev. T. R. Malthus, Dr. Chalmers, John Bright, [Lord] Brougham, &c.

Adam Smith, author of 'The Wealth of Nations';
General Thompson, author of the 'Catechism of
the Corn Laws'; Malthus, a writer on 'Population.'

Philosophical Transactions
(*The*). Published by the Royal Society
of London. First started Monday, 9
March, 1665, and ordered to be continued
the first Monday of every month. The
volumes contain memoirs of scientific
men, reports of the 'progress of science,'
and of 'new discoveries,' &c. The first
number was by Oldenburg, and, up to the
47th volume, the publications were left
to the secretaries of the society, but since
then they have been under the superintendence of a committee of the council.

The society's rooms were first in Crane's
Court; in 1780 they were removed to
Somerset House; and in 1857 to Bur-
lington House.

Philosophy (*The Father of*).
I. Roger Bacon (1214–1292).

II. Albrecht von Haller of Berne
(1708–1777).

The Father of Roman Philosophy,
Cicero the orator (B.C. 106–43).

Philoxen'ian Version (*The*). A
Syriac version of the Old and New Testa-
ments by Philoxĕnus bishop of Hierapŏlis,
A.D. 508. About a century afterwards
the New Testament portion was revised
by Thomas of Harkel [Heraclĕa], and is
called the Harklen'sian version.

Phœbus. Gaston III. comte de Foix (1331–1391). So called for his beautiful face and profusion of golden hair.

Phœnician Stone (*The*). A hoax. In 1824 the learned Raoul Rochette, professor of archæology and keeper of the Cabinet of Antiquities in Paris, received from Malta, 'for the Academy of France,' a stone with a bilingual inscription in Greek, and in what purported to be Phœnician. The stone was dated in 'the 85th Olympiad' (*i.e.* B.C. 436). Professor Rochette gave the inscription credit for the antiquity it pretended to, and sent a copy thereof to every savant in Europe for decipherment and translation. The giant scholar Gesēnius of Halle, and the hardly less learned Hamaker of Leyden, agreed with Rochette, and published comments upon the stone. Yet it turned out to be an impudent hoax and modern forgery. *See* 'Literary Forgeries,' &c.

Phœnix of Spain (*The*). Lope de Vega, 'whom no one could pass or equal in verse or rhyme' (1562–1635).

Phœnix Park Murder (*The*), 6 May, 1882. Lord Frederick Cavendish, the newly-appointed Secretary for Ireland, and Mr. Thomas A. Burke, the Under-Secretary, were stabbed to death while walking in Phœnix Park, Dublin, by assassins in the employ of the Irish Land League. Carey, one of the gang, gave queen's evidence, and it was found that there were twenty-one persons implicated in the cowardly murder. 10,000*l*. was offered for the arrest of the assassins.

C. S. Parnell, Dillon, and O'Kelly were released from Kilmainham Gaol only four days before this murder. They had been imprisoned by order of Mr. Gladstone for seditious speeches and conspiracy.

Phœnix Society (*The*), or 'The Phœnix National and Literary Society,' 1858, established in Skibbereen by O'Donovan Rossa to insure the separation of Ireland from the crown of England. *See* 'Irish Associations.'

The oath was : 'I do solemnly declare in the presence of God that I renounce all allegiance to the Queen of England, and will do my utmost, at every risk, to make Ireland an independent democratic republic. . .

Photin'ians. Heretics of the 4th cent. So denominated from Photīnus bishop of Sirmich, who taught that Jesus was born a mere human being, but began to be the Messiah or Christ when the Holy Ghost descended on Him in the Jordan.

Phrenology (*Founder of*). Gall (1758–1828) ; with whom Spurzheim (1766–1833) is inseparably connected.

Phrygian Cap (*The*). *See* 'Cap of Liberty in France.'

Physcon (Big-belly), Ptolemy VII. king of Egypt (B.C. 145–116). Aged 74.

Physical Club (*The*). An association in Moscow organised in the reign of Catherine II. (1762–1796). Physical excellence was essential for membership. The club consisted of men and women in the prime of life. 'Husbands introduced their wives, brothers their sisters. The requisites of men were health and vigour, of women youth and beauty.' The members belonged to the best families of Russia. This club was dissolved in the French Revolution, when the police had orders to ferret out all secret societies.

Physical Geography (*Father of*). Alexander von Humboldt (1769–1859).

Physicians (*College of*). London, 1510, founded by Dr. Thomas Linacre of Canterbury.

Physico-Historical   Society (*The*), 1745. Afterwards merged into the Royal Dublin Society for the improvement of agriculture, husbandry, and the useful arts.

Phys'iocrates (4 syl.), 18th cent. French political economists who advocated perfect freedom of trade, and insisted that land ought to bear all the taxes of a nation, as land only is naturally productive. The head of this school was Quesnay, but it was supported by Beaudeau, Larivière, Mercier, Mirabeau, Turgot, &c. *See* 'Economists.'

The term 'real property' applied to land is a phase of the same delusion. All other property may take to itself wings and fly away, not so land; but 1887 and some preceding years have taught us that land does not always pay the expenses of the landlord. Sahara is land, but certainly it would not pay for cultivation.

Physiognomy (*Founder of*). Lavater (1741–1801) of Zürich, who taught the art of reading character by the expression and marks of the face.

Y Y

Physiology (*Father of*). Albert von Haller (1708–1777).

Piagno'ni (*The*), or 'The Weepers.' The party of Savonarola were so called from the penitential character which they professed. The party of the Medici was called the *Arrabbiati* or the Enraged.

Piagno'ni Painters (*The*). Painters of Florence, friends of Savonarola. They were Botticelli, Lorenzo di Credi, Fra Bartolommeo (Baccio della Porta), and his friend Mariotto.

Piano Regolatore (*The*), 1889. A system introduced by the Italian Government by which the seven hills of old Rome are to be levelled and the valleys between them filled up, to facilitate the construction of squares and rectangular streets.

Piano'ri (*Giovanni*), 28 April, 1855. Shot at the Emperor Napoleon III. in the Champs Elysées. *See* 'Napoleon III.'

Piaristes. Called by the French 'Pauvres de la mère de Dieu.' A congregation devoted to the gratuitous education of poor children. Their houses were called 'Ecoles Pieuses.' Joseph Calasanzio started the idea in 1621, by assembling at his own house street arabs. The order of Piaristes was sanctioned by the Pope in 1624. Austria and Hungary are the chief countries where they exist.

Dr. Barnardo with his homes is a familiar example of the same benevolent zeal in our own land. In Dr.Barnardo's homes the waifs and strays are not only educated, but taught to earn their living, and placed out.

Piasts (*Dynasty of the*), 842–1370. The first dynasty of Poland; so called from Piast, a wheelwright of Cruswitz, chosen duke of Poland, its founder. It gave eight sovereigns, the first five of which were styled dukes; Boleslaus I. assumed the title of king in 1000, and his predecessor Miecislaus I. introduced Christianity into Poland. In 1037 a period of anarchy succeeded, and Silesia was severed from Poland. The descendants of Piast continued to reign in Poland thus mutilated till 1370, giving seventeen more monarchs : and a branch subsisted in Silesia till 1675.

The house of Piast was succeeded by the dynasty of Anjou.

Pica (*A*), or 'Pie.' A directory of the order to be observed in reciting the daily service.

Incipit ordo Breviarii seu portiforii secundum morem et consuetudinem ecclesiæ Sarum Anglicanæ una cum ordinali, seu quod usitato vocabulo dicitur Pica, sive directorium sacerdotum : Pica de dominica prima Adventus.—DU CANGE, vol. v. p. 288, col. 1.

Picards (*The*), 15th cent. A Christian sect founded by Picard, who called himself the Son of God and the New Adam. He taught like the Adamites that men and women ought to go about naked, and that God had sent him to restore the 'law of nature.' He also taught the rule of the community of women as wives.

Picares'co Romance. The romance of knavery, like 'The Adventures of Gil Blas.' Begun in Germany in the 17th cent. The romance called 'Simplicius Simplicissimus,' by Christopher von Grimmelshausen, is the best. It gives us a graphic picture of society in the Thirty Years' War.

Pichegru's Conspiracy, 1804. This was a Chouan or royalist conspiracy headed by Pichegru and George Cadoudal. It was discovered. Pichegru strangled himself in prison ; Cadoudal and twelve others were guillotined.

Pici'nists, 1774–1780. A French musico-political faction, who contended that pure Italian music is higher art than the mixed German school. In other words, that music is the alpha and omega of opera, and the dramatic part of very minor account. This is the most celebrated of all the contests in musical annals. Niccolo Piccini was the great exponent of the Italian school, and Christopher Gluck of the German school, his adherents being called Gluckists.

Niccolo Piccini of Naples, 1728-1801 ; Christopher Gluck of Bohemia, 1712 1787. In this paper contest of the two parties at Paris, the ordinary question asked of everyone was 'Etes-vous Picciniste ou Gluckiste ?' Arnaud and Suard were Gluckists, but Marmontel and Laharpe were Piccinists. The contest extended to England and raged with undiminished fury. Marie Antoinette, being a German by birth, patronised Gluck, and this was quite sufficient to raise up a host of opponents. Wagner renewed the contention of Gluck, insisting that the dramatic part of opera is quite as important as the musical part.

Picpus (*The*), or 'Order of Picpus,' 1601. A religious society of the Third order of St. Francis; so called from Picpus, anciently a part of the Faubourg St. Antoine. The order was suppressed in 1790, but was re-established at the restoration in 1814. The members are largely missionaries in heathen lands.

Picts. Ancient inhabitants of the north-east of Scotland. They were a Celtic race. Probably the word means much the same as Caledonians (dwellers in woods). The Scots were a Celtic colony from Ulster, in Ireland, which (about B.C. 400) settled in the south-western parts of Scotland, then called Caledonia. If so, the Picts were the more ancient inhabitants.

As the people were called Picts before the Romans called them Picti (painted people), the Latin word is merely a coincidence of sound, and is wholly without etymological value. The language of the Scoti was Earish (*Erse*), *i.e.* Irish or Western, still preserved in the Western Islands and Highlands. These Highlanders bear the same relation to Scotland generally as the Welsh do to the English.

Pietists (*The*), or ' Separatists,' 1689. A Lutheran sect who preferred private to public worship. Spener of Leipsic was the founder, whose house was *Collegia Pietatis*, because his disciples met there. Ordained clergymen had no marked precedence, but anyone was allowed to address the assembly, as among the Quakers.

Among the Jews the Chasidim (*q.v.*) were called ' Pietists.'

Pigeons. The priestesses of the oracle of Dodōna (*q.v.*), so called by a play on the words *peleiai* (πέλειαι), ' pigeons,' and *palaiai* (παλαιαί) old, aged [women].

It is said that Zeus (1 syl.) presented to his daughter Thēbē two black pigeons endowed with the gift of human speech ; that one of them flew into Libya, in Africa, and the other to Dodōna in Epirus ; and that he commanded the inhabitants of both places to raise a temple to his honour. Hence the temple of ' Jupiter Ammon ' in Libya, and that of Dodōna in Epirus. The two black pigeons may have been two gipsies or Egyptian fortune-tellers.

Pigeon's Blood. The poor nobility of Venice were called *I Barnaboti* from the quarter San Barnabo, where they dwelt. The wealthy nobles were called Blue Blood (*Sangue Colombin* and *Sangue Blù*).

Pigott Diamond (*The*). Brought from India by Lord Pigott, weighs 82¼ carats. In 1801 it was sold in a lottery for 750,000 francs (30,000*l.*) ; and in 1818 it passed into the possession of Messrs. Rundell and Bridge. *See* ' Diamonds.'

Pilate (*Mount*), in Switzerland, has no connection whatever with Pontius Pilate. It is a corruption of ' Mons Pileātus,' *the hatted mountain*, or mountain with a cap of snow.

Pilati (*Acta*). I. Said to be Pilate's despatch sent to the Emperor Tiberius of the crucifixion of Jesus. It is a mere forgery. *See* ' Literary Forgeries.'

II. Eusebius (book ix. 5) speaks of another *Acta Pilāti* ' full of blasphemy against Christ,' and sent by the emperor to every part of his dominion. Certain women who had once been Christians declared they had themselves been privy to criminal acts. These declarations (says Eusebius) were appended by order of the emperor to the ' Acts ' of the procurator.

No doubt Pilate sent a despatch to Rome, but whether either of these ' Acts ' is genuine is quite another matter.

Pilgrim Fathers (*The*). 102 Puritans who went, in 1620, to North America, in a ship called the ' Mayflower,' and colonised what are now the North-Eastern States, called New England, and consisting of (1) Maine, (2) New Hampshire, (3) Vermont, (4) Massachusetts, (5) Rhode Island, and (6) Connecticut. This was the second English settlement in the New World, and was planted at New Plymouth near Boston. The tyranny of the Ecclesiastical Commission raised up a host of dissenters, and in 1580 they chose John Robinson for their leader. Their independence soon drew upon them the heavy hand of the law, and they left the kingdom. The larger part settled at Leyden, whence 102 of them went to America, and many others followed later.

Pilgrimage of Grace (*The*). The insurrection of 1537 against the ' King's Supremacy,' headed by Lord Darcy and ' Captain ' Aske. Some 30,000 men, ' tall and well horsed,' demanded the redress of wrongs, reunion with Rome, the restoration of the Princess Mary to her rights as heiress of the crown, dismissal of Thomas Cromwell the lord chancellor, and restoration of all confiscated church property. The leaders of this rebellion wore for a badge ' the Five Wounds.' The king, Henry VIII., sent an army of 10,000 men against the rebels, and quelled the insurrection. Aske, Darcy, and a large number of others, both priests, nobles, and gentlemen, were executed as traitors.

This rising was supported by the Archbishop of York, and hundreds of priests who marched in the van with crosses, banners, and other ecclesiastical insignia.

Pillar of Northern History (*The*). ' Rei historicæ columen.' Snorre son of Sturla, or Snorre-Sturleson (1178–1241). His history begins with Odin and continues to his own times.

Pillar of the Doctors (*The*). 'La Colonne des docteurs,' William de Champeaux (died 1121).

Pillars of Hercules (*The*). Calpé (now Gibraltar rock), and Abỹla, opposite to it in Africa, which Greek story says were torn asunder and separated by Herculês about B.C. 1220 (while Gideon was Judge of Israel). Before Herculês tore these rocks or mountains asunder the Mediterranean was an inland sea, like the Caspian [hence the name Mediterraneum Mare].

Pilnitz (*The Convention of*), 27 Aug., 1791. To put down the French revolution by force of arms, restore the king, and dissolve the Constituent Assembly. The Kaiser-King of Germany, the King of Prussia, the Comte d'Artois, the Marquis de Bouillé, and the ex-minister Calonne signed the convention, and threatened France with invasion, unless the demands were at once conceded. Of course the convention was mere waste paper.

Pilot who weathered the Storm (*The*), 1801. William Pitt was so called on his retirement from office. The nation in 1797 was almost reduced to bankruptcy by war, when Pitt introduced paper payment for the nonce, whereby the nation soon righted itself again.

Pindar (*Peter*). The pen-name of Dr. John Wolcot (1738–1819).

Pindar (*The British*). Thomas Gray (1716–1771).

No more the Grecian muse unrivalled reigns ;
To Britain let the nations homage pay :
She felt a Homer's fire in Milton's strains,
A Pindar's rapture in the lyre of Gray.
Westminster Abbey (on the monument of Gray).

Pindar (*The Italian*). Gabriello Chiabrera (1552–1637).

Pindar of England (*The*). Abraham Cowley (1618–1667).

The Duke of Buckingham preposterously called him 'The Pindar, Horace, and Virgil of England.'

Pindar of France (*The*).
I. Jean Dorat (1507–1588).
II. Ponce Denis Lebrun (1719–1807). This title bestowed on Lebrun is simply absurd, but the French are not happy in their eponyms, of which they are especi-

ally fond. Also called 'The Poet of Liberty.'

Pindari War (*The*), 1817–18. The Pindaris attacked Madras 1817, the Marquis of Hastings marched against them, and a treaty of peace was concluded 5 Nov., 1818.

Pinda'ris (*The*) of India were exactly like the Grand Companies of Europe. They were bodies of mercenary horse who served any prince for hire, and in times of peace lived by plunder. In the early part of the 19th cent. the Pindāris aided Holkar, the Mahratta prince, against the British, but wholly without success. *See* 'Great Company,' 1353.

Pinerolo, or **Pignerolo** (*The Charter* or *Treaty of*), Aug. 1656. A charter granted by Charles Emmanuel II. the duke of Savoy to his Vaudois subjects after the savage attack of the Marquis of Pianezza. The treaty defined where the Vaudois might exercise their worship without being molested, but reserved to the duke himself the right of celebrating mass where he chose. It also confirmed the prerogatives and privileges previously granted, but in 1685 the Duke Victor Amadeus was made by Louis XIV. of France to extirpate, as far as possible, the 'heretics' in his dominions.

Pink (*Knights of the*), or 'Chevaliers de l'Œillet,' 1793. A society organised to save the queen and the young dauphin son of Louis XVI. It had its ramifications in Germany and Prussia, but its headquarters, of course, were Paris. The attempt to save the queen failed, and the failure was communicated to the conspirators by one of them pulling a pink to pieces and casting the stalk on the ground. *See* 'Louis XVII.'

Piombi (*The*). The terrific dungeons of Venice under the leaden roofs. Those under the canals were called *I Pozzi* (*q.v.*).

If he relapsed he was to be imprisoned for at least three years in the Piombi.—*Hist. of Venice*, vol. ii. p. 107 (Murray, 1838).

Pipe Office (*The*). An English law office in which a person called the 'Clerk of the Pipe' makes out leases of crown-lands and enters all debts to the crown in the 'Great Roll' made of parchment and kept in the exchequer. Abolished by 3, 4 Will. IV. c. 99.

Piph'les (2 syl.). So the Waldenses (*q.v.*) of Flanders were called. Etymology unknown, but probably connected with the Greek πιστικός and the Latin *pistis*, meaning ' the faithful' or 'true believers.' Sometimes called ' Pisti.'

Pisa, Genoa. *Those who want to see Pisa must go to Genŏa.* (An Italian saying.) In 1282 began the fourth war between Pisa and Genoa. The Pisans were almost extirpated. 3 000 were slain or drowned, and 13,000 were carried prisoners to Genoa, so that there were more Pisan captives in Genoa than there were left in the city itself.

Piscine Baptism. ' La piscine baptismale.' A term derived from *piscis*, the Latin word for ἰχθύς, a fish, an anagram of ' Iesous Christos Theou Uios, Sotèr' [I–Ch–Th–U–S]. A *notarica* used by the early Christians under persecution. It is a secret way of saying ' Christian baptism.'

Pishdad'ian Dynasty (*The*), or 'Paishdadians.' The first dynasty of the Parsees. Firdusi tells us it lasted 2,450 years, and was founded by Kayomurz, who was succeeded by his son Hoshung ; Hoshung was succeeded by Tahmuras, who was succeeded by his son Djemshid, who reigned 500 years. After Djemshid came his son Feridoun. Those who seek to reduce mythical history within Bible limits place these kings thus : Kayomurz B.C. 1990; Hoshung B.C. 1960; Tahmuras B.C. 1920; and Djemshid B.C. 1890. Djemshid was dethroned by Zohâk, an Arabian described as a most merciless tyrant, who was slain in a rebellion led by Kâwân the blacksmith, who raised Feridoun to the throne. The Pishdadian kings were succeeded B.C. by the Kaianian dynasty, called by the Greeks the Achimenidês. It was preceded by the Mahabadian dynasty (*q.v.*). The Pishdads were mythical kings. Capital : first Balk, then Istakar, and then Segestan.

Pisis'tratos of Rome (*The*). Julius Cæsar (B.C. 100–44).

Pitt Diamond (*The*), or ' The Regent Diamond,' found in Golconda, the most perfect brilliant in existence, about the size of a pigeon's egg. It was bought in 1702 by Thomas Pitt (grandfather of the great Earl of Chatham) for 20,400*l.*, and sold by him in 1717 to the Duke of Orleans regent of France for 135,000*l.* It weighed originally 410 carats, but was reduced by cutting to 136⅞ carats. This diamond decorated the hilt of Napoleon's sword of state, but now belongs to the king of Prussia. It was stolen by ' an honest factor,' and pawned to Thomas Pitt, who refused to give it back again, and the thief did not dare to vindicate his claim. It came from the mines of Parteal, near Golconda.

> Asleep and naked as an Indian lay,
> An honest factor stole a gem away ;
> He pledged it to the knight, the knight had wit
> So kept the diamond, and the rogue was bit.
>   POPE, *Sir Balaam.*

Pitt Scholarship for Classics, in the University of Cambridge. Founded out of a fund raised by subscribers to the statue of William Pitt, 1813. *See* ' Regius Professor of Greek.'

Pitt's Bridge. Blackfriars Bridge, the foundation of which was laid in 1770, was so called originally, in honour of Pitt earl of Chatham.

Pittsburg, when taken from the French by Brigadier Forbes in 1758, was called by him Fort Pitt, in honour of William Pitt (Earl of Chatham), but when it grew populous it was called Pittsburg, and is now the Birmingham of the United States.

Placards, 1534. So the protestations of the reformers against the mass were called. They were disseminated by thousands by one Féret from Switzerland, and on 18 Oct. the inhabitants of Paris found them attached to every public place, in all crossways, on the doors of churches, and even on the palace walls. François I. was furious, and many reformers were put to death.

Place de Grève (*La*). The place formerly used in Paris for executions, like our Tyburn; it is in the vicinity of the Hôtel de Ville. Grève means the bank of a river or shore of the sea where ' les eaux sont couverts de *gravier* et de cailloux roulés.'

Place de Louis Quinze. *See* ' Place de la Concorde.'

Place de la Concorde. The spot where Louis XVI. was executed, then called the ' Place de la Révolution,' and prior to the revolution called the ' Place de Louis Quinze.'

Place du Carrousel (*La*). A part of Paris where carrousels or mock tournaments were held, between the reign of Henri IV. and the 18th cent.

Place of Oak-trees (*The*), in Preussen (*i.e.* ancient Prussia). The Holy of Holies of the Druids, into which none might enter but the Druid priests. When Adalbert of Prague, a zealous Christian missionary, forced his way into this sanctuary he was instantly put to death.

Placemakers' Bible, or 'The Whig Bible,' so called because Matt. v. 9 is printed 'Blessed are the placemakers [peacemakers], for they shall be called the children of God.' *See* 'Bibles.'

Placita, A.D. 598. The first French parlements, convened by Clotaire III., were so called. They were ambulatory; that is, held sometimes in one town and sometimes in another.

From 'Placita' come our words plead, pleadings, &c.

Plague of Florence (*The*). *See* 'Black Vomit.'

Plague of London (*The*), 1665. Introduced by some Dutch merchants. It had been off and on in Holland ever since 1654; in Leyden 13,000 died; in 1655, in Amsterdam, 13,287 died of it. It was carried to London in bales of cotton, and 100,000 died in one year. Its symptoms were sudden delirium, when those attacked rolled about as if intoxicated, then followed profuse perspiration. In 1666 it spread to France, but died out in the winter.

The Plague was followed in 1666 by the Great Fire, and when London was rebuilt the streets were made wider, the drainage improved, and thatch for the roofs of houses was forbidden. Before then the Plague was constantly cropping up in London every few years.

Plague of Marseilles (*The*), 1720-1726. Brought from Syria in a merchant vessel. It spread to Arles, Aix, and Toulon, and above 80,000 fell victims to it. Henri François Xavier de Belsunce, bishop of Marseilles, exerted himself day and night to comfort the afflicted and take them spiritual consolation. By his devotion he gained the appellation of the *Good Bishop.* After the plague promotion was offered to him, but he resolved to remain bishop of Marseilles. He died in 1755, but it was not till 1853 that the inhabitants of Marseilles erected a statue to his memory.

Plagues, Epidemics, &c. *See* under

Antony's Fire (St.)	Feu Ardent
Belsunce	Great Plague
Black Death	Influenza (*Russian*)
,, Vomit	Loup-garou
Borromeo	Mazzuolo
Burning Fever (*Yellow Fever*)	Plague of London
	Plique
Coccoluccio (*see* 'Coqueluche')	Poitou Colic
	Scurvy
Coqueluche	Small-pox
Cholera Morbus	Sweating Sickness
Convulsionists	Tabardillo
Dance of St. Guy	Tac
Dancing Mania	Trousse-galant
English Sweat	Vomito Prieto
Febris Flamma (*Yellow Fever*)	(*Yellow Fever*)
	Yellow Fever

There have been thirty-three different pests in Europe since the founding of Rome, but a pest of some kind has visited Europe ninety-seven times since the birth of Christ. There were fourteen visitations in the 17th cent., and only eight in the 18th cent. Since then the visitations have greatly declined.

Plaine (*La*), 1791. The floor of the hall occupied by the National Convention of France. From the floor benches were raised on grades. These grades were called the Mountain. The red-hot Jacobins seated themselves on the raised benches and were called the Montagnards or Mountaineers, and the Girondists occupied the seat below them, called the Plaine. Both these parties formed the *côté gauche*; the *côté droit* was appropriated by the Constitutionalists. In 1794 the 'Plaine' was called the Marais (*q.v.*), or the Marsh.

Plaine des Vertus (*The*). This plain, which is in France, not far from Châlons-sur-Marne, is notorious for the review held there 10 Sept., 1814, of 160,000 Russian soldiers, before the diplomatic corps of Europe. 'Vertus' is the name of a town. It was taken by the English in 1422.

Plan of Campaign (*The*), Oct., 1886-1889. A device adopted by the Irish 'National party' for compelling Irish landlords to reduce their rents. The tenants were to offer what they thought proper for the rent of their holdings, and if the agents refused to accept their offer, the tenants were to lodge the money in the hands of trustees of the Land League. If evicted, they were, by boycotting, to prevent any other tenant from taking the farm. The plan was devised by Messrs. Dillon and W. O'Brien. It gave place in July, 1889, to the 'Tenants' Defence League' (*q.v.*).

The Solicitor-General said, 'One of the principal objects of the Plan was to get wealthy tenants, who could pay their rents, to lodge their money under the Plan, and once having done so they would not afterwards expose themselves to the risk which would follow its withdrawal. The meaning was this: The tenants were to fix their own rents, having first agreed among themselves the amount of reduction they intended to demand. If the landlord refused to grant the reduction, the tenants were to lodge the money as the Plan advised. If evicted, they were by boycotting to prevent anyone taking the farm.' 16 Feb., 1887. Forbidden by the Pope April, 1888.

No greater swindle was ever openly propounded, and, strange as it may seem, there were gentlemen and landlords of England who coquetted with it to gain the Irish vote.

Planets. *See* 'Bode's Law.'

Plantagenet. Geoffrey son of Fulk earl of Anjou was so surnamed, it is said, because he bore in his helmet a sprig of yellow broom instead of a feather (Lat. *planta-genistæ*); and this we are told was from penitential humility. Some say he was scourged with a rod of broom for his sins, as Henry II. is represented being scourged with birch-broom for the murder of Thomas Becket.

This Geoffrey married Maud daughter of Henry I., and their son was Henry Plantagenet, who succeeded the Norman dynasty in England. The Plantagenet race was succeeded by the Tudor dynasty. Fulk was son-in-law of Baldwin II. king of Jerusalem, whom he succeeded in 1131.

Plantation of Ulster (*The*), 1610. The colonising of the six counties of Ulster with Englishmen and Scotchmen. At the death of Queen Elizabeth, Sir Cahir O'Dogherty, chief of Inishowen, broke out into rebellion, but the rebellion was crushed in June 1608, when O'Dogherty fell in battle. Almost all Ulster now lay at the disposal of the crown. The lands of O'Dogherty were given to the deputy, and all the rest was divided into 3 lots. Lot 1 contained 2,000 acres; lot 2 contained 1,500 acres; and lot 3 contained 1000 acres. The parcels of lot 1 were sold to Englishmen and Scotchmen only; the parcels of lot 2 were distributed among servants of the crown. Neither of these could be alienated to the Irish. The parcels of lot 3 were held by Irishmen. The lands of Tyrone and O'Donnell were given by the crown to the corporation of London to be sold to Englishmen and Scotchmen. Husbandry and the arts being

introduced, Ulster, from being the most wild and disorderly province of Ireland, became the most civilised, the best cultivated, and the most prosperous.

The chief seat of this enforced colonisation was Londonderry, from the lands given to the Corporation of London. This land is still managed by twenty-six of the Common Council. The charter dates from 1619.

Tyrone [*i.e.* O'Neill], the principal chieftain of Ireland, wanted to be made king of the whole island, and promised to give all Ireland to Philip II. of Spain, and hold under him as a tributary prince, if Philip would help him to drive out the English. Philip sent money, arms, and men, under Don Juan d'Aguila, but the allied Spanish and Irish army was completely routed. Tyrone and Tyrconnell (O'Donell) soon quitted Ireland. Tyrone (O'Neill) settled in Rome, where the Pope and King of Spain allowed him a pension. O'Neill died there, and his son being assassinated, the race became extinct. Sir Cahir O'Dogherty the young chief of Inishowen now rose in insurrection, and was slain in battle. Thus the lands of O'Neill, O'Donell, and O'Dogherty all lapsed to the crown.

Planters (*The*). The colonists sent in the reign of James for the plantation of Ulster' (*q.v.*).

Plantin Polyglot Bible (*The*), 1569–1572. So called because it was printed by Christopher Plantin of Antwerp. It was edited by Arius Montãnus. *See* 'Polyglot.'

Plato (*The English*). The Rev. John Norris (1657–1711).

Plato (*The German*). Friedrich Heinrich Jacobi (1743–1819).

Plato (*The Jewish*). Philo-Judæus (flo. 20–40).

Plato (*The Scottish*). Dugald Stewart, born at Edinburgh 1753, died 1828.

Plato of the 18th cent. Voltaire (1694–1778).

The sage Plato of the 18th cent.—CARLYLE, *Friedrich II. of Prussia* (vol. ii. p. 597).

Platonic Puritan (*The*). John Howe (1630–1706). Author of 'The Good Man the Living Temple of God,' which occupies one of the highest places in Puritan literature.

Platonists. Dr. Joseph Priestley, in his 'Corruptions of Christianity,' maintains that the doctrine of the Trinity is due to Platonism, and it is certain that the Platonists taught a sort of Trinity. There was first the Unity, that abstract existence without form or personality of any kind. From this *ens* proceeded what St. John calls *Logos*, and the author of 'Proverbs' calls *Wisdom*. 'By Wisdom God established the heavens and founded the earth' (iii. 19); and from these two proceeded the Word-Soul, which constitute the Triad. So in Gen. i. we have first God in Unity, then the Word 'God said Let there be ' so and so, and then the Spirit which moved on the face of chaos to reduce matter into order. Certainly the Christians of Alexandria were correct in tracing a striking resemblance between the language of Moses, the Christian Trinity, and the Platonic Triad.

Platonists and Cartesians. The new departure in the Church of England in 1666, led by Henry More, and supported by Cudworth, Wilkins, Tillotson, Stillingfleet, Patrick, and others, who extended the principles of philosophy and divinity, and were the fathers of the Latitudinarian school of theology.

Cartesians were followers of the French philosopher Descartes.

Platonop'olis. The city of Plotin the neoplatonic philosopher, in Campania, where he intended to carry out his socialistic ideas and philosophical system. It does not appear that he was able to complete his project, for we hear nothing more about it except that the Emperor Galen granted him permission to build the city.

Plautus (*The Portuguese*). Gil Vicente (1480-1557).

Plea (*The Army's*), 1659, was a paper drawn up by the officers of the army left by Cromwell to vindicate their conduct in driving the Rump Parliament from power for a time, and endeavouring to place England under a military government.

Pleas of the Crown (*The Four*). Murder, fire, rape, and robbery.

Pleasant Willy. William Shakespeare (1564-1616).

Pleiadês, sing. *Pleïad.* Seven contemporaneous poets. The Alexandrine Pleiadês consisted of Lycophron, Theocritês, Arâtos, Nicander, Apollonios, Callimachos, and Philiscos (called Homer the Younger).

The *first* French Pleiade in the reign of Henri III. was composed of Ronsard, Dubellay, Remi Belleau, Jodelle, Baïf, Pontus de Thiard, and Amadis Jamyn (or else Dorat).

The *second* French Pleiade, in the

reign of Louis XIII., was composed of Rapin, Commire, Larue, Santeuil, Ménage, Dupérier, and Petit.

The Pleiades of Greek mythology were the seven sisters named Electra, Maia, Taygêtê (4 syl.), Alcyônê, Celæno, Sterôpê, and Merôpê, who died of grief, and were afterwards placed as stars in the back of Taurus.

Pliny (*The German*). Konrad von Gesner, styled by Boerhaave that 'Monstrum Eruditiônis.' He wrote the 'Historia Animalium,' &c. (1516-1565).

Pliny of the East. Zakarija-ibn-Muhammed, called Kâzwînî, from Kazwin, the place of his birth (1200-1283).

Plique (*Le*), or Plica Polonica, 1599. An endemic very common in Poland. 'Les médecins prétendent que le siège du mal est dans les cheveux, qui se mêlent d'abord sans causer beaucoup de douleur; mais ensuite la suppuration s'établit, et fait sortir une innombrable vermine qui cause des tiraillements et de picotements insupportables. La chevelure ne forme plus alors qu'une masse compacte.' It was called by the Poles *Gozdziec*, and it is said to have been caused by drinking the water of the Borysthênês. This disease is common in India. See 'Plagues,' &c.

Plogpenning, 'Plough-penny.' So Eric VI. of Denmark was called because he laid a tax on ploughs (1274, 1286-1319).

Plon-Plon. The sobriquet of Prince Napoleon Joseph Charles Bonaparte, son of Jerome Bonaparte. It is a euphonic corruption of *Craint-plomb* (Fear-bullet), given to the prince in the Crimêan war (1854-1856).

Plots (*The Three*). In the reign of Charles II. called Oates's Plot (*q.v.*), the Meal-tub Plot (*q.v.*), and the Rye-house Plot (*q.v.*), or Oates, Meal, and Rye. Oates's Plot 1678, Meal-tub Plot 1679, the Rye-house Plot 1683.

Ploughgates   in   demesne. Lands reserved in the lord's own hand, in contradistinction to lands held by homagers, villeins, cottars, and serfs in the manor.

Plug-drawers. A term invented by Peel, applied to stump-orators who drew the plug of their declamation, and let loose the waters of ' radical humanity,' *ad captandum vulgus.* There are plenty of such plug-drawers still, who let loose their 'humanity' in sympathy with rebels, like the French jury who acquitted the murderer of his father and mother, poor man, 'because he was an orphan.' The Luddite orators, 1811, the Chartist orators, 1848, &c., and the Home Rule orators, 1890, &c., are your plug-drawers who waste their sympathy 'in one weak, washy, everlasting flood.'

Plu'mean Professor of Astronomy and Experimental Philosophy. Stipend 800*l*. a year. Founded in the University of Cambridge by Dr. Plume, archdeacon of Rochester, 1704.

Plymouth Adventurers (*The*). A company chartered by James I. authorising them to plant all North America from 41° to 45° N. lat., which includes what we now call Pennsylvania, New Jersey, New York, and New England.

Plymouth Brethren (*The*), 1828. 'Brethrenism' began in Dublin, where certain Christians met together to partake of the Lord's Supper without a minister. In 1832 John H. Darby, a curate of the Anglican Church, joined the society, and afterwards became its head, but in time removed to Switzerland. The members call themselves merely 'Brethren,' but they are sometimes called Darbyites. They have no written creed, but believe Christianity is on its decline.

The religious system of the society is called Brethrenism.' They reject clericalism, insist on the equal standing and privilege of every member of Christ's Church, believe in the doctrine of election, and deem church-membership necessary for salvation. Called Plymouth because at Plymouth the society was first developed.

Plymouth Sound. James White, member for Plymouth, who spoke with a very loud voice.

Pneumatics, or 'Macedonians,' 4th cent. Those who denied the divinity of the Holy Ghost. Πνεῦμα, the spirit.

Pocket Borough (*A*). A borough in which the freemen were all controlled by the pocket of the candidate. This was in the 'good old days' before parliamentary reform abolished the freemen's absurd privilege of election.

Pocket Judgment. Statute-merchant is so called. It was a bond of record under the hand and seal of a debtor, authenticated by the king's seal.

On failure of payment, execution was at once awarded without further charge or trouble. This process is no longer in use.

Po'codena'rio, or Lack Penny. Maximilian I. (1493–1519); he failed well nigh in all his projects for want of money.

Poet-laureate. Petrarch appears to have been the first of modern poets crowned with laurels, 1341. Warton shows there were royal poets about our English kings before the time of Richard I., whose court poet Blondel is said to have discovered the place of the king's captivity and to have been the means of his release. Chaucer as royal poet was allowed a gallon of wine a day, and before that time a harper to Henry III. had an allowance of wine. Charles I. in 1630 made the office patent and settled both a stipend and wine on the laureate. Till Tennyson was made poet the stipend was 127*l*. plus 27*l*. for the purchase of a cask of canary.

The term arose thus: the king chose a laureated student of Oxford or Cambridge, that is a student to whom a laurel crown had been presented for the best Latin ode in praise of Alma Mater. In France crowning with laurels is continued still.

Poets' Corner (*The*), in Westminster Abbey, the South Corner. This is merely a popular name. As a Valhalla of British poets, one would be ashamed of the list. The poets represented are: Addison, Beaumont, S. Butler, Campbell, Cowley, Davenant, Drayton, Dryden, Gay, Goldsmith, Gray, Dr. Johnson, Ben Jonson, Longfellow of America, Macaulay, Mason, Milton, Philips, Prior, Rowe, Shakespeare, Shadwell, Sheridan, Spenser, and Thomson.

But there is no memorial to such poets as the following: Akenside, Mrs. Browning, BYRON, BURNS, Carew, Cartwright, CHAUCER, Churchill, Coleridge, Collins, Cotton, COWPER, Crabbe, Denham, Donne, Fletcher, Mrs. Hemans, Herbert, Herrick, HOGG, Hood, Keats, Miss Landon, Lee, Lovelace, Marlowe, Marston, Massinger, MOORE, Parnell, Pollok, POPE, Raleigh, Ramsay, Rossetti, SCOTT, SHELLEY, Shenstone, Southern, Southey, Waller, Wither, Wolfe, WORDSWORTH, Young, and several others.

** Why not place the name in a cartouch with date of birth and death? Let first-class men, like Chaucer, Shake-

speare, and Milton have a statue ; second-class poets, like Dryden, Byron, Words-worth, &c., have a cameo profile; the rest a simple cartouch with name. And no name inscribed till twenty-five years after death. The cloisters might be utilised for the purpose.

Poetical Milkmaid (*The*), or ' The Poetical Milkmaid of Bristol,' Ann Yearsley (1756–1806).

Pogon'atus, *i.e.* the bearded. The agnomen of Constantine IV. emperor of the East (648–685). Greek πωγώνατος.

Poinding. Taking an inventory of the effects of a debtor; taking goods by way of distress; the act of transferring a debtor's goods to his creditors in default or in payment of debt. The same was ' pounding ' or putting stray cattle into the parish pound. Ang.-Sax. *pynd-an*, to confine, to pound, our word ' impound-ing.'

The retainers of the law went from place to place, making an inventory of the goods and chattels falling under their warrant of distress, or poinding, as it is called in the law of Scotland. —Sir W. SCOTT, *The Antiquary*, chap. xlii.

'Pointed Arrow.' So General Jackson was called by the Indians against whom he fought in 1813 (1767–1845).

Poissy (*The Colloquy of*), 1561 (Sept. 9 to Oct. 9). A disputation between Catholics and reformers held at Poissy, under the expectation of proving which was right—Catholic faith or that of the reformers. Théodore de Bèze was the chief of the reform representatives, which consisted of twelve pastors and twenty-two laymen. The Catholic disputants were the cardinals of Tournon, Lorraine, Châtillon, Bourbon, Guise, and Arma-gnac, with about forty bishops and doctors. On the first day Bèze stated the reformers' creed of the eucharist, whereupon Cardinal de Tournon prayed that the blasphemer might be silenced, but no notice was taken of the cardinal's request. On the 16th Sept. Cardinal de Lorraine answered that the church could not err, and the church had decided that the real presence was the right faith. Bèze craved leave to reply, but the pre-lates rose and the conference was ad-journed. Other meetings were held, but on 9 Oct. the conference was broken off, each party being more embittered against

the other and more self-opinionated than before.

Generally called ' Beza' in English.

Poitiers (*The Edict of*), 8 Oct., 1577, granting to the Huguenots of France the exercise of the reformed religion, but only in the places where it was professed at the time of signing this treaty. Henri III. used to boast of this edict as ' My edict, my treaty.' It never was observed, and never would have been granted ex-cept out of spite to the Guises.

Poitou Colic (*The*), 1572–1606, appeared in France. It is said to have been caused by ergot (a sort of fungus) in the wheat; but some regard it as lead-poisoning. *See* ' Plagues,' &c.

Poland (*Father of*). Boleslas I. (960,992–1025) called the Great, certainly the greatest sovereign of the age.

Poland (*The Golden Age of*). The reign of Casimir IV. (1444–1492). Others call the reign of Sigismund I. (1506–1548) the ' golden age of Poland.' Perhaps it would be more correct to join the two and say 1444 to 1548 was the golden age. Lithuania, Smolensk, and the vast territories beyond the Euxine and the Baltic obeyed Sigismund; while his nephew Louis possessed Hungary, Bohemia, and Silesia.

Pole Star (*Knights of the*), 1741. A military order of Sweden instituted by King Frederick. The decoration is a Latin cross with four crowns ; the le-gend being ' Nescit Occasum,' in allusion to the pole star, which never sets.

Police Strike (*The London*), 5 July, 1890. The constables at Bow Street and the Metropolitan Police refused to go on duty. They complained of insuffi-cient pay (22*s.* a week), and demanded two-thirds of their pay as a superannua-tion pension after 25 years' service. The chief commissioner, Sir Edward Brad-ford, dismissed or removed above 400 of the force, and the strike collapsed.

At the same time the 2nd Grenadier Guards, some of the London postmen, and telegraph clerks struck for less work and more wages. Probably the insubordination of the Irish Home Rule party was responsible for these disturbances. The Grenadier Guards were relieved of the extra duty which they complained of, but were sent off im-mediately on colonial service to the islands of Bermuda for ' change of air ' ; and the telegraph clerks were told that they were free to go with proper notice.

Police System (*The*), 1814. Originated by Sir Robert Peel, chief secretary for Ireland; perfected in 1836. Providing a complete and efficient constabulary force both day and night for the United Kingdom.

Poliorce'tes (5 syl.), 'Besieger of cities.' Demetrius the Phalērean, historian, philosopher, poet, and king of Macedonia (B.C. 337, 294–287, died 283).

Political Handkerchief (*Berthold's*), 1831, price 4*d*. Printed and published by H. Berthold, No. 1 Bouverie Street, Fleet Street, and 14 Duke Street, Lincoln's Inn Fields. ' It was a pocket-handkerchief or book printed on cotton to avoid the paper tax. It contained various political articles, as the prophecy of Napoleon on various European States, &c.'

In 1832 an untaxed almanac, price 7*d*., was printed on linen by John Smith, No. 1 Bouverie Street, &c.

Politiques (*Les*). 'The Politicans,' the 'malcontents in the religious wars in the reign of Charles IX. and Henri III. The leaders were François d'Alençon (the king's brother), Henri king of Navarre, the Prince de Condé, and the Montmorencys. They were part Catholics, part Huguenots, recommended mutual tolerance, and proposed terms of peace between the Catholics and Protestants. In 1574 some of the Politiques conspired against Charles IX., and two of the conpirators (La Mole and Coconas) were beheaded. At the death of Charles IX. they took up arms, but were defeated by Henri de Guise at Dormans in 1575. The party melted away after the treaty of Beaulieu in 1576.

Called *Politicians*, because they advocated new maxims of politics and political liberty, such as the lawfulness of deposing bad kings. And called *Malcontents*, because they were not content with either the Catholic or Protestant party of France.

Polyglot Bibles. 1. The *Hexapla*, attempted by Origen (220–250) ; and projected by Aldus 1501.

2. The *Complutensian* (*q.v.*), under the patronage and at the expense of Cardinal Ximenês (1502–1517).

3. The *Plantin*, or Antwerp, printed by Christopher Plantin, and edited by Arius Montānus (1569–1572).

4. The *Paris*, by Le Jay (1628–1645).

5. The *London*, edited by Walton (1654–1657), in nine languages—Hebrēw, Syriac, Chaldee, Samaritan, Ethiopic, Arabic, Persian, Greek, and Latin.

6. *Hutter's*, published at Nürnberg (1599).

7. *Baxter's*, London, 1831. *See* ' Bible.'

Complutum is Alcălá de Henâres (3 syl.), a town near Madrid in New Castile.

Pomfret Marbles (*The*). A part of the Arundel collection, given to Oxford University in 1755.

Pons Subli'cius. The first Roman bridge. It was built over the Tiber by Ancus Martius on wooden piles (*sublicæ*), whence its name.

Pontifical (*The*). The service-book of the Romish bishops, embracing all that pertains to their several functions, as the 'Ceremonial' describes the various functions of the pope. It is attributed to Pope Gelasius (492–496) and Gregory the Great (590–604). *See* ' Ceremonial' and ' Ritual.'

Pontifical Indiction (*The*). Begins 25 Dec., B.C. 3.

Poor Brothers of St. John (*The*), 1048. Some Italian merchants obtained permission of the Kalif to build a hospital at Jerusalem for the protection of pilgrims. The hospital was dedicated to St. John the Almoner. During the first crusade many of the wounded were taken to this hospital, and after restoration to health dedicated themselves to a life of charity, under the designation of the Poor Brothers of St. John, consisting of knights, clergy, and serving brothers. Their dress was a black robe, on which was embroidered a white cross with eight points. These Poor Brothers were called 'Knights Hospitallers,' from the 'Hospital of St. John the Almoner.' They are also called ' White Cross Knights,' in contradistinction to the Knights Templars, who were Red Cross Knights.

Poor Clares, or Clarisses, 1224. Founded by St. Francis of Assisi, and placed under the charge of Clare or Clarisse of Assisi, his favourite nun.

Poor Knights (*The*), 1348. Instituted by Edward III. Twenty-four in number, maintained in St. George's chapel. The charity was instituted to provide a comfortable home for valiant soldiers fallen into poverty and decay. The number was increased by James I. to twenty-six, and each knight had a pension of 18*l*. 5*s*., paid quarterly.

Now called 'Military Knights,' and no longer limited to soldiers who have *fallen* into poverty and decay, but, like college sizars, often awarded to poor gentlemen still in the service. There are two foundations, the Royal and the Lower. The Lower Foundation consists of five knights, added by Sir Peter Lemaire and Sir Francis Crane.

Poor Law Amendment Act

(*The*), 1834 (4, 5 Will. IV. c. 76). Commissioners appointed for the better administration of the '.Poor Laws.' It repealed the law of settlement, united parishes into unions, each union being placed under a Board of Guardians elected annually by the ratepayers. It created 585 unions, including 13,964 parishes, in England and Wales. Besides these there are 21 unions by Local Acts, 12 by Gilbert's Act (*q.v.*), and the 89 parishes of the Scilly Isles included in a union. These, with 37 single parishes, make up the whole number of 14,610 parishes. Each union has a clerk, an auditor, a chaplain, a medical officer, relieving officers, a master and matron, schoolmaster and schoolmistress.

The principle embodied in the Act was to make the parish the hardest taskmaster, so as to drive able-bodied men to seek honest work elsewhere, and not hang in laziness on parish relief. The effects have been to reduce parochial expenditure, to diminish crime, and to encourage thrift.

Poor Men of Lyons (*The*), 12th

cent. Religious reformers of the Cevennes, or Mont de Lyonnais, who probably were organised by Peter Waldo, a rich merchant of Lyons. Though they held similar religious views to those of the Waldenses, they must not be confounded with them, seeing the Waldenses existed 350 years before the Lyonists. The Poor Men of Lyons dressed in mean attire, made a vow of voluntary poverty, and during the persecutions of the Waldenses and Albigenses also were involved in the same massacres. Those who escaped the fire and the sword hid themselves in the mountains of Provence and Piedmont, where they lived in concealment till 1545, when those of Provence were extirpated. In 1686-7 the survivors lurking about Piedmont were driven into Switzerland, and there still exist from sixteen to twenty thousand of these reformers.

Poor Priests (*The*). The preaching disciples of Wyclif, who went about barefoot, in plain frieze gowns.

Pope (*The Huguenot*). Philippe de Mornay, sieur du Plessis, so called from his 'Treatise on the Sacrament of the Eucharist,' published in 1598. He died in 1623, at the age of 74.

Pope (*The Worst*). Alexander VI., father of Cesare Borgia, his sister Lucrezia, and several other sons and daughters of inferior notoriety. Simony, treason, murder, poisoning, are amongst the crimes attributed to him (1431, 1492–1503).

Pope Joan (*Papissa Joanna*). 'John VIII.,' said to have held the chair of St. Peter from 853 to 855, between Leo IV. and Benedict III. To make this statement good the death of Leo IV. is placed in the year 853 (not 855). The tale is that she was an English girl, educated at Cologne, who assumed man's clothes in order to elope with a monk of Fulda. While at Rome she earned such high reputation for her learning that she was chosen to succeed Pope Leo IV., and assumed the name of John VIII. Her sex was discovered by the birth of a child as she was going from the Coliseum to the church of St. Clement. Being strangled, the time of her pontificate was added to that of her predecessor.

PRO.

Anastatius (886), in his 'Liber Pontificālis,' mentions the story, and as this was only thirty years after the death of Leo, if the passage is genuine, it is proof positive of the fact.

Mariānus Scotus (1083), in his 'Universal Chronicle,' repeats the story.

Sigebert of Gemblours (1030-1113), in his 'Chronicles,' does the same.

In the 'Augustan Annals' (1135) we are told that this papissa in 855 consecrated Louis II. of France.

Etienne de Bourbon (1225) states the tale as an historic fact.

Otto of Freisingen, and Godefroid of Viterbo, both mention her in their histories.

Martīnus Polōnus (1278), in his 'Chronicles of the Popes and Emperors,' tells us that John, an Englishman, succeeded Leo IV., and that this pope was said to be a woman, whose sex was discovered by the birth of a child on her way from the Coliseum to St. Clement's Church.

Thomas de Elmham repeats the story in 1422.

Platina (1479), in his 'Lives of the Popes,' repeats the story.

William Occam alludes to the story.

John Huss tells us her baptismal name was not Joan, but Agnes. Others say her baptismal name was Gilberta.

Spanheim (1600-1649) tells the same tale in his 'Exercit. de Papa Fæmina,' ii. 577.

Lenfant (1661-1728) wrote a 'History of the Female Pope.' He was the author of a 'History of the Council of Constance,' a 'History of Pisa,' a 'History of the Hussite Wars,' &c.

Prof. Kist of Leyden believed the tale to be true. Mosheim (1694-1755), in his 'Ecclesiastical History,' seems inclined to credit the story, though he acknowledges that it is doubtful.

Indubitably a statue of Pope Joan occupied a place among the accredited popes in the cathedral church of Sienna. *See* Pagi, 'Critica,' vol. iii. p. 624.

At least 150 authors, on every variety of subject, in the 13th, 14th, 15th, 16th cents. repeat the tale as an accredited fact.

Till the time of the Reformation it was undoubtedly considered to be a genuine historic fact.

CON.

Allatius, or Allatus, contradicts the story in his 'Confutatio Fabulæ de Johanna Papissa' (17th cent.).

Lequien does the same in his 'Oriens Christianus,' iii. 777 (18th cent.).

Blondel, a Calvinist divine (1649), wrote a book in confutation of the story.

Gibbon (1737-1794), in his 'Decline,' &c., chap. xlix., calls the story a 'fable,' and thinks that the appointment of popes by such prostitutes as Marozia and Theodora may have suggested the tale.

Bayle (1760-1815), in his 'Dictionnaire Critique,' article 'Papisse,' gives arguments pro and con, but decides against the story.

It is said that the clause in Anastatius ('Liber Pontificalis') is a forgery.

Pagi, Muratöri, and Leibnitz fix the date of the death of Leo IV. in the year 857.

Photius (9th cent.) and Luitprand, or Liutprand, omit all mention of Papissa Joanna (10th cent.).

. Arguments on both sides of the question are given in Cunningham's translation of 'Geiseler Lehrbuch,' ii. 21, 22.

The last person who critically examined the question was Döllinger in 1863.

It is strange that no Catholic of note has written to confute the story, but that the *contra* has been left to a Calvinist minister, an atheist, and a line or two of Gibbon, an infidel.

After all, it would be well indeed if the worst thing that could be said against the popes of Rome is that once a woman in male attire was mistaken for a man. Undoubtedly for a century, about the same period, there was a succession of popes of most infamous reputation (*see* 'Popes of the Tenth Cent.'). There was more than one *boy* pope, and a host of antipopes.

N.B.—I cannot think that Blondel's book has settled this vexed question, or anything like it. Of course the supposed date of Leo's death is wholly worthless unless it can be proved by independent testimony.

Pope of Rome (*The*).

In 597 John IV., the Jejunätor, patriarch of Constantinople, assumed the title of Œcumenical Patriarch, or Universal Bishop. This excited the indignation of the bishop of Rome against both the patriarch and the emperor. Soon after this, Mauricius the emperor was murdered and his successor (Phocas), in 602, was induced by Boniface III. to confer on the pope of Rome the title of the 'Universal Bishop,' which occurred in 666.

There seems something ominous in the strange date 666, connecting it with the 666 of Revelation xiii. 18. 'Here is wisdom. Let him that hath understanding count the number of the beast, for it is the number of a man, and the number is six hundred three score and six' (*i.e.* 666).

. Before this the episcopal titles of *Papa, Apostolicus, Vicarius Christi, Summus Pontifex*, and *Patriarcha* were very loosely applied to all sorts of bishops, &c.

Popes.

Presuming that Peter was in Rome, and that he was the first of the popes, there have been 297 popes, 24 of whom were anti-popes and one female (if indeed 'Pope Joan' was not wholly a myth). Of the rest, 19 quitted Rome, and 35 reigned elsewhere.

Eight of the reigns did not exceed a month in duration, 40 extended over *one* year, 22 over *two* years, 54 over *five* years, 51 over *fifteen* years, 18 over *twenty* years, and 9 have exceeded that duration.

Of the 297 popes, 31 were declared usurpers and heretics, 2 were young boys, 64 met with violent deaths (18 being poisoned and 4 strangled).

Independently of the Avignon popes, 26 of the Roman popes were deposed, expelled from Rome, or banished ; and 28 maintained their power only by foreign aid.

Very sad indeed is the history of the Popes as Vicars of Christ on earth.

Popes and Kings.

The 10th cent. was the era of impious popes and pious kings.

Good Kings, the last quarter of the 10th to the last quarter of the 11th cent. :—

963–969. Nicephorus II., emperor of the east, who united the hero with the saint.

996–1031. Robert the Pious of France.

997–1038. St. Stephen of Hungary.

1000–1030. St. Olaus II. of Norway.

1002–1024. Heinrich II., called the Saint and the Lame of Germany.

1012–1052. St. Boniface II. duke of Tuscany.

1016–1035. Canute the Great of England, a deeply religious man.

1024–1039. Konrad II. the Sage of Germany.

1039–1056. Heinrich III. the Black King of Germany. A model prince.

1041–1066. Edward the Confessor.

1080–1086. St. Knut IV. the Great of Denmark.

Popes of the 10th cent., the darkest period of the papacy. There were twenty-five popes in the century, which gives the average of four years to a pope.

Benedict IV. (900-903). Il ne put corriger la dépravation des mœurs.

Leo V. (903, 40 days), imprisoned by his chaplain

Christophorus, who usurped the office for nine months, and was then deposed.

Sergius III. (904-911), the *protégé* of Marozia, a licentious woman of Rome. He lived criminally with Theodora.

Anastasius III. (911-913). Rome was still under the influence of infamous women.

Lando (913-914), appointed by the intrigues of Theodora. He died in six months.

John X. (914-928), appointed by the intrigues of Theodora, his courtesan, and cast into prison by the harlot Marozia, daughter of Theodora. John X. died in prison, probably by poison.

Leo VI. (928 929, seven months), probably poisoned by Marozia.

Stephen VII. (929-931). A nonentity.

John XI. (931-936), son of Marozia the harlot. Cast into prison by another son of Marozia, and left to die there.

Leo VII. (936-939). Not a bad pope.

Stephen VIII. (939-942), father of Otho.

Martin III. (942-946). A nonentity.

Agapetus (946-956). Not a bad pope.

John XII. (956-963), grandson of the infamous Marozia, was only eighteen when made pope. His life was so licentious that he was deposed, and probably assassinated. Leo was anti-pope 963-964.

Benedict V. (964-965) was elected pope 964, but was detained at Hamburg by the emperor, and died there.

John XIII. (965-972). He was imprisoned in an insurrection.

Benedict VI. (972-974), strangled in the Castle of Angelo by Boniface VII., who usurped the pontifical office, but was driven from Rome in two months.

Domnus or Donus II. (974-975), died suddenly, probably by foul means.

Benedict VII. (975-983). His dead body was dragged by the heels about the streets, and then flung into the Tiber.

John XIV. (983-985), murdered in prison.

Boniface VII. (984-985), called anti-pope, murdered his rivals Benedict VI. and John XIV.

John XV. (985), died before he was inaugurated.

John XVI. (985-996). A nonentity.

Gregory V. (996-999), driven from Rome by the soldiers of his uncle, John XVII., who usurped the office.

Sylvester (999-1003). A Frenchman of considerable mechanical genius, and accused of magic.

John XVII. (1003), anti-pope, the mere tool of Crescentius the Roman demagogue.

A blacker century cannot be shown than this tenth century of the Roman popes. Of three or four of the names nothing whatever is known. These popes were names and nothing else. *See* 'Popes (*The Boy*).'

*** Yet was the doctrine of apostolic succession first maintained in this bad era.

Popes (*The Boy*). John XII. (956-963) was only 18 when he was made pope. Benedict IX. was made pope in 1033 at the age of 10. Both were profligate, extravagant, and licentious. John XII. was probably assassinated; and Benedict IX. was deposed in 1044.

In the Greek Church Theophylactos, a son of Romānus (Emperor of the East), was made patriarch when a mere lad, but it would be hard to find a more infamous character (933-956).

Giovanni de' Medici, son of Lorenzo (afterwards Leo X.), was made a cardinal at the age of 14.

Popes (*The Two*). While there were two popes, France, Scotland, Spain, Sicily, and Cyprus supported the French pope,

who resided at Avignon; but the Italians, with England, Flanders, and the rest of Europe, supported the Italian pope, who resided at Rome. The former were called Clementines and the latter Urbanists, from Clement VII. and Urban VI., the first of the two contemporaneous popes.

Pope's Cap. *See* under 'Tiara.'

Pope's Kaiser (*The*), 'Pfaffen Kaiser.' Karl IV. (*q.v.*), nominated to the crown by Pope Clement VI. without consulting the electors (1347-1378).

Popelitans, 'Populicans,' or 'Poplicans' (*q.v.*).

Popish Plot (*The*). I. 1678. A plot which Titus Oates affirmed the Roman Catholics had devised to murder the king (Charles II.), to restore the United Kingdom to the pope, and to massacre the Protestants as they were massacred in France in the St. Bartholomew slaughter. Oates said 20,000 Catholics were in the league. The king believed the whole story to be a hoax, but many strange discoveries were brought to light which gave some colour to a secret plot, and the whole nation was in a panic.

There was a scandalous rumour which charged the king himself, the Duke of York, and Louis XIV. of France with being the secret conspirators. They were quite capable of being so.

II. May 1798. An Irish insurrection in which Wolfe Tone induced the French to lend a hand under golden promises to the Directory. Some 14,000 Irish under the lead of Father Murphy attacked Wexford, and put to death a number of prisoners. They then took Enniscorthy, but being attacked by General Lake, both Wexford and Enniscorthy were retaken. At Scullabogue the insurgents massacred 100 Protestants in cold blood. The massacre of Protestants by the insurgents obtained for the rebellion the name of the Popish Plot, but the leading Catholics protested against the name, and offered their aid to government to put it down. When all seemed over, General Humbert landed from France with 900 men in three French frigates, but was defeated by Lord Cornwallis and surrendered. A few days afterwards Sir John Warren fell in with a French line-of-battle ship and 8 frigates. He captured the ship and 3 of the frigates. Wolfe Tone was executed, and so ended this absurd revolt.

Wolfe Tone was a mere unprincipled adventurer, who offered his services, as a buccaneer,

both to Pitt and to the Duke of Richmond.
Pitt did not condescend even to answer him,
and Tone, out of spite, turned 'patriot' (or
rebel). Incredible as it may seem, Mr. Gladstone,
in 1889, wrote a letter, published in the Scotch
newspapers, containing this sentence: 'I am
glad an effort has been made to do justice (!) to
Wolfe Tone. It is one of the most grievous facts
of Irish history that, at the close of the last century, her rebels were in many cases the very
flower of her children' (!!). Only read the 'Memoirs' of Wolfe Tone, written by himself, and see
if there is one single redeeming feature in his
whole life. He was an idle scamp, who deserted
his wife, and turned rebel, as he would have
turned buccaneer, from the grossest motives.
Read 'Nineteenth Century,' May 1890, pp. 733-756.

Popish Wind (A). A west wind.
See 'Protestant,' &c.

31 Oct. I was present when James received
letters from Newport, informing him, with extravagant exaggeration, of the dispersion of the
Prince of Orange's fleet. At dinner he said to the
French ambassador, 'At last the wind has declared
itself popish. You must know ' (he added ' for these
three days I have caused the Holy Sacrament to
be carried in procession.'—MISSON.

Pop'licans, 1160. So the Waldenses
(q.v.) who passed over to England from
Aquitaine were called. The word is a
contraction of Populicani, a corrupt form
of Publicani, so called because they
imitated the publican more than the
pharisee who went to the temple to pray.

Popola'ri (The). The Venetian plebeians, exercising small industries.

Porch (The). Zeno's school was so
called because the disciples of this Greek
philosopher met in the porch Pœcilê.
The Stoics were meant (στοά, a porch).
Similarly we have the Garden sect, and so on.

Por'cian Law (The). That no Roman citizen shall be scourged (Acts xvi.
22, 25-30, 37).

Por'phyrogen'itus. So Constantine VII. was called. Gibbon (chap.
xlviii.) says the word means 'born to the
purple'; but this etymology is by no
means certain.

There was an island called Porphyris between
Crete and Peloponnesus; if he was born there the
word would mean 'born in Porphyris,' but is it
certain he was born there?

Porphyry's 'Oracles of Philosophy'
proved by Dr. Lardner to be a literary
imposition. See 'Literary Forgeries.'

Porson Prize (The). For the best
translation into Greek verse of a given
passage from Shakespeare, Ben Jonson,
Massinger, or Beaumont and Fletcher.
Given in Greek books to an undergraduate
of the University of Cambridge. Value
about 12l. Founded by the trustees of

a fund raised for the benefit of Richard
Porson, professor of Greek, 1816. See
'Regius Professor of Greek.'

Porson Scholarship for Classics.
Value 65l. a year, and tenable for 4 years.
Founded in the University of Cambridge
out of a fund raised for the benefit of
Richard Porson, professor of Greek, 1855.

Porson died in 1808, but the fund was left to
accumulate.

Port Act (The), 1774. See p. 115,
'Boston Port Bill.'

Port Royal. An abbey founded in
1204 of the rule of St. Benedict; it had
for its object the education of youths. In
1625, the abbey being too small, the seminary was transferred to Paris, and on the
publication of Jansen's 'Augustīnus' (q.v.)
became fervent supporters of Jansenism
(q.v.) against the Sorbonne (q.v.). From
1636 the monastery of Port Royal was the
retreat of scholars who worked with their
hands and taught youths. In 1790 the
monastery was suppressed with most
others, and was converted into the prison
called Port Libre.

The most illustrious members were Arnauld,
Andilly (two brothers), Lemaistre de Sacy, Nicole,
Lancelot, Fontaine, and Lenain de Tillemont.
Pascal visited it often, and was a Jansenist. It
produced some first-class educational books, and
the Bible de Sacy.

Port Royal (Doctrines of the).
These doctrines were in accordance with
those of the Jansenists. The chief
authors of Port Royal in defence of the
'Augustīnus' of Cornelius Jansen were
the brothers Arnauld, Lemaistre de Sacy
and his two brothers, Nicole, Lancelot,
Fontaine, Lenain de Tillemont, and
Pascal.

Portcullis. One of the four pursuivants of England. See 'Heralds.'

Porte (The). Originally meant Bagdad or its caliphate. Mostasem, last of the
Abbasside califs, set in the threshold of
the principal gate of his palace at Bagdad
a small piece of the famous Black Stone,
'given to Ishmael by the angel Gabriel,'
and built into the shrine of Mecca, called
the 'Caaba.' This gate was called La
Porte by excellence. Mostasem was calif
1243-1258. See next article.

Porte (The), or 'The Sublime Porte,'
1324. The court of the sultan of the
Ottoman empire. Orchan, called the
'Padishah' (i.e. the 'Shah defender),

succeeded his father Othman in 1324, and built offices for the transaction of public business at the great gate of the palace. In the language of diplomacy ambassadors are distinguished by the court or locality where they perform their functions, and those in Turkey are ambassadors to 'La Porte,' for French was for many years the language of diplomacy. The 'Sublime Porte' means the 'lofty gate.' Bagdad had been called 'The Porte' nearly a hundred years before the reign of Orchan.

Porte Libre, 1790. A prison in Paris, formerly the famous Port Royal monastery.

Porteous Riot (*The*), 1736. Two smugglers from Fife (Wilson and Robertson) were condemned to death, and confined in the Tolbooth of Edinburgh, popularly styled 'The Heart of Midlothian.' They tried to escape, but Wilson, a strong stout man, got wedged in the gap they had made, and the two prisoners were secured. When they attended service in the Tolbooth church they were guarded by four soldiers. Wilson seized two in his hands and one with his teeth, calling to Robertson to escape. Robertson shook off the remaining soldier, escaped, and was never again captured. When Wilson was executed Captain Porteous was ordered with his city guard to attend, and being assailed by stones he fired on the mob. His men also fired, killing four and wounding eleven of the mob. Porteous was tried for his life and found guilty, but received a reprieve. On 7 Sept., the day on which the reprieve expired, the mob broke into the Tolbooth, seized Porteous, and hanged him in the Grass Market, the place where Wilson was executed, on a dyer's pole, to which a new rope was suspended. This being done, the mob quietly dispersed, and did no mischief to any other person nor injury to any property. (*See* Sir Walter Scott, 'Heart of Midlothian.')

Portiforium (*A*). 'Liber vocatus Portiforium antiquum, secundum usum Sarum,' &c. That is, a breviary with running annotations; a portable manual.

Portland Vase (*The*). The famous Barberi'ni vase purchased from Sir William Hamilton by the Duchess of Portland for 1,000 guineas, and presented in 1810 to the British Museum by the Duke of Portland.

This Greek vase was for more than two centuries the principal ornament of the Barberini palace. The material is glass. It was a cinerary urn, but neither the maker nor date is known.

In 1845 it was wantonly smashed by William Lloyd, but has been very carefully repaired. It is ten inches high, and six in diameter at the broadest part.

Portugal (*The Golden Age of*). The reign of Emanuel (1495–1521). Vasco da Gama lived in this reign.

Portuguese Livy (*The*). João da Barros (1496–1570), author of 'Asia Portugueza.'

Positivism. The system of Auguste Comte (1799–1857). Discarding the possibility of knowing the beginning and the end of anything, it concerns itself only with what lies between. It accepts neither atheism, theism, nor pantheism. It may be divided into two parts: the historic conception and the co-ordination of the sciences. The former is this: that the human mind passes through three states, viz. the theological, the metaphysical, and the positive. In all subjects capable of experiment it passes from metaphysics to experimental verification or exact science. In regard to the co-ordination of the sciences the basis is mathematics; then follow astronomy, physics, chemistry, biology, and sociology. Take the last: The science of society is impossible without the science of life. The science of life is impossible without chemistry. Chemistry presupposes physics, physics astronomy, and astronomy mathematics.

Posse Comita'tus, *i.e.* the power of the county, meaning the persons whom a sheriff is empowered to raise in his county in case of rebellion, riot, or invasion. They are all the able-bodied men between fifteen and seventy years of age. Any peace officer can raise a posse to assist in quieting a rebellion or opposing an invasion.

It used to be customary for the high sheriff to meet the judge or judges a mile from the assize town, accompanied by a train of servants, yeomen, or others on horseback, called his 'posse-men.' After the assize the judges were similarly escorted out of the town; but since the introduction of railways these pageants have been discontinued.

Post Office (*The*), London. Established by ordinance of parliament 1656.

Remodelled in Queen Anne's reign 1710 by the Act of Settlement. Cross-posts projected by Ralph Allen, post-master of Bath, who obtained a licence to establish them, for which he paid the government 6,000*l.* a year, and made a profit of 10,000*l.* annually. At his death the government added the cross-posts to the general post. Rowland Hill's reform was carried into effect in 1839, and the 'penny post' system was introduced.

This Ralph Allen is the 'Allworthy' of Fielding's 'Tom Jones.' A most benevolent man, of whom Pope says:

Let humble Allen, with an awkward shame,
Do good by stealth, and blush to find it fame.

Post Office Orders for the trans-mission of money were introduced in 1840. These orders require the names of sender and recipient, so a departure has been permitted in Postal Orders, which circulate like small notes.

Post Office Savings Bank, 1861. For investing small sums of money, from 1*s.* to 30*l.,* for which Government pays 6*d.* in the pound interest. Not more than 30*l.* can be deposited in any one year, and interest is not allowed for more than 150*l.*

Postage Stamp (*The*), 6 May, 1840. Invented by James Chalmers of Dundee [1782–1853]. His tablet records the event: 'To the memory of JAMES CHALMERS, Bookseller, Dundee. Born 1782. Died 1853. Originator of the Adhesive Postage Stamp, which saved the Penny Postage Scheme of 1840 from collapse, rendering it an unqualified success, and which has since been adopted throughout the postal systems of the world. This me-morial was erected by his son Patrick Chalmers, Wimbledon, 1888.'

Adopted in America in 1847.

Postmaster. A 'scholar' is so called at Merton College, Oxford.

Postmastership, 1370. The tenure of the rights and privileges of a post-master; a kind of scholarship in Merton College, Oxford, founded by Dr. Wyllyott for poor students called 'portionistæ,' but called 'postmasters' since 1380. The institution is peculiar to Merton.

Potato Disease (*The*), 1845. First a brown spot was observable on the skin of the potato; then the spot became darker, the leaves and flowers of the plant shrivelled up, and then in a short time the potato and stalk became putrid.

Potato Famine (*The*), 1846. The Irish famine produced by the almost utter failure of the potato crop from what was called 'potato-rot.' It is generally admitted that 200,000 persons died of famine in Ireland in the year of the potato-rot.

This fearful calamity has proved one of the greatest blessings to Ireland. It hurried on the introduction of free-trade. It indirectly brought about the arterial drainage of many of the main rivers of Ireland. It created the Land Improve-ment Act. It brought into existence the Incum-bered Estates Court, one of the most important acts ever passed in Ireland. It drove some mil-lions of Irish to the other side of the Atlantic. It broke up to a great extent the very small farms of Ireland. It relieved the plethora of the labour market. It removed the needy country gentle-men, and forced them to sell their estates to capitalists. It brought over hundreds of Scotch-men and Englishmen, who have introduced more scientific farming than had been hitherto practised in Ireland. And, in short, it has pro-duced a revolution in the country which has continued to the present day.—W. S. TRENCH, *Realities of Irish Life,* p. 105.

Potato Snuff-boxes. Snuff-boxes made of mashed potatoes; the material resembled *papier mâché.* They were adorned with paintings and designs. Such snuff-boxes were common enough in the first half of the 19th cent.

Pothi (*The*). The Bible of the Sikhs (*q.v.*).

Potsdam, in Prussia (*Treaty of*), Oct. 1805. A treaty of alliance solemn-ised by Czar Alexander I. and Frederick William III. of Prussia by an oath sworn on the tomb of Frederick the Great. The object of this alliance was directed against Napoleon. The result was the battle of Austerlitz on 2 Dec. Russia lost 30,000 warriors, buried under the ice of a lake which broke beneath their feet, and 15 of her generals were taken prisoners, or slain on the field of battle.

Potteries (*The*). North Stafford-shire is so called from the numerous pottery manufactories established there.

Potteries (*The Father of the*) Josiah Wedgwood (1730–1795).

Pouch (*Captain*). The assumed name of John Reynolds, head of the Levellers in the Midland counties in the May of 1607. Being captured, he was executed the same year.

Z Z

Pougatcheff the Pretender.
Emilian Pougatcheff, a Cossack of the
Don, who had served during the Seven
Years' war in the armies of Russia,
Prussia, and Austria. On his return to
his own country he incited a rebellion in
1773, and assumed to be Peter III., who
had been assassinated in 1762. Defeated
in 1774 on the banks of the Volga, he
was captured, and beheaded at Moscow
in 1775. *See* 'Otrepieff.'

Powis Medal. *See under* 'Camden and Powis Medals.'

Powys Land. One of the three
divisions of Wales made by Roderick
Mawr among his sons. Powys Land
fell to the lot of Mawr's youngest son,
Mervyn. (Powys, in Welsh, means 'the
state of being at rest or peace.')

Poyning's Act, or 'Poyning's
Law,' or 'Statute of Drogheda,' 10 Hen.
VII. c. 22, A.D. 1495, which declared that
all general statutes before then made in
England shall be of force in Ireland
also; and that no Irish act shall be
valid unless first submitted to the king
and council of England. The Irish parliament might reject a bill so approved,
but could not alter it. Repealed 1782.

(Sir Edward Poyning was lord deputy of Ireland
at the time.)
He [Charles I.] therefore authorised him to
grant the suspension of Poyning's act, and to
remove all the penal acts against the Catholics.—
HOWITT, *History of England*, Charles I., p. 253.

Pozzi (*The*). Venetian dungeons
beneath the level of the canals, in the
hollow walls of the doge's palace. *See*
'Piombi.'

Præfectus Præto'rio. In the
old Roman Empire. Augustus created
two; but Tiberius reduced them to one:
Commodus re-established the original
number; but Diocletian created four,
one for each quarter of his empire. The
prætorian prefect was the commanding
officer of the prætorian guard. In the
second and third centuries they gradually
usurped all authority and became virtually the masters even of the emperors.
Constantine reduced their civil power,
but gave each præfect authority in his
own quarter, called his præfecture. The
four were then called 'Præfectus prætorio
per Gallias,' 'Præfectus prætorio per
Illyricum,' 'Præfectus prætorio per

Italiam,' and 'Præfectus prætorio per
Orientem.'

There were many other officers called præfects:
as *præfectus annonæ, præfectus classi, præfectus
legionibus, præfectus ærario*, &c.

Præmunire (*Statute of*), 27 Edw.
III. s. 1, c. 1, A.D. 1353. An act of
Parliament specifying what things are to
be denounced as marks of contempt of
the king's kingship, such as the pope
presuming to appoint church dignitaries
instead of the sovereign; holding a royal
court in the realm—it was for holding
such a court as the pope's legate that
Cardinal Wolsey was prosecuted—maintaining that the sovereign has no right to
the crown, or that someone else has a
better claim to it; to assist at the marriage of a royal prince or princess, contracted in violation of the established
laws. The offences are short of treason,
but show directly or indirectly a contempt for the king or queen. Martin V.
called this statute 'execrabile illud
statutum.'

'Præmunire' is dog Latin for *præmoneri*. The
writ begins thus: Præmunire facias M or N . . .
(i.e. you shall cause M or N to be forewarned that
. . . &c.) The sta ut×s are 35 Edw. I. 1306; 25
Edw. III. 1364; 16 Rich. II. 1393; 2 Hen. IV. 1401;
26 Hen. VIII. 1532; 5 Eliz. 1563, and many others.
Some were repealed in 1846.

The most important points of these
statutes besides those stated above are
these prohibitions:

1. To prohibit the introduction into
England of papal provisions.

2. To prohibit the intervention of the
pope in ecclesiastical elections.

3. To prohibit English subjects being
called to Rome on points which may be
settled in the royal courts of our own
land.

4. To prohibit foreigners being presented to English livings.

Gregory XI. convened a conference at
Bruges in 1375 to discuss these statutes.

Prætor. A Roman magistrate with
the function of a supreme judge in one
of the provinces. He was the chief
military, civil, legislative, and financial
functionary. His legislative manifesto
was called *edictum prætōris*. There
were always at Rome two prætors, the
prætor urbānus and the *prætor pere-
grīnus*, elected by the centuries. They
were seated on a curule chair and arrayed
with the *toga prætexta*.

The 'sella curūlis' was like a camp-stool, used
by kings, consuls, prætors, and curule ædiles, who

carried their chair about with them. Originally they were made of ivory, but latterly they were inlaid with gold.

The ' toga prætexta ' was a bordered robe worn by aristocratic children, chief magistrates, dictators, consuls, prætors, and ædiles.

Prætorian Guard *(The)*. Originally the cohorts of the prætor, then the imperial guard. They received higher pay than other soldiers, and enjoyed several important privileges. There were originally nine prætorian cohorts; Vitellius increased the number to sixteen; Septimus Sevërus still further increased the number. For many years they acted as dictators, and their insolence, want of discipline, avidity, and insubordination became proverbial.

Pragmatic Sanction. 'Sanctio Pragmatica.' An ordinance relating to the State or to the Church. The Latin word *sanctio* means a decree or ordinance with a penalty attached, in other words 'a penal statute.' The word *pragmaticus* means relating to the state. Hence a pragmatic sanction is a 'penal statute relating to the state.'

In civil law a 'pragmatic sanction' means the response of the king to his *council*; the response to an *individual* was called a 'rescript.'

Historically a pragmatic sanction means a statute limiting or defining the power of the pope in foreign countries; or a statute fixing the succession of the crown in a certain line. What is generally meant by the term is the arrangement made by Karl VI. in 1713, whereby the crown of Germany was made hereditary in the house of Austria.

The most important pragmatic sanctions are the following:—

I. That of *St. Louis* in 1268, forbidding the pope to levy taxes in France, or to interfere in the appointment of the clergy.

This important ordinance did for France what the 'Constitutions of Clarendon' did for England.

The authenticity of this ordinance is doubtful, and certainly it is wholly out of harmony with the sainted king, who was canonised by Boniface III. only twenty-seven years after his decease. It is mentioned for the first time in the fifteenth century in the 'Bibliothèque des Conciles,'and is generally supposed to be a forgery.

II. *Of Rense*, in 1338, by which instrument an elected king of Germany was made *ex officio* kaiser or emperor of the holy Roman empire, independent of the pope's sanction, and without the neces-

sity of going to Rome to be crowned by him.

Rens or Rense will not be found in ordinary maps. It is on the Rhine, five miles from Coblentz, and close by is the very famous Thronus Regalis *(q.v.).*

III. *Of Bourges*, called the 'Palladium of France,' 7 July, 1438, published by Charles VII. of France. This also had for its scope the limitation of the power of the papal authority in France. It forbade the pope to present to any dignity or any church living in the kingdom. It is called the Magna Charta of the Gallican Church.

It declares the authority of councils to be superior to that of the popes. Insists on the free election of abbots and bishops by the chapters and monks. It suppresses annates or first fruits and other taxes claimed by Rome. It greatly restricted the effects of excommunication and interdicts. François I. in 1516 suppressed this pragmatic sanction, and substituted 'The Concordat of Bologna ' instead *(q.v.),* 1516.

IV. *Of the Emperor Karl VI.* (17 Apr. 1713), to secure the hereditary succession of the states of Austria in the female line. This was in order to transmit the crown to his eldest daughter, Maria Theresa. It was guaranteed by most of the great powers of Europe, but not by Spain till 1731. Karl VI. died in 1740.

This is the pragmatic sanction of historic eminence, and is meant unless some qualifying date or word is added to restrict it to some other instrument.

V. 1723, whereby Hungary and the Austrian provinces were declared inseparable, and the ruler of both was always to be one and the same person and of the Habsburg dynasty, in the regular order of succession in the male and female lines; but, otherwise, Hungary was to remain perfectly independent, and was to be governed by its own laws.

VI. *Of Carlos III.* of Spain (1759), to regulate the succession to the throne of the Two Sicilies.

VII. *Of Don Ferdinand,* 2 April, 1767, declaring all papal bulls and briefs to be null and void in the duchy of Parma and Piacenza, unless sanctioned by a ducal exequatur. Declared void by papal brief 1 Feb., 1768.

Our Constitutions of Clarendon, 1164, compelling the clergy to submit to the civil laws, were virtually a *pragmatic sanction.*

Prague *(Peace of).*
I. 1635, between Kaiser Ferdinand II. and the electors of Saxony and Brandenburg.

z z 2

II. 23 Aug., 1866. At the close of the Sevèn Weeks' War, Austria was entirely excluded from Germany, and in 1870 the King of Prussia was declared German Emperor in addition to his other titles.

Praguerie (*La*), 1440. A revolt and conspiracy in France to dethrone Charles VII. and place Louis the Dauphin (Louis XI.) on the throne. The conspirators were Alexander, the natural son of Bourbon, Charles and Louis de Bourbon, Jean d'Alençon, La Trémoille, Dunois, La Hire, and Xaintrailles. Their head-quarters were Prague in Bohemia, whence the name; but the enterprise was badly conducted, and Charles, marching to Prague, crushed out the revolt before the end of six months. The conspirators tendered their submission, and were graciously pardoned.

Prairial 1, 2, 3, An. III. *i.e.* 20, 21, 22 May, 1795. Noted for the insurrection against the Convention, the last effort of the Jacobins against the Thermidorian reaction. The populace of the faubourg seized the *Salle de la Convention*, presided over by Boissy d'Anglas, and assassinated the deputy Féraud. The troops being called out dispersed the mob. The convention ordered the arrest of thirteen deputies who had taken part in the plot, six of whom were executed.

Prairial 30 An. VII. *i.e.* 18 June 1799. When the directors La Réveillière-Lepeaux and Merlin were turned out of office in favour of Roger Ducos and Moulins.

Pras'ina Factio. The Green Coats, a faction of Byzantium; so called from the green-coated charioteers in the circus. They were opposed to the Emperor Justinian, who was a Blue Coat, or favourer of the Venèta Factio (*q.v.*).

Prason is the Greek for a ' leek,' and Prāsīnus means green as a leek.

Prayer Book of Edward VI. (*The First*), published 1549. Compiled by Cranmer and Ridley, assisted by other divines. The Communion Service was drawn up for administration to the laity in both kinds; offices for holidays as well as for Sundays, for baptism and confirmation, were included ; and the marriage and

burial services were considerably altered. *See* ' King's Primer.'

It began with the Lord's Prayer; it retained prayers for the dead ; it enjoined anointing of the sick. In 1550 the Ordination Service was added.

The Second, 1552. The First Prayer Book, revised by Cranmer, Martin Bucer, and Peter Martyr. The opening sentences, exhortation, confession, and absolution were added. The use of oil in baptism was discontinued, so was anointing the sick, and the prayers for the dead were struck out. In 1559 the book was revised, and the Elizabethan version is sometimes called ' The Third Common Prayer Book.' After the Hampton Court Conference (*q.v.*) in the reign of James I. the book was again revised, and some prayers for special occasions were introduced. In 1662, after the Restoration, when the new authorised version of the Scriptures was adopted, except in the Psalms, where Coverdale's version was followed, the sentences in the Communion Service, the General Thanksgiving, the Form of Prayer to be Used at Sea, the State Services (viz. for Gunpowder Treason, 5 Nov.; King Charles's Martyrdom, 30 Jan.; for the Restoration, 29 May; and the King's Accession) were annexed. The first three of these State Services were omitted by an order in council given by Queen Victoria in 1859.

Preacher (*The*). Juan Grandé of Andalusia (1546–1600).

Preaching Crosses. Generally either quadrangular or hexagonal, open on one or more sides, and raised on steps. They were used for the delivery of sermons in the open air. St. Paul's Cross was very celebrated, and the collection of sermons preached there is still known and highly appreciated.

Queen Elizabeth, we are told, once went in state to St. Mary's Cross to hear one of the Reformers preach. Besides a vast train of lords and ladies, she was ' accompanied by 1,000 soldiers, ten great cannons, hundreds of drums and trumpets, a party of morris-dancers, and two white bears.' She delighted in loud music, for even when she went to dinner twelve trumpets, two kettle-drums, and various other noisy instruments amused her with thundering uproar.

Preaching Friars, 1215. The idea of this order was suggested by Dominic at the Council of Lateran, with a view of stamping out the Vaudois and other enemies of ' the Church.' At a later period these preaching friars were called Dominicans, from Dominic their founder.

St. Francis of Assisi about the same time founded the order of Franciscans or Minor Friars, worthy rivals of the Dominicans.

Pre-Adamite Sovereign (*The*). So the bankers of England nicknamed the Georgian sovereigns called in by Mr. Goschen in April 1890.

The pre-Adamite sovereign is now very much in evidence, for everywhere there are notices posted up to the effect that they cannot be received. The Georgian gold is, in fact, as carefully avoided as were French coppers a couple of years ago.— *Newspaper paragraph* in April 1890.

Prebend, Prebendary. A prebend is a provision in land or money given to a church *in præbendam, i.e.* for the support of a clergyman whose title is either prebendary or canon. There are numerous honorary prebendaries and canons without any stipend at all, but they are provided with a prebendal stall in the cathedral church of the diocese, and are expected to preach in the cathedral occasionally, or to supply a substitute.

Preceptor. The master of a preceptory, that is, a manor of the Knights Templars. His duty was to take care of the lands and collect the rents. Sometimes the word preceptor is applied to the 'Magni Priores cujusque provinciæ, penes quos erat summa potestas.' Du Cange makes the word equivalent to 'Dominus Princeps, Supremus Magistratus,' and in A.D. 950 to 'Abbas.'

Præceptories were benefices . . . possessed by the more eminent of the Templers [*sic*], whom the Chief Master by his authority created and called 'Præceptores Templi.' — STEPHEN, *De Jurisdictione,* bk. iv. chap. x. No. 27.

Precious Blood (*The Feast of the*). The 1st Sunday in July. There are other days dedicated to the Precious Blood—for example, the fourth Friday in Lent. Sometimes Corpus Christi (the Thursday after Trinity Sunday) is so called. Hence the hymn of St. Thomas Aquīnas. *See* 'Sunday.'

Pange lingua gloriosi Corporis mysterium Sanguinisque pretiosi, quem in mundi pretium Fructus ventris generosi Rex effudit gentium.

Precis'ian (*A*), 1572. One of that section of the Puritan party who considered obedience to the civil government a matter of indifference. Or one who professes a *precise* or thorough puritan code of faith and conduct.

Since that [the burning of Latimer and Ridley] Tony married a pure Precisian, and is as good a Protestant as the best.—Sir W. SCOTT, *Kenilworth,* ch. ii.

Here is what neither Papist nor Puritan, Latitu-

dinarian nor Precisian, ever . . . makes mouths at.—*Ibid.* chap. vi.

Precursor Association (*O'Connell's*), or 'Precursor Society,' 1838. So called because it was designed to be the precursor of the Repeal of the Union. O'Connell said he had 2,000,000 'Precursors' to second his efforts.

Predestinarian Controversy (*The*), 1594–1600. The question was, which was correct, Calvin or Arminius. Calvin asserted that God from all eternity predestinated certain men unto eternal life, wholly irrespective of the works or faith of those individuals. Arminius asserted that God predestinated certain persons to eternal life because by His foreknowledge He foresaw they would be meet for salvation. The matter was debated at Lambeth Palace, and the result was the nine Lambeth Articles (*q.v.*), which are doubtlessly Calvinistic.

Those who wish to know what view the Church of England takes on this question, must consult Article XVII. of the Thirty-nine Articles.

Predestinarians. A religious sect, headed by John Calvin. They held that the elect are predestined to be saved, and cannot sin away grace.

The Predestinarians preached that the elect could not sin, nor the regenerate fall from grace. —BLUNT, *Reformation in England,* p. 158.

Pre-established Harmony. A term used by Leibnitz (1646–1716) to explain the dual nature of man. He supposed there are in man two sorts of monads or protoplasms, one spiritual and the other material, and that they act together by 'pre-established harmony.' He compared man to two clocks, one the mind clock and the other the body clock. The mind clock determines, and the body clock by simultaneous action does the very thing that the mind determined on. Not because soul and body are one, but only because they work together in perfect harmony. Locke denied the fact of 'innate ideas'; Leibnitz maintained that the seeds of ideas are in the mind, as the seeds of plants are in the plants.

Préfet. A French administrator of a department called his *préfecture*. Each préfet has his *sous-préfets* with authority in an arrondissement.

Prega'di (*The*). The Venetian senate, between the Forty and the Grand Council. To this senate was assigned all deliberations upon peace and war, the voting of supplies, and the confirmation of laws. Both the Forty and the Pregadi were elected by the Grand Council (*Consiglio Grande*).

Pre'latists. So the Scotch, in 1643, &c., called the royalists in contempt, because they tried to force Episcopacy on the people. In 1647 'Presbyterianism was declared to be the established religion of Scotland.'

Premonstratensian Order (*The*), or 'Norbertines,' 1119. Instituted by St. Norbert in the diocese of Laon, during the reign of Louis le Gros. The spot, which was a *meadow*, was pointed out to him in a vision, and was therefore called *Pratum Monstrātum*, in French *Pré Montré*. They are White Canons of the rule of St. Augustine, wear a white soutane and scapular, and wholly abstain from animal food.

Pre-Raphaelitism, 1849. A school of painting which originated in England with W. Holman Hunt, D. G. Rossetti, Alma Tadēma, and J. E. Millais. So called because it was supposed to be the style of painting anterior to Raphael. Raphael painted as he thought persons and things ought to be. The pre-Raphaelites are supposed to copy nature exactly.

Prerogative Court (*The*). A court in which wills were proved and administrations taken out. So called because it belonged to the prerogative of the archbishop to take charge of these matters. There was one in the province of Canterbury, and another in the province of York. This jurisdiction was transferred to the Probate Court in 1858.

Presburg (*Diet of*), 1687. Declared the crown of Hungary no longer elective, but hereditary in the Austrian male line.

Presburg, in Hungary (*Treaty of*), 26 Dec., 1805. A treaty of peace between France and Austria, soon after the battle of Austerlitz, and breaking up the third coalition against Napoleon. By this treaty Austria ceded Venice to France, and the Tyrol to Bavaria, the ally of France.

Presbyterian Synod of Munster (*The*). Formed about 1660. *See* 'Synod of Munster.'

Presbyterians. Christians who disavow the office of bishop and acknowledge instead certain delegated elders or presbyters, of whom the 'minister' of each of the Presbyterian congregations is one. The affairs of each of their congregations are administered by a court, styled in Scotland the 'kirk session,' and consisting of the minister or ministers, and the other elders. The appeal from this court is to the presbytery, which is constituted of the ministers of a certain number of congregations and one 'ruling elder' from each congregation. Further appeal may be made to the General Assembly. Presbyterianism prevails chiefly in Scotland.

The Presbyterian Church of England was founded by the Puritans. There are also Presbyterian Baptists, Reformed Presbyterians or Covenanters, the United Presbyterians, the Welsh Presbyterians, Free Church Presbyterians, and Unitarian Presbyterians.

Presbytery (*A*). A synod in the Presbyterian Church of Scotland, composed of all the ministers in a given district, the professors of divinity, and an elder from each 'kirk session' (*q.v.*). The chairman is called the 'moderator.' *See* 'Provincial Synod.'

Presbytery (*The*), 1689. The second of the four ecclesiastical governing bodies of the Kirk of Scotland. It is composed of the ministers of several contiguous parishes, who sit in it *ex officio*, and of an elder from each of the kirk sessions (*q.v.*) in the district, who is chosen for six months. It licenses and inducts ministers, and has a veto on those presented by patrons. Manses and churches are under their supervision, and an appeal may be made to this body from the judgment of the kirk session. *See also* 'Synod,' and 'General Assembly.'

Presbytery of Antrim (*The*). A body of Presbyterians who separated from the 'Synod of Ulster' in 1727, and from the 'Remonstrant Synod' (*q.v.*) in 1827.

Presentment of Englishry (*The*). In the case of murder the hundred was fined by the Danes and Normans unless it could be proved that the murdered person was an Englishman.

A presentment is a presumption from observation, as the presentment of a nuisance, the presentment of a libel, upon which the officer of the court frames an indictment. Englishry means the law respecting the English, or the state of being English-born.

Preserver of his Country (*The*). The Duc de Guise, called 'Le Balafré,' had this title conferred upon him by the Parlement of Paris in 1540.

President. In Oxford University the title of the head of four of the colleges : Corpus, Magdalen, St. John's, and Trinity. In Cambridge University the head of Queens' College is called the president, of King's College the provost, and of all the other colleges the master.

President and Council of the North (*Court of*). 31 Henry VIII. To try rioters against the suppression of the lesser monasteries. It also included all the powers vested in the king's own council, and had power to arraign all offenders against the king's prerogatives.

Prestation. Road rate. Nominally every ratepayer in France is bound to give three days'labour to keep the parish roads in repair; these are called 'journées de prestation,' and for the most part are compounded for by a money payment. The 'agents voyers cantonaux,' or road surveyors, in each parish determine what must be done.

In Saxon times one of the three exactions of *Trinoda Necessitas* was ' Bryge-bot,' for keeping roads as well as bridges in repair.

Prester John. Togrul Wang Khan, chief of the Mongol tribe of the Keraïtes, who held his court at Karakorum and established a sovereignty over those pastoral regions. He was slain in battle by his son-in-law Ghengis Khan (12th cent.).

Called Prester because he tolerated and perhaps favoured the Nestorian Christians. Ghengis Khan was called at the time Timurghen, but after the death of Togrul Wang his father-in-law he called himself the 'Great Khan.'—*History of Ghengis Khan*, chap. i. p. 24-26.

Preston Affair (*The*). The surrender of Preston, in Lancashire, 13 Nov., 1715, when 1,700 Jacobite insurgents yielded to General Carpenter. Amongst them were Thomas Forster (the commander), Brigadier Mackintosh of Boreland, Lord Derwentwater, Lord Kenmure, and Lord Widdrington with his two brothers (Charles and Peregrine).

The Hon. Peregrin[e] Widdrington, died 4 Feb., 1748-9. . . . he was with his brother in the Preston affair.

A mural monument in the Sherburne Chapel.

Pretender (*The*), in English history. The Old Pretender was the Chevalier de St. George, son of James II., who 'pretended' that he had a right to be king of Great Britain after the death of his father.

The Young Pretender was Charles Edward son of the Chevalier de St. George.

Of course these two princes were rightful heirs to the crown if the crown went by inheritance, but in England it is the people or parliament who appoint the king or queen, and the line from William I. has been broken over and over again ; for example, John ; Henry IV., V., VI. ; Henry VII., and all the Tudors ; Richard III. ; William III., and all the Hanoverians.

Pretio'sus (*The Bull*), by Benedict XIII., to explain that of Unigĕnĭtus (*q.v.*), and the doctrine of grace. So called from the first word in the bull. Benedict was pope 1724–1730.

Prêtre Insermenté (*Un*). A priest during the French Revolution who refused to take the oath ' à la constitution civile du clergé' decreed in 1790. Hundreds of these priests were put to death, and their names have been duly canonised.

Those who agreed to take the oath were called *prêtres assermentés*.

Pride's Purge, 2 Dec., 1648. Purging the House of Commons of all members favourable to the king and willing to abet his return to power. This was done by Colonel Pride, who blockaded the house with Rich's regiment of cavalry, and his own regiment of foot. He imprisoned 41 (some say 47) of the leading Presbyterian members in a sort of cellar belonging to the house and called ' Hell '; and next day other members were removed, leaving only 60 to form the house. These 60, being the fag-end of the Long Parliament, went by the name of the ' Rump.' The emasculated parliament complied with the Remonstrance (*q.v.*), removed the king (Charles I.) to Windsor, resolved on his immediate trial for 'treason against his people,' and nominated a court of 150 commissioners with Bradshaw at their head to conduct the trial. See ' Parliaments.'

Priest of Nature (*The*). Sir Isaac Newton (1642–1727).

Priests. ' Primi ordĭnis sacerdōtes,' bishops. ' Secundi ordĭnis sacerdōtes,' ordinary priests (' Pontificale Romanum ').

Priests
　Of the BUDDHISTS are called *Bonzes*.
　Of the GAULS, BRITONS, &c., were called *Druids*.
　Of the JEWS, *Cohenim* (singular *cohen*). All of the tribe of Levi.

Priests

Of the HINDÛS, *Brahmans.*

Of the MOSLEMS, *Imâms, Dervishes,* &c. In TARTARY, *Mullas.* N.B. Mollahs are not priests, but Turkish *judges.*

In Japan there is a spiritual emperor, called the Mikádo, who is also at present (1890) the temporal one.

Priests (*Greek*). Neŏkŏroi. The Eumolpĭdês of Athens were hereditary priests. Each separate divinity had its special priests, as the Idêan Daktŭloi, the Korybantês, the Bacchantês (priestesses of Bacchus or Dionŷsos), the priests of Zeus, &c. &c.

The pontiff who presided over the priests of Herăklês was called *Dadouchos.*

The pontiff who presided over the priests of Pallas was called *Stephanoph'oros.*

'Parasites' were priests who gathered in the corn and wine for the temple services.

The Korybantês were priests of Rhea. Called at Rome Galli, or priests of Cybĕlĕ.

The Daktuloi of Ida were so called because they were ten in number.

The Technītes were sorcerers.

Priests (*Roman*) were chosen only from the most distinguished citizens, and were divided into three classes :—

(*a*) The four great colleges, called Pontiffs, Augurs, Epulŏnés (4 syl.), and Quindecemvĭri.

(*b*) The three inferior colleges, called Arvāles Fratres, Curiōnes (4 syl.), Feciāles (4 syl.).

(*c*) The priests of special deities, as the Flamens, the Salii, the Luperci, the Galli, the Pinarii, the Politians, and some few others.

I. The four great colleges :

The *Pontiffs*, originally four, but subsequently nine. They had the supreme supervision of all the priests, and of all religious rites. The head of the college was entitled 'Pontifex Maximus.'

Augurs included Auspĭces and Haruspĭces. 'Augurs' were those who foretold future events from any sort of prodigy or omen. 'Auspĭces' were those who foretold future events from the inspection of birds. 'Haruspĭcés' were those who foretold future events by inspecting the entrails of beasts sacrificed, or from the smoke and flame of sacrifices, as in the sacrifices of Cain and Abel.

Epulōnes (4 syl.), a college of seven priests, whose duty it was to superintend the sacred feasts (*epŭla*), and more especially the 'epulum Jovis.'

Quindecemvĭri, a college of fifteen priests, who had charge of the Sibylline books (*q.v.*).

II. The three inferior colleges :

Arvāles Fratres, a college of twelve priests, who offered sacrifice to secure the fertility of the fields (*arva*).

Curiōnes (4 syl.), a college of thirty priests, one for each curia or district of Rome. Each curio was expected to perform the sacred rites of his own special curia or district.

Feciāles (4 syl.), a college of twenty priests, whose duty it was to see to the honour of Rome in all dealings with foreign states. They declared war, and dictated terms of peace.

III. Special priests :

Flamens, priests devoted to the service of some particular deity.

Salii, priests of Mars, who had charge of the twelve sacred shields. They were always patricians of high rank, and on the 1st March every year carried the sacred shields through the city in grand procession.

The *Luperci* were priests of Pan. The great festival was called the Lu'percal. Shakespeare makes Antony say :

You all do know that on the Lu'percal
I thrice presented him [Cæsar] a kingly crown,
Which he did thrice refuse. Was that ambition ?
Julius Cæsar.

The *Galli*, or priests of Cybĕlĕ (3 syl.).

The *Pinarii*, or priests of Hercules, and some few others.

Priest's Hole (*The*). A secret contrivance in old Catholic mansions for the concealment of the priest in times of persecution. Several still exist as curiosities.

Priests of the Mission. Same as Lazarists. Instituted 1625 by Vincent de Paul; organised for training young missionaries. *See* 'Lazarus.'

Priests of the Saviours (*The*), B.C. 307–287, and nominally till A.D. 264. Officers of Athens who superseded the archons eponymic.

Primate of All England (*The*). The Archbishop of Canterbury.

Primate of England (*The*). The Archbishop of York.

Prime. One of the eight daily services of the Catholic Church, and second of the four lesser ones, at six in the morning. The first hour of the day. *See* 'Canonical Hours.'

Primer Seizin. A whole year's profits of an estate paid by a king's tenant on first coming to his new tenement. Introduced by William the Conqueror, and abolished by 12 Car. II. c. 24.

Primitive Fathers of the Christian Church. Those who succeeded the Apostolic Fathers. The latter were born in the *first* cent., and were more or less contemporary with the apostles. The Primitive Fathers were not born till after the 1st cent., and were not contemporary with the apostles. These nine are the Primitive Fathers, and with Clemens, Hermas, Ignatius, Polycarp (and Barnabas) make up the Fathers of the first two cents. :—

Died	Died
167. Justin Martyr.	253. Origen.
190. Theophilus of Antioch.	258. Cyprian bishop of Carthage.
200. Irenæus.	265. Dionysius of Alexandria.
220. Clement of Alexandria.	270. Gregory Thaumaturgus.
240. Tertullian.	

Primitive Methodists, 1810. Reformed Methodists originated in Staffordshire and led by Hugh and J. Bourne, W. Clowes, and others, who thought the Connection too rigid in not allowing camp-meetings and women to preach. They advocate field preaching and street preaching of an emotional character. Sometimes called 'Ranters' by way of disrespect.

Primitive Wesleyans of Ireland (*The*), 1816. They seceded because they did not approve of the administration of the Lord's Supper by their preachers, but considered that they should receive the holy communion from the hands of a clergyman of the Church of England.

Primrose (*The*). The flower-emblem of the political adherents of Benjamin Disraeli (Lord Beaconsfield), 1805–1881. The tale is that when young he made a bet of a pair of gloves respecting a wreath of primroses. The point in doubt was whether the primroses were real or artificial. Mr. Disraeli staked that they were real, and won the bet. The lady competitor presented the successful guesser with one of the primroses, and Disraeli, with the gallantry of a young man, vowed he would preserve the flower faithfully and adopt it as his badge. For another derivation *see note to* 'Primrose League.'

Primrose Day, 19 April. The anniversary of the death of the Earl of Beaconsfield, founded by Sir George Birdwood in memory of the great Conservative leader, who died 19 April, 1881. He suggested to the St. Stephen's Club that the dining-tables of the club should be decorated with primroses on 19 April. Next year it was suggested that an

annual festival should be adopted, and Sir George Birdwood made arrangements with a large firm of Covent Garden florists to advertise largely at his expense the supply of primroses to any extent for 19 April. It was a complete success, and was soon followed by the establishment of Primrose Leagues throughout the United Kingdom.

Primrose League (*The*), 1883. An association of men and women to carry out the policy of Benjamin Disraeli, Lord Beaconsfield: 'The maintenance of true religion, of the three estates of the realm, and of the imperial ascendency of Great Britain.' The lodges are called 'habitations,' and a habitation consists of thirteen or more knights companions, knights harbingers, or knights almoners, and each knight has his squire. The chief ladies are called 'dames' (lady patronesses). A certain number of district habitations form a central habitation, by which the ruling council is elected. The Marquis of Abergavenny was the first 'grand councillor of the league.' *See* 'Primrose Day.'

The league was first organised in 1884, and inaugurated with a banquet 19 April, under the expectation of a general election, which took place between Nov. and Dec., 1885. The primrose is Beaconsfield's flower, as the violet is the Napoleonic flower.

⁂ A Primrose Order of Knights existed in Spain at the beginning of the 18th cent. (before 1717).

A rumour was very current for two or three years that the Queen, on the day of Lord Beaconsfield's funeral, sent a primrose wreath on which was written 'His favourite flower,' meaning the favourite flower of the late Prince Consort. Happily this error has been stamped out by the following letter :—

'Windsor Castle, 1 May, 1888.

'Sir,—The Queen did not send a wreath of primroses to Lord Beaconsfield's funeral, and consequently there could have been no inscription of the nature you describe.—I have the honour to be, sir, your obedient servant,

'HENRY PONSONBY.

'*To John Churchill Sikes (50 Agate Road, The Grove, Hammersmith, W.).*'

Primrose Pilgrimage (*The*), 19 April. A visit to the statue of Lord Beaconsfield in Parliament Square in order to decorate it with primrose wreaths. Of course it is a Conservative demonstration.

Prince (*The*). 'Del Principe.' The great work of Niccolò Machiavelli of Florence (1469–1527), setting forth his political principles.

The student of Machiavelli had not studied 'The Prince' in vain.—GREEN, *Hist. of the English People*, p. 335.

Prince Consort Prize (*The*). For original historic research. Given every alternate year to graduates of not more than four years' standing. Value about 100*l.* Founded from the surplus of a memorial fund of Prince Albert, chancellor of the University of Cambridge, 1888. *See* 'Modern History,' &c.

Prince Florizel. George IV. Also called 'Fum the Fourth,' 'The Fat Adonis of Fifty.' But the bitterest satire of all was 'The First Gentleman of Europe.'

Prince Tite. The nickname of George II.

Prince of Fools (*The*). The manager of the 'Enfans sans Souci.' (*q.v.*).

Prince of German Poets (*The*). Goethe (1749–1832).

Prince of Lyric Poets (*The*). Charles Dupérier, born at Aix (1620–1692). So called by Menage. One of the French Pléiade poets.

Prince of Music (*The*). J. Pierluigi Palestrīna (1529–1594).

Prince of Peace (*The*). A pun or abbreviation of 'Prince of the Peace.' Manuel de Godoy, duke of Alcudia, the cavalier of Maria Luiza, wife of Carlos IV. of Spain, was so called because he effected the pacification of Bâle, 22 July, 1795 (4 Thermidor, Year III.).

In one year this obscure garde-de-corps received the titles of lieutenant-general, admiral of the Spanish fleet, duke of Alcudia, knight of the Golden Fleece; and on his marriage with the king's niece he was created 'Prince of the Peace.' Born at Badajos 1767, died at Paris 1828.

Prince of Priests (*The*), 1420. Henry V. of England, who on his wedding tour visited the shrine of every saint on his way. He was most assiduous in his devotions, most profusely liberal in his contributions, and most severe in repressing Lollardism.

Prince of Quarrellers (*The*). Beaumarchais (1732–1799). A first-rate duellist and universal genius. Now best known by his two comedies, the 'Barber of Seville,' in four acts, and the 'Marriage of Figaro,' in five acts.

Prince of the Youth (*The*). Gonzalvo di Cordŏva, the great captain (1453–1515).

Prince's Metal. A metal like gold invented by Prince Rupert of Bavaria, nephew of Charles I. It is a mixture of copper and zinc.

Prince's Peers (*The*), 1456. Tradesmen, farmers, and even mechanics, ennobled for money by Louis the Dauphin (Louis XI.), when he revolted against his father, Charles VII.

Prince'ites (2 syl.). The members of the Agapĕmŏnê, in Somersetshire, established by Henry James Prince. Letters to Prince are addressed 'The Lord.' He said to Mr. Hepworth Dixon, 'You see in me Christ in the flesh, Christ in my flesh.' He calls his wife 'the bride of his soul.' He says 'Christ came to redeem the soul, I am come to redeem the body.' Mr. Prince in 1851 took a party to the Great Exhibition. He drove about like a prince, with outriders bareheaded. Prince was born in 1811.

Principal. In Oxford University; the title of the head of three colleges (Brasenose, Jesus, and Hertford), and of the four halls (New Inn, St. Alban's, St. Edmund, and St. Mary).

Principality (*The*). In Roman history means the first three centuries of the empire, from Augustus to Diocletian (B.C. 29 to A.D. 287), when the emperor had no other title except *princeps.* Diocletian introduced the title of *Augustus,* which had been occasionally loosely applied before his time, but not definitely.

Principia of Newton (*The*). 'Philosophiæ Naturalis Principia Mathematica,' in three books, by Isaac Newton.

Book I. (1686). The motion of bodies in free space. Every particle of matter attracts every other particle with a force which varies directly as the masses, and inversely as the square of the distance between them.

Book II. (3 months later). Of motion in a resisting medium. Hydrostatics and hydrodynamics. With a confutation of the Cartesian theory of vortices.

Book III. (1687). The solar system. The motion of the moon, the theory of the tides, the proof that comets belong to the solar system.

It is an inquiry into the truth of Kepler's 'Laws of Motion.'

Printer's Bible (*The*). Makes David pathetically complain that the 'printers [princes] have persecuted me without a cause.' *See* 'Bible.'

Prior (*A*), or 'Prior of the Arts.' A magistrate in the republic of Florence who superseded the Anziani or seniors in 1282. At first there were three priors, then six, and finally eight.

Priori (*Six*), 1293. The executive government of Florence placed in the hands of six presidents. Dante the poet was one of the six priori in 1300.

Prisage of Wine (*The*). The right of taking two casks out of each vessel for the crown.

Priscil'lianists (*The*). Followers of Priscillian (4th cent.). A learned Spaniard, bishop of Avila in Spain. Their doctrines were substantially those of the Manichæans, who taught that there were two principles, one of good and the other of evil. Priscillian said that the good principle in its descent from God to Earth fell into the power of the evil principle, and got corrupted. He also taught what is called *Docētism*; that is, that the actions and sufferings of Christ were not real, but only phenomenal.

Prison Authors and Literature.

BACON (*Roger*) imprisoned in 1278 in France by order of Pope Nicholas IV. During confinement he wrote his treatise 'On the Means of Avoiding the Infirmities of Old Age.'

BOETHIUS (*Anicius Manlius Torquātus Severīnus*) wrote his 'De Consolatione Philosophiæ' in his prison at Pavia, about 522; he was beheaded in 524.

BRIENNE (*Le Comte de*) wrote his 'Memoirs' during his eighteen years' incarceration at St. Lazare. He died 1698.

BUNYAN wrote his 'Grace Abounding' (1666) and Part I. of his 'Pilgrim's Progress' while confined in Bedford Gaol (1660–1672).

.*. *Part I. of 'Pilgrim's Progress' was printed* 1678, *and Part II. in* 1684.

CARLILE (*Richard*), during his ten years' imprisonment, edited various journals, and won the right of a free press.

COBBETT (*William*) carried on his 'Political Register' while in prison (1810–1812).

COMBE (*William*) wrote his 'Tour of Dr. Syntax' during his twenty years' imprisonment in the King's Bench (1743–1823).

COOPER (*Thomas*), born 1805, wrote in Stafford Gaol the 'Purgatory of Suicides' (1845) in Spenserian verse; published under the patronage of Benjamin Disraeli; and 'Wise Saws and Modern Instances.'

DAVITT (*Michael*) while confined in Portland wrote 'Leaves from a Prison Diary, or Lectures to a Solitary Audience,' which was published in 1884.

DEFOE wrote his celebrated 'Review' in prison (1704), and again (1713).

DIDEROT was imprisoned at Vincennes in 1749, when he began his famous 'Mémoires.'

HALL (*Thomas*) wrote in the Debtors' Ward, Winchester, a volume of 'Poems' towards the close of the 18th cent.

HARPSFIELD (*Nicholas*), Regius Professor of Greek, Oxford, was imprisoned in the Tower in 1562, and died there in 1583. He wrote in the Tower his bulky controversial work entitled 'Dialogi sex contra summi pontificatus, &c., oppugnatores, &c.,' published 1566; and a 'History of the Anglican Church,' published after his death in 1622.

HETHERINGTON in prison composed political and poetical ephemera.

JONES (*Ernest*) composed in gaol his political novel in which he attacked Feargus O'Connor, and parodied the Chartist agitation (1848–1850).

LOVELACE (*Richard*) wrote some beautiful ditties to his 'Divine Althea' (Lucy Sacheverell) while in prison for presenting from Kent a petition to the Long Parliament in behalf of the king (Charles II.).

LOVETT composed in prison poetical and political ephemera.

MIRABEAU was imprisoned in Vincennes three years and a half (beginning 7 June, 1777); during which confinement he wrote his 'Lettres à Sophie,' and ' Les Lettres de Cachet et les Prisons d'État.' He also translated in prison part of 'The Elegies of Tibullus,' 'Boccaccio's Decameron,' his 'Mémoires du Ministère du Duc d'Aiguillon,' and several other works.

OASTLER (*Richard*) kept up a fusillade of pamphlets in favour of the Ten Hours' Bill while in the Fleet Prison (born 1789, died 1861).

O'BRIEN (*William*) wrote the main part of his novel ' When We Were Boys ' while imprisoned for inciting to Irish disturbances. It was published in April 1890.

ORLÉANS (*Charles d'*) comte d'Angoulême during his twenty-five years' captivity in the 15th cent. wrote, among other poetry, his charming ode to Spring, beginning ' Le tems a laissié son manteau.'

PAGANO (*Mario*) wrote his 'Saggi Politici' in prison (1783–1792). He was executed at Naples in 1800.

PAINE (*Thomas*) wrote the second part of his 'Age of Reason' while imprisoned in Paris by command of Robespierre, 1794–5.

PAMPHILUS bishop of Cæsarea composed his 'Five Books in Defence of Origen' during the two years of his imprisonment. Eusebius completed the sixth book after the death of Pamphilus.

PELLISON wrote his two ' Discours au Roi ' and a ' Mémoire ' of his friend Fouquet while a prisoner in the Bastille (1661–1666).

PENN (*William*), 1644–1718, while in the Tower, where he was confined at the instigation of the Bishop of London, wrote his famous 'No Cross, no Crown' (1668-9).

RALEIGH (*Sir Walter*) wrote his 'History of the World' (down to B.C. 170) during his thirteen years' imprisonment in the Tower (1552-1618). He was beheaded 1618.

SACY'S Bible, the Port Royal translation into French, was made by Isaac Lemaistre [Sacy] (1666-1670) during his imprisonment in the Bastille.

TAYLOR (*Robert*) composed his 'Devil's Pulpit' while in Oakham Gaol.

THOMAS (*F.*) of Jesus, while confined in a dungeon in Morocco composed his 'Sufferings of Christ' (16th cent.).

VINCENT composed in prison poetical and political ephemera.

WOLLETT composed his 'Black Dwarf' in prison.

VOLTAIRE in 1717 spent eleven months in the Bastille, during which time he wrote two cantos of his 'Henriade,' and revised his tragedy of 'Œdipe.'

.*. Luther translated the Bible into German while he was lying perdu in the old castle of Wartburg. This was not strictly speaking a prison, but it was virtually so.

Similarly : The crypt under the church of St. Maria, in Via Lata, is said to have been the place where Paul was held in captivity when he wrote his 'Epistles' to the Hebrews, Ephesians, Philippians, Philemon, and 2 Timothy.

There is also a tradition that St. Peter dictated

the 'Gospel of Mark' while a prisoner at Rome; and some say that Luke wrote his 'Acts' in Rome.

Prison Dress. A third-class man, that is, a man who has completed his first year satisfactorily, has *black* facing to his jacket, and begins to earn something. In twelve months more he is promoted to the second class, and his jacket is faced with *yellow*. In twelve months more, if still on the good-conduct list, his jacket is faced with *blue*. If still under prison discipline at the end of four and a half years, he may receive a distinctive blue dress which will entitle him to a bonus of 3*l*. at his discharge. *See* 'Breeches Martyrs.'

A black facing may earn 1*d*. for 20 good marks; a yellow facing 1½*d*.; and a blue facing 2 *d*., credited to him, and given him at his discharge. Twenty good marks may be earned in about two days and a half. This allowance continues till it reaches the sum of 3*l*.

Private Wars. Those everlasting and wretched contests of the middle ages, between different barons, such as our war of the Two Roses, those of the Capulets and Montagues of Italy, the Armagnacs and Burgundians of France, the Guelfs and the Ghibellines, and so on. Charlemagne introduced a law to put a stop to these feuds, but it was powerless. The Church introduced the *Paix de Dieu* (*q.v.*), which suspended hostilities on certain days; but St. Louis established the Quarantaine-le-Roi (*q.v.*), and punished with death those who violated it. *See* 'Vendetta.'

Privilege of Union in Aragon. A brotherhood or confederacy for obtaining redress of grievances by armed force, as the barons of England obtained Magna Charta from King John. This privilege was granted by Alfonso III. in 1287, and confirmed by Alfonso X. as a right of the nobility.

The law runs thus: 'The duty of subjects towards their king enjoins them not to suffer him knowingly to endanger his salvation . . . or produce mischief to his kingdom. This may be done in two ways: one by good advice . . . and the other by preventing him from running to his own ruin.'

Privy Council (*The*). The 'Curia Regis' existed under Henry III.; the Concilium Privātum or Privy Council arose in the reign of Henry VI., but it was Charles II. who first appointed a cabinet of fifty members because he found the council unworkable. Its number now is indefinite, the members are 'Right Hon.' for life. It works by committees, except

when the sovereign issues 'orders in council.'

In the reigns of James I. and Charles I., the 'Star Chamber' was formed from the Privy Council. The chief committees of the Privy Council are the 'Committee of Trade and Plantations, 1688'; the 'Judicial Committee'; the 'Committee of Education, 1839'; the 'Local Government Board, 1871,' &c.

Privy Council of Ireland (*The*) consists of some fifty or sixty members. Almost all the judges are members.

Processio Plenaria.

Stent in ordine suo singuli in ecclesiam expectantes donec veniat pontifex cum processione plenaria ad Missam, sicut diebus solemnibus solet cum septem diaconibus, totidemque subdiaconibus et ceroferariis, et duobus thuribulis cum incenso.—*Quoted by* DU CANGE, vol. v. p. 467, col. 1.

Procession of the Black Breeches (*The*), 20 June, 1792. Carlyle says in the procession led by Santerre to the Tuileries were 'tricolour ribands streaming from pike-head; iron-shod bâtons; a bull's heart transfixed, and with this inscription, "Heart of an Aristocrat"; and, more striking still, a pair of old black silk breeches, extended on a cross-staff, with this inscription, "Tremble, tyrants; here are the Sans-culottes."' The chapter is headed 'Procession of the Black Breeches' (CARLYLE, 'French Revolution,' last chap. of book v.).

One of the standards consists of a pair of black silk breeches on a pole with the motto, 'Without breeches, but free.'—HOWITT, *Hist. of England* (Geo. III. p. 617).

They shut their gates after the day of the Black Breeches.—CARLYLE, *French Revolution*, vol. ii. book vi. 4.

Procession to Hernals (*The*). The estate of the Jörgers, 'where the Catholic doctrine had been first profaned by a Lutheran sermon,' established by the Jesuits in the reign of Kaiser Ferdinand II. (1619-1637).

Processional (*A*). A book containing all that pertains to ecclesiastical processions (1600).

Proc'lidæ (*Dynasty of the*), B.C. 1100-219. One of the two contemporaneous dynasties of Sparta. The other was the dynasty of the Agīdæ. The former received its name from Proclès, son of Aristodēmus, and the latter from Agis son of Eurysthēnês.

Proconsul. In the Roman empire was the quasi-consul of a province. The first was Titus Quintius Barbātus (B.C.

464). Pompey was for three years proconsul of the sea. Julius Cæsar was for five years proconsul of Gaul. As a rule they were avaricious, tyrannical, and immoral. The name is a hissing and a byword.

Proconsuls, 1793. French commissioners appointed by the Convention, with uncontrolled power to arrest persons suspected of being counter-revolutionists, or those who murmured at the new state of things. They had the power of taxing the rich, making compositions with them, and of seizing private horses for the use of the army. These commissioners were most arbitrary and insolent.

Proctors (*The*), 1629, of our universities. Two annually, elected in Oxford by the House of Convocation, and in Cambridge by the Senate. Their duties are to act as peace officers to maintain good behaviour of all persons *in statu pupillari*. Each proctor names a pro-proctor, who (in Oxford) must be an M.A. of three years' standing. The proctors are chosen by cycles. In Oxford from 1620 to 1859 the cycle was 23 years; in 1859 it was extended to 30 years. In Cambridge the cycle is 50 years. (Trinity and St. John's have eleven turns each; Christ's, Clare, Caius, Pembroke, Queen's, and Peter House six turns each; Emmanuel, Magdalene, Jesus, Sidney Sussex, Corpus and St. Catharine's five turns each; Trinity Hall three turns, with the right of nomination if a vacancy occurs within the year; and Downing two turns.

In Oxford the stipend of proctor is 350*l.* and of pro-proctor 80*l.* In Cambridge there are two assistant pro-proctors.

Procu'lians. In Latin ' Proculiāni.' A law school so called from Procŭlus, a jurist; opposed to the Sabinians (*q.v.*). Proculus is often cited, and there are thirty-seven extracts from him in the Digest. The Proculians were 'radicals,' but interpreted law literatim and verbatim. The Sabinians were courtiers and equity lawyers.

Procura'tor. A functionary in the Roman empire created by Augustus. Procurators were of two classes; those in the senatorial provinces, who were proxies of the senate; and those in the great imperial provinces, who were appointed by the emperor. The former were viceroys; the latter were fiscal officers.

Procura'tors of St. Mark. Nine magistrates in the republic of Venice who administered the effects of orphans and of those who died intestate.

Prodigy of France (*The*). Budé was so called by Erasmus (1467–1540). He introduced into France the study of Greek, and was learned in all the sciences.

Prodigy of Learning (*The*). Samuel Hahnemann, the German, is so called by J. P. Richter (1755–1843).

Profound Doctor (*The*). ' Doctor Profundus,' Thomas Bradwardine archbishop of Canterbury (1848–1349).

Egidius de Colonna [Giles of Cologne] is called 'The Most Profound Doctor ' (died 1316).

Progresses. Royal visits were so called in the reign of Elizabeth.

Elizabeth was in the habit of making visits to the houses of her nobles. . . . These visits were called progresses.—PRINCE, *Parallel History*, vol. ii. p. 106.

Progressives. So the Home Rule party began to call themselves in the December of 1889.

Projector (*The*). John Law of Edinburgh (1681–1729), the projector of the Mississippi Scheme or French bubble company.

Propaganda Fide (*The College of the Congregation de*), 1622. Established by Urban VIII. A great nursery of missionaries of all sorts and for all parts of the world: Gregorians, Persians, Nestorians, Jacobites, Melchites, Copts, Abyssinians, and Armenians.

Propaganda Fide (*The Congregation de*), 1572. Originated by Gregory XIII., and instituted at Rome by bull of Gregory XV. in 1622. It has the direction of missions, and consists of thirteen cardinals, three prelates, and a secretary,

Propagation of the Faith (*Society for the*). Established at Lyons in 1829.

Propagators of the Faith. Same as ' Converters ' (*q.v.*).

Prophecy of St. Laser'ian (*The*). ' The Church of Rome will surely fall when the Catholic faith is overthrown in Ireland.' St. Laserian was an ancient archbishop of Cashel.

Prophesyings suppressed, 1577. Prophesyings, in 1569, were meetings held once a fortnight by the puritans, under the guidance of Cartwright and Travers, and supported by several of the bishops, nominally for the edification of the clergy. They were under a moderator appointed by the bishop of the diocese or his deputy 'to discuss theological subjects and expound scripture.' They were called *prophesyings* from the text, 'Ye may all prophesy one by one, that all may learn, and all may be comforted' (1 Cor. xiv. 31). Queen Elizabeth, feeling convinced that this platform was a mere pretence, and that the true object of the meetings was political, commanded them to be suppressed. As Edmund Grindal, recently elevated to the see of Canterbury, favoured the 'prophesyings,' he was ordered to 'keep his house,' and never regained the queen's favour.

Prophetess of Exeter (*The*). Joanna Southcott (1750–1814).

Proprætor. A Roman officer who discharged in a province the functions of a prætor. Like a prætor he was attended by six lictors.

Propre, in English *A Proper*, is either a 'propre du temps,' a 'propre des saints,' or a 'propre d'une église.' The first is a clause in a liturgy introduced for special days and religious festivals; the second for special saints; and the third for special churches.

In the English Prayer Book there are 'Propers' in the 'Communion Service' for the great festivals, just before the canticle 'Therefore with Angels and Archangels we . . .' In bidding prayers the clause beginning 'and as in duty bound . . .' is a 'proper' of the third sort.

Pro-proctors. Instituted in the Cambridge University by a grace of the senate 29 April, 1818. They are nominated by the colleges according to the cycle of 'Proctors' (*q.v.*), but appointed by the senate.

6 June, 1878, two 'additional pro-proctors' were added by a grace of the senate. They must be masters of arts of not less than three years' standing, and are in office for one year.

Proscription. In Roman history, a list of persons proscribed stuck up in places of public resort. Sulla was the first to publish 'Tables of Proscription.' The triumvirs (Octavius, Antony, and Lepidus) followed his example. Informers received a part of the confiscated property, so that avarice and private vengeance were rewarded and encouraged.

Proselytes of the Covenant. Such Gentiles as received the covenant or law of Moses.

Proselytes of the Gate. Those Gentiles who worshipped the true God, but received not the law of Moses. The proselytes were only allowed to enter the outer court of the temple. In Solomon's time there were 153,000 of these proselytes who were compelled to hew wood, to draw water, to cut stones, and to carry burdens for the building of the temple (2 Chron. ii. 17, 18). These men were Canaanites who had continued in the country since the time of Joshua. They were proselytes of the *gate* because they were allowed to dwell 'within the gates' of Jerusalem.

Naaman the Syrian, Nebuzaradan (general of Nebuchadnezzar's army), Cornelius the centurion, the eunuch of Queen Candăce (3 syl.), the Kenites and Rechabites were proselytes of the gate.

Protection of British Industry. Acts of Parliament to compel people to purchase only home produce. This was done by laying a tax on all foreign commodities to make them dearer than similar commodities produced at home. Free trade in corn was introduced in 1846 by the abolition of the Corn Laws (*q.v.*), and in most other articles since.

In Oct. 1890 came into operation in the United States of North America the 'McKinley Tariff Bill,' which imposed a tax on imported articles of enormous magnitude, 'to protect native industry against foreign competition.' This battle with England will determine once for all whether Free Trade or Protection is the sounder policy.

Protector. In English history a kind of regent. The Duke of Bedford was protector of England under Henry VI.; the Duke of Gloucester [Richard III.] was protector under Edward V. *See next article.*

Protector of the Commonwealth of England, Scotland, and Ireland. Oliver Cromwell, 16 Dec., 1653. Reinaugurated with all the pomp of a coronation 26 June, 1656; died 3 Sept., 1658, aged 59.

His son Richard succeeded him, but retired into private life in 1660.

Protestant and Popish Wind. In court and city, says Misson, in the reign of James II., an east wind was called Protestant, and a west wind a Popish one.

October 23. James II., being extremely restless and uneasy, ordered a weathercock to be placed where he might see it from his apartment, that he might learn with his own eyes whether the wind is Protestant or Popish. This weathercock, at one end of the Banqueting House, is still to be seen there (1719).—MISSON.

Protestant Duke (*The*). James duke of Monmouth, said to be a love-child of Charles II. So called because he renounced the Catholic faith in which he had been brought up, and became a Protestant (1619–1685). *See* 'Monmouth.'

Protestant Flail (*A*). A kind of life-preserver, worn by timid magistrates in the reign of Charles II. The handle resembled a farrier's blood-stick, and the flail was joined to the end by a strong ligature, so short as to avoid the hand. It was made of lignum vitæ wood.

It [the Protestant flail] was for street and crowd work ; and the instrument lurking perdu in a coat pocket, might readily sally out to execution, and by clearing a great hall . . . carry an election, by a choice way of polling, called ' knocking down.'—ROGER NORTH.

Protestant Joiner (*The*). Colledge, in whose defence Titus Oates appeared in 1681. He was accused of treason, but there was not the slightest proof of the charge. ' State Trials,' vol. viii. p. 628.

Protestant Livy (*The*). John Sleidan of Cologne (1506-1556). His great work is ' The State of Religion in the reign of Kaiser Karl V.'

Protestant Patent (*The*), 1859. It granted to the communes of Hungary the free administration of their religious and educational matters.

Protestant Pope (*The*). Gian Vincenzo Ganganelli, Pope Clement XIV.: so called from his enlightened policy, and more especially for his bull suppressing the Jesuits (1705, 1769–1774).

Protestant Religion (*The*), 1675. When the Earl of Shaftesbury asked in the House of Lords, ' What is the Protestant religion [of England] ? ' The Bishop of Winchester replied, ' The 39 articles, the liturgy, the catechism, the canons, and the homilies.'

Not very logical, nor very orthodox. A better answer would have been, ' the Bible, the whole Bible, and nothing but the Bible.' The bishop's response at best can only apply to the Anglican Church, but the Anglican Church is not Protestantism.

Protestants, 1592. Those Christians who belonged to the reformed Church, as Episcopalians, Presbyterians, Huguenots, Lutherans, Calvinists, and all dissenters of every denomination. Called Protestants from those who protested against the decree of the second diet of Speyer, which pronounced Lutheranism to be heretical, and revoked the decree of the previous diet, which conceded liberty of conscience.

The second diet was presided over by Ferdinand, the brother of Karl V., and the dissentients appealed to Karl V.

Protesters. One of the 'religious' parties into which Scotland was divided after the death of Charles I. The other party was called the Resolutioners (*q.v.*). The Resolutioners adhered to Charles II., but the Protesters were inclined to a union with the republicans. *See* Sir W. Scott, ' Old Mortality,' ch. v.

Proteus (*The German*). Melanchthon (1497–1560). So called because he so often changed his religious views. He was a disciple of Luther, but followed Zwinglius in some points and Calvin in others.

Protevangelion (*The*), or 'Protevangelium.' A gospel falsely ascribed to St. James the Less, first bishop of Jerusalem. It is noted for its minute details of the Virgin and Jesus. Some ascribe it to L. Carīnas, who died 362.

First of all we shall rehearse .
The nativity of our Lord,
As written in the old record
Of the protevangelion.
LONGFELLOW, *The Golden Legend.*

Proto-Martyr (*The*).
I. St. Stephen. The first Christian martyr. Stoned to death about nine months after the Crucifixion.

II. Of the *British Isles*. [St.] Alban, A.D. 285. Condemned to death by Constantius for refusing to offer sacrifice to the gods of Rome, according to the edict of the Emperor Diocletian.

It must not be forgotten that these executions, called ' persecutions,' were political, not religious, except so far as state religion can be so called. Christian persecutions, on the other hand, are religious, not political, except, perhaps, in England, where churchmanship and dissent have a special political bias.

Protonotaries Apostolic. A college of twelve notaries, secretaries of the Roman chancellery instituted by Clement I. to write the lives of martyrs and assist at canonisations.

Proto-Syncell. The first syncell or domestic of the patriarchal palace of

Constantinople. He was one of the first ecclesiastical dignitaries of Constantinople.

Proud Duke (*The*). Charles Seymour duke of Somerset (1662–1748).

Prout (*Father*). The pen-name of the Rev. Francis Mahōney, a writer in 'Fraser's Magazine,' in the 'Globe' newspaper, &c. (1805–1866).

Provant Rapier. A sword supplied by the provant master, or officer who provided for the soldiers. Such a sword was very inferior to a Tolĕdo blade. In 'Kenilworth' Wayland Smith speaks of his sword as a ' poor provant rapier,' and contrasts it with Varney's special Toledo. Similarly we read of ' provant apparel,' that is, apparel provided to soldiers by the provant-master; ' provant-breeches,' &c. Provant also means ' common ' or ' ordinary,' as ' provant rogue.' We see also the expressions ' provant breeches,' ' provant swords,' &c., and the person employed to provide soldiers with their kit is called the ' provant master.'

Provedito're (5 syl.). The governor of a province in the ancient republic of Venice. There was the ordinary proveditore, charged with the supervision of streets, buildings, and police; and the marine proveditore, who was to provide for the payment, &c., of the fleet.

Providence. Alexander I. of Russia considered himself ' *La Providence libérale* of Europe, and the protector of the independence of the peoples '; but his good intentions for mankind took the form of the Holy Alliance, which stifled freedom all over Europe, re-established the old despotisms, and put back the world a generation at least (' Nineteenth Century,' June 1889, p. 834).

Provincial (*A*). The superior of all the religious houses in a province, subordinate to the general of the order.

By a ' province' is meant a ' division of the order,' containing all the houses of a certain district, or all those which speak the same language.

Provincial Letters or Provinciales, 1656–1657. The famous letters of Blaise Pascal under the pseudonym of ' Louis de Montalte,' in defence of the Jansenists and against the Jesuits, whom he accuses of lax morals, want of piety, equivocation, mental reservation, simony,

and so on. The letters are eighteen in number, and one fragment. Lemaistre added a twentieth. They are full of irony, very vigorous, and models of their kind. They were censured at Rome and condemned in France.

The objection that his necessity did not leave him the power to contract freely would apply equally to the discontented servant of the ' Provincial Letters.'—*The World* (2 May, 1888).

Provincial Synod (*A*) in the Presbyterian Church of Scotland consists of three ·or more presbyteries (*q.v.*) The chairman is called the ' moderator.'

Provincials of Lyndwood (*The*), 1444. A collection of papal constitutions drawn from the canon law by fourteen archbishops (from Langton 1206 to Chichele 1443). Lyndwood, or Lyndwode, was an ecclesiastical lawyer and bishop of St. David's.

Provisions. Reversionary grants of benefices during the lifetime of present incumbents. This followed as a consequent on the maxim of Clement V. that the pope has the free right of disposing of all ecclesiastical benefices. In consequence of this claim all the best livings of Europe were held by Italians wholly ignorant of the language of the people over whom they had charge. In 1350 Edward III. caused the Statute of Provisors (*q.v.*) to be passed, which enacted that, if the pope made a reversionary grant to anyone, the king should have the collation of such benefice. Subsequently it was enacted that no alien should be capable of holding any ecclesiastical preferment in England.

Provisions of Merton (*The*), the day after the coronation of Henry III. This is the first enactment on the English statute-book. ' Provisions' are acts of parliament to curb the arbitrary power of the crown. Merton, in Surrey, is the place where the parliament was held. These provisions are the most ancient body of laws after Magna Charta, and consist of eleven articles.

Provisions of Oxford (*The*), 11 June, 1258. Sworn to by Henry III. and his son Edward on one side, and by the citizens of London on the other. They provided that a council of twelve 'honest men ' shall assist the king as his privy council; that the great officers and treasurer shall give in their accounts at the close of every year; that sheriffs shall be appointed from the chief tenants of each county; that no fee shall be given directly or indirectly for the administration of justice; that three parliaments shall assemble every year.

A 'provision' is an act of parliament to curb the arbitrary power of the crown. These provisions are further noteworthy in that the royal proclamation which ordered their observance was in the English tongue, and this, as far as we know, is the first instance of the use of the English language for such a purpose.

Provisors. Persons in whose favour provisos had been made in the Acts for the Settlement of Ireland after the Restoration. To the English provisors 477,873 acres were awarded, and to the Irish provisors 491,001 statute acres, out of the 7,778,037 acres forfeited under the Commonwealth.

Provisors (*Statute of*), 25 Edward III., s. 6, A.D. 1350, &c. To prohibit anyone from making a reversionary grant of a benefice, or from receiving any fee or reward out of a living 'as a provision' for foreign cardinals. This act was followed by others of a like character, and the pope of Rome was deprived of presenting to any bishopric or living in England, or of receiving directly or indirectly any portion of the church revenues.

In the 14th cent. in England the imposts and taxes received by the pope were fivefold the amount of those received by the crown.

Provost. In Oxford University; the title of the head of three of the colleges, Oriel, Queen's, and Worcester. In Cambridge University the master of King's College only is called the Provost, the principal of Queen's College is called the President, but of all the other colleges the Master.

Provost and Bailies (*The*) in Scotland correspond to our English mayor and aldermen. They are chosen by the councilmen, and invested with the powers of magistrates in the burgh. The Scotch Municipal Reform Act passed in 1840 (18 August).

Provost of Paris (*The*). 'Le Prévôt de Paris,' magistrat d'épée, chef du Châtelet. Charged with the *gouvernement politique*, and also with the finances of Paris. He is the Viscount of Paris. This officer dates from the reign of Hugues Capet [*You Cap-pay*].

Provost of the Army. 'Le Prévôt de l'Armée,' a French officer charged

31

to administer justice between military men, to adjust differences between officers and privates, military men and civilians. Also called 'Les Prévôts des Bandes.'

Provost of the Constabulary, or **Grand Provost of France** (*The*). 'Le Prévôt de la Connétablie.' This office was in 1572 united to that of the 'Provost of the Hotel' (*q.v.*).

Provost of the Hotel (*The*). 'Le Prévôt de l'Hôtel, 1572.' A French officer who joined to his functions that of Provost of France, the chief military commander. The King of the Ribalds was also absorbed in the same office.

Provost of the King's Hotel (*The*). 'Le Prévôt de l'Hôtel du Roi,' judge in all crown cases. He moved from place to place with the court. The duties subsequently passed to the tribunal of the *Maîtres d'Hôtel du Roi*, and in 1573 the office was submerged in that of the Provost of France.

Provost of the Marshals (*The*). 'Le Prévôt des Maréchaux.' The Marshals' Provost adjudicated only between the upper officers. Under Charles VI. and VII. this provost was attached to the court.

Provost of the Merchants (*The*). 'Le Prévôt des Marchands.' Elected every three years. At first these provosts were only excise officers, who visited and taxed ships exporting or importing goods; but subsequently they had the jurisdiction of all mercantile affairs, were charged with public ceremonies, and capitation imposts.

Provvedito'ri (*The*). Officers appointed for the guardianship of St. Mark, at Venice.

Prox'enus (pl. *Prox'eni*). The host of a stranger or ambassador. Before public houses of entertainment were known travellers had to depend on the hospitality of strangers, who expected in return similar civilities if required. That the obligation might be recognised, the host and guest parted a white stone, and writing their name on the two halves, the host gave his portion to the guest, and vice versâ (*see* Rev. ii. 17). In time, certain houses were selected for the entertainment of ambassadors. These public entertainers were called 'Proxĕni,'

3 A

and voluntary entertainers were called 'Ethelo-proxĕni.'

> To him that overcometh I . . . will give a white stone, and on the stone a new name written, which no man knoweth saving he that receiveth it.—Rev. ii. 17.

Prussia. The Elector Friedrich III. raised his electorate to a kingdom in 1701. From this date it has been constantly increasing in power and extent, till in 1866, in a war of seven weeks, it overmastered Austria, and in 1870 in the seven months' war it triumphed over France, when the King of Prussia added to his other titles that of ' German Emperor.'

> In 1876 the Queen of England, by the advice of Lord Beaconsfield, then premier, added the title 'Empress of India' to her other titular designations.

Prussia (*Titles of the King of*) [*German Emperor*], since 1888.

> His Imperial and Royal Majesty * * King of Prussia and German Emperor, Margrave of Brandenburg, Burgrave of Nuremburg, Count of Hohenzollern, Premier Duke and Sovereign of Silesia and of the County of Glatz, Grand Duke of the Lower Rhine and of Posen, Duke of Saxony, of Westphalia, of Engern, of Pomerania. of Luneberg, of Holstein and Schleswig, of Magdeburg, of Bremen, of Gelderland, of Cleves, of Juliers, and of Berg, Duke of the Wends and of the Cassubes, Duke of Crossen, of Lauenberg, and of Mecklenburg, Landgrave of Hesse and Thuringia, Margrave of Upper and Lower Lusatia, Prince of Orange, Lord of Rügen, Lord of Eastern Frisia, of Paderborn and Pyrmont, of Halberstadt, Münster, Minden, Osnabrück and Hildesheim, of Verdun, Kammin, Fulda, Nassau and Moers, Princely Count of Henneberg, Count of the Marches, and of Ravensberg, Hohenstein, Tecklenburg, Lingen, Mansfeld, Sigmaringen and Veringen, and Lord of Frankfort.

Prussian Boot (*The*). Prince Bismarck, chancellor of Prussia (1813–   ), or more correctly the imperious domination and insolent arrogance of the prince chancellor.

> In the course of these unfortunate discussions . . . Prince Bismarck himself has revealed a doubt whether all the states of Germany rejoice in the domination of Prussia. The truth is . . . a vast number of Germans do not share the Berlinese idolatry of the Prussian Boot. They know the Boot; they are aware that it has been a serviceable aid to diplomacy; but they do not like it.—*Nineteenth Century* (Feb. 1889, p. 263).

Prussian Evangelical Church (*The*), 1828. A union of Calvinism and Lutheranism. Frederick William III., assisted by Bunsen his minister, compiled a new liturgy for Prussia and a new church organisation. The Calvinistic and Lutheran ministers were then invited to conform on a given day, and so many agreed to do so, that the few dissentients were compelled either to conform or to abandon their pastorates.

Prussian Orders. The highest is the 'Black Eagle.'

Pruth (*Treaty of the*), 23 July, 1711. A treaty of peace between Russia and Turkey, in which Czar Peter the Great was obliged to restore Azof and all of his other dominions on the Black Sea to Turkey.

Pryt'anes (3 syl.). Officers in ancient Greece entrusted with the chief magistacy in Corcӯra, Corinth, Rhodes, and Mitylēnê. At Athens they were of second rank, next to the archons, and acted with them as judges, sitting in the prytanĕum or hall of the prytănês. Their number was fifty, and all lived at the public expense.

Prytane'um. I. A common hall in a Greek state for a given district, containing (1) a law court for the prytănês; (2) granaries; and (3) restaurants for citizens and strangers also.

II. The *Prytanée Française* was the college of Louis le Grand set apart by the republic for a treasury office. In 1803 it was transferred to St. Cyr; and since 1852 to the military college of La Flèche.

Psalmanazar (*George*). A literary impostor born in France in 1679. He pretended to be a Japanese, born in the island of Formosa; and he wrote for the 'Universal History' what he called a 'History of Formosa,' altogether fabulous, but which thoroughly imposed on the learned world. The man died in London in 1763, but what was his real name nobody knows. *See* ' Literary Forgeries.'

Psalmo'rum Codex, 1457. The first book printed in movable metal type bearing a *date*; the printing firm was Fust and his son-in-law Peter Schaeffer. *See* ' Biblia Sacra Latīna.'

Psalter na Rann (*The*), by Ængus, is a hagiography of the saints of all nations including British, Welsh, Irish, and even Egyptian (9th cent.). *See* p. 7, ' Acta Sanctorum.'

Psalter of Cashel (*The*). A psalter is a provincial register of events, &c., briefly recorded for a national history. The oldest is the Psalter of Tara, which is lost. The Psalter of Cashel (in verse) was the work of MacCulinan bishop of Cashel and king of Munster, who died in the beginning of the 10th cent.

Psalter of Mainz (*The*), 1457. The first book ever printed.

Psalter of Tara (*The*). The great national register of the ancient Irish in which was briefly entered provincial annals as materials for national history. The Psalter of Tara has been long lost, but parts of the Psalter of Cashel (compiled in the 10th cent.) are supposed to have been transcribed from it.

It began B.C. 900 in the reign of Ollam Fodlah of the family of Ia.

> Their tribe, they said, their high degree,
> Was sung in Tara's Psaltery.
> CAMPBELL, *O'Connor's Child.*

Psaltery (*A*). ' Sacbut, harp, and psaltery.' The sacbut is a corruption of sambuc, a stringed instrument, ' genus citharæ rusticæ.' The psaltery is a trapezium with ten or thirteen strings, run over two bridges, struck with a plectrum.

The nablium or psaltery . . . is called in Psalm XXXIII. 2, and CXLIV. 9, a ten-stringed instrument . . . Josephus . . . assigns to it twelve strings. . . . There was another instrument of this kind used in Babylon. It was triangular in form. In Greek it is called σαμβύκη, in Hebrew סַבְּכָא. It had originally only four strings, but subsequently twenty (Dan. iii. 7, 10, 15).—JAHN, *Archæologia Biblica*, No. 94.

Psylli. Jugglers of Egypt and Libya who pretended to neutralise the poison of serpents, and even to kill them, merely by fixing their eyes on them.

Ptolemaic System (*The*). Ptolemy of Alexandria about A.D. 160 published his ' Great System,' called by the Arabians ' Almagest.' It presumed that our earth was stationary in the midst of the system, and that the heavenly bodies revolved round it. He adopted the theory of the epicycles.

Here E is the earth. The planets, including sun and moon, moved first round the little circle, and the centre of that little circle described in its revolution the large circle round E. The large circle was called the ' deferent.' Epicycle means ' upon the circle.'

Public Good (*The*), about 1820–1825. A Muscovite secret league, ostensibly for improving the education of the Russian empire by introducing the English Lancastrian plan, but really a political organisation to republicanise Russia, and introduce a ' constitution.' Colonel Pestel was head of the league, but was aided and abetted by 122 men of rank,

among whom were several princes. On the death of Alexander in 1825 the Grand-duke Constantine relinqu⸱shed the crown to his brother Nicholas, and when the troops were drawn up to administer to them the oath of fidelity, the cry was raised of ' Constantine and the Constitution !' Instantly the leaguers were seized; Pestel and four others were hanged, and 118 were banished to Siberia.

Public Good (*League of the*). ' Ligue du Bien Public,' 1465. An alliance against Louis XI. It consisted of the Duc de Bretagne, the Duc de Bourbon, the Duc de Calabre, the Duc de Nemours, Charles the king's brother, the Comte de Dunois, the Comte d'Armagnac, and the Comte Dammartin. At the head of the league was Charles le Téméraire. The nominal object of this formidable league was the relief of the people, but the real object was vengeance on the king for taking away from the aristocracy certain privileges. An indecisive battle was fought at Montlhéry in July 1465, after which Louis XI. contrived to break up the league by fair promises, which he never intended to fulfil, and the league was nicknamed *La Ligue du Mal Public.*

Public Health Act (*The*), 1875. This act embodies all the sanitary acts passed since 1848, and provides for the removal of all things injurious to health : the overcrowding of houses ; the ventilation of factories ; and either the consumption of smoke or its being carried high into the air by long chimneys.

Public Orator (*The*), of our universities. Elected in Cambridge by the senate from one of two persons nominated by the council. In Oxford he is elected by the House of Convocation (*q.v.*), and he must be either an M.A. or a B.C.L. He writes official letters, delivers in Latin an oration on great public festivals, presents to the vice-chancellor those on whom an honorary degree is to be conferred, and (in Oxford) delivers the Creweian Oration alternately with the professor of poetry. The Public Orator is the official voice of the legislative body.

The first Public Orator of Oxford was appointed in 1584 when Queen Elizabeth visited the university, and his salary was 20 nobles (6l. 13s. 4d.). This has been increased by Lord Crewe's benefaction by 20l., and 130l. from the university chest. Total 156l. 13s. 4d.

3 A 2

Public Safety (*The Committee of*), 1642. A committee appointed by the Long Parliament as its administrative organ. Its guiding spirits were Hampden, Hollis, and Pym. English and Scotch officers were drawn from the Low Countries, and Lord Essex was appointed commander-in-chief, with an army of 20,000 foot and 4,000 horse.

Pucelle (*La*), or 'La Pucelle d'Orléans.' 'The Maid,' that is, Jeanne d'Arc (1412-1431).

Puck. The nickname of William Ryan, an Irish ruffian of detestable character. Brought to trial in January 1848 for the murder of John Kelly, whom he shot deliberately in the presence of his family and in his own house. He was executed 8 Feb., 1848.

Pudsha Be'gum (East Indies). Queen-mother.

Pueri Regis. King's-men, or vassals of a king, who owed him homage and service. The service was help in time of war. King's-men had their vassals, who were called grafs. The lands held of a lord were called *fiefs*. The fiefs of king's-men were called *immediate*, because held immediately under the king.

Every king's-man was expected to furnish the king with a certain number of men in time of war, and every man was to be furnished by the vassal with 'a shield, spear, bow, 12 arrows, and a breast-plate.'

Pugilistic Club in Bond Street (*The*). In the time of the regency. Of this club not only the chief nobility, but even the Prince Regent and the Duke of York, were members. The ceaseless question was which school of boxing was the better, the Bristolian or the Hebrew. The Prince Regent was a Bristolian, but Frederick duke of York was for the Hebrews. Mendoza was the crack Hebrew prize-fighter; Jem Belcher, Thomas Cribb, and Molineux were the crack Bristolians. The members of the club were called Corinthians. Thomas Cribb was most unwisely attached to the household of the Prince Regent.

The following names are famous in the ring: Jim Belcher (*Bristolian*) champion (he had but one eye), and his brother Tom, Bendigo, Ben Burns, Cohen, Tom Cribb, champion, Dick Curtis, Figg, Fuller, Gardolio (of the Hebrew school), Bob Gregson (*the Pot of Pork*), Gully, John C. Heenan (*the Benicia Boy*), Hudson, Humphries, Gentleman Jackson (Lord Byron was his pupil), Jim Mace, Jack Martin, Daniel Mendoza the Jew, Molineux the Negro, Oliver, Painter, Randal (*the Nonpareil*)

noted for his pink cheeks, Caleb Rann (Mendoza's crack pupil, and called *The Pink* [of Bow]), Alec Reed, Richmond, Scroggins (a sailor), Tom Sayers (who fought the 'Benicia Boy' in 1860), Slack, Cyrus Smalley (*the Sprig of Myrtle*), Cribb's crack pupil, Spring (so called by Cribb, but whose real name was Tom Winter), Sutton, Tomkins, Jim Ward (*the Nestor of the Ring*), &c. The era of boxing was 1719-1860.

Punic Wars (*The*). Three wars carried on between the Carthaginians and the Romans, in all of which the Romans had the mastery. The first B.C. 263-241; the second 218-216, 215-211, 210-207, 206-202; the third 150-146, which ended in the fall of Carthage.

From *Pœni* (Carthaginians) comes the adjective *punic-us*; so from *mœnia* comes *munire*, and from *pœna* comes *punire*.

Punjab. Persian for five rivers. The five rivers are the Sutlej, the Beeas, the Ravee, the Chenab, and the Jhelum. These five rivers, uniting in succession, form ultimately a single stream called the Punjnud, which carries the collected water into the Indus.

The united Sutlej and Beeas form the Gharra; and the three rivers Chenab, Ravee, and Jhelum form the Trinab (three rivers). Ultimately the Gharra unites with the Trinab, and flows into the Indus.

Pura'nas, or 'Purani.' Eighteen poems in Sanskrit containing the Hindû traditions of creation, mythology, and the stories of Indian heroes. These poems serve as a commentary on the Vedas (*q.v.*).

Purchase (*The Abolition of*), 20 July, 1871. To prevent persons obtaining commissions or grades in the army by money payments. Before this law was passed the price of promotion was:

	£		£	
Lieutenant-colonel	. 4,500	price	1,300	difference
Major	. . .	3,200	„	1,400	„
Captain	. . .	1,800	„	1,100	„
Lieutenant	. . .	700	„	250	„
Cornet or Ensign	. .	450			

Suppose a lieutenant-colonel wished to retire, the senior major might purchase the rank for 1,300*l.*; the senior captain might purchase the majority for 1,400*l.*, and so on, the cornet paying 250*l.* for his lieutenancy, and a new man giving 450*l.* for the vacant cornetcy or ensigncy. Fancy prices were often given as bribes, but always *sub rosa*.

Purgers, 1793. In the French Revolution the great purgers commissioned by the Convention were—

BARRAS. See 'Fréron.'

CARRIER was sent to extirpate the anti-revolutionists of Nantes, and murdered 32,000 men, women, and children (*Prud-homme*).

COLLOT D'HERBOIS was sent to extirpate the anti-revolutionists of Lyons, and murdered 31,000 men, women, and children (*Prudhomme*).

FRÉRON and Barras were sent to extirpate the anti-revolutionists of Toulon.

KLÉBER, Westermann, Moreau, &c. were sent to extirpate the anti-revolutionists of Vendée, and murdered 337,000 men, women, and children (*Prudhomme*).

LEBON was sent to extirpate the anti-revolutionists of Arras, St. Pol, and St. Omer.

MAIGNET was sent to extirpate the anti-revolutionists of Orange in Vaucluse.

TALLIEN was sent to extirpate the anti-revolutionists of Bordeaux.

VICTOR HUGUES was sent to extirpate the anti-revolutionists of St. Domingo.

Purification of the Virgin Mary, 2 Feb. Instituted in 542.

Purists. An English translation of Cathāri (*q.v.*).

Puritans, 1565. First applied by way of reproach to the Nonconformists, but subsequently adopted by them. They maintained that they adopted the pure Word of God as their guide, and desired the church to be purified or rid of all things else. They maintained that the Church of England still retained many things not to be found in the Word of God : *i.e.* the clerical dresses, the book of common prayer, kneeling at the sacrament, the cross in baptism, sponsors, lay baptism, the ring in marriage, bowing at the name of Jesus, episcopacy, forms of prayer, church organs, chanting, and intoning.

The Cathāri of the 3rd cent. were 'Puritāni.'

Purple (*The*). 'To be raised to the purple,' in the Catholic Church, means to be made a cardinal ; but purple was the colour of the imperial robe of the Romans, and to be raised to the purple or to wear the purple signified to be made emperor or to be emperor. Hence such terms as *purpuram adorāre, purpurā-tōrum socius,* and so on.

Purple Cap. In primitive times young women who professed a state of virginity as a religious function had a purple cap, somewhat like a small mitre, given them at their consecration. *See* 'Cap.'

Purple Laws (*The*). The Roman rescripts (*q.v.*), grants, and pragmatic sanctions written in purple ink.

A compound of vermilion and cinnabar. White laws were the edicts of prætors, and red laws the *jus civile.*

Pursuivants. The four English pursuivants are Rouge-dragon, Portcullis, Blue-mantle, and Rouge-croix.

The four Irish are Athlone the chief, and the other three are pursuivants of St. Patrick.

The chief Scotch pursuivant is entitled Unicorn. *See* 'Heralds.'

Purveyor, Purveyance. A purveyor was one who provided for the royal household. Purveyance was the providing of necessaries for the sovereign ; sometimes they were bought at a valuation, and sometimes they were taken without the consent of the owner and without compensation. Thus, in war, horses, wagons, and food were purveyed.

Eadmer says : 'Those who attended the court plundered and destroyed the whole country through which the king passed without any control. Some . . . . when they could not consume all the provisions which they had taken, either sold or burnt what was left. After having washed their horses' feet with the liquors they could not drink, they threw it in the streets.' Time : Rufus.

Pusey and Ellerton Scholarships. Three for Hebrew. Value 50*l.* a year, and tenable for three years, in the University of Oxford. Founded by Philip Pusey, of Pusey, Berkshire ; Dr. Pusey, regius professor of Hebrew ; and Dr. Ellerton, fellow of Magdalen, in 1822.

Puseyism, 1833. The doctrinal and ritual tenets of Dr. Pusey of Oxford. This party of the Anglican Church was started by Mr. Perceval, who with some others met at the house of the Rev. Hugh James Rose, domestic chaplain to the archbishop of Canterbury. Probably the views of Charles Simeon, fellow of King's College, Cambridge, instigated the movement. The Pusey party was soon joined by many men of great learning, who introduced stricter ritual observances, more frequent services, and enforced the doctrines of apostolic succession, priestly absolution, and church sanctity, in opposition to Calvinism and the 'evangelical' party called Simeonites. A very large number of the Puseyites have joined the Roman communion.

Pushtû. The Afghan language, a dialect of the Persian, but very much changed by copious foreign elements.

Putrid Plain (*The*). The plain or field in Provence where the battle of Aix was fought B.C. 102. In this battle Caius Marius, the Roman general, almost extirpated the Teuton army led by Teutobod, and the people of Marseilles (we are told) employed the bones of the slain ' to make fences for their vineyards.'

Pyrenees (*Peace of the*). I. 7 Nov. 1659, between France and Spain. By this treaty it was stipulated that the crowns of France and Spain should never be united under one family. This stipulation was the pretext of the War of the Spanish Succession (*q.v.*), 1701–1714.

II. 1660. A peace made after the united armies of Mazarin and Cromwell had defeated the Great Condé in the *Dunes*. This peace stipulated that England should retain Dunkirk ; that Spain should cede Roussillon and Artois to France ; and that France should restore Catalonia to Italy.

Pyrrhonists. The disciples of Pyrrho of Elis, who died B.C. 280, aged 90. He taught that nothing is what it seems to be, and therefore we know nothing as matter of fact. *Pyrrhonism* now means religious scepticism.

Pyrrhonists have of late revived in Germany and England.

Pythagore'an Diet (*The*). Vegetable diet. Pythagoras taught that it is cruel and unjust to put any animal to death for food. And the only animal foods that he would sanction are milk, butter, cheese, and eggs.

Pythagore'an League (*The*). B.C.* overthrown B.C. 504. The only secret political society of ancient times known of. The ultras of the Carbonari of Naples, in the 19th cent., called themselves Pythagoreans. The object of the Pythagorean league was to introduce the aristocratic element, but at the same time to make it an aristocracy of talent and not of birth only.

Pythagorean Philosophers (*The*). Of ancient Greece, so called from Pythagoras (B.C. 481–411), a native of Samos, and often called the Samian Sage. His disciples were divided into two classes, the *exoterics* and *esoterics*. The latter must have attended his lectures for five years at least. The ' exoterics' were also divided into two classes —those who lived in the college, who were called *cænobitæ*—and those who merely attended his lectures, who were called *acusmatici*. The average number of the former was about 600 and of the latter about 2,000. *See* ' Golden Verses.'

Quaderno de las Leyes nuevas de la Hermandad. The laws of the Her'mandad (*q.v.*) compiled in 1485.

Quadrages'ima of St. Martin (*The*). At Milan, in Spain, and in Gaul, the number of Advent Sundays used to be six, beginning on the Sunday after Martinmas, from which it was styled the ' Quadragesima of St. Martin,' or 'Little Lent.'

At Rome the number was originally 5, in the East it was 40 days.

Quadrages'ima Sunday (1st Sunday in Lent), the Sunday next to Ash Wednesday. Quadragesima originally meant the day on which the forty hours' fast is to commence. Gregory I. extended the forty hours to forty days, and, including the four days from Ash Wednesday, the Sunday is forty days before Easter. *See* ' Sunday.'

Quadrilateral (*The*). The four fortresses of Italy : namely, Peschiëra and Mantua on the Mincio, Verona and Legnano on the Adige. Here the Austrians entrenched themselves after the battle of Solferîno, 24 June, 1859 ; but hostilities were suddenly put an end to by a treaty of peace.

Quadril'ogus. A biography of Thomas Becket, so-called because drawn up from his four contemporary biographers (bk. i. chap. ii.).

Quadrivium. In the 12th and part of the 13th cent. what we now call university students spent four years in the study of the ' Trivium ' (*q.v.*), when they took their degree of Bacheler. The next three years were given to the Quadrivium, which included—

1. Numbers absolute, or arithmetic, chiefly confined to the abacus.

2. Numbers applied to music, chiefly church music.

3. Magnitudes at rest, or geometry, some five or six propositions of Euclid.

4. Magnitudes in motion, or astronomy, which was only astrology, and the way of finding out the movable church festivals.

Quadruple Alliance.

1666. 28 Oct., between the States-General of Holland, Denmark, the Grand Elector, and the Duke of Brunswick-Luneburg, for mutual defence.

1674. Between Denmark, Holland, Germany, and Spain against France; because Louis XIV. had laid claim to Flanders and Franche-Comté. Finding the allies too strong, Louis then abandoned his claim on Flanders, but seized on Franche-Comté, which has ever since remained an integral part of the kingdom, empire, or republic of France.

1718. 2 August, between England, Austria, France, and the United Provinces, against Spain. It was a continuance of the Triple Alliance (*q.v.*), only with the addition of Austria, the fourth power. The immediate cause of this alliance was the effort made by Cardinal Alberōni of Spain to bring about the union of Spain and France, contrary to the terms of the Treaty of Utrecht, and subversive of the balance of power in Europe. This alliance guaranteed the succession of England in the house of Hanover, and that of France in the house of Bourbon; and it furthermore guaranteed that Spain and France should not be united under one crown. Spain accepted the conditions in 1720, when she resigned Sicily to Austria, and Sardinia was settled on the Duke of Savoy.

1745. Between England, Austria, Holland, and Saxony, in support of Maria Theresa queen of Austria, who was attacked by the King of Bavaria and the King of Prussia (Frederick II. the Great).

1834. Between England, Belgium, France, and Spain ; to put down the Carlists in Spain, and maintain Isabella on the Spanish throne.

1840. Between England, France, Portugal and Spain, to support Maria da Gloria on the throne of Portugal, Queen Isabella on the

throne of Spain, and to compel Mehemet Ali pasha of Egypt to withdraw from an attack on Turkey by the bombardment of Acre.

Quæsto'res Classici. Roman magistrates who had the charge of the public treasury. Called *classics* because they were originally elected by the centuries. Their number at first was *two* ; increased to *four* in B.C. 421 ; to *eight* soon after the Punic war ; to *twenty* in the time of Sulla ; and to *forty* in the time of Julius Cæsar.

Quæsto'res Parricidii, *i.e.* trackers of murder. The most ancient of the quæstorial magistrates of Rome. They were, later on, made public assessors, and ceased to exist in B.C. 366, when their duties were transferred to the 'Triumviri Capitāles.'

Quaker Poet (*The*). Bernard Barton (1784–1849).

Quakers, 1650. A religious sect founded by George Fox. Their great doctrine is that all religion consists in the inward operation of the Holy Spirit. They have no sacraments, no ordained ministers, are very serious in deportment, sober in dress, reject oaths, refuse the payment of tithes, use *thou* and *thee* instead of *you*, and call the days of the week and the months 1st, 2nd, and 3rd, &c. instead of Monday, Tuesday, &c., January, February, March, &c. They call themselves 'Friends.' The word 'Quaker' is used as a term of disrespect. *See* 'Nicolites.'

It is said that they were called Quakers because Fox, who had been imprisoned by the Puritans, when brought before Gervas Bennet, bade his judge 'quake and tremble at the judgments of God.' Be this as it may, no body of Christians even approach them in morality.

Quakers' 'Confession of Faith' (*The*) contains twenty-three articles by Robert Barclay (Evans, 'Exposition,' p. 67).

Quakers of Germany (*The*). The Moravians (*q.v.*).

Qualification (*Property*). Before Locke King's bill in 1859 all members of parliament were obliged to swear that they possessed a clear estate in perpetuity of 501*l.* a year (if a county member), and of 300*l.* a year (if a borough member), unless the son of a peer.

The argument that the abolition of the qualification test would encourage men of straw to set up as candidates at elections was met by the fact that this did not happen in Scotland, where no qualification was required.—HOWITT, *History of England* (1859), p. 526.

Qualification Act (*The*). A bill passed in the reign of Queen Anne, obliging every candidate for a seat in the House of Commons to show that he is worth 501*l*. a year in land if for a county, 300*l*. a year if for a borough. Abolished by 29 Vict. c. 22 (1866).

There is another Qualification Act, but that is for *killing game*, 22, 23 Car. II. c. 25. Abolished by 1, 2 Will. IV. c. 32.

Qualifiers. Officials in the 'Congregation of the Holy Office' (*q.v.*), whose duty it is to report on each case of suspected heresy for the information of the cardinals.

Quarantaine-le-Roi (*La*), 1245. An ordinance by St. Louis which rendered it a capital offence for an 'avenger of blood' to seek the death of the offender till full forty days had elapsed. In other words, there was to be a truce of forty days between the offence and the license of the kinsmen of the murdered person to avenge the death. This ordinance put an end to the *guerres privées* of France.

Quaranti. The forty. Three tribunals of Venice were composed of forty members: (1) The tribunal of appeal from the judgment of the *city* magistrates; (2) the tribunal of appeal from the sentences of the magistrates *extra muros*; and (3) the criminal tribunal for all crimes except high treason.

Quare Impedit. A writ to inquire why a bishop has refused to institute to a living a legal presentee.

Pronounce *Quair'-re im'-pe-dit.*

Quarrel of Friars (*The*), 1518. So the Lutheran controversy was contemptuously termed at Rome.

Quarta Luna Nati. Born to ill-luck, like Herculês, who was so born. According to tradition Abel was born on the fourth day of the moon, and was slain by his brother on the seventh day of the moon.

Quarter Licence (*A*). A marriage licence after banns, limited to three calendar months. After the expiration of three months new banns must be asked if marriage has not been solemnized.

Quarter Sessions. A court of justices of the peace held every three months in each county or borough for judicial and other business. The meetings are fixed by statute for the first full week after 28 Dec. (Epiphany), the first full week after 31 March (Easter), the first full week after 24 June (Trinity), and the first full week after 11 Oct. (Michaelmas) Sessions.

The jurisdiction of the Court of Quarter Sessions is confined to criminal business, not including treason, murder, capital felony, blasphemy, perjury, forgery, arson, bigamy, abduction, bribery, sedition, &c.

Quarterings. Subdividing an armorial shield so that the son of an heiress or co-heiress at her death may marshal the coat of their mother or their own paternal coat.

Besides the maternal arms the arms of all those to which the mother was entitled may be quartered according to seniority:

Quartermaster (*The*). An officer on the staff of each regiment, in which he ranks as lieutenant. His duties are to superintend the quarters, barracks, and kits of the regiment; to assign to each officer his rooms, and act as regimental storekeeper. After ten years' service he may retire with the honorary rank of captain.

In the navy the quartermaster is appointed by the captain, and his duties are to take charge of the stowage of ballast and provisions, coiling of ropes, keeping time by the sand-glasses, &c. The ship's quartermaster receives 41*l*. 1*s*. 3*d*. a year.

Quartermaster-General (*The*). A staff-officer whose duty it is to arrange the marches, quarters, and internal arrangements of the army to which he belongs. His salary is 173*l*. 7*s*. 6*d*. besides his pay.

Quartermaster-Sergeant. A non-commissioned officer whose duty it is to assist the quartermaster. He receives daily 2*s*. 8*d*. in the infantry of the line, 3*s*. 2*d*. in the cavalry, and 3*s*. 9¼*d*. in the artillery.

Quartodec'iman Pasch. The Easter of the Quartodecĭmans (*q.v.*).

Quartodec'imanism. The heresy of the Quartodecĭmans (*q.v.*).

Quartodec'imans (*The*), or 'Paschites' (2 syl.) 2nd cent. Christians who celebrated Easter on the fourteenth day of the first moon, whether Sunday or not, in imitation of the Jews. In 196

Pope Victor excommunicated all those who held Easter on any day but Sunday. The dispute was not finally settled till 325 in the Council of Nice, which prescribed the rule that 'the festival of Easter shall be held on the Sunday next after the fourteenth day of the first lunar month.'

The Asiatic churches followed the quartodecuman practice, which they traced to the apostles John and Philip.

The Western churches supported their views on the authority of Peter and Paul.

Reperimus quosdam . . . quartodecima luna cum Hebræis celebrare nitentes [i.e. celebrate the 'immolation of Christ'].—BEDE, ii. ch. 19.

Quasimo'do Sunday. The first Sunday after Easter. The introïtus (or beginning of the mass) commences with the word 'Quasimodo.' See 'Sunday.'

Sometimes called 'Dominica in albis,' because the neophytes who had been baptized at Easter wore their white dresses for the last time on Quasimodo Sunday, the octave of Easter Day.

Quatre Nations (*Les*), 1661. An ancient college of Paris founded by Mazarin for the gratuitous education and bringing up of sixty sons of poor gentlemen of Spain, Italy, Germany, or Flanders. It is now 'Le Palais de l'Institut.'

Quatre Premières Filles de Citeaux (*Les*). The four chief Cistercian abbeys of France, viz. La Ferté, Pontigny, Clairvaux, and Morimond.

Quatre Temps (*Les*). The three days' fast (Wednesday, Friday, and Saturday) at the beginning of each of the four seasons. These are ordination times. These fasts were introduced into France in 769, and Gregory VII. fixed the weeks in which the four fasts were to be held; called also Ember-days.

The Greek Church does not keep the Quatre Temps.

Queen (*The White*). 'La Reine Blanche.' Mary queen of Scots was so called by the French because she dressed in *white mourning* for her husband, François II. king of France.

Queen Anne's Bounty, 2, 3 Anne, c. 11, 7 Feb., 1704. An act of parliament by order of the queen to appropriate her revenue arising from the tenths and first-fruits to the augmentation of small livings and to aid the poor of the clergy. The income was 17,000*l.* a year, to which parliament added an annual grant of 100,000*l.*, and private individuals have still further increased the fund.

These first-fruits and tenths were originally sent to Rome. Henry VIII. added them to the crown revenue. They are calculated according to the value set down in the 'Liber Regis.'

Queen Anne's Dead. Addison announced this in the 'Spectator' long after it was public property, and in 1889 his letter containing the announcement was sold by Sotheby & Wilkinson at a literary sale.

Queen Bess's Day, 18 Nov., when the pope and the devil were burnt in effigy. In Queen Anne's reign the 'Pretender' was added.

Queen Dick. Richard Cromwell was so called from his want of spirit and manliness (1626, 1658–1660, died 1712).

Queen Eleanor Crosses. Nine crosses erected by the executors of Queen Eleanor, the wife of Edward I. (1) Lincoln, (2) Northampton, (3) Stony Stratford, (4) Woburn, (5) Dunstable, (6) St. Albans, (7) Waltham, (8) Cheap in London, and (9) Charing Cross in London. Of these the crosses at Northampton and Waltham have been restored, and the cross of Charing Cross, pulled down by the Long Parliament 1647, has been built in facsimile in Charing Cross Station. There are two other Queen Eleanor crosses not included in the nine, one at Geddington and one at Newark.

Holinshed's story is contradicted by the MS. discovered in 1841. See p. 287, 'Eleanor Crosses.'

Queen Henry. Henrietta Maria, wife of Charles I., was so prayed for in the royal chapel, her French name Henriette being distasteful to English ears.

Queen Margaret's Cave, Northumberland. After the battle of Hexham in 1464, Queen Margaret and her son Prince Edward were concealed in a cave on the south bank of a little stream which runs at the foot of Blockhill. Here they lay concealed till they escaped to Scotland.

Queen Sarah. The imperious Sarah Jennings duchess of Marlborough, the queen of Queen Anne (1660–1744).

Queen Anne only reigned, while Queen Sarah governed.—*Temple Bar*, 208.

Queen Square Hermit (*The*). Jeremy Bentham, who lived at No. 1 Queen Square, London (1748–1832).

Queen Victoria. Her name according to Lodge's 'Peerage' is Alexan-

drina-Victoria, but according to ' Men of
the Time,' Victoria-Alexandrina [Guelf].
Her husband's name was Francis Albert
Augustus Charles Emanuel [Wetter];
whence the queen is sometimes jocosely
called ' Mrs. Wetter.'

Some add Busiri to the prince's name.

Queen of Beauty (*The*). The
Duchess of Somerset, grandmother of
Lady Houghton, who died 1887.

Queen of Hearts (*The*). Elizabeth
Stuart, daughter of James I. of England,
was so called by her friends, but her
enemies called her the Snow Queen (*q.v.*).
She was not only lovely, but of a most
kindly disposition, and was by her own
mother called the ' Good Palatine.' She
married Friedrich, the elector palatine
[king of Bohemia], by whom she had
eight sons and five daughters. One of
her sons was the famous Prince Maurice,
and her youngest daughter was Sophia,
mother of George I. (1596–1662).

Queen of Heaven (*The*).
I. So Kao-tsong emperor of China
called his wife (Voo-chee). Kao-tsong
reigned in China 650–684.

Voo-Chee was a most infamous woman, the
Catharine de' Medici of China.

II. The Virgin Mary is so called by
Catholics, but not by Protestants.

Queen of Sheba (*The*). ' Nicaulis '
is the name given in the church of Allhallows, London, where is a large painting on cloth, with the effigy of Queen
Elizabeth lying on her tomb. The first
two lines of the inscription are :—

Read but her reign, this princess might have been
For wisdom called Nicaulis, Sheba's queen.

. The Arabs call her ' Balkis ' or ' Belkis '; the
Abyssinians call her ' Macqueda '; others call her
' Aazis.' It is said, on her return to Sheba [or
Azal], that she changed her son's name ' Menilek '
into ' David.'

Queen of Tears (*The*). Mary of
Mo·ĕna, second wife of James II. of
England, who was for ever weeping for
the crown which her own ill policy contributed to lose (1658–1718).

Queen of the Adriatic (*The*).
Venice.

Queen of the Ægean. Lesbos.

Queen of the Antilles [*An-teel*].
Cuba.

Queen of the Desert. The foolish
title which Lady Hester Lucy Stanhope
tried to assume (1776–1839).

Queen of the East. Zenobia
queen of Palmyra (reigned 266–273).

**Queen of the Eastern Archi-
pel'ago.** Java.

Queen of the Euxine (*The*).
Sebastopol.

Queen of the Lakes (*The*).
Windermere, partly in Lancaster and
partly in Westmoreland. The largest
lake in England.

Queen of the Mediterranean
(*The*). Carthage, during her maritime
supremacy—that is, before the Punic
Wars had discrowned her.

**Queen of the Mississippi
Valley.** St. Louis, Missouri.

Queen of the North. Edinburgh.

Queen of the Northern Seas.
Queen Elizabeth was so called because
of her powerful navy (1533, 1558–1603).

Great Britain, for a similar reason, is called
' Queen of the Ocean' or ' Queen of the Seas.'
Hence the pun ' If Britannia rules the waves, I
wish she'd rule them a little straighter.'
Tyre was also called ' Queen of the Sea.'

Queen of the South. Queen
of Sheba or Saba (*q.v.*).

The queen of the south . . . . came from the
uttermost parts of the earth to hear the wisdom
of Solomon.—Matthew xii. 42; 1 Kings x. 1.

Queens' College. I. In *Cambridge* University, founded by Queen
Margaret of Anjou, consort of Henry VI.,
in 1448, and refounded in 1465 by Elizabeth Woodville, consort of Edward VI.
The head of Queens' College is called the
president.

II. *Oxford*, 1340, founded by Robert
de Eglesfield, chaplain to Queen Philippa,
wife of Edward III. The headmaster is
called the provost.

Queen's Day, 17 Nov. The day of
the accession of Queen Elizabeth (1533,
1558–1603).

Queen's Evidence, or ' King's
Evidence.' The disclosure of a guilty
transaction by one of the guilty party on
the assurance of freedom from punishment. Such an impeacher of his accomplices is said ' to turn queen's evidence.'

Queen's Gap (*The*) at Hampden.
So called because Griffith Hampden, Esq.,
cut this passage through his wood when
Queen Elizabeth went to visit him.

Evelyn did the same when Peter the Great
visited his seat at Wotton, in Surrey.

Queen's Herb (*The*). Snuff was so called, at least in France, in the 16th cent. in compliment of Catherine de' Medici, who was passionately fond of it.

Queen's Men (Scotch history). *See* p. 490, 'King's and Queen's Men.'

Queen's Poisoner (*The*). Master René, employed by Catherine de' Medici, the queen-mother of Charles IX. He poisoned Jeanne d'Albret, mother of Henri [IV.] of France, on her visit to the court to be present at the marriage of her son Henri to the Princess Marguerite, the sister of Charles IX. Jeanne d'Albret arrived at the court on 15 May; fell ill 4 June, died 9 June, being poisoned by a pair of gloves sent to her by the Florentine perfumer.

Queen's University (Ireland), 1850, founded by Queen Victoria.

Queen's Ware, 1763. A durable earthenware first manufactured by Wedgwood, and patronised by Queen Charlotte.

Queenstown (Ireland), 1848. 'Cove' was so named from the visit of Queen Victoria accompanied by Prince Albert, the Prince of Wales, Prince Alfred, the Princess Royal, and the Princess Alice. Just as 'Dunleary' was christened *Kingstown* in honour of the visit of George IV. in 1821.

Queries (*Constitutional*), 1750. Papers aimed against the Duke of Cumberland, and distributed through the penny post to each member of both houses of parliament. These papers are generally attributed to Lord Egmont. Burnt by the common hangman.

Horace Walpole says the imputations made in the 'Queries' were: (*a*) that the Duke of Cumberland had disgraced or dismissed old officers, men of family and property, to make way for slaves, boys, and beggars; (*b*) that he had acquired absolute power over the army, and was trying to make himself master of the fleet; (*c*) that he had shown in Scotland an army superior to law; (*d*) that the right of succession was endangered by him.

Queries (the second paper), 1751, respecting the imprisonment in Newgate of Mr. Murray, M.P., who was accused by the bailiff of threatening his life during the election. Murray refused to receive on his knees the judgment of the house, saying he would kneel to no mortal man or set of men, and was committed to Newgate for contempt, where he remained till the close of the sessions. The 'Queries' condemned the Commons for acting *ultra vires*.

Qui tam. An action partly at the suit of the crown and partly at that of an informer. So called from the first two words, 'Qui tam pro domina regina, quam pro se ipso, sequitur.'

Quia Empto'res (*The Statute of*), 18 Edw. I. st. 1, c. 1, A.D. 1290. Making it lawful for every freeman to sell at pleasure his lands and tenements, or any part of them, under the proviso that the new feofee shall hold them of the chief lord thereof by the same service as the previous one held them. In other words, the sub-tenant was to hold of the lord or proprietor, not of the tenant. Emptōres (3 syl.).

Qui'etists. Those Christians who consider the highest state of man is stoical indifference to all temporal matters, and an unremitted contemplation of religious subjects. Like the Buddhists they place perfection in divine repose. Mme. Guyon, the mystic, was the founder of *Quietism* in France in the reign of Louis XIV. *See* 'Molinos.'

The Hesychasts or monks of Mount Athos would pass whole days looking at their own navels. Mme. Guyon of France was a very celebrated Quietist, and so was Molinos in Spain.

Quindecemviri. A college of priests instituted by Tarquinius Superbus to take charge of the Sibylline books, and they alone could consult them. It was Sylla who increased the number to 15; originally there were only 2, and the intermediate number was 10; they wore the toga prætexta, and were elected for life. This college continued to the time of Theodosius.

Quini-sext. A supplemental council to the fifth and sixth general councils. The fifth was held in 553 on the subject of the 'Three Chapters'; and the sixth held in 660 to condemn the Monoth'elites (4 syl.) (*q.v.*). In 692 some 211 bishops met in a hall (called Trullus) of the imperial palace at Constantinople. It laid down a law respecting celibacy which greatly displeased the Western Church, and prohibited fasting on Saturday even in Lent. The Pope of Rome reprobated the acts of the Quinisext Council, which pronounced the 'Apostolic Constitutions' to be apocryphal.

Quinque five, *sex* six. The council is by the

Greeks called the Πεντεκτη, from πεντε five, and εκτος sixth.

Quinquagesi'ma Sunday. The fiftieth day before Easter Sunday, or rather the period when fifty special services will be held before Easter. In all such ecclesiastical terms as Septuagesima, Sexagesima, Quinquagesima, and Quadrigesima, the week is reckoned as a ten-day week, because its octave and two eves are reckoned in. Quinquagesima Sunday precedes Ash Wednesday. *See* ' Sundays.'

1 Eve of Sunday, 2 Sunday, 3 Monday, 4 Tuesday, 5 Wednesday, 6 Thursday, 7 Friday, 8 Saturday, 9 Octave eve, 10 Octave. So in music 7 notes with the octave of the 1st we call an ' octave,' and the 3 days of the entombment were 1 eve of Saturday, 2 Saturday, 3 eve of Sunday.

Quin'quartic'ularControversy (*The*), 1618–1619. The controversy of the five points of dispute between Calvin and Arminius. The Synod of Dort was convened to settle this controversy, but, as it excluded all Arminians, it was a one-sided synod of no authority.

Quin'quartic'ular Grace, consisting of five articles. That is the five articles representing justification and grace, and in which reformers did not agree, but which the Synod of Dort met to settle.

The door was thrown wide by a lackey in lace,
Saying, ' What may you please to want with his Grace ?'
' His Grace!' quoth Jerome, for posed was he
To guess of what kind this Grace could be—
Whether Grace *preventive*, or Grace *particular*,
Or Grace of that sort called *quinquarticular*.
THOMAS MOORE, *St. Jerome's Visit to Earth*.

Quinquatria. A Roman festival of five days in honour of Minerva, opened on the 14th of the calends of April (*i.e.* 19th March), the birthday of the goddess. On the first day all went to the temple of Minerva to pay their adorations, the next three days were given to games and gladiatorial exhibitions, and the fifth day was devoted to the purification of the sacred trumpets. The festival was a school holiday time.

Quinta'na, or ' Quadrages'ima Sunday,' the 1st in Lent, ' quinta a paschate.'
This is the ' Dominica Brandônum,' or ' Dominica Barârum.' *See* ' Sunday.'

Quintus Cur'tius (*The ·Modern*). René de Vertot (1655–1735), author of the histories of the ' Revolution of Rome,' the ' Revolution of Portugal,' the ' Revolution of Sweden,' ' History of the Bretons,' ' History of Malta,' &c.

Quinze-Vingts. A hospital founded in Paris in 1254 by St. Louis for 300 ' gentilhommes à qui les Sarrasins avaient crevé les yeux,' and whom the king brought home with him from the Holy Land. It stood between the Louvre and the Palais Royal.

Quinze-vingts means 15 twenties, *i.e.* 300. The French numerals are the very acme of absurdity. Can anything exceed the folly of such a number as ' Four-twenty sixteen,' &c. ?

Quiri'tes (3 syl.). So the Sabines were called; but when the Sabines became fused with the Romans, the civilians of the united people were called Quirites. The soldiers never by any chance were addressed as Quirītes except by way of reproach. A general always addressed his troops as *milites* (3 syl.) ; hence Cæsar greatly mortified his rebellious legions on one occasion by calling them *Quirites* instead of *milites*.

In 1890 the Duke of Cambridge snubbed the rebellious 2nd Grenadier Guards in a similar way.

Quit Rent. A small rent paid by tenants of old manors to acquit them ' of service.' Also called ' White Rent ' (*q.v.*).

Quo Warranto. A writ demanding to be shown by what right a person holds an office, estate, &c. Regulated by Edward I. Charles II. made great use of these writs to evict Nonconformists, that the old Church livings might return to the Anglican clergy. Corporations were served by *quo warrantos*, and received back their charters shorn of their privileges.

Quoad Sacra. A term applied in Scotland to auxiliary churches built in large parishes, which already contain parish kirks. These chapels of ease have no territorial jurisdiction, and are usually supported by private or voluntary subscriptions.

Quorndon Pack. Mr. Osbaldeston's pack of hounds, one of the three packs of the old Melton Mowbray Hunt, established in 1759. The other two were the Duke of Rutland's hounds, and the Earl of Lonsdale's pack called the Cottesmore. The Melton Mowbray Hunt is a thing of the past, but the Rutland hounds, the Quorn and the Cottesmore hounds are still celebrated (1890).

Quorndon is in Leicestershire, and Cottesmore Park in Rutlandshire. Quorndon is always shortened into Quorn.

Quorum (*A*). The minimum legal number of a board, sufficient to discharge the business. Sometimes those who are to form the quorum are selected out of the general number. Thus if the general number is represented by the letters of the alphabet, a statute might direct that the five vowels should constitute the quorum or acting members.

R. Placed against a sailor's name in the muster-book of a man-of-war, stood for ' run ' [away] or deserter. Technically they were said to be *prickt run*, and so long as the letter remained uncrossed, the man was not entitled to bounty-money or promotion. *See* ' C. P.'

R. *The Pope marked with* 3 *R's.* Silvester II. who held the sees of Reims, Ravenna, and Rome.

Race of Stenkil (*The*). The third line of Swedish kings, so called from Stenkil, who reigned from 1056–1066. This race, which furnished five kings, succeeded that of Ivar, and was followed by the race of Sverker. It continued from 1056–1129.

Race of Sverker (*The*). In Sweden ; so called from Sverker the founder (1129-1155). It succeeded the race of Stenkil, and continued alternating with it from 1129–1250, when the ' Folkungs ' or *Jarls* succeeded.

Racine's Monkey. ' Le Singe de Racine.' So J. G. de Campistron was called (1636-1723).

Radcliffe Library (*The*). In the University of Oxford, 1747, founded by Dr. John Radcliffe, Fellow of Lincoln. The building is now used as a reading-room in connection with the Bodleian Library (*q.v.*), and the books on natural science have been removed to the University museum. The librarian has a salary of 150*l.* a year.

Radcliffe Travelling Fellowships. Three of the annual value of 200*l.* each, tenable for three years. Candidates must have passed their B.A. degree, and must travel abroad with a view of studying medicine. Founded in the University of Oxford by Dr. Radcliffe, 1858.

Radical. A political party. The word came into use in England about 1816 ; the general character of radicalism is democratic and republican.

Radom (*The Confederation of*), 1767. A confederation of the dissidents of Poland, who applied to Russia for aid against the patriots, called the Confederation of Bar (*q.v.*). This interference of Russia led to the partition of Poland. *See* ' Dissidents.'

Russia, glad to have a pretence for getting a footing in Poland, supported the Confederation of Radom. She pressed on the whole line of the Polish frontier with her armies, inundated the kingdom with her troops, and levied contributions for their support, as if she had been in a conquered country. France supported the confederates of Bar.—HOWITT, *Hist. of England* (Geo III. chap. iv. p. 96).

Radstadt (*Peace of*), 1714. Between Germany and France. It preserved to France its frontiers, and gave to Germany, Naples, Sardinia, Milan, and the Netherlands all taken from Spain. This treaty ended the war of the Spanish Succession, which had lasted twelve years.

Raffael. *See* ' Raphael.'

Rag (*The*). Episcopacy was so called in the 17th cent. by the Presbyterians. The term is a contracted form of ' the rag of the woman of Babylon.'

Though Leighton restored many of the Scotch ministers to vacant parishes, the most violent gloried in the name of Covenanters, and persisted in preaching in conventicles against ' the rag.'— PRINCE, *Parallel History*, vol. ii. p. 303.

Rag (*The*). A familiar name of the Army and Navy Club. The rag, of course, is the flag.

Ragged Schools. Opened in London 1838 ; in Aberdeen 1841. The *Union* established in 1844.

Ragman Roll (*The*), 1296. A list of all the Scotch barons and men of note who subscribed the submission to Edward I. It contains the largest and most authentic enumeration extant of the nobility, barons, landholders, burgesses, and clergy of Scotland prior to the 14th cent., and only genuine statistical notices of Scotland of the period. There are four rolls consisting of thirty-five pieces sewn together. A copy is preserved in the Rolls House, Chancery Lane, but the original no longer exists.

Ragman is a corruption of Ragimund, the name of a legate of Scotland who compelled the clergy of Scotland to give a true account of their benefices, that they might be duly taxed.

Ragmans. Long written documents, such as bulls, charters, patents, lists of names, &c. Rymer, in the ' Fœdera,' speaks of *literas patentes, vocata ragge-*

mans, sive blank chartres. Piers Plow-man says 'Rede on this ragman, and rewle you theraftur.'

Henry IV. issued a proclamation commanding all the blank bonds, called ragmans, which had been extorted from the people by Richard and his courtiers, to be made null and committed to the flames.—HOWITT, *Hist. of England*, vol. i. p. 481.

Raid (*The*), 1468. In Scotch history means the removal to Edinburgh of James III. at the age of fourteen by Robert lord Boyd and his two sons. His guardian Kennedy archbishop of St. Andrews being dead, the estates of Scotland appointed a new regency. The king wished to act for himself, and the Boyds helped him. The parliament sanctioned the raid.

According to Prof. Skeat. *raid* is from *ride*. Its usual meaning is a foray, or predatory excursion in border warfare.

Raid of Carlisle (*The*), 1596. This was the seizure of Kinmont Willie, a noted depredator upon the English border, during a day of truce. Sir Walter Scott of Buccleuch, warden of the Scottish border, held a day of truce for meeting the deputy of Lord Scroope, governor of Carlisle Castle. When the meeting broke up, the English on their return home saw Willie, and took him prisoner. Buccleuch sent a challenge to Lord Scroope, which was insolently declined. Whereupon he assembled his clansmen, forced his way into the castle, and set Willie free. Elizabeth demanded that Buccleuch should be delivered into her hands; this the Scotch parliament refused to do, but Buccleuch consented to appear before the queen to explain the whole matter. The queen was so pleased with his manly bearing and bold spirit, that she dismissed him with tokens of honour and regard.

Raid of Leith (*The*), 2 April, 1594. An attack of the Earl of Bothwell to get possession of the king's person on his return from church at Leith, on Sunday morning 2 April, 1594. Bothwell failed in this attempt.

In his proclamation, distributed at the raid of Leith, the Catholic lords were designated 'enemies of the true religion, and the practisers for bringing in of strangers; a company of lewd persons crept into the state to the high contempt of God and dishonour of the king.'—Sir W. SCOTT, *Hist. of Scotland*, xxxviii.

Raid of Ruthven (*The*), 1582. The forcible detention of James VI. at Ruthven Castle, to which he had been invited in a hunting expedition, by Alexander Ruthven earl of Gowrie. The object of this detention was to compel the king to dismiss his favourites, the Duke of Lennox and Stewart earl of Arran. *See* p. 380, 'Gowrie Conspiracy.'

Raid, in Scotland, was applied to any assembly met together in arms to enforce their will. Thus the barons who forced from John the Magna Charta would be called in Scotland the Raid of Runnymede.

Raid of Stirling (*The*), 1585. An armed attack on Stirling Castle, where James Stewart earl of Arran and chief minister of James VI. was cooped up. He defended the castle for a time, but had neither men, arms, nor provisions for a siege. Arran, therefore, fled, and having the key of Stirling Bridge, made good his escape by locking the gates behind him to prevent pursuit. Arran was dismissed the public councils, and lived in private as James Stewart.

Rail Splitter (*The*). President Abraham Lincoln. So called because at one time he earned his bread by splitting rails (1809–1865).

Railway King (*The*). George Hudson (1800–1871).

Railway Mania (*The*), 1845, when all the country went mad on railway speculations. The advertisements of projected railways in the 'Times' newspaper were from 3,000*l.* to 6,000*l.* weekly in the months of September, October, and November. Railways proper (with Robert Stephenson's locomotives) were first opened in England and America in 1830, between Manchester and Liverpool. Brunel introduced the *broad gauge* in 1833. Railways were not practically introduced into France till 1845, when the Chemin de fer du Nord was opened. The Chemin de fer de l'Ouest was opened in 1846; and that between Paris and Lyons in 1851.

'Chemin de fer' pronounce *Shmand fair.* 'Shmand' to rhyme with *darned* (silent).

Rajah of Mattan (*The*). If the Braganza is *not* a diamond, the Rajah of Mattan is the largest diamond known. Its original weight was 787 carats; but being given to Borgis, a Venetian, to cut, it was reduced to $379\frac{9}{10}$ carats. Borgis was fined 10,000 rupees for his waste, and received nothing for his cutting. *See* 'Diamonds.'

Raleigh Conspiracy (*The*), 1603. This was the 'Main Plot' (*q.v.*) to seize James I. and set Arabella Stuart on the throne. Raleigh and others were arrested. Clarke and Watson were hanged; Brooke was beheaded; Cobham, Grey, and Markham were pardoned; and Raleigh was reprieved and released from the Tower 30 Jan., 1616. He then sailed for Guiana, returned in 1618, was again arrested for complicity in the 'Main Plot,' and beheaded 29 Oct., 1618.

Ramadan. The ninth month in the Moslem year. It is a kind of Lent or fast in commemoration of the first revelation received by Mohammed. A strict Moslem must not eat or drink, smoke or bathe, smell any perfume, or even swallow his own spittle till after sunset. This fast is followed by the festival called 'Bairam' (*q.v.*).

The word 'Ramadan ' means the 'hot month,' from the Arabic *ramidāh*, or *ramaddh*, ' to be hot.'

Rambam. A sonant of 'R. M. B. M.,' that is, Rabbi Moses Ben Maimon, born at Cordŏva in 1135. He wrote commentaries on the Talmuds (Babylonian and Jerusalem), and a work on the Calendar. He is generally called ' Maimonides,' ' the doctor, the great sage, the glory of the West and light of the East, second only to Moses.'

Rambouillet (*L'Hôtel de*), 1600. The society which met in the mansion of the Marquis de Rambouillet, Rue St. Thomas, near the Louvre, Paris. The society consisted of the most distinguished persons in the city. The palmy days of these reunions were from 1635 to 1665. Cardinal Richelieu, Prince Condé, and Montausier were among the magnates, while Racan, Voiture, Benserade, Balzac, Ménage, Chapelain, La Calprenède, Scudéry, D'Urfé, Sarrasin, Desmarets, St. Sorlin, and the Abbé Cottin represented the *beaux esprits*. The ladies who usually attended were the Duchess of Longueville, the Marchioness of Lafayette, Madame de Sévigné, Madame Deshoulières, and the Duchess Montausier (the life and soul of the society). Each guest was nicknamed by some Greek or Roman celebrity, and the ladies were called *Les Précieuses*. At first this society was the arbiter of taste and literature, but it lapsed into prudery and affectation, gibbeted by the 'Précieuses Ridicules' of Molière.

Ramillies Wig (*A*). Introduced in the reign of George I., and so named from the famous battle of Ramillies. It had a long, gradually diminishing, plaited tail, called the ' Ramillie tail,' which was tied with a great bow at the top and a smaller one at the bottom. In 1736 the officers of the horse and foot guards were commanded to wear Ramillie periwigs.

This [the buzz wig] was the paragon of the three yet remaining wigs of the parish, which differed, as Monkbarns used to remark, like the three degrees of comparison—Sir Arthur's Ramillies being the positive, his own bob-wig the comparative, and the overwhelming grizzle [*i.e.* buzz wig] of the clergyman figuring as the superlative.—Sir W. SCOTT, *The Antiquary*, ch. xvii.

Ramists. Those who followed Pierre Ramus in his new pronunciation of Latin. This novelty especially affected such words as contained *qu*, pronounced *k*; as 'quisquis,' pronounced *kiskis*. This innovation produced riots in Paris, just as Sir John Cheke's innovation in the pronunciation of Greek produced riots in Cambridge a few years before. *See* 'Greeks and Trojans.'

Sir John Cheke died 1557; Pierre Ramus fell in the massacre of Barthélemi in 1572.

Ramnes. A Roman gentleman. (*See* Propertius, iv. 1, 31.) A contraction of ' Ramnenses.' Livy (i. 13) says ' a Romulo,' and tells us it was one of the three tribes or centuries into which Romulus divided his people. If ' Roma ' is from ' Romulus,' as we are told by Varro, then, with a little shuffling of the cards, we can get ' Romanenses ' (natives of Rome), contracted into ' Rom'nenses,' and corrupted into ' Ramnes.'

'Tatienses,' the Sabine tribe, from Tatius the Sabine king (Ovid, ' Fast.' iii. 131). The third century or tribe was called ' Luceres ' (strangers). Plutarch says 'a luco, ubi Romuli asylum fuit, ut sint advenæ in hac tribu.'

Ramorantin (*The Edict of*), 1560. Issued by François II. after the conspiracy of Amboise, constituting the bishops judges of heresy, and depriving Huguenots of the right of holding religious assemblies.

Ramparts. Those great masses of earth, about $7\frac{1}{2}$ feet in height, which are thrown up from the ditch inwards in fortification, in order to give the defenders in a siege a commanding surface for their cannon and musketry. The first range of ramparts is called the *body* of the place (or *enceinte*); and all the works between the enceinte and the covered way are called *outworks*. Those constructed beyond the covered way and the glacis, but within the range of the musketry of the main-works, are termed *advanced works*; and those beyond that range are called *detached works*. In the outline or 'tracing of a fortress,' if the angle points outwards towards the country it is called a *salient* angle; if inwards towards the place fortified, it is a *re-entering* angle.

Ramsden Sermon (*The*). On Church Extension. To be preached in full term in St. Mary's Church, Cambridge. Fee, five guineas. A fund was left for the purpose by Mrs. Charlotte Ramsden, of Bath, 1848.

Ranche'ros (*The*). The half-Indian and half-Spanish breed in Mexico. They form by far the best part of the Mexican army. They are a thin muscular race, temperate, daring, and hardy.

Rank and File. The technical phrase for privates and corporals of infantry, often spoken of as 'Bayonets,' from the instrument which they carry.

Ranstadt (*Treaties of*). I. 24 Sept., 1706. A treaty of *peace* between Charles XII. of Sweden and Frederick Augustus of Poland.
II. 22 Aug., 1707, a *Convention* signed at Alt Ranstadt between Charles XII. of Sweden and the kaiser Joseph I.

Ranters. The Primitive Methodists are sometimes so called. They seceded from the Methodists because, in their opinion, the true spirit of Methodism was no longer preserved in the body. By this they meant that too much attention was paid to formality, and that not sufficient fervour was manifested. Field-preaching and street-preaching of an emotional character was strongly advocated. Hugh and J. Bourne, with W. Clowes, were the chief instruments of this separation.

Ranz des Vaches (*The*). Simple melodies played on the Alphorn in the Swiss Alps, or sung by the herdsmen, or both, when they drive their cattle to and from the pasture.

Ranzelman (*A*). A petty magistrate in the Zetland islands, whose office

it is to divide the spoil of wrecks cast on the coast.

> The Ranzelman was dividing with all due impartiality the spoils of the wrecked vessel . . . and, if the matter in hand had not been, from beginning to end, utterly unjust and indefensible, discharging the part of a wise and prudent magistrate.—Sir W. SCOTT, *The Pirate*, chap. viii.

Rape of the Sabines, 8th cent. B.C. Romulus, wishing to find wives for his new city, invited the Sabines and other neighbouring towns to come and see his *consualia*, or public games, in honour of the god Consus, and when the spectators were intent on the show, a number of Roman youths rushed in among them, and seized all the marriageable maidens on whom they could lay hands.

> A very similar incident is recorded in Judges xxi. 19-23.

Raphael (*The Flemish*). Frans Floris. His chief works are 'St. Luke at his Easel,' and the 'Descent of the Fallen Angels,' both in Antwerp Cathedral (1520–1570).

Raphael (*The French*). Eustace Lesueur (1617–1655).

Raphael the Divine. Raffaello Sanzio il Divino (1483–1520), the greatest of all painters. His first works were under the influence of Perugīno, such as the 'Coronation of the Virgin,' in the Vatican, and the 'Marriage of the Virgin,' at Milan. His second class of paintings (1504–1508) were of the Florentine school, of which class is 'St. Catharine,' in the National Gallery, London. The cartoons in Hampton Court are of the third or Roman class.

Raphael of Cats (*The*). Godefroi Mind, a Swiss painter (1768–1814).

Raphael of Holland (*The*). Martin van Hemskerck (1498–1574).

Raphael of Opera or of **Music** (*The*). J. C. Wolfgang Mozart (1756–1791).

Raphael's Sketch Book ought to be called the 'Venice Sketch Book,' as Morelli has proved them to be sketches by Pinturicchio, the Umbrian artist, before Raphael was born. It is preserved in the Accademia delle Belle Arti, in Venice.

Rapparees, 17th cent. Wild Irish plunderers, so called from their being armed with a *rapary*, or half-pike. They were especially numerous in the Bog of Allan, if we may trust Lord Macaulay, who, speaking of newspaper leaders, refers to the 'Rapparees of the Bog of Allan' as one of the items which helped to furnish journals in their early days.

They commonly wear little woollen jackets, breeches close to their thighs, and over them a . . . shag rugg, deeply fringed. They go, for the most part, bareheaded, wear their hair long, and count it the greatest ornament. . . . They count it no infamy to commit robberies, and when they go to rob they make prayers to God that they may obtain booty. . . . They also suppose that violence and murder are in no wise displeasing to God.— GAY MIEGE, *New State of England* (second edition, 1711; Ireland added).

Raskolniks (*The*), 1654. Russian schismatics who opposed the revised translation of the Bible and Liturgies.

Rat, Cat, and the Dog. William Collingham was author of the rhyme (1483)

The rat, the cat, and Lovel the dog,
Rule all England under the hog.

The rat was Rat-cliffe, the cat was Cat-esby, Lovel was Francis viscount Lovel the king's 'spaniel,' and the hog was the blue boar, the crest of Richard III. Collingham was put to death for his too pregnant wit.

Rats. When the Assyrians, B.C. 692, invaded Egypt, Sethos the king raised an army of artisans and labourers. But no battle was fought; for during the night a swarm of rats gnawed to pieces the quivers, bowstrings, and shield-straps of the Assyrians, who at once fled. In honour of this event Sethos had a statue of himself, holding a rat in one hand, erected in the temple of Memnon.

Was not the rat in the hand of Sethos the water-rat, or ichneumon, the god of the people of Heracleopolis?

Rate in Aid (*A*), 1849. Sixpence in the pound to be levied in every county of Ireland towards a general fund for the relief of the poor of that country. The potato disease had reappeared, and this rate more equally divided the burden of supporting the poor by placing a portion of it on shoulders better able to bear it.

Rath (*A*). A hill-fortress, the dwelling of an old Irish chief, built on a natural elevation and surrounded by a rampart. The whole enclosure was the rath, and the chief's dwelling stood within

the area. It was made of wood, mud, and hurdles.

Rational School (*The*), in theology, revived in Germany by Paulus, who produced his 'Commentary of the New Testament' (1800–1804). His object is to show that miracles and all that is beyond man's reason and experience must be discarded.

Rationalism, in theology, is the rejection of everything in religion which cannot be supported by reason, as miracles; and the explaining away of miracles by ascribing the phenomena to natural causes. Thus, in the passage of the Red Sea, the Rationalists maintain that Moses and his host passed when the tide was out, but that Pharaoh and his host were overwhelmed by the returning tide.

Like King John and Lynn Wash.

Rationalists. A fanatical party which arose during the civil war, afterwards called 'Levellers' (1647). John Lilburne (afterwards Colonel Lilburne) was a leading spirit of these republicans. They said the election of Saul by the Jews plainly teaches that kings usurp the place of God, and that lords and princes are denounced in scripture, which teaches the equality of man. Their platform was religious equality; biennial parliaments; six-monthly sessions; a widely extended franchise; and a more equally distributed representation. These Rationalists or Levellers were pretty well the same as the Agitators. *See* Rom. xiii.

Ratisbon, in Bavaria (*Truce of*), 15 Aug., 1684. Between France and Spain on the one hand and the kaiser on the other.

Ratisbon Interim (*The*), in 1541· A provisionary arrangement between the Roman Catholic and Lutheran *ad interim*—that is, till the matters in dispute could be laid before a general council. In the Ratisbon Interim 3 Roman Catholics and 3 Lutherans were appointed to make provisionary measures of agreement. The Roman Catholic deputies were Eck, Pflug, and Gropper; the Lutheran deputies were Melanchthon, Bucer, and Pistorius. They agreed on all points except the sacraments and the power of the Church.

Raven Knight (*The*). John Hunyádi, whose shield had a black raven

3 B

holding a gold ring in his beak painted on it (1400–1456).

Never before had they witnessed fighting as gallant as that of the Raven Knight at the head of his small troop.—VAMBÉRY, *Hungary*, chap. ix.

Rawandians (*The*), A.D. 759. A Saracenic sect believing in metempsychosis.

Rawlinsonian Professorship (*The*) of Anglo-Saxon, in Oxford University. Stipend 300*l.* a year. Founded by Richard Rawlinson, D.C.L., of St. John's College, in 1750.

Rayleigh d'Isgustin (*Sir*). A punning toast (*Really disgusting, Sir*), by way of reproof.

Re Galantuomo, Victor Emmanuel II. (1820–1878), king of Sardinia 1849, king of Italy 1861.

'Here' (said Garibaldi), 'in the presence of our Re Galantuomo, I must be permitted to speak my mind.'—HOWITT, *History of England* (year 1859), p. 539.

Readers = 'Lectores' in the Greek and Latin Churches, were young men studying for the priesthood. They served as secretaries to the bishops, and were promoted according to merit; some, however, never graduated to any higher degree. Tertullian is the first who mentions this office. The readers had charge of all the sacred books, and acted as messengers. By the Fourth Council of Carthage the bishop, on ordaining a reader, had to place a Bible in the hand of the candidate, and say: 'Receive this book, and be a reader of the Word of God. If thou exercise thy ministry faithfully, thou wilt have part with those who administer God's word.'

The lectors used to read the Epistles till Innocent III. appointed the office of sub-deacon in the 10th cent.; but after that the lector only read the lessons at matins.

Reading (*The Council of*), 1279. It enacted that two representatives chosen by the clergy of each diocese shall attend the national synod, to consult respecting the redress of grievances, granting subsidies, and whatever else relates to the well-being of the Church. This is called the nucleus of 'Convocation.'

Pronounce *Red'-ding*.

Real Estate. Land and houses, in opposition to personal property, such as cash, jewels, and furniture. The Romans divided property into immovable (real) and movable (personal). Lands and houses are real because they cannot be carried away; personal property can be moved by the possessor from place to place.

Real Laws. Laws for the regulation of property without interfering with the state of persons.

Les lois réelles n'ont point d'extension directe ni indirecte hors la juridiction et la domination du législateur.—STORY, *Conflict of Laws*, 610.

Real Presence. The dogma that the bread and wine in the eucharist, after consecration, become the veritable and real body and soul, humanity and divinity of Christ. This is called the doctrine of transubstantiation, and is held by the Roman and Eastern Churches. Luther taught the same doctrine with a difference. By transubstantiation is meant that the wine is no longer wine, and the bread is no longer bread after consecration; Luther taught that the bread and wine remained bread and wine, but that the body and soul, humanity and divinity of Christ were incorporated with those elements. This is called the doctrine of con-substantiation. Calvin taught that the body and soul of Christ were taken only by faith, and not substantially by communicants in the eucharist.

Luther's word was *impanation*. As God was incarnate in Christ, so Christ was *impanated*, or introduced into the elements of bread and wine, and incorporated with them.

Real Right. A *jus in re* or right in the thing itself, and not its equivalent; in opposition to *jus ad rem*, or a right to enforce an obligation or the performance of something.

A servant has a *jus in re*, a master a *jus ad rem*. A master must pay his servant *wages*, and cannot instead of wages substitute work. A servant, on the other hand, must give his master *work*, and cannot be allowed to pay money instead. Thus a master, by paying a month's wages in advance, can dismiss a servant; but a servant cannot, by forfeiting a month's wages, quit a master's service. The master's obligation to a servant is *money*; a servant's obligation to a master is *work*.

Realists. Those who believe in realism, or the independent existence of universals. Tree in the abstract is a universal; an oak-tree, an elm, a fir-tree, are particular trees. Now realists maintain that tree exists in the abstract, and is not the hypothetical creature inferred from particular objects. Nominalists say *universalia post rem*, universals are *à posteriori*, and particulars come first. Realists say *universalia ante rem*, that universals precede sensible objects.

In theology we are told that Father, Son, and Holy Ghost are one God. There were certain divines who insisted that these three persons were only three names (*nomina*) of the same Being, as father, son, and husband are three names of the same person. Other theologians insisted that they are not only three names, but three real persons. Guillaume de Champeaux (1053–1120) was the founder of the realistic school.

There is yet a third sort of realism, or belief—viz. that the phenomenal world has an objective existence, quite independent of our perception thereof. To me or you the phenomenal world is what our senses cognise; but even if we were deprived of our senses, and there was no phenomenal world to us, still (say the realists) the phenomena would exist. This realism is opposed to Berkeley's 'Idealism.'

Traced to its origin we come to Plato and Aristotle. Plato insisted that the divine idea is a *real* something, a mould or matrix in which creation was fashioned. Aristotle contended that the Divine *word* was enough; 'he commanded, and it was done.'

** We also speak of realism in art and letters, meaning an imitation of nature, not a fanciful ideal.

Rosceline seems to have raised the question whether the personal distinctions of the Deity are real or only nominal.

St. Anselm of Canterbury, Albertus Magnus, Thomas Aquinas, and Duns Scotus were Realists.

Abelard, William Occam, Buridan, Hobbes, Locke, Bishop Berkeley, Condillac, and Dugald Stewart were Nominalists.

The Realist (as opposed to the Idealist) holds that the phenomenal world has an objective existence. The Idealist contends that it has only a subjective existence. The whole contest may be settled thus: To an individual every phenomenon is only subjective to *him*; that is, his perception of a phenomenon depends upon his senses, but independent of himself the phenomenon is real, or there is a real phenomenon.

Realm of St. Stephen (*The*). Hungary.

Croatia is still a member of the realm of St. Stephen.—VAMBERY, *Hungary*, chap. vii.

Rebecca Riots (*The*), 1843. A crusade against toll-gates begun in Wales. *See* next article.

Rebeccaites, or ' Children of Rebecca,' 1839. Welsh rioters who went about destroying turnpike gates. So called from Rebekah, the bride of Isaac. When she left home her father and friends said to her (Gen. xxiv. 60), ' Let thy seed possess the gate of those which hate thee.' *See* ' Rebecca Riots.'

Also called ' Rebecca's Daughters,' and ' Re-

beccas.' The word has been revived of late in reference to illegal fishing.

'Rebekah's Camels' Bible (*The*), 1823. So called because in Gen. xxiv. 61 the word ' damsels' is misprinted *camels*. Thus: ' And Rebekah arose, and her camels' [damsels]. *See* ' Bibles.'

Rebel Crown (*The*). A silver 5s. piece struck at Kilkenny in the reign of Charles I. There are seven varieties, distinguished by the size of the crown, and the shape of the letter S.

Rebellion (*The Great*). That of the Parliamentarians against Charles I. of England. It began in August, 1642, when Charles set up his standard at Nottingham, and terminated with the Restoration of Charles II., 29 May, 1660.

Rebellion of Paraguay (*The*), 1750. The Spanish Jesuits succeeded in forming a flourishing colony, amounting to 200,000 individuals, in Paraguay and Parâna, which for a century and a half enjoyed both peace and happiness; then Spain gave up seven districts of Paraguay to Portugal in exchange for certain territory on the left bank of the river Plate, and ordered the colony to remove. The Indians resisted, and this resistance was called rebellion. Ultimately the matter was arranged, and the colony remained undisturbed.

Rebellion of Shane O'Neil, in Ulster, 1561. On the death of O'Neil earl of Tyrone a dispute arose respecting the succession. England acknowledged the eldest son as heir to the earldom, while the sept maintained their right of choosing a chief from any of the family, and selected a younger son. Shane O'Neil made good his claim by the sword, and having defeated the lord deputy invaded Connaught. He was defeated by Colonel Randolph in 1566, took refuge in Antrim, and was hewn to pieces, June 1567, in a drunken squabble by his Scotch retainers.

Rebellion of 1715 (*The*), when the Chevalier de St. George landed in Scotland. James Francis Edward, son of James II., was defeated at Preston Nov. 1715, and the cause was resumed in 1745 by his son Charles Edward. *See* below, ' Rebellion of 1745.'

These were reasons which unquestionably operated to prevent [in 1708] that bloody retaliation which followed the rebellions of 1715 and 1745.—HOWITT, *Hist. of Eng.* (Anne, 245).

Rebellion of 1745 (*The*), when Charles, afterwards the 'Young Pretender,' landed in Scotland. Charles Edward Stuart proclaimed his father 'James VIII. of Scotland,' and defeated the royal troops at Prestonpans (22 Sept., 1745), and at Falkirk (28 Jan., 1746), but was defeated at Culloden (16 April, 1746), and returned to France. At his father's death (31 Jan., 1788) he became 'the Young Pretender.'

Rechabites (3 syl.). The posterity of Jonadab, son of Rechab, who were forbidden to build houses, to plant vineyards, to possess lands, to dwell in tents, and to drink wine. They continued to observe these injunctions for 300 years. (Jer. xxxv. 6, 7.)

They were probably carried away captive by the Chaldeans, as the title of Psalm lxx. is 'Sung by the sons of Jonadab and the principal captives.' They returned from captivity, and settled in the city of Jabez, beyond Jordan.

Reciprocity Acts, 1823 (4 Geo. IV. c. 77; 5 Geo. IV. c. 1), empowering the king, by order in council, to authorise the importation and exportation of goods in foreign ships, provided the foreign country in whose favour the order is made places British ships on the same footing as its own ships. *See* 'Navigation Act.'

Reciprocity Treaty (*The*), 7 June, 1854 (18 Vict. c. 3). Between Great Britain and the United States, regulating British American coast-fisheries, and the navigation of the St. Lawrence and the lakes. Terminated by notice from the United States 17 March, 1866.

Recluse of Edgbaston (*The*). John Henry Newman, created cardinal (1801–1890), author of Tract No. 90, the hymn 'Lead, kindly Light,' and a dramatic poem called 'Gerontius,' with numerous other works.

Recognition (*The Act of*), 1531. That the king and not the pope is 'unicus et supremus dominus' of the English Church; not in the same sense as Christ is head of the Church, but in the sense that he is head of all his subjects, with a right to their allegiance, obedience, and submission in all legalised matters.

Thus the Convocation of York, 1534, unanimously agreed that the Pope of Rome has no

'greater jurisdiction in these realms' than any other foreign bishop. In the Convocation of Canterbury thirty-four assented, one doubted, and four denied the Act as interpreted by the Convocation of York. *See* Article XXXVII.

N.B.—The words 'quantum per Christi legem licet' were afterwards added.

Recognitions (*The*). Quoted by Origen as a work of Clement's; was a romance in ten books embodying the Christian doctrines and history. It was translated by Rufi'nus into Latin and called 'The Acts and Travels of St. Peter.'

Called *Recognitions* because it supposes Clement to recognise his father, mother, and brother, who had been lost.

Récollets (Reformed Franciscans). Established in Spain in 1484, introduced into France in 1592, and into Paris in 1603. Like the Soccolanti they adopted sandals. Reformed Clares and Colettes are called 'Recollettines' (4 syl.).

The word is *Recollecti*, that is *recueillis*. It has reference to spiritual *recollection*—that is, the complete devotion of all the powers to a spiritual life.

Reconciliation (*The Bill of*), 1554. An Act of Parliament repealing the whole ecclesiastical legislation of Henry VIII. and Edward VI. It, however, rejected all proposals for the restoration of church lands, and refused to change the succession from Elizabeth to Philip.

Reconciliation (*The Feast of the*), 25 Jan. (*St. Andrew's Day*), 1555. To commemorate the return of England to the see of Rome in the reign of Mary. It was celebrated by a grand religious procession, and ordered to be kept as an anniversary for ever.

When the pope heard thereof he ordered a jubilee in honour of the event.

Recopilacion (*The*). The code of Castilian law.

The deputies in 1525 obtained a general law, inserted in the Recopilacion, enacting that the king shall answer all the petitions before he dissolves the assembly [Cortes].—HALLAM, *Middle Ages*, vol. ii. p. 43.

Rector. In Oxford University; the title of the head of Exeter College and Lincoln College.

In the Church of England the rector has the great tithes; a vicar merely represents the owner of a living, and receives either an annual stipend or the small tithes.

Recusants. Persons who wilfully absented themselves from their parish church on Sundays and other days appointed by the ordinary. This absence was made a legal offence by 1 Eliz. c. 2,

A.D. 1558. Popish recusants for wilfully hearing mass were fined 66l. 13s. 4d. (100 marks); and for saying mass double that sum, with a year's imprisonment in both cases. They could inherit no real estate, purchase no land, teach in no school, hold no public office, were not permitted to have arms in their houses, could not appear within ten miles of London under a penalty of 100l., could not travel above five miles from home without a licence, could bring no action at law or equity. These enactments were partly removed in 1791, and more fully by the Emancipation Act of 1829.

Recusants (*Statute of*), 25 Henry VIII. c. 20, transferred the annates and tenths from the pope to the crown.

Red and Black Lists (*The*). In the Irish parliament it was customary to publish lists of the Ayes and Noes on every important division. In the Union debates (1799, 1800) this custom was followed. These lists were printed in red and black. Hence the Red and Black Lists are lists of how the Irish members voted on the bills referred to.

Red and Blue Cockade (*The*), 1789. The cockade given to the French militia at the outbreak of the great French Revolution. Red and blue were the Parisian colours. White was the royal colour. Before the militia (or national guard) was organised the insurgents wore a green cockade (*q.v.*). The tricolour was adopted after the fall of the Bastille.

Red and Blue Hoods (*The*). In 1356, during the captivity of Jean le Bon, the Commune of Paris, as opposed to the dauphin (afterwards Charles V.), wore party-coloured hoods, *mi-partie* (*rouges et bleues*); but at the death of the provost Marcel in 1358 this faction died away.

Red or **Cardinal Band** (*The*), 1572. The companies of assassins organized at Bordeaux for the massacre of the Huguenots at the general slaughter begun on Sunday, St. Bartholomew's Day.

Red Beard.
I. Friedrich I. kaiser of Germany, called *Barbarossa* (1121, 1152–1190).

II. Horush or Horuc sultan of Algiers (1474, 1516–1518).
III. Khair Eddin sultan of Algiers (reigned 1518–1546).

Red Book (*The*).
I. In *England* is a register of all persons under government in every department, legal, civil, military, and naval. This register in the American government is termed their 'Blue Book.' The words Red and Blue refer to the colour of the wrappers, but even those parts issued without wrappers retain the generic name. See 'Blue Book.'
II. In *China* (so called from its red cover), contains the name, birthplace, and other particulars of the 14,000 officials of the Chinese empire. It is in six small volumes, and is printed quarterly.

No individual can hold a magistracy in his own province, and no public officer may make alliances with those under his own government; nor can a son, brother, or other near relative hold office under a near kinsman.

Red Book of Hergest (*The*). Includes the Mabinogion (*q.v.*), copies of some of the poems of Taliesin and of Llywarch Hen, a brief chronology from Adam to 1318, and a chronological history of the English to 1376. The MSS. are preserved in the library of Jesus College, Oxford, and are of the 14th cent.

Red Book of Maximilian I. of Germany (*The*). A manual which Maximilian always carried about him, and in which he set down all the injuries which he received from the French, a nation he hated with deadly hatred.

Red Book of the Exchequer (*The*). 'Liber Rubens Scaccarii' (in the Record Office), compiled in the reign of Henry III., 1246, by Alexander de Swereford archdeacon of Shrewsbury. It contains the returns of all tenants *in capite* in the reigns of Henry II., Richard I., John, and part of the reign of Henry III., certifying how many knights' fees they held, and the names of those who held them. It also contains much other matter from the Pipe Rolls and other sources. It has never been printed (1890). The other book is called the Black Book of the Exchequer, 'Liber Niger Scaccarii.' The Red Book derives its name from the colour of its cover, which was originally a pinkish-red leather.

The Red Book contains the only known fragment of the Pipe Roll of 1 Henry II., and copies of the important Inquisition returned into the Exchequer in 13 John.

Red Books of Spain (*The*).

Similar to our Blue Books (*q.v.*). All sorts of official reports, papers, and documents printed for government and laid before the legislative houses. Red and blue refer to the colours of the covers. *See* 'Yellow Books.'

Red Boots (*A Pair of*).

A Tartar phrase referring to a custom of cutting the skin of a victim round the upper part of the legs, and then stripping it off at the feet. A Tartar will say, ' When you come my way again, I will give you a pair of red boots to go home in.'

Red Branch (*Knights of the*).

An early military order of Ireland. So called from their chief seat, ' The School of the Red Branch,' in Emania, adjoining the palace of the Ulster kings. T. Moore refers to these knights in his ' Irish Melodies,' and subjoins a note of explanation :—

Let Erin remember the days of old . . . .
When her kings, with standard of green unfurled,
  Led the Red-branch Knights to danger;—
Ere the emerald gem of the western world
  Was set in the crown of a stranger.

Red Button (*A*).

A mandarin of the first class, whose badge of honour is a red button on his cap.

An interview was granted to the admiral [Elliot] by Kishen, the imperial commissioner, the third man in the empire, a mandarin of first class and red button.—HOWITT, *Hist. of England*, 1841, p. 471.

Red Coat in Fox-hunting.

Henry II. made fox-hunting a royal sport, and enjoined by mandate that all who took part in that royal sport should wear also the royal livery.

Red Columns of Venice (*The*).

Two magnificent columns of red granite erected in the Piazzetta of St. Mark in 1180. They were brought in 1125 from Palestine by Dominico Michielli, the doge, but for more than fifty years were left on the quay because no one knew how to erect them. At length Nicolo Barattiero, a Lombard, succeeded in rearing them. One column is surmounted with the winged lion of St. Mark, and the other with a full-length statue of St. Theodore, armed with sword and lance, and trampling on a serpent. The space between was the site of executions.

St. Theodore carries his shield on his *right* arm and his lance in the left hand.
    Between the pillars of St. Mark's, where 'tis
    The custom of the State to put to death
    Its criminals.—BYRON, *Marino Faliero*, v. 2.
Recanati expiated his treason between the Red Columns.—*History of Venice*, vol. i. p. 350.

Red Comyn (*The*).

Son of John Comyn of Badenoch and Margery sister of John Baliol.

David Earl of Huntingdon had two daughters— Margery and Isabella.
    Margery s son was named Baliol, and Baliol's son was BALIOL (the king). The king's daughter was Margery the mother of John, the ' Red Comyn.'
    Isabella (David's younger daughter) was the mother of BRUCE (the Competitor); the ' Competitor ' had a son named Bruce, whose son was ROBERT BRUCE, the great hero.

Red Cross (*The*).

The Badge of the royal banner of England till those of St. Patrick and St. Andrew were added.

The fall of Rouen (1419) was the fall of the whole province . . . and the red cross of England waved on all the towers of Normandy.—HOWITT, *Hist. of England*, vol. i. p. 545.

Red Cross Knights (*The*).

The Knights Templars, whose badge was a red cross on a white robe in contradistinction to the Knights Hospitallers, who wore a black robe with a white cross. *See* ' Templars.'

Red Cross Society (*The*), 1870.

For the relief of those wounded in battle. It recognises no distinctions of rank, friend, or foe. To be wounded is enough to call forth all its sympathy, all its skill, all its nursing care. The red cross on the field of battle is quite sufficient to command immunity from both belligerent armies. *See* ' Geneva Convention.'

Red Earl (*The*).

Richard Burke or Burgo (1227–1229), earl of Ulster.

Red Flag (*A*).

I. In the *Roman* empire signified war ; and when displayed on the capitol it was a call to arms.

** As a railway signal it intimates danger, and warns the engine driver to stop. A *green* flag is displayed by way of caution, and a white flag signifies that the rails are clear and all things in order.

II. Hoisted by *British seamen*, it indicates that no concession will be made. Thus, previous to the mutiny at the Nore, the sailors at Portsmouth hoisted the red flag, and when Lord Bridport promised redress the crew of every ship hauled down the red flag.

On the 23rd May [1797] the mutineers hoisted the red flag, and all the ships of war lying near

Sheerness dropped down the Nore.—HOWITT,
Hist. of England, Geo. III. 1797, p. 158.

III. In *France*. 'Le Drapeau Rouge,'
since 1791, has been made the symbol of
insurrection and terrorism. By a decree
of the Constituent Assembly the red flag
was unfurled to indicate that martial
law was established, and that all gatherings of the people would be dispersed by
force of arms. Usually, a red flag signifies defiance.

Black flag betokens a *pirate*; white flag, *peace*;
red flag, *defiance*; yellow flag signifies that the
vessel is in quarantine.

IV. A symbol or synonym of radicalism.

Mr. Chamberlain sticks to the red flag, and
apparently believes in its future success.—*Newspaper paragraph*, January 1886.

Red Flag with a White Flag
(*A*) indicates that unless the besieged
request peace without delay they will
receive no quarter.

De Feuquières planted a cannon on a level with
the castle, on the mountain of Guignevert, and
then hoisted a white flag, and after that a red
one.—ANT. MONASTIER, *Hist. of the Vaudois Church*,
pp. 371-2.

Red Hand of Ulster (*The*). It
is said that in an expedition to Ireland
the leader thereof gave out that whoever
first touched the Irish shore should be
made possessors of the territory. One
of the O'Neills, in order to be the first,
cut off his hand and threw it on the
coast. The badge of the O'Neills is the
'Red Hand.'

Red Hat. First presented by Innocent IV. to cardinals, 25 Dec., 1244, called
'the Sun's birthday,' and red is the symbolical colour of the sun. The notion
that it indicates a willingness in a cardinal to shed his blood for the church is
mythical.

David Beatoun was born of good family, had
been made privy-seal by James V., and was raised
to a red hat by Pope Paul III.—PRINCE, *Parallel
History*, vol. ii. p. 81.

Red Heads (*The*). The regular soldiers of the Persian empire, so called
from their red caps.

The Persian word is 'Kuzzilbashes.' They were
80,000 in the reign of Shah Abbas, but were afterwards reduced to 30,000.

Red Hoods. The party colour of
Paris. Blue hoods, the party colour of
Navarre. Red and blue, the party colour
of Charles [V.] when dauphin. White
hoods, the party colour of the Burgundians.

Red Hugh. Hugh O'Donell. So
called from a red birth-mark on his face
(reign of Elizabeth).

Red Indians of Newfoundland. So
called because they daub their skin,
garments, canoes, weapons, and almost
everything with red ochre mixed with
grease. Probably red has a religious
significance, as the Maōris of New Zealand regard red as a sacred colour. It
will be remembered that when the banner
of St. Ambrose, the sacred oriflamme of
Milan, was taken to a battle-field, it was
drawn in a red car by red bullocks harnessed with red trappings.

Whether it was merely a custom, or whether
they daubed their skin with red ochre to protect
it from the attacks of mosquitos and black flies,
which swarm by myriads in the woods and wilds
during the summer, it is not possible to say.—
Lady BLAKE, *Nineteenth Century* (Dec. 1888, p. 905).

Red King (*The*).
I. Otto II. of Germany (955, 973–983).
II. William II. [*Rufus*] of England
(1057, 1087–1100).
III. Amadeus VII. count of Savoy
(1360, 1383–1391). *See* 'Red Beard.'

Red Land (*The*). The jurisdiction
over which the Vehmgericht of Westphalia extended. The court was called
a 'Free Session'; the judges were 'Free
Grafs' or 'Free Burghers.' *See* 'Child
of the Cord.'

Red Laws (*The*). The civil code.
Juvenal says 'perlege rubras majorum
leges' ('Satires,' xiv. 193). The civil
laws, being written in vermilion, were
called *rubrīca*, and 'rubrica vetavit'
means 'it is forbidden by the civil laws.'
The prætors' laws were inscribed in *white*
letters, as Quintilian informs us (xii. 3),
'prætores edicta sua in albo propone-
bant.' Imperial rescripts were written
in purple.

Red-Letter Days. Saints' days,
Sundays, and festivals. Non-working
days, printed at one time in red letters
in almanacs.

Red Peter. Pierce earl of Ormond,
deputy to the Earl of Surrey, lord-
lieutenant of Ireland in the reign of
Henry VIII.

Red Prince (*The*). Prince Friedrich Karl of Germany (born 1828). So
called because wherever he has made
his appearance a red-letter day has been

added to the *fasti* of Fatherland. His daughter Louise married the Duke of Connaught. Prince Friedrich Karl was one of the most successful generals of the age.

Red Republicans. Extreme democrats who scruple not to dye their hands in blood. In France they used to wear red caps. This was taken from the old Roman custom of manumission. When a slave was manumitted a small red cloth cap, called *pileus*, was placed on his head. Their journals had red wrappers. *See* p. 406, 'Hats.'

The red cap of the French Republicans was a Phrygian cap, but the red cap given to the Roman slave was sack-shaped. *See* p. 142, 'Cap.'

Red Scarfs (*The*). The party of Henri and Charles IX.

White scarfs, the badge of the Crusaders, Armagnacs, and Huguenots. Green scarfs, the badge of Mazarin, Isabella, and the Condé family. Tricolour scarfs, still worn in France by the municipal magistrates and the commissaires of police. White *hoods*, the badge of the Burgundians.

Red-Shanks, 1327. So the English called the Scotch, who covered their feet and shanks with the raw hides of the beasts which they looted from the English, wearing the hair inside.

In 1273 the Scots and Redshanks out of the Highlands made a sudden incursion into Ireland, and, committing the most cruel murders and depredations, escaped with their booty before the inhabitants had time to rally in their defence.— THOMAS MOORE, *Hist. of Ireland*, ch. xxxv.

Red Standard (*The*). This was the Roman signal for battle.

Red Triumvirate (*The*), **1849.** Three cardinals sent by the pope from Gaëta to Rome after the Restoration to conduct the civil affairs of the Papal States during his voluntary exile. Della Genga was one of the Triumvirate. These commissioners robbed the people to the amount of 35 per cent. of all the money which bore the stamp of the republic, but promised liberal institutions so far as they were consistent with absolute power founded on divine right.

Red Turbans, Green Turbans. The Shiahs or Shiites of Persia wear the *red* turban, as all the Fatimites of Egypt did, to distinguish themselves from the Sunis or Sunnites of Turkey. The descendants of Fatima in Turkey, called 'emirs' or 'sherecfs,' wear *green* turbans.

Shiites the unorthodox Sunnites the orthodox party. The former dc not allow the Kalifates of Aboubekr, Omar, or Othman.

Reds and Blacks, or 'I Rossi,' and 'I Neri.' The Signory or privy council of the Doge were termed 'I Rossi' (the Reds) from their red robes of office. The Council of Ten was called 'I Neri' from their black official robes.

N.B.—Red, white, blue, and green were livery colours worn in the chariot races of Constantinople, just as light and dark blue are worn as distinctive colours in our university athletic contests, such as boat-racing, cricket, football, &c. In Constantinople the Reds merged into the Greens, and the Whites into the Blues. *See* 'Blues and Greens.'

Rede's Lecturer (*Sir Robert*). On natural history, antiquarian history, literature, science, &c., in the University of Cambridge. One lecture to be given in full term. Fee nine guineas. Fund left for the purpose by Sir Robert Rede, lord chief justice of the Common Pleas in the reign of Henry VII. Founded 1524.

Redemptionists (*The*), **1199.** An order of monks, founded by Jean de Matha and Felix de Valois, for the redemption of Christian captives from slavery in Barbary. These monks were originally called *Trinitaires*, and *Religieux de la Ste Trinité*. Subsequently they were called *Maturins*, from a church in Paris (St. Maturin) given to the order in 1226. Suppressed in 1790.

Redemptorists (*The*), or 'The Redemptorist Fathers,' **1732.** A Roman Catholic missionary fraternity founded by St. Alphonso Maria de Liguori. Their object is to supply preachers for rural districts, and to instruct the peasantry.

Also called Liguorians or Liguorians, from Liguori, their founder.

Redpath Boys. An Irish secret society, connected with the Moonlighters and Land-leaguers (*q.v.*). *See* 'Irish Associations.'

Reduction of Paraguay (*The*), **1690.** An exchange of territory between Spain and Portugal by which the sovereignty of that country was transferred to Portugal. At the time of these 'reductions' the Jesuits were virtually the dominant power in Paraguay.

Reed (*The*) connected with the 'Crucifixion' of Jesus was not found by the Empress Heléna with the three crosses, but was discovered subsequently. It was sent in 614 to Constantinople, when

Jerusalem was taken by the Persians. A part of it is said to be in Florence, a part in St. Julian's church of Lunegarde, a longer piece is in the convent of Andeschs in Bavaria, and a still larger piece in the convent of Vatopedi on Mount Athos. We are not, however, told which of the reeds is meant, whether the *roseau de la royauté dérisoire*, or the reed which held the sponge dipped in vinegar, or whether the same reed was used on both occasions. *See* p. 231, ' Crucifixion, *Relics of the.*'

Referendary (A). A public officer whose duty was to procure, execute, and despatch diplomas and charters. The office of grand referendary of France is now merged in that of the chancellor.

Reform Banquet (*The*), of the 12th arrondissement of Paris, 1848. Organised by 92 members of the opposition, and on Feb. 22 began the ' nouvelle révolution de trois jours.'

Reform Bill (*The*), 1832. Prepared by Lord John Russell for the better representation of the United Kingdom in the House of Commons.

1. It changed the voters from freemen (*q.v.*) to persons having stated money qualifications.

2. It disfranchised rotten boroughs and pocket boroughs, such as Gatton and Old Sarum (which had no inhabitants), and gave members to large boroughs, such as Birmingham and Brighton, which were unrepresented.

3. It reduced or increased the number of members according to a numerical scale of inhabitants.

4. It shortened the time of elections.

Reform Club (*The*) was established in London 20 May, 1835.

Reform League (*The*), 1866, dissolved 1869. President, Mr. Edmond Beales, a barrister. The ostensible object of the league was the extension of the suffrage, but it is best known by its breaking down the railings of Hyde Park July 23, 1866, in vindication of a public right to enter the London parks and address the people there. The committee of the league had publicly announced their intention of delivering an address in the park, and the authorities of the park ordered the gates to be shut. The mob broke down the railings and forced

32

their way in. In 1872 a law was passed to regulate the right of speaking to the people in public.

Reform Pope (*The*). John Calvin, 1509–1564. He established a consistory at Geneva invested with power to censure and even excommunicate; and made the church a corporation independent of the state.

Reformatio Legum, 1571. A digest of the ecclesiastical laws of England into a code, begun in 1534, renewed in 1536, 1549, but not completed till the reign of Elizabeth, 1571, when it appeared under the fuller title of ' Reformatio Legum Ecclesiasticārum.' *See* next article.

Reformatio Legum Eccle'siastica'rum, 1571. The *Reformatio legum* completed and passed into law in the reign of Elizabeth. This code of ecclesiastical laws deals with the doctrine of the Trinity, the powers of the church, the general councils, heresies, the sacraments, confirmation, ordination, witchcraft, marriage, simony, dilapidations, church parish officers, synods, visitations, excommunication, and ecclesiastical courts. Cranmer was the chief compiler.

Reformation (*The*). That great spiritual and ecclesiastical ' reform ' which took place in Europe in the 16th cent.

In *France*, 1512, begun by Lefevre and Farel.

In *Switzerland*, 1516, begun by Zwingli.

In *Germany*, 1517, begun by Luther.

In *Denmark*, 1527, introduced by Frederick I.

In *Scotland*, 1527, introduced by Patrick Hamilton.

In *Sweden*, 1529, established by Gustavus Vasa.

In *England*, 1534, begun under Henry VIII.

In *Geneva*, 1535, established by Farel.

Reformation Tree, or Oak (*The*). An old oak on Mousehold [heath], near Norwich, under which Robert Ket, the tanner, sat to meet the rebels in 1549. Under this tree the insurgents aired their grievances and concocted their schemes of redress. Here it was that Ket, or Kett, sat as a Judge Lynch to try offenders, and here he and other stump orators addressed the people.

Aldrich the Mayor of Norwich, several clergymen both of the old and new learning, and even Matthew Parker, the future Archbishop of Canterbury, ascended the tree to address the people. Mousehold, pronounce *Muscle*; Norwich, pronounce *Nor'ridge*.

Reformationes. 'Inquisitiones Reformatōrum in provincias missorum. Literæ Philippi VI. Franc. Regis, 1340, vol. iii.' (Du Cange, vol. v. p. 638).

Reformatory Schools, 1834. Schools where young misdemeanants are sent instead of being sent to prison. The greatest reformatory in England is at Redhill.

Reformed Church (*Second Parent of the*). John the Constant, elector of Saxony (1407–1532). He succeeded his brother Frederick the Wise in 1525, and in 1530 presented to Karl V. (Charles Quint) the Augsburg Confession of Faith, drawn out by Melanchthon.

Reformed Churches. Those of the Zwinglians, Swiss, Upper Rhine Provinces, and Holland, which were 'reformed' without accepting Lutheranism.

There is a German-Swiss 'Reformed Church' and also a Dutch 'Reformed Church' in the U.S.

Reformed European Patriots (*The*), 1821, or Philadelphians. A branch of the Carbonāri.

Reformed Presbyterian Church (*The*). A remnant of the old Cameronians, who have more than thirty congregations in Scotland, and about as many in Ireland. There are some also in the United States and in Canada.

Reformed Presbyterian Synod of Ireland (*The*). Unconnected with the General Assembly, it does not therefore participate in the parliamentary grant.

Reformers (*The*) of Hungary, 1794. A secret political society to insure the introduction of the principles of the French Revolution. This society was in alliance with the more aristocratic one called 'The Friends of Liberty and Equality.'

Reformers' Bible (*The*). The 'Black Book.' An exposition of crown revenues, with lists of pluralists, placemen, pensioners, and sinecurists. Effingham Wilson, 1833

Refreshment Sunday. The fourth Sunday in Lent, when the Gospel of the day is about Christ feeding the multitude, and the first lesson (Gen. xliii.) is about Joseph feasting his brother. *See* 'Sunday.'

Regalia, or 'Right of Regale.' A right in ecclesiastical things claimed by sovereigns as royal prerogatives : such as presentation to benefices, the revenues of vacant benefices and sees, &c. The most memorable conflict on the subject was that between Pope Innocent XI. and Louis XIV., which was only terminated by the death of the pope.

Regality (*A*). A territorial jurisdiction formerly existing in Scotland, resembling our palatinate. The holder, called a 'Lord of Regality,' exercised the rights of a king in his own jurisdiction. Abolished by 20 Geo. II. c. 50.

Regarders. Forest rangers, who made their regard or range through royal forests.

Regardes. Visitations held by the king's justiciaries to correct encroachments on crown lands, impose and assess fines, determine suit and service, and regulate forest ordinances. The 'Great Regarde' was held once in every fifty years, and was entrusted to the highest baron of the realm, who empanelled juries, summoned witnesses, required the attendance of all forest officers, and made all appointments.

Edward I., Aug. 1282, and Henry VII. undertook these inspections.

And early rising from his couch, with scant reflection done,
Soon from his woodland towers, I trow, had the good Abbot gone,
And with his white-frocked monks that day rode o'er the grassy sward,
Oblivious of the bleating fold, to join the Great Regarde.
            Hayward Oaks, at the Regarde of Brian d'Insula, the King's Justiciarie, 1209.

Regent and Non-regent. A regent was a professor or university lecturer. *See* Rymer, 'Fœdera,' vol. iv. page 411, col. 1 ; and again, p. 413, col. 1. A non-regent is a master of arts or doctor, no longer bound to give lectures. The terms were retained in the University of Cambridge till 1858, though the duties of giving lectures had long passed to what are called 'professors.'

Regent Diamond (*The*). *See* 'Pitt Diamond.'

Regent House (*The*) originally meant the governing body of the university. It was strictly confined to those graduates who were actively engaged in teaching, and those who had ceased to teach formed, in 1400, a second assembly called the Non-regent House, whose consent was needful to the more important graces. The two houses formed the Senate. The master's hood for the regent house was lined with white, for the non-regent house the black hood had no lining. In 1595 professors were substituted for regents as teachers. In 1570 the regency of masters was extended to five years, when a master became necessarily non-regent, and in 1858 both regents and non-regents ceased to exist.

The Regents were Masters of Arts of less than five years' standing, and Doctors of less than two; the non-Regents were Masters of Art of more than five years' standing, with the Doctors of two years' standing, who belonged to either of the houses.

Regent's Park, London, 1838. Planned and given to the public during the regency of George, afterwards the fourth of that name.

Regiam Majestatem. An ancient collection of laws said to have been compiled by order of David I. of Scotland (1124–1153), but probably not older than the reign of our Edward I. (1272–1307).

Regiam Potestatem. A compilation of laws by Ranulph Glanvil, chief justice of England, who died 1190.

Regicides (*The*). I. In *English* history the party which favoured the execution of Charles I.

Thirteen suffered death for the part they took in this affair, viz., Axtell, Barkstead, Carew, Clement, Cook, Corbet, Hacker, Harrison, Jones, Okey, Peters, Scott, and Scrope.

II. In *Russian* history, 1881, means those Terrorists, or political confederates, who combined to assassinate Czar Alexander II.

Régime de la Calotte (*Le*). The régime of priests. So the priestly administrator of affairs, at the restoration, was called in France.

The *calotte* is the skull-cap worn by monks over their tonsure.

Régiment de la Calotte (*Le*). See 'Calottistes.'

Regimen of Factors (*The*), 1745. The 'Factors' were the dukes of Devonshire, Bedford, Rutland, and Montague

with the lords Herbert, Halifax, Cholmondeley, Falmouth, Malton, Derby, and some others of less note belonging to the great Whig party. Subscriptions were given to a large amount for the raising of troops, both horse and foot, to oppose the Young Pretender after his victory at Prestonpans; but the Whig lords, 'fearing that their relations and friends would lose a magnificent job,' proposed in the House of Lords that all the regiments should be paid by the king only.

The 'Regiment-factors,' as they were called, thus loaded the army list with a swarm of lordlings and lazy young fellows of high family, whom the men in various cases refused to follow.— HOWITT, *Hist. of Eng.* (Geo. II.), 507.
Cholmondeley, pronounce *Chum'-ly.*

Regiomontanus. A Latinised form of Königsberger. 'Königs-berg' = king's-mount, like 'Regius-mons'; and Königs-berger = Regio-montanus. Regiomontānus was really John Müller of Königsberg, in Franconia (1436–1476), the restorer of the science of astronomy, and archbishop of Ratisbon.

Regiomontanus was also noted for his mechanical toys. Hence, says Sir T. Brown, 'who admires not Regiomontanus—his fly more than his eagle.'
A foolish fashion existed about the time of the Reformation, especially with German and Dutch scholars, of converting their names into Greek or Latin. As Melanchthon for Schwarzerdt, &c., &c. *See* p. 599, 'Names Classicised.'

Registrar (*The*), in the Oxford University, is elected by the House of Convocation (*q.v.*), and must be either an M.A. or a B.C.L. He has to attend all meetings of both Congregations, of Convocation, and of the Hebdomadal Council (*q.v.*); and registers all acts and documents to which the university seal is affixed. His stipend is 600*l.* a year. *See* 'Registrary.'

Registrar-General (*The*), 1837. Appointed under the Great Seal, with his central office at Somerset House. Under him is a chief clerk, six superintendents, and a large staff of clerks appointed by the lords of the treasury. From the office of the registrar-general emanate instructions to all superintendent registrars, registrars of births and deaths, and registrars of marriages. A copy of any registry may be obtained by anyone for 3*s.* 6*d.*, which includes search.

Registrary (*The*), in the Cambridge University, is elected by the senate from one of two persons nominated by the council. His duties are to attend all congregations of the senate, and to register all Graces (*q.v.*) in the University Records. This officer, in the University of Oxford, is called the registrar (*q.v.*).

Registration of Aliens Act (*The*), 6, 7 Will. IV. c. 11, A.D. 1836. This was the repeal of 7 Geo. IV. c. 54, A.D. 1827, which obliged all aliens or foreigners who visited the British Isles to present themselves at the Alien Office to be registered. By the new act, masters of vessels arriving from foreign parts are required to declare what number of foreign passengers are on board, and every foreigner on landing is required to show his passport to the chief officer of customs at the port of debarkation. This registration and showing of passports is never exacted; and no return is kept of vessels landing, nor have they been registered since 1842.

Registration of Copyright (*The*), 5, 6 Vict. c. 45, A.D. 1842, authorizing the registration at Stationers' Hall of the title of copyright property. The omission to register will not affect the copyright, but will bar any action being brought for its infringement.

Registration of Death (*The*), 1874. 37, 38 Vict. c. 88, s. 8 enacts that the death of every person dying in England shall be registered within five days of the decease, and the cause of death stated on a certificate to be handed to the officiating minister before interment. It devolves on the nearest relatives present at the death or in attendance at the time to give the registrar notice and to sign the register. In default of relatives the duty devolves on the occupier and inmates of the house.

Registration of Electors Act (*The*). 2 William IV. c. 45, s. 26, A.D. 1832, making it requisite for a voter in the election of members of Parliament to be registered before exercising the franchise.

This is sometimes called 'The Registration of Voters Act.'

Regium Donum. An annual grant of public money for the maintenance of dissenting ministers in Ireland. It began in 1672, when Charles II. gave 600*l*. of secret service money to be distributed annually among the Presbyterian clergy in Ireland. William III. in 1690 increased the grant to 1,200*l*. a year. George III. in 1784 raised it to 2,200*l*., and in 1792 to

5,000*l*. In 1863 the grant was 39,746*l*.; and in 1869 it was abolished.

In 1793 commenced an annual grant to dissenting ministers in England.

Regius Professor of Civil Law (*The*), in the University of Cambridge, 1540, founded by Henry VIII. Original stipend 40*l*. a year. Present stipend 534*l*. 18*s*., and 10 guineas a head from each of the students who attend his lectures. *See* 'Downing Professorship of the Laws of England,' 'International Law, &c.,' 'Chancellor's Medal, &c.,' 'Battie's Scholarship,' 'Browne Scholarship,' 'Craven Scholarship,' 'Whewell Scholarship of International Law.'

Regius Professorship of Civil Law (*The*), in Oxford University. Founded in 1546 by Henry VIII. at 40*l*. a year. The present stipend is 440*l*. a year.

Regius Professorship of Divinity (*The*), in the University of Cambridge, 1540, founded by Henry VIII. Original stipend 40*l*. a year, but now considerably augmented. *See* 'Lady Margaret Professorship of Divinity,' 'Norrisian Professor of Divinity,' and 'Hulsean Professor of Divinity,' 'Crosse Scholarship,' 'Evans's Prize,' 'Jeremie Prize,' 'Burney Prize,' 'Hulsean Prize,' 'Kaye Prize,' 'Norrisian Prize.'

Regius Professorship of Divinity (*The*), in Oxford University. Founded in 1535 by Henry VIII. at 40*l*. a year. Augmented by James I. in 1605.

Regius Professorship of Greek (*The*), of the University of Cambridge, 1540. Founded by Henry VIII. The original stipend was 40*l*. a year, but the present endowment includes a canonry of Ely Cathedral. *See* 'Chancellor's Classical Medal,' 'Porson Scholarship, 'Davies Scholarship,' 'Pitt's Scholarship,' 'Waddington Scholarship,' 'Scholefield Prize,' 'Porson Prize,' 'Browne's Medals.'

Regius Professorship of Greek (*The*), in Oxford University. Founded in 1547 by Henry VIII. at 40*l*. a year. Increased in 1865 to 500*l*. a year.

Regius Professorship of Hebrew (*The*), in the University of Cambridge, 1540. Founded by Henry VIII. Original stipend 40*l*. a year, now endowed with a canonry of Ely Cathedral. *See* 'Tyrwhitt Hebrew Scholarship.'

Regius Professorship of He-brew (*The*), in Oxford University. Founded in 1540 by Henry VIII. at 40*l*. a year. Augmented by Charles I. in 1630.

Regius Professorship of Medicine (*The*), in Oxford University. Founded in 1540 by Henry VIII. at 40*l*. a year. Augmented by Charles I. in 1630.

Called in the Cambridge University the 'Regius Professorship of Physic' (*q.v.*).

Regius Professorship of Modern History, &c., in Oxford University. Stipend 620*l*. a year. Founded by George I. in 1724.

In the University of Cambridge there is a Professor of Modern History, who holds his appointment during the sovereign's pleasure. Stipend 371*l*. a year, paid by the University.

Regius Professorship of Physic (*The*), in the University of Cambridge, 1540. Founded by Henry VIII. Original stipend 40*l*. a year. Present stipend 300*l*. a year and a house in Market Street. *See* 'Downing Professorship of Medicine.'

Regular Abbot (*A*). An abbot who discharged the duties of an abbey held by a secular abbot. As a secular abbot is a layman, he is not qualified to undertake clerical duties.

Regular Canons. 'Canonici Regulares,' canons who lived in community, bound by the 'rule' of the house. Secular canons were exempt from the 'rule.'

Regulars (*The*). I. 'Regular Clergy' (*Regularēs*, from *regula*, a rule), Catholic clergymen of some monastic order, who live according to the rule of their order, always including obedience, chastity, and poverty. The secular clergy are those, engaged in parochial duties, who are not bound by monastic rules.

Archbishops, bishops, rectors, vicars, and curates are not usually regulars but seculars.

II. In the *British army*. All troops except the militia, yeomanry, and volunteers. They are regular all the year, and not called out for certain days or weeks only.

Regulation Act (*The*), 1773. Relative to the East India Company. It established a governor-general and a Supreme Court of Judicature for all British possessions in India; prohibited judges and members of council from trading; forbade any receipt of presents from natives; and ordered that every

act of the East India Directors should be submitted to the House of Commons for approval before it was enforced.

Regulators.
I. In 1687. A committee of seven Catholics and Jesuits appointed by James II. to send deputations to different corporations and report on them. The board was at Whitehall, and they were empowered to introduce into the corporations new rules and new men as they thought fit. Of course the object was to prepare for the reintroduction of Roman Catholicism by returning members to the parliament about to be convened favourable to the king's views.

II. In 1770. A body of men who took the law into their own hands, and inflicted bodily punishment according to their own discretion and on their own authority upon offenders. The difficulty of bringing offenders in the back settlements of North America to justice induced orderly people to institute this rough and ready method of proceeding.

III. In 1776. Backwoodsmen collected together by Governor Martin to recover North Carolina in the American War of Independence. They were decoyed into a swamp, and such as escaped made again for the backwoods.

Regulators were, later on, especially active in Texas and California, where the population suddenly outgrew the constituted authorities.

Reichstag, 1871. The diet of the German empire. Since the establishment of the empire under the king of Prussia the legislative council has consisted of one representative to every 100,000 inhabitants. As the entire population is about 47 millions, this will give 470 members to the legislative assembly. The delegates of the confederated governments form the 'Bundesrath,' and whatever passes the two houses and is signed by the king-emperor becomes binding on all the twenty-six states.

Reign of Tears (*The*), 1871. The French Revolution terminated with the 'Reign of Terror'; the Franco-German war terminated with the 'Reign of Tears' [*Thiers*].

Reign of Terror (*The*).
I. In *Algiers*, 1509. That of Barbarossa, the Turkish chief who put to death Salem-Aben-Toumi, the Arab

sheik whom he came to assist against the Christians.

II. 'Le Régime de la Terreur' (from 31 May, 1793, to 27 July, 1794). It began with the triumph of the Mountain over the Girondists in the National Convention, and terminated with the execution of Robespierre. While Robespierre and his Committee of Public Safety (*q.v.*) dominated, France was filled with scaffolds.

Among its victims were Louis XVI., the Queen Marie Antoinette, the Duc d'Orléans (Philippe Egalité), twenty-one Girondists, and many thousands of others. It lasted 420 days.

III. In *Ireland*, 1881-1887. Under the domination of Charles Stewart Parnell, M.P. for Cork. Mr. Parnell, in order to obtain the severance of Ireland from Great Britain, was at the head of an organization which terrorized the Irish by shooting at the legs of those who refused to support their league, boycotting them, pouring pitch on the bare heads of their wives and daughters, maiming their cattle, and rendering their lives a ceaseless terror. In 1886 he contrived to get eighty-six of his partisans elected to the Imperial Parliament, and block the business of the house. Some of his American friends tried to terrorize the English by blowing up public buildings by dynamite, and denouncing death on the public servants of Ireland. *See* p. 679, 'Phœnix Park Murder.'

Reis-Effendi. A Turkish secretary of foreign affairs.

Relics (*Christian*). Excepting those connected with the crucifixion, which are noticed each *in loco*, the following may be mentioned :—

The famous *Manus de cœlo missa*, which even Pope Pius IX., in 1852, acknowledged to be genuine (!!) William of Oulx was a peasant who had lost his right hand, and for his piety an angel brought him one from heaven. When he died the 'hand' refused to be buried, and persistently pushed itself through the coffin. So the Archbishop of Embrun ordered it to be cut off and stored among the holy relics. This was done, and certain days were set apart when it was to be shown to the people. This is one of the best attested relics of the Catholic Church.

In a monastery of Calabria is the hood which an angel from heaven brought Francis of Paula, and put upon his head.

In half a dozen places is shown some of the milk of Mary while she was nursing the infant Jesus; but we are not informed how this 'spilt milk' was gathered up and preserved.

Part of one of the stones cast at Stephen is preserved at Toul. So Father Benedict informs us in his 'Life of St. Gerard' (1700).

Harmer, in his 'Observations,' tells us he was shown 'a prodigious tooth,' wrapped in three covers of paper, on one of which was written, *A tooth of the holy St. Paul.*

Peter himself told St. Longis where to find one of his teeth. The tooth was taken to Boisselière, and Harduin says that a great crowd of people flocked thither 'pour vénérer ce gage de la protection du prince des Apôtres.'

The girdle of Joseph the carpenter is preserved in Notre Dame, Joinville-sur-Marne; his walking stick at Florence; one of his hammers at the church of St. Anastasia, Rome; and one of his cloaks in the same place.

Brady gives us the following list: One of the coals that broiled St. Lawrence; a finger of St. Andrew, another of John the Baptist, and a thumb of St. Thomas; the hem of Christ's garment touched by the woman suffering from the issue of blood; a lock of Mary Magdalen's hair, with which she wiped her tears from the feet of Jesus; a phial of the sweat of St. Michael when he contended with Satan; some of the rays of the guiding star which appeared to the Wise Men of the East; a rib of the *Verbum caro factum*; a pair of Enoch's slippers; the pap-spoon of the infant Jesus; St. Michael's sword and buckler; one of the tears shed by Jesus at the tomb of Lazarus; and one of the water-pots used at the marriage feast of Cana of Galilee. *See* 'Clavis Calendaria,' p. 240.

There was an 'age of relics,' and it would require many pages even to tabulate them. Some could not even be set down without seeming to cast ridicule on a subject far too sacred to be trifled with. They have, however, an historic value, as they show a very important phase of religious thought and pious sentimentality in the middle ages, though in this matter-of-fact age they are much discredited.

Relics not Christian.

In one of the visits of the Prince of Wales to Germany, the English ladies staying at the hotel bought as relics the cherry-stones left by him at dessert. This surely was the very crest unto the crest of snobbism.

At Salamis was shown the sacred stone on which Telamon the father of Ajax sat.

In one of the Spartan temples was suspended one of the eggs of Leda, who had been transformed by Zeus into a swan. Probably it was an ostrich's egg.

At Panôpĕus, in Phocis, was shown some of the clay out of which Prometheus made man, and we are assured that it had a strong smell of human flesh.

Mazois, a French architect and archæologist, published in 1819 a work entitled 'The Palace of Scaurus,' in which were plates of the bones of the sea-monster which Perseus slew.

At Ceylon is preserved a tooth of Buddha; doubtless, from its great size, the tooth of some extinct saurian, for no animal with a mouth smaller than a horse could possibly have had such a huge molar.

From 1424, for many years, the *Heiltum* was exhibited at Nuremberg, the second Friday after Easter, together with the sword of Charlemagne, his crown and sceptre, as well as a piece of the true cross, a nail used at the crucifixion, the lance which pierced the dead body of Christ, part of the manger of Bethlehem, and portions of the several chains with which Peter, Paul, and John were bound.

Relief. A sum of money paid by a vassal to his baron on his coming of age, when he took up his right and paid his fee to the king.

Relief Bill (*The*), or 'Catholic Relief Bill,' 13 April, 1829. A bill to relieve Catholics from religious and civil disabilities. The same as the 'Catholic Emancipation Act' (*q.v.*).

The pastoral [of Dr. Doyle] besought the people to promote the end which the legislature contemplated in passing the Relief Bill.—HOWITT, *Hist. of Eng.* (year 1829, p. 146).

Relief Church (*The*), 1752.

Seceders from the Kirk of Scotland who choose their own pastors.

Relief Synod (*The*), 1752.

A secession from the Scotch Church led by the Rev. Thomas Gillespie, who was afterwards joined by the Rev. Thomas Boston. They allowed greater freedom of communion than any other sect in Scotland, and, next to the Associate Synod, are the most numerous of the Scotch Dissenters.

Reliefs.

Fines paid to the lord by a new tenant on his entering on the tenement of his predecessor at death. Introduced by William the Conqueror, and abolished by 12 Car. II. c. 24.

Religieux de Citeaux, 1098.

Twenty inmates led by St. Robert from the abbey of Molesme to the neighbourhood of Nuits, in the department of Côte d'Or, and so called from the *citernes* or subterraneous pits which they found there. Commonly called Cistercians.

Religieux de la Merci (*Les*),

1218. Confirmed by Gregory IX. in 1235. An order under the rule of St. Augustine for the redeeming of captives.

Religionists (*The*).

So the Huguenots or Calvinists were often called in France.

The universities and colleges . . . invented difficulty upon difficulty against conferring academic degrees upon the Religionists.—FÉLICE, *Hist. of the Protestants of France*, bk. iii. 7.

Religio'si.

Monks or Regulāres (4 syl.) were so called. Nuns were Religiōsæ. Called Regulars because they followed some regūla or rule; and called Religiosi because their entire life was spent in religious duties or observances.

Religious Peace (*The*), or 'The Treaty of Passau,' 1552.

Imposed on Karl V. by Maurice. It was agreed :

1. That both belligerents should lay down their arms, and assist Ferdinand against the Turks.

2. That the landgraf of Hesse should be set at liberty.

3. That the ' Interim ' (*q.v.*) should be revoked, and Protestants be free till the Diet met, which was to be within six months.

4. That those banished for their alliance with the Smalcaldic League (*q.v.*) should be recalled and reinstated.

5. That Protestants and Catholics should be on an equal footing.

Religious Peace of Augsburg (*The*), 26 Sept., 1555.

This was supplemental to the Treaty of Passau in 1552. By this ' Peace,' full liberty of worship, granted by the Treaty of Passau, was confirmed. Lutherans and Catholics were declared alike eligible to all offices of state ; and every ruler might sanction in his own province whatever form of religion he chose, but all were to tolerate those who held different religious views from those favoured by the state.

Religious Statistics, 1890.

Assuming the entire population of the globe to be 1,450 millions, of these, 1,050 millions are non-Christians, 400 millions are nominally Christians.

1. *Non-Christians—*

Buddhists	.	. 400	millions.
Brahmins	.	. 250	,,
Mahometans	.	. 180	,,
Fetish Worshippers	150		,,
Jews	.	. . 8	,,
Various	.	. . 62	,,
	Total	1,050	,,

2. *Christians—*

Roman Catholics	.	175	millions.
Protestants	.	. 110	,,
Greek Church	.	. 90	,,
Various	.	. 25	,,
	Total	400	,,
		1,050	,,

Entire population 1,450 ,,

Religious Wars (*The*), 1562–1598.

In the reigns of Charles IX. and Henri III. of France.

First, 1562–1563. The Catholic leaders were François duc de Guise, St. André, and the Comte de Montmorency; the Protestant leaders were Louis prince de Condé, and the Sire de Coligny. The chief events of this war were the siege of Rouen, the battle of Dreux, and the siege of Orleans.

Second, 1567–1568. The only event of note was the battle of St. Denis, in which Anne duc de Montmorency lost his life.

Third, 1569–1570. The chief events were (1) the battle of Jarnac (1569), in which the Catholics were victorious, and the Prince de Condé, the great Huguenot leader was slain; and (2) the battle of Moncontour, also won by the Catholics.

On 24 Aug., 1572, occurred the great slaughter of the Huguenots, called the Massacre of St. Bartholomew's Eve.

Fourth, 1573. The Catholics besieged La Rochelle, but were obliged to raise the siege.

Fifth, 1575–1576. The Catholic leader was Henri of Guise; the Protestant leaders were the prince de Condé and Henri of Navarre.

Sixth, 1577. The Protestants were overmastered, but Henri III. coquetted with them through fear of the Guises.

Seventh, 1577–1578. In which Henri of Navarre carried Cahors with a *coup-de-main*, and peace ensued.

The last of the Catholic triumvirate lost his life. The command of the Catholic army was now given to Henri duc d'Anjou.

Remember the Vase of Soissons.

Kings never forgive or forget. After the battle of Soissons (A.D. 486), Clovis wished to appropriate a valuable vase, but one of the warriors stepped forwards and broke it to atoms with his battle-axe, saying, 'Thou shalt have thy share only, like the rest of us.' Clovis dissembled his anger, but did not forget the insult; and one day, finding the same warrior had neglected to clean his axe, he snatched it out of the man's hand and split his skull with it, saying, 'Remember the vase of Soissons.'

Remembrance (*The*). This was the first document which openly avowed an intention of bringing the king (Charles I. of England) to a personal judgment, and of changing the monarchical form of government.

Remembrancer. An officer of the Exchequer, who reminds the lord treasurer and the justices of that court of such things as are to be called on and dealt with for the benefit of the crown. The clerks are called the 'Clerks of the Remembrancers.' The office of lord treasurer was abolished by Act 3, 4 William IV. chap. 99 (28 Aug., 1833), and its duties transferred to the lord high treasurer.

Remembrancers (*Clerks of the*). First mentioned in 1363. *See above.*

Reminiscere (5 syl.) **Sunday.** The second Sunday in Lent, so called in the Catholic Church from the introïtus (or beginning of the mass), the first word of which is *Reminiscere.*

Remish Bible (*The*), 1584. A translation of the Bible by the Roman Catholics at Reims. Printed on large paper. The great objection to this version is its retention of so many Hebrew and Greek terms untranslated, as Azymes, Tunike, Holocaust, Prepuce, Pasche, &c. *See* ' Bible.'

When any doctrine or dispute hangs on the word, without doubt it is better to retain the original Greek or Hebrew, as baptism, schism, and so on.

Remonstrance. From the council of officers, 1648, called for the election of a new parliament; for electoral reform; for the recognition of the supremacy of Parliament; for the change of kingship into a parliamentary magistracy; and that Charles I. should be brought to justice for treason, blood, and ill-government. *See* next article.

Remonstrance (*Grand*). On the state of the kingdom, 22 Nov., 1641. Clarendon says it was 'a very bitter representation of all the illegal things that had been done by the king [Charles I.] from the first hour of his coming to the crown to that minute.' It contained 206 clauses, and led to the arrest of the five members (*q.v.*).

Among the charges were these : The war against the French Protestants, the innovations in the Church, the illegal imposition of ship-money, forced loans, the cruelties of the Star Chamber and High Commission, the forcing of episcopacy on Scotland, the forcing of it on the Irish by Strafford, and other illegal proceedings.—HOWITT, *Hist. of England*, Charles I. chap. iv. p. 220.

Remonstrance (*The*), 1610. The petition presented to the States of Holland by the Arminians. It contained these five points : (1) Predestination is conditional on faith. Those who believe are predestined to be saved, those who refuse to believe are predestined to perish; (2) Christ died for all, but only believers will receive the benefits of redemption; (3) all must be born again, as no man is otherwise capable of exercising a saving faith; (4) though grace may be resisted, yet without grace no man can think or will any good thing; (5) believers are able by the aid of the Holy Ghost to resist sin.

Remonstrance (*The Irish*), 1318. In reply to a letter from Pope John XXII. to the Irish clergy, commanding them to censure all those who rebelled against the ruling powers. The remonstrance gives a sketch of Irish history ' for 4,000 years'; expresses irreconcilable bitterness against the English rulers; states that they had given Ireland to Edward Bruce, brother of the Scotch hero; and concludes with a threat of war *à outrance* against every Englishman who holds an inch of land in the whole island. *See* 'Irish Associations.'

Remonstrance of Grievances

(*The*), 1640. Sixteen articles. These were Irish grievances laid before the British Parliament, such as the arbitrary decision of pleas by the lord deputy; the perversion of law by the judges; the punishments inflicted for freedom of speech; the exorbitant powers of the court of commission; want of security for persons or property; the increase of monopolies; exorbitant fees extracted by the clergy, and so on.

Remonstrant Synod of Ulster

(*The*), 1830. Formed in consequence of the separation of seventeen ministers with their congregations from the General Synod of Ulster, on the ground that it required from its members in 1827 and 1828 submission to certain doctrinal acts not in accordance with the code of discipline and contrary to previous usage.

Remonstrants, 1610.

Arminians were so called from their humble petition or 'remonstrance' against Calvinism, addressed to the states of Holland. *See* 'Remonstrance,' 1610.

The anti-remonstrants were called Gomarists. The two leaders were Barneveldt (remonstrant) and Maurice of Nassau (Gomarist).

Remonstrators or 'Remonstrants,'

1650. A break from the general body of Presbyterians after the battle of Dunbar. They consisted, at first, of some 4,000 Scotchmen, under Kerr and Strachan, giving out that the defeat of Dunbar was a divine punishment on the Presbyterians for joining with Engagers (*q.v.*) and Malignants (*q.v.*) in espousing the royal cause. They were inclined to unite with the republicans.

The royalists obtained the name of Public Resolutioners; their opponents, of Protestors or Remonstrants.—Dr. LINGARD, *History of England*, viii. 4.

Strachan, pronounce *Strawn.*

Renaissance Period (*The*).

Began in France with the reign of François I. (1515). In Italy it began under the patronage of the Medici (1453). The Greeks, driven from Constantinople by Mahomet II., took refuge in Italy, and were the chief cause of this renaissance.

In architecture the Gothic was supplanted by the Renaissance, which was itself succeeded by imitation Greek. The Renaissance architecture is conspicuous for its high roofs, crowded ornamentation, fanciful chimneys, statues introduced into walls, parapets, and vestibules, for its doors and windows, and its general bad taste.

Repairs of Church Images.

The subjoined is an extract from an old account-book in the Muniment Room of Winchester Cathedral, A.D. 1450.

For work done as follows :	*s.*	*d.*
Item : For soldering and repairing ye St. Josef		8
Item : For cleaning and ornamenting ye Holy Ghost		6
Item : For repairing ye Virgin Mary before and behind, and making a new Child	4	8
Item : For repairing ye Nose of Devil, putting a new Horn on his head, and glueing a piece on his tail	5	6
	11	4

Repeal Agitation (Ireland).

Organised in 1842; reached its culmination in 1843. Its objects were to agitate for a resident parliament in Dublin, and to sever Ireland from the crown of Great Britain. It was distinguished for its monster meetings under the leadership of Daniel O'Connell; the largest was that held at Tara, in Meath, when above 250,000 persons assembled. Happily at this period the temperance cause under Father Mathew was in full force, so these vast meetings were not riotous. *See* 'Irish Associations.'

Repeal Association (*The*). I. 1829.

Followed the Catholic Association of 1824 (*q.v.*). The object was the repeal of the union of the two parliaments effected in 1801. Daniel O'Connell was the great agitator of this repeal. When the Repeal Association was proclaimed in 1830 a new society rose under the name of the Anti-Union Society. *See* 'Irish Associations.'

II. 1840, or 'National Association for the Repeal of the Union,' set on foot by Daniel O'Connell, who held his monster meetings in 1843.

Repeal Cap (*The*).

Green, gold, and velvet. Green for Ireland. It was worn by O'Connell and his party on their release from prison in 1844.

Repeal Year (*The*), 1843.

So called from the monster meetings held in Ireland for the repeal of the union. The first was held at Trim, in Meath; the largest was that on Tara hill, 15 Aug.,

3 C

under the auspices of Daniel O'Connell, and the last was at Mullaghmast, 1 Oct., 1843. *See* 'Irish Associations.'

Repeal of the Union (between Great Britain and Ireland). Resolutions in its favour passed by a meeting at Dublin, 1 Sept., 1810. Associations organised to promote the repeal in 1829. O'Connell brought forward his motion for the repeal in 1834, but it was rejected by the House of Commons. The National Association for the Repeal was established in 1840, and monster meetings were held for the object on Tara hill in Aug. 1843. In 1881–1890 the question again agitated Ireland under the leadership of Mr. Parnell. *See* 'Irish Associations.'

Representers (*The*), 1721. The twelve 'Marrow-men' (*q.v.*) were so called because they signed a 'representation' or protest against the judgment of the General Assembly on the subject of the book entitled 'The Marrow of Modern Divinity.' *See* 'Marrow Controversy.'

Republica Parthenope'a, 1799. The republic of Naples was so named by Championnet, who took possession of it.

Neapolis was anciently called Parthenôpê, from one of the syrens who was said to have lived there. Naples, a contraction of Neapolis, means the New City, referring to the new city built by a colony of Cumæans.

Republican Calendar. I. The Months, beginning 22 Sept. Each month 30 days.

AUTUMN.

Vendémiaire (Vintage month) ...	Sept. 22—Oct. 21.	
Brumaire (Foggy month)	Oct. 22—Nov. 20.	
Frimaire (Sleety month)	Nov. 21—Dec. 20.	

WINTER.

Nivose (Snowy month)	Dec. 21.—Jan. 19.	
Pluviose (Rainy month)	Jan. 20—Feb. 18.	
Ventose (Windy month)	Feb. 19—Mar. 20.	

SPRING.

Germinal (Budding month) ...	Mar. 21—April 19.	
Floréal (Flowery month) ...	April 20—May 19.	
Prairial (Pasture month)	May 20—June 18.	

SUMMER.

Messidor (Harvest month)... ...	June 19—July 18.	
Thermidor (Hot month)	July 19—Aug. 17	
Fructidor (Fruit month)	Aug. 18—Sept. 16	

From Sept. 16 to Sept. 22 are five days. These were called *Sans culottides* (4 syl.), and were national holidays ; 17 dedicated to Venus, 18 to Genius, 19 to Labour, 20 to Opinion, and 21 to Rewards.

II. The Years.

Year					
" I.	From 22 Sept., 1792 to 21 Sept., 1793.				
" II.	"	"	1793 "	"	1794.
" III.	"	"	1794 "	"	1795.
" IV.	"	"	1795 "	"	1796.
" V.	"	"	1796 "	"	1797.
" VI.	"	"	1797 "	"	1798.
Year VII.	From 22 Sept., 1798 to 21 Sept., 1799.				
" VIII.	"	"	1799 "	"	1800.
" IX.	"	"	1800 "	"	1801.
" X.	"	"	1801 "	"	1802.
" XI.	"	"	1802 "	"	1803.
" XII.	"	"	1803 "	"	1804.
" XIII.	"	"	1804 "	"	1805.
" XIV.	"	"	1805 to the close of the		

year, when the reckoning was abolished by Napoleon.

Republican Calendar of Brazil, 1890, beginning with Sunday: Humanidi, Maridi, Patridi, Filidi, Fratidi, Domidi, and Matridi. This ridiculous list of names is called the 'Positivists' Calendar,' and the twelve months are equally absurd.

Moses—January	Charlemagne—July
Homer—February	Dante—August
Aristotle—March	Gutenberg—September
Archimêdês—April	Shakespeare—October
Cæsar—May	Descartes—November
St. Paul—June	Frederick the Great—Dec.

Republican Marriages, 1794. A device by Carrier for putting to death those persons in Nantes supposed to be disaffected towards the republic. It consisted in tying men and women together by their hands and feet and casting them into the Loire. No people in the world have shown such refinement of savage cruelty as the French. *See* p. 236, 'Damiens,' as one example out of many.

Republican Martyr (*The*). Jean Paul Marat, murdered in his bath by Charlotte Corday (1744–1793).

Requests by the Captain of the Great Assembly in Kent (*The*), June 1450. A paper of grievances and requests handed in by Jack Cade for the consideration of the king and his advisers. It demanded that the king should resume the crown grants, so that his subjects might be relieved of too heavy taxation ; that the false progeny of the Duke of Suffolk be dismissed from the king's council; and that the Duke of York be restored.

Jack Cade was an illegitimate son of the Duke of York.

Rescessory Act (*The*), 1661. Whereby Charles II. revoked his oath taken in Scotland to be true to the 'Engagement' (*q.v.*). The revocation was grounded on the plea of moral compulsion.

The Rescessory Act at one blow levelled with the ground every legal prop of the Scottish Kirk.—Dr. LINGARD, *History of England*, ix. 1.

Rescript (*A*). The response of a king to an individual on some question officially submitted to him. If the response is made to a council, corporation, or community, it is called a 'Pragmatic Sanction.'

Rescripts (*The*) are replies of the Roman emperors to questions of law put to them by magistrates and colonial governors. They were written in purple ink. The edicts of prætors were in white, and the jus civile in red ink.

Reservatum Ecclesiasticum. A provision of the religious Peace of Westphalia (1549), whereby the church claimed the territorial property annexed to any dignity if the holder thereof changed his religion. This enactment led to the Thirty Years' War (*q.v.*).

Residences of the kings of France. *See* p. 492, 'Kings of France,' &c.

Resolutioners (*The*), or 'Public Resolutioners,' 1650, who were inclined to treat the conduct of the deceased king, Charles I., with leniency in opposition to the Remonstrants, who 'protested' against his conduct in unmeasured terms. In Scotch law a resolutioner is one who does something prejudicial to an estate, and if found guilty the estate is forfeited and passes to the next heir.

The kingdom of Scotland was divided into Resolutioners and Protesters, the former of whom adhered to Charles II., after his father's death upon the scaffold, while the Protesters inclined rather to a union with the triumphant Republicans.—Sir W. Scott, *Old Mortality*, ch. v.

Respublica Binepsis, 14th cent. A social order founded by some Polish noblemen, and so called from Binepsis, the seat of its founder. It was a *multum in parvo* of Poland itself, with its king, council, chamberlain, master of the chase, and other officers. Any of the members conspicuous for a foible was created to some office or title in ridicule thereof. Thus a great lover of hunting was made 'Master of the Chase,' a boaster was made 'Field Marshal.' But no one was allowed to chaff or ridicule these officers. At one time the order contained well-nigh all the court of Poland. The objects of the order were to promote charity, good feeling, and sociability, and to repress immorality and affectations of all kinds.

Restitution Edict (*The*), 1630. Published by Kaiser Ferdinand II., when the king of Denmark retired from the Thirty Years' War. It enjoined restitution to the Catholics of the two archbishoprics, the twelve bishoprics, and all the parish churches, lands, and other properties which had been confiscated by Protestants since the 'Treaty of Passau.' Compliance with this edict was well-nigh impossible, so the Protestants applied to Gustavus Adolphus of Sweden, and thus began the second part of this long religious war.

Restoration (*The*).
I. In *English* history, 29 May, 1660. The restoration of monarchical government interrupted at the death of Charles I. by a Commonwealth. The old form was restored by the recall and return of Charles II., who had been living in exile.
II. In *French* history. The restoration of Louis XVIII. to the throne after the abdication of Napoleon and his banishment to Elba, 3 May, 1814. On 21 March, 1815, Napoleon broke from Elba, and Louis XVIII. fled; but after the battle of Waterloo Louis was restored a second time, and entered Paris 8 July, 1815.

Restorationists. A religious sect which believes that all persons will ultimately be restored, after a due time of purgation proportionate to their sins. Origen was a Restorationist.

Restorer of Cities, and Father of his Country. Sancho I. of Portugal, who repaired the cities which had suffered greatly in the recent wars (1154, 1185–1212).

Restorer of French Liberty (*The*). 'Le Restaurateur de la Liberté Française,' 13 Aug., 1789. A title conferred on Louis XVI. when he signed the 19 articles formulated on the 4th by the National Assembly. *See* 'August 4.'

Restorer of Learning (*The*). Lorenzo de Medicis the Magnificent (1448–1492). Also called the 'Patron of the Fine Arts.'

Restorer of Letters (*The*). Alexander Heigius of Westphalia (18th cent.).

Restorer of the Protestantism of France (*The*). Antoine Court (1696–1760).

Restorers of Astronomy (*The*) John Müller (better known as 'Regiomontănus,' *q.v.*), 1436–1476, and his pupil Georg Purbach of Austria (1423–1461).

3 c 2

Resumption Bill (*The*), 1700 (11, 12 Will. III. c. 2). For the resumption of grants of land in Ireland by William III. to foreigners, as Keppel of Guelderland (Earl of Albemarle); William Bentinck, son of the Earl of Portland (a Dutch favourite of William's), created Viscount Woodstock; Ginckel, another Dutchman, created Earl of Athlone; and Ruvigny, a French Huguenot, created Earl of Galway. To these four foreigners William granted above 300,000 acres of land in Ireland. The land was sold to the highest purchasers, and the money employed in paying the arrears of the army.

He granted also to Elizabeth Villiers, his mistress, above 95,000 acres, valued at 25,995*l.* a year !!
The first *duke* of Portland was Henry Bentinck, 1716.

Resurrection (*The*). Tertullian says the Crucifixion occurred on 25 March, and the Calendar of the Arbuthnott Missal places the Resurrection on 27 March. If so the year must have been A.D. 29, when 25 March fell on a Friday.

Tertullian says that Christ suffered under Tiberius Cæsar in the consulate of Rubellius Geminus and Fufius Geminus, in the month of March, at the time of the passover, on the 8th day before the Kalends of April [25 March], on the first day of unleavened bread, on which they slew the lamb at even.—*Adversus Judæos,* c. 8.
The next year on which 25 March was Friday was A.D. 40, and not again till A.D. 119, 124, 214, &c.

Resurrection Men. Men who stole buried bodies out of cemeteries and churchyards, and sold them to surgeons for dissection. They were also called 'body snatchers.' In 1829 Burke and Hare made themselves conspicuous by this infamous traffic, and added to it the suffocation [burking] of living persons by strangulation, or smothering them by pitch-plasters placed over the mouth and nose. Bishop and Williams, in 1831, burked a poor Italian boy named Carlo Ferrari, and were both executed.

Retreat of the 10,000 (*The*), B.C. 401–399. Conducted by Xenophon, the historian, who had joined the expedition of Cyrus. In the battle of Cunaxa Cyrus lost his life, and the Greeks were left without a leader. Xenophon volunteered to lead them back to Greece, and has left an historical narrative of this famous retreat, called Xenophon's *Anabâsis.*

Return of the Heracli'dæ (*The*), B.C. 1103. The migration of the descendants of Heraclês (*Herculês*) and the Dorians to the Peloponnesus, which they conquered. Heraclês was promised the land of Argos by Zeus, but was kept out by Hera (*Juno*). Five times the descendants of Heraclês attempted to take possession of the promised land, but were driven out four times. The fifth invasion was 110 years after the first by Hyllos, son of Heraclês, and 80 years after the siege of Troy. It was completely successful, and the peninsula was divided by lot among the three leaders (*Mythic History*).

Revised Bible (*The*). Published in May 1885. The Revised New Testament was published 17 May, 1881. The work was begun 30 June, 1870, by twenty-five scholars, ten of whom died before the revision was completed, 20 June, 1884. The revisers had eighty-five sessions, which extended over fourteen years. *See* 'Bible.'

There seems no likelihood that the Revised Bible will ever supersede the Authorised Version. Whatever its critical value, it is sadly defective in style, and is not to be compared to the older book in rhythm and simplicity. It is equally defective in arrangement, and we greatly miss the tables of contents at the heads of the chapters.

Revised Code of 1862 (*The*). By Lord Sherbrooke. The minutes of the Committee of Council established by government in 1846 on the education of the children of the labouring poor, with government grants based on 'results.'

The three grades of the results are 'fair, good, and excellent,' as tested by government inspectors on examination, and the grant varies accordingly. In 1890 a change was made in the grant by results, by which 'cramming' was greatly checked, and general information was encouraged.

Revising Barrister (*A*). A barrister annually appointed by the English judges to revise the lists of voters for members of Parliament, and to settle who are qualified to vote.

Revival in Belfast (*The*), 1859. A strange religious movement in which the preacher produced hysteria, especially among the mill girls. When any girl was 'struck' the preacher evoked from her a wild continued scream, which of course was catching. Those struck were removed from the church to a darkened room, and there told 'what they had seen and heard.' This experience was in all cases a rigmarole based more or less on the Revelation

Revocation of the Edict of Nantes (*The*), 18 Oct., 1685. It prohibited all exercise of the reformed religion in the kingdom of France. Pastors were to quit France within fifteen days; if, however, they abjured, they were to be endowed with pensions one-third more than their previous salaries, with the reversion of one-third to their widows. If pastors wished to enter the legal profession they might dispense with academic studies. Parents were forbidden to teach their children the reformed religion, and were to bring them to be baptized in the Catholic Church, under a penalty of 500 livres (20*l.*) Refugees who did not return within four months were to suffer confiscation of all their property. Reformers caught in the act of emigrating were to be sent to the galleys (if men), and if women to be imprisoned for life.

By the Edict of Nantes granted by Henri IV. French Protestants enjoyed full freedom of their religion and were placed on the same level in all civil rights as Catholic subjects. It was Louis XIV. who revoked this Edict, whereby 80,000 Protestants fled the country, and 20,000 were slain or driven into the fields houseless and homeless.

Revolt of Egypt (*The*), 1835. A large body of Egyptians having taken refuge in Syria in 1832, · Mehemet Ali sent his son Ibrahim to punish the pacha of Acre for taking them under his protection. Ibrahim was wholly victorious, and, being opposed by a Turkish army, conquered it and took the vizier prisoner. The great powers now interfered, and Syria was added to the pachalik of Egypt, but in 1840 Syria was restored to the Porte by the intervention of the great powers.

Revolt of Hugh O'Neill (*The*), 1597–1599. After the death of Shane O'Neill, Hugh obtained the title of Earl of Tyrone. He was brought up in the English court, and was apparently in the queen's interest; but immediately he returned to Munster he took up an attitude of open defiance and offered Ireland to the King of Spain. In 1597 he defeated the English forces in Tyrone, but in 1601 he was obliged to surrender to Lord Mountjoy. Being brought to England, O'Neill was pardoned, retired to Brussels in 1607, and died at Rome in 1616.

Revolt of the Desmonds, in Ireland, 1579. Rome and Spain thinking Ireland oppressed by Queen Elizabeth, and hoping, through Ireland, to overthrow the great heretic queen, landed on the shores of Kerry a force of 700 men, which was supported by the Earl of Desmond. The invaders were cut to pieces at Smerwick, and Desmond declared a traitor. He was discovered in a hovel, and put to death by his pursuers.

There is a well-known legend that this old man is not dead, but keeps his state under the waters of Lough Gur, and that every seventh year he reappears fully armed, rides round the lake early in the morning, and will ultimately return in the flesh to claim his own again.

Revolution (*The American*), 1775. By which the United States of America threw off their dependence on Great Britain.

Revolution (*The Glorious*), 1688, in English history means the accession of William III., whereby the Stuart dynasty was set aside, and a new dynasty introduced.

William III. was grandson of Charles I., his mother being Mary, eldest daughter of Charles I. He married Mary, eldest daughter of James II. So that the choice of the nation fell on these two from their alliance to the Stuarts both by blood and marriage; but James II. was alive, and his son and grandson were set aside. On the death of William without offspring Anne, another daughter of James II., succeeded.

Revolution (*The Great French*), 1789–1794. A great reaction against absolutism, which began with the destruction of the Bastille. The king, Louis XVI., was beheaded 21 Jan., 1793. The Christian religion was set aside, and the worship of Reason substituted in its place. The Revolution terminated with the death of Robespierre.

Revolution (*The Italian*), 1859–1860. In which the various minor sovereigns of Italy were driven into exile, and the whole Italian peninsula (except the Roman and Venetian territory) was subjected to one ruler styled the 'King of Italy.'

The Roman and Venetian territories were added subsequently—the Venetian States in Oct. 1866, after the Seven Weeks' War; and the Papal States in Oct. 1870.

Revolution (*Victims of the French*). Prudhomme gives the following statistics: 18,603 nobles, priests, artisans, and others; that is 13,623 commoners, 1,467 wives of operatives, 1,278 nobles, 1,125 priests, 750 noblewomen, and 350 religieuses. Besides these 18,603 persons guillotined, we have 403,748 destroyed in various ways at Vendée, Nantes, Lyons, &c. Of these the victims of Vendée were 337,000, of Carrier at Nantes 32,000, of Lyons 31,000; of women who died of grief, &c. 3,748. This does not include those massacred at Versailles, the Abbaye, the Carmelites, the September victims, the victims of the Glacière d'Avignon, of Toulon, of Marseilles, and the whole town of Bedouin.

Revolution of Denmark (*The*), 8 Sept., 1660. By this revolution the kings of Denmark, who had hitherto been feudal chiefs, elected and controlled by the barons, were made hereditary and unlimited sovereigns, both in the male and female line. By the constitution granted by Frederick III., in 1665, the monarch of Denmark was declared to be hereditary and absolute, holding the whole legislative, executive, and judicial power of the state. It vested in him the unlimited power of appointing all public offices and dignities; of commanding the forces of the kingdom by sea and land; of making war, peace, and alliances. It gave him the supreme jurisdiction in ecclesiastical affairs, subject only to the obligation of professing the Protestant religion as expounded by the Confession of Augsburg.

Revolution of February (*The*), 1848. By which the Orleans dynasty was overthrown in France. Eighteen years before (1830) the Bourbon dynasty in the person of Charles X. had been overthrown. The revolution of 1848 occurred on 22, 23, 24 Feb.; on the last of these three days Louis Philippe fled from Paris, and abdicated. *See* p. 538, 'Louis-Philippe.'

Revolution of July (*The*), 1830, when Charles X. was obliged to flee from Paris, and abdicate.

Revolution of the 17th Cent., 1660, began with the restoration of Charles II. It transferred the crown from Cromwell and his party to Charles; it transferred the power of the crown from the king to the House of Commons; it overthrew Puritanism and introduced freedom of religious thought; it changed the manners and customs of the nation; it changed the fashion of dress and domestic life; it even introduced the study of experimental philosophy in place of dogmatism and tradition.

Revolution Society (*The*), 1792. A society numbering many of the highest

names in the Whig aristocracy, which met on the 4th Nov. to celebrate the anniversary of the landing of William III. This society sent a glowing address to the French National Assembly, which was carried over by Lord Stanhope and Dr. Price. In their address they vowed that they 'would never again fight with France at the command of any despot.'

The 4th Nov. was William's day. He was born 4 Nov., 1650; he took Bonn 4-12 Nov., 1673; he married the Princess Mary 4 Nov., 1677; and the 4th Nov. was the anniversary of his landing at Torbay in 1688.

Revolutionary Army (*The*), Sept. 1793. A Parisian guard, raised by the Convention at the instigation of Barère, to clear Paris of all enemies of the Republic, or (in other words) to massacre all who differed in opinion from the leaders of the revolution. The property of these victims was seized and confiscated to the state.

Revolutionary Committees (1793) were appointed by the Convention to act under the Committee of Public Safety, to receive denunciations and report them. *See* 'Revolutionary Tribunal.'

Revolutionary Parties in France between '93 and '95. *See* 'Partis en France.'

Revolutionary Tribunal (*The*), March 1793. A court of judgment instituted by the French Convention (*q.v.*) to quash conspiracies against the revolutionary government. This infamous court sat in judgment on all persons accused of disaffection to the state. During the Reign of Terror, when Fouquier Tinville was 'public accuser,' it acquired a horrible notoriety, being a mere official tool in the hands of Robespierre.

Revolver Boys, about 1885. Irish moonlighters, land-leaguers, and others, supplied with revolvers to shoot at those obnoxious to the secret societies. Generally the legs were aimed at. *See* 'Irish Associations.'

Rex Gentis Anglorum. The over-king of the English heptarchs, the first being Hengist king of Kent (457), and the last Egbert king of Wessex (who in 827 became bretwalda or king of all England).

Rhapsodists. Greek minstrels who wandered from place to place reciting in musical chant the epic ballads of Homer and other poets. After Peisistratos reduced the Homeric ballads into a connected epic, the occupation of the rhapsodists rapidly declined.

A rhapsody means a single canto, ballad, or part, suitable for one sitting or entertainment.

Rhode Island (U.S. America). So named, in 1663, from the isle of Rhodes in the Mediterranean. There seems no special reason for this name, but it is so called in the charter of Charles II. An old nickname of the people is *Gunflints.*

Rhodian Law (*The*). The earliest known code of marine law ; it was compiled by the Rhodians about B.C. 900. Probably the marine laws of Justinian were based on the Rhodian code.

Rhodian School of Sculpture (*The*). Famous for (1) the Colossus, by Charês, one of the seven wonders of the world ; (2) the Laocoön group, by Agesander, Polydōrus, and Athenodōrus ; and (3) the Farnesian bull, in the museum of Naples. This group represents Zethus and Amphīon binding Dircê to a wild bull in order to revenge their mother. It was the work of Apollonius and Tauriscus, and was discovered in 1546. Called Farnesian because it was set up in the palace of Farnesê at Rome.

Rhone of Christian Eloquence (*The*). St. Hilary (A.D. 300–368), bishop of Poitiers.

Rhuddlan (*Statute of*), 10 Edw. I. 1282. In Rhuddlan (North Wales) Edward I. held a parliament, which secured to the Welsh certain rights ; and in this town, in 1284, the infant Edward was acknowledged as ' the Prince of Wales.' The statute of Rhuddlan is the statute confirming to the Welsh the rights conferred on them by Edward I. Amongst other grants conferred by this statute, Anglesey was erected into a county.

It is said that Edward was born at Carnarvon.

Rialto (*The*) of Venice. A contraction of *Rivo alto*, the deep stream. First the name of an island in the Lagune, called ' Isola di Rialto ' ; then of the bridge called ' Il Ponte di Rialto,' connecting the island with the opposite shore ; and lastly of the exchange called the Rialto which stands on the island, and is so familiar from Shakespeare's ' Merchant of Venice.'

Ribalds (*The*), 1189. A militia raised by Philippe II. Auguste of France.

The captain was called the ' king of the Ribalds,' united by Charles V. of France to the ' Provost of the Hotel.' Disbanded on account of their unbridled licentiousness.

Ribalds or Ribauds, from the Latin *ripalis*, from *ripa*, a bank or border. The licentiousness of these soldiers gave birth to our word *ribald*, obscene.
Prof. Skeat derives ribald from the French *riber*, to dally with women.

Ribbonism. The political principles of the Ribbonmen of Ireland. *See next article.*

Ribbonmen, 1808. A secret association among the lowest classes in Ireland opposed to the Orange confederation. It originated in Armagh, spreading into Down, Antrim, Tyrone, Mon'aghan, and Fermānagh (where Protestants most abounded), but either under the same or some other name it had affiliated societies in King's County, Queen's County, Meath, Louth, and Tipperary. The members had their secret signs and pass-words, and though at first confined to the lowest classes, embraced later on farm-labourers, artisans, and even clergymen and merchants. The main object of the society was to prevent landlords from evicting or changing their tenants, or new tenants from taking the farms of evicted tenants. ' Tenant right ' or fixity of tenure was also an essential part of their demand which they determined to carry out to the death ; and general interference between employers and the employed. Ribbonism was suppressed by Act of Parliament in 1871, but only to break out again under some other name. From 1840 it was in the fullest operation. *See* ' Irish Associations.'

It is supposed that the name refers to some badge worn by the members.
The Ribbonmen apparently branched from the ' Defenders,' a Catholic counter-organisation to the Orangemen, who were Protestants, and are so still.
The Defenders being proclaimed changed their name in 1806 into ' Threshers,' who for the most part appeared in Sligo, Mayo, Leitrim, Longford, and Ca'van.
Next appear the Ribbonmen in 1808, first in Armagh, and thence spreading north and north-west.
Other societies sprang up in other parts of Ireland, i.e.—
The *Carders* in East and West Meath, Roscommon, and part of Mayo.
The *Shanavests* and *Caravats* in Tipperary, Kilkenny, Cork, and Limerick.
The *Phenicians*, the *Brotherhood of St. Patrick*, the *Fenians*, &c. follow in rapid succession. *See each of these.*

Rice Christians. Hindûs and Chinese who profess to be converted for the sake of the rice given by the missionaries to converts. Followers of Christ, not for his doctrines, but for the loaves and fishes.

Richard Cœur de Lion. *See* 'Richard I.'

Richard of Bordeaux. *See* 'Richard II.'

Richard surnamed Crookback. *See* 'Richard III.'

Richard I., surnamed 'Cœur de Lion' for his great daring and courage in the Holy Land during the crusade against Saladin. He was the third son of Henry II. of England, and married Berengaria, daughter of Sancho, king of Navarre, but had no lawful issue. Richard I. was the first to adopt the words '*Dei gratia*' before his titles. His style was 'Richardus, D.G. rex Angliæ et dux Normandiæ et Aquitaniæ [*Guienne*], et comes Andegaviæ [Anjou].'

When he travelled through Germany from the Holy Land, he assumed the name of Hugh the Merchant.

The youth who shot him with an arrow discharged from the castle of Chaluz was Bertrand de Gurdun or Gourdon. Being asked why he shot the king, the lad replied, 'Because he slew my father and two brothers.' Richard commanded that Bertrand should be set free, but Marcadee, leader of the Brabançons, flayed him alive, and then hanged him.

Richard II., of England, called Bordeaux,' because he was born there (1366, reigned 1377–1399, died 1400). He was the only son of the Black Prince and the Fair Maid of Kent (his wife). Richard II. married twice, but left no issue. His first wife was Anne of Luxembourg, daughter of the kaiser-king Karl IV., aged 15. His second wife was a mere child of 7, viz. Isabelle, daughter of Charles VI. of France.

His style was 'Richardus, D.G. rex Angliæ et Franciæ, et dominus Hiberniæ.'

It is generally asserted that when Richard was deposed he was imprisoned in Pontefract Castle, and murdered there or starved to death; but it has been also said that he made his escape, and lived many years disguised as an ordinary man. They say that the person exhibited to the people as the deceased king was his chaplain, Maudelain. This rumour was still rife in the reign of Henry V., when Thomas de Trumpington, in 1415, was induced to palm himself off as the deposed king.

In 1402 the French court sent Creton, the page of Richard II., into Scotland to ascertain if Richard was indeed alive, and Creton declared the Scotch Richard to be an undoubted impostor. The French ordinance for the payment of Craton still exists, and may be seen in the Archæologia. Serle before he was executed confessed that the Scotch Richard was Thomas Warde, Richard's court fool.

Richard III., of England, surnamed 'Crookback' (1452, 1483–1485), was the younger brother of Edward IV., and uncle of Edward V., whom he succeeded. He married Anne, widow of Edward prince of Wales (son of Henry VI.), and was slain in the battle of Bosworth Field.

His style was 'Richardus, D.G. rex Angliæ et Franciæ, et dominus Hiberniæ.'

EDWARD III.'s third son was Lionel, who had a daughter named Philippa. Philippa married Edward Mortimer, and their son was Roger Mortimer.

Roger Mortimer's daughter (Lady Anne) married Richard (son of Edmund duke of York), and their son was the famous Richard duke of York, 'the White Rose,' slain in the battle of Wakefield, leaving behind him two sons, EDWARD IV. and RICHARD III.

Whether Richard III. had a 'crookback' is very doubtful. Shakespeare makes him deformed, but this might be out of flattery to Queen Elizabeth, who was of the Lancastrian or Red Rose House. Stowe says of Richard III., 'He was comely enough, though low of stature.'

Richard IV., of England. Peter or Perkin Warbeck, who was put forward to personate Richard duke of York, younger son of Edward IV., and one of the two princes murdered in the Tower of London in 1492. Charles VIII. of France received the pretender as the true prince and paid him regal honours (1492). Margaret duchess of Burgundy acknowledged him as her nephew in 1493 ; James IV. of Scotland received him as the prince, and gave him to wife Lady Catherine Gordon, granddaughter of James I. (1493). 'Richard' invaded England in 1496, and assumed the royal title of Richard IV. (7 Sept. 1497), but he soon surrendered, and was committed to the Tower in Oct. 1497. He made his escape on 9 June, 1498, was retaken and put to death 23 Nov., 1499. His wife Lady Catherine received an appointment in the queen's household, was three times married, and died at Fyfield, Berks, 1537.

It is said that Perkin Warbeck was son of John Warbeck, or Osbeck, a renegade Jew of Tournaye, with whom Edward IV. did business. Some, however, maintain that he was the son of Edward IV. and the beautiful Catherine de Faro. Without doubt he bore a striking likeness to the king.

Richmondism. That the higher the price of corn the higher will be the wages of agricultural labourers. This was an axiom of the Chartists. When Joseph Lankaster, in 1844, was arrested for setting fire to wheat-stacks in order to raise the price of wages, the act was called by the free-traders 'Richmondism put in practice.'

Ricimer. A Roman general of Suevian origin, grandson of Walha the Goth. He rose to the highest rank, and for eighteen years was the 'king-maker' of the west. In 456 he dethroned Avītus and gave the crown to Majorian. Majorian being assassinated in 461, Ricīmer gàve the purple to Libius Sevērus (467), and married his daughter. In 472 (Severus being murdered) Ricimer placed Olybius on the throne. But the king-maker died forty weeks afterwards.

In the decrepitude of the western empire . . . . the Ricimers and Odoäcers put up and pulled down at pleasure a succession of insignificant princes, dignified with the names of 'Cæsar' and 'Augustus.'—PRINCE, *Parallel History*, vol. ii. p. 627.

Riding the Marches. 'Beating the bounds' of a parish. Saxon *mearc*, a boundary.

Ridley Hall, Cambridge, 1882. For training young men in the 'evangelical principles' of the Church of England.

Rienzi the Tribune (1310–1354). A man of mean birth invited by Pope Clement VI. to Rome, then in a state of anarchy. Rienzi proclaimed in 1347 a new constitution, drove away the turbulent barons, and put a stop to brigandage. He then received the title of Tribune with dictatorial power, and formed a design of making all Italy one united republic. He lost his popularity and was driven from Rome in 1348, returned in 1352, but was slain in 1354 in an insurrection.

Right and Fact, 1653. This distinction arose from a book called 'Augustīnus' by Cornelius Jansen, who died in 1638, just as the book was finished. The Jesuits condemned the book, and Urban VIII. pronounced it heretical. The friends of the book admitted that the five propositions condemned as heretical were in point of *right* justly condemned, but declared that in point of *fact* no such doctrines were taught or could be deduced from the book in question. That is, the doctrines condemned by the bull were heretical doctrines, but they were not the doctrines taught in Jansen's book.

In consequence of the bull of Urban VIII. against 'the five propositions,' the Jansenists maintained that though the pope is infallible in points of *faith*, he is not infallible in points of *fact*.

Right, Left, Centre (*The*). In the French Parliament. The Right, *i.e.* the conservatives or landed gentry. The Left, *i.e.* the rich wine merchants and other radicals. The Centre, *i.e.* the moderate party or Laodiceans.

Right-boys, 1787. An offshoot of the White-boys or agrarian rebels, who rose in defence of Irish 'rights,' and waged uncompromising war for a time against the exaction of tithes from Roman Catholics in support of the Anglican church in Ireland, and against various grievances connected with the tenure of lands. See 'Irish Associations.'

Right Honourable. Honourable by legal right. The younger children of earls and the children of viscounts and barons are called 'Honourable,' but have no legal right to the peerage. A peer, being Right Honourable, has such a right. Members of the privy council, even if commoners, and the mayors of London and York are right honourable because they are *lords* ex officio, and not by courtesy only. The former are, by right of office, 'Lords of H.M. Privy Council,' and the latter are by legal right 'lord mayors of London and York.'

Not only members of the privy council, but all who have been members. The Lord Mayor of Dublin and the Lord Provost of Edinburgh are also called 'Right Honourable.'

Right of Way. The right of passing over or through the grounds of another person, as over a path in a field or park which has been tacitly permitted by immemorial usage.

It is still thought in some places that a funeral procession passing over a field gives a right of way. I know a village where the man who walks at the head of the procession sticks a pin in the gate-post by way of fee or acknowledgment that there is no free 'right of way' through the field.

Rights (*The Bill of*). The statute 1 William and Mary, st. 2, chap. 2, A.D. 1689, in which is embodied the Declaration of Rights presented by both houses to William and Mary in the banqueting-house at Whitehall, 13 Feb., 1689. The bill contains thirteen clauses: (1) No law shall be suspended or held in abeyance without consent of parliament; (2) it is illegal for the crown to dispense with a law or suspend its operation; (3) courts of commission for ecclesiastical causes are illegal; (4) it is illegal to levy money by royal prerogative or without consent of parliament; (5) subjects shall have free right to petition the king; (6) it is illegal to keep a standing army without consent of parliament; (7) Protestants may carry arms in self-defence; (8) elections for members of parliament shall be free and unrestrained; (9) freedom of debate shall not be tampered with; (10) excessive bail and excessive fines are illegal; (11) jurors shall be duly empanelled and returned, only freeholders shall be jurors for high treason; (12) fines before conviction are illegal; (13) parliaments shall be called together frequently. N.B. It transferred the sovereignty from the king to the House of Commons. *See* 'Petition of Rights.'

Rights of Man (*The*), 1795. Published by the Batavian Republic.

1. All men are born with equal rights.

2. Each man has a right to serve God or not as he chooses

3. All the men of a state are eligible to office in that state.

4. Every functionary ought to give an account of his administration.

5. The people have a right to choose and change their rulers and magistrates.

Rights of Man (*The Society of the*), 1791. The name adopted by the club of the Cordeliers, after Bailly, the mayor, shut them out of their hall, because Danton denounced both him [Bailly] and Lafayette as traitors. The members removed to the Paris tennis-court and changed their name.

Rimbecco. The reproach by the relatives of a murdered man that the next akin has not followed up the blood-feud according to the custom of the vendetta. In Genöa the uttering of such reproach was punishable, but in Corsica the vendetta is considered so sacred a duty that the *rimbecco* is practically unknown.

Ring. At Rome the different orders of citizens were distinguished by a ring; in the early days of the republic only senators wore rings of gold, subsequently knights wore them, and later on anyone who chose wore one or more of them. Slaves wore an iron ring. The man in marriage gives the bride a ring to show that he confides in her the seal of his rights in his possessions. A ring with the cross is the symbol of pastoral power; it is given by the pope to cardinals, archbishops, and bishops; sometimes the ring is enchased with an amethyst. The pope's ring, called the 'Fisher's Ring,' with which he signs his briefs, has the image of St. Peter sitting in his boat. At the death of the pope the ring is broken.

Ring (*A*). Juvenal, speaking of Hannibal, says—

No sword his death, no dart, nor suchlike thing,

Rings he at Cannæ reaped, his death a ring.

At the battle of Cannæ 5,630 Roman knights were slain, and three bushels of gold rings were sent to Carthage (B.C. 216). In 183 the great hero poisoned himself with the contents of a ring which he wore.

Ring and Crozier, 1052. First given to a bishop on his consecration by Kaiser Heinrich III. as a symbol of investiture (*q.v.*). After the settlement of the moot point of investiture, the pope invested the bishop with ring and crozier, and the king invested him with a sceptre. *See* 'Hallam,' vol. ii. p. 266.

Ring-money. A very ancient coinage in use with the Egyptians. Cæsar mentions both gold and iron rings as used in Gaul and Britain for money. Sometimes a number of these rings were strung together into a chain, one or more being detached when required in payment of service. In 1805 a silver chain of thirty-three such rings was dug up near Inverness, and is now in the museum of the Scottish Antiquaries.

Ring of the Fisherman (*The*). The papal official seal. *See* 'Ring.'

Rings. Military encampments. Low Latin, *rinca* or *ringa*. The Avars lived in camps called *rings*, because they were disposed in concentric circles, and when Charlemagne in 796 exterminated these Huns, he took possession of their *rings*, where he found rich plunder which they had been accumulating for many years.

Rings of the Avars (*The*). Wooden fortifications which encompassed their villages and districts. Destroyed by Charlemagne, A.D. 796.

Ringan (*St.*), *i.e.* St. Ninian.

Their devotion to this church of St. Ninian, or, as she was popularly termed, St. Ringan.—Sir W. SCOTT, *The Pirate*, chap. xxv.

Ripaille Fraternity (*The*). A brotherhood of aged knights founded by Amadeus VIII., noted for their luxurious living, and giving rise to the phrase *faire ripaille*, to live jollily. Ripaille is the château of Savoy, and the Duke Amadeus was afterwards Pope Felix V. He abdicated his dukedom in 1434, when he retired to Ripaille, and left it when he was pope, 1440–1449.

Ritchie's Act (*Mr.*), 1888. The Local Government Act, of which Mr. Ritchie was the sponsor. *See* p. 220, 'County Councils, 1889,' and p. 529, 'Local Government Act.'

Ritual or **Pastoral** (*The*). A book containing directions for all the pastoral duties of the inferior clergy of the Roman Catholic Church, such as the administration of the sacraments and the celebration of the daily services. The book, which contains all that pertains to the celebration of the mass, is usually called the Missal. The two chief rituals are those of Rome and Paris. *See* 'Ceremonial' and 'Pontifical.'

Ritualism now means that stricter observance of church rites and ceremonies introduced by what is called the 'Oxford Party,' or 'High Church.' *See* p. 421, and 'Tractarians.'

Ritualism abjured. In 1890 was introduced in Suffolk the 'Besom Pledge,' to sweep from the land ritualism and Romanism. The phrase was suggested by the words of Isaiah, 'I will sweep it with the besom of destruction.'

River of Paradise (*The*). St. Bernard, abbot of Clairvaux (1091–1153). Also called the 'Mellifluous Doctor.'

Robber Synod (*The*), A.D. 449. A council held at Ephesus against Flaviānus. This council declared in favour of Eutychianism, and was called *Latrocinium*, or the Assembly of Thieves and Robbers.

Robbers of the Bristol Mail (*The*). John Hawkins and George Sympson, executed on Hounslow Heath, 1722.

Robe (*The*), worn by Jesus at the crucifixion (John xix. 23). Two robes claim pre-eminence—viz. ' the holy robe of Trèves' and 'the holy robe of Argenteuil.' The former is by far the more

delicate fabric, the latter being a tissue of goat's hair without seam. We are told that the robe of Trèves was the one worn as a shirt, and that of Argenteuil was the tunic for which the soldiers cast lots. Gregory of Tours tells us that this tunic was bought of the soldier who won the lot, and, being packed in a wooden box, was sent to Galatia, then removed for safety to Jaffa, then to Jerusalem. When Jerusalem was taken by the Persians, this tunic was removed to Persia; then, in 627, to Constantinople. It was given by Irene empress of Constantinople to Charlemagne, who sent it in 800 to his daughter Theodrada abbess of Argenteuil. A curé of Argenteuil cut the robe into several pieces, so that it is not now possible to piece the parts together.

The *White Robe* in which the soldiers of Herod arrayed Jesus is said to be at Venice.

The *Purple*, or *Scarlet Robe*, in which he was arrayed by the Roman soldiers, was divided (we are told) between the churches of St. Francis of Philip Anagni, St. John Lateran, and Santa Maria Maggiore. *See* 'Crucifixion, *Relics of the*.'

Moscow claims to have a robe of Christ, and so do several other places, as St. Prassada, Rome, St. Roch, &c.

Christ is always represented in the Gospels as a very poor man, but the shirt of Trèves is that of a prince, and must have been of fabulous price. The same inconsistency is remarkable in numerous other sacred 'relics.'

Robe of the Disdain (*The*). A robe given to the court-bard of Wales, at Christmas, Easter, and Whitsuntide. The bard sat next to the prefect of the palace and received from him his harp. When, however, the bard sang to the troops before a battle, the king himself handed to him his harp, and the queen a gold ring.

Robes of State. Peers have the privilege of wearing in parliament robes of scarlet cloth, differenced by bars of ermine. DUKES have 4 bars on each side; MARQUISES have 4 bars on the right side and 3 on the left; EARLS have 3 bars on each side, but VISCOUNTS and BARONS have on each side 2 rows of plain white fur, not ermine.

Robert Emmett. *See* 'Sons of Freedom.'

Robervallian Lines, 1646. Certain curves in geometry, invented by Gilles Persone de Roberval, delimiting the boundaries of lines infinitely extended in length, yet equal to other spaces which are terminated on all sides.

Robespierre's Soldiers, 1794. The French soldiers were so called by foreign potentates, intimating that Robespierre was virtually king of France. The term occurs in a proclamation by the Duke of York.

Robespierre's Weavers, 1793. The rowdy women, consisting of fishwives and other females of the lowest grade, who joined Henriot's *sans-culottes* called the Parisian Guard. This miscellaneous riff-raff lined all the avenues of the chamber during the session of the National Assembly, and never ceased yelling 'Down with the Girondists!'

Robin Bluestring. Sir Robert Walpole (1676–1745), so called because as knight of the garter he wore a blue ribbon. He was also called the 'Grand Corruptor,' because bribery was practised by him on all occasions.

Robin Hood's Day. 1 May, the anniversary of the death of Robin Hood (1247).

Robin of Redesdale, Robert Hilyard, an insurgent in the reign of Edward IV.; executed in 1469. He seems to have been a political tool of the Nevilles, who played him off against the Woodvilles.

Robinsonians. Followers of John Robinson of Leyden, a puritan divine (1575–1625). He seceded from the Church of England in 1604; escaped to Amsterdam in 1608; removed to Leyden in 1609; and conducted the service at the embarkation of the *Pilgrim Fathers,* 21 July, 1620.

The Robinsonians were only semi-Separatists, the Brownists were rigid Separatists.

Rob Roy. Robert king of freebooters was Robert M'Gregor Campbell, a Highland chief, born about 1657, and died after 1733.

Rock of Lamentation (*The*). Craigchonichen, in Kincardine, where the Marquis of Montrose fought his last battle, April 1650.

Rockites, in Ireland. Followers of 'Captain Rock,' a name assumed by the leader of the Irish insurgents in 1822.

Letters so signed were sent to persons opposed or obnoxious to the league, threatening death, or personal injury, or loss of property, unless the person addressed subscribed to the league, or did something specified, or forbore to do something. The threats held out were not vain words, and a warning from 'Captain Rock' was a real terror. The Rockites made themselves conspicuous in the sanguinary tithe-war (*q.v.*) 1830–1832. *See* p. 455, 'Irish Associations.'

Rogation Days prescribed by the first Council of Orleans in 511 are the Monday, Tuesday, and Wednesday preceding Ascension Day. The term means the Days of Supplication, and on these days the Catholic Church enjoins that the Litanies be recited or sung in public procession. In the Anglican Church the days are only faintly observed; but 'Beating the Bounds,' or the 'Perambulation of Parishes' was very general to the middle of the 19th cent., and even still survives in some parts of Great Britain.

Rogations (*Day of the*), 10 May, 1790 (French history). The day selected by the Municipal Council to visit the convents about to be suppressed. Extinct.

Rogations (*Fête of the*), A.D. 474. Instituted by St. Mamert bishop of Vienne, in Dauphiné, to invoke God's blessings on the fruits of the earth. It is celebrated three days before the Ascension.

Roger Bold. Robert Harley first Earl of Oxford of the name of Harley (1661–1724).

The De Veres were created earls of Oxford in the reign of Stephen, and the earldom became extinct in 1702 on the death of Aubrey de Vere, the twentieth earl.

Rogue-money, Scotland. Imposed by 11 Geo. II. c. 28 (1737), and abolished in 1868. It was an annual cess for defraying the expenses of apprehending offenders, maintaining them in gaol, and prosecuting them.

Roi Panade. Louis XVIII. of France (1755, 1814–1824).

A *panade* is a pipkin for babies' pap.

Roi de Pâques. The boy or man who draws by lot the bean in the Twelfth-night cake. This person is 'king' for the nonce, according to the rules of the game.

The word *pâque* in this case means the Epiphany, the 'Pascua de Epifania.'

Roi de Théâtre (*Un*). Joachim Murat king of Naples, who used to parade the streets of Naples in silks and satins, like a stage-king (1771–1815).

Roi des Halles (*Le*). François de Vendôme duc de Beaufort (1616–1669), grandson of Henri IV. and Gabrielle d'Estrées, idolised by the common people, and one of the leaders of the Fronde against the court party.

Roi des Versailles (*Le*). Nickname of M. Thiers the French historian (1797–1877). *See* 'Attila le Petit.'

Rois Chevelures (*Les*). The long-haired kings. So the successors of Clodion in Gaul were designated. Clodion introduced from Germany the custom of wearing long hair.

It will be remembered that Homer calls the magnates of the confederate Greek army 'the Long-haired Greeks.' St. Paul denounces long hair for men (1 Cor. xi. 14).

Rois Fainéants (*Les*), 638–742. Clovis II. and his ten successors. These worthless kings were all parents at 15, and old men at 30, to which age only one of them attained. Clotaire IV. died at the age of 12; Clovis III. and Dagobert III. at 15; Clotaire III. at 18; Chilpéric II. at 20; Clovis II. at 23; Thierry IV. at 25; Childebert II. at 28; and Thierry III. was the only one who outlived the age of 30.

Louis V., the last of the Carlovingian kings, was also surnamed 'Le Fainéant.'

Roll of Arms (*The*). An heraldic record of arms which goes back to the reign of Henry III. The original vellum roll is lost, but a copy made in 1586 by Glover, Somerset herald, is preserved in the English College of Arms.

Roll of Caerlaverock (*The*). An heraldic poem in Norman French, reciting the names and arms of the knights present at the siege of Caerlaverock in 1300.

Roll of Court. The court-roll in a manor, wherein the business of the court, the admissions, surrenders, names, rents, and services of the tenants, are copied and enrolled.

Rolls (*Master of the*). 'Magister Rotulorum.' The chief of a body of officers called 'Masters of Chancery.' He is judge of the Equity court, and ranks next to the Lord Chancellor. The Master of the Rolls has the keeping of the rolls and grants which pass the great seal, and the records of Chancery. Since 1838 he has been charged with the direction of the Public Record Office.

Rolls Court (*The*). The Chancery Court of the Master of the Rolls in Chancery Lane. The house was originally called *Domus Conversōrum*, being appointed by Henry III. for the use of converted Jews; but Edward II. converted it into a place for the custody of the rolls. In 1838 the Master of the Rolls was placed in charge of the Public Record Office, and under his superintendence have been translated, printed, and published a large number of MS. rolls; a magnificent historic work, which still goes on with great judgment and activity.

Rolls of Court (*The*). In Scotch law. The lists of causes depending on the Court of Session.

Rolls of Parliament. The MS. registers of the proceedings of our old parliament.

Rolls of the Exchequer. Rolls relating to the revenue of the country.

Rolls of the King's Court (*The*). Reports of legal processes from the 6 Rich. I. to 1 John. A very valuable document still extant giving great information on the status of the people, wages paid, their wealth, their legal rights, &c.

Rolls of the Temple, or 'Calves-head rolls,' in which every bencher, barrister, and student is taxed yearly in consideration of a dinner of calves-head, provided in Easter term.

Rolled Bacon. A consignment of dynamite from America to London. So called from being packed in barrels of what was invoiced as 'Rolled Bacon.' Sometimes these consignments were invoiced as 'American Apples' (1884–1885).

Rolliad (*The*). A series of political satires, the first of which appeared in a London newspaper in 1784, and was a humorous criticism on Colonel Rolle (afterwards Lord Rolle), member for Devonshire. The most important of the series was a pretended review of an imaginary epic poem.

Roman Achilles (*The*). Lucius Sicinius Dentātus. Assassinated B.C. 450.

Roman Catholic Hierarchy of England and Wales since 1850, constituted by Pius IX. The 'Province of Westminster' consists of the archiepiscopal See of Westminster and fourteen Suffragan Sees of

Birmingham	Northampton
Clifton	Nottingham
Hexham and Newcastle	Plymouth
Leeds	Portsmouth
Liverpool	Salford
Middlesborough	Shrewsbury
Newport and Menevia	Southwark

In 1890 there were 2,635 Catholic priests in Great Britain under the hierarchy, and 1,030 places having churches or chapels, with resident clergy, independent of those places which have weekly services, but no resident priest.

The hierarchy of Scotland was appointed in 1878 by Leo XIII., and comprises (1) the Province of St. Andrews and Edinburgh, with four suffragan sees (viz. Aberdeen, Argyll and the Isles, Dunkeld, and Galloway); and (2) the archiepiscopal See of Glasgow without suffragan sees.

Roman Catholicism (*Development of*).

	A.D.
Prayers for the dead began	200
Paul, the first hermit	251
Sunday made by Constantine the Christian Sabbath	321
First General Council, at Nice in Bithynia...	325
Celibacy of the clergy recommended ...	325
The Scriptures called the Bible by Jerome	340
SAINTS, MARTYRS, and ANGELS (*adoration of*)	360
Christmas Day a religious festival	375
Bells used in churches	390
The Nicene Creed introduced	391
(Except the word 'Dead,' and 'Communion of Saints.')	
MARY called the MOTHER OF GOD ...	431
Sprinkling of Ashes, in Lent (Felix III.) ...	487
Canon of Scripture completed	494
Priests began to wear a distinctive dress ...	500
Stone altars enjoined	506
EXTREME UNCTION introduced by Felix IV.	525
Lenten Fast extended to forty days (Council of Orleans)	547
PRAYERS addressed to the Virgin MARY ...	593
Worship in an unknown tongue	600
(It was in Latin as far back as 547.)	
The title of POPE first assumed by Boniface III.	606
PAPAL SUPREMACY assumed at the same time	606
All-Saints' Day introduced	625
Holy Bread first distributed	655
Athanasian Creed introduced	670
(Athanasius died 373)	
CRUCIFIXES used as talismans	680
HOLY WATER introduced	682
Kissing the Pope's toe introduced	708
(Abolished in 1773)	
VENERATION OF IMAGES imposed	788
Tithes exacted	789
Rogation days established by Leo III. ...	801
ASSUMPTION FESTIVAL introduced	813
Cardinals created ... ... ••	817

	A.D.
THE 'FILIOQUE' DOGMA introduced	830
Baptism of bells introduced	965
CANONISATION OF SAINTS introduced by John XVI. ... ... ••	993
All-Souls' Day appointed	998
Advent Sunday appointed..	1000
CELIBACY OF PRIESTS made obligatory .	1000
Prayers for souls in purgatory introduced ...	1000
INDULGENCES first bestowed by Ponce, bishop of Arles	1002
INTERDICTS introduced	1073
INFALLIBILITY OF THE ROMAN CHURCH taught	1076
EXCOMMUNICATION introduced by Gregory VII.	1077
SALE OF INDULGENCES sanctioned ...	1087
PLENARY INDULGENCE 'in this life and in the life to come,' authorised by the Council of Clermont	1095
Office of the Virgin Mary appointed by ditto	1095
TRANSUBSTANTIATION made a Church dogma	1215
AURICULAR CONFESSION officially imposed ...	1215
ADORATION OF THE HOST enjoined ...	1218
The INQUISITION established	1229
The CUP WITHHELD from the LAITY	1263
The Angelus announced by a bell	1316
The dogma of PURGATORY officially recognised	1439
HOLY OIL in chrism first used	1540
TRADITION declared authoritative ...	1540
VENERATION OF RELICS enjoined by the Council of Trent	1563
Marriage made a sacrament	1563
Confirmation made a sacrament ...	1563
The Festival of the Seven Sorrows introduced by Benedict XIII.	1725
The festival of the Sacred Heart introduced	1732
The IMMACULATE CONCEPTION proclaimed ..	1854
PAPAL INFALLIBILITY proclaimed ...	1870

. A glance down this list will give a better history of the Catholic Church than many volumes, whether from the Catholic or Protestant standpoint.

Roman Catholics, or, as they call themselves, 'Catholics.' Those Christians who acknowledge the supremacy of the Church of Rome. They believe that St. Peter was appointed by Christ head of the Apostolic College, that this same apostle founded the Roman diocese, and that the present pope comes in direct line by ordination from the first founder. All Roman Catholics accept seven sacraments (*q.v.*), believe in the doctrine of transubstantiation, withhold the cup from the laity as unnecessary, admit the infallibility of the pope when he speaks *ex cathedra*, believe in the doctrine of purgatory, in the efficacy of masses and prayers for the dead, in works of supererogation, the advocacy of saints, the sanctity of relics, and, above all, the power and exaltation of the Virgin Mary, whom they call 'the Mother of God' and 'Queen of Heaven.' In the Eastern rite the cup is given to the laity.

As the Roman Church seceded from the Eastern Church they are in reality schismatics. They rent the robe in two, the Protestants merely tore the rent a little further.

Roman Era (*The*). This era began 24 April, B.C. 753.

Roman Hercules (*The*). The Emperor Commŏdus (A.D. 161, 180–192). So he styled himself, and the club and lion's hide were placed by the side of his throne among the ensigns of sovereignty.

Roman Literature (*The Four Ages of*).

1. The *Golden* Age, B.C. 217 to A.D. 14. It includes Plautus, Ennius, Terence, Cato, Catullus, Cæsar, Cicero, Nepos, Sallust, Virgil, Tibullus, Propertius, Horace, Phædrus, Ovid, and Livy.

2. The *Silver* Age (A.D. 14–117), includes Celsus, Persius, Seneca, Lucan, Pliny, Juvenal, Martial, Quintilian, Statius, Tacitus, and Florus.

3. The *Brazen* Age (A.D. 117–476), includes Justin, Eutropius, Vegetius, Ausŏnius, Macrŏbius, Symmachus, Victor, Claudian, and Orŏsius.

4. The *Iron* Age, from 476, includes Sulpicius, Apollinaris, Boëthius, Priscian, Festus, Jornandes, and Cassiodŏrus.

Roman Liturgy (*The*). The oldest forms of this liturgy are to be found in the three Sacramentaries (viz. those of Leo, Gelasius, and Gregory the Great). That of Gregory the Great is most pronounced in the modern Roman missal, brought into its present shape by a commission appointed by the Council of Trent (16th cent.). Revised first by Pius V., then by Urban VIII., and thirdly by Clement VIII.

Said to have been the work of Peter the apostle, but without a shadow of proof. The Roman, the Milan, the Gallican, and the Spanish liturgies are the four chief ones of the Latin Church.

Roman Obedience. In ecclesiastical history means adherence to the Roman pope in opposition to the Avignon pope in the great Western Schism (*q.v.*). Sometimes it implies adherence to Latin Christianity, instead of Greek, Anglican, &c.

Roman Republic (*The*). The name, after the transfer of the seat of government to Constantinople, was confined to the Latin provinces.

Roman Tribes (*The*). The three original tribes were: (1) The 'Ramnenses,' so called (says Livy, i. 13) 'a Romulo'; (2) 'Tatienses,' from Tatius king of the Sabines; and (3) 'Luceres' (people of the grove), *i.e.* those received into the grove which Romulus turned

into a sanctuary. (Virgil, 'Æneid,' viii. 342.)

Ramnenses. Of course '-enses' is a mere termination, meaning 'a man or men of.' This leaves 'Ram-' as the crude form. 'Rem-us' is another variant. 'Ram-,' 'Rem-,' 'Rom-,' 'Romanus,' with *-ensis*, will explain the derivation of Livy. We have 'Catanensis' for 'Caithness,' 'Elfin-ensis' for 'Elphin,' 'Imelacensis' for 'Emley,' 'Midensis' for 'Midd,' *i.e.* 'Meath,' 'Osti-ensis' for 'Ostia,' 'Palensis' for 'Palencia,' 'Sabi-ensis' for 'Siben,' 'Uticensis' for 'Utica,' and hundreds of others.

Roman Type. The upright type used in the printing of this book, first used at Rome in 1467 by Sweynheim and Pannartz. The type previously used was what is called 'black letter.' Sloping letters are called 'italics' (*q.v.*), and type used in the heading of these articles is termed 'Clarendon type.'

Romans (*Emperor of the*), and 'Emperor-Elect of the Romans.' *See* under ' Emperor,' &c.

Romans (*King of the*), and 'King of Rome.' *See under* 'King,' &c.

Romans (*Last of the*).
I. Cato, called ' Uticensis ' (B.C. 95–46).
II. Caius Cassius was so called by Brutus.

The last of all the Romans fare thee well!
It is impossible that ever Rome
Should breed thy fellow.
    SHAKESPEARE, *Julius Cæsar*, v. 8.

III. Rienzi, last of the Tribunes (1310–1354).
IV. Horace Walpole, *Ultimus Romanorum* (1717–1797).
V. Charles James Fox (1749–1806).

Romance Languages (*The*) Languages based on the Latin.
1. Italian.
2. The Wallachian or Roumanian.
3. Spanish (mixed with Arabic).
4. Portuguese, a dialect of Spanish.
5. Provençal, south of France, called the *Langue d'oc*.
6. French, *i.e.* the northern portion, with Belgium and Switzerland. There are also minor Romance tongues, as Catalan, Valaque, Rhetian, Ladinique, &c.

'Valaque' is the Valacian dialect, 'Rhetian' is the language of the Grisons, and 'Ladinique,' spoken in the Engadine, is the Romance.

Romance of the Rose (*The*). An allegorical romance in verse begun by Guillaume di Lorris in the latter part of the 13th cent., and continued by Jean de Meung in the former half of the 14th cent. The sequel alone is longer than

Homer's 'Iliad.' The part by Guillaume di Lorris contains 4,000 lines; the sequel by Meung contains 18,000.

The poet dreams that dame Idleness conducts him to the palace of Pleasure, where he meets Love, whose attendants are Sweetface, Courtesy, Youth, Jollity, and Competence, who lead the poet to a bed of roses. He singles out one, and was about to pluck it, when an arrow from Love's bow stretches him fainting on the ground, and he is carried off. When he comes to himself he resolves to seek out the rose of his choice, and Welcome promises to aid him ; but Shyness, Fear, and Slander obstruct him, and Reason advises him to give up the pursuit. Pity and Liberality now show him the object of his desire, but Jealousy seizes the guide Welcome, and locks her in Fear Castle. Here the original poem ends. It is called the French *Iliad*.

Jean de Meung, pronounce *Jahnd Muhng*.

Romanov (*The Dynasty of*). The second Russian dynasty. The first five of this line of czars were scarcely acknowledged. Boris Godounov usurped the throne in 1598, and till 1613 it was a constant struggle with Poland and Sweden. In 1613 Michael III. [Romanov] put an end to these troubles, and from him dates the third dynasty; but it was still Romanov, and continued to 1762. Peter the Great (1613–1686) was the third successor of Michael, and there were four queens, Sophia, Catherine, Anne Ivanovna (Joanna), and Elizabeth Petrovna. It was succeeded by the dynasty of Holstein-Gottorp.

Romantic School of France (*The*), or *Romanticists*, 1830–1840. Lemercier, Victor Hugo, and Alexandre Dumas are the chief exponents of the French *Romantic School*, which sought to free the stage from the Aristotelian unities, and to introduce the English, Spanish, and German freedom. Delavigne attempted a compromise, and founded the *Classico-romantic* school of French tragedy. The Romantic School was not confined to tragedy ; all poetry discarded the classic affectations introduced at the revolution even into names and dress.

Romantic School of Germany (*The*), 1800–1810. Its founders were Schlegel, Novālis, and Ludwig Tieck. The next three names of the same school are Hoffman, De la Motte Fouqué (author of ' Undine '), and Chamisso (author of ' Peter Schlemil, the shadowless man ').

Novalis is the pen-name of Friedrich von Hardenberg of Saxony.

Rome of the African World (*The*). Carthage, a long time the rival of Rome.

Though Carthage might yield to the royal prerogatives of Constantinople, and perhaps to the trade of Alexandria or the splendour of Antioch, she still maintained the second rank in the west, as the 'Rome' of the African world.—GIBBON, chap. xxxiii.

Romescot, A.D. 720. When Ina king of Wessex abdicated he went to Rome, where he founded a Saxon school, to provide for which he imposed a penny on every family. This tax was called Romescot, and sometimes Peter-pence, because it was collected on the festival of St. Peter ad Vincula (Sharon Turner, ' History of the Anglo-Saxons ').

It was also called *Hearth-money*, being a tax on each hearth or family. Offa in 790 settled the tax on the pope. It was discontinued by Edward III., A.D. 1365, and prohibited by Act of Parliament, 25 Hen. VIII. c. 21, A.D. 1534.

Romorantin (*The Edict of*), 1560. A law passed through the influence of Michel de l'Hôpital, chancellor of France, to keep out the Inquisition, which the Guises wanted to introduce. By this edict the crime of heresy was entrusted to the bishops, and parliament was forbidden to interfere in matters of faith.

Romulus (*The Second*). Marcus Furius Camillus, four times Dictator of Rome ; died in retirement B.C. 360. After the Gauls had burnt Rome Camillus both repelled the invaders and restored the city.

Ronsard School (*The*). A school of French poetry founded by Ronsard (1524–1584) ; his sonnets were modelled on those of Petrarch ; his epic on the ' Æneid ' and his odes were in imitation of Horace, Pindar, and Anacreon. Pedantry was the characteristic of this school. Ronsard was the Cowley of France.

Rood of Grace (*The*). At Boxley in Kent. An image of Christ on the cross, which hung its lip when silver was offered it, but shook its beard merrily when the offering was of gold. At the dissolution of the smaller monasteries in England Thomas Cromwell (1538) had the rood taken to Paul's Cross, and Hilsey bishop of Rochester, before a large crowd of the citizens of London, exposed the wires, wheels, and springs by which this was done, and the image was broken to pieces. *See* ' Darvel Gatheren,' ' Blood of Christ,' &c.

Root and Branch Party (*The*), 1640. The Independents in the reign of

Charles I., hostile alike to the 'root,' that is Episcopacy, and to the 'branch,' that is Presbyterianism. A compromise was made by 16 Car. I. c. 27, A.D. 1642, when the bishops were deprived of their suffrages in the House of Lords; but the *status quo* was restored by 13 Car. II. c. 2, A.D. 1661.

Root and Branch Petition

(*The*), 1641. A petition containing 15,000 signatures in favour of the abolition of Episcopacy in England and the establishment of Presbyterianism.

Rope Dancer (*The*).

Yvo de Grantmesnil the Crusader, one of the leaders of Robert duke of Normandy's party against Henry I. of England. Yvo was one of those who escaped from Antioch when it was besieged. He was let down by a rope over the wall, and was hence called 'The Rope Dancer.'

Rope Dancers (*The*).

The deserters from Antioch in the first crusade, who dropped in the night from the walls, and fled. (Gibbon, chap. lviii.)

Rory o' the Hill (*Captain*), 1880.

The signature adopted by the writer of threatening letters to landlords, tenants who paid their rent, those who took the farms of evicted tenants, &c., under the authority of the Irish Land League. *See* p. 435, 'Irish Associations.'

Like the Fenians, the Land Leaguers wanted to sever Ireland from the British crown. Rory =Roderick, a common name in Ireland, as Rory O'More.

Rosamond.

Daughter of Walter Clifford, a Hertfordshire baron, mistress of Henry II. of England, was the mother of William Longsword, who married the daughter of the Earl of Salisbury, and of Geoffrey archbishop of York. She retired to the convent of Godestow, near Oxford, where she died. The tale of the labyrinth and the poisoned bowl forced upon her by Queen Eleanor is not mentioned by any contemporary, and probably is a mere invention of romance.

Rosary (*A*).

Either a sacred office in honour of the Virgin Mary or a string of beads, 15 of which are large ones. The 15 large beads tell off the *Pater Nosters*; the 150 smaller beads tell off the *Ave Marias*. Instituted by St. Dominic (1170-1221).

33

Rosary.

The *office* so called consists of three parts, each of which contains five mysteries. The entire rosary consists, therefore, of fifteen mysteries. The rosary begins by making the sign of the cross thrice : (1) to ward off the devil; (2) to implore the help of the Holy Trinity; and (3) to bring to mind that the cross is man's salvation.

After crossing comes the 'Apostles' Creed,' or Symbol, then the Lord's Prayer, and then 'Hail Mary' is repeated thrice : once in honour of God, the Virgin's 'Father-in-law'; once in honour of the Virgin's son; and once in honour of the Holy Ghost, the Virgin's spouse.

These being done, the rosary proper commences. The rosary proper consists of fifteen decades or dizains, divided into threes, five recounting the 'Five Joyous Mysteries' (*q.v.*), five recounting the 'Five Dolorous Mysteries' (*q.v.*), and five recounting the 'Five Glorious Mysteries' (*q.v.*). In each mystery 'Hail Mary' is repeated 50 times, *i.e.* 150 times in the three mysteries.

As each mystery begins with a *Pater Noster*, and as there are fifteen mysteries, it follows that the Lord's Prayer is repeated fifteen times and 'Ave Maria' is repeated 150 times.

There is supposed to be a meditation after the repetition of each mystery, a private prayer, and a doxology.

*** There is something revolting in the idea that God is the 'father-in-law' of a peasant girl, that this villager is 'mother of God,' and also the 'wife' of God. It may be logical, but it certainly anthropomorphoses Deity most shockingly.

Rosary (*The Festival of the*), 1573.

Instituted by Gregory XIII. to commemorate the victory of Lepanto, when in 1571 Don John of Austria defeated the Turks.

Rosary (*The Greater*)

includes all the three parts or fifteen mysteries with their component prayers. *See* 'Rosary, the Office.'

Rosary (*The Lesser*).

Takes in one of the three decades or mysteries. *See* 'Rosary, the Office.'

That is, five mysteries [the joyous mysteries, the dolorous mysteries, and the glorious mysteries. *See* under the word 'Five,' p. 329].

Rosary (*The Living*).

A recital by fifteen persons of the entire rosary, each person saying daily one of the fifteen mysteries.

3 D

Roscius (*The British*). I. Richard Burbage (1566-1619).

Richard Burbage is famous as our 'English Roscius.'

II. Thomas Betterton (1635-1710).

III. David Garrick (1716-1779).

Roscius (*The Irish*). Spranger Barry, the 'Silver-tongued' (1719-1777).

Roscius (*The Modern*). William Henry West Betty, who appeared at Covent Garden Theatre 1 Dec., 1804, at the age of 13, in the character of Achmet in the play entitled 'Barbarossa.' He received 50 guineas a night for the first three nights, and 100 guineas a night for the next twenty-five nights. In fifty nights with benefits he realised 34,000*l.*, and retired from the stage. He died in 1874, at the age of 84.

He is called sometimes the 'Infant Roscius,' and sometimes the 'Youthful Roscius.' The great Roman comic actor was Quintus Roscius, who died B.C. 62, having realised an immense fortune. His contemporary Æsopus was a tragic actor equally celebrated.

Roscius of France (*The*). Michel Baron (1653-1729). Roscius was a comedian of Rome, but the word in modern times is generally applied to tragic actors. Shakespeare says: 'What scene of death hath Roscius now to act!' Baron, however, was both a comedian and a tragedian.

Rose. The plucking of white and red roses by the Yorkists and Lancastrians, which (according to Shakespeare) gave the name to the great civil contest in the reign of Henry VI., was paralleled in the French Revolution, when Camille Desmoulins, after addressing the mob, tore a green leaf off a tree and placed it in his hat. 'Others' (says Carlyle, 'French Revolution,' vol. i. p. 160) 'followed his example, until the trees were stripped, and the " wearing of the green " became general.'

Rose of Derrinsalla (*The*), in Tipperary. She came into the Cleburne family by the marriage of Ellen Palmer to Edward Cleburne (grandson of Richard Cleburne, of Ballycullatan Castle, Tipperary).

Rose of Raby (*The*). The mother of Richard III. She was Cicely, daughter of Ralph de Neville of Raby, earl of Westmoreland.

Rose of Sharon (*The*), Cant. ii. 1. Solomon says : ' I am the Rose of Sharon.' Jesus Christ is also called the Rose of Sharon, *i.e.* the wild rose.

Rose of York (*The*). The Princess Elizabeth, eldest child of Edward IV. She married Henry VII., and thus united the Rose of York to the Rose of Lancaster.

Rose's Act, 1812, on clerical fees, &c. It directs ' that all customary fees for making entries in the register and giving copies shall remain in force.' In 1836 a uniform scale of fees for searches and certificates was fixed by act of parliament.

Roses (*Wars of the*), between the Houses of York (*q.v.*) and Lancaster (*q.v.*). Began with the battle of St. Albans, 23 May, 1455, and terminated with the battle of Bosworth Field, 22 Aug., 1485. The chief battles were those of Northampton, Wakefield, Towton, Hexham, Barnet, and Tewkesbury. A red rose was the badge of Edmund earl of Lancaster, brother to King Edward I.; and a white rose was the badge of the Black Prince. Tradition says that Somerset, in the Temple Gardens, plucked a red rose, saying, ' Let all the friends of Lancaster follow my example;' and Warwick, the friend of York, plucked a white rose, saying, ' Let all the friends of York wear a white rose for their badge.' The two tales are quite consistent, and it seems that ribbons and rosettes of red and white were worn by the partisans of Lancaster and York.

Rosicrucians. A secret society of the 17th cent., involved in much mystery. Mosheim and others derive the word from *ros* (dew) and *crux* (+ symbol of LVX, light). ' Lux,' we are told, is that which produces gold, and ' ros' is its greatest solvent.

In 1614 appeared a book entitled the ' Brotherhood of the illustrious Order of the R. C.' (*Rosy Cross*), which is the story of Brother Christian Rosenkreux, a German who is represented as living in the 14th cent., and who was the founder of the society.

F. R. C. stand for *Fratres Roris Coacti*, the philosopher's stone being supposed to be congealed dew.

That there was a secret society called

Rosicrucians in the 17th cent. may be admitted, but the tale about Brother Rosenkreux is mere romance.

Amongst other foolish things attributed to the Rosicrucians is a belief in the possibility of perpetual motion, and also of a perpetually burning lamp.

Rosin Bible (*The*), printed 1609. So called because the word *rosin* is substituted for 'balm' in Jer. viii. 22. Thus: 'Is there no rosin in Gilead?' *See* 'Bible.'

Roskild (*Treaty of*), 28 Feb., 1658, between Sweden and Denmark. Charles X. of Sweden had invaded Poland in 1655, and subjugated that country, when Frederick III. of Denmark unwisely espoused the Polish cause. On this interference Charles at once invaded Holstein, overran it, and proceeded to Zealand, which no doubt would have fallen into his power if Frederick had not sued for peace. By the treaty signed at Roskild, the Danish provinces beyond the Sound, Scania, Halland, and Bleking, were ceded to Sweden, together with the district of Trontheim, the northern part of Norway, and the island of Bornholm.

The district of Trontheim and island of Bornholm were restored to the Danes 10 June, 1660, by the Treaty of Copenhagen.
Trontheim, pronounce *Tron-yem*.

Rosse's Telescope, 1844. A telescope of 6 ft. aperture and 54 ft. focal length, erected by Lord Rosse in his grounds at Parsonstown, King's County, Ireland. The speculum weighs 4 tons. This telescope cost Lord Rosse as much as 20,000*l*.

Rossi (*I*) and 'I Neri.' *See* under 'Reds and Blacks.'

Rotten Borough System (*The*). The old ' free-men system ' which held in elections for members of parliament before it was abolished by the Reform Bill. These boroughs were rotten or corrupt because the electors were venal.

Rotten Boroughs. Places which returned members to the House of Commons, the only electors being tenants or subservients of the lord of the soil, who virtually nominated the member, while the electors merely gave effect to his nomination.

Rotulus Wintoniæ. The Winchester Roll. So Doomsday Book was called; because it was anciently preserved under three locks and keys, in the royal treasury of that city.

Rouge-croix. One of the four pursuivants of England. So called from the red cross of St. George. *See* p. 415, ' Heralds.'

Rouge-dragon. One of the four pursuivancies of England founded by Henry VII. on the day before his coronation. It was the ensign of Cadwaladyr, the last king of the Britons, from whom Henry was crookedly descended. Sometimes Henry VII. used a red dragon as a supporter. *See* p. 415, ' Heralds.'

Round Table (*The*). I. A.D. 540. King Arthur is said to have founded this order of knighthood at Winchester. So called because Arthur and his knights sat on state occasions at a round table, in order that no dispute about rank might arise.

II. A.D. 1884. The modern departure of this phrase hails from America, and is in no wise connected with the famous table round of King Arthur. The Chautauqua Reading Circle, near Lake Erie (instituted 1871), has given birth to a large number of similar societies in America and Canada. Members meet together occasionally at each other's houses to talk over given subjects, and these gatherings are called ' Round Tables,' or ' Round Table Conferences.'

I was present at one of Dr. Vincent's ' Round Table Conferences,' which was attended by several hundred members, . . . questions were asked and opinions invited respecting the choice of books, and the best mode of reading them.—*Nineteenth Century*, Oct. 1888, p. 490.

Round Table Conference (*Harcourt's*), Dec. 1886 to March, 1887. Held at the house of Sir Wm. Harcourt, where the members assembled. *See above.* The object was to unite, if possible, the Liberal party, which had been broken up by Mr. Gladstone's Irish policy. Mr. Chamberlain, who had been one of Mr. Gladstone's ministers, had left the party, and was invited by Sir Wm. Harcourt to join the Conference. In March a quarrel between Mr. Gladstone and Mr. Chamberlain broke up the Conference. The members were three Liberals (Lord Herschel, Sir William Harcourt, and John Morley), and two Unionists (Sir George Trevelyan and Joseph Chamberlain).

The platform was to give Ireland an Irish

executive, dependent on Irish legislation, with regular departments, including a Home Rule office. Irish members were to be admitted to Westminster to vote on Irish questions. The great stumbling-block was Ulster, the most wealthy and loyal part of Ireland, which strongly objected to 'Home Rule' (*q.v.*).

The whole history of Ireland shows that the Irish would invite over Spanish or French armies to strengthen their own if they were free to act for themselves, thus rendering the island a perpetual menace to Great Britain. On the other hand, Ireland would lose infinitely by separation; for, if cut off from England, of course no Irishmen could hold office in Great Britain, and Ireland itself would be a poor field for Irish genius and enterprise. Mr. Gladstone's notion of the Irish managing 'their own affairs' is silly, unless he will show that their 'own affairs' do not mean their government, which indubitably the Irish intend by the phrase. There can be no objection to extending County Councils to Ireland, but an Irish parliament is quite another matter.

Round World (*The*).

The rotundity of the world was not believed in by the early Christians, and was thought to be antagonistic to Mosaic teaching. In A.D. 200 Tertullian held that the 'Books of Moses [were] not only all truth, but that all truth was contained in them,' and as the globular form of the earth is not part of that revelation, the tenet is heretical. Lactantius about a century later, referring to the globosity of the earth and its revolution, says: 'Is it possible that men can be so absurd as to believe that the crops and trees on the other side of the earth hang downwards?' And St. Augustine, about A.D. 400, says: 'Is it possible there should be inhabitants on the other side of the earth, since there is no such race mentioned in Scripture among the descendants of Adam?' And then he adds: 'In the day of judgment men on the other side of the earth could not see the Lord descending through the air.' (!)

Cosmas, in the 6th cent., published his 'Christian Topography,' the object of which was to denounce the heathen doctrine of the rotundity of the earth, and to show that the tabernacle in the wilderness is the pattern or model of the universe. 'The earth,' he says, ' is a rectangular plane, 400 days' journey east and west, and half that distance north and south. It is surrounded by mountains, on which the sky rests. The heavens come down to the earth on all four sides, like the wall of a room. All below the firmament is the world, the story above is heaven, and below the earth is hell. Beyond ocean, bordering on the edge, is Paradise. Here, too, on a barren and thorny soil, outside the walls of Paradise, dwelt man from the Fall to the Deluge. The ark floated the survivors across the great ocean belt to the lands which we inhabit. This plain lies a little tilted to the south, so that the rivers (like the Tigris and the Euphrates) running south run rapidly, while those running north (like the Nile) run more slowly, because they have to run uphill.' (!) This notion prevailed for above 1,000 years in the Christian Church.

⁎⁎ Even so late as 25 Feb., 1616, the Holy Office, presided over by the pope, declared it to be absurd and contrary to Holy Writ to teach that the sun does not move from its place, that the earth is not the centre of the universe, that it moves round the sun, and has also a diurnal motion. These heretical notions were laid to the charge of Galileo, and he was threatened with imprisonment unless he abjured them. The judgment is signed by seven cardinals.

Roundabout Raid (*The*), 1565.

A military insurrection headed by Murray, the duke of Chatelherault, Argyle, Glencairn, and Rothes, at the marriage of Mary queen of Scots with Henry Darnley. Mary, arrayed in light armour, and wearing pistols in her saddle-bow, rode at the head of her troops, and the insurgents retreated from place to place to dodge the royal troops, without coming to a combat. Murray applied to Queen Elizabeth for aid, but Elizabeth dismissed the envoys, calling them traitors, and the insurgents dispersed, making the best terms they could, each for himself.

Morton and his associates [after the murder of Rizzio] went to occupy those quarters in Northumberland which had been lately tenanted by the lords concerned in the Roundabout Raid.— Sir W. SCOTT. *Hist. of Scotland.* xxviii.

Roundheads (*The*), 1641.

The Independents or Puritans in the reign of Charles I. The royalists were nicknamed 'The Cavaliers.' The former wore their hair short, and dressed with great simplicity; the latter wore their hair flowing over their shoulders, and dressed showily and expensively. The two came into collision about the expulsion of the bishops from the House of Lords. The Roundheads insisted on their expulsion, and the severance of the clergy from all secular and state offices. It was in this brawl that the two parties gave each other the nicknames of Roundheads and Cavaliers.

Clarendon says, when Williams archbishop of York was hustled by the mob, one David Hide, an officer who had been with the army in the North, drew his sword and swore that he would 'cut the throats of those Roundhead dogs,' and by this expression gave the first utterance to the name Roundheads.

Rousseauism.

The political theory of Jean-Jacques Rousseau as set forth in the 'Contrat Social' and his 'Discours sur l'origine de l'inégalité parmi les hommes.' In the state of nature man was strong, healthy, contented, and good; all the evils which have befallen him (such as feebleness, sickness, poverty, and inequality of social life) result from civilisation; and the first step to this Avernus

is 'the right of property.' His axioms
are :—
  I. All men are born free, politically
equal, and good, and in a 'state of nature'
remain so. Consequently, it is their
natural right to be free, equal, and good.
  II. If all are equal, none have any
right to disturb that equality by appropriating property or usurping authority.
The former is robbery, the latter tyranny.
  III. If so, the spoliation of wealth is
simply restitution, and the disregard of
all authority not delegated by social contract is simply a vindication of natural
rights.

The reply is:—I. No child is born free, but from
the moment of birth is under control and restraint.
  II. Children are not born equal, but some are
stronger and more intelligent than others, so
that in the nursery some lead and others follow.
  III. They are not born 'good,' in any sense of
the word.
  IV. In regard to authority, on board ship who
would take the votes of the sailors and crew
in regard to the steerage or trimming of the
vessel? Applied to politics, this practical rule
goes far to upset the popular theory of universal
suffrage.
  V. Historically, no people ever did exist in
Rousseau's hypothetical 'state of nature'; such
a state of existence is morally impossible.
  VI. All nature, from the stars of heaven to the
worm and rush, shows the greatest inequality;
and as for independence, there is no such thing
in heaven above, the earth beneath, or the waters
under the earth.
  . 'Born politically equal' is unmitigated nonsense. Political means that which pertains to
civil government, and government of necessity
implies rulers and subjects. Some to command,
and others to obey.

Rout of Moray (*The*), 1746. Lord
Loudoun, hearing that Charles Edward
(the son of the Pretender) was living in
easy security at Moray, sent out a nocturnal party to surprise him and carry
him off captive; but the 'surprise party'
were met in a wood by the Macintoshes,
who caused them to retreat. This flight
of Lord Loudoun's surprise party is called
'The Rout of Moray.'

Rout of Rosbach (*The*), 5 Nov.,
1757. A household phrase for a disgraceful rout. Its reference is to the
battle of Rosbach, won by Frederick II.
over the allied Austrian and French
army. The Prussian loss was 300, that
of the allies was 1,300 slain and 6,000
prisoners.

Routes, Chemins. Routes are
high-roads, chemins are common roads.
There are two sorts of Routes: (1)
Routes *Nationales*, the great high-roads
which lead to Paris, or which join two

principal towns, as Lyons and Bordeaux;
(2) Routes *Départementales*, which connect the principal towns of a department
one with another.
  There are three sorts of Chemins : (1)
Chemins de grande communication, the
network of the routes *départmentales*.
Originally the routes were kept up by
government and the chemins by rates;
(2) *Chemins d'intérêt commun*, country
roads connecting villages; (3) *Chemins
vicinaux ordinaires*, bye-roads.

Route=*root*. Chemins, pronounce *Shma[r]n*.

Routiers. Bands of French adventurers confederated in 1147, soon
after the departure of Louis VII. on his
crusade. They were so called from the
old French word *route*. These adventurers were put down in 1183 by the
Pacifici near Dun-le-Roi. Those who
survived enlisted in the militia called
the 'Ribalds' (*q.v.*).

The Pacifici were the 'Confrérie du charpentier
Durand du Puy.'

Rowdy Parliament (*The*), 1887.
Lord Salisbury was prime minister and
Mr. W. H. Smith leader of the House
of Commons. Eighty-one of the Irish
members, led by Mr. Parnell, resolved
to obstruct the business of the house
by long speeches, endless amendments,
and disorderly conduct. The most conspicuous in insolence and vulgarity were
Dr. Tanner and two members named
Healy. A Mr. Dillon, a Mr. Conybeare
member for Camborne, and a Mr. Labouchere senior member for Northampton,
were also especially conspicuous. Certainly the conduct of the house was never
so disgraceful. *See* 'Parliaments.'

In 1890, in six months, six members of the
House made above 750 speeches, or an average of
125 each. Chief of the six were Sir William Harcourt, Mr. Labouchere, and Sir George Campbell.
Now in six months, supposing parliament sits
five hours a day (with only four days' holiday),
this would give them 700 hours for business.
Some of the obstructive speeches lasted over an
hour. So 750 speeches by six Opposition members
in 700 hours certainly look very much like obstruction of public business.

Rowley. Applied to Charles II.
Rowley was the name of a goat which
used to run about the Priory garden.
The animal was lecherous, good-
humoured, and familiar, certainly typical
of the good-humoured royal libertine.

It is said that a famous stone-horse of that time
was called 'Old Rowley.'

Rowley's Poems. A volume of
poems said by Chatterton to have been

found by him in the muniment room of
the church of St. Mary Redcliffe, Bristol,
written on yellow parchment in very
antiquated style. Horace Walpole believed them to be genuine, but they
were the productions of Chatterton himself, a lad only 16 years of age. Besides
the poems of Rowley were those of
his friend Canynge (15th cent.). *See*
p. 525, ' Literary Forgeries.'

Roxalana. So Elizabeth Davenport (decoyed by Lord Oxford into a
mock marriage) was called from ' Roxalana,' in the ' Siege of Rhodes,' her
great part.

Roxburghe Club (*The*), 1812. A
literary club founded in London to
print, for members only, works hitherto
unedited or extremely rare. The idea
was started by the sale of the Duke of
Roxburghe's library in 1812, which contained several rare books, as an edition
of Boccaccio, bought by the Marquis of
Blandford for 260*l.*, afterwards purchased
by Lord Spencer for 918*l.* 15*s.*

Other similar clubs are the Camden Society, the
Percy, the Shakespeare, the Cheetham, the Whar-
ton, the Surtees (in England) ; and the Bannatyne,
the Maitland, the Abbotsford, and the Spalding
Club (in Scotland).
Roxburghe, pronounce *Rox-burrah.*

Royal Academy of Arts (*The*),
1768. To promote the cultivation of
painting, drawing, engraving, sculpture,
modelling, and other fine arts. There
are forty academicians and twenty associates, and six associate engravers. The
first attach to their names the letters
R.A. (Royal Academician) ; the second
attach to their names the letters A.R.A.
(Associate of the Royal Academy). They
first exhibited (1761) in Somerset House.
In 1836 they occupied part of the National Gallery in Trafalgar Square ; but
in 1869 they moved to Burlington House.

That members of the Academy should be allowed to hang on the line eight pictures each is
preposterous, and hundreds of excellent pictures
are discarded every year for want of room. Two
pictures should be the first limit to members,
then the best of the pictures of the general public. If room still remained, begin again with the
members, and go on to non-members, one each.
The exhibition is now a mere clique, and very
often most disappointing. We want to see *national
progress*, not what forty men can do (1890).

Royal Arms of Great Britain. Our
earliest kings bore for a lion an heraldic
figure purely hypothetical—a mixture
between a lion and a leopard. Scott, in
his ' Talisman,' makes the Duke of

Austria refer to the change of this funny
animal into a lion.
Edward III. quartered the arms of
France with those of England.
Mary united those of Spain, after her
marriage with Philip II.
James I. added the arms of Scotland
and Ireland ; the first and fourth
quarters representing France and England, the second Scotland (represented
by the lion rampant), and the third
Ireland (represented by a harp).
Anne had England and Scotland impaled in the first and fourth quarters,
France in the second, and Ireland in
the third.
George III. renounced the absurd
titular assumption of ' King of France.'
Victoria omitted the arms of Hanover
from the escutcheon, because by the
Salic law a female could not be monarch
of Hanover, and no sovereign of Great
Britain ought to covet such a white elephant.

Royal Arms in Churches (*The*),
1547. Shortly after the date of Henry
VIII. General in the reign of Elizabeth
(1558–1603).
' Whereas it is generally enjoined by the Great
Counsell of England that in all churches thorow-
out the kingdoms of England his Maiesties Armes
shalbe sett up.'—*Parish Register of Warrington*, 30
July, 1660.
. Surely this mixture of ' His Maiesties armes
and the Tenne Commandments ' is only an unseemly recognition of that divinity which doth
hedge a king,' and ought to be utterly and entirely discontinued.

Royal Assent (*The*) in parliamentary matters.
I. To a public bill the words are ' Le
roy (or la reyne) le veult.'
II. To a private bill the words used
are ' Soit fait comme il est désiré.'
III. To a bill of supply the words used
are ' Le roy remercie ses bons sujets,
accepte leur bénévolence, et ainsi le
veult.' *See* ' Royal Refusal.'

This was all very well with such kings as George
I. and II., who could not speak English, and before them, when the Court thought it more courtly
to talk French ; but it is now full time to speak
English, and to discontinue this ridiculous and
spperannuated pedantry. Must aristocratic England go to republican France for royal speech ?
It is full time for English monarchs to speak English to their British subjects (1890).

Royal Assurance (*The*). In
Swedish history. An act passed in 1720,
which limited the power of the king. He
could in future make no laws without
the consent of the states, nor could he

proclaim either peace or war. The counsellors of the king were in future to be called the Senate, and the number limited to sixteen. The king was to have two votes and the casting vote in the senate.

Royal Butcher (*The*). Henry VIII. (1491, 1509–1547).

Royal Chamber (*The*). A substitute for the Paris parliament which Louis XV. dissolved, and gave to the new chamber full jurisdiction in all civil and criminal matters. The barristers and councillors refused to plead before the Royal Chamber, and the king was obliged to give way.

Royal Collection of MSS. (*The*), 1757, in the Britsh Museum, presented by George II. These MSS. date from the reign of Richard III. to Charles II. One of the most remarkable is the *Codex Alexandrīnus*, a present from Cyril patriarch of Constantinople to Charles I. It is in four quarto volumes, written on fine vellum in uncial characters, is ascribed to some period between the 4th and 6th cents., and is supposed to be the oldest Greek Text extant. This collection contains many illuminated MSS., the *Basilicon Doron* of James I. in his own handwriting, several volumes executed for Edward IV., a volume of French romances presented by Talbot earl of Shrewsbury to Queen Margaret, and many other richly illuminated books.

'**Royal George**' (*Loss of the*), 1782. The 'Royal George' was an old ship of 100 guns, fitted out at Portsmouth for the relief of the garrison at Gibraltar. Before starting a gang of carpenters were sent to careen the vessel, and heeled her over too far, so that the sea ran into the portholes, and the ship went down suddenly. Admiral Kempenfelt (aged 70) and 900 or 1,000 others were drowned, and not above 300 were saved.

Royal Literary Fund (*The*), 1790, incorporated 1818 in Great Russell Street, Bloomsbury, London. For the relief of authors and literary men who have published works of merit, but who, from age or infirmity, are reduced to poverty.

Royal Marriage Act (*The*), 1772. It prohibits any descendant of George

II. from marrying till the age of twenty-five without the king's consent. After the age of twenty-five the person must apply to the privy council; and if within a year of such application both houses of parliament assented the marriage might be solemnized.

The bill was introduced because the Duke of Cumberland had recently married Mrs. Horton at Calais, and the Duke of Gloucester had married the Countess-Dowager Waldegrave.

Royal Medals of the Royal Society of London, 1825. Instituted by George IV. for scientific discoveries.

Royal Oak (*The*). The oak at Boscobel in which Charles II. hid himself in his flight after the battle of Worcester, 1651. From this circumstance oak leaves were worn on the birthday of Charles II. (May 29), especially when he returned to his kingdom, which he did on his birthday 1660.

Royal Refusal (*The*). In parliamentary matters. The words of dissent are ' Le roy (*or* La reyne) s'avisera.' *See* p. 774, ' Royal Assent.'

The last instance of royal refusal to a bill was in 1707, when Queen Anne refused to sign a bill for settling the militia of Scotland.

Royal Salute (*A*). Consists of 21 guns, *i.e.* 3×7. Three is the Trinity, seven the sacraments.

Royal Society (*The*).
I. Of *London*, founded 1660 for the promotion of mathematical and physical science.

• The *Copley* Medal was instituted in 1709 by Sir Godfrey Copley for scientific discoveries.
The *Rumford* Medal was instituted in 1796 by Count Rumford for discoveries in light and heat.
Royal Medals were instituted in 1825 by George IV. for scientific discoveries.
The 'Philosophical Transactions' (*q.v.*) were published 1665, to be continued monthly.

II. Of *Edinburgh*, founded 1783, on the model of the Berlin Academy, for the investigation and discussion of subjects in every branch of science, erudition, and taste.

The *Keith* prize was founded by Alexander Keith of Dunnottar.
The M'Dougal *Brisbane* prize was founded by Sir Thomas M'Dougal Brisbane.
The *Neill* Prize was founded by Dr. Patrick Neill.
All for communications on subjects connected with the society.

Royal Society of Literature (*The*). Founded in 1823, and chartered 1826.

Royal Style and Titles of the sovereigns of England since the Conquest.

1066 WILLIAM I.	'Rex Anglorum.'
1100 WILLIAM II.	'Ænglelandes King.'
1135 STEPHEN.	'Rex Anglorum, Dux Normannorum.'
1154 HENRY II.	'Rex Angliæ, Dux Normanniæ et Aquitaniæ.'
1199 JOHN.	'Rex Angliæ, Dominus Hiberniæ, Dux Normanniæ et Aquitaniæ.'
1265 HENRY III.	'Rex Angliæ, Dominus Hiberniæ, Dux Aquitaniæ.'
1341 "	'Rex Angliæ et Franciæ, et Dominus Hiberniæ.'
1421 HENRY V.	'Rex Angliæ, Hæres et Regens Franciæ, et Dominus Hiberniæ.'
1429 HENRY VI.	'Rex Angliæ et Franciæ, et Dominus Hiberniæ' (as Henry III.).
1544 HENRY VIII.	'Angliæ Franciæ et Hiberniæ Rex, Fidel Defensor et in terrâ Ecclesiæ Anglicanæ et Hiberniæ supremum caput.'
1559 ELIZABETH.	'Queen of England, France, and Ireland, Defender of the Faith.'
1603 JAMES I.	'King of Great Britain, France, and Ireland, Defender of the Faith.'
1702 ANNE.	'Queen of Great Britain, France, and Ireland, Defender of the Faith.'
1801 GEORGE III.	'Britanniarum Rex, and of the United Kingdom of Great Britain and Ireland King, Defender of the Faith.'
1877 VICTORIA.	'Of the United Kingdom of Great Britain and Ireland Queen, Defender of the Faith, Empress of India. Or, 'Victoria, Dei Gratia, Britanniarum Regina Fid. Def.'

Royal [*English*] **Subsidy** (*The*). The interest of a fund formed from a grant by Mary the wife of William III. of England for Vaudois pastors of the valleys and of the Würtemberg colony. This colony consisted of the French subjects expelled from the valleys by the secret treaty of Loretto. *See* 'Treaty of 1696.' The royal subsidy was augmented in 1770 by the 'National Subsidy' (*q.v.*).

Royalists and Cardinalists, 1642. The friends and adherents of Cinq-Mars, the friend and favourite of Louis XIII., called themselves Royalists. The adherents of Richelieu, whom the king hated, were called 'Cardinalists.'

Roydamna. The heir presumptive of the over-lord of Ireland. The heirs presumptive of the under-lords or dynasts were called tanists. The heir presumptive was elected in the lifetime of the ruler, and was generally one of the sons, brothers, or cousins of the blood royal.

He was ex-officio commander-in-chief of the forces.

Rubens's Women. The portrait of Helena Forman (or Fourment), his second wife, married at the age of sixteen, is introduced into several of his historical pictures; but in the painting called *Rubens and his Wife* in the Munich gallery the woman is the artist's first wife, Isabella Brandt of Antwerp.

Rubicon (*The*). Now the 'Pisatello,' a small river which flows into the Adriatic, and separates Cisalpine Gaul from Italy proper. It was an act of treason for a Roman to enter Italy proper with an army; when therefore Julius Cæsar, B.C. 49, crossed the Rubicon at the head of his army, it was a declaration of revolt, and the commencement of the civil war.

From this passage of the Rubicon by Cæsar, the phrase ' To pass the Rubicon ' became proverbial, meaning to take a decisive step and abide the consequences, or to enter on an undertaking from which there is no retreat.

Rubric (*The*). The directions to the minister and congregation given at the heads of divers parts of the liturgy. These were originally printed in red letters, the office itself being in black letters. (Latin *ruber*, red.)

Rubrics. The Romans called the *jus civile* 'Rubrica,' because these laws were written in vermilion. The prætors' edicts were written in white, the imperial rescripts in purple ink.

Rudel (*Geoffrey*). The king of minstrels, to whom Henry II., on one occasion, gave four manors in reward for a song.

Rudmas-day. The feast of the *rode* or holy cross. There were two of these feasts, one on 3 May (the invention of the cross), and the other 14 Sept. (the exaltation of the cross). The latter is called the Holy Rood-day.

Rudolph I. of Habsburg king of Germany, but never kaiser or 'Emperor of the Holy Roman Empire' (1218, 1273 –1291).

Father, Albrecht count of Habsburg; *Mother,* ——; *Wives,* (1) Gertrude of Hohenberg, (2) Elizabeth of Burgundy. *Contemporary* with Edward I.

After the close of the Hohenstauffen dynasty in 1254 to the accession of the Austrian dynasty in 1438, nearly 200 years, the rulers of Germany were promiscuous. After an interregnum of seventeen years came Rudolph I. of Habsburg, Adolph of Nassau, Albrecht I. of Austria, Heinrich VII. of Luxemburg, Friedrich III. of Austria, Ludwig V. of Bavaria, Gunther of Schwarzburg, Karl IV. of Luxemburg, Wenzel [Wenceslaus] the Worthless, Ruprecht the Elector Palatine of the Rhine, and Siegmund of Brandenburg, altogether eleven kings, besides the three nominal ones during the interregnum.

Rudolph II. Kaiser-king of Germany of the House of Austria (1552, 1576–1612).

Father, Maximilian II.; *Mother*, Mary. It was in honour of this monarch the 'Tabulæ Rudolphīnæ' were so named. *Contemporary* with Elizabeth and James I.

Rudolphine Tables (*The*). 'Tabulæ Rudolphīnæ,' 1627. Astronomical calculations begun by Tycho Brahé, and continued by Kepler under the immediate patronage of Kaiser Rudolf II., after whom Kepler named the work. *See* 'Ilkanian and Alfonsine Tables.'

Rudolph gave Tycho Brahé an annuity of 1,500l. sterling.

Ruel (*The Treaty of*), April, 1649. Terms of peace made by Mazarin and Anne of Austria with the Frondeurs or Parlementarians. Scarcely was the treaty signed when the Prince de Condé headed the party called 'La Jeune Fronde.' The queen-mother arrested the Prince de Condé, the Prince de Conti, and the Duc de Longueville while assembled in council in the Palais Royal, and sent them prisoners to Vincennes (18 Jan., 1650). All the nobility flew to arms. Anne of Austria stood out for a time, but Mazarin fled. In the autumn of 1651 Louis XIV. came of age, took the government into his own hands, and the nation quieted down.

Rufus Stone (*The*). A stone, now enclosed in an iron casing, near a by-road to Bramshaw, to commemorate the spot where Purkis picked up the body of William II. after he was shot. The traditional cottage stands some 100 yards off, in the hamlet of Canterton.

Rule Nisi. An order of the law court that something stated shall be done, *unless* the opposite party, within a certain time (say three or six days) show cause why it should not be done.

Rule of Faith (*The*). The dogmas and doctrines binding on Christians:

Dissenters say 'the Bible, the whole Bible, and nothing but the Bible is binding as a rule of faith.'

Catholics say the practices and doctrines recorded in the 'Fathers' show the rule held in their days, and this 'tradition' supplements the written Scriptures, the two together making the rule of faith.

The Church of England adds to the Bible the decisions of the first four general councils, and admits other practices 'not contrary to Holy Scriptures,' as the change of the Sabbath for Sunday, infant baptism, &c.

Rule of Monastic Houses. Certain laws to be observed by the order referred to. Originally there were but four orders (Augustine, Basil, Benedict, and Francis of Assisi); but these four have given rise to a large number of subordinate orders.

Every religious order was bound to the four vows of Obedience, Poverty, Charity, and Chastity; but history must very much wrong them if these vows were generally observed.

I. Rule of St. Augustine (*The*). St. Augustine, bishop of Hippo, in Africa, lived 354–430, and founded a society of hermits; but what is called 'Augustine or Austin Friars' is a society organised in 1256 by Pope Alexander IV., who appointed Lanfranc the 'general.' The Augustine Friars wore originally a gray habit, but afterwards a black and white one, with a leathern girdle about the waist.

There were also Augustine canons.

In 1567 Pius V. made the Augustine friars one of the four mendicant orders, the others being the Dominicans, the Franciscans, and the Carmelites.

In 1574 Thomas of Jesus, a Portuguese, founded the Barefooted Augustines (Augustins Déchaussés).

What is technically called 'The Rule of St. Augustine' is a set of laws appointed to be observed by those who belong to the order; but who was the author of these laws nobody knows. There were, in fact, three sets of rules; the chief items were :

1 CLASS : *Absolute and holy poverty.* To possess no worldly goods of any kind. Even articles of personal use to be in common. *See* IV.

If any novice had property he must sell it all, and give the proceeds to the poor, before he could be admitted into the order. *See* IV.

Never to receive money from anyone, nor any present except food, which must be taken untouched to the monastery for general distribution. *See* IV.

2 CLASS : *Monastic duties.*

To recite daily the psalms and appointed offices.

To employ the first part of the morning and afternoon in manual labour.

To wash their own clothes.

To observe strict silence at meals ; to attend to what was read; and never to eat out of the monastery.

Whenever they left the monastery, to go two together; and not even to go to the baths separately. *See* IV.

Never to utter an idle word.

Never to receive a private letter.

Never to engage in a lawsuit.

On a Sunday a little wine was allowed.

3 CLASS : *Religious duties.*

To love God and their neighbour man.

To attend prayer at the canonical hours.

To sing only what is appointed.

To fast with discretion.

To be modest in look, word, and deed.

Never to look immodestly on any woman, or harbour an immodest thought.

. Augustine himself, one of the four doctors of the Church, is called, ' Le Miroir des prélats, le Maître de la théologie, l Ornement des évêques. l'Eclat de tout l'ordre sacerdotal, la Lumière des docteurs, le Soleil de l'Afrique, le Bouclier de la foi, le Fléau des hérétiques. le Temple de la religion, le Firmament de l'église, et la Colonne inébranlable de la vérité.'

The following were branches of the Augustine order, and observed the same rule with a difference—viz. the Austin Friars, the Brigettines, DOMINICANS, GILBERTINES, Praemonstratensians or NORBERTINES, TABENNITES, TRINITARIANS, &c. *See* those in capitals ' Rule of . . . ' each name.

II. **Rule of St. Basil** (*The*). St. Basil lived 329–379. He retired into a desert in the province of Pontus, and founded there a monastery, for the better government of which he drew up a series of laws, called the ' Rule of St. Basil,' even to the present day universally followed by all Oriental monks, even by those who call themselves of the order of St. Antony. There were two sets of rules, the Longer and the Shorter. All that St. Basil himself enjoined are the following :—

No monk of this order to return to his parents without express permission of his superiors.

Use hospitality to strangers, but avoid dainty fare. Let even your hospitality teach your guests temperance and sobriety.

Communicate your most secret thoughts to your superior.

Never omit the service of prime, but always consecrate ' the firstfruits ' of your thoughts to God.'

St. Basil's day is 14 June.

III. **Rule of St. Benedict** (*The*). Absolute and holy humility. St. Bennet or Benedict (480–542) was the founder of the Benedictine Order. Gregory the Great preferred the Benedictine Rule to all others. Some ascribe the rule to Gregory III. (731–741). It contains twelve degrees of humility.

The following are the chief items of the Benedictine Rule :—

The monks to serve by turns in kitchen and at table, and the monks in service to wash the feet of the other monks, and on Saturday to clēan the plate and linen ; seven hours a day to be given to manual labour, four in the morning and three in the afternóon ; service seven times a day ; two hours to be given to pious reading.

Total abstinence from meat and fowls. The allowance of bread per day to be 1 lb. and a *hemina* of wine. Fast all Lent till 6 p.m. ; but no voluntary austerities allowed. Perfect silence to be observed at meals.

Avoid singularity, never give way to loud laughter, and never at any time speak in a loud voice.

Always to keep their eyes fixed towards the ground.

Renounce your own will ; bear injuries patiently ; think meanly of yourself and most highly of God.

Train yourself to continual penitence ; do all lowly offices ; be modest in look, word, and thought.

Know your own will ; obey promptly ; show your most secret thoughts to your director. *See* II., IV.

Never go abroad except in pairs; all to sleep in one dormitory, but never two in one bed ; all to sleep in their day-dress and girdle, with a lamp burning in the dormitory all night.

Small offences to be punished by loss of meals, great ones by expulsion from chapel.

No vows to be perpetual.

The dress to be a black gown with wide sleeves and a pointed cowl. Every monk to have two of each, but to prefer old clothes to new ones.

St. Bennet's Day is March 21.

The following observed the Benedictine Rule with a difference—viz.

The Bernardines, Camaldules, CARTHUSIANS, Celestines, CISTERCIANS, monks of Cluny or CLU-NIACS, Feuillants, TRAPPISTS, &c. *See* those in capitals under ' Rule of . . .' each name.

IV. Rule of St. Francis (*The*).

Absolute poverty. St. Francis of Assisi (1182-1226) was the founder of three orders: (1) the Fratres Minōres in 1206; (2) the nuns in 1212; and (3) what was far more important (in 1221) the secular order called Tertiaries—that is, men and women who lived in ordinary life (married and given in marriage), but promised to live religiously, and to abandon frivolity of dress, needless extravagance, and self-indulgence. The Franciscans were allowed to have nothing they could call their own, not even the clothes they wore, their convents or churches. Their right extended only to the use of these things. (*See* I.) They had to work for their living, and, when provisions ran short, to beg alms; but under no consideration were they allowed to take goods or money. *See* I. If a novitiate had property he was bound to sell all and give the proceeds to the poor, not one farthing might be invested even for the convent or the order. *See* I.

There are at present many conventual ter-tiaries.

The following are the chief of the twelve articles of the Rule of St. Francis:

Never to leave the convent except in twos. *See* I.

Never to preach without permission of the ordinary of the diocese.

Never to ride on a journey; and never to go into any foreign country.

Never to stand godfather to a child; and never to enter a nunnery.

To fast all Lent, and from All Saints' Day (Nov. 1) to Christmas Day.

To confess to their superior their most secret thoughts. *See* II., III.

This apostrophe of St. Francis is given in the ' Petits Bollandistes,' vol. xii. p. 29: ' Seigneur Jésus, montrez-moi les voies de votre très-chère pauvreté! Ayez pitié de moi et de ma dame la Pauvreté; car je l'aime avec tant d'ardeur, que je ne puis trouver de repos sans elle, et vous savez, O mon Dieu, que c'est vous qui m'avez donné ce grand amour.'

When some persons complained to St. Francis that his rule was too austere, Mgr. Guérin says (p. 86), 'Ils furent surpris d'entendre la voix de Jésu-Christ même qui lui dit en leur présence ces paroles distinctes: " François, cette Régle n'est point ton ouvrage, mais le mien; j'entends

qu'elle soit gardée à la lettre, à la lettre, à la lettre, sans glose, sans glose, sans glose. Si quelques-uns ne la veulent pas garder, qu'ils soient rejetés de la compagnie comme des difficiles, des mutins, des scandaleux, et des incorrigibles. Je sais la capacité de l'homme et je sais les grâces et les secours que je veux lui donner." Ces supérieurs, saisis de frayeur, tombèrent par terre et n'osè-rent ouvrir la bouche.' Notwithstanding, the rule was greatly modified by Elias (the successor of St. Francis), and the society was split in two, those who were strict Franciscans and those who followed a greatly modified rule.

St. Francis's Day is 4 Oct.

The following were Franciscans, and observed the Franciscan Rule with a difference—viz.

The Capucins or Capuchins, Clarisses, Minims, Picpus, Récollets, &c.

St. Francis of Paula, who founded the Minims, said that no monk who died without his cord of two knots would ever go to heaven.

Rule of St. Chrodegand [Franciscans], 763.

By this rule canons were bound to manual labour, silence, and confession twice a year. Chrodegand's day is 7 March.

Rule of St. Dominic [Augustines].

St. Dominic (1170-1221) was the founder of preaching friars; his rule of abstinence and poverty was similar to that of St. Francis, with this exception—the order might accept small rents in money.

The motto of his order was ' Perfect self-distrust, but perfect trust in God.'

Not only individual monks had no personal property, even the collective society had none. They entirely depended on alms.

St. Dominic's great object was to multiply churches and train zealous preachers.

The occupations of his monks were preaching, contemplation, severe study, and acts of charity. Retirement and self-denial were strictly enforced.

St. Dominic's day is 14 Aug.

Rule of St. Fintan of Leinster, 6th cent. [Benedictines].

The Rule of St. Fintan and that of the Trappists are unusually austere.

The monks of St. Fintan lived only on roots and vegetables, in many cases not even cooked. They tilled their own land.

St. Fintan's Day is 10 May.

Rule of St. Macarius [Augustines] 304-404.

The monks fasted every day except Sunday, and from Easter Day to Whit Sunday.

They divided the day between manual labour and prayer.

Hospitality was enforced by this rule.

No monk was allowed to speak a word to a stranger without express permission of the superior.

The abbots of this order wore no insignia.

St. Macarius's Day is 2 Jan.

Rule of the Carthusians [Benedictines], 1170, composed by Guido, the

fifth prior. They had nineteen articles in their rule:

> To fast all Lent till six o'clock at night; never at any time to eat flesh, fowl, or fish. Their bread to be made of bran. Sunday and Thursday their diet to be bread and cheese; Tuesday and Saturday pulse; all the rest of the week bread and water.
>
> Each monk to have a separate cell, where he was to sleep, work, and eat in silence his solitary meals.
>
> Each monk to have a hair shirt at all times.
>
> All to work at agriculture, to be hospitable, and given to hospitality.

Rule of the Cistercians [Benedictines], an order of monks founded by Robert of Molême (1018–1110). The Virgin Mary was the protectress of this order. The Cistercians were reformed Bernardines, who affected the severest simplicity.

> The rule enjoined four hours' sleep, four for choir singing, and four for manual labour in the morning.
>
> The diet was roots and herbs, which were not served on a table. but on the bare ground. They slept also on the bare ground.

Rule of the Cluniacs, or 'Monks of Cluny,' founded by St. Hugues, abbot of Cluny (1024–1109). Reformed Benedictines. The rule was very austere. St. Hugues abolished the law of manual labour, but enjoined total abstinence from animal food, and restricted the diet to bread and pulse.

> Mgr. Paul Guérin, camérier de sa Sainteté Léon XIII., says in his 'Petits Bollandistes,' vol. v. p. 76, 'Un moine de Cluny, plusieurs disent Hildebrand qui fut plus tard Gr goire VII., vit un jour Jésus-Christ s'asseoir dans une stalle du chœur, à côté de Hugues, et lui dicter les décrets et les règles monastiques.'

Rule of the Norbertines [Augustines]. The monks who followed this rule were called Norbertines, Premonstratensians, or White Canons. Robert Norbert lived 1092–1134.

> His rule enjoined total abstinence from flesh, constant fasts, and avoiding linen.
>
> St. Norbert's Day is 6 June.

Rule of the Tabennites. Founded by St. Pachomius (292–348), who was the first to draw up a monastic rule in writing. St. Jerome's version of it is still extant. Mgr. Guérin, cámerier de sa Sainteté Léon XIII., says in his 'Petits Bollandistes,' vol. v. p. 526 : 'Pacôme allait quelquefois dans un vaste désert, nommé Tabenne, situé sur les bords du Nil. Un jour qu'il y faisait son oraison, il entendit une voix qui lui ordonnait de bâtir, à l'endroit où il était, un monastère destiné à recevoir tous ceux qui y seraient envoyés de Dieu pour le

servir fidèlement. Vers le même temps, un ange lui donna la Règle que devaient suivre ses religieux, appelés depuis Tabennites.'

> These monks ate in common and in dead silence, having their hoods over their faces that they might not see each other. Their tunic was made of white linen, with a cowl, but no sleeves. Over their shoulders they wore a white goat-skin called a *méiotes*. They communicated the first and last day of every week. There was not one minute of the day which had not some duty awarded to it. The law of silence was so severe that a monk was allowed to express what he wanted only by signs.
>
> His day is 14 May.

Rule of the Trappists [Benedictines]. The most austere of the Cistercian order, reformed by Jean le Bouthillier de Rancé (1626–1700).

> The monks are not allowed to speak either to a stranger or to one another.
>
> They may never visit or even write to their friends or relatives, nor may they receive any communication whatever either from them or of them. If a father or mother, sister or brother, dies, the superior may be informed of it, and all that he says is, 'The prayers of the brotherhood are requested for the soul of one who has departed this life.'
>
> No monk of this order can possess any property of any sort, nor give any at any time to the monastery.
>
> They may never look on a stranger, but are bound to keep their eyes constantly on the ground.
>
> Their diet is weak cider and herb soup, with a raw radish, carrot, or a few lentils; but never meat, fowls, fish, or eggs. On fast days their allowance is two ounces of the coarsest bread.
>
> They work in the fields and lie upon straw.
>
> These monks not only obey the superior, but must obey the slightest sign of a brother-monk instantly, no matter how employed, even if their work is ruined by the interruption.
>
> The very slightest fault is most severely punished, and yet withal they seem cheerful and contented.
>
> In fact, it is not self-denial but self-indulgence, ambition, and uncertainty which are the chief seeds of man's unhappiness.

Rule of the Trinitarians [Augustinians]. Their special function was the redemption of captives. They divided their income into three parts: one for their own maintenance; another for the poor; and the third part for the redemption of Christian captives.

> *⁎* There are a multitude of sub-orders, but the instances given above will suffice to show the nature of their rules.

Rumford Medal (*The*), 1796. Instituted in the Royal Society of London by Count Rumford for discoveries in light and heat.

Rump (*The*). The fag-end of the Long Parliament after 'Pride's Purge' (*q.v.*), 6 Dec., 1648. It was dissolved by Cromwell, 20 April, 1653. The members of the Rump were only 100, and the usual attendance did not exceed 50. It refused

to dissolve, and therefore on 20 April, 1653, Cromwell stationed 50 musketeers within call, and after sitting awhile as if listening to the debate, rose and said, ' Come, come, we have had enough of this, I will put an end to your prating.' The musketeers then entered, and the members rushed out. ' Take away this bauble,' he said, referring to the mace, and locking the door he walked away, and the Rump was dissolved.

In 1849, from 6 to 18 June, was the German Rump Parliament in Stuttgart. We want a Cromwell to stop some of ' the prating ' in our present House of Commons (1890).

Rumpers. Members of the Rump Parliament (*q.v.*).

Rundale (*In*). In patches: sale of land in small separate patches. Sometimes, in Ireland, half an acre or an acre of land is held in thirty or forty little patches, too small to be enclosed, and thus subject to depredations from cattle. Sometimes the patches are so far asunder, it is no easy matter for a tenant to know what is his and what is another's. This is because he ' conacres ' (*q.v.*) to two or more different farmers.

Running Footmen were footmen who ran in front of their master's coach, to help it out of ruts, and to serve as couriers. The costume was a light black cap, a jockey coat, white linen trousers, and a staff some six feet long. The staff had a ball at the top containing a hard-boiled egg and a little white wine, to serve as refreshment. The last in England was in the service of the Duke of Queensberry (1810), but in Saxony there were running footmen even so late as 1845.

Running Parliament (*The*). A Scotch parliament, so called from its constantly being shifted from place to place. *See* ' Parliaments.'

Rupert [Ruprecht] surnamed Klemm, *i.e.* pinched or straitened in circumstances, last but one of the promiscuous kaiser-kings of Germany (1352, 1400–1410). He married Elizabeth of Nürnberg, and was contemporary with Henry IV.

Rupert (*Prince*). Grandson of James I. of England. His mother Elizabeth, daughter of James I., married Friedrich V. the elector palatine. Charles I. was his uncle.

Rupert's Land (1670). All the lands that pour water into Hudson's Bay. So called from Prince Rupert, who, with certain specified associates, formed the original Hudson's Bay Company (*q.v.*).

Rural Dean (*A*). A person (generally a beneficed clergyman) appointed to supervise in a certain district, called a deanery, the condition of the churches, the church furniture, the glebe houses, the schools, the appliances of public worship, and all other things pertaining to the church services, and to report on all to the bishop as occasion seems fit.

Rural Labourers' League (*The*), 12 May, 1888. A society which superseded the Allotments Association of 1882; its object being to deal with every practical grievance of the rural population, such for example as footpaths, commons, local charities, allotments, rights of labour, and so on.

Rurik (*The Dynasty of*). The first Russian dynasty, 862–1598. They were not kings of Russia, but rulers of a part of Russia, over-lords of other princes, and held their courts at Novogorod, Kiev (1154–1240), Moscow (1154–1240), Vladimir (1240–1339), Moscow again (1339–1584). The seventh of the line, Vladimir I. the Great, introduced Christianity; the ninth, Jaroslav I., was a great legislator; Ivan (or John) III. the Great unified the kingdom (1462–1505), and assumed the title of *czar*. This is called ' The Great Dynasty '; it gave sixty-seven sovereigns, and continued 736 years.

Russell's Cairn. A spot on the farm of Auldton-burn, on the march between England and Scotland, where Sir Francis Russell, eldest son of the Earl of Bedford, was mortally wounded in 1584 by a party of Scotch raiders led by Sir Thomas Kerr, of Ferniherst.

Russia, four dynasties.
1. The dynasty of Rurik (862–1598) gives 67 sovereigns.
2. The dynasty of Godunoff (1598–1613) gives 5 sovereigns.
3. The dynasty of Romanoff (1613–1762) gives 11 sovereigns.
4. The dynasty of Holstein-Gottorp (1762–   *)

Russia. The Scythians, we are told, called the Scandinavians *Russes, i.e.* warriors. This may be, but it is quite certain that the Norwegian *Rus* means a new or fresh-man; *Rus-land* the new-man's land; *Russia* is the freshman's land. The notion that ' Russia ' is derived from ' Rurik ' is absurd.

Russia (*The Seven Crowns of*). Three in Europe : Russia proper, Poland, and Finland. Four in Asia : Caucasus, Trans-Caspian, Central Asia, and Siberia. Population about 105 millions.

Russia Company (*The*). Formed in the reign of Edward VI., and chartered by Mary, in 1555, under the name of the ' Company of Merchant Adventurers of England for the Discovery of Lands, Territories, Islands, &c. unknown or unfrequented.' Their privileges were to have ' a governor, four consuls, and twenty-four assistants ; to make laws, inflict penalties, send out ships to make discoveries, take possession of them in the king's name, set up the royal banner of England, and enjoy the exclusive privilege of trading to Archangel and other parts of Russia, not yet frequented by the English.' The company still exists for social gatherings, but not for commercial purposes.

Russian Afghan Treaty, 1881. A treaty between Alexander II. of Russia and the Ameer of Afghanistan, in which the Russian Government engaged to be the perpetual friend of the government of Afghanistan, and to assist it against any enemy which the Ameer might be unable to subdue. The Ameer, on the other hand, engaged not to make war on any foreign power without first obtaining the consent of Russia ; and to report to Russia whatever goes on in Afghanistan. The secret object of the treaty was to win the Ameer from the British alliance, and make Afghanistan a standpoint to threaten our Indian empire, if at any time England and Russia should be at war.

Russian Byron (*The*). Alexander Sergeivitch Pushkin (1799–1837).

Russian Church Catechisms (*The*). The larger one was the Greek Church catechism prepared in 1642 by Peter Mogilas. The shorter one was the catechism prepared by the order of Peter the Great.

Russian History (*Father of*). Nestor, a monk of Kiev. His ' chronicle ' is from 862–1116. Nestor died in the 12th cent.

Russian Influenza. 20 Jan., 1837, was called Black Sunday, because 1,000 persons died in London of influenza, and numerous churches were closed from want of a congregation. Of the London police force 800 men were incapacitated for duty.

1832 and 1833 were influenza years. The next prevalence occurred in Jan. 1890. It was called 'The Russian Influenza,' and in France, where it was very fatal, it was called *La Grippe.*

Russian Laws. The *code* was compiled in 1497, by order of Ivan III. the Great. It was revised and completed in 1550 by Ivan IV. (the Terrible). Called *Sûdebnik.*

The New Code was compiled in 1649 by order of Alexis. It was called the *Sobornoe Ulajenie.*

The corpus juris (*Svod Zakonov*) was published 1826–1833.

Ivan III. the Great was the first to assume the title of ' czar.'

Russian Messali'na (*The*). Catharine, wife of Peter III. of Russia. Her paramour when Peter was alive was Gregory Orloff, officer of the guards.

Russian Murat (*The*). Michel Miloradowitch (1770–1820).

Russian Rebels. *See* ' Decembrists,' ' Nihilists,' ' Propagandists,' ' Terrorists.'

Russias (*All the*).

BALTIC RUSSIA, that part which borders on the Baltic Sea.

BLACK RUSSIA, the western part of Lithuania, which forms the governments of Minsk and Grodno. Called black from the black caps and vestments which the inhabitants used to wear.

GREAT RUSSIA, the north and middle portions of Russia in Europe ; formerly called Moscovia when Moscow was its capital.

LITTLE RUSSIA, the south-west region, the Ukraine.

NEW RUSSIA, the southern region, comprehending the governments of Kerson, Jekaterinoslav, Tauris, Bessarabia, the territory of the Cossacks of the Don, that of the Black Sea, and all the parts recently added.

RED RUSSIA, the part occupied by the Ruthenians (or Russniaks) and Poles of the Austrian frontier. It is said that they wore a red cap, like the Turkish fez.

WHITE RUSSIA, that part of Lithuania detached from Poland in 1772, forming the governments of Smolensk, Moholev, and Vitebsk. It is said that they wore white caps and dresses; the Austrian soldiers wear white.

Rus is Norwegian for *new*; Russers=the new men; and Rusland=the new man's land.

Russo-German War (*The*), 1812–1815, against Napoleon Bonaparte. It began with the Russian campaign of Napoleon, and ended with the battle of Waterloo.

Rustic War (*The*), 1525. Waged by the Elector of Saxony and the German princes against Munzer and the Anabaptists. The battle of Frankenhausen put an end to the Anabaptist rebellion. Munzer, being taken prisoner, was ignominiously put to death.

Rye House Plot (*The*), 1683. After the failure of the Mealtub plot, James duke of York was taken into the king's councils, and directed the affairs of government without a parliament. The nation grew alarmed, and a plot was set on foot for the assassination of the king on his way home from Newmarket. As the house in which the king lodged accidentally caught fire, he left Newmarket sooner than was expected, whereby his life was preserved ; but the conspirators were hunted up, and amongst others Lord William Russell and Algernon Sidney were executed.

Called the Rye House Plot, because the conspirators met at a farm belonging to Rumbold, a maltster, called the Rye House, on the river Lea, near Hoddesdon, in Hertfordshire, to concert their plans. Whether Lord William Russell was guilty has been much disputed.

Ryswick (*Peace of*), 20 Sept., 1697. Signed by England, France, Spain, and Holland ; 30 Oct., 1697, by the Emperor of Germany. To establish the peace of Europe disturbed by Louis XIV. The treaty consisted of four parts: (1) Between France and England ; (2) between France and Holland ; (3) between France and Spain ; (4) between France and Germany. By the 1st, Louis XIV. engaged to abandon the cause of James II., and to

acknowledge William III. as lawful king of England. By the 3rd, Louis restored to Spain Garonne, Roser, Barcelona, Luxembourg, Charleroi, Mons, Courtrai, and all the fortresses he had taken in Namur, Brabant, Hainault, and Flanders.

This important treaty closed the conspiracy between Louis XIV. and the Stuarts, begun at Dover ; the object of which was to make England a dependency of France and to restore Catholicism.

Sabathai Sevi (1625-1676). A false Messiah who went to Jerusalem in 1665, and, joining an ally named Nathan, gave out himself to be the *Messiah* and Nathan his *Precursor*. He collected a large following, but was arrested by Kiuperli (minister of Mohammed IV.), and, being brought before the sultan, confessed his imposition, consented to embrace Islamism, and became a public laughing-stock.

Sabbatarian Controversy (*The*), 1630. A controversy in the early part of Charles I.'s reign respecting the observance of the Sunday and its being called the 'Sabbath' or the 'Lord's Day.' The 'Book of Sports' (*q.v.*), published in the last reign, and appointed by Charles I. to be read in churches, gave great offence. Prynne printed his 'Histriomastix' in ridicule of Sunday sports, and spared neither king nor queen from his merciless castigation. For this he lost his ears, was fined, imprisoned, and struck off the Rolls.

Sabbatarians. Those Christians who observe the seventh day (our Saturday) as the true Sabbath. They are chiefly Baptists, and are sometimes called the 'Seventh-day Baptists.'

There are also Seventh-day Adventists both in America and in Europe.

Sabbata'ti, 12th cent. The Waldenses. Prat'eõlus says 'quod qui inter eos perfectiores erant, signum quoddam in superiore parte sui sotularis, quod *sabbatem* appellabant, deferre solebant.' Ebrardus Bethuniensis says : 'Sotulares cruciant, cum membra potius debeant cruciare ; calceamenta coronant, caput autem non coronant.' They were also called 'Insabbatati' (*q.v.*).

It is quite certain that the word is not connected with *Sabbath*, though it may be with *Sabot*.

Sabbath, or Day of Rest.
1st day, Sunday—Christians.
2nd day, Monday—Greeks.

3rd day, Tuesday—Persians.
4th day, Wednesday—Assyrians.
5th day, Thursday—Egyptians; Jesids (*q.v.*).
6th day, Friday—Turks.
7th day, Saturday—Jews.

Sabbat'ical Year (*The*). Every seventh year, when the Jews abstained from husbandry.

Sab'batum in Albis. The Saturday following Easter Sunday. So called because on that day those baptized on Holy Saturday (*i.e.* Saturday preceding Easter Sunday) laid aside the white robes or stoles assumed on their baptismal day.

Sab'batum in Traditio'ne Sym'boli. The Saturday preceding Palm Sunday. So called in the Ambrosian ritual, because on that day the Mediolani gave the creed (or symbol) to the catechumens, who appeared in white stoles on Palm Sunday.

Sabbatum Magnum, in the Catholic Church, means the Sabbath which occurs in the Paschal Week. The day when Christ lay in the grave, between Good Friday and Easter Sunday. Of course the day was the Saturday following Good Friday.

Sabbatum Vacat. The fifth Sunday in Lent. ' Diem Dominicum ita dictum, qui Pascha præcedit ; quia proprio officio caret. Propterea quod papa, ipso die, occuparetur eleemosyna eroganda' (Du Cange). *See* ' Sunday.'

Sabbatum XII. Lectionum. 'Ita appellatum Sabbatum Quatuor Temporum, auctor est Amalarius'(bk. ii. ch. 1).

Sabeism. Worship of the sun, moon, and stars. So-called from the Sabeans, a people of Arabia Felix.

Sabel'lianism, about A.D. 252. The heresy of Sabellius of Libya, who maintained that there is but one person of the Godhead: According to Sabellius, Father, Son, and Holy Ghost are not three distinct persons, but only three functions or manifestations of the one God. Before the incarnation there was only the One God ; this One God descended into the Virgin and became the Son, and on the Day of Pentecost this son diffused himself on the apostles, and that is the Holy Ghost. So that Father, Son, and Holy Ghost are only three names of the one hypostasis. The Sabellians also believed in the eternity of matter. Condemned by the Council of Alexandria in 261.

According to Sabellius the Son or Word and the Holy Ghost or Comforter are functions or operations of God, as light and heat are emanations of the sun.

. The Orthodox are those who accept the creed of the dominant state church. Heretics are those who choose for themselves their own religious tenets, or form their own opinions of religious truths. (Greek, mid. voice of αιρεω, to select for one's self.)

Sabian'ism. The religious system of the Sabians. They prayed thrice a day, and the temple of the moon at Haran was the term of their pilgrimage. Their traditions of the creation, deluge, and patriarchs were very similar to the Bible stories; they appealed to the secret books of Adam, Seth, and Enoch; and had a slight infusion of Christianity. It was not, however, as Sale says, 'the primitive religion of the Arabs,' but a graft of Chaldeanism. They are now called Mandæans, or St. John's Christians. The sect still exists (1890).

Sa'bians (*The*). A people and sect of Turkey. The same as the 'Nabathēans.'

Sabin'ians. In Latin, *Sabiniani*. A law school which derived its name from Massurius Sabīnus, a jurist in the time of Tiberius. He was opposed to the Proculēans (*q.v.*). The Sabinians were orthodox equity lawyers, attached to the court and aristocracy. The Proculeans were radicals.

Saccharissa. Dorothy Sydney is so called by Waller, who made love to her in vain.

In the meantime Sydney paced to and fro with him [Hugo Warncliffe] in the avenue which was called ' Saccharissa's Walk,' in memory of Sydney's beautiful sister Dorothy, immortalised by Waller under that name.—EDNA LYALL, *In the Golden Days*, ch. x.

Sache'verel (*Dr.*), 1709–1710. He preached two sermons on passive obedience and non-resistance : one 15 Aug., 1709, at the Derby assizes, before the judge and sheriff, and the other 5 Nov., 1709, before the lord mayor and corporation in St. Paul's Cathedral, on the text ' Perils from false brethren.' The gist of these sermons was against toleration in religion. He was tried in Westminster Hall in Feb. 1710, and condemned. But his sentence was suspension for two years, and the sermons to be burnt by the common hangman.

There was a large mob of Sachēverelites (5 syl.), who went about London pulling down the chapels of Dissenters and burning the hymn-books, Bibles, and furniture. The whole of this disgraceful riot was as much political as anything, the object being to oust the Whigs and bring the Tories into power.

Sacrament of the Mass, or 'Elevation of the Host.' That part of the mass in which the officiating priest holds up the consecrated bread and shows it to the people (A.D. 1373).

Sacramenta′rian Confession (*The*). The confession of faith presented by the Sacramentarians (*q.v.*) in the Diet of Augsburg (1530).

Sacramentarians, or 'Sacramentaries,' 1524. Certain reformers who separated from Luther on the doctrine of the eucharist. Luther believed in consubstantiation, but the Sacramentarians rejected the doctrine of a corporal presence, and admitted only a spiritual presence of Christ with the truly devout. Zwingli was a Sacramentarian ; so were Carlostadt, Œcolampadius, Muncer, Storck, and Martin Bucer.

M. Félice, in his 'History of the Protestants of France,' tells us that Lutherans were so called. 'Many Lutherans, or Sacramentarians as they were then called, were cast into prison' (iv. p. 34); but whether he means *all* Lutherans or *some* is not evident. Certainly Luther's 'impanation' means something *added to* the bread, or *incorporated* with it, or the word is senseless.

Sacramen′tary, or 'Sacramentarian.' One who rejects the doctrine of the real presence as taught in the Roman Catholic and Lutheran churches [that is, transubstantiation and consubstantiation].

The only thing which he [the Duke of Norfolk] thought his enemies might bring against him was for 'being quick against such as had been accused for sacramentaries' [1546],—HOWITT, *Hist. of Eng.,* vol. ii. p. 293.

*** The book used by Catholics in celebrating mass is called a 'Sacramentary.'

Sacred Art (*The*). *Ars Sacra.* Chemistry, which in Alexandria was limited to the priests.

Sacred Band (*The*). A Theban band of 300 hoplites of the best families, enrolled under Epaminondas. The special duty of this ἱερὸς λοχος was to defend the Cadmea. In 1821, 500 Greek students enrolled themselves into a 'Sacred Band' to resist the Turks. They fought most bravely, but, overpowered by numbers, they were all slain at Drageschan.

The motto of their standards was 'Death or Freedom,' or 'This, or Upon this' (ἤ τὰν, ἤ ἐπὶ ταν), the motto inscribed in the shields of the ancient Spartans.

Sacred College (*The*), A.D. 311. The Roman Church agreed to appoint seventy of their clergy into a sacred college. The number was in imitation of the Jewish Sanhedrim and the seventy disciples appointed by Christ. It was composed of six bishops, fifty priests, and fourteen deacons, to be called ' cardinals,' out of which one was to be elected chairman or head of the hierarchy. The assemblies of the college were called *conclaves,* and each of the members now wears a red hat.

The full number is not strictly kept up. Thus, in 1841, there were but 61 (38 instead of 50 being cardinal priests, and 11 instead of 14 being cardinal deacons).

Sacred Geese. Geese kept by the ancient Romans in the temple of Juno on the Capitoline Hill. These geese are especially noted in Roman story, because when a party of Gauls climbed stealthily up the steep rock, unobserved by the sentinels, and even without disturbing the watch-dogs, the geese gave the alarm by their cackling, and Manlius, being aroused, reached the rampart just in time to push over the foremost Gaul and thus saved the capitol.

Sacred Heart (*The*). There are two fêtes so called in the Catholic Church : (1) ' Le Sacré Cœur de Jésus,' instituted in 1698, from the revelations of Marie Alacoque, and celebrated the third Sunday after Pentecost, but in 1822 transferred to the second Sunday in July. And (2) the *Sacré Cœur de Marie,* instituted in 1661, and celebrated 8 February.

We are told as an historic truth that Jesus allowed this visionary to repose on his bosom, and one day said to her: 'Mary, my sacred heart is full of love to man, but to thee especially, to whom I enjoin the privilege of making known the treasures of sanctification and salvation, which alone can redeem from hell.' Then taking his heart, he put it into hers. She saw it distinctly, and says it was like a burning coal. Every Friday this was repeated, till she consented to establish the festival of the Sacred Heart (!). *See* 'Life and Works of Margaret Mary Alacoque' ; BRETON, 'Instruction sur le Sacré Cœur de Jésus,' and 'Les Petits Bollandistes,' vol. xii. p. 421.

Sacred Island (*The*). Ireland was so called long before the introduction of Christianity into the island. Probably it

3 E

was the seat of Spanish-Phœnician missions. Festus Avienus says that two days will bring you

> .... in sacram sic insulam
> Dixere prisci ....
> Eamque late gens Hibernorum colit.

Plutarch refers to the Magi of Ireland, and Diodorus Siculus to its sun-worship.

Sacred Month (*The*), 1838, of the Chartists. In which the Chartists swore to abstain from all work and all drink, 'in order to secure the charter of their political salvation.' *See* 'Six Articles, &c.' In some places the 'Sacred Month' began in July, in others in August.

From the despatch of the Sacred Ship (*q.v.*) to its return was a Sacred Month in Attica.

Sacred Mount (*The*), or Mons Sacer, a hill about two miles from Rome, commanding the junction of the Tiber and Anio. Called the *Sacred* Hill because it was here that the Roman army encamped with the intention of forming themselves into a free and independent community when they found that Appius and the senate refused to fulfil the promises twice made to them when enemies were at the gates. Ultimately a compromise was effected, and two popular officers were granted to the revolters. The terms of this treaty were called the Sacred Laws, or *Leges Sacratæ*.

Sacred Shields (*The*). Of the Salian priests, in the reign of Numa. These twelve shields, we are told, fell down from heaven, and became the palladium of Rome.

Sacred Ship (*The*). The ship in which Theseus (2 syl.) sailed to Crete to deliver Attica from the tyranny of Minos. It was preserved ever afterwards, and sent by the Athenians every year to the island of Delos with offerings. From the dispatch of the ship to its return no criminals were put to death.

It so happened that Socratês was condemned to death the night before the sacred ship weighed anchor, and consequently his death was deferred for thirty days, till the ship returned.

Sacred Spring (*A*). Ver Sacrum, a dedication of all the produce of the spring to the gods. Even the children born during a sacred spring were devoted, and had to leave the city of their birth. It was a Sabine custom; but when Hannibal invaded Italy, Quintus Fabius Maximus advised the Roman senate to decree a 'Sacred Spring.'

Sacred Standard (*The*). The 'standard of green silk,' unfolded by Mussulmans in times of imminent danger, and said to have been borne by the prophet himself. When Selim I., in 1517, conquered Egypt, this standard went to the Osmanlis, and has ever since been regarded as a palladium. In 1595 it was displayed in the war of Hungary. Mohammed III. confided it to the custody of 300 emirs. At present the sacred standard is enveloped in four coverings of green taffeta, and inclosed in a case of green cloth. In the same case is a small Koran written by the hand of the Calif Omar, and the keys of the Caaba (*q.v.*).

The pole of the standard is twelve feet high, and is surmounted with a closed hand. In times of peace it is preserved in the 'Hall of the Noble Vestments,' which also contains the prophet's tunic, the sacred teeth, beard, stirrup, sabre, and bow of the prophet.

Sacred War (*The*). There were two sacred wars in Grecian history—the *first* from 595 to 586, and the second from 356 to 346, each therefore of ten years' duration. The first of these broke out in Phocis soon after the establishment of Solon's laws in Athens. The Crisseans levied grievous taxes on those who went to consult the oracle of Delphi, and even seized the sacred treasures of that temple. Solon induced the Amphictyonic league to avenge the sacrilege, so the lands of the Crisseans were laid waste. In the ninth year of the war the city of Crissa was taken, and the spoil consecrated to Apollo. As many of the Crisseans had taken refuge in Cirrha, that city was attacked and shared the fate of Crissa; the whole territory of both Crissa and Cirrha was consecrated to Apollo, and was henceforth uncultivated.

The cause of the *second* sacred war was that the Phocians cultivated a part of the Cirrhæan territory which had been dedicated to Apollo. The offenders were cited before the Amphictyons, and, fined, but they refused to pay the fine. War broke out. Thebes, Locris, Thessaly, and several other states joined the Amphictyons; but Athens and Sparta joined the Phocians. At length Philip king of Macedonia joined the Amphictyons, and compelled Phocis to surrender at discretion, B.C. 352.

It was on the interference of Philip of Macedon in this war that Demosthênês spoke his first Philippic and Olynthiac orations.

Sacrifica'ti (*The*). Those lapsed Christians who, to avoid persecution, consented to offer sacrifice to heathen gods. They were very numerous.

Sacrificial Mass, or Sacrifice of the Mass. 'Missa Perfecta,' τελεία θυσία. The 'Missa Imperfecta' was that in which the body and blood of Christ were not administered. The 'Missa Perfecta' contained the perfect sacrifice. *See* 'Mass.'

Sacy's Bible. 'Bible de Sacy.' The Port Royal translation of the Bible, so called from Isaac Lemaistre (Sacy), director of the Port Royal monastery. He was imprisoned for three years in the Bastille for his Jansenist opinions, and during his captivity translated the Bible into French (1666-1670). *See* 'Bible.'

Saci (now written Sacy) is an anagram of Isaac. *See* ' Prison Literature.'

Sadducees, B.C. 250. A sect of the ancient Jews who took their name from ' Zadoc,' one of the followers of Antigŏnus Sochæus, president of the Sanhedrim. They rejected tradition, believed only in the pentateuch, disbelieved in a future state, in angels, and spirits. They were very rich and very influential.

Sadle'rian Professorship. Of pure mathematics, in the University of Cambridge, founded in 1710 by Lady Sadler. In 1886 an alteration was made, and the stipend increased to 850*l*. *See* ' Mathematics (Professorship of).'

Saffron Hue (*The*). The royal colour of the ancient Irish kings; thus Murkertach is described by the Four Masters (*q.v.*) as ' a warrior of the saffron hue.'

Henry VIII. forbade by statute any Irishman ' to wear or use any shirt, smocke, kerchor, bendol, neckerchour, mocket, or linnen cap, coloured or died with saffron.' The two chieftains, Lord Roche and the White Knight, having by their incessant quarrels wasted each other's lands, were both seized by order of Henry VIII., and in prison slept amicably in one bed. After a time they were released apparelled as Englishmen, and no longer wearing 'their saffron shirts and kernoghe's coats.'

Saffron Veil. The Greek and Roman brides wore a *flammeum* or yellow veil which wholly enveloped them (Pliny, ' Natural History,' xxi. 22). When the bride was taken home, it was the husband's part to take off her veil (Lucan, ii. 361).

We call a sweetheart ' a flame.' The coincidence is worth noting, if of no other value.

Sagas, 11th to 16th cent. Poetical compositions by the Scalds or Scandinavian bards. The subjects are mythological and historic traditions of Norway, Sweden, Denmark, and Iceland.

Sage of Syracuse (*The*). Archimēdês.

So Tully paused, amid the wrecks of time,
On the rude stone to trace the truth sublime:
When at his feet, in honoured dust disclosed,
The immortal sage of Syracuse reposed.
ROGERS, *Pleasures of Memory*, pt. 1

Sahidic Version (*The*) of the Scriptures, also called ' the Thebaidic,' in the dialect of Upper Egypt, and supposed to be of the 2nd cent. *See* ' Scriptures.'

Sailor King (*The*). William IV. of the British Empire (1765, 1830-1837). He entered the navy 15 June, 1779 ; was captain of royal navy 10 April, 1786 ; created rear-admiral 1790, vice-admiral 1793, admiral 1799, lord high-admiral 1827.

The great seal of William IV. represents him on horseback with ships in the background; and seated in a chair of state with Neptune and sea-nymphs, Minerva and sailors. Minerva holds a spear and Neptune the trident.

St. Andrew (*Order of*). Instituted by Hungus king of the Picts. It took its name, because after the battle with Athelstane of England, Hungus and his soldiers went barefooted to St. Andrews, and there vowed that they and their posterity would ever afterwards use his cross as their ensign in every warlike enterprise (Peter Heylyn, ' Cosmography,' p. 340).

St. Augustine's Oak. At Aust in Gloucestershire, where the conference was held in 601 under an oak on the banks of the Severn, to secure the co-operation of the British in the missionary work of St. Augustine, and to effect a complete uniformity of religious usages in the island. The British bishops utterly refused to accept Augustine as their archbishop, or to accept his platform.

His platform was this: (1) To keep Easter on the first Sunday after the 14th of Nisan; (2) to baptize by 'trine immersion;' and (3) to join Augustine in missionary work.

St. Bartholomew's Day, 24 Aug., 1572. A day never to be forgotten, on which at midnight began in Paris the diabolical massacre of the Huguenots. Those employed in this slaughter wore a

3 E 2

scarf on their left arm, and a white cross on their hat. For three days and three nights the butchery went on, and as many as 6,000 were massacred in Paris alone. The whole number murdered in France has been estimated at 50,000, some say 80,000. The day after St. Bartholomew's Day the king went in state to Notre Dame to assist at a *Te Deum*, or service of praise to God, and all the bells of the city rang out their joy peals, but the massacre was still going on and still were heard the shrieks of the dying and the roar of burning houses.

The massacre was planned by Catherine de' Medici, the queen-mother, in the reign of her son Charles IX. It seems past belief, but is nevertheless true, that Pope Gregory XIII. went in solemn state to the church of St. Louis to offer thanksgiving to Almighty God for this butchery; and yet dared to talk of the persecutions of the Roman emperors.

St. Brice's Day, 13 Nov., 1002, noted for the massacre of the Danes in England, at the instigation of Ethelred the Unready.

'**St. Cecilia,** the beautiful mother of beautiful daughters,' mentioned by Macaulay, was Mrs. Sheridan and her three daughters—the Duchess of Somerset, Lady Dufferin, and the Hon. Mrs. Norton.

St. Germain-en-Laye (*The Treaty of*), 8 Aug., 1570. Gave liberty of worship in all places under the French crown ; it gave furthermore two towns in each province for the celebration of the Protestant service; an amnesty for the past, equal right of admission to all public offices, permission to reside in any part of France, and four hostage towns—viz. La Rochelle, La Charité, Cognac, and Montauban.

St. Guy's Dance, 1374. Same as St. John's Dance (*q. v.*).

St. Guy's dance is another name for St. Vitus's dance (*q.v.*).

St. John's Dance, 1374. So the Dancing Mania was originally called. When it appeared at Strasburg in 1418 it was called St. Vitus's Dance. Whether St. John's or St. Vitus's Dance, the saint was the one applied to by the afflicted, who made small offerings on the altar of the favourite saint.

Not St. John the Evangelist but St. John the Baptist, to whose day was transferred several heathen customs. The dancing mania broke out on St. John the Baptist's Day (June 24).

St. Louis. Louis IX. of France (1215, 1226-1270).

St. Margaret's, the church of the House of Commons, is noted in history as being the place where the Commons swore to the Solemn League and Covenant in Sept. 1642. Mr. Nye read the Covenant from the pulpit; all present, consisting of members of both houses, the Assembly of Divines, and Scottish Commissioners, signified their assent to it by holding up their hands. The members afterwards signed the parchment-roll, and then Dr. Gouge implored a blessing upon the act.

St. Mark, Venice.

The glory, nay perhaps the very existence, of St. Mark must pass away for ever. These cities [mentioned in the text] still owed fealty to St. Mark.—*History of Venice*, vol. i. p. 331 ; vol. ii. p. 379 (Murray).

St. Mary Overie, Southwark, now St. Saviour's. It was founded by Mary Overie, a nun, on the site of her father's house. John Overie (it is said) was a ferryman, who used to ferry passengers from Southwark to the city and back again.

Shakespeare's brother (Edmond), Fletcher and Massinger (the dramatists) were buried in the churchyard ; and there are monuments to Gower the poet, Andrews bishop of Winchester, Lockyer (the quack doctor in the reign of Charles II.), and other historic characters.

St. Nicolas Shambles, London. A flesh-market, east of Greyfriars. So called from the church of St. Nicolas. The Butchers' Hall was close by. The lane of the shambles and hall used to be called Stinking Lane, but is now named King Edward Street.

St. Patrick's Purgatory. The place of penance on an island, now called Station Island, in Lough Derg, Ireland. It was a kind of cave dug up in the reign of Charles I.

St. Petersburg (*Treaties of*).

I. 30 Oct., 1715, between Peter I. and the King of Prussia, respecting the war in Pomerania.

II. 10 Aug., 1726, between the Czarina Catherine and the King of Prussia.

III. 16 Dec., 1740, a defensive alliance between the regent Anne of Russia and Frederick II. of Prussia.

IV. 4 Feb., 1744, a treaty of alliance between Russia and Poland.

V. 22 May (2 June), 1746, a defensive alliance between Great Britain and Russia.

VI. 9 March, 1759, a treaty between

Russia and Sweden to protect the navigation of the Baltic.

VII. 5 May, 1762, a treaty of peace between Czar Peter III. and Frederick II. of Prussia.

VIII. 11 April, 1764, an alliance between the Czarina Catherine and Frederick II. of Prussia.

IX. 20 June, 1766, a treaty of commerce between Great Britain and Russia.

X. 5 Aug., 1772, for the partition of Poland between Austria, Prussia, and Russia.

XI. 1 Aug., 1773, an alliance between Russia and Denmark.

XII. 1 Aug., 1780, an alliance between Russia and Sweden for the protection of commerce.

XIII. 11 Jan., 1787, a treaty of commerce with France.

XIV. 12 July, 1792, a defensive alliance between Russia and the King of Hungary and Bohemia.

XV. 18 Feb., 1795, a treaty of alliance between Russia and Great Britain.

XVI. 15 Jan., 1797, a treaty between Czar Paul I. and the Order of Malta.

XVII. 29 Nov., 1798, an alliance between Russia and the Two Sicilies.

XVIII. 28 Sept., 1799, an alliance between Russia and Portugal.

XIX. 21 May, 1800, between Russia and Turkey, constituting the Ionian Isles a republic.

XX. 18 Dec., 1800, an alliance between Russia and Prussia.

XXI. 13 March, 1801, a treaty of commerce between Russia and Sweden.

XXII. 8 April, 1805, a treaty for a third coalition against Napoleon, between Great Britain and Russia.

XXIII. 24 March, 1812, an alliance between Sweden and Russia against Napoleon.

XXIV. 1 Aug., 1812, a treaty of peace and union between Great Britain and Russia.

St. Salvator's College. Better 'San Salvător.' *See* p. 27, 'Andrews, *University of St.*'

Saint-Simo'nianism, 1814. A non-communistic socialism, in which industry is to be regulated in obedience to a self-constituted authority; production is first to be accumulated to excess, and then distributed in the ratio of merit; all transmission of property is to be abolished; marriage is to be abolished, all grades of rank, all family ties, and each individual is to belong to the one universal family of man. With all this communism there is to be a head called the 'Supreme Father,' whose authority is to be wholly absolute. *See* 'Supreme Father.'

A scheme which does not contemplate an equal but an unequal division of the produce. It does not propose that all should occupy alike, but differently, according to the vocation or capacity of each individual; the function and salary of each being assigned by the directing authority.—MILL, *Political Economy*, 258.

St. Simo'nians (*The*), 1825. The school of the Industrialists (*q.v.*) founded by St. Simon, for the amelioration of the working classes, perverted after his death into a communistic society, advocating the aristocracy of toil, the perfect equality of man, community of property, and the abolition of inheritance and marriage. Abolished by law in 1833.

'The aristocracy of toil and perfect equality,' indeed! This is mere clap-trap of the silliest kind. Where is the 'aristocracy' of digging a few potatoes, cobbling old boots, or crying 'Dust, oh!'? Stuff! And where is the equality of the infant and its father, the idiot of an asylum and Shakespeare and Newton? It is a mere perversion of language, and most misleading. The very stars differ in glory.

St. Stephen's. The British Houses of Parliament: thus we say, 'T. e parliaments called by Edward I. were identical with those which still sit in St. Stephen's.' St. Stephen's Chapel was built 1150 by King Stephen, rebuilt by Edward II. and III. and finally destroyed by fire in 1834. It was fitted up for the use of the House of Commons in the reign of Edward IV. In order to enter 'the palace of Westminster,' we pass through St. Stephen's porch into St. Stephen's Hall, and north and south of this hall corridors lead to the House of Peers and House of Commons; hence it is, that, by a figure of speech, the House of Commons is called 'St. Stephen's,' and even the House of Lords is sometimes so called, but not often, as a separate house. The two together are not unfrequently called St. Stephen's.

St. Stephen's originally formed part of the palace of Edward the Confessor.

St. Stephen's Crown. The Hungarian crown. St. Stephen (979, 997–1038) received a royal crown from Pope Sylvester II., and the title of apostolic king, which the emperors of Austria bear to the present day.

If Hungarian independence should be secured

through the help of Prince Napoleon, the prince himself should accept the crown of St. Stephen.
—KOSSUTH, *Memoirs of my Exile*, 1880.

St. Vitus's Dance. Chorea, a disease marked by an involuntary and irregular contraction of the muscles of the face and limbs; a kind of jerking movement, and in some cases a mere fidgetiness. In Germany the 'dancing mania' was called ' St. Witt's Dance,' in Italy called 'Tarantism' (*q.v.*).

St. Witt's Dance, 1374. So the dance of the dancing mania was called in Germany. *See* also 'St. Guy's Dance.'

Sainte Ampoule (*La*). The cruse containing the sacred oil with which the French kings were anointed at Reims.

Henri IV. and Louis XVIII. were not anointed at Reims. Nor, of course, were Napoleon I. and III.

Saints. Henry Garnet (Father Garnet), the English Jesuit (1555–1606), born at Nottingham, and educated at Winchester, is reckoned among the 'martyrs.' He confessed his implication in the Gunpowder Plot, and was executed for high treason.

Martyrdom and high treason should certainly never be made synonymous terms; yet the name of Henry Garnet is duly enrolled in the hagiography of the Bollandists, under 3 May.
At best the word 'Saint' applied to any man is most objectionable; and Irish agitators have reduced the word 'Martyr' to utter ridicule. If traitors and rebels are 'saints and martyrs,' the title dishonours the head that wears it.

Saka Era (*The*) of Hindûstan begins from the death of Salivâhana, A.D. 76. The Sakas or Scythians gained a footing in Hindûstan in 76, and gradually extended their empire. They were the ancestors of the numerous tribes of Rajputs from Oude to Marwar.

Sal'adin Tax (*The*), 1200. A tax imposed on Christendom by Pope Innocent III. for the prosecution of the fourth crusade.

Saladin himself died in 1194.

Sal'adine Tithe (*The*), 1187. A general tax of the tenth of all movable estate, imposed by the kings of France and England upon all their subjects, whether ecclesiastic or lay, towards the expense of their intended crusade (the third). This tax was sanctioned by the pope and prelates as well as by the kings and barons.

This is the first eminent instance of a general tax. Church property as a rule paid no tax, as it would have been deemed sacrilegious to take church property for civil purposes.

Salic Law (*The*). The code of the Salian Franks, introduced into France (Gaul) by the Franks. It contained 400 articles, chiefly concerning debt, theft, murder, and battery, the penalty in every case being a fine. The most famous article of the code is Title lxii. 6, according to which only males could succeed to the Salic land or *lod*, *i.e.* to the lands given for military service. In 1316, at the death of Louis le Hutin, the law was extended to the crown, and continued to be observed to the end of the monarchy.

Salii (*The*). Twelve priests of Mars chosen from high patrician families and appointed to guard the twelve sacred *ancilia* which were kept in the Temple of Mars on the Palatine hill. The great festival of Mars began on 1 March and continued several days. They were called Salii, from *salio* (to dance), from their dancing in procession. Their dance was called the 'Salic Dance,' and their hymns or chants the 'Salic Songs.'

Varro says *a salitando*.

Salisbury, or Sarum Missal (*The*), or 'Salisbury Hours,' A.D. 1078. A liturgy drawn up by Oswald or Osmund bishop of Salisbury *in usum Sarum*. It was in Latin and based on those of Rome. This Missal was used throughout the whole kingdom.

'Sarum' is the better word, as 'Salisbury' is 'New Sarum.' Our Common Prayer-Book is almost a translation of this Missal, and the Litany is almost word for word the same.

Sallust of France (*The*). L'Abbé de St. Real (1639–1692), author of ' Spanish Conspiracies against the Republic of Venice,' from which Otway borrowed his 'Don Carlos' and his 'Venice Preserved.'

Salt. At the accession of James I. the people of Grâce Dieu (within the liberties of Waterford) closed their gates against Mountjoy, the English lord-lieutenant of Ireland; but Mountjoy warned the people if they compelled him to enter by force he would utterly destroy the town, and ' spread salt upon the ruins.' In allusion to an ancient custom of drawing a plough over the walls of a conquered city and strewing salt over the place. Thus when Abimelech 'took the city of Shechem he sowed the place with salt (Judges ix. 15). (*See also* Judges ii. 9; Psalms cvii. 34; Jer. xvii. 6.)

Salters' Hall Controversy

(*The*), 1719. A Baptist controversy on the question whether toleration is or is not to be extended to Unitarians.

Salvation Army (*The*), 1873.

A home missionary organization set on foot by William Booth, who was called the 'General' of the army. The plan of operation is for a company to march about cities, towns, and villages, singing popular sacred songs and speaking between whiles for about five minutes. The army has also a large number of religious periodicals and small books.

Mr. Booth was a minister of the Methodist New Connexion, which he left in 1861, and began 'revivalistic services' in a tent in Whitechapel. In 1865 his little band of followers called themselves 'The East London Christian Revival Society,' afterwards changed to 'The Christian Mission.' In 1869 the Mission made expeditions to provincial towns. Lastly, in 1873, the name was changed to 'The Salvation Army.'

Their literary organ, called 'The Christian Mission,' first appeared monthly in 1874. In 1879 it was called 'The Salvationist,' and in the same year its title was changed into 'The War-Cry.'

Salvationism, Ecclesiasticism.

Ecclesiasticism is dogmatic religion, the doctrine that the church is the ark, out of which there is no salvation. Salvationism is the doctrine that the church is simply a name for all believing Christians, and that salvation is a gift wholly independent of an hierarchy or community of any kind called 'a church.' Ritualists are strong believers in ecclesiasticism; Dissenters and what are called 'Evangelicals' are salvationists.

Samaneans (*The*), or 'Samanæi,'

were distinct from the Brahmins and Gymnosophists (the latter were probably Jains), yet equally austere and living in solitude. They were apparently Buddhist priests. All the worshippers of the Dalaï-Lama have been also called 'Samanéans.'

Not to be mistaken for the Chamaneans. See 'Chamanism.'

Sama'nides (3 syl.).

A Persian dynasty while Persia was a province of the Califs. Founded by Ismail al Samäni. Lasted only 97 years (902–999). It succeeded the Sof'farides (3 syl.), and was overthrown by the Ghaz'nevides (3 syl.). It reigned only over Transoxiana, Khorasan, Balkh, and Seistan.

The Samanides reigned over Seistan, Korasan, Balkh, and Tabaristan. The Bowides in 932 obtained a part of Persia. Gibbon (ch. lvii.) says the dynasty lasted 125 years (874 999).

Samaritan Pentateuch (*The*),

2nd cent. A translation of the Hebrew Pentateuch into the Samaritan dialect. It bears a strong resemblance to the Targum of Onkelos. *See* 'Scriptures.'

It must not be confounded with the 'Pentateuch of the Samaritans,' which is a copy of the Hebrew Pentateuch in Samaritan characters. The Samaritan Pentateuch is a *translation.*

Samaritan War (*The*), A.D. 529.

A war carried on by Justinian against the Samaritans, who had risen in arms to retaliate their wrongs. In this war 20,000 Samaritans were slain and as many more were sold as slaves to the Arabs and Persians. Gibbon (xlvii.) says 100,000 Roman subjects were extirpated in this war, by which the fruitful province of Samaria was converted into a wilderness. 'But,' he adds, 'in the creed of Justinian, the guilt of murder could not be applied to the slaughter of unbelievers.'

Samaritans (*The*).

Not Israelites, but Assyrian and Medish colonists sent thither by Shalmanezer, when he had carried the native population to Nineveh. They received 'the books of the law.' The division into Israelites and Judæans had ceased long before the Incarnation.

Sa'mian Sage (*The*).

Pythagŏras of Samos (B.C. 481–411). One of the most astounding geniuses ever born.

Samnite Wars (*The*).

A series of wars between the Romans and the Sam'-nites (2 syl.), which lasted, with few interruptions, for fifty-three years. The three great wars were: (1) 343–341; (2) 326–304; (3) 298–290.

Samos'atans.

Followers of Paul of Samŏsăta, bishop of Antioch, who denied the doctrine of the Trinity and the divinity of Jesus the Christ. He was excommunicated by the Synod of Antioch in 270. His followers are also called Paulianists, or Paulinists.

Samp'sicera'nus, Alabar'ches, the Jerusalemite.

So Cicero designates the haughty Pompey, the great eastern conqueror (B.C. 106–48).

Sampsicerănus was king of Emesa in Syria. *Alabarches* is an oriental name for a tax-gatherer. *Jerusalemite* refers to his taking Jerusalem, B.C. 63, when he entered the Holy of Holies out of curiosity and found nothing.

Samson (*The Greek*).

Her'aklês, called by the Romans Her'culês.

Samson (*The Italian*). Milo of Crotōna, the athlete.

Samson (*The Turkish*). Ozdemir or the Iron Ogli (16th cent.) So called by Cantemir.

Sancho (*The Crowned*). Louis XVI. was so called by Camille Desmoulins, 'because he was always thinking of his stomach, and at Varennes lost the time in which he might have escaped by staying to eat pig's pettitoes.' So it is said.

Sanchoni'atho. In nine vols. A literary forgery by Wagenfeld of Hanover, published at Bremen in 1837. It was said that the MS. of this work had been discovered in the convent of St. Maria de Merinhão by a Colonel Pereira in the Portuguese army; but it was ascertained that there was no such convent nor any such colonel, and that the paper of the MS. bore the water-mark of Osnabrück paper-mills. *See* 'Literary Forgeries.'

There was a 'history' said to be by Sanchoniatho published bv Herennius Philon Byblius, a translation from the original Phœnician work, fragments of which are preserved in Eusebius; but considerable doubt exists as to the authenticity of this work also.

Sancy Diamond (*The*). Picked up on the field of battle near Granson. It belonged to Charles le Téméraire of Burgundy, who was routed there and fled. Sixteen years after the battle it was sold at Lucerne for 1,250*l.* It fell into the hands of the house of Braganza; was subsequently purchased by Nicholas de Sancy [*Sahn-se*], and under the name of the Sancy diamond was set in the crown of France. During the Revolution it was sold, but Napoleon I. rebought it. In 1825 it was sold to Prince Paul Demidoff for 80,000*l.* The prince sold it in 1830 to M. Levrat, administrator of the Mining Society; but, Levrat being unable to pay the money, it was returned in 1832 to the prince. We next hear of it in Bombay. In 1867 it was transmitted to England by the firm of Forbes & Co. In 1873 it formed part of the crown necklace worn by Mary of Sachsen-Altenburg on her marriage with Albert of Prussia. In 1876 it was worn as a pendant by the Maharajah of Puttiala; but in 1877 it belonged to the Czar of Russia.

Sandal-wood Gates (*The*), or Sandal Gates ' of the temple of the great idol Somnat in Somnauth, in Guzerat. This temple was built in the 5th cent., and in 1024 the city of Somnauth was stormed, the idol was broken by the Sultan Mahmud, and the Sandal Gates were sent to Ghuznee. In 1842 the gates were carried off by the British. Lord Ellenborough, governor-general of India, wanted to restore them to Somnauth, but the British Government would not allow it to be done for fear of provoking religious strife between Mahrattas and Moslems. So they were taken to Agra, where they still are (1890).

The stone idol, Somnat, an avatar of Siva or Mahades, was fifteen feet in height, six of whicn were sunk in the ground. When Mahmud took the town of Somnauth and entered the temple he knocked off the nose of the idol with his mace, and ordered two pieces of the idol to be sent to Ghuznee, where they still are. His next stroke was against the belly of the idol, and the opening revealed an enormous quantity of diamonds, rubies, and pearls. Som-nat=Somalord. Soma was the sacred drink of the gods.
. The old belief or prophecy was that when the gates should leave Ghuznee the Sikh rule would cease. This proved true.

Sandema'nians, 1728, or Glassists, from Mr. John Glass, the founder, expelled from the Church of Scotland for maintaining that national churches are 'kingdoms of this world,' and therefore unlawful. The word Sandemanian is from Robert Sandĕman, who published a series of letters on the subject in 1755.

San-kou-e, or ' San-Kou,' (221–317). Three states of China, collectively so called. The source of Chinese romance, and the fount from which they draw their historical plays. In 265 the three states (after being divided for forty-five years) were united under one ruler, who lived at Honan, and the Salic law was introduced; in 416 the Honan state merged again into the Chinese empire.

The ' Three states ' were (1) the sixth imperial dynasty ; (2) the kingdom of Oey or Wei; and (3) the kingdom of Ou or Woo.

Sanquhar Declaration (*The*), 1680. A deed renouncing the authority of Charles II., drawn up by Richard Cameron, Cargill, Douglas, and others. So called from Sanquhar, a town in Dumfries.

Sanquhar, pronounce *Sang-ker*.

Sans-culottes (*Les*). A name of contempt given to the democrats in the French Revolution; as much as to say, they were only the tag-rags or ragamuffins of society. Subsequently, like the *Gueux* (*q.v.*), they gloried in the name, and even affected negligence of dress, going about in a blouse, red cap, and wooden shoes. The red nightcap adorned with a tricoloured cockade was called the 'bonnet-rouge.' Blouse = blooze.

The Sans-culottes had a host of songs and a dance (called the Carmagnole) of their own. Pronounce *Lay Sahn' ku-lot'*.

Sans-culotte Cabinet (*The*), 1792. Consisting of Duranthon (minister of justice), De Grave (minister of war), Clavières, a deaf man (minister of finance), Lacoste (minister of marine), Roland (minister of the interior), and Dumouriez (minister of foreign affairs). None of these men, except Dumouriez, was distinguished, and the court called them the Sans-culotte Cabinet from their total insignificance. Pronounce *Sahn' ku-lot'*.

When Roland presented himself at court, the master of the ceremonies refused to admit him till Roland explained that he was minister of the interior. The astonished master observed to Dumouriez, who entered next, 'Ah, sir, no buckles in his shoes!' To which Dumouriez in affected amazement replied, 'Bon Dieu! then all is lost!'

Sans-culottides, 1793. The five supernumerary days of the Revolutionary Calendar. Romme divided the year into 12 equal months of 30 days, beginning 22 Sept., 1792. This gives only 360 days. The 5 days over were festival days—1 to Genius, 2 to Labour, 3 to Actions, 4 to Rewards, 5 to Opinion. In leap year a sixth Sans-culottide was added and called the Festival of the Revolution. The Convention Calendar ceased 1 Jan., 1806. The months, beginning with September, were called— (Autumn) Vendémiaire, Brumaire, Frimaire (wine-ary, fog-ary, frost-ary); (Winter) Nivôse, Pluviôse, Ventôse (snow-ous, rain-ous, wind-ous); (Spring) Germinal, Floréal, Prairial (bud-all, bloom-all, mead-all); (Summer) Messidor, Thermidor, Fructidor (reap-time, heat-time, fruit-time).

No one, however, was allowed to hold any opinion on politics, theology, sociology, or indeed any other subject of public interest not in accordance with the Convention. Such is liberty!

The ancient Irish calendar contained only 360 days, the other five or six were days in which they celebrated their Taltine games, *i.e.* to the sun and moon.

Sans Peur et sans Reproche. Chevalier Bayard is called the knight sans peur et sans reproche (1476–1524).

Pronounce *Sahn Puh'r a sahn R'prosh'*.

Santa Casa (*The*). The reputed house of Joseph and Mary in Nazareth

34

where Jesus was brought up. It was transported first in 1291 by angels to Fiume, in Dalmatia, but in 1294 angels removed it to Loreto at midnight 10 Dec. In eight months' time it shifted its place from the laurel grove, which was infested by brigands, to the hill, and in four months more,(1295) it again shifted its place from the hill to a heap of stones near the high road leading to Recanati, near the sea-coast, where it is still. *See* p. 149, ' Casa, &c.'

Pronounce *Sahn'-tah Kah'-sah*.

Santa Fedis, 1799. Members of the Secret Association of the Holy Faith, organised by Cardinal Ruffo to exterminate all Jansenists, Molinists, Economists, Illuminists, Freemasons, and Carbona'ri. A deadly hatred existed between those societies and the Fedists [Fa-dists]; and the Fedists, in 1816, committed most frightful slaughter, especially on the Carbona'ri and their families.

Santa Hermandad (*The*), or 'Holy Brotherhood.' An association which executed summary justice on all offenders without distinction of rank. It was established in Spain by Ferdinand the Catholic (1481–1516).

Santo Ben'ito. The robe worn by those who were punished by the inquisitors. It was a straight yellow coat without sleeves, with sundry devices. If it contained only a St. Andrew's cross, the wearer paid a fine and was discharged. If it was decorated with flames made of red serge, but without a cross, the wearer was discharged, but warned if ever he relapsed that he would be delivered to the flames. If besides the 'flames' it was decorated with devils, the wearer was condemned to die.

Santons. A mendicant tribe of Moslems which profess poverty and the complete sacrifice of all temporal interests to devote themselves to spiritual matters. Yet they have not unfrequently filled the chief offices of the state. When acting simply as ' prophets' they live in retired grottoes, like hermits, or in tents. The Osmanli consider Abdal, called ' Santone Kalenderi,' contemporary with Mahomet, as the founder. He never pronounced the name of God, but sounded it on his pipe. *See* p. 136, ' Calenders.'

Sappho (*The English*). Mrs. Mary D. Robinson (1758–1800).

Sappho (*The French*). Mdlle. Scudéri (1607–1701).

Sappho (*The Scotch*). Catherine Cockburn (1679–1749).

Sappho of Toulouse. Clémence Isaure (2 syl.), who instituted in 1490 *Les Jeux Floraux*. She is the authoress of a beautiful ' Ode to Spring ' (1463–1513).

Sarabaïtes. Monks who live two or three together in one cell.

Hermits or Eremites live alone, *Cenobites* (3 syl.) live socially in common, in a monastery, or convent, &c. All are *Ascetics*.

Sarace'nic Empire (*The Golden Age of the*). That of Haroun al Raschid, *i.e.* Haroun the Just (786–809).

Sardanapa'lus of China (*The*). Cheou-sin, the last of the Châng dynasty (B.C. 1154–1122). Like Sardanapalus, he burnt himself and his queen to death in his palace to escape falling into the hands of Woo-wong. Chopsticks were first used in this reign.

Sardanapa'lus of Germany (*The*). Wenceslas VI. (or IV.) king of Bohemia and kaiser of Germany (1359, 1378–1419).

Sardin'ians for Sale. ' Sardi venāles ' (Livy, xl. 19), rubbish for sale. The Sardinians rose against Rome in the Second Punic War, and again B.C. 181. Tiberius Gracchus checked the insurrection, and so numerous were the prisoners that the market was glutted, and slaves were an unsaleable drug.

Sargon was originally only a high priest for the year B.C. 721, but was afterwards king of Assyria. His name was Sarru-gina, and he was father of Sennacherib or Sin-akhi-erba, who began to reign B.C. 707.

Sarma'tia. Russia in Europe. Russia in Asia was called Scythia.

Sarum Missal (*The*), or ' Use of Sarum,' compiled by Osmund, 1085. Printed at Paris 1487, and at Rouen 1492. Only one perfect copy is known to exist, and that is in the British Museum.

Mr. Blades gives a description of the Sarum Missal printed at Paris in 1487 (' Athenæum,' 21 March, 1874). There is an imperfect copy of the edition of 1492 in the Bodleian Library.

Sassan'ian Dynasty (*The*), or the ' Sas'sanides ' (3 syl.). A Persian dynasty which succeeded the Arsacides (3 syl.), and was itself succeeded by the Samanides (3 syl.). So named from Sassan, father of Ardeshir [Babegan], called by the Greeks Artaxerxes, the first of the line. It lasted 426 years, and terminated with Yezdijird or Yezdedjerd III. (226–653). Title : Shah-an-Shah (king of kings). Capital : Madan.

This was the most glorious of the Persian dynasties. Artaxerxes or Ardeshir the founder, Shapûr I. and II., Baharam I. and V., Khosroo (Chosroes), Noorshirwan, were kings equal to any that history records.

Satire (*Father of*). Archilŏchos of Paros (B.C. 7th cent.).

Satire (*Father of French*). Mathurin Regnier (1573–1613).

Satire (*Father of Roman*). Lucilius (B.C. 148–103).

Satisfaction. In the Scotch Church is about equal to penance in the Roman Catholic Church, any disgrace suffered, or bodily distress inflicted, or sum of money paid, to obtain absolution of sin. Thus in Scotland the ' Stool of Repentance ' was called a satisfaction; sackcloth and ashes, money paid *ad pios usus*, and so on, were satisfactions or atonements for misdeeds.

Saturday Review (*The*). A London weekly journal, commenced 3 Nov., 1855.

Savage (*Richard*) claimed to be the son of the wife of Lord Brandon [afterwards Earl of Macclesfield] and Richard Savage earl of Rivers. His mother disowned him, had him baptized ' Richard Smith,' and then committed to the charge of a Mrs. Portlock, a baker's wife (1698–1743).

Savil'ian Professorship of Geometry in Oxford University. Open to all nations. Stipend 675*l.* a year. Founded by Sir Henry Savile (Warden of Merton) in 1619. Remodelled in 1857.

Saviour of the Nation (*The*). So Cromwell was called after the second battle of Newbury, 27 Oct., 1644, where his valour and military genius were most distinguished.

Saviour of the People (*The*), or ' King of the Poor.' William Fitz-

Osbert, surnamed Longbeard, executed with great barbarity in 1199.

Savoy Conference (*The*), 1661, between the Episcopalian and Presbyterian divines of England respecting the Liturgy. There were twelve bishops and twelve Presbyterian ministers, with nine assistants on each side. It was held in the Savoy, London, the residence of the Bishop of London. Richard Baxter was chief of the Nonconformists and Dr. Gunning his chief opponent. The Presbyterians objected to (1) the use of the surplice; (2) the cross in baptism; (3) to calling the baptized *regenerate*; (4) to the posture of kneeling at the Lord's Supper; (5) to the administration of the eucharist to the sick; (6) to the absolution; (7) to the words *sure and certain hope* in the burial service; and (8) to subscription to the 'Book of Common Prayer' and the 'Thirty-nine Articles.' The conference ended in nothing.

Saxo Grammaticus, died 1204. He was a Danish chronicler, and wrote in Latin a 'history of the Danish kings and heroes,' beginning from the foundation of the Danish monarchy, B.C. 1038. It is based on the Scaldic lays, Icelandic sagas, and local traditions. Much of it, historically, is about equal in value to Geoffrey of Monmouth's 'British History.'

Saxon Line of Kings. The first dynasty of Germany, 919–1024. It gave five kings—Heinrich I. (Henry the Fowler); Otto I., the Great; Otto II., the Red King; Otto III., the Wisdom of the World; and St. Heinrich II., the Lame. The Saxon dynasty was succeeded by the House of Franconia. In 1133–1137 reigned Lothair II., also of the House of Saxony.

Saxon Mirror (*The*), or 'Sachsen Spiegel,' between 1215 and 1218. The local laws of Saxony compiled into a digest. In the 15th cent. it had the same authority in Germany as the common law has in our own country. *See* 'Suabian Mirror.'

Saxony, in Scotch history, means the Lowlands, between the Forth and the Tweed. Hence we read of 'the Picts making raids upon Saxony,' the Picts being the Highlanders south of the Forth.

Saxony (*House of*). *See* 'Saxon Line,' &c.

Scalds. Scandinavian poets who wrote about gods, kings, and heroes. Each prince had his scald, who followed him to war to celebrate his deeds of fight. These chants were collected into the *Edda* and the *Sagas*.

Scan'dina'via. A name given by the ancients to Norway, Sweden, Denmark, Lapland, Finland, &c., supposed to constitute an island (Plin. iv. 13).

So called from the ancient province of Scandia in the south of Sweden.

Scandinavian Alps (*The*). The Dofrine mountains, a chain running between Norway and Sweden. The Sneehættan (*Snow-cap*) is the highest.

Scan'dina'vian   Semir'amis (*The*). Margaret, daughter of Valdemar III., king of Denmark (1353, 1388–1412).

Scarlet and Blue. The colours of the Scotch covenant.

Scarlet Days. Christmas Day, Easter Day, Ascension Day, Whit Sunday, Trinity Sunday, All Saints' Day, the first Sunday in November (the day for the commemoration of benefactors), Commencement Tuesday (the Tuesday next preceding 24 June), and any other days for which the Vice-Chancellor gives notice, are so called in the University of Cambridge, because on those days all doctors wear their scarlet robes.

On all Litany days the doctors and noblemen wear their robes, and the proctors their congregation ruffs.

Scarpine (*A*). An iron shoe, an instrument of torture, heated red-hot. Also a boot made of wood, torture being inflicted by driving wedges between the leg of the victim and the walls of the boot.

French *escarpin*, Ital. *scarpa*.

I was put to the scarpines.
            KINGSLEY, *Westward Ho!* chap. vii.

Sceptics, *i.e.* men of thought, searchers or examiners into the truth or falsehood of a statement. The Bereans, who searched the Scriptures to see if what was said by Christians was genuine and worthy of credit, were true 'sceptics.' The disciples of Pyrrho are called *Pyrrhonists* or *Sceptics.* The most famous sceptics of antiquity were Protagoras, Gorgias, Pyrrho, Timon, Enesidēmos, Sextus Empiricus, and, of the New Academy, Arcesilas and Carneâdês. The most famous sceptics of modern times are Montaigne, Lamothe-Levayer, Bayle, Sanchez, Huet, Berkeley, Hume, Kant, Schulze, &c.

Sceptre depart from Judah

(*The*). 'The sceptre shall not depart from Judah, nor a lawgiver from between her feet, until Shiloh [the Messiah] come.'

The Asmonæan dynasty terminated with Aristobūlus II., whose daughter Mariam'nê was married to Herod the Great, an Idumæan; and in this reign Jesus was born.

Every Jewish ruler up to this time had been of the race of Isaac. And Judah in the prophecy means a Jew, not a particular tribe. Herod was the first Jewish ruler not a Jew.

Herod was an Edomite, and therefore of the race of Esau.

Schamir.

A magic stone used by Satan, when compelled to assist in building the Temple. It cut the stones employed in the edifice as a diamond cuts glass; and in consequence 'no hammer, axe, or other instrument of iron' was required.

Schiltrons,

hollow squares. The Scotch infantry was disposed in *schiltrons* at Falkirk, their spears pointed obliquely outwards against the charging cavalry.

Schism Bill

(*The*), 10 June, 1714 (13 Anne, c. 7). Repealed 1718 (5 Geo. I. c. 4). Forbidding dissenters to educate their children. No person, unless he subscribed a declaration that he conformed to the Church of England, and obtained a licence from the archbishop or bishop of the diocese, was allowed to keep a school or become a private tutor. The penalty was three years' imprisonment; and even if licensed, if a teacher of youth neglected to teach the Church Catechism he forfeited his licence, and made himself subject to three years' imprisonment.

Schism of the East, A.D. 862.

The separation of the Western Church from communion with the Greek Church. It was provoked by Photius, and consummated in 1053 by the patriarch Cerularius.

Photius patriarch of Constantinople anathematised Nicholas I. ' pope ' of Rome, and Nicholas anathematised the patriarch, who advised his clergy to separate from communion with Rome.

Photius was a man of extraordinary erudition. Cerularius positively refused all intercourse with the Western Church.

Schism of the Mohammedans

(*The*), A.D. 632, after the death of Mahomet. The question was whether Ali, the son-in-law, or Abou-bekr, the father-in-law, ought to succeed the prophet. Those who thought Ali the proper successor were called Shiites (factious); those who thought Abou-bekr the true Imaum were called Sunnites (traditionists). The Turks, Arabs and Egyptians are Sunnites; the Persians are Shiites. The califs are Abou-bekr, 632-634; Omar, 634-644; Othman, 644-656; Ali, 656-661, &c. The Shiites reject the first three, and begin with Ali.

In India the Moslems are partly Sunnite and partly Shiah.

Schism of the Twelve Tribes

(*The*), B.C. 962, when ten of the tribes revolted from Rehoboam, son of Solomon, and formed the new kingdom of Israel. The tribes of Judah and Benjamin, which remained under Rehoboam, then formed the kingdom of Judah. Each kingdom had its own kings.

Schism of the West (*The Great*),

1378-1449. A period of seventy-one years, during which time two popes, and sometimes more than two, were elected—one at Rome, a**d** one at Avignon in France, or somewhere else. It began by the Italian cardinals electing Urban VI. in opposition to the French cardinals, who had elected Clement VII. The Roman clergy called the popes who were not of their own election 'anti-popes.'

This ' schism ' is not the same as the ' captivity' of the popes, meaning the residence of the popes at Avignon instead of Rome. The ' captivity ' began with Clement V., who in 1309 removed his court to Avignon, and ended in 1376 by Gregory XI. removing his court back to Rome. At the death of Gregory XI. the Italian cardinals chose Urban VI. and the French chose Clement VII., and for many years there were two simultaneous popes. *See* p. 31, ' Anti-Popes.'

Schism of the Western Church

(*The*), 324-334, in the reign of Constantine. The rivalry showed itself in 341.

I. The two churches differed in respect to the doctrine of the Holy Ghost about 400, and in 589 the Latin Church introduced into the creed the phrase ' filioque ' (*q.v.*).

II. In 484, Felix II. bishop of Rome and Acacius bishop of Constantinople excommunicated each other. In 648 Pope Theodore pronounced the patriarch

Paul II. to be deposed. In 867 Photius and Pope Nicholas I. excommunicated each other. In 1054 the legates of Leo IX. went to Constantinople to excommunicate Michael Cerularius, and then Cerularius excommunicated Leo IX.

III. In 588 the Patriarch of Constantinople assumed the title of 'Ecumenical (or universal) Patriarch'; and in 835 the Pope of Rome, by the False Decretals, claimed the right of universal jurisdiction.

Schleswig-Holstein Question

(*The*), 1848. That is, did the two duchies belong to Denmark or Germany? They were at the time parts of the kingdom of Denmark. Holstein belonged to Denmark only as a fief, and, though the duke owed homage to Denmark, he was an independent ruler. In 1846 the King of Denmark, who was then Duke of Holstein, declared the two duchies to be united to the crown of Denmark; but Holstein objected, and appealed to the German Confederation, of which it was a member. In 1848 the king sent troops to put down a revolt in Holstein, and the German diet sent troops to defend the duchy. In 1852 the great powers of Europe signed in London a protocol guaranteeing to Denmark the possession of the duchies, but neither Holstein nor the German diet would consent to the protocol. The quarrel smouldered on till 1863, when Austria and Prussia sent troops into the duchies, and Denmark armed for war; Denmark, of course, was powerless against these two great powers, was forced to crave peace and to give up the duchies. Prussia now quarrelled with Austria, conquered her in war, and the duchies fell to Prussia.

Schleswig-Holstein War (*The*).

I. 1848–52. On the accession of Frederick VII. to the throne of Denmark, the duchies of Schleswig and Holstein revolted, and declared their independence. Prussia entered Holstein, and Denmark defeated the Prussians and Holsteiners near Flensborg, 7 April, 1848. The war continued till the Treaty of London, 8 May, 1852, when Holstein was transferred to the Danes, and Schleswig was declared independent.

II. 1864–1866, Prussia and Austria demanded that Denmark should evacuate Schleswig and abolish the constitution; and Prince Frederick of Augustenburg

was proclaimed Duke of Kiel, 30 Dec., 1863. Austria and Prussia both interfered, and hostilities continued till 1864, when, by the Treaty of Vienna, Lunenberg, Schleswig, and Holstein were ceded by Denmark to the two powers. Austria evacuated Holstein 12 July, 1866. After the Seven Weeks' War, 23 Aug., 1866, Schleswig-Holstein was added to the kingdom of Prussia.

No war was ever more fruitful of consequences than this petty Schleswig-Holstein war. Out of it arose the war between Austria and Prussia called the 'Seven Weeks' War,' and the Franco-Prussian war or 'Seven Months' War,' by which Austria was severed from Germany, and Prussia was made the head of the German states. In 1870 the King of Prussia was declared to be the 'German Emperor' also.

Schola Palati'na.

The school established by Charlemagne in his own household. It accompanied the court wherever it went, and was attended by the king himself, his sons and daughters, and the high officers of the realm.

Transcribing MSS. was a fashionable occupation of the day, both in the schola palatina and in private families.

Scholars,

in the universities of Cambridge and Oxford. Students elected for the most part by competitive examinations in their respective colleges. They enjoy certain emoluments from their college from the time of their election.

At Merton College, Oxford, the 'scholars' are called *Postmasters*.

At Magdalen College, Oxford, the 'scholars' are called *Demies* [de-mize].

Scholastic Theology,

'Scholastic Divinity,' or 'Scholastic Philosophy,' may be divided into four periods.

I. The Preparatory period, from the 9th to the 11th cent. This period included Gerbert of Aurillac (afterwards Pope Sylvester II.), Berengarius of Tours, and Lanfranc archbishop of Canterbury.

II. The *First* period of Scholasticism proper, 12th cent., opened by Roscelinus, who broached the dispute concerning Nominalism and Realism. This period included Peter Lombard (*   –1164) and Alexander Hales (*   –1245). In this period it was pithy and logical.

III. The *Second* and Golden Age of Scholasticism, in which Aristotelian metaphysics were applied to the elucidation of Christian doctrines. This period began with Albertus Magnus (1193–1280), who was contemporary with one of the greatest of the Schoolmen, Thomas

Aquīnas (1224–1274). John Bonaventura died the same year as Aquīnas.

The great opponent of Thomas Aquīnas was Duns Scotus, a realist (1265–1308); the followers of Thomas Aquinas were called Thomists, and those of Duns Scotus were called Scotists. In this period the school was subtle and sophistical.

IV. The *Third* period dates from Durandus bishop of Meaux [*Mo*].

Called 'scholastic' because it was taught in the schools established by Charlemagne.

Scholefield Prize for knowledge of the Greek Testament and the Septuagint. Value about 15*l.* Founded in the University of Cambridge by the friends of the Rev. James Scholefield [*Skole-field*] regius professor of Greek, 1856. *See* 'Regius Professor of Greek.'

School Boards. The boards are due to the Elementary Education Act of 1870; the object of which act is to bestow elementary education upon every child in England and Wales. Where there does not exist a sufficient supply for the purpose, 'a school board shall be formed to supply the deficiency.' The boards are elected every three years, and the expenses of the education provided by these boards are defrayed partly by rates and partly by government grants.

The ratepayers appoint the board, but the directors are not paid.

Schoolmen. Those who taught in the schools established by Charlemagne. *See* 'Scholastic Divinity.'

Schwarz-gelber (*Ein*). In 1848 the Austrian Imperialists were called 'Black-yellows,' because the imperial cockades, sentry-boxes, and boundary posts were all black and yellow.

Sciences. The six sciences, according to Comte (1797–1857), are mathematics, astronomy, physics, chemistry, biology, and sociology; of these six, according to Comte, the last is the chief.

Sclavonic Version (*The*) of the Scriptures, by Cyril of Thessalonīca and his brother Methodius, in the 9th cent. Translated for the Sclavonians of Moravia. It embraced the whole Bible. *See* 'Scriptures.'

Scorpion Stanley. So Daniel O'Connell designated Edward Geoffrey Smith Stanley, chief secretary for Ireland in 1830–1832, afterwards fourteenth earl of Derby. Very obnoxious to the Irish agitation from his great firmness in administering the law (1799–1864).

No matter who the chief secretary may be, if he resists lawlessness, rebellion, and crime, he is bespattered as a 'scorpion Stanley,' a 'malignant Forster,' or a 'bloody Balfour.' Such dishonour is the proof and the reward of even-handed justice.

Scot and Lot include at the present day all parochial assessments for the poor, the church, lighting, cleansing, washing, roads, &c. Scot and lot are Swedish terms, both signifying *tax*, and originally were applied to assessments made for liquidating necessary debts of the crown, levied, not by an equal rate, but according to the capacity of the contributor.

Scota. When the Scotch barons in 1320 answered the bull of Pope John XXII., they began by stating that the Scots were lineal descendants of Scota, daughter of Pharaoh king of Egypt, and were converted to Christianity by St. Andrew the apostle.

Scotch Guard. *See* p. 357, 'Gardes du corps.'

Scotch Marriage (*A*). A consent to live together, without any legal or church ceremony.

Consent makes marriage [in Scotland]. No form or ceremony, civil or religious, no notice before or publication after, no cohabitation, no writing, no witnesses even are essential to . . . this contract.—Lord DEAS.

Scoti (*The*). Prehistoric invaders of Ireland, from whom the island was called Scotia. They conquered the five provincial kings and became their overlords. O'Connor ('History of the Irish People,' p. 30) says they were Scythi of the Scandinavian race. *See* 'Scots.'

Scotia. Applied exclusively to Ireland from the 4th to the 11th cent. The Scoti were a branch of the Teutons. North Britain was called Albany or Albania. It was not till the English, in the reign of Henry II., invaded Ireland that the island forces were called 'Irish.' *See* 'Scotland.'

Finibus occiduis describitur optima tellus,
  Nomine et antiquis Scotia dicta libris.
                                    DONATUS.

Far westward lies an isle of ancient fame
By nature blest, and Scotia is her name.

Scotists. A theological school so called from [John] Duns Scotus ('doctor *subtilissimus*'—'most subtle doctor'). This school was opposed to the Thomists or disciples of Thomas Aquinas. The Scotists were Realists, the Thomists were Nominalists (*q.v.*). Duns was a Franciscan, and therefore the natural opponent of Aquinas, who was a Dominican.

Scotland (*Kings of*). See p. 135, 'Caledonia.'

In the 9th cent. Kenneth II. (MacAlpin) united in his own person the two crowns of the Picts and Scots, and was, therefore, in reality the first king of Scotland; but the Scotch annalists count sixty-six kings before Kenneth MacAlpin, and head the list with Fergus, B.C. 330. Omitting all the names up to Fergus II., the list runs thus :—

FERGUS II.	410-427	CONSTANTINE IV.	994-995
EUGENE I.	427-449	GRIM	995-997
DONGARD	449-453	MALCOLM II.	997-1033
CONSTANTINE I.	453-469	DUNCAN	1033-1040
CONGAL I.	469-501	MACBETH	1040-1057
GONRAN	501-535	MALCOLM III.	1057-1093
EUGENE II.	535-568	DONALD VII.	1093-1094
CONGAL II.	568-572	DUNCAN II.	1094-1095
KINATHAL	572-580	(Donald VI. restored,	
AIDAN	580-604	1095 1098).	
(Columba converts the Scots).		EDGAR	1098-1107
		ALEXANDER I.	1107-1114
KENNETH I.	604-606	DAVID I.	1114-1143
EUGENE III.	606-622	MALCOLM IV.	1143-1157
FERCHARD I.	622-632	WILLIAM I.	1157-1214
DONALD II.	632-647	ALEXANDER II.	1214-1219
FERCHARD II.	647-668	ALEXANDER III.	1219-1286
MALDVIN	668-688	*Interregnum.*	
EUGENE IV.	688 692	JOHN BALIOL	1292-1306
EUGENE V.	692 699	EDWARD I.	
AMBERCHELET	699-700	ROBERT I.	
EUGENE VI.	700-702	(Bruce)	1306-1329
(Amberchelet restored, 702 704).		DAVID II.	
		(Bruce)	1329-1332
EUGENE VII.	704 717	EDWARD	
MORDAC	717 730	BALIOL	1332-1333
ERFINIUS	730-761	(David II. restored,	
EUGENE VIII.	761 764	1333-1370).	
FERGUS III.	764-767	ROBERT II.	1370-1390
SOLVATIUS	767-787	ROBERT III.	
ANCHAIUS	787-809	(called JOHN) 1390-1406	
CONGAL III.	809-814	*Robert the Regent,*	
DOUGAL	814-820	*1406-1409.*	
ALPIN	820-823	*Duke Murdoch,*	
KENNETH II.	823-854	*1409-1424.*	
DONALD V.	854-858	JAMES I.	1424-1437
CONSTANTINE II.	858-874	JAMES II.	1437-1460
ETHEUS	874-875	JAMES III.	1460 1488
GREGORY	875-893	JAMES IV.	1488-1513
DONALD VI.	893-904	JAMES V.	1513 1542
CONSTANTINE III.	904-943	MARY	1542 1567
MALCOLM I.	943-958	JAMES VI.	1567 1607
INDULPH	958-968	When he became	
DUFF	968 973	JAMES I. of Great	
CULEN	973 978	Britain (by royal pro-	
KENNETH III.	978-994	clamation).	

Scotland.

Till the 11th cent. North Britain was called Albany. The name Scotia from the 4th to the 11th cent. belonged exclusively to Ireland. A.D. 258 a colony of Irish-Scots settled in Argyllshire, and gave a line of Dalriadic kings. From the 11th cent. we read of Irish-Scots and Albanian-Scots. The Romans called the southern part of Scotland Caledonia, a name which disappears in the 4th cent.

Quod ut ante undecimum post Christi nativitatem sæculum haudquaquam factum, in fine præcedentis capitis declaravimus : ita neminem, qui toto antecedentium annorum spatio scripserit produci posse arbitramur qui *Scotiæ* appellatione Albaniam unquam designaverit.—USHER, *Eccles. Primord.* cap. xvi.

Scotland a Fief of England.

During the reign of Malcolm I. (successor of Constantine III.), Edmund king of England bestowed on him part of the Cumbrian kingdom [Cumberland and part of Westmoreland]. It was this grant which was the foundation of the claim of homage made by the English kings on the Scottish sovereigns.

Scots, *i.e.* Irish.

A prehistoric colony of Scythians which settled in Ireland about B.C. 400. Subsequently a colony from Ireland went to Argyllshire and reigned there as a race of Scottish kings. The famous Milesians were Scots, and as the Scoti conquered the five provincial kings, and became overlords, Ireland was called Scotia. The Scoti of Caledonia (Scotland) spoke Earish (Ersh), *i.e.* Irish or Western.

Totam cum Scotus Iernen
Movit et infesto spumavit remige Tethys.
    CLAUDIAN, *Iu I. Cons. Stilich.* Book I.

When Scots came thundering from the Irish shores,
The Atlantic trembled, struck with hostile oars.

Scottish Crown (*The*).

'It cam' wi' a lass, and will gang wi' a lass.' So said James V. a few days before his death when informed of the birth of a daughter, afterwards Mary queen of Scots. The Stuarts descended from Margery (daughter of Robert Bruce), who married Walter [the 6th] Steward or Seneschal of Scotland.

MALCOLM IV. was the father of WILLIAM the Lion (who succeeded him), and of David earl of Huntingdon. William the Lion had no issue.

David earl of Huntingdon was the father of Margaret, Isabella (who married Robert Bruce), and Ada.

First take Margaret; she was the mother of Devoirgoil, and JOHN BALIOL was the son of Devoirgoil (great-great-grandson of Malcolm IV.).

Now take Isabella (wife of Robert Bruce); their son was THE BRUCE (Robert I.).

The Bruce (ROBERT) was the father of Margery Bruce (who married Walter the Steward or Seneschal), and their son was DAVID II. (Steward or Stuart in French spelling).

Scottish Petitioners (*The*),

Aug. 1775, who prayed the Virginia convention that they might be allowed to stand neutral in the war between America and Great Britain. The licence was first granted and then revoked, the Scots being largely enrolled in the royal militia.

Scottish Plato (*The*).

Dugald Stewart (1753-1828).

Scottish Security Bill (*The*), 1704, for the separation of Scotland and England. Authorising the Scotch on the death of Anne to set up a monarch of their own choice, independent of the English choice of a sovereign. The Bill was brought in by Godolphin.

The English tories printed and circulated the Scottish Security Bill to show that the two countries were really separated in the most absolute manner.—HOWITT, *History of England* (Anne, 194).

Scotus (*John*), entitled Erigĕna [Erin-gena], an Irishman by birth. Died 875. North Britain was not called Scotland (*q.v.*) till the 11th cent.

Scourers. A set of dissolute young rips in London in the 18th cent., especially in the reign of Queen Anne, opposed to the Mohocks, but quite as infamous and lawless. They were organised to ' scour the streets of Mohocks,' but like other street bullies they considered it capital fun to break windows, upset sedan chairs, beat quiet citizens, rudely caress young women, and make other ones scream with terror. *See* ' Street Bullies.'

Who has not heard the Scourers' midnight fame?
Who has not trembled at the Mohocks' name?
Was there a watchman took his hourly rounds,
Safe from their blows and new-invented wounds?
GAY, *Trivia*, III.

*** The nephew of Prince Eugene, who accompanied his uncle on an embassage to Queen Anne, was so savagely assaulted by these street bullies in 1712 that he died from the treatment he received.

Denham bottled up his wrath till he was out of Newgate; but then, finding it no longer controllable, he joined a band of Scourers, and spent the evening in wrenching off knockers, assaulting defenceless shop signs, frightening the chapmen into fits, and hustling everything that was capable of being hustled (1684).—EDNA LYALL, *In the Golden Days*, xxxiv.

Scourge (*The*) used at the Crucifixion, we are told by Alexis Comnēnus, was preserved at Constantinople. *See* ' Crucifixion, *Relics of the*.'

Scourge of Christians (*The*). Noureddin-Mahmûd of Damascus (1116–1174).

Scourge of Europe (*The*). Napoleon Bonaparte (born 1768, foreign wars 1796–1815, died 1821).

Scourge of Germany (*The*). So the Swedes were called (1630–1635) for their extraordinary success in the Thirty Years' War.

Scourge of God (*The*). ' Flagellum Dei.' So a Gaulish hermit called

Attila, and the king delighted in the appellation (died 453).

Gensĕric king of the Vandals was called ' Virga Dei ' (reigned 429–477).

Scourge of Princes (*The*). Pietro Aretīno of Arezzo, a merciless satirist of kings and princes (1492–1557).

Thus Aretin of late got reputation
By scourging kings, as Lucian did of old
By scourging gods.
Lord BROOKE, *Inquisition upon Fame.*

Scourge of Scotland (*The*). ' Scotorum Malleus.' Edward I. (1239, 1272–1307).

Also called the ' Scourge of Wales.'

Scourge of the Propagators of the Faith (*The*). The pastor, Charles Drelincourt, who, in his ' Abrégé des Controverses,' refuted the arguments brought forward by the Converters (*q.v.*) to turn Huguenots to the Catholic Communion (1595–1669).

Scriptores Decem. A collection of ten ancient chronicles of English history in one folio vol. 1652, edited by Roger Twysden and John Selden.

1. Simeon Dunelmensis (of Durham). ' Historia.'

2. Johannes Hagustaldensis (John of Hexham). ' Historia Continuata.'

3. Richardus Hagustaldensis. ' De Gestis Regis Stephani.'

4. Ailredus Rievallensis (Ailred of Rieval or Rievaulx). ' Historia,' being a genealogy of the kings.

5. Radulphus de Dicĕto. ' Abbreviationes Chronicorum ' and ' Ymagines Historiarum.'

6. Johannes Brompton. ' Chronicon.'

7. Gervasius Dorobornensis (Gervais of Dover). ' Chronica,' &c. : the burning and repairs of Dover Church ; lives of the Archbishops of Canterbury ; and contentions between the monks of Canterbury and Archbishop Baldwin.

8. Thomas Stubbs, a Dominican. ' Chronica Pontificum Ecc. Eboraci ' (York).

9. Guilielmus Thorn Cantuariensis (of Canterbury). ' Chronica.'

10. Henricus Knighton Leicestrensis (of Leicester). ' Chronica.'

8, 9, 10 are chronicles of pontiffs or archbishops.

Scriptores Quinque, or ' Scriptores post Bedam,' 1 fol. vol., containing :—

1. Willielmus Malmesburiensis, ' De Gestis Regum Anglorum,' ' Historiæ

Novellæ,' and 'De Gestis Pontificum Anglorum.'

2. Henricus Huntindoniensis. 'Historia.'

3. Roger Hovedeni (Hoveden). 'Annales.'

4. Ethelwerd. 'Chronica.'

5. Ingulphus Croylandensis. 'Historia.'

Scriptores Tres, or in full thus: 'Britannicarum Gentium Historiæ Antiquæ Scriptores tres.' Then follow the names :—

1. Richardus Coriensis (of Cirencester). 'De Situ Britanniæ.'

2. Gildas Badonicus (of Bath).

3. Nennius Banchoriensis (of Bangor).

Dr. Bertram professed to have discovered these MSS. between the years 1747 and 1757; but J. E. Mayor, in his preface to 'Richardi de Cirencestria Speculum Historiale,' has laid bare this literary forgery. *See* 'Literary Forgeries.'

Scriptu'ra. A tax on cattle. So called because the collectors ' set down in writing ' a description of the number and kind of cattle on which the tax was levied.

Scriptu'ra Thesau'ri Regis. The 'Record of the King's Treasury.' So Doomsday Book was anciently called, because it was kept, together with the king's seal, under three locks and keys in the royal treasury.

Scripture Interpolations. Critics say a ' reading is to be rejected as genuine when there is plain evidence that it has undergone a *designed* alteration,' such as the following :—

1. From *doctrinal* reasons: Matt. i. 18; Mark viii. 31, xiii. 32, xvi. 14 to the end; and 1 John v. 7, 8.

2. From moral and practical reasons: as Matt. v. 22.

3. From historical and geographical doubts : Matt. viii. 28; compare Mark v. 1.

4. From a desire of reconciling texts inconsistent with each other: as Mark viii. 31.

5. From a desire to make a discourse more intensive.

6. From the manifest amalgamation of different MSS. or parallel passages.

See Ernesti, ' Principles of Interpreta-

tion,' vol. ii. p. 114 ; Horne's ' Introduction ' ; Davidson, Michaelis, &c.

Scriptures. To the article ' Bible,' p. 90, add the following :—

    The Discharge Bible.
    „ Ears to ear Bible.
    „ Rebekah's Camels Bible.
    „ Rosin * Bible.
    „ Standing fishes Bible.
    „ To-remain Bible.
    „ Unrighteous Bible.

⁎ These are typographical errors which have occurred in different Bibles, all but one (marked*) printed in the 19th cent. *See also* 'Peschito Version ' (the Syriac Bible).

Scriptures (*Spurious*).

Part I. The Old Testament.

1. *Apocryphal Books* received by some Christians and rejected by others :—

1 and 2 Esdras . . in 9+16 chapters.
Tobit . . . . „   14   „
Judith . . . . „   16   „
The rest of Esther . „   6   „
Wisdom . . . „   19   „
Ecclesiasticus . . „   51   „
Baruch and   }   „   6   „
Epistle of Jeremiah }
Song of the Three Children.
Story of Susanna.
Bel and the Dragon.
Prayer of Manasseh.
1 Maccabees, in 16 chapters.
2   „   „ 15   „

⁎ These and several others are canonical in the Abyssinian Church. Book of Enoch translated by Dr. Kenealy, *see* p. 296.

2. The following are not even accepted in the Apocrypha. They are called Pseudepigraphœ :—

The 3 and 4 of Maccabees (in the Septuagint Bible).
The Genealogy of Job and his Wife's speech (at the end of the Greek text of the Book of Job).
CLI. Psalm (at the end of the Greek psalms).
A discourse of King Solomon (at the end of the ' Book of Wisdom ').
The preface to the Book of Lamentations (in the Vulgate).

3. The following, referred to in the Old Testament, form no part of our Canon :—

The Book of the Acts of Solomon (1 Kings xi. 41).
   „   of the Acts of Uriah (2 Chron. xxvi. 22).
   „   of the Chronicles of David (1 Chron. xxvii. 24).
   „   of the Chronicles of the Kings of Israel (often).
   „   of the Chronicles of the Kings of Judah (often).
   „   of the Covenant (Jos. x. 13 ; 2 Sam. i. 18).
   „   of the Kings of Judah and Israel (often).
   „   of Gad the Seer (1 Chron. xxix. 20).
   „   of Iddo the Seer (2 Chron. xii. 15).
   „   of Jasher (Joshua x. 13; 2 Sam. i. 18).
   „   of Jehu (2 Chron. xx. 34).
   „   of Nathan the Prophet (1 Chron. xxix. 29).
   „   of Samuel the Seer (1 Chron. xxix. 29 2 Chron. ix. 29).
   „   of Shemaiah (2 Chron. xii. 15).
The Books of Jason (2 Maccabees ii.).
   „   of the Wars (Numbers xxi. 14).
The Memoirs of Hircānus (2 Macc. ii.).
   „   of Jeremiah (1 Macc. ii.).

3 F

The Prophecy about Babylon (Jer. ii.).
,,   of Ahijah (2 Chron. ix. 29).
,,   of Jeremiah (Jer. li.).
,,   of Jonah (Jonah).
Story of the Prophet Iddo (2 Chron. xiii. 22).
The Thousand and Five Songs of Solomon (1 Kings iv. 32).
Three Thousand Proverbs of Solomon (1 Kings iv. 32).
Visions of Iddo the Seer (2 Chron. ix. 29).

3. The following are sometimes referred to, but are no longer extant:—

The Assumption of Abraham.
,,   ,,   of Moses.
,,   ,,   of the Twelve Patriarchs.
,,   Book of King Og.
,,   Creation of Adam.
,,   Discourses of Jacob and Joseph.
,,   Generation of the Sons, &c., of Adam.
,,   Gospel of Eve.
,,   Ham's (or Cham's) Book of Magic.
,,   Jacob's Ladder.
,,   Jetsira.
,,   Prophecy of Eldad and Medad.
,,   Revelation of Adam.
,,   Secrets of Elias.
,,   Secrets of Jeremiah.
Seth.
,,   Treatise of Jannes and Jambres.

Part II. The New Testament.

The Book of Acts (ascribed to Peter).
The Gospel of Andrew, Apelles, Barnabas, Cerinthus, James the Elder, Judas Iscariot, Lucianus, Lucius, Matthew (the false gospel of), Matthias, Marcion, Nicodemus, Peter (Eusebius vi. 12). Philip, Tatian (The Diatessaron), Thaddeus, Thomas, Valentinus, &c.
The Gospel of Perfection.
,,   ,,   of the Ebionites (4 syl.).
,,   ,,   of the Infancy of Christ.
,,   ,,   of the Nativity of Mary.
,,   ,,   of the Twelve Apostles.
,,   ,,   according to the Egyptians.
,,   ,,   ,,   to the Hebrews.
,,   ,,   ,,   to the Syrians.
The Everlasting Gospel (13th cent.).
The Four Gospels of the Manichæans.
The Hebrew Gospel or Logia of Matthew, referred to by Papias.
The History of Joseph the Carpenter.
The Preaching and Revelation of Peter.
The Protevangelium of James.
Paul and Thekla.

, Irenæus (i. 17) speaks of the multitude of spurious books in the 2nd cent. In the 4th cent. there were at least eighty spurious gospels.
Mahomet apparently derived his knowledge of Jesus from 'the Gospel of the Infancy,' 'the Book of the Nativity of Mary,' and the 'Protevangelium of St. James.'

Part III. Books accepted by the Gnostics, which form no part of our canon.

Book of Adam, Enoch, Moseh, Elijah, Isajah.
Book of Armagil, Barbelon, Balsamum, Lensiboras, Matthias, and Glaucias.
Hymns of Marcos.
Prophecies of Barcobas, Barcoph, Cain, Ham, Parchor, &c.
Psalms of Valentinus, Bardesanés.

, Basilides chiefly relied on some prophecies which bore the names of Ham, Parchor, Barcobas, and Barcoph, with an esoteric tradition which he professed to derive from St. Matthias and from Glaucias.—ROBERTSON, History of the Church, vol. i. p. 72.

Part IV. The following, though admitted into our canon, are (on the authority of Eusebius, iii. 2) disputable.

Second and Third Epistles of John.
Second Epistle of Peter.
The Epistle of James.
The Epistle to the Hebrews.

, The Book of the Revelation was long disputed. Jerome, Amphilochius and Sulpitius Severus tell us that in their time many churches did not accept it; and certainly it is not in the catalogue of the Council of Laodicea or in that of Cyril of Jerusalem; nor in the Codex Vaticanus (q.v.). In more modern times Luther and Lücke deny its authenticity. (This is not the place to enter on the pros and cons of the subject, but simply to state a fact.)

Part V. Parts of our Canonical Scriptures are not to be found in some of the best MSS. It would take up too much space to jot down omitted words and short clauses, and the entire New Testament would be too wide a field. Confining ourselves to the four gospels (except in two cases), it may be remarked:—

I. The Apocalypse is omitted in the Codex Vaticānus, &c.
II. 1 John v. 51, 52 ('the three witnesses') are admitted by all scholars to be interpolated.
III. The Ascension, as described by Mark xii., the last twelve verses, is admitted in the Revised Version to be at least doubtful; and, what is more remarkable still, vv. 51, 52 of the last chapter of Luke are also omitted in many of the best MSS.
IV. In John ix. 35 our version makes Jesus say to the man cured of his blindness, 'Dost thou believe on the Son of God?' but many MSS. read, 'Dost thou believe on the Son of Man?'

The following are omitted in many MSS.:—

Matthew: vi. 15, the last clause of the 'Lord's Prayer'; xvi. 2, 3; xvii. 21; xviii. 11; xix. 9, the latter half.
Mark: x. 44, 46; xi. 26; xv. 28.
Luke: xvii. 36; xxii. 19, 'This is my body,' &c.; xxii. 43, 44; xxiii. 34, 'Father forgive them, for they know not what they do'; xxiv. 6, 12, 51, 52.
John: iii. 13, last clause; iv. 9, last clause; vii. 53; viii. 2-11 (inserted in brackets in the Revised Edition); ix. 36, for 'God' many read man.

Every iota of information on the subject is valuable and important, and the utmost candour should be encouraged. The Bereans were highly commended for searching to see how far the teaching of the Apostles accorded with the written word. Truth fears neither microscope, telescope, probe, nor scalpel.

Scriptures (Versions of the).
Oriental versions.

Arabic.	Memphitic (q.v.).
Armenian.	Persic (q.v.).
Basmuric.	Peschito.
Coptic. See Memphitic,	Sahidic (q.v.).
Thebaidic, Basmuric,	Samaritan Pentateuch
and Sahidic.	(q.v.).
Egyptian (q.v.).	Thebaidic (q.v.).
Ethiopic (q.v.).	

ARABIC (The) includes the Pentateuch and Isaiah. Translated by Rabbi Saadias in the 10th cent.
ARMENIAN (The) made by Miesrob in the 5th cent. Somewhat interpolated from the Vulgate.
BASMURIC (The), a version in the dialect of Bashmur, &c., east of the Nile.

Western versions. *See* ' Codex,' &c.

I. *Greek* : The Septuagint (*q.v.*).
II. *Latin* : Anglo-Saxon versions.
    Gothic version (*q.v.*).
    Slavonic version (*q.v.*).
    Vulgate (*q.v.*).

ANGLO-SAXON version. It is supposed that the Psalter was rendered into Saxon, in 709, by Aldhelm bishop of Sherborne. The Venerable Bede translated the whole Bible into Anglo-Saxon (died 735), and about 200 years later King Alfred translated the Psalter. In 995 it is supposed that Ealfric archbishop of Canterbury translated the Pentateuch, Joshua, Esther, and a part of Kings.

Scrutin d'Arrondissement.
Voting by districts.

Scrutin de Liste.   Voting in mass.

Scullabogue Barn (*Massacre at*),
1798, in the Great Irish Rebellion. This massacre by the rebels and that at Wexford Bridge were the most infamous of all the outrages in this fearful rebellion.

Scurvy.
At one time very common in England and Holland. It is described by Hippocrătês as a ' tumour of the spleen produced by drinking cold water.' Pliny calls it *stomacace* and prescribes the herb ' cochlearia ' (*herba Britannica*) as a remedy. It broke out in the army of Germanicus encamped on the Rhine, and is mentioned by Tacitus. It was accompanied with the loss of the teeth and paralysis in the knees. In Thorstein's expedition to Greenland, in 1002, it carried off Thorstein himself and his twenty-five companions. It caused great ravages in the army of St. Louis. Its first appearance in Germany was in 1481, when it was called Schorbuck (*i.e.* inflammation or tearing of the bowels). Freind says it was first introduced into Europe in the 15th cent. by the Portuguese, and that it came from the East Indies. In the year 1498 it committed frightful ravages in the crew of Vasco da Gama, when he lost fifty-five of his men ; in 1535 it broke out in the crew of Cartier in his voyage to Canada ; and in Lord Anson's memorable voyage (account published in 1746) whole crews were prostrated by this scourge.

Poupart the surgeon in 1699 says the plague of Athens described by Thucydides was the scurvy : so also was that described by Lucretius, book xvi.

Scutage,
or ' shield money,' a money payment in lieu of knight's service in the field. It consisted of one, two, or three marks (13*s.* 4*d.*) for each knight's fee (*i.e.* land to the value of 20*l.*, or as much more as the king chose to grant). THE GREAT

SCUTAGE, 1159, was a reform passed in the reign of Henry II. soon after the death of Thomas Becket. It greatly diminished the military power of the nobles, and gave the king instead a military force of mercenary soldiers entirely under his control.

As there were 60,000 knights' fees in England, scutage would amount to 180,000*l.*=at least 5½ millions according to the present value of money.

Scythia.
Russia in Asia. Russia in Europe was called by the Romans ' Sarmatia.'

Sea of Darkness (*The*).
The Black Sea.

Silesia and Little Poland, thirty days' journey, according to the Greek computation, from the Sea of Darkness.—GIBBON, lv.

Sea-dogs,
1577. Seamen of the southern coast who accepted letters of marque from the Prince of Condé and the French Protestants. These bold freebooters took no heed of the complaints of the French court, nor of Elizabeth's efforts at repression, for the connivance of every man along the coast, even of the crown port-officers, insured them immunity. Francis Drake was a sea-dog, and thought it a glory to sell negroes to the planters, to kill Spaniards, and to sack their gold-ships. Philip of Spain demanded that the freebooter should be given up, but instead of so doing Elizabeth knighted him.

Seagreen Incorruptible (*The*).
Robespierre is so called by Carlyle in his ' French Revolution.'

Not even the Seagreen Incorruptible but shall have some pity.—Vol. iii. book iii. 1.
There is in the incorruptible Seagreen himself . . . . a heartfelt knowledge of this latter fact.—Vol. iii. book iii. 2.

Seal of Confession (*The*).
' Sigillum Confessiŏnis,' the obligation of a confessor not to divulge to any human being what is told him in the confessional. The custom can be traced to the 5th cent. ; but it was made binding by Innocent III. in the 12th cent.

The confessional is the concealed seat on which the priest sits to hear confession in the Catholic church.

Seal of the Three Lions (*The*).
The Anglo-Norman official seal.

A few years afterwards the archdeacon [Becket] was raised to the office of chancellor of England, or keeper of the seal of the three lions, the symbol of Anglo-Norman power.—*Cassell's Hist. of Eng.*, vol. i. p. 183.

Sealed Prayer Book (*The*). Both the Universities of Oxford and Cambridge and the crown printers are bound by the Act of Uniformity to print the 'Book of Common Prayer' from a sealed prayer-book, a copy of which ought to be kept in each cathedral, and of course where the book is officially printed.

Séance Royale (*Une*). A variety of the 'Lit de Justice' (*q.v.*), in which the king of France took his seat and told the *parlement* what law or laws he requested them to pass. The parlement had no voice in the matter, but simply registered the royal edict.

Seato'nian Prize (*The*), for an English poem on some sacred subject. Value 40*l.*; given annually to an M.A. of the University of Cambridge. The same person is qualified to take the prize any number of times. Founded by the Rev. Thomas Seaton of Clare College in 1741.

Seceders, 1730. Dissenters from the kirk of Scotland led by Ralph and Ebenezer Erskine of Stirling. They are divided into burghers and anti-burghers, that is, those who did not object to take the 'Burgess oath' (*q.v.*), and those who refused to take it.

Secession (*The*), 1733. The body of seceders from the General Assembly of Scotland. *See* 'Seceders.'

Secession of Non-Jurors (*The*), 5 March, 1689. Sancroft archbishop of Canterbury and the seven bishops of Bath and Wells, Chichester, Ely, Gloucester, Norwich, Peterborough, and Worcester refused to take the oaths to William and Mary, and were suspended. On 1 Feb., 1691, they were all deprived of their sees.

Secession Synod of Ireland (*The*), 1780. Formed by seceders from the Presbyterian Assembly of Ireland.

Second Advent Brethren (*The*). A Protestant religious sect which keeps a watchful look-out for the second coming of the Messiah.

Second Book (*The*). King Edward's liturgies reformed under Queen Elizabeth. *See* p. 523, 'Liturgy.'

Second Catechism of Edward VI. (*The*), 1553. Called 'The Larger Catechism'; ascribed to Poynet bishop of Winchester, but recommended to the young king by Cranmer. It was in Latin and English, in question and answer. It was afterwards revised and enlarged by Noel dean of St. Paul's, and published in 1570. This is not the catechism inserted in our Book of Common Prayer. That formulary was drawn up by Dr. Nowell, afterwards bishop of Ely, and was enlarged by Dr. Overall, at the command of James I., and is based on Cranmer's Shorter Catechism.

According to Canon Luckock ('On the Book of Common Prayer') the greater part is by Nowell. Overall wrote the Explanation of the Sacraments.

Second Founder of Rome (*The*). Sixtus V., who greatly embellished Rome with beautiful edifices, brought water to the city by an aqueduct 22 miles long, constructed the cupola of St. Peter's, enlarged the Vatican library, fixed the number of cardinals at 70, and recreated both the city and constitution of the Church (1521, 1585–1590).

Second Grand Alliance (*The*), 7 Sept., 1701, between the kaiser, Great Britain, Holland, Prussia, and Hanover, against Louis XIV. Signed at the Hague. The object was to prevent France succeeding to Spain, and to secure Spain to Germany. If negotiations failed, the allies agreed to make war on France till they recovered Spanish Flanders, the kingdoms of Sicily and Naples, with all other Spanish territories in Italy. No peace was to be made till the absolute severance of Spain and France was effected. *See* p. 381, 'Grand Alliance.'

Second Plebe'ian War (*The*), A.D. 126, in Irish history, is the rising of the Attacots or proletariat of Ireland, aided by the sub-kings, to dethrone Tuathal, son of Feredach the Just. Tuathal took refuge with the king of the Picts, but a famine induced the insurgents to invite him back, and he was called Tuathal the Acceptable.

The first plebeian war was the Massacre at Magh-Cru (*q.v.*).

Second Prayer Book of Edward VI. (*The*), 1552. The second revision of the 'King's Primer' (*q.v.*); the first revision was 1549. King Edward's Prayer Book was augmented and revised in the reigns of Elizabeth and James I. In 1662 it assumed the present form of our 'Book of Common Prayer.'

Second Probation. The *dernier ressort* of the prison governor to an incorrigible offender. It consists of solitary confinement for 9 months, as at the commencement of a sentence, with deduction of one-third of the ordinary prison allowance of food and the loss of all remission marks.

Secret Articles (*The*), 1647. A secret treaty entered into by Charles I. with the Confederates or Catholics of Ireland. Edward lord Herbert persuaded the Confederates to make a double treaty, one public and one private. In the private treaty the Catholics had large concessions made to them, but if they had been generally known the king's cause would have been greatly prejudiced among Protestants. This secret treaty was accidentally discovered amongst the baggage of the Archbishop of Tuam and published. The king denied its authenticity, but no one believed him, and the documents are preserved still in the public libraries of England.

The secret treaty provided that the members of the Catholic Church should pay their fees to the Catholic clergy, and that the churches then in possession of Catholics should remain so.

Secret Association of the Holy Faith (*The*), 1799. Founded by Cardinal Ruffo, as a counterpoise to the Carbonàri. This society was sworn to exterminate all Jansenists, Molinists, Economists, Illuminists, Freemasons, and Carbonari. The members were called 'Santa Fedists.'

Secret Chancery (*The*). A kind of 'Star Chamber' introduced by Alexis Michailowitz czar of Russia. It was a species of state inquisition whereby the czar could get rid of all persons dangerous or obnoxious without any apparent interference on his part.

Karamsin says the Secret Chancery was founded by Peter I., and that the court founded by Alexis was only a private chancery.

Secret Committee (*The*), 1721. *See* 'Committee of Secrecy.'

Secret Device (*The*), 1 July, 1543. A private agreement between Henry VIII. and the Douglas faction to bamboozle the Scotch in regard to the projected alliance between the royal children Edward (son of Henry VIII.) and Mary (daughter of James V.). The promise was that Mary should remain in Scotland till her 11th year, but that an English nobleman and

his wife should form part of her suite. The secret device was that Douglas should throw Scotland virtually into the hands of Henry, to get possession of Mary, and to induce Scotland to repudiate her allegiance to the pope.

Secret Select (*The*), 1837. Persons who hired themselves out to the trades union of Glasgow to assassinate, mutilate, or injure persons obnoxious to the union. They belonged to what was called No. 61, and when the secret committee had resolved upon a deed of darkness the name of one of this No. 61 was written on paper and given to the secretary. The Secret Select being sent for was ushered into a dark room and told what he was appointed to do; then stretching out his hand in the dark, a purse of money was put into it. After the deed of darkness he was smuggled out of the kingdom. *See* 'Nobs.'

Secret Treaty (*The*), Jan. 1672, ratified in June, between Charles II. and Louis XIV.

I. Charles should publicly profess himself a Catholic at such time as might appear most expedient.

II. To enable Charles to quash insurrections, Louis should grant him 2,000,000 livres after the ratification of the treaty.

III. Both agree to observe the treaty of Aix-la-Chapelle.

IV. If any new rights on the Spanish monarchy should accrue to Louis, the King of England agrees to aid him in recovering them.

V. Both agree to make war on the United Provinces, and neither shall make peace without the other's consent.

VI. Louis agrees to take on himself the whole expense of the war, but England shall furnish him with 6,000 men.

VII. Charles shall equip fifty ships, and Louis thirty, and the united fleet shall be under the command of James duke of York.

VIII. Charles to receive Walcheren, Luys (2 syl.), and the island of Cadsand as his quota; Louis all the rest.

IX. A mutual treaty of commerce shall be concluded without delay.

No 'right divine' can palliate such infamy.

Secret Tribunal (*The*). I. A.D. 783, of Westphalia. A kind of inquisition established by Charlemagne to prevent a relapse into paganism.

II. The *Vehm-Gericht* of Westphalia (12th cent.), recognised 1371; general in Germany 1400, suppressed 1438, but did not wholly cease to exist till 1811.

Its judges and officers were all muffled, its summonses were delivered in secret, and everyone connected with the tribunal was sworn to secrecy. It exerted a wholesome restraint on the unruly barons, for anyone of them might at any time be dragged blindfold before the judges, and hung on the first tree. *See* 'Red Land.'

It was no single court, but a society, which could hold a court in any place within the Red Land.

Secular Abbots. Laymen who possessed monasteries; their vicars, who discharged the duties of the abbey, were styled 'Regular Abbots.'

Secular Canons. Canons not conventual. Laymen who out of honour or respect are admitted into some chapter of canons. They mixed more or less with the world, but observed the rules of the order to which they attached themselves.

Secular Clergy (*The*). The clergy generally who live in private houses. Nearly all archbishops, bishops, deans, canons, and parochial clergymen are Seculars, in contradistinction to the Regulars, who, having vowed obedience, chastity, and poverty, live in some religious house, dead to the world and the 'civil law' by their 'entrance into religion.' Called 'Regulars' because they live under the *Regula* or rule of some religious house.

Secularism, 1846. A system of ethics which teaches that conduct should be based on reason and knowledge, wholly ignoring the Christian doctrine of divine guidance and interference. It regards happiness as the proper aim of man, utility his highest duty, and progress as the only gauge of right living. Of course it considers perfect liberty of thought as essential to progress, and therefore objects to creeds, and what is termed 'orthodoxy,' that is, certain set dogmas and doctrines enforced by the authority of a dominant party. It regards this present life as the main concern of man, experience his best guide, the promotion of the well-being of society his highest duty, the Book of Nature his

only Bible, and science its best interpreter. *See* 'Agnosticism.'

Secularists. Freethinkers who believe that the affairs of this world should be the chief concern of man. They are generally Agnostics, but some are Materialists, and some few are Atheists. However, religious views have no part nor lot in Secularism except indirectly.

Sedan-day, 1 Sept. A school holiday in Hamburg in commemoration of the battle of Sedan in 1870, when Napoleon III. delivered up his sword to William king of Prussia.

Sedantaire, or 'Man of Sedan,' a sobriquet of Napoleon III. after he resigned his sword to the King of Prussia at Sedan, in the Franco-Prussian war, 1870. The pun is Sedan-terre.

Sede'runt (*The Acts of*). Acts whereby judges are empowered to make rules for the regulation of legal procedure and the expedition of justice in the Scotch Court of Session. Scotch Act, 1540, c. 93.

Sedgwick Prize (*The*), for geology. Given every third year to any graduate of the University of Cambridge who has resided sixty days during the year of his candidature. Value about 80*l.* Founded in 1865 in honour of the Rev. Adam Sedgwick, Woodwardian Professor (*q.v.*).

Sed'leyan Professor of Natural Philosophy in Oxford University. Stipend 570*l.* a year. Founded by Sir William Sedley, 1621.

Seekers, 1628. A religious sect in New England, which denied the churches and ordinances of Christ.—John Harvard.

II. During the civil wars between Charles I. and his parliament the sect spread into England. They believed that no true church was in existence; that a true church could be founded and administered only by men who had the supernatural gift conferred on the founders and members of the primitive churches. They were 'seeking and waiting' for such manifestation of the Holy Ghost as would render it possible for true churches to be constituted. George Fox was at one time a 'Seeker,' believing, as he said, that 'those who sought the truth would surely find it.' *See* Barclay,

'Inner Life,' which contains an excellent sketch of the Seekers.

Under the head of Independents. . . . were the Arminians, Millenaries, Baptists, Anabaptists, Familists, Enthusiasts, Seekers, Perfectists, Socinians, Arians, and others.—HOWITT, *Hist. of Eng.* (Charles I.), chap. vi. p. 273.

Segretario (*Il*). Machiavel is meant, if no proper name is added.

Seiads (*The Government of the*), 1414, succeeded in Delhi the 'House of Toghlak.' Khiza Khan expelled from the throne Doulat Khan Lodi.

Seicentis'ti. The Italian worthies of the 17th cent., or in the decline of Italian poetry and art. It is applied to the men of note in any debased period. *See* p. 174, 'Cinque Centisti.'

Se:gneur of Sark (*The*), 1565. Sir Helier de Carteret, appointed by Queen Elizabeth, was the first seigneur. In 1721 Sark passed by sale into the hands of James Milner, and in 1730 passed into the possession of Susannah Le Pelley; but in 1852 the seigneurie was transferred to Mr. T. G. Collings of Guernsey. The parliament or assembly of Sark is called the Chefs Plaids.

Seja'nus of England (*The*). So Sir John Elliot styled the Duke of Buckingham when he was impeached in 1627, and truly the resemblance between the favourite of Tiberius and the favourite of Charles I. is very striking. Both were equally unscrupulous, both equally licentious, both popular in a way for their dash, beauty, and extravagance; both favourites of two princes: Sejanus of Caius Cæsar and the Emperor Tiberius—Buckingham of James I. and Charles I.; and both met an untimely end.

Select Preachers (of our Universities). Ten clergymen selected to supply the place of those who decline to preach in St. Mary's Church in their regular turn. Five of the preachers are nominated annually by the Vice-Chancellor, the Regius and Margaret Professors of Divinity, and the two proctors. No substitute is permitted except those thus selected.

Select Vestry Act (*The*), 1663. By which a person was prohibited from being a vestryman unless he abjured the 'Covenant,' swore not to take up arms against the King's majesty, and promised by oath to conform to the Liturgy.

Seleucides (4 syl.), or 'Dynasty of the Seleucidæ,' B.C. 312–64 (247 years). A Macedonian dynasty which reigned in Syria and Upper Asia after the death of Alexander the Great. So called from Seleucus, one of Alexander's generals, its founder. Six of the dynasty were named Seleucus, thirteen were named Antiochus, and three were named Demetrius. It was succeeded by the Arsacĭdês.

The 'Era of the Seleucides' begins with this dynasty. Seleukos I. is surnamed *Nicâtor* (the Conqueror).

Self-denying Ordinance (*The*). *See* 'Self-renouncing Ordinance.'

Self-renouncing Ordinance (*The*), or 'Self-denying Ordinance,' 3 April, 1645. A measure moved by Zouch Tate and seconded by Sir Harry Vane in the House of Commons for the removal of the Earl of Essex from the command of the parliamentary army. Tate said, 'There is but one way of ending so many evils, and that is for everyone freely to renounce himself.' The ordinance was that no member of either house shall hold any office, civil or military, during the war. When the bill passed, Essex, Warwick, and Manchester resigned, and Fairfax was made commander. Cromwell ought to have been excluded as an M.P., but a special exception was made in his case 'for his brilliant achievements.' Cromwell really introduced the measure to the attention of the parliament, for he saw plainly that the aristocracy were only half-hearted in the war. On the death of Essex in 1647 this ordinance fell into abeyance.

Zouch, pronounce *Zootch*.

Seljuks (*The*), or 'Seljukian Dynasty.' An Oriental dynasty founded by Togrûl Bey, grandson of Seljûk of Turkestan. He took possession of the empire of the Ghaznevides (3 syl.), and put an end to the Bowides (2 syl.) in Ispahan. The Seljûks of Persia began with Togrûl I. and went out with Togrûl II. It gave twelve sovereigns, lasted 156 years (1038–1194), and was succeeded by the Gourides (2 syl.) or Khans of Kharizm (1155–1225).

It will be seen that the Gourides were for thirty-nine years contemporary with the Seljûks. Togrûl Bey, Alp Arslan, and Malek Shah are kings to be proud of in any nation.

Selkirk Island. Juan Fernandez is so called from Alexander Selkirk, a buccaneer from the fishing town of Largs in Fifeshire, who resided there in solitude for four years (1704–1708). The story of Selkirk probably suggested to Defoe that of 'Robinson Crusoe.'

Selwyn College, Cambridge, 1882. Built by public subscription in memory of George Augustus Selwyn, late bishop of Lichfield, to provide an economical education of 'high culture of the mind combined with Christian training based on the principles of the Church of England.'

Selwyn Divinity School (*The*). Founded in 1856 by William Selwyn, D.D., of St. John's College, Cambridge. Lady Margaret Professor of Divinity.

Sem'inarists, 1583 (Queen Elizabeth). The name given to the Roman Catholic clergy who were trained at Dr. Allen's College at Douay for the purpose of being sent over to England as missionaries of the Pope. These were afterwards treated by Elizabeth's officers as being on the same footing as Jesuits.

Sem'ipela'gians, A.D. 430. Pelāgius denied the doctrine of original sin, or the taint of Adam. He maintained that all men can, if they choose, keep all the laws of God; that God gives grace to those who deserve it; that good acts are due to the liberty of the will as well as bad acts. The Semipelāgians agreed with Pelagius in the freedom of the will to choose either good or evil, but after having made the choice then they maintained that God's grace is indispensable for justification and righteousness. Man can walk to the palace door, but must be ushered into the presence chamber.

Semir'amis of the North (*The*). I. Margaret de Valdemar, queen of Norway, Sweden, and Denmark. She was the daughter of Valdemar III. king of Denmark (1353–1412).

II. Catharine of Russia, a powerful ambitious sovereign, but licentious, sensual, and immoral (1729, 1762–1796).

Semitic Languages (*The*). Ancient Arabic, Hebrew, Syriac, Phœnician, Chaldaic, Æthiopic, and perhaps ancient Egyptian and Coptic.

Semitic Nations (*The*). The Hebrews, Syrians, old Æthiopians, Ara-

bians, and Phœnicians. *See* 'Turanian' and 'Aryan.'

Sempach (*Convention of*), 1393. An act of confederation between the Austrians and Swiss.

'Semper sub Sextis perdita Roma fuit.' •
NERO was the sixth Cæsar. (Julius, Augustus, Tiberius, Caligula, Claudius, Nero.)
STEPHEN VI. (pope 896–897) was a monster. He caused the body of his predecessor to be exhumed; and then, cutting off the head of the dead body with a hatchet, threw it into the Tiber. The people, disgusted, seized him, cast him into prison, and there strangled him.
BONIFACE VI. (pope 896) died within fifteen days.
BENEDICT VI. (972–974) was confined in St. Angelo by Boniface, called 'Antipope,' and died there.
GREGORY VI. (1044–1046) had three rival claimants, and when he had bribed them to retire Kaiser Heinrich III. and his cardinals obstructed all his reforms. Driven to despair, he abdicated.
CLEMENT VI. (1342–1352) resided at Avignon. It was in this pontificate that Rienzi the tribune troubled Rome.
URBAN VI. (1378–1389). With this pontificate began the 'Great Schism of the West' (*q.v.*).
PIUS VI. (1775–1799) was ill-starred. In France the National Assembly confiscated the property of the church and suppressed all religious orders; in Germany the Congress of Ems abolished the Nunciature; in Naples the papal tribute was withheld; and in 1791 Avignon and Venaissin were added to France. France invaded the papal dominions, Bonaparte attacked the Roman States, compelled Pius to sign the Treaty of Tolentino, by which he gave up the best pictures and statues of Rome, introduced his republic there, and the old pontiff, torn from his palace, was transferred successively to Sienna, Florence, Grenoble, and Valence, where he died at the age of eighty-two.

To Rome if *six* hath always brought mischance,
Three, without doubt, has fatal proved to France.
See 'Three Fatal to France.'

Sempro'nian Law (*The*), B.C. 123. That the state is to furnish corn at a low price to all Roman citizens (25 ases per bushel). At one time it cost the state a million a year to make up this deficit. It was carried by Caius Sempronius Gracchus.

There were several other Sempronian laws, the object of which was to lessen the power of the oligarchy and make the constitution more democratic.

Senate (*The*) of the University of Cambridge used to be divided into two Houses: (1) The regents or white-hoods, and (2) the non-regents or black-hoods. The Upper or White-hood House consisted of masters of arts of less than five years' standing and doctors of less than two years' standing. The Lower or Black-hood House consisted of masters of arts of more than five years' standing and doctors of more than two years' standing. All doctors of the Upper House and the public orator could vote in either house. This arrangement was wholly changed in 1857-58.

'Regents' originally meant 'tutors, lecturers, and professors.' 'Non-regents' were those who had served their time and were exempt from these duties. Masters of arts took off the white lining of their hoods to show they were no longer regents or tutors and lecturers. The stripping of the white lining has long been discontinued.
The Council of the Senate is called a 'Caput' (*q.v.*). An assembly in term-time is called a 'Congregation,' but out of term-time it is a 'Convocation.' By a 'Grace' a convocation may be converted into a congregation.
** There is no senate in the Oxford University. *See* 'House of Convocation.'

Senate (*The Present*). The legislative body of Cambridge University. Great changes were made in 1857 (19, 20 Vict. c. 88), and in 1882 an entire new code of statutes was approved by Queen Victoria in council. The senate now consists of one house only, which assembles in the senate-house. The members are the chancellor and vice-chancellor, and the following graduates, provided their names remain on the university register, viz.: All doctors of the five faculties (*i.e.* divinity, law, medicine, science, and letters). There is a Council of the Senate (*q.v.*), and there is also an Electoral Roll (*q.v.*).

Bachelors of divinity are members of the senate only in virtue of their M.A. degree.

Senate (*The Conservative*) of France, 1799. 'Le Sénat Conservateur' created by the Constitution of Year VIII. was not a legislative body. Its duties were to see the laws enforced, and to elect the future consuls. They appointed the tribunes and legislators, and even filled up vacancies in their own body.

The original number of Conservative senators was 60, elected for life; afterwards increased to 137. Under the empire the senate was quite powerless, and in 1814, on the restoration, the senate was replaced by the *Chambre des Pairs*.

Senate (*The French*). 'Le Sénat Français' (14 Jan., 1852) was composed of cardinals, marshals, and admirals, of princes over the age of eighteen, and of members nominated by the *chef de l'Etat*. The number was 150, and the election for life. A decree of the senate was called a *sénatus-consulte* (plu. *sénatus-consultes*).

Senate of Lilliput (*The*). In the reign of George II. (26 Feb., 1729), it was made illegal to print reports of the discussions of the House of Commons. To evade this law the debates were printed under *initials*, as debates of the 'Senate of Lilliput.'

Senate of Rome (*The*). Instituted by Romulus to deliberate on peace and war, appoint the imposts, distribute the provinces, render justice, and enact the laws. In the empire it lost all independence, and at the partition of the empire there were two senates—one at Constantinople and the other at Rome. The Roman senate ceased in 552, during the domination of Theodoric.

The original number was 100, called *Patres*. Tullus Hostilius doubled the number, and Tarquinius Priscus increased the number to 300. Brutus, on the expulsion of the kings, supplied the places of those senators who sided with Tarquin with new men whom he called *Conscripti*, and the body was addressed as *Patres* [et] *Conscripti*. Under the republic the number generally mounted up to 600, and at the death of Julius Cæsar the number was 1,000. Augustus reduced the number to 600. All senators wore the toga, with a large band of purple called the *laticlave*, from its being embroidered with a wide stripe, or border, *Clavus latus*.

Senate of Venice, 1173. A committee of 60 chosen from the Great Council (*q.v.*), which numbered 480 members. In 1435 the number was doubled, and later still it was increased to 300. It was deliberative. The college was executive.

The college consisted of 26 members: the Doge, the privy council of Signory (6), the 3 chief members of The Forty, and 16 representatives of the Senate. *See* 'Pregadi.'

Sénatus-consulte Organique de la Constitution (Year X.), 2 Aug., 1802. A modification of the Constitution of Year VIII. (*q.v.*), still less democratic. Instead of three consuls

Napoleon was appointed consul for life. In 1804 the consul was emperor.

Sénatus-consulte Organique de l'Empire Français (Year XII.), 18 May, 1804, conferring on Napoleon the power and title of emperor.

From the ANCIENT RÉGIME five constitutions brought the French back again to a monarchy. A constitutional monarchy, a pure democracy, a directory, three consuls and a conservative senate, a consulate, an EMPIRE.

Seneca (*The English*). Joseph Hall bishop of Norwich (1574–1656).

Seneca of the East (*The*). Buzurg-Mihir, who imported into Persia the game of chess and the fables of Pilpay (6th cent.).

Sénéchal (*The*). A subaltern officer of France who acted as a crown judge; the district over which he had jurisdiction was called a *sénéchaussée*. These sénéchaussées were established chiefly in the south of France; they were called *bailliages* in the north. All France was subdivided into sénéchaussées or bailliages.

Every grand feudatory had his sénéchal, who was his major domo. In England a sénéchal is temporarily created for a coronation ceremony, and when a peer is accused of a capital offence.

Sénéchal (*The Grand*) of France. He was master of the royal household, the chief lord of the treasury, commander-in-chief of the army, and lord chief justice. It was the highest rank in the kingdom, and in the 10th cent. was made hereditary in the house of Anjou. Suppressed in 1191 by Philippe II. Auguste, who divided the dignity and duties between the constable and grand master of the king's palace. *See above*, ' Sénéchal.'

Senior Students of Christ Church, Oxford, correspond to fellows in other colleges. What in other colleges are called Scholars are termed Junior Students in Christ Church. The head of Christ Church is called the ' Dean.'

Sennacherib, King of Assyria, was Sin-akhi-erba, son of Sarru-gina [Sargon]. He began to reign B.C. 707. He was high priest for eighteen years of his reign. His war with Hezekiah was not the third year of his reign, but his ' third expedition,' and his son Esar Haddon—that is, Asshur-akhi-dinna—did not succeed till B.C. 683.

Sensational School (*The*). I. A school of *philosophy* in the latter half of the 18th cent. Condillac (1715–1780) was its chief exponent. This school taught that all the functions usually ascribed to the soul are mere exhibits of the senses. Knowledge is obtained by the senses only; intelligence, conscience, ' mind,' and so on are from the brain. The disciples of this school were of course materialists.

II. In French *romance writers*, followed the Romantic. The first of the sensational novels was ' Indiana,' by George Sand (Mme. Dudevant, 1804–1877).

Bad as the sensual novels of the ' Sensational School' of France undoubtedly are, the Realistic School is ten times worse. They pander to the most prurient passions of man, and uncover sensuality in all its nastiness; for, laid bare, it is both disgusting and revolting.

Sensualists. In philosophy means those who believe that we depend on our senses for all our knowledge of the material world. These philosophers are also called ' Empirics,' from a Greek word meaning *experience*. The chief of these philosophers among the ancients were Democritus, Leucippos, Aristippos, Epicūros, and Lucretius; and among the moderns Hobbes, Gassendi, Condillac, Helvetius, Cabanis, De Tracy, Broussais, Hartley, and Priestley. Those who contend for intuitive ideas and an inner sense or perception are called Dogmatists. The system of Sensualists is called ' Sensualism.'

Some rank Aristotle, Bacon, and Locke among Sensualists, but they distinctly teach that the five senses are not of themselves sufficient to explain all ideas.

Cabanis, pronounce *Cah-bah-nee*.

Separatists (*The*). I. 1580. Those who withdrew from the Church of England in consequence of the tyranny and dogmatism of the Ecclesiastical Commission. They objected to an established church as contrary to the word of God; to the use of the cross in baptism as a rag of popery; to kneeling at the Lord's Supper as a semi-adoration of the elements; and to the use of the surplice. Persecution greatly increased their number and confirmed their opposition, so that they quickly mounted to 20,000 souls, and became a power in the state.

II. Or ' Pietists' (*q.v.*), 1689. Founded by Spener of Leipsic.

III. In 1886, &c. Those in favour of giving the Irish a separate parliament, supreme in Irish matters, but subordinate to the British parliament in all matters affecting the United Kingdom. The bill was brought in by Mr. Gladstone, the prime minister, but was thrown out, and led to the break-up of the Whig party, those Whigs and Radicals who opposed the bill being called Unionists. Lord Hartington was the leader of the Whig Unionists, and Mr. Chamberlain of the Radical Unionists. *See* 'Irish Associations.'

An *imperium in imperio* is proverbially dangerous, and would be especially so with the impulsive Irish, who are ready to follow any demagogue, and apply to foreign nations for support. What the Irish want is to be a 'separate nation,' and have its voice in the councils of Europe. To effect this it must have its consuls, ambassadors, and army. And fatal collision with England could not be long delayed.

Sepoy War (*The*), 1857–1858, or Indian Mutiny (*q.v.*).

September Massacres (*The*). 2, 3, 4, 5 Sept., 1792, when between eight and ten thousand persons, chiefly noblemen and priests, were massacred in cold blood at the instigation of Marat. *See* 'Septembrisers.'

September 9. The day appointed for the National Thanksgiving for the king's escape from the Rye-house plot in favour of the Duke of Monmouth and the assassination of Charles II., 1683. Lord William Russell and others were executed as being implicated in this plot.

You hypocrites, forbear your pranks,
To murder men and then give thanks ;
Forbear, your tricks pursue no further,
For God accepts no thanks for murder.
          LUTTRELL'S *Journal*.

The 'murder' referred to is that of Lord William Russell, &c.

Septembrisers. I. 'Septembriseurs.' Those engaged in the massacres of September (*q.v.*), Sept. 1792. Three hundred hired assassins wearing tricoloured scarfs round their waists went to Les Carmes, L'Abbaye, and La Force to assassinate those suspected of favouring the royal cause. In Les Carmes 163 ecclesiastics were executed without even a mockery trial. In the other two prisons a few questions were asked. If the judges said *à Coblentz* the ' suspect ' was acquitted, but if the sentence was *à l'Abbaye*, or *à la Force*, he was led into the yard and put to death. Truchat stated to the Legislative Assembly that the number which fell in the four days was 4,000, but the real number was double that or more. *See above.*

Billaud-Varennes promised each of the assassins 24 louis for his work (a total of about 5,000*l.*), but money enough could not be raised, and the sum of 1,463 livres (70*l.*) is set down in the books of the Commune as still due. This surely is some blunder, for it is incredible that the government should be unable to lay hands on such a paltry sum of money.

II. The revolutionary mob of France in the first revolution was so called because they began their annual calendar in September instead of January.

Certainly it was most unscientific to *begin* the year in September, when its end is so near at hand for all nations north of the equator.

Septennial Act (*The*), 1 Geo. I. c. 38, 7 May, 1716, extending the duration of parliament to seven years, instead of three, as it had been since 1641. By this act it was provided that the interval between two parliaments should in no wise exceed four years.

Sep'tuagesima Sunday. Seventy days before Easter, Church way of reckoning, which gives ten days to the week. Thus : 1 eve of Sunday, 2 Sunday, 3 Monday, 4 Tuesday, 5 Wednesday, 6 Thursday, 7 Friday, 8 Saturday, 9 eve of the Octave, 10 the Octave. *See* ' Sunday.'

So the entombment was 1 eve of Saturday, 2 Saturday, 3 eve of Sunday. Septuagesima, often, but incorrectly, pronounced *Sep'-t'a-jes'y-may.*

Septuagint (*The*). A Greek version of the Scriptures, and called ' the Alexandrian.' It was produced in the reign of Ptolemy Philadelphus (B.C. 284–247). The Pentateuch, which contains many Coptic words, was probably the work of Egyptian Jews. *See* ' Scriptures.'

No one believes the tradition repeated by Philo, Justin, Clement of Alexandria, Epiphanius, and others : That Ptolemy, by the advice of his librarian, employed seventy-two men of learning to translate the Hebrew Scriptures into Greek. The seventy-two met in the Isle of Pharos, and in seventy-two days produced that translation. It is furthermore added that each of the seventy-two was shut up in a separate room, and when they delivered in their translations all most minutely agreed. Not a word, not a letter differed. Richard Simon informs us that it was called the Septuagint, because it was approved and authorised by the Jewish Sanhedrim. The language is Greek, but many of the words are Aramaic. Often, but incorrectly, pronounced *Sep'-t'a-jint.*

Seraphic Doctor (*The*). John Bonaventura (1221–1274). A Franciscan, chiefly distinguished for his adoration of the Virgin Mary. He distorted everything, by the help of allegory and analogy, to Christian theology. This *Doctor Seraphicus* is placed by Dante among the saints in Paradise.

Serbo'nian Bog (*The*). The lake Serbōnis in Egypt, near the isthmus of

Suez, and the border of Syria, which, when the south wind prevailed, was covered with sand, and looked like dry land. Artaxerxes Ochus lost troop after troop in this bog, on his way to Egypt.

Serene Highness (*His Most*). In Germany is the title of the collateral branches of the sovereign or emperor. In the reign of Louis XIV. the title was given to the Prince de Condé.

Ser′geanty. Service rendered to the crown for lands. It was divided into Grand Sergeanty and Petit Sergeanty. The service in Grand Sergeanty was personal service, as following the king in battle. The service of Petit Sergeanty was some real or nominal payment by way of rent.

Pronounce *Sar′-jent-ty*.

Serpent, as a Standard (*The*). The kings of Assyria and of Babylon adopted as a standard a 'Great Red Dragon,' and Cyrus introduced a similar standard into the armies of the Medes and Persians. *See* Ezek. xxix. 3.

One of the Roman standards was a serpent. The Tartars carried a serpent standard, and it will be remembered that a serpent was the standard of the tribe of Dan, allusion to which is made in Gen. xlix. 17.

The ancient Britons adopted the dragon both as a crest and as a standard. Geoffrey of Monmouth tells us : 'When Aurēlius was at Winchester there appeared to him in the sky a star of wonderful magnitude and brilliancy, from which there darted forth a ray ending in a fiery dragon.' He adds that 'Uther had two golden dragons made, one of which he presented to Winchester and the other he carried with him as a royal standard.' A rattlesnake flag, with the motto 'Don't tread on me,' was one of the first standards adopted in the American revolution.

Probably this is a pure invention of the romancing chronicler to account for the title of *pendragon* given to King Uther. But *dragon* is the British word for 'leader,' and *pen-dragon* means simply 'leader-in-chief.'

The Greek δρακων is derived from δραω, to be active, and the Welsh *dragon* is allied to the word *draig*, lightning. Both express the essential characteristics of a good general, quick-eyed and quick in execution. Probably the astronomical symbol of the planet Jupiter (a serpent on a cross), and the coiled dragon at the base of Satan, refer to similar vigilance and activity.

Serpent Homer (*The*). A copy of Homer's 'Iliad' on a roll of serpent skin

120 feet in length. This ancient MS. was kept in the royal college of Constantinople, but was lost in a fire which destroyed the library. *See* Gibbon, chap. liii.

Serpent of Old Nile (*The*). Cleopatra queen of Egypt (B.C. 69, 51–30).

Serventese. A popular sort of mediæval ballad like 'Chevy Chase,' divided into stanzas.

Poemata in quibus Servientium seu Militum facta et servitia referuntur.—DU CANGE.

Serve′tus (*Michael*). The learned theologian, who embraced the Arian doctrine, persecuted to death by Calvin. He published a book anonymously, but Calvin ferreted out the author, and had the book burnt at the gallows. Not long afterwards, as he was passing through Geneva in disguise, Calvin had him arrested, and acted as informer, prosecutor, and judge, and Servetus was burnt to death by a slow fire. No more infamous act ever disgraced the memory of man (1509–1553).

Service Book (*The*), 1637. So the Scotch called the Common Prayer Book, which Charles I. tried to force the people of Scotland to use in their places of worship.

The term was common enough in England also, but they were more often called 'Uses' (*q.v.*). These eleven were consulted by the Commissioners who compiled our Common Prayer Book, viz. the Missal, the Graduale or Grayle, the Processionale, the Ordinale, the Portiforium or Breviary, the Legenda, the Pica or Pie, the Finale, the Antiphonarium, the Manuale, and Pontificale. *See* each of these words *in loco*.

Servile or Slave War (*The*). The first in Sicily, B.C. 133–131 ; the second in Sicily, B.C. 103.

Ser′vites (2 syl.), or 'Servitors of the Virgin.' A religious order founded in Florence in 1232. Called 'White Mantles' from their dress. The order still subsists in Italy, but was abolished in France 1274.

There are a few houses of Servites in the United States ; also some of Servite ladies (nuns). There is one house of Servites in England (Fulham Road, S.W.), one of Servite Sisters (St. Anne's Road, Stamford Hill, N.). 1890.

Servitors. Students of Christ Church College, Oxford University, received at reduced fees, like the 'Bible Clerks' of Oriel College, Oxford, and the sizars of Cambridge. At one time each fellow had his servitor to wait on him at dinner, and these servitors dined on what was left at the fellows' table.

Servus servi. A slave's drudge, who helped him to cultivate his *peculium* (*q.v.*).

Since the time of Gregory the Great the pope has styled himself *Servus servorum Dei* (the drudge of God's ministers).

Sessional School (*The Edinburgh*), 29 April, 1813. A normal or training school to educate teachers in the principles and art of teaching. This was the first of the training colleges in Great Britain, but they had been established in France in 1795, and in Germany even earlier (1748). *See* 'Normal Schools.'

The Sessional Schools were in 20 Feb., 1838, adopted as an appendage of the ecclesiastical establishment under the name of the General Assembly's Normal Institution.

Sestiere (*A*) (plural *Sestieri*). A division of the city of Florence for legislative purposes. It was a sixth part, and each sestiere elected two anziani or seniors. In 1282 the city was divided into quarters, and the anziani were superseded by priors (*q.v.*).

Sethos. King of Egypt, 19th dynasty, father of Sesostris, reigned five centuries before the Christian era. There is a statue of this king holding a rat in his hand, and containing this inscription : ' Learn from my example to honour the gods.'

The explanation given is this, according to Herodotus: His soldiers refused to contend with Sennacherib the Assyrian, and Sethos invoked the god whose minister he was to aid him. At night a crowd of rats invaded the Assyrian camp and gnawed the bowstrings of the sleeping men, so that next morning Sennacherib was obliged to draw off his army. No doubt this account is wholly mythical, and the rat held in the king's hand was the god he ' delighted to honour.'

Settlement (*The Act of*). The statute 12, 13 William III. c. 2 whereby the crown was limited to the family of William. If William and his successor Anne died without issue the succession was to pass to the descendants of Princess Sophia, a daughter of James I., provided they were Protestants (1702). This, of course, is the ground of the Hanoverian Succession. *See* ' Act of Settlement.'

Settling Day. The day on which stockbrokers settle or balance time bargains (*q.v.*). Once a fortnight.

Seven. A magic number in Brussels. Seven noble families, springing from seven ancient castles, supplied the stock from which was selected the seven senators who composed the upper council of the city. There were seven great squares and seven gates (Motley, ' Dutch Republic,' chap. i.).

Seven a Sacred Number.

Pythagoras, 500 years before the Christian era, tells us that the number 7 belongs especially to sacred things.

Hippocratès (B.C. 460–357) divided the life of man into 7 ages, a division adopted by Shakespeare.

The Egyptian priests enjoined rest on the 7th day, because it was held to be a *dies infaustus*. In Egyptian astronomy there were 7 planets, and hence 7 days in the week, each day ruled by its own special planet. The people of Peru had also a 7-day week.

The Persians and Mexicans have a tradition of a flood from which 7 persons saved themselves in a cave, and by whom the world was subsequently repeopled.

The Jews considered 7 the perfect number: hence we have the 7 days of the creative week ; 7 days' respite before the flood came ; 7 of all clean animals saved in the ark; the years of famine and plenty were in cycles of 7 ; every 7th year, like every 7th day, was a sabbath; the feasts of unleavened bread and of tabernacles lasted 7 days ; the golden candlestick had 7 branches; 7 priests blew with their trumpets when the walls of Jericho fell down, after being encompassed for 7 days, and 7 times on the 7th day; Jacob served 7 years for each of his wives; Samson kept his nuptials 7 days, was bound with 7 green withes, and 7 locks of his hair were cut off; Nebuchadnezzar was a ' beast' for 7 years; and the furnace for the three Jews was heated 7 times more than it was wont; the righteous are like gold 7 times purified in the furnace.

In the New Testament nearly everything occurs by sevens : there were 7 churches in Asia; 7 spirits symbolised by 7 candlesticks; 7 stars; 7 seals; 7 vials.

3×7 is an important factor among ourselves: thus, 3×7 constitutes a royal salute; 3×7 is the time that man ' comes of age,' &c. The 7th son of a 7th son was at one time supposed to possess wonderful powers. Man consists of 7 parts (2 legs, 2 arms, a stomach, chest, and head), and his head has 7 apertures (2 for the eyes, 2 for the ears, 2 for the nose, and one for the mouth).

Seven Articles of Islâm (*The*).

1, There is one only God; 2, Mohammed is his prophet; 3, Prayer is the key of paradise; 4, almsgiving; 5, fasting the whole month of Ramadán; 6, a pilgrimage to Mecca; and, 7, observance of the festivals, viz. the first three days of Shawál (which immediately follow the month of Ramadán) and the three or four days beginning on the tenth of Dsu'l Heggeh.

Friday is the sabbath, but, service being over, the rest of the day is at every man's disposal.

Seven Bibles (*The*). 1, The Christian's Bible; 2, the Korân or Mahometan's Bible; 3, the Eddas of the Scandinavians; 4, the Try Pitikes or Tripitaka, *i.e.* 'Triple basket' (viz. the *Soutras* or discourses (literally 'strings'), *Vinaya* or discipline, and *Abhidharma* or metaphysics); 5, the Chinese five kings (viz. *Yih-king*, cosmogony, *Shu-king*, or deliberations of the 'ancient kings,' the *Shi-king*, or book of psalms, the *Le-king*, or book of rites, the *Chun-tsien*, or history of China); 6, the Three Vedas of the Hindûs; and, 7, the Zendavesta of the Persians. Of these the Korân is the most modern.

The five kings do not mean five monarchs, but five webs of cloth or five warps.

Seven Bishops (*The*), committed to the Tower by Chief Justice Jeffreys, 10 June, 1688, were Sancroft archbishop of Canterbury, Lloyd bishop of St. Asaph, Ken bishop of Bath and Wells, Turner bishop of Ely, Lake bishop of Chichester, White bishop of Peterborough, and Trelawney bishop of Bristol. These seven bishops were deputed to wait on James II. and inform him that the bishops of the diocese declined to read the king's Declaration of Indulgence according to his command, or to instruct their clergy so to do. The object of the declaration was the removal of all disqualifications from Roman Catholics in church and state offices. The bishops, when brought to trial, were acquitted, and this tyrannical proceeding was the last offence which brought about the overthrow of James II. The declaration was to be read in London 20 May and elsewhere 27 May, 1688.

Seven Bodies in Alchemy (*The*). 1, the sun is *gold*; 2, the moon is *silver*; 3, Mars is *iron*; 4, Mercury is *quicksilver*; 5, Saturn is *lead*; 6, Jupiter is *tin*; and, 7, Venus is *copper*.

The bodies seven, eek, lo hem heer anoon:
Sol *gold* is, and Luna *silver* we threpe,
Mars *yren*, Mercurie *quyksilver* we clepe,

Saturnus *leed*, and Jubitur is *tyn*,
And Venus *coper*, by my fader kyn.
CHAUCER, *Canterbury Tales* (Prologue to the 'Chanounes Yemanes Tale ').

Seven Champions of Christendom (*The*). 1, St. George of *England*; 2, St. Andrew of *Scotland*; 3, St Patrick of *Ireland*; 4, St. David of *Wales*; 5, St. Denys of *France*; 6, St. James of *Spain*; and, 7, St. Anthony of *Italy*.

Seven Clerical Orders (*The*). Ostiarii, lectors, exorcists, acolytes, subdeacons, deacons, and priests. Bishops are dignified priests.

Docendum igitur erit hosce omnes ordines septenario numero contineri, semperque ita a Catholica Ecclesia traditum esse; quorum nomina hæc sunt: Ostiarius, Lector, Exorcista, Acolytus, Subdiaconus, Diaconus, Sacerdos.—*Cat. Concil. Trident.*, pt. ii. c. 24.

St. Caius, who succeeded Eutychiānus in 283, made it a law of the church that all clerici should pass through the seven inferior orders before they were capable of being ordained bishops.—PRINCE, *Parallel History.*

Seven Corporal Works of Mercy (*The*). 1, to bury the dead; 2, to clothe the naked; 3, to feed the hungry; 4, to give drink to the thirsty; 5, to harbour the houseless; 6, to visit those in prison; and, 7, to administer to the sick. *See* 'Seven Spiritual,' &c.

Seven Crosses (*The*). Seven crosses mark the tomb of a bishop, five of a priest, and one of an ordinary Christian.

There are also seven forms of the ecclesiastical cross.

+   The Greek cross, the oldest form. Symbol of the word LVX., *lux* (light).

†   The Latin cross.

✠   The Maltese cross.

X   St. Andrew's cross, or reliquary cross.

✚   The Lorrainese cross, or cardinal's cross, carried before a cardinal. The pope's cross has three transoms.

T   The Tau or Egyptian cross, or the marking cross.

☧   Constantine's cross ☧, *i.e.* XP, for Chr[istos].

Some other forms are occasionally seen, as the 'Lambeaux,' which is a Maltese cross on a Latin stem, standing on a lambel with three pendants. The rectoral cross consists of two spears crossed; the Agnus Dei cross is a spear · ᵣmounted with a Maltese cross: and the heraldıc crosses.

Seven Days' King (*The*). Masaniello (*i.e.* Tommaso Aniello), born 1622. Headed a revolt against the Duke of Arcos, at Naples, 7 July, 1647, forced him to abolish the tax on provisions, and for seven days was master of Naples. He was most arrogant and bloodthirsty, and was assassinated 16 July.

He is the hero of two operas: one by Caraffa called 'Masaniello,' and the other by Auber (libretto by Scribe) called 'La Muette de Portici.'

Seven Deadly Sins (*The*). Covetousness, envy, gluttony, lechery or lust, pride, sloth, wrath. *See* 'Seven Virtues.'

Seven Deposed Ministers of Scotland (*The*), 1843. A Mr. Edwards was presented to a church in Scotland, and, being refused ordination by the presbytery of Strathbogie, he appealed to the civil court and gained the verdict; whereupon seven ministers united in ordaining him, contrary to the principle of the 'veto' (*q.v.*) adopted in 1834. These seven ministers were now deposed by the presbytery, their churches declared vacant, and Mr. Edwards was deprived of his licence as a minister. The seven ministers petitioned the House of Lords, which justified them, and insisted on their restoration. This split up the Church of Scotland, and the seceding members formed what is called the 'Free Church of Scotland' (*q.v.*).

Seven Dolours (*The*), 1725. 'The seven dolours, or sorrows, of the Blessed Virgin' is a modern festival of the Catholic Church celebrated on the Friday preceding Palm Sunday. They refer to: 1, the prediction of St. Luke (ii. 34); 2, the flight into Egypt; 3, the loss of Jesus in Jerusalem; 4, the sight of Jesus bearing his cross; 5, the sight of Jesus on the cross; 6, the piercing of his side with the lance; and, 7, the burial. The festival was instituted by Pope Benedict XIII. *See* 'Seven Joys,' &c.

Instead of piercing the side we have the betrayal in the right place in some lists; and instead of the burial is given the Ascension, 'Let not your hearts be sorrowful, &c.' No. 1 was not a sorrow, but a prediction only; the 'sorrows' were the incidents which fulfilled it.

Seven Gifts of the Holy Ghost (*The*). 1, counsel; 2, the fear of the Lord; 3, fortitude; 4, piety; 5, understanding; 6, wisdom; and, 7, knowledge.

Philip said to the eunuch, 'Understandest thou what thou readest,' this is the first step to a knowledge of God.

'The fear of the Lord is the beginning of wisdom,' this is understanding carried into practice.

'I know whom I have believed,' this is the experience of a ripe Christian.

Seven-hilled City (*The*). 'Urbs Septicollis,' Rome, built on seven hills:

1, the Palatīnus; 2, the Capitolīnus; 3, the Quirinālis; 4, the Cælius; 5, the Aventīnus; 6, the Viminālis; and, 7, the Esquilīnus.

Seven Joys of Mary (*The*). 1, the annunciation; 2, the visitation; 3, the nativity; 4, the adoration of the wise men; 5, the presentation in the temple; 6, finding Christ among the doctors; and, 7, the assumption. *See* 'Seven Dolours,' &c.

Strange that the 'resurrection' should be omitted. One would have supposed it would have been the joy of joys next to the nativity.

Seven Liberal Sciences (*The*). Divinity, astronomy, geometry, music, law, physic, and rhetoric.

Seven Men of Moidart (*The*), 1745. The seven persons who accompanied Charles Edward, the young pretender, on his expedition to conquer Great Britain and win back the crown abandoned by his grandfather James II. So called because their first muster in Scotland was at Kinloch Moidart, Invernessshire. They were the old marquess of Tullibardine (called by the Jacobites the duke of Athol), Sir Thomas Sheridan (Charles Edward's tutor), Sir John Macdonald, Kelly (the nonjuring clergyman), Francis Strickland, Æneas Macdonald (banker in Paris), and Buchanan.

Seven Months' War (*The*), the Franco-Prussian War. War was declared by Napoleon III. against Prussia 19 July, 1870, and peace was signed at Frankfort 10 May, 1871. The first half consisted of a series of battles won by Prussia; the second half consisted of a series of sieges, ending with the siege of Paris, in all of which Prussia was successful.

The day after the battle of Sedan, Sept. 1, Napoleon III. surrendered his sword to the king of Prussia. On 18 January, 1871, Wilhelm I. king of Prussia was created emperor of Germany, and on 28 January Paris surrendered to the conquerors.

Seven Mortal Sins (*The*). Pride, wrath, envy, lust, gluttony, avarice, and sloth.

Seven Nations of Canaan (*The*). The Hittites, the Girgashites, the Amorites, the Canaanites, the Perizzites, the Hivites, and the Jebusites.

The Canaanites were also called the Philistines, and by the Hebrews 'Cherethites,' because they were supposed to be a colony from Cherith (Crete) The people called themselves Palishthines, and their country Palisthan (whence Philistines and Palestine).

Seven Orders of the Anglo-Saxon Church.

1. The *ostiary*, a kind of sexton, whose duty it was to ring the bells and keep the church doors.

2. The *exorcist*, whose function was to exorcise those possessed.

3. The *lector*, or ' reader,' who read the lessons at church.

4. The *acolyth*, or 'acolythist,' who held the candles while the priest read the Gospel in the celebration of the mass.

5. The *subdeacon*, who prepared the holy vessels, and attended on the deacon at the altar.

6. The *deacon*, who assisted the priest, laid the oblations on the altar, baptized children, and gave the eucharist to the laity.

7. The *priest*, or 'presbyter,' who preached, consecrated and administered the elements, &c. Bishops and archbishops are merely grades of the priesthood.

The Catholic Church has the same seven orders.

Seven Preexistences (*The*). Subscribed to by the Daruschists. They are Law and Throne of Glory, which existed before the creation of the world. The other five existed in contemplation only, viz. the Fathers, Israel, the Sanctuary, the Messiah, and Repentance.

Seven Religions (*The*), according to the Ismaëlites, are these : (1) that of Adam and his companion Soos (*Seth*); (2) Noah, with Shem; (3) Abraham, with Ismaël; (4) Moses, with Aaron; (5) Jesus, with Simon; (6) Mahomet, with Ali; (7) the Chief, or Master, in whom culminated ' the Sciences of the Primeval Ones.'

Seven Sacraments (*The*), of the Roman Catholic Church : (1) Baptism; (2) Confirmation ; (3) the Lord's Supper ; (4) Penance; (5) Holy Orders; (6) Matrimony; and (7) Extreme Unction. Of these, Confirmation and Orders can be administered only by bishops.

Baptism, Matt. xxviii. 19; Eucharist, Matt. xxvi. 26; Confirmation, Acts viii. 17 ; Penance. Matt. xvi. 19; Orders, Tim. iv. 4, 22 ; Matrimony, Eph. v. 32 ; Extreme Unction, Mark vi. 13, James v. 14.

Seven Sciences (*The*). The Trivium and Quadrivium—viz. grammar, rhetoric, and logic, music, arithmetic, geometry, and astronomy. Called by

mine host of the Black Bear the ' seven damnable sciences ' ; theology being held by the church the one and only true science (' Kenilworth,' chap. iii.).

Seven kinds of Sectaries (*The*), in New England in the 17th cent. GORTONISTS (who, it is said, denied the humanity of Christ) ; PAPISTS (who consider their own merits and works equal with Christ's invaluable death and suffering); FAMILISTS (looking for rare revelations, and forsaking the sure revealed word) ; SEEKERS (who deny the churches and ordinance of Christ); ANTINOMIANS (who deny the moral law to be the rule of Christ) ; ANABAPTISTS (who deny the civil government to be proved of Christ) ; PRELATISTS (who will have their own injunctions submitted unto in the churches of Christ) (John Harvard, 1628).

Seven Sisters (*The*). I. The old yew-trees, close to Fountain Abbey, at least 1,200 years old. Only two now remain, one of which is 25 feet in circuit.

II. 1513. Seven cannons cast by Robert Borthwick, master of artillery, and employed by the Scotch in the battle of Flodden Field. An official report says they were ' the neatest, the soundest, the best fashioned, the smallest in the touchhole, and the most beautiful of their size and length ever seen.' Borthwick fell on the field while directing their operations.

Seven Sleepers (*The*). Noircarmes and his six officers in the siege of Valenciennes (1566) were so called, on account of the sleepy way in which they conducted the siege (Motley, ' The Dutch Republic,' pt. ii. 9).

Of course, the legendary seven sleepers referred to in the Koran XVIII., the Golden Legends, and Gregory's 'De Gloria Martyrum' were seven noble youths of Ephesus who fled in the Decian persecution to a cave in Mount Celion, and slept for 230 years. Their names are differently given.

Seven Spiritual Works of Mercy (*The*). (1) to admonish sinners; (2) to bear wrongs patiently ; (3) to comfort the afflicted; (4) to counsel the doubtful ; (5) to forgive offences; (6) to instruct the ignorant; and (7) to pray for the living and the dead. See ' Seven Corporal, &c.'

Seven times Christ spoke on the Cross.

1. Father forgive them, for they know not what they do.

2. To day shalt thou be with me in paradise.

3. Woman, behold thy son.

4. My God, my God, why hast thou forsaken me?

5. I thirst.

6. It is finished.

7. Father, into thy hands I commend my spirit.

Seven Towers (*The*), or 'Heptapyrgium,' of Constantinople, clustered in the southern end of the wall, not far from the gate of Marmora. Within these Seven Towers is the Golden Gate. The Seven Towers were used as a state prison.

Supposing the top margin of this page to represent the port of Constantinople, the bottom of the page would be the site of the Tower of Marmora, and a little higher up would stand in a cluster (on the right hand side) the Seven Towers and Golden Gate. And about as far from the top margin as the Seven Gates would be from the bottom margin would stand the palace of Constantine. The wall connecting these is called the Western Wall.

Seven United Provinces (*The*). Seven provinces of the Netherlands under the yoke of Spain, leagued in 1579 under the leadership of William the Silent (prince of Orange-Nassau), aided by Count Hoorn and Count Egmont, to throw off their subjugation. In 1609 they succeeded in establishing themselves into a republic, by an armistice for twelve years. The struggle was renewed and carried on till 1648, when all the powers acknowledged the independence of the provinces by the Treaty of Münster.

The seven provinces were (1) Holland; (2) Zeeland; (3) Utrecht; (4) Guelderland, with Zutphen; (5) Over-Yssel; (6) Friesland; and (7) Groningen, with Drenthe. In 1795 the United Provinces became the Batavian Republic, paying 8½ millions sterling for a French army of 25,000 men, and in 1806 Louis Bonaparte was made king of Holland. In 1830 Belgium was broken off and the Netherlands became an independent kingdom.

Seven Virtues (*The*). Faith, hope, charity, prudence, justice, fortitude, and temperance.

The first three are called the 'Holy Virtues.'

Seven Weeks' War (*The*). From 8 June to 26 July, 1866, between Prussia and Austria for German supremacy. Italy was allied to Prussia. Prussia declared the Gastein Convention invalidated 4 June, and the Prussian troops entered Holstein 8 June. Hostilities between Austria and Italy ceased 25 July, but the Bavarians were defeated 26 July, and a preliminary treaty was agreed to by the belligerents. The Treaty of Prague was

35

signed 23 Aug., 1866, and the Treaty of Vienna between Italy and Austria on 3 Oct. By these treaties, Austria was entirely excluded from Germany; Prussia was placed at the head of the German states; and Venetia was added to the new-formed kingdom of Italy.

The battles were (1) Custozza (24 June), won by Victor Emmanuel; (2) Langensalza (27 June), in which Hanover, an ally of Austria, was defeated: (3) Nachod, same day, won by the Crown Prince; (4) Trautenau, same day, won by Prince Friedrich Karl; (5) Munchengrat, won 28 June; (6) Skalitz, same day; (7) Sadowa, won 3 July; (8) Olmütz, won 15 July; (9) Lissa, won 20 July; and (10) the defeat of the Bavarians, 26 July.

Seven Whistlers (*The*). The 'Gabriel Hounds,' a yelping or whistling sound heard in the air, and supposed to forebode bad luck. Called 'Gabriel Hounds' from the notion that they are the souls of the unsaved hunted by Gabriel, and shrieking from the smart of his whip as he lashes them along.

N.B.—The cry really arises from birds, such as teal, widgeons, and wild geese, flying by night to new feeding grounds.

Seven Years' War (*The*), or 'Third Silesian War,' the third period of the War of the Austrian Succession between Maria Theresa of Austria and Friedrich II. of Prussia. The object was to determine to which of these two crowns should Silesia belong. It was divided into seven campaigns.

First campaign, 1756. Dresden captured by Friedrich II. Battle of Lobositz indecisive. The Saxons surrendered.

Second campaign, 1757. Three battles won by Friedrich; those of Prague, Rosbach, and Leithen; one lost, that of Kolin.

Third campaign, 1758. Battle of Zorndorf won by Friedrich; that of Hochkirchen lost by him.

Fourth campaign, 1759. Both Kunersdorf and Maxen were won by the Austrians.

Fifth campaign, 1760. Both battles (Leignitz and Torgau) won by Friedrich II.

Sixth campaign, 1761. In which the French allies of Austria were defeated.

Seventh campaign, 1762. The Prussians victorious throughout. Peace of Hubertsburg, and end of the war (15 Feb., 1763).

The Seven Years' War began because Prussia claimed Silesia. After seven years' fighting, and the loss of a million

3 G

lives, Silesia was handed over to Prussia; but what was far more important is this: at the beginning of the war Prussia was only an insignificant kingdom; at the close of it, it was one of the great powers, and the rival of Austria.

In 1866 another contest arose between the two rival powers. This contest did not last seven years, but only seven weeks, and Austria yielded the palm to Prussia. After the Franco-Prussian war, in 1870-1871, the King of Prussia was universally acknowledged to be 'the German Emperor' also, and Austria was a separate dominion.

Seven Years' War with Sweden (*The*), 1563-1570. Erik XIV. of Sweden remonstrated with Frederick II. of Denmark for continuing in the national arms ' The Three Crowns,' commemorative of the Calmar Union. As Frederick gave no satisfactory answer, Erik retaliated by inserting the arms of Denmark in the royal banner of Sweden. The King of Poland and the city of Lübeck made common cause with Denmark. The Swedes, weary of the useless war and disgusted with their king, deprived him of his crown (1568) and confined him in prison, where he was poisoned by his brother and successor John, Feb. 1577. The first act of the new sovereign was to put an end to the war, but negotiations drawled on till 1570, when a treaty of peace was signed at Stettin by the belligerents.

Seventeen Provinces (*The*) of Karl V. (Charles-quint): Franche-Comté, Flanders, Artois, Malines (Mechlin), Anvers (Antwerp), Hainaut, Namur, Brabant, Limbourg, Luxemburg, Holland, Zeeland, Gueldre-with-Zutphen, Utrecht, Over-Yssel, Friesland, Groningen. Afterwards Cambray was added. In 1609 these provinces were divided into two parts, one of which was called the seven provinces of Holland, or the ' United Provinces,' and the other ten formed the Spanish Netherlands.

Seventh Day Baptists (*The*). A section of the Christian Baptist sect founded for the express purpose of restoring the Jewish sabbath, or making Saturday ' the Lord's Day.' There are also ' Seventh Day Adventists' both in America and in Europe.

Seventy (*The*). I. The Jewish Sanhedrim or national council, which consisted of a president called *Nasi*, a deputy, sub-deputy, and seventy ordinary members. Their place of meeting was

called *The Pavement.* The seventy sat in the form of a crescent, thirty-five on each side of the throne.

II. A.D. 32. The seventy sent forth by Jesus to spread his mission. They were to go two by two, without purse, scrip, or change of shoes, but were endowed with the power of working miracles.

III. The seventy elders who were appointed to assist Moses in the wilderness (Num. xi. 16, 17).

Seventy Years' Captivity (*The*). I. B.C. 584-515. The captivity of the Jews in Babylon, which lasted seventy years. They were carried into captivity by Nebuchadnezzar, and released by Cyrus. Also called ' The Babylonish Captivity.'

II. 1305-1376. The time when the popes fixed their chair at Avignon, in France. It began with Clement V., and led to the Great Schism of the West (1378-1429).

Seventy Weeks (*Daniel's*). Supposing it to begin with the decree of Darius given to Ezra B.C. 491, and seventy weeks to mean 70 times 7 years (*i.e.* 490), this would bring us to the birth of Christ, ' when a finish was made to transgression, and an end put to sins by the reconciliation of the Messiah, the prince.'

Several Lands, lands enclosed, and separate from common lands. ' Nos pascua et campos seorsim ab aliis separatos *Severels* dicimus ' (Minsheu, Dictionary, 1617).

My lips are no common, though several they be (*i.e.* My lips are not common property, though they are not inclosed or hedged in).—SHAKESPEARE, *Love's Labour's Lost*, ii. 1.

Severians, a religious sect of the 2nd Christian cent. So named from Sevērus their leader. They were exaggerated Encratites (3 syl.) who abstained from marriage, animal food, and wine; denied the salvation of Adam and Eve, and taught the existence of æons (Eusebius, book iv. 29).

Seville (*Treaty of*), 9 Nov., 1729, between Great Britain, France, Holland, and Spain. In 1731 the kaiser joined, and the five powers coalesced in the Treaty of Vienna.

Sex Viri (*The*). In the University of Cambridge. There are two courts, one to hear accusations against members of the University not *in statu pupillari*; and the other a court of discipline for those who are *in statu pupillari.* The latter court consists of the chancellor and six heads of houses appointed by grace of the Senate. The former, also elected by grace, held office for two years. The Sex Viri can deprive of a degree, but there is the liberty of appeal to the Senate.

Sexages'ima Sunday, 60 days before Easter. In all such ecclesiastical terms as Septuagesima, Sexagesima, Quinquagesima, and Quadrigesima (Sunday), the week is reckoned as a ten-day week, because the octave and the two eves equal ten. *See* 'Sunday.' Thus:

1 eve of Sunday, 2 Sunday, 3 Monday, 4 Tuesday, 5 Wednesday, 6 Thursday, 7 Friday, 8 Saturday, 9 Octave Eve, and 10 Octave. So in music, 7 notes with the octave of the first note we call an 'Octave,' and the 3 days of the entombment were 1 eve of Saturday, 2 Saturday, 3 eve of Sunday.

Sext (*The*). A continuation of the Decretals of Raymond de Penafort. Like the Decretals, the Sext is in 5 books. It was compiled by order of Boniface VIII., and contains the rescripts from Gregory IX. to Boniface VIII. *See* 'Decretum.'

The 3rd part of the Corpus Juris Canonici is the Extravagantes Communes, containing the Clementines and Extravagantes Joannis (*i.e.* Clement V. and John XXII.).

Sforza the More, or 'Moor.' Ludovico Sforza was called 'the More,' from *morus*, a mulberry. Either from a mulberry-spot or stain on his right arm, or from his armorial bearing (1451–1508).

Sforzes'chi (*The*), 1409. The partisans or company of Sforza, formed after the death of Barbiano. *See* 'Bracces'-chi.'

Shadower (*The*). Apollodōrus, the Athenian painter (* –440 B.C.). Zeuxis was his pupil.

Shah (*The*). A diamond about half the size of the Orloff, given to the Emperor of Russia by Prince Cosroes, younger son of the Abbas Mirza, when he was in St. Petersburg. It weighs 86 carats, but is without a flaw or cloud.

Shah-zada, a king's son (Afghanistan).

Shakers, 1747. Reformed Quakers, led by James Wardley and his wife. They believe that the second coming of Christ is at hand. They are Unitarians, deny the doctrine of original sin, and the eternity of punishment. They say that baptism is the resurrection, and after baptism there is no marriage or giving in marriage, hence the married are then divorced, and the single must remain so. Anne Lee was their apostle, whom they called 'Mother'—that is, the mother of all living in the new creation. They are called Shakers from the shaking of their bodies in religious exercises. 'The fundamental principles of Shakerism are virgin purity, non-resistance, peace, equality in inheritance, and unspottedness from the world.'

The Lord promised He would shake the earth with terror (*Isa.* ii. 19). 'In that day there shall be a great shaking in the land of Israel' (*Ezek.* xxxviii. 19, 20). 'I will shake the heavens and the earth.' 'I will shake all nations, and the desire of all nations [*Anne Lee*] shall come.' 'Yet once more I will shake not the earth only, but also heaven' (*Heb.* xii. 26).

Shakespeare (*The Spanish*). Calderon [de la Barca], 1601–1687.

Shakespeare Cipher (*The*). In 1886 Mr. Donnelly, of Hastings, Minnesota, U.S., gave out that he had discovered by ciphers that Lord Francis Bacon was the author of the plays attributed to Shakespeare. The 'cipher' he referred to consisted of the blunders in pagination, hyphenation, bracketing of the great Folio edition of 1623, to which must be added capitalling words without any ostensible reason (thus the word Bacon is capitalised even in such compounds as 'Bacon-fed'), and in the use of italics. In regard to italics he says: In '1 Henry IV.' there are 7 italic words in the first column, p. 53; by multiplying these 2 ciphers we get 53 × 7 = 371, and the 371st word is 'Bacon.' Again. On p. 67 of the same play the first column contains 6 words in italics, and 67 × 6 = 402, which word is 'St. Albans.' In this sort of way Mr. Donnelly reads a minute history of Lord Bacon in cipher, and affirms that all the blunders and irregularities of the printed plays were designed. The secret writing was adopted out of fear of the jealousy of Queen Elizabeth, who looked on some of the plays, as for example 'Richard II.,' as no better than high treason.

Shakespeare du Boulevard. Guilbert de Pixérécourt (1773–1844).

Shakespeare of Divines (*The*). Jeremy Taylor, bishop of Down (1613 -

3 G 2

1667). So called by Emerson from the fertility of his mind and the extent of his imagination.

Shakespeare of Eloquence (*The*), the Comte de Mirabeau (1749–1791). So called by Barnave.

Shakespeare of Germany (*The*). August Friedrich Ferdinand von Kotzebue (1761–1819).

We may parody the words of Coleridge on Klopstock, the German Milton, 'A very German Milton indeed.' Certainly Kotzebue is a very German Shakespeare indeed.

Shakespeare of Harmony (*The*). Richard Wagner (1813–1864).

This is a very exaggerated comparison.

Shakespeare of Painting (*The*). Salvator Rosa (1615–1673). So called by Garrick.

Shakespeare of Prose Fiction (*The*). Richardson the novelist (1689–1761). So called by D'Israeli.

Shaking Hands.
To confirm a bargain, mentioned 2 Kings x. 15.

As a salutation, mentioned by Homer, by Aristophanês ('Nubes,' 18), and by Virgil ('Æn.' i. 403).

In modern times the custom is English; most continental nations salute with kisses.

Shalmaneser, that is, Shalman of Assyria, son and successor of Tiglath Pileser. He reigned 14 years (A.M. 3276–3290, *i.e.* B.C. 724–710).

Sham'anism. The religious doctrines of the ancient Hungarians, and of many modern North Asiatics. The Shaman worshippers adored one supreme god called *Isten* with sundry inferior spirits, as the gods of the mountains, the woods, the springs, the rivers, fire, thunder, and so on. They offered sacrifice, especially white horses. Their priests were called *Táltos, Kam,* or *Shaman,* who were like the Roman augurs.

Shan'avests and **Car'avats,** 1808, the Ribbon-men of Tipperary, Kilkenny, Cork, and Limerick. They were rival factions. *See* 'Irish Associations.'

Neither the persons executed for these outrages nor anyone else could tell what was the dispute. It was notorious who were Caravats and who were Shanavests, and this was all.—ARNOLD.

Shâng Dynasty. *See* 'Chang.'

'Sharp Knife.' So General Jackson was called by the Indians against whom he fought in 1813 (1767–1845).

Shas'tras. A compilation of books in Sanskrit, containing the Upa-Vedas, the Up-Angas, and the Ved-Angas (*q.v.*), books upon the religious tenets of the Hindûs, their laws, the sciences, and the Sanskrit language, with two heroic poems. The Shastras teach that there is one supreme god called Brahm, but a triad deity consisting of Brahma, Vishnu, and Shiva.

She - majesty - generalissimo (*The*). Marie Henrietta, wife of Charles I., so called herself in 1643. At the death of Charles she married Lord Jermyn, and died 1669, at Colombe Castle, near Paris.

It is said she had a child by Lord Jermyn while Charles was alive.

She-wolf of France. I. Isabelle, wife of Edward II., who, according to a tradition, being in love with Mortimer, murdered her husband by thrusting a red-hot iron into his body. Hence Gray says, ' She-wolf of France, who tear'st the bowels of thy mangled mate.' She was the daughter of Philippe IV. of France.

II. Margaret wife of Henry VI. is so called by Shakespeare, '3 Hen. VI.' act i. sc. 4. She was the daughter of René le Bon, titular king of Sicily, but was brought up in the French court. In the war of the Two Roses she sided with the Lancastrians or Red-Rose faction. She is generally called Marguerite d'Anjou.

As a rule the French wives of our English sovereigns have not turned out well.

Sheb'sen. A Jewish sect founded by Sabathai Sevi of Smyrna (1625–1676). He proclaimed himself to be the Messiah, and found numerous followers in Germany, Poland, Italy, and Holland; but Sultan Mohammed IV. cast him into prison. They put a mystical meaning on the Bible and rejected wholly the Talmud. The last of the sect died in 1791.

Sheepshanks Exhibition. Astronomy. For undergraduates in the University of Cambridge. Value about 50*l.* a year, tenable for three years. The successful candidate must be or must become a student of Trinity College. Founded by the Rev. Richard Sheepshanks, fellow of Trinity, 1858.

Sheffield Trade Outrages, 1866–

1867. Mainly connected with the Saw-grinders', Saw-makers', and Saw-handle-makers' Unions, and brought to a head in Oct. 1866 by the murder of one Fearne-hough of Hereford Street, whose house was blown up with gunpowder because he refused to conform to the rules of the union of his trade. A reward of 1240l. was offered for the discovery of the per-petrator of this outrage, but without effect. At length the government sent down three Royal Commissioners to in-quire into the matter, and they sat for twenty-five days, from 3 June to 8 July, 1867. Their report states that there were sixty unions in Sheffield, thirteen of which encouraged outrages.

Several centuries ago the artisans of Sheffield had their trade laws, which in 1624 were revised. By these laws—

Every artisan was bound to contribute to the union of his trade.

The number of men allowed to be employed was stated, their wages fixed, and the masters allowed to be employers were named.

The enforced holidays were every Monday, a month at Christmas time, and twenty-eight days from 8 Aug.

No person was allowed to work without serving a seven-years' apprenticeship.

The chief of the gang of outragers was William Broadhead, an innkeeper, at whose house the committee met, and his tools were Samuel Crookes (employed to shoot people and throw gunpowder into obnoxious houses) and James Hallam, who revealed the whole matter.

Charles Reade, in his novel 'Put Yourself in his Place,' gives a most powerful and graphic descrip-tion of the organisation, management, and doings of these unions.

Sheik ul Gebel (*The*). Hussun

Subah, called the 'Old Man of the Mountain' (*q.v.*).

Sheldo'nian Theatre (*The*), 1669.

Erected by Gilbert Sheldon, archbishop of Canterbury and chancellor of the University of Oxford. It corresponds with the Cambridge Senate-house (*q.v.*).

Shemham-phorasch (*The*). A

talisman made of parchment on which the sacred names were written.

A juggler came to Albert duke of Saxony and offered to impart to him the gift of infallibility. 'Well,' quoth the duke, 'that I may make sure of it, I will make the first trial on you.' So saying, he drew his sword and so hacked the impostor that not even the Shemham-phorasch could cure him.

Shepherd Earl of Cumberland

(*The*). Henry de Clifford, the tenth baron by writ (died 1523). His mother, to save him from the Yorkists, sent him to be brought up by a shepherd; but in 1485 Henry VII. 'restored him in blood and honours,' and he was summoned to

Parliament the same year (15 Sept.). His son and successor was the first to discontinue the *de* before the name.

Henry de Clifford was not earl of Cumberland The first Clifford who bore that title was Henry Clifford his son, created earl of Cumberland 18 July, 1525, 'uppon the joyefull newes of the Emperours victorie at Pavie, in Italy.'

Shepherdess of Dauphiny

(*The*). Isabeau Vincent, who was only sixteen when she first appeared as a Camisard prophetess. She could neither write nor read, but was believed to be a worker of miracles, and prophesied 'without the slightest appearance of convulsion, and with a scarcely per-ceptible movement of the lips.'

Shere or Sheer Thursday.

Maundy Thursday, or day preceding Good Friday. The Northern 'Skyre Thursday,' Icelandic 'Skíri-þórsdagr,' Maundy Thursday. Anglo-Saxon *scír*, sheer; Icelandic *skíra*, to cleanse. *See* SKEAT, 'Etymological Dictionary,' ar-ticle *Sheer*. Miles Phillips (1583) quaintly says: 'In olde fader's dayes the people wolde that day shere theyr hedes, and clyppe theyr berdes, and polle theyr hedes, and so make theym honest ayenst Ester day.'

Sheridan's Begums Speech,

1787. One of the impeachments of Warren Hastings, governor-general of India (1774–1785). This speech lasted five hours, and produced such an effect that the house arose and adjourned till the next day. It is said that Sheridan wrote the best comedy ('The School for Scandal'), made the best speech (the third charge against Warren Hastings), and composed the best convivial song ('Here's to the Maiden of Bashful Fifteen') in the language. *See* 'Hast-ings' and 'Begums.'

Sheriff is a 'shire-reve' and the

chief officer of the county, who does all the crown business thereof. The judges, on the morrow of St. Martin (12 Nov.), meet in the Exchequer and propose three persons for each county, whose names are presented to the sovereign, who pricks one of them, and the person selected remains in office for one year or till a successor is appointed. The sheriff superintends the election of knights of the shire, coroners, and verderers. He is in the commission of the peace, and is *ex-officio* the first man in the county.

Every sheriff appoints a deputy or under-sheriff. It is customary for the high sheriff to receive and escort the judges to the assize court ; and in cases of disturbance it is his duty to summon the *posse comitatus* (*i.e.* all the people of the county) to assist him in keeping the peace.

Some cities (like Norwich) are both cities and counties, and then the borough sheriff is part of the municipal corporation (addressed as Mr. Sheriff So-and-so). The county sheriff is termed the 'high sheriff.'

Sheriff-tooth. A tenure by the service of providing entertainment for the sheriff at his county court. A tax for the sheriff's diet. Obsolete.

Sherrardian Professorship (*The*) of Botany in Oxford University. Stipend 200*l.* a year. Founded by Dr. Sherrard in 1728.

Sherwood Forester (*The*). Dr. Spencer T. Hall.

Shibboleth. When the Ephraimites, after their defeat by Jephthah, tried to pass the Jordan, a guard stationed on the banks of the river tested everyone who came to the ford by asking him to pronounce the word ' Shibboleth,' which the men of Ephraim called *sibboleth.* Everyone who said ' sibboleth ' was immediately cut down by the guard, and there fell in one day 42,000 Ephraimites (Judges xii. 1–6).

Shield of Rome (*The*). Quintus Fabius Maximus, died 203, called the Lingerer (Cunctator), and the Lamb (Ovicula) for his mild apathetic disposition.

Shi'ites (2 syl.), or ' Shiahs.' A Musulman sect opposed to the Sunnites. They recognise Ali as the real successor of Mahomet, and his descendants as the true imams. The word means *heretics,* and of course was given to them by the Sunnites, who call themselves the Orthodox party. The Musulmans of Persia, and some of those in India, Mesopotamia, Syria, and north of Asia are Shiites ; but those of the Ottoman empire, Arabia, Egypt, Afghanistan, Malaya, &c., are Sunnites.

In India the majority are Sunnites.

Shin'toism. A religious system which prevails, side by side with Buddhism, in Japan. It is a 'religion of reason,' requiring no temples, but having a sanctuary into which nobody but the Mika'do and his priests ever enter. The Shintos profess to worship nature, ancestors, and the Mikado. Their code of duty is to obey natural instincts and the laws of the state. Since 1868 Shintoism has been restored in Japan, and now overpowers Buddhism.

Shintoism is a sort of Agnosticism, which it resembles in many respects. Neither doctrine nor dogma can find place in either system, nor anything that does not commend itself to reason.

Ship Money. A tax to supply and fit out ships to protect our coast and our merchant vessels from corsairs and hostile states. In 1007 all proprietors of 310 hides of land were taxed to equip a fleet against the Danes. Queen Elizabeth required various ports to fit out a certain number of ships against the armada. Charles I. levied ship money to restore the palsgrave to his throne. The attorney-general Noye put the king up to the dodge, and it was given out that our commerce needed protection from pirates, Turkish corsairs, and the French and Dutch mariners ; so all the counties were taxed without consent of parliament, and the king was furnished with 218,500*l.* for his personal use, the tax being a money payment of 3,300*l.* per ship, instead of ι ps themselves. It was first levied on London in May, 1634 ; in the spring following on other maritime counties ; later on it was demanded from the inland counties. In 1636 the judges determined it was legal, but so great was the outcry that it was abolished (17 Car. I. c. 14).

Ship of Fools (*The*), or ' Narenschiff,' 1494, by Sebastian Brandt, a Strasburg lawyer (1458–1520). An allegorical satire in verse, in the Suabian dialect, and divided into 110 chapters, immensely popular at the time. It does not attack religious and moral delinquencies so much as social gaucheries. The tale is, a transport-ship of this world, laden with fools, and bound for Fools' Paradise (*Narrgonia*), was capsized by Antichrist. The voyagers, tossed on the surface of the waves, sought safety, some by prayer, some by scrambling into a crazy boat, and some by clinging to parts of the wreck. The sea was also strewn with books of an heretical character. The moral to be drawn from this allegory is that the abuse of printing will wreck the earth. The superstitious, he says, waste their lives watching the jumps of grasshoppers, knights enter church with hawk and hound, tradesmen have no honesty, manners at table are most gauche—carvers choose the best parts for themselves, some eat too fast, some talk too loud, and some engross the general conversation.

In 1860 an English translation by R. H. Mackenzie was published, with illustrations by Crowquill, and in 1880 another by Thomas Roscoe.

Shire'men (2 syl.)., now called earls. In Saxon times they had shires committed to their supervision.

Shire-mote was an assembly in Anglo-Saxon England of the county or shire, held twice a year, and presided over by the shire-reeve or sheriff. In this court all the rights of the crown and church, connected with the shire, were settled, and all disputes about land were adjudicated. Our county courts are shire-motes, and the judge or presiding magistrate of these courts is a shire-man. The shire-motes were often held under a tree in the open air. In these motes the king's writs were published; demands of aid were announced, the presentment of criminals was received, local jurors were pricked, the taxes of each district were adjusted, and appeals from the 'soke,' or lesser courts of the hundred, were heard. It was inferior to the Witenagemote, but superior to the Folk-mote (*q.v.*).

Shorn Moss (*The*), in Weardale, Scotland. A pathway cut through a great bog, which was filled with fagots, over which the Scotch army made a backward movement when they wished to retreat from the army of Edward III. in 1327.

Short Parliament (*The*), or the Three-week Parliament. From 13 April to 3 May, 1640. There were three shorter ones, but this • Three-week Parliament was called the 'Short Parliament' because it was followed by the 'Long Parliament.' *See* 'Parliaments, the Six Short.'

The Scots had made demands for triennial parliaments and for freedom both of elections and of debate, but the Earl of Strafford advised that the rogues should be whipped back into their senses, and the king summoned a parliament to raise money to stamp out 'the Scotch treason.' The new parliament distinctly declared that redress of grievances must precede a grant of supplies, and the parliament was summarily dissolved. It was the last that Charles I. dissolved.

Short Swords of Livonia (*The*), or 'Order of Christ,' 1205. Instituted in Livonia by Albert bishop of Riga, and incorporated with the Teutonic Knights in 1237.

Shortest Parliament (*The*). 7 days, from 21 to 28 March, 1681. The fifth and last of Charles II. It was held at Oxford. *See* 'Parliaments.'

Shrove Tuesday. The day before Ash Wednesday, the first day of Lent. So called because Catholics confess on that day and obtain absolution. To *shrive* is to absolve from sin.

Sibylline Prophecies. Twelve in number, manifestly a clumsy forgery of the 16th cent. They are as follows:—

1. The *Agrippīnan*, Sibylla Agrippīna: 'Jesus Christ shall be outraged and scourged.'

Emblem, a whip.

2. The *Cumæan*, Sibylla Cumæa: 'God shall be born of a pure virgin, and commune with sinners.'

Emblem, a cradle.

3. The *Cumānian*, Sibylla Cumāna: 'Jesus Christ shall descend from heaven, and live in poverty on earth.'

Emblem, a crown.

4. The *Delphic*, Sibylla Delphīca: 'The prophet born of the virgin shall be crowned with thorns.'

Emblem, a crown of thorns.

5. The *Erythræan*, Sibylla Erythræa: 'Jesus Christ, son of God, the Saviour of the world.'

Emblem, a horn.

6. The *Europæan*, Sibylla Europæa: 'A virgin and her son shall flee into Egypt.'

Emblem, a sword.

7. The *Hellespontic*, Sibylla Hellespontīca: 'Jesus Christ shall suffer shame upon the cross.'

Emblem, a T (tau).

8. The *Libyan*, Sibylla Libўca: 'The day shall come when men shall see the universal king.'

Emblem, a lighted taper.

9. The *Persian*, Sibylla Persīca: 'Satan shall be subdued by the true prophet.'

Emblem, a lantern, and a dragon under the sibyl's feet.

10. *Phrygian*, Sibylla Phrygĭca: 'Our Lord shall rise again.'

Emblem, a cross and a banner.

11. The *Samian*, Sibylla Samia: 'The rich one shall be born of a pure virgin.'

Emblem, a rose.

12. The *Tiburtine*, Sibylla Tiburtīna: 'The Highest shall descend from heaven, and a virgin shall be shown in the valleys of the desert.'

Emblem, a dove.   *See below.*

Sibylline Verses. These go back probably to the 2nd cent., when enthusiasts of Alexandria 'prophesied' oracularly. Whatever merit might be attached to the originals, it is quite certain the 'prophecies' were interpolated and falsified to assist the views of those interested in the propagation of the Christian faith. The utterances of these sibyllists form a special department of early ecclesiastical literature, and are a mixture of Jewish, Pagan and Christian doctrines.

Sibyllists. Those Christians who corroborated the Christian religion by references to what they termed 'Sibylline prophecies.' These verses were the forgeries of a Jew of Alexandria, added to from time to time by Christians, as they wanted to corroborate certain doctrines.

It is most regretable that for many centuries the Catholic clergy and their learned adherents thought it no shame to interpolate, mutilate, and falsify books at pleasure, in order to make them instruments of ecclesiastical dogmas and traditions. But so it was, and they actually defended the practice, as it 'caught men by guile,' as St. Paul did.

Sicilian Expedition (*The*), B.C. 415–410. In the seventeenth year of the Peloponnesian War, Alcibiădēs induced the Athenians to send a powerful armament to Sicily in order to re-establish the Ionian interest in the island. A magnificent fleet was equipped, and a large land force prepared, but the expedition was most disastrous; the fleet was ruined, and most of the land forces were either slain or taken prisoners. The Lacedæmonians joined the Syracusians against the Athenians. This terrible affair was the Moscow of Athenian greatness.

Sicilian Ox (*The*). Thomas Aquīnas (1224–1274). Called *ox* from his great size, and Sicilian because he was a native of Naples and allied to the Sicilian kings.

Sicilian Table (*A*). A table spread with aldermanic luxuries. Mithæcos tells us that the Sicilians were as remarkable for their luxurious living as the Spartans for their simplicity of diet.

Sicilian Vespers (*The*), 30 March, 1282 (Easter Monday). The massacre of the French in Sicily out of hatred to Charles of Anjou, king of the Two Sicilies. A Sicilian bride, going to vespers, happened to pass with her train by a house where some Frenchmen were holding the festival of Easter. One of them, named Drouet, advanced towards the bride under pretence of seeking for arms (which no Sicilian was allowed to carry), and in so doing behaved rudely to her. A young Sicilian instantly stabbed him with his sword. This led to a riot, in which the Sicilians put to death 8,000 of the French. A war ensued in which Charles of Anjou was over and over again defeated, and he died in 1285.

It is somewhat remarkable that a similar outrage occurred on the 4th of April, the same year, at Catania. In this case the young Frenchman was Jean Viglemada, the young lady was Julia Villamelli, whose husband was slain by the libertine.

Sicilies (*The Two*). The island of Sicily is one, and the kingdom of Naples is the other. United under Roger II. 1130. In 1062 Robert Guiscard and his brother Roger commenced the subjugation of Sicily, and in ten years drove the Saracens out of the island, when Roger was made count of Sicily (1072). He died 1102, and was succeeded by his son Roger II. Meantime Robert Guiscard, as sovereign of Naples, Puglia, and Calabria, added Corfu and a great part of Romania to his dominions. He died 1185, leaving his son, Roger Bursa, his successor. Roger Bursa died 1130 without issue, when his cousin Roger II., count and king of Sicily, succeeded to the kingdom of Naples, and called himself king of the Two Sicilies.

After the Sicilian Vespers in 1282 Sicily was severed for a time from Naples; but the kingdom of the Two Sicilies was restored, and was at last destroyed by Garibaldi in 1860.

Corfu, pronounce *Kor-foo*.

Sicyon'ian School of Painting (*The*). Chief representatives were Eupompos, Pamphĭlos, and Apellês.

Sicyon'ian School of Sculpture (*The*). Chief representatives were Euphrānon and Lysippos. The characteristics of this school were the representation of heroic strength and the forms of athletes. Alexander allowed only Lysippos and Apellês to represent him.

Side'tes (3 syl.). Antīŏchus VII., so called from Sidê in Pamphylia, where he was brought up (B.C. 137-128).

Sidmouth's and Castlereagh's Five Acts, Nov. and Dec. 1819. I. An Act to prevent the training of persons to the use of arms; II. An Act to punish blasphemous and pernicious libels; III. An Act to authorise magistrates to seize arms collected and kept for purposes dangerous to the public peace; IV. An Act to prevent seditious assemblies; V. Castlereagh's bill for stamps on newspapers. Called 'The Five Acts' by the partisans of Sir F. Burdett, William Hunt, and William Hone, because they aimed especially to cripple them in their proceedings.

Castlereagh, pronounce *Castle-ray.*

Sidney Sussex College, in Cambridge University. Founded by Lady Frances Sidney, countess dowager of Sussex, in 1594.

Sidonian Era (*The*). This era began Oct. B.C. 110. *See* 'Era.'

Siege or Obsidional Pieces. Coins for the nonce issued by Charles I. during the parliamentary wars. They were, for the most part, articles of silver clipped into pieces, and stamped with some rude device of a castle the letters O B S, the date, and the nominal value of the piece.

Siete Partidas (*Las*), 1260. A code of Alfonso X. which in 1501 became the universal law of the land.

No deputies were present from the kingdom of Leon in the cortes of Alcala in 1348 when the code of the Siete Partidas first obtained a legislative recognition.—HALLAM, *Middle Ages,* vol. ii. p. 30.

Sigillum Confessionis. 'The Seal of Confession,' the obligation of a confessor under no condition whatsoever to divulge to any living creature the secrets of the confessional. This rule of secrecy may be traced back to the 4th cent., but was not rendered obligatory till the 12th, when Innocent III. made its violation the most heinous of offences, and he who was proved guilty was punished by the severest penalties which the church could inflict.

Sigismund, properly 'Siegmund.' 'The Light of the World,' last of the promiscuous kaiser-kings of Germany (1368, 1410-1437). In this reign Huss and Jerome of Prague were burnt alive as 'heretics.' The house of Habsburg succeeded him.

Father, Karl IV.(the pope's kaiser); *Mother,* Anne of Schweidnitz; *Wives,* (1) Maria of Anjou, queen of Hungary, (2) Barbara called the Messalina of Germany. *Contemporary* with Henry V. and Henry VI.

Wenceslaus the Worthless was his brother.

. Sigismund was called 'Supra Grammaticam,' from his bad Latinity. Being one day reminded of a solecism, he replied: 'Ego sum Imperator Romanorum et supra grammaticam.'

Signory (*The*), or 'Signoria,' of Venice, 1173. The privy council of the doge; it consisted of six members, one for each district or *sestiere.* The college consisted of twenty-six members, viz. the Doge, the Signory, the three *Capi dei Quaranta* (chief members of the Forty), and sixteen Savii chosen by the Senate.

In Florence it consisted of eight priors with a Gonfalonier of Justice, who dwelt at the public charge in the palazzo, and held office for only two months.

Signs removed, 1766. Shop signs projecting over the footpaths were ordered to be removed from the streets of London, because their dripping in rainy weather and thaws was a nuisance to passengers.

Si-Han, or Western Hân. The first sixteen kings of the Hân dynasty of China (B.C. 202-25). These were about the best of the Chinese emperors. The second half of the dynasty was the Tong or Eastern Hân.

'Si j'avance, suivez-moi; si je recule, tuez-moi; si je tombe, vengez-moi.' The address of Henri de Larochejaquelein in the Vendean war 1794.

Sikhism. A compromise between Brahmanism and Mahometanism, advocated by Nânak (1469-1539) of Lahore. To him succeeded nine pontiffs called gurus (or teachers), the last of whom was Govind, who was assassinated in 1708. *See* 'Sikhs.'

It was Govind who called the Sikhs 'singhs,' or lions.

Sikhs, 1494, *i.e. disciples* [of Nânak the Neo-Brahman]. Nânak of Lahore (1469-1539) was their first pontiff, or 'guru,' and was succeeded by nine others. The sixth, named Har-govind, rebelled against the Great Mogul and the tenth, or last guru, named Govind, taught that the duty of a sikh is ' to be humble and sincere, to eschew superstition, to practise strict morality, and to live by the sword.' On the decline of the Mogul empire, the power of the sikhs rapidly increased, and in 1764 they assumed the state of a distinct nation, or rather federation of twelve states. In 1805 Runjit Singh became head of the federation. After the death of Runjit Singh, a series of battles occurred against the British—as that of Moodkee, 18 Dec., 1845; that of Ferozeshah, 21, 22 Dec., 1845; Aliwal, 28 Jan., 1846; Sobrāon, 10 Feb., 1846; Chillianwallah, 13 June, 1846; Goojĕrāt, 21 Feb., 1849, when the Punjab was annexed to British India.

The Sikhs worship one God, without image or mediator ; they eat all kinds of meat except beef, the ox being too useful to be eaten. They dress in blue, even to their turbans ; but other Hindûs consider blue to be unlucky. Their sacred book is called ' Pothi,' which means ' Bible.'

Silent (*The*). William I. the stadtholder of the United Provinces.

Our own king, William III., like his father and grandfather, was noted for his silence. After the battle of Wierden, in 1672, one of his officers asked him what next. ' Can you keep a secret ?' asked William. ' Yes,' said the officer. ' And so can I,' replied the Prince, drily.

Silent Week, or ' Holy Week '—that is, the week beginning with Palm Sunday and ending with Holy Saturday. So called because no bells are rung in churches during the Hebdomada Muta.

Silent'iary (*The*). Anastāsius I., emperor of the east (491–518), was so called because he had been the chief officer whose duty it was to maintain peace and silence in the precincts of the palace.

Sile'sia was divided into three governments—viz. Liegnitz, Breslau, and Oppeln. At the death of Kaiser Karl VI. numerous claimants put in claims for parts of the empire. Prussia demanded Silesia ; Sardinia demanded Milan ; Spain demanded Bohemia and Hungary ; and Bavaria claimed the whole empire.

Maria Theresa, daughter of Karl VI., was Queen of Hungary, and nominally Kaiserin. It was from this sovereign that Friedrich the Great claimed Silesia, and, after seven years' war it was added to the kingdom of Prussia.

In 1537 the Duke of Leignitz made an agreement with the Elector of Brandenburg that if either died without issue, the survivor should have both realms. In 1675 the Duke of Leignitz died without issue, but Kaiser Leopold I. claimed the dukedom as a forfeited fief. At the death of Karl VI., the Elector of Brandenburg (then Friedrich II. the Great, king of Prussia) claimed Silesia as his right, and this led to the three Silesian wars (1740–1763).

Sile'sian Poets (*The*), of the 17th cent. Martin Opitz (1597–1639), ' the father of modern German poetry ' ; Paul Flemming (1609–1640), the ' German Herrick ' ; Andrew Gryph (1616–1664), the ' father of the modern German drama ' ; and Gaspar Lohenstein (1635–1683), the ' blood and thunder ' dramatist.

Sile'sian Wars (*The*). Three wars between Maria Theresa of Austria and Friedrich II. the Great of Prussia, for the possession of Silesia. *First* war 1740–1742, when, by the treaty of Berlin, Silesia was handed over to Prussia. *Second* war : Prussia having made alliance with France broke the treaty, and a second war broke out in 1744. This was concluded by the treaty of Dresden, 25 Dec., 1745, when Silesia was again confirmed to Prussia. The *Third* was the Seven Years' War, and consisted of seven campaigns (1756–1763). By the Peace of Hubertsburg Silesia was finally confirmed to Prussia.

Field-Marshal Daun was by far the best general on the Austrian side, and Friedrich II. the Great on the Prussian side.

Silk Armour. A sort of armour worn by timid magistrates in the troublous times of Charles II. It consisted of a doublet and breeches of quilted silk, so closely stitched, and of such thickness, as to be proof against either bullet or steel ; while a thick bonnet of the same materials, with ear-flaps attached to it, and resembling a nightcap in shape, completed the equipment, and assured the wearer security from head to knee. Roger North describes this sort of armour, and Sir W. Scott avails himself of North's description in ' Peveril of the Peak,' chap. xxxii.

Silken Lord (*The*). Lord Thomas Fitzgerald (1513–1536), son of the Earl of Kildare. So called from the richness of his caparisons. He threw up his office of vice-deputy of Ireland in 1534, and was hanged at Tyburn for treason 3 Feb., 1535. Also called ' Silken Thomas.'

During his confinement he was lacking in the commonest necessaries of life ; and the ' silken lord,' bare-footed and bare-legged, was indebted to the charity of his fellow-prisoners for the few tattered garments that hardly covered him. ' I have never had since I came into pryson eny other garment but a syngyll fryse gowne, nothyr hosyn,

dublet, shoys, nor shyrt but on—and so I go bare-
foote and barelegyd, and shuld have don styll,
but that som pore prysoners have geven me old
hosyn and shoys and shyrtes.'—*Letter to Rothe*,
S.P. clviii.

Silly. Nickname of the Duke of
Marlborough, from his constant use of
this word when he disapproved of a sug-
gestion: as 'Will your Grace besiege
Lisle?' 'Oh, silly.' 'Will you besiege
Ypres?' 'No! silly, silly!' (1650–1722).

Silly Billy. I. The nickname of
William IV. of Great Britain, sometimes
called *The Sailor King*, because he was
lord high admiral of the navy (1765,
1830–1837).

II. William Frederick duke of Glou-
cester, chancellor of the university of
Cambridge. He was the son of William
Henry, a younger brother of George III.,
and died 1834. He married his cousin
Mary, a daughter of George III.

It is said that William duke of Gloucester was
shown one day over an asylum, and one of the inmates said ' Why, here is Silly Billy.' The duke
in amazement said to the keeper, ' The man
knows me.' 'Yes,' said the keeper, 'like all
lunatics he has his lucid intervals.'

Silver Book (*The*). The MS. of the
four gospels in Mæso-Gothic by Ulfilas
bishop of the Goths in the 4th cent., preserved in the library of Upsåla, in Sweden.
All the letters are silver except the
initials, which are gold. The leaves are
vellum; some purple, and others of a
violet colour.

Silver Captain (*The*). Admiral
Sir Henry Digby, who, 14 Oct., 1790, fell
in with a Spanish vessel while shaping
his course for Cape St. Vincent. It is said
that each captain received 40,000*l.*, and
each seamen 200*l.* as his share of this
prize, and 63 artillery wagons were
employed to convey the treasure to Plymouth citadel.

Another account states that each midshipman
received 10,000*l.* as his share of this rich prize.

Silver Casket (*The*), 1568. A casket
found in Edinburgh Castle after Mary
(queen of Scots) delivered it up to Murray
and Sir John Balfour. This casket contained letters of the queen to Balfour, and
love sonnets. When Mary fled to England, and was in the hands of Elizabeth,
commissioners were appointed to examine
into the recent murder of Lord Darnley
(Mary's husband), and this casket with
its contents was laid before them. The
originals have disappeared, but copies of

the letters and sonnets are still extant.
Whether these copies have been tampered
with is a question *sub judice*, but they
certainly are most discreditable to Mary.

Silver Code (*The*), or 'Codex Ar-
gentĕus' (*q.v.*). *See* ' Silver Book.'

Silver Crown (*The*). The crown of
the King of Germany. As king of Lombardy, he was crowned with the iron crown
(*q.v.*), and as kaiser of the Holy Roman
Empire he was crowned with the imperial
crown, which was a small episcopal mitre
cleft in the *front* and not at the sides.
He was crowned with the silver crown at
Aix-la-Chapelle; with the iron crown at
Monza; and with the imperial crown at
Rome.

The kings of Germany did not go to Rome to be
crowned latterly. Karl V. was the last kaiser who
received his imperial crown from the hands of the
pope.

Silver Hand. I. Nuad, the chieftain who led back the tribe of the Danaans from Scotland to Ireland, from
which they had migrated. Nuad of the
Silver Hand had an artificial hand made
of silver by Cred the goldsmith, to supply the loss sustained from a wound
received in the battle of Moytura. Miach
son of Dian Kect set it on the wrist.
So says O'Flaherty, ' Ogygia,' part iii.
chap. x.

The battle of Moytura was long a favourite
theme of Irish song. In the library of Stowe are
five metrical chronicles of this famous fight.

II. An order instituted by Abd-el-Kader
for ' the most worthy.' The hand was
fastened to the camel's bridle. The order
contained three ranks or degrees, the
highest having seven fingers, and the
lowest five. *See* ' Golden Hand.'

Silver People (*The*). So the Arabs
call the inhabitants of the Tell, or cultivated lands of the northern slope from
the Mediterranean to the Atlas mountains; the inhabitants of the towns they
term the *Gold* people; and those of the
Sahāra they call the *Camel* people.

Silver Stick. An officer of the
Second Life Guards, who carries an
ebony staff surmounted by a silver head,
and relieves Gold Stick when on duty in
attendance on the royal person. For
particulars *see* p. 371, ' Gold Stick.'

Silver Tongue. Daniel Finch 2nd
earl of Nottingham (1647–1730).

Silver-tongued (*The*). Spranger Barry, the Irish Roscius (1719–1777).

Simcha Thora (joy for the law). Last of the eight days of Succoth, or Feast of Tabernacles, held by the Jews in the month Tisri (Sept.). This day was, and still is, a day of joy.

Simeons of Van or **Ormia** (*The*). One of the three branches of the Nestorians. The other two are the 'Elijahs of Mosul,' and the 'Josephs of Amïda.'

Simmes' Hole. *See* 'Symmes' Hole.'

Simnel Conspiracy (*The*), 1486. A plot concocted by Richard Simons, a priest of Oxford, to palm off his ward, Lambert Simnel, a lad of about 11 years of age, and the son of an Oxford joiner, as Edward earl of Warwick, son of George duke of Clarence, and heir to the throne of England. Supported by many of the Anglo-Irish lords in the Pale, he was crowned in St. Mary's Abbey by the Bishop of Meath, with a diadem borrowed for the occasion from a statue of the Virgin Mary, as 'Edward VI., king of England and France, and lord of Ireland.' He invaded England, and was made prisoner by Henry VII. at the battle of Stoke near Newark ; but, instead of being put to death, he was made turnspit boy in the royal kitchen, and afterwards falconer.

Simon the Righteous (*Sir*). Simon de Montfort earl of Leicester, and brother-in-law of Henry III. (1200–1265). He was very popular, and his death was deemed almost a martyrdom, for few kings have been more detested than Henry III. and his father John.

Simo'nians (*The*). So called from Simon Magus, who believed that the body of Jesus Christ was not a real body, but a mere phantom, like any other visible form of God or angel spoken of in the Old Testament.

Simon'ides (*Constantine L. Philip*). A literary impostor (1824–1867). While on a visit in the monastery of Khosos in Mount Athos, he fell in with some Greek MSS. greatly damaged by mildew, and taught himself Greek manuscript writing. He soon afterwards succeeded in imposing spurious MSS. on the learned of Athens

and Constantinople, but, being detected, he fled to England. In 1854 he offered some genuine MSS. to the British Museum, and then tried to pass off his forgeries; but was found out by Sir Frederick Madden, and of course foiled. However, Sir T. Phillips bought of him a spurious MS. of Homer on serpent's skin, which he professed to have belonged to Chios Hipparchos, son of Pisistrãtos. He then sold some genuine MSS. to the Bodleian, but was again detected when he offered his forgeries. Some time after he sent to Berlin a palimpsest MS. in Greek of Egyptian kings, said by him to be the work of Uranios of Alexandria. Professor Dindorf began to publish this work, but Ehrenberg discovered that it was only a bad translation of the writings of Bunsen and Lepsius. Simonïdês was now imprisoned, but, being released, retired to Alexandria, where he died of leprosy. *See* 'Literary Forgeries.'

Si'nait'ic MS. (*The*) of the Bible. So called from the place where it was discovered by Dr. Tischendorf, at St. Catherine Convent, foot of Mount Sinai, in May 1844. On his first visit the monks allowed him to take away eleven sheets. At his second visit only one sheet remained, the rest having been used for lighting fires. Fifteen years later he was shown a bundle of waste paper, which to his delight contained parts of the Old Testament and all the New. This MS. is now preserved in the library of St. Petersburg. The date is supposed to be the middle of the 4th cent. *See* 'Vatican MS.' and 'Alexandrine MS.'

Singeing the King of Spain's Beard, 1587. So Sir Francis Drake called his raid upon Spain when the Armada was in active preparation. On 18 April he entered the road of Cadiz and destroyed upwards of 80 vessels ; he then ran over to Cape St. Vincent, and demolished above 100 more, with 4 forts ; and he next captured in the Tagus the magnificent ship called 'St. Philip.' All these vessels were designed to take part in the invasion.

Singh (a lion). An Indian title of royalty. In 1695 Govind abolished the system of castes, and changed the title of sikh (*deist*) into 'singh,' as Runjeet Singh of Lahore.

Single Bill Session (*A*). The autumn session of the British parliament in 1884, called by Mr. Gladstone to pass his Franchise Bill, rejected by the House of Lords in the preceding session the same year.

Single-speech Hamilton, 1755. This speech was delivered by William Gerald Hamilton upon the king's (George II.) speech demanding subsidies for Hesse and Russia. Legge and Pitt ranged themselves against the king, and even against their colleagues in the ministry. In the Commons the debate began at 2 and continued till 5 next morning (15 hours), the longest except one up to that period. The longest was on the Westminster election in 1741. Hamilton spoke in favour of the subsidies, and in 1761 was made Secretary of State (Ireland), and in 1763 Chancellor of the Exchequer in Ireland.

His speech in 1768 against Lord Townshend's proposal to tax America by import duties was both far-seeing and eloquent.

Singular and Invincible Doctor (*The*). William of Ockham or Occam, who died 1347.

Sinking Fund (*The*), 1716. Established by Sir Robert Walpole. It was to consist of the surpluses of the other funds, and to be employed in reducing the national debt.

The other funds were the South Sea Fund, established in 1711; the Aggregate Fund, established in 1714, and the General Fund, established in 1716.

Sino'pe (3 syl.), 30 Nov., 1853. The Russian admiral Nachimoff signalled to the Ottoman squadron to surrender. The Russian force was ten times as strong as the Turkish, and, as the Turks did not surrender, Nachimoff set the whole fleet on fire, and then, entering Sinope, set that on fire also. This butchery was called by the Russians a 'brilliant victory,' for which they 'thanked the Lord of battles' in solemn religious thanksgiving.

Sintu'ism. The primitive religion of Japan. It recognises a supreme deity (Tien)—*i.e.* heaven or the sun—and a host of inferior gods; deifies great men, and renders divine homage to virtue. The priests abstain from animal food. The Sintû religion teaches that there is a supreme god from whom issued two creator gods. Then succeed seven gods,

the last of which created a part of Japan by dipping his spear in the ocean. Sintûism existed 600 years, at least, before the advent of Christ.

The word *Sin* means a 'hero,' and *Sintû-ism* means 'hero-worship.'

Sir Bullface Doubleface. Sir Norton Fletcher, for eleven years Speaker of the House of Commons.

Sir Dynamite, 1885. The signature of threatening letters issued by the Irish Land League. *See* 'Irish Associations.'

Sirdar (India). A general, a chief. The generalissimo is the Sirdar-i-sirdar.

Sirventes (2 syl.). Lays of war and chivalry by the Provençals or troubadours. The erotic poems were called 'Chanzos.'

Sister Reform Association, 5 July, 1819. A society of women at Blackburn to co-operate with the men in bringing about parliamentary reform. These associated women took upon themselves to instil into the minds of children what we now call radical ideas.

Sisters of Charity (*The*), 1634. Unmarried Christian women associated to nurse the sick, and relieve the sufferings of all inmates of hospitals. The society was founded in France by Vincent de Paul and the widow Legras. It was suppressed at the revolution, but restored by Napoleon in 1807, under the presidency of the empress-mother.

Si'vanism. The religion of the votaries of Siva. One of the three great divisions of the Hindû sects.

Six Acts (*The*), Nov. and Dec., 1819. The first by Lord Eldon, the last by Castlereagh, and the others by Lord Sidmouth. [*Castle-ray.*]

1. 29 Nov. An act to prevent delay in the administration of justice in cases of misdemeanour. (*Eldon.*)

2. An act to prevent the training of persons to the use of arms. (To continue till 1822.)

3. An act to punish blasphemous and pernicious libels. (*Sidmouth.* Aimed at W. Hone. To continue till 1822.)

4. An act to authorise magistrates to seize arms collected and kept for purposes dangerous to the public peace. (*Sidmouth.* To continue till 1822.)

5. 17 Dec. An act to prevent seditious assemblies (like those in St. Peter's

Field, Manchester—*see* 'Peterloo'). (To continue for five years.)

6. An act for stamping newspapers.

Six Articles (*The*). A statute enacted in 1541 (33 Henry VIII.) commonly called 'The Bloody Statute.' Its object was to compel all British subjects to a uniform profession of six church dogmas, viz.: (1) The real presence of Christ in the eucharist; (2) the all-sufficiency of communion in one kind only; (3) the unlawfulness of the marriage of priests; (4) the indissoluble obligation of vows of chastity; (5) the propriety of retaining private masses; and (6) the obligation of auricular confession. Refusal to subscribe to these six articles was punished by death or imprisonment at the king's pleasure. Repealed in 1549. *See* p. 48, 'Articles on Theology.'

Six Articles of the People's Charter (*The*), 1838. (1) Manhood suffrage; (2) voting by ballot; (3) equal electoral districts; (4) annual parliaments; (5) no money qualification for members; (6) paid members.

Six Chroniclers (*The*). Dr. Giles compiled and edited six Old English Chronicles for Bohn's series in 1848.

1. Ethelwerd's 'Chronicle.'
2. Asser's 'Life of Alfred.'
3. Geoffrey of Monmouth's 'British History.'
4. Nennius's 'History of the Britons.'
5. Gildas Badonīcus (*i.e.* of Bath).
6. Richard of Cirencester, 'On the Ancient State of Britain.'

The last three belong to Dr. Bertram's 'Scriptores Tres' (*q.v.*).

Six Days' Battle, A.D. 327. The battle between Colla usurper of Ulster and Muredach Tiry the rightful successor. 'Six successive suns went down on this fight.' Muredach was the conqueror.

Six Errors, 1413. The 'Six Errors' ascribed to John Huss, and exposed to public view at the chapel of Bethlehem. (1) That he denies to the priesthood the power of absolution; (2) he condemns the doctrine of absolute obedience in all things to a superior; (3) he maintains that an unjust excommunication is not binding; (4) he condemns as heretical all simony, of which offence he charges many of the clergy; (5) he asserts that prayers for the dead are useless; and (6)

that money charged for ransoming souls from purgatory, for prayers for the dead, and for the sale of pardons are simply devices invented by the avarice of the clergy.

Six Nations (*The*), or 'The Indians of the Six Confederated Nations on the South-East of the Great Lakes,' called by the French the 'Iroquois,' viz.: The Mohawks, Oneidas, Onandagos, Cayugas, Sennekas, and Tuscaroras. In 1783 the flight of the Mohawks and Cayugas to Canada broke up the confederacy, and rendered the name no longer applicable.

The British, after the battle of Bunker's Hill, secured the Six Nations as allies.—GREEN, *Hist. of the English People.*

Six Sages of Venice (*The*). The doge's privy council. Every matter was first submitted to this grand jury, and, if approved, was next sent to the Forty, who were the council of state; and was finally sent to the 450 representatives who formed the legislative assembly, the members of which were annually chosen in the six quarters of the city.

Six-stringed Whip (*The*). The Six Articles (*q.v.*) were so called from their severity. Penalties were imposed for writing or even speaking against them.

Six unlucky to Rome. *See* p. 808, 'Semper sub Sextis, &c.'

Three is the French Fatal Number. *See* p. 313, 'Fatal Three.' To which might be added:

LOUIS III. *the Blind*. Had his eyes put out by Bérenger, who usurped the crown (880–923).

CHARLES III. *le Simple*. Was deposed in 887; reigned a short time with Eudes, but at the death of that prince had to abandon Normandy (Neustria) to Rollo; was imprisoned in the Château de Péronne, and died there (879–929).

PHILIPPE III. *le Hardi*. Went to Sicily to avenge the Sicilian Massacre (*q.v.*), was attacked by an epidemic, and died (1245–1285).

HENRI III. *le Mignon*. Beneath contempt, was assassinated by J. Clément (1551–1589).

NAPOLEON III. Being utterly vanquished by the allied Germans, resigned his sword, died in England, and with him ended the French empire. There was neither a Jean III. nor a François III.

Si dicitur semper sub sextis perdita Roma, Francia sub tribus indubitanter perdita semper.

Old Rome found 6 her number of mischance, But 3 the fatal numeral of France.

Sixteen (*The*). The standard-bearers of Florence. *See under* 'Gonfalons.'

Sixteen (*The*). 'La faction des Seize.' An insurrectional committee formed at Paris during the League (*q.v.*) consisting of 16 members, one to each of the 16 'quartiers de Paris,' Bussy-Leclerc being the principal. In 1587 to 1588 the Sixteen drove Henri from Paris and prepared the Day of the Barricades. In 1590 they offered great resistance to Henri IV. In 1591 they declared for Charles duc de Guise (son of Henri, 'Balafré'); but Mayenne sent Bussy-Leclerc to the Bastille, and the power of the Sixteen ceased.

Sixty Club (*The*). An Athenian club containing 60 members, who held their weekly meetings in the Temple of Herculès, in the time of Philip of Macedon.

Sizars, in Cambridge and Durham Universities, are students similar to the 'Servitors' of Christ Church, Oxford, and the ' Bible-clerks' of Oriel, Oxford, received at reduced fees. They are generally sons of the poorer clergy.

Sizings, in University parlance, means an allowance of food. Sizars have this allowance free. There are other privileges allowed them. Sometimes their rooms are free. There used to be duties attached to these sizarships, such as waiting on the Fellows, whence they dined at the Fellows' table (free) after the Fellows had left. In some cases they had to read the Bible lessons at chapel. The duties are now *nil*, but in some colleges they still dine as before.

Ski' Thursday. Maundy Thursday, that is, the day before Good Friday, meaning *pure, clean,* in allusion to the words of Christ when he washed the feet of his disciples. ' Ye are clean, but not all' (John xiii.). The Icelandic *skir-dagr,* 'clean day,' our Anglo-Saxon *scine,* brightness, splendour, our modern *sky* and *shine.* Corrupt for 'Skire Thursday.'

Skinless Prince of Wales (*The*). Richard, afterwards Richard II., son of Edward the Black Prince, was born absolutely skinless, according to a volume in French and Latin on ' Magna Charta ' (1556). Under the head *Nomina Regum et eorum coronatio* we read this observation : ' Richardus II., filius Ed. principis Walliæ, natus sine pelle, et nutritus in pellibus caprarum, incepit regnare XXIII Junii, anno domini MCCCLXXVII.'

Skioldungs (*The*). A semi-historical race of kings in Denmark, so called from Skiold, son of Odin, who, at the death of his father, established a colony of Goths at Ledra, in Zealand, and ruled there as a chief, B.C. 40–23. From Skiold descended the Skioldungs, which

furnished Denmark with 35 kings, the last of whom was Horda Knut II. (*Harde Canute*), 1047. The Skioldungs were succeeded by the Estrithides.

Magnus king of Norway laid claim to the crown of Denmark; but it was agreed between him and Horda Knut that whichever survived the other should have both kingdoms. Horda Knut died first, but the right of Magnus was disputed by Svend Estrithson, founder of the second dynasty. *See* ' Ynglings.'

Skirmishing Fund (*The*), for the use of the Fenian organisation. Michael Davitt was charged with appropriating this money for the purpose of outrage and crime in Ireland. The verdict of the three Royal Commissioners in 1889 was—

We have shown . . . that Mr. Davitt was a member of the Fenian organisation and was convicted as such—that he received money from a fund which had been contributed for the purpose of outrage and crime, namely the Skirmishing Fund. It was not, however, for the formation of the Land League (*q.v.*) this fund was raised, but for the promotion of the agitation which led up to it.

Skotkönung, *i.e.* the tax-king. Olaus II. of Sweden . was so called, because of his grant of an annual tribute to the pope, called Romskot or Rome-tax. He was also called 'the Fat' and ' the Saint' (992, 1000–1030).

Slade Professorship of Fine Art. I. Founded 1869, in the University of *Cambridge,* by Felix Slade. The professor must give 12 lectures a term free of charge.

II. Founded 1869, in the University of *Oxford,* by Felix Slade, who bequeathed for the purpose the sum of 12,000*l.* Chair held for three years, but the holder is eligible for re-election.

Slaughter of the Innocents (*The*). The murder of the children of Bethlehem and its coasts from two years old and under by order of Herod the Great, in order to cut off Jesus, who was born in Bethlehem about the same time Jesus escaped the slaughter because Joseph, from a warning dream, fled with him and his mother into Egypt. *See* p. 572, ' Massacre of the Innocents.'

Slave-carrying Act (*The*). Commanding that a certain given space between decks shall be allowed for each slave, and a certain stated supply of food and water shall be compulsory.

Slave Emancipation Act (*The*), 1807 (47 Geo. III. c. 36). African slavery abolished by the United States in 1808 ;

in France, 1815. Traffic in slaves declared to be felony by 51 Geo. III. c. 23 (1811); declared to be piracy by the United States in 1820; by Venezuela in 1825; by Brazil in 1850.

Slave Kings of Delhi (*The*), A.D. 1186. This was 'The First Gaurian Dynasty' (*q.v.*).

Slave Ship. The first English slave ship in 1562 commanded by Sir John Hawkins was named the 'Jesus,' and Queen Elizabeth allowed Sir John to wear as his crest a manacled negro slave.

In heraldic language ' a demy Moor in his proper colour, bound with a cord.'

Slave Trade (*Abolition of the*), 47 Geo. III. c. 36 (25 March, 1807); declared felony 14 May, 1811.

Slavery has existed from the earliest ages. It spread from Chaldēa into Egypt, Arabia, and all over the East.

It existed in Greece in Homeric times, and Lacedæmonjan lads were trained to ill-treat, deceive, and murder slaves. On one occasion as many as 3,000 slaves were massacred in one night by way of amusement.

Alexander, when he destroyed Thebes, sold the entire population, old and young of both sexes, for slaves. This was B.C. 335.

Among the Jews slavery was recognised by the Mosaic laws. Abraham had his slaves, and so probably had the antediluvians. Among the Jews slaves were either captives taken in war, or purchased as Joseph was, or born slaves, or men reduced to slavery for debt, theft, or some other offence. Masters had full power over their slaves, to scourge them, or even put them to death; but a bought Hebrew slave had to serve for only six years, when he became free (Exod. xxi.). If, however, he wished to remain in servitude, the master bored his ear with an awl (Deut. xv. 17), and he continued in his service till the year of Jubilee. Girls were sold for concubines; a man might sell himself or his children, and kidnapping was not uncommon among the Jews.

Slavery abolished in the United States, 31 July, 1865, the close of the American Civil War. Disputes respecting slavery gave rise to the secession of the Southern States in 1860. In 1861 President Lincoln allowed each state to maintain and regulate its own

laws about slavery, but 6 March, 1862, he proposed the entire abolition of slavery in all the United States. The northern states ultimately prevailed, and slavery was abolished by proclamation of the President, January 1863. At the close of the civil war it was wholly abolished.

No compensation was given to the slave-holders, but it cost them 460 millions sterling; it cost the Federals in war against the Union 940 millions sterling. Total, 1,400 millions sterling.
It was abolished in Vermont in 1777, in New York 4 July, 1827.

Slavery in Ancient Greece.
I. ATHENS. If they lived under the government of a master slaves in Athens were called οἰκέται (domestics); but after their freedom was granted them they were called δοῦλοι, and sometimes νόθοι (bastards, *i.e.* not genuine free-born citizens).

Slaves in Argos were called Gymnitæ.
  ,,   Crete were called Clarotæ and Mnoitæ.
  ,,   Sicyon were called Corynephori (κορυνη-φόροι) club-bearers in battle.
  ,,   Sparta were called Helots (Εἱλωτες). See ' Slavery,' *note*.
  ,,   Thessaly were called Penestæ (πενεσται),

Thessalian serfs, said to be from Penestia, a district of Macedonia, but more likely from πενομαι, to work for one's living, whence πενης, a day labourer.
. Our English word 'slave,' we are told, means Slavonian, and comes to mean a bondman because the Italians at one time bought Slavonians for serfs. Vossius derives the word from *Slaef*, now Sklàve, one of the Slavonic tribes reduced to slavery by Charlemagne. Probably, however, it is connected with the Latin *servus* (one who serves), Ital. *schiavo*, French *esclave*.

II. SPARTA. Slaves in Sparta were called ' Helots.' The tale is that the people of Helos, B.C. 883, refused to pay the Spartans tribute, so the Spartans in vengeance destroyed their city, reduced all the inhabitants to abject slavery, and degraded their name by calling all slaves ' Helots.'

This is most improbable. The town was called Ἑλος, which could not possibly be perverted into Εἱλωτες, Helots. The verb ἑλειν (an infinitive of αἱρεω) means to *seize*, to *take captive*, and the tale referred to is most likely an etymological myth. There are thousands of such like etymologies.
. In the Peloponnesian War the Helots behaved with such bravery that they were rewarded with liberty, B.C. 424. But, alas! for the villainy of the Spartans, 2,000 of the bravest and best were murdered. See p. 572, ' Massacre of the Helots.'

Slavery in Ancient Rome.
Men became slaves among the Romans in three ways: (1) being taken captives in war; (2) by sale and purchase; and (3) by way of punishment. The children of slaves were all born slaves.

Slaves were always sold naked. Those not warranted sound wore a cap, and were called *pileati*. Those from beyond seas had their feet chalked and ears bored. Some slaves were domestic servants, some followed trades, and some were instructed in literature and the arts. Masters had absolute power over their slaves ; they might scourge them, and even put them to death. We are told that C. Pollio threw such slaves as offended him into his fish-ponds, to his lampreys, B.C. 42. They were extremely numerous. Indeed Cæcilius Isidōrus left 4,116 slaves to his eldest son, B.C. 12.

Slavery in England.
Captain [Sir] John Hawkins was the first Englishman who made a traffic of slaves. He procured negroes on the coast of Africa, and sold them in the West Indies, Oct. 1563.

In 1786 England employed 130 slave ships, and carried off annually some 40,000 slaves, and in 1833 the number of slaves in British colonies exceeded 770,000.

European avarice has been glutted with the murder of 180 millions of our fellow creatures. For every slave procured 10 are slaughtered in their own land by war, a fifth die on the passage, and a third in the seasoning.—COOPER, *Letters on the Slave Trade.*

Lord Mansfield's Judgment. The famous judgment of Lord Mansfield, 22 June, 1772, that 'slavery cannot exist in England.'

The case tried in the court of King's Bench was this : a poor slave named Somerset, brought to England, was, from ill-health, turned adrift by his master. Mr. Granville Sharpe took pity on him, fed him, housed him, and restored him to health. His old master now came forward, and claimed his slave as his own, but Mr. Sharpe resisted the claim, and law proceedings were taken by the master for the recovery of his property. Lord Mansfield was the judge, and gave judgment in favour of the slave, as English law does not recognise such a status.

Abolished in the British Colonies, 28 Aug., 1833 (3, 4 Will. IV.). By this Act slavery was abolished in British colonies, and the slave-owners were compensated for their loss by a grant of 30 millions sterling voted by the British Parliament.

1 Aug., 1834, as many as 770,280 slaves were bought off and set free.

Slavery in France.
The holding of negro slaves was regulated in the reign of Louis XIV., 1685, by Colbert's ' Black Code.'

Abolished in the French Colonies. Slavery was abolished in French colonies by the National Assembly, 15 May, 1791. It was restored by Napoleon I. in all French colonies except Hayti, 1804 ; but was again abolished by the Provisional Government, 1848.

Slavery abolished in other Colonies.
In *Danish* colonies in 1848.

In *Dutch* colonies in 1860.
In *Swedish* colonies in 1746.
The trade in slaves was abolished by Austria in 1782.

Slavon'ic Liturgy (*The*).
The Liturgy used in the Russian and Russo-Greek Church. It is also called the Liturgy of Constantinople.

Slavon'ic Nations (*The*).
Poland, Russia, and Bohemia. *See* ' Celtic Nations,' ' Teutonic Nations.'

Slingsby Lawrence.
The pseudonym adopted by G. H. Lewes in his play called ' Speculation ' (or the ' Game of Speculation ').

Sloane Collection (*The*),
in the British Museum Library, consists of 4,100 volumes, chiefly MSS., on natural history, voyages, travels, and medicine. Also thirty volumes of Dr. Sloane's correspondence. Some of the drawings of animals are both rich and accurate, and two volumes of the insects of Surinam are from the pencil of Maria Sibylla Mérian, the great Swiss artist and naturalist. Collected by Dr. Hans Sloane.

Slobodisza (*Battle of*), 1665.
Won by Sobieski, the Polish general, over the Cossacks.

Smalkal'dic League (*The*), 1530.
A league signed at Schmalkald in Germany by the Protestant princes, by which they bound themselves and their heirs, for ten years, to assist each other by arms and money in defence of the reformed religion, and to act unitedly in all religious questions and movements.

Smalkaldic War (*The*), 1546–1547.
Charles V., being threatened by the Turks, tried to win over the Protestant states to support him in the war, but they thought this a ripe time to stand at bay, and raise the standard of revolt. Charles put the Smalkaldic League to the ban of the empire, raised a new army, and marched against the revolters. In April 1547 was fought the battle of Mühlberg, in which the Protestants were defeated, and the Elector of Saxony and the Landgrave of Hesse were taken prisoners. This is called ' The First Religious War of Germany.'

Smallest Bible (*The*)
in the world was one printed 1875.

In 1889 was printed at the Oxford Press the ' Finger Prayerbook,' weighing only three-quarters

3 H

of an ounce. A 'Finger New Testament' was published in 1890.

Smallpox, called by the French 'la petite vérole,' is said to have appeared in Europe in the 10th cent., being introduced from the East by the Saracens; but it was not common till the 16th cent., when it was introduced by a negro slave in the suite of Panfilo de Narvaez, who commanded the expedition against Cortez in Mexico. Robertson reports that it proved fatal to fifty per cent. of those attacked. Dr. Guy, 'Public Health,' p. 197, says, 'Smallpox certainly attacked the Arabian army at the siege of Mecca in 569, and soon after reached Alexandria. By the 8th cent. all Europe was infected by it. . . . Anglada proves that the disease had shown itself in France and Italy as early as 570.'

It appeared in England and in Rouen in 1521. In Normandy four men called *marquers* were employed to look after the sick of each house. They wore a blue gown with a white cross. In 1520 and 1528 it broke out afresh in Italy, and was especially fatal in Rome. Paul Jove and Theodor Zwinger tell us that a Greek, named Demetrius, authorised by the magistrates, had an ox led through the streets, one horn being cut off, and a filet hung on the other horn. After it had promenaded the town, it was slain, and the smallpox disappeared. *See* 'Plague,' &c.

This was evidently a parody of the Jewish scapegoat.

.Severe attacks occurred in 1174, 1365, 1440, 1556, 1564, and 1613.

In 1720 there died in Paris of smallpox 20,000 persons; in 1733 the inhabitants of Greenland were reduced by it from 30,000 to 7,000; in 1738 it committed great ravages in Russia: in 1743 as many as 75,000 died of it in Messina (Sicily). Baldwin king of Jerusalem died of it.
. The Chinese tried inoculation in the 11th cent.: and Timotheus, a Greek, in 1713 communicated this safeguard to the Universities of Oxford and Padua. It was first tried in England in 1721.

Smectym'nuus, 1641. An anagram of the five Puritan divines who controverted Bishop Hall's two books, entitled 'Episcopacy by Divine Right,' and 'An Humble Remonstrance.' Their names are Stephen Marshall, Edmund Calamy, Thomas Young, Matthew Newcome, William Spurstow.

Smith (*King*). Louis Philippe of France, who assumed the name of Smith when he fled to England.

'Mr. Smith!' exclaimed the king. 'That is curious indeed, and very remarkable that the first to welcome me to England should be a Mr. Smith, since the assumed name by which I escaped from France was *Smith*; and look! this is my passport made out in the name of Smith.'—*The Times,* 6 March, 1848.

Smith's Prizes for mathematics. Two of 23*l.* each for commencing bachelors of arts in the University of Cambridge. Founded by the Rev. Robert Smith, D.D., master of Trinity, 1768.

Smiths and Artists (*Patron Saint of*). St. Eloi (588–659), master of the mint in the reign of Clotaire II. Eloi= Eligius.

There was also a Nonne, a prioresse,
That of hire smylyng was ful symple and coy,
Hire grettest ooth nas but by Seynt Eloy.
    CHAUCER, *Canterbury Tales* (Prologue, 118, &c.).

Smock Marriages. Marriages in which the bride divested herself in church of all her clothes except her 'smock,' under the notion that the husband would not then be responsible for any of her debts.

When a man designs to marry a woman who is in debt, if he take her from the hands of the priest clothed only in her shift, it is supposed he will not be liable to her engagements.—BRAND, *Popular Antiquities* (Vulgar Errors).

Sneakers, 1741. Those lords who refused to vote on the motion for the removal of Walpole from the ministry and counsel of the king. The motion was made in the Commons by Pulteney, and in the Upper House by Carteret, supported by the Dukes of Argyll and Bedford, the Earls of Sandwich, Westmoreland, Berkshire, Carlisle, Abingdon, and Halifax; and the Lords Haversham and Bathurst.

Sneezing and Yawning. The European custom of saying 'God bless you' when a person sneezes, and the Catholic custom of making the mark of the cross on the mouth when a person yawns, dates from A.D .589, when a plague broke out in which people expired either sneezing or yawning. Pelagius died of the affection in 590.

The Catholic custom of making the sign of the cross when a person sneezes or yawns is attributed to Gregory of Tours (544 595). The ancient Romans considered sneezing a bad omen, and to avert the threatened evil cried *Absit omen.* Aristotle tells us that sneezing was accounted sacred among the Greeks (τὸν πταρμὸν θεὸν ἡγούμεθα); and Casaubon proves out of Xenophon that the Greek soldiers worshipped sneezing as a god, and averted evil consequences with the prayer, Ζεῦ σῶσον (God bless me). Ammian, in an epigram upon a man who had a very long nose, says:

Οὐδέ λέγει, Ζεῦ σῶσον, ὅταν πταρῇ, οὐ γὰρ ἀκούει
Τῆς ῥινός, πολὺ γὰρ τῆς ἀκοῆς ἀπέχει.

He never says 'God bless me!' when he sneezes,
Because his ear so far is from his nose
It cannot catch the sound.

Several of the native Indian tribes look on sneezing as ominous, and utter their *Absit omen* or *Ζεῦ σῶσον* also. The Germans say ' Gesundheit ' (' health ') when one sneezes.

Snow King (*The*). So the German Catholic party named Gustavus Adolphus king of Sweden, who in 1630 interfered in the Thirty Years' War. They called him the 'Snow King' because he came from Sweden, the land of snow, and they thought he would melt away like Frederick V. of Bohemia, nicknamed the 'Winter King' (*q.v.*).

At Vienna he (Gustavus Adolphus) was called ' The Snow King,' who was kept together by the cold, but would melt and disappear as he approached a warmer soil.—Dr. CRICHTON, *Scandinavia* (Gustavus Adolphus II., 61).

Snow Queen (*The*). I. Christina queen of Sweden (1626, 1633–1689).

II. Elizabeth queen of Bohemia. She was crowned with her husband Friedrich V. elector palatine, 25 Oct., 1619, but fled in Nov. 1620. She was queen during the winter 1619–20.

Soapy Sam. Samuel Wilberforce, bishop of Oxford, and afterwards of Winchester (1805–1873). It is somewhat remarkable that the floral decorations above the stalls of the bishop and principal of Cuddesdon were S. O. A. P. (the initials of Sam. Oxon and Alfred Pott). When Soapy Sam went to inspect the building he was dismayed at seeing his sobriquet thus perpetuated.

Someone asking why the Bishop of Oxford was so called, the bishop himself replied: 'Because I am often in hot water, and always come out with clean hands.'

Socage. Tenure by fixed and determinate service. Almost all free lands in England are held by socage tenure.

Soccolanti (*The*). An order in the Catholic Church akin to the Franciscans. It was established by St. Paulet de Foligny (Foligno) in 1568. St. Paulet was a hermit who, seeing that the mountaineers in his neighbourhood wore wooden sandals or sabots (Ital. *socco*), adopted them himself, and hence his followers were called the Soccolanti.

Social Circle (*The*), 1790. A society founded by the Abbé Fauchet, having for its object the establishment of ' truth, liberty, and happiness.' Fauchet was elected ' Attorney-General of Truth ';

Paris was appointed the centre of civilisation, and the Palais Royal was to be the place of assembly. At the inaugural address, 13 Oct., some 5,000 persons attended, and nearly double that number on 22 Oct., the day of the second meeting. This society soon gave way to the Theophilanthropists (*q.v.*).

Social Democratic Federation (*The*), 1886. The heads of which were Hyndman, Burns, Champion, and Williams. They inaugurated their society by riots, and frightful destruction of London club and shop property in the second week of February.

Social Reform Committee (*The*), 17 May, 1888. To push forward social reforms.

Social Science (*The National Association of*), 1857. For the promotion of cheap popular literature, called *Sixpenny Science*, because that was the price of the treatises produced once a fortnight.

Social War (*The*). I. B.C. 358–353. A war between Athens and her allies. Artaxerxes supported the allies, and Athens was compelled to make a disadvantageous peace.

Another (B.C. 220–217) between Philip of Macedonia and the Ætolians. A peace was patched up by Philip, who was the conqueror.

Social = confederate, and social war means war of several confederate or associated states.

II. B.C. 90–89, between the eight allied nations called the Italian Confederation and the Romans. The complaint was that they furnished two-thirds of the army, and were yet treated as aliens.

This war is also called *Bellum Italicum* and *Bellum Marsicum* from Pompædius the brave Marsian general. It is said that 300,000 men in the vigour of life fell in this war.

Socialism. A system for the regulation of labour by co-operation without competition. Louis Blanc was the father of the system, and his ' Organisation du Travail' was published in 1840. In this book he denounces the plan of ' individualism,' and advocates ' solidarity,' in which each workman is to be paid according to his need—a bachelor 2 francs a day, a married man 2½, and a man with a family 3 francs. In 1848 national workshops were tried in Paris on the Louis Blanc principle. Government was the employer of labour, and private enter-

3 H 2

prise was abolished as far as possible. It was soon found that the national workshops were overcrowded, work was ill-done, idle hands multiplied, and profitless work had to be invented to keep the men out of mischief. Some 1,500 tailors were set to work in the Hôtel Clichy at 2 francs a day, but the scheme was a total failure.

Plato's 'Republic' is an ideal communism. Minos and Lycurgos were communists. The early Christians had 'all things in common,' but the notion of government being the sole employer of labour, and paying each, not according to the work done, but according to individual necessity, was left to the device of Louis Blanc.
Bellamy's novel entitled 'Looking Backward' is based somewhat on the same idea.

Società degli Arcadi, or the 'Arcadians,' 1690.
A literary society of Rome in which each member was called a shepherd of Arcady. Founded by J. M. Crescimbeni with the view of introducing 'good taste.' A history of the Arcadians was published by the society.

Société des Egalitaires (La).
See 'Society of the Rights of Man.'
Pronounce So-ce'a-tay days a-gal'-e-tare'.

Société des Familles (La).
See 'Society of the Rights of Man.'
Pronounce So-ce'-a-tay day fah-meel'.

Société des Saisons (La).
See 'Society of the Rights of Man.'
Pronounce So-ce'-a-tay day Say'-zon (n nasal).

Société des Travailleurs (La), 1825.
The 'Industrialists' (q.v.), after the death of St.-Simon. The foundation departed from its original principles, and became communistic, advocating the absolute equality of man, the community of property, and the aristocracy of toil. Abolished by law in 1833.

Société en Commandite.
A limited liability partnership. A sleeping partner puts money in a concern, and is responsible only to the amount he agrees to be responsible for.

Society for Constitutional Information in London (The), 1792.
A corresponding society with the Jacobins of Paris. Its real object was to establish a republic in Great Britain. It numbered among its members several red-hot Americans.

Society for Constitutional Information in Sheffield (The), 1792.
A society in strong sympathy with the French Revolutionists. In May it called on the 'Society of the Friends of the People' (q.v.) to establish a convention in London ; but the latter society announced that they had no other object in view except parliamentary reform by strictly legal means, and that this end once secured they should forthwith dissolve themselves.

Society for Promoting Christian Knowledge (The), 1699.
In 1701 a branch called the 'Society for the Propagation of the Gospel in Foreign Parts' was established. These societies distribute bibles and common prayer-books at very cheap rates, and sometimes gratuitously. The original society limits its operations to home, the branch society extends to the colonies.

Society for Promoting the Education of the Poor (The), 2 Dec., 1811, in Ireland.
Commonly called the Kildare Place Society. A voluntary institution for the instruction of children, the instruction to be uninfluenced by religious distinctions. The Bible was not to be made a class book for teaching reading and spelling, and when read by pupils sufficiently advanced was to be without either note or comment. No religious catechism was to be taught, and no book introduced of a controversial character, that 'the religious tenets of the pupils might not be disturbed or interfered with.' A public grant was given in 1819, but withdrawn in 1830.

Society of Grütli (The).
Mentioned in the report of the government of Zürich, 1844, as then existing in Switzerland. Its object was the abolition of the federation principle in the Swiss constitution.
Grütli is a meadow in the canton of Uri, at the foot of the Seelisberg, and is famous for the oath sworn on the night of 7 Nov., 1307, by Werner, Stauffacher, Walter Furst, and Arnold Melchthal to liberate Switzerland from the Austrian yoke.

Society of Jesus (The).
The title under which the Jesuits were originally enrolled by Paul IV. in 1540. See 'Jesuits.'

Society of Progress (The).
A secret democratic society of France in the reign of Louis Philippe. By the decree of 10 April, 1834, secret societies were forbidden, and therefore when a particular society was pounced upon and declared illegal, it changed its name and

was reorganised. The interdiction of these secret societies led to the riots of Lyons and Paris (9, 10, 11 April, 1834), and prepared the way of the revolution of 1848.

Society of United Irishmen
(*The*), 1793–1800. This egg was hatched by the French Revolution, and the Irish came nigh to rival the French in savagery and lawlessness. The ostensible object of the society was parliamentary reform, but its real design was anarchy. The soldier was taught to betray the king, the servant to rebel against his master, and the tenant to cheat his landlord. Magistrates, witnesses, jurors, all who attempted to support the laws were marked for destruction. Assassins spared neither sex nor age, and spread terror and dismay throughout the island. In 1796 a communication was opened with the French Directory, who promised invasion, and in December a French fleet anchored in Bantry Bay, but was forced to retire; a second attempt was equally abortive; at last by vigorous measures the rebellion was stamped out, and in 1800 the Irish parliament was abolished. *See* 'Irish Associations.'

Society of the Black Pin (*The*),
or 'Conjuration de l'Epingle Noire.' A French secret society which arose from the Carbonari after the unsuccessful outbreak of 24 June, 1817.

Conspiration qui se forma sur la Restauration, et dans laquelle les conjurés avaient pris pour signe de ralliement une épingle noire.—LITTRÉ, vol. ii. p. 1463, col. 2.

. There was another secret society at the same period called 'The Society of the Red Pin, or La Conjuration de l'Epingle Rose.'

Society of the Friends of the People (*The*).
I. 28 April, 1792. An *English* parliamentary reform society, supported by the Lords Lauderdale, John Russell, Dare, Stanhope, and Fitzgerald. Many of the members were enthusiastic admirers of the French Revolution.

II. 1793. A society organized in *Scotland* in sympathy with the French revolutionists. • Their standing toast was 'George the Third and Last, and damnation to all crowned heads.'

Society of the Rights of Man
(*The*). 'La Société des Droits de l'Homme.' A secret political society formed in France during the reign of

Louis Philippe. By the decree of 10 April, 1834, secret societies were interdicted in France, and therefore when a society was dissolved by the government it was soon re-organised under another name. Thus we have 'La Société des Familles,' 'La Société des Saisons,' 'La Société des Travailleurs,' 'La Société des Egalitaires,' and so on, all of republican or communistic tendencies. The prohibition of secret societies led to the revolution of 1848 and the expulsion of Louis Philippe from the throne.

Socinians.
The followers of Faustus Socīnus, an Italian (1539–1604), nephew of Lælius Socinūs. He taught that God is one person, and denied the divinity of the Word and Holy Ghost, which he called 'expressions' and not 'persons'; he also taught that Jesus is no mediator, but only a perfect example of holy life; he furthermore taught that the punishment of hell is not eternal.

Socinians and Unitarians differ considerably in their views of Jesus Christ. The Socinians say he ought to be worshipped not as God, but as the Saviour of the world; and though a man, yet was He born through the operation of the Holy Ghost. The Unitarians admit neither of these dogmas. There are many Unitarians in England, but probably no Socinians. Trinitarians believe in the triple personality of the One God; Socinians and Unitarians both believe in the single personality of the One God.

Socratês (*The English*).
Dr. Johnson is so called by Boswell (1709–1784).

Mr. South's amiable manners and attachment to our Socratês at once united me to him.—*Life of Johnson.*

Socratês (*The Mad*).
So Plato denominated Diogenês the cynic (B.C. 419–324).

Socratês of the Musulmans
(*The*). Abou-Hanifa, born at Cousa, died in prison at Bagdad in A.D. 757. He was chief of the Han'ifites (3 syl.).

Sodality of the Blessed Sacrament (*Brothers of the*).
Certain fanatics which sprang up at Caen, in 1659, and gave out that their smell was so nice they could distinguish a Jansenist by the mere scent, and that all the clergy in Caen, except two, were Jansenists.

Sodor.
A small village in Iona or St. Columba's Isle, corruptly called 'Icolmkill.' Magnus king of Norway, in 1098, obtained possession of this isle, with the rest of the Hebridês, and united it to the Isle of Man under one bishop. In 1333

England took possession of the Isle of Man.

Sodor and Man. The Hebridês were called by the Norsemen the ' Sudrejar,' *i.e.* ' Southern Islands,' corrupted and shortened into ' Sud'ar,' ' Sodor.' The bishop of Sodor and Man is (titulary) bishop of the Hebridês and the Isle of Man. *See* ' Orkney Islands.'

Sœur Louise de la Miséricorde. Mdlle. de la Vallière, the mistress of Louis XIV., was so called in her retirement (born 1644, mistress of the king 1661, retired 1674, died 1710).

Soffa'rian Kings (*The*), or ' Sof'farides ' (3 syl.). A Persian dynasty which supplanted the Ta'herides (3 syl.) in many of their possessions. The founder was the brigand Yacoub the Soffar (or blacksmith). Yacoub reigned thirty years (872–902), and was succeeded by the Samanides (3 syl.).

The Ta'herides (3 syl.), Sof'farides (3 syl.), Sam'-anides (3 syl.), and Bou'ides (2 syl.), were concurrent with the Califs, and reigned only over parts of Persia, as Seistan, Khorasan, Balk, and Tabaristan.

Sof'farides (3 syl.). *See above.*

Sofi or **Soffee Dynasty** (*The*). *See* ' Suffavean.'

Soissons (*Plot of the Comte de*), 1641. Louis de Bourbon, comte de Soissons, had been proscribed by Richelieu for rebellion, and had taken refuge at Sedan, then the principality of the Duc de Bouillon. Here he entered into a plot with Spain, assembled troops, and assumed a defiant position. Richelieu sent an army against him ; gave him a crushing defeat at Marfée, near Sedan ; Louis de Bourbon was shot, and the plot fell through. *See* p. 752, ' Remember the Vase of Soissons.'

Soke or **Soc.** A privilege of administering justice and of executing laws in Anglo-Saxon times. The lord had the liberty of holding a court or mote of his ' soc-men ' or tenants, who held under him by a fixed determinate service called ' soccage.'

Soldier. About 1214 Philippe II. Auguste of France kept a large standing army, and the pay was called their *solde* ; hence ' sold-at,' and ' sold-ier,' a military servant who receives government pay.

Soldiers' Friend (*The*). Frederick duke of York and Albany (1763-1827), second son of George III., made colonel in the British army 1780 ; commander-in-chief in Flanders 1793 ; commander-in-chief 1798.

Sol'ecism. An impropriety in language, either of syntax or idiom. The Athenian colonists of Soloi, by their long expatriation, forgot their pure native language (Suidas, ' Soloi ').

Solemn League and Covenant (*The*). I. 3 Dec., 1557, whereby the Scotch reformers bound themselves to stand unflinchingly to the Calvinistic reform, and to fight, if necessary, in its defence. The bond was signed by the Earls of Glencairn, Argyll, and Morton, Lord Lorn, Erskine of Dun, and many others, who assumed the title of ' Lords of the Congregation.' And from this hour to flinch or fall from the covenant was an unpardonable sin in Scotland.

II. 1 March, 1638, the Scotch agreed to join the parliamentary army against the king (Charles I.) provided both popery and episcopacy in the two kingdoms were extirpated. The league was modified 25 Sept., 1643, by Sir Harry Vane, and the terms were ' the kirk should preserve its purity and freedom, and the church of England should be reformed *according to the Word of God.*' Charles I. in 1647 coquetted with the league, promising to establish presbytery and to concur in the extirpation ' of the sectaries ' ; but he dallied too long and disgusted the league. Charles II. subscribed to the league 16 June, 1650 ; but it was declared to be illegal by 14 Car. II. c. 4.

The Solemn League and Covenant, the Magna Charta of the Presbyterian Church.—Sir W. SCOTT, *Old Mortality*, ch. xxxvii.

III. 1774, a confederation entered into at Philadelphia to abstain from the use of English goods. This was in abhorrence of the Boston Port Bill (*q.v.*), which the colonists described as ' a barbarous, cruel, bloody, and inhuman murder.'

' Solicitudo Omnium Ecclesiarum,' 7 Aug., 1814. A bull issued by Pius VII. for the rehabilitation of the Jesuit order.

Solomon Avon, 3 November, meaning the Eve of the Summer-close.

'Avon' a corruption of even or eve, and 'Solomon' a corruption of the Irish *samhuin* = end of summer.

Solomon of China (*The*). Tae-tsong (* , 626–650), one of the most enlightened monarchs that ever reigned. He was the son of Kao-tsou, founder of the Tang dynasty (*q.v.*). This reign was the Augustan age of China. His wife was a lady also of singular wisdom and virtue.

Tae-tsong may be favourably compared with Antoninus the Roman emperor.

Solomon of his Age (*The*). Robert I. of Naples, 1309–1343. Pious, generous, and just; a great patron of learning and promoter of science. He died at the age of 64.

Solon of French Prose (*The*). Balzac (1596–1655), famous for his 'Letters.'

Solon of Parnassus. Boileau (1636–1711) was so called by Voltaire. He was the Alexander Pope of France, and his 'Art of Poetry' obtained for him Voltaire's cognomen.

Somnauth Proclamation (*The*), 1843, by Lord Ellenborough, governor-general of India. A pompous and foolish declaration that he restored to the Temple of Somnauth the sandal-wood gates which had been taken away 800 years ago. Now these gates were in ruins, and the people to whom they were promised had become Mahometans, who hated the Hindû religion of the Temple of Somnauth. So that the gates were worthless, and the Mahometans to whom they were promised would feel insulted, not honoured, by the gift. Again, the Hindûs, being a subjected race, the restored trophy of their subjection would be no more acceptable to them than to their conquerors.

Besides, it had been foretold that the restoration of the gates would be a forerunner of the end of the Sikh dominion. This prophecy proved true.

Son of Heaven (*The*) and 'The Ten Thousand Years' are the titles of the emperor of China.

Sons of Freedom (*The*). A Fenian organisation in North America opposed to Donovan Rossa. These 'Sons of Freedom,' also called 'The Robert Emmett,' have their head centre resident in Philadelphia. *See* 'Irish Associations.'

Sons of Liberty (*The*), 1765. An association of the colonists of North America, called into existence by Lord Grenville's Stamp Act. They combined to throw off allegiance to Great Britain and make North America independent. The association began in New York and Connecticut. The term 'Sons of Liberty' was suggested by a speech of Colonel Barré's.

The 'Daughters of Liberty' mutually bound themselves to drink no tea and wear no article of apparel imported from England while the import duties were unrepealed.

Sons of the Precept. Jewish children, who at the age of 13, having learnt the law and their daily prayers, were made answerable for their sins; for which, up to that time, their fathers had been held responsible. This evidently is the *fons et origo* of the Christian rite of confirmation.

Son'derbund (*The*), 1846. A league of the seven Catholic cantons of Switzerland [Friburg, Lucerne, Schwytz, Unterwalden, Uri, Valais, and Zug] to resist the federal diet, which had proclaimed the Jesuits, the Liguorians (*q.v.*), and other religious congregations. Sonderbund means 'separate league.'

Sonna (*The*), or 'Suna,' *i.e.* tradition. A collection of the Mahometan traditions, forming a supplement to the Koran. Those who accept these traditions are called Sonnites.

At the end of 200 years the Sonna or oral law was fixed by the labours of Al Bochazi, who had discriminated 7,275 genuine traditions from a mass of 300,000 reports.—GIBBON, chap. 1.

Sophis (*The*), or 'Sophees,' *i.e.* Mystics. A Moslem sect inclined to pantheism. They look on the Koran only as a book of morals. The sect was founded in the 8th cent. by Abu Said Abul Cheir. The system is called Sophiism or Sopheeism. The four stages are (1) Humanity or obedience to the established religion; (2) the Path, *i.e.* of piety, virtue, and fortitude; (3) Knowledge, when man is equal to the angels; and (4) Truth or union with deity.

To a Mahometan the word Sophi is about equal to 'infidel.'

So'phive'an (or Safawi) **Dynasty** (*The*), 1499–1736. Founded in Persia by Ismail grandson of Sheik Sophi u Dien Izhak, a lineal descendant of Ali. These kings were called saints.

'Saints' applied to these 13 kings seems like a

mockery. (2) Tamasp was poisoned; (3) Ismail II. his fourth son murdered all the princes of the blood royal and died of intoxication or poison; (5) Mohammed Murza was deposed; (6) Mir Hamzah was assassinated; (7) Ismail III. was assassinated; (9) Sefi, the Nero of Persia, had not one redeeming point; (11) Soliman was dethroned; (12) Tamasp was deposed and murdered; (13) Abbas III. was an infant set aside by the Affshars.

Sorbonne (*The*), 1252. The college founded in Paris by Robert de Sorbon (in the reign of St. Louis) for secular ecclesiastics (*q.v.*), who lived together in common, and devoted all their time to the study of theology. From the 14th to the close of the 17th cent. this college enjoyed a European reputation; its decisions on religious questions were deemed final; and it went by the flattering name of the *Perpetual Council of the Gallic Nation*. It is now used as a university, where the course in instruction includes, besides theology, science and general literature.

Soro'res de Pœnitentia. The same as the Beginæ (*q.v.*). They are spoken of in the bull of John XXII. (7 Kal. Martii, anno 3).

Sortês Bib'licæ, introduced during the reign of Charlemagne, was a method of telling fortunes by opening a book containing the Four Evangelists and the Psalms. The book was opened at random, and the finger laid promiscuously upon a passage, which was supposed to be prophetic. In the age of Clovis the book of the Acts of the Apostles was similarly employed. The Greeks used the poems of Homer and the Latins the 'Æneid' of Virgil as books of fate.

Sortês Sancto'rum. Consulting the Bible to know whether or not to do some stated thing, or how it will turn out if done. The Bible is opened at random, and the finger laid at random on any point. The passage pointed out is the answer. Mr. Berridge consulted the Bible on the question whether he should marry, and his finger touched Jer. xvi. 2: 'Thou shalt not take thee a wife.' I myself in a fit of curiosity consulted the oracle as to whether or not I should publish my 'Dictionary of Miracles,' and my finger touched Ezra iv. 22, 'Take heed now that ye fail not to do this.'

In the reign of Charlemagne, the Sortês Sanctorum was confined to the Four Evangelists and the Psalms. In the reign of Clovis the Acts of the Apostles.

Sortês Virgilia'næ. Consulting the Æneid of Virgil in the manner described in *Sortês Sanctorum* (*q.v.*).

In Persia the works of the poet Hafiz are employed in a similar way. The Greeks used the Epics of Homer.

Sosii (*The*), the publishers. The Sosii were two brothers, booksellers and publishers of Rome in the time of Horace.

He [Carlyle] could not throw his thoughts into a shape for which the Sosii of the day would give him money.—J. A. FROUDE, *Thomas Carlyle*, vol. ii. p. 114.

Soter (Preserver). Ptolemy I. king of Egypt was so called by the Rhodians B.C. 304, because he rescued them from Demetrios, surnamed Poliorkêtês, king of Macedonia, by whom they were besieged.

Poliorketes means the taker of cities by sieges. Demetrios the besieger. It is rather remarkable that this very Demetrios was called Soter (Preserver) by the Athenians. 'Soter,' pronounce *So-teer*.

Sothic Period (*A*), 1461. Egyptian years. So called from Sothis, the Egyptian word for the Dog-star, and the Sothic or Canicular period began with the heliacal rising of the Dog-star.

Soulouque (2 syl.). A nickname given to Louis Napoleon at the *coup d'état* of 1851. Soulouque was the negro who was president of St. Domingo, called himself emperor, and established in that island (1849) a parody of Napoleon and his empire in France. By 'Soulouque' was meant that Louis Napoleon was making a burlesque imitation of his uncle; but the *coup d'état* proved a reality, and the second empire is not to be despised either in its duration, its power in Europe, or its influence on France. Certainly Napoleon III. was an Augustus of Paris, for he beautified it more than any of its crowned heads, and kept it tolerably in hand.

Soul-shot, 'Pecūnia Sepulchrālis,' or 'Symbolum Animæ,' a mortuary or oblation made at a person's death. In Saxon times it was a funeral fee, and became a right settled on the church. It differed from a 'corse-present,' which was an oblation made at funerals.

Southcott (*Joanna*), 1810, declared herself about to be the mother of the promised Shiloh. She wrote a vast quantity of 'prophecy,' and sold seals which were to secure salvation to the purchasers. We are told that more than

100,000 persons believed in her, and a cradle of most costly materials was made for the expected babe, but in 1814 she died. Some, however, believed that she would rise from the grave and restore all things.

South-sea Bubble (*The*), 1720. The scheme of Sir John Blount, a leading director of the South Sea Company, to pay off the national debt (about 31 millions sterling) within twenty-six years. The proposal was accepted by the House of Commons 1 Feb., 1720, when 100*l.* stock rose to about 1,000*l.* By August 1,000,000*l.*of the new stock was subscribed for, but by the close of the month the stock began to fall. 22 Jan., 1721, Knight, the cashier, absconded, carrying the register of the company with him. The conduct of the company was inquired into by the House of Lords in June 1721. *See* 'South Sea Company.'

Blount's scheme was to buy up the unredeemable annuities, which amounted to 800,000*l.*, and reduce all the different public securities into one uniform fund, making the best arrangements he could with the present holders. *See* 'Committee of Secresy,' 'Assiento,' and 'Mississippi Bubble.'

South-sea Company (*The*), 9 Anne c. 21, 6 May, 1710. A company projected by Robert Harley for the purpose of relieving the nation of its floating debt, which amounted at the time to ten millions. The plan was to sell this debt to a number of merchants, who were to be guaranteed 6% interest, and to have a monopoly of the South-sea trade. The buyers of the debt were incorporated by royal charter as the 'South-sea Company,' and certain taxes were set aside to pay the annual interest, which amounted to 600,000*l.* 27 June, 1711, a capital of four millions was raised for the company under a royal commission. 18 Feb., 1715, the Prince of Wales was made a governor, and 3 Feb., 1718, the king himself, George I., was a governor. 7 April, 1720, the company offered to parliament to take into its hands the whole national debt, amounting to nearly 31 millions. *See* 'South Sea Scheme.'

South-sea Fund (*The*). Established in 1711 to pay the interest of that part of the National Floating Debt advanced by the South-sea Company and its annuitants. The debt was 10 millions sterling, and the interest at 6 per cent. amounted to 600,000*l.* a year.

36

South-sea Year (*The*), 1720. *See* 'South-sea Bubble.'

Sow has farrowed (*The*), 1319. When the English besieged Berwick they sent a testudo against the walls to undermine them. This movable penthouse was called a sow, because its roof resembled a sow's back. John Crab, a Fleming, erected a huge catapult, and one of the stones discharged from it smashed the wooden shed, and the soldiers under it ran as fast as they could to save themselves. 'The English sow has farrowed!' shouted the besieged, and by hurling lighted torches from the walls they set fire to the sundry machines of assault.

This jest was repeated, 7 Oct., 1337, by Black Agnes of Dunbar. Edward III. sent the Earl of Salisbury to besiege the castle of Dunbar, and a 'sow' was driven to the walls, when Agnes called out, 'Beware Montagow, for farrow shall thy sow,' and a huge rock falling on it, dashed it to pieces.

Sowars, native Indian troopers. In the Indian mutiny, 1857, the sowars were conspicuous for their bloodthirstiness.

Spa Fields (*The Affair of*), 2 Dec., 1816. A great crowd, led by Orator Hunt and Mr. Watson, met in Spa Fields. They called themselves Spencean Philanthropists or Spenceans (*q.v.*), and rushed to the Tower, demanding its surrender. The sentinel laughed at them, when they followed Watson to Snow Hill and ransacked a gunsmith's shop. The Lord Mayor and Sir James Shaw dispersed the mob, making several prisoners, but only one was executed. Capital was made of this riot in the House of Commons to urge the necessity of parliamentary reform.

Spahees, holders of military fiefs in Turkey. In war they are bound to arm at their own cost.

Spahis (*The*). The Arab cavalry in Algiers. The infantry are called *Turcos.*

Spain (*Kings and Queens of*). Ferdinand [Fernando] of Aragon and Isabel of Castile, 1479.
Then the house of Austria gives five kings, 1516-1700. Then follows the house of Bourbon.

House of *Austria*: Karl V., called Cárlos I. (1516-1556); Felipe II., his son (1556-1598); Felipe III., his son (1598-1621); Felipe IV., his son (1621-1665); Cárlos II., his son (1665-1700), no issue.
House of *Bourbon*: Felipe V., son of Louis the

Dauphin. grandson of Louis XIV. (1700-1724); Louis I.; Fernando VI.; Carlos IV.; [Joseph Bonaparte 1808 1813]; Fernando VII.; Isabél (deposed 1868); Amadeus 1870; Alfonso XII.; Alfonso XIII. (born 1886).

Spalding MS. (*The*). A MS. romance written by the Rev. Solomon Spalding, who died in 1816. The 'Book of Mormon' (*q.v.*) is said to be a verbatim copy of this romance, first published in 1830.

Span-counter. Strutt (p. 384) informs us that this was a game similar to our chuck-penny. One of the players throws a counter and another tries to hit it, or to place his counter so near as to be able to span both (as in marbles), and in either case he wins both counters. In French : ' Jouer au tapper,' and in Italian, 'Meglio al muro. *See* ' BLOW-POINT.'

> Shortly boys shall not play
> At span-counter or blow-point, but shall pay
> Toll to some courtier.
>   Dr. DONNE, *Satire*, iv.

Spanish Donkey (*The*), or ' Equileus,' an instrument of torture employed by the Inquisitors. It consisted of a saddle mounted on a post, but the saddle was sharpened to a point. The victim was seated on this point, and heavy weights being attached to his feet, the point was slowly and gradually driven into the victim's body.

Spanish Era (*The*). This era begins with 1 Jan. B.C. 38. *See* ' Era.'

Spanish Fury (*The*), 1576. The Spanish soldiers under the Duke of Parma garrisoned in Antwerp mutinied in 1576 on account of their pay, joined the rebels, surprised the city, and made dreadful havoc of the inhabitants. The town-house and many other magnificent buildings, with 600 houses, were burnt to the ground, and upwards of 6,000 persons were killed or severely wounded. The 'fury,' which lasted three days, began 4 Nov. *See* p. 348, ' French Fury.'

Spanish Inquisition (*The*). Instituted by Ferdinand and Isabella in 1480 and suppressed in 1820. There had existed an Inquisition ever since 1203, when Innocent III. appointed a commission to ' convert ' the Albigenses. Even in 382 Theodosius appointed inquisitors to search out and punish heretics; but what is generally understood by the Holy Office of the Inquisition is the modern Spanish Inquisition.

Spanish Liturgy (*The*). A Greek liturgy altered by Isidore of Seville (570–636). It remained in use till the 11th cent.

Spanish Liturgy (*The Old*), or ' Mozarabic Liturgy,' consists of the liturgy of Rome, mingled with the oriental liturgies of the Arian Goths. Its use was suspended by the council of Braga ; and it was only saved from oblivion by Cardinal Ximenes, who reprinted it in 1500, and endowed a chapel and canons to use it daily in Toledo.

Spanish Main (*The*). The coast along the north part of South America.

There was a loud demand upon Walpole (1733) to insist on plain terms for throwing open the trade to the Spanish main, and for satisfaction for past damages, but Walpole knew that such a course rendered a war hazardous.—HOWITT, *Hist. of England* (Geo. II. p. 418).

Spanish Marriages (*The*). I. That of Isabella II., who came of age in 1843 and who married against her will her imbecile cousin Don Francisco d'Assis 10 Oct., 1846.

II. The marriage of Louis Philippe's youngest son (the Duke de Montpensier) with the Infanta Luisa Maria, sister of Queen Isabella, also 10 Oct., 1846. These marriages were brought about by the intrigues of Louis Philippe under the hope of securing to his son the Spanish throne.

Spanish Phœnix (*The*). Lope de Vega (1562-1635) is so called by G. H. Lewis.

Spanish Shakespeare (*The*). Calderon is so called by the brothers Schlegel. Sismondi calls him the ' Poet of the Inquisition.'

Spanish Succession (1700). A question which led to a war of thirteen years' duration. Carlos II. had no child, and four crowned heads of Europe had pretty nearly equal claims to the succession, viz. the King of France, the Kaiser-King of Germany, the Elector of Bavaria, and the King of Savoy. The last two retired, and left the field to France and Germany. Louis XIV. was the cousin of Carlos and son-in-law of Felipe IV. (whose eldest daughter he had married), and Carlos left the crown to Philippe d'Anjou, second son of the dauphin. The kaiser argued that France could not accept the Spanish crown, as she had renounced all claim to it by the treaty of the Pyrenees, and Karl, a grandson of Felipe IV., was the rightful heir. Louis XIV. proclaimed his grandson 'Felipe V.' of Spain, and Leopold proclaimed his second son 'Carlos III.' of Spain. War ensued, and England joined Germany. After a long contest, the French claimant was acknowledged by all parties. See 'War of the Spanish Succession.'

Spanish Tyrtæus (*The*). Manuel José Quintana (1772–1857).

Spear (*The*), or 'Lance' which pierced the side of Jesus on the cross, is thus accounted for. St. Andrew of Crete affirms that it was found by the Empress Helĕna in the cave of the temple of Venus at Jerusalem, with the cross and other relics. The shaft is in the basilica of St. Peter's at Rome; but Baldwin II. king of Jerusalem sent the head of it to Venice, and St. Louis (IX.) took it thence to Paris, where it was carefully preserved in the Holy Chapel till the French Revolution. *See* 'Crucifixion, *Relics of the*.'

St. Andrew of Crete died in 722, and he speaks of the spear in his 'De Exaltatione Crucis'; but certainly it is not included in any of the early lists of the relics discovered by the Empress Helĕna.

Special Purposes and Sanitary Committee (*The Metropolitan*). Responsible for the inspection and control of the 15,403 premises in which animals are slaughtered, or offensive trades are carried on; where petroleum and other explosives are stored; where cows are kept and milk sold; and where babies are farmed out. The committee has an inspecting staff of ten persons. It also presides over the testing of gas and gas-meters, for which it employs fifty chemists, examiners, and inspectors. Every alternate Tuesday it acts as the Contagious Diseases Act Committee.

Speculum (*Dr. Dee's*). A mirror which Dr. John Dee asserted was brought to him by the angels Raphael and Gabriel. At the Doctor's death it passed into the possession of the Earl of Peterborough at Drayton; then to Lady Betty Germaine, who gave it to John duke of Argyll. The duke's grandson (Lord Frederick Campbell) gave it to Horace Walpole; and in 1842 it was sold, at the dispersion of the curiosities of Strawberry Hill, to Mr. Smythe Pigott. At the sale of Pigott's library in 1853 it passed into the

possession of Lord Londesborough, and is now in the British Museum.

It is a flat polished mineral, like cannel coal, of a circular form, and fitted with a handle.

Spec'ulum Hu'manæ Salva-tio'nis. A sacred picture book in rhyme. This book and the 'Biblĭa Pauperum' (*q.v.*) were immensely popular before the Reformation.

Speculum Majus (*The*). A kind of encyclopædia in four parts by Vincent de Beauvais, who died 1264. Part i. containing a description of nature; part ii. containing philosophy, rhetoric, grammar, law, medicine, and theology; part iii. containing history, and part iv. moral philosophy.

Spencean   Philanthropists (*The*), or 'Spenceans,' 1816. A society established in London by a Mr. Spence, a Yorkshire schoolmaster, assisted by Preston (a workman), Watson (father and son, surgeons), and Castles, who turned out to be an informer against them. Their platform was a common property in all land, the destruction of all machinery, and parliamentary reform. On 2 Dec. they met in Spa Fields, and went in a crowd to the Tower, when Preston summoned the sentinel to surrender, at which he laughed. The mob was dispersed, and one man was tried and condemned to death. Hunt made capital of this silly affair towards reform in parliament. The Spenceans were connected with the Green Bag Plot (*q.v.*).

Spenerism, 1690. A prototype of Methodism, or the establishment of 'collegia pietatis,' that is leavening confraternities. The whole community was divided into sections, each section had a centre of life, an earnest leader whom the section was to obey. There were exhorters to stir up the flagging, converts were placed under the eye of trusty overseers, and sections were vitalised by class meetings. So named from Philippe Jacques Spener, of Alsace, the founder of the sect (1635–1705).

Sphinx (*The Egyptian*) at Gizeh is attributed to the third Egyptian dynasty, but there are several of later date.

Spino'zaism. The philosophical system of Baruch de Spinoza, of Amsterdam (1622–1677), who taught that the universe is all one with a mundane soul.

That there is only one substance which is infinite, with two essential attributes—thought and extension. This substance is, in fact, Spinoza's deity, and all finite beings are merely parts or modifications of this one eternal whole. Spinoza died 1677, aged 45.

According to this system, the universe was not *created* by God, but the universe *is* God. God is everything, and everything is God ; that is to say, God is ' the all in all.'

Spires, or 'Speyer' (*Diet of*). *See* under ' Diet.'

Spiritualists, or ' Spiritists ' (*The*). Those who believe that men and women have intercourse with the spirits of the other world. Roman Catholics believe that holy men and women have communion with the spirits of the just, made perfect ; but spiritualists believe that any spirit may be invoked, and questioned by the living. Originated in America in 1848.

Splendour of Reason or Wisdom (*The*). Mian-ning emperor of China, son of Kia-king. In 1840 he declared war with England for importing opium into his empire. In 1842 the war terminated, and five ports were thrown open to English traders.

Spoilt Child of Fortune (*The*). André Massĕna, who, next to Napoleon, was the greatest of the French generals in the first empire. It was Napoleon who called him ' the Spoilt Child of Fortune ' and made him prince of Eslingen, for his distinguished valour at Eslingen in 1809 (1758–1817).

Spolia Opi'ma. Spoils taken by a Roman general from an enemy slain in single combat. Only thrice obtained : (1) by Romulus from Acron king of the Cæninenses ; (2) by Cossus from Tolumnius king of the Veientes, B.C. 318 ; and (3) by Marcellus from Virodomărus king of the Gauls, B.C. 222.

Sponge (*The*), filled with vinegar and presented to Jesus on the cross, when He cried ' I thirst,' is said to be in the basilica of St. John de Lateran of Rome. The Venerable Bede assures us that he saw it in the silver tankard used by our Lord in the Last Supper. *See* 'Crucifixion, *Relics of the*.'

A part of the sponge is said to be preserved at St. James of Compiègne, another piece at St. Sylvester, another piece at St. Maria Maggiore, another at St. Mary in Trastevere, another at St. Mark's, another at St. Mary's in Campitelli. St. Louis (IX.) we are told bought a part of the sponge of Baldwin with other ' sacred relics.'

Spot Ward. Joshua Ward, one of the physicians who attended the court of George II. So called from a claret spot (*nævus maternus*) on his cheek. He was famous for his blue, red, and purple pills containing antimony or arsenic.

Of late, without the least pretence to skill, Ward's grown a famed physician by a pill.

Spread-eagleism in America corresponds to *chauvinism* in France, and *jingoism* in England.

Spring Captains are officers of the militia summoned for duty in their respective regiments for about six weeks in the spring of the year. Also young officers who come to London in the spring to attend the Epsom and Ascot races, where they go ' to cut a dash,' and risk their money in bets. All well-dressed bet men were, at one time, called ' captain' by bookmakers, and are so still to a great extent. *See* p. 858, ' Summer Lieutenants.'

Spring-heeled Jack (1837–1838). Some one or party of confederates who assumed sundry diabolical shapes, and for six months kept London and its suburbs in perpetual fright. Robbery was not their game, but simply to scare. Spring-heeled Jack first appeared at Barnes as a white bull ; then at East Sheen as a white bear ; then at Richmond, Ham, Kingston, and Hampton as a man in brass armour ; then at Teddington, Twickenham, Hounslow, and Sion Park. Afterwards at Uxbridge, Hanwell, and Brentford ; then at Ealing, in steel armour ; then at Hammersmith, as a gigantic baboon, &c. He attacked travellers and caused them bodily injuries, then with a somersault disappeared over a wall or hedge. Rumour said that the ringleader of this gang was the Marquis of Waterford, but no proof was ever adduced in support of this surmise. In the spring of 1838 these silly pranks ceased.

Even so late as 1877-78 an officer of her Majesty's service caused no little excitement at Colchester, Aldershot, and other garrison towns, by springing suddenly on passers-by.

Spurious Scriptures (*The*). *See* p. 801, 'Scriptures, *Spurious*.'

Spy Wednesday. The Wednesday of Holy Week, or the day before Maundy Thursday. The sanhedrim first sent a deputation to pry into the credentials of Jesus ; then wily hypocrites to put questions to entrap him; at last they agreed with Judas to betray his private haunts during the hours of the night, and sent with the faithless disciple officers to apprehend his master.

Square Caps, in French 'Bonnets Carrés' (15th cent.). First made in France by Patrouillet, but used in England by ecclesiastics long before. The familiar name of a university cap is a mortar-board, which some affirm to be a playful corruption of the French *mortier*. This is doubtful, as the *mortier* is a round velvet cap, still worn in France by the présidents des cours de justice. It has not a flat square board, like a mortar-board, but resembles an inverted mortar used by chemists and druggists. As a rule *mortier* means a velvet cap, *bonnet* a woollen one.

Still the French mortar-cap may have suggested the playful name. St. Louis (1215-1270), in a window of Sainte Chapelle, is represented with a *mortier* on his head, and numerous MSS. and miniatures represent Louis XI. with the same sort of cap. All members of the French parlement wore scarlet robes and mortars.

Square the Circle (*To*). To find a square exactly equal to the area of a given circle, or (which is probably the same thing) to find the exact proportion between the diameter and the circumference of a circle. Roughly speaking, three times the diameter = the circumference, but the exact measure has never been discovered.

Anaxagoras died in prison while attempting to square the circle. B.C. 428.

Squares of a Right-angled Triangle (Euclid, i. 47). 'The square of the greatest side = the sum of the squares of the other two sides. This famous proposition is attributed to Pythagōras; but the Chinese have had from time immemorial a somewhat similar one. If the three sides are respectively equal to 3, 4, 5 (or their multiples), then the square of the greatest side will equal

the sum of the squares of the other two sides. This is obvious from the diagram. The square of 5 contains 25 equal parts, the square of 3 contains 9, and the square of 4 contains 16. As $9 + 16 = 25$, the sum of the squares of the two smaller

sides = the square of the greatest side of the right-angled triangle.

Squire Letters (*The*). Thirty-five letters sent to Carlyle in 1847 respecting Oliver Cromwell, purporting to have been written by Samuel Squire, a subaltern in the Ironsides. This Squire had served with Oliver from the 'first mount' of that indomitable corps, and had kept a journal (1642-1643). Carlyle requested to see the originals of these letters or this journal, and received for answer that the correspondent had 'gathered all the old Puritan papers, the Ironside Journal, and all Cromwell's autographs together, and burnt them,' adding 'Much evil hereby lies buried.' *See* p. 524, 'Literary Forgeries.'

Squitti'no (*The*) of Florence. A corruption of Scrutinio, a special council for the appointment of magistrates. The act of election was termed *squittinare*, *i.e. scrutinium*, because minute investigation was made into the qualities of the eligible burghers.

Sse-ki (*The*), or 'Book of Annals,' in five parts, begins the history of China from B.C. 2697, but no dates are given to the annals till B.C. 827, the reign of Siuen-wâng. It was the work of Sse-ma-Thsian, the Herodotus of China, who lived in the reign of Hân Ho-lee (89-106).

The Shu-king, a book of morals and history, is said to have been written in the mythical reign of Ya-u, who reigned 102 years (B.C. 2357-2255).

Stabat Mater Doloro'sa. This Latin hymn is sometimes attributed to Innocent III., but with greater probability was composed by Jacopone of Todi.

It has been set to music by Pergolēse (4 syl.), Haydn, Handel, Rossini, and others.

Stable-stand (in forest law) is when a person is found at his stand in a forest with a bow in his hand, or close to a tree with a greyhound ready to slip. It is one of the four presumptive evidences of deer-stealing. The other three are—

Back-berond, or back-berind; that is, having a deer on his back.

Bloody-hand, when his hands or clothes are stained with blood.

Dog-draw, drawing after a deer by the scent of a hound led in hand.

Stadtholder. A high functionary in the republic of the Seven United

Provinces of the Netherlands. Originally the word was given to the commander of the forces, then to the governor of a province, and to the general governor of the united provinces called his stadtholderate. The office was abolished at the death of William II., in 1650, but was restored in 1672 in favour of William III. (who received the crown of Great Britain). It was again abolished at the death of William III. in 1702, but was reconstituted in 1747 in favour of William IV. of Nassau, who was created ' General and Hereditary Stadtholder.' This continued till 1795, when France conquered Holland.

Staff of Jesus (*The*). Said to have belonged to St. Patrick. It was covered with gold and set with precious stones. It was kept in the Cathedral of Armagh till Fitz-Aldelm, the English governor of Ireland, removed it to the church in Dublin, in 1178.

Stagi'rite (*The*). Greek *σταγειρίτης*. Aristotle, born in Stagīra, in Macedonia (B.C. 384–322).

Staircase (*The*) of Pilate's judgment hall, up which Jesus ascended, was sent by the Empress Helĕna to Rome in 356, and it was deposited in St. John de Lateran. It consists of twenty-eight stairs of white marble, now cased in wood for preservation. *See* p. 231, ' Crucifixion (*Relics of the*).'

Pope Leo IV., in 850, established the practice of mounting these stairs on one's knees. If they had not been cased with wood they would assuredly have been worn through.

Stalwarts (*The*), 1889. The new Radical party in the House of Commons. In the U.S. the more out-and-out members of the Republican party have been called ' Stalwarts ' for fourteen or fifteen years (1890).

Stambool, *i.e.* Constantinople, is a corruption of *εἰς τὴν πόλιν* (Greek, ' to the city '), pronounced by the Turks *Stan-bolin*, shortened into *Stambool*.

Is it not rather a corrupt abbreviation of Constantinople into Stanti-pol, Stan-pol, Stambool?

Stamp Act (*The*), 1764, by Lord Grenville. The imposition of stamp duties on our American colonies. Repealed, after several riots in Boston and other parts of North America, in 1766.

All that Grenville expected to obtain by this act was barely 1s. a head from the North Americans, which would have produced at the utmost only 100,000*l*. a year.—HOWITT, *Hist. of Eng.* (Geo. III. chap. iii. p. 83).

** The principal *Stamp Acts* since are 55 Geo. III. c. 184 ; 13, 14 Vict. c. 97 ; 16, 17 Vict. cc. 59, 63 ; and the 17, 18 Vict. c. 83. The acts provide that a tax be imposed on all papers on which legal proceedings or private instruments are written, and also upon licences for retailing wines, letting horses on hire, cards, dice, cheques, receipts, and numerous other purposes.

Standard (*Battle of the*), 22 Aug., 1183, won by Stephen over the Scotch.

Standard (*The*) of the ' Battle of the Standard ' consisted of the banners of St. Cuthbert of Durham, St. John of Beverley, and St. Wilfrid of Ripon, brought from their churches. This combination banner, raised on a tall mast, was set on a four-wheeled car. The mast was surmounted with a cross, attached to which was a pyx containing the sacramental wafer. This standard was erected by the English army which fought for Stephen against the Scotch, who took the part of Matilda daughter of Henry I., and niece of David king of Scotland at the time. The battle was fought at Northallerton 22 Aug., 1138. *See above.*

Standard (*The Black*). That of the Abbaside califs.

The dress, the turbans, and the standards of the Abbaside califs were all black.—Dr. HERBELOT.

Standard (*The Celestial*). The great green silk flag of the Turks, said to have been given to Mohammed by the angel Gabriel. It is now preserved in four coverings of green taffeta, enclosed in a case of green cloth. It is twelve feet in height, and the golden hand which surmounts the pole holds a copy of the Koran. In times of peace this palladium is guarded in the ' hall of the noble vestments,' in which hall are preserved relics of the ' prophet,' as his teeth, beard, stirrup, sabre, and bow.

Standard Doctrines (*The*) of the Wesleyans, imposed by the Conference on every minister in the connexion, are contained in Wesley's four volumes of sermons, and his ' Notes on the New Testament.'

Standard of Augustus (*The*). A globe, to indicate his empire of the world.

Standard of Cheap (opposite Honey Lane). A substantial building for the supply of water, in existence in the reign of Edward I. Stow, in his 'Survey,' tells us it was made in the mayoralty of John Wells, grocer.

In the reign of Edward III. two fishmongers were beheaded at the Cheapside Standard for riot. And Henry IV. caused 'the blank charter' of Richard II. to be burnt at the same standard.

Standard of Constantine (*The*) was called the 'Labărum,' and the bearers were denominated *Labariféri*. It was purple, with a gold fringe, and only unfurled when the emperor himself was in the field. This standard was decorated with the sacred monogram **XP** (Chr-istos). *See* Gibbon, 'Decline and Fall,' xx., *note* (1788).

Standard of Cornhill (*The*), 1582. A water conduit with four spouts made by Peter Morris, a German, and supplied with Thames water conveyed by leaden pipes over the steeple of St. Magnus's Church. It stood at the east end of Cornhill, at its junction with Gracechurch Street, Bishopsgate Street, and Leadenhall Street. The water ceased to run between 1598–1603, but the standard itself remained long after. Distances from London were measured from this spot.

Standard of Great Britain (*The Royal*). A red banner with the national arms covering the entire field.

The standard of Edward I. was a flag with the arms of England, St. George, St. Edmond, and St. Edward.

Standard of the ancient *Danes*: A flag fringed, and bearing a raven. Sometimes mounted on a stand with wheels. Since the 13th cent. the *Dannebrog* has been the Danish standard.

  Egyptians: An eagle stripped of its feathers.

  Franks: A tiger or wolf on a pole. After they became Romanized they adopted the Roman eagle, and later still a large flag with fleurs-de-lis.

  Gauls: A lion, bull, or bear on a pole.

  Greeks: *See lower down.*

  Jews: *See lower down.*

  Persians: In the time of Cyrus, a golden eagle with outspread wings. The blacksmith's apron; said to be the apron of Kawah, or Gao, who headed a rebellion against Biver, and used his apron for a standard (B.C. 800).

  Romans: *See lower down.*

Standard of the Anglo-Saxons (*The*) was an ensign. It was a white horse on a pole. Later on it was a flag bearing a white horse.

Standard of the Greeks (*The*). The ancient Greeks had no national banners, but they had ensigns, called *semeia* [se-mī-ah].

The *Athenian* ensign was an owl on the top of a pole, in honour of Athênê [Minerva], their protector.

The *Corinthian* ensign was a pegăsus or winged horse.

The *Messenian* ensign was the letter M.

The *Lacedemonian* ensign was a Greek L [Λ].

The *Theban* ensign was a sphinx, in commemoration of the monster overcome by Œdipus.

The signal for battle was hoisting on a spear a purple coat or white cloth. Polybius tells us that the Illyrians received orders to begin the fight by the hoisting of a *white* flag; the Megalopolitans by hoisting a *purple coat*. And Homer says that Agamemnon hoisted a *purple cloth* as a telegraph to begin fighting. When the ensign was taken down the fighting was to cease.

Standard of the Jews (*The*).
1. Of Judah: A *lion*.
2. „ Reuben: A *man*.
3. „ Ephraim: A *bull*.
4. „ Dan: The *cherubim* (Gen. xlix. 3–22). *See* p. 306, 'Evangelical Symbols.' (Jahn, 'Archeologia Biblica,' No. 287.)

There are three words—*degel*, *oth*, and *nes*—meaning a standard. The *nes* was not borne from place to place, but the pole of the flag was fixed in the earth (Jer. iv. 6, 21; Il. 12, 27; Ezek. xxvii. 7). It seems to have been used as a call to arms. The *oth* appears to have been a long pole with a bunch of leaves fastened on the top.

Standard of the Prophet (*The*), A.D. 632. When Mahomet was dying, at Medīna, on the eve preceding the conquest of Syria, the chief officers entered to hear his last orders. Ayesha, to save the prophet from further exhaustion, tore down the green curtain which screened one end, threw it to the officers, and told them to preserve it as a rallying-point for Islam. This standard floated over the walls of Vienna in 1683, but is never unfurled except at times of grave emergency. In battle it is borne to the front, where all may see it.

Standard of the Romans (*The*) was not a flag, but a pole surmounted with an eagle, horse, or some other device. A flag was always the proper and only ensign of the Roman cavalry. Under the empire a distinct body of soldiers, called ' Vexillārii ' (flag-bearers), were embodied, to render assistance to the army if required and guard the frontiers. They were mounted, and carried a special flag or ' vexillum.'

Neither the Romans nor the Greeks had standards—*i.e.* large flags—but only ensigns.

Standard of the Turks.

The Sanjak Cherif of *green* silk. *See above*, ' Standard of the Prophet.'

The Sanjak Cherif of *red* silk.

The Tug, consisting of one, two, or three horse-tails fastened to the end of a gilt lance. Beys have one horse-tail carried before them. Pachas have three horse-tails.

The *Alem*, a broad standard with a silver crescent in the middle.

See ' Flags.'

Standards of Royalty, &c., in the Middle Ages.

The great standarde to be sett before the *kinge's* pavilion [not to be borne in battle] is to be of the length of eleven yardes, [but] the standarde to be borne [to battle] is to be slitte at the end, and vii. yardes long.

The *erle's* standarde is to be vi. yardes long.

The *baron's* standarde v. yardes long.

The *bannerett's* standarde iiij. yardes and the haulfe long.

The *knighte's* standarde iv. yardes longe.

Every standarde to have in the chiefe the crosse of St. George, to be slitte at the end, and to contayne the creast wyth the posy and device of the owner.

Standing Council of the Church (*The*), 1596. A permanent Scotch committee of Presbyterians, with supreme authority in the Presbyterian Church, whenever it was thought there was any danger to the ecclesiastical establishment. They were very dogmatical and most rancorous against Catholics.

Standing-fishes Bible (*The*), 1806. ' And it shall come to pass that the fishes [fishers] shall stand upon it from Engedi.' *See* ' Bible ' and ' Scriptures.'

Stanhope Historical Essay (*The*), Oxford University. Value 20*l.* in books. The range is limited to the dates, 1800–1815. Founded by Lord Stanhope in 1855.

Stapleton College, 1315. The original name of Exeter College, Oxford. Founded by Walter Stapleton, bishop of Exeter.

Star (*The Order of the*), 1350. A French military order, established by Jean le Bon. It consisted of warriors who had received wounds in battle. The knights of the Star vowed never to retreat before an enemy more than one mile, after which they had to make a stand and either conquer, be taken prisoners, or be cut down. Extinct about 1460.

Star and Luminary of Law and Lantern of Equity (*The*). Bartoli the Italian civilian (1312–1356).

Star Chamber (*The*). *Chambre des Estoylles*. In Latin, ' Camera Stellata,' 3 Henry VII. c. 1 (1486). Abolished 16 Car. I, c. 10 (1641). Green says, in his ' History of the English People,' ' the bonds of the Jews were deposited for greater security in a chamber of the royal palace at Westminster, which, from their Hebrew name of ' starrs,' gained the title of the Star Chamber.' The Latin equivalent, ' Camera Stellata,' does not support this hypothesis, but seems to refer to some ' starry decoration ' of the chamber. We have the *Painted* Chamber, the *White* Chamber, &c., and, if Mr. Green's suggestion were correct, the Latin phrase would be ' Camera *Stellarum*,' not ' Camera *Stellata*.' We are told that part of the decorations of the Star Chamber may still be seen in Leasowe Castle, West Cheshire, the seat of Sir Edward Cust, baronet.

The jurisdiction of this court was without appeal in the hands of the treasurer and the keeper of the privy seal, assisted by a bishop, a temporal lord of the privy council, the chief justice, and two other justices.

The reason why the Court of the Star Chamber was so hated in Charles I.'s time is because Charles used it as a general law court to exact fines for his own exchequer. Amongst other cases were the following: A gentleman who had married his niece was fined 12,000*l.* Brawlers were fined 4,000*l.* or 5,000*l.* John Hampden was prosecuted in this court for refusing to pay ship-money. Chambers, an alderman of London, was fined 2,000*l.* for saying that men in England were worse off than those in Turkey. The judges in the court of the Star Chamber were the king's privy council. It was held in the palace of Westminster without jury.

The Star Chamber took cognizance of forgery, perjury, riots, frauds, libels, conspiracies, misconduct of judges and of other officers connected with the law-courts, contempt of the king's authority, and even treason, felony, and murder ; but capital punishment could not be awarded by this court. Its power was restricted to fines, pillory, torture, mutilation, and incarceration for a term of years or for life. It dated back to very ancient times, but its powers were abridged by Edward III., and it was wholly abolished by 16 Car. I. c. 10.

Star of India (*The*), 1869. For distinguished merit or service in our colonial possessions. Originally it consisted of 25 knights of the grand cross,

60 knights commanders, and 100 companions; but in 1880 the numbers were increased to 35, 120, and 200.

Star of South Africa (*The*).

A South African diamond, weighing in the rough 83½ carats, and after being cut 46½ carats.

Star of the North (*The*).

Gustavus Adolphus, king of Sweden, was so called after his great victory at Leipzig, 7 Sept., 1631, over Tilly and the Catholic League. This was the first great battle of the Thirty Years' War.

The other two great battles of this war were Lützen (1632), also won by Gustavus; and Nordlingen, in 1634, won by the kaiser's son over the Protestants. This son was afterwards Friedrich III. of Germany.

Star of the South (*The*)

weighs 254 carats, and is the largest diamond hitherto found in Brazil. It is a brilliant of purest water, and was found in July 1853 by a poor negress working in the mines of Bogagen.

Star-spangled Banner (*The*).

The national banner of the United States of America. First applied to the American flag by Francis S. Key on the morning after the British attack on Fort McHenry, at Baltimore, in 1814.

Oh! say, does that star-spangled banner yet wave O'er the land of the free and the home of the brave?

Star Tables (*The*), 1437.

Compiled by Ulugh Begh, sultan of Samarcand and astronomer. They are still highly esteemed and referred to. *See* p. 284, 'Eelkhanee Tables.'

Starch.

It is said that Mrs. Anne Turner invented the yellow starch which stiffened the ruffs so fashionable at one time in the *haut monde*. This Mrs. Turner also compounded love-philters, and was condemned to death 15 Nov., 1615, for poisoning Sir Thomas Overbury. On the day of execution Mrs. Turner wore a ruff stiffened with yellow starch, and the fashion went out of vogue.

The legend that Mrs. Turner was hanged *by* her collar is, of course, nonsense. She might appear on the scaffold *in* such a collar, that is, wearing one, but that is a very different thing from being suspended *by* it to the gallows.

In 13 Nov., 1849, Maria Manning wore a black satin dress when she was executed on the roof of Horsemonger Lane Gaol, and black satin gowns instantly disappeared from society.

Star'keyites (3 syl.).

Faith-healers so called from Mr. Starkey, a clergyman, who joined James Prince, the founder of the Agapemŏnê at Charlynch, near Bridgewater.

Starosts (2 syl.).

Dignitaries of Poland who held in the name of the king either a fort or royal domain. They taxed their own people, but paid one-fourth to the king.

Stars and Bars.

The flag of the Confederate States of North America (1861–65).

Stars and Stripes.

The national banner of the North American United States. The stars are white on a blue canton; the stripes are alternately red and white running horizontally. Said to represent the mullets and bars of the Washington coat of arms.

Start (*The*), 1650.

The escape of Charles II. from Perth, during a hawking expedition, after the battle of Dunbar. He rode forty-two miles and passed the night in a miserable hovel at Clova, a village in Forfarshire, in the braes of Angus. Next day Colonel Montgomery induced him to return, and he was crowned by the Scotch parliament 1 Jan., 1651.

First the officers refused to serve under Leslie. . . . Next, they hinted doubts of the lawfulness of the war. . . . Then came the accident of 'The Start' which embittered and emboldened the zeal of the fanatics.—Dr. LINGARD, *Hist. of Eng.*, viii. 4.

State Services (*The*), 1661.

Four services annexed to the Book of Common Prayer after the Restoration: viz. one for Gunpowder Treason, 5 Nov.; one for King Charles's Martyrdom, 30 Jan.; one for the Restoration, 29 May; and one for the King's Accession. The first three were expunged from the book by order of council given by Queen Victoria.

Stately Sunday.

Trinity Sunday is so called, because the mystery of the Trinity is the most stately of all. *See* 'Sunday.'

States-General (*The*). I.

In *French* history was a deliberative assembly, consisting of deputies from the nobility, clergy, and commonalty. The first was convoked by Philippe IV. on 10 April, 1302, and the last by Louis XVI. in May, 1789, when the number of deputies was 1,145.

There was a states-general under Louis XIII., 27 Sept., 1614.

3 I

II. Of the *united provinces*. The legislative body consisting at first of only five members, but subsequently increased to seven. The states-general of Holland ceased to exist in 1795 when the republic was broken up.

The legislative body of the present kingdom of the Netherlands is so called.

Statesmen *(The)*, in the Commonwealth of England were the civilians of the House of Parliament in contradistinction to the 'Grandees of the Army' *(q.v.).*

The grandees of the army felt that they no longer [in 1653] possessed the chief sway of the government. War had called them away to their commands in Scotland and Ireland; and during their absence the conduct of affairs had devolved on those who, in contradistinction, were denominated the statesmen.—Dr. LINGARD, *Hist. of Eng.,* viii. 5.

Statics *(Father of).* Archimēdēs of Syracuse, slain B.C. 212, aged 75.

Statics is the science of forces *in æquilibrio,* which produce rest. Dynamics is the science of forces which produce motion. To Archimēdēs we owe also the principal laws of hydrostatics.

Statue of William III. This equestrian statue on College Green, Dublin, was inaugurated in 1701, in commemoration of the battle of the Boyne in 1690. Twice a year, viz. 1 July, the anniversary of the battle, and 4 Nov., the birthday of William (the Orangemen's festivals), the statue used to be whitewashed, the king being decorated with a scarlet coat and orange sash, while a bunch of green ribbons and shamrocks was placed under the uplifted left foot of the horse. Garlands of orange lilies, and streamers of orange ribbons decked the horse, and any person passing the statue who neglected to take off his hat was knocked down, and then kicked for presuming to fall in the presence of the hero. In 1822 these biennial decorations were prohibited by law, and in 1836 the statue was blown to pieces by gunpowder. Daniel O'Connell, during his year of mayoralty, had the statue repaired and bronzed. The original statue was of iron, faced with lead.

Statuesque School of French artists. The school of painting founded by David (1748–1825).

David, pronounced *Dah-veed.*

Statu'ta Gui'gonis, 1134. The written rules of the Carthusians made by the fifth prior Guigo. Also called *Consuetudines Cartusiæ.*

Statu'ta Sabau'diæ. The code of laws by Amadeus III. of Savoy (1391–1451).

Statute Caps. Cloth caps enjoined by statute (13 Eliz. c. 19) to be worn by all apprentices. Similar to the caps of the Bluecoat boys. James I. had the size, shape, colour, and price of such caps fixed by Act of Parliament.

Better wits have worn plain statute caps.
Love's Labour's Lost, Act v. 2.

Statute-merchant, 12 Oct., 1283. A bond of record under the hand and seal of the debtor, authenticated by the king's seal. If the debtor failed to pay on the date assigned, execution was summarily awarded. *See* p. 8, 'Acton Burnel, &c.'

Statute of Labourers *(The),* 1349, fixing the wages to be given; and another 1360 which enacted that labourers, who absented themselves from their work or quitted their place of abode without permission, should be imprisoned for fifteen days and branded on their forehead with a hot iron. Trades unions were decreed to be unlawful. Every labourer was to work at a rate of wages fixed by statute.

Statute 6 George I. *(The).* Enacted that 'the crown of Ireland be inseparably annexed to that of Great Britain; that Ireland be bound by British acts of Parliament, if named therein; that the Irish House of Lords have no appellate jurisdiction; and that final appeals, in all cases of law and equity, be to the British House of Peers.' In 1782 Henry Grattan induced the British legislature to repeal this act, and the Irish parliament voted him a donation of 50,000*l.*

Statutes of Io'na *(The),* 1603 (James I. of England). The object of these laws was to bring the Hebridēans in line with the rest of Scotland.

The principal men of the M'Leods, the Macdonalds, Macleans, and Macneils (also Mackinnons, &c.) were Hebridean chiefs.

Statutum de Milit'ibus, 1307 (1 Edw. II.), defining and regulating the obligation to receive knighthood in England. It is now a coveted honour, but in the middle ages it was shirked, and laws were passed to compel those qualified to assume the honour. The compulsory obligation was abolished in 1642 (16, 17 Car. I. c. 30).

Steel Boys (*The*), 1760. Irish rebels who went about armed to rescue from the constables those taken up for refusing to pay rent, or who committed acts of violence in opposing the law. *See* 'Irish Associations.'

The cause of this armed rebellion was this: The estates of Lord Donegal (an absentee Irish landlord) being out of lease, he proposed to accept fines from his tenants in the place of rent. Many tenants were unable to pay the fine imposed, and some did not choose to do so. Evictions followed, the vacant estates were let to merchants of Belfast, whole districts were partly depopulated, and insurrection followed insurrection. When these uprisings were put down by the military, thousands of Irish migrated to America. Ireland continued in a state of turbulence more or less to the close of the century, the great grievance being the restrictions imposed by the British parliament on Irish commerce.

** During the 'Home Rule' trouble there was a gang of Irish robbers called Steelboys in the county of Mayo, but they had no connection with the agrarian agitators. *See* p. 428, 'Home Rule.'

Steel Hand. The founder of the race of Clephane of Carslogie was so called because, when he lost one of his hands, his feudal lord supplied him with a hand made of steel (SCOTT, 'Border Antiquities,' vol. ii. p. 206). *See* 'Duke with the silver hand,' 'Golden Hand,' and 'Iron Hand.'

Steelyard (*The*). The English branch and depôt of the Hanseatic League, on the banks of the Thames, and near London Bridge. It was a solid imposing structure, surrounded by a strong wall, and with three massive gates. There was a large garden, orchard, and vineyard attached for the delectation of the merchants and their apprentices.

Stee'nie (2 syl.). George Villiers (subsequently duke of Buckingham). When first introduced to James I. as cupbearer, at a supper entertainment at Baynard's Castle, the king (weary of Carr, who had grown spiritless) was much struck with the looks of the youth, and pointed out his imagined likeness to a beautiful head of St. Stephen at Whitehall, whence he gave him the pet name of 'Steenie,' which he ever after retained. He was furthermore called by the king 'his dog Steenie,' because the queen said he must be her watchdog, and whenever the king was about to make a fool of himself he was to pull the old sow by the ear. I fear his office was no sinecure.

Steenkirk (*A*). I. A wig. We have also a Ramillies wig. The battle of Steenkirk was in 1694. *See* 'Wigs.'

I hope your lordship is pleased with your Steenkirk?—VANBRUGH, *The Relapse* (1697).

II. A cravat or neckcloth carelessly tied and worn, 1692, by French ladies, in imitation of the lace cravats worn by the young French nobles surprised by William III. in the Netherlands. These young nobles, not having time to change their dress, rushed to battle just as they were, 'with lace cravats loosely tied.' As William was repulsed by Marshal de Luxembourg in the battle of Steenkirk in the Netherlands, 3 August, 1692, the furore in France was boundless, and every sort of article was called a Steenkirk something. There were Steenkirk collars, bracelets, and chains, Steenkirk perfumes, confections, and sauces. In short, 'Steenkirk' was the slang of the day. William III. is usually represented with a Steenkirk cravat round his neck.

Good chance saved me from this extremity of wretchedness. For just as I had yielded up my cravat (a smart Steinkirk, by the way, richly laced) enter Dougal, and the scene was changed. —Sir W. SCOTT, *Rob Roy*.

Stella, the pen-name of Mrs. Bowen-Graves, authoress of 'My Queen.'

Stella (*Sir Philip Sidney's*), Lady Penelope Devereux. Edmund Spenser called Sir Philip 'Astrophel,' 'lover of Stella'—formed from Phil (Greek φίλος, lover), and ἄστρον (=Latin *stella*), a star. Hence Astro-philos, Astrophel.

'Stella' (*Swift's*) was Esther daughter of W. Johnson, steward to Sir William Temple. Some say she was Sir William's natural daughter. Swift was her tutor, and in 1716 privately married her, but she went by the name of Mrs. Johnson, and never lived under the same roof as Swift. In 1728 she died 'of a broken heart' at the age of 44.

While the husband of Stella he became an admirer of Miss Vanhomrigh ('Vanessa'), leading her to suppose that he was unmarried. In 1717 she discovered the fact, and soon after died. Swift died 1745, aged 78.

Stella is Latin for a star=the Greek *αστηρ*, phonetically near enough to Esther for a lover's pun. It is rather strange that Miss Vanhomrigh's name was also Esther, which Swift fondled into 'Essa,' and adding Van[homrigh] before it, made the poetical name Van-essa. A third flame of his was 'Varina,' a Miss Waring. *Esther*, in old Persian, means *a star*.

Stenkill (*The Dynasty of*). A dynasty of Sweden. It succeeded the Ivarian, gave five kings, and was followed by the race of Sverker. Stenkill race 1056–1129.

The Swedes chose Stenkill, but the Goths chose Hako the Red. The rival monarchs came to an amicable arrangement, stipulating that Hako should reign during his life, but that Gothland should revert to Sweden when he died.

Stephen, King of England, usurped the crown which by regular descent should have gone to Maud, daughter of the last king (Henry I.), wife of Geoffrey, Count of Anjou (Plantagĕnet). Maud was actually crowned in 1141, but Stephen was the recognised sovereign till his death, when the crown descended to the son of Maud (Henry II.). Stephen was the grandson of William the Conqueror by Adela, who married the Count of Blois (1104, 1135–1154).

Father: Stephen count of Blois; *Mother*: Adela, daughter of William I.; *Wife*: Matilda or Maud, daughter of Eustace count of Boulogne. (His son William inherited his estates and his title 'count of Blois.')
Style and Title.—Stephanus rex Anglorum.

Stephen (*Order of St.*), 1764. A military order of Hungary revived by Queen Maria Theresa, the decoration being an Hungarian cross hung on a cerise-coloured ribbon edged with green. The legend is 'Sancto Stephano regi Apostolico.'

Stephen I. (*St.*), king of Hungary (979, 997–1038). His name was Vayik, and he was the son of Duke Geyza. St. Adalbert, in 993, on the baptism of Vayik changed his name to Stephen. He was called 'the Apostle of Hungary' and 'S. Stephanus rex Apostolicus.' His day is 20 Aug., still held sacred, and his embalmed right hand is carried in procession through the streets of Buda. The crown given him by Gregory V. is still called St. Stephen's crown, and with it the emperor of Austria is still crowned as king of Hungary.

He died and was crowned on Ascension Day, and five centuries after his death was canonised.

Stephen's Crown (*St.*). The crown of Hungary presented by Pope Gregory V. to King Stephen of Hungary. The present crown consists of two parts, but it is the upper part which was presented by the pope.

Sterco'rians. Those Christians who believe that the Eucharistic elements are digested and turn to corruption like other food. Of course, with those who believe in the dogma of transubstantia-

tion, the difficulty is the promise: 'Thou wilt not suffer thy Holy One to see corruption.'

Stercorianism. The dogma that the Eucharistic elements are digested like other food. (Latin *stercus*, dung.)

Sterling Gold consists of 22 parts (called carats) of pure gold and two parts of alloy, either silver or copper. But fancy gold articles may be manufactured with only 15, 12, or even 9 carats of gold and the rest alloy. 1 lb. Troy of standard gold is coined into 46 sovereigns. There remains a small fraction over; but 46 sovereigns will do for a pound Troy weight.

A sovereign weighs 5 dwts. 3·27447 grains; but 5 dwts. 2½ grains is a legal tender.

The Bank of England gives 46l. 14s. 6d. a pound for gold, and 3l. 17s. 10½d. per ounce.

Sterling Silver consists of 37 parts of silver and three of copper. 1 lb. Troy of silver is coined into 66 shillings.

A shilling from the mint weighs 3 dwts. 15·27272 grains.

The standard value of silver is very variable. In 1870 it was 5s. an ounce. In 1875 about 4s. In 1878 it was 4s. 2d. In 1890 it varied from 4s. to 4s. 4d.

Stettin, in Prussia (*Treaty of*), 13 ·Dec., 1570. A treaty of peace after the Seven Years' War.

Steward of the Household (*Lord*). An officer in the royal household of England, head of the 'Board of Green Cloth.' He has no formal grant of office, but receives his charge from the sovereign, who presents him with a white wand, saying: 'Seneschal, tenez le bâton de notre maison.' The salary is 2,000l. a year.

These tags of French put into the mouth of our English monarchs are quite out of date, and ought to be abolished. Surely an English sovereign ought to speak the English language. English is fifty times a better language than French, and quite able to express the mystic phrase 'tenez le bâton de notre maison.'

Steward ˙of the Marshalsea (*Court of the*). For the trial of treason, murder, manslaughter, and blows· by which blood was shed in any of the palaces or houses of the king during his residence there (Henry VIII.).

Stewart Diamond (*The*). A South African diamond discovered in 1872, and weighing 288¾ carats (nearly 2 ounces Troy). It is of a light yellow colour. *See* ' Diamonds.'

'Stir-up' Sunday. The last or 25th Sunday after Trinity. So called from the first two words of the collect. *See* p. 858, ' Sunday.'

Still Christmas, 1525. The festivities of this Christmastide were forbidden on account of the illness of the king (Henry VIII.).

Stockholm (*Treaties of*). I. 11 Sept., 1640, of alliance between Sweden and the States-General.

II. 20 Nov., 1719, an accommodation between Sweden and George I., in right of his Hanoverian dominions. George agreed to pay a million crowns on condition that Bremen and Verden were ceded to him in perpetuity.

Bremen and Verden had been ceded to Sweden by the Peace of Westphalia (1648).

III. 21 Jan., 1720. By this treaty, enforced by Great Britain, the King of Prussia got the town of Stettin, with the Isles of Usedom and Wollin, and a part of Pomerania.

Stettin was occupied by the Swedes 1630-1648, and after much contention was restored to Sweden in 1679.

Stoic Sect (*The*) of ancient Greece. Founded by Zeno of Cyprus (B.C. 358–260). He lectured in the ' Stoa Pœcĭlê ' of Athens, whence his disciples were called *stoics*, or frequenters of the *porch*. The main doctrines of this sect were fatalism, perfect subjection of the passions, and the freedom of the will. Zeno considered the earth to be a sentient animal, of which God is the living soul. His contemporaries were Persæos, Aristo, Herillos, and Sphæros. Their successors were Cleanthês, Chrysippos, Zeno and Athenodōros of Tarsus, Panælĭos, Diogĕnês the Babylonian, and Posidonĭos.

The *New School* consisted of Epictêtos of Phrygia (A.D. 50–120), Arrĭan the historian (A.D. 90–182), and Marcus Aurēlius the Roman emperor (A.D. 130–180), author of ' Meditations ' written in Greek, and for style, humility, and piety unrivalled among heathen writers. The poet Senĕca was a Stoic.

Stolbowa (*Peace of*), Feb. 27, 1617, between Sweden and Russia, by which

Russia gave up Carelia, Ingria, Novgorod, and Narva to Sweden; renounced all pretensions on Livonia; and paid Sweden 200,000 roubles (8,000*l.*).

Stone Age (*The*). The period of stone implements, preceding the bronze age. *See* p. 14, ' Ages.'

Stone Staircase (*The*), Venice. A flight of forty-five stone steps leading up to the doge's palace. *See* p. 366, ' Giant's Stairs.'

Stone of Destiny (*The*). The Lia Fail of Ireland, better known as the Scone Stone, removed by Edward I. from Scotland and enclosed in our coronation chair, in Westminster Abbey, where it still remains. It was called the ' Fatale Marmor,' or ' Stone of Destiny,' from the notion, inscribed on it, that wherever this stone is, the Scots shall be the dominant power ; and the succession of the Stuarts is thought to be sufficient to justify the prophecy. *See* ' Lia Fail.'

Ni fallat fatum, Scoti, quocunque locatum
Invenient lapidem, regnare tenentur ibidem.

Where'er this stone may be, such is the Fates' decree,
There the Scottish race will fill the highest place.

It is a great pity it was not sent back again, for a worse dynasty than that of the Stuarts could not be easily found.

Stone of Infamy (*The*). A large flagstone on which bankrupts were bumped on Shrove Tuesday. There is still one to be seen in Venice near St. Mark's church, another in Verona, a third in Florence in the old market place. One by one the bankrupts were brought to the stone, partially stripped, and then, being lifted into the air by two or three stout men, bumped twelve times ' in honour of the twelve apostles.' At each bump the creditors crowed like cocks.

Stone of the Swede (*The*). Gustavus Adolphus was slain at Lützen 16 Nov., 1632. His body was found the next day not far from the great stone between Lützen and the canal. This stone has ever since been called ' The Stone of the Swede.'

In 1832 the German nation erected a noble monument to the memory of the Swedish king.

Stonewall Jackson. Thomas Jefferson Jackson, general of the southern or confederate army in the great American Civil War. He contributed to the defeat of the federals at Bull Run 21 July, 1861; distinguished himself in the battles of Chickahominy June, 1862; defeated General Banks at Cedar Mountain 9 Aug., 1862; captured Harper's Ferry 15 Sept., 1862; fought in the battle of Antietam 17 Sept., 1862; contributed to the defeat of Hooker at Chancellorsville 2 May, 1863, and here he received his death wound. It was General Bee who said, in the battle of Bull Run, 'There is Jackson, standing like a stone-wall.' *See* p. 119, 'Brazen Wall.'

Stony Waste (*The*). Between Marseilles and the mouths of the Rhône, 'about 100 furlongs from the sea.' Here Hercules, passing through Gallia, encountered Albion and Bergion, who had united their powers near the mouth of the river Rhosne (Rhône), and a great battle was fought. Hercules, seeing that his men were worsted, commanded them to pick up stones and cast them against the foe. This did they, and gained the victory, leaving Albion and his brother dead on the field.

Stool of Repentance (*The*). An ecclesiastical punishment in which the offender was placed 'directly over against the pulpit, there to stand bareheaded with a sheet, or other accustomed note of difference, on a board raised a foot and a half at least above the church floor, that they may be *in loco editiore, et eminentiores omni populo*. This was repeated sometimes for 'six preaching days,' or even more, and the preacher spoke at the 'penitent' or to the penitent as he thought proper. The satisfaction being finished, the offender put on his usual clothes and entered the church purified and absolved.

Storm (*The Great*), 26 Nov., 1703. The most terrible that ever raged in England. It was this storm which supplied Addison with the celebrated lines—

So when an angel by divine command
With rising tempests shakes a guilty land,
Such as of late o'er pale Britannia past,
Calm and serene he drives the furious blast;
And pleased the Almighty's orders to perform,
Rides on the whirlwind and directs the storm.

Storm of Nov. 14 (*The Memorable*), 1854, in the Black Sea, where an English fleet was moored during the Crimean War. It blew down six of the minarets of the Grand Mosque, tore off many roofs, blew down almost all the tents, dispersed the men's clothes in all directions—blankets, hats, great-coats, tables, chairs, tubs, bed-clothes, flew through the air like autumn leaves. Several ships were wrecked, and all the fleet more or less injured.

In the 'Prince' were lost 2,500 watch-coats, 16,000 blankets, 3,700 rugs, 53 000 woollen frocks, 19,000 lambswool drawers, 36,700 socks, 12,880 pairs of boots, 1,800 pairs of shoes, besides drugs of all sorts.
In 14 wrecked transports were lost 859,714 lbs. of biscuit, 74,880 lbs. of salt meat, 157 head of cattle, 645 sheep, 8,000 gallons of rum, 73,986 lbs. of rice, 11,200 lbs. of coffee, 1,116,172 lbs of forage corn, 800,000 lbs, of pressed hay.
With the 'Resolute' were lost several million rounds of ball cartridge, and all the reserve ammunition for the artillery.

Stormy Petrel (*The*). John Scott, Earl of Eldon (1751–1838). So called because he was in the habit of hastening up to London, when any rumour of a dissolution of the cabinet reached him. He did so at the death of Lord Liverpool, under the expectation that the king would call on him to form a ministry, but the task was assigned to Canning. Again, when Canning died, he was in full expectation of being sent for, but the king applied to Lord Goderich. Again, when Goderich resigned, Eldon felt sure of being sent for, but the king asked Wellington to form a ministry.

Stormy Petrel of Politics (*The*). Lord Brougham. In a H.B. sketch, No. 694, 22 June, 1841, Lord Brougham is represented as a stormy pet'rel flying over the Channel. The words 'France' and 'England' appear on opposite sides of the picture, and his lordship's flight is towards England.

Stormy Petrel of European Politics (*The*). Giuseppe Mazzīni (1808–1872).

Storthing, or Storting (*The*). The two legislative houses of Norway combined. It is elected once in three years, and for business purposes divides itself into two chambers—the Lagthing and the Odelsthing (the legislative house and 'house of commons'). All bills originate in the Odelsthing, and are sent up to the Lagthing for approval or disapproval. If assented to they are submitted to the king. If the king dissents, they are returned to the Storthing (or combined house), and whatever passes the Storthing thrice becomes law, whether the king approves it or not.

Thing, or *ting,* a diet; *Stor-thing,* the great diet; *Lag-thing,* the law diet; *Odels-thing,* the landed diet. Storthing, pronounce *Stoor-ting.*

Strabo of Germany (*The*). Sebastian Munster (1489–1552).

Stradiots.

A kind of light cavalry raised by the Venetians in their Dalmatian possessionš. They dressed in a semi-European and semi-Eastern fashion. They wore short hauberks, but over the hauberks a parti-coloured tunic of rich stuff; their legs were clad in wide pantaloons and half-boots. On their head they wore a straight upright cap, like a Greek cap, and their weapons were a target, a bow and arrows, a scimitar, and a poniard. Their horses were the best obtainable, being employed for skirmishing. Greek, στρατιώτης, a soldier.

Scarcely had Charles (VIII.) dismounted at Fornovo when his quarters were beaten up by the Stradiots, who retired as soon as the French took to arms.—*History of Venice,* vol. ii. p. 144 (Murray, 1830).

Straffor'dians, 1641.

The fifty-nine members of the House of Commons who voted against the bill of Strafford's attainder. In fact Strafford was not guilty of treason against the king, that is quite certain, and treason against the sovereignty of the people was a crime hitherto unheard of.

Strangers from Rome.

So Augustine and his party announced themselves when they landed in England, at Ebbsfleet, about 596.

The 'Strangers of Rome,' spoken of in Acts ii. 10, means Jews who had taken up a temporary residence in Rome. It was to these 'Strangers of Rome' that the 'Epistle to the Romans' was written.

Strate'gi.

The Board of generals in the Athenian republic, consisting of ten officers, who in war took the command of the army alternately, each for one day. Later on a chairman, called the Polemarch, was added, who had the casting vote in the board.

Towards the decline of Roman greatness the chief magistrate of Athens was called Stratègos (*duke*). Constantine the Great honoured him with the title of ' Megas Strategos ' (*Grand Duke*).

, Before the battle of Marathon 'The Ten Strategi' met in council, and the opinion was divided. The casting vote was given by the polemarch. Kallimåchos, in favour of battle.

Strawberry Leaves (*The*).

Emblem of a duke's crown. To 'desire the strawberry leaves' means to wish to be created a duke. The duke's coronet is adorned with eight strawberry leaves. The coronet of a marquis has only four leaves (either strawberry or oak) and four pearls, alternating.

The queen offered Lord Salisbury a dukedom, but he does not desire the strawberry leaves.— *Truth,* 11 Feb., 1886.

Strawberry Preachers.

So Latimer called those clergymen who strayed from their parishes. Some stray as stars, some for pleasure, some from idleness and indifference. The strawberry is the plant which *strays* (Anglo-Saxon *streowan,* to stray, whence *streow-berie*).

Street Bullies,

in London. At the Restoration they were called Muns and Tityre Tus [pronounce *tuze*].

They were next called Hectors and Scourers.

Later still they were called Nickers and Hawcabites.

Then Mohocks.

The last of this ill-famed notoriety was Spring-heeled Jack.

See each of these words *in loco.*

Street of Trip'ods (*The*),

in ancient Athens. These tripods had been won by musical competitions between different tribes. The chorāᵍos, or leader, received a tripod for prize, but was expected to build a shrine over it. The best known is that of Lysicrătês, popularly known as the ' Lantern of Demosthĕnês.'

Strelitzes (*The*),

that is, Russian musketeers. A militia raised by Ivan IV., and armed with muskets instead of bows and arrows. The word *strelitz* means ' one who fires a musket.' The militia ceased to exist in the reign of Peter the Great. Ivan = our English name John.

Strict Communionists.

See p. 180, ' Close Communionists.'

Strongbow.

Richard de Clare earl of Pembroke, to whom Dermot [M'Murrough] king of Leinster gave in marriage his daughter Eva and the succession to the crown, for having recovered the kingdom from which he had been driven by Tiernan O'Ruarc lord of Breffny, whose wife Dermot had abducted. Strongbow was brave, munificent, and of ruined fortune. His father Gilbert (who died 1149) was also called Strongbow. Died 1176.

Struck Bruce.

Midnight. Lord Aberdare (whose family name was

Bruce), as Home Minister, was the father of the bill for the closing of public houses at midnight. So when the clock has struck twelve, publicans say it has ' struck Bruce.'

Stuart Dynasty (*The*), in England, gave James I., Charles I., Charles II., James II., Mary wife of William III., and Anne. (With the two Pretenders, James and Charles Edward.)

HENRY VII. was the father of Margaret, who married James IV. of Scotland, and their son was James V. of Scotland. James V. was the father of Mary queen of Scots, and Mary queen of Scots was the mother of JAMES I. of England.

, The Scotch as a nation are radicals, but no kings could possibly be less democratic than the Stuarts. The Scots are Presbyterians and puritans, but the Stuart kings were Catholics, in heart, at least, and anything but puritans either in morals or religion. Perhaps Charles I. was the best of the bad lot, the worst of all our dynasties.

Stuart Papers (*The*), 1712. Negotiations carried on between the British ministry and the Old Pretender respecting his succession to the throne, on the death of Queen Anne. The chief correspondent was St. John lord Bolingbroke. These papers were obtained by George IV. from Rome, and are now preserved in Cumberland Lodge, Windsor.

Stuarts (*The*). The old Scottish way of spelling stewards. The royal Stuarts of Scotland were descended from Walter, the 6th steward or seneschal of Scotland. The first of the dynasty was David II., son of Margery and Walter, and grandson of ' The Bruce.'

ROBERT I. (The Bruce) was the father of Margery, who married Walter the Steward or Seneschal, and their son was David II.

Stuarts (*The*). Ill-starred for 400 years. The house of Stuart was as unlucky as the house of the Theban Laius.

ROBERT III. died of grief because his eldest son Robert had been starved to death, and his younger son James was taken captive by Henry IV.

JAMES I. (his son), after spending his youth in imprisonment, was assassinated by his uncle.

JAMES II. was struck dead by the plug of a bursting cannon.

JAMES III. flying from the field of battle, was thrown from his horse, and murdered in a cottage into which he had been conveyed.

JAMES IV. fell at Flodden Field.

JAMES V. died of grief for the ruin of his army at Solway Moss.

MARY his daughter was beheaded by Queen Elizabeth.

HENRY STUART lord Darnley, her cousin and husband (the titular king), was blown up in his own lodging-house.

JAMES I. of England died, not without suspicion of being poisoned by Lord Buckingham.

(His daughter Elizabeth Stuart was the ill-starred ' Winter Queen ' of Bohemia.)

(His cousin Arabella died insane in the Tower of London)

CHARLES I. was beheaded.

CHARLES II. passed many years in exile after the fatal battle of Worcester. (The slave of Louis XIV.)

JAMES II., being driven from his throne, died in a foreign land, a pensioner of Louis XIV.

The two Pretenders, James and Charles Edward Stuart, vainly tried to recover the throne, and both died in exile.

MARY, daughter of James II., died childless.

ANNE, sister of Mary, lost all her seventeen children in infancy.

HENRY the cardinal called himself Henry IX. ' by the grace of God, but not by the grace of man.'

It has been facetiously said that ' a cousin of Queen Anne ' may be found in every family of maiden ladies in every cathedral city of England.

Sturm und Drang Period, 1750 to 1800. The volcanic era of German literature, when French and Latin patches were banished from the language, and German was left unadulterated.

The Sturm und Drang period of life is between 20 and 25, all enthusiasm and cram full of radical reform. All abuses are to be swept away, and a Utopian millennium is to be introduced. So in this literary period the language was to be purified, and German literature was to be made the model literature of the world. Old things were to be done away, and all things to become new.

Styli'tes (3 syl.). ' Sancti Columnārês ' (Latin), ' Pillar-saints ' (English). Religious enthusiasts who followed the example of Simeon the Syrian, who lived 47 years on the top of a pillar, and died 460, aged 69, of an ulcer. He first lived on a pillar only 12 feet high, then on one 22 feet high, then on a pillar 56 feet high, and lastly on one 40 feet in height. This foolery continued in the East for 600 years.

When Vulfilacius erected a pillar near Trèves, the bishop had it pulled down.

Suabian League (*The*). ' Schwabischer Bund,' 1376, opposed to the ' League of Marbach ' (*q.v.*). In 1384 it was extended and converted into the *Grand Union* at Heidelberg. In 1499 Würtemberg joined, and thus formed the *Great Suabian Confederation*. It was dissolved in 1533.

At first it contained 32 towns, afterwards as many as 41.

Suabian Mirror (*The*), or Schwabenspiegel (13th cent.). The local laws of Suabia compiled into a digest. *See* ' Saxon Mirror.'

Suabian Poets (*The*). The Minnesingers (1150–1250). The modern school is headed by Uhland (1787–1862), universally known by his song called ' The Lad of the Mountain.'

Su'adæ Medulla. The Marrow of Persuasion; irresistible persuasion. So

Ennius calls Marcus Cethēgus, the curule, edile, and pontifex maximus, B.C. 213. Persuasion is here personified.

Subdeacon. He does not receive from the bishop imposition of hands, but receives from him the patera and cup empty, and from the archdeacon the cruises of wine, of water, and the towel. He must be 22 years of age. His duties are (1) the custody of the sacred vessels used in the mass; (2) to pour out the wine and the water; (3) to intone the epistle; (4) to hold the book of the Gospels while the priest reads; (5) to carry the cross in solemn processions; (6) to pour water for the priest's washing of his hands; and (7) to assist the deacon in receiving the offerings of the congregation.

Subjectivity of Knowledge (*The*). The question whether our knowledge of phenomena is merely subjective or mental. Does the outward world (in relation to any individual) really exist, except in the brain of that individual? Protagōras (B.C. 480–411) said, ' Man is the measure of all things, to himself'.; Heraclītos believed the same; so did Aristippos of Cyrēnê. This was the prevailing belief in old Rome at the close of the 2nd Christian cent., and has cropped up again in Germany, France, and England within the last few years. The argument is this : If man cannot get out of himself, all he knows must be *in* himself. Even his thoughts can never be divorced from his ego, but must be always a part of himself.

Sublapsa′rians, Supralapsari-ans. The Supralapsarians maintain that God decreed the fall of Adam and its consequences before the creation of Adam (*supra lapsum*, before the fall). The Sublapsarians maintain that God did not *decree*, but only *permitted* the fall, and *after* man had fallen, God's judgments against disobedient Adam were carried out (*sub lapsum*, after the fall).

Illustrate thus. I lay a log over a rail, and the train is smashed; that is one thing. The passengers themselves lay a log over a rail, and I do not interfere to prevent it ; that is another thing. In both cases the train is smashed, but in one case I am the active agent of the mischief, in the other I am the passive permitter of it.

Sublime Porte (*The*). French for the ' Lofty Gate.' Name given to the Turkish government. Bagdad, the capital of the caliph, was called ' the Porte ' (*q.v.*). Constantinople has 12 gates, and near one of these gates is a building with a lofty gateway (called ' Bab-i-humajun). In this building resides the vizier, and in the same are the offices of all the chief ministers of state. The French phrase has been adopted because French was, at the time, the language of European diplomacy.

Sublime Society of Beefsteaks (*The*). Established in London 1735.

Submission of the Clergy (*The*), 1531. Henry VIII. insisted on being acknowledged supreme head of the Church and clergy of England, next immediately after Christ. Convocation objected, but at length submitted, with the limitation ' quantum per Christi leges licet.' The Convocation of York gave in, and offered a subsidy also. It was then agreed that no new canons or constitutions should be enacted without the king's authority. The king agreed to the limitation, and the clergy were restored to royal favour. The Submission of the Clergy was confirmed by Act of Parliament in 1534 (25 Hen. VIII. c. 19).

Subtle Doctor (*The Most*). Docteur Subtil. So Duns Scotus was called by the French. He was regent of the theological schools of Paris from 1304 to 1310, when he died of apoplexy in the 34th year of his age.

Succession (*The Acts of*). Acts of Parliament to authorise a change in the hereditary succession of the British or English sovereigns.

(1) Henry IV. who possessed himself of the crown to the prejudice of Lionel duke of Clarence (second son of Edward III.), declared the succession should run in his own son Henry [V.] and his descendants.

(2) Henry VII. had no hereditary right to the crown, but Parliament passed an Act whereby his son Henry [VIII.] was made heir, and the succession was placed in his regular heirs.

(3) Henry VIII. changed the succession first from Mary to Elizabeth and then from Elizabeth to Edward VI.

(4) Charles II. was by parliament held to succeed Charles I., by which Act the Commonwealth was wholly ignored.

(5) On the ' abdication ' of James II.

the succession was settled on William and Mary; and if they died without issue, on the Protestant line, or issue of the Electress Sophia of Hanover.

Suf'fave'an or **Sofi dynasty** (*The*), lasted 237 (1499–1736). A Persian dynasty founded by Ismail, third son of Hyder, fifth in descent from Sheik Sofi or Suffee, a very holy man. It was overthrown by Nadir Shah.

Suffolk Resolutions (*The*), 9 Nov. 1774. That is the county of Suffolk in Massachusetts, of which Boston is the capital. They were made against the attempts of Great Britain 'to enslave America.' They enjoined officers who had public money in their hands to retain it till the wrongs of the people were redressed; and called on all public officers appointed by the British Government to resign before the 20th of Sept., or to be held as enemies of the American colonies. They called upon all Americans to attend military drill and prepare themselves for war. They advised the people to imprison all government servants if Government attempted to lay hands on the insurgents.

Suffragan Bishops. Assistant bishops. Twenty-six were appointed by 26 Hen. VIII. c. 14, A.D. 1534. So called because they were allowed the *jus suffragii* or right of suffrage in the synods. Discontinued and the Act repealed by 1, 2 Phil. & Mary c. 8, A.D. 1554. Revived by 1 Eliz. c. 1, A.D. 1559.

Su'liots. A number of families who fled from their Turkish oppressors to the mountains of Suli in the 17th cent. They were partly Hellēnic and partly Albanian in origin. Their descendants mostly live in Greece.

Sulpic'ians. The company of priests founded at Vaugirard by J. J. Olier, curé of St. Sulpice. The object of this college is the instruction of young ecclesiastics.

The great seminary at Montreal, Canada, is conducted by the Sulpicians, but their main establishment is in Paris.

Summer King. When Robert Bruce was boasting of his sovereign rank and great success, his wife said to him, 'You are, indeed, a summer king; but you will scarcely be a winter one.'

Summer Lieutenants. In the Prussian army are officers of the Land-

wehr and reserves summoned for duty in their respective regiments for six weeks in summer.

Summoned (*The*). Ferdinand IV. of Castile and Leon (1285, 1295–1312), so called because the brothers Peter and John Carvajal, being condemned to death without trial, ' summoned ' him to appear before the tribunal of God within thirty days. Ferdinand was quite well on the thirtieth day, but was found dead in his bed next morning.

Sun of Austerlitz (*The*). A promise of success, a good omen. Napoleon I. remembered that the sun broke out just before the battle of Austerlitz (2 Dec. 1805), which he won over the Emperors of Austria and Russia; and in subsequent campaigns looked on sunshine as a good omen.

Quelques instants avant la bataille de la Moskowa, le soleil se montra dans son éclat : ' Soldats (s'écrie Napoléon) c'est le soleil d'Austerlitz ! ' et ces seuls mots électrisèrent la grande armée.— LA ROUSSE, *Dictionnaire Universel*.

Sunday. *See under—*

ADVENT four weeks before Christmas.
Second Sunday after the EPIPHANY, Festum Architriclini.
Third Sunday before Lent, SEPTUAGESIMA Sunday.
Second Sunday before Lent, SEXAGESIMA Sunday.
First Sunday before Lent, QUINQUAGESIMA Sunday; Dominica Brandōnum; Sunday next before Lent.
1st Sunday of LENT, Quadragesima Sunday, next to Ash Wednesday; Day of the Buræ.
2nd Sunday of Lent, Reminiscēre Sunday.
3rd Sunday of Lent, Ocūli Sunday.
4th Sunday of Lent, Lætāre Sunday. Dominica de Rosa, Refreshment Sunday, Mothering Sunday, Mid-Lent.
5th Sunday of Lent, Passion Sunday, Carl Sunday, Sabbatum vacat.
6th Sunday of Lent, Palm Sunday; Festum Broncheriæ; Festum Olivārum; Sunday next before Easter.
EASTER DAY.
1st Sunday after Easter, Quasimodo Sunday, Low Sunday, Alb Sunday.
2nd Sunday after Easter, Balaam's Ass Sunday (*q.v.*).
3rd Sunday after Easter, Fête du Patronage de St. Joseph.
Sunday after ASCENSION, Expectation Sunday, the Sunday next before Whit Sunday.
Sunday after the Octave of Ascension, Fête of the Holy Relics.
WHIT SUNDAY or Pentecost.
TRINITY SUNDAY, called Stately Sunday.
Sunday next after Trinity Sunday, Fête Dieu, in France.
25th, or Last Sunday of Trinity, called ' Stir up ' Sunday and Fragment Sunday.
Sept. (Second Sunday in), Fête du saint nom de B. V. Marie.
Oct. (Fifth Sunday in). Fête du Patronage de la Sainte Vierge.
See also 'Panic Sunday,' ' Precious Blood ' (Feast of the).
** For explanation, see each word under its proper letter.

Sunday Fine (*The*). A fine of 1*s.* levied upon all the Irish who neglected to attend the Protestant church. This levy was made first in the reign of Elizabeth, and, with fees, amounted (says Hume) to 20*l.* a month. The shilling was supposed to go to the poor, but this was evaded, at least in the case of the Catholic poor, who (it was said) ought to pay and not receive the shilling.

Sunday Sabbath, 321. It was Constantine who, by an imperial decree, consecrated the Sun-day [*dies solis*], as the Christian sabbath, to be observed throughout Christendom as a day of rest and religious observances. And from this decree it was called ' The Lord's Day.' *See* 'Day of Rest.'

τὴν σωτήριον ἡμέραν, ἣν καὶ φωτὸς εἶναι καὶ ἡλίον ἐπώνυμον συμβαίνει.—EUSEBIUS, *Life of Constantine*, iv. 18.

Sung or **Song Dynasty.** *See* ' Tsong.'

Sunnites (2 syl.), or ' Sonnees ' or ' Sunis.' A Musulman sect so called from the Arabic word *sunnah* (tradition), because they professed to preserve the true tradition. They recognised as the real descendants of Mahomet, the califs Aboubekr, Omar, and Othman, and were opposed to the Shiites or Shiahs who insisted that Ali was the legitimate descendant of Mahomet. The Sunnites now prevail in the Ottoman Empire, Arabia, Egypt, &c., while the Shiites prevail in Persia, exist to some extent in India, and to a much less extent in Syria.

The Sunnites are divided into four sects, called the Hanbalites, the Shafeites, the Malekites, and the Hanefites, so called from their leaders, Hanbal, Hanefa, Shafei, and Malek. *See* ' Shiites.'

Superior Person (*The*). Edward Horsman, M.P. (1807–1876), was so called by Mr. Disraeli in his speech upon Denmark and Germany, 8 July, 1864.

We know in private life there is always in every circle some person who is regarded as a ' superior person.' They [*sic*] decide on everything, they lecture everybody, all acknowledge their transcendent qualities, but everyone gets out of their way. The right hón. member for Stroud is the ' superior person' of the House of Commons.

Su′perlapsa′rians, or ' Su′pralapsa′rians.' Those who believe that God from all eternity decreed the fall of man. The Sublapsarians, on the other hand, maintain that God did not foreordain and predetermine the fall, but only per-

mitted it—that Adam was free to stand and free to fall.

Supplementary Act (*The*), 1 June, 1815, added in the French Constitutional Charter to the Imperial Constitution as a codicil. This was done by Napoleon in the famous ' Hundred Days.'

Supplicat (*A*). In the University of Cambridge is a grace of the senate duly signed to confer a degree on the person signified in the writ.

Supporters to an heraldic shield are, in England, confined to corporations and to peers and knights either of the Garter or of the Bath. In Scotland Lord Lyon (*q.v.*) has the privilege of granting this honour to others ; not so the Garter king of Arms (*q.v.*) in England.

Supremacy (*The Act of*), 26 Hen. VIII. c. 1, A.D. 1534, constitutes the reigning monarch of England supreme head of the English church, and reduces the ' courts spiritual ' into king's courts. By this Act the bishops were virtually made responsible for the loyalty of their clergy ; the clergy were mere exponents of the Royal will ; and the king had the power of prescribing the form of faith, doctrine, and discipline, which should be taught throughout the land.

Fisher bishop of Rochester, Sir Thomas More the ex-lord chancellor, and several others were beheaded in 1535, for denying the king's supremacy. Before this Act was passed, the pope of Rome exercised supremacy in the churches of England and Scotland.

Supreme Being (*The*), 7 May, 1794. Robespierre proposed to the Convention that the republic should acknowledge Wisdom as the Supreme Being of all created things, not as a personal fact, but as a most useful political bogie. Accordingly, the painter David was employed to make in the garden of the Tuileries a suitable symbol of the Supreme Being. He made a mound surmounted with a tree of liberty. On the top of this mound Robespierre, as the high priest of the Supreme Being, was to set fire to the statues of Atheism and Deism, and to unveil the statue of Wisdom. Dressed in a sky-blue coat and most showy waistcoat, and carrying in his hand a monster bouquet, the ' Incorruptible ' headed the procession on 8 June. All Paris was mad with joy at this new change and

every church adopted the new motto TO
THE SUPREME BEING.

The babyism of such foolery seems quite inconsistent with the 'philosophy' of the Encyclope-
dists, and the many really wise and practical laws
passed at the time.

Supreme Father (*The*). The
grand master or chief potentate of the
St. Simonians. Barthélemy Prosper Enfantin, usually called Père Enfantin, was
elected Supreme Father in 1830. In
1831 a split in the 'family' was made by
Bazard, chief of the dogma department,
who wished to keep his wife to himself,
and also that his daughter should marry;
but Enfantin insisted there was no such
thing as marriage in the St. Simonian
Family. The contest grew so high that
Enfantin established 'a model community' at Ménilmontant, near Paris.
Here he was arrested for social inde-
cency, imprisoned for a year, fined 4*l*.,
and the family at Ménilmontant, which
had lasted only two years, was dispersed.
Enfantin, as Supreme Father of the world
both in spiritual and temporal matters,
summoned Louis Philippe, king of the
French, to appear before him, and answer
for his usurpation of the authority due
to the 'Supreme Father' only. The
family wore a blue robe with a leather
girdle, white trousers, and a red cap;
their neck was left bare, and they had
long flowing beards.

**Supreme Governor of the
Church.** When the 'Royal Supremacy' was restored (1 Eliz. c. 1), 1559,
the queen insisted that the words 'Supreme Governor of the Church, &c.'
should be substituted for 'Supreme Head
of the Church.'

Surgery (*Father of English*).
Richard Wiseman (17th cent.). He introduced ligatures in amputation instead of
hot pitch, or strong acids, or branding
the wound with burning iron. The ligature was invented by Ambroise Paré, a
French surgeon in the 16th cent.

Surgery (*Father of French*). Ambroise Paré (1517-1590).

Surintendant. A title of honour
in the old French monarchy.

I. Le surintendant *des finances* was
created in 1300 by Philippe IV. le Bel
for Enguerrand de Marigny; but the office
was suppressed in 1661 on the disgrace
of Fouquet.

II. Le surintendant général *de la
navigation* created by Louis XIII. for
Cardinal de Richelieu, but suppressed in
1669 on the death of the Duke of Beaufort, the third holder of the office.

III. Le surintendant *des bâtiments de
la couronne* created by Louis XV. for the
Marquis de Marigny, brother of Mme. de
Pompadour.

IV. In the empire there was a *surin-
tendante de la maison impériale.*

Surrender by a straw. Surrenders are made in various forms. In some
manors by a rod, in others by a straw,
in others by glove, delivered by the sur-
renderor to the steward or some other
person taking the surrender in the name
of seisin. In practicé a pen or penholder,
a walking-stick or umbrella, or, more
commonly still, an office ruler is employed
for surrenders and admissions to copyhold property.

Surtees Forgeries (*The*), 1806.
Mr. Surtees palmed off on Sir Walter
Scott certain ballads of his own composition as ancient ballads discovered by
him, and Sir Walter Scott inserted them
in his 'Border Minstrelsy.' One was
'On a feud between the Ridleys and the
Featherstones,' which Mr. Surtees says
he took down from the recitation of an
old woman on Alston Moor. Another was
a ballad of 'Lord Ewrie,' which he says
he took down from an old woman named
Rose Smith of Bishop Middleham (aged
91). A third was 'Barthram's Dirge,'
obtained from Ann Douglas, 'a withered
crone who weeded in his garden.' A
whole series of legends were professedly
obtained from a Mrs. Brown of Falkland,
and another series from Mrs. Arnut of
Arbroath. *See* 'Literary Forgeries.'

**Suspension of the Habeas
Corpus.** In old Rome the phrase was,
*Videant Consules, ne quid detrimenti
capiat Respublica* (Let the Consuls see
that the Commonwealth suffers no injury), by which the *appeal* to the Centuries (in the empire *to Cæsar*) was held
in abeyance, and dictatorial power was
vested in the consuls without appeal.
This suspension of appeal was enforced
against the Gracchi and against the Catiline conspirators.

When *habeas corpus* is suspended,
suspected persons may be arrested

without assigning any reason, and persons arrested are not allowed bail.

Sussex (*Kingdom of*). Founded A.D. 491 by Ella, who came from Holstein, the land of the Saxoni, landed at West Wittering near Chichester (477), and in 491 took Anderïda, the capital of the Regni. Chichester is a phonetic spelling of Cissa-ceaster, the campground of Cissa, son of Ella.

Sutin'ians. Same as Photin'ians (*q.v.*).

Sutras. Aphoristic rules in Sanskrit. The word means *strung together*, because the leaves on which they were written were strung together on a thread.

Suttee. The voluntary immolation of a Hindû widow on the funeral pile of her husband. Declared illegal by the governor-general of British India in 1829.

Swan. '*By heaven and the swans,*' an oath of Edward I.'s. On the day when King Edward I. conferred the dignity of knighthood on his son, the Prince of Wales, 300 others were also knighted. In the course of the high festival two swans richly adorned with gold network were placed on the table, and the king made a vow to God and the swans that he would start forthwith to Scotland and never sheathe sword till he had avenged the death of John [Red] Comyn.

Edward, in fulfilment of his romantic vow to heaven and the swans, advanced as far as Carlisle . . . . but was detained there by . . . . dysentery. —Sir W. SCOTT, *History of Scotland*, viii.

Sweating-sickness (*The*), in 1485 (Henry VII.'s reign), first appeared in England. It lasted a month and carried off 20,000 persons in London. Persons died from extreme exhaustion caused by profuse perspiration. It appeared a second time in England during the year 1506 (Henry VII.); again between July and Dec., 1517; for a fourth time in 1528 (Henry VIII.), and lastly in April and Sept., 1551 (Edward VI.). It raged in Holland, Germany, Denmark, Sweden, Poland, and Russia, 1525–1530.

Swechat, near Vienna, is the place where in 1848 the Hungarian patriots were defeated by the Austrians, led on by Jellachich.

Sweden. Nine dynasties.
1. The race of Ivar and Sigurd, *— 1056, gives twelve sovereigns.
2. The race of Stenkill, 1056–1129, gives seven sovereigns.
3. The races of Sverker and Eric, 1129–1250, gives eight sovereigns.
4. The Folkungians, 1250–1389, gives seven sovereigns.
5. The period of the Union of Calmar.
6. The dynasty of Vasa, 1523–1654, gives seven sovereigns.
7. The dynasty of Deux-Ponts, 1654–1751, gives five sovereigns.
·8. The dynasty of Holstein-Gottorp, 1751–1818, gives four sovereigns.
9. The French dynasty, 1818– *.

Swedenbor'gians, or 'The New Jerusalem Church' (*Rev.* xxi.10),followers of Dr. Emanuel Swedenborg (1688–1772). They hold peculiar views respecting salvation, inspiration, and the Trinity. In regard to the Trinity, they believe it to be centred in the person of Jesus Christ.

Swedes' Stone (*The*). A large stone placed by Jacob Erichsson on the night after the battle of Lützen (17 Nov., 1632) to mark the spot where Gustavus Adolphus fell. In 1830 the German nation replaced the stone by a noble monument in memory of this 'Star of the North.'

Sweet Singer of the Temple (*The*). George Herbert, the poet, who wrote 'The Temple' (1633) and 'The Priest to the Temple' (1652). Born 1593, died 1633.

Swi or **Sooy Dynasty** (*The*). The twelfth imperial dynasty of China, in which China was again united, after being divided for 167 years (420–587). It gave three emperors, and lasted thirty-seven years (587–618). The city of the court was Ho-nân. It was succeeded by the Tang dynasty.

Yang-kien, who assumed the name of Wentee, the founder of this dynasty, was prince of Swi.

Swing (*Captain*). 1830–1833. A name assumed by certain persons who sent threatening letters to those who used threshing machines. The letters ran thus : ' Sir, if you do not lay by your threshing machine, you will hear from SWING.'

Swing and his myrmidons were abroad in the counties, and could scarcely be kept down by the yeomanry and poor-law guardians.—T. Hughes, *Tom Brown at Oxford*, chap. xxxix.

Swing-fires. Incendiary fires for the burning of machinery. So called from ' Captain Swing ' (*see above*).

He [Mr. Gladstone] quoted the Swing-fires as an example of an evil which may have averted greater evil.—*The World*, 2 May, 1888.

Swiss Blood, or ' Sang des Suisses.' Wine of St. Jacques, near Basel, where 1,600 Switzers resisted 22,000 French commanded by the Dauphin (afterwards Louis XI. of France). All the Swiss but ten were slain. This is called the ' Swiss Thermopylæ,' A.D. 1444.

Swiss Thermop'ylæ (*The*), 1444. *See above.*

Sword, in the arms of the city of London.

The usual hypothesis is that this emblem was adopted on the first quarter of the arms of this corporation to commemorate the act of Sir William Walworth, who cut down with his sword the rebel Wat Tyler in the reign of Richard II. We are told in ' Notes and Queries ' (23 July, 1887) it had been adopted some ' few months previously.'

Another solution is that it is the sword of St. Paul, the patron saint of London.

A third is that Stow mistook the letter L in the first quarter for a sword.

Sword (*Order of the*). I. Created 1522 in Sweden by Gustavus I. as the ' Star of the North,' and reconstructed in 1748 by Frederick I. for ' fidelity to the king and the Lutheran faith.' The decoration is a St. Andrew's cross formed by two swords, &c.

II. An order of chivalry instituted 1449 by Alfonso V. of Portugal.

Sword-bearers (*Knights*), or Ensiferi, 1204. An order of knighthood in Livonia. Their habit was white, with two swords crossed, in red. They acquired sovereign power in Livonia. The order ceased in 1562.

Also called 'Brothers of the Sword.'

Sword of God (*The*). Khaled, Mahomet's lieutenant (582–642); also called 'The Scourge of Infidels.' It was by the valour of Khaled that the empire of the califs was founded in Arabia and Syria. He used to say, 'As long as I wear this cap, which has been blessed by the prophet himself, I am invulnerable to all the darts and swords of the infidel.'

Sword of Mars (*The*). Attila (died 453).

Sword of Rome (*The*). Marcus Claudius Marcellus, B.C. 270–280, famous in the second Punic war.

Sydrack. A philosopher and astronomer, who lived 847 years after Noah, of ' whose book of astronomy he held possession.' He converted King Boccus to the Christian faith (!!) and was invited by him to build a mighty tower against the invasions of a rival king ('The History of Boccus and Sydrack ').

Symbol (*The Twelve Articles of the*), *i.e.* the twelve articles of the Apostles' Creed, said, in legend, to have been suggested by the apostles themselves in a grotto of Mount Olivet, before their final separation. It was received into the Latin church, in its present form, in the 11th cent., but there was a formula extant in the 2nd cent. ; items were added in the 4th and 5th cent., and verbal alterations much later. It has as much right to be attributed to the apostles as the twelve sibylline ' prophecies ' to the ancient sibyls. Tradition assigns the items thus : To

1. PETER: 'I believe in God the Father Almighty, maker of heaven and earth,'
2, JOHN: [And] ' in Jesus Christ, his only Son, our Lord.'
3. JAMES, the Greater : [who was] ' conceived of the Holy Ghost ; born of the Virgin Mary ;'
4. ANDREW : ' Suffered under Pontius Pilate ;'
5. PHILIP : ' Was crucified and buried.'
  ' *Dead* ' *is a modern innovation, and is very shaky English.* ' *Mortuus est* ' *means* ' *died,*' *and not* ' *was dead.*' ' *Was crucified, was dead, and was buried.*' *Was dead ? when ? We should hardly say* ' *Charles I. was beheaded, dead, and buried.*'
  ⁂ ' Descended into Hell' is not in the older formulas.
6. THOMAS : 'The third day he rose again from the dead.'
7. JAMES the Less : ' He ascended into heaven, and sitteth on the right hand of God the Father Almighty.'
8. MATTHEW : [From thence] ' He shall come to judge the quick and the dead.'
9. NATHANIEL ; ' I believe in the Holy Ghost ;'
10. SIMON : ' The Holy Catholic Church ;'
  ' *The Communion of Saints' is not in the old formulas.*
11. MATTHIAS : ' The forgiveness of sins ;'
12. JUDE :' The resurrection of the dead.'
  ' The life everlasting' was added in the 4th cent.

Symbols (*The Four*).

I. The symbol of the apostles, called by us the ' Apostles' Creed,' because each of the twelve clauses is attributed by legend to one of the apostles.

II. The Symbol of Nicæa, called by us

the 'Nicene Creed,' because it was formulated in the Council of Nice A.D. 325.

III. The Symbol of Constantinople, so called because it was formulated at the Council of Constantinople in 331. It is nearly the same as the original Nicene Creed. This is the creed recited by the priest in the mass.

The phrase ' and the Son' (*filioque*) was added by a Council of Tolèdo in 589.
N.B. The original creed has been condensed in some parts and expanded in others.

IV. The Symbol of Athanāsius, called by us the 'Athanasian Creed,' directed mainly against Arianism. It did not exist till 670, nearly three centuries after the death of Athanasius, who died in 373, but it is supposed to express his teaching.

Symmes' Hole. The hole about the poles. Captain John Cleves Symmes propounded the theory that the earth about the poles is hollow, and his theory in ridicule is spoken of as Symmes' or Symmes's Hole.

Sym'pathi'sers, 1837-1838. Filibustering citizens of the United States of North America who 'sympathised' with and joined the democrats of Canada in the rebellion. They issued proclamations in the name of the Provisional Government, offering 100 dollars and 300 acres of the best land in Canada to everyone who joined the republicans. Their headquarters were on Navy Island, in the Niagara river, about two miles above the ' falls.'

Syncretists. I. In *philosophy.* So the Eclectics are called in contempt.

II. In *theology.* The Calixtines (*q.v.*) are so called.

Syndics, of the Cambridge University, are the members of special committees. They must be members of the Senate and are appointed, when required, by grace of the Senate.

Synergists, in theology. Those 'heretics' who maintain that man co-operates with grace, as a 'fellow-worker together with God ' in salvation, and that good works must be joined to grace. Melanchthon was a Synergist, so was Pfeffinger, and so was Strigel. This dogma caused a schism in the Lutheran party.

Synod (*The*), 1689, of the Scotch kirk, is a superior court to the Presby-tery, and consists of ministers and elders of contiguous presbyteries. It is a court of review.

The four ecclesiastical bodies are; 1. The Kirk Session; 2. The Presbytery; 3. The Synod; and 4. The General Assembly. The first is limited to one parish, the next extends to contiguous parishes, the third to contiguous presbyteries, and the fourth to the entire body in all Scotland.

Synod convened by Pole (*The*), 1555. A legatine synod convened in London by Cardinal Pole for the ' correction of abuses and making of canons.'

I. The Feast of Reconciliation (*q.v.*) was to be strictly observed.

II. Instructions were to be issued to the clergy for the proper administration of the eucharist.

III. Ecclesiastics were to resign all pluralities, and not engage in secular cares.

IV. Bishops were to restrain their ostentation and luxurious living.

V. Bishops were to examine candidates for holy orders personally.

Simony was forbidden, schools were to be established, and visitations enforced.

Synod of Dort (*The*), 1618-1619. A synod convened at Dort, to which James I. sent deputies to decide upon the five points of difference between Calvinists and Arminians. As the synod excluded the Arminians their judgment was one-sided. *See* 'Five Articles of Dort.'

Synod of Gap (*The*), 1603, is remarkable for giving out ' we believe and maintain that the pope of Rome is properly the Antichrist, and the " son of perdition" prophesied of in the Word of God, under the emblem of the scarlet woman.'

Synod of Lambeth (*The*), 1281. Convened for the correction of ecclesiastical abuses. Canons were passed in this synod against pluralities and non-residence, for the better teaching of the people, for enforcing the doctrine of Transubstantiation, and for communion in one kind only.

Synod of Merton (*The*), 1236. An assembly which attempted to introduce into England Roman Canon Law, in order to legitimise natural children by a subsequent marriage, and to prevent the interference of the secular power in ecclesiastical matters. The legitimation of children was warmly supported by the clergy, but was overruled by the barons.

Synod of Presbyters. A general
council composed of two or more presbyteries, convened for religious purposes.

1. Of *Antrim*, 1727. This 'presbytery' was an offshoot of the 'Synod of Munster.'

2. Of *Munster*, 1660. The same as the 'United Presbytery' (*q.v.*).

3. Of *Ulster*, 1642. Formed originally at Carrickfergus. This was the first presbytery of Ireland.

A 'Presbytery' is a religious court formed of the respective pastors of a given district, and a ruling elder, or the *district* itself so represented.

Synod of Ulster (*The*). *See above.*

Synod of the Oak (*The*). A villa
near Chalcēdon, to which Theophilus summoned Chrysostom to appear. The president was the bishop of Heraclēa, and a long list of charges was brought against the archbishop, relating to faulty administration of the church and its funds, his habits in private life, his ritual irregularities, and his heretical sermons. (Robertson, 'Hist. of the Christian Church,' vol. ii. p. 110.)

Synods of the Church. There
have been twenty-three altogether, or twenty-four if the apostolic one is reckoned in. Six are called Ecumenical Councils (*q.v.*), between 325 and 680. Seven other synods were held before the Eastern and Western Churches separated, and ten have been held since that division.

The seven synods, not Ecumenical, before the severance of the Eastern and Western Churches, are :—

1. Held at Sardīca, in 347, to restore the bishops deposed by Arius.

2. Held at Ariminium, in 360, to alter the wording of the Nicene Creed at the instance of the Arians.

3. Held at Ephesus, in 449, to depose Flavianus for condemning Eutỹchēs, who taught that the body of Christ was not strictly speaking human.

4. Held at Constantinople, in 754, commanding the disuse in churches of pictures and images.

5. Held at Nicæa, in 787, to reverse the decision of the previous council (No. 4).

6. Held at Constantinople, in 869, to depose Photius, the originator of the severance of the Eastern and Western churches.

7. Held at Constantinople, in 879, to restore Photius.

Synods of the Western Church
(*The*). Since the separation.

1. The first Lateran, summoned by Calixtus II. in 1123. To settle the question of investitures (*q.v.*).

2. The second Lateran, summoned by Innocent II. in 1139. To condemn the Manichēans, who believed there are two principles, one of good and one of evil.

3. The third Lateran, summoned by Alexander III. in 1179. To regulate the election of popes.

4. The fourth Lateran, summoned by Innocent III. in 1215. To publish a profession of faith, specially condemnatory of Manichæism.

5. Held at Lyons, summoned by Innocent IV. in 1245. To depose Kaiser Friederich II.

6. Held at Lyons, summoned by Gregory X. in 1274. To declare that the Holy Ghost proceeds *Patre Filio-quo* (not from the Father only).

7. Held at Constance, summoned by John XXIII. in 1414. To condemn the doctrines of Wyclif, and enforce the one element to the laity in the eucharist.

8. Held at Basle, summoned by Martin V. in 1431. To declare the authority of a council paramount over that of a pope.

9. Held at Florence, summoned by Eugenius IV. in 1437. To confirm the doctrine of purgatory, and the supremacy of the pope.

10. Held at Trent, summoned by Paul III. in 1545. To fix the doctrines of the church, and condemn Protestantism. This synod sat for eighteen years. The first session was held 13 Dec., 1545, and the last 3 Dec., 1563.

11. The Vatican Council, 1870, summoned by Pius IX. to render the 'Immaculate Conception' an article of faith.

Syrian War (*The*). I. B.C. 192–190,
between the Romans and Antiochus, king of Syria. It was brought to an end by the battle of Magnesia, won by Scipio, who was now called Asiaticus.

II. 1840. Mehemet Ali, pasha of Egypt, laid claim to Syria in 1839, but Great Britain, Russia, and Austria joined forces with Turkey to wrest it from him. After taking Beyrout, Acre, and Sidon, the pacha came to terms, and by the Treaty of London, in 1841, Syria was restored to Turkey.

Syro-Macedonian Era (*The*). This era began with 1 Sept., B.C. 312.

Szatmas (*The Compact of*), 1711, whereby an amnesty was granted to the Rakoczy insurgents, who rose in arms against the Austrians in 1703, and constitutional and religious liberty was secured to Hungary.

Szegedin (*Treaty of*), 12 July, 1444, between Hunya'dês, the Hungarian general, and the Sultan Amurath II. By this treaty of peace the sultan recognised the independence of Servia, and ceded Wallachia to Hungary.

Tabardillo, 1627. A contagious pest which ravaged Mexico, the year after it had been visited by the plague of locusts. The fever lasted seven days, but most persons died between the third and fifth day. The mouth and tongue became black as a coal. It began in Mexico and spread to Guatemala and thence to all the regions round about. *See* p. 694, ' Plagues,' &c.

Taberdarship. The rights and privileges of a Taberdar, a kind of scholarship in Queen's College, Oxford. So called from the taberds or tabards, or long gowns.

Tabernacle Connexion (*The*), 1770. A split from the Calvinistic Methodists after the death of George Whitfield. These Methodists hold that election has been from all eternity according to the sovereign will of God, and is not a choice on God's foreknowledge of the fitness of the elect to be numbered with the saints in light.

Tabernacles (*Feast of*), or ' Festum Canabārum ' (*Lev.* xxiii. 33–36). A Hebrew feast lasting seven days. It began on the fifteenth day of the seventh month (Tishri), and commemorated the sojourn in the wilderness.

Table. *See also*

Alfonsine Tables.	Theodosian Table.
Rudolphine Tables.	Twelve Tables.

Table (*The*) used at the last supper is said to be preserved in St. John de Lateran of Rome. Nothing is known about it. *See* ' Crucifixion, *Relics of the.*'

Table of Abydos (*The*). *See* ' Tablet,' &c.

Table of Emerald (*The*). The table on which Hermês engraved, before the flood, the secret of alchemy. It is said to be hid under the great pyramid.

Table of Peutinger. ' Tabula Peutingeriana,' also called the ' Theodosian Table,' one of the most valuable literary relics of the world. It traces all the military roads of the empire called ' Theodosian,' because they were made in the reign of Theodosius the Great. The table was discovered at Speyer [Spires] in 1500 by Conrad Peutinger, who lived 1465–1547.

Tables. The Scotch committees established in 1637 to resist an imposition of the Anglican system of religion on Scotland. In the burghs were four tables, each of four members, and each table sent one representative to a fifth table in the capital. All complaints were to be made to the tables. These tables soon spread through the length and breadth of the land, whereby a united decision was speedily come to, and the whole weight of the country was brought to bear on the unpopular measures of the king [Charles I.]. For the provincial Fifth Tables, meeting in Edinburgh on a summons, made a committee of the whole soul, strength, and life of the religious party of the entire country.

They next elected as clerk-register Archibald Johnstone, clerk of the Edinburgh Tables.— HOWITT, *Hist. of Eng.* (Charles I., ch. iii. p. 178).

Tables (*Lunar*). Tabular lists of the values of the elements of the moon's orbit. Also the tabulated angular distances of the moon from certain stars at fixed epochs, as given in the ' Nautical Almanac.'

Tables (*Planetary*). Tabular lists of the elements of the planets' paths.

Table - money. An allowance granted to general officers in the army, and to flag officers in the navy, to enable them to fulfil the duties of hospitality within their respective commands. It varies, but the maximum is three guineas a day.

Table-turning, 1848, with table-rapping, the card process of spelling, spirit drawings, and other manifestations of the spirit world, originated in America. It is said Andrew Jackson Davis, the 'Seer of Poughkeepsie,' a cobbler, who professed to hear spirit verses in the air, was the precursor of 'spiritism' or spiritualism.

Tablet of Aby'dos (*The*), B.C. 1355. A series of royal rings, each containing the name of an Egyptian king. It was found on a wall in a temple of Abydos. Three rows of these rings remain still, and the names correspond with those given by Manêtho. This valuable tablet, now in the British Museum, was discovered by W. Bankes, in 1818, on an inner wall of the Temple of Osīris at Abȳdos in Upper Egypt.

Similar lists (though not so extensive) have been found in Thebes (Egypt), and these names correspond with those on the tablet of Abydos, with some important additions.

Another valuable source of ancient Egyptian history is the list of names hewn in the solid rock in the Grottoes of Ben Hassan, on the east bank of the Nile.

Tabor (*Light of Mount*). In the 14th cent. a dispute of considerable acrimony arose respecting the Light of Mount Tabor, the scene of the Transfiguration. The question was this: What was the nature of the Light there seen by the three apostles: was it the uncreated and eternal light in which the divine essence dwells, or was it created and temporal? The monks of Mount Athos violently protested it was the light of God. Barlaam maintained the contrary, and so great was the angry feeling he excited by this 'heresy,' that he was obliged to quit Constantinople; and a synod, presided over by Cantacuzene, established the dogma as an article of faith, that the Light of Mount Tabor was uncreated and divine.

Also called the 'Taboritic Light.'

Ta'borites (3 syl.), 1419–1436. The insurgents of Bohemia after the treacherous martyrdom of John Huss and Jerome of Prague. So called from Mount Tabor where they pitched their tents. Under the leadership of Zisca they often defeated the armies of the church, insomuch that in 1433 the council of Basel called the leaders to a conference. Certain concessions were made, which split up the party, and in 1436 the church and the kaiser succeeded in gaining the ascendency.

Tac (*Le*), 1411. A pestilence which appeared in Paris of a very strange character. It was marked by loss of appetite and insomnia, a trembling of the limbs, and a violent cough night and day. It lasted three weeks, but no one died. At the end of three weeks the sufferer bled profusely, and then recovered. *See* p. 694, 'Plague,' &c.

Ta'hérides (3 syl.), or 'Ta'herites' (3 syl.). A dynasty in Persia which reigned over Khorassan (813–872). So called from Taher, an Arabian general (in the service of Haroun al Raschid), who assassinated Amyn, and received this government in reward. This was the first of the contemporary kings, and was succeeded by the Soffarides. Persia was at the time a province of the califs.

Tai-Ping Rebellion (*The*), 1850–1864. A schoolmaster named Hung, having renounced Buddhism, founded the society of the Taï-Pings (Universal Peace), which came into collision with the imperial army in 1850. Hung then gave out that he was an instrument sent by God to root out Buddhism and establish the dynasty of Universal Peace. He also assumed the title of Taï-ping Wang (Prince of Universal Peace). Nankin was made his capital in 1860. Colonel Gordon, since called Chinese Gordon, quelled the insurrection, and overthrew the armies of Hung. Hung himself committed suicide, and Gordon returned to England, having received the titles and privileges of the *Ti-Tu*, the Yellow Jacket, and the Peacock's Feather.

Taking of the Covenant (*The*), 1643. In the civil war Charles I. sought assistance from the Irish, who in 1641 had massacred 50,000 Englishmen in a diabolical manner in the north of Ireland. This was so hateful to the English, that officer after officer in his army laid down his commission, and Scotland, to secure its own safety, hastened to take or sign the covenant. The covenant pledged them to 'bring the churches of God in the three kingdoms to a uniformity of faith, church government, and form of worship; to extirpate popery, prelacy, schism, and profaneness; to preserve the rights and privileges of the parliament, and the liberties of the kingdom; to punish malignants; to unite England and Scotland in peace and lasting union;

and to vow both in public and private to live as God-fearing Christians.'

Talbotype (*The*), 1839. So called from W. H. Fox Talbot, who took permanent pictures on papers, which he called calotypes, but his 'instantaneous process' is more wonderful still. An image is formed in a camera, and a revolving-wheel which turns 200 times in a second, being illuminated by an electric spark, records a legible impression of what is printed on a bill affixed to the wheel.

Daguerre in 1839 took impressions on copper; Talbot the same year took impressions on paper; in 1848 Joseph Nicéphore Niepce de St. Victor took impressions on glass coated with a film of albumen; Mons. le Gray in 1850 introduced the use of collodion.

Talkmotes, places used by the old Saxons for conference. In these places they would also defend themselves when attacked unawares. In Ireland they are called *Bannes*; some are square and some round.

Tallage. Arbitrary impositions imposed by the Anglo-Norman kings on the demesne lands of the crown and all royal towns. Abolished by Edward III. by his famous statute *De tallagio cum concidendo.* The tax called *la taille* prevailed in France also, but Turgot, the French minister, substituted for it a fixed tax towards the close of the 18th cent.

Talmud (*The*). The code of the Jewish civil and canonical law. It is composed of the Mishna or decisions of the doctors, and the Gemāra or the reasons thereof. The Mishna was compiled in A.D. 180 by Jehūda the Saint. There are two Gemāras, that of Jerusalem completed A.D. 400; and that of Babylon a century later and four times the size of the former commentary. The language is Aramaic. *See* 'Targum.'

The former is called 'The Jerusalem Talmud,' and the latter 'The Babylonian Talmud.'

Talmudists. Those Israelites who accept the Talmud as authority. Those who reject its authority are called Caraïtes or Karaites.

'Talpra Magyar,' 'Up, Hungarians,' 1848. The Marseillaise of Hungary, written impromptu by Petöfi. The first verse runs thus:

Magyars, obey your country's call,
Be slaves, or break the Austrian thrall.
We swear on our forefathers' graves,
Mágyars no longer shall be slaves.

(Magyars pronounced *Mah-yars*, with a slight *d* sound in the first syllable.)

Tamerlan à Lunettes. A nickname of Mons. Thiers, the historian (1797–1877). *See* p. 57, 'Attila le Petit.'

Tamerlane. A corruption of Timur leng (*i.e. lame*), 1336–1408.

Tang Dynasty (*The*). The 13th imperial dynasty of China. It gave 22 emperors and lasted 289 years (618–907). The court was held at Sia-gan-fu, in Shen-si. In no dynasty was China more prosperous than in this. It succeeded the Swi dynasty, and at its close the empire was again divided.

This was the Augustan or Golden Age of China.

Tanist. Heir presumptive of an Irish provincial or sub-king. He was chosen by the people from the blood royal (either son, brother, or cousin) for the most part in the lifetime of the king, and was *ex officio* head of the army and chief judge of the province. The heir presumptive of the monarch or over-king bore the title of Roydamna.

Tanist Stone (*The*), or 'Heir-apparent's Stone.' A Celtic monolith used as a coronation seat. Thus we read in Judges ix. 6 of Abimelech, that 'a pillar was erected in Shechem' when he was made king. Again, in 2 Kings xi. 14 it is said that a pillar was raised when Joash was made king, 'as the manner was.'

Tanistry (in Ireland). A tenure of lands for life only, the successor being appointed from the family by election. The tenant of such a holding is called a tanist. By tanistry the 'inheritance of land was given to the most worthy,' and not to the next heir. The 'most worthy' was virtually the strongest, and this led to endless family feuds. Abolished in 1605.

They were bound not to alienate their lands to the mere Irish. Tanistry and Gavelkind were abolished in the 5th year of James I.—O'CONOR *Hist. of the Irish People*, p. 155.

Tan'simas. The organic laws of the Turkish empire, published in 1844 by the Sultan Abdul Medjid. Part 1 is the political organisation of the empire; part 2, finance; part 3, legal matters; and part 4, military affairs.

Tantivies (*The*), 1680. The Anti-Birmingham party, opposed to the Ex-

3 K 2

clusion Bill (*q.v.*). A royalist or cavalier, so called from tantivy, the note of a hunting-horn, and therefore a fox-hunter. The country gentlemen were almost all tories and royalists.

Those who took the king's side were Anti-Birminghams, Abhorrers, and Tantivies.—MACAULAY, *Hist. of England*, ch. ii.

Tantra. The Bible of the worshippers of Siva. Its subjects are the creation and destruction of the world; the worship of the gods; magical rites; and the modes of hypostatic union. There are several Tantras.

Tantum Ergo. The most popular of all the Eucharistic hymns in the Catholic Church. It is sung at benediction with the Holy Sacrament.

It consists of the last two stanzas of the 'Pange Lingua.' The first runs thus:

> Tantum ergo sacramentum
> Veneremur cernui:
> Et antiquum documentum
> Novo cedat ritui;
> Præstat fides supplementum
> Sensuum defectui.

(The second stanza is a mere Gloria Patri, &c.)

Tao-tsee. A religious sect in China who adore Tao, founded by Lao-Tseu in the 6th cent. B.C. Their sacred book is called 'Tao-te-King.'

Taouism [*Tao-tse*, primitive reason]. A religious system in China founded by Lao-Tseu, who was born B.C. 604. It has degenerated into a sort of polytheism. Its priests, who are looked on as magicians and astrologers, are consulted about the sites of houses, burial grounds, fortunate days, and other responses of the fortune-teller's character.

There are three religious systems in China. That of Yu, restored by Koun-fou-tse (Confucius); the state religion, in which the emperor acts as the priest and intermediator; and the third is Buddhism. There are, however, Moslems, Christians, and even a few Jews in China. The Christians are, for the most part, disciples of the Jesuits.

Tappent-durs (Strike-hards). A species of guard that Robespierre had always about his door, or guarding him through the streets. They were armed with clubs or heavy sticks.

Robespierre went, surrounded by his *Tappent-durs*, first to the Jacobin club, and then to the convention.—HOWITT, *Hist. of England* (Geo. III., 1794, p. 122).

Tara Meetings (*The*). Tara is a hill in the county of Wexford (Ireland)

where the ancient Irish held assemblies. These musters were not popular meetings, but conventions of the kings and chiefs of the Milesian line.

Taran'tism or **Tarentism** (16th cent.). The Dancing Mania. In 1374 a similar hysteria appeared in Germany. Probably the Bacchanalian orgies of the Greeks and Romans are to be attributed to similar hysteria.

The epidemic called *Tarentismus*, from Tarentum or Taranto, in Naples, was said to be caused by a small spider, the Tarentula (in Italian *tarantula*). It provoked an irresistible desire to dance. Hence the dance called *Tarantella*.

Tard-Venus (*Les*), 1361. Companies of adventurers who formed themselves into gangs, in France, after the Peace of Brétigny (1360). They were composed of the offscouring of all nations and disbanded soldiers. The utter destruction of property was prevented only by the payment of black mail. They defied the army of Jean which was under the command of Jacques de la Marche, made themselves masters of the Pont St. Esprit, and made Urban V. tremble in Avignon. The Marquis of Monferrat enrolled them in the pope's army, and drilled them into discipline.

Of course the word *venus* in this compound has nothing to do with the goddess so called, but is the participle of *venir*. Tard-venu, pl. Tard-venûs.

Targums (*The*). Translations of the Hebrew Scriptures into Aramaic, made for the Jews because they had forgotten the Hebrew language by their long residence in Chaldea. The oldest dates between the 3rd and 4th cent.; the latest in the early part of the 11th cent. The most noted Targums are those of Onkelos, of Jonathan ben Uziel, and of Joseph the Blind. *See* 'Talmud.'

A portion of Daniel and Ezra with verse 11 chap. x. of Jeremiah have no Hebrew original. Aramaic, the language of the Jews in the time of Christ, was a mixture of Chaldee, Syriac, and Hebrew.

There are three Targums of the Pentateuch, one on the prophets, two on Esther, one on Chronicles, one on Daniel, besides those on the Psalms, Job, the Proverbs, Solomon's Song, Ruth, Lamentations, Ecclesiastes, &c.

Tar'leton's Dash at Charlottesville, 4 June, 1781. During the American War of Independence, Colonel Tarleton at the head of his cavalry rode at a dash into this town of Virginia, took seven of the assembly prisoners, and destroyed a large quantity of stores.

Tascodrugi'tæ, or 'Tascod'rygites' (4 syl.). Du Cange (vol. vi. p. 487, col. 1) says: 'Hæretici ita appellati a τασχὸς, quod illis *paxillum* sonabat, et δροῦγγος, *nasus,* quod inter orandum indicem digitum naso apponerent, ut animi tristitiam et affectatam quandam sanctitatem præ se ferrent.' Also called 'Passalorinchitæ a Græco πάσσαλος, *paxillus,* et ῥίν, *nasus,* vel ῥύγχος, *rostrum, rictus.*'

Tatian. A name common to several persons, but especially noted in church history for two authors often confounded together. One was a Platonic philosopher, born in Syria, converted to Christianity by Justin the Martyr. He lived in the 2nd cent., and was the author of a 'Discourse to the Greeks.' In 172 he became a Gnostic, and was the founder of the Encratistês.

The 'Discourse' of this Tatian was published in 1545 by C. Gessner, and by Otto of Jena in 1851.

The other Tatian was a native of Mesopotamia, and lived a century or more after the Platonic philosopher. He wrote in very inferior Greek a book called 'Diatessaron.' The original is lost, but there is extant a Latin translation by Victor of Capua, inserted in the 'Bibliothèque des Pères.'

M. Bouillet says this latter Tatian 'vivait au Vᵉ siècle,' but this is an error, as the 'Diatessaron' is mentioned by Eusebius. The 'Diatessaron' is an heretical book supposed to be based on the Gospels. During the lifetime of the second Tatian Syria belonged to Persia; and the Emperor Julian went thither to prepare for his war against the Persians.

Tavernier's Diamond. The first blue diamond known in Europe was bought by Tavernier in India, in 1642,

THE GREAT 'TABLE DIAMOND, 242½ carats. (N.B. 151½ carats = 1 ounce.)

and sold to Louis XIV. in 1668. It is described as *d'un beau violet.* It was flat and ill formed. The cut given is from an old French engraving. It was apparently cut after it came into the possession of 'Le Grand Monarque,' for we read of a blue diamond in the regalia of 67⅛ carats. In August 1792 this 'blue diamond' was seized and deposited in the Garde Meuble. Of course it was abstracted and never heard of again. However, in 1830, a Daniel Eliason was in possession of a blue diamond weighing 44¼ carats, without a history, which afterwards **became** the property of Henry Hope, and was called the 'Hope Diamond.' Probably the Great Table Diamond was made into two brilliants. A model of the blue diamond was shown in the first French Exhibition, 1862. *See* p. 254, 'Diamonds.'

The other part of the great diamond was sold at the sale of the Duke of Brunswick's jewels in 1874, and is called the 'Brunswick Diamond.' Its weight is from 6 to 7 carats, and it was purchased in Geneva.

Taylor Institution (*The*). In the University of Oxford, 1848, erected from the bequest of Sir R. Taylor. It consists of a library and reading-room supplied with the chief periodicals of France, Germany, and Italy, accessible to all members of the university. It is well supplied with atlases, dictionaries, encyclopædias, biographical dictionaries, and reviews. There is also a Taylorian scholarship, and Taylorian scholars have certain privileges similar to graduates.

Taylor Scholarship and Exhibition, for modern languages. The Scholarship is worth 50*l.* a year and the Exhibition 25*l.* Called 'Taylor' because the candidates will be examined according to what is taught in the Taylor Institution, Oxford.

Tchew or **Chow Dynasty** (*The*), B.C. 1122–256. The third imperial dynasty, and last of the semi-historic period. It was preceded by the Chang dynasty, and followed by the Tshin or first historical dynasty. It gave thirty-four emperors, and the seat of government was Yn. This was the dynasty of the 'kings combatant.'

Tcin Dynasty (*The*). The seventh imperial dynasty of China. It gave fifteen emperors, and lasted 155 years (from 265 to 420). The seat of government was Ho-nân. It followed the San Kuo (or three States) period, and was succeeded by the Woo-tae, or five races.

Most of these rulers were bad emperors and met with violent deaths.

Te Deum of Handel was composed to commemorate the wonderful escape of George II. at Dettingen 15 June, 1743. The Earl of Stair had led the English into a trap, in which there seemed no escape; but George cut his way through the French, and ultimately drove them across the Main. The whole affair seems more like romance than sober history.

The 'Te Deum' is called the *Ambrosian Hymn* from a tradition that St. Ambrose composed it by sudden inspiration at the baptism of St. Augustine.

Te igitur. One of the service-books of the Catholic Church, used by prelates and other church dignitaries. So called from the first words of the canon *Te igitur, clementissime Pater*.

Tearless Victory (*The*), B.C. 367. The victory of Archidämos III. king of Sparta, over the Arcadians and Argives. So called because not one of the Spartans fell in the battle.

Not one of the British army fell in the Abyssinian expedition under Sir Charles Napier, 1867-1868.

Tellers. In the division lists of the House of Commons are a remnant of the old *talliers*, officers who kept one part of the tallies in the public archives, the corresponding part being given to the claimant. The tally system existed in England till 1826 in our public accounts. The tally was a wand cut with notches to represent certain sums. In 1834 the old tallies, of which there were two cart-loads, were burnt in the stores of the House of Lords, and it was this confla-gration which set fire to and destroyed both Houses of Parliament, with their offices and a large part of the old palace of Westminster.

Temperance Movement (*The*). The movement in Scotland began 1828. John Dunlop J.P. formed the first temperance society in 1829. The first English total abstinence society was formed 1830. A temperance society was formed in Ireland by the Rev. G. W. Carr in 1829. In England the first society was formed in 1830 by Henry Forbes, a merchant of Bradford, and the first total abstinence so-ciety, at Preston, in 1832. In 1838 Father Mathew began his crusade at Cork.

In 1808 a total abstinence society (which still exists (1890) was formed in Greenfield (New York). The American Temperance Society was founded in 1826.

Templars, or 'Knights Templars,' 1118. A secret society founded by Hugues de Payens and eight other knights then in Syria, and uniting the monastic with the military character. Its nominal ob-ject was to defend the Holy Sepulchre at Jerusalem, and the pilgrims who came to visit it. The red cross was assigned to them in 1146 by Pope Eugenius III. They were organised to defend the Holy Land and protect pilgrims; but on the loss of Palestine, in 1192, they took refuge in Cyprus. Their dissolution in England, France, and other countries occurred in 1312, when their lands were transferred to the Hospitallers, but in Spain to 'Our Lady of Montesa.' 'Le crime des Tem-pliers est encore un problème.' Lejeune in 1789 wrote a history in their defence, but Raynouard, in 1813, wrote a history in their condemnation.

Their dress was a white mantle with a red cross. In 1314 the master of the Order, James de Molay, was condemned to the stake.

Temple of Glory (*The*). Paris. *See* p. 548, 'Madeleine.'

Temporalisti, 1870. Those who advocate the temporal power of the pope, like M. Thiers; and after Rome had been added to the kingdom of Italy be-lieved in the possibility of its being restored to the pope.

M. Thiers to his last hour was unable to under-stand why the abolition of the pope's civil autho-rity should be an irrevocable fact: and he died belonging to the sect of the Temporalisti.—*Nine-teenth Century*, Sept. 1889, p. 395.

Temporary Relief Work, 1847. Ireland, during the potato famine. This relief was given in the spring to a large number of labourers employed on ' pub-lic works,' such as road-making, that they might go and cultivate their own plots of land for ensuing crops.

Ten (*The*), or 'I Dieci,' 1310. A criminal court of Venice invested with plenary inquisitorial powers, and entire sovereignty over every individual in the State from the doge downwards. At first the tribunal was appointed for 10 days, but was prolonged first for 3 months, then a year, then for 5 years, then for 10 years, and in 1325 for per-petuity. They were called *I Neri* (the black), from the colour of their official robes. The ten controlled every branch of government, were despotic in peace and war, had sole control over all fiscal enactments, annulled at pleasure even the decrees of the Grand Council, and were in power for five centuries. Long before the invasion of Napoleon, in 1796, the government of The Ten had become a veritable Reign of Terror.

The actual number of this council was seventeen, because the signoria (consisting of the doge and his six councillors) was associated with it.

Ten Articles (*The*), 1536.

Agreed to by the Convocation to settle the religious differences of the Protestant party at the reformation: (1) The Christian faith as comprised in the Bible, the three creeds, and first four general councils to be accepted; (2) baptism is essential for salvation; (3) penance is a sacrament; (4) the real corporal presence in the eucharist is to be believed; (5) justification and remission of sins is a gift of God, through the merits of Christ; (6) saints are to be honoured as examples of holy life; (7) prayers may be addressed to saints as intercessors; (8) vestments, holy water, candles, palms, ashes, &c., are excellent helps to devotion; (9) images aid devotion; (10) prayers for the dead are useful, though purgatory is uncertain. *See* p. 48, 'Articles.'

Ten Kings of Darkness (*The*),

or the She-ming-wâng, the ten judges of hell in Buddhism.

Ten Men's Tale, or 'Tenmentale.'

So the freeborg was called in Yorkshire. Tenmentale consisted in the responsibility of ten men for the good conduct of each other. If one of the ten committed a fault, the other nine were bound to produce him, and stand bail for him. If he fled from justice, and his estate proved insufficient, the nine had to make good the penalty.

Everyone above the age of twelve was required to be enrolled in some tything according to the laws of Canute.

Ten Numerations (*The*).

A cabalistic doctrine. Three are called the superior, and seven the inferior numerations. The three superior are the supreme diadem, wisdom, and understanding. These existed from all eternity. The seven inferior numerations are mercy, severity or might, beauty, victory, glory, stability, and sovereignty.

Ten per cent. and No Surrender, 1854.

The watchword of the trades-unions who commenced the great wages movement (*q.v.*).

Ten Persecutions (*The*).

Under the Roman emperors. 'The ten horns are ten kings which shall make war with the lamb' (Rev. xvii. 12–14).

First century.

1. Under Nero 64–68, in which Peter and Paul are said to have been slain.
2. Domitian, 81–96.

Second century.

3. Trajan, Hadrian, and Antonīnus Pius, 107–161.
4. Marcus Aurelius, 161–181, in which Justin Martyr, Polycarp, and Pothīnus were put to death.
5. Septimus Sevērus, 202–211, in which Irenæus was put to death.
6. Decius, 250–251.
8. Valerian, 257–260, in which Cyprian was put to death.
9. Aurelian, 272–275.
10. Diocletian, 298–305.

Before the Roman persecutions were those—
1. By the Zealots, A.D. 34, in which Stephen was stoned.
2. By Herod Agrippa, A.D. 44, in which James son of Zebedee was beheaded.
3. By Annas the High Priest, A.D. 62, in which James the Less was put to death. *See* 'Persecutions,' and 'Milan, Edict of.'

Ten Thousand (*The*), B.C. 370.

A confederation of Arcadians, a synod of which met periodically at Megalopŏlis. *See* p. 756, 'Retreat of the 10,000.'

Ten Virtues of the Virgin (*The*).

In Catholic theology.

(1) Chastity. Because she is the queen of virgins.

(2) Prudence. Shown in the Annunciation.

(3) Humility. Even when chosen for the mother of the Messiah, she called herself 'the handmaid of the Lord.'

(4) Faith. She believed and doubted not what the angel announced.

(5) Piety. Shown by her retirement, silence, and submission.

(6) Obedience. She submitted to the will of God.

(7) Poverty. She despised the grandeur and wealth of the world.

(8) Patience. In bearing the pain of her travail.

(9) Charity. In offering her son a sacrifice for the salvation of man.

(10) Compassion. In that a sword pierced her own heart out of compassion to her son.

Ten Years' War (*The*), or 'Sacred War,' B.C. 356–346. This was the *second* of the sacred wars. The *first*, called the Cirrhæan War, was B.C. 595–586; and the *third*, or Amphissian War, was from Feb. to Aug. of 338 B.C.

Tenaille (*The*). In fortification, a low work in the main ditch before the curtain (*q.v.*) and between the flanks of the half bastions of a front of fortification (*q.v.*). Usually about 16 yards in thickness, and riveted with masonry all round.

Tenant at Will. One who occupies without a lease, whose occupancy may be terminated at any time the proprietor thinks fit.

Proper time must be allowed for removal, and if crops have been sown the outgoing tenant has a right to them or can claim compensation.

Tenant in Fee Simple. An absolute owner, who by a fiction of law is a tenant of the crown.

Tenant-right, in the north of Ireland, was either the custom ensuring a permanence of tenure in the same occupier, without liability of any increase of rent, except such as might be sanctioned by the general community,—or else the right of the farm-tenant, on the transfer of his farm to another, to receive purchase-money, amounting to 10*l.* or 12*l.* an acre. In this latter case a schedule of the tenants' debts is made out. His back rent is first paid, and then the different creditors as far as the money goes. The reason of this custom is this. Large tracts of land, the property of absentees, were let, but the owner did nothing whatever either for the land or for the tenant; so the tenant claimed the right of selling his tenancy.

The legality of tenant-right in Ulster was established by 33, 34 Vict. c. 46 (1870).

Tenants' Defence Association (*The*), 1885. A society in connection with the anti-landlord platform and the 'Plan of Campaign' (*q.v.*). As the banks refused to renew the bills which the Irish tenants had taken out to pay their rents, the tenants formed themselves into a society, each contributing to a fund for defence of the whole tenantry. *See* 'Irish Associations.'

Tenants' Defence League (*The*), July 1889. An Irish League the object of which is 'by litigation and other constitutional methods to make the lives of Irish landlords as miserable as possible.' It is a tenants' protection league and an agrarian trade-union with an executive and sustentation fund. *See* p. 455, 'Irish Associations.'

Tenants'-right, in Ireland. The right of a tenant to his improvements, and giving him a property in his holding and a saleable interest. A provision of the Land Act.

This was a deadly blow to professional agitators, who did all they could to thwart the sale and purchase by denouncing the transaction as 'land-grabbing.'

Tenants in Socage. Tenants by hereditary right.

Tennessee (U.S. America) means a 'Curved Spoon,' an Indian name for its river. The state received its name in 1796. The inhabitants were at one time nicknamed *Whelps* (a nickname now seldom heard).

Tennis-ball of Fortune (*The*). Pertinax, the Roman emperor. He was first a charcoal-seller, then a schoolmaster, then a soldier, then emperor of Rome. Within three months he was dethroned and murdered (126–193).

Tenson (meaning a contention). A poetical dialogue, not unlike those eclogues of Virgil in which two or more shepherds contend in song. Spenser, in his eclogues, has several *tensons*. The word is applied to a class of Troubadour poetry.

Tenth Mazarine (*The*). One of the twelve diamonds set in the French crown. It was a brilliant, and was so called because Cardinal Mazarin in 1660 was the first person who had the diamond polished.

Tenth Muse (*The*).
I. Sappho of Lesbos, who flourished B.C. 600.
II. Margaret queen of Navarre, sister of François I. of France.

Tenth of April (*The*), 1848. The day when the Chartists determined to present their monster petition to parliament, and carry it to the house by a procession. The Chartists met on Kennington Common under the leadership of Feargus O'Connor, but the idea of a procession was abandoned, and the petition was sent in three cabs. The term 'Tenth of April' became proverbial of an apprehended danger averted by judicious forethought.

The 10th of April, 1848, has been a beneficial crisis, not merely in the temper of the working men, so called, but in the minds of those who are denominated by them 'the Aristocracy.' —C. KINGSLEY, *Alton Locke* (Preface addressed in 1854 to the Working-men of Great Britain).

Tephilim (*The*) or Frontlet. Four pieces of parchment containing four texts of scripture, worn by the ancient Jews on the left wrist or middle of the forehead. The texts are Exod. xiii. 10; Exod. xiii. 11–16; Deut. vi. 4–9; and Deut. xi. 13–21.

The Tephilim which these old pedants wore on their left wrists, and the Mezuzah which they fixed on the right side of their doors to keep off devils.—KINGSLEY, *Hypatia*, ch. xxi.

Ter Sex, aut Tres Tesseræ. Three sixes or three aces. The Romans played dice with three tesseræ, marked like our dice, and the highest throw was three sixes, the lowest throw was three aces. Technically the highest throw was called 'Venus' or 'king' (*basilicus*), and the lowest *canés, caniculæ, vulturii,* or 'tres tesseræ.'

There was another game played with four *tali*, in which the highest throw was when all four of the dice came different, and the lowest throw was when they all came alike.

Terminable Annuities. Sums of money borrowed and so paid back that both interest and principal are cancelled in a certain number of years, and the obligation terminates. Suppose I buy 1,000*l.* 3 per cent. of the Treasury Stock. If the government pays me only 30*l.* a year, it merely pays the interest, and the capital sum (1,000*l.*) remains unreduced; but suppose the government pays 60*l.* a year instead of 30*l.*, then it pays back every year both interest and part of the principal, and in about twenty years it would have paid back the entire interest and principal, so that the obligation would terminate.

Between 1889 and 1904 more than 70 millions of our National Debt will be thus cancelled.

Termors. Persons having only a chattel interest in their estates.

Terra Firma, applied to the former territories of Venice, means those possessions in Italy not in the Lagune, as the provinces of Bergãmo, Brescia, Crema, Verona, Vicenza, and so on.

Terreur Blanche (*La*), 1815. The bloody reaction of the Royalists. Marshal Brune was massacred by a Royalist mob at Avignon; Marshal Berthier committed suicide; Labedoyère was executed; Fouché and Talleyrand were dismissed; Marshal Ney was shot; Murat was shot; and 4,556,000 Frenchmen were slain in battle.

Terrible Tenth of May (*The*), 1857, when the British in India were fearfully massacred in Delhi during the Indian Mutiny.

Terror (*The*). A period in French history between the extirpation of the Girondists and the death of Robespierre, 1793–1794.

Terror of the Greeks (*The*). Dominico Michieli, or Micheli, the 36th doge of Venice (died 1130). His tomb bears this inscription: 'Terror Græcorum jacet hic.'

Terrorists.
I. 1793. The party headed by Robespierre after the death of Marie Antoinette. Those who tried to check the sanguinary fury were nicknamed the 'Moderates.'
II. 1879. Revolutionists of Russia who in 1881 assassinated Czar Alexander II. *See* 'Decembrists,' 'Propagandists,' and 'Nihilists.'

Terry Alts, in Ireland. Insurgents of Clare, who appeared after the Union, and committed great outrages. They were similar to the 'Thrashers' of Connaught, the 'Garders,' the 'Rockites,' the 'Fenians,' &c. They made themselves very conspicuous in the sanguinary tithe war 1830–1835 (*q.v.*). *See* p. 455, 'Irish Associations.'

Tertiaries, or Tiers Ordre. Seculars who followed their ordinary callings, and lived the ordinary life, but promised to conform to certain religious and moral rules drawn out by the order under which they lived.
The Tertiaries of St. Francis were founded in 1221.
Those of St. Augustine were founded in 1401.
Those of St. Dominic were founded in 1422.
Others have been founded since, such as the Carmelites, Servites, &c.

At present many tertiaries live in convents.

Tertiary Canons. Such as received only a third part of the revenue of the canonate.

Tertium Quid, which Abelard called 'Conceptualism.' The realists, like Plato, insisted that there is a real something in abstract ideas; thus *beauty* is not a mere notion, but a reality. Nominalists, like Aristotle, insist that abstract words are merely names of abstract ideas, that *beauty* is nothing *per se*, but simply expresses our general idea of the beautiful in objects. Abelard held a third or intervening theory, that after our conception has been formed, then there is reality in abstract ideas, but not before. Thus when we have made up our mind on what makes beauty, that conception of beauty is a reality, a reality *post rem* (after the conception), and not *ante rem*. It is a 'conceptual' reality, or *tertium quid*.

Teschen, in Silesia (*Peace of*), 13 May, 1779, between Prussia, Austria, and Saxony, terminating the war of Bavarian succession.

Test Act (*The*). I. 1562. The first of a series of penal statutes which weighed on the Roman Catholics of England for about 200 years. By these acts the oath of allegiance and the abjuration of the temporal authority of the pope was exacted of all persons holding office, whether lay or spiritual, with the exception of peers.

What is popularly known as the Test Act is not this statute of Elizabeth, but the one below.

II. 25 Car. II. cc. 1, 2 (1673), an enlargement of the Corporation Act (*q.v.*), obliging all persons whatsoever, before being allowed to accept any place of trust under the crown, to take the oaths of allegiance and supremacy, to subscribe a declaration against transubstantiation, and to receive the sacrament of the Lord's Supper in a parish church. Repealed 828.

After 'The Popish Plot' (Oct., 1678) another Test Act was passed to exclude all Roman Catholics from the House of Lords as well as from the House of Commons, and to declare the Church of Rome to be idolatrous.

Testament (*King Robert's*), in Latin leonines. Thus given by Mr. Tyler :—

On foot should be all Scottish weire [*war*]
By hill and moss themselves to bear :
Let wood for walls be ;—Bow and spear
And battle-axe their fighting-gear.—
That enemies do them no drear [*harm*].
In strait place cause to keep all store,
And burn the plain land them before ;
Then shall they pass away in haste
When that they nothing find but waste ;
With wiles and wakening of the night,
And mickle noises made on height,
Them shall they turn with great affray,
As they were chased with sword away.—
This is the council and intent
Of good King Robert's testament.

The Scots kept King Robert s [Bruce] testament in recollection, and lurking among the woods and valleys they fell upon such English as separated themselves from the main body.—Sir W. Scott, *Hist. of Scotland*, xiii.

Tête Morte of Würtemberg (*Order of the*), 1806. Established by Frederick William duke of Brunswick, on the death of his father, at Jena, in 1806. When the duke's father had received his death-wound Napoleon refused to allow the dying man to be conveyed to Brunswick, to die there. He wrote these words in reply to the request: ' Qu'il s'en aille en Angleterre, y chercher son salut. Je veux l'écraser lui et toute sa famille.' The young duke then arrayed all his soldiers in mourning, as members of the order of the Tête Morte. He placed on their military caps, in front, the device of a skull and cross-bones, and instead of a feather adopted flowing black horse-hair. This gloomy costume was to be continued till the death of Napoleon. It was called 'The Black Legion.'

Tetrad, according to Pythagoras, is the fourth mathematical quantity, viz. depth. The monad is the indivisible and impartible point ; length is the duad, and breadth the triad. Physically, intellectual capacity is the monad, scientific knowledge the duad, opinion the triad, and perception through the senses the tetrad.

Tetrapolitan Confession (*The*), 1531. The confession of faith of the four cities, Strasburg, Constance, Lindau, and Memmingen. This was the Sacramentarian confession presented in the diet of Augsburg, 1530. *See* p. 785, ' Sacramentarian.'

Tetrarchy (*A*). An independent fourth part of a kingdom. Thus at the death of Herod the Great the kingdom of Judæa was divided into four parts, of which Judæa, Galilee, and Iturea were given to his three sons, Archelaus, Antipas, and Philip. Samaria was the remaining part. In 56 the division was abolished again, and Herod II. (Agrippa) was made sole king of Judæa.

Herod II. was great-grandson of Herod the Great. His father, Herod Agrippa, ruled over three of the tetrarchies, Judæs, Galilee, and Samaria, but resided at Rome.

Herod the Great and Mariamne the Asmonæan
|
Aristobulus tetrarch of Judæa
|
Agrippa, who put James to death
|
Herod II. (Agrippa), who heard Paul make his defence.

Tetrarchy (*The Roman*), 304–311. Constantius Chlorus (the pale) was maximus imperator, and died at York A.D. 306. The four then were Constantius, Galerius, Sevērus, and Maximinus.

Severus put an end to his life in 307, and Maxentius became a tetrarch.

Constantine put an end to the tetrarchy, and became sole emperor A.D. 311.

Maximinus killed himself 313. He dispossessed Galerius in 308.

Teutonic Knights (*The*), or 'Order of Teutonic Knights,' 1190, confirmed by Celestine III. in 1192. They wore white robes with a black cross of eight points. Suppressed by Napoleon I. in 1809.

Called the 'Knights of the Virgin Mary,' or 'Brothers of the Teutonic House of Our Lady of Jerusalem,' or the 'Teutonic Knights of St. Mary of Jerusalem,' or 'German Knights of the Cross.'

Teutonic Knights (*The*), 1190. Organised by Frederick duke of Suabia, in Palestine, and invested in 1192 with the privileges of the Hospitallers and Templars. In 1237 incorporated with the Short-swords of Livonia. Prussia was given to them in 1243 by Innocent IV., and in 1255 they founded Königsberg. They lost Prussia in 1525, which was given to Albert of Brandenburg by the peace of Cracow. The order was abolished by Napoleon in 1809; but still subsists in Austria as an honour.

Teutonic Nations (*The*). The Germans, Danes, Swedes, Norwegians, Frisians, Dutch, Jutes, and Normans. England was Celtic, but after the Saxon and Danish invasions it became largely Teutonic, and the Normans (after the conquest) added to this predominance. *See* p. 154, ' Celts.'

Wales and Ireland are Celtic, and the north of Scotland, and Cornwall largely so.

Teutons. So the German races are called, from the Teutŏnês or Teutŏni, an ancient horde of Germany which, with the Cimbri, invaded the Roman dominions B.C. 113.

Tewkesbury Mustard Pills. Seven hundred fire-balls, which Titus Oates asserted the Roman Catholics had employed to set fire to London. Oates furthermore asserted that these Roman Catholics had made a good thing out of the conflagration by carrying off diamonds to the value of 14,000*l*. Ten years afterwards, in 1676, said Oates, the same persons had set fire to Southwark, by which they gained 2,000*l*. above their expenses.

Texas (U.S. America). It was so called (it is believed) from an Indian confederation called *Texas*, *Tejas*, or *Friends*. The inhabitants were once nicknamed BEEF-HEADS.

Texerans or **Tesserands** (weavers). So the Waldenses (*q.v.*) in the south of France were called, because they were for the most part weavers.

Thaborit'ic Light (*The*). A heavenly light supposed to emanate from the 'navel soul.' Certain quietists seat themselves on the ground and fix their eyes on their navel (the seat of the soul). After a time a light beams forth upon them which fills them with rapture and ecstasy. This is the Thaborit'ic Light.

See 'Tabor, Light of,' because it was believed to be identical with the light seen on Mount Tabor at the Transfiguration.

Thalami'tæ. The lowest bank of rowers in a Greek galley; the uppermost bank were the *Thranītæ*, and the middle bank the *Zeugītæ*.

Thames Tunnel (*The*), 1824–1841. Constructed by Marc Isambard Brunel to connect Rotherhithe with Wapping. A bridge was not practicable, not so much on account of the width of the river as the obstruction it would offer to our shipping. The Tunnel is 1,200 feet long, and 63 feet below the bed of the Thames. It has two arched ways and two footways, one for those going from Wapping and Rotherhithe, and one for those going in the opposite direction.

Thanes (1 syl.) were of two sorts, *Messe Thegnes* and *World Thegnes*. Bishops were ' Messe Thanes,' and by the laws of King Athelstan ranked with earls or secular Thanes. Other priests were 'World Thanes,' and hence were subsequently entitled ' Sir.' The bishop still retains the title of *Lord*, but the wife of a bishop has no title, not even that of a common knight's wife.

Thannaim (*The*). Jewish doctors, authors of the ' Mishnah.' They lived from the time of Malachi to B.C. 21. *See* p. 291, 'Emoraïm.'

The 'Mishnah' was closed by Rabbi Judah the Nachi four years before. The annotations, &c., form the 'Gemāra,' and both together the 'Talmud.'

Thaumaturga of the Nineteenth Century (*The*). Filumĕna, of whom nothing is known except that three tiles were disinterred in 1802 in the cemetery of Priscilla, inscribed thus:

| LVMENA | PAXTE | CVMFI |.

By changing the position of the tiles we get PAXTE CUMFI LUMENA, and by dividing the words *Pax tecum Filumena*. The miracles, of course, were those attributed to the disinterred body.

We are gravely told as an historic fact that the 'Virgin Martyr' took the trouble to reveal to a priest and a nun in a dream that her name was really Filumĕna, because she was Fi[lia] *Lumena*, the daughter of the 'Light of the World.' In confirmation of this revelation, when her bones were taken to Magnāno, she repaired her own skeleton, made her hair grow, and performed many other wonderful works! This silly stuff is told as an historic fact in the 19th cent., and is actually believed by many. Filumena is duly registered in the hagiography of the Petits Bollandistes.

Thaumaturgists. Workers of miracles. (Greek θαυματουργέω, to work wonders, or perform tricks of jugglery.)

From the Old Testament the greatest wonder-workers were *Moses, Jannes* and *Jambres* (Pharaoh's magicians), and *Elisha.*

Dositheus, who taught Simon Magus, was a great thaumaturgist.

Simon Magus was called 'The Great Power of God' (Acts viii. 10).

A most graphic account of the ascent of Simon Magus, in imitation of that of Elijah, is given in ' Notes and Queries,' 8 Dec., 1883, pp. 441-2. It was in the presence of Nero and an immense crowd. Simon Magus applied to himself many of the words uttered by Christ, such as 'Behold I go to the Father. . . I will prepare a seat for you at the foot of my throne. . . . I will pour out upon my elect people my celestial treasures.' And again, ' Verily, verily, I say unto you, whose believeth in me shall not see death; for in me is eternal life.' And again, 'Remember that your eyes have seen the Word of God. I am the Beautiful One, the Paraclete, the Omnipotent, the great Pan, the divine All.'

	Fête Day.	
I. *Apollōnius* of Tyăna. ' Life' by Philostrātos in 8 books	—	3-98
Philostrātos says : ' He raised the dead, healed the sick, cast out devils, uttered prophecies, and saw at Ephesus the assassination of Domitian.		
Plotīnus, the Neo-Platonic philosopher. ' Life' by Porphyry	—	205-270
Gregory, bishop of Neocæsarēa, in Cappadocia. Called emphatically ' The Thaumaturgus '	17 Nov.	212-270
Dionysius, or Denys, patron saint of France	9 Oct.	3rd cent
Quintus of Æolia, in Asia Minor	2 March	died 283
Rŏmānus of Antioch, martyr	9 Feb.	died 303
Asclepias, the Sabine. Martyred at Antinŏe, in Egypt	23 Jan.	died 311
Nicolas, bishop of Myra, in Lycia	6 Dec.	died 342
Macarius the Elder, of Egypt. Solitary of Scetê	15 Jan.	310-395
Martin of Tours, who divided his cloak with a beggar. 'Life' by N. Gervais	11 Nov.	316-397
Titus, martyr, while Rome was under the Goths	16 Aug.	died 410
Germānus, bishop of Auxerre, ccnfessor	31 July	330-448
Proclus. ' Life' by Marīnus, and by Eunapius	24 Oct.	412-485
Brigit, or Brigida, of Ireland. Her cell was called ' Kill-Dara'	1 Feb.	436-523
Linus, pope and martyr	23 Sept.	570-667
Cuthbert, the ' British Thaumaturgus '	20 March	died 668
Jonas, priest of St. Sabas, in Palestine. Of the Greek Church	21 Sept.	7th cent.
Hesychius, solitary of St. Andrew's, in Bithynia. Of the Greek Church	6 March	8th cent.
John, bishop of Polўbŏtos, in Asia	5 Dec.	8th cent.
Isaac of Cordŏva, martyr	3 June	died 851
Aldric, bishop of Mans	7 Jan.	800-856
Bernard of Clairvaux, called ' The True Thaumaturgus of the West '	20 Aug.	1091-1153

		Fête Day.	
Isidore of Seville, farm labourer. 'Life' by John of Damascus	. 10 May	1110–1170	
Dominic, founder of the Dominicans	. 22 Jan.	1170–1221	
Francis of Assisi, founder of the Franciscans . . .	. 4 Oct.	1182–1226	
Hyacinth, called 'Thaumaturgus of the Thirteenth Century'.	16 Aug.	1182–1256	
Anthony of Padua, who preached to the fishes . .	. 13 June	1195–1231	
Catherine of Siena. (Not the Catherine famous for the wheel)	30 April	1347–1380	
Vincent Ferrer, a Spanish Dominican	. 5 April	1357–1419	
Francis of Paula, founder of the Minims . . .	. 2 April	1416–1507	
Francis Xavier, apostle of the Indians . . .	. 3 Dec.	1506–1552	
Charles Borroméo, archbishop of Milan . . .	. 4 Nov.	1538–1554	
Vincent of Paul, founder of the Lazarists and 'Sisters of Charity'	. 19 July	1576–1660	

II. Of these neither the time of birth nor of death is known :—

	Fête Day.
Aninas, or Ananias, anchorite and prophet. In Greek menology	17 Feb.
Attalus, honoured in the Greek Church . . .	6 June
Dius, archimandrite and thaumaturgist of Constantinople	19 July
Elisabeth, virgin of Constantinople	24 April
Eustratius of Nicomedia. Honoured in the Greek Church . . 2 &	18 April
Felix of Spoleto . . .	16 June
Filuměna, called 'Thaumaturga of the Nineteenth Century,' of whom nothing whatever is known .	10 Aug.

In 1802 three tiles were found which made this name; and since then her ghost has told her story. L'Abbé Migne says : 'Ces révélations particulières paraissent réunir sous les caractères d'une source divine' !!! ('Encyclopédie Théologique,' vol. xii. p. 719).

	Fête Day.
Georgius the Younger. Honoured at Constantinople	23 March
Georgius-Theophŏrus, of the Greek Church . . .	11 March
Illyrius, of the Greek Church	3 April
Jasimus, of the Greek Church	4 Feb.
Maurus of Sopeto. (Not the great Maurus of Glanfeuille)	16 June
Memnon, of the Greek Church	28 April
Onesimus, of the Greek Church . . .	14 July
Peter, bishop of Argos . .	3 May
Peter of Gallia Cisalpīna .	*
Philotheus, founder of the monastery of Mermecium, on the Bosphŏrus . .	15 Sept.

	Fête Day.
Ritza, a virgin of Coblentz .	30 Aug.
Rufīnus, deacon of Sinōpê, martyr	7 April
Sebastiăna, Greek Church .	7 June
Stephen, Thaumaturgus of the laura of St. Sabas, in Palestine	13 July
Tharasius of Lycaonia. (Not the patriarch of Constantinople)	25 Feb.
Theoclěta, Greek Church .	21 Aug.
Titus, of the Greek Church .	2 April
Zanaïs, called 'Thaumaturgus of Constantinople' . .	6 June

III. The following were miracle workers, but not entitled 'Thaumaturgi' by the Catholic Church :—

Prince *Alexander* of Hohenlohe, titular bishop of Sardica. His miracles made a great noise in 1820–1821. He healed by prayer only.

J. Joseph *Gassner* of Bratz, in the Tyrol, who exorcised the sick. His cures were considered to be miraculous (1727–1779).

Jambiicus. When he prayed, we are told, his body 'rose in the air at least 10 cubits, and his face became luminous'; so says Eunāpius (4th cent.).

Jannes and *Jambres*, Pharaoh's magicians, who imitated the miracles of Moses.

Mohammed is said to have performed no miracles, yet rode he to heaven on the back of Albōrak, made the moon pass up one sleeve and down the other, and took a scroll of the Koran out of the horns of a bull (570–632).

Blaise *Pascal*, philosopher and mathematician (quite sufficient to account for his 'deeds of wonder'), 1623 1662.

Simon *Magus* of Samaria, called 'The Great Power of God' (Acts viii. 10).

Sospitra, who, says Eunapius, 'had the power of seeing what was done in any part of the world.'

Vespasian, the Roman emperor, we are told, 'cured a blind man and a cripple by his touch while staying at Alexandria.'

*** Gaspar Schott published a treatise on natural magic, entitled 'Thaumaturgus Physïcus' (1657–9).

Apparently thaumaturgy did not hold a very high place in the Christian Church. It was extremely common, and nothing whatever is known of many thauma-turgists beyond the name and *fête* day.

Thaumaturgus.

The following are given as thaumaturgi by Mgr. Guérin, 'Petits Bollandistes,' xvii. p. 757.

Antony of Padua . . .	1195–1231
Bridget or Brigit of Ireland	436–523
Francis de Paula . . .	1416–1507
Gregory of Neocæsarēa .	212–270
Hyacinth (of the 13th cent.).	1182–1257
Martin of Tours . . .	316–397
Vincent Ferrier . . .	1357–1419
Francis Xavier . . .	1506–1552

Hundreds of others are said to have worked miracles, but the eight given above are recognised thaumaturgi.

Thaumaturgus of the West

(*The*). St. Bernard of Clairvaux (1091–1153).

The before a proper name in Scotland and Ireland means the head of a clan, as: The MacLeod, The Chisholm, in Scotland; The O'Donoghue, The O'Connor Don, in Ireland. The assumption of 'the' was forbidden and declared treasonable because the head of a clan, like The O'Neill, also claimed a right to sovereignty. Thus when O'Neill threw off his allegiance to Queen Elizabeth, he called himself 'The O'Neill of Ulster,' meaning that he was king of Ulster.

The'atines

(3 syl.), 1524. Confirmed by Clement VII. in 1524. Settled in France by Cardinal Mazarin in 1644, and suppressed in France in 1790. The order was founded by the Archbishop of Chieti (in Latin, *Theāte*), who afterwards was pope (Paul IV.). The object of the order was to reform the lives of the clergy, and restore the priesthood to apostolic purity. They wore a black soutane, and black robe with white sleeves.

Theatines of the Congrega-tion,

1583. An order of nuns founded at Naples by Ursula Benincasa. Made subject to the Theatines by Clement IX. in 1668.

Theatines of the Hermitage,

1610. Founded in Naples by Ursula Benincasa, and confirmed by Urban VIII. in 1624.

Thebaidic.

See p. 787, 'Sahidic.'

Thellusson Act

(*The*), 39 & 40 Geo. III. c. 98. For checking the disposition of testators to restricting the use of their fortunes till they had accumulated to very large amounts. So called from Mr. Thellusson, who had directed in his will that his personal property should be left to accumulate during the lives of his three sons, and the lives of their sons, and then to be inherited by the eldest male descendant of his three sons. No testator can now tie up his property for more than twenty-one years, dating from the death of the testator.

Mr. Thellusson died 21 July, 1797. It was decided in the House of Lords that his 'stock' might accumulate for 120 years, when it would amount to 140 millions sterling. Should no heir then exist, the whole should be applied to the discharge of the national debt.

Themistians,

535. Monophysites, originated by Themistius, deacon at Alexandria. Also called Agnoites (*q.v.*).

Themis'toclês of Modern Greece.

Constantine Kanaris (1795–1855).

Theodor'ici Infernum.

The crater at Lipāri.

Theodosian Code (*The*).

Said to have been compiled by command of Theodosius the Younger, Emperor of the East (401, 402–450). The reputed date of the code is 438; but nine years later the 'Novellæ Constitutiones' were promulgated in the Western empire. The codex consists of 16 books, sub-divided into titles and sections. The 262 laws are imperial Rescripts (*q.v.*) consecrating the wisdom of Christian princes from the reign of Constantine to the year 447. One of the edicts ascribed to Constantine, extending the jurisdiction of bishops to all causes, has been proved to be a forgery; it is, however, inserted in the capitularies of Charlemagne. *See* p. 524,'Literary Forgeries.'

Another edict, ascribed to the same emperor [Constantine], and annexed to the Theodosian code, extended the jurisdiction of the bishops to all causes which either party chose to refer to it, even where they had already commenced in a secular court, and declared the bishop's sentence not subject to appeal. This edict has clearly been proved to be a forgery.—HALLAM, *Middle Ages*, vol. ii. p. 211.

Theodosian Table (*The*).

Same as the Peutingerian Table (*q.v.*).

Theoph'ilan'thropists

(Lovers of God and man), 1796–1800. Philanthropic deists who rose in France during the revolution. They believed in God and the immortality of the soul, but not in the Christian scheme of salvation through faith or by the atonement. They considered that the duty of man is doing good, and their rule was, 'Worship God, cherish your kind, and render yourself useful to your country.' Thomas Paine was one of the founders of this society, and one of its most active members.

These Theophilanthropists superseded the social circle of Paris. Its chief authors were Aubermesnil, Chemin, Mandar, and Valentin Haüy. The cult was professed in many of the French churches, but was forbidden in 1800.

Theoph'oron, Christot'okos, and Theot'okos. Nestorius (5th cent.) declared that Mary was not θεοτόκος (mother of God), but only χριστοτόκος (mother of Christ), for God cannot be born of a woman. Jesus of Nazareth he called θεοφόρον (possessed of God). These distinctions were condemned by the Council of Ephesus in 431.

Theos'ophy, 1889, means 'the wisdom of the gods,' or the divine wisdom which underlies all religions. It professes to pick out the grains of wisdom from all the divers religious systems of the world, and to amalgamate them into one consistent whole.

Theot (Catherine), 1725–1793. A French visionary, who called herself sometimes the Mother of God and sometimes the new Eve.

Theotokos. See 'Theophoron.'

Therapeutæ (The), Greek θεραπευταί. Greek Jews of Egypt, more rigid than the Essenes, as they avoided towns and dwelt only in deserts or 'commons,' where they gave themselves up to contemplation. Like the Essenes they had all things in common, but unlike the Essenes they abjured all possessions beyond the barest necessities. When anyone entered the society he 'sold all that he had and gave to the poor.' The Therapeutæ were all celibates, like the Essenes, although women were allowed to join their society. On Sabbath days all dined 'together, the women on one side, the men opposite, and the fare was bread and salt, with a little hyssop (Philo, 'De Vita Contemplativa').

The Therapeutæ believed that God is the author of all good, but not of evil.
That the soul is immortal. That the good are rewarded after death, and the wicked punished.
They objected to animal sacrifice, as no man could be justified in taking life.
Seven was their sacred number.

Ther'midor (The 9th), Year II. 27 July, 1794. The day when Robespierre was accused by Tallien in the Convention, and arrested in the Hôtel-de-Ville, Paris. He and 22 of his partisans were guillotined next day (10 Thermidor, Year II.).

Amongst these partisans were St. Just, Lebas, Henriot, Robespierre jeune, &c. The month called Thermidor was from 19 July to 18 Aug.

Thermido'rian Government (The), 1795–1799. The French Directory was so called because it was established in the month Thermidor (July).

Thermido'rian Reign of Terror (The), 1795. The period which immediately succeeded the fall of Robespierre, when the Anti-Jacobins were in power, and guillotined the Jacobins with the same relentless vengeance as Robespierre had shown against the Anti-Jacobins.

Thermido'rians. Partisans of the 9th Thermidor. See 'Thermidor.' Originally applied to Tallien, Legendre, Lecointre, Fréron, Thuriot, Bourdon de l'Oise, and Barras, but afterwards (1794) applied to all the Anti-Jacobin party, which rose into power on the downfall of Robespierre (9 Thermidor, Year II.), i.e. 27 July, 1794. There were a host of young Thermidorians called 'Fréron's Gilded Youth.' See 'Jeunesse Dorée.'

Generally speaking, the term Thermidorians was applied to those who wanted to restore the monarchy.

Thermopylæ of France (The), 1792. The Forest of Argonne, which Thouvenot was assigned by General Dumouriez to hold against the army of Brunswick, who was marching on towards Paris. Whilst planning how he was to prevent the allied Prussian and Austrian armies, which had just taken Verdun (2 Sept., 1792), from advancing on Paris, he wrote to the French ministers, 'Grand-Prey and Islettes are our Thermopȳlæ.' He meant that the enemy would be penned up in the desolate, muddy, and sterile fields of Campagne, if his army held Grand-Prey and Islettes. If not the enemy would winter in the fertile country of the Trois Evêches.

[Dumouriez] beckons a certain young Thouvenot, the fire of whose looks had pleased him, to wait a moment. Thouvenot waits: 'Voila (says Polymetis, pointing to the map) that is the Forest of Argonne, that long strip of rocky mountain and wild wood—40 miles long . . , this might one . . . seize . . . [and] once seized '. . . [it] might be the

Thermopylæ of France.'—CARLYLE, *French Revolution*, vol. iii., book i., 3.

Thes'mophor'ia.

A festival of the ancient Greeks in honour of Demēter, the thesmoph'oros or law-giver. It lasted three days of October, and only married women could take part in the ceremonies. The last day, called Kalligenei'a, was spent in jollity and raillery.

Thiers (*Mons.*).

His nicknames were 'Attila le Petit,' 'Tamerlan à lunettes,' 'Caméléon,' 'Général Bonne,' 'Le Roi des Versailleux.' Louis Adolphe Thiers, born at Marseilles 1797; first president of the French Republic 1871-1873; died 1877.

Thiggers and Sorners of Scotland.

Similar to the 'sturdy rogues' of England. Vagabonds who preferred begging to work, and collected alms by menacing the timid. James 1. of Scotland tried to put them down, and ordered licensed beggars to wear a badge. These licensed beggars were called 'Gaberlunzies.'

To thig is to beg. Ancient German *thigen*. Thiggers also written Thigsters. A Sorner, in Scotch law, is one who takes meat and drink from others by force or threats. Sorn or Sorehon was an arbitrary exaction or servile tenure in Scotland and Ireland. Purveyance was a similar exaction in England, that is food and free quarters for king or chief and all his retinue on passage.

Thimble League (*The*), 1886.

To provide work at fair wages for women whose only means of livelihood is needlework.

Thinæ.

An hypothetical city of ancient geographers, situated, as Ptolemy says (book vii., 3), 'on or near the vast ocean which bounds Asia. It is enclosed by brazen walls.' The following is the description given in the Periplus of this city: 'It is situated under the Lesser Bear, and is reported to border on the opposite part of Pontus and the Caspian Sea, by which the Mæōtis Palus flows into the ocean' ('Periplus Maris Erythræi,' ap. Hudson, 'Geogr. Vet. Scrip-Græci Minores,' vol. i., p. 36).

Some identify Thinæ with China.

Third Founder of Rome (*The*).

Caius Marius, the victor of the Teutons and Cimbrians (B.C. 101); the second founder was Camillus, who overthrew the Gauls that invaded Rome under Brennus (B.C. 367). Romulus is called the original founder (B.C. 753).

Third Order of Religionists (*The*).

See p. 873, 'Tertiaries.'

Third Romulus (*The*).

See above, 'Third Founder of Rome.'

Thirlwall Prize (*The*),

for original historical research. A prize given every alternate year. Part of the prize is a bronze medal. Open to all graduates of the University of Cambridge of not more than four years' standing. Founded out of the Thirlwall memorial fund 1884; first award 1889.

Thirteen United Colonies (*The*),

1775. The style assumed by the American Congress after Georgia sent in her adhesion. For the other twelve colonies, see 'Patres Patriæ.' See also 'Congress of the United Colonies.'

Thirty (*Battle of the*), 1351.

The defiance of Jean sire de Beaumanoir to the English châtelain Bemborough to decide a contest by thirty Bretons pitted against thirty Englishmen. It is said by French historians that after eight of the Englishmen had been slain, the rest surrendered; and that Jean sire de Beaumanoir quenched his thirst with a draught of blood. The fight took place between the castles of Josselin and Ploermel in France.

Thirty Tyrants (*The*).

I. Of Athens, B.C. 404. After the battle of Ægospotămos, the government of Athens was changed into an oligarchy. The political clubs named a committee of five who called themselves the Athenian ephors; and this committee nominated thirty persons to draw up the new constitution and to undertake the temporary administration of the city. The chief names were Theramĕnês and Critĭas. The committee thus appointed soon obtained the unenviable name of the Thirty Tyrants.

II. Of Rome, B.C. 200. A term loosely applied to a number of usurpers who assumed the rank and title of Augustus in different Roman provinces after the death of Valerian. The phrase applied to a list of independent rivals, only nineteen in number, is ridiculous, and these rivals in no wise resembled the council of thirty set by Sparta over Athens.

The nineteen pretenders to the Roman throne were Cyriădês, Macriānus, Balista Odenāthus, and Zenōbia (in the East); Posthumus, Lollian,

Victorīnus and his mother Victōria, Marīus, and Tetrīcus (in Gaul and the western provinces); Ingennus, Regelliānus, and Aureolus (in Illyricum and the confines of the Danube); Saturnīnus, in Pontus; Trebellīan, in Isauria; Piso, in Thessaly; Valens, in Achaia; Æmilian, in Egypt; and Celsus, in Africa. They all died a violent death. Perhaps the thirty was made up of the wives and children involved in the deaths of the pretenders.

Thirty Years' Peace of Venice (*The*). From 1538 to 1570, when Selim II. sultan of Turkey declared war against Venice wholly without provocation.

Thirty Years' Truce (*The*), B.C. 445-415. This truce preceded the great Peloponnesian war.

Thirty Years' War (*A*). The War of the Roses lasted thirty years; and in this civil war more than 100,000 Englishmen lost their lives. The first battle was that of St. Albans 23 May, 1455, and the war ended with the death of Richard III. in Bosworth Field 23 Aug., 1483. The other historic battles were : Northampton, in which Henry VI. was made prisoner a second time 19 July, 1460 ; Wakefield, in which Richard duke of York was slain 31 Dec., 1460; Towton, in which Henry VI. was a third time made prisoner—this was one of the bloodiest domestic battles ever fought, 29 March, 1461. Hexham, won by the Yorkists 15 May, 1463; Barnet, in which the Earl of Warwick was slain, fought Easter Day, 14 April, 1471 ; Tewkesbury, in which Margaret and her son were taken prisoners 4 May, 1471. Altogether eight noted battles.

Thirty Years' War (*The*), 1618-1648. A war to extirpate the Protestants of Germany set on foot by Kaiser Ferdinand II. It may be divided into four parts, thus—

I. From the commencement to the Danish intervention. A period of seven years (1618-1625).

II. From the beginning of the Danish intervention to the peace of Lübeck, when Christian IV. of Denmark retired from the contest. A period of five years (1625-1630).

III. From the intervention of the Swedes under Gustavus Adolphus to the battle of Nordlingen. Another period of five years (1630-1634).

IV. From the French intervention to the peace of Westphalia, a period of thirteen years, in which the character of the war was wholly changed. It was no longer a religious war, but a fight by France and Sweden for German ascendency (1635-1648).

Thistle (*Knights of the*), 809, said to have been founded in Scotland by Archaïcus. Revived by James II. of Great Britain in 1687 ; again by Anne 31 Dec., 1703. The badge is a collar composed of sixteen gold thistles interlaced with golden sprigs of rue ; and a small golden image of St. Andrew in a gold badge attached to the collar. The motto is ' Nemo me impune lacessit.'

The 'rue' is a pun. Thistles And-rew (*rue*).

Thistlewood's Conspiracy, 1820, to assassinate all the ministry. Arthur Thistlewood had been arrested for taking part in the Spa Fields riots (*q.v.*), Dec. 1816. He challenged Lord Sidmouth (secretary of state for the Home Department) 1817. Sixteen of the ministers were to die at Lord Harrowby's house in Grosvenor Square on 19 Feb. One of the conspirators was to call with a note, and when the door was opened the rest were to rush in and murder all the ministers, bringing off in bags the heads of Sidmouth and Castlereagh. They were then to throw fireballs into the straw-sheds of the cavalry barracks and set them on fire; and then to take the Bank and the Tower. Edwards informed against the conspirators, so the whole affair ended in smoke. Thistlewood and four others were executed 1 May, 1820.

The four others were Ings, Brunt, Tidd, and Davidson. Castlereagh, pronounce *Castle-ray*.

Thomas (*Christians of St.*). A very early sect settled on the coast of Malabar, and said to have been planted by Thomas the apostle. They lapsed into the Nestorian heresy ; that is, they believed in the co-existence of the two natures of Christ, but not in their union. At present they are chiefly Monophysites, but many are Romanists of the Eastern rite.

It is certainly remarkable that the churches said to have been founded by apostles were, as a rule, not what is now called ' orthodox.' These were the Seven Churches of Asia, the St, Thomas Christians, the Church of Pella presided over by James and his brother, and so on.

Thomasites. *See* p. 169, ' Christadelphians.'

Thomists. Disciples of Thomas Aquinas (1224-1274), who applied the Aristotelian philosophy to Christianity. Aquinas was a Dominican, and therefore

3 L

was hated by the Franciscans, their natural enemies. In the 14th cent. Duns Scotus, a Franciscan, came forward as the avowed opponent of Thomas Aquinas, and hence arose the two sects, the Thomists and the Scotists. The Thomists leaned to 'Nominalism' (q.v.); the Scotists to 'Realism' (q.v.). The Thomists, like Augustine, denied the 'Immaculate Conception'; the Scotists maintained it. The Thomists believed in the doctrine of Condignitism (q.v.); the Scotists were Semi-pelagians (q.v.). The points of grace and predestination were always bones of contention.

See 'Christians of St. Thomas,' a large body of Christians in Malabar. See p. 170.

Thomites (The) of Kent, 1838. Followers of John Nicholl Thom, a native of Cornwall, who went to Kent, assumed the name of Sir William Courtenay, gave out that he was the Messiah, and wholly invulnerable by fire or steel. This lunatic had a large following of respectable middle-class men and women, who were guilty of rioting. The military being called out, Thom was shot, and buried at Herne Hill 5 June, 1838.

Mr. Wyse referred to the ignorance revealed in the county of Kent by the delusion of the Thomites. —HOWITT, Hist. of Eng. year 1839, p. 441.

Thorn (Treaty of), 1466, which closed the wars between the Poles and the Teutonic Knights of Preussen. By this treaty all the western part of Preussen was ceded to Poland, and the rest of Preussen (or ancient Prussia) was held as a fief by the knights.

Thorough (The). A system adopted by Wentworth and Archbishop Laud, which would (by the aid of the church) have rendered Charles I. the most absolute of all monarchs. It was the 'thorough' subjection of all law to the royal will.

The hearers had not forgotten the 'Thorough,' nor the utter suppression of all forms of religion but his own, the sweeping away utterly of the faith of Scotland, and the substitution of Arminianism and the liturgy.—HOWITT, Hist. of Engl. (Charles I., chap. iv. p. 249).

Thoulounides (3 syl.). A Turcoman dynasty of Egypt (869–905), so called from Thouloun of the tribe of the Oïgours. He was a slave, but made Egypt independent.

Thrani'tæ, the uppermost bank of rowers in a Greek galley. The lowest bank was called the Thalamîtæ and the middle bank the Zeugîtæ. As the oars of the Thranitæ were the longest, their labour was greatest, and they had higher wages.

Three Articles (The), 1584. The three things which Archbishop Whitgift required the clergy to subscribe to, viz. (1) the royal supremacy in matters ecclesiastical as well as temporal; (2) the legality of the Book of Common Prayer and the Ordinal; and (3) the Thirty-nine Articles. See p. 48, 'Articles.'

Three Branch Men (The). A term applied to those politicians who in the reign of Charles I. used to speak of the king, lords, and commons as the three estates, or the three branches of the legislature. The phrase originated with John Reeves at the close of the 16th cent.

Lord Clarendon says: 'The three branches is not only unsound in point of law, but is wholly false as a metaphor. Nobody talks of branches, but relatively to something else. If you speak of branches of a canal, you always have in your mind the grand trunk; but if king, lords, and commons are three branches, where is the trunk?'

(Of course the three estates of the kingdom are the nobility, the clergy, and the commons.)

Three Chapters (The). In Greek Κεφάλαια. Schedules setting forth the heresies of Theodore of Mopsuestia, Theodoret of Cyrrhus, and Ibas of Edessa, accused of the Nestorian and Pelagian taint. They had been cut off and restored to church communion, and were dead and buried, when Justinian revived the controversy and submitted the 'Three Chapters' to the fifth general council held at Constantinople in 553. The three 'heretics' and all their defenders were then delivered over to the prince of darkness.

Dean Milman (vol. ii. p. 343) says: 'The controversy of "the Three Chapters" was idle and frivolous; yet how many pages of church history does it not fill!' Gibbon says: 'The dispute has filled more volumes than it deserves lines.'—See ROBERTSON, Hist. of the Christian Church, vol. ii. p. 301.

Three-cornered Constituencies. A political device for representing minorities. In 1867 it was enacted that if any place returned more than two members, the constituents should be allowed to vote for one less than the entire number: thus if, as in the city of London, there are four members, the constituents could vote for only three. By this arrangement the three most popular candidates would represent the majority, and the fourth choice would lie between the least popular of the majority and the most popular of the minority, and in almost every case the latter would be elected.

Three Days of July (*The*), or ' The Three Days,' July 27, 28, 29 (Tuesday, Wednesday, and Thursday) of 1830, in which the revolution of France culminated in the abdication of Charles X.

The famous Three Days of July had as thrilling an effect in Transylvania as elsewhere.—GODKIN, *Hist. of Hungary.*

Three Emperors (*The*), B.C. 2953– 2598. The 10th ki of Chinese 'history.' This mythic period followed the allegorical. The three mythic emperors were Fo-hi, Chin-nông, and Hoâng-li, *i.e.* son of heaven, divine husbandman, and emperor of earth.

Three Fatal to France. The fatal number to Rome has been six; and three has proved singularly fatal to France.

I. Take the kings. The third of any name has been uniformly either worthless or unlucky : Childebert III., Clotaire III., Clovis III., Dagobert III., and Thierry III. were *rois fainéants.*

CHILDERIC III., the last king of France of the first race, was confined in a cloister that Pepin le Bref might reign in his stead.

PEPIN le Bref was the *third* Pepin : (1) Pepin de Landen ; (2) Pepin d'Héristal, his grandson, and (3) Pepin le Bref, grandson of Pepin d'Héristal, who was succeeded by the Carlovingian dynasty.

CHARLES III. le Simple was wholly under the thumb of favourites, and after a most inglorious reign was poisoned by the Comte de Vermandois.

HENRI III. le Mignon, 'weaker than woman and worse than 'harlot,' was assassinated by Jacques Clément.

LOUIS III., joint king with Carloman, reigned about a year and was killed by an accident at the age of 22.

PHILIPPE III. le Hardi was singularly unfortunate, and singularly misnamed ' The Bold.' This tool of Labrosse went on a crusade, and brought home the dead bodies of five near relatives : his father, his wife, his son, his brother, and his brother-in-law. The 'Sicilian Vespers' (*q.v.*) occurred in his reign. He died of an epidemic at Perpignan.

NAPOLEON III. lost his imperial crown at Sedan, and died in exile at Chiselhurst, in Kent.

II. The succession of three brothers has always proved fatal :

The CAPETIAN dynasty terminated with the succession of three brothers : Louis X., Philippe V., and Charles IV. (sons of Philippe le Bel).

The VALOIS line came to an end by the succession of three brothers : François II., Charles IX., and Henri III. (sons of Henri II.).

The BOURBON dynasty terminated with the succession of three brothers : Louis XVI., Louis XVIII., and Charles X. (sons of Louis the Dauphin).

III. The *monarchy* of France was brought to an end by the third of these triplets.

The *empire* of France consisted of Napoleon I., Napoleon II., and Napoleon III.

Ut dicitur, semper sub sextis perdita Roma,
Sic quoque sub numero tres perdita Francia semper.

If *six* to Rome hath always brought mischance,
Three hath a fatal number proved to France.
     See p. 796, ' Semper sub Sextis.'

Three Glorious Days, or ' La grande semaine.' The insurrection of 27, 28, 29 July (1830), in Paris, which drove Charles X. from the throne. The days were Tuesday, Wednesday, and Thursday.

The political world was shaken by the three glorious days in Paris.—J. A. FROUDE, *Thomas Carlyle,* vol. ii. p. 124.

Three Great Military Orders (*The*). The Knights Templars, the Knights Hospitallers, and the Teutonic Knights of St. Mary of Jerusalem.

Three Hundred (*The*), of Milan. The band in charge of the banner of St. Ambrose, the sacred oriflamme of Milan, sworn to die in its defence. The three hundred were supported by a guard of three times three hundred, the elect soldiers of Lombardy. Three was a sacred number, and three times three was thrice sacred.

Three in English history. Our line of kings never exceeds three reigns without interruption or catastrophe.

William I., II., Henry I.
    A usurper, Stephen.
Henry II., Richard I.
    A usurper, John.

Henry III., Edward I.
Edward II. murdered.
Edward III.
Richard II. deposed.
Henry IV., V., VI.
Line of Lancaster changed.
Edward IV., V., Richard III.
Dynasty changed.
Henry VII., VIII., Edward VI.
Lady Jane Grey.
Mary, Elizabeth.
Dynasty changed.
James I.
Charles I. beheaded.
Charles II.
James II. dethroned.
William III., Anne.
Dynasty changed.
George I., II., III.
Regency.
George IV., William IV., Victoria.
Indirect successions.

** Except in one case, that of John, we have never had a *great-grandchild* as sovereign in direct descent. See 'Three Fatal to France.'

Three Kings (*The*). The three Kings of Cologne are the supposed Magians who offered gifts to the infant Jesus in Bethlehem. The 'Feast of the Three Kings' is the Feast of Epiphany or Twelfth Night. There was a famous dramatic spectacle so called, once extremely popular. The representation in 1336 by the monks of Milan is historic.

The names usually given in Cologne Cathedral are Gaspar, Melchīor, and Balthăzar ; but other traditions give other names, as Apellios, Ameros, and Damascos ; Magălath, Galgălath, and Sară- sin,—Ator, Sator, and Peratōras.

Three Kings' Day. Twelfth Day, so called because the visit of the 'Three Kings' or wise men of the East who came to honour the infant Jesus is commemorated on that day (the Epiphany).

Three per cent. Reduced Annuities (*The*), 1747. Several funds borrowed at a higher rate of interest reduced to a three per cent. interest. In 1749 by Act of Parliament it was declared that all such holders of the fund as did not choose to accept the reduced interest should be paid off in full. Very few embraced the alternative.

Three Popes.
I. In the 11th cent. there were three simultaneous popes : Benedict IX. (1033 –1048), Silvester III. (1044), and Gre-

gory VI., who bought the pontificate (1044–1046). Kaiser Henry III. in 1046, having set aside Benedict and Gregory, appointed Clement II., a German, who died the following year. Benedict still held on, and in the two next years two other Germans were appointed by the kaiser.

II. In the 15th cent. there were three simultaneous popes : Gregory XII. (1406 –1415, died 1417), held his court at Friuli ; Benedict XIII., the Avignon pope, held his court at Peniscola, in Spain (1394– 1424) ; and Alexander V., the Roman pope (1409–1410), succeeded by John XXIII. (1410–1415). While Gregory and Benedict were still alive the Council of Pisa appointed Martin V. (1417), and at the death of Benedict Clement VIII. took his chair.

Three Questions (*The*), 1687. The lords-lieutenants of counties and mayors of boroughs were requested by James II. to make a return of persons who answered the following questions in the affirmative : (1) If chosen to sit in the next parliament will you vote for the repeal of the Test Act and of the Penal Laws ? (2) Will you give your vote to candidates favourable to those repeals ? (3) Will you support the declaration for liberty of conscience by living peaceably with Christians of a different creed to your own ? The answers received were not favourable to the king's views.

Three Rejected Articles (*The*). The original number of the articles of the Church of England was 42, drawn up in 1551, but the present number is 39, three having been omitted by Convocation, 29 Jan., 1563. The three articles rejected are these : (1) The resurrection of the dead is not passed already ; (2) the soul does not perish with the body ; and (3) not all men will be saved.

Three Sacraments (*The*).
I. 1520. *Luther* acknowledged only three sacraments, viz. baptism, the eucharist, and penance. Roman Catholics have seven sacraments, but English Protestants since 1553 have admitted but two, baptism and the Lord's supper, as may be gathered from the church catechism published that year.
II. In 'Cranmer's Catechism' (*q.v.*) three sacraments are authorised :
1. Baptism, the bath of regeneration,

or instrument of the second birth (pp. 182, 206).

2. Absolution, or the authority of the keys, by virtue of which pardon is obtained for sins after baptism.

3. The holy communion, which supplies fresh grace to the worthy recipient, and enables him to go on from strength to strength.

Three States or Stages (*The*). Comte says the mind passes through three stages, the theological, the metaphysical, and the positive. In the infancy of thought the mind attributes phenomena to the arbitrary will of some spirit, fairy, or pervading providence, which says and it is done. In the second stage it attributes the causes of phenomena to some abstract or hypothetical principle, as law and force. In the third stage it relies on science and data. Thus plague and famine by the first is attributed to God; by the second to eclipses or some other hypothesis; by the third to bad sanitary arrangements. Most educated men are in all the three stages: on some subjects they are in the theological stage; on others in the metaphysical; and on others in the positive. Thus Faraday was remarkable for his theological and positive stages.

Three States (*Period of the*), called by the Chinese San-kuo (221–226). The states were (1) Heou-Hân, or Sho-Hân, the continuation of the Hân or 6th imperial dynasty. It gave two kings, and lasted forty-four years. The seat of government was Shen-see; (2) the kingdom of Oey or Wei, which gave five kings, lasted forty-five years, and had Honân for the seat of government; (3) the kingdom of Ou or Woo, which gave four kings, lasted forty-four years, and had its seat of government first at Ou-chang, and afterwards at Nankin.

Three Tailors of Tooley Street (*The*). Only two of these busybodies were tailors. They were John Grose (tailor, Tooley Street), Thomas Satterley (tailor, Weston Street), and George Sandham (grocer, Bermondsey Street), who met after business at a public-house, to smoke their pipes and talk politics. During the movement of Catholic Emancipation they resolved to petition parliament, and commenced their document

with these words: 'We, the people of England.' Canning was prime minister.

A correspondent of 'Notes and Queries' (21 Jan., 1888, p. 55) avouches this to be a fact.

Three Test Articles (*The*), 1554, introduced in the reign of Mary in proof of orthodoxy, were :—

1. Is the natural body of Christ really present in the elements after consecration, or not?

2. Does any substance, except the body and blood, remain in the eucharist?

3. Is the Mass a propitiatory sacrifice for the sins of the living and dead, or is it not? *See* p. 48, 'Articles.'

Three Theological Virtues (*The*). Faith, Hope, and Charity.

Three-way Leet. A three-way road, a cross-road where suicides used to be buried with a stake thrust through their body. These cross-ways were the terror of 'old women and old maides.'

Lædan, zelædan · lád, gelád. Junius says, 'Trivium, quadrivium, ita dicunt, in quibusdam Angliæ tractibus.

'Three Ws' (*The*), 1837. Three great American houses in London. The amount paid from June to December by Wilson & Co. was 935,300*l.*; by Wigan & Co. 674,700*l.*; and by Wildes & Co. 505,000*l.*; total acceptances in six months, 2,116,000*l.*

Three Writers (*The*). *See* p. 801, 'Scriptores Tres.'

'Five Writers,' *see* 'Scriptores Quinque'; 'Ten Writers,' *see* 'Scriptores Decem'; the 'Six Chronicles,' *see* 'Six.'

Threshers (*The*), 1806. An Irish secret treaty formed by Roman Catholics of Ireland in opposition to the Orangemen or Protestant association. They appeared in Sligo, Mayo, Leitrim, Longford, Roscommon, and Cavan. One of their articles was the resistance to the payment of tithes, even when voluntarily paid to Roman Catholic priests. Their chief called himself 'Capt. Thresher,' and his gangs used to thrash or beat unmercifully all collectors of tithes and their clerks, as well as those who paid tithes. *See* p. 455, 'Irish Associations.'

Throne and Altar (*The*). 'Le Trône et l'Autel,' the motto of the Legitimists and Carlists. It really means the divine right of kings and priests, both 'the Lord's Anointed.' The absolute king and infallible Church.

Throne of Jamshēd (*The*). Persepŏlis is so called because founded by Jamshēd (shēd means *illustrious*). This mythical king of Persia began to reign B.C. 2240 and reigned twenty years. The Blue-ribbonites will be glad to know that the art of making wine is ascribed to this king.

Throne of the Barricades (*The*). That of Louis Philippe of France (1830–1848), founded on the Revolution of July, when Paris was barricaded for three days.

Thronus Regalis (Königstuhl). A round vault on the Rhine, five miles south of Coblentz. The vault is built of freestone, and rests on nine stone pillars, one of which stands in the middle. It is eighty feet in circumference, furnished above with seven seats, one for each elector. The ascent to it is by stairs consisting of twenty-eight stone steps, and it has two stout doors. On this thronus regalis the original electors consulted respecting their choice of a king. Heinrich VII. in 1308 was elected in this manner, and in 1338 the electoral league was established here. Maximilian I. was the last of the kaisers brought to the thronus regalis.

Thugs (*The*). A religious fraternity in India in honour of Khali, wife of Siva, but addicted to murder. In some provinces they are called Phansīgars or stranglers.

Phansīgars means those who 'employ the noose' or *phansi*. Thug means deceiver or cheat.

Thunderbolt of Italy (*The*). Gaston de Foix, nephew of Louis XII., who fell at Ravenna in the moment of victory (1489–1512).

Thunderer (*The*). The 'Times' newspaper, so called from an expression used by Captain Edward Stirling while Thomas Barnes was editor : ' We thundered forth the other day an article on the subject of social and political reform.'

Thundering Legion (*The*), A.D. 174. In Latin 'Legio Fulminatrix.' While Marcus Aurelius was engaged in a war with the Quadi and Marcomanni his army suffered severely from want of water. Eusebius says the 12th legion (*Legio Melitīna*) fell on their knees and prayed for rain, when forthwith a storm broke overhead, supplying the Roman army with water, and dealing destruction to the foe. From this storm the Legio Melitīna was ever after called the Thundering Legion.

The assertion of Eusebius (v. 5), be it remembered, is only one-sided, for others ascribe the storm to the prayers of Marcus Aurelius to Jupiter, and under this impression the emperor raised a pillar in gratitude to 'Jupiter the Thunderer.' Others ascribe it to the incantations of Arnuphis, an Egyptian magician. Then, again, Dio Cassius informs us that the twelfth legion had been called 'Legio Fulminatrix' ever since the time of Augustus (Book vii., v. 23).

Thurificati (*The*). Those lapsed Christians who, to avoid persecution, consented to burn incense to heathen gods.

Tiara (*The*). The triple crown of the pope, symbolising his civil rank, as the keys symbolise his ecclesiastical power. The most ancient head-dress of the bishop of Rome was a high round cap. In 1053 Pope Damasus II. adopted a cap more like that of the Jewish high-priest or a mitre. In 1276 Pope John XIX. encompassed his mitre with a crown ; in 1295 Boniface added a second crown ; and in 1411 John XXII. added a third crown, completing the tiara or triple crown to signify the power of the pope over the church ' souffrante, militante, et triomphante,' or else his power over three parts of the world (Europe, Asia, and Africa).

Surely the pope cannot claim power over the church triumphant.

Tiberius (*The French*). Louis XI. (1423, 1461–1483). Both were cruel, crafty, and deceitful. Their rule of government was, 'He who knows not how to deceive knows not how to rule.'

Tibullus of France (*The*). Evariste Désiré Desforges Parny (1753–1814). The 'dame de sa plume' was a Creole, who, however, preferred in marriage a rich planter to a poor poet.

Tiedge Verein (*The*), 1842. An institution founded in Berlin in honour of Christoph August Tiedge, 'the Nestor of German poesy ' (1752–1841). It gives every fifth year a literary prize to some youthful candidate, and makes provision for needy meritorious authors.

Tien-teh. The pretender to imperial power in China, and leader of an insurrection which lasted sixteen years. There were five chiefs, all of whom acknowledged his supremacy (1850–1866).

His proper name was Hung sieu-tseuen. He

was a native of Quang-si of low origin, and assumed the titular names of Tien-teh (*celestial virtue*) and Tae-ping-wang (*prince of peace*).

Tien-tsin (*Treaty of*), 26 June, 1858, between Great Britain and China. Ratified 24 Oct., 1860. Provided for ambassadors on the part of the two contracting parties to reside at each other's court; for the establishment of a British minister at Pekin, and the liberty of trading without restriction.

Tierce. One of the eight daily services of the Catholic Church, and third of the four lesser ones. At nine in the morning—the third hour of the day. *See* p. 140, 'Canonical Hours.'

Tiers Consolidé, 1797. A name given in France during the Directory to the public debt, 'dont le tiers seul était garanti,' the nation being bankrupt at the time.

Tiers État (*Le*), or 'Le Tiers.' The third order of the state, the other two being the noblesse and the clergy. The three orders combined form the Etats Généraux. In the reign of Louis le Gros (1108–1137), the commons were admitted into the legislative assembly, which then took the name of the 'Assemblée des trois états.' 27 Dec., 1788, it was determined that the deputies of Le Tiers should equal those of the other two orders combined. This is called 'Le doublement du Tiers.' The name of *Tiers Etat* was abolished in 1789, and the *Etats Généraux* became the *Assemblée Nationale.*

Pronounce *Tears-a-tah'*.

Tiers Ordre, or 'Tiercelins,' or 'Tertiaries.' Seculars of a religious order who observe the rules of the order to which they attach themselves without renouncing their civil life. The 'Third Order of St. Francis' was founded in 1221; the 'Tertiaries of St. Augustine' in 1401; the 'Third Order of St. Dominic' in 1422; &c.

Some tertiaries who live in common.

Tigernach. The oldest of the Irish annalists (died 549). His annals were published in O'Connor's *Rerum Hibernicarum Scriptores Veteres* at the expense of the Duke of Buckingham, 1814–1826.

Tiglath-pileser. *See* p. 485, 'Kileh-Shergat.'

Tigretier. The dancing mania of Abyssinia, which occurs most frequently in the Tigré country, whence its name.

Tilsit (*Peace* or *Treaty of*), 7 July, 1807, between France and Russia. This was a most disgraceful affair, as Russia was at the time an ally of Great Britain, and they were acting together against Turkey and the French. Napoleon by this treaty won over Alexander, and secretly provided that he should make common cause with France against Great Britain, and sign the Berlin Decree (*q.v.*). It was secretly agreed between the two signatories that France should be allowed to make itself master of the Danish fleet and Russia to seize Finland. Turkey was to be divided between them: France to have Macedonia, Dalmatia, and Greece; and Russia all the rest of Turkey. 9 July Prussia signed the treaty, but was not informed of the *secret provisions* above referred to.

'Times' (*The*), newspaper. Commenced 1 January, 1788.

'Times' (*The*) and the *Irish Land League,* 1889. The 'Times' newspaper had used its gigantic influence to put down the crimes committed in Ireland for several past years connected with the Land League. The Irish were compelled by the leaguers to join the league on pain of death or personal injury, and those who joined the league were forbidden to pay their rents or to occupy a holding from which a defaulting tenant had been evicted. In 1889 three judges, called Commissioners, were appointed to examine into the merits of these charges made by the 'Times.'

Whatever may be said respecting the position taken up by the 'Times' in 1888-1889 against Charles S. Parnell and the Irish party, one thing is indisputable, the motive was noble and patriotic. Mr. Gladstone as prime minister had said that 'crime dogged the Parnellite party in every movement,' and if so, the movement ought to be put down. In fact, the phrase 'Parnellism and crime' is only Gladstone's *dictum* in another form. The conduct of the 'Times' in seconding Mr. Gladstone was a most disinterested act, with only one fault—the editors trusted too implicitly to an adventurer named Pigott, who betrayed them.

'Times' Fund (*The*), 1854. A sum of 10,000*l.* raised by private subscription and sent to Printing-house Square for the relief of the sick and wounded in the hospitals of Scutári, tended by Miss Florence Nightingale and a staff of lady volunteers in the Crimean war. The 'Times' newspaper undertook to superintend this fund.

'Times' Memorial (*The*), 1841. Mr. O'Reilly, the 'Times' correspondent at Paris, having received secret information of a gigantic fraud projected on the continent, exposed it in the 'Times' newspaper, and saved the bankers the loss of a million sterling. A testimonial was set on foot, and the 'Times' declining any money recompense, a 'Times' scholarship was founded at Oxford for boys educated at Christ's Hospital, and another at Cambridge for boys educated in the City of London School. The rest of the money was spent on four tablets, to be set up in the Royal Exchange, in Christ's Hospital, in the City of London School, and in the 'Times' printing office.

The swindle was to have been a simultaneous issue of forged letters of credit on the chief bankers of Europe. The attempt to expose the Irish Land League was equally noble, but miscarried through the villainy of one Pigott.

'Times' Testimonial (*The*), 1842. The Bishop of London headed a subscription to the 'Times' newspaper for the interest taken by that journal in the School of Christ's Hospital. The money collected was funded to create exhibitions in that school to either of the Universities, and to found 'Times' Scholarships.' *See above* 'The "Times" and the Irish Land League.'

Timothy Sparks. The *nom de guerre* of Charles Dickens in his pamphlet of 'Sunday under Three Heads': (1) As it is; (2) As Sabbath bills have made it; and (3) As it might be made (1836).

Timothy Titcomb. The penname of Josiah Gilbert Holland, an American author.

Tineman, *i.e.* lose-man, the man who loses his men. So Archibald Douglas was called, because after the death or murder of the Duke of Rothesay, fortune deserted him, and he lost most of his followers in each action he undertook (died 1424).

Tintamarresque. Burlesque history: as 'Le Trocadéroscope, Revue Tintamárresque de l'Exposition Universelle.' Paris, 1878. Par Touchatout.
' Histoire de France Tintamarresque.' Par Touchatout. Paris (to the flight of Louis-Philippe in 1848).
' Histoire Tintamarresque de Napoléon

III.' Par Touchatout. Paris, 1877 (from 1848).
' La Dégringolade Impériale ' (a second part to the above). Paris, 1878.
' Grande Mythologie Tintamarresque.' Par Touchatout.
' Histoire Populaire et Tintamarresque de la Belgique.' Par F. Delisle. Brussels.

Tintoret of Switzerland (*The*). John Rudolph Huber (1722–1790). He painted 3,065 portraits, besides other subjects.

Tippling Act (*The*). 24 Geo. II. ch. 40. So called because it allowed no action to be maintained for the sale of spirituous liquors, retailed on credit, unless the debt amounted to 20*s.* or upwards at one time. Now in part repealed.

Tire'sias. Milton is called 'the blind Tiresias of modern times' (1608–1674).

Tirshatha. A governor appointed over the Assyrian kings.

Tirzah (*The House of*). In the language of the Roundheads, the Episcopalians were of the house of Tirzah. Any persons who differ from our own religious faith. Tirzah was the royal city of the revolted tribes of Israel.

He liked not this going to feast in high places with the uncircumcised in heart, and looked on the whole . . . as a making merry in the house of Tirzah.—Sir W. SCOTT, *Peveril of the Peak*, chap. 4.

Tisserands (weavers). The French name of the Cathári, or Puritans of the 12th cent. *See* p. 150, ' Cathari.'

Tithe Agitation (*The*). In Ireland, 1831. The Catholic Irish combined to resist the payment of tithes to Protestant clergymen. The rebellion was stirred up by Daniel O'Connell, who hated Mr. Stanley, the chief secretary. Many of the clergy in Ireland were reduced to pauperism. At Newtownbarry, in Wexford, cattle were impounded by a tithe-proctor, and the peasantry who went to release them came into collision with the yeomanry, who fired and killed twelve. At Carrickshock, however, there was a more frightful tragedy. The peasantry armed with scythes and pitchforks killed eighteen of the police, including the commanding officer. At Castlepollard, in Westmeath, the police fired on the peasants and shot ten. At Gortroche, near Rathcormack (Cork), Archdeacon Ryder, supported by a number of the military, ordered the soldiers to fire, when eight were killed and thirteen wounded. Among the slain was the son of widow Ryan. Government now took the matter up. Mr. Stanley, chief secretary, insisted that the law must be respected; Daniel O'Connell sided with the tithe recusants. It was found that the amount of arrears was 104,285*l*., but all that could be collected was 12,000*l*., and the cost of collecting it was 15,000*l*., so the contest was given up, as the game was not worth the candle. *See* 'Irish Church Temporalities Bill.'

Tithe Bill, or Commutation Act, 1836. As a tenth of the produce of land would in many cases swallow up the profits of improvement, the bill enacted that a rent-charge should be levied equal to the average amount received for wheat, barley, and oats, during the seven preceding years. The rent-charge removed the vexatious custom of taking tithes in kind. The measure was devised by Mr. Jones.

Many landlords let their lands tithe free, and pay the rent-charge themselves. This should always be done under all circumstances. When tithe was collected in kind, a green bough was stuck into every tenth shock of corn on the field to mark the property of the tithe-owner.

Tithe Commissioners of England and Wales (*The*). 6, 7 Will. IV. c. 71 appointed to convert the tithes into a rent-charge payable in money, but varying in amount, according to the average price of corn (*i.e.* wheat, barley, and oats), for the seven preceding years.

Tithe Commutation Act (*The*), 1832. Ireland. This act enabled the tenant to pay a yearly sum of money in lieu of tithes, if the rector was willing to accept the commutation. Above 1,000 parishes accepted the change, but some rectors stood out, and this led to the Anti-tithe War (*q.v.*).

Tithe Composition Bill (*The*), 1832. Introduced by Lord Stanley. In 1838 composition for tithes in Ireland was changed for a fixed charge, which was only three-fourths of the former composition, to be paid by the landlords and not by the tenants (1, 2 Vict. c. 109).

Tithe War (*The*). In Ireland (1830-1835). A most sanguinary rebel-

38

lion ostensibly for the abolition of tithes. The Whitefeet, the Blackfeet, the Terryalts, the Lady Clares, the Molly Maguires, and the Rockites overran Ireland during these years. And in 1842, 1846, the Repeal movement roused the country to a state of enthusiasm bordering on frenzy, if not actual revolt. *See* p. 455, 'Irish Associations.'

Tithes (*Commutation of*). In England and Wales, 1836 (6, 7 Will. IV. c. 71), whereby the tithes hitherto collected in kind were commuted for a fixed sum of money. Amended by 1 & 2 Vict. c. 64 (1837), and several times since.

Titi (*Prince*). Frederick prince of Wales, eldest son of George II. Seward, a contemporary, tells us that Prince Frederick was a great reader of French memoirs, and that he wrote memoirs of his own times under the pseudonym of 'Prince Titi.' These memoirs were subsequently found amongst the papers of Ralph the historian.

Correspondents of 'Notes and Queries' in 1884 inform us that there is a political fairy tale by St. Hyacinthe (1684-1746) called the 'History of Prince Titi,' the four chief characters of which are KING GINGUET, mean, stingy, and hating his son (like George II.); the QUEEN TRIPASSE, his wife, haughty, very fond of money, and also hating her son (like Queen Caroline); PRINCE TITI, a good, kind-hearted, affable prince, handsome and brave, but ill-used by his royal parents (like Frederick prince of Wales); and PRINCE TRIPTILLON, a younger brother, made much of by both his parents (like the Duke of Cumberland). Ralph also wrote a 'History of Prince Titi,' in which the page L'Eveille by fairy help gets to know all that passes in royal councils, and keeps the prince advised of everything. The page made a journal in cipher of these matters, which was printed in 1736.

Titian (*The French*). Jacques Blanchard (1600-1638).

Titian (*The Portuguese*). Alonzo Sanchez Coello (1515-1590).

Titian (*The Spanish*). Juan Fernandez Ximenes, generally called 'El Mudo' (the Dumb), 1598-1666.

Title, or 'Titūlus,' means 'pastor,' as the 'Title of St. Mary,' *i.e.* the pastor of the church so called.

Title of Accusation, (*The*), nailed to the cross, we are told, is deposited with one of the nails in the Santa Croce of Rome. Bozio asserts that it was found in the cave where the three crosses were buried. The letters are red, and the slab of wood. Lipsius informs us that the slab shown to him was 9 inches long; but, as it contained only a small part of the inscription, the entire slab, he thinks, must have been about 4 feet. *See* p. 231, 'Crucifixion, *Relics of the.*'

Father Durand (1282-1296) tells us that he saw in *Paris* the title of the accusation in full. The monk Antonine (1389-1459) asserts that he held in his own hands the slab bearing the full accusation when he visited the Holy Sepulchre at *Jerusalem.*
The title on the Roman slab contains two Latin words, NAZARINVS RE[X], and one Greek word written *backwards* and spelt with two blunders, ΣYONEΡAZAN, where E should be H, and -OYΣ should be -OΣ. Surely this must be a most clumsy forgery, for the writer ignorantly supposed that Greek was written like Hebrew from right to left.

Tit'ulars of Tithes. Scotchmen

to whom the king made grants of abbey lands and tithes, on condition of their providing suitable stipends to the reformed clergy. Also called the 'Lords of Erection.'

Titus of Germany (*The*). Joseph II. (1741–1765–1790), son of Maria Theresa. So called because hardly a day passed which was not distinguished by some act of munificence, some private deed of charity, or something done for the good of others; yet was he almost always unfortunate.

Titus, or the Delight of Mankind of Germany (*The*). Maximilian II. Coxe, in his 'House of Austria,' says : 'If ever a Christian and philosopher filled the throne, that Christian and philosoper was Maximilian II.' (vol. i. part ii. p. 649). Born 1527, reigned 1564–1576.

Tityre Tus (pronounce *Tit'-e-re tuze*). The name assumed in the 17th cent. by a clique of young blades in London, of the upper class, whose delight was to break windows, upset sedan-chairs, rudely caress young women, molest the watch, and annoy quiet citizens. *See* 'Street Bullies.'

The reference is to the first line of Virgil's first 'Eclogue,' *Tityre, tu patula recubans sub tegmine fagi,* implying that they were men of leisure who delighted to 'recline at ease under their paternal beeches.'

To Remain Bible. In Gal. xxiv. 29 an editorial note in the margin, 'to remain' [*stet*], is inserted in the text: 'But as then he that was born after the flesh persecuted him that was born after the spirit to remain, even so it is now.' *See* p. 90, 'Bible,' and 'Scriptures.'

Tobacco Revolt (*The*), 1848. *See* p. 32, 'Anti-tobacconists.'

Toeplitz, in Bohemia (*Treaty of*), Sept. 1813, between Austria and Great Britain. This treaty of alliance was effected between the battle of Dresden and that at Leipsic. A few days previously (9 Sept.) Austria, Russia, and Prussia had entered into an alliance against Napoleon.

Toga'ted Nation (*The*). The ancient Romans, whose distinguishing dress was a toga or white robe bordered with purple for magistrates. Women as well as men wore the toga.

The children who were free-born wore a *toga prætexta* (white bordered with purple) till they were seventeen, when they changed it for the *toga virīlis,* made of white wool without ornament or border.

Toga'ti et Pallia'ti. The Romans and Greeks. The dress of a Roman was the toga, of a Greek the pallīum, whence the Romans were called the *gens togāta,* and the Greeks the *gens palliāta.*

Toghlak (*The House of*). Founded in Delhi by Tóghlak in 1321. This line of kings succeeded the second Gaurian dynasty, which reigned from 1288 to 1321. The house of Toghlak was succeeded in 1414 by the government of the Seiads.

Toleration Act (*The*), 1 William & Mary, c. 18 (24 May, 1689). For the relief of Protestant Dissenters. All persons dissenting from the Church of England (except Papists, Unitarians, and Arians) were allowed to assemble for religious worship according to their own forms, provided they took the oaths of allegiance and supremacy, and also subscribed a declaration against transubstantiation. The exception of Unitarians and Arians was repealed by 53 Geo. III. c. 160. The Roman Catholics were relieved by the Emancipation Act, 10 Geo. IV. c. 7, 1829, and 1844.

Tolosa (*Gold of*). Tolōsa—*i.e.* Toulouse—was a large and wealthy city with a famous temple, where great riches were deposited. In this temple was preserved the booty taken by 'Brennus' from Delphi. In 106 this temple was plundered by Quintus Servilius Cæpio on his way to meet the Cimbrian army. Cæpio was utterly defeated by the Cimbri, and it was said that his defeat was a judgment of the gods for his sacrilege. Hence the Latin proverb *Aurum Tolo-*

sănum habet ('Ill-gotten wealth never prospers ').

Toltecan Nations (*The*). The Mexicans and Peruvians are so called by Morton. The Toltecans, he says, were the builders of that series of mounds found throughout North America.

Tom Moore of France (*The*). Chaulieu (1639–1720). Called 'The Anacreon of the Temple.'

Tom of Ten Thousand. Thomas Thynne, of Longleat Hall. So called not only from his great wealth, but for his unbounded hospitality. He married Elizabeth Percy (countess of Ogle), heiress of Joscelyne earl of Northumberland, and was murdered on his wedding day (12 Feb., 1682) by three assassins hired by Charles count Konigsmark, a disappointed suitor of Lady Ogle.

In Dryden's 'Absalom and Achitophel' Thomas Thynne is introduced as 'Issachar.'

Tome of St. Leo (*The*). That is his 'Dogmatic Letter' 449. Leo set aside the Council of Ephesus, which had pronounced in favour of Eutўchês, and summoned a new council of Chalcēdon, in which his 'Tome' was accepted 'as the voice of St. Peter,' and adopted as the orthodox exposition of the doctrine of the person of Christ. It declared that his body was not a celestial body, as Eutychês maintained, nor yet a mere human body into which the Godhead descended at baptism, as the Nestorians taught, but a human and divine nature like the union of body and soul. This of course led to the dogma that Mary was the mother of God, and to the more modern dogma of the Immaculate Conception.

Tomlins Prælector of Anatomy in Oxford University. Founded by Richard Tomlins in 1626. Now annexed to the Linacre professorship of Physiology, the stipend being 200*l.* a year.

Tong-Hân. The last fourteen kings of the Hân dynasty (B.C. 25 to A.D. 220).

The first 16 kings of this dynasty were the western or Si-Hân. The second half the eastern or Tong-Hân.

Tong-Oeï Dynasty (*The*), A.D. 534. The northern empire of China was split into the eastern or Tong-Oeï, and the western or Si-Oeï. The first dynasty of

the eastern kingdom had but one sovereign, who reigned 16 years (534–550).

Tonnage and Poundage. A duty per ton or per pound on goods imported into England. First imposed by Edward III. by vote of parliament for a fixed number of years, and renewed at the expiry of the time. It was to furnish the sovereign with ready money for the defence of his realm. In the reign of Henry V. the grant was made for life, but on the accession of Charles I. the parliament limited the grant to a year, and when the grant was not renewed, as was usual, Charles levied it without the authority of a grant. The amount was about 3*s.* per tun on imported wines, 10 per cent. on goods sold by the pound of less value than 100*l.*, and 5 per cent. on goods above that value. In the reign of Queen Anne these imposts were made perpetual, and mortgaged for the public debt, and in 1787 (27 Geo. III. c. 13) tonnage and poundage was abolished, a duty being substituted according to tariff on each article subjected to duty.

Of course, since 1846, when free rade in corn was established, the principle has spread to the free importation of well-nigh every article of commerce; but no nation in the world follows the example (1890). The United States of N. America, in Oct. 1890, ran to the extreme of protection. And now the nations will learn whether Free Trade or Protection is the true principle of national prosperity.

Tonnage Bank (*The*), 1694. So the Bank of England was called when it was first established in the reign of William III., because the Bank company was to lend government 1,200,000*l.* at 8 per cent., and to receive in repayment the proceeds of a new duty on tonnage.

Tonsure. The shaven part of the head indicative in the Catholic Church of holy orders. Probably it represents the halo of sanctity, or else the crown of the royal priesthood.

1. *St. Peter's tonsure.* The shaven part is the whole crown of the head, with a fringe of hair left to represent the crown of thorns. This is the tonsure of the Latin Church.

2. *St. Paul's tonsure,* when the whole head is shaven. This is the tonsure of the Greek or Oriental Church.

Simon Magus's tonsure. A semicircle shaven from ear to ear above the forehead, but not reaching to the hinder part of the head, where the hair was suffered to remain. This is sometimes called St. James's tonsure. It was adopted by the Irish missionaries.

Tonsures are mentioned by St. Dionysius the Areopagite, who died A.D. 95, 'De Hierarchia,' p. 2; and they were general in the 4th and 5th cents. See Bede, 'Church Hist.,' book v. ch. 22.

Toom Tabard (Empty Jacket). So John Baliol was called by the Scotch for his silly opposition to Edward I. (Baliol born 1259, king 1292–1296, died 1314.) ' Vox et prætera nihil.'

Torch of Pengwern (The). Gwenwyn, prince of Powysland, was so called from his constantly laying Pengwern in Flintshire, part of the ' province of Shrewsbury,' in conflagration.

Torches, Links, and Lanterns. In the reigns of James I. and Charles I. courtiers (proceeding home after dark) were conducted with torches, merchants with links, and mechanics with lanterns.

Torgau (The Book of), 1574. A celebrated confession of faith, the object of which was to establish unanimity between the reformers. Torgau is in Prussia (Saxony). Also called the ' Formula of Concord.'

Torgau, pronounce Tor-gow (ow as in 'now ').

Tories (in Irish history), 1653, rapparees, or freebooters. They were the Irish Catholics driven by Cromwell from their homes into Connaught, who, instead of settling down, lived by blackmail, or by plundering those planted on their estates. Tory-hunting was a regular business after the Restoration, and was continued to the latter part of the 18th cent. In 1695 a law was made that any Tory killing two other Tories, ' proclaimed and on their keeping,' should be entitled to pardon for all former offences, except murder. In 1718 it was declared a sufficient claim for pardon if a Tory could plead that he had killed one Tory. These acts expired in 1776. The word is from *toruighim*, to pursue for the sake of plunder.

The word Tory has completely changed its meaning: it no longer means the anti-government party, but the Church and State party. So in Italy the Guelfs and Ghibellines (q.v.) in 1818 completely changed their meanings. From the accession of William III. to the reign of George II. the Jacobites or anti-government party were the Tories: since then they have been the strong Church and State party.

Tories and Whigs, 1781, in the American War of Independence. Those colonists who adhered to the British interest called themselves *Tories, Royalists,* or *Loyalists*; those in the American interest called themselves *Whigs* or *Patriots.* They were nearly equal in numbers, and showed a savage hostility to each other.

Torné (Bishop), 1792, in the National Hall of Paris, demanded that all religious costumes and such like caricatures should be abolished. Then he flung on the floor of the house his pontifical cross, skull-cap, and frill-collar. Fauchet and other prelates followed his example, till all insignia were stripped off (' Moniteur,' 7 April, 1792).

Torquema'da. A bigoted inquisitor. The reference is to Thomas de Torquemada, the first Inquisitor-General of Spain, born at Valladolid' (1420–1498). He was a Dominican, and made Inquisitor-General of Castile in 1483. He greatly augmented the number of persecutions against ' heretics,' consisting of confiscations, condemnations, punishments of all kinds, and autos-da-fé, insomuch that even the popes [Sixtus IV. and Alexander VI.] were obliged to moderate his excessive zeal. Torquemada had the chief hand in the banishment of the Jews and Moors of Spain in the time of Ferdinand and Isabella.

Tor'tura Torti (Tortus confuted), 1609. A book by Lancelot Andrews, written at the request of James I. to confute the attack of Bellarmine, who, under the assumed name of Matthew Tortus, had attacked that monarch. Andrews was rewarded for his book with the see of Chichester, 1605.

Tory. A political party in England opposed to the Whigs. They are the most remote from the democratic or republican party, and are for the most part attached to the monarchy, the established church, and the landed interest. They are called Conservatives from their desire to preserve these, which the Radicals wish to root out. For etymology see ' Tories and Whigs,' ' Whig and Tory.'

Toryism, in the latter part of Queen Anne's reign, and the earlier days of George I., meant the peace party, and the party of free-trade. This party was opposed to the pretensions of the crown, and endeavoured to override the authority of the House of Lords by the creation of new peerages. Their sympathies were with the Catholics of Ireland, and some of them were for the repeal of the Scotch Union. The reason is plain enough; they were Jacobites, and opposed to the innovations of Anne and the house of Hanover.

To'temism. An American Indian superstition; the belief in totems or guardian angels, whether animal, vegetable, or mineral. A totem is the image of this guardian spirit. For not only human beings have souls, but all animals, plants, inanimate beings, stars, sun, moon, earth, sky, and even thunder, which the totem is supposed to represent.

Tottenham in his Boots, 1748. The Irish patriot toast. The Irish House of Commons incurred great public debts, and was charged with extravagance. An attempt was made to change the annual vote for the discharge of the national debt into a grant either for perpetuity or for a term of years. The ayes and noes were equal, when a member named Tottenham entered the house in his riding dress, and gave the preponderance of votes to the anti-ministerialists. Hence the toast.

Touch-piece (*A*). A medal which the king hung on the neck of a person touched for the 'king's evil.' It was called an Angel, and contained the legend, 'He touched them, and they were healed.' In the Stuart Exhibition, 1889, nine of these tokens were exhibited. Those of Charles II. were gold pieces; those of James I. and the two Pretenders were silver.

Of course the legend shows the prevalence of the notion of the 'divinity' of kings.

Tou'lunites (3 syl.), 868–905. A dynasty of califs in Syria and Egypt, founded by Ahmed Ibn Toulun, a Turkish slave.

Tower of Famine (*The*). The tower on the Piazza del Anziana, in which Ugolino of Pisa, with Gaddo, Ugoccione (his sons), and Nino and Anselmuccio (his grandsons), was confined. The archbishop threw the key of the dungeon into the Arno. Ugolino survived five days after the death of the other four. Dante refers to this in his 'Inferno.'

Town Clerk (*The*). Since the Municipal Corporations Act of 1835 the town clerk acts in obedience to the directions of the town council. His duties are to preserve minutes of the transactions, and to make out the freemen's roll, the burgess list, and the ward list; he is responsible for the safe keeping of all charter deeds and municipal records; and is subject to various fines in cases of neglect. He is a lawyer by profession.

Townley Marbles (*The*). Sculptures which Charles Townley collected at Rome between 1765 and 1772. He died in 1805, when his collection was purchased by the nation for the British Museum.

Toyshop of Europe (*The*). Birmingham.

I look upon Birmingham as being the great toyshop of Europe.—BURKE, *speaking on a Bill for licensing the New Street Theatre, Birmingham.*

Tract No. 90 (1841), by the Rev. J. H. Newman, was intended to show that much of the Roman Catholic doctrine might be held consistently with subscription to the Thirty-nine Articles of the Anglican Church. This led to the termination of the series, and the resignation by Mr. Newman of the vicarage of St. Mary's, Oxford, and subsequently, in 1845, to his secession to the Church of Rome. Many of his friends and associates followed him.

Dr. Newman was made a Cardinal in 1879, and died in 1890.

Tracts for the Times, or 'The Oxford Tracts,' 1833–1841. A series of tracts published in Oxford having for their object the revival of church principles, greater attention to all the rites, ceremonies, and externals of religion, and checking the latitudinarian tendency of the day. The chief promoters of the movement were the Rev. John Keble (author of the 'Christian Year'), the Rev. J. H. Newman (author of Tract No. 90) (*q.v.*), the Rev. E. B. Pusey, the Rev. Isaac Williams, the Rev. Hugh J. Rose, &c., all men of great scholarship and literary honours.

The Apostolic succession, priestly absolution, baptismal regeneration, the real presence, the authority of the Church, the value of tradition, and a discountenancing of Protestant principles are the chief tenets of the Tractarian party.

Tractarianism. The system contained in a series of papers called 'Tracts for the Times' (*q.v.*). The effect of which have been :

1. A revival of the High Church party.

2. A great development of church ritual. The preacher no longer wore his college gown and Geneva bands, pews were abolished, intoning became general, and bowing at the name of Jesus.

3. A great impulse was given to church restoration and building, and the style of church architecture has been carefully studied.

4. Many hundreds of churchmen have seceded to the Roman Catholic Church.

5. The Pope has taken advantage of the movement to establish in England and Scotland a regular hierarchy. 1852.

Tractarians. Those who uphold the doctrines and practices advocated by the 'Tracts for the Times.'

Trades-Unions. Declared unlawful in 1360. The law abolished 1824. Regulated by Act of Parliament 1825, and again 1859. These unions are combinations of artisans to compel masters to pay such wages as the union thinks they ought to give. Commission on outrages at Sheffield, 1867; at Manchester, 1867; law amended, 1871. If masters refuse to obey the demand, the men 'strike,' *i.e.* refuse to work, and the masters are unable to fulfil their contracts.

So long as the members of a union do not interfere with the liberty of non-unionists, these combinations are lawful, but the moment they overstep that limit they are most despotic. Any man may fix the price at which he will work, but it is tyranny to prevent another man from working at a lower or higher wage.

In 1834 as many as 30,000 Dorchester labourers marched through London to Whitehall to present a petition of grievances to the throne. This, of course, was a moral threat, and meant to be so.

Tradu'cianism. A theory to account for the procreation of the soul in human beings, ascribed to Tertullian. Tertullian taught that souls are procreated by souls as bodies are by bodies.

Somewhat allied to Tertullian's theory are the theories called *Generationism* and *Creationism.* The former explains the production of soul as analogous to corporeal generation ; the latter supposes that the Creator sends a soul into every human body at birth.

Tragedy (*Father of French*). Robert Garnier (1534-1590). Also P. Corneille (1606-1684), generally called 'Le grand Corneille.'

Tragedy (*Father of Greek*). I. Thespis, the Richardson of Athens.

II. Æschylos is also called the 'Father of Greek Tragedy' (B.C. 525-426).

Trailbaston. A law term applied to certain lawless men, probably armed with clubs. *See below,* 'Court of Trailbaston.'

Circa hæc tempora processit in publicum novæ inquisitionis breve, quod Anglice dicitur *Trailbaston,* contra intrusores, conductitios, hominum vapulatores, conductitios seisinæ captores, pacis infractores, raptores, incendiarios, murduratores, pugnatores. Multi hoc perempti, multi redempti, multi noxii, pauci innoxii sunt inventi. Adeo quidem rigide processit hujus coercitionis justitia, quod pater proprio filio non parceret, &c., dira multa.—Hist. Roffens. folio 200, de anno 1305. *See* 'Notes and Queries,' 10 Dec., 1887, p. 470n.

Trailbaston (*Court of*), 1305. 'Justices of Traylbaston' were appointed by Edward I. upon occasions of great disorders in the realm during his absence in the Scotch and French wars. We should now call them 'justices in eyre.' Riley tells us that the offenders themselves were styled Trailbastons from the bastons or clubs with which they were armed. The courts were for the trials of these rebels, who 'lurked in woods and parks to rob, murder, and molest the unwary.'

Justices in eyre are itinerant magistrates. Eyre a French word from the Latin *iter,* a journey.

Train-band. A militia force substituted by James I. for the old English fyrd. In the civil wars the train-bands sided with the parliament. Charles II. restored the militia to their ancient footing. Everyone will call to mind that John Gilpin was a 'train-band captain.'

Trajan's Column, at Rome. Made of marble, A.D. 114, by Apollodŏrus. It is 132 feet in height, and has inside it a spiral staircase of 185 steps, with 40 windows to let in light. It was surmounted by a statue of the Emperor Trajan, but the original statue was (by Sixtus V.) most incongruously supplanted by that of St. Peter. As in the column of the Place Vendôme, Paris, the battles of Napoleon form the spiral reliefs, so the battles of Trajan are represented spirally in bas-relief in the older Roman column. It still stands amid the ruins of Trajan's Forum.

Trajan's Column is made of 24 huge pieces of marble so closely united that they seem like one block. It is about 12 feet in diameter.

Trajan's Rescript. This was a letter to Pliny the Younger, proprætor of Bithynia, telling him how to act towards Christians. 'They are not to be hunted up; but if brought before you and convicted of crime, they must be punished as the law directs.' *See* p. 397, 'Hadrian's Rescript.'

Trajan's Wall. A line of fortifications across the Dobrudscha.

Trampling on the Crucifix. *See* p. 468, 'Jefume.'

Transcendental and **Transcendent.** Kant means by transcendental the various ideas, forms, and categories assumed to be native elements of human thought. These are not products of experience, though manifested only in experience. Such, for example, as space, time, causality, &c.

Transcendent he reserves for those transcendental elements that transcend experience, as God, the immaterial soul, spirits, and so on. *See below.*

Kant says: 'I call all knowledge transcendental which occupies itself not so much with objects as with the way of knowing those objects so far as it is possible *à priori.*'

Transcen'dentalism. The system of certain schoolmen, like Duns Scotus, who taught the existence of conceptions which, by their universality, *transcend* or rise above the ten Aristotelian categories. Thus God exists and the world exists, so that existence bears the same relation to particular existences as summum genus does to genera. Kant uses the word transcendental differently, though analogously. *See above.*

Kant means (I think) that there are certain mental data which are innate, and thus *transcend* mere experience.

Transfiguration (*Day of*). Matt. xvii. 1–13. Instituted 6 Aug., 1498.

Transfiguration (*Mount of*). Supposed to be Tabor, in the plain of Esdraelon, in Galilee. On its summit is a plain of about a mile in circumference. The Mount is about 1,000 feet in height.

Transubstantiation. The change which takes place in the Eucharist by consecration, when the whole substance of the bread is changed into the body of Christ, and the whole substance of the wine into the blood of Christ. The fact that the bread and wine phenomenally appear to be unchanged is a sensual deception. By consecration the bread

ceases to be bread and the wine ceases to be wine, the phenomenal appearance is mere 'accident,' the noumenon, or real substance, is the body and blood of Christ.

The Lutheran doctrine is that the bread remains bread and the wine remains wine, but that the body and blood of Christ by consecration are transfused into them, 'as heat into hot iron'; so that the bread is bread *plus* the body of Christ, and the wine is wine *plus* the blood of Christ. This is called 'Consubstantiation,' or 'Impanation.'

It has been denied that Luther taught the doctrine of Consubstantiation; but what e'se did he mean by impanation and the 'he it of hot iron'?

Trappists, 1140. Founded in Normandy by Rotrou, comte de Perche. Refounded by Abbé de Rancé in 1636. A reformed Benedictine order. The female order call themselves Trappistines, instituted 1822. When driven out of France in 1791 they went to Switzerland and built the monastery called *Val-Sainte,* which was suppressed in 1811. Fifty-nine monks of La Trappe migrated from England to France in 1817, and settled in La Loire Inférieure. In 1822 the Trappists had sixteen houses in France. Their chief monastery was burnt to the ground in August, 1871. They have several houses in the United States.

Travaux Forcés, Code Napoléon, called *travaux publics* in republican euphemism. Hard labour of criminals in public works, instead of the punishment of the galleys, which was abolished in 1748.

Travelling Bachelors, in the University of Cambridge, 1861. Two bachelors to travel for three years to investigate the religion, learning, laws, politics, customs, manners, and rarities of foreign countries. Stipend, 100*l.* each per annum.

Travendhal (*Treaty of*), 5 Aug., 1700, between Charles XII. of Sweden and Frederick IV. of Denmark. Frederick IV. of Denmark, regardless of the treaty of Altŏna (1689), revived the disputes with the Duke of Holstein, who had married the eldest sister of Charles XII. Charles immediately attacked Denmark by sea and land, and so furious was the attack that Frederick of Denmark was obliged to sue for peace. By the mediation of England and France a treaty of peace was signed at Travendhal, and Denmark had to pay the expenses of the war.

Treacle Bible (*The*) is Beck's Bible of 1549, in which the word balm is rendered treacle. The Bishops' Bible has *tryacle* (Jer. iii. 22; xlvi. 11; and Ezek. xxvii. 17). *See* 'Bible.'

Treasurer (*The*), since the Municipal Corporations Act of 1835, is appointed by the council, of which he must be a member, and he must give security for the proper discharge of his duties. The treasurer of the corporation is bound to keep accounts of all receipts and disbursements, and these accounts must be open to the inspection of the members of the council. He is to pay no money except by written order, and is to submit his accounts with vouchers every half-year.

Treasury Devil. A law phrase meaning clerk to the Solicitor-General of government business.

Treasury Remembrancer, or 'Treasurer's Remembrancer.' He whose charge it is to put the lord treasurer and the rest of the judges of the exchequer in remembrance of such things as are called on and dealt with in the sovereign's behoof. In England the office was in 1833 allied to the queen's remembrancer, but in Scotland and Ireland the office remains.

Mr. Goschen met Mr. R. W. Arbuthnot-Solmes, Treasury Remembrancer, and other officials.— *Newspaper paragraph* (on Mr. Goschen's visit to Dublin), 8 Dec., 1887.

Treaties, Conventions, &c.
See also

Aarau	Blois
Abo	Bologna
Abrantes	Breda
Adrianople	Bretigny
Ainaly Cavak	Bromsberg
Aix-la-Chapelle	Bucharest
Afghan	Cambray
Akerman	Campo Formio
Alcacebas	Capriano
Almorah	Carlovitz
Altenberg	Cateau Cambresis
Altmark	Chaumont
Altöna	Closter Seven
Amboise	Cognac
Amiens	Conflans
Anagni	Constantinople
Ancenis	Constance
Andelot	Copenhagen
Andrussow	Edinburgh
Augsburg	Falezy
Bagdad	Ferrara
Bartenstein	Fontainebleau
Bergen	Frankfort

Frederikshamn	Poitiers
Ghent	Potsdam
Gisors	Prague
Gulestan	Presburg
Hamburg	Pruth
Hanover	Pyrenees
Hubertsburg	Ranstadt
Jassy	Ratisbon
Jonko'ping	Roskild
Kalnardji	Ryswick
Kardis	Sempach
Kiel	Seville
Knærod	Stettin
Lahore	Stockholm
Lambeth	Teschen
Laybach	Tilsit
Limerick	Toeplitz
London	Travendhal
Lubeck	Troppeau
Lunéville	Troyes
Madrid	Turchomancho
Mersen	Turin
Moss	Unkiar Skelessi
Münster	Utrecht
Nertschinsk	Verdun
Nimeguen	Verôna
Northampton	Versailles
Nottingham	Vervins
Noyon	Viasma
Nystadt	Vienna
Oliva	Villafranca
Orebro	Vordingborg
Paris	Wallingford
Passarowitz	Widmore
Passau	Weliki Luki
Pequigny	Westphalia
Perth	Wilna
Peronne	Würtzburg
Petersburg	Zürich

Treaty of 1841 (*The*), signed 29 Aug., 1842. Made with the Chinese after the war with that country. *Its provisions were*:—The payment by the Chinese of 21,000,000 dollars (about 4½ million £ sterling). The opening of the new ports, Canton, Amoy, Foo-Chow, Ningpo, and Shanghai to British merchants; the cession of the island of Hong Kong to England; correspondence to be opened and continued between the Chinese and British Governments, and the islands Chusan and Kolangsoo to be held until the money was paid.

Treaty of 2 Dec., 1854 (*The*). Between Austria, Great Britain, and France, against Russia. Austria engaged to defend the frontier of the Principalities against Russia; if Russia made war on Austria the three powers would act in concert; if the Crimêan War lasted beyond 1 Jan., 1855, the three powers would unite to bring it to an end.

Treaty of Partition (*The*), B.C. 205. At the peace of Dyrrhachium Philip V., king of Macedon, made a bargain with Antiochus, king of Syria, to divide the dominions of Ptolemy Epiphânês, the boy-king of Egypt. This scandalous treaty induced Ptolemy to place himself under the guardianship of Rome.

Treaty of 1696 (*The*). In this treaty it was secretly stipulated at Loretto: (1) That the Vaudois valleys should have no communication or connection with the subjects of the great king [Louis XIV.] in matters of religion; and (2) that the subjects of his most Christian Majesty [Louis XIV], who had taken refuge in the valley, should be banished.

This was a mere evasion of the famous Edict of 13 May (*q.v.*), to which Victor Amadeus (whose daughter was betrothed to the heir of France) was forced by Louis XIV.

Treaty Stone (*The*), 3 Oct., 1691, Limerick, Ireland. A large stone on which the capitulation of Limerick was signed by General Ginkell and the leaders of the Irish insurgents. It still stands near Thomond Bridge, in the county of Clare, beside the river-bank.

Trecentisti. The Italian worthies of the 14th cent. *See* 'Cinquecentisti' and 'Seicentisti.'

This was the golden period, of which Dante was the representative.

Tree of Feudalism (*The*), 14 July, 1792. An immense tree erected in the Champ de Mars, Paris, on which were hung crowns, blue ribbons, tiaras, cardinals' hats, St. Peter's keys, ermine mantles, doctors' caps, law-bags, titles of nobility, escutcheons, coats of arms, and so on, to which the king (Louis XVI.) was to set fire. Louis refused to do so, saying there was no such thing as feudalism in France.

Champ de Mars, pronounce *Sharnd Mar* (r of 'Sharnd' silent).

Trees of Liberty. Trees or green boughs set up as symbols of liberty. The idea came from America. In 1790 the Jacobins planted a tree of liberty in Paris, and soon every village in France had its tree, crowned with the cap of liberty, round which the people danced singing revolutionary songs, as English villagers used to sing and dance round the May-pole. In the Reign of Terror thousands were guillotined for injuring these trees. During the empire the trees were suppressed, but in July, 1830, they were again set up, and again in 1848. These trees were adorned with *rings* as symbols of unity, with *triangles* as symbols of equality, with tricoloured ribbons

as the revolutionary badge, and a cap of liberty. The last was rooted up in 1872.

In Italy, during the revolution of 1848 and 1849, numerous trees of liberty were planted in the peninsula.

Trent (*Council of*), begun 1545 and closed 1563. Its object was to correct, confirm, and fix for ever the doctrines and discipline of the Catholic Church, and to reform the lives of the Catholic clergy. Hence Catholics are called *Tridentines* (3 syl.), from Tridentum, the ancient name of Trent, in Lombardy.

Trêve de Dieu (*La*), 1040. Suspension of arms during sacred days, divine service, and the intervals between Advent and Epiphany, Quinquagesima and Pentecost.

Triad, according to Pythagoras, is the third mathematical quantity; the monad or point is the first, length is the duad, breadth the triad or third mathematical quantity, and the fourth or tetrad is the solid. Physically, intellectual capacity is the monad, scientific or certain knowledge is a duad, opinion a triad, and perception by the senses a tetrad.

Triad Society (*The*). A secret society in China during the reign of Kiaking (1796–1820). Organised for plunder. Ostensibly, however, for the expulsion of the Manchoos from the throne and country.

Triads (*Welsh*). Mythological traditions, moral rules, historic fragments of the British, &c., in the Welsh language, disposed in groups of three.

Trial by Battel, or 'Wager of Battle.' Recognised in the laws of Liutprand, about 720. In use in England before the reign of Henry I., and not abolished till 1819. The combatants fought on horseback, fully armed. Being duly marshalled, they entered the lists saying, 'May God defend the right.' The king presided: if he threw down his warder, the combat ceased; if not, it went on till one of the combatants was vanquished or slain. The notion was that God would defend the innocent party.

Abraham Thornton in 1818, charged with the murder of Mary Ashford, refused to be tried by a jury, and insisted on a wager of battle. Lord Chief Justice Ellenborough allowed the appeal, and as Thornton was a very strong and athletic

3 M

man, and his accuser a mere stripling, the trial was declined, and Thornton released.

Trial of the Pyx (*The*). A very ancient ceremony, spoken of in the reign of Edward I. as 'a well-known custom.' It is the final trial, by weight and assay, of the gold and silver coins of the United Kingdom prior to their issue. The proceedings, which now occur every year, are conducted by the Lords Commissioners of the Treasury with much solemnity, and constitute a public attestation of the standard purity of the coin. The wardens of the Goldsmiths' Company act as the jury, and after making a careful examination, deliver to the king's or the queen's remembrancer a verdict that they can discover no variation from the standard specified in the Coinage Act, 1870.

Triarchy (*The Roman*), 337–361. Constantine the Great, at his death, divided his empire into three parts between his three sons:

To his eldest son, Constantine [II.], he left Gaul, Spain, and Britain.

To his second son, Constans, he left Italy, Illyricum, and Africa.

To his third son, Constantius, he left the East.

Constantine attacked his brother Constans, and was slain A.D. 340, aged 25.

Constans was slain by Magnentius A.D. 350.

Constantius died at Tarsus A.D. 361, aged 41. And the empire came to Julian.

Tribes (*Roman*). The original followers of Romulus were called Ramnés, or Ramnians. After the Sabine war the Sabines had a share in the new state, and were called Tities, or Titians. And after the conquest of Rome by Porsěna, the Etruscans had a share in the state, and were called Lucěres.

Ramnes, the original Romans. *See* Ramnes.
Tities, so called from Tatius, the Sabine king.
Lucěres, so called from Lucěrum, a town of Etruria.
It has been suggested by modern scholars that these are primitive clan-names long before Rome was founded.

Tribunal Extraordinaire, or 'Tribunal Révolutionnaire,' 1792. Decreed by the Mountain for the trial and dispatch of suspects. It had five judges and a standing jury, was subject to no appeal, and was virtually free from any law forms.

Tribunal Révolutionnaire (*Le*), 10 March, 1793. An 'exceptional tribunal' created by the Convention of France, and consisting of three judges at least, a jury, and a public accuser. Its decisions were without appeal.

Tribunal de Première Instance (*Le*), 1810. A jurisdiction established in each arrondissement of France for 'toutes les affaires civiles et correctionnelles' which are not specially assigned to other tribunals.

Tribunal of Blood (*The*), 1567. The organisation under Margaret, governor of the Netherlands, under which 18,000 persons were put to death in three years. Also called 'The Council of Trouble.'

Tribunal of the Faith (*The*), 1823. A revival in Spain of the 'Holy Inquisition.' Extinct in 1868.

Tribunal of the 17th of August (*The*), 1792. A French revolutionary tribunal demanded of the Convention by Robespierre, for the trial of 'traitors against the people.' It consisted of one deputy from each section. This tribunal was succeeded by the more awful 'Tribunal Révolutionnaire' (*q.v.*).

Tribunat (*Le*), 1799. In France, established for discussing the merits of the laws presented by the government. Orators were appointed to speak pro and con, and the corps législatif decided. The tribunat entered on its functions in 1801. It was originally composed of 100 members, not above 25 years of age. In 1802 the number was reduced to 50, and in 1807 it was wholly suppressed.

Tribunaux Correctionnels (*Les*), 1810. Under this title the tribunals of 'première instance' take cognizance of appeals from the decisions of the police court, and all minor offences limited to five days' imprisonment or a fine not exceeding 15 francs (12s. 6d.).

Pronounce *Tre-bu-no cor'rek'-se-o-nel.*

Tribune of the People. So François Noel Babeuf called himself (1764–1797). He assumed the name of Gracchus, and tried to make himself a second Robespierre, but his rebellion was soon crushed by the Directory, and Babeuf was guillotined.

Tribunes (*French*), 1799. In the Consulate 100 tribunes formed part of the government. Their sole province was discussion. The first consul submitted a motion to the corps législatif ; whereupon the state councillors advocated its adoption, and the tribunes pleaded against it. In 1807 the tribunate was abolished, and the ' Corps Législatif ' was addressed by the *Conseil d'État.*

Tributum was the Roman property tax, an extraordinary levy in times of war. The censors made the assessment, and it was called *tribute* because it was exacted from *all the tribes.* The collectors were called Tribuni Ærarii.

Tricolour (*The*), 1789. Clovis, after his baptism, adopted the *blue* standard of St. Martin de Tours for the national banner. The successors of Hugues Capet, who made Paris their capital, changed the blue standard of St. Martin for the *red* standard of St. Denis. As red was the English colour, Charles VII. discarded it, and chose *white* (in honour of the Virgin Mary), for the national colour. Hence blue, red, and white have all in turns been the national colours of France. In the revolution, 1789, *blue and red* were adopted, being the colours of the commune of Paris, and Lafayette added *white* (the lilies of France), to represent the French nation.

Long before this, Mary Stuart, wife of François II. (afterwards queen of Scotland), had adopted the tricolour as the livery of her Swiss guards: *white* for France, *blue* for Scotland, and *red* for Switzerland, in compliment to the nationality of the guards themselves.

There is no reason to suppose that Lafayette introduced white (the monarchical colour) to conciliate the Bourbon king.

Tricolour Scarfs. Still worn in France by the municipal magistrates and commissaires of police.

Tricolours (*European*). Indicative of national liberty :
In FRANCE : Blue, red, white, divided vertically.
In ITALY : Green, white, red, divided vertically.
In BELGIUM : Black, yellow, red, divided vertically.
In HOLLAND : Red, white, blue, divided horizontally.

Tricoteuses (*Les*). Women who frequented the public clubs and revolutionary tribunal in Paris, where they sat knitting, while they listened to what was going on, and expressed audibly their approval or disapprobation. With the fall of the Jacobins in 1794 they ceased to appear. They were called ' The Furies of the Guillotine.'

Pronounce *Trick'-ko-teuze.* No combination of letters in the English language can convey the sound of the French *euse.* It almost rhymes with *hers.*

Tricoteuses de la Guillotine (*Les*). Knitters of the guillotine. Women of Paris who daily went to the Place de la Révolution, Paris, to witness the executions, and passed their time there knitting.

Tridentine Catechism (*The*), 1566. Prepared in accordance with the decrees of the Council of Trent by Archbishop Leon, the Bishop Ægidius Foscorari, and the Portuguese Dominican Francis Fureiro. It was revised by the Cardinals Borromēo, Sirlet and Antonian, and sanctioned by Pius V.

Tridentine Council (*The*), *i.e.* the Council of Trent, called in Latin ' Tridentum,' 1545-1563.

Tridentine Decrees. Decrees issued by the Council of Trent (16th cent.). *See above.*

Tridentines (3 syl.). Bigoted Roman Catholics whose religious views are rigidly circumscribed by the decrees of the Council of Trent [*Tridentum*], 1537-1563.

Triennial Bill (*The*), 1694. It provided two things : (1) That no parliament shall continue longer than three years, and (2) that a new parliament shall always be called within three years of the dissolution of the preceding one.

Triennial Parliaments, 1694 to 1715. Appointed to be held by Act 16 Car. I. c. 1 (1641), by 16 Car. II. c. 1 (1664), and by 6, 7 Will. & Mar. c. 2 (1694). Septennial Act was passed 1716 (1 Geo. I. c. 38). *See* ' Parliaments.'

Triers of Petitions. Edward I. granted leave for everyone who thought himself unduly assessed, rated, charged to aids, subsidies, or taxes, to deliver a petition to receivers who sat in the Great Hall of the Palace of Westminster. The petitions were forwarded to the king's council. This gave rise to the ' Triers of Petitions ' at the opening of every new

3 M 2

parliament by the House of Lords, a usage which is still continued. *See* 'Tryers.'

Trimmers, in the reigns of Charles II. and William III., were those whose political opinions were neither hot nor cold. Charles Montagu (earl of Halifax) called himself a 'trimmer' or medium man, half Whig and half Tory. They were friendly to the monarchy, but opposed to James duke of York; and pleased neither party.

Trimurti is the inseparable unity in the three gods Brahma, Vishnu, and Siva in one person. The Christian dogma is the inseparable unity of three Persons (Father, Son, and Holy Ghost) in one God.

Son, husband, and father may be one and the same person, or trimurti ; and Antony, Octavianus, and Lepidus may be three separate persons, but one triumvirate. This is not meant to be an explanation of the Trinity, but merely to show the difference between three gods equal to one person, and three persons equal to one god.

Tringlo (*A*). A soldier of the Arab commissariat and baggage trains in Algiers.

Trinita′rian Controversy (*The*), 17th and 18th cents. This controversy had many phases : (1) The Arian, answered by Dr. Bull in his 'Defensio Fidei Nicenæ,' 1685–1688. This is termed the 'Patristic' phase. (2) The Metaphysical phase, controverted by Dr. Thurlock and Dr. South. (3) The Scriptural phase, set forth by Dr. Samuel Clarke, Sykes, Whitby, and Jackson, and answered by Dr. Waterland in his 'Vindication of Christ's Divinity,' 1719, 1723. (4) The Free-thinkers led by Lord Shaftesbury, Collins's 'Free-thinking,' Woolston's 'Discourse on Miracles,' Tindal's 'Christianity'; replied to by Waterland, Zachary Pearce, and Warburton.

Trinitarians. Those who believe that there are three distinct Persons (Father, Son, and Holy Ghost) in the one undivided Godhead.

The word 'persons' is very misleading applied to deity, as we use the word to signify an objective individual, and cannot divest our thoughts of some such idea. In no sense is God an individual or objective person, but simply an entity, or, to use the Hebrew phrase, an 'I am.' No one on earth would call the human soul a *person*.

Trinity (*Confraternity of the*), or 'Fathers of the Oratory,' 1550. A religious order founded in Rome by Philip Neri to aid and succour pilgrims. When it undertook to instruct the young the brotherhood changed their original name to *Oratorians*. In 1611 P. de Bérille instituted a branch of the society in France, and called it 'L'Oratoire de Jésus,' a normal school for young priests. Suppressed in 1790, but re-established in 1853 under the title of *L'Oratoire de l'Immaculée Conception.*

Some of the greatest Christian orators of France were Oratorians ; as Malebranche, Massillon, Mascaron, Richard Simon, Lelong, La Bletterie, Foncemagne, Dotteville, Daunou, &c. Cardinal Newman was an Oratorian.

Trinity College.
I. *Cambridge* University. Is the consolidation of several foundations : (1) Of St. Michael house, founded by Hervey of Stanton in 1324; (2) of King's Hall, founded by Edward III. in 1337; (3) of Phiswick's Hostel and Oving's Inn ; (4) augmented and largely endowed by Henry VIII. in 1546, when its present name was given to the College. It is the largest and richest foundation in the University. The head of the college is called the Master, and is appointed by the crown.

II. *Dublin* University, 1591. Founded by Queen Elizabeth. Statutes revised 31 June, 1855.

III. *Oxford* University, 1554. Founded by Sir Thomas Pope. It was originally called 'Durham College,' being endowed by the priors and bishops of Durham. The headmaster is called the 'president.'

Trinity Hall. A college in the University of Cambridge, founded by William Bateman, bishop of Norwich in 1350.

William Bateman was the second founder of Gonville and Caius College also. *See* 'Caius College.'

Trinity Sunday. Instituted in 1287. It is next to Whitsunday, and is called 'Stately Sunday.' *See* 'Sunday.'

Statuimus quod Festum Trinitatis Dominicæ post octavam Pentecostes, quæ vocatur octava Trinitatis, cum ix lectionibus et debita solemnitate fiat.—*The Bull for its institution.*

Christmas Day is the day of the birth of Jesus, Whitsunday is the day of the outpouring of the Holy Ghost, and Trinity Sunday is the day dedicated to Father, Son, and Holy Ghost, 'One in Three and Three in One.'

Trinity Week. Hebdomada Trinitatis, the week which begins with Trinity Sunday.

Trino′da Neces′sitas. Three imposts or taxes to which all lands (not excepting church lands) were subject in Anglo-Saxon times : (1) *Bryge-bót*, for keeping bridges and highways in repair ; (2) *Burg-bót*, for keeping the burgs or fortresses in repair ; and (3) *Fyrd*, for the payment of the military and naval forces of the kingdom.

Fyrd means an army, or the military force of a country ; *fyrdung* means military service ; and *fyrd-wite* the fine for neglecting to join the fyrd.

Tripartite (*The*). The Jus Ælianum (*q.v.*).

Tripartite Decree (*The*), or 'Decretum tripartitum juris consuetudinarii,' by Verböczy of Hungary, 1514.
I. It established equal rights to all the Hungarian nobility, who were exempt from all taxation.
II. It limited the authority of the clergy, and deprived the pope of the disposal of church benefices in Hungary.
III. It took from the peasantry all liberty and every species of property, reducing them to the state of serfs.

Tripit'aka, or 'Three Baskets.' The sacred books of the Buddhists ; the books altogether being between two and three thousand. A complete series was presented to the India Office by the Japanese ambassador, Iwakura-Tomomi, from the Mika'do, some years ago. The collection was originally published by the Emperor Wan-lich of China, at the close of the 16th cent., and it was reproduced in Japan in the sixth year of Nengo Impo (*i.e.* 1679).

Triple Alliance (*The*). I. 28 Jan., 1668, between Great Britain, the Netherlands, and Sweden, against France. It was a *ruse* of Arlington's to force Louis XIV. to accept the peace of Aix-la-Chapelle. William III. was king of England, and his heart was bent on checking the conquests of Louis that his beloved Holland might be aggrandized, and to this end he wanted to protect from France the Spanish Netherlands.
II. 4 Jan., 1717. Between Great Britain, Holland, and France, against Spain, or rather against the designs of Cardinal Alberōni of Spain, whose object was to re-establish the monarchy of Charles V. In order to annoy the English the Spanish cardinal favoured the pretender, and in order to annoy France he favoured the Huguenots. He tried to

induce Charles XII. of Sweden and Peter I. of Russia to join him ; to plunge Austria into a war with Turkey, to stir up insurrection in Hungary, and actually effected the arrest of the regent Duc d'Orléans. The platform of the alliance was (*a*) that the Pretender should be made to quit France ; (*b*) that the fortifications of Dunkirk should be abolished according to the treaty of Utrecht ; and (*c*) that the Protestant succession of Great Britain should not be disturbed.
III. 1789, between Great Britain, Holland, and Russia, against Catharine of Russia, in defence of Turkey.

Triple Tree (*The*). The gallows, which was a permanent erection resting on three posts ; first at Smithfield, then at Tyburn. *See* ' Elms.'

Tripod of Life (*The*). The brain, the lungs, and the heart. All natural death in the human animal proceeds from one of these three organs.

Tripos, in the University of Cambridge. In the 15th cent. an ' ould bachelour,' as representative of the university, had to sit on a three-legged stool ' before Mr. Proctours ' to test the abilities of the candidates for degrees by arguing some question with the ' eldest son ' of them as their representative. There were three occasions on which questionists were admitted to degrees : (1) the *Comitia priora* on Ash-Wednesday, for the best men ; (2) the *Comitia posteriora*, a few weeks later, for the second-best men ; and (3) the *Comitia minora* for the ' poll-men.' Hence the word tripos meant the stool and the ' ould Bachelour,' then the three classes of questionists, and lastly the examination system.

The Classical Tripos was established in 1824, and the Historical Tripos, the Science Tripos, &c., in 1858.

*** The word now means the classification into three classes of graduated merit adopted in the University of Cambridge, Class I. being the highest.
The Triposes are : The Classical Tripos, the Historical Tripos, the Indian Languages Tripos, the Law Tripos, the Mathematical Tripos, the Mediæval and Modern Languages Tripos, the Natural Science Tripos, the Semitic Languages Tripos, and the Theological Tripos.

Trisag'ion (*The*), or 'First Religious War,' A.D. 508–518. The Trisagion is the repetition of the word 'Holy' three times, as 'Holy, holy, holy, Lord God of Hosts,' supposed to indicate a Trinity. The Greeks maintained that it is the song sung by the angels before the throne of God, and that it was miraculously revealed to the church at Constantinople in the middle of the 5th cent. The Manichæans objected, and a sedition was caused which filled the streets day and night with men, women, and children, shouting and fighting. Churches were destroyed, the statues of the Emperor Anastasius were thrown down, and at length Vitalian, with an army of Huns and Bulgarians, interfered for the Catholic party. Such, says Gibbon (xlvii.), was the event of the first religious war waged in the name of the God of peace.

Triumphal Arches. The most celebrated are the following:—

Constantine's Arch, in Rome, to commemorate the triumph of Constantine over Maxentius.

The Arch of Septimus Sevērus, at the foot of the capitol.

Galliēnus's Arch, erected A.D. 260.

Titus's Arch, to commemorate his taking of Jerusalem.

Arc de Bénévent, in honour of Traj'an. A copy of Titus's Arch. Another, dedicated to the same emperor, called the 'Arch of Ancōna.'

The Arch of Rimĭni, dedicated to Augustus. This is the most ancient of the Roman arches. Another, dedicated to the same emperor, at the foot of Mont Cenis, and called the 'Arch of Suza.'

In PARIS there is an arc de triomphe at the Porte St. Denis, erected in 1673 to commemorate the passage of the Rhine by Louis XIV. There is another dedicated to the same king at the Porte St. Martin, to commemorate his conquest of the Franche-Comté.

The arch in the *Carrousel* was raised to the honour of Napoleon in 1806. The splendid *Arc de Triomphe* in the Champs Elysées was begun in 1806 and finished in 1835. It is the work of Chalgrin and Huyot.

Triumvirate (*The*). I. The *British* Triumvirate (1763), consisting of George Grenville and the Lords Egremont and Halifax, who succeeded the Earl of Bute and Sir Francis Dashwood. Grenville took both Bute's and Dashwood's office (lord of the treasurer and chancellor of the exchequer), while Egremont and Halifax were the two secretaries of state.

. In the reign of Queen Anne the triumvirate was the Duke of Marlborough, Lord Godolphin, and Sarah duchess of Marlborough. The first controlled foreign affairs, the second controlled the council and parliament, and the third controlled the Court and queen.

II. The *First French* (1561). The Guise family leagued against the Huguenots. The triumvirate was the Duc de Guise, the Constable de Montmorency, and Marshal de St. André. This league was supported by the Pope, the Cardinal de Lorraine, and the clergy generally, the people of the north and west, and by Philip II. of Spain.

III. The *Second French* Triumvirate (1685) for the extirpation of Huguenots in the reign of Louis XIV. The triumvirate was Father la Chaise (the king's confessor), Madame de Maintenon (the king's wife), and the Marquis de Louvois. *See below*, No. IV., 'Triumvirate' (*The Thermidorian*),' and 'Reign of Terror.'

IV. The *Thermidorian* Triumvirate (1795), consisting of Barras, Rewbell, and La Réveillère. As in all other triumvirates one of the three is dominant, so in the Thermidorian Triumvirate Barras was infinitely more powerful than the other two.

V. *First Roman* (B.C. 60). A cabal formed by Crassus, Pompey, and Cæsar. Crassus was the wealthy partner, Pompey the most powerful, Cæsar the most popular.

VI. The *Second Roman* Triumvirate (B.C. 43–31). Lepidus, Antony, and Octavianus. After the assassination of Cæsar.

VII. Of the *Commonwealth* (1659). General Lambert having put down the Rump Parliament, after the death of Cromwell, introduced a military form of government. Its three heads were Lambert, Fleetwood, and Monk. In April, 1660, the king (Charles II.) was recalled.

Fleetwood was Cromwell's son-in-law, and Monk was governor of Scotland.

VIII. Of the *Reign of Terror* (1794). Robespierre, Couthon, and St. Just.

IX. Of the *Roman Government* (30 March, 1848) Mazzini, Armellini, and Suffi. These representatives of the people formed a constitutional assembly, with a design of converting Italy into a republic like France; but it was republican France which prevented it by an army of occupation.

Triumvirate of England (*The*). Gower, Chaucer, and Lydgate (poets).

Triumvirate of Italian Poets. Danté, Boccaccio, and Petrarch.

Boccaccio is now known chiefly as the 'Father of Italian Prose.' His 'Decameron' has outlived his poetry.

Triv'ium. The three sciences: Grammar, rhetoric, and logic. The QUADRIVIUM were the four sciences: Music, arithmetic, geometry, and astronomy. Up to the 14th cent. called the seven sciences or seven liberal arts, and all taught in Latin.

Trois Chapîtres (*Les*). Three theological works on the Incarnation of Christ and his dual nature, by Theodore of Mopsuestia, Theodoret of Cyrrhus, and Ibas of Edessa, condemned as heretical in 553.

Trojans and Greeks in the University of Cambridge. Partisans of Sir John Cheke, regius professor of Greek in the University, and of Gardiner the chancellor. Sir John introduced a new pronunciation of Greek, against which the chancellor protested. As Sir John was a Protestant and Gardiner a Catholic, the feud was more than half of a religious character. Those who took the side of the Regius professor were called 'Trojans'; those who sided with the chancellor called themselves 'Greeks.' Many a street row ensued, till at last the king in council commanded the innovation of Sir John to be discontinued. *See* p. 735, 'Ramists.'

Troppau, in Silesia (*Congress of*), from 20 Oct. to 20 Dec., 1820. Its object was to resist the revolutionary movement in Russia, Austria, and Prussia.

Trottiera (*La*). The bell which summoned the 'riders' or nobles to the Grand Council in Venice.

Trou'badours (*The*). Minstrels of Southern France in the 11th, 12th, and 13th cents. They were the first to discard Latin and use the native tongue in their compositions. Their poetry was either about love and gallantry or war and chivalry. *See* 'Trouvères.'

The poetry of the provençals or troubadours was of two sorts: *cansos*, or poems of love and gallantry, and *sirventese*, or lays of war and chivalry, politics and morals. The word is from *troubar*, to invent, as 'poetry' is from the Greek verb meaning 'to make' or 'create.'

Trousse-galant (*Le*), 1445. An epidemic which ravaged France, and was so called 'de la rapidité avec laquelle elle enlevait les malades. Elle affectait surtout le bas-ventre et la tête.' *See* 'Plague,' &c.

Trouvères (*The*). Minstrels of the north of France in the 12th, 13th, and 14th cents. The language they employed was the 'Walloon' or 'Langue d'oïl' (*q.v.*). The subjects of these minstrels were satires and romances, tales of knavery and adventure, legends and historical traditions. It had three periods. In the *first* period the subjects were Gothic, Frankish, and Burgundian heroes. In the *second* period the subjects were Charlemagne and his paladins. In the *third* period they were traditions of British story, such as the fabulous Brute, King Arthur and his knights, King Horn, and so on.

Sir Walter Scott's 'Marmion,' 'Lady of the Lake,' 'Rokeby,' &c., are excellent imitations of the old Trouvère minstrelsy. The word is the Walloon verb *trouver*, to find out or invent. The same as *troubar*. *See* 'Troubadours.'

Troy (*The Destruction of*). This was 12 June, B.C. 1184.

Troyes, in France (*Treaties of*). I. 21 May, 1420. Between Charles VI. of France, Henry V. of England, and Philippe le Bon of Burgundy, for the marriage of Henry V. with the Princess Katharine of France. By this treaty Henry was declared regent and heir of France.

II. 1 April, 1564. A treaty of peace between England and France.

Truce of God (*The*), 1040. A modification of the 'Peace of God' (*q.v.*). The latter was an ecclesiastical prohibition of war altogether, under the general expectation of the Second Advent of Christ, the Prince of Peace (1035). The truce limited the prohibition to Thursday, Friday, Saturday, Sunday, and Church festivals, such as Easter, Lent, and Christmas, and absolutely forbade anyone to molest a man working in the fields. The penalty of breaking the truce was death or outlawry.

Truck Act (*The*), 1, 2 Will. IV. c. 37 (1831), forbids employers to pay wages in whole or in part by goods instead of money. Orders on a truck-shop or store are likewise forbidden as a set-off against wages.

'Truck' is the French *troquer*, to barter.

Truck System (*The*). The mode of paying wages in part or wholly either by goods or by an order on some store. Very common before it was prohibited by law in 1831.

True as Bicknell. Bicknell was a hosier who supplied George III. with gloves. In the Gordon riots, 1780, a notion got abroad that the Roman Catholics designed to kill the king by poisoned gloves, as Catherine de Medicis killed Jeanne d'Albret, mother of Henri IV. of France, and many others. The 'London Courant' and other newspapers, to lull this suspicion, inserted the following paragraph: ' We are authorised to assure the public that Mr. Bicknell, his majesty's hosier, is as true and faithful a Protestant as any in his majesty's dominions.'

True Blue, in a theological sense, means a Presbyterian in contradistinction to an Episcopalian. Butler says that his knight Hudibras was 'Right Presbyterian true blue.' In the time of George I., and probably before that reign, ' True Blue,' in a political sense, meant a Whig in contradistinction to a Tory. Lord George Gordon, in 1780, and his adherents appeared in the House of Commons with blue cockades in their hats.

'True Blues'; so the Palatines of Limerick called themselves when they mustered into the yeomanry service. 'True Blues' have always been associated with Orangeism.

Trumpet (*Murder of the*), 1403. This refers to an incident in Venetian history. A Venetian trumpet (herald) appeared before Vicenza and announced to Francesco Terzo that the city had placed itself under the protection of Venice. Francesco ordered the trumpet to retire, and not return without a safe conduct. In the evening he returned, bearing the pennon of Vicenza, and commanded the Paduans to raise the siege. Francesco denied the authority of the trumpet, and said if he had been sent by the Venetians he would have borne the

Venetian pennon. Next morning the trumpet again appeared, this time with a Venetian pennon. The guards seized him, cut off his nose and ears, and sent him back with a declaration of war. ' Let us make this trumpet,' said the guards, ' the Lion of St. Mark.' The point was this : the Lion of St. Mark has both nose and ears, but shall henceforth be mutilated like this trumpet by the indignant Paduans.

Trumpet of Sedition (*The*). So George III. spoke of William Pitt, the statesman, afterwards the earl of Chatham, because he protested so strongly against the American war, which George as strongly desired. While Britain was glorying in the victories of Lord Howe, he said :—

You cannot conquer America. If I were an American, as I am an Englishman, while a foreign troop was landed in my country, I never would lay down my arms—never, never, never.'

Trumpets (*Feast of*). A Jewish festival held the first day of the civil year, which was in September, and instituted in commemoration of the thunder heard on Mount Sinai at the giving of the Law.

Tryers, or Triers, 20 March, 1654. Commissioners appointed by Cromwell and his council to examine into the ' sufferings of the clergy.' Francis Rous, with thirty-seven others, part laymen and part ministers, were appointed. A list of the names is given by Neal in his ' History of the Puritans,' iv. p. 93. *See* p. 899, ' Triers of Petitions.'

Tse Dynasty (*The*). The ninth imperial dynasty of China. Like the eighth, tenth, and eleventh dynasties, it had dominion only over Southern China, the court being held at Nankin. It lasted twenty-three years (479–502), and gave five sovereigns.

Tshin Dynasty (*The*). The first historic dynasty of China (B.C. 256–201). Also called the fourth imperial dynasty. It gave five emperors who held their court at Yn; and lasted fifty-four years. It was succeeded by the dynasty of Hân. It was Tchao, the first of this dynasty, who built the great wall of China.

This dynasty must not be confounded with that of *Tsin* (the seventh), nor with that of *Tchin* (the eleventh), nor with that of *Tsing* (the twenty-second). It is spelt and pronounced differently.

Tsin Dynasty (*The*), 265-420. The seventh imperial dynasty of China. It was preceded by the San-kuo or Three States, and succeeded by the duplex empire called Southern and Northern. It gave fifteen kings, all of whom were either dethroned or put to death. This dynasty is known by its exodus or grand migrations.

It is thought that the word China is derived from Tsin, but Fo-hi was said to hold his court at Shensi or the country of Tsin or Chin, whence Tsin-a, Sina, China, and this was B.C. 2953, the mythic period of the empire. No dates are introduced in the Chinese annals till B.C. 827.

Tsing Dynasty (*The*) of China (1644-*) succeeded the Mings, founded by Choun-tchi. This is sometimes called the Manchou dynasty. The present reigning family of China is of this dynasty.

Tsong Dynasty (*The*) or Pih Sung. The eighth imperial dynasty of China, and first of the Woo-tae or ' five races.' These five races ruled only over the southern empire, and held their court at Nankin. The eighth dynasty gave seven emperors and lasted fifty-nine years (420-479). The founder, Noo-tee, was a cobbler.

Tuatha-na-Danans (*The*), a semi-historical very early Irish dynasty. It is said that the five sons of Dela established in Ireland the five principalities of Leinster, Munster, Ulster, Connaught, and Meath, and this pentarchy continued for eighty years, when the three sons of Danan invaded the island and established themselves there, till they were driven out by the eight sons of Milesius, who came from Spain. Five of the sons perished, and the whole island was divided between two of the surviving sons, Heremon and Heber. Heremon took Connaught and Leinster, and fixed his residence at Tarah, in Meath. Heber ruled over the southern provinces, but being slain in battle, Heremon became sole monarch of the island.

Tuatha=commander.

Tübingen School (*The*), of theology in Germany, also called 'The Historical School,' founded by Baur, to investigate the historical correctness of the New Testament. Baur wrote a book to prove that the Gospel of St. John was not written till some considerable time after the other three gospels ; and another to show that St. Mark's Gospel was not written till many years after the supposed date. The bases of his criticisms are the undoubted historic facts of the New Testament.

Tuchins, or Touchins, 1385. Peasant rebels of France who committed most frightful massacres. The verb *tuchinare* (rebellare) and the noun *tuchinatus* (rebellio) are used in ancient French charters.

La ville de Nismes est bonne ville . . . les habitans sont . . . obéissans au roy, et ils ne furent onques Tuchins, mais ont toujours eu les fleurs de lys sur les portes de la ville.—*Placitum*, 21 Jan., 1387.

Tudor, a corruption of Theodore. Owen Tudor, a yeoman in the guards in Bedford's army, married Catherine, widow of Henry V., and had three sons. The eldest son Edmund, who was made by Henry VI. earl of Richmond, married Margaret Beaufort, heiress of the house of Somerset. He died at the age of 20, leaving one son, afterwards Henry VII.

Catherine fell in love with the Welsh guardsman while he was keeping guard at Windsor. It is said that he stumbled and fell upon her lap at a dancing party, whence their acquaintance began. He had but 40l. a year. No proof of the marriage was ever traced. The Duke of Gloucester, lord protector, seized Tudor and committed him to Newgate, whence he escaped, and after a while Henry VI. made him keeper of his park in Denbigh, Wales.

Tudor Rose (*The*), or ' Union Rose,' a combination of the Lancastrian red rose and the Yorkist white rose. The red rose has two rows of five alternate petals ; the white rose is represented with three rows of five alternate petals ; the Tudor or Union rose has four rows of alternate petals, one containing 10, one 8, one 7, and one 6 (counting from the exterior), with centre. The Tudor rose, between sprigs of shamrock and thistle on one stalk, forms the badge of England.

Tudors (*Line of the*). Henry VII., Henry VIII., Edward VI., Mary, and Elizabeth.

Henry VII. descended from John of Gaunt, duke of Lancaster, 4th son of Edward III. (*q.v.*). He married Elizabeth of York, daughter of Edward IV., son of Richard duke of York slain at the battle of Wakefield, 1466. *See* 'York.'

Henry VII. had no hereditary right to the crown. He was the illicit and adulterous son of Edmund Tudor by Margaret Beaufort, daughter of the Duke of Somerset. Elizabeth of York was heir to the crown, but even in the Lancastrian line there were many who had a much cleaner title than Henry. It is not even certain that he was born in wedlock at all. He was a despicable money-grubber, and very 'indifferent honest.'

Tudors' Crest *(The).* A crown in a bush of fruited hawthorn to commemorate the incident of a soldier finding the crown of Richard III. hid in a hawthorn bush on the day of battle. It was given to Lord Stanley, who placed it on the head of Richmond, saying 'Long live King Henry!'

Tugendbund *(Der),* or 'League of Virtue,' 1813. A secret society set on foot by the Prussian minister Von Stein, and supported especially by the students. It had for its object the total expulsion of the French from German soil, and embodied the seething hatred of Germany for France. It gave umbrage to the allies and was dissolved in 1815.

Tulchan Bishops, 1574. Bishops who took a small part of their stipends and gave the rest to their patrons. When a cow had lost her calf, it was customary in Scotland to flay the calf and stuff the skin with straw, that, being placed before the mother, she might be induced to part with her milk freely. This stuffed calf was called a Tulchan, and the stipendiary bishop parted with his revenues to the patron freely, his see being only nominal. The first skimmed-milk bishop was John Douglas, appointed archbishop of St. Andrews by the Earl of Morton, who claimed the cream.

The regent Morton, affecting zeal for the Protestant doctrines, disobliged the Church of Scotland by a device which he had invented to secure to the secular nobility the lands and revenues of the Catholic clergy. To this end he nominated to the archbishopric of St. Andrews a poor clergyman named Douglas, taking his obligation to rest satisfied with a very small annuity out of the revenues of the see, and to hand over the rest to his patron, the regent himself. This class of bishops . . . was facetiously called Tulchan prelates.—Sir W. SCOTT, *Hist. of Scotland,* xxxi.

Tuileries *(The),* a garden and palace in Paris, built on the site of an ancient *fabrique de tuiles.* It was composed of three great pavilions, called *Le pavillon de Marsan* (north), the *pavillon de Flore* (south), and the *pavillon de l'Horloge* (centre). It was joined to the Louvre by Napoleon III. (1851-6). The land was bought by François I. in 1564, and the original palace was made for Catherine de Medicis, after the design of Philibert Delorme. Louis XIV., Napoleon I., Louis-Philippe, and Napoleon III. made great improvements, especially the last.

In the republic the convention held their meetings there, afterwards it was used by the *Conseil des Anciens.* The First Consul made it his residence in 1800. In 1848 it was converted into an asylum for invalid workmen; it was the imperial residence of Napoleon III. from 1852; and was burnt by the Communists 24 May, 1871.

Tulip Mania *(The),* 1634–1637. An extraordinary rage for tulip-bulbs, which prevailed in Holland and spread through Europe. The tulip called the *Viceroy* fetched 250*l.*, and the *Semper Augustus* as much as 1,700*l.* Thousands were sold on Exchange merely as articles of speculation, and when the rage subsided thousands of persons were ruined.

Tullia'num *(The).* A loathsome dungeon in Rome. This dismal subterranean dungeon was built by Servius Tullius, and was a part of the Carcer Mamertinus built by Ancus Martius on the slope of the Capitoline hill. The Tullianum is especially noted, as it was in this dungeon, twelve feet underground, that several of the Catiline conspirators were put to death.

Mamers is the Sabine form of Mars, and Ancus Marcius was a Sabine. Jugurtha was starved to death in the Carcer Mamertinus.

Tully, *i.e.* Cicero. The Tullii were of Alban descent, transplanted to Rome in the reign of Tullus Hostilius. Cicero made the word a generic name for a legal orator.

Tumble-down Dick. Richard Cromwell, son of the Protector. He was proclaimed Protector after his father's death, but resigned office within seven months. 'Tumble-down Dick' was a common public-house sign affected by royalists.

Tumults and Disorders *(Act against),* 1661. This Act made it an offence punishable with a fine of 100*l.* and three months' imprisonment to solicit a signature to a petition to king or parliament which had more than twenty names signed, unless the petition was sanctioned by three justices of the peace, or by the majority of the grand jury of the county. Whoever presented such petition was liable to the same punishment also; and whoever was present at the presentation of a *sanctioned* petition, if there were more than ten persons attending it.

Turanian Languages (*The*). The agglutinate orders of languages, divided into North and South. The *Northern* division falls into five sections, viz. the Tungusic, Mongolic, Turkic, Finnic, and Samoyedic. The *Southern* division comprises the Tamulic, the Gangetic, the Taic, the Malaic, and some other Polynesian tongues or dialects. *See* 'Semitic' and 'Aryan.'

Turcomanchi (*Peace of*), Feb., 1828, between Persia and Russia, making the river Araxes the boundary of the two kingdoms. Persia had also to pay the expenses of the war.

Turcos (*The*). The native Algerian foot-soldiers. The horse-soldiers are called *Spahis*. Cf. SEPOY.

Turin (*Treaty of*). I. 8 Aug., 1381, terminating the war of Chiozza between the Venetians and the Genoese. The turning-point of Genoa's greatness, from which she began to decline.
II. 29 Aug., 1696, for separate peace between France and Savoy.

Turin Papy′rus (*The*), or 'Book of Kings.' A fragmentary list of Egyptian kings brought from Thebes by an Italian named Drovetti. At one time it was supposed that this was a complete list in chronological order, but it does not point out contemporary or double kings. A facsimile is preserved in the Royal Society of Literature, 21 Delahay Street, London.

Turkish Trilateral (*The*). Silistria, Shumla, and Varna in Bulgaria and on the flank of every possible line of operation upon the Balkan.

Turkish War of 1683-1697. Principally noted for the siege of Vienna by Mustapha, the Turkish vizier, in 1683. When, on the eve of success, Sobieski, king of Poland, arrived with reinforcements, Mustapha decamped, leaving behind him the sultan's standard, many splendid dresses, and the harnesses of several Turkish horses adorned with silver, gold, and precious stones; besides the money for the siege, the pay of the soldiers, the baggage, tents, cannons, and chariots.

The war dragged on after this till 1697, and was brought to an end by the 'Peace of Carlovitz.'

Turlupins, 1372. Heretics analogous to the Begards (*q.v.*). They taught the perfectionability of man; and, it is said, went about nude. They were excommunicated by Gregory XI. in 1372, and were extirpated by the order of Charles V. of France. They called themselves the *Fraternité des pauvres*. Called Turlupins 'quod ea tantum habitarent loca, quæ lupis exposita erant.' (An etymology most unsatisfactory.)

A turlupin means a sorry jester, a fool. Whence *turlupinade* and the verb *turlupiner*, to play the fool.

Turneys, 1339. A base coin made in Ireland and circulated 'to the injury of the king's sterling money.' *See* p. 99, 'Black Money.'

Turpin's Chronicle, 'Chronique de l'archevêque Turpin.' Turpin was a monk of St. Denis, and afterwards archbishop of Reims, contemporary of Charlemagne. The chronicle referred to is an historic romance having Charlemagne for its hero, and is full of marvels, such as enchanted castles, winged horses, magical horns, incantations, and so on. Historically it is worthless, and probably Turpin had no hand at all in it. Some say it was the work of Gui de Bourgogne (Calixtus II.) in the 12th cent.; others ascribe it to a monk of St. André de Vienne, in Dauphiné, who lived in the 11th cent.

Tweeddale's Act (*The Earl of*), 1668. It restored to their livings those ministers who had been ejected, provided they would accept collation from the bishop, and would attend the presbyteries and synods.
'Collation' means induction and institution, or investing a clergyman with the temporalities and spiritualities of his living.

Twelfth (*The*), *i.e.* the 12th August. The commencement of grouse-shooting.

Twelve Articles of the Symbol (*The*). Said to have been suggested by the Apostles in a grotto of Mount Olivet just before their final separation.
1. PETER: I believe in God the Father Almighty, maker of heaven and earth.
2. JOHN: [And] in Jesus Christ, his only son, our Lord.
3. JAMES the Greater: Who was conceived of the Holy Ghost, born of the Virgin Mary.

4. ANDREW: Suffered under Pontius Pilate; was crucified and buried.

'Dead' was subsequently added, and is bad English. We should not say (A B) was hanged, dead, and buried.

5. PHILIP: He descended into hell.

6. THOMAS: The third day he rose again from the dead.

7. JAMES the Less: He ascended into heaven, and sitteth on the right hand of God the Father Almighty.

8. MATTHEW: [From thence] He shall come to judge the quick and the dead.

9. NATHANIEL: I believe in the Holy Ghost.

10. SIMON: The Holy Catholic Church.

'The Communion of Saints' was added in the 6th cent.

11. MATTHIAS: The forgiveness of sins.

12. JUDE: The resurrection of the dead, and the life everlasting.

The twelve Apostles were anciently delineated, each holding a banderole inscribed with the words attributed to him. Of course the tradition is historically worthless. The Apostles had no hand whatever in the creed.

See 'Articles.'

Twelve Brethren (*The*). The Twelve 'Marrowmen' (*q.v.*).

Twelve Fruits of the Holy Ghost (*The*) in Catholic theology.

(1) Chastity; (2) faith; (3) gentleness; (4) goodness; (5) joy; (6) longsuffering; (7) love or charity; (8) meekness; (9) modesty; (10) patience; (11) peace; and (12) temperance.

Compare these with Gal. v. 22, 23.

Twelve Peers of France (*The*). Philippe Auguste fixed the number of peers to six seculars and six ecclesiastics. The secular peers were: (1) the Duke of Normandy; (2) the Duke of Burgundy; (3) the Duke of Guyenne; (4) the Count of Flanders; (5) the Count of Toulouse; and (6) the Count of Champagne.

The ecclesiastical peers were: (1) the Archbishop of Reims; (2) the Bishop of Laon; (3) the Bishop of Langres; (4) the Bishop of Beauvais; (5) the Bishop of Châlons; and (6) the Bishop of Noyon.

Twelve Remembrancers (*The*). (1) Unity of the Godhead; (2) the hypostatic union of God and man; (3) the Trinity; (4) the Evangelists; (5) the wounds of Christ, two in the hands, two in the feet, and one in the side; (6) the six days of creation; (7) the seven words

uttered on the cross; (8) the Beatitudes; (9) the heavenly host; (10) the commandments; (11) the Apostles after Judas the traitor had 'gone to his place'; (12) the Apostolic college when completed. Called 'The Twelve.'

Twelve Tables (*The*), or *Leges Duŏdĕcim Tabularum*. The Magna Charta of Old Rome drawn up by the Decemvirs. Ten of them B.C. 451, and the other two B.C. 450.

Twenty (*The*). See p. 367, 'Giunta.'

Twenty Years' War (*The*), 1794–1815. The wars against Napoleon. 1 June, 1894, the French fleet was defeated and crippled by Lord Howe off Brest, and 18 June, 1815, the battle of Waterloo gave the *coup de grâce* to the great disturber of nations and enduring enemy of England.

Twenty-two (*The*), 30 Oct., 1793. The twenty-two Girondin deputies were sentenced to death, with confiscation of goods.

Two Hundred (*The*). On the day of subscription to the Bill of Uniformity, in the reign of Charles II., 200 of the Scotch Presbyterian clergy relinquished their livings. Calamy, Baxter, and Reynolds, chief of the Nonconformist leaders, were offered bishoprics, but only Reynolds accepted the bribe. *See* 'Seven Bishops.'

Charles II. said to Lauderdale that a Scotchman's religion 'is not fit for a gentleman.' It is much to be feared the king's religion was not fit for any man, gentle or simple.

Two Thousand (*The*). *See* 'Memorable,' &c.

Tyburn Dick. Richard Savage, lord Rivers; made by Queen Anne lieutenant of the Tower in 1710.

Tyndale's Bible. English translation of the New Testament, published at Wittenberg in 1526. English translation of the Pentateuch, published at Hamburg in 1530. This translation was the basis of the Great Bible (1539–1541) in the reign of Henry VIII.; of the Bishops' Bible (1568–1572) in the reign of Elizabeth; of the King's Bible (1611) in the reign of James I.; and of the Revised Version (1870–1884) in the reign of Victoria. *See* 'Bible.'

Tynwald (*The Court of*). The court of the three estates of the Isle of Man, consisting of the governor, the council of ten, and the House of Keys. It is the supreme court of the island. All new Manx laws must be proclaimed in English and Manx, in the presence of the people, at the Tynwald Hill.

The laws of Man still retain much of their ancient peculiarity of character, though modified by occasional acts of the Tynwald.—PRINCE, *Parallel History*, vol. iii. p. 285.

Type (*The*), A.D. 648. An edict published by Constans II. of the Eastern empire under the hope of burying in silence the dissentient views of the orthodox Christians and the Monothelites (*q.v.*). It imposed silence on both parties on all points of religious differences.

Tyran de Blanc. Frederick baron Grimm (1723–1807). So called from his free use of cosmetics to repair the ravages of increasing age in his face. He was so called when he took up his abode in Paris.

Tyranny of the Thirty (*The*), B.C. 404, lasted eight months. After the overthrow of the Athenians at Ægospotāmos the Lacedæmonians insulted them by setting over them thirty magistrates, called 'Tyrants.' These magistrates behaved with such arrogance and cruelty that Thrasybūlus easily got possession of the city and expelled the tyrants.

To the honour of the Spartans be it said, when they were informed of the rebellion, instead of punishing the conspirators, they passed a bill of amnesty, and re-established in Athens the democratic form of government upon its ancient foundation.

Tyrant Basili'des (*The*). Ivan IV. of Russia, surnamed the 'Terrible' by the Russians. 'Basili' is only another spelling of 'Vassili,' and Ivan IV. was the fourth of the Vassili who had reigned in Russia. 'Basili-ides' or 'Vassili-ides' means 'a descendant of Vassili.'

Among the writers of the history of the north, Ivan IV. is famous as 'The tyrant Basilides.'—DUNCAN, *Hist. of Russia*, vol. i. p. 89.

Tyrants of Sparta (*The*), B.C. 219–192. They were, first, Lycurgus, nine years; then Machanīdas, four years; and lastly Nabis, fourteen years. Called tyrants because they did not belong to either of the royal dynasties, but were usurpers.

Tyrconnel—now Donegal, Tyrone, Derry, Fermānagh, Armagh, and Ca'van

(500,000 acres)—was the land planted by James I. The lands were portioned out into estates varying from 1,000 to 2,000 acres, and the proprietors were bound to build substantial houses in the English fashion, and to people them with English and Scotch tenantry. A company of London merchants, called 'The Irish Society,' contracted (1619) for large tracts of land, which are still held under this tenure.

Tyrian Era (*The*). This era began 19 Oct., B.C. 125.

Tyrolese Insurrection (*The*), 1809. Tyrol had been 442 years under Austria, and was happy and prosperous ; but Napoleon placed it under Bavaria, with a promise that nothing should be changed. Immediately, however, Maximilian changed its name to South Bavaria, and conformed its laws to those of his own kingdom. André Hofer, proprietor of the inn of Sand, now induced Austria to join them in freeing the Tyrol ; battle after battle was won by the insurgents, and then Austria made peace with France. Hofer was taken prisoner by the French and shot 20 Feb., 1810.

Tyrtæos (*The English*). Laurence Minot, who celebrated the exploits of Edward III. in English verse (died 1352).

In 1878 the music hall jingo-song, 'We don't want to fight,' almost roused England into a war with Russia.

Tyrtæos of Attica in the second Messēnian War was by command of an oracle appointed leader of the Spartan army, and by his war-songs led them to victory. The following is a free translation of the first of his three extant elegies :—

Oh ! 'tis joyful to fall in the face of the foe,
  For country and altar to die ;
But a lot more ignoble no mortal can know
Than with parents and children, heart-broken
  with woe,
From home as an exile to fly.

Unrecompensed travail, starvation, and scorn,
  The fugitive's footsteps attend ;
Dishonoured his race, and his children forlorn,
Himself by temptation and shame overborne,
  Never hear the sweet voice of a friend.

To the field, then ! Be strong, and acquit ye like
  men !
  Who shall fear for his country to fall ?
Ye younger, in ranks firmly serried remain ;
Ye elders, though weak, look on flight with disdain,
  And honour your fatherland's call.

Tyrtæos of France. Rouget de Lisle (1760–1836), whose 'Marseillaise' stirred the French revolutionary party almost to madness. The refrain of this spirit-stirring hymn runs thus :—

Aux armes, citoyens ! Formez vos bataillons !
Marchons! marchons ! qu'un sang impur abreuve
  nos sillons.

Tyrtæos of Germany (*The Youthful*). Karl Theodore Körner (1791-1813), killed in a skirmish with Walmoden's outposts at Godebusch. His 'Lyre and Sword Songs' stirred his countrymen like a trumpet. Perhaps the 'Wacht am Rhein,' by Max Schneckenburger, who died 1851, may be called the German 'Marseillaise.' The fifth verse runs thus:

While there's a drop of blood to run,
While there's an arm to bear a gun,
While there's a hand to wield a sword,
No foe shall dare thy stream to ford.
Dear fatherland, no fear be thine,
Thy sons stand firm to guard the Rhine.

Tyrtæos of Spain. Manuel José Quintāna, whose odes stimulated the Spaniards to vindicate their liberty at the war of independence (1772-1857).

Tyrwhitt Scholarships, for Hebrew. Two for bachelors of arts of the respective values of 30*l.* and 20*l.*, tenable for three years. Founded in the University of Cambridge by the Rev. Robert Tyrwhitt, 1818. *See* 'Hebrew Prize,' 'Mason Prize.'

U and V. The ancient use of these two letters was this: U before vowels, especially the vowels *a, e,* and *i*; V before consonants, especially the consonants *n, r, p, s.*
  As meruailed, aduantage, conuaye; leaue, haue, gaue, moued, reueal, gouern, deserues, diuers, forgiue ; deuise, hauing, deuil, sauiour, seruice.
  vnto, vnite, vnmannerly, covntry; discovrse, Oedipvs.
  It must not be supposed that *u* was never set before consonants, nor *v* before vowels. In the book now before me, dated 1604, hundreds of examples might be gathered, as very, rule, mouse, foure, houre, &c.

Ubiqua'rians (*The*). A social club which existed in Barbadoes, and probably elsewhere, in the latter half of the eighteenth cent. Their tenets were called Ubiquarianism.

Ubiquita'rians or **Ubiquists** (*The*), 1560. A small German religious sect, originating with John Brentius, who maintained that the body of Christ was present everywhere (*ubique*), in the eucharist, by virtue of his divine ubi-

quity. They were opposed to the Sacramentarians (*q.v.*).

Udaller (*A*), an allodial possessor of Zetland. A Udaller holds his possession under an old Norwegian law, instead of the feudal tenures introduced from Scotland. Hence a Udaller had no feudal lord or superior. Icelandic *odal,* an hereditary estate.

Uhlan King (*The*). King Alfonso XII. of Spain was so called in contempt by the French, in 1883, because he accepted a colonelcy in Germány of a Uhlan regiment.

Uhlans, Prussian hussars, 1813. They are mounted on fleet horses, are lightly clad, and armed with sword, pistol and lance. Every battalion of the Landwehr (*q.v.*) has its squadron of Uhlans. In the Franco-German War, 1870, these Uhlans did admirable service, especially as scouts.

Ukase (*Emanoi*), that is, a 'personal order,' meaning an edict signed by the czar. These edicts, as various as the opinions, whims, or prejudices of the czar, are the laws of Russia. Alexei Michailowitz (1645-1676) had a selection of such edicts for the preceding century made into a digest called the Sobornoe Ulajenie, which is the common law of Russia. In 1670 he collected all the royal ukāses held by private individuals as personal licences, and burnt them, so that one and the same law prevailed through his whole dominion. Ukase = *Ou'-kase.*

Ulaj'enie (*The*). A Russian code of jurisprudence, amended and codified by Alexei Michailowitz, czar of Russia (1646). *See above,* 'Ukase.'

Ule'ma, a powerful corporation in Turkey, consisting of the Mufti, who presides, the Imaums, the Mollahs, and the Kadis. Their functions extend to the religion of the country, the administration of justice, and the general government. It serves as an equipoise to the despotism of the sultan.

Ulid'ia, in Ireland, comprised the present county of Down and part of Antrim.

Ulster Custom (*The*), 1870. It was a custom up to 1870, but was then made a law. It is a sort of 'free sale' which prevails in Ulster. Suppose A is the tenant of B, and does not wish to continue so, instead of throwing up his tenancy, he can sell it to C, and then C is the tenant of B. Certain restrictions are made. For example, the landlord can prevent A's asking an exorbitant price, because this would be to the prejudice of the landlord. The new tenant C must be accepted by the landlord before the transfer is made. And, lastly, A (the old tenant) must pay up all rents and taxes before C can take his place.

Mr. Lowther, chief secretary of Ireland, in 1879, protested against the extension of Ulster custom to the rest of Ireland; but in 1881 this demand, together with 'fixity of tenure' and 'fair rent,' was duly recognised.

Ulster King-of-arms, chief of the Irish staff of heralds. The first was appointed by Edward VI. (1 June, 1552). That of Scotland is styled Lord-Lyon. *See* p. 415, 'Heralds.'

Ul'timus Anglo'rum. William Bedell (Protestant bishop of Kilmore and Ardagh), who died 1642, aged 70. The Irish insurgents fired a volley over his grave in Kilmore churchyard, and parted saying 'Requiescat in pace ultimus Anglorum.'

Ul'timus Romano'rum. Dr. Johnson was so called by Thomas Carlyle. I think he might be more aptly called the last of the Catos (1709-1784).

Sometimes Horace Walpole is so called (1717-1797).

Ulto'nian Kings (*The*). The kings of Ulster, in Ireland.

Emania, the seat of the old Ultonian kings.— T. MOORE, *Hist. of Ireland*, vii. p. 143.

Ultramontane Doctrines, or 'Ultramontanism.' Extreme views of papal supremacy and the rights of the popes. These partisans of the pope are so called in France because the pope resides on the other side of the Alps, *ultra montes.* They are opposed to the Gallicans (*q.v.*).

Ultramontane Party (in Ireland), 1825. The anti-English and anti-Protestant party. The Duke of Wellington made a great distinction between 'Orangemen and Papists' [Ultramontanists] and 'Protestants and Catholics.'

Ultramontanes. So the Vaudois who settled beyond the Apennines, after they were driven from their valley homes in the 13th cent., were called by the natives, because they originally dwelt on the other side of the mountain range. They first founded, in the vicinity of Montalto, the town of Borgo d'Ultramontani, subsequently the walled town of Guadia.

O Florence, what does the word Florence mean? The flower of Italy. And so thou wast till these Ultramontanes persuaded thee that man is justified by faith and not by works; and herein they lie.—GILLES, p. 20.

Ulysses of Brandenburg (*The*). Albrecht III., elector of Brandenburg. Also called the 'German Achilles' (1414-1486).

Ulysses of the Highlands. Sir Evan Cameron lord of Lochiel. Also called 'The Black' (died 1719).

It was the son of Sir Evan who was called the 'Gentle Lochiel.'

Umbrella (*Mr. Gladstone's*). Mr. Gladstone's policy. When in September 1885 he issued his manifesto to the electors of Midlothian it was said that he 'opened his umbrella.' His ministry were said to take shelter or stand under his umbrella. In caricature he is often drawn with a 'Sarah Gamp' under his arm.

Unam Sanctam, 1302. The famous constitution of Boniface VIII., setting forth that 'the church is one body and has one head. Under its sway are two swords, one spiritual and the other temporal. The former to be used by the supreme pontiff himself, and the latter by temporal powers at his bidding, but at all times the lesser sword must be in subjection to the greater, the temporal power to the spiritual . . . Every human being on the earth is the subject of the see of Rome ('Extravagantes,' book i., title viii. c. 1).

This constitution ends thus: ' Dicimus, definimus, et pronunciamus, omnino esse de necessitate fidei.'

Uncorruptible Commoner (*The*). Andrew Marvell, also called 'The British Aristidês' (1620-1678). *See* p. 43, 'Aristides,' *n.*

Uncrowned Monarch (*The*), of Ireland. Daniel O'Connell, also called 'The Agitator.' With Sheil he founded the new Catholic Association in 1825; he began the agitation for the repeal of the Union in 1842, held monster meetings in 1843, was arrested for sedition in 1844 and found guilty, but the sentence passed on him was reversed by the House of Lords. He lost his supremacy, and died at Genoa, on his way to Rome (1775–1847).

Under the Yoke (*Sent*). In Roman history to be sent under the yoke was a sign of subjection. The yoke consisted of an arch made with three spears, two upright ones, and one forming a transom. The conquered army was made to lay down their arms, and march *sub jugum* in token of subjugation.

Undertakers. I. In *English* history, 1614. Men of influence who undertook for a consideration to ' get such persons returned to parliament as would prove submissive to the royal will [James I.].

Bacon, Somerset, and Neville were the three chief, and are sometimes called 'undertakers' because they undertook by bribes to win over the chief speakers and men of influence in the parliament of 1614.

A generation about the court that, to please and humour greatness, undertook a parliament, as men presuming to have friends in every county and borough, who by their power among the people would combine to return such members as should comply solely to (*sic*) the king's desires.—WILSON.

In his [James I.] opening speech he admitted what he had so sturdily denied before, the existence of *Undertakers* in the last parliament, ' a strange kind of beast which had done mischief.—HOWITT, *Hist. of Eng.* (James I., vol. iii., p. 83).

II. In *Irish* history, 1608. Those English or Scotch colonists sent by James I. in the northern counties of Ca'van, Fermānagh, Armagh, Derry, Tyrone, and Tyrconnell, who were allotted 2,000 acres each. They were men of capital, and *undertook* to pay a mark a year for every 60 acres, and to admit no recusant for tenant.

James confiscated 2,000,000 acres in these counties, and divided them in lots of 2,000, 1,500, 1,000 acres. Elizabeth tried to plant Ulster with an English colony.

. In the early part of George III.'s reign a party which played off the British Government against the Irish Parliament were called Undertakers. They had two objects in view: (1) To make the crown, so far as Ireland was concerned, dependent on themselves: (2) To check the spirit of liberty in the people, but throw the odium on the government. This party was broken up by making the lord-lieutenant reside in Ireland and distribute the patronage himself.

Undertakers (*Fife*), 1600. An association of gentlemen, chiefly proprietors of Fife, who undertook to settle in the Lewis, Uist, and other isles convenient for the fisheries, in order to bring

these islands into a more civilised state. They expelled the natives, built towns, and introduced manufactories. The attempt did not succeed, and three years later was tried again, but with no better success.

Unfair Preacher (*The*). Isaac Barrow, D.D. (1630-1677). So Charles II. called him ' because his sermons were so exhaustive that he left nothing for others to say who came after him.'

Unfunded Debt (*The*). Loans to the British government which are paid off in a given number of years. Sometimes these loans are for a few months only, and sometimes for a few years. Thus a war, such as that in Egypt, may increase the government expenditure, say 10 millions, more than the Chancellor of the Exchequer has provided for, and instead of adding this sum to the National Debt, the Treasury may think proper to borrow the money at 3 per cent., and pay off 2 millions every year for 5 years, and so cancel the debt. Such a debt is not 'funded,' but is only temporary.

Unicorn. One of the pursuivants of Scotland. *See* p. 415, 'Heralds.'

Uniformity (*Statutes of*), 3 Edw. VI. c. 1 (1549); 5, 6 Edw. VI. c. 1; 1 Eliz. c. 2; 13, 14 Car. II. c. 4. Dissenters relieved of all penalties of nonconformity by the Act of Toleration (1689).

Uniformity (*Act of*), 1661. Enacted that the revised Book of Common Prayer shall be used in all places of public worship; that the ordination of ministers therein prescribed shall be alone lawful; that all beneficed clergymen shall read the service therein contained within a given time, shall subscribe to the 39 articles, and shall profess in a set form of words their unfeigned assent and consent to these Articles and to everything else contained in the said Book of Common Prayer. Above 2,000 ministers refused to be bound by this act. All schoolmasters, all who entered our universities, and all persons who took any office, civil or military, were required to give on oath their assent and consent to this act.

By the Act of Uniformity all ministers who refused to comply were to be imprisoned for six months for the first offence, to lose their livings for the second offence, and to be imprisoned for life for the third offence.

Unigen'itus (*The Bull*), 1713, passed by Clement XI. in condemnation of the Jansenists. This bull condemns 101 passages extracted from the famous book of Quesnel, called 'Moral Reflections on the New Testament,' and set the whole kingdom of France in an uproar.

The Jansenists were Calvinistic Roman Catholics who maintained the doctrines of free grace, predestination, and the non-freedom of the will.

Union (*The*), 22 July, 1706. The union of Scotland and England under the name of Great Britain. The terms were: (1) The succession to the throne of Great Britain shall be vested in the Princess Sophia and her heirs; (2) All the subjects shall enjoy the same rights and privileges; (3) the court of session and all other courts of judicature in Scotland shall remain as at present constituted; (4) Scotland shall be represented in parliament by 16 peers and 45 commoners, &c.

Union (*Act of*), 1799. An Act of Parliament by which Ireland was united to Great Britain. It came into operation 1 Jan. 1801, when the Dublin parliament was suppressed.

Union (*L'Arrêt d'*), 13 May, 1648. The abolition of the Act of Union. Mazarin proposed to keep back for four years the salaries of all the crown courts of France except those of the Paris parlement. The Paris parlement refused to be made an exception, and immediately passed the *Act of Union*, declaring that all crown courts should be treated alike. Mazarin stopped the Act from passing, declaring it to be illegal, and this was 'l'arrêt d'Union.' The parlement would not give way, and civil war broke out. This civil war was called *la guerre de la Fronde*, which was between Mazarin and the Paris parlement.

Union (*The Edict of*), 1588. An Act proclaimed at Blois, by which Henri III. was declared chief of the league or confederation of the Catholics in France against the Huguenots. *See* 'Holy Union.'

Union (*The Evangelical*), 1608. An alliance formed at Auhausen in Bavaria, and confirmed at Halle in 1610, between the Protestant states of the Palatinate, Würtemberg, Hesse-Cassel, and Baden-Dourlach, against the Holy League formed in 1609 at Wurtzburg.

Union Brigade (*The*), at Waterloo, 1815, was composed of the 1st Royal Dragoons [*England*]; the 2nd Dragoons [the Royal Scots Greys] for *Scotland* and the 6th [Inniskillings] for *Ireland*.

Union of Calmar (*The*). The union of the three crowns of Denmark, Norway, and Sweden, agreed to in the Conference of Calmar in Sweden. From the overthrow of Albert king of Sweden in the battle of Falkoping, Margaret queen-regent of Denmark and Norway had acted as regent of Sweden; but the Diet held at Calmar on 17 June, 1397, conferred the crown of the three kingdoms on Eric, her grand-nephew, because no woman could reign. The union was only nominal at any time, and was formally abolished in 1523.

Margaret had the provinces of Wermland, East and West Gothland, with several contiguous de pendencies, assigned to her as a life settlement.
. From 1471 to 1523 Sweden had separate administration, but Wasa or Vasa united the two kingdoms.

Union of Public Good (*The*). The reorganised 'Association of Russian Knights.' A Russian secret society in the reign of Czar Alexander I. Their ostensible object was the welfare of Russia, but all their schemes were to be worked secretly to prevent envy, hatred, and opposition. There were several sections; the duty of the first was philanthropy; it had to watch over all charitable institutions, and report abuses. The business of the second section was educational; it had to keep watch on all schools and colleges, and see that the scholars were taught to love Russia and hate foreigners. The third section was devoted to the law-courts, and reported all grievances. The fourth section was to study political economy, the sources of national wealth, and the development of industry.

Union of Safety, or the True and Faithful Sons of the Country (*The*). A secret society organised in Russia in 1816 by young officers who had served in the campaigns of 1813, 1814, 1815. The members were divided into (1) Brothers, (2) Men, and (3) Boyars. The Boyars were superior in grade to the Men and Brothers, and from them three directors were chosen monthly, viz. a president, a superintendent, and a secretary. Solemn ceremonies were observed at their meetings, and all members were sworn to absolute secrecy.   Dissolved 1821.

Union of Scotland and Ireland (*The*), 1651, effected by the Rump Parliament. Eight commissioners were sent to Scotland, and in spite of much opposition, procured a vote in favour of the union, and 30 members were admitted in the parliament of 1654 for Scotland, and 30 for Ireland. But the legislation of the Protectorate was ignored by Charles II., and the permanent Union was effected in the reign of Queen Anne, 1707, when the Scotch parliament was abrogated, and the nation was permitted to send 16 lords and 45 commoners to the British parliament.

Union of Utrecht (*The*), 1579. A league under the influence of William (prince of Orange-Nassau), aided by Count Hoorn and Count Egmont, to throw off the Spanish yoke. It was joined by seven of the South Belgian provinces, which succeeded in 1594 in erecting themselves into an independent state, called the 'Republic of the Seven United Provinces.'

The seven provinces were Holland, Zealand, Utrecht, Gelderland with Zutphen, Over-Yssel, Friesland, and Groningen with Drenthe.

Union with Ireland (*The*). The act passed for this Union 2 July, 1800 (39, 40 George III. c. 67).

Unionists, 1885, &c. The Radicals and Whigs who united with the Conservatives, in Lord Salisbury's administration, to preserve the integrity of the United Kingdom, which Mr. Gladstone (the preceding premier) would have sacrificed to please the Irish Home Rule party led by Mr. Parnell. Mr. Gladstone's bill utterly demoralised the Whig party, and split from it its richest, most talented, and most influential members. George Joachim Goschen, a Whig, joined the ministry as chancellor of the exchequer; Lord Hartington and Joseph Chamberlain, important members of Gladstone's ministry, abandoned the Whig party and became Unionist leaders; about seventy-five M.P.'s did the same, leaving the Gladstone party an utter wreck. See 'Broad-bottom Administration.'

Mr. Gladstone, by giving independent parliaments to Ireland, Scotland, and Wales, would have reduced the United Kingdom into a mere federation. In 1890 the Gladstone or Whig party was nicknamed the 'demoralised.'

Lord Salisbury's parliament, formed in 1886 on the downfall of the Gladstonian house, consisted of 670 members, of which 303 were Conservatives and 75 Liberal-Unionists who voted with the Conservatives=378. The opposition consisted of 205 Gladstonians and 86 Nationalists, chiefly Irish members=291. Conservative majority 87, often increased to 100 and more.

Unitarians, 16th cent. Protestant Dissenters who believe in the monarchy of God, and disbelieve that the one God has three persons. Arians, Socinians, Mussulmans, and Jews are in one sense Unitarians, but, of course, the sect so called disavow the identity of the five creeds. Unitarians disbelieve the doctrine of the Trinity, the vicarious atonement of Christ, the doctrine of original and transmitted sin, and everlasting punishment. They baptize, however, and celebrate the eucharistic sacrament as a memorial of the crucifixion.

Milton, Newton, Priestley, Locke, and Dr. Lardner were Unitarians.

U'nitas Fratrum. The Moravian brotherhood (1500).

United Armenians (*The*). A sect in Italy, Poland, Galicia, Persia, Russia, and Marseilles, which recognise the spiritual sovereignty of the pope and hold the doctrines of the Catholics, but have their own church government.

United Brethren (*The*), or, as they call themselves, 'Unitas Fratrum.' More generally called 'Moravians' (*q.v.*) or 'Moravian Brethren,' 1500.

The 'United Brethren in Christ' (1800) are German Methodists of North America.

United Brotherhood (*The*). The American Irish League. They were called 'V.C.' (*q.v.*). The object was to bring about an Independent Irish Republic in Ireland by force of arms. Called in Ireland 'I.R.B.' (Irish Revolutionary Brotherhood).

The Irish, in their jargon, were called 'Jajti,' and Ireland was called 'Jsfmboe.'

The executive body was known as 'F.C.' which was merely removing the initial letters (like V.C.) one letter in advance. F.C. for E.B., and V.C. for U.B.

The secretary was known as 'Y,' the treasurer as 'Z,' and the chairman as 'X.'

Letters were addressed 'To the F.C. of the V.C.,' *i.e.* the 'Executive Body of the United Brotherhood.' See 'Irish Associations.'

United Diet of Prussia (*The*), 1847. A union of the provincial diets created in the previous reign. It was no organ of the national will, like the British Parliament. It levied taxes, except in time of war, but the kingdom of Prussia was ruled like a military camp by the king as commander-in-chief, and his diet took the place of field officers.

United East India Company (The), 1708.

The original company chartered in 1600 by Queen Elizabeth, and granted a monopoly for fifteen years of trading to India, united with a rival company chartered in 1698. In 1759 the united company obtained from parliament the political management of the acquired countries, subject to certain restrictions, and was denominated the 'East India Company,' and twenty-four members were appointed directors, their acts being subject to the revisal of the Board of Control. In 1858 the government of India was transferred to the crown.

The original company was formed in 1599, and consisted of four ships. The charter had to be renewed every fifteen years.

United Empire Loyalists (The), 1783.

Those lovers of Old England who gave up everything they had rather than abide in the revolted American colonies under a new and alien flag. They settled in Nova Scotia, the wilderness of Ontario, the West Indies, New Brunswick, and elsewhere. The centenary of their departure from the United States was held in the Dominion in 1883, when the quaint costumes and old coaches of the previous century were paraded.

United Free Church Methodists (The), about 1850.

The Wesleyan Association and Wesleyan Reform Association united.

United Free Gospel Churches, or 'Band Room Methodists,' 1806,

who first met in the Band Room, Manchester. They do not pay their ministers, they ignore class meetings, and they admit non-members into their society.

United Irishmen (The).

I. In 1793. Projected in 1791 by Samuel Neilson, a draper of Belfast, to unite Protestants and Catholics in a constitutional agitation for reform and Catholic emancipation. The principal leaders of the people were Wolfe Tone, Hamilton Rowan, and James Napper Tandy, whose violence was so great that they were obliged to expatriate themselves. When the Earl of Camden, who

succeeded the Earl Fitzwilliam, returned to the old system of coercion, the United Irishmen advocated a separation from England and the establishment of a republic in Ireland in alliance with the French Republic, and a well-organized system of secret confederacy was spread over the country, the heads of which issued orders for enlisting, combining, and arming their adherents. In the northern and midland counties were two associations at the same time, one of Catholics called 'Defenders,' and the other of Protestants called 'Orangemen.' The Defenders joined the United Irishmen, and the Orangemen were the opponents. See 'Irish Associations.'

II. In 1846. An Irish newspaper edited by Mr. Mitchel; the organ of a party which split from the Young Irelanders, whose organ was called the 'Nation.' The 'Nation' advocated the 'combination of all classes, and the exercise of all political and social influences' to carry Repeal; the United Irishmen advocated revolution, bloodshed, and civil war. Mitchel every week addressed the lord lieutenant as 'Her Majesty's Executioner-general and Butcher-general of Ireland'; and women were exhorted to throw vitriol on the police and the Queen's soldiers.

United Kingdom.

That of Ireland added to Great Britain. The Act of Union took effect 1 Jan., 1801.

The union of the four kingdoms, Wales, Ireland, and Scotland, added to England, make the anagram W.I.S.E.

United Kingdoms (The Four).

England, the Heptarchy united under Egbert	802
Ireland, united under Anlaf . .	853
Scotland, one kingdom under Kenneth MacAlpin	850
Wales, the several princes of Wales and Powisland united under Howel Dha	907
England and Ireland, Henry II. .	1172
England and Wales (with Ireland), Edward I.	1283
Great Britain (England, Wales, Scotland, and Ireland), under James VI. of Scotland, called 'James I. of England' . .	1603

United Methodist Free Churches (The), 1857.

An amalgamation of the Protestant Methodists

(formed 1828), the Wesleyan Methodist Association (1834), and the Wesleyan Reform Association (founded in 1849).

The Wesleyans have 7,310 chapels, the Primitives 4,486, and the United Methodist Free Churches 1,242. Their chief differences are the disapproval of a theological seminary, the exclusion of instrumental music, the place they give to laymen in church administration, which is much larger than in the original body, and the greater freedom from control in the circuits.

United Presbyterian Church

(*The*), 1847, is composed of the 'Secession' and the 'Relief,' the former instituted in 1733 and the latter in 1752.

United Presbytery (*The*), or

'Synod of Munster,' formed in 1809 by the junction of the Southern Presbytery of Dublin with the Presbytery of Munster. It is one of the three non-subscribing Presbyterian bodies of Ireland.

The other two are the 'Remonstrant Synod of Ulster' (*q.v.*), and the 'Presbytery of Antrim' (*q.v.*). These three bodies subsequently united and formed the 'General Non-subscribing Presbyterian Association of Ireland' (*q.v.*).

United States (*The*). There are

somewhat more than 2,700 counties. Of these 10 per cent. are named after presidents, and 35 per cent. after Americans who have not been presidents (1890).

1. Counties, &c., named from presidents:—

27 counties named Washington, besides cities and towns innumerable.
48 Jefferson.
21 Jackson.
17 Lincoln, Madison, and Monroe.
12 Polk.
10 Grant.
9 Adams and Harrison.
4 Garfield, Pierce, and Van Buren.

2. Counties, &c., named from Americans who have not been presidents:—

Boone.	Putnam.
Calhoun.	Randolph.
Clay.	Scott.
Hancock.	Webster, and many more.

3. The following names are enough to Nicodemus any place from ever rising into a bishopric. Only fancy a dignified clergyman signing himself 'Yours faithfully, John . . . . ,' followed by one of the following names:—

Alkaliburg.	Eurekapolis.
Bleeder's Gulch.	Eurekaville (!)
Bloody Bend.	Fighting Cocks.
Boanerges Ferry.	Good Thunder.
Breeches Fork.	Hell and Nails Crossing.
Bludgeonsville.	
Bugville.	Hezekiahville.
Butter's Sell.	Hide and Seek.
Buried Pipe.	Jack Pot.
Cairoville.	Joker.
Clean Deck.	Murderville.
Daughter's Loss.	Nettle Carrier.
Euchreville.	Numaville.

Peddlecake.	Starvation.
Poker Flat.	Stuck-up-Canon.
Pottawattomieville.	Thief's End.
Plumpville.	Tombstone.
Roaring Fox.	Ubet.
Sharper's Creek.	Villa Realville.
Skeletonville Agency.	Yellow Medicine.
Soaker's Ranche.	Yuba Dam.
Spottedville.	&c.

United States (*The*), 4 July, 1776.

At the 'Declaration of Independence' the name of the American Colonies was changed into 'The United States.' At that time eleven of the states signed the declaration, and formed the nucleus of the United States.

The War of Independence did not terminate till 1782.

Unitive Life. Quietism.

Molinos in 1681 published his 'Spiritual Guide,' in which he spoke of bringing the soul to a degree of perfection which he called 'Unitive Life'; and 'Quietism' became the appellation of his mystic doctrine.—PRINCE, *Parallel History* (vol. ii. p. 290).

Universal Agent (*The*). That

subtle and all-pervading something of which light, heat, electricity, and life are the phenomena and sensible manifestations.

She struggled to take her eyes from his, but I was of no use. The subtle power of the Universal Agent had got hold upon her, and she was riveted to the spot so long as he kept his eyes upon her.—CRAWFORD, *Zoroaster*, chap. xviii.

Universalists, or 'The Universal

Christians,' 3rd cent. Those who believe that Christ died for all, and that no one will ultimately be cast away for ever. He shall see of the travail of his soul and be satisfied. The wicked. shall be cast into hell only till they are purified, when (cleansed from sin) they will join the saints in light.

The Philadelphian Universalists are the followers of Mr. James Kelly, who was connected with Mr. Geo. Whitfield. His congregation met in the Philadelphian Chapel, Windmill Street, Finsbury Square, London. There are a goodly number of these Christians at Boston, Philadelphia, and other parts of the U. S. of America.

See 'Paulinists.'

University.

Paris, founded about 1109; its degrees were recognized 1200.

Oxford, founded about 1150; its degrees were recognized 1214.

Cambridge, founded about 1209; its degrees were recognized 1231.

Glasgow, founded about 1450.

Aberdeen	„	„	1506.
Edinburgh	„	„	1582.
Dublin	„	„	1591.
London	„	„	1828.

University College, 872. The oldest in the University of Oxford, founded by Alfred the Great. Probably the real founder was William of Durham, rector of Wearmouth 1249. The head of the college is called the Master.

University Counsel (*The*), Cambridge. These officers have no connection whatever with the Council of the University (*q.v.*). They are counsellors-at-law consulted upon occasions of doubt, and appointed by grace of the Senate.

University Fight (*The*). In the reign of Elizabeth, when that queen in 1564 visited Cambridge, the public orator declared in his harangue that Cambridge was the older University. Oxford at once took up the cudgel, and when in 1566 the queen visited that university, she was told that Oxford, not Cambridge, was the older foundation.

Caius in 1574 published a goodly quarto in defence of Cambridge. He countenances the preposterous assertion that the first stones of Cambridge University were laid 178 years after the flood!! and gravely tells us that Cambridge derives its name from Cantaber, a royal Spanish emigrant, who in the 4th Christian cent. sent for Greek philosophers from Athens as professors in the Cantaber or Cambridge University. Brian Twyne in 1608 published a similar folio on behalf of Oxford, stating its foundation was laid when Brute came to the island. This 'Trojan' colony laid the university at Cricklade—*i-e.* Bello Situm—where Oxford now stands. And as for Cambridge, it was a mere offshoot of Oxford in the reign of Henry I.

University Museum (*The*), 1855, erected for the study of natural science. There are lecture-rooms, work-rooms, and laboratories, a dissecting-room, a library, and a reading-room. The keeper has 80*l.* a year (University of Oxford).

The nearest approximative institution of Cambridge is the museum in the old Botanical Gardens; but there are other museums, as the Woodwardian for geology, another for zoology, others for comparative anatomy, botany, mechanics, optics and astronomy, chemistry, &c. *See* p. 328, 'Fitzwilliam Museum.'

Unkiar Skelessi (*Treaty of*), 26 June (July 8), 1833. A secret treaty between Russia and Turkey of alliance, offensive and defensive, for eight years. It provided the establishment of a perpetual peace between Russia and Turkey. Each was to defend the other's territory against all invaders. The treaty was for eight years positive, with the hope of its being perpetual. The alliance was made when Egypt threatened Turkey with war, and Russia feared that Constanti-

nople would fall into the hands of Egypt. This alliance was annulled by the Treaty of London 13 July, 1841.

Unlearned Parliament (*The*). 'Parliamentum Indoctum,' 1404, from which all lawyers were excluded. So called by Sir E. Coke. *See* p. 664, 'Parliaments.'

It advised the king to seize the revenues of the church. More than one-third of all the land of England was church property. It also advised the king (Henry IV.) to repeal the statute De Hæretico Comburendo, but he feared the clergy.

Unrighteous Bible (*The*). Cambridge Press, 1653, contains this query: 'Know ye not that the unrighteous shall inherit the kingdom of God?' *See* 'Bible' and 'Scriptures.'

Up-Angas (*The*). Written in Sanskrit by the sage Vyasa, on the subjects of cosmogony, chronology, and geography. Two heroic poems are also included, viz. the Ramayâna and the Mahabhârata. *See* p. 820, 'Shastras.'

The Purânas, or sacred poems of Up-Angas, tell of virtue, good works, and the soul.

Upa-Vedas (*The*), delivered by Brahma, treat of medicine, archery, architecture, music, and sixty-four mechanical arts. *See* p. 820, 'Shastras.'

Upsetters. The college companions of St. Augustine. *See* his 'Confessions,' iii. 3.

They formed themselves into tumultuous bands
Which wandered through the city streets with noise,
Fright'ning the old, the peaceful, and the weak
And hence, from acts upsetting decency,
Were called 'Upsetters,' nor refused the name.
      HENRY WARWICK COLE, Q.C., *St. Augustine.*

Urbanists and Clem'entines (3 syl.), 1378. The followers of Urban VI., pope of Rome, and Clement VI., pope of Avignon. For fifty-one years there were two simultaneous popes.

Urbanists and Damianists. Nuns of the order of St. Claire. In 1264 Urban IV. mitigated the austerity of the Franciscan rule observed by these nuns. Those who followed the rule thus modified were called Urbanists, but those who continued the more austere rule were called *Damianists* from St. Pietro Damian, noted for his extreme austerity.

The nuns of St. Claire devote themselves chiefly to the education of the young.

Urbarial Dues. The labour and produce due to the landlord for an Urbarial Tenure (*q.v.*).

Urbarial Tenure. A free tenure in Hungary according to the provisions of the Urbarium. By this charter a Hungarian peasant was no longer attached to the soil, but could leave his landlord and farm whenever he thought fit. Every peasant had as his own an acre of land, with a house and garden; and also could possess a farm, varying from fourteen to sixty acres, the rent of which was paid by labour and produce. One-ninth of the produce belonged to the landlord, and the labour varied from 18 days to 104 days, according to the size of the holdings.

In 1848 the nobles of Hungary abolished, of their own free will, their right to exact either labour or produce in return for lands held by urbarian tenure. Thus were the peasants invested with the absolute ownership of twenty millions of acres among them.—GODKIN, *History of Hungary*, p. 319.

Urbarium (*The*). A code of laws made in the reign of Maria Theresa of Austria, regulating the relations between landlord and tenant. This was an admirable measure, passed in 1764, and remaining in force till 1835. It was called 'the People's Charter.'

Ursulins, 1537. A religious society founded by St. Angela of Brescia, and dedicated to St. Ursula. Their speciality is the gratuitous education of the young. They followed the rule of St. Augustine. Abolished in France in 1790, but subsequently re-established. They have some houses in the U.S.

Uscocchi, or **Uskoks.** Dalmatian fugitives, swelled by the offscouring of all nations, who infested the Adriatic for about a century as pirates. They consisted of Turks, Austrians, Croats, Dalmatians, Venetians, and English, who lived in Segni; and 'God save you from the Uskoks' was a proverbial expression. By the Treaty of Madrid, 16 Sept., 1617, the extermination of the pirates was an article stipulated by Venice and Austria, and the horde disappeared.

Uskoks, Russian *uskakat*, fugitives.

Use. Meaning the prayer-book used, or the 'services' of the mediæval church. Several large dioceses had their own prayer-book, which contained services for local saints and holidays, and special modes of singing and saying the service. The preface of our Common Prayer Book tells us 'there [had] been [hitherto] great diversity in singing and saying in churches within this realm, some following `Salisbury` Use, some *Hereford* Use, and some the Use of *Bangor*, some of *York*, some of *Lincoln*. Now, from henceforth, all the whole realm shall have but one Use.'

The Sarum or Salisbury Use was compiled by Osmund about 1085, and of this missal there have been several reprints and translations.

The dates and authors of the other five Uses are unknown, but it is generally thought that they were older than the Sarum. There is a MS. of the *Hereford* Missal in University College, Oxford, of the 14th cent., and it was printed at Rouen in 1502; copies of the printed Missal are preserved in the British Museum and in the Bodleian.

The *Bangor* Missal was never printed, but from a MS. of the 15th cent. of this book Mr. Maskell printed the Ordinary and Canon in the Ancient Liturgy of the Church of England in 1844.

The *York* Missal was printed at Rouen in 1509, and a copy of it is preserved in the Bodleian Library. Nothing of the *Lincoln* Missal remains except a MS. fragment of the 15th cent., preserved in the Bodleian.

Sometimes the term Use was applied to the local usage of a particular parish. Thus there were offices and a mass of St. Wilfrid *secundum usum Riponiæ*.

In the northern parts was generally observed the Use of the archiepiscopal Church of York, in South Wales the Use of Hereford, in North Wales the Use of Bangor, and in other places the Use of the principal sees, as Lincoln, Sarum, &c.— STEPHENS, *On the Common Prayer*, p. 121.
See 'Notes and Queries,' 28 June, 1890, pp. 509, 510.

Use of Sarum ('In Usum Sarum'), 1078. A liturgy or service-book drawn up by Osmund bishop of Salisbury, which was generally adopted throughout the entire kingdom. It was in Latin, and based on the Roman Missals.

There were other liturgies besides that of Sarum, as the 'Use of Bangor,' the 'Use of Hereford,' the 'Use of Lincoln,' and the 'Use of York.' These 'Uses' contained eleven different services, as the Missal, Graduale or Grayle, Processionale, Ordinale, Portiforium or Breviary, Legenda, Pica or Pie, Finale. Antiphonarium, Manuale, and Pontificale.

Uses. A legal device to elude the statutes of mortmain. As no lands could be left to religious houses, donors granted their property in trust for the *use* of a stated religious house. Other property was transferred by a similar fiction during the wars of the Roses. As a *use* was not a tenure, such property could not be forfeited for treason or any other offence.

Uses (*The Statute of*), 27 Henry VIII. c. 10. To prevent the ecclesiastical evasion of the statute of mortmain. It laid down the rule that there cannot be 'a use upon a use.' In other words, that a third person cannot be nominally held for a church or other society, so as to enable that church or that society to evade the statute of mortmain.

Useful Knowledge (*The Society for the Diffusion of*), 1827. Designed to give information on useful subjects generally. Lord Brougham, Professor De Morgan, Sir David Brewster, Professor Lindley, &c., contributed to the series of books issued by the Society.

Useless Parliament (*The*). Convened 18 June, 1625, by Charles I., adjourned to Oxford 1 Aug., and dissolved 12 Aug., having done nothing but offend the king. *See* p. 664, 'Parliaments.'

Utah Mormons (*The*). The Polygamist Mormons. Sometimes called Brighamites, from Brigham Young, who practised polygamy. Utah was first occupied by the Mormons in 1847.

Polygamy was declared unlawful in 1870 by the 'Mormon Disabilities Bill,' and in 1890 was abandoned by the Mormons.

Utas of Easter (*The*). Utas are the octaves of a festival. Old French, oitauves, octaves.

Utilitarian School (*The*). 'To be as useful as possible,' 'to give the least possible pain to others,' and 'to give the greatest possible happiness to the greatest number.' A system of ethics founded by Jeremy Bentham (1747–8—1832).

On his death-bed he gave his body to his physician, Dr. Southwood Smith, for dissection, that he might do the most useful thing possible with it. He forbade calling his friends to his bedside, that he might give them the least possible pain. The two were in accordance with his principle of *maxima felicitas*.
.•. His body was, however, embalmed, and is now kept in University College, London.

U'traquists. A sect of the Hussites, also called Calix'tines (3 syl.). Called Calixtines from *calix* (a cup), because they insisted on the cup being given to communicants; and called **U**traquists from *utraque* (both kinds), because they insisted that both bread and wine should be administered in the eucharistic sacrament.

Utrecht (*The Treaty of*), 1713, between France and the following allies, viz. Great Britain, Savoy, Portugal, Prussia, and the states of Holland, signed 11 April. Spain, which, of course, was allied with France, did not sign till 18 Sept. Peace was concluded after a war of eleven years, noted for the brilliant victories of the Duke of Marlborough and the Prince Eugene. The treaty of Utrecht is generally considered most dishonourable to England, as it ignored all Marlborough fought for. Philip still remained king of Spain, and the interests of the allies were almost entirely ignored. Bolingbroke, Oxford, and Ormonde, parties to this treaty, were (1715) charged by the House of Commons with high treason. Bolingbroke and Ormonde fled, but Oxford was brought to trial and acquitted. However, it confirmed to England the island of Newfoundland and Nova Scotia, with the possession of Gibraltar and Minorca, St. Kitts, and Hudson's Bay.

In 1708 Newfoundland was attacked and partly conquered by the French.
Nova Scotia was given to France by the treaty of St. Germain in 1632, was reconquered by the British in 1654, and again ceded to France by the treaty of Breda in 1667, was again taken by Britain 1711, and confirmed to the British crown in 1713.
These were but small concessions, it is true, but they tended to confirm the peace between France and England.

V. C. The cryptogram used in Ireland to designate the 'United Brethren.' It consists simply of shifting the initials one letter forwards. V comes next to U, and C comes next to B. The 'Clanna-Gael' (*q.v.*) was a secret organisation known as 'V. C.' *See* p. 455, 'Irish Associations.'

V and **S** (*branding with*). V = vagrant, S = slave.

A runaway, or anyone who lives idly for three days, shall be brought before two justices of the peace, and marked V with a hot iron on his breast, and shall be adjudged the slave of him who brought him for two years. . . . If within that space he absents himself fourteen days, he shall be marked on the forehead or cheek by a hot iron with an S, and be his master's slave for ever. (Edward VI.)

Vacca (*Tower of the*), in the Palazzo Pubblico or Della Signoria of Florence. The great bell-tower or campanile in the middle of the edifice. Arnolfo designed and began it, but it was completed by *altri maestri.* Why called the Cow Tower is not known, but the 'lowing' of the bell is a part of the city wit.

Vakeel. A Persian satrap, or prince of a small state. In India an envoy or inferior ambassador is called a Vakeel.

Aga Mohammed was soon set aside by Luft Ali Khan of the Zend tribe, and a relative of the late Vakeel, 1789.—PRINCE, *Parallel History*, vol. iii. p. 132.

Valdenses. Separatists from the Catholic Church in the 11th cent. Probably *vallenses* from the Latin *vallis*, a valley. Hence commonly called the 'Church of the Valleys,' the chief being the valleys of Piedmont and Embrun. Other valleys where they abounded were the 'Valley of San Martino,' the 'Valley of Perosa,' the 'Vale of Pragela,' the 'Valley of Lucerna,' the High Valley of the Durance and the adjacent glens, and many others. The followers of Peter Valdo were 'The Poor Men of Lyons.'

Eberard de Bethune says: 'They call themselves Vallenses because they live in a Vale of Tears.'— *Maxima Biblioth. P. P.* vol. xxiv.

Valentia. One of the five provinces into which Britain was divided in the reign of the Emperor Sevērus. It included the land from the Wall of Severus to the Forth and Clyde. It had its own ruler, but that ruler was subject to the præfect or governor-general of the island.

Valentin'ians (*The*), 2nd cent. Followers of Valentīnus, an Egyptian, a Platonist, who taught that Depth is the first principle, and the trinity of Depth, Thought, and Silence existed from all eternity. From this triune sprang Wisdom and Truth. Thought and Silence, Wisdom and Truth, Valentinus called the first quaternity of eons, the source of all the rest. The second quaternity was the offspring of Wisdom, viz. the Word (or Logos) and Life, Man and the Church. Logos and Life produced five couples of eons, Man and the Church formed six couples, and the thirty eons compose the Plerōma of deity. Wisdom wanting to pry into depth (or Bythos) gave herself much trouble, and from this sprang matter. Horos restored Wisdom to the Pleroma, and then she brought forth Christ and the Holy Ghost. Irenæus, Justin the Martyr, Tertullian, and others

were avowed opponents of the mixture of Christianity and Platonism.

Eon, in Platonic philosophy, means a divine attribute existing without beginning or end. In Gnostic theology it means an emanation from deity anterior to time. The Son is an eon of the Father, the Holy Ghost is an eon from the Father and Son. The word is also used to signify a period of time of immeasurable duration.

Vale'sians, A.D. 198. Heretics, so called from Valesius, an Arabian. They admitted only eunuchs into their society, insisting that this crucifixion of the flesh is essential to salvation.

Valley of Death (*The*). Balaklava, famous for the charge of Lord Cardigan's Light Brigade, consisting of 607 sabres, which advanced right into the Russian centre with the view of taking thirty Russian guns directed against them. When Lord Raglan perceived the mistake, he ordered a retreat to be sounded. 25 Oct., 1854.

Certainly a worse choice than Lord Raglan as leader of a great war could hardly have been made. He had neither the energy, the dash, nor the lightning speed of a military hero.

Valley of Heroes (*The*). So the Persians call the Plain of Oujan, the famous royal hunting-ground.

Valley of Waters (*The*). The Mediterranean Sea.

The Valley of Waters, widest next to that Which holds the earth engarland, shapes its course Between discordant shores [*Europe and Africa*].
DANTE, *Paradise,* ix.

Valley of the Shadow of Death (*The*). The Koord Cabul Pass, where in 1839 the Afghans annihilated the British army. *See* p. 485, 'Khyber Pass,' and p. 13, 'Afghan War.'

Valois Branch (*The*). The younger branch of the Capētian race of French kings (1328–1498). In 1498 came a branch of the Valois called the Orleans-Orleans, and in 1515 a branch called the Orleans-Angoulème. Called Valois from Philippe VI. de Valois (1328–1350).

Valois-Angoulème Branch of the Capētian dynasty gave to France five kings: François I., Henri II., François II., Charles IX., and Henri III. (1515–1589).

Valois-Orleans Branch of the Capētian dynasty gave to France one king, Louis XII., *le père du peuple* (1462, 1498–1515).

Valor Ben'eficio'rum, 1512. Drawn up by the clergy in council at Edinburgh, and known by the title of 'Bagimont's' or 'Bajimont's Roll.' *See* p. 66.

Vandyck (*The Caledonian*). George Jameson (1586–1644).

Vandyck (*The English*). William Dobson, painter (1610–1647).

Vandyck of France (*The*). Hyacinthe Rigaud (1659–1743), the founder of the Pre-Raphaelites.

Vandyck of Sculpture (*The*). Antoine Coysevox (1640–1720).

Va'nists. Followers of the religious opinions of Sir Harry Vane (1612–1662), which were almost identical with Antinomianism. He detested episcopacy, and though he promoted the Solemn League and Covenant, he abhorred both it and the presbytery. Vane was a fifth-monarchy man, and a great believer in 'unknown tongues,' so that his prayers were utterly unintelligible. He wrote several theological treatises, but all mark him out as a wild visionary.

Varan'gians. All Northmen were so denominated by the Greeks; but, strictly speaking, the Varangians were the Norse bodyguard of their emperors.

Varēla (*Peace of*), 3 Aug., 1790, between Sweden and Russia.

Vasa (*Order of*), 1772. A Swedish order instituted by Gustavus III. in honour of Gustavus Vasa, founder of the dynasty.

Vassy (*Massacre of*), 1 March, 1652. Some 1,200 reformers had assembled in a barn on Sunday morning, when François duc de Guise with sixty horsemen and bowmen rode by, and all began to insult the worshippers by calling them 'rebels! dogs! heretics!' &c. Some of the reformers shut the doors, when the duke shouted 'Mort-dieu! slay the vermin!' A scuffle ensued, in which a stone struck the duke on the cheek. His horsemen now fell foul cutting and slashing. Sixty were slain and above 200 wounded. When called upon to answer for this unprovoked attack, the duke declared that the reformers were the aggressors, and that he only acted in self-defence. He died the following year, and the matter ended for a time, but it led to the long 'Religious Wars of France.'

A Bible was shown to the duke, and he handed it to his brother the cardinal, who said, 'There is no harm in this book. It is the Holy Scriptures.' 'How! (cried the duke) sang-dieu! Call you that the Holy Scriptures? Why, they were written more than 1,000 years ago, and this was written last year, as you may see by the date.'

Vatican (*The*). 'Vaticānus Mons' is a hill at Rome; but is now chiefly noted for its magnificent palace of the popes, with its superb gardens, its museums, celebrated library, and basilica of St. Peter. The palace was constructed in 498, but has been often enlarged, especially by the popes Nicolas V., Paul II. and III., Sixtus IV., Leo X., Sixtus V., Benedict XIV., Clement XIV., Pius VI., &c.

In the Vatican are the celebrated Sixtine Chapel, the Pauline Chapel, and the Raphael room.

Vatican (*Council of the*), 1870, to render the dogma of the Immaculate Conception an article of faith.

Of course the New Testament does not give the remotest hint of such a dogma, nor does it remove the difficulty of 'bringing a clean thing out of an unclean,' or, in other words, the entail of sin. It merely removes it one stage further back, and helps to destroy the proper manhood of Christ. The dogma is a grand theological mistake.

Vatican MS. (*The*) of the Bible. *See* p. 184, 'Codex Vaticanus.'

Vauban de la Marine (*Le*). Baron Sané, the shipbuilder, born at Brest (1740–1832).

Vaudois (*The*) must not be confounded with the followers of Peter Waldo, or 'Poor Men of Lyons,' who were a revival of the Paulicians; but the Vaudois, mentioned by Jerome, were Valentinians, and were confined to the Cottian Alps.

Ved-Angas (*The*), revealed by Hindû inspired saints, are devoted to astronomy, grammar, prosody, pronunciation, charms, incantations, religious rites, and religious ceremonies. Written in Sanskrit. *See* 'Shastras.'

Vedas. The sacred books of the Hindûs written in Sanskrit. They are four in number: (1) The *Rig*, containing hymns, and in verse; (2) The *Yadjour*, prayers in prose; (3) The *Sama*, designed to be chanted; and (4) The *Atharvan*, containing formulas for consecration, expiation, and imprecation. Said to have been written in the 15th cent. B.C.

Of the commentaries the most celebrated are the *Purânas* and the *Sutras*. See these words.

Veduto. *See* p. 286, ' Eighty ' (The).

Vehmgerichte (*The*), ' The Holy Vehm.' A secret tribunal of Germany, death being the penalty of a betrayal thereof.

It had its origin in Westphalia in the 13th cent. The members consisted of the initiated and the ignorants, but every member must be free born and in lawful wedlock. There were secret signs of recognition. The names and charges of persons brought before the tribunal were entered in the ' Blood Book ' together with the sentence of the tribunal. There were three modes of proceeding— the summary, the secret, and the open. Death was by hanging on the nearest tree, but a knife stuck in the tree announced to the world that the victim was not hanged by highwaymen. Towards the close of the 16th cent. the Vehmgerichte dwindled and died. *See* p. 743, ' Red Land.'

See Walter Scott's 'Anne of Geierstein' and Reynolds's 'Bronze Statue.'

Vella (*Giuseppe*), an abbot and literary impostor (1751–1814). He confessed his frauds and was sentenced to fifteen years' imprisonment. His books are ' Codex Diplomaticus Siciliæ,' 1791, and ' Libro del Consiglio di Egitto,' 1798. *See* p. 524, ' Literary Forgeries,' &c.

Velvet. *The little gentleman in velvet*, the mole. The Jacobites used to drink to the ' little gentleman in velvet,' meaning the mole which threw up the mound against which Sorel (King William III.'s horse) stumbled, whereby, being thrown to the ground, he broke his collarbone, which caused his death.

Velvet Book (*The*). The Russian peerage and official lists.

Velveteen Plot (*The*), 1842. A trick played upon Sir Robert Peel by a Lancashire manufacturer in order to forward the anti-corn law interests. It was the present of a piece of cotton velvet so dressed as to look like silk velvet, and ostensibly made in New York. Sir Robert thanked the donor, and said that Lady Peel would have part made into a cloak and he himself would have the rest

made up for his own use. After a more careful inspection Sir Robert found that the design consisted of wheat-ears about a scroll on which was inscribed the word FREE. So he returned the present, stating that he was unaware of its political symbolism.

Vendéan Massacres (*The*), or Vendéan war, May 1793 to 19 Feb., 1795. That is the resistance of the Vendéans to the republican Jacobins. Prudhomme says the slaughter of the Vendéans in this contest was 337,000, distributed thus :—

Women killed in La Vendée 15,000 ; children killed 22,000 ; men killed 300,000.

Vendéan Wars (*The*), 1793–1800. Divers wars between royalists of the west of France and the republicans. The insurgents were the nobles, priests, and peasantry combined. The first encounter was in March 1793 in the Bocage. Lazarus Hoche brought the contest to an end in 1796, and was called the *Pacificateur de la Vendée*. In 1799 the Vendéans again took up arms. Brune brought this insurrection to an end in the early part of 1800. In 1815, during the Hundred Days (*q.v.*), the Vendéans would have taken up arms if General Lamarque had not interfered to prevent it. In 1832 insurrections were again planned, but came to nothing. Prudhomme estimates the death of the Vendéans in their resistance to the republican Jacobins at 337,000, of which 37,000 were women and children. *See* ' Chouans.'

Vendémiaire (Days 12, 13), Year IV. That is 3, 4 Oct., 1795 ; the days when the troops under Barras and General Bonaparte triumphed over the insurgents against the Convention. The combat before the church of St. Roch was most murderous.

Vendetta. The blood-feud, or duty of the nearest akin of a murdered man to slay the murderer. The custom prevails in Corsica, Sicily, Sardinia, Calabria, among the Montenegrins and Albanians, the Druses, Circassians, Arabs, natives of Australia, and in central Asia. In the play of ' Romeo and Juliet ' the two houses of Montague and Capulet ' suffered the vendetta.' Moses appointed cities of refuge to break down the vengeance of the vendetta.

The vendetta is called by the Bedouins *Tar* = retaliation. It existed in ancient times among the Greeks. In the summer of 1889 in Corsica both the slayer and the avenger in a blood-feud were slain in a duel fight with each other.

Vendetta Transversale, a cross blood-feud. That is, each set of two relatives has a murder to avenge, A has a blood-feud with B, but B has a blood-feud with A.

Vendidad Sadê. A sacred book of the Parsees attributed to Zoroaster. It forms part of the Zend-Avesta, and is in the form of a dialogue between Ormuzd and Zoroaster.

Venerable (The) Bede, the author of an 'Ecclesiastical History.' A native of Wearmouth. He died 735, aged 62.

Ven'eta Factio. The Blue Coats. A faction in Byzantium, so called because their livery was Venice blue. The Veneti were simply charioteers in the circus dressed in blue, but the blue coats ultimately formed into a political party of royalists, opposed to the Prasina Factio (q.v.), which were opposed to Justinian, and tried to assassinate him. See 'Blues and Greens.'

Venĕti is Latin for Venetians, Venice is 'Venetiæ,' and Venetus, the adjective, means 'of Venice,' or 'Venice Blue,' the livery of the common soldiers and seamen of Rome.

Vengeance de Jeanne de Castille (La), a box on the ears. Jeanne de Castille out of jealousy boxed the ears of a maid of honour she had brought from Portugal, and who developed into a rival.

Vengeance for the Lamb torn by the Wolf. The war-cry and motto of Capobianco, the leader of the Carbonari.

Vengeur (Le), 1 June, 1794. A French man-of-war immortalised by a romantic fiction. It was one of the fleet engaged against the English fleet under Lord Howe. The English gained a signal victory, but Jean Bon St.-André, the Jacobin commissioner on board the 'Vengeur,' announced to the Convention that the French had won a most splendid victory, and the 'Vengeur' went down all the men shouting 'Vive la République! Vive la France!' and continued these cries even at the bottom of the ocean. Barère added to the fiction that the 'Vengeur' was not sunk by the English, but was engulfed by the waves. Chénier

the revolutionary poet wrote a panegyric on the 'Vengeur,' containing these lines :—

Les voix des braves expirans
Qui chantent au fond des abîmes !

The sinking of 'Le Vengeur' described by Barère, and Napoleon crossing the Alps, a painting by David, are what Carlyle would call 'masterpieces of blague.' Napoleon, who really crossed the mountains on a plodding mule, and buttoned to the chin in a grey greatcoat, is represented in full military costume spurring a prancing charger, and pointing with his right hand towards Italy. But strangely the wind blows the tail and mane of the charger one way, and the military cloak of the rider in an opposite direction.

The 'Vengeur' was one of the ships of the French Convention, which encountered Howe in the Brest waters. Six of the French fleet had been taken, and the battle was lost. The 'Vengeur,' disabled, sank with all its crew, to the number of 200. The men were picked up by British boats, and saved from a watery grave, for which they were very grateful. This is how Barère describes the incident (the translation is by Carlyle, who spells the name Barrère) :—

Twelve hours of raging cannonade ; sun now sinking westward through the battle-smoke. Six French ships taken ; the battle lost; what ship soever can still sail, making off ! But how is it with 'Le Vengeur' ? she neither strikes [sail] nor makes off ? She is lamed ; she cannot make off, [and] strikes she will not. Fire rakes her fore and aft from victorious enemies : the 'Vengeur' is sinking. Strong are ye, tyrants of the sea ; yet we also, are we weak ? Lo ! all flags, streamers, jacks, every rag of tricolour that will yet run on rope, fly rustling aloft. The whole crew crowd to the upper deck, and with universal, soul-maddening yell, shouts 'Vive la République !' Sinking, sinking. She staggers, she lurches, her last drunk whirl. Ocean yawns abysmal. Down rushes 'Le Vengeur,' carrying 'Vive la Républiques' along with her, unconquerable, into eternity. (He gives as authority Barrère, 'Choix des Rapports,' xiv., 416-421, and refers to Lord Howe's report for the simple truth, 'Annual Register,' 1794, p. 86). See p. 368, 'Glorious First of June,' and 'Fire First.'

Veni, Vidi, Vici, B.C. 47. Cæsar's despatch to the Roman senate when he vanquished Pharnācēs, king of the Cimmerian Bosphorus in the battle of Zela.

Karl V. imitated this despatch when he announced his victory at Mühlberg, in April 1547. 'I came, I saw, God conquered.'

Venice of the East. Bangkok, capital of Siam.

Venice of the North (The). I. Amsterdam, built on 95 small islands, and its canals are crossed by 290 bridges. II. Stockholm, capital of Sweden.

Venice of the West. Glasgow.

Another element in the blazon of the Venice of the West is the fish laid across the stem of the tree.—BURTON.

Venice Sketch-Book (The), or 'Raphael's Sketch Book,' preserved in the Accademia delle Belle Arti, in Venice. Long considered to be a collection of sketches by Raphael, but proved by Morelli to be sketches by Pintoricchio,

the Umbrian artist, and executed before Raphael was born.

Ver Sacrum. When the whole produce of a spring-time was devoted to the gods. This was done by the Sabellians in times of famine and public calamities. Even the children born during the ver sacrum were devoted to Mamers, the war god, and had to leave the city of their birth.

Verbena'lia. Annual rites held by the Romans when the altars were decorated with verbena or vervain, called the *herba sacra.*

Verdun (*Treaty of*), A.D. 843, by which the empire of Charlemagne was divided into three parts. Lothaire I., as emperor, received Italy and Lorraine; Charles the Bald received France; and Louis or Ludwig received Germany. So that by this treaty Germany was created into a separate kingdom.

Vergobret [*Vergob'retus*]. A temporary king chosen by the Druids in times of danger. Like the Roman dictator a vergobret laid down his office when the war was ended.

Vergognosi (*I*). 'The Shamefaced,' or begging nobles of Venice, 16th cent. Many of the nobles of Venice from the 16th cent. were so utterly penniless that 'begging licences' were granted them. These begging nobles assumed a particular dress, viz. an old black linen frock falling to the feet. The head was covered with a hood, and a thick veil fell over the face with two eye-holes. They carried in their hands a little conical box made of paper, for alms. *See* p. 84, 'Begging Licences.'

Veriss'imus. So the Emperor Hadrian used to call Marcus Aurelius [Antonīnus], a pun on the name of his adopted son, Lucius Verus. Lucius the son was *Verus*; Marcus the father was *Verissimus* (the philosopher).

Vermilion Pencil. The pencil used by the Chinese in royal edicts and despatches.

On the 25th day of the 1st moon [16 Feb.], and 21st year of Tao-Kwang [1841], the following despatch, written with the vermilion pencil, was received in reply [to Commissioner Keshen's despatch].—*First Chinese War.*

Vermilion Towers. To the right of the Alhambra in Granāda. So called from their very ruddy hue. Built by Mohammed II., who reigned 1273–1302.

Vermont (U.S. America), means 'Green Mountains.' So called in 1777 from a range of mountains which traverses the state (French *Verd-mont*). The inhabitants are called *Green-mountain Boys.*

Verner's Law. The law of the interchanges of *s* and *r* in the Teutonic languages.

Vernier. A sliding scale by which linear and angular magnitude may be read off with much greater accuracy than by mechanical division and subdivision.

A B is part of a scale; *a b* is the vernier made to slide along the edge of the scale, Ten divisions of the vernier = eleven of the scale. Invented by Pierre Vernier, a Burgundian, who died 1637, aged 59.

Verona (*Congress of*), from 25 Aug. to 15 Dec., 1822. It was a congress of European sovereigns.

Versailles (*Congress of*), opened 8 Dec., 1784. Between France and the States-General of Holland.

Versailles (*Treaties of*).
1. 9 March, 1701, between the elector of Bavaria and Louis XIV.

2. 5 April, 1715, between Louis XIV. and Charles XII. of Sweden.

3. 5 June, 1744, between Louis XV. and Frederick II. the Great of Prussia.

4. 1 May, 1756, of alliance, between France and Austria.

5. 30 Dec., 1758, of alliance, between France and Austria.

6. 16 July, 1782, between France and America.

7. 3 Sept., 1783, of peace, between Great Britain and the United States of America, admitting the Independence of the United States.

8. 26 Feb., 1871, of peace, between France and Prussia, after the Franco-German War.

Versailles (*The German*). Cassel is so called from its gardens, conservatories, fountains, and colossal statue of Herculês.

Versailles of Poland (*The*). The palace and grounds of the counts of Braniski, which now belong to the municipality of Bialystok.

Versailles of Prussia (*The*). Potsdam.

Vervins (*Peace of*), 2 May, 1598, between Henri IV. of France and Felipe II. of Spain.

Vespers. One of the eight daily services of the Catholic Church, and one of the four greater ones. At eventide or sunset. *See* p. 140, 'Canonical Hours.'

Veto (*Monsieur*). Louis XVI., so called in mockery by the revolutionists, because at one time he had the power of annulling by a simple veto the decrees of the National Assembly. His queen, Marie Antoinette, was nicknamed Madame Veto (*q.v.* p. 548).

Veto Law (*The*) or 'Veto Act,' 1834, in Scotland. The General Assembly gave it out as a fundamental principle of the Scotch Church that no minister shall be placed in any parish against the will of the congregation—*i.e.* against the consent of the majority of the male communicants. This law was based on the practice of the 'minister's call,' or invitation of the people to become their pastor.

Viasma (*Peace of*), 1634, between Russia and Poland, in which Russia, on one part, renounced all pretensions to Livonia, Esthonia, and Courland; and Vladislas of Poland, on the other part, abandoned his rights to the throne of Poland, and recognised the dynasty of Romanov.

Vicar of Bray. 'Let whoever will be king, I will be Vicar of Bray.' Several vicars have held their livings through shifting creeds. Some say the vicar referred to was Simon Alleyn; others tell us it was Pendleton. Ray says Simon Symonds lived under the Protectorate, Charles II., James II., and William III., and that he was at one time Independent, then Anglican, then Papist, then moderate Churchman. The vicar referred to

in the song lived in the reigns of Charles II., James II., William III., Anne, and George I.

Vicars Apostolic (*of England*). Catholic dignitaries appointed by the Pope over the 'Vicariates' (*q.v.*).

Vicar'iates (4 syl.). Divisions of England into Catholic governments, presided over by 'Vicars Apostolic.' From the revolution of 1688 up to 1840 there were four vicariates; but Gregory XVI. doubled the number. They were the London, the Western, the Eastern, the Central, the Welsh, the Lancastrian, the York, and the Northern districts. In 1850 Pius IX. re-established in England the regular episcopal system of the Church of Rome; and since then the converts from the Anglican to the Roman rite have been very numerous indeed, especially in the upper classes of society. It looks very much as if Catholicism was about to become dominant in England again.

What else can be expected with the wretched organisation of the Anglican Church ? No authority to appeal to, powerless bishops, curates without any certain promotion, vicars taxed far higher than the squirarchy, and their widows virtually turned out of house and home the moment their husbands cease to breathe. It is a most pitiful system, hardly possible to be worse.

Vice-Chancellor (*The*). In our universities. The deputy of the chancellor, by whom, in Oxford, he is chosen annually from the heads of the colleges; but in Cambridge he is chosen annually by the Senate from two heads of colleges nominated by the council. In 1855 the stipend of the vice-chancellor, at Oxford, was fixed at 600*l.* a year from the university chest. At Oxford it has been usual of late to hold the office for four years, and the first vice-chancellor was William Farrendon (1400–1403). In Cambridge the office is an annual one.

In Cambridge the vice-chancellor is elected Nov. 1 or 3, and enters on his functions Jan. 1) or 11.

Victims of the Unstamped (*The*). Persons imprisoned or heavily fined for publishing unstamped newspapers. The duty was 4*d.* on each paper, and the Government stamp was in red, at one corner of each sheet. Stamp abolished 1855.

The prisons of London and the provincial towns of Manchester, Liverpool, Leeds, Hull, Birmingham, Bristol, Edinburgh, and Glasgow were seldom untenanted by some of the persons popularly called the 'Victims of the Unstamped.' Large numbers of women and very young persons were put in prison for selling by retail papers without a stamp.—HOWITT, *History of England*, year 1841, p. 518.

Victor (*Canons Regular of St.*), 1113. Established in Paris by Guillaume de Champeaux. *See* 'Victorins.'

Victor of a Hundred Battles (*The*). Napoleon the Great (born 1768, emperor 1804–1815, died 1821).

Victoria. Queen of Great Britain and Ireland, and Empress of India. The 5th sovereign of the house of Hanover. Born 24 May, 1819, began to reign 20 June, 1837. Proclaimed Empress of India 1 January, 1877.

Father: Edward duke of Kent, 4th son of George III.; *Mother*: Louisa Victoria of Saxe-Coburg; *Consort*: Albert of Saxe-Coburg-Gotha; *Children*: 1. Victoria, the princess royal (who married Frederick William, crown prince of Prussia); 2. Albert Edward, prince of Wales (who married Alexandra of Denmark); 3. Alice Maud (who married Louis of Hesse-Darmstadt), she died 1878; 4. Alfred duke of Edinburgh (who married Marie-Alexandrovna of Russia); 5. Lelēna (who married Christian of Schleswig-Holstein); 6. Louise (who married the Marquis of Lorne); 7. Arthur duke of Connaught (who married Louise Margaret, daughter of Prince Frederick Charles of Prussia); 8. Leopold duke of Albany (who married Helen, daughter of the Prince of Waldeck), died 1884; 9. Beatrice (who married Henry Maurice of Battenberg).

Style: Victoria, by the Grace of God, of the United Kingdom of Great Britain and Ireland, Queen, Defender of the Faith, Empress of India [Kaisar-i-Hind]. Or Victoria, Dei Gratia, Britanniarum Regina, Fid. Def. [Empress of India is added only to documents which extend to India.]

** The Queen Victoria is lineally descended from Egbert. Omitting the Normans, we come to Henry II., whose mother was Maud wife of Geoffrey Plantagenet. Maud's mother was Matilda wife of Henry I. of England. Matilda's mother was Margaret wife of Malcolm III. of Scotland. Margaret's father was Prince Edward, son of Edmund. King Edmund was son of Ethelred, Ethelred of Edgar, Edgar of Edmund, Edmund of Edward the Elder, Edward the Elder of Alfred, Alfred of Ethelwolf, and Ethelwolf of EGBERT.

From Henry II. the Plantagenets

continued to the Tudors. Henry VII. descended from John of Gaunt, 4th son of Edward III., and he married Elizabeth of York, daughter of Edward IV. Henry VII.'s daughter Margaret married James IV. of Scotland, and their son was James V. of Scotland. The daughter of James V. was Mary Queen of Scots, whose son was James I. of England. Elizabeth, daughter of James I., married Frederick king of Bohemia, whose daughter Sophia was the wife of Ernest Augustus duke of Brunswick. And their son was George I.

Victoria and Albert (*Royal Order of*). Instituted 1862. In 1878 was instituted 'The Imperial Order of the Crown of India.'

Victoria Cross (*The*), 19 Jan., 1856. A Maltese cross of bronze, with the inscription FOR VALOUR. It is given to any person who has performed an act of distinguished courage, such as rescuing from fire or water, acts of great bravery in battle, and so on. V.C.

Victorieux (*Le*). Charles VII. of France (1403, 1422–1461). So called because in his reign the English lost all their possessions in France except Calais. He won the battle of Gravelle in 1423, and of Montarges in 1427, and, by the aid of Joan of Arc raised the siege of Orleans in 1429; he took Metz, conquered the English at Formigni, got possession of Normandy and Guienne, and in 1451 drove the English out of France, leaving only Calais in their power.

Victorins (*The*), or ' Canons of St. Victor,' 1113, Paris; especially those of them who accepted and extended the mystical views of Hugo of St. Victor. St. Victor contended that the objects of religious contemplation are partly above reason and partly contrary to reason (*e.g.* the dogma of the Trinity). The Victorins were opposed to dialectical theology.

Victory of Victories (*The*). So the great battle of Nehavend (A.D. 637) is called by the Arabs. In this battle Yzdegerd III. king of Persia was defeated and afterwards murdered by the Saracens.

Vienna Conference (*The*). I. 6 Jan.–21 April, 1853. Between

Great Britain, France, Austria, and Prussia, on a device of Count Buol, chief minister of Austria, to prevent war with Russia. Great Britain and France could not agree to Count Buol's plan, and the conference fell through. *See* 'Vienna Note.'

II. in 1855. Between Austria, Great Britain, France, and Russia, for the purpose of bringing to an end the Crimēan war. It came to nothing.

Vienna (*Congress of*), from 1 Oct., 1814, to March, 1815, of the allied princes, to distribute the spoils of the French empire, after the banishment of Napoleon I. to Elba. It was found impossible to satisfy the greed of the different powers, and probably war would have broken out between the allies had they not been startled by the alarming news that Napoleon had escaped from Elba and was gathering around him the best strength of France (7 March, 1815).

In this congress England was represented by Lord Castlereagh, Russia by Czar Alexander, Austria by Prince Metternich, Prussia by Baron Hardenberg, and France by Prince Talleyrand.

It was arranged to give to England the Cape of Good Hope, the Mauritius, Malta, and Corfu; to Russia was assigned Finland and Poland; to Austria was assigned Lombardy and the Venetian States; to Prussia was allotted Saxony, Franconia, and Swedish Pomerania; to the Archduke Ferdinand was allotted Tuscany; to the King of Sardinia was allotted Genoa; to Marie Louise, wife of Napoleon, was assigned Parma and Placentia; to Sweden was assigned Norway: and to Ferdinand IV. of the Bourbon line was allotted the Two Sicilies.

Vienna (*Treaties of*). The treaties of Vienna are numerous. The three subjoined are the most important :—

I. 18 Nov., 1738, which gave Lorraine to France after the death of Stanislaus, Tuscany to Francis husband of Maria Theresa, and Naples to Don Carlos. It concluded the War of the Polish Succession (*q.v.*).

II. 14 Oct., 1809, which put an end to the war carried on by the fifth coalition against Napoleon I. By this treaty the emperor of Germany ceded the Tyrol and Dalmatia to France, and agreed to adopt the 'Continental System,' *i.e.* to hold no commercial intercourse with Great Britain.

III. 9 June, 1815, in which the boundaries of France were defined by the allied powers of Europe.

The other treaties of Vienna were :—
27 May, 1657. An alliance between the kaiser, Poland, and Denmark, against Sweden.
16 March, 1731. An alliance between the kaiser, Great Britain, and Holland, to guarantee the **Pragmatic Sanction.**

8 Oct., 1735. To agree upon preliminaries of peace between France and Germany.
20 June, 1800. To agree upon subsidies between Austria and Great Britain.
23 March, 1815. Between Great Britain, Austria, Russia, and Prussia, confirming the Treaty of Chaumont and effecting the union of Holland and Belgium.
31 May, 1815. Between the king of the Netherlands, Great Britain, Austria, Russia, and Prussia, agreeing to the enlargement of Dutch territories, and vesting the sovereignty of the Netherlands in the House of Orange.
4 June, 1815. Between Denmark and Prussia, for the cession of Swedish Pomerania and Rügen to Prussia in exchange for Lauenburg.
2 Dec., 1854. A treaty of alliance between Great Britain, France, and Austria.
30 Nov., 18 4. Between Denmark, Prussia, and Austria, for the cession of the duchies of Schleswig-Holstein to the allies.
11 Oct., 1866. A treaty of peace between Austria and Prussia.

Vienna Note (*The*), 1853. A scheme of Count Buol to prevent war with Russia. It proposed a compromise between the czar and the sultan. Russia claimed a protectorate over the Christian subjects of Turkey. This, of course, the sultan could not and would not concede. Count Buol suggested that the Christian subjects should have protection not only as Ottoman subjects, but over and above that as Christians.

The Vienna Note was as huge a diplomatic blunder as could possibly have been devised. 'Such a concession [wrote Lord Stratford 20 Aug.] would leave Russia nothing to desire as to the means of exercising a powerful influence on all the concerns of the Greek clergy, and of interfering on behalf of the Greek laity, subjects of the Porte.'—HOWITT, *Hist. of Eng.* (year 1853, p. 153).

Vigilance Society (*The*), 1885. A secret Irish society, similar to the Moonlighters, Fenians, &c., for the murder, mutilation, and destruction of the property of those who refused to obey the league. *See* p. 455, 'Irish Associations.'

Vigilants (*The*). Irish rebels similar to the Invincibles. *See* p. 455, 'Irish Invincibles.'

Vigin'ti-virat of Rome. The office of the Vigin'tivirs or Committee of Twenty. They had charge of the public ways, the minting of money, and the prisons. It was a most honourable office.

Villafranca, in Italy (*Treaty of*), 11 July, 1859. Between Francis Joseph emperor of Austria and Napoleon III. emperor of the French, for the creation of the Italian Confederation and the cession of Lombardy. Austria ceded Lombardy to France, and France gave it to Sardinia. Lombardy and Sardinia soon afterwards formed parts of the kingdom of Italy (14 March, 1861).

Villeins in Gross. Villeins were farm labourers and domestic servants, not exactly slaves nor yet exactly freemen, but something between the two. 'Villeins in Gross' were, for the most part, domestic servants, who moved from place to place with their master and his family. See 'Villeins Regardant.'

Villeins Regardant. Farm labourers who could not be shifted from place to place, but had a fixed habitation. If a master died or his tenement changed hands from any other cause the villeins remained, like other fixtures, with the new lord.

'Villeins in Gross' were those attached to the person of the lord, and, like personal property, might be sold or otherwise transferred. 'Villeins Regardant' were attached to the land, and were fixtures.

Vinegar Bible (*The*), 1617, Clarendon Press. In this Bible the 'Parable of the Vineyard' was printed the 'Parable of the Vinegar.' See p. 90, 'Bibles.'

Vinegar Hill. An eminence near the town of Enniscorthy in Ireland, famous for being a station of the rebels called 'White Boys' and 'Peep o' Day Boys,' &c. Here was fought what is called the 'Battle of Vinegar Hill' in 1798.

Vinerian Professorship (*The*) of English law, in the University of Oxford, 1758. Founded by Charles Viner. The professor is called the 'Vinerian Reader.'

Vinerian Scholarships. Three for law. Of the value of 80*l.* a year for three years. Founded in the University of Oxford by Charles Viner in 1755.

Vinzaglio (*Battle of*), 30 May, 1859, in which the allied army led by Victor Emmanuel and Napoleon III. defeated 200,000 Austrians. The honour of this day was due to General Cialdini.

Violets, worn by partisans of the French empire in compliment to Napoleon I. He was called 'Father Violet,' because he said, when leaving France for Elba, 'I will return with the violets.' Those partisans who were in the secret of his return wore a violet on their breasts, and always toasted Napoleon as 'Caporal la Violette.' Prints containing profiles of Napoleon and Maria Louisa in two violets were common in 1814, and

beneath was written 'En printemps il reviendra.' In 1815 a popular song refers to Napoleon as 'Le père de la Violette.'

Farewell to thee, France; but when liberty rallies
 Once more in thy regions, remember me then—
The violet still grows in the depth of thy valleys,
 Though withered, thy tear will unfold it again.
                                                        BYRON.

Violets (*The Day of the*), 1 March, 1815. The day when Napoleon I., having escaped from Elba, landed at Cannes, and with 800 soldiers began his march towards Paris.

Virgil of the race of Scota (*The*). Flann MacLonan, 'chief poet of all Ireland' (ninth cent.).

It must not be forgotten that Scota is Ireland. North Britain was called Albany till the 12th cent.

Virgin City (*A*), or 'Maiden City.' One which has never changed masters or been conquered. Bayonne, in France, boasts of being a 'Virgin City.' Metz was a 'Maiden Fortress' before it fell into the hands of the Germans in the Franco-German War, 1870.

Virgin Mary's Guard (*The*). The Corps Ecossais, or 'Gardes du Corps du Roi,' organised in 1448 by Charles VII. of France. Louis XI. made the Virgin Mary their colonel. Disbanded in 1830. See 'Gardes du Corps du Roi.'

Virgins (*The Eleven Thousand*). Ursul [Ursŭla], or Hörsel, in Suabia, means the moon, and her eleven thousand virgins are the stars. But in Cologne Cathedral is shown a pile of bones of all sorts, men, women, and children, taken from an old Roman cemetery, across which the wall of Cologne ran. These bones are exhibited as the veritable bones of St. Ursula and her eleven thousand virgin companions, said to have fallen martyrs to the Huns.

Virgins offered to dragons. When, in 786, Abdalrahman of Cordŏva entered the Asturias in the reign of Mauregato, he utterly defeated his army, and would make peace only on condition of an annual tribute of 100 Spanish virgins. Alfonso II., 'the Chaste,' has the credit of compelling the Moors to relinquish this tribute, about 800.

Virgins of the Shield. In Danish *Skioldmeyar*, female warriors of ancient Denmark.

Virginia (U.S. America), so called, in 1584, by Sir Walter Raleigh in compliment to the ' Virgin ' queen Elizabeth. The inhabitants are nicknamed *Beadies*.

Viri Galilæi. The north summit of the Mount of Olives, about three furlongs from the middle summit, from which Christ ascended. So called from the words of the angels, ' Ye men of Galilee.'
It is also called Galilee. *See Matt.* xxviii. 16.

Virtuous Genevese (*The*). Jacques Necker, the French statesman and financier (1732-1804).

Visigoths (*The*). The Western Goths, who came from Scandinavia, and settled in Mœsia, A.D. 376. They established themselves in Gaul, A.D. 412, and, passing into Spain, founded a kingdom there in 414, which was overthrown by the Moors in 712. The names of the kings were—

Ataulfus ..	... to 414	Gundemar	... 610-612
Wallia	... 415-418	Sisebut ...	... 612-620
Theodorês	... 418- ?	Recaréd II.	... 620-621
Theudis ..	... 531-548	Suintella	... 621-631
Theudisele	548-550	Sisenand	... 631-636
Agila (at Merida)	550-556	Tulca ...	... 636-642
Atharagild	556-567	Chindasvindé	642-649
(*Toledo his capital*)		Recesvindé	... 649-672
Liuva (at Narbonne)...	... 567-568	Wamba ...	... 672-680
		Ervigé ...	... 680-687
Leovigild	... 568-572	Egiza ...	... 687-701
Recaréd...	... 572-586	Witiza ...	... 701-710
Liuva II.	... 586-603	Roderic ...	... 710-711
Vitteric ...	... 603-610		

Visitandines (4 syl.), or ' Religieuses de la Visitation,' 1610. An order of females instituted by St. Francis of Sales and the Baroness of Chantal, in commemoration of the visitation of the Virgin Mary. They wore a black dress and a silver cross.

Visitation (*The*), or ' Festum Visitationis,' 2 July, instituted 1263 in commemoration of Mary's visit to her cousin Elizabeth (*Luke* i. 39-56). The ' Congregation of the Visitation ' was founded in 1610 by the Baroness de Chantal at Annecy, and the order was confirmed by Urban VIII. in 1626.

Vitry Disaster (*The*), 1143. Louis VII. (le Jeune) persuaded the Comte de Vermandois to divorce his wife and marry the princess (Louis's sister). The Comte de Champagne, father of the divorced countess, to resent this interference, stirred up a rebellion against the king, and Louis, to punish the revolt, set fire to the castle of Vitry. The flames spread to the town. The inhabitants fled to the church, which also caught fire, and 1,300 persons were burnt to death. The king,

horrified by the shrieks of the sufferers, gave up the war, and made peace with the count.

Vizier of Sultan Selim. The greatest curse which a Turk can utter against a foe is this, ' May you be vizier of Sultan Selim ! ' Few of his viziers lived more than a month (1512-1519).

Volpone (3 syl.), 1709. So Dr. Sacheverell called Lord Godolphin in his two sermons, one at Derby and another in St. Paul's, London. For this offence he was brought to trial before the Lords, and suspended for three years. The mob took the doctor's side, and shouted ' High Church and Sacheverell ! ' and Queen Anne gave him the living of St. Andrew's, Holborn. The first sermon he preached there was sold for 100*l.*, and 40,000 copies were sold in a few days.
' Volpone ' is the title of a comedy by Ben Jonson. It means ' old fox.'

Voltaire. His name was Marie François Arouet. He was confined in the Bastille for satirising the Duke of Orleans, and on his release from prison assumed the name of Voltaire from a small property left him by his mother. He retired to Ferney, a little village near Geneva. At one time he lived for fifteen years with Madame du Châtelet at Cirey, in Champagne, a lady of fortune, the wife of a marquis, and here he composed his best works. He set up *reason* as the guide and rule of everything, and whatever could not be squared with human reason he rejected in religion and politics.

Voltaire of Germany (*The*). I. Christoph Martin Wieland (1733-1813), author of ' Oberon ' and the romance of ' Agathon.'
II. Johann Wolfgang von Göthe (1749-1838), also called ' The German Voltaire.'
VOLTAIRE (*The Polish*). Ignatius Krasicki (1774-1801).
VOLTAIRE (*The Russian*). Alexander P. Sumorokof (1727-1777).

Voluntary Controversy (*The*), 1834, in Scotland. One of the most intensely pronounced controversies that Scotland ever witnessed. The question was this : Is a congregation to exercise the right of giving a ' call ' or invitation to its pastor, or has the kirk the right of presenting any minister it thinks proper ? The question was tried on the celebrated

'Auchterarder Case' (*q.v.*), and terminated in the great schism of the Free Church.

Volunteers (*The*), 1852. The Victorian movement sprang into existence, and Dr. J. C. Buckuill of Exeter was the originator. The corps first mustered in uniform 6 Oct., 1852, when the oath of allegiance was taken. Consolidated 21 July, 1863, by Act 26, 27 Vict. c. 65, which Act was amended 9 Aug., 1869.
Rifle corps organised 1859.

Volunteers as volunteers have no regimental colours, but several of the Volunteer corps have had special colours presented to them by persons interested in the movement. Thus the Duchess of Gloucester and her daughter Sophia presented colours to the Kensington Volunteers.

First raised in Great Britain March, 1794; again in the spring 1803. George III. reviewed them in Hyde Park, 26 and 28 Oct., 1803.

Vordingborg (*Peace of*), 1435, terminating the long war of twenty-six years between the counts of Holstein and the Hanse Towns. By this treaty it was stipulated that the Hanse republics should continue to enjoy all their immunities in the Sound and in the harbours of the three united kingdoms of Scandinavia; and that Adolphus count of Holstein should be secured in the possession of the duchy of Sleswig during his life and his heirs two years after.

Votaries of Celestial Reason (*The*), or Tien-le, a brotherhood in China during the reign of Kea-king (1796–1820). They broke into the palace and kept possession of it for several days.

Vote of Non-address (*The*), 1647. After the escape of Charles I. from Holmby House, a vote was passed in both houses that no further application or addresses to the king should be permitted under the penalty of high treason, and that neither the House of Lords nor House of Commons should receive from him any letter or message.

The vote of non-address amounted to a declaration that all attempts at reconciliation were at an end, and that the Independents meant to proceed to put the doctrines of the army in force, and put the king to death.—Howitt, *Hist. of Engl.* (Charles I., chap. vi. p. 290).

Votive Mass. 'Missa Votiva,' a mass 'quæ ex proprio voto dicitur.' *See* p. 565, ' Mass.'

Vow of the Swan (*The*), or Vow of the *peacock, heron, pheasant*, or some other bird. A fantastic vow made during some banquet in Mid-Lent to perform some feat during the year. The bird, profusely ornamented, was brought into the banquet-room in great ceremony, a herald trumpeted its approach, and a body of knights, squires, and pages attended it. The person who made the vow stood up, laid his hand on the bird, and vowed before the year was out to perform some feat in honour of the bird and some lady.

10 Feb., 1306, Edward I., then an old man, rising at the royal board, swore on the dish before him (*a swan*) to avenge on Scotland the murder of John Comyn by Robert Bruce.
Edward III. said, 'Hey! the White Swan! By God's soul I am thy man!'
Henry V. vowed in a similar manner to traverse France from sea to sea with flying banners.

Vulgate (*The*). A Latin version of the Scriptures by Jerome, the third of the Latin Fathers (*q.v.*), sanctioned by the Council of Trent. It was translated from the Hebrew, and received the approval of Gregory the Great. *See* p. 801, ' Scriptures.'

There was a 'New Latin Version' executed by Jerome, 390–405. Wiclif rendered it into English, 1324–1384. *See* ' Bibles.'

There was an earlier version called 'the Itala,' of which some few fragments remain. Jerome in the 4th cent. revised parts of the *Itala*, but his MSS. are lost. The Vulgate is quite a new translation.

Waddington Scholarship. Classics. For undergraduates in the University of Cambridge, tenable for five years. It is the interest of 3,000*l.* in the 3 per cent. consolidated Bank annuities. Founded by Miss Waddington and her sister in memory of their two brothers, 1870.

Wadham College, Oxford, 1609. Founded by Nicholas Wadham of Maryfield, Somersetshire. The headmaster is called the ' Warden.'

Wager of Battle. In this ordeal the challenger faced the west; the one challenged faced the east. If the defeated party craved his life he was a craven, but had his life spared.

Wages in England.

			d.
1352, a thresher	...	a dåy	1
reaper	...	,,	2 to 3*d.*, not less than 3*d.* in 1445.
master carpenter		,,	3, advanced to 5*d.* in 1445.

1352, a carpenter	... a day	*d.* 2, advanced to 4*d.* in 1445.
master mason bricklayer's ⎱ labourer ⎰	... ,, ...	4 1½, bricklayer, 4*d.* in 1445.
1568, farm labourer	... ,,	4
1620, ,, ,,	... ,,	4½
1632, ,, ,,	... ,,	6
1647, ,, ,,	... ,,	10
1662, ,, ,,	... ,,	6
1688, ,, ,,	... ,,	8
1698, ,, ,,	... ,,	8
1716, ,, ,,	... ,,	9
1740, ,, ,,	... ,,	10
1760, ,, ,,	... ,,	12
1788, ,, ,,	... ,,	16
1827, ,, ,,	... ,,	from 9*s.* to 15*s.* a week.
1890, ,, ,,	... ,,	,, 12*s.* to 15*s.* ,,

Wages Movement (*The*), 1854. A combination of artizans for a sliding scale of wages equal to a tenth of the profit of their production. The men went out on strike only in one or two places at a time, and those employed subscribed to support those on strike. The woollen manufacturers of Preston and Burnley led the way. The movement came to an untimely end in April 1854. The loss to workmen was 500,000*l.*, and to masters many millions.

Wahab'ites (3 syl.), or 'Wahabbees,' or 'Wah'abees,' 1759. Reformed Moslems, founded by the son of Abd-el Wahab, and dominant over the greater part of Arabia. They are firm believers in the Koran, and want to bring back the faithful to the primitive precepts and practices of the first kalifs. They deny the sacred character of Imaums, advocate the perfect equality of man, and call their muftis 'brothers.' These strictest and straitest of the Moslem sects are great brigands and pirates.

Mohammed Abd-el Wahab was born in Arabia 1696, and died about 1764. He preached universal toleration, and taught that Moses, Christ, and Mahomet were three gifted men who taught the will of God, and that the faiths of all three are reconcilable.

Waits. Musical serenaders, who play or sing between midnight and four or five in the morning about Christmas time, and call afterwards on the inhabitants for a Christmas-box. They used to wish greeting to the master, mistress, children, and all, before parting. The thing has now dwindled down to a carol or popular tune or two. Originally they were musical watchmen. Rymer, in the 'Fœdera,' tells us they 'piped the watch nightly in the king's court from Michaelmas to Shrove Thursday, and to make the bon gayte at every chamber-door and office, for fear of pyckeres and pillers.'

Wakes and **Lyke-wakes.** These are very different things. A *lyke* or *liche* wake is a watching of a dead body (Ang.-Sax. *lic*) all night by the friends and neighbours of the deceased. It used to be a scene of revelry and mourning, the object being to watch the body from being interfered with by evil spirits. The other 'wake' is about equal to 'vigil,' and every church had its wake on the anniversary of the saint. A religious service was given, but, as the crowd became great, hawkers and minstrels assembled, and the wake became a fair, held in the churchyard. In 1285 Edward I. forbade fairs to be held in churchyards, but the practice continued to the Reformation.

Walburgis. *See* 'Walpurgis.'

Wal'cheren Expedition (*The*), 1809. Under the charge of the Earl of Chatham and Sir Richard Strachan. The design was to destroy the French fleet in the Scheldt and take Antwerp; but the expedition was so ill-planned and executed that only the fortress of Flushing was taken and the isle of Walcheren. When the British seamen landed in the pestilential marshes of Walcheren they died by thousands. Napoleon said we might as well 'have thrown our men into the sea as land them at Walcheren.'

It was a magnificent fleet, consisting of 37 men-of-war, 23 frigates, 115 sloops, &c., and carrying 41,000 men. The Earl of Chatham resigned to prevent being brought before a court-martial.

.*.* Strachan, pronounce *Strawn.*

Waldemar (*Knights of St.*), 1783. A Russian order conferred on both military men and civilians for merit. The ribbon is red, edged with black.

Waldenses (*The*), or 'Vaudois,' 9th cent. By Mosheim traced to Peter Waldo of Lyons, who died 1197; but this is an error, as they are mentioned as early as 1100, and had a regular confession of faith in 1120. They seem to have been early reformers dwelling in the valleys of the Cottian Alps, called *Vaux,* and the inhabitants *Vaudois*—in Latin *Vallenses.* These were the ancient 'Subalpini.' The Lyonists or 'Poor Men of Lyons' seem to have followed in the same footsteps, and therefore the two are very often confounded. The Waldenses, the Wiclifites, and the Lutherans were very similar in their reforms. Their original limits were the districts of Angrogna, Villaro, Bobbio, and Rorata. *See* 'Lyonists.'

They were condemned by the Council of the Lateran in 1179, and Innocent VIII. in 1487 enjoined their extirpation. The crusade included the Waldenses and Lyonists (or Poor Men of Lyons) in one general slaughter. The similarity of Valdo and Valdenses led to the mistake, but the Waldenses were the followers of Claudius of Turin, who died 839—that is, 858 years before the death of Waldo.

The Waldenses or Valdenses were also called : Apostolicians (in the 12th cent.), Arnaldists, Arnoldists, Bagnolens, Cathäri (after the 12th cent.), Consoläti, Good Men (in Germany), Insabbates, Lionists, Montani, Passagins, Patarins or Paterins, Perfecti, Petrobrusians, Piphles (in Flanders), Poor Men of Lyons, Poplicans, Purists, Texerans or Tesserands (in some parts of France), Ultramontanes, Vaudois (in France), Xabatatenses. *See each of these words.*

A Miss Jane Waldo, of Clapham and Hever Castle, daughter of Sir Timothy Waldo, died 1841, aged ninety-six. This was the last of the direct descendants of Peter Waldo of Lyons.

Wales (*The Statute of*), 12 Edw. I., A.D. 1284, which abolished the most barbarous of the Welsh customs, established guilds, introduced English jurisprudence, and divided the land into shires and hundreds after the English model.

Walker Exhibition (*John Lucas*), for discoveries in pathology. Value 50*l.* a year ; in the University of Cambridge. Founded by John Lucas Walker, 1887.

Walker Studentship (*John Lucas*). Original research in pathology. It may be held by either sex, and not necessarily a member of the University. Value 200*l.* a year, tenable for three years, and the holder eligible for re-election for two more years. Founded in the University of Cambridge by John Lucas Walker, 1887.

Wall of Seve'rus, the Roman emperor, extending from the German Ocean to the Solway Firth. This was built because the emperor, when he visited Britain A.D. 208, viewed with alarm the enormous encroachment of the Scots southwards. This emperor died at York in 211, aged sixty-six.

The Wall of Sevērus was for the most part, but not invariably, parallel with Hadrian's rampart. It was further north, and extended somewhat further at each end.

Wallace of Switzerland (*The*). Andreas Hofer, the Tyrolese patriot (1767–1810). He was a man of gigantic stature and strength ; brave as a lion, but gentle as a lamb.

Wallace of Wales (*The*). Owen Glendower (1350–1415).

Wallach Rebellion (*The*). In Hungarian history, 1784. The Wallachs are a people of Hungary, but chiefly of Wallachia in Roumania. These insurgents, led by Hora and Kloska, assassinated the government commissioners, destroyed six villages and 182 private houses, killed 4,000 Hungarians, and did other acts of violence before they could be put down.

Wallingford, in Berkshire (*Treaty of*), 7 Nov., 1153. Between Stephen king of England and Henry (afterwards Henry II.), son of Matilda, 'the Lady of England.' Henry, by the death of his father, having succeeded to Normandy and Anjou, and holding Aquitaine in right of his wife (Eleanor of Poitou), was invited by the archbishop of Canterbury to make his appearance in England. On his arrival the treaty of Wallingford was agreed to by the rival claimants. The castles were to be razed, the crown lands resumed, the foreign mercenaries dismissed, Stephen to continue on the throne during life, and Henry to succeed as his heir. Stephen died within twelve months of this treaty.

Walloons (*The*). The French-speaking inhabitants of Artois, Hainault, Namur, Luxemburg, Flanders, and Brabant. These six provinces constituted Catholic Netherlands. The seven united provinces constituted Protestant Netherlands.

There are speakers of the Walloon dialect of French in Belgium, Luxembourg, the Netherlands, and Germany.

Walpurgis Night. The eve of May-day, when the old pagan witch-world was supposed to hold high revelry under its chief on certain high places. The Brocken, in Germany, was an especially favourite spot for these revelries. Walpurgis was a female saint concerned in the introduction of Christianity into Germany.

Walpurgis or Walburgis was the daughter of St. Richard, king of the West Saxons, and was educated in the monastery of Wimborne in Dorsetshire. She was sent to Germany in 752 to assist in the conversion of the Germans, and in 754 was made abbess of Heidenheim. She died 25 Feb., 779, and the day of her death is held in her honour.

> Already do I feel the power,
> The fun and frolic of the hour ;
> The advent of Walpurgis Night
> Bids every limb thrill with delight.
> Another night, another day,
> And then the glorious First of May.
>   GOETHE, *Faust* (Anster).

Walter the Pennyless. 'Gautier sans avoir' of Burgundy, joint leader of the First Crusade with Peter the Hermit in 1096.

Wapentake. A term in Yorkshire similar to *ward* or *hundred*. The word means weapon-touch, and refers to the vassals touching the spear of their feudal lord in token of homage. The word passed from the assembly to denote the district tenanted by the vassals.

Wappenschaws. The feudal array of a county, when each crown-vassal was required to appear with such muster of men and armour as he was bound to make by his fief, under high penalties.

War Cries.

I. Of ENGLAND, in the Middle Ages, 'St. George!'

  ,, FRANCE, 'Montjoye St. Denis!' [pronounce *Sahn Dnee*]. Montjoye referred to the little mounds surmounted with a cross between Paris and St. Denis, either to guide travellers or to console the pious wayfarer. In the French empire it was *Vive l'Empereur!*

  ,, GERMANY, during the long contention between the Dukes of Bavaria and the House of Hohenstauffen, it was *Guelf* and *Ghibelline! See* p. 394.

  ,, SCOTLAND, it was frequently the name of some clan or chief, as *A Douglas! A Home!*

  ,, SPAIN, 'St. Jago! [St. James] and close, Spain!' Cervantes says it was 'St. Jago! and charge, Spain!' or 'Santiagomata moros!' (II. ii. 4.)

> Mount, chivalrous hidalgo! Not in vain
> Revive the cry, 'St. Jago! and close, Spain!'
>   BYRON, *Age of Bronze*, vii.

  ,, the IRISH, 'Aboo!'

  ,, the WELSH, 'Alleluia!'

> Loud shrieks of 'Alleluia!' blended with those of 'Out! Out! [*Ouct! Ouct!*] Holy Cross.'—LORD LYTTON, *Harold*.

II. Of the BOURBONS, the word 'Bourbon!'

  ,, the CRUSADERS, 'Dieu le veut!' Not of the First Crusade.

Of the Counts of HAINAULT, 'Hainault the Noble!'

  ,, JEHOSHAPHAT, in his war against Ammon, Moab, and Seir, 'Praise the Lord, for His mercy endureth for ever!' (2 Chron. xx. 21.)

  ,, the Dukes of MILAN, 'Milan the Valiant!'

  ,, the Lords of MONTMORENCY, 'Dieu aide au premier Chrétien!'

III. In battle of MARKFELD, 1278. Of the Bohemians, 'Praga!' of the Germans, 'Christ!'

  ,, battle of NASEBY, 1645. Of the Royalists, 'God and Queen Mary!' of the Parliamentarians, 'God our strength!'

  ,, battle of PHARSALIA, B.C. 48. Of Pompey, 'Herculês Invictus!' of Cæsar, 'Venus Victrix!'

At *Senlac* the English had two war cries, 'God Almighty!' and 'Holy Cross!' The latter was the cry of Harold's own men, and referred to Waltham Cross, which he held in special reverence. The Norman shout was 'Dieu aidois à nos!' (*God help us!*).

Of Capobianco, leader of the Carbonâri, it was 'Vengeance for the Lamb torn by the Wolf!'

Nelson's *mot* at the battle of the Nile was 'Victory or Westminster Abbey.' At Trafalgar it was 'England expects that every man will do his duty.'

Several others are given *in loco.*

War Poet (*The*). G. H. Boker, rendered famous in the American antislavery war. *See* p. 100, 'Black Regiment.'

War Songs (*National*).

AUSTRIAN, Haydn's *Hymn to the Emperor.*

BELGIAN, the patriotic *Brabançonne.*

DANISH, the *Song of Danebrog.* The danebrog is the flag with a white cross which fell from heaven in the 13th cent. at the prayer of Waldemar II., and which ensured him the victory.

ENGLISH, *Rule Britannia.* Words by Thomson, music by Handel.

FRENCH (ancient), the *Chanson de Roland.*

FRENCH (modern), the *Marseillaise* and the *Chant du Départ.*

GERMAN (modern), Arndt's *Des Deutschen Vaterland* and *Heil Dir im Sieges-*

kranz, Watch on the Rhine, Sword-song of Körner, &c.

HUNGARIAN, the *Rakoczy March*.

ITALIAN, Garibaldi's warlike hymn, composed by Mercantino, and Godfredo Mameli's *Italian brethren, Italy has awaked!*

RUSSIAN, *God protect the Czar!*

SCOTCH Jacobite Songs: *The king shall enjoy his own again*, and *When the king comes o'er the water*. The *Lilli-bulero* of 1688 created a most marvellous furore.

War in Algeria (*The*), 1827–1847. France owed two Jewish merchants of Algiers 100,000*l.*, the balance due for the Egyptian expedition. Hussein dey of Algiers pressed for payment, and asked the French consul why his master did not reply to the letter sent. The consul insolently replied, 'The king of France holds no correspondence with the dey of Algiers.' Whereupon the dey struck him on the face. This insult could not be overlooked, and war ensued, which ended in France taking Algeria, and annexing it to France.

War of Calmar (*The*), 1611–1613. This war was carried on between Christian IV. king of Denmark and Charles IX. of Sweden, and, after the death of Charles, with Gustavus Adolphus. The real cause of the war was jealousy with Sweden, which had broken away from the 'Union.' The ostensible reason was interruption of Danish commerce in the ports of the Gulf of Riga. The war consisted in destroying each other's towns and ports. It was brought to an end by the mediation of James I. of England.

War of Candia (*The*), 1667–1668, between the Venetians and the Turks. So relentless was this war, that the expression 'Una Guerra di Candia' became in Venice synonymous with 'war to the knife.' In this terrible siege 30,000 Christians were slain, and although the Turks ultimately became masters of the island, yet they lost in the siege more than 120,000 men.

War of Chiozza (*The*), 1378–1381, between Venice and Genoa. Chiozza was taken by the Genoese under Pietro Doria 16 Aug., 1379, but recovered by the Venetians June 24, 1380. The recovery of Chiozza is one of the most marvellous of all the romances of history.

War of Devolution (*The*). 'Guerre de Dévolution,' 1667. The war proclaimed by Louis XIV. against Spain to enforce his pretension, to a part of the Spanish Netherlands, founded on an old custom of the Netherlands called 'Le droit de Dévolution.' The law was this: 'Les immeubles apportés en mariage par l'un des époux devinssent la propriété des enfants du premier lit lorsque le père ou la mère contractaient un second mariage.' Now Maria Theresa was the daughter of the first wife of Philippe IV., but Carlos II. of the second wife. The war was brought to a close by the Treaty of Aix-la-Chapelle, 2 May, 1668, by which treaty all Flanders was ceded to France.

Louis XIV. married Maria Theresa of Austria, daughter of the King of Spain.

War of Honain (*The*), A.D. 629–632, between Mahomet and the Arabian idolaters of Mecca. So called from the Valley of Honain, where the great conflict was decided. The battle was first lost by Mahomet and then recovered by his uncle Abbas. After this victory and the siege of Fayef, Mecca was lastingly converted to the winning side of the Koran.

War of Independence. I. In *North America* (1774–1782), *see* p. 24, 'American War of Independence.'

II. In *Scotland* (1297–1328). The wars carried on by Wallace and Bruce to liberate Scotland from the English crown. Bands of Scotch insurgents rose against Edward I. before 1297, but in that year the insurrection became general. The independence of Scotland was recognised in a parliament at Northampton, 4 March, 1328.

This recognition was due to the great Scotch victory at Bannockburn (24 June, 1314), the defeat of the army of Edward II. at Biland Abbey, in Yorkshire, in 1328, and a victory over Edward III. in 1827.

III. In *Hungary* (1848–1849). Through the treachery of General Goergey this struggle terminated fatally to the Hungarians. Austria called in the aid of Russia.

War of La Radde (*The*), 1573. A war against the Vaudois by the French. The Vaudois showed so determined a front that the French were glad to come to terms of peace. La Radde was the officer who commanded the French troops.

This was a continuance of the St. Bartholomew slaughter, begun in Aug. 1572.

War of Liberation (*The*). The war between Germany and Napoleon I.

to throw off the French yoke. It began in 1813 and ended in 1815. First Prussia and Russia made an offensive and defensive alliance, 27 Feb., 1813. Sweden joined on 14 March, and on 16 March Prussia declared war on Napoleon. Austria joined the alliance 27 June, and declared war with France on 12 Aug. Bavaria joined 8 Oct. (all in the year 1813). It terminated with the Treaty of Kiel, 14 Jan., 1814, in favour of national independence.

The French won the battles of Lützen, 2 May; Bautzen, 19–21 May; and Dresden, 26, 27 Aug.
They were defeated at Grossbeeran, 23 Aug.; Katzbach, 21 Aug.; Kulm, 29, 30 Aug.; Dennewitz, 6 Sept.; Wartenberg, 2 Oct.; and at Leipsic, 16-19 Oct.

War of Mityle'ne (*The*), B.C. 606, between the Athenians and Mitylenians. Phrynon the Athenian attacked Mitylenê, which was defended by Pittăcos. The two leaders agreed to decide the battle by single combat. Pittacos threw a net over his antagonist, and while Phrynon was struggling to extricate himself, despatched him and won the victory. Mitylēnê (4 syl.).

War of Proclamations (*The*), between General Burgoyne on the side of the English and General Schuyler on the side of the United States.

1. General Burgoyne issued in June a pompous proclamation threatening to punish with the utmost severity those who refused to side with the British government.

2. At Skenesborough, in July, he issued a second proclamation summoning the people to send deputies to deliberate on the measures to be adopted to save from destruction those who had not yet conformed to his former proclamation.

3. General Schuyler issued a counter-proclamation assuring the people they would be accounted traitors if they obeyed the proclamations of General Burgoyne.

War of Schmalkald (*The*), 1547, by the Kaiser against the 'Schmalkaldic League' (*q.v.*), under a plea made to the pope of extirpating heresy, and to the Germans of putting down rebellion. The real object of the war was the lust of dominion. The Protestant princes, alive to the danger of this alliance between kaiser and pope, assembled at Ratisbon and determined on resistance, but were overthrown.

War of the Amorous (*The*), or 'The War of the Lovers,' 1577–1578. The seventh religious war of France; so called because it arose out of some scandalous intrigues of the French court. In fact, Catharine de Medicis, in order to break up the Huguenot party, invited many of them to balls and *fêtes*, where she surrounded herself with maids of honour more beautiful and fascinating than moral. Gallantries and intrigues naturally took place. One effect of this was to detach the Duc d'Alençon from the court party and ally him to the reformers.

It is said that the real motive of this change was the hope of marrying the English queen, Elizabeth. He died in 1584.

War of the Austrian Succession (*The*), 1740–1745. On the death of Kaiser Karl VI. the question was who had a right to succeed him. Properly, females could not occupy the throne of Austria; but Karl VI., by a decree called the 'Pragmatic Sanction,' made his only child Maria Theresa his heir. Bavaria, Saxony, Prussia, Sardinia, and Naples all made rival claims, but Karl Albert elector of Bavaria had the best claim, and next Frederick Augustus elector of Saxony. Prussia demanded Silesia, Sardinia demanded Milan, and Spain demanded Bohemia and Hungary. Ultimately the war was left to Bavaria and Prussia; the Elector of Bavaria was crowned kaiser in 1744, lost his electorate, and was kaiser only in name. He died in Jan. 1745. Maria Theresa agreed to restore the electorate of Bavaria to his son Maximilian Joseph, and the elector agreed to give up all claim to the crown of Austria. This being settled, the husband of Maria Theresa was crowned kaiser 4 Oct., 1745 (the same year).

In 1756 broke out the Seven Years' War between Maria Theresa and Frederick II. (the Great) of Prussia.

War of the Bastards (*The*). 'La Guerre des Bâtards,' 1324. A war between Charles IV. of France and Edward II. of England, supported by the Gascons. 'Dite *La Guerre des Bâtards*, parce que les Gascons avaient pour chefs des bâtards de la noblesse.'

War of the Cam'isards (*The*), 1702–1704. The Count de Broglie began it with horrible savagery, but in 1703 he was recalled, and the war was conducted by Marshal de Montrevel.

War of the Giants (*The*), B.C. 1842. The third revolt of the Titans or sons of the earth. These revolters were ultimately overcome by Heräklês (Herculês).

The battle of Marignano, 1515, is called the 'battle of the Giants,' from the great valour displayed by the combatants. It was won by François I.

War of the Mercenaries, B.C. 241-238. A terrible war which Carthage had to sustain in Africa with the mercenaries because they were not paid. It occurred between the first and second Punic Wars, the leaders being Mathos and Spendius. Hamilcar was sent against the insurgents, and massacred some 40,000 entrapped in a defile.

War of the Peasants (*The*), 1525. Waged by the Elector of Saxony and the German princes against the Anabaptists, headed by Munzer, Stubner, Storck, and others. Munzer was taken prisoner and beheaded.

War of the Polish Succession (*The*), 1733-1738. The case was this: On the death of Sobieski king of Poland, in 1674, Frederick elector of Saxony was chosen king. At the death of Frederick, in 1733, two claimants were put forward, Stanislaus, a Pole, and Frederick Augustus elector of Saxony. As Stanislaus was the father-in-law of Louis XV. his claim was backed by France, but Germany took the side of the elector. The war ended in a compromise: Germany gave up Lorraine to Stanislaus, and agreed to exchange Naples and Sicily for Tuscany and Parma. This being done, Frederick Augustus was allowed to keep the throne of Poland.

War of the Rustards (*The*), also called 'The War of the Peasants,' 1525. A rising of the peasants of Alsatia, excited by the Anabaptists. The leader was Erasmus Gerbert of Molsheim. Chased from Alsatia by the Duc de Lorraine, they took refuge in Germany and amalgamated with the Anabaptists.

War of the Sacramentaries (*The*), 1524. The paper war or controversy between the followers of Luther and those of Zwingli, the Swiss reformer, on the subject of the Eucharist. Luther maintained that, though the bread remained bread and the wine remained wine after consecration, yet the body of Christ was transfused into the elements and was taken into the mouth by communicants. Zwingli maintained that no such transfusion took place at all, but that the bread and wine were simply symbols of the body and blood of Christ, well calculated to remind communicants of the sacrifice of Christ and nothing more.

Carlostadt, Œcolampadius, Muncer, Storck, and Martin Bucer sided with Zwingli.

War of the Spanish Succession (*The*), 1700-1714. Carlos II. had no child, and at his death four claimants to the throne of Spain arose—viz. the King of France, the Emperor of Germany, the Elector of Bavaria, and the King of Savoy. The last two retired and left the field to the other two. Louis XIV. was the cousin of Carlos and son-in-law of Philip IV., whose eldest daughter he had married. Carlos had recognised this claim by leaving the crown to Philippe d'Anjou second son of the dauphin, but Louis XIV. by the Treaty of the Pyrenees had renounced all claim to the Spanish crown. Leopold of Germany claimed the crown for his second son Karl, whose mother was also a daughter of Philip IV. War succeeded, and lasted for twelve years. England opposed France, and was joined by Holland, Portugal, Savoy, Brandenburg, and of course Germany.

The French won the battles of *Almanza, Villaviciosa*, and *Denain*; but lost those of Blenheim, Ramillies, Turin, Oudenarde, and Malplaquet. The Treaty of Utrecht left France in possession of Spain.

War of the Three Henris (*The*), 1584-1589—*i.e.* Henri III. of France, Henri of Navarre, and Henri duc de Guise. On the death of the Duc d'Alençon in 1584, Henri of Navarre was leader of the Protestant party in France; whereupon Henri duc de Guise put himself at the head of the Catholic league; Henri III., jealous of both parties, resolved to bring them to obedience. The king was driven from Paris, the Duc de Guise was assassinated, Henri III. was also assassinated, and Henri of Navarre succeeded to the crown of France, under the name and title of Henri IV., but he also was assassinated.

War of the Uscocchi (*The*), or 'Uskoks,' 1592-1617. The Uskoks were pirates who for a century infested the Adriatic. They first settled in Clissa, then removed to Zara, and finally to Segna. They were Dalmatian fugitives who gave sanctuary to the proscribed of all nations, and were both numerous and formidable. By the treaty of Madrid, 16 Sept., 1717, the Venetians and Austrians stipulated to extirpate the Uskoks, and the horde disappeared.

Uskoks means fugitives. The Russian *uskakat*, to run away, is the key to the word.

Wars of Cappel, 1529-1531. *See* p. 143, 'Cappel.'

Wars of the Roses (*The*), 1455-1485. Between the Houses of York (*white*) and Lancaster (the *red* rose). It began with the battle of St. Albans, 23 May, 1455, and ended with the battle of Bosworth Field, 22 Aug., 1483. The chief battles were Wakefield, 1460, won by the Lancastrians (in this battle fell Richard duke of York, claimant of the crown), and those of St. Albans, Northampton, Towton, Hexham, Barnet, and Tewkesbury, won by the Yorkists.

A *white rose* formed the badge of the House of York, and a red rose was the cognizance of the House of Lancaster. The political effects of the war were—(1) the ruin of the ancient baronage; and (2) the growth of monarchical power, being relieved of the baronial check.

Wars of the Silesian Succession. Between Frederick II. of Prussia and Maria Theresa of Austria for the possession of Silesia.

The first war (1740-1742). Maria Theresa ceded Silesia to Frederick II. of Prussia by the treaty of Berlin.

The second war (1744-1745). Maria Theresa confirmed Silesia to Prussia by the treaty of Dresden.

Between the first and second Silesian war was fought the battle of Dettingen, 27 June, 1743.

The third war (the 'Seven Years' War,' 1756-1763), when Silesia was finally ceded to Prussia by the treaty of Hubertsburg.

Wars of the Tributary Princes (*The*). An intestine commotion of China, which lasted with short intervals 450 years (B.C. 770-320); called by the Chinese the Chen-kuo (fighting kings).

The most powerful of these states were OEY, founded by Nang-lee-wàng; TCHAO, by Heao-tching-wàng; HAN, by Huon-hocj; TSEE, by Wàng-kin; and TSIN, by Tchao-siang-wàng.

Wars with the Albigenses (*The*). The *first* was from 1208 to 1229,

40

in the reign of Philippe Auguste. It was entrusted to Simon de Montfort, called 'The French Maccabæus.'

The *second* was in 1226, in the reign of Louis VIII., the Lion. Louis himself was the leader, instigated by Pope Honorius III. to 'purge the land of heretics.'

The *third* was from 1545-1547, in the reign of François I.

Warbeck Plot (*The*), 1490-1499, of which Margaret duchess of Burgundy was the prime mover. The person she selected to personate her nephew, Richard duke of York, second son of Edward IV., who (she said) had made his escape from the Tower, was a Flemish lad named Peter Osbeck, generally called Perkin Warbeck. The lad was invited to the French court, but soon abandoned. He then made his appearance in Ireland, in what is termed the Pale (*q.v.*), and in 1495 started for Scotland. He was received by the Scotch king James IV., who gave to him in marriage Catherine Gordon, granddaughter of James I. In 1497 he returned to Ireland, fled to Cornwall; and in 1499 was executed at Tyburn.

Warbeck of the North (*The*), 1598. Otrepieff, who personated Demetrius, the prince murdered by Boris. As Warbeck married Catherine Gordon, so this mock Demetrius married Marina, daughter of the Palatine Sandomir. He was murdered in an insurrection in 1605. Warbeck was hanged for insurrection. *See* 'Richard IV.'

Warden, in Oxford University. The title held by the head of five of the colleges: All Souls, Keble, Merton, New College, and Wadham.

Warden of the Cinque Ports. The custodian of Dover Castle was created by William the Conqueror warden of the Cinque Ports (*q.v.*). The jurisdiction of this office was very greatly abridged by 18, 19 Vict. c. 48.

Warden of the Stannaries (*Lord*). An officer who has the administration of the metal mines of Devon and Cornwall. When Edward III. created his infant son 'prince of Wales,' he conferred on him these stannaries.

Wardship. Custody of the body and estate of minors holding under the king, till the minor, if a male, was 21, and, if a female, was 16 years of age.

The lord gave no account to anyone of his stewardship. Introduced by William the Conqueror, and abolished by 12 Car. II. c. 24.

Warming-pans. Jacobites, so called because Mary d'Este, wife of James II., says rumour, never had a living child of her own, but, wishing for an heir, she had a male child brought to her in a warming-pan, which she substituted for her own still-born babe. This 'warming-pan heir' was James III. the Pretender, called 'The Warming-pan Hero.' *See* Macaulay, 'Hist. of England,' ii. 308; and Miss Strickland, 'Queens of England,' vi. 213, 243.

What gave some colour to the scandal are the facts that the child was born at least a month before its time, and at its birth none of the persons most interested in the matter were present. Thus the Princess Anne was not present, nor yet the Archbishop of Canterbury, nor yet the Dutch Ambassador, nor any one of the Hyde family. William of Orange, in his manifesto, openly refers to 'the son and heir' of James II. as spurious; but yet the probability is that there was really no collusion.

Warren's Cavalry, 1887. Mounted London police. Sir Charles Warren was Commissioner of the Metropolitan Police Force.

' "Warren's Cavalry" armed to the teeth.'— *Newspaper paragraph,* 30 Jan., 1888.

Warrior Lady of Latham (*The*). Charlotte countess of Derby, daughter of Claude de la Tremouille (peer of France) and of Charlotte daughter of William I. prince of Orange. Born 1601, died 1664. The earl joined the king's troops, and left his house at Latham in charge of his wife. The Parliamentary army demanded its surrender, but the countess returned answer, 'It does not suit me.' For eight months she held out, when Sir T. Fairfax retired, leaving Colonel Rigby in command of the besieging troops. At length Prince Rupert came to the rescue, and Rigby raised the siege.

Warrior of Freedom (*The*). Giuseppe Garibaldi (1807–1882).

Wartburg Contests (*The*), or 'Battles of the Minnesingers.' An annual prize given by Hermann margraf of Thuringia for the best minne-song. It was given in honour of his wife Sophia, and all the best minstrels attended. About 150 of these prize-songs are still extant. Those by Walter of Vogelwerde are the best. *See* 'Minnesingers.'

There is a poem so called. It is by Wolfram, and records the contests of the Thuringian and Suabian poets.

Wasa (*The Dynasty of*), or 'Vasa.' Gustavus Vasa broke off Sweden from Denmark, to which it had been united for 126 years—that is, from the 'Union of Calmar' (1497–1523). Norway still remained in the union till 1813, when it was taken from Denmark by the allies and attached to Sweden.

Wasa (*Knights of*), Sweden, 1772. Decoration is a gold sword hung on watered blue ribbon. The name of the founder is inscribed in a purple cartouche.

Wat Tyler's Insurrection, 1381. A rising of the peasantry against serfage. It was a servile war produced by oppression and misery. John Ball, a Kentish priest, was the stump orator of the day, and told the people that as all men came from Adam and Eve all men had equal rights, and it was gross oppression that some should be gentlemen and others serfs. The real cause of the insurrection was a poll-tax to defray the expenses of the war in France. The insurgents mustered in great force on Blackheath, where they had an interview with Richard II. The king invited Wat Tyler to a conference in Smithfield, when Sir William Walworth, lord mayor of London, despatched him with a dagger, and the king induced the rioters to disperse. The tax especially objected to was one to enable John of Gaunt to dispute with Henry of Trastamare the crown of Castile in right of his wife Constance, a natural daughter of Pedro the Cruel.

The mayors of London were created 'lord mayors' by Edward III. Walsingham calls Wat Tyler 'Wat the helier' (Ang.-Sax. *hel-an,* 'to cover').

Watches. It is said that Robert I. (Bruce) had a watch about 1310. Watches were used by Purbach in astronomical observations in 1500. Those made at Nuremberg in 1477 were egg-shaped. Cornelius van Dreble and James Torrianellus introduced great improvements in 1580. Henry VIII. (1509–1547) certainly had a watch. In 1572 the Earl of Leicester presented one to Queen Elizabeth. It is thus spoken of :—

One armelet or shakell of golde all over fairly garnished with small diamondes and fower score and one smaller peeces fully garnished with like diamondes, and hanginge thereat a rounde clocke fullie garnished with diamondes and an appendant of diamondes hanging thereat.

Pretty common in Shakespeare's time, and often alluded to in plays.

Watchwords. Of course military watchwords are frequently changed; still, it is interesting to know the watchwords of great military men. The following are well known: Brutus, *Libertas*; Cæsar, *Venus genitrix*; Marius, *Lar deus*; Sylla or Sulla, *Apollo Delphicus.*

Waterlanders (*The*). Mild Mennonites, who split off from the general body in 1554, and are so called from Waterland, in Holland.

Watling Street. A great Roman road running from Dover to Caernarvonshire in Wales. A branch ran to Scotland.

It passed through Canterbury and Rochester to London, then ran to Uriconium and Chester into Wales. From Uriconium a branch ran to Manchester, Lancaster, and Kendal.

Wattier's Club, at the corner of Bolton Street. In the time of the regency this was the club for all the marriageable young heirs to ancestral honours, and all the penniless younger sons whose dowry was their animal spirits. It is best known to fame for the masquerade attended by the prince regent, into which Caroline forced her way and created a fresh scandal.

Waynflete Professorships (*The*). One of moral philosophy, and one of chemistry, in Oxford University. Formed from three prælectorships of Magdalen College in 1854. Annual stipend 600*l.* each.

William of Waynflete, bishop of Winchester, founded Magdalen College, Oxford, in 1448.

Waywode (2 syl.). 1. A farmer of the revenue of a district in the Ottoman empire.

2. A former military title of Russia and Poland.

3. A former ruler in the Danubian provinces of Turkey.

Weapons of War and Armour.

Battle-axes:	the best were Danish.		
Casques:	,,	,,	of Poitiers.
Hauberks:	,,	,,	of Rouen.
Swords:	,,	,,	of Damascus, Cologne, and Toledo, in Spain.

Wec'habites (3 syl.). Generally called 'Wahabites' (*q.v.*).

Wedmore, in Somersetshire (*Peace of*), 878. Between Alfred king of England and Guthrum the Dane, settled in East Anglia. This treaty followed Alfred's great victory at Edington, and by its terms Guthrum consented to be baptized.

Week of Expectation (*The*). 'Hebdomada Expectationis.' The sixth week after Easter, when our Lord said to his apostles: 'Manete in hac civitate, et expectate usque dum induamini virtute ex alto' (*Luke* xxiv. 49).

Week of the Cross (*The*), or 'Hebdomada Crucis,' is Rogation week.

Weeping Crosses. So called because, in Catholic times, penances were finished before them.

Weeping Philosopher (*The*). Heraclitos the Ephesian, who died B.C. 495, aged sixty. So called because he was ever mourning over the follies and frailty of man, and the vicissitudes of all human affairs. *See* p. 630, 'Obscure Philosopher.'

Weliki-Luki (*Treaty of*), 20 July, 1812. Of alliance between Spain and Russia.

Well-beloved (*The*). 'Le Bienaimé.' Louis XV. (1710, 1715–1774).

The contest was carried into the reign of the 'Well-beloved.'—*Hist. of France.*

*** How such a licentious, heartless, and singularly immoral man could be 'well-beloved' is past all human understanding.

Wellington Administration (*The*), 1829–1830. That of Prince Polignac was so called by the French. It was a retrograde Tory administration, contemporary with the administration of the Duke of Wellington in England.

Wellington Statues.
I. By Boehm at Hyde Park Place, unveiled 21 Dec., 1888. The figures round the pedestal represent the four nationalities engaged in the battle of Waterloo in 1815—viz. (1) The British Guardsmen; (2) the 42nd Highlanders; (3) the Inniskilling Dragoons; and (4) the 23rd Welsh Fusiliers.

II. The bronze statue of Achilles, 18 June, 1822, by the women of England, and made of the cannons taken at Salamanca, Vittoria, Toulouse, and Waterloo. It was originally placed in the south-east angle of Hyde Park, near Apsley House.

III. Equestrian statue of the Duke of Wellington surmounting the Marble Arch, Hyde Park Corner, set up in 1846, taken down 24 Jan., 1883. *See* p. 131, 'Burton Arch.'

Wellington's Assassin. Cantillon, to whom Napoleon I. left a legacy for his base attempt, and to whom Napoleon III. paid the legacy. Whether Napoleon hired this villain or not to do the damning deed is not of the slightest moment. He certainly set his hand and seal to the full approval thereof, and it is but charity to believe that both Napoleon I. when he made the legacy and Napoleon III. when he paid it were 'politically insane.' Cantillon was alive and in Paris in 1859.

Welsh Calvinistic Methodists,

1743. Organised by Charles of Bala, a clergyman of the Church of England. They believe in the 'Thirty-nine Articles' taken in a Calvinistic sense. In church government they are Presbyterian.

Welsh Mortgage (A).

A pledge of land in which there is no day fixed for redemption. Such a mortgage is redeemable at any time on payment of the loan.

A 'vif-gage' (*vivum vadium*) is a conveyance of property to a creditor and his heirs till he has (out of the profits of the estate) satisfied the debt with interest. As neither debt nor interest is lost, such a gage is *living—i.e.* does not lapse or fail.

Wenceslaus the Worthless.

One of the promiscuous kaiser-kings of Germany (1357, 1378–1400, deposed and died 1419).

It was a frightful period. In Germany was Wenceslaus the Worthless, in France Charles VI. the idiot, in England Richard II. the fop. There were two popes anathematising each other, one at Rome and the other at Avignon.

Werela (Peace of),

14 Aug., 1790. Between Sweden and Russia. In this treaty the limits of both states were re-established according to the provisions of former treaties.

Wesleyan Conference (The),

1744. The original conference consisted of six Methodist clergymen of the Church of England and four lay preachers, who met together in London to consult on the continuance of the work. Subsequent conferences have been annually held since.

Wesleyan Methodist Association (The),

1835. Seceders from the old Methodist Connection from an objection to the Conference, which they thought to be tyrannical, especially in excluding laymen from any share in the general management.

Wesleyan Methodist Reformers (The).

Seceders from the Methodist Connection, who object to the overbearing authority of the Conference, and especially to the exclusion of those who dared to censure their proceedings. (19th cent.; about 1840.)

Wesleyan Methodists, 1738.

The Arminian Methodists organized by John Wesley.

The Calvinistic Methodists led by Whitfield separated in 1752. The 'Wesleyan Methodist Church,' 1843, was formed at Utica, and object to Episcopal titles.

Wesleyan Reform Union (The),

1849. Those Reformed Methodists who did not join the United Methodist Free Church.

Western Church (The),

or 'Latin Church'; as they call themselves, 'The Catholic Church'; as others call them, 'The Roman Catholic Church,' separated from the Eastern Church about 324–334. In 606 the word 'pope' was limited to the Bishop of Rome; the Bishop of Constantinople being called 'patriarch' since 588.

Of course the Eastern Church was established before the Western, and the Western Church separated on the moot point whether the bishop of Rome or patriarch of the East were the higher office. As the Western Church severed itself from the Eastern, in the language of the church, it was 'schismatic,' and remains so still.

Western Empire (The).

I. *Rome*, or the western portion of the ancient Roman empire after its division by Valentinian and Valens, A.D. 364. Valentinian had the western portion, with Rome for his capital, and Valens, his brother, had the eastern portion, with Constantinople for his capital. The Western empire ended in 476, when Odoäcer, king of the Herüli, took Rome, and assumed the title of 'king of Italy.'

The Eastern empire continued nearly 1,000 years longer, till 1453.

II. 960–1268. The united empire of *Germany and Italy*. Otto I. the Great took Italy from the usurper Berengarius II. and added it to the German empire. In 1268 the Germans were driven out of Italy, and several republics were formed there.

Western Schism (The),

or 'Great Schism of the West.' Variously reckoned 39 years, 50 years, and 71 years.

1. 39 years, from the double election of Urban VI. in Rome and Clement VII. in Avignon, 1378 to 1417, when Martin V. was elected by the Council of Pisa.

2. 50 years, from 1378 to 1429, when Clement VIII., elected to succeed Gregory XII. at Avignon, resigned the tiara.

3. 71 years, from 1378 to 1449, when Felix V. was elected by the Council of Basel to succeed Eugenius IV.

See p. 31, 'Anti-popes.'

Westminster (*The Conference of*), 1559. Summoned by Queen Elizabeth to settle these three questions: (1) Should the public worship be conducted in Latin or English? (2) What power should be allotted to each particular church in the matter of rites and ceremonies? (3) Is the Mass a propitiatory sacrifice or not? The bishops of Lincoln and Winchester threatened to excommunicate the queen and conference if they could not have their own way, were arrested and sent to the Tower for high treason, and the conference was dissolved.

Westminster Assembly of Divines (*The*), 1643–1649. A convocation appointed by the Long Parliament for settling the doctrine, liturgy, and government of the Church of England. It consisted of 121 clergymen and 30 laymen (10 of whom were lords). This assembly wanted dogmatically to dictate what articles of faith should be compulsory, and even what form of worship should be established, but Cromwell demanded toleration and independence.

Westminster Catechisms (*The*). The Shorter Catechism, 5 Nov., 1647; the Longer Catechism, 18 Sept., 1648. They were drawn up by the Westminster Assembly of Divines (*q.v.*), and are still used by the Presbyterians as standard catechisms, but are not accepted by the Church of England as of any authority.
The Shorter Assembly Catechism was probably drafted by Mr. Palmer.

Westminster Confession of Faith (*The*), 1646. A confession of faith contained in 33 articles drawn up by the Westminster Assembly of Divines (*q.v.*), and still considered a standard of faith in the Presbyterian churches of the United Kingdom; but, never having received the royal sanction, it is of no authority in the Church of England.

Westminster School, 1560. Founded by Queen Elizabeth.

Westphalia (*Peace of*), 24 Oct., 1648. One of the most important in European history, as it closed the Thirty Years' War. By the terms of this treaty 'the balance of power' in Europe was first recognised. Alsace was ceded to France; part of Pomerania to Sweden; the Swiss cantons were declared independent; perfect religious freedom was granted, and German Protestants were

admitted to equal rights with their Catholic fellow-countrymen. No one could henceforth be put under the ban of the empire but by the diet alone.
Lusatia and Alsace were taken from Austria, and Austria received instead Transylvania and Croatia. Upper Pomerania, Rugen, with Stettin, Gratz, Damme, Golnau, the Isle of Wollin, Peine Schiveine, the Divenau in Lower Pomerania, Wismar, the Duchy of Bremen, and the principality of Verdun were given to Sweden.

Wetter (*Mrs.*), the Queen Victoria. The family name of her husband was Wetter. A playful pseudonym.
Some say Wettin, which is Prussian; but Wetter or Vetter, is Swedish.

Wharncliffe Meetings. Meetings of public companies held in conformity with the Wharncliffe Order (*q.v.*).

Wharncliffe Order. A provision introduced into the House of Lords that no meeting of a public company shall have power to change the constitution of the company unless seven days' notice has been given to the subscribers and the meeting represents at least three-fourths of the paid-up capital.

Wharton. Philip Wharton, duke of Wharton (1698–1731). Pope calls him 'the scorn and wonder of our days.' His talents were brilliant, and his power of oratory electric; but his life was most licentious, and he turned traitor. He fought against his countrymen at the siege of Gibraltar, and joined the Pretender, from whom he accepted the worthless title of 'Duke of Northumberland.'

Whewell Scholarships for international law. Two yearly, value respectively 100*l.* and 50*l.*, tenable for four years. Founded in the University of Cambridge by the Rev. William Whewell, D.D., master of Trinity College. *See* p. 748, 'Regius Professor of Civil Law.'
Whewell, pronounce *You-el*.

Whig and Tory, modified continuations of the terms Roundhead and Cavalier, which arose, in 1680, on the introduction of the Exclusion Bill. Tory was the name by which ruined adherents of King James were known when he lived in a state of outlawry in Ireland. It was applied in derision to those who held the doctrine of 'the divine right of kings,' subsequently applied to those who stood by 'church and state.' Whig was applied to an opposite class of men in Scotland, but similarly circumstanced as the Irish Tories. They were vagabonds collected by the Marquis of Argyll to oppose certain government measures in the reign of James I. As the Irish Tories were church and state men, the Scotch Whigs were nonconformists, who repudiated the doctrine of 'divine right' and the right of an established church.

Scotch Covenanters were nicknamed Whigs (vagabonds) as far back as 1648; the *Abhorrers* (*q.v.*) slanged the *Petitioners* (*q.v.*) as Whigs. The term was not used in England as a political designation till 1680. Tory is about equal to Rapparee. As Abhorrers called the Petitioners by way of contempt *Whigs*, so the Petitioners returned the contumely by calling the Abhorrers *Tories*.

Tory is from an Irish verb, meaning to pursue for plunder.

Whig of the Revolution (*A*). So George III. called himself. Not the French but the English revolution. He abhorred the former, but owed his crown to the latter.

Whig Bible. *See* 'Placemakers' Bible' and 'Bible.'

Whig Club (*The*), 1793, in Irish history, was instituted to promote reform by pressure from without, through the agency of voluntary associations. It was afterwards superseded by the society of the United Irishmen (*q.v.*). *See* p. 455, 'Irish Associations.'

Whigs' Vault (*The*). A subterranean dungeon in the castle of Dunnottar where the Privy Council of Scotland, in 1685, shut up a number of prisoners supposed to be hostile to the government.

In this prison . . . . still termed the Whigs' Vault, several died of the diseases incidental to such a situation.—Sir W. SCOTT, *Old Mortality* (Introduction).

Whigamores (*The*). The rigid Presbyterian party, under the leadership of the Marquis of Argyll. After the defeat of the Duke of Hamilton, leader of the Engagers (*q.v.*) or moderate Presbyterians, the Marquis of Argyll, with 6,000 followers, marched to Edinburgh and made himself head of the government (1648). The word contracted into 'Whigs' was applied to the Presbyterians of Scotland opposed to the Royalists or Malignants, and was subsequently applied to all those who denied the divine right of kings, the supremacy of royal prerogatives, and the dogma of passive obedience.

The etymology of the word is doubtful. Some derive it from *Ugham-more*, pack-saddle thieves; others from *whig*, in horse language, meaning 'get on'; others more wittily than truly from an anagram 'We Hope In God.'

In the 'Encyclopædia Britannica' we read: The Whigs were so denominated from a cant name given to the Presbyterian conventiclers: "whig," milk turned sour; and Tories received that honourable appellation from the Irish banditti so called—the Irish word *toree* being equal to "stand and deliver!"' Whig or Whey is buttermilk.

Whigamores' Inroad (*The*), or 'The Whigamore Raid,' 1648. Cromwell with 8,000 men having defeated Langdale, whose army amounted to 20,000 men, made his way into Scotland, when the Marquis of Argyll, and the Earls Cassilis and Eglintoun, at the head of the Presbyterians of the west country and the Highlands, marched to Edinburgh, and conducted Cromwell to the metropolis in triumph. This expedition of the Covenanters to Edinburgh gave the finishing blow to the royal cause in Scotland, and is known in history as the 'Whigamore's Inroad' or 'Whigamore Raid.' ('Encyclop. Britannica,' v. 411.)

The Duke of Hamilton supported what is called 'the Engagement' (*q.v.*) in the Scotch parliament. The Marquis of Argyll opposed it. The Duke of Hamilton was defeated at Warrington (1648), and surrendered to Cromwell.

Whip with six strings (*The*), 31 Hen. VIII. c. 14, A.D. 1539. 'The Bloody Statute.' *See* the 'Six Articles.'

Whipping Boy (*A*). A boy kept to be whipped when a prince deserved chastisement.

EDWARD VI. Barnaby Fitzpatrick stood for Edward VI.

HENRI IV. of France. D'Ossat and Du Perron, afterwards cardinals, were whipped by Clement VIII. for Henri IV.—FULLER, *Church History*, ii. 342.

CHARLES I. Mungo Murray stood for Charles I.

JAMES I. of England. We are told that George Buchanan would not punish the Scotch by substitution, and when the Countess of Mar complained of his whipping the prince, he stoutly confessed it, and said he would do it again if the boy blundered over his Latin declensions.

Lesage, in his 'Gil Blas' makes Raphael to be flogged for the son of the Marquis de Leganez; but Raphael, not seeing the justice of this arrangement, ran away (v. 1).

Whipping Post (*The*), to which Jesus was fastened at the scourging, is now shown at Rome through iron railings in a little chapel in the church of St. Praxedés; and over it is inscribed words to the effect that John de Colonna brought it to Rome in 1223. The socle of the post, however, is in St. Mark's Cathedral, Venice. The post is of grey marble, a foot and a half long, one foot in diameter at the base and eight inches at the top, where an iron ring is inserted, to which the victim was tied. *See* p. 231, 'Crucifixion, *Relics of the.*'

White and Black Face, in Turkish phraseology, are terms of praise and reproach, meaning bright and downcast.

When the Janizaries were enrolled, a dervish blessed the new levies and said, 'Wheresoever they go, may they return with *white faces.*' Gibbon tells us that the Romans had the sentence 'Hic *niger* est, hunc tu, Romane, caveto.'—*Decline and Fall*, chap. lxiv., and *note.*

We also speak of a downcast leaden look. And say he looked black in the face; looked black at me; you need not look so black.

White and Black Factions
(*The*). The Ommiades (whose colour was white) and the Abbassides (whose colour was black). Green was the colour of the Fatimites (3 syl.).

From the Indus to the Euphratès the east was convulsed by the quarrels of the White and Black factions.—GIBBON, chap. lii.

White and Crimson.
In the Valois-Angoulême dynasty Protestant soldiers wore white jackets and scarfs, but the Catholic soldiers wore crimson jackets and scarfs. The Swiss guard wore a grey uniform.

White Battle
(*The*), 20 Sept., 1319. The battle of Mytton, in Yorkshire, was so called from the number of clerks who fell. It was between the Scots (under Douglas and Randolph) and the forces of William of Melton archbishop of York. It is said that at least 300 men in holy orders were slain, and many were taken prisoners, among whom was William de Ayremyn (afterwards bishop of Norwich). Bishop Hotham of Ely narrowly escaped being taken captive. The battle is sometimes jocosely spoken of as 'The Chapter of Mitton.'

Of tha yhet thre hundreth war
Prestis that deit [died] intill that chas :
Tharfore that bargane callit was
'The Chaptour of Mytoun,' for thare
Slain so many prestis war.
  BARBOUR, *The Brus.*

White Books.
The official reports of both Germany and Portugal are stitched in white wrappers. *See* 'Blue Books,' 'Black Books,' 'Red Books,' 'Yellow Books.'

White Brotherhood
(*The*). The adventurers led by John Hawkwood (14th cent.).

An English mercenary, John Hawkwood, with a band of adventurers, the White Brotherhood, had ravaged Italy from the Alps to Calabria.—GIBBON, chap. xlvi.

White Camisards,
1703. Catholic volunteers, under the name of Cadets of the Cross or White Camisards, joined the regular troops of Marshal Montrevel as auxiliaries to extirpate the Camisards

of the Cevennes, called by Pope Clement XI. ' a cursed brood from the execrable race of the Albigenses.' *See* p. 96, ' Black Camisards.'

A military night surprise is a *camisade.* Thus the taking of Pontoise in 1419 was a camisade, and the battle of Pavia in 1524 began with a camisade.

White Canons.
Canons, like the Premonstratensians, who wore white habits. *See* 'Canons,' 'Black Canons.'

White Caps
were worn by the Volones or volunteer slaves as a token of liberty.

Then Gracchus fulfilled his promise to the Volones, and celebrated their enfranchisement by a public festival, in which they all appeared wearing white caps in token of liberty.—*The Student's Rome*, p. 256.

White Caps
(in the U.S., 1889–1890), bodies of self-constituted 'regulators' and correctors of morals.

White Caps
(*The*), 1758. A seditious faction in China put down by the Emperor Kien-lông. They were zealous Mahometans. *See* p. 120, 'Brethren of the White Caps.'

White City
(*The*). Belgrade, called *Alba Græcia* by the Franks in the 9th cent.

White Coats
(*The*). I. The trainbands, as the 'Red Coats' were the regular soldiers, and the 'Blue Jackets' the sailors.

II. The Earl of Newcastle's pikemen, chiefly Roman Catholics, in the time of Charles I. They wore white coats.

White Company
(*The*). A company of adventurers which, after the wars of Edward III. in France, passed into the service of the Marquis of Montferrat. When they were employed by the Pisans against Florence the famous Sir John Hawkwood was their commander.

White Cross Knights
(*The*). The Knights Hospitallers, who had a white cross on their black robes. The Knights Templars were the Red Cross Knights, their badge being a red cross on a white robe. *See* 'Poor Brothers of St. John.'

White Eagle
(*Knights of the*), 1325. A Polish order instituted by Ladislas king of Poland on the marriage of his son Casimir with Anne, daughter of the Grand Duke of Lithuania. The ribbon was blue. Extinct.

White Flag
(*The*). Emblem of legitimacy in France. The flag of the

Bourbon monarchs. Ordinarily, the white flag craves for truce and peace ; a black flag indicates a pirate ; a red flag, defiance ; a yellow flag, that the vessel is in quarantine.

Those who reverence the symbol of the White Flag may feel that its latest upholder [the Comte de Chambord] did nothing to sully its purity.— *Daily News*, Sept. 3, 1883.

** A white flag as a railway signal means the rail is clear, and everything in order ; a red flag signifies danger, and means stop ; a green flag intimates that caution is required.

White Flagellants (*The*). So called from their white mantles. *See* 'Flagellants,' and 'Blancs Battus.'

White Friars (*The*), 1171. The Carmelites. So called from the colour of their dress, as the Dominicans were called 'Black Friars' and the Franciscans 'Grey Friars.'

White Hats (*The*). I. In *Flanders*, were in the 14th cent. the badge of the democratic party, led by Jacob van Artevelde, the great brewer of Ghent, who was elected their captain in 1338, and was assassinated in 1345. Their next captain was John Lyon, who was supposed to be poisoned by the court party in 1381. Philip van Artevelde, son of the great brewer, next assumed the white hat of the party. He was slain in the battle of Rosebeque, Nov. 1382.

II. White hats were used in *England* to denote radical proclivities, because Orator Hunt (1773-1835), the great demagogue, during the Wellington and Peel administration, used to wear a white hat. Lord Liverpool, who was prime minister for fifteen years (1812-1827), rendered the badge no longer distinctive by adopting a white hat himself.

White Hood House (*The*). The Regents' or Upper House of the University of Cambridge. So called because the Masters of Arts wore hoods lined with white silk. It consisted of Masters of Arts of less than five years' standing, and of Doctors of less than two. If of longer standing, they belonged to the Black Hood House (*q.v.*), called the non-regent or Lower House. All this was abolished in 1858. *See* 'Senate.'

Regents originally meant tutors, lecturers, and professors. Members of the University having served their time were exempt from these duties, and Masters of Arts took off the white lining of their hoods to show they were non-regents.

White Hoods (*The*), or 'Les Chaperons Blancs.' I. 1379. The work-men of Ghent, when they revolted against the Duke of Burgundy, adopted as their badge a white hood.

II. 1407-1415. All Paris, on the assassination of the Duc d'Orléans, was divided into two factions—the Burgundians under Jean-sans-Peur duke of Burgundy, and the Armagnacs, who were partisans of the Orleanists. The Burgundians adopted for their badge a St. Andrew's cross on a white *hood*, the Armagnacs adopted a St. George's cross. After a time the Cabocians were enlisted by Jean-sans-Peur, and wore as their badge white hoods. So violent were these rowdies that they compelled the doctors of the Sorbonne to wear the white hood, and, having got the dauphin into their power, made him also adopt the same badge. *See* p. 348, 'French Brigands.'

White Huns (*The*), or the 'Hiatilla.' The Huns of Sogdiana.

Called White Huns by the Greeks, 'à cause de leur civilisation et de leur douceur.'—BOUILLET.

Gibbon says, chap. xxvi., they were called *White Huns* from the change of complexions. The Huns of the North are the black Calmucks.

White Knight (*The*), or 'Chevalier Blanc de Valaigne' (*i.e.* Valachia), John Corvīnus Hunniādês, the Hungarian general (1400-1456). The Turks, who employed his name to frighten their perverse children, called him Jancus Lain (or the Wicked).

The white knight fought with the hand rather than the head.—GIBBON, lxvii.

White Knight of Wallachia (*The*). Same as the preceding.

White Laws. The Jus Honorarium, or Edicts of the Roman prætors. Red Laws or Rubrics were the Civil Law.

Alii se ad Album [*i.e.* jus prætorium, quia Prætores edicta sua in *albo* proponebant] ac Rubricas [*i.e.* jus civile] transtulerunt.—QUINTILIAN, xii. 3, 11. The Imperial Rescripts were written in purple ink.

White Mantles (*The*). I. The Servites (2 syl.), or 'Servitors of the Virgin.' A religious order founded in Florence in 1232. So called from their white mantles. The order was suppressed in France in 1274, but still subsists in Italy.

II. *Williamites* (3 syl.), or 'Guillemites' (3 syl.), were also called 'White Mantles' from their large white mantles. This was a religious order founded by

William of Malavalle, which spread through all Italy, Germany, and France.

White Monks. The Bernardines or Cistercians. So called from the colour of their habit.

The Dominicans wore a *black* habit, the Franciscans a *grey* one.

White Penitents, 1399. These were men, women, girls, boys, townsfolk and countryfolk, nobles and burghers, laity and clergy, all with bare feet and dressed in white sheets from head to foot, who visited in succession the towns and villages of every district of Milan. Whenever they came to a cross road or to a cross, they threw themselves on the ground, crying 'Misericordia' three times; then recited the Lord's Prayer and the Ave Maria. On entering a town or city, they walked singing the 'Stabat Mater.' Corio, in his 'History of Milan,' assures us that the number was between 10,000 and 15,000 at a time. 'However (he adds), the people returned to a worse course of life than ever after the excitement was over.'

White Poet (*The*). Olaf, younger brother of Sturla, and nephew of Snorro the historian (13th cent.).

White Rent. Rent paid in silver or white money instead of corn. Quit-rents were so called. Anglo-Saxon, *Hwit-rent*, white-rent.

White Rose (*The*). Elizabeth of York; she married Henry VII., and thus united the rival houses of York and Lancaster.

White Rose of England (*The*), 1490. So Margaret duchess of Burgundy called Perkin Warbeck, appointed by her to personate Richard duke of York, younger son of Edward IV.

White Rose of Scotland (*The*). Lady Catherine Gordon, daughter of the Earl of Huntly, and grand-daughter of James I. Her first husband was Perkin Warbeck the pretender, her second husband was Sir Matthew Cradock. Called the 'White Rose' because Warbeck pretended to be the representative of the House of York (the White Rose party).

White Russia. Muscovy. The king of Muscovy was called the 'White King' from his *alba tegumenta*.

White Scarfs and White Hoods (*The*), 1407–1415. The Armagnac and Burgundian factions, after the assassination of the Duc d'Orléans. The Orleanists or Armagnacs adopted as their cognizance a St. George's cross on a white *scarf*. The Burgundians, led by Jean-sans-Peur duke of Burgundy, adopted a St. Andrew's cross on a white *hood*.

The Crusaders, the Armagnacs, and the Huguenots all adopted as their badge the white *scarf ;* but the Burgundian badge was a white *hood*. A red scarf was the badge of Henri III. and Charles IX. ; a green scarf of Mazarin, Isabella, and the Condé family. A tricolour scarf is still worn in France by municipal magistrates and the commissaires of police.

White Sheep (*The*), 1468–1497. Certain Turkomans who on the decay of Timur's dynasty fixed themselves (under the leadership of Uzun Hussun) in Armenia, Mesopotamia, and part of Asia Minor. They afterwards drove out the Black Sheep and made themselves masters of all Western Persia. They were utterly stamped out by Ismael, a native prince, who founded the Suffavĕan or Sofi dynasty.

At the decay of the Timur dynasty the dominions of Timur were divided into three parts: Hussein Mirza, a descendant of Timur, had Khorassan, and held his court at Herat; the Black Sheep acquired Azerbijan, Irak, Fars, and Kerman; and the Turkomans of the White Sheep held the third part. Called the White Sheep from the effigy displayed on their standard.

White Ship (*The*). *La Blanche Nef*, the ship in which Prince William, son of Henry Beauclerc, embarked at Barfleur, and was wrecked with 140 passengers and 50 sailors, by striking on the Ras de Catte (now Catteville), 25 Nov., 1120. It is said that the king fainted when he heard the news and 'never smiled again.'

White Staff (*The*). The staff of office presented by the sovereign to her privy council. Thus the premier, the lord chamberlain, the treasurer of the household, the lord steward, &c., bear white wands or staffs.

Shrewsbury refused to take the white wand [of chief minister], except from her majesty's own hand. It was therefore handed to her [Queen Anne], and she extended it towards Shrewsbury, saying, 'For God's sake, use it for the good of my people.' Shrewsbury was already chamberlain, and he presented the staff of that office in resignation of it, but the queen bade him retain both.—HOWITT, *Hist. of England* (Anne, p. 322).

Lord Harley of Wigmore will have the white staff given him to-morrow by the queen herself, and be declared lord high treasurer.—DEFOE (29 May, 1711).

3 P

White Standard, that of Charles Edward the Young Pretender. The white cockade was the badge of his followers. The Bourbons also adopted the white cockade and standard.

When the white standard is again displayed, it shall not be turned back so easily.—Sir W. Scott, *Redgauntlet*, chap. xxii.

White Strangers, or 'White Gentiles.' Norwegians, who took possession of Dublin in 838. Dublin and northwards was the territory of the White Strangers. From Dublin southwards was the territory of the Black Strangers.

Dublin and settlements in Leinster constituted the territory of the Fin-gall or White Foreigners. Called by the Four Masters Fionn-gentie (White Gentiles).

White Town (*The*). Belgorod, the third circle of Moscow. So called from the white wall with which it was encompassed.

Moscow had four concentric circles. Beginning with the innermost they were—(1) the Kremlin, (2) Kilaigorod or the Chinese Town, (3) Belgorod or the White Town, and (4) Semilangorod, which was defended by ramparts.

White Water-flower (*The*), or Pe-lien-kaou. An association at the close of the 18th cent. formed in China against Kea-king, the emperor. This brotherhood excited in Shan-tung an insurrection, which spread over three of the neighbouring provinces. The leader was designated San-hwang, and maintained his ground for eight years.

Or White Water Lotus. Kea-king reigned 1796-1820.

Whites and Blacks (*The*), 13th cent. Rival factions in Italy at the close of the 13th cent. and the first four years of the 14th. The *Blacks* were the *noblesse*, the *Whites* the rich *bourgeois*. The Whites were Guelfs, the Blacks were Ghibelins. Dante in 1302 was exiled for being a *White*.

Whites and Blues (*The*). 'Les Blancs et Bleus' in the great French Revolution mean the royalists, whose flag and livery were white; the republican troops wore a blue uniform.

Whites, Reds, Blues, and Greens were colour factions of Constantinople, being the liveries worn in chariot races, and party colours as formerly in our elections for members of parliament; but the Whites merged into the Blues, and the Reds into the Greens. *See* p. 108, 'Blues and Greens.'

Whites and Reds (*The*). 'Albati' and 'Russati.' The original liveries of

the Roman charioteers, in the chariot races. Afterwards two more liveries, the Green and the Blue, were added, and the latter ultimately absorbed the original colours. In Rome, the colours were a Capulet and Montague standing faction, which led to street brawls and not unfrequently death; and such emperors as Caligula, Nero, Vitellius, Verus, Commodus, Caracalla, and Elagabālus, were Greens or Blues, and made their livery party questions as we do Whig and Tory, Church and Dissent. The same rage prevailed in Constantinople; the Greens were the partisans of Anastasius, the blues of Justinian. In fact, the whole empire was divided into Greens and Blues. Even religion had its Orthodox Blues and Heterodox Greens.

Whiteboy Acts (*The*), 1762. Laws against the Whiteboys, many of which are still in force.

Whiteboy Riots. It would be difficult to tabulate all the riots of these turbulent Irish since the formation of the society in 1760. Lord Drogheda was charged in 1762 with the task of suppressing the society, but he only scotched it. Outrages were renewed in 1822; and in 1828 Queen's County, Carlow, and Kilkenny were scenes of disgraceful 'Whiteboy riots.' These rioters robbed and murdered in every direction, much the same as the Moonlighters, as agents of the more secret leaders of the Land or National League, Home Rule, and Plan of Campaign (*q.v.*). *See* p. 455, 'Irish Associations.'

Whiteboys (*The*). I. Protestant rioters in the reign of Queen Elizabeth. *See* 'The Abbot,' chap. xvi., by Sir W. Scott.

II. 1760. An illegal association of Irishmen, so called because, in their nightly expeditions, they disguised themselves in white smocks. Their object was to resist the enclosure of commons, in order to increase the number of cattle required by the murrain which began in Germany and spread to England. They existed some time before 1760 under the name of Levellers (*q.v.*), and soon after 1760 became noted for agrarian aggressions. In 1762 Lord Drogheda was charged with the suppression of this riotous society. Outrages were renewed in 1807, and in

1811, 1812 spread to Tipperary, Waterford, Kilkenny, Westmeath, Roscommon, and Queen's County. The Whiteboys called themselves the agents of Captain Right.

In 1784 and the three following years houghing, tarring and feathering, and other personal molestations prevailed to a great extent. The Protestant clergy, especially in the south of Ireland, were subjects of especial persecution by the Whiteboys. Riotous assemblies were next organised, so that in 1787 an act was passed to prevent tumultuous assemblies.'

In 1822 the rioters became so violent that the ' Insurrection Act' was passed, and continued in force for three years. Similarly in 1807 an Insurrection Act had been passed which remained in force for four years; when withdrawn, two years of turbulence ensued of a very aggravated character. *See* p. 455, ' Irish Associations.'

* Parnellism and crime have had a long spell of late years. In 1890 it was thought 'patriotic' to insult the judges, slang the ministers, defy the laws, ruin the landlords, and obstruct the police in their attempts to keep order.

Whiteboyism. The political and agrarian platform of the Whiteboys of Ireland. In 1762 the outrages of this association were greatly repressed, but they reappeared soon afterwards in the south of Ireland. *See* ' Whiteboys.'

Whitefeet (*The*). One of the disturbing factions of Ireland in the Tithe War (*q.v.*). They were associated with the Blackfeet, Terryalts, Lady Clares, Molly Maguires, and Rockites. *See* each of these *in loco*, and ' Irish Associations.'

Whitefeet and Blackfeet. Illegal associations formed in Ireland during the sanguinary Tithe War (1830-1835) (*q.v.*). The names were in conformity with the colour of their shoes, assumed as badges of the associations.

Whitefieldites (3 syl.), 1739. Followers of the Rev. George Whitefield [*Whit-field*], an ordained clergyman of the Anglican Church, who separated from that communion and established a hyper-Calvinistic system of religion in opposition to Wesley, whose tenets were Arminian (*q.v.*). Whitefield insisted on the doctrines of predestination and unconditional election. Wesley founded the Wesleyan Methodist connexion.

Whitehall Preachers (*The*), 1724. Established by George I. One from the University of Oxford and one from the University of Cambridge. Appointed for two years. Originally there were twenty-four preachers, twelve resident fellows of each university. The two are

now appointed by the Bishop of London, as dean of the royal chapel.

White-hood House (*The*), in Cambridge University, is the Regent or Upper House of the Senate, composed of masters of arts of less than five years' standing and doctors of less than two years' standing. *See* ' Black-hood House.' Abolished 1858.

So called because the hood of a Cambridge M.A. is lined with white silk. Called ' regent ' because they were the tutors and professors, and as such were the ' rulers ' of the university. After the time stated they were released from these duties, and stripped off the white lining of their hoods. This has been discontinued for many years.

Whit-Sunday. The Sunday which commemorates the descent of the Holy Ghost on the day of Pentecost on the disciples, in the form of ' tongues of fire,' after which they were all inspired to speak in foreign tongues, as the Spirit gave them utterance. Verstegan says: ' We yet say hallowed for *halih-wied*; also we hereof retain the name of Whitsonday, which more rightly should be written *Weid-Sonday*, *i.e.* "Sacred Sonday." So called by reason of the descending down of the Holy Ghost . . . .' (' Restitution of Decayed Intelligence,' p. 188).

Robert of Gloucester, under the article ' Wytte-Sonetyd,' says: ' Good men and wymmen, this day is called Wyt-sonday, because the Holy Ghost brought wytte and wisdom into Cristis disciples, and so by her preching after in all cristendom, and fylled hem full of ghostly wytte.'

Another derivate is ' White-Sunday,' from the white dresses anciently worn by the newly baptized catechumens, to whom the sacrament of the Eucharist was administered on the vigil of Pentecost. Whitsuntide includes the white octave, but is now in England almost restricted to Whit-Sunday, Whit-Monday, and Whit-Tuesday.

Whitsuntide Dancers. At Echternach, in Luxemburg, thousands of pilgrims take an active part in a ' sacred ' dance, singing at the same time litanies in honour of St. Willebrod. The dancers take three springs forwards and one backwards, or five forwards and two backwards, to bands of music. The space traversed is about a mile and takes above an hour.

Le mardi de pentecôte une procession de sauteurs parcourt encore les rues d'Echternach du pont de la Sure à l'église, et cela, dit-on, pour conjurer la danse de St.-Guy, qu'une tradition locale

3 P 2

dit avoir été très-commune dans le pays vers le huitième siècle.'—RECLUS, *Nouvelle Géographie Universelle.*

('St. Guy' or 'Gui' is the French form of our St. Vitus.)

Whitsun Week.

'Hebdomăda Pentecostês.' Beginning with Whit-Sunday; the week which commemorates the descent of the Holy Spirit.

Whyte's Professorship of Moral Philosophy

(*Dr.*), in Oxford University, at 100*l.* a year. Founded by Thomas Whyte, D.D., in 1621. The stipend has been raised to 400*l.* a year.

Wicked Bible

(*The*), 1632. Printed in London by Richard Barker and Martin Lucas, the king's printers, in the reign of Charles I. The printing was bad, and the paper bad, and there were two monstrous errors. The seventh commandment, by the omission of *not*, ran thus: 'Thou shalt commit adultery'; and in one case 'greatnesse' got converted into 'great asse.' The printers were fined 500*l.*, and the edition of 1,000 copies was ordered to be burnt. *See* p. 90, 'Bibles.'

When the case was brought into the Court of High Commission, Laud said : 'The printeing is soe bad and the paper too, that, if it be not mended shortlie, they wilbe put downe by those of Amsterdam, and the trade spoyled.' *See* 'Raw. linson MS.,' printed by the Camden Society, N.S. 39.

Wicked Street

(*The*) of ancient Rome, at the foot of the Esquiline Hill. So called because here Tullia, the daughter of Servius Tullius, drove her chariot over the murdered body of her old father, who had been king of Rome forty-four years.

Wic'lifites

(3 syl.). Disciples of Wiclif. Also called 'Lollards.' They denied the dogma of transubstantiation. Wiclif lived 1324–1384.

Wigs.

In the middle of the 18th cent. there were thirty-three different sorts of wigs in use :—

The Artichoke wig.	The Half-natural.
Bag wig.	Jansenist bob.
Barrister's wig.	Judge's wig.
Bishop's wig.	Ladder wig.
Brush wig.	Long bob.
Bush wig.	Louis' wig.
Buckle wig.	Periwig.
Chain wig.	Pigeon's wing.
Chancellor's wig.	Rhinoceros wig.
Corded wolf's paw.	Rose.
Count Saxe's mode.	Scratch wig.
Crutch wig.	She dragon.
Cut bob wig.	Small black wig.
Detached buckle wig.	Spinage [*sic*] seed wig.
Drop wig.	Staircase.
Dutch wig.	Welsh wig.
Full wig.	Wild boar's back.

His periwig was large enough to have loaded a camel, and he bestowed upon it at least a bushel of powder.—BROWN, *Letters* (time Charles II.).

Sing [? singe] old Rose and burn the bellows (burn *libellos*).

Wigs were worn by bishops in the House of Lords till 1830, when Blomfield bishop of London obtained permission of William IV. for bishops to discontinue their use.

The oldest wig in the world is of ancient Egyptian manufacture. It was found in a tomb at Thebes, and is now in the British Museum.

Wilburites

(3 syl.). A new sect of Quakers of great strictness, founded by John Wilbur, who insisted most rigidly on the traditions and peculiarities of the society. This movement was the counter-action of the Hicksite movement in 1827.

Wild Scots of Galway

(*The*). The Galwegians, a mixed race, partly Irish-Scots of Argyllshire, partly Picts.

Wilfrid's Needle

(*St.*). The crypt of Ripon Cathedral. The eye of this 'needle' is a hole in a wall through which women suspected of unchastity were required to 'thread themselves,' as evidence of their innocence.

There is a 'Wilfrid's Needle' in Belvoir Castle, spoken of by Bishop [Joseph] Hall. Others are also referred to occasionally.

Wilkes's Riots,

1768. In No. 45 of the 'North Briton,' conducted by Wilkes, member for Aylesbury, the king was charged with telling a deliberate lie in his speech from the throne. The royal party was so infuriated that Wilkes fled to France, but returned in 1768, and was sentenced to imprisonment for twenty-two months. The mob rose in insurrection on behalf of their champion, and resolved to conduct him in triumph to Westminster. The yeomanry were called out. Wilkes was expelled from the house, but was re-elected by an over-whelming majority. Soon afterwards he was made a London alderman, lord mayor, and eventually member for Middlesex, and chamberlain of London—a very lucrative office.

William I.

'Wilhelm' king of Prussia and German emperor; born 1797, died 1888.

King of Prussia, 1861–1888.

German Emperor, 1871–1888.

Father, Friedrich Wilhelm III. (second son); *Mother*, Louisa Augusta of Mecklenburg-Strelitz; *Wife*, Louisa Augusta, daughter of Karl Friedrich of Saxe-Weimar. *Contemporary* with Victoria.

. His son, Friedrich Wilhelm [Nicholas], born 1831, married Victoria princess royal of England in 1858. He succeeded his father in March, but died in June 1888.

William I. the Conqueror (1025, 1066–1087). First of the Norman dynasty of England, which supplied four sovereigns—viz. William I., William II. (his son), Henry I. (brother of William II.), and Stephen (brother-in-law of the last two kings).

Father, Robert le Diable duke of Normandy (William was a natural son). His *mother* was Arlete, Harlotta, or Herleva='beloved,' and her father was a tanner of Falaise, *Wife*, Matilda, daughter of Baldwin V. count of Flanders. His daughter Adela married Stephen count of Blois, and it was their son Stephen who usurped the crown.

Style and title: Gulielmus rex Anglorum, comes Normannorum et Cenomanentium.

. The Cenomani were a people in what is now called Mans, in France.

William II., Rufus, or 'The Red King' (1056, 1087–1100), the second king of England from the Conquest. He was the second son of William I. (*q.v.*), and usurped the crown of his elder brother Robert.

Father, William I.; *Mother*, Matilda, daughter of Baldwin V. count of Flanders. Never married; shot in New Forest while hunting by Sir Walter Tyrell, whether by accident or design was never known. His *style and title*: Gulielmus rex Anglorum. Sometimes 'Gulielmus monarchicus Britanniæ.'

William III. and Mary. Fifth of the Stuart dynasty of Great Britain. William III. (1650, 1689–1702), Mary (1662, 1689–1694). No issue.

Father of William, William II. of Orange; *Mother*, Mary, eldest daughter of Charles I.; *Wife* (see below).

Father of Mary, James II. of Great Britain; *Mother*, Mary d'Este of Modéna; *Husband* (see above).

Style and Title: William and Mary, D. G. of England, Scotland, France, and Ireland, King and Queen; Defenders of the Faith, &c. After the death of Mary in 1694 the needful alterations were of course made.

The horse on which William III. was riding when he received his fatal accident was named Sorrel.' Pope says:—

Angels who watched the guardian oak so well,
How chanced ye slept when luckless Sorrel fell?

. The principality of Orange consisted of a part of the present department of Vaucluse; and the House was founded in the 9th cent, In 1530 Nassau was added by the marriage of Otto of Nassau with Claude de Chalon of Orange. In 1599 William of Orange and Nassau was elected stadtholder of Holland. After the death of William III. of England the line of Orange and Nassau became extinct, whereupon Louis XIV. claimed the principality of Orange and added it to France.

William IV. (1765, 1830–1837). Third son of George III., and brother of George IV., the preceding king. His brother, Frederick duke of York, the second son of George III., died in 1827.

William was duke of Clarence. Being brought up in the navy service, he became Lord Admiral of England, and was called 'The Sailor King.' By Mrs. Jordan he had eight children: George Fitzclarence, Frederick Fitzclarence, Augustus, and the five daughters Sophia, Mary, Elizabeth, Augusta, and Amelia.

Father, George III.; *Mother*, Charlotte Sophia of Mecklenburg-Strelitz; *Wife*, Adelaide, daughter of the Duke of Saxe-Meiningen; two children, both died in infancy. *Next heir to the crown*, Victoria, daughter of his brother Edward duke of Kent. *Style and title*, William IV., D.G. of England, Scotland, and Ireland, King, Defender of the Faith, &c.

William the Bad (*, 1154–1166). William I. of Sicily.

William the Conqueror. William I. (*q.v.*). So called because he conquered Harold in the battle of Senlac, and thus became king of England.

He had four sons and six daughters. His *sons* were Robert (twice supplanted by his younger brothers); WILLIAM II. (Rufus), who succeeded his father; Richard, who was killed by an accident; and HENRY I., who succeeded his brother William II.

His *daughters* were Cecilia, Constance, Adela who married Stephen count of Blois (whose son STEPHEN succeeded Henry I.), Adeliza, Agatha, and Gundred.

William the Conqueror's Comet, 1066. This comet was visible in China from 2 April for 67 days; it was visible in Europe from May for 40 days. Never comet excited such attention. In the famous tapestry of Queen Matilda several figures are represented gazing at this comet, and the inscription below is 'Isti mirantur stellam.'

William the Good (1154, 1166–1189). William II. king of Sicily, son of William the Bad.

William the Lion of Scotland (1166–1214). So called because he was the first who introduced a lion in the armorial bearings of Scotland. The chief of the Scottish heralds is called Lyon king of arms.

William the Silent (1533, 1544–1584), prince of Orange. Assassinated by Balthasar Gerard at Delft.

Williamites (3 syl.), in French 'Guillemites' (3 syl.), in Italy 'Guglielmotes,'1153. A religious institution founded by St. William of Malavalle, which rapidly spread through all Italy, Germany, and France. They were called *White Mantles* because they wore large white mantles.

Williams Prize (*The George*). Theology. Given to the best student in the theological tripos. Value about 9*l.* Founded in the University of Cambridge by friends of the Rev. George Williams, formerly fellow of King's College, 1882.

Will's Coffee House. In the reign of Charles II. near Covent Garden, at the western corner of Bow Street. It was the great emporium of libels and scandals, but was one of the best in London, and had acquired the sobriquet of 'the Wits' Coffee-house.' Here the frequenters heard the talk of the town about the poets, authors, and other celebrities, and here was the 'Observator,' and all the Tory and Whig journals of the day; and here would be found Matthew Prior, John Dryden, Betterton the tragedian, and other celebrities.

Wills and Uses (*The two Statutes of*), 1634. Passed by the Irish parliament, giving to the crown of England a share and interest in the education of the heirs-apparent of the great families of Ireland. Of course, the object was to bring them up Protestants, like the son of the Earl of Ormond, formerly the king's ward.

Winchester. Henry III. of England was surnamed Winchester from the place in which he was born (1206, 1216–1272).

Winchester (*The Statute of*), 1285. A renewal of the 'Assize of Arms' (*q.v.*), *i.e.* basing the preservation of public order on the strict enforcement of the local system of frank-pledge. By this statute every man was bound to hold himself in readiness for the king's service, every man was to join in the hue and cry after felons, every district was held responsible for all crimes committed within its bounds, the gates of every town were required to be closed at nightfall, every stranger was required to give an account of himself to a magistrate, and all brushwood and cover for thieves was to be destroyed for 200 feet on each side of a high road.

Winchester Book (*The*). The register of King Alfred's survey of England drawn up by his council at Winchester.

Winchester College [Seinte Marie College of Wynchestre], 1387. Founded by William of Wykeham, bishop of Winchester.

The famous *dulce domum* is still sung in the courts of the college before the breaking up of the school for long vacation. It is very funny that the solecism should have so caught the fancy.

Winchester Reading Prizes (*The*). For reading classical English poetry and prose, the scriptures and liturgy. Two prizes of the value of 40*l.*, two-thirds to be given to the best reader, and one-third to the second best. Founded in the University of Cambridge by an anonymous donor in 1886.

Wind, Protestant and Popish. See p. 718, 'Protestant.'

Windsor Prophecy (*The*), 1712. A scurrilous set of verses by Swift, afterwards dean of St. Patrick's, Dublin. In this 'prophecy' Elizabeth duchess of Somerset is called 'Carrots' for her red hair, and is accused of assassinating Thomas Thynne of Longleat, her second husband. She was daughter and heiress of Joceline duke of Northumberland, and married Lord Ogle, son of the Duke of Newcastle, when only 11 years old. She was a widow at 13, and married Thomas Thynne, who was shot by Count Königsmark, a German adventurer. Being thus a widow again at the age of 14, she took for her third husband the Duke of Somerset, who died 1748.

But England, dear England, if I understand,
Beware of *Carrots* from Northumberland (*daughter of . . .*)
Carrots, however *Thynne*, a deep root may get (*second husband*),
If so be they are in *Summer-set* (*third husband*).
Their *Cunning's-mark* thou, for I have been told (*shot Thynne*)
They *assassine* when young and poison when old.
Root out those Carrots, thou whose name
Spelt backwards and forwards is always the same (*Anna* or Queen Anne),
And keep close to thee always that name
Which backwards and forwards is almost the same (Mrs. *Masham*).
And England, wouldst thou be happy still,
Bury those Carrots under a *Hill*.
(Mrs. Masham s maiden name was Abigail Hill).

When Swift's name was given to the queen for the vacant see of Hereford the Duchess of Somerset set her face against the appointment, and Swift lost his bishopric. The ostensible plea against him was his 'Tale of a Tub.'

Windsor Soap. 'Soapy Sam,' Bishop of Oxford. Called 'Soap' from an inscription on the porch of Cuddesdon College. S. Oxon was the founder and Alfred Potts the first principal. The bishop himself observed the curious combination of letters S.O., A.P. 'Windsor' was added because Samuel Wilberforce was a great favourite with the court at Windsor (1805–1873).

Samuel Wilberforce was transferred to Winchester.

Windy Cap. Eric king of Sweden, second to none, says Olaus Magnus, in magical arts, was so familiar with evil spirits that what way soever he turned his cap the wind would presently blow that way. *Historia de Gentibus Septentrionalibus*, Romæ, 1555.

Wines of Africa and Asia. *Bithynian* wine from the Mersites grape was of a very choice quality. The wines of *Byblos*, in Phœnicia, vied in fragrancy with Lesbian wine. The white wines of *Mareotis* and *Tænia*, in Lower Egypt, were of unrivalled excellence; the former was sometimes called *Alexandrian*. The wine of *Meröe* resembled Falernian (Lucan, 'Pharsalia,' x. 161). *Tæniotic* wine was greenish, luscious, and aromatic. The wine of *Antylla*, in the vicinity of Alexandria, and the *Sebennytic* wines were also commended.

On the mountain of Tmölus, in Lydia, was produced a brown wine, described as first rate by Virgil and Galen. The *Scybellités* of Galatia was thick and sweet. The *Ahatés* of Cilicia was a sweet red wine. The *Tibenum*, the *Arsynium*, and the *Titucazenum* were of lighter growth, the first two being dry red wines, and the last a sweet wine of paler colour.

Wines of Ancient Greece. The earliest wine was the *Maronëan*, a sweet black wine, so called from the district where it was made, which was on the coast of Thrace. Usually mixed with twenty parts of water; in Pliny's time with only eight parts of water; *Sciathos*, another black wine of lighter quality, being drunk half and half. *Pramnian*, a dry red wine, made from grapes grown on the Pramnian hill, in the island of Icaros. *Corinthian* wine, so astringent that Alexis declares it was real torture to drink it ('Athen.' i. 24). The luscious sweet wines were *Lesbian*, *Chian*, *Thasian*, *Corcyrian*, *Cyprian*, *Cretan*, *Cnidian*, and *Rhodian*, all white wines. The *Saprian* (qy. Chian) wine was famous for its aroma; the *Lesbian* had less aroma, but was very delicious. Pliny places the *Clazomenian* wine of Ionia in the first rank. Virgil

calls the *Phanean* the king of wines. Of light wines we have the *Mendean* (from Mende, in Thrace), a white wine; the *Argitis* ('Georgics,' ii. 99), and *Omphacités*.

Winter King (*The*). Frederick V. (who married Elizabeth, daughter of James I. of England), who was crowned at Prague king of Bohemia, 25 Oct., 1619, and was driven from the throne by the Catholics, 8 Nov., 1620. He was king for one winter and no more.

Frederick, elector palatine, was made king of Bohemia in opposition to Kaiser Ferdinand II.

Winter Queen (*The*). Elizabeth, daughter of James I. of Great Britain, and wife of Frederick V. the 'Winter King.'

Winters (*Cold*). 1709, the severest winter on record. The following were cold winters:

1067. Thousands of travellers in Germany were frozen to death.
1133. Wine casks in France and Spain were frozen, and many trees in Italy were split by the frost.
1179. The snow up to Easter was eight feet deep in Austria.
1233. The Po was frozen over.
1236. The Danube was frozen to the very bottom. The Cattegat between Norway and Jutland was also frozen.
1281. Many houses in Austria were actually buried in snow.
1292. Travellers passed on the ice from Norway to Jutland. The Rhine was frozen over.
1314. All the rivers of Italy were frozen.
1323. Travellers passed on the ice from Dantzic to Denmark.
1364. The sea at Venice was frozen.
1408. Travellers passed on the ice from Norway to Denmark.
1434. It snowed forty days and forty nights in Germany without intermission.
1468. Wine in casks and bottles throughout all Europe was frozen.
1580. The Great and Little Belt were frozen over.
1622. The Hellespont was frozen over.
1658. Charles X. led his whole army over the ice from Holstein to Denmark.
1692. The Zuyder-Zee was entirely frozen over.
1684. Coaches plied on the Thames.
1709-10 was infinitely colder than any of the preceding. The frost penetrated three yards (!) into the ground. The olive plantations in France were utterly destroyed. Birds died by thousands, and trees with vegetables were killed in all directions. The Adriatic was frozen over, so was the coast of the Mediterranean about Genoa.
1729 was a continued frost from October to May 1730.
1740 was the coldest winter known except that of 1709.
1744 was a severe winter.
1776. Wine was frozen in the cellars in France and Holland. And in England the destruction of birds and fishes was frightful.
1794 was a continuous frost from 24 Dec. to 14 Feb., 1795.
1796. Dec. 25 was the coldest day ever known in London. Fahr. thermom. was 16° below zero (!).
1814. A fair was held on the Thames.

1848. On one occasion the mercury in the thermometer was frozen.

1860 was one of the severest winters ever known in Britain. On Christmas Day the thermometer on the grass stood 13° below zero Fahrenheit. The three coldest days were 24, 25, 26 Dec.

.·. Remember 32° is freezing, so that—16°=46° of frost. Apparently a correct observation.

Winton Domesday (*The*). Containing two surveys of the city of Winchester: one made between 1107 and 1128, and the other made in 1148. Published by Sir Henry Ellis in the second of the supplementary volumes of Domesday Book, 1816.

Wire Age (*The*). The Golden Age, the Silver Age, the Age of Bronze, and the Iron Age have had their day, and we now live in the Wire Age. Every street and almost every road is crowded with telegraph wires, which are stretched over our houses and sunk under our seas. Our books are stitched with wire, our clocks set by wire, our watches run by wire, our politics are managed by wire; we announce our wants, our news, our going and coming by wire; use wire covers for our meat, wire sieves, and wire pulls for our gongs; we sleep on wire mattresses, and indeed in every department of life wire is our slave (1890).

Wisconsin (U.S. America). So called in 1836 from its river of the same name. The inhabitants are nicknamed *Badgers*.

Wisest Fool in Christendom (*The*). James I. of England was so called by Sully, the French politician (1566, 1603–1625).

Witch of Eye (*The*). Marjory Jourdemain, with whom Dame-Eleanor Cobham, the mistress and afterwards wife of the 'Good duke Humphrey [Duke of Gloucester], protector of the realm in the minority of his nephew Henry VI., Dame Eleanor was accused of sorcery with intent to bewitch the king and raise her husband to the throne.' Marjory was burnt as a witch at Smithfield, 1441.

Witchcraft. So late as 1805 a woman was tried at Kirkcudbright for witchcraft, and actually sentenced to a year's imprisonment, and to be set once a quarter in the pillory. Elspeth Rule in 1709 was tried in Dumfries in the Court of Justiciary, and condemned for witchcraft to have her cheek branded with a hot iron. Documents referring to Elspeth M'Ewen, who was burnt to death in a tar-barrel for witchcraft in 1697 at Kirkcudbright, have recently been unearthed, in which is this item: 'Payed to Robert Creighton . . . 8 shill Scots for beating the drum at Elspet M'Queen's funeral, and to James Carsson his wife threeten shillings drunken by Elspet's executioner at seall times.'

That is, James Carsson's wife.

Witches' Hammer (*The*), 15th cent. An infamous document drawn up by John Gremper, an ecclesiastic, laying down with great minuteness the characteristics of witches and wizards, the skin-marks to be sought for, the familiar which clung to them in the shape of cat, dog, goat, or other pet animal, and the questions to be asked in order to convict them out of their own mouths.

Pope Innocent VIII. led the way to this witch persecution by his bull of 1484, which charged the inquisitors and all true Catholics diligently to search out and put to death all who practised the diabolical arts of witchcraft, magic, sorcery, and enchantment.

Wit'ena-gemo'te (*The*). The mote or council of wise men. In Saxon times each kingdom, before 827, had its separate gemote, but after that date there was one general assembly composed of ecclesiastics, aldermen, and large landholders, held every Christmas, Easter, and Whitsuntide. In the year 934 the gemote (2 syl.) was attended by King Athelstan, 4 Welsh princes, 2 archbishops, 17 bishops, 4 abbots, 12 dukes, and 52 thanes. The Witena-gemote ordained the king's succession, made laws and treaties, levied taxes, regulated military and church affairs, and was a supreme court of justice. *See* 'Shire-mote.'

Witena is the gen. plural of the Anglo-Saxon *wita*, a wise man (verb *witan*, 'to know'—our 'wit'), and *gemote* is an assembly, from the verb *metan*, 'to meet together.' The king presided in his robes of state.

Witling of Terror (*The*). Bertrand Barère de Vieuzac, president of the National Convention in 1792. So called from the flowery language in which he spoke on all measures of the reign of terror. Also called the 'Anacreon of the Guillotine.'

Wives of the English Kings.

I. *Before the Conquest* :—

Egbert	... ..	Lady Redburga.
Ethelwolf	... ...	Lady Osburga, whose father was the Great Butler of England (mother of Alfred the Great).

Alfred	1. Judith daughter of Charles the Bald of France. 2. Ethelswitha or Answinta daughter of the Earl of Mercia.
Edward the Elder	1. Lady Eguina. 2. Elfleda. 3. Edgiva mother of Edmund.
Edmund	Lady Elgiva.
Edgar	1. Ethelfled. 2. Elfrida daughter of Ordgarus duke of Devonshire.
Ethelred	1. Elgiva daughter of Duke Thored. 2. Emma daughter of Richard II. duke of Normandy.
Edmund Ironside	Algitha widow of Segeforth, a Dane.
Edward the Confessor	Edgitha daughter of Earl Godwine.

II. Since the Conquest :—

William I. the Conqueror	Matilda daughter of Baldwin V. count of Flanders.
Henry I.	Matilda or Maud daughter of Malcolm III. of Scotland.
Stephen	Matilda daughter of Eustace count of Boulogne.
Henry II.	Eleanor of Guienne, divorced wife of Louis VII. of France.
Richard Cœur de Lion	Berengaria daughter of Sancho VI. of Navarre.
John	1. A daughter of the Earl of Mortagne. 2. Avisa daughter of William earl of Gloucester, mother of Henry III. 3. Isabella of France.
Henry III.	Eleanor daughter of Raymonet earl of Provence.
Edward I.	Eleanor sister of Alfonso XI. king of Castile.
Edward II.	Isabella daughter of Philippe IV. of France.
Edward III.	Philippa of Hainault.
Richard II.	1. Anne daughter of Kaiser Karl IV. of Germany. 2. Isabella, aged seven, daughter of Charles VI. of France.
Henry IV.	1. Mary le Bohun daughter of the Earl of Hereford. 2. Jane daughter of Charles the Bald of Navarre and widow of John duke of Brittany.
Henry V.	Catherine daughter of Charles VI. of France.
Henry VI.	Margaret daughter of the Duke of Anjou.
Edward IV.	Elizabeth daughter of Sir Richard Woodville of Grafton, Northamptonshire.
Richard III.	Anne Neville widow of Edward prince of Wales.
Henry VII.	Princess Elizabeth daughter of Edward IV.
Henry VIII.	1. Catharine of Aragon mother of Mary, who married Philip [II.] of Spain. 2. Anne Boleyn mother of Elizabeth. 3. Jane Seymour mother of Edward VI. 4. Anne of Cleves. 5. Catharine Howard. 6. Catharine Parr.
James I.	Ann of Denmark.
Charles I.	Henrietta daughter of Henri IV. of France.

Charles II.*	The Infanta Katharine of Portugal.
James II.	1. Ann Hyde daughter of the Earl of Clarendon, mother of Mary and Anne. 2. Mary d'Este of Modĕna.
William III.	Mary daughter of James II. and Anne Hyde.

(Anne married Prince George of Denmark.)

George I.	Sophia daughter of George William duke of Brunswick and Zell.
George II.	Wilhelmina daughter of John Frederick margrave of Anspach.
George III.	Charlotte of Mecklenburgh-Strelitz.
George IV.	Caroline princess of Brunswick.
William IV.	Adelaide daughter of the Duke of Saxe-Meiningen.

(Victoria married Albert second son of Ernest duke of Saxe-Coburg and Gotha.)

* Cromwell married Elizabeth daughter of Sir James Bouchier of Essex.

Wizard of the Sea (*The*). Capt. Kidd, 17th cent. Executed for piracy 12 May, 1701.

Wolf of America (*The*). Montgomery, who led the attack on Quebec in 1775. The English Wolfe took Quebec, and fell in the hour of victory; Montgomery tried to take it, but failed, being killed in the hour of defeat.

Wolf of Badenoch (*The*). Sir Alexander Stewart, fourth son of Robert II. by his first wife Elizabeth, daughter of Sir William Mure of Rowallan, who was related to him within the prohibited degrees and was divorced. Sir Alexander, who was earl of Buchan, was fierce and savage as a wolf.

Some say he was grandson of Robert II., and third son of Robert duke of Albany.

Wolf of Plinlimmon (*The*). Gwenwyn prince of Powys Land during the reign of Henry II.

Wolsey of Hungary (*The*). The Cardinal Martinuzzi (16th cent.).

Wolsey's Foundation at Oxford, 1524. Called 'Cardinal College.' In 1546 the name was changed to 'Christ Church College.'

Woman-flogger (*The*). Julius Jakob baron von Haynau (1786–1853). An Austrian general who signalized himself during the Italian campaigns of 1848–1849 by ruthless cruelty. His flogging of women refers to his treatment of the defeated Hungarians, and his infamy excited the detestation of all Europe. In 1850 he came to England and visited the brewery of Barclay &

Perkins in London, when he was assaulted by the draymen and narrowly escaped with his life. He afterwards visited Belgium and France, and was received with strong demonstrations of popular hatred.

Women (*The Four Perfect*). Miriam sister of Moses, Mary mother of Jesus, Cadijah the first wife of Mahomet, and Fatima his daughter.

Women's Rights. A political movement first started in 1851 by the 'Westminster Review.' It includes the right of suffrage, for which a petition was presented to parliament in 1866. Their *industrial* rights include admission to the Universities and the right of engaging in the higher professions. The third claim is the right of married women to hold and bequeath property.

In 1869 the municipal franchise was conferred on women. Several colleges for women have been opened in Cambridge and Oxford ; and the Women's Property Act enables them both to hold and bequeath property.

Wonderful Boy of Devizes (*The*). Sir Thomas Lawrence, born at Bristol, the great painter of portraits. Died 1830 at the age of sixty.

Wonderful Boys.

BARATIER (*Johann Philip*), 1721–1740. German. At the age of five he knew Greek, Latin, and French, besides his native German. At nine he knew Hebrew and Chaldee, and could translate German into Latin. At thirteen he could translate Hebrew into French, or *vice versâ*. His life was written by Formey, and an account of him is inserted in most biographical dictionaries.

BASSLE (*Gustave Adolph*). In the first half of the 19th cent. exhibited his wonderful powers at Willis's Rooms under the patronage of the Duke of Sussex. About 20,000 questions had been prepared by the duke's authority, and were circulated amongst the audience. These questions were in sacred and profane history, chronology, physical science, mythology, statistics, arithmetic, geography, cosmography, and natural history. Any one of the audience might put any question to the boy, or as many as he pleased, in any order, and the boy instantly answered without a mistake. Several members of the British Association were present, and took part in the function.

It was said that much of this was due to the science of 'sunemonics,' a predecessor of 'mnemonics.'

BETTY (*William Henry West*). Made his *début* in London as an actor in 1803, being about twelve years of age. In fifty-six nights he realised 34,000*l.*, and with wonderful sagacity retired into private life. He died in 1874 at the age of 84.

The greatest mark of genius was his retirement in the full tide of his popularity.

BIDDER (*George Parker*). At the age of six amused himself by counting up to a million. He became an engineer, and baffled the parliamentary counsel on contested railway bills by confuting their statements of figures before the words were out of their mouths. In 1856 he showed to the members of the Institution of Civil Engineers that these calculations were not made by dodges, but seriatim, only with inconceivable rapidity (b. 1800).

BUXTON (*Jedediah*), son of a schoolmaster. On hearing a sermon he would tell at once how many words the preacher had spoken. If a period of time was mentioned, he would instantly calculate how many seconds had elapsed since then to the time. He was taken to see Garrick in 'Richard III.,' but his sole amusement was to count the number of words he uttered. He once set himself to reckon how much a farthing would amount to if doubled 140 times ; the answer contained thirty-nine figures representing pounds. In 1750 he reckoned how many grains of eight different kinds of corn and pulse would cover 200,000 miles, and how many hairs would make an inch. What is strange is this—he could suspend a calculation at any moment, and take it up again hours or days afterwards. (1704–1775.)

CANDIAC (*Jean Louis Elizabeth de Montcalm de*), we are told, knew his letters when an infant in arms. At three years he could read fluently both Latin and French either in print or MS. At four he could translate Latin. At five he could translate the most difficult Latin authors. At six he could read Greek and Hebrew, was good at arithmetic, history, heraldry, geography, and the science of medals. At seven years of age he had read the chief poets, orators, historians, philosophers, grammarians, &c. But he died before he had completed his seventh year. (1719–1726.)

Dictionnaire d'Education, 1819, and most biographical dictionaries, under the word 'Montcalm.'

His elder brother **Louis Joseph marquis de Mont-calm** (born 1712) commanded the French army in Canada and defeated Abercromby; but was mortally wounded in 1759 under the walls of Quebec.

COLBURN (*Zerah*). A native of Vermont, in the United States; came to London in 1812, being eight years old, and answered most complicated problems, such as raising 8 to the sixteenth power; giving the square root of 106,929, the cube root of 268,336,125; and how many seconds in fifty years. He never required above a second or two for his answer, but knew nothing of arithmetic. Zerah had more than the usual number of fingers and toes, so had his father and brothers. Later, his mathematical powers disappeared to a great extent. (1804–1840.)

HEINECKEN (*Christian Heinrich*). At one year old knew the chief events of the Pentateuch! At thirteen months he knew the history of the Old Testament! At fourteen months he knew the history of the New Testament! At two-and-a-half years of age he could answer any ordinary question of history or geography. And at three years old he knew French and Latin, as well as his native German. The life of this boy was written by Schœneich, his tutor, and his name, like that of Baratier, is inserted in most biographical dictionaries. (1721–1725.)

MANGIAMETE (*Nito*). A Sicilian, son of a shepherd. At eleven years old (July, 1839) he was examined by Arago, Lacroix, Libri, Sturm, and others, sent for the purpose by the Academy of Science in Paris. He was asked to give the cube root of 3,796,416, which he answered in one minute; he gave the 10th root of 282,475,249 in three minutes. He was then asked by M. Arago, 'What number has the following proportions: if the cube is added to five times its square, and then 42 times the number, and the number 42 be subtracted from the result, the remainder will be 0?' Before M. Arago had finished his question the boy answered 5.

VISCOUNT (*Ennius*), we are told, could 'read Greek and Latin, as well as his own language [Italian], before he was four years old. He was exhibited as a prodigy between the age of four and five, and submitted to a public examination. Viscount died in 1818, aged sixty-seven.

Wonderful Castle (*The*). The palace built of stone at Tuam by Roderic

O'Connor (1161). Castles were till the 12th cent. built of wood in Ireland.

Probably there were stone or brick structures in Ireland before the 12th century, as, for example, the Round Towers, but they were so rare that the palace of Tuam was called 'Wonderful.'

Wonderful Doctor (*The*). 'Doctor Mirabilis,' Roger Bacon (1214–1292). A Franciscan monk, born at Ilchester, in Somersetshire. His chief work is called 'Opus Majus.' He looked with contempt on 'Scholastic Theology.'

Wonderful Parliament (*The*), or 'Wonder-making Parliament,' 3 Feb., 1388. Convened by Thomas [Plantagenet] duke of Gloucester in the reign of his nephew Richard II. The chancellor, De la Pole, having been impeached in 1386 by the commons, the duke proceeded to establish a permanent council of fourteen, consisting of his own partisans, to inquire into everything in the king's household, the ministry, the law courts, and the condition of the people. Gloucester was at the head, and the king, now nearly twenty-one years of age, was virtually deposed. All sovereign prerogatives for five months lay with the council. The king protested, the judges declared the proceedings unconstitutional and the parliament guilty of treason. The king impeached the chief members, but Gloucester, at the head of 40,000 men, compelled the king to give way, and resolved to depose him. Several of the king's friends were arrested, and some were put to death. Strangest of all, it declared that its judgments should never be reversed, nor its acts repealed. It was dissolved 3 June, 1388. *See* p. 664, 'Parliament.'

Wood of the Cross (*The*). There is an ingenious legend that when Adam was buried at Hebron three trees sprang from his dead body. David transplanted these trees to Jerusalem, they amalgamated into one. Solomon felled the tree, intending to use it for the principal of the Temple, but being too short it was laid on one side. The Jews used this very tree for the Cross, and after the crucifixion it was buried for more than 200 years, when it was discovered in a cave during the visit of Helěna, the emperor's mother, to Jerusalem.

This can hardly be called a legend; it is a mere allegory, to connect the first with the second

Adam; the trinity with unity; and the short coming of the law with the everlasting gospel.

Wood Silver. A payment of money instead of wood for the manor fires by a tenant farmer (14th cent.).

Wood's Halfpence, 1724. Halfpence coined for Ireland by William Wood, an iron and copper founder of Wolverhamptom. There had long been a deficiency of copper coin in Ireland, and the government contracted with Mr. Wood to supply 108,000 pounds' worth of halfpence and farthings, of stated weight and fineness. Sir Isaac Newton, master of the mint, was fully satisfied with the way the contract had been carried out, and said that, although the weight of the Irish coin was a trifle less than that of the English copper money, yet Wood had fully compensated for this difference by superior fineness. Dean Swift, for political purposes, ran down the new coin both in prose and verse. One of his verses runs thus—

The halfpence are coming, the nation's undoing,
There's an end of your ploughing, and baking,
   and brewing,
In that you must all go to rack and to ruin.
          See ' Drapier's Letters.'

Woodland Party (*The*). The Bianchi faction (*q.v.*), so called from the Cerchi, who lived in woodland (= rural) districts when Dante in exile was thrown amongst them.

Woodstock Ghost (*The*), 1649. A trick played on the commissioners sent by the Long Parliament to take possession of the house. The ghost was one of the commissioners' clerks, named Giles Sharp, who played his part so well that his companions fled from Woodstock in terror. The secret was kept till the Revolution.

The real name of Giles Sharp was Joseph Collins, a concealed Royalist, who had lived at Woodstock and knew every hole and cranny intimately.

Woodwardian Professor of Geology. Value 500*l.* a year. Founded in the University of Cambridge by Dr. Woodward, 1727. *See* ' Harkness Scholarship,' ' Sedgwick Prize.'

Woo-taë in Chinese history means ' The period of the Five Races.' During the first part of this period the empire was divided into southern and northern; the imperial line reigned in the southern empire, with Nankin as the seat of government. The seat of government

of the northern empire was Ho-nân. In A.D. 534 the northern empire was split into the eastern or Tong-Oeï, and the western or Si-Oeï. In 587 the three empires were united again under the 12th imperial dynasty, that of Swi. The founder was a cobbler named Lieu-yu, and when he usurped the throne he was named Voo-tee III. The contemporary kings of the northern empire were Tao-Voo-tee and Ming-yuen-tee. The capital of the southern empire was Nân-kin, and of the northern empire Ho-nân.

The five races were Tsong, Tsee, Lëang, Tchin, and Swi, including the 8th, 9th, 10th, 11th, and 12th imperial dynasties.
. Voo means *warrior*, and tee means *ruler*.

Worcester College, Oxford, 1714. Founded by Sir Thomas Cookes. The head-master is called the Provost. It was originally called Gloucester Hall, and was used by the monks of St. Peter, Gloucester.

Working-men's Association (*The*), 1838. A title assumed by the Chartists (*q.v.*).

Works of Supererogation, 1274. The belief that our Saviour's sufferings were more than sufficient for the sins of the world, and hence good works were an extra stock which might be applied to balance off evil works. As saints abounded in good works they accumulated a stock of merits which could be applied for the benefit of others or for redemption of souls from purgatory.

Workshop Regulation Act (*The*), 1867 (30 & 31 Vict. c. 146), provides:

1. That no child under the age of 8 shall be employed in any handicraft.

2. That no child under 13 shall be employed for more than 6½ hours a day, between 6 a.m. and 8 p.m.

3. That no young person under 18 and no woman shall be employed more than 12 hours, between 5·a.m. and 9 p.m., with an hour and a half interval at least for meals.

4. Except in retail business no child or woman shall be employed after 2 o'clock on Saturdays.

5. No child under 11 shall in any wise be employed in grinding or fustian cutting.

Worms (*The Diet of*), 1521. Convened by Karl V. to put down the new opinions in religion. Luther was summoned, and defended himself; but the diet convicted him of heresy, and issued an edict for his apprehension, and the committal of his books to the flames. The Elector of Saxony concealed him for nine months, and he escaped.

Worship of Reason (*The*), 1793. A substitute for Christianity in the first French republic. It was the beauty of virtue and the arbitrament of reason. 7 Nov., 1793, Mgr. Gobet, archbishop of Paris, with a multitude of other ecclesiastics, went to the Hall of the Convention, and there solemnly resigned their functions and renounced the Christian religion. It was then decreed that the deities of France should thenceforth be Liberty, Equality, and Reason. The word 'God' was prohibited, and all Christian rites were abolished. A procession was then made to Notre Dame, where an actress was seated on the altar to represent the Goddess of Reason.

Worsley's Act (*Lord*), 1836 (6 & 7 Will. IV.). The General Enclosure Act. Nine years after came a more general Act for the enclosure of commons (1845).

Wranglers, 1753. In the University of Cambridge. Originally the Tripos consisted of Senior Optimes (3 syl.), Junior Optimes, and the Poll-men, or Oἱ πολλοί. But in 1753 the first class was divided, and the best men were made into a new division called Wranglers. The Poll-men were then cut off, and the Tripos consisted only of the three honour classes called Wranglers, Senior Optimes, and Junior Optimes. The first word referred to the disputations, or acts held in the school, which, being highly satisfactory, the moderator complimented the respondent by saying to him *Summo ingenii acumine disputasti* ('You have wrangled excellently'). To the other honour men he said *Optime disputasti* (for Junior Optimes), and *Optime quidem disputasti* (for Senior Optimes).

'Wright of Derby.' Joseph Wright (1734–1797), a celebrated landscape painter born at Derby. His landscapes are noted for elegance of outline and judicious management of light and shade.

Writ of Habeas Corpus (16 Car. I. c. 10), A.D. 1641. It enacts (1) that any person arrested for a bailable offence shall be set at liberty upon giving the awarded bail, with an assurance to appear and answer the charge when duly called upon so to do; (2) that officers shall not evade this law by shifting about the custody of a prisoner under a penalty of 100*l*. for the first offence and 200*l*. for the second; (3) no person delivered by *habeas corpus* shall be re-committed; (4) 'every person charged with an offence shall, if he requires it, be tried in the next session; (5) no prisoner shall be sent out of his own country to be tried. Thus an Englishman cannot be sent to Scotland, Ireland, the Channel Isles, or to any of the Colonies.

There are four other provisions, but they rather pertain to the legal profession than to the general public.

Writer to the Signet, or 'Clerk to the Signet.' A Scotch attorney of the highest class. At one time the clerks so called were in the office of the Secretary of State, where writs that passed under the royal signet were prepared.

Würzburg (*Patron Saint of*). St. Kilian, an Irishman, who converted a duke of Würzburg, and was assassinated by Geila, who was his brother's wife. Kilian told the duke it was unlawful to live with Geila, and the exasperated woman sent an assassin to murder Kilian while he was celebrating midnight service. Geilah = *Gy-lah*.

Wyatt's Rebellion, 1553–1554. Sir Thomas Wyatt the Younger formed a confederacy to oppose the marriage of Queen Mary with Philip II. of Spain. He marched on London, and the trainbands who were sent against him under the command of the Duke of Norfolk deserted in a mass to the rebel. Wyatt pushed on to Temple Bar, which was closed against him. He surrendered to Sir M. Berkeley, was committed to the Tower, tried, convicted, and beheaded.

Xabatatenses (Wooden shoes), so the Waldenses (*q.v.*) were called from xabatata (a wooden sandal), worn in imitation of the apostles.

Yankee. A name of badinage applied to the North Americans by the English, but accepted with pride and satisfaction by all true-hearted Americans. It was originally the corruption of the word Anglois by the American Indians. Jonathan Hastings, a farmer of Cambridge, in New England, in 1713, used the word as a synonym of excellence. 'It is Yankee good,' or good as if English made; and the people of the other colonies jocosely called the New Englanders 'Jonathan Yankees,' and sometimes shortened the phrase either into Jonathan or into Yankee.

Yankee Doodle. The name of a well-known tune, one of the 'national airs' of the U.S.; also a doggerel song set to that tune.

Yassanian Dynasty (*The*). The fourth of the fabulous dynasties of Persia. The two names given are Shah Yassan the founder, and Yassan Ajem the last of the race. It was preceded by the Kuleev dynasty, and followed by the Paishdadians (*q.v.*).

Yatagan, a Turkish sabre worn in the sash.

Year I. of the Revolutionary Calendar, from 22 Sept., 1792, to 21 Sept., 1793. The French Convention announced that in future the Christian era was to be abolished, and all dates were to be taken from the Revolution era.

The Republican calendar was first used 26 Nov., 1793, and was discontinued 31 Dec., 1805.
Royalty abolished, 22 Sept., 1792.
The King Louis XVI. guillotined, 21 January, 1793; and the Committee of Public Safety instituted.
Fall of the Girondists, 2 June, 1793.
Assassination of Marat by Charlotte Corday, 13 July, 1793.
New constitution proclaimed, 10 Aug., 1793.

Year II. of the Revolutionary Calendar, from 22 Sept., 1793, to 21 Sept., 1794.

The Queen Marie Antoinette guillotined, 16 Oct., 1793.
The Girondists put to death, 31 Oct., 1793.
Worship of the goddess of Reason introduced, 10 Nov., 1793.
The *noyades* of Nantes in Dec., 1793.
Danton and others guillotined, 5 April, 1794.
Robespierre president of the convention, 4 June, 1794.
Revolution of 9 Thermidor and end of the Reign of Terror, 27 July, 1794.

Year III. of the Revolutionary Calendar, from 22 Sept., 1794, to 21 Sept., 1795.

Jacobin Club closed, Nov., 1794.
Revolt in La Vendée, July, 1795.
New constitution (the Directory) appointed, 22 Aug., 1795.

Year IV. of the Revolutionary Calendar, from 22 Sept., 1795, to 21 Sept., 1796.

Close of the convention, 26 Oct., 1795.

Napoleon commander-in-chief of the army of Italy, 23 Feb., 1796.
Napoleon marries Josephine Beauharnais, 9 March, 1796.
Napoleon defeats the Austrians at Montenotte, 12 April, 1796.
Napoleon defeats the Piedmontese at Millesimo, 13 April; at Dego, 15 April; at Mondovi, 22 April, 1796.
Napoleon defeats the Austrians at the bridge of Lodi, 10 May, 1796.
Napoleon enters Milan, 15 May, 1796.
Napoleon defeats Wurmser at Castiglione, 5 Aug., 1796.
Napoleon defeats the Austrians at Roveredo, 4 Sept., and at Bassano, 8 Sept., 1796.

Year V. of the Revolutionary Calendar, from 22 Sept., 1796, to 21 Sept., 1797.

Alvinzi defeats Napoleon at the bridge of Arcōla, 15-17 Nov., 1796.
The Cispadane Republic formed, Dec., 1796.
Napoleon defeats the Austrians at Rivoli, 14 January, 1797.
Treaty of Tolentino, 19 Feb., 1797.
Napoleon defeats the Archduke Charles on the Tagliamento, 16 March, 1797.

Year VI. of the Revolutionary Calendar, from 22 Sept., 1797, to 21 Sept., 1798.

Treaty of Campo Formio, 17 Oct., 1797.
Napoleon takes Malta, 11 June, 1798.
Napoleon takes Alexandria, 4 July; wins the battle of the Pyramids, 23 July, 1798.

Year VII. of the Revolutionary Calendar, from 22 Sept., 1798, to 21 Sept., 1799.

Napoleon takes Jaffa by storm, 6 March, 1799.
Napoleon orders the massacre of his prisoners, March, 1799.
Napoleon wins the battle of Aboukir, 25 July, 1799.

Year VIII. of the Revolutionary Calendar, from 22 Sept., 1799, to 21 Sept., 1800.

Napoleon abolishes the Directory and seizes the supreme power, 9, 10 Nov., 1799.
Napoleon made first consul, 24 Dec., 1799.
Napoleon passes over the Alps, May, 1800.
Napoleon wins the battle of Marengo, 14 June, 1800.

Year IX. of the Revolutionary Calendar, from 22 Sept., 1800, to 21 Sept., 1801.

The infernal machine directed against Napoleon, 24 Dec., 1800.
Treaty of Lunéville, 9 Feb., 1801.
Concordat concluded with the pope, Sept., 1801.

Year X. of the Revolutionary Calendar, from 22 Sept., 1801, to 21 Sept., 1802.

Peace of Amiens, 25 March, 1802.
Napoleon first consul for life, 2 Aug., 1802.
Piedmont annexed to France, Sept., 1802.

Year XI. of the Revolutionary Calendar, from 22 Sept., 1802, to 21 Sept., 1803.

Napoleon declares war against England, 22 May, 1803.

Napoleon establishes the censorship of the press, Sept., 1803.

Year XII. of the Revolutionary Calendar, from 22 Sept., 1803, to 21 Sept., 1804.

The Duc d'Enghien shot at Vincennes, 21 March, 1804.
Napoleon assumes the title of Emperor, 18 May, 1804.
Napoleon prepares for the invasion of England during the summer of 1804.

Year XIII. of the Revolutionary Calendar, from 22 Sept., 1804, to 21 Sept., 1805.

Napoleon crowned by the pope, 2 Dec., 1804.
Napoleon crowned at Milan as king of Italy, 26 May, 1805.
Napoleon breaks up the camp of Boulogne, 16 Aug., 1805.

Year XIV. of the Revolutionary Calendar, from 22 Sept., 1805, to 31 Dec., 1805.

This was a year of 466 days, *i.e.* nine extra days in September, with the three months of October, November, and December, which, of course, were duplicates. But Napoleon, who abolished the calendar, returned to the old system on 1 Jan., 1806.

Napoleon wins the battle of Austerlitz, 2 Dec., 1805.
Peace of Presburg, 25 Dec., 1805.
Napoleon dethrones the King of Naples, Feb. 1806.
Napoleon makes his brother Joseph king of the Two Sicilies, March, 1806.
Napoleon makes his brother Louis king of Holland, 6 June, 1806.
Napoleon defeats the Prussians at Jena and Auerstadt, Oct., 1806.
Napoleon publishes his Berlin decree, 21 Nov., 1806.

Year Books.

Reports. These year-books are extant in an unbroken series from Edward II. to Henry VIII., and were made by the court scribes (protho-notaries) at the expense of the crown, and published annually.

Year of Confusion (*The*), B.C. 46,

which consisted of sixteen months (445 days). It was the year A.U.C. 708 when Julius Cæsar inserted (beside the inter-calary month of twenty-three days) two extraordinary months between Nov. and Dec., one of thirty-three days and the other of thirty-four days, in order to ad-just the year according to the course of the sun. To prevent the recurrence of any future confusion, he reformed the calendar, making it to consist of 365 days and a leap year of 366 days, instead of 355 and the *mensis intercalaris* attri-buted to Numa.

The reform was the work of Sosigĕnēs of Alex-andria, who introduced the terms kalends, nones, and ides, to designate certain divisions of the Roman month. Kalends the first day of the month, when the priest *called out* or announced to the people the day of the new moon. Nones, nine days before the Ides. The Ides were the 15th of March, May, July, and October, but the 13th of the other eight months.

Year of Death (*The*), A.D. 637,

is so called by the Arabian historians be-cause of the terrible plague which deso-lated Syria. As many as 25,000 men of the army of the Kalif Omar, encamped before Jerusalem, fell victims. Next year it desolated Aleppo and Antioch.

Year of Destruction (*The*), A.D. 639,

is so called by the Arabs from the dreadful plague which broke out at Medīna. It was preceded by violent hailstorms which destroyed enormous quantities of corn.

Year of Jubilee (*The*).

Every fiftieth year among the Jewish race, when all lands returned to their original owners and all slaves were set free.

Year of Liberty (*The*), 1648.

After the execution of Charles I. his statues in the Royal Exchange and in other places were taken down, and the following in-scription was substituted by Act of Par-liament: 'Exit Tyrannus, Regum ulti-mus, Anno Libertatis Angliæ restitutæ primo, A.D. 1648, Jan. 30' (old style).

Year of Revolutions (*The*), 1848.

The Chartist demonstration in this country; the third of France; the in-surrections of Italy; revolutions in Hun-gary and Austria.

Year of the Deputations (*The*).

The eighth of the Hedjrah (A.D. 630), when, after the victory near Taïf, deputa-tions flocked from various tribes to pay homage to Mohammed.

Year of the Revolutionary Calendar.

1.	From 22 Sept., 1792, to 21 Sept., 1793
2.	„	1793	„	1794
3.	„	1794	„	1795
4.	„	1795	„	1796
5.	„	1796	„	1797
6.	„	1797	„	1798
7.	„	1798	„	1799
8.	„	1799	„	1800
9	„	1800	„	1801
10.	„	1801	„	1802
11.	„	1802	„	1803

12. From 22 Sept., 1803, to 21 Sept., 1804
13.   „   1804   „   1805
14.   „   1805 to 31 Dec., 1805
When the practice was discontinued.

Yellow and Blue, in China. The followers of Lamaism wear yellow robes, the imperial colour, because Lamaism was promulgated in China by a son-in-law of the emperor. The other twelve sects wear blue.

Yellow Book (*The*). Reports of the inspectors of schools for England, Wales, and Scotland. So called from the yellow cover.

Yellow Books (*The*). In France, the government reports, papers, and other official documents are stitched in yellow covers. So are the government reports of foreign affairs. *See* p. 106, ' Blue Books.'

Yellow Caps. The caps worn in France before the 15th cent. were round and of a yellow colour, like the stockings of our Blue-coat boys.
In Italy Jews were obliged to wear yellow caps as a badge. And Shylock ought to have such a head-dress.

Yellow Caps (*Rebellion of the*). In China in the reign of Han-ling-tee (168–189). This formidable insurrection, headed by Tchang-keo, received its distinctive name from the caps worn by the insurgents, which were all of the imperial colour. Till 220 rebellion followed rebellion in quick succession, and between 220 and 266 China was divided into three states, called the San Kuo period.
Yellow in China is the imperial colour, which these insurgents adopted.

Yellow Division (*The*), or Brigade of Pentonville Prison. A convict goes through three grades during his sentence after the probation : (1) the third class, when he wears black facings on his jacket ; (2) the yellow division or second class, when he can, if he likes, have tea for supper instead of ' skilly ' or gruel; and (3) the first class, when he may have roast instead of boiled beef.

Yellow Dress (*The*). A dress worn by convicts who have attempted to escape, but have been captured and brought back. One half is a bright canary yellow and the other half a sombre drab. If the man has used violence, the penalty is a ' yellow dress and stangs' [irons], while the drab half is changed to deep black.

Yellow Fever (*The*). So called from the yellow tint which extends over the whole body, varying from a pale lemon to a deep orange colour. Havannah and Vera Cruz may be termed nurseries of this fatal disease, which attacks Europeans in Sept. and Oct. It seems to reappear in Europe about thirty times in a century.

It ravaged Antigua in 1816.
    „   Barbadoes in 1647 and 1691, where it was called the ' New Distemper.'
    „   Barcelona in 1821. Above 5,000 died.
    „   Cadiz for the first time in 1705, brought by a ship from America; since then in 1730, 1733, 1744, 1753, 1764, 1819, when it also attacked the dogs, cats, cattle, birds (even canaries), and was most fatal.
    „   Carthagena in 1792, where it produced dreadful havoc.
    „   Domingo (St.) in 1730, 1740, 1791, 1792-3, 1798, when 15,000 Englishmen and nearly the whole French garrison fell victims to it.
    „   Gaudeloupe in the autumn of 1816-7, 1819.
    „   Gibraltar in 1804, 1814, 1828.
    „   Guayaquil in 1740 and often since.
    „   Havannah is its nursery.
    „   Isla de Leon in 1819, 1828-9.
    „   Livorno in 1803, where it carried off 1,560 persons out of 5,500 who were attacked by it.
    „   Malaga in 1741, 1803, when 6,884 persons died ; in 1804, when 18,582 persons were attacked.
    „   Massachusetts in 1618, but not severe.
    „   Mauritius in 1815.
    „   Mexico in 1545, 1576, 1736-7, 1761-2, 1867.
    „   New York in 1791.
    „   North America eight times between 1790 and 1805 (sundry parts).
    „   Philadelphia in 1699, 1762, when its violence was unparalleled ; in 1793, 1797, 1802.
    „   Spain (various parts) in 1800, 1803, 1813. Vera Cruz, like Havannah, is a nursery of the disease.
    „   Virginia in 1699 and 1855, where its havoc was horrible.
    „   West Indies in 1732, 1739, 1745, 1763, and often since.

Yellow Flag (*A*). A yellow flag flying from a mast indicates that the vessel is in quarantine.

A black flag indicates a *pirate*, a red flag *defiance*, a white flag craves a truce.

Yellow Flags (*The*), or 'Yellow Flag Troops.' The Anamese mercenaries. In the Tonquin war, 1883, they were for a time French auxiliaries. Their standard was a yellow ensign, and their headquarters was Ho-Tang. *See* p. 97, ' Black Flags.'

Yellow Palace (*The*), or Khoosk e Zurd, one of the hunting-seats of Baharam Gour in Persia.

The Yellow Mountain, or 'Koh e Zurd,' is the source of the Zeinderood, on which Ispahan stands.

The Yellow Sea, or 'Whang Hai,' is an arm of the North Pacific, on the north-east of China.

Yellow River (*The*), or 'Hoang Ho.' Known generally as 'China's Sorrow.'

Yellow Robe (*Order of the*). A religious order founded by Buddha. The founder himself wore a yellow robe and carried an alms bowl.

But to his own, them of the Yellow Robe,
He taught how they should dwell;
How live, free from the snares of love and wealth;
What eat, and drink, and carry: three plain cloths,
Yellow, of stitched stuff, worn with shoulder bare—
A girdle, almsbowl, strainer. Thus he laid
That noble order of the Yellow Robe
Which to this day standeth.
    EDWIN ARNOLD, *The Light of Asia*, bk. viii.

Yellow Stick (*Religion of the*). Scotland. The reformed religion.

[Livingstone] has . . . recorded a tradition that the people of [Ulva Isle] were converted from being Roman Catholics by the laird coming round with a man having a yellow staff . . [and] the new religion went long afterwards . . . by the name of the 'Religion of the Yellow Stick.'— BLAIKIE, *Personal Life of David Livingstone*.

Dr. Blaikie adds: 'The same story is told of perhaps a dozen other places in the Highlands.' *See* 'Notes and Queries,' 13 July, 1889, p. 29.

Y'en Dynasty (*The*) of China (1279–1368) succeeded the dynasty of Song, and was succeeded by the Mings. Kublaï Khan was the founder. It was the twentieth imperial dynasty—that of the Moguls—gave ten kings, and lasted ninety years. The seat of government was Pe-kin.

China was at the time divided into two kingdoms, north and south of the Yellow River. The Song kings reigned in the south. It was the old, old tale. The reigning kings. threatened by the Tartars, called in the aid of the Moguls. Kublaï Khan repelled the Tartars, then dethroned the Song kings, and then made himself master of the north also, thus uniting again North and South China.

Kublaï Khan was called by the Chinese 'Ho-pee-lie.' His regnal name in China was 'Shee-tsu,' and his reign is still called 'the Wise Government.'

Yeoman Usher (*The*). The deputy of the Gentleman Usher of the Black Rod. *See* 'Black Rod.'

Yeomen of the Guard, or 'Beef-eaters,' 1485. Instituted by Henry VII. It was a corps of fifty soldiers, whose duty it was to attend upon the king and wait on him at meals.

It used to be generally supposed that 'Beefeater' was a corruption of the English-French *buffet-er* or *buffetier*, 'one who waits at the buffet.' That there is no such French word as *buffetier* is no argument against such a perversion. We have a small host of English-French words equally ignored in Paris. Take, for example, *encore*=the French *bis*, *surtout*=*pardessus*, while the French *surtout*=the English *epergne*. *Nom de plume* is English-French, in imitation of *nom de guerre*.

Yn (*Dynasty of*), B.C. 1401–1122. The latter part of the Chang dynasty was so called from the city Yn, where the court was held. The court had been previously held at Yang-tching, but Poan-keng, the seventeenth emperor of the Chang dynasty, moved his court to Yn (B.C. 1401), and changed the name of the dynasty from Chang to Yn.

This must not be confounded with the Y'en Dynasty. *See above*.

Ynglings of Norway (*The*). It is said that a family of Ynglings reigned in Norway from 863 to 1136, but the whole of this part of Norwegian history is very doubtful. The Ynglings of Norway were contemporaneous with the Skioldungs of Sweden, as will appear from the following lists :—

Norway Ynglings.		*Swedish Skioldungs.*	
	A.D.	A.D.	
Harald Haarfagen		859 Emund of the race	
I.	... 863	of Ivar.	
Eric I. Blodæxe	... 933	873 Erik Emundson.	
Hako I. the Good	936	923 Biorn Erikson.	
Harald II. Graafel	960		
Hako II. Jarl	962		
Olaf I. king of Denmark, Trygveson	—		
Eric II.	... 1000	993 Erik the Victorious.	
Olaf II. (*Saint*)	... 1015		
Sueno II. king of Denmark	—	1026 Olof Skotkonung.	
Magnus I. the Good	1036		
Harald III. ...	... 1047	1056 Stenkill, founder of the race of Stenkill.	
Magnus II. ...	... 1066	1066 Halstan.	
Olaf III. ...	... 1069	1080 Inge I.	
Magnus III...	... 1087		
Olaf IV. ...	... 1103	1112 Philip.	
Sigurd I. ...	. 1122	1118 Inge II.	
Magnus IV. ...	... 1130	1122 Sverker, founder of the race of Sverker.	
Harald IV. ...	1135–1136		

Ynglings of Sweden (*The*). A semi-historic race of Swedish kings from B.C. 70 to A.D. 647. So called from Yngve, son of Odin, to whom at death he assigned Sweden. The Ynglings of Sweden were not kings of all Sweden, but chiefs of Upsāla, and overlords of the other chiefs. They gave twenty-four chiefs, and were succeeded by the Skioldungs.

Yoke of Infamy. Three spears arranged like a gallows, under which conquered troops were made to march in token of subjection. (A Roman custom.)

Yorick. The pen-name of Laurence Sterne, who died in 1768, at the age of fifty-five.

York (*Frederick Duke of*), son of George III., commander-in-chief. He was obliged to resign his office owing to the exposure of a wholesale traffic in army commissions, carried on by his mistress Mrs. Clarke.

York (*The Line of*) gives England three kings, viz. Edward IV., Edward V., and Richard III., through Lionel duke of Clarence, third son of Edward III.

Lionel was the father of Philippa, who married Edward Mortimer earl of March, and their son was *Roger Mortimer* earl of March, who was slain in Ireland 1398.

This *Roger Mortimer* was father of EDMUND MORTIMER earl of March, and of ANN MORTIMER who married Richard duke of York.

.* At the death of Richard II. EDMUND MORTIMER was heir to the throne. He died 1424. It was in Sept. 1399 that Henry IV. deposed Richard II. and usurped the throne, being succeeded by Henry V. (his son) and Henry VI.

Now take ANN MORTIMER. She was the mother of Richard duke of York (slain, in 1466, at the battle of Wakefield), leaving two sons, EDWARD IV. and RICHARD III. Edward V. was the son of Edward IV., and was murdered by his uncle Richard.

York (*The Statute of*), 12 Edward II., A.D. 1318. Ordered that all black money (*noir monnoie*) lately current in the realm be excluded. This base coin was introduced from foreign countries, and probably from Ireland also, for in 1339 black money, called *turneys*, was current in Ireland.

York (*Trial of the Duke of*), 1809. Colonel Wardle accused the Duke of York in the House of Commons of promoting improper persons to military rank through the influence of a Mrs. Clarke. An inquiry was made and the duke acquitted. Such things were common enough till the middle of the nineteenth century. ' Douceurs ' [to mistresses] were even advertised in the daily press. I well remember when the ' Times ' discontinued these advertisements.

This was Frederick duke of York, second son of George III.

York Prize (*The*) for an essay on the law of primogeniture. For any graduate of the University of Cambridge of not more than seven years' standing. The same person may receive the prize

more than once. Value about 90*l*. Founded by Edmund York of St. Catharine's Hall, 1875.

Young Chevalier (*The*). The Prince Charles Edward [Stuart]. Also called the ' Young Pretender ' [*i.e.* to the British throne], 1720-1788.

Young Clerical School (*The*), 1890. To draw more closely together the religious party and the masses. M. de Mun (in France), M. Decurtius (in Switzerland), and a large number of German and Austrian Catholics have made numerous journeys to Rome, and have succeeded in forming a very influential party at the Vatican. The pope (Leo XIII.) is in favour of the movement, and hopes thereby to solve the great labour question.

A man who styled himself 'General' Booth, because he was head of a religious society termed by him ' the Salvation Army,' said, in the autumn of 1890, that if he was entrusted with 100,000*l*. he would solve the great 'labour question.' In December, 1890, above 80,000*l*. had been subscribed. Mr. (General) Booth issued a book to explain his scheme, but it has not yet been put in operation (1891).

Young England, about 1840. A group of clever politicians with fantastic ideas who for a time commanded considerable attention. The chief of the party were Benjamin Disraeli [Lord Beaconsfield], Lord John Manners, George Sydney Smithe [Lord Strangford], Cochrane-Wishart-Baillie [Lord Lamington], and many others distinguished in oratory and literature. Their platform was laughed at by practical men as Utopian, and quietly sank out of notice.

Young Englanders. A set of young men who tried to revive the formality and court manners of the Chesterfield school. They wore white waistcoats, patronised the pet poor, looked down upon shopkeepers, and were altogether Red Tape Knights.

In 1882-3 Oscar Wilde made himself ridiculous by trying to introduce the ' esthetic foolery ' both in taste, dress, and manners.

Young Europe, 1834. An Italian journal which took the place of 'Young Italy' (*q.v.*), and tried to propagate the same Utopian system.

Young German School (*The*) of literature followed the emancipation of Germany from the Napoleonic yoke.

Headed by Karl Gutzkow. The other chief authors of this school are Theodor Mundt, Gustav Kühne, Heinrich Laube, Ludolf Wienberg, Robert Heller, Ernst Kossak, and Heinrich Heine (the best of all).

Young Germany. A secret society mentioned in the report of the Government of Zürich, 1844, and said to be then in existence in Switzerland. This society aimed at a United Germany with a republican form of government.

Young Ireland, 1848. A party nursed by the newspaper called the 'Nation.' It differed from the Old Ireland party headed by Daniel O'Connell chiefly in this respect. The old party was a religious one and sought the supremacy of the Catholics; the young party wanted to unite both Protestants and Catholics in the great object of the severance of Ireland from the British crown. Though the Young Irelanders disclaimed warlike intentions, many of their speeches were very inflammatory. O'Connell headed the old repealers; the young repealers were led by William Smith O'Brien. The Young Irelanders gave birth to the United Irishmen (q.v.), a war party. See 'Irish Associations.'

In December, 1890, the Irish 'Nationalists,' who had been under the leadership of Charles S. Parnell for ten years, were split up into two parties, because Mr. Gladstone refused to co-operate with Mr. Parnell. Those who fell off from Mr. Parnell placed themselves under Justin M'Carthy, and the two Irish 'Nationalist' parties went by the name of Parnellites and M'Carthyites.

Young-Ireland Rising (The), 1848. This was the sequel of Daniel O'Connell's repeal agitation. The members called themselves the 'Patriots of the Nation.' They were quite ripe for active rebellion, but the ravings of Mitchel were of a piece with the stump orations of a music hall; and the Young-Ireland rising was easily suppressed. The 'Nation,' an Irish newspaper, was their organ, but the 'Nation' never had the slightest influence on public opinion. See 'Irish Associations.'

Young Italy, or 'The Young Italian Party,' 1831. Formed by Mazzini. The object of this party was 'the unification of Italy,' or 'Italy under one ruler.' At the time spoken of part of Italy belonged to Austria, part to France. Genoa and Lucca were a republic, Tuscany a grand duchy, Parma and Placentia were under a duke of the Bourbon line, Naples and Sicily were a kingdom, the States of the Church were under the pope, and so on. Young Italy wanted all the several parts to be united under one ruler, to be called the 'king of Italy.' In 1860, by the arms of Garibaldi, Victor Emmanuel was hailed 'king of Italy'; in 1866 Venice was added, and in 1870 Rome was made the capital of the new kingdom.

Mazzini lived till 1872; Garibaldi died in 1882; and Victor Emmanuel in 1878.

Young Pretender (The). Charles Edward, after the fatal battle of Culloden in 1746, made his escape to France, and his adventures resemble those of Charles II. after the battle of Worcester. The heroic lady who assisted him was Miss Flora Macdonald; and Charles Edward, dressed in woman's clothes, went by the name of 'Betty Bourke.' When Miss Macdonald left him, his guide was Malcolm Macleod; and the prince, as Macleod's man servant, assumed the name of 'Louis Caw of Crieff.' Ultimately he arrived at Roseau, near Morlaix, in Bretagne, and died at Florence in 1788.

Young Roscius (The). William Henry West Betty (1790–1874). He made his début in 1803, and in fifty-six nights realised 34,000l., when he wisely withdrew from public life.

Young Switzerland, 1835. An association in Switzerland organized by Joseph Mazzini on the same platform as 'Young Italy' (q.v.). Mazzini was banished from Switzerland in 1836, and his association melted into air.

Mazzini's motto was not the French 'Liberty, Fraternity, and Equality,' but the word 'Humanity.' Abstract humanity is not a workable quantity.

Yuen or **Y'en Dynasty** (The). The twentieth imperial dynasty of China. Founded by Kublaï Khan, emperor of the Mongols. It gave ten emperors, and lasted ninety years (1278–1368). Pekin was rebuilt and made the seat of government. It was succeeded by the Ming dynasty.

Yuen-Oeï Dynasty (The). The first dynasty of the Northern Empire of China. Founded by the Goli Tartars. Chief city Ho-nân. It gave eleven kings, when the Northern Empire was split into

3 Q 2

two, called 'Tong-Oeï' and 'Si-Oeï,' or 'Eastern and Western Oeï' (386–534).

'Oeï' is written 'Goeï' by many authors.

Zadigism. The science of observation, or the practice of observation in scientific research. 'Zadig' is the hero and title of a novel by Voltaire. He describes a lost camel, which he had never seen, as blind of the left eye, as having lost two of its front teeth, and being slightly lame in the near fore-foot. When pressed to explain how he knew all this, never having seen the animal, he replied: 'I knew it was blind of the left eye because I noticed it browsed only on the right side of the road. I knew it had lost two of its front teeth because some of the leaves and some of the grass was bitten and some not. I knew it was lame of the near fore-foot because the marks of this foot in the sand were shorter than those of the other feet,' &c.

Zampieri. Better known as 'Domenichino' (1581–1641).

Zegris (*The*), or 'Zegries.' A Mauritanian dynasty. *See* 'Zeirides.'

Zeirides (*The*), or 'Zeirites.' A tribe and dynasty of Moors which furnished many kings to Fez, Tlemçen, Algiers, Tunis, Kairouan, Mahadia, and Tripoli. The chief were the Sanhadjides or Zeirides Badissides, and the Zeirides Zenates. The former rendered themselves independent of the Fatimite califs in 972, and their dominion continued to 1050. The latter was from 988 to 1070.

Called after Zeïri ben Mounad, chief of the tribe of the Badissides, who conquered Algiers and Tripoli. He founded Achir, and died A.D. 971. In the proper names given above the *-es* does not form a syl., but Ze-i-rides is trisyllabic.

Ze′lotes (3 syl.). Simon is called 'the Canaanite'—*i.e.* Κανανίτης and also Ζηλωτής. Probably 'Kananite' is from the Hebrew root *kana*, whence *kanani* = 'zealous'; so that 'Simon Kananite' is merely the Aramaic translation of 'Simon Zēlōtês.' The Zelotæ were Hebraists—that is, great sticklers for the Mosaic law.

Zemindary. The jurisdiction of a zemindar or officer who superintends the lands, protects the landowners, and sees that government receives its legal share. (*Indian.*)

Zendavesta (*The*) is said to have been written by Zoroaster in letters of gold on 12,000 skins of parchment, and to have been deposited by Darīus Hystaspês in the Castle of Persepŏlis, about B.C. 500.

'Zend' is the language, and 'avesta' = text. The compound word means the sacred books of Zoroaster in the Zend tongue.

Zendicism, 8th cent. A Saracenic heresy resembling that of the Jewish Sadducees.

Zeugi′tæ. The middle bank of rowers in a Greek galley. The uppermost bank was the *Thanītæ*, and the lowest bank the *Thalamītæ*.

Zeyds (*The*). One of the numerous Shiite sects who profess to follow the tenets of Zeyd son of Ali, who is supposed to have received, through his father, some of the prophet's last injunctions. *See* 'Imaumians,' 'Khattabians.'

The Shiites reject the first three kalifs (Abubeker, Omar, and Othman), and also the traditions concerning the prophet and his will. The Sunis accept both. The Persians and Afghans are Shiites.

Ziobbagrassa. *Read* 'Zobia Grassa.' The last Thursday of carnival. *See* p. 559, 'Mardi Gras.'

Zisca ('one eye'). His name was John of Trockznov; he was born in Bohemia, and lost one eye in battle when a boy. In the Huss persecution he built a fort, which he called 'Tabor,' a place of refuge for the Hussites, who were thence called 'Taborites' (3 syl.). At the siege of Rabi, Zisca lost his other eye, and still continued to head his troops and win victories (1380–1424).

Zisca's Drum. Zisca, chamberlain to Wenceslaus, was the first leader of the Hussite War (*q.v.*), and died 1424. The tale is that he ordered his skin to be tanned and made into a drum-head. Byron, in his 'Werner,' and also in his 'Age of Bronze,' refers to this tradition.

But be it as it is, the time may come
His name [*i.e.* Napoleon's] shall beat th' alarm,
like Zisca's drum.
          Age of Bronze.

Zollverein (*The*), or 'Custom Union,' 1819. Hesse-Darmstadt joined it 14 Feb., 1828 ; Saxe-Meiningen and Saxe-Coburg-Gotha in 1829 ; Waldeck and Hesse-Cassel in 1831 ; Bavaria, Würtemberg, Saxony, Saxe-Weimar, Saxe-Altenberg,

and the two Schwarzburgs in 1833;
Hesse-Homburg, Baden, and Nassau, in
1835; Frankfort in 1836; Lippe-Detmold
and Brunswick in 1841; Luxemburg in
1847; Hanover, Oldenburg, and Schaumburg-Lippe in 1851; Mecklenburg-
Schwerin, Mecklenburg-Strelitz, and Lübeck in 1868. The effect of this union
has been a greatly increased demand for
German goods in foreign markets, and
diminished imports. Pronounce *Zol'-
ve-rine.*

Zoolactaf, or Dsulaktaf. So
Sapor II. was called (A.D. 310–379), be-
cause he dislocated the shoulders of all
Arabs capable of bearing arms.

Zoroaster. In Greek, ZOROASTRES;
in the Zendavesta, ZARATHUSTRA; in
Persian, ZERDUSHT. Founder of the
Magian religion.

Zoroas'trianism. The religious
system of Zoroaster, now called the Parsee religion. It was originally monotheism, but subsequently the dualism of
good and evil. The Magi remained
faithful to the monotheism of Zoroaster,
while the Zendiks believed in the dualism
as taught in the 'Zend-Avesta.' As
'Zoroaster' is also written 'Zarathustra,'
so 'Zoroastrianism' is called 'Zarathus-
traism.'

John Malcolm, who died in 1833, attempted to
prove that Zoroaster was the Jewish Ezra.

Zseklers, or Szeklers. A people who
occupy the highlands of Transylvania,
and belong to the Magyar stock, all
noble and free. Some are Magyar Unitarians and some Catholics. They are
spread over five districts, called Udvar-
hely, Haromszek, Csik, Maros, and Aran-
yos, and are about 350,000 in number.

Zürich (*Treaty of*), 11 Nov., 1859.
For the ratification of the Treaty of
Villafranca.

APPENDIX

THE CHIEF BATTLES OF THE WORLD

ALPHABETICALLY ARRANGED

Aboukir (*Battle of*), 1 Aug., 1798. Nelson defeated François Paul de Brueys, the French admiral, in the Bay of Aboukir. The French admiral was killed by a cannon-shot.

Generally called, in English history, 'The Battle of the Nile.'

Aboukir (*Battle of*), 25 July, 1799, won by Bonaparte over the Turks.

Next year (1800) Kléber was assassinated by a young Turk, and Egypt was lost to France.

Abu Klea (*Battle of*), 17 Jan., 1885, won by General Stewart with 1,500 men over an army of Arabs of 10,000 in the service of the Mahdi.

Abȳdos (*Naval battle of*), B.C. 411, won by the Athenians over the Lacedæmonians.

Aclea (*Battle of*), 851, in which Ethelwulf, the son of Egbert king of England, defeated the Danes. Aclēa is Ockley, in Surrey.

Actium (*Battle of*), 2 Sept., B.C. 31, gained by Octavian (Augustus Cæsar) over Antony and Cleopatra, both of whom killed themselves to prevent being made captives by the conqueror. Octavian dated the years of his imperial monarchy from the day of this battle.

Adrianople (*Battle of*), 3 July, A.D. 323. This battle obtained for Constantine the empire.

Ægatian Islands (*Naval battle of*), B.C. 241, won by the Roman consul Quintus Lutatius Catŭlus over Hanno the Carthaginian, off the Ægātēs. This victory brought to an end the First Punic War, which had lasted twenty-three years.

Ægospot'amos, or 'Goat's River' (*Naval battle of*), B.C. Sept. 405. This was scarcely a battle, it was rather a surprise, for no fighting was needed. The Athenians left their fleet unguarded, and most of the men were on shore when Lysander captured above 150 of their ships, and put to death above 3,000 Athenian

prisoners. This disaster virtually brought the Peloponnesian war to a close.

Aghrim, in Ireland (*Battle of*), 12 July, 1691, where William III. and General Ginkell defeated James II. and St. Ruth.

Agincourt (*Battle of*), 25 Oct., 1415, won by Henry V. of England over the French, led by D'Albret constable of France. The French army was five times greater than the English. The English loss did not exceed 1,600 men, but the French was 10,000 slain, and 15,000 taken prisoners.

Agnadello (*Battles of*). I. 14 May, 1509, in which Louis XII. defeated Petigliano and D'Alviano. This to the Venetians was one of the most disastrous battles in all their history.

II. 16 Aug., 1705, in which the Duc de Vendôme defeated Prince Eugene. Also called the 'Battle of Cassāno.'

Agosta (*Naval battle of*), 1676, won by Duquesne over the Dutch. Here Ruyter, the Dutch admiral, lost his life.

Ai'rolo, in Italy (*Battle of*), 23 Sept., 1799, in which Suwarrow, the Russian general, defeated Gudin, the French general.

Aix (*Battle of*), July, B.C. 101, in which the Teuton host was annihilated by Marius the Roman consul.

Aiznaden (*Battle of*), 13 July, A.D. 633, in which Khaled, commander of the Koreish cavalry, defeated Werdan, general of Heraclius, commander of the Greeks.

Aland, in the Baltic (*Battle of*), 27 July, 1714, in which Peter I. the Great defeated the Swedish fleet. Pronounce O-land.

Alarcon, in Spain (*Battle of*), autumn 1195, in which Yacub ben Yussef defeated Alfonso VIII. of Castile.

Albans (*Battles of St.*). I. 22 May, 1455. This was the first battle of the Two Roses, and was won by Richard duke of York (the White Rose) over Henry VI.

II. 2 Feb., 1461, between the same factions. In this battle Warwick, the king-maker, joined the royal side of Queen Margaret, and defeated the Yorkists.

Albuera, in Spain (*Battle of*), 1811, in which Marshal Beresford defeated Soult, one of Napoleon's marshals. Pronounce *Al-boo-a'-rah.*

Albufera da Valencia (*Battle of*), 1811, in which Suchet marshal of France defeated Blake and the Spaniards. For this victory Napoleon created Suchet ' Duke of Albufèra.'

Alcañiz', in Spain (*Battle of*), 23 May, 1809, in which Blake and the Spaniards defeated Suchet, one of the marshals of Napoleon.

Alcazar-quivir (*Battle of*), 4 Aug., 1578, in which Muley Moluc of Morocco defeated and slew Sebastian of Portugal.

Aldenhoven, in Belgium (*Battle of*), 1 March, 1793, in which Clairfait, the Austrian general, defeated Francisco Miranda.

Alessandria (*Battle of*), 17 May, 1799, in which Suwarrow, the Russian general, defeated the French under Moreau.

Alexandria (*Battle of*), 21 March, 1801, won by the British army under Sir Ralph Abercrombie over the French under the command of Menou.

Alford (*Battle of*), 2 July, 1645, in which General Baillie, with an army of Covenanters, was defeated by the Marquis of Montrose.

Alia, or Allia, in Italy (*Battles of*). I. 16 July, B.C. 390, where the Gauls under [their] Brennus defeated the Romans.

II. B.C. 374 or 377, when Cincinnātus, the dictator, defeated the Prænestines and their allies.

Aliwal', in India (*Battle of*), 28 Jan., 1846, won by Sir H. Smith over the Sikhs.

Aljubarota, in Portugal (*Battle of*), 14 Aug., 1385, in which Joam I. of Portugal defeated Juan I. of Castile.

Alkmaar (*Battle of*), 1799. A blooay but indecisive battle between the allied English and Russian on the one hand and the allied French and Dutch armies on the other.

Allīfæ, in Italy (*Battle of*), B.C. 307, in which the proconsul Q. Fabius Maximus defeated the Samnites.

Alma, in the Crimēa (*Battle of the*), 20 Sept., 1854, in which Lord Raglan, the English commander, and Marshal St. Arnaud, the French commander, defeated Prince Menschikoff, the Russian general.

Almanza, in Spain (*Battle of*), 25 April, 1707, in which the French Marshal Berwick defeated the Archduke Karl, and thus secured the throne to Philip V. (14 April, Old Style.)

Almarez, in Spain (*Battle of*), 24 Dec., 1808, in which Marshal Lefebvre defeated the Spaniards.

Almeida (*Battle of*), 5 Aug., 1811, won by Lord Wellington, commanding the Anglo-Spanish army, over the French commanded by Marshal Massena. Pronounce *Al-ma-e'-dah.*

Almenara, in Spain (*Battle of*), 27 July, 1710, in which the Earl of Stanhope and Count Stahremberg (or Starhemberg) defeated the Marquis de Bay.

Almham (*Battle of*), 723, in which Fergall (overlord of Ireland) with 21,000 men (who had invaded Leinster to enforce the Boarian Tribute (*q.v.*), remitted by Finactha) was utterly defeated by 9,000 Lagenians. As many as 7,000 were slain, among whom were 200 kings [chiefs] and Fergall with all his bodyguard.

Almonacid, in Spain (*Battle of*), 11 Aug., 1809, in which General Sebastian, a marshal of France, defeated Venegras (3 syl.).

Alney (*Battle of*), 1016. This was a single combat between Edmund Ironside and Canute in sight of their armies. When Canute was wounded he proposed a division of the kingdom, and the south part fell to Edmund ; but Edmund was murdered soon afterwards at Oxford, by Edric Streon.

Alsenz, in Germany (*Battle of*), 8 Dec., 1795, in which Clairfait, the Austrian general, repulsed the French under Pichegru (2 syl.).

Altdorf, in Switzerland (*Battle of*), 5 May, 1799. The Swiss peasants were here defeated by Marshal Soult, the French general.

Altenberg, in Germany (*Battle of*), 24 Sept., 1813, in which Lefebvre Desnouettes, the French cavalry officer, defeated Thielmann, commander of the Russian forces.

Altenheim, in Germany (*Battle of*), 29 Ju'y, 1675, in which Montecuculi, the Austrian general, defeated the French armies under Comte de Lorges. Here the Marquis de Vaubrun fell in battle.

Altenkirchen, in Germany (*Battles of*). I. 4 June, 1796, where Kléber, the French general, defeated the Archduke Karl of Austria.

II. 19 Sept., 1796, in which the Archduke Karl of Austria defeated the French led by Jourdan. In this battle the French general Marceau was slain.

Altura, in Spain (*Battle of*), 25 June, 1838, where the Carlists defeated Amor.

Amberg (*Battle of*), 24 Aug. 1796. The Archduke Karl defeated Moreau, the French general.

American Civil War, 1861–1865. Brought to a close 10 May, 1865, by the surrender of General Johnston.

Amis'ia, or the Ems, in Germany (*Battle of the*), B.C. 12, where Nero Claudius Drusus defeated the Bructĕri in a naval engagement.

Ancrum Muir, in Scotland (*Battle of*), 17 Feb., 1545, in which Archibald Douglas earl of Angus defeated Sir R. Eyre and Sir Brian Latoun.

Ancy'ra or **Ango'ra** (*Battle of*), 20 July, 1402, in which Bajazet I. sultan of the Otto-

mans, was defeated and taken prisoner by
Timour the Tartar.

Andernach (*Battle of*), 939, near Coblenz,
won by Otto I. over his rebellious half-brother
Tankmar and several disaffected nobles. Tankmar was slain and the rebellion quashed.

Andredes-lea, the Weald of Sussex
(*Battle of*), .477, where Ella and his sons defeated the Britons.

Ango'ra (*Battle of*). *See above,* ' Ancyra.'

Anjou (*Battle of*), or ' Battle of Beaugé,'
3 April, 1421, won by the Dauphin of France
over the Duke of Clarence. This battle turned
the tide of success against the English.

Antietam, in Maryland (*Battle of*), 17
Sept., 1862, between the Federals under General
McClellan and the Confederates under General
Lee. Indecisive.

Antium (*Battle of*), May 1378, between 14
Venetian galleys under the command of Victor
Pisani and 10 Genoese galleys under Luigi
Fiesco. The Venetians won the victory. One
of the Genoese galleys was dashed to pieces on
the rocky shore, five surrendered, and the other
four escaped.

Antoigné (*Battle of*), 13 Aug., 1792, won
by the French over the allied Austrians and
Prussians.

Aquæ Sextiæ (*Battle of*), B.C. 102, in
which Caius Marius defeated the Teutons.

Arbēla (*Battle of*), B.C. 1 Oct., 331, in which
Alexander the Great overthrew Darius Codo-
manus for the third time. It was fought near
Gaugamēla, and is sometimes called the ' Battle
of Gaugamela.'
  One of Sir Edward Creasy's *Fifteen Decisive
Battles of the World.*
  At Arbela the united Egyptian and Syrian
army defeated the Ottoman troops in the reign
of Bajazet II. (1482).

Arcis-sur-Aube (*Battle of*), 20 March,
1814, between Napoleon's French army and
Schwartzenberg's Austrian army. It was quite
indecisive.

Ar'cola (*Battle of*), 15 and 17 Nov., 1796, in
which Bonaparte defeated the Austrians under
Alvinzy.

Argentorātum (*Battle of*), A.D. 357, in
which Julian defeated the Alemanni.
  ⁎⁎⁎ Argentorātum, now Strassburg.

Arginūsæ (*Naval battle of*), B.C. 406, won
by the Athenians over the Lacedæmonians.

Arklow (*Battle of*), 10 June, 1798, where
a sma l British force utterly defeated 31,000
Irish insurgents.

Arles (*Battle of*), A.D. 508, in which Clovis,
founder of the French monarchy, was defeated
by Theodore the Great king of Italy, and
father-in-law of Alaric king of the West Goths.

Armageddon (*Battle of*), *Rev.* xvi. 16,
where God will collect together his enemies for
destruction. Ar-ma-geddon is supposed to be

the ' city of Megiddo,' and Megiddo is a typical
word for a battle-field. *Zech.* xii. 11 speaks of
' the mourning of Hadadrimmon in the valley
of Megiddon.' The vicinity of Megiddo was
noted as a great battle-field in Bible history.
It was here Pharaoh-necho overcame and slew
Josiah (2 *Kings* xxiii. 29, 30). The great
slaughter of Jabin's and Sisera's army was at
' the waters of Megiddo ' (*Judges* v. 19). It
was in this plain that Gideon overthrew the
Midianites (*Judges* vi. 33, vii. ; here was the
fight between Saul and the Philistines, and
between Tryphon and Jonathan Maccabæus
(1 *Mac.* xii.). . In later times it was the battle-
field of the Tartars and Saracens.

Armagh' (*Battle of*), 1318, in which Edward Bruce was defeated and taken prisoner.
He was beheaded at Dundalk.

Arginūsæ (*Naval battle of*), July B.C. 407,
won by the Athenians over the Lacedæmonians. What is especially noteworthy in this
victory is that six of the ten admirals who
commanded the Athenian fleet were put to
death, for not picking up those swimming
for their lives. The excuse was, they were
prevented by a sudden storm.

Argoed, or Argoed Llyvain (*Battle of*),
A.D. 547, won by Urien over Ida the Saxon invader.

Arques (*Battle of*), 21 Sept., 1589, in which
Henri IV. with 7,000 men defeated the Duc de
Mayenne at the head of 30,000 men.

Ascalon (*Battles of*). I. 12 Aug., 1099, in
which Godfrey of Bouillon defeated the Sultan
of Egypt.
  II. 1192, in which Richard I. defeated the
Soldan's united army, numbered at 300,000 men.
It is said that 40,000 of the Saracens were left
dead on the field.

Aschaffenburg (*Battle of*), 16 Sept., 1796.
The Archduke Karl of Austria defeated
Moreau, the French general. This was his
third victory since August.

Ashdown (*Battle of*), or Æscesdun, or
Ash-tree Hill, A.D. 870. The great battle in
which Ethelred and Alfred overthrew the
Danes and slew their king, Bacseg. This victory is commemorated by the famous White
Horse. The town now called Ashbury used to
be called Ayshesdown. The downs are still
called Ashdown, and not far off is Ashdown
Park.

Aspern (*Battle of*), 21 May, 1809, in
which the Archduke Karl of Austria was defeated by Napo'eon. Called by the French the
battle of Essling.

Assandun (*Battle of*), 1016. A decisive
victory of Canute over Edmund Ironside. The
death of Ironside left Canute master of the
realm.

Assaye, in India (*Battle of*), 23 Sept.,
1803, in which Arthur Wellesley (afterwards
Duke of Wellington) defeated Scindia and the
Rajah of Berar. The forces opposed to the
English were fully ten times the more nume-

rous. This battle is especially noteworthy as being the first great victory of the Iron Duke.

Athenry' (*Battle of*), 1316, in which Ferdlim O'Connor was utterly defeated by William de Burgh and Richard de Bermingham. It is said that 11,000 Irish fell in this battle, which gave a final blow to the restless O'Connors.

Audelay' (*Battle of*), 1118, in which Henry I. (Beauclerc) defeated Louis VI. of France. The object of this battle was to regain the dukedom of Normandy, which Henry had taken, for William, son of the deposed Robert.

Auerstadt (*Battle of*), 14 Oct., 1806, won by the French Marshal Davoust over the Prussians the same day as Napoleon won the battle of Jena. [Pronounce *Ya-nah.*]

Aughrim, in Ireland (*Battle of*), 12 July, 1691. Same as Aghrim (*q.v.*).

Augsburg (*Battles of*). I. 955, won by Otto I. (the Great) of Germany over the Hungarians.
II 24 Aug., 1796, by Moreau, who commanded the French army, over the Imperialists.
III. Again 2 Sept., and again 7 Sept., 1796, won by the same general (Moreau).

Austerlitz, in Moravia (*Battle of*), 2 Dec., 1805, in which Napoleon defeated the Emperors of Austria and Russia. This great victory led to the treaty of Presburg. It is called ' The Battle of the Emperors.'
The Emperor of Austria was Francis, and the Czar of Russia was Alexander I. It was won by Napoleon on the anniversary of his coronation.

Aylesford, in Kent (*Battle of*), A.D. 449, between the Angles and the Britons. Horsa fell in this battle, and the victory gave Kent to Hengist the invader. The massacre which followed the batt'e was merciless, and drove the conquered Britons over sea or to lurking-places in the forests, where many were cut down ¬nd many were made slaves to the conquerors.

Badon, *i.e.* Bath (*Battle of Mount*), 520. Called in Latin *Mons Badonicus.* This legendary battle was the 12th won by Arthur over the West Saxons, and checked for a time their progress.

Ballinahinch (*Battle of*). 13 June, 1798, against the insurgent Irish. The royal army was, of course, victorious, but suffered very severely.

Baltimore (*Battle of*), 12 Sept., 1814, won by General Ross over the Americans, but Ross was slain, and the attack on Baltimore failed.

Bannockburn (*Battle of*), 24 June, 1314, in which Robert Bruce of Scotland defeated Edward II. In this battle the flower of the English knighthood fell into the hands of the conquerors, while the Irishry and foot soldiers were ruth'essly cut down as they fled. For centuries afterwards, the rich p'under of the English camp left its traces on the vestment rolls of Scottish castle and abbey.

Banos di Toloso (*Battle of*), 1210, in which Alfonso IX. of Leon, &c. defeated the Moors. The loss of the Moors is stated to have been 180,000 men. They never recovered from this tremendous defeat.

Bantry Bay (*Battle of*), 1 May, 1689. This was merely an indecisive engagement with a French squadron. The English admiral was Herbert earl of Torrington, noted for his indolence and total want of seamanship.

Barbury Hill, in Wiltshire (*Battle of*), A.D. 552, in which the Angles defeated the Britons.

Barnet, in Hertfordshire (*Battle of*), 14 April, 1471, in which the Earl of Warwick was defeated and slain by Edward IV. This battle was a medley of carnage and treachery. It lasted six hours, and ended with the fall of Warwick, the 'king-maker,' as he fled for hiding to the woods. One more battle, that of Tewkesbury, three weeks afterwards, left Queen Margaret a captive in the victor's power.

Barrosa (*Battle of*), 6 March, 1811, won by General Graham, leader of the British army, over Marshal Victor and his French army. In this sanguinary conflict was captured the first eagle that the British army had ever taken.

Bassano (*Battle of*), 8 Sept., 1796, in which Bonaparte defeated the Austrians. In this battle Marshal Augereau and Marshal Massena greatly distinguished themselves.

Bassorah (*Battle of*), 4 Nov., A.D. 657. The first civil war of the Moslems. In this battle Ali, the calif, defeated Ayesha, Telha, and Zobeir.
⁎ Generally pronounced Bassorah, but it should be called Bas'sorah or Bas'rah.

Bath. *See* ' Badon.'

Batowitz (*Battle of*), 1653, in which the army of John II. of Poland suffered a crushing defeat from Bogdan the Cossack and his son.

Battlefield (*Battle of*), 1402, won by Henry IV. over Percy, surnamed Hotspur.

Bautzen (*Battle of*), 21 May, 1813, won by Napoleon over the allied Russian and Prussian armies. Pronounce *Bowl-zn.*

Baylen (*Battle of*), 19 July, 1808, in which the Spanish General Castanos utterly defeated Dupont and his French army.

Bazabde (*Battle of*), A.D. 360, in which Sapor the king of Persia repulsed Constantius II.

Beachy Head (*Battle of*), 30 June, 1690, in which the English and Dutch allied fleet was defeated by the French.

Beauge (*Battle of*), 1420, won by the French over the Duke of Clarence, brother of Henry V. In this battle Clarence was slain, and the Earls of Somerset, Dorset, and Huntingdon were taken prisoners. The victory is ascribed to a contingent of Scotch mercenaries.

Beaumont (*Battle of*), 28 Aug., 1870, in the Franco-German war. Won by the Prussians.

Bedr (*Battle of*), A.D. 624, the famous battle in which Mahomet defeated the Koreishites. He ascribed his victory to Gabriel, who fought on his white horse for the 'prophet.'

Belgrade (*Battle of*), 1456, in which the Turks were defeated by a German army. The famous Siege of Belgrade was in May, 1717, by Prince Eugene. The Turks went to relieve the city, Aug. 5, with 200,000 men, and, after a very sanguinary battle, Belgrade surrendered.
₀ This city has often been besieged.

Bellair, or Moorfields (*Battle of*), in Maryland, 30 Aug., 1814. A small British force under Sir Peter Parker attacked the town, but, after an obstinate fight, were repulsed with loss, Sir Peter being slain.

Belle Isle (*Naval battles of*), 25 Oct., 1747, in which Admiral Hawke well nigh annihilated the French fleet. In 1759 Admiral Hawke obtained a second victory over the French near the same spot.

Benacus (*Battle of Lake*), 268, in which Claudius defeated the Alemanni.

Benburb (*Battle of*), 5 June, 1646, in which Owen O'Neill the Irish chieftain completely defeated the Scotch and English, led b.' Monroe. Of the Scotch and English, 3,243 were slain in battle and many more on the road; of the Irish army, only 70 men were slain and 200 wounded. Owen Roe O'Neill died soon after the battle, the last of the Irish chiefs.

Bennington, Vermont, U.S. (*Battle of*), 16 July, 1777. Here the Americans defeated the Germans in the American War of Independence. These Germans were British mercenaries. The American general was Stark.

Bensington, in Oxfordshire (*Battle of*), in which Offa king of Mercia defeated Cynewulf king of the West Saxons.

Beresina (*Battle of*), 28 Nov., 1812, in which the French were attacked by the Russians, and lost 20,000 men. It was a most terrible disaster on their retreat from Moscow.

Bergen (*Battles of*). I. 14 April, 1759, won by the French over the allies.
II. 19 Sept., 1799, won also by the French over the allies.
III. 2 Oct., 1799, won by the French over the allies.

Biberach (*Battle of*), April,1799, in which Marshal Moreau, the French general, defeated the Austrians.

Bibracte (*Battle of*), B.C. 58, in which Julius Cæsar overthrew the Gauls.
Bibractê is Autun, in Burgundy.

Bicocco (*Battle of*), 1521, in which Charles V. defeated Lautrec, the French general. This defeat involved the loss of Milan to the French nation.

Bilbāo (*Battle of*), 25 Dec., 1836, won by Espartēro over the Carlists. (Christmas Day.)

Blackheath (*Battle of*), 22 June, 1497, in which the Cornish insurgents led by Lord Audley, Michael Joseph, and Thomas Flammock, met a crushing defeat from the army sent against them by Henry VII. Above 2,000 of the insurgents were slain and 1,500 taken prisoners.

Bladensburg (*Battle of*), 24 Aug., 1814, in which General Ross defeated the Americans commanded by General Winder in the second American war.

Blenheim, in Bavaria (*Battle of*), 13 Aug., 1704, in which Marlborough and Prince Eugene defeated the French and Bavarians. The great benefit of this victory was that it broke the spell of French invincibility. The many victories that the French had won induced Europe to believe they were irresistible; but the fate of Blenheim dispelled the delusion and raised the fame of England in proportion.
This is one of Sir Edward Creasy's *Fifteen Decisive Battles of the World.*

Borodi′no, in Russia (*Battle bf*), 7 Sept., 1812, between the French commanded by Napoleon, and the Russians under Kutusoff. This was one of the most sanguinary battles on record, and both sides claimed the victory; but as the Russians retreated, the advantage was with Napoleon, to whom the road to Moscow was left open.
This battle is also called 'The Battle of Moskwa.'

Boroughbridge (*Battle of*), 16 March, 1323, in which the royal troops of Edward II. led by Sir Simon Ward and Sir Andrew Barclay defeated the Earls of Lancaster and Hertford, two of the lords ordainers who had risen against the royal favourites Hugh le Despenser and his father. Lancaster, being taken prisoner, was hanged, drawn, and quartered as a traitor.
Fourteen bannerets and fourteen knights bachelors were hanged, drawn, and quartered, with the earl.

Borysthenes (*Battle of the*), 1508, won by Sigismund I. of Poland over the Muscovites. It is said that the Muscovites lost 80,000 men in this battle. Pronounce *Bo-ris′-then-eze.*

Bosworth Field, in Leicestershire (*Battle of*), 22 Aug., 1485, in which Richard III. was defeated and slain by the Earl of Richmond (Henry VII.). This battle brought the Plantagenet dynasty to an end, and established that of Tudor.
The Tudors were descendants of John of Gaunt's il egitimate offspring, born of Catherine Swynford. The last of this line, called Beaufort, was Lady Margaret, who married Edmund Tudor, and became the mother of our Henry VII.

Bouvines, in Flanders (*Battle of*), 27 July, 1217, in which Phi.ippe Auguste king of France defeated the Kaiser Otto and his allies, the Flemish and English. The Flemish were the first to fly, then the German centre gave way, and lastly the English on the right wing, led by the Earl of Salisbury. This was a very important battle. If Philippe had lost it, France would have been partitioned among the conquerors. As King John was one of the defeated allies, his vengeance against the English barons was powerless, and hence the grant of Magna Charta.

Boxtel (*Battle of*), 17 Sept., 1794, in which the British allied army commanded by the Duke of York was defeated by the French republican army. The Duke retreated across the Meuse.

Boyne, in Ireland (*Battle of the*), 1 July, 1690, where William III. defeated James II., who the parliament declared had abdicated.

Bradford on the Avon (*Battle of*), A.D. 657, in which Cenwalh defeated the Britons.

Brandywine, a river in the U.S. (*Battle of the*), 11 Sept., 1777. Won by Lord Howe over Washington, in the American War of Independence. Philadelphia fell to the possession of the victors.

Breslau. Between 1757–60, in the 'Seven Years' War,' it was taken and retaken by the Prussians under Frederick the Great and the Austrians ; but in 1763 Silesia passed definitively into the hands of the Prussians. It was besieged and surrendered to the French 5 Jan., 1807 ; and again 31 May, 1813. Pronounce *Bres-low* (*ow* as in *now*).

Bretigny (*Treaty of*), 1360, after the battle of Poitiers. It stipulated that Edward III. should renounce all claim to the crown of France ; but should retain Calais, and be the independent lord of Poitou, Aunis, Angoumois, Saintonge, the Limousin, and Guyenne. The French also paid in money 366,000*l*. and gave 40 hostages.

Briar's Creek, in South Carolina (*Battles of*). I. 16 March, 1779, won by the English army led by General Prevost over the Americans commanded by General Ashe.
II. 3 May, 1779, by the same belligerents and with the same results.

Brienne (*Battle of*), 29 Jan., 1814, won by Napoleon over the allied Russians and Prussians led by Blücher.

Brooklyn, U.S. (*Battle of*), 27 Aug., 1776, where General Howe defeated the Americans in the American War of Independence. This is sometimes called ' The Battle of Flatbush.'

Brunanburh (*Battle of*), 937, won by Athelstan king of England over a confederacy organised by Anlaf king of Ireland. The confederated chiefs who joined Anlaf were from Scotland, Cumberland, together with some Welsh or British chiefs, and some of the Danes settled by Alfred in the Five Boroughs.

Bull Run, Virginia (*Battles of*), 21 July, 1861. I. The first of the conflicts in the American Civil War. The Federals, under General Irwin M'Dowell, were successful at first ; but when some Confederate reinforcements arrived, being seized with a panic, they fled to Washington, leaving their baggage and ammunition behind. The Confederate generals were Beauregard and Jackson.
II. 30 Aug., 1862. A desperate conflict which also ended in the triumph of the Confederates, commanded by General [Stonewall] Jackson. The Northern army was under General Pope.
*** It was General [Bernard] Bee who gave Jackson this cognomen at Bull Run.

Bulla (*Battle of*), 15 Sept., A.D. 533, in which Belisarius defeated Gelimer, last of the Vandal kings of Carthage. Gelimer was made captive, and Carthage became a Roman province.

Bunker's Hill, near Boston, U.S. (*Battle of*), 17 June, 1775, two months after the battle of Lexington. Nominally the result was favourable to Lord Howe and the British troops, but the real victory was on the side of the American insurgents, led by Colonel Prescot. The British loss of men was double that of the Americans.

Burford, Oxfordshire (*Battle of*), 752, in which Cuthred king of Wessex defeated Ethelbald king of Mercia. In a second defeat at Secandum, in 755, Ethelbald was slain.
This battle between Wessex and Mercia was one of the best contested battles of the heptarchy.

Burkersdorf (*Battle of*), 21 July, 1762, in which the Prussians drove the Austrians from their entrenchments. (In the seventh campaign of the Seven Years' War.)

Burlington Heights (*Battle of*), 6 June, 1813, won by the British, who carried the heights, but the Americans defended them with great valour.

Busaco, in Portugal (*Battle of*), 27 Sept., 1810, in which Lord Wellington, the British commander, defeated the French, commanded by Massēna. After the battle, Wellington retreated to Torres Vedras.

Buttington, in Wales (*Battle of*), A.D. 894, in which Ethelred defeated the Danes.

Byland, in Yorkshire (*Battle of*), 1328, in which Robert the Bruce routed the chivalry of England and of France under Edward III.

Cadesia (*Battle of*), A.D. 636, in which Ysdegerd (king of Persia) was defeated by Khaled, commander of the Saracen army. The battle lasted three days. The first was called the *Day of Succour*, from a reinforcement of 30,000 which arrived on that day. The second day was called the *Day of Concussion*, from the conflict of the two armies on that day. The third day was called the *Day of Barking*, from the discordant noises of the Persian camp when a high wind drove clouds of dust into their faces. In this battle the famous standard called ' Durufsh e Kawanee,' better known as the ' Blacksmith's Apron,' fell into the hands of the Saracens.

Cambuskenneth (*Battle of*), 10 Sept., 1297, in which William Wallace defeated the English army under the Earl of Surrey. By this victory Scotland was lost to Edward I.

Cambuskenneth is close to Stirling Bridge. Wallace allowed half the English army to cross the bridge, then fell on them, and, taking possession of the bridge, prevented the rest of the English from crossing it.

Camden, South Carolina, U.S. (*Battles of*). I. 16 Aug., 1780. Here Lord Cornwallis defeated the American General Gates in the American War of Independence.

II. 25 April, 1781, won by Lord Rawdon, the British general, over General Greene of America.

III. 13 May, 1781, won by the same general over the same opponents. Camden was burnt.

Camperdown (*Battle of*), 11 Oct., 1797, in which Admiral Duncan defeated the Dutch.

Cannæ (*Battle of*), 2 Aug., B.C. 216, in which Hannibal the Carthaginian utterly defeated the Romans led by the Consul Varro. This was one of the most disastrous defeats ever suffered. At least 40,000 Roman foot and 3,000 horse were left dead on the field.

Cape St. Vincent (*Battles of*). I. 17 June, 1693, in which Sir George Rooke was defeated by Tourville the French admiral.

II. 14 Feb., 1797, in which Sir John Jervis defeated the Spanish fleet.

Caravaggio (*Battle of*), 1448, in which Sforza defeated the Venetians, took all their stores and 15,000 prisoners.

Caristo (*Battle of*), 29 Aug., 1351, a great naval victory of Venice over the Genoese.

Carthagena, South America (*Naval battle of*), 1747. It was seized by the French in 1544; taken by Sir Francis Drake in 1585; retaken by the French in 1697; and unsuccessfully besieged by Admiral Vernon in 1747.

Casal Secco (*Battle of*), 12 July, 1426. This was scarcely a battle. It was rather an affray between the Venetians led by Carmagnuola and the Milanese under the leadership of Francesco Sforza. It was not decisive, but the Venetians had the advantage in that they compelled the Milanese to retire to their lines.

Casalecchio (*Battle of*), 26 June, 1402, in which Visconti signally defeated the Bolognese.

Cassa'no (*Battle of*), 28 April, 1799, in which Suwarrow, the Russian general, defeated Marshal Moreau and took 5,000 French prisoners.

Cassel (*Battle of*), 1677, won by the Duc d'Orléans over the Dutch.

Castel Nuovo (*Battle of*), 29 Sept., 1806, in which the Russians were defeated by the French.

Castiglione (*Battle of*), from 2 to 5 Aug., 1796, in which Bonaparte defeated the Austrians under Wurmser. Here Marshal Augereau greatly distinguished himself, and was created Duc de Castiglione (5 syl.).

Castillon (*Battle of*), 17 July, 1453. The most signal defeat suffered by the English. Here the Earl of Shrewsbury and his son were slain. This victory put an end to the dominion of the English in France.

Castlebar, in Ireland (*Battle of*), 27 Aug., 1798. This was not strictly a battle. In 1798 the Irish rose in revolt, and were suppressed on Vinegar Hill, near Wexford, by General Lake, 21 June, 1798. Scarcely was this done, when General Humbert landed with 1,000 French soldiers, and defeated Lake and Hutchinson, who had some 3,000 men under them, at Castlebar. The lord-lieutenant, Lord Cornwallis, now marched against the invaders and Irish revolters, at the head of 30,000 men, and compelled Humbert to surrender.

Catalaunian Plains (*Battle of the*), A.D. 451. Here Attila king of the Huns was vanquished by the Gallic Mer-wig, or Merovēus, who united with the Roman army.

Cattraeth (*Battle of*), A.D. 547, won by Ida the Saxon over the British Confederacy. In this confederacy there were 363 Britons distinguished by golden torques.

Cerignōla (*Battle of*), 1503, won by Gonzalvo of Cordŏva over the French.

Chæroneia (*Battles of*). I. B.C. 447, in which the Athenians were defeated by the Bœōtians, and their general Tolmidas was slain.

II. 2 Aug. B.C. 338, won by Philip of Macedon over the allied Theban and Athenian army. This battle made Greece a province of the Macedonian monarchy.

It was in this battle that Demosthenēs the orator served as a foot-soldier, and fled.

III. B.C. 81, in which Sylla, or Sulla, overthrew Archelāos, the best general of Mithridātēs VI. king of Pontus, sent to aid the Athenians who had revolted against Rome. The army of Mithridates (4 syl.) consisted of 100,000 men, with 10,000 horse, and 90 scythed cars. The whole army of Scylla did not exceed 30,000 men. Pronounce *Ke-ro-ne'-ah.*

Chalgrove, in Oxfordshire (*Battle of*), 18 June, 1643. This was a skirmish between the parliamentarians and royalists, which is only noteworthy because it was here that Hampden was mortally wounded. Generally called 'Chalgrove Field.'

Châlons (*Battle of*), A.D. 451, in which Aëtius and Theodoric utterly overthrew Attila. This is one of Sir Edward Creasy's *Fifteen Decisive Battles of the World.*

Champ-Aubert (*Battles of*), 10 Feb., 1814, won by Napoleon over the Prussians led by Blücher. And again 14 Feb., 1814.

Chancellorsville, U.S. (*Battle of*), 2 May, 1863, won by the Confederates under Lee and Jackson. The Northern army was commanded by General Joseph Hooker.

Charford (*Battle of*), A.D. 519, in which a band of Saxons under Cerdic defeated the Britons. This victory set the crown of the West Saxons on the conqueror's head.

Charmouth (*Battle of*), A.D. 850, in which Ethelwulf king of Wessex was defeated by the Danes.

Charræ (*Battle of*), B.C. 53, in which the Roman army under Crassus the triumvir was defeated by Surēnas, a principal officer of Urōdēs, 'king of kings.' Crassus was treacherously seized in a conference, and killed by molten gold being poured down his throat.
Charræ is Haran [Harran] where Abraham once dwelt.

Château Thierry (*Battle of*), 13 Feb., 1814, won by Napoleon over the Prussians led by Blücher.

Chesapeake (*Battle of the*), 1781, in which the British admiral, Graves, was repulsed by the French admiral, De Grasse, fighting for the Americans in their struggle for independence. *See* 'Shannon and Chesapeake,' &c.

Chester (*Battle of*), 607, won by Ethelfrith over the North Britons. In this battle 2,000 monks of Bangor, who had invoked divine vengeance on the invaders, were the first to fall.

Chickahominy (*Battle of*), 25 June to 1 July, 1862, in the American Civil War. 'Stonewall' Jackson, a Confederate general, greatly distinguished himself in these conflicts.

Chickamauga, U.S. (*Battle of*), 19, 20 Sept., 1863, won by the Confederates under General Bragg. The Northern army was commanded by General Rosecrans.

Chillianwallah (*Battle of*), in India, 13 January, 1849, in which the Sikhs were completely routed by General Lord Gough.
   *** Gough, pronounce *Goff*.

Chippewa (*Battles of*). I. 5 July, 1814, in which the British forces under General Riall were defeated by the Americans led by General Browne.
II. 25 July, 1814. Between the English and North Americans. Both claimed the victory. The British were led by General Drummond and General Riall ; the Americans by Winfield Scott and General Browne. Riall was wounded and taken prisoner. *See* 'Lundy (*Battle of*).'

Chrysop'olis, Scutāri (*Battle of*), A.D. 323, won by Constantine over Licinius.

Clontarf (*Battle of*), Good Friday, 23 April, 1014, in which Brian Boru king of Munster and Connaught utterly defeated the confederated Danes of England, Wales, Ireland, and Denmark. This battle, which lasted all day, was one of the most decisive ever fought. It is said that 14,000 Danes were slain, and 7,000 Irish. Brian fell by assassination in his tent, aged 88.

Cnidus (*Naval battle of*), B.C. 394, won by Conon, the commander of the allied Phœnician and Grecian fleet, over Pisander the Lacedæmonian. This defeat deprived Lacedæmon of her recently gained maritime ascendency.

Coblenz (*Battle of*), B.C. 55, in which Julius Cæsar annihilated the German swarms.

It is said that 150,000 of them were either slain or drowned in the Rhine.

Cocherel, near Evreux (*Battle of*), 1364, in which Charles V. le Sage of France, by his General Duguesclin, defeated Charles the Bad king of Navarre.

Cold Harbor (*Battle of*), in Virginia, 3 June, 1864, between the Federals under Gen. Grant and the Confederates under Gen. Lee. It was very bloody, but indecisive.

Colline Gate (*Battle of the*), 23 Aug., B.C. 82, in which Pontius, leader of the Samnites, was defeated by Crassus. Sylla massacred the 6,000 captive Samnites taken in this battle.

Conquereux or **Conqueruëil**, in France (*Battles of*). I. A.D. 981, in which Geoffrey count of Anjou was defeated by Conan comte de Rennes.
II. A.D. 992, in which Conan comte de Rennes was defeated and slain by Foulques Nerra duke of Anjou.

Copenhagen (*Battle of*), 2 April, 1801, won over the Danish fleet by Admiral Lord Nelson and Admiral Parker.

Corinth (*Battle of*), B.C. 394, won by the Lacedæmonians over the allied Corinthian army.

Coronëa (*Battles of*). I. B.C. 447, won by the Bœōtians over the Athenians. This great disaster caused the death of Isocrătês, 'the old man eloquent.'
II. B.C. 394, in which Agesilāos king of Sparta defeated the allied Athenians, Thebans, Argives (2 syl.), and Corinthians.

Corrichie (*Battle of*), between the Earl of Huntley (a Catholic) and the Earl of Mar (a Protestant). The bone of contention was the earldom of Murray, which Mary the Queen first gave to the Earl of Huntley, and then recalled, that she might give it to her brother, the Earl of Mar. The feud culminated in the battle of Corrichie, in which the Earl of Huntley fell.
The houses of Huntley and Murray were mortal enemies. The fatal battle of Corrichie was an event not to be forgotten nor forgiven. Sir W. SCOTT, *Hist. of Scotland*, xxxviii.

Cortenuōva (*Battle of*), 17 Nov., 1237, in which Kaiser Frederick II. defeated the Milanese.

Corunna (*Battle of*), 16 January, 1809. This was not a battle, but a fight to keep the enemy at bay while the British troops were safely embarked. Sir John Moore had to retire before a French force, and repulsed the foe, which pressed hard upon him. The British loss was very great, and amongst the slain was Sir John Moore. The French say, 'Il y perdit le 16 Jan., 1809, la bataille, qui lui coûta la vie, et qui força ses troupes à abandonner toute l'Espagne.' Of course, after the British troops ha l set sail, Marshal Soult occupied Corunna, and therefore claimed the victory.

Corupedion, near Salamis (*Battle of*), B.C. 281, in which Lysimachus was defeated, and Macedonia, with most other parts of Alexander's vast empire, fell under the hands of Seleucus.

Courtray (*Battles of*). I. In 1302, in which the French were defeated by the Flemings, commanded by Count John of Namur [*Na-moor'*] and William de Juliers. This was 'The Battle of the Spurs,' so called because more than 4,000 gilt spurs were picked up on the field. These were the spurs of French knights slain in the battle.

II. In 1793, in which the French defeated the English.

₀ Courtray has been often lost and won.

Coutras (*Battle of*), 20 Oct., 1587, in which Henri (afterwards the IV. of France), at the head of the Huguenot army, utterly routed the Leaguers or Catholics led by the Duc de Joyeuse.

Cowpens, South Carolina, U.S. (*Battle of*), 11 Jan. 1811. Here the Americans defeated the British, in the American War of Independence. The English troops were led by Colonel Tarleton, the Americans by Colonel Morgan. The colours, cannons, and baggage waggons fell into the hands of the victors, and the loss of the British amounted to at least 600 men, while that of the Americans was trifling.

Cran'on (*Battle of*), B.C. 322, in which the Macedonians led by Antipăter and Cratěros defeated the confederated Greeks both by sea and land. We are told that Hyperīdês, being taken prisoner, was put under torture, and bit or cut off his tongue that he might betray no secrets.

Crayford (*Battle of*), A.D. 457, in which the Saxons triumphed over the Britons, who abandoned Kent and fled to London.

Probably the same as the battle of the Darent. The river Cray runs into the Darent.

Cressy or **Crêci,** in France (*Battle of*), Saturday, 26 Aug., 1346, in which Edward III. of England defeated Philippe VI. of France. The victory was mainly due to the Black Prince, who in this battle won his spurs. In this great victory 1,200 French knights and 30,000 foot-soldiers (a number equal to the whole English army) lay dead on the field. The siege of Calais followed, and its surrender to the victorious king.

This is the greatest victory ever won. The French were at least four times more numerous than the English, but they lost two kings, eleven great princes, eighty bannerets, 1,200 knights, and 30,000 rank and file. The English lost three knights one squire, and an insignificant number of inferior rank. After the battle, King Edward sent Lords Cobham and Surrey, with a number of secretaries and heralds, to take a record of the slain; and their record is still extant.

Cropredy Bridge, near Banbury (*Battle of*), 29 June, 1644, in which Charles I. defeated

Sir W. Waller, one of the Parliamentary officers.

Cullod'en, near Inverness (*Battle of*), 16 April, 1746, in which the Duke of Cumberland completely overthrew the Young Pretender, Charles Edward, and stamped out Jacobitism for ever. Charles Edward escaped to France, three Scotch nobles were beheaded, fifty of Charles's followers were hanged, and forty persons of rank attainted.

Cunax'a (*Battle of*), B.C. 401, between Cyrus the Younger and his brother Artaxerxes Mnemon. Cyrus was slain. This event has been rendered especially famous by 'the retreat of the 10,000' Greeks, led by Xenophon the historian, who also wrote an account of it in his 'Anabāsis.'

Cunersdorf (*Battle of*), 12 Aug., 1759, won by the Russians over the King of Prussia.

Cunobizza (*Battle of*), 1444, won by Hunyādês over the Sultan Amurath II.

Cynosceph'alæ, or the Dogheads (*Battle of*), B.C. 197, in which Philip V. of Macedon was utterly defeated by Flaminius the Roman consul. By this defeat Macedonia lost her supremacy in Greece.

Cynossēma (*Naval battle of*), B.C. 411, won by the Athenians over the Lacedæmonians. 'Cynossēma means 'dog's tomb,' so called from being the traditional tomb of Hecūba, who had been metamorphosed into a dog.

Cyzĭcum (*Battle of*), B.C. 410, won by the Athenians over the Lacedæmonian fleet commanded by Mindăros and assisted by Pharnabăsus the Persian.

Czaslau (*Battle of*), 17 May, 1742, in which Frederick II. of Prussia defeated Prince Charles of Lorraine. In the War of the Austrian Succession. Pronounce *Tshas-low* (ow as in *now*).

Dægsaslan, north of the river Tees (*Battle of*), 603, won by Ethelfrith over the forces of the Northern Britons. By this great victory the rule of Northumbria, from the Humber to the Forth, was established. Dægsaslan is Dalton, in Yorkshire.

Danbury, Connecticut, U.S. (*Battle of*), 26 April, 1777, won by the English, who set fire to the town. In the American War of Independence.

Dego (*Battle of*), 15 April, 1796, in which Bonaparte repulsed the Austrians.

Delium (*Battle of*), B.C. 424, won by the Bœotians over the Athenians in the eighth year of the Peloponnesian war. This battle was the most disastrous and most decisive of all the battles fought in the first eight years of the war.

Denain (*Battle of*), 1712, won by the French, commanded by Marshal Villars, over Prince Eugene.

Dennewitz (*Battle of*), 6 Sept., 1813, won by Marshal Bernadotte [afterwards Charles

Deorham, in Gloucestershire (*Battle of*), 577, in which the West Saxons conquered the Britons. Gloucester, Cirencester, and Bath, which had leagued under the British king in this contest, became the spoil of the conquerors. Three British kings, viz. Conmail, Condidan, and Farinmail, fell in this battle.

Dessau (*Battle of*), 1626, won by Wallenstein in the Catholic interest. This was one of the battles of the Thirty Years' War.

⁎ Pronounce *Des-sow* (ow as in *now*).

Dettingen (*Battles of*) I. 27 June, 1743, in which George II. defeated the French under Marshal Noailles. In a military point of view this battle was a very small matter, consisting of extricating Lord Stair from a position in which his blundering had placed him. George II. cut his way out. The effect of this success was considerable, for the French evacuated Germany, and the fortunes of Maria Theresa revived. This battle, which was in the War of the Austrian Succession, was the last in which an English sovereign engaged in person.

II. 26 July, 1866, in which the Prussians defeated the Bavarians in the Austro-Prussian war.

Diamond (*Battle of the*), Sept., 1795. A battle in Ireland between the Orangemen and Catholics ; so-called from the place where it was fought, county Antrim.

Dolabella (*Battle of*), A.D. 24, in which Tacfarinas the African freebooter was defeated by a Roman army and slain.

Donnington (*Battles of*). I. in 1643, in which the parliamentarians were defeated by Colonel Cavendish.

II. in 1645, in which the royalists, led by Lord Ashton, were defeated by Colonel Morgan.

These are not the same places. The former is in Lincolnshire ; the latter in Gloucestershire.

Douro (*Battle of the*), 12 May, 1809, won by Sir Arthur Wellesley (duke of Wellington) over Sou t, the French marshal.

For this exploit Sir Arthur was created Baron Douro.

Dresden (*Battles of*). I. 28 Oct., 1806, where Napoleon defeated the Prussians.

II. 26, 27 Aug., 1813, won by Napoleon over the allies, led by the Prince of Schwarzenberg. Marshal Moreau was slain in this battle.

Dreux (*Battle of*), 1562, between the Catholics and Huguenots, in the first religious war of France. Marshal St. André, one of the French Triumvirate (*q.v.*), was slain ; but the Catholics claimed the victory as Prince Condé was taken prisoner.

Dryfe Sands (*Battle of*), 1593. Between the Maxwells and Johnstones, the former of whom was left dead on the field. This was the last great clan battle fought on the borders.

Dunbar (*Battles of*). I. 27 April, 1296, in which the English, under John Earl of Warrenne, defeated Baliol's army with great slaughter.

II. 3 Sept., 1650, in which Cromwell utterly defeated the Scotch, led by Leslie. After this victory, Edinburgh Castle and several other strong fortresses fell into the hands of Cromwell.

Ten thousand prisoners fell into Cromwell's hands in this victory, with all the baggage and guns ; and as many as 3,000 were slain. Spain instantly recognised the commonwealth, and Holland offered its alliance.

Dunes (*Battle of the*), 4 June, 1658, in which the English and French defeated the Spaniards.

Dungan Hill (*Battle of*), 10 July, 1647, in which the Irish were defeated by Colonel Jones.

Dunsin'nane (*Battle of*), 1057, won by Seward over the army of Macbeth. Macbeth fled and was slain at Lumphanan, in Aberdeenshire.

⁎ Called by Shakespeare Dunsināne.

Dupplin Moor (*Battle of*), 1332, in which an army of 40,000 Scots was utterly defeated by some 3,000 Englishmen. Above 13,000 of the Scotch were slain, and not above 30 of the English.

Durham (*Battle of*), 17 Oct., 1346, in which Queen Philippa defeated David Bruce king of Scotland, who was taken prisoner.

Durham Station, North Carolina, the 'Sedan' of the American Civil War. Here (10 May, 1865) General Johnston, who had the chief command of the Confederates, surrendered to General Sherman, and thus brought the war to an end. The war began in 1861.

Durrenstein (*Battle of*), 11 Nov., 1805, in which the French were defeated by the Russians.

Ebersberg (*Battle of*), 13 May, 1809, in which the French Marshal Massēna defeated the Austrians.

Eckmühl in Bavaria (*Battle of*), 22 April, 1809, won by Napoleon over the Archduke Karl, leader of the Austrians. All the Austrian artillery, fifteen standards, and 20,000 prisoners fell to the French in this battle.

April 23, Napoleon was wounded in the heel.

Ec'nomus (*Naval battle of*), B.C. 256, in the first Punic war. The Roman fleet was victorious over the Carthaginian.

⁎ Econmus, now Monteserrato.

Eddington or Ethandun, near Westbury in Wilts (*Battle of*), May 11, A.D. 878, in which Alfred completely overthrew the Danes and recovered his throne. Finding it impossible to drive the Danes out of the kingdom, he allowed them to settle in East Anglia, &c., provided they became Christians.

Edgecote (*Battle of*), 26 July, 1469, in which the royal forces were defeated by Lancastrian insurgents.

Edgehill (*Battle of*), 23 Oct., 1642. An indecisive battle between the royalists led by Prince Rupert and the parliamentary party led by the Earl of Essex. This was the first battle between Charles I. and his subjects. The king himself was personally present in this battle.

Elchingen (*Battle of*), 14 Oct., 1805, in which the French under Marshal Ney defeated the Austrians.

Ellandun (*Battle of*), 823, in which Egbert defeated Beornwulf of Mercia. Ellandun is Wilton, close by Salisbury, a little to the south-east of Ethandun or Eddington, famous for one of Alfred's victories.

Elster (*Battle of*), 5 Oct., 1080, won by Heinrich IV. of Germany over Rudolf, the pseudo-emperor appointed by the diet of Forscheim. Rudolf died of his wounds.

Emmendingen (*Battle of*), 19 Oct., 1796. The Archduke Karl of Austria defeated Moreau the French general.

Engen (*Battle of*), April, 1799, in which Moreau the French general defeated the Austrians.

Enghien (*Battle of*), 3 Aug., 1692, won by the French under Marshal Luxembourg over William III. Enghien (3 syl.).

Epila (*Battle of*), 1348, in which the Union of Aragon was overthrown. This was the last battle of Aragon fought in defence of public liberty. The 'Privilege of Union' was abolished, Peter himself cutting to pieces with his sword the original charter.

Espierres (*Battle of*), 22 May, 1794, in which the French were repulsed by the allied English and Austrians.

Essling (*Battle of*), 21, 22 May, 1809, won by Karl archduke of Austria over Napoleon. This was the greatest defeat that Napoleon himself had hitherto sustained. Marshal Lannes fell in the fight, and 30,000 French were made prisoners.

Here Kaiser Rudolf, in 1276, overthrew Ottokar king of Bohemia.

Eurymēdon (*Battle of*), B.C. 470, won by Cimon, son of Miltiadēs, over the Persians.

Eutaw Springs, U.S. (*Battle of*), 8 Sept., 1781, in which Colonel Stewart and General Arnold (a renegade American) defeated the Americans in the American War of Independence.

Evesham (*Battle of*), 3 Aug., 1265, in which Simon de Montfort and his son were defeated and slain by Prince Edward son of Henry III. It is said that at one period of the battle the king was on the point of being cleft down by a common soldier, and saved his life by exclaiming, 'Don't kill me, soldier; I am Henry of Westminster, the king.' *See* Hexham.

Eylau (*Battle of*), 8 Feb., 1807, a doubtful battle between Napoleon and the combined Russian and Prussian armies. Napoleon claimed the victory because the allied army decamped during the night. It was a most bloody fight. The French were 54,000 strong, the allied Prussians and Russians were 72,000.

⁎⁎ Pronounce *Ey-low* (ow as in *now*).

Falkirk (*Battles of*). I. 22 July, 1298, in which Edward I. defeated Wallace, who was afterwards captured and beheaded.

II. 17 Jan., 1746, in which the 'Young Pretender' defeated General Hawley.

Farnham, in Surrey (*Battle of*), A.D. 894, in which Alfred defeated the Danes under Hastings their leader.

Fère - champenoise (*Battle of*), 25 March, 1814, in which Marmont's French army was defeated by the Austrians led by Schwartzenberg.

Ferozeshah (*Battle of*), in the Punjab, 22, 23 Dec., 1845, in which Sir Hugh Gough defeated the Sikhs.

Hugh Gough was created a baronet in 1842 and a baron in 1846. (Gough = *Goff*.)

Flat-bush (*Battle of*), Long Island, 27 Aug., 1776, in which the Americans were defeated by the British forces.

Fleurus (*Battle of*), 17 June, 1794, in which the allied army, consisting of 100,000 men, under the command of the Prince of Coburg, marching to the relief of Charleroi, was signally defeated by the French revolutionary army commanded by Jourdan. In this battle the French made use of balloons to reconnoitre the enemy's army.

Flodden Field (*Battle of*), 9 Sept., 1513, in which the Earl of Surrey defeated the Scots.

Fontenoy (*Battle of*), 11 May, 1745, in which Marshal Saxe defeated the Duke of Cumberland at the head of an allied army of English, Dutch, and Hanoverian troops.

Formigny, in Normandy (*Battle of*), 18 April, 1450, in which the Constable of Richemont defeated an army of 3,000 Englishmen. This battle was the *coup de grâce* of our claim upon France. A monument on the field of battle records the victory.

Fornovo (*Battle of*), 6 July, 1495, in which Charles VIII. of France defeated the Italian allies. This was a most marvellous victory: the French did not number above 9,000, the allies exceeded 40,000. Yet the loss of the French was only 200, but that of the allies 3,500. Paulus Jovius terms this battle 'the extinction of Cisalpine military glory, an ignominious rout which made Italy contemptible, and the beginning of countless miseries.' This battle is also called 'The Battle of the Taro.'

Frankenhausen (*Battle of*), 1525, in which the Elector of Saxony utterly defeated the Anabaptists, and took their leader, Munzer, prisoner. Munzer was ignominiously beheaded.

Fredericksburg, in the United States (*Battle of*), 13 Dec., 1862, in which the Confederates under General Lee defeated the Northern army led by General Burnside.

3 R

Freiburg (*Battle of*), 1644, in which the French led by the Great Condé defeated François de Merci, a general in the service of the Elector of Bavaria.

It was in this battle that Condé flung his bâton into the enemy's trenches.

Friedland (*Battle of*), 14 June, 1807, won by Napoleon over the Russian army which had fought at Eylau, 8 Feb., 1807. The peace of Tilsit was the result of this victory.

Friedlingen (*Battle of*), 1702, won by the French commanded by Marshal Villars over the imperialists commanded by the Prince of Baden.

Frithern (*Battle of*), A.D. 584, won by the Saxons over the Britons. Cealwin was the Saxon chief.

Fuentes de Onoro (*Battle of*), 5 May, 1811, between the British and Spanish forces under Wellington and the French under Masséna. It was an indecisive battle, but the French retreated out of Portugal on the 10th, and therefore the advantage was on the side of Wellington. The Anglo-Spanish loss was 1,500, the French loss nearly 5,000.

Gallip'oli (*Battle of*), 1294, a great naval victory won by the Genoese over the Venetians.

Garigliăno (*Battle of*), 27 Dec., 1503, won by Gonsalvo, the great captain, over the French.

Gaugaměla (*Battle of*), 1 Oct., B.C. 331. Same as the 'Battle of Arbela' (*q.v.*).

Gemblours (*Battle of*), Jan., 1578, in which the Dutch were defeated by Don John of Austria.

Genestrello (*Battle of*), 20 May, 1859, the first of the battles fought by the Sardinians against the Austrians. The allied army, consisting of Sardinians, Italians, and French, defeated the Austrians.

Germantown, U.S. (*Battle of*), 4 Oct., 1777. Here General Howe defeated the Americans in the American War of Independence.

Gettysburg, Pennsylvania (*Battle of*), 3 July, 1863, in which the Confederates under the command of General Lee were defeated by the Northern army. This was one of the great battles of the Civil War.

Ghuznee (*Battle of*), 23 July, 1839, won by the English, led by Sir J. Keane, over the Afghans. The citadel was attacked at 2 A.M. ; at 3 the gates were blown in, and at 5 the English colours were flying on the towers.

Glenlivet (*Battle of*), 3 Oct., 1594, a trial of strength between the Highlanders and the Lowlanders. The Earl of Argyll led the Highlanders and the Earl of Huntley the Lowlanders. Victory rested with the latter.

The encounter came to resemble that of Harlaw (*q v.*), where the force of the ancient Gael had been tried in mortal contest with that of the Low-country Saxons (Sir W. Scott, 'History of Scotland,' xxxviii.).

Goo'jerat, or **Gûjerat** (*Battle of*), 21 Feb., 1849, won by Lord Gough over the Sikhs. A magnificent affair.

..* Gough, pronounce *Goff*.

Gorey (*Battle of*), 4 June, 1798, in which the king's troops were defeated by the Irish insurgents.

Grampian Hills (*Battle of the*), A.D. 79 or 82, in which the Romans, under Agricola, utterly defeated the Caledonians led by Galgac.

Grani'cus (*Battles of the*). I. May B.C. 334, in which Alexander the Great defeated Darius Codoman'us.

II. B.C. 73, in which Lucullus defeated Mithridătes.

Granson (*Battle of*), 1476, in which the Swiss fell upon the army of Charles le Téméraire duke of Burgundy, and put it to utter rout.

Gravelotte (*Battle of*), 18 Aug., 1870, in the Franco-Prussian war ; won by the Prussians.

Grochow (*Battle of*), 20 Feb., 1831, won by the Poles over the Russians.

Gross Beeren (*Battle of*), 23 Aug., 1813, when the French were repulsed by the Swedes.

Guildford, or **Guilford** (*Battle of*), 1781, in which Lord Cornwallis with 1,600 men utterly defeated Greene, the American general, who had 6,600 or 7,000 men. Marshall, in his 'Life of Washington,' says : 'No battle in the whole course of the war reflects more honour on the courage of the British troops than this of Guildford' (in North Carolina).

Guinegate, near Calais (*Battle of*), 18 Aug., 1513, won by the allied armies of Henry VIII. of England, the Kaiser Maximilian, and the Swiss, over the French. Called the 'Battle of the Spurs,' because the French used their spurs in flight more than their swords in fight.

Guzerat. '*See* Goojerat.'

Gwenystrad (*Battle of*), A.D. 547, won by Urien over Ida the Saxon invader.

Hadrian'ple (*Battles of*). I. 3 July, A.D. 323, in which the Roman emperor Licinius was defeated by Constantine.

II. 9 Aug., A.D. 378, in which the Roman emperor Valens was utterly defeated by the Goths, and lost his life. No battle, except that of Cannæ, could be compared to this in its fatal consequences on the Romans.

Halidon Hill (*Battle of*), near Berwick, 19 July, 1333, in which Edward III. defeated the Regent Douglas (brother of the famous 'Good Sir James'). By this victory Berwick-upon-Tweed remained to the English, and Baliol was restored to the throne as sub-king to the English crown, but the wars with France drew Edward out of the country, Baliol fied, and David Bruce returned to his kingdom.

It is said that 30,000 Scots were killed ; but only 1 knight, 1 esquire, and 13 privates on Edward's side.

Halle (*Battle of*), 16, 17 Oct., 1806. Here Bernadotte defeated the Prussians.

Hanau (*Battle of*), 29 Oct., 1813. The French claim the victory because the Austrians were compelled to retreat. The French were led by Napoleon and the Austrians by General Wrede. The affair was doubtful, though the French army was double that of the adversary.

Harlaw (*Battle of*), 24 July, 1411, a trial of strength between the Gaels and Saxons. The Saxons, or Lowlanders, were led by the Earl of Mar; the Gaels, or Highlanders, by Donald of the Isles. The latter army was considerably more in number, but all the benefits of victory remained with the Saxons. On 3 Oct., 1594, a similar trial occurred at Glenlivet, when the Earl of Argyll led the Highlanders and Huntley the Lowlanders. In this case also the victory rested with the Lowlanders.

Hastings (*Battle of*), 14 Oct., 1066, where William duke of Normandy conquered and slew Harold II., and thus won, by conquest, the throne of England. Also called the 'Battle of Senlac.'

Hatfield, in Yorkshire (*Battle of*), 14 Oct., 633. Called the 'Battle of Hatfield Chase,' in which Edwine king of Northumbria was defeated and slain by Penda of Mercia.

Havenfeld, or **Hefenfield** (*Battle of*), 634, in which the Welsh under Cadwallon were utterly defeated by Oswald king of Northumbria. Havenfeld means 'heaven's field,' so called because Oswald just before the battle threw himself on his knees in the midst of the army, and asked God to give him the victory. Cadwallon fell fighting in this battle. Havenfeld was in Durham, not far from Hexham.

Hefenfield. *See* **Havenfeld.**

Heights of Romainville (*Battle of the*), 30 March, 1814, in which the French army under Joseph Bonaparte, Marmont, and Mortier was defeated by the allies, who entered Paris the next day.

Heilsberg (*Battle of*), 10 June, 1807, in which the Prussians were defeated by the French.

Hengestesdun (*Battle of*), 835, in which Egbert king of England defeated the Danes. Hengestesdun is now called Hengston Down, in Cornwall.

Heraclea (*Battle of*), B.C. 280. In which the Romans were defeated by Pyrrhus.

Heracleum (*Battle of*), B.C. 38, where Ventidius (Antony's legate) defeated the Parthians under Pacorus.

Herara (*Battle of*), in Aragon, 24 Aug., 1837, in which Don Carlos of Spain defeated General Buerens.

Hermanstadt (*Battle of*), 1442, won by Hunyades over the Turks.

Hexham, in Northumberland (*Battle of*), 15 May, 1464, in which the Lancastrians were defeated by Lord Montacute. There is a current legend that after the battle Queen Margaret, in her flight, encountered a brigand, and said to him, 'Man, I trust to your loyalty the son of your king.' We are furthermore assured that Margaret and her son escaped over the border under this robber's guidance. *See* Evesham.

Hobkirk's Hill, South Carolina, U.S. (*Battle of*), 25 April, 1781, where Lord Rawdon defeated the American General Greene in the American War of Independence.

Hochkirchen (*Battles of*). I. 14 Oct., 1758, when Marshal Daun defeated Frederick II. the Great of Prussia. (In the Third Campaign of the Seven Years' War.) II. 22 May, 1813, when Napoleon defeated the combined Russian and Prussian armies.

Höchst (*Battle of*), 11 Oct., 1795, in which the Austrians defeated Marshal Jourdan, and compelled the French to cross the Rhine.

Hochstadt (*Battle of*), 19 June, 1800, won by Marshal Moreau, the French general, over the Austrians.

Hogue (*Naval battle off Cape la*), 1692, in which the French were defeated by the League (consisting of England, Germany, Holland, Spain, and Savoy).

Hohenlinden (*Battle of*), 3 Dec., 1800, won by Marshal Moreau for the French over the Austrian Archduke John. In this battle he took 100 pieces of cannon and 11,000 prisoners.

Holmedon Hill (*Battle of*), 14 Sept., 1402, between the Scots headed by the Earl of Douglas and the Percys. Hotspur, one of the Percys, was the victor; Douglas was taken prisoner, and so were the earls of Angus, Fife, Murray, and Orkney, with many more of the Scotch nobility and gentry.

Iconium (*Battle of*), 1387, won by Amurath the Turkish sultan over the Caramanians. Here Prince Bajazet greatly distinguished himself, and acquired the epithet of *Yilderim* (Lightning).

Ingolstadt (*Battle of*), 20 April, 1809, won by Napoleon.

Inkermann, in the Crimea (*Battle of*), 5 Nov., 1854, won by the allied British and French armies over the Russians.

Inverlochy, in Scotland (*Battle of*), 2 Feb., 1645, in which the Marquis of Montrose, commander of the royal army in Scotland, defeated Argyll.

Ipsus (*Battle of*), B.C. 301, a decisive battle which closed the great contest between the generals of Alexander the Great for the succession to the empire. Antigonus being defeated and slain, Seleucus was confirmed in his kingdom.

Irun (*Battle of*), 17 May, 1837, in which the Carlists of Spain were defeated by the British auxiliary legion under General Evans.

Islip Bridge, Oxfordshire (*Battle of*), 22 April, 1645, in which Cromwell routed four regiments of cavalry convoying the king's artillery from Oxford to Worcester.

Issus (*Battles of*), Nov. B.C. 333, won by Alexander the Great over Darius Codoman'us king of Persia. The Persian army consisted of 600,000 men. Alexander's army did not amount to 30,000 men. In this battle Sisygamia, the mother of Darius, and Statira his wife, fell into the hands of the conqueror.

A.D. 194, Severus conquered Pescennius Niger in a decisive battle on the same plains. The loss of Pescennius Niger was 20,000 men and his own life. His head was sent to Rome.

Ivry (*Battle of*), 1590, in which Henry IV. gained a brilliant victory over the Duc de Mayenne.

Jalula (*Battle of*), A.D. 637, won by the Saracens over Yzdegerd king of Persia.

Janvilliers (*Battle of*), 14 Feb., 1814, won by the French over the Prussians under Blücher.

Jarnac (*Battle of*), 13 March, 1569, in the third religious war of France. The Catholics were victors, and the Prince de Condé, the great Huguenot leader, was killed in cold blood by Moncontour.

Jemappes, in Belgium (*Battle of*), 5 Nov., 1792. This battle lasted four days; it was between the French revolutionary army led by General Dumouriez and 28,000 Austrians entrenched in woods and hills. Dumouriez was the victor; but he lost 12,000 men, the loss of the Austrians being 10,000.

Jena, in Saxe-Weimar (*Battle of*), 14 Oct., 1806, in which Napoleon defeated the King of Prussia and advanced at once to Berlin. Here the Duke of Brunswick lost his life. On the same day Marshal Davoust routed the Prussians at Auerstadt.

*** Jena pronounce *Ya-nah.*

Jsaszeg (*Battle of*), 5 April, 1849, in the War of Independence. It was won by the Hungarians. With this battle the demoralisation of the Austrian army was complete.

June 1st (*Battle of*), 1794, a naval victory in which Lord Howe defeated and crippled the French fleet off the coast of Brest. The battle is called that of the 'First of June.' The French admiral was Villaret-Joyeuse.

Kadesiah (*Battle of*), or 'Kudseah,' A.D. 636, won by the Mahometans over the Persians. This battle decided the character of the Persian empire.

Kainardji, or Kutschuk-Kainardji (Treaty of), 21 July, 1774. A treaty of peace between Russia and Turkey. By this treaty the Azof was ceded to Russia, and the freedom of the Black Sea. The Crimea was severed from Turkey and declared free.

Kaiserlautern (*Battle of*), 30 Nov., 1793, won by the Duke of Brunswick over the French.

Kalitsch (*Battle of*), 13 Feb., 1813, in which the French were defeated by the Russians. The French general was Regnier and the Russian general was Winzingerode.

Kalusz (*Battle of*), 15 Oct., 1667, won by Sobieski, the Polish general, after seventeen days' fighting, over the Cossacks and Tartars.

Kapolna (*Battle of*), 1848, one of the battles of the War of Independence. Lost by the Hungarians, who were led by Dembinski. It is said that the jealousy of Görgey, who refused to obey orders, was the cause of this defeat.

Kars (*Battle of*), 29 Sept., 1855, won by the Turks, commanded by General Williams, over the Russians, commanded by General Mouravieff. Certainly, the Russians were thrice the number of the Turks. The Turks lost 1,094 men, the Russians lost 6,500. Kars was invested by Mouravieff, 16 June, 1885 ; after the battle it was obliged to capitulate, 12 Dec., 1855 ; but when peace was restored Kars was by the treaty of Paris restored to Turkey, 1856.

Katzbach (*Battle of*), 26 Aug., 1813, won by Blücher over the French.

Kesseldorff (*Battle of*), 15 Dec., 1745, in which Prince Leopold of Anhalt-Dessau defeated the Saxons under Prince Charles of Lorraine. (In the War of the Austrian Succession.)

Kiblene (*Battle of*), St. Andrews' day, 1335, won by the Scotch (led by Liddesdale) over the English, under the command of the Earl of Athol.

Kilcullen (*Battle of*), 23 May, 1798, in which General Dundas was routed by the Irish insurgents.

In a subsequent engagement General Dundas overthrew the rebels near Kilcullen Bridge.

Killiecrankie (*Battle of*), 17 July, 1689, in which John Graham viscount of Dundee (Claverhouse), a Jacobite, defeated General Mackay, who commanded an army in the service of the Prince of Orange (William III.) Claverhouse fell early in the battle.

Kilsyth, in Scotland (*Battle of*), 15 Aug., 1645, in which the Marquis of Montrose, commander of the royal forces in Scotland, defeated the Scots under Baillie.

Knoc-Auadh (*Battle of*), 1504, in which Kildare governor of Ireland (*i.e.* the Pale) utterly routed the confederated Irish. It is said that from 4,000 to 9,000 of the Irish fell, but not one single English soldier in Kildare's army.

Kolin, in Bohemia (*Battle of*), 18 June, 1757, where Marshal Daun defeated Frederick II. (the Great) of Prussia. (The Second Campaign of the Seven Years' War.)

Ko'nieh (*Battle of*), 20 Dec., 1832, in Turkey. The Turks were defeated by Ibrahim Pasha.

Königgrätz (*Battle of*), same as Sadowa (*q.v.*).

Koncvics (*Battle of*), 28 Nov., 1443, in which Hunyádi defeated the Turks.

Kossova (*Battle of*), 27 Aug., 1369, won by Amurath, the Turkish sultan, over the allied

Christian army. Amurath was slain, probably by treachery, after the battle was won.

Kotzim or **Choczim** (*Battle of*), 10 Nov., 1673, won by Sobieski, the Polish general, over Capitan Pasha, the Turkish general. This was a truly marvellous victory, and 40,000 Turks were slain.

Kowno (*Battle of*), 14 Dec., 1812, in which the French were defeated by the Russians.

Krasnoi (*Battle of*), 16 Nov., 1812, in which Marshal Davoust (Prince of Eckmühl) and his French army were defeated by the Russians under the command of Kutusoff.

Krefeld (*Battle of*), 23 June, 1758, in the third campaign of the Seven Years' War. Here the Duke of Brunswick, fighting on the side of Frederick II. (the Great) of Prussia, drove the French army across the Rhine.

Kulm (*Battle of*), 31 Aug., 1813, won by the allied armies of Austria and Russia over the French.

Kunersdorf (*Battle of*), 12 Aug., 1759, the fourth campaign of the Seven Years' War. Here Frederick II. (the Great) of Prussia suffered from the combined Austrian and Russian armies the greatest defeat in all his reign. He wrote in pencil to his chief minister, 'All is lost, save the royal family.' Strange to say, after this great victory, the Austrian and Russian generals fell to loggerheads, and Prussia was saved.

La Hogue (*Battle of*), 19 May, 1692, in which the French fleet, under Admiral Tourville, was utterly destroyed by the English and Dutch. This was a most important victory, won by the Admirals Russell and Rooke, as it not only put an end to the threatened French invasion, and overthrew the hopes of James II. of recovering his throne, but so crippled the navy of France that it ceased to be formidable.

La Rothière (*Battle of*), 1 Feb., 1814, won by Napoleon over the combined Prussian and Russian armies.

Lake Champlain, in North America (*Battles of*). I. 11 and 13 Oct., 1776, when the American flotilla was defeated by the English.
II. 11 Sept., 1814, when the Americans defeated the English squadron.

Lake Erie, in Canada (*Battle of*), 10 Sept., 1813, in which the Americans captured the British squadron.
Fort Erie, in Canada, was taken by General Brown from the British, 3 July, 1814; but 5 Nov. the same year was abandoned by the captors.

Lake Lemānus, in Geneva (*Battle of*). B.C. 108, in which Cassus Longinus the consul was slain, and his whole army cut to pieces by the Cimbrians.

Lake Merom (*Battle at the*), B.C. 1450, where the kings of the hill country and their allies were defeated by Joshua.

Lake Regillus. *See* 'Regillus.'

Landau, or Pirmasens (*Battle of*), 14 Sept.' 1793, won by the Duke of Brunswick over the French.
⁎ Pronounce *Lahn-dow* (ow as in *now*).

Landen (*Battle of*), 29 July, 1693, in which Marshal Luxembourg defeated William III. of England.

Langensalza, in Prussia (*Battles of*). I. 14 Feb., 1761, · in which the Hanoverians defeated the French (in the sixth campaign of the Seven Years' War.)
II. 27 June, 1866, in which General Flies defeated the Hanoverians in the Austro-Prussian war (in the Seven Weeks' War.)

Langport, in Somersetshire (*Battle of*), June, 1645, in which Fairfax routed the royal forces.

Langside, in Scotland (*Battle of*), 13 May, 1568, in which the Hamiltons, who supported the cause of Mary Queen of Scots, were defeated by the Earl of Murray. After this defeat Mary crossed the Solway and took refuge in the castle of Carlisle. Here she demanded one of two things—either her restoration to the throne of Scotland or a safe passage to France.

Lansdowne Hill, near Bath (*Battle of*), 5 July, 1643, in which the royalist army, under Sir Bevil Granville, defeated Sir William Waller and his parliamentarian forces.

Laon (*Battle of*), 9 March, 1814, won by the allied armies of Bernadotte of Sweden and Blücher over Napoleon.

Laufeld or **Lawfield** (*Battles of*). I. 1747, in which the French, under Marshal Saxe, defeated the allied English and Dutch, under the command of the Duke of Cumberland.
II. 1794, in which the French were victorious.

Laupen, Berne (*Battle of*), 1339, in which the Bernois, commanded by Rudolph d'Erlach, defeated the Austrians.

Lech (*Battle of*). 1632, won by Gustavus Adolphus over the German Catholic League. Here Tilly was mortally wounded. This was one of the battles of the Thirty Years' War.

Lechfeld (*Battles of*). I. A.D. 743 Pepin defeated the Bavarians and Saxons.
II. 794 Charlemagne defeated the Huns.
III. 910 the Hungarians defeated the Franks and Bavarians.
IV. 955 Otto I. of Germany defeated the Hungarians.

Legnāno, near Como (*Battle of*), 29 May, 1176, in which Frederick Barbarossa was defeated by the Milanese, and the independence of Lombardy was recognised by him in the treaty of Constance, 1183.

Leipzig (*Battles of*). I. 7 Sept., 1631, in which Gustavus Adolphus defeated Tilly. This was in the Thirty Year' War, and was one of the three great battles.
The other two were Lützen, won by Gusta-

vus Adolphus in 1632 ; and Nordlingen, won by the Kaiser's son (afterwards Ferdinand III.) in 1634.

II. 16, 18, 19 Oct., 1813, won by the allied Russian, Austrian, and Prussian armies over Napoleon.

The bridge over the Elster, blown up by a mine, was the most disastrous part of this sanguinary battle. The French numbered 180,000 men, the allied army 300,000. The 17 German battalions in the French army deserted to the allies.

Lens, in the Pas-de-Calais (*Battle of*), 1648, in which the great Condé defeated Leopold brother of the Kaiser of Germany.

Lepanto (*Naval battle of*), 7 Oct., 1571, in which Don John of Austria defeated the Turks. It was recaptured by the Venetians in 1678, and restored to the Turks by the treaty of Carlowitz in 1699.

The naval victory of Lepanto was one of the most splendid ever achieved. 25,000 Turks were slain, 4,000 were taken prisoners; 12,000 Christian slaves were released ; 130 ships were captured, 130 others were abandoned and destroyed, and 80 were sunk during the battle.

Leuctra (*Battle of*), 8 July, B.C. 371, in which the Lacedæmonians, led by Cleombrŏtus, received a crushing defeat from the Thebans, led by Epaminondas and Pelopĭdas.

Leuthen, in Silesia (*Battle of*), 5 Dec., 1757, in which Frederick II. of Prussia defeated the Austrians under Prince Charles of Lorraine. This was just one month after the rout of Rosbach (in the second campaign of the Seven Years' War).

Lewes (*Battle of*), in Sussex, 14 May, 1264, in which Simon de Montfort and his Londoners defeated and captured both King Henry III. and Richard earl of Cornwall, king of the Romans. Prince Edward escaped, and subsequently surrendered.

Lexington (*Battle of*), in Massachusetts.
I. 19 April, 1775. The first skirmish in the American War of Independence. Gage, the British general, had the worst of it, and so far it may be scored as an American victory; but the affair, though honourable to the American militia, was not important, and was not a battle, but a mere skirmish.

II. Lexington, in Missouri, is noted for a battle between the Federals (or. Northern States) and the Confederates (or Southern States) in Sept., 1861. In this case the town remained in the hands of the Confederates.

Liegnitz, in Silesia (*Battles of*). I. 9 April, 1241, in which Batou Khan defeated Duke Henry of Silesia and the Christian allies.

II. 3 May, 1634, in which the Saxons, under Arnheim, defeated Jerome Colloredo, commander of the Bohemians.

III. 16 Aug., 1760, in which Frederick II. (the Great) of Prussia, defeated the Austrians under Laudon (in the fifth campaign of the Seven Years' War).

Ligny (*Battle of*), 16 June, 1815, won by Napoleon over Blücher ; but the defeat was not sufficiently grave to prevent Blücher from assisting at the field of Waterloo on the 18th.

Lincoln (*Battles of*). I. 2 Feb., 1141, where Stephen king of England was both defeated and captured by Ralph and Robert of Gloucester. After this victory Matilda (the wife of Geoffrey the Handsome, or Geoffrey Plantagenet, and daughter of Henry I.) entered London, and was received as ' the Lady of England.'

II. 19 May, 1217, in which Louis the dauphin of France was utterly defeated by the army of Henry III.

Linlithgow Bridge (*Battle of*), 1525, won by Sir James Hamilton over the Earl of Lenox, who wanted to obtain possession of the King (James V. of Scotland). Lenox was slain by Hamilton.

Lippstadt (*Battle of*). See ' Lützen.'

Lissa (*Battle of*), in Silesia, 5 Dec., 1757, in which Frederick II. of Prussia defeated Prince Charles of Lorraine.

Llongborth (*Battle of*), 530, won by Cerdic over the Britons. In this battle Arthur was the commander of the British army, and Geraint prince of Devonshire united with him against the Saxons. Geraint was slain.

Lobositz (*Battle of*), Oct., 1756, between Frederick II. of Prussia and the Austrians under General Brown. It was indecisive, but Frederick claimed the victory. (First campaign of the Seven Years' War.)

Loch Gary (*Battle of*), 26 July, 1654, in which General Middleton and his Highlanders were defeated by the Protector's army.

Lodi (*Battle of*), 10 May, 1796. At the bridge of Lodi Bonaparte beat the Austrians, and on the 15th entered Milan without opposition.

Logron'o (*Battle of*), 10th century, in the reign of Ramiro II. king of Asturias, when the Arabs under Abderrahman II. were overthrown. This was the famous battle in which St. James on his white horse fought, as we are told, for Spain.

Lonäto (*Battle of*), 3 Aug. 1796, in which Bonaparte vanquished the Austrians led by Wurmser.

Long Island (*Battle of*), North America, 27 Aug., 1776, in which Sir William Howe defeated the American troops. Same as Flatbush.

Lundy (*Battle of*), 25 July, 1814, between the United States and the United Kingdom. The American generals were Winfield Scott and General Brown ; but the British forces were commanded by General Drummond and General Riall. The victory was doubtful.

Sometimes called the battle of Bridgewater, battle of Niagara, battle of Lundy's Lane, &c.

Lützen (*Battles of*). I. 6 Nov., 1632, won by the Swedes over the German Catholic League. Gustavus Adolphus king of Sweden

died of wounds received in this battle ; some say foully in the moment of victory. This was one of the battles of the Thirty Years' War. Also called the battle of Lippstadt.
II. 2 May, 1813, won by Napoleon I. over the allied armies of Prussia and Russia.

Macato (*Battle of*), 11 Oct., 1427, in which Carmagnuola defeated the Milanese forces led by Carlo Malatesta.

Macziewice (*Battle of*), 10 Oct., 1794, in which the Polish general Kosciusko was defeated and taken prisoner by Suwarof, the Russian general.

Mag'dolon (*Battle of*). So Herodotus calls the battle of Megiddo (*Hist.* ii. 159). The Romans called Megiddo ' Legio,' and it is still called ' Lejjun.' The battle referred to by Herodotus is that in which Josiah was overcome and slain by Pharaoh-Necho king of Egypt (2 *Kings* xxiii. 29, 30).

Magenta (*Battle of*), 4 June, 1859, won by the French Marshal M'Mahon over the Austrians. For this brilliant action M'Mahon was created 'Duc de Magenta' by Napoleon III. The Austrian general was Gyulay.

Magheracloon (*Battle of*), 1843. This was no battle in the usual sense of the word, but an affray between the police and some Irish rioters. A Mr. Shirley, being unable to obtain his rents, obtained an order for 'substitution of service;' the process was to be attached to the walls of the Catholic chapel of Magheracloon. When the bailiff attempted to attach the process to the chapel wall, he was assailed by a volley of stones, and he ordered the police to fire on the rioters. One man was shot dead and others wounded, but the rioters became so violent that the bailiff and the police had to make off with all speed in order to save their lives. This the rioters called a victory, and the affray is still called in Ireland ' the Battle of Magheracloon.'
Magheracloon is near Carrickmacross, in Mon'aghan.

Magnano (*Battle of*), 5 April, 1799 ; won by the Austrian General Kray over Schérer the French general.

Magnesia (*Battle of*), B.C. 190, in which Antiochus king of Syria was utterly defeated by the two Scipios, and lost all his conquests in Asia Minor.

Maida (*Battle of*), 4 July, 1806. Sir John Stuart routed the French under the command of Regnier.

Makla (*Battle of*), in Algeria, 1834, in which the French were defeated by Abd-el-Kader.

Mal'aga (*Naval battle of*), 1704, won by Admiral Rooke over the French.

Malplaquet, in France (*Battle of*), 11 Sept., 1709, where the Duke of Marlborough and Prince Eugène defeated the French under Marshal Villars. The French lost 12,000, the allies many more, though they won the victory. The cause of this battle was this : the allies

insisted that Louis XIV. should compel his grandson to give up the crown of Spain. Louis replied, ' If I must wage war, it shall be with my enemies and not with my own children.'
   ⁎⁎⁎ Pronounce *Mal-pla-ka'*.

Mantine'a (*Battles of*). I. B.C. 418, won by Agis the Spartan general over the Argive League.
II. B.C. 362, won by the Thebans, led by Epaminondas, over the Lacedæmonians and Arcadians.
III. B.C. 207, won by Philopœmen, head of the Achæan League, over the Lacedæmonians.

Marathon (*Battle of*), 28 Sept., B.C. 490, in which Miltiadès the Athenian defeated the Persians under Datis and Artaphernès. This was one of the most important and decisive battles of the world—the ' Waterloo ' of ancient history. If the Persians had been victorious, Attica would have been a mere satrapy of Persia, but as the Athenians were victorious they became one of the most brilliant people of all history.
One of Sir Edward Creasy's *Fifteen Decisive Battles of the World*.

Marengo, in Italy (*Battle of*), 14 June, 1800, in which Napoleon Bonaparte defeated the Austrians under General Melas. The French army was retreating, when General Dessaix arrived with reinforcements and turned the fortunes of the day.

Marignano, in Italy (*Battles of*). I. 14, 15 Sept., 1515, in which François I. of France defeated the allied Italian-Swiss armies, called by Trivulzio 'The battle of the giants,' from the great valour displayed on both sides. As many as 6,000 French and 10,000 of the allies were left dead on the field.
II. 8 July, 1859, in which the Austrians were driven from their position by Napoleon III. Also called the battle of Melegnano.

Maritza (*Battle of the*), 1375, won by Amurath, the Turkish sultan, over the crusaders. This was the first of a long series of Turkish victories.

Markfeld, near Vienna (*Battle of*), 1278, in which Ottokar king of Bohemia was utterly defeated by Rudolf I. king of Germany, and was slain in the battle.
Here, 5 July, 1809, was fought the battle of Wagram, in which Napoleon defeated the Austrians, and took 20,000 prisoners.

Marsala (*Battle of*), 11 May, 1860, certainly the most marvellous and heroic battle in all history. Garibaldi, with 1,000 Italian volunteers, 6 small cannons, and 1,200 peasants, utterly defeated 50,000 Austrian troops with numerous artillery, posted in strong fortresses, and supported with a fleet of 500 guns. After this victory, he crossed the mountains and took Palermo on the 27th of the same month. The thing seems wholly incredible, but is yet an historic fact without hyperbole or exaggeration.

Marston Moor, in Yorkshire (*Battle of*), 2 July, 1644, in which Cromwell defeated Prince

Rupert. The whole of the Prince's artillery fell into the hands of Cromwell, and the royalists never afterwards recovered the loss of that disastrous day.

Maserfeld (*Battle of the*), 655, in which Oswald king of Northumbria was defeated and slain by Penda king of Mercia.

Maxen, in Saxony (*Battle of*), 20 Nov., 1759, where Marshal Daun took Fink, a Prussian general, prisoner. (In the fourth campaign of the Seven Years' War.)

Meg'aletaph'ros, the 'Great Ditch' (*Battle of*), in which Aristoménês and the Messenians were completely defeated by the Spartans. In this battle the Arcadians deserted in a body from the Messenians.

Megiddo (*Battles of*). I. The overthrow of Jabin and Sisera was 'at the waters of Megiddo' (*Judges* v. 19).
II. Here Pharaoh-necho overthrew and slew Josiah (2 *Kings* xxiii. 29, 30).

Melitênê (*Battle of*), A.D. 576, in which Chosroes I. king of Persia was defeated by Justinian, general of Tiberias emperor of the East. This was the last conflict of the Persians with the Romans.

Meloria (*Battle of*), 1284, in which the whole navy of Pisa was utterly destroyed by the Genoese, and Pisa ceased to be a maritime power.

Merseburg, in Saxony (*Battle of*), 934, in which Heinrich I. the Fowler of Germany conquered the Hungarians with great slaughter.

Méry-sur-Seine (*Battle of*), 24 Feb., 1814, won by Napoleon over the Austrian army under Schwartzenberg.

Metaurus (*Battle of*), B.C. 207, in which the consuls Livius and Nero utterly cut to pieces the army of Hasdrubal sent to reinforce Hannibal in the south of Italy.
This is one of Sir Edward Creasy's *Fifteen Decisive Battles of the World.*

Mexico (*Battle of*), A.D. 1521, won by the Spaniards, because St. James on his white horse fought for them. Bernal Diaz, who was present and saw the mysterious rider, tells us he thought it was Francisco de Morla, but it might be St. James notwithstanding.

Meyenfels (*Battle of*), 8 Oct., 876, where Louis the Younger of Saxony defeated Charles the Bald of France.

Milazzo, or **Melazzo** (*Battle of*), 20 June, 1860, in which Garibaldi defeated the Neapolitan General Bosco.

Millesimo (*Battle of*), 14 April, 1796, in which Bonaparte repulsed the Piedmontese.

Minden, in Prussia (*Battle of*), 1 Aug., 1759, in which Prince Ferdinand of Brunswick with six English regiments defeated the French under Marshal Contades. (In the fourth campaign of the Seven Years' War. Ferdinand's army consisted principally of British and Hanoverian troops.)

Marshal Contades said : ' I have seen this day what I never thought possible, viz. a single line of cavalry break through three lines of cavalry ranked in order of battle, and tumble them all to ruins.' Contades (2 syl.).

Minorca (*Naval battle off*), 20 May, 1756. This was no battle, but a shameful retreat of Admiral Byng, who had been sent to the relief of Port Mahon. Byng was shot for his cowardice by sentence of court-martial 14 March, 1757.

Mockern (*Battles of*). I. April 1813, in which the Prussian army was defeated by the French under Eugène Beauharnais.
II. 14 Oct. 1813, between the French and the allies. The town of Mockern was taken and retaken five times in this conflict.

Mohatz (*Battles of*), in Lower Hungary. I. 29 Aug., 1526, in which the Turks under Solyman II. defeated Ludwig of Hungary, with the loss of 22,000 men. Ludwig after the battle was suffocated with his horse in a muddy brook called Csele.
II. A.D. 1687, in which a Christian army, commanded by Prince Charles of Lorraine, defeated the Turks, who lost 10,000 men.

Mohilow (*Battle of*), 23 July, 1812. A sanguinary battle between the Russians under Prince Bagration and the French under Marshal Davoust. The Russians were defeated, and their loss in killed and wounded was immense.

Moinmor (*Battle of*), 1151, in which Tordelvach O'Connor utterly defeated Thomond king of Munster with great slaughter, and became king of Ireland.

Molwitz (*Battle of*), 30 March, 1741, won by Friedrich III. of Prussia over the Austrian army sent against him by Maria Theresa. This was the first battle in the War of the Austrian Succession.

Moncontour (*Battle of*), 1570, in the third religious war of France. The Huguenots were defeated by Henri duc d'Anjou, brother of Charles IX.

Mondôvi (*Battle of*), 22 April, 1796, in which Bonaparte defeated the Piedmontese.

Monmouth Court House, U.S. (*Battle of*), 28 June, 1778. Here Washington won his third victory over the British in the American War of Independence : (1) Trenton, (2) Princeton. At Brandywine he was defeated (*q.v.*).

Mons en Puelle, in Flanders (*Battle of*), 18 Aug., 1304, in which Philippe le Bel defeated the Flemings.

Mont St. Jean (*Battle of*), 18 June, 1815, called in English history the 'Battle of Waterloo' (*q.v.*).

Montebello (*Battle of*), 6 June, 1800, won by Napoleon Bonaparte over Ott, the Austrian general. General Lannes for his valour in this battle was created Duc de Montebello.

Montenotte (*Battle of*), 11 April, 1796, in which Bonaparte defeated the Austrians, commanded by Beaulieu. This was the first of his series of brilliant victories.

Montereau (*Battle of*), 18 Feb., 1814, in which the allied armies were defeated by Napoleon.

Montlhéry (*Battle of*), 1465, between Louis XI. and the ' League for the Public Weal.' The battle was indecisive, but led to the treaty of Conflans, and the league was soon broken up.

Montmirail (*Battle of*), 11 Feb., 1814, won by Napoleon over the Prussians led by Blücher.

Moodkee, in Hindustan (*Battle of*), 18 Dec., 1845, in which Sir Hugh Gough defeated the Sikhs. Sir Robert Sale was mortally wounded in this battle.

Hugh Gough was created a baronet in 1842, and a baron in 1846.

₊ Gough, pronounce *Goff*.

Mooltan (*Battle of*), 7 Nov., 1848, won by the British over the Sikhs.

The town was taken 2 Jan., 1849, and the citadel 22 Jan.

Mopsuestia (*Battle of*), A.D. 838, called by Arabian writers ' Mamuriyah,' in which 30,000 Greeks were left dead on the field.

Morat, or **Murden**, Switzerland (*Battle of*), 22 June, 1476, in which the Swiss defeated the brilliant army of Charles le Téméraire. The celebrated Ossuaire of Morat was made of the bones of the Burgundians slain in this battle.

Moravian Town (*Battle of*), 5 Oct., 1813, won by General Harrison over Proctor.

Morgarten (*Battles of*). I. 25 Oct., 1315, between 1,300 Switzers and 20,000 Austrians under the command of Duke Leopold. The Swiss army was made up of 600 men of Schwitz, 400 of Uri, and 300 of Unterwalden. These 1,300 slew 15,000 Austrians, and not a few of the army of Leopold were drowned in the Egrer See. This and Marsala (*q.v.*) are, perhaps, the most extraordinary battles of history, if we except that of Gideon, who with 300 men put to flight the allied Midianites and Amalekites. Gideon's victory, however, was from panic, the other two the result of indomitable valour.

II. A.D. 1798, between the French and the Switzers. The French loss was 2,754 dead, exclusive of wounded ; the Switzers' loss was 431 men and women ; but the Assembly thought it prudent to come to terms with the French and not renew the fight.

III. In 1799 the French defeated the Austrians on the same battlefield.

Mortemer, in ancient Normandy (*Battle of*), 1054, where William (afterwards called the Conqueror) defeated Henri I. king of France.

Mortimer's Cross, near Hereford (*Battle of*), 2 Feb., 1461, in which Edward duke of York defeated the Lancastrians under the command of Jasper Tudor earl of Pembroke.

Moskirch (*Battle of*), April 1799, in which Marshal Moreau, the French general, defeated the Austrians.

Moskwa (*Battle of*), 7 Sept., 1812, between the French under Napoleon and the Russians led by Kutusoff. Each claimed the victory. It was one of the most sanguinary conflicts in history. Also called the Battle of Borodino.

Mosul (*Battle of*), also called 'The Battle of Nineveh,' 1 Dec., A.D. 627, won by Heraclius emperor of Constantinople over Chosroes II. of Persia. Elmacin says 500,000 Persians fell in this battle, but Gibbon thinks 50,000 too high a number. Twenty-seven standards were taken by the victorious Romans.

Motta (*Battle of*), 7 Oct., 1513, in which the Venetians led by D'Alviano were defeated by the Spaniards.

Mount Tabor (*Battle of*), 1799, won by Bonaparte over the Mamelukes.

Muhlberg (*Battle of*), 1547, in which the Smalkaldic League was utterly defeated by Karl V. The Elector of Saxony and the Landgrave of Hesse were both taken prisoners.

Muhldorf (*Battle of*), in Bavaria, 1322, between Friedrich the Handsome and Ludwig V., rivals for the throne of Germany. The latter was victorious, and Friedrich was taken prisoner.

Münchengrätz (*Battle of*), 28 June, 1866, in the Seven Weeks' War. The Prussians defeated the Austrians.

Mursa (*Battle of*), 28 Sept., A.D. 351, in which Constantius II. defeated the usurper Magnentius. Constantius lost 30,000 men out of an army of 80,000 ; and Magnentius lost 24,000 men out of an army of 36,000.

Muta (*Battle of*), A.D. 629, in which Khaled, commander of the Khoreish cavalry, saved the army of Mohammed.

Mӱcălĕ (*Battle of*), 22 Sept., B.C. 479, in which the Persians were completely defeated by the Greeks. On the same day Mardonius was defeated at Platēa.

Naas (*Battle of*), in Ireland, 24 May, 1798, in which the Irish rebels were defeated by the king's troops.

Nachod, in Bohemia (*Battle of*), 27–29 June, 1866, in the Seven Weeks' War. The Crown Prince of Prussia defeated the Austrians.

Nafels (*Battle of*), 6 April, 1388, in which 350 of the men of Glaris withstood 15,000 Austrians with such terrible slaughter that the Austrians were obliged to retreat.

Nahavund or Nehavend (*Battle of*), 637, in which Yzdegerd III. king of Persia was defeated by the Saracens, and subsequently murdered. His loss is stated at 100,000 men. This battle, called by the Arabs 'The Victory of Victories,' brought to an end the famous dynasty of the Sassanides (3 syl.) and also the religion of the Magi, which had existed in Persia more than 1,200 years.

Naïssus (*Battle of*), A.D. 270, won by the Emperor Claudius over 320,000 Goths, of whom 50,000 were left dead on the field. For this great victory Claudius was called *Gothicus*.

Najara, in Spain (*Battle of*), 3 April, 1367, in which Henry of Trastamare was defeated by his brother Pedro the Cruel assisted by the Black Prince. In this battle Duguesclin constable of France was taken prisoner.

Narva (*Battle of*), 30 Nov., 1700, in which Peter the Great of Russia was defeated by Carl XII. of Sweden.

While dictating despatches, a bomb fell through the roof of the house, whereupon his secretary dropped his pen in a fright. ' What's the matter ? ' asked Carl. 'The bomb, the bomb, sire !' said the secretary. ' The bomb ? ' replied the king, 'what have we to do with the bomb ? Pray write on.'

Naseby (*Battle of*), north-west of North-ampton, 14 June, 1645, in which Charles I. was defeated by Cromwell and Fairfax. The main body of the royal army was commanded by Lord Astley, the right wing by Prince Rupert, and the left by Sir Marmaduke Lang-dale. The king himself headed the reserves. In this battle the king lost all his cannon and baggage, and 5,000 of his army were made prisoners. This battle ended the war.

Fairfax led the centre of the parliamentary army, Ireton the right wing, and Cromwell the left. Ireton was therefore opposite Rupert, and Cromwell was opposite Sir Marmaduke. Ireton was routed, Fairfax fell back, but Cromwell overthrew his opponents and redeemed the day.

Navarete (*Battle of*). Same as 'Najara' (*q.v.*). The battle was fought between Najara and Navarete.

Navari'no (*Battle of*), 20 Oct., 1827, won over the Turkish navy by the combined fleets of England, France, and Russia, under the com-mand of Lord Codrington. The Turkish navy was well-nigh annihilated.

This 'untoward event' occurred under Canning's administration. The weakening of Turkey and an alliance for such a purpose with Russia was certainly one of the greatest blunders ever committed.

Navas de Tolosa (*Battle of Las*), 1214, in which Alfonso III. of Castile defeated the Almohades, and destroyed one of the largest armies that ever crossed the Straits of Gibraltar.

Naxos (*Naval battle of*), B.C. 376, won by the Athenians, led by Chabrias, over the Lace-dæmonian fleet. This victory restored to Athens the supremacy at sea.

Nechlansmere, in Scotland (*Battle of*), 20 May, 685, in which Egfrith king of Northumbria was defeated and slain by the Picts. 'A solitary fugitive alone escaped the slaughter to tell how Egfrith and the flower of his nobles lay dead on the field.' With this battle fell for ever the supremacy of Northum-bria; and Mercia succeeded to the overlordship.

Neerwinden (*Battles of*), I. 19 July, 1693, in which the French Marshal de Luxembourg defeated William III.

II. 18 March, 1793, in which the Austrians defeated General Dumouriez.

Nehavend. *See* 'Nahavund.'

Neresheim (*Battle of*), 10 Aug., 1796, in which the Archduke Karl defeated Marshal Moreau, the French general.

Netad (*Battle of*), A.D. 453, a great battle won by various dependent nations over the sons of Attila, after his death. Ellak, his eldest son, and above 30,000 of his people were slain. The great empire of Attila soon after this defeat crumbled away.

Neumarkt (*Battle of*), 22 Aug., 1796, in which the Archduke Karl defeated the French.

Neville's Cross (*Battle of*), near Durham, 12 Oct., 1346, in which David II. of Scotland was both defeated and taken prisoner. Aug. 26 the same year is noted for the battle of Cressy.

This battle was won by Philippa while Edward III. (her husband) was in France. King David was taken prisoner, and between 15,000 and 20,000 Scots were slain. Of the English, only one leader (Lord Hastings) fell.

New Orleans, in Louisiana (*Battle of*), 8 June, 1815, in which the American general Jackson defeated the English, and their gene-ral, Sir Edward Pakenham, was slain.

This, of course, was not the General Jackson who was one of the Confederate leaders in the American Civil War, 1861–1865.

Newark (*Battle of*), 21 March, 1644, in which the royal army, under Prince Rupert, was defeated by the parliamentarians.

Newburn (*Battle of*), 28 Aug., 1640. This was no battle at all, but a stampede. Lord Conway with 6,000 English troops was sent by Charles I. to resist the Scotch covenanters, but immediately the covenanters crossed the river the English fled without offering any resistance.

Newbury, in Berkshire (*Battle of*). 20 Sept., 1643, in which Charles I. repulsed the Earl of Essex, commander of the parliamentary army. Next year (27 Oct., 1644), was an indecisive engagement at Newbury between Charles I. and the Earl of Manchester.

In the former of these battles fell Lord Falk-land.

Newtown Butler, in Ireland (*Battle of*), 1689, between James II. aided by French troops and the army of William III. The Protestants were besieged in Londonderry, and had food only for two days, when the men of Enniskillen came to their relief, and drove the besiegers before them like wild geese ; the panic spread through Hamilton's whole army, which took refuge in Dublin, where James lay helpless. His French ally, Comte d'Avaux, advised the general massacre of all Protestants in the districts which remained still in James's interest ; but James revolted from the proposal, whereupon the Frenchman sullenly replied, 'Mercy to Protestants is cruelty to Catholics.'

Nicop'olis, in Turkey (*Battles of*). I. 28 Sept., 1396, in which Kaiser Sigismund was defeated by Bajazet.

II. A.D. 1799, in which the French were defeated by the Albanians.

Nile (*Battle of the*), 1 Aug., 1798, in which Admiral Nelson defeated the French fleet. This victory obtained for the admiral a peerage, under the title of Baron Nelson of the Nile. His battle cry was ' Victory or Westminster Abbey !' The French admiral was Brueys.

Often called, especially in French history, the Battle of Aboukir (*q.v.*).

Nineveh (*Battle of*),1 Dec., A.D. 627, won by Heraclius the emperor of the East over Chosroes II. the Great King. The slaughter was very great.

Nisbet (*Battle of*), 7 May, 1402, won by the English over the Scotch. It is said that as many as 10,000 Scots fell in this encounter.

Nordlingen, in Franconia (*Battles of*). I. 6 Nov., 1634, won by Ferdinand, son of Kaiser Ferdinand II. over the Protestants. This was one of the battles of the Thirty Years' War.

II. 6 Sept., 1645, won by the Duc d'Enghien over the imperial German army. (Ferdinand III. was kaiser.) This also was one of the battles of the Thirty Years' War.

Noreïa (*Battle of*), B.C. 113, in which Cneius Papirius Carbo the consul was slain by the Cimbrians and his whole army was cut to pieces.

Northallerton (*Battle of*), in Yorkshire, 22 Aug., 1138, in which David I. of Scotland was defeated by Stephen king of England. The battle is generally called ' The Battle of the Standard.'

Northampton (*Battle of*), 10 July, 1460, in which Henry VI. was defeated and captured by the Yorkists. Margaret the queen fled to Scotland.

Novāra (*Battle of*), 23 March, 1849, in which the Sardinians (under Charles Albert) were defeated by the Austrians led by Marshal Radetzky (a Bohemian).

Novi (*Battles of*). I. 15 Aug., 1799, in which Suwarrow, general of the allied Russian and Austrian armies, defeated Marshal Joubert and the French army. Joubert was slain in this battle and 4,000 French were taken prisoners.

II. 8 Jan., 1800, in which the French were defeated by the Austrians.

Nürnberg (*Battle of*), 1456, in Bavaria, between the barons and the townsmen. Eight times the barons were victors, but in the ninth contest the townsmen were the conquerors and Nürnberg vindicated its freedom.

In this battle Albrecht the Achilles and Ulysses of Germany was taken captive by the citzen soldiers.

Œnoph'yta (*Battle of*), B.C. 456, won by the Athenians over the Bœotians. The Athenian general was Myronīdês.

Ohud (*Battle of*), A.D. 623, in which Khaled, commander of the Koreish cavalry, defeated Mohammed.

Olmütz (*Battle of*), 15 July, 1866, the last battle of the Seven Weeks' War, won by the Prussians over the Austrians.

Oltenitza (*Battle of*), 4 Nov., 1853, won by Omar Pasha, the Turkish general, over the Russians.

Orthes (*Battle of*), 27 Feb., 1814, in which the French under Marshal Soult were defeated by the Marquis of Wellington, commander of the allied British and Spanish armies.

Ostrach (*Battle of*), 20 March, 1799, in which the Archduke Karl defeated Marshal Jourdan, the French general.

Ostrolenca (*Battle of*), 26 May, 1831, between the Russians and the Poles. It was a most sanguinary affair, and both sides claimed the victory.

Otford (*Battle of*), on the Derwent, 773, in which Offa king of Mercia defeated the Kentish men. By this victory Offa became lord of Kent and all East Anglia.

Otterburn (*Battle of*), 10 Aug., 1388, in which the Scots under Sir William Douglas defeated the English under the Earl of Northumberland and his two sons. Douglas was slain by Henry Percy, surnamed Hotspur, but both the Percys were made prisoners. *See* p. 165, ' Chevy Chase.'

Oudenarde (*Battle of*), in Belgium, 11 July, 1708, in which the Duke of Marlborough and Prince Eugene defeated the French under the Dukes of Burgundy and Vendôme. Louis XIV. gave up ten Flemish fortresses to the Dutch, surrendered to the empire all that France had gained since the peace of Westphalia, acknowledged Anne, offered to banish the pretender from his dominions and to demolish the fortifications of Dunkirk.

By the peace of Ryswick, in 1697, Louis XIV. agreed to recognise William III. ; but on the death of James II. in 1701 he recognised James the pretender as the lawful king of England, under the name and title of James III. This, in fact, involved him in the wars with Marlborough, so disastrous to France.

Oulart (*Battle of*), 27 May, 1798, in which the North Cork Militia were cut to pieces by the Irish insurgents.

Ourique (*Battle of*), 25 July, 1139, in which Alfonso of Portugal defeated a prodigious army of Moors, in which were five Saracen kings.

Palestro (*Battle of*), 31 May, 1859, in which the Austrians were defeated by the allied army of Sardinians and French.

Panormus (*Battle of*), B.C. 254, in which the Romans conquered the Carthaginians. Metellus was the Roman general and Hasdrubal the Carthaginian. This was the chief battle of the First Punic War.

Parret (*Battle of the*), 845, in which Ealstan (bishop of Sherborne) and Osric defeated the Northmen.

Patay (*Battles of*). I. 18 June, 1429. Talbot defeated by the Maid of Orleans and taken prisoner. This was the first battle lost by the English since their victory at Cressy in 1346. Talbot was taken prisoner.

II. 1 Dec., 1870, the Bavarians were repulsed.

Pa'via (*Battle of*). I. A.D. 774, where Charlemagne overthrew Desiderius, whom he afterwards confined in the monastery of Corbie, in France.

II. 24 Feb., 1525, in which François I. of France was taken prisoner, and all the flower of his army was cut to pieces. François, it is said, wrote to his mother, ' All is lost, Madam, except honour ' (*Tout est perdu, Madame, fors l'honneur*).

Peterwaradin (*Battles of*). I. 1691, won by the Austrians over the Turks. Kaprioli, son and brother of two former viziers, fell in this fight.

II. A.D. 1711, in which Prince Eugene defeated the Turks with great slaughter.

Pfaffendorf (*Battle of*), 15 Aug., 1760, in which the Austrians were defeated by the Prussians.

Pharsa'lia (*Battle of*), 12 May, B.C. 48, won by Julius Cæsar over Pompey the Great. This victory made Cæsar the foremost man of Rome.

Philiphaugh, in Scotland (*Battle of*), Sept., 1645, in which Montrose, called ' the Great Marquis,' commander of the royal forces in Scotland, sustained a crushing and irretrievable defeat. This was ten months after the defeat of Charles at Marston Moor.

Philippi (*Battle of*), Oct., B.C. 42, in which Brutus and Cassius both met their death, and Antony and Octavian became masters of Rome.

Pinkie, in Scotland (*Battle of*), 10 Sept., 1547, in which the Lord Protector Somerset defeated the Scotch with such great slaughter that the day was called ' Black Saturday.'

Plains of Abraham (*Battle of the*), 13 Sept., 1759, in which the French of Canada were defeated by the English under General Wolfe, who fell dead at the moment of victory.

Plassey (*Battle of*), in Hindustan, 23 June, 1757, in which Colonel Clive defeated Surajah Dowlah, and laid the foundation of our empire in the East. Clive's army consisted of 1,000 Englishmen and 2,000 sepoys ; the Surajah's army numbered 50,000 foot and 14,000 horse. The victory was complete, and Surajah Dowlah was one of the slain.

Platæa (*Battle of*), 22 Sept., B.C. 479, in which the Grecian army (110,000 men) under Pausanias utterly defeated the Persian army, which amounted to 300,000 men, under the command of Mardonius. Mardonius was slain at the very onset, and it is said that 200,000 of the Persians were left dead on the field. On the same day was won the battle of Mycălê.

Plattsburg (*Battle of*), 11 Oct., 1814, won by the Americans, under Gen. Macomb, over the English under Sir George Prevost.

Podaic (*Battle of*), 1672, won by Sobieski, the Polish general, over the Tartars.

Poitiers (*Battles of*). I. Oct., A.D. 732, in which Charles le Martel utterly defeated the Saracens under the command of Abd-el-Rahmah, viceroy of Spain.

II. 19 Sept., 1356, in which Edward the Black Prince defeated and took captive Jean II. le Bon of France. The English force was 8,000, the French 60,000. It is almost incredible, but we are assured on good authority, that 8,000 of the French were slain and 2,000 taken prisoners. Never was victory so unexpected, never was victory more complete.

Pola (*Battle of*), May, 1379, between a fleet of 22 Genoese galleys commanded by Luciano Doria and 20 galleys of the Venetians under Pisani. Doria was slain, but the Genoese won the victory, taking 15 galleys and 1,900 prisoners.

Pollentia, in Italy (*Battle of*), 29 March, A.D. 403 (Easter Day). In this battle Stilicho attacked Alaric, and caused him to retreat.

Polotsk (*Battle of*), 30, 31 July, 1812, in which the Russians, under Wittgenstein, defeated the French under Marshal Oudinot.

Portlevoi (*Battle of*), 1016, won by Fulc, called the Black Count, over the Count of Blois. This great victory crushed the rival house of Blois.

Porto Bello (*Naval battle of*), 1739, won, with six ships, by Admiral Vernon over the Spaniards. All the fortifications of the port were demolished.

Porto Novo (*Battle of*), 1 July, 1781, in which Sir Eyre Coote defeated Hyder Ali regent of Mysore.

Also called the battle of Cuddalore (3 syl.).

Potsdam (*Battle of*), 25 Oct., 1806, where Napoleon defeated the Prussians.

Praga (*Battles of*). I. 10 Oct., 1794, in which 30,000 Poles were butchered by the Russian general Suwarrow or Suwarof.

II. 31 March, 1831, won by the Poles, led by Skrznecki, over the Russians under the command of General Giesmar. Above 6,000 Russians were taken prisoners.

Prague (*Battles of*), in Bohemia. I. 8 Nov., 1620, when Maximilian of Bavaria defeated Frederick V. the Elector Palatine. This was the first of the battles of the Thirty Years' War. Prague (1 syl.).

II. 6 May, 1757, when Frederick II. (the Great) of Prussia defeated Prince Charles of Lorraine. This victory was followed (June 18) by a crushing defeat at Kolin by Marshal Daun. (Second campaign of the Seven Years' War). This is the great and memorable battle of Prague.

Prescott (*Battle of*), in Upper Canada, 17 Nov., 1838, in which the Canadian rebels were defeated by Lieutenant-Colonel Dundas.

Preston (*Battles of*), in Lancashire. I. 17 Aug., 1648, in which Cromwell defeated the Scotch royalist army, led by the Duke of Hamilton.

II. 12, 13 Nov., 1715, after the 'clap of Sheriff-muir.' A very poor affair, where the Jacobites were cooped up, and driven to a most cowardly surrender. (Reign of George I.)

All that is known of James the Pretender only confirms the wisdom of setting him aside.

Preston-pans (*Battle of*), in Scotland, 21 Sept., 1745, in which the 'Young Pretender' Charles Edward (grandson of James II.) defeated Sir John Cope.

Never was a battle so quickly decided. It is said not to have lasted more than five or six minutes. Never was a defeat more absolute.— HOWITT, *Hist. of England*, George II. p. 501.

Princeton, New Jersey, U.S. (*Battle of*), 2 Jan., 1777. Here Washington defeated Lord Cornwallis in the American War of Independence. This was Washington's second victory. *See* 'Battle of Trenton.'

Pultowa or **Pultawa** (*Battle of*), 9 July, 1709, in which Czar Peter the Great utterly defeated Charles XII. of Sweden.

This is one of Sir Edward Creasy's *Fifteen Decisive Battles of the World*.

Pultusk (*Battles of*). I. 1 May, 1703, in which the Saxons were defeated by the Swedes.

II. 26 Dec., 1806, between the French under Napoleon and the allied Prussians and Russians. Both sides claimed the victory.

Pydna (*Battle of*), B.C. 168, in which Perseus, last of the Macedon kings, was utterly defeated and his army annihilated by Æmilius Paulus, the Roman consul. Perseus was taken captive, and Macedonia was made a Roman province.

Pyramids (*Battle of the*), 21 July, 1798, in which Bonaparte defeated the Mamelukes.

Pyrenees (*Battle of the*), 28 July, 1813, won by Lord Wellington over the French under the command of Marshal Soult. Soult was sent by Napoleon to supersede Jourdan, who had been utterly defeated at Vittoria on the 21st, and to drive Wellington across the Ebro, but the French marshal met with a series of defeats between 25 July and 2 Aug., with the loss of 20,000 men.

Quatre-Bras, in Brabant (*Battle of*), 16 June, 1815. Two days before the battle of Waterloo. It was a combat between the British allied army and the French under Marshal Ney. The British under the Duke of Brunswick, the Prince of Orange, and Sir Thomas Picton, held their ground, but the Duke of Brunswick was slain and the Prince of Orange was taken prisoner. At the close of the day the French marshal withdrew his men.

Quebec, in Canada (*Battle of*), 13 Sept., 1759, where General Wolfe defeated the Marquis de Montcalm, commander-in-chief of the French armies in Canada. The taking of Quebec was the conquest of Canada. Wolfe died on the day of battle, and Montcalm the day after from his wounds. *See below* 'Quiberon Bay.'

Queenstown, Upper Canada (*Battle of*), 13 Oct., 1812, in the Second American War, where General Sheaffe defeated the Americans commanded by Van Rensselaer.

Quesnoy (*Battle of*), 11 Sept., 1793, in which the British forces defeated the French.

⁎ Pronounce *Keen-wah*.

Quiberon Bay (*Naval battle of*), 20 Nov., 1795, where Lord Hawke defeated the French fleet, which was utterly ruined. The commander of the French fleet was Marshal Conflans. In one year the English won three great victories over the French, viz. Minden, Quebec, and Quiberon Bay.

Raab (*Battles of*). I. 1 Aug., 1664, won by Montecuculi, general of the imperial army, over the Turks.

II. June, 1809, in which the Austrian Archduke John was totally defeated by Eugène Beauharnais, and the country bordering on the Adriatic was annexed to the French empire. Raab (1 syl.).

Raclawice (*Battle of*), 4 April, 1794, in which Kosciusko the Polish general defeated the Russians.

Ram-hormuz (*Battle of*), B.C. 226, in which Artaxerxes (called by the Persians Ardeshur Babegan, or Ardeschir ben Babek) utterly defeated Artabânês IV., shook off the Parthian yoke, and restored the empire of Persia Proper.

Ramillies, in Belgium (*Battle of*), 23 May, 1706, where the Duke of Marlborough defeated the French and Bavarians. The French general was Marshal Villeroý. France lost Flanders, and soon afterwards Italy.

⁎ This word is often called *Ram'-e-liz* in English, but it is called by Belgians *Ra-mel-ya'*.

Rathmines (*Battle of*), 2 Aug., 1649, between Ormond the royalist and Colonel Jones governor of Dublin. The royalists were defeated, and 2,000 of them were taken prisoners.

Ravenna, in Italy (*Battle of*), 11 April, 1512, between the French under Gaston de Foix (nephew of Louis XII.) and the combined Spanish and Papal armies. De Foix won the battle, but was left dead on the field.

Gaston de Foix was called 'The thunderbolt of Italy.'

Regillus (*Battle at the Lake*), B.C. 499, between the Romans and the allies who sought to restore Tarquin. In this battle it is said that Castor and Pollux on their white horses fought for the Romans and won the battle.

Rigomago (*Battle of*), 1447, lost by Hunyâdi, governor of Hungary through the treachery of the voivod of Wallachia. This was one of the bloodiest battles ever fought.

Riv'oli (*Battle of*), 14, 15 Jan., 1797, where Bonaparte defeated the Austrians led by Wurmser and Alvinzy.

Rocroy (*Battle of*), 1643, in which the French, led by the Great Condé, sustained a most crushing defeat.

Roliça (*Battle of*), 16 Aug., 1808, the first encounter of Sir Arthur Wellesley (afterwards Duke of Wellington) with the French in Portugal. The French under Delaborde were defeated.

Roncesvalles (*Battle of*), A.D. 778. It was here that the rear-guard of Charlemagne's army on their return from Spain were attacked by the Moors and annihilated. Among the slain was Roland, the famous paladin, the king's nephew.
Roland in Italian romance is called Orlando.

Rosbach, in Prussia (*Battles of*). I. 17 Nov., 1382, in which 40,000 insurgent Flemings were cut to pieces by the French.
II. 5 Nov., 1757, where Frederick II. defeated the allied Austrian and French armies. This defeat was so disgraceful to the French that the 'Rout of Rosbach' is still a proverb and a byword. The loss of the Prussians was only 300 men, that of the allies was 1,300 slain and 6,000 prisoners. (In the second campaign of the Seven Years' War.)

Rosbecque (*Battle of*), Nov. 1382, in which Charles VI. of France defeated the republican army of Flanders, and re-established the earl who had been deposed. Philip van Artevelde, leader of the democratic party, fell in this battle.

Ross, in Ireland (*Battle of*), 4 June, 1798, in which the Irish insurgents, commanded by General Beauchamp Bagenel Harvey, were defeated by the royal troops under the command of General Johnston.

Rothière (*Battle of*), 1 Feb., 1814, won by Napoleon over the combined armies of Blücher and Schwartzenberg.

Roucoux, or **Raucoux** (*Battle of*), 11 Oct., 1746, in which the French, under Marshal Saxe, defeated the allied English and Dutch armies.

Roundway Down, near Devizes (*Battle of*), 13 July, 1643, in which the royalists under Prince Rupert defeated Sir W. Waller, a parliamentary officer.

Roverēdo (*Battle of*), 4 Sept., 1796, in which Bonaparte defeated the Austrians.

Saalfeld (*Battle of*), 10 Oct., 1806, won by Napoleon over the confederates.

Saarbrück (*Battle of*), 2 Aug., 1870. In the Franco-Prussian war. Won by the Prussians the same day as they won the battle of Wörth.
31 July, 1870, it was seized by Napoleon III., and here the young Prince Imperial received his 'baptism of fire;' a battle was fought 2 Aug., in which the French were dislodged,

and on 6 Aug. it was occupied by the German allies.

Sadowa, in Bohemia (*Battle of*), 3 July, 1866, in the Seven Weeks' War. King William I. of Prussia defeated Benedek, the Austrian general.

St. Albans, Herts (*Battles of*). I. 22 May, 1455, in which Richard duke of York defeated and took prisoner Henry VI. of England.
II. 7 Feb., 1461 (*Shrove Tuesday*), in which battle Queen Margaret defeated the Earl of Warwick.

St. Denis (*Battle of*), 1567, in the Second Religious War of France. Here Anne de Montmorency, the last of the French Triumvirate (*q.v.*), lost his life, but the Huguenots were defeated.
St. Denis, pronounce *Sahn Dnee.*

St. Dizier (*Battle of*), 27 Jan., 1814, won by Napoleon over Blücher.
Pronounce *Sahn De-ze-a.*

St. Jacob's (*Battle of*), in the vicinity of Basle, 1444. Here 1,600 Swiss kept 32,000 French soldiers at bay for ten hours, and would not surrender till their number was reduced to ten men only.

St. Quintin (*Battle of*), 10 Aug., 1557, won by Philip II. of Spain over the French. This was their most severe defeat since the battle of Agincourt.
Pronounce *Sahn Kahn-tohn* (nasal).

St. Sebastian (*Battles of*). I. 5 May, 1836, won by General Evans, commander of the English Auxiliary Legion, against the Carlists of Spain.
II. 1 Oct., 1836, the Carlists were repulsed by De Lacy Evans.

St. Vincent, in Portugal (*Battles of*). I. 17 June, 1693, in which Admiral Tourville marshal of France defeated the allied English and Dutch fleets under the command of Sir G. Rooke. The allies lost 12 men-of-war and 80 merchantmen in this great naval battle.
II. 16 Jan., 1780, in which Admiral Rodney defeated Juan de Langara the Spanish admiral, who was also taken prisoner.
III. 14 Feb., 1797, in which Admiral Jervis defeated and won a great victory over the Spanish fleet, for which he was raised to the peerage under the name and title of John Jervis earl of St. Vincent.
IV. 2 July, 1833, in which Admiral Napier captured the Miguelite squadron.

Salamanca (*Battle of*), 22 July, 1812, won by Lord Wellington over the French forces led by Marshal Marmont. This was the seventh French marshal defeated by Lord Wellington in four years. In this battle 7,141 prisoners fell into the victor's hands, 11 cannons, 6 stand of colours, and 2 eagles.

Sal'amis (*Naval battle of*), 20 Oct., B.C. 480, in which the Greeks, under Themistoclês, with only 371 triremes, defeated the Persian fleet, which consisted of 928 sail of much larger size. Of this formidable fleet only 300 ships escaped destruction. The Persian loss must have been very great indeed, that of the Greeks was only 40 men all told.

Xerxes, who was a spectator of the fight, returned at once to Asia.

Saminara (*Battle of*), north-east of Reggio, 21 April, 1503, won by Gonzalvo of Cordova over the French.

Santes (*Battle of*), in which St. Louis of France defeated the insurgents under the Comte de la Marche. Santes (1 syl.).

Sapienza (*Battles of*), 4 Nov.,1354, in which the Venetian fleet under Niccolo Pisani was surprised and captured by the Genoese fleet under Paganini Doria.

II. 6 Oct., 1403, in which the Venetian fleet under Zeno defeated the Genoese fleet commanded by Boucicault.

Saratoga, New York, U.S. (*Battle of*), 11 Oct., 1777. Here the American General Gates defeated the British General Burgoyne. This was the worst disaster hitherto sustained by the English in the American War of Independence. General Burgoyne surrendered to General Gates, and, on capitulation, had a free passage to Great Britain, on condition of not serving again against America. After this terrible overthrow, France at once recognised the independence of America. Sir John Burgoyne, of course, retired from the army, and spent his time in writing for the stage.

This is one of Sir Edward Creasy's *Fifteen Decisive Battles of the World.*

Sasbach (*Battle of*), 1675, between Montecuculi on the German side and Marshal Turenne on the side of the French. Turenne was killed by a cannon ball, and victory was claimed by the Germans.

Scearstan (*Battle of*), 1016, won by Canute over Edmund Ironside ; but Canute retreated at night towards London, unwilling to renew the fight.

Schellenberg (*Battle of*), 2 July, 1704. Here Marlborough defeated the Bavarians, and returned to England with 121 standards, 179 colours, the Bavarian general, and twenty-six officers of high distinction.

Schleitz (*Battle of*), Oct., 1806, won by Napoleon over the confederates.

Schliengen (*Battle of*), 20 Oct., 1796. The Archduke Karl of Austria defeated Moreau, the French general. He had defeated him the day before at Emmendingen.

Secandun (*Battle of*), A.D. 755, in which the Mercians were defeated by the West Saxons. Ethelbald was slain in this battle.

Sedan (*Battle of*). I. 11 Sept., 1870, in the Franco-Prussian war, won by the Prussians. On 2 Sept. the Emperor Napoleon III. gave up his sword to William I. king of Prussia.

This was just a month after the war began. The occupation of Saarbrück and 'baptism of fire' was 2 Aug., and Napoleon gave up his sword 2 Sept.

II. 10 May, 1865, General Johnston, at Durham's Station, North Carolina, surrendered to General Sherman, and thus brought the American civil contest to a close. This was the American 'Sedan.'

Sedgemoor (*Battle of*), 5 July, 1685, in which the Duke of Monmouth was completely defeated by the army of James II. The duke was made prisoner, and was soon afterwards beheaded.

Seidlitz (*Battle of*), in Poland, 10 April, 1831, won by the Poles over the Russians.

Sellasia (*Battle of*), B.C. 221, in which Cleomenes the Spartan was utterly defeated by Antigonus and the Achæan League.

Semincas (*Battle of*), A.D. 938, won by Ramirez II. king of Leon and the Asturias over the Moors. It is said that 80,000 of the Moors were slain in this conflict.

Sempach (*Battle of*), 9 July,1386, in which 1,400 Switzers utterly defeated the Austrian army under Duke Leopold. The Austrian army consisted of 4,000 knights of high rank, and a numerous well-appointed host of foot soldiers. The duke and most of the knights were slain. It was in this battle that Arnold Struthan von Winkelried of Unterwalden rushed on the advancing spears of the Austrians, grasped as many of them as he could reach, buried them in his bosom and bore them to the ground ; thus making a gap into which the Swiss rushed and slaughtered the Austrians right and left. The loss of the Swiss was about 200, of the Austrians at least 6,000.

Probably a part of this tale is only legendary.

Senef (*Battle of*), 1674, a drawn battle between William prince of Orange and the Great Condé.

Senlac (*Battle of*), 14 Oct., 1066, where William duke of Normandy conquered Harold II., and thus won, by conquest, the throne of England. Also called 'The Battle of Hastings.'

This is one of Sir Edward Creasy's *Fifteen Decisive Battles of the World.*

Serin'gapatam' (*Battles of*). I. 15 May, 1791. Lord Cornwallis defeated Tippoo Saib sultan of Mysore. In 1799 the city was assigned to the British.

II. 4 May, 1799, won by Major-General Baird. In this battle Tippoo Saib was slain.

Shannon and Chesapeake (*Battle of the*), 1 June,1813. The 'Shannon' was an English ship, commanded by Captain Broke ; the 'Chesapeake' was an American vessel, commanded by Captain Lawrence. In the second American war Captain Broke sent a challenge to Captain Lawrence to meet him, in order to prove whether the English or Americans were the better men. The two combatants met ; and, after a most furious and murderous engagement, which lasted about fifteen minutes, the English seamen hauled down the American colours. Captain Lawrence was slain, and Captain Broke was made a baronet, under the style and title of Sir Philip Bowes Vere Broke, of Nacton, Suffolk.

Sheriffmuir (*Battle of*), in Dumblane, 13 Nov., 1715, in which the Duke of Argyll defeated the Jacobites led by the Earl of Mar. The worthless Pretender, James, arrived too late for the battle, and proved a more incompetent leader than even the Earl of Mar. James left England, and the clans dispersed like a dream.

Both claimed the victory; but, as the Pretender lost the battle of Preston on the same day, his cause hopelessly collapsed.

Shiloh, Tennessee (*Battle of*), 6 Feb., 1862, in the American Civil War. Won by the Federals.

Shrewsbury (*Battle of*), 23 July, 1403, in which Henry IV. defeated the Percys.

Shropshire (*Battle of*), A.D. 51, in which the Britons were completely subjugated to the Romans, and Caradoc [Caractacus] king of the Silûrês was made a prisoner.

Silverhausen (*Battle of*), 1553, in which Maurice elector of Saxony was slain. His antagonist was Albert of Brandenburg.

Sin'gara (*Battle of*), A.D. 348, between Constantius II. the emperor of the East and Sapor the Persian. The Romans had won the battle, and had given themselves up to joy and revelry; but Sapor crept upon them in the darkness of night, recovered the victory, and made most dreadful havoc of the panic-stricken Romans.

Sinōpê (*Naval battle of*), 30 Nov., 1853, won by the Russians over the Turks.

Sluys (*Naval battle of*), in the Netherlands, 24 June, 1340, in which Edward III. defeated the French fleet, which for a time was utterly ruined. (Pronounce *Slu-iz*).

Smolensko (*Battle of*), 17 Aug., 1812, won by the French over the Russians, led by Barclay de Tolli.

Sobrāon (*Battle of*), in the Punjab, 10 Feb., 1846, won by General Gough and Sir Henry Hardinge over the Sikhs. In this battle a bridge of boats over the Sutlej broke, and thousands of the Sikhs in their flight were drowned. It was the greatest battle ever fought in India.

Gough = *Goff*.

Soczawa (*Battle of*), 1676, won by John III. (Sobieski) of Poland over the Turks.

Soissons (*Battle of*), A.D. 486, in which Clovis, founder of the French monarchy, defeated Syagrius, son of Ægidius. After this victory Clovis made Soissons the capital of his kingdom. In 507 he removed to Paris.

Solebay (*Naval battle of*), 28 May, 1672, in which the Dutch were defeated by the English under the command of James duke of York [James II.].

Solferi'no, in Italy (*Battle of*), 24 June, 1859, in which Napoleon III. and Victor Emmanuel defeated Francis Joseph emperor of Austria.

Solonium (*Battle of*), B.C. 61, in which C. Pomptinus the prætor defeated the Allobrôgês.

Solway Moss, in Cumberland (*Battle of*), 25 Nov., 1542, in which the Scots under Oliver Sinclair were defeated by the Duke of Norfolk.

Somerton (*Battle of*), A.D. 733, in which the royal town of Somerton was captured by Ethelbald king of Mercia. This great victory ended the war with the West Saxons.

Sommershausen (*Battle of*), 17 April, 1648, won by Turenne and Wrangel. This was the last of the battles of the Thirty Years' War.

Spurs (*Battle of the*), 18 Aug., 1513, won by the English over the French, who used their spurs in flight more than their swords in fight.

Stamford Bridge, near York (*Battle of*), 25 Sept., 1066, in which Tostig, son of Earl Godwin, was defeated and slain by Harold II. king of England, his brother.

Steinkerke (*Battle of*), 4 Aug., 1692, in which the French Marshal de Luxembourg defeated William III. and his allies. The loss on both sides was about equal.

Stillwater (*Battle of*), 19 Sept. and 7 Oct., 1777, won by the British over the Americans. The loss of the British was 350 killed and wounded, of the Americans 1,500 slain.

Stillwater is a town on the river Hudson, belonging to the State of New York.

Stirling Bridge (*Battle of*), 10 Sept., 1297, in which William Wallace utterly defeated the English under the command of Warenne earl of Surrey.

Stockach (*Battle of*), 25 March, 1799, in which Marshal Jourdan, the French general, was defeated by the Archduke Karl, and Germany was lost to France.

Stoke, near Newark (*Battle of*), 1487, in which the conspiracy of Simnel was utterly crushed by Henry VII.

Stonar (*Battle of*), A.D. 465, in which Vortimer defeated Hengist, and drove the Saxons to their ships. They did not return till the death of Vortimer, five years afterwards.

Stony Creek, U.S. (*Battle of*), 6 June, 1813, where General Vincent surprised and defeated the American General Winder, in the Second American War.

Stony Point (*Battle of*), 1779. Stony Point, in New York, 30 May, was taken by Clinton. An engagement took place 20 June at Stone Ferry. General Wayne recovered Stony Point 15 July, but abandoned it to the British next day.

Stowe, in Bucks (*Battle of*), 1645, in which the Irish royalists, under the command of Lord Astley, were defeated by the parliamentary troops led by Colonel Morgan. Lord Astley was taken prisoner.

Strasburg (*Battle of*), Aug., A.D. 357, won by Julian over the Alemanni. In this battle

Chnodomar or Gundomar, the huge leader of the Germans, was taken prisoner.

Stratton Hill (*Battle of*), in Devonshire, 16 May, 1643, in which the royalists defeated the parliamentary army led by the poet Waller.

Ström'boli (*Naval battle of*), 1676, won by Duquesne over the Dutch.

Duquesne=*Duh-kān.*

Sukoro (*Battle of*), 29 Sept., 1848, between the Croats led by Baron Je'lachich, and the Magyars, led by Moga. The former numbered 50,000, and were well armed ; the latter not above 5,000, armed with scythes, pitchforks, and old muskets. The Hungarians, however, were completely victorious. This was the first battle in the War for Independence.

Tagina (*Battle of*), July, A.D. 552, in which Totila the Gothic king was defeated and slain by Narses the eunuch, commander-in-chief of Justinian's army.

Tagliamento (*Battle of*), 16 March, 1797, in which Bonaparte defeated the Austrians, led by the Archduke Karl.

Talavĕra, in Spain (*Battle of*), 27, 28 July, 1809, won by Sir Arthur Wellesley (Duke of Wellington), commander of the united British and Spanish forces, over Victor and Jourdan, marshals of France. The French loss was 10,000 men and 20 pieces of cannon ; the allied British and Spanish forces lost 800 killed and 4,000 wounded or missing.

For this victory Sir Arthur (already Baron Douro) was created Viscount Wellington of Talavera.

Taillebourg (*Battle of*), 1242, in which St. Louis of France defeated the insurgents under the Comte de la Marche.

Taliacot'a, or Tagliacozzo, in Italy (*Battle of*), 23 Aug., 1268, in which Charles of Anjou overthrew Conradin.

Tara (*Battles of*), I. 980, in which Malachy monarch of Ireland defeated the Danes. This was the most decisive of all the battles fought by the Irish against the Danes, except the battle of Clontarf in 1014.

(II.) 26 May, 1789, in which the Irish rebels were defeated by the royal troops.

Tarbes (*Battle of*), in France, 20 March, 1814, in which the French army under Marshal Soult was defeated by the Duke of Wellington. Tarbes (1 syl.).

Taro (*Battle of the*), 6 July, 1495, won by Charles VIII. with 9,000 men over an allied Italian, German, and Spanish army of 40,000. Of the French not above 200 fell, of the allies 15,000. The Venetians called this a victory, and erected a tablet to one of the Provveditori with this barefaced lying inscription : 'Here lies Melchior Trivisano, who fought successfully against Charles [VIII.] king of France at the battle of the Taro.'

Tchernaya (*Battle of the*), 16 Aug., 1855, in which the French and Sardinians defeated the Russians. This was one of the great battles of the Crimĕan War (*q.v.*).

Tel-el-Kebir (*Battle of*), 13 Sept., 1882, won by the English under General Wolseley over Arabi the Egyptian rebel.

Temesvar (*Battle of*), 1849. One of the battles of the War of Independence. The Hungarians were utterly routed by the allied Russian and Austrian armies.

Tenna (*Battle of*), 9 Nov., 1439, in which the Venetians led by Sforza utterly defeated the Milanese under the command of Piccinino.

Tewkesbury (*Battle of*), in Gloucestershire, 4 May, 1471, in which Edward IV. defeated and took prisoner Queen Margaret. Her son either fell on the field or was stabbed after the battle ; and the death of Henry VI. in the Tower, some eighteen days afterwards, left Edward IV. of the House of York the undisputed sovereign of the kingdom.

Thapsus (*Battle of*), 4 Feb., B.C. 46, in which Julius Cæsar utterly defeated Juba king of Numidia and the senatorial army which befriended the cause of Pompey.

Thermop'ylæ (*Battles of*), I. 7 Aug., B.C. 480, between the Greeks and the Persians. Leonidas king of Sparta was sent with 300 Spartans to withstand the whole Persian army at the defile of Thermopylæ. He held his ground for three days, when Ephialtĕs perfidiously led the enemy by a secret path to the rear of the Greeks, who were thus hemmed in between two forces. All but one man perished fighting gloriously, leaving 20,000 Persians dead in the pass. This was one of the most heroic acts in all history.

II. B.C. 191, in which Antiochus III. king of Syria was utterly defeated by the Romans.

Thionville, or Diedenhofen (*Battle of*), June, 1639, one of the minor battles of the Thirty Years' War. General de Feuquières was defeated by Ottavio Piccolomini.

Pronounce *Te-on[g]-veel.*

Thrasymĕnus (*Battle of*), B.C. 217, in which the Romans under Flaminius were defeated by the Carthaginians under Hannibal. Of the Romans, 15,000 were slain and 10,000 taken prisoners.

Till (*Battle of the*), A.D. 556, in which the Asiatic Turks slew the Khan of the Ogors with 300,000 of his subjects (! !).

Tinchebrai (*Battle of*), 28 Sept., 1106 where Robert duke of Normandy (son of William the Conqueror) was utterly defeated by his younger brother Henry I. king of England. In consequence of this victory the duchy became a dependency of the English crown.

Tippermuir (*Battle of*), Sept., 1644, in which the Marquis of Montrose, commander of the royal forces in Scotland, defeated the Covenanters.

Toggenburg or **Tockemburg**, in Switzerland. This has been the site of two contests, called the 'first' and 'second war of

3 S

Tockemburg.' The *first* in 1436 was a contest between the Count of Zürich and the Count of Schwitz for the succession. The *second*, in 1712, was the revolt of the Tockemburgers against the abbot of St. Gall their ruler, ending in favour of the revolters.

Tolbiac (*Battle of*), A.D. 496, in which Clovis, founder of the French monarchy, repulsed the Alemanni, a Teutonic league, with great slaughter.

Tolbiac is now called Zulpich; it is near Cologne.

Töplitz (*Battle of*), 1762, in which the Prussians were defeated by the Austrians.

Torgau (*Battle of*), in Prussia, 3 Nov., 1760, in which Frederick II. of Prussia encountered Marshal Daun. The battle was indecisive; but Frederick claimed the victory, because Marshal Daun decamped during the night. (In the fifth campaign of the Seven Years' War.)

Pronounce *Tor-gow* (ow as in *now*).

Torres Vedras, in Portugal. The French marshal arrived before the ' Lines ' constructed by Wellington in Oct., but retreated Nov. 14, 1810. *See* p. 521, ' Lines of Torres Vedras.'

Toulon, in France (*Battles of*). 1. 22 Feb., 1744, when Admiral Matthews was repulsed by the allied French and Spanish fleets.

II. 15 Nov., 1793, a conflict between the English and the French, in which the French were repulsed.

Toulouse (*Battle of*), 10 April, 1814, won by the Duke of Wellington over the French, led by Marshal Soult. This was the last of Wellington's peninsular battles.

Tours (*Battle of*), 10 Oct., A.D. 732, in which Charles Martel, mayor of the palace, leader of the Franks, utterly defeated the Saracens under Abderahman. This was one of the most important and decisive of victories. If the Saracens had succeeded, without doubt they would have planted in France the religion of Mahomet, and there, as in Spain, it would have dominated, at least for a time. It was the battle between the Crescent and the Cross.

This is one of Sir Edward Creasy's *Fifteen Decisive Battles of the World.*

Towton (*Battle of*), in Yorkshire, 29 March, 1461 (Palm Sunday), in which Edward IV. defeated Henry VI. This was one of the most terrible struggles in English history, second only to the battle of Hastings or Senlac. The number brought into the field on either side was about 60,000 men, and for six hours the fight lasted in the midst of a severe snow-storm. The loss on each side was more than 20,000. The Lancastrians lost six barons, the Earls of Devon and Wiltshire were taken prisoners and beheaded, the Lords Oxford and Aubrey were subsequently executed. An enormous number of the Lancastrians were charged with treason, and all their lands were confiscated.

Trafalgar (*Battle of*), 21 Oct., 1805, won by Admiral Lord Nelson over the combined French and Spanish fleets, commanded by Admiral Villeneuve (French) and two Spanish admirals. All the three admirals were taken prisoners. Nelson commanded in the ship called the ' Victory,' and lost his life in the battle. It was in this engagement he is credited with the signal, ' England expects every man to do his duty.' This is our most glorious naval victory.

Trasimēnê (*Battle of Lake*), same as Thrasymēnus (*q.v.*).

Trautenau (*Battle of*), 27 June, 1866, in the Seven Weeks' War. Prince Frederick Charles defeated the Austrians.

** Trautenau, pronounce *Trow'-ta-now*.

Tre'bia (*Battles of the*). I. B.C. 218, in which Hannibal the Carthaginian defeated Publius Scipio and Sempronius. This great battle ended Hannibal's first campaign.

II. 17–19 June, 1799, Suwarof, the Russian general, defeated Macdonald and his French army.

Trenton, in New Jersey, U.S. (*Battle of*), 26 Dec., 1776. Here Washington won his first victory over the British and Hessian troops in the American War of Independence.

Tricamarum (*Battle of*), A.D. 534, in which Belisarius defeated Gelimer, last of the Vandal kings of Africa.

Turin (*Battle of*), 1706, won by Prince Eugene over the French commanded by La Feuillade.

Ushant (*Naval battle of*), 27 July, 1778, in which the British fleet under Admiral Keppel defeated the French fleet commanded by the Comte d'Orvilliers. It was not a defeat, but the French withdrew their ships under cover of the night.

Val-ès-Dunes, near Caen (*Battle of*), 1047, in which William duke of Normandy defeated his revolted nobles.

Valmy', in France (*Battle of*), 20 Sept., 1792, in which the French Marshal Kellermann defeated the Duke of Brunswick. The duke looked on the French revolution as a contemptible riot, and was thunderstruck with the reception he met with at Valmy.

This is one of Sir Edward Creasy's *Fifteen Decisive Battles of the World.*

Varna (*Battle of*), 10 Nov., 1444, won by Amurath II. sultan of Turkey over the Hungarians, led by Ladislaus and Hunyādi. Ladislaus had sworn to preserve peace with Amurath for ten years, but, persuaded by Cardinal Julian and other churchmen, had scandalously broken his oath, and the defeat of Varna was the fruit of his perjury.

Vasag (*Battle of*), 1422, won by Hunyādi the Hungarian general over the Turks under Amurath II.

Vascape (*Battle of*), 1441. The greatest of all the victories of Hunyādi, won over the

Turks under the command of Sciabedin Bey. The Turks were 80,000, the Hungarians not 15,000.

Vercellæ (*Battle of*), 30 July, B.C. 101, in which the Cimbrian host was annihilated by Marius the Roman consul.

Verneuil, in France (*Battle of*), 16 Aug. 1424, in which the Duke of Bedford defeated the allied French and Scotch. This battle was hardly less disastrous to the French than that of Agincourt, for full one-third of the knighthood were left dead on that fatal field. The loss of the French was 4,000, that of Bedford's army 1,600.
Among the slain were the Earl of Buchan, Earl Douglas, Lord James Douglas (the earl's son), Sir Alexander Meldrum, &c.

Verona (*Battle of*), 30 March, 1799, in which the Austrian General Kray defeated the French.

Veszprem (*Battle of*), 997, won by St. Stephen king of Hungary, soon after his baptism, over Kopán, a nobleman of the old Shaman faith. By this victory Christianity was established in the land.

Vienna (*Battle of*), 12 Sept., 1683, in which Sobieski king of Poland, with a relief force of 40,000 men, utterly defeated Kara Mustapha vizier of the Sultan Mahomet II., whereby the siege of Vienna was raised. This is one of the most important and decisive victories ever won. If the Turks had been victorious, probably Vienna, like Constantinople, would have been subject to the Crescent, and the Eastern and Western empires would have been united again, but under the power and religion of the sultan.

Villa Viciosa (*Battle of*), 1710, won by the French, commanded by the Duc de Vendôme, over the Archduke Karl.

Villafranca, in Sicily (*Battles of*), I. 1718, in which the Spaniards won over the Austrians.
II. 10 April, 1812, in which the British cavalry, led by Sir Stapleton Cotton, defeated Marshal Soult. Napoleon greatly blamed Soult for this defeat.

Villingshausen (*Battle of*), 15 July, 1761, in which Ferdinand duke of Brunswick defeated the French. (In the sixth campaign of the Seven Years' War.)

Vimeira, in Portugal (*Battle of*), 21 Aug., 1808, in which Sir Arthur Wellesley (afterwards Duke of Wellington) defeated the allied French and Spanish forces under Marshal Junot. This was the first of his peninsular victories.

Vindalum (*Battle of*), B.C. 121, in which Cn. Domitius the pro-consul defeated the Allobróges.

Vinegar Hill, near Wexford (*Battle of*), 21 June, 1798. This could hardly be called a battle. The Irish had risen in revolt, and mustered 15,000 strong on Vinegar Hill. General Lake was sent to put down the revolt. He took their camp, and utterly suppressed the rebellion. In the autumn 1,000 French soldiers,

under General Humbert, landed in Mayo, and defeated Lake and Hutchinson, who had about 3,000 men under them, at Castlebar, 27 Aug., 1798 ; and then Lord Cornwallis, the lord-lieutenant, with 30,000 men, forced Humbert to surrender.

Vionville (*Battle of*), 16 Aug., 1870, in the Franco-Prussian war, won by the Prussians.

Vittoria (*Battle of*), 21 June, 1813, won by Lord Wellington over the French army commanded by Joseph Bonaparte and Marshal Jourdan. This was one of the most brilliant victories in the British annals. Marshal Jourdan lost 151 pieces of cannon, 451 ammunition waggons, all his baggage and treasure, and even his marshal's bâton.

Voglade. *See below* ' Vouglé.'

Volturno (*Battle of the*), 17 Sept., 1860, won by Garibaldi over the Neapolitan troops of Francis II.

Vouglé, near Poitiers (*Battle of*), A.D. 507, in which Clovis, founder of the French monarchy, overthrew Alaric II. king of the West-Goths. Alaric himself was slain on the field.

Wagram, in Austria (*Battle of*), 6 July, 1809, in which the French, led by Napoleon, overthrew the Austrians, led by the Archduke Karl. This battle led to a treaty of peace, in which Austria ceded all her sea-coast to France; the kingdoms of Saxony and Bavaria were also enlarged at the expense of Austria.

Wakefield, in Yorkshire (*Battle of*), 31 Dec., 1460, in which Queen Margaret defeated Richard duke of York. This was the only great victory of the Lancastrians in the long War of the Roses.

Walcourt, in Holland (*Battle of*), 27 Aug., 1689. Here Marshal d'Humières was defeated by the Prince of Waldeck. Marlborough was present in this battle, and laid the foundation of his future fame.

Wandewash, in Hindustan (*Battle of*), Jan., 1760, in which Thomas Arthur comte de Lally, the French governor in India, was defeated by Sir Eyre Coote, and Pondicherry fell into the hands of the English.

Wareham (*Battle of*), A.D. 876, in which the Danish fleet was repulsed by King Alfred. The Danes then allied themselves with the Welsh. Being hard pressed, the Danes swore to leave Wessex, but reappeared at Chippenham in the winter of 878.

Warna (*Battle of*), 10 Nov., 1444, in which Amurath II. defeated Ladislaus V. king of Hungary, who was also slain.

Warsaw (*Battles of*). I. 10, 12 Oct., 1794, in which the Poles were defeated by the Russians.
II. 20 Feb., 1831, in which the Russians were defeated. This is also called the battle of Growchow.
III. 7, 8 Sept., 1831, won by the Russians over the Poles.

Wartenburg, in Prussia (*Battle of*), 3 Oct., 1813, won by the allies over the French.

Waterloo (*Battle of*), 18 June, 1815, the most momentous victory ever won by the British arms, and the most happy in its results. Napoleon commanded the French and the Duke of Wellington the British and their allies. The battle lasted from seven in the morning till nine at night. Napoleon's career ended with this battle. He delivered himself into the hands of Captain Maitland, 3 July, and was banished to Longwood in St. Heléna, where he landed, 16 Oct., 1815.

The Duke of Marlborough won a battle over the French at Waterloo, 17 Aug., 1705.

₊ The battle of Waterloo, 18 June, 1815, was exactly six centuries to a day of the signature of Magna Charta by King John, 18 June, 1215. *See* Colonel Gurwood's 12th vol. Creasy's 'Fifteen Decisive Battles.'

Wattignies, near Lille (*Battle of*), 15, 16 Oct., 1793. The Austrians defeated Jourdan, the French marshal, here.

Wawz (*Battle of*), 31 March, 1831, in which the Russians were defeated by the Poles under the command of Skrzynecki.

Weissenburg (*Battles of*). I. A.D. 1620, won by the Roman Catholics over the Protestants of Bohemia. Maximilian duke of Bavaria affirms that his success was due to the aid of St. John Nepomuk.

II. 4 Aug., 1870. The first 'battle' of the Franco-Prussian war. Won by the Crown Prince of Prussia.

Wertingen (*Battle of*), 8 Oct., 1805, in which the French defeated Mack, general of the Austrian army.

White Plains, near New York, U.S. (*Battle of*), 28 Oct., 1776, where General Howe defeated the Americans in the American War of Independence.

Wig'an (*Battles of*). I. 1643, in which the royal forces, under the Earl of Derby, were defeated by the parliamentary army led by Sir John Smeaton.

II. 1651, in which the Earl of Derby was again defeated by the parliamentary army, led by Colonel Lilburne.

Wilhelmsthal (*Battle of*), 24 June, 1762, won for Prussia by the two Dukes of Brunswick. This was the last battle of the Seven Years' War.

Wilton (*Battle of*), A.D. 823, which Egbert king of Wessex won over Beornwulf king of Mercia. This victory led to the absorption of Mercia into the kingdom of Wessex.

Winceby-on-the-Wolds, Lincolnshire (*Battle of*), 1643, won by Cromwell and Fairfax over the Marquis of Newcastle. Here Cromwell had a horse shot under him.

Winwœd, near Leeds (*Battle of*), 665, also called Winwidfeld. In this battle Penda was slain by Oswi of Northumbria. Winwœd is Weewood in York.

In this battle Oswi vowed, if God gave him the victory, he would dedicate his daughter to the Lord and build twelve monasteries.

Witepsk (*Battle of*), 11 Nov., 1812, in which the French, under Marshal Victor, were defeated by the Russians commanded by General Wittgenstein.

Wittstock (*Battle of*), 4 Oct., 1636, won by the Swedes, in the Protestant interest, over the German Catholic League. This was one of the battles of the Thirty Years' War.

Wodensfield (*Battle of*), A.D. 910, in which Edward, son of Alfred, defeated the Anglo-Danes with great slaughter.

Wodnesbeorgh (*Battles of*). I. A.D. 591, in which Cealwin the Saxon was defeated by his nephew Ceolric, who had allied himself with the Cymry and Scoti. The death of Cealwin soon followed, in the thirty-third year of his reign.

II. 714, in which Ina, the greatest of the kings of Wessex, defeated and slew Ceobred king of Mercia. Wodnesbeorgh is Woodbury in Devonshire.

Woerden (*Battle of*), in Holland, June, 1672. Marshal de Luxembourg defeated the Hollanders.

Worcester (*Battle of*), 3 Sept., 1651, in which Cromwell utterly routed Charles II. Some 3,000 royalists were slain and 10,000 were taken prisoners, who were sent as slaves to the plantations. Charles made his escape to France, and his adventures make one of the most marvellous romances of history.

Cromwell says for four or five hours this battle was 'the stiffest contest he had seen.' The Scotch lost all their baggage and artillery, with 6,000 men, amongst whom was the Duke of Hamilton, their leader.

Wörth (*Battle of*), 6 Aug., 1870, in the Franco-Prussian war. Won by the Prussians over MacMahon, the French marshal.

Wurtschen (*Battle of*), 1813, in which Napoleon defeated the allied Russian and Prussian armies. The carnage on both sides was terrible.

Würtzburg (*Battle of*), 3 Sept., 1796. Archduke Charles of Austria defeated Moreau, the French general.

Wyppeds Fleot (*Battle of*), A.D. 465, won by Hengist over the Britons.

Xeres (*Battle of*), A.D. 1237, won by Alfonso, 'infant' of Ferdinand III., over Abenhud, the Moorish king of Seville. In this battle, we are told, St. James on his white horse fought for Spain.

Ximera (*Battle of*), 10 Sept., 1811, in which the Spaniards, under General Ballasteros, defeated the French under the command of General Regnier.

Yermuk, in Syria (*Battle of the*), Nov. A.D. 638, in which Khalid and Abu Obeidah, with their Saracen troops, defeated the Greeks under Heraclius.

York (*Battle of*), A.D. 867, in which the two sons of Ragnar Lodbrog the Dane defeated Osbert and Ella, the Saxons, with great slaughter. Both Osbert and Ella fell.

Yvres (*Battle of*), 1591, won by Henri IV. king of France over the Catholic League.

Zalaca, in Spain (*Battle of*), 23 Oct., 1086, in which Alfonso VI. of Castile was defeated by Jussef ben Taxfyn or Taschfin of Morocco.

Zama (*Battle of*), B.C. 202, in which Scipio defeated Hannibal, and ended the Second Punic War. Zama is called the Waterloo of Hannibal, as Cannæ is called his Austerlitz.

Zelïa, or Zeleia, in Mysia (*Battle of*), B.C. 47, where Cæsar defeated Pharnâces IV. king of Pontus. Cæsar announced his victory in the famous despatch VENI, VIDI, VICI.

Zelichow (*Battle of*), 6 April, 1831, in which the Russians, led by General Diebitsch, were defeated by the Poles with great slaughter.

Zenta, in Hungary (*Battle of*), 1697, won by Prince Eugene over the Turks. The prince fought contrary to orders; but so judicious were his plans and so well carried out, that he received a written licence from the kaiser to act ever after entirely on his own judgment. Certainly a most extraordinary licence.

Zingara (*Battle of*), A.D. 350, between the Persians, led by Shapûr Zoolaclaf, and the Romans, led by the Emperor Julian. The Romans won the field, but Shapûr recovered his advantage in a night attack.

Zlotzow (*Battle of*), won by John III. (Sobieski) of Poland over the Tartars.

Zorndorf (*Battle of*), 25, 26 Aug., 1758, in which Frederick II. of Prussia defeated the Russians under General Fermor, who retreated into Poland (in the third campaign of the Seven Years' War). This was one of the most tenaciously contested fields ever fought. It began at 9 A.M., and continued long after the moon had risen. As many as 19,000 Russians and 11,000 Prussians were slain.

Zutphen, in the Netherlands (*Battle of*), 22 Sept., 1586. Zutphen was under the power of Spain from 1572, but the States twice besieged it, in 1584 and in 1586, but without success. The second of these sieges is well known, because it was there that Sir Philip Sidney, 'the Marcellus of England,' and author of the prose-poem called 'Arcadia,' met his death. This was a mere skirmish, not a battle, Lord Leicester, with 8,000 men, being sent to assist the Flemish.

The tale is that he was mortally wounded in this batt'e; and, as he was raising a small bottle of wine to his lips, he cast his eyes upon a common soldier dying beside him. 'Poor fellow!' said Sir Philip, 'thy necessity is greater than mine;' so saying, he handed to the man the bottle, and died.

*** For battles named incidentally, or circumstantially—as the 'Battle of the Standard,' the 'Battle of the Forty,' &c.—and not geographically, see the word 'Battle,' pp. 78, 79, 80.